P9-DWJ-214

Library of Congress Cataloging in Publication Data
Main entry under title:

Webster's collegiate thesaurus.

1. English language—Synonyms and antonyms.
PE1591.W38 423'.1 75-45167
ISBN 0-87779-069-8 (indexed)
ISBN 0-87779-070-1 (deluxe)

Made in the United States of America

1112RMcN8180

Webster's Collegiate Thesaurus

A Merriam-Webster®

G. & C. Merriam Company, *Publishers*
Springfield, Massachusetts, U.S.A.

Preface

WEBSTER'S COLLEGIATE THESAURUS is a wholly new book resulting from long study and planning and differing from existent thesauruses in a number of significant respects. It may be worth mentioning that the idea of a thesaurus has been a viable notion in the Merriam offices since at least 1898 — in which year one of the responsibilities assigned the late Dr. William Torrey Harris when he was appointed Editor in Chief was to do preliminary planning for an improved thesaurus. Over the years that have passed since then, much testing has been done and much information accumulated. Now we are able to issue a thesaurus which, we are satisfied, eliminates many of the defects that impair both past and still existent books of this character.

What does the user look for in a thesaurus? The consensus agrees that he is seeking a more appropriate term than the one he has in mind. This very broad concept is scarcely consonant with the typical thesaurus presentation of "synonyms" and sometimes "antonyms". In point of fact, the user may be seeking a synonym, a word stronger or weaker in force, one of slightly different meaning, a more starchy or more folksy word, an idiomatic phrase that conveys the same idea, or a word that to a greater or less degree contrasts with his starting point. Patently, all these possible uses cannot be subsumed reasonably under the rather unitary notions of "synonym" and "antonym". Perhaps the longevity of

Roget's *Thesaurus* rests on the simple fact that in spite of its complexity and lack of guidance, it does spread before the user a greater body of material to browse through than any comparable book heretofore available. Webster's Collegiate Thesaurus is designed to present a similar range of material but in a readily available and highly structured form that minimizes the consultant's need to grope and guess.

In earlier Merriam-Webster publications the pattern of supplementing synonym lists with lists of related and contrasted words, words that were relevant to the group under study yet not quite synonyms or antonyms respectively, was extensively tested. This favorably received feature not only allowed more precise delineation of synonyms and antonyms but provided the user with much additional significant and pertinent assistance. The same plan of supplementing synonyms and antonyms with genuinely germane collateral material has been made a feature of this new thesaurus.

Additional features of Webster's Collegiate Thesaurus designed to facilitate its use are the provision at each main entry of a concise statement of the segment of denotation in which a group of words can be construed as synonyms, a strictly alphabetical organization, and the entry at its own alphabetical place of each word that appears as a synonym at a main entry. The absence or inadequate handling of the first of these features is a major flaw in most existent thesauruses. Though many justifications have been offered for avoiding the second, they all boil down to the implausible notion that the members of a group of words are synonymous but some are more synonymous than others! Perhaps unfairly, one can't help feeling that the only valid explanation for non-alphabetical listing of properly chosen synonyms appears in one specialized dictionary of synonyms whose author comments, "Apologies are in order, however, for my inability to maintain alphabetical order within the categories, the plea being of course lack of time." Finally, since no one can anticipate where the user's search may start, it seems only logical to enter each synonym in such a way that it can serve as a convenient starting point in his searching.

The material in Webster's Collegiate Thesaurus has been drawn primarily from Webster's Third New International Dictionary, the Merriam-Webster

unabridged dictionary containing more than 460,000 entries. This basic lexicographic reference has been reviewed page by page, entry by entry, and sense by sense in selecting the groups of terms to be entered in the thesaurus. The editors have not restricted themselves, however, to this one source but have freely consulted existent thesauruses and Webster's New Collegiate Dictionary and have not hesitated to draw on the resources of the more than 12,000,000 citations of the massive Merriam-Webster file of English usage to settle doubtful points. Entries of multisense words ordinarily follow the sequence of senses in, though not necessarily the identical numbering of, Webster's Third.

The editor of Webster's Collegiate Thesaurus has been assisted by Michael G. Belanger, William P. Black, Kathleen M. Doherty, Kathryn K. Flynn, Kerry W. Metz, Anne H. Soukhanov, and Raymond R. Wilson, assistant editors. Cross-referencing has been done under the supervision of Grace A. Kellogg, associate editor. The Merriam clerical and typing staff under the supervision of Evelyn G. Summers provided invaluable support in the preparation of this work.

Mairé Weir Kay, Editor

Introduction

Evolution of the Thesaurus

With its intricate interweaving of strands of Celtic, earlier Roman and later ecclesiastical Latin, northern and western Germanic tongues, and, through Norman-French, the whole body of Romance languages, it is scarcely surprising that English is a language peculiarly rich in synonyms. Equally, it is scarcely strange that with so much to work with, users of this language have long been interested in synonyms as an element both in precision and in elegance of expression. Though the word *synonym* had certainly been in use at least a century earlier, its first appearance with essentially its modern meaning seems to be that in the dedicatory epistle of John Palsgrave's translation of the Latin *Comedye of Acolasius* (1540) in which he castigates self-important and incompetent masters who

> *... do oppress and overlaye the tender wyttes, the whiche they wold so fayne further, with their multitude of sondry interpretations, confusedly by them uttered. So that fynally theyr yong scholers, ... be forced to falle a glosynge ... and as their chyldyshe judgement dothe for the time serve them, of dyvers englishe werdes in our tongue beinge synonymes ... they chuse moste commonly the very worste, and therewith scryble the bokes of theyr latyne auctours.*

To pass from awareness of synonyms as a usage problem to organized consideration of them as an organic factor in rhetorical excellence is no very long stride. This

is demonstrated by Henry Cockeram's *English Dictionarie* (1623). This engaging little work, though the first English dictionary in name, comes closer in some respects to being a thesaurus in fact. Its first book purports to define difficult words, but a good half of the "definitions" are simple lists of equivalents (as at *condigne* — worthy, due, deserved; at *luxurie* — lecherie, riotousnesse; at *sordid* — base, filthy). The second book contains in its author's words

The vulgar words, which whensoever any desirous of a more curious explanation by a more refined and elegant speech shall looke into, he shall there receive the exact and ample word to express the same.

Entries such as "to Behead one, *Decollate,* Obtruncate", "to put Over, *Adiourne,* Prorogue, Procrastine", "Youth, *Puerilitie,* Infancie, Adolescentie, Juvenilitie, Minoritie" are typical of this section. At some stretch of credibility one might suggest that Cockeram here anticipated Roget in assembling word lists matched to ideas rather than to other words.

After this vigorous beginning, English synonymy languished until the eighteenth century. It then was given a new impetus by the appearance in 1719 of the Abbé Gabriel Girard's book of discriminative synonymies of the French language. This was translated and adapted to English use, apparently by John Trusler, who brought out a book *The Distinction between Words esteemed Synonymous in the English Language* (1766) which is patently based on Girard and which unquestionably influenced the later discriminative synonymies of Mrs. Piozzi (1794) and George Crabb (1816). Thus, the discriminative or descriptive or prescriptive synonymy became established as an accepted literary and didactic form by the early years of the nineteenth century.

Slower in blooming in spite of its head start in Cockeram's work was the essentially mnemonic approach to synonymy, the *Thesaurus* of modern usage. The first book that undertook the orderly presentation of synonyms as a primary function was William Perry's *Synonymous, Etymological, and Pronouncing English Dictionary* (1805). With respect to the assembling of synonyms in readily available lists the author notes:

It is a matter of no small astonishment that a work of this kind, one among the desiderata *of literature, should have been so long neglected. Every person accustomed to write, whether on private concerns, or for public instruction, must have felt the want of such an assistant, not only to guard him against the tiresome repetition of the same words, but to enable him to select terms to express his ideas with greater clearness and precision.*

This first "thesaurus", produced nearly half a century before Peter Mark Roget gave that word its current meaning, offers a clear and concise explication of the purpose of such a volume as distinguished from the discriminative synonymy, which seeks to impose to varying degrees an author's notions of appropriateness, propriety, and correctitude on a user.

During succeeding years several synonym-listing books appeared, some of greater and some of less worth and degree of popular appeal. Formally organized word-finding lists became a feature of the general dictionary with the publication in 1847 under the editorship of Chauncey A. Goodrich of the royal octavo abridgment of Noah Webster's American Dictionary of the English Language (1828). Finally, with the publication of Peter Mark Roget's *Thesaurus of English Words and Phrases* in 1852, a new force entered the field.

This last was and remains a unique work. The product of nearly fifty years of collecting and testing to meet the author's own needs, it is organized primarily in terms of words related to concepts. For the scholarly user it opens a very real treasury of language, but Roget's impression, expressed in his introduction, that the user

scarcely ever need engage in any critical or elaborate study of the subtile distinctions existing between synonymous terms; for if the materials set before him be sufficiently abundant, an instinctive tact will rarely fail to lead him to the proper choice

is probably far too optimistic with regard to the person who needs guidance most — the person of average or limited vocabulary. In fact, Barnas Sears, editor of the first American edition of *The Thesaurus of English Words* (1854) makes the point in his "Editor's Preface" that

apprehending that many who may consult this work would regard the plan of the author for the distribution of his topics as too obscure for ordinary reference, the editor has caused the index to be greatly enlarged.

It has long been recognized that Roget is far more often

recommended by instructors than it is used by students. Nonetheless, *The Thesaurus of English Words and Phrases* is the only word-finding book to remain viable in various editions for well over a century, and one cannot help feeling that in spite of its complexity and elaborate structural plan the sheer wealth of relevant material that it offers a sophisticated user is the explanation of its survival.

Understandably enough, most thesaurists of the post-Roget period have sought an approach that would combine the wealth of material available in Roget's work with the indubitably simpler alphabetical organization of a dictionary. While differing levels of success have been attained, the underlying problem — that a dictionary dealing in synonyms and antonyms of specific words cannot honestly cover the same ground as a thesaurus devoted to the presentation of all pertinent terms about specific concepts — can scarcely be said to have been solved in an entirely satisfactory manner. It is the hope and belief of the editors of Webster's Collegiate Thesaurus that, by pinpointing the exact segment of meaning in which word groups are synonymous and by supplementing synonym and antonym lists in this book with lists of related and contrasted words and of pertinent idiomatic equivalents, they have gone far toward solving the problem without doing violence to the basic concepts of *synonym* and *antonym*.

The Synonym

The early lexicographers had a clear and precise awareness of the concept *synonym*. Thus, Johnson enters in his *Dictionary of the English Language* (1755) "SYNONYMA . . . Names which signify the same thing," George Mason in his *Supplement to Johnson's English Dictionary* (1803) adds "SYNONYME . . . A word of the same meaning as some other word" (an entry taken over verbatim in Todd's 1818 revision of *Johnson's English Dictionary*), and Webster (1828) includes "SYNONYM . . . a name, noun or other word having the same signification as another is its *synonym*. Two words containing the same idea are *synonyms*." Similarly, the eighteenth century discriminative synonymists implicitly followed the lead of Abbé Girard, whose title *La Justesse de la langue françoise ou les différentes significations des mots qui passent pour être synonymes* makes it clear that he was discriminating "words reputed to be synonyms" rather than words that are precisely such. His imitator Trusler refers in like manner to "Words esteemed Synonymous in the English Language," while Mrs. Piozzi in her *British Synonymy* (1794) almost routinely qualifies her discriminations with such statements about her "synonym" groups as that the words "are verbs very nearly yet not strictly synonymous," or "are not I believe exactly synonymous." There can be no doubt that the early discriminators were perfectly aware that they were not dealing with synonyms in the then generally accepted meaning of that word.

In course of time, the distinction between the synonymous words of the early lexicographers and the nearly synonymous words of the discriminative synonymists, appropriately called *pseudosynonyms* by Miss Whately (1851), gradually became eroded. As early as 1864 we find in Webster's American Dictionary of the English Language the entry "SYNONYM . . . One of two or more words in the same language which are the precise equivalents of each other or which have very nearly the same signification and therefore are liable to be confounded together." The trend toward a broad and loose definition of *synonym* has continued, especially as synonymists have striven for ever longer lists of ever more remotely related "synonyms." Indeed, there are those who compile "synonym" lists while denying the existence of synonyms.

All the varied definitions, both narrow and broad, somehow pass over what seems to the editors of Webster's Collegiate Thesaurus a fundamental point: *synonymy is a relation between meanings.* True, it can only be expressed in terms of words since meaning is an attribute of words. Nonetheless, synonymy must be thought of as a property of meanings and it must be identified through careful analysis of these meanings. With this in mind, it early became apparent that a fresh approach to the study of synonyms was essential if Webster's Collegiate Thesaurus was to be more than another compilation of vaguely related terms.

One lead was offered by Alfred Dwight Sheffield in his introductory discussion in the third edition of Soule's *Dictionary of English Synonyms* (1938), where he makes the point that *words can be displayed together in a synonym cluster to be chosen from when they share a basic meaning such that each synonym can be felt as offering this "core-sense" expressively enriched by further distinctions of sense, feeling, or tone.*

Unfortunately, in his revision of Soule, Sheffield failed to carry over his eminently sound approach and did not make such core-senses available to the users of the book. Nor is it always apparent that his synonym lists consistently share such a basic meaning. Nonetheless, his approach pointed to the need for more thorough analysis in identifying synonyms for use in Webster's Collegiate Thesaurus.

For practical purposes of analysis it became necessary to view synonymy as a relationship not between words nor even between lexicographic senses of words. It was essential to seek out discrete objective denotations uncolored by such peripheral aspects of meaning as connotations, implications, or quirks of idiomatic usage. Only by dissecting senses is it possible to isolate ultimate meanings and reach something which goes a little beyond Sheffield's core-sense and which for simplicity's sake will be here designated *elementary meaning.* Perhaps this approach needs to be examined more specifically to clarify the object in view. For example, there is a sense of the noun *input* in Webster's Third New International Dictionary that reads

> : power or energy put into a machine or system for storage (as into a storage battery) or for conversion in kind (as into a mechanically driven electric generator or a radio receiver) or conversion of characteristics (as into a transformer or electric amplifier) usu. with the intent of sizable recovery in the form of output

Obviously much of this definition is, as it should be from the lexicographic point of view, peripheral matter designed to guide and orient the consultant of the dictionary rather than a fundamental part of the denotation of the word in the sense in question. Stripped of this peripheral matter the sense can be restated denotationally as

> power or energy put into a machine or system for storage
> or for conversion in kind
> or conversion of characteristics.

When this in turn is expressed graphically

power		machine		storage
	put into a		for	conversion in kind
energy		system		conversion of characteristics

it becomes plain that there are twelve simple statements of denotation or individual elementary meanings associated in this single sense. Of these twelve only one, "energy put into a system for storage," could reasonably be considered as a synonym of *charge* as applied to a storage battery. For the purposes of Webster's Collegiate Thesaurus a word is construed as a synonym if and only if it or one of its senses shares with another word or sense of a word one or more elementary meanings.

When the synonymous relationship is viewed in terms of elementary meanings, the process of selecting synonyms is both simplified and facilitated. For example, it is immediately apparent that no term narrower in scope than the pertinent meaning of the headword can be its synonym, i.e., *sedan* cannot be a synonym of *automobile, biceps* cannot be a synonym of *muscle,* and *imply* cannot be a synonym of *communicate,* even though a very definite relation exists between the members of each pair. On the other hand, a term (such as *input* above) more broadly defined than another by the lexicographers is nonetheless a valid synonym of the latter if the two share one or more elementary meanings. In order to pin down the area of synonymity for the user, each main entry in Webster's Collegiate Thesaurus prefixes to its synonym list a *meaning core* (see pp. 22a) which states the elementary meaning or meanings and any peripheral notions common to all the members of the synonym group.

The Antonym

The term *antonym* was introduced by C. J. Smith in *Synonyms and Antonyms* (1867) as a term correlative to *synonym.* He identified the word somewhat ambiguously in his preface by stating that

words which agree in expressing one or more characteristic ideas in common he [the author] has regarded as Synonyms, those that negative one or more such ideas he has called Antonyms.

However, in his discussion of the etymology of the word *antonym* he elaborates the idea that though basically expressing the notion of a word used *in substitution for another,* this can be construed practically as one used *in opposition to another.* The idea of opposition is further stressed by his suggestion of *counterterm* as an alternative to *antonym.* The evidence clearly indicates that Smith in presenting the concept of *antonym* had in mind words that constitute the *negative opposite* of a term toward which they are antonymous. Unfortunately, the vagueness of his presentation and the looseness of his own usage within the body of his book have allowed great variation in subsequent application of the term. As a result, many synonymists have come to view antonyms as in some vague way converse to or contradictory of words toward which they are antonymous rather than as sharply, exactly, and completely opposed to such words in a manner that negates the implications of the latter.

In one collection or another various classes of terms have been construed as antonyms. Among these are several that, though of questionable validity, merit some consideration.

1 *Relative terms* have such a relationship one to the other that one can scarcely be used without suggesting the other (as *husband* and *wife, father* and *son, buyer* and *seller*), yet there is neither real opposition nor real negation between such pairs. Their relation is reciprocal or correlative rather than antonymous under any reasonably strict interpretation of the antonymous relationship.

2 *Complementary terms* in a similar way are normally paired and exhibit a reciprocal relationship such that one is likely to seem incomplete without its mate (as in such pairs as *question* and *answer, seek* and *find*). This reciprocal relation which involves no negation is better viewed as sequential than antonymous.

3 *Contrastive terms* differ sharply from their "opposites" only in some parts of their meaning. They neither oppose nor negate full force, since they differ significantly in range of meaning and applicability, in emphasis, and in the peripheral suggestions they convey. For example, *destitute* (an emphatic term carrying strong suggestions of misery and distress) is contrastive rather than antonymous with respect to *rich* (a rather neutral and matter-of-fact term), and *poor* (another neutral and matter-of-fact term) is the appropriate antonym of *rich.* Essentially, contrastive words are only tangentially opposed.

There can be no question that the inclusion of words like those just discussed whittles away at the basic notion of the antonym as an antithetical negative correlative of a term and that such whittling is undesirable. Certainly the treatment in dictionaries and manuals which indulge in this practice has become increasingly haphazard, uninformative, and unhelpful to the user of these works.

The editors of Webster's Collegiate Thesaurus feel that a reappraisal of the antonym concept is long overdue. As in the case of synonyms, the relation needs to be viewed as one between isolable segments of meaning rather than between words or lexicographic senses of words. For the purposes of this book, a word which in one or more of its elementary meanings precisely opposes a corresponding area of meaning of another word and which through its implications negates each implication that gives its individuality to its opposite is an antonym of the latter word.

This definition effectively excludes from consideration those classes of words previously discussed which either imperfectly oppose or incompletely negate their "opposites". There remain, however, three classes of words from which antonyms may reasonably be drawn. These are:

1 *Opposites without intermediates.* Such words are so opposed as to be mutually exclusive and to admit of no middle ground between them. They deny, point by point and item by item, whatever their opposites affirm. Thus, what is *perfect* can be in no way *imperfect* and what is *imperfect,* to however slight a degree, by no shift or twist can be viewed as *perfect;* one cannot in any way at once *accept* and *reject* or *agree* and *disagree.*

2 *Opposites with intermediates.* Such words constitute the terminal elements in a range of divergence and are so genuinely and diametrically opposed that the language admits of no wider divergence. Thus, a scale of excellence might include *superiority, adequacy, mediocrity,* and *inferiority,* but only the first and last are so totally opposed that each precisely negates what its opposite affirms. Similarly, in the sequence *prodigal, extravagant, careless, careful, frugal, parsimonious* there are three antonymous pairs. *Prodigal* (stressing excessive extravagance) and *parsimonious* (stressing excessive frugality) effectively cancel one another, as do *extravagant* (stressing disregard of conservation) and *frugal* (stressing

attention to conservation), or *careless* (stressing imprudence in expenditure) and *careful* (stressing prudence in expenditure). In such sequences the antonymous relation exists only between those members that are genuinely and precisely opposed. Other members (as *prodigal* and *frugal* or *careless* and *parsimonious*) may contrast sharply, but they do not clash full force; they are contrastive rather than antonymous.

3 *Reverse opposites.* These are terms that are opposed in such a way that each expresses the undoing or nullification of what the other affirms. Perhaps it is technically questionable practice to accept *nullification* as the equivalent of *negation;* yet the words overlap significantly in their range of meaning. Is it unreasonable, then, to accept two kinds of negation, one of which connotes privation (as, *bad* is the negation, or privation, of *good*) and the other of which connotes undoing or nullification (as, *reclamation* is the negation, or nullification, of *abandonment*)? Surely, these reverse opposites are entitled equally to consideration as antonyms when they precisely oppose and fully negate the special features of their opposites. Thus, *disprove* and its close synonym *refute* so perfectly oppose and so clearly negate the implications of *prove* that they fit the character of antonyms as effectively as does *unkind* with respect to *kind* or *come* with respect to *go.*

So, then, for the purposes of Webster's Collegiate Thesaurus, words that are opposites without intermediates, opposites with intermediates, or reverse opposites, and only these will be construed as antonymous.

Related and Contrasted Words

Though the editors of Webster's Collegiate Thesaurus are committed to a rigorous policy in the identification of synonyms and antonyms, they have no intention of evading their responsibility to those interested in a wider range of material for use in word finding or vocabulary building. In order to make relevant additional matter available without doing violence to reasonably restricted concepts of synonymity and antonymity, the book features lists of related and contrasted words wherever these seem appropriate and likely to be helpful. *Related words* (often misdescribed as synonyms) and *contrasted words* (often misdescribed as antonyms) are actually near-synonyms and near-antonyms respectively. They are words which do not quite qualify as synonyms or antonyms under a strict definition of these terms but which are so closely related to or so clearly contrastable with the members of a synonym group that the user of the book has a right to have them brought to his attention under appropriate headings.

Phrases and Idiomatic Equivalents

In the search for ever longer synonym lists thesaurists increasingly have included phrases among their synonyms. These phrases fall into three classes:

1 *word equivalents.* These are phrases that function as if they were single words. More often than not they are combinations of noun and attributive noun (as *county agent*) or noun and adjective (as *hard sell*) or of verb and adverb (as *make up*). However, such phrases may be made up of any kinds of verbal elements and may perform the function of any part of speech (as *with one accord,* adverb; *except for,* preposition; *Near Eastern,* adjective; *insofar as,* conjunction). These firmly fixed combinations that act as if they were single words and fulfill the grammatical functions of single words can scarcely be entirely excluded from synonym lists. The editors of Webster's Collegiate Thesaurus have taken a conservative position and only include such combinations when they are so firmly fixed in usage as to be accorded part-of-speech labels in major modern dictionaries.

2 *glosses.* These are phrases that restate the meaning of a word. Essentially, they are brief, sometimes cryptic definitions. There is no definition of *synonym* that reasonably can be construed to justify the inclusion of restatements or definitions in synonym lists. Thus, "do heavy menial service" is a gloss rather than a synonym of *drudge,* "have an opinion" is a gloss of *opine,* and "in a state of inferiority to" is a gloss of *under.* In the opinion of the editors of Webster's Collegiate Thesaurus, there is no place in a synonym list for such phrases since they contribute nothing useful to the vocabulary of the user of a thesaurus.

3 *idioms.* These are phrases that have a collective meaning other than the additive meaning of the constituent words. For example, there are no literal meanings of *compare* and *note* that allow the phrase "compare notes" to mean "to exchange observations and views"; yet, this is what it does mean. There are no literal meanings of the constituent words that allow "come a long way" to mean "make progress, succeed"; nonetheless, it does mean this. When idiomatic phrases mean the same thing as particular words the temptation to include them in relevant synonym lists is strong. Such phrases, however, lack the qualities that excuse addition of word equivalents to synonym lists — they do not function as words but, rather, as different ways of conveying the notions that particular words convey. As in the case of glosses there is no definition of synonym that justifies the inclusion of idioms in a synonym list. Nonetheless, such *idiomatic equivalents* are of potential value to the user of a thesaurus since they can add force, variety, and sprightliness to his expression. The editors of Webster's Collegiate Thesaurus have effected a compromise and included selected *idiomatic equivalents* of synonym groups or of particular words in synonym lists in separate lists that follow the pertinent synonym lists.

Explanatory Chart

***ant*onym(s)** page 27a

alpha *n* ***syn*** BEGINNING, commencement, dawn, dawning, genesis, opening, outset, outstart, setout, start
ant omega

asterisk page 32a

bleeding *adj* **1** ***syn*** DAMNED 2, blessed, blighted, blinding, ‖blinking, *‖bloody, ‖blooming, cursed, damnable, *‖ruddy

capitalization page 29a

Canaan *n* ***syn*** HEAVEN 2, bliss, Civitas Dei, elysium, empyrean, happy hunting ground, kingdom come, nirvana, paradise, Zion

comma page 30a

compare cross-reference page 23a

design *vb* . . . **3** to work out the arrangement of the parts of < *design* an urban center >
syn arrange, lay out, map (out), plan, set out; *compare* PLAN 2
rel delineate, diagram, draft, outline, sketch

***con*trasted words** page 27a

everyday *adj* **1** ***syn*** COMMON 4, customary, familiar, frequent
con distinctive, singular, unique; uncommon, unusual
ant exceptional

double bars page 32a

fag *n* ***syn*** CIGARETTE, ‖butt, ‖cig, ‖coffin nail, ‖gasper, ‖pill, ‖skag, smoke

headword page 21a

guest *n* **1** ***syn*** VISITOR 1, caller, visitant
2 guests *pl* ***syn*** COMPANY 2, visitors

***idiom*atic equivalent(s)** page 26a

handy *adj* **1** ***syn*** CONVENIENT 2, adjacent, close-at-hand, close-by, near-at-hand, nearby
idiom at one's hand (*or* elbow), ready to hand

main entry page 22a

itemize *vb* **1** to set down in detail or by particulars < *itemize* deductions on a tax form >
syn enumerate, inventory, list, particularize, specialize, specify; *compare* SPECIFY 3
rel circumstantiate, document; count, number; cite, instance, mention; spell out
ant summarize

meaning core page 22a

jingle *vb* to make a repeated sharp light ringing sound <the coins *jingled* in his pocket>
syn chink, chinkle, clink, tingle, tinkle
rel clack, clatter, rattle

part-of-speech label page 22a

keenly *adv* ***syn*** HARD 6, bitterly, hardly, rancorously, resentfully, sorely

plural label page 29a

lashings *n pl* ***syn*** MUCH, barrel, lot, lump, mass, ‖mess, mountain, peck, ‖power, ‖sight

minutia *n, usu* **minutiae** *pl* ***syn*** INS AND OUTS, ropes

notice *vb* ***syn*** SEE 1, descry, discern, distinguish, espy, mark, note, observe, perceive, remark
rel acknowledge, recognize; advert, allude, refer
con disregard, ignore, neglect, overlook, slight

***rel**ated word(s)* page 25a

order *n* ... **12** ***syn*** COMMAND 1, behest, bidding, charge, dictate, injunction, mandate, word
rel authorization, permission

secondary entry page 24a

parallel *n* one that corresponds to or closely resembles another <we seek in vain a *parallel* for this situation>
syn analogue, correlate, correspondent, counterpart, countertype, match; *compare* COUNTERPART 1, EQUAL
rel equivalent; double, duplicate, duplication

semicolon page 30a

quibble *vb* **1** to find fault with something usually on minor grounds <was a peevish critic, always ready to *quibble*>
syn cavil, chicane, hypercriticize
rel carp, criticize
idiom split hairs
con applaud, commend, compliment, recommend; approve, endorse, sanction

sense number page 22a

right *n* ... **3** *usu* **rights** *pl* ***syn*** DUE 1, comeuppance, desert(s), deserving, lumps, merit

subhead page 22a

set *vb* ... **12** *of a celestial body* to pass below the horizon <the sun *set* at seven o'clock>
syn decline, dip, go down, sink
rel descend, drop
con ascend, climb, come up
ant rise

subject guide phrase 30a

***syn**onym(s)* 23a

tab *n* ... **3** ***syn*** CHECK 2, bill

syn cross-reference page 24a

take down *vb* ***syn*** DISMOUNT, disassemble, dismantle, dismember

two-word verb page 21a

yes *adv* **1** — used as a function word to express assent, agreement, understanding, or acceptance <*yes,* I can do that>
syn agreed, all right, aye, OK (*or* okay), okeydoke, yea, ‖yep

usage note page 23a

variant spelling pages 22a, 31a

zero *n* **1** a numerical symbol 0 denoting the absence of all magnitude or quantity <wrote a row of *zeros* after the decimal point>
syn aught (*or* ought), cipher, goose egg, naught (*or* nought), nothing, zilch
rel blank, nil, void

verbal illustration page 23a

zero (in) *vb* ***syn*** DIRECT 2, address, aim, cast, head, lay, level, point, train, turn,

verb + particle page 21a

Explanatory Notes

How to Use Webster's Collegiate Thesaurus

Every thesaurus user should read these Explanatory Notes because a thorough understanding of the scope, content, and structure of the book is essential to its effective employment. The Explanatory Chart (pages 18a-19a) that depicts and spotlights the book's basic components is keyed to those sections of the Explanatory Notes where detailed discussions of particular features may be found. The key lines at the bottom of the text pages also direct the user to these Explanatory Notes.

Since the English lexicon contains an incalculable number of fixed combinations, senses, subsenses, and nuances of meaning (for example, Webster's Third New International Dictionary records some 251 distinguishable meanings for the verb *set* and its fixed combinations), *it is essential that the thesaurus be used in conjunction with an adequate dictionary.*

Scope of Webster's Collegiate Thesaurus

This book is concerned with the general vocabulary of the English language. Since the user may actually be hindered rather than helped by a vocabulary diluted with obsolete, archaic, or extremely rare terms or with specialized or technical jargon, such words have been omitted.

Structure and Content

Entry Order The body of the book consists of main and

secondary entries introduced by alphabetically ordered boldface headwords, as

raid *vb* **1** to make a raid on < Indians *raided* the settlers frequently >
syn foray, harass, harry, maraud
rel despoil, devastate, ravage, sack, spoliate, waste; loot, plunder, rifle, rob
2 *syn* INVADE 1, foray, inroad, overrun, overswarm

raider *n* *syn* MARAUDER, forager, freebooter, looter, pillager, plunderer, ravager, ravisher, sacker, spoiler

rail *n* *syn* RAILING, balustrade, banister

where *raid, raider,* and *rail* are the headwords introducing either a main entry (as **raid** *vb* **1**), or a secondary entry (as **raid** *vb* **2, raider** *n,* or **rail** *n*).

Homograph headwords are entered in historical order: the one first used in English is entered first, as

till *prep*
till *conj*
till *vb*

Verbs used predominantly with one or two prepositions or adverbs may be headwords introducing main or secondary entries; in this case, they are entered with the verb segment in boldface type followed by the parenthetical element or elements in lightface type. Such verb + particle combinations immediately follow their base verb in alphabetical order:

put *vb* —— base-verb homograph
put (back) *vb*
put (on) *vb* —— verb + particle combinations
put (on *or* upon) *vb*
put *n* —— noun homograph

Fixed verb + adverb collocations commonly entered in dictionaries as two-word verbs have boldface entry at their appropriate alphabetical positions in this book. However, they follow any verb + particle combinations occurring in the same alphabetical sequence:

take *vb* —— base verb
take (from) *vb* —— verb + particle combinations
take (to) *vb*
take away *vb*
take back *vb* —— two-word verb collocations
take down *vb*
take in *vb*
take off *vb*

Headwords ordinarily conform to normal dictionary practices: for instance, they are styled as singular nouns or infinitive verbs. Special situations (as plural usage or variant spellings) are signaled by the use of boldface subheads, as

crossroad *n, usu* **crossroads** *pl but sing or pl in constr* ***syn*** JUNCTURE 2, . . .

woe *n* . . . **3** *usu* **woes** *pl* ***syn*** DISASTER, . . .

catercorner (*or* **catty-corner** *or* **kitty-corner**) *adv* ***syn*** DIAGONALLY, . . .

where **crossroads** and **woes** are subheads indicating plural usage, and **catty-corner** and **kitty-corner** are subheads showing variant spellings of the headwords.

The Main Entry and Its Basic Elements Each main entry consists of a headword followed by a part-of-speech label, a sense number when needed, a meaning core with a brief verbal illustration, and a list of synonyms. Lists of related words, idiomatic equivalents, contrasted words, and antonyms follow the synonym list if they are called for. A typical main entry is

calm *adj* **1** free from storm or rough activity <the wind died and the sea became *calm*>
syn halcyon, hushed, placid, quiet, still, stilly, untroubled
rel inactive, quiescent, reposing, resting; pacific, smooth, tranquil, unruffled
idiom calm as a millpond, still as death
con agitated, disturbed, perturbed, restless, turbulent, uneasy
ant stormy

where the italic part-of-speech label *adj* indicates that the headword is an adjective. Other such labels used in the book are: *adv* (adverb), *conj* (conjunction), *interj* (interjection), *n* (noun), *prep* (preposition), *pron* (pronoun), and *vb* (verb).

Individual senses of multisense entries (as **calm** *adj*) are introduced by a boldface sense number (as **1**).

The meaning core, as at **calm 1**

free from storm or rough activity

indicates the area of meaning in which a group of words (in this case *calm, halcyon, hushed, placid, quiet, still, stilly,* and *untroubled*) are considered to be synonymous (see Introduction, page 12 a).

In other words, the meaning core pinpoints the exact relationship between the main-entry headword and its synonyms.

A meaning core may be supplemented by a usage note introduced by a lightface dash when additional information or comments on syntax or usage are required:

yet *adv* **1** beyond this — used as an intensive to stress the comparative degree

Some interjections express feelings but otherwise are untranslatable into substitutable meaning; in such cases, the meaning core itself may be replaced by a usage note:

good-bye *interj* — used as a conventional expression of good wishes at parting

Each meaning core is followed by a verbal illustration enclosed by angle brackets, as

<the wind died and the sea became *calm*>

that exemplifies a typical use of the headword (here, **calm**) in its pertinent sense (**1**). The verbal illustration also offers the thesaurus user a frame for testing the suitability of the synonyms and/or related words with regard to his particular needs. Two verbal illustrations may appear after a meaning core that is broad enough to subsume alternatives (as both a literal and an extended use):

see *vb* **1** to take cognizance of by physical or mental vision <*saw* that the boat was being driven ashore> <the only one who *saw* the truth>

Such double illustrations have been chosen with discretion and are used sparingly in this book.

The boldface italic abbreviation ***syn*** introduces a synonym list that appears at each main entry on a line below the meaning core and the verbal illustration. This list may consist of only one synonym (as *here* at **hitherto** *adv* **2**) or of many (as *halcyon, hushed, placid, quiet, still, stilly,* and *untroubled* at **calm** *adj* **1**). Each synonym in a main-entry list has a boldface entry at its own alphabetical place. For a detailed discussion of synonyms, see Introduction, pages 9a-12a.

A compare cross-reference may appear at the end of a main-entry ***syn*** list. This cross-reference introduced by the italic word *compare* is used (1) when two or more groups of synonyms are very closely related and it is felt that the user examining one list should be aware of the existence of the other list or lists:

assassin *n* a person hired or hirable to
commit murder <found out who paid the *assassin*>
syn bravo, cutthroat, gun, gunman, ‖gunsel, gunslinger, hatchet man, hit man, torpedo, triggerman; *compare* MURDERER

murderer *n* one who kills a human being
<a *murderer* who wouldn't hesitate to kill in cold blood>
syn homicide, killer, manslayer, slayer; *compare* ASSASSIN

and (2) when the user should be warned that certain words have evolved derivative senses that tend to blur precise sense boundaries and consequently cause an overlapping of senses or of meaning, thus making those words somewhat less desirable choices for the user in terms of preciseness than other words in their lists. A comparison of the main entries

ration *n* an amount allotted or made available
especially from a limited supply <saved up their gasoline *ration* for a vacation trip>
syn allotment, allowance, apportionment, measure, part, portion, quantum, quota, to, share; *compare* SHARE 1

share *n* **1** something belonging to,
assumed by,
or falling to one (as in division or apportionment)
<wanted his *share* of the prize money>
syn allotment, allowance, bite, cut, lot,
part, partage, portion, quota, slice; *compare* RATION

reveals the usage overlap of the synonyms *allotment, allowance, part, portion, quota,* and *share* which are indeed valid synonyms at both entries.

The Secondary Entry and Its Basic Elements

A secondary entry consists of a boldface headword followed by a part-of-speech label, a boldface sense number when needed, a ***syn*** cross-reference in small capitals directing the user to the appropriate main entry in whose ***syn*** list the secondary entry appears (followed when needed by a lightface sense number of the main entry), and a list of the other synonyms appearing at the main entry. Lists of related words, idiomatic equivalents, contrasted words, or antonyms that are specifically applicable to the secondary-entry headword in the relationship indicated by the ***syn*** cross-reference may be included as well. A typical secondary entry is

placid *adj* **1** ***syn*** CALM 1, halcyon, hushed, quiet, still, stilly, untroubled
rel irenic, peaceful, serene, unagitated, unstirring
ant roiled

where **placid** is the headword, *adj* is the part-of-speech label, **1** is the sense number of the secondary entry, and ***syn*** CALM 1 is the ***syn*** cross-reference directing the user to the main entry **calm 1** where *placid* is a synonym. The terms *halcyon, hushed, quiet, still, stilly,* and *untroubled* comprising the secondary-entry ***syn*** cross-reference list are the synonyms at **calm 1.** As such, each of these terms is entered at its own alphabetical position with at least one sense that is cross-referred to **calm 1,** as

still *adj* **1** ***syn*** MOTIONLESS, . . .
2 ***syn*** CALM 1, halycon, hushed, placid, quiet, stilly, untroubled
rel peaceful, unperturbed
3 devoid of or making no stir . . .
syn . . .

where only sense **2** of **still** is the secondary entry of **calm 1.**

If a main-entry ***syn*** list contains more than ten terms (as at **notable** *n* **1**), the secondary entries cross-referred to that main entry include only nine synonyms selected from the entire list. This space-saving convention is illustrated at

high-muck-a-muck *n* ***syn*** NOTABLE 1, big boy, ‖big cheese, ‖big chief, big shot, ‖big wheel, ‖bigwig, mugwump, nabob, VIP

where nine synonyms of the thirty-four at the main entry have been selected for inclusion at the secondary entry.

Main and Secondary Entries: Elements Common to Both

All, some, or none of the following lists may appear at both main and secondary entries in this order: related words, idiomatic equivalents, contrasted words, and antonyms.

The boldface abbreviation ***rel*** introduces a list of related words. The related words — words that are almost but not quite synonymous with the headword — are included at an entry next after the synonym list. For example, at the main entry

splendid *adj* . . .
2 extraordinarily or transcendently impressive . . .
syn glorious, gorgeous, magnificent, proud, resplendent, splendiferous, splendorous, sublime, superb
rel eminent, illustrious; grand, impressive, lavish,

luxurious, royal, sumptuous; divine, exquisite, lovely; incomparable, matchless, peerless, superlative, supreme, unparalleled, unsurpassed; surpassing, transcendent

the ***rel*** list is composed of twenty terms separated into five subgroups that each share a common likeness or relation with the headword and its synonyms. On the other hand, at the secondary entry

splendiferous *adj* ***syn*** SPLENDID 2, . . .
rel dazzling, marvelous; smashing, walloping; rattling, ripping, screaming, terrific

three subgroups of eight terms were selected as being distinctively related to *splendiferous* rather than to the whole synonym group in the context indicated by the ***syn*** cross-reference to **splendid 2.** Related words appearing at a main entry are not ordinarily repeated at the secondary entries. The user should therefore check the main entry when seeking the most complete groupings of related words. Related words as such are not entered in boldface at their own alphabetical places. They may, of course, be synonyms in other lists or head their own main entries.

The boldface italic abbreviation ***idiom*** introduces a list of idiomatic equivalents that are essentially the same in meaning as the members of a synonym group. An ***idiom*** list at a main entry includes phrases that are generally pertinent to the entire ***syn*** list and the headword, as the ones at

speak *vb* **1** to articulate words in order to express thoughts . . .
syn talk, utter, verbalize, vocalize, voice
rel . . .
idiom break silence, give voice (*or* tongue *or* utterance) to, let fall, make public (*or* known), open one's mouth (*or* lips), put in (*or* into) words, say one's say, speak one's piece

while a secondary-entry list, as the one at

retaliate *vb syn* RECIPROCATE, recompense, requite, return
rel . . .
idiom even the score, get back at, get even with, give in kind, give one a dose of his own medicine, give one tit for tat, pay one in his own coin, settle (*or* square) accounts, turn the tables on

features idioms that are particularly appropriate equivalents of its headword in the context indicated by the ***syn*** cross-reference. Idiomatic equivalents, including those fixed verb + preposition combinations that function as idioms rather than as literal meanings of the verb are not entered in boldface at their own alphabetical places in this book.

The boldface italic abbreviation ***con*** introduces a list of contrasted words — words that are strongly contrastable but not quite antonymous with the headword — that may appear at an entry:

> **watchful** *adj* paying close attention usually with a view to anticipating approaching danger or opportunity . . .
> ***syn*** . . .
> ***rel*** . . .
> ***idiom*** . . .
> ***con*** careless, heedless, thoughtless inadvertent; absentminded, abstracted, faraway

> **alert** *adj* **1** ***syn*** WATCHFUL, open-eyed, unsleeping, vigilant, wakeful, wide-awake
> ***rel*** . . .
> ***idiom*** . . .
> ***con*** inattentive, unmindful; aloof, detached, indifferent, unconcerned

At the main entry **watchful** *adj* the ***con*** list is composed of seven words separated into three subgroups that each share at least one aspect of contrast to the headword and its ***syn*** list, while the ***con*** list at the secondary entry **alert 1** comprises six words separated into two such subgroups. Contrasted words appearing at a main entry are not ordinarily repeated at the secondary entries. The thesaurus user should therefore check the main entry when seeking the most complete groupings of contrasted words. Contrasted words as such are not entered in boldface at their own alphabetical places. They may, of course, be synonyms in other lists or head their own main entries.

The boldface italic abbreviation ***ant*** introduces the last possible element of a main or secondary entry: an antonym or list of antonyms, as at the entry

> **perfect** *adj* . . . **2** . . .
> ***ant*** imperfect

or at the entry

quiet *adj*. . . **4** not showy or obtrusive . . .
ant gaudy, loud

When antonyms are drawn from more than one of the accepted classes of opposites (see Antonym, page 12a), members of the two groups are separated by a semicolon, as at the entry

assistance *n* ***syn*** HELP 1, aid, assist, comfort, hand, lift, relief, secours, succor, support
rel . . .
con . . .
ant impediment, impeding; obstructing, obstruction

antonyms that are opposites with intermediates
antonyms that are reverse opposites

Like related and contrasted words, antonyms as such are not entered in boldface at their own alphabetical places. They may, of course, be synonyms in other lists or head their own main entries.

Main and Secondary Entries: The One Arbitrary Rule

Ideally, a book such as this should be free of all arbitrary restraints and curtailments. In practice, however, its editors found that one rule was essential: *No word may appear in more than one list at a main or secondary entry.* For example, *nice* is a synonym at **pleasant** *adj* **1.** The applicable sense of *nice* is found in Webster's Third New International Dictionary at the entry [1]**nice** . . . *adj*. . . **7** (binding substitute) + **7b,** where the definitions are

: pleasant and satisfying: as . . . **b** : ENJOYABLE, PLEASING, DELIGHTFUL <a *nice* time at the party> <*nice* and warm by the fire> <we have four *nice* bedrooms upstairs to make them comfortable —Willa Cather>

However, one might reasonably construe senses **7e** (: MILD, CLEMENT, PLEASING <the *nice* weather of late spring> <the *nice* old days of the past>) and **7g** (: FITTING, APPROPRIATE, SUITABLE <the *nice* clothes she wears> <not a *nice* word for use in church>) as a basis for entering *nice* as a related word as well as a synonym at **pleasant 1,** while sense **8** in Webster's Third New International Dictionary

: most inappropriate : UNPLEASANT, UNATTRACTIVE, TREACHEROUS — used ironically <a chronic alcoholic is certainly a *nice* one to talk about temperance> <a *nice* friend, who would have me . . . cover myself with eternal infamy —J.A. Froude> <got himself in a *nice* fix>

could be construed as evidence for entering *nice* as both a contrasted word and an antonym at **pleasant 1.** Obviously, the thesaurus user would not be helped by an entry showing any word in such an involved relationship with itself.

Labels, Punctuation, and Symbols

Labels Words that are labeled *cap* or *usu* [ally] *cap* in Webster's Third New International Dictionary are capitalized in this book. Thus, the synonyms *Gehenna, Pandemonium, Sheol,* and *Tophet* are so styled at the main entry **hell** *n* as are the related words *Styx* and *Tartarus.* A term that is capitalized in a main-entry ***syn*** list is also capitalized when it appears as a boldface secondary entry at its own alphabetical position:

Gehenna *n* ***syn*** HELL, . . .

If only one entered sense of a word is capitalized, an italic *cap* label followed by a boldface capitalized subhead is attached to the affected sense:

pandemonium *n* **1** *cap* **Pandemonium** ***syn*** HELL, . . .
2 ***syn*** SINK 1, . . .
3 ***syn*** DIN, . . .

In addition to the part-of-speech label, an italic plural label may be added when a word or a sense of a word is sometimes, often, usually, or always used in the plural. Typical examples of these labels are found at

years *n pl* ***syn*** OLD AGE, age, caducity, elderliness, senectitude, senescence

where *pl* indicates that the headword **years** is always plural in form and construction in this particular application, and at

road *n* **1** *often* **roads** *pl* ***syn*** HARBOR 3, anchorage, ||chuck, harborage, haven, port, riding, roadstead
2 ***syn*** WAY 1, artery, avenue, boulevard, ||drag, highway, path, street, thoroughfare, track
3 ***syn*** WAY 2, course, line, passage, path, route

where sense **1** (and only that sense) of the headword **road** is often but not always used in the plural, and at

minutia *n, usu* **minutiae** *pl* **1** ***syn*** INS AND OUTS, ropes
2 ***syn*** TRIVIA, small beer, small change, small potato(es), triviality

where the label preceding both senses indicates that the headword **minutia** is usually used in the plural in both of these applications, and at the main entry

trivia *n pl but sometimes sing in constr*

where the label is qualified to show that this plural noun may sometimes be used with a singular verb, and at

common *n* **1 commons** *pl but sing or pl in constr* ***syn*** COMMONALTY, commonage, commoners, common men, people, plebeians, plebs, populace, rank and file, third estate

which indicates that **common** occurs as a plural noun in sense **1** but may occur with either singular or plural verbs, and at

outdoors *n pl but sing in constr* the space where air is unconfined <every night he let the dog run in the *outdoors*>

whose label indicates that while the word *outdoors* is a plural noun, it consistently takes a singular verb. Use of these labels conforms to the treatment of plurals in Webster's Third New International Dictionary.

An italic subject guide phrase pointing to something with which the headword is associated may precede a meaning core in a very few instances, as at

set *vb*. . . **11** *of a fowl* to incubate eggs by crouching upon them . . .

Punctuation A comma links items (as synonyms, idiomatic equivalents, members of a single group or subgroup of related or contrasted words or of antonyms) that are alike in their relation to the headword, as at

conservative *adj*. . . **2** . . .
syn controlled, discreet, moderate, reasonable, restrained, temperate, unexcessive, unextreme
rel cautious, chary, wary; circumspect, politic, proper, prudent
con expansive, unconstrained; excessive, freewheeling, uncontrolled, unrestrained

A semicolon signals a break in continuity and is used in ***rel*** and ***con*** lists (as between the two subgroups in the ***rel*** and ***con*** lists at **conservative 2** above) to separate subgroups of words which differ in their relation to the headword. A semicolon is also used to separate antonyms that belong to different classes of opposites, as

> **arise** *vb* **1** ***syn*** RISE 4, ascend, aspire, lift, mount, soar, up, uprear
> ***ant*** recline; slump

where the two antonyms are so separated. A semicolon may also appear at the end of a main-entry ***syn*** list to introduce a compare cross-reference, as shown at **honorable** *adj* **1**:

> ***syn*** estimable, high-principled, noble, sterling, worthy; *compare* VENERABLE 1

Parentheses enclose variant spellings, as at the main entry **cake** *vb* **1** where

> encrust (*or* incrust)

is a synonym, and at the secondary entries, where that particular synonym is styled

> **encrust** (*or* **incrust**) *vb* ***syn*** CAKE 1, . . .

Parentheses also enclose a particle or particles usually associated with a base word, as

> **adore** *vb*. . . **3** to love, admire, or enjoy excessively . . .
> ***syn*** dote (on *or* upon), idolize, worship

> **dote** (on *or* upon) *vb* ***syn*** ADORE 3, . . .

Similarly, parentheses may indicate usage alternatives in idiomatic expressions, as at **slavery** *n* **2** where

> ***idiom*** the yoke (*or* chains) of slavery

alerts the user that he may choose one of two noun elements when employing this particular idiom. Parentheses are also used in main-entry ***syn*** lists to enclose plural suffixes of words that are sometimes, often, or usually but not always used in the plural:

> **scad** *n, usu* **scads** *pl* a great number or abundance . . .
> ***syn*** gob(s), heap, jillion, load(s), million, oodles, quantities, . . .

Parentheses enclose material indicating a typical, or occasionally, a sole object of reference, as in the meaning core of **express** *vb* **2**

> to give expression to (as a thought, an opinion, or an emotion)

where they enclose an adjunct, or at entries such as
abrogate *vb* **2**

ant establish, fix (*as a right, a quality, or a custom*)

where an antonym or a group of antonyms are associated with a particular object or objects of reference — a restriction or limitation to which the thesaurus user should be alerted.

Symbols Two warning symbols are used in this book: the asterisk * and the double bars ‖.

The asterisk prefixes terms that are generally or often considered vulgar and that are appropriately stigmatized in Webster's Third New International Dictionary. Examples of such terms may be found at the main entries **fool** *n* **1** and **nonsense** *n* **2.** If an asterisk prefixes a term in a main-entry ***syn*** list, it also prefixes that term at its secondary entry. When only one sense of an entry is considered vulgar, the asterisk precedes only the affected sense of the entry.

The double bars prefixing some terms in this book warn the user that the employment of such a term may involve a problem of diction too complex for presentation in a thesaurus, or a restriction in usage. Consequently, the thesaurus user should consult a dictionary if he is in doubt about the stylistic level or appropriateness of the word or if he is unfamiliar with its meaning. For example, ‖**fat cat** (a synonym of **notable** *n* **1**), ‖**chuff** (a synonym of **sullen** *adj*), and ‖**puxy** (a synonym of **swamp** *n*) are all double-barred in this book because they carry stigmatizing or regional labels in Webster's Third New International Dictionary.

A Thesaurus of the English Language

A

aback *adv* ***syn*** UNAWARES, short, sudden, suddenly, unanticipatedly, unaware, unawaredly, unexpectedly

abaft *adv* toward or at the stern (of a vessel) <headed *abaft* for a smoke>
syn aft, astern
rel after, back, behind
ant forward

abaft *prep* to the rear of <huddled in a nook *abaft* the chimney>
syn back of, behind

abalienate *vb* ***syn*** TRANSFER 4, alien, alienate, assign, cede, convey, deed, make over, remise, sign (over)

abandon *vb* **1** to give up without intent to return or re-claim <*abandoned* his family>
syn chuck, desert, forsake, quit, renounce, throw over
rel cast (off), discard, disuse, drop, junk, scrap; reject, repudiate
idiom have done with, leave flat, quit cold, run out on, turn one's back on (*or* upon), walk out on
con hold, keep, possess, retain; redeem, rescue, save; acquire, gain, get, procure, win; cherish, foster
ant re-claim
2 ***syn*** RELINQUISH, cede, give up, hand over, leave, resign, surrender, ||turn up, waive, yield
ant retain

abandon *n* **1** ***syn*** UNCONSTRAINT, ease, naturalness, spontaneity, unrestraint
2 carefree disregard for consequences <behave with *abandon*>
syn impulsiveness, uninhibitedness, unrestraint; *compare* UNCONSTRAINT
rel freedom, liberty, license; exuberance, heedlessness, laxity, laxness, looseness, unruliness, wildness; incontinence, licentiousness, wantonness; fun, games, play, sport
con constraint, inhibitedness, inhibition, restraint; repression, suppression
ant self-restraint

abandoned *adj* **1** ***syn*** DERELICT 1, deserted, desolate, forsaken, lorn, solitary, uncouth
2 free from moral restraint <led a thoroughly *abandoned* life>
syn dissolute, licentious, profligate, reprobate, self-abandoned, unprincipled
rel debased, debauched, depraved, perverted, riotous; incorrigible; lascivious, lecherous, lewd, wanton; corrupt, degenerate
idiom dead to honor, gone to the bad, lost to shame, rotten (to *or* at) the core
con ethical, high-principled, moral, reputable, virtuous; correct, decent, decorous, proper, seemly
ant scrupulous, upright

abase *vb* ***syn*** HUMBLE, bemean, cast down, debase, degrade, demean, humiliate, lower, sink
rel demote, diminish, downgrade, reduce; fawn, grovel, toady; cower, cringe, truckle
con elevate, lift, raise

---

syn synonym(s)   *rel* related word(s)
idiom idiomatic equivalent(s)   *con* contrasted word(s)
ant antonym(s)   * vulgar
|| use limited; if in doubt, see a dictionary
The first word in a synonym list when printed in SMALL CAPITALS shows where there is more information about the group. For a more efficient use of this book see Explanatory Notes.

ant exalt; extol

abash *vb* ***syn*** EMBARRASS 1, confound, confuse, discomfit, disconcert, discountenance, faze, rattle
rel abase, demean, humble, humiliate
idiom make one eat humble pie
ant embolden, reassure

abashment *n* ***syn*** EMBARRASSMENT, confusion, discomfiture, discomposure, disconcertion, disconcertment, unease, uneasiness

abate *vb* **1** ***syn*** ABOLISH 1, abrogate, annihilate, annul, invalidate, negate, nullify, quash, undo, vitiate
2 ***syn*** ANNIHILATE 2, abolish, blot out, eradicate, exterminate, extinguish, extirpate, root out, uncreate, wipe (out)
3 ***syn*** DECREASE, close, diminish, drain (away), dwindle, lessen, recede, reduce, taper, taper off
4 to lessen in force or intensity <the storm *abated* slowly>
syn ‖bate, die (down *or* away), ease off, ebb, fall, let up, lull, moderate, relent, slacken, subside, wane
rel decrease, diminish, dwindle, lessen, weaken
idiom run its course
con augment, expand, extend, increase; mount, rage, soar, surge
ant revive; rise

abatement *n* ***syn*** DEDUCTION 1, discount, rebate, reduction, subtraction
con enlargement, increase
ant addition

abbreviate *vb* ***syn*** SHORTEN, abridge, curtail, cut, cut back, retrench, slash
rel attenuate, extenuate
con enlarge, increase; amplify, dilate, expand
ant lengthen; extend

ABC *n* **1** *usu* **ABC's** *pl* ***syn*** ALPHABET 1, christcross-row, letters
2 *often* **ABC's** *pl* ***syn*** ALPHABET 2, elements, fundamentals, grammar, principles, rudiments

abdicate *vb* **1** to part formally or definitely with a position of honor or power <the king *abdicated* the throne in order to marry a commoner>
syn demit, renounce, resign; *compare* RELINQUISH
rel abandon, leave, relinquish, surrender; drop; withdraw
con appropriate, arrogate, confiscate; grab, seize, take over, wrest
ant assume, usurp
2 ***syn*** DISCARD, cashier, cast, jettison, reject, scrap, shed, slough, throw away, throw out
con keep, retain, treasure

abdomen *n* the part of the body between the chest and the pelvis <intense pain in the lower *abdomen*>
syn belly, ‖gut, paunch, stomach, tummy, venter
rel bay window, ‖breadbasket, corporation, pod, pot, potbelly; middle, midriff, midsection

abduct *vb* ***syn*** KIDNAP, ‖snatch, spirit (away)
rel grab, seize

abecedarian *n* ***syn*** AMATEUR 2, dabbler, dilettante, nonprofessional, smatterer, tyro, uninitiate

aberrant *adj* **1** ***syn*** ABNORMAL 1, anomalous, atypical, deviant, deviative, heteroclite, preternatural, unrepresentative, untypical
rel different, disparate, divergent; eccentric, odd, peculiar, strange; exceptional, unusual
con natural, normal, regular, typical; customary, usual, wonted
ant true (*to a type*)
2 ***syn*** ERRANT 2, devious, erring

aberration *n* **1** ***syn*** DEVIATION 1, deflection, departure, divergence, diversion, turning
rel abnormality; mistake, slip; curiosity, oddity, prodigy, rarity
con average, mean, norm; normality
ant conformity; regularity
2 ***syn*** INSANITY 1, alienation, derangement, distraction, insaneness, lunacy, madness, psychopathy, unbalance
ant soundness (*of mind*)

abet *vb* **1** ***syn*** INCITE, foment, instigate, provoke, raise, set, set on, stir (up), whip (up)
rel egg, exhort, goad, prod, spur, urge; advocate, countenance, encourage, endorse
con forbid, prevent, prohibit; debar, deter, discourage
2 ***syn*** HELP 1, aid, assist, benefact, do for, help out, stead

abettor *n* ***syn*** CONFEDERATE, accessory, accomplice, coconspirator, conspirator

abeyance *n* a state of temporary inactivity <the warm dry weather kept his asthma in *abeyance*>
syn abeyancy, cold storage, doldrums, dormancy, intermission, interruption, latency, quiescence, quiescency, suspension
rel break, interval, pause, respite
con activeness, activity, stir
ant continuance

abeyancy *n* ***syn*** ABEYANCE, cold storage, doldrums, dormancy, intermission, interruption, latency, quiescence, quiescency, suspension
ant continuancy

abeyant *adj* ***syn*** LATENT, dormant, lurking, potential, prepatent, quiescent
rel deferred, intermitted, postponed, stayed, suppressed; repressed
con refreshed, renewed, restored
ant active, operative; revived

abhor *vb* **1** ***syn*** HATE, abominate, detest, execrate, loathe
2 ***syn*** DESPISE, contemn, disdain, look down, scorn, scout
con dote (on *or* upon), like, love
ant admire

abhorrence *n* ***syn*** ABOMINATION 2, aversion, detestation, hate, hatred, horror, loathing, repugnance, repulsion, revulsion
rel distaste, repellency; dismay, horror
con affection, attachment, love

---

syn synonym(s)	*rel* related word(s)
idiom idiomatic equivalent(s)	*con* contrasted word(s)
ant antonym(s)	* vulgar

‖ use limited; if in doubt, see a dictionary
The first word in a synonym list when printed in SMALL CAPITALS shows where there is more information about the group. For a more efficient use of this book see Explanatory Notes.

ant admiration; enjoyment

abhorrent *adj* **1** ***syn*** HATEFUL 2, abominable, detestable, hateable, horrid, odious
ant admirable
2 ***syn*** REPUGNANT 1, invidious, obnoxious, repellent, revulsive
rel antipathetic; uncongenial, unsympathetic
con alluring, attractive, captivating; enticing, seductive, tempting
ant congenial

abide *vb* **1** ***syn*** STAY 2, bide, linger, remain, stick around, tarry, wait
rel adhere, cleave, cling, stick; dwell, live, reside
con go, leave, quit; move, remove, shift
ant depart
2 ***syn*** CONTINUE 1, carry through, endure, last, perdure, persist
rel linger; exist, subsist
con avoid, elude, escape, evade
ant pass
3 ***syn*** BEAR 10, brook, endure, go, stand, stomach, suffer, swallow, take, tolerate
rel accept, receive; accede, consent
idiom put up with
4 ***syn*** RESIDE 1, bide, ‖dig, dwell, hang out, live

abiding *adj* ***syn*** SURE 2, enduring, firm, never-failing, steadfast, steady, unfaltering, unqualified, unquestioning, wholehearted
rel durable, lasting, perdurable, persistent
con ephemeral, impermanent, short-lived, transient, transitory

ability *n* **1** physical, mental, or legal power to perform <he has the *ability* to accomplish whatever he sets his mind to>
syn adequacy, capability, capacity, competence, might, qualification, qualifiedness
rel address, adroitness, cleverness, dexterity; aptitude, aptness, facility, knack
idiom what it takes
con impotence, inadequacy, incapability, incompetence
ant inability
2 natural or acquired proficiency especially in a particular activity <he has unusual *ability* in planning and designing>
syn command, expertise, expertism, expertness, knack, know-how, mastership, mastery, skill
rel adroitness, deftness, efficiency, handiness, proficiency; ingenuity, resourcefulness; talent
con inadequacy, incompetence, ineffectualness, unfitness; fatuity, futility, inanity

abject *adj* ***syn*** DOWNTRODDEN, underfoot

abjure *vb* to give up (something formerly adhered to) irrevocably and usually solemnly or formally <an immigrant solemnly *abjuring* allegiance to his former country>
syn forswear, palinode, recall, recant, retract, take back, unsay, withdraw
rel disavow, disown, renounce, repudiate; abandon, desert, forsake; cede, relinquish, surrender
idiom eat one's words

ablaze *adj* **1** ***syn*** BURNING 1, afire, aflame, alight, blazing, conflagrant, fiery, flaming, flaring, ignited
2 ***syn*** ALIGHT 2, afire, aflame, aflicker, aglow

able *adj* possessed of or marked by a high level of efficiency and ability <an *able* student always near the head of his class>
syn au fait, capable, competent, good, proper, qualified, wicked
rel efficient, effective, effectual; expert, proficient, skilled, skillful; alert, clever, keen, sharp; brainy, brilliant, intelligent, smart; enterprising, go-ahead, up-and-coming
con ineffective, ineffectual, inefficient; incapable, incompetent, unqualified; fair, indifferent, mediocre; lackluster, maladroit
ant inept; unable

abnegation *n* ***syn*** RENUNCIATION, denial, renouncement, self-abnegation, self-denial, self-renunciation

abnormal *adj* **1** departing significantly from the normal or a norm <the *abnormal* rains caused flooding>
syn aberrant, anomalous, atypical, deviant, deviative, heteroclite, preternatural, unrepresentative, untypical
rel divergent, offtype; irregular, unnatural; uncustomary, unusual, unwonted; heteromorphic; paratypic
con common, familiar, natural, ordinary, regular, typical; customary, usual, wonted
ant normal
2 ***syn*** IRREGULAR 1, anomalous, deviant, divergent, off-key, unnatural, unregular

abode *n* ***syn*** HABITATION 2, commorancy, domicile, dwelling, home, house, residence, residency

abolish *vb* **1** to bring to an end often by formal or concerted action <*abolish* a tax>
syn abate, abrogate, annihilate, annul, circumduct, invalidate, negate, nullify, quash, undo, vitiate
rel cancel, disallow, disannul, repeal, rescind, revoke, vacate
idiom bring to naught, make void, set aside
con conserve, preserve, save; keep, retain
2 ***syn*** ANNIHILATE 2, abate, blot out, eradicate, exterminate, extinguish, extirpate, root out, uproot, wipe (out)
con found, institute
ant establish

abominable *adj* ***syn*** HATEFUL 2, abhorrent, detestable, hateable, horrid, odious
rel accursed, cursed; loathsome, offensive, repugnant, revolting
con applaudable, commendable
ant laudable (*as practices, customs*); delightful, enjoyable

abominate *vb* ***syn*** HATE, abhor, detest, execrate, loathe
rel curse, damn, objurgate
idiom hold in abomination, take an aversion to
con admire, regard
ant enjoy; esteem

---

syn synonym(s) — ***rel*** related word(s)
idiom idiomatic equivalent(s) — ***con*** contrasted word(s)
ant antonym(s) — * vulgar
‖ use limited; if in doubt, see a dictionary
The first word in a synonym list when printed in SMALL CAPITALS shows where there is more information about the group. For a more efficient use of this book see Explanatory Notes.

abomination *n* **1** one that is a source of utter disgust or intense dislike <found the new tax form an *abomination* of confused complexity>

syn anathema, bête noire, black beast, bugbear, detestation, hate

rel annoyance, pest, plague, trial; bogey, bugaboo, incubus

con delectation, delight, joy, pleasure; treasure

2 a feeling of extreme disgust and dislike <they hold every indulgence in *abomination*>

syn abhorrence, aversion, detestation, hate, hatred, horror, loathing, repugnance, repugnancy, repulsion, revulsion

rel contempt, despite, disdain, scorn; disfavor, dislike, disrelish, distaste

con admiration, regard, respect; fondness, liking, relish, taste; approbation, approval, countenance, favor; acceptance, tolerance

ant esteem; enjoyment

aboriginal *adj* ***syn*** NATIVE 2, autochthonous, endemic, indigenous

rel primeval, primitive, primordial, pristine; barbarian, barbaric, barbarous, savage

con advanced, progressive; civilized, cultured; sequent, successive

abortion *n* ***syn*** FREAK 2, lusus, miscreation, monster, monstrosity

abortive *adj* ***syn*** FUTILE, bootless, fruitless, ineffective, ineffectual, unavailable, unavailing, unproductive, useless, vain

rel unformed; immature, unmatured, unripe

con accomplished, completed, concluded, finished

ant consummated

abound *vb* ***syn*** TEEM, crawl, flow, pullulate, ‖sny, swarm

abounding *adj* ***syn*** ALIVE 5, overflowing, replete, rife, swarming, teeming, thronged

rel full, jammed, packed, stuffed

about *adv* **1** in every direction <looked carefully *about*>

syn around, round, round about

2 in a circuitous way or course <took the long way *about*>

syn circuitously, round about

3 ***syn*** NEARLY, all but, almost, approximately, most, much, ‖nearabout, nigh, practically, well-nigh

4 here or there without plan or order <left his tools lying *about*>

syn anyhow, any which way, anywise, around, at random, haphazard, haphazardly, helter-skelter, random, randomly

rel back and forth, hither and thither, to and fro; aimlessly, carelessly, casually

5 in the vicinity <talked to the people standing *about*>

syn near, near-at-hand, nearby

idiom close by

6 in the opposite direction <he turned *about* and saw her>

syn again, around, back, backward, in reverse, round, round about

idiom in one's course

about *prep* **1** in the vicinity of <*about* five miles to go>

syn around, circa, close on, near, nearby, nigh

idiom hard by, not far from

2 ***syn*** APROPOS, anent, as regards, as respects, as to, concerning, in re, re, respecting, touching

idiom in point of, with regard to

3 ***syn*** OVER 3, on, upon, with

4 here and there upon or within <traveled *about* the country>

syn round, through, throughout

idiom all over

about–face *n* ***syn*** REVERSAL 1, changeabout, reverse, reversement, reversion, right-about, right-about-face, turn, turnabout, volte-face

above *adv* **1** ***syn*** OVER 4, aloft, overhead

ant below

2 higher on the same page or on a preceding page <earlier examples appear *above*>

syn supra

ant below, infra

above *prep* **1** ***syn*** OVER 1, o'er

ant below

2 ***syn*** BEYOND 2, past

aboveboard *adj* ***syn*** STRAIGHTFORWARD 2, forthright, plain dealing, straight

rel open, scrupulous; artless, ingenuous, unsophisticated

con clandestine, covert, furtive, secret, surreptitious; deceitful; crooked, devious, oblique

ant underhand, underhanded

abracadabra *n* ***syn*** GIBBERISH 3, hocus-pocus, mumbo jumbo, mummery

rel mystification; argot, cant, jargon

abrade *vb* **1** to injure or flaw by frictional action <wind-driven sand *abraded* the glass>

syn chafe, corrade, erode, gall, graze, rub, ruffle, wear

rel corrode, eat away, fret; grate, rasp, scrape

2 ***syn*** CHAFE 3, excoriate, fret, gall, rub

rel burn

3 ***syn*** ANNOY 1, bother, ‖bug, chafe, exercise, fret, gall, irk, provoke, ruffle

rel disorganize, disturb, flurry, rattle; confuse, distract, perturb

con calm, relieve, soothe

Abraham's bosom *n* ***syn*** HEAVEN 2, bliss, Canaan, Civitas Dei, elysium, empyrean, New Jerusalem, nirvana, paradise, Zion

abreast *adj* **1** ***syn*** UP-TO-DATE, au courant, contemporary, down-to-date, red-hot, up, up-to-the-minute

2 ***syn*** FAMILIAR 3, acquainted, au courant, au fait, conversant, informed, up, versant, versed

abridge *vb* **1** to make less by in some manner restricting <laws that *abridge* freedom of speech>

syn curtail, diminish, lessen, minify

---

syn synonym(s) | *rel* related word(s)
idiom idiomatic equivalent(s) | *con* contrasted word(s)
ant antonym(s) | * vulgar
‖ use limited; if in doubt, see a dictionary

The first word in a synonym list when printed in SMALL CAPITALS shows where there is more information about the group. For a more efficient use of this book see Explanatory Notes.

rel limit, narrow, reduce, restrict; minimize
con augment, broaden, enlarge, extend
ant amplify
2 *syn* SHORTEN, abbreviate, curtail, cut, cut back, retrench, slash
con amplify, augment, enlarge, increase
ant expand, extend

abridgment *n* a shortened version of a larger work or treatment produced by condensing and omitting without basic alteration of intent and language <an *abridgment* of a dictionary>
syn abstract, boildown, breviary, breviate, brief, condensation, conspectus, epitome, synopsis
rel aperçu, compendium, digest, outline, précis, sketch, syllabus; capsule, summary; sum, summation, summing-up
con elaboration; paraphrase
ant expansion

abroad *adv syn* OVERSEAS

abrogate *vb* **1** *syn* ANNUL 4, discharge, dissolve, quash, vacate, void
rel abate, extinguish
con establish, found; confirm, ratify
ant institute (*as by enacting or decreeing*)
2 *syn* ABOLISH 1, abate, annihilate, annul, invalidate, negate, nullify, quash, undo, vitiate
rel extinguish; blot out, cancel, obliterate; ruin, wreck
con support, uphold
ant establish, fix (*as a right, a quality, or a custom*)

abrupt *adj* **1** *syn* PRECIPITATE 1, hasty, headlong, hurried, impetuous, precipitant, precipitous, rushing, subitaneous, sudden
rel hastened; casual, informal, unceremonious; quick, speedy
con dilatory, laggard; easy, relaxed
ant deliberate, leisurely
2 *syn* BLUFF, blunt, brief, brusque, crusty, curt, gruff, short, short-spoken, snippy
rel brisk, crisp, sharp; impetuous, quick, ready
con calm, easy, relaxed
3 *syn* STEEP 1, arduous, precipitate, precipitous, sheer, sideling, steepdown, steep-to, steep-up, ‖stickle
rel perpendicular, plumb, vertical
con inclined, slanting; flat, level, plane, smooth
ant sloping

abruptly *adv syn* SHORT 1, asudden, forthwith, sudden, suddenly

abscess *n* a localized swollen area of infection containing pus <had an *abscess* on his leg>
syn boil, carbuncle, furuncle, pimple, pustule
rel lesion, sore, trauma; botch, ulcer

abscond *vb syn* ESCAPE 1, break, ‖bunk, decamp, flee, fly, scape
rel go, leave, quit, withdraw
idiom do the disappearing act, skip out, take French leave
con render, surrender, yield
ant give (oneself) up

absence *n* the state of being absent or missing <the *absence* of news was disturbing>
syn dearth, default, defect, lack, ‖miss, privation, want; *compare* FAILURE 3
rel deficiency, drought, inadequacy, insufficiency; exigency, necessity, need; vacuum, void; nonappearance, nonattendance
con abundance, copiousness, plenty
ant presence

absent *adj* **1** not now present <all missed their *absent* friend>
syn away, gone, lacking, missing, omitted, wanting
ant present
2 *syn* ABSTRACTED, absentminded, bemused, distrait, faraway, inconscient, lost, preoccupied
rel absorbed; forgetful, heedless
con attending, hearkening, listening; considerate, thoughtful
ant attentive

absentminded *adj syn* ABSTRACTED, absent, bemused, distrait, faraway, inconscient, lost, preococupied
rel unnoticing, unobserving, unperceiving, unseeing; heedless, inattentive
idiom lost in thought
con alert; aware
ant wide-awake

absolute *adj* **1** *syn* PERFECT 2, flawless, fleckless, impeccable, indefectible, note-perfect, unflawed
rel pure, sheer, simple
con circumscribed, limited, partial, restricted
2 *syn* PURE 2, perfect, sheer, simple, unadulterated, unalloyed, undiluted, unmitigated, unmixed, unqualified
rel abstract, ideal; real, true
con imperfect, incomplete
ant mixed, qualified
3 *syn* UTTER, complete, consummate, downright, out-and-out, outright, perfect, positive, thoroughgoing, unmitigated
4 exercising power or authority without external restraint <an *absolute* monarch>
syn arbitrary, autarchic, autocratic, despotic, monocratic, tyrannical, tyrannous; *compare* TOTALITARIAN 1
rel dictatorial, magisterial; authoritarian, totalitarian; domineering, imperious, masterful; plenipotential, plenipotentiary, unlimited
con circumscribed, limited, restrained, restricted; constitutional, lawful
5 *syn* ACTUAL 2, factual, genuine, hard, positive, sure-enough
6 *syn* ULTIMATE 3, categorical
rel ideal, transcendent, transcendental; autonomous, free, independent, sovereign; boundless, eternal, infinite
con circumscribed, limited, restricted; conditional, contingent, dependent

absolutely *adv syn* EASILY 2, definitely, doubtless, doubtlessly, positively, unequivocally, unquestionably

absolution *n syn* PARDON, amnesty

---

syn synonym(s) *rel* related word(s)
idiom idiomatic equivalent(s) *con* contrasted word(s)
ant antonym(s) * vulgar
‖ use limited; if in doubt, see a dictionary
The first word in a synonym list when printed in SMALL CAPITALS shows where there is more information about the group. For a more efficient use of this book see Explanatory Notes.

rel condonation
con censure, reprehension, reprobation
ant condemnation
absolve *vb* **1** *syn* EXEMPT, discharge, dispense, excuse, let off, privilege (from), relieve, spare
2 *syn* EXCULPATE, acquit, clear, disculpate, exonerate, vindicate
rel discharge, free, release
con condemn, doom, sentence; chasten, discipline, punish
ant charge (with), hold (to)
absorb *vb* **1** to take in and make a part of one's being < *absorb* knowledge from reading >
syn assimilate, imbibe, incorporate, inhaust, insorb
rel embody, imbue, impregnate, infuse, permeate
con disgorge, eject, expel, vomit; discharge, eliminate, emit, give off, pass
ant exude, give out
2 *syn* MONOPOLIZE, consume, engross, sew up
rel concern, engage, immerse, involve, preoccupy
con diffuse, disperse, scatter
ant dissipate (*as time, attention*)
absorbed *adj* *syn* INTENT, deep, engaged, engrossed, immersed, preoccupied, rapt, wrapped, wrapped up
rel involved
idiom caught up in, up to the elbows (*or* ears) in
con apathetic, disinterested, indifferent, unconcerned; uninterested; absent, abstracted
ant distracted
absorbing *adj* *syn* ENGROSSING, consuming, monopolizing
ant irksome
abstain *vb* **1** *syn* DENY 3, constrain, curb, hold back, refrain
rel abnegate, eschew, forgo; decline, refuse, reject, spurn
idiom dispense with, do without, let alone
con pamper; gratify, regale; sate, satiate, surfeit
ant indulge
2 *syn* REFRAIN 1, forbear, keep, withhold
abstemious *adj* marked by restraint in satisfying desires (as for food, drink, or pleasure) <an *abstemious* man, little given to self-indulgence>
syn abstentious, abstinent, continent, self-restraining, sober, temperate; *compare* SOBER 3
rel self-abnegating, self-denying; ascetic, austere; sparing
con greedy, rapacious, voracious; epicurean, sybaritic, voluptuous
ant gluttonous
abstentious *adj* *syn* ABSTEMIOUS, abstinent, continent, self-restraining, sober, temperate
ant gluttonous
abstinence *n* *syn* TEMPERANCE 2, continence, sobriety

---

syn synonym(s) — *rel* related word(s)
idiom idiomatic equivalent(s) — *con* contrasted word(s)
ant antonym(s) — * vulgar
‖ use limited; if in doubt, see a dictionary
The first word in a synonym list when printed in SMALL CAPITALS shows where there is more information about the group. For a more efficient use of this book see Explanatory Notes.

rel renunciation
con gorging, sating, surfeiting; immoderateness, overdoing, unrestraint; crapulence, excess, extravagance
ant self-indulgence
abstinent *adj* *syn* ABSTEMIOUS, abstentious, continent, self-restraining, sober, temperate
ant gluttonous
abstract *adj* **1** having conceptual rather than concrete existence <the *abstract* perfect society>
syn hypothetical, ideal, theoretical, transcendent, transcendental
rel academic, impractical, utopian, visionary; speculative, undemonstrable; conceptual, notional; inconcrete
con corporeal, material, objective, phenomenal, physical; actual, factual, real
ant concrete
2 *syn* NEUTRAL, colorless, detached, disinterested, dispassionate, impersonal, poker-faced, unpassioned
abstract *n* *syn* ABRIDGMENT, boildown, breviary, breviate, brief, condensation, conspectus, epitome, synopsis
con enlargement, expansion
ant amplification
abstract *vb* **1** *syn* DETACH, disassociate, disconnect, disengage, dissociate, uncouple, unfix
rel divide, part, separate
con insinuate, interpolate, interpose
ant insert, introduce
2 *syn* STEAL 1, annex, appropriate, ‖cop, filch, lift, pilfer, pinch, purloin, swipe
abstracted *adj* withdrawn in mind and inattentive to external matters <seemed *abstracted* and remote>
syn absent, absentminded, bemused, distrait, faraway, inconscient, lost, preoccupied
rel engrossed, intent, rapt; oblivious, unmindful, unminding; heedless, inattentive
idiom in a brown study, lost in thought, lost to the world
con attentive, vigilant, watchful, wide-awake; noticing, noting, observant, seeing
ant alert
abstruse *adj* *syn* RECONDITE, acroamatic, deep, esoteric, heavy, hermetic, occult, orphic, profound, secret
rel complex, complicated, intricate, knotty; abstract, hypothetical, ideal
con clear, evident, manifest, palpable; clear, lucid, perspicuous; easy, facile, simple
ant obvious, plain
absurd *adj* *syn* FOOLISH 2, ‖balmy, crazy, harebrained, insane, loony, ‖potty, preposterous, silly, wacky
rel comic, droll, funny; asinine, fatuous, simple; irrational, unreasonable
con logical, ratiocinative, subtle
ant rational, sensible
absurdity *n* *syn* FOOLISHNESS, craziness, dottiness, folly, inanity, insanity, preposterousness, senselessness, silliness, witlessness
abundance *n* *syn* PROSPERITY 2, ease, easy street, prosperousness, thriving, well-being
rel adequacy, competence, enough, plenty, sufficiency; lavishness, prodigality
idiom enough and to spare
con deficiency, inadequacy, insufficiency, lack, paucity
abundant *adj* *syn* PLENTIFUL, ample, bounteous, bountiful, copious, generous, liberal, plenteous, plenty

rel lavish, lush, luxuriant, profuse; crammed, crowded, thick; common
idiom in good supply
con infrequent, rare, uncommon; inadequate, scanty
ant scarce

abuse *vb* **1** ***syn*** DECRY 2, belittle, depreciate, derogate, detract (from), discount, disparage, dispraise, minimize, write off
ant praise
2 to put to a bad or improper use < *abuse* the prerogatives of office >
syn misapply, misemploy, mishandle, misimprove, misuse, pervert, prostitute
rel mar, spoil; corrupt, debase, desecrate, profane
idiom make ill use of
con esteem, honor, respect
3 ***syn*** EXPLOIT 2, impose (on *or* upon), use
4 to treat without compassion and usually in a hurtful manner < parents who *abuse* children >
syn ill-treat, ill-use, maltreat, mistreat, misuse, outrage
rel damage, harm, hurt, impair, injure; oppress, persecute, wrong; manhandle, mess (up)
idiom do one dirt, do violence to
con cherish, prize, treasure; esteem, revere, reverence, venerate
ant honor, respect

abuse *n* vehemently and usually coarsely expressed condemnation or disapproval < had an unequaled vocabulary of *abuse* >
syn billingsgate, contumely, invective, obloquy, scurrility, vituperation
rel calumny, defamation, malignment, mud, vilification; cursing, profanity, swearing; berating, railing, rating, reviling
con acclaim, laudation, praise; applause, commendation, compliment
ant adulation

abusive *adj* coarse, insulting, and contemptuous in character or utterance < an *abusive* denunciation >
syn contumelious, invective, opprobrious, scurrile, scurrilous, truculent, vituperative, vituperatory, vituperous
rel affronting, insulting, offending, outraging; dirty, odious, offensive; aspersing, maligning, vilifying
con acclaiming, extolling, lauding, praising; eulogistic, panegyrical; flattering
ant complimentary; respectful

abut *vb* ***syn*** ADJOIN, border, butt (on *or* against), communicate, join, line, march, neighbor, touch, verge

abutting *adj* ***syn*** ADJACENT 3, adjoining, approximal, bordering, conterminous, contiguous, juxtaposed, touching
rel connecting, joining; impinging
con detached, disengaged; disassociated, disconnected, disjoined, parted, separated

abysm *n* ***syn*** GULF 2, abyss, chasm

abysmal *adj* **1** ***syn*** BOTTOMLESS 2, fathomless, plumbless, plummetless, soundless, unfathomable
2 ***syn*** DEEP 1, profound
rel illimitable, infinite

abyss *n* **1** ***syn*** HELL, Gehenna, hades, inferno, netherworld, perdition, pit, Sheol, Tophet, underworld
2 ***syn*** GULF 2, abysm, chasm
3 ***syn*** DEPTH 2, deepness, profoundness, profundity

academic *adj* **1** ***syn*** PEDANTIC, bookish, book-learned, booky, quodlibetic, scholastic
con ignorant, illiterate, unlettered; down-to-earth, everyday, practical, realistic, straightforward
2 ***syn*** THEORETICAL 1, closet, speculative
rel impractical, utopian, visionary; chimerical, imaginary

accede *vb* ***syn*** ASSENT, acquiesce, agree, consent, subscribe, yes
rel concur, cooperate; allow, let, permit
con decline; balk, shy, stick; expostulate, kick, object, protest; fight, oppose, resist, withstand
ant demur

accelerate *vb* ***syn*** SPEED 3, hasten, hurry, quicken, shake up, step up, swiften
rel drive, impel
idiom get going, make up for lost time
con clog, hamper; delay, detain, slow
ant decelerate; retard

accent *n* **1** ***syn*** INFLECTION, intonation, tone
2 ***syn*** EMPHASIS, accentuation, stress
rel cadence, meter, rhythm; beat, pulsation, pulse, throb

accentuation *n* ***syn*** EMPHASIS, accent, stress
con evenness, sameness, steadiness, uniformity
ant inaccentuation

accept *vb* **1** ***syn*** APPROVE 1, approbate, countenance, favor, go (for), hold (with)
rel fancy, like, relish; admire, esteem
con discountenance, disesteem, dislike, disrelish
ant reject
2 to take or sustain without protest or repining < a losing candidate must *accept* the decision of the electorate >
syn bear (with), endure, pocket, swallow, tolerate, tough (out); *compare* BEAR 10
rel acquiesce (in), agree (to *or* with), assent (to), subscribe (to); respect; bow, capitulate, yield
idiom put up with
con disavow, disown; brush (aside), deny, reject, repudiate
3 ***syn*** BELIEVE 1, ‖buy, swallow
4 ***syn*** APPREHEND 1, catch, compass, comprehend, follow, grasp, see, take, take in, understand

acceptable *adj* ***syn*** DECENT 4, adequate, all right, good, satisfactory, sufficient, tolerable, unexceptionable, unexceptional, unimpeachable
rel average, commonplace, ordinary; bearable, endurable, supportable
con insupportable, intolerable, unbearable, unendurable
ant unacceptable

---

syn synonym(s) ***rel*** related word(s)
idiom idiomatic equivalent(s) ***con*** contrasted word(s)
ant antonym(s) * vulgar
‖ use limited; if in doubt, see a dictionary
The first word in a synonym list when printed in SMALL CAPITALS shows where there is more information about the group. For a more efficient use of this book see Explanatory Notes.

acceptably *adv* ***syn*** WELL 4, adequately, amply, appropriately, becomingly, fittingly, properly, right, satisfactorily, suitably

acceptant *adj* ***syn*** RECEPTIVE 1, acceptive, influenceable, persuadable, persuasible, responsive, suasible, swayable

acceptation *n* ***syn*** MEANING 1, import, intendment, message, purport, sense, significance, significancy, signification, understanding

accepted *adj* **1** ***syn*** USUAL 1, accustomed, chronic, customary, habitual, routine, wonted
rel conventional, established, recognized; correct, orthodox, proper, right
idiom according to custom (*or* use)
con irregular, questionable, unacceptable, unconventional; incongruent, unconformable, unorthodox
2 ***syn*** ORTHODOX 1, authoritative, canonical, received, sanctioned, sound

acceptive *adj* ***syn*** RECEPTIVE 1, acceptant, influenceable, persuadable, persuasible, responsive, suasible, swayable

access *n* **1** ***syn*** ATTACK 3, fit, seizure, spell, throe, turn
rel onset; taking; pang, stitch, twinge
2 ***syn*** OUTBURST 1, burst, eruption, explosion, flare-up, gust, sally
3 ***syn*** DOOR 2, adit, admission, admittance, entrance, entrée, entry, ingress, way
rel passage, route
con departure, retreat, withdrawal
ant egress; outlet

accessible *adj* **1** ***syn*** OPEN 4, open-door, public, unrestricted
rel approachable
con limited, restricted; remote
2 ***syn*** OPEN 5, employable, operative, practicable, usable
ant inaccessible

accession *n* ***syn*** ADDITION, accretion, augmentation, increase, increment, raise, rise
ant discard

accessory *n* **1** ***syn*** APPENDAGE, adjunct, appendix, appurtenance
rel accompaniment, concomitant; accretion, addition, increment
2 ***syn*** CONFEDERATE, abettor, accomplice, coconspirator, conspirator
ant principal

accessory *adj* ***syn*** AUXILIARY, adjuvant, ancillary, appurtenant, collateral, contributory, subservient, subsidiary
rel secondary, subordinate, tributary; coincident, concomitant, concurrent; adventitious, incidental
con constitutional, ingrained, inherent, intrinsic; cardinal, fundamental, vital; essential, indispensable, necessary
ant constituent, integral

accident *n* **1** absence of positive plan or intent <we stopped there by *accident*>
syn chance, fortuity, hap, luck
rel fluke, fortune, hazard
con design, premeditation
ant intent
2 a chance event bringing injury, loss, or distress <the school was closed by an *accident* to the heating system>
syn casualty, misadventure, mischance, mishap
rel calamity, catastrophe, disaster, tragedy; misfortune; chance, destiny, fate, kismet
con foreordination, predestination

accidental *adj* resulting from chance <an *accidental* meeting>
syn casual, chance, contingent, fluky, fortuitous, incidental, odd; *compare* RANDOM, UNINTENTIONAL
rel conditional, dependent; coincident, coincidental; inadvertent, undesigned, unintended, unintentional, unmeant, unplanned, unpurposed, unwitting
con designed, intended, purposed; constitutional, inherent, intrinsic; innate
ant planned; essential

accidentally *adv* ***syn*** INCIDENTALLY 1, casually, fortuitously

acclaim *vb* ***syn*** COMMEND 2, applaud, compliment, hail, kudize, praise, recommend, ‖roose
rel cheer, root (for); exalt, magnify; glorify, honor
con berate, rate, revile; damn, execrate, objurgate; censure, denounce
ant vituperate

acclaim *n* ***syn*** APPLAUSE, acclamation, plaudits
rel homage, honor, reverence; éclat, glory
con abuse, invective, obloquy; censure, condemnation, denunciation, reprobation
ant vituperation

acclamation *n* ***syn*** APPLAUSE, acclaim, plaudits

acclimate *vb* ***syn*** HARDEN 2, acclimatize, climatize, season, toughen

acclimatize *vb* ***syn*** HARDEN 2, acclimate, climatize, season, toughen

accolade *n* ***syn*** HONOR 2, award, badge, bays, decoration, distinction, kudos, laurels

accommodate *vb* **1** ***syn*** ADAPT, adjust, conform, fit, quadrate, reconcile, square, suit, tailor, tailor-make
rel bow, defer, submit, yield; alter, change, modify, vary
con alienate, estrange
ant constrain
2 ***syn*** HARMONIZE 3, attune, conform, coordinate, integrate, proportion, reconcile, reconciliate, tune
3 ***syn*** OBLIGE 2, convenience, favor
rel cater (to), humor, indulge
con annoy, harass, harry; irk, vex, worry
ant incommode
4 ***syn*** CONTAIN 2, hold
rel encase, enclose
5 ***syn*** HARBOR 2, bestow, billet, domicile, domiciliate, entertain, house, lodge, put up, quarter

accommodations *n pl* shelter, food, and services (as at a hotel) <searched for *accommodations* as night drew near>

---

syn synonym(s)	***rel*** related word(s)
idiom idiomatic equivalent(s)	***con*** contrasted word(s)
ant antonym(s)	* vulgar

‖ use limited; if in doubt, see a dictionary

The first word in a synonym list when printed in SMALL CAPITALS shows where there is more information about the group. For a more efficient use of this book see Explanatory Notes.

syn lodging, lodgment, room and board
rel bed, room; keep; housing, shelter
idiom bed and breakfast

accompaniment *n* **1** something added to a principal thing usually to increase its impact or effectiveness <her song had a soft orchestral *accompaniment*>
syn augmentation, complement, enhancement, enrichment
rel accessory, addition, supplement; aid, assistance, help
2 an accompanying individual, situation, or occurrence <smog is an inevitable *accompaniment* of excessive numbers of automobiles>
syn associate, companion, concomitant, consort, fellow, mate
rel attendant, colleague, comrade, partner; corollary, equivalent

accompany *vb* to go or be together with <*accompanied* his wife to the theater>
syn attend, bear, ||bring, ||carry, chaperon, companion, company, conduct, consort (with), convoy, escort
rel associate, combine, join, link; defend, guard, protect, safeguard, shield; guide, lead, pilot, steer
idiom bear one company, go along with, go hand in hand with
con leave, quit, withdraw; abandon, forsake

accompanying *adj syn* CONCOMITANT, ancillary, attendant, attending, coincident, collateral, incident, satellite

accomplice *n syn* CONFEDERATE, abettor, accessory, coconspirator, conspirator
rel aider, assistant, helper; flunky, stooge

accomplish *vb syn* GAIN 1, achieve, attain, rack up, reach, realize, score, win

accomplished *adj syn* CONSUMMATE 1, finished, perfected, ripe, virtuosic
rel adept, expert, masterly, proficient; all-around, many-sided, versatile

accomplishment *n* **1** *syn* ACQUIREMENT, achievement, acquisition, attainment, finish
rel art, craft, skill; adeptness, expertise, expertness, proficiency
2 *syn* ACTION 1, act, deed, doing, thing

accord *vb* **1** *syn* AGREE 4, conform, correspond, dovetail, fit (in), go, harmonize, jibe, square, tally
rel coincide, concur; blend, coalesce, fuse, merge
con differ, disagree; compare, contrast
ant conflict
2 *syn* GRANT 1, award, concede, vouchsafe
rel allot
con deny, gainsay; refuse; detain, hold, reserve
ant withhold
3 *syn* GIVE 2, award, confer, grant

accord *n* **1** *syn* HARMONY 2, agreement, chime, concord, concordance, consonance, tune
rel affinity, attraction, empathy, sympathy; solidarity, union
idiom community of interest(s)
con conflict, contention, difference; animosity, antipathy, hostility
ant dissension, strife; antagonism
2 *syn* AGREEMENT 2, deal, understanding
3 *syn* HARMONY 1, chorus, concert, concord, consonance, tune

accordant *adj syn* HARMONIOUS 2, concordant, congruous

accordingly *adv syn* THEREFORE, consequently, ergo, hence, so, then, thereupon, thus
idiom by reason of that (*or* this), for that (*or* this) reason

according to *prep syn* BY 5, as to

accost *vb* **1** *syn* ADDRESS 7, call (to), greet, hail, salute
rel buttonhole
con ignore, overlook, slight; avoid, elude, evade, shun
2 to approach boldly or in a challenging or sometimes a defensive manner <*accosted* by a beggar who demanded money>
syn confront, face, front
rel affront, insult, offend, outrage; annoy, bother; challenge, dare, outface
idiom come face to face with, meet face to face
3 *syn* ADDRESS 4, apply (to), approach, bespeak, memorialize
rel call (to), hail, halloo; buttonhole; dog, hound, pester, worry

accouchement *n syn* CONFINEMENT 2, childbed, lying-in

account *n* **1** *syn* BILL 1, invoice, reckoning, score, statement, tab
2 *syn* USE 3, advantage, applicability, appropriateness, avail, fitness, relevance, service, usefulness, utility
con immateriality, inconsequence, insignificance, unimportance; bootlessness, fruitlessness, futility
3 *syn* WORTH 1, valuation, value
4 *syn* REGARD 4, admiration, consideration, esteem, estimation, favor, respect
rel consequence, dignity, distinction, note; reputation, repute
5 *syn* EXPLANATION 2, justification, rationale, rationalization, reason
6 *syn* SCORE 4
7 a statement of real or purported events, occurrences, or conditions <wrote an *account* of his travels>
syn chronicle, history, narrative, report, story, version; *compare* STORY 2

account *vb* **1** *syn* CONSIDER 3, deem, reckon, regard, view
rel appraise, assess, estimate, evaluate, rate; esteem
con underestimate, underrate, undervalue
2 *syn* EXPLAIN 3, explain away, justify, rationalize
rel answer, elucidate, expound, interpret

accountable *adj syn* RESPONSIBLE, amenable, answerable, liable
con absolute, arbitrary, autocratic; imperious, magisterial, masterful
ant unaccountable

accouter *vb syn* FURNISH 1, appoint, arm, equip, fit out, gear, outfit, rig, turn out

---

syn synonym(s) *rel* related word(s)
idiom idiomatic equivalent(s) *con* contrasted word(s)
ant antonym(s) * vulgar
|| use limited; if in doubt, see a dictionary
The first word in a synonym list when printed in SMALL CAPITALS shows where there is more information about the group. For a more efficient use of this book see Explanatory Notes.

rel attire, dress; adorn, deck, decorate, embellish; fix (up), prepare, ready
accouterment *n, usu* **accouterments** *pl* ***syn*** EQUIPMENT, apparatus, gear, habiliments, machinery, matériel, outfit, paraphernalia, tackle, tackling
rel appointment(s); furnishing(s); bravery, regalia, trappings
accredit *vb* **1** ***syn*** APPROVE 2, certify, endorse, OK (*or* okay), sanction
rel commend, recommend; attest, certify, vouch (for)
con belittle, deprecate, depreciate, disapprove; reject, repudiate
2 ***syn*** ASCRIBE, assign, attribute, charge, credit, impute, lay, refer
3 ***syn*** AUTHORIZE 1, commission, empower, enable, license
rel introduce, present
accretion *n* ***syn*** ADDITION, accession, augmentation, increase, increment, raise, rise
rel enlargement; attachment, joining, uniting; adjunct, appendage
accroach *vb* **1** ***syn*** ARROGATE 1, appropriate, assume, commandeer, preempt, usurp
2 ***syn*** APPROPRIATE 1, annex, arrogate, commandeer, confiscate, expropriate, preempt, seize, sequester, take
accumulate *vb* to bring together and form a store of < *accumulate* knowledge >
syn amass, cumulate, garner, hive, lay up, roll up, stockpile, store (up), uplay; *compare* HOARD
rel assemble, collect, gather, lay by, lay down, lay in; heap, mass, pile, stock; fund, hoard, treasure
idiom squirrel away
con decrease, diminish, lessen; deal, dispense, distribute, dole (out); dispel, disperse, scatter; consume, expend, spend, use, use up
ant dissipate
accumulation *n* a mass, quantity, or number that has accumulated < an *accumulation* of rubbish >
syn agglomeration, aggregation, amassment, collection, colluvies, conglomeration, cumulation, hoard, trove
rel bank, heap, mass, pile; cumulus, reserve, stock, store
con dispersal, dispersion, scattering
accumulative *adj* ***syn*** CUMULATIVE, additive, additory, chain, summative
rel aggregative, conglomerative; augmentative, multiplicative
con contractile, contractive, reducing, reductive; dispelling, dispersing, dispersive, dissipative, scattering
accuracy *n* ***syn*** PRECISION, correctness, definiteness, definitiveness, definitude, exactitude, exactness, preciseness
accurate *adj* **1** ***syn*** CORRECT 2, exact, nice, precise, proper, right, rigorous
con slipshod, slovenly; careless, heedless, lax
ant inaccurate
2 ***syn*** CERTAIN 3, authentic, dependable, reliable
accurately *adv* ***syn*** JUST 1, bang, exactly, precisely, right, sharp, ‖smack-dab, spang, square, squarely
accursed *adj* ***syn*** EXECRABLE 1, cursed, damnable
rel abhorrent, abominable, detestable, hateful, odious; offensive, repugnant, revolting
con admirable, estimable; honorable; divine, holy, sacred
ant blessed
accuse *vb* to declare one guilty of a fault or offense < *accused* her daughter of neglecting her children >
syn arraign, charge, criminate, impeach, incriminate, inculpate, indict, tax
rel blame, censure, criticize, denounce, reprobate; complain
idiom bring charges (against), point the finger at, prefer charges (against)
con absolve, acquit, exonerate, vindicate; accept, approve, endorse, sanction
ant exculpate
accustom *vb* to make something familiar or acceptable through use or experience < *accustom* oneself to city life >
syn familiarize, habituate, inure, use, wont
rel accommodate, adapt, adjust; acclimatize, harden, season
con alienate, estrange, wean; abjure, reject, repudiate; rebuff, repel, repulse, scorn
ant disaccustom
accustomed *adj* **1** ***syn*** HABITUAL 2, chronic, confirmed, habituated
2 ***syn*** USUAL 1, accepted, chronic, customary, habitual, routine, wonted
rel commonplace, everyday; conventional, regulation, standard
con infrequent, occasional, uncommon; erratic, odd, peculiar, queer, singular
ant unaccustomed
ace *n* **1** ***syn*** HAIR, hairbreadth, whisker
2 ***syn*** PARTICLE, atom, bit, crumb, iota, jot, minim, mite, molecule, speck
acedia *n* ***syn*** SLOTH 2
acerb *adj* **1** ***syn*** SOUR 1, acerbic, acetose, acid, acidulous, dry, tart
2 ***syn*** SARCASTIC, acerbic, archilochian, caustic, corrosive, ‖sarky
acerbate *vb* ***syn*** EXACERBATE, embitter, envenom
acerbic *adj* **1** ***syn*** SOUR 1, acerb, acetose, acid, acidulous, dry, tart
2 ***syn*** SARCASTIC, acerb, archilochian, caustic, corrosive, ‖sarky
acerbity *n* **1** ***syn*** ACRIMONY, asperity, mordancy
rel acidity, sourness, tartness; crabbedness, dourness, saturninity, surliness; acridity, bitterness; harshness, roughness
con blandness, gentleness, mildness, smoothness; amiability, complaisance, good nature
ant mellowness
2 ***syn*** SARCASM, causticity, corrosiveness, sarcasticness
acetose *adj* ***syn*** SOUR 1, acerb, acerbic, acid, acidulous, dry, tart

---

ache *vb* **1** ***syn*** HURT 4, pain, ‖suffer
2 ***syn*** COMPASSIONATE, commiserate, feel (for), pity, sympathize (with)
rel deplore; sorrow (over); comfort, console, solace
3 ***syn*** LONG, crave, hanker, hunger, lust, pine, sigh, thirst, yearn, yen

ache *n* ***syn*** PAIN 1, ‖misery, pang, stitch, throe, twinge
rel injury; rack
con alleviation, assuagement, mitigation, relief; comfort, ease

acheronian *adj* ***syn*** GLOOMY 3, acherontic, black, bleak, cheerless, desolate, dismal, drear, funereal, joyless

acherontic *adj* ***syn*** GLOOMY 3, acheronian, black, bleak, cheerless, desolate, dismal, drear, funereal, joyless

achieve *vb* **1** ***syn*** PERFORM 2, do, execute
rel complete, conclude, finish; conquer, overcome, surmount
idiom bring to a happy issue, bring to pass
con begin, commence, start
ant fail (in *or* to do)
2 ***syn*** GAIN 1, accomplish, attain, rack up, reach, realize, score, win
rel acquire, get, obtain, secure; actualize; arrive, come
idiom gain one's end
con depart, deviate, swerve; avoid, elude, escape, shun
ant miss

achievement *n* **1** ***syn*** FEAT 2, deed, exploit, tour de force
con omission, slighting
ant failure
2 ***syn*** ACQUIREMENT, accomplishment, acquisition, attainment, finish

Achilles' heel *n* ***syn*** SOFT SPOT 2

aching *adj* ***syn*** PAINFUL 1, afflictive, algetic, hurtful, hurting, sore
rel achy

acicular *adj* ***syn*** POINTED 1, aciculate, acuminate, acuminous, acute, cuspidate, peaked, peaky, piked, sharp

aciculate *adj* ***syn*** POINTED 1, acicular, acuminate, acuminous, acute, cuspidate, peaked, peaky, piked, sharp

acid *adj* ***syn*** SOUR 1, acerb, acerbic, acetose, acidulous, dry, tart
con bland, mild, neutral
ant sweet; alkaline, basic

acidulous *adj* ***syn*** SOUR 1, acerb, acerbic, acetose, acid, dry, tart
rel biting, cutting, sharp; piquant, pungent
con bland, mild, neutral; mellow, smooth, suave
ant saccharine

acknowledge *vb* **1** to show often grudgingly by word or deed that one knows of and agrees to or with something < *acknowledge* the justice of a complaint >
syn admit, allow, avow, concede, confess, fess (up), grant, let on, own, own up
rel disclose, divulge, reveal, tell; announce, declare, proclaim, publish
con disallow, disavow, disown, ‖nix, reject; contradict, gainsay, impugn, negate, negative
ant deny
2 to take notice of and accept as being as stated <he is generally *acknowledged* to be the leader in his profession>
syn admit, agree, recognize
rel accept, receive; concede, consider, deem, hold, view
con disregard, neglect, slight; reject, repudiate, spurn
ant ignore

acknowledgment *n* ***syn*** CREDIT 4, recognition

acme *n* ***syn*** APEX 2, apogee, capstone, climax, culmination, meridian, peak, pinnacle, summit, zenith

acoustic *adj* ***syn*** AUDITORY, audile, aural

acquaint *vb* **1** ***syn*** INTRODUCE 4, present, ‖quaint
idiom make acquainted
2 ***syn*** INFORM 2, advise, apprise, clue (*or* clew), fill in, notify, post, tell, warn, wise (up)
rel disclose, divulge, reveal; accustom, habituate
con hold, hold back, reserve, withhold; conceal, hide

acquaintance *n* **1** knowledge of something based on personal exposure <had a considerable *acquaintance* with modern poetry>
syn experience, familiarity, intimacy, inwardness
rel apprehension, grasp, ken; appreciation, awareness, consciousness
con inexperience, unfamiliarity; greenness, verdancy
2 ***syn*** FRIEND, amigo, cater-cousin, confidant, familiar, intimate, mate
rel associate, companion, comrade, crony
con outsider, stranger

acquainted *adj* ***syn*** FAMILIAR 3, abreast, au courant, au fait, conversant, informed, up, versant, versed

acquiesce *vb* ***syn*** ASSENT, accede, agree, consent, subscribe, yes
rel accommodate, adapt, adjust, reconcile; bow, coincide, concur
con balk, demur, shy (away); kick, protest, remonstrate; differ, dissent
ant object

acquiescence *n* weak or passive agreement to what is asked or demanded <his childish *acquiescence* to all claims on his time>
syn compliance, conformity, resignation
rel complaisance; submissiveness; deference
con contumaciousness, insubordination; independence, self-assurance
ant rebellion, rebelliousness

acquiescent *adj* ***syn*** PASSIVE 2, nonresistant, nonresisting, resigned, submissive, unresistant, unresisting, yielding

acquire *vb* **1** ***syn*** GET 1, annex, gain, have, land, obtain, pick up, procure, secure, win
rel achieve, reach; add
con alienate, convey, transfer; abandon, relinquish, surrender, yield
ant forfeit
2 ***syn*** EARN 1, bring in, ‖drag down, draw down, gain, get, knock down, make, win
rel accumulate, amass, collect, cumulate, garner

---

syn synonym(s) *rel* related word(s)
idiom idiomatic equivalent(s) *con* contrasted word(s)
ant antonym(s) * vulgar
‖ use limited; if in doubt, see a dictionary
The first word in a synonym list when printed in SMALL CAPITALS shows where there is more information about the group. For a more efficient use of this book see Explanatory Notes.

3 ***syn*** DEVELOP 4, form

acquirement *n* a power or skill that results from persistent endeavor and cultivation <proud of his scholastic *acquirements*>
syn accomplishment, achievement, acquisition, attainment, finish
rel accretion, addition; advance, advancement; education, erudition, knowledge
con dearth, defect, lack, privation, want

acquisition *n* ***syn*** ACQUIREMENT, accomplishment, achievement, attainment, finish
rel accession, increment; assets, belongings, means, possessions

acquisitive *adj* ***syn*** COVETOUS, desirous, grabby, grasping, greedy, itchy, prehensile
rel demanding, exacting, exigent
con eschewing, forbearing, forgoing; sacrificing
ant abnegating, self-denying

acquit *vb* **1** ***syn*** EXCULPATE, absolve, clear, disculpate, exonerate, vindicate
rel discharge, free, liberate, release; justify
con condemn, damn, doom, proscribe, sentence
ant convict
2 ***syn*** BEHAVE 1, act, bear, carry, comport, conduct, demean, deport, go on, quit

acres *n pl* ***syn*** ESTATE 3, land, manor, quinta

acrid *adj* having or being a noticeable, persistent, and usually unpleasant flavor or sometimes odor <the tonic had an *acrid* aftertaste>
syn amaroidal, astringent, austere, bitter, harsh, sharp
rel biting, caustic, cutting; piquant, pungent; cloying, oversweet, saccharine
con palatable, sapid, tasty, toothsome; delectable, delicious, luscious
ant savory

acrimonious *adj* ***syn*** ANGRY, indignant, irate, ireful, mad, wrathful, wrathy, wroth, wrothful, wrothy
rel cranky, cross, irascible, splenetic, testy; belligerent, contentious, quarrelsome
con benign, benignant, kind, kindly
ant irenic, peaceable

acrimony *n* sharpness or rancor manifested in words, manner, or disposition <the dispute was renewed with increasing *acrimony*>
syn acerbity, asperity, mordancy
rel bitterness, ill will, malevolence, malice, malignity, spite, spleen; animosity, animus, antipathy, rancor
con civility, courtesy, graciousness, politeness; diplomacy, urbanity
ant suavity

acroamatic *adj* ***syn*** RECONDITE, abstruse, deep, esoteric, heavy, hermetic, occult, orphic, profound, secret

across *adv* **1** so as to intersect the length of something <cut the board *across*>
syn athwart, crossways, crosswise
2 ***syn*** OVER 1, athwart, beyond, transversely

across *prep* from one side to the other <drew the curtain *across* the window>
syn athwart, cross, over

act *vb* **1** to present a role or performance on or as if on the stage <*acted* the part of Hamlet's father>
syn discourse, do, enact, impersonate, perform, personate, play, playact
rel characterize, portray, represent; masquerade; counterfeit, feign, sham, simulate
2 ***syn*** ASSUME 4, affect, bluff, counterfeit, fake, feign, pretend, put on, sham, simulate
idiom act a part, put on an act (of)
3 ***syn*** BEHAVE 1, acquit, bear, carry, comport, conduct, demean, deport, go on, quit
rel perform
4 to perform the duties or function of <he *acted* as president for over a year>
syn function, officiate, serve
idiom do duty (as), discharge the office (of), serve in the office (*or* capacity) of
5 to perform especially in an indicated way <the laxative *acted* quickly>
syn behave, function, operate, perform, react, take, work
idiom take effect
6 ***syn*** FUNCTION 3, go, run, work

act *n* ***syn*** ACTION 1, accomplishment, deed, doing, thing
rel exploit, feat

actify *vb* ***syn*** VITALIZE, activate, activize, energize

acting *adj* ***syn*** TEMPORARY, ad interim, interim, pro tem, pro tempore, supply

action *n* **1** something done or effected <a kindly *action*>
syn accomplishment, act, deed, doing, thing
rel discharge, effectuation, execution, fulfillment, performance; activity, behavior, operation, reaction, work; procedure, proceeding, process
2 ***syn*** BATTLE, engagement
rel affray, combat, conflict, fray
3 ***syn*** SERVICE 1, combat
4 ***syn*** SUIT 1, case, cause, lawsuit

activate *vb* ***syn*** VITALIZE, actify, activize, energize
rel arouse, awaken, rally, rouse, stir, wake, waken
ant arrest

active *adj* **1** being at work or in effective operation <marginal mines that are *active* only when prices are high>
syn alive, dynamic, functioning, live, operative, running, working
rel assiduous, busy, diligent, industrious; energetic, strenuous, vigorous; alert, wide-awake; rushing
con dormant, latent, quiescent; idle, inert, passive, supine; dead, dull, slow
ant inactive; abeyant
2 ***syn*** AGILE, brisk, brisky, catty, lively, nimble, sprightly, spry, yare, zippy
rel animated, spirited, vivacious; flexible, graceful, supple
con inert, lumpish, torpid
ant inactive
3 ***syn*** ENERGETIC 2, driving, enterprising, lively

---

syn synonym(s) | *rel* related word(s)
idiom idiomatic equivalent(s) | *con* contrasted word(s)
ant antonym(s) | * vulgar
|| use limited; if in doubt, see a dictionary
The first word in a synonym list when printed in SMALL CAPITALS shows where there is more information about the group. For a more efficient use of this book see Explanatory Notes.

rel expeditious, prompt, ready
con disinterested, indifferent, unconcerned

actively *adv* ***syn*** SERIOUSLY 1, down, earnestly, for real

activity *n* ***syn*** EXERCISE 2, exercising, exertion

activize *vb* ***syn*** VITALIZE, actify, activate, energize

actor *n* **1** one who takes part in an exhibition simulating happenings in real life <had been an *actor* on the stage and in television>
syn impersonator, mime, mimic, mummer, performer, playactor, player, thespian, trouper
2 ***syn*** PARTICIPANT, partaker, participator, party, sharer
rel mainstay, supporter, sustainer, upholder
con abettor, backer, patron, promoter

actual *adj* **1** existing in act <our *actual* intentions>
syn existent, extant
ant possible, potential
2 existing in or based on fact <problems of *actual* life>
syn absolute, factual, genuine, hard, positive, sure-enough
rel commonplace, everyday, ordinary, routine, usual; concrete, real, tangible
con conjectural, hypothetical, theoretical; putative, reputed, supposititious
ant apparent, nominal
3 ***syn*** REAL 3, indisputable, true, undeniable, unfabled, veridical
rel material, objective, phenomenal, physical; authentic, bona fide, legitimate
con abstract, transcendent, transcendental; academic, speculative, theoretical; fabulous, fictitious, mythical
ant ideal; imaginary

actuality *n* **1** ***syn*** EXISTENCE 1, being
rel actualization, externalization, incarnation, materialization; achievement, attainment
con abstraction, ideality, transcendence
ant possibility, potentiality
2 something that has existence <the *actualities* of daily life>
syn materiality, reality
rel basis, essence, substance; embodiment, incarnation
3 ***syn*** FACT 1, reality

actually *n* ***syn*** VERY 2, de facto, genuinely, really, truly, veritably

actuate *vb* **1** ***syn*** MOVE 5, drive, impel, mobilize, propel
2 ***syn*** MOBILIZE 1, circulate, set off
rel excite, galvanize, provoke; arouse, rouse, stir; vitalize

act up *vb* ***syn*** CUT UP 2, carry on, horse, horseplay

acumen *n* ***syn*** WIT 3, astucity, astuteness, discernment, discrimination, keenness, penetration, percipience, perspicacity, shrewdness
rel acuteness, sharpness
con denseness, density, slowness
ant obtuseness, obtusity

acuminate *adj* ***syn*** POINTED 1, acicular, aciculate, acuminous, acute, cuspidate, peaked, peaky, piked, sharp

acuminous *adj* ***syn*** POINTED 1, acicular, aciculate, acuminate, acute, cuspidate, peaked, peaky, piked, sharp

acute *adj* **1** ***syn*** POINTED 1, acicular, aciculate, acuminate, acuminous, cuspidate, peaked, peaky, piked, sharp
rel barbed, prickly, spiky, spined, spiny
ant blunt
2 ***syn*** SHARP 4, keen, penetrating, penetrative, quick-sighted, quick-witted, sharp-sighted, sharp-witted
rel cutting, incisive, trenchant; piercing
con crass, dense, dull, slow, stupid
ant obtuse
3 perceiving clearly and sensitively <an *acute* ear>
syn keen, perceptive, sensitive, sharp
rel observant, penetrating, probing; accurate, meticulous, precise
con imperceptive, insensitive; imprecise, inaccurate; inexact, uncritical
ant dull
4 elevated in pitch <an *acute* note>
syn argute, high, piercing, piping, sharp, shrill, thin, treble
rel penetrating; reedy, screechy, shrieky, shrilly, squeaky; tinny
con bass, deep, low
ant grave
5 ***syn*** SHARP 8, knifelike, piercing, shooting, stabbing
6 serious to the point of approaching a crisis <an *acute* housing shortage>
syn climacteric, critical, crucial, desperate, dire
rel afflictive, grave, serious; aggravated, intensified; dangerous, hazardous, menacing, perilous, precarious, threatening; exigent, urgent

adage *n* ***syn*** SAYING, byword, proverb, saw, word

adamant *adj* ***syn*** INFLEXIBLE 2, inexorable, obdurate, relentless, rigid, unbendable, unbending, uncompromising, unswayable, unyielding
rel immobile, immovable; unsubmitting
con placable, relenting, submitting; complaisant, obliging; subdued, submissive
ant yielding

adamantine *adj* ***syn*** INFLEXIBLE 2, inexorable, obdurate, relentless, rigid, unbendable, unbending, uncompromising, unswayable, unyielding
rel immobile, immovable; unsubmitting
con placable, relenting, submitting; complaisant, obliging; subdued, submissive
ant yielding

adapt *vb* to bring into correspondence or make suitable <*adapted* himself easily to the company he found himself with>
syn accommodate, adjust, conform, fit, quadrate, reconcile, square, suit, tailor, tailor-make
rel qualify, temper; acclimate, acclimatize
ant unfit

adaptable *adj* **1** ***syn*** VERSATILE, all-around, ambidextrous, many-sided, mobile, myriad-minded
2 ***syn*** PLASTIC, ductile, malleable, moldable, pliable, pliant, supple

---

syn synonym(s)	***rel*** related word(s)
idiom idiomatic equivalent(s)	***con*** contrasted word(s)
ant antonym(s)	* vulgar

‖ use limited; if in doubt, see a dictionary
The first word in a synonym list when printed in SMALL CAPITALS shows where there is more information about the group. For a more efficient use of this book see Explanatory Notes.

con intractable, irreconcilable, nonconforming, refractory, unaccommodating
ant inadaptable, unadaptable

adapted *adj* ***syn*** ASSORTED 2, conformable, fitted, matched, suited

add *vb* **1** to bring in or join on something more so as to form a larger or more inclusive whole < *added* music to his accomplishments >
syn annex, append, subjoin, superadd, take on
rel affix, attach, fasten, superimpose, tack (on); augment, enlarge, increase; burden, clutter, cumber, encumber, saddle
con abstract, detach; curtail, decrease, diminish, lessen, reduce
ant deduct, subtract
2 to combine numbers or quantities into one sum < *add* up a column of figures >
syn cast, figure, foot, sum, summate, tot, total, totalize, tote
rel calculate, compute, estimate, reckon; score, tally

added *adj* ***syn*** ADDITIONAL, another, else, farther, fresh, further, more, new, other

addendum *n, sometimes* **addenda** *pl but sing or pl in constr* ***syn*** APPENDIX 1, codicil, rider, supplement

addict *vb* ***syn*** HABITUATE 2, adjust, confirm (in), devote (to), take (to)
rel bias, dispose, incline, predispose; address, apply, direct
con alienate, estrange; detach, disengage, disincline, indispose
ant wean

addict *n* a person who by habit or strong inclination indulges in something < a science fiction *addict* >
syn aficionado, buff, devotee, fan, habitué, hound, lover, votary
rel enthusiast, fanatic, zealot; hobbyist, putterer, tinkerer

addition *n* something that tends to increase something else (as in size, number, or content) < there are several new *additions* to our staff >
syn accession, accretion, augmentation, increase, increment, raise, rise
rel accessory, adjunct, appanage, appurtenance, supplement; continuation, extension, rider; accrual, accruement, accumulation
con deduction, lessening, reduction

additional *adj* being or coming by way of addition < gave *additional* reasons to justify his position >
syn added, another, else, farther, fresh, further, more, new, other
rel accessory, adscititious, collateral, extra, supplemental, supplementary

additionally *adv* **1** ***syn*** ALSO 2, as well, besides, furthermore, likewise, more, moreover, too, yea, yet
2 ***syn*** AGAIN 4, also, besides, further, in addition, then

additive *adj* ***syn*** CUMULATIVE, accumulative, additory, chain, summative
rel component, constituent, elemental

additory *adj* ***syn*** CUMULATIVE, accumulative, additive, chain, summative

addle *vb* ***syn*** CONFUSE 2, ball up, befuddle, bewilder, ‖bumfuzzle, distract, fluster, fuddle, mix up, throw off
rel confound, dumbfound, nonplus; amaze, astound, flabbergast
idiom addle one's wits
con animate, enliven, quicken, vivify
ant refresh (*mentally*)

address *vb* **1** ***syn*** DIRECT 2, aim, cast, incline, lay, level, point, train, turn, zero (in)
2 ***syn*** SEND 1, consign, dispatch, forward, remit, route, ship, transmit
3 to occupy (oneself or one's attention or efforts) with something < *addressed* himself to the job and soon finished it >
syn apply, bend, buckle (down), devote, direct, give, throw, turn
rel associate, connect, couple, link, relate; aim, level, point
idiom bring (oneself) into relation with something, tax (one's energies) with something
con disregard, ignore, overlook
4 to communicate directly to or with < *addressed* the governor with his petition >
syn accost, apply (to), approach, bespeak, memorialize
rel speak (to), talk (with); appeal (to); apostrophize; petition
con ignore, overlook, pass up, slight; avoid, cut, disregard
5 ***syn*** TALK 7, lecture, prelect, speak
6 to affix directions for delivery < *address* a letter >
syn direct, superscribe
7 to seek the attention of usually orally and in order to gain recognition < *address* a stranger to ask directions >
syn accost, call (to), greet, hail, salute
rel converse, speak, talk
idiom attract one's attention
8 to direct one's attention to in the role of a suitor < ready to marry the first man that *addressed* her >
syn court, make up (to), pursue, spark, sue, sweetheart, woo
rel attend, escort, squire; neck, pet, romance, rush, smooch, spoon
idiom make a play for, pay (one's) addresses to, run after

address *n* **1** the quality or state of being ready or skillful < to bring off such a coup requires *address* >
syn adroitness, deftness, dexterity, dexterousness, prowess, readiness, skill, sleight; *compare* TACT
rel competence, efficiency, expertise, know-how, proficiency; craft, finesse; ingeniousness, ingenuity, resourcefulness
con inadequacy, ineptitude, ineptness, unskillfulness; awkwardness, clumsiness, gawkiness, lubberliness, stupidity

---

syn synonym(s) ***rel*** related word(s)
idiom idiomatic equivalent(s) ***con*** contrasted word(s)
ant antonym(s) * vulgar
‖ use limited; if in doubt, see a dictionary
The first word in a synonym list when printed in SMALL CAPITALS shows where there is more information about the group. For a more efficient use of this book see Explanatory Notes.

2 *syn* TACT, delicatesse, diplomacy, poise, savoir faire, tactfulness
rel dexterity, ease, facility; cleverness, readiness; affability, graciousness
con awkwardness, clumsiness, gaucheness; boorishness, churlishness
ant maladroitness
3 *syn* BEARING 1, air, comportment, demeanor, deportment, mien, port, presence, set
4 *syn* SPEECH 2, allocution, lecture, talk

adduce *vb* to bring forward for consideration <*adduce* evidence in support of a hypothesis>
syn advance, allege, cite, lay, offer, present
rel animadvert, comment, commentate, remark; document, exemplify, illustrate; prefer, proffer, propose, submit, suggest, tender

add up *vb* *syn* AMOUNT 1, aggregate, come, number, run (to *or* into), sum (to *or* into), total

add up (to) *vb* *syn* MEAN 2, connote, denote, express, import, intend, signify, spell

adept *n* *syn* EXPERT, artist, ‖dabster, master, past master, professional, proficient, virtuoso, whiz, wizard
ant bungler, incompetent

adept *adj* *syn* PROFICIENT, crack, crackerjack, expert, master, masterful, masterly, skilled, skillful
rel clever; adroit, deft, dexterous
con amateurish, dabbling, dilettantish; awkward, clumsy, maladroit
ant bungling, inapt, inept

adequacy *n* 1 *syn* ABILITY 1, capability, capacity, competence, might, qualification, qualifiedness
rel equality, satisfactoriness, sufficiency
idiom enough on the ball
ant inadequacy, inadequateness
2 *syn* ENOUGH, competence, sufficiency, sufficient

adequate *adj* 1 *syn* SUFFICIENT 1, comfortable, competent, decent, enough, satisfactory, sufficing
con meager, scanty, sparse
ant inadequate, unadequate
2 *syn* DECENT 4, acceptable, all right, common, satisfactory, sufficient, unexceptionable, unexceptional, unimpeachable, unobjectionable

adequately *adv* 1 *syn* ENOUGH 1, sufficiently
2 *syn* WELL 4, acceptably, amply, appropriately, becomingly, fittingly, properly, right, satisfactorily, suitably

adequation *n* *syn* EQUIVALENCE, equality, equatability, equivalency, par, parity, sameness

adhere *vb* *syn* STICK 2, cleave, cling, cohere
rel combine, join, link, unite
con disjoin, disunite

adherence *n* 1 a physical adhering <the close *adherence* of scales to a plant bud>
syn adhesion, bond, cling, clinging, coherence, cohesion, stickage, sticking
rel agglutination, cementation, concretion, conglutination; congelation, set, setting, solidification
con detachment, disjunction, parting, separation
2 *syn* ATTACHMENT 1, adhesion, constancy, faithfulness, fidelity, loyalty
con fickleness, inconstancy

adherent *n* *syn* FOLLOWER, cohort, disciple, henchman, partisan, satellite, sectary, sectator, supporter
rel backer, champion, upholder
con apostate, recreant; deserter, forsaker; adversary, antagonist, opponent
ant renegade

adhesion *n* 1 *syn* ADHERENCE 1, bond, cling, clinging, coherence, cohesion, stickage, sticking
ant nonadhesion
2 *syn* ATTACHMENT 1, adherence, constancy, faithfulness, fidelity, loyalty
con fickleness, inconstancy

adhesive *adj* *syn* STICKY 1, ‖claggy, ‖clarty, cloggy, gluey, gooey, gummy, stodgy

adieu *interj* *syn* GOOD-BYE, by, bye-bye, ‖cheerio, farewell, so long, ‖toodle-oo

adieu *n* *syn* PARTING, congé, farewell, good-bye, leave-taking

ad interim *adj* *syn* TEMPORARY, acting, interim, pro tem, pro tempore, supply
ant permanent

adipose *adj* *syn* FATTY 1, fat

adiposity *n* *syn* OBESITY, corpulence, fatness, fleshiness

adit *n* *syn* DOOR 2, access, admission, admittance, entrance, entrée, entry, ingress, way

adjacent *adj* 1 *syn* NEIGHBORING, close-at-hand, close-by, contiguous, near-at-hand, nearby
ant remote
2 *syn* CONVENIENT 2, close-at-hand, close-by, handy, near-at-hand, nearby
3 having a common border <the brothers built on *adjacent* lots>
syn abutting, adjoining, approximal, bordering, conterminous, contiguous, juxtaposed, touching
rel closest, nearest, next; consecutive, successive; attached, connected, joined, linked
con distant, far, remote, removed; parted, separated
ant nonadjacent

adjoin *vb* to be contiguous or adjacent to <the new suburb *adjoins* farmland>
syn abut, border, butt (on *or* against), communicate, join, line, march, neighbor, touch, verge
rel meet, run (into); end

adjoining *adj* *syn* ADJACENT 3, abutting, approximal, bordering, conterminous, contiguous, juxtaposed, touching
ant detached

adjourn *vb* 1 *syn* DEFER, delay, hold off, hold over, hold up, postpone, put off, shelve, stay, suspend
rel curb, hold back, restrain
con advance, expedite, further, promote
2 to bring to a formal close <*adjourn* the legislature>
syn dissolve, prorogate, prorogue, recess, rise, terminate
rel break up, close, disband, discontinue, disperse; stay, suspend

---

syn synonym(s) — *rel* related word(s)
idiom idiomatic equivalent(s) — *con* contrasted word(s)
ant antonym(s) — * vulgar
‖ use limited; if in doubt, see a dictionary
The first word in a synonym list when printed in SMALL CAPITALS shows where there is more information about the group. For a more efficient use of this book see Explanatory Notes.

con open; mobilize, muster, rally
ant convene, convoke

adjudge *vb* ***syn*** JUDGE 1, adjudicate, arbitrate, referee, umpire
rel accord, allot, assign, award, grant

adjudicate *vb* ***syn*** JUDGE 1, adjudge, arbitrate, referee, umpire

adjunct *n* ***syn*** APPENDAGE, accessory, appendix, appurtenance
rel accretion, addition; appanage; affix, attachment, fixture

adjust *vb* **1** ***syn*** ADAPT, accommodate, conform, fit, quadrate, reconcile, square, suit, tailor, tailor-make
rel accord, correspond; attune, harmonize
2 to alter so as to make efficient or more efficient < *adjust* a carburetor >
syn fix, regulate, tune (up)
rel correct, rectify, right; balance, stabilize, steady, trim, true; arrange, order, rig
idiom make right, put (*or* set) in order, put right (*or* to rights), set right (*or* to rights)
con disarrange, disorder, disturb, upset
ant derange
3 ***syn*** HABITUATE 2, addict, confirm (in), devote (to), take (to)

adjuvant *adj* ***syn*** AUXILIARY, accessory, ancillary, appurtenant, collateral, contributory, subservient, subsidiary
rel synergistic
con antagonistic, negating, negativing, neutralizing; hindering, impeding, obstructing
ant counteractive

ad–lib *vb* ***syn*** IMPROVISE, extemporize, improvisate

admeasure *vb* ***syn*** ALLOT, allocate, allow, apportion, assign, give, lot, mete (out)

admeasurement *n* ***syn*** SIZE 1, dimension(s), dimensionality, extent, magnitude, measure, proportion

adminicular *adj* ***syn*** CORROBORATIVE, collateral, confirmative, confirmatory, corroboratory, verificatory

administer *vb* **1** to supervise the affairs or the provision, use, or conduct of especially in the capacity of an agent or steward < *administer* justice >
syn administrate, carry out, execute, govern, render
rel conduct, direct, manage, run, supervise
2 to provide in appropriate amount < *administer* a laxative >
syn apportion, deal (out), dispense, dole (out), mete (out), portion (out), share out
rel distribute, give, give out, issue; allot, assign, consign; allocate, ration
3 ***syn*** GIVE 10, deal, deliver, inflict, strike

administrate *vb* ***syn*** ADMINISTER 1, carry out, execute, govern, render

administrator *n* ***syn*** EXECUTIVE, exec, manager, officer, official

admirable *adj* ***syn*** WORTHY 1, commendable, deserving, estimable, laudable, meritable, meritorious, praisable, praiseworthy, thankworthy

admiration *n* **1** ***syn*** WONDER 2, amaze, amazement, marveling, wonderment
rel surprise; ecstasy, rapture, transport
con aloofness, indifference, unconcern
2 ***syn*** REGARD 4, account, consideration, esteem, estimation, favor, respect
rel appreciation; adoration, reverence, veneration, worship
con detestation, hate, hatred, loathing; dislike, disrelish, distaste
ant abhorrence

admire *vb* **1** to view with an elevated feeling of pleasure < *admired* the scene that spread out before them >
syn appreciate, cherish, delight (in), relish; *compare* APPRECIATE 1
rel adore, revere, reverence, venerate, worship
idiom go into raptures over, take delight in
con disesteem, disfavor, dislike, disrelish, mislike
ant disdain
2 to hold in high esteem < *admired* his ability to get things done >
syn consider, esteem, regard, respect
rel appreciate, cherish, prize, treasure, value
idiom have (*or* hold) a high opinion of, rate highly, set (great) store by, think much (*or* highly) of
con abominate, detest, hate, loathe; contemn, despise, disdain, scorn
ant abhor

admirer *n* ***syn*** AMATEUR 1, devotee, fan, fancier, votary

admissible *adj* ***syn*** PERMISSIBLE, allowable

admission *n* ***syn*** DOOR 2, access, adit, admittance, entrance, entrée, entry, ingress, way

admit *vb* **1** ***syn*** TAKE 10, receive, take in
rel allow, permit, suffer; entertain, harbor, house, lodge, shelter
con debar, exclude, shut out; bar, block, hinder, obstruct
ant eject, expel
2 ***syn*** ACKNOWLEDGE 1, allow, avow, concede, confess, fess (up), grant, let on, own, own up
rel acquiesce, agree, assent, subscribe
ant gainsay
3 ***syn*** ENTER 2, introduce
rel induct, initiate, install; insert, interject, interpose
con debar, shut out; eject, expel, oust
ant exclude
4 ***syn*** ACKNOWLEDGE 2, agree, recognize

admittance *n* ***syn*** DOOR 2, access, adit, admission, entrance, entrée, entry, ingress, way

admix *vb* ***syn*** MIX 1, comingle, commingle, commix, immingle, immix, intermingle, intermix, merge, mingle

admixture *n* **1** an added ingredient that alters the character of something < her love had a marring *admixture* of selfishness >
syn adulterant, alloy, denaturant
rel doctor, fortification, taint; accretion, addition; bit, dash, shade, smack, spice, tinge

---

syn synonym(s)	*rel* related word(s)
idiom idiomatic equivalent(s)	*con* contrasted word(s)
ant antonym(s)	* vulgar

‖ use limited; if in doubt, see a dictionary
The first word in a synonym list when printed in SMALL CAPITALS shows where there is more information about the group. For a more efficient use of this book see Explanatory Notes.

2 ***syn*** MIXTURE, amalgam, amalgamation, commixture, composite, compound, immixture, intermixture, mix, mix-up

admonish *vb* ***syn*** REPROVE, call down, chide, lesson, monish, ‖rack back, rebuke, reprimand, reproach, tick off
rel caution, forewarn, warn
idiom have a word with
con applaud, approve, compliment
ant commend

admonishing *adj* ***syn*** MONITORY, admonitory, cautionary, cautioning, monitorial, warning

admonishment *n* ***syn*** REBUKE, admonition, chiding, rap, reprimand, reproach, reproof, wig

admonition *n* **1** ***syn*** REBUKE, admonishment, chiding, rap, reprimand, reproach, reproof, wig
2 ***syn*** WARNING, caution, caveat, commonition, forewarning, monition

admonitory *adj* ***syn*** MONITORY, admonishing, cautionary, cautioning, monitorial, warning

ado *n* ***syn*** STIR 1, bustle, flurry, furore, fuss, pother, whirl, whirlpool, whirlwind
rel effort, exertion, pains, trouble; confusion, hurly-burly, turmoil, uproar
con calm, peace, serenity, tranquillity; quiet, silence, stillness

adolescence *n* ***syn*** YOUTH 1, greenness, juvenility, puberty, pubescence, spring, springtide, springtime, youthfulness, youthhood
ant senescence

adopt *vb* to make one's own what in some fashion one owes to another < *adopt* a new style >
syn embrace, espouse, take on, take up
rel affect, assume; appropriate, arrogate, take, usurp; domesticate, naturalize
idiom adapt to one's own ends, go in for
con reject, spurn; abjure, forswear, renounce
ant discard; repudiate

adoption *n* ***syn*** ESPOUSAL 4, embracement, embracing

adorable *adj* **1** ***syn*** LOVABLE, lovesome
2 ***syn*** DELIGHTFUL, ambrosial, darling, delectable, delicious, heavenly, luscious, lush, scrumptious, yummy

adoration *n* deep, ardent, and often excessive attachment or love <the *adoration* given popular heroes>
syn idolatry, idolization, worship
rel affection, attachment, devotion, love; crush, infatuation, passion, weakness
con antipathy, aversion; disfavor, dislike, distaste
ant detestation

adore *vb* **1** ***syn*** REVERE, reverence, venerate, worship
rel extol, laud, praise
con curse, execrate
2 ***syn*** LOVE 2, affection, worship
3 to love, admire, or enjoy excessively <she *adores* and spoils her grandchildren>
syn dote (on *or* upon), idolize, worship
rel admire, esteem, love; coddle, indulge, pamper, spoil
idiom be silly over
con abhor, abominate, hate, loathe; contemn, despise, disdain, scorn
ant detest
4 ***syn*** LOVE 1, delight (in), ‖eat up

adorn *vb* to add something nonessential to enhance the appearance or beauty of <a hat *adorned* with feathers>
syn beautify, bedeck, deck, decorate, dress (up), embellish, garnish, ornament, prank, trim
rel enrich, furbish, smarten, spruce (up); bedizen, dandify, fancy up; enhance, heighten, intensify
con clear, divest, expose, strip, uncover; deface, mar, scar, spoil
ant disfigure

ad rem *adj* ***syn*** RELEVANT, applicable, applicative, applicatory, apposite, apropos, germane, material, pertinent, pointful

adroit *adj* **1** ***syn*** DEXTEROUS 1, clever, deft, handy, neat-handed, nimble
ant maladroit
2 ***syn*** SKILLFUL 2, clever, good, pretty, ‖skilly, wicked, workmanlike, workmanly
3 ***syn*** CLEVER 4, canny, ‖coony, cunning, dexterous, ingenious, ‖sleighty, slim, sly
rel astute, perspicacious, shrewd; intelligent, quick-witted, smart; artful, subtle
con dense, dull, stupid; apathetic, heavy, impassive, phlegmatic, stodgy
ant stolid

adroitness *n* **1** ***syn*** ADDRESS 1, deftness, dexterity, dexterousness, prowess, readiness, skill, sleight
2 ***syn*** ART 1, craft, cunning, dexterity, expertise, know-how, skill

adscititious *adj* ***syn*** ADVENTITIOUS, advenient, adventitial, supervenient

adulation *n* ***syn*** FLATTERY, blandishment, blarney, incense, oil, soft soap
rel acclaim, applause
ant abuse

adult *adj* ***syn*** MATURE 1, full-blown, full-fledged, full-grown, grown, grown-up, matured, ripe, ripened
rel aged
con adolescent, pubescent
ant juvenile, puerile

adulterant *n* ***syn*** ADMIXTURE 1, alloy, denaturant

adulterate *vb* to alter fraudulently usually for profit <sausage *adulterated* with cereal products>
syn debase, doctor, dope (up), load, sophisticate, weight
rel cut, dilute; denaturalize, denature, manipulate, tamper (with); defile, impurify, pollute, taint; deacon
con better, improve; augment, fortify, supplement
ant refine

adumbrate *vb* **1** to give a hint or indication of something to come <social unrest that *adumbrated* the revolt>
syn foreshadow, hint, prefigurate, prefigure, shadow (forth); *compare* SUGGEST 5

---

syn synonym(s) ***rel*** related word(s)
idiom idiomatic equivalent(s) ***con*** contrasted word(s)
ant antonym(s) * vulgar
‖ use limited; if in doubt, see a dictionary
The first word in a synonym list when printed in SMALL CAPITALS shows where there is more information about the group. For a more efficient use of this book see Explanatory Notes.

rel augur, bode, forebode, foretell, portend, presage; lower, menace, threaten; symbolize, typify
idiom cast its shadow before
2 ***syn*** FORETELL, augur, call, forecast, portend, predict, presage, prognosticate, prophesy, vaticinate
rel argue, bespeak, betoken, indicate
3 ***syn*** SKETCH, block (out), chalk (out), characterize, draft, outline, rough (out), skeleton, skeletonize
4 ***syn*** SUGGEST 5, shadow (forth)
rel denote, mean, signify
5 ***syn*** OBSCURE, becloud, cloud, darken, dim, fog, mist, murk, obfuscate, shadow

adumbration *n* ***syn*** SHADE 1, penumbra, shadow, umbra, umbrage
rel hint, intimation, suggestion; sign, symptom, token; emblem, symbol, type
con disclosure, discovery, divulgence
ant revelation

advance *vb* **1** to cause to proceed or progress toward a goal <warm rains *advanced* the crops>
syn encourage, forward, foster, further, promote, serve
rel aid, assist, help; accelerate, quicken, speed
con hinder, impede; delay, slow; curb, restrain
ant retard; check
2 to raise in rank or position <was *advanced* to the presidency>
syn elevate, prefer, promote, upgrade
rel aggrandize, exalt, raise, uplift; glorify, immortalize, magnify
ant hold back; reduce (*in rank*)
3 ***syn*** LEND, loan
4 ***syn*** ADDUCE, allege, cite, lay, offer, present
rel air, broach, expose
5 to go forward in space or time or toward an objective <prices *advanced* sharply>
syn get along, get on, march, move, proceed, progress
rel heighten, increase, intensify; develop, mature
idiom forge ahead, gain ground, get ahead, make headway (*or* progress), make one's way, make rapid strides
con retire, retreat, retrograde, withdraw
ant recede

advance *n* **1** ***syn*** PROGRESS 2, course, progression
2 forward movement especially on a course of action or development <the recent *advance* of technology>
syn advancement, anabasis, headway, march, ongoing, proficiency, progress
rel betterment, furtherance, improvement; development, evolution; breakthrough
con retreat, retrogression; ebbing, retiring, withdrawal
ant recession
3 ***syn*** OVERTURE 1, approach
rel offer, proffer

advanced *adj* **1** ***syn*** PRECOCIOUS, forward
con retrograde, retrogressive
ant backward
2 ***syn*** LIBERAL 3, broad, broad-minded, progressive, radical, tolerant, wide
rel adventurous, daring, venturesome
ant conservative

advancement *n* **1** the act of raising or the status of being raised in grade, rank, or dignity <his *advancement* in his profession was rapid>
syn elevation, preference, preferment, prelation, promotion, upgrading
rel aggrandizement, dignification, magnification, raising, uplifting
con demotion, downgrading, reduction
ant degradation
2 ***syn*** ADVANCE 2, anabasis, headway, march, ongoing, proficiency, progress

advantage *n* **1** ***syn*** BETTER 2, superiority, upper hand, victory, whip hand
2 ***syn*** WELFARE, benefit, good, interest, prosperity, well-being
3 something giving one person or side a position of superiority (as in a contest) <he had the *advantage* of greater height>
syn allowance, bulge, ‖deadwood, draw, edge, handicap, head start, odds, ‖overhand, start, vantage; *compare* BETTER 2
rel drop, jump, lead, running start; ascendancy, domination, leadership; mastery, superiority, upper hand, whip hand
idiom ace in the hole, inside track
con embarrassment, hamper, hindrance, impediment, inconvenience
ant disadvantage
4 ***syn*** USE 3, account, applicability, appropriateness, avail, fitness, relevance, service, serviceability, usefulness
rel betterment, improvement; enhancement; heightening
con damage, harm, hurt, injury
ant detriment
5 ***syn*** GOOD 1, benediction, benefit, blessing, boon, godsend

advantage *vb* ***syn*** BENEFIT, avail, profit, serve, work (for)

advantageous *adj* **1** yielding a profit <sold on very *advantageous* terms>
syn gainful, good, lucrative, moneymaking, paying, profitable, remunerative, well-paying, worthwhile
rel acceptable, agreeable, desirable, pleasing, satisfactory, satisfying
idiom in the black, paying its (own) way
con disadvantageous, unfavorable, unprofitable; damaging, hurtful
2 ***syn*** GOOD 1, benefic, beneficial, brave, favorable, favoring, helpful, propitious, toward, useful
rel remedial, salutary; conducive, contributory, implemental, instrumental; advisable, expedient
con unfavorable; inconvenient; deleterious, detrimental
ant disadvantageous

advenient *adj* ***syn*** ADVENTITIOUS, adscititious, advential, supervenient

advent *n* ***syn*** ARRIVAL 1, coming
rel approach, nearing

---

syn synonym(s) | *rel* related word(s)
idiom idiomatic equivalent(s) | *con* contrasted word(s)
ant antonym(s) | * vulgar
‖ use limited; if in doubt, see a dictionary
The first word in a synonym list when printed in SMALL CAPITALS shows where there is more information about the group. For a more efficient use of this book see Explanatory Notes.

ant exit

advential *adj* ***syn*** ADVENTITIOUS, adscititious, advenient, supervenient

adventitious *adj* coming from without and not participating in the fundamental nature of something <*adventitious* notions that have corrupted the primitive doctrine>
syn adscititious, advenient, advential, supervenient
rel accidental, casual, contingent, fortuitous, incidental
con constitutional, essential, intrinsic; inborn, inbred, innate
ant inherent

adventure *n* an undertaking or experience that involves hazard and requires boldness <recounted the *adventures* of his solitary voyage>
syn emprise, enterprise, exploit, feat, gest, venture
rel hazard, peril, risk; quest; achievement

adventure *vb* ***syn*** VENTURE 1, chance, hazard, risk, wager

adventuresome *adj* ***syn*** ADVENTUROUS, audacious, daredevil, daring, foolhardy, rash, reckless, temerarious, venturesome, venturous
ant unadventurous; cautious

adventurous *adj* courting danger or exposing oneself to danger beyond the call of duty or courage <*adventurous* boys scrambled over the cliff face>
syn adventuresome, audacious, daredevil, daring, foolhardy, rash, reckless, temerarious, venturesome, venturous
rel bold, doughty, intrepid; brash, harebrained, hotheaded, impetuous, imprudent, madcap, overconfident
con shrinking, timid, timorous; afraid, alarmed, fearful, scared; apprehensive, uneasy
ant unadventurous; cautious

adversary *n* ***syn*** OPPONENT, antagonist, anti, con, match, opposer, oppugnant
rel assaulter, attacker
con backer, supporter, upholder
ant ally

adverse *adj* **1** acting against or in a contrary direction <hindered by *adverse* forces>
syn antagonistic, anti, antipathetic, opposed, opposing, oppugnant
rel contrary, counter, counteractive; hindering, impeding, obstructive; hostile, unfriendly
con coactive, collaborative, cooperative; adjuvant, synergistic; favorable, propitious
2 being opposed to one's interests <an *adverse* balance of trade>
syn detrimental, negative, unfavorable
rel deleterious, harmful, hurtful, injurious; disadvantageous, prejudicial, unpropitious, unsatisfactory
con advantageous, favorable, positive, propitious, satisfactory

adversity *n* ***syn*** MISFORTUNE, contretemps, ‖dole, mischance, mishap, tragedy, ‖unluck
rel distress, misery, suffering; deprivation, destitution, indigence, poverty
con bliss, felicity, happiness; comfort, ease
ant prosperity

advert *vb* ***syn*** REFER 3, allude, bring up, point (out)
rel animadvert, note, notice, observe, remark
con disregard, ignore, neglect, overlook

advertent *adj* ***syn*** ATTENTIVE 1, arrect, heedful, intentive, observant, regardful

advertise *vb* **1** ***syn*** DECLARE 1, announce, annunciate, blazon, broadcast, bruit (about), proclaim, promulgate, publish, sound
rel recount, relate, report; communicate, impart; ballyhoo, promote, propagandize, publicize
con conceal, repress, suppress; bury, hide, obscure
2 ***syn*** PUBLICIZE, build up, cry, press-agent, puff
3 ***syn*** PROMOTE 3, boost, plug, push

advertisement *n* ***syn*** DECLARATION, announcement, broadcast, proclamation, promulgation, pronouncement, pronunciamento, publication
rel ballyhoo, promotion, propaganda, publicity

advertising *n* ***syn*** PUBLICITY, buildup, press-agentry, promotion, puffery

advice *n* **1** recommendation regarding a decision or course of conduct <benefited from his *advice* on study habits>
syn advisement, counsel
rel direction, guidance, instruction, teaching; admonition; caution, cautioning, forewarning, warning
2 ***syn*** NEWS, information, intelligence, speerings, tidings, word

advisable *adj* ***syn*** EXPEDIENT, politic, prudent, tactical, wise
rel commendable, desirable; becoming, seemly, suitable; sensible
ant inadvisable

advise *vb* **1** ***syn*** COUNSEL, recommend
rel caution, forewarn, warn; coax, induce, persuade, win (over)
con bedazzle, misadvise, mislead
2 ***syn*** CONFER 2, collogue, confab, confabulate, consult, huddle, parley, powwow, treat
rel deliberate
3 ***syn*** INFORM 2, acquaint, apprise, clue (*or* clew), fill in, notify, post, tell, warn, wise (up)
rel disclose, let out, reveal; communicate, impart

advised *adj* ***syn*** DELIBERATE 1, aforethought, considered, designed, premeditated, prepense, studied, studious, thought-out
rel intended, intentional, meant; knowing, purposeful, willful

advisement *n* ***syn*** ADVICE 1, counsel

advocate *n* ***syn*** EXPONENT, champion, expounder, proponent, supporter

advocate *vb* **1** ***syn*** ENCOURAGE 2, countenance, favor
2 ***syn*** SUPPORT 2, back, backstop, champion, side (with), uphold
rel justify, vindicate; advance, forward, promote
idiom hold a brief for
con assail, attack; combat, fight, oppose
ant impugn

---

syn synonym(s) ***rel*** related word(s)
idiom idiomatic equivalent(s) ***con*** contrasted word(s)
ant antonym(s) * vulgar
‖ use limited; if in doubt, see a dictionary
The first word in a synonym list when printed in SMALL CAPITALS shows where there is more information about the group. For a more efficient use of this book see Explanatory Notes.

aegis *n* **1** ***syn*** DEFENSE 1, armament, armor, guard, protection, safeguard, security, shield, ward
2 ***syn*** BACKING, auspices, patronage, sponsorship

aeneous *adj* ***syn*** BRAZEN 4, brassy

aeon *n* ***syn*** AGE 2, blue moon, coon's age, dog's age, donkey's years, eternity, long

aerial *adj* **1** ***syn*** AIRY 1, atmospheric, pneumatic
2 ***syn*** LOFTY 6, airy, skyscraping, soaring, spiring, topless, towering, towery
3 ***syn*** AIRY 3, ethereal, vaporous, vapory
rel immaterial, incorporeal; impalpable, imperceptible, imponderable

aesthete *n* ***syn*** CONNOISSEUR, cognoscente, dilettante
rel perfectionist, stickler; fussbudget, old maid
con barbarian; clod, lout, oaf

affable *adj* **1** ***syn*** GRACIOUS 1, congenial, cordial, genial, sociable, ‖sonsy
rel courteous, polite; suave, urbane; loquacious, talkative
con crabbed, glum, surly; reticent, withdrawn; silent, taciturn, uncommunicative
ant reserved
2 ***syn*** GENTLE 2, amiable, genial

affair *n* **1** something done or dealt with <trying to get at the truth of the *affair*>
syn business, concern, matter, shooting match, thing
rel care, lookout, responsibility; pie, proceeding
idiom cup of tea
2 ***syn*** BUSINESS 8, concern, lookout, occasions, palaver
3 ***syn*** LOVE AFFAIR, amour, love, romance
4 ***syn*** AMOUR 2, intrigue, liaison

affect *vb* **1** ***syn*** ASSUME 4, act, bluff, counterfeit, fake, feign, pretend, put on, sham, simulate
2 ***syn*** FREQUENT, hang around, hang out, haunt, resort

affect *vb* to produce a usually mental or emotional effect on one capable of reaction <much *affected* by the touching scene>
syn carry, get, impress, influence, inspire, move, strike, sway, touch
rel actuate, draw, drive, impel; penetrate, pierce
idiom work on

affectation *n* ***syn*** POSE 2, air(s), lugs, mannerism, prettyism
rel ostentation, pretentiousness
con ingenuousness, naiveté, naturalness, simplicity, unsophistication
ant artlessness

affected *adj* **1** ***syn*** INTERESTED, concerned, implicated, involved
2 ***syn*** SELF-CONSCIOUS, conscious, mannered
3 ***syn*** GENTEEL 3, la-di-da, ‖lardy-dardy, mincing, pretentious, stilted, too-too
4 ***syn*** PRECIOUS 4, alembicated, chichi, la-di-da, overnice, overrefined, précieux
5 ***syn*** ARTIFICIAL 3, assumed, feigned, put-on, spurious

affecting *adj* ***syn*** MOVING 2, impressive, poignant, touching
rel piteous, pitiable, pitiful; distressful, distressing, disturbing, troubling

affection *n* **1** ***syn*** FEELING 3, affectivity, emotion, passion, sentiment
rel leaning, penchant, propensity; bias, predilection; bent, faculty, turn
con aversion, hate, hatred; dislike, distaste
ant antipathy
2 ***syn*** LOVE 1, attachment, devotion, fondness
rel sympathy, tenderness, warmth; attention, concern, interest; doting, enjoying
con coolness, frigidity
ant coldness

affection *vb* ***syn*** LOVE 2, adore, worship

affection *n* **1** ***syn*** DISEASE 1, ailment, complaint, condition, disorder, ill, infirmity, malady, sickness, syndrome
rel access, attack, paroxysm, spell; derangement, disordering, disturbance
2 ***syn*** QUALITY 1, attribute, character, characteristic, feature, mark, property, savor, trait, virtue

affectionate *adj* ***syn*** LOVING, dear, devoted, doting, fond, lovesome
rel sympathetic, tender, warm
con apathetic, impassive, stolid; remote, uninterested, withdrawn
ant cold; undemonstrative

affective *adj* ***syn*** EMOTIONAL 2, emotive, moving

affectivity *n* ***syn*** FEELING 3, affection, emotion, passion, sentiment

affianced *adj* ***syn*** ENGAGED 2, betrothed, contracted, intended, plighted, ‖promised

affianced *n* ***syn*** BETROTHED, intended

affiche *n* ***syn*** POSTER, bill, handbill, placard

affiliated *adj* ***syn*** RELATED, agnate, akin, allied, cognate, connate, connatural, consanguine, incident, kindred
con autonomous, free, independent
ant unaffiliated

affiliation *n* ***syn*** ASSOCIATION 1, alliance, cahoots, combination, conjointment, conjunction, connection, hookup, partnership, tie-up

affinity *n* **1** ***syn*** ATTRACTION 2, sympathy
con antipathy, aversion; dislike, distaste; repugnance, repellency, repulsion
2 ***syn*** LIKENESS, alikeness, analogy, comparison, resemblance, semblance, similarity, simile, similitude
rel accord

affirm *vb* ***syn*** ASSERT 1, aver, avouch, avow, constate, declare, depose, predicate, profess, protest
rel attest, certify, guarantee, vouch, witness; say, state
con debate

affirmative *adj* ***syn*** POSITIVE 6

affix *vb* ***syn*** FASTEN 1, attach, fix, rivet
rel add, annex, append, subjoin
con disengage, disjoin
ant detach

afflation *n* ***syn*** INSPIRATION, afflatus, inflatus

---

syn synonym(s) ***rel*** related word(s)
idiom idiomatic equivalent(s) ***con*** contrasted word(s)
ant antonym(s) * vulgar
‖ use limited; if in doubt, see a dictionary
The first word in a synonym list when printed in SMALL CAPITALS shows where there is more information about the group. For a more efficient use of this book see Explanatory Notes.

afflatus *n* ***syn*** INSPIRATION, afflation, inflatus

afflict *vb* to inflict upon one something hard to endure <he was *afflicted* with boils>
syn agonize, crucify, excruciate, harrow, martyr, martyrize, rack, smite, strike, torment, torture, try, wring
rel annoy, harass, harry, pester, plague, press, worry; bother, irk, vex; lacerate, wound
con console, delight, gladden, please, rejoice; ease, relieve, solace
ant comfort

afflicted *adj* ***syn*** WOEFUL 1, doleful, dolent, dolorous, miserable, rueful, ruthful, sorrowful, wretched

affliction *n* **1** ***syn*** TRIAL 1, calvary, cross, crucible, ordeal, tribulation, visitation
rel mischance, mishap
con alleviation, assuagement, easement, relief
ant consolation, solace
2 ***syn*** SORROW, anguish, care, ‖dole, grief, heartache, heartbreak, regret, rue, woe
3 ***syn*** SICKNESS 1, diseasedness, disorder, illness, indisposition, infirmity, unhealth

afflictive *adj* **1** ***syn*** PAINFUL 1, aching, algetic, hurtful, hurting, sore
2 ***syn*** DEPLORABLE, calamitous, dire, distressing, grievous, heartbreaking, lamentable, regrettable, unfortunate, woeful
3 ***syn*** BITTER 2, distasteful, galling, grievous, painful, unpalatable

affluent *adj* ***syn*** RICH 1, moneyed, ‖oofy, opulent, wealthy
rel acquisitive, grasping
con poor; bankrupt, impoverished
ant impecunious; straitened

affranchise *vb* ***syn*** ENFRANCHISE, franchise

affray *n* **1** ***syn*** BRAWL 2, broil, donnybrook, fight, fracas, fray, melee, row, ruction, scuffle
2 ***syn*** CLASH 2, brush, fray, melee, mellay, scrimmage, skirmish

affright *vb* ***syn*** FRIGHTEN, alarm, awe, fright, scare, ‖spook, startle, terrify, terrorize
rel bewilder, confound
con animate, fire, inspire
ant embolden, nerve

affront *vb* **1** ***syn*** OFFEND 3, insult, outrage
rel criticize, dispraise
con compliment; laud, praise; dignify, honor
2 ***syn*** CONFRONT 1, encounter, face, meet

affront *n* a speech or an action designed to impugn the honor or worth of someone or something <her costume was an *affront* to the solemnity of the occasion>
syn contumely, despite, indignity, insult, slap
rel dishonor, flouting, offense, outrage, slight; aspersion, barb, defamation, dig
idiom slap in the face
con deference, homage, honor; adulation, compliment, flattery

aficionado *n* ***syn*** ADDICT, buff, devotee, fan, habitué, hound, lover, votary

afield *adj* ***syn*** AMISS 2, astray, awry, badly, unfavorably, wrong

afire *adj* **1** ***syn*** BURNING 1, ablaze, aflame, alight, blazing, conflagrant, fiery, flaming, flaring, ignited
2 ***syn*** ALIGHT 2, ablaze, aflame, aflicker, aglow

aflame *adj* **1** ***syn*** BURNING 1, ablaze, afire, alight, blazing, conflagrant, fiery, flaming, flaring, ignited
2 ***syn*** ALIGHT 2, ablaze, afire, aflicker, aglow

aflicker *adj* ***syn*** ALIGHT 2, ablaze, afire, aflame, aglow

à fond *adv* ***syn*** WELL 3, altogether, completely, entirely, fully, perfectly, quite, thoroughly, utterly, wholly

aforementioned *adj* ***syn*** SUCH 1, aforesaid, said

aforesaid *adj* ***syn*** SUCH 1, aforementioned, said

aforethought *adj* ***syn*** DELIBERATE 1, advised, considered, designed, premeditated, prepense, studied, studious, thought-out

afraid *adj* **1** suffering the effects of apprehension, fear, or terror <too *afraid* to even cry for help>
syn aghast, anxious, ‖ascared, fearful, frightened, scared, scary, terrified; *compare* FEARFUL 2
rel shrinking, shy, timid, timorous; cautious, chary, wary; jumpy, skittish
idiom frightened out of one's wits, in a (blue) funk, scared to death, terror stricken
con confident, dauntless, fearless; assured, collected, poised, self-possessed
ant unafraid
2 ***syn*** FEARFUL 2, apprehensive
idiom all of a twitter (*or* flutter)
ant unafraid; sanguine
3 ***syn*** DISINCLINED, averse, backward, hesitant, indisposed, loath, reluctant, uneager, unwilling, unwishful

afresh *adv* **1** ***syn*** OVER 7, again, anew, de novo, once more
2 ***syn*** NEW, anew, lately, newly, of late, recently

‖African dominoes *n pl* ***syn*** DICE, bones, ‖cubes, ‖devil's bones, ‖ivory, ‖tats

aft *adv* ***syn*** ABAFT, astern
rel hind, posterior
con ahead, before, forward
ant fore

after *adv* so as to follow in time or space <*after*, we turned toward home>
syn afterward, afterwhile, behind, by and by, infra, later, latterly, next, subsequently
rel abaft, aft, astern
idiom after a time (*or* while), in the wake of
con ahead, forward
ant before

after *prep* **1** so as to resemble or follow in some respect <named *after* his father>
syn for, from
2 later in time or lower in place or rank <*after* our discussion>
syn behind, below, following, next, since, subsequent to
con ante, ere, in advance of, preceding, prior to
ant before
3 ***syn*** BEYOND 1, outside, past, without

---

syn synonym(s) *rel* related word(s)
idiom idiomatic equivalent(s) *con* contrasted word(s)
ant antonym(s) * vulgar
‖ use limited; if in doubt, see a dictionary
The first word in a synonym list when printed in SMALL CAPITALS shows where there is more information about the group. For a more efficient use of this book see Explanatory Notes.

after *adj* **1** ***syn*** SUBSEQUENT 1, ensuing, later, posterior, postliminary, subsequential
2 ***syn*** POSTERIOR 2, back, hind, hinder, hindmost, rear, retral
con antecedent, preceding, prior

after all *adv* ***syn*** HOWEVER, howbeit, nevertheless, nonetheless, notwithstanding, still, still and all, though, withal, yet

aftereffect *n* ***syn*** EFFECT 1, aftermath, causatum, consequence, event, eventuality, issue, outcome, result, upshot
rel remainder, residual, residuum

afterlife *n* **1** ***syn*** ETERNITY 2, everlastingness, eviternity, immortality, world-without-end
2 ***syn*** HEREAFTER 2, afterworld, beyond, otherworld

afterlight *n* ***syn*** REVIEW 5, reconsideration, reexamination, retrospect, retrospection, revision

aftermath *n* ***syn*** EFFECT 1, aftereffect, causatum, consequence, event, eventuality, issue, outcome, result, upshot
rel remainder, residual, residuum

aftertime *n* ***syn*** FUTURE, afterward, by-and-by, hereafter, offing, to-be

afterward *adv* ***syn*** AFTER, afterwhile, behind, by and by, infra, later, latterly, next, subsequently

afterward *n* ***syn*** FUTURE, aftertime, by-and-by, hereafter, offing, to-be

afterwhile *adv* ***syn*** AFTER, afterward, behind, by and by, infra, later, latterly, next, subsequently

afterword *n* ***syn*** EPILOGUE 1

afterworld *n* ***syn*** HEREAFTER 2, afterlife, beyond, otherworld

again *adv* **1** ***syn*** ABOUT 6, around, back, backward, in reverse, round, round about
2 ***syn*** OVER 7, afresh, anew, de novo, once more
3 ***syn*** THEN 1, anon, when
4 as another point, fact, or instance <*again,* consider taxes>
syn additionally, also, besides, further, in addition, then; *compare* ALSO 2
idiom by the same token, into the bargain, on top of that
5 as an alternative and especially a converse <he may win and *again* he may not>
syn contra, contrariwise, contrary, contrawise, conversely, oppositely, vice versa; *compare* HOWEVER
idiom at the same time, be that as it may, just the same, on the other hand

again and again *adv* ***syn*** OFTEN, frequently, much, oft, oftentimes, ofttimes, over and over, repeatedly, time and again

against *prep* **1** directly opposite <stood *against* the crowd and shouted for order>
syn contra, facing, fronting, over against, toward, vis-à-vis
idiom counter to, face to face with
2 so as to touch <vines trained *against* the wall>
syn to, touching
idiom in contact with, next to
3 ***syn*** VERSUS 1
4 without being prevented or obstructed by <succeeded *against* grave handicaps>
syn despite, in spite of, notwithstanding, regardless of
idiom in the face of
5 ***syn*** FROM 2
6 ***syn*** APROPOS, about, as for, as to, concerning, re, respecting, touching, toward, with respect to

agape *adj* ***syn*** AGHAST 2, confounded, dismayed, dumbfounded, overwhelmed, shocked, thunderstruck

age *n* **1** ***syn*** OLD AGE, caducity, elderliness, senectitude, senescence, years
ant youth
2 *often* **ages** *pl* a long or seemingly long period of time <haven't seen her for *ages*>
syn aeon, blue moon, coon's age, dog's age, donkey's years, eternity, long
idiom month of Sundays, ‖right smart spell
con flash, instant, minute, moment, second, split second, trice
3 ***syn*** PERIOD 2, day(s), epoch, era, time

age *vb* ***syn*** MATURE, develop, grow, grow up, maturate, mellow, ‖ripe, ripen

aged *adj* **1** being in the declining phase of life <*aged* pensioners>
syn ancient, elderly, old, olden
rel pensioned (off), retired, superannuated; senior; hoary, patriarchal, venerable; doddering, senescent, senile, tottery
idiom along in years, getting on, getting on (*or* along) in years, gray with age, on one's last legs, stricken with years
con juvenile, puerile
ant youthful
2 ***syn*** ANCIENT 1, age-old, antediluvian, antique, hoary, Noachian, old, timeworn, venerable
3 ***syn*** RIPE 3, matured, mellow, ripened

ageless *adj* ***syn*** ETERNAL 4, dateless, intemporal, timeless

agency *n* ***syn*** MEAN 2, agent, channel, instrument instrumentality, instrumentation, medium, ministry, organ, vehicle
rel antecedent, cause, determinant; gear

agenda *n* ***syn*** PROGRAM 1, calendar, card, docket, programma, schedule, sked, timetable

agent *n* **1** ***syn*** MEAN 2, agency, channel, instrument, instrumentality, instrumentation, medium, ministry, organ, vehicle
rel doer, executive, executor, performer; actor, worker; activator, energizer
2 one who acts for another <diplomatic *agents* serving abroad>
syn assignee, attorney, deputy, factor, proxy; *compare* DELEGATE
rel go-between, middleman; instrument, minister, tool; commissioner, institor, proctor, procurator, representative, steward; buyer, commissionaire

---

syn synonym(s) | *rel* related word(s)
idiom idiomatic equivalent(s) | ***con*** contrasted word(s)
ant antonym(s) | * vulgar
‖ use limited; if in doubt, see a dictionary
The first word in a synonym list when printed in SMALL CAPITALS shows where there is more information about the group. For a more efficient use of this book see Explanatory Notes.

ant principal
3 ***syn*** SPY, spook, undercover man
age–old *adj* ***syn*** ANCIENT 1, aged, antediluvian, antique, hoary, Noachian, old, timeworn, venerable
agglomerate *n* ***syn*** AGGREGATE 1, agglomeration, aggregation, conglomerate, conglomeration
rel heap, mass, pile
agglomeration *n* **1** ***syn*** ACCUMULATION, aggregation, amassment, collection, colluvies, conglomeration, cumulation, hoard, trove
rel association, combination
2 ***syn*** AGGREGATE 1, agglomerate, aggregation, conglomerate, conglomeration
aggrandize *vb* **1** ***syn*** INCREASE 1, augment, beef (up), boost, enlarge, expand, extend, heighten, magnify, multiply
rel amplify, build up
2 ***syn*** EXALT 1, dignify, distinguish, ennoble, erect, glorify, honor, magnify, sublime, uprear
ant belittle
aggrandizement *n* ***syn*** APOTHEOSIS 2, deification, dignification, exaltation, glorification
aggravate *vb* **1** ***syn*** INTENSIFY, deepen, enhance, heighten, intensate, magnify, mount, redouble, rise, rouse
rel augment, enlarge, increase, multiply; aggrandize
con extenuate, palliate
ant alleviate
2 ***syn*** IRRITATE, burn (up), exasperate, gall, get, grate, nettle, peeve, pique, provoke
rel disturb, perturb, upset; annoy, bedevil
con calm, tranquilize
ant appease
aggravation *n* ***syn*** ANNOYANCE 2, bother, botheration, exasperation, pother
aǵgregate *vb* ***syn*** AMOUNT 1, add up, come, number, run (to *or* into), sum (to *or* into), total
aggregate *n* **1** a mass or body formed of particles or parts that retain their individuality <an *aggregate* of ill-planned arguments>
syn agglomerate, agglomeration, aggregation, conglomerate, conglomeration; *compare* ACCUMULATION
ant constituent, element
2 ***syn*** BODY 5, amount, budget, bulk, quantity, quantum, total
ant individual, unit; particular
3 ***syn*** WHOLE 1, all, be-all and end-all, entirety, gross, sum, sum total, total, totality, ‖tote
aggregation *n* **1** ***syn*** AGGREGATE 1, agglomerate, agglomeration, conglomerate, conglomeration
ant constituent, element
2 ***syn*** ACCUMULATION, agglomeration, amassment, collection, colluvies, conglomeration, cumulation, hoard, trove
rel backlog, reserve, stockpile
3 ***syn*** GATHERING 2, assemblage, assembly, collection, company, congeries, crowd, group, muster, ruck
aggress *vb* ***syn*** ATTACK 1, assail, assault, beset, fall (on *or* upon), storm, strike
aggression *n* **1** ***syn*** ATTACK 1, assailment, assault, offense, offensive, onfall, onset, onslaught
2 ***syn*** ATTACK 2, aggressiveness, belligerence, combativeness, fight, pugnacity
rel incursion, inroad, invasion, raid; irruption
ant resistance
aggressive *adj* marked by bold determination and readiness for conflict <an *aggressive* fighter>
syn assertive, assertory, militant, pushful, pushing, pushy, self-assertive
rel belligerent, combative, contentious, scrappy; domineering, imperious, masterful, tough; energetic, hard-hitting, strenuous, vigorous
con passive, unassertive; meek, submissive, yielding
aggressiveness *n* ***syn*** ATTACK 2, aggression, belligerence, combativeness, fight, pugnacity
aggrieve *vb* **1** ***syn*** DISTRESS 2, constrain, grieve, hurt, injure, pain
rel abuse, misuse, outrage; pain
con delight, gladden, please
2 ***syn*** WRONG, oppress, outrage, persecute
rel afflict, torment, try; annoy, harass, harry, plague, worry
con benefit, profit
aghast *adj* **1** ***syn*** AFRAID 1, anxious, ‖ascared, fearful, frightened, scared, scary, terrified
rel appalled, horrified, horror-struck; undone, unmanned
idiom scared stiff (*or* white)
2 struck by an intense emotional reaction (as surprise, disgust, or bewilderment) <*aghast* at the lack of discipline>
syn agape, confounded, dismayed, dumbfounded, overwhelmed, shocked, thunderstruck
rel agog, amazed, startled; awed, awestricken; astonished, flabbergasted, surprised
idiom struck all of a heap, taken aback, unable to believe one's eyes (*or* senses)
con acceptant, acquiescent, tolerant
agile *adj* acting or moving with easy alacrity <an *agile* mind>
syn active, brisk, brisky, catty, lively, nimble, sprightly, spry, volant, yare, zippy
rel adroit, deft, dexterous; fleet, quick, speedy; limber, lissome, lithe, supple; light-footed, tripping
con inactive, inert, passive; heavy, lethargic, logy; dull, slow, sluggish
ant torpid
agitable *adj* ***syn*** EXCITABLE, alarmable, combustible, edgy, skittery, skittish, startlish, volatile
agitate *vb* **1** ***syn*** SHAKE 4, concuss, convulse, rock
rel bounce, joggle, jounce; actuate, drive, impel, move
con lull, quiet, still
2 ***syn*** DISCOMPOSE 1, bother, discombobulate, disturb, flurry, fluster, perturb, unhinge, untune, upset
rel exasperate, irritate, peeve, provoke, rile, ruffle
ant calm, tranquilize

---

syn synonym(s) *rel* related word(s)
idiom idiomatic equivalent(s) *con* contrasted word(s)
ant antonym(s) * vulgar
‖ use limited; if in doubt, see a dictionary
The first word in a synonym list when printed in SMALL CAPITALS shows where there is more information about the group. For a more efficient use of this book see Explanatory Notes.

3 ***syn*** DISCUSS 1, argue, canvass, debate, discept, dispute, ||kick around, moot, thrash out, toss (around)
rel air, broach, ventilate; consider; assail, attack

agitation *n* ***syn*** COMMOTION 2, confusion, dither, flap, lather, pother, stew, tumult, turbulence, turmoil
rel ado, bustle, disturbance, stir
ant tranquillity

agitator *n* ***syn*** INSTIGATOR, fomenter, inciter, mover

aglow *adj* ***syn*** ALIGHT 2, ablaze, afire, aflame, aflicker
rel gleaming, glowing, shining; lucent, luminous, radiant

agnate *adj* **1** ***syn*** RELATED, affiliated, akin, allied, cognate, connate, connatural, consanguine, incident, kindred
2 ***syn*** LIKE, akin, alike, analogous, comparable, corresponding, parallel, similar, undifferentiated, uniform

agog *adj* ***syn*** EAGER, anxious, appetent, ardent, athirst, avid, breathless, impatient, keen, thirsty
rel aroused, roused, stirred; excited, galvanized, stimulated; restive; zestful
ant aloof

agonize *vb* **1** ***syn*** AFFLICT, crucify, excruciate, harrow, martyr, rack, torment, torture, try, wring
rel distress, trouble; chafe, fret, gall
2 ***syn*** WRITHE 1, squirm, toss
rel bear, endure, suffer

agonizing *adj* ***syn*** EXCRUCIATING, harrowing, racking, tearing, tormenting, torturing, torturous
rel exquisite, fierce, intense, vehement, violent

agony *n* ***syn*** DISTRESS, dolor, misery, passion, suffering
con repose, rest

agrarian *adj* ***syn*** WILD 1, agrestal, native, natural, uncultivated, undomesticated

agree *vb* **1** ***syn*** ACKNOWLEDGE 2, admit, recognize
rel allow, concede, grant, own
con except, exclude
ant deny
2 ***syn*** ASSENT, accede, acquiesce, consent, subscribe, yes
rel allow, concede, grant; receive; acknowledge, admit
con expostulate, kick, object, remonstrate; balk, demur, jib; oppose, resist, withstand
ant protest (against); differ (with)
3 to achieve harmony (as of opinion, feeling, or purpose) <they *agreed* finally on all major issues>
syn coincide, concert, concord, concur, harmonize
rel coact, cooperate, unite
idiom fall in with, hit it off with
con bicker, quarrel, squabble, wrangle; argue, debate, dispute, hassle
ant differ; disagree
4 to exist or go together without conflict or incongruity <his conclusion *agrees* with the evidence>
syn accord, check, check out, cohere, comport, conform, consist, consort, correspond, dovetail, fit (in), ||gee, go, harmonize, jibe, march, quadrate, rhyme, square, suit, tally
rel approach, equal, match, rival, touch; complete, fulfill, round out, supplement
idiom go hand in hand
con negate, negative, nullify; clash, conflict, jar
ant differ (from)

agree (with) *vb* ***syn*** SUIT 4, become, befit, fit, go (together *or* with)

agreeability *n* ***syn*** AMENITY 1, agreeableness, amiability, cordiality, enjoyableness, geniality, gratefulness, pleasance, pleasantness, sweetness and light

agreeable *adj* **1** ***syn*** PLEASANT 1, congenial, favorable, grateful, gratifying, nice, pleasing, pleasurable, pleasureful, welcome
rel delectable, delightful
ant disagreeable
2 ***syn*** CONSONANT 1, compatible, congenial, congruous, consistent, sympathetic
con conflicting, inharmonious, jarring, uncongenial

agreeableness *n* ***syn*** AMENITY 1, agreeability, amiability, cordiality, enjoyableness, geniality, gratefulness, pleasance, pleasantness, sweetness and light

agreed *adv* ***syn*** YES 1, all right, aye, OK (*or* okay), ||okeydoke, yea, ||yep

agreement *n* **1** ***syn*** HARMONY 2, accord, chime, concord, concordance, consonance, tune
ant disagreement
2 a settlement reached by parties to a dispute or negotiation <the company has reached an *agreement* with the striking workers>
syn accord, deal, understanding; *compare* CONTRACT
rel cartel, concordat, convention, entente, pact; compact, contract, covenant, treaty; engagement
3 ***syn*** TREATY, concord, convention, pact
4 ***syn*** CONTRACT, bargain, bond, compact, convention, covenant, pact, transaction

agrestal *adj* ***syn*** WILD 1, agrarian, native, natural, uncultivated, undomesticated

agrestic *adj* ***syn*** RURAL, bucolic, campestral, countrified, country, out-country, outland, pastoral, provincial, rustic

agriculture *n* the science or business of raising useful plants and animals <opening the country for *agriculture*>
syn farming, husbandry

aground *adj* being or becoming forced onto the ground or shore <the boat is *aground* and breaking up>
syn beached, grounded, stranded
idiom high and dry, on the rocks
ant afloat

ahead *adv* **1** ***syn*** BEFORE 1, ante, antecedently, beforehand, fore, forward, in advance, precedently, previous
con after
ant behind
2 further on in the direction in question <the road stretched *ahead* toward the west>
syn alee, forth, forward, onward

ahead of *prep* ***syn*** BEFORE 1, ante, ere, in advance of, preceding, prior to, to

aid *vb* ***syn*** HELP 1, abet, assist, benefact, do for, help out, stead

---

syn synonym(s) ***rel*** related word(s)
idiom idiomatic equivalent(s) ***con*** contrasted word(s)
ant antonym(s) * vulgar
|| use limited; if in doubt, see a dictionary
The first word in a synonym list when printed in SMALL CAPITALS shows where there is more information about the group. For a more efficient use of this book see Explanatory Notes.

rel alleviate, lighten, mitigate, relieve
ant impede

aid *n* **1** ***syn*** HELP 1, assist, assistance, comfort, hand, lift, relief, secours, succor, support
2 ***syn*** HELP 2, support
rel alleviation, assuagement, mitigation; backing, support
idiom a leg up
con check, curb, restraint; bar, obstacle, obstruction
ant impediment
3 ***syn*** HELPER, ancilla, assistant, attendant, help, striker
4 ***syn*** ASSISTANT 2, aide, aide-de-camp, coadjutant, coadjutor, lieutenant
rel aider, befriender, benefactor, ministrant, succorer; striker

aidant *adj* ***syn*** HELPFUL 1, aiding, assistive, serviceable

aide *n* ***syn*** ASSISTANT 2, aid, aide-de-camp, coadjutant, coadjutor, lieutenant

aide–de–camp *n* ***syn*** ASSISTANT 2, aid, aide, coadjutant, coadjutor, lieutenant

aiding *adj* ***syn*** HELPFUL 1, aidant, assistive, serviceable

ail *vb* ***syn*** TROUBLE 1, cark, distress, upset, worry
rel afflict, try
idiom be the matter (with), give one trouble
con alleviate, ease, relieve; comfort, console, solace

ailing *adj* ***syn*** UNWELL, ‖donsie, indisposed, low, mean, off-color, offish, poorly, sickly, underly
rel debilitated, enfeebled, gone, strengthless, weak; droopy, limp, sapless, spiritless
con hale, lusty, robust, rugged, vigorous

ailment *n* **1** ***syn*** DISEASE, affection, complaint, condition, disorder, ill, infirmity, malady, sickness, syndrome
2 ***syn*** UNREST, disquiet, disquietude, ferment, inquietude, restiveness, restlessness, storm and stress, Sturm und Drang, turmoil

aim *vb* **1** ***syn*** DIRECT 2, address, cast, head, lay, level, point, train, turn, zero (in)
rel concentrate, fix, focus
idiom draw a bead on, take aim
2 to have as a controlling desire something that transcends one's present capacity for attainment <from a boy he had *aimed* at high office>
syn aspire, pant
rel attempt, endeavor, essay, strive, try; design, intend, propose, purpose; covet, crave, yearn (for)
idiom have an eye to, reach for the stars, set one's eyes upon
3 ***syn*** INTEND 2, contemplate, design, mean, ‖mind, plan, propose, purpose
rel choose, desire, want, wish; expect
idiom have (*or* keep) in view, promise oneself (to)
4 ***syn*** SLANT 2, angle

aim *n* ***syn*** AMBITION 2, goal, mark, objective, quaesitum, target
rel desideratum, desire, idol, urge
idiom end in view

aimless *adj* ***syn*** RANDOM, designless, desultory, haphazard, hit-or-miss, indiscriminate, irregular, purposeless, unaimed, unplanned

air *n* **1** ***syn*** BEARING 1, address, comportment, demeanor, deportment, mien, port, presence, set
rel manner, style
2 *usu* **airs** *pl* ***syn*** POSE 2, affectation, lugs, mannerism, prettyism
rel loftiness, ostentation, pretentiousness, show; complacency, self-importance, vainglory, vanity
3 a pervading influence that colors outward appearance or apparent character <the village had an *air* of decay>
syn atmosphere, aura, feel, feeling, mood, semblance
rel character, property, quality
con basis, essence, reality
4 ***syn*** MELODY, descant, diapason, lay, measure, melisma, melodia, strain, tune, warble

air *vb* ***syn*** EXPRESS 2, give, put, state, vent, ventilate
rel discover, divulge, reveal; broadcast, declare, proclaim, publish
idiom make public, noise (*or* sound) abroad, spread far and wide

airless *adj* ***syn*** STUFFY 1, breathless, close, stifling, stivy, suffocating, sultry

airman *n* ***syn*** PILOT 2, aviator, birdman, flier, fly-boy

airy *adj* **1** of or relating to air <clouds drifting on *airy* currents>
syn aerial, atmospheric, pneumatic
rel gaseous, vaporous
2 ***syn*** LOFTY 6, aerial, skyscraping, soaring, spiring, topless, towering, towery
rel exposed, windswept; supernal
3 resembling or suggesting air especially in lightness or lack of substance <*airy* persiflage>
syn aerial, ethereal, vaporous, vapory
rel frivolous, light, volatile; rare, rarefied, tenuous, thin; dainty, delicate, diaphanous, exquisite, spirituel
con corporeal, material, physical; bulky, massive, massy
ant substantial
4 ***syn*** ELASTIC 2, bouncy, buoyant, effervescent, expansive, resilient, volatile
rel animated, high-spirited, spirited
5 ***syn*** WINDY 1, blowy, breezy, gusty

akin *adj* **1** ***syn*** RELATED, affiliated, agnate, allied, cognate, connate, connatural, consanguine, incident, kindred
2 ***syn*** LIKE, alike, analogous, comparable, consonant, corresponding, parallel, similar, undifferentiated, uniform
rel kindred; according, agreeing, conforming, harmonizing
con extraneous, foreign
ant alien

alacrity *n* promptness in responding or acting <accepted the invitation with *alacrity*>
syn dispatch, expedition, goodwill, promptitude, readiness

---

syn synonym(s) ***rel*** related word(s)
idiom idiomatic equivalent(s) ***con*** contrasted word(s)
ant antonym(s) * vulgar
‖ use limited; if in doubt, see a dictionary
The first word in a synonym list when printed in SMALL CAPITALS shows where there is more information about the group. For a more efficient use of this book see Explanatory Notes.

rel briskness, eagerness; enthusiasm, fervor, heartiness, zeal; promptness, quickness
con hesitation, procrastination, temporization, vacillation; apathy, indifference, lethargy, phlegm, sluggishness
ant dilatoriness

a la mode *adj* *syn* STYLISH, chic, dashing, exclusive, fashionable, in, modish, tonish, tony, ‖trendy

alarm *n* **1** a signal that warns or calls to action <the door's squeak gave the *alarm*>
syn alert, SOS, tocsin
rel caution, forewarning, prenotice, warning
2 *syn* FEAR 1, cold feet, consternation, dismay, dread, fright, horror, panic, terror, trepidation
rel upset; strain, stress, tension
con calm, calmness, serenity, tranquillity; equanimity, sangfroid
ant assurance; composure

alarm *vb* *syn* FRIGHTEN, affright, awe, fright, scare, ‖spook, startle, terrify, terrorize
rel amaze, astonish, surprise
idiom give one a turn
con comfort, console, solace
ant assure, relieve

alarmable *adj* *syn* EXCITABLE, agitable, combustible, edgy, skittery, skittish, startlish, volatile

albeit *conj* *syn* THOUGH, although, howbeit, much as, when, whereas, while

album *n* *syn* ANTHOLOGY, ana, analects, florilegium, garland, miscellany, omnibus, posy

alcohol *n* *syn* LIQUOR 2, aqua vitae, booze, drink, firewater, grog, ‖hooch, ‖juice, spirit(s), tipple

alcoholic *adj* *syn* SPIRITUOUS, ardent, hard, strong

alcoholized *adj* *syn* INTOXICATED 1, ‖boozy, ‖canned, disguised, drunk, inebriated, ‖lushed, muddled, pixilated, ‖plastered

alcove *n* *syn* SUMMERHOUSE, belvedere, garden house, gazebo, pagoda

alee *adv* *syn* AHEAD 2, forth, forward, onward

alehouse *n* an establishment serving primarily beer and ale <warm country *alehouses*>
syn beer garden, beer hall, ‖beerhouse, bierstube, mughouse, stube; *compare* BAR 4
rel barrelhouse, bistro, bottle club, brasserie, cabaret, café, honky-tonk, nightclub, rathskeller, roadhouse, wineshop

alembicated *adj* *syn* PRECIOUS 4, affected, chichi, la-di-da, overnice, overrefined, précieux

alert *adj* **1** *syn* WATCHFUL, open-eyed, unsleeping, vigilant, wakeful, wide-awake
rel attentive, heedful, mindful; careful
idiom all eyes and ears, on (one's) guard, on the alert
con inattentive, unmindful; aloof, detached, indifferent, unconcerned
2 *syn* INTELLIGENT 2, brainy, bright, brilliant, clever, knowing, quick-witted, ready-witted, sharp, smart
rel apt, prompt, quick, ready
con lackadaisical, languid, listless
3 *syn* LIVELY 1, animated, ‖cant, ‖canty, gay, keen, spirited, sprightly, unpedantic, vivacious
rel frisky; mercurial
idiom full of life
con inactive, indolent
ant inert

alert *n* *syn* ALARM 1, SOS, tocsin

alfresco *adj* *syn* OUTDOOR, hypaethral, open-air, out-of-door, outside

algetic *adj* *syn* PAINFUL 1, aching, afflictive, hurtful, hurting, sore

alias *n* *syn* PSEUDONYM, anonym, nom de guerre

alibi *n* *syn* EXCUSE 1, plea, pretext, ‖right

alien *adj* *syn* EXTRINSIC, extraneous, foreign
rel exotic, outlandish, strange; incompatible, incongrous, inconsonant
con cognate, kindred, related; compatible, congenial, congruous, consonant; germane, material, pertinent, relevant
ant akin; assimilable

alien *n* *syn* STRANGER, auslander, foreigner, inconnu, outcomer, outlander, outsider
con national, subject
ant citizen

alien *vb* **1** *syn* ESTRANGE, alienate, disaffect, disunify, disunite, wean
rel alter, change, convert
con accommodate, adjust, conform, reconcile
ant unite; reunite
2 *syn* TRANSFER 4, abalienate, alienate, assign, cede, convey, deed, make over, remise, sign (over)
rel give up, hand over, relinquish

alienate *vb* **1** *syn* TRANSFER 4, abalienate, alien, assign, cede, convey, deed, make over, remise, sign (over)
rel give up, hand over, relinquish
2 *syn* ESTRANGE, alien, disaffect, disunify, disunite, wean
rel alter, change, convert
con accommodate, adjust, conform, reconcile
ant unite; reunite

alienation *n* **1** *syn* ESTRANGEMENT, disaffection
2 *syn* INSANITY 1, aberration, derangement, distraction, insaneness, lunacy, madness, psychopathy, unbalance

alight *vb* to come to rest after or as if after a flight, a descent, or a fall <snowflakes *alighting* on the bare trees>
syn land, light, perch, roost, set down, settle, sit down, touch down
rel drop, fall, tumble
con arise, ascend, rise, soar

alight *adj* **1** *syn* BURNING 1, ablaze, afire, aflame, blazing, conflagrant, fiery, flaming, flaring, ignited
2 made bright by or as if by fire <her face *alight* with joy>
syn ablaze, afire, aflame, aflicker, aglow
rel bright, effulgent, fulgent, refulgent; blazing, flaming, flaring, glowing
con dark, dusky, gloomy, heavy, lowery, shadowed, shadowy

---

syn synonym(s) — *rel* related word(s)
idiom idiomatic equivalent(s) — *con* contrasted word(s)
ant antonym(s) — * vulgar
‖ use limited; if in doubt, see a dictionary
The first word in a synonym list when printed in SMALL CAPITALS shows where there is more information about the group. For a more efficient use of this book see Explanatory Notes.

align *vb* ***syn*** LINE 1, allineate, line up, range
rel adjust, fix, regulate
con unsettle

alike *adj* ***syn*** LIKE, akin, analogous, comparable, consonant, corresponding, parallel, similar, undifferentiated, uniform
con separate
ant unlike; different

alikeness *n* ***syn*** LIKENESS, affinity, analogy, comparison, resemblance, semblance, similarity, simile, similitude

aliment *n* ***syn*** FOOD 2, nourishment, nutriment, pabulum, pap, sustenance

alimentary *adj* ***syn*** NUTRITIVE 1, alimentative, nutritional

alimentation *n* ***syn*** LIVING, alimony, bread, bread and butter, keep, livelihood, maintenance, subsistence, support, sustenance

alimentative *adj* ***syn*** NUTRITIVE 1, alimentary, nutritional

alimony *n* ***syn*** LIVING, alimentation, bread, bread and butter, keep, livelihood, maintenance, subsistence, support, sustenance

alive *adj* **1** ***syn*** LIVING 1, animate, animated, vital, zoetic
con inactive, inert
ant dead, defunct
2 ***syn*** EXTANT 1, around, existent, existing, living
3 ***syn*** ACTIVE 1, dynamic, functioning, live, operative, running, working
rel fresh, green, verdant
con dormant, inactive, quiescent
ant dead, extinct
4 ***syn*** AWARE, apprehensive, au courant, awake, cognizant, conscious, knowing, sensible, sentient, witting
rel vigilant, watchful, wide-awake; intelligent, quick, quick-witted
con heedless, inattentive, oblivious, unmindful; careless, neglectful, negligent
ant blind (to)
5 full of vigorous life, animation, or activity <the streets were *alive* with shoppers>
syn abounding, overflowing, replete, rife, swarming, teeming, thronged
rel crowded, populous, thick; filled, flush, full
con barren, empty, vacant, void; unoccupied, unpopulated, untenanted

all *adj* **1** ***syn*** WHOLE 4, complete, entire, gross, outright, total
rel full, plenary
2 each member or individual of <*all* my friends came with me>
syn each, every
ant no

all *adv* **1** without exception <the money was *all* spent>
syn all in all, altogether, exactly, in toto, just, purely, quite, stick, totally, utterly, wholly
idiom in its entirety
2 ***syn*** APIECE, aside, each, ‖per, per capita, per caput

all *pron* **1** ***syn*** EVERYTHING
2 ***syn*** EVERYBODY, everyman, everyone

all *n* ***syn*** WHOLE 1, aggregate, be-all and end-all, entirety, gross, sum, sum total, total, totality, ‖tote

all–around *adj* **1** ***syn*** VERSATILE, adaptable, ambidextrous, many-sided, mobile, myriad-minded
rel complete, consummate
2 not narrowly particularized <taking an *all-around* view of the problem>
syn comprehensive, general, global, inclusive, overall, sweeping
rel broad, extensive, panoramic, wide; all-inclusive, unexcluding, unexclusive, wide-ranging; synoptic
con express, particular, specific; narrow, precise, restricted; individual, singular

allay *vb* **1** ***syn*** RELIEVE 1, alleviate, assuage, ease, lighten, mitigate, mollify
con arouse, rouse, stir; excite, provoke, stimulate; aggravate, enhance
ant intensify
2 ***syn*** CALM, balm, compose, lull, quiet, ‖quieten, settle, soothe, still, tranquilize
rel ease, soften, subdue; deaden, dull, temper; disburden, disembarrass, disencumber; deliver, free, release
con aggravate, enhance, heighten, magnify, worsen
ant intensify

all but *adv* **1** ***syn*** NEARLY, about, almost, approximately, most, much, ‖nearabout, nigh, practically, well-nigh
2 ***syn*** ALMOST 2, as good as, as much as, essentially, practically, well-nigh

allege *vb* ***syn*** ADDUCE, advance, cite, lay, offer, present
rel affirm, assert, avouch, avow, declare, profess; recite, recount, rehearse, state
con contradict, deny, gainsay, impugn, negate, negative; controvert, disprove, rebut, refute
ant contravene

alleged *adj* of questionable truth or genuineness <had doubts of the *alleged* miracle>
syn ostensible, pretended, professed, purported, so-called, supposed; *compare* SUPPOSED 1
rel credible, plausible, specious; doubtful, dubious, questionable; self-styled, soi-disant, would-be
idiom in name only
con authentic, bona fide, genuine, veritable; actual, real, true; delusory, erroneous, fallacious, false, illusory, imaginary, unreal

allegiance *n* ***syn*** FIDELITY 1, ardor, devotion, faithfulness, fealty, loyalty, piety
rel firmness; consecration, dedication; deference, homage, honor
con alienation, disaffection; disloyalty, treason

allegiant *adj* ***syn*** FAITHFUL 1, ardent, constant, ‖dinky-di, liege, loyal, resolute, staunch, steadfast, true

allegory *n* **1** a method of indirect representation (as in literature or art) of ideas or truths <by *allegory* such abstractions as love and fear can be depicted>
syn figuration, symbolism, symbolization, typification

---

syn synonym(s) ***rel*** related word(s)
idiom idiomatic equivalent(s) ***con*** contrasted word(s)
ant antonym(s) * vulgar
‖ use limited; if in doubt, see a dictionary
The first word in a synonym list when printed in SMALL CAPITALS shows where there is more information about the group. For a more efficient use of this book see Explanatory Notes.

2 a literary form that tells a story to present a truth or enforce a moral <Orwell's *Animal Farm* is a well-known English *allegory*>
syn apologue, fable, myth, parable; *compare* MYTH 1
allergy *n* ***syn*** ANTIPATHY 2, aversion, dyspathy
rel rejection, repulsion, revulsion
con affinity, attraction, sympathy
alleviate *vb* ***syn*** RELIEVE 1, allay, assuage, ease, lighten, mitigate, mollify
rel cure, remedy
idiom temper the wind to the shorn lamb
con augment, heighten, intensify
ant aggravate
alleviation *n* ***syn*** EASE 3, easement, mitigation, relief
all–fired *adj* ***syn*** UTTER, blamed, blasted, blessed, dashed, deuced, doggone, goldarn, hell-fired, infernal
alliance *n* **1** ***syn*** ASSOCIATION 1, affiliation, cahoots, combination, conjointment, conjunction, connection, hookup, partnership, tie-up
2 an association (as of nations) for a common object <a world *alliance* in support of peace>
syn anschluss, coalition, confederacy, confederation, federation, league, union; *compare* UNIFICATION
rel association, club, order, society
allied *adj* ***syn*** RELATED, affiliated, agnate, akin, cognate, connate, connatural, consanguine, incident, kindred
rel linked, united; parallel, similar
con alien, extraneous, foreign; discrete, separate, several
ant unallied
all in *adj* ***syn*** EFFETE 2, bleary, depleted, drained, exhausted, far-gone, spent, used up, washed-out, worn-out
idiom at last gasp
all in all *adv* **1** ***syn*** ALL 1, altogether, exactly, in toto, just, purely, quite, totally, utterly, wholly
2 ***syn*** ALTOGETHER 3, by and large, en masse, generally, on the whole
allineate *vb* ***syn*** LINE 1, align, line up, range
allness *n* ***syn*** ENTIRETY 1, completeness, entireness, oneness, totality, wholeness
allocate *vb* **1** ***syn*** ALLOT, admeasure, allow, apportion, assign, give, lot, mete (out)
con reserve, sequester, stockpile
2 ***syn*** DESIGNATE 3, earmark
allocution *n* ***syn*** SPEECH 2, address, lecture, talk
allot *vb* to give as one's share, portion, role, or place <*allotted* himself a daily hour for exercise>
syn admeasure, allocate, allow, apportion, assign, give, lot, mete (out)
rel deal (out), dispense, distribute, dole (out); equip, fit out, furnish; accord, grant, vouchsafe; appoint, ordain, prescribe

---

syn synonym(s) | *rel* related word(s)
idiom idiomatic equivalent(s) | *con* contrasted word(s)
ant antonym(s) | * vulgar
‖ use limited; if in doubt, see a dictionary
The first word in a synonym list when printed in SMALL CAPITALS shows where there is more information about the group. For a more efficient use of this book see Explanatory Notes.

con detain, hold, hold back, keep, retain, withhold; appropriate, arrogate, confiscate
allotment *n* **1** ***syn*** SHARE 1, allowance, bite, cut, lot, part, partage, portion, quota, slice
2 ***syn*** RATION, allowance, apportionment, measure, meed, part, portion, quantum, quota, share
all–out *adj* ***syn*** TOTAL 5, full-blown, full-out, full-scale, totalitarian, unlimited
all over *adv* ***syn*** EVERYWHERE 1, all round (*or* all around), everyplace, far and near, far and wide, high and low, overall, throughout
allover *adj* ***syn*** OMNIPRESENT, ubiquitous, universal
‖**all–overs** *n pl* ***syn*** JITTERS, dither, heebie-jeebies, ‖jim-jams, ‖jimmies, jumps, shakes, shivers, whim-whams, willies
allow *vb* **1** ***syn*** ALLOT, admeasure, allocate, apportion, assign, give, lot, mete (out)
rel bestow, confer
con refuse
2 ***syn*** ACKNOWLEDGE 1, admit, avow, concede, confess, fess (up), grant, let on, own, own up
rel accede, acquiesce, assent
con confute, refute, reject
ant disallow
3 ***syn*** LET 2, have, leave, permit, suffer
rel brook, endure, stand, tolerate; defer, submit, yield
con avert, prevent, ward (off)
ant inhibit
allowable *adj* ***syn*** PERMISSIBLE, admissible
allowance *n* **1** ***syn*** RATION, allotment, apportionment, measure, meed, part, portion, quantum, quota, share
rel assignment; appropriation, grant, subsidy
2 ***syn*** SHARE 1, allotment, bite, cut, lot, part, partage, portion, quota, slice
3 ***syn*** ADVANTAGE 3, bulge, ‖deadwood, edge, handicap, head start, odds, ‖overhand, start, vantage
rel aid, assistance, help; bounty, grant, subsidy
4 ***syn*** PERMISSION, authorization, consent, leave, permit, sanction, sufferance
rel countenance, favor; indulgence, toleration
con refusal, rejection; contradiction, contravention, negation
5 a taking into account of extenuating circumstances or of contingencies <we must make *allowance* for the inexperience of youth>
syn concession
rel accommodation, adaptation, adjustment; extenuation, mitigation, palliation
alloy *n* **1** ***syn*** ADMIXTURE 1, adulterant, denaturant
2 ***syn*** MIXTURE, admixture, amalgam, amalgamation, blend, composite, compound, fusion, interfusion, intermixture
all–powerful *adj* ***syn*** OMNIPOTENT, almighty
all right *adv* ***syn*** YES 1, agreed, aye, OK (*or* okay), ‖okeydoke, yea, ‖yep
all right *adj* ***syn*** DECENT 4, acceptable, adequate, good, satisfactory, sufficient, tolerable, unexceptionable, unexceptional, unimpeachable
all round (*or* **all around**) *adv* ***syn*** EVERYWHERE 1, all over, everyplace, far and near, far and wide, high and low, overall, throughout
all there *adj* ***syn*** SANE 2, compos mentis, lucid, normal, right

all told *adv* ***syn*** ALTOGETHER 3, in all, quite

allude *vb* ***syn*** REFER 3, advert, bring up, point (out)
rel hint, imply, intimate, suggest

allure *vb* **1** ***syn*** ATTRACT 1, bewitch, captivate, charm, draw, enchant, fascinate, magnetize, take, wile
rel delude; woo
con avoid, elude, eschew, shun; alienate, disaffect, estrange, wean
2 ***syn*** LURE, bait, decoy, entice, entrap, inveigle, lead on, seduce, tempt, toll

allure *n* ***syn*** CHARM 3, appeal, charisma, fascination, glamour, magnetism, witchcraft, witchery

allurement *n* **1** ***syn*** ATTRACTION 1, appeal, attractiveness, call, draw, drawing power, lure, pull, seduction
2 ***syn*** LURE 2, bait, come-on, decoy, enticement, inveiglement, seducement, snare, temptation, trap

alluring *adj* ***syn*** ATTRACTIVE 1, appealing, bewitching, captivating, charming, enchanting, fascinating, glamorous, seductive, siren
rel appetizing; beguiling, delusive
con repellent; disagreeable, displeasing, uninviting, unlikable, unpleasant
ant repulsive

almighty *adj* ***syn*** OMNIPOTENT, all-powerful

almost *adv* **1** ***syn*** NEARLY, about, all but, approximately, most, much, ‖nearabout, nigh, practically, well-nigh
2 not actually but in effect <he paid *almost* nothing for it>
syn all but, as good as, as much as, essentially, practically, well-nigh; *compare* VIRTUALLY
idiom for all practical purposes, in effect, just about, to all intents and purposes

alms *n pl* ***syn*** DONATION, benefaction, beneficence, charity, contribution, offering

aloft *adv* ***syn*** OVER 4, above, overhead
rel high; skyward, upward
idiom in the clouds

alone *adj* **1** separated from others <the house was *alone* on a windy ridge>
syn apart, detached, isolate, isolated, removed, unaccompanied
rel out-of-the-way, private, remote, retired, secluded, withdrawn
idiom off the beaten track
con adjacent, close-by, near-at-hand, nearly, neighboring, nigh
2 ***syn*** LONE 1, lonely, lonesome, solitary
3 having no equal or rival and being single in kind or excellence <a drug *alone* in its curative powers>
syn matchless, only, peerless, unequaled, unique, unmatched, unparalleled, unrivaled; *compare* SUPREME
rel inimitable; incomparable, unexcelled, unsurpassed; excellent, good, superior
idiom second to none
con common, commonplace, everyday, ordinary, usual; accustomed, conventional, customary, regular
4 ***syn*** ONLY 2, lone, singular, sole, solitary, solo, unexampled, unique, unrepeatable

alone *adv* ***syn*** ONLY 1, but, entirely, exclusively, solely

aloneness *n* ***syn*** SOLITUDE, isolation, loneness, solitariness

along *adv* **1** so as to make forward progress <hurrying *along* toward town>
syn forth, forward, on, onward; *compare* AHEAD 2
2 ***syn*** ALSO 2, additionally, as well, besides, furthermore, likewise, moreover, too, yea, yet

alongside *prep* ***syn*** BESIDE 1, by, ‖fornent, next to

aloof *adj* **1** ***syn*** INDIFFERENT 2, casual, detached, disinterested, incurious, remote, unconcerned, uncurious, uninterested, withdrawn
rel arrogant, disdainful, haughty, proud; chilly, cold, cool, frigid; constrained, reserved, restrained, reticent, standoffish
con affable, companionable, gregarious, sociable, social; friendly, neighborly
ant familiar; outgoing
2 ***syn*** UNSOCIABLE, cool, distant, reserved, solitary, standoffish, unapproachable, unbending, uncompanionable, withdrawn

alp *n* ***syn*** MOUNTAIN 1, mount, peak

alpha *n* ***syn*** BEGINNING, commencement, dawn, dawning, genesis, opening, outset, outstart, setout, start
ant omega

alphabet *n* **1** a set of characters in which a language can be written <the Greek *alphabet*>
syn ABC(s), christcross-row, letters
2 the simplest fundamental part or level <learning the *alphabet* of science>
syn ABC's, elements, fundamentals, grammar, principles, rudiments
rel beginning, commencement, start; outset
idiom first steps
con entirety, total, whole; details, minutiae, trivia

already *adv* **1** ***syn*** BEFORE 2, earlier, erstwhile, formerly, heretofore, once, previously
2 ***syn*** EVEN 2

also *adv* **1** in the same manner <those *also* serve who support the workers>
syn correspondingly, likewise, similarly, so
idiom in like manner
2 in addition to that <he was stern but *also* just>
syn additionally, along, as well, besides, futhermore, item, likewise, more, moreover, still, too, withal, yea, yet
idiom into the bargain, on top of that, to boot
3 ***syn*** AGAIN 4, additionally, besides, further, in addition, then

alter *vb* **1** ***syn*** CHANGE 1, modify, mutate, refashion, turn, vary
rel accommodate, adapt, adjust, moderate, modulate, temper; doctor
idiom work a change (in)
con conserve, keep, preserve, retain
ant fix
2 ***syn*** STERILIZE, castrate, change, desexualize, fix, geld, mutilate, neuter, unsex

---

syn synonym(s)	***rel*** related word(s)
idiom idiomatic equivalent(s)	***con*** contrasted word(s)
ant antonym(s)	* vulgar

‖ use limited; if in doubt, see a dictionary
The first word in a synonym list when printed in SMALL CAPITALS shows where there is more information about the group. For a more efficient use of this book see Explanatory Notes.

alteration *n* **1** ***syn*** CHANGE 1, modification, mutation, turn, variation
rel accommodation, adaptation, adjustment; conversion, metamorphosis, transformation; fluctuation, shilly-shally, vacillation, wavering
con perdurability, permanence, stability; continuance, endurance, persistence
ant fixation, fixity
2 ***syn*** TRANSITION, passage, shift, transit
3 ***syn*** CONVERSION 2, changeover, shift, transformation

altercate *vb* ***syn*** QUARREL, bicker, brabble, caterwaul, row, scrap, spat, squabble, tiff, wrangle
rel agitate, argue, debate, dispute
con accord, get along; accommodate, adapt, adjust, conform
ant concur

altercation *n* ***syn*** QUARREL, bickering, controversy, dispute, embroilment, falling-out, fracas, squabble, tiff, wrangle
rel argument; combat, contest
con agreement, concord, consonance, harmony; empathy, like-mindedness, sympathy, understanding
ant accord; concurrence

alterity *n* ***syn*** DISSIMILARITY, difference, discrepancy, dissemblance, dissimilitude, distinction, divergence, divergency, otherness, unlikeness

alternate *adj* **1** ***syn*** INTERMITTENT, isochronal, isochronous, periodic, periodical, recurrent, recurring
rel alternant, alternating, rotating; complementary, corresponding, reciprocal
con sequent, successive
ant consecutive
2 ***syn*** SUBSTITUTE 1, alternative, surrogate
rel equivalent, proxy, replacing; exchangeable· interchangeable; makeshift, provisional, tentative

alternate *vb* ***syn*** ROTATE 2
rel fluctuate, oscillate, sway, waver; recur, return, revert
con follow, succeed

alternate *n* ***syn*** SUBSTITUTE, fill-in, locum tenens, pinch hitter, replacement, stand-in, sub, succedaneum, surrogate

alternately *adv* ***syn*** INSTEAD, alternatively, in lieu, rather

alternation *n* ***syn*** SUCCESSION 2, chain, consecution, order, progression, row, sequel, sequence, series, train
rel recurrence, return, reversion; reappearance, repetition

alternative *adj* ***syn*** SUBSTITUTE 1, alternate, surrogate
rel equivalent, proxy, replacing; exchangeable, interchangeable; makeshift, provisional, tentative

alternative *n* ***syn*** CHOICE 1, ‖druthers, election, option, preference, selection
rel attainable, contingency, possibility

alternatively *adv* ***syn*** INSTEAD, alternately, in lieu, rather

although *conj* ***syn*** THOUGH, albeit, howbeit, much as, when, whereas, while

altitude *n* ***syn*** HEIGHT, elevation
rel apex, eminence, peak, summit
con depth

altitudinous *adj* ***syn*** HIGH 1, tall

altogether *adv* **1** ***syn*** WELL 3, completely, entirely, perfectly, ‖plumb, quite, right, thoroughly, utterly, wholly
2 ***syn*** ALL 1, all in all, exactly, in toto, just, quite, stick, totally, utterly, wholly
3 as a total < *altogether* it cost over a thousand dollars >
syn all told, in all, quite
idiom taken together
4 with minor exceptions or flaws < *altogether* the party was a success >
syn all in all, by and large, en masse, generally, on the whole
idiom all things considered, as a whole, for the most part, generally speaking, in the main

altruistic *adj* ***syn*** CHARITABLE 1, benevolent, eleemosynary, good, humane, humanitarian, philanthropic
rel considerate, kind, unselfish; bounteous, bountiful, generous, liberal, open-handed; bighearted, magnanimous, noble-minded
con egotistic, self-centered, selfish, self-seeking; illiberal, mean, niggardly, stingy, ungenerous
ant egoistic

always *adv* **1** on every relevant occasion < *always* made the same mistake >
syn constantly, continuously, ever, invariably, perpetually
rel frequently, often, regularly, usually
idiom in every case (*or* instance), without exception
con rarely, seldom
ant never
2 ***syn*** EVER 2, eternally, evermore, forever, forevermore, in perpetuum

‖amah *n* ***syn*** NURSEMAID, ‖ayah, nana, ‖nanny, nurse, nurserymaid

amalgam *n* ***syn*** MIXTURE, admixture, alloy, amalgamation, blend, composite, compound, fusion, immixture, interfusion

amalgamate *vb* ***syn*** MIX 1, admix, compound, fuse, interfuse, intermingle, intermix, meld, merge, mingle
rel compact, consolidate, unify
con crumble, decompose, disintegrate; disperse, dissipate, scatter

amalgamation *n* **1** ***syn*** MIXTURE, admixture, alloy, amalgam, blend, commixture, composite, compost, compound, fusion
2 ***syn*** CONSOLIDATION 2, merger

amaranthine *adj* ***syn*** EVERLASTING 1, ceaseless, endless, eternal, immortal, never-ending, unending, world-without-end

amaroidal *adj* ***syn*** ACRID, astringent, austere, bitter, harsh, sharp

amass *vb* ***syn*** ACCUMULATE, cumulate, garner, hive, lay up, roll up, stockpile, store (up), uplay
ant distribute

---

syn synonym(s)	***rel*** related word(s)
idiom idiomatic equivalent(s)	***con*** contrasted word(s)
ant antonym(s)	* vulgar

‖ use limited; if in doubt, see a dictionary
The first word in a synonym list when printed in SMALL CAPITALS shows where there is more information about the group. For a more efficient use of this book see Explanatory Notes.

amassment *n* ***syn*** ACCUMULATION, agglomeration, aggregation, collection, colluvies, conglomeration, cumulation, hoard, trove

amateur *n* **1** one having a marked and usually informed taste or liking for something <an *amateur* of fine fabrics>
syn admirer, devotee, fan, fancier, votary
rel crank, enthusiast, faddist, infatuate, ‖nut, zealot; aesthete, cognoscente, connoisseur, dilettante; illuminato, illuminist
con abecedarian, dabbler, tyro; adept, expert
2 one who follows a pursuit without attaining mastery or professional status <a nation handicapped by *amateurs* in high office>
syn abecedarian, dabbler, dilettante, nonprofessional, smatterer, tyro, uninitiate
rel beginner, greenhorn, neophyte; apprentice, novice, probationer; potterer, putterer, tinker
con adept, virtuoso, wizard
ant expert, master; professional

amateurish *adj* lacking or marked by lack of expert skill or finish <an *amateurish* actor>
syn dabbling, dilettante, dilettantish, dilettantist, jackleg, unaccomplished, unfinished, ungifted, unskilled
rel clumsy, crude, green, raw, untutored; defective, deficient, faulty, flawed
con accomplished, expert, gifted, skilled
ant professional

amative *adj* ***syn*** EROTIC, amatory, amorous, aphrodisiac

amatory *adj* ***syn*** EROTIC, amative, amorous, aphrodisiac
rel admiring, attracted, yearning

amaze *vb* ***syn*** SURPRISE 2, astonish, astound, dumbfound, flabbergast
rel affect, impress, move, strike, touch

amaze *n* ***syn*** WONDER 2, admiration, amazement, marveling, wonderment
rel confoundment; surprise

amazement *n* ***syn*** WONDER 2, admiration, amaze, marveling, wonderment
rel confoundment; surprise

amazing *adj* ***syn*** MARVELOUS 1, astonishing, astounding, miraculous, prodigious, strange, stupendous, surprising, wonderful, wondrous

amazon *n* ***syn*** VIRAGO, fishwife, harpy, ogress, scold, shrew, termagant, vixen, Xanthippe

ambidextrous *adj* **1** ***syn*** TWO-HANDED 2, bimanal
2 ***syn*** VERSATILE, adaptable, all-around, many-sided, mobile, myriad-minded
3 ***syn*** INSINCERE, double, double-dealing, double-faced, doublehearted, double-minded, double-tongued, hypocritical, left-handed, mala fide

ambience *n* ***syn*** ENVIRONMENT, ambient, atmosphere, climate, medium, milieu, mise-en-scène, surroundings

ambient *n* ***syn*** ENVIRONMENT, ambience, atmosphere, climate, medium, milieu, mise-en-scène, surroundings

ambiguity *n* expression or an expression obscure because subject to more than one interpretation <a speech full of *ambiguities*>
syn amphibology, double entendre, double meaning, equivocality, equivocation, equivoque, tergiversation
rel dodge, evasion, hedge, quibble, shift, subterfuge; cavil, haggling, hair-splitting, quibbling; obscurity, uncertainty, vagueness
con definiteness, expressness, specificity; clearness, exactness, precision
ant explicitness; lucidity

ambiguous *adj* **1** ***syn*** OBSCURE 3, amphibological, equivocal, opaque, tenebrous, uncertain, unclear, unexplicit, unintelligible, vague
rel doubtful, dubious, questionable
con clear, lucid, perspicuous; categorical, express, specific
ant explicit
2 ***syn*** DOUBTFUL 1, dubious, equivocal, fishy, problematic, suspect, uncertain, unclear, unsettled, unsure

ambit *n* **1** ***syn*** CIRCUMFERENCE, circuit, compass, perimeter, periphery
2 ***syn*** RANGE 2, compass, extension, extent, orbit, purview, radius, reach, scope, sweep

ambition *n* **1** strong desire for advancement <a life ruled by *ambition*>
syn ambitiousness, aspiration, pretension
rel drive, go-ahead, push; anxiety, avidity, eagerness, keenness; energy, enterprise, spirit; goad, incentive, motive, spur
con contentment, satisfaction; faineance, indolence, lethargy, sloth
2 an object of desire or intent <his *ambition* was to have enough to live on without working>
syn aim, goal, mark, objective, quaesitum, target; *compare* INTENTION
rel design, intent, purpose; desire, fancy, hope, wish; dream, ideal, nirvana
3 ***syn*** ENTERPRISE 4, drive, get-up-and-go, initiative, push

ambitious *adj* **1** marked by intense desire for advancement (as in power, fame, or wealth) <a ruthlessly *ambitious* politician>
syn aspiring, emulous, vaulting
rel aggressive, enterprising, go-ahead, pushing, up-and-doing; energetic, hard-working, indefatigable; anxious, avid, eager, keen
con apathetic, phlegmatic, stolid; faineant, indolent, lazy, slothful
2 of a kind to try or exceed one's powers of performance <an *ambitious* scheme to recover gold from seawater>
syn grandiose, lofty, pretentious, utopian, visionary
rel audacious, bold, daring; chimerical, extravagant, high-flown, impractical, unrealistic
con easy, plain, straightforward; feasible, practicable, realistic; unpretentious
ant modest

ambitiousness *n* ***syn*** AMBITION 1, aspiration, pretension

ambivalent *adj* ***syn*** EQUIVOCAL 2

---

syn synonym(s)	***rel*** related word(s)
idiom idiomatic equivalent(s)	***con*** contrasted word(s)
ant antonym(s)	* vulgar

‖ use limited; if in doubt, see a dictionary
The first word in a synonym list when printed in SMALL CAPITALS shows where there is more information about the group. For a more efficient use of this book see Explanatory Notes.

amble *vb* ***syn*** SAUNTER, bummel, drift, linger, mope, mosey, ||muck, stroll

rel dally, dawdle, dillydally, loiter

ambrosial *adj* **1** ***syn*** DELIGHTFUL, adorable, darling, delectable, delicious, heavenly, luscious, lush, scrumptious, yummy

2 ***syn*** SWEET 2, aromal, aromatic, balmy, fragrant, perfumed, perfumy, redolent, savory, spicy

ambulant *adj* ***syn*** ITINERANT, ambulatory, deambulatory, nomadic, perambulant, perambulatory, peripatetic, roving, vagabond, vagrant

ant bedfast, bedridden

ambulate *vb* ***syn*** WALK 1, foot (it), hoof, pace, step, traipse, tread, troop

ambulatory *adj* ***syn*** ITINERANT, ambulant, deambulatory, nomadic, perambulant, perambulatory, peripatetic, roving, vagabond, vagrant

ambuscade *n* ***syn*** AMBUSH, ambushment

ambush *vb* ***syn*** SURPRISE 1, lay (for), waylay

rel assail, assault, attack; ensnare, entrap, snare, trap

ambush *n* a device to entrap an enemy by lying in hiding until a surprise attack is feasible <planned an *ambush* on the cliff above the trail>

syn ambuscade, ambushment

rel lure, snare, trap; blind, cover, hideout, retreat

ambushment *n* ***syn*** AMBUSH, ambuscade

ameliorate *vb* **1** ***syn*** IMPROVE 1, amend, better, help, meliorate

rel alleviate, lighten, mitigate, relieve

con damage, harm, hurt, impair, injure, mar, spoil; aggravate, intensify

ant worsen; deteriorate

2 ***syn*** IMPROVE 3, convalesce, gain, look up, mend, perk (up), recuperate

amenable *adj* **1** ***syn*** RESPONSIBLE, accountable, answerable, liable

rel open, subject; dependent, subordinate

con autarchic, free

ant independent (of); autonomous

2 ***syn*** OBEDIENT, biddable, docile, ||docious, tractable

rel subdued, tame; receptive, responsive, willing; adaptable, impressionable, malleable, plastic, pliable, pliant

con fierce, mulish, obstinate, stubborn, truculent

ant recalcitrant, refractory

amend *vb* **1** ***syn*** CORRECT 1, emend, mend, rectify, right

rel repair; elevate, lift, raise

con corrupt, debauch, deprave, pervert, vitiate

ant debase

2 ***syn*** IMPROVE 1, ameliorate, better, help, meliorate

rel advance, forward, promote

ant worsen; impair

---

syn synonym(s) ***rel*** related word(s)
idiom idiomatic equivalent(s) ***con*** contrasted word(s)
ant antonym(s) * vulgar
|| use limited; if in doubt, see a dictionary
The first word in a synonym list when printed in SMALL CAPITALS shows where there is more information about the group. For a more efficient use of this book see Explanatory Notes.

---

amends *n pl* ***syn*** REPARATION, compensation, indemnification, indemnity, quittance, recompense, redress, reprisal, restitution

amenity *n* **1** the quality of being pleasant or agreeable <a discussion conducted in perfect *amenity*> <the *amenity* of the climate>

syn agreeability, agreeableness, amiability, cordiality, enjoyableness, geniality, gratefulness, pleasance, pleasantness, sweetness and light

rel attractiveness, charm, delightfulness; fascination, pleasingness

con disagreeableness, distastefulness, unattractiveness, unpleasantness

2 a feature that makes for pleasantness or ease <among the *amenities* of the house is central air-conditioning>

syn comfort, convenience, facility

rel betterment, enhancement, enrichment, improvement; excellence, merit, quality, virtue

con difficulty, hardship, trial, vicissitude

3 *pl* **amenities** ***syn*** MANNER 5, civilities, decorum(s), etiquette, mores, proprieties

4 ***syn*** LUXURY, extravagance, frill, luxus, superfluity

5 ***syn*** COURTESY 1, attention, gallantry

rel civility, courteousness, politeness; affability, cordiality, geniality, graciousness, sociability

con discourtesy, impoliteness, incivility; affront, indignity, insult; acrimony

ant rudeness

ament *n* ***syn*** FOOL 4, cretin, ||feeb, half-wit, idiot, imbecile, moron, natural, simpleton, zany

amerce *vb* ***syn*** PENALIZE, fine, mulct

amercement *n* ***syn*** FINE, forfeit, mulct, penalty

amiability *n* ***syn*** AMENITY 1, agreeability, agreeableness, cordiality, enjoyableness, geniality, gratefulness, pleasance, pleasantness, sweetness and light

amiable *adj* **1** of a generally agreeable nature especially in social interaction <the meeting ended on an *amiable* note>

syn complaisant, easy, good-humored, good-natured, good-tempered, lenient, mild, obliging

rel affable, cordial, genial, gracious; courteous, mannerly; benign, benignant, kind, kindly; responsive, warm, warmhearted

idiom easy to get along with

con discourteous, ill-mannered, ill-natured, impolite, rude; crabbed, dour, unsociable

ant unamiable; surly

2 ***syn*** GENTLE 2, affable, genial

amicable *adj* **1** characterized by peaceableness and goodwill <the negotiators joined in *amicable* discussion>

syn friendly, neighborly

rel empathic, like-minded, sympathetic, understanding; accordant, agreeing, concordant, frictionless, harmonious; pacific, peaceable, peaceful

con bellicose, belligerent, combative, contentious, pugnacious, quarrelsome; antipathetic, hostile, suspicious, uncooperative

2 ***syn*** HARMONIOUS 3, amical, congenial, friendly

amical *adj* ***syn*** HARMONIOUS 3, amicable, congenial, friendly

amid *prep* **1** in or into the central part of <the bomb burst *amid* the crowd>

syn among, mid, midst
idiom in (*or* into) the middle of, in (*or* into) the midst of, in (*or* into) the thick of
2 *syn* AMONG 1, mid, midst
3 *syn* DURING, mid, midst, over, throughout

amigo *n* *syn* FRIEND, acquaintance, cater-cousin, confidant, familiar, intimate, mate

amiss *adv* **1** in a mistaken, inappropriate, or reprehensible way <I feel you judge him *amiss*>
syn faultily, incorrectly, wrongly
rel inaccurately; indiscreetly, unwisely
con accurately, correctly, properly, rightly; cleverly, wisely
ant right
2 out of the proper course <our planning had gone *amiss*>
syn afield, astray, awry, badly, unfavorably, wrong; *compare* HARD 5
idiom beside (*or* off) the mark
con auspiciously, famously, favorably, promisingly, propitiously, well
ant aright

amiss *adj* **1** *syn* BAD 1, ||bum, ||crappy, dissatisfactory, poor, ||punk, rotten, unsatisfactory, up, wrong
2 *syn* FAULTY, defective, flawed, imperfect, sick
3 *syn* BLAMEWORTHY, blamable, blameful, censurable, culpable, demeritorious, guilty, reprehensible, sinful, unholy

amity *n* *syn* GOODWILL 1, benevolence, comity, friendliness, friendship, kindliness
rel accord, agreement, concord, harmony; amicableness, neighborliness
con animosity, antagonism, antipathy, hostility; conflict, contention, discord, dissension, strife
ant enmity

amnesty *n* *syn* PARDON, absolution

among *prep* **1** surrounded by <the valley nestled *among* high mountains>
syn amid, mid, midst
2 *syn* AMID 1, mid, midst
3 *syn* BETWEEN

amorist *n* *syn* GALLANT 2, Casanova, Don Juan, lothario, paramour, Romeo

amorous *adj* *syn* EROTIC, amative, amatory, aphrodisiac
rel enamored, infatuated; lustful
con aloof, detached, indifferent; cold, cool; apathetic, impassive, unconcerned
ant frigid

amorousness *n* *syn* LOVE 2, amour, passion

amorphous *adj* *syn* FORMLESS, inchoate, shapeless, unformed, unshaped

amount *vb* **1** to make up as a total <their expenses *amounted* to just a hundred dollars>
syn add up, aggregate, come, number, run (to *or* into), sum (to *or* into), total
rel comprehend, comprise, embody, include, incorporate, reach, subsume
2 to be essentially equivalent <that utter terror that *amounts* to madness>
syn approach, correspond (to), equal, match, partake (of), rival, touch
rel hint, imply, intimate, smack (of), suggest
idiom be near to, come to the same thing as, have all the earmarks (*or* features) of

amount *n* **1** *syn* BODY 5, aggregate, budget, bulk, quantity, quantum, total
2 *syn* SUBSTANCE 2, body, burden, core, matter, purport, sense, short, thrust, upshot

amour *n* **1** *syn* LOVE AFFAIR, affair, love, romance
2 an illicit or informal sexual relation <memoirs devoted to accounts of his *amours*>
syn affair, intrigue, liaison
rel entanglement, intimacy, relationship; love affair, romance
3 *syn* LOVE 2, amorousness, passion

amour propre *n* **1** *syn* PRIDE 2, self-esteem, self-regard, self-respect
2 *syn* CONCEIT 2, conceitedness, narcissism, self-admiration, self-conceit, self-esteem, self-love, vainglory, vainness, vanity
rel complacency, self-complacency, self-satisfaction, smugness; pride

amphibological *adj* *syn* OBSCURE 3, ambiguous, equivocal, nubilous, tenebrous, uncertain, unclear, unexplicit, unintelligible, vague

amphibology *n* *syn* AMBIGUITY, double entendre, double meaning, equivocality, equivocation, equivoque, tergiversation

ample *adj* **1** *syn* SPACIOUS, capacious, commodious, roomy, wide
rel distended, expanded, inflated, swollen
con scant, skimpy, spare; cramped, exiguous, narrow, strait
ant meager; circumscribed
2 *syn* PLENTIFUL, abundant, bounteous, bountiful, copious, generous, liberal, plenteous, plenty
rel lavish, prodigal, profuse; handsome
idiom enough and to spare
con scrimpy, spare, sparse; beggarly, miserable, niggardly
ant meager, scant

amplify *vb* **1** *syn* EXPAND 4, develop, elaborate, enlarge
rel augment, extend, increase; unfold
con abbreviate, shorten
ant abridge, condense
2 *syn* EXPAND 3, dilate, distend, inflate, swell

amplitude *n* **1** *syn* SIZE 2, bigness, greatness, largeness, magnitude, sizeableness
2 *syn* BREADTH 2, comprehensiveness, fullness, scope, wideness
con closeness, limitation, restriction, straitness
ant narrowness
3 *syn* EXPANSE, breadth, distance, expansion, space, spread, stretch
rel bigness, greatness, largeness; capaciousness, commodiousness, roominess, spaciousness
con circumscription, restriction
ant straitness; limitation

---

syn synonym(s) *rel* related word(s)
idiom idiomatic equivalent(s) *con* contrasted word(s)
ant antonym(s) * vulgar
|| use limited; if in doubt, see a dictionary
The first word in a synonym list when printed in SMALL CAPITALS shows where there is more information about the group. For a more efficient use of this book see Explanatory Notes.

amply *adv* ***syn*** WELL 4, acceptably, adequately, appropriately, becomingly, fittingly, properly, right, satisfactorily, suitably

amulet *n* ***syn*** CHARM 2, fetish, juju, luck, mascot, periapt, phylactery, talisman, zemi
rel lucky piece, rabbit-foot

amuse *vb* to pass or cause to pass time in pleasant or agreeable activity <simple toys to *amuse* children on long trips>
syn divert, entertain, recreate
rel absorb, distract, engross; animate, enliven, fleet, quicken; beguile, charm, delight, enchant, fascinate, wile; while
con fatigue, irk, jade, pall (on), tire, wear (on), weary; bore, ennui

amusement *n* ***syn*** ENTERTAINMENT, dissipation, distraction, diversion, divertissement, recreation

ana *n* ***syn*** ANTHOLOGY, album, analects, florilegium, garland, miscellany, omnibus, posy

anabasis *n* ***syn*** ADVANCE 2, advancement, headway, march, ongoing, proficiency, progress

anachronism *n* **1** a chronological error <*anachronisms* of several centuries mar some earlier chronicles>
syn misdate, misdating, mistiming, parachronism
rel antedate, anticipation, prochronism, prolepsis; metachronism, postdate
2 one that is inappropriately situated especially in time <born centuries too late, he was an *anachronism* in modern urban society>
syn solecism
rel bevue, faux pas, gaffe; defect, flaw, mistake, slip

anadem *n* ***syn*** WREATH, chaplet, coronal, coronet, crown, garland

anagogic *adj* ***syn*** MYSTICAL 1, mystic, telestic
rel esoteric, occult, recondite; allegorical, symbolical

analects *n pl* ***syn*** ANTHOLOGY, album, ana, florilegium, garland, miscellany, omnibus, posy

analgesic *n* ***syn*** ANODYNE 1, anesthetic, pain-killer
ant irritant

analogous *adj* ***syn*** LIKE, akin, alike, comparable, consonant, corresponding, parallel, similar, undifferentiated, uniform
rel convertible, corresponding, interchangeable; kindred

analogue *n* ***syn*** PARALLEL, correlate, correspondent, counterpart, countertype, match
rel cognate, congener

analogy *n* **1** ***syn*** LIKENESS, affinity, alikeness, comparison, resemblance, semblance, similarity, simile, similitude
2 expression or an expression involving explicit or implied comparison of things basically unlike but with some striking similarities <God can be described only by *analogy*>
syn metaphor, simile, similitude
rel ambiguity, equivocation, equivoque, tergiversation
con demonstration, description, formulation

analphabet *n* ***syn*** ILLITERATE

analysis *n* **1** separation of a whole into its fundamental elements or constituent parts <*analysis* of a problem>
syn breakdown, breakup, dissection, resolution
rel division, separation; decomposition, disintegration
con combination, union; concatenation, integration, unification
ant synthesis
2 ***syn*** EXAMINATION, audit, checkup, inspection, perlustration, review, scan, scrutiny, survey, view

analytic *adj* ***syn*** LOGICAL 2, analytical, ratiocinative, subtle
rel deep, profound; acute, keen, sharp; penetrating, piercing
con constructive, creative, inventive

analytical *adj* ***syn*** LOGICAL 2, analytic, ratiocinative, subtle

analyze *vb* to divide a complex whole into its constituent parts or elements <*analyze* the plot of a novel>
syn anatomize, break down, decompose, decompound, dissect, resolve
rel divide, part, separate; assort, classify, pigeonhole; examine, inspect, investigate, scrutinize
con articulate, concatenate, integrate
ant compose, compound; construct

anamnesis *n* ***syn*** MEMORY 2, recall, recollection, remembrance, reminiscence

Ananias *n* ***syn*** LIAR, falsifier, fibber, fibster, perjurer, prevaricator, storyteller

anarch *n* ***syn*** REBEL, anarchist, frondeur, insurgent, insurrectionist, malcontent, mutineer, revolter

anarchism *n* **1** a political theory opposed to all forms of government and advocating voluntary cooperation and interaction of individuals and groups in satisfying their common needs <the doubtful premises of *anarchism* about human nature>
syn anarchy
rel utopianism; communism, Marxism, syndicalism
con absolutism, authoritarianism, dictatorship; elitism
2 ***syn*** DISORDER 2, anarchy, distemper, misrule, riot

anarchist *n* ***syn*** REBEL, anarch, frondeur, insurgent, insurrectionist, malcontent, mutineer, revolter

anarchy *n* **1** absence of effective government or the resulting social disorder <complete *anarchy* followed the breakdown of communications>
syn chaos, lawlessness, mobocracy, ochlocracy
rel confusion, disorder, disorganization
idiom mob rule (*or* law), reign of terror
2 ***syn*** ANARCHISM
3 ***syn*** DISORDER 2, anarchism, distemper, misrule, riot

anastomose *vb* ***syn*** INTERJOIN, interconnect, interlink, intertie

anathema *n* **1** ***syn*** CURSE 1, commination, imprecation, malediction, malison
rel censure, condemnation, denunciation, reprehension, reprobation, reproof
con eulogy, laudation, praise
2 ***syn*** ABOMINATION 1, bête noire, black beast, bugbear, detestation, hate
rel leper, pariah, outcast, untouchable

---

syn synonym(s) ***rel*** related word(s)
idiom idiomatic equivalent(s) ***con*** contrasted word(s)
ant antonym(s) * vulgar
‖ use limited; if in doubt, see a dictionary
The first word in a synonym list when printed in SMALL CAPITALS shows where there is more information about the group. For a more efficient use of this book see Explanatory Notes.

anathematize *vb* ***syn*** EXECRATE 1, curse, damn, objurgate
rel impugn, reproach
con approbate, approve, countenance, endorse, favor

anatomize *vb* ***syn*** ANALYZE, break down, decompose, decompound, dissect, resolve

ancestor *n* **1** a person from whom one is descended <proud of his pioneer *ancestors*>
syn antecedent (used in pl.), ascendant, forebear, forefather, primogenitor, progenitor
ant descendant
2 ***syn*** FORERUNNER 2, antecedent, antecessor, foregoer, precursor, predecessor, prototype

ancestry *n* one's progenitors or their character or quality as a whole <a man of noble *ancestry*>
syn blood, descent, extraction, lineage, origin, pedigree
rel family, kindred, line, race, stock; derivation, source; breed, breeding
ant descendants; posterity

anchor *vb* ***syn*** FASTEN 2, catch, fix, moor, secure
rel imbed, plant
idiom make fast (*or* secure)

anchorage *n* ***syn*** HARBOR 3, ||chuck, harborage, haven, port, riding, road(s), roadstead

ancient *adj* **1** persisting from the distant past <an *ancient* monument>
syn aged, age-old, antediluvian, antique, hoary, Noachian, old, timeworn, venerable; *compare* OBSOLETE
rel primal, primeval, primordial, pristine; forgotten, immemorial, remote, traditional; ageless, dateless
idiom old as time, older than God (*or* the hills), out of the dim past
con current, fresh, new, novel, prevailing, up-to-date
ant modern
2 ***syn*** AGED 1, elderly, old, olden
rel doddering, doting, fading, sinking, waning, wasting
idiom old as Methuselah (*or* the hills)

ancient *n* ***syn*** OLDSTER, elder, golden-ager, old-timer, senior, senior citizen

ancilla *n* ***syn*** HELPER, aid, assistant, attendant, help, striker

ancillary *adj* **1** ***syn*** AUXILIARY, accessory, adjuvant, appurtenant, collateral, contributory, subservient, subsidiary
2 ***syn*** CONCOMITANT, accompanying, attendant, attending, coincident, collateral, incident, satellite

androgynous *adj* ***syn*** BISEXUAL, hermaphrodite, hermaphroditic

android *n* ***syn*** ROBOT 1, automaton

anecdote *n* ***syn*** STORY 2, narration, narrative, tale, yarn
rel recital, relation; episode, event, incident

anemic *adj* ***syn*** PALE 2, bloodless, pallid, waterish, watery

anent *prep* ***syn*** APROPOS, about, as for, as regards, concerning, in re, re, touching, toward, with respect to

anesthetic *adj* ***syn*** INSENSIBLE 5, bloodless, dull, hard, impassible, insensate, insensitive, rocky
rel impenetrable, impermeable, impervious; obtuse
con responsive, sensitive

anesthetic *n* ***syn*** ANODYNE 1, analgesic, pain-killer
ant stimulant

anesthetized *adj* ***syn*** NUMB 1, asleep, benumbed, dead, deadened, insensible, insensitive, numbed, senseless, unfeeling

anew *adv* **1** ***syn*** OVER 7, afresh, again, de novo, once more
2 ***syn*** NEW, afresh, lately, newly, of late, recently

anfractuous *adj* ***syn*** WINDING, convoluted, flexuous, meandering, meandrous, serpentine, sinuous, snaky, tortuous

angel *n* ***syn*** SPONSOR, backer, backer-up, guarantor, patron, surety
rel ||butter-and-egg man

angelic *adj* ***syn*** SAINTLY, godly, holy

anger *n* emotional excitement induced by intense displeasure <a man easily aroused to *anger*>
syn fury, indignation, ire, mad, rage, wrath
rel ||dander, dudgeon, ||Dutch, huff, ||monkey, pet, pique, temper; annoyance, exasperation, infuriation, irritation
ant forbearance

anger *vb* **1** to make angry <their constant heedless interruptions *angered* her>
syn enrage, incense, infuriate, ire, mad, madden, steam up, umbrage
rel annoy, irk, vex; aggravate, exasperate, irritate, nettle, provoke, rile; affront, offend, outrage
idiom burn one up, make one hot under the collar, put (*or* get) one's dander up, set one by the ears
con appease, conciliate, mollify, placate, propitiate, soothe
ant gratify; pacify
2 to be or become angry <he *angers* easily>
syn blow up, boil, boil over, bristle, burn, flare (up), fume, rage, seethe
rel chafe, fret, stew; rant, rave, storm
idiom breathe fire, fly into a rage, get hot under the collar, get one's blood (*or* dander) up, hit the ceiling, lose one's temper, see red
ant calm (down)

angle *vb* ***syn*** HINT 4, fish

angle *n* **1** ***syn*** VIEWPOINT 2, direction, outlook, side, slant, standpoint
2 ***syn*** PHASE, aspect, facet, hand, side
rel detail, item, particular
3 ***syn*** TURN 4, bend, bow, flection, flexure, turning

angle *vb* **1** ***syn*** SLANT 2, aim
2 ***syn*** SLANT 3, bias, skew

angry *adj* feeling or showing strong displeasure or bad temper <*angry* at the children's lack of consideration>
syn acrimonious, choleric, heated, indignant, irate, ireful, mad, ||pissed, ||pissed off, shirty, waxy, wrathful, wrathy, wroth, wrothful, wrothy
rel aggravated, exasperated, perturbed, put out, riley, upset, uptight, worked up, wrought (up); angered, enraged, incensed, infuriate, infuriated, maddened, sore, vexed; orey-eyed, red-faced, wild-eyed

---

syn synonym(s) ***rel*** related word(s)
idiom idiomatic equivalent(s) ***con*** contrasted word(s)
ant antonym(s) * vulgar
|| use limited; if in doubt, see a dictionary
The first word in a synonym list when printed in SMALL CAPITALS shows where there is more information about the group. For a more efficient use of this book see Explanatory Notes.

idiom foaming at the mouth, hot under the collar, in a taking, in a temper (*or* rage), mad as a hornet (*or* wet hen)
con calm, placid, tolerant; content, pleased, satisfied

anguish *n* ***syn*** SORROW, affliction, care, ‖dole, grief, heartache, heartbreak, regret, rue, woe
rel anxiety, worry; ache, pain, pang, throe; torment, torture
con comfort, consolation, solace; alleviation, assuagement, mitigation
ant relief

angular *adj* **1** ***syn*** RUDE 1, crude, raw, rough, rough-hewn, undressed, unfashioned, unfinished, unpolished, unworked
2 ***syn*** LEAN, bony, gaunt, lank, lanky, rawboned, scraggy, scrawny, skinny, spare
rel lathy, ribby, weedy
con chubby, chuffy
ant rotund

anima *n* ***syn*** SOUL 1, animus, élan vital, pneuma, psyche, spirit, vital force

animadversion *n* a remark or statement that constitutes an adverse and usually uncharitable criticism <her spiteful *animadversions* on her neighbors' children>
syn aspersion, obloquy, reflection, slam, slur, stricture
rel censure, criticism, reprehension; accusation, imputation, insinuation; captiousness, carping, caviling, faultfinding
con acclaim, extolling, laudation, praise; approbation, approval
ant commendation

animadvert *vb* ***syn*** REMARK 2, comment, commentate, observe
rel declare, say, state, tell, utter; descant, dilate, expatiate, perorate; adduce, offer, present
con disregard, ignore, overlook

animal *n* ***syn*** BEAST, brute, creature, ‖critter

animal *adj* **1** ***syn*** BRUTISH, beastly, bestial, brutal, brute, feral, ferine, swinish
2 ***syn*** CARNAL 2, fleshly, sensual
rel bestial, brutal, brutish
con intellectual, mental, psychic; reasoning, thinking; nonphysical, spiritual
ant rational

animalism *n* ***syn*** ANIMALITY, carnality, fleshliness
rel lasciviousness, lecherousness, lechery, licentiousness, lustfulness, unchastity; sensualism, sensuality, voluptuousness

animality *n* the animal aspect or quality of human beings or human nature <his violent reaction was sheer *animality*>
syn animalism, carnality, fleshliness
rel maleness, masculinity, virility; sensuality; brutishness, coarseness, grossness

ant spirituality

animalize *vb* ***syn*** DEBASE 1, bastardize, bestialize, brutalize, corrupt, demoralize, deprave, pervert, vitiate, warp

animate *adj* **1** ***syn*** LIVING 1, alive, animated, vital, zoetic
rel breathing, viable
ant inanimate
2 ***syn*** LIVELY 1, alert, animated, ‖cant, ‖canty, gay, keen, spirited, sprightly, vivacious
rel active, dynamic, live; activated, energized, vitalized
con dead, inanimate, lifeless; passive
ant inert

animate *vb* **1** ***syn*** ENCOURAGE 1, cheer, chirk (up), embolden, enhearten, hearten, inspirit, nerve, steel, strengthen
rel invigorate, refresh, renew; fortify, reinforce, strengthen
idiom give a lift (to), put on (*or* upon) one's mettle, raise the spirits of
2 ***syn*** QUICKEN 1, enliven, liven, vivificate, vivify
3 ***syn*** FIRE 2, exalt, inform, inspire
rel activate, actuate, motivate; drive, impel, move
con check, curb, restrain; frustrate, thwart
ant inhibit

animated *adj* **1** ***syn*** LIVING 1, alive, animate, vital, zoetic
rel activated, energized, vitalized
con passive
ant inert
2 ***syn*** LIVELY 1, alert, animate, ‖cant, ‖canty, gay, keen, spirited, sprightly, vivacious
rel exuberant, high-spirited, zestful
con enervated, spiritless; comatose
ant dejected, depressed

animating *adj* ***syn*** INVIGORATING, bracing, exhilarating, exhilarative, quickening, stimulating, stimulative, tonic, vitalizing

animation *n* ***syn*** SPIRIT 5, brio, dash, élan, esprit, life, oomph, verve, vim, zing

animosity *n* ***syn*** ENMITY, animus, antagonism, antipathy, hostility, rancor
con amity; esteem
ant goodwill

animus *n* **1** ***syn*** INTENTION, design, intendment, intent, meaning, plan, purpose
2 ***syn*** SOUL 1, anima, élan vital, pneuma, psyche, spirit, vital force
3 ***syn*** ENMITY, animosity, antagonism, antipathy, hostility, rancor
rel grudge; bias, discrimination, prejudice
con partiality, predilection; sympathy
ant favor

annals *n pl* ***syn*** HISTORY 2, chronicle

annex *vb* **1** ***syn*** ADD 1, append, subjoin, superadd, take on
rel associate, connect, join, link, unite
con disengage; divorce, part, separate
2 ***syn*** GET 1, acquire, gain, have, land, obtain, pick up, procure, secure, win
3 ***syn*** APPROPRIATE 1, accroach, arrogate, commandeer, confiscate, expropriate, preempt, seize, sequester, take

---

syn synonym(s) *rel* related word(s)
idiom idiomatic equivalent(s) *con* contrasted word(s)
ant antonym(s) * vulgar
‖ use limited; if in doubt, see a dictionary
The first word in a synonym list when printed in SMALL CAPITALS shows where there is more information about the group. For a more efficient use of this book see Explanatory Notes.

4 ***syn*** STEAL 1, abstract, appropriate, cabbage, collar, ‖cop, hook, nim, pinch, purloin

annex *n* a subsidiary structure associated with a main building <built an *annex* to the museum to hold a new collection>
syn arm, block, ell, extension, wing
rel addition, continuation

annihilate *vb* **1** ***syn*** ABOLISH 1, abate, abrogate, annul, invalidate, negate, nullify, quash, undo, vitiate
2 to destroy utterly <matter cannot be *annihilated*>
syn abate, abolish, blot out, eradicate, exterminate, extinguish, extirpate, murder, root out, uncreate, uproot, wipe (out)
rel cancel, efface, erase, expunge, obliterate
con renew, restore; create, discover, invent; fashion, forge, form, make, shape
3 ***syn*** DESTROY 1, decimate, demolish, raze, ruin, unbuild, undo, unframe, wrack, wreck
4 ***syn*** SLAUGHTER 3, decimate, exterminate, massacre, wipe (out)
rel rout
5 ***syn*** CRUSH 5, extinguish, put down, quash, quell, quench, squash, suppress

annihilative *adj* ***syn*** DESTRUCTIVE, ruinous, shattering, wrackful, wreckful

annotate *vb* to add or append comment <*annotate* a volume of poems>
syn gloss
rel construe, elucidate, explain, expound; comment, commentate, remark

announce *vb* **1** ***syn*** DECLARE 1, advertise, annunciate, blazon, broadcast, bruit (about), proclaim, promulgate, publish, sound
rel communicate, impart
con hush (up), smother, stifle, suppress
2 to point to as a future occurrence or development <the shortening days *announce* the coming of winter>
syn forerun, foreshow, harbinger, herald, preindicate, presage
rel augur, forebode, forecast, foretell, predict
3 ***syn*** INDICATE 2, argue, attest, bespeak, betoken, testify, witness
rel present, set forth, show (forth)

announcement *n* ***syn*** DECLARATION, advertisement, broadcast, proclamation, promulgation, pronouncement, pronunciamento, publication
rel affirmation, assertion, averment, statement

annoy *vb* **1** to disturb and upset nervously <her persistent prying soon *annoyed* her hostess>
syn abrade, bother, ‖bug, chafe, exercise, fret, gall, irk, provoke, ruffle, vex; *compare* IRRITATE
rel agitate, disturb, perturb, upset
idiom get in one's hair
con comfort, console, solace; content, gratify, please, satisfy
ant soothe
2 ***syn*** WORRY 1, bedevil, beleaguer, gnaw, hagride, harass, harry, pester, plague, tease
rel badger, bait, chivy, heckle, hector; chafe, distress, gall, rub
idiom get (*or* grate) on one's nerves, rub one the wrong way
con disregard, ignore, overlook; appease, calm, dulcify, mollify; cool, lull, subdue

annoyance *n* **1** the act of annoying <devoted himself to the *annoyance* of his patient wife>
syn bothering, harassment, irking, provocation, provoking, vexation, vexing
rel pestering, teasing
2 the state or feeling of being annoyed <her *annoyance* increased as he continued to pester her>
syn aggravation, bother, botheration, exasperation, pother
rel anger, indignation, ire, wrath; aversion, repugnance, repulsion, revulsion; disgust, dislike, distaste
con appreciation, enjoyment, liking, pleasure
3 something that causes an annoyed state or feeling <his constant baiting was an *annoyance* to her>
syn besetment, bother, botheration, botherment, exasperation, irritant, nuisance, pest, pester, ‖pesterment, plague
rel affliction, aggravation, distress, provocation, trial; riding

annual *n* ***syn*** YEARBOOK, annuary

annuary *n* ***syn*** YEARBOOK, annual

annul *vb* **1** ***syn*** ERASE, black (out), blot out, cancel, delete, efface, expunge, obliterate, wipe (out), x (out)
rel abstract, dispose (of), eliminate, remove
2 ***syn*** NEUTRALIZE, cancel (out), counteract, countercheck, frustrate, negate, negative, redress
rel outweigh, overbalance
3 ***syn*** ABOLISH 1, abate, abrogate, annihilate, invalidate, negate, nullify, quash, undo, vitiate
rel counteract, negative, neutralize; blot out, cancel, efface, obliterate; extinguish
idiom make void, set aside
con enact, ordain, pass
4 to deprive of legal validity, force, or authority <*annul* a marriage>
syn abrogate, discharge, dissolve, quash, vacate, void
rel abolish, cancel, countermand, invalidate, nullify, undo
idiom make void

annunciate *vb* ***syn*** DECLARE 1, advertise, announce, blazon, broadcast, bruit (about), proclaim, promulgate, publish, sound
rel affirm, assert, asseverate, aver; profess, protest; pronounce, state

anodyne *n* **1** something used to relieve or prevent pain <opium and its derivatives are still our most potent *anodynes*>
syn analgesic, anesthetic, pain-killer
rel calmative, depressant, sedative, tranquilizer; hypnotic, somnifacient, soporific, stupefacient

---

2 something that soothes or, often, dulls or deadens the senses or sensibilities <the kind of religion that is no more than an *anodyne*>
syn narcotic, nepenthe, opiate
ant energizer, stimulant; irritant

anomalous *adj* **1** ***syn*** IRREGULAR 1, abnormal, deviant, divergent, off-key, unnatural, unregular
rel monstrous, prodigious
2 ***syn*** ABNORMAL 1, aberrant, atypical, deviant, deviative, heteroclite, preternatural, unrepresentative, untypical
rel foreign, peculiar, singular, strange; monstrous, prodigious
con accustomed, customary, usual, wonted

anon *adv* **1** ***syn*** PRESENTLY 1, by and by, directly, shortly, soon
2 ***syn*** THEN 1, again, when

anonym *n* ***syn*** PSEUDONYM, alias, nom de guerre

anonymous *adj* not identified by name <saved by an *anonymous* hero>
syn innominate, nameless, undesignated, unnamed
rel incognito, unidentified, unknown, unrecognized, unspecified
ant named, onymous

another *adj* **1** ***syn*** THAT 1
2 ***syn*** ADDITIONAL, added, else, farther, fresh, further, more, new, other
rel second

anschauung *n* ***syn*** INTUITION, insight, intuitiveness

anschluss *n* ***syn*** ALLIANCE 2, coalition, confederacy, confederation, federation, league, union

answer *n* **1** something spoken or written by way of return to a question or demand <a sullen *answer*>
syn antiphon, rejoinder, reply, respond, response, retort, return
rel comment, observation, remark; defense, justification; rebuttal, refutation; replication
con inquiry, interrogation, query, question, quiz
2 something attained by mental effort and especially by computation <got the *answer* by trial-and-error methods>
syn result, solution

answer *vb* **1** to say, write, or do something in response (as to a question) <*answered* his critics with documented facts>
syn come in, rejoin, reply, respond, retort, return
rel acknowledge, recognize; disprove, rebut, refute; countercharge, recriminate
idiom come back (at), make reply (to)
con ask, inquire, interrogate, query, question, quiz
2 ***syn*** SATISFY 5, fill, fulfill, meet

answerable *adj* ***syn*** RESPONSIBLE, accountable, amenable, liable

---

syn synonym(s) | *rel* related word(s)
idiom idiomatic equivalent(s) | *con* contrasted word(s)
ant antonym(s) | * vulgar
|| use limited; if in doubt, see a dictionary
The first word in a synonym list when printed in SMALL CAPITALS shows where there is more information about the group. For a more efficient use of this book see Explanatory Notes.

rel bound, compelled, constrained, duty-bound, obligated, obliged

Antaean *adj* ***syn*** HUGE, Brobdingnagian, colossal, cyclopean, gargantuan, giant, gigantic, Herculean, heroic, titanic

antagonism *n* **1** ***syn*** ENMITY, animosity, animus, antipathy, hostility, rancor
rel opposition, oppugnancy, resistance, withstanding; clashing, conflict, difference, disagreement, discord, friction
con concord, consonance, harmony; agreement, understanding
ant accord; comity
2 an opposing state, action, or position <the natural *antagonism* of predators and prey>
syn antithesis, con, contradistinction, contraposition, contrariety, opposition, opposure
rel disagreement, discrepancy, disparity, incongruity; annulling, negation, nullification; counteraction
con agreement, congruity; alliance, association, rapport; empathy, sympathy

antagonist *n* ***syn*** OPPONENT, adversary, anti, con, match, opposer, oppugnant
con adherent, henchman, partisan
ant supporter

antagonistic *adj* **1** ***syn*** BITTER 3, hostile, rancorous, virulent, vitriolic
2 ***syn*** ADVERSE 1, anti, antipathetic, opposed, opposing, oppugnant
rel discordant, incompatible, inconsonant; averse, disinclined, indisposed, unwilling; conflicting, hostile
con advantageous, beneficial; auspicious, benign, propitious
ant favorable
3 ***syn*** ANTIPATHETIC 1, clashing, conflicting, contrariant, contrary, discordant
rel adverse, counter, counteractive, reactive; discordant; antonymous, opposing, oppugnant

ante *adv* ***syn*** BEFORE 1, ahead, antecedently, beforehand, fore, forward, in advance, precedently, previous

ante *prep* ***syn*** BEFORE 1, ahead of, ere, in advance of, preceding, prior to, to

ante *n* ***syn*** BET, pot, stake, wager

antecede *vb* ***syn*** PRECEDE 2, antedate, forerun, pace, predate

antecedence *n* ***syn*** PRIORITY, precedence, precedency, previousness

antecedent *n* **1** ***syn*** CAUSE 1, determinant, occasion, reason
rel forebear, forerunner, precursor; agency, instrumentality, means
con sequel; upshot
ant consequence
2 ***syn*** FORERUNNER 2, ancestor, antecessor, foregoer, precursor, predecessor, prototype
3 — used in pl. ***syn*** ANCESTOR 1, ascendant, forebear, forefather, primogenitor, progenitor

antecedent *adj* ***syn*** PRECEDING, anterior, foregoing, former, past, precedent, previous, prior
ant consequent; subsequent

antecedently *adv* ***syn*** BEFORE 1, ahead, ante, beforehand, fore, forward, in advance, precedently, previous

antecessor *n* ***syn*** FORERUNNER 2, ancestor, antecedent, foregoer, precursor, predecessor, prototype

antedate *vb* ***syn*** PRECEDE 2, antecede, forerun, pace, predate

antediluvian *adj* ***syn*** ANCIENT 1, aged, age-old, antique, hoary, Noachian, old, timeworn, venerable

antediluvian *n* ***syn*** FOGY, fogram, fossil, fuddy-duddy, mid-Victorian, mossback, square, stick-in-the-mud

anterior *adj* ***syn*** PRECEDING, antecedent, anterior, foregoing, former, past, precedent, previous, prior
con after, back, hind, hinder, rear
ant posterior

anthology *n* a collection of selected artistic and especially literary pieces or passages <an *anthology* of sacred music>
syn album, ana, analects, florilegium, garland, miscellany, omnibus, posy
rel collection, compilation; delectus, treasure-house, treasury

anthropoid *adj* resembling man <*anthropoid* apes>
syn anthropomorphic, anthropomorphous, humanoid, manlike

anthropomorphic *adj* ***syn*** ANTHROPOID, anthropomorphous, humanoid, manlike

anthropomorphous *adj* ***syn*** ANTHROPOID, anthropomorphic, humanoid, manlike

anti *n* ***syn*** OPPONENT, adversary, antagonist, con, match, opposer, oppugnant

anti *adj* ***syn*** ADVERSE 1, antagonistic, antipathetic, opposed, opposing, oppugnant
ant pro

antic *n* ***syn*** PRANK, caper, dido(es), frolic, lark, monkeyshine, shenanigan, shine(s), tomfoolery, trick
rel artifice, wile; romp

antic *adj* **1** ***syn*** FANTASTIC 2, bizarre, grotesque
rel foolish; comic, comical, farcical, laughable, ludicrous
con prudent, sensible, wise; conventional, formal; grave, sedate, serious, solemn, somber
2 characterized by a light gay quality <a briskly *antic* and delightful tale>
syn frolicsome, playful, rollicking, sprightly
rel gay, lively, spirited; light, whimsical; casual, easy, suave
con constrained, controlled, curbed, guarded, inhibited, restrained
3 ***syn*** PLAYFUL 1, frisky, frolicsome, gamesome, ‖mischieffful, mischievous, prankful, prankish, pranky, roguish

anticipant *adj* ***syn*** EXPECTANT 1, anticipative, anticipatory, atiptoe, expecting

anticipate *vb* **1** ***syn*** PREVENT 1, forestall
rel forecast, foretell, presage
idiom be one step ahead of
con disregard, ignore, neglect, overlook, slight
2 ***syn*** FORESEE, apprehend, divine, forefeel, foreknow, preknow, previse, prevision, see, visualize
rel await, contemplate, expect; foretaste
idiom be on the lookout (*or* watch) for, look forward to, look (*or* watch) out for

anticipation *n* ***syn*** EXPECTANCY 1, expectation

anticipative *adj* ***syn*** EXPECTANT 1, anticipant, anticipatory, atiptoe, expecting

anticipatory *adj* ***syn*** EXPECTANT 1, anticipant, anticipative, atiptoe, expecting

antidote *n* ***syn*** REMEDY 2, corrective, counteractant, counteractive, counteragent, countermeasure, counterstep, cure
rel negator, neutralizer, nullifier, offset; backfire

antipasto *n* ***syn*** APPETIZER, hors d'oeuvre, whet, zakuska

antipathetic *adj* **1** having a natural or inherent opposition <national needs *antipathetic* to peace>
syn antagonistic, clashing, conflicting, contrariant, contrary, discordant
rel antipodal, antithetical, antonymous, contradictory, opposite
idiom at cross purposes, at daggers drawn, at war with one another
con agreeing, consonant, correspondent, harmonious; coactive, collaborative, cooperative
ant concordant
2 arousing marked aversion or dislike <found his sister's husband in every way *antipathetic*>
syn aversive, kindless, repellent, repugnant, uncongenial, ungenial, unsympathetic
rel abhorrent, obnoxious; disgustful, disgusting, distasteful, loathsome, repulsive
con compatible, consonant, sympathetic; alluring, attractive, charming; agreeable, pleasant, pleasing, satisfying, soothing
ant congenial
3 ***syn*** ADVERSE 1, antagonistic, anti, opposed, opposing, oppugnant

antipathy *n* **1** ***syn*** ENMITY, animosity, animus, antagonism, hostility, rancor
rel disrelish, distaste, repellency, repugnance; avoidance, escape, eschewal, evasion
con liking, partiality, predilection, prepossession; attachment, love; attraction, taste (for)
ant affection (for)
2 the state of mind induced by what is antipathetic <a strong *antipathy* to modern art>
syn allergy, aversion, dyspathy
rel abhorrence, dislike, disrelish, distaste, repellency, repugnance; avoidance, escape, eschewal, evasion
con liking, partiality, predilection, prepossession; affection, attachment, love; attraction
ant taste (for)

antiphon *n* ***syn*** ANSWER 1, rejoinder, reply, respond, response, retort, return

antipodal *adj* ***syn*** OPPOSITE, antipodean, antithetical, contradictory, contrary, converse, counter, diametric, polar, reverse

antipode *n* ***syn*** OPPOSITE, antipole, antithesis, contra, contradictory, contrary, converse, counter, counterpole, reverse

---

syn synonym(s) — ***rel*** related word(s)
idiom idiomatic equivalent(s) — ***con*** contrasted word(s)
ant antonym(s) — * vulgar
‖ use limited; if in doubt, see a dictionary
The first word in a synonym list when printed in SMALL CAPITALS shows where there is more information about the group. For a more efficient use of this book see Explanatory Notes.

antipodean *adj* ***syn*** OPPOSITE, antipodal, antithetical, contradictory, contrary, converse, counter, diametric, polar, reverse

antipole *n* ***syn*** OPPOSITE, antipode, antithesis, contra, contradictory, contrary, converse, counter, counterpole, reverse

antiquate *vb* ***syn*** OUTDATE, obsolesce, obsolete, outmode, superannuate

antiquated *adj* ***syn*** OLD-FASHIONED, antique, archaic, dated, fusty, moldy, oldfangled, old-timey, outmoded, passé
con modern, new, novel
ant modernistic

antique *adj* **1** ***syn*** ANCIENT 1, aged, age-old, antediluvian, hoary, Noachian, old, timeworn, venerable
rel ancestral, dateless, immemorial, legendary, time-honored, traditional
con advanced, current, recent
2 ***syn*** OLD-FASHIONED, antiquated, archaic, dated, oldfangled, old-timey, outdated, outmoded, out-of-date, passé

antisocial *adj* averse to the society of others <a pure scholar, remote and *antisocial*>
syn eremitic, misanthropic, reclusive, reserved, solitary, standoffish
rel ascetic, austere, cold, remote; cynical, introverted, withdrawn
con affable, friendly, gregarious; communicative, outgoing, sociable
ant social

antithesis *n* **1** ***syn*** ANTAGONISM 2, con, contradistinction, contraposition, contrariety, opposition, opposure
2 ***syn*** OPPOSITE, antipode, antipole, contra, contradictory, contrary, converse, counter, counterpole, reverse

antithetical *adj* ***syn*** OPPOSITE, antipodal, antipodean, contradictory, contrary, converse, counter, diametric, polar, reverse

anxiety *n* ***syn*** CARE 2, concern, concernment, disquiet, disquietude, solicitude, unease, uneasiness, worry
rel doubt, mistrust, uncertainty; distress, misery, suffering; dread; panic
con composure, equanimity, sangfroid; aplomb, confidence, self-possession; certainty, certitude, faith, trust
ant security

anxious *adj* **1** ***syn*** AFRAID 1, aghast, ||ascared, fearful, frightened, scared, scary, terrified
rel agitated, apprehensive, jittery, perturbed, upset, worried; alarmed, bothered, disquieted, troubled, uneasy
idiom ill at ease
con calm, collected, cool, easy, imperturbable, unruffled; assured, confident, sanguine, sure
2 ***syn*** EAGER, agog, appetent, ardent, athirst, avid, breathless, impatient, keen, thirsty
rel importunate, pressing, urgent
idiom all agog, bursting to
con averse, disinclined, hesitant, indisposed, reluctant
ant loath

anyhow *adv* ***syn*** ABOUT 4, any which way, anywise, around, at random, haphazard, haphazardly, helter-skelter, random, randomly

anytime *adv* ***syn*** EVER 4, at all

anyway *adv* ***syn*** EVER 5, anywise, at all, once

any which way *adv* ***syn*** ABOUT 4, anyhow, anywise, around, at random, haphazard, haphazardly, helter-skelter, random, randomly

anywise *adv* **1** ***syn*** ABOUT 4, anyhow, any which way, around, at random, haphazard, haphazardly, helter-skelter, random, randomly
2 ***syn*** EVER 5, anyway, at all, once

A1 *adj* ***syn*** EXCELLENT, blue-ribbon, first-class, first-rate, five-star, front-rank, Grade A, number one, prime, superior

apace *adv* ***syn*** FAST 2, expeditiously, flat-out, hastily, lickety-split, posthaste, quickly, rapidly, speedily, swiftly

apart *adv* **1** as a discrete item <taken *apart,* his view seemed sound enough>
syn independently, individually, one by one, separately, severally, singly
idiom one at a time
2 excluded from consideration <these slips *apart,* he had done very well>
syn aside
idiom to one side
3 in or into parts <tore the sheets *apart*>
syn asunder, sky-high
idiom all to pieces, to bits (*or* flinders)

apart *adj* ***syn*** ALONE 1, detached, isolate, isolated, removed, unaccompanied

apart from *prep* ***syn*** EXCEPT, aside from, bar, barring, besides, but, exclusive of, outside of, save, saving

apartheid *n* ***syn*** SEGREGATION, separateness, separation, separatism

apartment *n* **1** a set of rooms (as in a private house or a block) rented or leased for use as a dwelling place <had a tiny top-floor *apartment*>
syn ||chambers, flat, lodging(s), rental, rooms, suite, tenement
2 ***syn*** ROOM 1, chamber

apathetic *adj* ***syn*** IMPASSIVE 1, dry, matter-of-fact, phlegmatic, stoic, stolid
rel dull, inert, languid, sluggish, torpid; anesthetic, impassible, insensible, insensitive; callous, unmoved, untouched; limp, spiritless
con aroused, awake, aware, conscious, impressionable, perceptive, receptive; vigilant, watchful, wide-awake
ant alert

apathy *n* **1** lack of emotional responsiveness <hid her sorrow behind a dull brooding *apathy*>
syn impassivity, insensibility, phlegm, stoicism, stolidity, unresponsiveness
rel inertness, passivity, supineness; aloofness, detachment, indifference, unconcern; lethargy, torpidity, torpor; listlessness, numbness, stupefaction, stupor
con ardor, fervor, passion, responsiveness, warmth; alertness, awareness, concern, solicitude

---

syn synonym(s) ***rel*** related word(s)
idiom idiomatic equivalent(s) ***con*** contrasted word(s)
ant antonym(s) * vulgar
|| use limited; if in doubt, see a dictionary
The first word in a synonym list when printed in SMALL CAPITALS shows where there is more information about the group. For a more efficient use of this book see Explanatory Notes.

ant zeal; enthusiasm
2 lack of interest or concern <public *apathy* toward the school crisis>
syn disinterest, disregard, heedlessness, indifference, insouciance, lassitude, lethargy, listlessness, unconcern, unmindfulness
rel callousness, hardness, insensitivity, obduracy, unawareness; coldness, halfheartedness, lukewarmness; calmness, dispassion, dispassionateness
con attentiveness, concern, heedfulness, interest; awareness, mindfulness, sensitivity, solicitude; ardency, fervency, passion, warmth, zeal

ape *vb* ***syn*** MIMIC, burlesque, imitate, mock, parody, take off, travesty
rel caricature; emulate, rival
idiom make like

aperçu *n* ***syn*** COMPENDIUM 1, digest, pandect, précis, sketch, survey, syllabus, sylloge

aperitive *adj* ***syn*** PALATABLE, appetizing, flavorsome, mouth-watering, sapid, saporous, savory, tasteful, tasty, toothsome

aperture *n* a discontinuity allowing passage <the mouse squeezed through a narrow *aperture* in the wall>
syn hole, opening, orifice, outlet, vent
rel discontinuity, gap, hiatus, interstice; bore, perforation, pinhole, prick, puncture; chasm, cleft, cut, gash, slash, slit; breach, break, rupture

apery *n* ***syn*** MIMICRY

apex *n* **1** ***syn*** TOP 1, crest, crown, fastigium, peak, roof, summit, vertex
rel extremity, limit, spire
ant nadir
2 the culminating point <the *apex* of his career>
syn acme, apogee, capsheaf, capstone, climax, comble, crescendo, crest, crown, culmen, culmination, meridian, ne plus ultra, noon, noontide, peak, pinnacle, sublimity, summit, zenith
rel last word, prime, quintescence, ultimate; achievement, attainment, consummation, realization
ant nadir
3 ***syn*** POINT 9, cusp, tip
rel cap, crest, peak, prominence, spire

aphorism *n* ***syn*** MAXIM, apothegm, axiom, brocard, dictum, gnome, moral, rule, truism

aphrodisia *n* ***syn*** LUST 2, concupiscence, desire, eroticism, itch, lickerishness, lustfulness, passion, prurience, pruriency

aphrodisiac *adj* ***syn*** EROTIC, amative, amatory, amorous
ant anaphrodisiac

apiarist *n* ***syn*** BEEKEEPER, apiculturist, beeman, beemaster

apical *adj* ***syn*** TOP 1, highest, loftiest, topmost, uppermost

apiculturist *n* ***syn*** BEEKEEPER, apiarist, beeman, beemaster

apiece *adv* by, for, or to each one <gave the boys a dollar *apiece*>
syn all, aside, each, ‖per, per capita, per caput
rel individually, one by one, respectively, severally, singly, successively

apish *adj* ***syn*** SLAVISH 3, emulative, imitative

aplomb *n* ***syn*** CONFIDENCE 2, assurance, self-assurance, self-assuredness, self-confidence, self-trust
rel poise, savoir faire; coolness, imperturbability, levelheadedness, nonchalance; composure, ease, easiness, equanimity, sangfroid
idiom presence of mind
con bewilderment, distraction, perplexity; befuddlement, confusion, fluster, fuddlement; discomfiture, embarrassment, perturbation
ant shyness

apocalypse *n* ***syn*** REVELATION, oracle, prophecy, vision
rel envisioning, foresight, precognition, prevision

apocalyptic *adj* **1** ***syn*** PROPHETIC, Delphian, fatidic, mantic, oracular, prophetical, sibylline, vatic, vaticinal
2 ***syn*** OMINOUS, baleful, baneful, dire, direful, fateful, ill-boding, inauspicious, threatening, unlucky

apocryphal *adj* ***syn*** SPURIOUS 3, bastard, unauthentic, ungenuine
rel false, erroneous, inaccurate, incorrect, untrue, wrong; doubtful, dubious, questionable
idiom open to question
con accurate, correct, established, factual, true, truthful, veracious; authentic

apogee *n* ***syn*** APEX 2, acme, capstone, climax, culmination, meridian, peak, pinnacle, summit, zenith

Apollyon *n* ***syn*** DEVIL 1, Beelzebub, diablo, fiend, Lucifer, Old Gooseberry, Old Nick, Old Scratch, Satan, serpent

apologetic *adj* ***syn*** REMORSEFUL, attritional, compunctious, contrite, penitent, penitential, regretful, repentant, sorry

apologetic *n* ***syn*** APOLOGY 1, apologia, defense, justification

apologia *n* ***syn*** APOLOGY 1, apologetic, defense, justification
rel clarification, elucidation, explanation, interpretation

apologue *n* ***syn*** ALLEGORY 2, fable, myth, parable

apology *n* **1** a presentation intended to justify or defend something <the white paper is essentially an *apology* for recent foreign policy>
syn apologetic, apologia, defense, justification; *compare* EXCUSE 1
rel excuse, extenuation, mitigation, palliation; advocating, advocation, championing, espousal, espousing, support
idiom pleading one's cause, putting in a good word for, speaking up for
con blame, censure, condemnation, decrial, reprehension, reprobation
2 an acknowledgment expressing regret for a wrong, improper, or discommoding act <murmured a brief *apology* for her lateness>
syn excuse, regrets; *compare* EXCUSE 1
rel amends, atonement; acknowledgment, admission, concession, confession, mea culpa; reparation, redress, satisfaction

---

syn synonym(s)	***rel*** related word(s)
idiom idiomatic equivalent(s)	***con*** contrasted word(s)
ant antonym(s)	* vulgar

‖ use limited; if in doubt, see a dictionary
The first word in a synonym list when printed in SMALL CAPITALS shows where there is more information about the group. For a more efficient use of this book see Explanatory Notes.

3 *syn* EXCUSE 3
aporetic *adj syn* INCREDULOUS, disbelieving, questioning, quizzical, show-me, skeptical, unbelieving
apostasy *n syn* DEFECTION, desertion, falseness, recreancy, tergiversation
rel perfidy, treacherousness
apostate *n syn* RENEGADE, defector, rat, recreant, runagate, tergiversator, turnabout, turncoat
rel bolter; dissenter, nonconformist, recusant
con adherent, follower, partisan; convert, proselyte
apostatize *vb syn* DEFECT, desert, rat, renounce, repudiate, tergiversate, tergiverse, turn
a posteriori *adj syn* INDUCTIVE, inducible
apostle *n syn* MISSIONARY, colporteur, evangelist, missioner, propagandist
apothecary *n syn* DRUGGIST, ‖chemist, pharmacist
apothegm *n syn* MAXIM, aphorism, axiom, brocard, dictum, gnome, moral, rule, truism
apotheosis *n* **1** the consummate form, example, or instance (as of a quality) <the *apotheosis* of vulgarity>
syn epitome, last word, quintessence, ultimate; *compare* EMBODIMENT
rel acme, culmination, height, peak, summit
idiom ‖the living end
2 a raising to a state of eminent triumph or glory <the *apotheosis* of a folk hero>
syn aggrandizement, deification, dignification, exaltation, glorification
rel elevation, ennoblement, enshrinement, idolization, immortalization, lionization
con debasement, defamation, degradation, denigration, sullying
appall *vb syn* DISMAY 1, consternate, daunt, horrify, shake
rel awe, faze, overawe
con brace (up), buck up, cheer (up); assure, hearten, inspire, inspirit
ant embolden, nerve
appalling *adj syn* FEARFUL 3, awful, dreadful, formidable, frightful, horrible, horrific, shocking, terrible, terrific
rel daunting, dismaying, horrifying; bewildering, confounding, dumbfounding
con assuring, heartening, inspiriting
ant reassuring
appanage *n syn* RIGHT 2, birthright, perquisite, prerogative, privilege
apparatus *n syn* EQUIPMENT, accouterment(s), gear, habiliments, machinery, matériel, outfit, paraphernalia, tackle, tackling
rel implement, instrument, tool, utensil; furnishings, provisions, supplies
apparel *vb syn* CLOTHE, array, attire, clad, dress, enclothe, garb, garment, raiment
rel appoint
con bare, denude
ant divest
apparel *n syn* CLOTHES, attire, attirement, clothing, dress, duds, habiliment(s), raiment, things, togs
apparent *adj* **1** *syn* CLEAR 5, distinct, evident, manifest, obvious, palpable, patent, plain, unambiguous, unequivocal
rel ponderable; noticeable, prominent; discernible, observable, perceivable
idiom plain as day, plain to be seen
con ambiguous, hidden, obscure
ant inapparent
2 being other than seems to be the case <her *apparent* goodwill masked an inner loathing>
syn Barmecidal, illusive, illusory, ostensible, seeming, semblant
rel deceptive, delusive, delusory, misleading; credible, plausible, specious; factitious, fake, false, pseudo, sham, suppositious, supposititious
con genuine, true, valid; basic, essential, fundamental, inherent, intrinsic
ant actual, real
apparently *adv syn* OSTENSIBLY, evidently, officially, outwardly, professedly, seemingly
apparition *n* a visible appearance of something not present and especially of a dead person <illusions that the superstitious see as *apparitions*>
syn bogey, eidolon, ghost, ‖haunt, phantasm, phantom, revenant, shade, shadow, specter, spectrum, spirit, ‖spook, umbra, wraith
rel delusion, hallucination, illusion; corposant, foxfire, ignis fatuus, jack-o'-lantern, marshfire, Saint Elmo's fire, will-o'-the-wisp
appeal *n* **1** *syn* PRAYER, application, entreaty, imploration, imprecation, orison, petition, plea, suit, supplication
rel asking, requesting, solicitation
con claim, demand, exaction; kick, objection, protest
2 *syn* ATTRACTION 1, allurement, attractiveness, call, draw, drawing power, lure, pull, seduction
3 *syn* CHARM 3, allure, charisma, fascination, glamour, magnetism, witchcraft, witchery
rel draw; pleasantness
con disagreeableness, unpleasantness
appeal *vb* **1** *syn* BEG, beseech, brace, crave, entreat, implore, importune, plead, pray, supplicate
2 *syn* PETITION, sue (for *or* to)
3 *syn* INTEREST, attract, excite, fascinate, intrigue
appealing *adj syn* ATTRACTIVE 1, alluring, attracting, bewitching, captivating, charming, enchanting, fascinating, seductive, siren
appear *vb* **1** to become visible <the sun *appeared* from behind a cloud>
syn emerge, loom, show
rel arrive, come; arise, emanate, issue, materialize, outcrop, rise, spring
idiom come in sight, come into view, meet (*or* strike) the eye, show one's face
con go, leave; depart, retire, withdraw
ant disappear, vanish
2 *syn* SEEM, look, sound
idiom give an appearance of, strike one as

appearance *n* **1** the state or form in which one appears <his disheveled *appearance* surprised his guests>
syn aspect, look, mien, seeming
rel air, bearing, countenance, demeanor, manner
2 *usu* **appearances** *pl* outward and often deceptive indication or look <to all *appearances* he was guilty>
syn face, guise, seeming, semblance, show, showing, simulacrum; *compare* MASK
rel fiction, make-believe, pretense, pretension; disguise, facade, front, masquerade, outside, pose
idiom outward show
con fact, reality, truth

appease *vb* **1** ***syn*** PACIFY, assuage, conciliate, mollify, placate, propitiate, sweeten
rel calm (down), ease, soothe; extenuate, gloss (over), palliate, whitewash
con annoy, bother, irk, vex; anger, enrage, incense, infuriate; discompose, disturb, perturb, upset
ant exasperate
2 ***syn*** SATISFY 3, content, gratify
rel ease, relieve; cater (to), coddle, pamper, spoil
ant aggravate

appellation *n* ***syn*** NAME 1, appellative, cognomen, compellation, denomination, designation, ||moniker, nomen, style, title

appellative *n* ***syn*** NAME 1, appellation, cognomen, compellation, denomination, designation, ||moniker, nomen, style, title

append *vb* ***syn*** ADD 1, annex, subjoin, superadd, take on

appendage *n* something accompanying or attached to another thing to which it is usually subordinate or nonessential <people to whom culture is a mere *appendage* to life>
syn accessory, adjunct, appendix, appurtenance
rel auxiliary, incidental, subsidiary, supplement; collateral, extra, nonessential

appendix *n* **1** additional material subjoined to a writing and especially a book <a dictionary with an *appendix* of new words>
syn addendum, codicil, rider, supplement
2 ***rel*** APPENDAGE, accessory, adjunct, appurtenance

apperception *n* ***syn*** RECOGNITION 1, assimilation, identification
rel apprehension, grasp, perception; comprehension, understanding

appertain *vb* **1** ***syn*** BELONG 2, pertain, vest
2 ***syn*** BEAR (on *or* upon), apply, pertain, relate

appetence *n* ***syn*** APPETITE 1, stomach, taste

appetent *adj* ***syn*** EAGER, agog, anxious, ardent, athirst, avid, breathless, impatient, keen, thirsty
rel craving, desirous, lusting, yearning
idiom consumed with desire

appetite *n* **1** a natural enjoyment of food <all fell to with a hearty *appetite*>
syn appetence, stomach, taste
rel gluttony, greed, hunger, voracity; epicurism, gourmandise
2 ***syn*** DESIRE 1, appetition, craving, itch, lust, passion, urge
rel cupidity, greed, urgency
con abnegation, asceticism, renunciation, self-denial; distaste, revulsion
3 an attraction toward something <had a great *appetite* for gossip>
syn fondness, inclination, liking, soft spot, taste, weakness
rel bent, bias, flair, leaning, penchant, proclivity, propensity
con disinclination, dislike, distaste; disinterest, unconcern

appetition *n* ***syn*** DESIRE 1, appetite, craving, itch, lust, passion, urge

appetizer *n* food or drink served before a meal to stimulate appetite <*appetizers* such as cocktails, and canapés>
syn antipasto, hors d'oeuvre, whet, zakuska
rel dainty, delicacy, goody, tidbit; savory

appetizing *adj* ***syn*** PALATABLE, aperitive, flavorsome, mouth-watering, relishing, sapid, saporous, savory, tasty, toothsome
ant disgusting, nauseating

applaud *vb* **1** ***syn*** COMMEND 2, acclaim, compliment, hail, kudize, praise, recommend, ||roose
rel boost, plug
ant censure; admonish
2 to express enthusiastic approval <*applauded* wildly when his team won a point>
syn cheer, rise (to), root
rel acclaim, extol, laud, praise; eulogize, glorify, magnify, panegyrize
con deride, mock, ridicule, taunt; contemn, disdain, scorn, scout
ant boo; hiss

applause *n* public expression of approbation <her appearance was greeted with *applause*>
syn acclaim, acclamation, plaudit(s)
rel cheers, hand, ovation, round; cheering, clapping, rooting
con derision, mockery, ridicule, taunting; Bronx cheer, raspberry
ant booing, hissing

||**apple knocker** *n* ***syn*** RUSTIC, bucolic, bumpkin, hayseed, hick, hoosier, jake, provincial, redneck, yokel

apple–polish *vb* ***syn*** FAWN, bootlick, ||brownnose, cower, cringe, grovel, honey (up), kowtow, toady, truckle

apple–polisher *n* ***syn*** SYCOPHANT, bootlick, bootlicker, ||brownnose, ||brownnoser, ||clawback, footlicker, groveler, lickspit, lickspittle

||**applesauce** *n* ***syn*** NONSENSE 2, ||baloney, blatherskite, bunkum, fudge, hooey, malarkey, poppycock, rubbish, twaddle

appliance *n* ***syn*** USE 1, application, employment, operation, play, usance

applicability *n* ***syn*** USE 3, account, advantage, appropriateness, avail, fitness, relevance, serviceability, usefulness, utility
con irrelevance, unsuitability

---

syn synonym(s)	***rel*** related word(s)
idiom idiomatic equivalent(s)	***con*** contrasted word(s)
ant antonym(s)	* vulgar

|| use limited; if in doubt, see a dictionary

The first word in a synonym list when printed in SMALL CAPITALS shows where there is more information about the group. For a more efficient use of this book see Explanatory Notes.

ant inapplicability

applicable *adj* **1** *syn* RELEVANT, ad rem, applicative, applicatory, apposite, apropos, germane, material, pertinent, pointful
rel alliable, associable, compatible, congenial, connective
con incompatible, uncongenial; inappropriate, unfit, unsuitable
ant inapplicable
2 *syn* FIT 1, appropriate, apt, befitting, felicitous, fitting, happy, just, meet, suitable
rel correct, good, seemly
idiom as it ought to be, as it should be
con improper, incorrect

applicant *n syn* CANDIDATE, aspirant, hopeful, seeker

application *n* **1** *syn* ATTENTION 1, concentration, consideration, debate, deliberation, heed, study
rel busyness, zeal; energy, indefatigability
con bemusement, wool-gathering; faineance, laziness, sloth
ant indolence
2 *syn* USE 1, appliance, employment, operation, play, usance
3 *syn* EXERCISE 1, employment, exercising, exertion, operation, use
4 *syn* PRAYER, appeal, entreaty, imploration, imprecation, orison, petition, plea, suit, supplication

applicative *adj syn* RELEVANT, ad rem, applicable, applicatory, apposite, apropos, germane, material, pertinent, pointful

applicatory *adj syn* RELEVANT, ad rem, applicable, applicative, apposite, apropos, germane, material, pertinent, pointful

apply *vb* **1** *syn* ADDRESS 3, bend, buckle (down), devote, direct, give, throw, turn
rel set about, take on, undertake; drudge, grind, toil
idiom burn the midnight oil, keep one's nose to the grindstone, work like a horse (*or* dog *or* ‖nigger); concern (oneself) with something, set (one's hand) to something
con let slide, neglect, pass over, slight
2 *syn* BEAR (on *or* upon), appertain, pertain, relate
idiom come into relation with
3 *syn* RESORT 2, go, recur, refer, repair, run, turn
rel appeal, petition; beg, beseech, entreat, implore, supplicate; importune, press, urge
idiom make application to
4 *syn* USE 2, bestow, employ, exercise, exploit, handle, utilize

apply (to) *vb syn* ADDRESS 4, accost, approach, bespeak, memorialize

appoint *vb* **1** *syn* DESIGNATE 2, finger, make, name, nominate, tap
rel accredit, authorize, commission
con cashier, discharge, dismiss; debar, exclude, reject
2 *syn* FURNISH 1, accouter, arm, equip, fit out, gear, outfit, rig, turn out
rel embellish, enrich, furbish, garnish; dress up, set off, spruce (up)
con denude, dismantle, divest, strip

appointment *n* **1** *syn* JOB 2, berth, billet, connection, office, place, position, post, situation, spot
2 *syn* ENGAGEMENT 3, assignation, date, rendezvous, tryst

apportion *vb* **1** *syn* ALLOT, admeasure, allocate, allow, assign, give, lot, mete (out)
rel divide, partition, share
con assemble, collect, gather
2 to separate something into shares with care and accuracy and distribute it among a number <Christ *apportioned* the loaves and fishes>
syn divide, ‖divvy, parcel, portion, prorate, quota, ration, share, ‖shift
rel accord, award, bestow, distribute; give, grant, present; part, separate, split
3 *syn* ADMINISTER 2, deal (out), dispense, dole (out), mete (out), portion (out), share out
rel dish out, serve

apportionment *n syn* RATION, allotment, allowance, measure, meed, part, portion, quantum, quota, share

apposite *adj syn* RELEVANT, ad rem, applicable, applicative, applicatory, apropos, germane, material, pertinent, pointful
rel felicitous, happy; opportune, pat, seasonable, timely
idiom to the point (*or* purpose)
con awkward, inept; casual, haphazard, hit-or-miss, random
ant inapposite, inapt

appositeness *n syn* ORDER 11, appropriateness, aptness, expediency, fitness, meetness, propriety, rightness, suitability, suitableness

appraisal *n* **1** *syn* ESTIMATE 1, appraisement, assessment, estimation, evaluation, valuation
2 *syn* ESTIMATION 1, appraisement, assessment, estimate, evaluation, judgment, stock

appraise *vb syn* ESTIMATE 1, assay, assess, evaluate, rate, set (at), survey, valuate, value
rel adjudge, deem, esteem, judge; audit, examine, inspect, scrutinize
idiom set (*or* place) a value on, take the measure of

appraisement *n* **1** *syn* ESTIMATE 1, appraisal, assessment, estimation, evaluation, valuation
2 *syn* ESTIMATION 1, appraisal, assessment, estimate, evaluation, judgment, stock

appreciable *adj syn* PERCEPTIBLE, detectable, discernible, observable, palpable, sensible, tangible
rel noticeable; apparent, clear, evident, manifest, obvious, plain; concrete, material, real, substantial
con impalpable, imperceptible, imponderable, insensible, intangible
ant inappreciable

appreciate *vb* **1** to hold in high estimation <*appreciate* the kindness of a friend>
syn apprize, cherish, esteem, prize, treasure, value; *compare* ADMIRE 1
rel admire, regard, respect; adore, ‖eat up, enjoy, like, love, relish

---

syn synonym(s) — *rel* related word(s)
idiom idiomatic equivalent(s) — *con* contrasted word(s)
ant antonym(s) — * vulgar
‖ use limited; if in doubt, see a dictionary
The first word in a synonym list when printed in SMALL CAPITALS shows where there is more information about the group. For a more efficient use of this book see Explanatory Notes.

idiom rate highly, set great store by, think much (*or* well) of
con contemn, disapprove, disdain, scorn; decry, depreciate, disparage
ant despise
2 *syn* ADMIRE 1, cherish, delight (in), relish
rel enjoy, like, savor
con contemn, disdain, scorn
3 *syn* KNOW 1, apprehend, cognize, comprehend, fathom, grasp, have, understand
rel catch, seize, take in

appreciation *n syn* TESTIMONIAL 3, salvo, tribute

apprehend *vb* **1** to recognize the existence or meaning of <as a child learns to *apprehend* the relation between naughtiness and punishment>
syn accept, catch, compass, comprehend, conceive, cotton (to *or* on to), ||dig, follow, grasp, make out, see, take, take in, tumble (to), twig, understand
rel realize, recognize, sense; absorb, digest, seize; catch on, wise (up); penetrate
idiom catch (*or* get) the drift of, get the idea, get through one's head, make head or tail of
ant misapprehend
2 *syn* ARREST 2, ||bust, detain, nab, pick up, pinch, pull in, run in
3 *syn* FORESEE, anticipate, divine, forefeel, foreknow, preknow, previse, prevision, see, visualize
rel dread, fear
idiom be on pins and needles, have one's heart in one's mouth, wait with bated breath
4 *syn* KNOW 1, appreciate, cognize, comprehend, fathom, grasp, have, understand
idiom be acquainted with, be cognizant of

apprehensible *adj syn* UNDERSTANDABLE, comprehendible, comprehensible, fathomable, graspable, intelligible, knowable, lucid, luminous

apprehension *n* **1** *syn* IDEA, conceit, concept, conception, image, impression, intellection, notion, perception, thought
2 *syn* ARREST, arrestation, arrestment, detention, ||nab, pickup, pinch
3 fear that something is going or will go wrong <had the strongest *apprehension* about her sister's health>
syn apprehensiveness, foreboding, misgiving, premonition, prenotion, presage, presentiment
rel agitation, angst, anxiety, care, concern, disquiet, disquietude, solicitude, unease, uneasiness, worry; alarm, dread, fear, panic
idiom the anxious seat
con assurance, composure, equanimity, sangfroid, self-possession; faith, reliance, trust
ant confidence

apprehensive *adj* **1** *syn* AWARE, alive, awake, cognizant, conscious, knowing, sensible, sentient, ware, witting
2 *syn* FEARFUL 2, afraid
ant confident

apprehensiveness *n syn* APPREHENSION 3, foreboding, misgiving, premonition, prenotion, presage, presentiment

apprentice *n syn* NOVICE, beginner, colt, freshman, neophyte, newcomer, novitiate, rookie, tenderfoot, tyro
rel starter; amateur
con adept, expert, specialist

apprenticed *adj syn* BOUND 2, articled, indentured

apprise *vb syn* INFORM 2, acquaint, advise, clue (*or* clew), fill in, notify, post, tell, warn, wise (up)
rel announce, communicate, declare, proclaim, publish; disclose, discover, divulge, reveal, tell
idiom make known to, serve (one) notice

apprize *vb syn* APPRECIATE 1, cherish, esteem, prize, treasure, value

approach *vb* **1** to come or go near or nearer <as a boy *approaches* manhood>
syn approximate, near, nigh
rel achieve, arrive (at), attain, gain, hit, make, reach; draw on
idiom come to close quarters with
con recede, retire, retreat, withdraw; depart, go, leave
2 *syn* ADDRESS 4, accost, apply (to), bespeak, memorialize
rel advise, confer, consult, counsel, negotiate, parley; beg, beseech, entreat, implore, plead, supplicate
3 *syn* REACH 3
4 *syn* AMOUNT 2, correspond (to), equal, match, partake (of), rival, touch
con depart, deviate, digress; differ, disaccord, disharmonize, vary
5 *syn* BORDER 3, trench, verge

approach *n syn* OVERTURE 1, advance
rel attempt, endeavor, essay, try; call, invitation
ant withdrawal

approaching *adj syn* FORTHCOMING, coming, nearing, oncoming, upcoming

approbate *vb syn* APPROVE 1, accept, countenance, favor, go (for), hold (with)

approbation *n* warmly commending acceptance or agreement <expressed *approbation* of their progress>
syn approval, benediction, blessing, favor, OK (*or* okay)
rel commendation, countenance, goodwill, sanction; admiration, esteem, liking, regard, respect; pleasure, satisfaction
con censure, condemnation, criticism, disapproval, disfavor, reprehension; annoyance, disgust, irritation; distress, regret, sorrow
ant disapprobation

approbative *adj syn* FAVORABLE 1, approbatory, approving

approbatory *adj syn* FAVORABLE 1, approbative, approving

appropinquity *n syn* PROXIMITY, contiguity, contiguousness, immediacy, propinquity

appropriate *vb* **1** to take over as if by preeminent right <limitations on the right of the state to *appropriate* private property>

---

syn accroach, annex, arrogate, commandeer, confiscate, expropriate, preempt, seize, sequester, take; *compare* ARROGATE 1
rel grab, grasp, snatch; claim, exact, extort, wrench; conscript, draft, press
idiom help oneself to, lay hold of, make free with, take possession of
2 *syn* STEAL 1, annex, ||cop, filch, lift, pilfer, pinch, purloin, snitch, swipe
rel despoil, spoil; forage, raid
3 *syn* ARROGATE 1, accroach, assume, commandeer, preempt, usurp

appropriate *adj* 1 *syn* FIT 1, applicable, apt, befitting, felicitous, fitting, just, meet, proper, suitable
rel apposite, germane, pertinent, relevant; opportune, pat, seasonable, timely
con incompatible, incongruous, inconsonant
ant inappropriate
2 *syn* GOOD 2, convenient, fit, meet, proper, suitable, useful
rel agreeable, desirable, enjoyable, pleasant; acceptable, admissible, eligible, entitled, right, worthy
con disagreeable undesirable, unpleasant; inadmissible, ineligible, unworthy, wrong
ant inappropriate
3 *syn* JUST 3, condign, deserved, due, merited, requisite, rhadamanthine, right, rightful, suitable
con unfair, unjustified, unmerited, unreasonable; unsuitable
ant inappropriate
4 *syn* TRUE 7, desired, fitting, proper
ant inappropriate

appropriately *adv syn* WELL 4, acceptably, adequately, amply, becomingly, fittingly, properly, right, satisfactorily, suitably

appropriateness *n* 1 *syn* USE 3, account, advantage, applicability, fitness, relevance, service, serviceability, usefulness, utility
2 *syn* ORDER 11, appositeness, aptness, expediency, fitness, meetness, propriety, rightness, suitability, suitableness

appropriation *n* property (as money) set apart or given by official or formal action for a predetermined use by others <an increased *appropriation* for public housing>
syn grant, subsidy, subvention
rel allotment, allowance, stipend; aid, assistance, grant-in-aid, help

approval *n syn* APPROBATION, benediction, blessing, favor, OK (*or* okay)
rel applause, commendation, compliment; acceptance, endorsement, sanction, suffrage
con depreciation, derogation, disparagement
ant disapproval

---

syn synonym(s) *rel* related word(s)
idiom idiomatic equivalent(s) *con* contrasted word(s)
ant antonym(s) * vulgar
|| use limited; if in doubt, see a dictionary
The first word in a synonym list when printed in SMALL CAPITALS shows where there is more information about the group. For a more efficient use of this book see Explanatory Notes.

approve *vb* 1 to find acceptable <they were unable to *approve* his behavior>
syn accept, approbate, countenance, favor, go (for), hold (with)
rel back (up), stand by, support, sustain, uphold; bear, endure, put up (with), tolerate
idiom be in favor of, pat on the back, take kindly to, think well (*or* highly) of, view with approval (*or* favor)
con deprecate, disfavor, dislike, frown (on *or* upon); object (to), oppose
ant disapprove
2 to give an often formal expression of approval and support <the committee *approved* the plans for the new clubhouse>
syn accredit, certify, endorse, OK (*or* okay), sanction
rel applaud, compliment, commend; confirm, initial, ratify; clear
con refuse, reject, repudiate, spurn; censure, condemn, criticize, reprehend, reprobate
ant disapprove

approving *adj syn* FAVORABLE 1, approbative, approbatory

approximal *adj syn* ADJACENT 3, abutting, adjoining, bordering, conterminous, contiguous, juxtaposed, touching

approximate *adj* 1 *syn* COMPARATIVE, near, relative
2 *syn* RUDE 3, proximate, rough

approximate *vb* 1 *syn* APPROACH 1, near, nigh
idiom be in the neighborhood of
2 *syn* ESTIMATE 3, call, judge, place, put, reckon

approximately *adv syn* NEARLY, about, all but, almost, most, much, ||nearabout, nigh, practically, well-nigh
idiom in round numbers, right about
ant exactly, precisely

appulse *n syn* IMPACT, bump, clash, collision, concussion, impingement, jar, jolt, percussion, shock

appurtenance *n syn* APPENDAGE, accessory, adjunct, appendix
rel appointment (*usu* appointments *pl*), equipment, furnishings, furniture

appurtenant *adj syn* AUXILIARY, accessory, adjuvant, ancillary, collateral, contributory, subservient, subsidiary

a priori *adj syn* DEDUCTIVE, deducible, derivable, dogmatic, reasoned

apriorism *n syn* ASSUMPTION 2, posit, postulate, postulation, premise, presumption, presupposition, supposition, thesis

apropos *adj syn* RELEVANT, ad rem, applicable, applicative, applicatory, apposite, germane, material, pertinent, pointful
rel meet, proper
con clumsy, gauche, inappropriate, inept
ant malapropos

apropos *prep* in reference to <it is impossible to reach a decision *apropos* this matter at present>
syn about, against, anent, as for, as regards, as respects, as to, concerning, in re, in respect to, re, regarding, respecting, touching, toward, with respect to

apt *adj* 1 having a tendency or inclination <it is *apt* to be cool late in the evening>
syn given, inclined, liable, likely, prone
rel disposed, minded, predisposed

con averse, disinclined, indisposed, loath; doubtful, improbable, unlikely
2 ***syn*** FIT 1, appropriate, befitting, felicitous, fitting, happy, just, meet, proper, suitable
rel apposite, apropos, pertinent, relevant; compelling, convincing, telling; exact, nice, precise
con awkward, clumsy, maladroit
ant inapt, inept
3 ***syn*** QUICK 2, prompt, ready
rel alert, brainy, bright; gifted, talented
con laggard

aptness *n* **1** ***syn*** ORDER 11, appositeness, appropriateness, expediency, fitness, meetness, propriety, rightness, suitability, suitableness
rel helpfulness, propitiousness
2 ***syn*** GIFT 2, bent, bump, faculty, flair, genius, head, knack, talent, turn

‖**apurpose** *adv* ***syn*** INTENTIONALLY, deliberately, designedly, on purpose, prepensely, purposedly, purposely, purposively

apyrous *adj* ***syn*** NONCOMBUSTIBLE, incombustible, nonflammable, noninflammable, uninflammable

aquake *adj* ***syn*** TREMULOUS, aquiver, quaking, quivering, shaking, shaky, shivering, trembling, tremorous, tremulant

aqua vitae *n* ***syn*** LIQUOR 2, alcohol, booze, drink, firewater, grog, ‖hooch, ‖juice, spirit(s), tipple

aqueduct *n* ***syn*** CHANNEL 1, canal, conduit, course, duct, watercourse

aquiculture *n* ***syn*** HYDROPONICS, nutriculture

aquiver *adj* ***syn*** TREMULOUS, aquake, quaking, quivering, shaking, shaky, shivering, trembling, tremorous, tremulant

arab *n* **1** ***syn*** VAGABOND, clochard, drifter, floater, hobo, roadster, street arab, tramp, vag, vagrant
‖**2** ***syn*** PEDDLER, ‖duffer, hawker, higgler, huckster, monger, mongerer, outcrier, packman, vendor

arable *adj* suitable for tilling and for growing crops <used their *arable* land intensively>
syn cultivable, cultivatable, tillable
rel fat, fertile, fruitful, productive
con barren, sterile, unfertile, unfruitful, unproductive

arbiter *n* ***syn*** JUDGE 1, arbitrator, referee, umpire
rel moderator

arbitrary *adj* **1** characterized by or given to willful and often unwise or irrational choices and demands <a proud fitful *arbitrary* nature>
syn capricious, erratic, freakish, vagarious, wayward, whimsical, whimsied
rel undisciplined, unruly, wild, willful; arrogant, unconstrained, unreasonable; careless, heedless, impetuous, indiscreet, precipitate, rash; kooky, screwball, zany
con circumspect, discreet, heedful, judicious, politic, reflective; calculating, discriminative, judicial, prudent, well-advised
2 ***syn*** ABSOLUTE 4, autarchic, autocratic, despotic, monocratic, tyrannical, tyrannous
rel authoritarian, dictatorial, magisterial, oracular
con lawful, legal, licit, rightful
ant legitimate

arbitrate *vb* ***syn*** JUDGE 1, adjudge, adjudicate, referee, umpire
rel intermediate, intervene, mediate; appease, placate, soothe

arbitrator *n* **1** ***syn*** MODERATOR, mediator
2 ***syn*** JUDGE 1, arbiter, referee, umpire

arbor *n* a shelter (as in a garden) formed of vines or branches or of latticework covered with climbing shrubs or vines <the children picnicked under the *arbor*>
syn bower, pergola
rel belvedere, casino, gazebo, summerhouse

arc *n* ***syn*** CURVE, arch, bend, bow, curvation, curvature, round

arcadia *n* ***syn*** UTOPIA, Cockaigne, fairyland, heaven, lubberland, paradise, promised land, Shangri-la, wonderland, Zion

arcane *adj* ***syn*** MYSTERIOUS, cabalistic, impenetrable, inscrutable, mysterial, mystic, numinous, unaccountable, unguessed, unknowable
rel eerie, uncanny, weird; anagogic, mystical

arced *adj* ***syn*** CURVED, arched, arciform, arrondi, bent, bowed, curvilinear, round, rounded

arch *n* ***syn*** CURVE, arc, bend, bow, curvation, curvature, round

arch *adj* **1** ***syn*** FIRST 3, champion, chief, foremost, head, leading, premier, principal
rel conspicuous, notable, noteworthy; extraordinary, extreme
2 ***syn*** SAUCY 1, bantam, ‖cocket, malapert, pert
rel impish, mischievous, playful, roguish, waggish; bold, cheeky, cocky, flippant, fresh; derisive, mocking, twitting
con modest, quiet, respectful, submissive
3 ***syn*** COY 2, coquettish, roguish

archaic *adj* **1** ***syn*** OLD-FASHIONED, antiquated, antique, bygone, dated, old, old-timey, outdated, out-of-date, passé
idiom behind the times, of the old school
con fresh, modern, new, novel; fashionable
ant up-to-date
2 ***syn*** PRIMITIVE 3, persistent, undeveloped, unevolved

arched *adj* ***syn*** CURVED, arced, arciform, arrondi, bent, bowed, curvilinear, round, rounded

archetypal *adj* ***syn*** TYPICAL 1, classic, classical, exemplary, ideal, model, paradigmatic, prototypal, prototypical, quintessential

archetype *n* **1** ***syn*** ORIGINAL 1, protoplast, prototype
2 ***syn*** MODEL 2, beau ideal, ensample, example, exemplar, ideal, mirror, paradigm, pattern, standard

archfiend *n* ***syn*** DEVIL 2, demon, fiend, Satan, succubus

archilochian *adj* ***syn*** SARCASTIC, acerb, acerbic, caustic, corrosive, ‖sarky

archimage *n* ***syn*** MAGICIAN 1, enchanter, mage, magian, magus, necromancer, sorcerer, voodoo, warlock, wizard

architect *n* ***syn*** FATHER 2, author, creator, founder, generator, inventor, maker, originator, patriarch, sire

---

syn synonym(s) | *rel* related word(s)
idiom idiomatic equivalent(s) | *con* contrasted word(s)
ant antonym(s) | * vulgar
‖ use limited; if in doubt, see a dictionary
The first word in a synonym list when printed in SMALL CAPITALS shows where there is more information about the group. For a more efficient use of this book see Explanatory Notes.

architecture *n* ***syn*** MAKEUP 1, composition, constitution, construction, design, formation
archive *n, usu* **archives** *pl* **1** ***syn*** LIBRARY, athenaeum
2 ***syn*** DOCUMENT, monument, record
rel papers, parchments, scrolls, writings; clippings, cuttings, excerpts, extracts, fragments, gleanings, remains
arciform *adj* ***syn*** CURVED, arced, arched, arrondi, bent, bowed, curvilinear, round, rounded
arctic *adj* ***syn*** COLD 1, chill, chilly, cool, freezing, frosty, gelid, glacial, icy, nippy
rel bitter, boreal, hyperborean; numbing, rigorous; hibernal, hiemal
idiom cold as charity, cold enough to freeze a brass monkey
ant torrid
ardent *adj* **1** ***syn*** IMPASSIONED, blazing, burning, fervent, fervid, fiery, flaming, hot-blooded, passionate, red-hot
rel enthusiastic, urgent; avid, desirous, eager, keen
con calm, composed, imperturbable, nonchalant; apathetic, impassive, phlegmatic; disinterested, dispassionate, impartial, uninterested
ant cool
2 very deep or moving <had an *ardent* longing for knowledge>
syn extreme, intense
rel crying, importunate, insistent, urgent; great, mighty, powerful, strong
con feeble, minimal, slight, trivial
3 ***syn*** EAGER, agog, anxious, appetent, athirst, avid, breathless, impatient, keen, thirsty
rel hasty, impetuous, impulsive, precipitate; fervid, fiery, hectic, hot; uncontrolled, ungoverned; earnest, intent, urgent, vehement
con dull, heavy, inert, leaden, lumpish; languid, lethargic, listless; apathetic, impassive, phlegmatic
ant easygoing
4 ***syn*** FAITHFUL 1, allegiant, constant, ‖dinky-di, liege, loyal, resolute, staunch, steadfast, true
5 ***syn*** HOT 1, broiling, burning, fiery, heated, red-hot, scorching, sizzling, torrid, white-hot
6 ***syn*** SPIRITUOUS, alcoholic, hard, strong
ardor *n* **1** ***syn*** PASSION 6, calenture, enthusiasm, fervor, fire, hurrah, zeal
rel avidity; gusto, spirit, verve, zest; excitement, galvanization, quickening, stimulation
con aloofness, detachment, disinterest, unconcern; apathy, lackadaisy, languor, listlessness
ant coolness; indifference
2 ***syn*** EAGERNESS, enthusiasm, zing
rel ardency, fervor, warmth
3 ***syn*** FIDELITY 1, allegiance, devotion, faithfulness, fealty, loyalty, piety
rel adoration, love, worship
arduous *adj* **1** ***syn*** HARD 6, difficult, effortful, labored, laborious, operose, rough, strenuous, toilsome, uphill
2 ***syn*** STEEP 1, abrupt, precipitate, precipitous, sheer, sideling, steepdown, steep-to, steep-up, ‖stickle
3 ***syn*** TIGHT 4, rough, tricksy, trying
arduously *adv* ***syn*** HARD 8, burdensomely, difficultly, hardly, laboriously, onerously, toilsomely
con easily, facilely
ant effortlessly
area *n* **1** a distinguishable extent of surface and especially of the earth's surface <a large wooded *area*>
syn belt, region, territory, tract, zone
rel expanse, stretch; district, locality, place; lot, plot, section; terrain; circuit
2 ***syn*** LOCALITY 1, district, neighborhood, vicinage, vicinity
arena *n* ***syn*** SCENE 4
arete *n* ***syn*** EXCELLENCE, excellency, merit, perfection, quality, virtue
argent *adj* ***syn*** SILVERY, argentate, argenteous, argentine, silvern
argentate *adj* ***syn*** SILVERY, argent, argenteous, argentine, silvern
argenteous *adj* ***syn*** SILVERY, argent, argentate, argentine, silvern
argentine *adj* ***syn*** SILVERY, argent, argentate, argenteous, silvern
argot *n* ***syn*** DIALECT 2, cant, jargon, lingo, patois, patter, slang, vernacular
arguable *adj* ***syn*** MOOT, debatable, disputable, doubtful, dubious, mootable, problematic, questionable, uncertain
argue *vb* **1** ***syn*** DISCUSS 1, agitate, canvass, debate, discept, dispute, ‖kick around, moot, thrash out, toss (around)
rel analyze, investigate, review, sift, study, ventilate; expostulate, object, protest, remonstrate
2 to contend in words <*arguing* about who should answer the phone>
syn argufy, bicker, dispute, hassle, quibble, squabble, wrangle; *compare* QUARREL
rel differ, disaccord, disagree, dissent; balk, demur, jib; clash, conflict
idiom bandy words, have it out, join (*or* take) issue
con accord, agree, concur
3 ***syn*** INDICATE 2, announce, attest, bespeak, betoken, testify, witness
4 ***syn*** MAINTAIN 2, assert, claim, contend, defend, justify, vindicate, warrant
argue (into) *vb* ***syn*** INDUCE 1, bring around, convince, get, persuade, prevail (on *or* upon), procure, prompt, talk (into), win (over)
argufy *vb* ***syn*** ARGUE 2, bicker, dispute, hassle, quibble, squabble, wrangle
argument *n* **1** ***syn*** REASON 3, ground, proof, wherefore, why, whyfor
rel basis, foundation; position, posture, stance, standpoint
2 a vigorous often heated discussion of a moot question <their continuing *argument* over household expenses>
syn contention, controversy, dispute, hurrah, rumpus

rel argumentation, debate, disputation, polemic; disagreement, dissension, squabbling; embroilment, fuss, hassle, wrangle
3 *syn* SUBJECT 2, head, matter, motif, motive, point, subject matter, text, theme, topic
rel position, proposition, statement, thesis
argumentation *n* the act or art or an exercise of one's powers of argument <noted for his skill in *argumentation*>
syn debate, dialectic, disputation, forensic, mooting
rel argument, controversy, dispute; declamation, elocution, eloquence, oratory, rhetoric
argumentative *adj syn* CONTENTIOUS 2, controversial, disputatious, litigious, polemical
argute *adj* 1 *syn* SHREWD, astucious, astute, cagey, heady, perspicacious, sagacious, ||savvy
2 *syn* ACUTE 4, high, piercing, piping, sharp, shrill, thin, treble
aria *n syn* SONG 2, descant, ditty, hymn, lay, lied
arid *adj* 1 *syn* DRY 1, bone-dry, droughty, moistureless, sere, thirsty, unwatered, waterless
rel barren, infertile, sterile, unfruitful
con fecund, fertile, fruitful
2 lacking in interest or liveliness <some of the most *arid* prose ever written>
syn bromidic, dry, dryasdust, dull, dusty, insipid, tedious, uninteresting, weariful, wearisome; *compare* TEPID 2, UNORIGINAL
rel drab, dreary, flat, heavy, lackluster, leaden, unanimated, unlively; academic, bookish, pedantic; boring, humdrum, monotonous, unimaginative, uninspired
con appealing, bright, lively, sparkling, stimulating, vigorous, vivid
aright *adv syn* WELL 1, correctly, decently, decorously, fitly, fittingly, justly, nicely, properly, rightly
arise *vb* 1 *syn* RISE 4, ascend, aspire, lift, mount, soar, up, uprear
ant recline; slump
2 *syn* ROLL OUT, get up, pile (out), rise, rise and shine, turn out, uprise
3 *syn* SPRING 1, derive (from), emanate, flow, head, issue, originate, proceed, rise, stem
rel ensue, follow, succeed
4 *syn* BEGIN 2, commence, originate, start
aristarch *n syn* CRITIC, carper, caviler, criticizer, faultfinder, knocker, momus, smellfungus, Zoilus
aristo *n syn* GENTLEMAN, aristocrat, blue blood, patrician
aristocracy *n* the highest stratum of a society <the self-centered attitude of some *aristocracies*>
syn aristoi, blue blood, carriage trade, crème de la crème, elite, flower, gentility, gentry, haut monde, optimacy, patriciate, quality, society, upper class, upper crust, who's who
rel nobility, noblesse, patricians; county; beau monde, bon ton, jet set, smart set
con canaille, mob, rabble, riffraff; commoners, commons, masses, people, plebeians
aristocrat *n syn* GENTLEMAN, aristo, blue blood, patrician
ant commoner
aristoi *n syn* ARISTOCRACY, elite, flower, gentility, gentry, optimacy, quality, society, upper class, upper crust
arithmetic *n syn* COMPUTATION, calculation, ciphering, estimation, figuring, reckoning
arm *n* 1 *syn* INLET, bay, bayou, bight, cove, ||creek, firth, gulf, harbor, slough
2 *syn* ANNEX, block, ell, extension, wing
3 *syn* POWER 4, beef, energy, force, muscle, sinew, steam, strength, strong arm, vigor
arm *vb syn* FURNISH 1, accouter, appoint, equip, fit out, gear, outfit, rig, turn out
rel prepare, ready
idiom put in (*or* into) shape
ant disarm
armament *n syn* DEFENSE 1, aegis, armor, guard, protection, safeguard, security, shield, ward
armamentarium *n syn* SUPPLY, fund, inventory, stock, store
armed forces *n pl syn* TROOP 2, forces, military, servicemen
armistice *n syn* TRUCE, cease-fire
armor *n syn* DEFENSE 1, aegis, armament, guard, protection, safeguard, security, shield, ward
rel cloak, mantle, shroud, veil; buckler, cover, screen, shelter
armory *n* a place where military arms and supplies are stored <the problem of weapon theft from *armories*>
syn arsenal, depot, dump, magazine
army *n syn* MULTITUDE 1, cloud, crowd, flock, host, legion, rout, scores
rel crush, horde, mob, press, throng
aroma *n* 1 *syn* FRAGRANCE, balm, bouquet, incense, perfume, redolence, scent, spice
2 *syn* SMELL 1, odor, scent
rel fetor, mephitis, reek, stench, stink
aromal *adj syn* SWEET 2, ambrosial, aromatic, balmy, fragrant, perfumed, perfumy, redolent, savory, spicy
rel penetrating, piquant, pungent
ant acrid
aromatic *adj syn* SWEET 2, ambrosial, aromal, balmy, fragrant, perfumed, perfumy, redolent, savory, spicy
ant acrid
aromatize *vb syn* SCENT 2, odorize, perfume
around *adv* 1 *syn* ABOUT 1, round, round about
2 *syn* THROUGH 1, over, round, throughout
3 *syn* ABOUT 4, anyhow, any which way, anywise, at random, haphazard, haphazardly, helter-skelter, random, randomly
4 *syn* ABOUT 6, again, back, backward, in reverse, round, round about
around *prep syn* ABOUT 1, circa, close on, near, nearby, nigh
around *adj syn* EXTANT 1, alive, existent, existing, living
around-the-clock *adj syn* CONTINUAL, constant, continuous, incessant, minutely, perpetual, unintermitted, unintermittent, uninterrupted, unremitting

---

arouse *vb* ***syn*** STIR 1, awaken, bestir, challenge, kindle, rally, rouse, wake, waken, whet
rel alert, excite, work up; electrify, thrill; fire, inflame
idiom fan the fire (*or* flame), raise to fever heat, set on fire, stir one's blood (*or* feelings)
con allay, alleviate, assuage, ease, mitigate, relieve; mollify, pacify, placate
ant calm, quiet

arraign *vb* ***syn*** ACCUSE, charge, criminate, impeach, incriminate, inculpate, indict, tax
rel cite, summon; test, try
idiom bring to book, call to account
con absolve, acquit, exculpate, exonerate, vindicate; defend, justify

arrange *vb* **1** ***syn*** ORDER 1, array, dispose, marshal, methodize, organize, systematize
rel assort, categorize, pigeonhole, sort
con disorder, disorganize, disturb, unsettle; confuse, jumble, muddle, tumble; disperse, scatter
ant derange, disarrange
2 ***syn*** DESIGN 3, lay out, map (out), plan, set out
3 ***syn*** PLAN 2, blueprint, cast, chart, design, devise, ‖dope out, project
4 ***syn*** NEGOTIATE 1, concert, settle
rel design, plan, project, scheme
5 ***syn*** HARMONIZE 4, blend, integrate, orchestrate, symphonize, synthesize, unify

arrangement *n* ***syn*** ORDER 3, disposal, disposition, distribution, ordering, sequence
rel layout, lineup, setup; method, system
ant disarrangement

arrant *adj* **1** ***syn*** UTTER, absolute, complete, downright, flat-out, gross, infernal, out-and-out, rank, total
rel plain, pure, regular, sheer
2 ***syn*** SHAMELESS, barefaced, blatant, brassy, brazen, brazenfaced, impudent, overbold, unabashed, unblushing

array *vb* **1** ***syn*** ORDER 1, arrange, dispose, marshal, methodize, organize, systematize
ant disarray
2 ***syn*** CLOTHE, apparel, attire, clad, dress, enclothe, garb, garment, raiment

array *n* **1** ***syn*** GROUP 3, batch, body, bunch, bundle, clump, cluster, clutch, lot, set
2 ***syn*** DISPLAY 2, fanfare, panoply, parade, pomp, shine, show
rel exhibition, exposing, showing; arranging, marshaling, ordering

arrear *n, usu* **arrears** *pl* ***syn*** DEBT 3, arrearage, due, indebtedness, liability

arrearage *n* **1** ***syn*** DEBT 3, arrear(s), due, indebtedness, liability
2 ***syn*** INDEBTEDNESS 1, debt, liability, obligation

---

syn synonym(s) ***rel*** related word(s)
idiom idiomatic equivalent(s) ***con*** contrasted word(s)
ant antonym(s) * vulgar
‖ use limited; if in doubt, see a dictionary
The first word in a synonym list when printed in SMALL CAPITALS shows where there is more information about the group. For a more efficient use of this book see Explanatory Notes.

arrect *adj* **1** ***syn*** ERECT, raised, stand-up, straight-up, upright, upstanding
2 ***syn*** ATTENTIVE 1, advertent, heedful, intentive, observant, regardful

arrest *vb* **1** to bring to a halt <science cannot yet *arrest* the process of aging>
syn check, halt, interrupt, stall, stay; *compare* STOP 3
rel balk, frustrate, thwart; choke, obstruct, stop (up); delay, detain, hamper, hinder, restrain, retard; interfere, interpose, intervene; contain, stem, withstand
idiom bring to a halt (*or* stand *or* standstill), bring up short, check in full career, cut short
con advance, forward, further, promote; expedite, hasten, quicken, speed
2 to take and hold in custody under authority of the law <*arrested* for murder>
syn apprehend, ‖bust, detain, nab, pick up, pinch, pull in, run in; *compare* CATCH 1
rel immure, imprison, incarcerate, jail, lock (up), ‖slough; attach
idiom lay by the heels, lay hands on
con discharge, free, liberate, release

arrest *n* the taking and holding of a person in custody under authority of the law <unwilling to submit to *arrest*>
syn apprehension, arrestation, arrestment, detention, ‖nab, pickup, pinch
rel capture, catch, collar, seizure, taking
con discharge, freeing, liberation, release

arrestation *n* ***syn*** ARREST, apprehension, arrestment, detention, ‖nab, pickup, pinch

arresting *adj* ***syn*** NOTICEABLE, arrestive, conspicuous, marked, outstanding, pointed, prominent, remarkable, salient, signal
rel attractive, enchanting, fascinating; affective, appealing, impressive, moving, touching
idiom enough to make one stop and take notice
con common, familiar, ordinary, run-of-the-mill; hackneyed, stereotyped, trite

arrestive *adj* ***syn*** NOTICEABLE, arresting, conspicuous, marked, outstanding, prominent, remarkable, salient, signal, striking

arrestment *n* ***syn*** ARREST, apprehension, arrestation, detention, ‖nab, pickup, pinch

arride *vb* ***syn*** PLEASE 2, delectate, delight, gladden, gratify, happify, pleasure
rel beguile, divert, entertain, recreate
idiom tickle one's fancy
con bore, ennui, jade, weary

arrival *n* **1** the reaching of a destination <the train was late in its *arrival*>
syn advent, coming
rel appearance, emergence, entrance, issuance, manifestation
con disappearance, going, leaving, withdrawal; recession, retirement, retreat
ant departure
2 ***syn*** SUCCESS, ‖do, flying colors, go, prosperity, successfulness

arrive *vb* **1** ***syn*** COME 1, ‖blow in, get, get in, reach, show, show up, turn up
con get away, go, retire
ant depart

2 ***syn*** SUCCEED 3, flourish, go, make out, prosper, score, thrive

arriviste *n* ***syn*** UPSTART, nouveau riche, parvenu, roturier

arrogance *n* ***syn*** PRIDE 3, disdain, disdainfulness, haughtiness, hauteur, loftiness, morgue, superbity, superciliousness
ant humility

arrogant *adj* **1** ***syn*** PROUD 1, cavalier, disdainful, haughty, high-and-mighty, insolent, lordly, overbearing, supercilious, superior
rel domineering, imperative, peremptory; affected, artificial, highfalutin, mannered, showy
idiom too big for one's britches
con humble; deferential, submissive; abject, obsequious, subservient, truckling
ant meek
2 ***syn*** POMPOUS 1, bloated, important, magisterial, pontifical, puffy, self-important, stuffy, wiggy

arrogate *vb* **1** to claim or take over in a high-handed manner < *arrogated* to himself the right to make all decisions >
syn accroach, appropriate, assume, commandeer, preempt, usurp; *compare* APPROPRIATE 1
rel annex, preempt, preoccupy, sequester; grab, seize, take, take over
idiom help oneself to, make free with, take into one's own hands
con cede, relinquish, resign, surrender, yield
ant renounce
2 ***syn*** APPROPRIATE 1, accroach, annex, commandeer, confiscate, expropriate, preempt, seize, sequester, take

arrondi *adj* ***syn*** CURVED, arced, arched, arciform, bent, bowed, curvilinear, round, rounded

arroyo *n* ***syn*** RAVINE, chasm, cleft, clough, clove, gap, gorge, gulch

arse** *n* ***syn BUTTOCKS, *ass, *bum, *butt, ‖can, ‖duff, *prat, rear, tail, ‖tokus

arsenal *n* **1** ***syn*** ARMORY, depot, dump, magazine
2 ***syn*** DEPOT 2, depository, magazine, repository, store, storehouse

arsonist *n* ***syn*** INCENDIARY, firebug, torch

arsy–varsy *adj* ***syn*** UPSIDE-DOWN 2, downside-up, topsy-turvy

art *n* **1** a usually acquired proficiency in doing or performing <there's an *art* to competent public speaking>
syn adroitness, craft, cunning, dexterity, expertise, know-how, skill
rel capability, competence, handiness, proficiency; address, finesse, ‖savvy
con clumsiness, maladroitness
2 ***syn*** CUNNING 2, artfulness, artifice, cageyness, canniness, craft, craftiness, foxiness, slyness, wiliness
rel acuteness, astuteness
con candor, frankness, sincerity; directness, straightforwardness; bluffness, bluntness
3 ***syn*** TRADE 1, calling, craft, handicraft, métier, profession, vocation

artery *n* ***syn*** WAY 1, avenue, boulevard, ‖drag, highway, path, road, street, thoroughfare, track

artful *adj* ***syn*** SLY 2, astute, crafty, cunning, deep, foxy, guileful, insidious, tricky, wily
rel diplomatic, oily, politic, smooth, suave; facile, specious, superficial; adroit, dexterous
ant artless

artfulness *n* ***syn*** CUNNING 2, art, artifice, cageyness, canniness, craft, craftiness, foxiness, slyness, wiliness

article *n* **1** ***syn*** POINT 1, detail, element, item, particular, thing
rel division, section, segment
2 ***syn*** ESSAY 2, composition, paper, theme
rel critique, manifesto, report, statement, study, survey
3 ***syn*** THING 3, object
rel detail, particular

articled *adj* ***syn*** BOUND 2, apprenticed, indentured

articulate *adj* **1** ***syn*** VOCAL 1, oral, sonant, spoken, viva voce, voiced
rel clear, distinct, intelligible
ant inarticulate; dumb
2 ***syn*** VOCAL 3, eloquent, fluent, smooth-spoken
rel meaningful, significant; garrulous, prolix, talkative; uttering, venting
ant inarticulate

articulate *vb* **1** ***syn*** INTEGRATE 3, concatenate
rel connect, join, relate; methodize, order, organize, systematize; adjust, coordinate, harmonize, regulate; assemble, collect, gather; unify
con dissect, resolve; divide, part, separate
2 to form speech sounds <regional differences in *articulating* the letter *r*>
syn enunciate, phonate, pronounce, say
rel sound, utter

articulation *n* ***syn*** VOCALIZATION, utterance, uttering, vocalism

artifice *n* **1** ***syn*** CUNNING 2, art, artfulness, cageyness, canniness, craft, craftiness, foxiness, slyness, wiliness
rel ingenuity, inventiveness, originality; adroitness, cleverness, keenness, quickness, shrewdness; adeptness, proficiency
2 ***syn*** TRICK 1, device, feint, gambit, maneuver, play, ploy, ruse, stratagem, wile
rel chicane, chicanery, trickery; knavery, rascality, skulduggery; deceit, dissimulation, duplicity, guile

artificial *adj* **1** ***syn*** SYNTHETIC, factitious, man-made
rel fabricated, fashioned, made
con native
ant natural
2 taking the place of something else and especially of something finer or more costly < *artificial* diamonds >
syn dummy, ersatz, false, imitation, mock, sham, simulated, spurious, substitute; *compare* FICTITIOUS 2, SPURIOUS 3
rel fake, papier-mâché, ‖pretend, unreal; hollow, painted
con authentic, bona fide, genuine, real, sure-enough, true, veritable

---

syn synonym(s) ***rel*** related word(s)
idiom idiomatic equivalent(s) ***con*** contrasted word(s)
ant antonym(s) * vulgar
‖ use limited; if in doubt, see a dictionary
The first word in a synonym list when printed in SMALL CAPITALS shows where there is more information about the group. For a more efficient use of this book see Explanatory Notes.

3 lacking in spontaneity and genuineness <exchanged *artificial* smiles>
syn affected, assumed, feigned, put-on, spurious
rel histrionic, insincere, overdone, quaint, stagy, theatrical, unnatural; cute, cutesy, goody-goody, mincing, overrefined, simpering; contrived, forced, labored
con genuine, sincere, spontaneous, unaffected

artist *n* ***syn*** EXPERT, adept, artiste, authority, master, past master, proficient, virtuoso, whiz, wizard
rel ace, crackerjack, first-rater, shark, topnotcher; genius, prodigy, wonder

artiste *n* ***syn*** EXPERT, adept, artist, authority, master, past master, proficient, virtuoso, whiz, wizard

artless *adj* ***syn*** NATURAL 5, ingenuous, naive, simple, unaffected, unartful, unartificial, unschooled, unsophisticated, unstudied
rel free, relaxed; aboveboard, forthright, straightforward; childlike, trusting, unsuspicious; untouched, virginal
con cunning, insidious, sly, wily; calculating, designing, intriguing, scheming; artificial, insincere
ant artful; affected

arty *adj* ***syn*** PRETENTIOUS 3, arty-crafty, big, high-sounding, imposing, overblown

arty-crafty *adj* ***syn*** PRETENTIOUS 3, arty, big, high-sounding, imposing, overblown

as *conj* ***syn*** BECAUSE, as long as, being, cause, considering, for, inasmuch as, now, since, whereas

as a rule *adv* ***syn*** USUALLY 2, by ordinary, commonly, frequently, generally, ordinarily

‖**ascared** *adj* ***syn*** AFRAID 1, aghast, anxious, fearful, frightened, scared, scary, terrified

ascend *vb* **1** to move upward to or toward a summit <*ascend* a mountain>
syn climb, escalade, escalate, mount, scale, upclimb, upgo
rel clamber, get up, scramble, shin; crest, surmount, top
idiom scale the heights, work one's way up
ant descend
2 ***syn*** RISE 4, arise, aspire, lift, mount, soar, up, uprear

ascendancy *n* ***syn*** SUPREMACY, dominance, domination, dominion, masterdom, preeminence, preponderance, prepotence, prepotency, sovereignty

ascendant *n* **1** ***syn*** SUPREMACY, ascendancy, dominance, domination, dominion, masterdom, preeminence, preponderance, prepotence, sovereignty
2 ***syn*** ANCESTOR 1, antecedent (used in pl.), forebear, forefather, primogenitor, progenitor
rel forerunner, precursor, predecessor
ant descendant

ascendant *adj* ***syn*** DOMINANT 1, master, overbearing, paramount, predominant, predominate, preponderant, prevalent, regnant, sovereign

---

syn synonym(s) — *rel* related word(s)
idiom idiomatic equivalent(s) — *con* contrasted word(s)
ant antonym(s) — * vulgar
‖ use limited; if in doubt, see a dictionary
The first word in a synonym list when printed in SMALL CAPITALS shows where there is more information about the group. For a more efficient use of this book see Explanatory Notes.

ascension *n* ***syn*** ASCENT, rise, rising

ascent *n* a moving upward or an upward movement <the slow *ascent* of the creaky old elevator>
syn ascension, rise, rising
rel elevation, raising, uplifting
ant descent

ascertain *vb* ***syn*** DISCOVER 3, catch on, determine, find out, hear, learn, see, tumble, unearth
rel ask, inquire, interrogate, query, question; appraise, inspect, observe, survey, view; consider, contemplate, study, weigh
con assume, presume; conjecture, guess, surmise

ascetic *adj* ***syn*** SEVERE 1, astringent, austere, mortified, stern
rel abstemious, abstinent, forbearing; self-abasing, self-abnegating, self-denying, self-forgetful, selfless; disciplined, restrained, schooled, trained
con epicurean, sensual, sensuous, sybaritic; abandoned, dissolute, licentious, self-indulgent
ant luxurious, voluptuous

ascribe *vb* to refer especially to a supposed cause, source, or author <a manuscript commonly *ascribed* to Saint Augustine>
syn accredit, assign, attribute, charge, credit, impute, lay, refer
rel attach (to), connect (with), fix (on *or* upon), pin (on), saddle (on *or* upon *or* with); affix, fasten; conjecture, guess, surmise; adduce, advance, allege, cite

aseptic *adj* ***syn*** UNDEMONSTRATIVE, restrained, retiring, shrinking, unaffable, unexpansive, withdrawn

as for *prep* ***syn*** APROPOS, as regards, as respects, as to, concerning, in re, re, regarding, respecting, touching

as good as *adv* **1** ***syn*** NEARLY, about, all but, almost, approximately, just about, ‖nearabout, nigh, practically, well-nigh
2 ***syn*** ALMOST 2, all but, as much as, essentially, practically, well-nigh

ash *n* the residue left when material is consumed by fire <cold whitened *ash* on the hearth>
syn ashes, cinders, clinkers
rel dross, scoria, slag; charcoal, coal(s), coke, ember(s); fumes, smoke, soot

ashake *adj* ***syn*** TREMULOUS, aquake, aquiver, ashiver, quaking, quivering, shaking, shaky, shivering, trembling

ashamed *adj* humiliated or disconcerted usually by feelings of guilt, disgrace, or impropriety <*ashamed* of her brother's noisy boasting>
syn chagrined, mortified, shamed
rel abashed, discomfited, embarrassed; abased, humbled, humiliated; abject, hangdog, mean; contrite, penitent, repentant
idiom unable to show one's face
con arrogant, assured, overbearing, self-assured; vain, vainglorious
ant proud

ashen *adj* ***syn*** PALE 1, ashy, blanched, colorless, doughy, livid, lurid, pallid, wan, waxen
rel corpselike, ghostly, macabre; blanched, bleached, decolorized, faded

ashes *n pl* ***syn*** ASH, cinders, clinkers

ashiver *adj* ***syn*** TREMULOUS, aquake, aquiver, ashake, quaking, quivering, shaking, shivering, shivery, trembling

ashy *adj* ***syn*** PALE 1, ashen, blanched, colorless, doughy, livid, lurid, pallid, wan, waxen

aside *adv* **1** in a slanting or sloping direction <his head hung *aside* as if he lacked the strength to hold it up>
syn aslant, aslope, obliquely, sideways, sidewise, slant, slantingly, slantingways, slantly, slantways, slantwise, ‖slaunchways, slopeways; *compare* SIDEWAYS 1
rel askance, askant, askew, awry; downgrade, downhill
con erectly, uprightly, vertically
2 ***syn*** APART 2
3 ***syn*** APIECE, all, each, ‖per, per capita, per caput

‖**aside** *prep* ***syn*** NEAR 2, beside, by, nearby, nigh, round

aside *n* ***syn*** DIGRESSION, discursion, divagation, excursion, excursus, parenthesis

aside from *prep* ***syn*** EXCEPT, bar, barring, bating, besides, excluding, exclusive of, outside of, save, saving

asinine *adj* ***syn*** SIMPLE 3, brainless, fatuous, foolish, mindless, silly, unwitty, weak-headed, weak-minded, witless
rel puerile; absurd, irrational, unreasonable
con prudent, sage, sane, sapient, wise; clever, intelligent, knowing, smart; rational, reasonable
ant judicious, sensible

ask *vb* **1** to call upon for an answer or information <*asked* him to explain his behavior>
syn catechize, examine, inquire, interrogate, query, question, quiz
rel argue, canvass, debate, deliberate, discuss, review, talk (over)
con answer, rejoin, reply, respond, retort
2 to seek to obtain by making one's needs or desires known <*asked* for time to consider the problem>
syn bespeak, desire, request, solicit
rel claim, demand, exact, require; beg, beseech, entreat, implore, importune
idiom put in for
3 ***syn*** DEMAND 2, call (for), crave, necessitate, require, take
4 ***syn*** INVITE, bid
rel canvass, request, seek

askance *adv* **1** ***syn*** AWRY 1, askant, askew, ‖cam, cock-a-hoop, cockeyed, crookedly
ant directly
2 with absence of approval or trust <a proceeding one must view more than a little *askance*>
syn distrustfully, doubtfully, mistrustfully, skeptically, suspiciously
rel captiously, critically, cynically, doubtingly; deprecatingly, depreciatively, disparagingly
con approvingly, favorably

askant *adv* ***syn*** AWRY 1, askance, askew, ‖cam, cock-a-hoop, cockeyed, crookedly
ant directly

asker *n* ***syn*** SUPPLIANT, beggar, petitioner, prayer, suitor, supplicant, supplicator

askew *adv* ***syn*** AWRY 1, askance, askant, ‖cam, cock-a-hoop, cockeyed, crookedly
ant straight

aslant *adv* ***syn*** ASIDE 1, aslope, obliquely, sideways, sidewise, slantingly, slantly, slantways, slantwise, ‖slaunchways

asleep *adj* **1** ***syn*** DEAD 1, cold, deceased, defunct, departed, exanimate, inanimate, late, lifeless, unanimated
2 ***syn*** NUMB 1, anesthetized, benumbed, dead, deadened, insensible, insensitive, numbed, senseless, unfeeling
3 ***syn*** INACTIVE, idle, inert, passive, quiet, sleepy

as long as *conj* ***syn*** BECAUSE, as, ‖being, 'cause, considering, for, inasmuch as, seeing, since, whereas

aslope *adv* ***syn*** ASIDE 1, aslant, obliquely, sideways, sidewise, slantingly, slantly, slantways, slantwise, ‖slaunchways

as much as *adv* ***syn*** ALMOST 2, all but, as good as, essentially, practically, well-nigh

asomatous *adj* ***syn*** IMMATERIAL 1, bodiless, discarnate, disembodied, incorporeal, insubstantial, nonmaterial, nonphysical, unphysical, unsubstantial

aspect *n* **1** ***syn*** APPEARANCE 1, look, mien, seeming
rel countenance, face, visage; air, bearing, port, presence
2 ***syn*** PHASE, angle, facet, hand, side
rel point of view, slant, standpoint

asperity *n* **1** ***syn*** DIFFICULTY 1, hardness, hardship, rigor, vicissitude
rel austerity, bitterness, grimness, harshness, inclemency, severity, stringency
con blandness, gentleness, mildness, softness
2 ***syn*** INEQUALITY 1, irregularity, roughness, unevenness
3 ***syn*** ACRIMONY, acerbity, mordancy
rel harshness, keenness, roughness, sharpness; irritability, snappishness, tartness, waspishness
con blandness, smoothness, suavity, urbanity; courtesy, gallantry
ant amenity

asperous *adj* ***syn*** ROUGH 1, craggy, harsh, jagged, rugged, scabrous, scraggy, uneven, unlevel, unsmooth

asperse *vb* **1** ***syn*** MALIGN, calumniate, defame, denigrate, libel, ‖scandal, scandalize, slander, slur, traduce
rel deride, mock, taunt; affront, insult, offend
con applaud, commend, compliment
2 ***syn*** BAPTIZE, christen, immerse, sprinkle

aspersion *n* ***syn*** ANIMADVERSION, obloquy, reflection, slam, slur, stricture
rel abuse, invective, muck, vituperation; backbiting, calumny, detraction, scandal, slander; lampoon, libel, pasquinade, skit, squib
con eulogy, extolling, laudation, praise; acclaim, acclamation, applause, plaudits; commendation, compliment

asphyxiate *vb* ***syn*** SUFFOCATE, choke, ‖quackle, smother, stifle

aspirant *n* ***syn*** CANDIDATE, applicant, hopeful, seeker

aspiration *n* ***syn*** AMBITION 1, ambitiousness, pretension
rel aim, direction, goal, objective; desire, lust, passion, urge

aspire *vb* **1** ***syn*** AIM 2, pant

---

syn synonym(s) ***rel*** related word(s)
idiom idiomatic equivalent(s) ***con*** contrasted word(s)
ant antonym(s) * vulgar
‖ use limited; if in doubt, see a dictionary
The first word in a synonym list when printed in SMALL CAPITALS shows where there is more information about the group. For a more efficient use of this book see Explanatory Notes.

rel hunger, long, pine, thirst; bid (for), strain (for *or* after), struggle (for), try (for)
idiom cry for the moon, have at heart, have one's heart set on, reach for (*or* keep one's eyes on) the stars
con condescend, deign, look down (on); grovel, stoop, wallow
2 ***syn*** RISE 4, arise, ascend, lift, mount, soar, up, uprear

aspiring *adj* ***syn*** AMBITIOUS 1, emulous, vaulting
rel desirous, impassioned, urgent; wanting, wishful, yearning

as regards *prep* ***syn*** APROPOS, as for, as respects, as to, concerning, in re, re, regarding, respecting, touching

as respects *prep* ***syn*** APROPOS, as for, as regards, as to, concerning, in re, re, regarding, respecting, touching

ass *n* **1** ***syn*** DONKEY 1, burro, donk, jackass, ‖moke, ‖neddy, ‖Rocky Mountain canary
2 ***syn*** FOOL 1, *damfool, donkey, idiot, imbecile, jackass, jerk, nincompoop, ‖schmo, ‖schmuck

ass** *n* ***syn BUTTOCKS, *arse, *bum, ‖butt, ‖can, ‖duff, *prat, rear, tail, ‖tokus

assail *vb* ***syn*** ATTACK 1, aggress, assault, beset, fall (on *or* upon), storm, strike
rel beat, belabor, buffet, pound, pummel
idiom round on

assailment *n* ***syn*** ATTACK 1, aggression, assault, offense, offensive, onfall, onset, onslaught

assassin *n* a person hired or hirable to commit murder <found out who paid the *assassin*>
syn bravo, cutthroat, gun, gunman, ‖gunsel, gunslinger, hatchet man, hit man, torpedo, triggerman; *compare* MURDERER
rel apache, desperado, goon, ‖gorilla, highbinder, strong arm, thug

assassinate *vb* ***syn*** MURDER 1, ‖bump off, cool, do in, ‖dust off, execute, finish, knock off, liquidate, put away

assault *n* ***syn*** ATTACK 1, aggression, assailment, offense, offensive, onfall, onset, onslaught
rel brush, clash, invasion, melee, skirmish; brawl, contest, fracas, set-to

assault *vb* ***syn*** ATTACK 1, aggress, assail, beset, fall (on *or* upon), storm, strike
rel battle, fight, war; clash, collide, encounter, engage; skirmish

assay *vb* **1** ***syn*** TRY 5, attempt, endeavor, essay, offer, seek, strive, struggle, undertake
rel venture
idiom make an effort to
2 ***syn*** ESTIMATE 1, appraise, assess, evaluate, rate, set (at), survey, valuate, value
rel demonstrate, prove, test, try; analyze, resolve; calculate, compute, reckon

assemblage *n* ***syn*** GATHERING 1, aggregation, assembly, collection, company, congregation, crowd, group, muster, ruck

assemble *vb* **1** ***syn*** CONVOKE, call, convene, summon
2 ***syn*** GATHER 6, collect, congregate, congress, forgather, muster, raise, rendezvous
rel associate, combine, unite; convene, convoke
con dispel, dissipate, scatter; leave, part, quit, separate
ant disperse
3 ***syn*** GROUP 1, cluster, collect, gather, round up
rel accumulate, aggregate, amass, garner; bunch, clump; bank, heap, mound, pile, stack
con dispel, dissipate, scatter; leave, part, quit, separate; break up, disband
ant disperse
4 ***syn*** MAKE 3, build, contrive, fashion, form, manufacture, mold, produce, put together, shape

assembly *n* **1** ***syn*** GATHERING 2, assemblage, collection, company, congeries, congregation, crowd, group, muster, ruck
rel association, band, conclave, party, troupe
2 ***syn*** GROUP 1, band, bevy, bunch, cluster, covey, crew, party
rel crowd, push; faction, interest, sect, wing; brotherhood, fellowship, fraternity
con masses, multitude; canaille, rabble, riffraff, ruck, trash

assent *vb* to give or express one's consent or concurrence <*assented* grudgingly to her plans for the evening>
syn accede, acquiesce, agree, consent, subscribe, yes
rel adopt, embrace, espouse; accept; abide, bear (with), endure, stand, suffer, tolerate; down, stomach, swallow, take; defer, relent, submit, yield
idiom be at one with, cast one's vote for, give the nod of approval, go along with, see eye to eye with
con rebuff, refuse, reject, scorn, scout, spurn; deny, gainsay
ant dissent

assert *vb* **1** to state firmly, positively, or assuredly <he continued to *assert* his innocence>
syn affirm, aver, avouch, avow, constate, declare, depose, predicate, profess, protest
rel adduce, advance, allege, cite, claim, pretend; announce, broadcast, disseminate, proclaim, promulgate, publish, spread
idiom have it
con contradict, contravene, dispute, gainsay, negate, negative, traverse; confute, disprove, rebut, refute
ant deny; controvert
2 ***syn*** MAINTAIN 2, argue, claim, contend, defend, justify, vindicate, warrant
rel declare, express, utter, voice; advance, state, stipulate, submit

assertive *adj* **1** ***syn*** EMPHATIC, forceful, insistent, resounding
2 ***syn*** AGGRESSIVE, assertory, militant, pushful, pushing, pushy, self-assertive
rel affirmative; arbitrary, dogmatic, peremptory, positive; assured, certain, cocksure, opinionated, opinionative, self-assured, sure; confident, presumptuous, sanguine, self-confident
con bashful, diffident, modest, shy; amenable, biddable, docile, submissive

---

syn synonym(s) ***rel*** related word(s)
idiom idiomatic equivalent(s) ***con*** contrasted word(s)
ant antonym(s) * vulgar
‖ use limited; if in doubt, see a dictionary
The first word in a synonym list when printed in SMALL CAPITALS shows where there is more information about the group. For a more efficient use of this book see Explanatory Notes.

ant retiring; acquiescent

assertory *adj* *syn* AGGRESSIVE, assertive, militant, pushful, pushing, pushy, self-assertive

assess *vb* **1** *syn* LEVY, exact, impose, put (on *or* upon)
2 *syn* ESTIMATE 1, appraise, assay, evaluate, rate, set (at), survey, valuate, value
rel calculate, compute; account, consider, deem, reckon, weigh

assessment *n* **1** *syn* ESTIMATION 1, appraisal, appraisement, estimate, evaluation, judgment, stock
2 *syn* ESTIMATE 1, appraisal, appraisement, estimation, evaluation, valuation
3 *syn* TAX 1, ||cess, duty, impost, levy, tariff

asset *n* **1** **assets** *pl* *syn* MEAN 3, capital, resources, wealth
rel bankroll, money; equity; principal
ant liabilities
2 *syn* CREDIT 3
rel distinction, glory, honor, ornament
con detriment, disadvantage, discredit, liability
ant handicap

asshead *n* *syn* FOOL 1, ass, *damfool, donkey, doodle, idiot, imbecile, jackass, jerk, nincompoop

assiduous *adj* marked by careful attention or persistent application <learned to speak French fluently by *assiduous* practice>
syn diligent, industrious, operose, sedulous; *compare* BUSY 1
rel hardworking, laborious, moiling; indefatigable, tireless, untiring, unwearied, zealous
idiom hard at it
con casual, haphazard, happy-go-lucky, hit-or-miss, intermittent, random; careless, lax, remiss, slack, sloppy, slovenly; indolent, lazy, slothful
ant desultory

assiduously *adv* *syn* HARD 3, dingdong, earnestly, exhaustively, intensely, intensively, painstakingly, thoroughly, unremittingly

assign *vb* **1** *syn* TRANSFER 4, abalienate, alien, alienate, cede, convey, deed, make over, remise, sign (over)
2 *syn* ALLOT, admeasure, allocate, allow, apportion, give, lot, mete (out)
rel establish, fix, set, settle
3 *syn* ASCRIBE, accredit, attribute, charge, credit, impute, lay, refer
rel associate, link, relate; classify, pigeonhole
4 *syn* PRESCRIBE 2, define, lay down
rel decide, determine; commit, consign, entrust, relegate

assignation *n* *syn* ENGAGEMENT 3, appointment, date, rendezvous, tryst
rel agreement, arrangement, understanding; get-together

assignee *n* *syn* AGENT 2, attorney, deputy, factor, proxy

assignment *n* *syn* TASK 1, chare, chore, devoir, duty, job, stint
rel incumbency, liability, obligation, responsibility

assimilate *vb* **1** *syn* ABSORB 1, imbibe, incorporate, inhaust, insorb
rel imbue, infuse, ingrain, inoculate, leaven, suffuse; adopt, embrace, espouse; corner, engross, monopolize
2 *syn* EQUATE 2, compare, liken, match, paragon, parallel

assimilation *n* *syn* RECOGNITION 1, apperception, identification
rel awareness, consciousness, mindfulness

assist *vb* *syn* HELP 1, abet, aid, benefact, do for, help out, stead
rel accompany, attend, escort; concur, cooperate
con clog, fetter, trammel; forestall, prevent; burden, encumber, handicap, tax, weigh down
ant hamper; impede

assist *n* *syn* HELP 1, aid, assistance, comfort, hand, lift, relief, secours, succor, support

assistance *n* *syn* HELP 1, aid, assist, comfort, hand, lift, relief, secours, succor, support
rel backing, supporting, upholding; advantage, avail, profit, use; appropriation, grant, subsidy, subvention
con checking, hampering, hindering, hindrance; balking, foiling, frustration, thwarting
ant impediment, impeding; obstructing, obstruction

assistant *n* **1** *syn* HELPER, aid, ancilla, attendant, help, striker
2 a person who takes over part of the duties of a superior <started as *assistant* to the secretary>
syn aid, aide, aide-de-camp, coadjutant, coadjutor, lieutenant
rel acolyte, attendant, second; flunky, henchman, minion, stooge; girl Friday, right-hand man; agent, attorney, deputy, factor, proxy; fall guy, patsy; co-worker, workfellow, yokemate

assistive *adj* *syn* HELPFUL 1, aidant, aiding, serviceable

assize *n* **1** *syn* LAW 1, canon, decree, edict, ordinance, precept, prescript, regulation, rule, statute
2 *syn* STANDARD 4

associate *vb* *syn* JOIN 1, bracket, combine, conjoin, connect, couple, link, relate, unite, yoke
rel amalgamate, blend, coalesce, merge, mingle, mix; ally, confederate, federate, league
con alienate, estrange; divide, divorce, part

associate *n* **1** *syn* PARTNER, cohort, confrere, consociate, copartner, fellow, mate, ||pard
rel affiliate, ally, confederate, leaguer; abettor, accomplice, collaborator
2 *syn* COLLEAGUE, compatriot, compeer, confrere
3 a person regularly frequenting the company of another <a man is judged by the *associates* he keeps>
syn buddy, chum, comate, companion, comrade, crony, ||cully, pal, running mate; *compare* FRIEND
rel acquaintance, friend, sympathizer; confidant, familiar, intimate; brother-in-arms, comrade-in-arms
4 *syn* ACCOMPANIMENT 2, companion, concomitant, consort, fellow, mate
rel complement, correlate, correlative, counterpart, match; correspondent
con competitor, rival; adversary, antagonist, opponent

---

syn synonym(s) — *rel* related word(s)
idiom idiomatic equivalent(s) — *con* contrasted word(s)
ant antonym(s) — * vulgar
|| use limited; if in doubt, see a dictionary
The first word in a synonym list when printed in SMALL CAPITALS shows where there is more information about the group. For a more efficient use of this book see Explanatory Notes.

association *n* **1** the quality or state of being associated <worked in close *association* with the courts>
syn affiliation, alliance, cahoots, combination, conjointment, conjunction, connection, hookup, partnership, tie-up, togetherness
rel coaction, collaboration, concert, cooperation, teamwork; conviviality, gaiety, joviality, sociability
con aloofness, apartness, disjunction, disunion, isolation, separation
ant disassociation, dissociation
2 an organization of persons sharing a common interest or purpose <a buyers' *association*>
syn brotherhood, club, congress, fellowship, fraternity, guild, league, order, society, sodality, union
rel alliance, axis, bloc, coalition, federation, organization; faction, interest, sect, wing; combine, gang, machine, ring
3 ***syn*** LEAGUE 4, circuit, conference, loop, wheel
4 something (as a feeling or recollection) associated in the mind with a particular person or thing <the thought of her childhood home always carried an *association* of loving warmth>
syn connotation, hint, implication, overtone, suggestion, undertone
rel image, picture, vision; appearance, fantasy, illusion, mirage

assort *vb* to arrange systematically <*assort* yarn by color>
syn categorize, class, classify, group, pigeonhole
rel arrange, methodize, order, systematize; distribute, divide, separate; screen, sift; stratify
con derange, disarrange, disorder, disorganize; commingle, jumble, mingle, mix, scramble

assorted *adj* **1** ***syn*** MISCELLANEOUS, chowchow, conglomerate, heterogeneous, indiscriminate, mixed, motley, multifarious, promiscuous, varied
con chosen, picked, preferred, selected
2 corresponding in such manner or degree as to be appropriately associated <they made a well-*assorted* pair>
syn adapted, conformable, fitted, matched, suited
rel chosen, picked, preferred, selected; associated, bracketed, coupled, linked
con confused, disordered, fouled-up, haywire, jumbled, muddled, scrambled

assortment *n* **1** ***syn*** VARIETY 2
2 ***syn*** MISCELLANY 1, gallimaufry, hodgepodge, jumble, medley, mélange, mishmash, olio, pastiche, potpourri

assuage *vb* **1** ***syn*** RELIEVE 1, allay, alleviate, ease, lighten, mitigate, mollify
rel placate
con augment, increase, recruit, reinforce; enhance, exaggerate, heighten, intensify, magnify, strengthen
ant exacerbate
2 ***syn*** PACIFY, appease, conciliate, mollify, placate, propitiate, sweeten
rel calm, ease, relax, slack, slacken, soothe
con annoy, inflame, nettle, provoke, ruffle, vex

as such *adv* ***syn*** PER SE, intrinsically

assumably *adv* ***syn*** PRESUMABLY, doubtless, likely, presumptively, probably

assume *vb* **1** ***syn*** DON 2, pull, put on, strike, take on
2 ***syn*** DON 1, draw on, get on, huddle (on), put on, slip (on), throw
3 ***syn*** ARROGATE 1, accroach, appropriate, commandeer, preempt, usurp
rel grab, seize, snatch, take
idiom take over the helm, take possession (*or* command)
4 to take on or present a false or deceptive appearance <their gaiety was *assumed*>
syn act, affect, bluff, counterfeit, fake, feign, pretend, put on, sham, simulate
rel camouflage, cloak, conceal, disguise, dissemble, hide, mask
idiom make believe
5 ***syn*** PRESUPPOSE, posit, postulate, premise, presume
rel affirm, assert, aver, predicate, profess; allow, concede, grant
6 ***syn*** UNDERSTAND 3, believe, expect, gather, imagine, ‖reckon, suppose, suspect, take, think

assumed *adj* ***syn*** ARTIFICIAL 3, affected, feigned, put-on, spurious
rel factitious, synthetic; deceptive, delusory, illusory, insubstantial, unreal
con authentic, bona fide, genuine, veritable; real, true

assumption *n* **1** ***syn*** PRESUPPOSITION, presumption
2 something that is taken for granted or advanced as fact <decisions based on *assumptions* about the nature of society>
syn apriorism, posit, postulate, postulation, premise, presumption, presupposition, supposition, thesis
rel conjecture, guess, surmise; hypothesis, theory; axiom, fundamental, law, principle, theorem

assurance *n* **1** ***syn*** WORD 8, guarantee, pledge, warrant
rel parole, promise, troth; plight; agreement, compact, covenant, pact, understanding
2 ***syn*** CERTAINTY, assuredness, certitude, confidence, conviction, sureness, surety
rel credit; dependence, reliance, trust
con suspicion, uncertainty; disbelief, incredulity, unbelief
ant mistrust; dubiousness
3 ***syn*** SAFETY, safeness, security
4 ***syn*** CONFIDENCE 2, aplomb, self-assurance, self-assuredness, self-confidence, self-trust
rel composure, equanimity, sangfroid
con agitation, disquiet, jumpiness, nervousness, shakiness, skittishness; anxiety, doubt, foreboding, funk, perturbation, trepidation
ant alarm
5 ***syn*** TEMERITY, audacity, brashness, hardihood, hardiness, nerve
rel brazenness, cockiness, presumption; conceit, self-conceit, self-importance, vanity

---

syn synonym(s) | *rel* related word(s)
idiom idiomatic equivalent(s) | ***con*** contrasted word(s)
ant antonym(s) | * vulgar
‖ use limited; if in doubt, see a dictionary
The first word in a synonym list when printed in SMALL CAPITALS shows where there is more information about the group. For a more efficient use of this book see Explanatory Notes.

con diffidence, modesty, shyness, timidity; self-depreciation, self-effacement, unassumingness, unpretentiousness

assure *vb* **1** ***syn*** ENSURE, cinch, insure, secure
con abash, discomfit, embarrass; buffalo, bulldoze, cow, daunt, intimidate, shake; demoralize, disquiet, unman, unnerve
ant alarm
2 to make one sure or certain of something <pinched his arm to *assure* himself he was awake>
syn convince, persuade, satisfy
idiom bring (*or* drive) home to, lead one to believe, sell one on something

assured *adj* **1** ***syn*** CONFIDENT 1, sanguine, secure, self-assured, self-confident, undoubtful
rel collected, composed, cool, imperturbable, unflappable, unruffled; game, plucky, resolute, spunky
con abashed, discomfited, disconcerted, embarrassed, rattled; hesitant, insecure, reluctant, uncertain; apprehensive, timorous
2 ***syn*** DECIDED 1, clear-cut, definite, pronounced
rel certain, fixed, set
con ambiguous, uncertain; enigmatic, mysterious, obscure

assuredness *n* ***syn*** CERTAINTY, assurance, certitude, confidence, conviction, sureness, surety

astern *adv* ***syn*** ABAFT, aft
rel rear
con ahead, before, forward

as to *prep* **1** ***syn*** APROPOS, as for, as regards, as respects, concerning, in re, re, regarding, respecting, touching
2 ***syn*** BY 5, according to

astonish *vb* ***syn*** SURPRISE 2, amaze, astound, dumbfound, flabbergast
rel overwhelm; affright, alarm, terrify

astonishing *adj* ***syn*** MARVELOUS 1, amazing, astounding, miraculous, prodigious, spectacular, stupendous, surprising, wonderful, wondrous

astound *vb* ***syn*** SURPRISE 2, amaze, astonish, dumbfound, flabbergast

astounding *adj* ***syn*** MARVELOUS 1, amazing, astonishing, miraculous, prodigious, staggering, stupendous, surprising, wonderful, wondrous

astral *adj* **1** ***syn*** STELLAR 1, sidereal, ‖starny, starry, stellular
2 ***syn*** DREAMY 1, daydreaming, daydreamy, otherworldly, unworldly, visionary
3 ***syn*** EXALTED 1, highest, highest-ranking, top-drawer, top-ranking

astray *adv* ***syn*** AMISS 2, afield, awry, badly, unfavorably, wrong

astricted *adj* ***syn*** CONSTIPATED, bound, costive, obstipated

astringent *adj* **1** ***syn*** ACRID, amaroidal, austere, bitter, harsh, sharp
rel puckery
con bland, mellow, mild
2 ***syn*** SEVERE 1, ascetic, austere, mortified, stern
rel biting, cutting, incisive, penetrating, piercing, stabbing; brisk, caustic, keen, sharp
con lax, loose, relaxed, slack, weak; unexacting
3 ***syn*** TONIC 1, restorative, roborant

astucious *adj* ***syn*** SHREWD, argute, astute, cagey, heady, perspicacious, sagacious, ‖savvy
rel discreet, foresighted, prudent; cunning, sly, wily
con ingenuous, naive, simple, unsophisticated; dull, heavy, obtuse, slow; arid, barren, staid, stuffy, uninspired
ant gullible

astucity *n* ***syn*** WIT 3, acumen, astuteness, clear-sightedness, discernment, discrimination, keenness, penetration, percipience, shrewdness

astute *adj* **1** ***syn*** SHREWD, argute, astucious, cagey, heady, perspicacious, sagacious, ‖savvy
rel discreet, foresighted, prudent; cunning, sly, wily
con ingenuous, naive, simple, unsophisticated; dull, heavy, obtuse, slow; arid, barren, staid, stuffy, uninspired
ant gullible
2 ***syn*** SLY 2, artful, crafty, cunning, deep, foxy, guileful, insidious, tricky, wily
rel subtile, subtle; keen, knowing, sharp
idiom slippery as an eel, too clever by half
con aboveboard, forthright, straightforward; ingenuous, naive, simple, unsophisticated

astuteness *n* ***syn*** WIT 3, acumen, astucity, discernment, discrimination, keenness, penetration, percipience, perspicacity, shrewdness

asudden *adv* ***syn*** SHORT 1, abruptly, forthwith, sudden, suddenly

asunder *adv* ***syn*** APART 3, sky-high
idiom all to pieces, one part from the other, to shreds

as usual *adv* ***syn*** USUALLY 1, consistently, customarily, habitually, wontedly

asweat *adj* ***syn*** SWEATY, perspiring, perspiry, ‖puggy, sweatful, sweating

as well *adv* **1** ***syn*** ALSO 2, additionally, besides, furthermore, likewise, more, moreover, too, yea, yet
idiom over and above
2 ***syn*** EVEN 1, exactly, expressly, just, precisely

as well as *prep* ***syn*** BESIDES 1, beside, beyond, over and above

as yet *adv* ***syn*** HITHERTO 1, earlier, so far, thus far, yet

asylum *n* **1** ***syn*** SHELTER 1, cover, covert, harbor, harborage, haven, port, refuge, retreat, sanctuary
2 ***syn*** REFUGE 1, harborage, sanctuary, shelter
rel inviolability; security
3 an institution for the care of the insane <demand for improved *asylums*>
syn booby hatch, ‖bughouse, crazy house, loony bin, madhouse, ‖nuthouse
rel farm, home, institution, sanatorium
idiom ‖funny farm, insane (*or* lunatic) asylum, mental hospital (*or* institution), state hospital

---

asymmetric *adj syn* LOPSIDED, disproportionate, irregular, nonsymmetrical, off-balance, overbalanced, unbalanced, unequal, uneven, unsymmetrical

at all *adv* **1** *syn* EVER 5, anyway, anywise, once
2 *syn* EVER 4, anytime

ataraxy *n syn* EQUANIMITY, calmness, composure, coolness, imperturbability, phlegm, sangfroid, self-possession

atavism *n syn* REVERSION 1, throwback

ataxia *n syn* CONFUSION 3, ‖ballup, chaos, clutter, disarray, disorder, huddle, muddle, snarl, topsy-turviness

at close hand *adv syn* CLOSE, hard, near, nearby, nigh

atelier *n syn* STUDIO, bottega

athenaeum *n syn* LIBRARY, archive(s)

athirst *adj* **1** *syn* THIRSTY 1, dry, thirsting
rel dehydrated, desiccated, dried up
2 *syn* EAGER, agog, anxious, appetent, ardent, avid, breathless, impatient, keen, thirsty
con lackadaisical, languid, listless; autistic, withdrawn

athletic *adj syn* MUSCULAR 2, brawny, sinewy
rel active, energetic, strenuous, vigorous
con delicate; decadent, effete, flabby, soft

athletics *n pl* physical activities engaged in for exercise or pleasure <went in heavily for *athletics*>
syn games, sports
rel calisthenics, exercise, gymnastics; drill, practice, workout; amusement, diversion, entertainment, pastime, recreation

athwart *adv* **1** *syn* ACROSS 1, crossways, crosswise
2 *syn* OVER 1, across, beyond, transversely

athwart *prep syn* ACROSS, cross, over

atiptoe *adj syn* EXPECTANT 1, anticipant, anticipative, anticipatory, expecting

atmosphere *n* **1** *syn* AIR 3, aura, feel, feeling, mood, semblance
rel character, flavor, property, quality; characteristic, individuality, peculiarity; impression, suggestion
2 *syn* ENVIRONMENT, ambience, ambient, climate, medium, milieu, mise-en-scène, surroundings

atmospheric *adj syn* AIRY 1, aerial, pneumatic

atom *n syn* PARTICLE, bit, iota, jot, minim, mite, modicum, ounce, smidgen, tittle
rel dash, touch, trace; shade, smack, spice, soupçon, suggestion, suspicion, tincture, tinge

atomize *vb syn* DESTROY 1, demolish, destruct, dynamite, rub out, ruin, shatter, smash, tear down, wreck

at once *adv* **1** *syn* TOGETHER 1, coincidentally, coincidently, coinstantaneously, concurrently, simultaneously
2 *syn* AWAY 3, directly, first off, forthwith, immediately, instanter, instantly, now, right away, straightway

atone *vb syn* EXPIATE
rel compensate, pay, recompense, satisfy; appease, conciliate, propitiate
idiom set one's house in order

atone (for) *vb syn* COMPENSATE 1, balance, counterbalance, counterpoise, countervail, make up, offset, outweigh, redeem, set off

atramentous *adj syn* BLACK 1, ebon, ebony, inky, jet, jetty, pitch-black, pitch-dark, raven, sable

at random *adv syn* ABOUT 4, anyhow, any which way, anywise, around, haphazard, haphazardly, helter-skelter, random, randomly

atrocious *adj* **1** *syn* OUTRAGEOUS 2, crying, desperate, heinous, monstrous, scandalous, shocking
rel flagitious, infamous, iniquitous, vicious; barbarous, savage; glaring, rank; abominable, contemptible, despicable, execrable, odious, vile
con fine, righteous, upright, virtuous; benign, gentle, kindly
ant humane
2 *syn* OFFENSIVE, disgusting, foul, horrid, icky, loathsome, noisome, obscene, repulsive, sickening
rel displeasing, distasteful
con alluring, magnetic

atrociousness *n syn* ENORMITY 1, atrocity, heinousness, monstrousness

atrocity *n syn* ENORMITY 1, atrociousness, heinousness, monstrousness

atrophy *n syn* DETERIORATION 1, decadence, declension, declination, decline, degeneracy, degeneration, devolution, downfall, downgrade

attach *vb syn* FASTEN 1, affix, fix, rivet
rel associate; add, annex, append; bind, tie
con disassociate, dissociate; disembarrass, disencumber, disengage, disentangle
ant detach

attachment *n* **1** the state of being firmly attached to someone or something (as by affection, sympathy, or self-interest) <his *attachment* to an outworn code>
syn adherence, adhesion, constancy, faithfulness, fidelity, loyalty
rel firmness, staunchness, steadfastness; allegiance, devotion, fealty
con disloyalty, faithlessness, infidelity, unfaithfulness; aloofness, distance, remoteness; disinterest, disregard, unconcern, unmindfulness
ant detachment
2 *syn* LOVE 1, affection, devotion, fondness
rel piety; devotedness
con antipathy, disinclination, dislike; alienation, disaffection, estrangement
ant aversion

attack *vb* **1** to act in violent opposition <cavalry *attacked* the Indian camp>
syn aggress, assail, assault, beset, fall (on *or* upon), storm, strike
rel invade, irrupt; charge, raid, rush; besiege, blockade, encompass, invest; beleaguer, beset, harass, harry, press; turn (on)
idiom gang up on, light into, sail into, set upon, take the offensive
con defend, guard, protect, shield; combat, oppose, resist, withstand
2 to begin to work vigorously (as at a task) <*attack* a problem>
syn bang away (at), tackle
rel buckle (to *or* down *or* down to), fall to, pitch in, wade (in *or* into)

---

syn synonym(s) *rel* related word(s)
idiom idiomatic equivalent(s) *con* contrasted word(s)
ant antonym(s) * vulgar
‖ use limited; if in doubt, see a dictionary
The first word in a synonym list when printed in SMALL CAPITALS shows where there is more information about the group. For a more efficient use of this book see Explanatory Notes.

idiom address (*or* apply *or* devote) oneself to, give oneself up to
con dawdle, lag, poke, putter

attack *n* **1** an act of attacking especially in the form of an attempt to injure, destroy, or defame <insecticides that are essential for successful *attack* on insect pests>
syn aggression, assailment, assault, offense, offensive, onfall, onset, onslaught
rel charge, descent, drive, foray, push, raid, sally, sortie; blitz, incursion, inroad, surprise; action, battle
con championing, justification, protection, support, vindication; opposition, resistance; defending, guarding, protecting, sheltering
ant defense
2 action or an attitude in a struggle that calls for or is opposed by defense <his policy had always been one of *attack*>
syn aggression, aggressiveness, belligerence, combativeness, fight, pugnacity
rel bellicosity, chauvinism, jingoism, warmongering; activation, militarization, mobilization, muster
con submissiveness, yielding
3 an episode of bodily or mental disorder <a sudden *attack* of dizziness>
syn access, fit, seizure, spell, throe, turn; *compare* SIEGE
rel outbreak, paroxysm, spasm; affection, ailment, complaint, disease, disorder

attain *vb* ***syn*** GAIN 1, accomplish, achieve, rack up, reach, realize, score, win
idiom gain one's end, make good

attainable *adj* ***syn*** AVAILABLE 1, disponible, gettable, obtainable, procurable, securable

attainment *n* ***syn*** ACQUIREMENT, accomplishment, achievement, acquisition, finish

attempt *vb* ***syn*** TRY 5, assay, endeavor, essay, offer, seek, strive, struggle, undertake
rel begin, commence, inaugurate, initiate, start; venture
idiom give (something) a try, take a crack (*or* whack) at
con accomplish, achieve, effect, execute, fulfill, perform; attain, compass, gain, reach
ant succeed

attempt *n* an effort made to do or accomplish something <made a determined *attempt* to improve her writing>
syn endeavor, essay, hassle, striving, struggle, trial, try, undertaking
rel care, effort, pains, trouble; beginning, commencement, initiation, offer, shy, start
con accomplishment, achievement, attainment, finish, fulfillment

attend *vb* **1** ***syn*** LISTEN, hark, hear, hearken, heed
idiom be attentive (to), give heed (to)
2 ***syn*** TEND 2, care (for), mind, watch
rel govern, oversee, supervise; direct, handle, manage, regulate, run; aid, assist, help
3 ***syn*** ACCOMPANY, bear, ‖carry, chaperon, companion, company, conduct, consort (with), convoy, escort
rel associate, fraternize, join, mingle, mix

attendant *adj* ***syn*** CONCOMITANT, accompanying, ancillary, attending, coincident, collateral, incident, satellite

attendant *n* ***syn*** HELPER, aid, ancilla, assistant, help, striker

attending *adj* ***syn*** CONCOMITANT, accompanying, ancillary, attendant, coincident, collateral, incident, satellite

attention *n* **1** a focusing of the mind on something <gave the problem careful *attention*>
syn application, concentration, consideration, debate, deliberation, heed, study
rel assiduity, diligence, industry, sedulity, sedulousness; notice, observation, regard, remark; absorption, engrossment, immersion, intentness
con absence, absentmindedness, abstraction, detachment, remoteness, withdrawal; disinterest, indifference, unconcern, unmindfulness
ant inattention
2 ***syn*** NOTICE 1, cognizance, heed, mark, ‖mind, note, observance, observation, regard, remark
rel awareness, consciousness, mindfulness, sensibility
con disregard, heedlessness, insensibility, unawareness, unconsciousness
3 ***syn*** COURTESY 1, amenity, gallantry
rel deference, homage, honor, reverence; benignity; considerateness, consideration, kindliness, solicitude
con neglect, negligence; aloofness, indifference, unconcern; discourtesy

attentive *adj* **1** concentrating one's attention on something <listeners *attentive* to the speaker's appeal>
syn advertent, arrect, heedful, intentive, observant, regardful
rel alert, aware, mindful; agog, eager, interested, keen; concentrating, earnest, intent; open-eared, open-eyed
idiom all ears (*or* eyes), on the ball, paying attention
con absorbed, abstracted, bemused, preoccupied; absentminded, daydreaming, faraway, oblivious, wandering, woolgathering
ant absent; inattentive
2 ***syn*** THOUGHTFUL 3, considerate
con aloof, indifferent
ant inattentive; neglectful

attenuate *vb* **1** ***syn*** THIN 1, extenuate, wiredraw
rel lessen; sap; dissipate; constrict, contract, deflate, shrink
con amplify, dilate, distend, expand, inflate, swell; augment, enlarge, increase; enrich
2 ***syn*** WEAKEN 1, blunt, cripple, debilitate, disable, enfeeble, sap, unbrace, undermine, unstrengthen
3 ***syn*** THIN 2, rarefy

attenuate *adj* **1** ***syn*** THIN 1, reedy, slender, slight, slim, squinny, stalky, tenuous, twiggy
2 ***syn*** THIN 2, attenuated, rare, rarefied, subtile, subtle, tenuous

attenuated *adj* ***syn*** THIN 2, attenuate, rare, rarefied, subtile, subtle, tenuous

attest *vb* **1** ***syn*** CERTIFY 1, vouch, witness

---

rel confirm, corroborate, substantiate, verify; support, sustain, uphold, warrant; affirm, asseverate, depone, swear, testify
con confute, controvert, disprove, refute; contradict, deny, gainsay
2 *syn* INDICATE 2, announce, argue, bespeak, betoken, testify, witness
rel authenticate, confirm, substantiate
con falsify, misrepresent; distort, garble, pervert, twist, warp
ant belie
3 *syn* TESTIFY 1, point (to)

attestation *n syn* TESTIMONY, confirmation, evidence, proof, testament, testimonial, witness

at times *adv syn* SOMETIMES, ‖betimes, ever and again, ever and anon, here and there, now and again, now and then, once and again, ‖otherwhile

attire *vb syn* CLOTHE, apparel, array, clad, dress, enclothe, garb, garment, raiment
rel accouter, appoint, arm, equip, outfit
con bare, denude, dismantle, strip
ant divest

attire *n syn* CLOTHES, apparel, attirement, clothing, dress, duds, habiliment(s), raiment, things, togs

attirement *n syn* CLOTHES, apparel, attire, clothing, dress, duds, habiliment(s), raiment, things, togs

attitude *n* 1 *syn* POSTURE 1, carriage, pose, positure, stance
rel air, demeanor, port, presence
2 *syn* POSITION 1, color, stance, stand
rel point of view; bias, predilection, prejudice, prepossession

attitudinize *vb syn* POSE 4, masquerade, pass (as *or* for), pass off, posture

attorney *n* 1 *syn* AGENT 2, assignee, deputy, factor, proxy
rel alternate, locum tenens, stand-in, substitute, supply
2 *syn* LAWYER, attorney-at-law

attorney-at-law *n syn* LAWYER, attorney

attract *vb* 1 to exert an irresistible or compelling influence on <her beauty *attracted* all eyes>
syn allure, bewitch, captivate, charm, draw, enchant, fascinate, magnetize, take, wile
rel entice, lure, seduce, tempt; beguile, draw (in), intrigue, inveigle, suck (in); enrapture, entrance; court, invite, solicit
con fend (off), hold (off *or* away), rebuff, repulse; disgust, offend, revolt
ant repel
2 *syn* INTEREST, appeal, excite, fascinate, intrigue

attracting *adj syn* ATTRACTIVE 1, alluring, appealing, bewitching, captivating, charming, drawing, enchanting, fascinating, magnetic

attraction *n* 1 a quality that elicits admiration or pleased responsiveness <yielding to the *attraction* of the balmy afternoon>
syn allurement, appeal, attractiveness, call, draw, drawing power, lure, pull, seduction
rel charm, glamour, interest; delight, pleasure; bait, hook, snare
con offensiveness, repulsiveness, ugliness
2 a relationship characteristic of individuals that are drawn together naturally or involuntarily and exert a degree of influence on one another <the *attraction* between iron and the magnet>
syn affinity, sympathy
rel accord, concord, harmony
idiom drawing together
con conflict, discord, friction, tension

attractive *adj* 1 having the power to attract <an area *attractive* to wildlife>
syn alluring, appealing, attracting, bewitching, captivating, charming, drawing, enchanting, engaging, fascinating, glamorous, magnetic, mesmeric, prepossessing, seductive, siren
rel beautiful, bonny, comely, fair, lovely, pretty; Circean, enticing, fetching, luring, tempting; interesting, taking, winning; beckoning, come-hither, inviting, provocative, tantalizing, teasing; likable, simpatico
con abhorrent, distasteful, obnoxious, repugnant; loathsome, offensive, repulsive, revolting; antipathetic, unsympathetic
ant repellent, repelling; forbidding
2 *syn* BEAUTIFUL, beauteous, ‖bonny, comely, fair, good-looking, handsome, lovely, pretty, pulchritudinous
rel agreeable, goodly, ‖likely, pleasing, sightly
con homely, ill-favored, plain, uncomely, unprepossessing
ant unattractive

attractiveness *n syn* ATTRACTION 1, allurement, appeal, call, draw, drawing power, lure, pull, seduction

attribute *n* 1 *syn* QUALITY 1, affection, character, characteristic, feature, mark, property, savor, trait, virtue
rel particularity, singularity, specialty; brand, earmark, impress, stamp
2 *syn* SYMBOL 1, emblem

attribute *vb syn* ASCRIBE, accredit, assign, charge, credit, impute, lay, refer
rel calendar, chronologize, date, place

attrition *n syn* PENITENCE, contriteness, contrition, penance, penitency, remorse, remorsefulness, repentance, rue, ruth

attritional *adj syn* REMORSEFUL, apologetic, compunctious, contrite, penitent, penitential, regretful, repentant, sorry

attune *vb syn* HARMONIZE 3, accommodate, conform, coordinate, integrate, proportion, reconcile, reconciliate, tune
rel balance, compensate, counterbalance; accord, agree; fix, rectify, regulate
idiom put in tune, set to rights (*or* in order)
con divide, separate, wean

‖**atween** *prep syn* BETWEEN 2, ‖atwixt, ‖betwixt, in between, tween, twixt

‖**atwixt** *prep syn* BETWEEN 2, ‖atween, ‖betwixt, in between, tween, twixt

---

syn synonym(s) *rel* related word(s)
idiom idiomatic equivalent(s) *con* contrasted word(s)
ant antonym(s) * vulgar
‖ use limited; if in doubt, see a dictionary
The first word in a synonym list when printed in SMALL CAPITALS shows where there is more information about the group. For a more efficient use of this book see Explanatory Notes.

atypical *adj* ***syn*** ABNORMAL 1, aberrant, anomalous, deviant, deviative, heteroclite, preternatural, unrepresentative, untypical
rel irregular, unnatural; different, divergent; exceptional, odd, peculiar, queer, strange
con customary, usual
ant typical; representative

auberge *n* ***syn*** HOTEL, caravansary, hospice, hostel, hostelry, inn, lodge, public house, roadhouse, tavern

au courant *adj* **1** ***syn*** AWARE, alive, apprehensive, awake, cognizant, conscious, conversant, knowing, sentient, witting
2 ***syn*** UP-TO-DATE, abreast, contemporary, down-to-date, red-hot, up, up-to-the-minute
3 ***syn*** FAMILIAR 3, abreast, acquainted, au fait, conversant, informed, up, versant, versed

audacious *adj* **1** ***syn*** BRAVE 1, bold, courageous, dauntless, fearless, intrepid, unafraid, undaunted, valiant, valorous
rel adventurous, daredevil, daring, foolhardy, rash, reckless, venturesome; brash, brazen, shameless
con calculating, cautious, chary, wary; judicious, prudent, sane, wise; careful, circumspect, discreet
2 ***syn*** ADVENTUROUS, adventuresome, daredevil, daring, foolhardy, rash, reckless, temerarious, venturesome, venturous
rel fearless, valiant, valorous
con careful, circumspect, discreet; calculating, cautious, chary, wary
3 ***syn*** INSOLENT 2, bold, ‖boldacious, brazen, contumelious, impertinent, impudent, procacious, saucy
4 free from constraint and formality <found life an *audacious* ever-changing adventure>
syn uncurbed, ungoverned, unhampered, uninhibited, unrestrained, untrammeled
rel emancipated, free, independent; easy, relaxed; careless, heedless, thoughtless; self-absorbed, self-centered, selfish
con checked, curbed, governed, hampered, inhibited, restrained, trammeled; careful, cautious, heedful, mindful, thoughtful; considerate, generous, self-abnegating, self-effacing; drab, dull, pedestrian

audacity *n* ***syn*** TEMERITY, assurance, brashness, hardihood, hardiness, nerve
rel cheek, effrontery, face, gall; brass, brazenness, cockiness; forwardness, impudence, resolution; courage, mettle, spirit
con calculation, caution, wariness; shyness, timidity, timorousness; agitation, disquiet, nervousness, perturbation, trepidation
ant circumspection

audible *adj* ***syn*** AURAL 1, auricular
ant inaudible

audience *n* **1** ***syn*** HEARING 2, audition
rel attention, consideration, ear
2 ***syn*** FOLLOWING 2, clientage, clientele, public
rel admirers, devotees, fanciers, fans, votaries

audile *adj* ***syn*** AUDITORY, acoustic, aural

audit *n* ***syn*** EXAMINATION, analysis, checkup, inspection, perlustration, review, scan, scrutiny, survey, view
rel investigation, probe; check, control, corrective

audition *n* ***syn*** HEARING 2, audience

auditory *adj* of, relating to, or experienced through the sense of hearing < *auditory* disorders>
syn acoustic, audile, aural; *compare* AURAL 1

au fait *adj* **1** ***syn*** ABLE, capable, competent, good, proper, qualified, wicked
2 ***syn*** FAMILIAR 3, abreast, acquainted, au courant, conversant, informed, up, versant, versed
3 ***syn*** DECOROUS 1, becoming, befitting, comme il faut, conforming, correct, decent, nice, proper, right

au fond *adv* ***syn*** ESSENTIALLY 1, basically, fundamentally, in essence

Augean stable *n* ***syn*** SINK 1, cesspit, cesspool, den, pandemonium, Sodom, sty

aught (*or* **ought**) *n* ***syn*** ZERO 1, cipher, goose egg, naught (*or* nought), nothing, zilch

augment *vb* **1** ***syn*** INCREASE 1, build, compound, enlarge, expand, extend, heighten, magnify, manifold, multiply
2 ***syn*** INCREASE 2, build, enlarge, expand, heighten, mount, multiply, rise, upsurge, wax

augment *n* ***syn*** INCREASE 1, aggrandize, beef (up), boost, enlarge, expand, extend, heighten, magnify, multiply
rel exalt, hike, raise
con attenuate, decrease, dwindle; abridge; alleviate, assuage, relieve
ant abate

augmentation *n* **1** ***syn*** ACCOMPANIMENT 1, complement, enhancement, enrichment
rel adjunct, annex, attachment, fixture, reinforcement; bonus, boot, extra, plus
2 ***syn*** ADDITION, accession, accretion, increase, increment, raise, rise
con subtraction

augur *n* ***syn*** PROPHET, auspex, forecaster, foreseer, foreteller, haruspex, Nostradamus, predictor, prognosticator, prophesier

augur *vb* **1** ***syn*** FORETELL, adumbrate, forecast, portend, predict, presage, prognosticate, prophesy, soothsay, vaticinate
rel argue, bespeak, indicate
2 to indicate or suggest a future probability <their enthusiasm *augurs* well for the success of the enterprise>
syn betoken, bode, forebode, foreshadow, foreshow, foretoken, omen, portend, presage, promise
rel hint, imply, intimate, suggest; prefigure, shadow (forth)
idiom bid fair to, give promise (*or* fair promise) of, hold out hope of, lead one to believe (*or* expect)

augury *n* ***syn*** FORETOKEN, bodement, boding, omen, portent, presage, prognostic
rel anticipation, premonition, presentiment
con accomplishment, effecting, effectuation, fulfillment; actualization, materialization, realization; appearance, emergence, forthcoming, issuance

---

syn synonym(s)	***rel*** related word(s)
idiom idiomatic equivalent(s)	***con*** contrasted word(s)
ant antonym(s)	* vulgar

‖ use limited; if in doubt, see a dictionary
The first word in a synonym list when printed in SMALL CAPITALS shows where there is more information about the group. For a more efficient use of this book see Explanatory Notes.

august *adj* *syn* GRAND 1, baronial, grandiose, imposing, lordly, magnificent, majestic, noble, princely, stately
rel splendid, sublime, superb; impressive, moving, striking; awe-inspiring, awful, fearful, overwhelming

au naturel *adj* *syn* NUDE 2, *bare-assed, buff-bare, naked, raw, stark-naked, stripped, unclad, unclothed, undressed

aura *n* *syn* AIR 3, atmosphere, feel, feeling, mood, semblance
rel appearance, aspect, suggestion; aureole, radiance

aural *adj* 1 heard or perceived with the ear <responded to *aural* stimuli>
syn audible, auricular; *compare* AUDITORY
2 *syn* AUDITORY, acoustic, audile

aureate *adj* *syn* RHETORICAL, bombastic, declamatory, euphuistic, flowery, grandiloquent, magniloquent, overblown, sonorous, swollen
rel baroque, rococo
con moderate, quiet, restrained, sober, temperate
ant austere

auricular *n* *syn* AURAL 1, audible

aurora *n* *syn* DAWN 1, cockcrow, cockcrowing, dawning, daybreak, daylight, light, morn, morning, sunrise

auslander *n* *syn* STRANGER, alien, foreigner, inconnu, outcomer, outlander, outsider

auspex *n* *syn* PROPHET, augur, forecaster, foreseer, foreteller, haruspex, Nostradamus, prognosticator, prophesier, soothsayer

auspices *n pl* *syn* BACKING, aegis, patronage, sponsorship

auspicious *adj* 1 *syn* FAVORABLE 5, benign, bright, dexter, fortunate, propitious, white
rel hopeful; golden, halcyon, roseate, rosy
con ominous, portentous, unpropitious; adverse, antagonistic
ant inauspicious; ill-omened
2 *syn* TIMELY 1, favorable, opportune, propitious, prosperous, seasonable, timeous, well-timed

austere *adj* 1 *syn* SEVERE 1, ascetic, astringent, mortified, stern
rel bald, bare, simple, unadorned, undecorated, unembellished, unornamented; earnest, grave, serious, sober, somber
con complicated, elaborate, fancy, flamboyant, fussy, ornate; frivolous, light, light-minded, shallow, superficial
2 *syn* ACRID, amaroidal, astringent, bitter, harsh, sharp
rel biting, keen, rough
con bland, mellow, smooth, soft
3 *syn* GRIM 2, bleak, dour, hard, harsh, severe, stringent

autarchic *adj* 1 *syn* ABSOLUTE 4, arbitrary, autocratic, despotic, monocratic, tyrannical, tyrannous
rel commanding, dogmatic, imperious; nonconstitutional, undemocratic
2 *syn* FREE 1, autarkic, autonomous, independent, separate, sovereign
rel self-dependent, self-reliant, self-sufficient

autarkic *adj* *syn* FREE 1, autarchic, autonomous, independent, separate, sovereign
rel self-dependent, self-reliant, self-sufficient

authentic *adj* 1 worthy of acceptance because of accuracy <an *authentic* portrayal of ancient customs>
syn convincing, credible, faithful, trustworthy, trusty
rel accurate, dependable, factual, reliable, sure; solid, sound, straight, valid; authoritative, cathedral, official, standard
idiom all wool and a yard wide; to be depended (*or* relied) on
con incredible, unconvincing, untrustworthy; equivocal, obscure, uncertain, vague; hypothetical, purported, putative, supposed, supposititious; debatable, doubtful, questionable; nonstandard
ant inauthentic
2 being exactly as appears or is claimed <an *authentic* masterpiece>
syn blown-in-the-bottle, bona fide, genuine, indubitable, pukka, questionless, real, right, simon-pure, sure-enough, true, undoubted, undubitable, unquestionable, veritable, very
rel cognizable, identifiable, knowable, recognizable; honest, pure, unadulterated, unalloyed
con deceptive, delusive, delusory, false, misleading, wrong; unidentifiable, unrecognizable
ant spurious
3 *syn* CERTAIN 3, accurate, dependable, reliable

authenticate *vb* 1 *syn* CONFIRM 2, bear out, corroborate, justify, substantiate, validate, verify
rel accredit, approve, endorse; demonstrate, prove, test, try; avouch, vouch (for)
con reject, repudiate, spurn; contradict, deny, negate
ant impugn

author *n* *syn* FATHER 2, architect, creator, founder, generator, inventor, maker, originator, patriarch, sire
rel origin, source; ancestor, parent, procreator

authoritarian *adj* 1 *syn* DICTATORIAL, authoritative, dictative, doctrinaire, dogmatic, magisterial
rel heavy-handed, high-handed, oppressive, strict, stringent
ant libertarian; anarchistic
2 *syn* TOTALITARIAN 1, total, totalistic
rel fascistic, nazi; patriarchal
ant democratic

authoritative *adj* 1 *syn* OFFICIAL, ex cathedra, ex officio
2 *syn* TRUE 9, dependable, trustable, trustworthy
rel attested, authenticated, circumstantiated, confirmed, proven, validated, verified; convincing, indisputable, irrefutable, sure, unrefutable; cathedral, cathedratic
con contestable, controversial, debatable, disputable, refutable; dubious, questionable, suspect, unreliable
3 *syn* DICTATORIAL, authoritarian, dictative, doctrinaire, dogmatic, magisterial
4 *syn* ORTHODOX 1, accepted, canonical, received, sanctioned, sound

---

syn synonym(s) · *rel* related word(s)
idiom idiomatic equivalent(s) · *con* contrasted word(s)
ant antonym(s) · * vulgar
‖ use limited; if in doubt, see a dictionary
The first word in a synonym list when printed in SMALL CAPITALS shows where there is more information about the group. For a more efficient use of this book see Explanatory Notes.

authority *n* **1** ***syn*** EXPERT, adept, artist, artiste, master, past master, professional, proficient, virtuoso, wizard
2 ***syn*** POWER 1, command, control, domination, jurisdiction, mastery, might, strings, sway
rel governance, government, rule
3 ***syn*** INFLUENCE 1, credit, prestige, weight
rel example, exemplar, ideal, model, pattern, standard; force, power, pressure

authorization *n* ***syn*** PERMISSION, allowance, consent, leave, permit, sanction, sufferance

authorize *vb* **1** to invest with power or the right to act <I did not *authorize* him to speak for me>
syn accredit, commission, empower, enable, license
rel approve, countenance, endorse; aid, assist, help, support, subserve; advance, facilitate, forward, further, promote
con bar, disallow, enjoin, forbid, interdict, prohibit
2 ***syn*** ENTITLE 2, qualify
rel allow, let, permit; approve, countenance, endorse
idiom give one the right to
3 ***syn*** INVEST 2, empower, vest

auto *n* ***syn*** CAR, autocar, automobile, buggy, ||bus, machine, motor, motorcar

auto *vb* **1** ***syn*** DRIVE 5, charioteer, motor, pilot, tool, wheel
2 ***syn*** RIDE 1, motor

autobiographer *n* ***syn*** BIOGRAPHER, autobiographist, Boswell, memoirist

autobiographist *n* ***syn*** BIOGRAPHER, autobiographer, Boswell, memoirist

autobiography *n* ***syn*** BIOGRAPHY, bio, confessions, life, memoir
rel diary, journal, letters

autocar *n* ***syn*** CAR, auto, automobile, buggy, ||bus, machine, motor, motorcar

autochthonous *adj* ***syn*** NATIVE 2, aboriginal, endemic, indigenous
con alien, extraneous, extrinsic, foreign; imported, introduced
ant naturalized

autocracy *n* ***syn*** TYRANNY, despotism, dictatorship, totalitarianism

autocratic *adj* ***syn*** ABSOLUTE 4, arbitrary, autarchic, despotic, monocratic, tyrannical, tyrannous
rel arrogant, haughty, overbearing, overweening
con deferential, submissive, yielding; forbearing, indulgent, lenient, tolerant

autodidactic *adj* ***syn*** SELF-TAUGHT, self-educated, self-instructed

autograph *vb* ***syn*** SIGN 1, ink, signature, subscribe

autognosis *n* ***syn*** SELF-KNOWLEDGE, self-understanding

autoist *n* ***syn*** MOTORIST, automobilist, driver, operator

automatic *adj* **1** ***syn*** SPONTANEOUS, impulsive, instinctive, involuntary, unmeditated, unpremeditated, unprompted, will-less
rel prompt, quick, ready; accustomed, confirmed, habitual, habituated
2 ***syn*** PERFUNCTORY, mechanical

automaton *n* **1** ***syn*** ROBOT 1, android
2 ***syn*** ROBOT 2, golem, machine

automobile *n* ***syn*** CAR, auto, autocar, buggy, ||bus, machine, motor, motorcar

automobilist *n* ***syn*** MOTORIST, autoist, driver, operator

autonomous *adj* ***syn*** FREE 1, autarchic, autarkic, independent, separate, sovereign
rel self-governed; unconstrained, uncontrolled, unsubordinated
con controlled, subordinated; governed, ruled; affiliated, allied

autopsy *n* examination of the body after death usually to determine the cause of death <the *autopsy* of a murder victim>
syn necropsy, ||post, postmortem, postmortem examination

autoschediasm *n* ***syn*** IMPROVISATION, extemporization, impromptu

autoschediastic *adj* ***syn*** EXTEMPORANEOUS, extemporary, extempore, impromptu, improvised, offhand, spur-of-the-moment, unrehearsed, unstudied

auxiliary *adj* capable of supplying or intended to supply aid or support <an *auxiliary* police unit>
syn accessory, adjuvant, ancillary, appurtenant, collateral, contributory, subservient, subsidiary
rel complementary, supplementary; peripheral, secondary, subordinate, tributary; backing, supporting, upholding; aiding, assisting, helping
con chief, leading, main, principal; sole, solitary, unique

avail *vb* ***syn*** BENEFIT, advantage, profit, serve, work (for)
rel answer, fill, fulfill, meet, satisfy
con damage, harm, hurt, injure

avail *n* ***syn*** USE 3, account, advantage, applicability, appropriateness, fitness, relevance, service, serviceability, usefulness
rel interest; appositeness, suitability
con inappropriateness, unsuitableness

available *adj* **1** that is accessible or may be obtained <the best pen *available* at the present time>
syn attainable, disponible, gettable, obtainable, procurable, securable
rel accessible, convenient, handy
idiom to be had
con unattainable, unobtainable; absent, deficient, lacking, missing
ant unavailable
2 ***syn*** PURCHASABLE 1, obtainable, on offer

avarice *n* ***syn*** CUPIDITY, avariciousness, avidity, greed, rapacity
rel frugality, parsimony, thrift; miserliness, niggardliness, parsimoniousness, stinginess; acquisitiveness, covetousness, graspingness, piggishness
con extravagance; bountifulness, bounty, generosity, liberality, munificence, openhandedness
ant prodigality

avariciousness *n* ***syn*** CUPIDITY, avarice, avidity, greed, rapacity

---

syn synonym(s) — ***rel*** related word(s)
idiom idiomatic equivalent(s) — ***con*** contrasted word(s)
ant antonym(s) — * vulgar
|| use limited; if in doubt, see a dictionary
The first word in a synonym list when printed in SMALL CAPITALS shows where there is more information about the group. For a more efficient use of this book see Explanatory Notes.

avenge *vb* to inflict punishment by way of repayment for < *avenge* an insult >
syn redress, revenge, venge, vindicate
rel compensate, pay (back), pay out, recompense, repay, requite, retaliate, retribute; chasten, chastise, punish; correct, right
idiom get an eye for an eye, get even with, settle accounts, wreak one's vengeance
con condone, disregard, ignore, overlook; absolve, amnesty, forgive, pardon, remit; bear, endure, stand, suffer, tolerate

avengement *n* *syn* RETALIATION, avenging, counterblow, reprisal, requital, retribution, revanche, revenge, vengeance

avenging *n* *syn* RETALIATION, avengement, counterblow, reprisal, requital, retribution, revanche, revenge, vengeance

avenue *n* **1** *syn* WAY 1, artery, boulevard, ||drag, highway, path, road, street, thoroughfare, track
||**2** *syn* DRIVEWAY, drive

aver *vb* *syn* ASSERT 1, affirm, avouch, avow, constate, declare, depose, predicate, profess, protest
rel defend, hold, justify, maintain
con deny

average *n* something (as a number, quantity, or condition) that represents a middle point between extremes < somewhat sweeter than *average* >
syn mean, median, norm, par
ant maximum; minimum

average *adj* *syn* MEDIUM, fair, fairish, indifferent, intermediate, mean, mediocre, middling, moderate, so-so
rel common, familiar, ordinary; customary, usual
idiom common or garden variety
con choice, excellent, exceptional, prime, superior; conspicuous, noticeable, outstanding, prominent; bad, inferior, low-grade, poor, punk

averagely *adv* *syn* ENOUGH 2, fairly, moderately, passably, rather, so-so, tolerably

avernal *adj* *syn* INFERNAL 2, cimmerian, hellish, pandemoniac, plutonian, plutonic, stygian

averse *adj* *syn* DISINCLINED, afraid, backward, hesitant, indisposed, loath, reluctant, uneager, unwilling, unwishful
rel balky, contrary, perverse; flinching, quailing, recoiling, resistant, shrinking; uncongenial, unsympathetic
ant avid (of *or* for)

aversion *n* **1** *syn* DISLIKE, bad books, disfavor, disinclination, disliking, displeasure, disrelish, dissatisfaction, distaste, indisposition
rel antagonism, antipathy, hostility; dread, fear, horror
con bias, partiality; leaning, propensity, taste
ant predilection
2 *syn* ANTIPATHY 2, allergy, dyspathy
rel abhorrence, distaste, repellency, repugnance, repulsion, revulsion; disgust, dread, loathing
con bias, partiality, penchant; flair, inclination, leaning, taste
ant attachment; predilection
3 *syn* ABOMINATION 2, abhorrence, detestation, hate, hatred, horror, loathing, repugnance, repulsion, revulsion
ant delight

aversive *adj* *syn* ANTIPATHETIC 2, kindless, repellent, repugnant, uncongenial, ungenial, unsympathetic

avert *vb* **1** *syn* TURN 6, deflect, divert, pivot, sheer, veer, volte-face, wheel, whip, whirl
rel remove, transfer
2 *syn* PREVENT 2, deter, forestall, forfend, obviate, preclude, rule out, stave off, ward
rel anticipate; balk, foil, frustrate, thwart; check, halt, stay, stop
con advance, further, promote

aviary *n* a house, enclosure, or large cage for confining live birds < the zoo's *aviary* >
syn birdhouse
rel dovecote, dovehouse; columbary, pigeon house

aviator *n* *syn* PILOT 2, airman, birdman, flier, fly-boy

avid *adj* *syn* EAGER, agog, anxious, appetent, ardent, athirst, breathless, impatient, keen, thirsty
rel covetous, craving, desirous, wanting, wishful; importunate, insistent, pressing, urgent; gluttonous, omnivorous
con aloof, disinterested, uninterested; disinclined, indisposed, loath
ant indifferent; averse

avidity *n* *syn* CUPIDITY, avarice, avariciousness, greed, rapacity

avoid *vb* *syn* ESCAPE 2, bilk, double, duck, elude, eschew, evade, shun, shy
rel avert, deflect, divert, obviate, prevent, ward (off); debar, exclude, preclude; forbid, prohibit
idiom give a miss (*or* a wide berth), have no truck with, set one's face against, steer clear of, turn one's back on
con court, invite, solicit
ant face; meet

avoidance *n* *syn* ESCAPE 2, come-off, elusion, escaping, eschewal, evasion, runaround, shunning

avouch *vb* *syn* ASSERT 1, affirm, aver, avow, constate, declare, depose, predicate, profess, protest
rel confirm, corroborate; acknowledge, admit, confess, own
con deny, impugn

avow *vb* **1** *syn* ASSERT 1, affirm, aver, avouch, constate, declare, depose, predicate, profess, protest
rel defend, maintain, vindicate; asseverate, swear, testify
2 *syn* ACKNOWLEDGE 1, admit, allow, concede, confess, fess (up), grant, let on, own, own up
con repudiate, withdraw

avowry *n* *syn* PATRON SAINT, patron

await *vb* *syn* EXPECT 1, count (on *or* upon), hope, look
rel abide, stay, wait
idiom bide one's time, sweat (*or* tough) it out

awake *vb* *syn* WAKE 1, awaken, rouse, stir, waken

awake *adj* ***syn*** AWARE, alive, apprehensive, au courant, cognizant, conscious, conversant, knowing, sensible, sentient

rel vigilant, watchful; aroused, awakened, roused, stirred up; excited

con drowsy, sleepy, slumberous, somnolent; inactive, inert, supine

awaken *vb* **1** ***syn*** WAKE 1, awake, rouse, stir, waken

2 ***syn*** STIR 1, arouse, bestir, challenge, kindle, rally, rouse, wake, waken, whet

rel fire, inflame; alert

idiom stir the feelings (*or* blood) of

con arrest, check, retard, subdue; calm, compose, restrain

awanting *prep* ***syn*** WITHOUT 2, lacking, minus, sans, wanting

award *vb* **1** ***syn*** GRANT 1, accord, concede, vouchsafe

rel allocate, allot, apportion, assign; dower, endow, endue

2 ***syn*** GIVE 2, accord, confer, grant

award *n* ***syn*** HONOR 2, accolade, badge, bays, decoration, distinction, kudos, laurels

aware *adj* marked by realization, perception, or knowledge often of something not generally realized, perceived, or known < *aware* of her own inner weakness>

syn alive, apprehensive, au courant, awake, cognizant, conscious, conversant, knowing, mindful, sensible, sentient, ware, witting

rel acquainted, apprised, informed; alert, heedful; impressionable, perceptive, receptive

con anesthetic, impassible, insensible, insensitive; ignorant, unknowing

ant unaware

awash *adj* ***syn*** FULL 1, brimful, brimming, chock-full, crammed, crowded, jammed, loaded, packed, stuffed

away *adv* **1** from this or that place <come *away* at once>

syn hence, thence

rel forth, out, therefrom

2 at some distance from a place expressed or implied <he lived several blocks *away*>

syn off, over

rel afar, far; apart, aside

3 without hesitation or delay <fire *away* when you see the target>

syn at once, directly, first off, forthwith, immediately, instanter, instantly, now, PDQ, right, right away, right off, straight, straight away, straight off, straightway

rel momentarily, promptly, ‖pronto, punctually; expeditiously, quickly, speedily, swiftly

away *adj* ***syn*** ABSENT 1, gone, lacking, missing, omitted, wanting

awe *n* ***syn*** REVERENCE 2, fear

rel esteem, regard, respect, veneration, worship; admiration, amazement, wonder, wonderment

con despite, scorn; arrogance, insolence, superciliousness

awe *vb* ***syn*** FRIGHTEN, affright, alarm, fright, scare, ‖spook, startle, terrify, terrorize

aweless *adj* ***syn*** BRAVE 1, bold, courageous, dauntless, fearless, intrepid, unafraid, undaunted, valiant, valorous

awful *adj* ***syn*** FEARFUL 3, appalling, dreadful, formidable, frightful, horrible, horrific, shocking, terrible, terrific

rel impressive, moving; august, imposing, majestic; splendid, superb; grave, serious, solemn; ominous, portentous

‖**awful** *adv* ***syn*** VERY 1, awfully, ‖big, damned, extremely, greatly, hugely, much, whacking, whopping

awfully *adv* ***syn*** VERY 1, ‖awful, ‖big, damned, extremely, greatly, hugely, much, whacking, whopping

awkward *adj* **1** ***syn*** CLUMSY 1, gawky, lumbering, lumpish, splathering, splay, ungainly

rel blundering, bumbling, bungling; clownish, lubberly, oafish; cumbrous, hulking, ponderous

idiom all thumbs

2 marked by a lack of grace, ease, skill, or fitness (as in action or speech) <his *awkward* approach to the problem>

syn bumbling, clumsy, gauche, halting, ham-handed, heavy-handed, inept, lumbering, maladroit, unhandy, unhappy, wooden; *compare* CLUMSY 1

rel rigid, stiff; discomfited, disconcerted, embarrassed; bunglesome, bungling, inefficient, inexpert, unskillful

con adept, adroit, dexterous, expert, finished, polished, proficient, skilled, skillful, smooth; easy, effortless, facile, simple

ant deft; graceful

3 ***syn*** INCONVENIENT, discommoding, discommodious, embarrassing, incommodious

4 ***syn*** INFELICITOUS, graceless, ill-chosen, inept, unfortunate, unhappy

awry *adv* (*or adj*) **1** deviating from a straight line or direction <the coverlet was pulled *awry*>

syn askance, askant, askew, ‖cam, cock-a-hoop, cockeyed, crookedly

rel aside, aslant, obliquely, slantways

con even, straight, true; directly, undeviatingly

2 ***syn*** AMISS 2, afield, astray, badly, unfavorably, wrong

rel erroneously, faultily, untruly; aside

ax *vb* ***syn*** DISMISS 3, boot (out), bounce, ‖can, cashier, discharge, fire, kick out, sack, terminate

axiom *n* **1** ***syn*** PRINCIPLE 1, fundamental, law, principium, theorem

2 ***syn*** MAXIM, aphorism, apothegm, brocard, dictum, gnome, moral, rule, truism

‖**ayah** *n* ***syn*** NURSEMAID, ‖amah, nana, ‖nanny, nurse, nurserymaid

aye *adv* ***syn*** YES 1, agreed, all right, OK (*or* okay), ‖okeydoke, yea, ‖yep

---

syn synonym(s) — *rel* related word(s)
idiom idiomatic equivalent(s) — *con* contrasted word(s)
ant antonym(s) — * vulgar
‖ use limited; if in doubt, see a dictionary
The first word in a synonym list when printed in SMALL CAPITALS shows where there is more information about the group. For a more efficient use of this book see Explanatory Notes.

B

Babbitt *n* ***syn*** PHILISTINE, boeotian, boob, middlebrow

babblative *adj* ***syn*** TALKATIVE, chatty, gabby, garrulous, loose-lipped, loose-tongued, loquacious, multiloquent, multiloquious, talky

babble *vb* **1** ***syn*** GIBBER, chatter, gabble, jabber
2 to talk nonsensically <silly people *babbling* on about trivia>
syn blabber, blather, drivel, drool, gabble, prate, prattle, twaddle, ‖waffle
rel clack, jaw, rattle, run on, yak, yammer, yap
idiom run off at the mouth
3 ***syn*** CHAT 1, chatter, clack, gab, jaw, patter, prate, prattle, yak, yammer

babble *n* **1** ***syn*** CHATTER, blab, blabber, chat, clack, gab, gabble, jabber, palaver, prattle
2 ***syn*** GIBBERISH 1, drivel, Greek, jabber, jabberwocky, nonsense, skimble-skamble

babe *n* ***syn*** BABY 1, bantling, infant, neonate, newborn

babel *n* ***syn*** DIN, clamor, hubbub, hullabaloo, jangle, pandemonium, racket, tintamarre, tumult, uproar
con hush, noiselessness; peace, quiet, silence

babushka *n* ***syn*** KERCHIEF 1, bandanna

baby *n* **1** a very young child esp. in the first year of life <the love of a mother for her *baby*>
syn babe, bantling, infant, neonate, newborn
rel bambino, little one, toddler, tot; nursling, suckling, weanling; bratling
idiom babe in arms
2 ***syn*** WEAKLING, doormat, invertebrate, jellyfish, milksop, Milquetoast, mollycoddle, namby-pamby, pantywaist, sissy
‖**3** ***syn*** GIRL FRIEND 2, beloved, flame, honey, inamorata, ladylove, steady, sweetheart, sweetie, truelove

baby *vb* to treat with special, excessive, or fond care <*baby* a sick husband>
syn cater (to), cocker, coddle, cosset, cotton, humor, indulge, mollycoddle, pamper, spoil
rel dry-nurse, wet-nurse; dote (on *or* upon), favor; gratify, please, satisfy
con control, discipline, restrain; abuse, ill-treat, ill-use, mistreat, oppress; neglect, overlook, slight

baby buggy *n* ***syn*** BABY CARRIAGE, bassinet, ‖perambulator, ‖pram

baby carriage *n* a four-wheeled push carriage with a folding top for a baby <used the *baby carriage* to wheel home firewood>
syn baby buggy, bassinet, ‖perambulator, ‖pram

babyhood *n* ***syn*** INFANCY 1, infanthood

babyish *adj* ***syn*** CHILDISH, immature, infantile, infantine, prekindergarten, puerile

bacchanal *n* ***syn*** ORGY 2, bacchanalia, debauch, party, saturnalia

bacchanalia *n* ***syn*** ORGY 2, bacchanal, debauch, party, saturnalia

back *n* **1** the surface or part most remote from the front <the *back* of his neck>
syn posterior, rear, rearward
rel extremity, tail; reverse
con anterior
ant front
2 ***syn*** SPINE, backbone, rachis, spinal column, vertebrae, vertebral column

back *adv* ***syn*** ABOUT 6, again, around, backward, in reverse, round, round about

back *adj* **1** distant from settled areas <*back* regions in the hill country>
syn frontier, outlandish, remote, unsettled
rel uncultivated, uninhabited, unoccupied, unpopulated, wild
con built-up, settled, urban
2 ***syn*** POSTERIOR 2, after, hind, hinder, hindmost, rear, retral
ant front

back *vb* **1** ***syn*** SUPPORT 2, advocate, backstop, champion, side (with), uphold
rel aid, assist, help; abet
2 ***syn*** CAPITALIZE, bankroll, finance, grubstake, stake
3 ***syn*** MOUNT 5, bestride
4 ***syn*** RECEDE 1, fall back, retract, retreat, retrocede, retrograde
con advance, progress

back answer *n* ***syn*** RETORT 2, comeback, repartee, riposte

backbiting *n* ***syn*** DETRACTION, backstabbing, belittlement, calumny, defamation, depreciation, disparagement, scandal, slander, tale
rel animadversion, reflection, stricture; abuse, invective, obloquy, vituperation
con accolade, commendation, encomium, eulogy, laudation, paean, panegyric, praise, tribute; adulation, blarney, compliment, flattery, soft soap

backbiting *adj* ***syn*** LIBELOUS, calumnious, defamatory, detracting, detractive, maligning, scandalous, slanderous, traducing, vilifying

backbone *n* **1** ***syn*** SPINE, back, rachis, spinal column, vertebrae, vertebral column
2 ***syn*** FORTITUDE, grit, guts, intestinal fortitude, ‖moxie, nerve, sand, spunk
rel hardihood; heart
con irresoluteness, irresolution
ant backbonelessness, spinelessness

---

syn synonym(s) ***rel*** related word(s)
idiom idiomatic equivalent(s) ***con*** contrasted word(s)
ant antonym(s) * vulgar
‖ use limited; if in doubt, see a dictionary
The first word in a synonym list when printed in SMALL CAPITALS shows where there is more information about the group. For a more efficient use of this book see Explanatory Notes.

3 ***syn*** MAINSTAY, pillar, sinew(s)

backchat *n* ***syn*** BANTER, badinage, ‖cross talk, persiflage, repartee, snip-snap

backcountry *n* ***syn*** FRONTIER 2, backland, backwash, backwater, backwoods, ‖boondocks, bush, hinterland, sticks, up-country

‖**backdoor trots** *n pl but sing or pl in constr* ***syn*** DIARRHEA, dysentery, flux, ‖runs, scour(s), *shits, ‖squirts, *trots

back down *vb* to withdraw from a previous agreement or stand <a politician *backing down* on an earlier promise>
syn back off, back out, backpedal, backwater, crawfish (out), cry off, declare off, renege, resile, welsh
rel disavow, recall, recant, retract, take back, withdraw; backtrack; beg off, weasel (out); balk, demur, hold back, stickle
idiom get out of, go back on

backer *n* ***syn*** SPONSOR, angel, backer-up, guarantor, patron, surety
rel ally, protagonist; bankroller, ‖grubstaker, ‖meal ticket, promoter

backer–up *n* ***syn*** SPONSOR, angel, backer, guarantor, patron, surety

backfire *vb* to have the reverse of the desired effect <the new policy *backfired* disastrously>
syn backlash, boomerang, bounce (back), kick back
rel fall (through), fizzle, miscarry, miss, ricochet
idiom come to grief, go on the rocks, ‖lay an egg
con come off, succeed, work out

backhouse *n* ***syn*** PRIVY 1, ‖biffy, ‖closet, *crapper, jakes, ‖necessary, ‖office, outhouse

backing *n* aid or support given to an undertaking <the project had the *backing* of the city fathers>
syn aegis, auspices, patronage, sponsorship
rel championship, cooperation, fosterage; guidance, tutelage; encouragement; assistance, help, support

backland *n* ***syn*** FRONTIER 2, backcountry, backwash, backwater, backwoods, ‖boondocks, bush, hinterland, sticks, up-country

backlash *vb* ***syn*** BACKFIRE, boomerang, bounce (back), kick back

backlog *n* ***syn*** RESERVE, hoard, inventory, nest egg, reservoir, stock, stockpile, store

back of *prep* ***syn*** ABAFT, behind

back off *vb* ***syn*** BACK DOWN, back out, backpedal, backwater, crawfish (out), cry off, declare off, renege, resile, welsh

back out *vb* ***syn*** BACK DOWN, back off, backpedal, backwater, crawfish (out), cry off, declare off, renege, resile, welsh

backpack *n* a carrying case (as of canvas or nylon) held on the back by shoulder straps <carried his supplies in a *backpack*>
syn haversack, knapsack, pack, packsack, rucksack

backpedal *vb* ***syn*** BACK DOWN, back off, back out, backwater, crawfish (out), cry off, declare off, renege, resile, welsh
rel dodge, duck, elude, evade, get around, shirk, sidestep

backset *n* ***syn*** SETBACK, check, reversal, reverse

backside *n* ***syn*** BUTTOCKS, behind, bottom, derriere, fanny, heinie (*or* hiney), posterior, rear, rump, seat

backslide *vb* ***syn*** LAPSE, recidivate, relapse
rel regress, retrovert, return, revert; defect, desert, tergiversate, turn
idiom fall away, fall (*or* sink *or* slide *or* slip) back into, give in to

backsliding *n* ***syn*** LAPSE 2, relapse

backstabbing *n* ***syn*** DETRACTION, backbiting, belittlement, calumny, defamation, depreciation, disparagement, scandal, slander, tale

backstage *adj or adv* off or away from the part of the stage visible to the audience <*backstage* sounds that gave the impression of a storm>
syn offstage
idiom behind the scenes
ant onstage

backstop *vb* ***syn*** SUPPORT 2, advocate, back, champion, side (with), uphold

back talk *n* impudent and insolent talk <do as you're told and no *back talk*>
syn guff, ‖jaw, ‖lip, mouth, sass, sauce
rel cheek, impudence, insolence

‖**backveld** *n* ***syn*** FRONTIER 2, backcountry, backland, backwash, backwater, backwoods, bush, hinterland, ‖outback, up-country

backward *adv* ***syn*** ABOUT 6, again, around, back, in reverse, round, round about

backward *adj* **1** directed, turned, or executed backward <the *backward* swimming of the crayfish>
syn retral, retrograde
rel inverted, reversed
ant advance, forward
2 ***syn*** DISINCLINED, afraid, averse, hesitant, indisposed, loath, reluctant, shy, uneager, unwilling
rel bashful, diffident
3 ***syn*** SHY 1, bashful, demure, diffident, modest, retiring, self-effacing, timid, unassertive, unassured
4 ***syn*** RETARDED, dim-witted, dull, feebleminded, half-witted, imbecile, moronic, simpleminded, slow, slow-witted
5 holding to outworn or traditional views, ideas, or principles <had a *backward* attitude toward social inferiors>
syn benighted, ignorant, unenlightened, unprogressive
rel conservative, reactionary; obtuse, stupid, thickheaded; bigoted, hidebound, narrow; blind; unenlightened, uninformed
con advanced, aware, enlightened, forward-looking, progressive, unbenighted
6 not developing or progressing especially in economic and social areas <*backward* nations using primitive farming methods>
syn behindhand, underdeveloped, undeveloped, unprogressive

---

syn synonym(s) ***rel*** related word(s)
idiom idiomatic equivalent(s) ***con*** contrasted word(s)
ant antonym(s) * vulgar
‖ use limited; if in doubt, see a dictionary
The first word in a synonym list when printed in SMALL CAPITALS shows where there is more information about the group. For a more efficient use of this book see Explanatory Notes.

rel poor, struggling; medieval; benighted, retarded, uncultivated, uncultured
idiom behind the times
con forward-looking, progressive; civilized, cultivated, cultured; modern
ant advanced

backwash *n* ***syn*** FRONTIER 2, backcountry, backland, backwater, backwoods, ‖boondocks, bush, hinterland, sticks, up-country

backwater *n* ***syn*** FRONTIER 2, backcountry, backland, backwash, backwoods, ‖boondocks, bush, hinterland, sticks, up-country

backwater *vb* ***syn*** BACK DOWN, back off, back out, backpedal, crawfish (out), cry off, declare off, renege, resile, welsh
rel dodge, duck, elude, evade, get around, shirk, sidestep

backwoods *n pl but sing or pl in constr* ***syn*** FRONTIER 2, backcountry, backland, backwash, backwater, ‖boondocks, bush, hinterland, sticks, up-country

‖**backwoodser** *n* ***syn*** RUSTIC, bumpkin, hick, hillbilly, hillman, jake, provincial, ‖ridge runner, ‖wayback, yokel

backwoodsman *n* ***syn*** RUSTIC, bumpkin, hick, hillbilly, hillman, jake, provincial, ‖ridge runner, ‖wayback, yokel

bad *adj* **1** falling short of a standard of what is satisfactory <a *bad* repair job>
syn amiss, ‖bum, ‖crappy, dissatisfactory, poor, ‖punk, rotten, unsatisfactory, up, wrong
rel deficient, inadequate, inferior; careless, slipshod; defective, disordered, off, unsound; execrable, ‖lousy, miserable, ‖pisspoor, wretched; inadmissible, objectionable, unacceptable; insufferable, intolerable
idiom below par, not up to snuff (*or* scratch)
con excellent, fine, meritorious; acceptable, adequate, sound
2 ***syn*** WRONG 1, evil, immoral, iniquitous, reprobate, sinful, vicious, wicked
rel arrant, peccant; graceless, improper, indecorous, untoward; disorderly, misbehaving, naughty, rowdy, ruffianly, unruly; froward, perverse
ant good
3 ***syn*** EVIL 5, ill, unfavorable
4 ***syn*** EVIL 6, inauspicious
5 having undergone decay <one *bad* apple can spoil the barrel>
syn decayed, putrid, rotten, spoiled
rel fusty, stale; mildewed, moldered, moldy, moth-eaten, musty, rancid, worm-eaten; decomposed, putrefied, putrifacted; tainted, turned
con crisp, dewy, fresh, sweet, unspoiled; choice, picked, prime
ant good
6 ***syn*** NAUGHTY 1, ill-behaved, misbehaving, mischievous, paw
7 ***syn*** TOUGH 8, rough
8 arousing discomfort or distaste <a *bad* smell>
syn ‖chiselly, disagreeable, displeasing, rotten, sour, unhappy, unpleasant
rel disgusting, foul, nauseating, noisome, noxious, offensive, repulsive, sickening; abhorrent, hateful, loathsome, obnoxious; uneasy; thankless, ungrateful; distasteful, distressing, sticky; ungracious, unhandsome
con agreeable, pleasant, pleasing, refreshing, soothing; unoffensive
9 ***syn*** HARMFUL, damaging, deleterious, detrimental, evil, hurtful, injurious, mischievous, nocent, nocuous
10 ***syn*** DOWNCAST, crestfallen, dejected, depressed, disconsolate, dispirited, down, downhearted, low, woebegone
11 ***syn*** NULL, invalid, null and void, void

bad actor *n* ***syn*** TROUBLEMAKER, mischief-maker

bad books *n pl* ***syn*** DISLIKE, aversion, disfavor, disinclination, disliking, displeasure, disrelish, dissatisfaction, distaste, indisposition

badge *n* **1** ***syn*** INSIGNIA, emblem
2 ***syn*** HONOR 2, accolade, award, bays, decoration, distinction, kudos, laurels

badger *vb* ***syn*** BAIT 2, bullyrag, chivy, heckle, hector, hound, ride
rel plague, tease, worry

badinage *n* ***syn*** BANTER, backchat, ‖cross talk, persiflage, repartee, snip-snap
rel chaffing, guying, japery, joshing, kidding, sport

badland *n* ***syn*** WASTE 1, barren, desert, wasteland, wild, wilderness, wild land, wildness

‖**bad lot** *n* ***syn*** WASTREL 1, good-for-nothing, ne'er-do-well, no-good, profligate, rounder, scapegrace, waster

badly *adv* **1** ***syn*** HARD 5, hardly, harshly, painfully, rigorously, roughly, severely
2 ***syn*** AMISS 2, afield, astray, awry, unfavorably, wrong
ant well

badman *n* ***syn*** OUTLAW, ‖bandido, bandit, desperado
rel criminal, villain; hood, hoodlum, hooligan, thug; blackguard, devil, knave, rascal, rapscallion, rascallion, rogue, scoundrel

bad-tempered *adj* ***syn*** ILL-TEMPERED, dyspeptic, hot-tempered, ill-humored, ill-natured, ‖rusty, tempersome
rel cantankerous, cranky, crusty, temperamental, touchy
con forbearing, long-suffering, patient
ant good-tempered

Baedeker *n* ***syn*** HANDBOOK, compendium, enchiridion, guide, guidebook, manual, vade mecum

baffle *vb* ***syn*** FRUSTRATE 1, balk, beat, bilk, circumvent, dash, disappoint, foil, ruin, thwart
rel confound, dumbfound, flummox, mystify, nonplus, puzzle; addle, ball up, befuddle, confuse, fog, mix up, muddle; discomfit, disconcert, embarrass, faze, rattle
con enlighten, illuminate

bag *n* **1** a container made of a flexible material and open or opening at the top <a grocery *bag*>
syn ‖poke, pouch, sack
‖**2** ***syn*** HAG 2, ‖bat, beldam, biddy, crone, drab, trot, witch

---

syn synonym(s) — *rel* related word(s)
idiom idiomatic equivalent(s) — *con* contrasted word(s)
ant antonym(s) — * vulgar
‖ use limited; if in doubt, see a dictionary
The first word in a synonym list when printed in SMALL CAPITALS shows where there is more information about the group. For a more efficient use of this book see Explanatory Notes.

bag *vb* ***syn*** CATCH 1, capture, collar, ‖cotch, get, nail, prehend, secure, take
rel clench, ‖cop, ‖glom, hook, land, nab, net, sack, scoop
idiom lay by the heels

baggage *n* ***syn*** WANTON, hussy, jade, slattern, slut, strumpet, tramp, trollop, trull, wench

‖bagged *adj* ***syn*** INTOXICATED 1, ‖boozy, ‖canned, disguised, drunk, inebriated, ‖lushed, muddled, pixilated, ‖plastered

bagnio *n* ***syn*** BROTHEL, bawdy house, bordello, cathouse, ‖hookshop, ‖joyhouse, parlor house, sporting house, stew, whorehouse

bail *n* ***syn*** GUARANTEE 1, bond, guaranty, security, surety, warranty

bail *vb* ***syn*** DIP 2, lade, ladle, scoop

bailiwick *n* ***syn*** FIELD, champaign, demesne, domain, dominion, province, sphere, terrain, territory, walk
rel district, jurisdiction, neighborhood, place, quarter, realm; beat, circuit, round, walk

bait *vb* **1** ***syn*** MOLEST, heckle, persecute, torment
2 to persist in tormenting or harassing another <*baiting* him with gibes about his humble origin>
syn badger, bullyrag, chivy, heckle, hector, hound, ride
rel annoy, bedevil, bother, devil, rag, worry; harass, harry, haze, vex; ‖bug, nag, pester, push around
3 ***syn*** LURE, allure, decoy, entice, entrap, inveigle, lead on, seduce, tempt, toll

bait *n* **1** ***syn*** LURE 2, allurement, come-on, decoy, enticement, inveiglement, seducement, snare, temptation, trap
‖**2** ***syn*** SNACK, ‖bever, bite, ‖chack, morsel, mug-up, ‖piece, tapa

bake *vb* **1** ***syn*** BURN 3, broil, cook, melt, roast, scorch, swelter
2 ***syn*** FIRE 6, burn, kiln

baking *adj* ***syn*** HOT 1, broiling, burning, fiery, red-hot, scalding, scorching, sizzling, torrid, white-hot

balance *n* **1** the stability resulting from the equalization of opposing forces <keeping his emotional *balance* when under stress>
syn counterpoise, equilibrium, equipoise, equiponderation, poise, stasis
rel collectedness, composure, cool, coolness, coolth, equanimity, repose, sangfroid; aplomb, assurance, self-assurance, self-possession; control, self-control, stability, steadiness; stagnancy, stagnation
con imbalance, unbalance; instability, nervousness, shakiness, uncontrol, unsteadiness
2 ***syn*** SYMMETRY, harmony, proportion
rel congruity, consistency, correspondence, sameness
con disbalance, disharmony, disproportion, incongruity, inconsistency, irregularity, overbalance, unbalance
ant imbalance
3 ***syn*** REMAINDER, heel, leavings, remains, remanet, remnant, residual, residue, residuum, rest

balance *vb* ***syn*** COMPENSATE 1, atone (for), counterbalance, counterpoise, countervail, make up, offset, outweigh, redeem, set off
rel adjust, attune, harmonize, tune; accord, agree, correspond; even, level, square
idiom strike a balance

bald *adj* **1** ***syn*** HAIRLESS, glabrous, smooth
rel bobbed, clipped, cropped, polled, shaven, sheared
con bushy, hairy, hirsute, shaggy; unshaven, unshorn; fleecy, furry, woolly; downy, fuzzy, pilose, pubescent
2 ***syn*** BARE 1, naked, nude
rel austere, severe; plain, unadorned, undecorated, unembellished, ungarnished, unornamented; colorless, lackluster, lifeless, lusterless, uncolored

balderdash *n* ***syn*** NONSENSE 2, bilge, blague, bosh, bushwa, claptrap, eyewash, malarkey, rot, rubbish

baldhead *n* one who has a bald head
syn baldpate, ‖baldy, ‖skinhead

baldpate *n* ***syn*** BALDHEAD, ‖baldy, ‖skinhead

‖baldy *n* ***syn*** BALDHEAD, baldpate, ‖skinhead

balefire *n* ***syn*** BEACON 1, watchfire

baleful *adj* ***syn*** SINISTER, malefic, maleficent, malign
rel deadly, evil, harmful, pernicious; bodeful, foreboding; unfavorable, unpromising
con auspicious, benign, favorable, promising, propitious; advantageous, beneficial
ant beneficent
2 ***syn*** OMINOUS, apocalyptic, baneful, dire, direful, fateful, ill-boding, ill-omened, threatening, unpropitious

balk *n* ***syn*** TIMBER 2, beam

balk *vb* **1** ***syn*** FRUSTRATE 1, baffle, beat, bilk, circumvent, dash, disappoint, foil, ruin, thwart
idiom stand in the way of
con back, support, uphold; aid, assist, help
ant forward
2 ***syn*** DEMUR, boggle, gag, jib, scruple, shy, stick, stickle, strain, stumble
rel decline, refuse, turn down; flinch, hang back, quail, recoil, shrink
con capitulate, give in

balky *adj* ***syn*** CONTRARY 3, cross-grained, froward, ornery, perverse, restive, wayward, wrongheaded
rel immovable, inflexible, unbending, unmanageable; averse, disinclined, hesitant, indisposed, loath, reluctant
con subdued, submissive, tame

ball *n* **1** a more or less spherical body or mass <a *ball* of string>
syn globe, orb, rondure, round, sphere
rel egg, oval, ovoid
con block, cube, dice; chunk, hunk, lump
2 balls** *pl* ***syn COURAGE, cojones, dauntlessness, guts, heart, mettle, ‖moxie, pluck, resolution, spirit

ball *vb* to form into a more or less spherical body or mass <*balled* the cookie dough with her hands>
syn conglobate, conglobe, ensphere, round, sphere
rel bead, pill; clot, wad
con disperse, spread, strew; cube, dice

balladmonger *n* ***syn*** POETASTER, bardlet, bardling, poeticule, rhymer, rhymester, verseman, versemonger, versesmith, versifier

---

syn synonym(s) — *rel* related word(s)
idiom idiomatic equivalent(s) — *con* contrasted word(s)
ant antonym(s) — * vulgar
‖ use limited; if in doubt, see a dictionary
The first word in a synonym list when printed in SMALL CAPITALS shows where there is more information about the group. For a more efficient use of this book see Explanatory Notes.

ball and chain *n* **1** ***syn*** RESTRICTION 1, circumscription, cramp, limitation, stint, stricture
‖**2** ***syn*** WIFE, lady, ‖little woman, ‖missus, Mrs., ‖old lady, ‖old woman, ‖rib, ‖squaw, woman

ballast *vb* ***syn*** STABILIZE, poise, stabilify, stabilitate, steady

ballerina *n* ***syn*** DANCER, ballet girl, coryphée, dancing girl, danseur, danseuse, figurant, figurante, hoofer

ballet girl *n* ***syn*** DANCER, ballerina, coryphée, dancing girl, danseur, danseuse, figurant, figurante, hoofer

ballot *n* **1** a piece of paper used to cast a vote in an election <deliberately spoiled his *ballot*>
syn ticket, vote
rel Australian ballot, Indiana ballot, Massachusetts ballot, office-block ballot, office-group ballot, party-column ballot, secret ballot
2 ***syn*** SUFFRAGE, franchise, vote

ballot *vb* ***syn*** ELECT 2, vote (in)

‖**ballup** *n* ***syn*** CONFUSION 3, ataxia, chaos, clutter, disarray, disorder, huddle, muddle, snarl, topsy-turviness

ball up *vb* ***syn*** CONFUSE 2, addle, befuddle, bewilder, ‖bumfuzzle, distract, fluster, fuddle, mix up, throw off

ballyhoo *vb* ***syn*** TOUT, herald, trumpet

balm *n* **1** ***syn*** OINTMENT, cerate, chrism, cream, salve, unction, unguent
2 ***syn*** FRAGRANCE, aroma, bouquet, incense, perfume, redolence, scent, spice

balm *vb* ***syn*** CALM, allay, compose, lull, quiet, ‖quieten, settle, soothe, still, tranquilize

balmy *adj* **1** ***syn*** SWEET 2, ambrosial, aromal, aromatic, fragrant, perfumed, perfumy, redolent, savory, spicy
rel musky; refreshing, rejuvenating, restorative; pleasant, pleasing
2 ***syn*** GENTLE 1, bland, faint, lenient, mild, smooth, soft
rel agreeable, delightful, gratifying, pleasant, pleasing; allaying, assuaging, balsamic, easing, lightening, relieving, soothing
con annoying, bothering, bothersome, irking, irksome, vexing
‖**3** ***syn*** FOOLISH 2, absurd, crazy, harebrained, insane, loony, ‖potty, preposterous, silly, wacky

‖**baloney** *n* ***syn*** NONSENSE 2, ‖applesause, bosh, ‖bull, ‖bunk, hogwash, hokum, ‖horsefeathers, rot, rubbish

balustrade *n* ***syn*** RAILING, banister, rail

bamboozle *vb* ***syn*** DUPE, befool, chicane, flimflam, fool, gull, hoax, hoodwink, hornswoggle, trick
rel bilk, diddle, swindle

ban *vb* ***syn*** FORBID, enjoin, inhibit, interdict, outlaw, prohibit, taboo
rel illegalize, outlaw
con approve, authorize; suffer, tolerate

ban *n* ***syn*** TABOO, forbiddance, interdiction, prohibition, proscription

banal *adj* ***syn*** INSIPID 3, bland, flat, milk-and-water, namby-pamby, sapless, vapid, waterish, watery, wishy-washy
rel hackneyed, pedestrian, trite, warmed-over; bromidic, commonplace, corny, platitudinous, stock; bewhiskered, hoary, old; asinine, fatuous, silly, simple
con fresh, new, novel; different, uncommon, unusual; stimulating, zesty; choice, rare, recherché
ant original

banality *n* ***syn*** COMMONPLACE, bromide, cliché, platitude, prosaicism, prosaism, rubber stamp, shibboleth, tag, truism

banausic *adj* **1** ***syn*** DULL 9, blah, ‖dim, dreary, humdrum, monotone, monotonous, pedestrian, poky, stodgy
2 ***syn*** MATERIALISTIC, earthy, mundane, sensual, temporal, worldly

band *n* ***syn*** STRIP 1, bandeau, banding, fillet, ribbon, stripe
rel belt, border, edge, line; tape; fascia, taenia; streak, vein

band *vb* **1** ***syn*** BELT 1, begird, begirdle, cincture, encincture, engird, engirdle, gird, girdle
2 ***syn*** UNITE 2, coadjute, combine, concur, conjoin, cooperate, league
rel amalgamate, unionize; consociate; club, team (up)
con disintegrate, disperse, dissolve, separate
ant break up, disband

band *n* **1** ***syn*** COMPANY 4, corps, outfit, party, troop, troupe
rel assembly, bevy, body, bunch, covey, group; detachment, detail
2 ***syn*** GROUP 1, assembly, bevy, bunch, cluster, covey, crew, party
3 ***syn*** ORCHESTRA, philharmonic, symphony

bandage *vb* to cover with a bandage <*bandage* wounds>
syn bind, dress

bandanna *n* ***syn*** KERCHIEF 1, babushka

bandar–log *n* ***syn*** CHATTERBOX, blabber, blabbermouth, blabmouth, chatterer, gabber, jabberer, magpie, prater, prattler

bandbox *adj* ***syn*** DAPPER, doggish, doggy, natty, sassy, sparkish, spiffy, spruce, sprucy, well-groomed

bandeau *n* ***syn*** STRIP 1, band, banding, fillet, ribbon, stripe

banderole *n* ***syn*** FLAG, banner, bannerol, burgee, color, ensign, jack, pennant, pennon, streamer

‖**bandido** *n* ***syn*** OUTLAW, badman, bandit, desperado
rel brigand, footpad, highwayman, holdup man; bravo, cutthroat, gunman, villain; gangster, mobster, racketeer

banding *n* ***syn*** STRIP 1, band, bandeau, fillet, ribbon, stripe

bandit *n* **1** ***syn*** OUTLAW, badman, ‖bandido, desperado
rel brigand, footpad, highwayman, holdup man; bravo, cutthroat, villain; gangster, mobster, racketeer; jayhawker
2 ***syn*** MARAUDER, brigand, cateran, forager, freebooter, pillager, plunderer, raider, ravager, sacker

bandwagon *n* ***syn*** FASHION 3, chic, craze, cry, dernier cri, fad, mode, rage, style, vogue

bandy *vb* ***syn*** EXCHANGE 3, interchange
rel chuck, flip, pitch, throw, toss; banter; answer, repay, retort

---

syn synonym(s) — ***rel*** related word(s)
idiom idiomatic equivalent(s) — ***con*** contrasted word(s)
ant antonym(s) — * vulgar
‖ use limited; if in doubt, see a dictionary
The first word in a synonym list when printed in SMALL CAPITALS shows where there is more information about the group. For a more efficient use of this book see Explanatory Notes.

idiom bat (*or* beat) back and forth

bandy *adj syn* BOWLEGGED, bandy-legged, bowed

bandy–legged *adj syn* BOWLEGGED, bandy, bowed

bane *n* **1** *syn* POISON, contagion, venom, virus
2 *syn* DOWNFALL 2, destroyer, destruction, ruin, ruination, undoing

baneful *adj* **1** *syn* PERNICIOUS, deadly, noxious, pestiferous, pestilent, pestilential
rel injurious; insalubrious, noisome, unhealthy, unwholesome
con benign, favorable, propitious; advantageous, helpful, profitable; healthful, salubrious, salutary, wholesome
ant beneficial
2 *syn* OMINOUS, apocalyptic, baleful, dire, direful, fateful, ill-boding, ill-omened, threatening, unpropitious

‖**bang** *vb syn* SURPASS 1, beat, best, better, ding, exceed, outdo, outgo, outshine, outstrip

bang *n* **1** *syn* BLOW 1, bash, bat, belt, crack, smack, sock, wallop, whack, whop
2 a loud percussive or explosive noise <slammed the book shut with a *bang*>
syn blast, boom, burst, clap, crack, crash, slam, smash, wham
rel noise, report, sound; discharge, explosion, pop, shot; howl, roar, roll, rumble, thunder
3 *syn* THRILL, boot, kick, wallop
4 *syn* SMASH 6, bell ringer, hit, succès fou, ten-strike, wow
5 *syn* VIGOR 2, drive, getup, go, pep, punch, push, snap, starch, vitality

bang *adv syn* JUST 1, accurately, exactly, precisely, right, sharp, ‖smack-dab, spang, square, squarely

bang away (at) *vb syn* ATTACK 2, tackle

bang–up *adj syn* EXCELLENT, capital, ‖dandy, first-class, first-rate, first-string, five-star, top, top-notch, whiz-bang

banish *vb* to eject by force or authority from a country, state, or sovereignty <*banish* an enemy of the king>
syn cast out, deport, displace, exile, expatriate, expel, expulse, ‖lag, ostracize, oust, relegate, run out, transport; *compare* EJECT 1
rel disfellowship, excommunicate, rusticate; debar, exclude, shut out; drive out, eject, evict, turn out; bump, can, cashier, discharge, dismiss, fire, put out, sack; blackball, blacklist, boycott

banishment *n syn* EXILE 1, deportation, displacement, expulsion, ostracism, relegation

banister *n syn* RAILING, balustrade, rail

bank *n* **1** *syn* PILE 1, drift, heap, hill, mass, mound, mountain, mow, pyramid, stack
rel snowbank, snowdrift; cloudage, fogbank
2 *syn* SHORE, beach, coast, strand
rel bankside, levee, riverfront, streamside; lakefront, lakeshore, lakeside, margin; oceanfront, seabank, seabeach, seaboard, seafront, sea frontage, sea line, sea sands, shingle
idiom water's edge

bank *vb syn* HEAP 1, cock, drift, hill, mound, pile, stack
rel compact, concentrate

bank *vb* to place money in a bank <*banks* half his paycheck every week>
syn deposit
rel invest, lay aside, lay away, salt away, salt down, save, set aside, sock away; cache, coffer, hoard, squirrel (away), stash
con draw out, take out, withdraw; disburse, expend, fork (over *or* out), lay out, pay (out), spend

bank (on *or* upon) *vb syn* RELY (on *or* upon), build (on), calculate (on *or* upon), count (on), depend (on *or* upon), ‖lot (on *or* upon), reckon (on), trust (in *or* to)
rel intend, plan; bet (on), gamble (on), stake, venture, wager
idiom bank the rent on, bet one's bottom dollar on, go bail on, lay money on

bankroll *vb syn* CAPITALIZE, back, finance, grubstake, stake

bankrupt *vb* **1** *syn* DEPLETE, drain, draw, draw down, exhaust, impoverish, use up
rel break, impair, incapacitate
con rebuild, repair, restore, revive; augment, bolster, fortify, strengthen
2 *syn* STRIP 2, bare, denudate, denude, deprive, dismantle, disrobe, divest
3 *syn* RUIN 3, break, bust, fold up, impoverish, pauper, pauperize
4 *syn* RUIN 2, dilapidate, do in, shipwreck, wreck

banned *adj* **1** *syn* FORBIDDEN, prohibited, verboten
2 *syn* CONTRABAND, hot

banner *n syn* FLAG, banderole, color, ensign, jack, pendant, pennant, pennon, standard, streamer
rel banneret

banner *adj syn* EXCELLENT, bang-up, blue-ribbon, champion, first-class, first-rate, first-string, five-star, front-rank, top-notch

bannerol *n syn* FLAG, banderole, banner, color, ensign, jack, pendant, pennant, pennon, streamer

banquet *n syn* DINNER, feast, regale, spread
rel bridale, feed, ‖gaudy, harvest home, repast, ‖tuck, ‖tuck-in, ‖tuck-out

bantam *adj* **1** *syn* SMALL 1, little, monkey, petite, smallish
2 *syn* SAUCY 1, arch, ‖cocket, malapert, pert

banter *vb* **1** to make fun of good-naturedly <the students resented their teacher's *bantering* them about mistakes>
syn chaff, fool, fun, jest, ‖jive, joke, jolly, josh, kid, rag, razz, rib
rel deride, guy, mock, quiz, rally, ridicule, satirize, taunt, tease, twit
idiom make fun of, make merry with, poke fun at
‖**2** *syn* FACE 3, beard, brave, challenge, dare, defy, ‖double-dog dare, front, outface, venture
‖**3** *syn* COAX, blandish, blarney, cajole, con, soft-soap, sweet-talk, wheedle

banter *n* animated back-and-forth exchange of remarks <entertained the group with their jolly *banter*>

---

syn backchat, badinage, ||cross talk, persiflage, repartee, snip-snap
rel chitchat, gossip, gossipry, small talk; rallying, teasing; exchange, give-and-take
con debate, deliberation, discussion

bantling *n* ***syn*** BABY 1, babe, infant, neonate, newborn

baptismal name *n* ***syn*** GIVEN NAME, Christian name, font name, forename, personal name, prename

baptize *vb* **1** to administer the rite of baptism <a child *baptized* in the Catholic Church>
syn asperse, christen, immerse, sprinkle
rel cleanse, purify, regenerate
2 ***syn*** NAME 1, call, christen, denominate, designate, dub, entitle, style, term, title

bar *n* **1** a solid piece of material usually rectangular and considerably longer than it is wide <a *bar* of gold>
syn billet, ingot, rod, slab, stick, strip
2 something that stands in the way of some objective <his religion was a *bar* to membership in that exclusive club>
syn barricade, barrier, blank wall, block, blockade, fence, roadblock, stop, wall
rel clog, encumbrance, hamper, hindrance, impediment; hurdle, obstacle, obstruction, stumbling block; check, checkrein, control, curb; bamboo curtain, iron curtain; difficulty, hardship, vicissitude
3 ***syn*** OBSTACLE, Chinese wall, hamper, hurdle, impediment, obstruction, rub, snag, stumbling block, traverse
rel check, checkrein, control, curb
con accommodation, convenience, facility, service
ant advantage
4 ***syn*** COURT 2, lawcourt, tribunal
5 a room or public establishment where alcoholic beverages are served <nightly discussions in the *bar*>
syn barroom, ||boozer, ||bucket shop, buvette, cantina, cocktail lounge, drinkery, drunkery, ||gin mill, ||groggery, ||grogshop, lounge, pothouse, pub, ||public house, ||rum-hole, rummery, ||rum-mill, rumshop, saloon, tap, taproom, tavern, watering hole, watering place; *compare* ALEHOUSE
rel barrelhouse, bistro, bottle club, cabaret, café, dive, honky-tonk, nightclub, rathskeller, roadhouse, wineshop

bar *vb* **1** ***syn*** LIMIT 2, circumscribe, confine, delimit, delimitate, prelimit, restrict
2 ***syn*** EXCLUDE, bate, count out, debar, eliminate, except, rule out, suspend
rel block, hinder; leave out, omit, pass over; banish, deport, exile, ostracize
con accept, receive, welcome; allow, let, permit
ant admit, include
3 ***syn*** HINDER, block, brake, dam, impede, obstruct, overslaugh
rel halt, stop
con back, support, uphold

bar *prep* ***syn*** EXCEPT, aside from, barring, bating, but, excluding, exclusive of, outside of, save, saving

barathrum *n* ***syn*** HELL, Gehenna, hades, inferno, netherworld, perdition, pit, Sheol, Tophet, underworld

barb *n* ***syn*** SHAFT 2, dart

barbarian *adj* **1** of, relating to, or characteristic of people that are not fully civilized <the *barbarian* tribes that sacked Rome>
syn barbaric, barbarous, Gothic, Hunnic, Hunnish, rude, savage, uncivil, uncivilized, uncultivated, wild
rel heathenish, vandal, vandalic; backward, coarse, crude, ill-mannered, primitive, rough; untamed; uncouth, uncultured; beastish, bloodthirsty, brutal, cruel, ferocious, inhuman
con gentle, peaceful, subdued, submissive, tame; cultured, enlightened, humane, sophisticated; genteel, refined, well-bred, well-mannered
ant civilized
2 ***syn*** BARBARIC 1, barbarous, graceless, outlandish, tasteless, vulgar, wild

barbaric *adj* **1** marked by a lack of restraint, cultivated taste, and refinement <the *barbaric* use of color and ornament>
syn barbarian, barbarous, graceless, outlandish, tasteless, vulgar, wild
rel coarse, crude, rough, rude, uncouth; flamboyant, florid, ornate, ostentatious, showy; blatant, flashy, garish, gaudy, loud, tawdry; cacophonous, harsh, raucous; aggressive
con quiet, restrained, soft, subdued; concinnous, cultivated, elegant, polished, refined; smooth, sophisticated, urbane
2 ***syn*** BARBARIAN 1, barbarous, Gothic, Hunnish, rude, savage, uncivil, uncivilized, uncultivated, wild

barbarism *n* a word or expression which in form or use offends against contemporary standards of correctness or purity in a language <many writers consider *irregardless* a *barbarism*>
syn corruption, impropriety, slangism, solecism, vernacularism, vernacularity, vulgarism
rel neologism; colloquialism, foreignism; shibboleth; Goldwynism, Irish bull, malaprop, malapropism, spoonerism; caconym; error, lapse, misuse, slip

barbarous *adj* **1** ***syn*** BARBARIAN 1, barbaric, Gothic, Hunnish, rude, savage, uncivil, uncivilized, uncultivated, wild
2 ***syn*** OUTRAGEOUS 1, unchristian, uncivilized, unconscionable, ungodly, unholy, wicked
3 ***syn*** BARBARIC 1, barbarian, graceless, outlandish, tasteless, vulgar, wild
rel backward, benighted, cretinous, ignorant, illiterate, lowbrow, philistine, uneducated, unlettered, unread, unschooled, untaught, untutored
con aware, informed, sophisticated, with-it; finished, polished, rounded; well-bred, well-mannered; educated, intelligent, learned, schooled; erudite, well-read
4 ***syn*** FIERCE 1, cruel, fell, ferocious, grim, inhuman, inhumane, savage, truculent, wolfish
rel heartless, uncompassionate, unmerciful; atrocious, monstrous, outrageous; bloody, butcherly, sanguinary; fiendish, sadistic

---

syn synonym(s) | *rel* related word(s)
idiom idiomatic equivalent(s) | *con* contrasted word(s)
ant antonym(s) | * vulgar
|| use limited; if in doubt, see a dictionary
The first word in a synonym list when printed in SMALL CAPITALS shows where there is more information about the group. For a more efficient use of this book see Explanatory Notes.

con forbearing, lenient, merciful, tolerant; compassionate, sympathetic, tender; benevolent, humane, humanitarian
ant clement

barbate *adj* *syn* BEARDED, bewhiskered, whiskered

barber *n* one whose occupation is primarily cutting hair
syn haircutter
rel coiffeur, coiffeuse, friseur, hairdresser, hair stylist; beautician, cosmetologist; clipper, cropper, shaver

bard *n* **1** a poet-singer who sang or recited verse to the accompaniment of a stringed instrument (as a harp) < *bards* were the theater of olden times >
syn jongleur, minstrel, troubadour
rel meistersinger, minnesinger, rhapsodist; gleeman; skald; conteur
2 *syn* POET, muse, Parnassian

bardlet *n* *syn* POETASTER, poeticule, poetling, rhymer, rhymester, verseman, versemonger, versesmith, versificator, versifier

bardling *n* *syn* POETASTER, poeticule, poetling, rhymer, rhymester, verseman, versemonger, versesmith, versificator, versifier

bare *adj* **1** lacking a natural or usual cover or finish <the room looked *bare* without curtains and pictures>
syn bald, naked, nude
rel denuded, dismantled, divested, peeled, stripped, uncovered; baldish, depilated, hairless; unattired, unclad, unclothed, undressed, unrobed; arid, bleak, desert, desolate
con attired, clad, clothed, dressed, garbed; furry, hairy; green, leafy, luxuriant, verdant; complete, consummate, finished, perfect
ant covered
2 *syn* OPEN 2, denuded, exposed, naked, peeled, stripped, uncovered
3 *syn* EMPTY 1, clear, stark, vacant, vacuous, void
rel barren, depleted, destitute, dried-up, emptied, exhausted; unfilled, unstocked, unsupplied
con bountiful, bursting, chock-full, complete, crammed, laden, overflowing, overfull, replete, stuffed; full, stocked, supplied
4 *syn* VERY 4, mere

bare *vb* *syn* STRIP 2, bankrupt, denudate, denude, deprive, dismantle, disrobe, divest
rel disclose, exhibit, expose, reveal, show, unveil
con camouflage, cloak, disguise, dissemble, mask; apparel, attire, dress, garb, invest, robe
ant cover

***bare–assed** *adj* *syn* NUDE 2, au naturel, buff-bare, naked, raw, stark-naked, stripped, unclad, unclothed, undressed

barefaced *adj* *syn* SHAMELESS, arrant, blatant, brassy, brazen, brazenfaced, impudent, overbold, unabashed, unblushing
rel blunt, candid, frank, open, plain, temerarious; indecent, indecorous, unseemly
con covert, secret, secretive, stealthy; cautious, circumspect, discreet, tactful
ant furtive

barefisted *adj or adv* *syn* BARE-HANDED, bareknuckle

barefoot *adj* **1** wearing no shoes or stockings <always went *barefoot* in the summer>
syn shoeless, unsandaled, unshod
con socked, stockinged; sockless; booted, sandaled, shod
2 *syn* DISCALCED, discalceate

bare–handed *adj or adv* without covering on the hands <box *bare-handed*>
syn barefisted, bareknuckle
ant gloved

bareknuckle *adj or adv* *syn* BARE-HANDED, barefisted

barely *adv* *syn* JUST 2, hardly, scarce, scarcely
con amply; adequately, enough, sufficiently

barf *vb* *syn* VOMIT, ||cascade, ||cast, disgorge, ||heave, *puke, spew, spit up, throw up, upchuck

bargain *n* **1** an advantageous purchase <at that price the car is a *bargain*>
syn buy, closeout, pennyworth, steal
rel deal; giveaway
con cheat, flimflam, gouge, sticking, sting
2 *syn* CONTRACT, agreement, bond, compact, convention, covenant, pact, transaction

bargain *vb* **1** *syn* HAGGLE 2, chaffer, dicker, higgle, huckster, palter
rel arrange, confer, negotiate; compromise
2 *syn* TRADE 1, barter, exchange, swap, traffic, truck

barge *vb* *syn* LUMBER, clump, galumph, stumble, stump

bark *vb* *syn* SNAP 1, snarl

barkeeper *n* **1** *syn* SALOONKEEPER, boniface, innholder, innkeeper, ||publican, saloonist, taverner
2 *syn* BARTENDER, ||barmaid, barman, mixologist, tapster

||**barmaid** *n* *syn* BARTENDER, barkeeper, barman, mixologist, tapster

barman *n* *syn* BARTENDER, barkeeper, ||barmaid, mixologist, tapster

Barmecidal *adj* *syn* APPARENT 2, illusive, illusory, ostensible, seeming, semblant

barnacle *n* *syn* PARASITE, bloodsucker, freeloader, hanger-on, leech, lounge lizard, ||spiv, sponger, sucker

||**barney** *n* *syn* QUARREL, altercation, beef, bickering, controversy, dispute, hassle, miff, row, run-in

barnyard *adj* *syn* OBSCENE 2, coarse, dirty, filthy, foul, indecent, nasty, raunchy, smutty, vulgar

baron *n* *syn* MAGNATE, czar, king, merchant prince, mogul, prince, tycoon

baronial *adj* *syn* GRAND 1, august, grandiose, imposing, lordly, magnificent, majestic, noble, royal, stately

baroque *adj* *syn* ORNATE, flamboyant, florid, luscious, rich, rococo
rel embellished, gilt, ornamented, scrolled
con austere, gray

barrage *n* a vigorous expulsion or projection of many things at once <the announcement was met with a *barrage* of protests>

---

syn synonym(s)	*rel* related word(s)
idiom idiomatic equivalent(s)	*con* contrasted word(s)
ant antonym(s)	* vulgar

|| use limited; if in doubt, see a dictionary
The first word in a synonym list when printed in SMALL CAPITALS shows where there is more information about the group. For a more efficient use of this book see Explanatory Notes.

syn bombardment, broadside, burst, cannonade, drumfire, fusillade, hail, salvo, shower, storm, volley
rel burst, eruption, flare, outburst, stream, surge, tornado

barrel *n* **1** ***syn*** CASK, butt, hogshead, keg, pipe, tun
2 ***syn*** MUCH, great deal, lashings, lot, lump, ‖mess, mountain, peck, ‖power, ‖sight

barrel *vb* ***syn*** HURRY 2, barrelhouse, fleet, fly, hasten, highball, run, rush, speed, whiz

barrelhouse *n* ***syn*** DIVE, hangout, honky-tonk, joint

barrelhouse *vb* ***syn*** HURRY 2, barrel, bucket, fly, hasten, hustle, rocket, rush, whiz, zip

barren *adj* **1** ***syn*** STERILE 1, effete, impotent, infecund, infertile, unfruitful
rel childless, fallow, heirless, issueless
con pregnant; fertile
ant fecund
2 deficient in production of vegetation and especially crops < *barren* deserts and wastelands >
syn hardscrabble, infertile, unbearing, unfertile, unproductive
rel fallow; irreclaimable, uncultivable, unhusbanded, untillable, wild; bleak, depleted, improverished, poor, worn-out; vegetationless, verdureless; arid, desert, dry, parched
con arable, fruitful, productive; fat, rich; lush, luxuriant; green, verdant, verdurous
ant fertile

barren *n* ***syn*** WASTE 1, badland, desert, wasteland, wild, wilderness, wild land, wildness

barricade *n* ***syn*** BAR 2, barrier, blank wall, block, blockade, fence, roadblock, stop, wall

barrier *n* ***syn*** BAR 2, barricade, blank wall, block, blockade, fence, roadblock, stop, wall

barring *prep* ***syn*** EXCEPT, aside from, bar, bating, but, excluding, exclusive of, outside of, save, saving

barroom *n* ***syn*** BAR 5, ‖boozer, cocktail lounge, drinkery, ‖gin mill, lounge, pub, saloon, taproom, tavern

bar sinister *n* ***syn*** STIGMA, black eye, blot, blur, brand, odium, onus, slur, spot, stain

bartender *n* one who serves alcoholic beverages at a bar < worked for some years as a *bartender* >
syn barkeeper, ‖barmaid, barman, mixologist, tapster; *compare* SALOONKEEPER

barter *vb* ***syn*** TRADE 1, bargain, exchange, swap, traffic, truck

basal *adj* **1** ***syn*** FUNDAMENTAL 1, basic, bottom, foundational, primary, radical, underlying
rel pedimental; bottommost, lowermost, lowest, nethermost, undermost
con highest, uppermost
2 ***syn*** ELEMENTARY 1, beginning, elemental, rudimental, rudimentary, simplest

---

syn synonym(s) *rel* related word(s)
idiom idiomatic equivalent(s) *con* contrasted word(s)
ant antonym(s) * vulgar
‖ use limited; if in doubt, see a dictionary
The first word in a synonym list when printed in SMALL CAPITALS shows where there is more information about the group. For a more efficient use of this book see Explanatory Notes.

base *n* **1** something on which another thing is reared or built or by which it is supported or fixed in place < the *base* of a lamp >
syn basement, basis, bed, bedrock, bottom, footing, foundation, ground, groundwork, hardpan, infrastructure, rest, seat, seating, substratum, substruction, substructure, underpinning, understructure; *compare* BASIS 1
rel bolster, buttress, framework, prop, stand, stay, support; foot
2 ***syn*** BASIS 1, bedrock, footing, foundation, ground, groundwork, infrastructure, root, substratum, underpinning, warrant
3 ***syn*** BOTTOM 3, foot, nadir

base *vb* to supply or to serve as a basis < *based* his accusation on sound evidence >
syn bottom, establish, found, ground, predicate, rest, stay
rel build, construct, fix, plant, seat, set up

base *adj* **1** ***syn*** IGNOBLE 1, baseborn, humble, low, lowborn, lowly, mean, plebeian, unennobled, unwashed
2 ***syn*** CHEAP 2, common, mean, paltry, poor, rubbishy, shoddy, sleazy, tatty, trashy
3 contemptible because beneath minimal standards of human decency < a *base* lying cheat >
syn despicable, ignoble, low, low-down, servile, sordid, squalid, ugly, vile, wretched; *compare* CONTEMPTIBLE
rel beggarly, lousy, sorry; abominable, disgraceful, loathsome; bad, evil, wicked; base-minded, low-minded, meanspirited; caitiff, cowardly, dastardly, recreant; unworthy; dirty, filthy; degrading, humiliating, ignominious
con honest, honorable, upright; virtuous; ethical, moral, righteous; fair, forbearing, open-minded, patient, reasonable, tolerant, understanding
ant noble

baseborn *adj* **1** ***syn*** IGNOBLE 1, base, humble, low, lowborn, lowly, mean, plebeian, unennobled, unwashed
2 ***syn*** ILLEGITIMATE 1, bastard, fatherless, misbegotten, natural, spurious, supposititious, unfathered

baseless *adj* being without cause or occasion < anxious old ladies with their *baseless* fears >
syn bottomless, foundationless, gratuitous, groundless, uncalled-for, unfounded, ungrounded, unwarranted
rel false, wrong; indefensible, reasonless, unjustifiable, unsolid, unsupported, unsustained, untenable; empty, idle, vain; needless, pointless, senseless, unnecessary, unneeded
con actual, real, reasonable, true; authentic, bona fide, genuine, valid

basement *n* ***syn*** BASE 1, bed, bottom, footing, foundation, ground, groundwork, substratum, substructure, understructure

bash *n* **1** ***syn*** BLOW 1, bat, belt, crack, slam, smack, smash, wallop, whack, whop
2 ***syn*** SHINDIG 1, ‖blowout, shindy

bashful *adj* ***syn*** SHY 1, coy, demure, diffident, modest, retiring, self-effacing, timid, unassertive, unassured
rel timorous; recoiling, shrinking; mousy; abashed, embarrassed; blushful
con assured, bold, intrepid; arrogant, barefaced, brazen, impudent, shameless; loquacious, talkative
ant brash, forward

basic *adj* **1** ***syn*** FUNDAMENTAL 1, basal, bottom, foundational, primary, radical, underlying
rel capital, chief, main, principal
2 ***syn*** ELEMENTAL 1, elementary, essential, fundamental, primitive, substratal, underlying

basic *n* ***syn*** ESSENTIAL 1, element, fundamental, part and parcel, rudiment

basically *adv* ***syn*** ESSENTIALLY 1, au fond, fundamentally, in essence

basin *n* ***syn*** DEPRESSION 2, concavity, dip, hollow, sag, sink, sinkage, sinkhole

basis *n* **1** something that supports or sustains anything immaterial <his argument rested on a *basis* of conjecture>
syn base, bedrock, footing, foundation, ground, groundwork, infrastructure, root, substratum, underpinning; *compare* BASE 1
rel axiom, fundamental, law, principle, theorem; assumption, postulate, premise, presumption, presupposition; essence, heart
2 ***syn*** BASE 1, bed, bottom, footing, foundation, ground, groundwork, rest, seat, substructure
3 something serving as a reason or justification for an action or opinion <resented such a challenge without *basis* or reason>
syn foundation, warrant
rel call, justification, right; ground(s), reason

bask *vb* **1** ***syn*** SUN, insolate
2 ***syn*** WALLOW 3, indulge, luxuriate, revel, roll, rollick, welter

bassinet *n* ***syn*** BABY CARRIAGE, baby buggy, ||perambulator, ||pram

bastard *n* **1** one born out of wedlock <bore a *bastard* before she was fifteen>
syn by-blow, catch colt, chance child, come-by-chance, filius nullius, filius populi, illegitimate, love child, natural child, whoreson, woods colt
2 ***syn*** HYBRID, cross, crossbred, crossbreed, half blood, half-breed, mongrel, mule
3** ***syn VILLAIN 1, blackguard, heel, knave, lowlife, miscreant, rascal, rogue, scoundrel, *son of a bitch

bastard *adj* **1** ***syn*** ILLEGITIMATE 1, baseborn, fatherless, misbegotten, natural, spurious, supposititious, unfathered
2 ***syn*** SPURIOUS 3, apocryphal, unauthentic, ungenuine

bastardize *vb* ***syn*** DEBASE 1, bestialize, brutalize, corrupt, debauch, demoralize, deprave, pervert, vitiate, warp

bastardy *n* ***syn*** ILLEGITIMACY 1, illegitimateness, supposititiousness

baste *vb* **1** ***syn*** BEAT 1, batter, belabor, drub, lambaste, paste, pelt, pummel, thrash, wallop
rel clobber, ||larrup, mill, whip
2 ***syn*** SCOLD 1, bawl out, berate, ||bless out, ||chew out, lash, rail, tell off, tongue-lash, wig

bastille *n* ***syn*** JAIL, bridewell, ||bucket, ||caboose, ||calaboose, ||can, ||carcel, ||chokey, ||hoosegow, jug

bastille *vb* ***syn*** IMPRISON, confine, constrain, immure, incarcerate, intern, jail, jug, ||prison, ||quod

bastinado *n* ***syn*** BLOW 1, bash, bat, crack, pound, smack, smash, thwack, wallop, whack

bastion *n* ***syn*** BULWARK, breastwork, parapet, rampart

bat *n* **1** ***syn*** BLOW 1, belt, biff, bop, crack, slam, smack, sock, thwack, whop
2 ***syn*** CUDGEL, baton, billy club, bludgeon, club, knobkerrie, mace, ||shillelagh, truncheon, war club
||**3** ***syn*** SPEED 2, celerity, gait, pace, quickness, rapidity, rapidness, swiftness, velocity
4 ***syn*** BINGE 1, bender, booze, bum, bust, drunk, jag, ran-tan, spree, tear

||**bat** *n* ***syn*** HAG 2, ||bag, beldam, biddy, crone, drab, trot, witch

bat *vb* ***syn*** WANDER 1, drift, gad, gallivant, meander, mooch, ramble, roam, rove, traipse

bat *vb* ***syn*** WINK, blink, nictate, nictitate, twinkle

batch *n* ***syn*** GROUP 3, array, bunch, bundle, clump, cluster, clutch, lot, parcel, set

bate *vb* ||**1** ***syn*** ABATE 4, die (down *or* away), ease off, ebb, fall, let up, moderate, slacken, subside, wane
||**2** ***syn*** DECREASE, abate, close, diminish, drain (away), dwindle, lessen, reduce, taper, taper off
3 ***syn*** EXCLUDE, bar, count out, debar, eliminate, except, rule out, suspend

bath *n, usu* **baths** *pl* ***syn*** SPA 1, ||hydro, springs, watering place, wells

||**bath** *vb* ***syn*** BATHE 1, shower, tub, wash

bathe *vb* **1** to clean oneself with a bath <*bathed* only on Saturday nights>
syn ||bath, shower, tub, wash
rel soap; douse, soak
2 to flow or splash against <waves *bathed* the rocky shore>
syn lap, lave, lip, wash
rel drench, soak, sop, souse; flush

bathetic *adj* **1** ***syn*** TRITE, cliché, clichéd, commonplace, hack, hackneyed, stale, stereotyped, stereotypical, tired
2 ***syn*** SENTIMENTAL, lovey-dovey, maudlin, mawkish, mushy, romantic, slushy, ||soppy, sticky, tear-jerking

bathtub gin *n* ***syn*** MOONSHINE 2, ||blockade, bootleg, ||busthead, ||hooch, mountain dew, white lightning

bating *prep* ***syn*** EXCEPT, aside from, bar, barring, but, excluding, exclusive of, outside of, save, saving

baton *n* ***syn*** CUDGEL, bat, billy, billy club, bludgeon, club, mace, nightstick, truncheon, war club

batter *vb* **1** to affect (as by repeated blows) so severely as to disfigure or damage <so *battered* in the fight he couldn't even crawl away> <a boat *battered* to pieces by stormy seas>
syn ||bung up, mangle, maul
rel disable, disfigure; maim, mutilate; cripple, lame; bruise, contuse, lacerate; baste, clobber, pummel; shatter, wreck
idiom beat black and blue, beat to pieces (*or* shreds), beat within an inch of one's life
2 ***syn*** BEAT 1, baste, belabor, buffet, drub, lambaste, pound, pummel, thrash, wallop

battery *n* ***syn*** GROUP 3, array, batch, body, bunch, bundle, clot, clump, cluster, lot

---

syn synonym(s) ***rel*** related word(s)
idiom idiomatic equivalent(s) ***con*** contrasted word(s)
ant antonym(s) * vulgar
|| use limited; if in doubt, see a dictionary
The first word in a synonym list when printed in SMALL CAPITALS shows where there is more information about the group. For a more efficient use of this book see Explanatory Notes.

battle *n* a hostile meeting between opposing military forces <the *battle* continued until nightfall>
syn action, engagement
rel brush, clash, encounter, pitched battle, scrimmage, skirmish; assault, attack, onset, onslaught, sortie; combat, conflict, contest, fight; hostilities

battle *vb* ***syn*** CONTEND 1, fight, oppugn, tug, war
rel clash, scrimmage; assail, assault, attack, bombard

battle cry *n* a word or phrase used as a slogan by a faction <"death to the invader" was the *battle cry*>
syn cry, motto, rallying cry, war cry; *compare* CATCHWORD

battlesome *adj* ***syn*** QUARRELSOME 2, brawling, brawlsome, brawly, scrappy

||**batty** *adj* ***syn*** INSANE 1, bedlamite, cracked, crazed, crazy, deranged, maniac, nuts, screwy, wacky

bauble *n* ***syn*** KNICKKNACK, bibelot, curio, gewgaw, gimcrack, novelty, objet d'art, trifle, trinket, whatnot

bavardage *n* ***syn*** SMALL TALK, by-talk, chitchat, chitter-chatter, trifling

bawd *n* ***syn*** PROSTITUTE, drab, harlot, ||hooker, meretrix, moll, nightwalker, poule, streetwalker, whore

bawdy house *n* ***syn*** BROTHEL, bagnio, bordello, cathouse, ||hookshop, ||joyhouse, parlor house, sporting house, stew, whorehouse

bawl *vb* **1** ***syn*** ROAR, bellow, bluster, clamor, rout
rel holler, scream, screech, shout, shriek, squall, yammer, yell
2 to cry and weep loudly or lustily especially from distress <the baby *bawled* and kicked when its bottle was taken away>
syn howl, squall, wail, yowl; *compare* CRY 2, ROAR
rel blubber, boohoo, cry, sob, weep

bawl out *vb* ***syn*** SCOLD 1, berate, ||bless out, ||carpet, ||chew out, lash, tell off, tongue-lash, upbraid, wig
rel condemn, denounce
idiom read a lecture (*or* lesson)

bay *n, usu* **bays** *pl* ***syn*** HONOR 2, accolade, award, badge, decoration, distinction, kudos, laurels

bay *vb* ***syn*** HOWL 1, quest, ululate, wail

bay *n* ***syn*** INLET, arm, bayou, bight, cove, ||creek, firth, gulf, harbor, slough

baygall *n* ***syn*** SWAMP, bog, fen, marsh, mire, morass, ||moss, quag, ||sump, swampland

bayou *n* ***syn*** INLET, arm, bay, bight, cove, ||creek, firth, gulf, harbor, slough

bay window *n* ***syn*** POTBELLY, corporation, paunch, pod, ||pot

bazoo *n* ||**1** ***syn*** MOUTH 1, gob, ||mush, ||row, ||trap, ||yap
2 ***syn*** RASPBERRY, bird, boo, ||Bronx cheer, catcall, hiss, hoot, pooh, pooh-pooh, ||razz

be *vb* to have actuality or reality <I think, therefore I *am*>
syn breathe, exist, live, move, subsist

---

syn synonym(s) ***rel*** related word(s)
idiom idiomatic equivalent(s) ***con*** contrasted word(s)
ant antonym(s) * vulgar
|| use limited; if in doubt, see a dictionary
The first word in a synonym list when printed in SMALL CAPITALS shows where there is more information about the group. For a more efficient use of this book see Explanatory Notes.

rel hold, obtain, stand; abide, continue, endure, go on, persist, prevail, remain; come

beach *n* ***syn*** SHORE, bank, coast, strand
rel oceanfront; lakeshore, lakeside

beach *vb* ***syn*** SHIPWRECK 1, cast away, pile up, strand, wreck

beached *adj* ***syn*** AGROUND, grounded, stranded

beacon *n* **1** a signal fire usually on an elevated place <a *beacon* on the hill to warn of danger>
syn balefire, watchfire
rel flare; bonfire
2 ***syn*** LIGHTHOUSE, pharos

beak *n* **1** ***syn*** BILL 1, neb, nib, pecker
2 ***syn*** NOSE 1, ||beezer, ||boko, ||conk, pecker, proboscis, ||schnozzle, ||sneezer, snoot, snout
3 ***syn*** PROMONTORY, bill, cape, foreland, head, headland, naze, point
||**4** ***syn*** JUDGE 2, court, justice, magistrate

beak *vb* ***syn*** PECK 1, pick

be–all and end–all *n* **1** ***syn*** ESSENCE 2, bottom, marrow, pith, quintessence, rock bottom, root, soul, stuff, substance
2 ***syn*** WHOLE 1, aggregate, all, entirety, gross, sum, sum total, total, totality, ||tote

beam *n* **1** ***syn*** TIMBER 2, balk
2 ***syn*** RAY 1, shaft, shoot
3 ***syn*** BUTTOCKS, backside, behind, bottom, ||can, derriere, fanny, posterior, rear, seat

beam *vb* **1** ***syn*** SHINE 1, burn, gleam, radiate
2 ***syn*** SMILE, grin

beaming *adj* ***syn*** BRIGHT 1, brilliant, effulgent, fulgent, incandescent, lambent, lucent, luminous, radiant, refulgent

||**bean** *n* ***syn*** HEAD 1, ||belfry, ||coco, ||conk, ||dome, headpiece, noddle, noggin, noodle, poll

beanery *n* ***syn*** EATING HOUSE, café, coffee shop, diner, ||greasy spoon, ||hashery, ||hash house, luncheonette, lunchroom, sandwich shop

beany *adj* ***syn*** SPIRITED 2, fiery, gingery, high-hearted, high-spirited, mettlesome, peppery, spunky

bear *vb* **1** ***syn*** CARRY 1, buck, convey, ferry, ||hump, ||jag, lug, pack, tote, transport
rel shoulder
2 ***syn*** BEHAVE 1, acquit, act, carry, comport, conduct, demean, deport, go on, quit
3 to have attached to one <the bottle *bears* the label "poisonous">
syn carry, have, possess
rel display, exhibit, show
con lack, need, want
4 ***syn*** ACCOMPANY, attend, ||bring, ||carry, chaperon, companion, conduct, consort (with), convoy, escort
5 to give birth to offspring <she has *borne* several children>
syn ||birth, ||born, bring forth, deliver
idiom bring abed, bring to bed, bring to birth, give birth to, have a baby
con abort, miscarry
6 ***syn*** PRESS 8, squeeze
7 ***syn*** PRESS 1, crowd, crush, jam, push, ||squab, squash, squeeze, squish, squush
8 ***syn*** PROCREATE 1, beget, breed, generate, multiply, produce, propagate, reproduce

9 to bring forth a product <the apple trees *bear* every year>
syn produce, turn out, yield
rel breed, engender, generate, propagate, reproduce; fructify, fruit; fabricate, fashion, form, make, shape; create, invent
10 to put up with something trying or difficult <can't *bear* the tension of the work>
syn abide, brook, digest, endure, go, lump, stand, ‖stick, stick out, stomach, suffer, support, sustain, swallow, sweat out, take, tolerate; *compare* ACCEPT 2
rel afflict, torment, torture, try; allow, condone, countenance, permit; acquiesce, bow, defer, submit, yield
idiom make do, put up with, take lying down
con decline, refuse, reject, spurn; avoid, bypass, elude, evade, shun
11 ***syn*** HEAD 3, light out, make, set out, strike out, take off

bear (on *or* upon) *vb* to have a connection especially logically <this situation *bears* directly upon the question under discussion>
syn appertain, apply, pertain, relate
rel refer; affect, concern, involve, touch; correspond, parallel
idiom have to do with, tie in with

bear (with) *vb* ***syn*** ACCEPT 2, endure, pocket, swallow, tolerate, tough (out)

bearable *adj* capable of being borne <his outrageous behavior is hardly *bearable*>
syn endurable, livable, sufferable, supportable, sustainable, tolerable
rel acceptable, admissible, allowable, satisfactory
con insufferable, insupportable, intolerable, unendurable, unsupportable
ant unbearable

beard *n* the natural growth of hair on a man's face <some men look better with *beards*>
syn beaver, whiskers; *compare* SIDE-WHISKERS
rel charley, galways, goatee, imperial, spade beard, Vandyke; fuzz

beard *vb* ***syn*** FACE 3, brave, challenge, dare, defy, ‖double-dog dare, front, outdare, outface, venture
idiom beard the lion in his den

bearded *adj* having a beard <an old *bearded* philosopher>
syn barbate, bewhiskered, whiskered
rel beardy; goateed; hairy; stubbed, stubbly, unshaven
con barefaced, clean-faced, clean-shaven, shaven, smooth-faced, whiskerless
ant beardless

bear down *vb* ***syn*** CONQUER 1, beat down, crush, defeat, overpower, reduce, subdue, subjugate, vanquish

bearer *n* **1** ***syn*** MESSENGER, carrier, courier, emissary, envoy, internuncio
2 a man who carries baggage and supplies for travelers <native *bearers* serving the safari>
syn carrier, drogher, porter
rel boy, cargador, coolie; redcap, skycap

bearing *n* **1** the way in which or the quality by which a person outwardly manifests his personality <a dowager with a regal *bearing*>
syn address, air, comportment, demeanor, deportment, mien, port, presence, set
rel aspect, brow, look; attitude, carriage, pose, posture, stand; poise; display, front; behavior, conduct
2 ***syn*** BIRTH 1, ‖birthing, childbearing, childbirth, delivery, parturition

bearish *adj* ***syn*** CANTANKEROUS, cankered, cranky, cross-grained, crotchety, ornery, vinegarish, vinegary, waspish, waspy

bear out *vb* ***syn*** CONFIRM 2, authenticate, corroborate, justify, substantiate, validate, verify

bear up *vb* ***syn*** SUPPORT 4, bolster, brace, buttress, carry, prop, shore (up), sustain, upbear, uphold

beast *n* a lower animal as distinguished from man <*beasts* of the field>
syn animal, brute, creature, ‖critter
rel beastie, varmint; quadruped

beastly *adj* ***syn*** BRUTISH, animal, bestial, brutal, brute, feral, ferine, swinish

beat *vb* **1** to strike repeatedly <robbed and *beaten* by thugs>
syn baste, batter, belabor, buffet, drub, ‖dump, hammer, lam, lambaste, paste, pelt, pound, pummel, thrash, tromp, wallop, whop
rel bastinado, baton, bludgeon, cudgel, fustigate, pistol-whip; flog, lace, lash, tan, whip; lay on, maul, muss up, rough (up)
idiom give one beans, rain blows on
2 ***syn*** WHIP 2, ‖clobber, curry, drub, lick, shellac, smear, smother, thrash, trim
3 ***syn*** SCOUR 2, comb, finecomb, fine-tooth-comb, forage, grub, rake, ransack, rummage, search
4 ***syn*** WHIP 3, whisk
5 ***syn*** WAG, lash, switch, waggle, wave, woggle
6 ***syn*** HAMMER 1, malleate, pound
7 ***syn*** SURPASS 1, best, better, exceed, excel, outdo, outshine, outstrip, top, transcend
idiom beat (all) hollow
8 ***syn*** NONPLUS 1, buffalo, get, stick, stump
9 ***syn*** CHEAT, bilk, chouse, cozen, defraud, diddle, do, flimflam, gyp, overreach
10 ***syn*** FRUSTRATE 1, baffle, balk, bilk, circumvent, dash, disappoint, foil, ruin, thwart
11 ***syn*** SCOOP 3
12 ***syn*** PULSATE, palpitate, pulse, throb
13 ***syn*** WIN 1, overcome, prevail, triumph

beat *n* **1** ***syn*** RHYTHM, cadence, cadency, measure, meter, rhyme, rhythmus, swing
2 ***syn*** SCOOP, exclusive

beat down *vb* ***syn*** CONQUER 1, bear down, crush, defeat, overpower, reduce, subdue, subjugate, vanquish

beating *n* ***syn*** DEFEAT 1, debacle, defeasance, drubbing, licking, overthrow, rout, shellacking, thrashing, vanquishment
rel lump(s)

---

beatitude *n* ***syn*** HAPPINESS, blessedness, bliss, blissfulness
rel ecstasy, rapture, transport
con affliction, trial, tribulation; anguish, grief, sorrow, woe; agony, suffering
ant despair, dolor

beau *n* **1** ***syn*** BOYFRIEND 1, gentleman friend, swain, young man
2 ***syn*** BOYFRIEND 2, beloved, flame, inamorato, lover, steady, sweetheart, truelove

Beau Brummel *n* ***syn*** FOP, blood, buck, coxcomb, dandy, dude, exquisite, lounge lizard, macaroni, petit-maître

beau ideal *n* ***syn*** MODEL 2, archetype, ensample, example, exemplar, ideal, mirror, paradigm, pattern, standard
idiom shining example

‖**beaut** *n* ***syn*** BEAUTY, eyeful, knockout, looker, lovely, stunner

beauteous *adj* ***syn*** BEAUTIFUL, attractive, ‖bonny, comely, fair, good-looking, handsome, lovely, pretty, pulchritudinous

beautiful *adj* very pleasing or delightful to look at <the most *beautiful* woman in the world>
syn attractive, beauteous, ‖bonny, comely, fair, good-looking, handsome, lovely, pretty, pulchritudinous, stunning, well-favored
rel choice, elegant, exquisite; glorious, resplendent, splendid, sublime, superb; eye-appealing, eye-filling, ‖proper; personable, pleasing
con offensive, repugnant, repulsive, revolting; homely, plain, ordinary, unattractive, unbeauteous, uncomely, unhandsome, unlovely, unpretty
ant ugly, unbeautiful

beautiful people *n pl* ***syn*** SMART SET, jet set, ton

beautify *vb* ***syn*** ADORN, bedeck, deck, decorate, dress (up), embellish, garnish, ornament, prank, trim
rel glamorize, prettify
con deface, disfigure; damage, mar, spoil
ant uglify

beauty *n* a physically attractive woman <a charming woman and a *beauty* to boot>
syn ‖beaut, eyeful, knockout, looker, lovely, stunner
rel charmer, dazzler, dream, eye-opener, good-looker, peach; belle, toast
idiom raving beauty
con dog, gorgon, hag, slattern, witch

beaver *n* ***syn*** BEARD, whiskers

becalm *vb* ***syn*** CALM, allay, compose, lull, quiet, ‖quieten, settle, soothe, still, tranquilize

because *conj* for the reason that <I left *because* I was bored>
syn as, as long as, ‖being, 'cause, considering, for, inasmuch as, now, seeing, since, whereas
idiom in view of the fact

because of *prep* ***syn*** OVER 6, due to, owing to, through

becloud *vb* **1** ***syn*** OBSCURE, bedim, befog, cloud, darken, dim, eclipse, fog, obfuscate, overcloud
rel befuddle, confuse, perplex, puzzle
con illuminate
2 ***syn*** CONFUSE 4, befog, blur, cloud, fog, muddy

become *vb* **1** to commence to be <*became* sick yesterday>
syn come, ‖come over, get, go, grow, run, turn, wax
rel arise, mount, rise, soar
idiom get to be, turn out to be
2 ***syn*** SUIT 4, agree (with), befit, fit, go (together *or* with)
3 ***syn*** FLATTER, enhance, suit

becoming *adj* ***syn*** DECOROUS 1, befitting, comme il faut, conforming, correct, decent, nice, proper, right, seemly
rel attractive, flattering; tasteful
con unattractive, unflattering; distasteful; inappropriate, unfitting, unrespectable, unsuitable
ant unbecoming

becomingly *adv* ***syn*** WELL 4, acceptably, adequately, amply, appropriately, fittingly, properly, right, satisfactorily, suitably

becrush *vb* ***syn*** CRUSH 2, bruise, mash, ‖mush (up), pulp, squash

bed *n* ***syn*** BASE 1, basis, bedrock, bottom, foundation, ground, rest, seat, substratum, understructure

bed *vb* **1** to put to bed <getting the children *bedded*>
syn tuck (in)
rel cradle
2 ***syn*** RETIRE 4, ‖flop, pile (in), roll in, turn in

bedamn *vb* ***syn*** SWEAR 3, curse, cuss, damn, execrate, imprecate

bedaub *vb* ***syn*** SMEAR 1, besmear, dab, daub, plaster, ‖smarm, smudge

bedaze *vb* ***syn*** DAZE 2, bemuse, benumb, paralyze, petrify, stun, stupefy

bedazzle *vb* ***syn*** DAZE 1, blind, dazzle

bedcover *n* ***syn*** BEDSPREAD, counterpane, coverlet, ‖coverlid, spread

bedeck *vb* ***syn*** ADORN, beautify, deck, decorate, dress (up), embellish, garnish, ornament, prank, trim
rel bedaub, bedizen

bedevil *vb* ***syn*** WORRY 1, annoy, hagride, harass, harry, pester, plague, tantalize, tease, ‖wherret

bedfast *adj* ***syn*** BEDRIDDEN

bedim *vb* ***syn*** OBSCURE, becloud, befog, cloud, darken, dim, eclipse, fog, gloom, obfuscate
con highlight, illuminate

bedlamite *n* ***syn*** LUNATIC 1, dement, loon, loony, madling, madman, maniac, non compos, nut, Tom o' Bedlam

bedlamite *adj* ***syn*** INSANE 1, ‖batty, cracked, crazy, demented, deranged, lunatic, mad, maniac, nuts

bedog *vb* ***syn*** TAIL, dog, shadow, tag, trail

bedraggled *adj* ***syn*** SHABBY 1, decrepit, dilapidated, down-at-heel, faded, run-down, seedy, tagrag, tattered, threadbare

bedridden *adj* confined to one's bed by illness or injury <a *bedridden* invalid>
syn bedfast

---

syn synonym(s) ***rel*** related word(s)
idiom idiomatic equivalent(s) ***con*** contrasted word(s)
ant antonym(s) * vulgar
‖ use limited; if in doubt, see a dictionary
The first word in a synonym list when printed in SMALL CAPITALS shows where there is more information about the group. For a more efficient use of this book see Explanatory Notes.

rel confined, incapacitated, laid up; feeble, infirm, sickly, weak
idiom flat on one's back
con healed, well; hale, healthy, whole
ant ambulant, ambulatory

bedrock *n* **1** *syn* BASE 1, bed, footing, foundation, ground, groundwork, substratum, substructure, underpinning, understructure
2 *syn* BASIS 1, base, footing, foundation, ground, groundwork, infrastructure, root, substratum, underpinning

bedspread *n* an often ornamental outer covering for a bed <an appliqued *bedspread*>
syn bedcover, counterpane, coverlet, ‖coverlid, spread

bee *n* *syn* CAPRICE, boutade, conceit, crotchet, fancy, freak, humor, megrim, vagary, whim
rel idea; impulse

beef *n* **1** *syn* MUSCLE 1, brawn, might, thew
2 *syn* POWER 4, arm, energy, force, muscle, sinew, steam, strength, strong arm, vigor
3 *syn* QUARREL, altercation, bickering, brawl, dispute, falling-out, miff, rhubarb, squabble, tiff

‖**beef** *vb* *syn* GRIPE, ‖bellyache, ‖bitch, bleat, ‖blow off, crab, fuss, squawk, yammer, yawp (*or* yaup)

beef (up) *vb* *syn* INCREASE 1, aggrandize, augment, boost, enlarge, expand, extend, heighten, magnify, multiply

beefheaded *adj* *syn* STUPID 1, beef-witted, beetleheaded, blockheaded, chuckleheaded, dense, dull, fatheaded, hammerheaded, thickheaded

beef–witted *adj* *syn* STUPID 1, beefheaded, beetleheaded, blear-eyed, blear-eyed, blockheaded, fatheaded, hammerheaded, thickheaded, thick-witted

beefy *adj* *syn* HUSKY 1, burly, hefty

beekeeper *n* one who engages in the production of and caring for bees and honey <special masks and gloves for *beekeepers*>
syn apiarist, apiculturist, beeman, beemaster

beeline *vb* *syn* HURRY 2, bullet, highball, hotfoot, hustle, ‖nip, rocket, speed, whiz, zip

Beelzebub *n* *syn* DEVIL 1, Apollyon, diablo, fiend, Lucifer, Old Gooseberry, Old Nick, Old Scratch, Satan, serpent

beeman *n* *syn* BEEKEEPER, apiarist, apiculturist, beemaster

beemaster *n* *syn* BEEKEEPER, apiarist, apiculturist, beeman

beer garden *n* *syn* ALEHOUSE, beer hall, ‖beerhouse, bierstube, mughouse, stube

beer hall *n* *syn* ALEHOUSE, beer garden, ‖beerhouse, bierstube, mughouse, stube

‖**beerhouse** *n* *syn* ALEHOUSE, beer garden, beer hall, bierstube, mughouse, stube

beetle *vb* **1** *syn* HANG 4, bend (over), jut, lean (over), overhang
2 *syn* BULGE, jut, overhang, poke, pouch, pout, project, protrude, stand out, stick out

beetlehead *n* *syn* DUNCE, blockhead, bonehead, chowderhead, chucklehead, dolt, dope, dumbbell, fathead, knucklehead

beetleheaded *adj* *syn* STUPID 1, beefheaded, blockheaded, chuckleheaded, dense, dull, fatheaded, hammerheaded, numskulled, thickheaded

‖**beezer** *n* *syn* NOSE 1, beak, ‖boko, pecker, ‖schnozzle, smeller, ‖sneezer, ‖snitch, snoot, snout

befall *vb* *syn* HAPPEN 1, betide, break, chance, come off, develop, fall out, go, hap, occur

befit *vb* *syn* SUIT 4, agree (with), become, fit, go (together *or* with)

befitting *adj* **1** *syn* FIT 1, appropriate, apt, felicitous, fitting, happy, just, meet, proper, suitable
ant unbefitting
2 *syn* DECOROUS 1, becoming, comme il faut, conforming, correct, decent, nice, proper, right, seemly

befittingly *adv* *syn* WELL 1, correctly, decently, decorously, fitly, fittingly, justly, nicely, properly, rightly

befog *vb* **1** *syn* OBSCURE, bedim, becloud, cloud, darken, dim, eclipse, fog, obfuscate, overcloud
2 *syn* CONFUSE 4, becloud, blur, cloud, fog, muddy
3 *syn* PUZZLE, bewilder, ‖cap, confuse, confound, metagrobolize, perplex, pose, stumble

befool *vb* *syn* DUPE, bamboozle, chicane, fool, gull, hoax, hoodwink, hornswoggle, trick, victimize

before *adv* **1** so as to precede something in order or time <racing on *before* to give warning>
syn ahead, ante, antecedently, beforehand, fore, forward, in advance, precedently, previous
con behind; abaft, aft, astern
ant after
2 in time past <had heard that joke *before*>
syn already, earlier, erstwhile, formerly, heretofore, once, previously; *compare* THEN 1
ant after
3 until now or then <you'll get it tomorrow and not *before*>
syn beforehand, earlier, sooner

before *prep* **1** coming before in space or time <be home *before* dark>
syn ahead of, ante, ere, in advance of, preceding, prior to, to; *compare* UNTIL
con since, subsequent to
ant after
2 in the presence of <stood *before* the court>
syn confronting, facing
idiom face to face with
3 *syn* UNTIL, in advance of, prior to, till, to, up till, up to

beforehand *adv* **1** *syn* BEFORE 1, ahead, ante, antecedently, fore, forward, in advance, precedently, previous
2 *syn* BEFORE 3, earlier, sooner

befoul *vb* **1** *syn* CONTAMINATE 2, foul, pollute
2 *syn* MALIGN, bespatter, blacken, defame, denigrate, slander, slur, smear, spatter, traduce

befuddle *vb* *syn* CONFUSE 2, addle, ball up, bewilder, ‖bumfuzzle, distract, fluster, fuddle, mix up, throw off
rel daze

---

syn synonym(s) *rel* related word(s)
idiom idiomatic equivalent(s) *con* contrasted word(s)
ant antonym(s) * vulgar
‖ use limited; if in doubt, see a dictionary
The first word in a synonym list when printed in SMALL CAPITALS shows where there is more information about the group. For a more efficient use of this book see Explanatory Notes.

befuddlement *n* ***syn*** HAZE 2, daze, fog, ||maze, muddledness, muddleheadedness, muddlement
rel confusion, mix-up
con clearheadedness, lucidness

beg *vb* to ask for or ask one for something urgently < *beg* one's life from an attacker > < *beg* a stranger for help >
syn appeal, beseech, brace, conjure, crave, entreat, implore, importune, invoke, plead, pray, supplicate
rel ask, call (on), request, solicit; petition, sue; besiege, demand, press; nag, worry
idiom throw oneself at the feet of (*or* on the mercy of)
con hint, intimate, suggest

||**begats** *n pl* **1** ***syn*** GENEALOGY, family tree, pedigree, stemma
2 ***syn*** OFFSPRING, brood, children, descendants, issue, posterity, progeniture, progeny, scions, seed

begem *vb* ***syn*** BEJEWEL, beset, enjewel, gem, jewel

beget *vb* **1** ***syn*** FATHER, breed, get, procreate, progenerate, sire
2 ***syn*** PROCREATE 1, bear, breed, generate, multiply, produce, propagate, reproduce

beggar *n* **1** one who begs especially habitually or as a livelihood < *beggars* crying out to tourists >
syn bummer, cadger, moocher, panhandler, ||schnorrer
rel deadbeat, freeloader, sponge, sponger; ||bindle stiff, hobo, tramp
2 ***syn*** SUPPLIANT, asker, petitioner, prayer, suitor, supplicant, supplicator
3 ***syn*** PAUPER, down-and-out

beggared *adj* ***syn*** POOR 1, broke, destitute, dirt poor, flat, fortuneless, impecunious, impoverished, indigent, needy

beggarly *adj* ***syn*** CONTEMPTIBLE, cheap, despicable, despisable, mean, pitiable, pitiful, scurvy, shabby, sorry
rel wretched; ||cheesy, trashy; measly, paltry

beggary *n* **1** ***syn*** POVERTY 1, destitution, impecuniousness, impoverishment, indigence, need, neediness, pauperism, penury, want
2 ***syn*** MENDICANCY, bumming, cadging, mendicity, mooching, panhandling

begin *vb* **1** to carry out the first act or step of an action or operation < *began* his lecture with a joke >
syn commence, embark (on *or* upon), enter, get off, inaugurate, initiate, jump (off), kick off, launch, lead off, open, set to, start, take up, tee off
rel establish, found, institute; introduce, usher in; broach; attack, tackle; prepare; break in; dig in
idiom get the show on the road, get to work, get underway
con cease, desist, discontinue, quit, stop; close, complete, conclude, finish, terminate; abandon, forsake, leave, quit; back out, renege, withdraw
ant end

2 to come into existence <not since civilization *began* has there been such distress>
syn arise, commence, originate, start; *compare* SPRING 1
rel spring; open
idiom raise its head
con end, finish, terminate

beginner *n* ***syn*** NOVICE, apprentice, colt, freshman, neophyte, newcomer, novitiate, rookie, tenderfoot, tyro

beginning *n* the first part or stage of a process or development <the first few chapters at the *beginning* of the novel>
syn alpha, birth, commencement, dawn, dawning, day spring, genesis, onset, opening, opening gun, outset, outstart, setout, start
rel creation, inception, origin, origination, root, source, spring; anlage, rudiment, sprout; prologue; appearance, emergence, rise; incipiency, infancy
idiom the word go
con consummation, termination; closing, completion, conclusion; omega
ant end, ending

beginning *adj* **1** ***syn*** INITIAL 1, inceptive, incipient, initiative, initiatory, introductory, nascent
2 ***syn*** ELEMENTARY 1, basal, elemental, rudimental, rudimentary, simplest

begird *vb* **1** ***syn*** BELT 1, band, begirdle, cincture, encincture, engird, engirdle, gird, girdle
2 ***syn*** SURROUND 1, beset, circle, encircle, encompass, gird, girdle, hem, ring, round

begirdle *vb* ***syn*** BELT 1, band, begird, cincture, encincture, engird, engirdle, gird, girdle

begone *vb* ***syn*** GET OUT 1, clear out, decamp, hightail, kite, scram, skedaddle, skiddoo, take off, ||vamoose

begrime *vb* ***syn*** SOIL 2, besoil, dirty, foul, grime, smirch, smooch, smudge, smutch, tarnish

begrudge *vb* ***syn*** ENVY, grudge

beguile *vb* **1** ***syn*** MANIPULATE 2, exploit, finesse, jockey, maneuver, play
2 ***syn*** DECEIVE, betray, bluff, delude, double-cross, humbug, illude, juggle, mislead, take in
rel entice, lure, seduce
3 ***syn*** WHILE, fleet, wile

beguiling *adj* ***syn*** MISLEADING, deceiving, deceptive, deluding, delusive, delusory, fallacious, false

béguin *n* ***syn*** INFATUATION, crush, ||pash, passion

behave *vb* **1** to act in a specified way < *behave* as people of good breeding should >
syn acquit, act, bear, carry, comport, conduct, demean, deport, disport, do, go on, move, quit
rel control, direct, manage
idiom make as if (*or* as though); be on one's best behavior, mind one's p's and q's
ant misbehave, misconduct
2 ***syn*** ACT 5, function, operate, perform, react, take, work

behavior *n* one's actions in general or on a particular occasion <his flustered *behavior* before women>
syn comportment, conduct, deportment, tenue
rel bearing, demeanor, mien; action, manner, way
con misbehavior, misconduct

behead *vb* to sever the head <nobles *beheaded* for treason>

---

syn synonym(s) ***rel*** related word(s)
idiom idiomatic equivalent(s) ***con*** contrasted word(s)
ant antonym(s) * vulgar
|| use limited; if in doubt, see a dictionary
The first word in a synonym list when printed in SMALL CAPITALS shows where there is more information about the group. For a more efficient use of this book see Explanatory Notes.

syn decapitate, decollate, guillotine, head, neck
idiom bring to the block

behemoth *n syn* GIANT, leviathan, mammoth, monster, whale

behemothic *adj syn* HUGE, colossal, elephantine, gargantuan, gigantic, Herculean, mammoth, mastodonic, monstrous, titanic

behest *n syn* COMMAND 1, bidding, charge, dictate, injunction, mandate, order, word
rel demand; prompting, request, solicitation

behind *adv syn* AFTER, afterward, afterwhile, by and by, infra, later, latterly, next, subsequently

behind *prep* **1** *syn* ABAFT, back of
2 *syn* AFTER 2, below, following, next, since, subsequent to

behind *n syn* BUTTOCKS, backside, bottom, ‖can, derriere, fanny, heinie (*or* hiney), posterior, *prat, rump

behindhand *adj* **1** *syn* NEGLIGENT, careless, delinquent, derelict, disregardful, lax, neglectful, regardless, remiss, slack
2 *syn* BACKWARD 6, underdeveloped, undeveloped, unprogressive
3 *syn* TARDY, belated, late, lated, overdue, unpunctual
ant beforehand

behold *vb syn* SEE 1, descry, discern, distinguish, espy, mark, note, notice, observe, view

beholden *adj syn* INDEBTED, obligated, obliged

beholder *n syn* SPECTATOR, by-sitter, bystander, eyewitness, looker-on, observer, onlooker, viewer, watcher, witness

being *n* **1** *syn* EXISTENCE 1, actuality
rel character, individuality, personality
ant nonbeing
2 *syn* THING 4, entity, individual, material, matter, object, stuff, substance
3 *syn* ENTITY 1, existence, existent, individual, something, thing
4 *syn* ESSENCE 1, essentia, essentiality, nature, texture
5 *syn* HUMAN, body, ‖character, creature, individual, man, mortal, person, personage, soul

‖**being** *conj syn* BECAUSE, as, as long as, 'cause, considering, for, inasmuch as, seeing, since, whereas

bejewel *vb* to ornament with or as if with jewels <a *bejeweled* headdress> <cobwebs all *bejeweled* with glittering morning dew>
syn begem, beset, enjewel, gem, jewel
rel bespangle, spangle; diamond; encrust

belabor *vb syn* BEAT 1, baste, batter, buffet, drub, lambaste, pound, pummel, thrash, wallop

belated *adj* **1** *syn* TARDY, behindhand, late, lated, overdue, unpunctual
2 *syn* OLD-FASHIONED, antiquated, antique, archaic, dated, oldfangled, outdated, outmoded, out-of-date, passé

belch *vb* **1** to expel gas suddenly from the stomach through the mouth <ate and ate until he *belched*>
syn burp, eruct, eructate
2 *syn* ERUPT 1, disgorge, eject, eruct, expel, irrupt, spew

beldam *n* **1** a woman of advanced years <a crotchety *beldam* hunched over the fire>
syn dame, gammer, grandam; *compare* GAFFER, OLDSTER
rel grandmother, granny; grand dame; matron; matriarch
idiom old girl
con damsel, lass, maid, miss
2 *syn* HAG 2, ‖bag, ‖bat, biddy, crone, drab, trot, witch

beleaguer *vb* **1** *syn* BESIEGE, beset, blockade, invest
rel siege, storm
idiom set upon from all sides
2 *syn* WORRY 1, annoy, bedevil, gnaw, hagride, harass, harry, pester, plague, tease

belfry *n* **1** *syn* BELL TOWER, campanile, carillon
‖**2** *syn* HEAD 1, ‖bean, ‖coco, ‖conk, ‖dome, headpiece, noddle, noggin, noodle, poll

belie *vb syn* MISREPRESENT, color, distort, falsify, garble, miscolor, misstate, pervert, twist, warp
rel contradict, contravene, negative; controvert, disprove; conceal, disguise, hide
con bespeak, betoken, indicate; disclose, discover, reveal
ant attest

belief *n* **1** the act of assenting intellectually to something proposed as true or the state of mind of one who so assents <offered ready *belief* to anyone he trusted>
syn credence, credit, faith
rel assurance, certainty, certitude, conviction, sureness; acquiescence, assent; trust; credibility, trustworthiness
con distrust, doubt, mistrust, uncertainty; incredulity; question
ant disbelief, unbelief
2 *syn* OPINION, conviction, eye, feeling, mind, persuasion, sentiment, view
rel doctrine, dogma, fundamental, law, precept, principle; concept, idea

believable *adj* worthy of belief <the author's bizarre characterizations are hardly *believable*>
syn colorable, credible, creditable, plausible
rel likely, possible, probable, tenable; conceivable, rational, reasonable; presumable, supposable; unquestionable; convincing, impressive, persuasive, satisfying; meaningful, solid, substantial
con improbable, unlikely; doubtable, doubtful, dubious, fishy, questionable, specious; implausible, incredible; inconceivable, untenable; fabulous, mythological
ant unbelievable

believe *vb* **1** to have a firm conviction in the reality of something <*believes* in ghosts>
syn accept, ‖buy, swallow
rel accredit, credit, trust; admit
idiom have no doubts about, hold the belief that, take (*or* accept) as gospel, take at one's word, take one's word for
con discredit, distrust, doubt, mistrust, question, suspect; challenge, dispute; reject, turn down

---

syn synonym(s) *rel* related word(s)
idiom idiomatic equivalent(s) *con* contrasted word(s)
ant antonym(s) * vulgar
‖ use limited; if in doubt, see a dictionary
The first word in a synonym list when printed in SMALL CAPITALS shows where there is more information about the group. For a more efficient use of this book see Explanatory Notes.

ant disbelieve, misbelieve
2 ***syn*** FEEL 3, consider, credit, deem, hold, sense, think
3 ***syn*** UNDERSTAND 3, assume, expect, gather, imagine, ‖reckon, suppose, suspect, take, think

belittle *vb* ***syn*** DECRY 2, depreciate, derogate, detract (from), diminish, discount, disparage, dispraise, minimize, write off
rel criticize, discredit; underestimate, underrate, undervalue
con intensify; boast, crow
ant aggrandize; magnify

belittlement *n* ***syn*** DETRACTION, backbiting, backstabbing, calumny, defamation, depreciation, disparagement, scandal, slander, tale

bell *vb* ***syn*** RING, bong, chime, knell, peal, toll

‖**bell cow** *n* ***syn*** LEADER 1, bellwether, dean, doyen, guide, lead, pilot

bellicose *adj* ***syn*** BELLIGERENT, combative, contentious, gladiatorial, militant, pugnacious, quarrelsome, scrappy, truculent, warlike
rel aggressive, assertive; factious, fighting, rebellious
idiom full of fight
con gentle, moderate, temperate
ant amicable; pacific

belligerence *n* ***syn*** ATTACK 2, aggression, aggressiveness, combativeness, fight, pugnacity

belligerent *adj* having or taking an aggressive or fighting attitude <a *belligerent* reply to a diplomatic note>
syn bellicose, combative, contentious, gladiatorial, militant, pugnacious, quarrelsome, ‖ructious, scrappy, truculent, warlike; *compare* QUARRELSOME 2
rel battling, fighting, warring; attacking, invading; aggressive, antagonistic, fierce, hostile; ardent, hot, hot-tempered
con neutral; pacific, pacifist, peaceable, peaceful; conciliatory; amicable
ant friendly

‖**belling** *n* ***syn*** SHIVAREE, ‖bull band, ‖callithump, charivari, ‖horning, ‖riding, ‖skimmelton

bellow *vb* ***syn*** ROAR, bawl, bluster, clamor, rout
rel bark, bay, yelp; cry, wail; low, moo

bell ringer *n* ***syn*** SMASH 6, bang, hit, succès fou, ten-strike, wow

bell tower *n* a tower that supports or shelters a bell or group of bells <a *bell tower* stood free from the church>
syn belfry, campanile, carillon

bellwether *n* ***syn*** LEADER 1, ‖bell cow, dean, doyen, guide, lead, pilot

belly *n* ***syn*** ABDOMEN, ‖gut, paunch, stomach, ‖tummy, venter

bellyache *n* ***syn*** STOMACHACHE, colic, collywobbles, gripe(s)

---

syn synonym(s) — *rel* related word(s)
idiom idiomatic equivalent(s) — *con* contrasted word(s)
ant antonym(s) — * vulgar
‖ use limited; if in doubt, see a dictionary
The first word in a synonym list when printed in SMALL CAPITALS shows where there is more information about the group. For a more efficient use of this book see Explanatory Notes.

‖**bellyache** *vb* ***syn*** GRIPE, ‖beef, ‖bitch, bleat, ‖blow off, crab, fuss, squawk, yammer, yawp (*or* yaup)

‖**bellyacher** *n* ***syn*** GROUCH, complainer, crab, crank, faultfinder, griper, grouser, grumbler, kicker, malcontent

belong *vb* **1** to be suitable, appropriate, or advantageous or to be in a proper or fitting place or situation <the boxes *belong* in the attic>
syn fit, go, set
rel become, befit, suit; accord, agree, chime, harmonize; correspond, match, tally
idiom have one's place
2 to be the property of (a person or thing) <the books *belong* to the library>
syn appertain, pertain, vest
3 to be an attribute, part, adjunct, or function (of a person or thing) <good humor and wit *belong* to his personality>
syn indwell, inhere
idiom run in one's blood (*or* family)

belongings *n pl* ***syn*** POSSESSION 2, chattels, effects, goods, lares and penates, movables, things

beloved *adj* ***syn*** FAVORITE 1, blue-eyed, darling, dear, fair-haired, loved, pet, precious, white-haired, white-headed

beloved *n* **1** ***syn*** SWEETHEART 1, darling, dear, flame, heartthrob, honey, love, loveling, sweet, sweetling
2 ***syn*** GIRL FRIEND 2, ‖baby, flame, honey, inamorata, ladylove, steady, sweetheart, sweetie, truelove
3 ***syn*** BOYFRIEND 2, beau, flame, inamorato, lover, steady, sweetheart, truelove

below *adv* **1** in or at a lower position than something expressed or implied <several business establishments were situated *below*>
syn beneath, under, underneath
ant above
2 lower on the same page or on a following page <for additional examples see *below*>
syn infra
ant above, supra

below *prep* **1** in a lower position relative to some other object or place <lives just *below* me>
syn beneath, under, underneath
con over
ant above
2 ***syn*** AFTER 2, behind, following, next, since, subsequent to

belt *n* **1** a strip of flexible material worn around the waist <a leather *belt*>
syn ceinture, cincture, girdle, sash, waistband
rel baldric, cummerbund; band
2 ***syn*** AREA 1, region, territory, tract, zone
rel stretch, strip

belt *vb* **1** to bind about or around with or as if with a belt <gold lamé *belting* the gown>
syn band, begird, begirdle, cincture, encincture, engird, engirdle, gird, girdle
rel tie (up); loop; sash; circle, encircle, ring
2 ***syn*** SLAM 1, blast, clobber, slug, smash, wallop

belt *n* ***syn*** BLOW 1, bash, bat, biff, bop, slam, smack, sock, wallop, whop

belvedere *n* ***syn*** SUMMERHOUSE, alcove, garden house, gazebo, pagoda

bemean *vb* ***syn*** HUMBLE, abase, cast down, debase, degrade, demean, humiliate, lower, sink

bemedaled *adj* having or wearing decorations especially as awarded by the military <the general's *bemedaled* uniform>
syn beribboned, decorated

bemired *adj* ***syn*** MUDDY 1, ‖claggy, ‖clarty, miry, oozy

bemoan *vb* ***syn*** DEPLORE 1, bewail, grieve, lament, moan, weep
rel regret; complain
con applaud, cheer, huzzah; delight, jubilate, rejoice
ant exult

bemuse *vb* ***syn*** DAZE 2, bedaze, benumb, paralyze, petrify, stun, stupefy
rel addle; perplex, puzzle
con enlighten, illuminate

bemused *adj* ***syn*** ABSTRACTED, absent, absentminded, distrait, faraway, inconscient, lost, preoccupied

benchmark *n* ***syn*** STANDARD 3, criterion, gauge, measure, touchstone, yardstick

bend *vb* **1** ***syn*** CURVE, bow, crook, round
rel arch, curl, double, hook
ant straighten
2 ***syn*** GIVE 12, break, cave, collapse, crumple, fold up, go, yield
3 ***syn*** INCLINE 3, bias, dispose, predispose
4 ***syn*** ADDRESS 3, apply, buckle (down), devote, direct, give, throw, turn

bend (over) *vb* ***syn*** HANG 4, beetle, jut, lean (over), overhang

bend *n* **1** ***syn*** TURN 2, deflection, deviation, double, shift, tack, yaw
2 ***syn*** TURN 4, angle, bow, flection, flexure, turning
3 ***syn*** CURVE, arc, arch, bow, curvation, curvature, round

bender *n* ***syn*** BINGE 1, bat, booze, brannigan, bum, bust, drunk, jag, soak, tear

bending *adj* ***syn*** CROOKED 1, curving, devious, twisting

beneath *adv* ***syn*** BELOW 1, under, underneath

beneath *prep* ***syn*** BELOW 1, under, underneath
ant above, over

benediction *n* **1** ***syn*** BLESSING 1, benison
2 ***syn*** GRACE 1, blessing, thanks, thanksgiving
3 ***syn*** APPROBATION, approval, blessing, favor, OK (*or* okay)
4 ***syn*** GOOD 1, advantage, benefit, blessing, boon, godsend

benefact *vb* ***syn*** HELP 1, abet, aid, assist, do for, help out, stead

benefaction *n* ***syn*** DONATION, alms, beneficence, charity, contribution, offering

benefic *adj* ***syn*** GOOD 1, advantageous, beneficial, brave, favorable, favoring, helpful, propitious, toward, useful
rel desirable, pleasing, satisfying
con damaging, harmful, injurious
ant malefic

beneficence *n* ***syn*** DONATION, alms, benefaction, charity, contribution, offering

beneficial *adj* ***syn*** GOOD 1, advantageous, benefic, brave, favorable, favoring, helpful, propitious, toward, useful
rel salutary, wholesome
con baneful, deleterious, noxious, pernicious
ant detrimental, harmful

benefit *n* **1** ***syn*** GOOD 1, advantage, benediction, blessing, boon, godsend
2 ***syn*** WELFARE, advantage, good, interest, prosperity, well-being
rel account, behalf, sake; gain, profit
con catastrophe, disaster, misfortune; detriment
ant harm, ill

benefit *vb* to be useful or profitable to <medicines that *benefit* mankind>
syn advantage, avail, profit, serve, work (for)
rel advance, ameliorate, better, contribute (to), favor, improve; relieve, succor; build, further, promote; aid, assist, help
idiom do a world of good
con hinder, impede; damage, impair, injure; distress, upset; afflict, anguish; oppose
ant harm, hurt

benet *vb* ***syn*** CATCH 3, catch up, ensnare, entangle, entrap, snare, tangle, trap

benevolence *n* **1** ***syn*** GOODWILL 1, amity, comity, friendliness, friendship, kindliness
con animosity, bitterness, ill will; antagonism, hostility; inimicality, unkindliness; stinginess
2 ***syn*** GIFT 1, boon, ‖compliment, favor, largess, present

benevolent *adj* **1** ***syn*** GENEROUS 1, big, chivalrous, considerate, greathearted, lofty, magnanimous
rel beneficent; charitable; humane; compassionate, tenderhearted
con cruel, inhuman, malicious, spiteful
ant malevolent
2 ***syn*** CHARITABLE 1, altruistic, eleemosynary, good, humane, humanitarian, philanthropic
rel bighearted, freehearted, generous, greathearted, largehearted, liberal, openhanded; public-spirited; do-good
con niggardly, stingy; callous, indifferent, insensitive, unconcerned, unfeeling

benighted *adj* **1** ***syn*** IGNORANT 1, empty-headed, illiterate, know-nothing, uneducated, uninstructed, unlettered, unschooled, untaught, untutored
rel backward, unenlightened; uninformed
idiom in the dark
con informed, intelligent
2 ***syn*** BACKWARD 5, ignorant, unenlightened, unprogressive

benightedness *n* ***syn*** IGNORANCE 1, illiteracy

benign *adj* **1** ***syn*** KIND, benignant, good-hearted, kindly
rel gracious
con malevolent, malicious, malignant, spiteful; acrid, caustic, mordant
ant malign

---

syn synonym(s) ***rel*** related word(s)
idiom idiomatic equivalent(s) ***con*** contrasted word(s)
ant antonym(s) * vulgar
‖ use limited; if in doubt, see a dictionary
The first word in a synonym list when printed in SMALL CAPITALS shows where there is more information about the group. For a more efficient use of this book see Explanatory Notes.

2 ***syn*** FAVORABLE 5, auspicious, bright, dexter, fortunate, propitious, white
rel gentle, mild; benevolent, charitable, humane; clement, forbearing, merciful
con menacing, threatening
ant malign

benignant *adj* ***syn*** KIND, benign, good-hearted, kindly
rel mild; gracious
con malevolent, malicious, spiteful; relentless
ant malignant

benison *n* ***syn*** BLESSING 1, benediction

bent *n* **1** ***syn*** LEANING 2, disposition, inclination, inclining, penchant, predilection, predisposition, proclivity, propensity, tendency
2 ***syn*** GIFT 2, faculty, flair, genius, head, knack, nose, set, talent, turn
con antipathy, aversion; inability, incapacity

bent *adj* **1** ***syn*** CURVED, arced, arched, arciform, arrondi, bowed, curvilinear, round, rounded
2 ***syn*** DECIDED 2, decisive, determined, intent, resolute, resolved, set, settled

benumb *vb* **1** ***syn*** DEADEN 1, blunt, desensitize, dull, mull, numb
2 ***syn*** DAZE 2, bedaze, bemuse, paralyze, petrify, stun, stupefy

benumbed *adj* ***syn*** NUMB 1, anesthetized, asleep, dead, deadened, insensible, insensitive, numbed, senseless, unfeeling

bequeath *vb* **1** ***syn*** WILL, devise, leave, legate
con disinherit, exheridate
2 ***syn*** HAND DOWN, hand on, pass (on), transmit

bequest *n* ***syn*** LEGACY 1, devise, inheritance

berate *vb* ***syn*** SCOLD 1, bawl out, ‖chew out, jaw, rail, rate, revile, tongue-lash, upbraid, vituperate
con acclaim, praise; applaud; commend, compliment

berceuse *n* ***syn*** LULLABY, cradlesong

bereave *vb* ***syn*** DEPRIVE 2, disinherit, dispossess, divest, lose, oust, rob

bereaved *adj* suffering the death of a loved one <the *bereaved* family>
syn bereft
rel distressed, sorrowing

bereft *adj* ***syn*** BEREAVED

beribboned *adj* ***syn*** BEMEDALED, decorated

berth *n* **1** ***syn*** WHARF, dock, jetty, levee, pier, quay, slip
2 ***syn*** JOB 2, appointment, billet, connection, office, place, position, post, situation, spot

beseech *vb* ***syn*** BEG, appeal, crave, entreat, implore, importune, invoke, plead, pray, supplicate

beset *vb* **1** ***syn*** BEJEWEL, begem, enjewel, gem, jewel
2 ***syn*** ATTACK 1, aggress, assail, assault, fall (on *or* upon), storm, strike
3 ***syn*** BESIEGE, beleaguer, blockade, invest
4 ***syn*** INFEST 1, overrun, overspread, overswarm
5 ***syn*** SURROUND 1, circle, compass, encircle, encompass, environ, gird, girdle, hem, ring
idiom come at from all directions (*or* sides)

besetment *n* ***syn*** ANNOYANCE 3, bother, botheration, botherment, exasperation, irritant, nuisance, pest, pester, plague

beside *prep* **1** at or by the side of <left the car *beside* the road>
syn alongside, by, ‖fornent, next to
rel near, opposite
2 ***syn*** NEAR 2, ‖aside, by, nearby, nigh, round
3 ***syn*** BESIDES 1, as well as, beyond, over and above
4 ***syn*** EXCEPT, aside from, bar, barring, besides, but, excluding, exclusive of, outside of, save

besides *adv* **1** ***syn*** ALSO 2, additionally, along, as well, furthermore, likewise, more, moreover, too, yet
idiom at that
2 ***syn*** AGAIN 4, additionally, also, further, in addition, then

besides *prep* **1** in addition to <*besides* being tall, he's thin>
syn as well as, beside, beyond, over and above
idiom along with, together with
2 ***syn*** EXCEPT, aside from, bar, barring, beside, but, excluding, exclusive of, outside of, save

besides *adj* ***syn*** ADDITIONAL, added, beyond, else, farther, further, more, new, other, otherwise

besiege *vb* to surround an enemy in a fortified or strong position so as to prevent ingress and egress <Troy was *besieged* by Greeks for ten years>
syn beleaguer, beset, blockade, invest
rel encircle, encompass, hem (in), surround; trap; assail, assault, attack

besmear *vb* **1** ***syn*** SMEAR 1, bedaub, dab, daub, plaster, ‖smarm, smudge
2 ***syn*** TAINT 1, besmirch, defile, discolor, smear, soil, stain, sully, tar, tarnish

besmirch *vb* ***syn*** TAINT 1, besmear, defile, discolor, smear, soil, stain, sully, tar, tarnish

besoil *vb* ***syn*** SOIL 2, begrime, dirty, foul, grime, smirch, smooch, smudge, smutch, tarnish

besotted *adj* ***syn*** INFATUATED, dotty, enamored, infatuate

bespangle *vb* ***syn*** SPANGLE 1, glitter

bespatter *vb* **1** ***syn*** SPOT 1, bespot, spatter
2 ***syn*** MALIGN, asperse, befoul, blacken, defame, denigrate, slander, slur, smear, traduce

bespeak *vb* **1** ***syn*** RESERVE 2, book, preengage
2 ***syn*** ADDRESS 4, accost, apply (to), approach, memorialize
3 ***syn*** ASK 2, desire, request, solicit
idiom put in for
4 ***syn*** INDICATE 2, announce, argue, attest, betoken, testify, witness

bespeckle *vb* ***syn*** SPECKLE 1, dot, freckle, pepper, speck, sprinkle, stipple

bespectacled *adj* having or wearing glasses <*bespectacled* thesaurists>
syn spectacled

bespot *vb* ***syn*** SPOT 1, bespatter, spatter

besprinkle *vb* ***syn*** SPRINKLE 1, dust, powder, ‖strinkle

best *adj* much more than half <passed the *best* part of a month at the shore>

---

syn synonym(s) — *rel* related word(s)
idiom idiomatic equivalent(s) — *con* contrasted word(s)
ant antonym(s) — * vulgar
‖ use limited; if in doubt, see a dictionary
The first word in a synonym list when printed in SMALL CAPITALS shows where there is more information about the group. For a more efficient use of this book see Explanatory Notes.

syn better, ‖bettermost, greater, largest, most

best *vb* **1** ***syn*** CONQUER 2, master, overcome, prevail, triumph
2 ***syn*** SURPASS 1, beat, better, exceed, excel, outdo, outshine, outstrip, top, transcend
3 ***syn*** DEFEAT 2, down, outdo, ‖pip, worst

best *n* the choicest one or part <always gave the *best* that she had>
syn choice, cream, elite, fat, flower, pick, pride, prime, primrose, prize, top
rel gem; nonesuch, nonpareil; exemplar, model, paragon, pattern
idiom cock of the walk, flower of the flock, one in a thousand (*or* million)
ant worst

bestain *vb* ***syn*** STAIN 1, blot, discolor, smut

‖**best bib and tucker** *n* ***syn*** FINERY, bravery, frippery, full dress, ‖glad rags, regalia, Sunday best, war paint

best girl *n* ***syn*** GIRL FRIEND 1, ‖chick, ‖doney, gal, girl, lady friend, lass, mouse, popsy

bestial *adj* ***syn*** BRUTISH, animal, beastly, brutal, brute, feral, ferine, swinish

bestialize *vb* ***syn*** DEBASE 1, bastardize, brutalize, corrupt, debauch, demoralize, deprave, pervert, vitiate, warp

bestir *vb* ***syn*** STIR 1, arouse, awaken, challenge, kindle, rally, rouse, wake, waken, whet

bestow *vb* **1** ***syn*** USE 2, apply, employ, exercise, exploit, handle, utilize
2 ***syn*** STOW, pack, store, warehouse
3 ***syn*** HARBOR 2, billet, board, bunk, domicile, entertain, house, lodge, put up, quarter
4 ***syn*** GIVE 1, devote, donate, give away, hand out, present

bestower *n* ***syn*** DONOR, conferrer, donator, giver, presenter

bestrew *vb* ***syn*** STREW 1, broadcast, disject, disseminate, scatter, sow, straw

bestride *vb* **1** ***syn*** MOUNT 5, back
2 to sit with one leg on each side <boys *bestriding* a fallen log>
syn straddle, ‖striddle, stride

bet *n* something of value (as money) staked on a winner-take-all basis on the outcome of an uncertainty <laid a *bet* at three to one on the champion>
syn ante, pot, stake, wager

bet *vb* ***syn*** GAMBLE 1, game, lay, play, put (on), set, stake, wager

bête noire *n* ***syn*** ABOMINATION 1, anathema, black beast, bugbear, detestation, hate

bethink *vb* ***syn*** REMEMBER, cite, ‖mind, recall, recollect, remind, reminisce, retain, retrospect, revive

betide *vb* ***syn*** HAPPEN 1, befall, break, chance, come off, develop, fall out, go, hap, occur

betimes *adv* **1** ***syn*** EARLY 1, seasonably, soon, timely
2 ***syn*** EARLY 2, oversoon, prematurely
‖**3** ***syn*** SOMETIMES, at times, ever and again, ever and anon, here and there, now and again, now and then, once and again, ‖otherwhile

betoken *vb* **1** ***syn*** INDICATE 2, announce, argue, attest, bespeak, testify, witness
2 ***syn*** AUGUR 2, bode, forebode, foreshadow, foreshow, foretoken, omen, portend, presage, promise

betray *vb* **1** ***syn*** DECEIVE, beguile, bluff, delude, double-cross, humbug, illude, juggle, mislead, take in
rel ensnare, entrap, snare, trap
2 to prove faithless or treacherous <*betrayed* his own people by going over to the enemy>
syn cross, double-cross, sell, sell out, ‖split
rel desert, renegade; give away, inform, turn in; collaborate; apostatize
idiom act (*or* play) the traitor, break faith, round on, sell down the river
3 ***syn*** REVEAL 1, blab (out), disclose, discover, divulge, give away, spill, tell, uncover, unveil
rel demonstrate, evidence, evince, manifest, show; betoken, indicate
con defend, guard, protect, safeguard, shield

betrayer *n* ***syn*** INFORMER, ‖fink, ‖nark, snitch, ‖squealer, stoolie, stool pigeon, talebearer, tattler, tattletale

betrothal *n* ***syn*** ENGAGEMENT 2, betrothing, betrothment, espousal, troth

betrothed *n* either member of a couple engaged to be married
syn affianced, intended
rel fiancé, husband-to-be; bride-to-be, fiancée, wife-to-be

betrothed *adj* ***syn*** ENGAGED 2, affianced, contracted, intended, plighted, ‖promised

betrothing *n* ***syn*** ENGAGEMENT 2, betrothal, betrothment, espousal, troth

betrothment *n* ***syn*** ENGAGEMENT 2, betrothal, betrothing, espousal, troth

better *adj* **1** ***syn*** BEST, ‖bettermost, greater, largest, most
2 more worthy or pleasing than an alternative <it is *better* to lose gracefully than to win arrogantly>
syn ‖bettermost, preferable, superior; *compare* GOOD
rel exceeding, exceptional, surpassing; choice, desirable, excellent
idiom more than a match for
ant worse

better *adv* ***syn*** MORE 2
ant worse

better *n* **1** ***syn*** SUPERIOR, brass hat, elder, higher-up, senior
2 a superior or winning position <had the *better* of the argument>
syn advantage, superiority, upper hand, victory, whip hand; *compare* ADVANTAGE 3
rel success, triumph, win
con collapse, defeat, disadvantage, loss; beating, drubbing, licking
ant worse

better *vb* **1** ***syn*** IMPROVE 1, ameliorate, amend, help, meliorate
ant worsen

---

syn synonym(s) — *rel* related word(s)
idiom idiomatic equivalent(s) — *con* contrasted word(s)
ant antonym(s) — * vulgar
‖ use limited; if in doubt, see a dictionary
The first word in a synonym list when printed in SMALL CAPITALS shows where there is more information about the group. For a more efficient use of this book see Explanatory Notes.

2 ***syn*** SURPASS 1, beat, best, exceed, excel, outdo, outshine, outstrip, top, transcend

‖**bettermost** *adj* **1** ***syn*** BETTER 2, preferable, superior
2 ***syn*** BEST, better, greater, largest, most

between *prep* **1** in common to (as in position, in a distribution, or in participation) <a treaty *between* three powers>
syn among
2 in the time, space, or interval that separates <*between* the ages 12 and 20>
syn ‖atween, ‖atwixt, ‖betwixt, in between, tween, twixt

‖**betwixt** *prep* ***syn*** BETWEEN 2, ‖atween, ‖atwixt, in between, tween, twixt

bevel *adj* ***syn*** DIAGONAL, beveled, bias, biased, slanted, slanting

beveled *adj* ***syn*** DIAGONAL, bevel, bias, biased, slanted, slanting

‖**bever** *n* ***syn*** SNACK, ‖bait, bite, ‖chack, morsel, mug-up, ‖piece, tapa

beverage *n* ***syn*** DRINK 1, drinkable, liquor, potable

bevy *n* ***syn*** GROUP 1, assembly, band, bunch, cluster, covey, crew, party

bewail *vb* ***syn*** DEPLORE 1, bemoan, grieve, moan, weep
ant rejoice

beware *vb* to be cautious <*beware* of the dog>
syn look out, mind, watch out
rel attend, heed, notice, watch
idiom be on one's guard, be on the lookout (*or* watch), keep at a safe distance, take care (*or* heed)
con disregard, ignore, neglect

bewhiskered *adj* ***syn*** BEARDED, barbate, whiskered

bewilder *vb* **1** ***syn*** PUZZLE, befog, ‖cap, confound, confuse, metagrobolize, perplex, pose, stumble
rel baffle, fuddle, muddle
2 ***syn*** CONFUSE 2, addle, ball up, befuddle, ‖bumfuzzle, distract, fluster, fuddle, mix up, muddle

bewitch *vb* **1** to practice witchcraft on <medicine men who *bewitch* ignorant tribesmen>
syn charm, enchant, ensorcell, hex, spell, voodoo, witch
rel bedevil, demonize, overlook, possess, sorcerize; beglamour, dazzle, trick
idiom cast a spell on (*or* over), give (*or* cast) the evil eye, put a curse on
2 ***syn*** ATTRACT 1, allure, captivate, charm, draw, enchant, fascinate, magnetize, take, wile
rel beglamour, ‖snow

bewitched *adj* ***syn*** ENAMORED 3, captivated, charmed, enchanted, entranced, fascinated

bewitching *adj* ***syn*** ATTRACTIVE 1, alluring, captivating, charming, enchanting, fascinating, magnetic, mesmeric, seductive, siren
con forbidding, grim

bewitchment *n* ***syn*** MAGIC 1, conjuring, enchantment, incantation, magicking, necromancy, sorcery, witchcraft, witchery, wizardry

beyond *adv* **1** on or to the farther side <a house with mountains *beyond*>
syn farther, further, ‖yon, yonder
2 ***syn*** OVER 1, across, athwart, transversely

beyond *prep* **1** on or to the farther side of <the store is just *beyond* the next house>
syn after, outside, past, without
2 out of the reach, sphere, or comprehension of <it's *beyond* me how he did it>
syn above, past
idiom beyond one's depth (*or* power), over (*or* above) one's head, too deep (*or* much) for
3 ***syn*** BESIDES 1, as well as, beside, over and above

beyond *adj* ***syn*** ADDITIONAL, added, besides, else, farther, further, more, new, other, otherwise

beyond *n* ***syn*** HEREAFTER 2, afterlife, afterworld, otherworld

‖**b'hoy** *n* ***syn*** TOUGH, bullyboy, mucker, punk, rough, roughneck, rowdy, ruffian, toughie, yahoo

bias *n* **1** ***syn*** LEANING 2, bent, disposition, inclination, inclining, partiality, penchant, predilection, predisposition, proclivity
2 ***syn*** PREJUDICE, one-sidedness, partiality
rel inclination, predisposition; slant, standpoint, viewpoint
con dispassionateness; fairness, justness

bias *adj* ***syn*** DIAGONAL, bevel, beveled, biased, slanted, slanting

bias *vb* **1** ***syn*** SLANT 3, angle, skew
2 ***syn*** INCLINE 3, bend, dispose, predispose
3 ***syn*** PREJUDICE 2, influence, prepossess

biased *adj* **1** ***syn*** DIAGONAL, bevel, beveled, bias, slanted, slanting
2 exhibiting or characterized by a highly personal and unreasoned distortion of judgment <a *biased* estimate of the book's worth>
syn colored, jaundiced, one-sided, partial, partisan, prejudiced, prepossessed, tendentious, unindifferent, unneutral, warped
rel bent, disposed, inclined, predisposed; influenced, interested, swayed; opinionated
con detached, dispassionate, impartial, neutral, open-minded; fair, honest, just
ant unbiased

bibber *n* ***syn*** DRUNKARD, boozehound, boozer, drunk, guzzler, inebriate, lush, tippler, toper, tosspot

bibble–babble *n* ***syn*** CHATTER, babble, blabber, chitter-chatter, clack, gibble-gabble, jabber, palaver, prattle, tittle-tattle

bibelot *n* ***syn*** KNICKKNACK, bauble, curio, gewgaw, gimcrack, novelty, objet d'art, trifle, trinket, whatnot

Bible *n* the sacred volume of Christians <students of the *Bible*>
syn Book, Holy Writ, Sacred Writ, Scripture
idiom Book of Books, Good Book, Word of God

bibliopole *n* ***syn*** BOOKDEALER, bookman, bookseller

bicker *vb* **1** ***syn*** ARGUE 2, argufy, dispute, hassle, quibble, squabble, wrangle
rel battle, contend, fight, war
2 ***syn*** QUARREL, altercate, brabble, caterwaul, fall out, row, scrap, spat, squabble, tiff

---

syn synonym(s) *rel* related word(s)
idiom idiomatic equivalent(s) *con* contrasted word(s)
ant antonym(s) * vulgar
‖ use limited; if in doubt, see a dictionary
The first word in a synonym list when printed in SMALL CAPITALS shows where there is more information about the group. For a more efficient use of this book see Explanatory Notes.

3 ***syn*** RATTLE 1, clack, clatter, clitter, ‖ruttle, shatter

bickering *n* ***syn*** QUARREL, altercation, dispute, embroilment, hassle, row, run-in, spat, squabble, wrangle

bicycle *n* a pedal-propelled vehicle with two wheels tandem, a steering handle, and a saddle seat <ten-speed *bicycles*>
syn bike, cycle, two-wheeler, velocipede

bid *vb* **1** ***syn*** COMMAND, charge, direct, enjoin, instruct, order, tell, warn
rel summon
con interdict, prohibit
ant forbid
2 ***syn*** INVITE, ask
rel request

biddable *adj* ***syn*** OBEDIENT, amenable, docile, ‖docious, tractable
rel amiable, good-natured, obliging
con mulish, obstinate, stiff-necked, stubborn
ant recalcitrant

bidding *n* ***syn*** COMMAND 1, behest, charge, dictate, injunction, mandate, order, word
rel call, summoning

biddy *n* **1** ***syn*** MAID 2, girl, handmaid, hired girl, housemaid, maidservant
2 ***syn*** HAG 2, ‖bag, ‖bat, beldam, crone, drab, trot, witch

bide *vb* **1** ***syn*** STAY 2, abide, linger, remain, stick around, tarry, wait
rel continue
2 ***syn*** RESIDE 1, abide, ‖dig, dwell, hang out, live

bierstube *n* ***syn*** ALEHOUSE, beer garden, beer hall, ‖beerhouse, mughouse, stube

biff *n* ***syn*** BLOW 1, belt, bop, pound, smack, sock, thwack, wallop, whack, whop

‖**biff** *vb* ***syn*** STRIKE 2, catch, clout, ‖devel, ding, hit, ‖nail, ‖slosh, sock, whack

‖**biffy** *n* ***syn*** PRIVY 1, backhouse, ‖closet, *crapper, jakes, ‖necessary, ‖office, outhouse

bifold *adj* ***syn*** TWOFOLD 1, binary, double, double-barreled, dual, dualistic, duple, duplex

big *adj* **1** of significant size or scope <a *big* expanse of mud> <*big* plans>
syn considerable, extensive, hefty, large, large-scale, major, sizable
rel bumper, hulking, whacking, whopping; clumsy, unwieldy; ample, biggish, capacious, commodious, comprehensive, copious, roomy, spacious, voluminous; distended, inflated, swollen
con paltry, piddling, trivial; slight, small; insignificant; minute, tiny, wee
ant little
2 ***syn*** LARGE 1, bull, fat, great, husky, oversize
3 ***syn*** PREGNANT 1, childing, enceinte, expectant, expecting, gone, gravid, heavy, parous, parturient
4 ***syn*** FULL 1, awash, brimful, brimming, chock-full, crammed, crowded, packed, replete, stuffed
rel flushed, overflowing; cloyed, glutted, sated, satiated, satisfied
idiom full to bursting (*or* overflowing), full to the ears, stuffed to the gills
con empty
5 ***syn*** IMPORTANT 1, consequential, considerable, material, meaningful, momentous, significant, substantial, weighty
6 ***syn*** PRETENTIOUS 3, arty, arty-crafty, high-sounding, imposing, overblown
7 ***syn*** GENEROUS 1, benevolent, chivalrous, considerate, greathearted, lofty, magnanimous

‖**big** *adv* ***syn*** VERY 1, ‖awful, awfully, damned, extremely, greatly, hugely, much, whacking, whopping

big *n* ***syn*** NOTABLE 1, big boy, ‖big cheese, ‖biggie, ‖big noise, big shot, bigwig, great gun, heavyweight, lion

big boy *n* ***syn*** NOTABLE 1, ‖big cheese, ‖big chief, ‖biggie, big gun, big shot, big-timer, bigwig, high-muck-a-muck, VIP

‖**big bug** *n* ***syn*** NOTABLE 1, big, big boy, ‖big cheese, ‖big chief, big gun, ‖big noise, big shot, ‖big wheel, bigwig

‖**big cheese** *n* ***syn*** NOTABLE 1, big boy, ‖big chief, ‖biggie, big gun, ‖big noise, big shot, ‖big wheel, bigwig, VIP

‖**big chief** *n* ***syn*** NOTABLE 1, big boy, ‖big bug, ‖big cheese, ‖biggie, big gun, big shot, ‖big wheel, bigwig, great gun

‖**biggety** *adj* ***syn*** WISE 5, bold, cheeky, forward, fresh, impudent, nervy, procacious, sassy, smart-alecky

‖**biggie** *n* ***syn*** NOTABLE 1, big boy, ‖big noise, big shot, big-timer, ‖big wheel, chief, heavyweight, leader, lion

big gun *n* ***syn*** NOTABLE 1, big boy, ‖big cheese, ‖big noise, big shot, ‖big wheel, chief, great gun, high-muck-a-muck, leader

‖**big house** *n* ***syn*** JAIL, ‖can, ‖clink, ‖hoosegow, jug, lockup, pen, penitentiary, prison, reformatory

bight *n* ***syn*** INLET, arm, bay, bayou, cove, ‖creek, firth, gulf, harbor, slough

big name *n* ***syn*** CELEBRITY 2, ‖celeb, luminary, name, notability, notable, somebody

bigness *n* ***syn*** SIZE 2, amplitude, greatness, largeness, magnitude, sizableness

‖**big noise** *n* ***syn*** NOTABLE 1, big boy, ‖big cheese, big gun, big shot, ‖big wheel, bigwig, great gun, heavyweight, lion

bigot *n* ***syn*** ENTHUSIAST, bug, fanatic, fiend, freak, maniac, nut, zealot
rel approver, liker, relisher; mumpsimus, racist, segregationist
con depreciator, disparager, knocker; disliker, disrelisher, hater, loather, misliker

bigoted *adj* ***syn*** ILLIBERAL, brassbound, hidebound, intolerant, narrow, narrow-minded, small-minded, unenlarged
rel lily-white; conservative

big shot *n* ***syn*** NOTABLE 1, big boy, ‖big cheese, ‖big wheel, bigwig, dignitary, ‖fat cat, high-muck-a-muck, nabob, VIP

big-timer *n* ***syn*** NOTABLE 1, big, ‖biggie, ‖big noise, chief, heavyweight, leader, lion, luminary, VIP

---

syn synonym(s) ***rel*** related word(s)
idiom idiomatic equivalent(s) ***con*** contrasted word(s)
ant antonym(s) * vulgar
‖ use limited; if in doubt, see a dictionary
The first word in a synonym list when printed in SMALL CAPITALS shows where there is more information about the group. For a more efficient use of this book see Explanatory Notes.

‖**big wheel** *n* ***syn*** NOTABLE 1, big boy, ‖big cheese, ‖biggie, big gun, ‖big noise, big shot, bigwig, chief, VIP

bigwig *n* ***syn*** NOTABLE 1, big boy, ‖big cheese, ‖biggie, big gun, ‖big noise, big shot, ‖big wheel, nabob, VIP

bike *n* ***syn*** BICYCLE, cycle, two-wheeler, velocipede

bilge *n* ***syn*** NONSENSE 2, balderdash, ‖bunk, bushwa, ‖crap, hogwash, hooey, malarkey, rubbish, trash

bilk *vb* **1** ***syn*** FRUSTRATE 1, baffle, balk, beat, circumvent, dash, disappoint, foil, ruin, thwart
con fulfill
2 ***syn*** CHEAT, beat, chouse, cozen, defraud, diddle, do, flimflam, gyp, overreach
3 ***syn*** ESCAPE 2, avoid, double, duck, elude, eschew, evade, shun, shy
rel dodge, shake

bill *n* **1** the jaws of a bird with their projecting horny covering <the huge *bill* of the toucan>
syn beak, neb, nib, pecker
2 ***syn*** PROMONTORY, beak, cape, foreland, head, headland, naze, point
3 ***syn*** VISOR 1, peak

bill *n* **1** a statement of the amount due a creditor <*bills* from the grocer and doctor>
syn account, invoice, reckoning, score, statement, tab
rel charges, damage
idiom statement of account
2 ***syn*** CHECK 2, tab
3 ***syn*** POSTER, affiche, handbill, placard
4 ***syn*** DOLLAR, ‖bone, ‖buck, ‖fish, ‖frogskin, ‖ironman, oner, ‖skin, ‖smacker, ‖smackeroo

billet *n* ***syn*** JOB 2, appointment, berth, connection, office, place, position, post, situation, spot

billet *vb* **1** to assign quarters to soldiers <the troops were *billeted* in private homes>
syn canton, quarter
rel bed, house, lodge, put up; bestow
2 ***syn*** HARBOR 2, bestow, board, domicile, entertain, house, hut, lodge, put up, quarter

billet *n* ***syn*** BAR 1, ingot, rod, slab, stick, strip

billet–doux *n* ***syn*** LOVE LETTER, mash note

billingsgate *n* ***syn*** ABUSE, contumely, invective, obloquy, scurrility, vituperation

billy *n* ***syn*** CUDGEL, baton, billy club, bludgeon, club, knobkerrie, nightstick, ‖shillelagh, truncheon, war club

billy club *n* ***syn*** CUDGEL, baton, billy, bludgeon, club, knobkerrie, nightstick, ‖shillelagh, truncheon, war club

‖**bim** *n* ***syn*** WANTON, hussy, jade, jezebel, slut, strumpet, tramp, trollop, trull, wench

bimanal *adj* ***syn*** TWO-HANDED 2, ambidextrous

bimanual *adj* ***syn*** TWO-HANDED 1

‖**bimbo** *n* ***syn*** WANTON, hussy, jade, jezebel, slut, strumpet, tramp, trollop, trull, wench

binary *adj* ***syn*** TWOFOLD 1, bifold, double, double-barreled, dual, dualistic, duple, duplex

bind *vb* **1** ***syn*** TIE 1, tie up
con release
ant unloose
2 ***syn*** BANDAGE, dress

‖**bindle stiff** *n* ***syn*** VAGABOND, bum, derelict, drifter, floater, hobo, street arab, tramp, vag, vagrant

‖**bing** *n* ***syn*** PILE 1, cock, heap, hill, mound, mow, rick, ‖ruck, shock, stack

binge *n* **1** a drunken revel <hung over after a weekend *binge*>
syn bat, bender, blowoff, booze, brannigan, bum; bust, carousal, carouse, compotation, drunk, jag, orgy, ran*tan, rowdydow, soak, souse, spree, tear, ‖time, toot, wassail
rel bacchanal, bacchanalia, debauch; blast, ‖blowout; ‖bun
2 ***syn*** SPREE 1, fling, orgy, rampage, splurge

bio *n* ***syn*** BIOGRAPHY, autobiography, confessions, life, memoir

biocide *n* ***syn*** PESTICIDE, economic poison

biographer *n* one who writes a biography <irresponsible *biographers* whose work is more fiction than fact>
syn autobiographer, autobiographist, Boswell, memoirist

biography *n* a more or less detailed account of the events and circumstances of a person's life <wrote a *biography* of his grandfather>
syn autobiography, bio, confessions, life, memoir
rel diary, journal, letters; adventures, history, story; profile; obit, obituary

biologic *n* ***syn*** DRUG 1, medicinal, pharmaceutic, pharmaceutical

bird *n* ***syn*** RASPBERRY, bazoo, boo, ‖Bronx cheer, catcall, hiss, hoot, pooh, pooh-pooh, ‖razz

birdbrain *n* ***syn*** SCATTERBRAIN, featherbrain, featherhead, flibbertigibbet, harebrain, rattlebrain, rattlehead, shatterbrain

birdhouse *n* ***syn*** AVIARY

birdman *n* ***syn*** PILOT 2, airman, aviator, flier, fly-boy

bird–witted *adj* ***syn*** GIDDY 1, dizzy, empty-headed, featherbrained, frivolous, harebrained, light-headed, rattlebrained, scatterbrained, silly

birr *n* ***syn*** ENERGY 2, go, hardihood, ‖moxie, pep, potency, tuck, vigor

birth *n* **1** the act or process of bringing forth young from the womb <had a very hard *birth* after a prolonged labor>
syn bearing, ‖birthing, childbearing, childbirth, delivery, parturition
rel abortion, miscarriage, slip
2 ***syn*** BEGINNING, commencement, dawn, dawning, genesis, onset, opening, outset, outstart, start

birth *vb* ‖**1** ***syn*** BEAR 5, ‖born, bring forth, deliver
2 ***syn*** SPRING 1, arise, derive (from), emanate, flow, issue, originate, proceed, rise, stem

birth control *n* control of the number of children born especially by preventing or lessening the frequency of conception <cultural and religious aspects of *birth control*>
syn contraception
rel rhythm method; planned parenthood; vasectomy; (the) pill

‖**birthing** *n* ***syn*** BIRTH 1, bearing, childbearing, childbirth, delivery, parturition

---

syn synonym(s) ***rel*** related word(s)
idiom idiomatic equivalent(s) ***con*** contrasted word(s)
ant antonym(s) * vulgar
‖ use limited; if in doubt, see a dictionary
The first word in a synonym list when printed in SMALL CAPITALS shows where there is more information about the group. For a more efficient use of this book see Explanatory Notes.

birthmark *n* **1** a congenital pigmented area on the skin < *birthmarks* often appear on the neck >
syn mole, nevus
2 *syn* CHARACTERISTIC 1, character, feature, point, trait

birth pang *n, usu* **birth pangs** *pl syn* LABOR 2, childbearing, childbirth, travail

birthright *n* **1** *syn* RIGHT 2, appanage, perquisite, prerogative, privilege
2 *syn* HERITAGE 1, heritance, inheritance, legacy, patrimony

bisexual *adj* being structurally and functionally both male and female < many lower animals are *bisexual* >
syn androgynous, hermaphrodite, hermaphroditic

bistered *adj syn* DARK 3, black-a-vised, brunet, dark-skinned, dusky, swart, swarth, swarthy

bistro *n syn* NIGHTCLUB, cabaret, café, discotheque, hot spot, nightery, night spot, nitery, supper club, watering place

bit *n* **1** *syn* MORSEL 1, bite, mouthful
2 *syn* PARTICLE, atom, drop, iota, jot, minim, mite, molecule, smidgen, speck
3 *syn* END 4, fragment, scrap
4 *syn* WHILE 1, space, spell, stretch, time, ||whet

bit *vb syn* RESTRAIN 1, bridle, check, constrain, curb, hold back, hold down, hold in, inhibit, withhold

bit by bit *adv syn* GRADUALLY, little by little, piecemeal

||**bitch** *vb* **1** *syn* GRIPE, ||beef, ||bellyache, bleat, crab, ||crib, fuss, squawk, yammer, yawp (*or* yaup)
2 *syn* DECEIVE, beguile, betray, bluff, delude, double-cross, four-flush, humbug, juggle, take in

bitch (up) *vb syn* BOTCH, blunder, bobble, bollix, bungle, goof (up), gum (up), louse up, mess, ||screw (up)

bitchy *adj syn* MALICIOUS, catty, despiteful, evil, hateful, malevolent, rancorous, spiteful, vicious, wicked

bite *vb* **1** to seize with the teeth so that they enter < *bite* into a pear >
syn champ, chomp
rel gnaw, nibble, tooth; ||chaw, chew, crunch, masticate, munch, scrunch; eat
idiom sink one's teeth into
2 *syn* EAT 3, corrode, eat away, erode, gnaw, scour, wear (away)
3 *syn* SMART, burn, ||stang, sting

bite *n* **1** *syn* MORSEL 1, bit, mouthful
2 *syn* SNACK, ||bait, ||bever, ||chack, morsel, mug-up, ||piece, tapa
3 *syn* SHARE 1, allotment, allowance, cut, lot, part, partage, portion, quota, slice

biting *adj syn* INCISIVE, clear-cut, crisp, cutting, ingoing, penetrating, trenchant

||**bitsy** *adj syn* TINY, lilliputian, minute, teensy, teensy-weensy, teenty, teeny, teeny-weeny, wee, weeny

bitter *adj* **1** *syn* ACRID, amaroidal, austere, harsh, sharp
rel acerb, acid, bitterish
con delicious; bland, flat, insipid
2 difficult to accept mentally < the *bitter* truth >
syn afflictive, distasteful, galling, grievous, painful, unpalatable
rel annoying, distressing, disturbing, woeful; bad, disagreeable, displeasing, offensive, unpleasant; galling, provoking, vexatious
con agreeable, gratifying, satisfying
3 marked by intense animosity < *bitter* contempt >
syn antagonistic, hostile, rancorous, virulent, vitriolic
rel alienated, divided, estranged; irreconcilable
4 *syn* SEVERE 3, brutal, hard, harsh, inclement, intemperate, rigorous, rugged
con mild, springlike, summery

bitter-ender *n syn* DIEHARD 1, conservative, fundamentalist, old liner, right, rightist, right-winger, standpat, standpatter, tory

bitterly *adv syn* HARD 6, hardly, keenly, rancorously, resentfully, sorely

bivouac *vb syn* CAMP, ||bivvy, encamp, ||laager, ||maroon, tent

||**bivvy** *vb syn* CAMP, bivouac, encamp, ||laager, ||maroon, tent

bizarre *adj* **1** *syn* STRANGE 4, curious, odd, oddball, outlandish, peculiar, queer, singular, unusual, weird
2 *syn* FANTASTIC 2, antic, grotesque
con normal, ordinary, regular

blab *n syn* CHATTER, babble, blabber, chat, clack, gab, gabble, jabber, palaver, yak

blab *vb syn* GOSSIP, noise (about *or* abroad), rumor, talk, tattle

blab (out) *vb syn* REVEAL 1, betray, disclose, discover, divulge, give away, ||let out, mouth, spill, tell

blabber *vb syn* BABBLE 2, blather, drivel, drool, gabble, prate, prattle, twaddle, ||waffle

blabber *n syn* CHATTER, babble, blab, chat, clack, gab, gabble, jabber, palaver, prattle

blabber *n syn* CHATTERBOX, bandar-log, blabbermouth, blabmouth, chatterer, gabber, jabberer, magpie, prater, prattler

blabbermouth *n syn* CHATTERBOX, bandar-log, blabber, blabmouth, chatterer, gabber, jabberer, magpie, prater, prattler

blabmouth *n syn* CHATTERBOX, bandar-log, blabber, blabbermouth, chatterer, gabber, jabberer, magpie, prater, prattler

black *adj* **1** having the color of soot or coal < a *black* hearse >
syn atramentous, ebon, ebony, inky, jet, jetty, onyx, pitch-black, pitch-dark, pitchy, raven, sable
rel blackish; charcoal, slate; piceous; dusky, swart, swarthy; brunet
idiom black as a crow (*or* a shoe *or* the ace of spades), black as hell (*or* night)
ant white
2 *syn* DIRTY 1, filthy, foul, grubby, impure, nasty, soily, squalid, unclean, uncleanly
3 *syn* GLOOMY 3, bleak, depressing, depressive, dismal, dispiriting, dreary, funereal, oppressive, somber
4 *syn* UTTER, absolute, complete, downright, out-and-out, outright, perfect, positive, regular, thoroughgoing

---

syn synonym(s) *rel* related word(s)
idiom idiomatic equivalent(s) *con* contrasted word(s)
ant antonym(s) * vulgar
|| use limited; if in doubt, see a dictionary
The first word in a synonym list when printed in SMALL CAPITALS shows where there is more information about the group. For a more efficient use of this book see Explanatory Notes.

black *vb* ***syn*** BRUISE 1, contuse

black (out) *vb* ***syn*** ERASE, annul, blot out, cancel, delete, efface, expunge, obliterate, wipe (out), x (out)

black and white *n* ***syn*** PRINT 2, writing

black–a–vised *adj* ***syn*** DARK 3, bistered, brunet, dark-skinned, dusky, swart, swarth, swarthy

black beast *n* ***syn*** ABOMINATION 1, anathema, bête noire, bugbear, detestation, hate

‖**blackcoat** *n* ***syn*** CLERGYMAN, churchman, cleric, clerical, clerk, divine, ecclesiastic, minister, parson, preacher

black dog *n* ***syn*** SADNESS, blues, dejection, depression, dumps, gloom, melancholia, melancholy

blacken *vb* ***syn*** MALIGN, asperse, calumniate, defame, libel, slander, slur, smear, traduce, vilify
idiom blacken one's good name, give one a black eye, throw mud at

black eye *n* **1** a bruise about the eye <got a *black eye* in a fight>
syn mouse, shiner
rel contusion
2 ***syn*** STIGMA, bar sinister, blot, blur, brand, odium, onus, slur, spot, stain

blackguard *n* ***syn*** VILLAIN 1, *bastard, heel, knave, lowlife, miscreant, rascal, rogue, scoundrel, *son of a bitch

black out *vb* ***syn*** FAINT, ‖crap out, pass out, ‖swarf, ‖swelt, swoon

blackout *n* ***syn*** FAINT, coma, swoon, syncope

blague *n* ***syn*** NONSENSE 2, balderdash, bilge, blatherskite, bosh, bunkum, bushwa, claptrap, hokum, rubbish

blah *n* ***syn*** NONSENSE 2, balderdash, blather, blatherskite, bosh, bunkum, eyewash, hooey, humbug, pish-posh

blah *adj* ***syn*** DULL 9, banausic, ‖dim, dreary, humdrum, monotone, monotonous, pedestrian, plodding, stodgy

blamable *adj* ***syn*** BLAMEWORTHY, amiss, blameful, censurable, culpable, demeritorious, guilty, reprehensible, sinful, unholy

blame *vb* ***syn*** CRITICIZE, censure, condemn, denounce, denunciate, knock, rap, reprehend, reprobate, skin
rel accuse, charge; impute
idiom lay at one's door (*or* doorstep), lay (*or* put) the blame on
con exculpate, vindicate; praise

blame *n* responsibility for misdeed or delinquency <accepted the *blame* for his foolish act>
syn culpability, fault, guilt, onus
rel accountability, answerability, liability; accusation, charge, imputation; censure, condemnation, denunciation, reprehension
idiom burden of guilt
con commendation, compliment; acclaim, applause, praise

---

syn synonym(s) — *rel* related word(s)
idiom idiomatic equivalent(s) — *con* contrasted word(s)
ant antonym(s) — * vulgar
‖ use limited; if in doubt, see a dictionary
The first word in a synonym list when printed in SMALL CAPITALS shows where there is more information about the group. For a more efficient use of this book see Explanatory Notes.

blamed *adj* **1** ***syn*** DAMNED 2, blankety-blank, blasted, blessed, confounded, ‖consarned, dad-burned, darn, doggone, goldarn
2 ***syn*** UTTER, blasted, blessed, confounded, downright, out-and-out, perfect, rank, regular, straight-out

blameful *adj* ***syn*** BLAMEWORTHY, amiss, blamable, censurable, culpable, demeritorious, guilty, reprehensible, sinful, unholy

blameless *adj* **1** ***syn*** INNOCENT 2, clean, crimeless, faultless, guiltless, inculpable, unguilty
2 ***syn*** GOOD 11, exemplary, guiltless, inculpable, innocent, irreprehensible, irreproachable, lily-white, pure, righteous
rel unimpeachable
ant blameworthy

blameworthy *adj* deserving reproach and punishment <though not criminal, his behavior was certainly *blameworthy*>
syn amiss, blamable, blameful, censurable, culpable, demeritorious, guilty, reprehensible, sinful, unholy
rel illaudable, uncommendable, unpraiseworthy, unpretty; delinquent, faultful; punishable; foolish, irresponsible, reckless
idiom at fault, to blame
con faultless, flawless, impeccable, irreproachable, unimpeachable; guiltless, innocent, sinless; creditable, high-principled, upright
ant blameless; unblamable

blanch *vb* ***syn*** WHITEN 1, bleach, blench, decolor, decolorize, white

blanch (over) *vb* ***syn*** PALLIATE, extenuate, gloss (over), gloze (over), sugarcoat, varnish, veneer, white, whiten, whitewash

blanch *vb* ***syn*** RECOIL, blench, flinch, quail, shrink, squinch, start, wince

blanched *adj* ***syn*** PALE 1, ashen, ashy, colorless, complexionless, doughy, livid, pallid, wan, waxen

bland *adj* **1** ***syn*** SUAVE, civilized, smooth, urbane
rel good-natured, ingratiating
con bluff, crusty, gruff
ant brusque
2 ***syn*** GENTLE 1, balmy, faint, lenient, mild, smooth, soft
3 ***syn*** INSIPID 3, banal, flat, milk-and-water, namby-pamby, sapless, vapid, waterish, watery, wishy-washy
con pungent, savory, spicy, zestful

blandish *vb* ***syn*** COAX, ‖banter, blarney, cajole, con, soft-soap, sweet-talk, wheedle
rel flatter; beguile, charm
con threaten

blandishment *n* ***syn*** FLATTERY, adulation, blarney, incense, oil, soft soap

blank *adj* **1** ***syn*** EXPRESSIONLESS, deadpan, empty, inexpressive, unexpressive, vacant
2 ***syn*** UTTER, absolute, black, complete, downright, out-and-out, perfect, regular, straight-out, thoroughgoing

blank *n* ***syn*** OMISSION, chasm, overlook, oversight, preterition, pretermission, skip

blank check *n* ***syn*** CARTE BLANCHE, free hand

blanket *vb* ***syn*** COVER 3, cap, crown, overcast, overlay, overspread

blankety–blank *adj* **1** *syn* DAMNED 2, blamed, blasted, blessed, ‖blooming, confounded, cursed, cussed, dad-burned, doggone
2 *syn* UTTER, all-fired, blamed, blasted, blessed, confounded, deuced, hell-fired, rank, ‖tarnation

blankness *n syn* VACUITY 2, emptiness, vacancy, vacuousness, voidness

blank wall *n syn* BAR 2, barricade, barrier, block, blockade, fence, roadblock, wall

blare *vb* **1** *syn* BLAZE, flame, flare, glare, glow
2 *syn* SCREAM 4, shout, shriek

blaring *adj syn* LOUD 1, earsplitting, full-mouthed, piercing, roaring, stentorian, stentorious, stentorophonic

blarney *vb syn* COAX, ‖banter, blandish, cajole, con, soft-soap, sweet-talk, wheedle

blarney *n syn* FLATTERY, adulation, blandishment, incense, oil, soft soap

blasé *adj syn* SOPHISTICATED 2, disenchanted, disentranced, disillusioned, knowing, mondaine, sophisticate, worldly, worldly-wise, world-wise
con awed, wide-eyed; artless, naive, natural, unsophisticated

blasphemous *adj syn* SACRILEGIOUS, profane

blasphemy *n* **1** impious or irreverent language <cursing God is *blasphemy*>
syn cursing, cussing, execration, imprecation, profanity, swearing
rel affront, indignity, insult; abuse, billingsgate, scurrility, vituperation
con reverence, veneration, worship
ant adoration
2 *syn* PROFANATION, desecration, sacrilege, violation
rel abuse, befouling, shaming

blast *n syn* BANG 2, boom, burst, clap, crack, crash, slam, smash, wham

blast *vb* **1** to ruin or to injure severely, suddenly, or surprisingly <we'll have no peaches; frost *blasted* the blossoms this year>
syn blight, dash, nip
rel destroy, ruin, wreck; damage, injure, spoil; shrivel, stunt, wither
2 *syn* SLAM 1, belt, clobber, slug, smash, wallop
3 *syn* WHIP 2, beat, ‖clobber, drub, dust, lambaste, ‖larrup, lick, overwhelm, shellac

blasted *adj* **1** *syn* DAMNED 2, blamed, blankety-blank, blessed, confounded, ‖consarned, cursed, cussed, dad-burned, doggone
2 *syn* UTTER, all-fired, blamed, confounded, gross, hell-fired, outright, positive, rank, unmitigated

blat *vb syn* EXCLAIM, blurt (out), bolt, cry out, ejaculate

blatant *adj* **1** *syn* VOCIFEROUS, boisterous, clamorous, ‖dinsome, loudmouthed, multivocal, obstreperous, openmouthed, strident, vociferant
rel screaming; obtrusive
con modest, soft-spoken
2 *syn* GAUDY, brazen, chintzy, flashy, garish, glaring, loud, meretricious, tawdry, tinsel
3 *syn* SHAMELESS, arrant, barefaced, brassy, brazen, brazenfaced, impudent, overbold, unabashed, unblushing

blather *vb syn* BABBLE 2, blabber, drivel, drool, gabble, prate, prattle, twaddle, ‖waffle

blather *n syn* NONSENSE 2, balderdash, blatherskite, bosh, bunkum, double-talk, flapdoodle, hokum, jazz, twaddle

blatherskite *n syn* NONSENSE 2, balderdash, bilge, blather, bosh, bunkum, bushwa, claptrap, pishposh, twaddle

‖**blatter** *n syn* CHATTER, babble, blab, blabber, clack, gabble, jabber, palaver, prattle, yak

blaze *vb* to burn or appear to burn brightly <the hot sun *blazed* down>
syn blare, flame, flare, glare, glow
rel illuminate, illumine, light; radiate, shine; coruscate, fulgurate, scintillate, sparkle; incandesce

blaze (abroad) *vb syn* DECLARE 1, advertise, announce, annunciate, blazon, broadcast, bruit (about), proclaim, promulgate, publish

blazes *n pl syn* HELL, abyss, Gehenna, hades, inferno, Pandemonium, perdition, pit, Sheol, Tophet

blazing *adj* **1** *syn* BURNING 1, ablaze, afire, aflame, alight, conflagrant, fiery, flaming, flaring, ignited
2 *syn* IMPASSIONED, ardent, burning, fervent, fervid, fiery, flaming, passionate, perfervid, red-hot

blazon *vb syn* DECLARE 1, advertise, announce, annunciate, broadcast, bruit (about), proclaim, promulgate, publish, sound

bleach *vb syn* WHITEN 1, blanch, blench, decolor, decolorize, white

bleak *adj* **1** *syn* GRIM 2, austere, dour, hard, harsh, severe, stringent
2 *syn* GLOOMY 3, depressing, disheartening, dismal, drear, dreary, funereal, morne, oppressive, somber

blear *vb syn* DULL 4, blur, dim

blear *adj syn* FAINT 2, bleary, dim, ill-defined, indistinct, obscure, shadowy, unclear, undetermined, vague

blear–eyed *adj syn* STUPID 1, beef-witted, blear-witted, blockheaded, blockish, dense, dull, dumb, duncical, thick-witted

blear–witted *adj syn* STUPID 1, beef-witted, blear-eyed, blockish, dense, doltish, dull, dumb, thick, thick-witted

bleary *adj* **1** *syn* FAINT 2, blear, dim, ill-defined, indistinct, obscure, shadowy, unclear, undetermined, vague
2 *syn* EFFETE 2, all in, depleted, drained, exhausted, far-gone, spent, used up, washed-out, worn-out

bleat *vb syn* GRIPE, ‖beef, ‖bellyache, ‖bitch, ‖blow off, crab, fuss, squawk, yammer, yawp (*or* yaup)

bleed *vb* **1** *syn* EXUDE, ooze, ‖screeve, seep, ‖sew, ‖sicker, strain, sweat, transude, weep
2 *syn* FLEECE 1, milk, mulct, rook, stick, sweat

bleeding *adj* **1** *syn* DAMNED 2, blessed, blighted, blinding, ‖blinking, *‖bloody, ‖blooming, cursed, damnable, *‖ruddy
2 *syn* UTTER, absolute, blessed, ‖blinking, downright, gross, outright, rank, straight-out, unmitigated

---

syn synonym(s) *rel* related word(s)
idiom idiomatic equivalent(s) *con* contrasted word(s)
ant antonym(s) * vulgar
‖ use limited; if in doubt, see a dictionary
The first word in a synonym list when printed in SMALL CAPITALS shows where there is more information about the group. For a more efficient use of this book see Explanatory Notes.

blemish *vb syn* INJURE 1, damage, harm, hurt, impair, mar, prejudice, spoil, tarnish, vitiate

blemish *n* an imperfection (as a spot or crack) <a *blemish* on the face>
syn defect, flaw, vice
rel fault, scar; blister, blotch, disfigurement, pockmark, wart; catch, snag, tear

blench *vb syn* RECOIL, blanch, flinch, quail, shrink, squinch, start, wince

blench *vb syn* WHITEN 1, blanch, bleach, decolor, decolorize, white

blend *vb* **1** *syn* MIX 1, amalgamate, commingle, commix, compound, fuse, interblend, interfuse, intermix, meld
rel combine, integrate
con resolve, separate
2 *syn* HARMONIZE 4, arrange, integrate, orchestrate, symphonize, synthesize, unify

blend *n syn* MIXTURE, alloy, amalgam, amalgamation, commixture, composite, compound, fusion, interfusion, intermixture

blending *adj syn* HARMONIOUS 1, chiming, consonant, harmonic, musical, symphonic, symphonious

bless *vb* **1** to make holy by religious rite or word <the priest *blessed* the water and wine>
syn consecrate, hallow, sanctify
rel dedicate
con defile, desecrate, profane
2 *syn* PRAISE 2, celebrate, cry up, eulogize, extol, glorify, hymn, laud, magnify, panegyrize

blessed *adj* **1** *syn* HOLY 1, consecrated, hallowed, sacred, sanctified, unprofane
2 *syn* DAMNED 2, blasted, ‖blooming, cursed, cussed, dad-burned, darn, dashed, doggone, infernal
3 *syn* UTTER, absolute, blasted, ‖blooming, downright, outright, perfect, positive, regular, unmitigated

blessedness *n syn* HAPPINESS, beatitude, bliss, blissfulness
con agony, suffering
ant misery

blessing *n* **1** an expression or utterance of good wishes <on departing, he received his father's *blessing*>
syn benediction, benison
rel Godspeed, valediction
2 *syn* APPROBATION, approval, favor, OK (*or* okay)
3 *syn* GOOD 1, advantage, benediction, benefit, boon, godsend
4 *syn* GRACE 1, benediction, thanks, thanksgiving

‖**bless out** *vb syn* SCOLD 1, bawl out, berate, ‖chew out, jaw, lash, rail, tell off, tongue-lash, upbraid

blight *vb syn* BLAST 1, dash, nip

blighted *adj* **1** *syn* DAMNED 2, blasted, blessed, confounded, cursed, cussed, dad-burned, damnable, execrable, infernal
2 *syn* UTTER, absolute, blasted, blessed, downright, gross, out-and-out, rank, straight-out, unmitigated

‖**blighter** *n syn* WRETCH 1, lowlife, mucker, no-good, worm, wormling

blimp *n* **1** *syn* FATTY, butterball, dumpling, ‖fatso, ‖tub
2 *syn* REACTIONARY, Bourbon, diehard, reactionarist, reactionist, royalist, ultraconservative, white
3 *cap syn* STUFFED SHIRT, Colonel Blimp, fuddy-duddy

blind *adj* **1** lacking the power to see <kittens are *blind* at birth>
syn ‖dark, eyeless, sightless, stone-blind, visionless
rel dim-sighted, purblind, short-sighted; blindish; blindfolded; unseeing
idiom blind as a bat
con seeing, sighted; keen, sharp
2 *syn* INTOXICATED 1, ‖boozy, ‖canned, disguised, drunk, inebriated, ‖lushed, muddled, pixilated, ‖plastered
3 *syn* DULL 7, dead, dim, flat, lackluster, lusterless, mat, muted

blind *vb syn* DAZE 1, bedazzle, dazzle

blind *n* **1** *syn* FRONT 3
2 *syn* DECOY 2, ‖bonnet, ‖booster, capper, shill, shillaber, stick

blind alley *n syn* DEAD END, cul-de-sac, impasse, pocket

blinding *adj* **1** *syn* DAMNED 2, bleeding, blessed, ‖blinking, ‖blooming, confounded, dad-burned, doggone, execrable, infernal
2 *syn* UTTER, absolute, blessed, ‖blooming, confounded, downright, gross, outright, rank, unmitigated

blink *vb* **1** *syn* WINK, bat, nictate, nictitate, twinkle
2 to shine intermittently <we'll signal by *blinking* the headlights>
syn flash, flicker, twinkle
rel glimmer, scintillate, shimmer

blink (at) *vb syn* CONNIVE 1, wink (at)

blink (at *or* away) *vb syn* NEGLECT, discount, disregard, fail, forget, ignore, omit, overlook, overpass, slight

‖**blinking** *adj* **1** *syn* DAMNED 2, blasted, bleeding, ‖blooming, cursed, cussed, dad-burned, damnable, execrable, infernal
2 *syn* UTTER, absolute, bleeding, ‖blooming, complete, downright, out-and-out, outright, perfect, unmitigated

blip *vb* **1** *syn* SLAP 1, box, buffet, cuff, smack, spank, ‖wherret
2 *syn* CENSOR, bowdlerize, expurgate, screen

bliss *n* **1** *syn* HAPPINESS, beatitude, blessedness, blissfulness
con dolor, misery, woe
ant anguish
2 *syn* HEAVEN 2, Abraham's bosom, Canaan, elysium, empyrean, happy hunting ground, New Jerusalem, nirvana, paradise, Zion

blissfulness *n syn* HAPPINESS, beatitude, blessedness, bliss
rel ecstasy, euphoria, exaltation; heaven, paradise

blister *vb syn* LAMBASTE 3, castigate, excoriate, flay, lash (into), scarify, scathe, scorch, scourge, slash

blistering *adj* **1** *syn* HOT 1, baking, boiling, broiling, burning, fiery, red-hot, scalding, scorching, sizzling
‖**2** *syn* DAMNED 2, blasted, bleeding, blessed, ‖blooming, cursed, cussed, dad-burned, execrable, infernal

---

syn synonym(s) *rel* related word(s)
idiom idiomatic equivalent(s) *con* contrasted word(s)
ant antonym(s) * vulgar
‖ use limited; if in doubt, see a dictionary
The first word in a synonym list when printed in SMALL CAPITALS shows where there is more information about the group. For a more efficient use of this book see Explanatory Notes.

blithe *adj* 1 ***syn*** CHEERFUL 1, cheery, ‖chirk, chirpy, chirrupy, lightsome, sunbeamy, sunny
2 ***syn*** MERRY, blithesome, boon, gay, gleeful, jocund, jolly, jovial, lighthearted, mirthful
ant atrabilious, morose

blithering *adj* ***syn*** UTTER, absolute, blasted, blessed, downright, gross, out-and-out, outright, positive, rank

blithesome *adj* ***syn*** MERRY, blithe, boon, festive, gay, gleeful, jocund, jolly, jovial, lighthearted

blitz *vb* ***syn*** BOMBARD, bomb, cannonade, shell

‖**bloat** *n* ***syn*** DRUNKARD, ‖blotter, boozehound, boozer, drunk, guzzler, inebriate, lush, ‖shicker, sponge

bloated *adj* ***syn*** POMPOUS 1, arrogant, important, magisterial, pontifical, puffy, self-important, stuffy, wiggy

bloc *n* ***syn*** COMBINATION 2, coalition, combine, faction, party, ring

block *n* 1 ***syn*** BAR 2, barricade, barrier, blank wall, blockade, roadblock, stop, wall
2 ***syn*** ANNEX, arm, ell, extension, wing

block *vb* 1 ***syn*** HINDER, bar, brake, dam, impede, obstruct, overslaugh
2 ***syn*** INTERCEPT, catch, cut off
3 ***syn*** FILL 1, choke, clog, close, congest, obstruct, occlude, plug, stop, stopper

block (out) *vb* ***syn*** SKETCH, adumbrate, chalk (out), characterize, draft, outline, rough (out), skeleton, skeletonize

blockade *n* 1 ***syn*** BAR 2, barricade, barrier, blank wall, block, roadblock, stop, wall
‖2 ***syn*** MOONSHINE 2, bathtub gin, bootleg, ‖busthead, ‖hooch, mountain dew, white lightning

blockade *vb* ***syn*** BESIEGE, beleaguer, beset, invest

block and block *adj* ***syn*** FULL 1, brimful, brimming, bung-full, chockablock, chock-full, crammed, crowded, jam-packed, packed

blockhead *n* ***syn*** DUNCE, bonehead, clodpate, hammerhead, knucklehead, muttonhead, numskull, thickhead, thickskull, woodenhead

blockheaded *adj* ***syn*** STUPID 1, beefheaded, beetleheaded, blockish, chuckleheaded, fatheaded, hammerheaded, numskulled, thick, thickheaded

blockish *adj* ***syn*** STUPID 1, blockheaded, chuckleheaded, dense, doltish, dull, dumb, hammerheaded, numskulled, thick

block out *vb* ***syn*** SCREEN 3, close, obstruct, shroud, shut off, shut out

‖**bloke** *n* ***syn*** MAN 3, boy, buck, chap, fellow, ‖gee, gent, gentleman, guy, he

blond *adj* 1 of a pale soft yellow color < *blond* hair >
syn flaxen, golden, straw
rel blondish; platinum; champagne, towheaded
con dark; brunet
2 ***syn*** FAIR 3, light

blood *n* 1 the fluid that circulates in the heart, arteries, capillaries, and veins of a vertebrate animal < *blood* covered the battlefield >
syn ‖claret, gore
rel ichor; humor
2 ***syn*** ANCESTRY, descent, extraction, lineage, origin, pedigree
3 ***syn*** MURDER, ‖bump-off, foul play, homicide, killing, manslaughter
4 ***syn*** FOP, Beau Brummel, buck, coxcomb, dandy, dude, exquisite, lounge lizard, macaroni, petit-maître

blood-and-guts *adj* ***syn*** INTENSIVE, deep, hard, intense, profound

bloodbath *n* ***syn*** MASSACRE, bloodshed, butchery, carnage, slaughter

bloodless *adj* 1 ***syn*** PALE 2, anemic, pallid, waterish, watery
rel colorless; lifeless
con alive; vigorous; florid
ant plethoric; sanguine
2 ***syn*** INSENSIBLE 5, anesthetic, dull, hard, impassible, insensate, insensitive, rocky

bloodshed *n* ***syn*** MASSACRE, bloodbath, butchery, carnage, slaughter

bloodstained *adj* ***syn*** BLOODY 1, ensanguined, gory, imbrued, sanguinary, sanguine, sanguineous

bloodsucker *n* ***syn*** PARASITE, barnacle, freeloader, hanger-on, leech, lounge lizard, ‖spiv, sponge, sponger, sucker

bloodthirsty *adj* ***syn*** MURDEROUS, bloody, homicidal, murdering, sanguinary, sanguine, sanguineous

bloody *adj* 1 affected by or involving the shedding of blood < a *bloody* knife > < when will this long and *bloody* conflict cease? >
syn bloodstained, ensanguined, gory, imbrued, sanguinary, sanguine, sanguineous
rel bloodthirsty, grim, murderous, slaughterous; cutthroat, red-handed
2 ***syn*** MURDEROUS, bloodthirsty, homicidal, murdering, sanguinary, sanguine, sanguineous
*‖3 ***syn*** DAMNED 2, bleeding, ‖blooming, cursed, cussed, damnable, dashed, execrable, infernal, *‖ruddy
*‖4 ***syn*** UTTER, bleeding, ‖blooming, complete, consummate, gross, out-and-out, rank, *‖ruddy, unmitigated

bloom *n* 1 ***syn*** FLOWER 1, blossom, posy
2 a state or time of beauty, freshness, and vigor < the *bloom* of youth >
syn blossom, flush
rel glow
3 a rosy appearance of the cheeks < recovered all her health and *bloom* >
syn blossom, blush, flush, glow

bloom *vb* ***syn*** BLOSSOM, blow, burgeon, effloresce, flower, outbloom

‖**blooming** *adj* 1 ***syn*** DAMNED 2, blamed, blankety-blank, bleeding, ‖blinking, *‖bloody, cursed, damnable, execrable, *‖ruddy
2 ***syn*** UTTER, absolute, blasted, complete, consummate, infernal, out-and-out, outright, rank, unmitigated

blooper *n* 1 ***syn*** ERROR 2, blunder, boner, bull, bungle, fluff, lapse, mistake, slip, trip
2 ***syn*** FAUX PAS, boner, ‖boo-boo, break, gaffe, impropriety, indecorum, solecism

blossom *n* 1 ***syn*** FLOWER 1, bloom, posy

---

syn synonym(s)	***rel*** related word(s)
idiom idiomatic equivalent(s)	***con*** contrasted word(s)
ant antonym(s)	* vulgar

‖ use limited; if in doubt, see a dictionary
The first word in a synonym list when printed in SMALL CAPITALS shows where there is more information about the group. For a more efficient use of this book see Explanatory Notes.

rel capitulum, corymb, cyme, inflorescence, panicle, raceme, spike, umbel

2 *syn* BLOOM 2, flush

3 *syn* BLOOM 3, blush, flush, glow

blossom *vb* to produce flowers or be in flower <lilacs *blossom* in the spring>

syn bloom, blow, burgeon, effloresce, flower, outbloom

rel bud; leaf; shoot; open, unfold

idiom burst into bloom, come into flower, put forth blossoms (*or* flowers *or* bloom)

con fade, fall, wither

blot *n* *syn* STIGMA, bar sinister, black eye, blur, brand, odium, onus, slur, spot, stain

rel blemish, flaw, defect

blot *vb* *syn* STAIN 1, bestain, discolor, smut

blotch *vb* *syn* SPLOTCH, mottle, ||splodge

blot out *vb* **1** *syn* ERASE, annul, black (out), cancel, delete, efface, expunge, obliterate, wipe (out), x (out)

2 *syn* ANNIHILATE 2, abate, abolish, eradicate, exterminate, extinguish, extirpate, root out, uncreate, wipe (out)

||**blotter** *n* *syn* DRUNKARD, ||bloat, boozehound, boozer, drunk, guzzler, inebriate, lush, ||shicker, sponge

||**blotto** *adj* *syn* INTOXICATED 1, ||boozy, ||canned, disguised, drunk, inebriated, ||lushed, muddled, pixilated, ||plastered

bloviate *vb* *syn* ORATE, declaim, harangue, mouth, perorate, rant, rave, soapbox

blow *vb* **1** to produce a current of air on <let the wind *blow* your hair dry>

syn fan, ruffle, wind, winnow

2 *syn* BOAST, brag, cock-a-doodle-doo, crow, gasconade, mouth, prate, puff, rodomontade, vaunt

3 *syn* PANT 1, gasp, heave, huff, ||pank, ||pegh, puff

4 *syn* WASTE 2, blunder (away), consume, dissipate, fool (away), fritter, frivol away, squander, throw away, trifle (away)

5 *syn* TREAT 3, set up, ||shout, stand

||6 *syn* BOTCH, bobble, bungle, flub, fumble, goof (up), louse up, mess, muff, ||screw (up)

||7 *syn* GO 2, depart, exit, get away, get off, leave, pull out, quit, retire, withdraw

blow *n* *syn* BREAK 4, breath, breather, breathing space (*or* breathing spell), respite, ten

blow *vb* *syn* BLOSSOM, bloom, burgeon, effloresce, flower, outbloom

blow *n* **1** a forceful sharp stroke (as with the fist or an instrument) <struck him a sudden *blow*>

syn bang, bash, bastinado, bat, belt, biff, bop, crack, ||ding, ||douse, pound, slam, slosh, smack, smash, sock, ||swap, thwack, wallop, ||welt, whack, whop; *compare* CUFF, HIT 1

rel recumbentibus, slug, ||souse; clip, pelt, plug, punch, swat

2 *syn* IMPACT, bump, collision, concussion, jar, jolt, percussion, shock, smash, wallop

blow–by–blow *adj* *syn* CIRCUMSTANTIAL, clocklike, detailed, full, itemized, minute, particular, particularized, thorough

blowen *n* *syn* HARLOT 1, courtesan, demimondaine, demimonde, demirep, fancy woman, hetaera, kept woman, paphian, whore

blower *n* *syn* BRAGGART, blowhard, boaster, braggadocio, bragger, ||gasbag, puckfist, rodomont, rodomontade, vaunter

blowhard *n* *syn* BRAGGART, blower, boaster, braggadocio, bragger, ||gasbag, puckfist, rodomont, rodomontade, vaunter

||**blow in** *vb* *syn* COME 1, arrive, get, get in, reach, show, show up, turn up

blown–in–the–bottle *adj* *syn* AUTHENTIC 2, bona fide, genuine, indubitable, real, sure-enough, true, undoubted, unquestionable, veritable

||**blow off** *vb* *syn* GRIPE, ||beef, ||bellyache, ||bitch, bleat, crab, fuss, squawk, yammer, yawp (*or* yaup)

blowoff *n* *syn* BINGE 1, bender, brannigan, bust, carousal, carouse, ran-tan, spree, tear, wassail

||**blowout** *n* *syn* SHINDIG 1, bash, shindy

blowsy *adj* *syn* SLATTERNLY, dowdy, draggletailed, frowsy, slattern, sordid

ant spruce

blow up *vb* **1** *syn* EXPLODE 1, burst, detonate, go off, mushroom

2 *syn* DISCREDIT 2, disprove, explode, puncture, shoot

3 *syn* ANGER 2, boil, boil over, bristle, burn, flare (up), fume, rage, seethe

blowy *adj* *syn* WINDY 1, airy, breezy, gusty

blub *vb* *syn* CRY 2, blubber, boohoo, ||pipe, sob, wail, weep

blubber *vb* *syn* CRY 2, blub, boohoo, ||pipe, sob, wail, weep

bludgeon *n* *syn* CUDGEL, bat, baton, billy, billy club, club, nightstick, ||shillelagh, truncheon, war club

bludgeon *vb* *syn* INTIMIDATE, bluster, ||bounce, browbeat, bulldoze, bully, bullyrag, cow, hector, strong-arm

blue *adj* **1** *syn* DOWNCAST, bad, dejected, depressed, disconsolate, dispirited, down, downhearted, low, woebegone

2 *syn* RISQUÉ, broad, off-color, purple, racy, salty, shady, spicy, suggestive, wicked

3 *syn* UTTER, absolute, black, complete, downright, infernal, out-and-out, perfect, positive, regular

blue *n* *syn* OCEAN, brine, ||briny, deep, drink, main, sea

blue blood *n* **1** *syn* GENTLEMAN, aristo, aristocrat, patrician

2 *syn* ARISTOCRACY, aristoi, elite, flower, gentility, gentry, optimacy, quality, society, upper class

||**bluebottle** *n* *syn* POLICEMAN, bluecoat, ||bobby, ||bull, ||constable, cop, ||copper, Dogberry, ||flatfoot, ||fuzz

bluecoat *n* *syn* POLICEMAN, ||bluebottle, ||bobby, ||bull, ||constable, cop, ||copper, Dogberry, ||flatfoot, ||fuzz

blue–eyed *adj* *syn* FAVORITE 1, beloved, darling, dear, fair-haired, loved, pet, precious, white-haired, white-headed

blue moon *n* *syn* AGE 2, aeon, coon's age, dog's age, donkey's years, eternity, long

---

syn synonym(s) *rel* related word(s)
idiom idiomatic equivalent(s) *con* contrasted word(s)
ant antonym(s) * vulgar
|| use limited; if in doubt, see a dictionary
The first word in a synonym list when printed in SMALL CAPITALS shows where there is more information about the group. For a more efficient use of this book see Explanatory Notes.

bluenose *n* ***syn*** PRUDE, comstock, goody-goody, Grundy, Mrs. Grundy, nice Nelly, prig, puritan, ‖wowser

bluenosed *adj* ***syn*** PRIM 1, prig, priggish, prissy, prudish, puritanical, straitlaced, stuffy, tight-laced, Victorian

blueprint *n* ***syn*** PLAN 1, design, game plan, project, scheme, strategy
rel outline, sketch

blueprint *vb* ***syn*** PLAN 2, arrange, cast, chart, design, devise, ‖dope out, project

blue–ribbon *adj* ***syn*** EXCELLENT, capital, first-class, first-rate, first-string, five-star, Grade A, prime, top, top-notch

blues *n pl but sometimes sing in constr* ***syn*** SADNESS, dejection, depression, (the) dismals, dumps, gloom, heavyheartedness, melancholy, mournfulness, unhappiness

bluff *adj* direct and unceremonious in speech or manner < *bluff* aggressive questions >
syn abrupt, blunt, breviloquent, brief, brusque, crusty, curt, gruff, rough, short, short-spoken, snippety, snippy
rel hearty, honest, sincere; barefaced, candid, direct, forthright, frank, no-nonsense, outspoken, plainspoken, straightforward; bearish, rude, tactless; sharp, tart; laconic, terse
idiom to the point
con civil, courteous, courtly, gallant, polite; diplomatic, urbane
ant smooth, suave

bluff *vb* **1** ***syn*** DECEIVE, beguile, betray, delude, double-cross, humbug, illude, juggle, mislead, take in
rel fool, joke, trick
2 ***syn*** ASSUME 4, act, affect, counterfeit, fake, feign, pretend, put on, sham, simulate

blunder *vb* **1** ***syn*** STUMBLE 3, bumble, lurch, ‖snapper
2 ***syn*** WALLOW 2, flounder, lurch, stumble
3 ***syn*** BOTCH, ‖blow, bobble, bollix, bungle, goof (up), gum (up), louse up, mess, ‖screw (up)

blunder (away) *vb* ***syn*** WASTE 2, blow, consume, dissipate, fool (away), fritter, frivol away, squander, throw away, trifle (away)

blunder *n* ***syn*** ERROR 2, blooper, boner, bull, bungle, fluff, lapse, mistake, slip, trip

blunderbuss *n* ***syn*** STUMBLEBUM, blunderer, bungler

blunderer *n* ***syn*** STUMBLEBUM, blunderbuss, bungler

blunt *adj* **1** ***syn*** DULL 6, obtuse
rel unpointed, unsharp; insensitive
con acuminate, acute
ant keen, sharp
2 ***syn*** BLUFF, abrupt, brief, brusque, crusty, curt, gruff, short, snippety, snippy
con politic, smooth, suave
ant subtle; tactful

blunt *vb* **1** ***syn*** DULL 3, disedge, obtund, turn
2 ***syn*** DEADEN 1, benumb, desensitize, dull, mull, numb
3 ***syn*** DULL 5, hebetate, stupefy
4 ***syn*** WEAKEN 1, attenuate, cripple, debilitate, disable, enfeeble, sap, unbrace, undermine, unstrengthen

‖**blunt** *n* ***syn*** MONEY, ‖brass, ‖bread, ‖cabbage, ‖chips, ‖dibs, ‖dinero, ‖do-re-mi, ‖jack, ‖long green

blur *n* ***syn*** STIGMA, bar sinister, black eye, blot, brand, odium, onus, slur, spot, stain

blur *vb* **1** ***syn*** TAINT 1, besmear, besmirch, discolor, smear, smudge, smutch, stain, tar, tarnish
2 ***syn*** CONFUSE 4, becloud, befog, cloud, fog, muddy
3 ***syn*** DULL 4, blear, dim

blurb *n* ***syn*** PUFF 3, plug, puffing, write-up

blurt (out) *vb* ***syn*** EXCLAIM, blat, bolt, cry out, ejaculate

blush *vb* to turn or glow red in the face < *blushed* from embarrassment >
syn color, crimson, flush, glow, mantle, pink, pinken, redden, rose, rouge

blush *n* ***syn*** BLOOM 3, blossom, flush, glow

bluster *vb* **1** ***syn*** ROAR, bawl, bellow, clamor, rout
rel blast, storm, rage
2 ***syn*** INTIMIDATE, bludgeon, ‖bounce, browbeat, bulldoze, bully, bullyrag, cow, dragoon, hector

blustering *adj* ***syn*** WILD 6, blustery, ‖coarse, furious, raging, rough, stormful, stormy, tempestuous, turbulent

blustery *adj* ***syn*** WILD 6, blustering, ‖coarse, furious, raging, rough, stormful, stormy, tempestuous, turbulent

board *vb* **1** to get aboard of < *boarded* the wrong bus >
syn embark
rel embus, emplane, entrain
idiom get on
con debus, deplane, detrain; land
ant debark, disembark, get off
2 ***syn*** HARBOR 2, bestow, billet, domicile, entertain, house, hut, lodge, put up, quarter
rel care (for), cherish, nurture, tend

board *n* **1 boards** *pl* ***syn*** DRAMA, footlights, (the) stage, theater
2 ***syn*** TABLE 1, dining table, dinner table, mahogany, ‖table-board

boast *vb* to express pride in oneself or one's accomplishments < *boasting* about all the girl friends he had >
syn blow, brag, cock-a-doodle-doo, crow, gasconade, mouth, prate, puff, rodomontade, vaunt
rel pique, plume, preen, pride, quack; gush, vapor; aggrandize, exalt, glory, triumph; bluster, ‖bounce, bully, ruffle, swash, swashbuckle, swagger; flaunt, parade, show off
idiom blow one's horn, congratulate oneself, hug oneself, pat oneself on the back
con belittle, decry, degrade, disparage, knock, minimize, run down
ant depreciate

boaster *n* ***syn*** BRAGGART, blower, blowhard, braggadocio, bragger, ‖gasbag, puckfist, rodomont, rodomontade, vaunter

boastful *adj* given to or characterized by boasting < a *boastful* old windbag >
syn braggadocian, braggart, braggy, rodomontade, self-glorifying, vaunting

---

syn synonym(s) — ***rel*** related word(s)
idiom idiomatic equivalent(s) — ***con*** contrasted word(s)
ant antonym(s) — * vulgar
‖ use limited; if in doubt, see a dictionary
The first word in a synonym list when printed in SMALL CAPITALS shows where there is more information about the group. For a more efficient use of this book see Explanatory Notes.

rel arrogant, pretentious; cock-a-hoop, exultant; bigheaded, conceited, swelled-headed; self-aggrandizing, self-applauding, self-flattering, vainglorious
idiom having a high opinion of oneself, seeing oneself larger than life
con self-depreciating, self-effacing, unassuming; bashful, demure, sheepish, shy, timid; quiet, reserved, restrained, retiring
ant modest

bob *vb syn* TAP 1, knock, rap, tunk

bobbery *n syn* BRAWL 2, affray, broil, donnybrook, fight, fracas, fray, melee, row, ruction

bobble *vb syn* BOTCH, ||blow, boggle, bollix, bungle, cobble, goof (up), gum (up), louse up, mess

||**bobby** *n syn* POLICEMAN, ||bluebottle, ||bull, ||constable, ||copper, ||flatfoot, ||gendarme, officer, ||paddy, ||peeler

||**bodacious** *adj syn* NOTEWORTHY, memorable, nameable, notable, observable, red-letter, rubric

bode *vb syn* AUGUR 2, betoken, forebode, foreshadow, foreshow, foretoken, omen, portend, presage, promise

bodement *n syn* FORETOKEN, augury, boding, omen, portent, presage, prognostic

bodiless *adj syn* IMMATERIAL 1, asomatous, discarnate, disembodied, incorporeal, insubstantial, nonphysical, unembodied, unfleshly, unphysical

bodily *adj* of or relating to the human body < *bodily* pain >
syn carnal, corporal, corporeal, fleshly, physical, somatic
rel animal, sensual
con intellectual, mental, psychic, psychological; spiritual, unworldly

boding *n syn* FORETOKEN, augury, bodement, omen, portent, presage, prognostic

body *n* **1** *syn* HUMAN, being, creature, individual, man, mortal, party, person, personage, soul
2 *syn* CORPSE, cadaver, carcass, ||cold meat, ||deader, mort, remains, stiff
3 the main, central, or essential part < the *body* of the discussion dealt with ways to ensure equal opportunities for all >
syn bulk, core, corpus, mass, staple, substance; *compare* ESSENCE 2, SUBSTANCE 2, TENOR 1
rel majority; sum, total, whole; basis, crux, fundamental, gravamen; gist, pith
con angle, aspect, facet, feature, side; accessory, extension, offshoot, side issue
4 a discrete portion of matter < unknown *bodies* in space >
syn bulk, mass, object, volume
5 a determinable or measurable whole < collected a large *body* of evidence >
syn aggregate, amount, budget, bulk, quantity, quantum, total
rel extent, range; number, stock, sum, whole
6 *syn* GROUP 3, array, batch, bunch, bundle, clump, cluster, lot, parcel, set
7 *syn* SUBSTANCE 2, amount, burden, core, gist, meat, pith, purport, sense, upshot

body (forth) *vb syn* REPRESENT 2, emblematize, embody, epitomize, exemplify, illustrate, mirror, personify, symbolize, typify

boeotian *n syn* PHILISTINE, Babbitt, boob, middlebrow

bog *n syn* SWAMP, fen, marsh, mire, morass, ||moss, quag, quagmire, ||sump, swampland

bog (down) *vb syn* DELAY 1, decelerate, detain, embog, hang up, mire, retard, set back, slacken, slow (up *or* down)

bogey *n syn* APPARITION, ghost, ||haunt, phantom, revenant, shade, specter, spirit, ||spook, wraith

boggle *vb* **1** *syn* DEMUR, balk, gag, jib, scruple, shy, stick, stickle, strain, stumble
2 *syn* BOTCH, ||blow, bobble, bollix, bungle, cobble, goof (up), gum (up), louse up, mess
3 *syn* STAGGER 5, dumbfound, nonplus

bogus *adj syn* COUNTERFEIT, brummagem, fake, false, phony, pinchbeck, pseudo, sham, snide, spurious
rel forged; imitation
con bona fide, good
ant authentic, genuine, real

Bohemian *n* a person (as an artist) who has an unconventional life-style that often reflects protest against or indifference to convention < a gathering place for radicals and *Bohemians* >
syn maverick, nonconformist
rel beat, beatnik, dropout, hippie; iconoclast; eccentric, original; recusant
con conformer, conventionalist, formalist, pedant

bohunk *n syn* OAF 2, ||gaum, gawk, klutz, looby, lout, lubber, lummox, lump, palooka

boil *n syn* ABSCESS, carbuncle, furuncle, pimple, pustule

boil *vb* **1** *syn* SEETHE 4, bubble, churn, ferment, ||moil, simmer, smolder, stir
2 to prepare (as food) in a liquid heated to the point that it begins to give off steam < *boil* eggs >
syn parboil, seethe, simmer, stew
rel coddle, poach; decoct; steam
3 *syn* ANGER 2, blow up, boil over, bristle, burn, flare (up), fume, rage, seethe
4 *syn* RUSH 1, bolt, charge, chase, dash, fling, lash, race, shoot, tear

boil down *vb syn* SIMPLIFY, streamline

boildown *n syn* ABRIDGMENT, abstract, breviary, breviate, brief, condensation, conspectus, epitome, synopsis

||**boiled** *adj syn* INTOXICATED 1, ||boozy, ||canned, disguised, drunk, inebriated, ||lushed, muddled, pixilated, ||plastered

boiling *adj syn* HOT 1, baking, blistering, broiling, burning, fiery, red-hot, scalding, scorching, sizzling

boil over *vb syn* ANGER 2, blow up, boil, bristle, burn, flare (up), fume, rage, seethe

boisterous *adj* **1** *syn* TURBULENT 1, disorderly, rambunctious, raucous, rowdy, rowdydowdy, rowdyish, termagant, tumultuous, unruly
2 *syn* VOCIFEROUS, blatant, clamorous, ||dinsome, loudmouthed, multivocal, obstreperous, openmouthed, strident, vociferant

---

rel brawling, noisy, riotous, rollicking, rowdy
con sedate, sober, staid; noiseless

||**boko** *n* ***syn*** NOSE 1, beak, ||conk, pecker, proboscis, ||schnozzle, smeller, ||sneezer, snoot, snout

bold *adj* **1** ***syn*** BRAVE 1, audacious, courageous, dauntless, doughty, fearless, intrepid, unafraid, undaunted, valiant
con pusillanimous, shrinking, timid, timorous
ant cowardly
2 ***syn*** WISE 5, cheeky, forward, fresh, impudent, nervy, pert, sassy, smart, smart-alecky
rel audacious; bluff
con mousy, quiet, shy
3 ***syn*** INSOLENT 2, audacious, ||boldacious, brazen, contumelious, impertinent, impudent, procacious, saucy

||**boldacious** *adj* ***syn*** INSOLENT 2, audacious, bold, brazen, contumelious, impertinent, impudent, procacious, saucy

bold-faced *adj* ***syn*** WISE 5, cheeky, forward, fresh, impudent, nervy, pert, sassy, smart, smart-alecky

boldhearted *adj* ***syn*** BRAVE 1, audacious, courageous, dauntless, doughty, fearless, intrepid, unafraid, undaunted, valiant

boldness *n* ***syn*** INSOLENCE, disrespect, hardihood, impertinence, impudence, insolency, insolentness

bollix *vb* ***syn*** BOTCH, ||blow, bobble, bungle, flub, fumble, goof (up), gum (up), louse up, mess

Bolshevik *n* ***syn*** COMMUNIST, ||Bolshie, commie, comrade, Red

||**Bolshie** *n* ***syn*** COMMUNIST, Bolshevik, commie, comrade, Red

bolster *vb* **1** ***syn*** SUPPORT 4, bear up, brace, buttress, carry, prop, shore (up), sustain, upbear, uphold
rel reinforce, strengthen
2 ***syn*** SUPPORT 5, buoy (up), prop, sustain, underprop, uphold

bolt *n* ***syn*** THUNDERBOLT, thunderstroke

bolt *vb* **1** ***syn*** START 1, jump, spring, startle
2 ***syn*** RUSH 1, boil, charge, chase, dash, fling, lash, race, shoot, tear
3 ***syn*** RUN 2, flee, fly, make off, scamper, scoot, ||screw, skedaddle, skip, skirr
4 ***syn*** EXCLAIM, blat, blurt (out), cry out, ejaculate
5 ***syn*** GULP, cram, englut, gobble, guzzle, ingurgitate, slop, slosh, wolf

bomb *n* **1** ***syn*** FAILURE 5, bust, dud, flop, lemon, loser
||**2** ***syn*** FORTUNE 4, boodle, bundle, mint, packet, pile, pot, ||roll, wad

bomb *vb* ***syn*** BOMBARD, blitz, cannonade, shell

bombard *vb* to assault with bombs or shells <cities *bombarded* by planes and artillery>
syn blitz, bomb, cannonade, shell
rel barrage, strafe, strike
idiom open up on, pour a broadside into

bombardment *n* ***syn*** BARRAGE, broadside, burst, cannonade, drumfire, fusillade, hail, salvo, shower, volley

bombast *n* pretentious inflated speech or writing <adolescent *bombast* about Youth and Destiny>
syn fustian, highfalutin, lexiphanicism, rant, rhapsody, rhetoric, rodomontade
rel grandiloquence, magniloquence; flatulence, orotundity, tumidity, turgidity; heroics, pyrotechnics, sesquipedality; Johnsonese; spread-eagleism; nonsense
idiom purple prose

bombastic *adj* ***syn*** RHETORICAL, aureate, declamatory, euphuistic, flowery, grandiloquent, magniloquent, overblown, sonorous, swollen
rel flatulent
con unimpassioned; unaffected

||**bombed** *adj* ***syn*** INTOXICATED 1, ||bagged, blind, ||blotto, ||boozed, ||canned, ||crocked, ||lit, stoned, tight

bombinate *vb* ***syn*** HUM, ||bum, bumble, buzz, drone, ||sowf, strum, thrum

bona fide *adj* ***syn*** AUTHENTIC 2, blown-in-the-bottle, genuine, indubitable, real, sure-enough, true, undoubted, unquestionable, veritable

bona fides *n* ***syn*** GOOD FAITH, sincereness, sincerity, uberrima fides

bonanza *n* a place of great abundance or a source of great wealth or opportunity <the town proved to be a *bonanza* for entrepreneurs>
syn eldorado, Golconda, gold mine, mine, treasure-house, treasure trove, treasury

bond *n* **1** *usu* **bonds** *pl* ***syn*** SHACKLE, chains, fetter(s), gyve(s), iron(s)
2 ***syn*** CONTRACT, agreement, bargain, compact, convention, covenant, pact, transaction
3 a uniting or binding element or force <the *bonds* of friendship>
syn knot, ligament, ligature, link, nexus, tie, vinculum, yoke
rel bridge, connection, connective, liaison; interrelationship, relationship
4 ***syn*** ADHERENCE 1, adhesion, cling, clinging, coherence, cohesion, stickage, sticking
5 ***syn*** GUARANTEE 1, bail, guaranty, security, surety, warranty

bondage *n* the state of subjection to an owner or master <prisoners sold into *bondage*>
syn enslavement, helotry, peonage, serfage, serfdom, servility, servitude, slavery, thrall, thralldom, villenage, yoke
rel subjection, subjugation
con freedom, independence, liberty

bondman *n* ***syn*** SLAVE 1, bondslave, bondsman, chattel, mancipium

bondslave *n* ***syn*** SLAVE 1, bondman, bondsman, chattel, mancipium

bondsman *n* ***syn*** SLAVE 1, bondman, bondslave, chattel, mancipium

bone *n* **1** **bones** *pl* ***syn*** DICE, ||African dominoes, ||cubes, ||devil's-bones, ||ivory, ||tats
||**2** ***syn*** DOLLAR, bill, ||buck, ||fish, ||frogskin, ||ironman, oner, ||skin, ||smacker, ||smackeroo

bone (up) *vb* ***syn*** CRAM 4, ||mug up

bone-dry *adj* **1** ***syn*** DRY 1, arid, droughty, moistureless, sere, thirsty, unwatered, waterless

---

syn synonym(s) — *rel* related word(s)
idiom idiomatic equivalent(s) — *con* contrasted word(s)
ant antonym(s) — * vulgar
|| use limited; if in doubt, see a dictionary
The first word in a synonym list when printed in SMALL CAPITALS shows where there is more information about the group. For a more efficient use of this book see Explanatory Notes.

2 *syn* DRY 3, teetotal

bonehead *n syn* DUNCE, blockhead, clodpate, hammerhead, knucklehead, muttonhead, numskull, thickhead, thickskull, woodenhead

boneless *adj syn* WEAK 4, emasculate, forceless, impotent, inadequate, ineffective, ineffectual, invertebrate, slack-spined, wan

boner *n* **1** *syn* ERROR 2, blooper, blunder, bull, bungle, fluff, lapse, mistake, slip, trip

2 *syn* FAUX PAS, blooper, ‖boo-boo, break, gaffe, impropriety, indecorum, solecism

‖**boneyard** *n syn* CEMETERY, ‖boot hill, burial ground, burying ground, God's acre, graveyard, memorial park, necropolis, polyandrium, potter's field

bong *vb syn* RING, bell, chime, knell, peal, toll

boniface *n syn* SALOONKEEPER, barkeeper, innholder, innkeeper, ‖publican, saloonist, taverner

‖**bonkers** *adj syn* INSANE 1, ‖batty, bedlamite, brainsick, ‖buggy, ‖bughouse, ‖bugs, crackbrained, ‖crackers, ‖cracky

bonne bouche *n syn* DELICACY, dainty, goody, kickshaw, morsel, tidbit (*or* titbit), treat

‖**bonnet** *n syn* DECOY 2, blind, ‖booster, capper, shill, shillaber, stick

‖**bonny** *adj syn* BEAUTIFUL, attractive, beauteous, comely, fair, good-looking, handsome, lovely, pretty, pulchritudinous

bon vivant *n syn* EPICURE, gastronome, gastronomer, gastronomist, gourmand, gourmet

rel bon viveur, boulevardier, high liver, man-about-town, sport

bony *adj syn* LEAN, angular, gaunt, lank, lanky, rawboned, scraggy, scrawny, skinny, spare

boo *n syn* RASPBERRY, bazoo, bird, ‖Bronx cheer, catcall, hiss, hoot, pooh, pooh-pooh, ‖razz

boo *n syn* MARIJUANA, cannabis, grass, ‖Mary Jane, moocah, pot, ‖tea, weed

boob *n* **1** *syn* DUNCE, booby, chump, dolt, dolthead, fathead, goof, ‖goon, lunkhead, oaf

2 *syn* PHILISTINE, Babbitt, boeotian, middlebrow

‖**boo–boo** *n syn* FAUX PAS, blooper, boner, break, gaffe, impropriety, indecorum, solecism

booby *n syn* DUNCE, boob, chump, dolt, dolthead, fathead, goof, ‖goon, lunkhead, oak

booby hatch *n syn* ASYLUM 3, ‖bughouse, crazy house, loony bin, madhouse, ‖nuthouse

booby trap *n syn* PITFALL, deadfall, mousetrap, springe, trapfall

boodle *n* **1** *syn* FORTUNE 4, ‖bomb, bundle, mint, packet, pile, pot, ‖roll, wad

2 *syn* SPOIL, booty, loot, plunder, plunderage, prize, ‖spreaghery, ‖spulzie, swag

boodle *vb syn* CHEAT, beat, bilk, chisel, chouse, cozen, defraud, diddle, do, flimflam

---

syn synonym(s) *rel* related word(s)
idiom idiomatic equivalent(s) *con* contrasted word(s)
ant antonym(s) * vulgar
‖ use limited; if in doubt, see a dictionary
The first word in a synonym list when printed in SMALL CAPITALS shows where there is more information about the group. For a more efficient use of this book see Explanatory Notes.

boohoo *vb syn* CRY 2, blub, blubber, ‖pipe, sob, wail, weep

book *n* **1** a collection of folded, cut, bound, and usually printed sheets <a *book* of poems>

syn tome, volume

rel publication, work, writing; scroll; booklet, brochure, folder, leaflet, magazine, pamphlet; compendium, handbook, manual, monograph, textbook, tract, treatise; codex; novel

2 *cap* **Book** *syn* BIBLE, Holy Writ, Sacred Writ, Scripture

book *vb* **1** *syn* LIST 3, catalog, enroll, inscribe

2 *syn* TIME 1, schedule

3 *syn* RESERVE 2, bespeak, preengage

bookdealer *n* one who deals in books <sold his library to a *bookdealer*>

syn bibliopole, bookman, bookseller

rel bouquiniste

bookie *n syn* BOOKMAKER, layer

bookish *adj syn* PEDANTIC, academic, book-learned, booky, quodlibetic, scholastic

rel booksy, highbrow

book–learned *adj syn* PEDANTIC, academic, bookish, booky, quodlibetic, scholastic

bookmaker *n* one who determines odds and receives and pays off bets <*bookmakers* who welsh on paying off winners>

syn bookie, layer

rel pricemaker; runner

bookman *n syn* BOOKDEALER, bibliopole, bookseller

bookseller *n syn* BOOKDEALER, bibliopole, bookman

booky *adj syn* PEDANTIC, academic, bookish, book-learned, quodlibetic, scholastic

boom *n* **1** *syn* BANG 2, blast, burst, clap, crack, crash, slam, smash, wham

2 *syn* PROSPERITY 4, prosperousness

boomerang *vb syn* BACKFIRE, backlash, bounce (back), kick back

booming *adj syn* FLOURISHING, prospering, prosperous, roaring, robust, thrifty, thriving

boon *n* **1** *syn* GIFT 1, benevolence, ‖compliment, favor, largess, present

2 *syn* GOOD 1, advantage, benediction, benefit, blessing, godsend

boon *adj syn* MERRY, blithe, blithesome, festive, gay, gleeful, jocund, jolly, jovial, mirthful

‖**boondocks** *n pl syn* FRONTIER 2, backcountry, backland, backwash, backwater, backwoods, ‖boonies, bush, hinterland, sticks

‖**boonies** *n pl syn* FRONTIER 2, backcountry, backland, backwash, backwater, backwoods, ‖boondocks, bush, hinterland, sticks

boor *n* an uncouth ungainly fellow <an ill-mannered *boor*>

syn ‖bosthoon, chuff, churl, clodhopper, clown, grobian, mucker

rel barbarian, vulgarian; looby, lubber; farmer, loon, rustic, swain; ‖carl; bohunk; boob, buffoon, oaf

con slicker, smoothy; gentleman; cosmopolitan, cosmopolite, sophisticate

boorish *adj* uncouth in manner or appearance <a *boorish* fellow lacking all grace>

syn churlish, cloddish, clodhopping, clownish, ill-bred, loutish, lowbred, lubberly, lumpish, robustious, rugged,

swainish, uncivilized, uncultured, unpolished, unrefined; *compare* COARSE 3
rel barbarian, barbaric, outlandish, tasteless, vulgar; bucolic, countrified, inurbane, provincial, rustic, yokelish; ill-mannered, impolite, rude, uncivil, ungracious; graceless, unpoised
con cultivated, cultured, refined; suave, urbane; courteous, courtly, genteel, polite, well-bred; graceful, gracious, poised

boost *vb* **1** *syn* RAISE 9, hike, increase, jack (up), jump, put up, up
2 *syn* INCREASE 1, aggrandize, augment, beef (up), enlarge, expand, extend, heighten, magnify, multiply
3 *syn* PROMOTE 3, advertise, plug, push
‖**4** *syn* SHOPLIFT

boost *n syn* RISE 3, breakthrough, hike, increase, upgrade, wax

‖**booster** *n syn* DECOY 2, blind, ‖bonnet, capper, shill, shillaber, stick

boot *n* **1** *syn* THRILL, bang, kick, wallop
2 *syn* NOVICE, apprentice, beginner, colt, freshman, neophyte, rookie, tenderfoot, tyro

boot (out) *vb* **1** *syn* EJECT 1, chase, chuck, dismiss, evict, extrude, kick out, out, throw out
2 *syn* DISMISS 3, ax, bounce, ‖can, cashier, discharge, fire, kick out, sack, terminate

‖**boot hill** *n syn* CEMETERY, ‖boneyard, burial ground, burying ground, God's acre, graveyard, memorial park, necropolis, polyandrium, potter's field

bootleg *n syn* MOONSHINE 2, bathtub gin, ‖blockade, ‖busthead, ‖hooch, mountain dew, white lightning

bootleg *vb syn* SMUGGLE, contraband, run

bootless *adj syn* FUTILE, abortive, fruitless, ineffective, ineffectual, unavailable, unavailing, unproductive, useless, vain
rel frustrating; profitless, worthless

bootlick *vb syn* FAWN, apple-polish, ‖brownnose, cower, cringe, grovel, honey (up), kowtow, toady, truckle

bootlick *n syn* SYCOPHANT, bootlicker, ‖clawback, footlicker, lickspit, lickspittle, toad, toadeater, toady, truckler

bootlicker *n syn* SYCOPHANT, bootlick, ‖clawback, footlicker, lickspit, lickspittle, spaniel, toad, toadeater, toady

bootlicking *adj syn* FAWNING, cowering, cringing, groveling, kowtowing, parasitic, sycophantic, toadying, toadyish, truckling

booty *n syn* SPOIL, boodle, loot, plunder, plunderage, prize, ‖spreaghery, ‖spulzie, swag

booze *vb syn* DRINK 3, guzzle, imbibe, liquor (up), soak, swig, swill, swizzle, tank up, tipple

booze *n* **1** *syn* LIQUOR 2, aqua vitae, drink, firewater, grog, ‖hooch, ‖juice, ‖sauce, spirit(s), tipple
2 *syn* BINGE 1, bat, bender, brannigan, bum, carouse, drunk, jag, soak, souse

‖**boozed** *adj syn* INTOXICATED 1, ‖boozy, ‖canned, disguised, drunk, inebriated, ‖lushed, muddled, pixilated, ‖plastered

boozehound *n syn* DRUNKARD, ‖bloat, ‖blotter, boozer, drunk, guzzler, inebriate, lush, ‖shicker, sponge

boozer *n* **1** *syn* DRUNKARD, ‖bloat, ‖blotter, boozehound, drunk, guzzler, inebriate, lush, soak, sot
‖**2** *syn* BAR 5, barroom, drinkery, ‖gin mill, lounge, pothouse, ‖rum-hole, saloon, tavern, watering hole

‖**boozy** *adj syn* INTOXICATED 1, ‖boozed, ‖canned, disguised, drunk, inebriated, ‖lushed, muddled, pixilated, ‖plastered

bop *n syn* BLOW 1, bash, bat, belt, biff, ‖douse, pound, smack, sock, whop

borasca *n syn* POVERTY 1, destitution, impecuniousness, impoverishment, indigence, need, neediness, pauperism, penury, want

bordello *n syn* BROTHEL, bagnio, bawdy house, cathouse, ‖hookshop, ‖joyhouse, parlor house, sporting house, stew, whorehouse

border *n* **1** a line or relatively narrow space that marks the outermost bound of something <the *border* of the rug>
syn brim, brink, edge, fringe, hem, margin, perimeter, periphery, rim, selvage, skirt, verge; *compare* CIRCUMFERENCE
rel butts and bounds, lines, metes and bounds; bound, circumference, confine, end, extremity, limit, termination; boundary, frontier, march, pale; beginning, door, entrance, threshold; sideline; lip
con inside, interior; recesses; center; body, bulk, mass, whole
2 *syn* FRONTIER 1, borderland, march, marchland

border *vb* **1** to form a border to <hedges *border* the park>
syn bound, define, edge, fringe, hem, margin, outline, rim, skirt, surround, verge
rel circumscribe, encircle, enclose, frame; contour, delineate, mark (off), outline, set off; flank, line, side; trim
2 *syn* ADJOIN, abut, butt (on *or* against), communicate, join, line, march, neighbor, touch, verge
3 to come to be closely similiar to a specified thing <ideas that *border* on the absurd>
syn approach, trench, verge
rel approximate, compare, near
idiom come close (*or* near) to

bordering *adj syn* ADJACENT 3, abutting, adjoining, approximal, conterminous, contiguous, juxtaposed, touching

borderland *n syn* FRONTIER 1, border, march, marchland

borderline *adj syn* DOUBTFUL 1, ambiguous, dubitable, equivocal, open, problematic, uncertain, unclear, undecided, unsettled

bore *vb* **1** *syn* PERFORATE, drill, prick, ‖pritch, punch, puncture
2 *syn* GAZE 1, gape, ‖gaup (*or* gawp), gawk, glare, gloat, goggle, peer, stare

bore *vb* to induce a state of boredom in <*bored* to death by his endless sermon>
syn ennui, pall, tire, weary

---

syn synonym(s) *rel* related word(s)
idiom idiomatic equivalent(s) *con* contrasted word(s)
ant antonym(s) * vulgar
‖ use limited; if in doubt, see a dictionary
The first word in a synonym list when printed in SMALL CAPITALS shows where there is more information about the group. For a more efficient use of this book see Explanatory Notes.

rel jade; fatigue, wear; annoy, irk, irritate; afflict, bother, discomfort
idiom put one to sleep
con amuse, entertain; excite, fascinate, intrigue; absorb, beguile, engross, enthrall, grip; enliven, freshen, invigorate, quicken, stimulate
ant interest

boreal *adj* ***syn*** COLD 1, arctic, chill, chilly, cool, freezing, frosty, gelid, glacial, icy

boredom *n* ***syn*** TEDIUM, doldrums, ennui, yawn
rel fatigue, weariness; disgust, distaste
con amusement, diversion, entertainment; excitement, fascination; engrossment, enthrallment

boresome *adj* ***syn*** IRKSOME, boring, drudging, tedious, tiresome, tiring
rel deadly, dreary, dull, humdrum, monotonous
con amusing, entertaining; exciting, fascinating, intriguing; absorbing, engrossing, enthralling, gripping, stimulating
ant interesting

boring *adj* ***syn*** IRKSOME, boresome, drudging, tedious, tiresome, tiring

born *adj* ***syn*** INHERENT, built-in, congenital, constitutional, deep-seated, essential, inborn, inbred, ingenerate, intrinsic

‖**born** *vb* ***syn*** BEAR 5, ‖birth, bring forth, deliver

borné *adj* ***syn*** LITTLE 2, ineffectual, limited, mean, narrow, paltry, set, small

bosh *n* ***syn*** NONSENSE 2, balderdash, ‖baloney, blatherskite, ‖bull, bunkum, claptrap, hokum, malarkey, rubbish

bosom *n* ***syn*** HEART 1, breast, soul

bosomy *adj* ***syn*** BUXOM, busty, chesty, full-bosomed

boss *n* ***syn*** LEADER 2, chief, chieftain, cock, dominator, head, headman, hierarch, honcho, master

‖**boss** *adj* ***syn*** EXCELLENT, bang-up, capital, champion, ‖dandy, famous, fine, first-rate, top, whiz-bang

boss *vb* ***syn*** SUPERVISE, chaperon, overlook, oversee, quarterback, superintend, survey

bossy *adj* ***syn*** MASTERFUL 1, domineering, high-handed, imperative, imperial, imperious, magisterial, overbearing, peremptory

‖**bosthoon** *n* ***syn*** BOOR, chuff, churl, clodhopper, clown, grobian, mucker

Boswell *n* ***syn*** BIOGRAPHER, autobiographer, autobiographist, memoirist

botch *vb* to do or proceed ineffectively or badly through clumsiness, stupidity, or lack of ability <a complete incompetent—*botches* everything he puts his hand to>
syn bitch (up), ‖blow, blunder, bobble, boggle, bollix, bugger up, bumble, bungle, cobble, dub, flub, fluff, foozle, *fuck up, fumble, goof (up), gum (up), louse up, mess, ‖muck, mucker, muff, ‖screw (up)
rel butcher, mangle, murder, mutilate; mar, ruin, spoil; destroy, wreck; hash; tinker; misconduct, mishandle, mismanage; confuse, disorder
idiom play (*or* wreak) havoc with, play hell with

botch *n* ***syn*** MESS 3, botchery, hash, mess-up, mix-up, muddle, mull, muss, shambles

botchery *n* ***syn*** MESS 3, botch, hash, mess-up, mix-up, muddle, mull, muss, shambles

botchy *adj* ***syn*** SLIPSHOD 3, careless, messy, slapdash, sloppy, slovenly, unthorough, untidy

bother *vb* **1** ***syn*** DISCOMPOSE 1, agitate, discombobulate, disquiet, disturb, flurry, fluster, perturb, unhinge, upset
2 ***syn*** ANNOY 1, abrade, ‖bug, chafe, exercise, fret, irk, provoke, ruffle, vex

bother *n* **1** ***syn*** ANNOYANCE 2, aggravation, botheration, exasperation, pother
2 ***syn*** ANNOYANCE 3, besetment, botheration, botherment, exasperation, irritant, nuisance, pest, pester, plague
3 ***syn*** INCONVENIENCE, bothersomeness, ‖disconvenience, troublesomeness

botheration *n* **1** ***syn*** ANNOYANCE 2, aggravation, bother, exasperation, pother
2 ***syn*** ANNOYANCE 3, besetment, bother, botherment, exasperation, irritant, nuisance, pest, pester, plague

bothering *n* ***syn*** ANNOYANCE 1, harassment, irking, provocation, provoking, vexation, vexing

botherment *n* ***syn*** ANNOYANCE 3, besetment, bother, botheration, exasperation, irritant, nuisance, pest, pester, plague

bothersomeness *n* ***syn*** INCONVENIENCE, bother, ‖disconvenience, troublesomeness

bottega *n* ***syn*** STUDIO, atelier

bottle (up) *vb* **1** ***syn*** RESTRAIN
2 ***syn*** CORNER, collar, tree

bottom *n* **1** the under surface as opposed to the top surface <gum was stuck to the *bottom* of her shoe>
syn sole, underneath, underside, undersurface
rel belly, underbelly, underbody; base, floor, foot, ground
con acme, apex, cap, crest, crown, tip, upper
ant top
2 ***syn*** BUTTOCKS, *ass, backside, behind, breech, derriere, fanny, heinie (*or* hiney), posterior, rear end
3 the lower or lowest point <the *bottom* of the page>
syn base, foot, nadir
rel basement, floor, ground; end; low
con acme, apex, pinnacle, zenith
ant top
4 ***syn*** BASE 1, basement, bed, bedrock, footing, foundation, ground, rest, seat, substructure
5 ***syn*** ESSENCE 2, essentiality, marrow, pith, quintessence, quintessential, soul, stuff, substance, virtuality

bottom *vb* ***syn*** BASE, establish, found, ground, predicate, rest, stay

bottom *adj* **1** ***syn*** BOTTOMMOST, lowermost, lowest, nethermost, rock-bottom, undermost
2 ***syn*** FUNDAMENTAL 1, basal, basic, foundational, primary, radical, underlying

bottom dog *n* ***syn*** VICTIM 2, casualty, prey, underdog

bottomless *adj* **1** ***syn*** BASELESS, foundationless, gratuitous, groundless, uncalled-for, unfounded, ungrounded, unwarranted

rel reasonless, unjustifiable, unsupportable
2 extremely deep <the *bottomless* sea>
syn abysmal, fathomless, plumbless, plummetless, soundless, unfathomable; *compare* DEEP 1
rel endless, infinite

bottommost *adj* that is at the very bottom <the ladder's *bottommost* rung>
syn bottom, lowermost, lowest, nethermost, rock-bottom, undermost
con top, upper, uppermost
ant topmost

bough *n* ***syn*** LIMB, branch

bought *adj* ***syn*** READY-MADE, ||boughten, ready-to-wear, store, store-bought, ||store-boughten

||**boughten** *adj* ***syn*** READY-MADE, bought, ready-to-wear, store, store-bought, ||store-boughten

boulevard *n* ***syn*** WAY 1, artery, avenue, ||drag, highway, path, road, street, thoroughfare, track

bounce *vb* **1** ***syn*** JUMP 1, bound, hop, hurdle, leap, lop, saltate, spring, vault
2 ***syn*** DISMISS 3, ax, boot (out), ||can, cashier, discharge, fire, kick out, sack, terminate
||**3** ***syn*** INTIMIDATE, bludgeon, bluster, browbeat, bulldoze, bully, bullyrag, cow, dragoon, hector

bounce (back) *vb* **1** ***syn*** RECOVER 3, rebound, snap back
2 ***syn*** BACKFIRE, backlash, boomerang, kick back

bouncer *n* ||**1** ***syn*** LIE, canard, falsehood, falsity, fib, misrepresentation, prevarication, tale, untruism, untruth
rel exaggeration, hyperbole, overstatement
idiom tall tale
2 a person employed to restrain or eject disorderly persons (as at a bar) <tossed out by the *bouncer*>
syn chucker, ||chucker-out, houseman
rel goon, muscleman, strong arm

bouncy *adj* ***syn*** ELASTIC 2, airy, buoyant, effervescent, expansive, resilient, volatile

bound *n* **1** *usu* **bounds** *pl* ***syn*** ENVIRONS 1, boundary, compass, confine(s), limits, precinct(s), purlieus
2 ***syn*** LIMIT 1, confine(s), end, limitation, term

bound *vb* **1** ***syn*** DEMARCATE 1, delimit, delimitate, determine, limit, mark (out), measure
2 ***syn*** BORDER 1, define, edge, fringe, hem, margin, rim, skirt, surround, verge

bound *adj* **1** ***syn*** FINITE, bounded, limited
2 obliged to serve a master or in a clearly defined capacity for a certain length of time by the terms of a contract or mutual agreement <brought to the American colonies as a *bound* servant>
syn apprenticed, articled, indentured
rel contracted; enslaved
con free, freed
3 ***syn*** CONSTIPATED, astricted, costive, obstipated

bound *vb* ***syn*** JUMP 1, bounce, hop, hurdle, leap, lop, saltate, spring, vault

boundary *n* ***syn*** ENVIRONS 1, bound(s), compass, confine(s), limits, precinct(s), purlieus

bounded *adj* ***syn*** FINITE, bound, limited
ant unbounded

bounder *n* ***syn*** CAD, cur, rotter, yellow dog

boundless *adj* ***syn*** LIMITLESS, endless, immeasurable, indefinite, infinite, measureless, unbounded, unlimited, unmeasured

bounteous *adj* **1** ***syn*** LIBERAL 1, bountiful, free, freehanded, generous, handsome, munificent, openhanded, unsparing
con cheap, illiberal, scant
ant niggardly
2 ***syn*** PLENTIFUL, abundant, ample, bountiful, copious, generous, liberal, plenteous, plenty
con insufficient, scant, sparse

bountiful *adj* **1** ***syn*** LIBERAL 1, bounteous, free, freehanded, generous, handsome, munificent, openhanded, unsparing
2 ***syn*** PLENTIFUL, abundant, ample, bounteous, copious, generous, liberal, plenteous, plenty

bouquet *n* **1** cut flowers arranged for wear or display <a *bouquet* of spring flowers>
syn nosegay, posy
rel arrangement; boutonniere, corsage; spray; wreath; garland, festoon; lei
2 ***syn*** COMPLIMENT 1, kudo, orchid(s)
3 ***syn*** FRAGRANCE, aroma, balm, incense, perfume, redolence, scent, spice

Bourbon *n* ***syn*** REACTIONARY, blimp, diehard, reactionarist, reactionist, royalist, ultraconservative, white

bout *n* **1** ***syn*** SPELL 1, go, shift, stint, time, tour, trick, turn
2 ***syn*** SIEGE, go

boutade *n* ***syn*** CAPRICE, bee, conceit, crotchet, fancy, freak, humor, megrim, vagary, whim

bow *vb* ***syn*** YIELD 2, buckle (under), capitulate, cave, defer, knuckle, knuckle under, submit, succumb

bow *n* **1** ***syn*** CURVE, arc, arch, bend, curvation, curvature, round
2 ***syn*** TURN 4, angle, bend, flection, flexure, turning

bow *vb* ***syn*** CURVE, bend, crook, round

bowdlerize *vb* ***syn*** CENSOR, blip, expurgate, screen

bowed *adj* **1** ***syn*** CURVED, arced, arched, arciform, arrondi, bent, curvilinear, round, rounded
2 ***syn*** BOWLEGGED, bandy, bandy-legged

bowel *vb* ***syn*** EVISCERATE, disembowel, draw, embowel, exenterate, gut, paunch

bower *n* ***syn*** ARBOR, pergola

bowery *n* ***syn*** SKID ROW, skid road

bowl *n* ***syn*** STADIUM, coliseum, stade

||**bowl** (down *or* out) *vb* ***syn*** WHIP 2, beat, ||clobber, drub, dust, lambaste, ||larrup, lick, overwhelm, shellac

bowl (down *or* over) *vb* ***syn*** FELL 1, bring down, down, flatten, floor, ground, knock down, knock over, lay low, level

bowlegged *adj* having legs bent outward <a *bowlegged* cowboy>
syn bandy, bandy-legged, bowed
rel bent, crooked, curved, misshapen

bowwow *n* ***syn*** DOG 1, canine, hound, ||pooch, tyke

---

syn synonym(s) ***rel*** related word(s)
idiom idiomatic equivalent(s) ***con*** contrasted word(s)
ant antonym(s) * vulgar
|| use limited; if in doubt, see a dictionary
The first word in a synonym list when printed in SMALL CAPITALS shows where there is more information about the group. For a more efficient use of this book see Explanatory Notes.

‖**box** *n* **1** ***syn*** HUT, cabin, ‖caboose, camp, cot, cottage, lodge, shack, shanty
2 ***syn*** PREDICAMENT, corner, fix, hole, impasse, jam, pickle, plight, scrape, spot

box *n* ***syn*** CUFF, buffet, chop, clout, haymaker, ‖paste, punch, slap, smack, sock

box *vb* ***syn*** SLAP 1, blip, buffet, cuff, smack, spank, ‖wherret

boxing *n* the art of attack and defense with the fists practiced as a sport <he liked *boxing*—at least as a spectator sport>
syn fisticuffs, prizefighting, pugilism, ring

boy *n* **1** a male person not fully matured <a *boy* of nine>
syn lad, laddie, shaveling, son, stripling, tad
rel gamin, ragamuffin, street arab, urchin; hobbledehoy, whippersnapper; schoolboy
idiom little shaver, small fry
2 ***syn*** MAN 3, ‖bloke, buck, chap, fellow, ‖gee, gent, gentleman, guy, he

boyfriend *n* **1** a man who is a woman's usual or preferred escort or companion <went to the movies with her *boyfriend*>
syn beau, gentleman friend, swain, young man
rel admirer
2 a man who shares with a woman a strong and usually sexually oriented mutual attraction <moved in with her *boyfriend*>
syn beau, beloved, flame, inamorato, lover, steady, sweetheart, truelove
rel crush, heartthrob; fiancé
3 ***syn*** LOVER 1, fancy man, man, master, paramour

brabble *vb* ***syn*** QUARREL, bicker, caterwaul, fall out, row, scrap, spat, squabble, tiff, wrangle

brabble *n* **1** ***syn*** QUARREL, altercation, beef, bickering, brannigan, dispute, falling-out, hassle, squabble, wrangle
2 ***syn*** CHATTER, babble, cackle, chat, clack, gab, jabber, palaver, prattle, tittle-tattle

brace *n* **1** ***syn*** COUPLE, doublet, duo, dyad, pair, twosome
2 ***syn*** SUPPORT 3, buttress, column, prop, shore, stay, underpinner, underpinning, underpropping
3 **braces** *pl* ***syn*** SUSPENDERS, ‖gallows, ‖galluses

brace *vb* **1** ***syn*** GIRD 3, fortify, prepare, ready, steel, strengthen
2 ***syn*** SUPPORT 4, bear up, bolster, buttress, carry, prop, shore (up), sustain, upbear, uphold
3 ***syn*** BEG, appeal, beseech, crave, entreat, implore, importune, plead, pray, supplicate

bracing *adj* ***syn*** INVIGORATING, animating, exhilarating, exhilarative, quickening, stimulating, stimulative, tonic, vitalizing

---

syn synonym(s) ***rel*** related word(s)
idiom idiomatic equivalent(s) ***con*** contrasted word(s)
ant antonym(s) * vulgar
‖ use limited; if in doubt, see a dictionary
The first word in a synonym list when printed in SMALL CAPITALS shows where there is more information about the group. For a more efficient use of this book see Explanatory Notes.

---

bracket *vb* **1** ***syn*** JOIN 1, associate, combine, conjoin, connect, couple, link, relate, unite, wed
2 ***syn*** COMPARE 2, collate, contrast

brag *vb* ***syn*** BOAST, blow, cock-a-doodle-doo, crow, gasconade, mouth, prate, puff, rodomontade, vaunt
con apologize, deprecate

braggadocian *adj* ***syn*** BOASTFUL, braggart, braggy, rodomontade, self-glorifying, vaunting

braggadocio *n* ***syn*** BRAGGART, blower, blowhard, boaster, bragger, ‖gasbag, puckfist, rodomont, rodomontade, vaunter

braggart *n* one who boasts <too much of a *braggart* about his strength>
syn blower, blowhard, boaster, braggadocio, bragger, ‖gasbag, puckfist, rodomont, rodomontade, vaunter
rel bluffer, blusterer, loudmouth, miles gloriosus, ranter, raver, windbag
con Milquetoast

braggart *adj* ***syn*** BOASTFUL, braggadocian, braggy, rodomontade, self-glorifying, vaunting

bragger *n* ***syn*** BRAGGART, blower, blowhard, boaster, braggadocio, ‖gasbag, puckfist, rodomont, rodomontade, vaunter

braggy *adj* ***syn*** BOASTFUL, braggadocian, braggart, rodomontade, self-glorifying, vaunting

Brahmin *n* ***syn*** INTELLECTUAL 2, double-dome, egghead, highbrow

brain *n* **1** ***syn*** MIND 1, gray matter, head, ‖upper story, ‖upperworks, wit
2 ***syn*** INTELLECT 2, intellectual, intelligence
3 *often* **brains** *pl* ***syn*** INTELLIGENCE 1, brainpower, mentality, mother wit, sense, wit

brainchild *n* ***syn*** INVENTION, coinage, contrivance

brainless *adj* ***syn*** SIMPLE 3, asinine, ‖buffle-headed, foolish, mindless, nitwitted, senseless, unwitty, weak-minded, witless

brainpower *n* ***syn*** INTELLIGENCE 1, brain(s), mentality, mother wit, sense, wit

brainsick *adj* ***syn*** INSANE 1, ‖batty, bedlamite, cracked, crazed, crazy, daft, demented, deranged, lunatic

brainwork *n* ***syn*** THOUGHT 1, cerebration, cogitation, deliberation, reflection, speculation

brainy *adj* ***syn*** INTELLIGENT 2, alert, bright, brilliant, clever, knowing, quick-witted, ready-witted, sharp, smart

brake *vb* ***syn*** HINDER, bar, block, dam, impede, obstruct, overslaugh
rel slow, stop

branch *n* **1** ***syn*** LIMB, bough
rel branchlet
2 ***syn*** CREEK 2, brook, ‖burn, gill, race, ‖rindle, rivulet, ‖run, runnel, stream

brand *n* **1** ***syn*** MARK 7, logo, logotype, trademark
2 ***syn*** STIGMA, bar sinister, black eye, blot, blur, odium, onus, slur, spot, stain

brandish *vb* ***syn*** SHOW 4, display, disport, exhibit, expose, flash, flaunt, parade, show off, trot out

brand-new *adj* conspicuously new and unused <a *brand-new* car right out of the showroom>
syn fire-new, mint, spang-new, spanking-new, span-new, spick-and-span
rel untouched, unused; clean, fresh, pristine
con hand-me-down, secondhand, used; outworn, shabby, worn, worn-out

ant old

brannigan *n* **1** ***syn*** BINGE 1, bat, bender, booze, bum, bust, carouse, drunk, spree, wassail

2 ***syn*** QUARREL, altercation, brabble, dispute, falling-out, fight, hassle, row, ruckus, wrangle

brash *adj* **1** ***syn*** RASH 1, hasty, hot-headed, ill-advised, incautious, inconsiderate, mad-brained, madcap, reckless, thoughtless

2 ***syn*** EXUBERANT 1, ebullient, effervescent, high-spirited, vivacious

3 ***syn*** TACTLESS, impolitic, maladroit, undiplomatic, unpolitic, untactful

4 ***syn*** PRESUMPTUOUS, forward, overweening, presuming, pushful, pushing, self-asserting, self-assertive, uppish, uppity

rel bold, brazen; rash, reckless; headlong, impetuous; cocksure

brashness *n* **1** ***syn*** TEMERITY, assurance, audacity, hardihood, hardiness, nerve

2 ***syn*** EFFRONTERY, brass, cheek, confidence, ‖crust, face, gall, nerve, presumption

brass *n* ‖**1** ***syn*** MONEY, ‖blunt, ‖bread, ‖cabbage, ‖chips, ‖dinero, ‖do-re-mi, ‖gelt, ‖jack, ‖long green

2 ***syn*** EFFRONTERY, brashness, cheek, confidence, ‖crust, face, gall, nerve, presumption

brass ankle** *n* ***syn MULATTO, high yellow

brassbound *adj* **1** ***syn*** ILLIBERAL, bigoted, hidebound, intolerant, narrow, narrow-minded, small-minded, unenlarged

2 ***syn*** INFLEXIBLE 2, adamant, inexorable, obdurate, relentless, rigid, single-minded, unbending, uncompromising, unyielding

3 ***syn*** PRESUMPTUOUS, brash, forward, overweening, presuming, pushful, self-asserting, self-assertive, uppish, uppity

brass hat *n* ***syn*** SUPERIOR, better, elder, higher-up, senior

brassy *adj* **1** ***syn*** SHAMELESS, arrant, barefaced, blatant, brazen, brazenfaced, impudent, overbold, unabashed, unblushing

2 ***syn*** BRAZEN 4, aeneous

brave *adj* **1** having or showing no fear when faced with something dangerous, difficult, or unknown <made a *brave* attempt to save the burning house>

syn audacious, aweless, bold, boldhearted, bravehearted, chin-up, courageous, dauntless, doughty, fearless, gallant, game, greathearted, ‖gutsy, heroic, intrepid, lionhearted, manful, manly, ‖plucked, plucky, soldierly, spunky, stalwart, stout, stouthearted, unafraid, unblenched, unblenching, undauntable, undaunted, unfearful, unfearing, valiant, valorous

rel daring, defiant, gritty, hardy, mettlesome, resolute, spirited, steadfast, unapprehensive, undismayed, unflinching, unfrightened, unquailing, unshrinking, unswerving, unwincing, unyielding, venturesome; chivalrous, noble, preux; confident

con cringing, flinching, frightened, pusillanimous, scared, shrinking, timid; chickenhearted, fainthearted, lily-livered, nerveless, soft, spineless, unmanly, weakhearted, weak-kneed, yellow

ant cowardly, craven

2 ***syn*** COLORFUL, bright, colory, gay, vivid

3 ***syn*** GOOD 1, advantageous, benefic, beneficial, favorable, favoring, helpful, propitious, toward, useful

brave *vb* ***syn*** FACE 3, ‖banter, beard, challenge, dare, defy, front, outdare, outface, venture

con avoid

bravehearted *adj* ***syn*** BRAVE 1, bold, boldhearted, courageous, dauntless, fearless, heroic, lionhearted, manly, plucky

bravery *n* ***syn*** FINERY, ‖best bib and tucker, frippery, full dress, ‖glad rags, regalia, Sunday best, war paint

bravo *n* ***syn*** ASSASSIN, cutthroat, gun, gunman, ‖gunsel, gunslinger, hatchet man, hit man, torpedo, triggerman

brawl *vb* ***syn*** QUARREL, bicker, brabble, caterwaul, row, scrap, spat, squabble, tiff, wrangle

brawl *n* **1** ***syn*** QUARREL, altercation, bickering, dispute, dust, dustup, feud, fight, hassle, squabble

2 a rough, noisy, and often prolonged hand-to-hand fight usually involving several people <windows and furniture were broken in the barroom *brawl*>

syn affray, bobbery, broil, dogfight, donnybrook, fight, fracas, fray, free-for-all, knock-down-and-drag-out, maul, melee, mellay, ‖muss, rough-and-tumble, row, rowdydow, ruction, scrap, scrimmage, scuffle, set-to; *compare* QUARREL

rel fistfight, fisticuffs, slugfest; struggle, tussle; conflict, contention, contest, riot; altercation, embroilment, imbroglio, quarrel, wrangle; commotion, disturbance, eruption, hubbub, pandemonium, ruckus, rumpus, turn-to, ‖turnup, upheaval, uproar; incident, ‖rumble

idiom a coming to blows, exchange of blows

brawling *adj* ***syn*** QUARRELSOME 2, battlesome, brawlsome, brawly, scrappy

brawlsome *adj* ***syn*** QUARRELSOME 2, battlesome, brawling, brawly, scrappy

brawly *adj* ***syn*** QUARRELSOME 2, battlesome, brawling, brawlsome, scrappy

brawn *n* ***syn*** MUSCLE 1, beef, might, thew

brawny *adj* ***syn*** MUSCULAR 2, athletic, sinewy

rel lusty, red-blooded, vigorous, vital; tough

con lanky, lean, rawboned, skinny, thin

ant scrawny

bray *vb* ***syn*** PULVERIZE 1, buck, comminute, contriturate, crush, powder, triturate

brazen *adj* **1** ***syn*** INSOLENT 2, audacious, bold, ‖boldacious, contumelious, impertinent, impudent, procacious, saucy

2 ***syn*** SHAMELESS, arrant, barefaced, blatant, brassy, brazenfaced, impudent, overbold, unabashed, unblushing

3 ***syn*** GAUDY, blatant, chintzy, flashy, garish, glaring, loud, meretricious, tawdry, tinsel

4 of the color of polished brass <a *brazen* sky at sunset>

syn aeneous, brassy

rel bronze

---

syn synonym(s) *rel* related word(s)
idiom idiomatic equivalent(s) ***con*** contrasted word(s)
ant antonym(s) * vulgar
‖ use limited; if in doubt, see a dictionary
The first word in a synonym list when printed in SMALL CAPITALS shows where there is more information about the group. For a more efficient use of this book see Explanatory Notes.

brazenfaced *adj* ***syn*** SHAMELESS, arrant, barefaced, blatant, brassy, brazen, impudent, overbold, unabashed, unblushing

breach *n* **1** the act or offense of failing to keep the law or to do what law, duty, or obligation requires <sued for *breach* of contract> <his behavior was a gross *breach* of good manners>
syn contravention, infraction, infringement, transgression, trespass, violation
rel disregard, nonobservance; delinquency, dereliction, neglect
con conformance, conformity, observance
ant observance
2 ***syn*** GAP 1, break, discontinuity, hole, opening
3 an interruption of accustomed friendly relations <a trivial misunderstanding caused a *breach* between the brothers>
syn break, fissure, fracture, rent, rift, rupture, schism, split; *compare* SCHISM 3
rel division, separation, severance; alienation, estrangement; difference, discord, disharmony, dissension, disunity, strife, variance; secession, withdrawal; falling-out, quarrel
idiom parting of ways
con integrity, solidarity, union, unity; communion, community; accord, concord, harmony
4 ***syn*** GAP 2, break, hiatus, interim, interruption, interval, lacuna

breach *vb* **1** ***syn*** OPEN 3, disrupt, hole, rupture
rel bore, penetrate
2 ***syn*** VIOLATE 1, break, contravene, infract, infringe, offend, transgress

bread *n* **1** ***syn*** FOOD 1, comestibles, edibles, feed, grub, nurture, provender, provisions, viands, victuals
2 ***syn*** LIVING, alimentation, alimony, bread and butter, keep, livelihood, maintenance, subsistence, support, sustenance
‖**3** ***syn*** MONEY, ‖cabbage, cash, ‖coin, dough, ‖greenbacks, ‖jack, ‖mazuma, ‖scratch, ‖shekels

bread and butter *n* ***syn*** LIVING, alimentation, alimony, bread, keep, livelihood, maintenance, subsistence, support, sustenance

breadth *n* **1** ***syn*** EXPANSE, amplitude, distance, expansion, space, spread, stretch
2 spaciousness of extent <the *breadth* of his knowledge on the subject is awesome>
syn amplitude, comprehensiveness, fullness, scope, wideness
rel compass, gamut, orbit, range, reach, sweep; expanse, spread, stretch
con limitation, restriction
ant narrowness

breadthen *vb* ***syn*** BROADEN, widen

---

syn synonym(s) ***rel*** related word(s)
idiom idiomatic equivalent(s) ***con*** contrasted word(s)
ant antonym(s) * vulgar
‖ use limited; if in doubt, see a dictionary
The first word in a synonym list when printed in SMALL CAPITALS shows where there is more information about the group. For a more efficient use of this book see Explanatory Notes.

break *vb* **1** ***syn*** GIVE 12, bend, cave, collapse, crumple, fold up, go, yield
2 ***syn*** PLOW, plow up, turn, turn over
3 ***syn*** VIOLATE 1, breach, contravene, infract, infringe, offend, transgress
ant observe
4 ***syn*** ESCAPE 1, abscond, ‖bunk, decamp, flee, fly, scape
5 ***syn*** FAIL 5, bust, crash, fold
idiom go broke
6 ***syn*** RUIN 3, bankrupt, bust, fold up, impoverish, pauper, pauperize
7 ***syn*** DEGRADE 1, bump, bust, declass, demerit, demote, disgrade, disrate, downgrade, reduce
8 ***syn*** DISPROVE 1, confound, confute, controvert, disconfirm, evert, rebut, refute
9 ***syn*** COMMUNICATE 1, convey, impart, pass on, transmit
10 ***syn*** SOLVE 2, ‖cipher, clear up, decipher, dissolve, puzzle out, resolve, unfold, unravel, unriddle
11 ***syn*** DECODE, crack, cryptanalyze, decipher, decrypt
12 ***syn*** HAPPEN 1, befall, betide, chance, come off, develop, fall out, go, occur, transpire
13 ***syn*** GET OUT 2, come out, leak, out, transpire
‖**14** ***syn*** CLEAR 9, burn off

break *n* **1** ***syn*** GAP 1, breach, discontinuity, hole, opening
2 ***syn*** GAP 3, breach, hiatus, interim, interruption, interval, lacuna
3 ***syn*** INTERLUDE, intermission, interregnum, interval, parenthesis
4 a usually short rest period <took a *break* for coffee>
syn blow, breath, breather, breathing space (*or* spell), respite, ten; *compare* PAUSE
5 ***syn*** BREACH 3, fissure, fracture, rent, rift, rupture, schism, split
6 ***syn*** FAUX PAS, blooper, boner, ‖boo-boo, gaffe, impropriety, indecorum, solecism
7 ***syn*** OPPORTUNITY, chance, look-in, occasion, opening, shot, show, squeak, time

breakable *adj* ***syn*** FRAGILE 1, delicate, fracturable, frail, frangible, shatterable, shattery

break down *vb* **1** ***syn*** ANALYZE, anatomize, decompose, decompound, dissect, resolve
2 ***syn*** DECAY, crumble, decompose, disintegrate, molder, putrefy, rot, spoil, taint, turn
3 ***syn*** COLLAPSE 2, cave (in), drop, ‖flake out, give out, peg out, succumb, wilt

breakdown *n* **1** ***syn*** NERVOUS BREAKDOWN, collapse, crack-up, nervous prostration
2 ***syn*** COLLAPSE 2, crack-up, crash, debacle, smash, smashup, wreck
3 ***syn*** ANALYSIS 1, breakup, dissection, resolution

break in *vb* **1** ***syn*** HOUSEBREAK
idiom break and enter
2 ***syn*** INTERRUPT 2, chime in, chip in

breakneck *adj* ***syn*** FAST 3, expeditious, expeditive, fleet, harefooted, hasty, quick, rapid, speedy, swift

break out *vb* ***syn*** ERUPT 2, burst (forth), explode

breakout *n* ***syn*** ESCAPE 1, escapement, escaping, flight, getaway, lam, ‖scape, slip

breakthrough *n* ***syn*** RISE 3, boost, hike, increase, upgrade, wax

break up *vb* **1** ***syn*** SEPARATE 1, disjoin, disjoint, dissever, disunite, divide, part, rupture, split (up), sunder
2 ***syn*** DISBAND, disperse, dissolve

breakup *n* ***syn*** ANALYSIS 1, breakdown, dissection, resolution

breast *n* ***syn*** HEART 1, bosom, soul

breast–feed *vb* ***syn*** NURSE 1, nourish, suckle

breastwork *n* ***syn*** BULWARK, bastion, parapet, rampart

breath *n* **1** ***syn*** HINT 2, dash, shade, soupçon, streak, suggestion, suspicion, touch, trace, whiff
2 ***syn*** BREAK 4, blow, breather, breathing space (*or* spell), respite, ten

breathe *vb* **1** ***syn*** BE, exist, live, move, subsist
2 ***syn*** REST 3, lay off, lie by, spell
3 to draw (as air) into and expel from the lungs < *breathe* clean air >
syn respire
rel exhale, inhale
4 ***syn*** CONFIDE 1, whisper

breathe (in) *vb* ***syn*** INHALE, inspire

breathe (out) *vb* ***syn*** EXHALE, expire, outbreathe

breather *n* ***syn*** BREAK 4, blow, breath, breathing space (*or* spell), respite, ten

breathing *n* ***syn*** INSTANT 1, crack, flash, ‖jiff, jiffy, minute, moment, second, shake, split second

breathing space (*or* **spell**) *n* ***syn*** BREAK 4, blow, breath, breather, respite, ten

breathless *adj* **1** ***syn*** EAGER, agog, anxious, appetent, ardent, athirst, avid, impatient, keen, thirsty
2 ***syn*** STUFFY 1, airless, close, stifling, stivy, suffocating, sultry

bred–in–the–bone *adj* ***syn*** INVETERATE 1, confirmed, deep-dyed, deep-rooted, deep-seated, dyed-in-the-wool, entrenched, hard-shell, settled, sworn

breech *n* ***syn*** BUTTOCKS, backside, behind, bottom, derriere, fanny, fundament, posterior, rear, rump

breed *vb* **1** ***syn*** PROCREATE 1, bear, beget, generate, multiply, produce, propagate, reproduce
2 ***syn*** FATHER 1, beget, get, procreate, progenerate, sire
3 ***syn*** GENERATE 3, cause, engender, get up, hatch, induce, muster (up), occasion, produce, work up
4 ***syn*** GROW 1, cultivate, produce, propagate, raise

breed *n* ***syn*** TYPE, character, class, feather, ilk, kind, nature, species, stripe, variety

breeding *n* ***syn*** CULTURE, cultivation, polish, refinement
rel civility, courtesy, gentility, grace
con barbarism, boorishness; coarseness, grossness; discourtesy, rudeness
ant vulgarity

breeding ground *n* a place or environment which favors growth <the slum was a *breeding ground* for crime>
syn forcing bed, forcing house, hotbed, hothouse

breeze *n* ***syn*** SNAP 1, child's play, cinch, duck soup, kid stuff, picnic, pie, ‖pipe, pushover, setup

breeze *vb* to proceed quickly and easily < *breezed* through customs >
syn waltz, zip
rel skim, slide, slip
con drag, falter, flag, lag, trail

breezy *adj* **1** ***syn*** WINDY 1, airy, blowy, gusty
2 ***syn*** EASYGOING 3, casual, ‖common, dégagé, informal, low-pressure, relaxed, ‖sonsy, unconstrained, unfussy

breviary *n* ***syn*** ABRIDGMENT, abstract, boildown, breviate, brief, condensation, conspectus, epitome, synopsis

breviate *n* ***syn*** ABRIDGMENT, abstract, boildown, breviary, brief, condensation, conspectus, epitome, synopsis

breviloquent *adj* **1** ***syn*** CONCISE, brief, compendious, curt, laconic, short, short and sweet, succinct, summary, terse
2 ***syn*** BLUFF, abrupt, blunt, brief, brusque, crusty, curt, gruff, rough, short

brew *vb* ***syn*** LOOM 2, forthcome, gather, impend

brew *n* ***syn*** MISCELLANY 1, hash, hodgepodge, mélange, mishmash, olla podrida, pastiche, potpourri, salad, stew

bribable *adj* ***syn*** VENAL 1, buyable, corruptible, purchasable

bribe *vb* to give or promise money or favor to a person in a position of trust to influence his judgment or conduct < *bribed* a building inspector >
syn buy, buy off, fix, have, ‖lubricate, sop, square, tamper (with)
rel approach; corrupt, instigate, suborn; soften (up), sweeten
idiom grease the palm (*or* hand), oil the palm (*or* hand), tickle the palm

bridal *n* ***syn*** WEDDING, espousal(s), marriage, nuptial(s), spousal

bridewell *n* ***syn*** JAIL, ‖calaboose, ‖can, ‖carcel, ‖clink, cooler, ‖hoosegow, jug, lockup, prison

bridle *vb* ***syn*** RESTRAIN 1, bit, check, constrain, curb, hold back, hold down, hold in, inhibit, withhold
rel repress, suppress; control, manage; govern, rule
con air, express, utter, ventilate, voice
ant vent

brief *adj* **1** ***syn*** SHORT 1
rel fleeting, momentary, passing, transient
ant long
2 ***syn*** CONCISE, breviloquent, compendiary, compendious, curt, laconic, short, short and sweet, succinct, terse
3 ***syn*** BLUFF, abrupt, blunt, brusque, crusty, curt, gruff, short, snippety, snippy

brief *n* ***syn*** ABRIDGMENT, abstract, boildown, breviary, breviate, condensation, conspectus, epitome, synopsis

briefly *adv* in a few words <he answered *briefly* and to the point>
syn concisely, in brief, in short, laconically, shortly, succinctly, tersely
rel accurately, crisply, exactly, precisely
idiom in a capsule, in a nutshell, in a word, to make a long story short
con diffusely, long-windedly, profusely, prolixly, protractedly, verbosely, wordily; at length, comprehensively, fully

---

syn synonym(s) ***rel*** related word(s)
idiom idiomatic equivalent(s) ***con*** contrasted word(s)
ant antonym(s) * vulgar
‖ use limited; if in doubt, see a dictionary
The first word in a synonym list when printed in SMALL CAPITALS shows where there is more information about the group. For a more efficient use of this book see Explanatory Notes.

‖**brig** *n* ***syn*** JAIL, ‖calaboose, ‖can, ‖clink, cooler, guardroom, keep, lockup, prison, stockade

brigand *n* ***syn*** MARAUDER, bandit, bummer, cateran, depredator, forager, freebooter, looter, pillager, plunderer

bright *adj* **1** shining or glowing with light <the *bright* sun>
syn beaming, brilliant, effulgent, fulgent, incandescent, lambent, lucent, lucid, luminous, lustrous, radiant, refulgent
rel clear, light, undimmed; illuminated, lighted; coruscating, flashing, gleaming, glistening, glittering, scintillating, shimmering, sparkling; blazing, flaming, glowing; burnished, polished, shiny; sunshiny
con dark, dusky, gloomy, murky, tenebrous; colorless, drab, dreary, lackluster, leaden; somber; cloudy, gray, overcast, shadowy; moonless, starless, sunless; faint, pale, weak
ant dim; dull
2 ***syn*** COLORFUL, brave, colory, gay, vivid
3 ***syn*** GLAD 2, cheerful, cheery, radiant
4 ***syn*** FAVORABLE 5, auspicious, benign, dexter, fortunate, propitious, white
5 ***syn*** INTELLIGENT 2, alert, brainy, brilliant, clever, knowing, quick-witted, ready-witted, sharp, smart
rel advanced, precocious
con retarded
ant dense, dull
6 ***syn*** LIVELY 1, alert, animate, animated, ‖cant, gay, keen, spirited, sprightly, vivacious

brilliant *adj* **1** ***syn*** BRIGHT 1, beaming, effulgent, fulgent, incandescent, lambent, lucent, luminous, radiant, refulgent
ant subdued
2 ***syn*** INTELLIGENT 2, brainy, bright, clever, knowing, knowledgeable, quick-witted, ready-witted, sharp, smart
rel erudite, learned; sage, wise

brim *n* ***syn*** BORDER 1, brink, edge, fringe, hem, margin, perimeter, periphery, skirt, verge

brimful *adj* **1** ***syn*** FULL 1, awash, brimming, chock-full, crammed, crowded, jammed, loaded, packed, stuffed
2 ***syn*** BIG 3, brimming, filled, replete, swelling, teeming, welling

brimming *adj* **1** ***syn*** FULL 1, awash, brimful, chock-full, crammed, crowded, jammed, loaded, packed, stuffed
2 ***syn*** BIG 3, brimful, filled, replete, swelling, teeming, welling

brine *n* ***syn*** OCEAN, blue, ‖briny, deep, drink, main, sea

bring *vb* **1** ***syn*** CONVERT 1, lead, move, persuade
‖**2** ***syn*** ACCOMPANY, attend, bear, ‖carry, chaperon, companion, conduct, consort (with), convoy, escort
3 ***syn*** SELL 4, bring in, fetch

---

syn synonym(s)
idiom idiomatic equivalent(s)
ant antonym(s)
rel related word(s)
con contrasted word(s)
* vulgar
‖ use limited; if in doubt, see a dictionary
The first word in a synonym list when printed in SMALL CAPITALS shows where there is more information about the group. For a more efficient use of this book see Explanatory Notes.

---

bring about *vb* ***syn*** EFFECT 1, cause, draw on, make, produce, secure

bring around *vb* ***syn*** INDUCE 1, argue (into), convince, draw, get, persuade, prevail (on *or* upon), prompt, talk (into), win (over)

bring down *vb* ***syn*** FELL 1, down, drop, floor, ground, knock down, level, prostrate, throw down, tumble

bring forth *vb* ***syn*** BEAR 5, ‖birth, ‖born, deliver

bring in *vb* **1** ***syn*** YIELD 5, pay, return
2 ***syn*** SELL 4, bring, fetch
3 ***syn*** EARN 1, acquire, ‖drag down, draw down, gain, get, knock down, make, win

bring off *vb* ***syn*** EFFECT 2, carry out, carry through, effectuate

bring out *vb* ***syn*** SAY 1, chime in, come out (with), declare, deliver, state, tell, throw out, utter

bring up *vb* **1** to give a child a parent's fostering care <the orphan was *brought up* by his aunt>
syn ‖fetch up, raise, rear
rel breed, cultivate, foster, nurture; feed, nourish, provide (for); discipline, educate, train
con abuse, ill-use, maltreat; neglect
2 ***syn*** STOP 4, draw up, fetch up, halt, haul up, pull up
3 ***syn*** REFER 3, advert, allude, point (out)
4 ***syn*** BROACH, introduce, moot, ventilate
5 ***syn*** VOMIT, barf, ‖cast, disgorge, ‖heave, *puke, spew, spit up, throw up, upchuck

brink *n* **1** ***syn*** BORDER 1, brim, edge, fringe, hem, margin, perimeter, periphery, skirt, verge
2 ***syn*** VERGE 2, edge, point, threshold

‖**briny** *n* ***syn*** OCEAN, blue, brine, deep, drink, main, sea

brio *n* ***syn*** SPIRIT 5, animation, dash, élan, esprit, life, oomph, verve, vim, zing

brisk *adj* ***syn*** AGILE, active, brisky, lively, nimble, sprightly, spry, volant, yare, zippy
rel adroit; quick
con inactive, torpid
ant sluggish

brisky *adj* ***syn*** AGILE, active, brisk, lively, nimble, sprightly, spry, volant, yare, zippy

bristle *vb* ***syn*** ANGER 2, blow up, boil, boil over, burn, flare (up), fume, rage, seethe

brittle *adj* ***syn*** SHORT 6, crisp, crumbly, ‖crump, crunchy, friable

broach *n* ***syn*** BROOCH, clip, pin

broach *vb* to open up (a subject) for discussion <would be awkward to *broach* the matter now>
syn bring up, introduce, moot, ventilate
rel interject, interpose; mention, speak (about); propose, suggest
con hush (up), quash, stifle, suppress; black out, censor

broad *adj* **1** ***syn*** LIBERAL 3, advanced, broad-minded, progressive, radical, tolerant, wide
2 ***syn*** EXTENSIVE 1, expansive, extended, scopic, scopious, wide
3 ***syn*** RISQUÉ, blue, off-color, purple, racy, salty, shady, spicy, suggestive, wicked

broadcast *n* ***syn*** DECLARATION, advertisement, announcement, proclamation, promulgation, pronouncement, pronunciamento, publication

broadcast *vb* **1** ***syn*** STREW 1, bestrew, disject, disseminate, scatter, sow, straw

2 ***syn*** DECLARE 1, advertise, announce, annunciate, blaze (abroad), blazon, bruit (about), proclaim, promulgate, publish
rel communicate, radio, televise, transmit
idiom spread a report, spread far and wide

broaden *vb* to grow or become broad or broader <the street *broadens* into an avenue>
syn breadthen, widen
rel expand; spread (out); open
con contract, shrink; slim, thin
ant narrow

broad–minded *adj* ***syn*** LIBERAL 3, advanced, broad, progressive, radical, tolerant, wide

broadside *n* ***syn*** BARRAGE, bombardment, burst, cannonade, fusillade, hail, salvo, shower, storm, volley

Brobdingnagian *adj* ***syn*** HUGE, Antaean, colossal, cyclopean, gargantuan, giant, gigantic, mammoth, monstrous, titanic

brocard *n* ***syn*** MAXIM, aphorism, apothegm, axiom, dictum, gnome, moral, rule, truism

‖**brogue** *vb* ***syn*** IDLE, dawdle, diddle-daddle, drone, ‖lallygag, laze, loaf, loiter, loll, lounge

broil *vb* ***syn*** BURN 3, bake, cook, melt, roast, scorch, swelter

broil *n* ***syn*** BRAWL 2, affray, bobbery, donnybrook, fight, fracas, fray, free-for-all, row, ruction

broiling *adj* ***syn*** HOT 1, baking, burning, fiery, red-hot, scalding, scorching, sizzling, sweltering, torrid

broke *adj* ***syn*** POOR 1, beggared, destitute, dirt poor, flat, indigent, needy, stone-broke, stony, strapped

broken–down *adj* ***syn*** SHABBY 1, decrepit, dilapidated, dingy, run-down, seedy, tacky, tagrag, tattered, threadbare

broker *n* ***syn*** GO-BETWEEN 2, entrepreneur, interagent, interceder, intercessor, intermediary, intermediate, intermediator, mediator, middleman

bromide *n* ***syn*** COMMONPLACE, banality, cliché, platitude, prosaicism, prosaism, rubber stamp, shibboleth, tag, truism

bromidic *adj* ***syn*** ARID 2, dry, dryasdust, dull, dusty, insipid, tedious, uninteresting, weariful, wearisome

‖**Bronx cheer** *n* ***syn*** RASPBERRY, bazoo, bird, boo, catcall, hiss, hoot, pooh, pooh-pooh, ‖raze

brooch *n* an ornament with a pin or clasp now worn usually by women <a diamond *brooch*>
syn broach, clip, pin

brood *n* ***syn*** OFFSPRING, ‖begats, children, descendants, issue, posterity, progeniture, progeny, scions, seed

brood *vb* 1 ***syn*** SET 11, ‖clock, cover, sit
2 ***syn*** MOPE 1, despond

brook *vb* ***syn*** BEAR 10, abide, endure, go, stand, stomach, suffer, swallow, take, tolerate

brook *n* ***syn*** CREEK 2, ‖branch, ‖burn, gill, race, ‖rindle, rivulet, ‖run, runnel, stream

brothel *n* an establishment where prostitutes ply their trade <madam of the local *brothel*>
syn bagnio, bawdy house, bordello, call house, cathouse, crib, disorderly house, fancy house, ‖hookshop, ‖joyhouse, lupanar, parlor house, seraglio, sporting house, stew, whorehouse
idiom house of ill fame (*or* repute), house of prostitution

brotherhood *n* ***syn*** ASSOCIATION 2, club, guild, fellowship, fraternity, league, order, society, sodality, union

brouhaha *n* 1 ***syn*** DIN, babel, clamor, hubbub, hullabaloo, jangle, pandemonium, racket, tumult, uproar
2 ***syn*** COMMOTION 3, ‖catouse, coil, foofaraw, furore, fuss, hurrah, ruckus, rumpus, shindy

brow *n* ***syn*** FOREHEAD, frons, front

browbeat *vb* ***syn*** INTIMIDATE, bludgeon, bluster, ‖bounce, bulldoze, bully, bullyrag, cow, dragoon, hector

browbeater *n* ***syn*** BULLY 1, bulldozer, harasser, harrier, hector, intimidator

brownie *n* ***syn*** FAIRY, elf, fay, nisse, pixie, sprite

‖**brownnose** *vb* ***syn*** FAWN, apple-polish, bootlick, cower, cringe, grovel, honey (up), kowtow, toady, truckle

‖**brownnose** *n* ***syn*** SYCOPHANT, bootlick, bootlicker, ‖clawback, footlicker, lickspit, lickspittle, spaniel, toadeater, toady

‖**brownnoser** *n* ***syn*** SYCOPHANT, apple-polisher, bootlick, bootlicker, ‖brownnose, ‖clawback, footlicker, groveler, lickspit, lickspittle

brown study *n* ***syn*** REVERIE, muse, study, trance

browse *vb* to read through, study, or examine cursorily <*browsed* through the book looking for illustrations>
syn dip (into), flip (through), glance (at *or* over), leaf (through), riff (through), riffle (through), run (through *or* over), scan, skim (through), thumb (through)
rel go (through *or* over), look (over), peruse, skip (through)
idiom give the once over, run the eye over
con examine, study; delve (into), dig (into)
ant pore (over)

bruise *n* an injury involving rupture of small blood vessels and discoloration without break in the overlying skin <got an ugly *bruise* when he fell>
syn contusion; *compare* BLACK EYE
rel ‖boo-boo; abrasion, scrape, scratch
idiom black-and-blue spot (*or* mark)

bruise *vb* 1 to inflict a bruise on <fell down and *bruised* his hip>
syn black, contuse
rel batter, ‖bung up
2 ***syn*** CRUSH 2, becrush, mash, ‖mush (up), pulp, squash

bruit (about) *vb* ***syn*** DECLARE 1, advertise, announce, annunciate, blaze (abroad), blazon, broadcast, proclaim, promulgate, publish
rel hint, intimate, rumor, suggest

bruja *n* ***syn*** WITCH 1, enchantress, hag, hex, lamia, sorceress, witchwoman

brume *n* ***syn*** HAZE 1, film, mist, smaze

brummagem *adj* ***syn*** COUNTERFEIT, bogus, fake, false, phony, pinchbeck, pseudo, sham, snide, spurious

brunet *adj* ***syn*** DARK 3, bistered, black-a-vised, dark-skinned, dusky, swart, swarth, swarthy

---

brush *vb* to touch or strike lightly (as in passing) <they *brushed* fenders but no real damage was done>
syn glance, graze, kiss, shave, skim
rel bump, clash, collide, sideswipe; clip, contact, scrape, touch

brush *n* **1** *syn* ENCOUNTER, run-in, set-to, skirmish, velitation
rel clash, engagement
2 *syn* CLASH 2, affray, fray, melee, mellay, scrimmage, skirmish

brush up *vb syn* TOUCH UP, retouch, tease up

brusque *adj syn* BLUFF, abrupt, blunt, brief, crusty, curt, gruff, short, snippety, snippy

brutal *adj* **1** *syn* BRUTISH, animal, beastly, bestial, brute, feral, ferine, swinish
2 *syn* SEVERE 3, bitter, hard, harsh, inclement, intemperate, rigorous, rugged

brutalize *vb syn* DEBASE 1, bastardize, bestialize, corrupt, debauch, demoralize, deprave, pervert, vitiate, warp

brute *adj syn* BRUTISH, animal, beastly, bestial, brutal, feral, ferine, swinish

brute *n syn* BEAST, animal, creature, ‖critter

brutish *adj* marked by animal traits and by a lack of man's dignity or refinement <a graceless *brutish* hulk of a man>
syn animal, beastly, bestial, brutal, brute, feral, ferine, swinish
rel animalistic; coarse, crude; base, low, mean, scurvy, vile

bubble *vb* **1** *syn* SLOSH 1, burble, gurgle, lap, swash, wash
2 *syn* SEETHE 4, boil, churn, ferment, ‖moil, simmer, smolder, stir

bubble *n syn* PIPE DREAM, chimera, dream, fantasy (*or* phantasy), illusion, ‖pipe, rainbow

buccaneer *n syn* PIRATE, corsair, freebooter, picaroon, rover, sea dog, sea robber, sea rover, sea wolf

buck *n* **1** *syn* MAN 3, ‖bloke, boy, chap, fellow, ‖gee, gent, gentleman, guy, he
2 *syn* FOP, Beau Brummel, blood, coxcomb, dandy, dude, exquisite, lounge lizard, macaroni, petit-maître
‖**3** *syn* DOLLAR, bill, ‖bone, ‖fish, ‖frogskin, ‖ironman, oner, ‖skin, ‖smacker, ‖smackeroo
4 *syn* SAWHORSE, horse, sawbuck, trestle, workhorse

buck *vb* **1** *syn* RESIST, combat, contest, dispute, duel, fight, oppose, repel, traverse, withstand
2 *syn* CARRY 1, bear, convey, ferry, ‖hump, ‖jag, lug, pack, tote, transport
3 *syn* PASS 9, hand, reach, ‖shoot

buck (off) *vb syn* THROW 2, pitch, unhorse, unseat

buck *vb syn* PULVERIZE 1, bray, comminute, contriturate, crush, powder, triturate

---

syn synonym(s) *rel* related word(s)
idiom idiomatic equivalent(s) *con* contrasted word(s)
ant antonym(s) * vulgar
‖ use limited; if in doubt, see a dictionary
The first word in a synonym list when printed in SMALL CAPITALS shows where there is more information about the group. For a more efficient use of this book see Explanatory Notes.

‖**bucket** *n syn* JAIL, ‖calaboose, ‖can, ‖clink, cooler, ‖hoosegow, jug, lockup, ‖pokey, prison

bucket *vb syn* HURRY 2, barrel, fly, hasten, highball, hustle, run, rush, speed, whiz

‖**bucket shop** *n syn* BAR 5, barroom, ‖boozer, drinkery, ‖gin mill, ‖groggery, ‖grogshop, pothouse, pub, ‖rum-hole

buckle (down) *vb* **1** *syn* ADDRESS 3, apply, bend, devote, direct, give, throw, turn
2 *syn* PITCH IN 1, fall to, jump (in *or* into), set to, wade (in *or* into)

buckle (under) *vb syn* YIELD 2, bow, capitulate, cave, defer, knuckle, knuckle under, submit, succumb

buckram *adj syn* STIFF 4, cardboard, muscle-bound, stilted, wooden

buck up *vb syn* COMFORT, cheer, console, solace, upraise

bucolic *adj syn* RURAL, agrestic, campestral, countrified, country, out-country, outland, pastoral, provincial, rustic
ant urbane

bucolic *n syn* RUSTIC, bumpkin, chawbacon, hayseed, hick, hillman, hoosier, jake, provincial, yokel

bud *n* **1** *syn* CHILD 1, chick, chickabiddy, juvenile, kid, moppet, ‖nipper, youngling, young one, youngster
2 *syn* SEED 2, embryo, germ, nucleus, spark

buddy *n syn* ASSOCIATE 3, chum, comate, companion, comrade, crony, ‖cully, pal, running mate

‖**buddy–buddy** *adj syn* INTIMATE 4, chummy, cozy, pally, ‖palsy-walsy

‖**budge** *n syn* LIQUOR 2, alcohol, aqua vitae, booze, drink, firewater, grog, ‖hooch, ‖juice, ‖sauce

budget *n syn* BODY 5, aggregate, amount, bulk, quantity, quantum, total

budtime *n syn* SPRING 5, springtide, springtime

buff *n syn* ADDICT, aficionado, devotee, fan, habitué, hound, lover, votary

buff *vb syn* POLISH 1, burnish, furbish, glance, glaze, gloss, rub, shine

buffalo *vb* **1** *syn* FRUSTRATE 1, baffle, balk, beat, bilk, circumvent, dash, disappoint, foil, ruin
2 *syn* NONPLUS 1, beat, get, stick, stump

buff–bare *adj syn* NUDE 2, au naturel, *bare-assed, naked, raw, stark-naked, stripped, unclad, unclothed, undressed

buffet *n syn* CUFF, box, chop, clout, ‖paste, poke, punch, slap, smack, sock

buffet *vb* **1** *syn* SLAP 1, blip, box, cuff, smack, spank, ‖wherret
2 *syn* BEAT 1, batter, belabor, drub, lambaste, paste, pound, pummel, thrash, wallop

‖**buffet** *n syn* EATING HOUSE, café, coffee shop, diner, lunch counter (*or* bar), luncheonette, lunch wagon (*or* cart), quick lunch, sandwich shop, snack bar (*or* counter)

‖**bufflehead** *n syn* DUNCE, blockhead, bonehead, chowderhead, chucklehead, dunderhead, fathead, knucklehead, muttonhead, numskull

‖**buffle–headed** *adj syn* SIMPLE 3, asinine, brainless, mindless, nitwitted, senseless, sheepheaded, weak-headed, weak-minded, witless

buffoon *n syn* CLOWN 3, harlequin, merry-andrew, zany

‖**buffy** *adj* ***syn*** INTOXICATED 1, ‖boozy, ‖canned, disguised, drunk, inebriated, ‖lushed, muddled, pixilated, ‖plastered

bug *n* ***syn*** ENTHUSIAST, bigot, fanatic, fiend, freak, maniac, nut, zealot

‖**bug** *vb* ***syn*** ANNOY 1, abrade, bother, chafe, exercise, fret, gall, irk, provoke, vex

bugbear *n* ***syn*** ABOMINATION 1, anathema, bête noire, black beast, detestation, hate

‖**bugger** *n* ***syn*** SNOT 1, louse, ‖prick, puke, scum, *shit, *shithead, sod, stinker, toad

‖**bugger** *vb* ***syn*** EXHAUST 4, fag, frazzle, knock out, outtire, outwear, ‖poop, prostrate, tucker, wear out

bugger up *vb* ***syn*** BOTCH, bollix, bungle, flub, fluff, goof (up), gum (up), louse up, mess, ‖screw (up)

‖**buggy** *adj* **1** ***syn*** ENTHUSIASTIC, ‖bugs, gung ho, keen, nutty, warm, zealous
2 ***syn*** INSANE 1, ‖batty, bedlamite, ‖bughouse, ‖bugs, cracked, crazed, crazy, daft, demented

‖**buggy** *n* ***syn*** CAR, auto, autocar, automobile, ‖bus, machine, motor, motorcar

‖**bughouse** *n* ***syn*** ASYLUM 3, booby hatch, crazy house, loony bin, madhouse, ‖nuthouse

‖**bughouse** *adj* ***syn*** INSANE 1, ‖batty, bedlamite, ‖buggy, ‖bugs, cracked, crazed, crazy, daft, demented

‖**bugs** *adj* **1** ***syn*** INSANE 1, ‖batty, bedlamite, ‖buggy, ‖bughouse, cracked, crazed, crazy, daft, demented
2 ***syn*** ENTHUSIASTIC, ‖buggy, gung ho, keen, nutty, warm, zealous

build *vb* **1** to form or fashion a structure <will *build* either a garage or carport>
syn construct, erect, put up, raise, rear, uprear; *compare* ERECT 3, MAKE 3
rel fabricate, fashion, frame, manufacture; run up, throw up; prefabricate
con demolish, destroy, dismantle, level, pull down, raze, take down, tear down, wreck
2 ***syn*** MAKE 3, assemble, construct, erect, fashion, forge, form, mold, produce, shape
3 ***syn*** INCREASE 1, aggrandize, augment, boost, compound, enlarge, expand, heighten, magnify, multiply
4 ***syn*** INCREASE 2, augment, enlarge, expand, heighten, mount, multiply, rise, upsurge, wax

build (on) *vb* ***syn*** RELY (on *or* upon), bank (on *or* upon), calculate (on *or* upon), count (on), depend (on *or* upon), ‖lot (on *or* upon), reckon (on), trust (in *or* to)

build *n* ***syn*** PHYSIQUE, constitution, habit, habitus
rel conformation

building *n* a usually roofed and walled structure built for permanent use <a *building* with four apartments>
syn fabric, structure; *compare* EDIFICE, HUT

build up *vb* **1** ***syn*** ERECT 5, construct, establish, hammer (out), set up
2 ***syn*** PUBLICIZE, advertise, cry, press-agent, puff

buildup *n* ***syn*** PUBLICITY, advertising, press-agentry, promotion, puffery

‖**built** *adj* ***syn*** CURVACEOUS, curvesome, curvilinear, curvy, Junoesque, rounded, ‖stacked, well-developed

built–in *adj* ***syn*** INHERENT, congenital, constitutional, deep-seated, essential, inborn, inbred, indwelling, ingrained, innate

bulge *vb* to extend outward beyond the usual or normal line <the box was so full that the sides *bulged*>
syn beetle, jut, overhang, poke, pouch, pout, project, protrude, protuberate, stand out, stick out
rel bag, belly, dilate, distend, expand, swell

bulge *n* **1** ***syn*** PROJECTION 1, jut, outthrust, protrusion, protuberance
rel bump, lump, swelling
con depression, hollow, pit
2 ***syn*** ADVANTAGE 3, allowance, ‖deadwood, edge, handicap, head start, odds, ‖overhand, start, vantage

bulk *n* **1** a body of usually material substance that constitutes a thing or unit <his industry was proven by the *bulk* of his accomplishment> <a great dark *bulk* blocked the alley>
syn mass, volume
rel bigness, greatness, largeness, magnitude, quantity, totality
2 ***syn*** BODY 4, mass, object, volume
3 ***syn*** BODY 5, aggregate, amount, budget, quantity, quantum, total
4 ***syn*** BODY 3, core, corpus, mass, staple, substance

bulk *vb* ***syn*** LOOM 3, stand out

bull *n* **1** ***syn*** ERROR 2, blooper, blunder, boner, bungle, fluff, lapse, mistake, slip, trip
‖**2** ***syn*** NONSENSE 2, balderdash, ‖baloney, bilge, blatherskite, *bullshit, bunkum, claptrap, ‖crap, hogwash
‖**3** ***syn*** POLICEMAN, ‖bluebottle, ‖bobby, ‖constable, ‖copper, ‖flatfoot, ‖fuzz, gumshoe, officer, ‖paddy

bull *adj* ***syn*** LARGE 1, big, fat, great, husky, oversize

‖**bull band** *n* ***syn*** SHIVAREE, ‖belling, ‖callithump, charivari, ‖horning, ‖riding, ‖skimmelton

bulldoze *vb* **1** ***syn*** INTIMIDATE, bludgeon, bluster, ‖bounce, browbeat, bully, bullyrag, cow, dragoon, hector
rel menace, threaten; harass, harry
2 ***syn*** PUSH 2, elbow, hustle, jostle, press, ‖shog, shoulder, shove

bulldozer *n* ***syn*** BULLY 1, browbeater, harasser, harrier, hector, intimidator

bullet *vb* ***syn*** HURRY 2, barrel, bucket, fleet, fly, highball, hotfoot, rocket, whiz, zip

bullfighter *n* one who fights bulls <moved with the grace of an experienced *bullfighter*>
syn matador, toreador, torero
rel banderillero; cuadrillero, picador; cuadrilla

bullheaded *adj* ***syn*** OBSTINATE, headstrong, intractable, mulish, pertinacious, perverse, pigheaded, refractory, self-willed, stiff-necked

bullshit** *n* ***syn NONSENSE 2, balderdash, ‖baloney, ‖bull, bunkum, ‖crap, hooey, *horseshit, malarkey, poppycock

bullwork *n* ***syn*** WORK 2, donkeywork, drudge, drudgery, grind, labor, moil, sweat, toil, travail

---

syn synonym(s) ***rel*** related word(s)
idiom idiomatic equivalent(s) ***con*** contrasted word(s)
ant antonym(s) * vulgar
‖ use limited; if in doubt, see a dictionary
The first word in a synonym list when printed in SMALL CAPITALS shows where there is more information about the group. For a more efficient use of this book see Explanatory Notes.

bully *n* **1** an insolent, overbearing person who persists in tormenting another <a big *bully* who picked on little kids>
syn browbeater, bulldozer, harasser, harrier, hector, intimidator; *compare* TOUGH
rel annoyer, antagonizer, heckler, persecutor, pest, tease, tormenter
2 *syn* PIMP 1, cadet, ||easy rider, fancy man, ||mack, macquereau, pander

bully *adj syn* EXCELLENT, bang-up, capital, champion, ||dandy, famous, fine, first-rate, front-rank, superior

bully *vb syn* INTIMIDATE, bludgeon, bluster, ||bounce, browbeat, bulldoze, bullyrag, cow, dragoon, hector
rel torment, torture; menace, threaten
ant coax

bullyboy *n syn* TOUGH, ||b'hoy, mucker, punk, rough, roughneck, rowdy, ruffian, toughie, yahoo

bullyrag *vb* **1** *syn* INTIMIDATE, bludgeon, bluster, ||bounce, browbeat, bulldoze, bully, cow, dragoon, hector
2 *syn* BAIT 2, badger, chivy, heckle, hector, hound, ride

bulwark *n* an aboveground defensive structure that forms part of a fortification <the *bulwarks* were woefully undermanned>
syn bastion, breastwork, parapet, rampart
rel citadel, fort, fortress, stronghold
con bunker, dugout

bulwark *vb syn* DEFEND 1, cover, fend, guard, protect, safeguard, screen, secure, shield

***bum** *n syn* BUTTOCKS, *arse, backside, bottom, *butt, derriere, fanny, hind end, posterior, rump

||**bum** *vb syn* HUM, bombinate, bumble, buzz, drone, ||sowf, strum, thrum

bum *vb syn* IDLE, dawdle, goldbrick, ||goof (off), laze, lazy, loaf, loiter, loll, lounge

bum *n* **1** *syn* VAGABOND, ||bindle stiff, derelict, drifter, floater, hobo, street arab, tramp, vag, vagrant
2 *syn* SLUGGARD, dolittle, do-nothing, faineant, idler, lazybones, loafer, slouch, slug, slugabed

||**bum** *adj syn* BAD 1, amiss, ||crappy, dissatisfactory, poor, ||punk, rotten, unsatisfactory, up, wrong

bum *n syn* BINGE 1, bender, booze, brannigan, bust, carouse, drunk, jag, soak, wassail

bumble *vb syn* HUM, bombinate, ||bum, buzz, drone, ||sowf, strum, thrum

bumble *vb* **1** *syn* BOTCH, ||blow, blunder, bobble, bollix, bungle, fumble, mucker, muff, ||screw (up)
2 *syn* STUMBLE 3, blunder, lurch, ||snapper

bumbling *adj syn* AWKWARD 2, gauche, halting, ham-handed, heavy-handed, inept, maladroit, unhandy, unhappy, wooden

||**bumfuzzle** *vb syn* CONFUSE 2, addle, ball up, befuddle, bewilder, distract, fluster, fuddle, mix up, throw off

bummel *vb syn* SAUNTER, amble, drift, linger, mope, mosey, ||muck, stroll

bummer *n* **1** *syn* BEGGAR 1, cadger, moocher, panhandler, ||schnorrer
2 *syn* MARAUDER, bandit, brigand, cateran, depredator, forager, freebooter, looter, pillager, plunderer

bumming *n syn* MENDICANCY, beggary, cadging, mendicity, mooching, panhandling

bump *vb* **1** to meet with or come up against forcibly <the two cars *bumped* with a great crumpling of fenders>
syn clash, collide, ||prang
rel bang, carom, crash, hit, knock, slam, strike; impinge; jar, jolt
idiom whang together
2 *syn* HAPPEN 2, chance, hit, light, luck, meet, stumble, tumble
3 *syn* DEGRADE 1, break, bust, declass, demerit, demote, disgrade, disrate, downgrade, reduce

bump *n* **1** *syn* IMPACT, clash, collision, concussion, crash, jar, jolt, percussion, shock, wallop
2 a swelling of tissue usually resulting from a blow <fell and got a *bump* on his head>
syn bunch, knot, lump, ||pumpknot
rel protuberance, swelling
3 a marked unevenness in a road surface likely to jolt a passing vehicle
syn ||cahot, thank-you-ma'am
rel chuckhole, mudhole, pothole, rut
4 *syn* GIFT 2, aptness, bent, faculty, flair, genius, head, knack, talent, turn

bumpkin *n syn* RUSTIC, bucolic, chawbacon, clodhopper, hick, hoosier, jake, joskin, provincial, rube

bump off *vb syn* MURDER 1, assassinate, cool, do in, ||dust off, execute, finish, knock off, liquidate, put away

||**bump–off** *n syn* MURDER, blood, foul play, homicide, killing, manslaughter

bunch *n* **1** *syn* BUMP 2, knot, lump, ||pumpknot
2 *syn* GROUP 3, batch, body, bundle, clump, cluster, clutch, lot, parcel, set
3 *syn* SET 5, circle, crowd, group, lot, push
4 *syn* GROUP 1, assembly, band, bevy, cluster, covey, crew, party

bunco steerer *n syn* SWINDLER, confidence man, con man, defrauder, diddler, double-dealer, ||grifter, gyp, sharper, trickster

bundle *n* **1** *syn* GROUP 3, array, batch, body, bunch, clump, cluster, lot, parcel, set
2 *syn* FORTUNE 4, ||bomb, boodle, mint, packet, pile, pot, ||roll, wad

bundle up *vb* to dress warmly <*bundle up,* it's cold outside>
syn ||hap, muffle, wrap (up)
rel envelop, mummify, swaddle, swathe

||**bung** *vb syn* THROW 1, cast, fire, fling, heave, hurl, launch, pitch, sling, toss

bung–full *adj syn* FULL 1, block and block, brimful, chockablock, chock-full, crammed, crowded, jam-full, jam-packed, packed

bungle *vb syn* BOTCH, ||blow, bollix, flub, fluff, goof (up), gum (up), louse up, muff, ||screw (up)

bungle *n syn* ERROR 2, blooper, blunder, boner, bull, fluff, lapse, mistake, slip, trip

---

syn synonym(s) *rel* related word(s)
idiom idiomatic equivalent(s) *con* contrasted word(s)
ant antonym(s) * vulgar
|| use limited; if in doubt, see a dictionary
The first word in a synonym list when printed in SMALL CAPITALS shows where there is more information about the group. For a more efficient use of this book see Explanatory Notes.

bungler *n* ***syn*** STUMBLEBUM, blunderbuss, blunderer

‖**bung up** *vb* ***syn*** BATTER 1, mangle, maul

bunk *vb* ***syn*** HARBOR 2, bestow, billet, board, domicile, house, hut, lodge, put up, quarter

‖**bunk** *vb* ***syn*** ESCAPE 1, abscond, break, decamp, flee, fly, scape

‖**bunk** *n* ***syn*** NONSENSE 2, ‖applesauce, balderdash, ‖baloney, ‖bull, eyewash, flimflam, hokum, jazz, poppycock

‖**bunk** *vb* ***syn*** DECEIVE, beguile, betray, delude, double-cross, four-flush, humbug, illude, mislead, sell out

bunkum *n* ***syn*** NONSENSE 2, ‖applesauce, balderdash, ‖baloney, ‖bull, eyewash, flimflam, hokum, jazz, poppycock

‖**bunkum** *adj* **1** ***syn*** EXCELLENT, bang-up, blue-ribbon, ‖boss, champion, first-string, Grade A, top, top-notch, whiz-bang
2 ***syn*** HEALTHY 1, fit, hale, right, sane, sound, well, well-conditioned, well-liking, wholesome

Bunyanesque *adj* ***syn*** HUGE, behemothic, colossal, gargantuan, gigantic, Herculean, mammoth, monstrous, prodigious, titanic

buoy (up) *vb* ***syn*** SUPPORT 5, bolster, prop, sustain, underprop, uphold

buoyancy *n* ***syn*** EBULLIENCE, effervescence, exuberance, exuberancy

buoyant *adj* ***syn*** ELASTIC 2, airy, bouncy, effervescent, expansive, resilient, volatile

burble *vb* **1** ***syn*** SLOSH 1, bubble, gurgle, lap, swash, wash
2 ***syn*** CHAT 1, babble, chatter, clack, gabble, prattle, rattle, run on, yak, yammer

burden *n* **1** ***syn*** LOAD 1, cargo, freight, haul, lading, payload
2 ***syn*** LOAD 3, charge, deadweight, duty, millstone, onus, task, tax, weight

burden *vb* to lay a heavy load on or to lie like a heavy load on a person or thing <*burdened* his men with needless heavy work> <I won't *burden* you with this lengthy story>
syn charge, clog, cumber, encumber, lade, load, lumber, saddle, task, tax, weigh, weight
rel overburden, overload, overweigh; handicap; afflict, oppress
idiom bear down on (*or* upon)
con alleviate, ease, lighten, relieve, unload; disburden, disencumber
ant unburden

burden *n* ***syn*** SUBSTANCE 2, amount, body, gist, matter, meat, pith, purport, thrust, upshot

burdensome *adj* ***syn*** ONEROUS, demanding, exacting, exigent, grievous, oppressive, superincumbent, taxing, tough, weighty

burdensomely *adv* ***syn*** HARD 8, arduously, difficultly, hardly, laboriously, onerously, toilsomely

bureaucrat *n* a member of a bureaucracy <*bureaucrats* were blamed for the error>
syn mandarin
rel civil servant, functionary, official

burg *n* a small, insignificant, remote town <the *burg* had only two stores and one gas station>
syn hick town, jerkwater town, mudhole, one-horse town, Podunk, tank town, whistle-stop
rel cowtown; crossroads; jumping-off place; hamlet, village
con city, metropolis

burgee *n* ***syn*** FLAG, banner, color, ensign, jack, pendant, pennant, pennon, standard, streamer

burgeon *vb* **1** ***syn*** INCREASE 2, augment, build, enlarge, expand, heighten, mount, multiply, run up, snowball
2 ***syn*** BLOSSOM, bloom, blow, effloresce, flower, outbloom

burghal *adj* ***syn*** URBAN, city, municipal

burgher *n* ***syn*** TOWNSMAN, cit, citizen, towner, townman, towny

burglarize *vb* to commit an act of breaking open and entering with a felonious purpose the dwelling house of another by night <that night several homes were *burglarized*>
syn burgle; *compare* HOUSEBREAK, ROB 1
rel knock over, rob; ransack, rifle; screw

burgle *vb* ***syn*** BURGLARIZE

burial *n* **1** ***syn*** GRAVE, ‖pit, sepulcher, sepulture, tomb
2 the act or ceremony of burying <his *burial* took place yesterday>
syn entombment, inhumation, interment, sepulture
rel burying, exequies, funeral, obsequies; deposition; deep six
con disinterment, exhumation

burial ground *n* ***syn*** CEMETERY, ‖boneyard, ‖boot hill, burying ground, God's acre, graveyard, memorial park, necropolis, polyandrium, potter's field

buried *adj* ***syn*** ULTERIOR, concealed, covert, guarded, hidden, obscured, privy, shrouded

burke *vb* **1** ***syn*** SUPPRESS 3, hush (up), stifle
2 ***syn*** SKIRT 3, bypass, circumvent, ‖polly-fox, sidestep

burlesque *n* **1** ***syn*** MOCKERY 2, caricature, farce, mock, sham, travesty
2 ***syn*** CARICATURE 2, parody, takeoff, travesty

burlesque *vb* ***syn*** MIMIC, ape, imitate, mock, parody, take off, travesty

burly *adj* ***syn*** HUSKY 1, beefy, hefty

‖**burn** *n* ***syn*** CREEK 2, ‖branch, brook, gill, race, ‖rindle, rivulet, ‖run, runnel, stream

burn *vb* **1** ***syn*** SHINE 1, beam, gleam, radiate
2 to undergo combustion <the wood is too green to *burn*>
syn combust
rel fire, flame, ignite, kindle, light; consume, use; smolder, sputter
3 to be hot as if on fire <sand *burning* in the blazing sun>
syn bake, broil, cook, melt, roast, scorch, swelter
rel parch, toast, warm; char
con chill, cool, freeze
4 ***syn*** ANGER 2, blow up, boil, boil over, bristle, flare (up), fume, rage, seethe

---

syn synonym(s) ***rel*** related word(s)
idiom idiomatic equivalent(s) ***con*** contrasted word(s)
ant antonym(s) * vulgar
‖ use limited; if in doubt, see a dictionary
The first word in a synonym list when printed in SMALL CAPITALS shows where there is more information about the group. For a more efficient use of this book see Explanatory Notes.

5 ***syn*** SMART, bite, ‖stang, sting

6 ***syn*** FIRE 6, bake, kiln

‖7 ***syn*** CHEAT, beat, bilk, chisel, chouse, cozen, gyp, overreach, ream, take

burn (up) *vb* ***syn*** IRRITATE, aggravate, exasperate, gall, get, grate, inflame, provoke, rile, roil

burnable *adj* ***syn*** COMBUSTIBLE 1, flammable, ignitable, inflammable

burning *adj* **1** on fire <the *burning* house>

syn ablaze, afire, aflame, alight, blazing, conflagrant, fiery, flaming, flaring, ignited, lighted

rel aglow, glowing, incandescent

idiom in flames

con burned-out, cold

2 ***syn*** HOT 1, ardent, broiling, fiery, heated, red-hot, scorching, sizzling, torrid, white-hot

ant icy

3 ***syn*** FEVERISH 2, fervid, fevered, heated, hectic

4 ***syn*** IMPASSIONED, ardent, blazing, fervent, fervid, fiery, flaming, passionate, red-hot, white-hot

5 ***syn*** PRESSING, clamant, clamorous, crying, dire, exigent, imperative, importunate, instant, urgent

burnish *vb* ***syn*** POLISH 1, buff, furbish, glance, glaze, gloss, rub, shine

burnished *adj* ***syn*** LUSTROUS 1, gleaming, glistening, glossy, polished, sheeny, shining, shiny

burn off *vb* ***syn*** CLEAR 9, ‖break

burnsides *n pl* ***syn*** SIDE-WHISKERS, dundrearies, muttonchops, sideboards, sideburns

burp *vb* ***syn*** BELCH 1, eruct, eructate

burro *n* ***syn*** DONKEY 1, ass, donk, jackass, ‖moke, ‖neddy, ‖Rocky Mountain canary

burrow *n* **1** ***syn*** LAIR 1, couch, den, lodge

2 ***syn*** HOVEL, hole

burrow *vb* ***syn*** SNUGGLE, ‖croodle, cuddle, nestle, nuzzle, ‖snudge, snug, ‖snuzzle

burst *vb* **1** ***syn*** EXPLODE 1, blow up, detonate, go off, mushroom

2 ***syn*** SHATTER 1, fragment, ‖pash, rive, shiver, smash, ‖smatter, splinter, splinterize, splitter

3 ***syn*** PLUNGE 2, dive, drive, lunge, pitch, ‖splunge

burst (forth) *vb* ***syn*** ERUPT 2, break out, explode

burst *n* **1** ***syn*** OUTBREAK 1, eruption, flare, outburst

2 ***syn*** OUTBURST 1, access, eruption, explosion, flare-up, gust, sally

3 ***syn*** BANG 2, blast, boom, clap, crack, crash, slam, smash, wham

4 ***syn*** BARRAGE, bombardment, broadside, cannonade, drumfire, fusillade, salvo, shower, storm, volley

bury *vb* **1** to deposit (a corpse) in or as if in the earth <the pharaohs were *buried* in pyramids> <*buried* at sea>

syn entomb, inhume, inter, lay away, plant, put away, sepulcher, sepulture, tomb; *compare* ENTOMB 1

rel inurn; coffin

idiom consign to the grave, lay to rest, put six feet under

con dig (up), disentomb, disinter, exhume, untomb; burn, cremate

2 ***syn*** HIDE, cache, conceal, cover, ensconce, occult, plant, screen, secrete, stash

burying ground *n* ***syn*** CEMETERY, ‖boneyard, ‖boot hill, burial ground, God's acre, graveyard, memorial park, necropolis, polyandrium, potter's field

‖**bus** *n* ***syn*** CAR, auto, autocar, automobile, buggy, machine, motor, motorcar

bush *n* ***syn*** FRONTIER 2, backcountry, backland, ‖backveld, backwash, backwater, backwoods, hinterland, ‖outback, up-country

‖**bush up** *vb* ***syn*** HIDE, bury, cache, conceal, cover, ‖ditch, ensconce, occult, screen, secrete, stash

bushwa *n* ***syn*** NONSENSE 2, balderdash, ‖baloney, bosh, bunkum, eyewash, flapdoodle, hooey, malarkey, poppycock

business *n* **1** ***syn*** FUNCTION 1, duty, office, province, role

2 ***syn*** PATRONAGE 2, custom, trade, traffic

3 ***syn*** WORK 1, calling, employment, job, line, occupation, pursuit, ‖racket

4 activity concerned with the supplying and distribution of commodities <the lumber *business* depends heavily on the housing *business*>

syn commerce, industry, trade, traffic

5 ***syn*** ENTERPRISE 3, company, concern, establishment, firm, house, outfit

6 ***syn*** AFFAIR 1, concern, matter, shooting match, thing

7 ***syn*** DOODAD, dingus, dofunny, doohickey, gadget, gizmo, ‖hootenanny, jigger, thingumajig, thingumbob

8 something personal to oneself <that is none of your *business*>

syn affair, concern, lookout, occasions, palaver

businessman *n* ***syn*** MERCHANT, dealer, merchandiser, trader, tradesman, trafficker

buss *vb* ***syn*** KISS 1, lip, osculate, peck, smack, smooch, ‖smoodge, ‖smouch

bust *vb* **1** ***syn*** RUIN 3, bankrupt, break, fold up, impoverish, pauper, pauperize

2 ***syn*** DEGRADE 1, break, bump, declass, demerit, demote, disgrade, disrate, downgrade, reduce

ant promote

3 ***syn*** FAIL 5, break, crash, fold

‖4 ***syn*** ARREST 2, apprehend, detain, nab, pick up, pinch, pull in, run in

bust *n* ‖**1** ***syn*** CUFF, box, chop, clout, haymaker, ‖paste, poke, punch, smack, sock

2 ***syn*** FAILURE 5, bomb, dud, flop, lemon, loser

3 ***syn*** BINGE 1, bat, bender, booze, brannigan, bum, carouse, drunk, jag, spree

4 ***syn*** RAID 2

‖**busthead** *n* ***syn*** MOONSHINE 2, bathtub gin, ‖blockade, bootleg, ‖hooch, mountain dew, white lightning

bustle *vb* ***syn*** HURRY 2, ‖dust, flit, fly, hasten, hustle, run, rush, whirl, whisk

bustle *n* **1** ***syn*** STIR 1, ado, flurry, furore, fuss, pother, whirl, whirlpool, whirlwind

2 ***syn*** COMMOTION 4, clamor, hassle, hubbub, hurly-burly, to-do, tumult, turmoil, uproar, whirl

---

syn synonym(s) ***rel*** related word(s)
idiom idiomatic equivalent(s) ***con*** contrasted word(s)
ant antonym(s) * vulgar
‖ use limited; if in doubt, see a dictionary
The first word in a synonym list when printed in SMALL CAPITALS shows where there is more information about the group. For a more efficient use of this book see Explanatory Notes.

bustling *adj* full of activity <a *bustling* frontier town>
syn busy, fussy, hopping, humming, hustling, lively, popping
rel active, brisk, energetic
idiom on its way, on the go (*or* move), up and doing

busty *adj* *syn* BUXOM, bosomy, chesty, full-bosomed

busy *adj* **1** engaged in activity <I can't stop to talk. I'm *busy*>
syn employed, engaged, occupied, working; *compare* ASSIDUOUS
idiom at work, on the fly
con idle, inactive
ant free
2 *syn* BUSTLING, fussy, hopping, humming, hustling, lively, popping
3 *syn* IMPERTINENT 2, intrusive, meddlesome, ||nebby, obtrusive, officious, polypragmatic

busy *vb* *syn* ENGAGE 4, engross, immerse, occupy, soak

busybody *n* one who concerns himself with affairs not his own <a meddlesome *busybody* who saw all and tattled all she saw>
syn butt-in, ||buttinsky, intermeddler, kibitzer, meddler, Meddlesome Mattie, nose, nosey Parker, Paul Pry, polypragmatist, pragmatic, pragmatist, prier (*or* pryer), quidnunc, rubber, rubberneck, snoop, ||stickybeak; *compare* GOSSIP 1, INFORMER
rel gossip, gossipmonger, newsmonger, rumormonger, scandalmonger, tabby, talebearer, telltale
idiom curiosity shop, question box

busybody *vb* **1** *syn* SNOOP, mouse, nose, ||piroot, poke, pry, ||snook
2 *syn* MEDDLE, butt in, fool, horn in, interfere, interlope, intermeddle, ||make, monkey (with), tamper (with)

but *conj* **1** *syn* ONLY, except, however, save, yet
2 *syn* EXCEPT 1, save, saving, unless, ||without

but *prep* *syn* EXCEPT, aside from, bar, barring, bating, besides, excluding, outside of, save

but *adv* **1** *syn* ONLY 1, alone, entirely, exclusively, solely
2 *syn* JUST 3, merely, only, simply

butcher *vb* **1** *syn* SLAUGHTER 1, slay
2 *syn* SLAUGHTER 2, slay

butchery *n* *syn* MASSACRE, bloodbath, bloodshed, carnage, slaughter

butt *n* **1** *syn* TARGET 1, mark, sitting duck
2 *syn* LAUGHINGSTOCK, derision, jest, jestee, joke, mock, mockery, pilgarlic, sport
3 *syn* FOOL 3, chump, dupe, fall guy, gudgeon, gull, mark, pigeon, sucker, victim

butt (on *or* against) *vb* *syn* ADJOIN, abut, border, communicate, join, line, march, neighbor, touch, verge

||**butt** *n* **1** *syn* BUTTOCKS, backside, behind, bottom, breech, derriere, fanny, posterior, *prat, rear
2 *syn* CIGARETTE, ||cig, ||coffin nail, fag, ||gasper, ||pill, ||skag, smoke

butt *n* *syn* CASK, barrel, hogshead, keg, pipe, tun

butterball *n* *syn* FATTY, blimp, dumpling, ||fatso, ||tub

butt in *vb* **1** *syn* INTRUDE 1, chisel (in), cut in, horn in, intertrude, obtrude
con abstain, forbear, restrain
2 *syn* MEDDLE, busybody, fool, horn in, interfere, interlope, intermeddle, ||make, monkey (with), tamper (with)

butt–in *n* *syn* BUSYBODY, ||buttinsky, intermeddler, kibitzer, meddler, pragmatist, prier (*or* pryer), quidnunc, rubberneck, snoop

||**buttinsky** *n* *syn* BUSYBODY, butt-in, intermeddler, kibitzer, meddler, pragmatist, prier (*or* pryer), quidnunc, rubberneck, snoop

buttocks *n pl* the part of the back on which a person sits <gave the boy a whack across the *buttocks*>
syn *arse, *ass, backside, beam, behind, bottom, breech, *bum, ||butt, ||can, cheeks, derriere, ||duff, fanny, fundament, hams, haunches, heinie (*or* hiney), hind end, ||hinder, hunkers, ||keister, nates, podex, posterior, *prat, rear, rear end, rump, seat, ||stern, tail, tail end, ||tokus, ||twat
idiom seat of one's pants

button–down *adj* *syn* CONVENTIONAL 1, orthodox, square, straight

buttress *n* *syn* SUPPORT 3, brace, column, prop, shore, stay, underpinner, underpinning, underpropping

buttress *vb* *syn* SUPPORT 4, bear up, bolster, brace, carry, prop, shore (up), sustain, upbear, uphold

buvette *n* *syn* BAR 4, barroom, cocktail lounge, drinkery, ||gin mill, lounge, pub, tavern, watering hole

buxom *adj* having an amply developed bosom <a *buxom* young woman>
syn bosomy, busty, chesty, full-bosomed; *compare* CURVACEOUS
rel ||stacked; full-figured, Junoesque, shapely, well-developed, well-proportioned

buy *vb* **1** to acquire something for money or the equivalent <*bought* a new car>
syn purchase, take
rel acquire, get, obtain, procure
ant sell
2 *syn* RANSOM, redeem
3 *syn* BRIBE, buy off, fix, have, ||lubricate, sop, square, tamper (with)
||**4** *syn* BELIEVE 1, accept, swallow

buy *n* *syn* BARGAIN 1, closeout, pennyworth, steal

buyable *adj* *syn* VENAL 1, bribable, corruptible, purchasable

buyer *n* *syn* PURCHASER, emptor, vendee

buy off *vb* *syn* BRIBE, buy, fix, have, ||lubricate, sop, square, tamper (with)

buzz *vb* **1** *syn* HUM, bombinate, ||bum, bumble, drone, ||sowf, strum, thrum
2 *syn* HISS, fizz, fizzle, sibilate, sizzle, wheeze, whish, whisper, whiz, whoosh
||**3** *syn* TELEPHONE, call, phone, ||ring (up)

buzz *n* *syn* REPORT 1, cry, gossip, grapevine, hearsay, on-dit, rumble, rumor, scuttlebutt, talk

||**buzzed** *adj* *syn* INTOXICATED 1, ||boozy, ||canned, disguised, drunk, inebriated, ||lushed, muddled, pixilated, ||plastered

---

syn synonym(s)	*rel* related word(s)
idiom idiomatic equivalent(s)	*con* contrasted word(s)
ant antonym(s)	* vulgar

|| use limited; if in doubt, see a dictionary
The first word in a synonym list when printed in SMALL CAPITALS shows where there is more information about the group. For a more efficient use of this book see Explanatory Notes.

by *prep* **1** ***syn*** BESIDE 1, alongside, ‖fornent, next to
2 ***syn*** NEAR 2, ‖aside, beside, nearby, nigh, round
3 ***syn*** VIA 1, by way of, through
4 ***syn*** VIA 2, by dint of, by means of, by virtue of, by way of, per, through, with
5 with reference to <sorted *by* color>
syn according to, as to

by *adv* ***syn*** OVER 5, through

by *interj* ***syn*** GOOD-BYE, adieu, bye-bye, ‖cheerio, farewell, so long, ‖toodle-oo

by all odds *adv* ***syn*** FAR AND AWAY, by a long shot, by far, by long odds, by odds, out and away

by a long shot *adv* ***syn*** FAR AND AWAY, by all odds, by far, by long odds, by odds, out and away

by and by *adv* **1** ***syn*** AFTER, afterward, afterwhile, behind, infra, later, latterly, next, subsequently
2 ***syn*** PRESENTLY 1, anon, directly, shortly, soon

by–and–by *n* ***syn*** FUTURE, aftertime, afterward, hereafter, offing, to-be

by and large *adv* ***syn*** ALTOGETHER 3, all in all, en masse, generally, on the whole

by–blow *n* ***syn*** BASTARD 1, catch colt, chance child, come-by-chance, filius nullius, filius populi, illegitimate, love child, natural child, woods colt

by dint of *prep* ***syn*** VIA 2, by, by means of, by virtue of, by way of, per, through, with

bye–bye *interj* ***syn*** GOOD-BYE, adieu, by, ‖cheerio, farewell, so long, ‖toodle-oo

by far *adv* ***syn*** FAR AND AWAY, by all odds, by a long shot, by long odds, by odds, out and away

bygone *adj* **1** ***syn*** FORMER 2, erstwhile, late, old, once, onetime, past, quondam, sometime, whilom
2 ***syn*** OLD-FASHIONED, antiquated, antique, archaic, belated, dated, oldfangled, old-time, old-timey, out-of-date
3 ***syn*** EXTINCT 2, dead, defunct, departed, gone, lost, vanished

by long odds *adv* ***syn*** FAR AND AWAY, by all odds, by a long shot, by far, by odds, out and away

by means of *prep* ***syn*** VIA 2, by, by dint of, by virtue of, by way of, per, through, with

byname *n* ***syn*** NICKNAME, byword, ‖handle, hypocorism, ‖moniker, sobriquet

by odds *adv* ***syn*** FAR AND AWAY, by all odds, by a long shot, by far, by long odds, out and away

by ordinary *adv* ***syn*** USUALLY 2, as a rule, commonly, frequently, generally, ordinarily

bypass *vb* **1** ***syn*** SKIRT 2, circumnavigate, circumvent, detour
2 ***syn*** SKIRT 3, burke, circumvent, ‖polly-fox, sidestep

byplace *n* ***syn*** NOOK, cranny, niche

by–product *n* ***syn*** OUTGROWTH 2, derivative, descendant, offshoot, spin-off

by–sitter *n* ***syn*** SPECTATOR, beholder, bystander, eyewitness, looker-on, observer, onlooker, viewer, watcher, witness

bystander *n* ***syn*** SPECTATOR, beholder, by-sitter, eyewitness, looker-on, observer, onlooker, viewer, watcher, witness

by stealth *adv* ***syn*** SECRETLY, clandestinely, covertly, furtively, hugger-mugger, in camera, privately, stealthily, sub rosa, surreptitiously

by–talk *n* ***syn*** SMALL TALK, bavardage, chitchat, chitter-chatter, trifling

by the bye *adv* ***syn*** INCIDENTALLY 2, by the way, in passing, obiter, parenthetically

by the way *adv* ***syn*** INCIDENTALLY 2, by the bye, in passing, obiter, parenthetically

by–the–way *adj* ***syn*** INDIFFERENT 2, aloof, casual, detached, disinterested, incurious, remote, unconcerned, uninterested, withdrawn

by virtue of *prep* ***syn*** VIA 2, by, by dint of, by means of, by way of, per, through, with

by way of *prep* **1** ***syn*** VIA 1, by, through
2 ***syn*** VIA 2, by, by dint of, by means of, by virtue of, per, through, with

byword *n* **1** ***syn*** SAYING, adage, proverb, saw, word
2 ***syn*** CATCHWORD, byword, catchphrase, phrase, shibboleth, slogan, watchword
3 ***syn*** NICKNAME, byname, ‖handle, hypocorism, ‖moniker, sobriquet

Byzantine *adj* ***syn*** COMPLEX 2, complicated, daedal, elaborate, gordian, intricate, involved, knotty, labyrinthine, sophisticated

---

syn synonym(s) ***rel*** related word(s)
idiom idiomatic equivalent(s) ***con*** contrasted word(s)
ant antonym(s) * vulgar
‖ use limited; if in doubt, see a dictionary
The first word in a synonym list when printed in SMALL CAPITALS shows where there is more information about the group. For a more efficient use of this book see Explanatory Notes.

C

cab *n* ***syn*** TAXICAB, hack, taxi

‖**cab** *n* ***syn*** CRUD, goo, gook, gunk

cabal *n* **1** ***syn*** CLIQUE, camarilla, camp, circle, clan, coterie, ingroup, mob, ring
2 ***syn*** PLOT 2, conspiracy, covin, intrigue, machination, practice, scheme

cabalistic *adj* ***syn*** MYSTERIOUS, arcane, impenetrable, inscrutable, mysterial, mystic, numinous, unaccountable, unguessed, unknowable

cabaret *n* ***syn*** NIGHTCLUB, café, discotheque, hot spot, nightery, night spot, nitery, supper club, watering hole, watering place

‖**cabbage** *n* ***syn*** MONEY, ‖blunt, ‖brass, ‖bread, ‖chips, ‖dibs, ‖dinero, ‖do-re-mi, dough, ‖greenbacks

cabbage *vb* ***syn*** STEAL 1, appropriate, collar, ‖cop, hook, lift, nab, nip, pinch, purloin

cabbagehead *n* ***syn*** DUNCE, blockhead, bonehead, chowderhead, chucklehead, dunderhead, fathead, knucklehead, muttonhead, numskull

cabin *n* ***syn*** HUT, ‖box, ‖caboose, camp, cot, cottage, lodge, shack, shanty

‖**caboose** *n* ***syn*** HUT, ‖box, cabin, camp, cot, cottage, lodge, shack, shanty

‖**caboose** *n* ***syn*** JAIL, bridewell, ‖can, ‖chokey, ‖hoosegow, jug, lockup, penitentiary, prison, ‖stir

‖**ca' canny** *n* ***syn*** SLOWDOWN 2

cache *vb* ***syn*** HIDE, bury, ‖bush up, conceal, cover, ensconce, plant, screen, secrete, stash
con discover, unearth

cachet *n* ***syn*** STATUS 2, consequence, dignity, position, prestige, rank, standing, state, stature

‖**cack** *vb* ***syn*** VOMIT, barf, ‖cascade, ‖cast, ‖cat, ‖heave, *puke, spew, spit up, throw up

cackle *vb* ***syn*** CHAT 1, babble, burble, chatter, clack, gab, ‖gas, jaw, prattle, run on

cackle *n* ***syn*** CHATTER, babble, blab, blabber, ‖blatter, chat, clack, gab, gabble, prattle

cacophonic *adj* ***syn*** DISSONANT 1, cacophonous, discordant, disharmonic, disharmonious, immusical, inharmonic, inharmonious, unharmonious, unmusical

cacophonous *adj* ***syn*** DISSONANT 1, cacophonic, discordant, disharmonic, disharmonious, immusical, inharmonic, inharmonious, unharmonious, unmusical

cad *n* a person without gentlemanly instincts <gloated over his rival's distress like the *cad* that he was>
syn bounder, cur, rotter, yellow dog
rel boor, churl, clown, lout; guttersnipe, mucker, vulgarian; ‖creep; bastard, heel, louse, rat, stinker
idiom Jack Nasty
ant gentleman

cadaver *n* ***syn*** CORPSE, body, carcass, ‖cold meat, ‖deader, mort, remains, stiff

cadaverous *adj* **1** ***syn*** GHASTLY 2, corpselike, deathlike, ghostlike, ghostly, shadowy, spectral
2 ***syn*** EMACIATED, gaunt, skeletal, wasted
rel careworn, haggard, pinched, worn

cadence *n* ***syn*** RHYTHM, beat, cadency, measure, meter, rhyme, rhythmus, swing
rel accent, accentuation, emphasis, stress; pulsation, pulse, throb

cadency *n* ***syn*** RHYTHM, beat, cadence, measure, meter, rhyme, rhythmus, swing

cadet *n* ***syn*** PIMP 1, bully, ‖easy rider, fancy man, ‖mack, macquereau, pander

cadger *n* ***syn*** BEGGAR 1, bummer, moocher, panhandler, ‖schnorrer

cadging *n* ***syn*** MENDICANCY, beggary, bumming, mendicity, mooching, panhandling

caducity *n* ***syn*** OLD AGE, age, elderliness, senectitude, senescence, years
rel childishness, dotardy, dotingness

café *n* **1** ***syn*** EATING HOUSE, beanery, coffee shop, cookshop, diner, ‖hashery, ‖hash house, luncheonette, lunchroom, quick-lunch
2 ***syn*** NIGHTCLUB, cabaret, discotheque, hot spot, nightery, night spot, nitery, supper club, watering hole, watering place

cage *vb* ***syn*** ENCLOSE 1, close in, coop, envelop, fence, hem, immure, mew, pen, shut in
rel imprison, incarcerate, jail

cagey *adj* ***syn*** SHREWD, argute, astucious, astute, heady, perspicacious, sagacious, ‖savvy

cageyness *n* ***syn*** CUNNING 2, art, artfulness, artifice, canniness, craft, craftiness, foxiness, slyness, wiliness

cahoots *n pl* ***syn*** ASSOCIATION 1, affiliation, alliance, combination, conjunction, connection, hookup, partnership, tie-up, togetherness

‖**cahot** *n* ***syn*** BUMP 3, thank-you-ma'am

cajole *vb* ***syn*** COAX, ‖banter, blandish, blarney, con, soft-soap, sweet-talk, wheedle
rel beguile, deceive, delude; tantalize; crowd, push

cake *vb* **1** to cover with a surface layer <the floor was *caked* with filth>
syn crust, encrust (*or* incrust), incrustate, rime
rel besmear, coat, smear, spread; cover, daub
2 ***syn*** HARDEN 1, concrete, congeal, dry, indurate, set, solidify
rel compress, condense, contract, shrink

cakewalk *n* ***syn*** RUNAWAY, romp, rout, walkaway, walkover

---

syn synonym(s) — ***rel*** related word(s)
idiom idiomatic equivalent(s) — ***con*** contrasted word(s)
ant antonym(s) — * vulgar
‖ use limited; if in doubt, see a dictionary
The first word in a synonym list when printed in SMALL CAPITALS shows where there is more information about the group. For a more efficient use of this book see Explanatory Notes.

calaboose *n* ***syn*** JAIL, ‖can, ‖clink, cooler, ‖hoosegow, jug, lockup, ‖pokey, prison, ‖stir

calamitous *adj* **1** ***syn*** FATAL 2, cataclysmic, catastrophic, disastrous, fateful, ruinous
2 ***syn*** DEPLORABLE, afflictive, dire, distressing, grievous, heartbreaking, lamentable, regrettable, unfortunate, woeful

calamity *n* ***syn*** DISASTER, cataclysm, catastrophe, misadventure, tragedy, woe(s)
rel collapse, ruin, wreck; affliction, cross, trial, tribulation, visitation
con fortune, luck; benefaction; favor, gift
ant boon

calamity howler *n* ***syn*** PESSIMIST, Cassandra, crepehanger, worrywart

calculate *vb* to determine or approximate a mathematical value (as speed, cost, or quantity) < *calculate* the cost of a new car >
syn cipher, compute, estimate, figure, reckon
rel consider, study, weigh; ascertain, determine, discover; appraise, evaluate, price, value; assess, prize, rate
con conjecture, guess, surmise

calculate (on *or* upon) *vb* ***syn*** RELY (on *or* upon), bank (on *or* upon), build (on), count (on), depend (on *or* upon), ‖lot (on *or* upon), reckon (on), trust (in *or* to)

calculating *adj* ***syn*** CAUTIOUS, careful, chary, circumspect, considerate, discreet, gingerly, guarded, safe, wary
rel artful, crafty, cunning, guileful, sly, wily
con improvident, imprudent, indiscreet
ant rash, reckless

calculation *n* ***syn*** COMPUTATION, arithmetic, ciphering, estimation, figuring, reckoning

calembour *n* ***syn*** PUN, paronomasia

calendar *n* ***syn*** PROGRAM 1, agenda, card, docket, programma, schedule, sked, timetable

calenture *n* ***syn*** PASSION 6, ardor, enthusiasm, fervor, fire, hurrah, zeal

caliber *n* **1** ***syn*** QUALITY 2, merit, stature, value, virtue, worth
rel ability, capability, capacity; force, power
2 ***syn*** QUALITY 3, class, grade

caliginous *adj* ***syn*** DARK 1, dim, dusk, dusky, gloomy, lightless, murky, obscure, tenebrous, unilluminated

call *vb* **1** to speak or utter in a loud distinct carrying voice < *call* for help >
syn cry, hallo, holler, hollo, shout, vociferate, yell; *compare* SHOUT 1
rel bawl, bellow, hoot, howl, roar, scream, screech, shriek, shrill, whoop, yowl
con murmur, whisper
2 ***syn*** DEMAND 1, challenge, claim, exact, postulate, require, requisition, solicit
3 ***syn*** SUMMON 2, call in, convene, summons
rel assemble, collect, gather, round up; bid, invite
4 ***syn*** CONVOKE, assemble, convene, summon
5 ***syn*** TELEPHONE, ‖buzz, phone, ‖ring (up)
6 ***syn*** NAME 1, baptize, christen, denominate, designate, dub, entitle, style, term, title
7 ***syn*** PREDICT 2, guess
8 ***syn*** ESTIMATE 3, approximate, judge, place, put, reckon
9 ***syn*** FORETELL, adumbrate, augur, forecast, portend, predict, presage, prognosticate, prophesy, vaticinate
10 ***syn*** VISIT 2, come by, come over, drop (in *or* by), look in, look up, pop (in), run in, see, stop (in *or* by)

call (for) *vb* ***syn*** DEMAND 2, ask, crave, necessitate, require, take

call (to) *vb* ***syn*** ADDRESS 7, accost, greet, hail, salute

call *n* **1** the natural vocal sound of an animal and especially a bird < the clear *call* of a bellbird >
syn cry, note, song
rel cheep, chirp, peep, twitter, warble
2 ***syn*** ATTRACTION 1, allurement, appeal, attractiveness, draw, drawing power, lure, pull, seduction
3 ***syn*** OCCASION 3, cause, necessity, obligation
4 ***syn*** VISIT 1, visitation

call down *vb* ***syn*** REPROVE, admonish, chide, lesson, monish, ‖rack back, rebuke, reprimand, reproach, tick off

caller *n* ***syn*** VISITOR 1, guest, visitant

‖**callet** *n* ***syn*** PROSTITUTE, bawd, call girl, ‖cruiser, harlot, ‖hooker, hustler, ‖joy girl, nightwalker, streetwalker

call girl *n* ***syn*** PROSTITUTE, bawd, drab, fille de joie, harlot, ‖hooker, hustler, poule, streetwalker, whore

call house *n* ***syn*** BROTHEL, bagnio, bordello, cathouse, ‖hookshop, ‖joyhouse, lupanar, sporting house, stew, whorehouse

calligraphy *n* ***syn*** HANDWRITING, chirography, ductus, fist, hand, penmanship, script

call in *vb* ***syn*** SUMMON 2, call, convene, summons

calling *n* **1** ***syn*** MISSION, lifework, vocation
2 ***syn*** TRADE 1, art, craft, handicraft, métier, profession, vocation
3 ***syn*** WORK 1, business, employment, job, line, occupation, pursuit, ‖racket

‖**callithump** *n* ***syn*** SHIVAREE, ‖belling, ‖bull band, charivari, ‖horning, ‖riding, ‖skimmelton

call off *vb* ***syn*** CANCEL 2, drop, scrub

callous *adj* ***syn*** UNFEELING 2, coldhearted, hardhearted, heartless, obdurate, stony, stonyhearted, uncompassionate, unemotional, unsympathetic
rel indurated, set

callow *adj* **1** ***syn*** YOUNG 1, green, immature, infant, juvenile, unfledged, unripe, youthful
2 ***syn*** INEXPERIENCED, fresh, green, raw, unexperienced, unpracticed, unseasoned, untried, unversed, young

callowness *n* ***syn*** INEXPERIENCE, freshness, greenness, rawness

call up *vb* to summon for active military duty < *called up* the army reserves >
syn order up; *compare* DRAFT 1
rel mobilize
idiom call to the colors
ant discharge, muster out

---

syn synonym(s) — ***rel*** related word(s)
idiom idiomatic equivalent(s) — ***con*** contrasted word(s)
ant antonym(s) — * vulgar
‖ use limited; if in doubt, see a dictionary
The first word in a synonym list when printed in SMALL CAPITALS shows where there is more information about the group. For a more efficient use of this book see Explanatory Notes.

calm *n syn* QUIET 1, hush, lull

calm *adj* **1** free from storm or rough activity <the wind died and the sea became *calm*>
syn halcyon, hushed, placid, quiet, still, stilly, untroubled
rel inactive, quiescent, reposing, resting; pacific, smooth, tranquil, unruffled
idiom calm as a millpond, still as death
con agitated, disturbed, perturbed, restless, turbulent, uneasy
ant stormy
2 free from mental or emotional distress or agitation <a man who remained *calm* under stress>
syn collected, composed, easy, easygoing, placid, poised, possessed, self-composed, self-possessed, serene, tranquil
rel cool, imperturbable, nonchalant, unflappable, unruffled; even-tempered, impassive, phlegmatic, steady; firm, stable, staunch
con discomposed, disturbed, perturbed, upset; anxious, bothered, confused, nervous; fidgety, jittery, jumpy, shaky, tense
ant agitated

calm *vb* to relieve from or bring to an end whatever distresses, agitates, or disturbs <that inner faith that *calms* the troubled spirit>
syn allay, balm, becalm, compose, lull, quiet, ‖quieten, settle, soothe, ‖soother, still, tranquilize
rel alleviate, assuage, mitigate, relieve; appease, mollify, pacify, placate; relax, steady
con bother, discompose, disquiet, disturb, flurry, perturb, stir up, upset
ant agitate; arouse

calmant *n syn* SEDATIVE, calmative, quietive

calmative *n syn* SEDATIVE, calmant, quietive

calmness *n syn* EQUANIMITY, ataraxy, composure, coolness, imperturbability, phlegm, sangfroid, self-possession

calumniate *vb syn* MALIGN, asperse, defame, denigrate, libel, scandalize, slander, traduce, vilify, villainize
ant eulogize; vindicate

calumnious *adj syn* LIBELOUS, backbiting, defamatory, detracting, detractive, maligning, scandalous, slanderous, traducing, vilifying

calumny *n syn* DETRACTION, backbiting, backstabbing, belittlement, defamation, depreciation, disparagement, scandal, slander, tale
rel animadversion, reflection, stricture
con encomium, panegyric, tribute; adulation, compliment, flattery
ant eulogy; vindication

calvary *n syn* TRIAL 1, affliction, cross, crucible, ordeal, tribulation, visitation

‖**cam** *adv syn* AWRY 1, askance, askant, askew, cock-a-hoop, cockeyed, crookedly

camaraderie *n* a spirit of friendly goodwill typical of comrades <the easy *camaraderie* of a cozy neighborhood bar>
syn comradery, good-fellowship
rel affability, friendliness, gregariousness, sociability; cheer, conviviality, jollity
con aloofness, coldness, frigidity, inaccessibility, reclusiveness, remoteness, self-containment; exclusiveness, self-sufficiency, unsociability

camarilla *n syn* CLIQUE, cabal, camp, circle, clan, coterie, ingroup, mob, ring

cameraman *n syn* PHOTOGRAPHER, camerist, photog, photographist, photoist

camerist *n syn* PHOTOGRAPHER, cameraman, photog, photographist, photoist

camouflage *vb syn* DISGUISE, cloak, dissemble, dissimulate, dress up, mask
rel becloud, befog, dim

camp *n* **1** a place where a number of people (as vacationers or soldiers) live temporarily together in usually more or less casual housing <planned to summer at a fishing *camp* in Maine>
syn campground, encampment
2 *syn* CLIQUE, cabal, camarilla, circle, clan, coterie, ingroup, mob, ring
3 *syn* HUT, ‖box, cabin, ‖caboose, cot, cottage, lodge, shack, shanty

camp *vb* to live temporarily in a camp or the outdoors <*camped* under the trees for the night>
syn bivouac, ‖bivvy, encamp, ‖laager, ‖maroon, tent
idiom rough it
con decamp

campanile *n syn* BELL TOWER, belfry, carillon

campestral *adj syn* RURAL, agrestic, bucolic, countrified, country, out-country, outland, pastoral, provincial, rustic

camp follower *n syn* PROSTITUTE, bawd, call girl, ‖cruiser, harlot, ‖hooker, hustler, nightwalker, streetwalker, whore

campground *n syn* CAMP 1, encampment

‖**cample** *vb syn* SCOLD 1, baste, berate, ‖carpet, lash, rail, rate, revile, tongue-lash, vituperate

‖**can** *n* **1** *syn* JAIL, ‖calaboose, ‖clink, ‖hoosegow, jug, lockup, pen, ‖pokey, prison, ‖stir
2 *syn* TOILET, ‖donicker, head, john, johnny, latrine, ‖pot, ‖potty, privy, ‖throne
3 *syn* BUTTOCKS, *arse, backside, behind, ‖butt, derriere, fanny, fundament, hind end, hunkers

‖**can** *vb syn* DISMISS 3, ax, boot (out), bounce, cashier, discharge, fire, kick out, sack, terminate

Canaan *n syn* HEAVEN 2, bliss, Civitas Dei, elysium, empyrean, happy hunting ground, kingdom come, nirvana, paradise, Zion

canaille *n syn* RABBLE 2, dreg(s), mass(es), mob, proletariat, ragtag and bobtail, riffraff, scum, trash, unwashed

canal *n syn* CHANNEL 1, aqueduct, conduit, course, duct, watercourse

canard *n syn* LIE, ‖bouncer, falsehood, falsity, fib, misrepresentation, prevarication, tale, untruism, untruth
rel hoax, humbug, mare's-nest, sell, spoof; artifice, dodge, trick

---

syn synonym(s)	*rel* related word(s)
idiom idiomatic equivalent(s)	*con* contrasted word(s)
ant antonym(s)	* vulgar

‖ use limited; if in doubt, see a dictionary

The first word in a synonym list when printed in SMALL CAPITALS shows where there is more information about the group. For a more efficient use of this book see Explanatory Notes.

‖**canary** *n* ***syn*** INFORMER, betrayer, ‖fink, ‖nark, snitch, ‖squeaker, squealer, stoolie, stool pigeon, tipster

cancel *vb* **1** ***syn*** ERASE, black (out), blot out, delete, efface, expunge, obliterate, wipe (out), x (out)
2 to give up something previously arranged or agreed on <decided to *cancel* his appointment with the dentist>
syn call off, drop, scrub
rel end, terminate; annul, invalidate, rescind, revoke; give up, relinquish, surrender

cancel (out) *vb* ***syn*** NEUTRALIZE, annul, counteract, countercheck, frustrate, negate, negative, redress

candid *adj* **1** ***syn*** FAIR 4, dispassionate, equal, equitable, impartial, just, objective, unbiased, uncolored, unprejudiced
rel aboveboard, forthright, straightforward; honest, scrupulous, upright
2 ***syn*** FRANK, open, openhearted, plain, straightforward, unconcealed, undisguised, undissembled, undissembling, unreserved
ant evasive

candidate *n* one who seeks an office, honor, position, or award <examining *candidates* for editorial positions>
syn applicant, aspirant, hopeful, seeker
rel nominee; dark horse; also-ran, has-been; campaigner, electioneerer, stumper, whistle-stopper

candy *vb* ***syn*** SUGARCOAT 1, honey, sugar (over), sweeten

canine *n* ***syn*** DOG 1, bowwow, hound, ‖pooch, tyke

canker *vb* ***syn*** DEBASE 1, animalize, bestialize, corrupt, debauch, demoralize, deprave, pervert, stain, vitiate

cankered *adj* ***syn*** CANTANKEROUS, bearish, cranky, cross-grained, crotchety, ornery, vinegarish, vinegary, waspish, waspy

cannabis *n* ***syn*** MARIJUANA, boo, grass, ‖Mary Jane, moocah, pot, ‖tea, weed

canned *adj* **1** ***syn*** CONDENSED, capsule, epitomized, pocket, potted
‖**2** ***syn*** INTOXICATED 1, ‖boozed, ‖boozy, disguised, drunk, inebriated, ‖lushed, muddled, pixilated, ‖plastered

cannibalic *adj* ***syn*** FIERCE 1, barbarous, cruel, ferocious, grim, inhuman, inhumane, savage, truculent, wolfish

canniness *n* **1** ***syn*** PRUDENCE 1, caution, discreetness, discretion, foresight, forethought, precaution, providence
2 ***syn*** CUNNING 2, art, artfulness, artifice, cageyness, craft, craftiness, foxiness, slyness, wiliness

‖**cannon** *n* ***syn*** PICKPOCKET, cutpurse, ‖dip, ‖diver, purse cutter, ‖wire

cannonade *n* ***syn*** BARRAGE, bombardment, broadside, burst, drumfire, fusillade, hail, salvo, shower, volley

cannonade *vb* ***syn*** BOMBARD, blitz, bomb, shell

canny *adj* **1** ***syn*** CLEVER 4, adroit, ‖coony, cunning, dexterous, ingenious, ‖sleighty, slim, sly
2 ***syn*** SPARING, chary, economical, frugal, provident, saving, Scotch, stewardly, thrifty, unwasteful
3 ***syn*** WISE 4, hep, knowing, nimble-witted, quick, quick-witted, sharp, sharp-witted, slick, smart

canon *n* **1** ***syn*** LAW 1, assize, decree, decretum, edict, ordinance, precept, regulation, rule, statute
2 ***syn*** DOCTRINE, dogma, tenet

canonical *adj* ***syn*** ORTHODOX 1, accepted, authoritative, received, sanctioned, sound

‖**cant** *adj* ***syn*** LIVELY 1, alert, animate, animated, ‖canty, gay, keen, spirited, sprightly, vivacious

cant *vb* ***syn*** SLANT 1, heel, incline, lean, list, recline, slope, tilt, tip

cant *n* **1** ***syn*** DIALECT 2, argot, jargon, lingo, patois, patter, slang, vernacular
rel diction, language, phraseology, vocabulary; idiom, speech
2 ***syn*** TERMINOLOGY, dictionary, jargon, language, lexicon, palaver, vocabulary
3 ***syn*** HYPOCRISY, hypocriticalness, pecksniffery, pharisaicalness, pharisaism, sanctimoniousness, sanctimony, Tartuffery, Tartuffism

cantankerous *adj* habitually ill-humored, irritable, and disagreeable <one of our more *cantankerous* fellow workers>
syn bearish, cankered, cranky, cross-grained, crotchety, ornery, rantankerous, vinegarish, vinegary, waspish, waspy; *compare* IRASCIBLE, IRRITABLE
rel dour, morose, sour; crabbed, cross, crusty, huffy, petulant, prickly, snappish; dyspeptic, ill-conditioned, ill-natured; liverish
idiom like a bear with a sore paw
con benign, kindly, mellow, mild; amiable, congenial, friendly, pleasant, well-disposed; benevolent, gracious, kind

canter *n* ***syn*** VAGABOND, ‖bindle stiff, bum, derelict, drifter, hobo, street arab, tramp, vag, vagrant

cantina *n* ***syn*** BAR 5, barroom, drinkery, ‖gin mill, ‖groggery, pothouse, pub, ‖rum hole, saloon, tavern

canting *adj* ***syn*** HYPOCRITICAL, pecksniffian, pharisaic, pharisaical, sanctimonious, self-righteous

canton *vb* ***syn*** BILLET 1, quarter

‖**canty** *adj* ***syn*** LIVELY 1, alert, animate, animated, ‖cant, gay, keen, spirited, sprightly, vivacious

canvass *vb* **1** ***syn*** SCRUTINIZE 1, ‖case, check over, check up, con, examine, inspect, study, survey, vet
2 ***syn*** DISCUSS 1, agitate, argue, debate, discept, dispute, ‖kick around, moot, thrash out, toss (around)
3 ***syn*** SOLICIT 1, drum, drum up

cap *vb* **1** ***syn*** SURMOUNT 3, crest, crown, top
‖**2** ***syn*** PUZZLE, befog, bewilder, confound, confuse, metagrobolize, perplex, pose, stumble
3 ***syn*** COVER 3, blanket, crown, overcast, overlay, overspread
4 ***syn*** SURPASS 1, best, cob, exceed, outshine, outstrip, pass, top, transcend, trump
5 ***syn*** CLIMAX, crown, culminate, finish off, round off, top off

capability *n* **1** ***syn*** ABILITY 1, adequacy, capacity, competence, might, qualification, qualifiedness
rel art, craft, cunning, skill

---

syn synonym(s) — ***rel*** related word(s)
idiom idiomatic equivalent(s) — ***con*** contrasted word(s)
ant antonym(s) — * vulgar
‖ use limited; if in doubt, see a dictionary
The first word in a synonym list when printed in SMALL CAPITALS shows where there is more information about the group. For a more efficient use of this book see Explanatory Notes.

con disability, inability
ant incapability, incompetence
2 *syn* EFFICACY 1, effectiveness, efficiency, potency

capable *adj* *syn* ABLE, au fait, competent, good, proper, qualified, wicked
ant incapable

capacious *adj* *syn* SPACIOUS, ample, commodious, roomy, wide
rel dilatable, distensible, expandable, expansive, extensile; abundant, copious, plentiful
ant exiguous

capacity *n* **1** *syn* ABILITY 1, adequacy, capability, competence, might, qualification, qualifiedness
rel bent, faculty, gift, knack, talent, twin; caliber, stature
con impotence, ineffectiveness, powerlessness
ant incapacity
2 *syn* STATUS 1, character, footing, place, position, rank, situation, standing, state, station

cape *n* *syn* PROMONTORY, beak, bill, foreland, head, headland, naze, point

caper *vb* *syn* GAMBOL, cavort, frisk, frolic, rollick, romp
idiom cut capers

caper *n* **1** *syn* ESCAPADE, lark, rollick
2 *syn* PRANK, antic, dido(es), frolic, lark, monkeyshine, shenanigan, shine(s), tomfoolery, trick
rel devilment, impishness, mischief, roguery, waggishness

‖**capernoited** *adj* *syn* INTOXICATED 1, ‖boozy, ‖canned, disguised, drunk, inebriated, ‖lushed, muddled, pixilated, ‖plastered

capital *adj* **1** *syn* EGREGIOUS, flagrant, glaring, gross, rank
2 *syn* CHIEF 2, ‖cock, dominant, main, major, number one, outstanding, predominant, preeminent, principal
rel cardinal, essential, vital; basic, fundamental, underlying
3 *syn* EXCELLENT, ‖dandy, famous, fine, first-class, first-rate, five-star, prime, top, top-notch

capital *n* *syn* MEAN 3, assets, resources, wealth

capitalize *vb* to supply capital for or to <agreed to *capitalize* the venture>
syn back, bankroll, finance, grubstake, stake
rel aid, assist, help, subsidize, support; fund; promote, sponsor

capitulate *vb* *syn* YIELD 2, bow, buckle (under), cave, defer, knuckle, knuckle under, submit, succumb

capitulation *n* *syn* SURRENDER, dedition, submission

capper *n* *syn* DECOY 2, blind, ‖bonnet, ‖booster, shill, shillaber, stick

caprice *n* an arbitrary, impulsive, and often illogical notion or change of mind <given to sudden *caprices* and random fancies>
syn bee, boutade, conceit, crank, crotchet, fancy, freak, humor, maggot, megrim, notion, vagary, whigmaleerie, whim, whimsy
rel mood, temper, vein; contrariety, inconsistency, perversity; characteristic, foible, habit, mannerism, peculiarity, trait, trick

capricious *adj* **1** *syn* ARBITRARY 1, erratic, freakish, vagarious, wayward, whimsical, whimsied
2 *syn* INCONSTANT 1, changeable, fickle, lubricious, mercurial, temperamental, ticklish, unstable, variable, volatile
rel humorsome, moody; effervescent
con constant, steady
ant steadfast
3 *syn* UNCERTAIN 1, chancy, erratic, fluctuant, iffy, incalculable, unpredictable, whimsical

capsheaf *n* *syn* APEX 2, acme, capstone, climax, culmination, meridian, peak, pinnacle, summit, zenith

capstone *n* *syn* APEX 2, acme, apogee, capsheaf, climax, culmination, meridian, peak, pinnacle, summit

capsule *adj* *syn* CONDENSED, canned, epitomized, pocket, potted

caption *n* an explanatory or identifying comment accompanying a pictorial illustration <the *captions* were under the wrong figures>
syn legend, underline

captious *adj* *syn* CRITICAL 1, carping, caviling, cavillous, censorious, critic, faultfinding, hypercritical, overcritical
rel demanding, exacting, finicky; contrary, perverse; irritable, peevish, petulant, snappish, snappy, testy
con judicious, sensible, wise; rational, reasonable; knowing, knowledgeable
ant appreciative

captivate *vb* *syn* ATTRACT 1, allure, bewitch, charm, draw, enchant, fascinate, magnetize, take, wile
rel delight, gratify, please; enthrall, grip, hold, mesmerize, spellbind
ant repulse

captivated *adj* *syn* ENAMORED 3, bewitched, charmed, enchanted, entranced, fascinated

captivating *adj* *syn* ATTRACTIVE 1, alluring, appealing, bewitching, drawing, enchanting, fascinating, glamorous, magnetic, seductive

capture *vb* *syn* CATCH 1, bag, collar, ‖cotch, get, nail, prehend, secure, take

Capuan *adj* *syn* LUXURIOUS 3, deluxe, luscious, lush, luxuriant, opulent, palatial, plush, sumptuous, upholstered

car *n* a usually private passenger-carrying automotive vehicle <drove a shabby old *car*>
syn auto, autocar, automobile, buggy, ‖bus, machine, motor, motorcar
rel coach, convertible, coupe, hardtop, limousine, phaeton, roadster, runabout, sedan, station wagon, touring car; ‖clunker, ‖crate, ‖heap, ‖jalopy, junker, ‖wreck

caravansary *n* *syn* HOTEL, auberge, hospice, hostel, hostelry, inn, lodge, public house, roadhouse, tavern

carbon *n* *syn* REPRODUCTION, carbon copy, copy, ditto, duplicate, facsimile, reduplication, replica, replication

carbon copy *n* *syn* REPRODUCTION, carbon, copy, ditto, duplicate, facsimile, reduplication, replica, replication

carbuncle *n* *syn* ABSCESS, boil, furuncle, pimple, pustule

---

syn synonym(s) — *rel* related word(s)
idiom idiomatic equivalent(s) — *con* contrasted word(s)
ant antonym(s) — * vulgar
‖ use limited; if in doubt, see a dictionary
The first word in a synonym list when printed in SMALL CAPITALS shows where there is more information about the group. For a more efficient use of this book see Explanatory Notes.

carcass *n* ***syn*** CORPSE, body, cadaver, ‖cold meat, ‖deader, mort, remains, stiff

‖**carcel** *n* ***syn*** JAIL, ‖brig, ‖calaboose, ‖can, ‖clink, cooler, lockup, ‖pokey, prison, ‖stir

card *n* **1** ***syn*** WAG 1, comedian, humorist, joker, zany
2 ***syn*** PROGRAM 1, agenda, calendar, docket, programma, schedule, sked, timetable
3 ***syn*** MENU, carte du jour

card *vb* ***syn*** SCHEDULE 1, sked

cardboard *adj* ***syn*** STIFF 4, buckram, muscle-bound, stilted, wooden
rel unlifelike, unreal, unrealistic

cardinal *adj* **1** ***syn*** ESSENTIAL 2, constitutive, fundamental, vital
2 ***syn*** CENTRAL 1, overriding, overruling, pivotal, ruling

care *n* **1** ***syn*** SORROW, affliction, anguish, ‖dole, grief, heartache, heartbreak, regret, rue, woe
rel strain, stress, tension
2 a burdened or disquieted state of mind <a mind full of *care* and sadness>
syn anxiety, concern, concernment, disquiet, disquietude, solicitude, unease, uneasiness, worry
rel apprehension, foreboding, misgiving, suspense; agitation, disturbance, perturbation; alarm, consternation, dismay, fear
con calm, ease, peace, quietude; assurance, comfort, easiness
3 ***syn*** TRIAL 2, trouble, worry
4 serious and heedful attentiveness <attended his words with *care*>
syn carefulness, concern, consciousness, heed, heedfulness, regard; *compare* ATTENTION 1
rel curiosity; enthusiasm, interest; consideration, solicitude, thoughtfulness; effort, exertion, pains, trouble; alertness, vigilance, watchfulness
con carelessness, disregard, heedlessness, unconcern; boredom, disinterest, ennui
5 ***syn*** OVERSIGHT 1, charge, conduct, handling, intendance, management, running, superintendence, superintendency, supervision
6 ***syn*** CUSTODY, guardianship, keeping, safekeeping, trust, ward

care (for) *vb* **1** ***syn*** TEND 2, attend, mind, watch
2 ***syn*** MINISTER (to), mother, nurse, serve, wait (on)
idiom take care of

careen *vb* ***syn*** LURCH 2, stagger, ‖stoit, ‖stoiter, ‖stot, sway, swing, weave, wobble

career *vb* ***syn*** COURSE, chase, race, rush, speed, tear

carefree *adj* **1** ***syn*** HAPPY-GO-LUCKY, free-minded, insouciant, lighthearted, lightsome
2 ***syn*** IRRESPONSIBLE, careless, feckless, incautious, reckless, uncareful, wild

careful *adj* **1** ***syn*** CAUTIOUS, calculating, chary, circumspect, considerate, discreet, gingerly, guarded, safe, wary
rel attentive, heedful, observant
2 closely attentive to details or showing such attention <*careful* workmanship>
syn conscientious, conscionable, exact, fussy, heedful, meticulous, painstaking, punctilious, punctual, scrupulous
rel accurate, nice, precise; deliberate, studied; foresighted, provident, prudent; critical, discriminating, finical, finicky; observant, particular, religious; duteous, dutiful, intent
con disorderly, lax, negligent, slack, slipshod, slovenly; heedless, neglectful, remiss
ant careless

carefulness *n* ***syn*** CARE 4, concern, consciousness, heed, heedfulness, regard

careless *adj* **1** lacking in or showing lack of care and attention <*careless* of the harm his neglect might do to others> <unwilling to accept such *careless* shoddy work>
syn feckless, heedless, inadvertent, irreflective, thoughtless, uncaring, unheeding, unrecking, unreflective, unthinking; *compare* INCAUTIOUS, RASH 1
rel forgetful, inattentive, oblivious, unmindful; lax, neglectful, negligent, slack, unconcerned, uninterested; inadequate, incapable, unfit, unqualified
con careful, heedful, thoughtful; concerned, considerate, punctilious, scrupulous
ant careful
2 ***syn*** IRRESPONSIBLE, carefree, feckless, incautious, reckless, uncareful, wild
3 ***syn*** NEGLIGENT, behindhand, delinquent, derelict, disregardful, lax, neglectful, regardless, remiss, slack
4 ***syn*** SLIPSHOD 3, botchy, messy, slapdash, sloppy, slovenly, unthorough, untidy
5 ***syn*** SLOVENLY 1, disheveled, messy, raunchy, slipshod, sloppy, unfastidious, unkempt, unneat, untidy

caress *vb* to express interest, affection, or love by touching or handling <*caress* a frightened child>
syn cosset, cuddle, dandle, fondle, love, pet
rel cocker, coddle, indulge, pamper; coquet, dally, flirt, toy, trifle; nuzzle, pat, stroke

careworn *adj* ***syn*** HAGGARD, drawn, pinched, worn
rel distressed, troubled; exhausted, fagged, jaded, tuckered
ant carefree

cargo *n* ***syn*** LOAD 1, burden, freight, haul, lading, payload

caricature *n* **1** ***syn*** MOCKERY 2, burlesque, farce, mock, sham, travesty
2 a grotesque or bizarre imitation <a doting attentiveness that was a sickly *caricature* of motherhood>
syn burlesque, parody, takeoff, travesty
rel lampoon, libel, pasquinade; laughingstock, mockery; cheat, fake, imitation, phony, sham; bosh, bunk, gammon, hokum, moonshine; clinquant, pinchbeck, shoddy, tinsel

carillon *n* ***syn*** BELL TOWER, belfry, campanile

caritas *n* ***syn*** MERCY, charity, clemency, grace, lenity

cark *vb* **1** ***syn*** TROUBLE 1, ail, distress, upset, worry
2 ***syn*** WORRY 3, fret, fuss, pother, stew, ‖tew

carnage *n syn* MASSACRE, bloodbath, bloodshed, butchery, slaughter

carnal *adj* **1** *syn* BODILY, corporal, corporeal, fleshly, physical, somatic
rel material, substantial; earthly, earthy
2 characterized by physical rather than intellectual or spiritual orientation <giving too much heed to the *carnal* aspects of day-to-day life>
syn animal, fleshly, sensual; *compare* SENSUOUS
rel bodily, corporal, corporeal, physical; coarse, gross, obscene, vulgar; earthly, earthy, mundane, temporal, worldly; lascivious, lewd, lustful, wanton; Pandemic, sensuous
con ethical, moral, noble, righteous, virtuous; aerial, ethereal, otherworldly, supernal; chaste, decent, modest, pure
ant spiritual; intellectual

carnality *n syn* ANIMALITY, animalism, fleshliness

carom *vb syn* GLANCE 1, dap, graze, ricochet, skim, skip

carousal *n syn* BINGE 1, bat, bender, blowoff, booze, brannigan, drunk, jag, spree, tear

carouse *n syn* BINGE 1, bat, bender, blowoff, booze, brannigan, drunk, jag, spree, tear

carouse *vb syn* REVEL 1, frolic, hell, riot, roister, spree, wassail

carp (at) *vb syn* NAG, fuss, henpeck, peck (at)

carper *n syn* CRITIC, aristarch, caviler, criticizer, faultfinder, knocker, momus, smellfungus, Zoilus

‖**carpet** *vb syn* SCOLD 1, berate, ‖cample, lash, rail, rate, tell off, upbraid, vituperate, wig
idiom call on the carpet, take to task

carpet knight *n syn* HEDONIST, pleasuremonger, sybarite

carping *adj syn* CRITICAL 1, captious, caviling, cavillous, censorious, critic, faultfinding, hypercritical, overcritical
rel blaming, criticizing, reprehending, reprobating; jawing, railing, upbraiding; blameful, condemnatory, damnatory, objurgatory, reproachful, reprobatory
con applauding, commendatory, complimentary; approving, endorsing; extolling, laudatory, praiseful
ant fulsome

carriage *n* **1** *syn* TRANSPORTATION 1, carrying, conveyance, transit, transport, transporting
2 *syn* POSTURE 1, attitude, pose, positure, stance

carriageable *adj syn* PORTABLE, portative, transportable

carriage trade *n syn* ARISTOCRACY, blue blood, elite, flower, gentility, gentry, quality, upper class, upper crust, who's who

carrier *n* **1** *syn* BEARER 2, drogher, porter
2 *syn* MESSENGER, bearer, courier, emissary, envoy, internuncio
3 *syn* VECTOR, vehicle

carrot *n syn* REWARD, dividend, guerdon, meed, plum, premium, prize

carry *vb* **1** to be the agent or means by which someone or something is shifted from one place to another <*carried* the child on his shoulder>
syn bear, buck, convey, ferry, ‖hump, ‖jag, lug, pack, tote, transport
rel bring, fetch, take; move, remove, shift, transfer; send, transmit
‖**2** *syn* ACCOMPANY, attend, bear, chaperon, companion, company, conduct, consort (with), convoy, escort
3 *syn* AFFECT, get, impress, influence, inspire, move, strike, sway, touch
4 *syn* BEAR 3, have, possess
5 *syn* CONDUCT 4, channel, convey, funnel, pipe, siphon, traject, transmit
6 *syn* BEHAVE 1, acquit, act, bear, comport, conduct, demean, deport, disport, quit
7 *syn* SUPPORT 4, bear up, bolster, brace, buttress, prop, shore (up), sustain, upbear, uphold
8 *syn* STOCK, keep

carrying *n syn* TRANSPORTATION 1, carriage, conveyance, transit, transport, transporting

carry off *vb syn* KILL 1, cut off, destroy, dispatch, down, finish, lay low, put away, slay, take off

carry on *vb* **1** *syn* CONDUCT 3, direct, keep, manage, operate, ordain, run
2 *syn* CUT UP 2, act up, horse, horseplay
3 *syn* PERSEVERE, go on, hang on, persist

carry out *vb* **1** *syn* ADMINISTER 1, administrate, execute, govern, render
rel complete, finalize; discharge, effect, effectuate, fulfill; prosecute, transact
idiom put in force (*or* into effect); sign, seal, and deliver
2 *syn* EFFECT 2, bring off, carry through, effectuate

carrytale *n syn* GOSSIP 1, clack, gossiper, gossipmonger, newsmonger, quidnunc, scandalmonger, tabby, talebearer, telltale

carry through *vb* **1** *syn* EFFECT 2, bring off, carry out, effectuate
2 *syn* CONTINUE 1, abide, endure, last, perdure, persist

carte blanche *n* full discretionary power <was given *carte blanche* to build, landscape, and furnish the house>
syn blank check, free hand
rel license, prerogative, right; authority, power; say, say-so
idiom power of attorney

carte d'entrée *n syn* TICKET 2

carte du jour *n syn* MENU, card

cartel *n* **1** *syn* DEFIANCE 1, challenge, dare, defi, defy, stump
rel gage, gauntlet, glove; blow, slap
2 *syn* SYNDICATE, chain, combine, conglomerate, group, pool, trust
rel corporation; multinational; consortium, merger

carve *vb* **1** *syn* CUT 5, cleave, dissect, dissever, sever, slice, split, sunder
2 *syn* SCULPTURE, chisel, sculp, sculpt

Casanova *n* **1** *syn* GALLANT 2, amorist, Don Juan, lothario, paramour, Romeo

---

syn synonym(s) — *rel* related word(s)
idiom idiomatic equivalent(s) — *con* contrasted word(s)
ant antonym(s) — * vulgar
‖ use limited; if in doubt, see a dictionary
The first word in a synonym list when printed in SMALL CAPITALS shows where there is more information about the group. For a more efficient use of this book see Explanatory Notes.

2 *syn* WOLF, chaser, Don Juan, ladies' man, lady-killer, masher, philander, philanderer, womanizer

cascade *n* *syn* WATERFALL, cataract, chute, fall(s), ‖force, sault, spout

‖**cascade** *vb* *syn* VOMIT, barf, bring up, disgorge, ‖heave, *puke, spew, spit up, throw up, upchuck

case *n* **1** *syn* EVENT 4, eventuality

2 *syn* ORDER 9, condition, estate, repair, shape

3 *syn* SUIT 1, action, cause, lawsuit

4 *syn* INSTANCE, case history, example, illustration, representative, sample, sampling, specimen

rel circumstance, episode, event, incident, occurrence; condition, situation, state

5 *syn* ECCENTRIC, character, ‖duck, oddball, oddity, original, quiz, ‖spook, ‖wack, zombie

case *n* *syn* HULL, husk, pod, shell, shuck, skin, ‖slough

‖**case** *vb* *syn* SCRUTINIZE 1, canvass, check over, check up, con, examine, inspect, study, vet, view

case history *n* *syn* INSTANCE, case, example, illustration, representative, sample, sampling, specimen

cash *n* *syn* MONEY, ‖bread, ‖coin, dough, ‖jack, legal tender, ‖mazuma, ‖scratch, ‖shekels, ‖wampum

cashier *vb* **1** *syn* DISMISS 3, ax, boot (out), bounce, ‖can, discharge, fire, kick out, sack, terminate

rel eject, expel, oust; bar, eliminate, exclude; pass over, shelve

con appoint, designate, elect, name; employ, engage, hire

2 *syn* DISCARD, abdicate, cast, jettison, reject, scrap, shed, slough, throw away, throw out

cash in *vb* *syn* DIE 1, ‖check out, conk, ‖croak, drop, ‖kick in, ‖kick off, pass away, pop off, succumb

cask *n* a vessel made of staves, headings, and hoops <a *cask* of cider>

syn barrel, butt, hogshead, keg, pipe, tun

Cassandra *n* *syn* PESSIMIST, calamity howler, crepe-hanger, worrywart

cassock *n* *syn* CLERGYMAN, churchman, cleric, clerical, clerk, divine, ecclesiastic, minister, parson, preacher

cast *vb* **1** *syn* THROW 1, ‖bung, fire, fling, heave, hurl, launch, pitch, sling, toss

rel broadcast, disperse, distribute, scatter

2 *syn* DIRECT 2, address, aim, incline, lay, level, point, train, turn, zero (in)

3 *syn* DISCARD, abdicate, cashier, jettison, junk, reject, scrap, shed, slough, throw away

rel abandon, leave, relinquish, surrender, yield; dismiss, drop

‖**4** *syn* VOMIT, barf, bring up, disgorge, ‖heave, *puke, spew, spit up, throw up, upchuck

5 *syn* ADD 2, figure, foot, sum, summate, tot, total, totalize, tote

6 *syn* PLAN 2, arrange, blueprint, chart, design, devise, ‖dope out, project

syn synonym(s) *rel* related word(s)
idiom idiomatic equivalent(s) *con* contrasted word(s)
ant antonym(s) * vulgar
‖ use limited; if in doubt, see a dictionary
The first word in a synonym list when printed in SMALL CAPITALS shows where there is more information about the group. For a more efficient use of this book see Explanatory Notes.

cast *n* **1** *syn* LOOK 2, countenance, expression, face, visage

2 *syn* PREDICTION, forecast, foretelling, prevision, prognosis, prognostication, prophecy, weird

3 *syn* COLOR 1, hue, shade, tinge, tint, tone

4 *syn* HINT 2, dash, intimation, shade, smack, soupçon, suggestion, suspicion, touch, trace

5 *syn* TYPE, character, class, description, kind, nature, sort, stripe, variety, way

6 *syn* FORM 1, configuration, conformation, figure, shape

cast about *vb* *syn* SEEK 1, ferret out, hunt, quest, search (for *or* out)

cast away *vb* **1** *syn* WASTE 2, blow, consume, dissipate, fool (away), fritter, frivol away, squander, throw away, trifle (away)

2 *syn* SHIPWRECK 1, beach, pile up, strand, wreck

castaway *n* *syn* OUTCAST, derelict, Ishmael, Ishmaelite, leper, offscouring, pariah, untouchable

cast down *vb* *syn* HUMBLE, abase, bemean, debase, degrade, demean, humiliate, lower, sink

cast down *adj* *syn* DOWNCAST, bad, crestfallen, dejected, depressed, disconsolate, dispirited, down, low, woebegone

castigate *vb* **1** *syn* PUNISH 1, chasten, chastise, correct, discipline

rel baste, beat, belabor, drub, pummel, thrash; berate, rail, rate, tongue-lash, upbraid, wig; penalize

2 *syn* LAMBASTE 3, blister, excoriate, flay, lash (into), scarify, scathe, scorch, scourge, slash

castigation *n* *syn* PUNISHMENT, chastisement, correction, discipline, punition, rod

castigatory *adj* *syn* PUNITIVE, disciplinary, punishing, punitory

castle *n* *syn* MANSION, chateau, manor, villa

castle-builder *n* *syn* DREAMER, idealist, ideologue, utopian, visionary

cast out *vb* **1** *syn* BANISH, deport, displace, exile, expatriate, expel, expulse, ostracize, oust, transport

‖**2** *syn* QUARREL, bicker, brabble, caterwaul, row, scrap, spat, squabble, tiff, wrangle

castrate *vb* **1** *syn* STERILIZE, alter, change, desexualize, fix, geld, mutilate, neuter, unsex

2 *syn* UNNERVE, emasculate, enervate, unman, unstring

rel bleed, drain, empty, exhaust

casual *adj* **1** *syn* ACCIDENTAL, chance, contingent, fluky, fortuitous, incidental, odd

rel unplanned, unpremeditated; extemporaneous, extempore, impromptu, improvised, offhand; impulsive, spontaneous

con advised, considered, deliberate, intentional, planned, premeditated, studied

ant deliberate

2 *syn* INDIFFERENT 2, aloof, detached, disinterested, incurious, remote, unconcerned, uncurious, uninterested, withdrawn

3 *syn* EASYGOING 3, breezy, ‖common, dégagé, informal, low-pressure, relaxed, ‖sonsy, unconstrained, unfussy

con ceremonial, conventional, formal

4 *syn* LITTLE 3, inconsiderable, insignificant, light, minor, petty, shoestring, small-beer, trivial, unimportant

casually *adv* ***syn*** INCIDENTALLY 1, accidentally, fortuitously

casualty *n* **1** ***syn*** ACCIDENT 2, misadventure, mischance, mishap
2 ***syn*** FATALITY 2, death, fatal
3 ***syn*** VICTIM 2, bottom dog, prey, underdog

casuistry *n* ***syn*** FALLACY 2, deception, deceptiveness, delusion, equivocation, speciousness, sophism, sophistry, spuriousness

||cat *n* ***syn*** MAN 3, ||bloke, boy, buck, chap, fellow, ||gee, gent, gentleman, guy

||cat *vb* ***syn*** VOMIT, barf, ||cack, ||cascade, ||cast, ||heave, *puke, spew, spit up, throw up

cataclysm *n* **1** ***syn*** FLOOD 2, cataract, deluge, flooding, inundation, niagara, overflow, pour, spate, torrent
2 ***syn*** DISASTER, calamity, catastrophe, misadventure, tragedy, woe(s)

cataclysmic *adj* ***syn*** FATAL 2, calamitous, catastrophic, disastrous, fateful, ruinous

catacomb *n* ***syn*** CRYPT, undercroft, vault

catalog *n* ***syn*** LIST, register, roll, roll call, roster, schedule
rel program, prospectus, syllabus

catalog *vb* **1** ***syn*** INVENTORY, itemize, tally
2 ***syn*** LIST 3, book, enroll, inscribe
rel admit, enter, introduce; count, enumerate, number

catalyst *n* ***syn*** STIMULUS, goad, impetus, impulse, incentive, incitation, incitement, motivation, spur, stimulant

cataplasm *n* ***syn*** POULTICE

cataract *n* **1** ***syn*** WATERFALL, cascade, chute, fall(s), ||force, sault, spout
2 ***syn*** FLOOD 2, cataclysm, deluge, flooding, inundation, niagara, overflow, pour, spate, torrent

catastrophe *n* ***syn*** DISASTER, calamity, cataclysm, misadventure, tragedy, woe(s)

catastrophic *adj* ***syn*** FATAL 2, calamitous, cataclysmic, disastrous, fateful, ruinous

catcall *n* ***syn*** RASPBERRY, bazoo, bird, boo, ||Bronx cheer, hiss, hoot, pooh, pooh-pooh, ||razz

catch *vb* **1** to obtain physical mastery and possession of <the cat *caught* a mouse>
syn bag, capture, collar, ||cotch, get, nail, prehend, secure, take; *compare* ARREST 2, SEIZE 2
rel clutch, grab, snatch; clasp, grasp, grip; ensnare, entangle, entrap, snare, tangle, trap
con free, release
ant miss
2 ***syn*** SEIZE 2, clutch, ||cotch, grab, grapple, nab, ||nail, snatch, take
3 to put at a disadvantage or bring under control by or as if by enmeshing in a net <*caught* in the fallacy of his own argument>
syn benet, catch up, ensnare, entangle, entrap, snare, tangle, trap; *compare* ENTANGLE 3
rel baffle, confound, nonplus, perplex, stick, stump; abash, disturb, embarrass, put out; confuse, flurry, fluster, rattle
4 ***syn*** DUPE, bamboozle, chicane, con, flimflam, fool, gull, hoax, hoodwink, trick
5 ***syn*** FIND 1, descry, detect, encounter, espy, hit (on *or* upon), meet (with), spot, turn up
6 ***syn*** MARRY 1, espouse, wed
7 to come up with often unexpectedly <the storm *caught* them unawares>
syn ||cotch, overhaul, overtake, take
rel reach
idiom come upon
8 ***syn*** SEIZE 3, strike, take
9 ***syn*** INTERCEPT, block, cut off
10 ***syn*** CONTRACT 1, come down (with), get, sicken (with *or* of), take
idiom fall ill (of *or* with), fall victim to
11 ***syn*** FASTEN 2, anchor, fix, moor, secure
12 ***syn*** STRIKE 2, ||biff, clout, ding, hit, ||nail, ||slosh, smite, sock, whack
13 ***syn*** APPREHEND 1, accept, comprehend, ||dig, follow, grasp, see, take, take in, understand

catch colt *n* ***syn*** BASTARD, by-blow, chance child, come-by-chance, filius nullius, illegitimate, love child, natural child, whoreson, woods colt

catching *adj* **1** ***syn*** INFECTIOUS 2, communicable, contagious
2 ***syn*** INFECTIOUS 3, contagious, taking

catch on *vb* ***syn*** DISCOVER 3, ascertain, determine, find out, hear, learn, see, tumble, unearth

catchphrase *n* ***syn*** CATCHWORD, byword, phrase, shibboleth, slogan, watchword

catchpole *n* ***syn*** DELEGATE, deputy, representant, representative

catch up *vb* **1** ***syn*** CATCH 3, benet, ensnare, entangle, entrap, snare, tangle, trap
2 ***syn*** ENTHRALL 2, fascinate, grip, hold, mesmerize, spellbind

catchword *n* a word or phrase that catches the eye or ear and is repeated so often that it becomes representative of a political party, school of thought, or point of view <"new deal" became the *catchword* of supporters and critics of Franklin Roosevelt>
syn byword, catchphrase, phrase, shibboleth, slogan, watchword; *compare* BATTLE CRY
rel household word; maxim, motto

catchy *adj* ***syn*** FITFUL, desultory, on-again-off-again, spasmodic, sporadic, spotty

catechize *vb* ***syn*** ASK 1, examine, inquire, interrogate, query, question, quiz

categorical *adj* **1** ***syn*** ULTIMATE 3, absolute
con conjectural, hypothetical, supposititious; conditional, contingent, dependent, relative
2 ***syn*** EXPLICIT, clean-cut, clear-cut, definite, definitive, express, specific, unambiguous
rel certain, positive, sure; direct, downright, forthright
con ambiguous; doubtful, dubious, problematic, questionable
3 ***syn*** POSITIVE 1, decided, definite, unequivocal

categorically *adv* ***syn*** EXPRESSLY 1, definitely, explicitly, specifically

---

syn synonym(s) ***rel*** related word(s)
idiom idiomatic equivalent(s) ***con*** contrasted word(s)
ant antonym(s) * vulgar
|| use limited; if in doubt, see a dictionary
The first word in a synonym list when printed in SMALL CAPITALS shows where there is more information about the group. For a more efficient use of this book see Explanatory Notes.

categorize *vb* ***syn*** ASSORT, class, classify, group, pigeonhole, sort
rel identify, nail down, peg, put down

category *n* ***syn*** CLASS 1, grade, group, grouping, league, pigeonhole, tier

cater (to) *vb* **1** ***syn*** BABY, cocker, coddle, cosset, cotton, humor, indulge, mollycoddle, pamper, spoil
idiom make much of
2 ***syn*** INDULGE 1, gratify, humor

cateran *n* ***syn*** MARAUDER, bandit, brigand, bummer, forager, freebooter, looter, pillager, plunderer, raider

catercorner (*or* **catty-corner** *or* **kitty-corner**) *adv* ***syn*** DIAGONALLY, cornerwise, slantingways, slantways, slantwise, ‖slaunchways

cater–cousin *n* ***syn*** FRIEND, acquaintance, amigo, confidant, familiar, intimate, mate

caterwaul *vb* ***syn*** QUARREL, bicker, brabble, fall out, row, scrap, spat, squabble, tiff, wrangle

catharsis *n* ***syn*** PURIFICATION, cleansing, expurgation, lustration, purgation

catholic *adj* **1** ***syn*** UNIVERSAL 2, cosmic, cosmopolitan, ecumenical, global, planetary, worldwide
rel comprehensive, inclusive; general, generic, indeterminate; extensive, large-scale
ant parochial; provincial
2 ***syn*** ECLECTIC 2

catholicon *n* ***syn*** PANACEA, cure-all, elixir, nostrum

cathouse *n* ***syn*** BROTHEL, bagnio, bawdy house, bordello, ‖hookshop, ‖joyhouse, parlor house, sporting house, stew, whorehouse

catlike *adj* ***syn*** STEALTHY 2, catty, feline, furtive

catnap *n* ***syn*** NAP, dog nap, ‖dover, forty winks, siesta, snooze

catnap *vb* ***syn*** NAP, ‖caulk (off), siesta, snooze

‖**catouse** *n* ***syn*** COMMOTION 3, brouhaha, coil, foofaraw, furore, ruckus, rumpus, shindig, shindy, uproar

cat's–paw *n* ***syn*** TOOL 2, pawn, puppet, stooge

catty *adj* **1** ***syn*** STEALTHY 2, catlike, feline, furtive
2 ***syn*** AGILE, active, brisk, lively, nimble, sprightly, spry, volant, yare, zippy
3 ***syn*** MALICIOUS, bitchy, despiteful, evil, hateful, malevolent, rancorous, spiteful, vicious, wicked

‖**caulk** (off) *vb* ***syn*** NAP, catnap, siesta, snooze

‖**caulker** *n* ***syn*** DRAM, drop, jolt, nip, shot, slug, snifter, snort, toothful, tot

causatum *n* ***syn*** EFFECT 1, aftermath, consequence, event, eventuality, issue, outcome, result, sequel, upshot

cause *n* **1** that (as a person, fact, or condition) which is responsible for an effect <the storm was the *cause* of all our difficulties>
syn antecedent, determinant, occasion, reason
rel goad, impulse, incentive, inducement, motive, spring; origin, prime mover, root, source; author, creator, generator, originator
con consequence, effect, issue, outcome, result
2 ***syn*** MOTIVE 1, consideration, reason, spring
3 ***syn*** OCCASION 3, call, necessity, obligation
4 ***syn*** SUIT 1, action, case, lawsuit

cause *vb* **1** ***syn*** GENERATE 3, breed, engender, get up, hatch, induce, muster (up), occasion, produce, work up
2 ***syn*** EFFECT 1, bring about, draw on, make, produce, secure
rel elicit, evoke, provoke
idiom be at the root of, give origin to, set on foot

'cause *conj* ***syn*** BECAUSE, as, as long as, ‖being, for, inasmuch as, now, seeing, since, whereas

causerie *n* ***syn*** CHAT 2, chin, prose, rap, talk, yarn

caustic *adj* **1** marked by sharp and often witty incisiveness <a *caustic* critic>
syn mordacious, mordant, salty, scathing, trenchant; *compare* SARCASTIC
rel biting, cutting, incisive; acrid, bitter, pungent, tart; acute, keen, sharp; ironic, sarcastic, satiric, stinging; harsh, rough, severe, stringent; crisp, pithy, succinct, terse
con gentle, mild; cordial, gracious; bland, diplomatic, suave, urbane
ant genial
2 ***syn*** SARCASTIC, acerb, acerbic, archilochian, corrosive, ‖sarky

causticity *n* ***syn*** SARCASM, acerbity, corrosiveness, sarcasticness

caution *n* **1** ***syn*** WARNING, admonition, caveat, commonition, forewarning, monition
2 ***syn*** PRUDENCE 1, canniness, discreetness, discretion, foresight, forethought, precaution, providence

caution *vb* ***syn*** WARN 1, forewarn

cautionary *adj* ***syn*** MONITORY, admonishing, admonitory, cautioning, monitorial, warning

cautioning *adj* ***syn*** MONITORY, admonishing, admonitory, cautionary, monitorial, warning

cautious *adj* marked by careful prudence especially in reducing or avoiding risk or danger <a *cautious* approach to marriage>
syn calculating, careful, chary, circumspect, considerate, discreet, gingerly, guarded, safe, wary
rel alert, vigilant, watchful; cagey, canny, cozy, foresighted, precautious, shrewd; forethoughtful, prethoughtful, provident, prudent; calculating, scheming, shrewd; expedient, judicious, politic
idiom on one's guard, on the safe side, playing it safe
con daring, rash, reckless, venturesome; headlong, impetuous, precipitate
ant adventurous, temerarious

cavalier *adj* ***syn*** PROUD 1, arrogant, disdainful, haughty, high-and-mighty, insolent, lofty, overbearing, supercilious, superior

cave *n* a usually natural underground chamber <the limestone *caves* of Kentucky>
syn cavern, grotto, subterrane, subterranean

cave *vb* **1** ***syn*** GIVE 12, bend, break, collapse, crumple, fold up, go, yield
2 ***syn*** YIELD 2, bow, buckle (under), capitulate, defer, knuckle, knuckle under, submit, succumb

---

syn synonym(s) ***rel*** related word(s)
idiom idiomatic equivalent(s) ***con*** contrasted word(s)
ant antonym(s) * vulgar
‖ use limited; if in doubt, see a dictionary
The first word in a synonym list when printed in SMALL CAPITALS shows where there is more information about the group. For a more efficient use of this book see Explanatory Notes.

cave (in) *vb* ***syn*** COLLAPSE 2, break down, drop, ‖flake out, give out, peg out, succumb, wilt

caveat *n* ***syn*** WARNING, admonition, caution, commonition, forewarning, monition

cavern *n* ***syn*** CAVE, grotto, subterrane, subterranean

cavernous *adj* **1** suggestive of a cave <a *cavernous* fireplace that gulped in wood>
syn chasmal, gaping, yawning
rel commodious, vast
2 ***syn*** HOLLOW 1, reverberant, sepulchral

cavil *vb* ***syn*** QUIBBLE 1, chicane, hypercriticize

caviler *n* ***syn*** CRITIC, aristarch, carper, criticizer, faultfinder, knocker, momus, smellfungus, Zoilus

caviling *adj* ***syn*** CRITICAL 1, captious, carping, cavillous, censorious, critic, faultfinding, hypercritical, overcritical
rel contrary, perverse; demanding, exacting; finicky, fussy, picky; mean, petty, small; hairsplitting, niggling, nitpicking
con amiable, complaisant, good-natured, tolerant; accommodating, easy, obliging

cavillous *adj* ***syn*** CRITICAL 1, captious, carping, caviling, censorious, critic, faultfinding, hypercritical, overcritical

cavity *n* ***syn*** HOLE 3, hollow, vacuity, void

cavort *vb* ***syn*** GAMBOL, caper, frisk, frolic, rollick, romp
rel carry on, cut up, horse (around), horseplay, roughhouse

caw *vb* ***syn*** SQUALL 1, ‖quawk, squark, squawk, yawp (*or* yaup)

cease *vb* ***syn*** STOP 3, desist, ‖deval, discontinue, give over, halt, knock off, leave off, quit, surcease
rel close, conclude, end, finish, terminate; intermit
con continue, persist; extend, prolong, protract; arise, originate, rise, spring

cease *n* ***syn*** END 2, cessation, close, conclusion, desistance, ending, finish, period, stop, termination

cease-fire *n* ***syn*** TRUCE, armistice

ceaseless *adj* **1** ***syn*** CONTINUAL, constant, continuous, endless, interminable, perpetual, unceasing, unending, uninterrupted, unremitting
2 ***syn*** EVERLASTING 1, amaranthine, endless, eternal, immortal, never-ending, unending, world-without-end

cede *vb* **1** ***syn*** RELINQUISH, abandon, give up, hand over, leave, resign, surrender, ‖turn up, waive, yield
rel accord, concede, grant, vouchsafe
con hold, hold back, keep back, retain, withhold
2 ***syn*** TRANSFER 4, abalienate, alien, alienate, assign, convey, deed, make over, remise, sign (over)

ceinture *n* ***syn*** BELT 1, cincture, girdle, sash, waistband

‖**celeb** *n* ***syn*** CELEBRITY 2, big name, luminary, name, notability, notable, somebody

celebrate *vb* **1** ***syn*** KEEP 2, commemorate, observe, solemnize
2 ***syn*** PRAISE 2, bless, cry up, eulogize, extol, glorify, hymn, laud, magnify, panegyrize

celebrated *adj* ***syn*** FAMOUS 2, celebrious, distinguished, eminent, famed, great, illustrious, notable, prominent, renowned

celebrious *adj* ***syn*** FAMOUS 2, celebrated, distinguished, eminent, famed, great, illustrious, notable, prominent, renowned

celebrity *n* **1** ***syn*** FAME 2, éclat, notoriety, renown, ‖rep, reputation, repute
ant obscurity
2 a widely known and popularly esteemed person <youngsters making a great to-do over sports *celebrities*>
syn big name, ‖celeb, luminary, name, notability, notable, somebody
rel hero, immortal, mahatma, star, superstar; lion; personage, worthy; cynosure
idiom center of attraction, person of note (*or* mark)
con back number; nobody

celerity *n* **1** ***syn*** HASTE 1, dispatch, expedition, expeditiousness, hurry, hustle, rustle, speed, speediness, swiftness
rel alacrity, briskness, legerity
2 ***syn*** SPEED 2, ‖bat, gait, pace, quickness, rapidity, rapidness, swiftness, velocity

celestial *adj* of, relating to, or befitting heaven or the heavens <*celestial* music from an angelic choir>
syn empyreal, empyrean, heavenly
rel ethereal, supernal, transcendental; otherworldly, unearthly, transmundane; beatific, blessed, elysian, Olympian
con earthly, earthy, mundane, sublunary, worldly; chthonian, hellish, infernal
ant terrestrial, uncelestial

cemetery *n* a piece of land used for burying the dead <the quiet peace of a country *cemetery*>
syn ‖boneyard, ‖boot hill, burial ground, burying ground, God's acre, graveyard, memorial park, necropolis, polyandrium, potter's field
rel churchyard; catacomb
idiom city of the dead

censor *vb* to remove matter considered objectionable by expurgation or alteration <*censor* a movie>
syn blip, bowdlerize, expurgate, screen
rel cut out, excise, exscind; blue-pencil, delete, edit, red-pencil; bleach, clean (up), purge, purify; narrow, restrain, restrict

censorious *adj* ***syn*** CRITICAL 1, captious, carping, caviling, cavillous, critic, faultfinding, hypercritical, overcritical
rel chiding, reproachful, reproaching; condemnatory, condemning, denouncing, denunciatory, reprehending; accusatory, culpatory
con acclaiming, acclamatory, extolling, laudatory, lauding, praising; adulatory, complimentary, flattering
ant eulogistic

censurable *adj* ***syn*** BLAMEWORTHY, amiss, blamable, blameful, culpable, demeritorious, guilty, reprehensible, sinful, unholy
rel improper, incorrect, objectionable, wrong, wrongful; discreditable, doubtful, questionable; inadmissible, unacceptable

---

syn synonym(s) — *rel* related word(s)
idiom idiomatic equivalent(s) — *con* contrasted word(s)
ant antonym(s) — * vulgar
‖ use limited; if in doubt, see a dictionary
The first word in a synonym list when printed in SMALL CAPITALS shows where there is more information about the group. For a more efficient use of this book see Explanatory Notes.

con correct, proper, right; acceptable, admissible; creditable
ant uncensurable

censure *vb* ***syn*** CRITICIZE, blame, condemn, denounce, denunciate, knock, rap, reprehend, reprobate, skin
rel rebuke, reprimand, reproach, reprove; contemn, disdain, scorn, scout, strafe; disallow, disapprove, oppose, reject, stigmatize
con applaud, compliment, recommend; allow, approve, support
ant commend

center *n* **1** a point or part in a surface or solid more or less equidistant from the periphery <the *center* of the earth>
syn core, middle, midpoint, midst
rel inside, interior
con circumference, compass, perimeter, periphery; bounds, confines, limits
2 one eminent in or central to a particular activity, condition, or interest <a *center* of international trade>
syn focal point, focus, heart, hub, nerve center, polestar, seat; *compare* ESSENCE 2
3 a source or point of origin (as of an influence, pressure, or effect) <the group proved a *center* of discontent>
syn core, heart, pith, quick, root
rel activator, dynamo, energizer, stimulant

center *adj* **1** ***syn*** MIDDLE 1, centermost, equidistant, halfway, medial, median, mid, middlemost, midmost
2 ***syn*** MIDDLE 2, central, intermediary, intermediate, mean, medial, median, mid

centermost *adj* ***syn*** MIDDLE 1, center, equidistant, halfway, medial, median, mid, middlemost, midmost

central *adj* **1** occupying a dominant or supremely important position <the *central* theme of American foreign policy>
syn cardinal, overriding, overruling, pivotal, ruling
rel dominant, paramount, predominant, preponderant; important, significant; outstanding, salient, signal; chief, essential, foremost, leading, main; all-absorbing, controlling, master; focal, key; basic, fundamental, primary, radical
con insignificant, minor, trivial, unimportant; borderline, marginal
ant peripheral
2 ***syn*** MIDDLE 2, center, intermediary, intermediate, mean, medial, median, mid

centralizing *adj* ***syn*** INTEGRATIVE, centripetal, compacting, concentrating, consolidating, unifying

centripetal *adj* ***syn*** INTEGRATIVE, centralizing, compacting, concentrating, consolidating, unifying

‖**cep** *prep* ***syn*** EXCEPT, apart from, aside from, bar, barring, beside, besides, excluding, outside of, save

---

syn synonym(s) ***rel*** related word(s)
idiom idiomatic equivalent(s) ***con*** contrasted word(s)
ant antonym(s) * vulgar
‖ use limited; if in doubt, see a dictionary
The first word in a synonym list when printed in SMALL CAPITALS shows where there is more information about the group. For a more efficient use of this book see Explanatory Notes.

cerate *n* ***syn*** OINTMENT, balm, chrism, cream, salve, unction, unguent

cerberus *n* ***syn*** CUSTODIAN, claviger, ‖custodier, custos, guardian, keeper, warden, watchdog

cerebral *adj* **1** ***syn*** MENTAL 1, intellective, intellectual, psychic, psychical, psychological
2 ***syn*** INTELLECTUAL 2, highbrow, highbrowed, intellectualistic

cerebrate *vb* ***syn*** THINK 5, cogitate, deliberate, reason, reflect, speculate

cerebration *n* ***syn*** THOUGHT 1, brainwork, cogitation, deliberation, reflection, speculation

ceremonial *adj* stressing or concerned with careful attention to form and detail <his *ceremonial* approach to everyday life>
syn ceremonious, conventional, formal, solemn, stately
rel mannered, studied, stylized; liturgical, ritual, ritualistic; august, courtly, imposing, lofty; fixed, rigid, set, starchy, stiff
con casual, easy, informal, relaxed; artless, ingenuous, open, sincere

ceremonial *n* **1** ***syn*** FORM 2, ceremony, formality, liturgy, rite, ritual
2 ***syn*** RITE 2, ceremony, formality, liturgy, observance, ritual, service

ceremonious *adj* ***syn*** CEREMONIAL, conventional, formal, solemn, stately
rel decorous, proper, seemly; impressive, moving, striking; grandiose, imposing, majestic
ant unceremonious

ceremony *n* **1** ***syn*** FORM 2, ceremonial, formality, liturgy, rite, ritual
2 ***syn*** RITE 2, ceremonial, formality, liturgy, observance, ritual, service

certain *adj* **1** ***syn*** FIRM 4, fixed, set, settled, stated, stipulated
rel assured, certified, guaranteed, warranted; ensured, insured, sure
2 constituting an indeterminate and otherwise unidentified part of a group or whole <*certain* students dispute this finding>
syn some, various
rel a, an, one; many, numerous; divers, several, sundry
con no; all
3 being such beyond a doubt <no *certain* likeness of this saint survives>
syn accurate, authentic, dependable, reliable
rel credible, plausible, well-grounded
con counterfeit, false, spurious; controversial, doubtful, dubious, questionable
ant uncertain
4 ***syn*** INFALLIBLE 2, sure, surefire, unfailing
5 ***syn*** POSITIVE 3, inarguable, incontestable, indisputable, indubitable, sure, uncontestable, uncontrovertible, undeniable, undoubtable
rel confirmable, demonstrable, establishable, provable, verifiable; doubtless, trustworthy, unerring
con controversial, iffy
ant uncertain
6 ***syn*** INEVITABLE, ineluctable, ineludible, inescapable, inevasible, necessary, returnless, unavoidable, unescapable, unevadable
rel indefeasible, irrevocable, unalterable, written; fated, predestinated, predetermined

ant uncertain
7 ***syn*** SURE 5, cocksure, confident, positive
rel assured, confident, sanguine
con hesitant, indecisive, vague, wavering; doubtful, dubious, questionable
ant uncertain

certainty *n* a state of mind in which one is free from doubt <answered with complete *certainty*>
syn assurance, assuredness, certitude, confidence, conviction, sureness, surety
rel belief, credence, faith; absoluteness, definiteness, dogmatism, positiveness, positivism; firmness, staunchness, steadiness
con doubt, mistrust, skepticism, unsureness; fluctuation, irresolution, shifting, trimming, vacillation, wavering; obscurity, vagueness
ant uncertainty

certify *vb* **1** to testify usually formally and in writing to the truth or genuineness of something <*certify* a student's college transcript>
syn attest, vouch, witness
rel assert, aver, avouch, avow, profess
2 ***syn*** WARRANT 2, guarantee, guaranty
3 ***syn*** APPROVE 2, accredit, endorse, OK (*or* okay), sanction
rel authorize, commission, license
con antagonize, counter, oppose

certitude *n* ***syn*** CERTAINTY, assurance, assuredness, confidence, conviction, sureness, surety
rel cocksureness
con uncertainty
ant doubt

‖**cess** *n* ***syn*** TAX 1, assessment, duty, impost, levy, tariff

cessation *n* ***syn*** END 2, cease, close, conclusion, desistance, ending, finish, period, stop, termination

cesspit *n* ***syn*** SINK 1, Augean stable, cesspool, den, pandemonium, Sodom, sty

cesspool *n* ***syn*** SINK 1, Augean stable, cesspit, den, pandemonium, Sodom, sty

‖**chack** *n* ***syn*** SNACK, ‖bait, ‖bever, bite, morsel, mug-up, ‖piece, tapa

chafe *vb* **1** ***syn*** ANNOY 1, abrade, bother, exercise, fret, gall, irk, provoke, ruffle, vex
2 ***syn*** ABRADE 1, corrode, erode, gall, graze, rub, ruffle, wear
3 to make sore or raw through friction <the high stiff collar *chafed* his neck>
syn abrade, excoriate, fret, gall, rub
rel damage, hurt, impair, injure; flay, peel, skin; inflame, irritate; graze, scrape, scratch
con ease, relieve, soothe

chaff *vb* ***syn*** BANTER 1, fun, jest, joke, jolly, josh, kid, rag, razz, rib
idiom make merry over

chaffer *vb* ***syn*** HAGGLE 2, bargain, dicker, higgle, huckster, palter
rel beg, coax, plead

chafing *adj* ***syn*** IMPATIENT 1, fretful, unpatient

chagrined *adj* ***syn*** ASHAMED, mortified, shamed
rel crushed, disconcerted; discomposed, perturbed, upset
idiom put out of countenance

chain *n* **1** **chains** *pl* ***syn*** SHACKLE, bond(s), fetter(s), gyve(s), iron(s)
2 ***syn*** SUCCESSION 2, alternation, consecution, order, progression, row, sequence, series, string, train
3 ***syn*** SYNDICATE, cartel, combine, conglomerate, group, pool, trust

chain *adj* **1** ***syn*** CUMULATIVE, accumulative, additive, additory, summative
2 ***syn*** TRITE, clichéd, commonplace, hackneyed, old hat, shopworn, stale, stereotyped, stereotypical, twice-told

chair *vb* ***syn*** PRESIDE

chair car *n* ***syn*** PARLOR CAR, club car, lounge car, palace car, tavern car

chalk (out) *vb* ***syn*** SKETCH, adumbrate, block (out), characterize, draft, outline, rough (out), skeleton, skeletonize

chalk up *vb* ***syn*** GET 1, acquire, annex, gain, have, obtain, pick up, procure, secure, win

challenge *vb* **1** ***syn*** DEMAND 1, call, claim, exact, postulate, require, requisition, solicit
2 ***syn*** QUESTION 2, dispute, doubt, mistrust
3 ***syn*** FACE 3, ‖banter, beard, brave, dare, defy, ‖double-dog dare, front, outdare, venture
rel question; dispute; strive, struggle, try
idiom throw down the (*or* one's) gage
con by-pass, evade
4 ***syn*** STIR 1, arouse, awaken, bestir, kindle, rally, rouse, wake, waken, whet

challenge *n* **1** ***syn*** DEMUR 2, demurral, demurrer, difficulty, objection, protest, question, remonstrance, remonstration
2 ***syn*** DEFIANCE 1, cartel, dare, defi, defy, stump
rel calling, claiming, demanding, exacting; importuning, insistence

chamber *n* **1** ***syn*** ROOM 1, apartment
‖**2** **chambers** *pl* ***syn*** APARTMENT 1, flat, lodging(s), rental, rooms, suite, tenement

chamber *vb* ***syn*** HARBOR 1, haven, house, roof, shelter, shield

champ *vb* **1** ***syn*** CHEW 1, ‖chaw, chomp, ‖chonk, chumble, crunch, masticate, munch, ruminate, scrunch
rel crush, macerate, mash, smash
2 ***syn*** BITE 1, chomp
rel nibble, nip; gum, mouth, mumble; peck, pick

champaign *n* ***syn*** FIELD, bailiwick, demesne, domain, dominion, province, sphere, terrain, territory, walk

champion *n* ***syn*** EXPONENT, advocate, expounder, proponent, supporter

champion *vb* ***syn*** SUPPORT 2, advocate, back, backstop, side (with), uphold
rel battle, contend, fight (for)
idiom put in a good word for, stand behind (*or* back of), stand up for
con resist, withstand; denounce, condemn
ant combat

---

syn synonym(s) — ***rel*** related word(s)
idiom idiomatic equivalent(s) — ***con*** contrasted word(s)
ant antonym(s) — * vulgar
‖ use limited; if in doubt, see a dictionary
The first word in a synonym list when printed in SMALL CAPITALS shows where there is more information about the group. For a more efficient use of this book see Explanatory Notes.

champion *adj* **1** ***syn*** EXCELLENT, bang-up, blue-ribbon, ‖boss, capital, ‖dandy, prime, superior, top-notch, whiz-bang
rel distinguished, illustrious, outstanding, splendid
2 ***syn*** FIRST 3, arch, chief, foremost, head, leading, premier, principal

chance *n* **1** ***syn*** ACCIDENT 1, fortuity, hap, luck
con certainty, inevitability, necessity; destiny, fate, foreordination, predestination
ant law
2 an unpurposed, unpredictable, and uncontrollable master force <the folly of depending on *chance* for success in life>
syn fortune, hazard, luck
rel advantage, break, fluke; fate, lot; contingency
3 ***syn*** OPPORTUNITY, break, look-in, occasion, opening, shot, show, squeak, time
rel likelihood, possibility, probability; outlook, prospect

chance *vb* **1** ***syn*** HAPPEN 1, befall, betide, break, come off, fall out, go, hap, occur, transpire
2 ***syn*** HAPPEN 2, bump, hit, light, luck, meet, stumble, tumble
3 ***syn*** GAMBLE 2, hazard, risk, venture
4 ***syn*** VENTURE 1, adventure, hazard, risk, wager
idiom put at (*or* in) hazard
con cherish, protect, safeguard, secure

chance *adj* ***syn*** ACCIDENTAL, casual, contingent, fluky, fortuitous, incidental, odd
rel careless, heedless, offhand

chance child *n* ***syn*** BASTARD 1, by-blow, catch colt, come-by-chance, filius nullius, illegitimate, love child, natural child, whoreson, woods colt

chancy *adj* **1** ***syn*** UNCERTAIN 1, capricious, erratic, fluctuant, iffy, incalculable, unpredictable, whimsical
rel hazardous, risky, speculative, unsound; precarious, ticklish, touchy, tricky
idiom hanging by a thread, on thin ice (*or* slippery ground)
con safe, secure, sound, stable
2 ***syn*** DANGEROUS 1, hairy, hazardous, jeopardous, perilous, risky, treacherous, unhealthy, unsound, wicked

change *vb* **1** to make or become different <*changed* her will again and again> <our needs *change* as we grow older>
syn alter, modify, mutate, refashion, turn, vary; *compare* TRANSFORM
rel convert, metamorphose, transform, transmute; diversify, variegate; exchange, interchange
idiom go (*or* pass through) a change
con establish, fix, set
2 ***syn*** TRANSFORM, commute, convert, metamorphose, transfigure, translate, transmogrify, transmute, transpose, transubstantiate
3 ***syn*** REVERSE 1, inverse, invert, revert, transplace, transpose, turn
4 ***syn*** STERILIZE, alter, castrate, desexualize, fix, geld, mutilate, neuter, unsex
5 to make substitution for or among <it's time to *change* the subject>
syn replace, shift
rel exchange, swap, trade; substitute
6 ***syn*** EXCHANGE 2, substitute, swap, switch, trade

change *n* **1** a making different <saw a gradual *change* of attitude in the community>
syn alteration, modification, mutation, turn, variation
rel aberration, deviation, divergence; diversification; shift; innovation
ant uniformity
2 a result of such change <amazed at the *changes* in the town>
syn innovation, mutation, novelty, permutation, sport, vicissitude
rel conversion, metamorphosis, transformation, transmutation; shift, substitute, surrogate; avatar

changeable *adj* **1** alterable or changing under slight provocation <*changeable* April weather>
syn changeful, fluid, mobile, mutable, protean, unsettled, unstable, unsteady, variable, weathery; *compare* INCONSTANT 1, MUTABLE 2
rel adaptable, impressionable, plastic, pliant; ever-changing, kaleidoscopic; restless, unfixed; inconstant, uncertain, vicissitudinous
con constant, invariable, permanent; certain, fixed, immutable, unalterable, unmodifiable; abiding, enduring, persistent
ant unchangeable; unchanging
2 ***syn*** MUTABLE 2, inconstant, shifty, slippery, uncertain, unstable, unsteady, variable
3 ***syn*** INCONSTANT 1, capricious, fickle, lubricious, mercurial, temperamental, ticklish, unstable, variable, volatile

changeabout *n* ***syn*** REVERSAL 1, about-face, reverse, reversement, reversion, right-about, right-about-face, turn, turnabout, volte-face

changeful *adj* ***syn*** CHANGEABLE 1, fluid, mobile, mutable, protean, unsettled, unstable, unsteady, variable, weathery
rel active, dynamic, live; lively, vigorous
con durable, lasting, perdurable, stable; steady, uniform
ant changeless, unchanging

changeover *n* ***syn*** CONVERSION 2, alteration, shift, transformation

channel *n* **1** passage through which a fluid (as water) flows or is led <the river cut a new *channel* to the sea>
syn aqueduct, canal, conduit, course, duct, watercourse
rel pass, passage, way
2 ***syn*** MEAN 2, agency, agent, instrument, instrumentality, instrumentation, medium, ministry, organ, vehicle
3 ***syn*** PIPELINE, conduit

syn synonym(s) | *rel* related word(s)
idiom idiomatic equivalent(s) | *con* contrasted word(s)
ant antonym(s) | * vulgar
‖ use limited; if in doubt, see a dictionary
The first word in a synonym list when printed in SMALL CAPITALS shows where there is more information about the group. For a more efficient use of this book see Explanatory Notes.

channel *vb syn* CONDUCT 4, carry, convey, funnel, pipe, siphon, traject, transmit

chant *vb syn* SING 1, tune, vocalize

chaos *n* **1** *syn* CONFUSION 3, ataxia, ‖ballup, clutter, disarray, disorder, huddle, muddle, snarl, topsyturviness
2 *syn* ANARCHY 1, lawlessness, mobocracy, ochlocracy
rel misrule, unruliness

chap *n syn* MAN 3, ‖bloke, boy, buck, fellow, ‖gee, gent, gentleman, guy, he

chaperon *vb* **1** *syn* ACCOMPANY, attend, bear, ‖bring, ‖carry, companion, conduct, consort (with), convoy, escort
rel guide, overlook, oversee, supervise
2 *syn* SUPERVISE, boss, overlook, oversee, quarterback, superintend, survey

chapfallen *adj syn* DOWNCAST, blue, cast down, crestfallen, dejected, depressed, disconsolate, down, downhearted, down-in-the-mouth

chaplet *n syn* WREATH, anadem, coronal, coronet, crown, garland

character *n* **1** an arbitrary or conventional device used in writing or printing <an inscription in runic *characters*>
syn mark, sign, symbol
rel cipher, device, monogram; letter
2 *syn* CHARACTERISTIC 1, birthmark, feature, point, trait
3 *syn* QUALITY 1, affection, attribute, characteristic, feature, mark, property, savor, trait, virtue
rel distinction, uniqueness, uniquity
4 *syn* TYPE, description, feather, ilk, kidney, kind, nature, sort, stripe, variety
5 *syn* DISPOSITION 3, complexion, humor, individualism, individuality, makeup, nature, personality, temper, temperament
rel soul, spirit; courage, mettle, resolution; intellect, intelligence, mind
6 *syn* ROLE 1, clothing
7 *syn* STATUS 1, capacity, footing, place, position, rank, situation, standing, state, station
8 *syn* CREDENTIALS, recommendation, reference, testimonial
9 *syn* NOTABLE 1, big shot, big-timer, bigwig, chief, dignitary, eminence, nabob, notability, VIP
10 *syn* ECCENTRIC, case, ‖duck, oddball, oddity, original, quiz, ‖spook, ‖wack, zombie
‖**11** *syn* HUMAN, being, body, creature, individual, man, mortal, party, person, wight
12 *syn* REPUTATION 2, fame, name, ‖rep, report, repute

character assassination *n syn* DETRACTION, backbiting, backstabbing, belittlement, calumny, defamation, depreciation, disparagement, scandal, slander

characteristic *adj* being or revealing a quality specific or identifying to an individual or group <her *characteristic* down-to-earth approach to a problem>
syn diacritic, diagnostic, distinctive, idiosyncratic, individual, peculiar, proper
rel especial, particular, special, specific; natural, normal, regular, typical
con general, generic, universal
ant uncharacteristic

characteristic *n* **1** something that marks or sets apart <*characteristics* that distinguish man from lower primates>
syn birthmark, character, feature, point, trait; *compare* QUALITY 1
rel badge, mark, sign, token; flavor, odor, savor, smack, tang; differentia; singularity
2 *syn* QUALITY 1, affection, attribute, character, feature, mark, property, savor, trait, virtue

characterize *vb* **1** *syn* SKETCH, adumbrate, block (out), chalk (out), draft, outline, rough (out), skeleton, skeletonize
2 to be a peculiar or significant quality or feature of something <a man *characterized* by quiet dignity>
syn distinguish, individualize, individuate, mark, qualify, signalize, singularize
rel define, describe, differentiate, identify; peculiarize, personalize
idiom be a feature of

characterless *adj* lacking in character or solid qualities <a drab *characterless* little man that no one ever seemed to notice>
syn namby-pamby, pantywaist, wishy-washy
rel childish, infantile; sissified, sissy, unmanly; futile, weak; impotent, powerless
con manly, strong, vigorous, virile

charade *n syn* PRETENSE 2, disguise, make-believe, pageant, pretension, pretentiousness

chare *n syn* TASK 1, assignment, chore, devoir, duty, job, stint

charge *vb* **1** *syn* BURDEN, clog, cumber, encumber, lade, load, saddle, tax, weigh, weight
2 *syn* LOAD 3, choke, fill, heap, pack, pile
3 *syn* PERMEATE, compenetrate, impenetrate, impregnate, interpenetrate, penetrate, percolate, pervade, saturate, transfuse
4 *syn* ENTRUST 1, trust
5 *syn* COMMAND, bid, direct, enjoin, instruct, order, tell, warn
rel ask, request, solicit; adjure
6 *syn* ACCUSE, arraign, criminate, impeach, incriminate, inculpate, indict, tax
rel impugn, reprehend, reproach
idiom bring (*or* prefer) charges
con excuse, forgive, pardon, remit; acquit
ant absolve
7 *syn* ASCRIBE, accredit, assign, attribute, credit, impute, lay, refer
8 *syn* RUSH 1, boil, bolt, chase, dash, fling, lash, race, shoot, tear

charge *n* **1** *syn* LOAD 3, burden, deadweight, duty, millstone, onus, task, tax, weight
rel business, devoir, place

---

syn synonym(s) | *rel* related word(s)
idiom idiomatic equivalent(s) | *con* contrasted word(s)
ant antonym(s) | * vulgar
‖ use limited; if in doubt, see a dictionary
The first word in a synonym list when printed in SMALL CAPITALS shows where there is more information about the group. For a more efficient use of this book see Explanatory Notes.

2 *syn* OBLIGATION 2, commitment, committal, devoir, duty, must, need, ought, ‖right
3 *syn* OVERSIGHT 1, care, conduct, handling, intendance, management, running, superintendence, superintendency, supervision
4 *syn* COMMAND 1, behest, bidding, dictate, injunction, mandate, order, word
5 *syn* PRICE 1, cost, price tag, rate, tab, tariff

chargeless *adj syn* FREE 5, complimentary, costless, gratis, gratuitous

charger *n syn* COURSER, war-horse

charioteer *vb syn* DRIVE 5, auto, motor, pilot, tool, wheel

charisma *n syn* CHARM 3, allure, appeal, fascination, glamour, magnetism, witchcraft, witchery

charitable *adj* 1 having or showing interest in or concern for the welfare of others <spent generously for *charitable* aid to the needy>
syn altruistic, benevolent, eleemosynary, good, humane, humanitarian, philanthropic
rel accommodating, helpful, obliging; benign, kindhearted, kindly, sympathetic
2 *syn* FORBEARING, clement, easy, indulgent, lenient, merciful, tolerant
rel benevolent, considerate, kindly, thoughtful
con cold, harsh, heartless, unfeeling
ant uncharitable

charity *n* 1 *syn* MERCY, caritas, clemency, grace, lenity
rel affection, attachment, love; altruism, benevolence, humaneness; kindliness; amity, friendliness, goodwill
con malevolence, malignancy, malignity, spite, spleen
ant ill will, malice
2 *syn* DONATION, alms, benefaction, beneficence, contribution, offering

charivari *n syn* SHIVAREE, ‖belling, ‖bull band, ‖callithump, ‖horning, ‖riding, ‖skimmelton

charlatan *n* one who pretends unscrupulously to knowledge or skill <the professions overrun with *charlatans* and rogues>
syn mountebank, quack, quacksalver, quackster, saltimbanque; *compare* IMPOSTER
rel bluff, four-flusher, sham

Charlie McCarthy *n syn* STOOGE 1, dummy, yes-man

charm *n* 1 *syn* SPELL, conjuration, ‖devil-devil, incantation, rune
2 an object worn or cherished to ward off evil or attract good fortune <the Indian medicine bag is essentially a *charm*>
syn amulet, fetish, juju, luck, mascot, periapt, phylactery, talisman, zemi
3 a quality or combination of qualities that is wholly attractive and irresistible <the *charm* of her smile>
syn allure, appeal, charisma, fascination, glamour, magnetism, witchcraft, witchery
rel allurement, attraction, attractiveness, lure; agreeableness, delightfulness, gratefulness
con hatefulness, obnoxiousness, odiousness, repulsiveness; distastefulness, unpleasantness

charm *vb* 1 *syn* ATTRACT 1, allure, bewitch, captivate, draw, enchant, fascinate, magnetize, take, wile
2 *syn* BEWITCH 1, enchant, ensorcell, hex, spell, voodoo, witch

charmed *adj syn* ENAMORED 3, bewitched, captivated, enchanted, entranced, fascinated

charmer *n syn* MAGICIAN 1, conjurer, enchanter, mage, magian, magus, necromancer, sorcerer, warlock, wizard

charming *adj syn* ATTRACTIVE 1, alluring, attracting, captivating, drawing, enchanting, glamorous, magnetic, seductive, siren
ant charmless

chart *n* 1 a stylized or symbolic depiction of something incapable of direct verbal or pictorial representation (as because of complexity or abstractness) <a *chart* of anticipated economic progress>
syn graph, map
rel plan, plat, plot, scheme
2 *syn* TABLE 2, tabulation

chart *vb syn* PLAN 2, arrange, blueprint, cast, design, devise, ‖dope out, project

charter *n syn* DEED 3, conveyance

charter *vb syn* HIRE 1, lease, let, rent

chary *adj* 1 *syn* CAUTIOUS, calculating, careful, circumspect, considerate, discreet, gingerly, guarded, safe, wary
rel disinclined, hesitant, loath, reluctant; economical, frugal, sparing, thrifty; constrained, inhibited, restrained
2 *syn* SPARING, canny, economical, frugal, provident, saving, Scotch, stewardly, thrifty, unwasteful

chase *vb* 1 *syn* FOLLOW 2, chivy, pursue, trail
con flee, fly
2 *syn* HUNT 1, run
3 *syn* EJECT 1, boot (out), chuck, dismiss, evict, extrude, kick out, out, throw out
4 *syn* RUSH 1, boil, bolt, charge, dash, fling, lash, race, shoot, tear
5 *syn* COURSE, career, race, rush, speed, tear

chase *n syn* HUNTING, venery
2 *syn* GAME 3, prey, quarry

chaser *n syn* WOLF, Casanova, Don Juan, ladies' man, lady-killer, masher, philander, philanderer, womanizer

chasm *n* 1 *syn* GULF 2, abysm, abyss
2 *syn* RAVINE, arroyo, cleft, clough, clove, gap, gorge, gulch
3 *syn* OMISSION, blank, overlook, oversight, preterition, pretermission, skip
4 *syn* SCHISM 3, cleavage, cleft, split

chasmal *adj syn* CAVERNOUS 1, gaping, yawning

chaste *adj* free from every trace of the lewd or salacious <was as *chaste* in language as in conduct>
syn clean, decent, immaculate, modest, pure, spotless, stainless, unblemished, undefiled, unsullied
rel ethical, moral, righteous, virtuous; maidenly, virgin, virginal; becoming, decorous, proper, seemly; abstinent, continent
con coarse, gross, obscene, ribald, vulgar; lascivious, lecherous, licentious, lustful; gluttonous, incontinent, self-indulgent

---

syn synonym(s) — *rel* related word(s)
idiom idiomatic equivalent(s) — *con* contrasted word(s)
ant antonym(s) — * vulgar
‖ use limited; if in doubt, see a dictionary
The first word in a synonym list when printed in SMALL CAPITALS shows where there is more information about the group. For a more efficient use of this book see Explanatory Notes.

ant unchaste

chasten *vb* ***syn*** PUNISH 1, castigate, chastise, correct, discipline
rel abase, humble, humiliate; afflict, try
con baby, humor, indulge, spoil
ant pamper

chastise *vb* ***syn*** PUNISH 1, castigate, chasten, correct, discipline
rel baste, beat, belabor, pummel, thrash

chastisement *n* ***syn*** PUNISHMENT, castigation, correction, discipline, punition, rod

chat *vb* **1** to emit a ready flow of inconsequential talk <*chats* on the phone for hours>
syn babble, burble, cackle, chatter, chin-chin, clack, clatter, ‖dish, dither, gab, gabble, ‖gas, jaw, ‖natter, patter, prate, prattle, rattle, run on, smatter, talk, tinkle, twaddle, twiddle, twitter, yak, yakety-yak, yammer, yatter; *compare* CONVERSE
rel yap; blab, gossip; gush, lallygag; confabulate
idiom beat one's gums, ‖chew the fat (*or* rag), ‖shoot (*or* bat) the breeze, ‖shoot (*or* sling) the bull
con discourse, expound; declaim, harangue, hold forth, orate, preach
2 *syn* CONVERSE, chin, colloque, talk, visit, yarn

chat *n* **1** ***syn*** CHATTER, babble, bibble-babble, clack, gab, jabber, palaver, prattle, tittle-tattle, yak-yak
2 an informal conversation <had a satisfactory little *chat* with the new assistant>
syn causerie, chin, prose, rap, talk, yarn; *compare* CONVERSATION 2
rel gossip, tête-à-tête
idiom bull session, rap session
con debate, deliberation, discussion
3 *syn* CONVERSATION 1, colloquy, confabulation, converse, dialogue, parley

chateau *n* ***syn*** MANSION, castle, manor, villa

chattel *n* **1 chattels** *pl* ***syn*** POSSESSION 2, belongings, effects, goods, lares and penates, movables, things
2 *syn* SLAVE 1, bondman, bondslave, bondsman, mancipium

chatter *vb* **1** ***syn*** GIBBER, babble, gabble, jabber
2 *syn* CHAT 1, babble, clack, gab, jaw, patter, prate, prattle, yak, yammer

chatter *n* idle and often loud and incessant talk <schoolgirl *chatter*>
syn babble, bibble-babble, blab, blabber, ‖blatter, brabble, cackle, chat, chin-chin, ‖chin music, chitchat, chitter-chatter, clack, gab, gabble, gibble-gabble, jabber, palaver, prate, prattle, stultiloquence, talkee-talkee, tittle-tattle, yak, yakety-yak, yak-yak, yatter
rel ‖bull, gossip, small talk
idiom tongue wagging

chatterbox *n* one who engages in chatter <that old *chatterbox* will talk your arm off>
syn bandar-log, blabber, blabbermouth, blabmouth, chatterer, chewet, gabber, jabberer, magpie, prater, prattler
rel busybody, gossip, newsmonger, quidnunc, scandalmonger, tabby, tattletale

chatterer *n* ***syn*** CHATTERBOX, bandar-log, blabber, blabbermouth, blabmouth, gabber, jabberer, magpie, prater, prattler

chatty *adj* ***syn*** TALKATIVE, babblative, gabby, garrulous, loose-lipped, loose-tongued, loquacious, multiloquent, multiloquious, talky

‖**chaw** *vb* **1** ***syn*** CHEW 1, champ, chomp, ‖chonk, chumble, crunch, masticate, munch, ruminate, scrunch
2 *syn* PONDER 2, deliberate, meditate, mull (over), muse, revolve, roll, ruminate, turn over

chawbacon *n* ***syn*** RUSTIC, ‖apple knocker, bucolic, bumpkin, clodhopper, hayseed, hick, jake, redneck, yokel

cheap *adj* **1** costing little <produce is usually *cheaper* in summer>
syn inexpensive, low, low-cost, low-priced, popular, reasonable, uncostly, undear
rel bargain-basement, bargain-counter, cut-rate, reduced; dirt-cheap
con dear, high, high-priced
ant costly, expensive
2 of inferior quality <*cheap* furniture is never a bargain>
syn base, cheesy, common, mean, ‖ornery, paltry, poor, rubbishing, rubbishly, rubbishy, shoddy, sleazy, tatty, trashy, trumpery; *compare* INFERIOR 2
rel cheap-jack, valueless, worthless; flashy, garish, meretricious, tawdry; brummagem, fake, phony, sham; bad, rotten, terrible
con capital, excellent, fine, good; first-class, first-rate, high-class, high-grade, superior, tip-top, top-notch
ant precious
3 *syn* CONTEMPTIBLE, beggarly, despicable, despisable, mean, pitiable, pitiful, scurvy, shabby, sorry
rel wrong; base, low, vile; measly, paltry, petty, trifling
ant noble

cheapen *vb* ***syn*** DEPRECIATE 1, decry, devaluate, devalue, downgrade, lower, mark down, undervalue, write down, write off

cheap–jack (*or* **cheap–john**) *n* ***syn*** PEDDLER, ‖arab, ‖duffer, hawker, higgler, huckster, monger, outcrier, packman, vendor

cheapskate *n* ***syn*** MISER, cheeseparer, chuff, muckworm, niggard, ‖nipcheese, skin, skinflint, stiff, tightwad

cheat *n* **1** ***syn*** DECEPTION 1, chicane, chicanery, dishonesty, double-dealing, fourberie, hanky-panky, highbinding, sharp practice, trickery
2 *syn* IMPOSTURE, deceit, deception, flimflam, fraud, gyp, hoax, humbug, put-on, sell
rel bamboozlement, cozening, hoaxing; chicane, chicanery, trickery
3 *syn* SWINDLER, cheater, confidence man, con man, defrauder, diddler, double-dealer, gyp, sharper, trickster

---

cheat *vb* to obtain something (as money) from or an advantage over by dishonesty and trickery < *cheated* out of his inheritance by a grasping lawyer >
syn beat, bilk, boodle, ‖burn, chisel, chouse, cozen, ‖crook, defraud, diddle, do, ‖doodle, ‖dry-shave, ‖duff, flimflam, gyp, ‖mace, ‖mump, overreach, ream, ‖screw, sucker, swindle, take; *compare* EXTORT 1, FLEECE 1
rel befool, dupe, fool, gull, slick; bunco, con, fudge, short; beguile, deceive, delude, double-cross, mislead

cheater *n* ***syn*** SWINDLER, cheat, confidence man, con man, defrauder, diddler, double-dealer, gyp, sharper, trickster

check *vb* **1** ***syn*** ARREST 1, halt, interrupt, stall, stay
rel cease, desist, discontinue, stop; repress, suppress; circumvent, foil, frustrate, thwart
ant expedite
2 ***syn*** RESTRAIN 1, bit, bridle, constrain, curb, hold back, hold down, hold in, inhibit, withhold
rel baffle, balk; obviate, preclude, prevent
ant accelerate (*of speed*); advance (*as of hopes, plans*); release (*of feelings, energies*)
3 ***syn*** TRY 1, examine, prove, test
4 ***syn*** AGREE 4, accord, conform, correspond, dovetail, ‖gee, go, jibe, square, tally

check *n* **1** ***syn*** SETBACK, backset, reversal, reverse
2 a statement of charges for food and drink consumed (as at a restaurant) <shocked at the size of the *check* >
syn bill, tab
rel damage, score

check out *vb* ‖**1** ***syn*** DIE 1, cash in, conk, ‖croak, drop, ‖kick in, ‖kick off, pass, pass away, pop off
2 ***syn*** AGREE 4, conform, correspond, dovetail, fit (in), ‖gee, harmonize, jibe, square, tally

check over *vb* ***syn*** SCRUTINIZE 1, canvass, check up, con, examine, inspect, study, survey, vet, view

check–over *n* ***syn*** EXAMINATION, analysis, audit, checkup, inspection, review, scan, scrutiny, survey, view

check up *vb* ***syn*** SCRUTINIZE 1, canvass, check over, con, examine, inspect, study, survey, vet, view

checkup *n* ***syn*** EXAMINATION, analysis, audit, check-over, inspection, review, scan, scrutiny, survey, view

cheek *n* **1 cheeks** *pl* ***syn*** BUTTOCKS, *arse, backside, behind, bottom, breech, ‖butt, ‖can, derriere, ‖duff
2 ***syn*** EFFRONTERY, brashness, brass, confidence, ‖crust, face, gall, nerve, presumption

cheeky *adj* ***syn*** WISE 5, bold, forward, fresh, impudent, nervy, pert, sassy, smart, smart-alecky

cheep *vb* ***syn*** CHIRP, chip, chipper, ‖chirm, chirrup, chitter, peep, tweedle, tweet, twitter

cheer *vb* **1** ***syn*** COMFORT, buck up, console, solace, upraise
2 ***syn*** ENCOURAGE 1, animate, chirk (up), embolden, enhearten, hearten, inspirit, nerve, steel, strengthen
3 ***syn*** APPLAUD 2, rise (to), root

cheerful *adj* **1** marked by or suggestive of lighthearted ease of mind and spirit <a *cheerful* smile>
syn blithe, cheery, ‖chirk, chirpy, chirrupy, lightsome, sunbeamy, sunny; *compare* LIVELY 1
rel airy, carefree, debonair, jaunty; animated, gay, lighthearted, lively, vivacious; buoyant, corky
idiom in good (*or* high) spirits, of good cheer
con blue, dejected, depressed, melancholy; dispirited, heavyhearted; joyless, mournful, sorrowful, woeful; dour, morose, saturnine, sullen; doleful, lugubrious; austere, forbidding, grim, stern
ant gloomy, glum
2 ***syn*** GLAD 2, bright, cheery, radiant
ant cheerless

‖**cheerio** *interj* ***syn*** GOOD-BYE, adieu, by, bye-bye, farewell, so long, ‖toodle-oo

cheerless *adj* ***syn*** GLOOMY 3, bleak, depressing, dismal, dispiriting, dreary, funereal, oppressive, somber, tenebrific
rel dejecting
ant cheerful

cheery *adj* **1** ***syn*** GLAD 2, bright, cheerful, radiant
2 ***syn*** CHEERFUL 1, blithe, ‖chirk, chirpy, chirrupy, lightsome, sunbeamy, sunny

cheeseparer *n* ***syn*** MISER, cheapskate, chuff, muckworm, niggard, ‖nipcheese, skin, skinflint, stiff, tightwad

cheeseparing *adj* ***syn*** STINGY, close, closefisted, miserly, niggardly, parsimonious, penny-pinching, penurious, tight, tightfisted
rel cheap, grudging, mean, shabby; illiberal

cheesy *adj* ***syn*** CHEAP 2, common, mean, ‖ornery, poor, rubbishy, shoddy, sleazy, tatty, trashy

chef d'oeuvre *n* **1** ***syn*** MASTERPIECE 1, classic, magnum opus, masterwork, tour de force
2 ***syn*** SHOWPIECE, masterpiece, pièce de résistance

‖**chemist** *n* ***syn*** DRUGGIST, apothecary, pharmacist

cherish *vb* **1** ***syn*** NURSE 2, cultivate, foster, nourish, nursle, nurture
rel conserve, preserve, save; entertain, harbor, keep, shelter; defend, guard, safeguard, shield
con reject, repudiate, scorn
ant abandon
2 ***syn*** APPRECIATE 1, apprize, esteem, prize, treasure, value
rel revere, reverence, venerate
idiom hold in high esteem
con disregard, forget, ignore, overlook, slight
ant neglect
3 ***syn*** ADMIRE 1, appreciate, delight (in), relish

‖**cherry** *n* ***syn*** VIRGINITY, maidenhead, maidenhood

chest *n* ***syn*** TREASURY 2, coffer, exchequer, war chest

chesty *adj* ***syn*** BUXOM, bosomy, busty, full-bosomed

chew *vb* **1** to crush or grind with the teeth < *chew* your food well >
syn champ, ‖chaw, chomp, ‖chonk, chumble, chump, crunch, masticate, munch, ruminate, scrunch
rel bite; gnaw, nibble; consume, devour, eat; gum, mumble
‖**2** ***syn*** SCOLD 1, bawl out, ‖bless out, ‖carpet, jaw, revile, tell off, tongue-lash, vituperate, wig

---

syn synonym(s) *rel* related word(s)
idiom idiomatic equivalent(s) *con* contrasted word(s)
ant antonym(s) * vulgar
‖ use limited; if in doubt, see a dictionary
The first word in a synonym list when printed in SMALL CAPITALS shows where there is more information about the group. For a more efficient use of this book see Explanatory Notes.

chewet *n* ***syn*** CHATTERBOX, bandar-log, blabber, blabbermouth, blabmouth, chatterer, gabber, magpie, prater, prattler

‖**chew out** *vb* ***syn*** SCOLD 1, bawl out, ‖bless out, ‖carpet, jaw, revile, tell off, tongue-lash, vituperate, wig

chiaus *n* ***syn*** SWINDLER, cheat, cheater, defrauder, mountebank, rogue, sharper, sharpie, skin, trickster

chic *n* ***syn*** FASHION 3, craze, cry, dernier cri, fad, furore, mode, rage, style, vogue

chic *adj* ***syn*** STYLISH, dashing, exclusive, fashionable, modish, smart, swank, swish, ‖trendy, with-it

chicane *vb* **1** ***syn*** QUIBBLE 1, cavil, hypercriticize
2 ***syn*** DUPE, bamboozle, befool, flimflam, fool, gull, hoax, hoodwink, trick, victimize

chicane *n* ***syn*** DECEPTION 1, chicanery, dishonesty, double-dealing, fourberie, fraud, hanky-panky, highbinding, sharp practice, trickery
rel artifice, feint, gambit, maneuver, ploy, ruse, stratagem, trick, wile; furtiveness, surreptitiousness, underhandedness
con forthrightness, straightforwardness

chicanery *n* ***syn*** DECEPTION 1, chicane, dishonesty, double-dealing, fourberie, fraud, hanky-panky, highbinding, sharp practice, trickery
rel intrigue, machination, plot; furtiveness, surreptitiousness, underhandedness
con forthrightness, straightforwardness; honesty, honor, integrity, probity

chichi *adj* **1** ***syn*** SHOWY, flamboyant, orchidaceous, ostentatious, peacockish, peacocky, pretentious, splashy, swank
2 ***syn*** PRECIOUS 4, affected, alembicated, la-di-da, overnice, overrefined, précieux

chick *n* **1** ***syn*** CHILD 1, bud, chickabiddy, juvenile, kid, moppet, ‖nipper, youngling, young one, youngster
‖**2** ***syn*** GIRL FRIEND 1, best girl, ‖doney, gal, girl, lady friend, lass, mouse, popsy

chickabiddy *n* ***syn*** CHILD 1, bud, chick, juvenile, kid, moppet, ‖nipper, youngling, young one, youngster

chicken *n* ***syn*** COWARD, craven, dastard, funk, funker, poltroon, quitter, yellowbelly

‖**chicken** *adj* ***syn*** COWARDLY, coward, craven, gutless, lily-livered, poltroonish, poor-spirited, pusillanimous, spunkless, unmanly

chide *vb* ***syn*** REPROVE, admonish, call down, lesson, monish, ‖rack back, rebuke, reprimand, reproach, tick off
rel berate, rate, scold, upbraid
con applaud, compliment; approve, endorse, sanction
ant commend

chiding *n* ***syn*** REBUKE, admonishment, admonition, rap, reprimand, reproach, reproof, wig

chief *n* **1** ***syn*** LEADER 2, boss, chieftain, cock, dominator, head, headman, hierarch, honcho, master
rel dictator, duce, führer
2 ***syn*** NOTABLE 1, big-timer, ‖big wheel, bigwig, dignitary, eminence, leader, lion, luminary, notability

chief *adj* **1** ***syn*** FIRST 3, arch, champion, foremost, head, leading, premier, principal
2 standing apart by reason of superior importance, significance, or influence <his *chief* claim to consideration is his unquestionable uprightness>
syn capital, ‖cock, dominant, main, major, number one, outstanding, predominant, preeminent, principal, star, stellar
rel primal, primary, prime; important, prominent, significant; consequential, momentous, weighty; effective, potent, telling; controlling, master, ruling
con inconsequential, minor, trivial, unimportant; collateral, contingent, secondary

chiefly *adv* ***syn*** GENERALLY 1, largely, mainly, mostly, overall, predominantly, primarily, principally

chieftain *n* ***syn*** LEADER 2, boss, chief, cock, dominator, head, headman, hierarch, honcho, master

chiffer *n* ***syn*** NUMBER, cipher, digit, figure, integer, numeral, whole number

child *n* **1** a young person <a movie for both *children* and adults>
syn bud, chick, chickabiddy, chit, juvenile, kid, moppet, ‖nipper, puss, youngling, young one, youngster, youth
rel minor; adolescent, teenager, teener, teenybopper; brat, bratling, dickens, runabout; cherub, innocent, lamb, sweetling
idiom a slip of a boy (*or* girl), small fry, young hopeful
ant adult, grown-up
2 children *pl* ***syn*** OFFSPRING, ‖begats, brood, descendants, issue, posterity, progeniture, progeny, scions, seed

childbearing *n* **1** ***syn*** BIRTH 1, bearing, ‖birthing, childbirth, delivery, parturition
2 ***syn*** LABOR 2, birth pang(s), childbirth, travail

childbed *n* ***syn*** CONFINEMENT 2, accouchement, lying-in

childbirth *n* **1** ***syn*** BIRTH 1, bearing, ‖birthing, childbearing, delivery, parturition
2 ***syn*** LABOR 2, birth pang(s), childbearing, travail

childing *adj* **1** ***syn*** PREGNANT 1, big, enceinte, expectant, expecting, gone, gravid, heavy, parous, parturient
2 ***syn*** FERTILE, fecund, fruitful, productive, proliferant, prolific, rich, spawning

childish *adj* significantly deficient in maturity <a *childish* and spiteful attitude>
syn babyish, immature, infantile, infantine, prekindergarten, puerile
rel asinine, fatuous, foolish, silly, simple; naive, unsophisticated; arrested, backward, moronic, retarded, slow, ‖wanting
ant adult

child's play *n* ***syn*** SNAP 1, breeze, cinch, duck soup, kid stuff, picnic, pie, ‖pipe, pushover, setup

chill *vb* ***syn*** DISCOURAGE 1, deject, demoralize, dishearten, disparage, dispirit

chill *adj* **1** ***syn*** COLD 1, arctic, chilly, cool, freezing, frosty, gelid, glacial, icy, nippy

---

2 ***syn*** COLD 2, emotionless, frigid, glacial, icy, indifferent, unemotional
rel distant, formal, reserved, solitary, standoffish, uncompanionable, withdrawn; abstracted, disinterested, uninterested
con easy, gregarious, informal; sociable

chiller *n* ***syn*** THRILLER, shocker, thriller-diller

chillsome *adj* ***syn*** COLD 1, arctic, chill, chilly, cool, freezing, frosty, gelid, glacial, icy

chilly *adj* ***syn*** COLD 1, arctic, chill, chillsome, cool, freezing, frosty, gelid, glacial, icy

chime *n* ***syn*** HARMONY 2, accord, agreement, concord, concordance, consonance, tune

chime *vb* ***syn*** RING, bell, bong, knell, peal, toll

chime in *vb* **1** ***syn*** INTERRUPT 2, break in, chip in
2 ***syn*** SAY 1, bring out, come out (with), declare, deliver, state, tell, throw out, utter

chimera *n* ***syn*** PIPE DREAM, bubble, dream, fantasy (*or* phantasy), illusion, ‖pipe, rainbow

chimerical *adj* ***syn*** FICTITIOUS 1, fanciful, fantastic, fictional, fictive, illusory, imaginary, suppositious, supposititious, unreal
rel ambitious, pretentious, utopian; deceptive, delusive, delusory; fabulous, mythical; absurd, preposterous
con believable, plausible, rational, reasonable; possible, practicable
ant feasible

chiming *adj* ***syn*** HARMONIOUS 1, blending, consonant, harmonic, musical, symphonic, symphonious

chin *n* ***syn*** CHAT 2, causerie, prose, rap, talk, yarn

chin *vb* ***syn*** CONVERSE, chat, colloque, talk, visit, yarn

chin–chin *vb* ***syn*** CHAT 1, chatter, clack, gab, ‖gas, jaw, prate, prattle, run on, yak

chin–chin *n* ***syn*** CHATTER, babble, blabber, cackle, chat, clack, gab, jabber, palaver, prattle

‖**chinchy** *adj* ***syn*** STINGY, cheeseparing, close, close-fisted, hardfisted, hardhanded, ‖narrow, narrow-fisted, niggardly, scrimpy

chine *n* ***syn*** RIDGE 1, crest, hogback

Chinese puzzle *n* ***syn*** MYSTERY, closed book, conundrum, enigma, mystification, puzzle, puzzlement, riddle, why

Chinese wall *n* ***syn*** OBSTACLE, bar, hamper, hurdle, impediment, obstruction, rub, snag, stumbling block, traverse

chink *n* ***syn*** CRACK 3, cleft, fissure, rift, rima, rimation, rime, split
rel interruption

chink *vb* ***syn*** JINGLE, chinkle, clink, tingle, tinkle

‖**chink** *n* ***syn*** MONEY, cash, ‖coin, currency, dough, filthy lucre, legal tender, ‖lettuce, loot, ‖wampum

chinkle *vb* ***syn*** JINGLE, chink, clink, tingle, tinkle

‖**chin music** *n* ***syn*** CHATTER, babble, blabber, cackle, clack, gab, gabble, jabber, palaver, yak

chintzy *adj* ***syn*** GAUDY, blatant, brazen, flashy, garish, glaring, loud, meretricious, tawdry, tinsel

chin–up *adj* ***syn*** BRAVE 1, aweless, bold, boldhearted, courageous, dauntless, fearless, intrepid, stalwart, valiant

chip *vb* ***syn*** CHIRP, cheep, chipper, ‖chirm, chirrup, chitter, peep, tweedle, tweet, twitter

chip in *vb* **1** ***syn*** CONTRIBUTE 1, come through, kick in, pitch in, subscribe
2 ***syn*** INTERRUPT 2, break in, chime in

chipper *vb* ***syn*** CHIRP, cheep, chip, ‖chirm, chirrup, chitter, peep, tweedle, tweet, twitter

chipper *adj* **1** ***syn*** LIVELY 1, alert, animate, animated, bright, gay, keen, spirited, sprightly, vivacious
2 ***syn*** NEAT 2, orderly, shipshape, snug, spick-and-span, tidy, trig, trim, uncluttered, well-groomed

‖**chippy** *n* ***syn*** DOXY 1, floozy, grisette, light-o'-love, nymph, nymphet, party girl, roundheel, tart, ‖tootsie

‖**chips** *n pl* ***syn*** MONEY, ‖bread, cash, ‖coin, currency, dough, ‖jack, legal tender, rocks, ‖scratch

‖**chirk** *adj* **1** ***syn*** LIVELY 1, alert, animate, animated, bright, chipper, gay, keen, sprightly, vivacious
2 ***syn*** CHEERFUL 1, blithe, cheery, chirpy, chirrupy, lightsome, sunbeamy, sunny

chirk (up) *vb* ***syn*** ENCOURAGE 1, animate, cheer, embolden, enhearten, hearten, inspirit, nerve, steel, strengthen

‖**chirm** *n* ***syn*** DIN, babel, brouhaha, clamor, hubbub, hullabaloo, jangle, pandemonium, racket, uproar

‖**chirm** *vb* ***syn*** CHIRP, cheep, chip, chipper, chirrup, chitter, peep, tweedle, tweet, twitter

chirography *n* ***syn*** HANDWRITING, calligraphy, ductus, fist, hand, penmanship, script

chirp *vb* to make a short, sharp, and usually repetitive sound <sparrows *chirping* on the lawn>
syn cheep, chip, chipper, ‖chirm, chirrup, clutter, peep, tweedle, tweet, twitter

chirpy *adj* ***syn*** CHEERFUL, blithe, cheery, ‖chirk, chirrupy, lightsome, sunbeamy, sunny

chirrup *vb* ***syn*** CHIRP, cheep, chip, chipper, ‖chirm, chitter, peep, tweedle, tweet, twitter

chirrupy *adj* ***syn*** CHEERFUL 1, blithe, cheery, ‖chirk, chirpy, lightsome, sunbeamy, sunny

chisel *vb* **1** ***syn*** SCULPTURE, carve, sculp, sculpt
2 ***syn*** CHEAT, beat, bilk, cozen, defraud, diddle, do, ‖dry-shave, gyp, overreach

chisel (in) *vb* ***syn*** INTRUDE 1, butt in, cut in, horn in, intertrude, obtrude

‖**chiselly** *adj* ***syn*** BAD 8, disagreeable, displeasing, rotten, sour, unhappy, unpleasant

chit *n* ***syn*** CHILD 1, bud, chick, chickabiddy, juvenile, kid, moppet, puss, young one, youngster

chit *n* ***syn*** NOTE 2, memo, memorandum, notandum, notation

chitchat *n* **1** ***syn*** CHATTER, babble, cackle, chat, chitter-chatter, clack, gabble, prattle, talkee-talkee, tittle-tattle
2 ***syn*** SMALL TALK, bavardage, by-talk, chitter-chatter, trifling

chitter *vb* ***syn*** CHIRP, cheep, chip, chipper, ‖chirm, chirrup, peep, tweedle, tweet, twitter

chitter–chatter *n* **1** ***syn*** CHATTER, babble, bibble-babble, chat, ‖chin music, gabble, gibble-gabble, jabber, palaver, tittle-tattle

---

syn synonym(s) ***rel*** related word(s)
idiom idiomatic equivalent(s) ***con*** contrasted word(s)
ant antonym(s) * vulgar
‖ use limited; if in doubt, see a dictionary
The first word in a synonym list when printed in SMALL CAPITALS shows where there is more information about the group. For a more efficient use of this book see Explanatory Notes.

2 ***syn*** SMALL TALK, bavardage, by-talk, chitchat, trifling

chivalrous *adj* ***syn*** GENEROUS 1, benevolent, big, considerate, greathearted, lofty, magnanimous
rel knightly, manly, noble
con churlish common, low

chivy *vb* **1** ***syn*** FOLLOW 2, chase, pursue, trail
2 ***syn*** BAIT 2, badger, bullyrag, heckle, hector, hound, ride
rel afflict, torment, try; chase, pursue, trail

choate *adj* ***syn*** WHOLE 3, complete, entire, full, integral, perfect

chockablock *adj* ***syn*** FULL 1, block and block, brimful, bung-full, chock-full, crammed, crowded, jam-full, jam-packed, packed

chock–full *adj* ***syn*** FULL 1, awash, brimful, brimming, crammed, crowded, jammed, loaded, packed, stuffed

choice *n* **1** the act, right, opportunity, or faculty of choosing or deciding <the *choice* lies with the electorate>
syn alternative, ‖druthers, election, option, preference, selection
rel decision, determination, finding, judgment, verdict; appraisal, evaluation, rating
2 ***syn*** BEST, cream, elite, fat, flower, pick, pride, prime, prize, top

choice *adj* having qualities that appeal to a fine or highly refined taste <a few *choice* spirits gathered nightly to discuss the day's events>
syn dainty, delicate, elegant, exquisite, rare, recherché, select, superior
rel incomparable, peerless, preeminent, prime, superlative, supreme, surpassing, transcendent, unsurpassed; chosen, culled, picked, selected
con common, ordinary; average, fair, mediocre, medium, middling, run-of-the-mill, second-rate; drab, dull, lackluster, lusterless
ant indifferent

‖**choicy** *adj* ***syn*** NICE 1, choosy, fastidious, finical, finicking, finicky, fussy, particular, persnickety, picky

choke *vb* **1** to check normal breathing especially by compressing or obstructing the windpipe <*choked* by a bone in the throat>
syn strangle, throttle; *compare* SUFFOCATE
2 ***syn*** SUFFOCATE, asphyxiate, ‖quackle, smother, stifle
3 ***syn*** FILL 1, block, clog, close, congest, obstruct, occlude, plug, stop, stopper
4 ***syn*** LOAD 3, charge, fill, heap, pack, pile

choke (off) *vb* ***syn*** SILENCE, hush, quiet, ‖quieten, shush, shut up, still

‖**chokey** *n* ***syn*** JAIL, bridewell, ‖caboose, ‖can, ‖hoosegow, jug, lockup, penitentiary, prison, ‖stir

choking *n* ***syn*** REPRESSION 1, extinguishment, quashing, quenching, smothering, squashing, squelching, stifling, strangling, suppression

choleric *adj* **1** ***syn*** IRASCIBLE, cranky, hot-tempered, quick-tempered, ratty, ‖stomachy, temperish, testy, tetchy, touchy
rel acrimonious, angry, fiery, indignant, irate, mad, spunky, wrathful, wroth; captious, carping, faultfinding
con calm, serene, tranquil; composed, cool, nonchalant
ant placid
2 ***syn*** ANGRY, acrimonious, heated, indignant, irate, ireful, mad, waxy, wrathful, wrathy

chomp *vb* **1** ***syn*** CHEW 1, champ, ‖chaw, ‖chonk, chump, crunch, masticate, munch, ruminate, scrunch
2 ***syn*** BITE 1, champ

‖**chonk** *vb* ***syn*** CHEW 1, champ, ‖chaw, chomp, chump, crunch, masticate, munch, ruminate, scrunch

choose *vb* **1** to fix upon one among alternatives as the one to be taken, accepted, or adopted <*chose* the largest apple but found it sour>
syn cull, elect, mark, opt (for), optate, pick, pick out, prefer, select, single (out), take
rel adopt, embrace, espouse; crave, desire, love, want, wish
con decline, refuse, repudiate, spurn; abnegate, forbear, forgo
ant reject; eschew
2 ***syn*** WILL, elect, like, please, wish
rel favor, prefer
‖**3** ***syn*** DESIRE 1, covet, crave, desiderate, want, wish

choosy *adj* ***syn*** NICE 1, delicate, fastidious, finical, finicking, finicky, fussy, particular, pernickety, persnickety

chop *vb* **1** ***syn*** FELL 2, cut, hew
2 to cut into fragments by repeated strokes <*chop* meat and onions for hash>
syn hash, mince
rel cut up, dice, fragment
idiom cut to bits, make mincemeat of

chop *n* ***syn*** CUFF, box, buffet, ‖bust, clout, ‖paste, poke, slap, smack, spank

chop–chop *adv* ***syn*** FAST 2, flat-out, full tilt, hastily, lickety-split, posthaste, promptly, quickly, rapidly, speedily

chore *n* **1** ***syn*** TASK 1, assignment, chare, devoir, duty, job, stint
2 ***syn*** TASK 2, effort, job, taskwork
rel trial, tribulation

chortle *vb* ***syn*** LAUGH, chuckle, giggle, guffaw, hee-haw, snicker, ‖sniggle, tehee, titter

chorus *n* ***syn*** HARMONY 1, accord, concert, concord, consonance, tune

chosen *adj* ***syn*** SELECT 1, elect, exclusive, pick, picked, selected

chouse *n* ***syn*** TRICK 1, artifice, feint, gambit, gimmick, jig, play, ploy, ruse, whizzer

chouse *vb* ***syn*** CHEAT, beat, bilk, cozen, defraud, diddle, do, flimflam, gyp, overreach

‖**chow** *n* **1** ***syn*** FOOD 1, comestibles, ‖eats, edibles, grub, nurture, provender, provisions, viands, victuals
2 ***syn*** MEAL, feed, refection, repast

chowchow *adj* ***syn*** MISCELLANEOUS, assorted, conglomerate, heterogeneous, indiscriminate, mixed, motley, multifarious, promiscuous, varied

chowchow *n* ***syn*** MISCELLANY 1, brew, hash, hodgepodge, jumble, medley, mélange, mishmash, potpourri, stew

---

syn synonym(s) ***rel*** related word(s)
idiom idiomatic equivalent(s) ***con*** contrasted word(s)
ant antonym(s) * vulgar
‖ use limited; if in doubt, see a dictionary
The first word in a synonym list when printed in SMALL CAPITALS shows where there is more information about the group. For a more efficient use of this book see Explanatory Notes.

chowderhead *n* ***syn*** DUNCE, chucklehead, dope, ‖dumbhead, dunderhead, lame-brain, noddy, noodle, ‖schnook, ‖stupe

chrism *n* ***syn*** OINTMENT, balm, cerate, cream, salve, unction, unguent

christcross–row *n* ***syn*** ALPHABET 1, ABC(s), letters

christen *vb* **1** ***syn*** BAPTIZE, asperse, immerse, sprinkle
2 ***syn*** NAME 1, baptize, call, denominate, designate, dub, entitle, style, term, title

Christian *adj* ***syn*** DECOROUS 1, becoming, befitting, civilized, decent, done, nice, proper, right, seemly

Christian name *n* ***syn*** GIVEN NAME, baptismal name, font name, forename, personal name, prename

Christmas *n* a festival or holiday commemorating the birth of Christ <gave presents on *Christmas*>
syn Nativity, noel, Xmas, yule, yuletide

chronic *adj* **1** ***syn*** HABITUAL 2, accustomed, confirmed, habituated
2 ***syn*** USUAL 1, accepted, accustomed, customary, habitual, routine, wonted

chronicle *n* **1** ***syn*** HISTORY 2, annals
2 ***syn*** ACCOUNT 7, history, narrative, report, story, version
rel narration, recital, recountal

chthonian *adj* ***syn*** INFERNAL 1, chthonic, Hadean, plutonian, plutonic, sulphurous, Tartarean

chthonic *adj* ***syn*** INFERNAL 1, chthonian, Hadean, plutonian, plutonic, sulphurous, Tartarean

chubby *adj* ***syn*** ROTUND 2, plump, plumpish, plumpy, podgy, pudgy, roly-poly, round, roundabout, tubby
ant slim

chuck *vb* **1** ***syn*** DISCARD, cast, ditch, jettison, junk, reject, scrap, shed, slough, throw away
2 ***syn*** EJECT 1, boot (out), chase, dismiss, evict, extrude, kick out, out, throw out
3 ***syn*** ABANDON 1, desert, forsake, quit, renounce, throw over

‖**chuck** *n* ***syn*** HARBOR 3, anchorage, harborage, haven, port, riding, road(s), roadstead

chucker *n* ***syn*** BOUNCER 2, ‖chucker-out, houseman

‖**chucker–out** *n* ***syn*** BOUNCER 2, chucker, houseman

chuckhole *n* ***syn*** POTHOLE, mudhole

chuckle *vb* ***syn*** LAUGH, chortle, giggle, guffaw, hee-haw, snicker, ‖sniggle, tehee, titter

chucklehead *n* ***syn*** DUNCE, chowderhead, dope, ‖dumbhead, dunderhead, lame-brain, noddy, noodle, ‖schnook, ‖stupe

chuckleheaded *adj* ***syn*** STUPID 1, beefheaded, beetleheaded, blockheaded, fatheaded, hammerheaded, numskulled, pinheaded, thickheaded, thick-witted

chuff *n* **1** ***syn*** BOOR, ‖bosthoon, churl, clodhopper, clown, grobian, mucker
2 ***syn*** MISER, hunks, moneygrubber, muckworm, nabal, niggard, ‖nipcheese, scrooge, skinflint, stiff

---

syn synonym(s) ***rel*** related word(s)
idiom idiomatic equivalent(s) ***con*** contrasted word(s)
ant antonym(s) * vulgar
‖ use limited; if in doubt, see a dictionary
The first word in a synonym list when printed in SMALL CAPITALS shows where there is more information about the group. For a more efficient use of this book see Explanatory Notes.

‖**chuff** *adj* ***syn*** SULLEN, ‖chuffy, crabbed, ‖dorty, gloomy, glum, morose, sulky, surly, ugly

‖**chuffy** *adj* ***syn*** STOCKY, ‖chumpy, chunky, dumpy, squab, squat, squdgy, stubby, ‖stuggy, stumpy

‖**chuffy** *adj* ***syn*** SULLEN, ‖chuff, crabbed, ‖dorty, dour, gloomy, glum, sulky, surly, ugly

chum *n* ***syn*** ASSOCIATE 3, buddy, comate, companion, comrade, crony, ‖cully, pal, running mate

chumble *vb* ***syn*** CHEW 1, champ, ‖chaw, chomp, ‖chonk, crunch, masticate, munch, ruminate, scrunch

chummy *adj* **1** ***syn*** FAMILIAR 1, close, confidential, intimate, thick
2 ***syn*** INTIMATE 4, ‖buddy-buddy, cozy, pally, ‖palsy-walsy

chump *n* ‖**1** ***syn*** HEAD 1, ‖bean, ‖coco, ‖conk, ‖dome, headpiece, noddle, noggin, noodle, poll
2 ***syn*** DUNCE, boob, booby, dolt, dolthead, fathead, goof, ‖goon, lunkhead, oaf
3 ***syn*** FOOL 3, butt, dupe, fall guy, gudgeon, gull, mark, pigeon, sap, sucker

chump *vb* ***syn*** CHEW 1, champ, ‖chaw, chomp, ‖chonk, crunch, masticate, munch, ruminate, scrunch

‖**chumpy** *adj* ***syn*** STOCKY, chunky, dumpy, heavyset, squat, stubby, ‖stuggy, stumpy, thick-bodied, thickset

chunk *n* ***syn*** LUMP 1, clod, clump, gob, hunch, hunk, nugget, wad

chunky *adj* ***syn*** STOCKY, ‖chumpy, dumpy, heavyset, squat, stubby, ‖stuggy, stumpy, thick-bodied, thickset
rel chubby, rotund

‖**chunter** *vb* ***syn*** MUMBLE, fumble, muddle, ‖mump, murmur, mutter, swallow

church *n* **1** ***syn*** HOUSE OF WORSHIP, house of God, house of prayer, tabernacle, temple
2 ***syn*** RELIGION 2, communion, connection, creed, cult, denomination, faith, persuasion, sect

church *adj* ***syn*** ECCLESIASTICAL, churchly, churchmanly, spiritual

churchly *adj* ***syn*** ECCLESIASTICAL, church, churchmanly, spiritual

churchman *n* ***syn*** CLERGYMAN, cleric, clerical, clerk, divine, ecclesiastic, minister, parson, preacher, reverend

churchmanly *adj* ***syn*** ECCLESIASTICAL, church, churchly, spiritual

churl *n* ***syn*** BOOR, ‖bosthoon, chuff, clodhopper, clown, grobian, mucker
ant aristocrat, gentleman

churlish *adj* ***syn*** BOORISH, cloddish, clodhopping, clownish, coarse, loutish, lowbred, uncivilized, uncultured, unpolished
rel crude, discourteous; blunt, brusque, crusty, curt, gruff; dour, surly; naive, unschooled
con bland, politic, smooth; polished, sophisticated
ant courtly

churn *vb* ***syn*** SEETHE 4, boil, bubble, ferment, ‖moil, simmer, smolder, stir

chute *n* ***syn*** WATERFALL, cascade, cataract, fall(s), ‖force, sault, spout

cicatrix *n* ***syn*** SCAR, scarification

cicatrize *vb* ***syn*** SCAR, scarify

‖**cig** *n* ***syn*** CIGARETTE, ‖butt, ‖coffin nail, fag, ‖gasper, ‖pill, ‖skag, smoke

cigarette *n* a paper-wrapped tube of finely cut smoking tobacco <dependence on *cigarettes*>

syn ‖butt, ‖cig, ‖coffin nail, fag, ‖gasper, ‖pill, ‖skag, smoke

cimmerian *adj syn* INFERNAL 2, avernal, hellish, pandemoniac, plutonian, plutonic, stygian

cinch *n syn* SNAP 1, breeze, child's play, duck soup, kid stuff, picnic, pie, ‖pipe, pushover, setup

cinch *vb syn* ENSURE, assure, insure, secure

cincture *n syn* BELT 1, ceinture, girdle, sash, waistband

cincture *vb syn* BELT 1, band, begird, begirdle, encincture, engird, engirdle, gird, girdle

cinders *n pl syn* ASH, ashes, clinkers

cine *n syn* MOVIE, ‖cinema, film, flick, motion picture, moving picture, photoplay, picture, picture show, show

‖**cinema** *n syn* MOVIE, cine, film, flick, motion picture, moving picture, photoplay, picture, picture show, show

cipher *n* **1** *syn* ZERO 1, aught (*or* ought), goose egg, naught (*or* nought), nothing, zilch
2 *syn* NUMBER, chiffer, digit, figure, integer, numeral, whole number
3 *syn* MONOGRAM
4 *syn* NONENTITY, insignificancy, nobody, nothing, nullity, whiffet, whippersnapper, whipster, zero, zilch

cipher *vb* **1** *syn* CALCULATE, compute, estimate, figure, reckon
‖**2** *syn* SOLVE 2, break, clear up, decipher, ‖dope out, figure out, puzzle out, resolve, unravel, unriddle

ciphering *n syn* COMPUTATION, arithmetic, calculation, estimation, figuring, reckoning

circa *prep syn* ABOUT 1, around, close on, near, nearby, nigh

Circean *adj syn* ENTICING, fetching, luring, tempting

circle *n* **1** *syn* RANGE 2, compass, dimension(s), extension, extensity, extent, length, orbit, radius, scope
2 *syn* CYCLE 1, round, wheel
3 *syn* SET 5, bunch, crowd, group, lot, push
rel acquaintance; cronies, friends, intimates; associates, companions, comrades
4 *syn* CLIQUE, cabal, camarilla, camp, clan, coterie, ingroup, mob, ring

circle *vb* **1** *syn* SURROUND 1, begird, compass, encircle, encompass, environ, gird, girdle, hem, ring
2 *syn* TURN 1, circumduct, gyrate, gyre, revolve, roll, rotate

circuit *n* **1** *syn* CIRCUMFERENCE, ambit, compass, perimeter, periphery
rel course, route, way; journey, tour, travels, trip
2 *syn* REVOLUTION 1, circulation, circumvolution, gyration, gyre, rotation, round, turn, wheel, whirl
3 *syn* TOUR 2, round, roundabout, round trip
4 *syn* LEAGUE 4, association, conference, loop, wheel

circuitous *adj syn* INDIRECT 1, circular, collateral, oblique, roundabout
ant straight

circuitously *adv syn* ABOUT 2, round about

circular *adj* **1** *syn* ROUND 1
2 *syn* INDIRECT 1, circuitous, collateral, oblique, roundabout

circulate *vb* **1** *syn* SPREAD 1, diffuse, disperse, disseminate, distribute, propagate, radiate, strew
rel exchange, interchange; flow; revolve, rotate
2 *syn* MOBILIZE 1, actuate, set off

circulation *n syn* REVOLUTION 1, circuit, circumvolution, gyration, gyre, rotation, round, turn, wheel, whirl

circulator *n syn* GOSSIP 1, carrytale, clack, gossiper, gossipmonger, ‖long tongue, newsmonger, quidnunc, rumormonger, sieve

circumambages *n pl syn* VERBIAGE 1, circumbendibus, circumlocution, periphrase, periphrasis, pleonasm, redundancy, roundabout, tautology, verbality

circumambulate *vb syn* WANDER 1, drift, meander, mooch, ramble, range, roam, rove, straggle, stray

circumbendibus *n syn* VERBIAGE 1, circumambages, circumlocution, periphrase, periphrasis, pleonasm, redundancy, roundabout, tautology, verbality

circumduct *vb* **1** *syn* TURN 1, circle, gyrate, gyre, revolve, roll, rotate
2 *syn* ABOLISH 1, abate, abrogate, annihilate, annul, invalidate, negate, nullify, quash, undo

circumference *n* a continuous line or course about an area <strolled along the *circumference* of the reservoir>
syn ambit, circuit, compass, perimeter, periphery; *compare* BORDER 1
rel boundary, bounds, confines, limits; border, margin, rim

circumlocution *n syn* VERBIAGE 1, circumambages, circumbendibus, periphrase, periphrasis, pleonasm, redundancy, roundabout, tautology, verbality
con conciseness, concision, pithiness, succinctness, terseness; compactness

circumnavigate *vb syn* SKIRT 2, bypass, circumvent, detour

circumscribe *vb syn* LIMIT 2, bar, confine, delimit, delimitate, prelimit, restrict
rel fetter, hamper, trammel
con amplify, distend, inflate, swell; enlarge
ant dilate, expand

circumscribed *adj syn* DEFINITE 1, determinate, fixed, limited, narrow, precise, restricted
rel bound, bounded, finite; confined, cramped, strait

circumscription *n* **1** *syn* RESTRICTION 1, ‖ball and chain, cramp, limitation, stint, stricture
2 *syn* RESTRICTION 2, confinement, constrainment, constraint, cramp, restraint

circumspect *adj syn* CAUTIOUS, calculating, careful, chary, considerate, discreet, gingerly, guarded, safe, wary
rel meticulous, punctilious, scrupulous
con adventurous, daredevil, foolhardy; careless, heedless; bold
ant audacious

circumstance *n* **1** *syn* OCCURRENCE, episode, event, go, happening, incident, occasion, thing
rel detail, item, particular; component, constituent, element, factor
2 *syn* FATE, destiny, doom, kismet, lot, moira, portion, weird

---

syn synonym(s)	*rel* related word(s)
idiom idiomatic equivalent(s)	*con* contrasted word(s)
ant antonym(s)	* vulgar

‖ use limited; if in doubt, see a dictionary
The first word in a synonym list when printed in SMALL CAPITALS shows where there is more information about the group. For a more efficient use of this book see Explanatory Notes.

circumstantial *adj* marked by careful attention to relevant details <gave a *circumstantial* account of his adventure>
syn blow-by-blow, clocklike, detailed, full, itemized, minute, particular, particularized, thorough
rel accurate, exact, nice, precise; complete, replete; close, strict
con compendious, concise, laconic, pithy, short, succinct, terse; abbreviated, curtailed, cut, pruned, shortened, trimmed
ant abridged; summary

circumvent *vb* **1** *syn* FRUSTRATE 1, baffle, balk, beat, bilk, dash, disappoint, foil, ruin, thwart
rel befool, dupe, hoodwink, trick; avoid, elude, escape, evade
ant conform (*to laws, orders*); cooperate (*with persons*)
2 *syn* SKIRT 2, bypass, circumnavigate, detour
3 *syn* SKIRT 3, burke, bypass, ‖polly-fox, sidestep

circumvolution *n syn* REVOLUTION 1, circuit, circulation, gyration, gyre, rotation, round, turn, wheel, whirl

cit *n syn* TOWNSMAN, burgher, citizen, towner, townman, towny

citadel *n syn* FORT, fastness, fortress, redoubt, stronghold

citation *n syn* ENCOMIUM, eulogy, panegyric, salutation, tribute
rel award, guerdon, reward

cite *vb* **1** *syn* REMEMBER, bethink, ‖mind, recall, recollect, remind, reminisce, retain, retrospect, revive
2 *syn* MENTION, instance, name, specify
3 *syn* ADDUCE, advance, allege, lay, offer, present
rel count, enumerate, number, tell

citizen *n* **1** *syn* TOWNSMAN, burgher, cit, towner, townman, towny
2 a person regarded as a member of a sovereign state, entitled to its protection, and subject to its laws <the subtle bond between the *citizen* and the nation>
syn national, subject
con foreigner, stranger
ant alien

city *adj syn* URBAN, burghal, municipal

civic *adj syn* PUBLIC 1, civil, national

civil *adj* **1** *syn* PUBLIC 1, civic, national
2 adequate in courtesy <made a *civil* inquiry about their health>
syn courteous, genteel, mannerly, polite, well-mannered; *compare* COURTLY
rel cultivated, refined, well-bred; accommodating, affable, cordial, obliging; bland, diplomatic, gracious, politic, suave, urbane
con boorish, churlish, loutish, uncouth; discourted, ill-mannered, impolite, ungracious
ant uncivil; rude

civilities *n pl syn* MANNER 5, amenities, decorum(s), etiquette, mores, proprieties

civilized *adj* **1** *syn* DECOROUS 1, becoming, befitting, Christian, comme il faut, conforming, correct, decent, done, nice
2 *syn* SUAVE, bland, smooth, urbane

Civitas Dei *n syn* HEAVEN 2, Abraham's bosom, bliss, Canaan, elysium, empyrean, New Jerusalem, nirvana, paradise, Zion

‖**clabber** *vb syn* CURDLE, ‖cruddle, curd, ‖lopper, turn

clack *vb* **1** *syn* CHAT 1, babble, chatter, gab, gabble, jaw, prate, prattle, yak, yakety-yak
2 *syn* RATTLE 1, bicker, clatter, clitter, ‖ruttle, shatter

clack *n* **1** *syn* CHATTER, babble, blab, blabber, chat, gabble, jabber, palaver, prattle, yak
2 *syn* GOSSIP 1, carrytale, ‖long tongue, quidnunc, rumormonger, scandalmonger, sieve, tabby, talebearer, telltale

clad *vb* **1** *syn* CLOTHE, apparel, array, attire, dress, enclothe, garb, garment, raiment
2 *syn* SHEATHE, face, side, skin

‖**claggy** *adj* **1** *syn* STICKY 1, adhesive, ‖clarty, cloggy, gluey, gooey, gummy, stodgy
2 *syn* MUDDY 1, bemired, ‖clarty, miry, oozy

claim *vb* **1** *syn* DEMAND 1, call, challenge, exact, postulate, require, requisition, solicit
rel adduce, advance, allege; assert, defend, justify, maintain, vindicate
con abnegate, forgo; refuse, reject, repudiate; disavow, disown
ant disclaim; renounce
2 *syn* MAINTAIN 2, argue, assert, contend, defend, justify, vindicate, warrant

claim *n* **1** a real or assumed right to demand something as one's own or one's due <his genial wit was his greatest *claim* to fame>
syn ‖dibs, pretense, pretension, title
rel birthright, prerogative, privilege, right; affirmation, assertion, declaration, protestation
2 *syn* INTEREST 1, share, stake

clamant *adj syn* PRESSING, burning, clamorous, crying, dire, exigent, imperative, importunate, instant, urgent

clamber *vb syn* SCRAMBLE 1, scrabble, ‖spartle, ‖sprauchle

clamor *n* **1** *syn* COMMOTION 4, bustle, hassle, hubbub, hurly-burly, to-do, tumult, turmoil, uproar, whirl
2 *syn* DIN, babel, hubbub, hullabaloo, jangle, pandemonium, racket, tintamarre, tumult, uproar
3 *syn* COMMOTION 1, convulsion, ferment, outcry, tumult, upheaval, upturn

clamor *vb syn* ROAR, bawl, bellow, bluster, rout
rel claim, demand; agitate, debate, dispute
idiom make the welkin ring, raise the roof

clamorous *adj* **1** *syn* VOCIFEROUS, blatant, boisterous, ‖dinsome, loudmouthed, multivocal, obstreperous, openmouthed, strident, vociferant
rel articulate, eloquent, vocal, voluble; adjuring, begging, imploring, importunate
ant taciturn
2 *syn* PRESSING, burning, clamant, crying, dire, exigent, imperative, importunate, instant, urgent

clamp *n syn* HOLD, clasp, clench, clinch, clutch, grapple, grasp, grip, gripe, tenure

---

syn synonym(s) — *rel* related word(s)
idiom idiomatic equivalent(s) — *con* contrasted word(s)
ant antonym(s) — * vulgar
‖ use limited; if in doubt, see a dictionary
The first word in a synonym list when printed in SMALL CAPITALS shows where there is more information about the group. For a more efficient use of this book see Explanatory Notes.

clampdown *n* ***syn*** REPRESSION 2, crackdown, suppression

clan *n* **1** ***syn*** FAMILY 1, folk, house, kindred, lineage, race, stock, tribe
2 ***syn*** CLIQUE, cabal, camarilla, camp, circle, coterie, ingroup, mob, ring

clandestine *adj* ***syn*** SECRET 1, covert, furtive, hugger-mugger, hush-hush, stealthy, surreptitious, undercover, ‖underneath, under-the-table
rel illegitimate, illicit; artful, foxy, sly
con aboveboard, forthright, straightforward
ant open

clandestinely *adv* ***syn*** SECRETLY, by stealth, covertly, furtively, hugger-mugger, in camera, privately, stealthily, sub rosa, surreptitiously

clangorous *adj* ***syn*** NOISY, clattery, noiseful, rackety, sonorous, uproarious

clap *n* ***syn*** BANG 2, blast, boom, burst, crack, crash, slam, smash, wham

claptrap *n* ***syn*** NONSENSE 2, ‖baloney, ‖bull, bunkum, drivel, flapdoodle, hokum, humbug, malarkey, twaddle

‖**claret** *n* ***syn*** BLOOD 1, gore

clarify *vb* **1** ***syn*** PURIFY 1, clean, cleanse, depurate
2 to make clear and understandable <felt a need to *clarify* his position on the question>
syn clear, clear up, elucidate, explain, illuminate, illustrate; *compare* EXPLAIN 1
rel settle, straighten out; define, delineate, formulate; analyze, break down, simplify
idiom make plain
con befog, cloud, obfuscate, obscure; confuse, foul up, muddle, ‖snafu

clarion *adj* ***syn*** FAIR 2, clear, cloudless, fine, pleasant, rainless, sunny, sunshiny, unclouded, undarkened

clarity *n* notable precision of thought or expression <*clarity* of expression depends on use of exactly the right words in precisely the right way>
syn clearness, limpidity, lucidity, perspicuity, plainness
rel articulateness, articulation; care, exactitude, fussiness, meticulousness, nicety, precision; accuracy, correctitude, propriety
con haziness, imprecision, indefiniteness, unclearness, vagueness; inexactness, laxity, looseness, sloppiness, slovenliness
ant obscurity

‖**clarty** *adj* **1** ***syn*** MUDDY 1, bemired, ‖claggy, miry, oozy
2 ***syn*** STICKY 1, adhesive, ‖claggy, cloggy, gluey, gooey, gummy, stodgy

clash *vb* **1** ***syn*** BUMP 1, collide, ‖prang
2 to be markedly out of harmony <garish colors that *clashed* almost painfully>
syn conflict, disaccord, discord, disharmonize, jangle, jar, mismatch
rel fret, gall, grate, try
idiom swear at one another
con accord, blend, conform, correspond; fit, meet, suit
ant harmonize

clash *n* **1** ***syn*** IMPACT, bump, collision, concussion, crash, jar, jolt, shock, smash, wallop
2 a sharp and usually brief conflict especially between military units <recurrent border *clashes*>
syn affray, brush, fray, melee, mellay, scrimmage, skirmish
rel brawl, broil, fracas, riot, row, rumpus, scrap, set-to; action, battle, conflict, engagement; embroilment, encounter
idiom clash of arms, passage at (*or* of) arms

clashing *adj* ***syn*** ANTIPATHETIC 1, antagonistic, conflicting, contrariant, contrary, discordant

clasp *n* ***syn*** HOLD, clamp, clench, clinch, clutch, grapple, grasp, grip, gripe, tenure

clasp *vb* **1** ***syn*** EMBRACE 1, ‖clinch, ‖clip, ‖coll, enfold, hug, press, squeeze
2 ***syn*** TAKE 4, grasp, grip

class *n* **1** a unit or a subunit of a larger whole made up of members sharing one or more characteristics <miniaturization of circuitry made possible a whole new *class* of small computers and calculators>
syn category, grade, group, grouping, league, pigeonhole, tier
rel brand, color, description, feather, genre, grain, ilk, kidney, kind, nature, order, sort, stamp, style, type; bracket, branch, denomination, division, head, section; genus, species
2 ***syn*** QUALITY 3, caliber, grade
3 ***syn*** TYPE, feather, ilk, kidney, kind, order, sort, species, stripe, variety

class *vb* **1** ***syn*** ASSORT, categorize, classify, group, pigeonhole, sort
2 to put into an appropriate class <he is generally *classed* among our leading theoretical physicists>
syn classify, evaluate, grade, rank, rate
rel appraise, gauge, judge; divide, part, separate; allot, assign; account, assess, consider, hold, reckon, regard; mark, score

classic *adj* **1** ***syn*** EXCELLENT, capital, champion, classical, famous, fine, prime, superior, top, top-notch
2 ***syn*** VINTAGE 1, classical
3 ***syn*** TYPICAL 1, classical, exemplary, ideal, model, paradigmatic, prototypal, prototypical, quintessential, representative

classic *n* ***syn*** MASTERPIECE 1, chef d'oeuvre, magnum opus, masterwork, tour de force

classical *adj* **1** ***syn*** EXCELLENT, capital, champion, classic, famous, fine, prime, superior, top, top-notch
2 ***syn*** VINTAGE 1, classic
3 ***syn*** TYPICAL 1, classic, exemplary, ideal, model, paradigmatic, prototypal, prototypical, quintessential, representative

classify *vb* **1** ***syn*** ASSORT, categorize, class, group, pigeonhole, sort
2 ***syn*** CLASS 2, evaluate, grade, rank, rate

‖**classy** *adj* ***syn*** STYLISH, dashing, fashionable, in, modish, sharp, swank, swish, tonish, tony

clatter *vb* **1** ***syn*** RATTLE 1, bicker, clack, clitter, ‖ruttle, shatter

---

syn synonym(s) ***rel*** related word(s)
idiom idiomatic equivalent(s) ***con*** contrasted word(s)
ant antonym(s) * vulgar
‖ use limited; if in doubt, see a dictionary
The first word in a synonym list when printed in SMALL CAPITALS shows where there is more information about the group. For a more efficient use of this book see Explanatory Notes.

2 *syn* CHAT 1, babble, chatter, clack, dither, gab, jaw, ‖natter, rattle, run on

clatter *n syn* COMMOTION 4, clamor, hassle, hubbub, hurly-burly, pother, to-do, tumult, turmoil, uproar

clattery *adj syn* NOISY, clangorous, noiseful, rackety, sonorous, uproarious

claviger *n syn* CUSTODIAN, cerberus, ‖custodier, custos, guardian, keeper, warden, watchdog

‖**clawback** *n syn* SYCOPHANT, bootlicker, footlicker, lickspit, lickspittle, spaniel, toad, toadeater, toady, truckler

clean *adj* **1** free from dirt <kept a *clean* house in a dirty neighborhood>
syn cleanly, immaculate, spotless, taintless, unsoiled, unsullied
rel bright, shining, sparkling; fresh, pure, untainted, wholesome
idiom clean as a whistle (*or* new penny)
con dingy, grimy, grubby, messy, mussy, slovenly; filthy, foul, noisome
ant dirty, unclean
2 *syn* INNOCENT 2, blameless, crimeless, faultless, guiltless, inculpable, unguilty
3 *syn* CHASTE, decent, immaculate, modest, pure, spotless, stainless, unblemished, undefiled, unsullied
ant unclean
4 *syn* FAIR 5, sportsmanlike, sportsmanly

clean *vb* **1** *syn* PURIFY 1, clarify, cleanse, depurate
2 to make clean <*cleaned* his car every week>
syn cleanse, clean up
rel do, neaten, order, police, spruce, straighten (up), tidy, trim; brighten, freshen, furbish, recondition; renew, renovate
idiom make spick-and-span
con begrime, daub, dirty, sully; besmirch, defile, foul, pollute
ant soil
3 *syn* DRESS 3, gut

clean–cut *adj syn* EXPLICIT, categorical, clear-cut, definite, definitive, express, specific, unambiguous

clean–limbed *adj syn* SHAPELY, shapeful, statuesque, trim, well-proportioned, well-turned

cleanly *adj syn* CLEAN 1, immaculate, spotless, taintless, unsoiled, unsullied
rel neat, orderly, spick-and-span, tidy, trim; dainty, fastidious, fussy, nice
con disheveled, disorderly, slipshod, sloppy, slovenly, unkempt
ant uncleanly

cleanse *vb* **1** *syn* CLEAN 2, clean up
rel disinfect, sanitize, sterilize
2 *syn* PURIFY 1, clarify, clean, depurate
3 *syn* PURIFY 2, expurgate, lustrate, purge

---

syn synonym(s) *rel* related word(s)
idiom idiomatic equivalent(s) *con* contrasted word(s)
ant antonym(s) * vulgar
‖ use limited; if in doubt, see a dictionary
The first word in a synonym list when printed in SMALL CAPITALS shows where there is more information about the group. For a more efficient use of this book see Explanatory Notes.

cleansing *n syn* PURIFICATION, catharsis, expurgation, lustration, purgation

clean up *vb* **1** *syn* CLEAR 6, gain, make, net
2 *syn* CLEAN 2, cleanse
3 *syn* SETTLE 7, wind up

‖**clean up** (on) *vb syn* WHIP 2, beat, ‖clobber, drub, dust, lambaste, ‖larrup, lick, overwhelm, shellac

clear *adj* **1** *syn* FAIR 2, clarion, cloudless, fine, pleasant, rainless, sunny, sunshiny, unclouded, undarkened
2 *syn* TRANSPARENT 1, limpid, pellucid, see-through, translucent
3 *syn* TRANSLUCENT 3, tralucent, translucid, transparent
rel milky, opalescent
4 free from obscurity or ambiguity <his account of the accident was perfectly *clear*>
syn clear-cut, crystal, lucent, lucid, luculent, luminous, pellucid, perspicuous, translucent, transparent, transpicuous, unambiguous, unblurred; *compare* UNDERSTANDABLE
rel apprehensible, comprehensible, graspable, knowable, understandable; plain, simple, straightforward, uncomplicated, unperplexed; defined, definite
idiom clear as day (*or* crystal), plain as the nose on one's face
con clouded, dark, mysterious, unclear; hazy, ill-defined, vague
ant obscure
5 readily perceived or apprehended <a *clear* case of embezzlement>
syn apparent, conspicuous, distinct, evident, manifest, obvious, open-and-shut, openhanded, palpable, patent, plain, straightforward, unambiguous, unequivocal, univocal, unmistakable; *compare* SELF-EXPLANATORY, UNDERSTANDABLE
rel appreciable, perceptible, recognizable, sensible, tangible; overt, public, published, unhidden, unobscured; exact, precise
con dim, dusky, gloomy, murky; cryptic, dark, enigmatic, equivocal, indistinct, vague; arcane, esoteric, mysterious, occult
ant obscure
6 *syn* EMPTY 1, bare, stark, vacant, vacuous, void

clear *adv syn* WELL 3, à fond, altogether, completely, entirely, fully, perfectly, quite, ‖slap, utterly

clear *vb* **1** *syn* EXCULPATE, absolve, acquit, disculpate, exonerate, vindicate
2 *syn* CLARIFY 2, clear up, elucidate, explain, illuminate, illustrate
3 *syn* VACATE 2, empty, void
4 *syn* RID, lose, shake (off), throw off, unburden
rel eliminate, rule out; clean, cleanse
5 to make right by presenting what is due <*clear* one's accounts>
syn clear off, discharge, liquidate, pay, pay up, quit, satisfy, settle, square
rel close, pay off, repay, sink, solve
6 to obtain as a profit or return <he *cleared* several thousand on the deal>
syn clean up, gain, make, net
rel acquire, get, obtain, secure; earn, win; accumulate, gather, glean, pick up

7 ***syn*** EXTRICATE 2, clear away, disencumber, disentangle, disentwine, unentangle, unscramble, untangle, untie, untwine

8 to pass over or by <*cleared* the hurdle with perfect form>

syn hurdle, leap, negotiate, over, overleap, surmount, vault

9 to become fair <the weather *cleared* later in the day>

syn ‖break, burn off

rel ameliorate, better, improve, meliorate; settle, stabilize

10 ***syn*** VANISH, disappear, evanesce, evanish, evaporate, fade

clear away *vb* 1 ***syn*** REMOVE 4, eliminate, take out

2 ***syn*** EXTRICATE 2, clear, discumber, disembarrass, disembroil, disencumber, disentangle, disentwine, unentangle, untangle

clear–cut *adj* 1 ***syn*** CLEAR 4, crystal, lucent, lucid, luminous, pellucid, translucent, transparent, transpicuous, unblurred

2 ***syn*** EXPLICIT, categorical, clean-cut, definite, definitive, express, specific, unambiguous

3 ***syn*** INCISIVE, biting, crisp, cutting, ingoing, penetrating, trenchant

rel clear, distinct, manifest, plain; definite, explicit, express; exact, nice, precise

con fogged, hazy, misty; confused, muddled; obscured, overcast

4 ***syn*** DECIDED 1, assured, definite, pronounced

rel indubitable, undisputed, undoubted, unquestioned

idiom beyond a shade (*or* shadow) of doubt, past dispute

clearness *n* ***syn*** CLARITY, limpidity, lucidity, perspicuity, plainness

clear off *vb* ***syn*** CLEAR 5, discharge, liquidate, pay, pay up, quit, satisfy, settle, square

clear out *vb* ***syn*** GET OUT 1, begone, decamp, hightail, kite, scram, skedaddle, skiddoo, take off, ‖vamoose

clear–sightedness *n* ***syn*** WIT 3, acumen, astucity, astuteness, discernment, discrimination, keenness, penetration, percipience, shrewdness

clear up *vb* 1 ***syn*** CLARIFY 2, clear, elucidate, explain, illuminate, illustrate

2 ***syn*** SOLVE 2, ‖cipher, decipher, dissolve, ‖dope out, figure out, puzzle out, resolve, unfold, unravel

cleavage *n* ***syn*** SCHISM 3, chasm, cleft, split

cleave *vb* ***syn*** STICK 2, adhere, cling, cohere

rel associate, combine, conjoin, join, link, unite

con alienate, disaffect, disunite, estrange, separate

cleave *vb* 1 ***syn*** CUT 5, carve, dissect, dissever, sever, slice, split, sunder

2 ***syn*** TEAR 1, rend, rip, rive, split

rel divide, divorce, separate; chop, hew

con join, link, unite; attach, fasten

cleft *n* 1 ***syn*** CRACK 3, chink, fissure, rift, rima, rimation, rime, split

2 ***syn*** RAVINE, arroyo, chasm, clough, clove, gap, gorge, gulch

3 ***syn*** SCHISM 3, chasm, cleavage, split

clemency *n* 1 ***syn*** MERCY, caritas, charity, grace, lenity

rel gentleness, mildness; equitableness, fairness, justness

con austerity, severity, sternness; rigidity, rigorousness, strictness; inexorableness, inflexibility, obduracy

ant harshness

2 ***syn*** FORBEARANCE 2, indulgence, lenience, leniency, mercifulness, tolerance, toleration

rel endurance, sufferance

con firmness, hardness, inflexibility, obdurateness, relentlessness, rigidity

ant harshness

clement *adj* ***syn*** FORBEARING, charitable, easy, indulgent, lenient, merciful, tolerant

rel compassionate, sympathetic, tender; benign, benignant, kind, kindly; benevolent, charitable, humane

con austere, severe, stern; rigid, rigorous, strict, stringent

ant harsh; barbarous

clench *n* ***syn*** HOLD, clamp, clasp, clinch, clutch, grapple, grasp, grip, gripe, tenure

clergyman *n* one duly ordained to the service of God in the Christian church <the responsibility of the *clergyman* to the whole community>

syn ‖blackcoat, cassock, churchman, cleric, clerical, clerk, ‖devil-dodger, divine, ‖dominie, ecclesiast, ecclesiastic, ‖Holy Joe, minister, parson, preacher, pulpitarian, pulpiteer, pulpiter, reverend, sermonizer, sky pilot

rel evangelist, missionary; chaplain, curate, pastor, vicar; father, priest, shepherd; predicant

idiom man of God, man of the cloth

cleric *n* ***syn*** CLERGYMAN, churchman, clerical, clerk, divine, ecclesiastic, minister, parson, preacher, reverend

clerical *n* ***syn*** CLERGYMAN, churchman, cleric, clerk, divine, ecclesiastic, minister, parson, preacher, reverend

clerisy *n* ***syn*** INTELLIGENTSIA, illuminati, intellectuals, literati

clerk *n* ***syn*** CLERGYMAN, churchman, cleric, clerical, divine, ecclesiastic, minister, parson, preacher, reverend

clerkish *adj* ***syn*** NICE 1, choosy, fastidious, finical, finicking, finicky, fussy, particular, picky, squeamish

clever *adj* 1 ***syn*** SKILLFUL 2, adroit, good, pretty, ‖skilly, wicked, workmanlike, workmanly

2 ***syn*** DEXTEROUS 1, adroit, deft, handy, neat-handed, nimble

3 ***syn*** INTELLIGENT 2, alert, brainy, bright, brilliant, knowing, quick-witted, ready-witted, sharp, smart

rel apt, prompt, quick, ready; able, capable, competent; all-around, many-sided, versatile

idiom quick as a flash, sharp (*or* smart) as a whip

con asinine, fatuous, foolish, simple

ant dull

4 highly skilled in devising or contriving <very *clever* about getting her own way>

syn adroit, canny, ‖coony, cunning, dexterous, ingenious, ‖sleighty, slim, sly; *compare* SKILLFUL 2

---

syn synonym(s) *rel* related word(s)
idiom idiomatic equivalent(s) *con* contrasted word(s)
ant antonym(s) * vulgar
‖ use limited; if in doubt, see a dictionary
The first word in a synonym list when printed in SMALL CAPITALS shows where there is more information about the group. For a more efficient use of this book see Explanatory Notes.

rel able, adept, expert, handy, masterly, proficient, skilled, skillful; capable, competent, qualified; crafty, deceitful, slick, tricky
con awkward, clumsy, gauche, inept, maladroit; dilatory, laggard, slow, sluggish; incapable, incompetent, inept, unqualified
5 pleasing because of aptness, sparkle, and usually wit <delighted her audience with a series of *clever* comparisons>
syn good, scintillating, smart, sprightly
rel bright, brilliant, coruscating, dazzling, sparkling; piquant, racy, salty; fanciful, whimsical; amusing, entertaining, pleasing; facetious, funny, humorous, witty; laughable, risible
con drab. dull, humdrum, monotonous, stodgy; barren, empty, inane; fatuous, pointless; absurd, foolish, nonsensical, ridiculous
ant stupid

||**cleverly** *adv* ***syn*** WELL 3, clear, completely, entirely, fully, ||plumb, quite, thoroughly, utterly, wholly

cliché *n* ***syn*** COMMONPLACE, banality, bromide, platitude, prosaicism, prosaism, rubber stamp, shibboleth, tag, truism

cliché *adj* ***syn*** TRITE, bathetic, clichéd, commonplace, hack, hackneyed, stale, stereotyped, stereotypical, time-worn

clichéd *adj* ***syn*** TRITE, bathetic, cliché, commonplace, hack, hackneyed, stale, stereotyped, stereotypical, time-worn

click *vb* ***syn*** SUCCEED 2, come off, go, go over, pan out, prove out

client *n* ***syn*** CUSTOMER, patron

clientage *n* ***syn*** FOLLOWING 2, audience, clientele, public

clientele *n* ***syn*** FOLLOWING 2, audience, clientage, public

climacteric *adj* ***syn*** ACUTE 6, critical, crucial, desperate, dire

climate *n* ***syn*** ENVIRONMENT, ambience, ambient, atmosphere, medium, milieu, mise-en-scène, surroundings

climatize *vb* ***syn*** HARDEN 2, acclimate, acclimatize, season, toughen

climax *n* ***syn*** APEX 2, acme, apogee, capsheaf, capstone, culmination, meridian, peak, pinnacle, summit

climax *vb* to bring to or come to a satisfying termination <the feast was *climaxed* by a glorious plum pudding>
syn cap, crown, culminate, finish off, round off, top off
rel content, please, satisfy; conclude, end, finish, terminate

climb *vb* ***syn*** ASCEND 1, escalade, escalate, mount, scale, upclimb, upgo

---

syn synonym(s)	***rel*** related word(s)
idiom idiomatic equivalent(s)	***con*** contrasted word(s)
ant antonym(s)	* vulgar

|| use limited; if in doubt, see a dictionary
The first word in a synonym list when printed in SMALL CAPITALS shows where there is more information about the group. For a more efficient use of this book see Explanatory Notes.

||**clinch** *vb* ***syn*** EMBRACE 1, clasp, ||clip, ||coll, enfold, hug, press, squeeze

clinch *n* ***syn*** HOLD, clamp, clasp, clench, clutch, grapple, grasp, grip, gripe, tenure

clincher *n* ***syn*** TRUMP CARD, trump

cling *vb* ***syn*** STICK 2, adhere, cleave, cohere

cling *n* ***syn*** ADHERENCE 1, adhesion, bond, clinging, coherence, cohesion, stickage, sticking

clinging *n* ***syn*** ADHERENCE 1, adhesion, bond, cling, coherence, cohesion, stickage, sticking

clink *vb* ***syn*** JINGLE, chink, chinkle, tingle, tinkle

||**clink** *n* ***syn*** JAIL, ||calaboose, ||can, cooler, coop, ||hoosegow, jug, lockup, ||pokey, ||stir

clinkers *n pl* ***syn*** ASH, ashes, cinders

||**clip** *vb* ***syn*** EMBRACE 1, clasp, ||clinch, ||coll, enfold, hug, press, squeeze

clip *n* ***syn*** BROOCH, broach, pin

clip *vb* **1** ***syn*** CUT 6, crop, pare, prune, shave, shear, skive, trim
2 ***syn*** MOW, crop, cut
3 ***syn*** REDUCE 2, cut, cut back, cut down, lower, mark down, pare, shave, slash
4 ***syn*** OVERCHARGE 1, fleece, skin, soak, stick

clique *n* a narrowly exclusive group of people usually held together by a common often selfish interest or purpose <there was a politically minded *clique* on the campus>
syn cabal, camarilla, camp, circle, clan, coterie, in-group, mob, ring; *compare* SET 5

clitter *vb* ***syn*** RATTLE 1, bicker, clack, clatter, ||ruttle, shatter

cloak *n* ***syn*** MASK 2, cover, disguise, facade, face, guise, semblance, show, veil, veneer

cloak *vb* ***syn*** DISGUISE, camouflage, dissemble, dissimulate, dress up, mask
rel blanket, curtain, screen, shroud, veil
ant uncloak

clobber *vb* ||**1** ***syn*** WHIP 2, beat, drub, lambaste, lick, shellac, smear, smother, thrash, trim
2 ***syn*** SLAM 1, belt, blast, slug, smash, wallop

clochard *n* ***syn*** VAGABOND, ||bindle stiff, canter, drifter, floater, hobo, roadster, tramp, vag, vagrant

clock *vb* ***syn*** TIME 2

||**clock** *vb* ***syn*** SET 11, brood, cover, sit

clocklike *adj* ***syn*** CIRCUMSTANTIAL, blow-by-blow, detailed, full, itemized, minute, particular, particularized, thorough

clockwise *adj* ***syn*** RIGHT-HANDED, dextrorotatory, positive

clod *n* **1** ***syn*** LUMP 1, chunk, clump, gob, hunch, hunk, nugget, wad
2 ***syn*** DUNCE, blockhead, boob, chump, dimwit, dolt, dope, dumbbell, dummy, lame-brain

cloddish *adj* ***syn*** BOORISH, churlish, clodhopping, clownish, ill-bred, loutish, uncivilized, uncultured, unpolished, unrefined

clodhopper *n* **1** ***syn*** RUSTIC, ||apple knocker, bumpkin, chawbacon, hayseed, hick, ||hodge, hoosier, redneck, yokel
2 ***syn*** BOOR, ||bosthoon, chuff, churl, clown, grobian, mucker

clodhopping *adj* ***syn*** BOORISH, churlish, cloddish, clownish, ill-bred, loutish, uncivilized, uncultured, unpolished, unrefined

clodpate *n* ***syn*** DUNCE, blockhead, bonehead, hammerhead, knucklehead, muttonhead, numskull, thickhead, thickskull, woodenhead

clodpoll *n* ***syn*** DUNCE, blockhead, bonehead, chowderhead, clod, clodpate, dimwit, dolt, dumbbell, numskull

clog *n* ***syn*** ENCUMBRANCE, cumbrance, hindrance, impedance, impediment

clog *vb* **1** ***syn*** BURDEN, charge, cumber, encumber, lade, load, lumber, saddle, tax, weigh

2 ***syn*** HAMPER, curb, entrammel, fetter, hobble, hog-tie, leash, shackle, tie, trammel

3 ***syn*** FILL 1, block, choke, close, congest, obstruct, occlude, plug, stop, stopper

cloggy *adj* ***syn*** STICKY 1, adhesive, ||claggy, ||clarty, gluey, gooey, gummy, stodgy

cloister *vb* ***syn*** SECLUDE, sequester

cloistered *adj* ***syn*** SECLUDED, hermetic, recluse, secluse, seclusive, sequestered

clonk *vb* ***syn*** THUD, clunk, thump

||**Cloot** *n, usu* **Cloots** *pl* ***syn*** DEVIL 1, Apollyon, Beelzebub, ||Clootie, diablo, fiend, Lucifer, Old Nick, Old Scratch, Satan

||**Clootie** *n* ***syn*** DEVIL 1, Apollyon, Beelzebub, ||Cloot(s), diablo, fiend, Lucifer, Old Nick, Old Scratch, Satan

close *vb* **1** to fill an opening with an appropriate closure <be sure to *close* the gate>

syn ||put to, shut

rel bang, clap, slam; block, choke, clog, obstruct, occlude, stop; debar, exclude

ant open

2 ***syn*** SCREEN 3, block out, obstruct, shroud, shut off, shut out

3 to bring or come to a limit or to a natural or appropriate stopping point <*closed* the meeting as soon as the discussion was over>

syn complete, conclude, consummate, determine, do, end, finish, halt, terminate, ultimate, wind up, wrap up

rel cease, desist, quit, stop; finalize, write off

idiom call it a day, set a period to

con begin, commence, enter (on *or* upon), inaugurate, initiate, start

4 ***syn*** FILL 1, block, choke, clog, congest, obstruct, occlude, plug, stop, stopper

5 ***syn*** DECREASE, abate, ||bate, diminish, drain (away), dwindle, lessen, reduce, taper, taper off

6 ***syn*** MEET 6, encounter, face, front

close *n* **1** ***syn*** END 2, cease, cessation, conclusion, desistance, ending, finish, period, stop, termination

2 ***syn*** FINALE, conclusion, end, ending, finish, windup

ant opening

||**close** *n* ***syn*** COURT 1, courtyard, curtilage, enclosure, quad, quadrangle, yard

close *adj* **1** ***syn*** SILENT 3, close-lipped, closemouthed, close-tongued, reserved, reticent, taciturn, tight-lipped, tight-mouthed, uncommunicative

idiom close as a clam

con candid, frank, plain

ant open

2 ***syn*** STUFFY 1, airless, breathless, stifling, stivy, suffocating, sultry

rel humid, muggy, sticky

3 ***syn*** STINGY, cheeseparing, closefisted, miserly, ||narrow, niggardly, parsimonious, penny-pinching, penurious, tight

ant liberal

4 having the constituent parts massed closely together <a paper of fine *close* texture>

syn compact, crowded, dense, thick, tight

rel compacted, compressed, condensed, consolidated, constricted, contracted; firm, solid, substantial; impenetrable, impermeable; close-grained

con lax, loose, slack; unconsolidated

5 ***syn*** TIGHT 3, taut, tense

6 not far removed (as in space, time, or relationship) from something stipulated or understood <true and veritable are *close* synonyms> <the park is very *close* to the river> <it is *close* to closing time>

syn immediate, near, near-at-hand, nearly, nigh, proximate; *compare* NEIGHBORING

rel abutting, adjacent, adjoining, contiguous; convenient, handy; nearest, nearmost, next

idiom at hand, at one's fingers' ends (*or* fingertips), under one's nose

con distant, far, faraway, far-off, removed

ant remote

7 ***syn*** FAMILIAR 1, chummy, confidential, intimate, thick

con cool, remote, withdrawn

ant aloof

close *adv* into proximity with respect to space, time, or approach <hoping to come *closer* to the truth of the matter>

syn at close hand, hard, near, nearby, nigh

rel almost, nearabout, nearly

idiom as near as no matter (*or* never mind), in hailing (*or* spitting) distance, within an inch (*or* an ace) of, within a stone's throw

con afar, distantly, far

ant remotely

close–at–hand *adj* **1** ***syn*** NEIGHBORING, adjacent, close-by, contiguous, near-at-hand, nearby

2 ***syn*** CONVENIENT 2, adjacent, close-by, handy, near-at-hand, nearby

close–by *adj* **1** ***syn*** NEIGHBORING, adjacent, close-at-hand, contiguous, near-at-hand, nearby

2 ***syn*** CONVENIENT 2, adjacent, close-at-hand, handy, near-at-hand, nearby

closed *adj* ***syn*** SELF-SUFFICIENT, independent, self-centered, self-contained, self-sufficing, self-supported, self-supporting, self-sustained, self-sustaining

closed book *n* ***syn*** MYSTERY, Chinese puzzle, conundrum, enigma, mystification, puzzle, puzzlement, riddle, why

closed–minded *adj* ***syn*** OBSTINATE, bullheaded, deaf, hardheaded, intractable, pigheaded, self-willed, unpliable, unpliant, unyielding

---

closefisted *adj* ***syn*** STINGY, close, hardfisted, hardhanded, miserly, ‖narrow, narrow-fisted, niggardly, penny-pinching, tightfisted
rel clinging, clutching, grasping, keeping, tenacious
close in *vb* ***syn*** ENCLOSE 1, cage, coop, corral, envelop, fence, hedge, hem, immure, mew
close–lipped *adj* ***syn*** SILENT 3, close, closemouthed, close-tongued, reserved, reticent, taciturn, tight-lipped, tight-mouthed, uncommunicative
closely *adv* ***syn*** HARD 4, intently, searchingly, sharply
rel carefully, heedfully, mindfully, thoughtfully; meticulously, minutely, punctiliously, scrupulously
con carelessly, heedlessly, thoughtlessly
closemouthed *adj* ***syn*** SILENT 3, close, close-lipped, close-tongued, reserved, reticent, taciturn, tight-lipped, tight-mouthed, uncommunicative
close off *vb* ***syn*** ISOLATE, cut off, enisle, insulate, island, segregate, separate, sequester
close on *prep* ***syn*** ABOUT 1, around, circa, near, nearby, nigh
close out *vb* ***syn*** SELL OUT 1, sell off, ‖sell up
closeout *n* ***syn*** BARGAIN 1, buy, pennyworth, steal
‖**closet** *n* ***syn*** PRIVY 1, backhouse, ‖biffy, *crapper, jakes, ‖necessary, ‖office, outhouse
closet *adj* **1** ***syn*** PRIVATE 2, confidential, hushed, inside
2 ***syn*** THEORETICAL 1, academic, speculative
close–tongued *adj* ***syn*** SILENT 3, close, close-lipped, closemouthed, reserved, reticent, speechless, tight-lipped, tight-mouthed, uncommunicative
closing *n* ***syn*** END 2, cessation, close, closure, desistance, ending, finish, period, stop, termination
closing *adj* ***syn*** LAST, concluding, eventual, final, hindmost, lag, latest, latter, terminal, ultimate
closure *n* ***syn*** END 2, cease, cessation, close, closing, conclusion, desistance, ending, stop, termination
clot *n* ***syn*** GROUP 3, array, batch, battery, body, bunch, bundle, clump, cluster, set
clot *vb* ***syn*** COAGULATE, congeal, gel, gelate, gelatinize, jell, jellify, jelly, set
clothe *vb* to cover with or as if with garments <forests *clothe* the rocky slopes>
syn apparel, array, attire, clad, dress, enclothe, garb, garment, raiment
rel costume, do up, dress up, tog (up *or* out); cloak, mantle, robe; accouter, equip, outfit, rig (out); bedrape, drape, swathe; endue, invest
con dismantle, divest, strip
ant unclothe
clothes *n pl* a person's garments as a whole <dressed in new *clothes* from the skin out>
syn apparel, attire, attirement, clothing, dress, duds, habiliment(s), rags, raiment, rigging, things, togs
rel array, garb, toggery, vestments, vesture; costume, getup, outfit, rig

---

syn synonym(s) ***rel*** related word(s)
idiom idiomatic equivalent(s) ***con*** contrasted word(s)
ant antonym(s) * vulgar
‖ use limited; if in doubt, see a dictionary
The first word in a synonym list when printed in SMALL CAPITALS shows where there is more information about the group. For a more efficient use of this book see Explanatory Notes.

clothing *n* **1** ***syn*** CLOTHES, apparel, attire, attirement, dress, duds, habiliment(s), rags, raiment, things
2 ***syn*** ROLE 1, character
cloud *n* ***syn*** MULTITUDE 1, army, crowd, flock, host, legion, rout, scores
cloud *vb* **1** ***syn*** OBSCURE, adumbrate, becloud, befog, dim, fog, gloom, overcast, overcloud, shadow
rel addle, befuddle, confuse, muddle; distract, perplex, puzzle
2 ***syn*** CONFUSE 4, becloud, befog, blur, fog, muddy
3 ***syn*** TAINT 1, besmear, besmirch, blur, discolor, smear, smudge, sully, tar, tarnish
clouded *adj* ***syn*** DOUBTFUL 1, ambiguous, dubious, equivocal, open, problematic, shady, uncertain, unclear, unsettled
cloudless *adj* ***syn*** FAIR 2, clarion, clear, fine, pleasant, rainless, sunny, sunshiny, unclouded, undarkened
cloudy *adj* **1** ***syn*** OVERCAST, ‖dowly, dull, heavy, lowering (*or* louring), nubilous, overclouded
2 ***syn*** HAZY, foggy, misty, mushy, vague, vaporous, vapory
3 ***syn*** MURKY 3, mucky
clough *n* ***syn*** RAVINE, arroyo, chasm, cleft, clove, gap, gorge, gulch
clout *n* **1** ***syn*** CUFF, box, buffet, chop, ‖paste, poke, punch, slap, smack, sock
2 ***syn*** PULL 2, ‖drag, in, influence
clout *vb* **1** ***syn*** STRIKE 2, ‖biff, ding, hit, ‖nail, slog, ‖slosh, smite, sock, whack
‖**2** ***syn*** STEAL 1, cabbage, ‖cly, collar, ‖cop, ‖heist, hook, ‖nail, ‖nick, nip
clove *n* ***syn*** RAVINE, arroyo, chasm, cleft, clough, gap, gorge, gulch
clown *n* **1** ***syn*** RUSTIC, ‖apple knocker, bucolic, bumpkin, clodhopper, hayseed, hick, hoosier, jake, rube
2 ***syn*** BOOR, ‖bosthoon, chuff, churl, clodhopper, grobian, mucker
3 a performer (as in a circus) who entertains by grotesque appearance and actions <children delighted by the antics of the *clowns*>
syn buffoon, harlequin, merry-andrew, zany
rel comedian; fool, jester, mountebank; mime, mummer
4 ***syn*** ZANY 2, cutup, farceur, joker, jokester, wag
clownish *adj* ***syn*** BOORISH, churlish, cloddish, ill-bred, loutish, lumpish, uncivilized, uncultured, unpolished, unrefined
rel awkward, clumsy, gauche; green, raw, rough, rude, uncouth
ant urbane
cloy *vb* ***syn*** SATIATE, fill, glut, gorge, jade, pall, sate, ‖stall, stodge, surfeit
con excite, pique, provoke, stimulate
ant whet
club *n* **1** ***syn*** CUDGEL, bat, baton, billy, billy club, bludgeon, knobkerrie, mace, nightstick, truncheon
2 ***syn*** ASSOCIATION 2, brotherhood, fellowship, fraternity, guild, league, order, society, sodality, union
club car *n* ***syn*** PARLOR CAR, chair car, lounge car, palace car, tavern car
‖**cluck** *n* ***syn*** DUNCE, dimwit, ‖dumb bunny, ‖dumb cluck, featherweight, lackwit, nitwit, pinhead, simp, wantwit

clue *n* ***syn*** HINT 1, cue, indication, inkling, intimation, notion, suggestion, telltale, wind

clue (*or* **clew**) *vb* ***syn*** INFORM 2, acquaint, advise, apprise, fill in, notify, post, tell, warn, wise (up)

clump *n* **1** ***syn*** GROUP 3, array, batch, body, bunch, bundle, cluster, lot, parcel, set
rel clutter, hodgepodge, jumble, omnium-gatherum
2 ***syn*** LUMP 1, chunk, clod, gob, hunch, hunk, nugget, wad

clump *vb* ***syn*** LUMBER, barge, galumph, stumble, stump

clumsy *adj* **1** lacking in physical ease and grace usually because of coarse cumbersome build or poor coordination <a *clumsy* boy constantly stumbling over his own feet> <the *clumsy* gait of a young puppy>
syn awkward, gawky, lumbering, lumpish, splathering, splay, ungainly; *compare* AWKWARD 2
rel butterfingered, heavy-handed, left-handed, unhandy; graceless, inelegant, uncouth; bulky, hulking, unwieldy
idiom all thumbs, fingers all thumbs
con comely, shapely, well-formed, well-proportioned; apt, deft, handy, quick, ready
2 ***syn*** AWKWARD 2, bumbling, gauche, ham-handed, heavy-handed, inept, maladroit, unhandy, unhappy, wooden

clunk *vb* ***syn*** THUD, clonk, thump

clunker *n* ***syn*** JALOPY, crate, dog, heap, junker, wreck

cluster *n* **1** ***syn*** GROUP 3, array, batch, body, bunch, bundle, clump, clutch, lot, set
2 ***syn*** GROUP 1, assembly, band, bevy, bunch, covey, crew, party

cluster *vb* ***syn*** GROUP 1, assemble, collect, gather, round up
rel accumulate, aggregate, associate, cumulate; bundle, package, parcel

clutch *vb* ***syn*** SEIZE 2, catch, ‖cotch, grab, grapple, nab, ‖nail, snatch, take
rel clench, clinch, gripe; cherish, harbor, hold, keep

clutch *n* ***syn*** HOLD, clamp, clasp, clench, clinch, grapple, grasp, grip, gripe, tenure

clutch *n* ***syn*** GROUP 3, array, batch, body, bunch, bundle, clump, cluster, parcel, set

clutter *n* **1** ***syn*** CONFUSION 3, ataxia, ‖ballup, chaos, disarray, disorder, huddle, muddle, snarl, topsy-turviness
2 a disordered nondescript mass or group <a *clutter* of ornaments on the mantel>
syn hash, hugger-mugger, jumble, jungle, litter, mash, mishmash, muddle, rummage, scramble, shuffle, tumble
rel hodgepodge, macédoine, medley, mélange; disarray, mess, muss, ruck
con arrangement, array, order; grouping, ordering, pigeonholing, ranking, sorting

‖**cly** *vb* ***syn*** STEAL 1, ‖clout, ‖cop, ‖heist, hook, lift, nail, nip, snitch, swipe

coact *vb* ***syn*** INTERACT, interplay, interreact

coacting *adj* ***syn*** COOPERATIVE, coactive, coefficient, conjoint, synergetic, synergic

coactive *adj* ***syn*** COOPERATIVE, coacting, coefficient, conjoint, synergetic, synergic

coadjutant *n* ***syn*** ASSISTANT 2, aid, aide, aide-de-camp, coadjutor, lieutenant

coadjute *vb* ***syn*** UNITE 2, band, combine, concur, conjoin, cooperate, league

coadjutor *n* ***syn*** ASSISTANT 2, aid, aide, aide-de-camp, coadjutant, lieutenant

coadunate *vb* ***syn*** JOIN 1, associate, coagment, coalesce, connect, link, one, relate, unite, wed

coadunation *n* ***syn*** UNIFICATION, coalition, combination, consolidation, melding, mergence, merger, merging, union

coagment *vb* ***syn*** JOIN 1, associate, coadunate, coalesce, combine, conjoin, connect, link, one, unite

coagulate *vb* to alter by chemical reaction from a liquid to a more or less firm jelly <the blood *coagulated* and closed the wound>
syn clot, congeal, gel, gelate, gelatinize, jell, jellify, jelly, set
rel concrete, harden, solidify; curdle, inspissate; compact, concentrate, consolidate; coalesce; freeze; dehydrate, dry; condense, thicken
con deliquesce, fluidify, liquefy, liquesce; flux, fuse, melt, run

coalesce *vb* ***syn*** JOIN 1, associate, bracket, combine, conjoin, connect, link, relate, unite, wed
rel adhere, cleave, cling, stick; blend, fuse, merge, mingle, mix

coalition *n* **1** ***syn*** UNIFICATION, coadunation, combination, consolidation, melding, mergence, merger, merging, union
2 ***syn*** COMBINATION 2, bloc, combine, faction, party, ring
3 ***syn*** ALLIANCE 2, anschluss, confederacy, confederation, federation, league, union

coarct *vb* ***syn*** RESTRAIN 1, bit, bridle, check, constrain, curb, hold back, hold down, hold in, inhibit

coarse *adj* **1** made up of relatively large particles <*coarse* sand>
syn grainy, granular
rel caked, cakey, lumpy, particulate
2 ***syn*** CRUDE 5, inexpert, prentice
3 deficient in refinement of manner and delicacy of feeling <a *coarse* practical man lacking all social graces>
syn crass, crude, gross, incult, inelegant, low, raw, rough, rude, uncouth, uncultivated, uncultured, unrefined, vulgar; *compare* BOORISH
rel raffish, roughneck, rowdy, vulgarian; common, tacky
con considerate, courtly, gracious; cultivated, polished, refined
4 ***syn*** OBSCENE 2, dirty, filthy, foul, indecent, nasty, raunchy, scatological, smutty, vulgar
‖**5** ***syn*** WILD 6, blustering, blustery, dirty, furious, raging, rough, stormy, tempestuous, turbulent

coast *n* ***syn*** SHORE, bank, beach, strand

coast *vb* ***syn*** SLIDE 6, drift

---

syn synonym(s) ***rel*** related word(s)
idiom idiomatic equivalent(s) ***con*** contrasted word(s)
ant antonym(s) * vulgar
‖ use limited; if in doubt, see a dictionary
The first word in a synonym list when printed in SMALL CAPITALS shows where there is more information about the group. For a more efficient use of this book see Explanatory Notes.

coax *vb* to influence or persuade by artful ingratiation < *coaxed* her friend to help her with her work >
syn ‖barter, blandish, blarney, cajole, con, soft-soap, sweet-talk, wheedle
rel pester, plague, tease; importune, press, urge; get, induce, persuade, prevail; entice, inveigle, lure, tempt; butter (up)
con coerce, compel, constrain, force, oblige; browbeat, bulldoze, cow, intimidate
ant bully

cob *vb syn* SURPASS 1, ‖bang, cap, ding, exceed, excel, outdo, outmatch, outshine, outstrip

cobble *vb syn* BOTCH, ‖blow, bobble, bollix, bungle, goof (up), louse up, mess, mucker, ‖screw (up)
rel confuse, foul up, snafu, snarl (up)

cobweb *n syn* WEB 2, entanglement, mesh(es), toil(s)

cock *n* **1** *syn* FAUCET, gate, hydrant, petcock, spigot, stopcock, tap, valve
2 *syn* LEADER 2, boss, chief, chieftain, dominator, head, headman, hierarch, honcho, master
‖**3** *syn* NONSENSE 2, ‖baloney, bilge, bosh, ‖bull, bunkum, ‖crap, guff, hokum, rot

‖**cock** *adj syn* CHIEF 2, capital, dominant, main, major, number one, outstanding, predominant, preeminent, principal

cock *vb syn* LORD, peacock, pontificate, swagger, swank, swell

cock *n syn* PILE 1, drift, heap, hill, mass, mound, mountain, pyramid, rick, stack

cock *vb syn* HEAP 1, bank, drift, hill, mound, pile, stack

cock-a-doodle-doo *vb syn* BOAST, blow, brag, crow, gasconade, mouth, prate, puff, rodomontade, vaunt

cock-a-hoop *adj* **1** *syn* EXULTANT, cock-a-whoop, exulting, jubilant, triumphal, triumphant
2 *syn* AWRY 1, askance, askant, askew, ‖cam, cockeyed, crookedly

Cockaigne *n syn* UTOPIA, arcadia, fairyland, heaven, lubberland, paradise, promised land, Shangri-la, wonderland, Zion

cock-and-bull story *n syn* LIE, ‖bouncer, canard, falsehood, falsity, fib, misrepresentation, prevarication, story, untruth

cock-a-whoop *adj syn* EXULTANT, cock-a-hoop, exulting, jubilant, triumphal, triumphant

cockcrow *n syn* DAWN 1, aurora, cockcrowing, dawning, daybreak, daylight, light, morn, morning, sunrise

cockcrowing *n syn* DAWN 1, aurora, cockcrow, dawning, daybreak, daylight, light, morn, morning, sunrise

cocker *vb syn* BABY, cater (to), coddle, cosset, humor, indulge, mollycoddle, ‖much, pamper, spoil

‖**cocket** *adj syn* SAUCY 1, arch, bantam, malapert, pert

cockeyed *adj* **1** *syn* AWRY 1, askance, askant, askew, ‖cam, cock-a-hoop, crookedly
2 *syn* INTOXICATED 1, ‖boozy, ‖canned, disguised, drunk, inebriated, ‖lushed, muddled, pixilated, ‖plastered

cockle *vb syn* RIPPLE, dimple, fret, riffle

cocksure *adj syn* SURE 5, certain, confident, positive

cocktail lounge *n syn* BAR 5, barroom, ‖gin mill, ‖groggery, lounge, pothouse, pub, saloon, taproom, tavern

‖**coco** *n syn* HEAD 1, ‖belfry, ‖coconut, ‖conk, ‖dome, headpiece, noddle, noggin, noodle, poll

coconspirator *n syn* CONFEDERATE, abettor, accessory, accomplice, conspirator

‖**coconut** *n syn* HEAD 1, ‖belfry, ‖coco, ‖conk, ‖dome, headpiece, noddle, noggin, noodle, poll

cocotte *n syn* PROSTITUTE, bawd, call girl, ‖cruiser, harlot, ‖hooker, hustler, nightwalker, streetwalker, whore

coddle *vb syn* BABY, cater (to), cosset, cotton, humor, indulge, mollycoddle, ‖much, pamper, spoil

codicil *n syn* APPENDIX 1, addendum, rider, supplement

coefficient *adj syn* COOPERATIVE, coacting, coactive, conjoint, synergetic, synergic

coerce *vb syn* FORCE 2, compel, concuss, constrain, make, oblige, shotgun
rel beset, push, urge; browbeat, bulldoze, bully, cow, intimidate; menace, terrorize, threaten

coercion *n syn* FORCE 4, compulsion, constraint, duress, violence
rel menace, menacing, threat, threatening

coetaneous *adj syn* CONTEMPORARY 1, coeval, coexistent, coexisting, concurrent, contemporaneous, simultaneous, synchronal, synchronic, synchronous

coeval *adj syn* CONTEMPORARY 1, coetaneous, coexistent, coexisting, concurrent, contemporaneous, simultaneous, synchronal, synchronic, synchronous

coexistent *adj syn* CONTEMPORARY 1, coetaneous, coeval, coexisting, concurrent, contemporaneous, simultaneous, synchronal, synchronic, synchronous

coexisting *adj syn* CONTEMPORARY 1, coetaneous, coeval, coexistent, concurrent, contemporaneous, simultaneous, synchronal, synchronic, synchronous

coffee shop *n syn* EATING HOUSE, café, cookshop, diner, ‖greasy spoon, ‖hash house, luncheonette, lunchroom, sandwich shop, snack bar (*or* counter)

coffer *n syn* TREASURY 2, chest, exchequer, war chest

‖**coffin nail** *n syn* CIGARETTE, ‖butt, ‖cig, fag, ‖gasper, ‖pill, ‖skag, smoke

cogency *n syn* POINT 3, effectiveness, force, punch, validity, validness
rel pertinence, relevance; bearing, concern, connection

cogent *adj* **1** *syn* VALID, convincing, satisfactory, satisfying, solid, sound, telling
rel compelling, constraining, forceful, forcible, potent, powerful, puissant; inducing, persuasive; justified, well-founded, well-grounded
con ineffective, ineffectual, inefficacious; feeble, forceless, impotent, powerless, weak
2 *syn* WELL-FOUNDED, good, just, justified, well-grounded
rel consequential, influential, momentous, weighty; meaningful, significant

cogitable *adj syn* THINKABLE 1

cogitate *vb* **1** *syn* THINK 5, cerebrate, deliberate, reason, reflect, speculate

rel conceive, envisage, envision, imagine
2 *syn* PLOT, ‖collogue, collude, connive, conspire, contrive, devise, intrigue, machinate, scheme (out)

cogitation *n syn* THOUGHT 1, brainwork, cerebration, deliberation, reflection, speculation

cogitative *adj syn* THOUGHTFUL 1, contemplative, meditative, pensive, pondering, reflecting, reflective, ruminative, speculative, thinking

cognate *adj syn* RELATED, affiliated, agnate, akin, allied, connate, connatural, consanguine, incident, kindred
rel common, general, generic, universal
con different, disparate, divergent, diverse, various

cognizance *n syn* NOTICE 1, attention, heed, mark, ‖mind, note, observance, observation, regard, remark

cognizant *adj syn* AWARE, alive, apprehensive, au courant, awake, conscious, knowing, sensible, sentient, witting
con forgetful, oblivious, unmindful; heedless, ignoring, neglectful, slighting, unmindful
ant ignorant

cognize *vb syn* KNOW 1, appreciate, apprehend, comprehend, fathom, grasp, have, understand

cognomen *n syn* NAME 1, appellation, appellative, compellation, denomination, designation, ‖moniker, nomen, style, title

cognoscente *n syn* CONNOISSEUR, aesthete, dilettante
rel ‖dab, proficient, specialist; authority, critic, judge

cohere *vb* **1** *syn* STICK 2, adhere, cleave, cling
rel blend, coalesce, fuse, merge; associate, combine, connect, join, unite
con disembarrass, disentangle, untangle
2 *syn* AGREE 4, accord, check, check out, comport, conform, correspond, dovetail, fit (in), go

coherence *n* **1** *syn* ADHERENCE 1, adhesion, bond, cling, clinging, cohesion, stickage, sticking
rel integrity, solidarity, union, unity
ant incoherence
2 *syn* CONSISTENCY, conformity, congruity, correspondence

cohesion *n* **1** *syn* ADHERENCE 1, adhesion, bond, cling, clinging, coherence, stickage, sticking
ant incohesion
2 *syn* SOLIDARITY, solidarism, togetherness

cohort *n* **1** *syn* PARTNER, associate, confrere, consociate, copartner, fellow, mate, ‖pard
2 *syn* FOLLOWER, adherent, disciple, henchman, partisan, satellite, sectary, sectator, supporter

coil *n syn* COMMOTION 3, brouhaha, ‖catouse, foofaraw, furore, ruckus, rumpus, shindig, shindy, uproar

coil *vb syn* WIND 2, corkscrew, curl, entwine, twine, twist, wreathe
rel revolve, rotate, turn

‖**coin** *n syn* MONEY, ‖bread, ‖chips, currency, dough, ‖jack, legal tender, ‖mazuma, ‖scratch, ‖shekels
idiom coin of the realm

coinage *n syn* INVENTION, brainchild, contrivance

coincide *vb syn* AGREE 3, concert, concord, concur, harmonize
rel accord, correspond, jibe, tally; equal, match
con deviate, divagate, divaricate, diverge; bias, skew, twist, warp
ant differ

coincident *adj syn* CONCOMITANT, accompanying, ancillary, attendant, attending, collateral, incident, satellite

coincidentally *adv syn* TOGETHER 1, at once, coincidently, coinstantaneously, concurrently, simultaneously

coincidently *adv syn* TOGETHER 1, at once, coincidentally, coinstantaneously, concurrently, simultaneously

coinstantaneously *adv syn* TOGETHER 1, at once, coincidentally, coincidently, concurrently, simultaneously

cojones *n pl syn* COURAGE, dauntlessness, guts, heart, mettle, ‖moxie, pluck, resolution, spirit, spunk

cold *adj* **1** marked by a deficiency of warmth <a *cold* day>
syn arctic, chill, chillsome, chilly, cool, freezing, frigid, frore, frosty, gelid, glacial, icy, nippy, shivery
rel biting, bleak, chilling, cutting, nipping, polar, raw, sharp; frozen, iced, wintry; bracing, brisk, crisp, snappy
con calid, genial, mild
ant warm
2 lacking cordiality or emotional warmth <a *cold* greeting>
syn chill, emotionless, frigid, glacial, icy, indifferent, unemotional
rel unenthusiastic, unresponsive, unsympathetic
con cordial, friendly, genial, hearty, warm; empathic, sympathetic
3 *syn* MATTER-OF-FACT 3, cold-blooded, emotionless, impersonal, unimpassioned
4 *syn* FRIGID 3, inhibited, passionless, undersexed, unresponsive
ant hot
5 *syn* GLOOMY 3, black, bleak, cheerless, dismal, dispiriting, drear, joyless, oppressive, somber
6 *syn* DEAD 1, asleep, deceased, defunct, departed, exanimate, extinct, inanimate, late, lifeless
7 *syn* INSENSIBLE 2, comatose, inconscious, senseless, unconscious

cold–blooded *adj* **1** *syn* UNFEELING 2, callous, coldhearted, hard-boiled, hardened, hardhearted, heartless, obdurate, stonyhearted, uncompassionate
2 *syn* MATTER-OF-FACT 3, cold, emotionless, impersonal, unimpassioned

cold feet *n syn* FEAR 1, alarm, consternation, dismay, dread, fright, horror, panic, terror, trepidation

coldhearted *adj syn* UNFEELING 2, callous, hardhearted, heartless, ironhearted, obdurate, stonyhearted, uncompassionate, unemotional, unsympathetic
ant warmhearted

‖**cold meat** *n syn* CORPSE, body, cadaver, carcass, ‖deader, mort, remains, stiff

cold–shoulder *vb syn* CUT 7, ostracize, snob, snub

---

cold storage *n* ***syn*** ABEYANCE, abeyancy, doldrums, dormancy, intermission, interruption, latency, quiescence, quiescency, suspension

colic *n* ***syn*** STOMACHACHE, bellyache, collywobbles, gripe(s)

coliseum *n* ***syn*** STADIUM, bowl, stade

‖**coll** *vb* ***syn*** EMBRACE 1, clasp, ‖clinch, ‖clip, enfold, hug, press, squeeze

collapse *vb* **1** ***syn*** GIVE 12, bend, break, cave, crumple, fold up, go, yield
rel break up, disintegrate, shatter
idiom fall to pieces
2 to lose energy, stamina, or control under stress <exhausted to the point of *collapsing* helplessly on the bed>
syn break down, cave (in), drop, ‖flake out, give out, peg out, succumb, wilt
rel droop, fail, languish, weaken; exhaust, fag, flag, play out, tire, weary
con enliven, invigorate, stimulate

collapse *n* **1** ***syn*** NERVOUS BREAKDOWN, breakdown, crack-up, nervous prostration
2 a sudden and grave failure <the *collapse* of an overextended market>
syn breakdown, crack-up, crash, debacle, smash, smashup, wreck
rel breakup, disorganization, disruption, undoing; cataclysm, catastrophe; destruction, ruination, ruining; failure

collar *vb* **1** ***syn*** CORNER, bottle (up), tree
2 ***syn*** CATCH 1, bag, capture, ‖cotch, get, nail, prehend, secure, take
3 ***syn*** STEAL 1, appropriate, cabbage, ‖clout, ‖cop, hook, lift, nab, ‖nail, nip

collate *vb* ***syn*** COMPARE 2, bracket, contrast

collateral *adj* **1** ***syn*** CONCOMITANT, accompanying, ancillary, attendant, attending, coincident, incident, satellite
2 ***syn*** INDIRECT 1, circuitous, circular, oblique, roundabout
3 ***syn*** CORROBORATIVE, adminicular, confirmative, confirmatory, corroboratory, verificatory
4 ***syn*** SUBORDINATE, dependent, secondary, sub, subject, tributary, under
rel allied, cognate, kindred, related; complementary, corresponding, reciprocal
con major, prominent
5 ***syn*** AUXILIARY, accessory, adjuvant, ancillary, appurtenant, contributory, subservient, subsidiary

‖**collateral** *n* ***syn*** REFUSE, debris, garbage, junk, kelter, litter, offal, outsweepings, riffraff, rubbish

colleague *n* one affiliated with another usually through a common office or profession <he claims to speak for his *colleagues* in the Senate>
syn associate, compatriot, compeer, confrere
rel consociate, copartner, fellow, partner; co-worker, workfellow; buddy, chum, companion, crony, pal; aide, assistant, helper

collect *vb* **1** ***syn*** GATHER 6, assemble, congregate, congress, forgather, muster, raise, rendezvous
con assort, sort; sever, sunder; deal, dispense, divide, dole
ant disperse; distribute
2 ***syn*** INFER, conclude, deduce, deduct, derive, draw, gather, judge, make, make out
3 ***syn*** COMPOSE 4, control, cool, re-collect, rein, repress, restrain, simmer down, smother, suppress
4 ***syn*** GROUP 1, assemble, cluster, gather, round up
rel align, array, dispose, marshal, order, rank
con broadcast, disperse, distribute, scatter

collected *adj* **1** ***syn*** CALM 2, composed, easy, easygoing, placid, poised, possessed, self-possessed, serene, tranquil
rel peaceful, quiet, still
ant distraught
2 ***syn*** COOL 2, composed, disimpassioned, imperturbable, nonchalant, unflappable, unruffled
rel assured, confident, sanguine, sure; complacent, self-satisfied, smug
con disordered, troubled

collection *n* **1** ***syn*** GATHERING 2, assemblage, assembly, company, congeries, congregation, crowd, group, muster, ruck
rel band, crew, outfit, party
2 ***syn*** ACCUMULATION, agglomeration, aggregation, amassment, colluvies, conglomeration, cumulation, hoard, trove
rel assortment, medley, miscellany, variety; bunch, clump, cluster, group; armamentarium; boiling, caboodle, kit, lot

‖**college** *n* ***syn*** JAIL, ‖caboose, ‖can, ‖chokey, ‖hoosegow, jug, lockup, prison, rock pile, ‖stir

collide *vb* ***syn*** BUMP 1, clash, ‖prang
rel atomize, fragment, pulverize, shatter, smash, splinter; break up, crunch, scrap

collimate *vb* ***syn*** PARALLEL 2, collocate, parallelize

collision *n* ***syn*** IMPACT, bump, clash, concussion, crash, jar, jolt, percussion, shock, smash
rel dilapidation, ruin, wreck; demolishment, destruction

collocate *vb* ***syn*** PARALLEL 2, collimate, parallelize

collogue *vb* ‖**1** ***syn*** PLOT, cogitate, collude, connive, conspire, contrive, devise, intrigue, machinate, scheme (out)
2 ***syn*** CONFER 2, advise, confab, confabulate, consult, huddle, parley, powwow, treat

colloque *vb* ***syn*** CONVERSE, chat, chin, talk, visit, yarn

colloquial *adj* ***syn*** VERNACULAR, vulgar, vulgate

colloquial *n* ***syn*** VERNACULAR 3, patois, vulgate

colloquium *n* ***syn*** CONFERENCE 2, colloquy, palaver, rap session, seminar

colloquy *n* **1** ***syn*** CONVERSATION 1, chat, confabulation, converse, dialogue, parley
2 ***syn*** CONVERSATION 2, confabulation, dialogue, talk
3 ***syn*** CONFERENCE 2, colloquium, palaver, rap session, seminar

---

syn synonym(s) ***rel*** related word(s)
idiom idiomatic equivalent(s) ***con*** contrasted word(s)
ant antonym(s) * vulgar
‖ use limited; if in doubt, see a dictionary
The first word in a synonym list when printed in SMALL CAPITALS shows where there is more information about the group. For a more efficient use of this book see Explanatory Notes.

collude *vb* ***syn*** PLOT, cogitate, ‖collogue, connive, conspire, contrive, devise, intrigue, machinate, scheme (out)

collusion *n* ***syn*** COMPLICITY, connivance

colluvies *n* **1** ***syn*** ACCUMULATION, agglomeration, aggregation, amassment, collection, conglomeration, cumulation, hoard, trove
2 ***syn*** MISCELLANY 1, assortment, hash, hodgepodge, jumble, medley, mélange, mishmash, pastiche, potpourri

collywobbles *n pl but sing or pl in constr* ***syn*** STOMACHACHE, bellyache, colic, gripe(s)

Colonel Blimp *n* ***syn*** STUFFED SHIRT, Blimp, fuddy-duddy

color *n* **1** a property of a visible thing recognizable only when rays of light fall upon it and serving to distinguish things otherwise visually identical (as in size, shape, or texture) <the green *color* of foliage turns rainbow-hued in autumn>
syn cast, hue, shade, tinge, tint, tone
2 ***syn*** MASK 2, coloring, disguise, facade, face, front, guise, put-on, semblance, show
3 ***syn*** VERISIMILITUDE, plausibility, verisimility
4 ***syn*** POSITION 1, attitude, stance, stand
5 ***syn*** FLAG, banner, ensign, gonfalon, jack, oriflamme, pennant, pennon, standard, streamer
6 something used to impart visible color to something <dyed her curtains with one of the new easy-to-use *colors*>
syn colorant, dye, dyestuff, pigment, stain, tincture

color *vb* **1** ***syn*** EMBROIDER, embellish, exaggerate, fudge, magnify, overcharge, overdraw, overpaint, overstate, pad
rel disguise, distort, fake, misrepresent
con constrain, minimize, reduce, soften, temper; blue-pencil, censor, edit
2 ***syn*** MISREPRESENT, belie, distort, falsify, garble, miscolor, misstate, pervert, twist, warp
3 ***syn*** BLUSH, crimson, flush, glow, mantle, pink, pinken, redden, rose, rouge

colorable *adj* ***syn*** BELIEVABLE, credible, creditable, plausible
rel cogent, compelling, convincing, sound, telling, valid

colorant *n* ***syn*** COLOR 6, dye, dyestuff, pigment, stain, tincture

colored *adj* ***syn*** BIASED 2, jaundiced, one-sided, partial, partisan, prejudiced, prepossessed, tendentious, unindifferent, warped

colorful *adj* making a fine display of usually showy color <a *colorful* bed of asters>
syn brave, bright, colory, gay, vivid
rel blatant, florid, garish, gaudy, loud; flashy, showy, splashy
con blanched, bleached, pallid, wan; dim, dull, faint, pale, weak
ant colorless

coloring *n* **1** ***syn*** MASK 2, color, disguise, facade, face, front, guise, put-on, semblance, show
2 ***syn*** EXAGGERATION, embellishment, embroidering, hyperbole, overstatement

colorless *adj* **1** ***syn*** PALE 1, ashen, ashy, blanched, doughy, livid, lurid, pallid, wan, waxen
2 lacking in sparkle and vitality <an accurate but *colorless* recital of facts>
syn drab, dull, flat, lackluster, lifeless, lusterless, prosaic, prosy
rel blurry, hazy, obscure, vague; feeble, insipid, milk-and-water, namby-pamby, weak, wishy-washy; unimaginative, uninspired
con clear, concise, exact, precise; exciting, provocative, rousing, stimulating, stirring
ant colorful
3 ***syn*** NEUTRAL, abstract, detached, disinterested, dispassionate, impersonal, poker-faced, unpassioned
rel aloof, remote, withdrawn

colory *adj* ***syn*** COLORFUL, brave, bright, gay, vivid

colossal *adj* ***syn*** HUGE, behemothic, cyclopean, elephantine, gargantuan, gigantic, mammoth, monstrous, titanic, vast

colporteur *n* ***syn*** MISSIONARY, apostle, evangelist, missioner, propagandist

colt *n* ***syn*** NOVICE, beginner, boot, fledgling, freshman, neophyte, newcomer, novitiate, rookie, tyro

coltish *adj* ***syn*** PLAYFUL 1, elvish, frisky, frolicsome, impish, kittenish, larkish, mischievous, puckish, waggish

columbary *n* ***syn*** DOVECOTE, culverhouse, dovehouse, pigeon house, pigeonry

column *n* **1** ***syn*** PILLAR 1, pier, pilaster
2 ***syn*** SUPPORT 3, brace, buttress, prop, shore, stay, underpinner, underpinning, underpropping

coma *n* **1** ***syn*** FAINT, blackout, swoon, syncope
2 ***syn*** LETHARGY 1, dullness, hebetude, languor, lassitude, sleep, slumber, stupor, torpidity, torpor

comate *n* ***syn*** ASSOCIATE 3, buddy, chum, companion, comrade, crony, ‖cully, pal, running mate

comatose *adj* **1** ***syn*** INSENSIBLE 2, cold, inconscious, senseless, unconscious
2 ***syn*** LETHARGIC, dopey, heavy, hebetudinous, sluggish, slumberous, stupid, torpid
rel anesthetic, impassible, insensitive
ant awake

comb *vb* **1** ***syn*** SORT 2, separate, sift, winnow
2 ***syn*** SCOUR 2, beat, finecomb, fine-tooth-comb, forage, grub, rake, ransack, rummage, search
rel examine, inspect, scrutinize; investigate, probe, sift

combat *vb* ***syn*** RESIST, buck, contest, dispute, duel, fight, oppose, repel, traverse, withstand
rel battle, contend, war

combat *n* ***syn*** SERVICE 1, action

combative *adj* ***syn*** BELLIGERENT, bellicose, contentious, gladiatorial, militant, pugnacious, quarrelsome, ‖ructious, truculent, warlike
rel energetic, strenuous, vigorous; manful, manly, virile
ant pacifistic

---

combativeness *n* ***syn*** ATTACK 2, aggression, aggressiveness, belligerence, fight, pugnacity

‖**combe** *n* ***syn*** VALLEY, dale, glen, vale

combination *n* **1** ***syn*** UNIFICATION, coadunation, coalition, consolidation, melding, mergence, merger, merging, union
2 individuals or organized interests banded together to further a common end <a *combination* of citizens devoted to holding down taxes>
syn bloc, coalition, combine, faction, party, ring
rel cartel, pool, syndicate, trust; cabal, circle, clique, coterie, set
3 ***syn*** ASSOCIATION 1, affiliation, alliance, cahoots, conjunction, connection, hookup, partnership, tie-up, togetherness

combine *vb* **1** ***syn*** JOIN 1, associate, bracket, coalesce, conjoin, connect, link, relate, unite, wed
rel amalgamate, blend, commingle, fuse, mingle, mix; consolidate, unify
con divide, divorce, part
ant separate
2 ***syn*** EMBODY 2, incorporate, integrate
3 ***syn*** UNITE 2, band, coadjute, concur, conjoin, cooperate, league
rel agree, coincide; merge, pool

combine *n* **1** ***syn*** COMBINATION 2, bloc, coalition, faction, party, ring
2 ***syn*** SYNDICATE, cartel, chain, conglomerate, group, pool, trust

comble *n* ***syn*** APEX 2, acme, apogee, capsheaf, capstone, climax, culmination, peak, pinnacle, summit

combust *vb* ***syn*** BURN 2

combustible *adj* **1** capable of catching or being set on fire <*combustible* materials should be stored away from open fire>
syn burnable, flammable, ignitable, inflammable
rel comburent, combustive; burning, firing, igniting, kindling
con fireproof; flameproof, nonflammable; fire-resistant, fire-resistive, fire-retardant
ant incombustible, noncombustible
2 ***syn*** EXCITABLE, agitable, alarmable, edgy, skittery, skittish, startlish, volatile

come *vb* **1** to attain to a destination <when will they *come*>
syn arrive, ‖blow in, get, get in, reach, show, show up, turn up
rel approach, near, nigh
con depart, leave, quit, retreat, withdraw
ant go
2 ***syn*** AMOUNT 1, add up, aggregate, number, run (to *or* into), sum (to *or* into), total
3 ***syn*** HAPPEN 1, befall, betide, break, chance, develop, fall out, hap, occur, transpire
4 ***syn*** BECOME 1, ‖come over, get, go, grow, run, turn, wax

come (from) *vb* **1** ***syn*** SPRING, arise, derive (from), emanate, flow, issue, originate, proceed, rise, stem
2 ***syn*** ORIGINATE 5, hail (from)

come (in) *vb* ***syn*** ENTER 1, go in, ingress, penetrate

comeback *n* ***syn*** RETORT 2, back answer, repartee, riposte

come by *vb* ***syn*** VISIT 2, call, come over, drop (in *or* by), look in, look up, pop (in), run in, see, step in

come–by–chance *n* ***syn*** BASTARD 1, by-blow, chance child, filius nullius, filius populi, illegitimate, love child, natural child, whoreson, woods colt

comedian *n* **1** ***syn*** HUMORIST 2, comic, droll, funnyman, jester, joker, jokester, quipster, wag, wit
2 ***syn*** WAG 1, card, humorist, joker, zany

come down (with) *vb* ***syn*** CONTRACT 1, catch, get, sicken (with *or* of), take

comedown *n* a loss of status <bitter over their *comedown* in the world>
syn descent, discomfiture, down; *compare* SETBACK
rel collapse, crash, downfall, fall, ruin, smash, undoing, wreck
con advance, headway, progress
ant rise

comedy *n* ***syn*** HUMOR 4, comicality, comicalness, drollery, drollness, funniness, humorousness, wittiness

come in *vb* ***syn*** ANSWER 1, rejoin, reply, respond, retort, return

comely *adj* **1** ***syn*** BEAUTIFUL, attractive, beauteous, ‖bonny, fair, good-looking, handsome, lovely, pretty, pulchritudinous
ant homely
2 ***syn*** DECOROUS 1, becoming, befitting, civilized, comme il faut, conforming, correct, nice, proper, seemly

come off *vb* **1** ***syn*** SUCCEED 2, click, go, go over, pan out, prove out
2 ***syn*** HAPPEN 1, befall, betide, break, chance, develop, fall out, go, hap, occur

come–off *n* ***syn*** ESCAPE 2, avoidance, elusion, escaping, eschewal, evasion, runaround, shunning

come–on *n* **1** ***syn*** LURE 2, allurement, bait, decoy, enticement, inveiglement, seducement, snare, temptation, trap
‖**2** ***syn*** FOOL 3, butt, chump, dupe, fall guy, gull, mark, pigeon, sap, sucker
3 ***syn*** SWINDLER, bunco steerer, cheat, confidence man, con man, double-dealer, flimflammer, gypper, rogue, trickster

come out *vb* **1** ***syn*** GET OUT 2, break, leak, out, transpire
2 ***syn*** DEBUT

come out (with) *vb* ***syn*** SAY 1, bring out, chime in, declare, deliver, state, tell, throw out, utter

come over *vb* **1** ***syn*** VISIT 2, call, come by, drop (in *or* by), look in, look up, pop (in), run in, see, step in
2 ***syn*** BECOME 1, come, get, go, grow, run, turn, wax

come round *vb* ***syn*** RECOVER 2, rally

comestible *adj* ***syn*** EDIBLE, eatable, esculent

comestibles *n pl* ***syn*** FOOD 1, ‖chow, ‖eats, edibles, feed, grub, provender, provisions, viands, victuals

come through *vb* **1** ***syn*** SURVIVE 2, pull through, ride (out)

---

syn synonym(s) ***rel*** related word(s)
idiom idiomatic equivalent(s) ***con*** contrasted word(s)
ant antonym(s) * vulgar
‖ use limited; if in doubt, see a dictionary
The first word in a synonym list when printed in SMALL CAPITALS shows where there is more information about the group. For a more efficient use of this book see Explanatory Notes.

2 ***syn*** CONTRIBUTE 1, chip in, kick in, pitch in, subscribe

comeuppance *n* ***syn*** DUE 1, desert(s), deserving, lumps, merit, right(s)

comfort *n* **1** ***syn*** HELP 1, aid, assist, assistance, hand, lift, relief, secours, succor, support
2 ***syn*** AMENITY 2, convenience, facility

comfort *vb* to make or try to make brighter a person overcome by grief or misery <*comforting* her widowed sister with words of hope>
syn buck up, cheer, console, solace, upraise
rel brighten, gladden, lighten; allay, alleviate, assuage, mitigate, relieve; refresh, renew, restore; reassure; commiserate, condole, sympathize
idiom give a lift to
con torment, torture, try; distress, trouble, worry; annoy, irk, vex
ant afflict; bother

comfortable *adj* **1** ***syn*** SUFFICIENT 1, adequate, competent, decent, enough, satisfactory, sufficing
2 enjoying or providing conditions that make for comfort and security <lived in a *comfortable* home on a quiet street>
syn comfy, cozy, cushy, easeful, easy, snug, soft
rel agreeable, grateful, gratifying, welcome; pleasant, pleasing; restful; comforting, consoling, solacing; content, pleased, satisfied
con distressing, perturbing, troubling; annoying, bothering, irking, vexing; inferior, miserable, poor, substandard, wretched
ant uncomfortable
3 ***syn*** PROSPEROUS 3, easy, ||snug, substantial, well, well-fixed, well-heeled, well-off, well-to-do
idiom in comfortable circumstances

||**comfortable** *n* ***syn*** QUILT, comforter, pouf, puff

comforter *n* ***syn*** QUILT, ||comfortable, pouf, puff

comfortless *adj* ***syn*** UNCOMFORTABLE, discomforting, harsh, uncomforting, uncomfy

comfy *adj* ***syn*** COMFORTABLE 2, cozy, cushy, easeful, easy, snug, soft

comic *adj* ***syn*** LAUGHABLE, comical, droll, farcical, funny, gelastic, ludicrous, ridiculous, risible
rel antic, fantastic, grotesque; mocking, ridiculing
ant tragic

comic *n* ***syn*** HUMORIST 2, comedian, droll, funnyman, jester, joker, jokester, quipster, wag, wit

comical *adj* ***syn*** LAUGHABLE, comic, droll, farcical, funny, gelastic, ludicrous, ridiculous, risible
rel absurd, foolish, silly; impish, roguish, sportive, waggish
con doleful, dolorous, lugubrious, melancholy
ant pathetic

comicality *n* ***syn*** HUMOR 4, comedy, comicalness, drollery, drollness, funniness, humorousness, wittiness

comicalness *n* ***syn*** HUMOR 4, comedy, comicality, drollery, drollness, funniness, humorousness, wittiness

coming *n* ***syn*** ARRIVAL 1, advent

coming *adj* **1** ***syn*** FORTHCOMING, approaching, nearing, oncoming, upcoming
2 ***syn*** NEXT, ensuing, following

coming in *n, usu* **comings in** *pl* ***syn*** REVENUE, income, receipts

comingle *vb* ***syn*** MIX 1, commingle, commix, compound, immingle, immix, intermingle, intermix, merge, mingle

comity *n* ***syn*** GOODWILL 1, amity, benevolence, friendliness, friendship, kindliness
rel accord, concord, harmony; camaraderie, companionship, comradeship, good-fellowship

comma *n* ***syn*** PAUSE, interval, lull, pausation

command *vb* to issue orders or an order to <the general *commanded* the troops to advance>
syn bid, charge, direct, enjoin, instruct, order, tell, warn
rel demand, exact, require; coerce, compel, constrain, force, oblige; conduct, control, manage; ask, call (on), request, say
ant comply, obey

command *n* **1** a direction that must or should be obeyed <failure to obey a direct *command* subjects the soldier to grave penalties>
syn behest, bidding, charge, dictate, injunction, mandate, order, word
rel direction, directive, instruction; canon, law, ordinance, precept, rule, statute; devoir, duty, obligation, responsibility
2 ***syn*** POWER 1, authority, control, domination, jurisdiction, mastery, might, strings, sway
rel rule
3 ***syn*** ABILITY 2, expertise, expertism, expertness, knack, know-how, mastership, mastery, skill
rel aplomb, assurance, confidence, poise
con incertitude, insecurity, uncertainty, unsureness; indecisiveness, vagueness

commandeer *vb* **1** ***syn*** APPROPRIATE 1, accroach, annex, arrogate, confiscate, expropriate, preempt, seize, sequester, take
2 ***syn*** ARROGATE 1, accroach, appropriate, assume, preempt, usurp

comme il faut *adj* ***syn*** DECOROUS 1, becoming, befitting, conforming, correct, decent, nice, proper, right, seemly

commemorate *vb* **1** ***syn*** KEEP 2, celebrate, observe, solemnize
2 ***syn*** MEMORIALIZE 2, monument, monumentalize

commemorative *adj* ***syn*** MEMORIAL, commemoratory

commemoratory *adj* ***syn*** MEMORIAL, commemorative

commence *vb* **1** ***syn*** BEGIN 1, embark (on *or* upon), enter, inaugurate, kick off, launch, lead off, open, start, take up
2 ***syn*** BEGIN 2, arise, originate, start
idiom come into being (*or* existence)

commencement *n* ***syn*** BEGINNING, alpha, birth, dawn, dawning, genesis, onset, opening, outset, outstart

commend *vb* **1** ***syn*** COMMIT 1, confide, consign, entrust, hand over, relegate, turn over

---

syn synonym(s) — *rel* related word(s)
idiom idiomatic equivalent(s) — *con* contrasted word(s)
ant antonym(s) — * vulgar
|| use limited; if in doubt, see a dictionary
The first word in a synonym list when printed in SMALL CAPITALS shows where there is more information about the group. For a more efficient use of this book see Explanatory Notes.

rel resign, yield; proffer, tender
2 to indicate one's warm approval <the teacher *commended* her pupils' studious attitude>
syn acclaim, applaud, compliment, hail, kudize, praise, recommend, ‖roose
rel eulogize, extol; approve, countenance, endorse, support
con blame, criticize, reprehend, reprobate; chide, rebuke, reprimand, reproach, reprove
ant censure; admonish

commendable *adj* ***syn*** WORTHY 1, admirable, deserving, estimable, laudable, meritable, meritorious, praisable, praiseworthy, thankworthy

commensurable *adj* ***syn*** PROPORTIONAL, commensurate, equal, symmetrical

commensurate *adj* ***syn*** PROPORTIONAL, commensurable, equal, symmetrical

comment *n* **1** ***syn*** REMARK 2, commentary, note, obiter dictum, observation
2 ***syn*** CRITICISM, critique, notice, review, reviewal

comment *vb* ***syn*** REMARK 2, animadvert, commentate, observe
rel construe, elucidate, explain, explicate, expound; annotate, gloss

commentary *n* ***syn*** REMARK 2, comment, note, obiter dictum, observation

commentate *vb* ***syn*** REMARK 2, animadvert, comment, observe

commerce *n* **1** ***syn*** CONTACT 2, communication, communion, intercommunication, intercourse
2 a situation characterized by mutual exchange (as of ideas) <those who feel that art should have no *commerce* with morality>
syn communion, dealings, intercourse, traffic, truck
rel communication, congress, contact, exchange, interchange, intercommunication; basis, common ground, takeoff
3 ***syn*** BUSINESS 4, industry, trade, traffic

commie *n* ***syn*** COMMUNIST, Bolshevik, ‖Bolshie, comrade, Red

commination *n* ***syn*** CURSE 1, anathema, imprecation, malediction, malison

commingle *vb* ***syn*** MIX 1, comingle, commix, compound, immingle, immix, intermingle, intermix, merge, mingle
rel integrate, unify

comminute *vb* ***syn*** PULVERIZE 1, bray, buck, contriturate, crush, powder, triturate

commiserable *adj* ***syn*** PITIFUL 1, pathetic, piteous, pitiable, poor, rueful

commiserate *vb* ***syn*** COMPASSIONATE, ache, feel (for), pity, sympathize (with)

commiseration *n* ***syn*** PITY, compassion, rue, ruth, sympathy

---

syn synonym(s) — *rel* related word(s)
idiom idiomatic equivalent(s) — *con* contrasted word(s)
ant antonym(s) — * vulgar
‖ use limited; if in doubt, see a dictionary
The first word in a synonym list when printed in SMALL CAPITALS shows where there is more information about the group. For a more efficient use of this book see Explanatory Notes.

commission *vb* **1** ***syn*** AUTHORIZE 1, accredit, empower, enable, license
rel appoint, designate, name, nominate; bid, charge, command, enjoin, instruct, order
2 ***syn*** DELEGATE, depute, deputize

commit *vb* **1** to assign (as to a person) especially for use or safekeeping <it is unwise to *commit* all power and authority to one man> <sainted beings who *commit* their spirits to God>
syn commend, confide, consign, entrust, hand over, relegate, turn over
rel allocate, allot, assign, destine, ordain; move, remove, shift, transfer; deliver, give, offer, submit; delegate, deputize
idiom give into the charge (*or* hands) of
2 to be responsible for or guilty of (an offense or wrongdoing) <*commit* a crime>
syn perpetuate, pull
rel accomplish, achieve, do, effectuate, execute, perform, pull off; contravene, transgress, trespass, violate; offend, scandalize, sin

commitment *n* ***syn*** OBLIGATION 2, charge, committal, devoir, duty, must, need, ought, ‖right

committal *n* ***syn*** OBLIGATION 2, charge, commitment, devoir, duty, must, need, ought, ‖right

commix *vb* ***syn*** MIX 1, admix, commingle, compound, immix, intermingle, intermix, meld, merge, mingle

commixture *n* ***syn*** MIXTURE, admixture, composite, compost, fusion, immixture, interfusion, intermixture, mix, mix-up

commodious *adj* ***syn*** SPACIOUS, ample, capacious, roomy, wide
con cramped, narrow, strait
ant incommodious

commodities *n pl* ***syn*** MERCHANDISE, goods, line, vendible(s), wares
rel articles, items, things

common *adj* **1** generally shared in or participated in by members of a community <our *common* civic responsibilities>
syn communal, conjoint, conjunct, intermutual, joint, mutual, public, shared
rel general, generic, universal; like, reciprocal, similar; corporate
con personal, private, restricted
ant individual
2 ***syn*** GENERAL 2, generic, universal
rel popular, public
3 ***syn*** IMPURE 3, defiled, desecrated, polluted, profaned, unclean
4 taking place often <a *common* occurrence>
syn customary, everyday, familiar, frequent
rel repetitious, routine, usual
con infrequent, occasional, unfrequent; casual, chance, incidental
ant rare, uncommon
5 ***syn*** GENERAL, commonplace, matter-of-course, natural, normal, prevalent, regular, typic, typical, usual
6 conforming to a type without noteworthy excellences or faults <just a *common* everyday sort trying to get by in life>
syn commonplace, ordinary, prosaic, uneventful, unexceptional, unnoteworthy

rel down-to-earth, matter-of-fact, prosy, unexciting; dull, flat, trite, stale, uninteresting
con exceptional, noteworthy, remarkable; excellent, marvelous, prodigious, wonderful; aberrant, divergent, eccentric
ant extraordinary
7 *syn* DECENT 4, adequate, all right, good, satisfactory, sufficient, tolerable, unexceptionable, unexceptional, unimpeachable
8 *syn* CHEAP 2, mean, ‖ornery, paltry, poor, rubbishy, shoddy, sleazy, tatty, trashy
9 *syn* INFERIOR 2, déclassé, hack, low-grade, mean, poor, second-class, second-drawer, second-rate
‖10 *syn* EASYGOING 3, breezy, casual, informal, low-pressure, relaxed, ‖sonsy, unconstrained, unfussy, unreserved

common *n* 1 **commons** *pl but sing or pl in constr syn* COMMONALTY, commonage, commoners, common men, people, plebeians, plebs, populace, rank and file, third estate
2 an often improved and ornamentally planted open space for public use in a built-up area <in summer a band played on the village *common*>
syn green, plaza, square
rel garden, park, pleasance, pleasure ground

commonage *n syn* COMMONALTY, commoners, common men, commune, people, plebeians, plebs, populace, rank and file, third estate

commonalty *n* persons without rank or authority or the political estate made up of these <laws that both the gentles and the *commonalty* recognized as just>
syn commonage, commoners, common men, commune, people, plebeians, plebes, plebs, populace, rank and file, third estate
rel masses, mob, multitude, proletariat, public
con aristocracy, elite, gentility, nobility; classes, gentry, nobs

commoners *n pl syn* COMMONALTY, commonage, common men, people, plebeians, plebes, plebs, populace, rank and file, third estate

commonition *n syn* WARNING, admonition, caution, caveat, forewarning, monition

commonly *adv syn* USUALLY 2, as a rule, by ordinary, frequently, generally, ordinarily
idiom more often than not

common men *n pl syn* COMMONALTY, commonage, commoners, people, plebeians, plebes, plebs, populace, rank and file, third estate

commonplace *n* an idea or expression deficient in originality or freshness <lazily exchanging *commonplaces* over their beer>
syn banality, bromide, cliché, platitude, prosaicism, prosaism, rubber stamp, shibboleth, tag, truism
rel chestnut, corn, prose, stereotype; inanity, shallowness, wishy-washiness; threadbareness, triteness
ant profundity

commonplace *adj* 1 *syn* COMMON 6, ordinary, prosaic, uneventful, unexceptional, unnoteworthy
2 *syn* GENERAL 1, common, matter-of-course, natural, normal, prevalent, regular, typic, typical, usual
3 *syn* PROSAIC 3, everyday, lowly, mundane, workaday, workday
4 *syn* TRITE, cliché, clichéd, shopworn, stereotyped, stereotypical, threadbare, timeworn, tired, well-worn
idiom a dime a dozen, as everyday as breakfast

common sense *n syn* SENSE 6, good sense, gumption, horse sense, judgment, wisdom

commorancy *n syn* HABITATION 2, abode, domicile, dwelling, home, house, residence, residency

commotion *n* 1 a state of often disorderly civic unrest <the whole city was in *commotion* over the new restrictions>
syn clamor, convulsion, ferment, outcry, tumult, upheaval, upturn
rel insurgence, insurrection, mutiny, rebellion, revolt, riot, uprising
2 a state of usually mental or emotional excitement <this challenge threw him into great *commotion* of mind>
syn agitation, confusion, dither, flap, lather, pother, stew, tumult, turbulence, turmoil
rel discomposure, disquiet, flurry, fluster, perturbation, upset; annoyance, bother, irritation, vexation; strain, tension
con calm, placidity, quietude, relaxation, serenity
3 a noisy and often unruly disturbance <the children created a *commotion* over missing the circus>
syn brouhaha, ‖catouse, coil, foofaraw, furore, fuss, hurrah, ruckus, rumpus, shindig, shindy, to-do, uproar
rel din, hubbub, hullabaloo, pandemonium, racket; fracas, ruction, row
4 a state of noisy confusion <never saw such *commotion* as the time the old sow got out and knocked the preacher into the midden>
syn bustle, clamor, clatter, hassle, hubbub, hurly-burly, lather, moil, pother, rowdydow, ruction, storm, to-do, tow-row, tumult, turmoil, uproar, whirl, whoopla; *compare* DIN, STIR 1
con calmness, order, peace, quiet

commove *vb syn* ELATE, excite, exhilarate, inspire, set up, spirit (up), stimulate

communal *adj syn* COMMON 1, conjoint, conjunct, intermutual, joint, mutual, public, shared

commune *n syn* COMMONALTY, commonage, commoners, common men, people, plebeians, plebes, plebs, populace, rank and file, third estate

communicable *adj* 1 *syn* INFECTIOUS 2, catching, contagious
2 *syn* COMMUNICATIVE, expansive

communicate *vb* 1 to make known <*communicated* the whole story under a pledge of secrecy>
syn break, convey, impart, pass on, transmit
rel betray, disclose, discover, divulge, ‖let out, reveal, tell; hint, imply, let on, suggest; broadcast, disseminate, publicize
con conceal, hide, obscure, screen, veil; dissemble; distort, garble, twist, warp; camouflage, disguise

---

syn synonym(s) *rel* related word(s)
idiom idiomatic equivalent(s) *con* contrasted word(s)
ant antonym(s) * vulgar
‖ use limited; if in doubt, see a dictionary
The first word in a synonym list when printed in SMALL CAPITALS shows where there is more information about the group. For a more efficient use of this book see Explanatory Notes.

2 ***syn*** ADJOIN, abut, border, butt (on *or* against), join, line, march, neighbor, touch, verge

communication *n* **1** ***syn*** MESSAGE 1, directive, word
2 ***syn*** CONTACT 2, commerce, communion, intercommunication, intercourse
3 interchange of thoughts or opinions through shared symbols <the difficulties of *communication* between people of different cultural backgrounds>
syn communion, converse, intercommunication, intercourse
rel exchange, interchange; conversing, discussing, talking; conversation, discussion, talk; advice, intelligence, news, tidings

communicative *adj* inclined to talk freely and sometimes indiscreetly <too *communicative* to be trusted with a secret>
syn communicable, expansive; *compare* FRANK
rel garrulous, loquacious, talkative, voluble; conversational; demonstrative, effusive, gushing
con constrained, guarded, inhibited, restrained; bridled, controlled, curbed

communion *n* **1** ***syn*** COMMERCE 2, dealings, intercourse, traffic, truck
2 ***syn*** COMMUNICATION 3, converse, intercommunication, intercourse
3 ***syn*** CONTACT 2, commerce, communication, intercommunication, intercourse
4 ***syn*** RELIGION 2, church, connection, creed, cult, denomination, faith, persuasion, sect

Communist *n* a member of the Russian Communist party <restructuring of Russia by the *Communists*>
syn Bolshevik, ‖Bolshie, commie, comrade, Red
rel fellow traveler, pink, pinko; Leninist, Marxist, Stalinist, Trotskyist; apparatchik

community *n* ***syn*** SOCIETY 3, people, public

commutable *adj* ***syn*** INTERCHANGEABLE, exchangeable, fungible, interconvertible, substitutable

commute *vb* ***syn*** TRANSFORM, change, convert, metamorphose, transfer, transfigure, translate, transmogrify, transmute, transpose

compact *adj* **1** ***syn*** PITHY, epigrammatic, marrowy, meaty
2 ***syn*** CLOSE 4, crowded, dense, thick, tight
rel hard; appressed, bunched, packed
con loose, slack, unconstrained; rare, tenuous, thin

compact *vb* ***syn*** UNIFY 1, concentrate, consolidate, integrate
rel compress, condense, contract; combine, unite; set, solidify
con disperse, dissipate; fluff, loosen

compact *n* ***syn*** CONTRACT, agreement, bargain, bond, convention, covenant, pact, transaction

compacting *adj* ***syn*** INTEGRATIVE, centralizing, centripetal, concentrating, consolidating, unifying

---

syn synonym(s) — ***rel*** related word(s)
idiom idiomatic equivalent(s) — ***con*** contrasted word(s)
ant antonym(s) — * vulgar
‖ use limited; if in doubt, see a dictionary
The first word in a synonym list when printed in SMALL CAPITALS shows where there is more information about the group. For a more efficient use of this book see Explanatory Notes.

companion *n* **1** ***syn*** ASSOCIATE 3, buddy, chum, comate, comrade, crony, ‖cully, pal, running mate
rel colleague, fellow, partner; chaperon, escort
2 ***syn*** MATE 5, coordinate, double, duplicate, fellow, match, reciprocal, twin
3 ***syn*** ACCOMPANIMENT 2, associate, concomitant, consort, fellow, mate

companion *vb* ***syn*** ACCOMPANY, attend, bear, ‖bring, ‖carry, chaperon, conduct, consort (with), convoy, escort

companionable *adj* ***syn*** SOCIAL 1, convivial, sociable
rel amiable, complacent, good-natured
con uncongenial, unsympathetic; reserved, taciturn, uncommunicative

companionship *n* ***syn*** COMPANY 1, fellowship, society

company *n* **1** association between individuals especially on pleasant or intimate terms <we always enjoyed his *company*>
syn companionship, fellowship, society
rel camaraderie, comradeship, consociation
2 persons visiting especially in one's house <invited *company* for dinner>
syn guests, visitors; *compare* VISITOR 1
3 ***syn*** GATHERING 2, aggregation, assemblage, assembly, collection, congregation, crowd, group, muster, ruck
4 a group of persons associated in a joint effort or for a common purpose <a *company* of thieves lay in wait by the highway>
syn band, corps, outfit, party, troop, troupe
rel crew, gang, pack, team; circle, clique, coterie, set; association, club, order, society; crowd, horde, mob, throng; group
5 ***syn*** ENTERPRISE 3, business, concern, establishment, firm, house, outfit

company *vb* ***syn*** ACCOMPANY, attend, bear, ‖bring, ‖carry, chaperon, companion, conduct, consort (with), convoy

comparable *adj* ***syn*** LIKE, agnate, akin, alike, consonant, corresponding, parallel, similar, undifferenced, uniform
ant disparate

comparative *adj* being such in comparison with an expressed or implied standard or absolute <living in *comparative* poverty>
syn approximate, near, relative
rel equivalent, like, similar
con genuine, real, true
ant absolute

compare *vb* **1** ***syn*** EQUATE 2, assimilate, liken, match, paragon, parallel
2 to examine side by side or point by point in order to establish likenesses and differences <*compare* the effects of two diets on weight loss>
syn bracket, collate, contrast
rel approach, equal, match, rival, touch; examine, inspect, observe, scan, scrutinize, size (up); consider, contemplate, ponder, study, weigh

comparison *n* ***syn*** LIKENESS, affinity, alikeness, analogy, resemblance, semblance, similarity, simile, similitude

compass *vb* **1** ***syn*** SURROUND 1, circle, encircle, encompass, environ, gird, girdle, hem, ring, round

2 ***syn*** GET 1, acquire, annex, gain, have, land, obtain, procure, secure, win
3 ***syn*** APPREHEND 1, accept, catch, comprehend, ‖dig, grasp, see, take in, twig, understand

compass *n* **1** ***syn*** CIRCUMFERENCE, ambit, circuit, perimeter, periphery
rel domain, field, sphere; enclosure
2 ***syn*** ENVIRONS 1, bound(s), boundary, confine(s), limits, precinct(s), purlieus
3 ***syn*** RANGE 2, ambit, extension, extent, orbit, purview, radius, reach, scope, sweep
rel bounds, limits; circumscription, limitation, restriction

compassion *n* **1** ***syn*** SYMPATHY 2, empathy, fellow feeling
rel charity, clemency, grace, lenity, mercy; benevolence, humaneness, humanity
con aloofness, indifference, unconcern; cruelty, harshness, mercilessness; implacability, relentlessness
2 ***syn*** PITY, commiseration, rue, ruth, sympathy

compassionate *adj* ***syn*** TENDER, kindhearted, responsive, softhearted, sympathetic, warm, warmhearted
rel clement, forbearing; piteous, pitiful
con grim, implacable, merciless, relentless, unrelenting; adamant, inexorable, inflexible, obdurate

compassionate *vb* to feel or express compassion for <a kindly man who *compassionated* all human misery>
syn ache, commiserate, feel (for), pity, sympathize (with)
rel grieve (over), regret, repine; lament, mourn, sorrow (for *or* over); deplore
con accept, endure, tolerate; disregard, ignore, overlook, pass over

compassionless *adj* ***syn*** UNFEELING 2, callous, cold-blooded, hardhearted, heartless, ironhearted, obdurate, stony, stonyhearted, uncompassionate

compatible ***syn*** CONSONANT 1, agreeable, congenial, congruous, consistent, sympathetic
rel appropriate, fit, fitting, meet, proper, suitable
ant incompatible

compatriot *n* ***syn*** COLLEAGUE, associate, compeer, confrere

compeer *n* ***syn*** COLLEAGUE, associate, compatriot, confrere

compel *vb* ***syn*** FORCE 2, coerce, concuss, constrain, make, oblige, shotgun

compellation *n* ***syn*** NAME 1, appellation, appellative, cognomen, denomination, designation, ‖moniker, nomen, style, title

compendiary *adj* ***syn*** CONCISE, breviloquent, brief, compendious, curt, laconic, short, short and sweet, succinct, summary

compendious *adj* ***syn*** CONCISE, breviloquent, brief, compendiary, curt, laconic, short, short and sweet, succinct, summary
rel close, compact
con amplified, elaborated, expanded, inflated; complete, full

compendium *n* **1** a condensed treatment of a subject <prepared a *compendium* of the state laws dealing with education>
syn aperçu, digest, pandect, précis, sketch, survey, syllabus, sylloge
rel abridgment, abstract, brief, conspectus, epitome; overview
con elaboration, expansion
2 ***syn*** HANDBOOK, Baedeker, enchiridion, guide, guidebook, manual, vade mecum

compenetrate *vb* ***syn*** PERMEATE, impenetrate, impregnate, interfuse, interpenetrate, penetrate, percolate, pervade, saturate, transfuse

compensate *vb* **1** to make good the defects of <her kind heart *compensated* for her nosy ways>
syn atone (for), balance, counterbalance, counterpoise, countervail, make up, offset, outweigh, redeem, set off
rel abrogate, annul, invalidate, negate, nullify; counteract, negative, neutralize; better, fix (up), improve, repair; redress
idiom make amends (*or* reparations), make matters right
2 ***syn*** PAY 1, guerdon, remunerate
3 to make proper payment to (as for injury, loss, or damage) <*compensated* a worker injured on the job>
syn indemnify, pay, recompense, reimburse, remunerate, repay, requite
rel recoup, refund
idiom make restitution (*or* reparation)

compensation *n* ***syn*** REPARATION, amends, indemnification, indemnity, quittance, recompense, redress, reprisal, restitution

compete *vb* **1** to strive to gain mastery or obtain a prize <students *competing* for a scholarship>
syn contend, contest, rival, vie
rel dispute; battle, fight, strive, struggle; attempt, essay, try
2 ***syn*** RIVAL 2, emulate, rivalize
rel approach, equal, match, touch

competence *n* **1** ***syn*** ENOUGH, adequacy, sufficiency, sufficient
2 ***syn*** ABILITY 1, adequacy, capability, capacity, might, qualification, qualifiedness
rel appropriateness, fitness, suitability
ant incompetence

competent *adj* **1** ***syn*** ABLE, au fait, capable, good, proper, qualified, wicked
rel adept, finished, masterly, polished
ant incompetent
2 ***syn*** SUFFICIENT 1, adequate, comfortable, decent, enough, satisfactory, sufficing

competition *n* **1** ***syn*** CONTEST 1, conflict, emulation, rivalry, strife, striving, tug-of-war, warfare
2 ***syn*** CONTEST 2, concours, conflict, meet, meeting, rencontre
3 ***syn*** RIVAL, competitor, corrival

competitor *n* ***syn*** RIVAL, competition, corrival

complacence *n* ***syn*** CONCEIT 2, amour propre, complacency, conceitedness, consequence, egoism, egotism, narcissism, pride, vainglory

---

syn synonym(s)	***rel*** related word(s)
idiom idiomatic equivalent(s)	***con*** contrasted word(s)
ant antonym(s)	* vulgar

‖ use limited; if in doubt, see a dictionary
The first word in a synonym list when printed in SMALL CAPITALS shows where there is more information about the group. For a more efficient use of this book see Explanatory Notes.

complacency *n* ***syn*** CONCEIT 2, amour propre, complacence, conceitedness, consequence, egoism, egotism, narcissism, pride, vainglory

complacent *adj* feeling or showing an often excessive or unjustified satisfaction and pleasure in one's status, possessions, or attainments <had the *complacent* air of superiority that often mars an ignorant self-made man>
syn priggish, self-complacent, self-contented, self-pleased, self-satisfied, smug
rel assured, confident, self-assured, self-confident, self-possessed; conceited, egoistic, egotistic
con humble, modest; diffident, shy

complain *vb* to express discontent, resentment, or regret usually peaceably and as if seeking sympathy <a nice girl but given to *complaining* over trifles>
syn fuss, kick, murmur, repine, wail, whine; *compare* GRIPE 2, GRUMBLE 1
rel fret, worry; nag, pester
idiom air a grievance, find fault, register a complaint, sing (*or* cry) the blues
con accept, condone, countenance, tolerate

complainer *n* ***syn*** GROUCH, crab, crank, faultfinder, griper, grouser, grumbler, kicker, malcontent, sourpuss

complaint *n* ***syn*** DISEASE 1, affection, ailment, condition, disorder, ill, infirmity, malady, sickness, syndrome

complaisant *adj* ***syn*** AMIABLE 1, easy, good-humored, good-natured, good-tempered, lenient, mild, obliging
rel accommodating, agreeable, generous, indulgent; submissive
con harsh, rigorous, stern; determined, firm, masterful

complement *n* **1** something that makes up a deficiency in another thing <bought the farm with its *complement* of equipment and livestock>
syn supplement
rel correlate, counterpart; makeweight
2 ***syn*** ACCOMPANIMENT 1, augmentation, enhancement, enrichment
3 ***syn*** COUNTERPART 1, correlate, pendant

complete *adj* **1** ***syn*** WHOLE 3, choate, entire, full, integral, perfect
2 ***syn*** UNABRIDGED, unabbreviated, uncondensed, uncut, undocked, whole-length
3 ***syn*** WHOLE 4, all, entire, gross, outright, total
4 brought to completion <each *complete* revolution of the earth>
syn completed, concluded, done, down, ended, finished, terminated, through
rel accomplished, achieved, effected, executed, realized; attained, compassed
idiom all over, done with, set at rest
ant incomplete
5 ***syn*** EXHAUSTIVE, full-dress, thorough, thoroughgoing, whole-hog
ant incomplete
6 ***syn*** UTTER, absolute, consummate, downright, out-and-out, outright, perfect, positive, thoroughgoing, unmitigated

complete *vb* **1** ***syn*** CLOSE 3, conclude, determine, end, finish, halt, terminate, ultimate, wind up, wrap up
rel accomplish, achieve, discharge, effect, execute, fulfill, perform
idiom carry through, go through with
2 ***syn*** FULFILL 1, execute, implement, perform

completed *adj* ***syn*** COMPLETE 4, concluded, done, down, ended, finished, terminated, through

completely *adv* **1** ***syn*** DOWN 2, fully, through-and-through
idiom down to the ground
2 ***syn*** THOROUGHLY 2, detailedly, exhaustively, in and out, inside out, up and down
3 ***syn*** WELL 3, à fond, altogether, entirely, fully, perfectly, quite, thoroughly, utterly, wholly

completeness *n* **1** ***syn*** ENTIRETY 1, allness, entireness, oneness, totality, wholeness
2 ***syn*** INTEGRITY 2, entireness, perfection, wholeness

complex *adj* **1** made up of two or more separable or identifiable elements <the *complex* vascular system of higher plants>
syn composite, compound
rel blended, compounded, mingled, mixed; heterogeneous, varied; elaborate, intricate, involved; complicated, confused, mixed-up
con homogeneous, uniform
ant simple
2 difficult to comprehend because of a multiplicity of interrelated elements <a *complex* plot to undermine the government by discrediting its leaders>
syn Byzantine, complicated, daedal, elaborate, gordian, intricate, involved, knotty, labyrinthine, sophisticated
rel bewildering, confusing, distracting, disturbing; baffling, confounding, mysterious, mystifying, perplexing, puzzling, equivocal, obscure, vague; involute, involuted, reticular
con clear, defined, definite, distinct, plain, recognizable, uncomplicated, uninvolved; comprehensible, explicable, intelligible, knowable
ant simple

complex *n* ***syn*** SYSTEM 1
con constituent, element, factor; member, part, piece, portion; detail, item, particular
ant component

complexion *n* ***syn*** DISPOSITION 3, character, humor, individualism, individuality, makeup, nature, personality, temper, temperament
rel kind, sort, style, type

complexion *vb* ***syn*** TINT, tincture, tinge

complexionless *adj* ***syn*** PALE 1, ashen, ashy, blanched, colorless, doughy, livid, lurid, pallid, waxen

compliance *n* ***syn*** ACQUIESCENCE, conformity, resignation
rel amenability, docility, obedience, tractability; deference, submission, submissiveness
con contumacy, obstinacy, stubbornness
ant frowardness

complicate *vb* to make complex, involved, or difficult <a disagreement *complicated* by intense personal animosities>

---

syn synonym(s) ***rel*** related word(s)
idiom idiomatic equivalent(s) ***con*** contrasted word(s)
ant antonym(s) * vulgar
‖ use limited; if in doubt, see a dictionary
The first word in a synonym list when printed in SMALL CAPITALS shows where there is more information about the group. For a more efficient use of this book see Explanatory Notes.

syn entangle, ‖muck, muddle, perplex, ravel, snarl, tangle
rel jumble, ‖snafu; derange, disarrange, disorder, mix up, upset
con arrange, order; disentangle, straighten (out), untangle
ant simplify

complicated *adj* **1** *syn* ELABORATE 2, fancy, intricate
2 *syn* COMPLEX 2, Byzantine, daedal, elaborate, gordian, intricate, involved, knotty, labyrinthine, sophisticated
rel arduous, difficult, hard; abstruse, recondite
con easy, facile, light; clear-cut, precise, straightforward
ant simple

complicity *n* association with an improper or unlawful activity <failed to prove his *complicity* in the cover-up>
syn collusion, connivance
rel implication, involvement; engineering, machination, manipulation, wire-pulling

compliment *n* **1** an expression of regard or praise <a man meriting the *compliments* and homage of his fellows>
syn bouquet, kudo, orchid(s)
rel trade-last; laud, laudation, praise; accolade, commendation, honor; blessing(s), congratulation(s), felicitation(s); encomium, eulogy, tribute
con dig, gibe, jeer, slam
ant taunt
‖**2** *syn* GIFT 1, benevolence, boon, favor, largess, present

compliment *vb* *syn* COMMEND 2, acclaim, applaud, hail, kudize, praise, recommend, ‖roose
idiom take off one's hat to
con belittle, decry, denigrate, depreciate, disparage, run down

complimentary *adj* *syn* FREE 5, chargeless, costless, gratis, gratuitous

comply *vb* *syn* OBEY, conform, follow, keep, mind, observe

component *n* *syn* ELEMENT 2, constituent, factor, ingredient
con admixture, amalgam, blend, compound, mixture
ant composite; complex

comport *vb* **1** *syn* AGREE 4, accord, check, correspond, dovetail, fit (in), ‖gee, go, square, tally
2 *syn* BEHAVE 1, acquit, act, bear, carry, conduct, demean, deport, go on, quit

comportment *n* **1** *syn* BEARING 1, address, air, demeanor, deportment, mien, port, presence, set
2 *syn* BEHAVIOR, conduct, deportment, tenue

compose *vb* **1** *syn* CONSTITUTE 1, comprise, form, make, make up
rel consist (of)
2 to bring into being by mental and especially artistic effort <*compose* a ballad or a history of England>
syn create
rel devise, invent, make up, originate; dream up
3 *syn* CALM, allay, balm, becalm, lull, quiet, settle, soothe, still, tranquilize
rel ease, lessen, soften; comfort, console, solace
con agitate, embroil, trouble, unsettle
ant discompose
4 to bring oneself or one's emotions under control <*composed* himself and turned to face the new attack>
syn collect, contain, control, cool, re-collect, rein, repress, restrain, simmer down, smother, suppress
rel down, mitigate, moderate, modulate, pocket, temper, tune down; bottle (up), check, hold in; ease (off *or* up), let up, relax, slacken
idiom calm down, control one's feelings (*or* emotions), get hold of oneself, master one's feelings, pull oneself together

composed *adj* **1** *syn* CALM 2, collected, easy, easygoing, placid, poised, possessed, self-possessed, serene, tranquil
2 *syn* COOL 2, collected, disimpassioned, imperturbable, nonchalant, unflappable, unruffled
rel quiet, still; sedate, serious, staid; repressed, suppressed
con concerned, worried
ant discomposed, ruffled

composite *adj* *syn* COMPLEX 1, compound

composite *n* *syn* MIXTURE, amalgam, amalgamation, commixture, compost, compound, immixture, intermixture, mix, mix-up
rel combination, union

composition *n* **1** *syn* MAKEUP 1, architecture, constitution, construction, design, formation
2 *syn* COMPROMISE
3 *syn* ESSAY 2, article, paper, theme

compos mentis *adj* *syn* SANE 2, all there, lucid, normal, right

compost *n* *syn* MIXTURE, admixture, commixture, composite, compound, fusion, immixture, interfusion, intermixture, mix

composure *n* *syn* EQUANIMITY, ataraxy, calmness, coolness, imperturbability, phlegm, sangfroid, self-possession
ant discomposure, perturbation

compotation *n* *syn* BINGE 1, bender, booze, brannigan, bum, bust, drunk, jag, soak, souse

compound *vb* **1** *syn* JOIN 1, associate, bracket, coadunate, coagment, coalesce, connect, couple, link, unite
2 *syn* MIX 1, admix, comingle, commingle, commix, immix, intermingle, intermix, make up, mingle
3 *syn* INCREASE 1, aggrandize, augment, boost, enlarge, expand, extend, heighten, magnify, multiply

compound *adj* *syn* COMPLEX 1, composite

compound *n* *syn* MIXTURE, admixture, alloy, amalgam, amalgamation, blend, commixture, composite, compost, fusion

comprehend *vb* **1** *syn* APPREHEND 1, accept, catch, compass, ‖dig, grasp, see, take in, twig, understand

---

syn synonym(s) *rel* related word(s)
idiom idiomatic equivalent(s) *con* contrasted word(s)
ant antonym(s) * vulgar
‖ use limited; if in doubt, see a dictionary
The first word in a synonym list when printed in SMALL CAPITALS shows where there is more information about the group. For a more efficient use of this book see Explanatory Notes.

2 ***syn*** KNOW 1, appreciate, apprehend, cognize, fathom, grasp, have, understand
rel envisage, envision, see
3 ***syn*** INCLUDE, contain, embody, embrace, encompass, have, involve, subsume, take in

comprehendible *adj* ***syn*** UNDERSTANDABLE, apprehensible, comprehensible, fathomable, graspable, intelligible, knowable, lucid, luminous
ant incomprehensible

comprehensible *adj* ***syn*** UNDERSTANDABLE, apprehensible, comprehendible, fathomable, graspable, intelligible, knowable, lucid, luminous
ant incomprehensible

comprehensive *adj* **1** ***syn*** ENCYCLOPEDIC, inclusive
2 ***syn*** ALL-AROUND 2, general, global, inclusive, overall, sweeping
idiom in depth

comprehensiveness *n* ***syn*** BREADTH 2, amplitude, fullness, scope, wideness

compress *vb* **1** ***syn*** CONTRACT 3, concentrate, condense, constrict, shrink
rel compact, consolidate; cram, crowd, press, squeeze
con disperse, dissipate, scatter
ant stretch; spread
2 ***syn*** PRESS 1, bear, crowd, crush, jam, push, ‖squab, squash, squeeze, squish

comprise *vb* ***syn*** CONSTITUTE 1, compose, form, make, make up

compromise *n* a settlement reached by mutual concession <the company and the union agreed to a *compromise* on fringe benefits>
syn composition
rel golden mean, mean, middle ground, middle way; agreement, compact, contract, pact; arrangement, bargain, understanding
idiom happy medium

compromise *vb* ***syn*** ENDANGER, hazard, imperil, jeopard, jeopardize, jeopardy, menace, peril, risk
rel blast, blight, mar, queer, ruin, spoil
idiom cook one's goose; play havoc (*or* hob) with, settle one's hash

compulsatory *adj* ***syn*** MANDATORY, compulsory, imperative, imperious, obligatory, required

compulsion *n* ***syn*** FORCE 4, coercion, constraint, duress, violence
rel driving, impelling, pressing; exigency, necessity, need; pressure, stress
con coaxing, inducing, persuasion; choice, election, option, preference

compulsory *adj* ***syn*** MANDATORY, compulsatory, imperative, imperious, obligatory, required

compunction *n* **1** ***syn*** PENITENCE, attrition, contriteness, contrition, penance, penitency, remorse, repentance, rue, ruth
rel conscience, conscientiousness, punctiliousness, scrupulosity, scrupulousness
con brazenness, callousness, hardness, insensitivity; disinterest, indifference, unconcern; obduracy, recalcitrance
2 ***syn*** QUALM, conscience, demur, scruple, squeam
rel disinclination; hesitancy, hesitation

compunctious *adj* ***syn*** REMORSEFUL, apologetic, attritional, contrite, penitent, penitential, regretful, repentant, sorry

computation *n* the act or action of calculating mathematically <by his *computation* they could not possibly afford a new car>
syn arithmetic, calculation, ciphering, estimation, figuring, reckoning

compute *vb* ***syn*** CALCULATE, cipher, estimate, figure, reckon

comrade *n* **1** ***syn*** ASSOCIATE 3, buddy, chum, comate, companion, crony, ‖cully, pal, running mate
rel consort, fellow, mate; adjunct, ally, auxiliary
2 ***syn*** COMMUNIST, Bolshevik, ‖Bolshie, commie, Red

comradery *n* ***syn*** CAMARADERIE, good-fellowship

comstock *n* ***syn*** PRUDE, bluenose, goody-goody, Grundy, Mrs. Grundy, nice Nelly, prig, puritan, ‖wowser

con *vb* **1** ***syn*** SCRUTINIZE 1, canvass, check over, check up, examine, inspect, study, survey, vet, view
2 ***syn*** MEMORIZE, get, learn

con *n* **1** ***syn*** OPPONENT, adversary, antagonist, anti, match, opposer, oppugnant
ant pro
2 ***syn*** ANTAGONISM 2, antithesis, contradistinction, contraposition, contrariety, opposition, opposure

con *vb* **1** ***syn*** DUPE, bamboozle, befool, chicane, flimflam, fool, hoax, hoodwink, hornswoggle, trick
2 ***syn*** COAX, ‖banter, blandish, blarney, cajole, soft-soap, sweet-talk, wheedle

‖**con** *n* ***syn*** CONVICT, jailbird, ‖lag, loser, prison bird

concatenate *vb* ***syn*** INTEGRATE 3, articulate

concavity *n* ***syn*** DEPRESSION 2, basin, dip, hollow, sag, sink, sinkage, sinkhole

conceal *vb* ***syn*** HIDE, bury, cache, cover, ‖ditch, ensconce, occult, screen, secrete, stash
rel camouflage, disguise, dissemble
idiom keep (something) dark
con betray, divulge; evidence, evince, manifest
ant reveal

concealed *adj* ***syn*** ULTERIOR, buried, covert, guarded, hidden, obscured, privy, shrouded

concede *vb* **1** ***syn*** ACKNOWLEDGE 1, admit, allow, avow, confess, fess (up), grant, let on, own, own up
rel cede, relinquish, waive
con agitate, argue, debate, discuss; answer, confute, refute; controvert
ant dispute
2 ***syn*** GRANT 1, accord, award, vouchsafe
con refuse, reject
ant deny

conceit *n* **1** ***syn*** IDEA, apprehension, concept, conception, image, impression, intellection, notion, perception, thought
2 an attitude of regarding oneself with favor <his constant boasting was an indication of *conceit*>

---

syn synonym(s) ***rel*** related word(s)
idiom idiomatic equivalent(s) ***con*** contrasted word(s)
ant antonym(s) * vulgar
‖ use limited; if in doubt, see a dictionary
The first word in a synonym list when printed in SMALL CAPITALS shows where there is more information about the group. For a more efficient use of this book see Explanatory Notes.

syn amour propre, complacence, complacency, conceitedness, consequence, egoism, egotism, narcissism, outrecuidance, pride, self-admiration, self-complacency, self-conceit, self-consequence, self-esteem, self-exaltation, self-glory, self-importance, self-love, self-opinion, self-pride, swelled head, swellheadedness, vainglory, vainness, vanity
rel assurance, pomposity, self-partiality, smugness, stuffiness
con humbleness, humility, self-depreciation, unpretentiousness
ant modesty
3 ***syn*** CAPRICE, bee, boutade, crotchet, fancy, freak, humor, megrim, vagary, whim

‖**conceit** *vb* ***syn*** UNDERSTAND 3, assume, believe, conceive, expect, gather, imagine, ‖reckon, suppose, think

conceited *adj* ***syn*** VAIN 3, ‖conceity, narcissistic, self-conceited, stuck-up, vainglorious

conceitedness *n* ***syn*** CONCEIT 2, amour propre, narcissism, self-admiration, self-conceit, self-esteem, self-love, vainglory, vainness, vanity

‖**conceity** *adj* ***syn*** VAIN 3, conceited, narcissistic, self-conceited, stuck-up, vainglorious

conceivable *adj* **1** ***syn*** THINKABLE 2, imaginable, supposable
2 ***syn*** PROBABLE, earthly, likely, mortal, possible

conceive *vb* **1** ***syn*** THINK 1, envisage, envision, fancy, feature, image, imagine, realize, vision, visualize
rel excogitate; cogitate, speculate; meditate, ponder, ruminate
2 ***syn*** APPREHEND 1, accept, catch, compass, comprehend, ‖dig, follow, grasp, twig, understand
rel heed, mark, note, notice, observe, remark
3 ***syn*** UNDERSTAND 3, assume, believe, expect, gather, imagine, ‖reckon, suppose, suspect, take
rel judge; deem, feel

concenter *vb* **1** ***syn*** FASTEN 3, concentrate, fix, fixate, focus, put, rivet
2 ***syn*** CONVERGE, concentrate, focus, meet

concentrate *vb* **1** ***syn*** FASTEN 3, concenter, fix, fixate, focus, put, rivet
rel establish, set, settle
2 ***syn*** UNIFY 1, compact, consolidate, integrate
rel assemble, collect, gather; heap, mass, pile
con dispel, disperse; attenuate, dilute, extenuate, rarefy, thin; dispense, distribute
ant dissipate
3 ***syn*** CONTRACT 3, compress, condense, constrict, shrink
4 ***syn*** CONVERGE, concenter, focus, meet

concentrated *adj* **1** ***syn*** STRONG 3, full-bodied, lusty, potent, robust
2 ***syn*** WHOLE 5, exclusive, fixed, undistracted, undivided, unswerving
rel complete, entire, total
3 ***syn*** INTENSE 1, desperate, exquisite, fierce, furious, terrible, vehement, vicious, violent

concentrating *adj* ***syn*** INTEGRATIVE, centralizing, centripetal, compacting, consolidating, unifying

concentration *n* ***syn*** ATTENTION 1, application, consideration, debate, deliberation, heed, study
rel enthrallment, raptness
ant distraction

concept *n* ***syn*** IDEA, apprehension, conceit, conception, image, impression, intellection, notion, perception, thought
con percept, sensation, sense-datum, sensum

conception *n* ***syn*** IDEA, apprehension, conceit, concept, image, impression, intellection, notion, perception, thought

conceptual *adj* existing or dealing with what exists only in the mind < *conceptual* analysis of a problem >
syn ideal, ideational, notional
rel abstract, transcendent, transcendental; absolute, categorical, ultimate; obscure, remote; fanciful, imaginary, visionary
con practical, pragmatic, realistic; concrete, material, substantial, tangible

concern *n* **1** ***syn*** INTEREST 3, curiosity, interestedness, regard
2 ***syn*** AFFAIR 1, business, matter, shooting match, thing
3 ***syn*** BUSINESS 8, affair, lookout, occasions, palaver
4 ***syn*** CARE 4, carefulness, consciousness, heed, heedfulness, regard
5 ***syn*** CONSIDERATION 3, considerateness, regard, solicitude
6 ***syn*** UNCERTAINTY, doubt, dubiety, dubiosity, incertitude, mistrust, skepticism, suspicion, uncertitude, wonder
rel faltering, irresolution; apprehension, misgiving; inquietude, suspense
7 ***syn*** CARE 2, anxiety, concernment, disquiet, disquietude, solicitude, unease, uneasiness, worry
rel attention, consideration, thoughtfulness
con aloofness, incuriousness, indifference
ant unconcern
8 ***syn*** ENTERPRISE 3, business, company, establishment, firm, house, outfit
9 ***syn*** GADGET 1, gimmick, gizmo, jigger, widget

concerned *adj* ***syn*** INTERESTED, affected, implicated, involved

concerning *prep* ***syn*** APROPOS, about, against, anent, as for, as regards, in re, re, regarding, respecting

concernment *n* ***syn*** CARE 2, anxiety, concern, disquiet, disquietude, solicitude, unease, uneasiness, worry

concert *vb* **1** ***syn*** NEGOTIATE 1, arrange, settle
rel argue, debate, discuss; concur, cooperate, unite
2 ***syn*** AGREE 3, coincide, concord, concur, harmonize

concert *n* ***syn*** HARMONY 1, accord, chorus, concord, consonance, tune

concession *n* ***syn*** ALLOWANCE 5

conciliate *vb* ***syn*** PACIFY, appease, assuage, mollify, placate, propitiate, sweeten
rel intervene, mediate; persuade, prevail; calm, quiet, soothe, tranquilize

---

syn synonym(s) — ***rel*** related word(s)
idiom idiomatic equivalent(s) — ***con*** contrasted word(s)
ant antonym(s) — * vulgar
‖ use limited; if in doubt, see a dictionary
The first word in a synonym list when printed in SMALL CAPITALS shows where there is more information about the group. For a more efficient use of this book see Explanatory Notes.

con alienate, disaffect, estrange; foment, incite; excite, pique, provoke, stimulate
ant antagonize

concise *adj* presented with or given to brevity of expression <a *concise* statement of the problem> <a very *concise* thinker>
syn breviloquent, brief, compendiary, compendious, curt, laconic, short, short and sweet, succinct, summary, terse; *compare* PITHY
rel abridged, compressed, condensed; marrowy, meaty, pithy; lean
con diffuse, long-winded, prolix, rambling, voluble, wordy
ant redundant; verbose

concisely *adv syn* BRIEFLY, in brief, in short, laconically, shortly, succinctly, tersely

conclude *vb* **1** *syn* DECIDE, determine, figure, resolve, rule, settle
2 *syn* CLOSE 3, complete, determine, end, finish, halt, terminate, ultimate, wind up, wrap up
idiom ring down the curtain
ant open
3 *syn* INFER, collect, deduce, deduct, derive, draw, gather, judge, make, make out

concluded *adj syn* COMPLETE 4, completed, done, down, ended, finished, terminated, through

concluding *adj syn* LAST, closing, eventual, final, hindmost, lag, latest, latter, terminal, ultimate
ant opening

conclusion *n* **1** *syn* INFERENCE 2, deduction, illation, judgment, ratiocination, sequitur
2 *syn* FINALE, close, end, ending, finish, windup
3 *syn* END 2, cease, cessation, close, closure, desistance, finish, period, stop, termination
4 *syn* DECISION 1, determination, resolution, settlement

conclusive *adj* putting an end to debate or question usually by reason of irrefutability <the evidence was *conclusive* and no defense was possible>
syn definitive
rel cogent, compelling, convincing, telling; incontrovertible, irrefragable, irrefrangible, irrefutable, unanswerable; deciding, decisive, determinant, determinate, determinative; clear, precise, unambiguous
con doubtful, dubious, problematic, questionable; credible, plausible, specious; ambiguous, cryptic, enigmatic, obscure
ant inconclusive

concoct *vb syn* CONTRIVE 2, cook (up), devise, dream up, formulate, frame, hatch (up), invent, make up, vamp (up)
rel conceive, envisage, envision; create, discover, originate

concomitant *adj* occurring in company with <good manners are likely to be *concomitant* with good behavior>
syn accompanying, ancillary, attendant, attending, coincident, collateral, incident, satellite
rel accessory, adjuvant, supplementary; correlative, corresponding

concomitant *n syn* ACCOMPANIMENT 2, associate, companion, consort, fellow, mate

concord *n* **1** *syn* HARMONY 2, accord, agreement, chime, concordance, consonance, tune
rel amity, comity, friendship, goodwill; calmness, peace, placidity, serenity, tranquillity
con conflict, contention, difference, dissension, strife, variance
ant discord
2 *syn* HARMONY 3, rapport, unity
3 *syn* HARMONY 1, accord, chorus, concert, consonance, tune
4 *syn* TREATY, agreement, convention, pact

concord *vb syn* AGREE 3, coincide, concert, concur, harmonize

concordance *n syn* HARMONY 2, accord, agreement, chime, concord, consonance, tune

concordant *adj syn* HARMONIOUS 2, accordant, congruous

concours *n syn* CONTEST 2, competition, conflict, meet, meeting, rencontre

concourse *n* a coming, flocking, or flowing together <they doubt the universe originated in a chance *concourse* of atoms>
syn concursion, confluence, gathering, junction, meeting
rel association, joining, linkage
con disassociation, parting, separation

concrete *vb* **1** *syn* HARDEN 1, cake, congeal, dry, indurate, set, solidify
2 *syn* JOIN 1, associate, bracket, coalesce, combine, compound, connect, couple, link, unite

concupiscence *n syn* LUST 2, aphrodisia, desire, eroticism, itch, lickerishness, lustfulness, passion, prurience, pruriency

concupiscent *adj syn* LUSTFUL 2, goatish, *horny, hot, lascivious, libidinous, lickerish, passionate, prurient, satyric

concur *vb* **1** *syn* UNITE 2, band, coadjute, combine, conjoin, cooperate, league
rel accord, agree, harmonize, jibe
2 *syn* AGREE 3, coincide, concert, concord, harmonize
rel accede, acquiesce, assent, consent
ant contend; altercate

concurrent *adj syn* CONTEMPORARY 1, coetaneous, coeval, coexistent, coexisting, contemporaneous, simultaneous, synchronal, synchronic, synchronous

concurrently *adv syn* TOGETHER 1, at once, coincidentally, coincidently, coinstantaneously, simultaneously

concursion *n syn* CONCOURSE, confluence, gathering, junction, meeting

concuss *vb* **1** *syn* SHAKE 4, agitate, convulse, rock
2 *syn* FORCE 2, coerce, compel, constrain, make, oblige, shotgun

concussion *n syn* IMPACT, bump, clash, collision, crash, jar, jolt, percussion, shock, smash

---

syn synonym(s) | *rel* related word(s)
idiom idiomatic equivalent(s) | *con* contrasted word(s)
ant antonym(s) | * vulgar
‖ use limited; if in doubt, see a dictionary
The first word in a synonym list when printed in SMALL CAPITALS shows where there is more information about the group. For a more efficient use of this book see Explanatory Notes.

rel beating, buffeting, jarring, jolting, pounding, shaking; blow, clip, clout

condemn *vb* **1** *syn* CRITICIZE, blame, censure, denounce, denunciate, knock, rap, reprehend, reprobate, skin
rel belittle, decry, depreciate, disparage; deprecate, disapprove
idiom damn with faint praise, find fault with
con applaud, commend, compliment; acclaim, eulogize, extol, laud, praise; condone, excuse, forgive, pardon
2 *syn* SENTENCE, damn, doom, proscribe
con deliver, redeem, rescue, save

condemned *adj syn* DAMNED 1, doomed, lost
rel fallen, fated

condensation *n syn* ABRIDGMENT, abstract, boildown, breviary, breviate, brief, conspectus, epitome, synopsis

condense *vb* **1** *syn* CONTRACT 3, compress, concentrate, constrict, shrink
rel compact, consolidate; curtail, minimize
con amplify
2 *syn* EPITOMIZE 1, digest, inventory, nutshell, sum, summarize, summate, sum up, synopsize
con broaden, expand, extend, widen
ant amplify

condensed *adj* made shorter and typically simpler <a *condensed* biography>
syn canned, capsule, epitomized, pocket, potted
rel abbreviated, abridged, bobbed, bobtail, bobtailed, curtailed, shortened
con elaborated, polished, refined; amplified, enlarged, expanded

condescend *vb syn* STOOP 1, deign

condign *adj syn* JUST 3, appropriate, deserved, due, merited, requisite, rhadamanthine, right, rightful, suitable
rel grim, rigorous, stern, strict, stringent; atrocious, awful, dreadful, horrible

condition *n* **1** something that limits or qualifies an agreement or offer <included the *condition* that any heir contesting the will would be automatically disinherited>
syn provision, proviso, reservation, stipulation, strings, terms
rel prerequisite, requirement, requisite; exception, exemption, limitation, modification, qualification, restriction, saving clause
2 *syn* ESSENTIAL 2, must, necessity, precondition, prerequisite, requirement, requisite, sine qua non
3 *syn* STATE 1, mode, posture, situation, status
4 *syn* ORDER 9, case, estate, repair, shape
5 *syn* ORDER 10, fettle, fitness, kilter, repair, shape, trim
6 *syn* DISEASE 1, affection, ailment, complaint, disorder, ill, infirmity, malady, sickness, syndrome

conditional *adj* **1** containing or dependent on a condition <our agreement is *conditional* on your raising the needed funds>
syn provisional, provisionary, provisory, tentative
rel iffy, obscure, uncertain; limited, modified, qualified, restricted
con fixed, set, sure
ant unconditional
2 *syn* DEPENDENT 1, contingent, relative, reliant
rel provisional, tentative; problematic, questionable; fortuitous, incidental
ant unconditional

condonable *adj syn* JUSTIFIABLE, defensible, excusable, tenable, vindicable, warrantable
rel acceptable, tolerable

condone *vb syn* EXCUSE 1, forgive, pardon, remit
rel disregard, forget, ignore, overlook
con deplore, deprecate, disapprove; impugn, reproach

conduce *vb syn* CONTRIBUTE 2, redound, tend

conduct *n* **1** *syn* OVERSIGHT 1, care, charge, handling, intendance, management, running, superintendence, superintendency, supervision
2 *syn* BEHAVIOR, comportment, deportment, tenue
rel bearing, demeanor, mien, posture, stance

conduct *vb* **1** *syn* GUIDE, direct, escort, lead, pilot, route, see, shepherd, show, steer
2 *syn* ACCOMPANY, attend, bear, ‖bring, ‖carry, chaperon, companion, company, convoy, escort
rel convey, transmit
3 to have the direction of and responsibility for <he had *conducted* a small market for many years>
syn carry on, direct, keep, manage, operate, ordain, run
rel administer, handle, head, oversee, supervise; arrange, control, keep up, order, regulate, rule; engineer, lead, pilot, steer
4 to act as a conduit for <shady transactions that *conducted* profits away from the stockholders>
syn carry, channel, convey, funnel, pipe, siphon, traject, transmit
rel remove, separate, take away, withdraw
5 *syn* BEHAVE 1, acquit, act, bear, carry, comport, demean, deport, go on, quit

conduit *n* **1** *syn* CHANNEL 1, aqueduct, canal, course, duct, watercourse
2 *syn* PIPELINE, channel

confab *vb syn* CONFER 2, advise, collogue, confabulate, consult, huddle, parley, powwow, treat

confabulate *vb syn* CONFER 2, advise collogue, confab, consult, huddle, parley, powwow, treat

confabulation *n* **1** *syn* CONVERSATION 1, chat, colloquy, converse, dialogue, parley
2 *syn* CONVERSATION 2, colloquy, dialogue, talk
3 *syn* CONFERENCE 1, deliberation, discussion, rap, ventilation

confederacy *n syn* ALLIANCE 2, anschluss, coalition, confederation, federation, league, union

confederate *n* one associated with another or others in a wrong or unlawful act <conspiring with his *confederates* to overthrow the government>
syn abettor, accessory, accomplice, coconspirator, conspirator
rel collaborator, fellow traveler; associate, colleague, fellow, partner

---

syn synonym(s) *rel* related word(s)
idiom idiomatic equivalent(s) *con* contrasted word(s)
ant antonym(s) * vulgar
‖ use limited; if in doubt, see a dictionary
The first word in a synonym list when printed in SMALL CAPITALS shows where there is more information about the group. For a more efficient use of this book see Explanatory Notes.

confederation *n* ***syn*** ALLIANCE 2, anschluss, coalition, confederacy, federation, league, union

confer *vb* **1** ***syn*** GIVE 2, accord, award, grant
rel allot, provide; vouchsafe
2 to carry on a conversation or discussion usually directed toward reaching a decision or settlement <the President *conferred* with his cabinet about the scandal>
syn advise, collogue, confab, confabulate, consult, huddle, parley, powwow, treat
rel bargain, chaffer, deal, negotiate; argue, debate, discuss; converse, speak, talk
idiom put one's head together with

conference *n* **1** an interchanging of views <took several hours of *conference* to find a solution to the problem>
syn confabulation, deliberation, discussion, rap, ventilation
2 a meeting for the purpose of serious discussion and interchange of views <the association held a *conference* on the problems of aging>
syn colloquium, colloquy, palaver, rap session, seminar
rel round robin, round table
3 ***syn*** TALK 4, meeting, parley, powwow
4 ***syn*** LEAGUE 4, association, circuit, loop, wheel

conferrer *n* ***syn*** DONOR, bestower, donator, giver, presenter

confess *vb* ***syn*** ACKNOWLEDGE 1, admit, allow, avow, concede, fess (up), grant, let on, own, own up
idiom make a clean breast, open one's heart

confessions *n pl* ***syn*** BIOGRAPHY, autobiography, bio, life, memoir

confidant *n* ***syn*** FRIEND, acquaintance, amigo, cater-cousin, familiar, intimate, mate

confide *vb* **1** to tell confidentially <shyly *confided* her secret>
syn breathe, whisper
rel hint, insinuate, intimate, suggest
con advertise, broadcast, proclaim, publish
2 ***syn*** COMMIT 1, commend, consign, entrust, hand over, relegate, turn over
rel bestow, present

confidence *n* **1** ***syn*** TRUST 1, dependence, faith, hope, reliance, stock
con distrust, mistrust; despair, hopelessness
ant doubt; apprehension
2 a feeling or showing of adequacy and reliance on oneself and one's powers <had serene *confidence* in his own ability to win through>
syn aplomb, assurance, self-assurance, self-assuredness, self-confidence, self-trust; *compare* EQUANIMITY
rel courage, mettle, resolution, spirit, tenacity; brashness, impudence, presumption
con apprehension, incertitude, misgiving, self-depreciation, self-doubt, uncertitude
ant diffidence
3 ***syn*** CERTAINTY, assurance, assuredness, certitude, conviction, sureness, surety
4 ***syn*** EFFRONTERY, brashness, brass, cheek, ‖crust, face, gall, nerve, presumption

confidence man *n* ***syn*** SWINDLER, bunco steerer, con man, defrauder, diddler, ‖grifter, gyp, sharper, sharpie, trickster

confident *adj* **1** marked by a strong, fearless, and bold belief in oneself and one's capacities <faced his accusers with a *confident* air>
syn assured, sanguine, secure, self-assured, self-confident, undoubtful
rel certain, cocksure, cocky, perky, positive, sure; self-possessed, self-reliant; bold, brave, courageous, dauntless, fearless, intrepid, unafraid, undaunted, valiant
con jittery, nervous, uneasy; afraid, daunted, fearful; doubtful, dubious
ant apprehensive
2 ***syn*** SURE 5, certain, cocksure, positive
3 ***syn*** PRESUMPTUOUS, brash, brassbound, overconfident, overweening, presuming, pushful, ‖pushy, self-assertive, uppity

confidential *adj* **1** ***syn*** PRIVATE 2, closet, hushed, inside
2 ***syn*** FAMILIAR 1, chummy, close, intimate, thick
rel secret; tried, trustworthy, trusty

configuration *n* ***syn*** FORM 1, cast, conformation, figure, shape

confine *vb* **1** ***syn*** LIMIT 2, bar, circumscribe, delimit, delimitate, prelimit, restrict
2 ***syn*** IMPRISON, bastille, constrain, immure, incarcerate, intern, jail, jug, ‖prison, ‖quod

confine *n, usu* **confines** *pl* **1** ***syn*** ENVIRONS 1, bound(s), boundary, compass, limit(s), precinct(s), purlieus
2 ***syn*** LIMIT 1, bound, end, limitation, term
rel circumference, compass, periphery
3 ***syn*** RANGE 2, compass, dimension(s), extent, orbit, purview, radius, reach, scope, sweep

confined *adj* ***syn*** CRAMPED, cramp, incommodious, squeezy, ‖tucked up

confinement *n* **1** ***syn*** RESTRICTION 2, circumscription, constrainment, constraint, cramp, restraint
2 the state attending and consequent to childbirth <had a long difficult *confinement*>
syn accouchement, childbed, lying-in
rel parturition; labor, travail

confirm *vb* **1** ***syn*** RATIFY
rel accede, acquiesce, assent, consent, subscribe; validate
idiom make good
con decline, refuse, reject
2 to attest to the truth, genuineness, accuracy, or validity of something <a surprise witness *confirmed* his account of the incident>
syn authenticate, bear out, corroborate, justify, substantiate, validate, verify
rel attest, certify, vouch, witness; back, support, underpin, uphold, warrant; check, check out
con confute, controvert, disprove, refute; contravene, gainsay, impugn, negative, traverse
ant deny; contradict

confirm (in) *vb* ***syn*** HABITUATE 2, addict, adjust, devote (to), take (to)

---

syn synonym(s) ***rel*** related word(s)
idiom idiomatic equivalent(s) ***con*** contrasted word(s)
ant antonym(s) * vulgar
‖ use limited; if in doubt, see a dictionary
The first word in a synonym list when printed in SMALL CAPITALS shows where there is more information about the group. For a more efficient use of this book see Explanatory Notes.

confirmation *n* ***syn*** TESTIMONY, attestation, evidence, proof, testament, testimonial, witness

confirmative *adj* ***syn*** CORROBORATIVE, adminicular, collateral, confirmatory, corroboratory, verificatory

confirmatory *adj* ***syn*** CORROBORATIVE, adminicular, collateral, confirmative, corroboratory, verificatory

confirmed *adj* **1** ***syn*** HABITUAL 2, accustomed, chronic, habituated

2 ***syn*** INVETERATE 1, bred-in-the-bone, deep-dyed, deep-rooted, deep-seated, dyed-in-the-wool, entrenched, hard-shell, settled, sworn

confiscate *vb* ***syn*** APPROPRIATE 1, accroach, annex, arrogate, commandeer, expropriate, preempt, seize, sequester, take

confiture *n* ***syn*** JAM, conserve, preserve

conflagrant *adj* ***syn*** BURNING 1, ablaze, afire, aflame, alight, blazing, fiery, flaming, flaring, ignited

conflagration *n* ***syn*** FIRE 1, holocaust, inferno

conflict *n* **1** ***syn*** CONTEST 1, competition, emulation, rivalry, strife, striving, tug-of-war, warfare

rel argument, controversy, dispute

2 ***syn*** CONTEST 2, competition, concours, meet, meeting, rencontre

3 ***syn*** DISCORD, contention, difference, disaccord, dissension, dissent, dissidence, disunity, strife, variance

conflict *vb* ***syn*** CLASH 2, disaccord, discord, disharmonize, jangle, jar, mismatch

rel differ, disagree, vary; disturb, interfere

idiom run against the tide

conflicting *adj* **1** ***syn*** ANTIPATHETIC 1, antagonistic, clashing, contrariant, contrary, discordant

2 ***syn*** INCONSONANT 1, disconsonant, discordant, discrepant, dissonant, incompatible, incongruent, incongruous, inconsistent, unmixable

confluence *n* ***syn*** CONCOURSE, concursion, gathering, junction, meeting

conform *vb* **1** ***syn*** ADAPT, accommodate, adjust, fit, quadrate, reconcile, square, suit, tailor, tailor-make

rel attune, harmonize, tune

2 ***syn*** AGREE 4, accord, correspond, dovetail, fit (in), ‖gee, go, harmonize, jibe, square

con conflict, differ, disagree

ant diverge

3 ***syn*** HARMONIZE 3, accommodate, attune, coordinate, integrate, proportion, reconcile, reconciliate, tune

4 ***syn*** OBEY, comply, follow, keep, mind, observe

idiom toe the line

conformable *adj* ***syn*** ASSORTED 2, adapted, fitted, matched, suited

rel appropriate, fitting, suitable; applicable, usable

conformation *n* ***syn*** FORM 1, cast, configuration, figure, shape

conforming *adj* ***syn*** DECOROUS 1, becoming, befitting, civilized, comme il faut, decent, done, nice, proper, seemly

conformity *n* **1** ***syn*** CONSISTENCY, coherence, congruity, correspondence

2 ***syn*** ACQUIESCENCE, compliance, resignation

confound *vb* **1** ***syn*** PUZZLE, befog, bewilder, ‖cap, confuse, metagrobolize, perplex, pose, stumble

idiom take aback

2 ***syn*** MISTAKE 1, confuse, misdeem, misidentify, mix, mix up

ant discriminate, distinguish

3 ***syn*** EMBARRASS, abash, confuse, discomfit, disconcert, discountenance, faze, rattle

4 ***syn*** DISPROVE 1, break, confute, controvert, disconfirm, evert, rebut, refute

confounded *adj* **1** ***syn*** AGHAST 2, agape, dismayed, dumbfounded, overwhelmed, shocked, thunderstruck

2 ***syn*** DAMNED 2, blamed, blasted, blessed, ‖consarned, cursed, cussed, dad-burned, execrable, infernal

3 ***syn*** UTTER, absolute, blasted, blessed, gross, out-and-out, outright, rank, straight-out, unmitigated

confoundedly *adv* ***syn*** EVER 6, consumedly, excessively, extremely, inordinately, over, overfull, overly, too, unduly

confrere *n* **1** ***syn*** COLLEAGUE, associate, compatriot, compeer

2 ***syn*** PARTNER, associate, cohort, consociate, copartner, fellow, mate, ‖pard

confront *vb* **1** to stand over against in the role of an adversary or enemy <he *confronted* his accusers with perfect aplomb>

syn affront, encounter, face, meet; *compare* MEET 6

rel beard, brave, challenge, defy; flout, scorn, scout; oppose, resist, withstand

idiom come to close quarters with, come up against

con avoid, elude, evade

2 ***syn*** ACCOST 2, face, front

confronting *prep* ***syn*** BEFORE 2, facing

confuse *vb* **1** ***syn*** EMBARRASS, abash, confound, discomfit, disconcert, discountenance, faze, rattle

2 to make unclear in mind or purpose <found the city hustle and noise very *confusing*>

syn addle, ball up, befuddle, bewilder, ‖bumfuzzle, discombobulate, distract, dizzy, fluster, fuddle, mix up, ‖mizzle, ‖momble, muddle, mull, throw off, throw out

rel misguide, mislead; agitate, bother, discompose, disquiet, flurry, perturb, upset

3 ***syn*** PUZZLE, befog, bewilder, ‖cap, confound, metagrobolize, pose, stumble

4 to make indistinct the elements or true character of (as a discussion) <*confuse* an issue in a debate>

syn becloud, befog, blur, cloud, fog, muddy

rel complicate, confound, involve, mix up

idiom lose in a fog

con clarify, elucidate; simplify

5 to throw into disorder <surging waves *confused* the waters> <her accounts were totally *confused*>

syn foul up, jumble, mix up, muddle, ‖snafu, snarl up, tumble; *compare* DISORDER 1

rel derange, disarrange, disorder, disorganize, disturb, mess (up), unsettle

idiom put in a flutter, throw into confusion

6 ***syn*** MISREPRESENT, color, distort, garble, miscolor, pervert, twist, warp, wrench, wrest

---

syn synonym(s) — *rel* related word(s)
idiom idiomatic equivalent(s) — *con* contrasted word(s)
ant antonym(s) — * vulgar
‖ use limited; if in doubt, see a dictionary
The first word in a synonym list when printed in SMALL CAPITALS shows where there is more information about the group. For a more efficient use of this book see Explanatory Notes.

7 ***syn*** MISTAKE 1, confound, misdeem, misidentify, mix, mix up
ant differentiate

confusion *n* **1** ***syn*** RUIN 3, destruction, devastation, havoc, loss, ruination
2 ***syn*** EMBARRASSMENT, abashment, discomfiture, discomposure, disconcertion, disconcertment, unease, uneasiness
3 a condition in which things are out of their normal or proper places or relationships <the room was in complete *confusion*>
syn ataxia, ‖ballup, chaos, clutter, disarray, disorder, huddle, misorder, muddle, ‖mullock, pell-mell, snarl, topsy-turviness
rel derangement, disarrangement, disturbance; foul-up, mess, mix-up, muck, ‖mux, ‖snafu; babel, din, hullabaloo, pandemonium
con methodization, ordering, organization, systematization; method, order, system
4 ***syn*** COMMOTION 2, agitation, dither, flap, lather, pother, stew, tumult, turbulence, turmoil
rel disorder, disorganization, disturbance; discomfiture, embarrassment

confute *vb* ***syn*** DISPROVE 1, break, confound, controvert, disconfirm, evert, rebut, refute

congé *n* ***syn*** PARTING, adieu, farewell, good-bye, leave-taking

congeal *vb* **1** ***syn*** HARDEN 1, cake, concrete, dry, indurate, set, solidify
rel chill, cool, freeze
2 ***syn*** COAGULATE, clot, gel, gelate, gelatinize, jell, jellify, jelly, set

congenial *adj* **1** ***syn*** HARMONIOUS 3, amicable, amical, friendly
ant uncongenial
2 ***syn*** CONSONANT 1, agreeable, compatible, congruous, consistent, sympathetic
rel companionable, cooperative, social; affable, cordial, genial, gracious, sociable; pleasant, pleasing
ant uncongenial; antipathetic (*of persons*); abhorrent (*of tasks, responsibilities*)
3 ***syn*** PLEASANT 1, agreeable, favorable, good, grateful, gratifying, nice, pleasing, pleasurable, welcome
4 ***syn*** GRACIOUS 1, affable, cordial, genial, sociable, ‖sonsy

congenital *adj* **1** ***syn*** INNATE 1, connate, connatural, inborn, indigenous, inherited, native, natural, unacquired
2 ***syn*** INHERENT, connate, deep-seated, essential, inborn, inbred, indwelling, ingrained, innate, intrinsic

congeries *n* ***syn*** GATHERING 2, aggregation, assemblage, assembly, collection, company, congregation, group, muster, ruck

---

syn synonym(s) ***rel*** related word(s)
idiom idiomatic equivalent(s) ***con*** contrasted word(s)
ant antonym(s) * vulgar
‖ use limited; if in doubt, see a dictionary
The first word in a synonym list when printed in SMALL CAPITALS shows where there is more information about the group. For a more efficient use of this book see Explanatory Notes.

congest *vb* ***syn*** FILL 1, block, choke, clog, close, obstruct, occlude, plug, stop, stopper

conglobate *vb* ***syn*** BALL, conglobe, ensphere, round, sphere

conglobe *vb* ***syn*** BALL, conglobate, ensphere, round, sphere

conglomerate *adj* ***syn*** MISCELLANEOUS, assorted, chowchow, heterogeneous, indiscriminate, mixed, motley, multifarious, promiscuous, varied

conglomerate *n* **1** ***syn*** AGGREGATE 1, agglomerate, agglomeration, aggregation, conglomeration
2 ***syn*** SYNDICATE, cartel, chain, combine, group, pool, trust

conglomeration *n* **1** ***syn*** ACCUMULATION, agglomeration, aggregation, amassment, collection, colluvies, cumulation, hoard, trove
2 ***syn*** AGGREGATE 1, agglomerate, agglomeration, aggregation, conglomerate

congratulate *vb* to express to another one's pleasure in his good fortune or success <*congratulate* a friend when he wins a race>
syn felicitate
rel applaud, laud, praise; bless, compliment
idiom pat one on the back, tender (*or* offer) congratulation, wish one joy, wish one well
con belittle, depreciate, disparage, knock, run down, slur

congregate *vb* ***syn*** GATHER 6, assemble, collect, congress, forgather, muster, raise, rendezvous
rel swarm, teem
ant disperse

congregation *n* ***syn*** GATHERING 2, aggregation, assemblage, assembly, collection, company, crowd, group, muster, ruck
rel audience, disciples, following, public

congress *n* ***syn*** ASSOCIATION 2, brotherhood, club, fellowship, fraternity, guild, league, order, society, union

congress *vb* ***syn*** GATHER 6, assemble, collect, congregate, forgather, muster, raise, rendezvous

congruity *n* ***syn*** CONSISTENCY, coherence, conformity, correspondence

congruous *adj* **1** ***syn*** CONSONANT 1, agreeable, compatible, congenial, consistent, sympathetic
rel appropriate, fit, fitting, meet; proper, seemly
ant incongruous
2 ***syn*** HARMONIOUS 2, accordant, concordant

conjectural *adj* ***syn*** SUPPOSED 1, hypothetical, putative, reputed, suppositional, suppositious, supposititious, suppositive, suppository
con demonstrated; unquestionable

conjecture *n* ***syn*** THEORY 2, perhaps, speculation, suppose, supposition
ant fact

conjecture *vb* to draw an inference from slight or inadequate evidence <when he failed to arrive on time she *conjectured* that he was drinking again>
syn guess, presume, pretend, suppose, surmise, think; *compare* INFER, UNDERSTAND 3
rel assume, expect, suspect; believe, deem, feel; conceive, fancy, imagine; conclude, estimate, gather, glean, infer, judge
idiom hazard a conjecture, take for granted
con demonstrate, prove, test, try; ascertain, determine, discover, learn

conjoin *vb* **1** ***syn*** JOIN 1, associate, combine, connect, couple, link, relate, unite, wed, yoke
2 ***syn*** UNITE 2, band, coadjute, combine, concur, cooperate, league

conjoint *adj* **1** ***syn*** COMMON 1, communal, conjunct, intermutual, joint, mutual, public, shared
2 ***syn*** COOPERATIVE, coacting, coactive, coefficient, synergetic, synergic

conjointly *adv* ***syn*** TOGETHER 3, jointly, mutually

conjointment *n* ***syn*** ASSOCIATION 1, affiliation, alliance, cahoots, combination, conjunction, connection, hookup, partnership, tie-up

conjugal *adj* ***syn*** MATRIMONIAL, connubial, hymeneal, marital, married, nuptial, spousal, wedded

conjugality *n* ***syn*** MARRIAGE 1, connubiality, matrimony, wedlock

conjugate *vb* ***syn*** JOIN 1, associate, bracket, coalesce, combine, conjoin, connect, couple, link, yoke

conjunct *adj* ***syn*** COMMON 1, communal, conjoint, intermutual, joint, mutual, public, shared

conjunction *n* ***syn*** ASSOCIATION 1, affiliation, alliance, cahoots, combination, conjointment, connection, hookup, partnership, tie-up

conjuration *n* ***syn*** SPELL, charm, ||devil-devil, incantation, rune

conjure *vb* ***syn*** BEG, appeal, beseech, brace, crave, entreat, implore, importune, pray, supplicate

conjurer *n* **1** ***syn*** MAGICIAN 1, enchanter, mage, magian, magus, necromancer, sorcerer, voodooist, warlock, wizard
2 ***syn*** MAGICIAN 2, illusionist, trickster

conjuring *n* **1** ***syn*** MAGIC 1, bewitchment, conjury, enchantment, necromancy, sorcery, thaumaturgy, witchcraft, witchery, wizardry
2 ***syn*** MAGIC 2, legerdemain

conjury *n* ***syn*** MAGIC 1, bewitchment, conjuring, enchantment, necromancy, sorcery, thaumaturgy, witchcraft, witchery, wizardry

||**conk** *n* **1** ***syn*** NOSE 1, beak, ||beezer, pecker, proboscis, ||schnozzle, smeller, ||snitch, snoot, snout
2 ***syn*** HEAD 1, ||belfry, ||chump, ||coco, ||dome, headpiece, noddle, noggin, noodle, poll

||**conk** *n* ***syn*** HIT 1, knock, lick, rap, swat, swipe, wipe

conk *vb* ***syn*** DIE 1, cash in, ||check out, ||croak, decease, ||kick in, ||kick off, pass, pass away, pop off

con man *n* ***syn*** SWINDLER, bunco steerer, confidence man, defrauder, diddler, ||grifter, gyp, sharper, sharpie, trickster
rel shill
con mark, sucker, victim; greenhorn

connate *adj* **1** ***syn*** INNATE 1, congenital, connatural, inborn, indigenous, inherited, native, natural, unacquired
2 ***syn*** INHERENT, congenital, constitutional, deep-seated, elemental, essential, inborn, indwelling, innate, intrinsic
3 ***syn*** RELATED, affiliated, agnate, akin, allied, cognate, connatural, consanguine, incident, kindred

connatural *adj* **1** ***syn*** INNATE 1, congenital, connate, inborn, indigenous, inherited, native, natural, unacquired
2 ***syn*** RELATED, affiliated, agnate, akin, allied, cognate, connate, consanguine, incident, kindred

connect *vb* ***syn*** JOIN 1, associate, combine, conjoin, couple, link, relate, unite, wed, yoke
ant disconnect

connection *n* **1** ***syn*** ASSOCIATION 1, affiliation, alliance, combination, conjointment, conjunction, hookup, partnership, tie-up, togetherness
2 ***syn*** JOINT 1, coupling, joining, junction, juncture, seam, union
3 ***syn*** JOB 2, appointment, berth, billet, office, place, position, post, situation, spot
4 ***syn*** RELIGION 2, church, communion, creed, cult, denomination, faith, persuasion, sect

connivance *n* ***syn*** COMPLICITY, collusion

connive *vb* **1** to secretly favor or sympathize with something improper or illicit <*connive* at treason>
syn blink (at), wink (at)
rel condone, disregard, ignore, overlook, tolerate
idiom close (*or* shut) one's eyes to, let go by (*or* get by) one's eye, regard with indulgence
con disapprove, disfavor, frown (at *or* upon); disallow, reject, repudiate; disdain, scorn, scout, spurn
2 ***syn*** PLOT, cogitate, ||collogue, collude, conspire, contrive, devise, intrigue, machinate, scheme (out)

connoisseur *n* a person who enjoys with discrimination and appreciation of subtleties and details especially in matters of culture or art <a *connoisseur* of fine wines>
syn aesthete, cognoscente, dilettante
rel bon vivant, epicure, gourmet; adept, authority, critic, expert
con abecedarian, amateur, dabbler, tyro

connotation *n* ***syn*** ASSOCIATION 4, hint, implication, overtone, suggestion, undertone

connote *vb* **1** ***syn*** MEAN 2, add up (to), denote, express, import, intend, signify, spell
2 ***syn*** SUGGEST 1, hint, imply, insinuate, intimate

connubial *adj* ***syn*** MATRIMONIAL, conjugal, hymeneal, marital, married, nuptial, spousal, wedded

connubiality *n* ***syn*** MARRIAGE 1, conjugality, matrimony, wedlock

conquer *vb* **1** to overcome or gain dominion over by force of arms <leaders who have tried and failed to *conquer* the world>
syn bear down, beat down, crush, defeat, overpower, reduce, subdue, subjugate, vanquish; *compare* DEFEAT 2, OVERTHROW 2, WHIP 2, WIN 1
rel baffle, balk, circumvent, foil, frustrate, outwit, override, thwart; bend, control, master, overmaster, subject, worst
idiom bring one to one's knees, trample in the dust, trample underfoot
con bow, cave, give up, succumb, yield; capitulate, submit, surrender

---

syn synonym(s) ***rel*** related word(s)
idiom idiomatic equivalent(s) ***con*** contrasted word(s)
ant antonym(s) * vulgar
|| use limited; if in doubt, see a dictionary
The first word in a synonym list when printed in SMALL CAPITALS shows where there is more information about the group. For a more efficient use of this book see Explanatory Notes.

2 to gain mastery over something by getting the better of obstacles and difficulties <trials faced by the men who *conquered* Mount Everest>
syn best, master, overcome, prevail, triumph; *compare* OVERCOME 1
3 ***syn*** OVERCOME 1, down, hurdle, lick, master, surmount, throw

conqueror *n* ***syn*** VICTOR 1, defeater, master, subduer, subjugator, vanquisher

conquest *n* ***syn*** VICTORY 1, triumph, win
rel defeating, overthrow, rout, routing, subdual

consanguine *adj* ***syn*** RELATED, affiliated, agnate, akin, allied, cognate, connate, connatural, incident, kindred

||**consarned** *adj* **1** ***syn*** DAMNED 2, blamed, blasted, blessed, confounded, cursed, cussed, dad-burned, execrable, infernal
2 ***syn*** UTTER, absolute, blasted, blessed, gross, outright, positive, rank, tarnation, unmitigated

conscience *n* ***syn*** QUALM, compunction, demur, scruple, squeam

conscienceless *adj* ***syn*** UNSCRUPULOUS, stick-at-nothing, unconscionable, unprincipled
rel devious, shifty, tricky, unfair
ant conscientious

conscientious *adj* **1** ***syn*** UPRIGHT 2, honest, honorable, just, right, scrupulous, true
ant conscienceless
2 ***syn*** CAREFUL 2, conscionable, exact, fussy, heedful, meticulous, painstaking, punctilious, punctual, scrupulous

conscionable *adj* ***syn*** CAREFUL 2, conscientious, exact, fussy, heedful, meticulous, painstaking, punctilious, punctual, scrupulous

conscious *adj* **1** ***syn*** AWARE, alive, au courant, awake, cognizant, conversant, mindful, sensible, sentient, witting
rel noticing, noting, observing, perceiving, remarking; vigilant, watchful
con forgetful, oblivious, unmindful; disregarding, ignoring, overlooking
ant unconscious
2 ***syn*** SELF-CONSCIOUS, affected, mannered

consciousness *n* ***syn*** CARE 4, carefulness, concern, heed, heedfulness, regard

conscribe *vb* ***syn*** DRAFT 1, conscript

conscript *vb* ***syn*** DRAFT 1, conscribe

consecrate *vb* **1** ***syn*** DEVOTE 1, dedicate, hallow
con desecrate, profane; defile, pollute
2 ***syn*** BLESS 1, hallow, sanctify

consecrated *adj* ***syn*** HOLY 1, blessed, hallowed, sacred, sanctified, unprofane

consecution *n* **1** ***syn*** ORDER 5, procession, sequence, succession
2 ***syn*** SUCCESSION 2, alternation, chain, order, progression, row, sequel, sequence, series, train

consecutive *adj* following one after another in orderly fashion <it rained for five *consecutive* days>
syn sequent, sequential, serial, subsequent, subsequential, succedent, succeeding, successional, successive; *compare* NEXT
rel after, ensuing, following, later; enlarging, increasing, progressive
con antecedent, preceding, prior

consecutively *adv* ***syn*** TOGETHER 2, continually, continuously, hand running, night and day, running, successively, unintermittedly, uninterruptedly

consent *vb* ***syn*** ASSENT, accede, acquiesce, agree, subscribe, yes
rel allow, let, permit; approve, sanction; concur
con decline; balk, demur, stick, stickle

consent *n* **1** ***syn*** PERMISSION, allowance, authorization, leave, permit, sanction, sufferance
2 ***syn*** AGREEMENT 2, accord, understanding

consentaneous *adj* ***syn*** UNANIMOUS, consentient, solid

consentient *adj* ***syn*** UNANIMOUS, consentaneous, solid

consequence *n* **1** ***syn*** EFFECT 1, aftereffect, aftermath, event, issue, outcome, result, sequel, sequence, upshot
con origin, root, source
ant antecedent
2 ***syn*** IMPORTANCE, import, magnitude, moment, momentousness, pith, significance, ||signification, weight, weightiness
rel exigency, need; fame, honor, renown, reputation, repute
3 ***syn*** STATUS 2, cachet, dignity, position, prestige, rank, standing, state, stature
4 ***syn*** CONCEIT 2, amour propre, complacence, complacency, conceitedness, egoism, egotism, narcissism, pride, vainglory

consequent *adj* ***syn*** RATIONAL, intelligent, logical, reasonable, sensible, sound

consequential *adj* ***syn*** IMPORTANT 1, big, considerable, material, meaningful, momentous, significant, substantial, weighty

consequently *adv* ***syn*** THEREFORE, accordingly, ergo, hence, so, then, thereupon, thus

conservancy *n* ***syn*** CONSERVATION 1, husbanding, preserval, preservation, salvation, saving

conservation *n* **1** a deliberate planned guarding and protecting of something felt as precious <*conservation* of our natural resources>
syn conservancy, husbanding, preserval, preservation, salvation, saving
rel attention, care, cherishing, protection; control, directing, governing, management, managing, supervising, supervision
con neglect, squandering, waste
2 ***syn*** PRESERVATION 1, keeping, safekeeping, salvation, saving, sustentation

conservative *adj* **1** tending to resist or oppose change <took a very *conservative* stance politically>
syn die-hard, fogyish, old-line, orthodox, reactionary, right, tory, traditionalistic
con modern, progressive, radical
ant advanced
2 kept or keeping within bounds <equally *conservative* in speech and action>

---

syn synonym(s)	***rel*** related word(s)
idiom idiomatic equivalent(s)	***con*** contrasted word(s)
ant antonym(s)	* vulgar

|| use limited; if in doubt, see a dictionary
The first word in a synonym list when printed in SMALL CAPITALS shows where there is more information about the group. For a more efficient use of this book see Explanatory Notes.

syn controlled, discreet, moderate, reasonable, restrained, temperate, unexcessive, unextreme
rel cautious, chary, wary; circumspect, politic, proper, prudent
con expansive, unconstrained; excessive, freewheeling, uncontrolled, unrestrained

conservative *n syn* DIEHARD 1, bitter-ender, fundamentalist, old liner, right, rightist, right-winger, standpat, standpatter, tory

conservatory *n syn* GREENHOUSE, ‖glasshouse

conserve *vb syn* SAVE 3, preserve
rel keep up, maintain, support, sustain
con dissipate, fritter, squander, waste

conserve *n syn* JAM, confiture, preserve

consider *vb* **1** to give serious thought to <*consider* the risk you would be taking>
syn contemplate, excogitate, mind, perpend, ponder, study, think (out *or* over), weigh
rel meditate, muse, ruminate; cogitate, reason, reflect, speculate, think; examine, inspect, look (at), scan, scrutinize, see
idiom bestow thought to, chew the cud over, revolve (*or* turn over) in one's mind
con disregard, ignore, neglect, overlook, slight
2 *syn* EYE 1, contemplate, gaze (upon), look (at *or* upon), view
rel envisage, envision
3 to come to view, judge, or classify <he *considered* thrift essential to success>
syn account, deem, reckon, regard, view; *compare* FEEL 3
rel conceive, fancy, imagine, think; conclude, gather, infer, judge, rule
4 *syn* ADMIRE 2, esteem, regard, respect
5 *syn* FEEL 3, believe, credit, deem, hold, sense, think

considerable *adj* **1** *syn* IMPORTANT 1, big, consequential, material, meaningful, momentous, significant, substantial, weighty
2 tending more to the large than the small <buckled down with his ax and made a *considerable* impression on the woodpile>
syn good, respectable, ‖right smart, sensible, sizable, ‖smart
rel able, capable, competent; active, effective, efficacious; important, notable, significant; goodly, pretty, substantial, tidy
con insignificant, meager, slight, trivial; big, grand, great, huge
3 *syn* BIG 1, extensive, hefty, large, large-scale, major, sizable

considerably *adv syn* WELL 8, far, quite, rather, significantly, somewhat

considerate *adj* **1** *syn* CAUTIOUS, calculating, careful, chary, circumspect, discreet, gingerly, guarded, safe, wary
2 *syn* THOUGHTFUL 3, attentive
rel kind, kindly; compassionate, sympathetic, tender, warmhearted; amiable, complaisant, obliging
ant inconsiderate
3 *syn* GENEROUS 1, benevolent, big, chivalrous, greathearted, lofty, magnanimous

considerately *adv syn* WELL 2, generously, heedfully, kindly, thoughtfully
rel solicitously, tenderly; altruistically, benevolently, charitably
con austerely, harshly, severely, strictly

considerateness *n syn* CONSIDERATION 3, concern, regard, solicitude

consideration *n* **1** *syn* ATTENTION 1, application, concentration, debate, deliberation, heed, study
2 *syn* MOTIVE 1, cause, reason, spring
3 thoughtful and sympathetic attention <showed great *consideration* to the needs of others>
syn concern, considerateness, regard, solicitude
rel awareness, heed, heedfulness, mindfulness; forbearance, mercy, quarter
con disregard, heedlessness, unconcern, unmindfulness; inconsiderateness; contempt, despite, disdain, disinterest, scorn
4 *syn* REGARD 4, account, admiration, esteem, estimation, favor, respect

considered *adj syn* DELIBERATE 1, advised, aforethought, designed, premeditated, prepense, studied, studious, thought-out
rel intentional, voluntary, willful
con impulsive, instinctive, spontaneous; headlong, impetuous, precipitate
ant unconsidered

considering *conj syn* BECAUSE, as, as long as, ‖being, 'cause, for, inasmuch as, now, seeing, since

consign *vb* **1** *syn* COMMIT 1, commend, confide, entrust, hand over, relegate, turn over
rel resign, surrender, yield
2 *syn* SEND 1, address, dispatch, forward, remit, route, ship, transmit

consist *vb* **1** to have existence or a place <our national strength *consists* not solely in military readiness>
syn dwell, exist, inhere, lie, reside
rel be, subsist; abide, repose, rest
idiom have one's (*or* a) place
2 *syn* AGREE 4, accord, comport, conform, consort, correspond, dovetail, fit (in), ‖gee, go

consistency *n* agreement or harmony of parts, traits, or features <his adversary had to admit the *consistency* of his position>
syn coherence, conformity, congruity, correspondence; *compare* HARMONY 2
rel agreement, concord, consonance; likeness, similarity; apposition, aptness, felicity, fitness, suitability
con incoherence, incongruity; impropriety, inappropriateness, unsuitability
ant inconsistency

consistent *adj* **1** *syn* SAME 3, constant, invariable, unchanging, unfailing, unvarying
2 *syn* CONSONANT 1, agreeable, compatible, congenial, congruous, sympathetic

---

syn synonym(s)　*rel* related word(s)
idiom idiomatic equivalent(s)　*con* contrasted word(s)
ant antonym(s)　* vulgar
‖ use limited; if in doubt, see a dictionary
The first word in a synonym list when printed in SMALL CAPITALS shows where there is more information about the group. For a more efficient use of this book see Explanatory Notes.

consistently *adv* ***syn*** USUALLY 1, as usual, customarily, habitually, wontedly

consociate *n* ***syn*** PARTNER, associate, cohort, confrere, copartner, fellow, mate, ‖pard

console *vb* ***syn*** COMFORT, buck up, cheer, solace, upraise
rel calm, relieve, tranquilize; animate, hearten, inspirit
idiom lift the spirits of
con agitate, discompose, disquiet, disturb, perturb, upset

consolidate *vb* ***syn*** UNIFY 1, compact, concentrate, integrate
rel amalgamate, blend, fuse, merge; set, solidify
con part, sever, sunder; liquefy, melt

consolidating *adj* ***syn*** INTEGRATIVE, centralizing, centripetal, compacting, concentrating, unifying

consolidation *n* **1** ***syn*** UNIFICATION, coadunation, coalition, combination, melding, mergence, merger, merging, union
2 a union of two or more businesses <*consolidation* is often accompanied by a new corporate name>
syn amalgamation, merger
ant dissolution

consonance *n* **1** ***syn*** HARMONY 2, accord, agreement, chime, concord, concordance, tune
con discrepancy, incompatibility, incongruousness
ant discord
2 ***syn*** HARMONY 1, accord, chorus, concert, concord, tune
ant dissonance

consonant *adj* **1** conforming (as to a pattern, a standard, or a relationship) without discord or difficulty <his performance was seldom *consonant* with his very real abilities>
syn agreeable, compatible, congenial, congruous, consistent, sympathetic; *compare* HARMONIOUS 2
rel accordant, conformable, harmonious; coincident, concurrent; en rapport
con discordant, discrepant; incompatible, incongruous, inconsistent
ant inconsonant
2 ***syn*** HARMONIOUS 1, blending, chiming, harmonic, musical, symphonic, symphonious
ant dissonant
3 ***syn*** LIKE, agnate, akin, alike, analogous, comparable, corresponding, parallel, similar, uniform
4 ***syn*** RESONANT, orotund, plangent, resounding, ringing, rotund, round, sonorant, sonorous, vibrant

consort *n* **1** ***syn*** ACCOMPANIMENT 2, associate, companion, concomitant, fellow, mate
2 ***syn*** SPOUSE, mate

consort *vb* ***syn*** AGREE 4, accord, comport, conform, correspond, dovetail, harmonize, march, square, tally

---

syn synonym(s) ***rel*** related word(s)
idiom idiomatic equivalent(s) ***con*** contrasted word(s)
ant antonym(s) * vulgar
‖ use limited; if in doubt, see a dictionary
The first word in a synonym list when printed in SMALL CAPITALS shows where there is more information about the group. For a more efficient use of this book see Explanatory Notes.

consort (with) *vb* ***syn*** ACCOMPANY, attend, bear, ‖bring, ‖carry, chaperon, companion, company, conduct, convoy

consortium *n* ***syn*** ASSOCIATION 2, club, congress, fellowship, fraternity, guild, league, order, society, union

conspectus *n* ***syn*** ABRIDGMENT, abstract, boildown, breviary, breviate, brief, condensation, epitome, synopsis

conspicuous *adj* **1** ***syn*** CLEAR 5, apparent, distinct, evident, manifest, obvious, open-and-shut, openhanded, patent, plain
2 ***syn*** NOTICEABLE, arresting, arrestive, marked, outstanding, pointed, prominent, remarkable, salient, striking
rel celebrated, eminent, illustrious; showy
con common, everyday, ordinary; covert, secret; concealed, hidden
ant inconspicuous

conspiracy *n* ***syn*** PLOT 2, cabal, covin, intrigue, machination, practice, scheme
rel sedition, treason; disloyalty, faithlessness, falsity, perfidiousness, perfidy, treacherousness, treachery
con faith, faithfulness, fealty, loyalty

conspirator *n* ***syn*** CONFEDERATE, abettor, accessory, accomplice, coconspirator

conspire *vb* ***syn*** PLOT, cogitate, ‖cologue, collude, connive, contrive, devise, intrigue, machinate, scheme (out)

‖**constable** *n* ***syn*** POLICEMAN, ‖bobby, ‖bull, ‖copper, ‖gendarme, John Law, officer, ‖paddy, ‖peeler, ‖police constable

constancy *n* ***syn*** ATTACHMENT 1, adherence, adhesion, faithfulness, fidelity, loyalty

constant *adj* **1** ***syn*** FAITHFUL 1, allegiant, ardent, ‖dinky-di, fast, liege, loyal, staunch, steadfast, true
rel abiding, clinging, enduring, lasting, persistent, persisting
con capricious, mercurial
ant fickle, inconstant
2 ***syn*** INFLEXIBLE 3, fixed, immovable, immutable, inalterable, invariable, unalterable, unchangeable, unmodifiable, unmovable
con fluctuant, fluctuating, fluctuational, unstable
ant inconstant, variable
3 ***syn*** SAME 3, consistent, invariable, unchanging, unfailing, unvarying
4 ***syn*** STEADY 2, equable, even, stabile, stable, unchanging, unfluctuating, uniform, unvarying
5 ***syn*** CONTINUAL, ceaseless, continuous, endless, everlasting, interminable, perpetual, unceasing, unending, unremitting
rel chronic, confirmed, inveterate; dogged, obstinate, pertinacious; persevering
con alternate, intermittent, recurrent; infrequent, occasional, sporadic
ant fitful

constantly *adv* ***syn*** ALWAYS 1, continuously, ever, invariably, perpetually
idiom day after day; day in, day out
ant occasionally

constate *vb* ***syn*** ASSERT 1, affirm, aver, avouch, avow, declare, depose, predicate, profess, protest

consternate *vb* ***syn*** DISMAY 1, appall, daunt, horrify, shake

consternation *n* ***syn*** FEAR 1, alarm, dismay, dread, fright, horror, panic, terror, trepidation, trepidity
rel confusion, muddle, muddlement; bewilderment, distraction, perplexity
con composure, equanimity, phlegm, sangfroid; aplomb, poise, self-command, self-possession

constipate *vb* ***syn*** STULTIFY, stagnate, stifle, trammel

constipated *adj* being unable to defecate regularly and without difficulty <complained that she was constantly *constipated*>
syn astricted, bound, costive, obstipated

constituent *n* ***syn*** ELEMENT 2, component, factor, ingredient
rel division, fraction, part, portion
con complex, economy, organism, system; amalgam, blend, composite, compound
ant aggregate, whole

constitute *vb* **1** to be all or a fundamental part of the substance of <water *constitutes* the greater part of the human body>
syn compose, comprise, form, make, make up
rel embody, incorporate, integrate; complement, complete, fill out, flesh (out)
2 ***syn*** ENACT 1, establish, make
3 ***syn*** FOUND 2, create, establish, institute, organize, set up, start

constitution *n* **1** ***syn*** PHYSIQUE, build, habit, habitus
2 ***syn*** MAKEUP 1, architecture, composition, construction, design, formation

constitutional *adj* ***syn*** INHERENT, built-in, congenital, deep-seated, essential, inborn, inbred, ingrained, innate, intrinsic
con anomalous, irregular, unnatural
ant advenient

constitutional *n* ***syn*** WALK 1, ramble, saunter, stroll, turn
rel ambulation, footwork, legwork, perambulation

constitutive *adj* ***syn*** ESSENTIAL 2, cardinal, fundamental, vital

constrain *vb* **1** ***syn*** FORCE 2, coerce, compel, concuss, make, oblige, shotgun
2 ***syn*** RESTRAIN 1, bit, bridle, check, curb, hold back, hold down, hold in, inhibit, withhold
3 ***syn*** DENY 3, abstain, curb, hold back, refrain
rel abridge, curtail, deprive; ban, bar, disallow, enjoin
4 ***syn*** IMPRISON, bastille, confine, immure, incarcerate, intern, jail, jug, ||prison, ||quod
5 ***syn*** PRESS 1, bear, crowd, crush, jam, push, ||squab, squash, squeeze, squish
6 ***syn*** DISTRESS 2, aggrieve, grieve, hurt, injure, pain

constrained *adj* ***syn*** RESERVED 1, incommunicable, noncommittal, restrained

constrainment *n* ***syn*** RESTRICTION 2, circumscription, confinement, constraint, cramp, restraint

constraint *n* **1** ***syn*** FORCE 4, coercion, compulsion, duress, violence
rel repression, suppression; driving, impelling, impulsion; goad, motive, spring, spur
2 ***syn*** RESTRICTION 2, circumscription, confinement, constrainment, cramp, restraint

constrict *vb* **1** ***syn*** CONTRACT 3, compress, concentrate, condense, shrink
rel curb, restrain; circumscribe, confine, limit, restrict
con enlarge, expand, increase, maximize
2 to make narrow or narrower <the muscles that *constrict* the sphincter>
syn constringe, narrow
rel gather, plait, pucker; compress, constrain, squeeze; astringe
con broaden, dilate, distend, widen
ant expand

constringe *vb* ***syn*** CONSTRICT 2, narrow

construal *n* ***syn*** EXPLANATION 1, construction, exegesis, explication, exposé, exposition, interpretation

construct *vb* **1** ***syn*** MAKE 3, assemble, build, fabricate, fashion, forge, form, frame, produce, put together
2 ***syn*** BUILD 1, erect, put up, raise, rear, uprear
3 ***syn*** ERECT 5, build up, establish, hammer (out), set up

construction *n* **1** ***syn*** MAKEUP 1, architecture, composition, constitution, design, formation
2 ***syn*** EXPLANATION 1, construal, exegesis, explication, exposé, exposition, interpretation

constructive *adj* ***syn*** IMPLICIT 2, practical, virtual
rel inferential, ratiocinative; construable, interpretable, renderable
con clear, evident, obvious, patent
ant manifest

construe *vb* ***syn*** EXPLAIN 1, explicate, expound, interpret, spell out

consuetude *n* ***syn*** HABIT 1, custom, habitude, manner, practice, praxis, trick, usage, use, wont

consult *vb* ***syn*** CONFER 2, advise, collogue, confab, confabulate, huddle, parley, powwow, treat
rel cogitate, counsel, deliberate; consider, examine, review

consume *vb* **1** to bring to an end by or as if by the action of a destroying force <the village was *consumed* by fire>
syn devour, eat, eat up, exhaust, use up
rel destroy, raze, ruin, wreck; annihilate, extinguish; crush, overwhelm, suppress
con bolster, brace, buttress, hold up, prop, stay, support, sustain; build, construct, create, make, produce; renew, restore
2 ***syn*** WASTE 2, blow, cast away, dissipate, drivel, fritter, frivol away, squander, throw away, trifle (away)
3 ***syn*** GO 4, exhaust, expend, finish, run through, spend, use up, wash up
4 ***syn*** EAT 1, devour, feed (on), ingest, meal, partake (of), take
5 to eat or drink usually gluttonously or without measure <*consumed* dozens of burgers and a case of beer>
syn polish off, punish, put away, put down, shift, swill; *compare* EAT 1

---

syn synonym(s) — ***rel*** related word(s)
idiom idiomatic equivalent(s) — ***con*** contrasted word(s)
ant antonym(s) — * vulgar
|| use limited; if in doubt, see a dictionary
The first word in a synonym list when printed in SMALL CAPITALS shows where there is more information about the group. For a more efficient use of this book see Explanatory Notes.

rel absorb, ingest; devour, gobble (up), gorge, wolf; down, gulp, guzzle, inhale, swallow
idiom dispose of
6 ***syn*** MONOPOLIZE, absorb, engross, sew up

consumedly *adv* ***syn*** EVER 6, confoundedly, excessively, extremely, immensely, inordinately, over, overly, super, too

consuming *adj* ***syn*** ENGROSSING, absorbing, monopolizing

consummate *adj* **1** brought to the highest possible point of perfection <the difficult allegro passages displayed her *consummate* skill>
syn accomplished, finished, perfected, ripe, virtuosic; *compare* PERFECT 2
rel faultless, flawless, impeccable, perfect; practiced, skilled, trained; able, gifted, talented; inimitable, peerless, superb, superlative, supreme, transcendent, unsurpassable
con callow, crude, green, raw, rough, uncouth; defective, deficient, inadequate
2 ***syn*** UTTER, absolute, complete, downright, out-and-out, outright, perfect, positive, thoroughgoing, unmitigated

consummate *vb* ***syn*** CLOSE 3, complete, conclude, end, finish, halt, terminate, ultimate, wind up, wrap up

consumption *n* ***syn*** TUBERCULOSIS, phthisis, TB, white plague

contact *n* **1** the state of being in or coming into close association or connection <shuddered at the *contact* of his icy hand>
syn contingence, touch
rel closeness, contiguity, nearness, propinquity, proximity; impingement, taction, touching; association, connection, relation; oneness, union, unity
con breach, break, rift, rupture, split; insularity, isolation, seclusion, segregation, separation; distance, farness, remoteness
2 a situation permitting exchange of ideas and opinions <tried for several days to get in *contact* with her brother>
syn commerce, communication, communion, intercommunication, intercourse
rel association, companionship, fellowship; oneness, union, unity; accord, concord, harmony, rapport; empathy, sympathy, understanding

contact *vb* ***syn*** REACH 4, get

contagion *n* ***syn*** POISON, bane, venom, virus
rel contamination, corruption, pollution, taint; miasma

contagious *adj* **1** ***syn*** INFECTIOUS 2, catching, communicable
2 ***syn*** INFECTIOUS 3, catching, taking

contain *vb* **1** ***syn*** COMPOSE 4, collect, control, cool, re-collect, rein, repress, restrain, simmer down, smother
2 to have or be capable of having within <the box *contained* family papers> <a mug that will *contain* a quart of ale>
syn accommodate, hold
rel harbor, house, lodge, shelter; admit, receive, take, take in
3 ***syn*** INCLUDE, comprehend, embody, embrace, encompass, have, involve, subsume, take in

contaminate *vb* **1** to debase by making impure or unclean <feared her child's morals would be *contaminated* by others>
syn defile, pollute, soil, taint; *compare* TAINT 1
rel corrupt, debase, debauch, deprave, pervert, vitiate; harm, injure, spoil
con better, elevate, improve
ant purify
2 to render unfit for use by the introduction of unwholesome or undesirable elements <water *contaminated* by sewage>
syn befoul, foul, pollute
rel infect; poison; dirty, soil
ant purify

contemn *vb* ***syn*** DESPISE, abhor, disdain, look down, scorn, scout

contemplate *vb* **1** ***syn*** EYE 1, consider, gaze (upon), look (at *or* upon), view
rel ponder, reflect, study; examine, inspect, scan, scrutinize
2 ***syn*** CONSIDER 1, excogitate, mind, perpend, ponder, study, think (out *or* over), weigh
rel drift, roam
3 ***syn*** INTEND 2, aim, design, mean, ‖mind, plan, propose, purpose
idiom have in view

contemplative *adj* ***syn*** THOUGHTFUL 1, cogitative, meditative, pensive, pondering, reflecting, reflective, ruminative, speculative, thinking
rel musing, weighing; reasoning
idiom in a brown study

contemporaneous *adj* ***syn*** CONTEMPORARY 1, coetaneous, coeval, coexistent, coexisting, concurrent, simultaneous, synchronal, synchronic, synchronous

contemporary *adj* **1** existing or occurring at the same time <the story has come down from several *contemporary* sources>
syn coetaneous, coeval, coexistent, coexisting, concurrent, contemporaneous, simultaneous, synchronal, synchronic, synchronous
rel accompanying, attendant, attending, coincident, concomitant; current, existing, present; associated, connected, linked, related
con antecedent, foregoing, preceding, previous, prior; ensuing, following, succeeding
2 ***syn*** PRESENT, current, existent, extant, instant, present-day, todayish
3 ***syn*** UP-TO-DATE, abreast, au courant, down-to-date, red-hot, up, up-to-the-minute

contempt *n* **1** ***syn*** DESPITE 1, despisal, despisement, disdain, disparagement, scorn
rel antipathy, aversion; distaste, repugnance
con awe, fear, reverence
ant regard

---

syn synonym(s) | *rel* related word(s)
idiom idiomatic equivalent(s) | *con* contrasted word(s)
ant antonym(s) | * vulgar
‖ use limited; if in doubt, see a dictionary
The first word in a synonym list when printed in SMALL CAPITALS shows where there is more information about the group. For a more efficient use of this book see Explanatory Notes.

2 ***syn*** DISGRACE, discredit, disesteem, disfavor, dishonor, disrepute, ignominy, infamy, opprobrium, shame
3 ***syn*** DEFIANCE 2, contumacy, despite, recalcitrance, stubbornness

contemptible *adj* arousing or meriting scorn or disdain <a *contemptible* attempt to blame his wife for his failure>
syn beggarly, cheap, despicable, despisable, mean, pitiable, pitiful, scummy, scurvy, shabby, sorry; *compare* BASE 3
rel abhorrent, abominable, detestable, hateful, odious; abject, ignoble, sordid; bad, inferior, poor, sad; disgusting, scrimy, shameful; outcast
con creditable, estimable, honorable, noble; high-minded, high-principled, principled, true, upright; honest, square, straight
ant admirable

contend *vb* **1** to strive in opposition to someone or something <*contending* against the temptation to look behind him>
syn battle, fight, oppugn, tug, war
rel combat, oppose, resist, withstand; contest, cope (with), vie
2 ***syn*** MAINTAIN 2, argue, assert, claim, defend, justify, vindicate, warrant
rel report, say, tell; charge, enjoin, urge; dictate, prescribe
3 ***syn*** COMPETE 1, contest, rival, vie
rel combat, oppose, resist, withstand; confront, encounter, face, meet, stand

content *vb* ***syn*** SATISFY 3, appease, gratify
rel delight, thrill, tickle; bewitch, captivate, charm, enrapture
con disappoint, dishearten, displease
ant discontent

contention *n* **1** ***syn*** DISCORD, conflict, difference, disaccord, dissension, dissent, dissidence, disunity, strife, variance
rel altercation, quarrel, squabble, wrangle; argument, controversy, dispute
con agreement, coincidence, concurrence
2 ***syn*** ARGUMENT 2, controversy, dispute, hurrah, rumpus
3 ***syn*** THESIS 1, contestation

contentious *adj* **1** ***syn*** BELLIGERENT, bellicose, combative, gladiatorial, militant, pugnacious, quarrelsome, ‖ructious, truculent, warlike
rel contrary, froward, perverse; captious, carping, caviling, faultfinding
con calm, serene, tranquil; amiable, complaisant, good-natured, obliging
ant peaceable
2 prone to wordy contention <a *contentious* old chap, always ready for an argument>
syn argumentative, controversial, disputatious, litigious, polemical
rel fiery, hasty, hotheaded, impetuous, peppery; belligerent, bellicose, scrappy
con amiable, complaisant, good-natured, obliging; agreeable, cooperative, understanding

conterminous *adj* ***syn*** ADJACENT 3, abutting, adjoining, approximal, bordering, contiguous, juxtaposed, touching

contest *vb* **1** ***syn*** COMPETE 1, contend, rival, vie
rel endeavor
2 ***syn*** RESIST, buck, combat, dispute, duel, fight, oppose, repel, traverse, withstand

contest *n* **1** earnest struggle for superiority or victory <the rival factions continued in *contest* for several years>
syn competition, conflict, emulation, rivalry, strife, striving, tug-of-war, warfare
rel brush, encounter, skirmish; action, battle, engagement
2 a competitive encounter between groups or individuals <there were *contests* of skill and of wit>
syn competition, concours, conflict, meet, meeting, rencontre
rel proving, testing, trial, trying

contestation *n* ***syn*** THESIS 1, contention

contiguity *n* ***syn*** PROXIMITY, appropinquity, contiguousness, immediacy, propinquity

contiguous *adj* **1** ***syn*** ADJACENT 3, abutting, adjoining, approximal, bordering, conterminous, juxtaposed, touching
rel close, near, nearby, nigh
con apart, separate; distant, remote
2 ***syn*** NEIGHBORING, adjacent, close-at-hand, close-by, near-at-hand, nearby

contiguously *adv* ***syn*** IMMEDIATELY 1, directly

contiguousness *n* ***syn*** PROXIMITY, appropinquity, contiguity, immediacy, propinquity

continence *n* ***syn*** TEMPERANCE 2, abstinence, sobriety
rel self-restraint; moderation, temperateness; chasteness, chastity, purity
con self-indulgence; excessiveness, inordinateness; lasciviousness, lecherousness, lewdness, licentiousness, wantonness
ant incontinence

continent *adj* ***syn*** ABSTEMIOUS, abstentious, abstinent, self-restraining, sober, temperate
rel bridled, curbed, inhibited, restrained; chaste, pure
con self-indulgent, spoiled
ant incontinent

contingence *n* ***syn*** CONTACT 1, touch

contingency *n* ***syn*** JUNCTURE 2, crisis, crossroad(s), emergency, exigency, pass, pinch, strait, turning point, zero hour
rel break, chance, occasion, opportunity

contingent *adj* **1** ***syn*** ACCIDENTAL, casual, chance, fluky, fortuitous, incidental, odd
rel unanticipated, unforeseeable, unforeseen; likely, possible, probable
con certain, inevitable, necessary
2 ***syn*** DEPENDENT 1, conditional, relative, reliant

---

syn synonym(s) — *rel* related word(s)
idiom idiomatic equivalent(s) — *con* contrasted word(s)
ant antonym(s) — * vulgar
‖ use limited; if in doubt, see a dictionary
The first word in a synonym list when printed in SMALL CAPITALS shows where there is more information about the group. For a more efficient use of this book see Explanatory Notes.

continual *adj* continuing without intermission and seemingly without end <they were tired of her *continual* nagging>
syn around-the-clock, ceaseless, constant, continuous, endless, everlasting, incessant, interminable, minutely, perpetual, timeless, unceasing, unending, unintermitted, unintermittent, uninterrupted, unremitting
rel abiding, enduring, persistent, persisting, staying; unvarying; unchanging, unfailing, unflagging, unwaning; relentless, running, steady
con ephemeral, evanescent, impermanent, short-lived, temporary, transient, transitory

continually *adv syn* TOGETHER 2, consecutively, continuously, hand running, night and day, running, successively, unintermittedly, uninterruptedly

continuance *n syn* RUN 2, continuation, duration, persistence
rel constancy, longevity, permanence; survival

continuation *n* 1 uninterrupted existence or succession <the *continuation* of political disorder in Northern Ireland>
syn continuity, duration, endurance, persistence
rel extension, prolongation, protraction
ant termination
2 *syn* RUN 2, continuance, duration, persistence
ant cessation

continue *vb* 1 to remain indefinitely in existence or in a particular state or course <many traditional beliefs still *continue*> <do you expect to *continue* in school for the rest of your life?>
syn abide, carry through, endure, last, perdure, persist
rel carry on, carry over, ride, run on; outlast, outlive, survive; remain, stay
con cease, desist, discontinue, quit; arrest, check, interrupt; defer, intermit, postpone, stay, suspend
ant discontinue
2 *syn* RESUME 2, pick up, recommence, renew, reopen, restart, take up

continuing *adj syn* OLD 2, enduring, inveterate, lifelong, long-lasting, long-lived, perennial

continuity *n syn* CONTINUATION 1, duration, endurance, persistence

continuous *adj syn* CONTINUAL, ceaseless, constant, endless, everlasting, interminable, perpetual, timeless, unceasing, unending
ant discontinuous

continuously *adv* 1 *syn* TOGETHER 2, consecutively, continually, hand running, night and day, running, successively, unintermittedly, uninterruptedly
2 *syn* ALWAYS 1, constantly, ever, invariably, perpetually

contort *vb syn* DEFORM, distort, misshape, torture, warp, wind
rel bend, curve, twist

---

syn synonym(s) *rel* related word(s)
idiom idiomatic equivalent(s) *con* contrasted word(s)
ant antonym(s) * vulgar
|| use limited; if in doubt, see a dictionary
The first word in a synonym list when printed in SMALL CAPITALS shows where there is more information about the group. For a more efficient use of this book see Explanatory Notes.

contour *n syn* OUTLINE, delineation, figuration, line, lineament, lineation, profile, silhouette

contra *prep syn* AGAINST 1, facing, fronting, over against, toward, vis-à-vis

contra *adv syn* AGAIN 5, contrariwise, contrary, contrawise, conversely, oppositely, vice versa

contra *n syn* OPPOSITE, antipode, antipole, antithesis, contradictory, contrary, converse, counter, counterpole, reverse

contraband *adj* prohibited or excluded by law or treaty <fur or feathers from endangered species are *contraband* in advanced nations>
syn banned, hot
rel disapproved, proscribed, taboo; forbidden, prohibited; excluded, shut out

contraband *vb syn* SMUGGLE, bootleg, run

contraception *n syn* BIRTH CONTROL

contract *n* a usually legally enforceable arrangement between two or more parties <a *contract* for a new roof>
syn agreement, bargain, bond, compact, convention, covenant, pact, transaction; *compare* AGREEMENT 2, TREATY

contract *vb* 1 to become affected by a disease or disorder <*contracted* a severe cold that later turned into pneumonia>
syn catch, come down (with), get, sicken (with *or* of), take
rel acquire, obtain; decline, fail, sink, weaken; afflict, derange, disorder, indispose, upset; bring on, cause, induce; succumb (to)
idiom be laid by the heels by, fall (a) victim to
2 *syn* INCUR
3 to make or become smaller in bulk or volume <*contract* a muscle>
syn compress, concentrate, condense, constrict, shrink
rel decrease, diminish, dwindle, lessen, reduce
con dilate, distend, inflate, swell
ant expand

contracted *adj syn* ENGAGED 2, affianced, betrothed, intended, plighted, ||promised

contradict *vb syn* DENY 4, contravene, cross, disaffirm, gainsay, impugn, negate, negative, traverse
rel dispute; belie, falsify, garble
con authenticate, substantiate, verify
ant corroborate; confirm

contradiction *n syn* DENIAL 2, gainsaying, negation

contradictory *n syn* OPPOSITE, antipode, antipole, antithesis, contra, contrary, converse, counter, counterpole, reverse

contradictory *adj syn* OPPOSITE, antipodal, antipodean, antithetical, contrary, converse, counter, diametric, polar, reverse
rel negating, nullifying; adverse, antagonistic, counteractive
con agreeing, jibing, squaring, tallying
ant corroboratory; confirmatory

contradistinction *n syn* ANTAGONISM 2, antithesis, con, contraposition, contrariety, opposition, opposure

contraposition *n syn* ANTAGONISM 2, antithesis, con, contradistinction, contrariety, opposition, opposure

contraption *n syn* DEVICE 2, contrivance

contrariant *n syn* ANTIPATHETIC 1, antagonistic, clashing, conflicting, contrary, discordant

contrariety *n* ***syn*** ANTAGONISM 2, antithesis, con, contradistinction, contraposition, opposition, opposure

contrariwise *adv* ***syn*** AGAIN 5, contra, contrary, contrawise, conversely, oppositely, vice versa
idiom on (*or* to) the contrary

contrary *n* ***syn*** OPPOSITE, antipode, antipole, antithesis, contra, contradictory, converse, counter, counterpole, reverse

contrary *adj* **1** ***syn*** OPPOSITE, antipodal, antipodean, antithetical, contradictory, converse, counter, diametric, polar, reverse
2 ***syn*** ANTIPATHETIC 1, antagonistic, clashing, conflicting, contrariant, discordant
3 obstinately self-willed in refusing to concur, conform, or submit <why be *contrary* about something that you cannot change>
syn balky, cross-grained, froward, ornery, perverse, restive, wayward, wrongheaded
rel headstrong, intractable, recalcitrant, refractory, unruly; contumacious, insubordinate, rebellious; dissentient, dissident, nonconforming, nonconformist, recusant; obstinate, stubborn
con amenable, biddable, docile, obedient, tractable; amiable, obliging; acquiescent, compliant; forbearing, long-suffering, tolerant
ant complaisant

contrary *adv* ***syn*** AGAIN 5, contra, contrariwise, contrawise, conversely, oppositely, vice versa

contrast *vb* ***syn*** COMPARE 2, bracket, collate

contravene *vb* **1** ***syn*** VIOLATE 1, breach, break, infract, infringe, offend, transgress
rel encroach, intrude, overstep, trespass
2 ***syn*** DENY 4, contradict, cross, disaffirm, gainsay, impugn, negate, negative, traverse
rel combat, fight, oppose, resist; abjure, disclaim, disown, exclude, reject, repudiate, spurn
con accept, agree, subscribe (to); admit, allow, own
ant uphold (*as a principle*); allege (*as a right or claim*)

contravention *n* ***syn*** BREACH 1, infraction, infringement, transgression, trespass, violation
rel crime, offense, sin, vice

contrawise *adv* ***syn*** AGAIN 5, contra, contrariwise, contrary, conversely, oppositely, vice versa

contretemps *n* ***syn*** MISFORTUNE, adversity, ‖dole, mischance, mishap, tragedy, ‖unluck

contribute *vb* **1** to give in common with others <*contribute* to a fund for handicapped children>
syn chip in, come through, kick in, pitch in, subscribe; *compare* GIVE 1
idiom put something in the pot, sweeten the kitty
2 to have a share in something (as an act or effect) <careful planning *contributed* greatly to the success of the project>
syn conduce, redound, tend
rel aid, help, assist; add (to), augment, supplement; fortify, recruit, reinforce, strengthen
idiom do one's bit, have a hand in
con detract, minus, subtract, take away

contribution *n* ***syn*** DONATION, alms, benefaction, beneficence, charity, offering

contributory *adj* ***syn*** AUXILIARY, accessory, adjuvant, ancillary, appurtenant, collateral, subservient, subsidiary

contrite *adj* ***syn*** REMORSEFUL, apologetic, attritional, compunctious, penitent, penitential, regretful, repentant, sorry

contriteness *n* ***syn*** PENITENCE, attrition, compunction, contrition, penance, penitency, remorse, remorsefulness, repentance, ruth

contrition *n* ***syn*** PENITENCE, attrition, compunction, contriteness, penance, penitency, remorse, repentance, rue, ruth

contriturate *vb* ***syn*** PULVERIZE 1, bray, buck, comminute, crush, powder, triturate

contrivance *n* **1** ***syn*** DEVICE 2, contraption
2 ***syn*** INVENTION, brainchild, coinage

contrive *vb* **1** ***syn*** PLOT, cogitate, ‖collogue, collude, connive, conspire, devise, intrigue, machinate, scheme (out)
rel develop, elaborate, work out
2 to use ingenuity in making or doing or achieving an end <*contrived* a useful camp stove from a few bricks and a piece of screen>
syn concoct, cook (up), devise, dream up, formulate, frame, hatch (up), invent, make up, vamp (up)
rel plan, plot, project, scheme; fabricate, fashion, make, manufacture; handle, manipulate, move; rig

control *vb* **1** ***syn*** COMPOSE 4, collect, contain, cool, recollect, rein, repress, restrain, simmer down, smother
rel adjust, regulate; curb, master, quell, subdue
2 ***syn*** GOVERN 3, direct, dominate, handle, manage
rel regulate, supervise; discipline
idiom put through the mill (*or* a course of sprouts), take in hand

control *n* ***syn*** POWER 1, authority, command, domination, jurisdiction, mastery, might, strings, sway

controlled *adj* ***syn*** CONSERVATIVE 2, discreet, moderate, reasonable, restrained, temperate, unexcessive, unextreme

controversial *adj* ***syn*** CONTENTIOUS 2, argumentative, disputatious, litigious, polemical

controversy *n* **1** ***syn*** ARGUMENT 2, contention, dispute, hurrah, rumpus
2 ***syn*** QUARREL, altercation, bickering, dispute, embroilment, falling-out, miff, squabble, tiff, wrangle

controvert *vb* ***syn*** DISPROVE 1, break, confound, confute, disconfirm, evert, rebut, refute
rel challenge, oppugn, question

contumacious *adj* ***syn*** INSUBORDINATE, factious, insurgent, mutinous, rebellious, seditious
rel contrary, froward, perverse; alienated, disaffected, estranged, irreconcilable
con acquiescent, compliant, resigned
ant obedient

contumacy *n* ***syn*** DEFIANCE 2, contempt, despite, recalcitrance, stubbornness

---

syn synonym(s) ***rel*** related word(s)
idiom idiomatic equivalent(s) ***con*** contrasted word(s)
ant antonym(s) * vulgar
‖ use limited; if in doubt, see a dictionary
The first word in a synonym list when printed in SMALL CAPITALS shows where there is more information about the group. For a more efficient use of this book see Explanatory Notes.

contumelious *adj* **1** ***syn*** ABUSIVE, invective, opprobrious, scurrile, scurrilous, truculent, vituperative, vituperatory, vituperous
2 ***syn*** INSOLENT 2, audacious, bold, ||boldacious, brazen, impertinent, impudent, procacious, saucy
ant obsequious

contumely *n* **1** ***syn*** ABUSE, billingsgate, invective, obloquy, scurrility, vituperation
rel animadversion, aspersion, reflection, stricture
idiom hard (*or* bitter) words
2 ***syn*** AFFRONT, despite, indignity, insult, slap

contuse *vb* ***syn*** BRUISE 1, black

contusion *n* ***syn*** BRUISE

conundrum *n* ***syn*** MYSTERY, Chinese puzzle, closed book, enigma, mystification, puzzle, puzzlement, riddle, why

convalesce *vb* ***syn*** IMPROVE 3, ameliorate, gain, look up, mend, perk (up), recuperate

convenance *n* ***syn*** FORM 3, convention, usage

convene *vb* **1** to begin a session (as of a legislature or conference) < the council *convened* at 10 o'clock >
syn meet, open, sit
idiom hold a meeting (*or* session)
2 ***syn*** SUMMON 2, call, call in, summons
rel convoke, muster
3 ***syn*** CONVOKE, assemble, call, summon

convenience *n* **1** ***syn*** AMENITY 2, comfort, facility
2 ***syn*** TOILET, head, john, johnny, latrine, lavatory, ||loo, privy, ||throne, water closet

convenience *vb* ***syn*** OBLIGE 2, accommodate, favor

convenient *adj* **1** ***syn*** GOOD 2, appropriate, fit, meet, proper, suitable, useful
2 situated within easy reach < left his glasses *convenient* to his book >
syn adjacent, close-at-hand, close-by, handy, near-at-hand, nearby
rel close, near, nigh; immediate, next
idiom at one's beck and call, at one's fingertips, in one's immediate neighborhood, under one's nose
ant inconvenient

convention *n* **1** ***syn*** TREATY, agreement, concord, pact
2 ***syn*** CONTRACT, agreement, bargain, bond, compact, covenant, pact, transaction
rel accord, understanding
3 ***syn*** FORM 3, convenance, usage
rel canon, law, precept, rule; custom, practice

conventional *adj* **1** according with or based on generally accepted and well-established usage < took a very *conventional* view of his duty >
syn button-down, orthodox, square, straight; *compare* TRADITIONAL 1
rel moderate, sober, temperate; constrained, restrained; dependable, reliable, responsible; conscientious, fastidious, nice, punctilious, scrupulous; conservative, traditionalistic
ant unconventional
2 ***syn*** TRADITIONAL 1, tralatitious
3 ***syn*** CEREMONIAL, ceremonious, formal, solemn, stately
rel decent, decorous, proper, seemly; correct, precise, right
con lax, negligent, remiss, slack; artless, ingenuous, naive, natural, simple, unsophisticated
ant unconventional

converge *vb* to come to or trend toward a common point < the main streets *converge* on a central square >
syn concenter, concentrate, focus, meet
idiom come to a center, come (*or* run) together

conversant *adj* **1** ***syn*** AWARE, alive, apprehensive, awake, cognizant, conscious, knowing, sensible, sentient, witting
ant ignorant
2 ***syn*** FAMILIAR 3, abreast, acquainted, au courant, au fait, informed, up, versant, versed
rel sensible; up-to-date; apprehending, comprehending, perceptive, percipient
con unfamiliar; nescient
ant unconversant

conversation *n* **1** oral exchange of information or ideas < leaned against the fence in casual *conversation* >
syn chat, colloquy, confabulation, converse, dialogue, parley
rel discussion; discourse, speech, talk
2 an instance of conversational exchange < had a long *conversation* about family problems >
syn colloquy, confabulation, dialogue, talk; *compare* CHAT 2
rel debate, deliberation, discussion, ventilation; comment, observation, remark; cross talk, repartee

conversation piece *n* ***syn*** CURIOSITY 2, oddity

converse *vb* to engage in conversation < they *conversed* quietly while waiting for their friend >
syn chat, chin, colloque, talk, visit, yarn; *compare* CHAT 1

converse (in) *vb* ***syn*** SPEAK 3, parley, talk, use

converse *n* **1** ***syn*** CONVERSATION 1, chat, colloquy, confabulation, dialogue, parley
2 ***syn*** COMMUNICATION 3, communion, intercommunication, intercourse

converse *adj* ***syn*** OPPOSITE, antipodal, antipodean, antithetical, contradictory, contrary, counter, diametric, polar, reverse

converse *n* ***syn*** OPPOSITE, antipode, antipole, antithesis, contra, contradictory, contrary, counter, counterpole, reverse

conversely *adv* ***syn*** AGAIN 5, contra, contrariwise, contrary, contrawise, oppositely, vice versa

conversion *n* **1** fundamental alteration in one's system of beliefs < Judaism does not encourage *conversion* of gentiles >
syn metanoia, rebirth
rel about-face, reversal, turning; reclamation, regeneration
idiom change of heart
2 change of one thing to another usually by substitution < *conversion* of locomotives from steam to diesel power >

---

syn synonym(s) ***rel*** related word(s)
idiom idiomatic equivalent(s) ***con*** contrasted word(s)
ant antonym(s) * vulgar
|| use limited; if in doubt, see a dictionary
The first word in a synonym list when printed in SMALL CAPITALS shows where there is more information about the group. For a more efficient use of this book see Explanatory Notes.

syn alteration, changeover, shift, transformation
rel change, modification, qualification; metamorphosis, mutation, permutation, transmutation; innovation, novelty

convert *vb* **1** to induce (another or others) to accept the validity of something (as a belief, course of action, or point of view) <Chinese missionaries *converted* many Japanese to Buddhism>
syn bring, lead, move, persuade
rel redeem, reform, save; bend, bias, incline, sway; actuate, budge, impel; proselyte, proselytize
2 *syn* TRANSFORM, change, commute, metamorphose, transfigure, translate, transmogrify, transmute, transpose, transubstantiate
rel fabricate, forge, make, manufacture; apply, employ, use, utilize

convey *vb* **1** *syn* CARRY 1, bear, buck, ferry, ‖hump, ‖jag, lug, pack, tote, transport
2 *syn* COMMUNICATE 1, break, impart, pass on, transmit
rel project, put across
3 *syn* TRANSFER 4, abalienate, alien, alienate, assign, cede, deed, make over, remise, sign (over)
rel commit, consign, relegate
4 *syn* CONDUCT 4, carry, channel, funnel, pipe, siphon, traject, transmit

conveyance *n* **1** *syn* TRANSPORTATION 1, carriage, carrying, transit, transport, transporting
2 *syn* DEED 3, charter
3 *syn* VEHICLE 3, transport, transportation

convict *n* a person serving time in prison after conviction as a criminal <mixing hardened *convicts* with juvenile offenders>
syn ‖con, jailbird, ‖lag, loser, prison bird
rel long-termer, longtimer; ‖stir bug; recidivist, repeater

conviction *n* **1** *syn* CERTAINTY, assurance, assuredness, certitude, confidence, sureness, surety
con dubiety, dubiosity, uncertainty; disbelief, incredulity, unbelief
2 *syn* OPINION, belief, eye, feeling, mind, persuasion, sentiment, view
rel doctrine, dogma, tenet

convince *vb* **1** *syn* ASSURE 2, persuade, satisfy
2 *syn* INDUCE 1, argue (into), bring around, draw, get, persuade, prevail (on *or* upon), prompt, talk (into), win (over)

convincing *adj* **1** *syn* AUTHENTIC 1, credible, faithful, trustworthy, trusty
2 *syn* VALID, cogent, satisfactory, satisfying, solid, sound, telling

convivial *adj syn* SOCIAL 1, companionable, sociable
rel lively, vivacious; jocund, jolly, merry
con grave, sedate, serious, sober, solemn, somber; reserved, reticent, silent
ant taciturn; stolid

convoke *vb* to bring together by or as if by summons <the ruler *convoked* his council>
syn assemble, call, convene, summon; *compare* SUMMON 2
rel collect, congregate, gather; ask, bid, invite, request; meet, sit
con adjourn, close, dissolve, prorogue, recess, suspend; disperse, scatter

convoluted *adj syn* WINDING, anfractuous, flexuous, meandering, meandrous, serpentine, sinuous, snaky, tortuous

convoy *vb syn* ACCOMPANY, attend, bear, ‖bring, ‖carry, companion, company, conduct, consort (with), escort
rel defend, guard, protect, safeguard, shield

convulse *vb syn* SHAKE 4, agitate, concuss, rock

convulsion *n syn* COMMOTION 1, clamor, ferment, outcry, tumult, upheaval, upturn
rel cataclysm, disaster; quaking, rocking, shaking, tottering, trembling

cook *vb* **1** to make ready or fit for eating by the use of heat <liked everything well-*cooked*>
syn do
2 *syn* BURN 3, bake, broil, melt, roast, scorch, swelter

cook (up) *vb syn* CONTRIVE 2, concoct, devise, dream up, formulate, frame, hatch (up), invent, make up, vamp (up)

cookshop *n syn* EATING HOUSE, beanery, café, ‖greasy spoon, ‖hash house, lunch counter (*or* bar), luncheonette, lunchroom, quick-lunch, snack bar (*or* counter)

cool *adj* **1** *syn* COLD 1, arctic, chill, chilly, freezing, frigid, frore, frosty, gelid, nippy
ant warm
2 freed or giving the impression of freedom from all agitation or excitement <they looked *cool* and very formidable>
syn collected, composed, disimpassioned, imperturbable, nonchalant, unflappable, unruffled; *compare* HAPPY-GO-LUCKY
rel calm, placid, serene, tranquil; aloof, detached, indifferent; impassive, phlegmatic, stolid; assured, confident, self-possessed
con fervent, fervid, impassioned, passionate, perfervid; discomposed, disturbed, flurried, flustered, perturbed, upset
ant ardent; agitated
3 *syn* UNSOCIABLE, aloof, distant, offish, reserved, solitary, standoffish, unapproachable, uncompanionable, withdrawn
‖**4** *syn* MARVELOUS 2, ‖dandy, divine, glorious, groovy, hunky-dory, ‖keen, nifty, sensational, swell

cool *vb* **1** *syn* COMPOSE 4, collect, control, re-collect, rein, repress, restrain, simmer down, smother, suppress
2 *syn* MURDER 1, assassinate, ‖bump off, do in, ‖dust off, execute, finish, knock off, liquidate, put away

cooler *n syn* JAIL, ‖calaboose, ‖can, ‖clink, coop, ‖hoosegow, lockup, ‖pokey, prison, ‖stir

coolness *n syn* EQUANIMITY, ataraxy, calmness, composure, imperturbability, phlegm, sangfroid, self-possession

‖**coon** *vb syn* STEAL 1, cabbage, ‖clout, ‖cly, ‖cop, ‖crook, filch, ‖heist, pinch, snitch

---

coon's age *n* ***syn*** AGE 2, aeon, blue moon, dog's age, donkey's years, eternity, long

‖**coony** *adj* ***syn*** CLEVER 4, adroit, canny, cunning, dexterous, ingenious, ‖sleighty, slim, sly

coop *n* ***syn*** JAIL, ‖calaboose, ‖can, ‖clink, cooler, ‖hoosegow, jug, lockup, ‖pokey, prison

coop *vb* ***syn*** ENCLOSE 1, cage, close in, corral, envelop, fence, hem, pen, shut in, wall
rel bar, block, hinder, impede, obstruct

cooperate *vb* ***syn*** UNITE 2, band, coadjute, combine, concur, conjoin, league
rel agree, coincide
con annul, negate, nullify; negative, neutralize
ant counteract

cooperative *adj* involving joint action in producing a result <the need of *cooperative* efforts to effect lasting social change>
syn coacting, coactive, coefficient, conjoint, synergetic, synergic
rel collaborative, concerted; noncompetitive, uncompetitive
con competitive, emulous, rivaling, vying; antagonistic, conflicting, oppugnant
ant counteractive

coordinate *vb* ***syn*** HARMONIZE 3, accommodate, atune, conform, integrate, proportion, reconcile, reconciliate, tune

coordinate *n* **1** ***syn*** OPPOSITE NUMBER, counterpart, vis-à-vis
2 ***syn*** MATE 5, companion, double, duplicate, fellow, match, reciprocal, twin

‖**cop** *vb* ***syn*** STEAL 1, annex, appropriate, cabbage, ‖clout, filch, lift, nab, pinch, purloin

cop *n* ***syn*** POLICEMAN, bluecoat, ‖copper, ‖flatfoot, ‖fuzz, gumshoe, ‖heat, man, officer, ‖pig

copartner *n* ***syn*** PARTNER, associate, cohort, confrere, consociate, fellow, mate, ‖pard

copious *adj* ***syn*** PLENTIFUL, abundant, ample, bounteous, bountiful, generous, liberal, plenteous, plenty
rel exuberant, lush, luxuriant
con exiguous, scant, scanty, scrimpy, spare, sparse; slender, slight, slim, tenuous, thin
ant meager

‖**cop out** *vb* ***syn*** DIE 1, cash in, ‖check out, conk, ‖croak, drop, go, ‖kick in, ‖kick off, peg out

‖**copper** *n* ***syn*** POLICEMAN, bluecoat, cop, ‖flatfoot, ‖fuzz, gumshoe, ‖heat, man, officer, ‖pig

copy *n* **1** ***syn*** IMITATION, ersatz, simulacrum
2 ***syn*** REPRODUCTION, carbon, carbon copy, ditto, duplicate, facsimile, reduplication, replica, replication
rel counterpart, parallel; impress, impression, imprint, print; effigy, image, likeness
ant original

---

syn synonym(s) *rel* related word(s)
idiom idiomatic equivalent(s) *con* contrasted word(s)
ant antonym(s) * vulgar
‖ use limited; if in doubt, see a dictionary
The first word in a synonym list when printed in SMALL CAPITALS shows where there is more information about the group. For a more efficient use of this book see Explanatory Notes.

copy *vb* to make a copy of <had her more valuable jewelry *copied*>
syn duplicate, imitate, reduplicate, replicate, reproduce
rel ditto, repeat; counterfeit, fake, sham, simulate; ape, burlesque, mock, parody, take off, travesty
ant originate

coquet *vb* ***syn*** TRIFLE 1, dally, flirt, fool, lead on, string along, toy, wanton

coquette *n* ***syn*** FLIRT, vamp

coquettish *adj* ***syn*** COY 2, arch, roguish

cordial *adj* ***syn*** GRACIOUS 1, affable, congenial, genial, sociable, ‖sonsy
rel responsive, sympathetic, tender, warm, warmhearted; heartfelt, hearty, sincere, wholehearted
con cold, cool, frigid, frosty; aloof, detached, disinterested, indifferent; reserved, silent, taciturn

cordiality *n* ***syn*** AMENITY 1, agreeability, agreeableness, amiability, enjoyableness, geniality, gratefulness, pleasance, pleasantness, sweetness and light
rel responsiveness, sympathy, understanding, warmth; mutuality, reciprocity; approbation, approval, favor
con cross-purposes, difference, disagreement, misunderstanding, odds, variance; disapprobation, disapproval, disfavor

core *n* **1** ***syn*** CENTER 1, middle, midpoint, midst
2 ***syn*** BODY 3, bulk, corpus, mass, staple, substance
3 ***syn*** SUBSTANCE 2, amount, body, burden, gist, meat, pith, purport, thrust, upshot
rel consequence, import, importance, significance
4 ***syn*** CENTER 3, heart, pith, quick, root
rel base, basis, foundation; beginning, commencement, origin, start

‖**corker** *n* ***syn*** ‖DILLY, crackerjack, ‖daisy, dandy, humdinger, jim-dandy, knockout, ‖lalapalooza, ‖lulu, nifty

corkscrew *vb* ***syn*** WIND 2, coil, curl, entwine, spiral, twine, twist, wreathe

corner *n* **1** ***syn*** PREDICAMENT, box, dilemma, fix, hole, impasse, jam, pickle, plight, scrape
2 ***syn*** MONOPOLY

corner *vb* to get into one's control or a position from which escape is difficult <*cornered* him at a party and tried to borrow a hundred dollars>
syn bottle (up), collar, tree
rel bother, disturb, put out, trouble; capture, catch, nab, seize, trap
idiom chase up a tree, drive (*or* run) into a corner, get (*or* have) on the ropes

cornerwise *adv* ***syn*** DIAGONALLY, catercorner (*or* catty-corner *or* kitty-corner), slantingways, slantways, slantwise, ‖slaunchways

corny *adj* ***syn*** TRITE, clichéd, commonplace, hackneyed, old hat, shopworn, stale, stereotyped, tired, warmed-over

corollary *n* ***syn*** EFFECT 1, aftereffect, consequence, end product, issue, precipitate, result, sequel, sequence, upshot

coronal *n* ***syn*** WREATH, anadem, chaplet, coronet, crown, garland

coronet *n* ***syn*** WREATH, anadem, chaplet, coronal, crown, garland

corporal *adj* ***syn*** BODILY, carnal, corporeal, fleshly, physical, somatic

corporation *n* ***syn*** POTBELLY, bay window, paunch, pod, ‖pot

corporeal *adj* **1** ***syn*** BODILY, carnal, corporal, fleshly, physical, somatic
2 ***syn*** MATERIAL 1, gross, objective, phenomenal, physical, sensible, substantial, tangible

corps *n* ***syn*** COMPANY 4, band, outfit, party, troop, troupe

corpse *n* a dead body especially of a human being <concealed the *corpse* under some rubbish>
syn body, cadaver, carcass, ‖cold meat, ‖deader, mort, remains, stiff
rel carrion; bones

corpselike *adj* **1** ***syn*** DEATHLY 1, corpsy, dead, deadened, deadly, deathful, deathlike
2 ***syn*** GHASTLY 2, cadaverous, deathlike, ghostlike, ghostly, shadowy, spectral

corpsy *adj* ***syn*** DEATHLY 1, corpselike, dead, deadened, deadly, deathful, deathlike

corpulence *n* ***syn*** OBESITY, adiposity, fatness, fleshiness

corpulent *adj* ***syn*** FAT 2, fleshy, gross, heavy, obese, overblown, overweight, portly, stout, weighty

corpus *n* **1** ***syn*** BODY 3, bulk, core, mass, staple, substance
2 ***syn*** OEUVRE, opera omnia

corrade *vb* ***syn*** ABRADE 1, chafe, erode, gall, graze, rub, ruffle, wear

corral *vb* ***syn*** ENCLOSE 1, cage, close in, coop, fence, hedge, hem, mew, pen, shut in

correct *vb* **1** to set right something that is wrong <*correct* a misstatement>
syn amend, emend, mend, rectify, right
rel ameliorate, better, improve; redress, remedy, revise; make over, reform; adjust, fix, regulate
con damage, harm, hurt, impair, injure, mar, spoil
2 ***syn*** PUNISH 1, castigate, chasten, chastise, discipline
con baby, coddle, cosset, humor, indulge, pamper, spoil

correct *adj* **1** ***syn*** DECOROUS 1, becoming, comme il faut, conforming, decent, done, nice, proper, right, seemly
rel careful, meticulous, punctilious, scrupulous
2 conforming to or agreeing with fact <the *correct* solution to the problem>
syn accurate, exact, nice, precise, proper, right, rigorous
rel faithful, true, undistorted, veracious, veridical; faultless, flawless, impeccable, perfect
con fallacious, false, wrong; defective, faulty, flawed, imperfect
ant incorrect

correction *n* ***syn*** PUNISHMENT, castigation, chastisement, discipline, punition, rod

correctitude *n* ***syn*** ORDER 7, correctness, decorousness, decorum, orderliness, properness, propriety, seemliness

corrective *n* ***syn*** REMEDY 2, antidote, counteractant, counteractive, counteragent, countermeasure, counterstep, cure

correctly *adv* ***syn*** WELL 1, befittingly, decently, decorously, fitly, fittingly, justly, nicely, properly, rightly

correctness *n* **1** ***syn*** ORDER 7, correctitude, decorousness, decorum, orderliness, properness, propriety, seemliness
2 ***syn*** PRECISION, accuracy, definiteness, definitiveness, definitude, exactitude, exactness, preciseness

correlate *n* **1** ***syn*** COUNTERPART 1, complement, pendant
2 ***syn*** PARALLEL, analogue, correspondent, counterpart, countertype, match

correspond *vb* ***syn*** AGREE 4, accord, conform, consort, dovetail, ‖gee, go, harmonize, jibe, square

correspond (to) *vb* ***syn*** AMOUNT 2, approach, equal, match, partake (of), rival, touch

correspondence *n* ***syn*** CONSISTENCY, coherence, conformity, congruity
ant divergence

correspondent *n* ***syn*** PARALLEL, analogue, correlate, counterpart, countertype, match

corresponding *adj* ***syn*** LIKE, agnate, akin, alike, analogous, comparable, consonant, parallel, similar, undifferentiated

correspondingly *adv* ***syn*** ALSO 1, likewise, similarly, so

corridor *n* ***syn*** PASSAGE 4, couloir, hall, hallway, passageway

corrival *n* ***syn*** RIVAL, competition, competitor

corroborate *vb* ***syn*** CONFIRM 2, authenticate, bear out, justify, substantiate, validate, verify
con invalidate, negate, nullify
ant contradict

corroborative *adj* serving or tending to corroborate <*corroborative* evidence>
syn adminicular, collateral, confirmative, confirmatory, corroboratory, verificatory
rel ancillary, auxiliary, supplementary, supportive; assisting, helping
con confutative, refutative, refutatory; contradictory, negatory

corroboratory *adj* ***syn*** CORROBORATIVE, adminicular, collateral, confirmative, confirmatory, verificatory

corrode *vb* ***syn*** EAT 3, bite, eat away, erode, gnaw, scour, wear (away)

corrosive *adj* ***syn*** SARCASTIC, acerb, acerbic, archilochian, caustic, ‖sarky

corrosiveness *n* ***syn*** SARCASM, acerbity, causticity, sarcasticness

corrugation *n* ***syn*** WRINKLE, crease, crinkle, fold, furrow, plica, ridge, rimple, rivel, ruck

corrupt *vb* **1** ***syn*** DEBASE 1, animalize, bastardize, debauch, demoralize, deprave, pervert, stain, vitiate, warp
rel abase, degrade; ruin, wreck
con amend, correct, reform
2 ***syn*** DECAY, break down, crumble, decompose, disintegrate, molder, putrefy, rot, spoil, taint, turn
rel befoul, defile, foul; smirch, tarnish

corrupt *adj* **1** ***syn*** VICIOUS 2, degenerate, depraved, flagitious, infamous, miscreant, nefarious, perverse, rotten, villainous
rel crooked, devious, oblique; baneful, deleterious, detrimental, noxious, pernicious; abased, degraded, low

---

syn synonym(s)	***rel*** related word(s)
idiom idiomatic equivalent(s)	***con*** contrasted word(s)
ant antonym(s)	* vulgar

‖ use limited; if in doubt, see a dictionary
The first word in a synonym list when printed in SMALL CAPITALS shows where there is more information about the group. For a more efficient use of this book see Explanatory Notes.

2 seeking sordid advantage with little regard to moral or legal bars <a *corrupt* politician>
syn mercenary, praetorian, unethical, unprincipled, unscrupulous, venal; *compare* CROOKED 2, VENAL 1
rel undependable, unreliable, untrustworthy; faithless, inconstant, unfaithful; double-dealing, perfidious, treacherous, two-faced; bribable, corruptible; blackguardly, knavish, reprobate
con ethical, principled, scrupulous, upright; dependable, reliable, trustworthy, trusty
3 ***syn*** CROOKED 2, dishonest, snide

corrupted *adj* ***syn*** DEBASED, debauched, depraved, perverted, vitiate, vitiated

corruptible *adj* ***syn*** VENAL 1, bribable, buyable, purchasable

corruption *n* **1** ***syn*** VICE 1, depravity, immorality, wickedness
2 ***syn*** BARBARISM, impropriety, slangism, solecism, vernacularism, vernacularity, vulgarism

corsair *n* ***syn*** PIRATE, buccaneer, freebooter, picaroon, rover, sea dog, sea robber, sea rover, sea wolf

coruscate *vb* ***syn*** FLASH 1, glance, gleam, glimmer, glint, glisten, glitter, scintillate, shimmer, sparkle

coruscation *n* ***syn*** FLASH 1, glance, gleam, glimmer, glint, glisten, glitter, scintillation, shimmer, sparkle

corybantic *adj* ***syn*** FURIOUS 2, delirious, frantic, frenetic, frenzied, mad, rabid, wild

coryphée *n* ***syn*** DANCER, ballerina, ballet girl, dancing girl, danseur, danseuse, figurant, figurante, hoofer

cosmic *adj* ***syn*** UNIVERSAL 2, catholic, cosmopolitan, ecumenical, global, planetary, worldwide

cosmopolitan *adj* **1** exhibiting or characterized by a sophistication and savoir faire arising from cultured urban life and wide travel <had a thoroughly *cosmopolitan* outlook on life>
syn metropolitan, urbane; *compare* SOPHISTICATED 2
rel civilized, polished, smooth; sophisticated, worldly-wise; cultivated, cultured
con boorish, cloddish, rude, rustic; insular, parochial, provincial
2 ***syn*** UNIVERSAL 2, catholic, cosmic, ecumenical, global, planetary, worldwide

cosmos (*or* **kosmos**) *n* ***syn*** UNIVERSE, creation, macrocosm, macrocosmos, megacosm, nature, world

cosset *vb* **1** ***syn*** CARESS, cuddle, dandle, fondle, love, pet
2 ***syn*** BABY, cater (to), cocker, coddle, humor, indulge, mollycoddle, ‖much, pamper, spoil

cost *n* **1** ***syn*** PRICE 1, charge, price tag, rate, tab, tariff
2 ***syn*** EXPENSE 1, disbursement, expenditure, outlay
3 ***syn*** EXPENSE 2, price, toll

costive *adj* **1** ***syn*** CONSTIPATED, astricted, bound, obstipated
2 ***syn*** STINGY, cheeseparing, close, hardfisted, mean, miserly, niggardly, parsimonious, penurious, tight

costless *adj* ***syn*** FREE 5, chargeless, complimentary, gratis, gratuitous

costly *adj* **1** commanding or being a large price <the scarcer an item becomes the more *costly* it is>
syn dear, expensive, high; *compare* PRECIOUS 1
rel excessive, exorbitant, extravagant, inordinate, steep, stiff; fancy, premium, top
con inexpensive, low, low-priced, reasonable
ant cheap
2 ***syn*** PRECIOUS 1, inestimable, invaluable, priceless, valuable

costume *n* style of clothing and adornment <her *costume* was always suitable to the occasion>
syn dress, getup, guise, outfit, rig, setout, turnout
rel fashion, mode, style

cot *n* ***syn*** HUT, ‖box, cabin, ‖caboose, camp, cottage, lodge, shack, shanty

‖**cotch** *vb* **1** ***syn*** SEIZE 2, catch, clutch, grab, grapple, nab, ‖nail, snatch, take
2 ***syn*** CATCH 1, bag, capture, collar, get, nail, prehend, secure, take
3 ***syn*** CATCH 7, overhaul, overtake, take

coterie *n* ***syn*** CLIQUE, cabal, camarilla, camp, circle, clan, ingroup, mob, ring

cottage *n* ***syn*** HUT, ‖box, cabin, ‖caboose, camp, cot, lodge, shack, shanty

cotton *vb* **1** ***syn*** BABY, cater (to), cocker, coddle, cosset, humor, indulge, mollycoddle, pamper, spoil
2 ***syn*** FAWN, apple-polish, bootlick, ‖brownnose, cower, cringe, grovel, honey (up), kowtow, toady

cotton (to *or* on to) *vb* ***syn*** APPREHEND 1, accept, catch, compass, comprehend, ‖dig, follow, grasp, see, take in

cottony *adj* ***syn*** SOFT 3, satiny, silken, silky, velvety

couch *vb* **1** ***syn*** WORD, express, formulate, phrase, put
2 ***syn*** LOWER 3, demit, depress, droop, let down, sink

couch *n* ***syn*** LAIR 1, burrow, den, lodge

couleur de rose *adj* ***syn*** HOPEFUL 2, encouraging, likely, promiseful, promising, roseate, rose-colored, rosy

couloir *n* ***syn*** PASSAGE 4, corridor, hall, hallway, passageway

counsel *n* ***syn*** ADVICE 1, advisement

counsel *vb* to give advice to or about <*counseled* him to wait for a more propitious occasion>
syn advise, recommend
rel admonish, reprehend, warn; direct, order, prescribe; charge, enjoin, prompt, urge; advocate, suggest

count *vb* **1** to ascertain the total of units in a collection by noting one after another <*counted* the sheep in the pasture>
syn enumerate, number, numerate, tale, tally, tell
rel add, cast, figure, foot, sum, tot, total; calculate, compute, estimate, reckon; tell off
2 ***syn*** MATTER, import, mean, signify, weigh
3 ***syn*** WEIGH 3, militate, tell

count (on) *vb* ***syn*** RELY (on *or* upon), bank (on *or* upon), build (on), calculate (on *or* upon), depend (on *or* upon), ‖lot (on *or* upon), reckon (on), trust (in *or* to)

count (on *or* upon) *vb* ***syn*** EXPECT 1, await, hope, look

countenance *n* **1** ***syn*** LOOK 2, cast, expression, face, visage

idiom (the) cut of one's jib
2 *syn* FACE 1, ‖dial, features, ‖kisser, ‖map, mug, ‖pan, phiz, ‖puss, visage

countenance *vb* **1** *syn* ENCOURAGE 2, advocate, favor
rel applaud, commend; back, champion, support, uphold
con deride, ridicule; criticize, reprehend, reprobate; reproach, reprove
ant discountenance
2 *syn* APPROVE 1, accept, approbate, favor, go (for), hold (with)

counter *vb syn* OPPOSE 1, match, pit, play (off), vie

counter *n syn* OPPOSITE, antipode, antipole, antithesis, contra, contradictory, contrary, converse, counterpole, reverse

counter *adj syn* OPPOSITE, antipodal, antipodean, antithetical, contradictory, contrary, converse, diametric, polar, reverse
rel hostile, inimical; adverse, antagonistic, anti, oppugnant; hindering, impeding, obstructive

counteract *vb syn* NEUTRALIZE, annul, cancel (out), countercheck, frustrate, negate, negative, redress
rel correct, fix, rectify, right
con cooperate, coordinate, synergize; back, reinforce, support

counteractant *n syn* REMEDY 2, antidote, corrective, counteractive, counteragent, countermeasure, counterstep, cure

counteractive *n syn* REMEDY 2, antidote, corrective, counteractant, counteragent, countermeasure, counterstep, cure

counteragent *n syn* REMEDY 2, antidote, corrective, counteractant, counteractive, countermeasure, counterstep, cure

counterbalance *vb syn* COMPENSATE 1, atone (for), balance, counterpoise, countervail, make up, offset, outweigh, redeem, set off
rel amend, correct, rectify
con overbalance, unbalance

counterblow *n syn* RETALIATION, avengement, avenging, reprisal, requital, retribution, revanche, revenge, vengeance

countercheck *vb syn* NEUTRALIZE, annul, cancel (out), counteract, frustrate, negate, negative, redress

counterfactual *adj syn* FALSE 1, erroneous, inaccurate, incorrect, specious, unsound, untrue, wrong

counterfeit *vb syn* ASSUME 4, act, affect, bluff, fake, feign, pretend, put on, sham, simulate
rel ape, copy, imitate, mimic

counterfeit *adj* being an imitation intended to mislead or deceive < *counterfeit* money > < *counterfeit* sympathy >
syn bogus, brummagem, fake, false, phony, pinchbeck, pseudo, sham, snide, spurious; *compare* SPURIOUS 3
rel feigned, pretended, simulated; deceptive, delusive, delusory, misleading; fraudulent
con authentic, veritable; actual, real, true; unquestionable, valid
ant bona fide, genuine

counterfeit *n syn* IMPOSTURE, deceit, deception, fake, fraud, gyp, hoax, humbug, phony, sell
rel copy, facsimile, reproduction; dummy, simulacrum

countermeasure *n syn* REMEDY 2, antidote, corrective, counteractant, counteractive, counteragent, counterstep, cure

counterpane *n syn* BEDSPREAD, bedcover, coverlet, ‖coverlid, spread

counterpart *n* **1** something that completes or complements < export controls as a *counterpart* of domestic distribution controls >
syn complement, correlate, pendant; *compare* PARALLEL
rel analogue, correlate, correspondent; equal, equivalent, like, match
con counterpoint, opposite
2 *syn* PARALLEL, analogue, correlate, correspondent, countertype, match
3 *syn* EQUAL, equivalent, like, match
4 *syn* OPPOSITE NUMBER, coordinate, vis-à-vis

counterpoise *n syn* BALANCE 1, equilibrium, equipoise, equiponderation, poise, stasis

counterpoise *vb syn* COMPENSATE 1, atone (for), balance, counterbalance, countervail, make up, offset, outweigh, redeem, set off
rel ballast, poise, stabilize, steady, trim
con capsize, overturn, upset

counterpole *n syn* OPPOSITE, antipode, antipole, antithesis, contra, contradictory, contrary, converse, counter, reverse

countersign *n syn* PASSWORD 1, watchword, word

counterstep *n syn* REMEDY 2, antidote, corrective, counteractant, counteractive, counteragent, countermeasure, cure

countertype *n syn* PARALLEL, analogue, correlate, correspondent, counterpart, match

countervail *vb syn* COMPENSATE 1, atone (for), balance, counterbalance, counterpoise, make up, offset, outweigh, redeem, set off
rel amend, correct, rectify; foil, frustrate, thwart; overcome, surmount

countless *adj syn* INNUMERABLE, innumerous, numberless, uncountable, uncounted, unnumberable, unnumbered, untold

count out *vb syn* EXCLUDE, bar, bate, debar, eliminate, except, rule out, suspend

countrified *adj syn* RURAL, agrestic, bucolic, campestral, country, out-country, outland, pastoral, provincial, rustic

country *n* the nation-state to which one belongs or from which one originated < returned to his own *country* after years of exile >
syn fatherland, home, homeland, land, mother country, motherland, soil

country *adj syn* RURAL, agrestic, bucolic, campestral, countrified, out-country, outland, pastoral, provincial, rustic

---

syn synonym(s)
idiom idiomatic equivalent(s)
ant antonym(s)
rel related word(s)
con contrasted word(s)
* vulgar
‖ use limited; if in doubt, see a dictionary
The first word in a synonym list when printed in SMALL CAPITALS shows where there is more information about the group. For a more efficient use of this book see Explanatory Notes.

country jake *n* ***syn*** RUSTIC, backwoodsman, bumpkin, clodhopper, clown, hayseed, hick, hillbilly, jake, rube

countryman *n* ***syn*** RUSTIC, ‖backwoodser, backwoodsman, bumpkin, clodhopper, clown, hayseed, hick, hillbilly, jake

couple *vb* **1** ***syn*** JOIN 1, bracket, coalesce, combine, conjoin, connect, link, marry, unite, yoke
2 ***syn*** HITCH 2, harness, yoke
rel hook up, ‖inspan

couple *n* two individuals of the same or a similar kind that occur, function, or are considered together <a *couple* of ideas for improving the book> <the happiest *couple* I know>
syn brace, doublet, duo, dyad, pair, twosome
rel span, team, yoke

coupling *n* ***syn*** JOINT 1, connection, joining, junction, juncture, seam, union

courage *n* a quality of mind or temperament that enables one to stand fast in the face of opposition, hardship, or danger <had the kind of *courage* that could appreciate a danger yet steadfastly face it>
syn *balls, cojones, dauntlessness, guts, heart, mettle, ‖moxie, pluck, resolution, spirit, spunk; *compare* FORTITUDE
rel audacity, boldness, bravery, doughtiness, fearlessness, intrepidity; gallantry, heroism, valor; backbone, fortitude, grit, sand; assurance, determination, firmness, persistence, tenacity
con chickenheartedness, faintheartedness, unmanliness, yellowness; baseness, cravenness, poltroonery, pusillanimity; timidity, timorousness
ant cowardice

courageous *adj* ***syn*** BRAVE 1, audacious, bold, dauntless, fearless, intrepid, unafraid, undaunted, valiant, valorous
rel fiery, high-spirited; strong, tenacious
con afraid, apprehensive, fearful
ant pusillanimous

courier *n* ***syn*** MESSENGER, bearer, carrier, emissary, envoy, internuncio

course *n* **1** ***syn*** WAY 2, line, passage, path, road, route
rel circuit, orbit, range, scope
2 ***syn*** CHANNEL 1, aqueduct, canal, conduit, duct, watercourse
3 way of acting or proceeding <hard to decide on the best *course* to follow>
syn line, policy, polity, procedure, program
rel design, pattern, plan, platform, scheme; manner, system, way
idiom course of action
4 ***syn*** PROGRESS 2, advance, progression
5 ***syn*** SUCCESSION 2, chain, consecution, order, progression, row, sequel, sequence, series, string

---

syn synonym(s) | *rel* related word(s)
idiom idiomatic equivalent(s) | *con* contrasted word(s)
ant antonym(s) | * vulgar
‖ use limited; if in doubt, see a dictionary
The first word in a synonym list when printed in SMALL CAPITALS shows where there is more information about the group. For a more efficient use of this book see Explanatory Notes.

---

course *vb* to proceed with great celerity (as in pursuing or competing) <the fox *coursed* after the hare>
syn career, chase, race, rush, speed, tear; *compare* RUSH 1
rel hasten, hurry, hustle; dart, dash, scamper, scoot, scurry; run, sprint
idiom step on the gas, stir one's stumps

courser *n* a strong vigorous horse formerly used in mounted combat <heroes mounted on great fiery *coursers*>
syn charger, war-horse

court *n* **1** an open space wholly or partly enclosed (as by buildings or walls) <the window looked on the *court*>
syn ‖close, courtyard, curtilage, enclosure, quad, quadrangle, yard
2 a place or the persons assembled for the administration of justice <the *court* was called to order>
syn bar, lawcourt, tribunal
3 ***syn*** JUDGE 2, ‖beak, justice, magistrate

court *vb* ***syn*** ADDRESS 8, make up (to), pursue, spark, sue, sweetheart, woo
rel allure, attract, captivate, charm

courteous *adj* ***syn*** CIVIL 2, genteel, mannerly, polite, well-mannered
rel attentive, considerate, thoughtful
con blunt, brusque, curt, gruff; insolent, overbearing, supercilious
ant discourteous

courtesan *n* ***syn*** HARLOT 1, blowen, demimondaine, demimonde, demirep, fancy woman, hetaera, kept woman, paphian, whore

courtesy *n* **1** courteous behavior or a courteous act <noted for her *courtesy* and graciousness> <such little *courtesies* take little time but often brighten lonely lives>
syn amenity, attention, gallantry
rel affability, cordiality, geniality, graciousness; comity, complaisance; chivalry, civility, courteousness, courtliness; attentiveness, considerateness, consideration, thoughtfulness
con boorishness, churlishness; impoliteness, incivility, rudeness, ungraciousness
ant discourtesy
2 ***syn*** FAVOR 4, dispensation, indulgence, kindness, service

courtly *adj* marked by elaborate and often ceremonious courtesy <this was indeed a *courtly* gentleman of the old school>
syn gallant, gracious, preux, stately; *compare* CIVIL 2
rel august, dignified, imposing, lofty; prim, starchy, stiff, stilted, studied; ceremonious, conventional, formal; civilized
con discourteous, ill-mannered, impolite, rude, uncivil, ungracious; boorish, coarse, gross, loutish, uncouth, vulgar
ant churlish

courtyard *n* ***syn*** COURT 1, ‖close, curtilage, enclosure, quad, quadrangle, yard

cousinage *n* ***syn*** KIN 2, cousinhood, kinfolk, kinsmen

cousinhood *n* ***syn*** KIN 2, cousinage, kinfolk, kinsmen

cove *n* ***syn*** INLET, arm, bay, bayou, bight, ‖creek, firth, gulf, harbor, slough

covenant *n* ***syn*** CONTRACT, agreement, bargain, bond, compact, convention, pact, transaction

covenant *vb* ***syn*** VOW, pledge, plight, swear
rel agree, concur

cover *vb* **1** ***syn*** DEFEND 1, bulwark, fend, guard, protect, safeguard, screen, secure, shield
2 ***syn*** HIDE, bury, ||bush up, cache, conceal, ||ditch, ensconce, screen, secrete, stash
3 to spread over or put something over <a smile *covered* her face> <*cover* the garden with manure>
syn blanket, cap, crown, overcast, overlay, overspread
rel conceal, hide, screen; defend, protect, shield; enclose, enfold, envelop, shroud, wrap; overspread, superimpose, superpose
con display, exhibit, expose
ant bare, uncover
4 ***syn*** TRAVEL 2, do, pass (over), track, traverse
5 ***syn*** SET 11, brood, ||clock, sit

cover *n* **1** ***syn*** SHELTER 1, asylum, covert, harbor, harborage, haven, port, refuge, retreat, sanctuary
rel concealment, hiding, screen; safety, security
ant exposure
2 ***syn*** MASK 2, cloak, disguise, facade, false front, guise, masquerade, put-on, semblance

coverlet *n* ***syn*** BEDSPREAD, bedcover, counterpane, ||coverlid, spread

||**coverlid** *n* ***syn*** BEDSPREAD, bedcover, counterpane, coverlet, spread

covert *adj* **1** ***syn*** SECRET 1, clandestine, furtive, hugger-mugger, hush-hush, stealthy, sub-rosa, surreptitious, undercover, under-the-table
rel camouflaged, cloaked, disguised, dissembled, masked
con candid, frank, open
ant overt
2 ***syn*** ULTERIOR, buried, concealed, guarded, hidden, obscured, privy, shrouded
con direct, forthright; honest, square, straight

covert *n* ***syn*** SHELTER 1, asylum, cover, harbor, harborage, haven, port, refuge, retreat, sanctuary

covertly *adv* ***syn*** SECRETLY, by stealth, clandestinely, furtively, hugger-mugger, in camera, privately, stealthily, sub rosa, surreptitiously

covet *vb* ***syn*** DESIRE 1, ||choose, crave, desiderate, want, wish
con abjure, forswear
ant renounce

covetous *adj* having or marked by an urgent and often unscrupulous desire for possessions <the *covetous* eye of an avid collector>
syn acquisitive, desirous, grabby, grasping, greedy, itchy, prehensile
rel esurient, gluttonous, rapacious, ravenous, voracious; hoggish, lickerish, piggish, swinish; avid, eager, keen; envious, jealous; grudging, selfish
con generous, liberal, munificent; ungrudging, unselfish; abstemious, abstinent, ascetic, austere; moderate, restrained, temperate

covey *n* ***syn*** GROUP 1, assembly, band, bevy, bunch, cluster, crew, party

covin *n* ***syn*** PLOT 2, cabal, conspiracy, intrigue, machination, practice, scheme

cow *vb* ***syn*** INTIMIDATE, bludgeon, bluster, browbeat, bulldoze, bully, bullyrag, dragoon, hector, strong-arm
rel appall, daunt, dismay; abash, discomfit, disconcert, embarrass, faze, rattle
con cower, cringe, fawn, toady, truckle

coward *n* one who shows or yields to ignoble fear <a treacherous *coward* who betrayed his friends to save his own skin>
syn chicken, craven, dastard, funk, funker, poltroon, quitter, yellowbelly
rel baby, fraidycat, invertebrate, jellyfish, milksop, scaredy-cat; caitiff, recreant
con gallant, hero, palladin, stalwart; ideal, model, pattern, standard

coward *adj* ***syn*** COWARDLY, ||chicken, craven, gutless, lily-livered, poltroonish, poor-spirited, pusillanimous, spunkless, unmanly

cowardly *adj* marked by or arising from a base lack of courage <a *cowardly* desertion>
syn ||chicken, coward, cowhearted, craven, gutless, lily-livered, milk-livered, poltroon, poltroonish, poor-spirited, pusillanimous, spunkless, unmanly, white-livered, yellow
rel afraid, chickenhearted, fainthearted, fearful, timid, timorous; funky, panicky; caitiff, dastardly, recreant, vile, worthless
con courageous, fearless, intrepid, valiant; daring, reckless, temerarious
ant brave

cower *vb* ***syn*** FAWN, apple-polish, bootlick, ||brownnose, cringe, grovel, honey (up), kowtow, toady, truckle
rel blench, flinch, quail, recoil, shrink, wince
con browbeat, bulldoze, bully, cow, intimidate; bristle, strut, swagger

cowering *adj* ***syn*** FAWNING, bootlicking, cringing, groveling, kowtowing, parasitic, sycophant, sycophantic, toadyish, truckling

cowhearted *adj* ***syn*** COWARDLY, ||chicken, coward, craven, gutless, lily-livered, poltroon, poor-spirited, pusillanimous, yellow

coxcomb *n* ***syn*** FOP, Beau Brummel, blood, buck, dandy, dude, exquisite, lounge lizard, macaroni, petit-maître

coy *adj* **1** ***syn*** SHY 1, bashful, demure, diffident, rabbity, retiring, self-effacing, timid, unassertive, unassured
rel decent, decorous, nice, proper, seemly
con brash, brazen, impudent
2 marked by a light playful artlessness <glanced up with a *coy* twinkle in her eye>
syn arch, coquettish, roguish
rel capricious, kittenish, lively, mischievous, playful, skittish
con serious, sober, thoughtful

cozen *vb* **1** ***syn*** CHEAT, beat, bilk, defraud, diddle, do, flimflam, gyp, overreach, swindle

---

2 *syn* DECEIVE, beguile, betray, delude, double-cross, humbug, illude, mislead, sell out, take in
cozy *adj* 1 *syn* COMFORTABLE 2, comfy, cushy, easeful, easy, snug, soft
rel safe, secure
2 *syn* INTIMATE 4, ‖buddy-buddy, chummy, pally, ‖palsy-walsy
crab *vb syn* GRIPE, ‖beef, ‖bellyache, ‖bitch, bleat, ‖crib, fuss, squawk, yammer, yawp (*or* yaup)
idiom fret and fume
crab *n syn* GROUCH, ‖bellyacher, complainer, crosspatch, faultfinder, griper, grouser, growler, grumbler, kicker
crabbed *adj syn* SULLEN, ‖chuff, ‖chuffy, dour, gloomy, glum, morose, saturnine, sulky, surly
rel blunt, brusque, crusty, gruff; choleric, cranky, splenetic, testy; huffy, irascible, irritable, snappish
con amiable, complaisant, good-natured, obliging; benign, benignant, kind, kindly; agreeable, pleasing; affable, genial, gracious
crabber *n syn* GROUCH, ‖bellyacher, complainer, crab, crank, crosspatch, faultfinder, griper, malcontent, sorehead
crabby *adj syn* SULLEN, ‖chuffy, crabbed, ‖dorty, dour, gloomy, glum, mumpish, sulky, surly
crabwise *adv syn* SIDEWAYS 1, laterally, sideling, ‖sidelings, sidelong, sideward, sidewise
crack *vb syn* DECODE, break, cryptanalyze, decipher, decrypt
rel puzzle out
crack *n* 1 *syn* BANG 2, blast, boom, burst, clap, crash, slam, smash, wham
rel splintering, splitting; percussion
2 *syn* JOKE 1, drollery, gag, jape, jest, quip, sally, wisecrack, witticism, ‖yak
rel dig, fling, potshot
idiom flash of wit
3 a usually narrow opening, break, or discontinuity made by splitting and rupture <a *crack* in the ice>
syn chink, cleft, fissure, rift, rima, rimation, rime, split
rel rent; discontinuity, interstice, interval; cranny, niche; crevasse, crevice
4 *syn* INSTANT 1, breathing, flash, ‖jiff, jiffy, minute, moment, second, shake, split second
idiom flash of lightning
5 *syn* BLOW 1, bang, bash, bastinado, belt, slam, smack, ‖welt, whack, whop
6 *syn* FLING 1, go, pop, shot, slap, stab, ‖stagger, try, whack, whirl
crack *adj syn* PROFICIENT, adept, crackerjack, expert, master, masterful, masterly, skilled, skillful
rel excellent, superior
crackbrain *n syn* CRACKPOT, crank, cuckoo, ding-a-ling, harebrain, kook, lunatic, nut, screwball
idiom cracked wit
crackbrained *adj syn* INSANE 1, cracked, ‖crackers, ‖cracky, ‖cranky, crazed, crazy, cuckoo, daffy, daft
crackdown *n syn* REPRESSION 2, clampdown, suppression
rel quashing
idiom lowering the boom
cracked *adj syn* INSANE 1, ‖batty, crazy, daft, demented, lunatic, mad, maniac, nuts, screwy
idiom ‖off in the upper story
crackerjack *n syn* ‖DILLY, ‖corker, ‖daisy, dandy, humdinger, jim-dandy, knockout, ‖lalapalooza, ‖lulu, nifty
crackerjack *adj syn* PROFICIENT, adept, crack, expert, master, masterful, masterly, skilled, skillful
‖**crackers** *adj syn* INSANE 1, crackbrained, cracked, ‖cracky, ‖cranky, crazed, crazy, cuckoo, daffy, daft
cracking *adj syn* MONSTROUS 1, fantastic, massive, monumental, mortal, prodigious, stupendous, towering, tremendous
crackpot *n* one given to extremely eccentric or lunatic ideas or actions <a *crackpot* who wrote threatening letters to public figures>
syn crackbrain, crank, cuckoo, ding-a-ling, harebrain, kook, lunatic, nut, screwball
rel case, character, ‖dingbat, eccentric, oddball, oddity, ‖wack; loon, loony, madman, maniac
crack-up *n* 1 *syn* NERVOUS BREAKDOWN, breakdown, collapse, nervous prostration
2 *syn* CRASH 3, pileup, ‖prang, smash, smashup, ‖stramash, wreck
3 *syn* COLLAPSE 2, breakdown, crash, debacle, smash, smashup, wreck
rel decline, deterioration
‖**cracky** *adj syn* INSANE 1, crackbrained, cracked, ‖crackers, ‖cranky, crazed, crazy, cuckoo, daffy, daft
cradlesong *n syn* LULLABY, berceuse
craft *n* 1 *syn* ART 1, adroitness, cunning, dexterity, expertise, know-how, skill
2 *syn* TRADE 1, art, calling, handicraft, métier, profession, vocation
rel job
3 *syn* CUNNING 2, art, artfulness, artifice, cageyness, canniness, craftiness, foxiness, slyness, wiliness
craftiness *n syn* CUNNING 2, art, artfulness, artifice, cageyness, canniness, craft, foxiness, slyness, wiliness
crafty *adj syn* SLY 2, artful, astute, cunning, deep, foxy, guileful, insidious, tricky, wily
rel adroit, clever, tidy; acute, keen, sharp; deceitful, fawning, ‖sleekit, ‖sleeky
cragged *adj syn* ROUGH 1, asperous, craggy, harsh, jagged, rugged, scabrous, scraggy, uneven, unsmooth
craggy *adj syn* ROUGH 1, asperous, harsh, jagged, rugged, scabrous, scraggy, uneven, unlevel, unsmooth
cram *vb* 1 to fill (a limited space) forcibly with more than is practicable or fitting <*crammed* the suitcase chock-full and had to sit on it to close it>
syn jam, jam-pack, ‖pang, ram, stuff, tamp; *compare* LOAD 3, PRESS 7
rel pack, stive; fill, heap; chock, choke; press, shove, thrust; drive, force; squeeze, wedge
2 *syn* PRESS 7, crowd, crush, jam, squash, squeeze
3 *syn* GULP, bolt, englut, gobble, guzzle, ingurgitate, slop, slosh, wolf

rel overeat

idiom pack it in

4 to study intensively or under pressure <had to *cram* all night before the exam>

syn bone (up), ‖mug (up)

rel study; review

idiom burn the midnight oil

cram–full *adj* *syn* FULL 1, brimful, bung-full, chock-full, crammed, crowded, jam-full, jam-packed, packed, stuffed

crammed *adj* *syn* FULL 1, awash, brimful, brimming, chock-full, crowded, jammed, loaded, packed, stuffed

idiom crammed full, crammed to the bursting point, fit (*or* ready) to burst

ant emptied

cramp *n* **1** *syn* RESTRICTION 1, ‖ball and chain, circumscription, limitation, stint, stricture

rel shackle

2 *syn* RESTRICTION 2, circumscription, confinement, constrainment, constraint, restraint

rel constipation, stultification

cramp *adj* *syn* CRAMPED, confined, incommodious, squeezy, ‖tucked up

cramped *adj* having insufficient size or capacity <a *cramped* cubbyhole of an office>

syn confined, cramp, incommodious, squeezy, ‖tucked up

rel close, narrow, tight, two-by-four; little, minute, small, tiny

con commodious, unconfined

ant spacious

crank *n* **1** *syn* CAPRICE, bee, boutade, conceit, crotchet, fancy, freak, maggot, notion, vagary

2 *syn* CRACKPOT, crackbrain, cuckoo, ding-a-ling, harebrain, kook, lunatic, nut, screwball

rel freak

3 *syn* GROUCH, ‖bellyacher, crab, crosspatch, faultfinder, griper, grouser, growler, grumbler, sourpuss

cranky *adj* **1** *syn* INSANE 1, crackbrained, cracked, ‖crackers, ‖cracky, crazed, crazy, cuckoo, daffy, daft

2 *syn* CANTANKEROUS, bearish, cankered, cross-grained, crotchety, ornery, vinegarish, vinegary, waspish, waspy

rel contrary, difficult, froward, perverse

3 *syn* IRASCIBLE, choleric, hot-tempered, quick-tempered, ratty, ‖stomachy, temperish, testy, tetchy, touchy

rel bad-humored, ill-humored; disagreeable; ugly

idiom out of sorts

cranny *n* *syn* NOOK, byplace, niche

‖**crap** *n* *syn* NONSENSE 2, ‖baloney, bilge, ‖bull, ‖bunk, claptrap, drivel, hogwash, rot, twaddle

‖**crap out** *vb* *syn* FAINT, black out, pass out, ‖swarf, ‖swelt, swoon

***crapper** *n* **1** *syn* TOILET, ‖can, ‖donicker, john, johnny, latrine, ‖loo, ‖pot, ‖potty, ‖throne

2 *syn* PRIVY 1, backhouse, ‖biffy, ‖closet, jakes, ‖necessary, ‖office, outhouse

‖**crappy** *adj* *syn* BAD 1, amiss, ‖bum, dissatisfactory, poor, ‖punk, rotten, unsatisfactory, up, wrong

crash *vb* *syn* FAIL 5, break, bust, fold

ant skyrocket

crash *n* **1** *syn* BANG 2, blast, boom, burst, clap, crack, slam, smash, wham

2 *syn* IMPACT, bump, clash, collision, concussion, jar, jolt, percussion, shock, smash

3 a wrecking or smashing especially of a vehicle <an air *crash*>

syn crack-up, pileup, ‖prang, smash, smashup, ‖stramash, wreck

rel accident; collision

4 *syn* COLLAPSE 2, breakdown, crack-up, debacle, smash, smashup, wreck

crashing *adj* *syn* UTTER, absolute, blasted, *‖bloody, confounded, consummate, downright, gross, infernal, positive

crass *adj* *syn* COARSE 3, crude, gross, inelegant, raw, rough, rude, uncouth, unrefined, vulgar

rel churlish, loutish

ant refined

crate *n* *syn* JALOPY, clunker, dog, heap, junker, wreck

crave *vb* **1** *syn* BEG, appeal, beseech, brace, entreat, implore, importune, plead, pray, supplicate

2 *syn* DESIRE 1, ‖choose, covet, desiderate, want, wish

con contemn, despise, disdain, scorn

ant spurn

3 *syn* LONG, ache, dream, hanker, hunger, lust, pine, sigh, suspire, thirst

idiom have a craving for

4 *syn* DEMAND 2, ask, call (for), necessitate, require, take

craven *adj* *syn* COWARDLY, ‖chicken, coward, gutless, lily-livered, poltroonish, poor-spirited, pusillanimous, spunkless, unmanly

craven *n* *syn* COWARD, chicken, dastard, funk, funker, poltroon, quitter, yellowbelly

craving *n* *syn* DESIRE 1, appetite, appetition, itch, lust, passion, urge

crawfish (out) *vb* *syn* BACK DOWN, back off, back out, backpedal, backwater, cry off, declare off, renege, resile, welsh

crawl *vb* **1** *syn* CREEP 1, slide, snake

rel grovel; worm

2 *syn* TEEM, abound, flow, pullulate, ‖sny, swarm

‖**3** *syn* LAMBASTE 3, blister, castigate, excoriate, flay, lash (into), roast, scathe, scorch, slam

craze *vb* *syn* MADDEN 1, derange, distract, frenzy, unbalance, unhinge

craze *n* *syn* FASHION 3, chic, cry, dernier cri, fad, furore, rage, style, thing, vogue

rel enthusiasm, fever

crazed *adj* *syn* INSANE 1, bedlamite, cracked, crazy, demented, deranged, mad, non compos mentis, unbalanced, unsound

craziness *n* *syn* FOOLISHNESS, absurdity, dottiness, folly, inanity, insanity, preposterousness, senselessness, silliness, witlessness

---

syn synonym(s) — *rel* related word(s)

idiom idiomatic equivalent(s) — *con* contrasted word(s)

ant antonym(s) — * vulgar

‖ use limited; if in doubt, see a dictionary

The first word in a synonym list when printed in SMALL CAPITALS shows where there is more information about the group. For a more efficient use of this book see Explanatory Notes.

crazy *adj* **1** ***syn*** INSANE 1, ‖batty, crazed, daft, lunatic, mad, maniac, nuts, screwy, unbalanced
rel doting, gaga, moonstruck; beeheaded, silly; erratic, possessed
idiom as crazy as a loon, having a screw loose, having bats in one's belfry, not having all one's marbles (*or* buttons)
ant sane
2 ***syn*** FOOLISH 2, absurd, ‖balmy, harebrained, insane, loony, ‖potty, preposterous, silly, wacky
rel goofy, senseless
idiom beyond the realm of reason, out of all reason
con practical, reasonable, reasoned, sensible
ant sane

‖**crazy** *adv* ***syn*** VERY 1, ‖awful, ‖big, damned, ‖dreadful, ‖larruping, ‖main, ‖monstrous, ‖mortacious, ‖right smart

crazy house *n* ***syn*** ASYLUM 3, booby hatch, ‖bughouse, loony bin, madhouse, ‖nuthouse

cream *n* **1** ***syn*** OINTMENT, balm, cerate, chrism, salve, unction, unguent
2 ***syn*** BEST, choice, elite, fat, flower, pick, pride, prime, prize, top
idiom (the) top cream

‖**cream** *vb* ***syn*** WHIP 2, beat, blast, ‖bowl (down *or* out), ‖clobber, drub, lambaste, lick, overwhelm, shellac

crease *n* ***syn*** WRINKLE, corrugation, crinkle, fold, furrow, plica, ridge, rimple, rivel, ruck

create *vb* **1** ***syn*** GENERATE 1, father, hatch, make, originate, parent, procreate, produce, sire, spawn
idiom call into being
2 ***syn*** FOUND 2, constitute, establish, institute, organize, set up, start
3 ***syn*** COMPOSE 2
rel conceive, formulate; imagine

creation *n* ***syn*** UNIVERSE, cosmos (*or* kosmos), macrocosm, macrocosmos, megacosm, nature, world

creative *adj* ***syn*** INVENTIVE, demiurgic, deviceful, ingenious, innovational, innovative, innovatory, original, originative
rel causal, institutive, occasional; Promethean
ant uncreative

creator *n* ***syn*** FATHER 2, architect, author, founder, generator, inventor, maker, originator, patriarch, sire
rel brain(s), brainpower, mastermind

creature *n* **1** ***syn*** BEAST, animal, brute, ‖critter
2 ***syn*** HUMAN, being, body, individual, man, mortal, party, person, personage, soul
3 ***syn*** SYCOPHANT, minion, reptile, spaniel, ‖suck, toad, toadeater, toadier, toady, truckler

credence *n* ***syn*** BELIEF 1, credit, faith
rel acceptance, accepting, admission, admitting; confidence, reliance, trust
con skepticism; distrust, mistrust; disbelief, incredulity, unbelief

credentials *n pl* something presented or held by one as proof that he is what or who he claims to be <her academic *credentials* were excellent>
syn character, recommendation, reference, testimonial
rel document(s), documentation, paper(s), voucher; accreditation, certification, endorsement, sanction

credible *adj* **1** ***syn*** BELIEVABLE, colorable, creditable, plausible
rel satisfying, satisfactory; solid, sound, straight, valid
idiom to be believed
con unsatisfactory; preposterous, ridiculous
ant incredible
2 ***syn*** AUTHENTIC 1, convincing, faithful, trustworthy, trusty
rel likely, probable; rational, reasonable; conclusive, determinative
ant incredible

credit *n* **1** ***syn*** BELIEF 1, credence, faith
rel confidence, reliance, trust
2 ***syn*** INFLUENCE 1, authority, prestige, weight
rel fame, renown, reputation, repute
con disrepute, ignominy, obloquy, opprobrium
ant discredit
3 one that enhances another <he is a *credit* to his family>
syn asset
rel honor
4 favorable notice or attention resulting from an action or achievement <took all the *credit* for the idea>
syn acknowledgment, recognition
rel attention, notice; distinction, fame, honor; glory, kudos

credit *vb* **1** ***syn*** FEEL 3, believe, consider, deem, hold, sense, think
con disbelieve, pooh-pooh
ant discredit
2 ***syn*** ASCRIBE, accredit, assign, attribute, charge, impute, lay, refer

creditable *adj* **1** ***syn*** BELIEVABLE, colorable, credible, plausible
ant discreditable
2 ***syn*** RESPECTABLE 1, estimable, reputable, reputed, well-thought-of
rel satisfactory; suitable
ant discreditable

credo *n* ***syn*** IDEOLOGY, creed, weltanschauung

credulous *adj* ready or inclined to believe especially on slight or insufficient evidence <deceiving the *credulous* young girls>
syn unsuspecting, unsuspicious, unwary
rel believing; accepting, unquestioning; trustful, trusting; green, inexperienced; naive, simple, unsophisticated; dupable, gullible
con mistrustful, suspecting, suspicious; careful, wary; doubtful, doubting, questioning
ant incredulous, skeptical

creed *n* **1** ***syn*** RELIGION 1, cult, faith, persuasion
2 ***syn*** RELIGION 2, church, communion, connection, cult, denomination, faith, persuasion, sect
3 ***syn*** IDEOLOGY, credo, weltanschauung

creek *n* ‖**1** ***syn*** INLET, arm, bay, bayou, bight, cove, firth, gulf, harbor, slogh

---

syn synonym(s) *rel* related word(s)
idiom idiomatic equivalent(s) *con* contrasted word(s)
ant antonym(s) * vulgar
‖ use limited; if in doubt, see a dictionary
The first word in a synonym list when printed in SMALL CAPITALS shows where there is more information about the group. For a more efficient use of this book see Explanatory Notes.

rel ria
2 a natural stream of water normally smaller than and often tributary to a river <went wading in the *creek*>
syn ‖branch, brook, ‖burn, ‖crick, gill, race, ‖rindle, ‖rithe, rivulet, ‖run, runnel, stream
rel ‖beck, brooklet, ‖rigolet, rill, rillet, runlet, streamlet; freshet; ditch, watercourse; wadi

creep *vb* **1** to move along a surface in a prone or crouching position <a cat *creeping* through the grass>
syn crawl, slide, snake
rel glide, slither; sneak, steal, tiptoe; edge, inch; sniggle, wriggle
2 *syn* STEAL 3, glide, mouse, slide, slip
3 *syn* SNEAK, glide, gumshoe, lurk, pussyfoot, shirk, skulk, slide, slink, steal

crème de la crème *n syn* ARISTOCRACY, aristoi, blue blood, carriage trade, elite, gentry, haut monde, optimacy, quality, upper crust

crepehanger *n syn* PESSIMIST, calamity howler, Cassandra, worrywart

crescendo *n syn* APEX 2, acme, apogee, capstone, climax, crest, culmen, culmination, meridian, peak

crest *n* **1** *syn* TOP 1, apex, crown, fastigium, peak, roof, summit, vertex
rel cap
2 *syn* RIDGE 1, chine, hogback
3 *syn* APEX 2, acme, apogee, climax, crescendo, culmination, noon, peak, pinnacle, summit

crest *vb syn* SURMOUNT 3, cap, crown, top

crestfallen *adj syn* DOWNCAST, blue, cast down, dejected, depressed, disconsolate, dispirited, down, downhearted, low
idiom ‖in a funk
ant elated

cretin *n syn* FOOL 4, ament, ‖feeb, half-wit, idiot, imbecile, moron, natural, simpleton, zany
rel zombie

crew *n syn* GROUP 1, assembly, band, bevy, bunch, cluster, covey, party
rel aggregation, collection, congregation; gang, retinue, set

crib *n* **1** *syn* BROTHEL, bagnio, bawdy house, bordello, cathouse, disorderly house, ‖hookshop, ‖joyhouse, stew, whorehouse
2 *syn* PONY, trot
rel plagiarism

‖**crib** *vb syn* GRIPE, ‖beef, ‖bellyache, ‖bitch, blast, ‖blow off, crab, fuss, squawk, yammer

‖**crick** *n syn* CREEK 2, ‖branch, brook, gill, race, ‖rindle, rivulet, ‖run, runnel, stream

crime *n* **1** a serious breach of the public law <armed robbery is a *crime*>
syn misdeed, offense
rel criminality, illegality, lawlessness; delict, delictum; breach, break, infringement, transgression, violation; wrong, wrongdoing; felony
2 *syn* EVIL 3, diablerie, iniquity, sin, tort, wrong, wrongdoing

crimeless *adj syn* INNOCENT 2, blameless, clean, faultless, guiltless, inculpable, unguilty

criminal *adj syn* UNLAWFUL, illegal, illegitimate, illicit, lawless, wrongful

criminal *n* one who has committed a usually serious offense <car thieves and other *criminals*>
syn felon, lawbreaker, malefactor, offender
rel scofflaw; transgressor, trespasser, wrongdoer; crook, ‖twicer; gangster, hood, mobster, racketeer, thug; fugitive, outlaw; convict, jailbird

criminate *vb syn* ACCUSE, arraign, charge, impeach, incriminate, inculpate, indict, tax
ant exonerate

crimp *vb* **1** *syn* CRUMPLE 1, crimple, crinkle, rimple, ruck (up), ‖ruckle, rumple, screw, scrunch, wrinkle
2 *syn* RESTRAIN 1, bit, bridle, check, constrain, hold back, hold down, hold in, inhibit, withhold

crimp *n syn* OBSTACLE, bar, Chinese wall, hamper, hurdle, impediment, mountain, obstruction, rub, snag

crimple *vb syn* CRUMPLE 1, crimp, crinkle, rimple, ruck (up), ‖ruckle, rumple, screw, scrunch, wrinkle

crimson *vb syn* BLUSH, color, flush, glow, mantle, pink, pinken, redden, rose, rouge
ant blanch

cringe *vb syn* FAWN, apple-polish, bootlick, ‖brownnose, cower, grovel, kowtow, slaver, toady, truckle
rel blench, flinch, quail, recoil, wince; ‖croodle, crouch, shrink
idiom bow and scrape, eat dirt

cringing *adj syn* FAWNING, bootlicking, cowering, groveling, kowtowing, parasitic, sycophant, sycophantic, toadying, truckling
rel obeisant, prostrate
idiom bowing and scraping, eating dirt, eating humble pie, on one's hands and knees

crinkle *vb syn* CRUMPLE 1, crimp, crimple, rimple, ruck (up), ‖ruckle, rumple, screw, scrunch, wrinkle

crinkle *n syn* WRINKLE, corrugation, crease, fold, furrow, plica, ridge, rimple, rivel, ruck
rel crimp

cripple *vb* **1** *syn* MAIM, dislimb, dismember, mayhem, mutilate
rel lame
2 *syn* PARALYZE 1, disable, disarm, immobilize, incapacitate, prostrate
3 *syn* WEAKEN 1, attenuate, blunt, debilitate, disable, enfeeble, sap, unbrace, undermine, unstrengthen

crisis *n syn* JUNCTURE 2, contingency, crossroad(s), emergency, exigency, pass, pinch, strait, turning point, zero hour

crisp *adj* **1** *syn* SHORT 6, brittle, crumbly, ‖crump, crunchy, friable
con flabby, flaccid, limp
2 *syn* INCISIVE, biting, clear-cut, cutting, ingoing, penetrating, trenchant
rel piquing, provoking, stimulating

crisscross *vb syn* INTERSECT, cross, crosscut, decussate, intercross

---

syn synonym(s) — *rel* related word(s)
idiom idiomatic equivalent(s) — *con* contrasted word(s)
ant antonym(s) — * vulgar
‖ use limited; if in doubt, see a dictionary
The first word in a synonym list when printed in SMALL CAPITALS shows where there is more information about the group. For a more efficient use of this book see Explanatory Notes.

criterion *n* ***syn*** STANDARD 3, benchmark, gauge, measure, touchstone, yardstick
rel adjudgment, judgment

critic *n* one given to harsh or captious judgment <chronic *critics* of the administration>
syn aristarch, carper, caviler, criticizer, faultfinder, knocker, momus, smellfungus, Zoilus
rel Monday morning quarterback; nitpicker, quibbler; belittler, disparager; complainer; censurer; muckraker, mudslinger
con backer, supporter; partisan; advocate, champion, protagonist

critic *adj* ***syn*** CRITICAL 1, captious, carping, caviling, cavillous, censorious, faultfinding, hypercritical, overcritical

critical *adj* **1** exhibiting the spirit of one who looks for and points out faults and defects <constant *critical* comments about her attire>
syn captious, carping, caviling, cavillous, censorious, critic, faultfinding, hypercritical, overcritical
rel discerning, discriminating, penetrating; finicky, fussy, particular; belittling, demeaning, disparaging, humbling, lowering
con cursory, shallow, superficial; encouraging, flattering, praising
ant uncritical
2 ***syn*** ACUTE 6, climacteric, crucial, desperate, dire
rel conclusive, decisive, determinative; consequential, important, momentous, significant, weighty

criticism *n* a discourse that evaluates or analyzes something (as a work of art or literature) <read every *criticism* of the new play>
syn comment, critique, notice, review, reviewal
rel analysis, examination, study; commentary, observation; opinion; appraisal, assessment, estimate, rating

criticize *vb* to make adverse comments about (someone or something) openly, often publicly, and with varying severity <*criticized* his opponent's liberal views>
syn blame, censure, condemn, cut up, denounce, denunciate, knock, pan, rap, reprehend, reprobate, skin; *compare* LAMBASTE 3, REPROVE, SCOLD 1
rel blast, castigate, fulminate (against), fustigate, roast, scathe
idiom find fault with, pull (*or* pick *or* tear) to pieces, take to task
con approve, countenance, endorse, OK (*or* okay)
ant praise

criticizer *n* ***syn*** CRITIC, aristarch, carper, caviler, faultfinder, knocker, momus, smellfungus, Zoilus

critique *n* ***syn*** CRITICISM, comment, notice, review, reviewal

‖**critter** *n* ***syn*** BEAST, animal, brute, creature

croak *vb* **1** ***syn*** GRUMBLE 1, grouch, grouse, ‖grunt, murmur, mutter, scold
rel complain, quarrel
‖**2** ***syn*** DIE 1, cash in, ‖check out, conk, expire, ‖kick in, ‖kick off, pass, pass away, pop off

‖**croaker** *n* ***syn*** PHYSICIAN, doc, doctor, MD, medical, mediciner, medico, ‖sawbones

croaking *adj* ***syn*** HOARSE 1, croaky, gruff, husky

croaky *adj* ***syn*** HOARSE 1, croaking, gruff, husky

‖**crocked** *adj* ***syn*** INTOXICATED 1, ‖boozed, ‖boozy, ‖canned, drunk, inebriated, ‖lushed, muddled, pixilated, ‖plastered

crone *n* ***syn*** HAG 2, ‖bag, ‖bat, beldam, biddy, drab, trot, witch
rel frump, slattern, sloven

crony *n* ***syn*** ASSOCIATE 3, buddy, chum, comate, companion, comrade, ‖cully, pal, running mate
idiom bosom buddy

‖**crooch** *vb* ***syn*** CROUCH, huddle, hunch, scrooch (down)

‖**croodle** *vb* ***syn*** SNUGGLE, burrow, cuddle, nestle, nuzzle, ‖snudge, snug, ‖snuzzle

crook *vb* **1** ***syn*** CURVE, bend, bow, round
‖**2** ***syn*** STEAL 1, appropriate, ‖clout, ‖cly, ‖coon, ‖cop, filch, ‖heist, nab, pinch
‖**3** ***syn*** CHEAT, beat, bilk, chisel, chouse, cozen, defraud, diddle, do, swindle

crooked *adj* **1** departing from a straight line or course <a *crooked* road>
syn bending, curving, devious, twisting; *compare* CURVED, WINDING
rel oblique; circuitous, indirect, roundabout; errant, meandering, rambling, serpentine, snaky, tortuous, winding; zigzag
con direct, undeviating
ant straight
2 deviating from rectitude <*crooked* police officers on the take>
syn corrupt, dishonest, snide; *compare* CORRUPT 2, VENAL 1
rel devious, indirect, shifty, underhand; double-dealing, fraudulent; deceitful, lying, untruthful; ruthless, unscrupulous
con aboveboard, forthright, straightforward; conscientious, honorable, just, proper, righteous, scrupulous, upright
ant honest, straight

crookedly *adv* ***syn*** AWRY 1, askance, askant, askew, ‖cam, cock-a-hoop, cockeyed
ant straight

crop *n* ***syn*** HARVEST 2, fruitage

crop *vb* **1** ***syn*** TOP 1, detruncate, pollard, truncate
rel chop, hew, slash; detach, disengage
2 ***syn*** MOW, clip, cut
3 ***syn*** CUT 6, clip, pare, prune, shave, shear, skive, trim
rel snip

cropping *n* ***syn*** HARVEST 1, gathering, harvesting, ingathering, reaping

cross *n* **1** ***syn*** TRIAL 1, affliction, calvary, crucible, ordeal, tribulation, visitation
idiom a cross to bear
2 ***syn*** HYBRID, bastard, crossbred, crossbreed, half blood, half-breed, mongrel, mule

cross *vb* **1** ***syn*** DENY 4, contradict, contravene, disaffirm, gainsay, impugn, negate, negative, traverse

---

syn synonym(s)	*rel* related word(s)
idiom idiomatic equivalent(s)	*con* contrasted word(s)
ant antonym(s)	* vulgar

‖ use limited; if in doubt, see a dictionary
The first word in a synonym list when printed in SMALL CAPITALS shows where there is more information about the group. For a more efficient use of this book see Explanatory Notes.

2 ***syn*** BETRAY 2, double-cross, sell, sell out, ‖split
idiom bite the hand that feeds one, stab in the back
3 ***syn*** TRAVERSE 4, transverse
4 to cause (an animal or plant) to breed with one of a different kind < *crossing* a horse with an ass results in a mule>
syn crossbreed, cross-mate, hybridize, interbreed, intercross
rel mongrelize
5 ***syn*** INTERSECT, crisscross, crosscut, decussate, intercross
idiom lie (*or* be) athwart

cross *adj* ***syn*** IRASCIBLE, choleric, cranky, quick-tempered, ratty, ‖stomachy, temperish, testy, tetchy, touchy
rel captious, carping, caviling, faultfinding
idiom cross as a bear

cross *prep* ***syn*** ACROSS, athwart, over

crossbred *n* ***syn*** HYBRID, bastard, cross, crossbreed, half blood, half-breed, mongrel, mule

crossbreed *vb* ***syn*** CROSS 4, cross-mate, hybridize, interbreed, intercross

crossbreed *n* ***syn*** HYBRID, bastard, cross, crossbred, half blood, half-breed, mongrel, mule

crosscut *vb* ***syn*** INTERSECT, crisscross, cross, decussate, intercross

cross–examination *n* a thorough, typically formal questioning for full information < *cross-examination* of a hostile witness>
syn grill, grilling, interrogation, third degree
rel debriefing; questioning

cross–grained *adj* **1** ***syn*** CANTANKEROUS, bearish, cankered, cranky, crotchety, ornery, vinegarish, vinegary, waspish, waspy
2 ***syn*** CONTRARY 3, balky, froward, ornery, perverse, restive, wayward, wrongheaded
rel difficult

crossing *adj* ***syn*** TRANSVERSE, crosswise, thwart, transversal, traverse

cross–mate *vb* ***syn*** CROSS 4, crossbreed, hybridize, interbreed, intercross

crosspatch *n* ***syn*** GROUCH, complainer, crab, crank, griper, grouser, growler, grumbler, sorehead, sourpuss

crossroad *n, usu* **crossroads** *pl but sing or pl in constr*
syn JUNCTURE 2, contingency, crisis, emergency, exigency, pass, pinch, strait, turning point, zero hour

‖**cross talk** *n* ***syn*** BANTER, backchat, badinage, persiflage, repartee, snip-snap

crossways *adv* ***syn*** ACROSS 1, athwart, crosswise
rel transversely; askew, awry, crisscross
con lengthwise
ant longways

crosswise *adv* ***syn*** ACROSS 1, athwart, crossways
con longways
ant lengthwise

crosswise *adj* ***syn*** TRANSVERSE, crossing, thwart, transversal, traverse
ant lengthwise

crotchet *n* ***syn*** CAPRICE, bee, boutade, conceit, fancy, freak, humor, megrim, vagary, whim
rel eccentricity, kink, kinkiness, quirk, twist
idiom bee in one's bonnet (*or* brain), flea in one's nose, kink in one's horn, maggot in one's brain

crotchety *adj* ***syn*** CANTANKEROUS, bearish, cankered, cranky, cross-grained, ornery, vinegarish, vinegary, waspish, waspy

crouch *vb* to stoop low with the limbs close to the body < *crouched* behind a rock and watched>
syn ‖crooch, huddle, hunch, scrooch (down); *compare* SQUAT
rel bend, bow, dip, duck; hunker (down), ‖quat, squat, stoop, ‖swat; cower, cringe, flinch, quail, wince; grovel

crow *vb* ***syn*** BOAST, blow, brag, cock-a-doodle-doo, gasconade, mouth, prate, puff, rodomontade, vaunt
rel cry, exult, jubilate

crowd *vb* **1** ***syn*** PRESS 1, bear, crush, jam, push, ‖squab, squash, squeeze, squish, squush
rel ram, shove
2 ***syn*** PRESS 7, cram, crush, jam, squash, squeeze
rel bunch, cluster

crowd *n* **1** a usually large group of people <a *crowd* gathered before the palace>
syn crush, drove, horde, multitude, press, push, squash, throng; *compare* MULTITUDE 1
rel army, host, legion; flock, gaggle, herd, swarm; mob, rabble, rout
2 ***syn*** GATHERING 2, aggregation, assemblage, assembly, collection, company, congeries, congregation, group, ruck
rel huddle, parley; troop; herd; rally
3 ***syn*** MULTITUDE 1, army, cloud, flock, host, legion, rout, scores
4 ***syn*** SET 5, bunch, circle, group, lot, push

crowded *adj* **1** ***syn*** FULL 1, awash, brimful, brimming, chock-full, crammed, jammed, loaded, packed, stuffed
rel overcharged, overloaded
ant uncrowded
2 ***syn*** CLOSE 4, compact, dense, thick, tight
ant uncrowded

crown *n* **1** ***syn*** TOP 1, apex, crest, fastigium, peak, roof, summit, vertex
2 ***syn*** WREATH, anadem, chaplet, coronal, coronet, garland
rel diadem, tiara
3 ***syn*** APEX 2, acme, climax, crest, culmination, meridian, peak, pinnacle, summit, zenith

crown *vb* **1** ***syn*** SURMOUNT 3, cap, crest, top
2 ***syn*** COVER 3, blanket, cap, overcast, overlay, overspread
3 ***syn*** CLIMAX, cap, culminate, finish off, round off, top off

crown (with) *vb* ***syn*** ENDOW 1, dower, endue

crucial *adj* ***syn*** ACUTE 6, climacteric, critical, desperate, dire

---

syn synonym(s) *rel* related word(s)
idiom idiomatic equivalent(s) *con* contrasted word(s)
ant antonym(s) * vulgar
‖ use limited; if in doubt, see a dictionary
The first word in a synonym list when printed in SMALL CAPITALS shows where there is more information about the group. For a more efficient use of this book see Explanatory Notes.

rel deciding, decisive, important; necessary, vital; clamorous, compelling, crying, imperative, insistent, pressing

crucible *n* ***syn*** TRIAL 1, affliction, calvary, cross, ordeal, tribulation, visitation

crucify *vb* ***syn*** AFFLICT, agonize, excruciate, harrow, martyr, rack, smite, torment, torture, try

rel bedevil, bother, browbeat

idiom kill by inches, nail to the cross, put on the rack

crud *n* a deposit or incrustation of something filthy, greasy, or sticky <machinery all covered with *crud*>

syn ‖cab, goo, gook, gunk; *compare* GOO 1

rel filth, muck, slime, sludge; debris, junk, rubbish, trash

‖**cruddle** *vb* ***syn*** CURDLE, ‖clabber, curd, ‖lopper, turn

crude *adj* **1** ***syn*** UNREFINED 3, impure, native, raw, run-of-mine, ungraded, unsorted

2 ***syn*** COARSE 3, crass, gross, inelegant, raw, rough, rude, uncouth, unrefined, vulgar

rel backward, ignorant, unenlightened; boorish, cloddish, clodhopping, ill-bred, loutish, lowbred; savage; insensible

3 ***syn*** RUDE 1, rough, roughhewn, undressed, unfashioned, unfinished, unformed, unhewn, unpolished, unworked

rel immature, unmatured; coarse, graceless

con cultivated, cultured, refined; developed, matured, ripened

ant consummate, finished

4 ***syn*** OBSCENE 2, barnyard, coarse, dirty, filthy, foul, gross, indecent, raunchy, smutty

rel blue, risqué

idiom rated X

5 rough in plan or execution <*crude* imitations, completely lacking in the original artistry>

syn coarse, inexpert, prentice; *compare* RUDE 1

rel amateurish, unproficient, unskilled, untaught, untrained; raw, rough, rude, unfinished, unpolished; inadequate, ineffective, inferior, poor

con finished, perfected, polished

ant expert

cruel *adj* ***syn*** FIERCE 1, barbarous, fell, ferocious, grim, inhuman, inhumane, savage, truculent, wolfish

rel atrocious, heinous, monstrous, outrageous; bestial, bloodthirsty, brutish; heartless, implacable, relentless; impiteous, unpitying

con compassionate, sympathetic, tender; clement, forbearing, lenient, merciful; humane, kindly

‖**cruise** *vb* ***syn*** GO 1, fare, hie, journey, pass, proceed, push on, repair, travel, wend

cruise *n* ***syn*** VOYAGE

rel sail

‖**cruiser** *n* ***syn*** PROSTITUTE, fille de joie, harlot, ‖hooker, hustler, nightwalker, poule, streetwalker, ‖tomato, whore

crumb *n* ***syn*** PARTICLE, bit, dram, drop, iota, jot, ounce, scrap, shred, smidgen

crumble *vb* ***syn*** DECAY, break down, decompose, disintegrate, molder, putrefy, rot, spoil, taint, turn

rel mush, squash

crumbly *adj* ***syn*** SHORT 6, brittle, crisp, ‖crump, crunchy, friable

rel rubbery

‖**crump** *adj* ***syn*** SHORT 6, brittle, crisp, crumbly, crunchy, friable

crumple *vb* **1** to press or twist into folds or wrinkles <*crumple* a piece of paper>

syn crimp, crimple, crinkle, ‖crunkle, rimple, ruck (up), ‖ruckle, rumple, screw, scrunch, wrinkle

rel crease, fold; buckle, cockle; wad

ant smooth

2 ***syn*** GIVE 12, bend, break, cave, collapse, fold up, go, yield

crunch *vb* ***syn*** CHEW 1, champ, ‖chaw, chomp, chumble, chump, masticate, munch, ruminate, scrunch

crunchy *adj* ***syn*** SHORT 6, brittle, crisp, crumbly, ‖crump, friable

‖**crunkle** *vb* ***syn*** CRUMPLE 1, crimp, crinkle, rimple, ruck (up), ‖ruckle, rumple, screw, scrunch, wrinkle

crusading *adj* ***syn*** EVANGELICAL, evangelistic

crush *vb* **1** ***syn*** PRESS 3, express

rel ‖scruze, squeeze

2 to reduce or be reduced to a pulpy or broken mass <*crushed* rose petals>

syn becrush, bruise, mash, ‖mush (up), pulp, squash

rel press, squeeze; contuse; batter, maim; beat, pound; dash, quash, ‖quat, smash; comminute, powder, pulverize, triturate

3 ***syn*** PULVERIZE 1, bray, buck, comminute, contriturate, powder, triturate

4 ***syn*** PRESS 1, bear, crowd, jam, push, ‖squab, squash, squeeze, squish, squush

5 to bring to an end by destroying or defeating <the police *crushed* the rebellion>

syn annihilate, extinguish, put down, quash, quell, quench, squash, suppress; *compare* SUPPRESS 2

rel ‖quelch, repress, squelch, strangle; beat down, conquer, defeat, subdue, subjugate; ruin, wreck; abolish, demolish, destroy; blot out, obliterate

idiom crush (*or* grind) under one's heel, ride down into the dust, roll (*or* trample) in the dust

6 ***syn*** CONQUER 1, bear down, beat down, defeat, overpower, reduce, subdue, subjugate, vanquish

idiom bring one to his knees

7 ***syn*** PRESS 7, cram, crowd, jam, squash, squeeze

crush *n* **1** ***syn*** CROWD 1, drove, horde, multitude, press, push, squash, throng

2 ***syn*** INFATUATION, béguin, ‖pash, passion

rel calf love, puppy love

‖**crust** *n* ***syn*** EFFRONTERY, brashness, brass, cheek, confidence, face, gall, nerve, presumption

crust *vb* ***syn*** CAKE 1, encrust (*or* incrust), incrustate, rime

crusty *adj* **1** ***syn*** BLUFF, abrupt, blunt, brief, brusque, curt, gruff, short, snippety, snippy

---

syn synonym(s) ***rel*** related word(s)

idiom idiomatic equivalent(s) ***con*** contrasted word(s)

ant antonym(s) * vulgar

‖ use limited; if in doubt, see a dictionary

The first word in a synonym list when printed in SMALL CAPITALS shows where there is more information about the group. For a more efficient use of this book see Explanatory Notes.

rel irritable, snappish, waspish; choleric, cranky, irascible, splenetic, testy; crabbed, dour, saturnine, surly
2 *syn* OBSCENE 2, barnyard, coarse, dirty, fescennine, filthy, foul, gross, rank, raunchy

crux *n syn* SUBSTANCE 2, core, gist, kernel, matter, meat, nub, pith, purport, thrust

cry *vb* **1** *syn* CALL 1, hallo, holler, hollo, shout, vociferate, yell
rel bleat
2 to show distress, grief, or pain by tears and usually incoherent utterances <the little girl *cried* when she fell down>
syn blub, blubber, boohoo, ‖pipe, sob, wail, weep; *compare* BAWL 2, WHIMPER
rel sniff, snivel, whimper, whine; break down, choke up; groan, moan, sigh; bemoan, bewail, keen, lament, mourn, sorrow; bawl, howl, squall, yowl
idiom cry one's eyes (*or* heart) out, ‖pipe one's eye, shed tears
3 *syn* SHOUT 1, whoop, yell
4 *syn* PUBLICIZE, advertise, build up, press-agent, puff

cry *n* **1** *syn* BATTLE CRY, motto, rallying cry, war cry
rel slogan
2 *syn* REPORT 1, buzz, gossip, grapevine, hearsay, on-dit, rumble, rumor, scuttlebutt, talk
3 *syn* FASHION 3, bandwagon, craze, dernier cri, furore, mode, rage, ton, trend, vogue
4 *syn* CALL 1, note, song
rel screech, squawk; squeak; caw

cry down *vb syn* DECRY 2, belittle, depreciate, derogate, detract (from), diminish, disparage, downcry, opprobriate, run down
ant cry up

crying *adj* **1** *syn* PRESSING, burning, clamant, clamorous, dire, exigent, imperative, importunate, instant, urgent
rel necessary, needed
2 *syn* OUTRAGEOUS 2, atrocious, desperate, heinous, monstrous, scandalous, shocking

cry off *vb syn* BACK DOWN, back off, back out, backpedal, backwater, crawfish (out), declare off, renege, resile, welsh

cry out *vb syn* EXCLAIM, blat, blurt (out), bolt, ejaculate

crypt *n* a subterranean chamber <a burial *crypt*>
syn catacomb, undercroft, vault
rel cell; chamber, compartment, room; cave, cavern, grotto

cryptanalyze *vb syn* DECODE, break, crack, decipher, decrypt

cryptic *adj* being intentionally obscure and mysterious <the senator made some *cryptic* statements about intelligence operations>
syn dark, Delphian, enigmatic, mystifying; *compare* OBSCURE 3
rel equivocal, murky, obscure, opaque, tenebrous, unclear, uninformative, vague; incomprehensible, inexplicable, strange, unfathomable; abstruse, mysterious; evasive, secretive

crystal *adj syn* CLEAR 4, clear-cut, lucent, lucid, luminous, pellucid, translucent, transparent, transpicuous, unblurred
idiom clear as crystal, crystal clear

cry up *vb syn* PRAISE 2, bless, celebrate, eulogize, extol, glorify, hymn, laud, magnify, panegyrize
idiom beat the drum for, praise to the skies
ant cry down

cubby *n syn* CUBBYHOLE, mousehole, pigeonhole

cubbyhole *n* an excessively small room or place <a cramped *cubbyhole* of an office>
syn cubby, mousehole, pigeonhole
rel recess; niche; cubicle
idiom hole in the wall

‖**cubes** *n pl syn* DICE, ‖African dominoes, bones, ‖devil's-bones, ‖ivory, ‖tats

cuckoo *n syn* CRACKPOT, crackbrain, crank, ding-a-ling, harebrain, kook, lunatic, nut, screwball

cuckoo *adj syn* INSANE 1, crackbrained, cracked, ‖crackers, ‖cracky, ‖cranky, crazed, crazy, daffy, daft

cuddle *vb* **1** *syn* CARESS, cosset, dandle, fondle, love, pet
rel embrace, enfold, hold
2 *syn* SNUGGLE, burrow, ‖croodle, nestle, nuzzle, ‖snudge, snug, ‖snuzzle

cudgel *n* a short solid stick used as a weapon or an instrument of punishment <beat the prisoner with a *cudgel*>
syn bat, baton, billy, billy club, bludgeon, club, knobkerrie, mace, nightstick, ‖shillelagh, spontoon, truncheon, war club
rel birch, cane, ferule, hickory, paddle, rattan, rod, switch; blackjack; quarterstaff; bastinado

cue *n syn* HINT 1, clue, indication, inkling, intimation, notion, suggestion, telltale, wind

cuff *vb syn* SLAP 1, blip, box, buffet, smack, spank, ‖wherret

cuff *n* a sharp blow typically delivered with the hand <gave him a good *cuff* in the face>
syn box, buffet, ‖bust, chop, clout, haymaker, ‖paste, poke, punch, slap, smack, sock, spank, ‖spat, ‖swack; *compare* BLOW 1, HIT 1
rel bat, blow, clip, wallop

cul-de-sac *n syn* DEAD END, blind alley, impasse, pocket
rel stalemate

cull *vb* **1** *syn* GLEAN, extract, garner, gather, pick up
rel accumulate, amass, collect, round up
2 *syn* CHOOSE 1, elect, mark, opt (for), optate, pick, prefer, select, single (out), take
rel discriminate
idiom separate the sheep from the goats, separate the wheat from the chaff

‖**cull** *n syn* FOOL 3, butt, chump, dupe, easy mark, fall guy, fish, gull, mark, sucker

‖**cully** *n syn* ASSOCIATE 3, buddy, chum, comate, companion, comrade, crony, pal, running mate

---

syn synonym(s) | *rel* related word(s)
idiom idiomatic equivalent(s) | *con* contrasted word(s)
ant antonym(s) | * vulgar
‖ use limited; if in doubt, see a dictionary
The first word in a synonym list when printed in SMALL CAPITALS shows where there is more information about the group. For a more efficient use of this book see Explanatory Notes.

culmen *n* ***syn*** APEX 2, acme, apogee, capsheaf, capstone, climax, culmination, ne plus ultra, peak, zenith

culminate *vb* ***syn*** CLIMAX, cap, crown, finish off, round off, top off

culmination *n* ***syn*** APEX 2, acme, apogee, climax, meridian, ne plus ultra, noon, peak, pinnacle, summit
rel extremity, limit, maximum

culpability *n* ***syn*** BLAME, fault, guilt, onus
con blamelessness, innocence
ant inculpability

culpable *adj* ***syn*** BLAMEWORTHY, amiss, blamable, blameful, censurable, demeritorious, guilty, reprehensible, sinful, unholy
rel impeachable, indictable
ant inculpable

cult *n* **1** ***syn*** RELIGION 1, creed, faith, persuasion
2 ***syn*** RELIGION 2, church, communion, connection, creed, denomination, faith, persuasion, sect

cultivable *adj* ***syn*** ARABLE, cultivatable, tillable
ant uncultivable

cultivatable *adj* ***syn*** ARABLE, cultivable, tillable
ant uncultivatable

cultivate *vb* **1** ***syn*** TILL, dress, ‖labor, tend, work
rel crop, farm, manage
2 ***syn*** NURSE 2, cherish, foster, nourish, nursle, nurture
rel raise, rear; educate, instruct, teach, train; ameliorate, better, improve
con disregard, ignore, neglect, slight
3 ***syn*** GROW 1, breed, produce, propagate, raise
rel develop, mature, ripen

cultivated *adj* ***syn*** GENTEEL 1, cultured, distingué, polished, refined, urbane, well-bred
rel courteous, polite
ant uncultivated

cultivation *n* ***syn*** CULTURE, breeding, polish, refinement

culture *n* enlightenment and excellence of taste acquired by intellectual and aesthetic training <a man of *culture* is known by his reading>
syn breeding, cultivation, polish, refinement
rel education, enlightenment, erudition, learning; gentility, manners; discrimination, taste; savoir-faire, sophistication, urbanity; class, elegance
con greenness, ignorance, inexperience, verdancy; crudeness, vulgarity

cultured *adj* ***syn*** GENTEEL 1, cultivated, distingué, polished, refined, urbane, well-bred
rel educated, enlightened, erudite, learned, literate; civilized
ant uncultured

culverhouse *n* ***syn*** DOVECOTE, columbary, dovehouse, pigeon house, pigeonry

cumber *vb* ***syn*** BURDEN, charge, clog, encumber, lade, load, lumber, saddle, task, tax

---

syn synonym(s) ***rel*** related word(s)
idiom idiomatic equivalent(s) ***con*** contrasted word(s)
ant antonym(s) * vulgar
‖ use limited; if in doubt, see a dictionary
The first word in a synonym list when printed in SMALL CAPITALS shows where there is more information about the group. For a more efficient use of this book see Explanatory Notes.

---

cumbersome *adj* ***syn*** UNWIELDY, cumbrous, ponderous, unhandy
rel irksome, tiresome, wearisome

cumbrance *n* ***syn*** ENCUMBRANCE, clog, hindrance, impedance, impediment
rel burden, charge, pressure

cumbrous *adj* ***syn*** UNWIELDY, cumbersome, ponderous, unhandy
rel clogging, hampering, hindering, impeding

cumshaw *n* ***syn*** GRATUITY, lagniappe, largess, ‖palm grease, ‖palm oil, ‖perk(s), perquisite, pourboire, tip

cumulate *vb* ***syn*** ACCUMULATE, amass, garner, hive, lay up, roll up, stockpile, store (up), uplay
rel obtain, secure
ant dissipate

cumulation *n* ***syn*** ACCUMULATION, agglomeration, aggregation, amassment, collection, colluvies, conglomeration, hoard, trove
rel stockpile; snowball

cumulative *adj* increasing or produced by addition of like or similar things <the *cumulative* effect of several drugs>
syn accumulative, additive, additory, chain, summative
rel accumulated, amassed; augmenting, increasing, multiplying; advancing, heightening, intensifying, magnifying, snowballing
con dispersed, dissipated, scattered

cunning *adj* **1** ***syn*** CLEVER 4, adroit, canny, ‖coony, dexterous, ingenious, ‖sleighty, slim, sly
rel well-devised, well-laid, well-planned; crackerjack, masterful
idiom too clever by half
2 ***syn*** SLY 2, artful, astute, crafty, deep, foxy, guileful, insidious, tricky, wily
rel acute, keen, sharp; knowing, smart; wary
idiom not to be caught with chaff
con artless, naive, unsophisticated

cunning *n* **1** ***syn*** ART 1, adroitness, craft, dexterity, expertise, know-how, skill
rel deftness, dexterousness; adeptness, expertness; cleverness, ingeniousness, ingenuity
2 skill in devising or using indirect or subtle methods <a woman able to maneuver people with great *cunning*>
syn art, artfulness, artifice, cageyness, canniness, craft, craftiness, foxiness, slyness, wiliness
rel savvy, sharpness, shrewdness; cleverness, ingeniousness, ingenuity; agility, facility, finesse, slickness; subtlety; insidiousness, shiftiness, trickiness
3 ***syn*** DECEIT 1, dissemblance, dissimulation, duplicity, guile
idiom satanic cunning, the cunning of the serpent

cupidity *n* intense desire for possessions and wealth <the sight of so much money aroused his *cupidity*>
syn avarice, avariciousness, avidity, greed, rapacity
rel acquisitiveness, greediness, possessiveness, rapaciousness; eagerness, voracity; craving, desire; lust; infatuation, passion

cur *n* **1** ***syn*** SNOT 1, dog, scum, *shit, *shithead, skunk, snake, stinkard, stinker, toad
rel riffraff
2 ***syn*** CAD, bounder, rotter, yellow dog

curative *adj* restoring or tending to restore to a state of normalcy or health <a *curative* drug>

syn curing, healing, remedial, remedying, restorative, sanative, sanatory, vulnerary, wholesome
rel medicable, medicative, medicinal; corrective, therapeutic; invigorating, tonic; beneficial, helpful, salutary, wholesome

curb *vb* **1** *syn* HAMPER, clog, entrammel, fetter, hobble, hog-tie, leash, shackle, tie, tie up
2 *syn* DENY 3, abstain, constrain, hold back, refrain
rel repress, suppress
ant goad
3 *syn* RESTRAIN 1, bit, bridle, check, constrain, hold back, hold down, hold in, inhibit, withhold
rel fetter, hamper, hog-tie, manacle, shackle
idiom hold in leash, keep a tight rein on
con unbridle, unleash
ant spur

curd *vb syn* CURDLE, ||clabber, ||cruddle, ||lopper, turn

curdle *vb* to cause to become coagulated or thickened and often sour <hot weather will *curdle* milk>
syn ||clabber, ||cruddle, curd, ||lopper, turn
rel clot, coagulate, condense, thicken; ferment; go off, sour, spoil

cure *n* **1** *syn* REMEDY 1, medicament, medicant, medication, medicine, pharmacon, physic
2 *syn* REMEDY 2, antidote, corrective, counteractant, counteractive, counteragent, countermeasure, counterstep

cure *vb* to rectify an unhealthy or undesirable condition <aspirin *cured* his headache>
syn heal, remedy
rel doctor, medicate; restore; ameliorate, better, improve

cure–all *n syn* PANACEA, catholicon, elixir, nostrum

cureless *adj syn* HOPELESS 2, immedicable, impossible, incurable, insanable, irremediable, irreparable, uncorrectable, uncurable, unrecoverable

curing *adj syn* CURATIVE, healing, remedial, remedying, restorative, sanative, sanatory, vulnerary, wholesome

curio *n syn* KNICKKNACK, bauble, bibelot, gewgaw, objet d'art, pretty-pretty, toy, trifle, trinket, whatnot

curiosity *n* **1** *syn* INTEREST 3, concern, interestedness, regard
rel inquisitiveness, questioning
ant disinterest
2 something that arouses interest especially because of uncommon or exotic characteristics <an architectural *curiosity*>
syn conversation piece, oddity
rel exception, nonesuch, rarity; marvel, prodigy, wonder; anomaly; freak, monstrosity
idiom something to write home about

curious *adj* **1** *syn* INQUISITIVE 1, disquisitive, inquiring, investigative, questioning
rel searching; analytical; prurient
ant incurious
2 interested in what is not one's personal or proper concern <a *curious* old woman prying into her neighbors' affairs>
syn inquisitive, inquisitorial, inquisitory, ||nibby, nosy, peery, prying, snoopy
rel interfering, intermeddling, meddling, tampering; examining, inspecting, scrutinizing; impertinent, intrusive, meddlesome
idiom consumed (*or* burning *or* eaten up) with curiosity, curious as a cat (*or* monkey)
con aloof, detached, disinterested, indifferent, unconcerned, uninterested; apathetic, impassive, phlegmatic, stolid
ant incurious
3 *syn* STRANGE 4, bizarre, odd, oddball, peculiar, quaint, queer, singular, unusual, weird

curl *vb syn* WIND 2, coil, corkscrew, entwine, spiral, twine, twist, wreathe
rel crook; roll; ringlet; kink
con straighten, unkink, unwind
ant uncurl

currency *n syn* MONEY, cash, ||coin, dough, filthy lucre, legal tender, ||lettuce, ||long green, lucre, needful

current *adj* **1** *syn* PRESENT, contemporary, existent, extant, instant, present-day, todayish
rel topical, up-to-date
con antiquated, antique, obsolete
2 *syn* PREVAILING, popular, prevalent, rampant, regnant, rife, ruling, widespread
rel accustomed, customary; a la mode, fashionable, modern, popular
ant antique

current *n* **1** *syn* FLOW, drift, flood, flux, rush, spate, stream, tide
2 *syn* TENDENCY 1, drift, run, tenor, trend

curry *vb syn* WHIP 2, ||clobber, drub, lick, overwhelm, shellac, smear, smother, thrash, trim

curse *n* **1** a denunciation that conveys a wish or threat of evil <the dying man's *curse* against his family>
syn anathema, commination, imprecation, malediction, malison
rel execration, objurgation; damning, denunciation; blasphemy, profanation, profanity, sacrilege
ant blessing
2 *syn* SWEARWORD, cuss, cussword, expletive, oath, swear
3 *syn* PLAGUE 1, pestilence, scourge

curse *vb* **1** *syn* EXECRATE 1, anathematize, damn, objurgate
rel blaspheme; blight; doom
idiom call down curses on the head of, call down evil on
ant bless
2 *syn* SWEAR 3, bedamn, cuss, damn, execrate, imprecate
idiom ||curse up a storm

cursed *adj* **1** *syn* DAMNED 2, blankety-blank, blasted, blessed, confounded, ||consarned, cussed, doggone, dratted, infernal
rel hateful
2 *syn* EXECRABLE 1, accursed, damnable
rel disgusting; odious

---

syn synonym(s) *rel* related word(s)
idiom idiomatic equivalent(s) *con* contrasted word(s)
ant antonym(s) * vulgar
|| use limited; if in doubt, see a dictionary
The first word in a synonym list when printed in SMALL CAPITALS shows where there is more information about the group. For a more efficient use of this book see Explanatory Notes.

ant blessed
cursing *n syn* BLASPHEMY 1, cussing, execration, imprecation, profanity, swearing
cursive *adj syn* EASY 9, effortless, flowing, fluent, running, smooth
cursory *adj syn* SUPERFICIAL 2, depthless, shallow, sketchy, uncritical
rel fast, hasty, hurried, quick, rapid, speedy, swift; brief, short; casual, desultory, haphazard, random
con careful, meticulous, scrupulous
ant painstaking
curt *adj* **1** *syn* CONCISE, breviloquent, brief, compendiary, compendious, laconic, short, short and sweet, succinct, summary
2 *syn* BLUFF, abrupt, blunt, brief, brusque, crusty, gruff, short, snippety, snippy
rel imperious, peremptory
ant voluble
curtail *vb* **1** *syn* SHORTEN, abbreviate, abridge, cut, cut back, retrench, slash
ant prolong, protract
2 *syn* ABRIDGE 1, diminish, lessen, minify
ant extend
curtains *n pl but sing in constr syn* DEATH 1, decease, defunction, demise, dissolution, (the) Pale Horse, passing, quietus, silence, sleep
curtilage *n syn* COURT 1, ‖close, courtyard, enclosure, quad, quadrangle, yard
curvaceous *adj* having a shapely figure marked by pronounced curves <*curvaceous* bikini-clad girls swarmed over the beach>
syn ‖built, curvesome, curvilinear, curvy, Junoesque, rounded, ‖stacked, well-developed; *compare* BUXOM, SHAPELY
rel shapeful, shapely, statuesque, well-proportioned; attractive, charming, pleasing
idiom ‖built (*or* stacked) like a brick outhouse
curvation *n syn* CURVE, arc, arch, bend, bow, curvature, round
curvature *n syn* CURVE, arc, arch, bend, bow, curvation, round
curve *vb* to swerve or cause to swerve from a straight line or course <the road *curves* to the right>
syn bend, bow, crook, round; *compare* WIND 2
rel deflect, divert, turn; deviate, swerve, veer; coil, curl, spiral, twist, wind; incurve
ant straighten
curve *n* something (as a line or surface) that curves or is curved <a slight *curve* to her eyebrows>
syn arc, arch, bend, bow, curvation, curvature, round
rel incurvation, incurvature; inflection; rondure; circuit, circumference, compass
curved *adj* having or characterized by a curve or curves <a *curved* vault>
syn arced, arched, arciform, arrondi, bent, bowed, curvilinear, round, rounded; *compare* CROOKED 1
rel declinate; embowed, incurvate, incurved; excurved; bending, twisted, twisting
ant straight
curvesome *adj syn* CURVACEOUS, ‖built, curvilinear, curvy, Junoesque, rounded, ‖stacked, well-developed
curvilinear *adj* **1** *syn* CURVED, arced, arched, arciform, arrondi, bent, bowed, round, rounded
2 *syn* CURVACEOUS, ‖built, curvesome, curvy, Junoesque, rounded, ‖stacked, well-developed
curving *adj syn* CROOKED 1, bending, devious, twisting
curvy *adj syn* CURVACEOUS, ‖built, curvesome, curvilinear, Junoesque, rounded, ‖stacked, well-developed
cushy *adj syn* COMFORTABLE 2, comfy, cozy, easeful, easy, snug, soft
cusp *n syn* POINT 9, apex, tip
cuspidate *adj syn* POINTED 1, acicular, aciculate, acuminate, acuminous, acute, peaked, peaky, piked, sharp
cuss *n* **1** *syn* SWEARWORD, curse, cussword, expletive, oath, swear
2 *syn* MAN 3, ‖bloke, boy, buck, chap, fellow, gent, guy, he, ‖mun
cuss *vb syn* SWEAR 3, bedamn, curse, damn, execrate, imprecate
idiom ‖cuss up a blue streak
cussed *adj syn* DAMNED 2, blankety-blank, blasted, blessed, confounded, ‖consarned, cursed, doggone, dratted, infernal
cussing *adj syn* BLASPHEMY 1, cursing, execration, imprecation, profanity, swearing
cussword *n syn* SWEARWORD, curse, cuss, expletive, oath, swear
custodian *n* one that guards, protects, or maintains (as property or records) <was the *custodian* of the manor for many years>
syn cerberus, claviger, ‖custodier, custos, guardian, keeper, warden, watchdog
rel curator, steward; castellan, governor; overseer, supervisor
‖**custodier** *n syn* CUSTODIAN, cerberus, claviger, custos, guardian, keeper, warden, watchdog
custody *n* the act or duty of guarding and preserving <the government has *custody* of all state gifts>
syn care, guardianship, keeping, safekeeping, trust, ward
rel caretaking; charge, management, supervision; protection
custom *n* **1** *syn* HABIT 1, consuetude, habitude, manner, practice, praxis, trick, usage, use, wont
rel precedent; ritual; mold; fixture, institution; prescription, rubric; canon, law, precept, rule
idiom matter of course
con departure, deviation, shift; exception; irregularity
2 *syn* PATRONAGE 2, business, trade, traffic
custom *adj syn* CUSTOM-MADE, custom-built, customized, custom-tailored, made-to-order, tailor-made
customarily *adv syn* USUALLY 1, as usual, consistently, habitually, wontedly
rel conventionally, traditionally; normally, ordinarily; routinely
idiom as a matter of course
con rarely; never

---

syn synonym(s) *rel* related word(s)
idiom idiomatic equivalent(s) *con* contrasted word(s)
ant antonym(s) * vulgar
‖ use limited; if in doubt, see a dictionary
The first word in a synonym list when printed in SMALL CAPITALS shows where there is more information about the group. For a more efficient use of this book see Explanatory Notes.

ant occasionally

customary *adj* **1** ***syn*** USUAL 1, accepted, accustomed, chronic, habitual, routine, wonted
rel acknowledged, recognized, understood; standard; conventional, orthodox, traditional; prescriptive, regulation, stipulated
idiom being the customary (*or* usual) thing
con occasional; infrequent, inhabitual, sporadic, uncommon; irregular
ant uncustomary
2 ***syn*** COMMON 4, everyday, familiar, frequent
rel household, popular; general, universal
ant uncustomary

custom–built *adj* ***syn*** CUSTOM-MADE, custom, customized, custom-tailored, made-to-order, tailor-made

customer *n* one that patronizes or uses the services of something (as a store or restaurant) <many *customers* in the shop>
syn client, patron
rel buyer, consumer, purchaser, shopper

customized *adj* ***syn*** CUSTOM-MADE, custom, custom-built, custom-tailored, made-to-order, tailor-made

custom–made *adj* made according to personal order and individual specifications <he always wore a *custom-made* suit>
syn custom, custom-built, customized, custom-tailored, made-to-order, tailor-made
ant mass-produced

custom–tailored *adj* ***syn*** CUSTOM-MADE, custom, custom-built, customized, made-to-order, tailor-made

custos *n* ***syn*** CUSTODIAN, cerberus, claviger, ‖custodier, guardian, keeper, warden, watchdog

cut *vb* **1** to penetrate with or as if with a sharp edge <*cut* his hand on a broken bottle>
syn gash, incise, pierce, slash, slice, slit
rel cleave, dissever, sever, sunder; rend, rip, rive, tear; lacerate, wound
2 ***syn*** SHORTEN, abbreviate, abridge, curtail, cut back, retrench, slash
3 ***syn*** REDUCE 2, clip, cut back, cut down, lower, mark down, pare, shave, slash
4 ***syn*** MOW, clip, crop
5 to penetrate and divide with an edged tool or instrument <*cut* the melon into slices>
syn carve, cleave, dissect, dissever, sever, slice, split, sunder
rel divide, part, separate; chop, dice, hash, mince, mow
idiom lay open
6 to reduce by severing parts <the barber *cut* his hair too short>
syn clip, crop, pare, prune, shave, shear, skive, trim
rel cut back, dock, lop, poll, pollard, shrub; amputate; curtail
7 to refuse social recognition especially by way of rebuke <his friends *cut* him after the scandal broke>
syn cold-shoulder, ostracize, snob, snub
rel disdain, ignore, rebuff, reject, slight, turn away; affront, insult, offend
idiom give the cold shoulder (to), show one his place, slam the door in one's face, slam the door on, slap one in the face, turn aside (*or* away) from, turn one's back (on *or* upon)
8 ***syn*** DILUTE, thin, weaken
9 ***syn*** FELL 2, chop, hew
10 ***syn*** OPERATE 2, open up

cut *n* **1** ***syn*** PART 1, division, member, moiety, parcel, piece, portion, section, segment
2 ***syn*** SHARE 1, allotment, allowance, bite, lot, part, partage, portion, quota, slice
3 ***syn*** TRENCH, ditch
4 ***syn*** TYPE, cast, description, feather, ilk, kind, lot, mold, sort, stamp

cut *adj* ***syn*** INTOXICATED 1, ‖bagged, ‖blotto, ‖boozed, ‖canned, cockeyed, ‖crocked, drunk, drunken, ‖lit

cut back *vb* **1** ***syn*** SHORTEN, abbreviate, abridge, curtail, cut, retrench, slash
2 ***syn*** REDUCE 2, clip, cut, cut down, lower, mark down, pare, shave, slash

cut down *vb* ***syn*** REDUCE 2, clip, cut, cut back, lower, mark down, pare, shave, slash

cut in *vb* ***syn*** INTRUDE 1, butt in, chisel (in), horn in, intertrude, obtrude

cut off *vb* **1** ***syn*** KILL 1, carry off, destroy, dispatch, finish, lay low, put away, scrag, slay, take off
2 ***syn*** INTERCEPT, block, catch
3 ***syn*** ISOLATE, close off, enisle, insulate, island, segregate, separate, sequester
4 ***syn*** DISINHERIT 1

cutoff *n* ***syn*** SHORTCUT

cut out *vb* **1** ***syn*** EXCISE, exsect, extirpate, resect
2 ***syn*** SUPPLANT 1, displace, usurp

cutpurse *n* ***syn*** PICKPOCKET, ‖cannon, ‖dip, ‖diver, purse cutter, ‖wire

cutthroat *n* ***syn*** ASSASSIN, bravo, gun, gunman, ‖gunsel, gunslinger, hatchet man, hit man, torpedo, triggerman

cutting *adj* ***syn*** INCISIVE, biting, clear-cut, crisp, ingoing, penetrating, trenchant
rel piercing, probing

cut up *vb* **1** ***syn*** CRITICIZE, censure, condemn, denounce, knock, pan, rap, reprehend, reprobate, skin
2 to behave in a boisterously comic or unruly manner <children *cutting up* in front of company>
syn act up, carry on, horse, horseplay
rel caper, cavort, romp; clown; show off; roughhouse; misbehave
idiom cut a dido (*or* shine), cut up rough, ‖kick up a shindy, raise Cain (*or* Ned), whoop it up

cutup *n* ***syn*** ZANY 2, clown, farceur, joker, jokester, wag

cycle *n* **1** a complete course of recurrent operations or events <a 24-hour *cycle* of medication>
syn circle, round, wheel; *compare* SUCCESSION 2
rel chain, sequel, sequence, series; course, run; circuit, loop, ring
2 ***syn*** BICYCLE, bike, two-wheeler, velocipede

cyclone *n* ***syn*** TORNADO, twister

---

syn synonym(s)	***rel*** related word(s)
idiom idiomatic equivalent(s)	***con*** contrasted word(s)
ant antonym(s)	* vulgar

‖ use limited; if in doubt, see a dictionary
The first word in a synonym list when printed in SMALL CAPITALS shows where there is more information about the group. For a more efficient use of this book see Explanatory Notes.

cyclopean *adj syn* HUGE, Antaean, colossal, elephantine, gargantuan, gigantic, Herculean, mammoth, monstrous, titanic
ant lilliputian

cynical *adj syn* SARDONIC, ironic, wry

cyprian *n syn* WANTON, hussy, jade, jezebel, ‖pig, slattern, slut, strumpet, tramp, trollop

czar *n syn* MAGNATE, baron, king, merchant prince, mogul, prince, tycoon

D

dab *vb* ***syn*** SMEAR 1, bedaub, besmear, daub, plaster, ‖smarm, smudge

‖**dab** *n* ***syn*** EXPERT, adept, authority, ‖dabster, master, professional, proficient, whiz, wiz, wizard

dabbler *n* ***syn*** AMATEUR 2, abecedarian, dilettante, nonprofessional, smatterer, tyro, uninitiate
con adept, artist, connoisseur; expert, master, professional

dabbling *adj* ***syn*** AMATEURISH, dilettante, dilettantish, dilettantist, jackleg, unaccomplished, unfinished, ungifted, unskilled
rel sciolistic, shallow, sophomoric, superficial
con adept, capable, competent

‖**dabster** *n* ***syn*** EXPERT, adept, authority, ‖dab, master, professional, proficient, whiz, wiz, wizard

dad *n* ***syn*** FATHER 1, dada, daddy, ‖governor, ‖old man, pa, ‖pap, papa, ‖pappy, pop

dada *n* ***syn*** FATHER 1, dad, daddy, ‖governor, pa, ‖pap, papa, ‖pappy, pop, poppa

dad–blamed *adj* **1** ***syn*** DAMNED 2, blankety-blank, blessed, ‖blooming, confounded, ‖consarned, dang, doggone, dratted, goldarn
2 ***syn*** UTTER, absolute, blessed, ‖blooming, downright, gross, out-and-out, outright, rank, unmitigated

dad–blasted *adj* **1** ***syn*** DAMNED 2, blankety-blank, blessed, ‖blooming, confounded, ‖consarned, dang, doggone, dratted, goldarn
2 ***syn*** UTTER, absolute, blessed, ‖blooming, downright, gross, out-and-out, outright, rank, unmitigated

dad–burned *adj* **1** ***syn*** DAMNED 2, blankety-blank, blessed, ‖blooming, confounded, ‖consarned, dang, doggone, dratted, goldarn
2 ***syn*** UTTER, absolute, blessed, ‖blooming, downright, gross, out-and-out, outright, rank, unmitigated

daddy *n* ***syn*** FATHER 1, dad, dada, ‖governor, ‖old man, pa, ‖pap, papa, ‖pappy, pop

daedal *adj* ***syn*** COMPLEX 2, Byzantine, complicated, elaborate, gordian, intricate, involved, knotty, labyrinthine, sophisticated

daffy *adj* ***syn*** INSANE 1, cuckoo, daft, demented, deranged, ‖fruity, ‖loco, lunatic, mad, maniac

daft *adj* ***syn*** INSANE 1, bedlamite, cracked, crazed, crazy, demented, deranged, mad, unbalanced, unsound

daily *adj* of each or every day < *daily* prayers for the dead >
syn diurnal, quotidian
con nocturnal; alternate, intermittent, periodic, recurrent, spasmodic; erratic, fitful, fluctuating, infrequent, irregular; occasional, sporadic
ant nightly

dainty *n* ***syn*** DELICACY, bonne bouche, goody, kickshaw, morsel, tidbit (*or* titbit), treat

dainty *adj* **1** ***syn*** CHOICE, delicate, elegant, exquisite, rare, recherché, select, superior
rel beautiful, bonny, fair, lovely, pretty; delectable, delicious, delightful; airy, diaphanous, ethereal, light
con coarse, vulgar
ant gross
2 ***syn*** NICE 1, delicate, fastidious, finical, finicking, finicky, fussy, particular, pernickety, persnickety
rel acute, penetrative, perceptive
con careless, neglectful, negligent, thoughtless

‖**daisy** *n* ***syn*** ‖DILLY, ‖corker, crackerjack, dandy, humdinger, jim-dandy, knockout, ‖lalapalooza, ‖lulu, nifty

dale *n* ***syn*** VALLEY, ‖combe, glen, vale

dally *vb* **1** ***syn*** TRIFLE 1, coquet, flirt, fool, lead on, string along, toy, wanton
rel frolic, gambol, play, rollick, romp, sport; caress, cosset, cuddle, dandle, fondle, pet
2 ***syn*** DELAY 2, dawdle, drag, lag, loiter, poke, procrastinate, put off, tarry, trail
con fleet, rush, scurry, skedaddle
ant hasten

dam *vb* ***syn*** HINDER, bar, block, brake, impede, obstruct, overslaugh
rel repress, suppress
con air, express, utter, vent

damage *n* ***syn*** INJURY 1, harm, hurt, mischief, outrage, ruin
rel impairment, marring; deterioration, dilapidation, disrepair, ruining, wrecking; deleteriousness, disadvantage, drawback
con amelioration, betterment, improvement; benefit, profit; advantage, service, use
ant repair

damage *vb* ***syn*** INJURE 1, blemish, harm, hurt, impair, mar, prejudice, spoil, tarnish, vitiate
rel demolish, destroy, raze, ruin, wreck; deteriorate, dilapidate; abuse, ill-treat, maltreat, mistreat, misuse, outrage
con ameliorate, amend, better, improve; mend
ant repair

damaged *adj* having been injured < *damaged* merchandise >
syn flawed, impaired, marred, spoiled
rel blemished, broken, imperfect, injured, unsound
con flawless, good, intact, unbroken, unhurt, unimpaired, uninjured, unmarred, whole; corrected, improved, rectified, repaired
ant undamaged

---

syn synonym(s) ***rel*** related word(s)
idiom idiomatic equivalent(s) ***con*** contrasted word(s)
ant antonym(s) * vulgar
‖ use limited; if in doubt, see a dictionary
The first word in a synonym list when printed in SMALL CAPITALS shows where there is more information about the group. For a more efficient use of this book see Explanatory Notes.

damaging *adj* ***syn*** HARMFUL, bad, deleterious, detrimental, evil, hurtful, injurious, mischievous, nocent, nocuous

dame *n* **1** ***syn*** MATRIARCH, dowager, grande dame, matron
2 ***syn*** BELDAM 1, gammer, grandam

damfool** *n* ***syn FOOL 1, ass, donkey, idiot, imbecile, jackass, jerk, nincompoop, ninny, tomfool

damn *vb* **1** ***syn*** SENTENCE, condemn, doom, proscribe
rel castigate, discipline, penalize, punish; banish, cast out, expel
con deliver, ransom, redeem, rescue; reward
ant save
2 ***syn*** EXECRATE 1, anathematize, curse, objurgate
rel abominate; vituperate
3 ***syn*** SWEAR 3, bedamn, curse, cuss, execrate, imprecate

damn *n* ***syn*** PARTICLE, ace, hoot, iota, jot, modicum, ounce, shred, whit, whoop

damnable *adj* **1** ***syn*** EXECRABLE 1, accursed, cursed
rel abhorrent, abominable, detestable, hateful, odious; damned
con admirable, commendable, estimable; laudable, praiseworthy
2 ***syn*** DAMNED 2, blamed, blasted, blessed, cursed, cussed, dad-burned, dang, darn, dratted
3 ***syn*** UTTER, absolute, blamed, blasted, complete, downright, gross, out-and-out, outright, unmitigated

damned *adj* **1** being doomed to eternal punishment <a *damned* soul>
syn condemned, doomed, lost
rel anathematized, cursed, reprobate; done for
idiom gone to blazes, hell bound
con delivered, ransomed, redeemed
ant saved
2 deserving censure or strong disapproval—often used as a generalized expression of annoyance <this *damned* door won't open>
syn blamed, blankety-blank, blasted, bleeding, blessed, blighted, blinding, ‖blinking, ‖blistering, *‖bloody, ‖blooming, confounded, ‖consarned, cursed, cussed, dad-blamed, dad-blasted, dad-burned, damnable, dang, darn (*or* durn), dashed, doggone, dratted, execrable, *fucking, *goddamn, goldarn, infernal, perishing, *‖ruddy, so-and-so
3 ***syn*** UTTER, absolute, complete, downright, gross, out-and-out, outright, rank, straight-out, unmitigated

damned *adv* ***syn*** VERY 1, ‖awful, awfully, ‖big, extremely, greatly, hugely, much, whacking, whopping

damp *adj* slightly or relatively wet <her dress was still *damp*>
syn dampish, dank, moist, moisty, wettish
rel drenched, saturated, soaked, soaking; soggy, water-logged
con arid, dry

dampen *vb* ***syn*** MUFFLE 2, deaden, mute, stifle

dampish *adj* ***syn*** DAMP, dank, moist, moisty, wettish

damsel *n* ***syn*** GIRL 1, gal, lass, lassie, maid, maiden, miss, missy, ‖quail, wench

dance *vb* **1** to perform a rhythmic and patterned succession of steps usually to music <the band was good enough to *dance* to>
syn foot (it), hoof (it), prance, step, tread
rel shuffle, trip, truck
idiom ‖cut a rug, trip the light fantastic
2 ***syn*** FLIT 2, flicker, flitter, flutter, hover
rel quaver, quiver, shake, tremble, wobble

dancer *n* a professional performer of dances <*dancers* performing a ballet>
syn ballerina, ballet girl, coryphée, dancing girl, danseur, danseuse, figurant, figurante, hoofer
rel chorine, chorus boy, chorus girl, chorus man; danseur noble, premier danseur, premiere danseuse, prima ballerina

dancing girl *n* ***syn*** DANCER, ballerina, ballet girl, coryphée, danseur, danseuse, figurant, figurante, hoofer

dandle *vb* ***syn*** CARESS, cosset, cuddle, fondle, love, pet
rel disport, play, sport

dandy *n* **1** ***syn*** FOP, Beau Brummel, blood, buck, coxcomb, dude, exquisite, lounge lizard, macaroni, popinjay
con clod, lout, lump, oaf, slob, slouch
ant sloven
2 ***syn*** ‖DILLY, ‖corker, crackerjack, ‖daisy, humdinger, jim-dandy, ‖lalapalooza, ‖lulu, nifty, peach

‖**dandy** *adj* **1** ***syn*** MARVELOUS 2, ‖cool, glorious, groovy, hunky-dory, ‖neat, nifty, peachy, swell, terrific
2 ***syn*** EXCELLENT, capital, famous, fine, first-class, first-rate, first-string, five-star, prime, superior
rel grand, hunky-dory, keen, nifty, swell
idiom fine and dandy
con ‖bum, ‖crummy, grim, ‖lousy, ‖putrid, rotten
ant blah

dang *adj* **1** ***syn*** DAMNED 2, blasted, blessed, ‖blooming, confounded, cursed, cussed, darn, dratted, goldarn
2 ***syn*** UTTER, absolute, blasted, blessed, consummate, darn (*or* durn), downright, outright, regular, unmitigated

danger *n* the state of being exposed to injury, pain, or loss <they are seeking a place where children can play without *danger*>
syn hazard, jeopardy, peril, risk
rel menace, precariousness, threat; emergency, exigency, pass; precipice
idiom dangerous ground, thin ice
con safety; exemption, immunity; defense, guard, protection, safeguard, shield
ant security

dangerous *adj* **1** attended by or involving the possibility of injury, pain, or loss <a *dangerous* crossing>
syn chancy, ‖dangersome, hairy, hazardous, jeopardous, parlous, perilous, risky, treacherous, unhealthy, unsound, wicked; *compare* GRAVE 3
rel insecure, precarious, uncertain, unsafe; chance, haphazard, hit-or-miss, random; critical, menacing, serious, threatening
idiom beset (*or* fraught) with danger, on a collision course

---

syn synonym(s) ***rel*** related word(s)
idiom idiomatic equivalent(s) ***con*** contrasted word(s)
ant antonym(s) * vulgar
‖ use limited; if in doubt, see a dictionary
The first word in a synonym list when printed in SMALL CAPITALS shows where there is more information about the group. For a more efficient use of this book see Explanatory Notes.

con certain, reliable; harmless, innocent
ant safe, secure
2 *syn* GRAVE 3, fell, grievous, major, serious, ugly

||**dangersome** *adj* *syn* DANGEROUS 1, chancy, hairy, hazardous, jeopardous, perilous, risky, treacherous, unsound, wicked

dangle *vb* *syn* HANG 1, depend, sling, suspend

dank *adj* *syn* DAMP, dampish, moist, moisty, wettish

danseur *n* *syn* DANCER, ballerina, ballet girl, coryphée, dancing girl, danseuse, figurant, figurante, hoofer

danseuse *n* *syn* DANCER, ballerina, ballet girl, coryphée, dancing girl, danseur, figurant, figurante, hoofer

dap *vb* *syn* GLANCE 1, carom, graze, ricochet, skim, skip

dapper *adj* trimly neat and tidy <a *dapper* dresser, always neat as a pin>
syn bandbox, doggish, doggy, natty, sassy, sparkish, spiffy, spruce, sprucy, well-groomed; *compare* NEAT 2, STYLISH
rel chichi; jaunty, rakish; showy
con dowdy, drab, unstylish; disheveled, disordered, slipshod, sloppy, slovenly, unkempt, untidy; blowsy, dowdy, frowsy, shabby, slatternly

dappled *adj* *syn* VARIEGATED, discolor, motley, multicolor, multicolored, multihued, parti-colored, varicolored, versicolor, versicolored
con pure, smooth, spotless, unbroken, uniform

dare *vb* *syn* FACE 3, beard, brave, challenge, defy, ||double-dog dare, front, outdare, outface, venture
rel change, hazard, risk
idiom take the bull by the horns
con avoid, evade; flee, run

dare *n* *syn* DEFIANCE 1, cartel, challenge, defi, defy, stump

daredevil *adj* *syn* ADVENTUROUS, adventuresome, audacious, daring, foolhardy, rash, reckless, temerarious, venturesome, venturous
con timid, timorous; cautious, chary, circumspect, wary; discreet, judicious, prudent, sane, sensible

daring *adj* *syn* ADVENTUROUS, adventuresome, audacious, daredevil, foolhardy, rash, reckless, temerarious, venturesome, venturous

dark *adj* **1** deficient in light <a *dark* room>
syn caliginous, dim, dun, dusk, dusky, gloomy, lightless, murky, obscure, somber, tenebrous, unilluminated
rel cloudy, dull, shadowy, shady; pitch-black, pitch-dark
con bright, brilliant, luminous, radiant; enlightened, illuminated, illumined, lighted
ant light
2 *syn* CRYPTIC, Delphian, enigmatic, mystifying
rel abstruse, esoteric, hidden, occult, recondite; anagogic, cabalistic, darkling, mystic, mystical; complicated, intricate, knotty
con clear, perspicuous; easy, facile, light, simple
ant lucid
3 of dark complexion <her *dark* good looks>
syn bistered, black-a-vised, brunet, dark-skinned, dusky, swart, swarth, swarthy
con blond, fair, light; ruddy, tawny
||**4** *syn* BLIND 1, eyeless, sightless, stone-blind, visionless

darken *vb* *syn* OBSCURE, cloud, dim, eclipse, fog, haze, murk, obfuscate, overcast, overshadow
ant illuminate

dark-skinned *adj* *syn* DARK 3, bistered, black-a-vised, brunet, dusky, swart, swarth, swarthy

darling *n* *syn* SWEETHEART 1, beloved, dear, flame, honey, honeybunch, love, loveling, sweet, sweetling

darling *adj* **1** *syn* FAVORITE 1, beloved, blue-eyed, dear, fair-haired, loved, pet, precious, white-haired, white-headed
2 *syn* DELIGHTFUL, adorable, ambrosial, delectable, delicious, heavenly, luscious, lush, scrumptious, yummy

darn (*or* **durn**) *adj* **1** *syn* DAMNED 2, blankety-blank, blasted, blessed, confounded, cursed, cussed, doggone, goldarn, infernal
2 *syn* UTTER, absolute, blamed, blasted, downright, infernal, outright, positive, straight-out, unmitigated

dart *n* *syn* SHAFT 2, barb

dart *vb* *syn* FLY 1, float, sail, scud, shoot, skim, skirr
rel hasten, hurry, precipitate, speed; run, scamper, scoot, scurry, sprint, spurt
con dally, dawdle, delay, linger, tarry; lumber, plod, slog, trudge

dash *vb* **1** *syn* RUSH 1, boil, bolt, charge, chase, fling, lash, race, shoot, tear
rel run, scamper, scoot, scurry, sprint
con dally, dawdle, delay, linger, tarry; lumber, plod, slog, trudge
2 *syn* RUN 1, scamper, scoot, scurry, skin, sprint
3 *syn* BLAST 1, blight, nip
4 *syn* FRUSTRATE 1, baffle, balk, beat, bilk, circumvent, disappoint, foil, ruin, thwart

dash *n* **1** *syn* SPIRIT 5, animation, brio, élan, esprit, life, oomph, verve, vim, zing
rel energy, force, might, power, strength; intensity, vehemence; impressiveness
con apathy, dullness, languor, lethargy, listlessness, sluggishness, stagnation, torpor
2 *syn* HINT 2, lick, smack, soupçon, sprinkling, streak, suggestion, tincture, trace, trifle
rel impress, impression, stamp

dashed *adj* **1** *syn* DAMNED 2, blasted, blessed, confounded, cursed, cussed, dad-burned, damnable, dratted, infernal
2 *syn* UTTER, absolute, blasted, blessed, confounded, deuced, downright, gross, outright, unmitigated

dashing *adj* **1** *syn* LIVELY 1, alert, animate, animated, bright, gay, keen, rousing, spirited, vivacious
2 *syn* STYLISH, chic, exclusive, fashionable, modish, smart, swank, swish, ||trendy, with-it
rel flashy, flaunting; dapper, jaunty, spiffy, spruce
idiom cutting a fine figure
con unfashionable, unstylish; modest, unostentatious, unpretentious
ant drab

---

syn synonym(s) — *rel* related word(s)
idiom idiomatic equivalent(s) — *con* contrasted word(s)
ant antonym(s) — * vulgar
|| use limited; if in doubt, see a dictionary
The first word in a synonym list when printed in SMALL CAPITALS shows where there is more information about the group. For a more efficient use of this book see Explanatory Notes.

dastard *n* ***syn*** COWARD, chicken, craven, funk, funker, poltroon, quitter, yellowbelly

date *vb* to go or take on a date <he *dated* her several times that winter>
syn see, take out
rel accompany, escort; court, woo
idiom go out with

date *n* **1** ***syn*** ENGAGEMENT 3, appointment, assignation, rendezvous, tryst
2 ***syn*** ESCORT 1

dated *adj* ***syn*** OLD-FASHIONED, antiquated, archaic, belated, démodé, old, old hat, outdated, outmoded, passé
ant up-to-the-minute

dateless *adj* ***syn*** ETERNAL 4, ageless, intemporal, timeless
ant ephemeral

daub *vb* ***syn*** SMEAR 1, bedaub, besmear, dab, plaster, ||smarm, smudge
rel spatter, speckle, spot; dapple, fleck, variegate

daunt *vb* ***syn*** DISMAY 1, appall, consternate, horrify, shake
rel browbeat, bully, cow, intimidate; baffle, foil, frustrate, thwart
con arouse, awaken, rally, rouse, stir, waken; actuate, drive, impel, move; activate, energize, vitalize
ant enhearten

dauntless *adj* ***syn*** BRAVE 1, aweless, bold, courageous, fearless, game, lionhearted, unafraid, unfearing, unfearful
rel indomitable, invincible, unconquerable
con hesitant, reluctant
ant poltroon

dauntlessness *n* ***syn*** COURAGE, cojones, guts, heart, mettle, ||moxie, pluck, resolution, spirit, spunk
ant poltroonery

dawdle *vb* **1** ***syn*** IDLE, bum, diddle-daddle, ||goof (off), laze, lazy, loaf, loiter, loll, lounge
2 ***syn*** DELAY 2, dally, drag, lag, loiter, poke, procrastinate, put off, tarry, trail
rel amble, saunter, stroll; stay, wait; toy, trifle; fritter, waste
idiom fritter away time
con arouse, rally, rouse, stir; hasten, hurry, speed

dawdler *n* ***syn*** LAGGARD, lingerer, loiterer, slow coach, slowpoke, straggler

dawn *n* **1** the first appearance of light in the morning <birds which sing at *dawn*>
syn aurora, cockcrow, cockcrowing, dawning, daybreak, daylight, light, morn, morning, sunrise, sunup
rel prime
idiom break of day, crack of dawn, first blush (*or* flush) of day, first light, peep of day, the wee small hours
2 ***syn*** BEGINNING, alpha, commencement, dawning, genesis, onset, opening, outset, outstart, start
ant sunset

dawning *n* **1** ***syn*** DAWN 1, aurora, cockcrow, cockcrowing, daybreak, daylight, light, morn, morning, sunrise
2 ***syn*** BEGINNING, alpha, commencement, dawn, genesis, onset, opening, outset, outstart, start
ant sunset

day *n* **1** the time of light between one night and the next <waiting for *day* to dawn>
syn daylight, daytime
rel light, sunlight, sunshine
con dark, nighttime
ant night
2 *usu* **days** *pl* ***syn*** PERIOD 2, age, epoch, era, time

daybreak *n* ***syn*** DAWN 1, aurora, cockcrow, cockcrowing, dawning, daylight, light, morn, morning, sunrise

daydream *n* ***syn*** FANCY 4, dream, fantasy (*or* phantasy), nightmare, phantasm, vision
rel conceiving, fancying, imagination, imagining
con substantiality, tangibility; authenticity, truth, verity

daydreaming *adj* ***syn*** DREAMY 1, astral, daydreamy, otherworldly, unworldly, visionary

daydreamy *adj* ***syn*** DREAMY 1, astral, daydreaming, otherworldly, unworldly, visionary

daylight *n* **1** ***syn*** DAWN 1, aurora, cockcrow, cockcrowing, dawning, daybreak, light, morn, morning, sunrise
syn DAY 1, daytime

dayspring *n* ***syn*** BEGINNING, alpha, birth, commencement, dawn, dawning, genesis, onset, opening gun, start

daystar *n* ***syn*** SUN 1, phoebus, Sol

daytime *n* ***syn*** DAY 1, daylight

daze *vb* **1** to confuse with light <the bright sunlight *dazed* him>
syn bedazzle, blind, dazzle
rel overcome, overpower, overwhelm; dizzy
2 to dull or deaden the powers of the mind through some disturbing experience or influence <*dazed* by the news of the accident>
syn bedaze, bemuse, benumb, paralyze, petrify, stun, stupefy
rel bewilder, confound, disorder, distract, dumbfound, mystify; befuddle, confuse, fuddle, muddle; dazzle, dizzy; rock
con enhance, expand, heighten, sharpen; alert, arouse, waken

daze *n* ***syn*** HAZE 2, befuddlement, fog, ||maze, muddledness, muddleheadedness, muddlement

dazzle *vb* ***syn*** DAZE 1, bedazzle, blind

dead *adj* **1** devoid of life <a *dead* person>
syn asleep, cold, deceased, defunct, departed, exanimate, extinct, inanimate, late, lifeless, spiritless, unanimated
rel bloodless, breathless; gone, reposing; inactive, inert; belowground, buried
idiom dead as a doornail, gone the way of all flesh, out of one's misery, pushing up daisies
con animate, animated, living, vital; being, existing; active, live
ant alive
2 ***syn*** DEATHLY 1, corpselike, corpsy, deadened, deadly, deathful, deathlike

---

syn synonym(s) ***rel*** related word(s)
idiom idiomatic equivalent(s) ***con*** contrasted word(s)
ant antonym(s) * vulgar
|| use limited; if in doubt, see a dictionary
The first word in a synonym list when printed in SMALL CAPITALS shows where there is more information about the group. For a more efficient use of this book see Explanatory Notes.

rel insensible, insentient, numb, unfeeling, unresponsive; inanimate, unconscious
con feeling, responsive, sensitive, sentient; animate, animated, living, spirited, vivacious
ant alive
3 *syn* NUMB 1, anesthetized, asleep, benumbed, deadened, insensible, insensitive, numbed, senseless, unfeeling
4 *syn* OBSOLETE, disused, extinct, outmoded, outworn, passé, superseded
ant living; viable
5 *syn* EXTINCT 2, bygone, defunct, departed, gone, lost, vanished
6 *syn* DULL 7, blind, dim, flat, lackluster, lusterless, mat, muted
rel bleak, dismal
con glorious, resplendent
7 *syn* UTTER, absolute, *‖bloody, complete, damned, downright, out-and-out, outright, perfect, unmitigated

dead *adv syn* DIRECTLY 1, direct, due, right, straight, straightly, undeviatingly

deaden *vb* **1** to impair in vigor, force, activity, or sensation <the news *deadened* his distress>
syn benumb, blunt, desensitize, dull, mull, numb
rel anesthetize, paralyze, unnerve; stun, stupefy
con animate, vivify; energize, invigorate; activate, vitalize
ant enliven
2 *syn* MUFFLE 2, dampen, mute, stifle

dead end *n* a course which leads to nothing further <had reached a *dead end* in negotiations>
syn blind alley, cul-de-sac, impasse, pocket
rel corner, hole; deadlock, halt, standstill; bottleneck

deadened *adj* **1** *syn* DEATHLY 1, corpselike, corpsy, dead, deadly, deathful, deathlike
2 *syn* NUMB 1, anesthetized, asleep, benumbed, dead, insensible, insensitive, numbed, senseless, unfeeling

‖deader *n syn* CORPSE, body, cadaver, carcass, ‖cold meat, mort, remains, stiff

deadfall *n syn* PITFALL, booby trap, mousetrap, springe, trapfall

deadliness *n syn* FATALITY 1, lethality, mortality

deadlock *n syn* DRAW 4, dogfall, stalemate, standoff, tie
rel condition, posture, situation, state; dilemma, plight, predicament, quandary
con decision, determination, resolution, solution

deadly *adj* **1** causing or causative of death <a *deadly* disease>
syn deathly, fatal, lethal, mortal, mortiferous, pestilent, pestilential; *compare* PERNICIOUS
rel destroying, destructive; killing, slaying; internecine; baneful, noxious, pernicious; poisonous, toxic, virulent
con healthful, healthy, wholesome; advantageous, beneficial, restorative, sanative
2 *syn* PERNICIOUS, baneful, noxious, pestiferous, pestilent, pestilential
con harmless, innocuous, inoffensive, unoffending
3 *syn* DEATHLY 1, corpselike, corpsy, dead, deadened, deathful, deathlike

deadpan *adj syn* EXPRESSIONLESS, blank, empty, inexpressive, unexpressive, vacant

dead to rights *adv syn* RED-HANDED, flagrante delicto

deadweight *n syn* LOAD 3, burden, charge, duty, millstone, onus, task, tax, weight

‖deadwood *n syn* ADVANTAGE 3, allowance, bulge, edge, handicap, head start, odds, ‖overhand, start, vantage

deaf *adj syn* OBSTINATE, bullheaded, headstrong, intractable, mulish, pertinacious, perverse, pigheaded, self-willed, stubborn

deal *vb* **1** *syn* DISTRIBUTE 1, disburse, dispense, disperse, divide, ‖divvy, dole (out), lot (out), measure (out), partition
rel partake, participate, share
con receive, take; detain, hold, hold back, keep, retain, withhold; appropriate, arrogate, confiscate
2 *syn* GIVE 10, administer, deliver, inflict, strike
rel impart, mete, render
con annul, cancel, remove, rescind, revoke

deal (out) *vb syn* ADMINISTER 2, apportion, dispense, dole (out), mete (out), portion (out), share out
rel dish, dish out, help, serve; offer, present, proffer, tender
con hold, hold back, keep, retain, withhold

deal (with) *vb syn* TREAT 2, handle, play, serve, take, use
rel control, direct; clear, rid, unburden
con misconduct, misdirect, mishandle, mismanage; disregard, ignore, neglect; burden, cumber, encumber

deal *n* **1** *syn* AGREEMENT 2, accord, understanding
2 treatment received in a transaction from another <a fair *deal*>
syn shake

dealer *n syn* MERCHANT, businessman, merchandiser, trader, tradesman, trafficker

dealings *n pl syn* COMMERCE 1, intercourse, traffic, truck
rel affairs, business, concerns, doings, matters, things; proceedings

deambulatory *adj syn* ITINERANT, ambulant, ambulatory, nomadic, perambulant, perambulatory, peripatetic, roving, vagabond, vagrant

dean *n syn* LEADER 1, ‖bell cow, bellwether, doyen, guide, lead, pilot

dear *adj* **1** *syn* FAVORITE 1, beloved, blue-eyed, darling, fair-haired, loved, pet, precious, white-haired, white-headed
2 *syn* LOVING, affectionate, devoted, doting, fond, lovesome
3 *syn* COSTLY 1, expensive, high
con inexpensive, low, moderate, modest, nominal
ant cheap

dear *n syn* SWEETHEART 1, beloved, darling, heartthrob, honey, honeybunch, love, loveling, sweet, sweetling

dearth *n syn* ABSENCE, default, defect, lack, ‖miss, privation, want

---

syn synonym(s) · *rel* related word(s)
idiom idiomatic equivalent(s) · *con* contrasted word(s)
ant antonym(s) · * vulgar
‖ use limited; if in doubt, see a dictionary
The first word in a synonym list when printed in SMALL CAPITALS shows where there is more information about the group. For a more efficient use of this book see Explanatory Notes.

rel infrequency, rareness, scarcity, uncommonness; exiguousness, meagerness, scantiness, scantness; paucity, insufficiency

con superfluity, surplus; lavishness, prodigality, profusion

ant excess

death *n* **1** the end or the ending of life <*death* of a man> <*death* of an enterprise>

syn curtains, decease, defunction, demise, dissolution, grim reaper, (the) Pale Horse, passing, quietus, silence, sleep

rel annihilation, ending, expiration, extinction, grave, termination

idiom crossing the bar

ant life

2 *syn* FATALITY 2, casualty, fatal

deathful *adj syn* DEATHLY 1, corpselike, corpsy, dead, deadened, deadly, deathlike

deathless *adj syn* IMMORTAL 1, undying

rel eternal; abiding, lasting, persisting

deathlike *adj* **1** *syn* DEATHLY 1, corpselike, corpsy, dead, deadened, deadly, deathful

2 *syn* GHASTLY 2, cadaverous, corpselike, ghostlike, ghostly, shadowy, spectral

deathly *adj* **1** suggesting death (as in inertness or appearance) <fell in a *deathly* faint>

syn corpselike, corpsy, dead, deadened, deadly, deathful, deathlike

rel cadaverous, haggard, wasted; ghastly, grisly, gruesome, macabre; appalling, dreadful, horrible

con healthy, hearty, robust; stout, sturdy; energetic, strenuous, vigorous

2 *syn* DEADLY 1, fatal, lethal, mortal, mortiferous, pestilent, pestilential

debacle *n* **1** *syn* DEFEAT 1, beating, defeasance, drubbing, licking, overthrow, rout, shellacking, trouncing, vanquishment

2 *syn* COLLAPSE 2, breakdown, crack-up, crash, smash, smashup, wreck

debar *vb syn* EXCLUDE, bar, bate, count out, eliminate, except, rule out, suspend

rel forbid, interdict; block, hinder, impede, obstruct

con accept, receive; allow, let, permit

ant admit

debark *vb syn* DISEMBARK, land

debase *vb* **1** to cause to become impaired in quality or character <vulgarly outrageous movies that *debase* the taste of the people>

syn animalize, bastardize, bestialize, brutalize, canker, corrupt, debauch, demoralize, deprave, pervert, poison, rot, stain, vitiate, warp; *compare* ADULTERATE

rel damage, harm, impair, injure, mar, spoil; contaminate, defile, dishonor, pollute, taint; commercialize

---

syn synonym(s) — *rel* related word(s)
idiom idiomatic equivalent(s) — *con* contrasted word(s)
ant antonym(s) — * vulgar
‖ use limited; if in doubt, see a dictionary
The first word in a synonym list when printed in SMALL CAPITALS shows where there is more information about the group. For a more efficient use of this book see Explanatory Notes.

con enhance, heighten; lift, raise; ameliorate, better, improve

ant elevate; amend

2 *syn* HUMBLE, abase bemean, cast down, degrade, demean, humiliate, lower, sink

rel cripple, debilitate, disable, enfeeble, sap, undermine, weaken

con acclaim, laud, praise; refresh, rejuvenate, renew, restore

3 *syn* ADULTERATE, doctor, dope (up), load, sophisticate, weight

rel damage, impair, worsen; corrupt, defile, spoil

idiom play the devil (*or* the mischief) with

con amend, upgrade

debased *adj* being lowered in quality or character <became *debased* in his greed for money>

syn corrupted, debauched, depraved, perverted, vitiate, vitiated

rel decadent, degenerate, degenerated, deteriorated; abandoned, dissolute, profligate, reprobate

con ameliorated, bettered, improved; elevated, lifted, raised

ant elevated

debatable *adj syn* MOOT, arguable, disputable, doubtful, dubious, mootable, problematic, questionable, uncertain

ant undebatable

debate *n* **1** *syn* ARGUMENTATION, dialectic, disputation, forensic, mooting

rel controverting, rebutting, refuting

2 *syn* ATTENTION 1, application, concentration, consideration, deliberation, heed, study

debate *vb syn* DISCUSS 1, agitate, argue, canvass, discept, dispute, ‖kick around, moot, thrash out, toss (around)

rel altercate, quarrel, wrangle; confute, controvert, disprove, rebut, refute; demonstrate, prove; contend, contest

con agree, coincide, concur; affirm, aver, maintain, profess

debauch *vb* **1** *syn* DEBASE 1, bastardize, bestialize, brutalize, corrupt, demoralize, deprave, pervert, vitiate, warp

rel decoy, inveigle, lure, seduce, tempt

con amend, remedy; clean, cleanse, purge, purify; preserve, reclaim, save

2 *syn* SEDUCE 2, undo

debauch *n syn* ORGY 2, bacchanal, bacchanalia, party, saturnalia

debauched *adj syn* DEBASED, corrupted, depraved, perverted, vitiate, vitiated

rel lascivious, lecherous, lewd, libertine, libidinous, licentious, wanton

con delivered, reclaimed, redeemed, rescued, saved; chaste, decent, pure; moral, virtuous; continent, temperate

debilitate *vb syn* WEAKEN 1, attenuate, blunt, cripple, disable, enfeeble, sap, unbrace, undermine, unstrengthen

rel devitalize; attenuate, extenuate; harm, hurt, mar, spoil

con energize, vitalize; fortify, reinforce, strengthen; refresh, rejuvenate, renew, restore; rally, rouse, stir

ant invigorate

debility *n* ***syn*** INFIRMITY 1, decrepitude, disease, feebleness, infirmness, malaise, sickliness, unhealthiness

debris *n* ***syn*** REFUSE, garbage, junk, litter, offal, riffraff, rubbish, spilth, trash, waste
rel dregs, dross, rubble

debt *n* **1** ***syn*** EVIL 2, sin, wickedness, wrong
2 ***syn*** INDEBTEDNESS 1, arrearage, liability, obligation
3 something (as money) that is owed <struggling to keep ahead of his *debts*>
syn arrear(s), arrearage, due, indebtedness, liability; *compare* INDEBTEDNESS 1
rel default, deficit, delinquency, nonpayment, outstandings; debit, demurrage
con asset, credit; compensation, refund, reimbursement, remuneration

debunk *vb* ***syn*** EXPOSE 4, discover, show up, uncloak, undress, unmask, unshroud

debut *vb* to make one's formal entrance into society <she *debuted* on her 20th birthday>
syn come out
idiom make one's bow

decadence *n* ***syn*** DETERIORATION 1, declension, declination, decline, degeneracy, degeneration, dégringolade, devolution, downfall, downgrade
rel regress, regression, regressiveness, retrogradation, retrograding, retrogression, retrogressiveness; debasement, degradation
con advance, progress, progression; amelioration, bettering, betterment, improvement
ant rise; flourishing

decadent *adj* ***syn*** EFFETE 3, decayed, degenerate, overripe

decamp *vb* **1** ***syn*** GET OUT 1, begone, clear out, hightail, kite, scram, skedaddle, skiddoo, take off, ‖vamoose
2 ***syn*** ESCAPE 1, abscond, break, ‖bunk, flee, fly, scape
rel exit, go, leave, quit, retire, withdraw; avoid, elude, evade, shun
con arrive, come

decapitate *vb* **1** ***syn*** BEHEAD, decollate, guillotine, head, neck
2 ***syn*** DESTROY 1, decimate, demolish, raze, ruin, unbuild, undo, unmake, wrack, wreck

decay *vb* to undergo or to cause to undergo destructive changes <apples *decaying* in the basket>
syn break down, corrupt, crumble, decompose, disintegrate, molder, ‖perish, putrefy, putresce, rot, spoil, taint, turn
rel deteriorate; debilitate, enfeeble, sap, undermine, weaken; contaminate, defile, pollute; dilapidate, ruin, wreck; curdle, ferment, sour, work; dry-rot
idiom go bad, go to pot, go to seed, go to wrack and ruin
con mature, ripen; refresh, renew, restore; activate, energize, vitalize; cleanse, purify; galvanize, quicken, stimulate, strengthen

decayed *adj* **1** ***syn*** EFFETE 3, decadent, degenerate, overripe
2 ***syn*** BAD 5, putrid, rotten, spoiled

decease *n* ***syn*** DEATH 1, curtains, defunction, demise, dissolution, (the) Pale Horse, passing, quietus, silence, sleep

decease *vb* ***syn*** DIE 1, cash in, depart, drop, expire, go, pass, pass away, perish, succumb

deceased *adj* ***syn*** DEAD 1, asleep, cold, defunct, departed, exanimate, extinct, inanimate, late, lifeless

deceit *n* **1** the act or practice of imposing upon the credulity of others by dishonesty, fraud, or trickery <he was full of *deceit* in his business dealings>
syn cunning, dissemblance, dissimulation, duplicity, guile
rel chicane, chicanery, deception, double-dealing, fraud, trickery; artifice, craft; cheating, cozening, defrauding, entrapping, overreaching, trapping
con honesty, scrupulosity, scrupulousness, uprightness; candidness, candor, frankness, openness; forthrightness, straightforwardness
2 ***syn*** IMPOSTURE, deception, flimflam, fraud, gyp, hoax, humbug, sell, sham, swindle

deceitful *adj* ***syn*** DISHONEST 1, knavish, lying, mendacious, roguish, shifty, unhonest, untruthful
rel artful, crafty, cunning, foxy, guileful, insidious, sly, tricky, wily; clandestine, furtive, stealthy, underhand, underhanded; deceptive, delusive, delusory, misleading
con assuring, convincing, reassuring
ant trustworthy

deceive *vb* to lead astray or frustrate by underhandedness <advertising that *deceives* the public>
syn beguile, betray, ‖bitch, bluff, ‖bunk, cozen, delude, double-cross, four-flush, humbug, illude, juggle, mislead, mock, sell out, suck in, take in, two-time
rel cheat, defraud, do, overreach; circumvent, outwit; bamboozle, befool, dupe, gull, hoax, hoodwink, spoof, trick, victimize; throw off
idiom pull one's leg, pull the wool over one's eyes, put something over (*or* across), take for a ride, take into camp, throw off the scent (*or* track)
con correct, disabuse, rectify, unblind; acquaint, advise, apprise, inform
ant undeceive; enlighten

deceiving *adj* ***syn*** MISLEADING, beguiling, deceptive, deluding, delusive, delusory, fallacious, false
ant undeceiving; enlightening

decelerate *vb* ***syn*** DELAY 1, bog (down), detain, embog, hang up, mire, retard, set back, slacken, slow (up *or* down)
ant accelerate

decency *n* ***syn*** DECORUM 1, dignity, etiquette, propriety, seemliness
rel appropriateness, fittingness, fitness, suitability; ceremoniousness, conventionality, formality
con impropriety, indecorousness, unseemliness; inappropriateness, unfitness, unsuitability; discourteousness, impoliteness, rudeness
ant indecency

decent *adj* **1** ***syn*** DECOROUS 1, becoming, befitting, comme il faut, conforming, correct, nice, proper, right, seemly

---

syn synonym(s) ***rel*** related word(s)
idiom idiomatic equivalent(s) ***con*** contrasted word(s)
ant antonym(s) * vulgar
‖ use limited; if in doubt, see a dictionary
The first word in a synonym list when printed in SMALL CAPITALS shows where there is more information about the group. For a more efficient use of this book see Explanatory Notes.

con awkward, clumsy, gauche, inept, maladroit; discomfiting, disconcerting, embarrassing; crude, rough, rude, uncouth
2 ***syn*** CHASTE, clean, immaculate, modest, pure, spotless, stainless, unblemished, undefiled, unsullied
rel noble; good, right; rigid, strict; ascetic, austere, severe
con lewd; libertine, wanton; abandoned, dissolute, profligate, reprobate
ant indecent; obscene
3 ***syn*** RESPECTABLE 5, presentable, tolerable
4 better than mediocre but less than excellent <the accommodations were *decent*>
syn acceptable, adequate, all right, common, good, respectable, right, satisfactory, sufficient, tolerable, unexceptionable, unexceptional, unimpeachable, unobjectionable; *compare* RESPECTABLE 5, SUFFICIENT 1
rel average, fair, mediocre, middling
con imperfect, inadequate, unacceptable, unsatisfactory; excellent, fine, superior
5 ***syn*** SUFFICIENT 1, adequate, comfortable, competent, enough, satisfactory, sufficing

decently *adv* ***syn*** WELL 1, befittingly, correctly, decorously, fitly, fittingly, justly, nicely, properly, rightly

deception *n* **1** the act of deliberately deceiving <resort to falsehood and *deception* in avoiding the tax>
syn cheat, chicane, chicanery, dipsy-doodle, dirt, dishonesty, double-dealing, dupery, fourberie, fraud, hanky-panky, highbinding, indirection, sharp practice, subterfuge, ||suck-in, trickery
rel cunning, deceit, dissimulation, duplicity, guile; cheating, cozening, defrauding, overreaching; bamboozling, befooling, duping, gulling, hoaxing, hoodwinking; manipulation; ride, ||snow job
con candidness, frankness, openness; honesty, integrity, probity; artlessness, ingenuousness, naiveté
2 ***syn*** IMPOSTURE, cheat, deceit, fraud, gyp, hoax, humbug, sell, sham, spoof
rel delusion, hallucination, illusion, mirage
3 ***syn*** FALLACY 2, casuistry, deceptiveness, delusion, equivocation, sophism, sophistry, speciousness, spuriousness

deceptive *adj* ***syn*** MISLEADING, beguiling, deceiving, deluding, delusive, delusory, fallacious, false
rel colorable, plausible, specious; apparent, illusory, ostensible, seeming
con authentic, bona fide, genuine, veritable; actual, real, true; dependable, reliable, trustworthy

deceptiveness *n* ***syn*** FALLACY 2, casuistry, deception, delusion, equivocation, sophism, sophistry, speciousness, spuriousness

decide *vb* to come or to cause to come to a conclusion <he *decided* how to solve the problem>
syn conclude, determine, figure, resolve, rule, settle
rel gather; adjudge, adjudicate, judge; conjecture, guess, surmise; establish, fix, set
idiom cast the die, make up one's mind, settle in one's mind
con falter, hesitate, vacillate, waver; fluctuate, oscillate; balk, demur, scruple, shy

decided *adj* **1** beyond any doubt or ambiguity <a *decided* advantage over her opponent>
syn assured, clear-cut, definite, pronounced
rel determined, resolved; certain, positive, sure; categorical, explicit, express, unequivocal; clear, obvious, unmistakable, runaway
con doubtful, dubious, problematic, uncertain; equivocal, obscure, vague
ant questionable
2 free from doubt or wavering <he had a *decided* manner>
syn bent, decisive, determined, intent, resolute, resolved, set, settled
rel certain, cocksure, positive, sure; iron-jawed; established, fixed; earnest, purposeful, serious; unfaltering, unhesitating, unwavering
con doubtful, dubious, irresolute, uncertain; faltering, hesitant, vacillating, wavering; undetermined, unresolved, unsettled, unsure
ant undecided
3 ***syn*** POSITIVE 1, categorical, definite, unequivocal

decidedness *n* ***syn*** DECISION 2, determination, firmness, purposefulness, purposiveness, resoluteness, resolution, resolve

decimate *vb* **1** ***syn*** DESTROY 1, demolish, raze, ruin, unbuild, undo, unframe, unmake, wrack, wreck
2 ***syn*** SLAUGHTER 3, annihilate, exterminate, massacre, wipe (out)

decipher *vb* **1** ***syn*** DECODE, break, crack, cryptanalyze, decrypt
ant cipher, encipher
2 ***syn*** SOLVE 2, break, ||cipher, ||dope out, figure out, puzzle out, resolve, unfold, unravel, unriddle
rel paraphrase, translate; analyze, break down
idiom find the key of
con misconstrue, misinterpret, misunderstand; confuse, muddle; bewilder, confound, mystify, puzzle; jumble, mix, scramble

decision *n* **1** a position arrived at after consideration <the *decision* of the committee remains firm>
syn conclusion, determination, resolution, settlement
rel accord, agreement, understanding; accommodation, adjustment, arrangement; compromise, reconciliation; choice, preference, selection
con deadlock, draw, stalemate, standoff, tie
2 freedom from doubt or wavering <a man of unusual *decision*>
syn decidedness, determination, firmness, purposefulness, purposiveness, resoluteness, resolution, resolve
rel doggedness, obstinacy, obstinance, perseverance, persistence, stubbornness; earnestness, seriousness; backbone, fortitude, grit, pluck
con changeableness, indetermination, irresolution; uncertainty, unsureness; faltering, fluctuation, hesitation, vacillation, wavering
ant indecision

decisive *adj* ***syn*** DECIDED 2, bent, determined, intent, resolute, resolved, set, settled

---

syn synonym(s) — *rel* related word(s)
idiom idiomatic equivalent(s) — *con* contrasted word(s)
ant antonym(s) — * vulgar
|| use limited; if in doubt, see a dictionary
The first word in a synonym list when printed in SMALL CAPITALS shows where there is more information about the group. For a more efficient use of this book see Explanatory Notes.

rel imperative, imperious, masterful, peremptory; assured, self-assured, self-confident; steadfast, unswerving, unwavering
con fluctuating, oscillating; hesitant, reluctant; doubtful, dubious, irresolute, uncertain, undecided
ant indecisive

deck *vb syn* ADORN, beautify, bedeck, decorate, dress (up), embellish, garnish, ornament, prank, trim
rel apparel, array, attire, clothe, dress; accouter, appoint, furnish
con deface, disfigure; impair, mar, spoil; contort, deform, distort; dismantle, divest, strip

deck (out) *vb syn* DRESS UP 1, doll out, doll up, fix up, gussy up, primp, slick, spiff, spruce (up), tog (out *or* up)

declaim *vb syn* ORATE, bloviate, harangue, mouth, perorate, rant, rave, soapbox

declamatory *adj syn* RHETORICAL, aureate, bombastic, euphuistic, flowery, grandiloquent, high-flown, magniloquent, oratorical, sonorous

declaration *n* the act of declaring, proclaiming, or publicly announcing <a *declaration* of war>
syn advertisement, announcement, broadcast, proclamation, promulgation, pronouncement, pronunciamento, publication
rel information, notice, notification; communication; disclosure, revelation; report, statement; acknowledgment, avowal
con concealment, hiding; denial, disaffirmation; recall, recantation, retraction, revocation

declare *vb* **1** to make known openly or publicly <*declared* his intention to run for the senate>
syn advertise, announce, annunciate, blaze (abroad), blazon, broadcast, bruit (about), disseminate, proclaim, promulgate, publish, sound, toot, vend
rel acquaint, advise, apprise, inform, notify; communicate, impart; pronounce; disclose, discover, divulge, reveal; report
idiom declare oneself, make public (*or* known)
con hold, hold back, keep back, reserve, withhold; recall, recant, retract, revoke
2 *syn* ASSERT 1, affirm, aver, avouch, avow, constate, depose, predicate, profess, protest
rel air, broach, express, utter, vent, ventilate, voice; acknowledge, admit, own
idiom have one's say
con controvert; deny; repress, suppress; conceal, hide
3 *syn* SAY 1, bring out, chime in, come out (with), deliver, state, tell, throw out, utter
rel broach, express, voice
idiom speak one's piece

declare off *vb syn* BACK DOWN, back off, back out, backpedal, backwater, crawfish (out), cry off, renege, resile, welsh

declass *vb syn* DEGRADE 1, break, bump, bust, demerit, demote, disgrade, disrate, downgrade, reduce
rel disbar, exclude, rule out; abash, discomfit, disconcert
con aggrandize, exalt, magnify

déclassé *adj syn* INFERIOR 2, common, hack, low-grade, mean, poor, second-class, second-drawer, second-rate

declension *n syn* DETERIORATION 1, decadence, declination, decline, degeneracy, degeneration, dégringolade, devolution, downfall, downgrade
rel regression, regressiveness, retrogression, retrogressiveness; dilapidation, ruination
con ascension, ascent; rise, rising; advance, progress, progression; development, maturation

declination *n* **1** *syn* DETERIORATION 1, decadence, declension, decline, degeneracy, degeneration, dégringolade, devolution, downfall, downgrade
2 *syn* FAILURE 4, decline, deterioration, ebbing, waning

decline *vb* **1** *syn* SET 12, dip, go down, sink
ant ascend
2 *syn* FAIL 1, deteriorate, ‖dwine, fade, flag, languish, weaken
rel backslide, lapse, relapse; slide; return, revert; recede, retrograde; abate, ebb, subside, wane
idiom go downhill, take a turn for the worse
con advance, progress; develop, mature; gain, recover
3 *syn* DETERIORATE 1, degenerate, descend, disimprove, disintegrate, retrograde, rot, sink, worsen
4 to turn away by not accepting, receiving, or considering <he *declined* the invitation>
syn disapprove, dismiss, refuse, reject, reprobate, repudiate, spurn, turn down
rel balk, boggle, demur, jib, scruple, shy, stick, stickle; abstain, forbear, refrain; deny, gainsay; abjure, renounce; bypass
idiom send regrets
con receive, take; accede, acquiesce, assent, consent; choose, select; adopt, embrace, espouse
ant accept

decline *n* **1** *syn* FAILURE 4, declination, deterioration, ebbing, waning
rel devitalization, weakening
con advancement, progress; recovery; development, maturation
2 *syn* DETERIORATION 1, decadence, declension, declination, degeneracy, degeneration, dégringolade, devolution, downfall, downgrade
rel comedown, descent, drop, fall, falling off, slump; ebb, wane; backsliding, lapse, relapse
con development, evolution
3 a downward movement (as in price or value) <stocks suffered a *decline* in the market>
syn dip, downslide, downswing, downtrend, downturn, drop, falloff, sag, slide, slip, slump
rel lapse, loss, lowering; depression; decrease, drop-off, sell-off
con upswing, uptrend, upturn
4 *syn* DESCENT 4, declivity, dip, drop, fall

declivate *adj syn* INCLINED 3, declivitous, inclining, leaning, oblique, pitched, sloped, sloping, tilted, tipped

declivitous *adj syn* INCLINED 3, declivate, inclining, leaning, oblique, pitched, sloped, sloping, tilted, tipped

declivity *n syn* DESCENT 4, decline, dip, drop, fall

---

ant acclivity

decode *vb* to convert code into ordinary language < *decode* a message >
syn break, crack, cryptanalyze, decipher, decrypt
rel anagram; render, translate; ‖dope out, figure out, make out; resolve, solve, unfold, unravel, unriddle, work, work out; elucidate, explain, interpret
con cipher, codify, encipher; anagrammatize
ant code, encode, encrypt

decollate *vb syn* BEHEAD, decapitate, guillotine, head, neck

decolor *vb syn* WHITEN 1, blanch, bleach, blench, decolorize, white
rel wash out; achromatize, fume, peroxide
con blacken; dye, imbue, stain, tinge, tint; paint, shade
ant color

decolorize *vb syn* WHITEN 1, blanch, bleach, blench, decolor, white
ant color

decompose *vb* **1** *syn* ANALYZE, anatomize, break down, decompound, dissect, resolve
con combine, join, link, write; synthesize, unify; amalgamate, merge, mix
ant compound
2 *syn* DECAY, break down, crumble, disintegrate, molder, putrefy, rot, spoil, taint, turn
rel deliquesce, liquefy, melt; break up, dissolve

decompound *vb syn* ANALYZE, anatomize, break down, decompose, dissect, resolve
ant compound

decorate *vb syn* ADORN, beautify, bedeck, deck, dress (up), embellish, garnish, ornament, prank, trim
rel accouter, appoint, equip, furnish, outfit
con impair, injure, mar, spoil; blot, blotch, foul, mutilate, scar, uglify; dismantle, divest, strip

decorated *adj syn* BEMEDALED, beribboned

decoration *n syn* HONOR 2, accolade, award, badge, bays, distinction, kudos, laurels

decorous *adj* **1** conforming to an accepted standard of propriety or good form < *decorous* behavior seems regrettably out of fashion >
syn au fait, becoming, befitting, Christian, civilized, comely, conforming, correct, decent, de rigueur, done, nice, proper, respectable, right, seemly
rel ceremonial, ceremonious, conventional, formal; dignified, elegant; appropriate, fit, fitting, meet, seasonable, suitable; prim, punctilious, rigid, stiff, stuffy
con blatant, clamorous, obstreperous, strident; aggressive, assertive, pushing, pushy; coarse, gross, vulgar; easy, fast, loose; improper, incorrect, unbecoming
ant indecorous
2 *syn* GOOD 13, well-behaved

decorously *adv syn* WELL 1, befittingly, correctly, decently, fitly, fittingly, justly, nicely, properly, rightly

decorousness *n syn* ORDER 7, correctitude, correctness, decorum, orderliness, properness, propriety, seemliness
rel ceremoniousness, conventionality, formality, solemnity; convenance, convention, form, usage
con inappropriateness, incorrectness; unfitness, unsuitability, unsuitableness; disorder, misbehavior, misconduct, misdeed, misdemeanor
ant indecorousness

decorticate *vb syn* SKIN 2, excorticate, peel, scale, strip
rel bark; scalp; denude, divest

decorum *n* **1** socially acceptable behavior or accepted standards of this < they found his conduct quite lacking in *decorum* >
syn decency, dignity, etiquette, propriety, seemliness
rel convenance, convention, form, usage
con laxity, laxness, license, slackness; carelessness, heedlessness, inconsiderateness, mannerlessness; inappropriateness, incorrectness
ant indecorum
2 *syn* ORDER 7, correctitude, correctness, decorousness, orderliness, properness, propriety, seemliness
rel ceremoniousness, conventionality, formality, solemnity; convenance, convention, form, usage
con inappropriateness, incorrectness; unfitness, unsuitability, unsuitableness; disorder, misbehavior, misconduct, misdeed, misdemeanor
ant indecorum; license
3 *usu* **decorums** *syn* MANNER 3, amenities, civilities, etiquette, mores, proprieties

decoy *n* **1** *syn* LURE 2, allurement, bait, come-on, enticement, inveiglement, seducement, snare, temptation, trap
rel chicane, chicanery, deception, trickery; drawing card
con rebuff, repellence, repellency, repellent, repugnance, repulse, repulsion
2 a person used as a lure < used the detective as a *decoy* to catch the pushers >
syn blind, ‖bonnet, ‖booster, capper, shill, shillaber, stick
rel lugger, roper, steerer; come-on, front, plant, stall

decoy *vb syn* LURE, allure, bait, entice, entrap, inveigle, lead on, seduce, tempt, toll
rel deceive, delude, mislead; ensorcell, wile
con disgust, repel, sicken; offend, repulse, revolt

decrease *vb* to grow less especially gradually < his influence *decreased* as a new generation grew up >
syn abate, bate, close, diminish, drain (away), dwindle, lessen, peak (out), peter (out), rebate, recede, reduce, taper, taper off
rel abbreviate, abridge, clip, curtail, retrench, shorten, trim; contract, shrink; allay, alleviate, ease, lighten, mitigate; ebb, subside; cut, cut back, cut down, lower; deduct, subtract
con augment, enlarge, multiply; elongate, extend, lengthen, prolong, protract; amplify, dilate, distend, expand, swell; accumulate, amass
ant increase

decree *n* **1** *syn* EDICT 1, directive, ruling, ukase
2 *syn* LAW 1, canon, decretum, edict, ordinance, precept, prescript, regulation, rule, statute
rel behest, bidding, injunction, order; charge, charging, direction, instruction; announcement, declaration, proclamation, promulgation, pronouncement

decree *vb* ***syn*** DICTATE, impose, lay down, ordain, prescribe, set

rel compel, constrain, force, oblige; demand, require

decrepit *adj* **1** ***syn*** WEAK 1, feeble, flimsy, fragile, frail, infirm, insubstantial, unsound, unsubstantial, weakly

rel haggard, wasted, worn; aged, old, superannuated; creaky, quavering, shaking, tottering

con strong; lusty; hale, healthy, hearty, robust, sound, well

ant sturdy

2 ***syn*** SHABBY 1, bedraggled, broken-down, down-at-heel, run-down, seedy, tacky, tagrag, threadbare, tired

rel damaged, impaired, injured, marred, spoiled; cast-off, ragged, used; slipshod, sloppy, unkempt

decrepitude *n* ***syn*** INFIRMITY 1, debility, disease, feebleness, infirmness, malaise, sickliness, unhealthiness

ant vigor

decretum *n* ***syn*** LAW 1, assize, canon, decree, edict, ordinance, precept, regulation, rule, statute

decry *vb* **1** ***syn*** DEPRECIATE 1, devaluate, devalue, downgrade, lower, mark down, underrate, undervalue, write down, write off

2 to indicate one's low opinion of something < *decrying* his opponent's character >

syn abuse, belittle, cry down, depreciate, derogate, detract (from), diminish, discount, disparage, dispraise, downcry, ‖low-rate, minimize, opprobriate, run down, take (from), take away, write off

rel deprecate, disapprove; censure, condemn, criticize, denounce, reprehend, reprobate; asperse, calumniate, defame, malign, traduce, vilify; discredit, disgrace

idiom bring into discredit, cast a slur upon, cast blame upon, throw stones at

con acclaim, eulogize, laud, praise; aggrandize, exalt, magnify; applaud, commend, compliment, recommend; endorse, sanction; approve, countenance, favor

ant extol, puff

decrypt *vb* ***syn*** DECODE, break, crack, cryptanalyze, decipher

decumbent *adj* ***syn*** PRONE 4, flat, procumbent, prostrate, reclining, recumbent

decussate *vb* ***syn*** INTERSECT, crisscross, cross, crosscut, intercross

dedicate *vb* ***syn*** DEVOTE 1, consecrate, hallow

rel address, apply, direct, give, surrender; commit, confide, consign, entrust; allot, appropriate, assign, set (aside)

idiom give over to

dedition *n* ***syn*** SURRENDER, capitulation, submission

deduce *vb* ***syn*** INFER, collect, conclude, deduct, derive, draw, gather, judge, make, make out

rel cogitate; consider, deem, regard; conceive, fancy, imagine; assume, presume, presuppose; read (into)

idiom take to mean

deducible *adj* ***syn*** DEDUCTIVE, a priori, derivable, dogmatic, reasoned

deduct *vb* **1** to take away one quantity from another < *deduct* the cost from his bill >

syn discount, draw back, knock off, substract, subtract, take, take away, take off, take out

rel decrease, diminish, lessen, reduce; roll back

con cast, figure, sum, tot, total

ant add

2 ***syn*** INFER, collect, conclude, deduce, derive, draw, gather, judge, make, make out

deduction *n* **1** an amount subtracted from a sum < *deductions* from gross income >

syn abatement, discount, rebate, reduction, subtraction

rel allowance, credit, cut; decrease, decrement, depreciation, diminution; charge-off, offtake, takeoff, write-off; dockage

con accession, accretion, augmentation, increase, increment, raise, rise; appreciation

ant addition

2 ***syn*** INFERENCE 1, illation, judgment, ratiocination

3 ***syn*** INFERENCE 2, conclusion, illation, judgment, ratiocination, sequitur

rel cogitation, deliberation, reasoning, reflection, speculation, thinking; consideration, contemplation; meditation, mulling, musing, pondering, rumination

deductive *adj* that can be deduced or developed from premises < *deductive* laws >

syn a priori, deducible, derivable, dogmatic, reasoned

rel illative, inferential, ratiocinative; conjectural, hypothetical, purported, putative, supposed, suppositious; academic, speculative, theoretical

con categorical, definite, explicit, express; instinctive, intuitive

deed *n* **1** ***syn*** ACTION 1, accomplishment, act, doing, thing

2 ***syn*** FEAT 2, achievement, exploit, tour de force

rel gaining, securing, winning; adventure, enterprise, quest; cause, crusade

idiom bold stroke

3 a written, signed, and usually sealed instrument that spells out some bargain, transfer, or contract <the *deed* to the property >

syn charter, conveyance

rel bargain, compact, contract, covenant, pact

deed *vb* ***syn*** TRANSFER 4, abalienate, alien, alienate, assign, cede, convey, make over, remise, sign (over)

deem *vb* **1** ***syn*** CONSIDER 3, account, reckon, regard, view

rel conjecture, guess, surmise, suspect, ‖suspicion, understand; ‖allow, assume, believe, ‖calculate, daresay, divine, expect, presume, suppose

idiom hold to be true

2 ***syn*** FEEL 3, believe, consider, credit, hold, know, sense, think

idiom take for granted

de-emphasize *vb* ***syn*** SOFT-PEDAL, play (down)

deep *adj* **1** having great extension downward or inward <a *deep* well> <a *deep* closet>

syn abysmal, profound; *compare* BOTTOMLESS 2

con depthless, shallow, superficial, unprofound; flat, level, plain, plane

ant shallow

---

syn synonym(s) — *rel* related word(s)
idiom idiomatic equivalent(s) — *con* contrasted word(s)
ant antonym(s) — * vulgar
‖ use limited; if in doubt, see a dictionary
The first word in a synonym list when printed in SMALL CAPITALS shows where there is more information about the group. For a more efficient use of this book see Explanatory Notes.

2 ***syn*** INTENSIVE, blood-and-guts, hard, intense, profound
3 ***syn*** RECONDITE, abstruse, acroamatic, esoteric, heavy, hermetic, occult, orphic, profound, secret
rel complex, complicated, intricate; arcane, mysterious; concealed, hidden
con easy, facile, simple; apparent, clear, distinct, evident, manifest, obvious; lucid, perspicuous; depthless, shallow, superficial, unprofound
4 ***syn*** SLY 2, artful, astute, crafty, cunning, foxy, guileful, insidious, tricky, wily
rel shrewd; acute, keen, knowing, sharp; contriving, intriguing, plotting
con ingenuous, naive, simple, unsophisticated; aboveboard, forthright, straightforward
5 ***syn*** INTENT, absorbed, engaged, engrossed, immersed, preoccupied, rapt, wrapped, wrapped up
rel abstracted, concentrated; centered, fixed, focused, set
con distracted, diverted; detached, disinterested, indifferent, unconcerned, uninterested

deep *n* ***syn*** OCEAN, blue, brine, ||briny, drink, main, sea

deep–dyed *adj* ***syn*** INVETERATE 1, bred-in-the-bone, confirmed, deep-rooted, deep-seated, dyed-in-the-wool, entrenched, hard-shell, settled, sworn

deepen *vb* ***syn*** INTENSIFY, aggravate, enhance, heighten, intensate, magnify, mount, redouble, rise, rouse

deepness *n* **1** ***syn*** DEPTH 1, drop
ant shallowness
2 ***syn*** DEPTH 2, abyss, profoundness, profundity

deep–rooted *adj* ***syn*** INVETERATE 1, bred-in-the-bone, confirmed, deep-dyed, deep-seated, dyed-in-the-wool, entrenched, hard-shell, settled, sworn

deep–seated *adj* **1** ***syn*** INHERENT, congenital, connate, constitutional, inborn, inbred, indwelling, ingrained, innate, intrinsic
2 ***syn*** INVETERATE 1, bred-in-the-bone, confirmed, deep-dyed, deep-rooted, dyed-in-the-wool, entrenched, hard-shell, settled, sworn
rel constitutional, immanent, indwelling, ingrained, inherent, intrinsic; deep, profound; inner, internal, inward; implanted; infixed
con peripheral, shallow, superficial, surface; adventitious, casual, chance, incidental
ant skin-deep

||**deep–six** *vb* ***syn*** DISCARD, cast, chuck, ||dice, ditch, jettison, junk, reject, scrap, throw away

deep water *n* ***syn*** PREDICAMENT, box, corner, dilemma, fix, hole, jam, pickle, plight, scrape

deface *vb* to mar the appearance of < *deface* the wall with graffiti >
syn disfashion, disfeature, disfigure
rel blemish, damage, harm, impair, injure, mar, spoil; contort, deform, distort, misshape; batter, mangle, mutilate; demolish, destroy; dilapidate, ruin, wreck
con mend, patch, repair; freshen, improve, refurbish, renew, restore; adorn, beautify, deck, decorate, embellish, ornament

defacer *n* ***syn*** VANDAL, despoiler, destroyer, ruinator, ruiner, wrecker

de facto *adv* ***syn*** VERY 2, actually, genuinely, really, truly, veritably

defalcation *n* ***syn*** FAILURE 3, deficiency, deficit, inadequacy, insufficience, insufficiency, lack, scantiness, shortage, underage
rel laxness, negligence, remissness, slackness; failing, fault
con discharge, effectuation, execution, fulfillment; completion, conclusion

defamation *n* ***syn*** DETRACTION, backbiting, backstabbing, belittlement, calumny, depreciation, disparagement, scandal, slander, tale
ant puffery

defamatory *adj* ***syn*** LIBELOUS, backbiting, calumnious, detracting, detractive, maligning, scandalous, slanderous, traducing, vilifying

defame *vb* ***syn*** MALIGN, asperse, calumniate, denigrate, libel, scandalize, slander, traduce, vilify, villainize
rel belie, misrepresent
idiom cast a slur on, throw mud at
con applaud, commend, compliment; exalt, magnify; back, champion, support, uphold
ant laud; puff

default *n* **1** ***syn*** FAILURE 1, delinquency, dereliction, neglect, oversight
rel deficiency, fault, imperfection, shortcoming; lapse, weakness; disregard, omission, overlooking, slight
2 ***syn*** ABSENCE, dearth, defect, lack, ||miss, privation, want

defeasance *n* ***syn*** DEFEAT 1, beating, debacle, discomfiture, drubbing, licking, overthrow, rout, shellacking, vanquishment

defeat *vb* **1** ***syn*** CONQUER 1, bear down, beat down, crush, overpower, reduce, subdue, subjugate, vanquish
rel bar, block, hinder, impede, obstruct; repress, suppress
idiom beat all hollow, get the better of, grind into the dust, ||have by the short hairs
con capitulate, defer, give in, submit; back down, withdraw
2 to win a victory over < *defeated* his opponent in the race >
syn best, down, outdo, ||pip, worst; *compare* CONQUER 1, WHIP 2
rel outfight, outgame; nose out
idiom get the better of

defeat *n* **1** an overthrow especially of an army in battle < the brigade suffered a *defeat* >
syn beating, debacle, defeasance, discomfiture, downcast, downthrow, drubbing, ||dusting, licking, overthrow, rout, shellacking, thrashing, trouncing, vanquishment, warming
rel bafflement, check, foil, frustration; rebuff, repulse, reversal, reverse, setback; ||cleaning, ||cleanup, clobbering, lambasting

syn synonym(s) ***rel*** related word(s)
idiom idiomatic equivalent(s) ***con*** contrasted word(s)
ant antonym(s) * vulgar
|| use limited; if in doubt, see a dictionary
The first word in a synonym list when printed in SMALL CAPITALS shows where there is more information about the group. For a more efficient use of this book see Explanatory Notes.

con conquest, triumph; gaining, securing, winning; ascendancy, supremacy
ant victory
2 *syn* FAILURE 2, insuccess, nonsuccess, unsuccess, unsuccessfulness

defeater *n syn* VICTOR 1, conqueror, master, subduer, subjugator, vanquisher
ant defeated

defect *n* **1** *syn* BLEMISH, flaw, vice
rel failing, fault, foible, frailty; infirmity, weakness; deficiency, imperfection, shortcoming
con excellence, faultlessness, impeccability; merit, perfection, virtue
2 *syn* ABSENCE, dearth, default, lack, ||miss, privation, want
rel scantiness, scarceness, scarcity, shortage
con overage, overplus, superfluity, surplus, surplusage
ant excess

defect *vb* to desert a cause or party often in order to espouse another <he *defected* from the Communist party>
syn apostatize, desert, rat, renounce, repudiate, tergiversate, tergiverse, turn
rel abandon, forsake; back out, renege, withdraw; depart, go, leave, quit; reject, spurn
idiom change sides, go back on, go over, turn one's coat, walk (*or* run) out on
con adhere (to), cling (to), hang on, stick (to *or* with); cherish, cultivate, foster

defection *n* conscious abandonment of allegiance or duty < *defection* from family responsibilities in times of trouble>
syn apostasy, desertion, falseness, recreancy, tergiversation
rel alienation, disaffection, estrangement; disloyalty, faithlessness; abandonment, forsaking; divorce, parting, runout, separation, sundering; disownment, rejection, repudiation
idiom running out on, ||taking a runout powder
con constancy, faithfulness, loyalty, resoluteness, staunchness, steadfastness; allegiance, fealty, fidelity; dependability, reliability, trustworthiness

defective *adj* **1** *syn* FAULTY, amiss, flawed, imperfect, sick
rel broken, damaged, impaired, injured
con faultless, flawless, impeccable, unblemished, undamaged
ant defectless
2 *syn* DEFICIENT 1, ||half-assed, inadequate, incomplete, insufficient, lacking, uncomplete, wanting
rel corrupted, debased, vitiated; deranged, disordered, disturbed, unsettled; unhealthy, unsound
con entire, perfect, whole; complete, full, plenary; healthy, sound
ant intact; defectless

defector *n syn* RENEGADE, apostate, rat, recreant, runagate, tergiversator, turnabout, turncoat

defend *vb* **1** to keep safe (as from danger or against attack) < *defend* the country from aggression>
syn bulwark, cover, fend, guard, protect, safeguard, screen, secure, shield
rel avert, prevent, ward; oppose, resist, withstand; battle, contend, fight, war; conserve, preserve, save
idiom stand on the defensive, stave off from
con aggress, assail, assault, fall (on *or* upon); bombard, storm; beset, besiege, overrun; capitulate, cave, submit, yield
ant attack
2 *syn* MAINTAIN 2, argue, assert, claim, contend, justify, vindicate, warrant
rel air, express, utter, vent, voice; account, explain, justify, rationalize; back, champion, support, uphold
idiom speak (*or* stand *or* stick) up for
con contradict, deny, gainsay, traverse; confute, controvert, disprove, rebut, refute

defendable *adj syn* TENABLE 1, defensible
ant undefendable

defense *n* **1** means or method of defending <the skunk's powerful *defense* against attackers>
syn aegis, armament, armor, guard, protection, safeguard, security, shield, ward
rel arms, munitions, weaponry, weapons; fastness, fort, fortress, stronghold
con aggression, offense, offensive
ant attack
2 *syn* APOLOGY 1, apologetic, apologia, justification
rel answer, rejoinder, reply, response, retort, return; exculpation, excuse, explanation, rationalization
con censure, condemnation, criticism, decrial, reprehension, reprobation, reproof; assault, attack, onset, onslaught

defenseless *adj syn* HELPLESS 1, unprotected

defensible *adj* **1** *syn* TENABLE 1, defendable
ant indefensible
2 *syn* JUSTIFIABLE, condonable, excusable, tenable, vindicable, warrantable
ant indefensible

defer *vb* to delay an action or proceeding <decided to *defer* voting until the next meeting>
syn adjourn, delay, hold off, hold over, hold up, intermit, lay over, postpone, prorogue, put off, put over, remit, shelve, stand over, stay, suspend, waive
rel detain, retard, slow; block, hinder, impede, obstruct; stall; extend, lengthen, prolong, protract
idiom hold up on, lay to one side, put on ice, set aside
con accelerate, hasten, hurry, speed; expedite, further, promote
ant advance

defer *vb syn* YIELD 2, bow, buckle (under), capitulate, cave, knuckle, knuckle under, submit, succumb
rel accede, acquiesce, agree, assent; accommodate, adapt, adjust, conform; cringe, fawn, truckle
con combat, fight, oppose, resist; object, remonstrate; balk, demur, stickle, strain
ant withstand

deference *n syn* HONOR 1, homage, obeisance, reverence

rel acquiescence, compliance; submission, submissiveness
con insolence, irreverence; disesteem, disfavor; discourtesy, incivility, rudeness
ant disrespect

deferential *adj* **1** ***syn*** RESPECTFUL, duteous, dutiful, regardful
2 ***syn*** INGRATIATING, disarming, ingratiatory, insinuating, insinuative, saccharine, silken, silky

defi *n* ***syn*** DEFIANCE 1, cartel, challenge, dare, defy, stump

defiance *n* **1** the act or an instance of defying <presented a *defiance* to his rival>
syn cartel, challenge, dare, defi, defy, stump
rel call, muster, summons; command, enjoinder, order
con capitulation, submission, surrender
2 disposition to resist or unwillingness to brook opposition <exhibited *defiance* toward his teacher>
syn contempt, contumacy, despite, recalcitrance, stubbornness
rel factiousness, insubordination, insurgency, rebelliousness; headstrongness, intractableness, unruliness; boldness, bravado, brazenness, impudence, insolence; audacity, effrontery, hardihood, temerity; contrariness, perversity
con acquiescence, compliance; amenableness, docility, obedience, tractableness; submissiveness

deficiency *n* **1** ***syn*** FAILURE 3, defalcation, deficit, inadequacy, insufficience, insufficiency, lack, scantiness, shortage, underage
rel absence, default, defect, want
con copiousness, plenty; great deal, heap, lot, much
2 ***syn*** IMPERFECTION, demerit, fault, shortcoming, sin
rel dearth, defect, lack, privation, want; default, dereliction, miscarriage, neglect
ant excess

deficient *adj* **1** showing lack of something necessary <*deficient* in judgment>
syn defective, ||half-assed, inadequate, incomplete, insufficient, lacking, uncomplete, wanting
rel faulty, flawed, imperfect, unsound; damaged, impaired, injured, marred; amiss, bad, unsatisfactory
idiom in want of
con complete, entire, intact, whole; acceptable, adequate, sufficient
2 ***syn*** SHORT 3, failing, inadequate, insufficient, scant, scanty, scarce, shy, unsufficient, wanting
rel infrequent, rare, uncommon
idiom found wanting
con excessive, extravagant, immoderate, inordinate; enough, satisfactory, sufficing
ant adequate, sufficient

---

syn synonym(s) *rel* related word(s)
idiom idiomatic equivalent(s) *con* contrasted word(s)
ant antonym(s) * vulgar
|| use limited; if in doubt, see a dictionary
The first word in a synonym list when printed in SMALL CAPITALS shows where there is more information about the group. For a more efficient use of this book see Explanatory Notes.

deficit *n* ***syn*** FAILURE 3, defalcation, deficiency, inadequacy, insufficience, insufficiency, lack, scantiness, shortage, underage
con copiousness, plenty; excess, surplus, surplusage

defile *vb* **1** ***syn*** CONTAMINATE 1, pollute, soil, taint
rel desecrate, profane; befoul, dirty, foul, sully, tarnish
con consecrate, hallow
ant cleanse; purify
2 ***syn*** RAPE, deflorate, deflower, force, outrage, ravish, spoil, violate
rel dishonor, shame, soil, sully
3 ***syn*** TAINT 1, besmear, besmirch, discolor, smear, soil, stain, sully, tar, tarnish

defiled *adj* ***syn*** IMPURE, common, desecrated, polluted, profaned, unclean

define *vb* **1** ***syn*** PRESCRIBE 2, assign, lay down
rel circumscribe, limit, mark (off), mark (out); designate; delineate, describe
con confound, confuse, mistake
2 ***syn*** BORDER 1, bound, edge, hem, margin, outline, rim, skirt, surround, verge
3 ***syn*** ETCH 2, delineate
rel explain, expound, interpret

definite *adj* **1** having distinct or certain limits <*definite* dimensions>
syn circumscribed, determinate, fixed, limited, narrow, precise, restricted
rel assigned, defined, prescribed; established, set; decided, determined, settled
con ambiguous, obscure, vague; unconditional, unlimited, unqualified, unrestricted; indeterminate, uncircumscribed; imprecise, loose, undefined
ant indefinite
2 ***syn*** EXPLICIT, categorical, clean-cut, clear-cut, definitive, express, specific, unambiguous
rel complete, full; downright, forthright; incisive
con doubtful, dubious, questionable; ambiguous
ant indefinite; equivocal
3 ***syn*** POSITIVE 1, categorical, decided, unequivocal
4 ***syn*** DECIDED 1, assured, clear-cut, pronounced
ant uncertain

definitely *adv* **1** ***syn*** EXPRESSLY 1, categorically, explicitly, specifically
2 ***syn*** EASILY 2, absolutely, doubtless, doubtlessly, positively, unequivocally, unquestionably

definiteness *n* ***syn*** PRECISION, accuracy, correctness, definitiveness, definitude, exactitude, exactness, preciseness
ant indefiniteness

definitive *adj* **1** ***syn*** CONCLUSIVE
rel determining, settling; concluding, final, last, terminal, ultimate; closing, completing, ending, finishing, terminating; absolute, categorical
con inconclusive, indecisive; temporary, transitory
ant provisional, tentative
2 ***syn*** EXPLICIT, categorical, clean-cut, clear-cut, definite, express, specific, unambiguous
rel actual, real
con doubtful, dubious, questionable; ambiguous
ant indefinitive

definitiveness *n* ***syn*** PRECISION, accuracy, correctness, definiteness, definitude, exactitude, exactness, preciseness

ant indefinitiveness, indefinitude

definitude *n* ***syn*** PRECISION, accuracy, correctness, definiteness, definitiveness, exactitude, exactness, preciseness

ant indefinitiveness, indefinitude

deflect *vb* **1** ***syn*** TURN 6, avert, divert, pivot, sheer, veer, volte-face, wheel, whip, whirl

rel disperse, swerve; hook, skew

2 ***syn*** WARD 1, fend, parry

rel hold off, keep off

deflection *n* **1** ***syn*** DEVIATION 1, aberration, departure, divergence, diversion, turning

rel bending, curving, twisting; departing, swerve, swerving, veer, veering

2 ***syn*** TURN 2, bend, deviation, double, shift, tack, yaw

deflorate *vb* ***syn*** RAPE, defile, deflower, force, outrage, ravish, spoil, violate

deflower *vb* **1** ***syn*** RAPE, defile, deflorate, force, outrage, ravish, spoil, violate

2 ***syn*** RAVAGE, depredate, desecrate, desolate, despoil, devast, devastate, devour, harry, havoc

deform *vb* to mar or spoil by or as if by twisting <a face *deformed* by bitterness>

syn contort, distort, misshape, torture, warp, wind

rel batter, cripple, maim, mangle, mutilate; deface, disfigure; damage, impair, injure, mar, spoil; blemish, flaw; screw (up), squinch

deformity *n* a physical blemish or disfigurement <the dwarf's humpback *deformity*>

syn distortion, malconformation, malformation, misshape

rel defacement, deformation, disfigurement; damage, impairment, injury; aberration, abnormality; irregularity, unnaturalness

defraud *vb* ***syn*** CHEAT, beat, bilk, chouse, cozen, do, flimflam, gyp, swindle, take

rel bamboozle, hoax, trick; circumvent, foil, outwit; fleece, milk, stick; take in

idiom do out of, put over a fast one, take to the cleaner's

defrauder *n* ***syn*** SWINDLER, cheat, confidence man, con man, diddler, double-dealer, flimflammer, gyp, sharper, trickster

deft *adj* ***syn*** DEXTEROUS 1, adroit, clever, handy, neat-handed, nimble

rel agile, brisk, fleet; apt, prompt, quick, ready; adept, crack, crackerjack; ingenious, neat

con heavy-handed, unskillful; blundering, bungling, butterfingered; rigid, stiff, wooden

ant awkward, unhandy

deftness *n* ***syn*** ADDRESS 1, adroitness, dexterity, dexterousness, prowess, readiness, skill, sleight

rel agility, fleetness, nimbleness; assuredness, confidence

con incompetence, inefficiency; clumsiness, heavy-handedness, maladroitness

ant awkwardness

defunct *adj* **1** ***syn*** DEAD 1, asleep, cold, deceased, departed, exanimate, extinct, inanimate, late, lifeless

rel inactive, inert

ant alive; live

2 ***syn*** EXTINCT 2, bygone, dead, departed, gone, lost, vanished

ant surviving

defunction *n* ***syn*** DEATH 1, curtains, decease, demise, dissolution, (the) Pale Horse, passing, quietus, silence, sleep

defy *vb* ***syn*** FACE 3, beard, brave, challenge, dare, ||double-dog dare, front, outdare, outface, venture

rel deride, mock, ridicule; gibe, flout; scorn, scout, spurn; disregard, ignore

idiom fling (*or* throw) down the gauntlet, hurl defiance at

con blench, flinch, quail, shrink

ant recoil

defy *n* ***syn*** DEFIANCE 1, cartel, challenge, dare, defi, stump

dégagé *adj* ***syn*** EASYGOING 3, breezy, casual, ||common, informal, low-pressure, relaxed, unconstrained, unfussy, unreserved

ant mannered

degeneracy *n* ***syn*** DETERIORATION 1, atrophy, decadence, declination, decline, degeneration, dégringolade, devolution, downfall, downgrade

degenerate *adj* **1** ***syn*** EFFETE 3, decadent, decayed, overripe

rel deteriorating, retrograde, retrogressive, worsening; failing, sinking

2 ***syn*** VICIOUS 2, corrupt, depraved, flagitious, infamous, miscreant, nefarious, rotten, unhealthy, villainous

rel degraded, demeaned

con ethical, moral, virtuous; honorable, just, upright

ant regenerate

degenerate *vb* ***syn*** DETERIORATE 1, decline, descend, disimprove, disintegrate, retrograde, rot, sink, worsen

rel corrupt, deprave, vitiate; backslide, lapse; return, revert

con improve, upgrade; lift, uplift

degeneration *n* ***syn*** DETERIORATION 1, atrophy, decadence, declination, decline, degeneracy, dégringolade, devolution, downfall, downgrade

rel regression, regressiveness, retrogression, retrogressiveness; depreciation; corruption, depravation, depravedness, depravity, perversion

con regeneracy, regenerateness; progress, progression

ant regeneration

degradation *n* ***syn*** DEMOTION, downgrading, reduction

ant advancement; elevation

degrade *vb* **1** to lower in station, rank, or grade <*degraded* in rank for misconduct>

syn break, bump, bust, declass, demerit, demote, disgrade, disrate, downgrade, put down, reduce

rel abase, debase, humble, humiliate, lower; disbar, rule out

con advance, further; boost, lift, raise; enhance, heighten

---

syn synonym(s) — *rel* related word(s)
idiom idiomatic equivalent(s) — *con* contrasted word(s)
ant antonym(s) — * vulgar
|| use limited; if in doubt, see a dictionary
The first word in a synonym list when printed in SMALL CAPITALS shows where there is more information about the group. For a more efficient use of this book see Explanatory Notes.

ant elevate
2 ***syn*** HUMBLE, abase, bemean, cast down, debase, demean, humiliate, lower, sink
rel belittle, decry, derogate, detract, disparage; diminish, lessen, reduce
con elevate, raise; acclaim, extol, laud, praise
ant uplift

degree *n* **1** a unitary component of a process, course, or order of classification <advanced by *degrees*>
syn grade, notch, rung, stage, step
2 relative size or character of the parts or components in a complex whole compared with other like things <the *degree* of difference between the two jobs> <his work demands a high *degree* of intelligence>
syn proportion, rate, ratio, scale
rel dimension; extent, magnitude, measure, size

dégringolade *n* ***syn*** DETERIORATION 1, atrophy, decadence, declension, declination, decline, degeneracy, degeneration, devolution, downfall

dehydrate *vb* ***syn*** DRY 1, desiccate, exsiccate, parch, sear
ant hydrate; rehydrate

deific *adj* **1** ***syn*** DIVINE 1, godly
2 ***syn*** DIVINE 2, godlike

deification *n* ***syn*** APOTHEOSIS 2, aggrandizement, dignification, exaltation, glorification

deign *vb* ***syn*** STOOP 1, condescend

deject *vb* ***syn*** DISCOURAGE 1, chill, demoralize, dishearten, disparage, dispirit
ant exhilarate; cheer

dejected *adj* ***syn*** DOWNCAST, blue, crestfallen, depressed, disconsolate, dispirited, down, downhearted, low, woebegone
idiom down in the dumps (*or* mouth), in the dumps
ant animated

dejection *n* ***syn*** SADNESS, blues, depression, (the) dismals, dumps, gloom, heavyheartedness, melancholy, mournfulness, unhappiness
rel despair, desperation
ant exhilaration

‖**dekko** *vb* ***syn*** SEE 2, look, watch

delay *vb* **1** to cause to be late or behind in movement or progress <was *delayed* by traffic>
syn bog (down), decelerate, detain, embog, hang up, mire, retard, set back, slacken, slow (up *or* down)
rel block, hinder, impede, obstruct; defer, hold over, hold up, intermit, postpone, put off, stay, suspend; arrest, check, interrupt
idiom hang fire
con accelerate, hasten, hurry, precipitate, quicken, speed; advance, forward, further, promote
ant expedite
2 to move or act slowly so that progress or work is retarded <their landlord kept *delaying* in making repairs>
syn dally, dawdle, dilly, dillydally, drag, lag, linger, loiter, mull, poke, procrastinate, put off, tarry, trail
rel hang back, idle, wait; drone; falter, hesitate, vacillate, waver
idiom take one's own sweet (*or* good) time
ant hasten, hurry
3 ***syn*** DEFER, hold off, hold over, hold up, postpone, prorogue, put off, shelve, stay, suspend

delectable *adj* ***syn*** DELIGHTFUL, adorable, ambrosial, darling, delicious, heavenly, luscious, lush, scrumptious, yummy
rel choice, dainty, delicate, exquisite, rare; palatable, sapid, savory, tasty, toothsome
con loathsome, offensive, repulsive, revolting
ant distasteful

delectate *vb* ***syn*** PLEASE 2, arride, delight, gladden, gratify, happify, pleasure

delectation *n* **1** ***syn*** PLEASURE 2, delight, enjoyment, fruition, joy, joyance
rel gratification, gratifying, regalement, regaling; enjoyment, relish
ant distaste
2 ***syn*** ENJOYMENT 1, diversion, pleasure, relish

‖**deleerit** *adj* ***syn*** INTOXICATED 1, ‖boozy, ‖canned, disguised, drunk, inebriated, ‖lushed, muddled, pixilated, ‖plastered

delegate *n* a person standing in the place of another or others <was a *delegate* to the convention>
syn catchpole, deputy, representant, representative; *compare* AGENT 2
rel agent, factor, proxy; alternate, replacement, stand-in, substitute, surrogate; mouthpiece, spokesman; emissary, envoy

delegate *vb* to appoint as one's representative <*delegated* her to watch the children>
syn commission, depute, deputize
rel ascribe, assign, charge; appoint, designate, name; choose, pick, select

delete *vb* ***syn*** ERASE, annul, black (out), blot out, cancel, efface, expunge, obliterate, wipe (out), x (out)
rel eliminate, exclude, rule out; omit

deleterious *adj* ***syn*** HARMFUL, damaging, detrimental, hurtful, injurious, mischievous, nocent, nocuous, prejudicial, prejudicious
rel destroying, destructive; ruining, ruinous
con advantageous, profitable; healthful, healthy, salubrious, wholesome
ant salutary

deliberate *adj* **1** arrived at after due thought <a *deliberate* judgment>
syn advised, aforethought, considered, designed, premeditated, prepense, studied, studious, thought-out
rel planned, projected, schemed; calculated; careful, meticulous, scrupulous; foresighted, forethoughtful, provident, prudent
con chance, chancy, desultory, haphazard, happy-go-lucky, hit-or-miss, random; aimless, designless, purposeless; hasty, hurried; abrupt, impetuous, sudden; automatic, instinctive, spontaneous
ant casual

---

syn synonym(s) *rel* related word(s)
idiom idiomatic equivalent(s) *con* contrasted word(s)
ant antonym(s) * vulgar
‖ use limited; if in doubt, see a dictionary
The first word in a synonym list when printed in SMALL CAPITALS shows where there is more information about the group. For a more efficient use of this book see Explanatory Notes.

2 ***syn*** VOLUNTARY, intentional, unforced, unprescribed, willful, willing, witting
rel intended, meant, meditated, purposed; determined, purposeful; aware, cognizant, conscious
con careless, heedless, inadvertent, thoughtless; unintended, unpurposed
ant impulsive
3 ***syn*** SLOW 2, dilatory, laggard, leisurely, unhasty, unhurried
rel calculating, cautious, chary, circumspect, wary; careful, heedful; collected, composed, cool, imperturbable
con hasty, headlong, impetuous, sudden
ant abrupt, precipitate

deliberate *vb* **1** ***syn*** PONDER 2, ‖chaw, meditate, mull (over), muse, revolve, roll, ruminate, turn over
2 ***syn*** THINK 5, cerebrate, cogitate, reason, reflect, speculate
rel excogitate, study, weigh; argue, debate, discuss, talk over

deliberately *adv* ***syn*** INTENTIONALLY, ‖apurpose, designedly, on purpose, prepensely, purposedly, purposely, purposively

deliberation *n* **1** ***syn*** ATTENTION 1, application, concentration, consideration, debate, heed, study
2 ***syn*** THOUGHT 1, brainwork, cerebration, cogitation, reflection, speculation
3 ***syn*** CONFERENCE 1, confabulation, discussion, rap, ventilation

delicacy *n* something special and delicious to eat <fresh fruit in the winter was once an uncommon *delicacy*>
syn bonne bouche, dainty, goody, kickshaw, morsel, tidbit (*or* titbit), treat
rel banquet, feast, regale; cosseting, indulgence, luxury
idiom choice bit, dish fit for a king

delicate *adj* **1** ***syn*** CHOICE, dainty, elegant, exquisite, rare, recherché, select, superior
rel delectable, delicious, delightful; balmy, gentle, lenient, mild, soft; aerial, airy, ethereal
con coarse, crude, vulgar
ant gross
2 ***syn*** FINE 1, finespun, hairline, hairsplitting, nice, refined, subtle
3 ***syn*** NICE 1, dainty, fastidious, finical, finicking, finicky, fussy, particular, persnickety, squeamish
rel perceptive, sensitive
con insensitive, undiscriminating, unperceptive
4 ***syn*** FRAGILE 1, breakable, fracturable, frail, frangible, shatterable, shattery
5 lacking in strength or substance <a *delicate* constitution>
syn flimsy, slight
rel feeble, fragile, frail, weak; sickly, unhealthy; decrepit, infirm
con stalwart, stout, strong, sturdy, tenacious, tough; hale, healthy, robust, sound, well, wholesome
6 ***syn*** TACTFUL, diplomatic, politic, tactical
rel adept, expert, masterly, proficient; discreet, foresighted, prudent; careful, heedful; cautious, wary
con impolitic; imprudent, indiscreet; awkward, clumsy, gauche, inept, maladroit; unskillful
7 marked by or requiring tact <a *delicate* situation>
syn precarious, sensitive, ticklish, touchy, tricky
rel uncertain, unpredictable; hair-trigger, volatile; sticky

delicatesse *n* ***syn*** TACT, address, diplomacy, poise, savoir faire, tactfulness
ant indelicacy

delicious *adj* ***syn*** DELIGHTFUL, adorable, ambrosial, darling, delectable, heavenly, luscious, lush, scrumptious, yummy
rel appetizing, palatable, sapid, savory, toothsome; choice, dainty, delicate, exquisite, rare
con banal, flat, inane, insipid, jejune, wishy-washy

delight *vb* **1** ***syn*** EXULT, glory, jubilate, triumph
2 ***syn*** PLEASE 2, arride, delectate, gladden, gratify, happify, pleasure
rel amuse, divert, entertain; allure, attract, charm, enchant, fascinate; enrapture, entrance, transport
con aggrieve, distress, pain, trouble; afflict, try; grieve; bother, irk; bore

delight (in) *vb* **1** ***syn*** ADMIRE 1, appreciate, cherish, relish
rel enjoy, like, savor; eat up, luxuriate (in)
con abhor, abominate, hate, loathe
2 ***syn*** LOVE 1, adore, ‖eat up

delight *n* ***syn*** PLEASURE 2, delectation, enjoyment, fruition, joy, joyance
rel glee, hilarity, jollity, mirth; ecstasy, rapture, transport; contentment, satisfaction; relish
con abhorrence, detestation, hate, hatred; dislike, distaste; discontent, dissatisfaction
ant aversion; disappointment

delightful *adj* highly pleasing to the senses or to aesthetic taste <a *delightful* view>
syn adorable, ambrosial, darling, delectable, delicious, heavenly, luscious, lush, scrumptious, yummy
rel charming, enchanting, fascinating; alluring, attractive; beautiful, fair, lovely; ineffable; agreeable, gratifying, pleasant, pleasing; satisfying
con miserable, wretched; distasteful, obnoxious, repellent, repugnant; abhorrent, detestable, hateful, odious; boring, irksome, tedious; distressing, troubling
ant abominable, horrid

delimit *vb* **1** ***syn*** DEMARCATE 1, bound, delimitate, determine, limit, mark (out), measure
rel decide
2 ***syn*** LIMIT 2, bar, circumscribe, confine, delimitate, prelimit, restrict

delimitate *vb* **1** ***syn*** DEMARCATE 1, bound, delimit, determine, limit, mark (out), measure
2 ***syn*** LIMIT 2, bar, circumscribe, confine, delimit, prelimit, restrict

delineate *vb* **1** ***syn*** REPRESENT 1, depict, describe, image, interpret, limn, picture, portray, render
rel design, plan; evoke, paint
2 ***syn*** ETCH 2, define

---

delineation *n* **1** ***syn*** REPRESENTATION, depiction, description, picture, portraiture, portrayal, presentment
rel design, plan; evocation, painting; account, story, version
2 ***syn*** OUTLINE, contour, figuration, line, lineament, lineation, profile, silhouette

delinquency *n* ***syn*** FAILURE 1, default, dereliction, neglect, oversight
rel nonobservance; nonfulfillment; lapse, weakness

delinquent *adj* ***syn*** NEGLIGENT, behindhand, careless, derelict, disregardful, lax, neglectful, regardless, remiss, slack

deliquesce *vb* ***syn*** LIQUEFY, dissolve, flux, fuse, liquesce, melt, run, thaw
rel decay, decompose, disintegrate
con cake, harden, indurate, set, solidify

delirious *adj* **1** disordered in mind especially temporarily < *delirious* from the fever >
syn raving, wandering
rel deranged, disarranged, disordered, disturbed, unsettled; bewildered, confused, distracted; rambling; irrational, unreasonable; crazed, crazy, demented, insane, lunatic, mad, maniac
idiom out of one's head (*or* mind)
con rational, reasonable; sane, sensible; comatose, unconscious
2 ***syn*** FURIOUS 2, corybantic, frantic, frenetic, frenzied, mad, rabid, wild
rel overexcited, overwrought; ecstatic, rapturous, transported; delighted, enthused, thrilled
idiom all agog, beside oneself
con collected, composed, easy, relaxed; unexcited, unmoved, unstimulated

delirium *n* frenzied excitement or wild enthusiasm <in a *delirium* of patriotic feeling>
syn frenzy, furor
rel ardor, enthusiasm, fervor, passion, zeal; ecstasy, rapture, transport
con nonchalance, sangfroid; indifference, unconcern
ant apathy

deliver *vb* **1** ***syn*** RESCUE, save
con immure, imprison, incarcerate, intern, jail; capture, catch, ensnare, entrap, snare, trap; condemn, damn, doom
2 ***syn*** GIVE 3, dispense, feed, find, hand, hand over, provide, supply, transfer, turn over
rel relinquish, resign, surrender, yield
con keep, retain
3 ***syn*** BEAR 5, ‖birth, ‖born, bring forth
4 ***syn*** SAY 1, bring out, chime in, come out (with), declare, state, tell, throw out, utter
rel broach, express, vent, voice; communicate, impart
5 ***syn*** GIVE 10, administer, deal, inflict, strike
rel dispatch, send, transmit; fling, hurl, pitch, throw

syn synonym(s) ***rel*** related word(s)
idiom idiomatic equivalent(s) ***con*** contrasted word(s)
ant antonym(s) * vulgar
‖ use limited; if in doubt, see a dictionary
The first word in a synonym list when printed in SMALL CAPITALS shows where there is more information about the group. For a more efficient use of this book see Explanatory Notes.

delivery *n* ***syn*** BIRTH 1, bearing, ‖birthing, childbearing, childbirth, parturition

Delphian *adj* **1** ***syn*** PROPHETIC, apocalyptic, fatidic, mantic, oracular, prophetical, sibylline, vatic, vaticinal
2 ***syn*** CRYPTIC, dark, enigmatic, mystifying

delude *vb* ***syn*** DECEIVE, beguile, betray, bluff, double-cross, humbug, illude, juggle, mislead, take in
idiom play tricks (*or* a trick) on
con enlighten, illume, illuminate, illustrate, light, lighten; elucidate, explain

deluding *adj* ***syn*** MISLEADING, beguiling, deceiving, deceptive, delusive, delusory, fallacious, false

deluge *n* ***syn*** FLOOD 2, cataclysm, cataract, flooding, inundation, niagara, overflow, pour, spate, torrent
rel flux; overrunning

deluge *vb* **1** to flow over so as to submerge or enclose <the lowlands were completely *deluged*>
syn drown, engulf, flood, inundate, overflow, overwhelm, submerge, swamp, whelm
rel overrun; flush, gush, pour, sluice, stream
2 ***syn*** WET, douse, drench, drown, soak, sop, souse
con dehydrate, desiccate, dry, parch
3 to affect overwhelmingly as if by a deluge of water <he was *deluged* by telephone calls>
syn flood, overwhelm, swamp, whelm
rel overcome; oversupply; abound, teem

delusion *n* **1** something accepted as true that is actually false or unreal <people who suffer from *delusions* of persecution>
syn hallucination, ignis fatuus, illusion, mirage, phantasm
rel chicane, chicanery, deception, trickery; cheat, counterfeit, deceit, fake, fraud, humbug, imposture, sham; daydream, dream, fancy, fantasy, figment, vision; apparition, eidolon, ghost, phantom, shade
ant reality
2 ***syn*** FALLACY 2, casuistry, deception, deceptiveness, equivocation, sophism, sophistry, speciousness, spuriousness
ant verity

delusive *adj* ***syn*** MISLEADING, beguiling, deceiving, deceptive, deluding, delusory, fallacious, false
rel chimerical, fanciful, fantastic, imaginary, quixotic, visionary; apparent, illusory, ostensible, seeming
con authentic, bona fide, genuine, veritable; actual, real, true

delusory *adj* ***syn*** MISLEADING, beguiling, deceiving, deceptive, deluding, delusive, fallacious, false

deluxe *adj* ***syn*** LUXURIOUS 3, Capuan, luscious, lush, luxuriant, opulent, palatial, plush, sumptuous, upholstered
rel choice, dainty, delicate, elegant, exquisite, rare, recherché
con coarse, common, ordinary; inelegant

delve *vb* ‖**1** ***syn*** DIG 1, excavate, grub, shovel, spade
rel gouge (out), hollow (out), scoop (out), quarry (out); burrow, tunnel; comb, ferret out, search, seek
2 ***syn*** MINE, quarry

delve (into) *vb* ***syn*** EXPLORE, dig (into), go (into), inquire (into), investigate, look (into), probe, prospect, sift

delve *n* ***syn*** HOLE 1, cavity, hollow, pocket, vacancy, vacuity, vacuum, void

delving *n* ***syn*** INQUIRY 1, inquest, inquisition, investigation, probe, probing, quest, research

demagogue *n* a leader who makes use of popular prejudices and false claims especially for political advantage < *demagogues* who endanger the orderly processes of democratic government >
syn rabble-rouser
rel fomenter, inciter, instigator; agitator, firebrand, hothead, incendiary, inflamer; troublemaker

demand *n* **1** ***syn*** REQUIREMENT 1, need, want
2 ***syn*** NEED 3, occasion, use

demand *vb* **1** to ask for something as or as if one's right or due <the physician *demanded* payment of his bill>
syn call, challenge, claim, exact, postulate, require, requisition, solicit
rel ask, request; bid, charge, command, direct, enjoin, order; cite, summon, summons; coerce, compel, constrain, force, oblige; necessitate
con cede, relinquish, resign, waive; allow, concede, grant; give, offer, tender
2 to have as a need or requirement <it *demands* considerable practice to master the piano>
syn ask, call (for), crave, necessitate, require, take
rel fail, lack, need, want
idiom need (*or* want), doing, stand in need of

demanding *adj* ***syn*** ONEROUS, burdensome, exacting, exigent, grievous, oppressive, taxing, tough, trying, weighty
rel rigid, rigorous, severe, stern, strict, stringent; crying, imperative, importunate, instant, pressing, urgent
ant undemanding

demarcate *vb* **1** to mark the limits of < *demarcate* the boundary between two countries>
syn bound, delimit, delimitate, determine, limit, mark (out), measure
rel establish, fix, set; assign, define, prescribe; circumscribe, confine, restrict
2 ***syn*** DISTINGUISH, differentiate, discriminate, separate, set apart, set off
rel insulate, isolate, seclude, segregate, sequester

demean *vb* ***syn*** BEHAVE 1, acquit, act, bear, carry, comport, conduct, deport, go on, quit

demean *vb* ***syn*** HUMBLE, abase, bemean, cast down, debase, degrade, humiliate, lower, sink
rel belittle, decry, derogate, detract, disparage; contemn, despise, scorn
con elevate, enhance, heighten

demeanor *n* ***syn*** BEARING 1, address, air, comportment, deportment, mien, port, presence, set
rel behavior, conduct

dement *n* ***syn*** LUNATIC 1, bedlamite, loon, loony, madling, madman, maniac, non compos, nut, Tom o' Bedlam

demented *adj* ***syn*** INSANE 1, crazed, crazy, deranged, lunatic, mad, maniac, non compos mentis, unbalanced, unsound
rel delirious, frenzied, hysterical

demerit *n* ***syn*** IMPERFECTION, deficiency, fault, shortcoming, sin

demerit *vb* ***syn*** DEGRADE 1, break, bump, bust, declass, demote, disgrade, disrate, downgrade, reduce

demeritorious *adj* ***syn*** BLAMEWORTHY, amiss, blamable, blameful, censurable, culpable, guilty, reprehensible, sinful, unholy
ant meritorious

demesne *n* ***syn*** FIELD, bailiwick, champaign, domain, dominion, province, sphere, terrain, territory, walk

demigod *n* ***syn*** SUPERMAN, superhuman

demimondaine *n* ***syn*** HARLOT 1, blowen, courtesan, demimonde, demirep, fancy woman, hetaera, kept woman, paphian, whore

demimonde *n* ***syn*** HARLOT 1, blowen, courtesan, demimondaine, demirep, fancy woman, hetaera, kept woman, paphian, whore

demirep *n* ***syn*** HARLOT 1, blowen, courtesan, demimondaine, demimonde, fancy woman, hetaera, kept woman, paphian, whore

demise *vb* ***syn*** DIE 1, cash in, decease, depart, drop, expire, go, pass, pass away, succumb

demise *n* ***syn*** DEATH 1, curtains, decease, defunction, dissolution, (the) Pale Horse, passing, quietus, silence, sleep
rel annihilation, ending, expiration, extinction

demit *vb* ***syn*** ABDICATE 1, renounce, resign

demit *vb* ***syn*** LOWER 3, couch, depress, droop, let down, sink

demiurgic *adj* ***syn*** INVENTIVE, creative, deviceful, ingenious, innovational, innovative, innovatory, original, originative

||**demob** *vb* ***syn*** DISCHARGE 7, demobilize, muster out, separate
ant mobilize

demobilize *vb* ***syn*** DISCHARGE 7, demob, muster out, separate
rel break up, disband, dispel, disperse, scatter; retire, withdraw
ant mobilize

democratic *adj* of or relating to a political system in which the supreme power is held and exercised by the people <a *democratic* government>
syn popular, self-governing, self-ruling
rel representative; libertarian
con totalitarian; absolute, arbitrary, autocratic, despotic; tyrannical, tyrannous; fascistic, nazi, patriarchal
ant authoritarian; undemocratic

démodé *adj* ***syn*** OLD-FASHIONED, antique, archaic, belated, dated, old-timey, outdated, outmoded, out-of-date, passé
ant a la mode

demoded *adj* ***syn*** OLD-FASHIONED, antique, archaic, belated, dated, old-timey, outdated, outmoded, out-of-date, passé
ant a la mode

demolish *vb* ***syn*** DESTROY 1, decimate, raze, ruin, unbuild, undo, unframe, unmake, wrack, wreck
rel dilapidate; crush, smash; break, burst, crack
con build, erect, frame, raise, rear
ant construct; rebuild

---

syn synonym(s)	***rel*** related word(s)
idiom idiomatic equivalent(s)	***con*** contrasted word(s)
ant antonym(s)	* vulgar

|| use limited; if in doubt, see a dictionary
The first word in a synonym list when printed in SMALL CAPITALS shows where there is more information about the group. For a more efficient use of this book see Explanatory Notes.

2 ***syn*** TOTAL 3, wreck

demon *n* ***syn*** DEVIL 2, archfiend, fiend, Satan, succubus

demoniac *adj* ***syn*** FIENDISH, demonian, demonic, devilish, diabolic, diabolonian, satanic, serpentine, unhallowed

rel crazed, crazy, insane, maniac; fired, inspired

con celestial, heavenly

ant angelic

demonian *adj* ***syn*** FIENDISH, demoniac, demonic, devilish, diabolic, diabolonian, satanic, serpentine, unhallowed

rel crazed, crazy, insane, maniac; fired, inspired

con celestial, heavenly

ant angelic

demonic *adj* ***syn*** FIENDISH, demoniac, demonian, devilish, diabolic, diabolonian, satanic, serpentine, unhallowed

rel crazed, crazy, insane, maniac; fired, inspired

con celestial, heavenly

ant angelic

demonstrate *vb* **1** ***syn*** SHOW 2, evidence, evince, exhibit, illustrate, manifest, mark, ostend, proclaim

rel display, exhibit, expose, flaunt, parade; explain, set forth

idiom go to show

con conceal, hide, secrete; camouflage, cloak, disguise, dissemble, mask

2 ***syn*** PROVE 1, test, try

rel authenticate, validate

3 ***syn*** ESTABLISH 6, determine, make out, prove, show

demonstration *n* ***syn*** EXHIBITION 1, display, show, spectacle

demonstrative *adj* marked by display of feeling <was *demonstrative* in his welcome>

syn expansive, outgoing, unconstrained, unreserved, unrestrained

rel affectionate, loving; effusive, outpouring, profuse; candid, frank, open, outspoken, plain

con constrained, reserved, restrained, reticent, taciturn; bashful, shy; retiring, shrinking; introverted; aloof, detached, indifferent, unconcerned; chilly, cold, frigid, glacial, icy

ant undemonstrative

demoralize *vb* **1** ***syn*** DEBASE 1, bastardize, bestialize, brutalize, corrupt, debauch, deprave, pervert, vitiate, warp

rel debilitate, undermine, weaken; damp, dampen

2 ***syn*** DISCOURAGE 1, chill, deject, dishearten, disparage, dispirit

rel agitate, disturb, upset; disarrange, disorder, disorganize, unsettle; confuse, jumble, muddle, snarl; debilitate, undermine, weaken; unman, unnerve

con arrange, order, organize; energize, fortify, invigorate, strengthen

syn synonym(s) ***rel*** related word(s)
idiom idiomatic equivalent(s) ***con*** contrasted word(s)
ant antonym(s) * vulgar
|| use limited; if in doubt, see a dictionary
The first word in a synonym list when printed in SMALL CAPITALS shows where there is more information about the group. For a more efficient use of this book see Explanatory Notes.

demote *vb* ***syn*** DEGRADE 1, break, bump, bust, declass, demerit, disgrade, disrate, downgrade, reduce

rel demean, lower

ant promote

demotion *n* the action or an instance of demoting <received a *demotion* from sergeant to corporal>

syn degradation, downgrading, reduction

rel debasement, humbling, humiliation; blackballing, disbarment, exclusion, suspension

con advancement, preferment, upgrading; aggrandizement; boost, elevation, lift, raise

ant promotion

demur *vb* to object or have scruples <he *demurred* at any horseplay>

syn balk, boggle, gag, jib, scruple, shy, stick, stickle, strain, stumble

rel falter, hesitate, vacillate, waver; combat, fight, oppose, resist; expostulate, object, protest, remonstrate; deprecate, disapprove

con accept, admit, receive, take; acquiesce, agree, assent, consent, subscribe, yes; concur; defer, relent, succumb, submit, yield

ant accede

demur *n* **1** ***syn*** QUALM, compunction, conscience, scruple, squeam

rel faltering, hesitancy, hesitation; aversion, disinclination, loathness; expostulation, protest

con promptness, quickness, readiness

2 the act of objecting or taking exception <accepted without *demur*>

syn challenge, demurral, demurrer, difficulty, objection, protest, question, remonstrance, remonstration

rel reluctance, unwillingness; faltering, hesitancy, hesitation; deprecation, disapproval; protestation; difference, disagreement, dissent, variance

con acquiescence, agreement, assent, consent; concurrence; submission

demure *adj* ***syn*** SHY 1, backward, bashful, coy, diffident, modest, retiring, timid, unassertive, unassured

rel decent, decorous, nice, proper, seemly; prim; earnest, serious, solemn; close, reserved, reticent, silent

con impertinent, intrusive, meddlesome, obtrusive, officious; brash, forward, unbashful, unretiring

demurral *n* ***syn*** DEMUR 2, challenge, demurrer, difficulty, objection, protest, question, remonstrance, remonstration

demurrer *n* ***syn*** DEMUR 2, challenge, demurral, difficulty, objection, protest, question, remonstrance, remonstration

den *n* **1** ***syn*** LAIR 1, burrow, couch, lodge

2 ***syn*** HIDEOUT, hideaway, lair

3 ***syn*** SINK 1, Augean stable, cesspit, cesspool, pandemonium, Sodom, sty

denaturant *n* ***syn*** ADMIXTURE 1, adulterant, alloy

denial *n* **1** refusal to satisfy a request or desire <*denial* of his visiting privileges>

syn disallowance, refusal, rejection

rel declination, nonacceptance

con allowing, conceding, grant, letting; leave, permission, sufferance

2 refusal to admit the truth <his *denial* that he took the money>

syn contradiction, gainsaying, negation

rel controversion, disproof, rebuttal, refutal, refutation; refusal, rejection, repudiation
con acknowledgment, avowal, confession; affirmation, assertion, confirmation
ant admission
3 ***syn*** RENUNCIATION, abnegation, renouncement, self-abnegation, self-denial, self-renunciation
rel abstaining, refraining
con indulgence, self-indulgence; overdoing, overindulgence

denigrate *vb* ***syn*** MALIGN, asperse, calumniate, defame, libel, scandalize, slander, tear down, traduce, vilify

denizen *n* **1** ***syn*** INHABITANT, dweller, habitant, indweller, liver, occupant, resident, ‖residenter, resider
rel citizen, national, subject
2 ***syn*** HABITUÉ 1, frequenter, haunter

denominate *vb* ***syn*** NAME 1, baptize, call, christen, designate, dub, entitle, style, term, title

denomination *n* **1** ***syn*** NAME 1, appellation, appellative, cognomen, compellation, designation, ‖moniker, nomen, style, title
2 ***syn*** RELIGION 2, church, communion, connection, creed, cult, faith, persuasion, sect

denotative *adj* ***syn*** INDICATIVE, denotive, designative, exhibitive, indicatory, indicial, significative

denote *vb* ***syn*** MEAN 2, add up (to), connote, express, import, intend, signify, spell
rel insinuate; announce, argue, bespeak, prove

denotive *adj* ***syn*** INDICATIVE, denotative, designative, exhibitive, indicatory, indicial, significative

denounce *vb* ***syn*** CRITICIZE, blame, censure, condemn, denunciate, knock, rap, reprehend, reprobate, skin
rel accuse, arraign, charge, impeach, incriminate, indict, tax; revile, vituperate; delate, inform
idiom cry harrow (*or* haro)
con panegyrize, praise
ant eulogize

de novo *adv* ***syn*** OVER 7, afresh, again, anew, once more

dense *adj* **1** ***syn*** CLOSE 4, compact, crowded, thick, tight
rel heaped, massed, piled; crammed, crowded, jam-packed
con dispersed, dissipated, scattered; rare, thin; exiguous, meager, scant, scanty, spare
ant sparse; tenuous
2 ***syn*** STUPID 1, blockheaded, blockish, doltish, dull, dumb, fatheaded, numskulled, thick, thickheaded
rel obtuse; impassive, phlegmatic, stolid; lethargic, sluggish, torpid
ant subtle; bright

denticulate *adj* ***syn*** SERRATE, saw-edged, sawtooth, saw-toothed, serrated, serried

denudate *vb* ***syn*** STRIP 2, bankrupt, bare, denude, deprive, dismantle, disrobe, divest

denude *vb* **1** ***syn*** STRIP 1, disrobe, unclothe, undress
2 ***syn*** STRIP 2, bankrupt, bare, denudate, deprive, dismantle, disrobe, divest

denuded *adj* ***syn*** OPEN 2, bare, exposed, naked, peeled, stripped, uncovered

denunciate *vb* ***syn*** CRITICIZE, blame, censure, condemn, denounce, knock, rap, reprehend, reprobate, skin
rel delate, inform; menace, threaten
ant eulogize

deny *vb* **1** ***syn*** DISCLAIM, disacknowledge, disallow, disavow, disown, repudiate
rel abandon, desert, forsake
con adopt, embrace, espouse; recognize
ant acknowledge; admit
2 to refuse to grant <he was unwilling to *deny* the child's request>
syn disallow, keep back, refuse, withhold
idiom say no to, turn thumbs down on
con allow, concede, let, permit; afford, give
ant grant
3 to restrain (as oneself) from or forgo what is pleasant or satisfying <decided to *deny* himself a second piece of pie>
syn abstain, constrain, curb, hold back, refrain
rel eschew, forbear, forgo, sacrifice; inhibit, restrain; avoid, shun
con overdo, overindulge
ant indulge
4 to refuse to accept as true, valid, or worthy of consideration <*denying* the existence of witches>
syn contradict, contravene, cross, disaffirm, gainsay, impugn, negate, negative, traverse
rel decline, refuse, reject, repudiate; confute, controvert, disprove, rebut, refute; downface
con affirm, assert, aver; allow, grant; authenticate, corroborate, substantiate, validate, verify; avow, confess; claim, submit
ant concede; confirm

depart *vb* **1** ***syn*** GO 2, ‖blow, exit, get away, get off, leave, pull out, quit, retire, withdraw
rel set out, start, strike out, toddle
con linger, stay, tarry, wait; come; approach, near
ant arrive; abide, remain
2 ***syn*** DIE 1, conk, ‖croak, decease, demise, expire, go, pass, pass away, succumb
con exist, live, survive
3 ***syn*** SWERVE 2, deviate, digress, diverge
rel abandon, desert, forsake; reject, repudiate; cast, discard; differ, disagree, dissent, vary
4 ***syn*** DIGRESS 2, divagate, diverge, excurse, ramble, stray, wander

departed *adj* **1** ***syn*** DEAD 1, asleep, cold, deceased, defunct, exanimate, extinct, inanimate, late, lifeless
idiom called home, gone to a better land
2 ***syn*** EXTINCT 2, bygone, dead, defunct, gone, lost, vanished

departing *adj* ***syn*** PARTING, farewell, good-bye, valedictory

departure *n* **1** the act of going, coming out, or leaving a place <the hasty *departure* of the refugees>
syn egress, egression, exit, exiting, exodus, offgoing, setting-out, withdrawal

---

syn synonym(s) | *rel* related word(s)
idiom idiomatic equivalent(s) | *con* contrasted word(s)
ant antonym(s) | * vulgar
‖ use limited; if in doubt, see a dictionary
The first word in a synonym list when printed in SMALL CAPITALS shows where there is more information about the group. For a more efficient use of this book see Explanatory Notes.

rel going, leaving, quitting, retreat; decampment, flight; farewell, leave-taking
con coming, entering, ingress
ant arrival
2 ***syn*** DEVIATION 1, aberration, deflection, divergence, diversion, turning
rel rambling, straying, wandering

depend *vb* ***syn*** HANG 1, dangle, sling, suspend

depend (on *or* upon) *vb* **1** to rest or to be contingent upon something uncertain, variable, or indeterminable <our trip *depends* upon the weather>
syn hang (on *or* upon), hinge (on *or* upon), ‖pend, stand (on *or* upon), turn (on *or* upon)
rel base, bottom, found, ground, rest, stay
idiom hang in the balance
2 ***syn*** RELY (on *or* upon), bank (on *or* upon), build (on), calculate (on *or* upon), count (on), ‖lot (on *or* upon), reckon (on), trust (in *or* to)
rel incline, lean

dependable *adj* **1** ***syn*** RELIABLE 1, secure, tried, tried and true, trustworthy, trusty
rel assured, confident, sure; responsible; constant, faithful, loyal, staunch, steadfast, steady
idiom as good as one's word, to be counted on
con capricious, fickle, inconstant, mercurial, unstable; dishonest, lying, mendacious, untruthful
ant independable, undependable
2 ***syn*** TRUE 9, authoritative, trustable, trustworthy
3 ***syn*** CERTAIN 3, accurate, authentic, reliable

dependence *n* ***syn*** TRUST 1, confidence, faith, hope, reliance, stock

dependent *adj* **1** determined or conditioned by another <a conclusion that is *dependent* on a premise>
syn conditional, contingent, relative, reliant
rel exposed, liable, open, subject, susceptible; iffy, provisional, provisory; uncertain; circumscribed, limited, restricted
con categorical, ultimate; boundless, eternal, illimitable, uncircumscribed; basal, basic, fundamental, primary, underived
ant absolute; infinite; original
2 ***syn*** SUBORDINATE, collateral, secondary, sub, subject, tributary, under
rel counting, depending, reckoning, relying, trusting; accessory, ancillary, appurtenant; abased, debased, humbled
con principal; paramount, predominant, preponderant, preponderating, sovereign
ant independent

depict *vb* ***syn*** REPRESENT 1, delineate, describe, image, interpret, limn, picture, portray, render
rel narrate, recite, recount, rehearse, relate, report, state; outline, sketch

---

syn synonym(s)	*rel* related word(s)
idiom idiomatic equivalent(s)	*con* contrasted word(s)
ant antonym(s)	* vulgar

‖ use limited; if in doubt, see a dictionary
The first word in a synonym list when printed in SMALL CAPITALS shows where there is more information about the group. For a more efficient use of this book see Explanatory Notes.

depiction *n* ***syn*** REPRESENTATION, delineation, description, picture, portraiture, portrayal, presentment

deplete *vb* to bring to a low estate by depriving of something essential <an epidemic which *depletes* an army of manpower>
syn bankrupt, drain, draw, draw down, exhaust, impoverish, use up
rel cripple, debilitate, disable, enfeeble, sap, undermine, weaken; decrease, diminish, lessen, reduce; bleed, draw off, dry up, empty, milk; consume, expend, finish, spend, wash up
idiom dig into
con augment, enlarge, increase; bolster, fortify, strengthen; rebuild, repair, restore, revive
ant renew, replace

depleted *adj* ***syn*** EFFETE 2, all in, bleary, drained, exhausted, far-gone, spent, used up, washed-out, worn-out
rel sapped, weakened
con augmented, enlarged, increased

deplorable *adj* of a kind to cause great distress <a *deplorable* loss of life>
syn afflictive, calamitous, dire, distressing, dolorous, grievous, heartbreaking, heartrending, lamentable, mournful, regrettable, unfortunate, woeful
rel awful, dreadful, terrible; horrifying, intolerable, overwhelming, sickening, unbearable; miserable, wretched; disastrous
idiom as bad as bad can be, as bad as can be
con beneficial, helpful, salutary; advantageous, favorable, propitious

deplore *vb* **1** to manifest grief or sorrow for something <*deplore* the death of a close friend>
syn bemoan, bewail, grieve, lament, moan, weep
rel deprecate, disapprove; mourn, sorrow; cry, keen, wail
con boast, brag, crow, vaunt; rejoice
2 ***syn*** REGRET, repent, rue

depone *vb* ***syn*** TESTIFY 2, depose, ‖mount, swear

deport *vb* **1** ***syn*** BEHAVE 1, acquit, act, bear, carry, comport, conduct, demean, go on, quit
2 ***syn*** BANISH, displace, exile, expatriate, expel, expulse, ‖lag, oust, relegate, transport

deportation *n* ***syn*** EXILE 1, banishment, displacement, expulsion, ostracism, relegation

deportment *n* **1** ***syn*** BEHAVIOR, comportment, conduct, tenue
2 ***syn*** BEARING 1, address, air, comportment, demeanor, mien, port, presence, set

depose *vb* **1** to remove from a throne or other high position <trying to *depose* the king in favor of his brother> <*deposed* industrial leaders>
syn dethrone, discrown, disenthrone, displace, disthrone, uncrown, unmake
rel overthrow, subvert, upset; chuck, dismiss, eject, oust, throw out
con inaugurate, induct, install, instate, invest; crown, enthrone, throne
2 ***syn*** ASSERT 1, affirm, aver, avouch, avow, constate, declare, predicate, profess, protest
3 ***syn*** TESTIFY 2, depone, ‖mount, swear

deposit *vb* ***syn*** BANK
rel put by, store, stow

deposit *n syn* SEDIMENT, dreg(s), grounds, lees, precipitate, precipitation, settlings

depository *n syn* DEPOT 2, arsenal, magazine, repository, store, storehouse

depot *n* **1** *syn* ARMORY, arsenal, dump, magazine
2 a place where something is deposited or stored <a gasoline *depot*>
syn arsenal, depository, magazine, repository, store, storehouse
rel storeroom, warehouse
3 *syn* RAILROAD STATION, station, station house
rel terminal, terminus

deprave *vb syn* DEBASE 1, bastardize, bestialize, brutalize, corrupt, debauch, demoralize, pervert, vitiate, warp
con elevate, ennoble, exalt, raise, uplift

depraved *adj* **1** *syn* DEBASED, corrupted, debauched, perverted, vitiate, vitiated
rel degenerate, infamous, vicious, villainous; degraded; twisted, warped
con scrupulous, upright
2 *syn* VICIOUS 2, corrupt, degenerate, flagitious, miscreant, nefarious, perverse, putrid, rotten, unhealthy

depravity *n syn* VICE 1, corruption, immorality, wickedness

deprecate *vb syn* DISAPPROVE 1, discommend, discountenance, disesteem, disfavor, frown, object
rel bemoan, bewail, deplore, lament; derogate, detract
ant endorse

depreciate *vb* **1** to reduce the value of <*depreciate* the dollar>
syn cheapen, decry, devalorize, devaluate, devalue, downgrade, lower, mark down, soften, underprize, underrate, undervalue, write down, write off
rel depress; abate, decrease, diminish, dwindle, lessen, reduce; erode
con augment, increase; bloat, blow up, expand, inflate; amplify, magnify
ant appreciate
2 *syn* DECRY 2, abuse, belittle, derogate, detract (from), diminish, discount, disparage, dispraise, minimize
rel underestimate, underrate, undervalue; discountenance, disfavor, disesteem
con cherish, prize, treasure, value; comprehend, understand
ant appreciate

depreciation *n syn* DETRACTION, backbiting, backstabbing, belittlement, calumny, defamation, disparagement, scandal, slander, tale

depreciative *adj syn* DEROGATORY, depreciatory, detracting, disadvantageous, disparaging, dyslogistic, pejorative, slighting, uncomplimentary
rel underestimating, underrating, undervaluing
ant appreciative

depreciatory *adj syn* DEROGATORY, depreciative, detracting, disadvantageous, disparaging, dyslogistic, pejorative, slighting, uncomplimentary
rel underestimating, underrating, undervaluing
ant appreciative

depredate *vb syn* RAVAGE, desecrate, desolate, despoil, devastate, devour, pillage, sack, spoliate, waste

depredator *n syn* MARAUDER, despoiler, forager, freebooter, looter, pillager, plunderer, raider, spoiler, spoliator

depress *vb* **1** *syn* LOWER 3, couch, demit, droop, let down, sink
2 to lower in spirit or mood <the thought of all his debts *depressed* him>
syn oppress, press, sadden, weigh down
rel ail, distress, trouble; afflict, torment, try; contrist, deject, discourage, dishearten, dispirit; bother, disturb, perturb, upset
con delight, gladden, gratify, please, rejoice; excite, inspire, stimulate; brighten, cheer up, encourage; buoy, elevate
ant elate, exhilarate; cheer

depressant *adj syn* GLOOMY 3, black, bleak, cheerless, depressing, depressive, dismal, dispiriting, dreary, oppressive

depressed *adj* **1** *syn* DOWNCAST, bad, blue, dejected, disconsolate, dispirited, down, low, spiritless, woebegone
rel lugubrious, melancholy
ant exhilarated; animated
2 *syn* UNDERPRIVILEGED, deprived, disadvantaged

depressing *adj* **1** *syn* GLOOMY 3, black, bleak, depressive, disheartening, dismal, dreary, funereal, oppressive, somber
con cheering, elevating, uplifting; exciting, inspiring
ant exhilarating
2 *syn* SAD 2, joyless, melancholic, melancholy, mournful, saddening, triste

depression *n* **1** *syn* SADNESS, blues, dejection, (the) dismals, dumps, gloom, heavyheartedness, melancholy, mournfulness, unhappiness
rel boredom, doldrums, ennui, tedium
con glee, hilarity, mirth
ant buoyancy; elation
2 a low spot <a *depression* in the land>
syn basin, concavity, dip, hollow, sag, sink, sinkage, sinkhole; *compare* NOTCH 1
rel cavity, hole, pocket, vacuity, vacuum, void; crater, pit; scoop
3 a period of lowered economic activity and extensive unemployment <indicators that warn of a coming *depression*>
syn recession, slump, stagnation
rel crash, decline, dislocation, drop; sag; paralysis; ‖stagflation
con expansion; booming, development, growth; advancement, progress
ant boom

depressive *adj syn* GLOOMY 3, black, bleak, depressing, disheartening, dismal, dreary, funereal, oppressive, somber

deprivation *n syn* PRIVATION 2, deprivement, dispossession, divestiture, loss

---

syn synonym(s) — *rel* related word(s)
idiom idiomatic equivalent(s) — *con* contrasted word(s)
ant antonym(s) — * vulgar
‖ use limited; if in doubt, see a dictionary
The first word in a synonym list when printed in SMALL CAPITALS shows where there is more information about the group. For a more efficient use of this book see Explanatory Notes.

deprive *vb* **1** ***syn*** STRIP 2, bankrupt, bare, denudate, denude, dismantle, disrobe, divest
2 to prevent one from possessing <to *deprive* a person of his civil rights>
syn bereave, disinherit, dispossess, divest, lose, oust, rob; *compare* STRIP 2
rel dock; bare, denude, dismantle, strip
con furnish, give, supply; clothe, endow, equip, fit (out), invest, outfit
ant provide

deprived *adj* ***syn*** UNDERPRIVILEGED, depressed, disadvantaged

deprivement *n* ***syn*** PRIVATION 2, deprivation, dispossession, divestiture, loss

depth *n* **1** the perpendicular extent or measurement downward from a surface <measured the *depth* of the river>
syn deepness, drop
rel profoundness, profundity; lowness; sounding; draft
con shallowness; altitude, elevation
2 the quality of being profound (as in insight) or full (as of knowledge) <her answer showed she had great *depth* in that subject>
syn abyss, deepness, profoundness, profundity
rel sense, wisdom, wiseness; brain, intellect, intelligence; keenness, sharpness
con shallowness, superficiality, unprofoundness; sciolism, smatter, smattering

depthless *adj* ***syn*** SUPERFICIAL 2, cursory, shallow, sketchy, uncritical

depurate *vb* ***syn*** PURIFY 1, clarify, clean, cleanse

depute *vb* ***syn*** DELEGATE, commission, deputize

deputize *vb* ***syn*** DELEGATE, commission, depute

deputy *n* **1** ***syn*** AGENT 2, assignee, attorney, factor, proxy
rel substitute, surrogate; replacement
2 ***syn*** DELEGATE, catchpole, representant, representative

derange *vb* **1** ***syn*** DISORDER 1, disarrange, disarray, discompose, disorganize, disturb, mess (up), rummage, unsettle, upset
rel perturb; discommode, incommode, inconvenience
con compose, settle
ant arrange; adjust
2 ***syn*** UPSET 5, disorder, sicken, turn, unhinge, unsettle
3 ***syn*** MADDEN 1, craze, distract, frenzy, unbalance, unhinge

deranged *adj* ***syn*** INSANE 1, cracked, crazed, crazy, demented, lunatic, mad, maniac, unbalanced, unsound
rel disarranged, disordered, disturbed

derangement *n* ***syn*** INSANITY 1, aberration, alienation, distraction, insaneness, lunacy, madness, psychopathy, unbalance

---

syn synonym(s) ***rel*** related word(s)
idiom idiomatic equivalent(s) ***con*** contrasted word(s)
ant antonym(s) * vulgar
‖ use limited; if in doubt, see a dictionary
The first word in a synonym list when printed in SMALL CAPITALS shows where there is more information about the group. For a more efficient use of this book see Explanatory Notes.

rel disarrangement, disorder; confusion; disturbance; unsoundness

derelict *adj* **1** given up especially by the owner or occupant <a *derelict* old home>
syn abandoned, deserted, desolate, forsaken, lorn, solitary, uncouth
rel dilapidated, dingy, faded, run-down, seedy, shabby, threadbare
con cherished, prized, treasured; attended, kept up, maintained
2 ***syn*** NEGLIGENT, behindhand, careless, delinquent, disregardful, lax, neglectful, regardless, remiss, slack
rel irresponsible, undependable, unreliable, untrustworthy
con dependable, reliable, responsible, trustworthy; careful, heedful, thoughtful
ant faithful

derelict *n* **1** ***syn*** OUTCAST, castaway, Ishmael, Ishmaelite, leper, offscouring, pariah, untouchable
2 ***syn*** VAGABOND, ‖bindle stiff, bum, drifter, floater, hobo, street arab, tramp, vag, vagrant

dereliction *n* ***syn*** FAILURE 1, default, delinquency, neglect, oversight
rel abuse, misuse, outrage
ant faithfulness

deride *vb* ***syn*** RIDICULE, lout, mock, quiz, rally, razz, scout, taunt, twit
rel banter, chaff, jolly, kid, rag, rib

de rigueur *adj* ***syn*** DECOROUS 1, au fait, becoming, comme il faut, correct, decent, done, nice, proper, right

derision *n* ***syn*** LAUGHINGSTOCK, butt, jest, jestee, joke, mock, mockery, pilgarlic, sport

derivable *adj* ***syn*** DEDUCTIVE, a priori, deducible, dogmatic, reasoned

derivate *adj* ***syn*** SECONDARY 2, derivational, derivative, derived

derivation *n* ***syn*** SOURCE, fountain, inception, origin, provenance, provenience, root, well, wellspring, whence

derivational *adj* ***syn*** SECONDARY 2, derivate, derivative, derived

derivative *adj* ***syn*** SECONDARY 2, derivate, derivational, derived
ant underivative

derivative *n* ***syn*** OUTGROWTH 2, by-product, descendant, offshoot, spin-off

derive *vb* **1** to reach (as a conclusion) as an end point of reasoning and observation <evidence from which he *derived* a startling new set of axioms>
syn educe, evolve, excogitate
rel conclude, deduce, gather, infer, judge; arrive (at), elicit, extract, reach; develop, elaborate, formulate, put (together), work out
2 ***syn*** INFER, collect, conclude, deduce, deduct, draw, gather, judge, make, make out
3 ***syn*** TAKE 14, draw

derive (from) *vb* ***syn*** SPRING 1, arise, emanate, flow, head, issue, originate, proceed, rise, stem

derived *adj* ***syn*** SECONDARY 2, derivate, derivational, derivative

dernier cri *n* ***syn*** FASHION 3, chic, craze, cry, fad, furore, mode, rage, style, vogue

dernier ressort *n* ***syn*** RESOURCE 3, expediency, expedient, makeshift, recourse, refuge, resort, shift, stopgap, substitute

derogate *vb* ***syn*** DECRY 2, belittle, depreciate, detract (from), diminish, disparage, dispraise, minimize, opprobriate, write off
rel decrease, lessen, reduce; discredit, disgrace
con enhance, heighten, intensify

derogatory *adj* designed or tending to belittle <*derogatory* comments about the actor's performance>
syn depreciative, depreciatory, detracting, disadvantageous, disparaging, dyslogistic, pejorative, slighting, uncomplimentary
rel belittling, decrying, minimizing; aspersing, calumnious, defamatory, maligning, vilifying; degrading, demeaning, humiliating; despiteful, malevolent, malicious, spiteful; contumelious, disdainful, scornful
con admiring, esteeming; acclaiming, laudatory, praising; appreciative
ant complimentary

derout *vb* ***syn*** ROUT 1, stampede

derriere *n* ***syn*** BUTTOCKS, backside, beam, behind, bottom, fanny, posterior, rear, rear end, seat

descant *n* **1** ***syn*** MELODY, air, diapason, lay, measure, melisma, melodia, strain, tune, warble
2 ***syn*** SONG 2, aria, ditty, hymn, lay, lied

descant *vb* ***syn*** DISCOURSE 1, dilate (on *or* upon), discuss, dissert, dissertate, expatiate, sermonize

descend *vb* **1** ***syn*** FALL 1, drop, lower
ant rise
2 ***syn*** STOOP 2, sink
3 ***syn*** DETERIORATE 1, decline, degenerate, disimprove, disintegrate, retrograde, rot, sink, worsen

descendant *n* **1 descendants** *pl* ***syn*** OFFSPRING, ‖begats, brood, children, issue, posterity, progeniture, progeny, scions, seed
ant ascendants, ancestors
2 ***syn*** OUTGROWTH 2, by-product, derivative, offshoot, spin-off

descent *n* **1** the act or process of passing from a higher to a lower level or state <a parachute *descent*> <his slow *descent* to the gutter>
syn drop, fall
rel plummeting, plunging, sinking
con rise, upswing, upturn; advance, headway, progress, progression; betterment, improvement
ant ascent
2 ***syn*** COMEDOWN, discomfiture, down
3 ***syn*** ANCESTRY, blood, extraction, lineage, origin, pedigree
4 an inclination downward <the steep *descent* of the mountain>
syn decline, declivity, dip, drop, fall
rel downgrade, grade, gradient, incline, slope; drop, drop-off
con acclivity, upgrade, uphill
ant ascent, rise

describe *vb* **1** ***syn*** RELATE 1, narrate, recite, recount, rehearse, report, state
rel communicate, impart; transmit; construe, elucidate, explain, explicate, expound; exemplify, illustrate; characterize, distinguish
2 ***syn*** REPRESENT 1, delineate, depict, image, interpret, limn, picture, portray, render

description *n* **1** ***syn*** REPRESENTATION, delineation, depiction, picture, portraiture, portrayal, presentment
2 a descriptive statement <a fascinating *description* of his adventures>
syn narration, recital, recountal, recounting
rel anecdote, narrative, story, tale, yarn; account, chronicle, version; report, statement
3 ***syn*** TYPE, character, feather, ilk, kidney, kind, nature, sort, stripe, variety

descry *vb* **1** ***syn*** SEE 1, behold, discern, distinguish, espy, mark, note, observe, perceive, view
2 ***syn*** FIND 1, catch, detect, encounter, espy, hit (on *or* upon), meet (with), spot, turn up
rel appreciate, comprehend, understand; realize

desecrate *vb* ***syn*** RAVAGE, depredate, desolate, despoil, devastate, devour, pillage, sack, spoliate, waste

desecrated *adj* ***syn*** IMPURE 3, common, defiled, polluted, profaned, unclean

desecration *n* ***syn*** PROFANATION, blasphemy, sacrilege, violation
ant consecration

desensitize *vb* ***syn*** DEADEN 1, benumb, blunt, dull, mull, numb
ant sensitize

desert *n* ***syn*** WASTE 1, badland, barren, wasteland, wild, wilderness, wild land, wildness

desert *n* *usu* **deserts** *pl* ***syn*** DUE 1, comeuppance, deserving, lumps, merit, right(s)
rel chastening, chastisement, discipline, disciplining, punishment
idiom just deserts

desert *vb* **1** ***syn*** ABANDON 1, chuck, forsake, quit, renounce, throw over
rel depart, go, leave
con adhere, cohere
ant cleave (to), stick (to)
2 ***syn*** DEFECT, apostatize, rat, renounce, repudiate, tergiversate, tergiverse, turn
rel abscond, decamp, escape, flee, fly
idiom go over the hill
con abide, remain, stay

deserted *adj* ***syn*** DERELICT 1, abandoned, desolate, forsaken, lorn, solitary, uncouth
rel empty, vacant; uninhabited, unoccupied; bare, barren

desertion *n* ***syn*** DEFECTION, apostasy, falseness, recreancy, tergiversation
rel perfidiousness, perfidy, treacherousness, treachery

deserve *vb* ***syn*** EARN 2, merit, rate
rel gain, get, win; demand
idiom have it coming

deserved *adj* ***syn*** JUST 3, appropriate, condign, due, merited, requisite, rhadamanthine, right, rightful, suitable
ant undeserved

---

syn synonym(s) — *rel* related word(s)
idiom idiomatic equivalent(s) — *con* contrasted word(s)
ant antonym(s) — * vulgar
‖ use limited; if in doubt, see a dictionary
The first word in a synonym list when printed in SMALL CAPITALS shows where there is more information about the group. For a more efficient use of this book see Explanatory Notes.

deserving *n* ***syn*** DUE 1, comeuppance, desert(s), lumps, merit, right(s)

deserving *adj* ***syn*** WORTHY 1, admirable, commendable, estimable, laudable, meritable, meritorious, praisable, praiseworthy, thankworthy
ant undeserving

desexualize *vb* ***syn*** STERILIZE, alter, castrate, change, fix, geld, mutilate, neuter, unsex

desiccate *vb* **1** ***syn*** DRY 1, dehydrate, exsiccate, parch, sear
2 to drain or be drained of emotional or intellectual vitality <this book is *desiccated* by undue concentration on statistics>
syn devitalize, dry up
rel deplete, drain, exhaust; divest; decay, fade, shrivel, wither, wizen
con brighten, enliven

desiderate *vb* ***syn*** DESIRE 1, ||choose, covet, crave, want, wish

desight *n* ***syn*** EYESORE, fright, mess, monstrosity, sight

design *vb* **1** ***syn*** INTEND 2, aim, contemplate, mean, ||mind, plan, propose, purpose
2 ***syn*** PLAN 2, arrange, blueprint, cast, chart, devise, ||dope out, project
rel delineate, diagram; create, invent; construct, fashion, form, frame, produce; contrive
con accomplish, achieve, effect, execute, fulfill, perform
3 to work out the arrangement of the parts of < *design* an urban center>
syn arrange, lay out, map (out), plan, set out; *compare* PLAN 2
rel delineate, diagram, draft, outline, sketch

design *n* **1** ***syn*** PLAN 1, blueprint, game plan, project, scheme, strategy
rel delineation, diagram, draft, outline, sketch, tracing; creation, invention
con accomplishment, achievement, execution, fulfillment, performance
2 ***syn*** INTENTION, animus, intendment, intent, meaning, plan, purpose
rel conation, volition, will; deliberation, reflection, thinking, thought; intrigue, machination, plot
con accident, chance, fortuity, hap; impulse
3 ***syn*** FIGURE 3, device, motif, motive, pattern
4 ***syn*** MAKEUP 1, architecture, composition, constitution, construction, formation

designate *vb* **1** ***syn*** NAME 1, baptize, call, christen, denominate, dub, entitle, style, term, title
2 to declare a person one's choice < *designated* him to fill the position>
syn appoint, finger, make, name, nominate, tap
rel choose, elect, opt, pick, select, single; assign, delegate, depute; dictate
con disapprove, disfavor, object (to), oppose; disallow, reject, turn down
3 to set aside (as funds) for a specific use < *designated* the income to be used for charity>
syn allocate, earmark
rel specify; appropriate, reserve; stipulate; allot, apportion, mete (out)

designation *n* ***syn*** NAME 1, appellation, appellative, cognomen, compellation, denomination, ||monicker, nomen, style, title
rel identification, recognition; classification, pigeonhole, pigeonholing

designative *adj* ***syn*** INDICATIVE, denotative, denotive, exhibitive, indicatory, indicial, significative

designed *adj* ***syn*** DELIBERATE 1, advised, aforethought, considered, premeditated, prepense, studied, studious, thought-out
rel decided, determined, resolved
con casual, chance, contingent, fluky, fortuitous, incidental; impulsive, spontaneous; natural, normal, regular, typical
ant accidental

designedly *adv* ***syn*** INTENTIONALLY, ||apurpose, deliberately, on purpose, prepensely, purposedly, purposely, purposively

designless *adj* ***syn*** RANDOM, aimless, desultory, haphazard, hit-or-miss, indiscriminate, purposeless, spot, unconsidered, unplanned

desire *n* **1** a longing for something that promises enjoyment or satisfaction <he had a strong *desire* for fame and fortune>
syn appetite, appetition, craving, itch, lust, passion, urge
rel hankering, hunger, hungering, longing, pining, thirst, thirsting, yearning; desideratum, desiderium; avarice, cupidity, greed, rapacity; concupiscence, eros
con abhorrence, repellency, repugnance, repulsion; aversion, disfavor, dislike
ant distaste
2 ***syn*** LUST 2, aphrodisia, concupiscence, eroticism, itch, lickerishness, lustfulness, passion, prurience, pruriency

desire *vb* **1** to have a longing for something <men who *desire* success>
syn ||choose, covet, crave, desiderate, want, wish
rel hanker, hunger, long, pine, thirst, yearn; enjoy, fancy, like; aim, aspire, pant
idiom set one's eyes (*or* heart) upon
con abhor, abominate, detest, hate, loath; decline, refuse, reject, repudiate, spurn
2 ***syn*** ASK 2, bespeak, request, solicit

desired *adj* ***syn*** TRUE 7, appropriate, fitting, proper

desirous *adj* ***syn*** COVETOUS, acquisitive, grabby, grasping, greedy, itchy, prehensile

desist *vb* ***syn*** STOP 3, cease, ||deval, discontinue, give over, halt, knock off, leave off, quit, surcease
rel abstain, forbear; abandon, relinquish, resign, yield
idiom have done with
con continue; persevere
ant persist

desistance *n* ***syn*** END 2, cease, cessation, close, conclusion, ending, finish, period, stop, termination

---

syn synonym(s) — *rel* related word(s)
idiom idiomatic equivalent(s) — *con* contrasted word(s)
ant antonym(s) — * vulgar
|| use limited; if in doubt, see a dictionary
The first word in a synonym list when printed in SMALL CAPITALS shows where there is more information about the group. For a more efficient use of this book see Explanatory Notes.

desk *n* a table, frame, or case with a sloping or horizontal surface especially for writing <sat meditating at her *desk*>
syn escritoire, secretaire, secretary, writing desk
rel lectern, reading desk

desolate *adj* **1** ***syn*** DERELICT 1, abandoned, deserted, forsaken, lorn, solitary, uncouth
rel empty, vacant; uninhabited, unoccupied
2 ***syn*** INCONSOLABLE, disconsolate, unconsolable
3 ***syn*** GLOOMY 3, acheronian, black, bleak, cheerless, dismal, drear, funereal, joyless, somber
rel bare, barren; destitute, poor, poverty-stricken; dark, murky

desolate *vb* ***syn*** RAVAGE, depredate, desecrate, despoil, devastate, devour, pillage, sack, spoliate, waste

despair *vb* to lose all hope or confidence < *despaired* of winning>
syn despond, give up
rel abandon, drop, relinquish, renounce, resign, surrender, yield
idiom lose heart (*or* courage *or* faith *or* hope)
con await, count (on), depend (on), hope, look (for); trust (in *or* to)
ant expect

despairing *adj* ***syn*** DESPONDENT, desperate, desponding, forlorn, hopeless
rel atrabilious, melancholic, melancholy; cynical, misanthropic, pessimistic; depressed, oppressed, weighed down
con optimistic, roseate, rose-colored; assured, confident, sanguine, sure
ant hopeful

desperado *n* ***syn*** OUTLAW, badman, ||bandido, bandit
rel convict, criminal, lawbreaker

desperate *adj* **1** ***syn*** DESPONDENT, despairing, desponding, forlorn, hopeless
rel foolhardy, rash, reckless, venturesome; headlong, precipitate; baffled, balked, circumvented, foiled, frustrated, outwitted, thwarted
con collected, composed, cool, nonchalant; assured, confident, sanguine, sure
2 ***syn*** ACUTE 6, climacteric, critical, crucial, dire
3 ***syn*** INTENSE 1, concentrated, exquisite, fierce, furious, terrible, vehement, vicious, violent
4 ***syn*** OUTRAGEOUS 2, atrocious, crying, heinous, monstrous, scandalous, shocking

despicable *adj* **1** ***syn*** CONTEMPTIBLE, beggarly, cheap, despisable, mean, pitiable, scummy, scurvy, shabby, sorry
rel disgraceful, disreputable, ignominious, infamous, loathsome
con applaudable, commendable
ant laudable, praiseworthy
2 ***syn*** BASE 3, abject, ignoble, low, mean, scurvy, sordid, ugly, vile, wretched

despisable *adj* ***syn*** CONTEMPTIBLE, beggarly, cheap, despicable, pitiable, pitiful, mean, scurvy, shabby, sorry

despisal *n* ***syn*** DESPITE 1, contempt, despisement, disdain, disparagement, scorn

despise *vb* to regard as beneath one's notice and unworthy of consideration or interest <he had always *despised* the weak>
syn abhor, contemn, disdain, look down, scorn, scout
rel abominate, detest, execrate, hate, loathe; reject, repudiate, spurn; avoid, eschew, renounce, shun; disregard, ignore, overlook, slight, snub
idiom have no use for, look down one's nose at
con apprize, cherish, prize, treasure, value; admire, regard, respect
ant appreciate, esteem

despisement *n* ***syn*** DESPITE 1, contempt, despisal, disdain, disparagement, scorn

despite *n* **1** the feeling or attitude of despising <felt *despite* toward the lowly>
syn contempt, despisal, despisement, disdain, disparagement, scorn
rel disdainfulness, insolence, superciliousness; abhorrence, abomination, detestation, hate, hatred, loathing; rejection, repudiation, spurning; aversion, disfavor, dislike, distaste; cold shoulder, rebuff, slight, snub; disgust, loathing
con admiration, esteem, honor, regard, respect; attraction, liking
2 ***syn*** MALICE, grudge, ill will, malevolence, maliciousness, malignancy, malignity, spite, spitefulness, spleen
rel contempt, disdain, scorn; abhorrence, abomination, detestation, hate, hatred, loathing
con admiration, esteem, respect; awe, fear, reverence
ant appreciation
3 ***syn*** DEFIANCE 2, contempt, contumacy, recalcitrance, stubbornness
rel harm, hurt, injury
4 ***syn*** AFFRONT, contumely, indignity, insult, slap
rel cut, discourtesy, incivility; rebuff, slight, snub

despite *prep* ***syn*** AGAINST 4, in spite of, notwithstanding, regardless of

despiteful *adj* ***syn*** MALICIOUS, bitchy, catty, evil, hateful, malevolent, rancorous, spiteful, vicious, wicked

despitefulness *n* ***syn*** MALICE, despite, grudge, malevolence, maliciousness, malignancy, malignity, spite, spitefulness, spleen

despoil *vb* ***syn*** RAVAGE, depredate, desecrate, desolate, devastate, devour, pillage, sack, spoliate, waste

despoiler *n* **1** ***syn*** MARAUDER, depredator, forager, freebooter, looter, pillager, plunderer, sacker, spoiler, spoliator
2 ***syn*** VANDAL, defacer, destroyer, ruinator, ruiner, wrecker

despond *vb* **1** ***syn*** DESPAIR, give up
rel droop, sag; languish
idiom reach the depths
con expect, hope, look
2 ***syn*** MOPE 1, brood

despondent *adj* having lost all or nearly all hope < *despondent* about his health>
syn despairing, desperate, desponding, forlorn, hopeless

---

syn synonym(s) *rel* related word(s)
idiom idiomatic equivalent(s) *con* contrasted word(s)
ant antonym(s) * vulgar
|| use limited; if in doubt, see a dictionary
The first word in a synonym list when printed in SMALL CAPITALS shows where there is more information about the group. For a more efficient use of this book see Explanatory Notes.

rel grieving, mourning, sorrowful; dejected, depressed, melancholy, sad; disconsolate, dispirited, downcast, woebegone; discouraged, disheartened
con cheerful, glad, happy, joyful, joyous; buoyant, elastic, resilient, volatile; hopeful, optimistic
ant lighthearted

desponding *adj* ***syn*** DESPONDENT, despairing, desperate, forlorn, hopeless

despot *n* ***syn*** TYRANT, dictator, duce, oppressor, strong man

despotic *adj* ***syn*** ABSOLUTE 4, arbitrary, autarchic, autocratic, monocratic, tyrannical, tyrannous

despotism *n* ***syn*** TYRANNY, autocracy, dictatorship, totalitarianism

despotize *vb* ***syn*** TYRANNIZE

desquamate *vb* ***syn*** SCALE 2, exfoliate, flake (off), peel

destine *vb* ***syn*** PREDESTINE 1, determine, doom (to), fate, foreordain, predetermine, preform, preordain

destiny *n* ***syn*** FATE, circumstance, doom, kismet, lot, moira, portion, weird
rel design, goal, intent, intention, objective

destitute *adj* **1** ***syn*** DEVOID, empty, innocent, void
rel deficient; bankrupt, bankrupted, depleted, drained, exhausted; divested, stripped
con complete, full, replete
2 ***syn*** POOR 1, dirt poor, impecunious, impoverished, indigent, necessitous, needy, penurious, poverty-stricken, stone-broke
rel depleted, drained, exhausted
idiom on one's uppers, on the rocks
con comfortable, prosperous, well-fixed, well-off, well-to-do
ant opulent

destituteness *n* ***syn*** POVERTY 1, destitution, impecuniousness, impoverishment, indigence, need, neediness, penury, privation, want
rel absence, dearth, lack; adversity, misfortune
con competence, sufficiency
ant opulence

destitution *n* ***syn*** POVERTY 1, destituteness, impecuniousness, impoverishment, indigence, need, neediness, penury, privation, want
rel absence, dearth, lack, privation, want; adversity, misfortune
con competence, sufficiency
ant opulence

destroy *vb* **1** to bring to ruin <the army *destroyed* the enemy village> <his health was finally *destroyed* by drink>
syn annihilate, atomize, decapitate, decimate, demolish, destruct, discreate, dismantle, dissolve, dynamite, pull down, pulverize, quench, raze, rub out, ruin, ‖ruinate, shatter, shoot, smash, tear down, unbuild, undo, unframe, unmake, wrack, wreck; *compare* TOTAL 3
rel abolish, extinguish; devastate, pillage, ravage, sack, waste; eradicate, exterminate, extirpate, wipe; mangle, mutilate; rubble; doom
idiom blow to bits, bring to an end, dispose of, tear to shreds
con establish, found, institute, organize; fabricate, fashion, forge, form, make, manufacture, shape; conserve, preserve, protect, save
2 ***syn*** KILL 1, carry off, cut off, dispatch, down, finish, lay low, put away, slay, take off

destroyer *n* **1** ***syn*** VANDAL, defacer, despoiler, ruinator, ruiner, wrecker
2 ***syn*** DOWNFALL 2, bane, destruction, ruin, ruination, undoing

destruct *vb* ***syn*** DESTROY 1, decimate, demolish, raze, ruin, unbuild, undo, unmake, wrack, wreck

destruction *n* **1** ***syn*** DOWNFALL 2, bane, destroyer, ruin, ruination, undoing
2 ***syn*** RUIN 3, confusion, devastation, havoc, loss, ruination

destructive *adj* having the capability, property, or effect of destroying <a *destructive* windstorm> <his brother was a *destructive* influence in his life>
syn annihilative, ruinous, shattering, wrackful, wreckful
rel calamitous, disastrous, deadly, fatal, lethal, mortal; consumptive; internecine; baneful, deleterious, detrimental
con creative, formative; harmless, innocuous, inoffensive; helpful, improving
ant constructive

desuetude *n* **1** ***syn*** END 2, cease, cessation, close, closing, closure, conclusion, discontinuance, discontinuation, ending
2 ***syn*** DISUSE, disusage

desultory *adj* **1** ***syn*** FITFUL, catchy, on-again-off-again, spasmodic, sporadic, spotty
rel erratic; shifting, vagrant, wavering
con constant, invariable, unchanging, unfailing
ant steady
2 ***syn*** RANDOM, aimless, casual, designless, haphazard, hit-or-miss, indiscriminate, purposeless, unconsidered, unplanned
rel fitful, spasmodic; disorderly, unmethodical, unsystematic; capricious, fickle, inconstant, mercurial
con orderly, systematic
ant assiduous; methodical

detach *vb* to remove one thing from another with which it is in union or association <*detach* sheets from a loose-leaf book>
syn abstract, disassociate, disconnect, disengage, dissociate, uncouple, unfix
rel cut off, divorce, part, separate, sever, sunder; disjoin, disunite; disassemble, dismantle, dismember, dismount; disaffiliate
idiom take apart
con fasten, fix; bind, tie; combine, conjoin, unite
ant affix, attach

detached *adj* **1** ***syn*** ALONE 1, apart, isolate, isolated, removed, unaccompanied
rel separate, unconnected
con abutting, adjacent; connected, joined, linked
ant adjoining; attached

---

syn synonym(s) | *rel* related word(s)
idiom idiomatic equivalent(s) | *con* contrasted word(s)
ant antonym(s) | * vulgar
‖ use limited; if in doubt, see a dictionary
The first word in a synonym list when printed in SMALL CAPITALS shows where there is more information about the group. For a more efficient use of this book see Explanatory Notes.

2 ***syn*** INDIFFERENT 2, aloof, casual, disinterested, incurious, remote, unconcerned, uncurious, uninterested, withdrawn
con anxious, concerned, solicitous; self-centered, selfish
ant interested
3 ***syn*** NEUTRAL, abstract, colorless, disinterested, dispassionate, impersonal, poker-faced, unpassioned
rel distant, remote, removed

detachment *n* ***syn*** SEPARATION 1, dissolution, disunion, division, divorce, divorcement, partition, rupture, split-up

detail *n* ***syn*** POINT 1, article, element, item, particular, thing
con anatomy, framework, skeleton, structure; bulk, mass; design, plan

detail *vb* ***syn*** SPECIFY 3, particularize, specificate, specificize, stipulate

detailed *adj* ***syn*** CIRCUMSTANTIAL, blow-by-blow, clocklike, full, itemized, minute, particular, particularized, thorough
rel abundant, copious; exhausting, exhaustive, thoroughgoing

detailedly *adv* ***syn*** THOROUGHLY 2, completely, exhaustively, in and out, inside out, up and down

detain *vb* **1** ***syn*** ARREST 2, apprehend, ‖bust, nab, pick up, pinch, pull in, run in
rel buttonhole, hold, restrain
2 ***syn*** KEEP 5, hold, hold back, keep back, keep out, reserve, retain, withhold
3 ***syn*** DELAY 1, bog (down), decelerate, embog, hang up, mire, retard, set back, slacken, slow (up *or* down)
rel check, curb, inhibit, restrain

detect *vb* ***syn*** FIND 1, catch, descry, encounter, espy, hit (on *or* upon), meet (with), spot, turn up

detectable *adj* ***syn*** PERCEPTIBLE, appreciable, discernible, observable, palpable, sensible, tangible

detection *n* ***syn*** DISCOVERY, espial, find, strike, unearthing

detective *n* one employed or engaged in detecting lawbreakers or in getting information that is not readily or publicly accessible <used *detectives* to locate the missing witness>
syn dick, ‖eye, gumshoe, hawkshaw, investigator, plainclothesman, Sherlock, Sherlock Holmes, sleuth, ‖tec; *compare* INFORMER, PRIVATE DETECTIVE
rel G-man; roper; shoofly

detention *n* ***syn*** ARREST, apprehension, arrestation, arrestment, ‖nab, pickup, pinch
rel imprisonment, incarceration, internment

deter *vb* **1** ***syn*** DISSUADE, disadvise, discourage, divert
rel prevent; block, hinder, impede, obstruct; debar, shut out; frighten, scare; inhibit, restrain
con abet, incite, instigate; excite, provoke, stimulate; actuate, motivate
2 ***syn*** PREVENT 2, avert, forestall, forfend, obviate, preclude, rule out, stave off, ward

deteriorate *vb* **1** to pass from a higher to a lower type or condition <the road quickly *deteriorated* into a bumpy path>
syn decline, degenerate, descend, disimprove, disintegrate, retrograde, rot, sink, worsen
rel crumble, decay, decompose; impair, mar, spoil; debilitate, undermine, weaken; depreciate, lessen
idiom be the worse for wear, go downhill, go to pot (*or* the dogs)
con better, improve; advance, progress; enhance, heighten
ant ameliorate
2 ***syn*** FAIL 1, decline, ‖dwine, fade, flag, languish, weaken

deterioration *n* **1** a falling from a higher to a lower level (as of quality or character) <the *deterioration* of business during the depression>
syn atrophy, decadence, declension, declination, decline, degeneracy, degeneration, dégringolade, devaluation, devolution, downfall, downgrade, ruin
rel impairment, spoiling; crumbling, decay, decaying, decomposition, disintegration, dissolution, dry rot, rotting; debasement, degradation; depreciation, lessening; dislocation, disruption
con betterment, help; enhancement, heightening, improvement
ant amelioration
2 ***syn*** FAILURE 4, declination, decline, ebbing, waning
con convalescence, recovering, recuperation
ant improvement

determinable *adj* ***syn*** TERMINABLE, endable

determinant *n* ***syn*** CAUSE 1, antecedent, occasion, reason
rel factor; authority, influence, weight

determinate *adj* **1** ***syn*** INFLEXIBLE 3, constant, fixed, immovable, immutable, inalterable, invariable, unalterable, unchangeable, unmodifiable
2 ***syn*** DEFINITE 1, circumscribed, fixed, limited, narrow, precise, restricted
ant indeterminate

determinate *vb* ***syn*** IDENTIFY, diagnose, diagnosticate, distinguish, finger, pinpoint, place, recognize, spot

determination *n* **1** ***syn*** DECISION 1, conclusion, resolution, settlement
2 ***syn*** DECISION 2, decidedness, firmness, purposefulness, purposiveness, resoluteness, resolution, resolve
ant indetermination

determine *vb* **1** ***syn*** ESTABLISH 6, demonstrate, make out, prove, show
rel fix, set; settle
2 ***syn*** PREDESTINE 1, destine, doom (to), fate, foreordain, predetermine, preform, preordain
3 ***syn*** DEMARCATE 1, bound, delimit, delimitate, limit, mark (out), measure
4 ***syn*** DECIDE, conclude, figure, resolve, rule, settle
rel bias, dispose, incline, predispose; actuate, drive, impel, move; induce, persuade
5 ***syn*** CLOSE 3, complete, conclude, end, finish, halt, terminate, ultimate, wind up, wrap up
6 ***syn*** DISCOVER 3, ascertain, catch on, find out, hear, learn, see, tumble, unearth

---

determined *adj* ***syn*** DECIDED 2, bent, decisive, intent, resolute, resolved, set, settled

rel earnest, purposeful, serious; unfaltering, unhesitating, unwavering

con unresolved, unsettled; hesitating, hesitant, wavering

ant undetermined

detest *vb* ***syn*** HATE, abhor, abominate, execrate, loathe

rel reject, repudiate, spurn

con love; appreciate, treasure, value

ant adore

detestable *adj* ***syn*** HATEFUL 2, abhorrent, abominable, hateable, horrid, odious

rel sorry; atrocious, heinous, monstrous, outrageous

ant adorable

detestation *n* **1** ***syn*** ABOMINATION 2, abhorrence, aversion, hate, hatred, horror, loathing, repugnance, repulsion, revulsion

rel antipathy, disgust

con affection, attachment, love; forbearance, indulgence, tolerance

ant adoration

2 ***syn*** ABOMINATION 1, anathema, bête noire, black beast, bugbear, hate

ant adoration

dethrone *vb* ***syn*** DEPOSE 1, discrown, disenthrone, displace, disthrone, uncrown, unmake

ant enthrone, throne

detonate *vb* ***syn*** EXPLODE 1, blow up, burst, go off, mushroom

detour *n* an indirect course often temporarily replacing part of a usual route <a *detour* around road construction> <took a *detour* to show him the lake>

syn roundabout, runaround

rel bypass

detour *vb* ***syn*** SKIRT 2, bypass, circumnavigate, circumvent

detract (from) *vb* ***syn*** DECRY 2, belittle, depreciate, derogate, diminish, discount, disparage, dispraise, minimize, write off

rel libel, slander; decrease, lessen, reduce

con enhance, heighten, intensify

detracting *adj* **1** ***syn*** DEROGATORY, depreciative, depreciatory, disadvantageous, disparaging, dyslogistic, pejorative, slighting, uncomplimentary

2 ***syn*** LIBELOUS, backbiting, calumnious, defamatory, detractive, maligning, scandalous, slanderous, traducing, vilifying

detraction *n* the expression of damaging or malicious opinions <his persistent *detraction* of his rival's motives was wholly unfair>

syn backbiting, backstabbing, belittlement, calumny, character assassination, defamation, depreciation, disparagement, scandal, slander, sycophancy, tale

rel damage, harm, hurt, injury; injustice, wrong; aspersion, calumniation, libel, libeling, maligning, slandering, traducing, vilification

con enhancement, heightening, laudation, praise; approbation, approval

ant commendation

detractive *adj* ***syn*** LIBELOUS, backbiting, calumnious, defamatory, detracting, maligning, scandalous, slanderous, traducing, vilifying

detractory *adj* ***syn*** LIBELOUS, backbiting, calumnious, defamatory, detracting, maligning, scandalous, slanderous, traducing, vilifying

detriment *n* ***syn*** DISADVANTAGE, disability, drawback, handicap

rel damage, harm, hurt, injury, mischief; impairment, marring, spoiling

ant advantage, benefit

detrimental *adj* ***syn*** HARMFUL, bad, damaging, deleterious, evil, hurtful, ill, injurious, mischievous, nocuous

con aiding, helpful, helping; harmless

ant beneficial

2 ***syn*** ADVERSE 2, negative, unfavorable

de trop *adj* ***syn*** SUPERFLUOUS, excess, extra, recrementitious, spare, superfluent, supernumerary, surplus

detruncate *vb* ***syn*** TOP 1, crop, pollard, truncate

deuced *adj* ***syn*** UTTER, absolute, blasted, confounded, consummate, damned, dashed, infernal, outright, unmitigated

‖**deval** *vb* ***syn*** STOP 3, cease, desist, discontinue, give over, halt, knock off, leave off, quit, surcease

devalorize *vb* ***syn*** DEPRECIATE 1, decry, devaluate, devalue, lower, mark down, underrate, undervalue, write down, write off

devaluate *vb* ***syn*** DEPRECIATE 1, decry, devalorize, devalue, lower, mark down, underrate, undervalue, write down, write off

devaluation *n* ***syn*** DETERIORATION 1, atrophy, decadence, declension, declination, decline, degeneracy, degeneration, devolution, downfall

devalue *vb* ***syn*** DEPRECIATE 1, decry, devalorize, devaluate, lower, mark down, underrate, undervalue, write down, write off

devast *vb* ***syn*** RAVAGE, depredate, desecrate, desolate, despoil, devastate, devour, pillage, sack, spoliate

devastate *vb* ***syn*** RAVAGE, depredate, desecrate, desolate, despoil, devast, devour, pillage, sack, spoliate

devastation *n* ***syn*** RUIN 3, confusion, destruction, havoc, loss, ruination

‖**devel** *vb* ***syn*** STRIKE 2, ‖biff, clout, ding, hit, ‖nail, ‖slosh, smite, sock, whack

develop *vb* **1** ***syn*** EXPAND 4, amplify, elaborate, enlarge

2 ***syn*** UNFOLD 3, elaborate, evolve

rel actualize, materialize, realize

3 ***syn*** MATURE, age, grow, grow up, maturate, mellow, ‖ripe, ripen

rel dilate, expand; enroot, establish; flourish, prosper, thrive

con shrivel, wither, wizen

4 to come to have usually gradually <*develop* a taste for dry wine>

syn acquire, form

rel gain, get, obtain; achieve, attain, reach

5 ***syn*** HAPPEN 1, befall, betide, break, chance, come off, fall out, go, occur, transpire

syn synonym(s) ***rel*** related word(s)
idiom idiomatic equivalent(s) ***con*** contrasted word(s)
ant antonym(s) * vulgar
‖ use limited; if in doubt, see a dictionary
The first word in a synonym list when printed in SMALL CAPITALS shows where there is more information about the group. For a more efficient use of this book see Explanatory Notes.

development *n* progressive advance from a lower or simpler to a higher or more complex form <*development* of a seed into a plant> <*development* of an industry>
syn evolution, evolvement, flowering, growth, progress, progression, unfolding, upgrowth
rel advance, advancement, ongoing
con decadence, declension, degeneration, deterioration, devolution
ant decline

deviant *adj* **1** ***syn*** ABNORMAL 1, aberrant, anomalous, atypical, deviative, heteroclite, preternatural, unrepresentative, untypical
con normal; natural
2 ***syn*** IRREGULAR 1, abnormal, anomalous, divergent, off-key, unnatural, unregular

deviate *vb* **1** ***syn*** SWERVE 2, depart, digress, diverge
2 ***syn*** ERR, stray, wander
idiom deviate from the path of virtue

deviation *n* **1** departure from a course or procedure or from a norm or standard <no *deviation* from traditional methods was permitted>
syn aberration, deflection, departure, divergence, diversion, turning
rel alteration, change, modification, variation; breach, transgression, violation; anomaly, failing, fault; blunder, error, lapse
con accordance, agreement, conformance, conformity, correspondence
2 ***syn*** TURN 2, bend, deflection, double, shift, tack, yaw

deviative *adj* ***syn*** ABNORMAL 1, aberrant, anomalous, atypical, deviant, heteroclite, preternatural, unrepresentative, untypical

device *n* **1** ***syn*** TRICK 1, artifice, feint, gambit, gimmick, maneuver, play, ploy, stratagem, wile
2 something (as a mechanical device) that performs a function or effects a desired end <invented many handy household *devices*>
syn contraption, contrivance; *compare* GADGET 1
rel appliance, implement, instrument, tool, utensil; apparatus, machine, mechanism; expedient, makeshift, resort, resource, shift; creation, invention; dingus, doohickey, hickey, thingumbob
3 ***syn*** FIGURE 3, design, motif, motive, pattern
rel attribute, emblem, symbol, type; insignia, motto

deviceful *adj* ***syn*** INVENTIVE, creative, demiurgic, ingenious, innovational, innovative, innovatory, original, originative

devil *n* **1** *often cap* the personal supreme spirit of evil and unrighteousness in Jewish and Christian theology
syn Apollyon, Beelzebub, ||Cloot(s), ||Clootie, diablo, fiend, Lucifer, Old Gooseberry, Old Nick, Old Scratch, Satan, serpent
rel cacodemon; dybbuk
idiom Prince of Darkness
2 an extremely and malignantly wicked person <he was a *devil* who would stop at nothing to get what he wanted>
syn Archfiend, demon, fiend, Satan, Succubus; *compare* SCAMP, VILLAIN 1
rel blackguard, caitiff, knave; scoundrel, villain; beast, brute
3 ***syn*** SCAMP, enfant terrible, limb, mischief, rapscallion, rascal, rogue, scalawag, skeezicks, villain

||**devil–devil** *n* ***syn*** SPELL, charm, conjuration, incantation, rune

||**devil–dodger** *n* ***syn*** CLERGYMAN, churchman, cleric, clerical, clerk, divine, ecclesiastic, minister, parson, preacher

deviling *n* ***syn*** IMP 1, devilkin

devilish *adj* **1** ***syn*** FIENDISH, demoniac, demonian, demonic, diabolic, diabolonian, satanic, serpentine, unhallowed
rel iniquitous, nefarious, villainous; accursed, cursed, damnable, execrable; bad, evil, wicked
ant angelic
2 ***syn*** SATANIC 1, diabolic, Mephistophelian

devilkin *n* ***syn*** IMP 1, deviling

devil–may–care *adj* ***syn*** WILD 7, fast, gay, raffish, rakehell, rakish, sporty
rel rash, reckless
con careful, heedful, responsible, thoughtful

devilment *n* ***syn*** MISCHIEVOUSNESS, devilry, deviltry, diablerie, mischief, roguery, roguishness, sportiveness, waggery, waggishness

devilry *n* ***syn*** MISCHIEVOUSNESS, devilment, deviltry, diablerie, mischief, roguery, roguishness, sportiveness, waggery, waggishness

||**devil's–bones** *n pl* ***syn*** DICE, ||African dominoes, bones, ||cubes, ||ivory, ||tats

deviltry *n* ***syn*** MISCHIEVOUSNESS, devilment, devilry, diablerie, mischief, roguery, roguishness, sportiveness, waggery, waggishness

devious *adj* **1** ***syn*** OBSCURE 2, lonesome, out-of-the-way, remote, removed, retired, secret
2 ***syn*** CROOKED 1, bending, curving, twisting
rel deviating, digressing, diverting
ant straightforward
3 ***syn*** ERRATIC 1, errant, stray, wandering
4 ***syn*** ERRANT 2, aberrant, erring
rel artful, crafty, cunning, foxy, insidious, sly, tricky
5 ***syn*** UNDERHAND, duplicitous, guileful, indirect, shifty, sneaking, sneaky, underhanded
ant straightforward

devise *n* ***syn*** LEGACY 1, bequest, inheritance

devise *vb* **1** ***syn*** PLAN 2, arrange, blueprint, cast, chart, design, ||dope out, project
2 ***syn*** CONTRIVE 2, concoct, cook (up), dream up, formulate, frame, hatch (up), invent, make up, vamp (up)
rel create, discover; forge, form, shape; design
3 ***syn*** PLOT, cogitate, ||collogue, collude, connive, conspire, contrive, intrigue, machinate, scheme (out)
4 ***syn*** WILL, bequeath, leave, legate

devitalize *vb* ***syn*** DESICCATE 2, dry up
rel deprive; eviscerate, weaken
ant vitalize

---

syn synonym(s) — ***rel*** related word(s)
idiom idiomatic equivalent(s) — ***con*** contrasted word(s)
ant antonym(s) — * vulgar
|| use limited; if in doubt, see a dictionary
The first word in a synonym list when printed in SMALL CAPITALS shows where there is more information about the group. For a more efficient use of this book see Explanatory Notes.

devoid *adj* showing a want or lack <a poem *devoid* of worth>
syn destitute, empty, innocent, void
rel bare, barren; lacking, wanting; deficient
con filled, full; furnished, provided, supplied
ant replete

devoir *n* **1** *syn* OBLIGATION 2, charge, commitment, committal, duty, must, need, ought, ||right
2 *syn* TASK 1, assignment, chare, chore, duty, job, stint

devolution *n* *syn* DETERIORATION 1, atrophy, decadence, declension, declination, decline, degeneracy, degeneration, dégringolade, downfall
rel regression, regressiveness, retrogression, retrogressiveness; receding, recession, retrogradation, retrograding
con development; progress, progression
ant evolution

devote *vb* **1** to set apart for a particular and often a better or higher use or end <a woman who *devotes* her life to helping others>
syn consecrate, dedicate, hallow
rel sanctify, vow; commit, confide, consign, entrust
idiom set apart
2 *syn* GIVE 1, bestow, donate, give away, hand out, present
3 *syn* ADDRESS 3, apply, bend, buckle (down), direct, give, throw, turn
rel attempt, endeavor, strive, struggle, try; employ, use, utilize

devote (to) *vb* *syn* HABITUATE 2, addict, adjust, confirm (in), take (to)
rel attach, wrap (up)

devoted *adj* *syn* LOVING, affectionate, dear, doting, fond, lovesome
rel constant, faithful, loyal, true; thoughtful; fervid, zealous

devotee *n* **1** *syn* ADDICT, aficionado, buff, fan, habitué, hound, lover, votary
2 *syn* AMATEUR 1, admirer, fan, fancier, votary

devotion *n* **1** *syn* FIDELITY 1, allegiance, ardor, faithfulness, fealty, loyalty, piety
rel enthusiasm, fervor, passion, zeal; affection, attachment, love; consecration, dedication, devotement
2 *syn* LOVE 1, affection, attachment, fondness

devour *vb* **1** *syn* EAT 1, consume, feed (on), ingest, meal, partake (of), take
2 *syn* EAT UP 1, dispatch, polish off
idiom eat like a horse, eat one's head off
3 *syn* CONSUME 1, eat, eat up, exhaust, use up
4 *syn* RAVAGE, depredate, desecrate, desolate, despoil, devastate, pillage, sack, spoliate, waste
rel demolish, destroy; ruin, wreck; dissipate, squander
5 to exhibit avid interest in or enjoyment of <the crowd *devoured* the lurid scene>
syn ||eat up
rel delight (in), enjoy, rejoice (in), relish, revel (in); feast (on), gloat (over *or* on)
con avoid, eschew, shun

devout *adj* showing fervor in the practice of religion <a *devout* churchgoer>
syn godly, holy, pietistic, pious, prayerful, religious
rel ardent, fervent, fervid, zealous; adoring, revering, venerating, worshiping
con impious, irreligious, ungodly, unholy; irreverent; apostate, backsliding
ant undevout

dexter *adj* *syn* FAVORABLE 5, auspicious, benign, bright, fortunate, propitious, white
ant sinister

dexterity *n* **1** *syn* ADDRESS 1, adroitness, deftness, dexterousness, prowess, readiness, skill, sleight
rel adeptness, skillfulness; effortlessness, smoothness
con awkwardness, maladroitness
ant clumsiness
2 *syn* ART 1, adroitness, craft, cunning, expertise, know-how, skill

dexterous *adj* **1** ready and skilled in physical movements <a *dexterous* worker>
syn adroit, clever, deft, handy, neat-handed, nimble
rel agile; adept, expert, masterly, proficient, skilled, skillful; easy, effortless, facile, smooth
con awkward, gauche, inept, maladroit
ant clumsy
2 *syn* CLEVER 4, adroit, canny, ||coony, cunning, ingenious, ||sleighty, slim, sly

dexterousness *n* *syn* ADDRESS 1, adroitness, deftness, dexterity, prowess, readiness, skill, sleight
ant clumsiness

dextrorotatory *adj* *syn* RIGHT-HANDED, clockwise, positive
ant levorotatory

diablerie *n* **1** *syn* MISCHIEVOUSNESS, devilment, devilry, deviltry, mischief, roguery, roguishness, sportiveness, waggery, waggishness
2 *syn* EVIL 3, crime, iniquity, sin, tort, wrong, wrongdoing

diablo *n* *syn* DEVIL 1, Apollyon, Beelzebub, fiend, Lucifer, Old Gooseberry, Old Nick, Old Scratch, Satan, serpent

diabolic *adj* **1** *syn* SATANIC 1, devilish, Mephistophelian
2 *syn* FIENDISH, demoniac, demonian, demonic, devilish, diabolonian, satanic, serpentine, unhallowed
rel evil, ill, wicked
ant angelic

diabolism *n* *syn* SATANISM

diabolonian *adj* *syn* FIENDISH, demoniac, demonian, demonic, devilish, diabolic, satanic, serpentine, unhallowed

diacritic *adj* *syn* CHARACTERISTIC, diagnostic, distinctive, idiosyncratic, individual, peculiar, proper

diagnose *vb* *syn* IDENTIFY, determinate, diagnosticate, distinguish, finger, pinpoint, place, recognize, spot

diagnostic *adj* *syn* CHARACTERISTIC, diacritic, distinctive, idiosyncratic, individual, peculiar, proper

diagnosticate *vb* *syn* IDENTIFY, determinate, diagnose, distinguish, finger, pinpoint, place, recognize, spot

---

syn synonym(s)	*rel* related word(s)
idiom idiomatic equivalent(s)	*con* contrasted word(s)
ant antonym(s)	* vulgar

|| use limited; if in doubt, see a dictionary
The first word in a synonym list when printed in SMALL CAPITALS shows where there is more information about the group. For a more efficient use of this book see Explanatory Notes.

diagonal *adj* between horizontal and vertical in direction <cloth with a *diagonal* stripe>
syn bevel, beveled, bias, biased, slanted, slanting; *compare* INCLINED 3

diagonally *adv* in a line running across from corner to corner <decided to place the couch *diagonally* at the end of the room>
syn catercorner (*or* catty-corner *or* kitty-corner), cornerwise, slantingways, slantways, slantwise, ‖slaunchways
idiom on the bias
con parallelly, square, straight

‖**dial** *n* ***syn*** FACE 1, countenance, features, ‖kisser, ‖map, mug, ‖pan, phiz, ‖puss, visage

dial *vb* ***syn*** TUNE 3

dialect *n* **1** ***syn*** LANGUAGE 1, idiom, speech, tongue, vernacular
2 a form of language that is not recognized as standard <the Doric *dialect* of ancient Greece>
syn argot, cant, jargon, lingo, patois, patter, slang, vernacular; *compare* TERMINOLOGY, VERNACULAR 3
rel localism, provincialism, regionalism

dialectic *n* ***syn*** ARGUMENTATION, debate, disputation, forensic, mooting

dialogue *n* **1** ***syn*** CONVERSATION 1, chat, colloquy, confabulation, converse, parley
2 ***syn*** CONVERSATION 2, colloquy, confabulation, talk

diametric *adj* ***syn*** OPPOSITE, antipodal, antipodean, antithetical, contradictory, contrary, converse, counter, polar, reverse

diapason *n* ***syn*** MELODY, air, descant, lay, measure, melisma, melodia, strain, tune, warble

diaphanous *adj* ***syn*** FILMY, flimsy, gauzy, gossamer, sheer, tiffany, transparent

diarrhea *n* abnormally frequent intestinal evacuations with more or less fluid stools <they were taken with severe *diarrhea*>
syn ‖backdoor trots, dysentery, flux, ‖runs, scour(s), *shits, ‖squirts, *trots
idiom Montezuma's revenge, summer complaint

diatribe *n* ***syn*** TIRADE, harangue, jeremiad, philippic

‖**dibs** *n pl* **1** ***syn*** MONEY, ‖blunt, ‖brass, ‖bread, ‖cabbage, ‖chips, ‖dinero, ‖do-re-mi, dough, ‖gelt
2 ***syn*** CLAIM 1, pretense, pretension, title

dice *n pl, sing* **die** a pair or set of small cubes marked on each face with from one to six spots and used in various games and in gambling by being shaken and thrown to come to rest at random <staked everything on a cast of the *dice*>
syn ‖African dominoes, bones, ‖cubes, ‖devil's-bones, ‖ivory, ‖tats

dice *vb* ***syn*** DISCARD, cashier, cast, jettison, reject, scrap, shed, slough, throw away, throw out

dichotomize *vb* ***syn*** SEPARATE 1, break up, disjoin, disjoint, dissect, disunite, divide, part, sever, sunder

dick *n* **1** ***syn*** DETECTIVE, ‖eye, gumshoe, hawkshaw, investigator, plainclothesman, Sherlock, Sherlock Holmes, sleuth, ‖tec

dicker *vb* ***syn*** HAGGLE 2, bargain, chaffer, higgle, huckster, palter

dickey *adj* ***syn*** WEAK 2, fluctuant, insecure, rootless, shaky, unstable, unsure, vacillating, wavering, wobbly

dictate *vb* to promulgate expressly something to be followed, observed, obeyed, or accepted <the commission *dictated* the policies to be followed>
syn decree, impose, lay down, ordain, prescribe, set
rel control, direct, manage; guide, lead; govern, rule; say, tell, utter; bid, charge, command, enjoin, instruct, order

dictate *n* ***syn*** COMMAND 1, behest, bidding, charge, injunction, mandate, order, word

dictative *adj* ***syn*** DICTATORIAL, authoritarian, authoritative, doctrinaire, dogmatic, magisterial

dictator *n* ***syn*** TYRANT, despot, duce, oppressor, strong man

dictatorial *adj* imposing one's will or opinions on others <the chief was inclined to be *dictatorial* with his subordinates>
syn authoritarian, authoritative, dictative, doctrinaire, dogmatic, magisterial; *compare* TOTALITARIAN 1
rel bossy, domineering, imperative, imperious, masterful, peremptory; absolute, arbitrary, autocratic, despotic, tyrannical; arrogant, haughty, overbearing, proud; firm, stern
con amenable, biddable, docile, obedient, tractable; menial, obsequious, servile, slavish, subservient

dictatorship *n* ***syn*** TYRANNY, autocracy, despotism, totalitarianism

diction *n* ***syn*** WORDING, parlance, phrase, phraseology, phrasing, verbalism, verbiage, wordage

dictionary *n* ***syn*** TERMINOLOGY, cant, jargon, language, lexicon, palaver, vocabulary

dictum *n* ***syn*** MAXIM, aphorism, apothegm, axiom, brocard, gnome, moral, rule, truism

‖**dicty** *adj* ***syn*** SNOBBISH, high-hat, potty, snobby, snooty

didactic *adj* overburdened with instruction and the proprieties <his speech to the new freshmen was painfully *didactic*>
syn moral, moralizing, preachy, schoolmasterish, sermonic, sermonizing, teachy
rel advisory, exhortative, hortative; preceptive
ant undidactic

‖**didder** *vb* ***syn*** SHAKE 1, dither, quake, quaver, quiver, shiver, shudder, tremble, tremor, twitter

diddle *vb* **1** ***syn*** IDLE, dawdle, diddle-daddle, drone, ‖lallygag, laze, loaf, loiter, loll, lounge
2 ***syn*** CHEAT, beat, bilk, chouse, cozen, defraud, do, gyp, overreach, take

diddle–daddle *vb* ***syn*** IDLE, dawdle, drone, goldbrick, ‖lallygag, laze, loaf, loiter, loll, lounge

diddler *n* ***syn*** SWINDLER, cheat, confidence man, con man, defrauder, double-dealer, ‖grifter, gyp, sharper, trickster

---

syn synonym(s) ***rel*** related word(s)
idiom idiomatic equivalent(s) ***con*** contrasted word(s)
ant antonym(s) * vulgar
‖ use limited; if in doubt, see a dictionary
The first word in a synonym list when printed in SMALL CAPITALS shows where there is more information about the group. For a more efficient use of this book see Explanatory Notes.

dido *n* **1** *usu* **didoes** *pl* ***syn*** PRANK, antic, caper, frolic, lark, monkeyshine, shenanigan, shine(s), tomfoolery, trick
2 ***syn*** KNICKKNACK, bauble, bibelot, curio, gewgaw, gimcrack, toy, trifle, trinket, whatnot

die *vb* **1** to pass from physical life <he *died* at an advanced age>
syn cash in, ‖check out, conk, ‖cop out, ‖croak, decease, demise, depart, drop, expire, go, ‖kick in, ‖kick off, pass, pass away, pass out, peg out, perish, pip, pop off, ‖snuff (out), succumb, ‖swelt
idiom be gathered to one's fathers, bite the dust (*or* ground), breathe one's last, cash in one's checks (*or* chips), give up the ghost, ‖kick the bucket, ‖kick up one's heels, meet one's end, shuffle off this mortal coil, ‖snuff it, turn up one's toes (to the daisies)
con be, exist, subsist; flourish, thrive
ant live
2 ***syn*** PERISH 2

die (down *or* away) *vb* ***syn*** ABATE 4, ‖bate, ease off, ebb, fall, let up, moderate, slacken, subside, wane
rel recede; disappear
con ascend, mount, rise
ant come up

die *n* **1** *see* DICE
‖**2** ***syn*** TOY 2, ‖play-pretty, plaything, ‖pretty

die–away *adj* ***syn*** LANGUID, enervated, lackadaisical, languishing, languorous, limp, listless, spiritless

diehard *n* **1** an irreconcilable opponent of change <party *diehards* who would make no concessions>
syn bitter-ender, conservative, fundamentalist, old liner, praetorian, pullback, right, rightist, right wing, right-winger, standpat, standpatter, tory; *compare* REACTIONARY
rel mossback, old fogy, stick-in-the-mud; intransigent; true blue; right-center
con liberal, progressive, radical
2 ***syn*** REACTIONARY, blimp, Bourbon, reactionarist, reactionist, royalist, ultraconservative, white

die–hard *adj* ***syn*** CONSERVATIVE 1, fogyish, old-line, orthodox, reactionary, right, tory, traditionalistic

differ *vb* **1** to be unlike or distinct in nature, form, or characteristics <the houses *differ* only in a few minor details>
syn disagree, vary
rel depart, deviate, diverge
con accord, conform, correspond
ant agree
2 to be of unlike or opposite opinion <men who *differ* on religious matters>
syn disaccord, disagree, discord, dissent, divide, vary
rel clash, conflict, jar; bicker, quarrel, squabble; argue, debate, dispute; oppose, protest (against)
idiom differ in opinion, hold opposite views
con coincide, concert, concur, harmonize; accord, conform, correspond
ant agree

difference *n* **1** ***syn*** DISSIMILARITY, alterity, discrepancy, dissemblance, dissimilitude, distinction, divergence, divergency, otherness, unlikeness
rel modification, variation
con equivalence, equivalency, sameness
ant resemblance
2 ***syn*** DISCORD, conflict, contention, disaccord, dissension, dissent, dissidence, disunity, strife, variance
rel clash, conflict
3 ***syn*** VARIANCE 1, variation

difference *vb* ***syn*** KNOW 4, differentiate, discern, discrepate, discriminate, distinguish, extricate, separate, sever, severalize

different *adj* **1** unlike in kind or character <could hardly be more *different*>
syn disparate, dissimilar, distant, divergent, diverse, other, otherwise, unalike, unequal, unlike, unsimilar, various
rel particular, single; distinctive, individual, peculiar; divers, sundry
con akin, analogous, comparable, like, parallel, similar, uniform; equal, equivalent, self-same
ant alike, identical, same
2 ***syn*** DISTINCT 1, discrete, diverse, separate, several, various

differential *adj* ***syn*** DISCRIMINATORY, discriminative, prejudiced

differentiate *vb* ***syn*** KNOW 4, difference, discern, discrepate, discriminate, distinguish, extricate, separate, sever, severalize
rel comprehend, understand
con confound, mistake
ant confuse

differently *adv* ***syn*** OTHERWISE 1, diversely, ‖othergates, variously

difficile *adj* ***syn*** HARD 6, arduous, difficult, formidable, heavy, laborious, severe, strenuous, toilsome, tough

difficult *adj* ***syn*** HARD 6, arduous, difficile, effortful, labored, laborious, operose, strenuous, toilsome, uphill
rel problem, problematic
idiom easier said than done, no picnic, tough sledding
ant simple

difficultly *adv* ***syn*** HARD 8, arduously, burdensomely, hardly, laboriously, onerously, toilsomely

difficulty *n* **1** something obstructing one's course and demanding effort and endurance if one's end is to be attained <he encountered great *difficulties* on his way to success>
syn asperity, hardness, hardship, rigor, vicissitude
rel impediment, obstacle, obstruction, snag; dilemma, fix, jam, pickle, plight, predicament, quandary, scrape; emergency, exigency, pass, pinch, strait; bother, inconvenience, problem, trouble
idiom hard nut to crack, hard row to hoe, heavy sledding
2 ***syn*** DEMUR 2, challenge, demurral, demurrer, objection, protest, question, remonstrance, remonstration
3 ***syn*** QUARREL, altercation, beef, bickering, controversy, dispute, falling-out, fight, hassle, squabble

diffident *adj* ***syn*** SHY 1, bashful, coy, demure, modest, retiring, self-effacing, timid, unassertive, unassured

---

syn synonym(s) — *rel* related word(s)
idiom idiomatic equivalent(s) — *con* contrasted word(s)
ant antonym(s) — * vulgar
‖ use limited; if in doubt, see a dictionary
The first word in a synonym list when printed in SMALL CAPITALS shows where there is more information about the group. For a more efficient use of this book see Explanatory Notes.

rel blenching, flinching, shrinking; hesitant, reluctant
con assured, presumptuous, sanguine, sure; self-assured, self-confident, self-possessed, self-reliant; brazen, impudent, shameless
ant confident

difform *adj syn* LOPSIDED, asymmetric, disproportional, disproportionate, nonsymmetrical, proportionless, unequal, uneven, unproportionate, unsymmetrical

diffuse *adj syn* WORDY, long-winded, palaverous, prolix, redundant, verbose, windy
rel exuberant, lavish, profuse; casual, desultory, random; lax, loose, slack; lengthy, long
con concentrated; condensed
ant succinct

diffuse *vb* **1** *syn* SPREAD 1, circulate, disperse, disseminate, distribute, propagate, radiate, strew
rel extend; expand
con compact, consolidate; center, centralize, focus
ant concentrate
2 *syn* INTERFUSE 2, infuse, interlard, intersow, intersperse, intersprinkle

dig *vb* **1** to loosen and turn over or remove (as soil) with or as if with a spade <*dig* for potatoes> <*dug* through her drawer looking for the scarf>
syn ‖delve, excavate, grub, shovel, spade
rel quarry; enter, penetrate, pierce, probe; dig up, root, rootle, root out
2 to form by digging <*dig* a trench>
syn dig out, excavate, scoop, shovel, spade
3 *syn* THRUST 2, drive, plunge, ram, run, sink, stab, stick
‖**4** *syn* RESIDE 1, abide, bide, dwell, hang out, live
5 *syn* POKE 1, jab, jog, nudge, prod, punch
‖**6** *syn* APPREHEND 1, accept, catch, comprehend, follow, grasp, see, take, take in, understand
7 *syn* ENJOY 1, go, like, ‖mind, relish

dig (into) *vb syn* EXPLORE, delve (into), go (into), inquire (into), investigate, look (into), probe, prospect, sift

dig *n* **1** *syn* POKE 1, jab, punch, stab
2 *syn* SITE 3

digest *n syn* COMPENDIUM 1, aperçu, pandect, précis, sketch, survey, syllabus, sylloge
rel abridgment, synopsis

digest *vb* **1** *syn* BEAR 10, abide, brook, endure, go, stand, stomach, swallow, take, tolerate
2 *syn* EPITOMIZE 1, condense, inventory, nutshell, sum, summarize, summate, sum up, synopsize

digit *n syn* NUMBER, chiffer, cipher, figure, integer, numeral, whole number

dignification *n syn* APOTHEOSIS 2, aggrandizement, deification, exaltation, glorification

dignify *vb syn* EXALT 1, aggrandize, distinguish, ennoble, erect, glorify, honor, magnify, sublime, uprear
con abase, debase
ant demean

dignitary *n syn* NOTABLE 1, chief, eminence, high-muck-a-muck, leader, lion, luminary, nabob, notability, VIP

dignity *n* **1** *syn* STATUS 2, cachet, consequence, position, prestige, rank, standing, state, stature
2 *syn* DECORUM 1, decency, etiquette, propriety, seemliness
rel excellence, merit, perfection, virtue; ethicalness, ethics, morality, nobleness, nobility
con impropriety, indecency, indecorum, unseemliness
3 *syn* ELEGANCE, grace
rel augustness, grandeur, grandness, magnificence, majesty, nobleness, nobility; address, poise

dig out *vb* **1** *syn* DIG 2, excavate, scoop, shovel, spade
2 *syn* RUMMAGE 3, hunt (down *or* out *or* up), rout

digress *vb* **1** *syn* SWERVE 2, depart, deviate, diverge
2 to turn aside from the main subject of attention or course of argument <he *digressed* into too many side issues>
syn depart, divagate, diverge, excurse, ramble, stray, wander
rel drift, roam
idiom get off the subject, go off on a tangent
con advance, proceed, progress

digression *n* a departure from a subject or theme <a *digression* from the main point of the speech>
syn aside, discursion, divagation, excursion, excursus, parenthesis
rel episode, excurse, incident, underaction; deflection, deviation, divergence; departure; drifting, rambling, straying, wandering

‖**dike** (out *or* up) *vb syn* DRESS UP 1, deck (out), doll out, doll up, ‖dude up, fix up, gussy up, slick, spiff, spruce (up)

dilapidate *vb syn* RUIN 2, bankrupt, do in, shipwreck, wreck
rel crumble, decay, decompose, disintegrate; disregard, forget, ignore, neglect, overlook, slight
con mend, rebuild, repair; rejuvenate, renew, renovate, restore

dilapidated *adj syn* SHABBY 1, broken-down, dingy, down-at-heel, faded, run-down, seedy, tacky, tagrag, threadbare
rel damaged, impaired, injured, marred; crumbled, decayed

dilate *vb syn* EXPAND 3, amplify, distend, inflate, swell
rel augment, enlarge, increase; extend, lengthen, prolong, protract; broaden, widen
con compress, condense, contract, shrink; attenuate
ant circumscribe; constrict

dilate (on *or* upon) *vb syn* DISCOURSE 1, descant, discuss, dissert, dissertate, expatiate, sermonize
rel describe, narrate, recite, recount, rehearse, relate
con abbreviate, abridge, curtail, shorten

dilatory *adj syn* SLOW 2, deliberate, laggard, leisurely, unhasty, unhurried
rel lax, neglectful, negligent, remiss, slack
con assiduous, busy, industrious, sedulous; prompt, quick, ready; hasty, impetuous, precipitate
ant diligent

---

syn synonym(s) *rel* related word(s)
idiom idiomatic equivalent(s) *con* contrasted word(s)
ant antonym(s) * vulgar
‖ use limited; if in doubt, see a dictionary
The first word in a synonym list when printed in SMALL CAPITALS shows where there is more information about the group. For a more efficient use of this book see Explanatory Notes.

dilemma *n* ***syn*** PREDICAMENT, box, corner, fix, hole, jam, pickle, plight, scrape, spot
rel bewilderment, mystification, perplexity
idiom horns of a dilemma

dilettante *n* **1** ***syn*** CONNOISSEUR, aesthete, cognoscente
2 ***syn*** AMATEUR 2, abecedarian, dabbler, nonprofessional, smatterer, tyro, uninitiate

dilettante *adj* ***syn*** AMATEURISH, dabbling, dilettantish, dilettantist, jackleg, unaccomplished, unfinished, ungifted, unskilled

dilettantish *adj* ***syn*** AMATEURISH, dabbling, dilettante, dilettantist, jackleg, unaccomplished, unfinished, ungifted, unskilled

dilettantist *adj* ***syn*** AMATEURISH, dabbling, dilettante, dilettantish, jackleg, unaccomplished, unfinished, ungifted, unskilled

diligent *adj* ***syn*** ASSIDUOUS, industrious, operose, sedulous
rel persevering, persistent, persisting; unflagging
con deliberate, laggard, leisurely, slow; desultory
ant dilatory

‖**dilly** *adj* ***syn*** FOOLISH 2, absurd, ‖balmy, crazy, harebrained, insane, loony, ‖potty, silly, wacky

‖**dilly** *n* one that is remarkable or extraordinary of its kind <came up with a *dilly* of an idea to sell the product>
syn ‖corker, crackerjack, ‖daisy, dandy, ‖dinger, ‖doozer, humdinger, jim-dandy, knockout, ‖lalapalooza, ‖lulu, nifty, peach, ‖pip, pippin, ripper, ripsnorter, rouser

dilly *vb* ***syn*** DELAY 2, dally, dawdle, dillydally, lag, linger, loiter, poke, put off, tarry

dillydally *vb* ***syn*** DELAY 2, dally, dawdle, dilly, lag, linger, loiter, poke, put off, tarry

dilute *vb* to make less strong or concentrated <*dilute* acid>
syn cut, thin, weaken
rel moderate, qualify, temper; deliquesce, liquefy; alter, modify
con enrich, fortify, richen, upgrade; condense, densify, evaporate, thicken
ant concentrate

dilute *adj* of relatively low strength or concentration <*dilute* acid>
syn diluted, thin, washy, watered-down, waterish, watery, weak
rel reduced; adulterated, sophisticated; impaired, impoverished, weakened
con condensed, densified, thickened
ant concentrated

diluted *adj* ***syn*** DILUTE, thin, washy, watered-down, waterish, watery, weak
ant concentrated

---

syn synonym(s) — ***rel*** related word(s)
idiom idiomatic equivalent(s) — ***con*** contrasted word(s)
ant antonym(s) — * vulgar
‖ use limited; if in doubt, see a dictionary
The first word in a synonym list when printed in SMALL CAPITALS shows where there is more information about the group. For a more efficient use of this book see Explanatory Notes.

dim *adj* **1** ***syn*** DARK 1, caliginous, dusk, dusky, gloomy, lightless, murky, obscure, tenebrous, unilluminated
ant bright
2 ***syn*** DULL 7, blind, dead, flat, lackluster, lusterless, mat, muted
‖**3** ***syn*** DULL 9, banausic, blah, dreary, humdrum, monotone, monotonous, pedestrian, poky, stodgy
4 ***syn*** FAINT 2, blear, bleary, ill-defined, indistinct, obscure, shadowy, unclear, undetermined, vague
con manifest, plain
ant distinct

dim *vb* **1** ***syn*** OBSCURE, becloud, bedim, befog, cloud, darken, eclipse, fog, haze, obfuscate
2 ***syn*** DULL 1, fade, muddy, pale, tarnish
3 ***syn*** DULL 4, blear, blur

dime novel *n* a usually paperback melodramatic novel <read mostly *dime novels*>
syn dreadful, penny dreadful, shilling shocker, shocker, yellowback
rel bloodcurdler, chiller, ‖killer-diller; thriller; pulp

dimension *n* **1** *usu* **dimensions** *pl* ***syn*** SIZE 1, admeasurement, dimensionality, extent, magnitude, measure, proportion
2 *usu* **dimensions** *pl* ***syn*** RANGE 2, ambit, circle, compass, confine(s), extension, extensity, extent, length, reach

dimensionality *n* ***syn*** SIZE 1, admeasurement, dimension(s), extent, magnitude, measure, proportion

diminish *vb* **1** ***syn*** ABRIDGE 1, curtail, lessen, minify
2 ***syn*** DECREASE, abate, ‖bate, close, drain (away), dwindle, lessen, reduce, taper, taper off
rel ebb, subside, wane; moderate, temper; attenuate, extenuate
con aggravate, enhance, heighten, intensify
3 ***syn*** DECRY 2, abuse, belittle, depreciate, derogate, detract (from), disparage, dispraise, minimize, write off

diminutive *adj* ***syn*** TINY, lilliputian, miniature, minute, teensy, teensy-weensy, teeny, teeny-weeny, wee, weeny

‖**dimmet** *n* ***syn*** EVENING 1, ‖dimps, ‖dimpsy, dusk, ‖dusk dark, eventide, gloaming, nightfall, owl-light, twilight

dimple *vb* ***syn*** RIPPLE, cockle, fret, riffle

‖**dimps** *n* ***syn*** EVENING 1, ‖dimmet, ‖dimpsy, dusk, ‖dusk dark, eventide, gloaming, nightfall, owl-light, twilight

dim–sighted *adj* ***syn*** PURBLIND, half-blind

‖**dimpsy** *n* ***syn*** EVENING 1, ‖dimmet, ‖dimps, dusk, ‖dusk dark, eventide, gloaming, nightfall, owl-light, twilight

dimwit *n* ***syn*** DUNCE, ‖cluck, ‖dumb bunny, ‖dumb cluck, featherweight, lackwit, nitwit, pinhead, simp, wantwit

dim–witted *adj* ***syn*** RETARDED, backward, dull, feebleminded, half-witted, imbecile, moronic, simpleminded, slow, slow-witted
con alert, keen

din *n* a welter of discordant sounds <the *din* of a machine shop>
syn babel, brouhaha, ‖chirm, clamor, hubbub, hullabaloo, jangle, music, pandemonium, racket, racketry, tintamarre, tumult, uproar; *compare* COMMOTION 4
rel blatancy, boisterousness, clamorousness, stridency; bedlam; clangor, clatter, rattle; clash, percussion; ‖row; noise, sound

con calm, lull, quietude, stillness; concord, consonance, harmony; melody, musicality, tunefulness

diner *n* ***syn*** EATING HOUSE, café, coffee shop, ‖greasy spoon, ‖hashery, ‖hash house, lunch counter (*or* bar), quick-lunch, sandwich shop, snack bar (*or* counter)

‖**dinero** *n* ***syn*** MONEY, ‖blunt, ‖brass, ‖bread, ‖cabbage, ‖chips, ‖dibs, ‖do-re-mi, dough, filthy lucre

ding *vb* **1** ***syn*** STRIKE 2, ‖biff, catch, clout, ‖devel, hit, ‖nail, ‖slosh, sock, whack

2 ***syn*** SURPASS 1, ‖bang, beat, best, better, exceed, outdo, outgo, outmatch, outshine

‖**ding** *n* ***syn*** BLOW 1, bash, belt, crack, ‖douse, slam, smack, sock, whack, whop

ding–a–ling *n* ***syn*** CRACKPOT, crackbrain, crank, cuckoo, harebrain, kook, lunatic, nut, screwball

dingdong *adv* ***syn*** HARD 3, assiduously, earnestly, exhaustively, intensely, intensively, painstakingly, thoroughly, unremittingly

dinge *n* ***syn*** SADNESS, blues, dejection, depression, dumps, gloom, heavyheartedness, melancholy, mournfulness, unhappiness

‖**dinger** *n* ***syn*** ‖DILLY, ‖corker, crackerjack, ‖daisy, dandy, humdinger, jim-dandy, knockout, ‖lalapalooza, ‖lulu

dingus *n* ***syn*** DOODAD, dofunny, doohickey, gadget, gizmo, ‖hootenanny, jigger, thingum, thingumajig, thingumbob

dingy *adj* ***syn*** SHABBY 1, broken-down, dilapidated, down-at-heel, faded, run-down, seedy, tacky, threadbare, tired

rel grimed, smirched, soiled, sullied, tarnished; dull; dusky, gloomy, murky

con bright, brilliant, luminous, shining; clean, cleanly

dining table *n* ***syn*** TABLE 1, board, dinner table, mahogany, ‖table-board

dinky *adj* ***syn*** MINOR 2, insignificant, lesser, minor-league, secondary, small, small-fry, small-time

‖**dinky–di** *adj* ***syn*** FAITHFUL 1, allegiant, ardent, constant, liege, loyal, resolute, staunch, steadfast, true

dinner *n* a usually elaborate meal served to guests or a group often to mark an occasion or honor an individual <the annual club *dinner*>

syn banquet, feast, regale, spread

rel ‖blowout, festival, fete, junket; breakfast, collation, luncheon

dinner table *n* ***syn*** TABLE 1, board, dining table, mahogany, ‖table-board

dinosauric *adj* ***syn*** HUGE, behemothic, colossal, cyclopean, elephantine, enormous, gargantuan, leviathan, mammoth, mastodonic

‖**dinsome** *adj* ***syn*** VOCIFEROUS, blatant, boisterous, clamorous, loudmouthed, multivocal, obstreperous, openmouthed, strident, vociferant

dint *n* ***syn*** POWER 4, energy, force, might, potency, puissance, sinew, strength, vigor, virtue

dip *vb* **1** to plunge or thrust momentarily or partially under the surface of a liquid <*dip* a dress in cleansing fluid>

syn douse, duck, dunk, immerse, souse, submerge, submerse

rel pitch, plunge

2 to lift a portion of by reaching below the surface with something shaped to hold liquid <*dip* drinking water from a spring>

syn bail, lade, ladle, scoop

rel dish, spoon; bucket (up *or* out), draw

‖**3** ***syn*** PAWN, hock, impignorate, mortgage, pledge, ‖pop, ‖spout

4 ***syn*** DUCK 2, stoop

5 ***syn*** PLUMMET, drop, fall, nose-dive, plunge, skid, tumble

6 ***syn*** SET 12, decline, go down, sink

7 ***syn*** SWERVE 1, sheer, skew, slue, train off, veer

dip (into) *vb* ***syn*** BROWSE, flip (through), glance (at *or* over), leaf (through), riff (through), riffle (through), run (through *or* over), scan, skim (through), thumb (through)

dip *n* **1** ***syn*** DESCENT 4, decline, declivity, drop, fall

2 ***syn*** DECLINE 3, downslide, downswing, downtrend, downturn, drop, falloff, sag, slip, slump

3 ***syn*** DEPRESSION 2, basin, concavity, hollow, sag, sink, sinkage, sinkhole

‖**4** ***syn*** PICKPOCKET, ‖cannon, cutpurse, ‖diver, purse cutter, ‖wire

diplomacy *n* ***syn*** TACT, address, delicatesse, poise, savoir faire, tactfulness

diplomatic *adj* ***syn*** TACTFUL, delicate, politic, tactical

rel bland, smooth; courteous, polite; astute, shrewd; artful, crafty, guileful, wily

ant undiplomatic

‖**dippy** *adj* ***syn*** FOOLISH 2, absurd, ‖balmy, crazy, fantastic, harebrained, insane, preposterous, silly, wacky

‖**dipsy–doodle** *n* ***syn*** DECEPTION 1, cheat, chicane, chicanery, double-dealing, fourberie, fraud, hanky-panky, highbinding, trickery

dire *adj* **1** ***syn*** FEARFUL 3, appalling, awful, direful, dreadful, frightful, horrible, shocking, terrible, terrific

2 ***syn*** DEPLORABLE, afflictive, calamitous, distressing, grievous, heartbreaking, lamentable, regrettable, unfortunate, woeful

rel depressing, oppressing

3 ***syn*** OMINOUS, apocalyptic, baleful, baneful, direful, fateful, ill-boding, inauspicious, threatening, unpropitious

4 ***syn*** PRESSING, burning, clamant, clamorous, crying, exigent, imperative, importunate, instant, urgent

5 ***syn*** ACUTE 6, climacteric, critical, crucial, desperate

direct *vb* **1** ***syn*** ADDRESS 6, superscribe

2 to turn something toward its appointed or intended mark or goal <*directed* his eyes to the door>

syn address, aim, cast, head, incline, lay, level, point, present, set, train, turn, zero (in)

rel beam; divert; fasten, focus

3 ***syn*** ADDRESS 3, apply, bend, buckle (down), devote, give, throw, turn

rel fix, set, settle

con deflect, divert; deviate, digress, diverge, swerve

---

syn synonym(s) — ***rel*** related word(s)
idiom idiomatic equivalent(s) — ***con*** contrasted word(s)
ant antonym(s) — * vulgar
‖ use limited; if in doubt, see a dictionary
The first word in a synonym list when printed in SMALL CAPITALS shows where there is more information about the group. For a more efficient use of this book see Explanatory Notes.

4 ***syn*** GUIDE, conduct, escort, lead, pilot, route, see, shepherd, show, steer
ant misdirect
5 ***syn*** GOVERN 3, control, dominate, handle, manage
6 ***syn*** CONDUCT 3, carry on, keep, manage, operate, ordain, run
7 ***syn*** COMMAND, bid, charge, enjoin, instruct, order, tell, warn
rel assign, define, prescribe

direct *adj* **1** being or passing in a straight line of descent from parent to offspring < *direct* ancestors >
syn lineal
2 admitting free or continuous passage <a *direct* route to the beach>
syn straight, straightforward, through, uninterrupted
rel linear; continuous, unbroken, undeviating, unswerving
con circuitous, roundabout
ant indirect
3 ***syn*** FRANK, candid, man-to-man, open, plain, straightforward, unconcealed, undisguised, undissembled, unreserved
ant devious
4 marked by absence of an intervening agency, instrumentality, or influence <he had no *direct* knowledge of the crime>
syn firsthand, immediate, primary
rel contiguous, next, proximate
ant indirect

direct *adv* **1** ***syn*** DIRECTLY 1, dead, due, right, straight, straightly, undeviatingly
2 ***syn*** VERBATIM, directly, literally, literatim, word for word

direction *n* **1** ***syn*** VIEWPOINT 2, angle, outlook, side, slant, standpoint

directive *n* **1** ***syn*** EDICT 1, decree, ruling, ukase
2 ***syn*** MEMORANDUM 2, memo, notice
3 ***syn*** MESSAGE 1, communication, word

directly *adv* **1** without deviation of course <the turnpike runs *directly* east and west>
syn dead, direct, due, right, straight, straightly, undeviatingly
idiom as the crow flies, in a beeline
con circuitously, deviously, round about; discursively, ramblingly
ant indirectly
2 ***syn*** VERBATIM, direct, literally, literatim, word for word
3 ***syn*** IMMEDIATELY 1, contiguously
4 ***syn*** AWAY 3, at once, first off, forthwith, immediately, instanter, instantly, right away, straight off, straightway
5 ***syn*** PRESENTLY 1, anon, by and by, shortly, soon

---

syn synonym(s) — *rel* related word(s)
idiom idiomatic equivalent(s) — *con* contrasted word(s)
ant antonym(s) — * vulgar
|| use limited; if in doubt, see a dictionary
The first word in a synonym list when printed in SMALL CAPITALS shows where there is more information about the group. For a more efficient use of this book see Explanatory Notes.

direful *adj* **1** ***syn*** FEARFUL 3, appalling, awful, dire, dreadful, frightful, horrible, shocking, terrible, terrific
2 ***syn*** OMINOUS, apocalyptic, baleful, baneful, dire, fateful, ill-boding, inauspicious, unlucky, unpropitious

dirt *n* **1** ***syn*** EARTH 2, dry land, ground, land, soil, terra firma
2 ***syn*** DECEPTION 1, chicane, chicanery, dishonesty, double-dealing, fourberie, fraud, hanky-panky, highbinding, sharp practice

dirt poor *adj* ***syn*** POOR 1, beggared, broke, destitute, flat, impoverished, indigent, penurious, poverty-stricken, stone-broke

dirty *adj* **1** soiled or begrimed with dirt <wash those *dirty* hands>
syn black, dungy, filthy, foul, grubby, impure, mucky, murky, nasty, soily, sordid, squalid, unclean, uncleanly
rel contaminated, defiled, polluted, tainted; dreggy; draggled, draggletailed, draggly
idiom dirty as a pig
con immaculate, spotless; unsoiled, unspotted, unsullied
ant clean
2 ***syn*** IMPURE 1, immoral, unchaste, unclean, uncleanly
ant clean
3 ***syn*** OBSCENE 2, coarse, filthy, foul, indecent, nasty, raunchy, scatological, smutty, vulgar
4 ***syn*** WILD 6, blustering, blustery, ||coarse, furious, raging, rough, stormful, stormy, tempestuous

dirty *vb* **1** ***syn*** SOIL 2, begrime, besoil, foul, grime, smirch, smooch, smudge, smutch, tarnish
ant clean
2 ***syn*** TAINT 1, besmear, besmirch, discolor, smear, soil, stain, sully, tar, tarnish
idiom dirty one's hands

disability *n* ***syn*** DISADVANTAGE, detriment, drawback, handicap

disable *vb* **1** ***syn*** DISQUALIFY, disenable, incapacitate
2 ***syn*** PARALYZE 1, cripple, disarm, immobilize, incapacitate, prostrate
3 ***syn*** WEAKEN 1, attenuate, blunt, cripple, debilitate, enfeeble, sap, unbrace, undermine, unstrengthen
rel harm, hurt, mar, spoil; batter, maim, mangle, mutilate; ruin, wreck
con restore, resuscitate, revive, revivify
ant rehabilitate

disabuse *vb* to set free from mistakes (as in reasoning or judgment) <he was *disabused* of his belief when the facts were presented>
syn purge, undeceive, undelude
rel amend, correct, emend, rectify, redress; disillude, disillusion, unblind; enlighten, illuminate; free, liberate, release
idiom open one's eyes, prick the (*or* one's) bubble, puncture one's balloon, set (*or* put) right (*or* straight)
con deceive, delude, mislead; dupe, gull

disaccord *vb* **1** ***syn*** CLASH 2, conflict, discord, disharmonize, jangle, jar, mismatch
2 ***syn*** DIFFER 2, disagree, discord, dissent, divide, vary
ant accord

disaccord *n* ***syn*** DISCORD, conflict, contention, difference, dissension, dissent, dissidence, disunity, strife, variance

ant accord

disacknowledge *vb* ***syn*** DISCLAIM, deny, disallow, disavow, disown, repudiate

disadvantage *n* an unfavorable or prejudicial quality or circumstance <the machine has two serious *disadvantages*>
syn detriment, disability, drawback, handicap
rel bar, impediment, obstacle, obstruction; blocking, hamper, hindrance, imposition
con aid, assistance, help; service, usefulness, utility, value, worth
ant advantage

disadvantaged *adj* ***syn*** UNDERPRIVILEGED, depressed, deprived
ant advantaged

disadvantageous *adj* ***syn*** DEROGATORY, depreciative, depreciatory, detracting, disparaging, dyslogistic, pejorative, slighting, uncomplimentary

disadvise *vb* ***syn*** DISSUADE, deter, discourage, divert

disaffect *vb* ***syn*** ESTRANGE, alien, alienate, disunify, disunite, wean
rel agitate, discompose, disquiet, disturb, upset
ant win (over)

disaffection *n* ***syn*** ESTRANGEMENT, alienation

disaffirm *vb* ***syn*** DENY 4, contradict, contravene, cross, gainsay, impugn, negate, negative, traverse

disagree *vb* **1** ***syn*** DIFFER 1, vary
ant agree
2 ***syn*** DIFFER 2, disaccord, discord, dissent, divide, vary
ant agree

disagreeable *adj* **1** ***syn*** BAD 8, ‖chiselly, displeasing, rotten, sour, unhappy, unpleasant
rel annoying, distressing, disturbing, woeful
ant agreeable
2 ***syn*** IRRITABLE, peevish, pettish, petulant, querulous, snappy, twitty, waspish, waspy, whiny
ant agreeable

disallow *vb* **1** ***syn*** DENY 2, keep back, refuse, withhold
con accede, acquiesce, assent
ant allow
2 ***syn*** DISCLAIM, deny, disacknowledge, disavow, disown, repudiate
rel debar, exclude, shut out
ant allow

disallowance *n* ***syn*** DENIAL 1, refusal, rejection

disappear *vb* ***syn*** VANISH, clear, evanesce, evanish, evaporate, fade
rel go, leave
ant appear

disappoint *vb* ***syn*** FRUSTRATE 1, baffle, balk, beat, bilk, circumvent, dash, foil, ruin, thwart

disapprove *vb* **1** to feel or express an objection <*disapprove* of his actions>
syn deprecate, discommend, discountenance, disesteem, disfavor, frown, object
rel blame, censure, condemn, criticize, denounce, reprehend, reprobate; decry, depreciate, detract, disparage, dispraise; expostulate, remonstrate
idiom look askance at, make a wry face at, not go for, take a dim view of, take exception to
con applaud, commend, compliment, recommend; accredit, certify, endorse, sanction; approbate, countenance, favor
ant approve
2 ***syn*** DECLINE 4, dismiss, refuse, reject, reprobate, repudiate, spurn, turn down

disarm *vb* **1** ***syn*** PARALYZE 1, cripple, disable, immobilize, incapacitate, prostrate
2 to influence favorably by persuasive words or acts <*disarmed* by her smile>
syn unarm, unsteel, win (over)
rel allure, attract, bewitch, captivate, charm, enchant, fascinate
con alert, caution, tip (off), warn
ant arm

disarming *adj* ***syn*** ingratiating, deferential, ingratiatory, insinuating, insinuative, saccharine, silken, silky

disarrange *vb* ***syn*** DISORDER 1, derange, disarray, discompose, disorganize, disturb, jumble, mess (up), rummage, unsettle
rel mislay, misplace; displace, replace; overturn
ant arrange

disarray *n* ***syn*** CONFUSION 3, ataxia, ‖ballup, chaos, clutter, disorder, huddle, muddle, snarl, topsy-turviness
con arrangement, marshaling

disarray *vb* ***syn*** DISORDER 1, derange, disarrange, discompose, disorganize, disturb, jumble, mess (up), rummage, unsettle
ant array

disassemble *vb* ***syn*** DISMOUNT, dismantle, dismember, take down

disassociate *vb* ***syn*** DETACH, abstract, disconnect, disengage, dissociate, uncouple, unfix

disaster *n* a sudden calamitous event bringing great damage, loss, or destruction <a flood *disaster* struck the valley>
syn calamity, cataclysm, catastrophe, misadventure, tragedy, woe(s)
rel accident, casualty, fatality, mishap; adversity, distress, misadventure, mischance, misfortune; rock(s)

disastrous *adj* ***syn*** FATAL 2, calamitous, cataclysmic, catastrophic, fateful, ruinous
rel hapless, luckless, unfortunate; destructive
con fortunate, happy, lucky, providential

disavow *vb* ***syn*** DISCLAIM, deny, disacknowledge, disallow, disown, repudiate
rel impugn, negate, negative
con allow, concede, grant; assert, justify, maintain
ant avow

disband *vb* to cease to exist as a unit <the dance group *disbanded* after a farewell concert>
syn break up, disperse, dissolve
rel dispel, dissipate, scatter; dichotomize, disjoin, disjoint, dissect, dissever, disunite, divide, divorce, part, separate, sever, sunder
idiom go their several ways, part company

---

con combine, concur, conjoin, cooperate, unite; assemble, collect, congregate, gather; call up, summon
ant band

disbelief *n* ***syn*** UNBELIEF, incredulity, unbelievingness, unfaith
rel atheism, deism; rejection, repudiation, spurning
con credence, credit, faith
ant belief

disbelieve *vb* to hold not to be true or real < *disbelieved* his professions of sincerity >
syn discredit, unbelieve
rel distrust, doubt, mistrust, question, suspect; eschew, reject, scorn, scout
con accept, ‖buy, swallow
ant believe

disbelieving *adj* ***syn*** INCREDULOUS, aporetic, questioning, quizzical, show-me, skeptical, unbelieving

disbodied *adj* ***syn*** IMMATERIAL 1, bodiless, discarnate, disembodied, incorporeal, insubstantial, metaphysical, nonmaterial, nonphysical, unembodied

disburden *vb* ***syn*** UNLOAD, discharge, off-load, unlade, unship, unstow

disburse *vb* **1** ***syn*** SPEND 1, expend, fork (out), give, lay out, outlay, pay, shell out
2 ***syn*** DISTRIBUTE 1, deal, dispense, disperse, divide, ‖divvy, dole (out), lot (out), measure (out), partition

disbursement *n* ***syn*** EXPENSE 1, cost, expenditure, outlay

discalceate *adj* ***syn*** DISCALCED, barefoot

discalced *adj* wearing only sandals on the feet < *discalced* monks >
syn barefoot, discalceate
con calced, shod

discard *vb* to get rid of < *discard* old clothes > < people who *discard* traditional values >
syn abdicate, cashier, cast, chuck, ‖deep-six, ‖dice, ditch, dump, jettison, junk, lay aside, reject, scrap, shed, ‖shoot, shuck (off), slough, throw away, throw out, wash out
rel abandon, desert, forsake; repudiate, spurn; dismiss, eject, oust
idiom do away with, let go by the board
con adopt, embrace, espouse, take on, take up; employ, use, utilize; hold, hold back, keep, retain; cherish, esteem, nurture

discarding *n* ***syn*** DISPOSAL 2, disposition, dumping, jettison, junking, relegation, riddance, scrapping, throwing away

discarnate *adj* ***syn*** IMMATERIAL 1, asomatous, bodiless, disembodied, incorporeal, insubstantial, nonphysical, unembodied, unfleshly, unphysical
ant carnate, incarnate

---

syn synonym(s) *rel* related word(s)
idiom idiomatic equivalent(s) *con* contrasted word(s)
ant antonym(s) * vulgar
‖ use limited; if in doubt, see a dictionary
The first word in a synonym list when printed in SMALL CAPITALS shows where there is more information about the group. For a more efficient use of this book see Explanatory Notes.

discept *vb* ***syn*** DISCUSS 1, agitate, argue, canvass, debate, dispute, ‖kick around, moot, thrash out, toss (around)

discern *vb* **1** ***syn*** SEE 1, behold, descry, distinguish, note, notice, observe, perceive, remark, view
rel ascertain, discover; anticipate, apprehend, divine, foresee
2 ***syn*** KNOW 4, difference, differentiate, discrepate, discriminate, distinguish, extricate, separate, sever, severalize

discernible *adj* ***syn*** PERCEPTIBLE, appreciable, detectable, observable, palpable, sensible, tangible
ant indiscernible

discerning *adj* ***syn*** WISE 1, gnostic, insighted, insightful, knowing, knowledgeable, perceptive, sagacious, sage, wisehearted
ant undiscerning

discernment *n* ***syn*** WIT 3, acumen, astuteness, clear-sightedness, discrimination, keenness, penetration, percipience, perspicacity, shrewdness
rel intuition, reason; sagaciousness, sagacity
con crassness, density, slowness; blindness

discharge *vb* **1** ***syn*** UNLOAD, disburden, off-load, unlade, unship, unstow
2 ***syn*** EXEMPT, absolve, dispense, excuse, let off, privilege (from), relieve, spare
3 ***syn*** SHOOT 1, fire, loose
4 ***syn*** FREE, emancipate, liberate, loose, loosen, manumit, release, unbind, unchain, unshackle
rel dismiss, eject, expel, oust; eliminate, exclude
5 to give outlet to < the river *discharges* its waters into the bay >
syn disembogue, emit, flow, give off, pour, void
rel eject, exude, release
6 ***syn*** DISMISS 3, ax, boot (out), bounce, ‖can, cashier, fire, kick out, sack, terminate
rel displace, replace, supersede, supplant
con hire; contract
ant engage
7 to release from service with the armed forces < *discharged* from the army with the rank of sergeant >
syn ‖demob, demobilize, muster out, separate
rel disenroll; deactivate, inactivate; bounce, cashier, dismiss, drop, fire, sack
8 ***syn*** CLEAR 5, clear off, liquidate, pay, pay up, quit, satisfy, settle, square
9 ***syn*** ANNUL 4, abrogate, dissolve, quash, vacate, void

discinct *adj* ***syn*** NEGLIGENT, behindhand, careless, delinquent, derelict, disregardful, lax, neglectful, remiss, slack

disciple *n* ***syn*** FOLLOWER, adherent, cohort, henchman, partisan, satellite, sectary, sectator, supporter
rel enthusiast, fanatic, zealot

disciplinary *adj* ***syn*** PUNITIVE, castigatory, punishing, punitory

discipline *n* **1** ***syn*** PUNISHMENT, castigation, chastisement, correction, punition, rod
2 ***syn*** WILL 3, self-command, self-control, self-discipline, self-government, self-mastery, self-restraint, willpower

discipline *vb* **1** ***syn*** PUNISH 1, castigate, chasten, chastise, correct
rel overcome, reduce, subdue, subjugate; bridle, check, curb, inhibit, restrain

2 ***syn*** TEACH, educate, instruct, school, train
rel guide, lead; conduct, control, direct, manage

disclaim *vb* to refuse to admit, accept, or approve <the senator *disclaimed* the comment attributed to him> <*disclaim* responsibility for a subordinate's mistake>
syn deny, disacknowledge, disallow, disavow, disown, repudiate
rel contradict, contravene, gainsay, traverse; refuse, reject, spurn; deprecate; belittle, disparage, minimize; abjure, forswear, recant, renounce, retract; challenge, criticize
idiom turn one's back on, wash one's hands of
con acknowledge, avow, own; accept, admit, receive, take
ant claim

disclose *vb* **1** ***syn*** OPEN 2, display, expose, reveal, unclothe, uncover, unveil
2 ***syn*** REVEAL 1, betray, blab (out), discover, divulge, give away, mouth, spill, tell, unclose
rel acknowledge, admit, avow, confess, own
idiom make public
con conceal, hide; camouflage, cloak, disguise, dissemble, mask

discolor *vb* **1** ***syn*** TAINT 1, besmear, besmirch, defile, smear, soil, stain, sully, tar, tarnish
2 ***syn*** STAIN 1, bestain, blot, smut

discolor *adj* ***syn*** VARIEGATED, dappled, motley, multicolor, multicolored, multihued, parti-colored, varicolored, versicolor, versicolored

discombobulate *vb* **1** ***syn*** DISCOMPOSE 1, agitate, bother, disquiet, disturb, flurry, fluster, perturb, unhinge, upset
2 ***syn*** CONFUSE 2, addle, ball up, befuddle, bewilder, distract, fuddle, muddle, mull, throw off

discomfit *vb* ***syn*** EMBARRASS, abash, confound, confuse, disconcert, discountenance, faze, rattle
rel annoy, bother, irk, vex; disturb, perturb, upset

discomfiture *n* **1** ***syn*** DEFEAT 1, beating, debacle, defeasance, drubbing, licking, overthrow, rout, shellacking, vanquishment
2 ***syn*** COMEDOWN, descent, down
3 ***syn*** EMBARRASSMENT, abashment, confusion, discomposure, disconcertion, disconcertment, unease, uneasiness
rel agitation, disquiet, perturbation, upset; commotion; prickles

discomforting *adj* ***syn*** UNCOMFORTABLE, comfortless, harsh, uncomforting, uncomfy
ant comforting

discommend *vb* ***syn*** DISAPPROVE 1, deprecate, discountenance, disesteem, disfavor, frown, object
rel admonish; criticize, reprehend; censure
con approve, endorse, sanction
ant commend; recommend

discommode *vb* ***syn*** INCONVENIENCE, ||disconvenience, disoblige, incommode, put about, put out, trouble
rel flurry, fluster, perturb, upset; bother, irk, vex

discommoding *adj* ***syn*** INCONVENIENT, awkward, discommodious, embarrassing, incommodious

discommodious *adj* ***syn*** INCONVENIENT, awkward, discommoding, embarrassing, incommodious

discompose *vb* **1** to destroy or impair one's capacity for collected thought or decisive action <*discomposed* by the rudeness of his friend>
syn agitate, bother, discombobulate, dismay, disquiet, disturb, flurry, fluster, perturb, unhinge, unsettle, untune, upset; *compare* EMBARRASS
rel disagree; annoy, irk, vex; harass, harry, pester, plague, worry
con calm, quiet, settle, soothe, tranquilize; allay, alleviate, assuage; appease, conciliate, mollify, pacify, placate, propitiate
ant compose
2 ***syn*** DISORDER 1, derange, disarrange, disarray, disorganize, disturb, mess (up), rummage, unsettle, upset
ant compose

discomposure *n* ***syn*** EMBARRASSMENT, abashment, confusion, discomfiture, disconcertion, disconcertment, unease, uneasiness
ant composure

disconcert *vb* ***syn*** EMBARRASS, abash, confound, confuse, discomfit, discountenance, faze, rattle
rel bewilder, nonplus, perplex, puzzle

disconcertion *n* ***syn*** EMBARRASSMENT, abashment, confusion, discomfiture, discomposure, disconcertment, unease, uneasiness

disconcertment *n* ***syn*** EMBARRASSMENT, abashment, confusion, discomfiture, discomposure, disconcertion, unease, uneasiness

disconfirm *vb* ***syn*** DISPROVE 1, break, confound, confute, controvert, evert, rebut, refute

disconnect *vb* ***syn*** DETACH, abstract, disassociate, disengage, dissociate, uncouple, unfix
ant connect

disconnected *adj* ***syn*** INCOHERENT 2, discontinuous, disjointed, disordered, inchoate, incohesive, muddled, unconnected, uncontinuous, unorganized
ant connected

disconsolate *adj* **1** ***syn*** DOWNCAST, bad, crestfallen, dejected, depressed, dispirited, down, downhearted, low, woebegone
rel comfortless, inconsolable; sorrowful, woeful; doleful, melancholy; unhappy
ant cheerful
2 ***syn*** INCONSOLABLE, desolate, unconsolable
3 ***syn*** GLOOMY 3, black, bleak, cheerless, cold, depressing, dismal, drear, joyless, somber
ant cheerful, cheery

disconsonant *adj* ***syn*** INCONSONANT 1, conflicting, discordant, discrepant, dissonant, incompatible, incongruent, incongruous, inconsistent, unmixable

discontent *adj* ***syn*** DISCONTENTED, disgruntled, dissatisfied, malcontent, malcontented, uncontent, uncontented, ungratified
ant content

discontented *adj* showing or expressing a sense of grievance or thwarted aspirations or desires <*discontented* with his position>

---

syn synonym(s)	*rel* related word(s)
idiom idiomatic equivalent(s)	*con* contrasted word(s)
ant antonym(s)	* vulgar

|| use limited; if in doubt, see a dictionary
The first word in a synonym list when printed in SMALL CAPITALS shows where there is more information about the group. For a more efficient use of this book see Explanatory Notes.

syn discontent, disgruntled, dissatisfied, malcontent, malcontented, uncontent, uncontented, ungratified
rel disquieted, disturbed, perturbed, restless, upset; displeased; unhappy
con satisfied; gratified, pleased; happy; elated, exultant, jubilant, triumphant
ant contented

discontinuance *n* ***syn*** END 2, cease, cessation, close, closing, desistance, desuetude, discontinuation, ending, termination
ant continuance, continuation

discontinuation *n* ***syn*** END 2, cease, cessation, closing, conclusion, desistance, desuetude, discontinuance, ending, finish
ant continuance, continuation

discontinue *vb* ***syn*** STOP 3, cease, desist, ‖deval, give over, halt, knock off, leave off, quit, surcease
ant continue

discontinuity *n* ***syn*** GAP 1, breach, break, hole, opening
ant continuity

discontinuous *adj* ***syn*** INCOHERENT 2, disconnected, disjointed, disordered, inchoate, incohesive, muddled, unconnected, uncontinuous, unorganized
ant continuous

‖**disconvenience** *n* ***syn*** INCONVENIENCE, bother, bothersomeness, troublesomeness
ant convenience

‖**disconvenience** *vb* ***syn*** INCONVENIENCE, discommode, disoblige, incommode, put about, put out, trouble
ant convenience

discord *n* the state of those who disagree and lack harmony <a household full of turmoil and *discord*>
syn conflict, contention, difference, disaccord, disharmony, dispeace, dissension, dissent, dissidence, dissonance, disunion, disunity, division, inharmony, mischief, strife, unpeace, variance
rel discrepancy, incompatibility, incongruity, inconsistency, inconsonance, uncongeniality; animosity, antagonism, antipathy, enmity, hostility, rancor; polarization; collision
con accord, consonance; agreement, concordance, concurrence
ant concord, harmony

discord *vb* **1** ***syn*** CLASH 2, conflict, disaccord, disharmonize, jangle, jar, mismatch
ant concord, harmonize
2 ***syn*** DIFFER 2, disaccord, disagree, dissent, divide, vary
ant accord

discordant *adj* **1** ***syn*** INHARMONIOUS 2, inconsonant, uncongenial, unharmonious
2 ***syn*** INCONSONANT 1, conflicting, disconsonant, discrepant, dissonant, incompatible, incongruent, incongruous, inconsistent, unmixable
con according, agreeing, congenial, harmonious, harmonizing
ant concordant
3 ***syn*** ANTIPATHETIC 1, antagonistic, clashing, conflicting, contrariant, contrary
ant concordant
4 ***syn*** DISSONANT 1, cacophonic, cacophonous, disharmonic, disharmonious, immusical, inharmonic, inharmonious, unharmonious, unmusical

discotheque *n* ***syn*** NIGHTCLUB, cabaret, café, hot spot, nightery, night spot, nitery, supper club, watering hole, watering place

discount *n* ***syn*** DEDUCTION 1, abatement, rebate, reduction, subtraction

discount *vb* **1** ***syn*** DEDUCT 1, draw back, knock off, substract, subtract, take, take away, take off, take out
con boost, hike, increase, mark up, raise
2 ***syn*** NEGLECT, blink (at *or* away), disregard, fail, forget, ignore, omit, overlook, overpass, slight
3 ***syn*** DECRY 2, abuse, belittle, depreciate, derogate, detract (from), diminish, disparage, dispraise, minimize

discountenance *vb* **1** ***syn*** EMBARRASS, abash, confound, confuse, discomfit, disconcert, faze, rattle
idiom put out of countenance
2 ***syn*** DISAPPROVE 1, deprecate, discommend, disesteem, disfavor, frown, object
rel reproach, reprove
con encourage, favor
ant countenance

discourage *vb* **1** to weaken the stamina, interest, or zeal of <the long winter and lack of fuel *discouraged* the settlers>
syn chill, deject, demoralize, dishearten, disparage, dispirit
rel depress, weigh; afflict, try; damp, dampen, droop; distress, trouble; bother, irk, vex
idiom take the heart out of
con cheer, embolden, hearten, inspirit, nerve, steel
ant encourage
2 ***syn*** DISSUADE, deter, disadvise, divert
rel check, inhibit, restrain; prevent; frighten, scare
idiom lay a wet blanket on, throw cold water on
con advocate, countenance, favor; approve, back, endorse
ant encourage

discouraging *adj* ***syn*** GLOOMY 3, black, bleak, depressing, depressive, disheartening, dismal, dispiriting, dreary, oppressive
rel deterring; hindering
ant encouraging

discourse *n* **1** ***syn*** SPEECH 1, speaking, talk, utterance, verbalization
2 a systematic, serious, and often learned exposition of a subject or topic <his *discourses* during the seminar were long remembered>
syn disquisition, dissertation, memoir, monograph, monography, thesis, tractate, treatise
rel article, essay, paper; lecture, sermon; rhetoric, speech, talk

discourse *vb* **1** to express oneself especially formally and at length <*discourses* knowledgeably about the laws of nature>
syn descant, dilate (on *or* upon), discuss, dissert, dissertate, expatiate, sermonize

---

syn synonym(s) *rel* related word(s)
idiom idiomatic equivalent(s) *con* contrasted word(s)
ant antonym(s) * vulgar
‖ use limited; if in doubt, see a dictionary
The first word in a synonym list when printed in SMALL CAPITALS shows where there is more information about the group. For a more efficient use of this book see Explanatory Notes.

rel converse, speak, talk, voice; argue, dispute; harangue, lecture, orate, perorate; amplify, develop, elaborate, enlarge, expand; explain, expound; comment, commentate, remark
2 ***syn*** ACT 1, do, enact, impersonate, perform, personate, play, playact

discourteous *adj* ***syn*** RUDE 6, disgracious, disrespectful, ill-bred, ill-mannered, impertinent, impolite, uncivil, ungracious, unmannerly
con chivalrous, civil, courtly, gallant
ant courteous

discover *vb* **1** ***syn*** EXPOSE 4, debunk, show up, uncloak, undress, unmask, unshroud
2 ***syn*** REVEAL 1, betray, blab (out), disclose, divulge, give away, mouth, spill, tell, unclose
rel advertise, proclaim, publish
con repress, suppress
3 to become or be made aware of something not previously known <*discover* a secret>
syn ascertain, catch on, determine, find out, hear, learn, see, tumble, unearth
rel descry, detect, encounter, espy, hit (on *or* upon), meet (with), spot; discern, note, observe, perceive
idiom get wise to
con miss, overlook; disregard, ignore

discovery *n* the gaining knowledge of or ascertaining the existence of something previously unknown or unrecognized <the *discovery* of a new chemical element>
syn detection, espial, find, strike, unearthing
rel disclosure, exposition, exposure, revelation, uncovering

discreate *vb* ***syn*** DESTROY 1, annihilate, decimate, demolish, destruct, dissolve, raze, ruin, smash, wreck

discredit *vb* **1** ***syn*** DISBELIEVE, unbelieve
ant credit
2 to deprive of credibility <he *discredited* the rumor immediately>
syn blow up, disprove, explode, puncture, shoot
rel expose, show up; destroy, ruin
idiom bring to naught, knock the bottom out of, not leave a leg to stand on
con accept, believe, credit

discredit *n* ***syn*** DISGRACE, disesteem, dishonor, disrepute, ignominy, infamy, obloquy, odium, opprobrium, shame
ant credit

discreditable *adj* ***syn*** DISREPUTABLE 1, disgraceful, dishonorable, ignominious, inglorious, shabby, shady, shameful, shoddy, unrespectable

discreet *adj* **1** ***syn*** CAUTIOUS, calculating, careful, chary, circumspect, considerate, gingerly, guarded, safe, wary
con foolhardy
ant indiscreet
2 ***syn*** PLAIN 1, dry, inelaborate, modest, simple, unadorned, unbeautified, unelaborate, unostentatious, unpretentious
3 ***syn*** CONSERVATIVE 2, controlled, moderate, reasonable, restrained, temperate, unexcessive, unextreme

discreetness *n* ***syn*** PRUDENCE 1, canniness, caution, discretion, foresight, forethought, precaution, providence
ant indiscreetness

discrepancy *n* ***syn*** DISSIMILARITY, alterity, difference, dissemblance, dissimilitude, distinction, divergence, divergency, otherness, unlikeness

discrepant *adj* ***syn*** INCONSONANT 1, conflicting, disconsonant, discordant, dissonant, incompatible, incongruent, incongruous, inconsistent, unmixable
rel different, disparate, divergent, diverse; disagreeing, varying
con agreeing, conforming, corresponding, jibing, squaring, tallying; alike, identical, like, parallel, similar, uniform

discrepate *vb* ***syn*** KNOW 4, difference, differentiate, discern, discriminate, distinguish, extricate, separate, sever, severalize

discrete *adj* ***syn*** DISTINCT 1, different, diverse, separate, several, various
con blended, fused, merged, mingled
ant indiscrete

discretion *n* ***syn*** PRUDENCE 1, canniness, caution, discreetness, foresight, forethought, precaution, providence
rel moderation, restraint; gumption, judgment, sense, wisdom
con asininity, fatuousness, foolishness, simplicity; foolhardiness, rashness, recklessness
ant indiscretion

discretionary *adj* ***syn*** OPTIONAL, elective, facultative, nonobligatory

discriminate *vb* ***syn*** KNOW 4, difference, differentiate, discern, discrepate, distinguish, extricate, separate, sever, severalize
rel note, perceive, remark; collate, compare, contrast
ant confound

discriminating *adj* ***syn*** ECLECTIC 1, select, selective
rel careful; judicious, prudent, wise
ant undiscriminating

discrimination *n* ***syn*** WIT 3, acumen, astucity, astuteness, discernment, keenness, penetration, percipience, perspicacity, shrewdness
rel judgment, sense
con crassness, density, slowness

discriminative *adj* ***syn*** DISCRIMINATORY
ant undiscriminative

discriminatory *adj* applying or favoring discrimination in treatment <*discriminatory* employment practices against women>
syn discriminative
rel biased, inequitable, partial, partisan, prejudiced, prepossessed, unfair, unjust
con dispassionate, equal, equitable, fair, impartial, just, objective, unbiased, uncolored, unprejudiced
ant nondiscriminatory

discrown *vb* ***syn*** DEPOSE 1, dethrone, disenthrone, displace, disthrone, uncrown, unmake

---

disculpate *vb* ***syn*** EXCULPATE, absolve, acquit, clear, exonerate, vindicate
ant inculpate

discumber *vb* ***syn*** EXTRICATE 2, disembarrass, disembroil, disencumber, disentangle, disentwine, unentangle, unscramble, untangle, untie

discursion *n* ***syn*** DIGRESSION, aside, divagation, excursion, excursus, parenthesis

discuss *vb* **1** to exchange views about something in order to arrive at the truth or to convince others <met to *discuss* community needs>
syn agitate, argue, canvass, debate, discept, dispute, ‖kick around, moot, pro and con, thrash out, toss (around)
rel deliberate, hash over, reason (out), talk over; consider, weigh
idiom consider pro and con, go into, reason the point
2 ***syn*** DISCOURSE 1, descant, dilate (on *or* upon), dissert, dissertate, expatiate, sermonize
rel elucidate, explicate, interpret

discussion *n* ***syn*** CONFERENCE 1, confabulation, deliberation, rap, ventilation

disdain *n* **1** ***syn*** DESPITE 1, contempt, despisal, despisement, disparagement, scorn
rel antipathy, aversion; arrogance, haughtiness, insolence, superciliousness
con awe, fear, reverence
2 ***syn*** PRIDE 3, arrogance, disdainfulness, haughtiness, hauteur, loftiness, morgue, superbity, superciliousness

disdain *vb* ***syn*** DESPISE, abhor, contemn, look down, scorn, scout
con accept, receive, take; acknowledge, admit, own; esteem, respect
ant admire

disdainful *adj* ***syn*** PROUD 1, arrogant, cavalier, haughty, high-and-mighty, insolent, lordly, overbearing, supercilious, superior
rel rejecting, repudiating, spurning; contemning, despising, scorning, scouting; antipathetic, averse, unsympathetic
ant admiring; respectful

disdainfulness *n* ***syn*** PRIDE 3, arrogance, disdain, haughtiness, hauteur, loftiness, morgue, superbity, superciliousness

disease *n* **1** a kind or instance of impairment of a living being that interferes with normal bodily function <tuberculosis has become a controllable *disease*>
syn affection, ailment, complaint, condition, disorder, ill, infirmity, malady, sickness, syndrome; *compare* INFIRMITY 1, SICKNESS 1
rel bug, ‖epizootic, ‖misery, virus
2 ***syn*** INFIRMITY 1, debility, decrepitude, feebleness, infirmness, malaise, sickliness, unhealthiness
ant health

syn synonym(s) *rel* related word(s)
idiom idiomatic equivalent(s) *con* contrasted word(s)
ant antonym(s) * vulgar
‖ use limited; if in doubt, see a dictionary
The first word in a synonym list when printed in SMALL CAPITALS shows where there is more information about the group. For a more efficient use of this book see Explanatory Notes.

diseasedness *n* ***syn*** SICKNESS 1, affliction, disorder, illness, indisposition, infirmity, unhealth

disedge *vb* ***syn*** DULL 3, blunt, obtund, turn

disembark *vb* to go ashore out of a ship <*disembark* at the next port>
syn debark, land
rel put in
con board, get on
ant embark

disembarrass *vb* ***syn*** EXTRICATE 2, discumber, disembroil, disencumber, disentangle, disentwine, unentangle, untangle, untie, untwine
rel clear, rid, unburden
ant embarrass

disembodied *adj* ***syn*** IMMATERIAL 1, asomatous, bodiless, discarnate, incorporeal, insubstantial, nonphysical, unembodied, unfleshly, unphysical

disembogue *vb* ***syn*** DISCHARGE 5, emit, flow, give off, pour, void

disembowel *vb* ***syn*** EVISCERATE, bowel, draw, embowel, exenterate, gut, paunch

disembroil *vb* ***syn*** EXTRICATE 2, discumber, disembarrass, disencumber, disentangle, disentwine, unentangle, unscramble, untangle, untwine
ant embroil

disemploy *vb* ***syn*** DISMISS 3, ax, boot (out), bounce, ‖can, discharge, drop, fire, let out, terminate

disenable *vb* ***syn*** DISQUALIFY, disable, incapacitate

disenchanted *adj* ***syn*** SOPHISTICATED 2, blasé, disentranced, disillusioned, knowing, mondaine, sophisticate, worldly, worldly-wise, world-wise

disencumber *vb* ***syn*** EXTRICATE 2, discumber, disembroil, disentangle, disentwine, unentangle, unscramble, untangle, untie, untwine
rel alleviate, lighten, relieve
con depress, oppress, weigh
ant encumber

disenfranchise *vb* ***syn*** DISFRANCHISE

disengage *vb* **1** ***syn*** DETACH, abstract, disassociate, disconnect, dissociate, uncouple, unfix
rel free, liberate, release
con associate, connect, join, link, unite
ant engage
2 ***syn*** LOOSE 3, unbind, undo, unfasten, unfix, unloose, unloosen

disentangle *vb* ***syn*** EXTRICATE 2, discumber, disembroil, disencumber, disentangle, unentangle, unscramble, untangle, untie, untwine
rel detach, disengage; part, separate, sever, sunder
con enmesh, involve
ant entangle, tangle

disenthrall *vb* ***syn*** FREE, discharge, emancipate, liberate, loose, loosen, manumit, release, unbind, unchain

disenthrone *vb* ***syn*** DEPOSE 1, dethrone, discrown, displace, disthrone, uncrown, unmake

disentranced *adj* ***syn*** SOPHISTICATED 2, blasé, disenchanted, disillusioned, knowing, mondaine, sophisticate, worldly, worldly-wise, world-wise

disentwine *vb* ***syn*** EXTRICATE 2, discumber, disembroil, disencumber, disentangle, unentangle, unscramble, untangle, untie, untwine

disesteem *vb* ***syn*** DISAPPROVE 1, deprecate, discommend, discountenance, disfavor, frown, object

disesteem *n* ***syn*** DISGRACE, discredit, dishonor, disrepute, ignominy, infamy, obloquy, odium, opprobrium, shame
ant esteem

disfashion *vb* ***syn*** DEFACE, disfeature, disfigure

disfavor *n* **1** ***syn*** DISLIKE, aversion, bad books, disinclination, disliking, displeasure, disrelish, dissatisfaction, distaste, indisposition
rel distrust, mistrust
con approbation, approval; admiration, esteem, liking, regard, respect
ant favor
2 ***syn*** DISGRACE, discredit, disesteem, dishonor, disrepute, ignominy, infamy, obloquy, odium, opprobrium

disfavor *vb* ***syn*** DISAPPROVE 1, deprecate, discommend, discountenance, disesteem, frown, object
con approve, accept, approbate, countenance, go (for), hold (with)
ant favor

disfeature *vb* ***syn*** DEFACE, disfashion, disfigure

disfigure *vb* ***syn*** DEFACE, disfashion, disfeature
ant adorn

disfranchise *vb* to deprive of a legal right and especially of the right to vote <people subtly *disfranchised* by community apathy>
syn disenfranchise
rel deprive, take away
ant affranchise, enfranchise, franchise

disgorge *vb* **1** ***syn*** VOMIT, barf, bring up, ‖cast, ‖heave, *puke, spew, spit up, throw up, upchuck
2 ***syn*** ERUPT 1, belch, eject, eruct, expel, irrupt, spew

disgrace *n* the state of one who has lost esteem and good repute <retired in *disgrace* after the scandal became public>
syn contempt, discredit, disesteem, disfavor, dishonor, disrepute, ignominy, infamy, obloquy, odium, opprobrium, shame
rel abasement, debasement, debasing, degradation, humbling, humiliation; black eye, blot, brand, spot, stain, stigma
con admiration, regard; awe, fear, reverence; fame, glory, honor, renown, repute
ant esteem, respect

disgraceful *adj* ***syn*** DISREPUTABLE 1, discreditable, dishonorable, ignominious, inglorious, shabby, shady, shameful, shoddy, unrespectable
ant respectable; respectworthy

disgracious *adj* ***syn*** RUDE 6, discourteous, disrespectful, ill-bred, ill-mannered, impertinent, impolite, incivil, uncivil, ungracious
ant gracious

disgrade *vb* ***syn*** DEGRADE 1, break, bump, bust, declass, demerit, demote, disrate, downgrade, reduce

disgruntled *adj* ***syn*** DISCONTENTED, discontent, dissatisfied, malcontent, malcontented, uncontent, uncontented, ungratified

disguise *vb* to alter so as to hide the true appearance or character of <*disguised* herself with a wig> <*disguised* his anger behind a false geniality>
syn camouflage, cloak, dissemble, dissimulate, dress up, mask
rel conceal, hide; obfuscate, obscure; belie, falsify, garble, misrepresent; affect, assume, counterfeit, feign, pretend, sham, simulate
con display, exhibit, expose, flaunt, parade, show; betray, disclose, discover, reveal

disguise *n* **1** ***syn*** MASK 2, color, coloring, facade, face, false front, front, put-on, show, veneer
rel deception, delusion; speciousness
2 ***syn*** PRETENSE 2, charade, make-believe, pageant, pretension, pretentiousness

disguised *adj* ***syn*** INTOXICATED 1, ‖boozed, ‖boozy, ‖canned, drunk, inebriated, ‖lushed, muddled, pixilated, ‖plastered

disguisement *n* ***syn*** MASK 2, cloak, color, coloring, cover, disguise, facade, face, false front, front

disgust *vb* to be offensive to the taste or sensibilities of <the sight of filth *disgusted* him>
syn nauseate, reluct, repel, repulse, revolt, sicken
rel offend, outrage
idiom make one sick, stick in one's craw (*or* crop *or* gizzard), turn one's stomach
con charm, entice, tempt; delight, gratify, please, rejoice, tickle

disgusted *adj* ***syn*** FED UP, sick, tired, weary

disgusting *adj* ***syn*** OFFENSIVE, foul, loathsome, nasty, repellent, repugnant, repulsive, revolting, sickening, vile

‖**dish** *vb* ***syn*** CHAT 1, babble, cackle, clack, dither, gab, ‖gas, jaw, prattle, yak

disharmonic *adj* ***syn*** DISSONANT 1, cacophonic, cacophonous, discordant, disharmonious, immusical, inharmonic, inharmonious, unharmonious, unmusical
ant harmonic, harmonious

disharmonious *adj* ***syn*** DISSONANT 1, cacophonic, cacophonous, discordant, disharmonic, immusical, inharmonic, inharmonious, unharmonious, unmusical
ant harmonic, harmonious

disharmonize *vb* ***syn*** CLASH 2, conflict, disaccord, discord, jangle, jar, mismatch
ant harmonize

disharmony *n* ***syn*** DISCORD, conflict, contention, difference, disaccord, dispeace, dissension, strife, unpeace, variance
ant harmony

dishearten *vb* ***syn*** DISCOURAGE 1, chill, deject, demoralize, disparage, dispirit
ant hearten

disheartening *adj* ***syn*** GLOOMY 3, black, bleak, depressing, depressive, dismal, dreary, funereal, oppressive, somber
rel despondent, pessimistic
con encouraging, optimistic
ant heartening

disheveled *adj* ***syn*** SLOVENLY 1, ill-kempt, messy, raunchy, slipshod, sloppy, uncombed, unfastidious, unkempt, untidy

dishonest *adj* **1** unworthy of trust or belief <made a *dishonest* report on their progress>

---

syn synonym(s)	***rel*** related word(s)
idiom idiomatic equivalent(s)	***con*** contrasted word(s)
ant antonym(s)	* vulgar

‖ use limited; if in doubt, see a dictionary
The first word in a synonym list when printed in SMALL CAPITALS shows where there is more information about the group. For a more efficient use of this book see Explanatory Notes.

syn deceitful, knavish, lying, mendacious, roguish, shifty, unhonest, untruthful
rel crooked, devious, furtive, oblique; faithless, false, perfidious, untrustworthy; cheating, cozening, ‖cronk, defrauding, double-dealing, fraudulent, swindling, two-faced; insidious, tricky
con conscientious, honorable, just, scrupulous, upright; aboveboard, forthright, straightforward; candid, fair, frank, open, plain; dependable, reliable, sure, trustworthy, trusty
ant honest
2 *syn* CROOKED 2, corrupt, snide

dishonesty *n syn* DECEPTION 1, chicane, chicanery, double-dealing, fourberie, fraud, hanky-panky, highbinding, sharp practice, trickery

dishonor *n syn* DISGRACE, discredit, disesteem, disrepute, ignominy, infamy, obloquy, odium, opprobrium, shame
con reverence, veneration; authority, credit, influence, prestige, weight
ant honor

dishonorable *adj syn* DISREPUTABLE 1, discreditable, disgraceful, ignominious, inglorious, shabby, shady, shameful, shoddy, unrespectable
ant honorable

dish out *vb syn* GIVE 3, deliver, dispense, furnish, hand, hand over, provide, supply, transfer, turn over

disillusioned *adj syn* SOPHISTICATED 2, blasé, disenchanted, disentranced, knowing, mondaine, sophisticate, worldly, worldly-wise, world-wise
con beguiled, deceived, deluded, misled

disimpassioned *adj syn* COOL 2, collected, composed, imperturbable, nonchalant, unflappable, unruffled
ant heated, impassioned

disimprison *vb syn* FREE, discharge, emancipate, liberate, loose, manumit, release, unbind, unchain, unshackle
ant imprison

disimprove *vb syn* DETERIORATE 1, decline, degenerate, descend, disintegrate, retrograde, rot, sink, worsen
ant improve

disinclination *n syn* DISLIKE, aversion, bad books, disfavor, disliking, displeasure, disrelish, dissatisfaction, distaste, indisposition
ant inclination

disinclined *adj* lacking the will or desire to do something < *disinclined* to accept his story>
syn afraid, averse, backward, hesitant, indisposed, loath, reluctant, shy, uneager, unwilling, unwishful
rel antipathetic, unsympathetic; doubtful, dubious; opposing, resisting; balking, boggling, shying, sticking, stickling; objecting, protesting
con anxious, avid, eager, keen; disposed, predisposed, ready, willing
ant inclined

disingenuous *adj* lacking in candor and often giving a false appearance of simple frankness <had a *disingenuous* way of asking for advice when he really wanted help>
syn uncandid, unfrank
rel false, feigned, insincere, left-handed; artful, crafty, cunning, foxy, guileful, insidious, sly, tricky, wily; devious, indirect, oblique
con artless, naive, natural, simple, unsophisticated; candid, frank, open, plain; sincere, unfeigned; aboveboard, direct, straightforward
ant ingenuous

disinherit *vb* **1** to deprive (an heir apparent) of the right to inherit <the father *disinherited* his wayward son in his will>
syn cut off
rel disown, repudiate; dispossess
idiom cut off without a cent
2 *syn* DEPRIVE 2, bereave, dispossess, divest, lose, oust, rob

disinhume *vb syn* EXHUME, disinter, exhumate, unbury, uncharnel
ant inhume

disintegrate *vb* **1** *syn* DECAY, break down, crumble, decompose, molder, putrefy, rot, spoil, taint, turn
rel deliquesce; disperse, dissipate, scatter
con articulate, concatenate; blend, coalesce, fuse, merge; associate, combine, conjoin, connect, join, link, unite
2 *syn* DETERIORATE 1, decline, degenerate, descend, disimprove, retrograde, rot, sink, worsen

disinter *vb syn* EXHUME, disinhume, exhumate, unbury, uncharnel
ant inter

disinterest *n syn* APATHY 2, disregard, heedlessness, indifference, insouciance, lassitude, lethargy, listlessness, unconcern, unmindfulness
ant interest

disinterested *adj* **1** *syn* INDIFFERENT 2, aloof, casual, detached, incurious, remote, unconcerned, uncurious, uninterested, withdrawn
rel negative, neutral
con concerned, curious; fervent, impassioned, passionate
ant interested
2 *syn* NEUTRAL, abstract, colorless, detached, dispassionate, impersonal, poker-faced, unpassioned
rel fair, just, impartial, unbiased
con biased, prejudiced; involved
ant concerned

disject *vb syn* STREW 1, bestrew, broadcast, disseminate, scatter, sow, straw

disjoin *vb syn* SEPARATE 1, break up, disjoint, dissever, disunite, divide, divorce, part, sever, sunder

disjoint *vb* **1** *syn* SEPARATE 1, break up, disjoin, dissever, disunite, divide, part, sever, sunder, uncombine
2 *syn* DISORDER 1, disarray, discompose, disorganize, disrupt, disturb, mess (up), muddle, rummage, upset

disjointed *adj syn* INCOHERENT 2, disconnected, discontinuous, disordered, inchoate, incohesive, muddled, unconnected, uncontinuous, unorganized

---

syn synonym(s) *rel* related word(s)
idiom idiomatic equivalent(s) *con* contrasted word(s)
ant antonym(s) * vulgar
‖ use limited; if in doubt, see a dictionary
The first word in a synonym list when printed in SMALL CAPITALS shows where there is more information about the group. For a more efficient use of this book see Explanatory Notes.

dislike *n* a state of mind or feeling marked by an inner avoidance of something usually felt as unpleasant or repugnant <a pronounced *dislike* for mathematics>
syn aversion, bad books, disfavor, disinclination, disliking, displeasure, disrelish, dissatisfaction, distaste, indisposition
rel detestation, hate, hatred; deprecation, disapproval; prejudice, scunner
idiom ‖a derry on
con affection, attachment, love; partiality, predilection, preference
ant liking

disliking *n* ***syn*** DISLIKE, aversion, bad books, disfavor, disinclination, displeasure, disrelish, dissatisfaction, distaste, indisposition
ant liking

dislimb *vb* ***syn*** MAIM, cripple, dismember, mayhem, mutilate

dislimn *vb* ***syn*** OBSCURE, adumbrate, becloud, bedim, cloud, darken, dim, gloom, obfuscate, overcast

dislocate *vb* **1** ***syn*** DISORDER 1, disarrange, disarray, discompose, disorganize, disrupt, disturb, jumble, mix up, rummage
2 ***syn*** MOVE 4, disturb, remove, shift, ship, transfer

disloyal *adj* ***syn*** FAITHLESS, false, perfidious, recreant, traitorous, treacherous, unfaithful, unloyal, untrue
rel alienated, disaffected, estranged
ant loyal

disloyalty *n* **1** ***syn*** INFIDELITY, faithlessness, falseness, falsity, perfidiousness, perfidy, unfaithfulness
ant loyalty
2 ***syn*** TREACHERY, faithlessness, perfidiousness, perfidy, treacherousness, treason
ant loyalty

dismal *adj* ***syn*** GLOOMY 3, black, bleak, depressing, depressive, disheartening, dreary, funereal, oppressive, somber
con animated, gay, lively; cheerful

dismals *n pl, used with* the ***syn*** SADNESS, blues, dejection, depression, dumps, gloom, heavyheartedness, melancholy, mournfulness, unhappiness

dismantle *vb* **1** ***syn*** STRIP 2, bankrupt, bare, denudate, denude, deprive, disrobe, divest
con appoint, equip, outfit
2 ***syn*** DESTROY 1, annihilate, decimate, demolish, raze, ruin, unbuild, undo, wrack, wreck
3 ***syn*** REVOKE 2, lift, recall, repeal, rescind, reverse
4 ***syn*** DISMOUNT, disassemble, dismember, take down

dismay *n* ***syn*** FEAR 1, alarm, cold feet, consternation, dread, fright, horror, panic, terror, trepidation
con aplomb, assurance, confidence, self-possession; mettle, resolution, spirit

dismay *vb* **1** to unnerve and check by arousing fear, apprehension, or aversion <*dismayed* by the task that lay ahead>
syn appall, consternate, daunt, horrify, shake
rel bewilder, confound, dumbfound, mystify, nonplus, perplex, puzzle; abash, discomfit, disconcert, embarrass, faze, rattle; discourage, dishearten; affright, alarm, frighten, scare, terrify
idiom set one back on one's heels, take aback
con assure, ensure, secure; excite, galvanize, pique, provoke, quicken, stimulate
2 ***syn*** DISCOMPOSE 1, agitate, bother, disquiet, disturb, flurry, fluster, perturb, unhinge, upset

dismayed *adj* ***syn*** AGHAST 2, agape, confounded, dumbfounded, overwhelmed, shocked, thunderstruck
rel discomfited, disconcerted, fazed, rattled
ant undismayed

dismember *vb* **1** ***syn*** MAIM, cripple, dislimb, mayhem, mutilate
rel part, separate, sever, sunder
2 ***syn*** DISMOUNT, disassemble, dismantle, take down

dismiss *vb* **1** ***syn*** DIVORCE 2, put away, unmarry
2 ***syn*** DECLINE 4, disapprove, refuse, reject, reprobate, repudiate, spurn, turn down
3 to let go from one's employ or service <during the recession thousands of employees were *dismissed*>
syn ax, boot (out), bounce, ‖can, cashier, discharge, disemploy, drop, fire, kick out, let out, sack, terminate, turn off
rel depose, displace, furlough, lay off, remove, retire, suspend, unseat; reject, turn away; riff
idiom give one the gate (*or* one's walking papers), let go; give the ax (*or* the can) to
con hire; contract, engage; get, obtain, procure, secure
ant employ
4 ***syn*** EJECT 1, boot (out), chase, chuck, evict, extrude, kick out, out, throw out
rel cast, discard, shed, slough
idiom send one to Coventry
5 to refuse to consider seriously <*dismisses* the other performers as mere amateurs>
syn kiss off, pooh-pooh
rel deride, mock, rally, ridicule, taunt, twit; flout, gibe, gird, jeer, scoff; contemn, despise, disdain, scorn, scout; reject

dismissive *adj* ***syn*** PROUD 1, arrogant, cavalier, disdainful, haughty, high-and-mighty, insolent, overbearing, supercilious, superior

dismount *vb* to take down or apart from an assembled position <*dismount* a revolver for cleaning>
syn disassemble, dismantle, dismember, take down
rel detach, disengage; disconnect, disjoin, disunite, separate
idiom take apart, take to pieces
con assemble, construct, put together; combine, unite

disobedient *adj* refusing or neglecting to obey <the *disobedient* child refused to come in>
syn naughty, obstreperous, unruly; *compare* CONTRARY 3, NAUGHTY 1
rel headstrong, recalcitrant, willful; contumacious, insubordinate, rebellious
con amenable, biddable, docile, tractable; decorous, good, well-behaved
ant obedient

---

syn synonym(s)	***rel*** related word(s)
idiom idiomatic equivalent(s)	***con*** contrasted word(s)
ant antonym(s)	* vulgar

‖ use limited; if in doubt, see a dictionary
The first word in a synonym list when printed in SMALL CAPITALS shows where there is more information about the group. For a more efficient use of this book see Explanatory Notes.

disoblige *vb* ***syn*** INCONVENIENCE, discommode, ‖disconvenience, incommode, put about, put out, trouble
con accommodate, convenience, favor
ant oblige

disorder *n* **1** ***syn*** CONFUSION 3, ataxia, ‖ballup, chaos, clutter, disarray, huddle, muddle, snarl, topsy-turviness
con orderliness; pattern, plan
ant order
2 breach of public order <the overthrow of the government caused *disorder* in the country>
syn anarchism, anarchy, distemper, misrule, riot
rel anomie; agitation, commotion, convulsion, tumult, turbulence, turmoil, upheaval
ant order
3 ***syn*** DISEASE 1, affection, ailment, complaint, condition, ill, infirmity, malady, sickness, syndrome
4 ***syn*** SICKNESS 1, affliction, diseasedness, illness, indisposition, infirmity, unhealth

disorder *vb* **1** to undo the fixed or proper order of something <*disorder* the carefully arranged contents of a drawer>
syn derange, disarrange, disarray, discompose, disjoint, dislocate, disorganize, disrupt, distemper, disturb, jumble, ‖mammock, mess (up), mix up, muddle, muss (up), ‖mux, rummage, shuffle, tumble, unsettle, upset; *compare* CONFUSE 5
rel ball up, embroil; dishevel, rumple
idiom make hay of
con arrange, marshal, methodize, organize, systematize; align, array, line, line up, range; adjust, fix, regulate
ant order
2 ***syn*** UPSET 5, derange, sicken, turn, unhinge, unsettle

disordered *adj* **1** ***syn*** INCOHERENT 2, disconnected, discontinuous, disjointed, inchoate, incohesive, muddled, unconnected, uncontinuous, unorganized
2 ***syn*** INSANE 1, ‖batty, bedlamite, cracked, crazed, crazy, daft, demented, deranged, lunatic

disorderly *adj* ***syn*** TURBULENT 1, boisterous, raucous, rowdy, rowdydowdy, rowdyish, rumbustious, termagant, tumultuous, unruly

disorderly house *n* ***syn*** BROTHEL, bagnio, bawdy house, bordello, call house, cathouse, ‖joyhouse, parlor house, sporting house, whorehouse

disorganize *vb* ***syn*** DISORDER 1, derange, disarrange, disarray, discompose, disturb, jumble, mess (up), unsettle, upset
ant organize

disown *vb* ***syn*** DISCLAIM, deny, disacknowledge, disallow, disavow, repudiate
ant own

disparage *vb* **1** ***syn*** DECRY 2, abuse, belittle, depreciate, derogate, detract (from), dispraise, downcry, minimize, write off
ant applaud
2 ***syn*** DISCOURAGE 1, chill, deject, demoralize, dishearten, dispirit

disparagement *n* **1** ***syn*** DETRACTION, backbiting, backstabbing, belittlement, calumny, defamation, depreciation, scandal, slander, tale
rel animadversion, aspersion, reflection, stricture
2 ***syn*** DESPITE 1, contempt, despisal, despisement, disdain, scorn

disparaging *adj* ***syn*** DEROGATORY, depreciative, depreciatory, detracting, disadvantageous, dyslogistic, pejorative, slighting, uncomplimentary
rel underestimating, underrating, undervaluing
con acclaiming, extolling, praising; exalting, magnifying

disparate *adj* ***syn*** DIFFERENT 1, dissimilar, distant, divergent, diverse, unalike, unequal, unlike, unsimilar, various
rel discordant, discrepant, incompatible, inconsistent, inconsonant; distinct, separate
ant analogous, comparable

disparity *n* the state of being different (as in degree, rank, excellence, or number) <the *disparity* between the rich and the poor> <their stories showed significant *disparity*>
syn disproportion, imparity, inequality, unevenness
rel alterity, difference, dissemblance, dissimilarity, dissimilitude, distinction, divergence, divergency, otherness, unlikeness
con adequation, equality, equatability, equivalence, equivalency, sameness; correlation, correspondence, likeness; evenness
ant parity

dispassionate *adj* **1** ***syn*** NEUTRAL, abstract, colorless, detached, disinterested, impersonal, poker-faced, unpassioned
rel imperturbable, unflappable, unruffled
con fervent, vehement; intemperate
2 ***syn*** FAIR 4, equal, equitable, impartial, just, nondiscriminatory, unbiased, uncolored, unprejudiced, unprepossessed
rel aloof, indifferent; frank, open; aboveboard, straightforward

dispatch *vb* **1** ***syn*** SEND 1, address, consign, forward, remit, route, ship, transmit
rel hasten, quicken, speed
2 ***syn*** KILL 1, carry off, cut off, destroy, finish, lay low, put away, scrag, slay, take off
3 ***syn*** EAT UP 1, devour, polish off

dispatch *n* **1** ***syn*** HASTE 1, celerity, expedition, expeditiousness, hurry, hustle, rustle, speed, speediness, swiftness
con dawdling, loitering, procrastination
ant delay
2 ***syn*** ALACRITY, expedition, goodwill, promptitude, readiness
rel diligence, industriousness

dispeace *n* ***syn*** DISCORD, conflict, contention, difference, disaccord, disharmony, dissension, strife, unpeace, variance

dispel *vb* ***syn*** SCATTER 1, disperse, dissipate
rel dismiss, eject, expel, oust; crumble, disintegrate

dispensable *adj* capable of being dispensed with <many household gadgets are readily *dispensable*>

---

syn synonym(s) | *rel* related word(s)
idiom idiomatic equivalent(s) | *con* contrasted word(s)
ant antonym(s) | * vulgar
‖ use limited; if in doubt, see a dictionary
The first word in a synonym list when printed in SMALL CAPITALS shows where there is more information about the group. For a more efficient use of this book see Explanatory Notes.

syn nonessential, unessential, unrequired
rel needless, unnecessary, unneeded; minor, trivial, unimportant
con essential, imperative, necessary, necessitous, required; vital
ant indispensable

dispensation *n* ***syn*** FAVOR 4, courtesy, indulgence, kindness, service

dispense *vb* **1** ***syn*** DISTRIBUTE 1, deal, disburse, disperse, divide, ‖divvy, dole (out), lot (out), measure (out), partition
2 ***syn*** GIVE 3, deliver, dish out, furnish, hand, hand over, provide, supply, transfer, turn over
rel portion, prorate
3 ***syn*** ADMINISTER 2, apportion, deal (out), dole (out), mete (out), portion (out), share out
4 ***syn*** HANDLE 2, maneuver, manipulate, ply, swing, wield
5 ***syn*** EXEMPT, absolve, discharge, excuse, let off, privilege (from), relieve, spare

disperse *vb* **1** ***syn*** SCATTER 1, dispel, dissipate
rel discharge, dismiss
con call, cite, convene, convoke, summon
ant assemble, congregate; collect
2 ***syn*** DISTRIBUTE 1, deal, disburse, dispense, divide, ‖divvy, dole (out), lot (out), measure (out), partition
3 ***syn*** SPREAD 1, circulate, diffuse, disseminate, distribute, propagate, radiate, strew
4 ***syn*** DISBAND, break up, dissolve

dispirit *vb* ***syn*** DISCOURAGE 1, chill, deject, demoralize, dishearten, disparage
idiom dampen (*or* lower) one's spirits
ant inspirit

dispirited *adj* ***syn*** DOWNCAST, blue, cast down, dejected, depressed, disconsolate, downhearted, low, spiritless, woebegone
rel melancholy, sad
ant high-spirited, inspirited

dispiriting *adj* ***syn*** GLOOMY 3, black, bleak, depressing, depressive, discouraging, disheartening, dismal, dreary, funereal
rel dejecting, distressing; oppressing
ant inspiriting

displace *vb* **1** ***syn*** BANISH, deport, exile, expatriate, expel, expulse, ‖lag, oust, relegate, transport
2 ***syn*** DEPOSE 1, dethrone, discrown, disenthrone, disthrone, uncrown, unmake
3 ***syn*** SUPPLANT 1, cut out, usurp

displaced person *n* ***syn*** REFUGEE, DP, émigré, evacuee, fugitive

displacement *n* ***syn*** EXILE 1, banishment, deportation, expulsion, ostracism, relegation

display *vb* **1** ***syn*** OPEN 2, disclose, expose, reveal, unclothe, uncover, unveil
rel demonstrate, evidence, evince, lay out, manifest, show
con camouflage, cloak, disguise, dissemble, mask; conceal, hide, secrete
2 ***syn*** SHOW 4, brandish, disport, exhibit, expose, flash, flaunt, parade, show off, trot out
3 ***syn*** SHOW 1, offer

display *n* **1** ***syn*** EXHIBITION 1, demonstration, show, spectacle
2 a striking or spectacular exhibition <a parvenu's *display* of wealth>
syn array, fanfare, panoply, parade, pomp, shine, show
rel ostentation, ostentatiousness, pretension, pretentiousness, showiness; setout

displeasing *adj* ***syn*** BAD 8, ‖chiselly, disagreeable, rotten, sour, unhappy, unpleasant
rel annoying, bothersome, irksome, vexing
con agreeable, gratifying, pleasant
ant pleasing

displeasure *n* ***syn*** DISLIKE, aversion, bad books, disfavor, disinclination, disliking, disrelish, dissatisfaction, distaste, indisposition
rel anger; vexation
con delight, enjoyment
ant pleasure

disponible *adj* ***syn*** AVAILABLE 1, attainable, gettable, obtainable, procurable, securable

disport *n* ***syn*** PLAY 1, diversion, fun, recreation, sport
rel jollity, merriment

disport *vb* **1** ***syn*** SHOW 4, brandish, display, exhibit, expose, flash, flaunt, parade, show off, trot out
2 ***syn*** BEHAVE 1, acquit, act, bear, carry, comport, conduct, demean, deport, go on
3 ***syn*** PLAY 1, recreate, sport

disposal *n* **1** ***syn*** ORDER 3, arrangement, disposition, distribution, ordering, sequence
2 the act of ridding oneself of something <incinerators used for the *disposal* of trash>
syn discarding, disposition, dumping, jettison, junking, relegation, riddance, scrapping, throwing away
rel chucking, clearance; demolishing, demolition, destroying, destruction
con acquirement, acquisition; accumulation, collection, cumulation, deposit, hoard, trove

dispose *vb* **1** ***syn*** INCLINE 3, bend, bias, predispose
ant indispose
2 ***syn*** ORDER 1, arrange, array, marshal, methodize, organize, systematize

disposed *adj* ***syn*** WILLING 1, fain, inclined, minded, predisposed, prone, ready
ant indisposed

disposition *n* **1** ***syn*** DISPOSAL 2, discarding, dumping, jettison, junking, relegation, riddance, scrapping, throwing away
rel control, controlling, direction, management
2 ***syn*** ORDER 3, arrangement, disposal, distribution, ordering, sequence
3 the complex of especially mental and emotional qualities that distinguish an individual <a man of irritable *disposition*>
syn character, complexion, humor, individualism, individuality, makeup, nature, personality, temper, temperament

---

syn synonym(s) — *rel* related word(s)
idiom idiomatic equivalent(s) — *con* contrasted word(s)
ant antonym(s) — * vulgar
‖ use limited; if in doubt, see a dictionary
The first word in a synonym list when printed in SMALL CAPITALS shows where there is more information about the group. For a more efficient use of this book see Explanatory Notes.

rel mood, tone, vein; cast, stamp, tenor, type; being; identity
idiom frame of mind
4 *syn* LEANING 2, bent, inclination, inclining, penchant, predilection, predisposition, proclivity, propensity, tendency

dispossess *vb syn* DEPRIVE 2, bereave, disinherit, divest, lose, oust, rob
con provide, supply

dispossession *n syn* PRIVATION 2, deprivation, deprivement, divestiture, loss

dispraise *vb syn* DECRY 2, belittle, depreciate, derogate, detract (from), diminish, discount, disparage, minimize, opprobriate
ant praise

disproportion *n syn* DISPARITY, imparity, inequality, unevenness

disproportional *adj syn* LOPSIDED, asymmetric, difform, disproportionate, nonsymmetrical, proportionless, unequal, uneven, unproportionate, unsymmetrical

disproportionate *adj syn* LOPSIDED, asymmetric, irregular, nonsymmetrical, off-balance, overbalanced, unbalanced, unequal, uneven, unsymmetrical
ant proportionate

disprove *vb* **1** to show by presenting evidence that something is not true <the defendant's claims were *disproved* by the testimony>
syn break, confound, confute, controvert, disconfirm, evert, rebut, refute
rel contravene, impugn, negative, traverse; overthrow, overturn
con evidence, show; demonstrate, display, illustrate, manifest; argue, bespeak, tell
ant prove
2 *syn* DISCREDIT 2, blow up, explode, puncture, shoot

disputable *adj syn* MOOT, arguable, debatable, doubtful, dubious, mootable, problematic, questionable, uncertain

disputation *n syn* ARGUMENTATION, debate, dialectic, forensic, mooting

disputatious *adj syn* CONTENTIOUS 2, argumentative, controversial, litigious, polemical

dispute *vb* **1** *syn* ARGUE 2, argufy, bicker, hassle, quibble, squabble, wrangle
con give in, surrender
2 *syn* DISCUSS 1, agitate, argue, canvass, debate, discept, ||kick around, moot, thrash out, toss (around)
rel confute, controvert, disprove, rebut, refute
con allow, grant
ant concede
3 *syn* QUESTION 2, challenge, doubt, mistrust
4 *syn* RESIST, buck, combat, contest, duel, fight, oppose, repel, traverse, withstand

dispute *n* **1** *syn* ARGUMENT 2, contention, controversy, hurrah, rumpus
rel conflict, discord, dissension, strife
2 *syn* QUARREL, altercation, bickering, controversy, embroilment, falling-out, miff, squabble, tiff, wrangle

disqualified *adj syn* UNFIT 2, incapable, incompetent, ineligible, unequipped, unfitted, unqualified
ant qualified

disqualify *vb* to deprive of a power, right, or privilege <a conviction of perjury *disqualified* him from being a witness>
syn disable, disenable, incapacitate
rel bar, bate, debar, eliminate, except, exclude, rule out, suspend
con empower, enable
ant qualify

disquiet *vb syn* DISCOMPOSE 1, agitate, bother, disturb, flurry, fluster, perturb, unhinge, untune, upset
rel distress, trouble
con calm, compose, lull, still
ant quiet, soothe, tranquilize

disquiet *n* **1** *syn* CARE 2, anxiety, concern, concernment, disquietude, solicitude, unease, uneasiness, worry
ant quiet
2 *syn* UNREST, ailment, disquietude, ferment, inquietude, restiveness, restlessness, storm and stress, Sturm und Drang, turmoil
ant quiet

disquietude *n* **1** *syn* CARE 2, anxiety, concern, concernment, disquiet, solicitude, unease, uneasiness, worry
2 *syn* UNREST, ailment, disquiet, ferment, inquietude, restiveness, restlessness, storm and stress, Sturm und Drang, turmoil
ant quietness, quietude

disquisition *n syn* DISCOURSE 2, dissertation, memoir, monograph, monography, thesis, tractate, treatise
rel inquiry, investigation; argumentation, debate, disputation

disquisitive *adj syn* INQUISITIVE 1, curious, inquiring, investigative, questioning

disrate *vb syn* DEGRADE 1, break, bump, bust, declass, demerit, demote, disgrade, downgrade, reduce

disregard *vb syn* NEGLECT, blink (at *or* away), discount, fail, forget, ignore, omit, overlook, overpass, slight
con attend, mind, tend, watch; note, notice, observe, remark
ant regard

disregard *n syn* APATHY 2, disinterest, heedlessness, indifference, insouciance, lassitude, lethargy, listlessness, unconcern, unmindfulness
rel forgetting, ignoring, neglecting, omission, omitting, overlooking, slighting
con consideration, thoughtfulness

disregardful *adj syn* NEGLIGENT, behindhand, careless, delinquent, derelict, lax, neglectful, regardless, remiss, slack
ant regardful

disrelish *n syn* DISLIKE, aversion, bad books, disfavor, disinclination, disliking, displeasure, dissatisfaction, distaste, indisposition
ant relish

disremember *vb syn* FORGET 1, ||misremember, unknow

disreputable *adj* **1** not reputable or decent <was punished for his *disreputable* conduct>
syn discreditable, disgraceful, dishonorable, ignominious, inglorious, shabby, shady, shameful, shoddy, unrespectable
rel abject, mean, sordid; beggarly, cheap, contemptible, despicable, pitiable, scurvy, sorry
con admirable, creditable, estimable, honorable, respectable
ant reputable
2 ***syn*** SHABBY 1, bedraggled, decrepit, dilapidated, dingy, down-at-heel, faded, run-down, seedy, threadbare

disrepute *n* ***syn*** DISGRACE, discredit, disesteem, dishonor, ignominy, infamy, obloquy, odium, opprobrium, shame
ant repute

disrespect *n* ***syn*** INSOLENCE, boldness, hardihood, impertinence, impudence, insolency, insolentness
ant respect

disrespectful *adj* ***syn*** RUDE 6, discourteous, disgracious, ill-bred, ill-mannered, impertinent, impolite, incivil, uncivil, ungracious
ant respectful

disrobe *vb* **1** ***syn*** STRIP 1, denude, unclothe, undress
2 ***syn*** STRIP 2, bankrupt, bare, denudate, denude, deprive, dismantle, divest

disrupt *vb* **1** ***syn*** OPEN 3, breach, hole, rupture
2 ***syn*** DISORDER 1, disarray, discompose, disorganize, disturb, mess (up), muddle, rummage, unsettle, upset

dissatisfaction *n* ***syn*** DISLIKE, aversion, bad books, disfavor, disinclination, disliking, displeasure, disrelish, distaste, indisposition
ant satisfaction

dissatisfactory *adj* ***syn*** BAD 1, amiss, ‖bum, ‖crappy, poor, ‖punk, rotten, unsatisfactory, up, wrong
ant satisfactory

dissatisfied *adj* ***syn*** DISCONTENTED, discontent, disgruntled, malcontent, malcontented, uncontent, uncontented, ungratified
rel annoyed, bothered, irked, vexed
con content, contented, gratified
ant satisfied

dissect *vb* **1** ***syn*** SEPARATE 1, break up, dichotomize, disjoin, disjoint, dissever, divide, part, sever, sunder
2 ***syn*** CUT 5, carve, cleave, dissever, sever, slice, split, sunder
rel penetrate, pierce, probe
3 ***syn*** ANALYZE, anatomize, break down, decompose, decompound, resolve

dissection *n* ***syn*** ANALYSIS 1, breakdown, breakup, resolution
rel examination, inspection, review, scrutiny; criticism, critique

dissemblance *n* ***syn*** DISSIMILARITY, alterity, difference, discrepancy, dissimilitude, distinction, divergence, divergency, otherness, unlikeness
ant resemblance, semblance

dissemblance *n* ***syn*** DECEIT 1, cunning, dissimulation, duplicity, guile

dissemble *vb* ***syn*** DISGUISE, camouflage, cloak, dissimulate, dress up, mask
con demonstrate, evidence, evince, manifest, show

dissembler *n* ***syn*** HYPOCRITE, dissimulator, lip server, pharisee, Tartuffe, whited sepulcher

disseminate *vb* **1** ***syn*** SPREAD 1, circulate, diffuse, disperse, distribute, propagate, radiate, strew
2 ***syn*** DECLARE 1, advertise, announce, annunciate, blaze (abroad), blazon, broadcast, proclaim, promulgate, publish
3 ***syn*** STREW 1, bestrew, broadcast, disject, scatter, sow, straw

dissension *n* ***syn*** DISCORD, conflict, contention, difference, disaccord, dissent, dissidence, disunity, strife, variance
rel altercation, bickering, quarrel, wrangle; argument, controversy, dispute
con amity, friendship, goodwill
ant accord; comity

dissent *vb* ***syn*** DIFFER 2, disaccord, disagree, discord, divide, vary
rel balk, boggle, demur, shy, stickle
con accede, acquiesce, agree, subscribe
ant assent; concur

dissent *n* **1** ***syn*** DISCORD, conflict, contention, difference, disaccord, dissension, dissidence, disunity, strife, variance
2 ***syn*** HERESY, dissidence, heterodoxy, misbelief, nonconformism, nonconformity, schism, unorthodoxy
rel disagreement, nonagreement, nonconcurrence

dissenter *n* ***syn*** HERETIC, dissident, misbeliever, nonconformist, schismatic, schismatist, sectary, separatist

dissert *vb* ***syn*** DISCOURSE 1, descant, dilate (on *or* upon), discuss, dissertate, expatiate, sermonize

dissertate *vb* ***syn*** DISCOURSE 1, descant, dilate (on *or* upon), discuss, dissert, expatiate, sermonize

dissertation *n* ***syn*** DISCOURSE 2, disquisition, memoir, monograph, monography, thesis, tractate, treatise
rel exposition; argumentation, disputation

dissever *vb* **1** ***syn*** SEPARATE 1, dichotomize, disjoin, disjoint, dissect, disunite, divide, divorce, sever, sunder
2 ***syn*** CUT 5, carve, cleave, dissect, sever, slice, split, sunder

dissidence *n* **1** ***syn*** DISCORD, conflict, contention, difference, disaccord, disharmony, dispeace, dissension, dissent, strife
2 ***syn*** HERESY, dissent, heterodoxy, misbelief, nonconformism, nonconformity, schism, unorthodoxy

dissident *adj* ***syn*** HERETICAL, heterodox, nonconformist, schismatic, sectarian, unorthodox

dissident *n* ***syn*** HERETIC, dissenter, misbeliever, nonconformist, schismatic, schismatist, sectary, separatist

dissimilar *adj* ***syn*** DIFFERENT 1, disparate, distant, divergent, diverse, unalike, unequal, unlike, unsimilar, various
rel antithetical, antonymous, contradictory, contrary, opposite

---

ant similar

dissimilarity *n* lack of agreement or correspondence or an instance of this <the *dissimilarities* in the cultures of the two countries>

syn alterity, difference, discrepancy, dissemblance, dissimilitude, distance, distinction, divarication, divergence, divergency, otherness, unlikeness

rel disparity, diversity; discordance, incongruity, inconsistency, inconsonance; discord, variance; severance; offset; margin

con affinity, analogy, likeness, resemblance, similitude; accordance, congruity, consistency, consonance; agreement, conformity, correspondence

ant similarity

dissimilitude *n* ***syn*** DISSIMILARITY, alterity, difference, discrepancy, dissemblance, distinction, divergence, divergency, otherness, unlikeness

ant similitude

dissimulate *vb* ***syn*** DISGUISE, camouflage, cloak, dissemble, dress up, mask

dissimulation *n* ***syn*** DECEIT 1, cunning, dissemblance, duplicity, guile

rel camouflaging, cloaking, disguising, dissembling, masking; concealing, hiding, secreting; feigning, pretending, pretense, shamming; hypocrisy, pharisaism, sanctimony

dissimulator *n* ***syn*** HYPOCRITE, dissembler, lip server, pharisee, Tartuffe, whited sepulcher

dissipate *vb* **1** ***syn*** SCATTER 1, dispel, disperse

rel crumble, disintegrate

ant accumulate; concentrate (*as efforts, thoughts*)

2 ***syn*** WASTE 2, blow, blunder (away), consume, fool (away), fritter, frivol away, squander, throw away, trifle (away)

rel disappear, evanesce, evaporate, vanish

ant absorb (*as time, attention*)

dissipation *n* ***syn*** ENTERTAINMENT, amusement, distraction, diversion, divertissement, recreation

dissociate *vb* ***syn*** DETACH, abstract, disassociate, disconnect, disengage, uncouple, unfix

rel alienate, estrange

ant associate

dissolute *adj* ***syn*** ABANDONED 2, licentious, profligate, reprobate, self-abandoned, unprincipled

rel lax, light, loose, slack, wanton, wayward; fast, raffish, rakish, wild

dissolution *n* **1** ***syn*** SEPARATION 1, detachment, disunion, division, divorce, divorcement, partition, rupture, split-up

2 ***syn*** DEATH 1, curtains, decease, defunction, demise, (the) Pale Horse, passing, quietus, silence, sleep

dissolve *vb* **1** ***syn*** DESTROY 1, annihilate, decimate, demolish, destruct, ruin, shatter, shoot, wrack, wreck

2 ***syn*** ADJOURN 2, prorogate, prorogue, recess, rise, terminate

3 ***syn*** ANNUL 4, abrogate, discharge, quash, vacate, void

4 ***syn*** LIQUEFY, deliquesce, flux, fuse, liquesce, melt, run, thaw

5 ***syn*** SOLVE 2, ‖cipher, clear up, decipher, ‖dope out, figure out, puzzle out, resolve, unfold, unravel

6 ***syn*** DISBAND, break up, disperse

dissonance *n* ***syn*** DISCORD, conflict, contention, difference, disaccord, disharmony, dissension, dissidence, strife, variance

dissonant *adj* **1** marked by a mingling of discordant sounds <the two bands playing different pieces at the same time sounded *dissonant*>

syn cacophonic, cacophonous, discordant, disharmonic, disharmonious, immusical, inharmonic, inharmonious, rude, unharmonious, unmusical

rel grating, harsh, hoarse, jarring, raucous, rugged, strident

con blending, chiming, concerted, harmonic, symphonious; euphonious, harmonious, mellifluous, mellow, melodious, musical; agreeable, pleasing

ant consonant

2 ***syn*** INCONSONANT 1, conflicting, disconsonant, discordant, discrepant, incompatible, incongruent, incongruous, inconsistent, unmixable

dissuade *vb* to turn one aside from a purpose, a project, or a plan <they tried to *dissuade* a friend from making a mistake>

syn deter, disadvise, discourage, divert

rel derail, throw off; advise, counsel; exhort, prick, urge

idiom talk out of

con get, induce, prevail; affect, influence, touch

ant persuade

distance *n* **1** an extent of areal or linear measure <he did not know the *distance* he had walked>

syn length, stretch

rel area, extent; ambit, compass, extension, orbit, purview, radius, range, reach, scope, sweep

2 the length of a literal or figurative course traversed or to be traversed <he had come a long *distance* from his pitiful beginnings>

syn way, ways

rel extent, size; piece, spell

3 ***syn*** EXPANSE, amplitude, breadth, expansion, space, spread, stretch

4 ***syn*** DISSIMILARITY, alterity, difference, dissemblance, dissimilitude, distinction, divergence, divergency, otherness, unlikeness

distance *vb* ***syn*** OUTSTRIP 1, outdistance, outpace, outrun, outspeed

distant *adj* **1** not close in space, time, or relationship <traveling to a more *distant* place> <the *distant* days of the Pilgrim fathers> <a *distant* cousin>

syn far, faraway, far-flung, far-off, off-lying, outlying, remote, removed

rel apart, isolated, obscure, out-of-the-way, retired, secret; secluded, sequestered

idiom at a distance

con close, near, nearby, next, nigh; adjacent, adjoining, contiguous

---

syn synonym(s) ***rel*** related word(s)
idiom idiomatic equivalent(s) ***con*** contrasted word(s)
ant antonym(s) * vulgar
‖ use limited; if in doubt, see a dictionary
The first word in a synonym list when printed in SMALL CAPITALS shows where there is more information about the group. For a more efficient use of this book see Explanatory Notes.

2 ***syn*** DIFFERENT 1, disparate, dissimilar, divergent, diverse, unalike, unequal, unlike, unsimilar, various

3 ***syn*** UNSOCIABLE, aloof, cool, insociable, reserved, solitary, standoffish, unapproachable, uncompanionable, withdrawn

rel arrogant, haughty, proud; modest, retiring, shy

con forward, presuming, ‖pushy, self-assertive

distaste *n* ***syn*** DISLIKE, aversion, bad books, disfavor, disinclination, disliking, displeasure, disrelish, dissatisfaction, indisposition

rel abhorrence, repugnance, repulsion, revulsion; antipathy, hostility

con relish, zest; appetite, desire; enjoyment

ant taste

distasteful *adj* **1** ***syn*** UNPALATABLE 1, flat, flavorless, ill-flavored, insipid, savorless, tasteless, unappetizing, unsavory

ant tasteful, tasty

2 ***syn*** BITTER 2, afflictive, galling, grievous, painful, unpalatable

rel obnoxious, repellent, repugnant, repulsive; abominable, detestable, hateful, odious

con agreeable, grateful, gratifying, pleasant, pleasing, welcome

distemper *vb* ***syn*** DISORDER 1, derange, disarrange, disarray, discompose, disjoint, disturb, mix up, muddle, rummage

distemper *n* ***syn*** DISORDER 2, anarchism, anarchy, misrule, riot

distend *vb* ***syn*** EXPAND 3, amplify, dilate, inflate, swell

rel augment, enlarge, increase; extend, lengthen

ant constrict

disthrone *vb* ***syn*** DEPOSE 1, dethrone, discrown, disenthrone, displace, uncrown, unmake

distill *vb* ***syn*** DRIP, drib, dribble, drop, trickle, trill, weep

distinct *adj* **1** capable of being distinguished as differing <the novel has two related, but nevertheless *distinct,* plots>

syn different, discrete, diverse, separate, several, various

rel distinctive, individual, peculiar; particular, single, sole; especial, individual, special, specific; disparate, dissimilar, divergent

con identical, same, selfsame; corresponding, equivalent, like, similar

ant indistinguishable

2 ***syn*** CLEAR 5, apparent, evident, manifest, obvious, palpable, patent, plain, unambiguous, unequivocal

rel defined, prescribed; categorical, definite, explicit, express, specific; lucid, perspicuous; clear-cut, incisive, trenchant

con faint, obscure

ant indistinct; nebulous

distinction *n* **1** ***syn*** DISSIMILARITY, alterity, difference, discrepancy, dissemblance, dissimilitude, divergence, divergency, otherness, unlikeness

con affinity, analogy, likeness, similarity, similitude

ant indistinction, resemblance

2 ***syn*** EMINENCE 1, illustriousness, kudos, preeminence, prestige, prominence, prominency, renown

3 ***syn*** HONOR 2, accolade, award, badge, bays, decoration, kudos, laurels

distinctive *adj* ***syn*** CHARACTERISTIC, diacritic, diagnostic, idiosyncratic, individual, peculiar, proper

rel separate, single, unique; discrete, distinct, several

con common, familiar, ordinary, popular, vulgar; alike, analogous, comparable, identical, like, parallel; equal, equivalent, same

distinctively *adv* ***syn*** ESPECIALLY 1, particularly, special, specially, specifically

distinctiveness *n* ***syn*** INDIVIDUALITY 3, individualism, particularity, singularity

distingué *adj* ***syn*** GENTEEL 1, cultivated, cultured, polished, refined, urbane, well-bred

distinguish *vb* **1** ***syn*** KNOW 4, difference, differentiate, discern, discrepate, discriminate, extricate, separate, sever, severalize

rel divide, part; detach, disengage; demarcate, set off

con confuse, mistake

ant confound

2 ***syn*** EXALT 1, aggrandize, dignify, ennoble, erect, glorify, honor, magnify, sublime, uprear

3 ***syn*** CHARACTERIZE 2, individualize, individuate, mark, qualify, signalize, singularize

idiom set apart

4 ***syn*** SEE 1, descry, discern, mark, note, notice, observe, perceive, remark, view

5 ***syn*** IDENTIFY, determinate, diagnose, diagnosticate, finger, pinpoint, place, recognize, spot

distinguished *adj* ***syn*** FAMOUS 2, celebrated, celebrious, eminent, famed, great, illustrious, notable, prominent, renowned

rel courtly, dignified, grand, imposing, stately

ant undistinguished

distort *vb* **1** ***syn*** MISREPRESENT, belie, color, falsify, garble, miscolor, misstate, pervert, twist, warp

rel misconstrue, misinterpret; alter, change

2 ***syn*** DEFORM, contort, misshape, torture, warp, wind

rel bend, curve, twist

distortion *n* ***syn*** DEFORMITY, malconformation, malformation, misshape

distract *vb* **1** ***syn*** CONFUSE 2, addle, ball up, befuddle, bewilder, ‖bumfuzzle, fluster, fuddle, mix up, throw off

2 ***syn*** MADDEN 1, craze, derange, frenzy, unbalance, unhinge

distracted *adj* ***syn*** DISTRAUGHT, distrait, distressed, harassed, tormented, troubled, worried

distraction *n* **1** ***syn*** INSANITY 1, aberration, alienation, derangement, insaneness, lunacy, madness, psychopathy, unbalance

2 ***syn*** ENTERTAINMENT, amusement, dissipation, diversion, divertissement, recreation

distrait *adj* **1** ***syn*** ABSTRACTED, absent, absentminded, bemused, faraway, inconscient, lost, preoccupied

2 ***syn*** DISTRAUGHT, distracted, distressed, harassed, tormented, troubled, worried

---

syn synonym(s) | ***rel*** related word(s)
idiom idiomatic equivalent(s) | ***con*** contrasted word(s)
ant antonym(s) | * vulgar
‖ use limited; if in doubt, see a dictionary
The first word in a synonym list when printed in SMALL CAPITALS shows where there is more information about the group. For a more efficient use of this book see Explanatory Notes.

distraught *adj* **1** agitated with doubt or mental conflict < *distraught* over the health of her child >
syn distracted, distrait, distressed, harassed, tormented, troubled, worried
rel agitated, concerned, discomposed, flustered, perturbed, upset; addled, confused, muddled; bewildered, nonplussed
idiom beside oneself
con composed, cool, imperturbable, nonchalant, unflappable, unruffled; calm, tranquil; unconcerned, undisturbed, unworried
ant collected
2 *syn* INSANE 1, ‖batty, cracked, crazed, crazy, daft, demented, deranged, mad, nuts

distress *n* the state of being in serious trouble or in mental or physical anguish <in great *distress* over the decision he had to make>
syn agony, dolor, misery, passion, suffering
rel affliction, cross, trial, tribulation, visitation; anguish, grief, heartbreak, sorrow, woe; exigency, pass, pinch, strait; difficulty, hardship, rigor, vicissitude; ache, pain, pang, throe, twinge
con comfort, comforting, consolation, solace, solacing; allaying, alleviation, assuagement, ease, relief, relieving; ease, peace, security

distress *vb* **1** *syn* TRY 2, harass, irk, pain, strain, stress, trouble
rel afflict, rack, torment, torture
con allay, alleviate, assuage, lighten, mitigate, relieve
2 to cause pain or suffering to <the death of his longtime friend *distressed* him deeply>
syn aggrieve, constrain, grieve, hurt, injure, pain
rel harass, strain, stress, try, trouble; depress, oppress, weigh
con comfort, console, solace; aid, assist, help
3 *syn* TROUBLE 1, ail, cark, upset, worry
rel annoy, harry, pester, plague

distressed *adj syn* DISTRAUGHT, distracted, distrait, harassed, tormented, troubled, worried

distressing *adj syn* DEPLORABLE, afflictive, calamitous, dire, grievous, heartbreaking, lamentable, regrettable, unfortunate, woeful

distribute *vb* **1** to give out, usually in shares, to each member of a group < *distributed* his possessions among his heirs>
syn deal, disburse, dispense, disperse, divide, ‖divvy, dole (out), lot (out), measure (out), partition
rel allocate, allot, apportion, assign, mete (out); parcel, portion, prorate, ration; administer; dribble; bestow, donate, give, present
con assemble, gather; accumulate, hoard
ant amass; collect
2 *syn* SPREAD 1, circulate, diffuse, disperse, disseminate, propagate, radiate, strew

---

syn synonym(s) | *rel* related word(s)
idiom idiomatic equivalent(s) | *con* contrasted word(s)
ant antonym(s) | * vulgar
‖ use limited; if in doubt, see a dictionary
The first word in a synonym list when printed in SMALL CAPITALS shows where there is more information about the group. For a more efficient use of this book see Explanatory Notes.

distribution *n syn* ORDER 3, arrangement, disposal, disposition, ordering, sequence

district *n* **1** *syn* QUARTER 2, precinct, section, sector
2 *syn* LOCALITY 1, area, neighborhood, vicinage, vicinity
rel division, parcel

distrust *vb* to have no trust or confidence in <he *distrusted* most politicians>
syn doubt, misdoubt, mistrust, suspect, ‖suspicion
rel disbelieve, discredit, unbelieve
con bank, count, depend, reckon, rely; commit, confide, consign, entrust
ant trust

distrustful *adj syn* SUSPICIOUS 2, jealous, mistrustful

distrustfully *adv syn* ASKANCE 2, doubtfully, mistrustfully, skeptically, suspiciously

disturb *vb* **1** *syn* MOVE 4, dislocate, remove, shift, ship, transfer
2 *syn* DISCOMPOSE 1, agitate, bother, discombobulate, disquiet, flurry, fluster, perturb, unhinge, upset
rel alarm, frighten, scare, terrify; bewilder, distract, perplex, puzzle; discommode, incommode, inconvenience, trouble
3 *syn* DISORDER 1, derange, disarrange, disarray, discompose, disorganize, jumble, mess (up), unsettle, upset
rel displace, replace; move, remove, shift; interfere, intermeddle, meddle, tamper
con establish, fix, set, settle; adjust, regulate

disunify *vb syn* ESTRANGE, alien, alienate, disaffect, disunite, wean

disunion *n* **1** *syn* SEPARATION 1, detachment, dissolution, division, divorce, divorcement, partition, rupture, split-up
2 *syn* DISCORD, conflict, contention, difference, disaccord, dissension, dissent, disunity, strife, variance

disunite *vb* **1** *syn* SEPARATE 1, dichotomize, disjoin, disjoint, dissever, divide, divorce, part, sunder, uncombine
2 *syn* ESTRANGE, alien, alienate, disaffect, disunify, wean

disunity *n syn* DISCORD, conflict, contention, difference, disaccord, dissension, dissent, disunion, strife, variance

disusage *n syn* DISUSE, desuetude

disuse *n* cessation of use, practice, or exercise <to keep the mind from falling into *disuse,* one must exercise one's reading abilities> <his muscles became atrophied from *disuse*>
syn desuetude, disusage
con appliance, application, employment, operation, play, usance; exercise
ant use

disused *adj syn* OBSOLETE, dead, extinct, outmoded, outworn, passé, superseded

ditch *n syn* TRENCH, cut

ditch *vb* **1** *syn* DISCARD, cashier, cast, chuck, jettison, junk, reject, scrap, throw away, throw out
‖**2** *syn* HIDE, bury, ‖bush up, cache, conceal, cover, ensconce, occult, screen, secrete

‖**dite** *n syn* PARTICLE, doit, dram, drop, iota, jot, mite, ray, ‖rissom, smitch

dither *vb* **1** *syn* SHAKE 1, ‖didder, quake, quaver, quiver, shiver, shudder, tremble, tremor, twitter
2 *syn* HESITATE, falter, halt, shilly-shally, stagger, vacillate, waver, whiffle, wiggle-waggle

3 ***syn*** CHAT 1, babble, cackle, clack, gab, ‖gas, jaw, ‖natter, run on, yak

dither *n* 1 ***syn*** JITTERS, ‖all-overs, heebie-jeebies, ‖jim-jams, ‖jimmies, jumps, shakes, shivers, whim-whams, willies

2 ***syn*** COMMOTION 2, agitation, confusion, flap, lather, pother, stew, tumult, turbulence, turmoil

dithyrambic *adj* ***syn*** IMPASSIONED, ardent, burning, fervent, fervid, fiery, flaming, perfervid, passionate, torrid

ditto *n* ***syn*** REPRODUCTION, carbon, carbon copy, copy, duplicate, facsimile, reduplication, replica, replication

ditty *n* ***syn*** SONG 2, aria, descant, hymn, lay, lied

diurnal *adj* ***syn*** DAILY, quotidian

ant nocturnal

diuturnal *adj* ***syn*** LASTING, durable, enduring, perdurable, perduring, permanent, stable

divagate *vb* ***syn*** DIGRESS 2, depart, diverge, excurse, ramble, stray, wander

divagation *n* ***syn*** DIGRESSION, aside, discursion, excursion, excursus, parenthesis

divarication *n* ***syn*** DISSIMILARITY, alterity, difference, dissemblance, dissimilitude, distinction, divergence, divergency, otherness, unlikeness

dive *vb* ***syn*** PLUNGE 2, burst, drive, lunge, pitch, ‖splunge

rel bound, jump, leap, spring; impel, move

dive *n* a shabby or disreputable place for drinking or entertainment <got a schooner of beer at the *dive* down the street>

syn barrelhouse, hangout, honky-tonk, joint

rel dump, hole; bar, barroom, lounge, pothouse, pub, saloon, taproom, tavern

‖**diver** *n* ***syn*** PICKPOCKET, ‖cannon, cutpurse, ‖dip, purse cutter; ‖wire

diverge *vb* 1 ***syn*** SWERVE 2, depart, deviate, digress

rel differ, disagree, vary; divide, part, separate

ant converge; conform

2 ***syn*** DIGRESS 2, depart, divagate, excurse, ramble, stray, wander

divergence *n* 1 ***syn*** DISSIMILARITY, alterity, difference, discrepancy, dissemblance, dissimilitude, distinction, divergency, otherness, unlikeness

rel diversity, variety

con accord, concord, consonance, harmony

ant conformity, correspondence

2 ***syn*** DEVIATION 1, aberration, deflection, departure, diversion, turning

rel division, parting, separation; differing, disagreeing, varying

con agreement, coincidence, concurrence

ant convergence

divergency *n* ***syn*** DISSIMILARITY, alterity, difference, discrepancy, dissemblance, dissimilitude, distinction, divergence, otherness, unlikeness

divergent *adj* 1 ***syn*** DIFFERENT 1, disparate, dissimilar, distant, diverse, unalike, unequal, unlike, unsimilar, various

rel antithetical, contradictory, contrary, opposite; aberrant, abnormal, atypical

con alike, identical, parallel, same

ant convergent

2 ***syn*** IRREGULAR 1, abnormal, anomalous, deviant, off-key, unnatural, unregular

divers *adj* ***syn*** SEVERAL 3, some, sundry, various

divers *pron, pl in constr* ***syn*** SUNDRY, many, ‖several, various

diverse *adj* 1 ***syn*** DIFFERENT 1, disparate, dissimilar, distant, divergent, unalike, unequal, unlike, unsimilar, various

rel contrasted, contrasting, contrastive; contradictory, contrary, opposite

con equal, equivalent, same

ant identical, selfsame

2 ***syn*** DISTINCT 1, different, discrete, separate, several, various

idiom of every description

3 ***syn*** MANIFOLD, diversiform, multifarious, multifold, multiform, multiplex, multivarious

diversely *adv* ***syn*** OTHERWISE 1, differently, ‖othergates, variously

diverseness *n* ***syn*** VARIETY 1, diversity, multeity, multifariousness, multiformity, multiplicity, variousness

diversiform *adj* ***syn*** MANIFOLD, diverse, multifarious, multifold, multiform, multiplex, multivarious

diversion *n* 1 ***syn*** DEVIATION 1, aberration, deflection, departure, divergence, turning

2 ***syn*** PLAY 1, disport, fun, recreation, sport

3 ***syn*** ENTERTAINMENT, amusement, dissipation, distraction, divertissement, recreation

rel frivolity, levity

4 ***syn*** ENJOYMENT 1, delectation, pleasure, relish

diversity *n* ***syn*** VARIETY 1, diverseness, multeity, multifariousness, multiformity, multiplicity, variousness

rel difference, dissimilarity, distinction, divergence, divergency, unlikeness

ant uniformity; identity

divert *vb* 1 ***syn*** TURN 6, avert, deflect, pivot, sheer, veer, volte-face, wheel, whip, whirl

rel swerve; alter, change, modify

con fix, set, settle

2 ***syn*** DISSUADE, deter, disadvise, discourage

rel abstract, detach, disengage

3 ***syn*** AMUSE, entertain, recreate

rel delight, gladden, please, regale, tickle

divertissement *n* ***syn*** ENTERTAINMENT, amusement, dissipation, distraction, diversion, recreation

divest *vb* 1 ***syn*** STRIP 2, bankrupt, bare, denudate, denude, deprive, dismantle, disrobe

ant invest, vest; apparel, attire, clothe

2 ***syn*** DEPRIVE 2, bereave, disinherit, dispossess, lose, oust, rob

rel despoil, plunder, spoil

ant invest, vest

divestiture *n* ***syn*** PRIVATION 2, deprivation, deprivement, dispossession, loss

divide *vb* 1 ***syn*** SEPARATE 1, break up, dichotomize, disjoin, disjoint, dissect, divorce, part, sever, sunder

---

rel carve, chop, cut
ant unite
2 *syn* DISTRIBUTE 1, deal, disburse, dispense, disperse, ‖divvy, dole (out), lot (out), measure (out), partition
3 *syn* APPORTION 2, ‖divvy, parcel, portion, prorate, quota, ration, share, ‖shift
rel allocate, allot, assign
4 *syn* DIFFER 2, disaccord, disagree, discord, dissent, vary
rel part, separate
con combine, concur, conjoin, cooperate
ant unite

dividend *n syn* REWARD, carrot, guerdon, meed, plum, premium, prize

divine *n syn* CLERGYMAN, churchman, cleric, clerical, clerk, ecclesiastic, minister, parson, preacher, reverend

divine *vb syn* FORESEE, anticipate, apprehend, forefeel, foreknow, preknow, previse, prevision, see, visualize

divine *adj* **1** of or relating to God or a god <the *divine* will>
syn deific, godly
rel chthonian
2 like or like that of God or a god <men who aspire to *divine* honors>
syn deific, godlike
rel extramundane, superhuman, superphysical, transmundane
3 *syn* MARVELOUS 2, ‖cool, ‖dandy, dreamy, groovy, ‖keen, ‖neat, nifty, sensational, swell

division *n* **1** *syn* PART 1, cut, member, moiety, parcel, piece, portion, section, segment
2 *syn* SEPARATION 1, detachment, dissolution, disunion, divorce, divorcement, partition, rupture, split-up
3 *syn* DISCORD, conflict, difference, disaccord, disharmony, dissension, dissent, dissidence, dissonance, variance

divorce *n syn* SEPARATION 1, detachment, dissolution, disunion, division, divorcement, partition, rupture, split-up

divorce *vb* **1** *syn* SEPARATE 1, break up, disjoin, disjoint, dissever, disunite, divide, part, sever, sunder
rel disaffect, wean
2 to end a marriage by legal action <unable to agree, they decided to *divorce*> <*divorced* his wife>
syn dismiss, put away, unmarry
rel break up, separate, split; annul, cancel

divorcement *n syn* SEPARATION 1, detachment, dissolution, disunion, division, divorce, partition, rupture, split-up

divulge *vb syn* REVEAL 1, betray, blab (out), disclose, discover, give away, mouth, spill, tell, unclose
rel proclaim; gossip, tattle

‖**divvy** *vb* **1** *syn* DISTRIBUTE 1, deal, disburse, dispense, disperse, divide, dole (out), lot (out), measure (out), partition
2 *syn* APPORTION 2, divide, parcel, portion, prorate, quota, ration, share, ‖shift

‖**dizzard** *n syn* DUNCE, blockhead, boob, chump, dimwit, dolt, dope, moron, nitwit, numskull

dizzy *adj* **1** *syn* GIDDY 1, bird-witted, empty-headed, featherbrained, flighty, frivolous, harebrained, scatterbrained, silly, skittish
rel asinine, fatuous, foolish; inane
2 affected by a sensation of being whirled about or around <the speed with which she dispatched her tasks made the onlookers *dizzy*>
syn giddy, light, light-headed, swimming, swimmy, vertiginous
rel reeling, whirling; bewildered, confounded, distracted, puzzled; addled, befuddled, confused, dazed, dazzled, fuddled, muddled
idiom with spots before one's eyes
3 *syn* EXCESSIVE 1, exorbitant, extravagant, extreme, immoderate, inordinate, towering, unconscionable, undue, unmeasurable

dizzy *vb syn* CONFUSE 2, addle, ball up, befuddle, bewilder, fluster, fuddle, mix up, muddle, throw off

do *vb* **1** *syn* PERFORM 2, achieve, execute
2 *syn* CLOSE 3, complete, conclude, determine, end, finish, halt, terminate, wind up, wrap up
3 *syn* ACT 1, discourse, enact, impersonate, perform, personate, play, playact
4 *syn* CHEAT, beat, bilk, chouse, cozen, defraud, diddle, flimflam, gyp, overreach
idiom do out of, sell one a bill of goods
5 *syn* COOK 1
6 *syn* BEHAVE 1, acquit, act, bear, comport, conduct, demean, deport, go on, quit
7 *syn* SHIFT 5, fare, get along, get by, get on, ‖make out, manage, muddle through, stagger (on *or* along)
8 *syn* HAPPEN 1, befall, betide, break, chance, come off, develop, fall out, occur, transpire
9 *syn* TRAVEL 2, cover, pass (over), track, traverse
10 *syn* SERVE 3, suffice, suit
11 *syn* SERVE 5

‖**do** *n syn* SUCCESS, arrival, flying colors, go, prosperity, successfulness

doable *adj syn* POSSIBLE 1, feasible, practicable, viable, workable

doc *n syn* PHYSICIAN, ‖croaker, doctor, MD, medical, mediciner, medico, ‖sawbones

docile *adj syn* OBEDIENT, amenable, biddable, ‖docious, tractable
rel adaptable, pliable, pliant
con obstinate, self-willed, stubborn, willful
ant indocile; ungovernable, unruly

‖**docious** *adj syn* OBEDIENT, amenable, biddable, docile, tractable

dock *n syn* WHARF, berth, jetty, levee, pier, quay, slip

docket *n syn* PROGRAM 1, agenda, calendar, card, programma, schedule, sked, timetable

doctor *n syn* PHYSICIAN, ‖croaker, doc, MD, medical, mediciner, medico, ‖sawbones

doctor *vb* **1** *syn* TREAT 4
2 *syn* MEND 2, do up, fix, overhaul, patch, rebuild, recondition, reconstruct, repair, revamp

---

syn synonym(s) *rel* related word(s)
idiom idiomatic equivalent(s) *con* contrasted word(s)
ant antonym(s) * vulgar
‖ use limited; if in doubt, see a dictionary
The first word in a synonym list when printed in SMALL CAPITALS shows where there is more information about the group. For a more efficient use of this book see Explanatory Notes.

3 ***syn*** ADULTERATE, debase, dope (up), load, sophisticate, weight

doctrinaire *adj* ***syn*** DICTATORIAL, authoritarian, authoritative, dictative, dogmatic, magisterial
rel bullheaded, dogged, mulish, obstinate, pertinacious, pigheaded, stiff-necked, stubborn
ant undoctrinaire

doctrine *n* a principle accepted as valid and authoritative <the *doctrine* of evolution>
syn canon, dogma, tenet
rel instruction, teaching; axiom, basic, fundamental, principle
idiom article of belief (*or* faith)

document *n* something preserved and serving as evidence (as of an event, a situation, or the culture of a period) <ceramic and flint artifacts provide our only *document* of this ancient people>
syn archive(s), monument, record
rel evidence, testimony

doddering *adj* ***syn*** SENILE, doddery, ||doted, doting

doddery *adj* ***syn*** SENILE, doddering, ||doted, doting

dodge *vb* **1** to avoid or evade by some maneuver or shift <*dodging* in and out among the crowd> <*dodged* his pursuer with ease>
syn duck, fence, parry, shirk, sidestep
rel malinger; avoid, elude, escape, evade, skirt; slide, slip; short-circuit
idiom fight shy of
con ||banter, beard, brave, challenge, dare, defy, front, venture; confront, encounter, meet
ant face
2 ***syn*** EQUIVOCATE 2, evade, hedge, pussyfoot, shuffle, sidestep, tergiversate, tergiverse, weasel

dodo *n* ***syn*** DUNCE, boob, dimwit, dolt, dummy, idiot, moron, nitwit, numskull, simpleton

||**dods** *n pl* ***syn*** SULK, ||dorts, grumps, mulligrubs, mumps, pouts, sullens

||**dodunk** *n* ***syn*** DUNCE, boob, clod, dimwit, dolt, dumbbell, ||goon, ignoramus, lame-brain, pinhead

doff *vb* ***syn*** REMOVE 3, douse, put off, take off

do for *vb* ***syn*** HELP 1, abet, aid, assist, benefact, help out, stead

dofunny *n* ***syn*** DOODAD, dingus, doohickey, gadget, gizmo, ||hootenanny, jigger, thingum, thingumajig, thingumbob

dog *n* **1** a highly variable carnivorous domesticated mammal <many households have *dogs* as pets>
syn bowwow, canine, hound, ||pooch, tyke
rel pup, puppy; cur, ||feist, mongrel, mutt
2 ***syn*** SNOT 1, cur, ||prick, scum, *shithead, skunk, snake, stinkard, toad, *turd
3 ***syn*** FRANKFURTER, frank, hot dog, wiener, wienerwurst, ||wienie
4 ***syn*** JALOPY, clunker, crate, heap, junker, wreck

dog *vb* ***syn*** TAIL, bedog, shadow, tag, trail

Dogberry *n* ***syn*** POLICEMAN, bluecoat, cop, ||copper, ||flatfoot, ||fuzz, ||heat, man, officer, police officer

dogfall *n* ***syn*** DRAW 4, deadlock, stalemate, standoff, tie

dogfight *n* ***syn*** BRAWL 2, broil, donnybrook, fracas, fray, free-for-all, melee, row, ruction, set-to

dogged *adj* **1** ***syn*** INFLEXIBLE 2, adamant, brassbound, inexorable, obdurate, relentless, rigid, single-minded, steadfast, unbending
2 ***syn*** PERSISTENT 1, insistent, perseverant, perseverative, persevering, persisting, persistive

doggery *n* ***syn*** RABBLE 2, canaille, hoi polloi, mass(es), mob, other half, proletariat, riffraff, trash, unwashed

doggish *adj* ***syn*** DAPPER, bandbox, doggy, natty, sassy, sparkish, spiffy, spruce, sprucy, well-groomed

doggone *adj* **1** ***syn*** DAMNED 2, blankety-blank, blasted, blessed, ||blooming, confounded, dad-burned, darn, dratted, infernal
2 ***syn*** UTTER, absolute, blasted, blessed, ||blooming, confounded, out-and-out, outright, rank, unmitigated

doggy *adj* ***syn*** DAPPER, bandbox, doggish, natty, sassy, sparkish, spiffy, spruce, sprucy, well-groomed

dogma *n* ***syn*** DOCTRINE, canon, tenet
rel belief, conviction, persuasion, view

dogmatic *adj* **1** ***syn*** DICTATORIAL, authoritarian, authoritative, dictative, doctrinaire, magisterial
2 ***syn*** DEDUCTIVE, a priori, deducible, derivable, reasoned

dog nap *n* ***syn*** NAP, catnap, ||dover, forty winks, siesta, snooze

dog's age *n* ***syn*** AGE 2, aeon, blue moon, coon's age, donkey's years, eternity, long

do in *vb* **1** ***syn*** RUIN 2, bankrupt, dilapidate, shipwreck, wreck
2 ***syn*** MURDER 1, assassinate, ||bump off, cool, ||dust off, execute, finish, knock off, liquidate, put away
3 ***syn*** EXHAUST 4, fag, frazzle, knock out, outtire, outwear, ||poop, prostrate, ||sew up, wear out

doing *n* ***syn*** ACTION 1, accomplishment, act, thing

doit *n* ***syn*** PARTICLE, damn, ||dite, dram, drop, hoot, iota, jot, whit, whoop

doldrums *n pl* **1** ***syn*** TEDIUM, boredom, ennui, yawn
rel blues, dejection, depression, dumps, gloom; apathy, disinterest, indifference, listlessness
con high spirits, spirits
2 ***syn*** ABEYANCE, abeyancy, cold storage, dormancy, intermission, interruption, latency, quiescence, quiescency, suspension
rel depression, retardation, slump, stagnation; inactivity

dole (out) *vb* **1** ***syn*** ADMINISTER 2, apportion, deal (out), dispense, mete (out), portion (out), share out
2 ***syn*** DISTRIBUTE 1, deal, disburse, dispense, disperse, divide, ||divvy, lot (out), measure (out), partition

||**dole** *n* **1** ***syn*** SORROW, affliction, anguish, care, grief, heartache, heartbreak, regret, rue, woe
2 ***syn*** MISFORTUNE, adversity, contretemps, mischance, mishap, tragedy, ||unluck

doleful *adj* **1** ***syn*** DOWNCAST, cast down, crestfallen, dejected, depressed, dispirited, down, downhearted, down-in-the-mouth, woebegone
2 ***syn*** WOEFUL 1, afflicted, dolent, dolorous, miserable, rueful, ruthful, sorrowful, wretched

---

syn synonym(s) *rel* related word(s)
idiom idiomatic equivalent(s) *con* contrasted word(s)
ant antonym(s) * vulgar
|| use limited; if in doubt, see a dictionary
The first word in a synonym list when printed in SMALL CAPITALS shows where there is more information about the group. For a more efficient use of this book see Explanatory Notes.

3 ***syn*** MELANCHOLY 2, dolesome, dolorous, lamentable, lugubrious, mournful, plaintive, rueful, sorrowful, woeful
rel grieving, mourning, sorrowing; piteous, pitiful
con blithe, blithesome, radiant, sparkling, sunny
ant cheerful, cheery

dolefuls *n pl, used with* the ***syn*** SADNESS, blues, dejection, depression, dinge, (the) dismals, dumps, gloom, heavyheartedness, melancholy

dolent *adj* ***syn*** WOEFUL 1, afflicted, doleful, dolorous, miserable, rueful, ruthful, sorrowful, wretched

dolesome *adj* ***syn*** MELANCHOLY 2, doleful, dolorous, lamentable, lugubrious, mournful, plaintive, rueful, sorrowful, woeful

dolittle *n* ***syn*** SLUGGARD, bum, do-nothing, faineant, idler, lazybones, loafer, slouch, slug, slugabed

dollar *n* a currency bill representing one hundred cents <had a single *dollar* left>
syn bill, ‖bone, ‖buck, ‖fish, ‖frogskin, ‖ironman, oner, rock, ‖skin, ‖smacker, ‖smackeroo

dollop *n* ***syn*** DRAM 1, drop, jolt, nip, shot, slug, snifter, snort, toothful, tot

doll out *vb* ***syn*** DRESS UP 1, deck (out), doll up, fix up, gussy up, primp, smarten (up), spiff, spruce (up), tog (out *or* up)

doll up *vb* ***syn*** DRESS UP 1, deck (out), doll out, fix up, gussy up, primp, smarten (up), spiff, spruce (up), tog (out *or* up)

dolor *n* ***syn*** DISTRESS, agony, misery, passion, suffering
con blessedness, bliss, felicity, happiness
ant beatitude

dolorous *adj* 1 ***syn*** DEPLORABLE, afflictive, calamitous, dire, distressing, grievous, heartbreaking, lamentable, regrettable, woeful
2 ***syn*** WOEFUL 1, afflicted, doleful, dolent, miserable, rueful, ruthful, sorrowful, wretched
3 ***syn*** MELANCHOLY 2, doleful, dolesome, lamentable, lugubrious, mournful, plaintive, rueful, sorrowful, woeful

dolt *n* ***syn*** DUNCE, boob, booby, chump, dolthead, fathead, goof, ‖goon, lunkhead, oaf

dolthead *n* ***syn*** DUNCE, boob, booby, chump, dolt, fathead, goof, ‖goon, lunkhead, oaf

doltish *adj* ***syn*** STUPID 1, beetleheaded, blockheaded, blockish, dense, dull, dumb, duncical, fatheaded, thick

domain *n* ***syn*** FIELD, bailiwick, champaign, demesne, dominion, province, sphere, terrain, territory, walk

‖**dome** *n* ***syn*** HEAD 1, ‖bean, ‖belfry, ‖coco, ‖conk, headpiece, noddle, noggin, noodle, poll

domestic *adj* 1 of or relating to the household or family <*domestic* chores required to maintain a home>
syn family, home, household
con civic, public; personal, private; business, occupational, professional

2 of, relating to, or carried on within an indicated or implied country <charts of *domestic* as well as foreign waters>
syn home, ‖inland, internal, intestine, municipal, national, native
ant foreign
3 ***syn*** TAME, domesticated, domitae naturae, subdued, submissive

domesticate *vb* to adapt (an animal or plant) to life in intimate association with and to the advantage of man <the man who *domesticated* the first dog>
syn domesticize, domiciliate, master, tame
rel gentle, subdue; housebreak; break, bust, train

domesticated *adj* ***syn*** TAME, domestic, domitae naturae, subdued, submissive

domesticize *vb* ***syn*** DOMESTICATE, domiciliate, master, tame

domicile *n* ***syn*** HABITATION 2, abode, commorancy, dwelling, home, house, residence, residency

domicile *vb* ***syn*** HARBOR 2, bestow, billet, board, entertain, house, hut, lodge, put up, quarter

domiciliate *vb* 1 ***syn*** HARBOR 2, billet, board, bunk, domicile, house, hut, lodge, put up, quarter
2 ***syn*** DOMESTICATE, domesticize, master, tame

dominance *n* ***syn*** SUPREMACY, ascendancy, domination, dominion, masterdom, preeminence, preponderance, prepotence, prepotency, sovereignty

dominant *adj* 1 superior to all others in power, influence, or importance <the Sumerians were a *dominant* race of ancient times>
syn ascendant, master, outweighing, overbalancing, overbearing, overweighing, paramount, predominant, predominate, preponderant, prevalent, regnant, sovereign
rel prevailing; preeminent, supreme, surpassing, transcendent; chief, first, foremost, leading, main, principal; governing, ruling
con collateral, dependent, secondary, subject, tributary; unimportant
ant subordinate
2 ***syn*** CHIEF 2, capital, ‖cock, main, major, number one, predominant, preeminent, principal, stellar

dominate *vb* 1 ***syn*** GOVERN 3, control, direct, handle, manage
2 ***syn*** RULE 2, domineer, predominate, preponderate, prevail, reign
3 ***syn*** OVERLOOK 2, look down, overtop, tower (above *or* over)

domination *n* 1 ***syn*** SUPREMACY, ascendancy, dominance, dominion, masterdom, preeminence, preponderancy, prepotence, prepotency, sovereignty
2 ***syn*** POWER 1, authority, command, control, jurisdiction, mastery, might, strings, sway

dominator *n* ***syn*** LEADER 2, boss, chief, chieftain, cock, head, headman, hierarch, honcho, master

domineer *vb* ***syn*** RULE 2, dominate, predominate, preponderate, prevail, reign

domineering *adj* ***syn*** MASTERFUL 1, bossy, high-handed, imperative, imperial, imperious, magisterial, overbearing, peremptory
rel arrogant, insolent, lordly
con obsequious, servile, slavish; bootlicking, groveling, sycophantic, toadying

---

syn synonym(s) ***rel*** related word(s)
idiom idiomatic equivalent(s) ***con*** contrasted word(s)
ant antonym(s) * vulgar
‖ use limited; if in doubt, see a dictionary
The first word in a synonym list when printed in SMALL CAPITALS shows where there is more information about the group. For a more efficient use of this book see Explanatory Notes.

ant subservient; fawning

‖**dominie** *n* ***syn*** CLERGYMAN, ‖blackcoat, churchman, cleric, clerical, ‖devil-dodger, divine, ecclesiastic, minister, parson

dominion *n* **1** ***syn*** SUPREMACY, ascendancy, ascendant, dominance, domination, masterdom, preeminence, prepotence, prepotency, sovereignty
2 ***syn*** FIELD, bailiwick, champaign, demesne, domain, province, sphere, terrain, territory, walk
3 ***syn*** OWNERSHIP, possession, possessorship, property, proprietary, proprietorship

domino *n* ***syn*** MASK 1, doughface, false face, visor, vizard

domitae naturae *adj* ***syn*** TAME, domestic, domesticated, subdued, submissive

don *vb* **1** to place on one's person (an article of clothing) < *donned* a raincoat for his trip >
syn assume, draw on, get on, huddle (on), put on, slip (on), throw
rel apparel, array, attire, clad, clothe, dress, enclothe, garb, garment, raiment
con cast, pull (off), remove, take off, throw off; unclothe, undress; disrobe
ant doff
2 to clothe or envelop oneself in <able to *don* a new personality at will>
syn assume, pull, put on, strike, take on
rel camouflage, color, disguise; belie, falsify, garble, misrepresent

donate *vb* ***syn*** GIVE 1, bestow, devote, give away, hand out, present

donation *n* a gift of money or its equivalent to a charity, humanitarian cause, or public institution <sought *donations* for victims of the flood>
syn alms, benefaction, beneficence, charity, contribution, offering
rel aid, assistance, help, relief; philanthropy; bequest, endowment; appropriation, grant, subsidy, subvention; allowance, dole, pittance, ration

donator *n* ***syn*** DONOR, bestower, conferrer, giver, presenter

done *adj* **1** ***syn*** DECOROUS 1, becoming, befitting, comme il faut, conforming, correct, decent, nice, proper, right
2 ***syn*** COMPLETE 4, completed, concluded, down, ended, finished, terminated, through
3 ***syn*** EFFETE 2, all in, depleted, done in, drained, exhausted, far-gone, spent, used up, worn-out
4 ***syn*** THROUGH 4, washed-up

done for *adj* ***syn*** THROUGH 3, finished, washed-up

done in *adj* ***syn*** EFFETE 2, all in, depleted, done, exhausted, far-gone, spent, used up, washed-out, worn-out

‖**doney** *n* ***syn*** GIRL FRIEND 1, best girl, ‖chick, gal, girl, lady friend, lass, mouse, popsy

‖**donicker** *n* ***syn*** TOILET, ‖can, *crapper, john, johnny, latrine, ‖loo, ‖pot, ‖potty, ‖throne

Don Juan *n* **1** ***syn*** GALLANT 2, amorist, Casanova, lothario, paramour, Romeo
2 ***syn*** WOLF, Casanova, chaser, ladies' man, lady-killer, masher, philander, philanderer, womanizer

donk *n* ***syn*** DONKEY 1, ass, burro, jackass, ‖moke, ‖neddy, ‖Rocky Mountain canary

donkey *n* **1** the domestic ass <the *donkey,* a typical pack animal>
syn ass, burro, donk, jackass, ‖moke, ‖neddy, ‖Rocky Mountain canary
rel ‖dickey, jack; hinny, mule; jennet, jenny, jenny ass
2 ***syn*** FOOL 1, ass, *damfool, idiot, imbecile, jackass, jerk, nincompoop, ‖schmo, ‖schmuck

donkeyish *adj* ***syn*** FOOLISH 2, absurd, ‖balmy, crazy, fantastic, harebrained, idleheaded, loony, silly, tomfool

donkey's years *n pl* ***syn*** AGE 2, aeon, blue moon, coon's age, dog's age, eternity, long

donkeywork *n* ***syn*** WORK 2, bullwork, drudge, drudgery, grind, labor, moil, plugging, slavery, toil

donnybrook *n* ***syn*** BRAWL 2, affray, bobbery, fight, fracas, fray, free-for-all, knock-down-and-drag-out, melee, ruction

donor *n* one that gives something to another <a *donor* of funds to research foundations>
syn bestower, conferrer, donator, giver, presenter
rel contributor, subscriber

do-nothing *n* ***syn*** SLUGGARD, bum, dolittle, faineant, idler, lazybones, loafer, slouch, slug, slugabed

‖**donsie** *adj* ***syn*** UNWELL, ailing, indisposed, low, mean, off-color, offish, poorly, sickly, underly

doodad *n* something trivial which is hard to classify or whose name is unknown <wondered what the little round *doodad* was for>
syn business, dingus, dofunny, doohickey, gadget, gizmo, ‖hootenanny, jigger, rigamajig, thingum, thingumajig, thingumbob, thingummy; *compare* GADGET 1, WHAT-DO-YOU-CALL-IT

doodle *n* ***syn*** FOOL 1, ass, *damfool, donkey, idiot, imbecile, jackass, jerk, nincompoop, ninny

‖**doodle** *vb* ***syn*** CHEAT, beat, bilk, chisel, cozen, defraud, do, flimflam, gyp, overreach

doodle *vb* ***syn*** FIDDLE 2, mess, mess around, potter, puddle, putter, tinker

doohickey *n* ***syn*** DOODAD, dingus, dofunny, gadget, gizmo, ‖hootenanny, jigger, thingum, thingumajig, thingumbob

doom *n* ***syn*** FATE, circumstance, destiny, kismet, lot, moira, portion, weird
rel calamity, cataclysm, catastrophe, disaster, tragedy

doom *vb* ***syn*** SENTENCE, condemn, damn, proscribe

doom (to) *vb* ***syn*** PREDESTINE 1, destine, determine, fate, foreordain, predetermine, preform, preordain

doomed *adj* ***syn*** DAMNED 1, condemned, lost

doomful *adj* ***syn*** OMINOUS, apocalyptic, baleful, baneful, dire, direful, ill-boding, inauspicious, unlucky, unpropitious

door *n* **1** an opening by which one can enter or leave a structure and especially a building <looked through the front *door*>

---

syn synonym(s) *rel* related word(s)
idiom idiomatic equivalent(s) *con* contrasted word(s)
ant antonym(s) * vulgar
‖ use limited; if in doubt, see a dictionary
The first word in a synonym list when printed in SMALL CAPITALS shows where there is more information about the group. For a more efficient use of this book see Explanatory Notes.

syn doorway, entrance, entranceway, entry, entryway, portal
2 a means or right of entering, approaching, or participating <viewed education as the *door* to success>
syn access, adit, admission, admittance, entrance, entrée, entry, ingress, way

doormat *n syn* WEAKLING, baby, invertebrate, jellyfish, milksop, Milquetoast, mollycoddle, namby-pamby, pantywaist, sissy

doorway *n syn* DOOR 1, entrance, entranceway, entry, entryway, portal

||**doozer** *n syn* ||DILLY, ||corker, ||daisy, dandy, ||dinger, humdinger, jim-dandy, ||lalapalooza, ||lulu, peach

dope *n* **1** *syn* DRUG 2, ||hop, narcotic, opiate
2 *syn* DUNCE, chowderhead, chucklehead, ||dumbhead, dunderhead, lame-brain, noddy, noddle, ||schnook, ||stupe

dope (up) *vb syn* ADULTERATE, debase, doctor, load, sophisticate, weight

doped *adj syn* DRUGGED, high, hopped-up, spaced-out, stoned, tripped out, turned on, ||wiped out, zonked

||**dope out** *vb* **1** *syn* SOLVE 2, ||cipher, clear up, decipher, dissolve, figure out, puzzle out, resolve, unravel, unriddle
2 *syn* INFER, collect, conclude, deduce, deduct, derive, gather, judge, make, make out
3 *syn* PLAN 2, arrange, blueprint, cast, chart, design, devise, project

dopey *adj syn* LETHARGIC, comatose, heavy, hebetudinous, sluggish, slumberous, stupid, torpid

||**do–re–mi** *n syn* MONEY, ||blunt, ||brass, ||bread, ||cabbage, ||chips, ||dibs, ||dinero, dough, filthy lucre

||**dorm** *vb syn* DOZE, drowse, ||sloom, slumber, ||snoozle, ||sog

dormancy *n syn* ABEYANCE, abeyancy, cold storage, doldrums, intermission, interruption, latency, quiescence, quiescency, suspension

dormant *adj syn* LATENT, abeyant, lurking, potential, prepatent, quiescent
ant active

||**dort** *vb syn* SULK, grump, ||mump, pet, pout, ||sull

||**dorts** *n pl syn* SULK, ||dods, grumps, mulligrubs, mumps, pouts, sullens

||**dorty** *adj syn* SULLEN, ||chuff, ||chuffy, crabbed, dour, gloomy, glum, sulky, surly, ugly

||**doss** *n syn* SLEEP 1, ||shut-eye, slumber

||**doss** *vb syn* SLEEP, slumber

dot *n syn* POINT 11, flyspeck, mote, speck

dot *vb* **1** *syn* SPECKLE 1, bespeckle, freckle, pepper, speck, sprinkle, stipple
2 *syn* SPOT 2, pimple, speckle, sprinkle, stud

dot *n syn* DOWRY, dower, marriage portion

---

syn synonym(s) *rel* related word(s)
idiom idiomatic equivalent(s) *con* contrasted word(s)
ant antonym(s) * vulgar
|| use limited; if in doubt, see a dictionary
The first word in a synonym list when printed in SMALL CAPITALS shows where there is more information about the group. For a more efficient use of this book see Explanatory Notes.

dotage *n* advanced age accompanied by a decline of mental poise and alertness <a doddering eighty-year-old entering his *dotage*>
syn second childhood, senility; *compare* OLD AGE
rel decrepitude, feebleness, infirmity; age, elderliness, senectitude
con adolescence, youth; maturity

dote (on *or* upon) *vb syn* ADORE 3, idolize, worship
rel enjoy, fancy, like
idiom be sweet on
ant loathe

||**doted** *adj syn* SENILE, doddering, doddery, doting

doting *adj* **1** *syn* SENILE, doddering, doddery, ||doted
2 *syn* LOVING, affectionate, dear, devoted, fond, lovesome
rel asinine, fatuous, foolish, silly, simple

dottiness *n syn* FOOLISHNESS, absurdity, craziness, folly, inanity, insanity, preposterousness, senselessness, silliness, witlessness

dotty *adj* **1** *syn* INFATUATED, besotted, enamored, infatuate
2 *syn* FOOLISH 2, absurd, ||balmy, crazy, fantastic, insane, loony, ||potty, preposterous, wacky

double *adj* **1** *syn* TWOFOLD 1, bifold, binary, double-barreled, dual, dualistic, duple, duplex
2 *syn* TWIN, dual, paired
3 *syn* TWOFOLD 2, double-barreled
4 *syn* INSINCERE, ambidextrous, double-dealing, double-faced, doublehearted, double-minded, double-tongued, hypocritical, left-handed, mala fide

double *n* **1** *syn* MATE 5, companion, coordinate, duplicate, fellow, match, reciprocal, twin
2 *syn* IMAGE 1, picture, portrait, ringer, simulacrum, spit, spitting image
3 *syn* TURN 2, bend, deflection, deviation, shift, tack, yaw
rel departure, digression, divergence, swerving, veering

double *vb* **1** to make twice as great or as many <*doubled* the amount of his salary>
syn dualize, dupe, duplicate
rel replicate; amplify, augment, enlarge, increase, magnify; supplement
con decrease, lessen, minimize
ant halve
2 to make of two thicknesses by turning or bending usually in the middle <he *doubled* the towel for better absorbency>
syn fold
rel pleat, plicate, turn over
3 *syn* ESCAPE 2, avoid, bilk, duck, elude, eschew, evade, shun, shy
4 *syn* DUB

double–barreled *adj* **1** *syn* TWOFOLD 2, double
2 *syn* TWOFOLD 1, bifold, binary, double, dual, dualistic, duple, duplex

double–cross *vb* **1** *syn* DECEIVE, beguile, betray, bluff, four-flush, humbug, illude, juggle, mislead, take in
2 *syn* BETRAY 2, cross, sell, sell out, ||split

double–dealer *n syn* SWINDLER, cheat, confidence man, con man, defrauder, diddler, flimflammer, gyp, mountebank, sharper

double–dealing *n syn* DECEPTION 1, chicane, chicanery, ||dipsy-doodle, fourberie, fraud, hanky-panky, highbinding, sharp practice, trickery

double–dealing *adj syn* INSINCERE, ambidextrous, double, double-faced, doublehearted, double-minded, double-tongued, hypocritical, left-handed, mala fide

double–distilled *adj syn* UTTER, absolute, blasted, blessed, complete, confounded, gross, infernal, out-and-out, rank

||**double–dog dare** *vb syn* FACE 3, ||banter, beard, brave, challenge, dare, defy, front, outdare, venture

double–dome *n syn* INTELLECTUAL 2, Brahmin, egghead, highbrow

double–dyed *adj syn* UTTER, absolute, blasted, blessed, complete, confounded, gross, infernal, out-and-out, rank

double–edged *adj syn* OBSCURE 3, ambiguous, amphibological, double-faced, equivocal, tenebrous, uncertain, unclear, unintelligible, vague

double entendre *n syn* AMBIGUITY, amphibology, double meaning, equivocality, equivocation, equivoque, tergiversation

double–faced *adj* **1** *syn* OBSCURE 3, ambiguous, amphibological, double-edged, equivocal, tenebrous, uncertain, unclear, unintelligible, vague
2 *syn* INSINCERE, ambidextrous, double, double-dealing, doublehearted, double-minded, double-tongued, hypocritical, left-handed, mala fide

doublehearted *adj syn* INSINCERE, ambidextrous, double, double-dealing, double-faced, double-minded, double-tongued, hypocritical, left-handed, mala fide

double meaning *n syn* AMBIGUITY, amphibology, double entendre, equivocality, equivocation, equivoque, tergiversation

double–minded *adj* **1** *syn* VACILLATING 2, halting, hesitant, hesitating, indecisive, irresolute, tentative, uncertain, undecisive, wavering
idiom of two minds
2 *syn* INSINCERE, ambidextrous, double, double-dealing, double-faced, doublehearted, double-minded, double-tongued, hypocritical, left-handed, mala fide

doublet *n syn* COUPLE, brace, duo, dyad, pair, twosome

double–talk *n* **1** *syn* NONSENSE 2, balderdash, ||baloney, ||bull, bunkum, drivel, flimflam, hokum, jazz, twaddle
2 *syn* GOBBLEDYGOOK, gibberish

double–tongued *adj syn* INSINCERE, ambidextrous, double, double-dealing, double-faced, doublehearted, double-minded, hypocritical, left-handed, mala fide

doubt *vb* **1** *syn* QUESTION 2, challenge, dispute, mistrust
2 *syn* DISTRUST, misdoubt, mistrust, suspect, ||suspicion
con accredit, credit, trust; accept, believe, ||buy, swallow

doubt *n syn* UNCERTAINTY, concern, dubiety, dubiosity, incertitude, mistrust, skepticism, suspicion, uncertitude, wonder
rel dubiousness, questionableness; disbelief, incredulity, unbelief
con dependence, faith, reliance, trust
ant certitude; confidence

doubtable *adj syn* DOUBTFUL 1, ambiguous, borderline, dubious, dubitable, equivocal, open, problematic, suspect, undecided
ant undoubtable

doubter *n syn* SKEPTIC, doubting Thomas, headshaker, Pyrrhonian, Pyrrhonist, unbeliever, zetetic

doubtful *adj* **1** not having or affording assurance of the certainty or soundness of something or someone <their chance of success is *doubtful*>
syn ambiguous, borderline, clouded, doubtable, dubious, dubitable, equivocal, fishy, impugnable, indecisive, open, precarious, problematic, queasy, shady, shaky, suspect, suspicious, uncertain, unclear, undecided, uneasy, unsettled, unstable, unsure; *compare* MOOT
rel question-begging; touch-and-go; chancy, insecure, questionable, speculative; hazy, obscure; unlikely; contingent, iffy
idiom at issue, in dispute, in doubt, in question
con decisive, open-and-shut, positive, sure; inarguable, incontestable, unarguable, undeniable, undoubted, unquestionable
ant indubitable
2 *syn* MOOT, arguable, debatable, disputable, dubious, mootable, problematic, questionable, uncertain
3 *syn* IMPROBABLE 1, dubious, questionable, unlikely

doubtfully *adv syn* ASKANCE 2, distrustfully, mistrustfully, skeptically, suspiciously

doubtfulness *n syn* UNCERTAINTY, concern, doubt, dubiety, dubiosity, dubitancy, mistrust, skepticism, suspicion, uncertitude

doubting Thomas *n syn* SKEPTIC, doubter, headshaker, Pyrrhonian, Pyrrhonist, unbeliever, zetetic

doubtless *adv* **1** *syn* EASILY 2, absolutely, definitely, doubtlessly, positively, unequivocally, unquestionably
2 *syn* PRESUMABLY, assumably, likely, presumptively, probably

doubtlessly *adv* **1** *syn* WELL 7, easily, indeed, really, truly, undoubtedly
ant doubtfully
2 *syn* EASILY 2, absolutely, definitely, doubtless, positively, unequivocally, unquestionably

dough *n syn* MONEY, ||bread, cash, ||chips, ||coin, currency, ||greenbacks, ||jack, legal tender, ||scratch

doughface *n syn* MASK 1, domino, false face, visor, vizard

||**doughhead** *n syn* DUNCE, blockhead, bonehead, dimwit, dumbbell, dummy, fathead, knucklehead, nitwit, numskull

doughty *adj syn* BRAVE 1, bold, dauntless, fearless, ||gutsy, manly, plucky, spunky, unafraid, undaunted

doughy *adj syn* PALE 1, ashen, ashy, blanched, colorless, complexionless, livid, lurid, pallid, waxen

do up *vb syn* MEND 2, doctor, fix, overhaul, patch, rebuild, recondition, reconstruct, repair, revamp

dour *adj* **1** *syn* GRIM 2, austere, bleak, hard, harsh, severe, stringent
rel rigid, rigorous, strict; implacable
2 *syn* SULLEN, crabbed, ||dorty, gloomy, glum, morose, saturnine, sulky, surly, ugly

---

‖**douse** *n* ***syn*** BLOW 1, bang, bash, bat, belt, bop, crack, slam, smack, smash

douse *vb* ***syn*** REMOVE 3, doff, put off, take off

douse *vb* **1** ***syn*** DIP 1, duck, dunk, immerse, souse, submerge, submerse
2 ***syn*** WET, deluge, drench, drown, soak, sop, souse
con bake, dehydrate, desiccate, dry, parch
3 ***syn*** SPLASH, plash, slop, slosh, spatter, splatter, splosh, splurge, spurtle, swash
4 ***syn*** EXTINGUISH 1, ‖dout, out, put out, quench, ‖squench

‖**dout** *vb* ***syn*** EXTINGUISH 1, douse, out, put out, quench, ‖squench

dove *n* ***syn*** PACIFIST, pacificist
ant hawk

dovecote *n* a small compartmented raised house or box for domestic pigeons <old countryseats with elaborate stone *dovecotes*>
syn columbary, culverhouse, dovehouse, pigeon house, pigeonry
rel aviary, birdhouse; perch, roost

dovehouse *n* ***syn*** DOVECOTE, columbary, culverhouse, pigeon house, pigeonry

‖**dover** *n* ***syn*** NAP, catnap, dog nap, forty winks, siesta, snooze

dovetail *vb* ***syn*** AGREE 4, accord, check out, correspond, fit (in), go, harmonize, jibe, square, tally

dowager *n* ***syn*** MATRIARCH, dame, grande dame, matron

dowd *n* ***syn*** SLATTERN 1, dowdy, drab, draggle-tail, ‖malkin, slut, ‖streel, traipse

dowdy *n* ***syn*** SLATTERN 1, dowd, drab, draggle-tail, ‖malkin, slut, ‖streel, traipse

dowdy *adj* **1** ***syn*** SLATTERNLY, blowsy, draggletailed, frowsy, slattern, sordid
con chic, fashionable, modish, stylish; flashy, garish, gaudy
ant smart
2 ***syn*** TACKY 2, frumpish, frumpy, outmoded, out-of-date, stodgy, unstylish
ant smart
3 ***syn*** OLD-FASHIONED, antiquated, archaic, bygone, dated, démodé, old hat, outdated, passé, vintage

dower *n* ***syn*** DOWRY, dot, marriage portion

dower *vb* ***syn*** ENDOW 1, crown (with), endue
rel accouter, appoint, equip, furnish, outfit

‖**dowly** *adj* ***syn*** OVERCAST, cloudy, dull, heavy, lowering (*or* louring), nubilous, overclouded

down *adv* **1** from a higher to a lower level <the land sloped *down* toward the sea>
syn downward, downwardly, downwards, netherwards
rel below, earthward, groundward; downgrade, downhill, downslope
con aloft, upward, upwardly, upwards
ant up
2 to completion <wash *down* the car>
syn completely, fully, through-and-through
idiom from top to bottom
3 ***syn*** SERIOUSLY 1, actively, earnestly, for real

down *adj* **1** ***syn*** SLOW 3, off, slack, sluggish
2 ***syn*** DOWNCAST, bad, blue, cast down, dejected, depressed, dispirited, downhearted, hipped, low
ant up
3 ***syn*** SICK 1, ill
4 ***syn*** LOWER, inferior, nether, subjacent, under
ant up
5 ***syn*** COMPLETE 4, completed, concluded, done, ended, finished, terminated, through

down *n* ***syn*** COMEDOWN, descent, discomfiture

down *vb* **1** ***syn*** SWALLOW 1, take
2 ***syn*** DEFEAT 2, best, outdo, ‖pip, worst
3 ***syn*** FELL 1, bowl (down *or* over), bring down, drop, flatten, floor, knock down, lay low, level, mow (down)
4 ***syn*** KILL 1, carry off, cut off, destroy, dispatch, finish, lay low, liquidate, scrag, take off
5 ***syn*** OVERCOME 1, conquer, hurdle, lick, master, surmount, throw

down *n* a soft fluffy material or covering <the *down* on a peach>
syn floss, flue, fluff, fur, fuzz, lint, pile

down–and–out *n* ***syn*** PAUPER, beggar

down–at–heel *adj* ***syn*** SHABBY 1, bedraggled, broken-down, dilapidated, run-down, seedy, tacky, tagrag, tattered, threadbare

downcast *n* ***syn*** DEFEAT 1, beating, debacle, defeasance, downthrow, drubbing, licking, overthrow, rout, shellacking

downcast *adj* low in spirits <felt *downcast* by the rejection>
syn bad, blue, cast down, chapfallen, crestfallen, dejected, depressed, disconsolate, dispirited, doleful, down, downhearted, down-in-the-mouth, downthrown, droopy, dull, heartsick, heartsore, hipped, low, low-spirited, mopey, soul-sick, spiritless, sunk, woebegone; *compare* SAD 1
rel discouraged, disheartened; oppressed, weighed down; distressed, troubled; despondent, forlorn; listless; broody, moody; gloomy, glum, morose
idiom in the depths
con cheerful, happy, joyous, lighthearted; excited, exhilarated, intoxicated; buoyed up, gladdened; encouraged, heartened; animated, gay, lively, sprightly, vivacious; delighted, pleased
ant elated

downcry *vb* ***syn*** DECRY 2, abuse, belittle, depreciate, derogate, detract (from), diminish, discount, disparage, dispraise

downfall *n* **1** ***syn*** DETERIORATION 1, atrophy, decadence, declension, declination, decline, degeneracy, degeneration, dégringolade, devolution
rel comedown, descent, discomfiture, down
2 something that causes a downfall <drink was his *downfall*>
syn bane, destroyer, destruction, ruin, ruination, undoing
rel headache, problem, trouble
idiom road to ruin

---

syn synonym(s) ***rel*** related word(s)
idiom idiomatic equivalent(s) ***con*** contrasted word(s)
ant antonym(s) * vulgar
‖ use limited; if in doubt, see a dictionary
The first word in a synonym list when printed in SMALL CAPITALS shows where there is more information about the group. For a more efficient use of this book see Explanatory Notes.

con aid, help, support

downgrade *n syn* DETERIORATION 1, atrophy, decadence, declension, decline, degeneracy, degeneration, dégringolade, devolution, downfall
ant upgrade

downgrade *vb* **1** *syn* DEPRECIATE 1, decry, devalorize, devaluate, devalue, lower, mark down, undervalue, write down, write off
ant upgrade
2 *syn* DEGRADE 1, break, bump, bust, declass, demerit, demote, disgrade, disrate, reduce
ant upgrade

downgrading *n syn* DEMOTION, degradation, reduction
ant upgrading

downhearted *adj syn* DOWNCAST, blue, dejected, depressed, disconsolate, dispirited, down, low, spiritless, woebegone

down–in–the–mouth *adj syn* DOWNCAST, bad, blue, crestfallen, dejected, depressed, disconsolate, down, downhearted, low

downright *adj* **1** *syn* UTTER, absolute, complete, damned, gross, out-and-out, outright, positive, thoroughgoing, unmitigated
2 being what is stated beyond any possibility of doubt <a *downright* lie>
syn flat, indubitable, unquestionable, up-and-down; *compare* POSITIVE 3
rel out-and-out, sure-enough; absolute, positive; certain, clear

downside–up *adj syn* UPSIDE-DOWN 2, arsy-varsy, topsy-turvy

downslide *n syn* DECLINE 3, dip, downswing, downtrend, downturn, drop, falloff, sag, slip, slump

downswing *n syn* DECLINE 3, dip, downslide, downtrend, downturn, drop, falloff, sag, slip, slump

downthrow *n syn* DEFEAT 1, beating, debacle, defeasance, drubbing, licking, overthrow, rout, shellacking, thrashing

downthrown *adj syn* DOWNCAST, bad, blue, cast down, crestfallen, dejected, depressed, disconsolate, down, downhearted

down–to–date *adj syn* UP-TO-DATE, abreast, au courant, contemporary, red-hot, up, up-to-the-minute

down–to–earth *adj syn* REALISTIC, hard, hard-boiled, hardheaded, matter-of-fact, practical, pragmatic, sober, unfantastic, unidealistic

downtrend *n syn* DECLINE 3, dip, downslide, downswing, downturn, drop, falloff, sag, slip, slump

downtrodden *adj* oppressed by superior power <the *downtrodden* peasants>
syn abject, underfoot
rel oppressed, persecuted; abused, maltreated, mistreated

downturn *n syn* DECLINE 3, dip, downslide, downswing, downtrend, drop, falloff, sag, slip, slump

downward *adv syn* DOWN 1, downwardly, downwards, netherwards
ant upward

downwardly *adv syn* DOWN 1, downward, downwards, netherwards
ant upwardly

downwards *adv syn* DOWN 1, downward, downwardly, netherwards
ant upwards

‖**downy** *adj syn* SLY 2, artful, astute, crafty, cunning, deep, guileful, insidious, tricky, wily

dowry *n* the money, goods, or estate that a woman brings to her husband in marriage <from a poor family, she came to her marriage with no *dowry*>
syn dot, dower, marriage portion
con bride-price, bridewealth; settlement

doxy *n* **1** a usually young woman who engages in promiscuous sexual intercourse <a *doxy* who frequented singles bars>
syn ‖chippy, floozy, grisette, light-o'-love, nymph, nymphet, party girl, roundheel, tart, ‖tootsie; *compare* HARLOT 1, PROSTITUTE, WANTON
idiom woman of easy virtue
‖**2** *syn* MISTRESS, girl friend, inamorata, lover, paramour, woman

doyen *n* **1** *syn* LEADER 1, ‖bell cow, bellwether, dean, guide, lead, pilot
2 *syn* EXPERT, artist, authority, master, master-hand, maven, passed master, proficient, virtuoso

doze *vb* to sleep lightly <he was inclined to *doze* at his desk>
syn ‖dorm, drowse, ‖sloom, slumber, ‖snoozle, ‖sog; *compare* NAP, SLEEP

doze (off) *vb* to fall into a light sleep <*dozed* off while sitting before the fire>
syn drop off, drowse (off)
idiom drift off

doze *n* a light sleep <was caught in a *doze* at his desk>
syn drowse, ‖sloom, slumber; *compare* NAP, SLEEP 1

dozy *adj syn* SLEEPY 1, drowsy, nodding, ‖peepy, ‖sloomy, slumberous, slumbery, snoozy, somnolent, soporific

DP *n syn* REFUGEE, displaced person, émigré, evacuee, fugitive

drab *n* **1** *syn* HAG 2, ‖bag, ‖bat, beldam, biddy, crone, trot, witch
2 *syn* SLATTERN 1, dowd, dowdy, draggle-tail, ‖malkin, slut, ‖streel, traipse
3 *syn* PROSTITUTE, bawd, ‖cruiser, fille de joie, harlot, ‖hooker, hustler, nightwalker, streetwalker, whore

drab *adj* **1** *syn* DULL 8, muddy, murky, subfusc
2 *syn* COLORLESS 2, dull, flat, lackluster, lifeless, lusterless, prosaic, prosy
rel bleak, desolate, dismal, dispiriting, dreary; dingy, faded
con bright, brilliant, luminous

draconian *adj syn* RIGID 3, ironhanded, rigorist, rigorous, strict, stringent, unpermissive

draffy *adj syn* WORTHLESS 1, drossy, good-for-nothing, inutile, ‖no-account, no-good, nothing, unworthy, valueless

draft *n* DRINK 3, drag, drain, drench, ‖peg, swig, swill

---

syn synonym(s) | *rel* related word(s)
idiom idiomatic equivalent(s) | *con* contrasted word(s)
ant antonym(s) | * vulgar
‖ use limited; if in doubt, see a dictionary
The first word in a synonym list when printed in SMALL CAPITALS shows where there is more information about the group. For a more efficient use of this book see Explanatory Notes.

draft *vb* **1** to enroll in the armed forces by compulsion <*drafted* when he was barely eighteen>
syn conscribe, conscript; *compare* CALL UP
rel induct; enlist, enroll, muster (in *or* out); impress, press
2 *syn* SKETCH, adumbrate, block (out), chalk (out), characterize, outline, rough (out), skeleton, skeletonize
3 to formulate and produce <*drafting* plans to meet an emergency>
syn draw up, formulate, frame, make, prepare
rel concoct, contrive, devise, invent; fabricate, fashion, forge, form, manufacture, shape; plan, project; outline, sketch
4 *syn* DRAIN 1, draw, draw off, pump, siphon, tap

drag *n* **1** *syn* DRAW 1, puff, pull
2 *syn* DRINK 3, draft, drain, drench, ‖peg, swig, swill
‖**3** *syn* PULL 2, clout, in, influence
‖**4** *syn* WAY 1, artery, avenue, boulevard, highway, path, road, street, thoroughfare, track

drag *vb* **1** *syn* PULL 2, draw, haul, lug, tow, tug
con propel, push, shove, thrust; drive, impel, move
2 *syn* DELAY 2, dally, dawdle, lag, loiter, poke, procrastinate, put off, tarry, trail
idiom drag one's feet (*or* heels)
con hasten, hurry
3 to hang down and be drawn behind <her dress *dragged* in the dust>
syn draggle, trail, traipse
rel droop, hang, sag

‖**drag down** *vb syn* EARN 1, acquire, bring in, draw down, gain, get, knock down, make, win

dragging *adj syn* LONG 2, drawn-out, ‖dreich, lengthy, long-drawn-out, longsome, overlong, prolonged, protracted

draggle *vb syn* DRAG 3, trail, traipse

draggle–tail *n syn* SLATTERN 1, dowd, dowdy, drab, ‖malkin, slut, ‖streel, traipse

draggletailed *adj syn* SLATTERNLY, blowsy, dowdy, frowsy, slattern, sordid

dragoon *vb syn* INTIMIDATE, browbeat, bulldoze, bully, bullyrag, cow, hector, ‖ruffle, strong-arm, terrorize

drain *vb* **1** to draw off (liquid) by degrees <*drain* the water from the swimming pool>
syn draft, draw, draw off, pump, siphon, tap
rel milk; bleed; suck; empty, exhaust
2 *syn* TIRE 1, fatigue, jade, wear, wear down, weary
3 *syn* DEPLETE, bankrupt, draw, draw down, exhaust, impoverish, use up
idiom bleed white

drain (away) *vb syn* DECREASE, abate, ‖bate, close, diminish, dwindle, lessen, reduce, taper, taper off

drain *n syn* DRINK 3, draft, drag, drench, ‖peg, swig, swill

---

syn synonym(s) | *rel* related word(s)
idiom idiomatic equivalent(s) | *con* contrasted word(s)
ant antonym(s) | * vulgar
‖ use limited; if in doubt, see a dictionary
The first word in a synonym list when printed in SMALL CAPITALS shows where there is more information about the group. For a more efficient use of this book see Explanatory Notes.

drained *adj syn* EFFETE 2, all in, bleary, depleted, exhausted, far-gone, spent, used up, washed-out, worn-out

dram *n* **1** a small quantity of something (as alcoholic liquor) to drink <a *dram* of brandy helped to break his chill>
syn ‖caulker, dollop, drop, jolt, nip, shot, slug, snifter, snort, snorter, spot, toothful, tot, ‖wet
rel draft, drink, ‖peg, potation, pull, swig, swill; finger; jigger; dash; ‖splash; snack; quick one
2 *syn* PARTICLE, bit, crumb, drop, hoot, iota, modicum, ounce, shred, smidgen

drama *n* dramatic art, literature, or affairs <was interested in *drama* during his college years>
syn boards, footlights, (the) stage, theater
rel show business

dramatic *adj* **1** of or relating to drama <made no objections to his son's *dramatic* ambitions>
syn dramaturgic, histrionic, theatral, theatric, theatrical, thespian
2 *syn* THEATRICAL 2
ant undramatic

dramatist *n syn* PLAYWRIGHT, dramatizer, dramaturge

dramatizer *n syn* PLAYWRIGHT, dramatist, dramaturge

dramaturge *n syn* PLAYWRIGHT, dramatist, dramatizer

dramaturgic *adj syn* DRAMATIC 1, histrionic, theatral, theatric, theatrical, thespian

drape *vb* **1** *syn* SWATHE, enswathe, envelop, enwrap, roll, swaddle, wrap (up)
2 *syn* SPRAWL 1, ‖scamble, ‖spelder, spraddle, spread-eagle

dratted *adj syn* DAMNED 2, blasted, blessed, ‖blooming, confounded, dang, darn, doggone, goldarn, infernal

draw *vb* **1** *syn* PULL 2, drag, haul, lug, tow, tug
rel bring, fetch; educe, elicit, evoke, extract
con propel, push, shove, thrust; drive, impel, move
2 *syn* DRAIN 1, draft, draw off, pump, siphon, tap
3 *syn* ATTRACT 1, allure, bewitch, captivate, charm, enchant, fascinate, magnetize, take, wile
4 *syn* INDUCE 1, argue (into), bring around, convince, draw in, draw on, get, persuade, prompt, win (over)
5 *syn* TAKE 14, derive
6 *syn* INFER, collect, conclude, deduce, derive, ‖dope out, gather, judge, make, make out
7 *syn* EXTEND 3, draw out, elongate, lengthen, prolong, prolongate, protract, spin (out), stretch
8 *syn* DEPLETE, bankrupt, drain, draw down, exhaust, impoverish, use up
9 *syn* EVISCERATE, bowel, disembowel, embowel, exenterate, gut, paunch

draw *n* **1** a sucking pull on something (as a sipping straw or cigarette) <took a long *draw* on his pipe before answering>
syn drag, puff, pull
rel smoke; inhale
2 *syn* ADVANTAGE 3, allowance, bulge, ‖deadwood, edge, handicap, head start, odds, start, vantage
3 *syn* ATTRACTION 1, allurement, appeal, attractiveness, call, drawing power, lure, pull, seduction
4 an indecisive ending to a contest or competition <the prizefight ended in a *draw*>
syn deadlock, dogfall, stalemate, standoff, tie
rel dead heat, photo finish; standstill

con loss; win

draw back *vb* ***syn*** DEDUCT 1, discount, knock off, substract, subtract, take, take away, take off, take out

drawback *n* ***syn*** DISADVANTAGE, detriment, disability, handicap
rel evil, ill; inconvenience, trouble
con advantage, edge

draw down *vb* **1** ***syn*** EARN 1, acquire, bring in, ‖drag down, gain, get, knock down, make, win
2 ***syn*** DEPLETE, bankrupt, drain, draw, exhaust, impoverish, use up

draw in *vb* ***syn*** INDUCE 1, argue (into), bring around, convince, get, persuade, prevail (on *or* upon), prompt, talk (into), win (over)

drawing *adj* ***syn*** ATTRACTIVE 1, alluring, appealing, attracting, bewitching, captivating, charming, enchanting, fascinating, magnetic

drawing power *n* ***syn*** ATTRACTION 1, allurement, appeal, attractiveness, call, draw, lure, pull, seduction

drawing room *n* ***syn*** SALON 1, saloon

drawn *adj* ***syn*** HAGGARD, careworn, pinched, worn
con hale, robust

drawn–out *adj* ***syn*** LONG 2, dragging, ‖dreich, lengthy, long-drawn-out, longsome, overlong, prolonged, protracted

draw off *vb* ***syn*** DRAIN 1, draft, draw, pump, siphon, tap
rel abstract; withdraw; move, remove, shift, transfer

draw on *vb* **1** ***syn*** EFFECT 1, bring about, cause, make, produce, secure
2 ***syn*** INDUCE 1, argue (into), bring around, convince, get, persuade, prevail (on *or* upon), prompt, talk (into), win (over)
3 ***syn*** DON 1, assume, get on, huddle (on), put on, slip (on), throw

draw out *vb* ***syn*** EXTEND 3, draw, elongate, lengthen, prolong, prolongate, protract, spin (out), stretch

draw up *vb* **1** ***syn*** DRAFT 3, formulate, frame, make, prepare
2 ***syn*** STOP 4, bring up, fetch up, halt, haul up, pull up

dray horse *n* ***syn*** SLAVE 2, drudge, galley slave, peon, slavey, toiler, workhorse

dread *n* ***syn*** FEAR 1, alarm, consternation, dismay, fright, horror, panic, terror, trepidation, trepidity

dreadful *adj* ***syn*** FEARFUL 3, appalling, awful, formidable, frightful, horrible, horrific, shocking, terrible, terrific

‖**dreadful** *adv* ***syn*** VERY 1, ‖awful, awfully, ‖big, damned, dreadfully, exceedingly, rattling, remarkably, strikingly

dreadful *n* ***syn*** DIME NOVEL, penny dreadful, shilling shocker, shocker, yellowback

dreadfully *adv* ***syn*** VERY 1, ‖awful, awfully, ‖big, damned, ‖dreadful, exceedingly, extremely, strikingly, surpassingly

dream *n* **1** ***syn*** FANCY 4, daydream, fantasy (*or* phantasy), nightmare, phantasm, vision
2 ***syn*** PIPE DREAM, bubble, chimera, fantasy (*or* phantasy), illusion, ‖pipe, rainbow

dream *vb* ***syn*** LONG, ache, crave, hanker, hunger, lust, pine, sigh, suspire, thirst

dreamer *n* one whose conduct is guided more by ideals than practicalities <a *dreamer* proposing glorious plans impossible to make work>
syn castle-builder, idealist, ideologue, utopian, visionary
rel daydreamer, illusionist, lotus-eater, wishful thinker; Don Quixote; theorist
con pragmatist, realist; Babbitt, Philistine; pedant

dream up *vb* ***syn*** CONTRIVE 2, concoct, cook (up), devise, formulate, frame, hatch (up), invent, make up, vamp (up)

dreamy *adj* **1** given to dreaming, reverie, or fancy <a *dreamy* and most impractical person>
syn astral, daydreaming, daydreamy, otherworldly, unworldly, visionary
rel fanciful, idealistic, romantic, whimsical
con down-to-earth, practical, pragmatic, realistic; actual, factual
2 ***syn*** MARVELOUS 2, ‖cool, ‖dandy, divine, glorious, groovy, ‖neat, nifty, peachy, super

drear *adj* ***syn*** GLOOMY 3, black, bleak, depressant, depressive, dismal, dispiriting, dreary, joyless, somber

dreary *adj* **1** ***syn*** GLOOMY 3, black, bleak, depressing, depressive, dismal, dispiriting, funereal, oppressive, somber
2 ***syn*** DULL 9, banausic, blah, ‖dim, humdrum, monotone, monotonous, pedestrian, poky, stodgy

dreck *n* ***syn*** REFUSE, garbage, junk, litter, ‖muck, offal, outsweepings, rubbish, ‖sculch, swill

dreg *n, usu* **dregs** *pl* **1** ***syn*** SEDIMENT, deposit, grounds, lees, precipitate, precipitation, settlings
2 ***syn*** RABBLE 2, canaille, mass(es), mob, proletariat, ragtag and bobtail, riffraff, scum, trash, unwashed

‖**dreich** *adj* ***syn*** LONG 2, dragging, drawn-out, lengthy, long-drawn-out, longsome, overlong, prolonged, protracted

drench *n* ***syn*** DRINK 3, draft, drag, drain, ‖peg, swig, swill

drench *vb* **1** ***syn*** WET, deluge, douse, drown, soak, sop, souse
rel dip, duck, dunk, immerse, submerge
2 ***syn*** SOAK 1, impregnate, saturate, seethe, sodden, ‖sog, sop, souse, steep, waterlog
3 ***syn*** POUR 3, lash, teem

drenched *adj* ***syn*** WET 1, dripping, saturated, soaked, soaking, sodden, sopping, soppy, soused, wringing-wet

dress *vb* **1** ***syn*** CLOTHE, apparel, array, attire, clad, enclothe, garb, garment, raiment
ant undress
2 ***syn*** BANDAGE, bind
3 to remove the entrails from <*dress* fish, fowl, or game>
syn clean, gut
rel butcher, slaughter

---

syn synonym(s) — ***rel*** related word(s)
idiom idiomatic equivalent(s) — ***con*** contrasted word(s)
ant antonym(s) — * vulgar
‖ use limited; if in doubt, see a dictionary
The first word in a synonym list when printed in SMALL CAPITALS shows where there is more information about the group. For a more efficient use of this book see Explanatory Notes.

4 ***syn*** TILL, cultivate, ||labor, tend, work
rel fertilize, topdress

dress (up) *vb* ***syn*** ADORN, beautify, bedeck, deck, decorate, embellish, garnish, ornament, prank, trim

dress *n* **1** ***syn*** CLOTHES, apparel, attire, attirement, clothing, duds, habiliment(s), raiment, things, togs
2 ***syn*** COSTUME, getup, guise, outfit, rig, setout, turnout

dress down *vb* ***syn*** SCOLD 1, bawl out, berate, ||bless out, ||chew out, lash, rail, ||ream out, tell off, tongue-lash

dress up *vb* **1** to attire in best or formal clothes <*dressed up* to go to the theater>
syn deck (out), ||dike (out *or* up), doll out, doll up, ||dude up, fix up, gussy up, prank, ||prick (up), primp, prink (up), slick, smarten (up), smug, spiff, spruce (up), tog (out *or* up), ||toggle, trick (off, out, *or* up)
rel prettify, pretty (up); apparel, array, attire, clad, clothe, dress, enclothe, garb, garment, raiment; overdress; preen; prim (up)
idiom dress fit to kill, dress to the nines, put on the dog
2 ***syn*** DISGUISE, camouflage, cloak, dissemble, dissimulate, mask

drib *vb* ***syn*** DRIP, distill, dribble, drop, trickle, trill, weep

drib *n* ***syn*** DROP 1, driblet, droplet, globule, gobbet

dribble *vb* **1** ***syn*** DRIP, distill, drib, drop, trickle, trill, weep
2 ***syn*** DROOL 2, drivel, salivate, slabber, slaver, slobber

dribble (away) *vb* ***syn*** WASTE 2, blow, blunder (away), consume, drivel, fritter, frivol away, squander, throw away, trifle (away)

dribble *n* ***syn*** PITTANCE, driblet, ||scrimption

driblet *n* **1** ***syn*** PITTANCE, dribble, ||scrimption
2 ***syn*** DROP 1, drib, droplet, globule, gobbet

drift *n* **1** ***syn*** FLOW, current, flood, flux, rush, spate, stream, tide
2 ***syn*** PILE 1, bank, heap, hill, mass, mound, mountain, pyramid, shock, stack
rel array, batch, bunch, bundle, clump, cluster, clutch, group, lot, parcel, set
||**3** ***syn*** DROVE 2, flock, herd
4 ***syn*** TENDENCY 1, current, run, tenor, trend
rel motion, movement, progress, progression; aim, intent, intention, purpose
5 ***syn*** LEANING 2, bent, disposition, inclination, inclining, partiality, penchant, predilection, propensity, tendency
6 ***syn*** TENOR 1, purport, substance
rel direction, line, set

drift *vb* **1** to become carried or floated along <cakes of ice *drifting* along the stream>
syn float, ride, wash
rel dart, fly, sail, scud, shoot, skim; dance, flicker, flit, flitter, flutter, hover
2 ***syn*** SAUNTER, amble, bummel, linger, mope, mosey, ||muck, stroll
3 ***syn*** WANDER 1, bat, gad, gallivant, maunder, meander, ramble, range, roam, stray
4 ***syn*** SLIDE 6, coast
5 ***syn*** HEAP 1, bank, cock, hill, mound, pile, stack

drifter *n* **1** ***syn*** ROVER, meanderer, rambler, roamer, rolling stone, wanderer
2 ***syn*** VAGABOND, ||bindle stiff, bum, derelict, floater, hobo, street arab, tramp, vag, vagrant

driftwood *n* vagrant impoverished people <the *driftwood* of skid row>
syn flotsam, jetsam, wreckage

drill *vb* **1** ***syn*** PERFORATE, bore, prick, ||pritch, punch, puncture
2 ***syn*** EXERCISE 3, practice, rehearse
rel accustom, habituate

drill *n* ***syn*** EXERCISE 3, drilling, practice

drilling *n* ***syn*** EXERCISE 3, drill, practice

drink *vb* **1** to take in (potable liquid) <the boys *drank* all the soda>
syn imbibe, quaff, sip, sup (off *or* up), swallow, toss
rel drain, gulp, guzzle, slosh, slurp, swig, swill; wash down
idiom wet one's whistle
2 to salute and wish honor and health to (a person) by raising and then drinking from a vessel <*drink* to the bride and groom>
syn pledge, toast
rel honor, salute; wet
3 to partake of alcoholic liquors especially habitually or to excess <he *drinks* but does not smoke>
syn booze, guzzle, imbibe, liquor (up), ||lush (up), nip, soak, swig, swill, swizzle, tank up, tipple, tope
idiom bend the elbow, cheer the inner man, drink like a fish, go on a binge, hit the bottle, take a nip

drink *n* **1** liquid suitable for swallowing <able to make palatable *drink* from seawater>
syn beverage, drinkable, liquor, potable
rel liquid; brew; potion
2 ***syn*** LIQUOR 2, aqua vitae, booze, firewater, grog, ||hooch, ||joy-juice, ||juice, spirit(s), tipple
3 a portion of potable liquid <took a *drink* from the cup>
syn draft, drag, drain, drench, ||peg, swig, swill
rel draw, pull; finger, jigger; libation
4 ***syn*** OCEAN, blue, brine, ||briny, deep, main, sea

drinkable *adj* ***syn*** POTABLE

drinkable *n* ***syn*** DRINK 1, beverage, liquor, potable

drinkery *n* ***syn*** BAR 5, barroom, ||bucket shop, cocktail lounge, ||gin mill, lounge, pub, saloon, taproom, tavern

drip *vb* to let fall drops of moisture or liquid <trees *dripping* after the rain>
syn distill, drib, dribble, drop, trickle, trill, weep
rel spatter, sprinkle, spurtle; gush, pour, sluice, stream

||**drip** *n* **1** ***syn*** NONSENSE 2, balderdash, ||baloney, ||bull, ||bunk, bushwa, drivel, ||gas, poppycock, twaddle
2 ***syn*** DUNCE, boob, chump, clod, dolt, dope, dullard, ||goon, moron, simpleton

dripping *adj* ***syn*** WET 1, drenched, saturated, soaked, soaking, sodden, sopping, soppy, soused, wringing-wet

---

drippy *adj* *syn* SENTIMENTAL, maudlin, mawkish, mushy, sappy, slushy, sobby, sobful, ‖soppy, soupy

drive *vb* **1** *syn* MOVE 5, actuate, impel, mobilize, propel
rel coerce, compel, force; incite, instigate
con check, curb, inhibit, restrain; guide, lead, pilot, steer
2 *syn* PUSH 1, propel, shove, thrust
3 to urge along (as cattle) <cowboys *driving* the great herds north>
syn ‖drove, herd, run
rel shepherd; wrangle; egg, exhort, goad, prick, prod, punch, sic, spur, urge
4 *syn* THRUST 2, dig, plunge, ram, run, sink, stab, stick
5 to operate and steer (a motor vehicle) <*drive* a car>
syn auto, charioteer, motor, pilot, tool, wheel
rel operate, run, work; guide, steer; roll; chauffeur
6 *syn* IMPRESS 3, grave, hammer, pound, stamp
7 *syn* PLUNGE 2, burst, dive, lunge, pitch, ‖splunge
8 *syn* LABOR 1, moil, strain, strive, toil, tug, work

drive *n* **1** a short trip in a vehicle <took a *drive* around town>
syn ride, spin, turn; *compare* TRIP 1
rel whirl; joyride; excursion, outing
2 *syn* DRIVEWAY, ‖avenue
3 *syn* ENTERPRISE 4, ambition, get-up-and-go, initiative, push
4 *syn* VIGOR 2, bang, getup, get-up-and-go, go, pep, punch, push, snap, vitality
rel impetus, momentum, speed, velocity

drivel *vb* **1** *syn* DROOL 2, dribble, salivate, slabber, slaver, slobber
2 *syn* BABBLE 2, blabber, blather, drool, gabble, prate, prattle, twaddle, ‖waffle
3 *syn* WASTE 2, blow, blunder (away), cast away, consume, fritter, frivol away, squander, throw away, trifle (away)

drivel *n* **1** *syn* NONSENSE 2, blatherskite, bosh, claptrap, double-talk, flapdoodle, hooey, pishposh, rubbish, twaddle
2 *syn* GIBBERISH 1, babble, Greek, jabber, jabberwocky, nonsense, skimble-skamble

driveling *adj* *syn* INSIPID 3, flat, inane, innocuous, jejune, milk-and-water, namby-pamby, sapless, vapid, wishy-washy

driver *n* *syn* MOTORIST, autoist, automobilist, operator

driveway *n* a private road giving access from a public way <the *driveway* to a house>
syn ‖avenue, drive
rel court, place, row, street

driving *adj* *syn* ENERGETIC 2, active, enterprising, lively

drizzle *vb* *syn* SPRINKLE 5, ‖mizzle

drogher *n* *syn* BEARER 2, carrier, porter

drôlerie *n* *syn* JOKE 1, crack, drollery, gag, jape, jest, quip, sally, wisecrack, witticism

droll *adj* *syn* LAUGHABLE, comic, comical, farcical, funny, gelastic, ludicrous, ridiculous, risible
rel absurd, preposterous

droll *n* *syn* HUMORIST 2, comedian, comic, funnyman, jester, joker, jokester, quipster, wag, wit

drollery *n* **1** *syn* JOKE 1, crack, gag, jape, jest, quip, waggery, wisecrack, witticism, ‖yak
2 *syn* HUMOR 4, comedy, comicality, comicalness, drollness, funniness, humorousness, wittiness

drollness *n* *syn* HUMOR 4, comedy, comicality, comicalness, drollery, funniness, humorousness, wittiness

drone *vb* **1** *syn* HUM, bombinate, ‖bum, bumble, buzz, ‖sowf, strum, thrum
2 *syn* IDLE, bum, dawdle, diddle-daddle, ‖lallygag, laze, loaf, loiter, loll, lounge

drony *adj* *syn* LAZY, easygoing, faineant, indolent, slothful, slowgoing, work-shy

drool *vb* **1** to secrete or become filled with saliva usually in anticipation of food <mouths *drooled* as we waited for dinner>
syn water
idiom water at the mouth
2 to let saliva or some other substance flow from the mouth <babies often *drool* uncontrollably>
syn dribble, drivel, salivate, slabber, slaver, slobber
3 *syn* ENTHUSE 2, rave, rhapsodize, rhapsody
4 *syn* BABBLE 2, blabber, blather, drivel, gabble, prate, prattle, twaddle, ‖waffle

drool *n* *syn* NONSENSE 2, balderdash, ‖baloney, bushwa, claptrap, drivel, guff, hot air, jazz, twaddle

droop *vb* **1** *syn* SLOUCH, loll, ‖lollop, lop, slump, trollop
2 *syn* LOWER 3, couch, demit, depress, let down, sink
3 to become literally or figuratively limp through loss of vigor or freshness <he walked along, his shoulders *drooping* from exhaustion>
syn flag, sag, swag, wilt
rel drop, fall, sink, slump, subside; dangle, hang, loll, lop, sling, suspend; decline, deteriorate, ‖dwine, fade, fail, languish, weaken

droopy *adj* *syn* DOWNCAST, bad, blue, cast down, dejected, depressed, dispirited, doleful, down, downhearted

drop *n* **1** the quantity of fluid that falls in one spherical mass <a *drop* of rain>
syn drib, driblet, droplet, globule, gobbet
rel dribble, drip, trickle
2 *syn* PARTICLE, crumb, dram, iota, molecule, ounce, shred, smidgen, smitch, speck
3 *syn* DRAM, ‖caulker, jolt, nip, shot, slug, snifter, snort, toothful, tot
4 *syn* DESCENT 4, decline, declivity, dip, fall
5 *syn* DESCENT 1, fall
6 *syn* DECLINE 3, dip, downslide, downswing, downtrend, downturn, falloff, sag, slip, slump
7 *syn* DEPTH 1, deepness

drop *vb* **1** *syn* FALL 2, go down, keel (over), pitch, plunge, slump, topple, tumble
2 *syn* FALL 1, descend, lower
ant mount
3 *syn* PLUMMET, dip, fall, nose-dive, plunge, skid, tumble
rel slide, slip
con rally, rebound; ascend, climb; soar

---

syn synonym(s)	*rel* related word(s)
idiom idiomatic equivalent(s)	*con* contrasted word(s)
ant antonym(s)	* vulgar

‖ use limited; if in doubt, see a dictionary
The first word in a synonym list when printed in SMALL CAPITALS shows where there is more information about the group. For a more efficient use of this book see Explanatory Notes.

ant mount
4 *syn* COLLAPSE 2, break down, cave (in), ||flake out, give out, peg out, succumb, wilt
rel backslide, lapse, relapse
5 *syn* DIE 1, cash in, decease, demise, depart, expire, pass, pass away, pop off, succumb
6 *syn* DRIP, distill, drib, dribble, trickle, trill, weep
7 *syn* FELL 1, bowl (down *or* over), bring down, down, floor, ground, knock down, lay low, prostrate, throw down
8 *syn* QUIT 6, leave, resign, terminate
9 *syn* CANCEL 2, call off, scrub
10 *syn* DISMISS 3, ax, boot (out), bounce, ||can, discharge, fire, let out, sack, terminate
11 *syn* LOSE 2, lose out
12 *syn* LOSE 1, forfeit, sacrifice

drop (in *or* by) *vb syn* VISIT 2, call, come by, come over, look in, look up, pop (in), run in, see, stop (in *or* by)

drop (off) *vb syn* SLIP 6, fall (off *or* away), sag, slide, slump

droplet *n syn* DROP 1, drib, driblet, globule, gobbet

drop off *vb syn* DOZE (off), drowse (off)

dropsical *adj syn* INFLATED, dropsied, flatulent, overblown, tumescent, tumid, turgid, windy

dropsied *adj syn* INFLATED, dropsical, flatulent, overblown, tumescent, tumid, turgid, windy

drossy *adj syn* WORTHLESS 1, draffy, good-for-nothing, inutile, ||no-account, no-good, nothing, unworthy, worthless

droughty *adj syn* DRY 1, arid, bone-dry, moistureless, sere, thirsty, unwatered, waterless

||**drouk** *vb syn* SOAK 1, drench, impregnate, saturate, sodden, ||sog, sop, souse, steep, waterlog

drove *n* **1** *syn* CROWD 1, crush, horde, multitude, press, push, squash, throng
2 a group of domestic animals reared or handled as a unit <a *drove* of cattle>
syn ||drift, flock, herd
rel drive; pack; school

||**drove** *vb syn* DRIVE 3, herd, run

drown *vb* **1** *syn* OVERWHELM 4, knock over, overcome, overpower, prostrate, whelm
2 *syn* DELUGE 1, engulf, flood, inundate, overflow, overwhelm, submerge, swamp, whelm
3 *syn* WET, deluge, douse, drench, soak, sop, souse

drowse *vb syn* DOZE, ||dorm, ||sloom, slumber, ||snoozle, ||sog

drowse (off) *vb syn* DOZE (off), drop off

drowse *n syn* DOZE, ||sloom, slumber

drowsy *adj syn* SLEEPY 1, dozy, nodding, ||peepy, ||sloomy, slumberous, slumbery, snoozy, somnolent, soporific
rel lackadaisical, languid, languorous

syn synonym(s) — *rel* related word(s)
idiom idiomatic equivalent(s) — *con* contrasted word(s)
ant antonym(s) — * vulgar
|| use limited; if in doubt, see a dictionary
The first word in a synonym list when printed in SMALL CAPITALS shows where there is more information about the group. For a more efficient use of this book see Explanatory Notes.

con alert, vigilant, watchful; active, dynamic, live; animated, lively, vivacious

drub *vb* **1** *syn* BEAT 1, baste, batter, belabor, buffet, lambaste, paste, pound, thrash, wallop
2 *syn* LAMBASTE 3, blister, castigate, excoriate, flay, lash (into), scorch, score, scourge, slash
3 *syn* WHIP 2, beat, ||clobber, lambaste, lick, overwhelm, shellac, smear, thrash, trim

drubbing *n syn* DEFEAT 1, beating, debacle, defeasance, licking, overthrow, rout, shellacking, trouncing, vanquishment

drudge *vb* to perform hard, menial, or monotonous work <*drudged* all day washing floors>
syn grind, grub, ||muck, plod, slave, slog, toil
rel hammer, peg (away *or* at *or* on), plow, plug, pound (away); perform, work
idiom keep one's nose to the grindstone
con idle, laze, loaf, lounge; dally, dawdle, potter, putter; cheat, chisel

drudge *n* **1** *syn* SLAVE 2, dray horse, galley slave, peon, slavey, toiler, workhorse
2 *syn* WORK 2, bullwork, donkeywork, drudgery, grind, labor, moil, plugging, slavery, toil
3 *syn* HACK 2, grub, grubber, hireling, mercenary, slavey

drudgery *n syn* WORK 2, bullwork, donkeywork, grind, labor, moil, plugging, sweat, toil, travail

drudging *adj syn* IRKSOME, boresome, boring, tedious, tiresome, tiring

drug *n* **1** a substance used by itself or in a mixture in the treatment or diagnosis of disease <a life-sustaining *drug*>
syn biologic, medicinal, pharmaceutic, pharmaceutical
rel cure, medicament, medication, medicine, physic, remedy, specific; simple
2 a narcotic substance or preparation <depended on *drugs* to make life bearable>
syn dope, ||hop, narcotic, opiate

drugged *adj* being under the influence of a drug taken for nonmedical purposes <was *drugged* on LSD>
syn doped, high, hopped-up, spaced-out, stoned, tripped out, turned on, ||wiped out, zonked
idiom on a trip
ant straight

druggist *n* one who deals in medicinal drugs
syn apothecary, ||chemist, pharmacist
rel pharmacologist

drum *vb syn* SOLICIT 1, canvass, drum up

drumfire *n syn* BARRAGE, bombardment, broadside, cannonade, fusillade, hail, salvo, shower, storm, volley

drumhead *adj syn* SUMMARY 2

drum up *vb syn* SOLICIT 1, canvass, drum

drunk *adj syn* INTOXICATED 1, drunken, inebriated, ||lushed, ||oiled, ||pie-eyed, ||plastered, ||stewed, tight, zonked
rel drinking, drinky
idiom roaring drunk
con bone-dry, dry
ant sober

drunk *n* **1** *syn* BINGE 1, bender, booze, brannigan, bust, jag, soak, souse, spree, tear
2 *syn* DRUNKARD, ||bloat, ||blotter, boozehound, boozer, guzzler, inebriate, lush, sot, tippler

drunkard *n* one who drinks alcoholic liquors to excess < *drunkards* lurching homeward when the bar finally closes >
syn bibber, ‖bloat, ‖blotter, boozehound, boozer, drunk, fuddler, guzzler, inebriate, lush, ‖lusher, rumdum, rummy, ‖rumpot, ‖shicker, soak, soaker, sot, sponge, stiff, swillbowl, swiller, tippler, toper, tosspot
rel alcoholic, dipsomaniac; wino; drammer
idiom elbow bender (*or* crooker)
ant teetotaler

drunken *adj* ***syn*** INTOXICATED 1, ‖boozy, drunk, inebriated, ‖oiled, ‖pie-eyed, ‖spiflicated, ‖stewed, tight, tipsy

drunkery *n* ***syn*** BAR 5, barroom, ‖boozer, ‖gin mill, ‖groggery, rumshop, saloon, tap, taproom, tavern

‖**druthers** *n* ***syn*** CHOICE 1, alternative, election, option, preference, selection

dry *adj* **1** devoid of or deficient in moisture < preferred a *dry* climate >
syn arid, bone-dry, droughty, moistureless, sere, thirsty, unwatered, waterless
rel baked, dehydrated, desiccated, parched; bald, bare, barren; depleted, drained, exhausted, impoverished; juiceless, sapless, sapped
con drenched, dripping, saturated, soaked, soaking, sodden, sopping, soppy, soused, wringing-wet; damp, dank, humid, moist; exuberant, lush, luxuriant, prodigal, profuse
ant wet
2 ***syn*** THIRSTY 1, athirst, thirsting
3 marked by the absence of or abstention from alcoholic beverages < a *dry* party >
syn bone-dry, teetotal
ant wet
4 ***syn*** IMPASSIVE 1, apathetic, matter-of-fact, phlegmatic, stoic, stolid
5 ***syn*** ARID 2, bromidic, dryasdust, dull, dusty, insipid, tedious, uninteresting, weariful, wearisome
6 ***syn*** PLAIN 1, discreet, inelaborate, modest, simple, unadorned, unembellished, unembroidered, ungarnished, unpretentious
7 ***syn*** SOUR 1, acerb, acerbic, acetose, acid, acidulous, tart
ant sweet
8 ***syn*** HARSH 3, grating, hoarse, jarring, rasping, raucous, rough, rugged, strident, stridulous

dry *vb* **1** to treat or affect so as to deprive of moisture < clothes *dried* in the wind >
syn dehydrate, desiccate, exsiccate, parch, sear
rel evaporate; anhydrate; deplete, drain, exhaust; shrivel, wither, wizen
con deluge, douse, drench, soak, sop, souse; damp, dampen, moisten
ant wet
2 ***syn*** HARDEN 1, cake, concrete, congeal, indurate, set, solidify

dryasdust *adj* ***syn*** ARID 2, bromidic, dry, dull, dusty, insipid, tedious, uninteresting, weariful, wearisome

dry land *n* ***syn*** EARTH 2, dirt, ground, land, soil, terra firma

‖**dry-shave** *vb* ***syn*** CHEAT, beat, bilk, cozen, defraud, diddle, do, gyp, overreach, ‖screw

dry up *vb* **1** ***syn*** DESICCATE 2, devitalize
2 ***syn*** WITHER, mummify, mummy, shrivel, welter, wilt, wizen
3 ***syn*** SHUT UP 2, dumb (up), ‖dummy (up), pipe down, ‖ring off

dual *adj* **1** ***syn*** TWOFOLD 1, bifold, binary, double, double-barreled, dualistic, duple, duplex
2 ***syn*** TWIN, double, paired

dualistic *adj* ***syn*** TWOFOLD 1, bifold, binary, double, double-barreled, dual, duple, duplex

dualize *vb* ***syn*** DOUBLE 1, dupe, duplicate

dub *vb* **1** ***syn*** NAME 1, baptize, call, christen, denominate, designate, entitle, style, term, title
2 ***syn*** BOTCH, ‖blow, blunder, bobble, boggle, bollix, flub, fluff, goof (up), muff

dub *vb* to provide (a motion-picture film) with a new sound track (as for substituting dialogue in a foreign language) < *dubbed* the Italian movie into English >
syn double

dubiety *n* ***syn*** UNCERTAINTY, concern, doubt, dubiosity, incertitude, mistrust, skepticism, suspicion, uncertitude, wonder
rel hesitancy; faltering, vacillation, wavering
con decidedness, decisiveness
ant decision

dubiosity *n* ***syn*** UNCERTAINTY, concern, doubt, dubiety, incertitude, mistrust, skepticism, suspicion, uncertitude, wonder
rel addlement, confusion, muddlement; faltering, vacillation, wavering
con cocksureness, positiveness
ant decidedness

dubious *adj* **1** ***syn*** MOOT, arguable, debatable, disputable, doubtful, mootable, problematic, questionable, uncertain
2 ***syn*** DOUBTFUL 1, dubitable, equivocal, fishy, open, problematic, suspect, uncertain, unclear, undecided
rel skeptical; mistrustful; disinclined, hesitant, reluctant
con dependable, tried, trustworthy, trusty; certain, positive, sure
ant cocksure; reliable
3 ***syn*** IMPROBABLE 1, doubtful, questionable, unlikely
4 ***syn*** UNRELIABLE 1, fly-by-night, questionable, trustless, undependable, unsure, untrustworthy, untrusty
ant trustworthy

dubitable *adj* ***syn*** DOUBTFUL 1, ambiguous, borderline, doubtable, dubious, fishy, open, suspect, uncertain, unsettled
ant indubitable

dubitancy *n* ***syn*** UNCERTAINTY, concern, doubt, dubiety, dubiosity, incertitude, mistrust, skepticism, suspicion, uncertitude

duce *n* ***syn*** TYRANT, despot, dictator, oppressor, strong man

‖**duck** *n* ***syn*** ECCENTRIC, case, character, oddball, oddity, original, quiz, ‖spook, ‖wack, zombie

---

syn synonym(s) — *rel* related word(s)
idiom idiomatic equivalent(s) — *con* contrasted word(s)
ant antonym(s) — * vulgar
‖ use limited; if in doubt, see a dictionary
The first word in a synonym list when printed in SMALL CAPITALS shows where there is more information about the group. For a more efficient use of this book see Explanatory Notes.

duck *vb* **1** ***syn*** DIP 1, douse, dunk, immerse, souse, submerge, submerse

2 to lower (as the head or body) quickly <had to *duck* his head to get through the door>

syn dip, stoop

rel bend; bow

3 ***syn*** DODGE 1, fence, parry, shirk, sidestep

rel avert, prevent, ward

4 ***syn*** ESCAPE 2, avoid, bilk, double, elude, eschew, evade, shun, shy

duck soup *n* ***syn*** SNAP 1, breeze, child's play, cinch, kid stuff, picnic, pie, ‖pipe, pushover, setup

duct *n* ***syn*** CHANNEL 1, aqueduct, canal, conduit, course, watercourse

ductile *adj* ***syn*** PLASTIC, adaptable, malleable, moldable, pliable, pliant, supple

rel responsive; submitting; fluid, liquid

con intractable, refractory; adamant, obdurate

ductus *n* ***syn*** HANDWRITING, calligraphy, chirography, fist, hand, penmanship, script

dud *n* ***syn*** FAILURE 5, bomb, bust, flop, lemon, loser

dude *n* ***syn*** FOP, Beau Brummel, blood, buck, coxcomb, dandy, exquisite, lounge lizard, macaroni, petit-maître

‖**dude up** *vb* ***syn*** DRESS UP 1, deck (out), ‖dike (out *or* up), doll up, gussy up, slick, smarten (up), spiff, spruce (up), tog (out *or* up)

dudgeon *n* ***syn*** OFFENSE 2, huff, miff, pique, resentment, ‖snuff, umbrage

rel fury, ire, rage, wrath; humor, mood, temper

duds *n pl* **1** ***syn*** CLOTHES, apparel, attire, attirement, clothing, dress, habiliment(s), raiment, things, togs

‖**2** ***syn*** RAGS 1, tatters

due *adj* **1** ***syn*** JUST 3, appropriate, condign, deserved, merited, requisite, rhadamanthine, right, rightful, suitable

rel good, right; equitable, fair, just; coming, earned

con excessive, exorbitant, extravagant, immoderate, inordinate; deficient

ant undue

2 having reached the date at which payment is required <a note that would become *due* after eighteen months>

syn mature, payable

3 ***syn*** UNPAID 2, mature, outstanding, overdue, owing, payable, unsettled

due *n* **1** what one fairly has coming <the artist has finally been accorded his *due*>

syn comeuppance, desert(s), deserving, lumps, merit, right(s)

rel deservedness, dueness, entitlement; compensation, payment, recompense, recompensing, repayment, satisfaction; reprisal, retaliation, retribution, revenge, vengeance; guerdon, need, reward

idiom what is coming to one

---

syn synonym(s) — *rel* related word(s)

idiom idiomatic equivalent(s) — *con* contrasted word(s)

ant antonym(s) — * vulgar

‖ use limited; if in doubt, see a dictionary

The first word in a synonym list when printed in SMALL CAPITALS shows where there is more information about the group. For a more efficient use of this book see Explanatory Notes.

---

2 ***syn*** DEBT 3, arrear(s), arrearage, indebtedness, liability

due *adv* ***syn*** DIRECTLY 1, dead, direct, right, straight, straightly, undeviatingly

duel *vb* ***syn*** RESIST, buck, combat, contest, dispute, fight, oppose, repel, traverse, withstand

due to *prep* ***syn*** OVER 6, because of, owing to, through

‖**duff** *vb* ***syn*** CHEAT, beat, bilk, cozen, defraud, diddle, do, gyp, overreach, ‖screw

‖**duff** *n* ***syn*** BUTTOCKS, *arse, behind, bottom, *butt, ‖can, fanny, *prat, rear, tail

duffer *n* ‖**1** ***syn*** PEDDLER, ‖arab, hawker, higgler, huckster, monger, outcrier, packman, roadman, vendor

2 ***syn*** DUNCE, blockhead, boob, dimwit, dolt, dope, dumbbell, idiot, ignoramus, numskull

dulcet *adj* **1** ***syn*** MELODIOUS 1, euphonic, euphonious, mellisonant, melodic, sweet, tuneful

con grinding, rasping, scraping, scratching

ant grating

2 ***syn*** SWEET 1, engaging, winning, winsome

dull *adj* **1** ***syn*** STUPID 1, beef-witted, blear-witted, dense, doltish, dumb, duncical, numskulled, thick, thick-witted

ant sharp

2 ***syn*** RETARDED, backward, dim-witted, feebleminded, half-witted, imbecile, moronic, simple, simpleminded, slow

con advanced, precocious

3 ***syn*** INSENSIBLE 5, anesthetic, bloodless, hard, impassible, insensate, insensitive, rocky

4 ***syn*** DOWNCAST, bad, blue, cast down, dejected, depressed, dispirited, down, downhearted, spiritless

5 ***syn*** COLORLESS 2, drab, flat, lackluster, lifeless, lusterless, prosaic, prosy

ant bright

6 lacking sharpness of edge or point <a knife with a *dull* blade>

syn blunt, obtuse

rel blunted, dulled, unsharpened

con honed, keen, razor-sharp, unblunted, whetted

ant sharp

7 lacking warmth, luster, or brilliance <a smooth *dull* finish>

syn blind, dead, dim, flat, lackluster, lusterless, mat, muted

rel cold, dingy, drab, dun, leaden, somber; deadened, lifeless

con beaming, bright, brilliant, effulgent, fulgent, incandescent, lambent, lucent, lucid, luminous, lustrous, radiant, refulgent; burnished, polished, shiny

8 cloudy in color <a *dull* brown>

syn drab, muddy, murky, subfusc

rel blurry, cloudy, hazy; flat, lackluster, lifeless, lusterless; mousy

ant clear; rich

9 being so unvaried or uninteresting as to provoke boredom or tedium <any routine constantly repeated can become *dull*>

syn banausic, blah, ‖dim, dreary, humdrum, monotone, monotonous, pedestrian, plodding, poky, stodgy

rel boring, irksome, tedious, tiring, wearisome; brainless; exhausting, fagging, fatiguing

con animating, exciting, stimulating; gay, spritely

ant lively

10 ***syn*** OVERCAST, cloudy, ‖dowly, heavy, lowering (*or* louring), nubilous, overclouded

11 ***syn*** ARID 2, bromidic, dry, dryasdust, dusty, insipid, tedious, uninteresting, weariful, wearisome

rel matter-of-fact, prosaic, prosy; bloodless

idiom dull as ditchwater

con exciting, stimulating

ant lively

dull *vb* **1** to make less clear, distinct, or bright <colors *dulled* by the sun>

syn dim, fade, muddy, pale, tarnish

rel discolor, wash out; blur

con brighten, freshen, intensify

2 ***syn*** DEADEN 1, benumb, blunt, desensitize, mull, numb

ant sharpen

3 to deprive of sharpness (as of edge or point) <*dull* a spade>

syn blunt, disedge, obtund, turn

idiom take the edge off

con edge, hone

ant sharpen

4 to impair one or more of the senses <age had *dulled* his hearing>

syn blear, blur, dim

rel debilitate, enfeeble, weaken; darken; retard, slow

ant sharpen

5 to make slow or obtuse <his mind had been *dulled* by drink>

syn blunt, hebetate, stupefy

rel becloud, befog, cloud, darken, dim; benumb, deaden, numb; retard, slow

con quicken, stimulate, whet

ant sharpen

dullard *n* ***syn*** DUNCE, dullhead, dumbbell, ‖dummkopf, dummy, idiot, ignoramus, moron, simpleton, stupid

dullhead *n* ***syn*** DUNCE, dullard, dumbbell, ‖dummkopf, dummy, idiot, ignoramus, moron, simpleton, stupid

dullness *n* ***syn*** LETHARGY 1, coma, hebetude, languor, lassitude, sleep, slumber, stupor, torpidity, torpor

rel denseness, stupidity

con edge, incisiveness, keenness

ant sharpness

dumb *adj* **1** lacking the power to speak <deaf and *dumb* from birth>

syn inarticulate, mute, silent, speechless, unarticulate, voiceless; *compare* SILENT 2

ant articulate

2 ***syn*** SILENT 2, mum, ‖mumchance, mute, speechless, wordless

rel incoherent, indistinct, maundering, tongue-tied

3 ***syn*** SILENT 3, closemouthed, close-tongued, reticent, speechless, taciturn, tight-lipped, tight-mouthed, uncommunicative, wordless

con speaking, talking; talkative, verbose

4 ***syn*** STUPID 1, blockheaded, dense, doltish, dull, duncical, fatheaded, numskulled, thick, thick-witted

idiom dumb as an ox

dumb (up) *vb* ***syn*** SHUT UP 2, dry up, ‖dummy (up), pipe down, ‖ring off

dumbbell *n* ***syn*** DUNCE, dullard, dullhead, ‖dummkopf, dummy, idiot, ignoramus, moron, simpleton, stupid

‖**dumb bunny** *n* ***syn*** DUNCE, ‖cluck, dimwit, ‖dumb cluck, featherweight, lackwit, nitwit, pinhead, simp, wantwit

‖**dumb cluck** *n* ***syn*** DUNCE, ‖cluck, dimwit, ‖dumb bunny, featherweight, lackwit, nitwit, pinhead, simp, wantwit

dumbfound *vb* **1** ***syn*** SURPRISE 2, amaze, astonish, astound, flabbergast

2 ***syn*** STAGGER 5, boggle, nonplus

dumbfounded *adj* ***syn*** AGHAST 2, agape, confounded, dismayed, overwhelmed, shocked, thunderstruck

‖**dumbhead** *n* ***syn*** DUNCE, chowderhead, chucklehead, dope, dunderhead, lame-brain, noddy, noodle, ‖schnook, ‖stupe

‖**dummkopf** *n* ***syn*** DUNCE, dullard, dullhead, dumbbell, dummy, idiot, ignoramus, moron, simpleton, stupid

dummy *n* **1** ***syn*** DUNCE, dullard, dullhead, dumbbell, ‖dummkopf, idiot, ignoramus, moron, simpleton, stupid

2 ***syn*** STOOGE 1, Charlie McCarthy, yes-man

dummy *adj* ***syn*** ARTIFICIAL 2, ersatz, false, imitation, mock, sham, simulated, spurious, substitute

‖**dummy** (up) *vb* ***syn*** SHUT UP 2, dry up, dumb (up), pipe down, ‖ring off

dump *vb* **1** ***syn*** DISCARD, cast, chuck, ‖deep-six, ditch, jettison, junk, scrap, throw away, throw out

‖**2** ***syn*** BEAT 1, baste, batter, belabor, buffet, drub, hammer, lam, lambaste, wallop

dump *n* **1** ***syn*** ARMORY, arsenal, depot, magazine

2 ***syn*** STY 1, pigpen, pigsty

dumping *n* ***syn*** DISPOSAL 2, discarding, disposition, jettison, junking, relegation, riddance, scrapping, throwing away

dumpling *n* ***syn*** FATTY, blimp, butterball, ‖fatso, ‖tub

dumps *n pl* ***syn*** SADNESS, blues, dejection, depression, (the) dismals, gloom, heavyheartedness, melancholy, mournfulness, unhappiness

idiom low spirits

dumpy *adj* ***syn*** STOCKY, ‖chumpy, chunky, heavyset, squat, squdgy, stubby, thick, thick-bodied, thickset

rel formless, shapeless, unformed

dun *adj* ***syn*** DARK 1, caliginous, dim, dusk, dusky, gloomy, lightless, murky, obscure, somber

dun *vb* ***syn*** WORRY 1, annoy, bedevil, beleaguer, gnaw, hagride, harass, needle, pester, plague

dunce *n* a dull-witted person <the traditional *dunce* in pointed cap>

syn beetlehead, blockhead, bonehead, boob, booby, ‖bufflehead, cabbagehead, chowderhead, chucklehead, chump, clod, clodpate, clodpoll, ‖cluck, dimwit, ‖dizzard, dodo, ‖dodunk, dolt, dolthead, dope, ‖doughhead, ‖drip, duffer, dullard, dullhead, dumbbell, ‖dumb bunny, ‖dumb cluck, ‖dumbhead, ‖dummkopf, dummy, dunderhead, dunderpate, fathead, featherweight, goof, ‖goon, hammerhead, idiot, ignoramus, ironhead, knot-

---

syn synonym(s) *rel* related word(s)
idiom idiomatic equivalent(s) *con* contrasted word(s)
ant antonym(s) * vulgar
‖ use limited; if in doubt, see a dictionary
The first word in a synonym list when printed in SMALL CAPITALS shows where there is more information about the group. For a more efficient use of this book see Explanatory Notes.

head, knucklehead, lackwit, lame-brain, lunk, lunkhead, ||moonraker, moron, muddlehead, mug, muggins, mutt, muttonhead, nitwit, noddy, noodle, numskull, oaf, pinhead, poke, prune, pumpkin head, put, ||schnook, simp, simpleton, ||spoon, squarehead, ||stunpoll, ||stupe, stupid, thickhead, thickskull, turnip, wantwit, woodenhead, zombie
rel lightweight; ass, donkey, fool, imbecile, jackass, jerk, nincompoop, ninny, ||schmo, ||schmuck; birdbrain, featherbrain, scatterbrain
idiom dumb ox, Simple Simon
con brain, highbrow, intellectual, thinker, wit; pundit, sage, savant, scholar, wise man; prodigy, wizard; genius, mastermind

duncical *adj* ***syn*** STUPID 1, blockheaded, blockish, dense, doltish, dull, dumb, numskulled, pinheaded, thickheaded

dunderhead *n* ***syn*** DUNCE, chowderhead, chucklehead, dope, ||dumbhead, lame-brain, noddy, noodle, ||schnook, ||stupe

dunderpate *n* ***syn*** DUNCE, blockhead, bonehead, chowderhead, dimwit, dolt, dope, dummy, dunderhead, numskull

dundrearies *n pl* ***syn*** SIDE-WHISKERS, burnsides, muttonchops, sideboards, sideburns

dungeon *n* a close dark prison or vault commonly underground <the prisoners were kept in lightless *dungeons*>
syn oubliette
rel vault; black hole; cell; jail, prison

dungy *adj* ***syn*** DIRTY 1, black, filthy, foul, grubby, nasty, soily, sordid, squalid, unclean

dunk *vb* ***syn*** DIP 1, douse, duck, immerse, souse, submerge, submerse
rel saturate, soak, sop

duo *n* ***syn*** COUPLE, brace, doublet, dyad, pair, twosome

dupe *n* ***syn*** FOOL 3, butt, chump, fall guy, gudgeon, gull, mark, pigeon, sap, sucker

dupe *vb* to delude by underhand methods <the public is easily *duped* by extravagant claims in advertising>
syn bamboozle, befool, catch, chicane, con, dust, flimflam, fool, gull, hoax, hoodwink, hornswoggle, job, kid, pigeon, ||rig, spoof, trick, victimize
rel beguile, betray, deceive, delude, double-cross, mislead; cheat, cozen, defraud, overreach; baffle, circumvent, outwit
idiom pull one's leg, put something over (*or* across)
con enlighten, inform, wise (up)

dupe *vb* ***syn*** DOUBLE 1, dualize, duplicate

dupery *n* ***syn*** DECEPTION 1, cheat, chicane, chicanery, dirt, dishonesty, double-dealing, fraud, hanky-panky, sharp practice

duple *adj* ***syn*** TWOFOLD 1, bifold, binary, double, double-barreled, dual, dualistic, duplex

syn synonym(s) — *rel* related word(s)
idiom idiomatic equivalent(s) — *con* contrasted word(s)
ant antonym(s) — * vulgar
|| use limited; if in doubt, see a dictionary
The first word in a synonym list when printed in SMALL CAPITALS shows where there is more information about the group. For a more efficient use of this book see Explanatory Notes.

duplex *adj* ***syn*** TWOFOLD 1, bifold, binary, double, double-barreled, dual, dualistic, duple

duplicate *adj* ***syn*** SAME 2, equal, equivalent, identic, identical, indistinguishable, tantamount

duplicate *n* **1** ***syn*** REPRODUCTION, carbon, carbon copy, copy, ditto, facsimile, reduplication, replica, replication
rel analogue, counterpart, parallel
2 ***syn*** MATE 5, companion, coordinate, double, fellow, match, reciprocal, twin

duplicate *vb* **1** ***syn*** DOUBLE 1, dualize, dupe
2 ***syn*** COPY, imitate, reduplicate, replicate, reproduce

duplicitous *adj* ***syn*** UNDERHAND, devious, guileful, indirect, shifty, sneaking, sneaky, underhanded

duplicity *n* ***syn*** DECEIT 1, cunning, dissemblance, dissimulation, guile
rel faithlessness, perfidiousness, perfidy, treacherousness, treachery

durable *adj* ***syn*** LASTING, diuturnal, enduring, perdurable, perduring, permanent, stable
rel stout, strong, tenacious
con feeble, fragile, frail, weak

duration *n* **1** ***syn*** CONTINUATION 1, continuity, endurance, persistence
2 ***syn*** RUN 2, continuance, continuation, persistence
3 ***syn*** TERM 2, span, time

duress *n* ***syn*** FORCE 4, coercion, compulsion, constraint, violence

during *prep* in the course of <*during* the disorder some men kept their heads>
syn amid, mid, midst, over, throughout

dusk *adj* ***syn*** DARK 1, caliginous, dim, dusky, gloomy, lightless, murky, obscure, tenebrous, unilluminated

dusk *n* ***syn*** EVENING 1, ||dimmet, ||dimps, ||dimpsy, ||dusk dark, eventide, gloaming, nightfall, owl-light, twilight

||**dusk dark** *n* ***syn*** EVENING 1, ||dimmet, ||dimps, ||dimpsy, dusk, eventide, gloaming, nightfall, owl-light, twilight

dusky *adj* **1** ***syn*** DARK 3, bistered, black-a-vised, brunet, dark-skinned, swart, swarth, swarthy
2 ***syn*** DARK 1, caliginous, dim, dusk, gloomy, lightless, murky, obscure, tenebrous, unilluminated
3 ***syn*** GLOOMY 3, acheronian, black, bleak, cheerless, desolate, dismal, drear, funereal, joyless
4 ***syn*** OBSCURE 3, ambiguous, amphibological, double-edged, double-faced, equivocal, murky, nubilous, opaque, sibylline

dust *n* **1** ***syn*** DUSTING, powdering, sprinkling
2 ***syn*** QUARREL, altercation, bickering, dispute, dustup, falling-out, fracas, hassle, row, run-in
||**3** ***syn*** REFUSE, ||collateral, debris, garbage, junk, litter, offal, riffraff, rubbish, trash

dust *vb* **1** ***syn*** SPRINKLE 1, besprinkle, powder, ||strinkle
2 ***syn*** WHIP 2, beat, ||clobber, drub, lambaste, ||larrup, lick, overwhelm, shellac, thrash
3 ***syn*** DUPE, bamboozle, chicane, flimflam, fool, gull, hoax, hoodwink, hornswoggle, trick
idiom throw dust in one's eyes
||**4** ***syn*** HURRY 2, barrel, beeline, flit, fly, hasten, hotfoot, hustle, run, speed

dusting *n* **1** a small quantity lightly applied to or sprinkled on <a *dusting* of sugar on the cake>

syn dust, powdering, sprinkling
||2 *syn* DEFEAT 1, beating, drubbing, licking, overthrow, rout, shellacking, thrashing, trouncing, warming

||**dust off** *vb syn* MURDER 1, assassinate, ||bump off, cool, do in, execute, finish, knock off, liquidate, put away

dustup *n syn* QUARREL, altercation, bickering, dispute, dust, falling-out, fracas, hassle, row, run-in

dusty *adj syn* ARID 2, bromidic, dry, dryasdust, dull, insipid, tedious, uninteresting, weariful, wearisome

Dutch *n syn* TROUBLE 3, hot water

duteous *adj syn* RESPECTFUL, deferential, dutiful, regardful

dutiful *adj syn* RESPECTFUL, deferential, duteous, regardful

duty *n* **1** *syn* OBLIGATION 2, charge, commitment, committal, devoir, must, need, ought, ||right
rel accountability, amenability, answerability, liability
2 *syn* FUNCTION 1, business, office, province, role
3 *syn* LOAD 3, burden, charge, deadweight, millstone, onus, task, tax, weight
4 *syn* TAX 1, assessment, ||cess, impost, levy, tariff
5 *syn* TASK 1, assignment, chare, chore, devoir, job, stint
6 *syn* USE 4, function, goal, mark, object, objective, purpose, target

dwarf *n* a very small person <she was a tiny little thing, almost a *dwarf*>
syn homunculus, hop-o'-my-thumb, Lilliputian, manikin, midge, midget, peewee, pygmy, runt, Tom Thumb
rel ||ribe, ||shrimp, wart; dwarfling; minimus
ant giant

dwarf *vb syn* STUNT, suppress

dwarf *adj syn* TINY, ||bitsy, diminutive, dwarfish, lilliputian, midget, miniature, minikin, teensy, wee

dwarfish *adj syn* TINY, ||bitsy, diminutive, dwarf, itsy-bitsy, itty-bitty, lilliputian, midget, miniature, minikin

dwell *vb* **1** *syn* RESIDE 1, abide, bide, ||dig, hang out, live
2 *syn* CONSIST 1, exist, inhere, lie, reside

dweller *n syn* INHABITANT, denizen, habitant, indweller, liver, occupant, resident, ||residenter, resider

dwelling *n syn* HABITATION 2, abode, commorancy, domicile, home, house, residence, residency

dwindle *vb* **1** *syn* DECREASE, abate, ||bate, close, diminish, drain (away), lessen, reduce, taper, taper off
rel ebb, subside, wane; attenuate, extenuate, thin; moderate; disappear
2 *syn* FAIL 3, fall short, shrink, wane, waste (away), weaken

||**dwine** *vb syn* FAIL 1, decline, deteriorate, fade, flag, languish, weaken

dyad *n syn* COUPLE, brace, doublet, duo, pair, twosome

dye *n syn* COLOR 6, colorant, dyestuff, pigment, stain, tincture

dyed-in-the-wool *adj syn* INVETERATE 1, bred-in-the-bone, confirmed, deep-dyed, deep-rooted, deep-seated, entrenched, hard-shell, settled, sworn

dyestuff *n syn* COLOR 6, colorant, dye, pigment, stain, tincture

dying *adj syn* MORIBUND

dynamic *adj* **1** *syn* ACTIVE 1, alive, functioning, live, operative, running, working
rel activating, energizing, vitalizing
ant static
2 *syn* VIGOROUS, energetic, lusty, red-blooded, strenuous, ||survigrous, vital
rel forceful, forcible; intense, vehement, violent
con idle, inactive, passive
ant inert

dynamite *vb syn* DESTROY 1, annihilate, decimate, demolish, destruct, dismantle, dissolve, raze, ruin, shatter

dynamo *n syn* HUSTLER 1, go-getter, live wire, peeler, rustler, self-starter

dysentery *n syn* DIARRHEA, ||backdoor trots, flux, ||runs, scour(s), *shits, ||squirts, *trots

dyslogistic *adj syn* DEROGATORY, depreciative, depreciatory, detracting, disadvantageous, disparaging, pejorative, slighting, uncomplimentary
ant eulogistic

dyspathy *n syn* ANTIPATHY 2, allergy, aversion

dyspeptic *adj syn* ILL-TEMPERED, bad-tempered, hot-tempered, ill-humored, ill-natured, ||rusty, tempersome

dysphoria *n syn* SADNESS, dejection, depression, gloom, heavyheartedness, melancholy, mopes, mournfulness, suds, unhappiness

---

E

each *adj* ***syn*** ALL 2, every
rel any, several, various; particular, respective, specific

each *adv* ***syn*** APIECE, all, aside, ‖per, per capita, per caput
idiom a shot, a throw, a whack

eager *adj* moved by a strong and urgent desire or interest <young executives *eager* to succeed>
syn agog, anxious, appetent, ardent, athirst, avid, breathless, impatient, keen, raring, solicitous, thirsty
rel enthusiastic, gung ho, heated, hot; ambitious, intent; acquisitive, covetous, craving, desirous, hankering, ‖honing, hungry, longing, pining, wishful, yearning; impatient, restive, restless
idiom champing at the bit, ready and willing
con aloof, disinterested, incurious, indifferent, unconcerned, uninterested; apathetic, detached, impassive, stolid
ant listless

eagerness *n* a strong and urgent desire or interest <an *eagerness* to learn>
syn ardor, enthusiasm, zing
rel alacrity, avidity, keenness, quickness; ambition; gusto, ‖mustard, zest
con lackadaisicality, languor, lethargy; aloofness, disinterest; apathy, deliberation, detachment, impassivity, stolidity
ant listlessness

eagle eye *n* ***syn*** EYE 3, scrutiny, surveillance, tab, watch

eagle–eyed *adj* ***syn*** SHARP-EYED, hawk-eyed, lyncean, lynx-eyed, sharp-sighted

ear *n* ***syn*** NOTICE 1, attention, heed, mark, ‖mind, note, observance, observation, regard, remark

earlier *adv* **1** ***syn*** BEFORE 2, already, erstwhile, formerly, heretofore, once, previously
2 ***syn*** HITHERTO 1, as yet, so far, thus far, yet
3 ***syn*** BEFORE 3, beforehand, sooner

earliest *adj* ***syn*** FIRST 2, initial, maiden, original, pioneer, primary, prime
con final, terminal, ultimate
ant latest

early *adv* **1** at or nearly at the beginning of a period, course, process, or series <it is much too *early* to guess the outcome>
syn betimes, seasonably, soon, timely
rel first
2 in advance of the expected or usual time <these apples bear *early* and heavy>
syn betimes, oversoon, prematurely
rel beforehand
idiom ahead of time, bright and early

early *adj* **1** of, relating to, or occurring near the beginning of a period of time, a development, or a series <*early* Renaissance> <*early* art forms>
syn primitive, primordial
rel original, pristine; ancient, antediluvian, antiquated, primal, primeval; antecedent, preceding, prevenient, prior
con conclusive, final, last, terminal, ultimate; eventual; intermediate, middle, midmost
ant late
2 occurring before the expected or usual time <an *early* death> <an *early* peach>
syn overearly, oversoon, premature, previous, ‖soon, untimely; *compare* PRECOCIOUS
rel anticipative, anticipatory, precipitant, precocious; unanticipated, unexpected
con slow, tardy; anticipated, expected
ant late

earmark *vb* ***syn*** DESIGNATE 3, allocate

earn *vb* **1** to receive as return for effort <*earn* a living wage>
syn acquire, bring in, ‖drag down, draw down, gain, get, knock down, make, win
rel attain, effect, obtain, procure, realize, receive, secure
2 to be or make worthy of <his devotion to duty *earned* him a promotion>
syn deserve, merit, rate
rel bag, come by, harvest, net, reap, score

earnest *n* ***syn*** EARNESTNESS, intentness, serious-mindedness, seriousness
rel attention, interest; enthusiasm, warmth, zeal
ant jest, play

earnest *adj* ***syn*** SERIOUS 1, grave, no-nonsense, sedate, sober, sobersided, solemn, somber, staid, weighty
rel ardent, enthusiastic, passionate, pressing, warm, zealous; assiduous, busy, diligent, industrious, perseverant, sedulous; sincere, wholehearted, whole-souled
con buoyant, effervescent, elastic, flippant, light
ant frivolous

earnest *n* ***syn*** PLEDGE 1, pawn, security, token, warrant

earnestly *adv* **1** ***syn*** HARD 3, assiduously, dingdong, exhaustively, intensely, intensively, painstakingly, thoroughly, unremittingly
rel seriously, soberly, solemnly, thoughtfully; zealously
2 ***syn*** SERIOUSLY 1, actively, down, for real

earnestness *n* a state of freedom from all jesting or trifling <he studied with great *earnestness*>
syn earnest, intentness, serious-mindedness, seriousness
rel doggedness, perseverance, persistence; decision, determination, firmness, purposefulness, resolve; absorp-

---

syn synonym(s) ***rel*** related word(s)
idiom idiomatic equivalent(s) ***con*** contrasted word(s)
ant antonym(s) * vulgar
‖ use limited; if in doubt, see a dictionary
The first word in a synonym list when printed in SMALL CAPITALS shows where there is more information about the group. For a more efficient use of this book see Explanatory Notes.

tion, attentiveness, concentration, engrossment; deliberation; gravity, sobriety
con levity, lightness; shallowness, superficiality; carelessness, slackness
ant frivolity

earnings *n pl* ***syn*** PROFIT, gain, lucre, proceeds, return

earshot *n* the range within which something (as a voice) may be heard <the gossips were still within *earshot* of her>
syn hearing, sound
idiom carrying (*or* hearing) distance

earsplitting *adj* ***syn*** LOUD 1, blaring, full-mouthed, piercing, roaring, stentorian, stentorious, stentorophonic
rel penetrating, shrill

earth *n* **1** the entire area in which man lives and acts <expect the destruction of the *earth*>
syn globe, (the) planet, world
rel orb, sphere; cosmos, creation, macrocosm, universe, vale
2 areas of land as distinguished from sea and air <clayey *earth*, difficult to drain>
syn dirt, dry land, ground, land, soil, terra firma
rel clay, gravel, humus, loam, mud, sand; fill, subsoil; terrain, turf; clod

earthlike *adj* ***syn*** EARTHY 1, terrene, terrestrial

earthly *adj* **1** of, relating to, or characteristic of this earth or man's life on earth <*earthly* pursuits>
syn earthy, mundane, sublunary, tellurian, telluric, terrene, terrestrial, uncelestial, worldly
rel carnal, corporeal, earthbound, physical; material, temporal; unspiritual
con celestial, empyreal, empyrean, heavenly; ideal, utopian; divine, spiritual
2 ***syn*** PROBABLE, conceivable, likely, mortal, possible
rel imaginable, potential

earthquake *n* a shaking or trembling of the earth that is volcanic or tectonic in origin <homes destroyed by *earthquakes*>
syn quake, ‖quaker, shake, shock, temblor (*or* tremblor), tremor

earthy *adj* **1** consisting of, resembling, or suggesting earth <a stale *earthy* smell>
syn earthlike, terrene, terrestrial
rel clayey, dusty, muddy, sandy
2 ***syn*** EARTHLY 1, mundane, sublunary, tellurian, telluric, terrene, terrestrial, uncelestial, worldly
3 ***syn*** MATERIALISTIC, banausic, mundane, sensual, temporal, worldly
4 ***syn*** REALISTIC, down-to-earth, hard-boiled, hard-headed, matter-of-fact, practical, pragmatic, unfantastic, unidealistic, unsentimental
ant impractical

ease *n* **1** ***syn*** REST 1, leisure, relaxation, repose, requiescence
rel idleness, inactivity, inertia, inertness, passivity, supinity; calmness, security
con labor, toil, travail; adversity, difficulty; burden, care, worry
2 ***syn*** UNCONSTRAINT, abandon, naturalness, spontaneity, unrestraint
3 freedom from or mitigation of pain <medication brought him instant *ease*>
syn alleviation, easement, mitigation, relief
rel decrease, diminishment, moderation, reduction; calming, soothing
con discomfort, unrest; agony, pain
4 ***syn*** READINESS 3, facility
rel adroitness, artfulness, cleverness, deftness, effortlessness, expertise, expertness, fluency, knack, poise, skillfulness, smoothness; efficiency, dispatch
con awkwardness, clumsiness, maladroitness, stiffness, woodenness; constraint; inconvenience, pains; exertion
ant effort
5 ***syn*** PROSPERITY 2, abundance, easy street, prosperousness, thriving, well-being

ease *vb* **1** ***syn*** RELIEVE 1, allay, alleviate, assuage, lighten, mitigate, mollify
rel deaden, dull; ameliorate, help
con afflict, torment
2 ***syn*** LOOSE 5, ease off, lax, loosen, relax, slack, slacken, untighten
rel disengage, free, release
con bind, restrain, tighten
3 to make less difficult <new laws that will *ease* voting requirements>
syn facilitate
rel aid, assist, better, help, improve; forward, further, promote, speed
idiom clear (*or* prepare) the way (for), grease the wheels, open the door (to *or* for)
con hinder, impede, retard

easeful *adj* ***syn*** COMFORTABLE 2, comfy, cozy, cushy, easy, snug, soft

easement *n* ***syn*** EASE 3, alleviation, mitigation, relief
rel allayment, appeasement, assuagement, mollification

ease off *vb* **1** ***syn*** LOOSE 5, ease, lax, loosen, relax, slack, slacken, untighten
2 ***syn*** ABATE 4, die (down *or* away), ebb, fall, let up, moderate, relent, slacken, subside, wane
3 ***syn*** RELAX 2, loosen up, unbend, unlax, unwind

easily *adv* **1** without discomfort, difficulty, or reluctance <*easily* translated the document>
syn effortlessly, facilely, freely, lightly, readily, smoothly, well
rel competently, dexterously, efficiently, fluently, handily, simply
idiom hands down, slick as a whistle
con awkwardly, clumsily, ineptly, stiffly; arduously, wearily
ant laboriously
2 without question <this is *easily* the best course of action>
syn absolutely, definitely, doubtless, doubtlessly, positively, unequivocally, unquestionably
rel actually, assuredly, certainly, clearly, decidedly, indeed, really, truly, undoubtedly

---

idiom no doubt
con apparently, perhaps, probably, seemingly; doubtfully, equivocally, questionably
3 ***syn*** WELL 7, doubtlessly, indeed, really, truly, undoubtedly

easy *adj* **1** causing or involving little or no difficulty <an *easy* solution>
syn effortless, facile, light, royal, simple, smooth, untroublesome
rel apparent, clear, distinct, evident, manifest, obvious, plain; clear-cut, straightforward, uncomplicated, uncompounded, uninvolved
idiom easy as falling off a log, easy as pie, nothing to it
con arduous, difficult, troublesome; abstruse, complex, complicated, intricate, knotty
ant hard
2 ***syn*** FORBEARING, charitable, clement, indulgent, lenient, merciful, tolerant
rel compassionate, condoning, excusing, forgiving, pardoning, sympathetic; benign, kindly; lax, moderate, soft; humoring, mollycoddling, pampering, spoiling
con austere, exacting, rigid, severe, stern, strict, stringent
3 easily taken advantage of or imposed upon <he was *easy* prey to her wiles>
syn fleeceable, gullible, naive, susceptible
rel credulous, trusting, unmistrusting, unsuspicious; deceivable, deludable, dupable, exploitable; artless, dewy-eyed, green, simple, unsophisticated
con critical, cynical, disbelieving, mistrustful, scoffing, skeptical, suspicious, unbelieving
4 ***syn*** FAST 7, light, loose, ‖riggish, unchaste, wanton, whorish
5 ***syn*** COMFORTABLE 2, comfy, cozy, cushy, easeful, snug, soft
rel secure
con discontented, dissatisfied; miserable
ant uncomfortable
6 ***syn*** AMIABLE 1, complaisant, good-humored, good-natured, good-tempered, lenient, mild, obliging
rel familiar, gregarious, informal; courtly, diplomatic, pleasant, polite, sociable; smooth, suave, urbane
con brusque, curt, unfriendly, unpleasant; constrained, embarrassed, formal, restrained; discourteous, impolite, undiplomatic, ungracious; stiff, unsocial, withdrawn, wooden
ant ill at ease
7 ***syn*** CALM 2, collected, composed, easygoing, placid, poised, possessed, self-possessed, serene, tranquil
rel relaxed; lethargic, unambitious
con agitated, tense, troubled, uptight
8 ***syn*** PROSPEROUS 3, comfortable, ‖snug, substantial, well, well-fixed, well-heeled, well-off, well-to-do
rel successful, thriving
idiom in easy circumstances, on easy street
con straitened
9 marked by ready facility (as of expression) <an *easy* style of writing>
syn cursive, effortless, flowing, fluent, running, smooth
rel facile; graceful
con effortful, labored
ant difficult

easygoing *adj* **1** ***syn*** CALM 2, collected, composed, easy, placid, poised, self-composed, self-possessed, serene, tranquil
con agitated, flurried, flustered, harassed; anxious, concerned, upset, worried
ant uptight
2 ***syn*** LAZY, drony, faineant, indolent, slothful, slow-going, work-shy
rel apathetic, careless, indifferent, unconcerned; unambitious
con active, ambitious, diligent, dynamic, energetic, industrious, live, vigorous
3 not constrained or bound by rigid standards <enjoyed the *easygoing* morality of a commune>
syn breezy, casual, ‖common, dégagé, informal, low-pressure, relaxed, ‖sonsy, unconstrained, unfussy, unreserved
rel affable, folksy; flexible, lax, moderate, offhand, off-handed, unaffected; carefree, devil-may-care, happy-go-lucky; outgiving; uninhibited
idiom free and easy
con ceremonious, decorous, formal, proper, stuffy; constrained, inflexible, inhibited, restrained, rigid, starchy, stiff

easy mark *n* **1** ***syn*** FOOL 3, butt, chump, dupe, fall guy, gull, mark, pigeon, sap, sucker
2 ***syn*** SOFT TOUCH 1

‖**easy rider** *n* **1** ***syn*** SYCOPHANT, apple-polisher, bootlicker, ‖brownnoser, footlicker, groveler, minion, spaniel, toadeater, toady
2 ***syn*** PIMP 1, bully, cadet, fancy man, ‖mack, macquereau, pander

easy street *n* ***syn*** PROSPERITY 2, abundance, ease, prosperousness, thriving, well-being

eat *vb* **1** to take in as food <they quickly *ate* a hearty breakfast>
syn consume, devour, feed (on), ingest, meal, partake (of), take; *compare* CONSUME 5
rel banquet, feast, gormandize; eat up, gobble (up *or* down), gorge (on), ‖mop (up), polish off, scoff; breakfast, dine, lunch, snack, sup; mouth, ‖muckamuck; nibble, pick
idiom break bread, get away with, have (*or* take) a bite, take nourishment, ‖put on the feed bag
2 ***syn*** CONSUME 1, devour, eat up, exhaust, use up
3 to consume gradually <the acid *ate* the surface of the copper>
syn bite, corrode, eat away, erode, gnaw, scour, wear (away)
rel nibble (away); consume, decompose, disintegrate, dissolve

eatable *adj* ***syn*** EDIBLE, comestible, esculent

eat away *vb* ***syn*** EAT 3, bite, corrode, erode, gnaw, scour, wear (away)

---

syn synonym(s) *rel* related word(s)
idiom idiomatic equivalent(s) *con* contrasted word(s)
ant antonym(s) * vulgar
‖ use limited; if in doubt, see a dictionary
The first word in a synonym list when printed in SMALL CAPITALS shows where there is more information about the group. For a more efficient use of this book see Explanatory Notes.

eating house *n* a cheap often small restaurant <grabbed a quick sandwich at a local *eating house*>
syn beanery, ‖buffet, café, coffee shop, cookshop, diner, ‖greasy spoon, ‖hashery, ‖hash house, lunch counter (*or* bar), luncheonette, lunchroom, lunch wagon (*or* cart), quick-lunch, sandwich shop, snack bar (*or* counter)
rel cafeteria, eatery, tearoom; trattoria

‖**eats** *n pl syn* FOOD 1, ‖chow, comestibles, edibles, grub, nurture, provender, provisions, viands, victuals

eat up *vb* **1** to eat completely and without delay <*eat up* your dinner before it gets cold>
syn devour, dispatch, polish off
rel down, eat; bolt, gobble (up *or* down), gorge (on), ‖mop (up), wolf
2 *syn* CONSUME 1, devour, eat, exhaust, use up
‖**3** *syn* DEVOUR 5
rel luxuriate (in), riot (in), wallow (in)
idiom be beside oneself over, be thrilled to death by, smack one's lips over, take delight in
‖**4** *syn* LOVE 1, adore, delight (in)

ebb *vb syn* ABATE 4, die (down *or* away), ease off, fall, let up, moderate, relent, slacken, subside, wane
rel decline, peter (out); recede, retreat, retrograde
con ascend, increase, mount, rise; advance, progress
ant flow

ebbing *n syn* FAILURE 4, declination, decline, deterioration, waning
rel declining, sinking

ebon *adj syn* BLACK 1, atramentous, ebony, inky, jet, jetty, pitch-black, pitch-dark, raven, sable

ebony *adj syn* BLACK 1, atramentous, ebon, inky, jet, jetty, pitch-black, pitch-dark, raven, sable

ebullience *n* lively or enthusiastic expression of thoughts or feelings <her bubbling *ebullience* was infectious>
syn buoyancy, effervescence, exuberance, exuberancy
rel animation, enthusiasm, gaiety, high-spiritedness, liveliness, vitality, vivaciousness vivacity; agitation, excitement, exhilaration, ferment
con apathy, impassivity, languor, lethargy, listlessness, passivity, sluggishness, stolidity, torpidity, torpor; enervation, inactivity, inertia, lifelessness; disinterest, unconcern, uninterest

ebullient *adj syn* EXUBERANT 1, brash, effervescent, high-spirited, vivacious

eccentric *adj* **1** not having the same center <*eccentric* spheres>
syn off-center
rel uncentered; off-balance, unbalanced
con centered; balanced
ant concentric
2 *syn* STRANGE 4, curious, erratic, idiosyncratic, odd, oddball, peculiar, queer, singular, weird
rel anomalous, irregular, unnatural; exceptionable, exceptional, quirky, quizzical; beeheaded, ‖dippy, wacky; fantastic, grotesque
con customary, habitual; natural, normal, regular, typical

eccentric *n* one who deviates from established patterns especially in odd or whimsical ways <an *eccentric* who filled his house with statues of himself>
syn case, character, ‖duck, oddball, oddity, original, quiz, ‖spook, ‖wack, zombie
rel bohemian, maverick, nonconformist, unconformist; dissenter, heretic; caution, coot, ‖geezer; crackpot, crank, freak, kook, screwball
idiom queer duck (*or* potato)
con conformer, conformist, conventionalist, traditionalist; bore, bromide, dullard

ecclesiast *n syn* CLERGYMAN, churchman, cleric, clerical, clerk, divine, ecclesiastic, minister, parson, preacher

ecclesiastic *n syn* CLERGYMAN, churchman, cleric, clerical, clerk, divine, minister, parson, preacher, reverend

ecclesiastical *adj* of, relating to, or belonging to a church especially as an established institution <*ecclesiastical* law>
syn church, churchly, churchmanly, spiritual
rel apostolic, canonical, episcopal, episcopalian, evangelistic, theological; clerical, ministerial, papal, pastoral, patriarchal, pontifical, prelatial, priestly, rabbinical, sacerdotal; cathedralesque, churchlike, pantheonic, synagogal, synagogical, tabernacular, templelike
con lay, secular

ecdysiast *n syn* STRIPTEASER, peeler, stripper, striptease, teaser

echelon *n syn* LINE 5, file, queue, rank, row, string, tier

echoic *adj syn* ONOMATOPOEIC, imitative, onomatopoetic

éclat *n syn* FAME 2, celebrity, notoriety, renown, ‖rep, reputation, repute
rel bang, brilliance, brilliancy, display, luster, noticeableness, prominence, remarkableness; distinction, standing; kudos
con oblivion, obscurity; contempt, derision, scorn

eclectic *adj* **1** selecting what appears to be the best from various doctrines, methods, or styles <an *eclectic* taste in music>
syn discriminating, select, selective
rel elective, selecting; choosing, choosy, discerning, fastidious, finicky, fussy, particular, picky
2 composed of elements drawn from various sources <an *eclectic* art incorporating romanticism and impressionism>
syn catholic
rel broad, comprehensive, inclusive; assorted, mingled, mixed; diverse, diversified, heterogeneous, multifarious, multiform, varied; derived, unoriginal
con distinctive, narrow; new, original

eclipse *vb syn* OBSCURE, adumbrate, becloud, bedim, darken, dim, murk, overcloud, overshadow, shadow

economical *adj syn* SPARING, canny, chary, frugal, provident, saving, Scotch, stewardly, thrifty, unwasteful
rel careful, forehanded, prudent; economizing, penny-wise; cheeseparing, close, mean, miserly, niggardly, penny-pinching, penurious, scrimping, skimping, spare, stingy
con generous, lavish, wasteful

---

syn synonym(s) *rel* related word(s)
idiom idiomatic equivalent(s) *con* contrasted word(s)
ant antonym(s) * vulgar
‖ use limited; if in doubt, see a dictionary
The first word in a synonym list when printed in SMALL CAPITALS shows where there is more information about the group. For a more efficient use of this book see Explanatory Notes.

ant extravagant

economic poison *n* ***syn*** PESTICIDE, biocide

economize *vb* to avoid unnecessary waste or expense < *economize* on food by using leftovers >
syn save
rel conserve; scrimp, skimp
con dissipate, scatter, waste
ant squander, throw away

economy *n* careful management of material resources < retired people often must learn to practice *economy* >
syn forehandedness, frugality, husbandry, providence, prudence, thrift, thriftiness
rel meanness, miserliness, niggardliness, parcity, parsimony, scrimping, skimping, stinginess; carefulness, discretion
con improvidence, lavishness, prodigality, squandering, thriftlessness, wastefulness
ant extravagance

ecstasy *n* intense exaltation of mind and feelings < was in *ecstasy* over flying >
syn heaven, rapture, rhapsody, seventh heaven, transport; *compare* EXHILARATION
rel beatitude, blessedness, bliss, blissfulness, felicity, gladness, happiness; delectation, delight, elation, joy, joyfulness, overjoyfulness, pleasure; enchantment, euphoria, intoxication, madness; exaltation, inspiration; paradise; afflatus, frenzy, fury
idiom cloud nine
con dejection, downheartedness, lowness, lowspiritedness, oppression; blues, dumps, melancholy
ant depression

ecumenical *adj* ***syn*** UNIVERSAL 2, catholic, cosmic, cosmopolitan, global, planetary, worldwide
rel heaven-wide; all-comprehending, all-comprehensive, all-covering, all-including, all-pervading; comprehensive, general, inclusive
con diocesan, local, parochial, provincial; circumscribed, insular, limited, narrow, restricted

edacious *adj* ***syn*** VORACIOUS, gluttonous, rapacious, ravening, ravenous

eddy *n* a swirling mass especially of water < dark *eddies* in the flooded stream >
syn maelstrom, vortex, whirl, whirlpool
rel gurge, surge, swirl, twirl, whirl; back current, back stream, countercurrent, counterflow, counterflux; backwash, backwater

eddy *vb* ***syn*** SWIRL, gurge, purl, swoosh, whirl, whirlpool, whorl

edge *n* **1** ***syn*** BORDER 1, brim, brink, fringe, hem, margin, perimeter, periphery, skirt, verge
rel end, extremity; ledge, side
con area, surface

---

syn synonym(s) ***rel*** related word(s)
idiom idiomatic equivalent(s) ***con*** contrasted word(s)
ant antonym(s) * vulgar
‖ use limited; if in doubt, see a dictionary
The first word in a synonym list when printed in SMALL CAPITALS shows where there is more information about the group. For a more efficient use of this book see Explanatory Notes.

2 a cutting quality < there was an *edge* to his voice as he answered >
syn incisiveness, keenness, sharpness
rel bite, cut, sting; knife-edge, razor-edge; acerbity, acidity, acridity, causticity; astringency, stringency; acuteness, penetration, shrillness, thinness
3 ***syn*** VERGE 2, brink, point, threshold
4 ***syn*** ADVANTAGE 3, allowance, bulge, ‖deadwood, draw, handicap, head start, odds, start, vantage
con bar, encumbrance, obstacle; disadvantage

edge *vb* **1** ***syn*** SHARPEN, hone, ‖sharp, whet
2 ***syn*** BORDER 1, bound, fringe, hem, margin, outline, rim, skirt, surround, verge
3 ***syn*** SIDLE, ‖slive

edge in *vb* ***syn*** INSINUATE 3, foist, infiltrate, work in, worm

edgy *adj* **1** ***syn*** TENSE 2, nervy, restive, uneasy, uptight
rel skittish; excitable, excited, high-strung, overstrung; irritable, touchy; impatient, restless
idiom on edge
con detached; peaceful, placid; patient
2 ***syn*** EXCITABLE, agitable, alarmable, combustible, skittery, skittish, startlish, volatile

edible *adj* suitable for use as food < *edible* plant products >
syn comestible, eatable, esculent
rel digestible; nourishing, nutritious, nutritive; palatable, savory, succulent, tasty, toothsome
ant inedible

edibles *n pl* ***syn*** FOOD 1, ‖chow, comestibles, ‖eats, grub, nurture, provender, provisions, viands, victuals

edict *n* **1** a publicly proclaimed order or rule of conduct by a competent authority < a government *edict* regarding curfew enforcement >
syn decree, directive, ruling, ukase
rel instrument; order; manifesto, proclamation, pronouncement, pronunciamento; bull
2 ***syn*** LAW 1, canon, decree, decretum, ordinance, precept, prescript, regulation, rule, statute

edifice *n* a large, magnificent, or massive building < a marble *edifice* now used as a museum >
syn erection, pile, structure; *compare* BUILDING, HUT

edify *vb* ***syn*** ILLUMINATE 2, enlighten, illume, illumine, improve, irradiate, uplift
rel better, enhance; elucidate; educate, instruct, teach
con debase, deprave

edition *n* the total number of copies of the same work printed during a stretch of time < the initial *edition* of 50,000 copies was exhausted in a month >
syn impression, printing, reissue, reprinting

educate *vb* ***syn*** TEACH, discipline, instruct, school, train
rel cultivate, nurture; brief, explain, inform

education *n* **1** the act or process of educating < devoted himself to the *education* of illiterate adults >
syn instruction, schooling, teaching, training, tuition, tutelage
rel coaching, pedagogy, tutorage, tutoring, tutorship; direction, guidance
2 the product or result of being educated < obtained his *education* in local schools and in college >
syn erudition, knowledge, learning, scholarship, science
rel culture, edification, enlightenment, learnedness, literacy

con ignorance, illiteracy

educational *adj* ***syn*** INFORMATIVE, educative, informational, informatory, instructional, instructive

educative *adj* ***syn*** INFORMATIVE, educational, informational, informatory, instructional, instructive

educe *vb* **1** to draw out something hidden, latent, or reserved < *educed* important information from the witness >
syn elicit, evince, evoke, extort, extract, milk
rel drag, draw, draw out, pull, wrest, wring; gain, get, obtain, procure, secure; distill
con miss, overlook, pass over
2 ***syn*** DERIVE 1, evolve, excogitate
rel reason (out), think (out)

eerie *adj* ***syn*** WEIRD 1, spooky, uncanny, unearthly
rel bizarre, fantastic, grotesque; arcane; crawly

efface *vb* ***syn*** ERASE, annul, black (out), blot out, cancel, delete, expunge, obliterate, wipe (out), x (out)
rel eradicate, extirpate; eliminate, exclude, rule out

effect *n* **1** a condition or occurrence traceable to a cause < the *effect* of the medicine was dizziness >
syn aftereffect, aftermath, causatum, consequence, corollary, end product, event, eventuality, issue, outcome, precipitate, result, sequel, sequence, upshot
rel pursuance; development, fruit, outgrowth, ramification; denouement, repercussion; conclusion, end; side effect
con antecedent, determinant, occasion, reason; base, basis, foundation, ground, groundwork
ant cause
2 effects *pl* ***syn*** POSSESSION 2, belongings, chattels, goods, lares and penates, movables, things

effect *vb* **1** to induce to come into being < specific genes *effect* specific bodily characters >
syn bring about, cause, draw on, make, produce, secure
rel conceive, create, generate; bring on, induce; enact, render, turn out, yield
con impede, limit, restrict; repress, suppress
2 to carry to a successful conclusion < found a pass that allowed them to *effect* passage through the mountains >
syn bring off, carry out, carry through, effectuate; *compare* FULFILL 1, PERFORM 2
rel actualize, realize; achieve, procure
con fail, fall down
3 ***syn*** ENFORCE, implement, invoke

effective *adj* producing or capable of producing a result < an *effective* rebuke >
syn effectual, efficacious, efficient, virtuous
rel adequate, capable, competent; cogent, compelling, convincing, sound, telling, valid; able, active, dynamic; operative, useful; direct
con abortive, bootless, fruitless, futile, vain; empty, hollow, idle, nugatory, otiose, pointless; inoperative, useless, worthless
ant ineffective

effectiveness *n* **1** ***syn*** POINT 3, cogency, force, punch, validity, validness
rel forcefulness, potency, power, strength, verve, vigor
con impotence, weakness
ant ineffectiveness
2 ***syn*** EFFICIENCY 1, efficacy, performance
3 ***syn*** EFFICACY 1, capability, efficiency, potency

effectual *adj* ***syn*** EFFECTIVE, efficacious, efficient, virtuous
rel accomplishing, achieving, effecting, fulfilling; practicable, sound, useful, valid, workable; conclusive, decisive, determinative, influential; authoritative, potent, powerful, strong, toothy
con impotent, weak
ant ineffectual

effectuate *vb* ***syn*** EFFECT 2, bring off, carry out, carry through

effeminate *adj* lacking manly strength and purpose < an *effeminate* preoccupation with trifles >
syn epicene, Miss-Nancyish, pansified, prissy, sissified, sissy, unmanly
rel chichi, old-maidish, overnice, precious; foppish, sappy, silken
ant manly, masculine

effervescence *n* ***syn*** EBULLIENCE, buoyancy, exuberance, exuberancy
rel bubbling, ebullition, fizzing, foaming
con deadness, flatness, staleness

effervescent *adj* **1** ***syn*** EXUBERANT 1, brash, ebullient, high-spirited, vivacious
2 ***syn*** ELASTIC 2, airy, bouncy, buoyant, expansive, resilient, volatile
rel animated, boiling, bubbly, excited, gay, lively, sparkling, sprightly, vivacious; gleeful, hilarious, jolly, mirthful
con lifeless, listless, subdued; earnest, sedate, serious, solemn

effete *adj* **1** ***syn*** STERILE 1, barren, impotent, infecund, infertile, unfruitful
2 having lost energy or drive < *effete,* weary, burned-out revolutionaries >
syn all in, bleary, depleted, done, done in, drained, exhausted, far-gone, spent, used up, washed-out, worn-out
rel consumed; debilitated, enfeebled, fatigued
idiom on one's last legs, out on one's feet
con alive, lively, vigorous, vital
3 having lost character < a soft, *effete* society >
syn decadent, decayed, degenerate, overripe
rel decaying, declining; soft, weak; dissolute, immoral

efficacious *adj* ***syn*** EFFECTIVE, effectual, efficient, virtuous
rel active, operative, productive; influential, potent, powerful, puissant, strong
con abortive; impotent, powerless, useless, vain, weak
ant inefficacious

efficacy *n* **1** the power to produce an effect < *efficacy* of the drug >
syn capability, effectiveness, efficiency, potency

---

syn synonym(s) — ***rel*** related word(s)
idiom idiomatic equivalent(s) — ***con*** contrasted word(s)
ant antonym(s) — * vulgar
‖ use limited; if in doubt, see a dictionary
The first word in a synonym list when printed in SMALL CAPITALS shows where there is more information about the group. For a more efficient use of this book see Explanatory Notes.

rel capableness, productiveness, use; adequacy, capacity, sufficiency
con ineffectiveness, inefficiency; uselessness, worthlessness
ant inefficacy
2 ***syn*** EFFICIENCY 1, effectiveness, performance

efficiency *n* **1** the capacity to produce desired results with a minimum expenditure of energy, time, or resources <demands a high degree of *efficiency* on the job>
syn effectiveness, efficacy, performance
rel ability, address, adeptness, competence, expertise, know-how, proficiency, prowess, skill; capability, resourcefulness; productivity
con inadequacy, incompetence, ineffectiveness; unproductiveness
ant inefficiency
2 ***syn*** EFFICACY 1, capability, effectiveness, potency

efficient *adj* ***syn*** EFFECTIVE, effectual, efficacious, virtuous
rel able, capable, competent, fitted, qualified; adept, expert, masterly, proficient, skilled, skillful
con incapable, incompetent, inexpert, unadept, unproficient, unqualified, unsuitable; unproductive; ineffectual
ant inefficient

effloresce *vb* ***syn*** BLOSSOM, bloom, blow, burgeon, flower, outbloom

effort *n* **1** the active use of energy in producing a result <thought the job wasn't worth the *effort*>
syn elbow grease, exertion, pains, trouble, while
rel labor, toil, travail, work; energy, force, might, power, puissance; attempt, endeavor, essay
idiom sweat of one's brow
con adroitness, facility, smoothness; do-nothingness, inaction, indolence, inertia, lackadaisicalness, languor, laziness
ant ease
2 ***syn*** TASK 2, chore, job, taskwork

effortful *adj* ***syn*** HARD 6, arduous, difficult, labored, laborious, operose, rough, strenuous, toilsome, uphill

effortless *adj* **1** ***syn*** EASY 1, facile, light, royal, simple, smooth, untroublesome
rel adept, expert, masterly, proficient, ready, skilled, skillful
con laborious, toilsome, trying
ant painstaking
2 ***syn*** EASY 9, cursive, flowing, fluent, running, smooth

effortlessly *adv* ***syn*** EASILY 1, facilely, freely, lightly, readily, smoothly, well
rel adeptly, adroitly, efficiently, expertly, proficiently, skillfully
con painstakingly
ant arduously, laboriously

---

syn synonym(s) — *rel* related word(s)
idiom idiomatic equivalent(s) — *con* contrasted word(s)
ant antonym(s) — * vulgar
|| use limited; if in doubt, see a dictionary
The first word in a synonym list when printed in SMALL CAPITALS shows where there is more information about the group. For a more efficient use of this book see Explanatory Notes.

effrontery *n* flagrant disregard of courtesy or propriety and an arrogant assumption of privilege <had the *effrontery* to insult her father>
syn brashness, brass, cheek, confidence, ||crust, face, gall, nerve, presumption; *compare* INSOLENCE
rel audacity, hardihood, temerity; assurance, self-assurance, self-confidence; brazenness, impudence; impertinence, insolence
con courtesy, grace, propriety

effulgent *adj* ***syn*** BRIGHT 1, beaming, brilliant, fulgent, incandescent, lambent, lucent, luminous, radiant, refulgent
rel vivid; glorious, resplendent, splendid
con dark, dusky, gloomy, murky

effusive *adj* unduly demonstrative <*effusive* assurances of undying love>
syn gushing, gushy, slobbering, slobbery, sloppy
rel expansive, fulsome, outpouring, profuse; demonstrative, unconstrained, unreserved, unrestrained; cloying, slushy; smarmy
con close, restrained, reticent, taciturn; bashful, modest, shy
ant reserved

egg (on) *vb* ***syn*** URGE, exhort, goad, prick, prod, prompt, propel, sic, spur
rel agitate, excite, pique, stimulate; instigate; arouse, drive, rally, stir up, whip (on *or* up)
con arrest, bridle

egghead *n* ***syn*** INTELLECTUAL 2, Brahmin, double*dome, highbrow

egocentric *adj* **1** concerned with the individual person rather than society <an *egocentric* approach to world problems>
syn individualist, individualistic
rel self-centered, selfish
2 concerned only with one's own activities or needs and usually tending to self-assertion or self-satisfaction <an *egocentric* man, lacking feeling for others>
syn egoistic, egomaniacal, egotistic, self-absorbed, self*centered, self-concerned, self-interested, self-involved, selfish, self-seeking, self-serving; *compare* POMPOUS 1
rel conceited, narcissistic, self-affected, self-applauding, self-conceited, self-concentered, self-indulgent, self-loving, stuck-up, vainglorious; megalomaniac
idiom wrapped up in oneself

egoism *n* **1** ***syn*** EGOTISM 1, self-importance
rel self-assurance, self-confidence, self-possession
ant altruism
2 ***syn*** CONCEIT 2, egotism, pride, self-consequence, self-glory, self-importance, self-opinion, self-pride, swellheadedness, vainglory
rel self-satisfaction
con meekness, modesty
ant humility

egoistic *adj* ***syn*** EGOCENTRIC 2, egomaniacal, egotistic, self-absorbed, self-centered, self-concerned, self-interested, self-involved, selfish, self-serving
rel individualistic; self-satisfied, swellheaded
con humble, modest
ant altruistic

egomaniacal *adj* ***syn*** EGOCENTRIC 2, egoistic, egotistic, self-absorbed, self-centered, self-concerned, self-interested, self-involved, selfish, self-serving *rel* self-exalting, self-glorifying, vainglorious

egotism *n* **1** an exaggerated sense of one's own importance <in believing that he was indispensable, he exhibited consummate *egotism*>
syn egoism, self-importance
rel conceit, conceitedness, narcissism, self-esteem, self-love, vainness; boastfulness, boasting, bragging, gasconade, gasconism, megalomania, vaunting
con humility, lowliness; bashfulness, diffidence, shyness; modesty
ant altruism
2 *syn* CONCEIT 2, egoism, pride, self-consequence, self-glory, self-importance, self-opinion, self-pride, swell-headedness, vainglory
rel arrogance, superiority; contempt
con humbleness, self-effacement
ant humility

egotistic *adj syn* EGOCENTRIC 2, egoistic, egomaniacal, self-absorbed, self-centered, self-concerned, self-interested, self-involved, selfish, self-serving
rel boastful, cocky, inflated, pretentious, proud, puffed up, self-satisfied; conceited, stuck-up
idiom in love with oneself, stuck on oneself
con humble, modest; self-effacing, shy

egregious *adj* conspicuously bad or objectionable <an *egregious* mistake>
syn capital, flagrant, glaring, gross, rank
rel arrant, outright, stark; infamous, nefarious, notorious; atrocious, deplorable, heinous, monstrous, outrageous, preposterous
con measly, minor, petty, piddling, slender, slight, trifling, trivial

egress *n* **1** *syn* DEPARTURE 1, egression, exit, exiting, exodus, offgoing, setting-out, withdrawal
rel emergence, emerging
con coming, entering; arrival
ant ingress
2 a place or means of going out <a gate providing *egress* from the pasture>
syn exit, outlet
rel opening, passage; escape
idiom way out
con entrance, entry, entryway
ant access, ingress

egression *n syn* DEPARTURE 1, egress, exit, exiting, exodus, offgoing, setting-out, withdrawal
con entrance, entering
ant ingression

eidolon *n syn* APPARITION, ghost, ‖haunt, phantasm, phantom, shade, shadow, specter, spirit, ‖spook

ejaculate *vb syn* EXCLAIM, blat, blurt (out), bolt, cry out
rel call (out), shout, vociferate, yell

eject *vb* **1** to drive or force (somebody) out <*eject* an intruder from one's home>
syn boot (out), chase, chuck, dismiss, evict, extrude, kick out, out, throw out; *compare* BANISH
rel displace, dispossess; drive off, rout, run off; debar, disbar, eliminate, exclude, rule out, shut out; bump, cashier, discharge, fire, sack; discard, shed; reject, repudiate, spurn
idiom give one his walking papers, send packing, show one the door
con accept, admit, install, receive; entertain, harbor, house, lodge, shelter
2 *syn* ERUPT 1, belch, disgorge, eruct, expel, irrupt, spew

elaborate *adj* **1** *syn* COMPLEX 2, Byzantine, complicated, daedal, gordian, intricate, involved, knotty, labyrinthine, sophisticated
2 marked by complexity of detail or ornament <an *elaborate* coiffure>
syn complicated, fancy, intricate
rel detailed, highly-wrought; decorated, dressy, embellished, ornate; elegant; busy, overdone, overworked, overwrought
con common, ordinary, plain, unpolished; inartificial, inornate, natural
ant simple

elaborate *vb* **1** *syn* EXPAND 4, amplify, develop, enlarge
rel comment, discuss, dwell (upon); clarify, explain, expound, interpret
2 *syn* UNFOLD 3, develop, evolve

élan *n syn* SPIRIT 5, animation, brio, dash, esprit, life, oomph, verve, vim, zing
rel impetus

élan vital *n syn* SOUL 1, anima, animus, pneuma, psyche, spirit, vital force

elapse *vb syn* PASS 3, expire, go, pass away
rel flow, glide, pass (by), slide, slip (by); lapse, run out

elastic *adj* **1** able to withstand strain without being permanently affected or injured <a rubber band is *elastic*>
syn flexible, resilient, springy, stretch, stretchy, supple, whippy
rel ductile, malleable, pliable, pliant, plastic, rubberlike, rubbery; adaptable, moldable, stretchable, yielding; bouncy, limber, lithe
con brittle; inflexible, stiff, tense
ant rigid
2 able to recover quickly from depression and maintain high spirits <had an *elastic* optimistic nature>
syn airy, bouncy, buoyant, effervescent, expansive, resilient, volatile
rel animated, gay, lively, sprightly, vivacious; ebullient, high-spirited, mettlesome, soaring, spirited; adaptable, recuperative
con blue, dejected, depressed, gloomy, melancholy, sad; flaccid, limp

elate *vb* to elevate the spirits of <the phenomenal sales record *elated* him>
syn commove, excite, exhilarate, inspire, set up, spirit (up), stimulate
rel brighten, cheer, cheer up, encourage; delight, gladden, gratify, overjoy; buoy, elevate, exalt, uplift
con distress; oppress, weigh; weary

---

syn synonym(s) *rel* related word(s)
idiom idiomatic equivalent(s) *con* contrasted word(s)
ant antonym(s) * vulgar
‖ use limited; if in doubt, see a dictionary
The first word in a synonym list when printed in SMALL CAPITALS shows where there is more information about the group. For a more efficient use of this book see Explanatory Notes.

ant depress

elated *adj* ***syn*** INTOXICATED 2, excited, exhilarated, turned-on
rel enchanted, enraptured, exalted, transported; delighted, ecstatic, euphoric, exultant, jubilant, overjoyed
idiom in heaven, in seventh heaven, on cloud nine
con blue, deflated, unhappy

elation *n* **1** the quality or state of being elated <felt great *elation* when he won the presidential nomination>
syn euphoria, exaltation, exhilaration
rel buoyancy; happiness, joy; excitement; rapture, transport
idiom stars in one's eyes
con blues, depression; distress, misery, sadness, unhappiness
ant deflation
2 ***syn*** EUPHORIA 2, exaltation, intoxication
ant depression

elbow *vb* ***syn*** PUSH 2, bulldoze, hustle, jostle, press, ‖shog, shoulder, shove

elbowroom *n* ***syn*** ROOM 3, latitude, leeway, margin, play, scope
rel space

elder *n* **1** ***syn*** SENIOR 2
2 ***syn*** OLDSTER, ancient, golden-ager, old-timer, senior, senior citizen
3 ***syn*** SUPERIOR, better, brass hat, higher-up, senior

elderliness *n* ***syn*** OLD AGE, age, caducity, senectitude, senescence, years

elderly *adj* ***syn*** AGED 1, ancient, old, olden
rel aging, declining
con juvenile, young
ant youthful

eldorado *n* ***syn*** BONANZA, Golconda, gold mine, mine, treasure-house, treasure trove, treasury

elect *adj* ***syn*** SELECT 1, chosen, exclusive, pick, picked, selected
rel choice, rare; hand-picked, singled out; designated, destined, ordained; delivered, redeemed, saved
con refused, rejected, repudiated, spurned; disdained, scorned; damned, doomed, reprobate

elect *vb* **1** ***syn*** CHOOSE 1, cull, mark, opt (for), optate, pick, prefer, select, single (out), take
rel decide, determine, resolve, settle; conclude, judge; accept, admit, receive
con reject; dismiss, eject, expel, oust
ant abjure
2 to select by or as if by ballot <the board of directors *elected* a new chairman>
syn ballot, vote (in)
rel choose, designate, name, opt, pick, select, single; nominate; appoint
3 ***syn*** WILL, choose, like, please, wish

---

syn synonym(s) *rel* related word(s)
idiom idiomatic equivalent(s) *con* contrasted word(s)
ant antonym(s) * vulgar
‖ use limited; if in doubt, see a dictionary
The first word in a synonym list when printed in SMALL CAPITALS shows where there is more information about the group. For a more efficient use of this book see Explanatory Notes.

election *n* ***syn*** CHOICE 1, alternative, ‖druthers, option, preference, selection

elective *adj* ***syn*** OPTIONAL, discretionary, facultative, nonobligatory

electrify *vb* ***syn*** THRILL, enthuse, send
rel provoke; jar, stagger, stun

eleemosynary *adj* ***syn*** CHARITABLE 1, altruistic, benevolent, good, humane, humanitarian, philanthropic
rel beneficent, generous, liberal, munificent, openhanded
con close, parsimonious, tight

elegance *n* impressive beauty of form, appearance, or behavior <the sumptuous *elegance* of the furnishings>
syn dignity, grace
rel beauty, charm; cultivation, culture, polish, refinement, sophistication, style, taste, tastefulness; lushness, magnificence, ornateness, poshness, richness, splendor, sumptuousness
con grotesqueness, ugliness; clumsiness, crudeness, roughness, rudeness; austerity, bareness, inornateness, severity

elegant *adj* ***syn*** CHOICE, dainty, delicate, exquisite, rare, recherché, select, superior
rel august, grand, majestic, noble, stately; beautiful, graceful, handsome, lovely; cultivated, cultured, finished, polished, refined, tasteful; luxurious, opulent, sumptuous
con crude, rough, rude, uncouth; grotesque

element *n* **1** ***syn*** ESSENTIAL 1, basic, fundamental, part and parcel, rudiment
2 one of the parts, substances, or principles that make up a compound or complex whole <analyzed the various *elements* of the problem>
syn component, constituent, factor, ingredient; *compare* POINT 1
rel fundamental, principle; item, member, part, particle, piece, portion; detail, particular; aspect, facet, feature, view
con bulk, mass, volume; entirety, whole; sum, total, totality
ant composite, compound
3 elements *pl* ***syn*** ALPHABET 2, ABC's, fundamentals, grammar, principles, rudiments
rel basics, basis, foundations, groundwork; outlines
4 ***syn*** POINT 1, article, detail, item, particular, thing
rel division, member, section, sector, segment

elemental *adj* **1** of, relating to, or being an ultimate and irreducible element <such *elemental* aspects of life as sex and nutrition>
syn basic, elementary, essential, fundamental, primitive, substratal, underlying
rel primary, prime, primordial; inherent, intrinsic, radical
con secondary, subordinate; casual, incidental, trivial, unimportant
2 ***syn*** ELEMENTARY 1, basal, beginning, rudimental, rudimentary, simplest
3 ***syn*** INHERENT, connate, constitutional, deep-seated, essential, inborn, ingrained, innate, intimate, intrinsic

elementary *adj* **1** of, relating to, or dealing with the simplest principles of something <can't handle the most *elementary* decision-making>
syn basal, beginning, elemental, rudimental, rudimentary, simplest

rel introductory, prefatory, preliminary; easy, simple; rude, unsubtle
con complex, complicated, elaborate, intricate, labyrinthine; sophisticated
ant advanced
2 *syn* ELEMENTAL 1, basic, essential, fundamental, primitive, substratal, underlying

elephantine *adj* 1 *syn* HUGE, behemothic, colossal, enormous, gargantuan, gigantic, mammoth, mastodonic, monstrous, prodigious
con slender, slight, slim, thin; dainty
2 *syn* PONDEROUS 2, heavy-footed, heavy-handed, uninspired
rel awkward, clumsy, graceless, maladroit, ungraceful
con graceful, nimble, quick

elevate *vb* 1 *syn* LIFT 1, hoist, pick up, raise, rear, take up, uphold, uplift, upraise, uprear
rel ensky, erect
con cut (down), deflate, depress, scale (down)
ant lower
2 *syn* ADVANCE 2, prefer, promote, upgrade
rel boost; enhance, glorify, heighten
con demote, downgrade, lower, reduce; abase, debase, degrade

elevated *adj* 1 being positioned above a surface <an *elevated* monorail>
syn lifted, raised, upheaved, uplifted, upraised, uprisen
rel high; aerial
con ground-level, low, lowered, low-lying, unelevated
ant sunken
2 being on a high moral or intellectual plane <*elevated* ideas>
syn high-minded, moral, noble
rel ethical, honorable, righteous, upright, upstanding, virtuous
con base, ignoble, mean; immoral, low, unethical; intolerable, unacceptable
3 *syn* GRAND 3, exalted, lofty, sublime, superb
4 being exceedingly dignified in form, tone, or style <an *elevated* prose style>
syn eloquent, high, lofty
rel dignified, formal; grand, grandiloquent, grandiose, high-flown, majestic, stately, towering
con informal; lowly, unassuming

elevation *n* 1 *syn* HEIGHT, altitude
rel acclivity, ascent, rise
con depression, descent; flatness, levelness
2 *syn* ADVANCEMENT 1, preference, preferment, prelation, promotion, upgrading
rel advance, boost, raise; ennoblement, exaltation, glorification, lionization; apotheosis, deification, immortalization, magnification
con downgrading; depreciation, detraction, disparagement
ant degradation

elf *n syn* FAIRY, brownie, fay, nisse, pixie, sprite

elicit *vb syn* EDUCE 1, evince, evoke, extort, extract, milk
rel bring, fetch
con eschew, forgo; abandon

elide *vb syn* NEGLECT, discount, disregard, fail, forget, ignore, omit, overlook, pass, slight

eligible *adj* qualified to be or worthy of being chosen <an *eligible* bachelor>
syn fit, suitable
rel acceptable, desirable, likely, preferable, seemly; capable, fitted, qualified, suited, worthy; marriageable, nubile; visitable
con undesirable; disqualified, unfit, unqualified, unsuitable, unworthy
ant ineligible

eliminate *vb* 1 *syn* EXCLUDE, bar, bate, count out, debar, except, rule out, suspend
rel freeze out, shut out; dismiss, ||dump, eject, evict, expel, oust; delete, erase, expunge
con accept, receive
2 *syn* REMOVE 4, clear away, take out
3 *syn* PURGE 3, liquidate, remove

elite *n* 1 *syn* BEST, choice, cream, fat, flower, pick, pride, prime, prize, top
rel elect, pink, select; ||hoi polloi
idiom cream of the crop, crème de la crème, pick of the bunch
2 *syn* ARISTOCRACY, aristoi, flower, gentility, gentry, optimacy, quality, society, upper class, upper crust
rel drawing rooms; Four Hundred; beautiful people, jet set, smart set
idiom high society, horsey set
con hoi polloi, (the) masses, mob, peasantry, people, proletariat, rabble

elixir *n syn* PANACEA, catholicon, cure-all, nostrum
rel balm, cure, therapy, therapeutic

ell *n syn* ANNEX, arm, block, extension, wing

elocution *n syn* ORATORY, rhetoric, speechcraft

elongate *vb syn* EXTEND 3, draw, draw out, lengthen, prolong, prolongate, protract, spin (out), stretch
rel drag (out); string
con contract, draw in; compress; curtail, retrench; shrink
ant abbreviate, shorten

elongate *adj syn* LONG 1, elongated, extended, lengthy
rel lengthened
ant abbreviated, shortened

elongated *adj syn* LONG 1, elongate, extended, lengthy
rel drawn (out), lengthened, prolongated, prolonged, protracted, stretched
con contracted, drawn (in), shrunken
ant shortened

elongation *n syn* EXTENSION 1, lengthening, production, prolongation, prolongment, protraction

elope *vb* to go away secretly usually with the intention of marrying <decided to *elope* rather than endure a big wedding>
syn run away
idiom go to Gretna Green

eloquence *n* discourse marked by force and persuasiveness suggesting strong feeling <read the poem with *eloquence*>

---

syn expression, expressiveness, expressivity, facundity
rel meaningfulness, persuasiveness; fervor, force, forcefulness, passion, power, spirit, vigor

eloquent *adj* **1** ***syn*** VOCAL 3, articulate, fluent, smooth-spoken
rel forceful, potent, powerful; ardent, fervent, fervid, impassioned, passionate; glib, silver-tongued, voluble
con inarticulate, ineffective, weak
2 ***syn*** EXPRESSIVE, facund, meaningful, pregnant, rich, sententious, significant
rel graphic, indicative, revealing, suggestive, telling; affecting, impressive, moving, poignant, touching
3 ***syn*** ELEVATED 4, high, lofty

else *adv* ***syn*** OTHERWISE 2, ‖elseways, elsewise, ‖otherways

else *adj* ***syn*** ADDITIONAL, added, another, farther, fresh, further, more, new, other

‖**elseways** *adv* ***syn*** OTHERWISE 2, else, elsewise, ‖otherways

elsewise *adv* ***syn*** OTHERWISE 2, else, ‖elseways, ‖otherways

elucidate *vb* ***syn*** CLARIFY 2, clear, clear up, explain, illuminate, illustrate
rel exemplify; demonstrate, prove; annotate, spell out; enlighten
con confuse; darken

elude *vb* ***syn*** ESCAPE 2, avoid, bilk, double, duck, eschew, evade, shun, shy
rel baffle, circumvent, foil, frustrate, outwit, thwart; flee, fly
idiom give the slip
con accost, face; chase, follow, pursue, tag, tail, trail

elusion *n* ***syn*** ESCAPE 2, avoidance, come-off, escaping, eschewal, evasion, runaround, shunning

elusive *adj* not easily perceived, grasped, comprehended, pinned down, or isolated <inspiration need not be forever *elusive*> <they finally isolated the *elusive* virus that caused the disease>
syn elusory, evasive, intangible
rel evanescent, fleeting, fugitive; baffling, imponderable, incomprehensible, mysterious; insubstantial, phantom

elusory *adj* ***syn*** ELUSIVE, evasive, intangible
rel nebulous, vague

elvish *adj* ***syn*** PLAYFUL 1, antic, coltish, frisky, impish, kittenish, larkish, prankish, puckish, roguish

elysium *n* ***syn*** HEAVEN 2, bliss, Canaan, Civitas Dei, empyrean, happy hunting ground, New Jerusalem, nirvana, paradise, Zion

emaciated *adj* being very lean through loss of flesh (as from hunger or disease) <*emaciated* bony hands clutched at him>
syn cadaverous, gaunt, skeletal, wasted
rel bony, lean, scrawny, skinny, wizened; starved, underfed, undernourished
idiom all skin and bones, thin as a rail
con fit, husky, solid, well-fed, well-nourished; chubby, plump, portly, rotund, stocky, stout; corpulent, obese
ant fleshy

emanate *vb* ***syn*** SPRING 1, arise, birth, derive (from), flow, issue, originate, proceed, rise, stem
rel initiate; emit, exude, radiate

emancipate *vb* ***syn*** FREE, discharge, liberate, loose, loosen, manumit, release, unbind, unchain, unshackle
ant enslave

emasculate *vb* ***syn*** UNNERVE, castrate, enervate, unman, unstring
rel debilitate, devitalize
con energize, vitalize

emasculate *adj* ***syn*** WEAK 4, boneless, forceless, impotent, inadequate, ineffective, ineffectual, slack-spined, spineless, wan

embark *vb* ***syn*** BOARD 1

embark (on *or* upon) *vb* ***syn*** BEGIN 1, commence, enter, get off, jump (off), open, set to, start, take up, tee off

embarrass *vb* to throw into a state of self-conscious distress <bawdy stories *embarrassed* her>
syn abash, confound, confuse, discomfit, disconcert, discountenance, faze, rattle; *compare* DISCOMPOSE 1
rel agitate, bother, discompose, flurry, fluster, perturb; nonplus; chagrin, distress, vex; queer
idiom put on the spot, put to the blush
con calm, relieve, soothe

embarrassing *adj* ***syn*** INCONVENIENT, awkward, discommoding, discommodious, incommodious

embarrassment *n* the quality, state, or condition of being embarrassed <felt great *embarrassment* when she fell down>
syn abashment, confusion, discomfiture, discomposure, disconcertion, disconcertment, unease, uneasiness
rel constraint, strain; agitation, discombobulation, perturbation; chagrin, distress, vexation; humiliation, mortification; difficulty, Queer Street
con assurance, calm, imperturbability, savoir faire

embed *vb* ***syn*** ENTRENCH 1, fix, infix, ingrain, lodge, root

embellish *vb* **1** ***syn*** ADORN, beautify, bedeck, deck, decorate, dress (up), garnish, ornament, prank, trim
rel apparel, array, ‖doll up, dress up, emblaze, embroider, enrich, furbish
con bare, denude, divest, strip
2 ***syn*** EMBROIDER, color, exaggerate, fudge, magnify, overcharge, overdraw, overpaint, overstate, pad

embellishment *n* ***syn*** EXAGGERATION, coloring, embroidering, hyperbole, overstatement
rel floridity, ostentation

embezzle *vb* to appropriate dishonestly and fraudulently to one's own use <*embezzled* a trust fund>
syn misappropriate, peculate
rel loot, pilfer, steal, thieve

embitter *vb* ***syn*** EXACERBATE, acerbate, envenom
rel bitter, sour

emblem *n* **1** ***syn*** SYMBOL 1, attribute, adumbration, coat of arms, crest, insignia, monogram
2 ***syn*** INSIGNIA, badge

---

emblematize *vb* ***syn*** REPRESENT 2, body (forth), embody, epitomize, exemplify, illustrate, mirror, personify, symbolize, typify

embodiment *n* a concrete or actual entity in which something (as an idea, principle, or type) is embodied <he is the *embodiment* of all our hopes>
syn incarnation, personification; *compare* APOTHEOSIS 1
rel manifestation; prosopopocia; archetype; apotheosis, epitome, quintessence

embody *vb* **1** to make an abstraction concrete or perceptible often by representation in human or animal form <Dickens *embodied* hypocrisy in his Uriah Heep>
syn exteriorize, externalize, incarnate, manifest, materialize, objectify, personalize, personify, personize, substantiate; *compare* REPRESENT 2
rel actualize, hypostatize, realize, reify, symbolize, typify; demonstrate, evince, exemplify, exhibit, illustrate, show (forth)
ant disembody
2 to cause to become a body or part of another body < *embodied* a revenue provision in the new law>
syn combine, incorporate, integrate
rel absorb, amalgamate, assimilate, blend, consolidate, fuse, merge, unify
3 ***syn*** INCLUDE, comprehend, contain, embrace, encompass, have, involve, subsume, take in
rel compose, consist (of), constitute
4 ***syn*** REPRESENT 2, body (forth), emblematize, epitomize, exemplify, illustrate, mirror, personify, symbolize, typify

embog *vb* ***syn*** DELAY 1, bog (down), decelerate, detain, hang up, mire, retard, set back, slacken, slow (up *or* down)

embolden *vb* ***syn*** ENCOURAGE 1, animate, cheer, chirk (up), enhearten, hearten, inspirit, nerve, steel, strengthen
rel impel; inspire; chance, hazard, venture
con deter, discourage
ant abash

embouchement *n* ***syn*** MOUTH 5, embouchure

embouchure *n* ***syn*** MOUTH 5, embouchement

embowel *vb* ***syn*** EVISCERATE, bowel, disembowel, draw, exenterate, gut, paunch

embrace *vb* **1** to gather into one's arms usually as a gesture of affection < *embraced* his wife>
syn clasp, ‖clinch, ‖clip, ‖coll, enfold, hug, press, squeeze
rel cling, grip, hold; encircle, entwine, envelop, enwind, fold, lock, twine, wrap; cuddle, fondle, nuzzle, snuggle; cradle, hold
idiom ‖go into a clinch
2 ***syn*** ADOPT, espouse, take on, take up
rel accept, accommodate, admit, incorporate, receive, take (over), take in; seize (upon), welcome
con reject; abjure, deny, forswear, renounce
ant spurn
3 ***syn*** INCLUDE, comprehend, contain, embody, encompass, have, involve, subsume, take in
rel compose, cover, enclose, hold

embracement *n* ***syn*** ESPOUSAL 4, adoption, embracing

embracing *n* ***syn*** ESPOUSAL 4, adoption, embracement

embrangle *vb* ***syn*** ENTANGLE 3, enmesh, ensnarl, trammel

embroider *vb* to give an elaborate account of, often with florid language and fictitious details < *embroidered* the story of his adventures in the army>
syn color, embellish, exaggerate, fudge, magnify, overcharge, overdraw, overpaint, overstate, pad, stretch
rel aggrandize, amplify, build up, distend, elaborate, enhance, enlarge (upon), expand; dramatize, hyperbolize, overdo, overelaborate, overembellish, overemphasize, overestimate
idiom lay it on thick, stretch (*or* strain) the truth
con deemphasize, minimize, play (down), underestimate, understate

embroidering *n* ***syn*** EXAGGERATION, coloring, embellishment, hyperbole, overstatement

embroil *vb* ***syn*** INVOLVE 1, implicate, mire, tangle

embroilment *n* **1** ***syn*** QUARREL, altercation, bickering, controversy, dispute, falling-out, fracas, squabble, tiff, wrangle
2 ***syn*** ENTANGLEMENT 1, enmeshment, involvement

embryo *n* ***syn*** SEED 2, bud, germ, nucleus, spark

emend *vb* ***syn*** CORRECT 1, amend, mend, rectify, right
rel alter, edit, emendate; polish, retouch

emerge *vb* ***syn*** APPEAR 1, loom, show
rel derive, originate, spring, stem; arise, materialize, rise; come (forth), come out, emanate, flow, issue (forth); proceed
idiom appear on the horizon, come on the scene, come out in the open, come to light, make its appearance
con disappear, fade, fade (out); evaporate; dissolve

emergency *n* ***syn*** JUNCTURE 2, contingency, crisis, crossroad(s), exigency, pass, pinch, strait, turning point, zero hour
rel difficulty, extremity; clutch, fix, hole, pinch, push, squeeze, vicissitude; climax
idiom turn of events

emigrant *n* one that leaves one place to settle in another <a city teeming with *emigrants* from many lands>
syn immigrant, migrant
rel alien, displaced person, DP, émigré, evacuee, exile, expatriate, fugitive, refugee; migrator, migratory
con aborigine, native

emigrate *vb* ***syn*** MIGRATE, transmigrate

émigré *n* **1** a person forced to immigrate usually for political reasons <a city filled with White Russian *émigrés*>
syn exile, expatriate, expellee
rel emigrant, immigrant; alien, displaced person, DP, evacuee, fugitive, refugee
2 ***syn*** REFUGEE, displaced person, DP, evacuee, fugitive

eminence *n* **1** a condition, position, or state of great importance or superiority <the *eminence* of the presidency>

---

syn synonym(s) ***rel*** related word(s)
idiom idiomatic equivalent(s) ***con*** contrasted word(s)
ant antonym(s) * vulgar
‖ use limited; if in doubt, see a dictionary
The first word in a synonym list when printed in SMALL CAPITALS shows where there is more information about the group. For a more efficient use of this book see Explanatory Notes.

syn distinction, illustriousness, kudos, preeminence, prestige, prominence, prominency, renown
rel greatness, loftiness, prepotency, significance, superiority; authority, credit, dignity, importance, influence, power, weight; fame, famousness, glory, honor, reputation, repute
con insignificance, unimportance; obscurity
2 *syn* NOTABLE 1, big-timer, bigwig, chief, dignitary, leader, lion, luminary, notability, VIP
3 a natural elevation <the house stood on an *eminence* overlooking the river>
syn projection, prominence
rel peak, raise, rise, uprise; altitude, elevation, height; highness, loftiness
con cavity, depression, dip

eminency *n syn* FORTE, long suit, medium, métier, oyster, strong suit

eminent *adj syn* FAMOUS 2, celebrated, celebrious, distinguished, famed, great, illustrious, notable, prominent, renowned
rel well-known; august, dominant, exalted, important, lofty, noble, preeminent; big league, big-name, big-time
con uncelebrated, unremarkable, unrenowned; common, lowly

eminently *adv syn* VERY 1, exceedingly, exceptionally, extremely, greatly, highly, notably, remarkably, strikingly, surpassingly

emissary *n syn* MESSENGER, bearer, carrier courier, envoy, internuncio

emit *vb* **1** *syn* DISCHARGE 5, disembogue, flow, give off, pour, void
2 to discharge something such as moisture, vapor, or fumes <a smokestack *emitting* effluents>
syn give off, give out, issue, release, throw off, vent
rel discharge, evacuate, expel; let out, loose, pass (off); pour (out), reek; drip, emanate, excrete, extrude, exude, ooze, secrete; exhale, expire

emolument *n syn* WAGE, fee, hire, pay, pay envelope, salary, stipend
rel guerdon

emote *vb* to give expression to emotion especially on or as if on the stage <she *emotes,* postures, and harangues at the slightest provocation>
syn emotionalize
rel gush, sentimentalize; carry on, rage, rant, storm, take on

emotion *n syn* FEELING 3, affection, affectivity, passion, sentiment
rel excitability, responsiveness, sensibility, sensitiveness, sensitivity, susceptibilities; sensation
con coldness, detachment, reserve, unfeelingness

emotionable *adj syn* EMOTIONAL 1, feeling, sensitive, sentient

---

syn synonym(s) *rel* related word(s)
idiom idiomatic equivalent(s) *con* contrasted word(s)
ant antonym(s) * vulgar
‖ use limited; if in doubt, see a dictionary
The first word in a synonym list when printed in SMALL CAPITALS shows where there is more information about the group. For a more efficient use of this book see Explanatory Notes.

emotional *adj* **1** dominated by, prone to, or moved by emotion <an irritable *emotional* woman who was easily upset by trivialities>
syn emotionable, feeling, sensitive, sentient
rel responsive, susceptible, susceptive; softhearted, sympathetic; ardent, fervent, passionate; rhapsodic, rhapsodical
con cold, detached, insensitive, reserved, taciturn, unfeeling
ant emotionless, unemotional
2 appealing to or arousing emotion <an *emotional* sermon>
syn affective, emotive, moving; *compare* MOVING 2
rel affecting, stirring, touching

emotionalize *vb syn* EMOTE

emotionless *adj* **1** *syn* COLD 2, chill, frigid, glacial, icy, indifferent, unemotional
rel nonemotional, undemonstrative; cool, dispassionate, distant, immovable, impassive, remote, reserved; heartless, unfeeling
con responsive, softhearted, sympathetic; ardent, fervent, passionate
ant emotional
2 *syn* MATTER-OF-FACT 3, cold, cold-blooded, impersonal, unimpassioned

emotive *adj syn* EMOTIONAL 2, affective, moving

empathy *n syn* SYMPATHY 2, compassion, fellow feeling
rel accord, affinity, communion, compatibility, concord, congeniality, fellow feeling, rapport, responsiveness, warmth; appreciation, comprehension, understanding
idiom community of interests
con animosity, animus, antagonism, antipathy, enmity

emphasis *n* force brought to bear on something to bring out what is important <the school's *emphasis* on discipline>
syn accent, accentuation, stress
rel attention; force, insistence; weight

emphasize *vb* to give emphasis to especially by displaying more or less prominently <the papers *emphasized* crime stories>
syn feature, italicize, play (up), stress, underline, underscore
rel accent, accentuate, charge, highlight, mark, pinpoint, point (up), punctuate, spotlight; assert, press
idiom bear down on (*or* upon)
con depreciate, minimize, play (down), shrug off, underrate, understate
ant de-emphasize

emphatic *adj* marked by, uttered with, or made prominent by stress or emphasis <made his point in an *emphatic* argument>
syn assertive, forceful, insistent, resounding
rel aggressive, energetic, insistive, vigorous; accented, accentuated, assertative, decided, emphasized, marked, pointed, stressed, underlined
con insipid, milk-and-water, unaggressive, unassertive, weak, wishy-washy; de-emphasized, played (down), understated
ant unemphatic

empirical *adj* originating in, relying on, or based on factual information, observation, or direct sense experience <an *empirical* basis for an ethical theory>

syn experient, experiential, experimental
rel observational; factual
con conjectural, speculative, unproved, unsubstantiated; ideal, imagined
ant theoretical

employ *vb* **1** ***syn*** USE 2, apply, bestow, exercise, exploit, handle, utilize
rel avail, exert, practice, work; devote, engross, monopolize
2 to provide with a job that pays wages <*employed* a new draftsman>
syn engage, hire, put on, take on
rel add, contract (for), obtain, procure, retain, secure, sign (on *or* up)

employable *adj* ***syn*** OPEN 5, accessible, operative, practicable, usable

employed *adj* ***syn*** BUSY 1, engaged, occupied, working

employment *n* **1** ***syn*** USE 1, appliance, application, operation, play, usance
rel purpose; disposition, exercise, exploitation, handling, utilization
2 ***syn*** EXERCISE 1, application, exercising, exertion, operation, use
3 ***syn*** WORK 1, business, calling, job, line, occupation, pursuit, ‖racket
rel assignment, mission; office, position, post, situation; function
4 the act of employing for wages <handled the *employment* of new workers>
syn engagement, engaging, hiring
rel enlistment, enrollment, recruitment, signing on

empower *vb* **1** ***syn*** INVEST 2, authorize, vest
2 ***syn*** AUTHORIZE 1, accredit, commission, enable, license
3 ***syn*** ENABLE 2
rel endow, invest; authorize, charge, commission, entitle, entrust, license, privilege, sanction
con debar, disallow, disbar, exclude, rule out, shut out

emprise *n* ***syn*** ADVENTURE, enterprise, exploit, feat, gest, venture

emptiness *n* ***syn*** VACUITY 2, blankness, vacancy, vacuousness, voidness

emptor *n* ***syn*** PURCHASER, buyer, vendee

empty *adj* **1** lacking contents that could or should be present <an *empty* apartment> <the whole book is *empty* of meaning>
syn bare, clear, stark, vacant, vacuous, void
rel barren, blank; abandoned, deserted, emptied, forsaken, godforsaken, unfilled, unfurnished uninhabited, untenanted, vacated; destitute, devoid; depleted, drained, exhausted
con complete, replete; filled, occupied, packed, teeming
ant full
2 ***syn*** VAIN 1, hollow, idle, nugatory, otiose
rel paltry, petty, trifling, trivial; banal, flat, inane, ineffectual, insipid, jejune, vapid; dumb, fatuous, foolish, ignorant, silly, simple
con meaningful, pregnant, significant; authentic, bona fide, genuine, veritable
3 ***syn*** EXPRESSIONLESS, blank, deadpan, inexpressive, unexpressive, vacant
4 ***syn*** DEVOID, innocent, void

empty *vb* ***syn*** VACATE 2, clear, void

empty–headed *adj* **1** ***syn*** GIDDY 1, dizzy, featherbrained, flighty, frivolous, harebrained, rattlebrained, scatterbrained, silly, skittish
rel brainless, rattleheaded; ignorant, simple
2 ***syn*** VACUOUS 2, vacant
3 ***syn*** IGNORANT 1, benighted, illiterate, know-nothing, rude, uneducated, uninstructed, unlettered, unschooled, untaught

empyreal *adj* ***syn*** CELESTIAL, empyrean, heavenly
rel aerial, airy; extraterrestrial; divine, holy, spiritual, sublime
ant terrestrial

empyrean *adj* ***syn*** CELESTIAL, empyreal, heavenly

empyrean *n* **1** ***syn*** HEAVEN 2, Abraham's bosom, bliss, Civitas Dei, elysium, happy hunting ground, New Jerusalem, nirvana, paradise, Zion
2 ***syn*** SKY, firmament, heaven(s), welkin

emulate *vb* ***syn*** RIVAL 2, compete, rivalize
rel challenge, outvie

emulation *n* ***syn*** CONTEST 1, competition, conflict, rivalry, strife, striving, tug-of-war, warfare

emulative *adj* ***syn*** SLAVISH 3, apish, imitative

emulous *adj* ***syn*** AMBITIOUS 1, aspiring, vaulting
rel aiming, striving; agog, athirst; competitive, vying
con unambitious, unaspiring; detached, disinterested, uninterested

enable *vb* **1** ***syn*** AUTHORIZE 1, accredit, commission, empower, license
rel allow, let, permit, sanction
2 to render able often by giving power, strength, or competence to <his education *enabled* him to find an excellent job>
syn empower
rel allow, let, permit; condition, fit, prepare, qualify, ready
con inhibit, preclude, prevent; disallow, enjoin, forbid, prohibit

enact *vb* **1** to cause to be by legal and authoritative act <*enact* a law>
syn constitute, establish, make
rel bring about, institute; authorize, decree, proclaim; accomplish, carry (through), effect, effectuate, execute, legislate, pass, put (through), ratify
con abolish, abrogate, annul, cancel, invalidate, nullify, rescind, revoke; overturn
ant repeal
2 ***syn*** ACT 1, discourse, do, impersonate, perform, personate, play, playact
rel depict, portray, represent

enamored *adj* **1** moved by intense sexual attraction <became more desperately *enamored* of the man every day>
syn mashed, smitten, soft (on), spoony (over *or* on)

---

syn synonym(s) | ***rel*** related word(s)
idiom idiomatic equivalent(s) | ***con*** contrasted word(s)
ant antonym(s) | * vulgar
‖ use limited; if in doubt, see a dictionary
The first word in a synonym list when printed in SMALL CAPITALS shows where there is more information about the group. For a more efficient use of this book see Explanatory Notes.

rel infatuated; crazy (over *or* about), mad (about), nuts (about), silly (over *or* about), wild (about); amorous, devoted, loving
idiom head over heels in love, stuck on, sweet on
2 *syn* INFATUATED, besotted, dotty, infatuate
3 taking great pleasure in something <found herself *enamored* of those huge English teas>
syn bewitched, captivated, charmed, enchanted, entranced, fascinated
rel fond

encamp *vb syn* CAMP, bivouac, ‖bivvy, ‖laager, ‖maroon, tent

encampment *n syn* CAMP 1, campground

enceinte *adj syn* PREGNANT 1, big, childing, expectant, expecting, gone, gravid, heavy, parous, parturient

enchant *vb* 1 *syn* BEWITCH 1, charm, ensorcell, hex, spell, voodoo, witch
2 *syn* ATTRACT 1, allure, bewitch, captivate, charm, draw, fascinate, magnetize, take, wile
rel delight, enthrall, please, send, thrill; mesmerize
idiom carry away, knock dead
con disillusion, dissatisfy, let down
ant disenchant

enchanted *adj syn* ENAMORED 3, bewitched, captivated, charmed, entranced, fascinated
rel delighted, pleased; pixilated
ant disenchanted

enchanter *n syn* MAGICIAN 1, charmer, conjurer, mage, magus, necromancer, sorcerer, voodooist, warlock, wizard

enchanting *adj syn* ATTRACTIVE 1, alluring, appealing, bewitching, captivating, charming, fascinating, glamorous, seductive, siren
rel attractive, pleasing; delectable, delightful; beguiling, enthralling, entrancing, intriguing, witching; exciting, sirenic
con repellent

enchantment *n syn* MAGIC 1, bewitchment, conjuring, incantation, magicking, necromancy, sorcery, witchcraft, witchery, wizardry

enchantress *n syn* WITCH 1, bruja, hag, hex, lamia, sorceress, witchwoman

enchiridion *n syn* HANDBOOK, Baedeker, compendium, guide, guidebook, manual, vade mecum
rel book, text

encincture *vb syn* BELT 1, band, begird, begirdle, cincture, engird, engirdle, gird, girdle

encircle *vb syn* SURROUND 1, begird, circle, compass, encompass, environ, gird, girdle, hem, ring
rel band, cincture, circuit, enring; halo, wreathe

enclose *vb* 1 to shut up or confine by or as if by barriers <a valley *enclosed* by mountains>
syn cage, close in, coop, corral, envelop, fence, hedge, hem, immure, mew, mure, pen, shut in, wall
rel bound, circumscribe, confine, contain, limit, restrict; circle, compass, encircle, encompass, surround; environ; enlock
2 *syn* ENFOLD 1, enshroud, envelop, enwrap, invest, shroud, veil, wrap

enclosure *n syn* COURT 1, ‖close, courtyard, curtilage, quad, quadrangle, yard

enclothe *vb syn* CLOTHE, apparel, array, attire, clad, dress, garb, garment, raiment

encomiastic *adj syn* EULOGISTIC, laudative, laudatory, panegyrical, praiseful

encomium *n* a formal expression of praise <an unstinted *encomium* of a national hero>
syn citation, eulogy, panegyric, salutation, tribute
rel approval, kudos, laud, laudation, magnification, praise; acclaim, acclamation, applause, plaudits; accolade, commendation, compliment
con abuse, invective, obloquy, vituperation; criticism, critique, faultfinding

encompass *vb* 1 *syn* SURROUND 1, beset, circle, compass, encircle, environ, gird, girdle, hem, ring
rel bound, delimit
2 *syn* INCLUDE, comprehend, contain, embody, embrace, have, involve, subsume, take in

encounter *vb* 1 *syn* CONFRONT 1, affront, face, meet
rel clash, collide, conflict
2 *syn* ENGAGE 5, face, meet, take on
3 *syn* MEET 6, close, face, front
rel ‖bump (into), come (across), run (across), run (into)
idiom cross the path of, fall in with, meet up with
con miss, pass (by)
4 *syn* FIND 1, catch, descry, detect, espy, hit (on *or* upon), meet (with), spot, turn up

encounter *n* a sudden, hostile, and usually brief confrontation or dispute between factions or persons <a sharp courtroom *encounter* between opposing lawyers>
syn brush, run-in, set-to, skirmish, velitation
rel conflict, contest; scrap; fray, fight; battle; argument, contention, quarrel

encourage *vb* 1 to fill with courage or strength of purpose especially in preparation for a hard task <the teacher's praise *encouraged* the student to try harder>
syn animate, cheer, chirk (up), embolden, enhearten, hearten, inspirit, nerve, ‖pearten (up), steel, strengthen; *compare* SUPPORT 5
rel assure, reassure; boost, excite, galvanize, pique, provoke, quicken, stimulate; buck up, buoy (up), energize, fortify, invigorate; rally, stir
idiom give a shot in the arm
con deject, depress, discourage, dishearten, dispirit; affright, caution, frighten
ant discourage
2 to give the support of one's approval to <the government openly *encouraged* East-West détente>
syn advocate, countenance, favor
rel approve, back, endorse, go (for), sanction, subscribe (to); abet, assist, reinforce, support, sustain; incite, instigate; induce, prevail
idiom lend one's countenance to, lend one's favor (*or* support) to, smile upon
con deter, dissuade, divert, hinder; inhibit, restrain; disapprove

ant discourage
3 ***syn*** ADVANCE 1, forward, foster, further, promote, serve
rel patronize, push, support; develop, improve, subsidize
con weaken; check, retard, slow
ant discourage

encouraging *adj* ***syn*** HOPEFUL 2, couleur de rose, likely, promiseful, promising, roseate, rose-colored, rosy

encroach *vb* ***syn*** TRESPASS 2, entrench, infringe, invade
rel barge (in), ||bust (in), butt (in), chisel (in), horn (in), muscle (in), worm (in); interfere, interpose, intervene, meddle; overstep
idiom foist oneself upon, stick one's nose in (*or* into)
con ignore, let (alone), pass over; avoid

encrust (*or* **incrust**) *vb* ***syn*** CAKE 1, crust, incrustate, rime

encumber *vb* ***syn*** BURDEN, charge, clog, cumber, lade, load, saddle, tax, weigh, weight
rel freight; discommode, incommode, inconvenience; fetter, hamper, handicap; block, impede, obstruct; oppress, overburden

encumbrance *n* something that impedes and makes action difficult <told his story simply without the *encumbrance* of unnecessary details>
syn clog, cumbrance, hindrance, impedance, impediment
rel disadvantage, handicap, load; difficulty, hardship, inconvenience
con aid; catalyst, impetus, stimulus
ant assist, assistance

encyclopedic *adj* embracing, comprehensively treating, or informed in a wide range of subjects <an *encyclopedic* article on world history>
syn comprehensive, inclusive
rel all-comprehensive, all-embracing, all-inclusive, complete; extensive, general; discursive

end *n* **1** ***syn*** LIMIT 1, bound, confine(s), limitation, term
rel borderline, tip; extreme, extremity
con center, hub, middle
2 ceasing of a course (as of action or activity) or the point at which something ceases <the *end* of the war>
syn cease, cessation, close, closing, closure, conclusion, desistance, desuetude, discontinuance, discontinuation, ending, finish, period, stop, termination, terminus; *compare* FINALE
rel consummation, culmination; expiration; coda, curtains, finale, finality, finis, terminal, windup
idiom cutoff point, end of the line, stopping point
con genesis, inception
ant beginning
3 ***syn*** FINALE, close, conclusion, ending, finish, windup
4 something residual <melted down candle *ends*>
syn bit, fragment, scrap
rel butt end, fag end, leaving, remainder, remnant, residue; part, particle, piece

end *vb* ***syn*** CLOSE 3, complete, conclude, determine, finish, halt, terminate, ultimate, wind up, wrap up
ant begin

endable *adj* ***syn*** TERMINABLE, determinable

endanger *vb* to bring into peril (as of harm or disaster) <conspirators who were *endangering* the cause of freedom>
syn compromise, hazard, imperil, jeopard, jeopardize, jeopardy, menace, peril, risk
rel expose, lay (open); chance, venture
con guard, protect, shelter, shield; preserve, save

endeavor *vb* ***syn*** TRY 5, assay, attempt, essay, offer, seek, strive, struggle, undertake
rel determine, intend, purpose; address, apply, bid (for), drive (at), go (for); strain

endeavor *n* ***syn*** ATTEMPT, essay, hassle, striving, struggle, trial, try, undertaking
rel exertion, push; labor, toil, travail, work

ended *adj* ***syn*** COMPLETE 4, completed, concluded, done, down, finished, terminated, through

endemic *adj* ***syn*** NATIVE 2, aboriginal, autochthonous, indigenous
rel home-bred, native-born
con pandemic; extraneous, extrinsic
ant exotic

ending *n* **1** ***syn*** END 2, cessation, close, closing, conclusion, desistance, finish, period, stop, termination
ant beginning
2 ***syn*** FINALE, close, conclusion, end, finish, windup

endless *adj* **1** ***syn*** LIMITLESS, boundless, immeasurable, indefinite, infinite, measureless, unbounded, unlimited, unmeasured
2 ***syn*** EVERLASTING 1, amaranthine, ceaseless, eternal, immortal, never-ending, unending, world-without-end
rel constant, continuous; deathless, immortal, undying; boundless, limitless, unbounded, unlimited; self-perpetuating
3 ***syn*** CONTINUAL, ceaseless, constant, continuous, everlasting, interminable, perpetual, unceasing, unending, uninterrupted
rel overlong

endorse *vb* ***syn*** APPROVE 2, accredit, certify, OK (*or* okay), sanction
rel attest, authenticate, pass (on *or* upon), vouch, witness; command, recommend; advocate, back (up), champion, stand by, support, uphold
con deprecate, disapprove; anathematize, denounce

endorsement *n* ***syn*** SANCTION, fiat

endow *vb* **1** to furnish or provide with a gift, talent, or good quality <poets *endowed* with genius>
syn crown (with), dower, endue
rel bestow, confer; accord, award, grant; empower, enable; enhance, enrich, heighten
con bare, denude, divest, strip; despoil, ravage, spoliate; deplete, drain, exhaust
2 to furnish, (as an institution) with a store of capital <*endowed* a hospital>
syn finance, fund, subsidize

---

rel found, organize; bequeath, contribute, donate, subscribe, support; award, grant; back, promote, sponsor; provide, supply
con beggar, impoverish, pauperize; drain, draw (on)

end product *n* *syn* EFFECT 1, aftereffect, aftermath, consequence, issue, outcome, result, sequel, sequence, upshot

endue *vb* *syn* ENDOW 1, crown (with), dower
rel clothe, invest, vest; accouter, equip, furnish, outfit

endurable *adj* *syn* BEARABLE, livable, sufferable, supportable, sustainable, tolerable

endurance *n* 1 *syn* CONTINUATION 1, continuity, duration, persistence
2 *syn* TOLERANCE 1, stamina, toleration

endure *vb* 1 *syn* CONTINUE 1, abide, carry through, last, perdure, persist
rel bide, linger
con crumble, decay, disintegrate; collapse, fall
ant perish
2 *syn* ACCEPT 2, bear (with), pocket, swallow, tolerate, tough (out)
rel stand, submit (to), suffer, sustain; undergo
con break, collapse, give in, resign
3 *syn* BEAR 10, abide, brook, go, stand, stomach, suffer, swallow, take, tolerate

enduring *adj* 1 *syn* LASTING, diuturnal, durable, perdurable, perduring, permanent, stable
ant fleeting
2 *syn* OLD 2, continuing, inveterate, lifelong, long-lasting, long-lived, perennial
3 *syn* SURE 2, abiding, firm, never-failing, steadfast, steady, unfaltering, unqualified, unquestioning, wholehearted
rel durable, resolute, solid, sound, stable, staunch, sturdy, substantial
con capricious, changeable, fickle, inconstant, mercurial, unstable, variable

endways *adv* *syn* LENGTHWISE, endwise, lengthways, longitudinally, longways, longwise

endwise *adv* *syn* LENGTHWISE, endways, lengthways, longitudinally, longways, longwise

enemy *n* an individual or group that is hostile toward another <the senator was blackmailed by a political *enemy*>
syn foe
rel adversary, antagonist, opponent; assailant, attacker, combatant, invader; competitor, contender, emulator, rival
con benefactor, friend, supporter; ally, collaborator, colleague, confederate, friendly; adherent, follower, partisan, upholder

energetic *adj* 1 *syn* VIGOROUS, dynamic, lusty, red-blooded, strenuous, ‖survigrous, vital
rel aggressive, emphatic, vibrant; indefatigable
con easygoing; faineant, idle, languorous, lethargic
2 disposed to or having a capacity for action <an *energetic* campaign worker>
syn active, driving, enterprising, lively
rel animated, breezy, brisk, fresh, kinetic, peppy, spirited, sprightly, spry, vivacious, zippy
idiom full of go (*or* life *or* pep *or* zip)
con apathetic, inert; lethargic, limp, listless, passive, phlegmatic, spiritless, spunkless
ant inactive

energetically *adv* *syn* HARD 1, forcefully, forcibly, hardly, might and main, mightily, powerfully, strongly, vigorously
rel firmly, strenuously; busily, industriously, zealously
idiom at full tilt
con idly, lazily, lethargically, listlessly; slowly
ant unenergetically

energize *vb* 1 *syn* VITALIZE, actify, activate, activize
idiom put pep (*or* zip) into
con emasculate, enervate; debilitate, enfeeble
2 *syn* STRENGTHEN 2, fortify, invigorate, reinforce
rel arm, empower, enable; build (up), sustain
con daunt

energy *n* 1 *syn* POWER 4, beef, force, might, muscle, potency, puissance, sinew, steam, strength
rel activity, operativeness; forcefulness, mightiness, powerfulness
con impotence; decrepitude, feebleness, weakness; powerlessness
ant inertia
2 vigorous and effectual application and operation of power <work with *energy*>
syn birr, go, hardihood, ‖moxie, pep, potency, tuck, vigor; *compare* VIGOR 2
rel application, effectiveness, efficacy; effort, operativeness; toughness
con kef, languor, lethargy, listlessness, sluggishness; ergophobia

enervate *vb* *syn* UNNERVE, castrate, emasculate, unman, unstring
rel debilitate, devitalize, disable; exhaust, fatigue, jade, tire, weary
con activate, energize, vitalize; galvanize, quicken, stimulate

enervated *adj* *syn* LANGUID, die-away, lackadaisical, languishing, languorous, limp, listless, spiritless
rel debilitated, devitalized, enfeebled, undermined, weakened; exhausted, fatigued, run-down, tired, weary; decadent, degenerate, degenerated, deteriorated
con active, animated, energetic, lusty, strenuous, vigorous, vital; strong, sturdy, tenacious, tough

enfant terrible *n* *syn* SCAMP, devil, limb, mischief, rapscallion, rascal, rogue, scalawag, skeezicks, villain

enfeeble *vb* *syn* WEAKEN 1, attenuate, blunt, cripple, debilitate, disable, sap, unbrace, undermine, unstrengthen
rel devitalize, exhaust
con galvanize; harden, strengthen
ant fortify

enfold *vb* 1 to surround or cover closely <a heavy fog *enfolded* the ships>
syn enclose, enshroud, envelop, enwrap, invest, shroud, veil, wrap; *compare* SWATHE

---

syn synonym(s) *rel* related word(s)
idiom idiomatic equivalent(s) *con* contrasted word(s)
ant antonym(s) * vulgar
‖ use limited; if in doubt, see a dictionary
The first word in a synonym list when printed in SMALL CAPITALS shows where there is more information about the group. For a more efficient use of this book see Explanatory Notes.

rel cover, drape; encase, ensheathe; encircle, encompass, environ, gird, girdle, surround
2 *syn* EMBRACE 1, clasp, ‖clinch, ‖clip, ‖coll, hug, press, squeeze

enforce *vb* to put something into effect or operation < *enforce* a law >
syn effect, implement, invoke
rel accomplish, administer, carry (out *or* through), discharge, execute, fulfill, perform; compel, force, oblige
con disregard, forget, ignore, neglect; relax

enfranchise *vb* to admit to full political rights as a freeman or citizen <slaves were emancipated in 1863 but were not *enfranchised* until the fifteenth amendment went into effect in 1870>
syn affranchise, franchise
rel emancipate, free, liberate, release; deliver, extricate, rescue
con enslave, oppress, subject
ant disenfranchise, disfranchise

engage *vb* 1 to come into contact and interlock with <the teeth of one gear wheel *engaging* those of another>
syn intermesh, mesh
rel interact, interlace, interlock, interplay
con free, release
ant disengage
2 *syn* PROMISE 1, pass, pledge, undertake
rel commit; bind, tie; affiance, betroth, troth
3 *syn* EMPLOY 2, hire, put on, take on
con dismiss, eject, fire
ant discharge
4 to hold the attention of <the puzzle *engaged* him all evening>
syn busy, engross, immerse, occupy, soak
rel absorb, imbue, involve; arrest, captivate, enthrall, fascinate, grip; monopolize, preengage, preoccupy
5 to enter into contest or conflict with <ordered to seek out and *engage* the enemy fleet>
syn encounter, face, meet, take on
rel assault, attack, strike; battle, fight
idiom do battle with, join battle with
con elude, escape, evade

engaged *adj* 1 *syn* BUSY 1, employed, occupied, working
ant unengaged
2 pledged in marriage <the *engaged* couple made a charming pair>
syn affianced, betrothed, contracted, intended, plighted, ‖promised
rel committed, pledged
con free, uncommitted, unpledged
ant unengaged
3 *syn* INTENT, absorbed, deep, engrossed, immersed, preoccupied, rapt, wrapped, wrapped up

engagement *n* 1 *syn* PROMISE, plight, word
2 the act or state of being engaged to be married <the couple recently announced their *engagement*>
syn betrothal, betrothing, betrothment, espousal, troth
rel pledge, plight, promise
ant disengagement
3 a promise to be in an agreed place at a specified time, usually for a particular purpose <had an *engagement* with him for nine that evening>
syn appointment, assignation, date, rendezvous, tryst
rel arrangement, invitation; interview, get-together, meeting, visit
4 *syn* EMPLOYMENT 4, engaging, hiring
5 *syn* BATTLE, action

engaging *adj* 1 *syn* ATTRACTIVE 1, appealing, bewitching, enchanting, fascinating, glamorous, magnetic, mesmeric, prepossessing, siren
2 *syn* SWEET 1, dulcet, winning, winsome
rel alluring, appealing, attractive, captivating, charming, enchanting, entrancing, fetching; fascinating, interesting, intriguing
con repellent, repelling, repulsive; unappealing, unattractive, uninteresting
ant loathsome

engaging *n* *syn* EMPLOYMENT 4, engagement, hiring

engender *vb* *syn* GENERATE 3, breed, cause, hatch, induce, muster (up), occasion, produce, provoke, work up
rel develop; excite, stimulate; arouse, quicken, rouse, stir

engineer *vb* to contrive or plan out usually with subtle skill or craft < *engineered* an agreement between the two rival governments>
syn finagle, machinate, maneuver, wangle; *compare* MANIPULATE 2
rel arrange, contrive, devise, mastermind, plan (out), set up; intrigue, plot, scheme; manage, manipulate, negotiate; put (over), put (through), swing
idiom pull strings (*or* wires)

engird *vb* *syn* BELT 1, band, begird, begirdle, cincture, encincture, engirdle, gird, girdle

engirdle *vb* *syn* BELT 1, band, begird, begirdle, cincture, encincture, engird, gird, girdle

englut *vb* *syn* GULP, bolt, cram, gobble, guzzle, ingurgitate, slop, slosh, wolf

engrave *vb* 1 to cut into a surface usually with a graving tool in order to form an inscription or a pictorial illustration < *engraved* a banknote design on the copper plate>
syn etch, grave, incise
rel chase, enchase; carve; inscribe
2 to impress deeply <the incident was *engraved* in his memory>
syn etch, impress, imprint, inscribe
rel carve; fix; instill; print; embed, entrench, infix, ingrain, root

engross *vb* 1 *syn* WRITE, indite, inscribe, scribe
rel enscroll, scroll; superscribe
2 *syn* MONOPOLIZE, absorb, consume, sew up
rel apply, fill, occupy, preoccupy; assimilate, take up; arrest, engage, grip, ‖hog, hold, immerse, involve; attract, captivate, enthrall
con bewilder, distract; disperse, dissipate, scatter
3 *syn* ENGAGE 4, busy, immerse, occupy, soak

---

syn synonym(s) *rel* related word(s)
idiom idiomatic equivalent(s) *con* contrasted word(s)
ant antonym(s) * vulgar
‖ use limited; if in doubt, see a dictionary
The first word in a synonym list when printed in SMALL CAPITALS shows where there is more information about the group. For a more efficient use of this book see Explanatory Notes.

engrossed *adj* ***syn*** INTENT, absorbed, deep, engaged, immersed, preoccupied, rapt, wrapped, wrapped up
rel consumed, monopolized, occupied; submerged; assiduous, busy, diligent, industrious, sedulous
idiom caught up in, lost in, taken up with
con detached, disinterested, indifferent, unconcerned, uninterested

engrossing *adj* gripping the attention completely so as to exclude everything else <the *engrossing* nature of his task made the time pass quickly>
syn absorbing, consuming, monopolizing
rel all-consuming, controlling, gripping; interesting, intriguing; exciting, provoking, stimulating; obsessing, preoccupying
con boring, drab, dull, monotonous; unentertaining, unexciting, uninteresting

engulf *vb* ***syn*** DELUGE 1, drown, flood, inundate, overflow, overwhelm, submerge, swamp, whelm

enhance *vb* **1** ***syn*** INTENSIFY, aggravate, deepen, heighten, intensate, magnify, mount, redouble, rise, rouse
rel elevate, lift, raise; enlarge (upon), exaggerate, strengthen; augment, build (up), increase; adorn, beautify, embellish, embroider
con belittle, deprecate, detract, minimize
2 ***syn*** FLATTER, become, suit

enhancement *n* ***syn*** ACCOMPANIMENT 1, augmentation, complement, enrichment
rel improvement, intensification

enhearten *vb* ***syn*** ENCOURAGE 1, animate, cheer, chirk (up), embolden, hearten, inspirit, nerve, steel, strengthen

enigma *n* ***syn*** MYSTERY, Chinese puzzle, closed book, conundrum, mystification, puzzle, puzzlement, riddle, why
rel crux, knot, puzzler, sticker; bewilderment, perplexity, question, question mark
idiom hard nut to crack

enigmatic *adj* ***syn*** CRYPTIC, dark, Delphian, mystifying

enisle *vb* ***syn*** ISOLATE, close off, cut off, insulate, island, segregate, separate, sequester

enjewel *vb* ***syn*** BEJEWEL, begem, beset, gem, jewel

enjoin *vb* **1** ***syn*** COMMAND, bid, charge, direct, instruct, order, tell, warn
rel decree, dictate, impose, prescribe, rule; adjure, advise, counsel; admonish, caution, forewarn
con acquiesce, agree, comply, conform, obey, submit, yield
2 ***syn*** FORBID, ban, inhibit, interdict, outlaw, prohibit, taboo
rel deny, disallow

enjoy *vb* **1** to take pleasure in or receive satisfaction from <*enjoyed* the meal>
syn ‖dig, go, like, ‖mind, relish
rel cotton (to); take (to); appreciate, dote (on *or* upon), fancy, love; delight (in), drink (in), eat up, luxuriate (in), savor
con abhor, abominate, detest, hate, loathe; condemn, despise, scorn
2 ***syn*** HAVE 1, hold, own, possess, retain
rel fill, occupy, maintain; boast, command

enjoyableness *n* ***syn*** AMENITY 1, agreeability, agreeableness, amiability, cordiality, geniality, gratefulness, pleasance, pleasantness, sweetness and light
rel attractiveness, pleasingness, pleasurableness; niceness

enjoyment *n* **1** an attitude, circumstance, or favorable response to a stimulus that tends to make one gratified or happy <gave himself up to vigorous *enjoyment* of his pipe>
syn delectation, diversion, pleasure, relish; *compare* PLEASURE 2
rel delight, joy; amusement, entertainment; indulgence, savor; recreation, relaxation; gratification, satisfaction
con abhorrence, antipathy, aversion; repugnance, repulsion
2 ***syn*** PLEASURE 2, delectation, delight, fruition, joy, joyance

enkindle *vb* ***syn*** LIGHT 1, fire, ignite, inflame, kindle

enlarge *vb* **1** ***syn*** INCREASE 1, aggrandize, augment, beef (up), boost, expand, extend, heighten, magnify, multiply
rel add (to), embroider, exaggerate; grow, stretch, widen
con attenuate; abridge; compress
2 ***syn*** EXPAND 4, amplify, develop, elaborate
3 ***syn*** INCREASE 2, augment, build, expand, heighten, mount, multiply, rise, upsurge, wax

enlargement *n* ***syn*** EXPANSION 2, extension, spread

enlighten *vb* ***syn*** ILLUMINATE 2, edify, illume, illumine, improve, irradiate, uplift
rel direct, educate, guide, inform, instruct, school, teach, train; acquaint, advise, apprise, inform
con bewilder, confuse, mystify, perplex, puzzle; addle, fuddle, muddle

enlightening *adj* tending to dissipate ignorance or increase knowledge and awareness <an *enlightening* glimpse of government in action>
syn illuminant, illuminating, illuminative, illumining
rel broadening, edifying, educational, instructive; clarifying, elucidative, explanatory
con unedifying, uninstructive; confusing, obfuscatory, obscuring

enlist *vb* ***syn*** ENTER 3, enroll, join (up), muster, sign on, sign up

enliven *vb* ***syn*** QUICKEN 1, animate, liven, vivificate, vivify
rel refresh, rejuvenate, renew, restore; excite, galvanize, invigorate, jazz (up), pep (up), provoke, stimulate; amuse, cheer, divert, entertain, recreate; exhilarate, fire, inspire
idiom give (new) life to
con depress, oppress, weigh
ant subdue

en masse *adv* ***syn*** ALTOGETHER 3, all in all, by and large, generally, on the whole

enmesh *vb* ***syn*** ENTANGLE 3, embrangle, ensnarl, trammel

---

syn synonym(s) *rel* related word(s)
idiom idiomatic equivalent(s) *con* contrasted word(s)
ant antonym(s) * vulgar
‖ use limited; if in doubt, see a dictionary
The first word in a synonym list when printed in SMALL CAPITALS shows where there is more information about the group. For a more efficient use of this book see Explanatory Notes.

rel drag (into), draw (in), hook, tangle; embarrass, implicate
idiom make party to
con disembarrass, disentangle
ant extricate

enmeshment *n* ***syn*** ENTANGLEMENT 1, embroilment, involvement

enmity *n* deep-seated dislike or ill will or a manifestation of such feeling <the country had experienced generations of racial *enmity*>
syn animosity, animus, antagonism, antipathy, hostility, rancor
rel uncordiality, unfriendliness; alienation, dead set, disaffection, estrangement; abhorrence, detestation, dislike, hate, hatred, loathing; aversion; bad blood, bitterness, daggers, gall, ill will, malevolence, malice, malignancy, malignity, spite, spleen
con amicability, cordiality, friendliness, neighborliness; comity, empathy, friendship, goodwill, sympathy, understanding
ant amity

ennoble *vb* ***syn*** EXALT 1, aggrandize, dignify, distinguish, erect, glorify, honor, magnify, sublime, uprear

ennui *n* ***syn*** TEDIUM, boredom, doldrums, yawn
rel blues, dejection, depression, dumps, melancholy, sadness; boredness; fatigue, languidness, languor, listlessness, spiritlessness, tiredness, weariness; satiety, surfeit

ennui *vb* ***syn*** BORE, pall, tire, weary
con enliven, stimulate, vitalize

enormity *n* **1** the quality or state of being abnormally, monstrously, or outrageously evil <the utter *enormity* of the crime>
syn atrociousness, atrocity, heinousness, monstrousness
rel grossness, outrage, outrageousness, rankness; depravity; flagrancy
con excusableness, remissibility, veniality; bearableness, tolerability
2 the quality or state of being huge <the *enormity* of the task confounded him>
syn enormousness, hugeness, immensity, magnitude, tremendousness, vastness
rel bigness, greatness, massiveness; graveness, seriousness, weightiness
con diminutiveness, minuteness, smallness, tininess; triviality, unimportance

enormous *adj* ***syn*** HUGE, colossal, gargantuan, gigantic, immense, mammoth, prodigious, titanic, tremendous, vast
rel stupendous
ant tiny

enormousness *n* ***syn*** ENORMITY 2, hugeness, immensity, magnitude, tremendousness, vastness
rel monstrousness, prodigiousness, stupendousness

enough *adj* ***syn*** SUFFICIENT 1, adequate, comfortable, competent, decent, satisfactory, sufficing

enough *adv* **1** in or to a degree or quantity that satisfies some condition <unstable *enough* to react with water>
syn adequately, sufficiently
rel abundantly, amply; acceptably, admissibly, satisfactorily; commensurately, proportionately
2 in a tolerable degree <she sang well *enough*>
syn averagely, fairly, moderately, passably, rather, so-so, tolerably
rel acceptably, decently, satisfactorily

enough *n* as much as is needed or wanted <we have *enough* for all of our needs>
syn adequacy, competence, sufficiency, sufficient
rel abundance, ampleness, plenty
con inadequateness; deficiency, deficit, lack, shortage, want; outage, ullage, wantage
ant inadequacy, insufficiency

enounce *vb* ***syn*** ENUNCIATE 1, state

enrage *vb* ***syn*** ANGER 1, incense, infuriate, ire, mad, madden, steam up, umbrage
idiom make one's blood boil, work up into a passion
ant placate

enrapture *vb* ***syn*** TRANSPORT 2, enravish, entrance, ravish, trance
rel elate, gladden, gratify, please, rejoice; allure, attract, captivate, charm, enchant, enthrall, fascinate

enravish *vb* ***syn*** TRANSPORT 2, enrapture, entrance, ravish, trance

enrich *vb* to make financially rich or richer <*enriched* himself through speculation>
syn richen

enrichment *n* ***syn*** ACCOMPANIMENT 1, augmentation, complement, enhancement

enroll *vb* **1** to take in (as a person) by entering identification in a list, catalog, or roll <the school *enrolls* about 800 students>
syn list, register
rel enter, insert; catalog, inscribe, record; enlist, line (up), recruit, sign (up); join, matriculate
con discard, omit, reject
2 ***syn*** LIST 3, book, catalog, inscribe
3 ***syn*** ENTER 3, enlist, join (up), muster, sign on, sign up

ensample *n* **1** ***syn*** MODEL 2, archetype, beau ideal, example, exemplar, ideal, mirror, paradigm, pattern, standard
2 ***syn*** EXAMPLE 3, illustration, problem

ensanguined *adj* ***syn*** BLOODY 1, bloodstained, gory, imbrued, sanguinary, sanguine, sanguineous

ensconce *vb* **1** ***syn*** HIDE, bury, ‖bush up, cache, conceal, ‖ditch, plant, screen, secrete, stash
2 to establish or place firmly, comfortably, or snugly <was happily *ensconced* on the sofa before the fire>
syn install, settle
rel establish, fix, locate, place, plant, seat, set, situate, station

ensepulcher *vb* ***syn*** ENTOMB 1, sepulcher, sepulture, tomb

enshroud *vb* ***syn*** ENFOLD 1, enclose, envelop, enwrap, invest, shroud, veil, wrap
rel cloak, conceal, curtain, hide

---

con disclose, display, illustrate, open (up), reveal, show, uncover, unveil

ensign *n* *syn* FLAG, banner, color, gonfalon, jack, oriflamme, pennant, pennon, standard, streamer

enslave *vb* to reduce to and hold in a state of servitude <free peasants reduced to serfdom or *enslaved*>
syn enthrall, subjugate
rel disenfranchise, disfranchise; subject; oppress, shackle, yoke
con affranchise, enfranchise; free, liberate
ant emancipate

enslavement *n* *syn* BONDAGE, helotry, peonage, serfdom, servitude, slavery, thrall, thralldom, villenage, yoke

ensnare *vb* *syn* CATCH 3, benet, catch up, entangle, entrap, snare, tangle, trap
rel decoy, entice, inveigle, lure; hook, net, snag; bag, capture

ensnarl *vb* **1** *syn* ENTANGLE 1, intertangle, perplex, snarl, tangle
2 *syn* ENTANGLE 3, embrangle, enmesh, trammel

ensorcell *vb* *syn* BEWITCH 1, charm, enchant, hex, spell, voodoo, witch

ensorcellment *n* *syn* MAGIC 1, bewitchment, conjuring, enchantment, incantation, necromancy, sorcery, witchcraft, witchery, wizardry

ensphere *vb* *syn* BALL, conglobate, conglobe, round, sphere

ensue *vb* *syn* FOLLOW 1, succeed, supervene
rel derive, emanate, issue, proceed, stem; attend, result
idiom be subsequent (to), come next
con antecede, forerun, preface

ensuing *adj* **1** *syn* SUBSEQUENT 1, after, later, posterior, postliminary, subsequential
2 *syn* NEXT, coming, following

ensure *vb* to make something certain or sure <provisions *ensuring* that the rank and file have a voice in union policy-making>
syn assure, cinch, insure, secure
rel certify, guarantee, warrant; arrange, establish, provide, set out

enswathe *vb* *syn* SWATHE, drape, envelop, enwrap, roll, swaddle, wrap (up)

entangle *vb* **1** to twist or interweave so as to make separation difficult <*entangled* the yarn>
syn ensnarl, intertangle, perplex, snarl, tangle
rel intertwine, interweave, ‖snirl, twist; ball up
2 *syn* COMPLICATE, ‖muck, muddle, perplex, ravel, snarl, tangle
3 to catch or hold as if in a net from which escape is difficult <a firm hopelessly *entangled* in financial difficulties>
syn embrangle, enmesh, ensnarl, trammel; *compare* CATCH 3, INVOLVE 1
rel burden, clog, fetter, hamper, impede; bag, capture, catch, ensnare, entrap, snare, trap; discomfit, embarrass, embroil
con extricate, untangle; detach, disengage; clear, free; disburden, unfetter
ant disentangle
4 *syn* CATCH 3, benet, catch up, ensnare, entrap, snare, tangle, trap

entanglement *n* **1** the condition of being deeply involved or closely linked often in an embarrassing or compromising way <*entanglements* with underworld figures tarnished his reputation>
syn embroilment, enmeshment, involvement; *compare* WEB 2
rel ensnarement; affair, intrigue, liaison; association, contact
2 *syn* WEB 2, cobweb, mesh(es), toil(s)

enter *vb* **1** to come or go into some place or thing <he *entered* the room>
syn come (in), go in, ingress, penetrate
rel pierce, probe
idiom set foot in
con egress, exit, go out, leave; come out, emerge, sally; escape, flee
ant issue
2 to cause or permit to go in or into <*enter* synonyms in a thesaurus>
syn admit, introduce
rel inject, insert, intercalate, interpolate, put (in), set down; docket, inscribe, list, post, record, register; enroll
3 to make or become a member of <decided to *enter* the army>
syn enlist, enroll, join (up), muster, sign on, sign up
rel come (into), go (into)
idiom get oneself into, take up (*or* out) membership (in)
4 *syn* BEGIN 1, commence, embark (on *or* upon), inaugurate, lead off, open, set to, start, take up, tee off

enterprise *n* **1** *syn* ADVENTURE, emprise, exploit, feat, gest, venture
rel attempt, effort, endeavor, striving, struggle; campaign, cause, project, pursuit, task, undertaking; deed
2 *syn* PROJECT 2, undertaking
rel speculation
3 a unit of economic or business organization or activity <an economy encouraging the expansion of small, privately owned *enterprises*>
syn business, company, concern, establishment, firm, house, outfit
rel interest; organization; corporation; industry
4 readiness to attempt or engage in what requires energy or daring <complained about his brother's lack of *enterprise*>
syn ambition, drive, get-up-and-go, initiative, push; *compare* VIGOR 2
rel ambitiousness, eagerness, energy, enthusiasm, ‖hustle, vigor; boldness, courage, daring, venturesomeness; inventiveness, self-reliance
con languor, lethargy; indolence, laziness, sloth; apathy, inertia

enterprising *adj* **1** *syn* ENERGETIC 2, active, driving, lively

---

syn synonym(s) *rel* related word(s)
idiom idiomatic equivalent(s) *con* contrasted word(s)
ant antonym(s) * vulgar
‖ use limited; if in doubt, see a dictionary
The first word in a synonym list when printed in SMALL CAPITALS shows where there is more information about the group. For a more efficient use of this book see Explanatory Notes.

rel aggressive, ambitious, busy, eager, hustling, pushing, up-and-coming; adventurous, venturesome
2 showing initiative, resolution, and determined effort (as in pursuing a course or a career) <an *enterprising* young man likely to go far>
syn go-ahead, gumptious, up-and-coming
rel aggressive, pushing; diligent, hardworking, industrious, zealous; ambitious, aspiring, craving, hungry, itching, lusting, yearning; audacious, daring, dashing, venturesome
idiom on one's toes
ant unenterprising

entertain *vb* **1** *syn* HARBOR 2, bestow, billet, board, domicile, house, lodge, put up, quarter, room
rel invite; admit, receive; cherish, cultivate, foster; feed, nourish
con banish, eject, throw out; ignore, neglect
2 *syn* AMUSE, divert, recreate
rel delight, enliven, gladden, gratify, please, regale, rejoice

entertainment *n* something diverting, amusing, or entertaining <staged a floor show as *entertainment* for her guests>
syn amusement, dissipation, distraction, diversion, divertissement, recreation
rel disport, play, sport; enjoyment, gaiety, pleasure; relaxation, relief

enthrall *vb* **1** *syn* ENSLAVE, subjugate
rel master, subdue
con emancipate
2 to hold spellbound <told mystery stories that *enthralled* his playmates>
syn catch up, fascinate, grip, hold, mesmerize, spellbind
rel absorb, engage, preoccupy; charm, enchant, engross, intrigue
con bore, ennui, weary

enthuse *vb* **1** *syn* THRILL, electrify, send
2 to show great enthusiasm <tourists *enthusing* over the medieval towns>
syn drool, rave, rhapsodize, rhapsody
con censure, criticize; belittle, depreciate, disparage, dispraise, knock, undervalue

enthusiasm *n* **1** *syn* PASSION 6, ardor, calenture, fervor, fire, hurrah, zeal
rel craze, fascination, infatuation, mania
con impassivity, phlegm, stolidity; aloofness, detachment, indifference, unconcern
ant apathy
2 *syn* EAGERNESS, ardor, zing
rel earnest, interest; ebullience, élan

enthusiast *n* a person who manifests extreme and often uncritical ardor, fervor, or devotion in an attachment <an increasing number of ecology *enthusiasts*>
syn bigot, bug, fanatic, fiend, freak, maniac, nut, zealot
rel addict, aficionado, buff, bum, devotee, fan, habitué, lover, votary; partisan, supporter; bear, extremist
con depreciator, detractor, disparager, knocker

enthusiastic *adj* filled with or marked by enthusiasm <was *enthusiastic* about golf>
syn ‖buggy, ‖bugs, gung ho, keen, nutty, warm, zealous
rel ardent, devoted, eager, fervent, hearty, spirited; gaga, ‖gone (on), hopped-up; hipped, obsessed; passionate, vascular; rabid
con apathetic, detached, indifferent, reluctant, uninterested
ant unenthusiastic

entice *vb* *syn* LURE, allure, bait, decoy, entrap, inveigle, lead on, seduce, tempt, toll
con alarm, fright, frighten (off), terrify
ant scare (off)

enticement *n* *syn* LURE 2, allurement, bait, come-on, decoy, inveiglement, seducement, snare, temptation, trap

enticing *adj* being extremely and often dangerously attractive <she looked at him with an *enticing* smile>
syn Circean, fetching, luring, tempting
rel attractive, beguiling, bewitching, enchanting, fascinating, intriguing, inviting, siren, witching; captivating; likable, pleasant, pleasing

entify *vb* *syn* MATERIALIZE 2, hypostatize, reify

entire *adj* **1** *syn* WHOLE 3, choate, complete, full, integral, perfect
rel all, gross; plenary
con incomplete, unfinished; limited, qualified
ant partial
2 *syn* WHOLE 1, intact, perfect, sound, unbroken, undamaged, unhurt, unimpaired, uninjured, unmarred
rel concatenated, integrated; compacted, consolidated, unified
con broken (up); faulty
ant impaired
3 *syn* WHOLE 4, all, complete, gross, outright, total

entirely *adv* **1** *syn* WELL 3, altogether, completely, fully, perfectly, ‖plumb, quite, thoroughly, utterly, wholly
2 *syn* ONLY 1, alone, but, exclusively, solely

entireness *n* **1** *syn* ENTIRETY 1, allness, completeness, oneness, totality, wholeness
con incompleteness
2 *syn* INTEGRITY 2, completeness, perfection, wholeness

entirety *n* **1** the state of being complete <the striking *entirety* and self-sufficiency of the feudal community>
syn allness, completeness, entireness, oneness, totality, wholeness
rel collectiveness, unity; integrity, plenitude; comprehensiveness, omneity, universality
con disunity, division, separateness; fragmentation, incompleteness
2 *syn* WHOLE 1, aggregate, all, be-all and end-all, gross, sum, sum total, total, totality, ‖tote
rel collectivity, complex, everything
con component, detail, element, item, part
ant particular

---

syn synonym(s) *rel* related word(s)
idiom idiomatic equivalent(s) *con* contrasted word(s)
ant antonym(s) * vulgar
‖ use limited; if in doubt, see a dictionary
The first word in a synonym list when printed in SMALL CAPITALS shows where there is more information about the group. For a more efficient use of this book see Explanatory Notes.

entitle *vb* **1** ***syn*** NAME 1, baptize, call, christen, denominate, designate, dub, style, term, title

2 to furnish with proper authority or grounds for seeking or claiming something <this ticket *entitles* the bearer to free admission>

syn authorize, qualify

rel empower, license; allow, enable, let, permit

entity *n* **1** one that has real and independent existence <each *entity* of the series requires separate study>

syn being, existence, existent, individual, something, thing

rel body, object

2 ***syn*** THING 4, being, individual, material, matter, object, stuff, substance

3 ***syn*** WHOLE 2, integral, integrate, sum, system, totality

entomb *vb* **1** to deposit in or as if in a tomb <relics *entombed* in pyramids>

syn ensepulcher, sepulcher, sepulture, tomb; *compare* BURY 1

rel bury, inhume, inter, ‖plant; inurn; enshrine, shrine

con dig (up), disinhume, disinter, exhume, unbury

ant disentomb

2 ***syn*** BURY 1, inhume, inter, lay away, plant, put away, sepulcher, sepulture, tomb

entombment *n* ***syn*** BURIAL 2, inhumation, interment, sepulture

entourage *n* one's attendants or subordinates <the queen's *entourage*>

syn following, retinue, suite, train

rel associates, attendants, courtiers, followers, retainers; hangers-on, sycophants, toadies

entrails *n pl* the internal organs of the body <some of the *entrails* are valued as food>

syn gut(s), innards, insides, internals, inwards, ‖pudding(s), stuffing, tripes, viscera

rel bowels, intestines; vitals; giblets, pluck, purtenance

entrammel *vb* ***syn*** HAMPER, clog, curb, fetter, hobble, hog-tie, leash, shackle, tie, trammel

con assist, expedite, facilitate; extricate

entrance *n* **1** the act or fact of going in or coming in <awaited the *entrance* of the army into the city>

syn entry, ingress, ingression

rel arrival, coming, incoming, ingoing; penetration

con departure, egress, emergence, emerging, emigration, exit

ant egression, exiting

2 ***syn*** DOOR 1, doorway, entranceway, entry, entryway, portal

rel access, aperture, opening, threshold

ant exit

3 ***syn*** DOOR 2, access, adit, admission, admittance, entrée, entry, ingress, way

rel open door

---

syn synonym(s) — *rel* related word(s)
idiom idiomatic equivalent(s) — *con* contrasted word(s)
ant antonym(s) — * vulgar
‖ use limited; if in doubt, see a dictionary
The first word in a synonym list when printed in SMALL CAPITALS shows where there is more information about the group. For a more efficient use of this book see Explanatory Notes.

entrance *vb* ***syn*** TRANSPORT 2, enrapture, enravish, ravish, trance

rel gladden, please, rejoice; attract, bewitch, captivate, charm, enchant, fascinate; enthrall, hypnotize, spellbind

con disappoint, disgust, repel, repulse; bore

entranced *adj* ***syn*** ENAMORED 3, bewitched, captivated, charmed, enchanted, fascinated

entranceway *n* ***syn*** DOOR 1, doorway, entrance, entry, entryway, portal

entrap *vb* **1** ***syn*** CATCH 3, benet, catch up, ensnare, entangle, snare, tangle, trap

2 ***syn*** LURE, allure, bait, decoy, entice, inveigle, lead on, seduce, tempt, toll

entreat *vb* ***syn*** BEG, appeal, beseech, crave, implore, importune, invoke, plead, pray, supplicate

rel blandish, coax, wheedle; pester, plague, press, urge

entreaty *n* ***syn*** PRAYER, appeal, application, imploration, imprecation, orison, petition, plea, suit, supplication

entrée *n* ***syn*** DOOR 2, access, adit, admission, admittance, entrance, entry, ingress, way

rel introduction; open door

entrench *vb* **1** to establish so solidly or strongly as to make dislodgment or change extremely difficult <prejudices *entrenched* for generations>

syn embed, fix, infix, ingrain, lodge, root

rel found, ground; implant; confirm, define, establish, settle, strengthen

con eliminate, eradicate, root out, uproot; banish, cast out, eject, expel; remove

ant dislodge

2 ***syn*** TRESPASS 2, encroach, infringe, invade

rel interfere, intervene

idiom break in upon, stick one's nose into

entrenched *adj* ***syn*** INVETERATE 1, bred-in-the-bone, confirmed, deep-dyed, deep-rooted, deep-seated, dyed-in-the-wool, hard-shell, settled, sworn

entrepreneur *n* **1** one who owns, launches, manages, and assumes the risks of an economic venture <theatrical *entrepreneurs* making fortunes from successful shows>

syn undertaker

rel organizer; backer, impresario; contractor; administrator, manager; producer; promoter

2 ***syn*** GO-BETWEEN 2, broker, interagent, interceder, intercessor, intermediary, intermediate, intermediator, mediator, middleman

entrust *vb* **1** to confer a trust upon <*entrusted* him with responsibility for completing the work>

syn charge, trust

rel confer, impose; delegate, relegate; allocate, allot, assign

2 ***syn*** COMMIT 1, commend, confide, consign, hand over, relegate, turn over

rel deliver, deposit, leave, trust; bank, count, depend, reckon, rely

idiom give in trust

entry *n* **1** ***syn*** ENTRANCE 1, ingress, ingression

2 ***syn*** DOOR 1, doorway, entrance, entranceway, entryway, portal

rel access, opening, threshold

con egress

ant exit

3 ***syn*** DOOR 2, access, adit, admission, admittance, entrance, entrée, ingress, way

entryway *n* ***syn*** DOOR 1, doorway, entrance, entranceway, entry, portal
rel threshold
con egress
ant exit

entwine *vb* ***syn*** WIND 2, coil, corkscrew, curl, spiral, twine, twist, wreathe
rel entangle, entwist, interlace, interplait, intertwine, interweave; enmesh
con uncoil, undo, unravel, untwine, untwist, unwind, unwrap; straighten (out)

enumerate *vb* **1** ***syn*** COUNT 1, number, numerate, tale, tally, tell
2 to specify one after the other < *enumerated* the advantages of his position >
syn list, numerate, tick off
rel run (over), tell off; identify, mention, recite, recount, relate, specify
3 ***syn*** ITEMIZE 1, inventory, list, particularize, specialize, specify

enunciate *vb* **1** to make a definite or systematic statement of < was the first to *enunciate* the modern principle of inertia >
syn enounce, state
rel develop, formulate, outline, postulate; advance, lay down, submit; announce, declare, proclaim; affirm; show
idiom set forth
2 ***syn*** ARTICULATE 2, phonate, pronounce, say
rel express, intone, modulate, vocalize, voice

envelop *vb* **1** ***syn*** ENFOLD 1, enclose, enshroud, enwrap, invest, shroud, veil, wrap
rel cloak, hide, mask
2 ***syn*** SWATHE, drape, enswathe, enwrap, roll, swaddle, wrap (up)
3 ***syn*** ENCLOSE 1, cage, coop, corral, fence, hedge, hem, immure, pen, shut in
rel guard, protect, shield

envenom *vb* ***syn*** EXACERBATE, acerbate, embitter

envious *adj* maliciously grudging another's advantages < *envious* of her rival's charm >
syn envying, green-eyed, invidious, jealous
rel coveting, covetous, grasping, greedy; begrudging, grudging; appetent, desirous, longing, yearning; resentful, umbrageous
idiom green with envy
con benign, benignant; generous, kind; tolerant; unconcerned, uninterested

enviousness *n* ***syn*** ENVY, invidiousness, jealousy

environ *vb* ***syn*** SURROUND 1, beset, circle, compass, encircle, encompass, gird, hem, ring, round
rel enclose, fence, go (around)

environment *n* surrounding or associated matters that influence or modify a course of development < the socioeconomic *environment* in Germany that produced Hitler >
syn ambience, ambient, atmosphere, climate, medium, milieu, mise-en-scène, surroundings
rel habitat; backdrop, background, context, setting; situation, status

environs *n pl* **1** an enclosing line or margin < several thousand businesses located within the *environs* of the city >
syn bound(s), boundary, compass, confine(s), limits, precinct(s), purlieus; *compare* LIMIT 1
rel fringes
2 the suburban areas or districts around a city or heavily populated area < a new system of parks for the national capital and its *environs* >
syn outskirt(s), purlieus, suburbs
rel locality, neighborhood, vicinity; surroundings

envisage *vb* ***syn*** THINK 1, conceive, envision, fancy, feature, image, imagine, realize, vision, visualize
rel behold, grasp, look (upon), picture, regard, survey, view; externalize, materialize, objectify; foresee
idiom form a mental picture of, have a picture of, picture to oneself, view in the mind's eye

envision *vb* ***syn*** THINK 1, conceive, envisage, fancy, feature, image, imagine, realize, vision, visualize
rel call up, conjure up, summon up; picture, view; foresee
idiom have a mental picture of, picture to oneself, view in the mind's eye

envoy *n* **1** a representative with a rank between an ambassador and a minister resident who is accredited to a foreign government < the President received the *envoy* from Spain >
syn envoy extraordinary, minister plenipotentiary
rel ambassador, attaché, chargé d'affaires, consul, councillor, internuncio, legate, minister, nuncio; diplomat
2 ***syn*** MESSENGER, bearer, carrier, courier, emissary, internuncio

envoy extraordinary *n* ***syn*** ENVOY 1, minister plenipotentiary

envy *n* spiteful malice and resentment over another's advantage < his lavish life-style provoked *envy* among his colleagues >
syn enviousness, invidiousness, jealousy
rel covetousness; grudging; resentment

envy *vb* to experience envy < while she outwardly criticized her sister's looks, she secretly *envied* them >
syn begrudge, grudge
rel covet, crave, desire, hanker, long, want, yearn
idiom be green with envy

envying *adj* ***syn*** ENVIOUS, green-eyed, invidious, jealous

enwrap *vb* **1** ***syn*** SWATHE, drape, enswathe, envelop, roll, swaddle, wrap (up)
2 ***syn*** ENFOLD 1, enclose, enshroud, envelop, invest, shroud, veil, wrap
rel enswathe, swaddle, swathe; sheathe

ephemeral *adj* ***syn*** TRANSIENT, evanescent, fleeting, fugacious, fugitive, momentary, passing, short-lived, transitory, volatile

---

syn synonym(s) ***rel*** related word(s)
idiom idiomatic equivalent(s) ***con*** contrasted word(s)
ant antonym(s) * vulgar
‖ use limited; if in doubt, see a dictionary
The first word in a synonym list when printed in SMALL CAPITALS shows where there is more information about the group. For a more efficient use of this book see Explanatory Notes.

rel brief, short, temporary, unenduring; episodic
idiom here today and gone tomorrow
con endless, enduring, eternal, everlasting, lasting
ant perpetual

epicene *adj* ***syn*** EFFEMINATE, Miss-Nancyish, pansified, prissy, sissified, sissy, unmanly

epicure *n* one who takes great and fastidious pleasure in eating and drinking <was a real *epicure,* and his dinners were excellent>
syn bon vivant, gastronome, gastronomer, gastronomist, gourmand, gourmet
rel amateur, connoisseur, epicurean; glutton, ravener; high liver

epicurean *adj* ***syn*** SENSUOUS, luscious, lush, luxurious, sensual, sensualistic, voluptuous

epidemic *n* the sudden widespread occurrence of something felt to resemble an epidemic disease <an *epidemic* of art forgeries>
syn outbreak, plague, rash; *compare* OUTBREAK 1

epigrammatic *adj* ***syn*** PITHY, compact, marrowy, meaty

epilogue *n* **1** the final part that rounds out or completes the design of a nondramatic literary work <the author wrote an *epilogue* to his book explaining that some of his earlier impressions were wrong>
syn afterword
rel postlude; conclusion, ending
con prelude; foreword, introduction, preface
ant prologue
2 something that resembles an epilogue in rounding out or giving point to something else <an incident that can be regarded as an *epilogue* to the history of Roman Britain>
syn sequel
rel follow-up, postscript
ant prologue

episode *n* ***syn*** OCCURRENCE, circumstance, event, go, happening, incident, occasion, thing

epistle *n* ***syn*** LETTER 2, missive, note
rel communication

epitaph *n* an inscription on a tombstone in memory of the one buried there
syn hic jacet

epitome *n* **1** ***syn*** ABRIDGMENT, abstract, boildown, breviary, breviate, brief, condensation, conspectus, synopsis
2 ***syn*** SUMMARY, recapitulation, résumé, sum, summation, summing-up, sum-up
3 ***syn*** APOTHEOSIS 1, last word, quintessence, ultimate

epitomize *vb* **1** to make or give an epitome of <a report which *epitomizes* one of the most complex theories of all time>
syn condense, digest, inventory, nutshell, sum, summarize, summate, sum up, synopsize
rel boil down, capsulize; outline, tabulate

---

syn synonym(s) · *rel* related word(s)
idiom idiomatic equivalent(s) · *con* contrasted word(s)
ant antonym(s) · * vulgar
‖ use limited; if in doubt, see a dictionary
The first word in a synonym list when printed in SMALL CAPITALS shows where there is more information about the group. For a more efficient use of this book see Explanatory Notes.

---

con elaborate, enlarge (on), expand
2 to serve as the typical representation or ideal expression of <he *epitomized* safe, dull conservatism>
syn exemplify, typify
rel embody, incarnate, incorporate, personify, represent, symbolize
3 ***syn*** REPRESENT 2, body (forth), emblematize, embody, exemplify, illustrate, mirror, personify, symbolize, typify

epitomized *adj* ***syn*** CONDENSED, canned, capsule, pocket, potted

epoch *n* ***syn*** PERIOD 2, age, day(s), era, time
rel interval, term

epochal *adj* uniquely or highly significant <had to make an *epochal* decision: whether or not to declare war>
syn momentous
rel consequential, far-reaching, important; unmatched, unparalleled
con inconsequential, minor, petty, small-time, trivial, unimportant

equable *adj* ***syn*** STEADY 2, constant, even, stabile, stable, unchanging, unfluctuating, uniform, unvarying
rel methodical, orderly, regular, systematic; immutable, invariable, unchangeable; equal, equivalent, same
con variable; fitful, spasmodic
ant inequable, unequable

equal *adj* **1** ***syn*** SAME 2, duplicate, equivalent, identic, identical, indistinguishable, tantamount
rel equable, even, uniform; alike, like; commensurate, corresponding, proportionate
idiom one and the same
con different, disparate, divergent, diverse, varied; unalike, unequable, uneven; irregular
ant unequal
2 ***syn*** FAIR 4, dispassionate, equitable, impartial, just, nondiscriminatory, objective, unbiased, uncolored, unprejudiced
idiom without distinction
con discriminating, discriminative, unfair
ant inequitable
3 ***syn*** EVEN 3, equitable, fair
4 ***syn*** EVEN 4, even-up, fifty-fifty
5 ***syn*** PROPORTIONAL, commensurable, commensurate, symmetrical

equal *n* one that is equal to another in status, achievement, value, meaning, or effect <he has no *equal* in common sense and honesty>
syn counterpart, equivalent, like, match; *compare* OPPOSITE NUMBER, PARALLEL
rel companion, fellow, mate, peer; alter ego, double, twin; competitor, rival; similar

equal *vb* **1** ***syn*** AMOUNT 2, approach, correspond (to), match, partake (of), rival, touch
rel compare, parallel; accord, agree, square, tally; reach
idiom amount to the same thing
2 ***syn*** EVEN 2, equalize
3 to make or produce something equal to (as in quality or value) < *equal* that if you can>
syn match, measure up, meet, rival, tie, touch
rel beat, top

equality *n* ***syn*** EQUIVALENCE, adequation, equatability, equivalency, par, parity, sameness

equalize *vb* **1** to make equal in amount, degree, or status < *equalize* educational opportunities >
syn equate, even
rel balance, level, square
2 ***syn*** EVEN 2, equal

equally *adv* **1** ***syn*** EVENLY 1, fifty-fifty, squarely
2 ***syn*** EVENLY 2, impartially

equanimity *n* the characteristic quality of one who is self-possessed and not easily disturbed or perturbed < faced disaster with bland *equanimity* >
syn ataraxy, calmness, composure, coolness, imperturbability, phlegm, sangfroid, self-possession; *compare* CONFIDENCE 2
rel balance, equilibrium, equipoise, poise; aplomb, assurance, confidence, self-assurance; detachment; placidity, serenity, tranquillity
con alarm, anxiety, apprehension; excitability, nervousness; agitation, discomposure, disquiet, disturbance, perturbation

equatability *n* ***syn*** EQUIVALENCE, adequation, equality, equivalency, par, parity, sameness

equate *vb* **1** ***syn*** EQUALIZE 1, even
2 to treat, represent, or regard as equal, equivalent, or comparable < *equated* retreat with cowardice >
syn assimilate, compare, liken, match, paragon, parallel
rel associate, relate, similize; consider, hold, regard, represent, treat

equidistant *adj* ***syn*** MIDDLE 1, center, centermost, halfway, medial, median, mid, middlemost, midmost

equilibrium *n* ***syn*** BALANCE 1, equipoise, equiponderation, poise, stasis
rel stabilization, steadiness, steadying; counterbalance, counterpoise
con top-heaviness

equip *vb* ***syn*** FURNISH 1, accouter, appoint, arm, fit out, gear, outfit, rig, turn out
rel provide, supply; fit (out), rig (up *or* out), turn (out); gear, prepare, qualify

equipment *n* items needed for the performance of a task or useful in effecting an end < the *equipment* for the polar expedition included ships, instruments, sleds, dogs, and supplies >
syn accouterment(s), apparatus, gear, habiliments, machinery, material(s), matériel, outfit, paraphernalia, tackle, tackling
rel accessories, appurtenances, attachments, fittings, trappings; baggage, belonging(s), impedimenta, rig, things, traps; equipage, provisioning, provisions

equipoise *n* ***syn*** BALANCE 1, equilibrium, equiponderation, poise, stasis
rel counterbalance, counterpoise, counterweight

equiponderation *n* ***syn*** BALANCE 1, equilibrium, equipoise, poise, stasis

equitable *adj* **1** ***syn*** FAIR 4, dispassionate, impartial, impersonal, just, nondiscriminatory, objective, unbiased, uncolored, unprejudiced
rel level, stable; equivalent, identical, same
idiom fair and square
con discriminatory
ant inequitable, unfair
2 ***syn*** EVEN 3, equal, fair

equity *n* ***syn*** JUSTICE 1
rel equitableness, justness
con bias, discrimination, partiality, unfairness
ant inequity

equivalence *n* the state or property of being equivalent or the result of making equivalent < the *equivalence* of paper money and coins >
syn adequation, equality, equatability, equivalency, par, parity, sameness
rel likeness; compatibility, correlation, correspondence; exchangeability, interchangeability
con discrepancy, disparity, divergence, incompatibility, inequality, unlikeness
ant difference

equivalency *n* ***syn*** EQUIVALENCE, adequation, equality, equatability, par, parity, sameness

equivalent *adj* **1** ***syn*** SAME 2, duplicate, equal, identic, identical, indistinguishable, tantamount
rel commensurate, proportionate; convertible, correlative, corresponding, parallel, reciprocal, substitute
con disparate, divergent, diverse, various; discordant, discrepant, incompatible, inconsonant
ant different
2 ***syn*** LIKE, agnate, akin, alike, analogous, comparable, corresponding, parallel, similar, undifferenced

equivalent *n* ***syn*** EQUAL, counterpart, like, match
rel obverse, reciprocal, substitute; parallel

equivocal *adj* **1** ***syn*** OBSCURE 3, ambiguous, amphibological, tenebrous, uncertain, unclear, unexplicit, unintelligible, vague
rel hazy, indistinct; doubtful, dubious, questionable; indeterminate, multivocal
idiom clear as mud
con clear, distinct, understandable; categorical, explicit, unambiguous, univocal; certain, conclusive
ant unequivocal
2 characterized by a mixture of opposing feelings < an *equivocal* attitude toward the expensive proposal >
syn ambivalent
rel uncertain, undecided
idiom having mixed (*or* divided) feelings
con assured, certain, decided, sure
3 ***syn*** DOUBTFUL 1, ambiguous, borderline, clouded, dubious, fishy, indecisive, open, problematic, suspect
rel disreputable
idiom open to question
con credible

equivocality *n* ***syn*** AMBIGUITY, amphibology, double entendre, double meaning, equivocation, equivoque, tergiversation

equivocate *vb* **1** ***syn*** LIE, falsify, fib, palter, prevaricate
rel elude, escape, evade
2 to avoid committing oneself by speaking evasively < he'd rather be brutally frank with them than *equivocate* on that issue >

---

syn synonym(s) — *rel* related word(s)
idiom idiomatic equivalent(s) — *con* contrasted word(s)
ant antonym(s) — * vulgar
‖ use limited; if in doubt, see a dictionary
The first word in a synonym list when printed in SMALL CAPITALS shows where there is more information about the group. For a more efficient use of this book see Explanatory Notes.

syn dodge, evade, hedge, pussyfoot, shuffle, sidestep, tergiversate, tergiverse, weasel; *compare* SKIRT 3
rel cavil, prevaricate, quibble; fence, parry; avoid, elude, eschew
idiom beat around (*or* about) the bush, beg the question, mince words

equivocating *adj* *syn* EVASIVE 1, prevaricative, prevaricatory, shifty, shuffling
rel deceptive, delusive, misleading

equivocation *n* **1** *syn* AMBIGUITY, amphibology, double entendre, double meaning, equivocality, equivoque, tergiversation
rel hedging; coloring, distortion, misrepresentation; deceit, dissimulation, duplicity
ant explicitness
2 *syn* FALLACY 2, casuistry, deception, deceptiveness, delusion, sophism, sophistry, speciousness, spuriousness
rel haggling, quibbling; fib, fibbing, lie, lying

equivoque *n* *syn* AMBIGUITY, amphibology, double entendre, double meaning, equivocality, equivocation, tergiversation

era *n* *syn* PERIOD 2, age, day(s), epoch, time
rel term; stage

eradicate *vb* *syn* ANNIHILATE 2, abate, abolish, blot out, exterminate, extinguish, extirpate, root out, uproot, wipe (out)
rel demolish, destroy, raze; liquidate, purge
con establish, fix, set; implant, inculcate, instill; breed, engender, generate, propagate

erase *vb* to eliminate or neutralize with or as if with a stroke of the pen <time has *erased* their sad memories> <*erase* an error>
syn annul, black (out), blot out, cancel, delete, efface, expunge, obliterate, wipe (out), x (out)
rel disannul, negate, nullify; abolish, blank (out), cross (off *or* out), cut out, dele, eliminate, excise, extirpate, rub out, scrape, sponge (out), strike (out); neutralize; remove, take out, withdraw
con impress, imprint, print, stamp; insert; reinstate, renew, restore

ere *prep* *syn* BEFORE 1, ahead of, ante, in advance of, preceding, prior to, to

erect *adj* standing up straight <the dog's *erect* ears pricked forward>
syn arrect, raised, stand-up, straight-up, upright, upstanding
rel erectile; elevated, lifted, upraised; perpendicular, standing, vertical
con decumbent, flat, prostrate, recumbent; drooping, hanging, pendent

erect *vb* **1** *syn* BUILD 1, construct, put up, raise, rear, uprear
2 *syn* MAKE 3, build, construct, fabricate, fashion, forge, form, frame, manufacture, produce
rel compose, create; make up, run up
con demolish, destroy, tear up, unbuild, wreck
3 to fix in an upright position <*erected* a flagpole>
syn put up, raise, rear, set up; *compare* BUILD 1
rel elevate, heighten, hoist, lift, upraise, uprear; upend
4 *syn* EXALT 1, aggrandize, dignify, distinguish, ennoble, glorify, honor, magnify, sublime, uprear
idiom put on a pedestal
ant abase
5 to bring into existence as if by raising a building <*erect* social barriers along religious lines>
syn build up, construct, establish, hammer (out), set up
rel fabricate, fashion, forge, form, shape; bring about, effect
con break down, tear down; liquidate, purge; dispose (of), eliminate, remove

erection *n* *syn* EDIFICE, pile, structure

eremitic *adj* *syn* ANTISOCIAL, misanthropic, reclusive, reserved, solitary, standoffish

ergo *adv* *syn* THEREFORE, accordingly, consequently, hence, so, then, thereupon, thus

erode *vb* **1** *syn* EAT 3, bite, corrode, eat away, gnaw, scour, wear (away)
rel crumble, decay, deteriorate, disintegrate; consume
2 *syn* ABRADE 1, chafe, corrade, gall, graze, rub, ruffle, wear
rel grate, rub (off *or* away), scrape (off *or* away)

erotic *adj* of, devoted to, affected by, or tending to arouse sexual love or desire <*erotic* art>
syn amative, amatory, amorous, aphrodisiac
rel ardent, fervent, fervid, impassioned, lovesome, passionate; earthy; carnal, epicurean, fleshly, voluptuous; bawdy, sexy, spicy; concupiscent, lecherous; lascivious, lewd, lickerish, prurient, salacious, sensual

eroticism *n* *syn* LUST 2, aphrodisia, concupiscence, desire, itch, lickerishness, lustfulness, passion, prurience, pruriency

err *vb* to depart from a standard (as of wisdom or morality) <the human tendency to *err*>
syn deviate, stray, wander
rel miscalculate; lapse, slip (up), stumble, trip; transgress, trespass; offend; sin
idiom go astray (*or* amiss *or* wrong), leave the straight and narrow

errable *adj* *syn* FALLIBLE, errant

errant *adj* **1** *syn* ERRATIC 1, devious, stray, wandering
rel drifting, itinerant, meandering, rambling, ranging, roaming, roving, shifting, straying
con static, unmoving
2 deviating from an accepted pattern or standard <a parent scolding his *errant* child>
syn aberrant, devious, erring
rel deviating, straying, wandering; misbehaving, mischievous, naughty
idiom off the straight and narrow
3 *syn* FALLIBLE, errable
rel aberrant, erring; unreliable
con perfect, trustworthy
ant inerrant

erratic *adj* **1** moving about aimlessly or irregularly without a fixed course <an *erratic* breeze barely stirred the leaves of the tree>

---

syn synonym(s)	*rel* related word(s)
idiom idiomatic equivalent(s)	*con* contrasted word(s)
ant antonym(s)	* vulgar

‖ use limited; if in doubt, see a dictionary
The first word in a synonym list when printed in SMALL CAPITALS shows where there is more information about the group. For a more efficient use of this book see Explanatory Notes.

syn devious, errant, stray, wandering
rel curving, meandering, roundabout, winding; shifting, undirected
con fixed, stable, unmoving; active, animated, brisk, lively, sprightly
ant static
2 ***syn*** UNCERTAIN 1, capricious, chancy, fluctuant, iffy, incalculable, unpredictable, whimsical
rel doubtful, dubious
ant stable
3 ***syn*** ARBITRARY 1, capricious, freakish, vagarious, wayward, whimsical, whimsied
rel changeable, inconsistent, inconstant, unpredictable, variable; mercurial, unstable, volatile
con consistent, conventional, predictable, stable
4 ***syn*** STRANGE 4, bizarre, eccentric, idiosyncratic, oddball, peculiar, queer, singular, unusual, weird
rel anomalous, irregular, unnatural
con natural, normal, regular, typical; customary, usual

erring *adj* ***syn*** ERRANT 2, aberrant, devious

erroneous *adj* **1** ***syn*** FALSE 1, counterfactual, inaccurate, incorrect, specious, unsound, untrue, wrong
rel amiss, askew, awry, off; defective; mistaken
idiom all off, all wrong, way off the mark
con right, true
ant accurate, correct
2 ***syn*** MISTAKEN, misguided, wrong

erroneousness *n* ***syn*** FALLACY 1, error, fallaciousness, falsehood, falseness, falsity, untruth
rel inaccurateness, mistakenness
con accuracy, accurateness, rightness
ant correctness

error *n* **1** an often unintentional deviation from truth or accuracy <made an *error* in adding the figures>
syn mistake, x
rel inaccuracy; miscalculation, miscomputation; oversight, slip
2 something (as an act, statement, or belief) that departs from what is or is generally held to be acceptable <spying on the opposing party proved to be a grave *error*>
syn blooper, blunder, boner, bull, bungle, fluff, lapse, miscue, misstep, mistake, rock, slip, slipup, trip; *compare* FAUX PAS
rel bevue, fault, misdoing, misjudgment, stumble; ‖boo-boo, botch, fumble, muff; howler, screamer; impropriety, indecorum
3 ***syn*** FALLACY 1, erroneousness, fallaciousness, falsehood, falseness, falsity, untruth
rel misreading, misunderstanding; delusion, illusion

errorless *adj* ***syn*** IMPECCABLE 1, exquisite, faultless, flawless, immaculate, irreproachable
con imprecise, inaccurate, incorrect, unexact, wrong

ersatz *adj* ***syn*** ARTIFICIAL 2, dummy, false, imitation, mock, sham, simulated, spurious, substitute
rel factitious, synthetic; fake

ersatz *n* ***syn*** IMITATION, copy, simulacrum

erstwhile *adv* ***syn*** BEFORE 2, already, earlier, formerly, heretofore, once, previously

erstwhile *adj* ***syn*** FORMER 2, bygone, late, old, once, onetime, past, quondam, sometime, whilom

eruct *vb* **1** ***syn*** BELCH 1, burp, eructate
idiom bring up gas
2 ***syn*** ERUPT 1, belch, disgorge, eject, expel, irrupt, spew

eructate *vb* ***syn*** BELCH 1, burp, eruct

erudite *adj* ***syn*** LEARNED, scholarly, scholastic
rel lettered, well-read; studious
ant illiterate

eruditeness *n* ***syn*** ERUDITION 2, learnedness, scholarliness, scholarship

erudition *n* **1** ***syn*** EDUCATION 2, knowledge, learning, scholarship, science
2 the quality or state of being erudite <a scholar of great cultivation and *erudition*>
syn eruditeness, learnedness, scholarliness, scholarship
rel cultivation, culture, education, intellectuality, literacy; bookishness, pedantry, studiousness
ant illiteracy

erupt *vb* **1** to give off or release (as something pent up) forcefully <the volcano *erupted* gouts of lava>
syn belch, disgorge, eject, eruct, expel, irrupt, spew
rel cast (out *or* up), hurl, throw off; boil, discharge, emit; jet, spout, spurt; extravasate
2 to break away or burst from limits or restraint <riots *erupted* in the ghetto>
syn break out, burst (forth), explode
rel detonate, touch off; go off

eruption *n* **1** ***syn*** OUTBURST 1, access, burst, explosion, flare-up, gust, sally
2 ***syn*** OUTBREAK 1, burst, flare, outburst

escalade *vb* ***syn*** ASCEND 1, climb, escalate, mount, scale, upclimb, upgo
con clamber (down), climb (down); go (down)

escalate *vb* **1** ***syn*** ASCEND 1, climb, escalade, mount, scale, upclimb, upgo
2 to increase in extent, volume, amount, number, intensity, or scope <a little war threatens to *escalate* into a huge, ugly one>
syn expand, grow
rel broaden, enlarge, heighten, increase, intensify, spread, widen
con decrease, limit, minimize; constrict, contract, narrow; collapse, shrink, shrivel
ant de-escalate

escapade *n* a usually adventurous action that runs counter to approved or conventional conduct <childish *escapades* on Halloween>
syn caper, lark, rollick; *compare* PRANK
rel antic, frolic, vagary; prank; fling, spree; mischief, roguery

escape *vb* **1** to run away especially from something that limits one's freedom and threatens one's well-being <trying to *escape* from prison>
syn abscond, break, ‖bunk, decamp, flee, fly, scape

---

syn synonym(s) *rel* related word(s)
idiom idiomatic equivalent(s) *con* contrasted word(s)
ant antonym(s) * vulgar
‖ use limited; if in doubt, see a dictionary
The first word in a synonym list when printed in SMALL CAPITALS shows where there is more information about the group. For a more efficient use of this book see Explanatory Notes.

rel get away, make off, mosey, run away; bail out, ‖ditch, double, duck out, flit, jump, skip; depart; disappear, vanish
idiom cut and run, cut loose, fly the coop, take it on the lam
con come back, return; abide, remain, stay; chase, follow, pursue, tag, trail
2 to get away or keep away from what one does not wish to incur, endure, or encounter <made every effort to *escape* suspicion>
syn avoid, bilk, double, duck, elude, eschew, evade, shun, shy; *compare* SHAKE 5, SKIRT 3
rel burke, bypass, circumvent; dodge, shake, shun, skit; miss
idiom fight shy of, give the slip
con catch, contract, incur; abide, bear, brook, endure, stand, suffer, tolerate; dare, face, meet

escape *n* **1** the act or fact of escaping or having escaped physically <succeeded in making his *escape* from the prison>
syn breakout, escapement, escaping, flight, getaway, lam, ‖scape, slip
rel departure; deliverance, liberation, release
con return; grasp, grip, hold, retention; imprisonment, incarceration
2 the act or fact of escaping or having escaped what one does not wish to incur, encounter, or endure <sought *escape* from responsibility>
syn avoidance, come-off, elusion, escaping, eschewal, evasion, runaround, shunning
rel bypassing, circumvention, dodging, ducking, sidestepping; elusiveness, evasiveness
con abidance, abiding, bearing, endurance, enduring, submission, submitting, toleration; facing

escapement *n* ***syn*** ESCAPE 1, breakout, escaping, flight, getaway, lam, ‖scape, slip

escaping *n* **1** ***syn*** ESCAPE 1, breakout, escapement, flight, getaway, lam, ‖scape, slip
2 ***syn*** ESCAPE 2, avoidance, come-off, elusion, eschewal, evasion, runaround, shunning

eschew *vb* **1** ***syn*** ESCAPE 2, avoid, bilk, double, duck, elude, evade, shun, shy
idiom shy away from, steer clear of
con adopt, embrace, espouse
ant choose
2 ***syn*** FORGO, forbear, sacrifice
rel abstain, refrain
idiom let well enough alone

eschewal *n* ***syn*** ESCAPE 2, avoidance, come-off, elusion, escaping, evasion, runaround, shunning
rel shirking; shying

escort *n* **1** a boy or man who goes on a date with a girl or woman <had her pick of *escorts* to the dance>
syn date
rel beau, boyfriend, fellow; cavalier, gallant, squire, vis-à-vis
2 a person who leads or directs another or others in a way or course (as through difficult terrain) <served as our *escort* when we drove through the desert>
syn guide
rel attendant, companion, guard

escort *vb* **1** ***syn*** ACCOMPANY, attend, bear, ‖carry, chaperon, companion, company, conduct, consort (with), convoy
2 ***syn*** GUIDE, conduct, direct, lead, pilot, route, see, shepherd, show, steer
rel bring; squire

escritoire *n* ***syn*** DESK, secretaire, secretary, writing desk

esculent *adj* ***syn*** EDIBLE, comestible, eatable

esoteric *adj* ***syn*** RECONDITE, abstruse, acroamatic, deep, heavy, hermetic, occult, orphic, profound, secret

especial *adj* **1** ***syn*** SPECIAL 1, individual, particular, specific
rel preeminent, supreme, surpassing; dominant, paramount, predominant, preponderant; exceptional, notable, singular, unusual
con unexceptional, usual
ant general
2 ***syn*** EXPRESS 2, set, special, specific

especially *adv* **1** in a special way <was *especially* good at math>
syn distinctively, particularly, special, specially, specifically
rel remarkably, unusually; exceptionally, markedly, peculiarly, singularly, uniquely; eminently, notably, preeminently, supremely
idiom before all else
2 ***syn*** EXPRESSLY 2, in specie, specially, specifically

espial *n* ***syn*** DISCOVERY, detection, find, strike, unearthing

espionage *n* systematic secret observation in order to accumulate information <agents engaged in industrial *espionage*>
syn spying
rel observation, reconnaissance, sleuthing, surveillance, watching

espousal *n* **1** ***syn*** ENGAGEMENT 2, betrothal, betrothing, betrothment, troth
2 *often* **espousals** *pl* ***syn*** WEDDING, bridal, marriage, nuptial(s), spousal
3 ***syn*** MARRIAGE
rel mating; union
idiom getting hitched, taking on the ball and chain, tying the knot
con estrangement, separation
4 ready acceptance of or the taking up of a cause or belief <his wholehearted *espousal* of left-wing philosophies worried his family>
syn adoption, embracement, embracing
rel acceptance, approval; advocacy; aid, promotion, support
con denial, rejection; disapproval, dislike, distaste; antipathy, aversion, intolerance
ant repudiation

espouse *vb* **1** ***syn*** MARRY 1, catch, wed
2 ***syn*** ADOPT, embrace, take on, take up
rel accept, approve; advocate, back, champion, support, uphold

---

syn synonym(s) | *rel* related word(s)
idiom idiomatic equivalent(s) | *con* contrasted word(s)
ant antonym(s) | * vulgar
‖ use limited; if in doubt, see a dictionary
The first word in a synonym list when printed in SMALL CAPITALS shows where there is more information about the group. For a more efficient use of this book see Explanatory Notes.

con abandon, desert, forsake; deny, reject; disapprove, dislike
ant repudiate

esprit *n* **1** ***syn*** SPIRIT 5, animation, brio, dash, élan, life, oomph, verve, vim, zing
rel acumen, acuteness, brains, brightness, cleverness, intelligence, mind, quick-wittedness, sharpness, wit; courage, mettle, tenacity; fervor, passion
2 ***syn*** MORALE, esprit de corps
rel camaraderie, fellowship; devotion, loyalty; enthusiasm, fervor, passion
3 ***syn*** WIT 5, humor

esprit de corps *n* ***syn*** MORALE, esprit
rel camaraderie, comradeship, fellowship; partisanism, partisanship; devotion, loyalty; enthusiasm, spirit

espy *vb* **1** ***syn*** SEE 1, behold, descry, discern, distinguish, mark, note, notice, remark, view
rel recognize, take in; sight, spot, spy; witness
idiom catch sight of, get a load of
2 ***syn*** FIND 1, catch, descry, detect, encounter, hit (on *or* upon), meet (with), spot, turn up
rel spy; make out; notice

essay *vb* ***syn*** TRY 5, assay, attempt, endeavor, offer, seek, strive, struggle, undertake
rel venture; labor, toil, travail, work
idiom give it a try (*or* fling *or* go), have at it, make a stab at, take a crack (*or* whack) at

essay *n* **1** ***syn*** ATTEMPT, endeavor, hassle, striving, struggle, trial, try, undertaking
rel exertion; labor, toil, travail, work; go, venture
2 a relatively brief discourse written for others' reading or consideration <an *essay* on free will>
syn article, composition, paper, theme
rel discourse, discussion, explication, exposition, study; piece; tract, treatise; dissertation, thesis

essence *n* **1** a basic underlying or constituting entity, substance, or form <succeeds in conveying completely the cruel *essence* of loneliness>
syn being, essentia, essentiality, nature, texture
rel entity, form, substance
2 the most basic, significant, and indispensable element, attribute, quality, property, or aspect of a thing <the very *essence* of Machiavellianism is the belief that in politics there is neither good nor evil>
syn be-all and end-all, bottom, essentiality, marrow, pith, quintessence, quintessential, rock bottom, root, soul, stuff, substance, virtuality; *compare* BODY 3, CENTER 2, SUBSTANCE 2
rel timber; element, fiber, property; aspect, attribute, quality, spirit; inwardness, significance; crux, gist, kernel, nub, nubbin; distillate, distillation

essentia *n* ***syn*** ESSENCE 1, being, essentiality, nature, texture

essential *adj* **1** ***syn*** INHERENT, congenital, connate, constitutional, deep-seated, elemental, inborn, inbred, innate, intrinsic
con conditional, contingent, dependent
ant accidental
2 so important to the nature and essence of a thing as to be indispensable <the *essential* ingredient in this medicine is a new drug>
syn cardinal, constitutive, fundamental, vital
rel basal, basic, underlying; capital, chief, foremost, leading, main, principal; primal, primary, prime
con dependent, secondary, subordinate; accessory, auxiliary, contributory, subsidiary
3 ***syn*** ELEMENTAL 1, basic, elementary, fundamental, primitive, substratal, underlying
4 urgently required <raw materials *essential* to industry>
syn imperative, indispensable, necessary, necessitous, prerequisite
rel needed, needful; required, requisite, wanted; right-hand; vital
con dispensable, unnecessary, unneeded, unrequired, unwanted
ant nonessential

essential *n* **1** something that forms part of the minimal body, character, or structure of a thing <prosperity is an *essential* of the good life>
syn basic, element, fundamental, part and parcel, rudiment
rel essence, stuff, substance; must, necessary, prerequisite, sine qua non
2 something necessary, required, or unavoidable <work was an *essential* to survival>
syn condition, must, necessity, precondition, prerequisite, requirement, requisite, sine qua non
idiom name of the game

essentiality *n* **1** ***syn*** ESSENCE 1, being, essentia, nature, texture
2 ***syn*** ESSENCE 2, bottom, marrow, pith, quintessence, quintessential, soul, stuff, substance, virtuality

essentially *adv* **1** in regard to the essential points <*essentially* the problem is this: he is unreliable>
syn au fond, basically, fundamentally, in essence
rel actually, really
idiom at bottom
2 ***syn*** ALMOST 2, all but, as good as, as much as, practically, well-nigh
rel substantially, virtually
idiom in the main

establish *vb* **1** ***syn*** SET 1, fix, lay, place, put, settle, stick
rel enroot, entrench, implant, inculcate, infix, instill, root; set down, set up; moor, rivet, secure; found, ground
con eradicate, exterminate, extirpate, uproot, wipe (out)
ant abrogate
2 ***syn*** BASE, bottom, found, ground, predicate, rest, stay
idiom lay the foundation for (*or* of)
3 ***syn*** ENACT 1, constitute, make
rel formulate; authorize, decree, legislate, prescribe
ant repeal
4 ***syn*** FOUND 2, constitute, create, institute, organize, set up, start
rel endow, provide; originate; build

---

syn synonym(s)	***rel*** related word(s)
idiom idiomatic equivalent(s)	***con*** contrasted word(s)
ant antonym(s)	* vulgar

|| use limited; if in doubt, see a dictionary
The first word in a synonym list when printed in SMALL CAPITALS shows where there is more information about the group. For a more efficient use of this book see Explanatory Notes.

con disestablish; demolish, tear down
ant abolish
5 *syn* ERECT 5, build up, construct, hammer (out), set up
6 to make clear beyond a reasonable doubt < *established* an alibi for the time of the crime >
syn demonstrate, determine, make out, prove, show
rel authenticate, confirm, corroborate, document, substantiate, verify; attest; clarify
idiom afford (*or* offer) proof of
con discredit, expose, show up; confute, invalidate, parry, rebut, refute
ant disprove

established *adj syn* FIRM 3, fixed, set, settled

establishment *n* **1** *syn* ENTERPRISE 3, business, company, concern, firm, house, outfit
rel workplace; institute, institution; foundation
2 *often cap* a group of influential leaders who represent an established order of society < the literary *establishment* >
syn Old Guard
rel conservative(s), diehard(s)
con liberal(s)

estate *n* **1** *syn* ORDER 9, case, condition, repair, shape
rel form, state
2 a class of people in a community distinguishable by social or political duties or privileges < a party platform appealing to people of every *estate* >
syn grade, rank
rel bracket, category; footing, level, order, standing; place, position, station; caste, class
3 an extensive landed property < spent the weekend at his country *estate* >
syn acres, land, manor, quinta
rel farm, ranch; plantation; villa

esteem *n syn* REGARD 4, account, admiration, consideration, estimation, favor, respect
rel approval, liking; appreciation, valuation
ant abomination

esteem *vb* **1** *syn* APPRECIATE 1, apprize, cherish, prize, treasure, value
rel idolize, revere, worship
idiom hold dear, think the world of
ant despise
2 *syn* ADMIRE 2, consider, regard, respect
rel revere, venerate
idiom hold in esteem (*or* high regard)
con abhor
ant abominate

estimable *adj* **1** *syn* WORTHY 1, admirable, commendable, deserving, laudable, meritable, meritorious, praisable, praiseworthy, thankworthy
2 *syn* RESPECTABLE 1, creditable, reputable, reputed, well-thought-of

---

syn synonym(s) *rel* related word(s)
idiom idiomatic equivalent(s) *con* contrasted word(s)
ant antonym(s) * vulgar
‖ use limited; if in doubt, see a dictionary
The first word in a synonym list when printed in SMALL CAPITALS shows where there is more information about the group. For a more efficient use of this book see Explanatory Notes.

rel admired, esteemed, respected
con disreputable, unworthy; bad
3 *syn* HONORABLE 1, high-principled, noble, sterling, worthy

estimate *vb* **1** to judge something with respect to its worth < *estimated* the value of the jewels >
syn appraise, assay, assess, evaluate, rate, set (at), survey, valuate, value
rel adjudge, adjudicate, judge; ascertain, determine, discover; price, prize; decide, settle
2 *syn* CALCULATE, cipher, compute, figure, reckon
rel cast, sum; count, enumerate
3 to fix some value (as size, distance, or composition) more or less accurately < *estimated* the rainfall at over six inches >
syn approximate, call, judge, place, put, reckon
rel round, round off; conjecture, guess, suppose, surmise; fancy, imagine; deduce, infer
con calculate, compute; measure

estimate *n* **1** the act of appraising or valuing the nature, character, quality, status, or worth of something < his influence as President is beyond *estimate* >
syn appraisal, appraisement, assessment, estimation, evaluation, valuation
rel calculation, measurement, reckoning; sizing up; projection
2 *syn* ESTIMATION 1, appraisal, appraisement, assessment, evaluation, judgment, stock
idiom point of view

estimation *n* **1** the result of evaluating something < his *estimation* of the man's ability proved incorrect >
syn appraisal, appraisement, assessment, estimate, evaluation, judgment, stock
rel impression; opinion
2 *syn* COMPUTATION, arithmetic, calculation, ciphering, figuring, reckoning
3 *syn* ESTIMATE 1, appraisal, appraisement, assessment, evaluation, valuation
4 *syn* REGARD 4, account, admiration, consideration, esteem, favor, respect

estrange *vb* to cause one to break a bond or tie of affection or loyalty < her arrogance *estranged* her children and friends >
syn alien, alienate, disaffect, disunify, disunite, wean
rel break up, divide, divorce, part, separate, sever, split, sunder
idiom set at odds
con appease, conciliate, pacify, propitiate; associate, espouse, join, link, unite
ant reconcile

estrangement *n* the act of estranging or the condition of being estranged < a petty dispute resulted in total *estrangement* >
syn alienation, disaffection
rel division, divorce, schism; withdrawal
con appeasement, conciliation, propitiation
ant reconciliation

etceteras *n pl syn* SUNDRIES, oddments, odds and ends, this and that(s)

etch *vb* **1** *syn* ENGRAVE 1, grave, incise
2 to set forth in a sharp, clear-cut manner with minute attention to detail < the most sharply *etched* character in the novel >
syn define, delineate

rel outline, set forth; depict, describe, picture, portray, represent
3 *syn* ENGRAVE 2, impress, imprint, inscribe

eternal *adj* 1 *syn* INFINITE 1, illimitable, perdurable, sempiternal, supertemporal
rel endless, interminable, unceasing, unending; lasting, permanent, perpetual; deathless, immortal, undying
con ephemeral, evanescent, momentary, passing, short-lived, temporary, transient
ant mortal
2 *syn* EVERLASTING 1, amaranthine, ceaseless, endless, immortal, never-ending, unending, world-without-end
rel deathless, undying
3 *syn* CONTINUAL, ceaseless, constant, endless, everlasting, interminable, perpetual, unceasing, unending, unremitting
con interrupted, sporadic
4 valid or existing unaltered at all times <right and wrong are *eternal* verities that cannot be changed>
syn ageless, dateless, intemporal, timeless
rel immemorial, lasting, perdurable, permanent, perpetual; immutable, inalterable, unalterable, unchangeable, unchanging
con alterable, changeable, changing, fluctuating, varying; debatable, questionable, suspect

eternalize *vb syn* PERPETUATE, eternize, immortalize

eternally *adv syn* EVER 2, always, evermore, forever, forevermore, in perpetuum

eternity *n* 1 a totality of infinite time <in *eternity* there is no change or passing away>
syn infinity, sempiternity
rel endlessness, infiniteness, infinitude, perpetuity, timelessness
con ephemerality, impermanence, transience; limitedness, restrictedness
ant finiteness
2 unending existence after death <belief in the *eternity* of our spiritual nature>
syn afterlife, everlastingness, eviternity, immortality, world-without-end
3 *syn* AGE 2, aeon, blue moon, coon's age, dog's age, donkey's years, long
idiom forever and a day, forever and ever

eternize *vb syn* PERPETUATE, eternalize, immortalize

ethereal *adj syn* AIRY 3, aerial, vaporous, vapory
rel celestial, empyreal, empyrean, heavenly; vaporish, vaporlike, unsubstantial; filmy, gossamer; delicate, fragile, light
con heavy, thick
ant substantial

ethic *n* 1 **ethics** *pl but usu sing in constr* the discipline dealing with what is good and bad and with moral duty and obligation <*ethics* has been called the science of the ideal of human character>
syn morals
2 a group of moral principles or set of values <the Christian *ethic*>
syn morality, morals, mores
3 **ethics** *pl* the code of conduct or behavior governing an individual or a group (as the members of a profession) <medical *ethics*>
syn principles
rel moralities, morals, mores; criteria, standards
4 the complex of ideals, beliefs, or standards that characterizes or pervades a group, community, or people <the American work *ethic*>
syn ethos
rel belief, ideal, standard, value

ethical *adj syn* MORAL 1, moralistic, noble, principled, righteous, right-minded, virtuous
rel high-principled; elevated; upright, upstanding
con flagitious, iniquitous, nefarious; improper, indecent, indecorous, unbecoming, unseemly; immoral, low

ethnic *adj* 1 *syn* HEATHEN, gentile, infidel, infidelic, pagan, profane
rel non-Christian, unchristian
2 of, relating to, or originating from the traits shared by members of a group as a product of their common heredity and cultural tradition <only a person thoroughly familiar with Yiddish can recognize the *ethnic* quality of the pun> <*ethnic* cookery>
syn racial
rel national; tribal

ethos *n syn* ETHIC 4

etiquette *n* 1 *syn* MANNER 5, amenities, civilities, decorum(s), mores, proprieties
2 *syn* DECORUM 1, decency, dignity, propriety, seemliness
rel behavior, conduct, deportment, manners; amenities, civilities, formalities; convention, form, protocol
idiom social graces

eulogistic *adj* of, relating to, characterized by, or bestowing praise <the speaker made *eulogistic* remarks on the group's accomplishment>
syn encomiastic, laudative, laudatory, panegyrical, praiseful
rel approbatory, approving, commendatory, complimentary
con uncomplimentary; critical, disapproving, disparaging; abusive
ant dyslogistic

eulogize *vb syn* PRAISE 2, bless, celebrate, cry up, extol, glorify, hymn, laud, magnify, panegyrize
rel applaud; belaud, bepraise
idiom praise to the skies, sing the praises of
ant vilify

eulogy *n syn* ENCOMIUM, citation, panegyric, salutation, tribute
rel adulation, glorification
con calumny, slander
ant vilification

euphemism *n* an agreeable or inoffensive expression that is substituted for one that might offend or suggest unpleasantness <vandalism that goes under the *euphemism* of souvenir hunting>
syn nice Nelly, nice-nellyism
ant dysphemism

---

euphonic *adj* ***syn*** MELODIOUS 1, dulcet, euphonious, mellisonant, melodic, sweet, tuneful

euphonious *adj* ***syn*** MELODIOUS 1, dulcet, euphonic, mellisonant, melodic, sweet, tuneful

euphoria *n* **1** ***syn*** ELATION 1, exaltation, exhilaration
ant deflation, dysphoria
2 an often groundless or excessive feeling of well-being and happiness <drug-induced *euphoria*>
syn elation, exaltation, intoxication
rel ecstasy, frenzy; madness; glee
con anxiety, unease, uneasiness
ant depression

euphuistic *adj* ***syn*** RHETORICAL, aureate, bombastic, declamatory, flowery, grandiloquent, magniloquent, overblown, sonorous, swollen
rel elaborate; colorful; verbose; elevated
con concise, simple, straightforward; lean

evacuee *n* ***syn*** REFUGEE, displaced person, DP, émigré, fugitive

evade *vb* **1** ***syn*** ESCAPE 2, avoid, bilk, double, duck, elude, eschew, shun, shy
rel flee, fly, slip (away); foil, outwit, thwart
idiom keep (*or* know) one's distance
con accost, confront, dare, face
2 ***syn*** EQUIVOCATE 2, dodge, hedge, pussyfoot, shuffle, sidestep, tergiversate, tergiverse, weasel
rel bypass, circumvent, duck; parry, turn (aside)
idiom give (someone) the runaround
con confront, face; elucidate, explain

evaluate *vb* **1** ***syn*** ESTIMATE 1, appraise, assay, assess, rate, set (at), survey, valuate, value
rel appreciate; class, gauge, rank; criticize
2 ***syn*** CLASS 2, classify, grade, rank, rate

evaluation *n* **1** ***syn*** ESTIMATE 1, appraisal, appraisement, assessment, estimation, valuation
rel interpreting; judging, rating
2 ***syn*** ESTIMATION 1, appraisal, appraisement, assessment, estimate, judgment, stock
rel appreciation; interpretation; decision

evanesce *vb* ***syn*** VANISH, clear, disappear, evanish, evaporate, fade
rel disintegrate, dispel, disperse, dissipate, dissolve, scatter
idiom go up in smoke, vanish into thin air
con appear; coalesce
ant materialize

evanescent *adj* ***syn*** TRANSIENT, ephemeral, fleeting, fugacious, fugitive, momentary, passing, short-lived, transitory, volatile
rel temporary; flying; dissolving, fading, melting; disappearing, vanishing

evangelical *adj* characterized by or reflecting a missionary, reforming, or redeeming impulse or purpose <a mood of *evangelical* nationalism>
syn crusading, evangelistic
rel ardent, fervid, impassioned, militant, zealous; missionary, propagandizing, proselytizing

evangelist *n* ***syn*** MISSIONARY, apostle, colporteur, missioner, propagandist

evangelistic *adj* ***syn*** EVANGELICAL, crusading
rel missionary, reforming

evangelize *vb* ***syn*** PREACH 1, homilize, sermonize

evanish *vb* ***syn*** VANISH, clear, disappear, evanesce, evaporate, fade
idiom pass out of the picture

evaporate *vb* ***syn*** VANISH, clear, disappear, evanesce, evanish, fade
rel escape, pass (away *or* off); weaken; vaporize
idiom go pouf

evasion *n* ***syn*** ESCAPE 2, avoidance, come-off, elusion, escaping, eschewal, runaround, shunning
rel dodging, equivocating, equivocation, evading, excuse, subterfuge; haggling, quibbling; escapism
con confrontation, confronting; daring
ant facing

evasive *adj* **1** tending to evade or avoid confrontation <his answers were ambiguous and *evasive*>
syn equivocating, prevaricative, prevaricatory, shifty, shuffling
rel ambiguous, equivocal, unclear, vague; sliding, slippery, sly
con categorical, definite, explicit, unambiguous, univocal; candid, forthright
ant direct
2 ***syn*** ELUSIVE, elusory, intangible

even *adj* **1** ***syn*** LEVEL, flat, flush, planate, plane, smooth
con bent, crooked, curved, twisted
ant uneven
2 ***syn*** STEADY 2, constant, equable, stabile, stable, unchanging, unfluctuating, uniform, unvarying
rel equal, identical, same; consistent, continual, continuous, undeviating, unvaried
3 giving no advantage to either side <an *even* exchange>
syn equal, equitable, fair
rel balanced, fair and square, square; honest, straightforward, unprejudiced
con inequitable, unequal, unfair
ant uneven
4 being nicely in balance <his chances for success or failure are *even*>
syn equal, even-up, fifty-fifty
rel balanced, comparable, proportionate
con disproportionate, unbalanced
ant uneven
5 being neither more nor less than the named or understood amount, extent, or number <an *even* mile>
syn exact, square
con approximate, imprecise, inaccurate

even *adv* **1** in a like manner <they can learn *even* as others do>
syn as well, exactly, expressly, just, precisely
2 at the very time <perhaps *even* now the moment has come to consider a retreat>
syn already
3 not this merely but also — used as an intensive to emphasize the identity or character of something <a huge, *even* monstrous animal>

---

syn synonym(s) | *rel* related word(s)
idiom idiomatic equivalent(s) | *con* contrasted word(s)
ant antonym(s) | * vulgar
‖ use limited; if in doubt, see a dictionary
The first word in a synonym list when printed in SMALL CAPITALS shows where there is more information about the group. For a more efficient use of this book see Explanatory Notes.

syn indeed, nay, truly, verily, yea
rel absolutely, positively; quite, really
4 — used as an intensive to indicate an extreme, hypothetical, or unlikely case or instance <refused *even* to look at her> <*even* if this were so, it should not change our plans>
syn so much as
idiom even so much as
5 *syn* YET 1, still

even *vb* **1** to make (as a surface) smooth, even, level, or flat <*even* the soil with a spade>
syn flatten, flush, lay, level, plane, smooth, smoothen
rel grade, roll; align; symmetrize; uniform; pancake
con rough, roughen
2 to make even or balanced in advantage <hoped to *even* the odds by training>
syn equal, equalize
rel balance, square
con unbalance, unequalize, upset; derange, disarrange
3 *syn* EQUALIZE 1, equate

evening *n* **1** the closing part of day and the early part of night <the last light of *evening*>
syn ‖dimmet, ‖dimps, ‖dimpsy, dusk, ‖dusk dark, eventide, gloaming, nightfall, owl-light, twilight
rel afternoon; sundown, sunset; duskiness, duskness
con sunrise; dawn
ant morning
2 a latter portion or a period of decline <in the *evening* of life>
syn sunset, twilight
3 a party taking place in the evening <their *evenings* were notable affairs>
syn soiree
rel reception; salon; party

evenly *adv* **1** in equal parts <a career divided *evenly* between stage and screen>
syn equally, fifty-fifty, squarely
rel commensurably, proportionately
con disproportionately, unequally
ant unevenly
2 in a just or fair manner <she was *evenly* polite to everyone>
syn equally, impartially
rel fairly, justly
con unfairly, unjustly
3 without variation or fluctuation <spread the paint *evenly*>
syn flatly, smooth, smoothly, uniformly
con irregularly, roughly
ant unevenly

event *n* **1** *syn* OCCURRENCE, circumstance, episode, go, happening, incident, occasion, thing
rel act, action, deed; achievement, exploit, feat; accident, chance, fortune
2 a matter worthy of remark <the trip was an *event* in their dull routine>
syn milepost, milestone, occasion
rel affair, landmark; delight, treat
idiom historic event
con insignificancy, trifle, triviality
3 *syn* EFFECT 1, aftereffect, aftermath, causatum, consequence, issue, outcome, result, sequel, upshot
rel offshoot, outgrowth; product, resultant, sequent
idiom end result
4 a postulated outcome, condition, or contingency <in the *event* of rain, we will not meet>
syn case, eventuality
rel chance, fortuity, hap, happenstance
5 any of the contests in a sports program <track-and-field *events*>
syn match, meet
rel competition, contest
6 *syn* FACT 2, phenomenon

eventide *n syn* EVENING 1, ‖dimmet, ‖dimps, ‖dimpsy, dusk, ‖dusk dark, gloaming, nightfall, owl-light, twilight

eventual *adj syn* LAST, closing, concluding, final, hindmost, lag, latest, latter, terminal, ultimate
rel consequent, ensuing, inevitable, succeeding; ending, endmost
con antecedent, beginning, inceptive, initial, original

eventuality *n* **1** *syn* EVENT 4, case
rel contingency, possibility
2 *syn* EFFECT 1, aftereffect, aftermath, consequence, event, issue, outcome, result, sequel, upshot
con antecedent, beginning, root

eventually *adv syn* YET 2, finally, someday, sometime, somewhen, sooner or later, ultimately
idiom in the long run

even–up *adj syn* EVEN 4, equal, fifty-fifty

ever *adv* **1** *syn* ALWAYS 1, constantly, continuously, invariably, perpetually
2 through all or an indefinite time <a name that will *ever* be respected>
syn always, eternally, evermore, forever, forevermore, in perpetuum
3 in each and every case <war and suffering have *ever* gone hand in hand>
syn invariably
rel consistently, regularly, usually
4 at any time or on any occasion <he is seldom if *ever* absent>
syn anytime, at all
5 in any way <nor was it *ever* important>
syn anyway, anywise, at all, once
6 — used as an intensive after an inverted verb-subject construction <is he *ever* proud of himself>
syn confoundedly, consumedly, excessively, extremely, immensely, inordinately, over, overfull, overly, overmuch, super, too, unduly
rel annoyingly, plaguey; grievously, mortally; consummately

ever and again *adv syn* SOMETIMES, at times, ‖betimes, ever and anon, here and there, now and again, now and then, once and again, ‖otherwhile

---

ever and anon *adv* ***syn*** SOMETIMES, at times, ‖betimes, ever and again, here and there, now and again, now and then, once and again, ‖otherwhile

everlasting *adj* **1** lasting or enduring through all time <*everlasting* laws governing the physical universe>
syn amaranthine, ceaseless, endless, eternal, immortal, never-ending, unending, world-without-end; *compare* IMMORTAL 1
rel lasting, perdurable, permanent, perpetual; boundless, infinite, limitless, termless
con ephemeral, evanescent, momentary, short-lived, transitory
2 ***syn*** CONTINUAL, ceaseless, constant, continuous, endless, perpetual, unceasing, unending, uninterrupted, unremitting
con off-and-on, interrupted, periodic, sporadic

everlastingness *n* ***syn*** ETERNITY 2, afterlife, eviternity, immortality, world-without-end

evermore *adv* ***syn*** EVER 2, always, eternally, forever, forevermore, in perpetuum

evert *vb* ***syn*** DISPROVE 1, break, confound, confute, controvert, disconfirm, rebut, refute

every *adj* ***syn*** ALL 2, each

everybody *pron* every person <*everybody* must do what his conscience dictates>
syn all, everyman, everyone
idiom all and sundry
ant nobody

everyday *adj* **1** ***syn*** COMMON 4, customary, familiar, frequent
con distinctive, singular, unique; uncommon, unusual
ant exceptional
2 ***syn*** PROSAIC 3, commonplace, lowly, mundane, workaday, workday
3 ***syn*** ORDINARY 1, plain, plain Jane, quotidian, routine, unremarkable, usual, workaday

everyman *pron* ***syn*** EVERYBODY, all, everyone
idiom the man in the street

everyone *pron* ***syn*** EVERYBODY, all, everyman
ant no one

everyplace *adv* ***syn*** EVERYWHERE 1, all over, all round (*or* all around), far and near, far and wide, high and low, overall, throughout
idiom all over the place

everything *pron* the whole amount <lost *everything* in the fire>
syn all
idiom all in all, the lot, the whole bit (*or* shebang), the whole kit and kaboodle, the works

everywhere *adv* **1** in every place or in all places <poverty anywhere is a danger to peace and prosperity *everywhere*>
syn all over, all round (*or* all around), everyplace, far and near, far and wide, high and low, overall, throughout
idiom in all quarters, in every quarter
2 ***syn*** WHEREVER, where

evict *vb* ***syn*** EJECT 1, boot (out), chase, chuck, dismiss, extrude, kick out, out, throw out
rel dislodge, dispossess, force (out), put out, shut out, turn out
idiom turn (*or* put) out bag and baggage, turn out of doors, turn out of house and home
con harbor, house, lodge, shelter

evidence *n* **1** ***syn*** INDICATION 3, index, indicia, mark, sign, significant, symptom, token
2 ***syn*** TESTIMONY, attestation, confirmation, proof, testament, testimonial, witness

evidence *vb* ***syn*** SHOW 2, demonstrate, evince, exhibit, illustrate, manifest, mark, ostend, proclaim
rel display, expose; attest, bespeak, betoken, confirm, indicate, prove, testify

evident *adj* ***syn*** CLEAR 5, apparent, distinct, manifest, obvious, palpable, patent, plain, straightforward, unambiguous
rel noticeable, prominent, pronounced
idiom as plain as the nose on one's face, plain as day
con inconspicuous; ambiguous, unapparent, unrecognizable; concealed, hidden
ant inevident

evidently *adv* ***syn*** OSTENSIBLY, apparently, officially, outwardly, professedly, seemingly

evil *n* **1** whatever is harmful, distressing, or disastrous <attempts to grasp the nature of *evil*>
syn ill
rel bad, badness, devilry, diablerie, diabolism, evilness, satanism, satanity, wickedness, wrong
con goodness, virtue
ant good
2 whatever is morally unacceptable <return good for *evil*>
syn debt, sin, wickedness, wrong
rel evildoing, misconduct, sinfulness, wrongdoing
con rectitude, righteousness, virtue
ant good
3 a particular thing (as an act) that is evil <choose the lesser of two *evils*>
syn crime, diablerie, iniquity, sin, tort, wrong, wrongdoing
rel badness, evilness, maleficence, vice, wickedness; misdeed, offense

evil *adj* **1** ***syn*** WRONG 1, bad, immoral, iniquitous, reprobate, sinful, vicious, wicked
rel base, low, vile; flagitious, nefarious; baneful, pernicious; black, damnable, execrable
con high, noble; exemplary, salutary
ant good
2 ***syn*** OFFENSIVE, atrocious, foul, hideous, loathsome, obscene, repugnant, repulsive, revolting, vile
rel distasteful, repellent; fetid, putrid, stinking
3 ***syn*** MALICIOUS, bitchy, catty, despiteful, hateful, malevolent, rancorous, spiteful, vicious, wicked
rel angry, disagreeable, ugly, unpleasant, wrathful; harmful, hurtful, injurious, mischievous; destructive

---

4 *syn* HARMFUL, bad, damaging, deleterious, detrimental, hurtful, injurious, mischievous, nocent, nocuous
rel calamitous, destructive, disastrous
con harmless, noninjurious
ant innocuous
5 reporting or predicting harm or misfortune <messengers bearing *evil* tidings>
syn bad, ill, unfavorable; *compare* OMINOUS
rel baleful, baneful, inauspicious; ill-boding, ill-omened, ominous
con auspicious, favorable
ant good
6 marked by misfortune or calamity <the family fell upon *evil* times>
syn bad, inauspicious
rel unfavorable, unfortunate, unlucky; difficult, hard, trying; calamitous, disastrous
con favorable; lucky; easy, prosperous; auspicious, halcyon, happy
ant good

evince *vb* 1 *syn* SHOW 2, demonstrate, evidence, exhibit, illustrate, manifest, mark, ostend, proclaim
rel argue, attest, bespeak, betoken, confirm, indicate, prove; display, exhibit, expose, illustrate, signify
con repress, suppress; conceal, hide
2 *syn* EDUCE 1, elicit, evoke, extort, extract, milk
rel bring (about), cause; provoke, stimulate

eviscerate *vb* to take out the entrails of <*eviscerate* a turkey>
syn bowel, disembowel, draw, embowel, exenterate, gut, paunch

eviternity *n syn* ETERNITY 2, afterlife, everlastingness, immortality, world-without-end

evocative *adj* serving or tending to call something (as a mood) forth <conduct *evocative* of the utmost contempt>
syn evocatory, suggestive
rel meaningful, pregnant, weighty; arousing, moving, stimulating, stirring; causing, effecting, inducing, producing

evocatory *adj syn* EVOCATIVE, suggestive

evoke *vb syn* EDUCE 1, elicit, evince, extort, extract, milk
rel excite, provoke, stimulate; arouse, awaken, rally, rouse, stir, waken; call forth, call up, conjure (up), raise, summon (forth *or* up)

evolution *n syn* DEVELOPMENT, evolvement, flowering, growth, progress, progression, unfolding, upgrowth
rel change, transformation

evolve *vb* 1 *syn* DERIVE 1, educe, excogitate
rel get (at), obtain; advance
2 *syn* UNFOLD 3, develop, elaborate
rel advance, progress; mature, open (up), ripen

evolvement *n syn* DEVELOPMENT, evolution, flowering, growth, progress, progression, unfolding, upgrowth
rel metamorphosis, transformation

evulse *vb syn* EXTRACT 1, pull, tear, yank

exacerbate *vb* to cause to become increasingly bitter or severe <foolish words that only *exacerbated* the quarrel>
syn acerbate, embitter, envenom
rel annoy, exasperate, irritate, provoke; aggravate, heighten, intensify; inflame
idiom add fuel to the flame, fan the flames, feed the fire, pour oil on the fire
con appease, mollify, pacify, placate, quell; lessen, moderate
ant assuage

exact *vb* 1 *syn* EXTORT 1, gouge, pinch, screw, shake down, squeeze, wrench, wrest, wring
2 *syn* LEVY, assess, impose, put (on *or* upon)
3 *syn* DEMAND 1, call, challenge, claim, postulate, require, requisition, solicit
rel coerce, compel, constrain, force, oblige; extort, extract, squeeze, wrest, wring

exact *adj* 1 *syn* CORRECT 2, accurate, nice, precise, proper, right, rigorous
2 *syn* EVEN 5, square
ant imprecise, inexact
3 *syn* SAME 1, identical, selfsame, very
4 *syn* CAREFUL 2, conscientious, conscionable, fussy, heedful, meticulous, painstaking, punctilious, punctual, scrupulous
5 *syn* PRECISE 4, very

exacting *adj syn* ONEROUS, burdensome, demanding, exigent, grievous, oppressive, taxing, tough, trying, weighty
rel rigid, rigorous, severe, stern, strict, stringent; finicky, fussy, particular; critical, hypercritical
con laissez-faire, lenient
ant unexacting

exactitude *n syn* PRECISION, accuracy, correctness, definiteness, definitiveness, definitude, exactness, preciseness

exactly *adv* 1 *syn* JUST 1, accurately, bang, precisely, right, sharp, ‖smack-dab, spang, square, squarely
rel ‖plumb, plunk; specifically
idiom on the dot (*or* nose), right on the nail
con about, around, more or less, roughly
ant approximately
2 *syn* ALL 1, all in all, altogether, in toto, just, quite, stick, totally, utterly, wholly
rel absolutely, expressly, positively; completely
3 as you say or state — used to express agreement or concurrence <"You are accusing me of lying?" he asked. "*Exactly*," she replied.>
syn precisely, yes
idiom quite so, (that's) for sure (*or* certain)
4 *syn* EVEN 1, as well, expressly, just, precisely

exactness *n syn* PRECISION, accuracy, correctness, definiteness, definitiveness, definitude, exactitude, preciseness

exaggerate *vb syn* EMBROIDER, color, embellish, fudge, magnify, overcharge, overdraw, overpaint, overstate, pad
rel hyperbolize, overcolor, romance, romanticize

---

syn synonym(s) *rel* related word(s)
idiom idiomatic equivalent(s) *con* contrasted word(s)
ant antonym(s) * vulgar
‖ use limited; if in doubt, see a dictionary
The first word in a synonym list when printed in SMALL CAPITALS shows where there is more information about the group. For a more efficient use of this book see Explanatory Notes.

idiom blow up out of (all) proportion, draw the long bow, make the eagle scream
ant understate

exaggeration *n* an overstepping of the bounds of truth <the passage shows the author's penchant for grotesque *exaggeration*>
syn coloring, embellishment, embroidering, hyperbole, overstatement
rel aggrandizement, amplification, enlargement; overcoloring, overdrawing, romance, stretching
idiom flight of fancy, tall talk
con minimizing, underestimation
ant understatement

exalt *vb* **1** to enhance the status of <propaganda that *exalts* nationalism to the level of religion>
syn aggrandize, dignify, distinguish, ennoble, erect, glorify, honor, magnify, pedestal, stellify, sublime, uprear
rel boost, build up, elevate, lift, promote, raise, upgrade, uplift; enhance, heighten, intensify; acclaim, enhalo, extol, laud, praise; apotheosize
con debase, degrade, demean, humble, humiliate; belittle, decry, depreciate, derogate, detract, disparage, downgrade, minimize
ant abase
2 ***syn*** FIRE 2, animate, inform, inspire
rel pique, stimulate, quicken; deepen, enhance, sharpen; encourage, inspirit, spirit (up), uplift

exaltation *n* **1** ***syn*** APOTHEOSIS 2, aggrandizement, deification, dignification, glorification
rel upgrading, uplifting; extolment, laudation, praise
con debasement, degradation, demeanment, humiliation; belittlement, depreciation, derogation, disparagement, downgrading
ant abasement
2 ***syn*** ELATION 1, euphoria, exhilaration
rel delectation, delight; bliss, joy, rapture
ant deflation
3 ***syn*** EUPHORIA 2, elation, intoxication
ant depression

exalted *adj* **1** raised to or having high rank <moved in *exalted* circles> <Alexander was *exalted* to the papal throne in 1492>
syn astral, highest, highest-ranking, top-drawer, top-ranking
rel august, noble; eminent, illustrious, prominent; high, high-ranking; foremost, number one; first, leading, outstanding
con low, lowly, low-ranking, unimportant; minor; humble, plebeian
ant abject
2 ***syn*** GRAND 3, elevated, lofty, sublime, superb
ant abject

examination *n* a careful, detailed, and often formal study designed to uncover pertinent information <the doctor gave him a physical *examination*>
syn analysis, audit, check-over, checkup, inspection, perlustration, review, scan, scrutiny, survey, view
rel assay, breakdown, diagnosis, dissection; sifting, winnowing; canvass, catechization, inquiry, questioning, quizzing, testing

examine *vb* **1** ***syn*** SCRUTINIZE 1, canvass, check over, check up, con, inspect, study, survey, vet, view
rel check (out), go (over), investigate, look (into); contemplate, look (at *or* over), observe
idiom give a going over, give the once-over, go over with a fine-toothed comb
2 ***syn*** TRY 1, check, prove, test
3 ***syn*** ASK 1, catechize, inquire, interrogate, query, question, quiz
rel cross-examine; grill; pump
idiom give the third degree to, put to the question

example *n* **1** ***syn*** INSTANCE, case, case history, illustration, representative, sample, sampling, specimen
2 ***syn*** MODEL 2, archetype, beau ideal, ensample, exemplar, ideal, mirror, paradigm, pattern, standard
idiom shining example
3 an instance that illustrates a rule or provides practice in its application <worked out his arithmetic *examples*>
syn ensample, illustration, problem
idiom case in point

exanimate *adj* ***syn*** DEAD 1, asleep, cold, deceased, defunct, departed, extinct, inanimate, late, lifeless

exasperate *vb* ***syn*** IRRITATE, aggravate, gall, get, huff, nettle, peeve, pique, rile, roil
rel agitate, work up
idiom try one's temper (*or* patience)
ant appease; mollify

exasperation *n* **1** ***syn*** ANNOYANCE 2, aggravation, bother, botheration, pother
rel irritation, vexation; displeasure; resentment
2 ***syn*** ANNOYANCE 3, besetment, bother, botheration, botherment, irritant, nuisance, pest, pester, plague

ex cathedra *adj* ***syn*** OFFICIAL, authoritative, ex officio

excavate *vb* **1** ***syn*** DIG 1, ‖delve, grub, shovel, spade
rel gouge (out), hollow (out), scoop (out), scrape (out), quarry (out)
2 ***syn*** DIG 2, dig out, scoop, shovel, spade

exceed *vb* **1** to go or be beyond a natural or set limit <the policeman *exceeded* his authority> <this task *exceeds* my powers>
syn outstep, overrun, overstep, surpass
rel outreach, overreach; dare, presume, venture
2 ***syn*** SURPASS 1, beat, best, better, excel, outdo, outshine, outstrip, top, transcend

exceedingly *adv* ***syn*** VERY 1, exceptionally, extremely, hugely, notably, parlous, remarkably, strikingly, surpassingly, vitally

excel *vb* ***syn*** SURPASS 1, beat, best, better, exceed, outdo, outshine, outstrip, top, transcend

excellence *n* something that gives especial worth or value <the particular *excellence* of this cake is its lightness>
syn arete, excellency, merit, perfection, quality, virtue
rel value, worth; distinction, fineness, superiority; goodness, niceness, superbness; class

---

syn synonym(s) — *rel* related word(s)
idiom idiomatic equivalent(s) — *con* contrasted word(s)
ant antonym(s) — * vulgar
‖ use limited; if in doubt, see a dictionary
The first word in a synonym list when printed in SMALL CAPITALS shows where there is more information about the group. For a more efficient use of this book see Explanatory Notes.

con blemish, defect, flaw; failing, foible, frailty, vice
ant fault

excellency *n* ***syn*** EXCELLENCE, arete, merit, perfection, quality, virtue

excellent *adj* meritoriously near the standard or model and eminently good of its kind <an *excellent* restaurant specializing in French cuisine>
syn A1, bang-up, banner, blue-ribbon, ‖boss, bully, ‖bunkum, capital, champion, classic, classical, ‖dandy, famous, fine, first-class, first-rate, first-string, five-star, front-rank, Grade A, number one, par excellence, prime, quality, royal, skookum, ‖slap-up, sovereign, stunning, superior, ‖swingeing, top, top-notch, whiz-bang; *compare* MARVELOUS 2; SUPREME
rel high-class, high-grade, proper; ‖rum; distinguished, exceptional, premium; brag, incomparable, magnificent, nobby, sensational, smart, superb, superlative, terrific, tip-top, unsurpassed
idiom all wool and a yard wide, beyond compare, out of this world
con mediocre; bad, inadequate, inferior, low, low-grade, low-quality, substandard; fourth-rate, second-class, second-rate; poor, shoddy, sorry, unsatisfactory, wretched; commonplace, mediocre, ordinary
ant execrable

except *vb* **1** ***syn*** EXCLUDE, bar, bate, count out, debar, eliminate, rule out, suspend
rel omit, pass over; exempt; reject
con incorporate, receive, work in
ant admit
2 ***syn*** OBJECT 1, expostulate, inveigh (against), kick, protest, remonstrate

except *prep* with the exclusion or exception of <*except* Christmas, we had no long holiday>
syn apart from, aside from, bar, barring, bating, beside, besides, but, ‖cep, except for, excluding, exclusive of, outside, outside of, save, saving

except *conj* **1** on any other condition than that <wouldn't go near that woman *except* I had to>
syn but, save, saving, unless, ‖without
2 ***syn*** ONLY, but, however, save, yet

except for *prep* ***syn*** EXCEPT, apart from, aside from, bar, barring, besides, but, excluding, exclusive of, save

exceptionable *adj* ***syn*** OBJECTIONABLE, ill-favored, inadmissible, unacceptable, undesirable, unwanted, unwelcome
con unimpeachable; exemplary
ant unexceptionable

exceptional *adj* **1** being out of the ordinary <an *exceptional* opportunity>
syn extraordinary, phenomenal, rare, remarkable, singular, uncommon, uncustomary, unimaginable, unique, unordinary, unthinkable, unusual, unwonted; *compare* STRANGE 4
rel infrequent, scarce; distinct, exceptional, notable, noteworthy
con frequent; common, commonplace, familiar, ordinary, usual
ant unexceptional
2 ***syn*** SUPERIOR 4, premium
rel good; excellent, marvelous, outstanding, phenomenal, wonderful; extraordinary, singular, special
con common, ordinary, run-of-the-mill
ant average

exceptionally *adv* ***syn*** VERY 1, exceedingly, extremely, hugely, notably, parlous, remarkably, strikingly, surpassingly, vitally
rel especially, particularly; extraordinarily, unusually; marvelously, phenomenally, stupendously, wonderfully

excerpt *vb* to select (passages or details) as typical of a larger store <quotations *excerpted* from many authors>
syn extract
rel cull, glean; choose, pick, pick out, select, single; cite, quote

excess *n* **1** whatever exceeds a limit, measure, bound, or accustomed degree <the proper balance between sufficiency and *excess*>
syn fat, overabundance, overflow, overkill, overmuch, overplus, plethora, superfluity, surfeit, surplus, surplusage
rel overbalance, overspill; oversupply; profusion; superabundance
idiom enough and then some, enough and to spare, too much of a good thing
con insufficiency, lack, scarcity
ant deficiency; dearth
2 the amount or degree by which a thing or number exceeds another <an *excess* of 10 bushels over what was needed>
syn overage, overstock, oversupply, plus, surplus, surplusage
rel overproduction; overmeasure
ant deficit, shortfall
3 *often* **excesses** *pl* undue or immoderate personal indulgence especially in eating and drinking <*excess* at table is seldom healthful> <his *excesses* led to his failure in business>
syn immoderation, inordinateness, intemperance, overindulgence
rel extravagance, overdoing; indulgence, self-indulgence; immoderacy, immoderateness; dissipation, prodigality, Saturnalia
con moderation; sobriety, temperatenes; restraint, self-discipline, self-restraint
ant temperance

excess *adj* ***syn*** SUPERFLUOUS, de trop, extra, recrementitious, spare, superfluent, supernumerary, surplus
rel redundant; unessential

excessive *adj* **1** going beyond a normal or acceptable limit <spend an *excessive* amount on clothes>
syn dizzy, exorbitant, extravagant, extreme, immoderate, inordinate, sky-high, steep, stiff, stratospheric, supernatural, towering, unconscionable, undue, unmeasurable
rel boundless, limitless, unbounded; over, overboard, overmuch, overweening; super

---

syn synonym(s)	***rel*** related word(s)
idiom idiomatic equivalent(s)	***con*** contrasted word(s)
ant antonym(s)	* vulgar

‖ use limited; if in doubt, see a dictionary
The first word in a synonym list when printed in SMALL CAPITALS shows where there is more information about the group. For a more efficient use of this book see Explanatory Notes.

idiom out of bounds
con exiguous, meager, narrow, scant, scanty, skimpy, sparse, tight
ant deficient
2 given to personal excesses <an *excessive* drinker, often drunk and never quite sober>
syn immoderate, inordinate, intemperate, overindulgent, unrestrained, untempered
rel extravagant; indulgent, self-indulgent; dissipated, prodigal
con conservative, moderate, sober, temperate
ant restrained

excessively *adv syn* EVER 6, extremely, immensely, inordinately, over, overfull, overly, overmuch, too, unduly

exchange *vb* **1** *syn* TRADE 1, bargain, barter, swap, traffic, truck
2 to give up, taking in return something else <*exchanged* his uniform for civilian clothes>
syn change, substitute, swap, switch, trade; *compare* TRADE 1
rel displace, replace
3 to give and receive reciprocally <*exchanged* a few words with his neighbor>
syn bandy, interchange
rel pay back, reciprocate
idiom give as much as one takes, give tit for tat, return the compliment

exchangeable *adj syn* INTERCHANGEABLE, commutable, fungible, interconvertible, substitutable

exchequer *n syn* TREASURY 2, chest, coffer, war chest

excise *vb* to remove by or as if by dissecting <*excise* a tumor> <*excised* some wordy passages>
syn cut out, exsect, extirpate, resect
rel amputate, cut off; elide, remove, strike out; eradicate, root out; delete, expurgate, exscind, slash

excitable *adj* easily excited <an *excitable* child who needs a firm hand>
syn agitable, alarmable, combustible, edgy, skittery, skittish, startlish, volatile
rel high-strung, mercurial, temperamental, unstable; touchy
idiom like a bundle of nerves, likely to go off at half cock, on edge, on the ragged edge
con calm, collected, cool, easy, easygoing, phlegmatic, placid, quiet
ant unexcitable

excite *vb* **1** *syn* PROVOKE 4, galvanize, innervate, innerve, motivate, move, pique, prime, quicken, stimulate
rel agitate, discompose, disquiet, disturb, perturb, stir up; impassion; charge (up), energize, touch off, turn on
idiom set astir, set on fire, stir the blood
con allay, placate, soothe
ant quiet
2 *syn* ELATE, commove, exhilarate, inspire, set up, spirit (up), stimulate
rel move; fire
con depress, dishearten
3 *syn* INTEREST, appeal, attract, fascinate, intrigue

excited *adj syn* INTOXICATED 2, elated, exhilarated, turned-on
rel animated, atwitter; agitated, charged (up), inflamed, pink; delighted, enthusiastic
idiom all fired up, all of a twitter, beside oneself
con apathetic, unmoved; deflated
ant unexcited

exciting *adj* absorbingly interesting <the most *exciting* day of her life> <an *exciting* personality>
syn exhilarant, exhilarating, exhilarative, eye-popping, inspiring, intoxicating, rousing, stimulating, stirring
rel arresting, interesting, intriguing; moving, provocative; heady, thrilling
con blah, dull, uninteresting, unintriguing; humdrum, monotonous, tedious
ant unexciting

exclaim *vb* to speak or utter suddenly and usually sharply, vehemently, or passionately <*exclaimed* in delight at the sight of the toy>
syn blat, blurt (out), bolt, cry out, ejaculate
rel burst (out); roar, snort

exclude *vb* to prevent the participation, consideration, or inclusion of <*excluded* that subject from discussion>
syn bar, bate, count out, debar, eliminate, except, rule out, suspend
rel ban; close out, estop, obviate, preclude, prevent, prohibit, ward (off); blackball, blacklist, ostracize; block; disbar; lock out, put out, shut out
idiom close (*or* shut) the door on
con comprehend, involve; embrace, take in
ant admit; include

excluding *prep syn* EXCEPT, bar, barring, bating, besides, but, exclusive of, outside of, save, saving

exclusionary *adj syn* EXCLUSIVE 1, exclusory

exclusive *adj* **1** having or exercising the power to limit or exclude <a tangle of *exclusive* laws>
syn exclusionary, exclusory
rel barring, debarring, excluding; limitative, limiting, restrictive; preclusive, prohibitive
con free, unlimited, unrestricted, unrestrictive
ant admissive
2 *syn* SELECT 1, chosen, elect, pick, picked, selected
rel aristocratic, elite, preferred, privileged, tony; aloof, clannish, cliquish, cliquy; high-hat, snobbish, standoffish
con catholic, cosmopolitan, universal; common, familiar, ordinary, popular, vulgar
ant inclusive
3 *syn* STYLISH, chic, dashing, fashionable, modish, smart, swank, swish, ||trendy, with-it
con tasteless; frumpy, unfashionable
4 *syn* SOLE 4, single, unshared
rel individual, lone, only
con common, general, public
5 *syn* WHOLE 5, concentrated, fixed, undistracted, undivided, unswerving
con divided, partial

exclusive *n syn* SCOOP, beat

exclusively *adv* ***syn*** ONLY 1, alone, but, entirely, solely
rel completely, wholly; particularly

exclusive of *prep* ***syn*** EXCEPT, aside from, bar, barring, bating, besides, but, excluding, outside of, save

exclusory *adj* ***syn*** EXCLUSIVE 1, exclusionary

excogitate *vb* **1** ***syn*** CONSIDER 1, contemplate, mind, perpend, ponder, study, think (out *or* over), weigh
2 ***syn*** DERIVE 1, educe, evolve
rel contrive, invent, think (up); develop, think (out)

excoriate *vb* **1** ***syn*** CHAFE 3, abrade, fret, gall, rub
2 ***syn*** LAMBASTE 3, blister, castigate, flay, lash (into), scarify, scathe, scorch, scourge, slash
idiom tear into

excorticate *vb* ***syn*** SKIN 2, decorticate, peel, scale, strip

excrescence *n* ***syn*** OUTGROWTH 1, excrescency, process, processus

excrescency *n* ***syn*** OUTGROWTH 1, excrescence, process, processus

excruciate *vb* ***syn*** AFFLICT, agonize, crucify, harrow, martyr, rack, torment, torture, try, wring
rel inflame, irritate; hurt, pain, wound; convulse
idiom prolong the agony

excruciating *adj* intensely or unbearably painful <his suffering was *excruciating*>
syn agonizing, harrowing, racking, tearing, tormenting, torturing, torturous
rel acute, extreme; piercing, sharp, shooting, stabbing; consuming, rending

exculpate *vb* to free from alleged fault or guilt <the court *exculpated* him after a thorough investigation>
syn absolve, acquit, clear, disculpate, exonerate, vindicate
rel explain, justify, rationalize; condone, excuse, forgive, pardon, remit; amnesty, free, let off
idiom clear the (*or* one's) record, wipe the slate clean
con blame, censure, denounce, reprehend, reprobate; incriminate; accuse, charge; arraign, indict; impeach; convict
ant inculpate

excurse *vb* ***syn*** DIGRESS 2, depart, divagate, diverge, ramble, stray, wander

excursion *n* **1** a trip not involving a prolonged or definite separation from one's usual abode or way of life <an afternoon *excursion* to the city>
syn jaunt, junket, outing, roundabout, sally
rel expedition, journey, trek, trip, safari; circuit, tour; one-way trip, pleasure trip, round trip; ||pasear, paseo, walk, ||walkabout
2 ***syn*** DIGRESSION, aside, discursion, divagation, excursus, parenthesis

excursus *n* ***syn*** DIGRESSION, aside, discursion, divagation, excursion, parenthesis

excusable *adj* **1** ***syn*** VENIAL, forgivable, pardonable, remittable
2 ***syn*** JUSTIFIABLE, condonable, defensible, tenable, vindicable, warrantable

excuse *vb* **1** to exact neither punishment nor redress for or from <she was much too ready to *excuse* her children's faults>
syn condone, forgive, pardon, remit
rel alibi, apologize (for), explain, justify, pretext, rationalize; absolve, acquit, clear, exculpate, exonerate, vindicate; extenuate, gloss (over), gloze, overlook, palliate, pass over, shrug off, whitewash, wink (at)
con blame, censure, criticize, reprehend, reprobate; castigate, chasten, chastise, correct, discipline; admonish, chide, rebuke, reprimand
ant punish
2 ***syn*** EXEMPT, absolve, discharge, dispense, let off, privilege (from), relieve, spare

excuse *n* **1** a justifying explanation of a fault or defect <what's your *excuse* for being late>
syn alibi, plea, pretext, ||right; *compare* APOLOGY 1, 2
rel defense; explanation, justification, rationalization; reason
2 ***syn*** APOLOGY 2, regrets
3 an inferior example of a specified kind <this heap is a sorry *excuse* for a car>
syn apology
rel makeshift, shift, stopgap, substitute
idiom a sorry specimen
con nonpareil, paragon; gem, jewel, treasure

exec *n* ***syn*** EXECUTIVE, administrator, manager, officer, official

execrable *adj* **1** so odious as to be utterly detestable <an *execrable* crime>
syn accursed, cursed, damnable
rel atrocious, heinous, horrific, horrifying, monstrous; base, despicable, foul, low, vile; detestable, loathsome, nauseating, repulsive, revolting
idiom beneath (*or* below) contempt, not to be put up with (*or* endured)
2 ***syn*** DAMNED 2, blasted, blessed, ||blinking, confounded, cursed, cussed, damnable, dashed, infernal

execrate *vb* **1** to denounce violently <*execrated* those responsible for the concentration camps>
syn anathematize, curse, damn, objurgate
rel censure, condemn, denounce, reprehend, reprobate, reprove; ban; revile; accurse, imprecate
con applaud, commend, compliment; acclaim, extol, laud, praise; admire
ant eulogize
2 ***syn*** HATE, abhor, abominate, detest, loathe
3 ***syn*** SWEAR 3, bedamn, curse, cuss, damn, imprecate

execration *n* ***syn*** BLASPHEMY 1, cursing, cussing, imprecation, profanity, swearing

execute *vb* **1** ***syn*** PERFORM 2, achieve, do
rel act; bring about, cause; carry out, complete, discharge, transact
2 ***syn*** ADMINISTER 1, administrate, carry out, govern, render
rel discharge, dispatch, transact; conduct, handle
3 ***syn*** FULFILL 1, complete, implement, perform
rel put through
4 ***syn*** MURDER 1, assassinate, ||bump off, cool, do in, ||dust off, finish, knock off, liquidate, put away
rel eliminate, purge
idiom put to death

---

syn synonym(s) ***rel*** related word(s)
idiom idiomatic equivalent(s) ***con*** contrasted word(s)
ant antonym(s) * vulgar
|| use limited; if in doubt, see a dictionary
The first word in a synonym list when printed in SMALL CAPITALS shows where there is more information about the group. For a more efficient use of this book see Explanatory Notes.

executive *n* one who holds an administrative or managerial position <a senior sales *executive*>
syn administrator, exec, manager, officer, official
rel businessman, businesswoman; entrepreneur; higher-up; director, leader, supervisor

exegesis *n syn* EXPLANATION 1, construal, construction, explication, exposé, exposition, interpretation

exegetic *adj syn* EXPLANATORY, explanative, explicative, explicatory, expositional, expositive, expository, interpretive

exemplar *n syn* MODEL 2, archetype, beau ideal, ensample, example, ideal, mirror, paradigm, pattern, standard
rel soul; exponent, illustration; prototype

exemplary *adj* **1** *syn* GOOD 11, blameless, guiltless, inculpable, innocent, irreprehensible, pure, righteous, unblamable, virtuous
rel ideal, model; admirable, commendable, praiseworthy, worthy
con evil, corrupt; unworthy
2 *syn* TYPICAL 1, classic, classical, ideal, model, paradigmatic, prototypal, prototypical, quintessential, representative

exemplify *vb* **1** to use examples in order to clarify <a good teacher *exemplifies* each complex point>
syn illustrate, instance
rel clarify, clear up, spell out; cite, quote; enlighten, illuminate
2 *syn* EPITOMIZE 2, typify
rel demonstrate; illustrate
3 *syn* REPRESENT 2, body (forth), emblematize, embody, epitomize, illustrate, mirror, personify, symbolize, typify

exempt *vb* to free from a liability or requirement <*exempt* a man from military service>
syn absolve, discharge, dispense, excuse, let off, privilege (from), relieve, spare
rel except; free
idiom give (one) exemption

exemption *n* freeing or the state of being free or freed from a charge or obligation to which others are subject <received a tax *exemption*>
syn immunity, impunity
rel exception; discharge, freedom, release

exenterate *vb syn* EVISCERATE, bowel, disembowel, draw, embowel, gut, paunch

exercise *n* **1** the act of bringing into play or realizing in action <one can usually avoid accidents by the *exercise* of foresight>
syn application, employment, exercising, exertion, operation, use; *compare* USE 1
con dereliction, disregard, neglect; carelessness, heedlessness, inattention, laxity
2 regular or repeated appropriate use of a faculty, power, or bodily organ <muscular atrophy from lack of *exercise*>
syn activity, exercising, exertion
rel action, movement; practice, use, workout
con inactiveness, inactivity; idleness, unemployment
3 something practiced or performed in order to develop, improve, or display a specific power or skill <spelling *exercises*>
syn drill, drilling, practice
4 a performance having a strongly marked secondary or ulterior aspect <his writing is an *exercise* in confusion>
syn lesson, study

exercise *vb* **1** *syn* USE 2, apply, bestow, employ, exploit, handle, utilize
idiom put into practice
2 *syn* EXERT, ply, put out, throw, wield
3 to use repeatedly in order to master or strengthen <beginning swimmers *exercising* their new skill> <games that *exercise* the muscles>
syn drill, practice, rehearse
rel break in, condition, groom, prepare, train; cultivate, develop, foster, improve; fix, set
4 *syn* ANNOY 1, abrade, bother, ||bug, chafe, fret, gall, irk, provoke, vex

exercising *n* **1** *syn* EXERCISE 1, application, employment, exertion, operation, use
2 *syn* EXERCISE 2, activity, exertion

exert *vb* to bring to bear especially with sustained effort or lasting effect <*exerted* tremendous influence over his son's development>
syn exercise, ply, put out, throw, wield
rel apply, employ, use
idiom put forth

exertion *n* **1** *syn* EXERCISE 1, application, employment, exercising, operation, use
2 *syn* EFFORT 1, elbow grease, pains, trouble, while
rel strain, striving, struggle
idiom hard (*or* long) pull
con ease, leisure, relaxation, repose, rest; inactivity, idleness
ant inertia
3 *syn* EXERCISE 2, activity, exercising

exfoliate *vb syn* SCALE 2, desquamate, flake (off), peel

exhale *vb* to let or force out of the lungs <*exhaled* a cloud of cigarette smoke>
syn breathe (out), expire, outbreathe
rel emit, let (out); blow
ant inhale, inspire

exhaust *vb* **1** *syn* DEPLETE, bankrupt, drain, draw, draw down, impoverish, use up
rel dispel, disperse, dissipate, scatter; run out
idiom suck dry
con conserve, preserve, save; renew, restore
2 *syn* CONSUME 1, devour, eat, eat up, use up
3 *syn* GO 4, consume, expend, finish, run through, spend, use up, wash up
4 to tire utterly <the 14-hour flight *exhausted* everyone>
syn ||BUGGER, do in, fag, frazzle, knock out, outtire, outwear, ||poop, prostrate, ||sew up, tucker, wear out; *compare* TIRE 1

---

syn synonym(s) *rel* related word(s)
idiom idiomatic equivalent(s) *con* contrasted word(s)
ant antonym(s) * vulgar
|| use limited; if in doubt, see a dictionary
The first word in a synonym list when printed in SMALL CAPITALS shows where there is more information about the group. For a more efficient use of this book see Explanatory Notes.

rel overdo, overdrive, overexert, overextend, overply, overwork; debilitate, enfeeble, weaken
idiom run one ragged, tire to death
con relax, rest, unlax

exhausted *adj* *syn* EFFETE 2, all in, bleary, depleted, drained, far-gone, spent, used up, washed-out, worn-out
rel run-down, weak, weakened; ||beat, dog-tired, tired, ||tucked up; limp; dead
idiom all done in (*or* for)

exhaustion *n* *syn* FATIGUE, lassitude, tiredness, weariness
rel collapse, prostration

exhaustive *adj* testing all possibilities or considering all the elements of <an *exhaustive* investigation was soon under way>
syn complete, full-dress, thorough, thoroughgoing, whole-hog
rel all-encompassing, all-out, comprehensive, full-blown, full-scale, out-and-out, profound, total; intensive, radical, sweeping
con cursory, shallow; incomplete, partial; slipshod, unthorough
ant superficial

exhaustively *adv* **1** *syn* HARD 3, assiduously, dingdong, earnestly, intensely, intensively, painstakingly, thoroughly, unremittingly
con cursorily, superficially; incompletely, partially
2 *syn* THOROUGHLY 2, completely, detailedly, in and out, inside out, up and down

exhibit *vb* **1** *syn* SHOW 2, demonstrate, evidence, evince, illustrate, manifest, mark, ostend, proclaim
2 *syn* LOOK 4, show
3 *syn* SHOW 4, brandish, display, disport, expose, flash, flaunt, parade, show off, trot out
idiom parade one's wares, strut one's stuff

exhibit *n* *syn* EXHIBITION 2, exposition, fair, show

exhibition *n* **1** an act or instance of showing, evincing, or showing off <she gave an incredible *exhibition* of bad manners>
syn demonstration, display, show, spectacle
rel manifestation, sight
2 a public display of objects of interest <a trade *exhibition*>
syn exhibit, exposition, fair, show
rel demonstration, display, offering, presentation, showing

exhibitive *adj* *syn* INDICATIVE, denotative, denotive, designative, indicatory, indicial, significative

exhilarant *adj* *syn* EXCITING, exhilarating, exhilarative, eye-popping, inspiring, intoxicating, rousing, stimulating, stirring

exhilarate *vb* *syn* ELATE, commove, excite, inspire, set up, spirit (up), stimulate
rel animate, enliven, invigorate, vitalize; boost, buoy, exhalt, inspirit, lift, pep (up), uplift; cheer, delight, gladden, ||send, thrill
idiom send into ecstasies
con deject, dishearten, dispirit, weigh down
ant depress

exhilarated *adj* *syn* INTOXICATED 2, elated, excited, turned-on
rel buoyed up, exalted, gladdened, pepped up, uplifted
idiom in ecstasies, on cloud nine
con blue, dispirited, down, low, unhappy, weighed down
ant depressed

exhilarating *adj* **1** *syn* EXCITING, exhilarant, exhilarative, eye-popping, inspiring, intoxicating, rousing, stimulating, stirring
rel animating, animative, enlivening, inspiriting, invigorating, quickening; cheering, elevating, uplifting; breathtaking, electric
con deflating, disheartening, dispiriting
ant depressing
2 *syn* INVIGORATING, animating, bracing, exhilarative, quickening, stimulating, stimulative, tonic, vitalizing

exhilaration *n* *syn* ELATION 1, euphoria, exaltation; *compare* ECSTASY
rel animation, enlivenment, firing, invigoration, quickening, stimulation, vitalization, vivification; electrification, excitation, excitement, galvanization; elevation, inspiration, uplift
ant dejection

exhilarative *adj* **1** *syn* EXCITING, exhilarant, exhilarating, eye-popping, inspiring, intoxicating, rousing, stimulating, stirring
2 *syn* INVIGORATING, animating, bracing, exhilarating, quickening, stimulating, stimulative, tonic, vitalizing

exhort *vb* *syn* URGE, egg (on), goad, prick, prod, prompt, propel, sic, spur
rel admonish, plead; call upon, insist; stimulate
con block, deter, discourage, impede

exhumate *vb* *syn* EXHUME, disinhume, disinter, unbury, uncharnel

exhume *vb* to take out of a place of burial <the body was *exhumed* and burned>
syn disinhume, disinter, exhumate, unbury, uncharnel
rel dig up, disentomb, unearth; disembalm
con bury, entomb, inter, ||plant
ant inhume

exigency *n* **1** *syn* JUNCTURE 2, contingency, crisis, crossroad(s), emergency, pass, pinch, strait, turning point, zero hour
rel difficulty, hardship, rigor, vicissitude; dilemma, fix, jam, pickle, scrape; pressure, urgency
2 *syn* NEED 4, necessity
rel demand, imperativeness, insistence, requirement; coercion, compulsion, constraint; duress, pressure, urgency
idiom matter of life and death

exigent *adj* **1** *syn* PRESSING, burning, clamant, clamorous, crying, imperative, importunate, insistent, instant, urgent
rel acute; necessary; menacing, threatening

---

2 ***syn*** ONEROUS, burdensome, demanding, exacting, grievous, oppressive, superincumbent, taxing, tough, weighty

exiguous *adj* ***syn*** MEAGER 2, poor, scant, scanty, scrimp, scrimpy, skimp, skimpy, spare, sparse
rel diminutive, little, small, tiny; slender, slight, tenuous, thin; confined, limited, narrow, restricted, straitened
ant ample

exile *n* **1** forced removal from one's native country <a deposed king living in *exile* in Rome>
syn banishment, deportation, displacement, expulsion, ostracism, relegation
rel exclusion; extradition; expatriation; diaspora, dispersion, migration, scattering
con recall, restoration
2 ***syn*** ÉMIGRÉ, expatriate, expellee
rel nonperson, outcast, unperson
idiom man without a country

exile *vb* ***syn*** BANISH, cast out, deport, displace, expatriate, expel, expulse, ‖lag, ostracize, transport
rel dispossess; evacuate; extradite; drive out
idiom turn out of house and home
con recall, restore

exist *vb* **1** ***syn*** BE, breathe, live, move, subsist
2 ***syn*** CONSIST 1, dwell, inhere, lie, reside

existence *n* **1** the state or fact of having independent reality <customs that have recently come into *existence*>
syn actuality, being
rel life; presence; reality; perseity
ant nonexistence
2 ***syn*** ENTITY 1, being, existent, individual, something, thing
rel essence; individuality

existent *adj* **1** ***syn*** ACTUAL 1, extant
rel existing; present
2 ***syn*** EXTANT 1, alive, around, existing, living
3 ***syn*** PRESENT, contemporary, current, extant, instant, present-day, todayish

existent *n* ***syn*** ENTITY 1, being, existence, individual, something, thing

existing *adj* ***syn*** EXTANT 1, alive, around, existent, living

exit *n* **1** ***syn*** DEPARTURE 1, egress, egression, exiting, exodus, offgoing, setting-out, withdrawal
ant entry
2 ***syn*** EGRESS 2, outlet
ant entrance, entry

exit *vb* ***syn*** GO 2, ‖blow, depart, get away, get off, leave, move, quit, retire, withdraw
idiom make an (*or* one's) exit
con arrive, come
ant enter

---

syn synonym(s) — ***rel*** related word(s)
idiom idiomatic equivalent(s) — ***con*** contrasted word(s)
ant antonym(s) — * vulgar
‖ use limited; if in doubt, see a dictionary
The first word in a synonym list when printed in SMALL CAPITALS shows where there is more information about the group. For a more efficient use of this book see Explanatory Notes.

exiting *n* ***syn*** DEPARTURE 1, egress, egression, exit, exodus, offgoing, setting-out, withdrawal
ant entering

exodus *n* ***syn*** DEPARTURE 1, egress, egression, exit, exiting, offgoing, setting-out, withdrawal
rel emigration, migration; flight
con immigration; ingress
ant influx

ex officio *adj* ***syn*** OFFICIAL, authoritative, ex cathedra

exonerate *vb* ***syn*** EXCULPATE, absolve, acquit, clear, disculpate, vindicate
rel disburden, free
ant incriminate

exorbitant *adj* ***syn*** EXCESSIVE 1, dizzy, extravagant, extreme, immoderate, inordinate, towering, unconscionable, undue, unmeasurable
rel overboard, overmuch; unwarranted; outrageous, preposterous; exacting, extortionate
idiom out of sight
con equitable, fair, just; rational, reasonable

exordium *n* ***syn*** INTRODUCTION, foreword, overture, preamble, preface, prelude, prelusion, proem, prolegomenon, prologue
rel preliminary
con afterword, conclusion, epilogue, postscript

exotic *adj* **1** not native to the place where found <*exotic* fish>
syn foreign
rel imported, introduced, naturalized; alien, extrinsic, strange
con aboriginal, autochthonous, endemic, native; domestic, local
ant indigenous
2 excitingly or enticingly different or unusual <he was moved by her *exotic* beauty>
syn romanesque, romantic, strange
rel different, unusual; alluring, enticing, fascinating, glamorous, mysterious

expand *vb* **1** ***syn*** OPEN 4, extend, fan (out), outspread, outstretch, spread, unfold
2 ***syn*** INCREASE 1, aggrandize, augment, beef (up), boost, enlarge, extend, heighten, magnify, multiply
3 to increase or become increased in bulk, volume, or size <water *expands* when heated>
syn amplify, dilate, distend, inflate, swell
rel grow; bulk (up), enlarge, fill (out); bolster; mushroom, ‖plim, puff (up)
con condense, decrease, deflate, shrink, shrivel; dwindle, lessen
ant contract
4 to express more fully and in greater detail <*expanded* his notes into an essay>
syn amplify, develop, elaborate, enlarge
rel detail, explicate; augment; discourse, expatiate
con compress, condense, contract
ant abridge
5 ***syn*** INCREASE 2, augment, build, enlarge, heighten, mount, multiply, rise, upsurge, wax
6 ***syn*** ESCALATE 2, grow
rel prolong, protract
con de-escalate; circumscribe
ant limit, restrict

expanse *n* a significantly large area or range <a trackless *expanse* of moor>

syn amplitude, breadth, distance, expansion, space, spread, stretch

rel compass, extent, orbit, range, reach, scope, sweep; area, domain, field, sphere, territory; immensity, magnitude

expansion *n* **1** ***syn*** EXPANSE, amplitude, breadth, distance, space, spread, stretch

2 the act or process of increasing in some way <the recent *expansion* of science>

syn enlargement, extension, spread

con contraction, decrease, shrinking

expansive *adj* **1** ***syn*** ELASTIC 2, airy, bouncy, buoyant, effervescent, resilient, volatile

rel communicative, demonstrative, extroverted, gregarious, unconstrained, unreserved, unrestrained; effusive, gushy, lavish; generous, liberal, openhanded

con austere, severe, stern; reserved, reticent, silent, taciturn

2 ***syn*** DEMONSTRATIVE, outgoing, unconstrained, unreserved, unrestrained

ant withdrawn

3 ***syn*** COMMUNICATIVE, communicable

4 ***syn*** EXTENSIVE 1, broad, extended, scopic, scopious, wide

rel ample, large; big, great

ant limited

expatiate *vb* ***syn*** DISCOURSE 1, descant, dilate (on *or* upon), discuss, dissert, dissertate, sermonize

rel narrate, recite, recount, rehearse, relate; ramble

expatriate *vb* ***syn*** BANISH, deport, displace, exile, expel, expulse, ‖lag, oust, relegate, transport

ant repatriate

expatriate *n* ***syn*** ÉMIGRÉ, exile, expellee

ant repatriate

expect *vb* **1** to anticipate in the mind <did not *expect* him for dinner>

syn await, count (on *or* upon), hope, look

rel anticipate, apprehend, divine, foreknow, foresee

idiom bargain on (*or* for), look for

ant despair (of)

2 ***syn*** UNDERSTAND 3, assume, believe, gather, imagine, ‖reckon, suppose, suspect, take, think

rel feel, sense; presume, presuppose

expectancy *n* **1** the state of one who looks forward to something <had an air of wistful *expectancy*>

syn anticipation, expectation

rel presensation, presentiment

2 ***syn*** EXPECTATION 2

expectant *adj* **1** characterized by expectation <an *expectant* crowd>

syn anticipant, anticipative, anticipatory, atiptoe, expecting

rel open-eyed, openmouthed; hopeful; eager; alert, watchful

con apathetic, indifferent, uninterested; unconcerned, unimpressed, unmoved

2 ***syn*** PREGNANT 1, big, childing, enceinte, expecting, gone, gravid, heavy, parous, parturient

idiom anticipating a blessed event, waiting for the stork

expectation *n* **1** ***syn*** EXPECTANCY 1, anticipation

2 something that is expected <each had his own dreams and *expectations*>

syn expectancy

rel design, hope, intention, motive, notion; prospect

expecting *adj* **1** ***syn*** EXPECTANT 1, anticipant, anticipative, anticipatory, atiptoe

2 ***syn*** PREGNANT 1, big, childing, enceinte, expectant, gone, gravid, heavy, parous, parturient

expediency *n* **1** ***syn*** ORDER 11, appositeness, appropriateness, aptness, fitness, meetness, propriety, rightness, suitability, suitableness

rel propitiousness; convenience

2 ***syn*** RESOURCE 3, dernier ressort, expedient, makeshift, recourse, resort, shift, stopgap, substitute, surrogate

rel design, strategy, tactic; measure, step

idiom card up one's sleeve, means to an end

expedient *adj* dictated by practical or prudential motives <decided it was not *expedient* to interfere yet>

syn advisable, politic, prudent, tactical, wise

rel advantageous, beneficial, convenient, practical, profitable, useful, utilitarian; opportune, seasonable, timely, well-timed; feasible, possible, practicable; appropriate, fit, fitting, suitable; judicious

con deleterious, detrimental; harmful, hurtful, injurious; fruitless, futile, vain; inappropriate, uncalled-for, unfitting, unsuitable; impolite, imprudent, inadvisable, injudicious, unwise

ant inexpedient

expedient *n* ***syn*** RESOURCE 3, dernier ressort, expediency, makeshift, recourse, refuge, resort, shift, stopgap, substitute

rel agency, instrument, instrumentality, means, medium

expedition *n* **1** ***syn*** JOURNEY, peregrination(s), travel(s), trek, trip

rel campaign; entrada, exploration

2 ***syn*** HASTE 1, celerity, dispatch, expeditiousness, hurry, hustle, rustle, speed, speediness, swiftness

rel alacrity, promptitude

con delay, retardation, slackening, slowing

ant procrastination

3 ***syn*** ALACRITY, dispatch, goodwill, promptitude, readiness

rel expeditiousness, speediness, swiftness; punctuality

con dawdling, delaying, faltering, hesitation

expeditious *adj* ***syn*** FAST 3, breakneck, expeditive, fleet, harefooted, hasty, quick, rapid, speedy, swift

rel effective, effectual, efficacious, efficient; prompt, ready

con ineffective, ineffectual, inefficacious, inefficient; dilatory, laggard, leisurely, slow

ant sluggish

expeditiously *adv* ***syn*** FAST 2, apace, flat-out, hastily, lickety-split, posthaste, quickly, rapidly, speedily, swiftly

---

rel effectively, efficaciously; punctually
con ineffectively; deliberately, dilatorily, leisurely, slowly
ant sluggishly

expeditiousness *n syn* HASTE 1, celerity, dispatch, expedition, hurry, hustle, rustle, speed, speediness, swiftness

expeditive *adj syn* FAST 3, breakneck, expeditious, fleet, harefooted, hasty, quick, rapid, speedy, swift

expel *vb* **1** *syn* ERUPT 1, belch, disgorge, eject, eruct, irrupt, spew
rel blow off, blow out, ejaculate, exhaust
2 *syn* BANISH, cast out, deport, displace, exile, expatriate, expulse, ‖lag, oust, transport
rel drum out, read out; eliminate, turn out; ‖bounce
idiom give (one) the boot, give the bum's rush, give the old heave-ho, send to Coventry, throw out on one's ear
ant admit

expellee *n syn* ÉMIGRÉ, exile, expatriate

expend *vb* **1** *syn* SPEND 1, disburse, fork (out), give, lay out, outlay, pay, shell out
rel dispense, distribute; blow, exhaust, use up
idiom loose (*or* untie) the purse strings, open one's purse
con hoard, lay up, save
2 *syn* GO 4, consume, exhaust, finish, run through, spend, use up, wash up

expenditure *n syn* EXPENSE 1, cost, disbursement, outlay

expense *n* **1** something expended to secure a benefit or bring about a result <spared no *expense* in furnishing their home>
syn cost, disbursement, expenditure, outlay
2 a loss incurred in the course of gaining something <won the war at the *expense* of many lives>
syn cost, price, toll
rel decrement, forfeit, forfeiture, sacrifice; deprivation, loss

expensive *adj syn* COSTLY 1, dear, high
rel immoderate, uneconomical; big-ticket, high-priced
con economical, moderate; bargain, low-cost, low-priced, thrifty; cheap
ant inexpensive

experience *n syn* ACQUAINTANCE 1, familiarity, intimacy, inwardness
rel background; observation; know-how, practice, skill; savoir faire, sophistication; wisdom
ant inexperience

experience *vb* **1** to meet with directly (as through participation or observation) <*experience* pain> <trying to *experience* the problems of a different culture>
syn have, know, see, suffer, sustain, undergo
rel encounter, meet; accept, receive
2 *syn* FEEL 2, know, savor, taste
rel behold, see, survey, view

experienced *adj* made skillful or wise through practice <an *experienced* sales executive>
syn old, old-time, practical, practiced, seasoned, skilled, versed, vet, veteran; *compare* PROFICIENT
rel broken in; accomplished, skillful; expert, qualified; old-line, wise
idiom having been around, knowing the score (*or* the ropes)
con apprentice, beginning, freshman, green, new, novice, raw, untested, untried
ant experienceless, inexperienced

experient *adj syn* EMPIRICAL, experiential, experimental

experiential *adj syn* EMPIRICAL, experient, experimental

experiment *n* an operation or process carried out to resolve an uncertainty <*experiments* that added much to our understanding of nutritional needs>
syn experimentation, test, trial, trial and error, trial run
rel probe, research, search; examination, investigation; analysis, study

experiment *vb* to engage in experimentation <*experimenting* with regional solutions to urban problems>
syn experimentalize, experimentize, test (out), try (out), try on
rel investigate, probe, research, search; analyze, scrutinize, study, weigh
idiom play around with

experimental *adj* **1** *syn* EMPIRICAL, experient, experiential
2 of, relating to, or having the characteristics of experiment <*experimental* missile flights>
syn experimentative, test, trial
rel preliminary, preparatory; developmental; provisional, temporary, tentative
con tested, tried; permanent, proved; accepted, established, standard

experimentalize *vb syn* EXPERIMENT, experimentize, test (out), try (out), try on

experimentation *n syn* EXPERIMENT, test, trial, trial and error, trial run

experimentative *adj syn* EXPERIMENTAL 2, test, trial

experimentize *vb syn* EXPERIMENT, experimentalize, test (out), try (out), try on

expert *adj syn* PROFICIENT, adept, crack, crackerjack, master, masterful, masterly, skilled, skillful
rel schooled, trained; adroit, deft, dexterous; pro, professional
con unpracticed; unschooled
ant amateur, inexpert

expert *n* one who has acquired special skill in or knowledge and mastery of something <a fingerprint *expert*>
syn adept, artist, artiste, authority, ‖dab, ‖dabster, doyen, master, master-hand, maven, passed master, past master, pro, professional, proficient, swell, virtuoso, whiz, wiz, wizard
rel ‖darb; specialist
con dabbler, dilettante, tyro; apprentice, novice, probationer
ant amateur

---

syn synonym(s) — *rel* related word(s)
idiom idiomatic equivalent(s) — *con* contrasted word(s)
ant antonym(s) — * vulgar
‖ use limited; if in doubt, see a dictionary
The first word in a synonym list when printed in SMALL CAPITALS shows where there is more information about the group. For a more efficient use of this book see Explanatory Notes.

expertise *n* **1** ***syn*** ABILITY 2, command, expertism, expertness, knack, know-how, mastership, mastery, skill
rel readiness; competence; skillfulness
2 ***syn*** ART 1, adroitness, craft, cunning, dexterity, know-how, skill
rel quickness; cleverness, ingeniousness; finesse; savvy

expertism *n* ***syn*** ABILITY 2, command, expertise, expertness, knack, know-how, mastership, mastery, skill

expertness *n* ***syn*** ABILITY 2, command, expertise, expertism, knack, know-how, mastership, mastery, skill
rel prowess; facility

expiate *vb* to make amends or give satisfaction for wrong done < *expiated* his crime with his life >
syn atone
rel amend, compensate (for), correct, rectify, redress, remedy
idiom make up for, put right

expiative *adj* ***syn*** PURGATIVE, expiatory, expurgatorial, expurgatory, lustral, lustratory, propitiatory, purgatorial

expiatory *adj* ***syn*** PURGATIVE, expiative, expurgatorial, expurgatory, lustral, lustratory, propitiatory, purgatorial

expire *vb* **1** ***syn*** DIE 1, conk, ‖croak, decease, demise, depart, go, ‖kick off, pass, pass away
idiom draw one's last breath; give up the breath of life
con live, thrive
2 ***syn*** PASS 3, elapse, go, pass away
3 ***syn*** EXHALE, breathe (out), outbreathe
ant inspire

explain *vb* **1** to make something comprehensible or more comprehensible <a commentary that *explains* the allegory>
syn construe, explicate, expound, interpret, spell out; *compare* CLARIFY 2
rel decipher, disentangle, undo, unravel, unriddle, unscramble, untangle; analyze, break down; clear up, resolve, solve
idiom put into plain English
con confound, confuse, puzzle
ant obfuscate
2 ***syn*** CLARIFY 2, clear, clear up, elucidate, illuminate, illustrate
3 to give the reason for or cause of <unable to *explain* his strange conduct>
syn account, explain away, justify, rationalize
rel condone, excuse; absolve, acquit, exculpate, exonerate, vindicate

explain away *vb* ***syn*** EXPLAIN 3, account, justify, rationalize

explanation *n* **1** something that makes clear what is obscure <sought some *explanation* of the difficult passage>
syn construal, construction, exegesis, explication, exposé, exposition, interpretation
rel disentanglement, unscrambling; enlightenment, illumination; definition, meaning; resolution, solution; demonstration, example, exemplification, illustration
2 a statement of causes, grounds, or motives <refused an *explanation* for his act>
syn account, justification, rationale, rationalization, reason
rel grounds; motive

explanative *adj* ***syn*** EXPLANATORY, exegetic, explicative, explicatory, expositional, expositive, expository, interpretive

explanatory *adj* serving to explain < *explanatory* notes in a book>
syn exegetic, explanative, explicative, explicatory, expositional, expositive, expository, interpretive
rel enlightening, illuminating; discursive; demonstrative, illustrative
con baffling, bewildering, confusing, misleading, mystifying, puzzling
ant obfuscatory

expletive *n* ***syn*** SWEARWORD, curse, cuss, cussword, oath, swear

explicate *vb* ***syn*** EXPLAIN 1, construe, expound, interpret, spell out
rel amplify, develop, dilate, enlarge (upon), expand, expatiate; demonstrate
idiom dot the *i*s (and cross the *t*s)

explication *n* ***syn*** EXPLANATION 1, construal, construction, exegesis, exposé, exposition, interpretation
rel amplification, development, enlargement, expansion, expatiation

explicative *adj* ***syn*** EXPLANATORY, exegetic, explanative, explicatory, expositional, expositive, expository, interpretive
rel annotative, exemplificative, scholiastic

explicatory *adj* ***syn*** EXPLANATORY, exegetic, explanative, explicative, expositional, expositive, expository, interpretive

explicit *adj* characterized by full precise expression <gave the guard *explicit* orders about whom to admit>
syn categorical, clean-cut, clear-cut, definite, definitive, express, specific, unambiguous
rel certain, clear, distinct, lucid, perspicuous, plain, sure, understandable, unequivocal; accurate, correct, exact, precise
con cryptic, dark, enigmatic, equivocal, obscure, unclear, vague; implicit, implied, inferred; imprecise, inaccurate, incorrect, inexact
ant ambiguous

explicitly *adv* ***syn*** EXPRESSLY 1, categorically, definitely, specifically

explode *vb* **1** to burst violently and noisily usually due to pressure within <the bomb *exploded*>
syn blow up, burst, detonate, go off, mushroom
rel blast, discharge
idiom blow sky-high, blow to kingdom come
con fail, fizzle, peter (out)
2 ***syn*** ERUPT 2, break out, burst (forth)
rel flame (up), flare (up)
idiom blow a fuse (*or* gasket)

---

syn synonym(s) — *rel* related word(s)
idiom idiomatic equivalent(s) — *con* contrasted word(s)
ant antonym(s) — * vulgar
‖ use limited; if in doubt, see a dictionary
The first word in a synonym list when printed in SMALL CAPITALS shows where there is more information about the group. For a more efficient use of this book see Explanatory Notes.

3 ***syn*** DISCREDIT 2, blow up, disprove, puncture, shoot
rel invalidate; deflate
idiom shoot full of holes

exploit *n* **1** ***syn*** ADVENTURE, emprise, enterprise, feat, gest, venture
rel effort, job; maneuver
2 ***syn*** FEAT 2, achievement, deed, tour de force
rel do, performance, stunt; blow, coup, stroke
idiom bold stroke

exploit *vb* **1** ***syn*** USE 2, apply, bestow, employ, exercise, handle, utilize
rel cultivate, work
2 to take unfair advantage of < *exploits* his friend's good nature >
syn abuse, impose (on *or* upon), use
rel manipulate; bleed, fleece, skin, soak, stick
3 ***syn*** MANIPULATE 2, beguile, finesse, jockey, maneuver, play

explore *vb* to search through or into < *explored* the possibilities of reaching an agreement >
syn delve (into), dig (into), go (into), inquire (into), investigate, look (into), probe, prospect, sift
rel burrow, mouse (out); quarry, search; examine, test, try; inquisite, question
idiom nose around

explosion *n* ***syn*** OUTBURST 1, access, burst, eruption, flare-up, gust, sally

exponent *n* one who actively promotes or backs something < an *exponent* of arbitration in labor disputes >
syn advocate, champion, expounder, proponent, supporter
rel backer, booster, partisan, promoter, protagonist; defender, upholder
con antagonist, enemy; opposition
ant opponent

expose *vb* **1** to make accessible to something detrimental or dangerous < he needlessly *exposed* his troops to enemy fire >
syn lay (open), subject, uncover
rel endanger, hazard, imperil, jeopard, jeopardize, jeopardy, peril, risk
idiom put (*or* leave) in harm's way
con cover, shelter; guard, protect
ant shield
2 ***syn*** OPEN 2, disclose, display, reveal, unclothe, uncover, unveil
rel unfold, unshroud
3 ***syn*** SHOW 4, brandish, display, disport, exhibit, flash, flaunt, parade, show off, trot out
rel advertise, air, broadcast, publish
4 to reveal the faults, frailties, unsoundness, or pretensions of < the monograph *exposed* the theory as being pure myth >
syn debunk, discover, show up, uncloak, undress, unmask, unshroud
rel disclose, reveal, uncover
idiom lay bare

exposé *n* ***syn*** EXPLANATION 1, construal, construction, exegesis, explication, exposition, interpretation

exposed *adj* **1** ***syn*** OPEN 2, bare, denuded, naked, peeled, stripped, uncovered
rel apparent, evident, manifest; unconcealed, unhidden; revealed; visible
idiom laid bare
con covered, enveloped, sheathed
2 ***syn*** LIABLE 2, obnoxious, open, prone, sensitive, subject, susceptible
rel likely; menaced, threatened
con defended, guarded, protected, safeguarded, shielded

exposition *n* **1** ***syn*** EXPLANATION 1, construal, construction, exegesis, explication, exposé, interpretation
rel presentation; discourse, discussion, disquisition, expounding; statement; delineation, enunciation
2 ***syn*** EXHIBITION 2, exhibit, fair, show
rel display, production

expositional *adj* ***syn*** EXPLANATORY, exegetic, explanative, explicative, explicatory, expositive, expository, interpretive

expositive *adj* ***syn*** EXPLANATORY, exegetic, explanative, explicative, explicatory, expositional, expository, interpretive
rel depictive, descriptive, graphic; illuminative; delineative

expository *adj* ***syn*** EXPLANATORY, exegetic, explanative, explicative, explicatory, expositional, expositive, interpretive
rel disquisitional; critical

expostulate *vb* ***syn*** OBJECT 1, except, inveigh (against), kick, protest, remonstrate
rel combat, fight, oppose, resist; argue, debate, discuss, dispute
idiom raise one's voice against

exposure *n* the condition of being exposed to something detrimental < *exposure* to attack >
syn liability, openness, vulnerability, vulnerableness
rel susceptibility, susceptiveness, susceptivity; defenselessness, helplessness, unprotection; danger, jeopardy, peril, risk
con bulwark, cover, protection, safeguard, shelter, shield, shielding

expound *vb* ***syn*** EXPLAIN 1, construe, explicate, interpret, spell out
rel express, present, state; comment, discourse; clarify, delineate, describe, exemplify, illustrate

expounder *n* ***syn*** EXPONENT, advocate, champion, proponent, supporter
rel explainer, expositor

express *adj* **1** ***syn*** EXPLICIT, categorical, clean-cut, clear-cut, definite, definitive, specific, unambiguous
rel expressed, uttered, voiced; out-and-out, unmistakable; unconditional, unqualified
con unexpressed, unsaid, unstated; ambiguous, equivocal; conditional, qualified
2 of a particular or exact sort < came for the *express* purpose of buying a car >

syn especial, set, special, specific
rel individual; definite, particular; explicit; intended, intentional, premeditated
ant vague

express *vb* **1** *syn* WORD, couch, formulate, phrase, put
2 to give expression to (as a thought, an opinion, or an emotion) <*expressed* his views freely>
syn air, give, put, state, vent, ventilate; *compare* SAY 1, WORD
rel broach, circulate, put about; disclose, tell; frame; enunciate, phrase; announce, declare, proclaim, pronounce; discharge, drain
con hint, insinuate, intimate, suggest
ant imply
3 *syn* MEAN 2, add up (to), connote, denote, import, intend, signify, spell
rel communicate, convey, impart
4 *syn* PRESS 3, crush

expression *n* **1** an act, process, or instance of expressing in words <his anger found *expression* in a string of oaths>
syn statement, utterance, vent, voice
rel issue; manifestation, representation; observation, reflection
con hint, insinuation, intimation, suggestion
2 *syn* PHRASE 2, locution
rel word; verbalism; idiom; clause
3 one thing that calls to mind another often symbolically <sent flowers as an *expression* of sympathy>
syn gesture, indication, reminder, sign, token
rel embodiment, manifestation, representation, symbol; demonstration, show
4 *syn* ELOQUENCE, expressiveness, expressivity, facundity
rel graphicness, vividness
5 *syn* LOOK 2, cast, countenance, face, visage

expressionless *adj* lacking expression <cold *expressionless* eyes>
syn blank, deadpan, empty, inexpressive, unexpressive, vacant
rel dull, lackluster, lusterless, vacuous; impassive, inscrutable, stolid, wooden; dead
con lustrous; responsive; alive, vital
ant expressive

expressive *adj* clearly conveying or manifesting something <a forceful and *expressive* word>
syn eloquent, facund, meaningful, pregnant, rich, sententious, significant
rel revealing, revelatory, suggestive; graphic, pictorial, vivid; alive, demonstrative, lively, responsive, senseful, spirited
con banal, commonplace, drab, dull, flat, jejune, inane, insipid, vacuous, vapid; impassive, indifferent; austere, severe, stern, stiff, wooden; blank, deadpan, empty, expressionless, vacant; dead
ant inexpressive, unexpressive

expressiveness *n* *syn* ELOQUENCE, expression, expressivity, facundity
ant inexpressiveness

expressivity *n* *syn* ELOQUENCE, expression, expressiveness, facundity

expressly *adv* **1** in direct and unmistakable terms <his beliefs *expressly* repudiate the church's teachings>
syn categorically, definitely, explicitly, specifically
rel directly; unmistakably
con ambiguously, equivocally; conditionally; likely, possibly, probably
2 for the express purpose <programs designed *expressly* to serve immediate political objectives>
syn especially, in specie, specially, specifically
3 *syn* EVEN 1, as well, exactly, just, precisely

expropriate *vb* *syn* APPROPRIATE 1, accroach, annex, arrogate, commandeer, confiscate, preempt, seize, sequester, take
rel dispossess; take (away)

expulse *vb* *syn* BANISH, cast out, deport, displace, exile, expel, ‖lag, oust, relegate, transport
rel ‖bounce; eject
con admit, receive

expulsion *n* *syn* EXILE 1, banishment, deportation, displacement, ostracism, relegation
rel driving out, forcing out; ejection, ousting; removal
idiom the boot, the old heave-ho

expunge *vb* *syn* ERASE, annul, black (out), blot out, cancel, delete, efface, obliterate, wipe (out), x (out)
rel discard, drop, exclude, omit; annihilate, eradicate

expurgate *vb* **1** *syn* PURIFY 2, cleanse, lustrate, purge
2 *syn* CENSOR, blip, bowdlerize, screen

expurgation *n* *syn* PURIFICATION, catharsis, cleansing, lustration, purgation

expurgatorial *adj* *syn* PURGATIVE, expiative, expiatory, expurgatory, lustral, lustratory, propitiatory, purgatorial

expurgatory *adj* *syn* PURGATIVE, expiative, expiatory, expurgatorial, lustral, lustratory, propitiatory, purgatorial

exquisite *adj* **1** *syn* CHOICE, dainty, delicate, elegant, rare, recherché, select, superior
rel consummate, finished; faultless, flawless, impeccable
2 *syn* IMPECCABLE 1, errorless, faultless, flawless, immaculate, irreproachable
rel superb, superlative
con faulty, flawed, imperfect
3 *syn* INTENSE 1, concentrated, desperate, fierce, furious, terrible, vehement, vicious, violent
rel acute, extreme; consummate, transcending

exquisite *n* *syn* FOP, Beau Brummel, blood, buck, coxcomb, dandy, dude, lounge lizard, macaroni, petit-maître

exsect *vb* *syn* EXCISE, cut out, extirpate, resect

exsiccate *vb* *syn* DRY 1, dehydrate, desiccate, parch, sear

extant *adj* **1** that is in existence <the most talented writer *extant*>
syn alive, around, existent, existing, living

---

con dead, defunct, destroyed, exterminated, extinct; departed, gone, lost
ant nonextant
2 ***syn*** ACTUAL 1, existent
rel current, immediate, present
con possible, potential
3 ***syn*** PRESENT, contemporary, current, existent, instant, present-day, todayish

extemporaneous *adj* composed, devised, or done at the moment rather than beforehand <made an *extemporaneous* speech after the dinner>
syn autoschediastic, extemporary, extempore, impromptu, improvised, offhand, spur-of-the-moment, unrehearsed, unstudied; *compare* UNINTENTIONAL
rel casual, informal; unprepared, unthought-out; impulsive, snap, spontaneous
idiom off the cuff, on the spur of the moment
con designed, planned, prepared, projected, schemed, thought-out; considered, deliberated, premeditated, studied

extemporary *adj* ***syn*** EXTEMPORANEOUS, autoschediastic, extempore, impromptu, improvised, offhand, spur-of-the-moment, unrehearsed, unstudied

extempore *adj* ***syn*** EXTEMPORANEOUS, autoschediastic, extemporary, impromptu, improvised, offhand, spur-of-the-moment, unrehearsed, unstudied

extemporization *n* ***syn*** IMPROVISATION, autoschediasm, impromptu

extemporize *vb* ***syn*** IMPROVISE, ad-lib, improvisate
rel dash off, knock off, toss off
idiom do offhand, play (it) by ear
con cook up, plan, prepare, think out

extend *vb* **1** ***syn*** OPEN 4, expand, fan (out), outspread, outstretch, spread, unfold
con close, fold
2 ***syn*** OFFER 1, give, hold out, pose, present, proffer, tender
rel allocate, allot; accord, advance, award, bestow, confer, grant; donate
idiom place at one's disposal
3 to make or become longer <*extended* his visit by a week>
syn draw, draw out, elongate, lengthen, prolong, prolongate, protract, spin (out), stretch
rel amplify, enlarge, expand, increase
con abridge; curtail
ant shorten
4 ***syn*** INCREASE 1, aggrandize, augment, beef (up), boost, enlarge, expand, heighten, magnify, multiply
5 ***syn*** RUN 8, go, make, reach, stretch
rel advance, proceed; continue
6 ***syn*** RANGE 3, go, run, vary
7 to reach a certain point <his education doesn't *extend* beyond elementary school>
syn go
rel reach, run; advance; attain

extended *adj* **1** ***syn*** LONG 1, elongate, elongated, lengthy
rel prolonged, protracted, spread out, stretched out (*or* forth)
ant contracted
2 ***syn*** EXTENSIVE 1, broad, expansive, scopic, scopious, wide
rel far-flung, widespread
con narrow; inextensive
ant unextended

extension *n* **1** the act or state of extending or being extended <a one-month *extension* of the price freeze seems likely>
syn elongation, lengthening, production, prolongation, prolongment, protraction
rel continuation, continuing; drawing out, stretch, stretch-out
con abridgment, shortening; contraction, curtailment, shrinking
2 ***syn*** EXPANSION 2, enlargement, spread
rel augmentation, increase; spreading out
con abridgment, curtailment; reduction
ant contraction
3 ***syn*** RANGE 2, ambit, compass, extent, orbit, purview, radius, reach, scope, sweep
rel magnitude, size, spread; comprehensiveness
4 ***syn*** ANNEX, arm, block, ell, wing

extensity *n* ***syn*** RANGE 2, ambit, compass, extent, orbit, purview, radius, reach, scope, sweep

extensive *adj* **1** widely ranging in scope or application <*extensive* privileges>
syn broad, expansive, extended, scopic, scopious, wide
rel comprehensive, general, inclusive; far-reaching, far-spreading, spacious, wide-ranging; all-encompassing, all-inclusive, blanket, boundless, indiscriminate, unrestricted, wholesale
con circumscribed, constricted, limited, narrow, restricted; unextended
2 ***syn*** BIG 1, considerable, hefty, large, large-scale, major, sizable
con little, small

extent *n* **1** ***syn*** RANGE 2, ambit, compass, extension, orbit, purview, radius, reach, scope, sweep
rel domain, field, province, sphere
2 ***syn*** SIZE 1, admeasurement, dimension(s), dimensionality, magnitude, measure, proportion
rel compass, extension, orbit, radius, reach, scope, sweep
3 ***syn*** ORDER 4, magnitude, matter, neighborhood, range, tune, vicinity

extenuate *vb* **1** ***syn*** THIN 1, attenuate, wiredraw
rel mitigate; moderate, qualify, temper
con aggravate, enhance, heighten
2 ***syn*** PALLIATE, blanch (over), gloss (over), gloze (over), sugarcoat, varnish, veneer, white, whiten, whitewash
rel explain, justify, rationalize; apologize
idiom put a gloss on (*or* upon *or* over), put a good face upon

exterior *adj* ***syn*** OUTER, external, outside, outward, over

---

syn synonym(s) — *rel* related word(s)
idiom idiomatic equivalent(s) — *con* contrasted word(s)
ant antonym(s) — * vulgar
‖ use limited; if in doubt, see a dictionary
The first word in a synonym list when printed in SMALL CAPITALS shows where there is more information about the group. For a more efficient use of this book see Explanatory Notes.

rel outermost, outmost
con inner, ingrained, inherent, intrinsic
ant interior

exteriorize *vb* ***syn*** EMBODY 1, externalize, incarnate, manifest, materialize, objectify, personalize, personify, personize, substantiate
ant interiorize

exterminate *vb* **1** ***syn*** ANNIHILATE 2, abate, abolish, blot out, eradicate, extinguish, extirpate, root out, uproot, wipe (out)
rel finish off; execute; kill (off)
idiom do away with, put an end to, put out of the way
2 ***syn*** SLAUGHTER 3, annihilate, decimate, massacre, wipe (out)
idiom wipe off the face of the earth, wipe off the map

external *adj* ***syn*** OUTER, exterior, outside, outward, over
rel out, outermost, outmost, peripheral
con ingrained, inherent, intrinsic
ant internal

externalize *vb* ***syn*** EMBODY 1, exteriorize, incarnate, manifest, materialize, objectify, personalize, personify, personize, substantiate
ant internalize

extinct *adj* **1** ***syn*** DEAD 1, asleep, cold, deceased, defunct, departed, exanimate, late, lifeless, unanimated
2 that has died out altogether <an *extinct* civilization>
syn bygone, dead, defunct, departed, gone, lost, vanished
rel nonexistent; collapsed, fallen, overthrown; disappeared
idiom gone from the face of the earth
con existent, existing, living; active; contemporary, current
ant extant
3 ***syn*** OBSOLETE, dead, disused, outmoded, outworn, passé, superseded
rel antiquated, archaic, old-fashioned
con modern; contemporary
ant current

extinguish *vb* **1** to cause to cease burning <firemen *extinguishing* the blaze>
syn douse, ||dout, out, put out, quench, ||squench
rel blow out, snuff out; smother
con fire, kindle, start; torch
ant ignite
2 ***syn*** ANNIHILATE 2, abate, abolish, blot out, eradicate, exterminate, extirpate, root out, uproot, wipe (out)
rel erase, expunge, obliterate
3 ***syn*** CRUSH 5, annihilate, put down, quash, quell, quench, squash, suppress
rel check; smother, stifle; snuff (out); choke (out), trample (down)
idiom put the lid (*or* the kibosh) on
con encourage, fire (up)
ant inflame

extinguishment *n* ***syn*** REPRESSION 1, choking, quashing, quenching, smothering, squashing, squelching, stifling, strangling, suppression

extirpate *vb* **1** ***syn*** ANNIHILATE 2, abate, abolish, blot out, eradicate, exterminate, extinguish, root out, uproot, wipe (out)
rel efface, erase, expunge, demolish, destroy, raze; kill off
con breed, engender, generate, propagate
2 ***syn*** EXCISE, cut out, exsect, resect

extol *vb* ***syn*** PRAISE 2, bless, celebrate, cry up, eulogize, glorify, hymn, laud, magnify, panegyrize
idiom beat the drum for, make much of
ant decry

extort *vb* **1** to obtain something by pressure or intimidation <racketeers *extorting* protection money>
syn exact, gouge, pinch, screw, shake down, squeeze, wrench, wrest, wring; *compare* CHEAT, FLEECE 1
rel demand; coerce, force; extract, get, obtain, secure; bleed, fleece, skin
idiom bleed one white, make one pay through the nose, put the screws to
2 ***syn*** EDUCE 1, elicit, evince, evoke, extract, milk

extra *adj* ***syn*** SUPERFLUOUS, de trop, excess, recrementitious, spare, superfluent, supernumerary, surplus
rel added, additional, supplemental, supplementary

extra *adv* to a degree or extent beyond the usual <she was *extra* smart>
syn extremely, rarely, ||uncommon, uncommonly, unusually
rel especially; particularly; considerably, markedly, noticeably
con barely, scarcely

extract *vb* **1** to draw out forcibly or with effort <*extract* a confession> <*extract* a tooth>
syn evulse, pull, tear, yank
rel pry; avulse
2 ***syn*** EKE OUT 3, scratch, squeeze, wring
3 ***syn*** GLEAN, cull, garner, gather, pick up
4 ***syn*** EDUCE 1, elicit, evince, evoke, extort, milk
5 ***syn*** EXCERPT
rel abridge, condense, shorten

extraction *n* ***syn*** ANCESTRY, blood, descent, lineage, origin, pedigree

extraneous *adj* **1** ***syn*** EXTRINSIC, alien, foreign
rel accidental, adventitious, incidental
con constitutional, ingrained, inherent; germane, material, pertinent
2 ***syn*** IRRELEVANT, foreign, immaterial, impertinent, inapplicable, inapposite, irrelative
rel incidental; unessential; unrelated; pointless; inappropriate
idiom beside the point
ant relevant

extraordinary *adj* ***syn*** EXCEPTIONAL 1, rare, singular, uncommon, unimaginable, unique, unordinary, unthinkable, unusual, unwonted

---

syn synonym(s) | ***rel*** related word(s)
idiom idiomatic equivalent(s) | ***con*** contrasted word(s)
ant antonym(s) | * vulgar
|| use limited; if in doubt, see a dictionary
The first word in a synonym list when printed in SMALL CAPITALS shows where there is more information about the group. For a more efficient use of this book see Explanatory Notes.

rel amazing; stupendous, terrific, wonderful
idiom out of the ordinary
con customary, normal, regular, usual
ant ordinary

extravagance *n* **1** *syn* LUXURY, amenity, frill, luxus, superfluity
2 the quality, state, fact, or an instance of being extravagant <by living simply and avoiding *extravagance* they saved enough for the trip>
syn extravagancy, lavishness, overdoing, prodigality, squander, unthrift, waste, wastefulness
rel improvidence, spendthriftness; excess, indulgence, overindulgence
con moderation, temperateness; care, forehandedness, frugality; austerity
ant economy

extravagancy *n* *syn* EXTRAVAGANCE 2, lavishness, overdoing, prodigality, squander, unthrift, waste, wastefulness

extravagant *adj* **1** grossly exaggerated <*extravagant* accusations>
syn fantastic, preposterous, wild
rel unbalanced, unrestrained; absurd, foolish, ludicrous, nonsensical, ridiculous, silly; bizarre, crazy; exaggerated, implausible
con plausible, sensible; restrained
ant reasonable
2 *syn* EXCESSIVE 1, dizzy, exorbitant, extreme, immoderate, inordinate, towering, unconscionable, undue, unmeasurable
rel exuberant, lavish, profuse; prodigal, profligate, wasteful
con economical, frugal, sparing
ant restrained

extreme *adj* **1** very great <the project demanded *extreme* secrecy>
syn utmost, uttermost
2 *syn* ARDENT 2, intense
rel deep, moving
3 departing sharply from the traditional or usual <*extreme* political views>
syn extremist, fanatic, rabid, radical, revolutional, revolutionary, revolutionist, ultra, ultraist; *compare* OUTLANDISH 3
rel excessive, immoderate; desperate, drastic; extravagant, unreasonable; violent, wild
con conservative, moderate, restrained; reasonable, sensible
4 *syn* EXCESSIVE 1, dizzy, exorbitant, extravagant, immoderate, inordinate, towering, unconscionable, undue, unmeasurable
rel intolerable, unwarranted
5 most distant from a center <the *extreme* edge of the city>
syn farthest, furthermost, furthest, outermost, outmost, remotest, utmost, uttermost

extreme *n* **1** an extreme state or condition <an *extreme* of poverty>
syn extremity
rel excess, inordinancy
2 something situated at or marking one end or the other of a range <*extremes* of heat and cold>
syn extremity, limit
rel climax, consummation, culmination; ceiling, crest, crown, height; peak, pinnacle, summit, top; maximum, utmost, uttermost

extremely *adv* **1** *syn* EVER 6, excessively, immensely, inordinately, over, overfull, overly, overmuch, too, unduly
2 *syn* VERY 1, exceedingly, exceptionally, hugely, notably, parlous, remarkably, strikingly, surpassingly, vitally
3 *syn* EXTRA, rarely, ‖uncommon, uncommonly, unusually

extremist *n* *syn* RADICAL, revolutionary, revolutionist, ultraist

extremist *adj* *syn* EXTREME 3, fanatic, rabid, radical, revolutional, revolutionary, revolutionist, ultra, ultraist

extremity *n* **1** *syn* EXTREME 2, limit
rel acme, apex, apogee, vertex, zenith
2 *syn* EXTREME 1

extricate *vb* **1** *syn* KNOW 4, difference, differentiate, discern, discrepate, discriminate, distinguish, separate, sever, severalize
2 to free from an undesirable situation or condition <*extricate* himself from financial difficulties>
syn clear, clear away, discumber, disembarrass, disembroil, disencumber, disentangle, disentwine, unentangle, unscramble, untangle, untie, untwine
rel unravel; abstract, detach, disengage; disburden, disemburden; deliver, disinvolve, free, liberate, release, rescue; resolve
con embroil, entangle, tangle; clog, fetter, hog-tie, manacle, shackle, trammel; block, hamper, hinder, impede, obstruct

extrinsic *adj* not properly part of a thing <a point *extrinsic* to his basic thesis>
syn alien, extraneous, foreign
rel acquired, gained; exterior, external, outer, outside, outward
con native; inner, inside, interior, internal, inward; individual, personal
ant intrinsic

extrude *vb* *syn* EJECT 1, boot (out), chase, chuck, dismiss, evict, kick out, out, throw out

exuberance *n* *syn* EBULLIENCE, buoyancy, effervescence, exuberancy
rel gayness; friskiness, life, liveliness, sprightliness, zest, zestfulness; abandon, ardor

exuberancy *n* *syn* EBULLIENCE, buoyancy, effervescence, exuberance

exuberant *adj* **1** joyously unrestrained and enthusiastic <his warm *exuberant* personality>
syn brash, ebullient, effervescent, high-spirited, vivacious
rel gay, lively, spirited, sprightly, zestful; frolicsome; ardent, passionate

---

syn synonym(s) — *rel* related word(s)
idiom idiomatic equivalent(s) — *con* contrasted word(s)
ant antonym(s) — * vulgar
‖ use limited; if in doubt, see a dictionary
The first word in a synonym list when printed in SMALL CAPITALS shows where there is more information about the group. For a more efficient use of this book see Explanatory Notes.

con constrained, inhibited, repressed, restrained, subdued; calm, impassive, quiet
ant austere
2 ***syn*** PROFUSE, lavish, lush, luxuriant, opulent, prodigal, profusive, riotous
rel fecund, fertile, fruitful, prolific; rampant, rank; diffuse
con scant, scanty, spare

exude *vb* to flow slowly out <a sticky resin *exuded* from the bark>
syn bleed, ooze, percolate, ‖screeve, seep, ‖sew, ‖sicker, strain, sweat, transude, weep
rel emanate; discharge, emit; trickle

exult *vb* to rejoice especially with feelings or display of triumph or self-satisfaction <the team were *exulting* in their victory>
syn delight, glory, jubilate, triumph
rel rejoice; celebrate; boast, brag, crow, show off
con lament, mourn
ant bemoan

exultance *n* ***syn*** EXULTATION, jubilance, jubilation, triumph

exultant *adj* manifesting proud elation <*exultant* over his successes>
syn cock-a-hoop, cock-a-whoop, exulting, jubilant, triumphal, triumphant
rel happy, joyous, overjoyed; delighting, rejoicing; elated, flushed
idiom in high feather
con depressed, mournful, unhappy

exultation *n* the act of exulting or the state of being exultant <the *exultation* of victory and the thrill of power>
syn exultance, jubilance, jubilation, triumph
rel delight, elation, satisfaction; celebration, rejoicing; gloating

exulting *adj* ***syn*** EXULTANT, cock-a-hoop, cock-a-whoop, jubilant, triumphal, triumphant

exuviate *vb* ***syn*** SHED 2, molt, slip, slough

eye *n* **1** an organ of sight <turned his *eyes* to the view>
syn lamp, ocular, oculus, ‖ogle, orb, peeper, winker
2 the faculty of seeing with or as if with the eyes <had a keen *eye* for details>
syn eyesight, seeing, sight, vision
3 very close watching or observation <kept an *eye* on him>
syn eagle eye, scrutiny, surveillance, tab, watch
4 *often* **eyes** *pl* a way of looking at something <in the *eyes* of the law, a man is innocent until proven guilty>
syn view, viewpoint; *compare* VIEWPOINT 2
rel attitude, position, thinking; conception, grasp; conclusion, judgment
5 ***syn*** OPINION, belief, conviction, feeling, mind, persuasion, sentiment, view
6 ***syn*** LOOP 1, ring
7 ***syn*** LOOP 2, ring, staple
‖**8** ***syn*** DETECTIVE, dick, gumshoe, hawkshaw, investigator, plainclothesman, Sherlock, Sherlock Holmes, sleuth, ‖tec

eye *vb* **1** to fix the eyes on <the child *eyed* the presents with delight>
syn consider, contemplate, gaze (upon), look (at *or* upon), view; *compare* LOOK 7
rel regard; stare (at)
2 to keep a close watch on <the detective *eyed* the suspect>
syn eyeball, scrutinize, watch; *compare* TAIL
rel stare (at); size up
idiom keep a close (*or* an eagle) eye on
3 ***syn*** LOOK 7, gape, ‖gaup (*or* gawp), gaze, goggle, ogle, rubberneck, stare

eyeball *vb* ***syn*** EYE 2, scrutinize, watch

eye–catching *adj* ***syn*** NOTICEABLE, arresting, conspicuous, marked, outstanding, pointed, prominent, remarkable, salient, signal

eyeful *n* ***syn*** BEAUTY, ‖beaut, knockout, looker, lovely, stunner

eyeless *adj* ***syn*** BLIND 1, ‖dark, sightless, stone-blind, visionless

eye–popping *adj* ***syn*** EXCITING, exhilarant, exhilarating, exhilarative, inspiring, intoxicating, rousing, stimulating, stirring

eyesight *n* ***syn*** EYE 2, seeing, sight, vision

eyesore *n* something offensive to the sight <the old abandoned house was a neighborhood *eyesore*>
syn desight, fright, mess, monstrosity, sight

eyewash *n* ***syn*** NONSENSE 2, ‖baloney, bilge, bunkum, hogwash, hooey, ‖horsefeathers, malarkey, rot, twaddle

eyewitness *n* ***syn*** SPECTATOR, beholder, by-sitter, bystander, looker-on, observer, onlooker, viewer, watcher, witness

---

F

fable *n* **1** ***syn*** FICTION, fabrication, figment
2 ***syn*** ALLEGORY 2, apologue, myth, parable

fabric *n* **1** ***syn*** BUILDING, structure
2 ***syn*** TEXTURE 2, fiber, web

fabricate *vb* ***syn*** MAKE 3, assemble, build, construct, fashion, form, frame, manufacture, produce, shape
rel turn out; create, formulate, invent; concoct, contrive, devise

fabrication *n* ***syn*** FICTION, fable, figment
rel creation; deceit, fib; artifact, opus, product, production, work

fabulous *adj* ***syn*** MYTHICAL, legendary, mythological
rel amazing, astonishing, astounding, incredible, marvelous, unbelievable, wonderful; exorbitant, extravagant, inordinate, outrageous, preposterous; monstrous, prodigious, stupendous
con believable, colorable, credible

facade *n* ***syn*** MASK 2, color, disguise, face, front, guise, pretense, put-on, show, veneer

face *n* **1** the front part of the head including the eyes, nose, mouth, cheeks, chin, and usually forehead <hid his *face* from the camera>
syn countenance, ||dial, features, ||kisser, ||map, mug, ||mush, muzzle, ||pan, phiz, ||puss, visage
rel lineaments, physiognomy
2 ***syn*** LOOK 2, cast, countenance, expression, visage
3 ***syn*** APPEARANCE 2, guise, seeming, semblance, show, showing, simulacrum
4 ***syn*** MASK 2, cloak, cover, disguise, facade, false front, front, masquerade, show, veil
5 ***syn*** EFFRONTERY, brashness, brass, cheek, confidence, ||crust, gall, nerve, presumption
6 a distortion of the face usually as an expression of contempt or distaste <the old man made a *face* at the flat beer>
syn grimace, moue, mouth, mouthing, mow, mug
rel frown, glower, lower, pout, scowl
idiom wry face, wry mouth
con grin, simper, smile, smirk
7 ***syn*** MAKEUP 3, maquillage, paint, war paint
8 ***syn*** TOP 2, superficies, surface

face *vb* **1** to have the face or front in a specified direction <the house *faces* toward the river>
syn front, look
rel border, meet
ant back
2 ***syn*** MEET 6, close, encounter, front
rel watch; gaze, glare, stare; await, expect, look (for)
3 to confront with courage or boldness <ready to *face* his accusers>
syn ||banter, beard, brave, challenge, dare, defy, ||double-dog dare, front, outdare, outface, venture
rel confront, encounter, meet; oppose, resist, withstand; contend, fight
idiom brazen it out, face the music, face up to, take the bull by the horns
con elude, escape, eschew, evade, shun
ant avoid
4 ***syn*** CONFRONT 1, affront, encounter, meet
5 ***syn*** ACCOST 2, confront, front
rel beard, brave, challenge, dare, defy
idiom stand up to
6 ***syn*** ENGAGE 5, encounter, meet, take on
7 ***syn*** SHEATHE, clad, side, skin

facet *n* ***syn*** PHASE, angle, aspect, hand, side
rel face, front

facetious *adj* ***syn*** WITTY, humorous, jocose, jocular
rel jesting, joking, quipping, wisecracking; blithe, jocund, jolly, jovial, merry; comic, comical, droll, funny, laughable, ludicrous
con grave, serious, sober, solemn, somber
ant lugubrious

facile *adj* ***syn*** EASY 1, effortless, light, royal, simple, smooth, untroublesome
rel adroit, deft, dexterous; fluent, glib, voluble; cursory, shallow, superficial, uncritical
con awkward, clumsy, constrained, cumbersome, labored, maladroit; tongue-tied; deep, profound, thorough
ant arduous

facilely *adv* ***syn*** EASILY 1, effortlessly, freely, lightly, readily, smoothly, well
ant arduously

facilitate *vb* ***syn*** EASE 3

facility *n* **1** ***syn*** READINESS 3, ease
rel skill, wit; aptitude, bent, leaning, propensity, turn; abandon, spontaneity, unconstraint; address, poise, tact; effortlessness, lightness, smoothness
con awkwardness, clumsiness, ineptness, maladroitness; rigidity, stiffness, woodenness; effort, exertion, pains
2 ***syn*** AMENITY 2, comfort, convenience
rel accommodation, advantage, aid, fitting
con difficulty, hardship, inconvenience

facing *prep* **1** ***syn*** AGAINST 1, contra, fronting, over against, toward, vis-à-vis
con side by side
2 ***syn*** BEFORE 2, confronting

facsimile *n* ***syn*** REPRODUCTION, carbon, carbon copy, copy, ditto, duplicate, reduplication, replica, replication

syn synonym(s) ***rel*** related word(s)
idiom idiomatic equivalent(s) ***con*** contrasted word(s)
ant antonym(s) * vulgar
|| use limited; if in doubt, see a dictionary
The first word in a synonym list when printed in SMALL CAPITALS shows where there is more information about the group. For a more efficient use of this book see Explanatory Notes.

con archetype, model, original, pattern, prototype, standard

fact *n* **1** the quality of being actual <the realm of *fact* is distinct from fancy>

syn actuality, reality

rel authenticity, genuineness, truth

con fancy, fantasy, fiction

2 something that has actual existence <stubborn *facts* that cannot be confuted>

syn event, phenomenon

rel circumstance, detail, episode, particular; happening, incident, occurrence; observable

con contingency, eventuality, hope, possibility, potentiality, probability

ant illusion

faction *n syn* COMBINATION 2, bloc, coalition, combine, part, ring

rel camp, offshoot, wing

idiom splinter group

factious *adj syn* INSUBORDINATE, contumacious, insurgent, mutinous, rebellious, seditious

rel contending, fighting, warring; belligerent, contentious, quarrelsome; alienated, disaffected, estranged

con companionable, gregarious, social; acquiescent, compliant; faithful, loyal, true

ant cooperative

factitious *adj syn* SYNTHETIC, artificial, man-made

rel affected, assumed, counterfeited, false, feigned, forced, pretended, sham, shammed, simulated

con authentic, bona fide, genuine, veritable; artless, naive, simple, spontaneous

ant natural

factor *n* **1** *syn* ELEMENT 2, component, constituent, ingredient

rel antecedent, cause, determinant; agency, agent, instrument, instrumentality, means

2 *syn* AGENT 2, assignee, attorney, deputy, proxy

rel bailiff, majordomo, seneschal, steward; adjutant, aid, assistant, coadjutor, helper

factory *n* an establishment for the manufacturing of goods <a shoe *factory*>

syn manufactory, mill, plant, works

factual *adj syn* ACTUAL 2, absolute, genuine, hard, positive, sure-enough

rel certain, undoubted, veritable; authentic, legitimate, unquestionable, valid

con erroneous, false, questionable, wrong

ant illusory

facultative *adj syn* OPTIONAL, discretionary, elective, nonobligatory

faculty *n* **1** *syn* GIFT 2, aptness, bent, bump, flair, genius, knack, nose, talent, turn

rel instinct; property, quality; leaning, penchant, proclivity, propensity; predilection

con inability, incapability, incapacity, ineptness

2 *syn* POWER 3, function

facund *adj syn* EXPRESSIVE, eloquent, meaningful, pregnant, rich, sententious, significant

facundity *n syn* ELOQUENCE, expression, expressiveness, expressivity

fad *n syn* FASHION 3, chic, craze, cry, dernier cri, furore, mode, rage, style, vogue

rel caprice, conceit, fancy, vagary, whim, whimsy

con custom, habit, practice, usage

fade *vb* **1** *syn* FAIL 1, decline, deteriorate, ‖dwine, flag, languish, weaken

2 *syn* DULL 1, dim, muddy, pale, tarnish

3 *syn* VANISH, clear, disappear, evanesce, evanish, evaporate

rel deliquesce, dissolve, melt; abate, diminish, dwindle, ebb, lessen, moderate, wane; attenuate, rarefy, thin

idiom fade like a shadow

con intensify; eternalize, immortalize, perpetuate

faded *adj syn* SHABBY 1, bedraggled, dingy, run-down, seedy, tacky, tagrag, tattered, threadbare, tired

rel haggard, washed-out, wasted, worn; dim, murky; achromatic, colorless; ashen, pale, pallid, wan

con energetic, lusty, vigorous; colorful; vivid

fag *n syn* CIGARETTE, ‖butt, ‖cig, ‖coffin nail, ‖gasper, ‖pill, ‖skag, smoke

fag *vb syn* EXHAUST 4, ‖bugger, frazzle, knock out, outtire, outwear, ‖poop, prostrate, tucker, wear out

con refresh, relax, rest, restore

fag *n syn* HOMOSEXUAL, faggot, ‖fruit, homo, invert, queer, uranian, uranist

faggot *n syn* HOMOSEXUAL, fag, ‖fruit, homo, invert, queer, uranian, uranist

fail *vb* **1** to lose strength, power, vitality, or intensity <his health *failed* and he retired early>

syn decline, deteriorate, ‖dwine, fade, flag, languish, weaken

rel jade, sink, slip, waste (away), worsen

idiom go downhill, hit the skids

con better, improve, strengthen

2 to become used up <food *failed* before they got back to civilization>

syn give out, run out

rel dwindle, shrink, wane

3 to be or become inadequate or deficient <the spring gradually *failed* as the drought persisted>

syn dwindle, shrink, wane, waste (away), weaken

rel decrease, diminish, lessen; give out, run out; short

idiom be found wanting

con appreciate, gain, grow, increase, wax

4 to be less than adequate or successful <the attack *failed*>

syn ‖flop, flummox, wash out

rel bankrupt, bomb, deplete, drain, exhaust, impoverish; bust out, flunk, ‖spin

idiom come to grief, fall flat (*or* short), go on the rocks, ‖lay an egg, ‖take the count

ant succeed

5 to be unable to meet financial engagements <the bank *failed*>

syn break, bust, crash, fold

rel gazette; close, end, finish, terminate

---

syn synonym(s) — *rel* related word(s)
idiom idiomatic equivalent(s) — *con* contrasted word(s)
ant antonym(s) — * vulgar
‖ use limited; if in doubt, see a dictionary
The first word in a synonym list when printed in SMALL CAPITALS shows where there is more information about the group. For a more efficient use of this book see Explanatory Notes.

idiom be ruined, go bankrupt, go broke, go on the rocks, go to the wall, go under
con boom, prosper
6 *syn* NEGLECT, blink (at *or* away), discount, disregard, forget, ignore, omit, overlook, overpass, slight
idiom be found wanting, come (*or* fall) short of

failing *n syn* FAULT 2, foible, frailty, vice
rel imperfection, shortcoming
idiom weak point

failing *adj syn* SHORT 3, deficient, inadequate, insufficient, scant, scanty, scarce, shy, unsufficient, wanting

failure *n* **1** omission of performance of an action or task <the mechanic's *failure* to adjust the brakes>
syn default, delinquency, dereliction, neglect, oversight
rel laxity, negligence, remissness, slackness; indifference, unconcern
con accomplishment, achievement, discharge, effectuation, fulfillment
2 lack of satisfactory performance or effect <the *failure* of the candidate in the election>
syn defeat, insuccess, nonsuccess, unsuccess, unsuccessfulness
rel failing, fault, imperfection, shortcoming
idiom no go
ant success
3 the fact or state of being inadequate <the crop *failure* brought on a near famine>
syn defalcation, deficiency, deficit, inadequacy, insufficience, insufficiency, lack, scantiness, shortage, underage; *compare* ABSENCE, SCARCITY
rel inferiority, meagerness, poorness, skimpiness; dearth, paucity
con abundance, adequacy, sufficiency
4 a marked weakening <felt a warning *failure* of physical strength>
syn declination, decline, deterioration, ebbing, waning
rel debilitation, enfeeblement, exhaustion, flagging, weakness
con improvement; invigoration, revitalization, strengthening
5 one that has failed <he is a *failure* in school because of inattention>
syn bomb, bust, dud, flop, lemon, loser
rel botch, fiasco, fizzle, hash, muddle, washout; might-have-been
ant success

fain *adj syn* WILLING 1, disposed, inclined, minded, predisposed, prone, ready

faineant *n syn* SLUGGARD, bum, dolittle, do-nothing, idler, lazybones, loafer, slouch, slug, slugabed

faineant *adj syn* LAZY, drony, easygoing, indolent, slothful, slowgoing, work-shy
rel apathetic, impassive, phlegmatic
con active, energetic, vigorous; busy, industrious

---

syn synonym(s) *rel* related word(s)
idiom idiomatic equivalent(s) *con* contrasted word(s)
ant antonym(s) * vulgar
‖ use limited; if in doubt, see a dictionary
The first word in a synonym list when printed in SMALL CAPITALS shows where there is more information about the group. For a more efficient use of this book see Explanatory Notes.

faint *adj* **1** *syn* GENTLE 1, balmy, bland, lenient, mild, smooth, soft
2 scarcely or imperfectly perceptible <he had only a *faint* idea of how he could help>
syn blear, bleary, dim, fuzzy, ill-defined, indistinct, obscure, shadowy, unclear, undefined, undetermined, undistinct, vague; *compare* OBSCURE 3
rel blurred, dusty, pale, wan, weak; hushed, inaudible, low, muffled, small, soft, stifled, thin
con bright, distinct, evident, obvious, patent, unmistakable; certain, sure
ant clear

faint *n* the act or condition of losing consciousness <was so frightened she fell into a *faint*>
syn blackout, coma, swoon, syncope
rel grayout, swim; dizziness, vertigo
idiom a dead faint

faint *vb* to lose consciousness <*fainted* at the sight of blood>
syn black out, ‖crap out, pass out, ‖swarf, ‖swelt, swoon
rel gray out
idiom faint dead away, fall in a faint, go out like a light, pass out cold

faintly *adv syn* SOTTO VOCE, mutedly, weakly

fair *adj* **1** *syn* BEAUTIFUL, attractive, beauteous, ‖bonny, comely, good-looking, handsome, lovely, pretty, pulchritudinous
rel dainty, delicate, exquisite; charming, enchanting; chaste, pure
con ill-favored, ugly
ant foul
2 not stormy <a *fair* day>
syn clarion, clear, cloudless, fine, pleasant, rainless, sunny, sunshine, sunshining, sunshiny, unclouded, undarkened
rel calm, placid, tranquil, unthreatening; balmy, clement, mild, pretty
con overcast, stormy, threatening
3 of light complexion <*fair* people often sunburn badly>
syn blond, light
rel ruddy, tawny
con brunet, dark, swarthy
4 characterized by honesty, justice, and freedom from improper influence <a *fair* decision by the judge>
syn candid, dispassionate, equal, equitable, impartial, impersonal, indifferent, just, nondiscriminatory, nonpartisan, objective, square, unbiased, uncolored, undistinctive, unprejudiced, unprepossessed
rel detached, disinterested; balanced, rational, reasonable, sane; open-minded, straight
con biased, inequitable, partial, partisan, prejudiced, prepossessed, unjust
ant unfair
5 observing the rules <a *fair* fight>
syn clean, sportsmanlike, sportsmanly
rel decent, honest, lawful
con dirty, dishonest, fixed
ant unfair
6 *syn* EVEN 3, equal, equitable
7 *syn* MEDIUM, average, fairish, indifferent, intermediate, mean, mediocre, middling, moderate, so-so

rel common, ordinary
con choice, good, prime, right; bad, poor, wrong

fair *n* ***syn*** EXHIBITION 2, exhibit, exposition, show
rel carnival, festival

fair–haired *adj* ***syn*** FAVORITE 1, beloved, blue-eyed, darling, dear, loved, pet, precious, white-haired, white-headed

fairish *adj* ***syn*** MEDIUM, average, fair, indifferent, intermediate, mean, mediocre, middling, moderate, so-so

fairly *adv* **1** ***syn*** ENOUGH 2, averagely, moderately, passably, rather, so-so, tolerably
2 ***syn*** SOMEWHAT 2, kind of, moderately, more or less, pretty, rather, ratherish, some, something, sort of

fairy *n* a benevolent mythical being <children who believe in *fairies*>
syn brownie, elf, fay, nisse, pixie, sprite
rel gremlin, imp, leprechaun, puck; dwarf, gnome, goblin, kobold
con ogre, troll

fairyland *n* ***syn*** UTOPIA, arcadia, Cockaigne, heaven, lubberland, paradise, promised land, Shangri-la, wonderland, Zion

faith *n* **1** ***syn*** BELIEF 1, credence, credit
con dubiety, dubiosity, skepticism, uncertainty
2 ***syn*** TRUST 1, confidence, dependence, hope, reliance, stock
con disbelief, incredulity, unbelief; apprehension, misgiving
3 ***syn*** RELIGION 1, creed, cult, persuasion
4 ***syn*** RELIGION 2, church, communion, connection, creed, cult, denomination, persuasion, sect
rel doctrines, dogmas, tenets

faithful *adj* **1** firm in adherence to whatever one is bound to by duty or promise <a *faithful* public official, conscientious and above reproach>
syn allegiant, ardent, constant, ‖dinky-di, fast, liege, loyal, resolute, staunch, steadfast, steady, true
rel dependable, reliable, tried, trustworthy; affectionate, devoted, loving; dyed-in-the-wool
con disloyal, false, perfidious, traitorous, treacherous; fickle, inconstant, unstable
ant faithless
2 ***syn*** TRUE 3, just, right, strict, undistorted, veracious, veridical
idiom at one with, on all fours with
3 ***syn*** AUTHENTIC 1, convincing, credible, trustworthy, trusty

faithfulness *n* **1** ***syn*** ATTACHMENT 1, adherence, adhesion, constancy, fidelity, loyalty
2 ***syn*** FIDELITY 1, allegiance, ardor, devotion, fealty, loyalty, piety

faithless *adj* not true to allegiance or duty <a *faithless* husband>
syn disloyal, false, perfidious, recreant, traitorous, treacherous, unfaithful, unloyal, untrue
rel capricious, fickle, inconstant, unstable; fluctuating, wavering; changeable, changeful
con constant, loyal, resolute, staunch, steadfast, true
ant faithful

faithlessness *n* **1** ***syn*** TREACHERY, disloyalty, perfidiousness, perfidy, treacherousness, treason
2 ***syn*** INFIDELITY, disloyalty, falseness, falsity, perfidiousness, perfidy, unfaithfulness

fake *vb* ***syn*** ASSUME 4, act, affect, bluff, counterfeit, feign, pretend, put on, sham, simulate

fake *n* **1** ***syn*** IMPOSTURE, counterfeit, fraud, gyp, hoax, humbug, phony, sell, sham, spoof
2 ***syn*** IMPOSTOR, faker, fraud, humbug, phony, pretender

fake *adj* **1** ***syn*** COUNTERFEIT, bogus, brummagem, false, phony, pinchbeck, pseudo, sham, snide, spurious
rel fabricated, forged; concocted, framed, invented
con bona fide, genuine
2 ***syn*** FICTITIOUS 2, mock, sham, simulated

faker *n* ***syn*** IMPOSTOR, fake, fraud, humbug, phony, pretender
rel cheat, cheater, cozener, defrauder, swindler

fall *vb* **1** to pass downward <fruit *falling* off a tree> <the temperature *fell* sharply>
syn descend, drop, lower
rel decline, dip, plummet, sink; decrease, diminish, lessen; dangle, drag, droop, trail
ant rise
2 to come down suddenly and involuntarily <*fell* on the ice>
syn drop, go down, keel (over), pitch, plunge, slump, topple, tumble
rel slip, sprawl, stumble, trip
idiom come a cropper, take a header, take a spill
con ascend, climb
3 to suffer ruin, defeat, or failure <the city *fell* after a long siege>
syn go down, go under, submit, succumb, surrender
rel give up, yield
con endure, prevail, resist; conquer, triumph, vanquish, win
4 ***syn*** ABATE 4, die (down *or* away), ease off, ebb, let up, moderate, relent, slacken, subside, wane
ant rise
5 ***syn*** PLUMMET, dip, drop, nose-dive, plunge, skid, tumble

fall (off *or* away) *vb* ***syn*** SLIP 6, drop (off), sag, slide, slump

fall (on *or* upon) *vb* ***syn*** ATTACK 1, aggress, assail, assault, beset, storm, strike

fall *n* **1** ***syn*** DESCENT 1, drop
2 ***syn*** DESCENT 4, decline, declivity, dip, drop
3 *usu* **falls** *pl but sing or pl in constr* ***syn*** WATERFALL, cascade, cataract, chute, ‖force, sault, spout

fallacious *adj* **1** ***syn*** ILLOGICAL, invalid, irrational, mad, nonrational, reasonless, sophistic, unreasonable, unreasoned
ant valid, sound
2 ***syn*** MISLEADING, beguiling, deceiving, deceptive, deluding, delusive, delusory, false
ant veritable

---

syn synonym(s) — *rel* related word(s)
idiom idiomatic equivalent(s) — *con* contrasted word(s)
ant antonym(s) — * vulgar
‖ use limited; if in doubt, see a dictionary
The first word in a synonym list when printed in SMALL CAPITALS shows where there is more information about the group. For a more efficient use of this book see Explanatory Notes.

fallaciousness *n* ***syn*** FALLACY 1, erroneousness, error, falsehood, falseness, falsity, untruth
rel ambiguity, equivocation; deception, deluding, misleading; faultiness, illogicality, unreasonableness
ant soundness, validity

fallacy *n* **1** a false or erroneous idea <his argument is based on a *fallacy*>
syn erroneousness, error, fallaciousness, falsehood, falseness, falsity, untruth
rel misconception, misconstrual, misinterpretation, misunderstanding
con comprehension, grasp, understanding; correctitude, correctness, truth
ant verity
2 unsound and misleading reasoning <the *fallacy* of his theory is clearly evident>
syn casuistry, deception, deceptiveness, delusion, equivocation, sophism, sophistry, speciousness, spuriousness
rel elusion, evasion, inconsistency, quibble, quibbling

fall back *vb* **1** ***syn*** RETREAT 2, give back, retire, withdraw
2 ***syn*** RECEDE 1, back, retract, retreat, retrocede, retrograde

fall flat *vb* ***syn*** FAIL 4, bust out, fall short, ||flop, flummox, flunk, ||spin, wash out

fall guy *n* **1** ***syn*** SCAPEGOAT, goat, patsy, whipping boy
2 ***syn*** FOOL 3, butt, chump, dupe, fish, gudgeon, gull, pigeon, sap, sucker

fallible *adj* liable or inclined to error <a *fallible* rule>
syn errable, errant
rel careless, faulty, heedless
con careful, heedful; inerrable, inerrant, unerring; exact, perfect, precise
ant infallible

falling–out *n* ***syn*** QUARREL, altercation, beef, bickering, controversy, dispute, feud, hassle, row, run-in

falloff *n* ***syn*** DECLINE 3, dip, downslide, downswing, downtrend, downturn, drop, sag, slip, slump

fall out *vb* **1** ***syn*** HAPPEN 1, befall, betide, break, chance, come off, develop, go, occur, transpire
2 ***syn*** QUARREL, bicker, brabble, caterwaul, row, scrap, spat, squabble, tiff, wrangle

fall to *vb* ***syn*** PITCH IN 1, buckle (down), jump (in *or* into), set to, wade (in *or* into)

false *adj* **1** not in conformity with what is true <the information turned out to be *false*>
syn counterfactual, erroneous, inaccurate, incorrect, specious, unsound, untrue, wrong; *compare* ILLOGICAL
rel deceptive, delusive, delusory, distorted, fallacious, misleading; deceitful, dishonest, fraudulent, lying, mendacious, untruthful
idiom contrary to fact, off the mark
con accurate, correct, established, factual, truthful, veracious, veridical
ant true
2 ***syn*** MISLEADING, beguiling, deceiving, deceptive, deluding, delusive, delusory, fallacious
3 ***syn*** FAITHLESS, disloyal, perfidious, recreant, traitorous, treacherous, unfaithful, unloyal, untrue
rel apostate, backsliding, renegade; crooked, devious; hollow
ant true
4 ***syn*** COUNTERFEIT, bogus, brummagem, fake, phony, pinchbeck, pseudo, sham, snide, spurious
rel apparent, ostensible, seeming
con bona fide, genuine
ant real
5 ***syn*** ARTIFICIAL 2, dummy, ersatz, imitation, mock, sham, simulated, spurious, substitute

false face *n* ***syn*** MASK 1, domino, doughface, visor, vizard

false front *n* ***syn*** MASK 2, cloak, cover, disguise, facade, face, front, masquerade, show, veil

falsehood *n* **1** ***syn*** FALLACY 1, erroneousness, error, fallaciousness, falseness, falsity, untruth
2 ***syn*** LIE, canard, falsity, fib, misrepresentation, prevarication, story, tale, untruism, untruth
rel fakery, feigning, pretense, sham; deceit, dissimulation, fraud
ant truth
3 ***syn*** MENDACITY, fibbery, mendaciousness, truthlessness, untruthfulness, unveracity

falseness *n* **1** ***syn*** FALLACY 1, erroneousness, error, fallaciousness, falsehood, falsity, untruth
2 ***syn*** INFIDELITY, disloyalty, faithlessness, falsity, perfidiousness, perfidy, unfaithfulness
3 ***syn*** DEFECTION, apostasy, desertion, recreancy, tergiversation

falsifier *n* ***syn*** LIAR, Ananias, fibber, fibster, perjurer, prevaricator, storyteller

falsify *vb* **1** ***syn*** LIE, equivocate, fib, palter, prevaricate
2 ***syn*** MISREPRESENT, belie, color, distort, garble, miscolor, misstate, pervert, twist, warp
rel alter, change; cook, doctor; contort; contradict, contravene, deny, traverse

falsity *n* **1** ***syn*** LIE, canard, falsehood, fib, misrepresentation, prevarication, story, tale, untruism, untruth
2 ***syn*** FALLACY 1, erroneousness, error, fallaciousness, falsehood, falseness, untruth
rel bluff, fabrication, fake, sham; disingenuousness, hypocrisy, insincerity, uncandidness
ant verity
3 ***syn*** INFIDELITY, disloyalty, faithlessness, falseness, perfidiousness, perfidy, unfaithfulness

falter *vb* **1** ***syn*** TEETER, lurch, stagger, ||stammer, stumble, topple, totter, wobble
2 ***syn*** HESITATE, dither, halt, shilly-shally, stagger, vacillate, waver, whiffle, wiggle-waggle
rel blench, flinch, quail, recoil, shrink; quake, quaver, shake, shudder, tremble; tick over
con persevere, persist; decide, determine, resolve

faltering *adj* ***syn*** VACILLATING 2, halting, hesitant, irresolute, shilly-shallying, tentative, uncertain, vacillatory, wiggle-waggle, wobbly

fame *n* **1** ***syn*** REPUTATION 2, character, name, ||rep, report, repute

---

syn synonym(s) ***rel*** related word(s)
idiom idiomatic equivalent(s) ***con*** contrasted word(s)
ant antonym(s) * vulgar
|| use limited; if in doubt, see a dictionary
The first word in a synonym list when printed in SMALL CAPITALS shows where there is more information about the group. For a more efficient use of this book see Explanatory Notes.

2 the state of being widely known for one's deeds <his *fame* was short-lived>
syn celebrity, éclat, notoriety, renown, ‖rep, reputation, repute
rel acclaim, acclamation, applause; acknowledgment, recognition; conspicuousness, prominence; distinction, eminence, glory, greatness, honor, illustriousness, note, preeminence
con disgrace, dishonor, disrepute, ignominy, obloquy, odium, opprobrium, shame
ant obscurity; infamy

famed *adj* ***syn*** FAMOUS 2, celebrated, celebrious, distinguished, eminent, great, illustrious, notable, prominent, renowned
ant obscure; ill-famed

familiar *n* ***syn*** FRIEND, acquaintance, amigo, cater-cousin, confidant, intimate, mate

familiar *adj* **1** closely associated <time and interests have made them *familiar*>
syn chummy, close, confidential, intimate, thick
rel amicable, friendly, neighborly; affable, boon, cordial, genial, gracious, sociable; comfortable, cozy, easy, snug; forward, fresh, impertinent, intrusive, obtrusive, officious
con detached, disinterested, incurious, indifferent, remote, unconcerned; ceremonial, ceremonious, conventional, formal
ant aloof
2 ***syn*** COMMON 4, customary, everyday, frequent
rel accustomed, habitual, wonted; commonplace, prosaic
con new, newfangled, new-fashioned, novel; rare, strange, uncommon; chimerical, fantastic
ant unfamiliar
3 well-informed especially through study or experience <*familiar* with what is being taught in the schools>
syn abreast, acquainted, au courant, au fait, conversant, informed, up, versant, versed
rel aware, cognizant, conscious, mindful
con unacquainted, unconversant, uninformed, unversed; insensible, unaware, unconscious, unmindful; ignorant, unenlightened, unknowing
ant unfamiliar

familiarity *n* ***syn*** ACQUAINTANCE 1, experience, intimacy, inwardness
rel awareness, cognition, comprehension, knowledge, understanding
ant unfamiliarity

familiarize *vb* ***syn*** ACCUSTOM, habituate, inure, use, wont
rel acquaint, adapt, adjust, condition, naturalize, season

family *n* **1** a group of persons of or regarded as of common ancestry <traditionally all men belong to the *family* of Noah>
syn clan, folk, house, kindred, lineage, race, stock, tribe
rel brood, dynasty, line, stirp, strain; issue, offspring, progeny
idiom kith and kin, one's own flesh and blood
2 a group of usually related persons living in one house and under one head <was the only child in her *family*>
syn folks, house, household, ménage

family *adj* ***syn*** DOMESTIC 1, home, household

family tree *n* ***syn*** GENEALOGY, ‖begats, pedigree, stemma

famished *adj* ***syn*** HUNGRY, ‖peckish, ravenous, starved, starving

famous *adj* **1** ***syn*** WELL-KNOWN, leading, noted, notorious, popular, prominent
2 widely known and honored for achievement <a *famous* physician>
syn celebrated, celebrious, distinguished, eminent, famed, great, illustrious, notable, prestigious, prominent, redoubtable, renowned; *compare* WELL-KNOWN
rel estimable, honorable, reputable, respectable, well-thought-of
idiom held in esteem
con humble, inconspicuous, undistinguished, unimportant, unknown
ant obscure; infamous
3 ***syn*** EXCELLENT, capital, ‖dandy, first-class, first-rate, first-string, five-star, superior, top, top-notch
ant wretched

fan *n* **1** ***syn*** ADDICT, aficionado, buff, devotee, habitué, hound, lover, votary
2 ***syn*** AMATEUR 1, admirer, devotee, fancier, votary

fan *vb* **1** ***syn*** BLOW 1, ruffle, wind, winnow
‖**2** ***syn*** SEARCH 2, frisk, shake down

fan (out) *vb* ***syn*** OPEN 4, expand, extend, outspread, outstretch, spread, unfold

fanatic *adj* ***syn*** EXTREME 3, extremist, rabid, radical, revolutional, revolutionary, revolutionist, ultra, ultraist

fanatic *n* ***syn*** ENTHUSIAST, bigot, bug, fiend, freak, maniac, nut, zealot

fancied *adj* ***syn*** IMAGINARY 1, fanciful, imagined, notional, shadowy

fancier *n* ***syn*** AMATEUR 1, admirer, devotee, fan, votary

fanciful *adj* **1** ***syn*** IMAGINARY 1, fancied, imagined, notional, shadowy
rel apocryphal, fabulous, fictitious, legendary, mythical; bizarre, fantastic, grotesque; absurd, preposterous; false, wrong
con matter-of-fact, prosaic; truthful, veracious
ant realistic
2 ***syn*** FICTITIOUS 1, chimerical, fantastic, fictional, fictive, illusory, imaginary, suppositious, supposititious, unreal
ant veridical

fancy *n* **1** ***syn*** WILL 1, inclination, liking, mind, pleasure, velleity
2 ***syn*** CAPRICE, bee, boutade, conceit, crotchet, freak, humor, megrim, vagary, whim
rel idea; irrationality, unreasonableness; contrariness, perverseness

---

syn synonym(s) ***rel*** related word(s)
idiom idiomatic equivalent(s) ***con*** contrasted word(s)
ant antonym(s) * vulgar
‖ use limited; if in doubt, see a dictionary
The first word in a synonym list when printed in SMALL CAPITALS shows where there is more information about the group. For a more efficient use of this book see Explanatory Notes.

3 *syn* IMAGINATION, fantasy (*or* phantasy), imaginativeness
rel envisagement, envisioning, objectification
idiom flight of fancy
con awareness, experience, perception
4 an idea or image present in the mind but having no concrete or objective reality <unable to tell fact from *fancy*>
syn daydream, dream, fantasy (*or* phantasy), nightmare, phantasm, vision
rel fable, fabrication, fiction, figment, invention; concept, conception, idea, notion; chimera, delusion, illusion; fata morgana, hallucination, mirage
idiom figment of the imagination
con actuality, fact, reality

fancy *vb* **1** *syn* LIKE
rel approve, endorse, sanction
idiom have a fancy (*or* hankering) for; have one's heart set on
con deprecate, disapprove; abhor, abominate, detest, dislike, hate, loathe
2 *syn* THINK 1, conceive, envisage, envision, feature, image, imagine, realize, vision, visualize
con demonstrate, prove, test, try

fancy *adj syn* ELABORATE 2, complicated, intricate

fancy–free *adj syn* FREE 6, heart-whole

fancy house *n syn* BROTHEL, bagnio, bawdy house, bordello, call house, cathouse, ||joyhouse, sporting house, stew, whorehouse

fancy man *n* **1** *syn* LOVER 1, boyfriend, man, master, paramour
2 *syn* PIMP 1, bully, cadet, ||easy rider, ||mack, macquereau, pander

fancy woman *n syn* HARLOT 1, blowen, courtesan, demimondaine, demimonde, demirep, hetaera, kept woman, paphian, whore

fanfare *n syn* DISPLAY 2, array, panoply, parade, pomp, shine, show

fanny *n syn* BUTTOCKS, backside, behind, bottom, derriere, heinie (*or* hiney), hind end, posterior, *prat, seat

fantastic *adj* **1** *syn* FICTITIOUS 1, chimerical, fanciful, fictional, fictive, illusory, imaginary, suppositious, supposititious, unreal
rel implausible, incredible, unbelievable; absurd, preposterous; irrational, unreasonable; deceptive, delusive, delusory, misleading
con common, commonplace, everyday, familiar, ordinary; customary, prevailing, universal, usual
2 conceived or made without reference to reality <their explanation was *fantastic*>
syn antic, bizarre, grotesque
rel adroit, clever, ingenious; eccentric, erratic, odd, queer, singular, strange; absurd, nonsensical, preposterous, ridiculous

con factual, solid, sound, valid, well-grounded; plausible, reasonable
3 *syn* FOOLISH 2, absurd, ||balmy, crazy, insane, loony, preposterous, silly, unearthly, wacky
4 *syn* MONSTROUS 1, cracking, massive, monumental, mortal, prodigious, stupendous, towering, tremendous
5 *syn* EXTRAVAGANT 1, preposterous, wild

fantasy (*or* **phantasy**) *n* **1** *syn* IMAGINATION, fancy, imaginativeness
rel conceiving, envisioning, fancying, imagining; externalizing, objectifying
2 *syn* FANCY 4, daydream, dream, nightmare, phantasm, vision
rel caprice, freak, vagary, whim, whimsy; bizarrerie, grotesquerie
con actuality, fact, reality
3 *syn* PIPE DREAM, bubble, chimera, dream, illusion, ||pipe, rainbow

far *adv syn* WELL 8, considerably, quite, rather, significantly, somewhat

far *adj syn* DISTANT 1, faraway, far-flung, far-off, offlying, outlying, remote, removed
idiom a long day's journey
ant near

far and away *adv* by a considerable margin <he was *far and away* the best man for the job>
syn by all odds, by a long shot, by far, by long odds, by odds, out and away
rel decidedly, definitely; doubtless, unconditionally, undoubtedly, unequivocally, unquestionably; absolutely, positively; just, quite, very
con barely; slightly; possibly

far and near *adv syn* EVERYWHERE 1, all over, all round (*or* all around), everyplace, far and wide, high and low, overall, throughout

far and wide *adv syn* EVERYWHERE 1, all over, all round (*or* all around), everyplace, far and near, high and low, overall, throughout

faraway *adj* **1** *syn* DISTANT 1, far, far-flung, far-off, offlying, outlying, remote, removed
ant near-at-hand
2 *syn* ABSTRACTED, absent, absentminded, bemused, distrait, inconscient, lost, preoccupied
rel disregardful, heedless, oblivious, stargazing, unheeding, unmindful
idiom off one's guard

farce *n syn* MOCKERY 2, burlesque, caricature, mock, sham, travesty

farceur *n syn* ZANY 2, clown, cutup, joker, jokester, wag

farcical *adj syn* LAUGHABLE, comic, comical, droll, funny, gelastic, ludicrous, ridiculous, risible
rel absurd, extravagant, nonsensical, outrageous, preposterous

fare *vb* **1** *syn* GO 1, hie, journey, pass, proceed, ||process, push on, repair, travel, wend
rel advance, progress
idiom make headway
con stay, stop
2 *syn* SHIFT 5, do, get along, get by, get on, ||make out, manage, muddle through, stagger (*on or* along)

farewell *interj syn* GOOD-BYE, adieu, by, bye-bye, ||cheerio, so long, ||toodle-oo

---

syn synonym(s) *rel* related word(s)
idiom idiomatic equivalent(s) *con* contrasted word(s)
ant antonym(s) * vulgar
|| use limited; if in doubt, see a dictionary
The first word in a synonym list when printed in SMALL CAPITALS shows where there is more information about the group. For a more efficient use of this book see Explanatory Notes.

farewell *n* ***syn*** PARTING, adieu, congé, good-bye, leave-taking

farewell *adj* ***syn*** PARTING, departing, good-bye, valedictory

farfetched *adj* ***syn*** FORCED, labored, strained
rel bizarre, fantastic, grotesque; eccentric, erratic, queer, strange
con accustomed, usual, wonted

far–flung *adj* ***syn*** DISTANT 1, far, faraway, far-off, off-lying, outlying, remote, removed

far–gone *adj* ***syn*** EFFETE 2, all in, bleary, depleted, drained, exhausted, spent, used up, washed-out, worn-out

farming *n* ***syn*** AGRICULTURE, husbandry
rel cultivation, tillage; agronomy, geoponics, hydroponics

far–off *adj* ***syn*** DISTANT 1, far, faraway, far-flung, off-lying, outlying, remote, removed
idiom behind the farthest range
ant nearby

far–out *adj* ***syn*** OUTLANDISH 3, kinky, outré, ultra

farther *adv* ***syn*** BEYOND 1, further, ‖yon, yonder

farther *adj* ***syn*** ADDITIONAL, added, another, else, fresh, further, more, now, other

farthest *adj* ***syn*** EXTREME 5, furthermost, furthest, outermost, outmost, remotest, utmost, uttermost
ant nearest

fascinate *vb* **1** ***syn*** ENTHRALL 2, catch up, grip, hold, mesmerize, spellbind
2 ***syn*** ATTRACT 1, allure, bewitch, captivate, charm, draw, enchant, magnetize, take, wile
rel affect, impress, influence, strike, sway, touch; delight, gladden, please, rejoice; absorb, engage, engross, occupy, preoccupy
con disgust, horrify, repel; affront, insult, offend, outrage, shame
3 ***syn*** INTEREST, appeal, attract, excite, intrigue

fascinated *adj* ***syn*** ENAMORED 3, bewitched, captivated, charmed, enchanted, entranced

fascinating *adj* ***syn*** ATTRACTIVE 1, alluring, appealing, bewitching, captivating, charming, enchanting, glamorous, seductive, siren
rel delectable, delightful; seducing

fascination *n* ***syn*** CHARM 3, allure, appeal, charisma, glamour, magnetism, witchcraft, witchery

fashion *n* **1** ***syn*** METHOD 1, manner, mode, modus, system, technique, way, wise
rel custom, habit, practice, usage, wont
2 ***syn*** VEIN 1, manner, mode, style, tone
3 the prevailing or accepted custom <follow the *fashion*>
syn bandwagon, chic, craze, cry, dernier cri, fad, furore, mode, rage, style, thing, ton, trend, ‖twig, vogue
rel drift, tendency; convention, form, usage
idiom the in thing, the last word, the latest thing

fashion *vb* ***syn*** MAKE 3, build, construct, erect, fabricate, form, frame, mold, produce, shape
rel contrive, devise; design, plan, plot; turn out

fashionable *adj* ***syn*** STYLISH, chic, dashing, exclusive, modish, smart, swank, swish, ‖trendy, with-it
rel current, popular, prevalent, up-to-the-minute
idiom all the rage
ant unfashionable

fast *adj* **1** ***syn*** SURE 1, firm, secure, stable, staunch, strong
rel fixed, held, inextricable, stuck, wedged
con insecure, loose, shaky, unstable
2 ***syn*** FAITHFUL 1, ardent, constant, ‖dinky-di, liege, loyal, resolute, staunch, steadfast, true
3 moving, proceeding, or acting with great celerity <a *fast* horse>
syn breakneck, expeditious, expeditive, fleet, hare-footed, hasty, posthaste, quick, raking, rapid, snappy, speedy, swift
rel active, alert, brisk, keen, lively
idiom quick as lightning, quick as thought, swift as an arrow
con lethargic, logy, poky, sluggish, tardy, torpid; languid, languorous; deliberate, gradual
ant slow
4 persistent in adhering to something <a *fast* grip>
syn firm, fixed, secure, set, tenacious, tight; *compare* STABLE 4, SURE 1
idiom stuck fast
con insecure, loose, relaxed, unfirm, weak; free, unattached, unfixed
5 ***syn*** WILD 7, devil-may-care, gay, raffish, rakehell, rakish, sporty
6 ***syn*** LICENTIOUS 2, incontinent, lascivious, lecherous, lewd, libertine, libidinous, lustful, salacious, satyric
7 sexually promiscuous—usually used of a woman <she's said to be *fast*>
syn easy, light, loose, ‖riggish, unchaste, wanton, whorish
rel careless, heedless, lax, slack; bawdy, indecent; lascivious, lecherous, lewd, libertine, licentious, lickerish, riotous
idiom no better than one should be, of easy virtue
con chaste, decent, decorous, modest, moral, pure, virtuous

fast *adv* **1** ***syn*** HARD 7, firm, firmly, fixedly, solidly, steadfastly, tight, tightly
2 in a rapid manner <run up the hill as *fast* as you know how>
syn apace, chop-chop, expeditiously, flat-out, fleetly, full tilt, hastily, lickety-split, posthaste, presto, promptly, pronto, quick, quickly, rapidly, soon, speedily, swift, swiftly
idiom by leaps and bounds, in a flash, in a twinkling, in nothing flat, in short order, like a bat out of hell, like a blue streak, like a flash, like a house afire, like a shot, like a streak, like greased lightning, like wildfire
con deliberately, leisurely; apathetically, lethargically, sluggishly
ant slow, slowly

fasten *vb* **1** to cause one thing to hold to another <*fasten* a feather to a hat>

---

syn synonym(s) ***rel*** related word(s)
idiom idiomatic equivalent(s) ***con*** contrasted word(s)
ant antonym(s) * vulgar
‖ use limited; if in doubt, see a dictionary
The first word in a synonym list when printed in SMALL CAPITALS shows where there is more information about the group. For a more efficient use of this book see Explanatory Notes.

syn affix, attach, fix, rivet
rel connect, join, link, unite; adhere, cleave, cling, cohere, stick
con divide, divorce, part, separate, sever, sunder; loose, loosen
ant unfasten
2 to fix in place or in a desired position <*fasten* the door>
syn anchor, catch, fix, moor, secure
rel bed, implant, infix, lodge, set, settle; embed, join, wedge; establish; bar, hitch, hook
idiom make fast (*or* secure *or* sure)
con loose, undo, unloose, unloosen
ant unfasten
3 to direct (as attention or hope) directly and steadily <*fastened* his whole mind on the problem>
syn concenter, concentrate, fix, fixate, focus, put, rivet
rel address, apply, devote, direct, train, turn
con falter, vacillate, waver

fastidious *adj* ***syn*** NICE 1, dainty, finical, finicking, finicky, fussy, particular, pernickety, persnickety, squeamish
rel demanding, exacting; captious, critical, hypercritical
con cursory, uncritical

fastigium *n* ***syn*** TOP 1, apex, crest, crown, peak, roof, summit, vertex

fastness *n* ***syn*** FORT, citadel, fortress, redoubt, stronghold
rel retreat, shelter; defense, guard, protection; adytum, sanctum

fat *adj* **1** ***syn*** FATTY 1, adipose
2 having excess adipose tissue <a *fat* woman overflowing her chair>
syn corpulent, fleshy, gross, heavy, obese, overblown, overweight, porcine, portly, pursy, stout, upholstered, weighty; *compare* ROTUND 2
rel beefy, bulky, chunky, dumpy, full-bodied, heavyset, squat, stocky, stubby, thick, thickset; paunchy, potbellied; brawny, burly, husky
idiom broad in the beam, fat as a pig
con angular, gaunt, lank, lanky, rawboned, scrawny, skinny, spare; slender, slight, slim, thin
ant lean
3 ***syn*** LARGE 1, big, bull, great, husky, oversize
rel broad, deep, wide
con narrow, skinny
4 ***syn*** RESONANT, consonant, orotund, resounding, ringing, rotund, round, sonorant, sonorous, vibrant
‖**5** ***syn*** REMOTE 4, negligible, off, outside, slender, slight, slim, small

fat *n* **1** ***syn*** BEST, choice, cream, elite, flower, pick, pride, prime, prize, top

---

syn synonym(s) *rel* related word(s)
idiom idiomatic equivalent(s) *con* contrasted word(s)
ant antonym(s) * vulgar
‖ use limited; if in doubt, see a dictionary
The first word in a synonym list when printed in SMALL CAPITALS shows where there is more information about the group. For a more efficient use of this book see Explanatory Notes.

2 ***syn*** EXCESS 1, overabundance, overflow, overkill, overmuch, overplus, plethora, superfluity, surfeit, surplus

fatal *adj* **1** ***syn*** DEADLY 1, deathly, lethal, mortal, mortiferous, pestilent, pestilential
2 bringing on an adverse fate <to accept his word was a *fatal* mistake>
syn calamitous, cataclysmic, catastrophic, disastrous, fateful, ruinous
rel baneful, pernicious; baleful, malefic, maleficent, malign, sinister; ill-fated, ill-starred, unlucky
con advantageous, beneficial, profitable; auspicious, benign, favorable, propitious

fatal *n* ***syn*** FATALITY 2, casualty, death

fatality *n* **1** the condition of causing death <the tuberculosis *fatality* remains high>
syn deadliness, lethality, mortality
rel malignancy, noxiousness, perniciousness, poisonousness, virulence
2 an instance of dying especially as the result of accident or disaster <two *fatalities* over the weekend>
syn casualty, death, fatal

‖**fat cat** *n* ***syn*** NOTABLE 1, ‖big cheese, ‖big chief, ‖biggie, big shot, big-timer, heavyweight, high-muck-a-muck, mugwump, nabob

fate *n* whatever is destined or inevitably decreed for one <the *fate* of the bill has not been decided>
syn circumstance, destiny, doom, kismet, lot, moira, portion, weird
rel consequence, effect, issue, outcome, result, upshot; end, ending, termination; ineluctability, inescapableness, inevitability, inevitableness, unavoidability
con accident, chance, fortune, hazard, luck

fate *vb* ***syn*** PREDESTINE 1, destine, determine, doom (to), foreordain, predetermine, preform, preordain

fateful *adj* **1** ***syn*** OMINOUS, apocalyptic, baleful, baneful, direful, doomful, ill-boding, inauspicious, threatening, unpropitious
rel important, momentous, significant; conclusive, decisive, determinative; acute, critical, crucial
con inconclusive, insignificant, trivial, unimportant
2 ***syn*** FATAL 2, calamitous, cataclysmic, catastrophic, disastrous, ruinous

fathead *n* ***syn*** DUNCE, boob, booby, chump, dolt, dolthead, goof, ‖goon, lunkhead, oaf

fatheaded *adj* ***syn*** STUPID 1, beefheaded, beetleheaded, blockheaded, chuckleheaded, dense, hammerheaded, numskulled, thick, thickheaded

father *n* **1** a male human parent <scarcely knew his *father*>
syn dad, dada, daddy, ‖governor, ‖old man, pa, ‖pap, papa, ‖pappy, ‖pater, pop, poppa; *compare* MOTHER 1
2 one that originates or institutes <the *father* of radiotelegraphy>
syn architect, author, creator, founder, generator, inventor, maker, originator, patriarch, sire
rel builder, encourager, motor, mover, organizer, prime mover, producer, promoter, promulgator, supporter; inaugurator, initiator, introducer
con disciple, follower

father *vb* **1** to be the male parent in reproduction <didn't know who *fathered* the child>
syn beget, breed, get, procreate, progenerate, sire

rel engender, generate, ingenerate; spawn
2 *syn* GENERATE 1, create, hatch, make, originate, parent, procreate, produce, sire, spawn

fatherland *n syn* COUNTRY, home, homeland, land, mother country, motherland, soil

fatherless *adj syn* ILLEGITIMATE 1, baseborn, bastard, misbegotten, natural, spurious, supposititious, unfathered

fathom *vb* **1** *syn* SOUND, plumb, plumb-line
2 *syn* KNOW 1, appreciate, apprehend, cognize, comprehend, grasp, have, understand
rel penetrate, pierce, probe; perceive, recognize; ‖dig, savvy

fathomable *adj syn* UNDERSTANDABLE, apprehensible, comprehendible, comprehensible, graspable, intelligible, knowable, lucid, luminous

fathomless *adj syn* BOTTOMLESS 2, abysmal, plumbless, plummetless, soundless, unfathomable

fatidic *adj syn* PROPHETIC, apocalyptic, Delphian, mantic, oracular, prophetical, sibylline, vatic, vaticinal

fatigue *n* complete depletion of strength <suffering from *fatigue*>
syn exhaustion, lassitude, tiredness, weariness
rel enervation, ennui, languor, listlessness; debilitation, faintness, feebleness, weakness
con briskness, energy, liveliness, vigor, vitality; endurance, strength

fatigue *vb syn* TIRE 1, drain, jade, wear, wear down, weary
rel deplete; exhaust, fag, tucker, wear out; debilitate, disable, weaken; annoy, bother, irk, vex
con refresh, rejuvenate, renew, restore; assuage, relieve

fatigued *adj syn* TIRED 1, jaded, wearied, weary, worn, worn down

fatness *n syn* OBESITY, adiposity, corpulence, fleshiness

‖**fatso** *n syn* FATTY, blimp, butterball, dumpling, ‖tub

fatty *adj* **1** containing fat especially in unusual amounts <a rather *fatty* steak>
syn adipose, fat
rel blubbery, lardy, suety
ant lean
2 having the qualities of fat <the constant frying left a *fatty* deposit on the kitchen woodwork>
syn greasy, oily, oleaginous, unctuous

fatty *n* a fat person <*fatties* trying to diet>
syn blimp, butterball, dumpling, ‖fatso, ‖tub
rel overweight; pudge, roly-poly, strapper; potbelly
idiom tons of fun
ant skinny

fatuous *adj syn* SIMPLE 3, asinine, brainless, foolish, sheepheaded, silly, unwitty, weak-headed, weak-minded, witless
rel idiotic, imbecile, moronic; besotted, fond, infatuated, insensate; absurd, dumb, silly, stupid
con judicious, prudent, sage, sane, sapient, wise
ant sensible

faucet *n* a fixture for controlling the passage of fluid <turn off the *faucet*>
syn cock, gate, hydrant, petcock, spigot, stopcock, tap, valve
rel bung, spile

fault *n* **1** *syn* IMPERFECTION, deficiency, demerit, shortcoming, sin
rel infirmity, weakness
con faultlessness, impeccability; meticulousness, preciseness, precision
2 an imperfection in character or an ingrained moral weakness <he has few *faults*>
syn failing, foible, frailty, vice
rel infirmity, weakness; blemish, defect, flaw
con excellence, perfection, virtue; desirability, goodness, rightness
ant merit
3 *syn* BLAME, culpability, guilt, onus
rel accountability, answerability, liability, responsibility; crime, error, offense, sin, transgression

faultfinder *n* **1** *syn* CRITIC, aristarch, carper, caviler, criticizer, knocker, momus, smellfungus, Zoilus
2 *syn* GROUCH, ‖bellyacher, complainer, crab, griper, grump, kicker, malcontent, sorehead, sourpuss

faultfinding *adj syn* CRITICAL 1, captious, carping, caviling, cavillous, censorious, critic, hypercritical, overcritical
rel particular, pernickety; ultracritical
con appreciative, cherishing, prizing, valuing

faultily *adv syn* AMISS 1, incorrectly, wrongly
rel erroneously, fallaciously, inaccurately, mistakenly, unfairly
con correctly, right

faultless *adj* **1** *syn* IMPECCABLE 1, errorless, exquisite, flawless, immaculate, irreproachable
rel entire, intact, perfect, whole; blameless
con defective, deficient, imprecise, inaccurate, inexact, uncorrect
ant faulty
2 *syn* INNOCENT 2, blameless, clean, crimeless, guiltless, inculpable, unguilty

faulty *adj* marked by a fault or defect <a *faulty* mechanism>
syn amiss, defective, flawed, imperfect, sick
rel imprecise, inaccurate, inexact, uncorrect; deficient, inadequate, incomplete; erroneous, fallacious, fallible, specious, wrong; blemished, damaged, defaced, disfigured, marred
con accurate, correct, exact, nice, precise, right; complete, entire, intact, perfect, whole; excellent, good; unflawed, unimpaired
ant faultless

faux pas *n* a breach of etiquette or of social convention <hustled him out of the room before he could commit another *faux pas*>
syn blooper, boner, ‖boo-boo, break, gaffe, impropriety, indecorum, solecism; *compare* ERROR 2
rel bungle, misstep, stumble; howler, screamer; indiscretion, misjudgment, oversight, pratfall

favor *n* **1** *syn* REGARD 4, account, admiration, consideration, esteem, estimation, respect

---

syn synonym(s) — *rel* related word(s)
idiom idiomatic equivalent(s) — *con* contrasted word(s)
ant antonym(s) — * vulgar
‖ use limited; if in doubt, see a dictionary
The first word in a synonym list when printed in SMALL CAPITALS shows where there is more information about the group. For a more efficient use of this book see Explanatory Notes.

ant disfavor
2 ***syn*** APPROBATION 1, approval, benediction, blessing, OK (*or* okay)
con depreciation, derogation, disparagement
ant disfavor
3 ***syn*** GIFT 1, benevolence, boon, ‖compliment, largess, present
rel aid, assistance, backing, encouragement, help, support
4 a special privilege <willing to grant a *favor* to a good friend>
syn courtesy, dispensation, indulgence, kindness, service
rel aid, assistance, cooperation, help

favor *vb* **1** ***syn*** APPROVE 1, accept, approbate, countenance, go (for), hold (with)
rel endorse, OK (*or* okay), sanction; appreciate, prize, value
idiom set great store by
con decry, depreciate, disparage
ant disfavor
2 ***syn*** OBLIGE 2, accommodate, convenience
rel humor, indulge, pamper
idiom do one a favor (*or* service), do right by
con baffle, circumvent, foil, frustrate, thwart
3 ***syn*** ENCOURAGE 2, advocate, countenance
4 ***syn*** RESEMBLE, ‖feature, simulate
con contradict, differ

favorable *adj* **1** expressing approval <a *favorable* recommendation>
syn approbative, approbatory, approving
rel benignant, kind, kindly; recommendatory, well-disposed; commendatory, complimentary, laudatory, praiseful
idiom in one's favor
con depreciative, disapprobatory, disapproving, disparaging, uncomplimentary; censorious, condemnatory, critical, faultfinding
ant unfavorable
2 ***syn*** PLEASANT 1, agreeable, good, grateful, gratifying, nice, pleasing, pleasurable, pleasureful, welcome
3 ***syn*** GOOD 1, advantageous, benefic, beneficial, brave, favoring, helpful, propitious, toward, useful
rel healthful, salutary, wholesome
con disadvantageous, unpropitious; damaging, hampering
ant unfavorable
4 ***syn*** TIMELY 1, auspicious, opportune, propitious, prosperous, seasonable, timeous, well-timed
5 indicative of a successful outcome <*favorable* conditions for opening a new business>
syn auspicious, benign, bright, dexter, fortunate, propitious, white

---

syn synonym(s) — *rel* related word(s)
idiom idiomatic equivalent(s) — *con* contrasted word(s)
ant antonym(s) — * vulgar
‖ use limited; if in doubt, see a dictionary
The first word in a synonym list when printed in SMALL CAPITALS shows where there is more information about the group. For a more efficient use of this book see Explanatory Notes.

rel advantageous, beneficial, profitable; happy, lucky, promising, providential; cheering, encouraging, reassuring
idiom full of promise
con calamitous, cataclysmic, catastrophic, disastrous, fatal, fateful, ruinous; baleful, malefic, maleficent, malign, sinister; ill-fated, ill-starred, unlucky; inauspicious, unpromising, unpropitious
ant unfavorable

favorably *adv* ***syn*** WELL 5, fortunately, happily, prosperously, satisfyingly, successfully, swimmingly

favored *adj* ***syn*** FAVORITE 2, popular, preferred, well-liked

favoring *adj* ***syn*** GOOD 1, advantageous, benefic, beneficial, brave, favorable, helpful, propitious, toward, useful

favorite *adj* **1** accorded special treatment or attention <a *favorite* daughter>
syn beloved, blue-eyed, darling, dear, fair-haired, loved, pet, precious, white-haired, white-headed
rel admired, adored, esteemed, revered; cherished, prized, treasured
idiom dear as the apple of one's eye, dear to one's heart, held dear
con contemned, despised, disdained; abhorrent, detested, hated
2 constituting a favorite <*favorite* melodies>
syn favored, popular, preferred, well-liked
rel laudable, pleasant, praiseworthy; cherished, prized, treasured
con despised, detested, disliked, hated, unpopular; eschewed, rejected

fawn *vb* to act or behave with abjectness in the presence of a superior <*fawn* on the master>
syn apple-polish, bootlick, ‖brownnose, cotton, cower, cringe, grovel, honey (up), kowtow, slaver, toady, truckle
rel blandish, cajole, coax, wheedle; butter (up), flatter, make up (to); cater (to), pander (to); crawl; abase, debase, demean; bow, cave, defer, submit, yield; court, invite, woo
idiom be at one's beck and call, curry favor, dance attendance, kiss one's feet, lick one's shoes (*or* boots), make a doormat of oneself, ‖suck up to
con contemn, despise, disdain, scorn, scout; reject, repudiate, spurn; flout, gibe, jeer, scoff; deride, mock, ridicule, taunt
ant domineer

fawning *adj* characteristic of one that fawns <sent *fawning* greetings>
syn bootlicking, cowering, cringing, groveling, kowtowing, parasitic, sycophant, sycophantic, sycophantical, sycophantish, toadying, toadyish, truckling
rel flunkyish, obsequious, servile, slavish, subservient; compliant, deferential, humble, submissive, yielding; ingratiating; adulatory, flattering, mealy-mouthed; crawling, spineless; abject, ignoble, mean
con arrogant, disdainful, haughty, insolent, lordly, overbearing, proud, supercilious; contemptuous, insulting, scathing, scornful; authoritative, imperious, magisterial, masterful
ant domineering

fay *n* ***syn*** FAIRY, brownie, elf, nisse, pixie, sprite

faze *vb* ***syn*** EMBARRASS, abash, confound, confuse, discomfit, disconcert, discountenance, rattle
rel confound, dumbfound, mystify, nonplus, perplex, puzzle; confuse, muddle; appall, daunt, dismay, horrify; annoy, bother, irritate, vex
con calm, compose, quiet, relax, soothe; ease, relieve

fealty *n* ***syn*** FIDELITY 1, allegiance, ardor, devotion, faithfulness, loyalty, piety
rel faith, trueness, truth; dependability, reliability, trustworthiness; devotedness, support
con disloyalty, traitorousness, treacherousness
ant perfidy

fear *n* **1** agitation or dismay in the anticipation of or in the presence of danger <living in *fear* of what the future might hold>
syn alarm, cold feet, consternation, dismay, dread, fright, horror, panic, terror, trepidation, trepidity
rel apprehension, foreboding, misgiving, presentiment; angst, anxiety, concern, worry; agitation, discomposure, disquietude, perturbation; chickenheartedness, cowardice, cowardliness, faintheartedness, timidity, timorousness; funk, scare
idiom cold sweat
con boldness, bravery, courage, courageousness, dauntlessness, fortitude, gallantry, intrepidity, prowess, valiancy, valor
ant fearlessness
2 ***syn*** REVERENCE 2, awe
rel esteem, respect
con contempt, scorn

fearful *adj* **1** ***syn*** AFRAID 1, aghast, anxious, ‖ascared, frightened, scared, scary, terrified
rel agitated, alarmed, discomposed, disquieted, disturbed, perturbed
con audacious, bold, brave, courageous, dauntless, unafraid, valiant
ant fearless
2 inspired or moved by fear <*fearful* of loud noises>
syn afraid, apprehensive; *compare* AFRAID 1
rel alarmed, disquieted, disturbed; aflutter, agitated, jittery, nervous, perturbed, uneasy; anxious, concerned, solicitous, worried
con assured, confident, sanguine, sure; collected, composed, cool, imperturbable, nonchalant, unflappable, unperturbed
ant unafraid
3 causing fear <a *fearful* sight>
syn appalling, awful, dire, direful, dreadful, formidable, frightful, horrible, horrific, redoubtable, shocking, terrible, terrific, tremendous
rel alarming, frightening, terrifying; ghastly, grim, grisly, gruesome, lurid, macabre; baleful, malign, sinister; overwhelming, sublime
con attractive, charming, delightful, enchanting, pleasant, pleasing
ant reassuring

fearless *adj* ***syn*** BRAVE 1, aweless, bold, courageous, dauntless, game, lionhearted, unafraid, unfearing, unfearful
rel assured, confident, sanguine, sure
con afraid, frightened, scared, terrified
ant fearful

feasible *adj* ***syn*** POSSIBLE 1, doable, practicable, viable, workable
rel practical; advantageous, beneficial, profitable; appropriate, fit, fitting, suitable
con impossible, impracticable, unachievable, unattainable, unworkable; ambitious, pretentious, utopian
ant infeasible, unfeasible

feast *n* ***syn*** DINNER, banquet, regale, spread
rel entertainment, festivity; refreshment, repast; meal

feat *n* **1** ***syn*** ADVENTURE, emprise, enterprise, exploit, gest, venture
idiom bold stroke, deed of derring-do
2 a remarkable act or performance <Washington's *feat* of tossing a dollar across the river>
syn achievement, deed, exploit, tour de force
rel act, action; accomplishment, consummation, execution, performance; conquest, triumph, victory
3 ***syn*** TRICK 3, stunt

feather *n* ***syn*** TYPE, breed, ilk, kidney, kind, order, sort, species, stripe, variety

featherbrain *n* ***syn*** SCATTERBRAIN, birdbrain, featherhead, flibbertigibbet, harebrain, rattlebrain, rattlehead, shatterbrain

featherbrained *adj* ***syn*** GIDDY 1, dizzy, empty-headed, flighty, frivolous, harebrained, rattlebrained, scatterbrained, silly, skittish
rel capricious, fickle, impulsive, whimsical; shallow, superficial, unprofound

featherhead *n* ***syn*** SCATTERBRAIN, birdbrain, featherbrain, flibbertigibbet, harebrain, rattlebrain, rattlehead, shatterbrain

featherlight *adj* ***syn*** LIGHT 1, featherweight, imponderous, lightweight, unheavy, weightless

featherweight *n* ***syn*** DUNCE, ‖cluck, dimwit, ‖dumb bunny, ‖dumb cluck, lackwit, nitwit, pinhead, simp, wantwit

featherweight *adj* ***syn*** LIGHT 1, featherlight, imponderous, lightweight, unheavy, weightless

feature *n* **1** ***syn*** QUALITY 1, affection, attribute, character, characteristic, mark, property, savor, trait, virtue
2 ***syn*** CHARACTERISTIC 1, birthmark, character, point, trait
rel article, detail, item, particular; component, constituent, element, factor, ingredient; individuality, particularity, peculiarity, speciality, specialty; attribute, property, quality
3 features *pl* ***syn*** FACE 1, countenance, ‖dial, ‖kisser, ‖map, mug, ‖pan, phiz, ‖puss, visage

feature *vb* ‖**1** ***syn*** RESEMBLE, favor, simulate
2 ***syn*** THINK 1, conceive, envisage, envision, fancy, image, imagine, realize, vision, visualize
3 ***syn*** EMPHASIZE, italicize, play (up), stress, underline, underscore

febrile *adj* ***syn*** FEVERISH 1, fevered, fiery

feckless *adj* **1** having no real worth or purpose <after years of *feckless* negotiations>

---

syn synonym(s) — *rel* related word(s)
idiom idiomatic equivalent(s) — *con* contrasted word(s)
ant antonym(s) — * vulgar
‖ use limited; if in doubt, see a dictionary
The first word in a synonym list when printed in SMALL CAPITALS shows where there is more information about the group. For a more efficient use of this book see Explanatory Notes.

syn fustian, good-for-nothing, meaningless, purposeless, unpurposed, useless, worthless
rel bootless, fruitless, futile, unavailing, vain; ineffective, ineffectual, inefficacious
con meaningful, purposeful, worthwhile; fruitful; effective, effectual, efficacious; consequential, important, momentous, significant, weighty
ant efficient, ‖feckful
2 ***syn*** CARELESS 1, heedless, inadvertent, irreflective, thoughtless, uncaring, unheeding, unrecking, unreflective, unthinking
rel carefree, easygoing, happy-go-lucky, lackadaisical, nonchalant; remiss; irresponsible, undependable, unreliable, untrustworthy
con attentive, considerate, thoughtful; meticulous, punctilious, punctual, scrupulous; dependable, reliable, responsible, trustworthy
3 ***syn*** IRRESPONSIBLE, carefree, careless, incautious, reckless, uncareful, wild
ant ‖feckful

fecund *adj* ***syn*** FERTILE, childing, fruitful, productive, proliferant, prolific, rich, spawning
rel breeding, generating, propagating, reproducing
con infertile, sterile
ant barren

fecundity *n* **1** ***syn*** FERTILITY, fruitfulness, prolificacy
rel productiveness, productivity; exuberance, lavishness, lushness, luxuriance, prodigality, profuseness, profusion
con infertility, sterility, unproductiveness
ant barrenness, infecundity
2 ***syn*** ELOQUENCE, expression, expressiveness, expressivity

federation *n* ***syn*** ALLIANCE 2, anschluss, coalition, confederacy, confederation, league, union

fed up *adj* disgusted and completely out of patience <*fed up* with her bad behavior>
syn disgusted, sick, tired, weary
rel bored; glutted, sated, satiated, surfeited
idiom fed to the gills (*or* teeth), full up to here with, sick and tired of, sick (*or* tired) to death
con enchanted, enraptured, enthralled; delighted, excited, exhilarated, pleased, thrilled

fee *n* ***syn*** WAGE, emolument, hire, pay, pay envelope, salary, stipend
rel consideration; charge, cost, expense, price

‖**feeb** *n* ***syn*** FOOL 4, ament, cretin, half-wit, idiot, imbecile, moron, natural, simpleton, zany

feeble *adj* **1** ***syn*** WEAK 1, decrepit, flimsy, fragile, frail, infirm, insubstantial, unsubstantial, ‖wanky, weakly
rel emasculated, enervated, unmanned, unnerved; helpless; aged, doddering, senile; ailing, sapless
con hale, healthy, sound; lusty, strenuous; strong
ant robust
2 ***syn*** TENUOUS 3, insubstantial, unsubstantial

feebleminded *adj* ***syn*** RETARDED, backward, dim-witted, dull, half-witted, imbecile, moronic, simpleminded, slow, slow-witted
ant strong-minded

feebleness *n* ***syn*** INFIRMITY 1, debility, decrepitude, disease, infirmness, malaise, sickliness, unhealthiness

feed *vb* ***syn*** GIVE 3, deliver, dish out, dispense, find, furnish, hand, hand over, provide, supply

feed (on) *vb* ***syn*** EAT 1, consume, devour, ingest, meal, partake (of), take
idiom have (*or* take) a bite, ‖put on the feed bag (*or* nose bag)

feed *n* **1** ***syn*** MEAL, ‖chow, refection, repast
2 ***syn*** FOOD 1, ‖chow, ‖eats, edibles, grub, nurture, provender, provisions, viands, victuals
rel banquet, feast, meal, repast

feel *vb* **1** ***syn*** TOUCH 1, finger, handle, palpate, paw
rel manipulate, ply, wield; explore, sound; fumble, grope
2 to have as an emotional response <*felt* pleasure in her company>
syn experience, know, savor, taste
rel apprehend; notice, observe, perceive; encounter, meet; endure, suffer, undergo
idiom be aware (*or* conscious) of, be sensible of
con disregard, ignore
3 to view as right or true <we *feel* that he should retire soon>
syn believe, consider, credit, deem, hold, sense, think; *compare* CONSIDER 3
rel assume, presume, suppose, suspect; conclude, deduce, gather, infer, judge; conjecture, guess, surmise; esteem; repute
idiom take (it) into one's head
con challenge, distrust, doubt, misdoubt, mistrust, question
4 ***syn*** GROPE, fumble, grabble

feel (for) *vb* ***syn*** COMPASSIONATE, ache, commiserate, pity, sympathize (with)

feel *n* **1** ***syn*** TOUCH 3, tactility
2 ***syn*** TOUCH 4, feeling
3 ***syn*** AIR 3, atmosphere, aura, feeling, mood, semblance
con basis, essence, reality

feeler *n* an attempt to ascertain opinion <the letter was a *feeler* to see how they would react>
syn trial balloon
rel query, question; inquiry, probe, test; leader, leading question; sounding board; intimation, representation; prospectus; kiteflying

feeling *n* **1** ***syn*** SENSATION 1, sense, sensibility, sensitivity
rel action, behavior, reaction; responsiveness; palpability, palpableness, perceptibility, perceptibleness, tangibility, tangibleness
con apathy, indifference, insensibility, numbness
2 ***syn*** TOUCH 4, feel
3 subjective response or reaction (as to a person or situation) <a *feeling* of sadness>
syn affection, affectivity, emotion, passion, sentiment
rel humor, mood, temper, vein; attitude, outlook; belief, opinion, view; concept, idea, impression, notion, thought

---

syn synonym(s) — *rel* related word(s)
idiom idiomatic equivalent(s) — *con* contrasted word(s)
ant antonym(s) — * vulgar
‖ use limited; if in doubt, see a dictionary
The first word in a synonym list when printed in SMALL CAPITALS shows where there is more information about the group. For a more efficient use of this book see Explanatory Notes.

4 ***syn*** OPINION, belief, conviction, eye, mind, persuasion, sentiment, view
5 ***syn*** AIR 3, atmosphere, aura, feel, mood, semblance
rel impress, impression, imprint

feeling *adj* ***syn*** EMOTIONAL 1, emotionable, sensitive, sentient
con numb, unmoved, unresponsive
ant unfeeling

feel out *vb* ***syn*** PROBE 2, sound (out)

feign *vb* ***syn*** ASSUME 4, act, affect, bluff, counterfeit, fake, pretend, put on, sham, simulate

feigned *adj* ***syn*** ARTIFICIAL 3, affected, assumed, put-on, spurious
rel counterfeit, false, sham
con heartfelt, hearty, sincere, wholehearted, whole-souled

feint *n* ***syn*** TRICK 1, gambit, jig, maneuver, play, ploy, ruse, stratagem, whizzer, wile
rel make-believe, pretense, pretension; befooling, hoax, hoodwinking; cheat, counterfeit, deceit, fake, humbug, imposture, sham; expedient, resort, shift

felicitate *vb* ***syn*** CONGRATULATE
rel commend, compliment, recommend; salute
con comfort, console, solace; commiserate, condole (with), pity; gibe, jeer, scoff; deride, mock, ridicule, taunt; contemn

felicitous *adj* ***syn*** FIT 1, applicable, appropriate, apt, fitting, happy, just, meet, proper, suitable
rel convincing, telling; opportune, pat, seasonable, timely, well-timed; apposite, apropos, germane, pertinent, relevant
con awkward, clumsy, gauche, inept, maladroit; unfortunate, unhappy, unlucky
ant infelicitous

feline *adj* ***syn*** STEALTHY 2, catlike, catty, furtive

fell *vb* **1** to force an opponent off his feet <*felled* the heckler with a single blow>
syn bowl (down *or* over), bring down, down, drop, flatten, floor, ground, knock down, knock over, lay low, level, mow (down), prostrate, throw down, tumble
rel shoot, shoot down
idiom lay level with the ground
con pick up, raise
2 to bring down by cutting <*felled* the great oak by the driveway>
syn chop, cut, hew
rel flatten, level, raze; cleave, rive, split; sever, sunder; gash, hack, mangle, slash

fell *adj* **1** ***syn*** FIERCE 1, barbarous, cruel, ferocious, grim, inhuman, inhumane, savage, truculent, wolfish
rel baleful, malefic, maleficent, malign, sinister; implacable, relentless, unrelenting; fearful, horrible, horrific, terrific
con compassionate, sympathetic, tender; clement, forbearing, lenient, merciful; humane
2 ***syn*** GRAVE 3, dangerous, grievous, major, serious, ugly

fell *n* ***syn*** HIDE, fur, jacket, pelt, skin

fellow *n* **1** ***syn*** PARTNER, associate, cohort, confrere, consociate, copartner, mate, ‖pard
2 ***syn*** ACCOMPANIMENT 2, associate, companion, concomitant, consort, mate
3 ***syn*** MATE 5, companion, coordinate, double, duplicate, match, reciprocal, twin
4 ***syn*** MAN 3, ‖bloke, boy, buck, chap, ‖gee, gent, gentleman, guy, he

fellow feeling *n* ***syn*** SYMPATHY 2, compassion, empathy

fellowship *n* **1** ***syn*** COMPANY 1, companionship, society
2 ***syn*** ASSOCIATION 2, brotherhood, club, fraternity, guild, league, order, society, sodality, union

felo–de–se *n* ***syn*** SUICIDE, hara-kiri, self-destruction, self-murder, self-slaughter, self-violence

felon *n* ***syn*** CRIMINAL, lawbreaker, malefactor, offender

femme fatale *n* ***syn*** SIREN, Lorelei, seductress, temptress

fen *n* ***syn*** SWAMP, baygall, bog, marsh, mire, morass, ‖moss, quag, slough, ‖sump

fence *n* ***syn*** BAR 2, barricade, barrier, block, blockade, roadblock, stop, wall

fence *vb* **1** ***syn*** ENCLOSE 1, cage, corral, hedge, hem, immure, mew, mure, pen, wall
2 ***syn*** DODGE 1, duck, parry, shirk, sidestep
rel feint, maneuver; baffle, foil, outwit

fend *vb* **1** ***syn*** DEFEND 1, bulwark, cover, guard, protect, safeguard, screen, secure, shield
2 ***syn*** WARD 1, deflect, parry

fend (off) *vb* to give a sharp check to <tried to *fend* off his attentions>
syn hold off, keep off, rebuff, rebut, repel, repulse, stave off, ward (off)
rel refuse, reject; snub, spurn; avert, avoid
idiom hold (*or* keep) at bay, keep at a distance, keep at arm's length
con allure, attract, captivate, charm, enchant, fascinate; embolden, hearten

feral *adj* **1** ***syn*** BRUTISH, animal, beastly, bestial, brutal, brute, ferine, swinish
rel barbaric, barbarous, ferocious, fierce, inhuman, savage, vicious
con gentle, mild, tame
2 ***syn*** SAVAGE 1, vicious, wild

ferine *adj* ***syn*** BRUTISH, animal, beastly, bestial, brutal, brute, feral, swinish

ferment *vb* ***syn*** SEETHE 4, boil, bubble, churn, ‖moil, simmer, smolder, stir

ferment *n* **1** ***syn*** UNREST, ailment, disquiet, disquietude, inquietude, restiveness, restlessness, storm and stress, Sturm und Drang, turmoil
2 ***syn*** COMMOTION 1, clamor, convulsion, outcry, tumult, upheaval, upturn

ferocious *adj* **1** ***syn*** FIERCE 1, barbarous, cruel, fell, grim, inhuman, inhumane, savage, truculent, wolfish
rel rapacious, ravening, ravenous, voracious; implacable, relentless
ant tender
2 ***syn*** SAVAGE, bestial, brutal, brute, feral, vicious

ferret out *vb* ***syn*** SEEK 1, cast about, hunt, quest, search (for *or* out)

---

syn synonym(s) ***rel*** related word(s)
idiom idiomatic equivalent(s) ***con*** contrasted word(s)
ant antonym(s) * vulgar
‖ use limited; if in doubt, see a dictionary
The first word in a synonym list when printed in SMALL CAPITALS shows where there is more information about the group. For a more efficient use of this book see Explanatory Notes.

rel elicit, extract; nose out, pry (out); penetrate, pierce, probe; chase, follow, pursue, trail; ascertain, determine, discover, learn
con conceal, hide, screen, secrete; camouflage, disguise; cover (up), hush (up), suppress
ant squirrel (away)

ferry *vb* ***syn*** CARRY 1, bear, buck, convey, ‖hump, ‖jag, lug, pack, tote, transport

fertile *adj* marked by abundant productivity <*fertile* soil> <a *fertile* mind>
syn childing, fecund, fruitful, productive, proliferant, prolific, rich, spawning
rel bearing, producing, yielding; abundant, bountiful, copious, exuberant, generous, lush, luxuriant, plenteous, plentiful, teeming; creative, ingenious, inventive, pregnant, resourceful; exciting, galvanizing, provoking, quickening, stimulating
con barren, impotent, unfruitful; dull, imitative, stupid, unproductive
ant infertile, sterile

fertility *n* the quality or state of being fertile <insure the *fertility* of the soil>
syn fecundity, fruitfulness, prolificacy
rel abundance, copiousness, plentifulness; creativity, ingenuity, inventiveness, resourcefulness
con barrenness, impotence, unfruitfulness
ant infertility, sterility

fervent *adj* ***syn*** IMPASSIONED, ardent, blazing, burning, fervid, fiery, glowing, hot-blooded, passionate, perfervid
rel devout, pious, religious; responsive, tender, warm, warmhearted; heartfelt, hearty, sincere, unfeigned, wholehearted, whole-souled; earnest, serious; eager, enthusiastic
con apathetic, impassive, phlegmatic; aloof, detached, indifferent, unconcerned

fervid *adj* **1** ***syn*** IMPASSIONED, ardent, blazing, burning, fervent, fiery, glowing, hot-blooded, passionate, perfervid
con collected, composed, cool, imperturbable, nonchalant
ant gelid
2 ***syn*** FEVERISH 2, burning, fevered, heated, hectic

fervor *n* ***syn*** PASSION 6, ardor, calenture, enthusiasm, fire, hurrah, zeal
rel devoutness, piety, piousness; earnestness, seriousness, solemnity; heartiness, sincerity, wholeheartedness; empressement, warmth
con apathy, impassiveness, impassivity; aloofness, detachment, indifference, unconcern; languor, lethargy, torpor

fescennine *adj* ***syn*** OBSCENE 2, coarse, dirty, filthy, foul, indecent, nasty, raunchy, smutty, vulgar

fess (up) *vb* ***syn*** ACKNOWLEDGE 1, admit, allow, avow, concede, confess, grant, let on, own, own up

---

syn synonym(s) *rel* related word(s)
idiom idiomatic equivalent(s) *con* contrasted word(s)
ant antonym(s) * vulgar
‖ use limited; if in doubt, see a dictionary
The first word in a synonym list when printed in SMALL CAPITALS shows where there is more information about the group. For a more efficient use of this book see Explanatory Notes.

fester *vb* ***syn*** RANKLE

festive *adj* ***syn*** MERRY, blithe, blithesome, gay, gleeful, jocund, jolly, jovial, lighthearted, mirthful

festivity *n* ***syn*** MERRYMAKING, gaiety, jollity, merriment, revel, reveling, revelment, revelry, whoopee

fetch *vb* ***syn*** SELL 4, bring, bring in

fetching *adj* ***syn*** ENTICING, Circean, luring, tempting

fetch up *vb* ‖**1** ***syn*** BRING UP 1, raise, rear
2 ***syn*** STOP 4, bring up, draw up, halt, haul up, pull up

fetid *adj* ***syn*** MALODOROUS 1, fusty, noisome, putrid, rancid, rank, reeking, smelly, stinking, strong
rel loathsome, repugnant, repulsive, revolting
con aromatic, balmy, odorous, redolent
ant fragrant

fetish *n* **1** ***syn*** CHARM 2, amulet, juju, luck, mascot, periapt, phylactery, talisman, zemi
2 irrational reverence or attachment <had a *fetish* for red hair>
syn fixation, mania, obsession, thing
rel preoccupation, prepossession; bias, partiality, predilection, prejudice; leaning, penchant, proclivity, propensity
con antipathy, aversion, repugnance, repulsion; dislike, disrelish, distaste

fetter *n, usu* **fetters** *pl* ***syn*** SHACKLE, bond(s), chains, gyve(s), iron(s)

fetter *vb* ***syn*** HAMPER, clog, curb, entrammel, hobble, hog-tie, leash, shackle, tie, trammel
con disembarrass, disencumber, disentangle, extricate, untangle; detach, disengage

fettle *n* ***syn*** ORDER 10, condition, fitness, kilter, repair, shape, trim

feud *n* **1** ***syn*** VENDETTA
2 ***syn*** QUARREL, altercation, bickering, controversy, dispute, falling-out, fracas, row, run-in, squabble
rel argument; combat, contest

fevered *adj* **1** ***syn*** FEVERISH 1, febrile, fiery
ant afebrile
2 ***syn*** FEVERISH 2, burning, fervid, heated, hectic

feverish *adj* **1** abnormally heated by fever <the child's forehead felt *feverish*>
syn febrile, fevered, fiery
rel burning, flushed, hectic, hot, inflamed, pyretic
ant afebrile
2 marked by intense emotion or activity <a *feverish* imagination>
syn burning, fervid, fevered, heated, hectic
rel excited, high-strung, nervous, overwrought; frenzied, furious, passionate
idiom keyed up
con calm, composed, cool, serene, tranquil; apathetic, languid, lethargic, listless, phlegmatic

few *adj* ***syn*** INFREQUENT, occasional, rare, scarce, seldom, semioccasional, sporadic, uncommon, unfrequent

few *n* a small quantity or number <sold a *few* of the books>
syn handful, scattering, smatch, smatter, smattering, spatter, spattering, sprinkling
con abundance, many, multitude, numbers

fiat *n* ***syn*** SANCTION, endorsement

fib *n* ***syn*** LIE, ‖bouncer, canard, cock-and-bull story, falsehood, falsity, prevarication, story, tale, untruth

rel equivocation, evasiveness; mendacity, untruthfulness
idiom tall tale

fib *vb* ***syn*** LIE, equivocate, falsify, palter, prevaricate
rel concoct, fabricate, make up, trump up
idiom draw the long bow, stretch the truth

fibber *n* ***syn*** LIAR, Ananias, falsifier, fibster, perjurer, prevaricator, storyteller

fibbery *n* ***syn*** MENDACITY, falsehood, mendaciousness, truthlessness, untruthfulness, unveracity

fiber *n* ***syn*** TEXTURE 2, fabric, web

fibrous *adj* ***syn*** MUSCULAR 1, ropy, sinewy, stringy, wiry

fibster *n* ***syn*** LIAR, Ananias, falsifier, fibber, perjurer, prevaricator, storyteller

fickle *adj* ***syn*** INCONSTANT 1, capricious, changeable, lubricious, mercurial, temperamental, ticklish, unstable, variable, volatile
rel unfaithful; undependable, unreliable
con stable, unchanging
ant constant, true

fiction *n* a story, account, explanation, or conception which is an invention of the human mind <his belief was based on a *fiction*>
syn fable, fabrication, figment
rel concoction, fantasy, invention; falsehood, lie, misrepresentation, untruth; anecdote, narrative, story, tale, yarn; fish story
con actuality, reality
ant fact

fictional *adj* ***syn*** FICTITIOUS 1, chimerical, fanciful, fantastic, fictive, illusory, imaginary, suppositious, supposititious, unreal

fictitious *adj* **1** suggestive of fiction especially in lacking a sound factual basis <*fictitious* values in logic>
syn chimerical, fanciful, fantastic, fictional, fictive, illusory, imaginary, suppositious, supposititious, unreal
rel concocted, created, invented, made; fabricated, fashioned; cooked-up, false, made-up, trumped-up, untrue; romantic
con actual, real, true; authentic, genuine; factual, veritable; truthful, veracious, verisimilar
2 not genuine <the gigolo wooed the heiress with *fictitious* ardor>
syn fake, mock, sham, simulated; *compare* ARTIFICIAL 2
rel deceptive, delusive, delusory, misleading; dishonest, unreal, untrue; artificial, ersatz, factitious, synthetic
con authentic, bona fide, veritable; actual, honest, real, true
ant genuine

fictive *adj* ***syn*** FICTITIOUS 1, chimerical, fanciful, fantastic, fictional, illusory, imaginary, suppositious, supposititious, unreal

fiddle *vb* **1** to handle something nervously or absently <always *fiddling* with his tie>
syn fidget, play, trifle, twiddle
rel feel, handle, touch
2 to work aimlessly, fruitlessly, or pointlessly <*fiddled* around with the engine for hours>
syn doodle, mess, mess around, potter, puddle, putter, tinker
rel dabble, fool, monkey

fiddle-faddle *n* ***syn*** NONSENSE 2, ‖applesauce, blatherskite, bosh, fiddlesticks, flapdoodle, flummadiddle, fudge, hooey, pishposh

fiddlesticks *n pl* ***syn*** NONSENSE 2, ‖applesauce, ‖baloney, bosh, bunkum, fiddle-faddle, fudge, hooey, piffle, pishposh

fidelity *n* **1** constancy to something to which one is bound by a pledge or duty <we must practice *fidelity* to our word>
syn allegiance, ardor, devotion, faithfulness, fealty, loyalty, piety
rel constancy, staunchness, steadfastness; dependability, reliability, trustworthiness
con disloyalty, falseness, falsity, perfidiousness, traitorousness, treacherousness, treachery; undependableness, unreliability, untrustworthiness
ant perfidy; faithlessness
2 ***syn*** ATTACHMENT 1, adherence, adhesion, constancy, faithfulness, loyalty
ant infidelity

fidget *vb* ***syn*** FIDDLE 1, play, trifle, twiddle

fidgety *adj* ***syn*** NERVOUS, goosey, high-strung, jittery, jumpy, nervy, spooky, twittery, unrestful

field *n* a limited area of knowledge or endeavor to which pursuits, activities, and interests are confined <a lawyer eminent in his *field*>
syn bailiwick, champaign, demesne, domain, dominion, precinct, province, region, sphere, terrain, territory, walk
rel bounds, confines, limits; area, department; compass, orbit, purview, range, reach, scope, sweep
con terra incognita

fiend *n* ***syn*** DEVIL 1, Apollyon, Beelzebub, diablo, Lucifer, Old Gooseberry, Old Nick, Old Scratch, Satan, serpent
2 ***syn*** DEVIL 2, archfiend, demon, Satan, succubus
3 ***syn*** ENTHUSIAST, bigot, bug, fanatic, freak, maniac, nut, zealot

fiendish *adj* having or manifesting qualities associated with devils, demons, and fiends <inflicted *fiendish* tortures on his captive>
syn demoniac, demonian, demonic, devilish, diabolic, diabolonian, satanic, serpentine, unhallowed
rel hellish, infernal; baleful, malefic, maleficent, malign, sinister; malevolent, malicious, malignant; atrocious, heinous, monstrous, outrageous; barbarous, cruel, ferocious, inhuman, savage, vicious
con benign, benignant, kind, kindly; gentle, mild; compassionate, sympathetic, tender

fierce *adj* **1** displaying fury or malignity in looks or actions <*fierce* native tribes>
syn barbarous, cannibalic, cruel, fell, ferocious, grim, inhuman, inhumane, savage, truculent, wolfish

---

rel menacing, threatening; enraged, infuriated, maddened; aggressive, bellicose, belligerent, pugnacious; brutal, merciless, pitiless, ruthless, vicious, wild
con benign, benignant, gentle, kind, kindly; peaceful; subdued, submissive, tame
ant mild
2 *syn* INTENSE 1, concentrated, desperate, exquisite, furious, terrible, vehement, vicious, violent
rel excessive, extreme, inordinate; penetrating, piercing; superlative, supreme, transcendent
con gentle, mild, subdued

fiercely *adv syn* HARD 2, frantically, furiously, hardly, madly, stormily, tumultuously, turbulently, violently, wildly

fiery *adj* **1** *syn* BURNING 1, ablaze, afire, aflame, alight, blaring, conflagrant, flaming, flaring, ignited
2 *syn* HOT 1, ardent, broiling, burning, heated, red-hot, scalding, scorching, sizzling, torrid
ant frigid, icy
3 *syn* FEVERISH 1, febrile, fevered
4 *syn* SPIRITED 2, beany, gingery, high-hearted, high-spirited, mettlesome, peppery, spunky
rel headlong, hotheaded, impetuous, madcap, precipitate; fervid, impassioned, perfervid; fierce, intense, vehement, violent; enthusiastic, excitable, impulsive, unrestrained; irascible, irritable
con deliberate, leisurely, slow; apathetic, dull, impassive, lethargic, phlegmatic, sluggish; enervated, listless, spiritless
5 *syn* IMPASSIONED, ardent, blazing, burning, fervent, flaming, passionate, perfervid, red-hot, white-hot
ant icy

fifty–fifty *adv syn* EVENLY 1, equally, squarely

fifty–fifty *adj syn* EVEN 4, equal, even-up

fight *vb* **1** *syn* CONTEND 1, battle, oppugn, tug, war
rel strive, struggle; rowdy, scuffle, tussle; debate, dispute; altercate, bicker, quarrel, scrap, spat, squabble, tiff, wrangle
idiom ‖mix it, mix it up, put up a fight
con bow, capitulate, submit, succumb, yield
2 *syn* RESIST, buck, combat, contest, dispute, duel, oppose, repel, traverse, withstand
con abide, bear, endure, suffer; advocate, back, champion, support, uphold; defend, guard, protect, shield

fight *n* **1** *syn* BRAWL 2, affray, broil, donnybrook, fracas, fray, knock-down-and-drag-out, row, scrap, scuffle
2 *syn* QUARREL, altercation, beef, bickering, brawl, feud, hassle, row, squabble, word(s)
3 *syn* ATTACK 2, aggression, aggressiveness, belligerence, combativeness, pugnacity

fighter *n syn* SOLDIER, fighting man, GI, man-at-arms, serviceman, swad, ‖swaddy, ‖sweat, warrior

fighting man *n syn* SOLDIER, fighter, GI, man-at-arms, serviceman, swad, ‖swaddy, ‖sweat, warrior

---

syn synonym(s) *rel* related word(s)
idiom idiomatic equivalent(s) *con* contrasted word(s)
ant antonym(s) * vulgar
‖ use limited; if in doubt, see a dictionary
The first word in a synonym list when printed in SMALL CAPITALS shows where there is more information about the group. For a more efficient use of this book see Explanatory Notes.

figment *n syn* FICTION, fable, fabrication
rel daydream, dream, fancy, nightmare; bubble, chimera, illusion; creation

figurant *n syn* DANCER, ballerina, ballet girl, coryphée, dancing girl, danseur, danseuse, figurante, hoofer

figurante *n syn* DANCER, ballerina, ballet girl, coryphée, dancing girl, danseur, danseuse, figurant, hoofer

figuration *n* **1** *syn* OUTLINE, contour, delineation, line, lineament, lineation, profile, silhouette
2 *syn* ALLEGORY 1, symbolism, symbolization, typification

figure *n* **1** *syn* NUMBER, chiffer, cipher, digit, integer, numeral, whole number
rel character, symbol
2 *syn* FORM 1, cast, configuration, conformation, shape
rel delineation; appearance, build, frame, physique
3 a unit in a decorative composition (as in a fabric) <a rug with geometrical *figures* in blue and red>
syn design, device, motif, motive, pattern
rel decoration, embellishment, ornamentation

figure *vb* **1** *syn* CALCULATE, cipher, compute, estimate, reckon
2 *syn* ADD 2, cast, foot, sum, summate, tot, total, totalize, tote
rel count, enumerate, number
3 *syn* DECIDE, conclude, determine, resolve, rule, settle

figure out *vb syn* SOLVE 2, ‖cipher, clear up, decipher, ‖dope out, puzzle out, resolve, unfold, unravel, unriddle
rel disentangle, unscramble, untangle; crack, decode
con obfuscate, obscure; conceal, hide, screen

figuring *n syn* COMPUTATION, arithmetic, calculation, ciphering, estimation, reckoning

filch *vb syn* STEAL 1, ‖cop, lift, nim, nip, pilfer, pinch, purloin, snitch, swipe

filcher *n syn* THIEF, larcener, larcenist, nimmer, pilferer, prig, purloiner, stealer

file *n syn* LINE 5, echelon, queue, rank, row, string, tier

filius nullius *n syn* BASTARD 1, by-blow, catch colt, chance child, filius populi, illegitimate, love child, natural child, whoreson, woods colt

filius populi *n syn* BASTARD 1, by-blow, catch colt, chance child, filius nullius, illegitimate, love child, natural child, whoreson, woods colt

fill *vb* **1** to make full in a way or to a degree that prevents further entry or passage <*fill* a cavity in a tooth>
syn block, choke, clog, close, congest, obstruct, occlude, plug, stop, stopper
rel bar, dam, jam; ‖bung, pug
con clear, free
2 *syn* LOAD 3, charge, choke, heap, pack, pile
3 *syn* SATISFY 5, answer, fulfill, meet
4 *syn* SATIATE, cloy, glut, gorge, jade, pall, sate, ‖stall, stodge, surfeit
rel overfeed, overfill, overstuff

fille de joie *n syn* PROSTITUTE, call girl, harlot, ‖hooker, hustler, meretrix, poule, streetwalker, ‖tomato, whore

fillet *n syn* STRIP 1, band, bandeau, banding, ribbon, stripe

fill in *vb* **1** *syn* INTRODUCE 6, insert, insinuate, intercalate, interject, interpolate, interpose, throw in

2 ***syn*** INFORM 2, acquaint, advise, apprise, clue (*or* clew), notify, post, tell, warn, wise (up)

fill–in *n* ***syn*** SUBSTITUTE, alternate, locum tenens, pinch hitter, replacement, stand-in, sub, succedaneum, surrogate

film *n* **1** ***syn*** HAZE 1, brume, mist, smaze
2 ***syn*** MOVIE, cine, ‖cinema, flick, motion picture, moving picture, photoplay, picture, picture show, show

filmy *adj* characterized by fineness and delicacy of texture <*filmy* curtains>
syn diaphanous, flimsy, gauzy, gossamer, sheer, tiffany, transparent
rel dainty, delicate, fine
con coarse, heavy, opaque, rough

filthy *adj* **1** ***syn*** DIRTY 1, black, foul, grubby, impure, nasty, soily, squalid, unclean, uncleanly
rel disheveled, slipshod, sloppy, slovenly, unkempt; loathsome, offensive, repulsive, revolting, verminous; coarse, gross, obscene, ribald, vulgar
con cleaned, cleansed; clean, cleanly; neat, shipshape, tidy, trig, trim
ant immaculate, spick-and-span
2 ***syn*** OBSCENE 2, coarse, dirty, foul, indecent, nasty, raunchy, scatological, smutty, vulgar

filthy lucre *n* ***syn*** MONEY, ‖bread, cash, ‖coin, currency, dough, legal tender, loot, lucre, pelf

finagle *vb* ***syn*** ENGINEER, machinate, maneuver, wangle

final *adj* ***syn*** LAST, closing, concluding, eventual, hindmost, lag, latest, latter, terminal, ultimate
rel crowning, ending, finishing; conclusive, decisive, definitive, determinative; irrefutable, unanswerable, unappealable
con earliest, maiden, original, primary; beginning, incipient, introductory; inaugural
ant initial

finale *n* a final part or element (as of a sequence, series, or action) <the solution of the mystery forms the *finale* of the play>
syn close, conclusion, end, ending, finish, windup; *compare* END 2
rel climax, consummation, culmination; denouement, payoff; cessation, termination
con beginning, genesis, initiation, rise, start; inception, origin, root, source
ant prologue

finally *adv* ***syn*** YET 2, eventually, someday, sometime, somewhen, sooner or later, ultimately
idiom at last, at length, at long last, in the long run, when all is said and done

finance *vb* **1** ***syn*** CAPITALIZE, back, bankroll, grubstake, stake
idiom put up the money, raise the dough
2 ***syn*** ENDOW 2, fund, subsidize
rel back, bank, bankroll, grubstake, stake, underwrite; patronize, promote, sponsor, support

financial *adj* of or relating to finance <the *financial* interests of the country>
syn fiscal, monetary, pecuniary, pocket
rel business, commercial, economic

find *vb* **1** to come upon <they soon *found* what they needed>
syn catch, descry, detect, encounter, espy, hit (on *or* upon), meet (with), spot, turn up
rel discern, discover, note, sight; distinguish, identify, recognize; dig up, scare up
idiom bring to light, come up with, fall in with, lay one's finger (on *or* upon), lay one's hand (on *or* upon)
con miss, overlook, pass (over)
ant lose
2 ***syn*** GIVE 3, dish out, dispense, furnish, hand, hand over, provide, supply, transfer, turn over

find *n* **1** one of unexpected worth or merit obtained or encountered more or less by chance <the young understudy proved to be a remarkable *find*>
syn treasure, treasure trove
rel boast, gem, jewel, pride
idiom one in a thousand (*or* million)
2 ***syn*** DISCOVERY, detection, espial, strike, unearthing

find out *vb* ***syn*** DISCOVER 3, ascertain, catch on, determine, hear, learn, see, tumble, unearth

fine *n* a pecuniary penalty exacted by an authority <paid a *fine* of ten dollars>
syn amercement, forfeit, mulct, penalty
rel damages, reparation; punishment; assessment

fine *vb* ***syn*** PENALIZE, amerce, mulct
rel distrain, exact, levy, tax; confiscate, sequestrate

fine *adj* **1** marked by subtlety of perception or discrimination <I cannot follow these *fine* distinctions>
syn delicate, finespun, hairline, hairsplitting, nice, refined, subtle
rel abstruse, esoteric, recondite; cryptic, enigmatic, obscure; minute, petty, trifling
con definite, explicit, express, specific; clear, lucid, perspicuous; broad, extensive, general, generic, indefinite, wide
2 consisting of small particles <*fine* sand>
syn impalpable, powdery, pulverized
rel light, loose, porous
ant coarse
3 ***syn*** EXCELLENT, capital, ‖dandy, first-class, first-rate, first-string, five-star, superior, top, top-notch
rel beautiful, splendid; enjoyable, pleasant
idiom fine and dandy
con miserable, wretched; atrocious, awful, objectionable, unpleasant
4 ***syn*** FAIR 2, clarion, clear, cloudless, pleasant, rainless, sunny, sunshiny, unclouded, undarkened

finecomb *vb* ***syn*** SCOUR 2, beat, comb, fine-tooth-comb, forage, grub, rake, ransack, rummage, search

finery *n* dressy clothing <decked out in all her *finery*>
syn ‖best bib and tucker, bravery, frippery, full dress, ‖glad rags, regalia, Sunday best, war paint
rel apparel, clothes; foofaraw, frill, gewgaw, ornament, trimming
con rags, tatters

finespun *adj* ***syn*** FINE 1, delicate, hairline, hairsplitting, nice, refined, subtle

---

finesse *vb* ***syn*** MANIPULATE 2, beguile, exploit, jockey, maneuver, play

fine–tooth–comb *vb* ***syn*** SCOUR 2, beat, comb, fine-comb, forage, grub, rake, ransack, rummage, search

finger *vb* **1** ***syn*** TOUCH 1, feel, handle, palpate, paw
2 ***syn*** DESIGNATE 2, appoint, make, name, nominate, tap
3 ***syn*** IDENTIFY, determinate, diagnose, diagnosticate, distinguish, pinpoint, place, recognize, spot

finical *adj* ***syn*** NICE 1, dainty, fastidious, finicking, finicky, fussy, particular, pernickety, persnickety, squeamish
con slipshod, sloppy, slovenly; blowsy, dowdy, frowzy, slatternly

finicking *adj* ***syn*** NICE 1, dainty, fastidious, finical, finicky, fussy, particular, pernickety, persnickety, squeamish

finicky *adj* ***syn*** NICE 1, dainty, fastidious, finical, finicking, fussy, particular, pernickety, persnickety, squeamish

finish *vb* **1** ***syn*** CLOSE 3, complete, conclude, determine, end, halt, terminate, ultimate, wind up, wrap up
rel accomplish, achieve, effect, fulfill
idiom have done with
2 ***syn*** GO 4, consume, exhaust, expend, run through, spend, use up, wash up
3 ***syn*** KILL 1, carry off, cut off, destroy, dispatch, down, put away, scrag, slay, take off
4 ***syn*** MURDER 1, assassinate, ‖bump off, cool, do in, ‖dust off, execute, knock off, liquidate, put away

finish *n* **1** ***syn*** END 2, cease, cessation, close, closing, desistance, ending, stop, termination, terminus
2 ***syn*** FINALE, close, conclusion, end, ending, windup
3 ***syn*** ACQUIREMENT, accomplishment, achievement, acquisition, attainment
rel correctness, discrimination, propriety, refinement; elegance, grace, polish; cultivation, taste

finished *adj* **1** ***syn*** COMPLETE 4, completed, concluded, done, down, ended, terminated, through
2 ***syn*** THROUGH 3, done for, washed-up
3 ***syn*** CONSUMMATE 1, accomplished, perfected, ripe, virtuosic
rel cultivated, cultured, refined; smooth, suave, urbane; elegant, exquisite; all-around, many-sided, versatile
con imperfect, incomplete
ant crude; unfinished

finish off *vb* ***syn*** CLIMAX, cap, crown, culminate, round off, top off

finite *adj* having definite or definable limits or boundaries <a *finite* thickness>
syn bound, bounded, limited
rel confined, restricted; definable, defined, definite, determinate, fixed, terminable; exact, precise, specific
con boundless, unbounded, unlimited; absolute, complete, total
ant infinite

‖**fink** *n* ***syn*** INFORMER, betrayer, ‖canary, ‖nark, snitch, squealer, stoolie, stool pigeon, talebearer, tipster

fire *n* **1** a destructive burning <the house was destroyed by *fire*>
syn conflagration, holocaust, inferno
rel blaze, flame, flare, glare; burning, charring, scorching, searing
idiom sea of flames, sheet of fire
2 ***syn*** PASSION 6, ardor, calenture, enthusiasm, fervor, hurrah, zeal
rel animation, exhilaration, liveliness; dash, drive, energy, ginger, gusto, heartiness, pep, punch, snap, spirit, starch, verve, vigor, vim, zest, zing, zip
con languor, lassitude, lethargy, listlessness, stupor, torpidity, torpor; apathy, impassivity, phlegm

fire *vb* **1** ***syn*** LIGHT 1, enkindle, ignite, inflame, kindle
idiom set fire to, set on fire
con extinguish, quench, smother
2 to stimulate (as mental powers) to higher or more intense activity <a painting that *fired* the viewer's imagination>
syn animate, exalt, inform, inspire; *compare* PROVOKE 4
rel arouse, enliven, rouse, stir; electrify, excite; heighten, intensify; enthuse, thrill
con appall, dismay; alarm, frighten, terrify
ant daunt
3 ***syn*** DISMISS 3, ax, boot (out), bounce, ‖can, discharge, drop, kick out, sack, terminate
rel eject, expel, oust
idiom give the pink slip, give the sack, strike off the rolls
con engage; appoint, designate, elect, name
ant hire
4 ***syn*** SHOOT 1, discharge, loose
5 ***syn*** THROW 1, ‖bung, cast, fling, heave, hurl, launch, pitch, sling, toss
6 to dry or harden by subjecting to heat <*fire* bricks>
syn bake, burn, kiln

firebug *n* ***syn*** INCENDIARY, arsonist, torch

fire–new *adj* ***syn*** BRAND-NEW, mint, spang-new, spanking-new, span-new, spick-and-span

firewater *n* ***syn*** LIQUOR 2, alcohol, aqua vitae, booze, drink, grog, ‖hooch, ‖juice, spirit(s), tipple

firm *adj* **1** ***syn*** FAST 4, fixed, secure, set, tenacious, tight
2 ***syn*** STABLE 4, secure, solid, sound
3 having a texture or consistency that resists deformation by external force <*firm* flesh>
syn hard, solid
rel close, compact, dense, thick; inelastic, inflexible, rigid, stiff, unyielding; sturdy, substantial, tough
con flaccid, flimsy, floppy, limp, loose, slack, sleazy, soft, squishy
ant flabby
4 that has been established and is not usually subject to change <a *firm* price>
syn certain, fixed, set, settled, stated, stipulated
rel established, going, prevailing; consistent, stable, steady, unwavering; definite, exact, explicit, specific, undeviating; flat

con changeable, fluctuating, shaky, shifting, unsteady, variable
5 ***syn*** SURE 1, fast, secure, stable, staunch, strong
6 ***syn*** SURE 2, abiding, enduring, fixed, never-failing, steadfast, steady, unfaltering, unqualified, unwavering

firm *adv* ***syn*** HARD 7, fast, firmly, fixedly, solidly, steadfastly, tight, tightly

firm *n* ***syn*** ENTERPRISE 3, business, company, concern, establishment, house, outfit

firmament *n* ***syn*** SKY, empyrean, heaven(s), welkin

firmly *adv* **1** ***syn*** HARD 7, fast, firm, fixedly, solidly, steadfastly, tight, tightly
2 ***syn*** HARD 9, hardly, solid, solidly

firmness *n* **1** ***syn*** STABILITY, security, soundness, stableness, steadiness, strength
2 ***syn*** DECISION 2, decidedness, determination, purposefulness, purposiveness, resoluteness, resolution, resolve

first *adj* **1** being number one in a series <the *first* day of the week>
syn foremost, headmost, inaugural, initial, leading
con final, terminal, ultimate; interjacent, intermediary, intermediate, intervenient, intervening
ant last
2 preceding all others <succeeded at his *first* try>
syn earliest, initial, maiden, original, pioneer, primary, prime
rel early, pristine; primal, primogenial, primordial
con derivative, imitative, secondary
ant final
3 exceeding all others <he was the *first* statesman of his era>
syn arch, champion, chief, foremost, head, leading, premier, principal
rel eminent, highest, preeminent, primary, prime, supreme; dominant, paramount, predominant, sovereign; main, outstanding
con ancillary, auxiliary, secondary, subsidiary
ant subordinate
4 most rudimentary <had not the *first* chance of success>
syn least, slightest, smallest
rel measly, slight, slim, trifling, trivial
con considerable, goodly, significant, substantial, tolerable, worthwhile

first *adv* ***syn*** FIRSTLY, initially

first–class *adj* ***syn*** EXCELLENT, capital, fine, first-rate, first-string, five-star, prime, superior, top, top-notch
idiom in a class by itself
con fair, indifferent, middling; unexceptional, unnoteworthy, unremarkable

firsthand *adj* ***syn*** DIRECT 4, immediate, primary

firstly *adv* as the first thing to be mentioned <*firstly,* we wish to consider the economic problem>
syn first, initially
rel incipiently, originally, primarily
idiom before all (*or* anything) else, first of all, first off, to begin with
con ultimately
ant finally, lastly

first off *adv* ***syn*** AWAY 3, at once, directly, forthwith, immediately, instanter, instantly, right away, straight off, straightway

first–rate *adj* ***syn*** EXCELLENT, capital, ‖dandy, fine, first-class, five-star, prime, superior, top, top-notch
con fair, indifferent, middling, poor; unexceptional, unnoteworthy, unremarkable

first–string *adj* ***syn*** EXCELLENT, capital, famous, first-class, first-rate, five-star, prime, superior, top, top-notch

firth *n* ***syn*** INLET, arm, bay, cove, ‖creek, gulf, harbor, ‖loch, ‖lough, slough

fiscal *adj* ***syn*** FINANCIAL, monetary, pecuniary, pocket

fish *n* **1** ***syn*** FOOL 3, butt, chump, dupe, fall guy, gudgeon, gull, pigeon, sap, sucker
‖**2** ***syn*** DOLLAR, bill, ‖bone, ‖buck, ‖frogskin, ‖ironman, oner, ‖skin, ‖smacker, ‖smackeroo

fish *vb* ***syn*** HINT 4, angle

fishwife *n* ***syn*** VIRAGO, amazon, harpy, ogress, scold, shrew, termagant, vixen, Xanthippe

fishy *adj* ***syn*** DOUBTFUL 1, ambiguous, doubtable, dubious, dubitable, equivocal, problematic, suspect, suspicious, uncertain

fissure *n* **1** ***syn*** CRACK 3, chink, cleft, rift, rima, rimation, rime, split
rel abyss, chasm, gorge, ravine; breach, rent, rupture; gash, hole, opening
2 ***syn*** BREACH 3, break, fracture, rent, rift, rupture, schism, split

fist *n* ***syn*** HANDWRITING, calligraphy, chirography, ductus, hand, penmanship, script

fisticuffs *n pl* ***syn*** BOXING, prizefighting, pugilism, ring

fit *n* ***syn*** ATTACK 3, access, seizure, spell, throe, turn

fit *adj* **1** adapted to an end or use by nature or art <food *fit* for a king>
syn applicable, appropriate, apt, befitting, felicitous, fitting, happy, just, meet, proper, right, rightful, suitable; *compare* JUST 3
rel adapted, adjusted; congruous, consonant; decent, decorous; acceptable, adequate, tolerable
con improper, inadequate, inappropriate, unsuitable; false, wrong
ant unfit
2 ***syn*** ELIGIBLE, suitable
rel able, competent
3 ***syn*** GOOD 2, appropriate, convenient, meet, proper, suitable, useful
4 ***syn*** HEALTHY 1, ‖bunkum, hale, right, sane, sound, well, well-conditioned, well-liking, wholesome
idiom fit as a fiddle
ant unfit

fit *vb* **1** ***syn*** SUIT 4, agree (with), become, befit, go (together *or* with)
2 ***syn*** BELONG 1, go, set
3 ***syn*** PREPARE 1, fix, get, make, make up, ready
4 ***syn*** ADAPT, accommodate, adjust, conform, quadrate, reconcile, square, suit, tailor, tailor-make

---

fit (in) *vb* ***syn*** AGREE 4, accord, conform, correspond, dovetail, go, harmonize, jibe, square, tally

fitful *adj* lacking steadiness or regularity in course, movement, or succession <a *fitful* breeze>
syn catchy, desultory, on-again-off-again, spasmodic, sporadic, spotty
rel intermittent, interrupted, irregular, periodic, recurrent; haphazard, hit-or-miss, random; changeable, variable; capricious, inconstant, unstable
con equable, even, steady, uniform; methodical, orderly, regular, systematic
ant constant

fitly *adv* ***syn*** WELL 1, befittingly, correctly, decently, decorously, fittingly, justly, nicely, properly, rightly

fitness *n* **1** ***syn*** ORDER 10, condition, fettle, kilter, repair, shape, trim
2 ***syn*** ORDER 11, appositeness, appropriateness, aptness, expediency, meetness, propriety, rightness, suitability, suitableness
rel decency, decorum, harmony
ant unfitness
3 ***syn*** USE 3, account, advantage, applicability, appropriateness, relevance, service, serviceability, usefulness, utility

fit out *vb* ***syn*** FURNISH 1, accouter, appoint, arm, equip, gear, outfit, rig, turn out

fitted *adj* ***syn*** ASSORTED 2, adapted, conformable, matched, suited

fitting *adj* **1** ***syn*** FIT 1, applicable, appropriate, apt, felicitous, happy, just, meet, proper, suitable
rel apposite, apropos, germane, pertinent, relevant, seemly; accordant, concordant, harmonious
2 ***syn*** TRUE 7, appropriate, desired, proper

fittingly *adv* **1** ***syn*** WELL 1, befittingly, correctly, decently, decorously, fitly, justly, nicely, properly, rightly
2 ***syn*** WELL 4, acceptably, adequately, amply, appropriately, becomingly, properly, right, satisfactorily, suitably

fivefold *adj* ***syn*** QUINTUPLE, quinary

five–star *adj* ***syn*** EXCELLENT, famous, fine, first-class, first-rate, first-string, prime, superior, top, top-notch

fix *vb* **1** ***syn*** SET 1, establish, lay, place, put, settle, stick
rel stabilize, steady; decide, determine, rule; specify
con change, modify, vary
ant alter; abrogate
2 ***syn*** ENTRENCH 1, embed, infix, ingrain, lodge, root
rel inculcate, instill
con overthrow, overturn, subvert, upset
3 ***syn*** FASTEN 1, affix, attach, rivet
4 ***syn*** FASTEN 2, anchor, catch, moor, secure
con dislodge, displace
5 ***syn*** FASTEN 3, concenter, concentrate, fixate, focus, put, rivet
6 ***syn*** PREPARE 1, fit, get, make, make up, ready
7 ***syn*** MEND 2, doctor, do up, overhaul, patch, rebuild, recondition, reconstruct, repair, revamp
8 ***syn*** ADJUST 2, regulate, tune (up)
rel mend, patch, rebuild, repair; amend, emend, revise
con disorganize, unsettle
9 ***syn*** SOLVE 1, resolve, work, work out
10 ***syn*** STERILIZE, alter, castrate, change, desexualize, geld, mutilate, neuter, unsex
11 ***syn*** BRIBE, buy, buy off, have, ||lubricate, sop, square, tamper (with)

fix *n* ***syn*** PREDICAMENT, box, corner, dilemma, hole, jam, pickle, plight, scrape, spot

fixate *vb* ***syn*** FASTEN 3, concenter, concentrate, fix, focus, put, rivet

fixation *n* ***syn*** FETISH 2, mania, obsession, thing
rel craze, fascination, infatuation
idiom bee in one's bonnet

fixed *adj* **1** ***syn*** FAST 4, firm, secure, set, tenacious, tight
2 ***syn*** IMMOVABLE 1, fixed, immobile, immotile, immotive, irremovable, ||sitfast, steadfast, unmovable
3 ***syn*** DEFINITE 1, circumscribed, determinate, limited, narrow, precise, restricted
4 ***syn*** INFLEXIBLE 3, constant, immovable, immutable, inalterable, invariable, unalterable, unchangeable, unmodifiable, unmovable
5 ***syn*** FIRM 4, certain, set, settled, stated, stipulated
con changing, variable, varying
6 ***syn*** SURE 2, abiding, enduring, firm, never-failing, steadfast, steady, unfaltering, unqualified, unwavering
7 ***syn*** WHOLE 5, concentrated, exclusive, undistracted, undivided, unswerving
con distracted, erratic, wandering

fixedly *adv* ***syn*** HARD 7, fast, firm, firmly, solidly, steadfastly, tight, tightly
rel stubbornly, tenaciously

fixture *n* ***syn*** INSTITUTION

fix up *vb* ***syn*** DRESS UP 1, deck (out), doll out, doll up, gussy up, primp, slick, smarten (up), spiff, spruce (up)

fizz *vb* ***syn*** HISS, buzz, fizzle, sibilate, sizzle, swish, wheeze, whisper, whiz, whoosh

fizzle *vb* ***syn*** HISS, buzz, fizz, sibilate, sizzle, swish, wheeze, whisper, whiz, whoosh

flabbergast *vb* ***syn*** SURPRISE 2, amaze, astonish, astound, dumbfound
rel overwhelm, shock

flabby *adj* ***syn*** LIMP 1, flaccid, flimsy, floppy, sleazy
rel soft, yielding; impotent, powerless; enervated, languid, listless, spiritless
con taut, tense, tight; strong, sturdy, tenacious, tough; gritty, plucky
ant firm

flaccid *adj* ***syn*** LIMP 1, flabby, flimsy, floppy, sleazy
rel emasculated, enervated, unnerved; debilitated, enfeebled, sapped, weakened
con elastic, flexible, springy, supple; limber, lithe; energetic, lusty, nervous, vigorous
ant resilient

flag *n* a piece of fabric that is used as a symbol (as of a nation) or as a signaling device <we respect the *flag* of our fathers>
syn banderole, banner, bannerol, burgee, color, ensign, gonfalon, gonfanon, jack, oriflamme, pendant, pennant, pennon, standard, streamer

flag *vb* ***syn*** SIGNAL, gesture, motion, sign, signalize
flag *vb* **1** ***syn*** FAIL 1, decline, deteriorate, ||dwine, fade, languish, weaken
2 ***syn*** DROOP 3, sag, swag, wilt
rel abate, ebb, wane
flagellate *vb* ***syn*** WHIP 1, flog, hide, ||larrup, lash, scourge, stripe, switch, thrash, whale
flagitious *adj* ***syn*** VICIOUS 2, corrupt, degenerate, depraved, infamous, miscreant, nefarious, perverse, rotten, villainous
rel criminal, scandalous, sinful, wicked; disgraceful, shameful; flagrant, glaring, gross
con good, upstanding, virtuous
flagrant *adj* ***syn*** EGREGIOUS, capital, glaring, gross, rank
rel bold, conspicuous, obvious, striking; heinous; flagitious, wicked; disgraceful, scandalous, shameful, shocking
con hidden, inconspicuous, obscure; excusable, unimportant
flagrante delicto *adv* ***syn*** RED-HANDED, dead to rights
flag-waver *n* ***syn*** PATRIOTEER, patriot, superpatriot
flair *n* ***syn*** GIFT 2, aptness, bent, bump, faculty, genius, head, knack, talent, turn
flake (off) *vb* ***syn*** SCALE 2, desquamate, exfoliate, peel
||**flake out** *vb* ***syn*** COLLAPSE 2, break down, cave (in), drop, give out, peg out, succumb, wilt
flam *n* ***syn*** IMPOSTURE, cheat, flimflam, gyp, hoax, humbug, phony, put-on, sell, spoof
flamboyant *adj* **1** ***syn*** ORNATE, baroque, florid, luscious, rich, rococo
2 ***syn*** SHOWY, chichi, orchidaceous, ostentatious, peacockish, peacocky, pretentious, splashy, swank
flame *n* **1** ***syn*** SWEETHEART 1, beloved, darling, dear, heartthrob, honey, honeybunch, love, loveling, turtledove
2 ***syn*** GIRL FRIEND 2, ||baby, beloved, honey, inamorata, ladylove, steady, sweetheart, sweetie, truelove
3 ***syn*** BOYFRIEND 2, beau, beloved, inamorato, lover, steady, sweetheart, truelove
flame *vb* ***syn*** BLAZE, blare, flare, glare, glow
rel coruscate, glint; fire, ignite, kindle, light
flaming *adj* **1** ***syn*** BURNING 1, ablaze, afire, aflame, alight, blazing, conflagrant, fiery, flaring, ignited
2 ***syn*** IMPASSIONED, ardent, blazing, burning, fervent, fiery, hot-blooded, passionate, red-hot, white-hot
flammable *adj* ***syn*** COMBUSTIBLE 1, burnable, ignitable, inflammable
ant incombustible, nonflammable
flap *n* ***syn*** COMMOTION 2, agitation, confusion, dither, lather, pother, stew, tumult, turbulence, turmoil
flapdoodle *n* ***syn*** NONSENSE 2, blatherskite, bosh, bunkum, fiddle-faddle, flummadiddle, fudge, malarkey, poppycock, rubbish
flare *vb* ***syn*** BLAZE, blare, flame, glare, glow
rel dart, shoot; flicker, flutter
idiom burst into flame
ant gutter out
flare (up) *vb* ***syn*** ANGER 2, blow up, boil, boil over, bristle, burn, fume, rage, seethe
idiom ||blow one's stack (*or* top *or* lid), fly into a passion, fly off the handle
con calm (down), cool (off *or* down), simmer down
flare *n* ***syn*** OUTBREAK 1, burst, eruption, outburst
flare–up *n* ***syn*** OUTBURST 1, access, burst, eruption, explosion, gust, sally
flaring *adj* ***syn*** BURNING 1, ablaze, afire, aflame, alight, blazing, conflagrant, fiery, flaming, ignited
flash *vb* **1** to shoot forth light (as in rays or sparks) <lightning *flashed* in the sky>
syn coruscate, glance, gleam, glimmer, glint, glisten, glitter, scintillate, shimmer, spangle, sparkle, twinkle
rel dart, shoot; blare, blaze, burn, flame, flare, glare, glow, incandesce; blink, flicker, spark; dazzle; beam, radiate, shine
2 ***syn*** BLINK 2, flicker, twinkle
3 ***syn*** SHOW 4, brandish, display, disport, exhibit, expose, flaunt, parade, show off, trot out
flash *n* **1** a sudden brief light <saw a *flash* sweep across the sky>
syn coruscation, glance, gleam, glimmer, glint, glisten, glitter, quiver, scintillation, shimmer, sparkle, twinkle
rel blare, blaze, flame, flare, glare, glow; flicker; beam, ray
2 ***syn*** INSTANT 1, breathing, crack, ||jiff, jiffy, minute, moment, second, shake, split second
idiom half a second (*or* shake), twinkling of an eye
flashy *adj* ***syn*** GAUDY, blatant, brazen, chintzy, garish, glaring, loud, meretricious, tawdry, tinsel
rel flamboyant, florid, ornate; flashing, glittering, sparkling
con dowdy, slatternly; natural, simple, unaffected; chic, modish, smart
flat *adj* **1** ***syn*** LEVEL, even, flush, planate, plane, smooth
idiom flat as a billiard table (*or* pancake)
con rugged, scabrous, uneven; hilly, mountainous
2 ***syn*** PRONE 4, decumbent, procumbent, prostrate, reclining, recumbent
3 ***syn*** DOWNRIGHT 2, indubitable, unquestionable, up-and-down
4 ***syn*** COLORLESS 2, drab, dull, lackluster, lifeless, lusterless, prosaic, prosy
5 ***syn*** INSIPID 3, banal, bland, inane, innocuous, jejune, milk-and-water, namby-pamby, sapless, vapid
rel dull, lifeless; flavorless, stale, tasteless
6 ***syn*** UNPALATABLE 1, distasteful, flavorless, ill-flavored, insipid, savorless, tasteless, unappetizing, unsavory
7 ***syn*** POOR 1, broke, destitute, dirt poor, needy, penurious, poverty-stricken, stone-broke, stony, strapped
8 ***syn*** DULL 7, blind, dead, dim, lackluster, lusterless, mat, muted
flat *n* ***syn*** APARTMENT 1, ||chambers, lodging(s), rental, rooms, suite, tenement
||**flatfoot** *n* ***syn*** POLICEMAN, ||bull, cop, ||copper, ||fuzz, ||heat, officer, ||pig, police, police officer
flatly *adv* ***syn*** EVENLY 3, smooth, smoothly, uniformly

---

flat-out *adj* ***syn*** UTTER, absolute, blasted, damned, goldarn, out-and-out, outright, rank, straight-out, unmitigated

flat-out *adv* ***syn*** FAST 2, apace, expeditiously, hastily, lickety-split, posthaste, quickly, rapidly, speedily, swiftly

flatten *vb* **1** ***syn*** EVEN 1, flush, lay, level, plane, smooth, smoothen
2 ***syn*** FELL 1, bring down, down, floor, ground, knock down, lay low, level, mow (down), prostrate

flatter *vb* to be becoming to <a neckline designed to *flatter* the stylishly stout>
syn become, enhance, suit
rel adorn, beautify, decorate, embellish, ornament; finish, perfect
idiom put in the best light
con deface, disfigure; distort; mar, spoil

flattery *n* flattering speech or attentions <*flattery* will get you nowhere>
syn adulation, blandishment, blarney, incense, oil, soft soap
rel compliments; laud, laudation, praise; cajolery, coaxing, wheedling; fulsomeness, unctuousness; bootlicking, fawning, ingratiation, obsequiousness, sycophancy, toadying, truckling
idiom honeyed words
con censure, condemnation, criticism, reprehension, reprobation; castigation, excoriation; aspersion, insult; contempt, disdain, scorn; belittling, depreciation, derogation, detraction, disparagement

flatulent *adj* ***syn*** INFLATED, dropsical, dropsied, overblown, tumescent, tumid, turgid, windy
rel empty, hollow, vain; shallow, superficial
con weighty; cogent, compelling, convincing, telling; forceful, forcible, potent

flaunt *vb* ***syn*** SHOW 4, brandish, display, disport, exhibit, expose, flash, parade, show off, trot out
rel boast, brag, gasconade, vaunt; disclose, discover, divulge, reveal; advertise, broadcast, declare, proclaim, publish; flourish, wave
idiom dangle before the (*or* one's) eyes
con camouflage, cloak, disguise, dissemble, mask; bury, conceal, hide, screen, secrete

flavor *n* ***syn*** TASTE 3, relish, sapidity, sapor, savor, smack, tang

flavorless *adj* ***syn*** UNPALATABLE 1, distasteful, flat, ill-flavored, insipid, savorless, tasteless, unappetizing, unsavory
ant flavorsome

flavorsome *adj* ***syn*** PALATABLE, aperitive, appetizing, good-tasting, mouth-watering, relishing, sapid, savory, tasty, toothsome

---

syn synonym(s)	***rel*** related word(s)
idiom idiomatic equivalent(s)	***con*** contrasted word(s)
ant antonym(s)	* vulgar

|| use limited; if in doubt, see a dictionary
The first word in a synonym list when printed in SMALL CAPITALS shows where there is more information about the group. For a more efficient use of this book see Explanatory Notes.

con flat, insipid, vapid, wishy-washy; bland, mild; displeasing, tasteless, unflavored, unpalatable, unpleasant, unsavory
ant flavorless

flaw *n* ***syn*** BLEMISH, defect, vice
rel cleavage, rent, rip, riving, split, tear

flawed *adj* **1** ***syn*** DAMAGED, impaired, marred, spoiled
ant flawless
2 ***syn*** FAULTY, amiss, defective, imperfect, sick
ant flawless

flawless *adj* **1** ***syn*** WHOLE 1, entire, intact, perfect, sound, unblemished, unbroken, undamaged, unimpaired, unmarred
ant flawed
2 ***syn*** PERFECT 2, absolute, fleckless, impeccable, indefectible, note-perfect, unflawed
3 ***syn*** IMPECCABLE 1, errorless, exquisite, faultless, immaculate, irreproachable
con defective, faulty, flawed, imperfect, unsound
4 ***syn*** IDEAL 3, indefectible, model

flaxen *adj* ***syn*** BLOND 1, golden, straw

flay *vb* ***syn*** LAMBASTE 3, blister, castigate, excoriate, lash (into), scarify, scathe, scorch, scourge, slash
rel assail, attack, berate, tongue-lash

fleckless *adj* ***syn*** PERFECT 2, absolute, flawless, impeccable, indefectible, note-perfect, unflawed

flection *n* ***syn*** TURN 4, angle, bend, bow, flexure, turning

fledgling *n* ***syn*** NOVICE, apprentice, beginner, boot, colt, freshman, neophyte, newcomer, rookie, tyro

flee *vb* **1** ***syn*** ESCAPE 1, abscond, break, ||bunk, decamp, fly, scape
rel avoid, elude, evade, shun
idiom take a (runout) powder
2 ***syn*** RUN 2, bolt, fly, make off, scamper, scoot, ||screw, skedaddle, skip, skirr
con stand, stay

fleece *vb* **1** to obtain something valuable from by improper means <a corrupt mayor who *fleeced* the town treasury>
syn bleed, milk, mulct, rook, stick, sweat; *compare* CHEAT, EXTORT 1
rel cheat, cozen, defraud, do, hustle, ||rope (in), swindle, take; pluck
idiom sell one a bill of goods, take for a sucker, take to the cleaner's
2 ***syn*** OVERCHARGE 1, clip, skin, soak, stick

fleeceable *adj* ***syn*** EASY 3, gullible, naive, susceptible

fleecy *adj* ***syn*** HAIRY 1, hirsute, pileous, pilose, whiskered, woolly

fleer *vb* **1** ***syn*** SNEER 1, leer, ||sleer
2 ***syn*** SCOFF, flout, gibe, gird, jeer, jest, quip (at), scout (at), sneer
rel grin, smile, smirk
idiom cast in one's teeth, curl one's lip at, laugh one out of court

fleet *vb* **1** ***syn*** WHILE, beguile, wile
rel dally, fritter, idle, potter, squander, waste
2 ***syn*** FLY 4, flit, sail, sweep, wing
idiom go like the wind (*or* lightning), make (good) time
3 ***syn*** HURRY 2, flit, fly, hasten, hustle, rocket, run, speed, ||tatter

fleet *adj* ***syn*** FAST 3, breakneck, expeditious, expeditive, harefooted, hasty, quick, rapid, speedy, swift
rel agile, brisk, nimble, spry; alert, animated, lively, spirited, sprightly, vivacious

fleeting *adj* ***syn*** TRANSIENT, ephemeral, evanescent, fugacious, fugitive, momentary, passing, short-lived, transitory, volatile
con abiding, enduring, persistent
ant lasting

fleetly *adv* ***syn*** FAST 2, flat-out, full tilt, hastily, lickety-split, posthaste, quickly, rapidly, speedily, swiftly

flesh *n* ***syn*** MANKIND, Homo sapiens, humanity, humankind, man, mortality

fleshiness *n* ***syn*** OBESITY, adiposity, corpulence, fatness

fleshliness *n* ***syn*** ANIMALITY, animalism, carnality

fleshly *adj* **1** ***syn*** BODILY, carnal, corporal, corporeal, physical, somatic
2 ***syn*** CARNAL 2, animal, sensual
rel epicurean, luxurious, sensuous, sybaritic, voluptuous; lay, profane, secular, temporal
con divine, religious, spiritual; intellectual, mental, psychic

fleshy *adj* ***syn*** FAT 2, corpulent, gross, heavy, obese, overweight, porcine, portly, stout, weighty
ant emaciated

flexible *adj* ***syn*** ELASTIC 1, resilient, springy, stretch, stretchy, supple, whippy
rel amenable, docile, manageable, tractable; acquiescent, compliant
con brittle, crisp, fragile, frangible; firm, hard, rigid, stiff, unyielding, wooden; intractable, recalcitrant, refractory, ungovernable; callous, hardened, indurated
ant inflexible

flexuous *adj* ***syn*** WINDING, anfractuous, convoluted, meandering, meandrous, serpentine, sinuous, snaky, tortuous

flexure *n* ***syn*** TURN 4, angle, bend, bow, flection, turning

flibbertigibbet *n* ***syn*** SCATTERBRAIN, birdbrain, featherbrain, featherhead, harebrain, rattlebrain, rattlehead, shatterbrain

flick *n* ***syn*** MOVIE, cine, ‖cinema, film, motion picture, moving picture, photoplay, picture, picture show, show

flicker *vb* **1** ***syn*** FLIT 2, dance, flitter, flutter, hover
2 ***syn*** BLINK 2, flash, twinkle
rel fluctuate, oscillate, swing, vibrate, waver; blaze, flame, flare, glare; coruscate, glance, gleam, glint, glitter, sparkle; quaver, quiver, tremble

flier *n* ***syn*** PILOT 2, airman, aviator, birdman, fly-boy

flight *n* ***syn*** ESCAPE 1, breakout, escapement, escaping, getaway, lam, ‖scape, slip

flightiness *n* ***syn*** LIGHTNESS, flippancy, frivolity, levity, light-mindedness, volatility
rel capriciousness, fickleness, inconstancy, instability, mercurialness
con constancy, equableness, steadfastness
ant steadiness

flighty *adj* ***syn*** GIDDY 1, dizzy, empty-headed, featherbrained, frivolous, harebrained, rattlebrained, scatterbrained, silly, skittish
rel changeable, inconstant, mercurial, unstable; buoyant, effervescent, volatile; gay, lively, sprightly; irresponsible
con constant, dependable, reliable, responsible, trustworthy; stable; sedate
ant steady

flimflam *n* **1** ***syn*** IMPOSTURE, cheat, deceit, fake, fraud, hoax, humbug, sell, sham, swindle
2 ***syn*** NONSENSE 2, balderdash, ‖bull, double-talk, drivel, eyewash, hokum, hot air, jazz, moonshine

flimflam *vb* **1** ***syn*** DUPE, bamboozle, befool, chicane, fool, gull, hoax, hoodwink, hornswoggle, pigeon
2 ***syn*** CHEAT, beat, bilk, chouse, cozen, defraud, diddle, do, gyp, overreach

flimflammer *n* ***syn*** SWINDLER, cheat, con man, defrauder, diddler, double-dealer, ‖grifter, gyp, sharper, skin

flimsy *adj* **1** ***syn*** FILMY, diaphanous, gauzy, gossamer, sheer, tiffany, transparent
2 ***syn*** IMPLAUSIBLE, improbable, inconceivable, incredible, thin, unbelievable, unconceivable, unconvincing, unsubstantial, weak
ant substantial
3 ***syn*** DELICATE 5, slight
4 ***syn*** WEAK 1, decrepit, feeble, fragile, frail, infirm, insubstantial, unsound, unsubstantial, weakly
ant sturdy
5 ***syn*** LIMP 1, flabby, flaccid, floppy, sleazy

flinch *vb* ***syn*** RECOIL, blanch, blench, quail, shrink, squinch, start, wince
rel avoid, elude, escape, eschew, evade, shun; retire, withdraw; recede, retreat

fling *vb* **1** ***syn*** RUSH 1, boil, bolt, charge, chase, dash, lash, race, shoot, tear
2 ***syn*** THROW 1, ‖bung, cast, fire, heave, hurl, launch, pitch, sling, toss
con catch, grab, receive

fling *n* **1** a casual attempt <I'm willing to take a *fling* at almost any job>
syn crack, go, pop, shot, slap, stab, ‖stagger, try, whack, whirl
rel attempt, effort, essay, trial
con best, limit, maximum
ant utmost
2 ***syn*** SPREE 1, binge, orgy, rampage, splurge

flip (through) *vb* ***syn*** BROWSE, dip (into), glance (at *or* over), leaf (through), riff (through), riffle (through), run (through *or* over), scan, skim (through), thumb (through)

flippancy *n* ***syn*** LIGHTNESS, flightiness, frivolity, levity, light-mindedness, volatility
rel archness, pertness, sauciness; impishness, mischievousness, playfulness, roguishness, waggishness; cheekiness, cockiness, freshness
con earnestness, gravity, soberness, solemnity
ant seriousness

---

flirt *vb* ***syn*** TRIFLE 1, coquet, dally, fool, lead on, string along, toy, wanton
rel disport, play, sport; caress, fondle, pet

flirt *n* a woman who trifles amorously <a charming girl but an outrageous *flirt*>
syn coquette, vamp

flit *vb* **1** ***syn*** HURRY 2, fleet, fly, hasten, run, rush, speed, ‖tatter, whiz, zip
2 to move briskly, irregularly, and usually intermittently <the hummingbird *flitted* from flower to flower>
syn dance, flicker, flitter, flutter, hover
rel dart, float, fly, scud, skim
3 ***syn*** FLY 4, fleet, sail, sweep, wing

flitter *vb* ***syn*** FLIT 2, dance, flicker, flutter, hover
rel quaver, quiver, teeter

float *vb* **1** ***syn*** DRIFT 1, ride, wash
2 ***syn*** HANG 3, hover, poise
3 ***syn*** FLY 1, dart, sail, scud, shoot, skim, skirr
rel drift, waft

floater *n* ***syn*** VAGABOND, ‖bindle stiff, bum, derelict, drifter, hobo, street arab, tramp, vag, vagrant

flock *n* **1** ***syn*** MULTITUDE 1, army, cloud, crowd, host, legion, rout, scores
2 ***syn*** DROVE 2, ‖drift, herd

flog *vb* ***syn*** WHIP 1, flagellate, hide, ‖larrup, lash, lather, scourge, stripe, thrash, whale

flood *n* **1** ***syn*** FLOW, current, drift, flux, rush, spate, stream, tide
2 a great or overwhelming flow of or as if of water <a *flood* of messages>
syn cataclysm, cataract, deluge, flooding, inundation, niagara, overflow, pour, spate, torrent
rel current, flow, stream, tide; excess, superfluity, surplus; outgushing, outpouring
con dribble, drip, dropping
ant trickle

flood *vb* **1** ***syn*** DELUGE 1, drown, engulf, inundate, overflow, overwhelm, submerge, swamp, whelm
2 ***syn*** DELUGE 3, overwhelm, swamp, whelm

flooding *n* ***syn*** FLOOD 2, cataclysm, cataract, deluge, inundation, niagara, overflow, pour, spate, torrent

floor *vb* ***syn*** FELL 1, bowl (down *or* over), bring down, down, drop, flatten, ground, knock down, lay low, level

floozy *n* ***syn*** DOXY 1, ‖chippy, grisette, light-o'-love, nymph, nymphet, party girl, roundheel, tart, ‖tootsie

‖**flop** *vb* **1** ***syn*** RETIRE 4, bed, pile (in), roll in, turn in
2 ***syn*** FAIL 4, flummox, wash out
con come off, go over, succeed

flop *n* ***syn*** FAILURE 5, bomb, bust, dud, lemon, loser

floppy *adj* ***syn*** LIMP 1, flabby, flaccid, flimsy, sleazy

florid *adj* **1** ***syn*** RHETORICAL, aureate, bombastic, declamatory, euphuistic, flowery, grandiloquent, magniloquent, overblown, sonorous
2 ***syn*** ORNATE, baroque, flamboyant, luscious, rich, rococo
rel ostentatious, pretentious, showy
con bald, bare, barren; austere, unadorned
3 ***syn*** RUDDY 1, flush, flushed, full-blooded, glowing, rubicund, sanguine
ant pallid

florilegium *n* ***syn*** ANTHOLOGY, album, ana, analects, garland, miscellany, omnibus, posy

floss *n* ***syn*** DOWN, flue, fluff, fur, fuzz, lint, pile

flotsam *n* ***syn*** DRIFTWOOD, jetsam, wreckage

flounce *vb* ***syn*** SASHAY, mince, prance, ‖prink, strut

flounder *vb* ***syn*** WALLOW 2, blunder, lurch, stumble
rel strive, struggle; labor, toil, travail

flourish *vb* ***syn*** SUCCEED 3, arrive, go, make out, prosper, score, thrive
rel bloom, blossom, flower; augment, increase, multiply; amplify, expand; develop, grow, wax
con shrivel, wither; contract, shrink; abate, ebb, subside, wane
ant languish

flourishing *adj* enjoying a vigorous growth <a *flourishing* economy>
syn booming, prospering, prosperous, roaring, robust, thrifty, thriving; *compare* SUCCESSFUL
rel vigorous; rampant, rank; exuberant, lush, luxuriant, profuse
idiom going strong, in full swing
con decadent, declining, deteriorating; failing; decreasing, dwindling
ant languishing

flout *vb* ***syn*** SCOFF, fleer, gibe, gird, jeer, jest, quip (at), scout (at), sneer
rel disregard, slight; repudiate, spurn; insult; defy
idiom thumb one's nose at
con admire, esteem, regard, respect
ant revere

flow *vb* **1** ***syn*** POUR 2, gush, roll, sluice, stream, surge
rel cascade, jet, spout, spurt; well; course, ripple, run
2 ***syn*** SPRING 1, arise, derive (from), emanate, head, issue, originate, proceed, rise, stem
3 ***syn*** TEEM, abound, crawl, pullulate, ‖sny, swarm
4 ***syn*** DISCHARGE 5, disembogue, emit, give off, pour, void

flow *n* something suggestive of running water <she expressed herself in a *flow* of words>
syn current, drift, flood, flux, rush, spate, stream, tide
rel progression, sequence, series, succession; continuance, continuation, continuity

flower *n* **1** the often showy part of a seed plant that bears reproductive organs <children picking *flowers* in the meadow>
syn bloom, blossom, posy
rel bud, floret; shoot, spray
2 ***syn*** BEST, choice, cream, elite, fat, pick, pride, prime, prize, top
3 ***syn*** ARISTOCRACY, aristoi, elite, gentility, gentry, optimacy, quality, society, upper class, upper crust

flower *vb* ***syn*** BLOSSOM, bloom, blow, burgeon, effloresce, outbloom

---

syn synonym(s) — *rel* related word(s)
idiom idiomatic equivalent(s) — *con* contrasted word(s)
ant antonym(s) — * vulgar
‖ use limited; if in doubt, see a dictionary
The first word in a synonym list when printed in SMALL CAPITALS shows where there is more information about the group. For a more efficient use of this book see Explanatory Notes.

flowering *n* ***syn*** DEVELOPMENT, evolution, evolvement, growth, progress, progression, unfolding, upgrowth
ant fading

flowery *adj* ***syn*** RHETORICAL, aureate, bombastic, declamatory, euphuistic, grandiloquent, magniloquent, overblown, sonorous, swollen
rel diffuse, prolix, redundant, verbose, wordy
con compendious, concise, laconic, pithy, succinct, summary, terse

flowing *adj* ***syn*** EASY 9, cursive, effortless, fluent, running, smooth

flub *vb* ***syn*** BOTCH, ||blow, bollix, bungle, fluff, goof (up), louse up, mess, muff, ||screw (up)

fluctuant *adj* **1** ***syn*** WEAK 2, dickey, insecure, rootless, shaky, unstable, unsure, vacillating, wavering, wobbly
2 ***syn*** UNCERTAIN 1, capricious, chancy, erratic, iffy, incalculable, unpredictable, whimsical

flue *n* ***syn*** DOWN, floss, fluff, fur, fuzz, lint, pile

fluent *adj* **1** ***syn*** VOCAL 3, articulate, eloquent, smooth-spoken
rel loquacious, talkative; easy, effortless, facile, smooth; apt, prompt, quick, ready
con stammering, stuttering; tongue-tied; dumb; fettered, hampered, trammeled
2 ***syn*** EASY 9, cursive, effortless, flowing, running, smooth

fluff *n* **1** ***syn*** DOWN, floss, flue, fur, fuzz, lint, pile
2 ***syn*** ERROR 2, blooper, blunder, boner, bull, bungle, lapse, mistake, slip, trip

fluff *vb* ***syn*** BOTCH, ||blow, bollix, bungle, flub, goof (up), louse up, mess, muff, ||screw (up)

fluid *adj* ***syn*** CHANGEABLE 1, changeful, mobile, mutable, protean, unsettled, unstable, unsteady, variable, weathery

fluky *adj* ***syn*** ACCIDENTAL, casual, chance, contingent, fortuitous, incidental, odd

flummadiddle *n* ***syn*** NONSENSE 2, balderdash, bilge, blatherskite, bushwa, malarkey, pishposh, poppycock, rubbish, twaddle

flummox *vb* ***syn*** FAIL 4, ||flop, wash out

flurry *n* ***syn*** STIR 1, ado, bustle, furore, fuss, pother, whirl, whirlpool, whirlwind
rel confusion, excitement, turbulence, turmoil; haste, hurry

flurry *vb* ***syn*** DISCOMPOSE 1, agitate, bother, discombobulate, disquiet, disturb, fluster, perturb, unhinge, upset
rel bewilder, distract, perplex; excite, galvanize, provoke, quicken, stimulate

flush *n* **1** ***syn*** BLOOM 3, blossom, blush, glow
2 ***syn*** BLOOM 2, blossom

flush *vb* **1** ***syn*** BLUSH, color, crimson, glow, mantle, pink, pinken, redden, rose, rouge
2 ***syn*** EVEN 1, flatten, lay, level, plane, smooth, smoothen

flush *adj* **1** ***syn*** RICH 1, affluent, moneyed, ||oofy, opulent, wealthy
2 ***syn*** RUDDY 1, florid, flushed, full-blooded, glowing, rubicund, sanguine
3 ***syn*** LEVEL, even, flat, planate, plane, smooth

flushed *adj* ***syn*** RUDDY 1, florid, flush, full-blooded, glowing, rubicund, sanguine

fluster *vb* **1** ***syn*** DISCOMPOSE 1, agitate, bother, discombobulate, disquiet, disturb, flurry, perturb, unhinge, upset
rel bewilder, confound, distract, mystify, nonplus, perplex, puzzle; addle, confuse, fuddle, muddle
ant steady
2 ***syn*** CONFUSE 2, addle, ball up, befuddle, bewilder, ||bumfuzzle, distract, dizzy, fuddle, muddle

flutter *vb* ***syn*** FLIT 2, dance, flicker, flitter, hover
rel quaver, quiver, shake, tremble, wobble; beat, palpitate, pulsate, throb; fluctuate, oscillate, swing, vibrate; flap

flux *n* **1** ***syn*** DIARRHEA, ||backdoor trots, dysentery, ||runs, scour(s), *shits, ||squirts, *trots
2 ***syn*** FLOW, current, drift, flood, rush, spate, stream, tide

flux *vb* ***syn*** LIQUEFY, deliquesce, dissolve, fuse, liquesce, melt, run, thaw

fly *vb* **1** to pass lightly or quickly over or above a surface <clouds *flying* across the sky>
syn dart, float, sail, scud, shoot, skim, skirr
rel dance, flicker, flit, flitter, flutter, hover; arise, ascend, mount, rise, soar; glide, slide, slip
2 ***syn*** RUN 2, bolt, flee, make off, scamper, scoot, ||screw, skedaddle, skip, skirr
rel hide; retreat, withdraw
3 ***syn*** ESCAPE 1, abscond, break, ||bunk, decamp, flee, scape
4 to pass swiftly as if on wings <how time *flies* when we are happy>
syn fleet, flit, sail, sweep, wing
rel soar; hasten, hurry, speed; barrel, skim, whisk, whiz, zip; breeze, dart, dash, rush, tear
idiom go like the wind (*or* lightning), outstrip the wind
con dally, dawdle, dillydally, drift; lag, linger, loiter, trail; crawl, creep, poke
ant drag
5 ***syn*** HURRY 2, flit, hasten, highball, hotfoot, hustle, run, rush, speed, whish

fly–boy *n* ***syn*** PILOT 2, airman, aviator, birdman, flier

fly–by–night *adj* ***syn*** UNRELIABLE 1, dubious, questionable, trustless, undependable, unsure, untrustworthy, untrusty

flying colors *n pl* ***syn*** SUCCESS, arrival, ||do, go, prosperity, successfulness

flyspeck *n* ***syn*** POINT 11, dot, mote, speck

foam *n* a mass of bubbles gathering in or on the surface of a liquid or something as insubstantial as such a mass <a *foam* of delicate lace at her throat>
syn froth, lather, spume, suds, yeast

fob off *vb* ***syn*** FOIST 3, palm (on *or* upon), palm off, pass off, work off

---

syn synonym(s) — ***rel*** related word(s)
idiom idiomatic equivalent(s) — ***con*** contrasted word(s)
ant antonym(s) — * vulgar
|| use limited; if in doubt, see a dictionary
The first word in a synonym list when printed in SMALL CAPITALS shows where there is more information about the group. For a more efficient use of this book see Explanatory Notes.

focal point *n* ***syn*** CENTER 2, focus, heart, hub, nerve center, polestar, seat

focus *n* ***syn*** CENTER 2, focal point, heart, hub, nerve center, polestar, seat
idiom center of attraction (*or* interest), focus of attention

focus *vb* **1** ***syn*** FASTEN 3, concenter, concentrate, fix, fixate, put, rivet
2 ***syn*** CONVERGE, concenter, concentrate, meet
idiom come to a focus

foe *n* ***syn*** ENEMY
con associate, companion, comrade
ant friend

fog *n* ***syn*** HAZE 2, befuddlement, daze, ||maze, muddledness, muddleheadedness, muddlement

fog *vb* **1** ***syn*** OBSCURE, becloud, bedim, befog, cloud, darken, dim, eclipse, obfuscate, overcloud
rel bewilder, distract, mystify, perplex, puzzle
2 ***syn*** CONFUSE 4, becloud, befog, blur, cloud, muddy
rel addle, muddle

foggy *adj* ***syn*** HAZY, cloudy, misty, mushy, vague, vaporous, vapory
idiom in a fog

fogram *n* ***syn*** FOGY, antediluvian, fossil, fuddy-duddy, mid-Victorian, mossback, square, stick-in-the-mud

fogy *n* a person who is behind the times or overconservative <his father is an old *fogy*>
syn antediluvian, fogram, fossil, fuddy-duddy, mid-Victorian, mossback, square, stick-in-the-mud
rel conservative, diehard; back number
idiom regular old fogy
ant modern

fogyish *adj* ***syn*** CONSERVATIVE 1, die-hard, old-line, orthodox, reactionary, right, tory, traditionalistic
ant up-to-the-minute

foible *n* ***syn*** FAULT 2, failing, frailty, vice
rel imperfection, shortcoming

foil *vb* ***syn*** FRUSTRATE 1, baffle, balk, beat, bilk, buffalo, circumvent, dash, disappoint, thwart
rel discomfit, disconcert, embarrass, faze, rattle; curb, restrain

foist *vb* **1** ***syn*** INSINUATE 3, edge in, infiltrate, work in, worm
2 ***syn*** IMPOSE 4, wish
3 to pass or offer (something spurious) as genuine or worthy <his theory was far more reasonable than many *foisted* on the public>
syn fob off, palm (on *or* upon), palm off, pass off, work off; *compare* IMPOSE 4
rel beguile, deceive, delude, mislead; bamboozle, dupe, gull, hoax, hoodwink, trick; cheat, defraud, overreach, swindle; impose, inflict, wish

fold *n* ***syn*** WRINKLE, corrugation, crease, crinkle, furrow, plica, ridge, rimple, rivel, ruck

fold *vb* **1** ***syn*** DOUBLE 2
2 ***syn*** FAIL 5, break, bust, crash

fold up *vb* **1** ***syn*** GIVE 12, bend, break, cave, collapse, crumple, go, yield
2 ***syn*** RUIN 3, bankrupt, break, bust, impoverish, pauper, pauperize

foliage *n* the leaves of plants <a tree with handsome *foliage*>
syn leafage, umbrage, verdure
rel greenness, herbage; growth, vegetation

folk *n* **1** ***syn*** FAMILY 1, clan, house, kindred, lineage, race, stock, tribe
2 folks *pl* ***syn*** FAMILY 2, house, household, ménage

folklore *n* ***syn*** LORE 2, legend, myth, mythology, mythos, tradition

follow *vb* **1** to come after in time <a juggling act *followed* the singer>
syn ensue, succeed, supervene
rel displace, replace, supersede, supplant; postdate
con herald, lead, preface, usher (in); antedate, predate
ant precede
2 to go after or on the track of <*followed* the boys to their hiding place>
syn chase, chivy, pursue, trail; *compare* TAIL
rel trace, track; hunt, search, seek; dog, hound, tag; accompany, attend, convoy; ape, copy, imitate; exercise, practice
con guide, lead, pilot, steer; elude, escape, evade; abandon, desert
ant precede; forsake
3 ***syn*** OBEY, comply, conform, keep, mind, observe
4 ***syn*** APPREHEND 1, accept, catch, comprehend, ||dig, grasp, see, take, take in, understand

follower *n* one who attaches himself to another <he is a born *follower*>
syn adherent, cohort, disciple, henchman, partisan, satellite, sectary, sectator, supporter
rel addict, devotee, freak, habitué, votary; admirer, fan, fancier; advocate; bootlicker, hanger-on, lickspittle, parasite, sycophant, toady
ant leader

following *adj* ***syn*** NEXT, coming, ensuing

following *n* **1** ***syn*** ENTOURAGE, retinue, suite, train
2 the body of persons who attach themselves to another especially as disciples, patrons, or admirers <he has a strong *following* in this country>
syn audience, clientage, clientele, public

following *prep* ***syn*** AFTER 2, behind, below, next, since, subsequent to

folly *n* ***syn*** FOOLISHNESS, absurdity, craziness, dottiness, inanity, insanity, preposterousness, senselessness, silliness, witlessness
rel fatuity, stupidity
ant wisdom

foment *vb* ***syn*** INCITE, abet, instigate, provoke, raise, set, set on, stir (up), whip (up)
rel goad, spur; cultivate, foster, nurse, nurture
con repress, suppress
ant quell

fomenter *n* ***syn*** INSTIGATOR, agitator, inciter, mover

fond *adj* **1** ***syn*** OPTIMISTIC, Pollyannaish, sanguine, upbeat
2 ***syn*** LOVING, affectionate, dear, devoted, doting, lonesome

---

syn synonym(s) — ***rel*** related word(s)
idiom idiomatic equivalent(s) — ***con*** contrasted word(s)
ant antonym(s) — * vulgar
|| use limited; if in doubt, see a dictionary
The first word in a synonym list when printed in SMALL CAPITALS shows where there is more information about the group. For a more efficient use of this book see Explanatory Notes.

rel responsive, romantic, sentimental, sympathetic, tender, warm; indulgent
idiom silly over

fondle *vb* *syn* CARESS, cosset, cuddle, dandle, love, pet
rel clasp, embrace, hug; nestle, snuggle

fondness *n* **1** *syn* LOVE 1, affection, attachment, devotion
2 *syn* APPETITE 3, inclination, liking, soft spot, taste, weakness
rel partiality, predilection; relish
con disgust; hate

font name *n* *syn* GIVEN NAME, baptismal name, Christian name, forename, personal name, prename

food *n* **1** things that are edible <conserve a nation's supply of *food*>
syn bread, ‖chow, comestibles, ‖eats, edibles, feed, foodstuff, grub, meat, ‖muckamuck, nurture, provender, provisions, scoff, ‖tuck, viands, victuals, vivres
2 material which feeds and supports the mind or spirit <*food* for thought>
syn aliment, nourishment, nutriment, pabulum, pap, sustenance

foodstuff *n* *syn* FOOD 1, bread, ‖chow, comestibles, ‖eats, edibles, feed, grub, nurture, provender

foofaraw *n* *syn* COMMOTION 3, brouhaha, ‖catouse, coil, furore, fuss, hurrah, ruckus, rumpus, shindy

fool *n* **1** a person lacking in judgment or prudence <stop acting like a *fool*>
syn ass, asshead, *damfool, donkey, doodle, idiot, imbecile, jackass, jerk, madman, mooncalf, nincom, nincompoop, ninny, ninnyhammer, poop, ‖schmo, ‖schmuck, tomfool
rel blockhead, dimwit, dope, dumbbell, dummy, nitwit, numskull, pinhead; birdbrain, featherbrain, featherhead, rattlebrain, scatterbrain; goose, silly
2 a retainer formerly kept to provide casual entertainment <a king's *fool*>
syn idiot, jester, motley
rel buffoon, clown, comedian, comic, merry-andrew
3 one who is victimized or made to appear foolish <he's nobody's *fool*>
syn butt, chump, ‖come-on, ‖cull, dupe, easy mark, fall guy, fish, gudgeon, gull, mark, monkey, ‖mug, patsy, pigeon, sap, saphead, ‖schlemiel, simple, sucker, victim
rel pushover; laughingstock; loser; instrument, tool
4 one who is mentally deficient <a badly retarded child, little more than a *fool*>
syn ament, cretin, ‖feeb, half-wit, idiot, imbecile, moron, natural, simpleton, softhead, underwit, zany

fool *vb* **1** *syn* TRIFLE 1, coquet, dally, flirt, lead on, string along, toy, wanton
2 *syn* MEDDLE, busybody, butt in, horn in, interfere, interlope, intermeddle, ‖make, monkey (with), tamper (with)
3 *syn* BANTER, fun, jest, ‖jive, jolly, josh, kid, rag, razz, rib
4 *syn* DUPE, bamboozle, befool, chicane, flimflam, gull, hoax, hoodwink, hornswoggle, trick

fool (around) *vb* *syn* PHILANDER, mess around, play (around), wolf, womanize

fool (away) *vb* *syn* WASTE 2, blow, blunder (away), consume, dissipate, fritter, frivol away, squander, throw away, trifle (away)

foolhardy *adj* *syn* ADVENTUROUS, adventuresome, audacious, daredevil, daring, rash, reckless, temerarious, venturesome, venturous
rel headlong, impetuous, precipitate
con calculating, cautious, circumspect; careful, prudent
ant wary

fooling *n* *syn* HORSEPLAY, high jinks, roughhouse, roughhousing, rowdiness, skylarking

foolish *adj* **1** *syn* SIMPLE 3, asinine, brainless, fatuous, senseless, silly, unwitty, weak-headed, weak-minded, witless
rel idiotic, imbecilic, moronic; daft, feebleminded, half-witted; ‖half-assed, half-cocked; irrational
con bright, clever, intelligent, quick-witted
ant smart
2 felt to be ridiculous because not exhibiting good or conventional sense <a *foolish* investment>
syn absurd, ‖balmy, crazy, ‖dilly, ‖dippy, donkeyish, dotty, fantastic, harebrained, idleheaded, insane, loony, loopy, lunatic, mad, ‖potty, preposterous, sappy, silly, tomfool, unearthly, wacky
rel laughable, ludicrous, ridiculous; half-baked, headless, jerky, nonsensical; offbeat, unacceptable, unconventional, unorthodox
con judicious, sage, sapient; discreet, foresighted, prudent; canny, shrewd, slick
ant sensible; wise

foolishness *n* the quality or state of being foolish <the *foolishness* of so many of her schemes>
syn absurdity, craziness, dottiness, folly, inanity, insanity, lunacy, preposterousness, senselessness, silliness, witlessness
rel imprudence, indiscretion, injudiciousness, insensibility, unwiseness; irrationality, unreasonableness; impracticality; absurdness, ludicrousness, ridiculousness; bull, bunk, nonsense
con discretion, judiciousness, prudence, sensibility, wiseness; rationality, reasonableness; practicality; soundness; canniness, shrewdness
ant sense, wisdom

foot *n* *syn* BOTTOM 3, base, nadir

foot *vb* *syn* ADD 2, cast, figure, sum, summate, tot, total, totalize, tote

foot (it) *vb* **1** *syn* DANCE 1, hoof (it), prance, step, tread
2 *syn* WALK 1, ambulate, hoof, pace, step, traipse, tread, troop

footing *n* **1** *syn* BASIS 1, base, bedrock, foundation, ground, groundwork, infrastructure, substratum, underpinning, warrant
2 *syn* STATUS 1, capacity, character, place, position, rank, situation, standing, state, station
3 *syn* BASE 1, basement, bottom, foundation, groundwork, seat, seating, substructure, underpinning, understructure

---

syn synonym(s) *rel* related word(s)
idiom idiomatic equivalent(s) *con* contrasted word(s)
ant antonym(s) * vulgar
‖ use limited; if in doubt, see a dictionary
The first word in a synonym list when printed in SMALL CAPITALS shows where there is more information about the group. For a more efficient use of this book see Explanatory Notes.

4 ***syn*** TERM 5, standing

footlicker *n* ***syn*** SYCOPHANT, bootlick, bootlicker, ‖clawback, lickspit, lickspittle, spaniel, toad, toadeater, toady

footlights *n pl* ***syn*** DRAMA, boards, (the) stage, theater

footprint *n* the mark or impression made by a foot <*footprints* in the sand>
syn footstep, spoor, step, track, tract, vestige
rel sign, trace; pug, pugmark

footslog *vb* ***syn*** PLOD 1, ‖plodge, plunther, slog, slop, stodge, toil, ‖trash, trudge

footstep *n* ***syn*** FOOTPRINT, spoor, step, track, tract, vestige

footstone *n* ***syn*** TOMBSTONE, grave marker, gravestone, headstone, ledger, monument

foozle *vb* ***syn*** BOTCH, bitch (up), blunder, bobble, boggle, bollix, bungle, fumble, gum (up), louse up

fop *n* a man who is conspicuously fashionable or elegant in dress or appearance <felt contempt for the mincing overdressed *fop*>
syn Beau Brummel, blood, buck, coxcomb, dandy, dude, exquisite, gallant, lounge lizard, macaroni, petit-maître, popinjay
rel fashion plate, silk stocking; blade, cavalier, man-about-town, spark, sport, swell; ladies' man, lady-killer, masher
idiom man of the world

for *prep* **1** ***syn*** TO 5
2 on the side of <I'm *for* Smith all the way>
syn in favor of, pro, with
con anti, contra
ant against
3 ***syn*** AFTER 1, from

for *conj* ***syn*** BECAUSE, as, as long as, ‖being, 'cause, considering, inasmuch as, now, since, whereas

forage *vb* ***syn*** SCOUR 2, beat, comb, finecomb, fine-tooth-comb, grub, rake, ransack, rummage, search

forager *n* ***syn*** MARAUDER, freebooter, looter, pillager, plunderer, raider, ravager, ravisher, sacker, spoiler

foray *vb* **1** ***syn*** INVADE 1, inroad, overrun, overswarm, raid
2 ***syn*** RAID 1, harass, harry, maraud

foray *n* ***syn*** INVASION, incursion, inroad, irruption, raid

forbear *vb* **1** ***syn*** FORGO, eschew, sacrifice
rel bridle, curb, inhibit, restrain; avoid, escape, evade, shun; cease, desist
2 ***syn*** REFRAIN 1, abstain, keep, withhold
rel bear, endure, suffer, tolerate

forbearance *n* **1** ***syn*** PATIENCE, longanimity, long-suffering, patientness, resignation, uncomplainingness
rel restraint, temperance; endurance
2 the quality of being forbearing <she is known for her *forbearance* with children>
syn clemency, indulgence, lenience, leniency, mercifulness, tolerance, toleration; *compare* MERCY
rel longanimity, long-suffering, patience; charity, grace, lenity, mercy
con firmness, inflexibility, rigidity, sternness, strictness; austerity, harshness, inexorability
ant vindictiveness

forbearing *adj* disinclined to be severe or rigorous <*forbearing* toward her husband's weaknesses>
syn charitable, clement, easy, indulgent, lenient, merciful, tolerant
rel gentle, mild; longanimous, long-suffering, patient; considerate, thoughtful
con grim, implacable, merciless, relentless; impatient, nervous, restive; firm, inflexible, rigid, stern, strict; austere, harsh
ant unrelenting

forbid *vb* to debar one from using, doing, or entering or something from being used, done, or entered <smoking is *forbidden* here> <security regulations *forbid* the entry of unauthorized persons>
syn ban, enjoin, inhibit, interdict, outlaw, prohibit, taboo
rel debar, exclude, rule out, shut out; estop, obviate, preclude, prevent; forestall; proscribe, veto; check, curb, halt, restrain, stop; bar, block, hinder, impede, obstruct
con allow, let, suffer; authorize, license; approve, endorse, sanction; command, order; abide, bear, endure, tolerate
ant permit; bid

forbiddance *n* ***syn*** TABOO, ban, interdiction, prohibition, proscription

forbidden *adj* not permitted or allowed <accepting bribes is *forbidden*>
syn banned, prohibited, verboten
ant permitted

force *n* **1** ***syn*** POWER 4, arm, beef, energy, might, muscle, potency, sinew, strength, strong arm
rel pressure, strain, stress, tension; headway, impetus, momentum, speed, velocity; vigor
2 ***syn*** POINT 3, cogency, effectiveness, punch, validity, validness
3 forces *pl* ***syn*** TROOP 2, armed forces, military, servicemen
4 the exercise of power in order to impose one's will on a person or to have one's will with a thing <move a huge boulder by main *force*>
syn coercion, compulsion, constraint, duress, violence
rel fierceness, intensity, vehemence; effort, exertions, pains, trouble
con compliance, submission, yielding; impotence, powerlessness, weakness
ant forcelessness

force *vb* **1** ***syn*** RAPE, defile, deflorate, deflower, outrage, ravish, spoil, violate
2 to cause a person or thing to yield to pressure <hunger *forced* him to steal the food>
syn coerce, compel, concuss, constrain, make, oblige, shotgun
rel drive, impel, move; command, enjoin, order; demand, exact, require; press, pressure, sandbag; cause, occasion

---

syn synonym(s) — *rel* related word(s)
idiom idiomatic equivalent(s) — *con* contrasted word(s)
ant antonym(s) — * vulgar
‖ use limited; if in doubt, see a dictionary
The first word in a synonym list when printed in SMALL CAPITALS shows where there is more information about the group. For a more efficient use of this book see Explanatory Notes.

con blandish, cajole, coax, wheedle; get, induce, persuade, prevail; entice, inveigle, lure, seduce, tempt

force (on *or* upon) *vb* ***syn*** INFLICT 2, impose, visit, wreak, wreck

‖**force** *n* ***syn*** WATERFALL, cascade, cataract, chute, fall(s), sault, spout

forced *adj* produced or kept up through effort <a *forced* laugh>
syn farfetched, labored, strained
rel coerced, compelled, constrained; artificial, factitious; unnatural; inflexible, rigid, stiff, wooden; exhausting, fatiguing
con easy, effortless, smooth; impulsive, instinctive, spontaneous; artless, natural, normal, unaffected, unsophisticated
ant unforced

forceful *adj* **1** ***syn*** POWERFUL 2, forcible, mighty, potent, puissant
rel compelling, constraining; manful, virile; cogent, telling
con decrepit, frail, infirm
ant feeble
2 ***syn*** EMPHATIC, assertive, insistent, resounding

forcefully *adv* ***syn*** HARD 1, energetically, forcibly, hardly, might and main, mightily, powerfully, strongly, vigorously

forceless *adj* ***syn*** WEAK 4, boneless, emasculate, impotent, inadequate, ineffective, ineffectual, invertebrate, slack-spined, spineless

forcible *adj* ***syn*** POWERFUL 2, forceful, mighty, potent, puissant
rel intense, vehement, violent; aggressive, assertive, militant, self-assertive; coercive

forcibly *adv* ***syn*** HARD 1, energetically, forcefully, hardly, might and main, mightily, powerfully, strongly, vigorously

forcing bed *n* ***syn*** BREEDING GROUND, forcing house, hotbed, hothouse

forcing house *n* ***syn*** BREEDING GROUND, forcing bed, hotbed, hothouse

fore *adv* ***syn*** BEFORE 1, ahead, ante, antecedently, beforehand, forward, in advance, precedently, previous

forebear *n* ***syn*** ANCESTOR 1, antecedent (used in pl.), ascendant, forefather, primogenitor, progenitor

forebode *vb* ***syn*** AUGUR 2, betoken, bode, foreshadow, foreshow, foretoken, omen, portend, presage, promise

foreboding *n* ***syn*** APPREHENSION 3, apprehensiveness, misgiving, premonition, prenotion, presage, presentiment
rel augury, foretoken, omen, portent, prognostic; forewarning, warning

forecast *vb* ***syn*** FORETELL, adumbrate, augur, portend, predict, presage, prognosticate, prophesy, soothsay, vaticinate
rel conjecture, guess, surmise; conclude, gather, infer

forecast *n* ***syn*** PREDICTION, cast, foretelling, prevision, prognosis, prognostication, prophecy, weird

forecaster *n* ***syn*** PROPHET, augur, auspex, foreseer, foreteller, haruspex, Nostradamus, predictor, prognosticator, prophesier

foredestine *vb* ***syn*** PREDESTINE 2, foreordain, predestinate, predetermine, preordain

forefather *n* ***syn*** ANCESTOR 1, antecedent (used in pl.), ascendant, forebear, primogenitor, progenitor

forefeel *vb* ***syn*** FORESEE, anticipate, apprehend, divine, foreknow, preknow, previse, prevision, see, visualize

foregoer *n* ***syn*** FORERUNNER 2, ancestor, antecedent, antecessor, precursor, predecessor, prototype

foregoing *adj* ***syn*** PRECEDING, antecedent, anterior, former, past, precedent, previous, prior
ant following

forehandedness *n* ***syn*** ECONOMY, frugality, husbandry, providence, prudence, thrift, thriftiness

forehead *n* the part of the face above the eyes <his broad noble *forehead*>
syn brow, frons, front

foreign *adj* **1** ***syn*** EXOTIC 1
ant native
2 ***syn*** EXTRINSIC, alien, extraneous
rel incompatible, incongruous, inconsistent, inconsonant; distasteful, obnoxious, repellent, repugnant; accidental, adventitious
con applicable, apposite, apropos, material, pertinent, relevant; akin, alike, uniform
ant germane
3 ***syn*** IRRELEVANT, extraneous, immaterial, impertinent, inapplicable, inapposite, irrelative

foreigner *n* ***syn*** STRANGER, alien, auslander, inconnu, outcomer, outlander, outsider

foreknow *vb* ***syn*** FORESEE, anticipate, apprehend, divine, forefeel, preknow, previse, prevision, see, visualize
rel conclude, gather, infer

foreland *n* ***syn*** PROMONTORY, beak, bill, cape, head, headland, naze, point

foremost *adj* **1** ***syn*** FIRST 1, headmost, inaugural, initial, leading
2 ***syn*** FIRST 3, arch, champion, chief, head, leading, premier, principal

forename *n* ***syn*** GIVEN NAME, baptismal name, Christian name, font name, personal name, prename

forenoon *n* ***syn*** MORNING 2, morn

forensic *n* ***syn*** ARGUMENTATION, debate, dialectic, disputation, mooting

foreordain *vb* **1** ***syn*** PREDESTINE 1, destine, determine, doom (to), fate, predetermine, preform, preordain
2 ***syn*** PREDESTINE 2, foredestine, predestinate, predetermine, preordain

forerun *vb* **1** ***syn*** PRECEDE 2, antecede, antedate, pace, predate
2 ***syn*** ANNOUNCE 2, foreshow, harbinger, herald, preindicate, presage

forerunner *n* **1** one that goes before and in some way announces the coming of another <a coma is often a *forerunner* of death>
syn harbinger, herald, outrider, precursor
rel anticipator; advertiser, announcer; advertisement, announcement, augury, foretoken, omen, portent, pres-

---

age, prognostic; forewarning, warning; mark, sign, symptom, token; foreshadow
2 one belonging to an early developmental period of something contemporary or fully developed <the water-driven dynamo that was a *forerunner* of present-day giant atomic power plants>
syn ancestor, antecedent, antecessor, foregoer, precursor, predecessor, prototype
rel example, exemplar, model, pattern; pioneer; author, initiator, originator
con consequence, result; effect, event, issue, outgrowth; conclusion, consummation, culmination
ant end product

foresee *vb* to know or expect in advance that something will happen or come into existence or be made manifest <he had not *foreseen* his present problems>
syn anticipate, apprehend, divine, forefeel, foreknow, preknow, previse, prevision, see, visualize
rel forebode, forecast, foretell, predict, presage, prognosticate, prophesy; descry, discern, espy, perceive
idiom look for, look forward to

foreseer *n* ***syn*** PROPHET, augur, auspex, forecaster, foreteller, haruspex, Nostradamus, predictor, prognosticator, prophesier

foreshadow *vb* **1** ***syn*** ADUMBRATE 1, hint, prefigurate, prefigure, shadow (forth)
2 ***syn*** AUGUR 2, betoken, bode, forebode, foreshow, foretoken, omen, portend, presage, promise

foreshow *vb* **1** ***syn*** AUGUR 2, betoken, bode, forebode, foreshadow, foretoken, omen, portend, presage, promise
2 ***syn*** ANNOUNCE 2, forerun, harbinger, herald, preindicate, presage

foresight *n* ***syn*** PRUDENCE, canniness, caution, discreetness, discretion, forethought, precaution, providence
rel clairvoyance, discernment, perception
ant hindsight

forest *n* a heavily wooded area
syn timber, timberland, weald, wood(s), woodland
rel coppice, copse, grove, thicket; wildwood, woodlot
con field, meadow, plain, prairie

forestall *vb* **1** ***syn*** PREVENT 2, avert, deter, forfend, obviate, preclude, rule out, stave off, ward
con court, invite, woo; advance, forward, further, promote
2 ***syn*** PREVENT 1, anticipate

foretell *vb* to tell something before it happens through or as if through special knowledge or occult power <the prophet *foretold* the fall of the city>
syn adumbrate, augur, call, forecast, portend, predict, presage, prognosticate, prophesy, soothsay, vaticinate
rel anticipate, apprehend, divine, foreknow, foresee; announce, declare, proclaim; disclose, divulge, reveal; forewarn, warn; bode, forebode, foreshadow, foreshow, foretoken, promise; prefigure

foreteller *n* ***syn*** PROPHET, augur, auspex, forecaster, foreseer, haruspex, Nostradamus, predictor, prognosticator, prophesier

foretelling *n* ***syn*** PREDICTION, cast, forecast, prevision, prognosis, prognostication, prophecy, weird

forethink *vb* ***syn*** PREMEDITATE, precogitate, predetermine

forethought *n* ***syn*** PRUDENCE 1, canniness, caution, discreetness, discretion, foresight, precaution, providence
rel deliberation, premeditation; gumption, judgment, sense
ant rashness; impetuosity

foretime *n* ***syn*** PAST, ‖lang syne, yesterday, yesteryear, yore

foretoken *n* something that serves as a sign of future happenings <they felt that his new job was a *foretoken* of good fortune>
syn augury, bodement, boding, omen, portent, presage, prognostic
rel badge, indication, mark, note, sign, symptom, token; forerunner, harbinger, herald, precursor; forewarning, shadow, warning; intimation, promise; ostent; hint, inkling, suggestion

foretoken *vb* ***syn*** AUGUR 2, betoken, bode, forebode, foreshadow, foreshow, omen, portend, presage, promise

forever *adv* ***syn*** EVER 2, always, eternally, evermore, forevermore, in perpetuum

forevermore *adv* ***syn*** EVER 2, always, eternally, evermore, forever, in perpetuum

forewarn *vb* ***syn*** WARN 1, caution

forewarning *n* ***syn*** WARNING, admonition, caution, caveat, commonition, monition

foreword *n* ***syn*** INTRODUCTION, exordium, overture, preamble, preface, prelude, prelusion, proem, prolegomenon, prologue

forfeit *n* ***syn*** FINE, amercement, mulct, penalty

forfeit *vb* ***syn*** LOSE 1, drop, sacrifice

forfend *vb* ***syn*** PREVENT 2, avert, deter, forestall, obviate, preclude, rule out, stave off, ward

forgather *vb* ***syn*** GATHER 6, assemble, collect, congregate, congress, muster, raise, rendezvous

forge *vb* ***syn*** MAKE 3, build, construct, fabricate, fashion, form, manufacture, mold, put together, shape
rel beat, pound, turn out; copy, imitate

forget *vb* **1** to lose the remembrance of <I soon *forgot* his name>
syn disremember, ‖misremember, unknow
rel misrecollect; blow up, fluff; unlearn
idiom clean forget, draw a blank
con recall, recollect
ant remember
2 ***syn*** NEGLECT, blink (at *or* away), discount, disregard, fail, ignore, omit, overlook, overpass, slight
con bethink, mind, recall, recollect
ant remember

forgetful *adj* tending to lose or let go from one's mind something once known or learned <she is growing *forgetful*>
syn oblivious, unmindful, unwitting
rel lax, neglectful, negligent, remiss, slack; careless, heedless, thoughtless; absent, absentminded, abstracted, bemused

---

syn synonym(s) ***rel*** related word(s)
idiom idiomatic equivalent(s) ***con*** contrasted word(s)
ant antonym(s) * vulgar
‖ use limited; if in doubt, see a dictionary
The first word in a synonym list when printed in SMALL CAPITALS shows where there is more information about the group. For a more efficient use of this book see Explanatory Notes.

con alert, alive, awake, aware, cognizant, conscious, sensible; attentive, considerate, thoughtful

forgetfulness *n* ***syn*** OBLIVION, lethe, obliviousness

forgivable *adj* ***syn*** VENIAL, excusable, pardonable, remittable

forgive *vb* ***syn*** EXCUSE 1, condone, pardon, remit
idiom forgive and forget

forgo *vb* to deny oneself something for the sake of an end <he vowed to *forgo* all luxuries until the debt was paid>
syn eschew, forbear, sacrifice
rel abandon, relinquish, surrender, waive; abdicate, renounce, resign; forsake, give up

fork (out) *vb* ***syn*** SPEND 1, disburse, expend, give, lay out, outlay, pay, shell out

forlorn *adj* **1** dejected and saddened especially by reason of being alone <a *forlorn* lost child>
syn lonely, lonesome, lorn
rel abandoned, deserted, desolate, forgotten, forsaken; miserable, wretched; friendless, homeless; defenseless, helpless; depressed, oppressed, weighed down; alone, solitary
2 ***syn*** DESPONDENT, despairing, desperate, desponding, hopeless
rel cynical, pessimistic; fruitless, futile, vain
con hopeful, optimistic, roseate, rose-colored

form *n* **1** outward appearance of something as distinguished from the substance of which it is made <the carefully graded *form* of the curves>
syn cast, configuration, conformation, figure, shape
rel contour, outline, profile, silhouette; anatomy, framework, skeleton, structure; economy, organism, scheme, system
2 conduct regulated by an external control (as custom or a formal protocol of procedure) <observing the *forms* of polite society>
syn ceremonial, ceremony, formality, liturgy, rite, ritual
rel procedure, proceeding, process; custom, habit, practice, usage; canon, law, precept, regulation, rule; method, mode; decorum, etiquette, propriety
3 a fixed or accepted way of doing or sometimes of expressing something <good *form* in swimming>
syn convenance, convention, usage
rel fashion, manner, mode, style, way

form *vb* **1** ***syn*** MAKE 3, construct, fabricate, fashion, forge, frame, manufacture, mold, produce, shape
rel devise; create, invent; turn out; design, plan, plot, project, scheme; establish, found, organize
con demolish, destroy, ruin, wreck
2 ***syn*** DEVELOP 4, acquire
3 ***syn*** CONSTITUTE 1, compose, comprise, make, make up

formal *adj* **1** ***syn*** CEREMONIAL, ceremonious, conventional, solemn, stately
rel methodical, orderly, regular, systematic; decorous, proper, seemly; prim, unbending; distant, reserved
ant informal
2 ***syn*** NOMINAL, so-called, titular

formality *n* **1** ***syn*** FORM 2, ceremonial, ceremony, liturgy, rite, ritual
rel convenance, convention
ant informality
2 ***syn*** RITE 2, ceremonial, ceremony, liturgy, observance, ritual, service

formation *n* ***syn*** MAKEUP 1, architecture, composition, constitution, construction, design

former *adj* **1** ***syn*** PRECEDING, antecedent, anterior, foregoing, past, precedent, preceding, previous, prior
con following, succeeding, supervening
ant latter
2 having been such at some previous time <*former* friends>
syn bygone, erstwhile, late, old, once, onetime, past, quondam, sometime, whilom
con current, present; future, prospective

formerly *adv* ***syn*** BEFORE 2, already, earlier, erstwhile, heretofore, once, previously

formidable *adj* **1** ***syn*** FEARFUL 3, appalling, awful, dreadful, frightful, horrible, horrific, shocking, terrible, terrific
ant comforting
2 ***syn*** HARD 6, arduous, difficult, effortful, labored, laborious, strenuous, toilsome, tough, uphill
ant simple

formless *adj* having no definite or recognizable form <a *formless* fear>
syn amorphous, inchoate, shapeless, unformed, unshaped
rel chaotic, orderless, unordered, unorganized; indistinct, obscure, unclear, vague; indefinite, indeterminate, undefined; crude, raw, rough, rude
con distinct, formed; definite, explicit, express, specific; ordered, organized

formulate *vb* **1** ***syn*** WORD, couch, express, phrase, put
2 ***syn*** CONTRIVE 2, concoct, cook (up), devise, dream up, frame, hatch (up), invent, make up, vamp (up)
3 ***syn*** DRAFT 3, draw up, frame, make, prepare

‖**fornent** *prep* ***syn*** BESIDE 1, alongside, by, next to

for real *adv* ***syn*** SERIOUSLY 1, actively, down, earnestly

forsake *vb* ***syn*** ABANDON 1, chuck, desert, quit, renounce, throw over
rel spurn; leave; abdicate, resign
ant return (to), revert (to)

forsaken *adj* ***syn*** DERELICT 1, abandoned, deserted, desolate, lorn, solitary, uncouth

forswear *vb* **1** ***syn*** ABJURE, palinode, recall, recant, retract, take back, unsay, withdraw
2 ***syn*** PERJURE

fort *n* a structure or place offering resistance to a hostile force <settlers fled to the *fort*>
syn citadel, fastness, fortress, redoubt, stronghold

forte *n* that in which one excels <cooking is her strongest *forte*>
syn eminency, long suit, medium, métier, oyster, strong suit

---

syn synonym(s) — ***rel*** related word(s)
idiom idiomatic equivalent(s) — ***con*** contrasted word(s)
ant antonym(s) — * vulgar
‖ use limited; if in doubt, see a dictionary
The first word in a synonym list when printed in SMALL CAPITALS shows where there is more information about the group. For a more efficient use of this book see Explanatory Notes.

rel ableness, effectiveness, efficiency; ability, competence; bag, thing
idiom cup of tea, dish of tea, strong point
con inadequacy, incapability, incompetence, inefficiency; greenness, rawness

forth *adv* **1** *syn* AHEAD 2, alee, forward, onward
2 *syn* ALONG 1, forward, on, onward

forthcome *vb syn* LOOM 2, brew, gather, impend

forthcoming *adj* being soon to appear or take place <the *forthcoming* holidays>
syn approaching, coming, nearing, oncoming, upcoming
rel future; imminent, impending, pending; anticipated, awaited, expected
con distant, far-off, remote; bygone, former, gone, gone-by, past

forthright *adj* **1** *syn* STRAIGHTFORWARD 2, aboveboard, plain dealing, straight
con covert, secret, stealthy, surreptitious, underhand; deceitful, mendacious, untruthful
ant furtive
2 *syn* FRANK, candid, direct, open, openhearted, plain, single, straightforward, undisguised, unvarnished

forthwith *adv* **1** *syn* AWAY 3, at once, directly, immediately, instanter, instantly, now, right away, straightaway, straightway
2 *syn* SHORT 1, abruptly, asudden, sudden, suddenly

fortify *vb* **1** *syn* STRENGTHEN 2, energize, invigorate, reinforce
rel arouse, rally, rouse, stir; refresh, renew, restore
con dilute, thin
ant enfeeble
2 *syn* GIRD 3, brace, prepare, ready, steel, strengthen

fortitude *n* a quality of character combining courage and staying power <she bore up under all her problems with admirable *fortitude*>
syn backbone, grit, guts, intestinal fortitude, ‖moxie, nerve, sand, spunk; *compare* COURAGE
rel courage, mettle, pith, resoluteness, resolution, spirit, stick-to-itiveness, tenacity; boldness, bravery, courageousness, dauntlessness, fearlessness, intrepidity, valiancy, valor, valorousness; endurance, stamina, strength; constancy, determination, perseverance; bottom
con cowardliness, fearfulness, timidity, timorousness; faintheartedness, milksoppiness, weakness; cowardice, yellowness
ant pusillanimity

fortress *n syn* FORT, citadel, fastness, redoubt, stronghold

fortuitous *adj syn* ACCIDENTAL, casual, chance, contingent, fluky, incidental, odd
con activated, actuated, motivated; projected, schemed
ant deliberate

---

syn synonym(s) — *rel* related word(s)
idiom idiomatic equivalent(s) — *con* contrasted word(s)
ant antonym(s) — * vulgar
‖ use limited; if in doubt, see a dictionary
The first word in a synonym list when printed in SMALL CAPITALS shows where there is more information about the group. For a more efficient use of this book see Explanatory Notes.

fortuitously *adv syn* INCIDENTALLY 1, accidentally, casually
ant deliberately

fortuity *n syn* ACCIDENT 1, chance, hap, luck
ant deliberation

fortunate *adj* **1** *syn* FAVORABLE 5, auspicious, benign, bright, dexter, propitious, white
ant disastrous
2 *syn* LUCKY, happy, providential, ‖sonsy, well
ant unfortunate

fortunately *adv syn* WELL 5, favorably, happily, prosperously, satisfyingly, successfully, swimmingly

fortunateness *n syn* LUCK 3, fortune, luckiness
ant unfortunateness

fortune *n* **1** *syn* CHANCE 2, hazard, luck
rel destiny, doom, portion
con design, intent, intention
2 *syn* LUCK 3, fortunateness, luckiness
ant misfortune
3 *syn* WEALTH 2, property, resources, riches, substance, worth
4 a very large amount of money <those furs must have cost a *fortune*>
syn ‖bomb, boodle, bundle, mint, packet, pile, pot, ‖roll, wad
idiom king's ransom, pretty penny, tidy sum

fortuneless *adj syn* POOR 1, beggared, destitute, impecunious, impoverished, indigent, needy, penurious, poverty-stricken, unprosperous

forty winks *n pl but sing or pl in constr syn* NAP, catnap, dog nap, ‖dover, siesta, snooze

forward *adj* **1** *syn* PRESUMPTUOUS, brash, overweening, presuming, pushful, pushing, self-asserting, self-assertive, uppish, uppity
2 *syn* WISE 5, bold, cheeky, fresh, impudent, nervy, pert, sassy, smart, smart-alecky
ant bashful
3 *syn* PRECOCIOUS, advanced
con regressive, retrograde, retrogressive
ant backward

forward *adv* **1** *syn* BEFORE 1, ahead, ante, antecedently, beforehand, fore, in advance, precedently, previous
2 *syn* AHEAD 2, alee, forth, onward
ant backward
3 *syn* ALONG 1, forth, on, onward

forward *vb* **1** *syn* ADVANCE 1, encourage, foster, further, promote, serve
rel back, champion, support, uphold
con baffle, circumvent, foil, frustrate, outwit, thwart
ant balk
2 *syn* SEND 1, address, consign, dispatch, remit, route, ship, transmit

fossil *n syn* FOGY, antediluvian, fogram, fuddy-duddy, mid-Victorian, mossback, square, stick-in-the-mud

foster *vb* **1** *syn* NURSE 2, cherish, cultivate, nourish, nursle, nurture
rel back, champion, support, uphold; entertain, harbor, house, lodge, shelter; accommodate, assist, favor, help, oblige
con combat, fight, oppose, resist, withstand; curb, inhibit, restrain; ban, forbid, interdict, prohibit; abuse, disregard, neglect
2 *syn* ADVANCE 1, encourage, forward, further, promote, serve

foul *adj* **1** ***syn*** OFFENSIVE, disgusting, horrid, loathsome, nasty, noisome, repellent, repugnant, repulsive, vile
2 ***syn*** DIRTY 1, black, filthy, grubby, impure, nasty, soily, squalid, unclean, uncleanly
rel fetid, malodorous, noisome, putrid, stinking; loathsome, offensive, repulsive, revolting
ant fair; undefiled
3 ***syn*** OBSCENE 2, coarse, dirty, filthy, indecent, nasty, raunchy, scatological, smutty, vulgar

foul *vb* **1** ***syn*** SOIL 2, begrime, besoil, dirty, grime, smirch, smooch, smudge, smutch, tarnish
rel contaminate, defile, pollute; desecrate, profane
2 ***syn*** CONTAMINATE 2, befoul, pollute

foul play *n* ***syn*** MURDER, blood, ||bump-off, homicide, killing, manslaughter

foul up *vb* ***syn*** CONFUSE 5, jumble, mix up, muddle, ||snafu, snarl up, tumble

found *vb* **1** ***syn*** BASE, bottom, establish, ground, predicate, rest, stay
rel support, sustain; erect, raise, rear
2 to set going or to bring into existence <*founded* a new school for graduate studies>
syn constitute, create, establish, institute, organize, set up, start
rel begin, commence, inaugurate, initiate; fashion, form
con close, conclude, end, finish, terminate; arrest, check, halt, stay, stop

foundation *n* **1** ***syn*** BASIS 1, base, bedrock, footing, ground, groundwork, infrastructure, substratum, underpinning, warrant
2 ***syn*** BASIS 3, warrant
3 ***syn*** BASE 1, basis, bottom, footing, groundwork, rest, substruction, substructure, underpinning, understructure

foundational *adj* ***syn*** FUNDAMENTAL 1, basal, basic, bottom, primary, radical, underlying

foundationless *adj* ***syn*** BASELESS, bottomless, gratuitous, groundless, uncalled-for, unfounded, ungrounded, unwarranted

founder *n* ***syn*** FATHER 2, architect, author, creator, generator, inventor, maker, originator, patriarch, sire

founder *vb* ***syn*** SINK 1, go down, go under, submerge, submerse

fount *n* ***syn*** SOURCE, fountain, fountainhead, origin, root, spring, well, wellhead, wellspring, whence

fountain *n* ***syn*** SOURCE, fountainhead, inception, origin, provenance, provenience, root, wellhead, wellspring, whence

fountainhead *n* ***syn*** SOURCE, fountain, inception, origin, provenance, provenience, root, wellhead, wellspring, whence

four *n* ***syn*** QUARTET, foursome, quartetto, quaternion, quatuor, tetrad

fourberie *n* ***syn*** DECEPTION 1, chicane, chicanery, dishonesty, double-dealing, fraud, hanky-panky, highbinding, sharp practice, trickery

four-flush *vb* ***syn*** DECEIVE, beguile, betray, ||bitch, bluff, delude, double-cross, humbug, juggle, take in

foursome *n* ***syn*** QUARTET, four, quartetto, quaternion, quatuor, tetrad

foursquare *adj* ***syn*** SQUARE 1, quadrate, quadratic, quadratical

fourth *n* ***syn*** QUARTER 1, quartern

foxiness *n* ***syn*** CUNNING 2, art, artfulness, artifice, cageyness, canniness, craft, craftiness, slyness, wiliness

foxy *adj* ***syn*** SLY 2, artful, astute, crafty, cunning, deep, guileful, insidious, tricky, wily
rel deceitful, dishonest
con aboveboard, forthright, straightforward

foyer *n* ***syn*** VESTIBULE, lobby

fracas *n* **1** ***syn*** QUARREL, altercation, bickering, dispute, feud, fight, hassle, run-in, set-to, squabble
2 ***syn*** BRAWL 2, affray, broil, donnybrook, fight, fray, knock-down-and-drag-out, melee, row, ruction

fractional *adj* ***syn*** INCOMPLETE 1, fragmentary, part, partial

fractious *adj* **1** ***syn*** UNRULY 1, indocile, indomitable, intractable, recalcitrant, undisciplinable, undisciplined, ungovernable, unmanageable, wild
ant orderly
2 ***syn*** IRRITABLE, fretful, huffy, peevish, pettish, petulant, querulous, snappish, waspish, waspy
ant peaceable

fracturable *adj* ***syn*** FRAGILE 1, breakable, delicate, frail, frangible, shatterable, shattery

fracture *n* ***syn*** BREACH 3, break, fissure, rent, rift, rupture, schism, split

fragile *adj* **1** easily broken <a *fragile* dish of the finest porcelain>
syn breakable, delicate, fracturable, frail, frangible, shatterable, shattery
rel brittle, crisp, crumbly, crunchy, friable, short
con infrangible, unbreakable; elastic, flexible, resilient; stout, strong, sturdy, tenacious
ant tough
2 ***syn*** WEAK 1, decrepit, feeble, flimsy, frail, infirm, insubstantial, unsound, unsubstantial, weakly
ant durable

fragment *n* **1** ***syn*** PARTICLE, ace, atom, bit, crumb, grain, iota, jot, minim, shred
2 ***syn*** END 4, bit, scrap

fragment *vb* ***syn*** SHATTER 1, burst, ||pash, rive, shiver, smash, ||smatter, splinter, splinterize, splitter

fragmentary *adj* ***syn*** INCOMPLETE 1, fractional, part, partial

fragrance *n* a sweet or pleasant odor <the *fragrance* of flowers>
syn aroma, balm, bouquet, incense, perfume, redolence, scent, spice
rel odor, smell
con fetidness, fetor, malodor, noisomeness, rancidness, rankness
ant stench, stink

fragrant *adj* ***syn*** SWEET 2, ambrosial, aromal, aromatic, balmy, perfumed, perfumy, redolent, savory, spicy
rel delectable, delicious, delightful
ant fetid

---

syn synonym(s)	*rel* related word(s)
idiom idiomatic equivalent(s)	*con* contrasted word(s)
ant antonym(s)	* vulgar

|| use limited; if in doubt, see a dictionary

The first word in a synonym list when printed in SMALL CAPITALS shows where there is more information about the group. For a more efficient use of this book see Explanatory Notes.

frail *adj* **1** ***syn*** WEAK 1, decrepit, feeble, flimsy, fragile, infirm, insubstantial, unsound, unsubstantial, weakly
rel slender, slight, slim, tenuous, thin; petty, puny
con hale, healthy, sound
ant robust
2 ***syn*** FRAGILE 1, breakable, delicate, fracturable, frangible, shatterable, shattery
con solid, substantial

frailty *n* ***syn*** FAULT 2, failing, foible, vice

frame *vb* **1** ***syn*** CONTRIVE 2, concoct, cook (up), devise, dream up, formulate, hatch (up), invent, make up, vamp (up)
2 ***syn*** DRAFT 3, draw up, formulate, make, prepare
3 ***syn*** MAKE 3, build, construct, erect, fabricate, fashion, forge, form, manufacture, produce

framework *n* ***syn*** STRUCTURE 3

franchise *n* ***syn*** SUFFRAGE, ballot, vote

franchise *vb* ***syn*** ENFRANCHISE, affranchise

frangible *adj* ***syn*** FRAGILE 1, breakable, delicate, fracturable, frail, shatterable, shattery

frank *adj* marked by free, forthright, and sincere expression <a *frank* answer>
syn candid, direct, forthright, man-to-man, open, openhearted, plain, plainspoken, single, single-eyed, single-hearted, single-minded, straightforward, unconcealed, undisguised, undissembled, undissembling, unmannered, unreserved, unvarnished; *compare* COMMUNICATIVE, STRAIGHTFORWARD 2
rel ingenuous, naive, natural, simple, unsophisticated; bluff, blunt; heart-to-heart, sincere; honest, scrupulous, upright; dispassionate, fair, impartial, just, unbiased; barefaced, brazen, outspoken, uninhibited
con reserved, reticent, secretive, silent, taciturn, uncommunicative; covert, furtive, secret, sneaking, underhand; deceitful, deceptive, dishonest, evasive, false, lying, mendacious, tricky, untruthful; insincere
ant reticent

frank *n* ***syn*** FRANKFURTER, dog, hot dog, wiener, wienerwurst, ‖wienie

frankfurter *n* a seasoned beef or beef and pork sausage
syn dog, frank, hot dog, wiener, wienerwurst, ‖wienie

frantic *adj* ***syn*** FURIOUS 2, corybantic, delirious, frenetic, frenzied, mad, rabid, wild

frantically *adv* ***syn*** HARD 2, fiercely, frenziedly, furiously, madly, stormily, tumultuously, turbulently, violently, wildly

fraternity *n* ***syn*** ASSOCIATION 2, brotherhood, club, fellowship, guild, league, order, society, sodality, union

fraud *n* **1** ***syn*** DECEPTION 1, cheat, chicane, chicanery, double-dealing, fourberie, hanky-panky, highbinding, sharp practice, trickery
2 ***syn*** IMPOSTURE, cheat, deceit, fake, hoax, humbug, phony, sell, sham, swindle
rel bamboozlement, bamboozling, dupery, duping, hoodwinking
3 ***syn*** IMPOSTOR, fake, faker, humbug, phony, pretender

fray *n* **1** ***syn*** BRAWL 2, affray, broil, donnybrook, fight, fracas, melee, row, ruction, scuffle
rel contention, discord, dissension, strife
2 ***syn*** CLASH 2, affray, brush, melee, mellay, scrimmage, skirmish

frayed *adj* ***syn*** RAGGED, frazzled, shreddy, tattered

frazzle *vb* ***syn*** EXHAUST 4, ‖bugger, fag, knock out, outtire, outwear, ‖poop, prostrate, tucker, wear out

frazzled *adj* ***syn*** RAGGED, frayed, shreddy, tattered

freak *n* **1** ***syn*** CAPRICE, bee, boutade, conceit, crotchet, fancy, humor, megrim, vagary, whim
2 one that is physically abnormal <pitiful *freaks* displayed in sideshows>
syn abortion, lusus, miscreation, monster, monstrosity
rel aberration, chimera, malconformation, malformation, misshape, mosaic, mutation, sport; abnormality, anomaly, curiosity, oddity; rara avis, rarity; androgyne, hermaphrodite
idiom freak of nature
3 ***syn*** ENTHUSIAST, bigot, bug, fanatic, fiend, maniac, nut, zealot

freakish *adj* ***syn*** ARBITRARY 1, capricious, erratic, vagarious, wayward, whimsical, whimsied

freckle *vb* ***syn*** SPECKLE 1, bespeckle, dot, pepper, speck, sprinkle, stipple

free *adj* **1** not subject to the rule or control of another <a *free* country>
syn autarchic, autarkic, autonomous, independent, separate, sovereign
rel free-born, unenslaved; delivered, emancipated, enfranchised, freed, liberated, released; democratic, self-directing, self-governing, self-ruling; sui juris; individualistic, unregimented
con coerced, compelled, constrained, forced, obliged; dependent, restricted, subject; inferior, subordinate, subservient; captive, enslaved, enthralled, subjugated
ant bond
2 not bound, confined, or detained by force <the prisoner was now *free*>
syn loose, unconfined, unrestrained
rel unbound, unchained, unfettered, unshackled, untied; clear, loose, scot-free; emancipated, freed, liberated; independent
idiom at liberty, free as a bird, free as air, free to come and go
con confined, restrained; impounded, imprisoned, incarcerated, interned, jailed; bound, chained, fettered, shackled, tied
3 ***syn*** LIBERAL 1, bounteous, bountiful, freehanded, generous, handsome, munificent, openhanded, unsparing
ant close
4 ***syn*** OUTSPOKEN, free-spoken, round, vocal
5 not costing or charging anything <a *free* public school>
syn chargeless, complimentary, costless, gratis, gratuitous
rel unpaid, unrecompensed, unremunerated
idiom for free, for love, for nothing, on the cuff, on the house

---

syn synonym(s) ***rel*** related word(s)
idiom idiomatic equivalent(s) ***con*** contrasted word(s)
ant antonym(s) * vulgar
‖ use limited; if in doubt, see a dictionary
The first word in a synonym list when printed in SMALL CAPITALS shows where there is more information about the group. For a more efficient use of this book see Explanatory Notes.

con charged, paid; costly, dear, expensive, high, high priced
6 not having the affections fixed on a particular object <she was happy to be *free* and in no hurry to fall in love again>
syn fancy-free, heart-whole

free *vb* to relieve from constraint or restraint <*free* an oppressed people>
syn discharge, disenthrall, disimprison, emancipate, liberate, loose, loosen, manumit, redeem, release, ‖spring, unbind, unchain, unshackle
rel clear, detach, disencumber, disengage, disentangle, extricate; deliver, ransom, redeem, rescue; affranchise, enfranchise
idiom cut loose
con fetter, hamper, hog-tie, manacle, shackle, trammel; immure, imprison, incarcerate, intern, jail; circumscribe, confine, limit, restrict; curb, inhibit, restrain; enslave, enthrall, subjugate

freebooter *n* **1** ***syn*** MARAUDER, bandit, brigand, bummer, cateran, forager, looter, pillager, plunderer, raider
2 ***syn*** PIRATE, buccaneer, corsair, picaroon, rover, sea dog, sea robber, sea rover, sea wolf

freedom *n* the power or condition of acting without compulsion <*freedom* of the press>
syn liberty, license
rel exemption, immunity; prerogative, privilege, right; compass, latitude, scope, sweep
con coercion, compulsion, constraint; restraint
ant necessity

free–for–all *n* ***syn*** BRAWL 2, affray, broil, donnybrook, fight, fracas, fray, knock-down-and-drag-out, melee, ruction

free hand *n* ***syn*** CARTE BLANCHE, blank check

freehanded *adj* ***syn*** LIBERAL 1, bounteous, bountiful, free, generous, handsome, munificent, openhanded, unsparing

freeloader *n* ***syn*** PARASITE, barnacle, bloodsucker, hanger-on, leech, lounge lizard, ‖spiv, sponge, sponger, sucker

freely *adv* EASILY 1, effortlessly, facilely, lightly, readily, smoothly, well

free–minded *adj* ***syn*** HAPPY-GO-LUCKY, carefree, insouciant, lighthearted, lightsome

free–spoken *adj* ***syn*** OUTSPOKEN, free, round, vocal

freezer *n* ***syn*** JAIL, ‖big house, bridewell, ‖brig, ‖calaboose, ‖can, ‖clink, cooler, coop, ‖hoosegow

freezing *adj* ***syn*** COLD 1, arctic, chill, chilly, frosty, gelid, glacial, icy, nippy, shivery
ant scorching

freight *n* ***syn*** LOAD 1, burden, cargo, haul, lading, payload

frenetic *adj* ***syn*** FURIOUS 2, corybantic, delirious, frantic, frenzied, mad, rabid, wild

frenzied *adj* ***syn*** FURIOUS 2, corybantic, delirious, frantic, frenetic, mad, rabid, wild

frenziedly *adv* ***syn*** HARD 2, fiercely, frantically, furiously, madly, stormily, tumultuously, turbulently, violently, wildly

frenzy *n* ***syn*** DELIRIUM, furor

frenzy *vb* ***syn*** MADDEN 1, craze, derange, distract, unbalance, unhinge

frequent *adj* ***syn*** COMMON 4, customary, everyday, familiar
ant infrequent, rare

frequent *vb* to go to or be in often <he *frequents* the bar down the street>
syn affect, hang around, hang out, haunt, resort
rel attend, go (to), visit; infest, overrun
con avoid, miss, sidestep
ant shun

frequenter *n* ***syn*** HABITUÉ 1, denizen, haunter

frequently *adv* **1** ***syn*** OFTEN, again and again, much, oft, oftentimes, ofttimes, over and over, repeatedly, time and again
ant infrequently
2 ***syn*** USUALLY 2, as a rule, by ordinary, commonly, generally, ordinarily

fresh *adj* **1** ***syn*** NEW 1, modern, modernistic, neoteric, newfangled, new-fashioned, new-sprung, novel, recent
rel gleaming, glistening, sparkling; striking, vital, vivid; virginal, youthful; crude, green, raw, uncouth; artless, naive, natural, unsophisticated
con hackneyed, shopworn, stereotyped, threadbare, trite
ant stale
2 ***syn*** ADDITIONAL, added, another, else, farther, further, more, new, other
3 ***syn*** INEXPERIENCED, callow, green, raw, unfleshed, unpracticed, unseasoned, untried, unversed, young
4 ***syn*** WISE 5, bold, cheeky, forward, impudent, nervy, pert, sassy, smart, smart-alecky

freshman *n* ***syn*** NOVICE, apprentice, beginner, colt, neophyte, newcomer, novitiate, rookie, tenderfoot, tyro

freshness *n* ***syn*** INEXPERIENCE, callowness, greenness, rawness

fret *vb* **1** ***syn*** WORRY 3, cark, fuss, pother, stew, ‖tew
rel chafe, fume; brood, mope
idiom eat one's heart out
2 ***syn*** ANNOY 1, abrade, bother, chafe, exercise, gall, irk, provoke, ruffle, vex
3 ***syn*** CHAFE 3, abrade, excoriate, gall, rub
4 ***syn*** RIPPLE, cockle, dimple, riffle

fretful *adj* **1** ***syn*** IRRITABLE, fractious, huffy, peevish, pettish, petulant, querulous, snappish, waspish, waspy
rel captious, carping, caviling, critical, faultfinding; contrary, perverse
con forbearing, long-suffering, patient, resigned; subdued, submissive, tame
2 ***syn*** IMPATIENT 1, chafing, unpatient

friable *adj* ***syn*** SHORT 6, brittle, crisp, crumbly, ‖crump, crunchy

fribble *adj* ***syn*** GIDDY 1, dizzy, featherbrained, flighty, fribbling, frivolous, harebrained, light, light-headed, scatter-brained

fribbling *adj* ***syn*** GIDDY 1, dizzy, featherbrained, flighty, fribble, frivolous, harebrained, light, light-headed, scatterbrained

---

syn synonym(s)	*rel* related word(s)
idiom idiomatic equivalent(s)	*con* contrasted word(s)
ant antonym(s)	* vulgar

‖ use limited; if in doubt, see a dictionary
The first word in a synonym list when printed in SMALL CAPITALS shows where there is more information about the group. For a more efficient use of this book see Explanatory Notes.

fried *adj* ***syn*** INTOXICATED 1, ‖boozy, ‖canned, disguised, drunk, inebriated, ‖lushed, muddled, pixilated, ‖plastered

friend *n* a person with whom one is on good and, usually, familiar terms <he is one of my closest *friends*>
syn acquaintance, amigo, cater-cousin, confidant, familiar, intimate, mate; *compare* ASSOCIATE 3
rel alter ego, best friend, bosom friend; ally, colleague, partner; nodding acquaintance
con enemy; adversary, antagonist, opponent; competitor, rival
ant foe

friendliness *n* ***syn*** GOODWILL 1, amity, benevolence, comity, friendship, kindliness
rel affability, amiability, congeniality, cordiality, neighborliness, sociability
ant unfriendliness

friendly *adj* **1** ***syn*** AMICABLE 1, neighborly
rel close, familiar, intimate; affectionate, devoted, loving
ant unfriendly; belligerent
2 ***syn*** HARMONIOUS 3, amicable, amical, congenial
3 ***syn*** SYMPATHETIC 2, receptive, ‖sib, well-disposed
ant unfriendly

friendship *n* ***syn*** GOODWILL 1, amity, benevolence, comity, friendliness, kindliness
rel affinity, attraction; empathy; accord, concord, consonance, harmony; alliance, coalition, federation, fusion, league
con antagonism, antipathy, hostility, rancor; hate
ant animosity

fright *n* **1** ***syn*** FEAR 1, alarm, consternation, dismay, dread, horror, panic, terror, trepidation, trepidity
2 ***syn*** EYESORE, desight, mess, monstrosity, sight

fright *vb* ***syn*** FRIGHTEN, affright, alarm, awe, scare, ‖spook, startle, terrify, terrorize

frighten *vb* to strike or to fill with fear or dread <the puppy was *frightened* by the unfamiliar noises>
syn affright, alarm, awe, fright, scare, ‖spook, startle, terrify, terrorize
rel appall, astound, daunt, disconcert, dismay, faze, horrify, shock; demoralize, unman, unnerve; browbeat, bulldoze, cow, intimidate; agitate, discompose, disquiet, perturb, upset
idiom curdle the blood, curl the hair, frighten one out of one's wits, freeze the blood, give one a scare, give one a turn, make one's blood run cold, make one's flesh creep, make one's hair stand on end, make one's teeth chatter, make one tremble, put one's heart in one's mouth, scare hell out of, scare one spitless, scare one stiff, scare the life out of, scare the pants off of, scare to death, strike terror into, take one's breath away
con embolden, encourage, hearten, reassure

---

syn synonym(s)	***rel*** related word(s)
idiom idiomatic equivalent(s)	***con*** contrasted word(s)
ant antonym(s)	* vulgar

‖ use limited; if in doubt, see a dictionary
The first word in a synonym list when printed in SMALL CAPITALS shows where there is more information about the group. For a more efficient use of this book see Explanatory Notes.

frightened *adj* ***syn*** AFRAID 1, aghast, anxious, ‖ascared, fearful, scared, scary, terrified
idiom in a fright
ant unfrightened

frightful *adj* ***syn*** FEARFUL 3, appalling, awful, dreadful, formidable, horrible, horrific, shocking, terrible, terrific

frigid *adj* **1** ***syn*** COLD 1, arctic, chill, chilly, cool, freezing, frosty, gelid, glacial, icy
2 ***syn*** COLD 2, chill, emotionless, glacial, icy, indifferent, unemotional
3 free from or deficient in passion <claimed his wife was a *frigid* woman>
syn cold, inhibited, passionless, undersexed, unresponsive
idiom as cold as an iceberg
con affectionate, demanding, loving
ant ardent; amorous

frill *n* ***syn*** LUXURY, amenity, extravagance, luxus, superfluity

fringe *n* ***syn*** BORDER 1, brim, brink, edge, hem, margin, perimeter, periphery, skirt, verge

fringe *vb* ***syn*** BORDER 1, bound, define, edge, hem, margin, rim, skirt, surround, verge

frippery *n* ***syn*** FINERY, ‖best bib and tucker, bravery, full dress, ‖glad rags, regalia, Sunday best, war paint

frisk *vb* **1** ***syn*** GAMBOL, caper, cavort, frolic, rollick, romp
2 ***syn*** SEARCH 2, ‖fan, shake down

frisky *adj* ***syn*** PLAYFUL 1, antic, frolicsome, gamesome, kittenish, larkish, prankish, sportive, waggish, wicked

fritter *vb* ***syn*** WASTE 2, blow, cast away, consume, dissipate, fool (away), frivol away, squander, throw away, trifle (away)

frivol away *vb* ***syn*** WASTE 2, blow, cast away, consume, dissipate, fool (away), fritter, squander, throw away, trifle (away)

frivolity *n* ***syn*** LIGHTNESS, flightiness, flippancy, levity, light-mindedness, volatility
rel coquetting, dallying, flirting, toying, trifling; fun, game, jest, play, sport
ant seriousness; staidness

frivolous *adj* ***syn*** GIDDY 1, bird-witted, dizzy, empty-headed, featherbrained, flighty, harebrained, rattlebrained, scatterbrained, silly
rel shallow, superficial, unprofound; gay, light, playful
ant serious

‖**frogskin** *n* ***syn*** DOLLAR, bill, ‖bone, ‖buck, ‖fish, ‖ironman, oner, ‖skin, ‖smacker, ‖smackeroo

frolic *vb* **1** ***syn*** REVEL 1, carouse, hell, riot, roister, spree, wassail
2 ***syn*** GAMBOL, caper, cavort, frisk, rollick, romp

frolic *n* ***syn*** PRANK, antic, caper, dido(es), lark, monkeyshine, shenanigan, shine(s), tomfoolery, trick

frolicsome *adj* **1** ***syn*** ANTIC 2, playful, rollicking, sprightly
2 ***syn*** PLAYFUL 1, antic, coltish, frisky, gamesome, impish, mischievous, roguish, sportive, waggish

from *prep* **1** ***syn*** AFTER 1, for
2 in the face of <protect them *from* exploitation>
syn against

frondeur *n* ***syn*** REBEL, anarch, anarchist, insurgent, insurrectionist, malcontent, mutineer, revolter

frons *n* ***syn*** FOREHEAD, brow, front

front *n* **1** ***syn*** FOREHEAD, brow, frons
2 ***syn*** MASK 2, color, coloring, disguise, facade, face, false front, put-on, show, veil
3 a person, group, or thing used to mask the identity or true character of a controlling agent <the export company was a *front* for illegal activities>
syn blind
rel disguise, facade, mask

front *vb* **1** ***syn*** FACE 1, look
2 ***syn*** FACE 3, ‖banter, beard, brave, challenge, dare, defy, outdare, outface, venture
3 ***syn*** MEET 6, close, encounter, face
4 ***syn*** ACCOST 2, confront, face

frontier *n* **1** a region between two countries <lived on the *frontier* between Mexico and the U.S.>
syn border, borderland, march, marchland
2 a rural region that forms the margin of settled or developed territory <settlers found living on the *frontier* was a hard life>
syn backcountry, backland, ‖backveld, backwash, backwater, backwoods, ‖boondocks, ‖boonies, bush, hinterland, ‖outback, sticks, up-country
idiom the back of beyond

frontier *adj* ***syn*** BACK 1, outlandish, remote, unsettled

fronting *prep* ***syn*** AGAINST 1, contra, facing, over against, toward, vis-à-vis

front–rank *adj* ***syn*** EXCELLENT, blue-ribbon, first-class, first-rate, first-string, five-star, Grade A, prime, superior, top-notch

frore *adj* ***syn*** COLD 1, arctic, chill, chilly, cool, freezing, frosty, gelid, glacial, icy

frosty *adj* ***syn*** COLD 1, chill, chilly, cool, freezing, gelid, glacial, icy, nippy, shivery

froth *n* ***syn*** FOAM, lather, spume, suds, yeast
rel flippancy, frivolity, levity, lightness

froward *adj* ***syn*** CONTRARY 3, balky, cross-grained, ornery, perverse, restive, wayward, wrongheaded

frown *vb* **1** to put on a dark or malignant countenance or aspect <he *frowned* at the naughty child>
syn gloom, glower, lower, scowl
rel glare; grimace; pout, sulk
idiom look black, look daggers
con grin, laugh
ant smile
2 ***syn*** DISAPPROVE 1, deprecate, discommend, discountenance, disesteem, disfavor, object

frowsy *adj* **1** ***syn*** SLATTERNLY, blowsy, dowdy, draggletailed, slattern, sordid
rel lax, neglectful, negligent, remiss, slack
ant trim; smart
2 ***syn*** MALODOROUS 1, funky, fusty, musty, noisome, rank, reeking, smelly, stale, stinking

frugal *adj* ***syn*** SPARING, canny, chary, economical, saving, Scotch, stewardly, thrifty, unwasteful, wary
rel careful, meticulous; discreet, prudent; conserving, preserving; cheeseparing, penny-pinching, scrimping, stinting
ant wasteful

frugality *n* ***syn*** ECONOMY, forehandedness, husbandry, providence, prudence, thrift, thriftiness

‖**fruit** *n* ***syn*** HOMOSEXUAL, fag, faggot, homo, invert, queer, uranian, uranist

fruitage *n* ***syn*** HARVEST 2, crop

fruitful *adj* ***syn*** FERTILE, childing, fecund, productive, proliferant, prolific, rich, spawning
rel breeding, propagating, reproducing; abounding
con abortive, bootless, futile, vain
ant unfruitful; fruitless

fruitfulness *n* ***syn*** FERTILITY, fecundity, prolificacy

fruition *n* ***syn*** PLEASURE 2, delectation, delight, enjoyment, joy, joyance
rel actualization, materialization, realization; accomplishment, fulfillment; achievement, attainment

fruitless *adj* ***syn*** FUTILE, abortive, bootless, ineffective, ineffectual, unavailable, unavailing, unproductive, useless, vain
rel barren, infertile, sterile, unfruitful; foiled, frustrated, thwarted; infructuous, unprofitable
con fecund, fertile, prolific
ant fruitful

‖**fruity** *adj* ***syn*** INSANE 1, ‖loco, lunatic, mad, maniac, ‖mental, mindless, non compos mentis, nuts, nutsy

frumpish *adj* ***syn*** TACKY 2, dowdy, frumpy, outmoded, out-of-date, stodgy, unstylish

frumpy *adj* ***syn*** TACKY 2, dowdy, frumpish, outmoded, out-of-date, stodgy, unstylish

frustrate *vb* **1** to come between a person and his aim or desire or to defeat another's plan <my efforts are *frustrated* at every turn>
syn baffle, balk, beat, bilk, buffalo, circumvent, dash, disappoint, foil, ruin, thwart; *compare* OUTWIT
rel annul, cancel, counteract, negative, neutralize, nullify; anticipate, forestall; conquer, defeat, lick, overcome; forbid, inhibit, prohibit; obviate, preclude, prevent; bar, block, hinder, impede, obstruct; arrest, check, halt, interrupt
idiom cut the ground from under one, dash one's hope, defeat expectation, throw a monkey wrench into the works, upset one's applecart
con accomplish, achieve, bring about, effect, perform; advance, forward, further, promote; abet, foment, incite, instigate
ant fulfill
2 ***syn*** NEUTRALIZE, annul, cancel (out), counteract, countercheck, negate, negative, redress

frying pan *n* a pan with a handle used for frying food <some still prefer the sturdy cast-iron *frying pan*>
syn skillet, spider

fucking** *adj* **1** ***syn DAMNED 2, blamed, blasted, blessed, *‖bloody, damnable, dratted, execrable, infernal, *‖ruddy
2 ***syn*** UTTER, absolute, *‖bloody, complete, consummate, downright, gross, out-and-out, rank, unmitigated

fuck up** *vb* ***syn BOTCH, bitch (up), ‖blow, blunder, bugger up, bungle, flub, louse up, ‖muck, ‖screw up

fuddle *vb* ***syn*** CONFUSE 2, addle, ball up, befuddle, bewilder, distract, fluster, mix up, muddle, throw off

---

syn synonym(s)	***rel*** related word(s)
idiom idiomatic equivalent(s)	***con*** contrasted word(s)
ant antonym(s)	* vulgar

‖ use limited; if in doubt, see a dictionary
The first word in a synonym list when printed in SMALL CAPITALS shows where there is more information about the group. For a more efficient use of this book see Explanatory Notes.

ant clarify, clear

fuddler *n* ***syn*** DRUNKARD, bibber, boozehound, boozer, drunk, guzzler, inebriate, lush, sot, tippler

fuddy–duddy *n* **1** ***syn*** FOGY, antediluvian, fogram, fossil, mid-Victorian, mossback, square, stick-in-the-mud
2 ***syn*** STUFFED SHIRT, Blimp, Colonel Blimp
3 ***syn*** FUSSBUDGET, fusser, fusspot, granny, old lady, old maid

fudge *vb* ***syn*** EMBROIDER, color, embellish, exaggerate, magnify, overcharge, overdraw, overpaint, overstate, pad

fudge *n* ***syn*** NONSENSE 2, ||applesauce, ||baloney, bilge, bosh, ||bull, bunkum, hogwash, hooey, poppycock

fugacious *adj* ***syn*** TRANSIENT, ephemeral, evanescent, fleeting, fugitive, impermanent, momentary, passing, short-lived, transitory

fugitive *adj* ***syn*** TRANSIENT, ephemeral, evanescent, fleeting, fugacious, momentary, passing, short-lived, transitory, volatile

fugitive *n* ***syn*** REFUGEE, displaced person, DP, émigré, evacuee

fulfill *vb* **1** to do what is required by the terms of so as to make effective <found themselves unable to *fulfill* their contract>
syn complete, execute, implement, perform; *compare* EFFECT 2
rel effect, effectuate; discharge
2 ***syn*** SATISFY 5, answer, fill, meet

fulgent *adj* ***syn*** BRIGHT 1, beaming, brilliant, effulgent, incandescent, lambent, lucent, luminous, radiant, refulgent

full *adj* **1** containing as much as is possible <the hamper is *full*>
syn awash, big, block and block, brimful, brimming, bung-full, chockablock, chock-full, cram-full, crammed, crowded, jam-full, jammed, jam-packed, loaded, packed, ||packed out, replete, stuffed, ||trig
rel abounding, teeming
idiom full to bursting (*or* overflowing), ready to burst
con blank, vacant, void; bare, barren
ant empty
2 ***syn*** CIRCUMSTANTIAL, blow-by-blow, clocklike, detailed, itemized, minute, particular, particularized, thorough
ant incomplete
3 ***syn*** WHOLE 2, choate, complete, entire, integral, perfect
con denuded, dismantled, divested, stripped
4 ***syn*** SATIATED, glutted, gorged, jaded, sated, satiate, surfeited

full–blooded *adj* **1** ***syn*** PUREBRED, pedigree, pedigreed, pureblood, thoroughbred
2 ***syn*** RUDDY 1, florid, flush, flushed, glowing, rubicund, sanguine

syn synonym(s) ***rel*** related word(s)
idiom idiomatic equivalent(s) ***con*** contrasted word(s)
ant antonym(s) * vulgar
|| use limited; if in doubt, see a dictionary
The first word in a synonym list when printed in SMALL CAPITALS shows where there is more information about the group. For a more efficient use of this book see Explanatory Notes.

full–blown *adj* **1** ***syn*** MATURE 1, adult, full-fledged, full-grown, grown, grown-up, matured, ripe, ripened
2 ***syn*** TOTAL 5, all-out, full-out, full-scale, totalitarian, unlimited

full–bosomed *adj* ***syn*** BUXOM, bosomy, busty, chesty

full–bodied *adj* ***syn*** STRONG 3, concentrated, lusty, potent, robust

full dress *n* ***syn*** FINERY, ||best bib and tucker, bravery, frippery, ||glad rags, regalia, Sunday best, war paint

full–dress *adj* ***syn*** EXHAUSTIVE, complete, thorough, thoroughgoing, whole-hog

full–fledged *adj* ***syn*** MATURE 1, adult, full-blown, full-grown, grown, grown-up, matured, ripe, ripened

full–grown *adj* ***syn*** MATURE 1, adult, full-blown, full-fledged, grown, grown-up, matured, ripe, ripened

full–mouthed *adj* ***syn*** LOUD 1, blaring, earsplitting, piercing, roaring, stentorian, stentorious, stentorophonic

fullness *n* ***syn*** BREADTH 2, amplitude, comprehensiveness, scope, wideness

full–out *adj* ***syn*** TOTAL 5, all-out, full-blown, full-scale, totalitarian, unlimited

full–scale *adj* ***syn*** TOTAL 5, all-out, full-blown, full-out, totalitarian, unlimited

full tilt *adv* ***syn*** FAST 2, expeditiously, flat-out, hastily, lickety-split, posthaste, quickly, rapidly, speedily, swiftly

fully *adv* **1** ***syn*** DOWN 2, completely, through-and-through
2 ***syn*** WELL 3, altogether, completely, entirely, perfectly, ||plumb, quite, thoroughly, utterly, wholly

fulsome *adj* too obviously extravagant or ingratiating to be accepted as genuine or sincere <offering sickeningly *fulsome* praise>
syn oily, oleaginous, slick, smarmy, soapy, unctious, unctuous
rel canting, holier-than-thou, hypocritical, pecksniffian, pharisaical, sanctimonious; bland, glib, honey-mouthed, honey-tongued, ingratiating, mealy-mouthed, oily-tongued, smooth, smooth-tongued, suave; buttery, flattering, wheedling; excessive, extravagant, exuberant, lavish, profuse; cloying, satiating, sating; bombastic, grandiloquent, magniloquent
con earnest, genuine, heartfelt, hearty, sincere, true, truthful, unfeigned, wholehearted, whole-souled

fumble *vb* **1** ***syn*** GROPE, feel, grabble
2 ***syn*** BOTCH, ||blow, bobble, bollix, bungle, flub, goof (up), louse up, mess, muff
rel flounder, stumble
3 ***syn*** MUMBLE, ||chunter, muddle, ||mump, murmur, mutter, swallow

fume *n* ***syn*** SNIT, stew, sweat, swivet, tizzy

fume *vb* ***syn*** ANGER 2, blow up, boil, boil over, bristle, burn, flare (up), rage, seethe

fun *vb* ***syn*** BANTER, fool, ||jive, joke, jolly, josh, kid, rag, razz, rib

fun *n* **1** action or speech intended to amuse or arouse laughter <you know he only said it in *fun*>
syn game, jest, joke, play, sport
rel amusement, diversion, entertainment, recreation; blitheness; jocundity, joviality, merriment; glee, hilarity, jollity, mirth; mischief, teasing
con soberness, thoughtfulness

ant earnestness, seriousness
2 ***syn*** PLAY 1, disport, diversion, recreation, sport
function *n* **1** the acts or operations expected of a person or thing <fulfill one's *function* as a mother>
syn business, duty, office, province, role
rel affair, concern; job, task, work
2 ***syn*** USE 4, duty, goal, mark, object, objective, purpose, target
3 ***syn*** POWER 3, faculty
rel action, behavior, operation
function *vb* **1** ***syn*** ACT 4, officiate, serve
2 ***syn*** ACT 5, behave, operate, perform, react, take, work
3 to operate in the proper or expected manner <finally succeeded in getting the motor to *function*>
syn act, go, run, work
rel do, operate, perform
functional *adj* ***syn*** PRACTICAL 2, handy, practicable, serviceable, useful, utile
functioning *adj* ***syn*** ACTIVE 1, alive, dynamic, live, operative, running, working
fund *n* ***syn*** SUPPLY, armamentarium, inventory, stock, store
fund *vb* ***syn*** ENDOW 2, finance, subsidize
fundament *n* ***syn*** BUTTOCKS, backside, beam, behind, bottom, derriere, posterior, rear, rump, seat
fundamental *adj* **1** forming or affecting the groundwork, roots, or lowest part of something <the *fundamental* rules of poetry>
syn basal, basic, bottom, foundational, primary, radical, underlying
rel primal, prime, primordial; elemental, elementary
con incidental
2 ***syn*** ELEMENTAL 1, basic, elementary, essential, primitive, substratal, underlying
3 ***syn*** ESSENTIAL 2, cardinal, constitutive, vital
rel indispensable, necessary, needful, requisite; dominant, paramount
fundamental *n* **1** ***syn*** PRINCIPLE 1, axiom, law, principium, theorem
rel component, constituent, factor, element
2 ***syn*** ESSENTIAL 1, basic, element, part and parcel, rudiment
3 *usu* **fundamentals** *pl* ***syn*** ALPHABET 2, ABC's, elements, grammar, principles, rudiments
fundamentalist *n* ***syn*** DIEHARD 1, bitter-ender, conservative, old liner, right, rightist, right-winger, standpat, standpatter, tory
fundamentally *adv* ***syn*** ESSENTIALLY 1, au fond, basically, in essence
ant superficially
funeral director *n* ***syn*** MORTICIAN, undertaker
funereal *adj* ***syn*** GLOOMY 3, black, bleak, depressing, depressive, disheartening, dismal, dreary, oppressive, somber
rel grave, solemn
con animated, gay, lively, sprightly, vivacious; blithe, jocund, jolly, jovial, merry
ant festive
fungible *adj* ***syn*** INTERCHANGEABLE, commutable, exchangeable, interconvertible, substitutable
funk *vb* ***syn*** SMELL 3, reek, stench, stink
funk *n* ***syn*** COWARD, chicken, craven, dastard, funker, poltroon, quitter, yellowbelly
funker *n* ***syn*** COWARD, chicken, craven, dastard, funk, poltroon, quitter, yellowbelly
funky *adj* ***syn*** MALODOROUS 1, frowsy, fusty, musty, noisome, rank, reeking, smelly, stale, stinking
funnel *vb* ***syn*** CONDUCT 4, carry, channel, convey, pipe, siphon, traject, transmit
funniness *n* ***syn*** HUMOR 4, comedy, comicality, comicalness, drollery, drollness, humorousness, wittiness
funny *adj* ***syn*** LAUGHABLE, comic, comical, droll, farcical, gelastic, ludicrous, ridiculous, risible
rel antic, bizarre, fantastic, grotesque
idiom too funny for words
con doleful, dolorous, lugubrious, melancholy, plaintive
ant unfunny
funnyman *n* ***syn*** HUMORIST 2, comedian, comic, droll, jester, joker, jokester, quipster, wag, wit
fur *n* **1** ***syn*** HIDE, fell, jacket, pelt, skin
2 ***syn*** DOWN, floss, flue, fluff, fuzz, lint, pile
furbish *vb* ***syn*** POLISH 1, buff, burnish, glance, glaze, gloss, rub, shine
furious *adj* **1** ***syn*** WILD 6, blustering, blustery, ‖coarse, dirty, raging, rough, stormy, tempestuous, turbulent
2 marked by uncontrollable excitement often under the stress of a powerful emotion <in a state of *furious* activity>
syn corybantic, delirious, frantic, frenetic, frenzied, mad, rabid, wild
rel excited, provoked, stimulated; enthusiastic, fanatic; desperate, feverish, hasty, impetuous; fierce, intense, vehement, violent; excessive, extravagant, extreme, inordinate; enraged, incensed, infuriated, maddened; hysterical, irrational, unreasonable; bewildered, distracted, upset; crazed, demented, insane, mad, maniac
con calm, composed, peaceful, placid, quiet, serene, subdued, tranquil; apathetic, impassive, imperturbable, inexcitable
3 ***syn*** INTENSE 1, concentrated, desperate, exquisite, fierce, terrible, vehement, vicious, violent
furiously *adv* ***syn*** HARD 2, fiercely, frantically, frenziedly, madly, stormily, tumultuously, turbulently, violently, wildly
furl *vb* ***syn*** ROLL 3
furnish *vb* **1** to supply one with what is needed (as for daily living or a particular activity) <*furnished* him the papers for his application>
syn accouter, appoint, arm, equip, fit out, gear, outfit, rig, turn out
rel dower, endow, endue; apparel, array, clothe; mount; give, provide, supply
con denude, dismantle, divest, strip; despoil, spoliate; relieve (of), take away
2 ***syn*** GIVE 3, deliver, dispense, feed, hand, hand over, provide, supply, transfer, turn over

furor *n* ***syn*** DELIRIUM, frenzy

furore *n* **1** ***syn*** STIR 1, ado, bustle, flurry, fuss, pother, whirl, whirlpool, whirlwind
2 ***syn*** FASHION 3, chic, craze, cry, dernier cri, fad, mode, rage, style, vogue
3 ***syn*** COMMOTION 3, ‖catouse, coil, foofaraw, fuss, ruckus, rumpus, shindig, to-do, uproar

furrow *n* ***syn*** WRINKLE, corrugation, crease, crinkle, fold, plica, ridge, rimple, rivel, ruck
rel channel, groove, rut

further *adv* **1** ***syn*** BEYOND 1, farther, ‖yon, yonder
2 ***syn*** AGAIN 4, additionally, also, besides, in addition, then

further *adj* ***syn*** ADDITIONAL, added, another, else, farther, fresh, more, new, other

further *vb* ***syn*** ADVANCE 1, encourage, forward, foster, promote, serve
rel engender, generate, propagate
con bar, block, impede, obstruct; forestall, prevent
ant hinder; retard

furthermore *adv* ***syn*** ALSO 2, along, as well, besides, likewise, moreover, too, withal, yea, yet

furthermost *adj* ***syn*** EXTREME 5, farthest, furthest, outermost, outmost, remotest, utmost, uttermost

furthest *adj* ***syn*** EXTREME 5, farthest, furthermost, outermost, outmost, remotest, utmost, uttermost

furtive *adj* **1** ***syn*** SECRET 1, clandestine, covert, hugger-mugger, hush-hush, stealthy, sub-rosa, surreptitious, ‖underneath, under-the-table
rel artful, crafty, cunning, foxy, guileful, insidious, scheming, shifty, sly, sneaky, tricky, wily; calculating, cautious, circumspect, wary; cloaked, disguised, masked
con brash, impudent, presumptuous
ant forthright; barefaced, brazen
2 ***syn*** STEALTHY 2, catlike, catty, feline
ant open

furtively *adv* ***syn*** SECRETLY, by stealth, clandestinely, covertly, hugger-mugger, in camera, privately. stealthily, sub rosa, surreptitiously
ant openly

furuncle *n* ***syn*** ABSCESS, boil, carbuncle, pimple, pustule

fury *n* ***syn*** ANGER, indignation, ire, mad, rage, wrath
rel passion; furor; acerbity, acrimony, asperity

fuse *vb* **1** ***syn*** LIQUEFY, deliquesce, dissolve, flux, liquesce, melt, run, thaw
2 ***syn*** MIX 1, amalgamate, blend, interblend, interfuse, intermingle, intermix, meld, merge, mingle
rel compact, consolidate, unify

fusillade *n* ***syn*** BARRAGE, bombardment, broadside, burst, cannonade, drumfire, hail, salvo, shower, volley

fusion *n* ***syn*** MIXTURE, admixture, alloy, amalgam, amalgamation, blend, compound, immixture, interfusion, intermixture

fuss *n* **1** ***syn*** STIR 1, ado, bustle, flurry, furore, pother, whirl, whirlpool, whirlwind
rel fluster, perturbation; bother, flap, stew; racket, rumpus; haste, hurry, speed
2 ***syn*** COMMOTION 3, ‖catouse, coil, furore, hurrah, ruckus, rumpus, shindig, shindy, to-do
3 ***syn*** QUARREL, altercation, beef, bickering, controversy, dispute, falling-out, fight, hassle, miff

fuss *vb* **1** ***syn*** WORRY 3, cark, fret, pother, stew, ‖tew
idiom fret and fume
2 ***syn*** COMPLAIN, kick, murmur, repine, wail, whine
3 ***syn*** GRIPE, ‖beef, ‖bellyache, ‖bitch, bleat, ‖blow off, crab, squawk, yammer, yawp (*or* yaup)
4 ***syn*** NAG, carp (at), henpeck, peck (at)

fussbudget *n* one who becomes upset over trifles <he is the biggest *fussbudget* I know, always going into a tizzy over nothing>
syn fuddy-duddy, fusser, fusspot, granny, old lady, old maid
rel perfectionist, precisionist, stickler

fusser *n* ***syn*** FUSSBUDGET, fuddy-duddy, fusspot, granny, old lady, old maid

fusspot *n* ***syn*** FUSSBUDGET, fuddy-duddy, fusser, granny, old lady, old maid

fussy *adj* **1** ***syn*** BUSTLING, busy, hopping, humming, hustling, lively, popping
2 ***syn*** CAREFUL 2, conscientious, conscionable, exact, heedful, meticulous, painstaking, punctilious, punctual, scrupulous
3 ***syn*** NICE 1, dainty, fastidious, finical, finicking, finicky, particular, pernickety, persnickety, squeamish
rel fretful, irritable, querulous

fustian *n* ***syn*** BOMBAST, highfalutin, lexiphanicism, rant, rhapsody, rhetoric, rodomontade

fustian *adj* ***syn*** FECKLESS 1, good-for-nothing, meaningless, purposeless, unpurposed, useless, worthless

fusty *adj* **1** ***syn*** MALODOROUS 1, fetid, musty, noisome, putrid, rancid, rank, smelly, stale, stinking
rel close, moldy; dirty, filthy, squalid; disheveled, slipshod, sloppy, slovenly, unkempt
2 ***syn*** OLD-FASHIONED, antiquated, archaic, bygone, dated, moldy, moth-eaten, old hat, outdated, passé

futile *adj* barren of results <efforts to convince him were *futile*>
syn abortive, bootless, fruitless, ineffective, ineffectual, unavailable, unavailing, unprevailing, unproductive, useless, vain
rel empty, hollow, idle, nugatory, otiose; inadequate, inefficacious, inefficient, insufficient; unsatisfactory, unsuccessful
idiom in vain, no dice, of no avail, to no effect
con effectual, efficacious, fruitful; advantageous, beneficial, profitable
ant effective

future *n* time that is to come <you must try to do better in the *future*>
syn aftertime, afterward, by-and-by, hereafter, offing, to-be; *compare* PRESENT
idiom time to come
ant past

fuzz *n* **1** ***syn*** DOWN, floss, flue, fluff, fur, lint, pile
‖**2** ***syn*** POLICEMAN, ‖bull, cop, ‖copper, ‖flatfoot, ‖heat, officer, ‖pig, police, police officer

fuzzy *adj* ***syn*** FAINT 2, bleary, dim, ill-defined, indistinct, obscure, shadowy, unclear, undefined, vague

---

syn synonym(s) *rel* related word(s)
idiom idiomatic equivalent(s) *con* contrasted word(s)
ant antonym(s) * vulgar
‖ use limited; if in doubt, see a dictionary
The first word in a synonym list when printed in SMALL CAPITALS shows where there is more information about the group. For a more efficient use of this book see Explanatory Notes.

G

gab *vb* ***syn*** CHAT 1, babble, chatter, clack, gabble, jaw, prate, prattle, yak, yakety-yak

gab *n* ***syn*** CHATTER, babble, blabber, chat, clack, gabble, jabber, palaver, prattle, yak

gabber *n* ***syn*** CHATTERBOX, bandar-log, blabber, blabbermouth, blabmouth, chatterer, jabberer, magpie, prater, prattler

gabble *vb* **1** ***syn*** GIBBER, babble, chatter, jabber
2 ***syn*** BABBLE 2, blabber, blather, drivel, drool, prate, prattle, twaddle, ‖waffle
3 ***syn*** CHAT 1, babble, chatter, clack, gab, jaw, prate, prattle, yak, yakety-yak

gabble *n* ***syn*** CHATTER, babble, blabber, chat, clack, gab, jabber, palaver, prattle, yak

gabby *adj* ***syn*** TALKATIVE, babblative, chatty, garrulous, loose-lipped, loose-tongued, loquacious, multiloquent, multiloquious, talky

gad *vb* ***syn*** WANDER 1, bat, gallivant, maunder, mooch, range, roam, rove, stray, traipse

gadget *n* **1** a usually small and often novel mechanical or electronic device or contrivance <a new kitchen *gadget* for separating egg whites>
syn concern, gimmick, gizmo, jigger, widget; *compare* DEVICE 2, DOODAD, WHAT-DO-YOU-CALL-IT
rel apparatus, appliance, contraption, tool, utensil
2 ***syn*** DOODAD, business, dingus, dofunny, doohickey, gizmo, ‖hootenanny, jigger, rigamajig, thingumajig

gaffe *n* ***syn*** FAUX PAS, blooper, boner, ‖boo-boo, break, impropriety, indecorum, solecism

gaffer *n* a man of advanced years <doddering *gaffers* on the park benches>
syn graybeard, patriarch; *compare* BELDAM 1, OLDSTER
rel duffer, geezer, grandfather, old boy, veteran

gag *vb* **1** ***syn*** RETCH, heave, keck
2 ***syn*** DEMUR, balk, boggle, jib, scruple, shy, stick, stickle, strain, stumble

gag *n* ***syn*** JOKE 1, crack, drollery, jape, jest, quip, sally, wisecrack, witticism, ‖yak
rel ruse, trick, wile

gaiety *n* **1** ***syn*** MERRYMAKING, festivity, jollity, merriment, revel, reveling, revelment, revelry, whoopee
2 ***syn*** MIRTH, festivity, glee, hilarity, jollity, joy
rel cheerfulness, gladness, happiness; geniality, pleasantness, winsomeness; animation, conviviality, entertainment, exhilaration, liveliness, merrymaking, radiance, spiritedness, vivacity
con blues, cheerlessness, dismalness, dreariness, gloom, grief, infelicity, joylessness, misery, moodiness, moroseness, pensiveness, solemnity, somberness, sorrow, sullenness, uncheerfulness, wistfulness, woe

gain *n* ***syn*** PROFIT, earnings, lucre, proceeds, return
rel cut, rake-off, share, take, winnings
ant loss

gain *vb* **1** to arrive at a goal, point, or end <*gained* success in the theater>
syn accomplish, achieve, attain, rack up, reach, realize, score, win
rel complete, consummate, fulfill, perfect, produce; succeed
con falter, flop, flounder, flunk, lose
2 ***syn*** IMPROVE 3, ameliorate, convalesce, look up, mend, perk (up), recuperate
rel invigorate, renew, strengthen; cure, heal, remedy
3 ***syn*** EARN 1, acquire, bring in, ‖drag down, draw down, get, knock down, make, win
4 ***syn*** GET 1, acquire, annex, have, land, obtain, pick up, procure, secure, win
ant lose
5 ***syn*** CLEAR 6, clean up, make, net
ant lose

gainful *adj* ***syn*** ADVANTAGEOUS 1, good, lucrative, moneymaking, paying, profitable, remunerative, well-paying, worthwhile
rel fat, fruitful, generous, lush, productive, rich; satisfying, substantial

gainsay *vb* ***syn*** DENY 4, contradict, contravene, cross, disaffirm, impugn, negate, negative, traverse
rel combat, fight, oppose, resist, withstand
ant admit

gainsaying *n* ***syn*** DENIAL 2, contradiction, negation
ant admission; admitting

gait *n* ***syn*** SPEED 2, ‖bat, celerity, pace, quickness, rapidity, rapidness, swiftness, velocity

gal *n* **1** ***syn*** GIRL 1, damsel, lass, lassie, maid, maiden, miss, missy, ‖quail, wench
2 ***syn*** GIRL FRIEND 1, best girl, ‖chick, ‖doney, girl, lady friend, lass, mouse, popsy

gall *n* ***syn*** EFFRONTERY, brashness, brass, cheek, confidence, ‖crust, face, nerve, presumption
rel arrogance, conceit, haughtiness, loftiness, lordliness, overbearance, pomposity, pride, priggishness, self-importance, smugness
con bashfulness, humbleness, humility, lowliness, modesty, shyness
ant meekness

gall *vb* **1** ***syn*** ABRADE 1, chafe, corrade, erode, graze, rub, ruffle, wear
rel bark, burn, file, fray, frazzle, grate, graze, scrape, scratch, scuff, skin
2 ***syn*** CHAFE 3, abrade, excoriate, fret, rub
rel distress, pain; cut, score, wound
3 ***syn*** ANNOY 1, abrade, bother, chafe, exercise, fret, irk, provoke, ruffle, vex
4 ***syn*** IRRITATE, aggravate, burn (up), get, grate, inflame, provoke, rile, roil

---

syn synonym(s)	***rel*** related word(s)
idiom idiomatic equivalent(s)	***con*** contrasted word(s)
ant antonym(s)	* vulgar

‖ use limited; if in doubt, see a dictionary
The first word in a synonym list when printed in SMALL CAPITALS shows where there is more information about the group. For a more efficient use of this book see Explanatory Notes.

rel chide, disturb, harass, harry, torment, worry; bedevil, needle, trouble

gallant *n* **1** ***syn*** FOP, Beau Brummel, blood, buck, coxcomb, dandy, dude, exquisite, lounge lizard, petit-maître
2 an individual who is amorously attracted to the opposite sex <his fiancee accused him of being a trifling *gallant*>
syn amorist, Casanova, Don Juan, lothario, paramour, Romeo
rel dirty old man, lecher, libertine, rake, satyr; admirer, adorer, beau, date, escort, lover, sparker, suitor, swain, wooer
idiom gay blade

gallant *adj* **1** ***syn*** COURTLY, gracious, preux, stately
rel urbane, suave; attentive, considerate, thoughtful
con heedless, inattentive, indifferent, thoughtless, unconcerned
ant ungallant
2 ***syn*** BRAVE 1, bold, bravehearted, dauntless, game, heroic, lionhearted, manful, manly, stouthearted
ant dastardly

gallantry *n* **1** ***syn*** COURTESY 1, amenity, attention
rel deference, duty, homage, honor; reverence, suavity, urbanity; address, poise, savoir faire, tact
con boorishness, churlishness, clownishness, loutishness; discourteousness
ant discourtesy
2 ***syn*** HEROISM, prowess, valiance, valiancy, valor, valorousness
rel bravery, dauntlessness; mettle, resolution, spirit
ant dastardliness

gallery *n* ***syn*** MUSEUM

galley slave *n* ***syn*** SLAVE 2, dray horse, drudge, peon, slavey, toiler, workhorse

gallimaufry *n* ***syn*** MISCELLANY 1, assortment, hodgepodge, jumble, medley, mélange, olio, pastiche, potpourri, salmagundi

galling *adj* ***syn*** BITTER 2, afflictive, distasteful, grievous, painful, unpalatable

gallivant *vb* ***syn*** WANDER 1, bat, gad, meander, mooch, ramble, range, rove, stray, traipse

‖**gallows** *n pl* ***syn*** SUSPENDERS, braces, ‖galluses

‖**galluptious** *adj* ***syn*** MARVELOUS 2, ‖cool, ‖dandy, divine, glorious, sensational, super, swell, terrific, wonderful

‖**galluses** *n pl* ***syn*** SUSPENDERS, braces, ‖gallows

galoot *n* ***syn*** MAN 3, ‖bloke, buck, chap, cuss, fellow, ‖gee, gent, guy, skate

galumph *vb* ***syn*** LUMBER, barge, clump, stumble, stump

galvanize *vb* ***syn*** PROVOKE 4, excite, innervate, innerve, motivate, move, pique, prime, quicken, stimulate
rel activate, energize, vitalize

---

syn synonym(s) ***rel*** related word(s)
idiom idiomatic equivalent(s) ***con*** contrasted word(s)
ant antonym(s) * vulgar
‖ use limited; if in doubt, see a dictionary
The first word in a synonym list when printed in SMALL CAPITALS shows where there is more information about the group. For a more efficient use of this book see Explanatory Notes.

gambit *n* ***syn*** TRICK 1, artifice, device, gimmick, jig, maneuver, play, ploy, ruse, whizzer
rel design, plan, plot

gamble *vb* **1** to engage in a game of chance for something of value <swore he would never *gamble* for high stakes again>
syn bet, game, lay, play, put (on), set, stake, wager
rel chance, hazard, lot, risk, speculate, venture
idiom buck the odds, take a flyer (on), try one's luck
2 to take a chance on something <*gambled* on the train being late>
syn chance, hazard, risk, venture; *compare* VENTURE 1
rel brave, challenge, dare, defy, face; endanger, imperil, jeopardize
idiom go it blind, take a chance (*or* one's chances), tempt fortune, trust to luck

gambol *vb* to leap or tumble about playfully <young lambs *gamboling* in the meadow>
syn caper, cavort, frisk, frolic, rollick, romp
rel lark, revel, roister; bound, leap, spring
idiom kick up one's heels, let off steam

game *n* **1** ***syn*** FUN 1, jest, joke, play, sport
con business, duty, labor, study, toil
2 games *pl* ***syn*** ATHLETICS, sports
3 animals under pursuit <hunting big *game* is a risky and expensive sport>
syn chase, prey, quarry
rel kill, ravin, victim

game *vb* ***syn*** GAMBLE 1, bet, lay, play, put (on), set, stake, wager

game *adj* ***syn*** BRAVE 1, bold, courageous, dauntless, fearless, intrepid, unafraid, undaunted, valiant, valorous

game plan *n* ***syn*** PLAN 1, blueprint, design, project, scheme, strategy

gamesome *adj* ***syn*** PLAYFUL 1, antic, frolicsome, larkish, mischievous, prankful, prankish, pranky, sportive, wicked

gamin *n* ***syn*** URCHIN, imp, monkey

gamine *n* ***syn*** TOMBOY, hoyden

gammer *n* ***syn*** BELDAM 1, dame, grandam

gamy *adj* ***syn*** MALODOROUS 1, fetid, funky, noisome, olid, rank, reeking, smelly, stinky, strong

‖**gander** *n* ***syn*** PEEP, glance, glimpse, peek

gangling *adj* being tall, thin, and usually loose-jointed <a *gangling* high-school boy>
syn gangly, lanky, rangy, spindling, spindly
rel bony, gaunt, lank, lean, scrawny, skinny, spare, tall, thin
con low, low-set, low-statured, short, squat, stocky, sturdy, thickset

gangly *adj* ***syn*** GANGLING, lanky, rangy, spindling, spindly

‖**gangrel** *n* ***syn*** VAGABOND, ‖bindle stiff, drifter, floater, hobo, runagate, ‖shack, ‖sundowner, ‖swagman, ‖traveler

gap *n* **1** an open space in a barrier <the sheep got through a *gap* in the fence>
syn breach, break, discontinuity, hole, opening
rel fracture, rupture; chink, cleavage, cleft, crack, crevice, fissure, slit, slot; division, interspace, interval, separation; aperture, cranny, orifice
2 ***syn*** RAVINE, arroyo, chasm, cleft, clough, clove, gorge, gulch

3 a period of discontinuity <a *gap* of an hour between speakers>
syn breach, break, hiatus, interim, interruption, interval, lacuna; *compare* PAUSE
rel caesura, intermission, lull, pause, respite, rest

gape *vb* **1** *syn* GAZE 1, bore, ‖gaup (*or* gawp), gawk, glare, gloat, goggle, peer, stare
2 *syn* LOOK 7, eye, ‖gaup (*or* gawp), gaze, goggle, ogle, rubberneck, stare
3 *syn* YAWN, yaw

gaping *adj syn* CAVERNOUS 1, chasmal, yawning

garb *vb syn* CLOTHE, apparel, array, attire, clad, dress, enclothe, garment, raiment

garbage *n syn* REFUSE, debris, junk, kelter, litter, offal, riffraff, rubbish, trash, waste
rel dregs, rubble; filth, sewage, slop

garble *vb syn* MISREPRESENT, belie, color, distort, falsify, miscolor, misstate, pervert, twist, warp
rel becloud, conceal, hide, obfuscate, obscure

garden house *n syn* SUMMERHOUSE, alcove, belvedere, gazebo, pagoda

gargantuan *adj syn* HUGE, Brobdingnagian, colossal, cyclopean, enormous, gigantic, leviathan, mammoth, monstrous, titanic
ant lilliputian

garish *adj syn* GAUDY, blatant, brazen, chintzy, flashy, glaring, loud, meretricious, tawdry, tinsel
rel overdone, overwrought
con dark, dim, dreary, dull, dusky, murky; quiet, unpretentious
ant somber

garland *n* **1** *syn* WREATH, anadem, chaplet, coronal, coronet, crown
2 *syn* ANTHOLOGY, album, ana, analects, florilegium, miscellany, omnibus, posy

garment *vb syn* CLOTHE, apparel, array, attire, clad, dress, enclothe, garb, raiment

garner *vb* **1** *syn* REAP, gather, harvest, ingather
2 *syn* GLEAN, cull, extract, gather, pick up
3 *syn* ACCUMULATE, amass, cumulate, hive, lay up, roll up, stockpile, store (up), uplay
rel gather, glean, harvest, reap; hoard, store
con disseminate, spread

garnish *vb syn* ADORN, beautify, bedeck, deck, decorate, dress (up), embellish, ornament, prank, trim

garrulous *adj syn* TALKATIVE, babblative, chatty, gabby, loose-lipped, loose-tongued, loquacious, multiloquent, talky, tonguey
rel blabbing, prattling, prolix, verbose, windy, wordy
con concise; terse; blunt, brusque, curt
ant taciturn

‖**gas** *n syn* NONSENSE 2, blather, ‖bull, bunkum, flapdoodle, hokum, hot air, jazz, malarkey, poppycock

‖**gas** *vb syn* CHAT 1, babble, chatter, clack, gab, jaw, prate, prattle, run on, yak

‖**gasbag** *n syn* BRAGGART, blower, blowhard, boaster, braggadocio, bragger, puckfist, rodomont, rodomontade, vaunter

gasconade *vb syn* BOAST, blow, brag, cock-a-doodle-doo, crow, mouth, prate, puff, rodomontade, vaunt

gash *vb syn* CUT 1, incise, pierce, slash, slice, slit
rel carve, split; injure, wound; furrow, mark, notch; lance, nip

gasp *vb syn* PANT 1, blow, heave, huff, ‖pank, ‖pegh, puff

‖**gasper** *n syn* CIGARETTE, ‖butt, ‖cig, ‖coffin nail, fag, ‖pill, ‖skag, smoke

gastronome *n syn* EPICURE, bon vivant, gastronomer, gastronomist, gourmand, gourmet
rel aesthete, connoisseur, dilettante

gastronomer *n syn* EPICURE, bon vivant, gastronome, gastronomist, gourmand, gourmet

gastronomist *n syn* EPICURE, bon vivant, gastronome, gastronomer, gourmand, gourmet

gate *n syn* FAUCET, cock, hydrant, petcock, spigot, stopcock, tap, valve

gather *vb* **1** *syn* GROUP 1, assemble, cluster, collect, round up
rel choose, cull, pick, select; accumulate, amass
idiom separate the wheat from the chaff (*or* the sheep from the goats)
con dispel, disperse, dissipate
ant scatter
2 *syn* REAP, garner, harvest, ingather
rel cull, pick, pluck; heap, mass, pile, stack
3 *syn* GLEAN, cull, extract, garner, pick up
4 *syn* INFER, collect, conclude, deduce, deduct, derive, draw, judge, make, make out
rel catch, fathom, follow, grasp, take in
idiom put two and two together
5 *syn* UNDERSTAND 3, assume, believe, expect, imagine, ‖reckon, suppose, suspect, take, think
6 to bring or come together <a crowd *gathered* to watch the fight>
syn assemble, collect, congregate, congress, forgather, muster, raise, rendezvous; *compare* GROUP 1
rel aggregate, troop; affiliate, ally, associate, league; encounter, meet
con break up, disband, disperse, part, separate; disintegrate, disorganize, dissolve
ant scatter
7 *syn* LOOM 2, brew, forthcome, impend

gathering *n* **1** *syn* CONCOURSE, concursion, confluence, junction, meeting
2 a number of individuals come or brought together <a *gathering* in the town park>
syn aggregation, assemblage, assembly, collection, company, congeries, congregation, crowd, group, muster, ruck; *compare* GROUP 1
rel bunch, crew, crush, flock, gang, horde, mass, press, rout, swarm, turnout
3 *syn* HARVEST 1, cropping, harvesting, ingathering, reaping

gauche *adj syn* AWKWARD 2, bumbling, clumsy, halting, ham-handed, heavy-handed, inept, maladroit, unhappy, wooden
rel crude, green, unpolished

---

syn synonym(s) *rel* related word(s)
idiom idiomatic equivalent(s) *con* contrasted word(s)
ant antonym(s) * vulgar
‖ use limited; if in doubt, see a dictionary
The first word in a synonym list when printed in SMALL CAPITALS shows where there is more information about the group. For a more efficient use of this book see Explanatory Notes.

con bland, smooth, suave, urbane
ant adroit

gaudy *adj* cheaply or vulgarly showy <*gaudy* sideshow posters>
syn blatant, brazen, chintzy, flashy, garish, glaring, loud, meretricious, tawdry, tinsel
rel obtrusive, ostentatious, pretentious, showy, tasteless; coarse, crude, gross, vulgar; brummagem, fake, phony, sham
con restrained, tasteful, unobtrusive; factual, illuminating, informative
ant quiet

gauge *n* *syn* STANDARD 3, benchmark, criterion, measure, touchstone, yardstick
rel check, mark, model, norm, pattern, rule, type

gauge *vb* *syn* MEASURE 2, scale

‖**gaum** *n* *syn* OAF 2, gawk, klutz, lobster, looby, lout, lubber, ‖lug, lummox, palooka

gaunt *adj* **1** *syn* LEAN, angular, bony, lank, lanky, rawboned, scraggy, scrawny, skinny, spare
2 *syn* EMACIATED, cadaverous, skeletal, wasted
ant bloated

‖**gaup** (*or* **gawp**) *vb* **1** *syn* LOOK 7, eye, gape, gaze, goggle, ogle, rubberneck, stare
2 *syn* GAZE 1, bore, gape, gawk, glare, gloat, goggle, peer, stare

gauzy *adj* *syn* FILMY, diaphanous, flimsy, gossamer, sheer, tiffany, transparent

gawk *vb* *syn* GAZE 1, bore, gape, ‖gaup (*or* gawp), glare, gloat, goggle, peer, stare

gawk *n* *syn* OAF 2, klutz, lobster, looby, lout, lubber, ‖lug, lummox, lump, palooka

gawky *adj* *syn* CLUMSY 1, awkward, lumbering, lumpish, splathering, splay, ungainly

gay *adj* **1** *syn* MERRY, blithe, blithesome, festive, gleeful, jocund, jolly, jovial, lighthearted, mirthful
2 *syn* LIVELY 1, alert, animate, animated, ‖cant, ‖canty, keen, spirited, sprightly, vivacious
rel frolicsome, playful, sportive
con earnest, sedate, serious, solemn, somber, staid; quiet, silent, still
ant grave, sober
3 *syn* COLORFUL, brave, bright, colory, vivid
4 *syn* WILD 7, devil-may-care, fast, raffish, rakehell, rakish, sporty
5 *syn* HOMOSEXUAL, homoerotic, homophile, inverted, queer, uranian
6 *syn* PRESUMPTUOUS, brash, brassbound, confident, forward, overweening, presuming, pushful, ‖pushy, self-assertive

gaze *vb* **1** to look long and usually attentively <*gazed* out the window>
syn bore, gape, ‖gaup (*or* gawp), gawk, glare, gloat, goggle, peer, stare; *compare* LOOK 7
rel look, see, watch; peek, peep; contemplate, inspect, observe, scrutinize, survey; admire, ogle, regard
con glance, skim, skip
2 *syn* LOOK 7, eye, gape, ‖gaup (*or* gawp), goggle, ogle, rubberneck, stare

gaze (upon) *vb* *syn* EYE 1, consider, contemplate, look (at *or* upon), view

gazebo *n* *syn* SUMMERHOUSE, alcove, belvedere, garden house, pagoda

gear *n* *syn* EQUIPMENT, accouterment(s), apparatus, habiliment(s), machinery, matériel, outfit, paraphernalia, tackle, tackling
rel accessories, adjuncts, appendages, appurtenances; belongings, effects, means, possessions

gear *vb* *syn* FURNISH 1, accouter, appoint, arm, equip, fit out, outfit, rig, turn out

‖**gee** *n* *syn* MAN 3, ‖bloke, boy, buck, chap, fellow, gent, gentleman, guy, he

‖**gee** *vb* *syn* AGREE 4, accord, conform, correspond, dovetail, go, harmonize, jibe, square, tally

Gehenna *n* *syn* HELL, abyss, hades, inferno, netherworld, perdition, pit, Sheol, Tophet, underworld

gel *vb* *syn* COAGULATE, clot, congeal, gelate, gelatinize, jell, jellify, jelly, set

gelastic *adj* *syn* LAUGHABLE, comic, comical, droll, farcical, funny, ludicrous, ridiculous, risible

gelate *vb* *syn* COAGULATE, clot, congeal, gel, gelatinize, jell, jellify, jelly, set

gelatinize *vb* *syn* COAGULATE, clot, congeal, gel, gelate, jell, jellify, jelly, set

geld *vb* *syn* STERILIZE, alter, castrate, change, desexualize, fix, mutilate, neuter, unsex

gelid *adj* *syn* COLD 1, arctic, chill, chilly, cool, freezing, frosty, glacial, icy, nippy
con ardent, burning, fervent, scorching, sweltering, torrid
ant fervid

‖**gelt** *n* *syn* MONEY, ‖bread, dough, filthy lucre, ‖lettuce, loot, lucre, ‖mazuma, ‖ooftish, ‖shekels

gem *vb* *syn* BEJEWEL, begem, beset, enjewel, jewel

‖**gendarme** *n* *syn* POLICEMAN, ‖bobby, ‖bull, ‖constable, cop, ‖flatfoot, ‖fuzz, ‖heat, ‖paddy, ‖peeler

genealogy *n* an account often in chart form recording a line of ancestors <decided to prepare a *genealogy* of his family>
syn ‖begats, family tree, pedigree, stemma

general *adj* **1** conforming to what is expected in the ordinary course of events <the *general* problems of everyday life>
syn common, commonplace, matter-of-course, natural, normal, prevalent, regular, run-of-the-mill, typic, typical, usual
rel everyday, popular; familiar, universal; habitual, humdrum, routine, uneventful
con abnormal, extraordinary, irregular, novel, strange, unexpected, unforeseeable, unusual
2 belonging or relating to the whole <a *general* change in the weather>
syn common, generic, universal
rel natural, normal, regular, typical; broad, inclusive, wide
con individual, particular, special; characteristic, distinctive, peculiar

---

syn synonym(s) — *rel* related word(s)
idiom idiomatic equivalent(s) — *con* contrasted word(s)
ant antonym(s) — * vulgar
‖ use limited; if in doubt, see a dictionary
The first word in a synonym list when printed in SMALL CAPITALS shows where there is more information about the group. For a more efficient use of this book see Explanatory Notes.

3 ***syn*** ALL-AROUND 2, comprehensive, global, inclusive, overall, sweeping
4 ***syn*** PUBLIC 4, popular, vulgar

generally *adv* **1** in a reasonably inclusive manner <the forest was *generally* coniferous>
syn chiefly, largely, mainly, mostly, overall, predominantly, primarily, principally
rel about, approximately, practically, roughly, roundly
con altogether, totally, wholly
2 ***syn*** ALTOGETHER 3, all in all, by and large, en masse, on the whole
3 ***syn*** USUALLY 2, as a rule, by ordinary, commonly, frequently, ordinarily

generate *vb* **1** to bring into existence <*generate* new business>
syn create, father, hatch, make, originate, parent, procreate, produce, sire, spawn
rel bring about, effect, impose, occasion; introduce; cause; found, inaugurate, institute, set up; develop, induce, whip (up)
idiom bring to pass, give birth to, give rise to
con demolish, destroy, extinguish, ruin; degenerate, deteriorate, impair, worsen
2 ***syn*** PROCREATE 1, bear, beget, breed, multiply, produce, propagate, reproduce
3 to be the cause or source of something immaterial <actions that *generated* a good deal of suspicion>
syn breed, cause, engender, get up, hatch, induce, muster (up), occasion, produce, provoke, work up
rel accomplish, achieve, perform
idiom give birth to, give rise to

generator *n* ***syn*** FATHER 2, architect, author, creator, founder, inventor, maker, originator, patriarch, sire

generic *adj* ***syn*** GENERAL 2, common, universal
ant specific

generous *adj* **1** marked by a noble or forbearing spirit <*generous* toward the weakness of others>
syn benevolent, big, chivalrous, considerate, greathearted, lofty, magnanimous
rel altruistic, charitable, kindhearted, kindly, thoughtful, ungrudging, unselfish; fair, honest; long-suffering, tolerant; helpful, willing
con base, ignoble, mean, self-centered, selfish; grim, hard, harsh, intolerant
ant ungenerous
2 ***syn*** LIBERAL 1, bounteous, bountiful, free, freehanded, handsome, munificent, openhanded, unsparing
ant stingy
3 ***syn*** PLENTIFUL, abundant, ample, bounteous, bountiful, copious, liberal, plenteous, plenty
rel lavish; luxuriant; affluent, wealthy
con scant, scanty, sparse

generously *adv* ***syn*** WELL 2, considerately, heedfully, kindly, thoughtfully

genesis *n* ***syn*** BEGINNING, alpha, commencement, dawn, dawning, opening, outset, outstart, setout, start
rel provenance, provenience
con cessation, conclusion, culmination, end, finish, termination

genial *adj* **1** ***syn*** GRACIOUS 1, affable, congenial, cordial, sociable, ‖sonsy
rel amicable, friendly, neighborly; blithe, cheerful, jocund, jolly, jovial, merry
con discourteous, rude, uncivil, ungracious; crabbed, morose, sullen; ironic, sarcastic, sardonic, satiric
ant caustic (*remarks, comments*); saturnine (*manner, disposition, aspect*)
2 ***syn*** GENTLE 2, affable, amiable

geniality *n* ***syn*** AMENITY 1, agreeability, aggreeableness, amiability, cordiality, enjoyableness, gratefulness, pleasance, pleasantness, sweetness and light

genitalia *n pl* the external components of the reproductive system <the gradual adolescent differentiation of the *genitalia*>
syn genitals, parts, private parts, privates, privities, privy parts, pudendum (*usu* pudenda *pl*), secrets

genitals *n pl* ***syn*** GENITALIA, parts, private parts, privates, privities, privy parts, pudendum (*usu* pudenda *pl*), secrets

genius *n* ***syn*** GIFT 2, aptness, bent, bump, faculty, flair, head, knack, talent, turn
rel creativity, ingenuity, inventiveness, originality; astuteness, brains, grasp, intellect, intelligence, understanding

gent *n* ***syn*** MAN 3, ‖bloke, boy, buck, chap, fellow, ‖gee, gentleman, guy, he

genteel *adj* **1** having characteristics or qualities befitting the upper classes <in those days croquet was a very *genteel* sport> <his manner was perfectly *genteel*>
syn cultivated, cultured, distingué, polished, refined, urbane, well-bred
rel elegant, fashionable, graceful, stylish; chivalrous, gentlemanly, knightly, ladylike, noble; mannerly, well-mannered
con coarse, common, crude, ill-bred, rough, rude, uncouth, uncultured, unpolished, vulgar
ant ungenteel
2 ***syn*** CIVIL 2, courteous, mannerly, polite, well-mannered
rel well-behaved; aristocratic, cultured
con crude, discourteous, inconsiderate, rough, rude
3 involving or excessively preoccupied with the airs and forms of middle-class or upper-class proprieties <a shy *genteel* girl terrified of blundering socially>
syn affected, la-di-da, ‖lardy-dardy, mincing, pretentious, stilted, too-too; *compare* PRECIOUS 4, PRIM 1
rel artificial, formal, high-falutin
con cultured, genuine, honest, refined; gracious, polished; gentlemanly, ladylike
4 ***syn*** PRIM 1, prig, priggish, prissy, prudish, puritanical, straitlaced, stuffy, tight-laced, Victorian
rel narrow; intolerant, uncharitable; confined, insular, parochial, provincial
idiom nasty nice
con charitable, tolerant, understanding; broad-minded, easy, relaxed

---

gentile *adj* ***syn*** HEATHEN, ethnic, infidel, infidelic, pagan, profane

gentility *n* ***syn*** ARISTOCRACY, aristoi, elite, flower, gentry, optimacy, quality, society, upper class, upper crust

gentle *adj* **1** free from all harshness, roughness, or intensity <a *gentle* summer breeze>
syn balmy, bland, faint, lenient, mild, smooth, soft
rel delicate, mellow, tender; hushed, low, soothing; calm, halcyon, peaceful, placid, quiet, serene, tranquil
con coarse, harsh, rough; exquisite, fierce, intense, savage, vehement, violent; forceful, forcible, powerful
2 having a pleasant easygoing nature <a *gentle* person in everything she does>
syn affable, amiable, genial
rel kind, pleasant, pleasing, tender; agreeable, benign, mild; compassionate, kindly, softhearted, sympathetic, warmhearted
con belligerent, cantankerous, contentious, ill-natured, petty, quarrelsome; aggressive, demanding, overbearing
ant harsh, stern

gentleman *n* **1** a person of good or noble birth <the contributions of the country *gentleman* to social stability>
syn aristo, aristocrat, blue blood, patrician
rel Brahmin; chevalier; nob, swell
con churl, clown, lout
ant boor
2 ***syn*** MAN 3, ‖bloke, boy, buck, chap, fellow, ‖gee, gent, guy, he

gentleman friend *n* ***syn*** BOYFRIEND 1, beau, swain, young man

gentry *n* ***syn*** ARISTOCRACY, aristoi, elite, flower, gentility, optimacy, quality, society, upper class, upper crust

genuine *adj* **1** ***syn*** AUTHENTIC 2, bona fide, indubitable, real, sure-enough, true, undoubted, unquestionable, veritable, very
con artificial, ersatz, factitious; counterfeited, sham, simulated; sophisticated
ant fraudulent
2 ***syn*** ACTUAL 2, absolute, factual, hard, positive, sure-enough
con uncommon, unordinary, unusual; alleged, apocryphal, apparent, fabulous, fictitious, mythical
3 free from hypocrisy or pretense <a *genuine* love for his fellowman>
syn heart-whole, honest, real, sincere, true, undesigning, undissembled, unfeigned; *compare* NATURAL 5, SINCERE 1
rel reliable, trustworthy, unaffected, unimpeachable, veritable
con affected, hyprocritical
ant insincere

---

syn synonym(s) | *rel* related word(s)
idiom idiomatic equivalent(s) | *con* contrasted word(s)
ant antonym(s) | * vulgar
‖ use limited; if in doubt, see a dictionary
The first word in a synonym list when printed in SMALL CAPITALS shows where there is more information about the group. For a more efficient use of this book see Explanatory Notes.

genuinely *adv* ***syn*** VERY 2, actually, de facto, really, truly, veritably

germ *n* ***syn*** SEED 2, bud, embryo, nucleus, spark

germane *adj* ***syn*** RELEVANT, ad rem, applicable, applicative, applicatory, apposite, apropos, material, pertinent, pointful
con incompatible, incongruous, inconsonant
ant foreign

gest *n* ***syn*** ADVENTURE, emprise, enterprise, exploit, feat, venture

gestapo *adj* ***syn*** TERRORISTIC

gestation *n* ***syn*** PREGNANCY, gravidity, pregnance, situation

gesture *n* ***syn*** EXPRESSION 3, indication, reminder, sign, token

gesture *vb* ***syn*** SIGNAL, flag, motion, sign, signalize

get *vb* **1** to come into possession of <hoped to *get* a fortune from his invention>
syn acquire, annex, chalk up, compass, gain, have, land, obtain, pick up, procure, pull, secure, win
rel educe, elicit, evoke, extort, extract, ‖promote; accept, receive; clutch, grab, grasp, take; accomplish, achieve, effect; capture, carry; draw
idiom come by
con abnegate, eschew, forbear, forgo, give up, sacrifice; abandon, forsake, renounce
2 ***syn*** EARN 1, acquire, bring in, ‖drag down, draw down, gain, knock down, make, win
3 ***syn*** BECOME 1, come, ‖come over, go, grow, run, turn, wax
rel achieve, attain, effect, realize
idiom get to be, turn out to be
4 ***syn*** CONTRACT 1, catch, come down (with), sicken (with *or* of), take
5 ***syn*** FATHER 1, beget, breed, procreate, progenerate, sire
6 ***syn*** PREPARE 1, fit, fix, make, make up, ready
rel arrange, order, right; adjust, coordinate, organize
7 ***syn*** CATCH 1, bag, capture, collar, ‖cotch, nail, prehend, secure, take
8 ***syn*** AFFECT, carry, impress, influence, inspire, move, strike, sway, touch
rel bend, bias, dispose, predispose, prompt
con benumb, deaden, numb; blunt, dull, harden
9 ***syn*** NONPLUS 1, beat, buffalo, stick, stump
rel bother, distress, disturb, perturb, upset; discomfit, disconcert, embarrass
10 ***syn*** IRRITATE, aggravate, burn (up), exasperate, gall, nettle, peeve, provoke, put out, rile
idiom try one's temper
con calm, compose, cool, lull, soothe, subdue
11 ***syn*** LEARN 1, master, pick up
idiom get into one's head
12 ***syn*** MEMORIZE, con, learn
13 ***syn*** INDUCE 1, argue (into), bring around, convince, draw, persuade, prevail (on *or* upon), prompt, talk (into), win (over)
rel provoke; beg, coax, press, pressure, urge
14 ***syn*** REACH 4, contact
15 ***syn*** COME 1, arrive, ‖blow in, get in, reach, show, show up, turn up

get along *vb* **1** ***syn*** ADVANCE 5, get on, march, move, proceed, progress

rel depart, go
con recede, regress, retreat, retrogress, reverse, revert
2 ***syn*** SHIFT 5, do, fare, get by, get on, ‖make out, manage, muddle through, stagger (on *or* along)
rel flourish, prosper, succeed, thrive

get away *vb* ***syn*** GO 2, ‖blow, depart, exit, get off, leave, pull out, quit, retire, withdraw

getaway *n* ***syn*** ESCAPE 1, breakout, escapement, escaping, flight, lam, ‖scape, slip

get back *vb* ***syn*** RECOVER 1, recoup, recruit, regain, repossess, retrieve

get by *vb* ***syn*** SHIFT 5, do, fare, get along, get on, ‖make out, manage, muddle through, stagger (on *or* along)

get in *vb* ***syn*** COME 1, arrive, ‖blow in, get, reach, show, show up, turn up

get off *vb* **1** ***syn*** GO 2, ‖blow, depart, exit, get away, leave, pull out, quit, retire, withdraw
rel advance, progress
2 ***syn*** BEGIN 1, commence, embark (on *or* upon), inaugurate, initiate, jump (off), kick off, launch, open, start

get on *vb* **1** ***syn*** DON 1, assume, draw on, huddle (on), put on, slip (on), throw
2 ***syn*** ADVANCE 5, get along, march, move, proceed, progress
3 ***syn*** SHIFT 5, do, fare, get along, get by, ‖make out, manage, muddle through, stagger (on *or* along)

get out *vb* **1** to go away quickly, immediately, and often secretly <had to *get out* before the police arrived>
syn begone, clear out, decamp, hightail, kite, scram, skedaddle, skiddoo, take off, ‖vamoose
rel depart, duck (out), egress, exit, go, leave, split
idiom beat it, be off, make tracks, take a powder, take a runout powder
con abide, remain, reside, stay
2 to become known <we can't let this story *get out*>
syn break, come out, leak, out, transpire
3 ***syn*** PUBLISH 2, issue, put out

gettable *adj* ***syn*** AVAILABLE 1, attainable, disponible, obtainable, procurable, securable

get up *vb* **1** ***syn*** ROLL OUT, arise, pile (out), rise, rise and shine, turn out, uprise
2 ***syn*** RISE 1, stand, up, uprise, upspring
3 ***syn*** GENERATE 3, breed, cause, engender, hatch, induce, muster (up), occasion, produce, work up

getup *n* **1** ***syn*** COSTUME, dress, guise, outfit, rig, setout, turnout
2 ***syn*** VIGOR 2, bang, drive, get-up-and-go, go, pep, punch, push, snap, vitality

get-up-and-go *n* **1** ***syn*** VIGOR 2, bang, drive, getup, go, pep, punch, push, snap, vitality
2 ***syn*** ENTERPRISE 4, ambition, drive, initiative, push

gewgaw *n* ***syn*** KNICKKNACK, bauble, bibelot, curio, gimcrack, novelty, objet d'art, trifle, trinket, whatnot

ghastly *adj* **1** disturbingly frightening or repellent in appearance or aspect <the *ghastly* sight of burned and rotting bodies>
syn grim, grisly, gruesome, hideous, horrible, horrid, horrifying, lurid, macabre, terrible, terrifying
rel appalling, awful, dreadful, frightening, frightful, shocking; disgustful, disgusting, nauseant, nauseating, sickening
con appealing, attractive, charming, pleasant, touching; acceptable, bearable; trivial, unimportant
2 resembling or suggestive of a ghost <a *ghastly* form slightly visible through the fog>
syn cadaverous, corpselike, deathlike, ghostlike, ghostly, shadowy, spectral
rel ashen, livid, lurid, pale; uncanny, weird; gruesome, haggard, macabre; dim, faint, weak; charnel, mortuary, sepulchral

ghost *n* ***syn*** APPARITION, ‖haunt, phantasm, phantom, shade, shadow, specter, spirit, spook, wraith
rel demon, devil

ghost *vb* ***syn*** GHOSTWRITE, ‖spook

ghostlike *adj* ***syn*** GHASTLY 2, cadaverous, corpselike, deathlike, ghostly, shadowy, spectral

ghostly *adj* ***syn*** GHASTLY 2, cadaverous, corpselike, deathlike, ghostlike, shadowy, spectral

ghostwrite *vb* to write for and in the name of another <a *ghostwritten* autobiography>
syn ghost, ‖spook

GI *n* ***syn*** SOLDIER, fighter, fighting man, man-at-arms, serviceman, swad, ‖swaddy, ‖sweat, warrior

giant *n* something of monstrous size, appearance, or power <a *giant* of a tractor>
syn behemoth, leviathan, mammoth, monster, whale
rel cyclops, polypheme

giant *adj* ***syn*** HUGE, behemothic, Brobdingnagian, colossal, cyclopean, gargantuan, gigantic, Herculean, mammoth, titanic
rel gross, hulking
con paltry, petty, puny, trifling, trivial
ant dwarf

gibber *vb* to utter or speak rapidly, inarticulately, and usually unintelligibly <a *gibbering* idiot>
syn babble, chatter, gabble, jabber
rel blather, drivel, prate, prattle, yammer; stammer, stutter; mumble, mutter; mow
idiom run off at the mouth
con articulate, enunciate, pronounce

gibberish *n* **1** unintelligible or meaningless talk <the *gibberish* of an imbecile>
syn babble, drivel, Greek, jabber, jabberwocky, nonsense, skimble-skamble; *compare* GIBBERISH 3
rel blather, bunkum, claptrap, twaddle; blabber, gabble, palaver, prattle
2 ***syn*** GOBBLEDYGOOK, double-talk
3 speech or actions that are esoteric in nature and suggest the magical, strange, or unknown <the shaman's strange *gibberish*>
syn abracadabra, hocus-pocus, mumbo jumbo, mummery
rel magic, sorcery, thaumaturgy

gibbet *vb* ***syn*** HANG 2, noose, scrag, string (up), turn off

gibble-gabble *n* ***syn*** CHATTER, babble, bibble-babble, chat, gab, jabber, palaver, prattle, tittle-tattle, yak-yak

---

syn synonym(s) — ***rel*** related word(s)
idiom idiomatic equivalent(s) — ***con*** contrasted word(s)
ant antonym(s) — * vulgar
‖ use limited; if in doubt, see a dictionary
The first word in a synonym list when printed in SMALL CAPITALS shows where there is more information about the group. For a more efficient use of this book see Explanatory Notes.

gibe *vb* ***syn*** SCOFF, fleer, flout, gird, jeer, jest, quip (at), scout (at), sneer
rel rail, rally, revile, scold, twit

giddy *adj* **1** having a lightheartedly silly nature <tried to teach a bunch of *giddy* Girl Scouts how to make a fire>
syn bird-witted, dizzy, empty-headed, featherbrained, flighty, fribble, fribbling, frivolous, harebrained, hoity-toity, light, lightheaded, rattlebrained, scatterbrained, silly, skittish, volage, yeasty
rel capricious, fickle, impulsive, whimsical; brainless, exuberant, thoughtless, witless
idiom giddy as a goose
con earnest, pensive, sedate, serious, sober, solemn, staid, thoughtful
2 ***syn*** DIZZY 2, light, light-headed, swimming, swimmy, vertiginous
rel bemused, flustered
idiom going around in circles, like a chicken with its head cut off, seeing double

gift *n* **1** something freely given by one person to another for his benefit or pleasure <the watch was a graduation *gift*>
syn benevolence, boon, ‖compliment, favor, largess, present
rel alms, benefaction, contribution, donation; award, bestowal, grant, presentation; legacy; offering, reward, tip; remembrance, souvenir, token
2 a natural or special facility or capableness <has a *gift* for electronics>
syn aptness, bent, bump, faculty, flair, genius, head, knack, nose, set, talent, turn; *compare* LEANING 2
rel ability, aptitude, capability; accomplishment, acquirement, attainment; instinct, numen, power; forte, leaning, propensity, specialty
con awkwardness, clumsiness, maladroitness

gigantean *adj* ***syn*** HUGE, behemothic, Brobdingnagian, colossal, cyclopean, elephantine, gargantuan, gigantic, leviathan, mammoth

gigantesque *adj* ***syn*** HUGE, Antaean, behemothic, colossal, cyclopean, gigantic, Herculean, mammoth, monstrous, titanic

gigantic *adj* ***syn*** HUGE, colossal, cyclopean, elephantine, enormous, gargantuan, immense, mammoth, monstrous, prodigious
rel hulking, stupendous
con paltry, petty, puny, trifling, trivial

giggle *vb* ***syn*** LAUGH, chortle, chuckle, guffaw, hee-haw, snicker, ‖sniggle, tehee, titter

gill *n* ***syn*** CREEK 2, ‖branch, brook, ‖burn, race, ‖rindle, rivulet, ‖run, runnel, stream

gimcrack *n* ***syn*** KNICKKNACK, bauble, bibelot, curio, gewgaw, novelty, objet d'art, trifle, trinket, whatnot

syn synonym(s) ***rel*** related word(s)
idiom idiomatic equivalent(s) ***con*** contrasted word(s)
ant antonym(s) * vulgar
‖ use limited; if in doubt, see a dictionary
The first word in a synonym list when printed in SMALL CAPITALS shows where there is more information about the group. For a more efficient use of this book see Explanatory Notes.

gimmick *n* **1** ***syn*** GADGET 1, concern, gizmo, jigger, widget
2 ***syn*** TRICK 1, artifice, feint, gambit, maneuver, ploy, ruse, stratagem, whizzer, wile
rel cheat, counterfeit, deceit, dodge, fake, humbug, imposture; fun, game, jest, method, sport

gimp *n* ***syn*** SPIRIT 5, brio, dash, élan, esprit, life, oomph, verve, vim, zing

gingerly *adj* ***syn*** CAUTIOUS, calculating, careful, chary, circumspect, considerate, discreet, guarded, safe, wary

gingery *adj* ***syn*** SPIRITED 2, beany, fiery, high-hearted, high-spirited, mettlesome, peppery, spunky
con lethargic, listless, poky, slow; dead, dull, flat, insipid, stuffy; dreary; blasé, lackadaisical, nonchalant

‖gin mill *n* ***syn*** BAR 5, barroom, ‖boozer, cocktail lounge, drinkery, lounge, pub, ‖rum-mill, saloon, tavern

gird *vb* **1** ***syn*** BELT 1, band, begird, begirdle, cincture, encincture, engird, engirdle, girdle
ant ungird
2 ***syn*** SURROUND 1, begird, beset, circle, encircle, encompass, girdle, hem, ring, round
rel wrap, wreathe
3 to prepare oneself for action <*girded* himself for the coming trial>
syn brace, fortify, prepare, ready, steel, strengthen
rel bolster, buttress, support, sustain; harden, reinforce, shore (up); invigorate; dispose, forearm, prepare
idiom gird one's loins, whet the knife

gird *vb* ***syn*** SCOFF, fleer, flout, gibe, jeer, jest, quip (at), scout (at), sneer

girdle *n* ***syn*** BELT 1, ceinture, cincture, sash, waistband

girdle *vb* **1** ***syn*** BELT, band, begird, begirdle, cincture, encincture, engird, engirdle, gird
2 ***syn*** SURROUND 1, begird, beset, circle, encircle, encompass, gird, hem, ring, round

girl *n* **1** a young unmarried female person <hired a *girl* to babysit>
syn damsel, gal, lass, lassie, maid, maiden, miss, missy, ‖quail, ‖quiff, wench
rel hoyden, tomboy; deb, debutante, subdeb, subdebutante; bobby-soxer; schoolgirl; gamine
2 ***syn*** MAID 2, biddy, handmaid, hired girl, housemaid, maidservant
3 ***syn*** GIRL FRIEND 1, best girl, ‖chick, ‖doney, gal, lady friend, lass, mouse, popsy

girl Friday *n* ***syn*** RIGHT-HAND MAN, man Friday, right hand

girl friend *n* **1** a woman who is a man's usual or preferred companion <took his *girl friend* out every weekend>
syn best girl, ‖chick, ‖doney, gal, girl, lady friend, lass, mouse, popsy
2 a woman who shares with a man a strong and usually sexually oriented mutual attraction <his wife caught him with his *girl friend*>
syn ‖baby, beloved, flame, honey, inamorata, ladylove, steady, sweetheart, sweetie, truelove
3 ***syn*** MISTRESS, ‖doxy, inamorata, lover, paramour, woman

gist *n* ***syn*** SUBSTANCE 2, burden, core, matter, meat, pith, sense, short, thrust, upshot
rel sap, soul, spirit; subject, theme, topic; bearing, drift, tenor

give *vb* **1** to provide gratuitously <*gave* their labor to rebuild the burned church>
syn bestow, devote, donate, give away, hand out, present; *compare* CONTRIBUTE 1
rel accord, award, confer, grant, hand; afford, contribute, furnish, provide; aid, assist, benefact, help
con keep, retain, withhold; lease, sell
2 to provide by or as if by formal action <he was *given* a diploma>
syn accord, award, confer, grant; *compare* GRANT 1
rel bestow, hand over, present; allocate, appropriate, assign
con decline, refuse; hold back, withhold
3 to put into the possession of another usually for use or consumption <*gave* the dog a drink of water>
syn deliver, dish out, dispense, feed, find, furnish, hand, hand over, provide, supply, transfer, turn over
rel administer, commit, offer; deal, disburse, disperse, distribute, divide, dole (out), lot (out); afford, lend
con have, hold, hold back, keep, keep back, reserve, retain, withhold
4 *syn* OFFER 1, extend, hold out, pose, present, proffer, tender
rel bestow, confer, render; administer, dispense, issue
5 *syn* EXPRESS 2, air, put, state, vent, ventilate
6 *syn* ALLOT, admeasure, allocate, allow, apportion, assign, lot, mete (out)
7 to furnish as a result or product <6 + 6 *gives* 12>
syn produce, yield
rel be, equal, make; afford, furnish, offer, supply
8 *syn* SPEND 1, disburse, expend, fork (out), lay out, outlay, pay, shell out
9 *syn* SELL 2, market, vend
10 to bestow or dispense by some action <*gave* him a punch in the nose>
syn administer, deal, deliver, inflict, strike
rel bestow, dispense; fetch
11 *syn* ADDRESS 3, apply, bend, buckle (down), devote, direct, throw, turn
12 to fail in response to physical stress <the bridge *gave* under the heavy load>
syn bend, break, cave, collapse, crumple, fold up, go, yield
rel fail, relax, relent, slacken, weaken
idiom cave in, give way
13 *syn* HAPPEN 1, befall, betide, break, chance, come, come off, fall out, go, hap

give away *vb* **1** *syn* GIVE 1, bestow, devote, donate, hand out, present
2 *syn* REVEAL 1, betray, blab (out), disclose, discover, divulge, mouth, spill, tell, unclose

give back *vb* **1** *syn* RETREAT 2, fall back, retire, withdraw
rel back out, backtrack, backwater; crumble, fail, falter, weaken
2 *syn* RESTORE 5, put (back), reinstate, replace, return

given *adj* *syn* APT 1, inclined, liable, likely, prone

given name *n* the name that precedes one's surname <arguing over the baby's *given name*>
syn baptismal name, Christian name, font name, forename, personal name, prename
rel first name, middle name; appellation, appellative, compellation, denomination, style; praenomen; epithet, label, tag

give off *vb* **1** *syn* EMIT 2, give out, issue, release, throw off, vent
2 *syn* DISCHARGE 5, disembogue, emit, flow, pour, void

give out *vb* **1** *syn* EMIT 2, give off, issue, release, throw off, vent
2 *syn* COLLAPSE 2, break down, cave (in), drop, ‖flake out, peg out, succumb, wilt
3 *syn* FAIL 2, run out

give over *vb* *syn* STOP 3, cease, desist, ‖deval, discontinue, halt, knock off, leave off, quit, surcease

giver *n* *syn* DONOR, bestower, conferrer, donator, presenter

give up *vb* **1** *syn* RELINQUISH, abandon, cede, hand over, leave, resign, surrender, ‖turn up, waive, yield
2 *syn* DESPAIR, despond

gizmo *n* **1** *syn* DOODAD, dingus, dofunny, doohickey, gadget, ‖hootenanny, jigger, thingumajig, thingumbob, thingummy
2 *syn* GADGET, concern, gimmick, jigger, widget

glabrous *adj* *syn* HAIRLESS, bald, smooth
rel beardless, shaven, smooth-shaven
con bristled, bristly, hairy, hirsute, stubbled, stubbly

glacial *adj* **1** *syn* COLD 1, arctic, chill, chilly, cool, freezing, frosty, gelid, icy, nippy
2 *syn* COLD 2, chill, emotionless, frigid, icy, indifferent, unemotional
rel aloof, distant, remote, reserved, standoffish, withdrawn; exclusive, inaccessible, seclusive, unapproachable
con affable, gregarious, sociable

glad *adj* **1** characterized by or expressing the mood of one who is pleased or delighted <he was *glad* to be on vacation>
syn happy, joyful, joyous, lighthearted
rel delighted, gratified, pleased, rejoiced, tickled; blithe, exhilarated, jocund, jolly, jovial, merry; gleeful, hilarious, mirthful
idiom filled with (*or* full of) delight
con blue, dejected, depressed, downcast, melancholy; despondent, dispirited, heavyhearted, sadhearted, unhappy; forlorn, joyless, sorrowful, woeful
ant sad
2 full of brightness and cheerfulness <a *glad* spring morning>
syn bright, cheerful, cheery, radiant
rel beaming, sparkling; beautiful; genial, pleasant
con dark, dim, dull, gloomy, somber

gladden *vb* *syn* PLEASE 2, arride, delectate, delight, gratify, happify, pleasure
rel comfort, console, solace; animate, enliven, exhilarate, invigorate, liven, quicken, vivify
con depress, oppress, weigh; discourage, dishearten, dispirit; damp, dampen; bother, irk

---

syn synonym(s) *rel* related word(s)
idiom idiomatic equivalent(s) *con* contrasted word(s)
ant antonym(s) * vulgar
‖ use limited; if in doubt, see a dictionary
The first word in a synonym list when printed in SMALL CAPITALS shows where there is more information about the group. For a more efficient use of this book see Explanatory Notes.

ant sadden
gladiatorial *adj syn* BELLIGERENT, bellicose, combative, contentious, militant, pugnacious, quarrelsome, ‖ructious, truculent, warlike
‖**glad rags** *n pl syn* FINERY, ‖best bib and tucker, bravery, frippery, full dress, regalia, Sunday best, war paint
glamorous *adj syn* ATTRACTIVE 1, alluring, bewitching, captivating, charming, enchanting, fascinating, magnetic, seductive, siren
glamour *n syn* CHARM 3, allure, appeal, charisma, fascination, magnetism, witchcraft, witchery
glance *vb* **1** to strike a surface obliquely so as to go off at an angle <the bullet *glanced* off the stone wall>
syn carom, dap, graze, ricochet, skim, skip
rel brush, kiss, scrape, shave, slant; contact, hit, strike, touch; bounce, careen, rebound
con center, focus
2 *syn* BRUSH, graze, kiss, shave, skim
3 *syn* FLASH 1, coruscate, gleam, glimmer, glint, glisten, glitter, shimmer, sparkle, twinkle
glance (at *or* over) *vb syn* BROWSE, dip (into), flip (through), leaf (through), riff (through), riffle (through), run (through *or* over), scan, skim (through), thumb (through)
glance *n* **1** *syn* FLASH 1, coruscation, gleam, glimmer, glint, glisten, glitter, shimmer, sparkle, twinkle
2 *syn* PEEP, ‖gander, glimpse, peek
glance *vb syn* POLISH 1, buff, burnish, furbish, glaze, gloss, rub, shine
glare *vb* **1** *syn* BLAZE, blare, flame, flare, glow
rel dazzle, flash, gleam, glisten, glitter
2 *syn* GAZE 1, bore, gape, ‖gaup (*or* gawp), gawk, gloat, goggle, peer, stare
rel frown, glower, lower, scowl
glaring *adj* **1** *syn* EGREGIOUS, capital, flagrant, gross, rank
rel conspicuous, noticeable, outstanding; excessive, extreme, inordinate; obtrusive
ant unnoticeable
2 *syn* GAUDY, blatant, brazen, chintzy, flashy, garish, loud, meretricious, tawdry, tinsel
rel cheap, coarse, crude, gross
con elegant, tasteful
glass *n syn* MIRROR 1, looking glass, ‖seeing glass
glass *vb syn* REFLECT 1, image, mirror
‖**glasshouse** *n syn* GREENHOUSE, conservatory
glassy *adj syn* SLEEK, glossy, polished, ‖sleekit, sleeky, smarmy
glaze *vb syn* POLISH 1, buff, burnish, furbish, glance, gloss, rub, shine
glaze *n syn* LUSTER, glint, gloss, polish, sheen, shine
gleam *n syn* FLASH 1, coruscation, glance, glimmer, glint, glisten, glitter, scintillation, sparkle, twinkle
gleam *vb* **1** *syn* SHINE 1, beam, burn, radiate
2 *syn* FLASH 1, glance, glimmer, glint, glisten, glitter, scintillate, shimmer, sparkle, twinkle
rel burn
gleaming *adj syn* LUSTROUS 1, burnished, glistening, glossy, polished, sheeny, shining, shiny
glean *vb* to gather by effort and usually bit by bit <evidence *gleaned* from various testimonies>
syn cull, extract, garner, gather, pick up
rel sift, winnow; ascertain, conclude, deduce, learn
con amass, heap, pile
glee *n syn* MIRTH, hilarity, jocularity, jocundity, jollity, joviality, merriment
rel delectation, delight, enjoyment, joy, pleasure; blitheness; joyousness
ant gloom
gleeful *adj syn* MERRY, blithe, blithesome, boon, gay, jocund, jolly, jovial, lighthearted, mirthful
glen *n syn* VALLEY, ‖combe, dale, vale
glib *adj* characterized by very fluent often superficial address toward others <*glib* chatter>
syn silver-tongued, vocative, voluble, well-hung; *compare* TALKATIVE
rel articulate, eloquent, facile, fluent, vocal
con inarticulate, unfluent
glide *vb* **1** *syn* SLIDE 1, glissade, slick, slip, slither
rel float, fly, sail, scud, shoot, skim
2 *syn* STEAL 3, creep, mouse, slide, slip
3 *syn* SNEAK, creep, gumshoe, pussyfoot, skulk, slide, slink, slip, ‖snake, steal
glimmer *vb syn* FLASH 1, coruscate, glance, gleam, glint, glisten, glitter, shimmer, sparkle, twinkle
glimmer *n syn* FLASH 1, coruscation, glance, gleam, glint, glisten, glitter, scintillation, shimmer, sparkle
glimpse *n syn* PEEP, ‖gander, glance, peek
glint *vb syn* FLASH 1, coruscate, glance, gleam, glimmer, glisten, glitter, shimmer, sparkle, twinkle
glint *n* **1** *syn* FLASH 1, coruscation, glance, gleam, glimmer, glisten, glitter, scintillation, sparkle, twinkle
2 *syn* LUSTER, glaze, gloss, polish, sheen, shine
glissade *vb syn* SLIDE 1, glide, slick, slip, slither
rel float, fly, sail, scud, shoot, skim
glisten *vb syn* FLASH 1, coruscate, glance, gleam, glimmer, glint, glitter, shimmer, sparkle, twinkle
glisten *n syn* FLASH 1, coruscation, glance, gleam, glimmer, glint, glitter, shimmer, sparkle, twinkle
glistening *adj syn* LUSTROUS 1, burnished, gleaming, glossy, polished, sheeny, shining, shiny
glitter *vb* **1** *syn* FLASH 1, coruscate, glance, gleam, glimmer, glint, glisten, shimmer, sparkle, twinkle
2 *syn* SPANGLE 1, bespangle
glitter *n syn* FLASH 1, coruscation, glance, gleam, glimmer, glint, glisten, scintillation, shimmer, sparkle
gloaming *n syn* EVENING 1, ‖dimmet, ‖dimps, ‖dimpsy, dusk, ‖dusk dark, eventide, nightfall, owl-light, twilight
gloat *vb syn* GAZE 1, bore, gape, ‖gaup (*or* gawp), gawk, glare, goggle, peer, stare
con begrudge, covet, envy, grudge
global *adj* **1** *syn* UNIVERSAL 2, catholic, cosmic, cosmopolitan, ecumenical, planetary, worldwide
ant parochial
2 *syn* ALL-ROUND 2, comprehensive, general, inclusive, overall, sweeping
rel all-inclusive, blanket, catholic, grand, universal

globe *n* **1** ***syn*** BALL 1, orb, rondure, round, sphere
2 ***syn*** EARTH 1, (the) planet, world
globule *n* ***syn*** DROP 1, drib, driblet, droplet, gobbet
gloom *vb* **1** ***syn*** FROWN 1, glower, lower, scowl
rel brood, mope
con smile; bubble, effervesce, enthuse, sparkle
2 ***syn*** OBSCURE, adumbrate, becloud, bedim, cloud, darken, dim, murk, overcast, overshadow
gloom *n* ***syn*** SADNESS, blues, dejection, depression, (the) dismals, dumps, heavyheartedness, melancholy, mournfulness, unhappiness
con hilarity, jollity, mirth; gaiety, gladness
ant glee
gloomy *adj* **1** ***syn*** DARK 1, caliginous, dim, dun, dusky, lightless, murky, obscure, tenebrous, unilluminated
rel bleak, dismal, dreary
ant brilliant
2 ***syn*** SULLEN, crabbed, ‖dorty, dour, glum, morose, saturnine, sulky, surly, ugly
rel cheerless, dejected, depressed, downcast, joyless, melancholy, oppressed, solemn, unhappy, weary
con glad, happy, joyful, joyous, lighthearted; blithe, jocund, jovial, merry
ant cheerful
3 causing or marked by gloom <the *gloomy* atmosphere of the dungeon>
syn acheronian, acherontic, black, bleak, cheerless, cold, depressant, depressing, depressive, desolate, disconsolate, discouraging, disheartening, dismal, dispiriting, drear, dreary, dusky, funereal, joyless, lugubrious, morne, oppressive, somber, tenebrific, unhappy, woebegone
rel despondent, mirthless, pessimistic; melancholy, mournful, sad; drab, dull, muzzy
con bright, cheerful, happy; cheering, emboldening, encouraging, heartening, optimistic
ant gloomless
glorification *n* ***syn*** APOTHEOSIS 2, aggrandizement, deification, dignification, exaltation
glorify *vb* **1** ***syn*** PRAISE 2, bless, celebrate, cry up, eulogize, extol, hymn, laud, magnify, panegyrize
2 ***syn*** EXALT 1, aggrandize, dignify, distinguish, ennoble, erect, honor, magnify, sublime, uprear
glorious *adj* **1** ***syn*** SPLENDID 2, gorgeous, magnificent, proud, resplendent, splendiferous, splendorous, sublime, superb
rel brilliant, effulgent, lustrous, radiant; imposing, impressive; majestic, noble; ravishing, stunning; beautiful
ant inglorious
2 ***syn*** MARVELOUS 2, ‖cool, ‖dandy, divine, ‖galluptious, groovy, hot, hunky-dory, ‖keen, ‖neat
glory *vb* ***syn*** EXULT, delight, jubilate, triumph
gloss *n* ***syn*** LUSTER, glaze, glint, polish, sheen, shine
rel glossiness, silkiness, sleekness, slickness; burnish
gloss *vb* ***syn*** POLISH 1, buff, burnish, furbish, glance, glaze, rub, shine
gloss (over) *vb* ***syn*** PALLIATE, blanch (over), extenuate, gloze (over), sugarcoat, varnish, veneer, white, whiten, whitewash
rel account, explain, justify, rationalize; belie, falsify, miscolor, misrepresent
gloss *vb* ***syn*** ANNOTATE
glossy *adj* **1** ***syn*** LUSTROUS 1, burnished, gleaming, glistening, polished, sheeny, shining, shiny
2 ***syn*** SLEEK, glassy, polished, ‖sleekit, sleeky, smarmy
glow *vb* **1** ***syn*** BLAZE, blare, flame, flare, glare
rel burn; ignite, kindle, light
2 ***syn*** BLUSH, color, crimson, flush, mantle, pink, pinken, redden, rose, rouge
glow *n* ***syn*** BLOOM 3, blossom, blush, flush
glower *vb* ***syn*** FROWN 1, gloom, lower, scowl
rel stare; look, watch
glowing *adj* **1** ***syn*** RUDDY 1, florid, flush, flushed, full-blooded, rubicund, sanguine
2 ***syn*** IMPASSIONED, ardent, blazing, burning, fervent, fervid, fiery, flaming, hot-blooded, passionate
rel enthusiastic; avid, desirous, eager, fierce, keen; burning, heated
gloze (over) *vb* ***syn*** PALLIATE, blanch (over), extenuate, gloss (over), sugarcoat, varnish, veneer, white, whiten, whitewash
rel account, explain, justify, rationalize; belie, falsify, miscolor, misrepresent
gluey *adj* ***syn*** STICKY 1, adhesive, ‖claggy, ‖clarty, cloggy, gooey, gummy, stodgy
glum *adj* ***syn*** SULLEN, ‖chuff, crabbed, ‖dorty, dour, gloomy, morose, saturnine, sulky, surly
rel close-lipped, silent, taciturn, tight-lipped; depressed, oppressed, weighed down
con glad, happy, joyful, joyous, lighthearted
ant cheerful
glut *vb* ***syn*** SATIATE, clog, fill, gorge, jade, pall, sate, ‖stall, stodge, surfeit
rel cram, feast, stuff
idiom make a pig of (oneself)
con scant, skimp
ant stint
glutted *adj* ***syn*** SATIATED, full, gorged, jaded, sated, satiate, surfeited
gluttonous *adj* ***syn*** VORACIOUS, edacious, rapacious, ravening, ravenous
rel hoggish, piggish; indulgent, intemperate
con sober, temperate; ascetic, austere; sparing
ant abstemious
gnaw *vb* **1** ***syn*** WORRY 1, annoy, bedevil, beleaguer, hagride, harass, harry, pester, plague, tease
rel haunt, irritate, rankle
2 ***syn*** EAT 3, bite, corrode, eat away, erode, scour, wear (away)
rel abrade, fret; consume, crumble
gnome *n* ***syn*** MAXIM, aphorism, apothegm, axiom, brocard, dictum, moral, rule, truism
gnostic *adj* ***syn*** WISE 1, discerning, insighted, insightful, knowing, knowledgeable, perceptive, sagacious, sage, sophic
go *vb* **1** to move on a course <they were glad to be *going* toward home>

---

syn synonym(s) ***rel*** related word(s)
idiom idiomatic equivalent(s) ***con*** contrasted word(s)
ant antonym(s) * vulgar
‖ use limited; if in doubt, see a dictionary
The first word in a synonym list when printed in SMALL CAPITALS shows where there is more information about the group. For a more efficient use of this book see Explanatory Notes.

syn ‖cruise, fare, hie, journey, pass, proceed, ‖process, push on, repair, travel, wend
rel advance; approach, near
idiom gain ground, get over the ground, make one's way
ant stay; stop
2 to move out of and away from where one is <it's time to *go* now>
syn ‖blow, depart, exit, get away, get off, leave, ‖mog, move, pop off, pull out, push off, quit, retire, run along, shove off, take off, withdraw
rel abscond, decamp, escape, flee, fly, hightail
idiom take a powder
con abide, remain, stay; arrive
ant come
3 *syn* RUN 8, extend, make, reach, stretch
4 to be brought to or toward an end <his money will soon be *gone*>
syn consume, exhaust, expend, finish, run through, spend, use up, wash up
rel deplete, devour, dissipate, fritter (away), overspend, squander, waste
con conserve, preserve, save
5 *syn* DIE 1, cash in, decease, demise, depart, drop, expire, pass, pass away, succumb
6 *syn* PASS 3, elapse, expire, pass away
7 *syn* GIVE 12, bend, break, cave, collapse, crumble, fold up, yield
8 *syn* HAPPEN 1, befall, betide, break, chance, come off, fall out, hap, occur, transpire
9 *syn* BECOME 1, come, ‖come over, get, grow, run, turn, wax
10 *syn* RANGE 3, extend, run, vary
11 *syn* SUCCEED 3, arrive, flourish, make out, prosper, score, thrive
12 *syn* SUCCEED 2, click, come off, go over, pan out, prove out
13 *syn* RESORT 2, apply, recur, refer, repair, run, turn
14 *syn* FUNCTION 3, act, run, work
15 *syn* EXTEND 7
16 *syn* AGREE 4, accord, conform, correspond, dovetail, fit (in), ‖gee, harmonize, jibe, square
17 *syn* BELONG 1, fit, set
18 *syn* BEAR 10, abide, brook, endure, stand, stomach, suffer, swallow, take, tolerate
19 *syn* ENJOY 1, ‖dig, like, ‖mind, relish

go (for) *vb syn* APPROVE 1, accept, approbate, countenance, favor, hold (with)

go (into) *vb syn* EXPLORE, delve (into), dig (into), inquire (into), investigate, look (into), probe, prospect, sift

go (together *or* with) *vb syn* SUIT 4, agree (with), become, befit, fit

---

syn synonym(s) *rel* related word(s)
idiom idiomatic equivalent(s) *con* contrasted word(s)
ant antonym(s) * vulgar
‖ use limited; if in doubt, see a dictionary
The first word in a synonym list when printed in SMALL CAPITALS shows where there is more information about the group. For a more efficient use of this book see Explanatory Notes.

go *n* **1** *syn* OCCURRENCE, circumstance, episode, event, happening, incident, occasion, thing
2 *syn* VIGOR 2, bang, drive, getup, get-up-and-go, pep, push, snap, starch, vitality
3 *syn* ENERGY 2, birr, hardihood, ‖moxie, pep, potency, tuck, vigor
4 *syn* FLING 1, crack, pop, shot, slap, stab, ‖stagger, try, whack, whirl
5 *syn* SPELL 1, bout, shift, stint, time, tour, trick, turn
6 *syn* SIEGE, bout
7 *syn* SUCCESS, arrival, ‖do, flying colors, prosperity, successfulness

goad *n syn* STIMULUS, catalyst, impetus, impulse, incentive, incitation, incitement, motivation, spur, stimulant
rel compulsion, drive, impulsion; desire, lust, passion, urge, zeal
ant curb

goad *vb syn* URGE, egg (on), exhort, prick, prod, prompt, propel, sic, spur
rel impel, move; coerce, compel, force; instigate

go–ahead *adj syn* ENTERPRISING 2, gumptious, up-and-coming

goal *n* **1** *syn* AMBITION 2, aim, mark, objective, quaesitum, target
2 *syn* USE 4, duty, function, mark, object, objective, purpose, target

goat *n syn* SCAPEGOAT, fall guy, patsy, whipping boy

goatish *adj syn* LUSTFUL 2, concupiscent, *horny, hot, lascivious, libidinous, lickerish, passionate, prurient, satyric

gob *n* **1** *syn* LUMP 1, chunk, clod, clump. hunch, hunk, nugget, wad
2 *usu* **gobs** *pl syn* SCAD, heap, load(s), million, oodles, quantities, ream(s), ‖rimption(s), slather(s), wad(s)

gob *n syn* MOUTH 1, ‖bazoo, ‖mush, ‖row, ‖trap, ‖yap

gobbet *n syn* DROP 1, drib, driblet, droplet, globule

gobble *vb syn* GULP, bolt, cram, englut, guzzle, ingurgitate, slop, slosh, wolf

gobbledygook *n* wordy unintelligible language <*gobbledygook* of bureaucrats>
syn double-talk, gibberish
rel double Dutch, Greek, jabberwocky; ‖bull, bunkum, claptrap, drivel, garbage, malarkey, nonsense, poppycock, twaddle

go–between *n* **1** *syn* MARRIAGE BROKER, matchmaker
2 an intermediate agent between individuals or groups <served as *go-between* in the labor dispute>
syn broker, entrepreneur, interagent, interceder, intercessor, intermediary, intermediate, intermediator, mediator, middleman
rel agent, attorney, deputy, factor, proxy; emissary, envoy, messenger; delegate, representative; arbitrator, negotiator

***goddamn** *adj* **1** *syn* DAMNED 2, blankety-blank, blasted, blessed, ‖blooming, damnable, darn, execrable, goldarn, infernal
2 *syn* UTTER, absolute, blasted, blessed, complete, consummate, dad-burned, goldarn, outright, unmitigated

godless *adj syn* IRRELIGIOUS, nonreligious, unreligious
rel agnostic, atheistic, infidel
ant godly

godlike *adj* ***syn*** DIVINE 2, deific
godly *adj* **1** ***syn*** DIVINE 1, deific
2 ***syn*** SAINTLY, angelic, holy
3 ***syn*** DEVOUT, holy, pietistic, pious, prayerful, religious
ant godless
go down *vb* **1** ***syn*** FALL 2, drop, keel (over), pitch, plunge, slump, topple, tumble
rel droop, sag, sink; cave (in), collapse, crumple, fold
2 ***syn*** SET 12, decline, dip, sink
3 ***syn*** SINK 1, founder, go under, submerge, submerse
4 ***syn*** FALL 3, go under, submit, succumb, surrender
God's acre *n* ***syn*** CEMETERY, ‖boneyard, ‖boot hill, burial ground, burying ground, graveyard, memorial park, necropolis, polyandrium, potter's field
godsend *n* ***syn*** GOOD 1, advantage, benediction, benefit, blessing, boon
go-getter *n* ***syn*** HUSTLER 1, dynamo, live wire, peeler, rustler, self-starter
goggle *vb* **1** ***syn*** LOOK 7, eye, gape, ‖gaup (*or* gawp), gaze, ogle, rubberneck, stare
2 ***syn*** GAZE 1, bore, gape, ‖gaup (*or* gawp), gawk, glare, gloat, peer, stare
go in *vb* ***syn*** ENTER 1, come (in), ingress, penetrate
Golconda *n* ***syn*** BONANZA, eldorado, gold mine, mine, treasure-house, treasure trove, treasury
goldarn *adj* **1** ***syn*** DAMNED 2, blamed, blasted, blessed, ‖blooming, ‖consarned, cursed, cussed, dratted, infernal
2 ***syn*** UTTER, absolute, blamed, blasted, blessed, complete, gross, outright, rank, unmitigated
goldbrick *n* ***syn*** SLACKER, shirker, slinker, ‖spiv
goldbrick *vb* ***syn*** IDLE, bum, dawdle, ‖goof (off), laze, lazy, loaf, loiter, loll, lounge
golden *adj* **1** ***syn*** BLOND 1, flaxen, straw
2 ***syn*** MELLIFLUOUS, honeyed, Hyblaean, liquid, mellifluent, mellow
golden-ager *n* ***syn*** OLDSTER, ancient, elder, old-timer, senior, senior citizen
gold mine *n* ***syn*** BONANZA, eldorado, Golconda, mine, treasure-house, treasure trove, treasury
golem *n* ***syn*** ROBOT 2, automaton, machine
gone *adj* **1** ***syn*** EXTINCT 2, bygone, dead, defunct, departed, lost, vanished
2 ***syn*** ABSENT 1, away, lacking, missing, omitted, wanting
3 ***syn*** LOST 2, missing
4 ***syn*** PREGNANT 1, big, childing, enceinte, expectant, expecting, gravid, heavy, parous, parturient
gonfalon *n* ***syn*** FLAG, banderole, banner, color, ensign, gonfanon, oriflamme, pendant, pennant, standard
gonfanon *n* ***syn*** FLAG, banderole, banner, color, ensign, gonfalon, oriflamme, pendant, pennant, standard
goo *n* **1** a sticky substance <slipped on a patch of greasy *goo* on the walk>
syn gook, goop, gumbo, gunk, muck; *compare* CRUD
rel dope
2 ***syn*** CRUD, ‖cab, gook, gunk
good *adj* **1** having a helpful or auspicious character <a *good* wind>
syn advantageous, benefic, beneficial, brave, favorable, favoring, helpful, propitious, toward, useful
rel convenient, suitable; desirable, needed; appropriate, proper, right
con disadvantageous, unfavorable; damaging, hampering, harmful; unwanted
ant ill
2 adapted to the end in view <they doubted that the fruit was *good* to eat>
syn appropriate, convenient, fit, meet, proper, suitable, useful
rel all right, apt, becoming, conformable, congruous, fitting, seemly
con inadequate, inappropriate, undesirable, unfit, unsuitable, useless
3 ***syn*** WHOLE 1, flawless, intact, perfect, sound, unblemished, undamaged, unhurt, unimpaired, unmarred
con blemished, damaged, defective, flawed, impaired, imperfect, unsound
ant bad
4 ***syn*** ADVANTAGEOUS 1, gainful, lucrative, moneymaking, paying, profitable, remunerative, well-paying, worthwhile
5 ***syn*** PLEASANT 1, agreeable, congenial, favorable, gratifying, nice, pleasing, pleasurable, pleasureful, welcome
6 ***syn*** HEALTHFUL, healthy, hygienic, salubrious, salutary, salutiferous, wholesome
7 ***syn*** CLEVER 5, scintillating, smart, sprightly
8 ***syn*** CONSIDERABLE 2, respectable, ‖right smart, sensible, sizable, ‖smart
9 ***syn*** WELL-FOUNDED, cogent, just, justified, well-grounded
10 ***syn*** DECENT 4, acceptable, adequate, all right, common, respectable, satisfactory, sufficient, tolerable, unobjectionable
11 conforming to a high standard of morality or virtue <if you can't be *good*, be careful>
syn blameless, exemplary, guiltless, inculpable, innocent, irreprehensible, irreproachable, lily-white, pure, righteous, unblamable, virtuous
rel incorrupt, sound, uncorrupted, untainted
con blameworthy, impure, unrighteous; evil, iniquitous, reprobate, sinful
ant bad
12 ***syn*** CHARITABLE 1, altruistic, benevolent, eleemosynary, humane, humanitarian, philanthropic
13 behaving in an acceptable or desirable manner <a *good* child>
syn decorous, well-behaved
rel polite, proper; considerate, kindly, thoughtful
con ill-behaved, indecorous, naughty; careless, heedless, inconsiderate, mischievous, thoughtless
ant bad
14 ***syn*** SKILLFUL 2, adroit, clever, pretty, ‖skilly, wicked, workmanlike, workmanly
ant bad

15 *syn* ABLE, au fait, capable, competent, proper, qualified, wicked

good *n* **1** something that is desirable or beneficial <it's an ill wind that blows no *good*>
syn advantage, benediction, benefit, blessing, boon, godsend
con bane, harm, misfortune; detriment, jinx
ant evil, ill
2 *syn* RIGHT 1, straight
3 *syn* WELFARE, advantage, benefit, interest, prosperity, well-being
4 goods *pl syn* POSSESSION 2, belongings, chattels, effects, lares and penates, movables, things
5 goods *pl syn* MERCHANDISE, commodities, line, vendible(s), wares

good–bye *interj* — used as a conventional expression of good wishes at parting <the party was over; the time had come to say *good-bye*>
syn adieu, by, bye-bye, ‖cheerio, farewell, so long, ‖toodle-oo
rel good day, good evening, good morning, good night
idiom be good, be seeing you, fare you well, keep in touch, see you (later)
con hello, how do, howdy, hullo

good–bye *n syn* PARTING, adieu, congé, farewell, leave-taking

good–bye *adj syn* PARTING, departing, farewell, valedictory

good faith *n* a state of mind characterizing one free from fraud, deceit, or misconduct <determined to act in *good faith*>
syn bona fides, sincereness, sincerity, uberrima fides
rel decency, decorum, propriety, seemliness; ethicality, morality, virtuousness

good–fellowship *n syn* CAMARADERIE, comradery

good–for–nothing *n syn* WASTREL 1, ‖bad lot, ne'er-do-well, no-good, profligate, rounder, scapegrace, waster

good–for–nothing *adj* **1** *syn* FECKLESS 1, fustian, meaningless, purposeless, unpurposed, useless, worthless
2 *syn* WORTHLESS 1, draffy, drossy, inutile, ‖no-account, no-good, nothing, unworthy, valueless
ant precious

good–hearted *adj syn* KIND, benign, benignant, kindly

good–humored *adj syn* AMIABLE 1, complaisant, easy, good-natured, good-tempered, lenient, mild, obliging
rel buoyant, cheerful, cheery, genial, smiling
ant ill-humored

good–looking *adj syn* BEAUTIFUL, attractive, beauteous, ‖bonny, comely, fair, handsome, lovely, pretty, pulchritudinous
ant ill-looking

good–natured *adj syn* AMIABLE 1, complaisant, easy, good-humored, good-tempered, lenient, mild, obliging
rel altruistic, benevolent, charitable; acquiescent, compliant
con choleric, cranky, cross, irascible, splenetic, touchy; crabbed, gloomy, glum, morose, splenetic
ant contrary; ill-natured

goodness *n* the quality or state of being morally excellent <that eternal *goodness* that burns away evil>
syn morality, probity, rectitude, righteousness, rightness, uprightness, virtue
rel honesty, honor, integrity; grace, merit, quality, superiority
ant badness, evil

good sense *n syn* SENSE 6, common sense, gumption, horse sense, judgment, wisdom

good–tasting *adj syn* PALATABLE, appetizing, flavorsome, mouth-watering, relishing, sapid, savory, tasteful, tasty, toothsome

good–tempered *adj syn* AMIABLE 1, complaisant, easy, good-humored, good-natured, lenient, mild, obliging
con crabbed, surly; snappish, touchy; irascible
ant bad-tempered, ill-tempered

goodwill *n* **1** benevolent interest or concern <trying to promote interracial *goodwill*>
syn amity, benevolence, comity, friendliness, friendship, kindliness
rel altruism, charity, favor, generosity, helpfulness, kindness, rapport, sympathy, tolerance
con animus, disfavor, enmity, hatred, intolerance, malevolence
ant animosity, ill will
2 *syn* ALACRITY, dispatch, expedition, promptitude, readiness

goody *n syn* DELICACY, bonne bouche, dainty, kickshaw, morsel, tidbit (*or* titbit), treat

goody–goody *n syn* PRUDE, bluenose, comstock, Grundy, Mrs. Grundy, nice Nelly, prig, puritan, ‖wowser

gooey *adj* **1** *syn* STICKY 1, adhesive, ‖claggy, ‖clarty, cloggy, gluey, gummy, stodgy
2 *syn* SENTIMENTAL, drippy, maudlin, mushy, sappy, slushy, sobby, ‖soppy, soupy, sticky

goof *n syn* DUNCE, boob, booby, chump, dolt, dolthead, fathead, ‖goon, lunkhead, oaf

‖**goof** (off) *vb syn* IDLE, bum, dawdle, goldbrick, laze, lazy, loaf, loiter, loll, lounge

goof (up) *vb syn* BOTCH, bitch (up), ‖blow, bobble, bollix, bungle, gum (up), louse up, mess, ‖screw (up)

go off *vb syn* EXPLODE 1, blow, burst, detonate, mushroom

gook *n* **1** *syn* GOO, goop, gumbo, gunk, muck
2 *syn* CRUD, ‖cab, goo, gunk
3 *syn* NONSENSE 2, ‖baloney, bilge, ‖crap, drivel, hogwash, hooey, malarkey, rot, trash

go on *vb* **1** *syn* PERSEVERE, carry on, hang on, persist
2 *syn* BEHAVE 1, acquit, act, bear, carry, comport, conduct, demean, deport, quit

‖**goon** *n syn* DUNCE, boob, booby, chump, dolt, dolthead, fathead, goof, lunkhead, oaf

goop *n syn* GOO 1, gook, gumbo, gunk, muck

goose egg *n syn* ZERO 1, aught (*or* ought), cipher, naught (*or* nought), nothing, zilch

goosey *adj* **1** ***syn*** STUPID 1, blockheaded, chuckleheaded, dense, doltish, dumb, fatheaded, numskulled, pinheaded, thick
2 ***syn*** NERVOUS, fidgety, high-strung, jittery, jumpy, nervy, spooky, twittery, unrestful

go over *vb* ***syn*** SUCCEED 2, click, come off, go, pan out, prove out

gordian *adj* ***syn*** COMPLEX 2, Byzantine, complicated, daedal, elaborate, intricate, involved, knotty, labyrinthine, sophisticated

gore *n* ***syn*** BLOOD 1, ‖claret

gorge *n* ***syn*** RAVINE, arroyo, chasm, cleft, clough, clove, gap, gulch

gorge *vb* ***syn*** SATIATE, cloy, fill, glut, jade, pall, sate, ‖stall, stodge, surfeit
rel bolt, devour, gobble, guzzle, raven, wolf; overeat, overindulge, stuff
idiom eat like a horse, eat one out of house and home

gorged *adj* ***syn*** SATIATED, full, glutted, jaded, sated, satiate, surfeited

gorgeous *adj* **1** ***syn*** SPLENDID 2, glorious, magnificent, proud, resplendent, splendiferous, splendorous, sublime, superb
rel elegant, luxurious, opulent, plush, sumptuous; flamboyant, garish, gaudy, ostentatious, pretentious, showy; beautiful, colorful
2 ***syn*** GRAND 2, impressive, lavish, luxurious, splendid, sumptuous

‖**gorilla** *n* ***syn*** THUG 1, ‖hood, hoodlum, hooligan, ruffian, strong arm

gory *adj* ***syn*** BLOODY 1, bloodstained, ensanguined, imbrued, sanguinary, sanguine, sanguineous

gospel *n* ***syn*** VERACITY 2, truism, truth, veracity

gossamer *adj* ***syn*** FILMY, diaphanous, flimsy, gauzy, sheer, tiffany, transparent

gossip *n* **1** a person who habitually retails private, scandalous, or sensational and often inaccurate information <her life ruined by a vicious old *gossip*>
syn carrytale, circulator, clack, gossiper, gossipmonger, ‖long tongue, mumblenews, newsmonger, quidnunc, rumorer, rumormonger, scandalizer, scandalmonger, sieve, tabby, talebearer, telltale; *compare* BUSYBODY, INFORMER
2 ***syn*** REPORT 1, buzz, cry, grapevine, hearsay, on-dit, rumble, rumor, scuttlebutt, talk
rel account, chronicle, conversation, story, tale; babble, banter, chatter, prate

gossip *vb* to disclose something, often of questionable veracity, that is better kept to oneself < *gossiped* about his neighbor's business>
syn blab, noise (about *or* abroad), rumor, talk, tattle
rel babble, chat, chatter, prate, prattle; hint, imply, insinuate, intimate, suggest
idiom dish the dirt, spill the beans, tell idle tales, tell tales out of school

gossiper *n* ***syn*** GOSSIP 1, carrytale, gossipmonger, newsmonger, quidnunc, rumorer, scandalmonger, tabby, talebearer, telltale

gossipmonger *n* ***syn*** GOSSIP 1, carrytale, gossiper, newsmonger, quidnunc, rumorer, scandalmonger, tabby, talebearer, telltale

Gothic *adj* ***syn*** BARBARIAN 1, barbaric, barbarous, Hunnic, Hunnish, rude, savage, uncivilized, uncultivated, wild
rel brutal, coarse, crude

gouge *vb* ***syn*** EXTORT 1, exact, pinch, screw, shake down, squeeze, wrench, wrest, wring
rel cheat, con, swindle; overcharge

go under *vb* **1** ***syn*** FALL 3, go down, submit, succumb, surrender
2 ***syn*** SINK 1, founder, go down, submerge, submerse

gourmand *n* ***syn*** EPICURE, bon vivant, gastronome, gastronomer, gastronomist, gourmet

gourmet *n* ***syn*** EPICURE, bon vivant, gastronome, gastronomer, gastronomist, gourmand

govern *vb* **1** to exercise sovereign authority <a dictator may *govern* in a thoroughly enlightened manner>
syn overrule, reign, rule, sway
rel captain, command, head; administer, conduct, control, direct, manage, master; regulate, supervise
2 ***syn*** ADMINISTER 1, administrate, carry out, execute, render
3 to exercise a decisive role in influencing the actions and conduct of <parents who *govern* their children wisely>
syn control, direct, dominate, handle, manage
rel directionalize, guide, lead, shepherd, steer; boss, oversee, supervise
idiom be at the helm (*or* wheel), be in the driver's seat, hold the reins

‖**governor** *n* ***syn*** FATHER 1, dad, daddy, ‖old man, pa, ‖pap, papa, ‖pappy, pop, poppa

grab *vb* ***syn*** SEIZE 2, catch, clutch, ‖cotch, grapple, nab, ‖nail, snatch, take

grabble *vb* ***syn*** GROPE, feel, fumble

grabby *adj* ***syn*** COVETOUS, acquisitive, desirous, grasping, greedy, itchy, prehensile

grace *n* **1** a short prayer either asking a blessing before or giving thanks after a meal <taught each child a *grace* of his own>
syn benediction, blessing, thanks, thanksgiving
rel invocation, petition
2 ***syn*** MERCY, caritas, charity, clemency, lenity
rel compassionateness, responsiveness, tenderness; forbearance, indulgence, leniency; goodness
3 ***syn*** ELEGANCE, dignity

graceless *adj* **1** ***syn*** BARBARIC 1, barbarian, barbarous, outlandish, tasteless, vulgar, wild
2 ***syn*** INFELICITOUS, awkward, ill-chosen, inept, unfortunate, unhappy
ant graceful

gracious *adj* **1** marked by kindly courtesy <her *gracious* attitude toward those around her>
syn affable, congenial, cordial, genial, sociable, ‖sonsy
rel amiable, complaisant, easy, obliging; benign, benignant, kind, kindly; chivalrous, courteous, courtly; approachable, bonhomous, clubby, forthcoming, forthgoing, outgoing

---

syn synonym(s) *rel* related word(s)
idiom idiomatic equivalent(s) *con* contrasted word(s)
ant antonym(s) * vulgar
‖ use limited; if in doubt, see a dictionary
The first word in a synonym list when printed in SMALL CAPITALS shows where there is more information about the group. For a more efficient use of this book see Explanatory Notes.

con boorish, churlish; blunt, brusque, crabbed, crusty, curt, gruff, short, sullen, surly
ant ungracious
2 *syn* COURTLY, gallant, preux, stately
rel mannered, starchy

gradation *n* the difference or variation between two things that are nearly alike <the *gradations* were too small to be seen with the unaided eye>
syn nuance, shade
rel difference, distinction, divergence; change, modification, variation

grade *n* **1** *syn* DEGREE 1, notch, rung, stage, step
2 *syn* ESTATE 2, rank
3 *syn* CLASS 1, category, group, grouping, league, pigeonhole, tier
4 *syn* QUALITY 3, caliber, class
5 *syn* SLOPE, gradient, inclination, incline, lean, leaning, slant, tilt

grade *vb syn* CLASS 2, classify, evaluate, rank, rate
rel arrange, order; assort, sort

Grade A *adj syn* EXCELLENT, capital, fine, first-class, first-rate, five-star, prime, superior, top, top-notch

gradient *n syn* SLOPE, grade, inclination, incline, lean, leaning, slant, tilt

gradual *adj* proceeding slowly usually by minute or imperceptible steps or degrees <his health showed *gradual* improvement>
syn piecemeal, step-by-step
rel deliberate, dilatory, lagging, poky, sluggish
con acute, sharp, sudden
ant abrupt

gradually *adv* by small degrees or amounts <*gradually* he learned the new job>
syn bit by bit, little by little, piecemeal
idiom a little at a time, by degrees
con quickly, rapidly, speedily; at once, immediately, suddenly

grain *n syn* PARTICLE, bit, crumb, iota, jot, mite, molecule, smidgen, speck, tittle

grainy *adj syn* COARSE 1, granular

grammar *n syn* ALPHABET 2, ABC's, elements, fundamentals, principles, rudiments

grand *adj* **1** large and impressive in size, scope, extent, or conception <the platform provided a *grand* view of the canyon>
syn august, baronial, grandiose, imposing, lordly, magnific, magnificent, majestic, noble, princely, royal, stately; *compare* HUGE
rel monumental, prodigious, stupendous, tremendous; towering; gorgeous, splendid, sublime, superb
con measly, paltry, petty, puny, trifling, trivial
2 marked by great magnificence, display, and usually ceremony or formality <delighted to attend the *grand* presidential fete>
syn gorgeous, impressive, lavish, luxurious, splendid, sumptuous
rel magnificent, majestic; flashy, garish, gaudy, ornate, ostentatious, showy
con crude, meretricious, obtrusive, vulgar; flimsy, tawdry
3 noble in character or spirit <a *grand* outlook on life>
syn elevated, exalted, lofty, sublime, superb
rel magnificent, splendid
con average, common, commonplace, ordinary; base, lowly, mean, poor

grandam *n syn* BELDAM 1, dame, gammer

grande dame *n syn* MATRIARCH, dame, dowager, matron

grandiloquent *adj syn* RHETORICAL, aureate, bombastic, declamatory, euphuistic, flowery, magniloquent, overblown, sonorous, swollen

grandiose *adj* **1** *syn* GRAND 1, august, imposing, lordly, magnificent, majestic, noble, princely, royal, stately
rel ostentatious, pretentious, showy; cosmic, overwhelming, unfathomable, vast
2 *syn* AMBITIOUS 2, lofty, pretentious, utopian, visionary

granny *n syn* FUSSBUDGET, fuddy-duddy, fusser, fusspot, old lady, old maid

grant *vb* **1** to give as a favor or right <*granted* him an extension of payments>
syn accord, award, concede, vouchsafe
rel bestow, confer, donate, give, present; allow, permit; cede, relinquish, yield
con decline, refuse, turn down
2 *syn* ACKNOWLEDGE 1, admit, allow, avow, concede, confess, fess (up), let on, own, own up
con differ, disagree, dissent; challenge, dispute, object, protest
3 *syn* GIVE 2, accord, award, confer

grant *n syn* APPROPRIATION, subsidy, subvention
rel gift; assistance, benefaction, contribution, donation; alms, charity, dole, handout

granular *adj syn* COARSE 1, grainy

grapevine *n syn* REPORT 1, buzz, cry, gossip, hearsay, on-dit, rumble, rumor, scuttlebutt, talk

graph *n syn* CHART 1, map
rel diagram, outline, sketch

graphic *adj* **1** giving a clear visual impression especially in words <gave a *graphic* description of the whole incident>
syn photographic, pictorial, picturesque, vivid
rel clear, lucid, perspicuous; clear-cut, incisive; cogent, compelling, convincing, telling; definite, explicit, precise, realistic, striking, visual
con confused, hazy, indistinct, obscure
2 *syn* PICTORIAL 1, iconographic, illustrational, illustrative, illustratory, pictoric

grapple *n syn* HOLD, clamp, clasp, clench, clinch, clutch, grasp, grip, gripe, tenure

grapple *vb* **1** *syn* SEIZE 2, catch, clutch, ‖cotch, grab, nab, ‖nail, snatch, take
2 *syn* WRESTLE, scuffle, tussle, ‖wraxle

grasp *vb* **1** *syn* TAKE 4, clasp, grip
2 *syn* APPREHEND 1, accept, catch, compass, comprehend, ‖dig, follow, take, take in, understand

rel envisage, fathom, perceive
3 *syn* KNOW 1, appreciate, apprehend, cognize, comprehend, fathom, have, understand

grasp *n syn* HOLD, clamp, clasp, clench, clinch, clutch, grapple, grip, gripe, tenure

graspable *adj syn* UNDERSTANDABLE, apprehensible, comprehendible, comprehensible, fathomable, intelligible, knowable, lucid, luminous
ant ungraspable

grasping *adj syn* COVETOUS, acquisitive, desirous, grabby, greedy, itchy, prehensile
rel extorting, extortionate

grass *n syn* MARIJUANA, boo, cannabis, ‖Mary Jane, moocah, pot, ‖tea, weed

grate *vb* **1** *syn* SCRAPE 1, rasp, scratch
rel abrade, bark, chafe, fray, gall, scuff, skin
2 *syn* IRRITATE, aggravate, burn (up), gall, get, nettle, peeve, pique, provoke, rile

grateful *adj* **1** feeling or expressing gratitude <was *grateful* for the gift>
syn obliged, thankful
rel appreciative, beholden; gratified, pleased
idiom filled with gratitude
ant ungrateful
2 *syn* PLEASANT 1, agreeable, congenial, favorable, good, gratifying, nice, pleasurable, pleasureful, welcome
rel comforting, consoling, solacing; refreshing, rejuvenating, renewing, restorative, restoring; delectable, delicious, delightful
ant obnoxious

gratefulness *n syn* AMENITY 1, agreeability, agreeableness, amiability, cordiality, enjoyableness, geniality, pleasance, pleasantness, sweetness and light

gratify *vb* **1** *syn* PLEASE 2, arride, delectate, delight, gladden, happify, pleasure
rel appease, baby, cater (to), coddle, favor, humor, indulge, oblige, pamper
con bother, irk; aggravate, exasperate, irritate, nettle, rile; agitate, disturb, perturb, upset
2 *syn* SATISFY 3, appease, content
3 *syn* INDULGE 1, cater (to), humor
idiom do one proud

gratifying *adj syn* PLEASANT 1, agreeable, congenial, favorable, good, grateful, nice, pleasurable, pleasureful, welcome
rel contenting, satisfying; delighting, gladdening, regaling, rejoicing
con invidious, obnoxious; offensive, revolting

grating *adj syn* HARSH 3, dry, hoarse, jarring, rasping, raucous, rough, strident, stridulent, stridulous

gratis *adj syn* FREE 5, chargeless, complimentary, costless, gratuitous

gratuitous *adj* **1** *syn* FREE 5, chargeless, complimentary, costless, gratis
rel voluntary, willing
2 *syn* SUPEREROGATORY, supererogant, supererogative, unasked, uncalled-for, wanton
3 *syn* BASELESS, bottomless, foundationless, groundless, uncalled-for, unfounded, ungrounded, unwarranted
rel indefensible, reasonless, unsupportable

gratuity *n* something given over and above what is due, generally in return for or expectation of good service <he found that an occasional *gratuity* smoothed his path>
syn cumshaw, lagniappe, largess, ‖palm grease, ‖palm oil, ‖perk(s), perquisite, pourboire, tip
rel alms, benefaction, contribution, donation; offering, reward

grave *vb* **1** *syn* ENGRAVE 1, etch, incise
2 *syn* IMPRESS 3, drive, hammer, pound, stamp

grave *n* a place of interment <his *grave* is in the church burial ground>
syn burial, ‖pit, sepulcher, sepulture, tomb
rel catacomb, crypt, vault; mausoleum; ossuary; cinerarium
idiom final resting place

grave *adj* **1** *syn* SERIOUS 2, heavy, severe, weighty
2 *syn* SERIOUS 1, earnest, no-nonsense, sedate, sober, sobersided, solemn, somber, staid, weighty
rel heavy, ponderous; grim, sad, saturnine; awful, dreadful, horrible, terrible
con flippant, light, light-minded
ant gay
3 involving marked risk of impairment or destruction <a *grave* illness>
syn dangerous, fell, grievous, major, serious, ugly; *compare* DANGEROUS 1
rel deadly, destructive, dire, fatal, killing, murderous; frightening, ghastly, terrible; afflictive, severe
con paltry, petty, trivial; harmless, innocuous; temporary, transitory

gravely *adv syn* SERIOUSLY 2, intensely, severely

grave marker *n syn* TOMBSTONE, footstone, gravestone, headstone, ledger, monument

gravestone *n syn* TOMBSTONE, footstone, grave marker, headstone, ledger, monument

graveyard *n syn* CEMETERY, ‖boneyard, ‖boot hill, burial ground, burying ground, God's acre, memorial park, necropolis, polyandrium, potter's field

gravid *adj syn* PREGNANT 1, big, childing, enceinte, expectant, expecting, gone, heavy, parous, parturient

gravidity *n syn* PREGNANCY, gestation, pregnance, situation

graybeard *n syn* GAFFER, patriarch

gray matter *n syn* MIND 1, brain, head, ‖upper story, ‖upperworks, wit

graze *vb* **1** *syn* BRUSH, glance, kiss, shave, skim
2 *syn* GLANCE 1, carom, dap, ricochet, skim, skip
3 *syn* ABRADE 1, chafe, corrade, erode, gall, rub, ruffle, wear
rel harm, hurt, injure; bruise, contuse, wound

greasy *adj* **1** *syn* FATTY 2, oily, oleaginous, unctuous
2 *syn* SLICK 1, lubricious, ‖sliddery, ‖slipper, slippery, slippy, slithery

‖**greasy spoon** *n syn* EATING HOUSE, beanery, café, coffee shop, diner, ‖hashery, ‖hash house, luncheonette, lunchroom, sandwich shop

great *adj* **1** *syn* LARGE 1, big, bull, fat, husky, oversize

---

syn synonym(s) | *rel* related word(s)
idiom idiomatic equivalent(s) | *con* contrasted word(s)
ant antonym(s) | * vulgar
‖ use limited; if in doubt, see a dictionary
The first word in a synonym list when printed in SMALL CAPITALS shows where there is more information about the group. For a more efficient use of this book see Explanatory Notes.

con measly, paltry, petty, puny, trifling, trivial
ant little
2 *syn* FAMOUS 2, celebrated, celebrious, distinguished, eminent, famed, illustrious, notable, prominent, renowned
rel superlative, supreme, surpassing, transcendent

great deal *n syn* MUCH, barrel, heap, lot, mass, mountain, multiplicity, peck, pile, ‖power

greater *adj* **1** *syn* BEST, better, ‖bettermost, largest, most
2 *syn* SUPERIOR 1, higher, over, overlying, superincumbent, superjacent

great gun *n syn* NOTABLE 1, big boy, ‖big cheese, ‖biggie, ‖big noise, big shot, leader, lion, nabob, VIP

greathearted *adj* **1** *syn* BRAVE 1, boldhearted, bravehearted, courageous, fearless, gallant, heroic, lionhearted, manly, stouthearted
2 *syn* GENEROUS 1, benevolent, big, chivalrous, considerate, lofty, magnanimous

greatly *adv syn* VERY 1, exceedingly, exceptionally, extremely, highly, hugely, notably, remarkably, strikingly, surpassingly

greatness *n syn* SIZE 2, amplitude, bigness, largeness, magnitude, sizableness

greed *n syn* CUPIDITY, avarice, avariciousness, avidity, rapacity
rel gluttonousness, gluttony, rapaciousness, ravenousness, voraciousness

greedy *adj syn* COVETOUS, acquisitive, desirous, grabby, grasping, itchy, prehensile
con bounteous, bountiful, generous, liberal, munificent, openhanded; exuberant, lavish, prodigal, profuse

Greek *n syn* GIBBERISH 1, babble, drivel, jabber, jabberwocky, nonsense, skimble-skamble

green *adj* **1** *syn* YOUNG 1, callow, immature, infant, juvenile, unfledged, unripe, youthful
2 *syn* INEXPERIENCED, callow, fresh, raw, unconversant, unpracticed, unseasoned, untried, unversed, young
con grown-up, ripe, mature, matured; educated, instructed, trained; proficient, skilled, skillful
ant experienced

green *n syn* COMMON 2, plaza, square

‖**greenbacks** *n pl syn* MONEY, ‖bread, cash, currency, dough, ‖jack, legal tender, ‖long green, ‖scratch, ‖wampum

green–eyed *adj syn* ENVIOUS, envying, invidious, jealous

greenhorn *n syn* RUSTIC, backwoodsman, bumpkin, clodhopper, clown, hayseed, hick, hillbilly, provincial, rube

greenhouse *n* a glass-enclosed structure for the cultivation and protection of tender plants <a small window *greenhouse* full of bloom>
syn conservatory, ‖glasshouse
rel coolhouse, hotbed, hothouse

greenness *n* **1** *syn* YOUTH 1, adolescence, juvenility, puberty, pubescence, spring, springtide, springtime, youthfulness, youthhood
2 *syn* INEXPERIENCE, callowness, freshness, rawness

greet *vb syn* ADDRESS 7, accost, call (to), hail, salute

greeting *n* the ceremonial words or acts of one who meets, welcomes, or formally addresses another <after the *greeting* the chairman called the roll>
syn salutation, salute
rel address, hail, hello, welcome
con farewell, good-bye
ant valediction

gregarious *adj syn* SOCIAL 2, sociable

grief *n syn* SORROW, affliction, anguish, care, ‖dole, heartache, heartbreak, regret, rue, woe
rel bemoaning, bewailing, deploring, lamenting
con comfort, comforting, consolation, solace, solacing
ant joy

grievance *n syn* INJUSTICE 2, injury, wrong
rel hardship, rigor; affliction, cross, trial, tribulation

grieve *vb* **1** *syn* DISTRESS 2, aggrieve, constrain, hurt, injure, pain
2 to feel or express deep distress <*grieved* at the loss of so many lives>
syn mourn, sorrow
rel bear, endure, suffer; bemoan, bewail, deplore, lament; cry, keen, wail, weep
ant rejoice
3 *syn* DEPLORE 1, bemoan, bewail, lament, moan, weep

grievous *adj* **1** *syn* ONEROUS, burdensome, demanding, exacting, exigent, oppressive, superincumbent, taxing, tough, weighty
2 *syn* BITTER 2, afflictive, distasteful, galling, painful, unpalatable
3 *syn* GRAVE 3, dangerous, fell, major, serious, ugly
4 *syn* DEPLORABLE, afflictive, calamitous, dire, distressing, heartbreaking, lamentable, regrettable, unfortunate, woeful

‖**grifter** *n syn* SWINDLER, cheat, confidence man, con man, defrauder, diddler, double-dealer, gyp, sharper, trickster

grill *n syn* CROSS-EXAMINATION, grilling, interrogation, third degree

grilling *n syn* CROSS-EXAMINATION, grill, interrogation, third degree

grim *adj* **1** *syn* FIERCE 1, barbarous, cruel, fell, ferocious, inhuman, inhumane, savage, truculent, wolfish
rel foreboding, ominous
2 forbidding in action or appearance <had a *grim* and determined expression on his face>
syn austere, bleak, dour, hard, harsh, severe, stringent
rel cold, forbidding, ‖off-putting; fixed, rigid, set; determined, firm, stern
con calm, mellow, mild, soft, warm; attractive, beautiful, pleasing
ant pleasant
3 being extremely obdurate or firm in action or purpose <fought with *grim* determination>
syn implacable, ironfisted, merciless, mortal, relentless, ruthless, unappeasable, unflinching, unrelenting, unyielding

rel adamant, inexorable, inflexible, obdurate, resolute, stubborn, unforgiving, vindictive; certain, inevitable; determined, dogged
con considerate, gentle, mild; clement, forbearing, indulgent
ant lenient
4 *syn* GHASTLY 1, grisly, gruesome, hideous, horrible, horrifying, lurid, macabre, terrible, terrifying
rel loathsome, offensive, repugnant, repulsive, revolting

grimace *n syn* FACE 6, moue, mouth, mouthing, mow, mug

grimace *vb* to distort one's face by way of expressing a feeling < *grimaced* with pain >
syn mop, mouth, mow, mug, ‖mump
rel contort, deform, distort, misshape
idiom make a face (*or* mouth), make a wry face (*or* mouth), pull a face, screw up one's face

grime *vb syn* SOIL 2, begrime, besoil, dirty, foul, smirch, smooch, smudge, smutch, tarnish

grim reaper *n syn* DEATH 1, curtains, decease, defunction, demise, (the) Pale Horse, passing, quietus, silence, sleep

grin *vb syn* SMILE, beam
con frown, gloom
ant grimace

grind *vb syn* DRUDGE, grub, ‖muck, plod, slave, slog, toil

grind *n* **1** *syn* WORK 2, bullwork, donkeywork, drudgery, labor, moil, plugging, sweat, toil, travail
2 *syn* ROUTINE, groove, pace, rote, rut, treadmill

grip *vb* **1** *syn* TAKE 4, clasp, grasp
2 *syn* ENTHRALL 2, catch up, fascinate, hold, mesmerize, spellbind

grip *n syn* HOLD, clamp, clasp, clench, clinch, clutch, grapple, grasp, gripe, tenure
rel coercion, constraint, duress, restraint

gripe *vb* to complain emphatically and often petulantly < students *griping* about the cafeteria food >
syn ‖beef, ‖bellyache, ‖bitch, bleat, ‖blow off, crab, ‖crib, fuss, squawk, yammer, yawp (*or* yaup); *compare* COMPLAIN
rel brawl, kick, take on; croak, grouch, grouse, grumble, murmur, mutter
con applaud, approve, cheer; rejoice; accept, bear, endure, tolerate

gripe *n* **1** *syn* HOLD, clamp, clasp, clench, clinch, clutch, grapple, grasp, grip, tenure
2 *usu* **gripes** *pl syn* stomachache, bellyache, colic, collywobbles

griper *n syn* GROUCH, ‖bellyacher, complainer, crab, growler, grumbler, kicker, malcontent, sorehead, sourpuss

grisette *n syn* DOXY 1, ‖chippy, floozy, light-o'-love, nymph, nymphet, party girl, roundheel, tart, ‖tootsie

grisly *adj syn* GHASTLY 1, gruesome, hideous, horrible, horrid, horrifying, lurid, macabre, terrible, terrifying
rel eerie, uncanny, weird

grit *n syn* FORTITUDE, backbone, guts, intestinal fortitude, ‖moxie, nerve, sand, spunk
con faltering, hesitation, vacillation, wavering
ant faintheartedness

grobian *n syn* BOOR 2, ‖bosthoon, chuff, churl, clodhopper, clown, mucker

grog *n syn* LIQUOR 2, alcohol, aqua vitae, booze, drink, firewater, ‖hooch, ‖juice, spirit(s), tipple

‖**groggery** *n syn* BAR 5, ‖boozer, ‖bucket shop, drinkery, ‖gin mill, ‖grogshop, pothouse, ‖rumhole, ‖rum-mill, saloon

‖**grogshop** *n syn* BAR 5, ‖boozer, ‖bucket shop, drinkery, ‖gin mill, ‖groggery, pothouse, ‖rumhole, ‖rum-mill, saloon

groove *n syn* ROUTINE, grind, pace, rote, rut, treadmill

groovy *adj syn* MARVELOUS 2, ‖cool, ‖dandy, divine, ‖galluptious, glorious, hot, hunky-dory, ‖keen, ‖neat

grope *vb* to reach out or about blindly (as in testing or searching) < *groped* along the wall in search of a door >
syn feel, fumble, grabble
rel poke, pry, root; examine, explore, search

gross *adj* **1** *syn* EGREGIOUS, capital, flagrant, glaring, rank
rel excessive, exorbitant, extreme, immoderate, inordinate
con paltry, trifling, trivial
ant petty
2 *syn* UTTER, absolute, complete, damned, downright, out-and-out, outright, perfect, rank, unmitigated
3 *syn* FAT 2, corpulent, fleshy, heavy, obese, overweight, porcine, portly, stout, weighty
4 *syn* WHOLE 4, all, complete, entire, outright, total
ant net
5 *syn* MATERIAL 1, corporeal, objective, phenomenal, physical, sensible, substantial, tangible
6 *syn* COARSE 3, crass, crude, inelegant, raw, rough, rude, uncouth, unrefined, vulgar
7 *syn* OBSCENE 2, barnyard, coarse, crude, foul, rank, ‖raw, scatological, smutty, vulgar
rel animal, carnal, fleshy, sensual; loathsome, offensive, repulsive, revolting; improper, unrefined
con decent, decorous, proper, refined

gross *n syn* WHOLE 1, aggregate, all, be-all and end-all, entirety, sum, sum total, total, totality, ‖tote

grotesque *adj syn* FANTASTIC 2, antic, bizarre
rel baroque, flamboyant, rococo; eerie, uncanny, weird; extravagant, extreme; comic, comical, droll, ludicrous

grotto *n syn* CAVE, cavern, subterrane, subterranean

grouch *n* an habitually irritable or complaining person < it's hard to live with a *grouch* >
syn ‖bellyacher, complainer, crab, crabber, crank, crosspatch, faultfinder, griper, grouser, growler, grumbler, grump, kicker, malcontent, sorehead, sourpuss
con optimist, Pollyanna

grouch *vb syn* GRUMBLE 1, croak, grouse, ‖grunt, murmur, mutter, scold

---

syn synonym(s) — *rel* related word(s)
idiom idiomatic equivalent(s) — *con* contrasted word(s)
ant antonym(s) — * vulgar
‖ use limited; if in doubt, see a dictionary
The first word in a synonym list when printed in SMALL CAPITALS shows where there is more information about the group. For a more efficient use of this book see Explanatory Notes.

ground *n* **1** ***syn*** BASIS 1, base, bedrock, footing, foundation, groundwork, infrastructure, root, substratum, underpinning
2 ***syn*** BASE 1, basement, basis, bed, bedrock, bottom, footing, foundation, seat, substratum
3 ***syn*** REASON 3, argument, proof, wherefore, why, whyfor
rel evidence, testimony; antecedent, cause, determinant; demonstration, test, trial
4 grounds *pl* ***syn*** SEDIMENT, deposit, dreg(s), lees, precipitate, precipitation, settlings
5 ***syn*** EARTH 2, dirt, dry land, land, soil, terra firma

ground *vb* **1** ***syn*** FELL 1, bring down, down, drop, flatten, floor, knock down, level, mow (down), throw down
2 ***syn*** BASE, bottom, establish, found, predicate, rest, stay
rel buttress, support, sustain

grounded *adj* ***syn*** AGROUND, beached, stranded

groundless *adj* ***syn*** BASELESS, bottomless, foundationless, gratuitous, uncalled-for, unfounded, ungrounded, unwarranted
ant well-founded, well-grounded

groundwork *n* **1** ***syn*** BASIS 1, base, bedrock, footing, foundation, ground, infrastructure, root, substratum, underpinning
2 ***syn*** BASE 1, basement, bed, bottom, footing, foundation, substruction, substructure, underpinning, understructure

group *n* **1** a usually comparatively small assemblage of individuals <people gathered in *groups* about the hall>
syn assembly, band, bevy, bunch, cluster, covey, crew, party; *compare* COMPANY 1, GATHERING
rel circle, clique, cotery, set
con crowd, crush, horde, mob, press, rout, throng
2 ***syn*** GATHERING 2, aggregation, assemblage, assembly, collection, company, congeries, crowd, muster, ruck
3 an assemblage of things constituting a unit <a *group* of houses behind the church>
syn array, batch, battery, body, bunch, bundle, clot, clump, cluster, clutch, lot, parcel, passel, platoon, set, sort, suite
rel assemblage, collection, mess, shooting match
4 ***syn*** SET 5, bunch, circle, crowd, lot, push
5 ***syn*** SYNDICATE, cartel, chain, combine, conglomerate, pool, trust
6 ***syn*** CLASS 1, category, grade, grouping, league, pigeonhole, tier

group *vb* **1** to make into or bring together in a group <*grouped* the children according to age>
syn assemble, cluster, collect, gather, round up; *compare* GATHER 6
rel adjust, arrange, harmonize, organize, systematize; allocate, dispose, distribute, place; bunch, crowd, huddle
idiom bring together, get together
con disband, disperse, scatter, separate
2 ***syn*** ASSORT, categorize, class, classify, pigeonhole, sort

grouping *n* ***syn*** CLASS 1, category, grade, group, league, pigeonhole, tier

grouse *vb* ***syn*** GRUMBLE 1, croak, grouch, ‖grunt, murmur, mutter, scold

grouser *n* ***syn*** GROUCH, ‖bellyacher, crab, crank, griper, growler, grumbler, grump, sorehead, sourpuss

grovel *vb* ***syn*** FAWN, apple-polish, bootlick, ‖brownnose, cower, cringe, honey (up), kowtow, toady, truckle
idiom lick the dust (*or* one's boots)

groveler *n* ***syn*** SYCOPHANT, bootlick, bootlicker, ‖brownnose, ‖brownnoser, ‖clawback, footlicker, lickspittle, ‖suck, toady

groveling *adj* ***syn*** FAWNING, bootlicking, cowering, cringing, kowtowing, parasitic, sycophantic, toadying, toadyish, truckling

grow *vb* **1** to cause (something living) to exist or flourish <*grew* a crop of wheat>
syn breed, cultivate, produce, propagate, raise
rel care (for), foster, nurse, nurture, rear, tend
2 ***syn*** MATURE, age, develop, grow up, maturate, mellow, ‖ripe, ripen
3 ***syn*** ESCALATE 2, expand
4 ***syn*** BECOME 1, come, ‖come over, get, go, run, turn, wax

growl *vb* ***syn*** RUMBLE, grumble, roll

growler *n* ***syn*** GROUCH, ‖bellyacher, crab, crank, griper, grouser, grumbler, grump, sorehead, sourpuss

grown *adj* **1** ***syn*** MATURE 1, adult, full-blown, full-fledged, full-grown, grown-up, matured, ripe, ripened
2 ***syn*** OVERGROWN, rank

grown–up *adj* ***syn*** MATURE 1, adult, full-blown, full-fledged, full-grown, grown, matured, ripe, ripened
ant childish; callow

growth *n* ***syn*** DEVELOPMENT, evolution, evolvement, flowering, progress, progression, unfolding, upgrowth

grow up *vb* ***syn*** MATURE, age, develop, grow, maturate, mellow, ‖ripe, ripen

grub *vb* **1** ***syn*** DIG 1, ‖delve, excavate, shovel, spade
rel burrow, poke, root
2 ***syn*** SCOUR 2, beat, comb, finecomb, fine-tooth-comb, forage, rake, ransack, rummage, search
3 ***syn*** DRUDGE, grind, ‖muck, plod, slave, slog, toil

grub *n* **1** ***syn*** HACK 2, drudge, grubber, hireling, mercenary, slavey
2 ***syn*** FOOD 1, ‖chow, ‖eats, edibles, feed, nurture, provender, provisions, viands, victuals

grubber *n* ***syn*** HACK 2, drudge, grub, hireling, mercenary, slavey

grubby *adj* ***syn*** DIRTY 1, black, filthy, foul, impure, nasty, soily, squalid, unclean, uncleanly
ant immaculate

grubstake *vb* ***syn*** CAPITALIZE, back, bankroll, finance, stake

grudge *vb* ***syn*** ENVY, begrudge
rel deny; refuse

---

syn synonym(s) ***rel*** related word(s)
idiom idiomatic equivalent(s) ***con*** contrasted word(s)
ant antonym(s) * vulgar
‖ use limited; if in doubt, see a dictionary
The first word in a synonym list when printed in SMALL CAPITALS shows where there is more information about the group. For a more efficient use of this book see Explanatory Notes.

grudge *n* ***syn*** MALICE, despite, ill will, malevolence, maliciousness, malignancy, malignity, spite, spitefulness, spleen
rel grievance, injury, injustice

gruesome *adj* ***syn*** GHASTLY 1, grisly, hideous, horrible, horrid, horrifying, lurid, macabre, terrible, terrifying
rel appalling, daunting; horrendous, horrific; baleful, sinister

gruff *adj* **1** ***syn*** BLUFF, abrupt, blunt, brusque, crusty, curt, short, short-spoken, snippety, snippy
rel crabbed, dour, morose, saturnine, sullen, surly; boorish, churlish; fierce, truculent
con bland, smooth, suave, urbane; fulsome, oily, slick, soapy, unctuous
2 ***syn*** HOARSE 1, croaking, croaky, husky

grumble *vb* **1** to complain in a low harsh voice and often in a surly manner <workers *grumbling* about the low wages>
syn croak, grouch, grouse, ‖grunt, murmur, mutter, scold; *compare* COMPLAIN
rel ‖beef, ‖bellyache, ‖bitch, brawl, crab, fuss, gripe, holler, squawk, whine; groan, moan; complain, kick
con applaud, cheer; rejoice
2 ***syn*** RUMBLE, growl, roll

grumbler *n* ***syn*** GROUCH, ‖bellyacher, complainer, crab, crosspatch, faultfinder, grouser, growler, malcontent, sorehead

grump *n* **1 grumps** *pl* ***syn*** SULK, ‖dods, ‖dorts, mulligrubs, mumps, pouts, sullens
2 ***syn*** GROUCH, ‖bellyacher, crab, crank, griper, growler, grumbler, kicker, sorehead, sourpuss

grump *vb* ***syn*** SULK, ‖dort, ‖mump, pet, pout, ‖sull

Grundy *n* ***syn*** PRUDE, bluenose, comstock, goody-goody, Mrs. Grundy, nice Nelly, prig, puritan, ‖wowser

‖**grunt** *vb* ***syn*** GRUMBLE 1, croak, grouch, grouse, murmur, mutter, scold

guarantee *n* **1** an assurance for the fulfillment of a condition <gave him a *guarantee* that the work would be done according to specifications>
syn bail, bond, guaranty, security, surety, warranty; *compare* PLEDGE 1
rel earnest, pledge, promise, token, undertaking, word; oath, vow
2 ***syn*** WORD 8, assurance, pledge, warrant

guarantee *vb* ***syn*** WARRANT 2, certify, guaranty

guarantor *n* ***syn*** SPONSOR, angel, backer, backer-up, patron, surety

guaranty *n* ***syn*** GUARANTEE 1, bail, bond, security, surety, warranty
rel bargain, contract

guaranty *vb* ***syn*** WARRANT 2, certify, guarantee

guard *n* **1** ***syn*** DEFENSE 1, aegis, armament, armor, protection, safeguard, security, shield, ward
2 a person or group on sentinel duty <posted six *guards* around the diamond necklace> <turned out the *guard*>
syn lookout, picket, sentinel, sentry, ward, watch, watchman
rel guardian, jailer, keeper, turnkey, warden, warder; patrolman; outguard, patrol

guard *vb* ***syn*** DEFEND 1, bulwark, cover, fend, protect, safeguard, screen, secure, shield
rel attend, mind, tend, watch; accompany, chaperon, conduct, convoy, escort

guarded *adj* **1** ***syn*** ULTERIOR, buried, concealed, covert, hidden, obscured, privy, shrouded
2 ***syn*** CAUTIOUS, calculating, careful, chary, circumspect, considerate, discreet, gingerly, safe, wary
ant unguarded

guardian *n* ***syn*** CUSTODIAN, cerberus, claviger, ‖custodier, custos, keeper, warden, watchdog

guardianship *n* ***syn*** CUSTODY, care, keeping, safekeeping, trust, ward

guardroom *n* ***syn*** JAIL, ‖can, ‖clink, cooler, lockup, pen, prison, reformatory, ‖stir, stockade

gudgeon *n* ***syn*** FOOL 3, chump, dupe, fall guy, fish, gull, pigeon, sap, saphead, sucker

guerdon *n* ***syn*** REWARD, carrot, dividend, meed, plum, premium, prize

guerdon *vb* ***syn*** PAY 1, compensate, remunerate

guerrilla *n* ***syn*** PARTISAN 2, irregular, patriot

guess *vb* **1** ***syn*** CONJECTURE, presume, pretend, suppose, surmise, think
rel reason, speculate; deduce; estimate, reckon
idiom venture a guess
2 ***syn*** PREDICT 2, call

guest *n* **1** ***syn*** VISITOR 1, caller, visitant
2 guests *pl* ***syn*** COMPANY 2, visitors

guff *n* **1** ***syn*** NONSENSE 2, balderdash, bunkum, claptrap, hogwash, hokum, hooey, malarkey, poppycock, trash
2 ***syn*** BACK TALK, jaw, lip, mouth, sass, sauce

guffaw *vb* ***syn*** LAUGH, chortle, chuckle, giggle, hee-haw, snicker, ‖sniggle, tehee, titter

guide *vb* to put or lead on a course or into the way to be followed <*guided* them safely through the minefields>
syn conduct, direct, escort, lead, pilot, route, see, shepherd, show, steer
rel accompany, chaperon, convoy; control, manage; contrive, engineer, maneuver
idiom set one on one's way
con bewilder, distract, mystify, perplex, puzzle; beguile, deceive, delude, mislead
ant misguide

guide *n* **1** ***syn*** LEADER 1, ‖bell cow, bellwether, dean, doyen, lead pilot
2 ***syn*** ESCORT 2
rel conductor, director, leader, pilot
3 ***syn*** HANDBOOK, Baedeker, compendium, enchiridion, guidebook, manual, vade mecum

guidebook *n* ***syn*** HANDBOOK, Baedeker, compendium, enchiridion, guide, manual, vade mecum

guild *n* ***syn*** ASSOCIATION 2, brotherhood, club, fellowship, fraternity, league, order, society, sodality, union

---

guile *n* ***syn*** DECEIT 1, cunning, dissemblance, dissimulation, duplicity
ant ingenuousness; candor

guileful *adj* **1** ***syn*** SLY 2, artful, astute, crafty, cunning, deep, foxy, insidious, tricky, wily
ant guileless
2 ***syn*** UNDERHAND, devious, duplicitous, indirect, shifty, sneaking, sneaky, underhanded

guileless *adj* ***syn*** NATURAL 5, artless, ingenuous, naive, unaffected, unartful, unschooled, unsophisticated, unstudied, untutored
ant guileful

guillotine *vb* ***syn*** BEHEAD, decapitate, decollate, head, neck

guilt *n* ***syn*** BLAME, culpability, fault, onus
rel crime, offense, sin; responsibility
ant innocence; guiltlessness

guiltless *adj* **1** ***syn*** GOOD 11, blameless, exemplary, inculpable, innocent, irreproachable, pure, righteous, unblamable, virtuous
2 ***syn*** INNOCENT 2, blameless, clean, crimeless, faultless, inculpable, unguilty
ant guilty

guilty *adj* ***syn*** BLAMEWORTHY, amiss, blamable, blameful, censurable, culpable, demeritorious, reprehensible, sinful, unholy
rel accountable, answerable, responsible; impeached, incriminated, indicted
ant innocent; guiltless

guise *n* **1** ***syn*** COSTUME, dress, getup, outfit, rig, setout, turnout
2 ***syn*** APPEARANCE 2, face, seeming, semblance, show, showing, simulacrum
3 ***syn*** MASK 2, cloak, color, coloring, cover, disguise, disguisement, facade, face, false front

gulch *n* ***syn*** RAVINE, arroyo, chasm, cleft, clough, clove, gap, gorge

gulf *n* **1** ***syn*** INLET, arm, bay, bayou, bight, cove, ‖creek, firth, harbor, slough
2 a hollow place of vast width and depth <a *gulf* extending deep into the earth>
syn abysm, abyss, chasm
rel cave, cavity, hollow; crevasse, gulch, ravine; pit, shaft, well

gull *vb* ***syn*** DUPE, bamboozle, befool, chicane, flimflam, fool, hoax, hoodwink, hornswoggle, pigeon

gull *n* ***syn*** FOOL 3, chump, dupe, fall guy, fish, gudgeon, pigeon, sap, saphead, sucker

gullible *adj* ***syn*** EASY 3, fleeceable, naive, susceptible
ant astute

gulp *vb* to swallow hurriedly or greedily or in one swallow <*gulped* his lunch and ran off>
syn bolt, cram, englut, gobble, guzzle, ingurgitate, slop, slosh, wolf
rel devour, glut, stuff
con nibble, pick

gum (up) *vb* ***syn*** BOTCH, bitch (up), ‖blow, bobble, bollix, bungle, goof (up), louse up, mucker, ‖screw (up)

gumbo *n* ***syn*** GOO 1, gook, goop, gunk, muck

gummy *adj* ***syn*** STICKY 1, adhesive, ‖claggy, ‖clarty, cloggy, gluey, gooey, stodgy

gumption *n* ***syn*** SENSE 6, common sense, good sense, horse sense, judgment, wisdom
rel astuteness, perspicaciousness, perspicacity, sagaciousness, sagacity, shrewdness

gumptious *adj* ***syn*** ENTERPRISING 2, go-ahead, up-and-coming

gumshoe *n* **1** ***syn*** DETECTIVE, dick, ‖eye, hawkshaw, investigator, plainclothesman, Sherlock, Sherlock Holmes, sleuth, ‖tec
2 ***syn*** POLICEMAN, ‖bull, cop, ‖flatfoot, ‖fuzz, ‖heat, officer, ‖peeler, ‖pig, police officer

gumshoe *vb* ***syn*** SNEAK, creep, lurk, pussyfoot, shirk, skulk, slink, slip, ‖snake, steal

gun *n* ***syn*** ASSASSIN, bravo, cutthroat, gunman, ‖gunsel, gunslinger, hatchet man, hit man, torpedo, triggerman

gung ho *adj* ***syn*** ENTHUSIASTIC, ‖buggy, ‖bugs, keen, nutty, warm, zealous

gunk *n* **1** ***syn*** GOO 1, gook, goop, gumbo, muck
2 ***syn*** CRUD, ‖cab, goo, gook

gunman *n* ***syn*** ASSASSIN, bravo, cutthroat, gun, ‖gunsel, gunslinger, hatchet man, hit man, torpedo, triggerman

‖**gunsel** *n* ***syn*** ASSASSIN, bravo, cutthroat, gun, gunman, gunslinger, hatchet man, hit man, torpedo, triggerman

gunslinger *n* ***syn*** ASSASSIN, bravo, cutthroat, gun, gunman, ‖gunsel, hatchet man, hit man, torpedo, triggerman

gurge *vb* ***syn*** SWIRL, eddy, purl, swoosh, whirl, whirlpool, whorl

gurgle *vb* ***syn*** SLOSH 1, bubble, burble, lap, swash, wash

gush *vb* ***syn*** POUR 2, flow, roll, sluice, stream, surge
rel flood, flush; emanate, issue, spring

gushing *adj* ***syn*** EFFUSIVE, gushy, slobbering, slobbery, sloppy

gushy *adj* ***syn*** EFFUSIVE, gushing, slobbering, slobbery, sloppy

gussy up *vb* ***syn*** DRESS UP 1, deck (out), doll out, doll up, ‖dude up, fix up, slick, smarten (up), spiff, spruce (up)

gust *n* ***syn*** OUTBURST 1, access, burst, eruption, explosion, flare-up, sally

gusto *n* ***syn*** TASTE 4, heart, palate, relish, zest
rel delectation, delight, enjoyment, pleasure; ardor, enthusiasm, fervor, passion, zeal

gusty *adj* ***syn*** WINDY 1, airy, blowy, breezy

‖**gusty** *adj* ***syn*** PALATABLE, appetizing, flavorsome, good-tasting, mouth-watering, relishing, savory, tasty, toothsome, toothy

gut *n* **1** *usu* **guts** *pl* ***syn*** ENTRAILS, innards, insides, internals, inwards, ‖pudding(s), stuffing, tripes, viscera
‖**2** ***syn*** ABDOMEN, belly, paunch, stomach, tummy, venter
3 guts *pl* ***syn*** COURAGE, *balls, cojones, dauntlessness, heart, mettle, ‖moxie, pluck, resolution, spirit
4 guts *pl* ***syn*** FORTITUDE, backbone, grit, intestinal fortitude, ‖moxie, nerve, sand, spunk

gut *vb* **1** ***syn*** EVISCERATE, bowel, disembowel, draw, embowel, exenterate, paunch

---

syn synonym(s) — *rel* related word(s)
idiom idiomatic equivalent(s) — *con* contrasted word(s)
ant antonym(s) — * vulgar
‖ use limited; if in doubt, see a dictionary
The first word in a synonym list when printed in SMALL CAPITALS shows where there is more information about the group. For a more efficient use of this book see Explanatory Notes.

2 ***syn*** DRESS 3, clean
gut *adj* ***syn*** INNER 2, interior, internal, intimate, visceral, viscerous
gutless *adj* ***syn*** COWARDLY, ||chicken, coward, craven, lily-livered, poltroonish, poor-spirited, pusillanimous, spunkless, unmanly
ant ||gutsy
||**gutsy** *adj* ***syn*** BRAVE 1, bold, courageous, intrepid, manful, manly, plucky, spunky, unfearful, valiant
guy *n* ***syn*** MAN 3, ||bloke, boy, buck, chap, fellow, ||gee, gent, gentleman, he
guzzle *vb* **1** ***syn*** DRINK 3, booze, imbibe, liquor (up), soak, swig, swill, swizzle, tank up, tipple
2 ***syn*** GULP, bolt, cram, englut, gobble, ingurgitate, slop, slosh, wolf
guzzler *n* ***syn*** DRUNKARD, bibber, boozehound, boozer, drunk, inebriate, lush, soak, sot, tippler
gyp *n* **1** ***syn*** SWINDLER, cheat, con man, defrauder, diddler, double-dealer, flimflammer, mountebank, sharper, trickster
2 ***syn*** IMPOSTURE, cheat, fake, fraud, hoax, humbug, phony, sell, spoof, swindle
gyp *vb* ***syn*** CHEAT, beat, bilk, chouse, cozen, defraud, diddle, do, overreach, swindle
gypper *n* ***syn*** SWINDLER, cheat, con man, defrauder, diddler, double-dealer, flimflammer, mountebank, sharper, trickster
gyrate *vb* **1** ***syn*** TURN 1, circle, circumduct, gyre, revolve, roll, rotate
2 ***syn*** SPIN 1, gyre, ||pirl, pirouette, ||purl, twirl, whirl, whirligig
gyration *n* ***syn*** REVOLUTION 1, circuit, circulation, circumvolution, gyre, rotation, round, turn, wheel, whirl
gyre *vb* **1** ***syn*** TURN 1, circle, circumduct, gyrate, revolve, roll, rotate
2 ***syn*** SPIN 1, gyrate, ||pirl, pirouette, ||purl, twirl, whirl, whirligig
gyre *n* ***syn*** REVOLUTION 1, circuit, circulation, circumvolution, gyration, rotation, round, turn, wheel, whirl
gyve *n, usu* **gyves** *pl* ***syn*** SHACKLE, bond(s), chains, fetter(s), iron(s)

H

habiliment *n* **1 habiliments** *pl* ***syn*** EQUIPMENT, accouterment(s), apparatus, gear, machinery, matériel, outfit, paraphernalia, tackle, tackling
2 *usu* **habiliments** *pl* ***syn*** CLOTHES, apparel, attire, attirement, clothing, dress, duds, raiment, things, togs

habit *n* **1** a mode of behaving or doing fixed by constant repetition <it was his *habit* to rise early>
syn consuetude, custom, habitude, manner, practice, praxis, trick, usage, use, way, wont
rel bent, disposition, inclination, proclivity, tendency, turn; convention, fashion, form, mode, pattern, style; addiction; groove, rote, routine, rut, set
2 ***syn*** PHYSIQUE, build, constitution, habitus
rel carcass; framework; contour, outline

habitable *adj* ***syn*** LIVABLE 1, inhabitable, lodgeable, occupiable, tenantable
ant unhabitable, uninhabitable

habitant *n* ***syn*** INHABITANT, denizen, dweller, indweller, liver, occupant, resident, ‖residenter, resider

habitat *n* the physical environment natural to a kind of being <the watery *habitat* of the eel>
syn haunt, home, locality, range, site, stamping ground
rel environment, locale, surroundings, territory

habitation *n* **1** the act of inhabiting or the state of being inhabited <places suitable for *habitation*>
syn inhabitancy, inhabitation, occupancy, occupation, residence, settlement
rel colonization, domiciliation, peopling; sojourning
2 the place where one lives <*habitations* unfit for human occupancy>
syn abode, commorancy, domicile, dwelling, home, house, residence, residency
rel apartment, flat, tenement; housing, lodging, lodgment, quarters; haunt, haven, homeplace, homestead, place, seat; ‖digs, nest, nook, ‖pad, ‖roost; astre, fireside, hearth, hearthside, hearthstone, roof, rooftree
idiom roof over one's head, where one hangs one's hat

habitual *adj* **1** ***syn*** USUAL 1, accepted, accustomed, chronic, customary, routine, wonted
rel constant, established, ingrained, inveterate, persistent, steady
con infrequent, irregular, sporadic, uncommon
ant occasional
2 acting by force of habit <*habitual* smokers who blue the air>
syn accustomed, chronic, confirmed, habituated
rel continual, inveterate, persistent, regular, steady; automatic, instinctive, involuntary; addicted; customary, wonted
con conscious, deliberate, premeditative, purposive, witting

habitually *adv* ***syn*** USUALLY 1, as usual, consistently, customarily, wontedly
ant occasionally

habituate *vb* **1** ***syn*** ACCUSTOM, familiarize, inure, use, wont
2 to make acceptable or desirable (as to oneself) through use <*habituate* oneself to poverty>
syn addict, adjust, confirm (in), devote (to), take (to)
rel bear, endure, inure, support, tolerate; condition, familiarize, season
con balk (at), object (to), resist

habituated *adj* ***syn*** HABITUAL 2, accustomed, chronic, confirmed

habitude *n* ***syn*** HABIT 1, consuetude, custom, manner, practice, trick, usage, use, way, wont
rel attitude, position, stand; condition, situation, state
con humor, mood, temper; caprice, freak, vagary, whim

habitué *n* **1** one who frequents a place <an *habitué* of libraries>
syn denizen, frequenter, haunter
rel customer, devotee, patron, sojourner; employer, user
2 ***syn*** ADDICT, aficionado, buff, devotee, fan, hound, lover, votary

habitus *n* ***syn*** PHYSIQUE, build, constitution, habit

hack *vb* to cut with repeated crude or ruthless blows <*hack* a path through the jungle>
syn hackle, haggle, slash
rel gash, mangle; chop, cut, fell, hew

hack *n* **1** ***syn*** TAXICAB, cab, taxi
2 one who surrenders intellectual or personal integrity for an assured reward (as a regular income) <party *hacks* and hangers-on>
syn drudge, grub, grubber, hireling, mercenary, slavey
rel grind, lackey, servant, slave; machine, plodder; potboiler

hack *adj* **1** ***syn*** INFERIOR 2, common, déclassé, low-grade, mean, poor, second-class, second-drawer, second-rate
rel commonplace, dull, ordinary, trite, usual; inconsequential, petty, trivial
con individual, original, uncommon, unusual
2 ***syn*** TRITE, cliché, clichéd, commonplace, stale, stereotyped, stereotypical, timeworn, tired, well-worn
rel antiquated, old, outmoded, outworn
con lively; unfamiliar

hackle *vb* ***syn*** HACK, haggle, slash

hackneyed *adj* ***syn*** TRITE, bathetic, clichéd, commonplace, hack, stale, timeworn, tired, well-worn, worn-out
rel antediluvian, antiquated, archaic, obsolete, outmoded, out-of-date; conventional, everyday, quotidian, stock; moth-eaten

---

ant unhackneyed

Hadean *adj syn* INFERNAL 1, chthonian, chthonic, plutonian, plutonic, sulphurous, Tartarean
rel gloomy, murky, stygian

hades *n syn* HELL, barathrum, Gehenna, netherworld, Pandemonium, perdition, pit, Sheol, Tophet, underworld

hag *n* **1** *syn* WITCH 1, bruja, enchantress, hex, lamia, sorceress, witch-woman
2 an ugly or evil-looking old woman <a pitiful homeless *hag*>
syn ||bag, ||bat, beldam, biddy, crone, drab, trot, witch
rel gammer, grandam; ||battle-ax, fishwife, gorgon, harpy, harridan, shrew, slattern, virago, vixen

haggard *adj* thin and contracted by or as if by fatigue or inner distress <*haggard* from their long vigil>
syn careworn, drawn, pinched, worn
rel angular, gaunt, lank, lean, scraggy, scrawny, skinny, spare; ashen, faded, pale, pallid, wan; exhausted, fagged, fatigued, tired, wearied, worn-down
con energetic, lusty, strenuous, vigorous; easy, relaxed

haggle *vb* **1** *syn* HACK, hackle, slash
2 to argue as to terms <*haggle* over prices>
syn bargain, chaffer, dicker, higgle, huckster, palter
rel barter, deal, horse-trade, trade; bicker, cavil, dispute, quibble, squabble, stickle, wrangle

hagridden *adj syn* OBSESSED, hipped, queer

hagride *vb syn* WORRY 1, annoy, bedevil, gnaw, harass, harry, pester, plague, tease, ||wherret

hail *n syn* BARRAGE, bombardment, broadside, cannonade, drumfire, fusillade, salvo, shower, storm, volley

hail *vb* **1** *syn* ADDRESS 7, accost, call (to), greet, salute
rel hallo, hallow, holler, shout
2 *syn* COMMEND 2, acclaim, applaud, compliment, kudize, praise, recommend, ||roose
con belittle, depreciate, disparage, downgrade; berate, censure, condemn, libel, rap; dismiss, reject

hail (from) *vb syn* ORIGINATE 5, come (from)

hair *n* a minute distance, degree, or margin <won the election by a *hair*>
syn ace, hairbreadth, whisker; *compare* HINT 2
rel bit, fraction, jot, mite, particle, trace, trifle

hairbreadth *n syn* HAIR, ace, whisker

haircutter *n syn* BARBER

hairless *adj* lacking hair <he had a shining *hairless* head>
syn bald, glabrous, smooth
rel baldish; shaved, shaven, shorn, tonsured
ant hairy

hairline *adj syn* FINE 1, delicate, finespun, hairsplitting, nice, refined, subtle

hairsplitting *adj syn* FINE 1, delicate, finespun, hairline, nice, refined, subtle

hair–trigger *adj syn* INSTANTANEOUS, immediate, instant

hairy *adj* **1** covered with or as if with hair <wore a *hairy* overcoat>
syn fleecy, hirsute, pileous, pilose, whiskered, woolly
rel bristly, bushy, downy, fluffy, fuzzy, lanate, nappy, pubescent, rough, shaggy, tomentose, tufted, unshorn, villous
con bald, barefaced, beardless, glabrous, shaved, shaven, shorn, smooth
ant hairless
2 *syn* DANGEROUS 1, chancy, hazardous, jeopardous, perilous, risky, treacherous, unhealthy, unsound, wicked
3 *syn* ROUGH 1, asperous, craggy, harsh, jagged, rugged, scabrous, scraggy, uneven, unsmooth

halcyon *adj syn* CALM 1, hushed, placid, quiet, still, stilly, untroubled
con blustery, fevered, foul, raging, rough, stormy, tempestuous, troubled, tumultuous, wild

hale *adj syn* HEALTHY 1, ||bunkum, fit, right, sane, sound, well, well-conditioned, well-liking, wholesome
rel husky, stout, strapping
idiom hale and hearty
ant infirm

haleness *n syn* HEALTH, healthiness, soundness, wholeness

||**half–assed** *adj syn* DEFICIENT 1, defective, inadequate, incomplete, insufficient, lacking, uncomplete, wanting

half–blind *adj syn* PURBLIND, dim-sighted

half blood *n syn* HYBRID, bastard, cross, crossbred, crossbreed, half-breed, mongrel, mule
ant full blood

half–breed *n syn* HYBRID, bastard, cross, crossbred, crossbreed, half blood, mongrel, mule
ant full blood

halfhearted *adj syn* TEPID 2, lukewarm, unenthusiastic

||**half–seas over** *adj syn* INTOXICATED 1, ||bagged, ||boozed, drunk, ||juiced, ||lit, ||smashed, ||stewed, stiff, wet

halfway *adj syn* MIDDLE 1, center, centermost, equidistant, medial, median, mid, middlemost, midmost

half–wit *n syn* FOOL 4, ament, cretin, ||feeb, idiot, imbecile, moron, natural, simpleton, zany

half–witted *adj syn* RETARDED, backward, dim-witted, dull, feebleminded, imbecile, moronic, simpleminded, slow, slow-witted

hall *n syn* PASSAGE 4, corridor, couloir, hallway, passageway

hallo *vb syn* CALL 1, cry, holler, hollo, shout, vociferate, yell

hallow *vb* **1** *syn* BLESS 1, consecrate, sanctify
2 *syn* DEVOTE 1, consecrate, dedicate
con defile, desecrate, pollute, profane

hallowed *adj syn* HOLY 1, blessed, consecrated, sacred, sanctified, unprofane

hallucination *n syn* DELUSION 1, ignis fatuus, illusion, mirage, phantasm
rel apparition, fata morgana, phantom, wraith

hallway *n syn* PASSAGE 4, corridor, couloir, hall, passageway

halt *vb syn* LIMP 1, hitch, hobble

halt *vb* **1** *syn* STOP 4, bring up, draw up, fetch up, haul up, pull up
ant proceed

---

syn synonym(s) *rel* related word(s)
idiom idiomatic equivalent(s) *con* contrasted word(s)
ant antonym(s) * vulgar
|| use limited; if in doubt, see a dictionary
The first word in a synonym list when printed in SMALL CAPITALS shows where there is more information about the group. For a more efficient use of this book see Explanatory Notes.

2 ***syn*** STOP 3, cease, desist, ‖deval, discontinue, give over, knock off, leave off, quit, surcease

3 ***syn*** ARREST 1, check, interrupt, stall, stay

4 ***syn*** HESITATE, dither, falter, shilly-shally, stagger, vacillate, waver, whiffle, wiggle-waggle

5 ***syn*** CLOSE 2, complete, conclude, determine, end, finish, terminate, ultimate, wind up, wrap up

halting *adj* **1** ***syn*** AWKWARD 2, bumbling, clumsy, gauche, inept, lumbering, maladroit, unhandy, unhappy, wooden

2 ***syn*** VACILLATING 2, faltering, hesitant, irresolute, shilly-shallying, tentative, uncertain, vacillatory, wiggle-waggle, wobbly

ham–handed *adj* ***syn*** AWKWARD 2, bumbling, clumsy, gauche, halting, heavy-handed, inept, maladroit, unhandy, wooden

hammer *vb* **1** to strike or shape with or as if with a hammer <brass *hammered* into bowls and trays>

syn beat, malleate, pound

rel elaborate, fashion, form, shape

2 ***syn*** BEAT 1, batter, belabor, drub, lambaste, pelt, pound, pummel, thrash, wallop

3 ***syn*** IMPRESS 3, drive, grave, pound, stamp

‖**4** ***syn*** STAMMER 1, ‖stut, stutter

hammer (out) *vb* ***syn*** ERECT 5, build up, construct, establish, set up

hammerhead *n* ***syn*** DUNCE, blockhead, bonehead, clodpate, knucklehead, muttonhead, numskull, thickhead, thickskull, woodenhead

hammerheaded *adj* ***syn*** STUPID 1, beefheaded, beetleheaded, blockheaded, chuckleheaded, dull, fatheaded, numskulled, thick, thickheaded

hamper *vb* to impede in moving, progressing, or acting freely <the long dress *hampered* her escape>

syn clog, curb, entrammel, fetter, hobble, hog-tie, leash, shackle, tie, tie up, trammel; *compare* HINDER, RESTRAIN 1

rel cumber, encumber, handicap, hinder, impede, lumber, obstruct; baffle, balk, bar, block, foil, frustrate, thwart; restrain, restrict, retard; discomfit, embarrass; check, inconvenience, inhibit

idiom tie one's hands

con free, liberate, loose, release, unfetter, unleash, unshackle

ant aid, facilitate

hamper *n* ***syn*** OBSTACLE 1, bar, Chinese wall, crimp, hurdle, impediment, obstruction, rub, snag, stumbling block

hams *n pl* ***syn*** BUTTOCKS, backside, behind, ‖butt, cheeks, ‖duff, fanny, haunches, hunkers, rump

hand *n* **1** ***syn*** SIDE 1

2 ***syn*** PHASE, angle, aspect, facet, side

3 ***syn*** HANDWRITING, calligraphy, chirography, ductus, fist, penmanship, script

4 ***syn*** HELP 1, aid, assist, assistance, comfort, lift, relief, secours, succor, support

5 ***syn*** WORKER, laborer, ‖mozo, operative, roustabout, workhand, workingman, workman

6 ***syn*** TOUCH 6

hand *vb* **1** ***syn*** GIVE 3, deliver, dish out, dispense, feed, find, provide, supply, transfer, turn over

2 ***syn*** PASS 9, buck, reach, ‖shoot

handbill *n* ***syn*** POSTER, affiche, bill, placard

handbook *n* a concise reference book <a *handbook* of wild flowers>

syn Baedeker, compendium, enchiridion, guide, guidebook, manual, vade mecum

con cyclopedia, encyclopedia

hand down *vb* to convey in succession <a skill *handed down* from father to son>

syn bequeath, hand on, pass (on), transmit

con get, obtain, receive

handful *n* ***syn*** FEW, scattering, smatch, smatter, smattering, spatter, spattering, sprinkling

handicap *n* **1** ***syn*** DISADVANTAGE, detriment, disability, drawback

rel burden, encumbrance, load; embarrassment

ant asset

2 ***syn*** ADVANTAGE 3, allowance, bulge, ‖deadwood, edge, head start, odds, ‖overhand, start, vantage

handicraft *n* ***syn*** TRADE 1, art, calling, craft, métier, profession, vocation

hand in *vb* ***syn*** SUBMIT 2, refer

handkerchief *n* a small usually square piece of cloth used especially for blowing the nose <carry a pocket *handkerchief*>

syn hankie, kerchief, *snot-rag, ‖wipe, ‖wiper

‖**handle** *n* **1** ***syn*** NAME 1, appellation, cognomen, compellation, denomination, designation, ‖moniker, nomen, style, title

2 ***syn*** NICKNAME, byname, byword, hypocorism, ‖moniker, sobriquet

handle *vb* **1** ***syn*** TOUCH 1, feel, finger, palpate, paw

rel test, try; manipulate

2 to deal with or manage usually with dexterity or efficiency <*handles* his tools with great skill>

syn dispense, maneuver, manipulate, ply, swing, wield

rel direct, guide, manage, operate, run, work; brandish, flourish, shake, wave; aim, lay, level, point

3 ***syn*** OPERATE 3, run, use, work

4 ***syn*** TREAT 2, deal (with), play, serve, take, use

rel conduct, control, direct, manage

5 ***syn*** GOVERN 3, control, direct, dominate, manage

6 ***syn*** USE 2, apply, bestow, employ, exercise, exploit, utilize

handling *n* ***syn*** OVERSIGHT 1, care, charge, conduct, intendance, management, running, superintendence, superintendency, supervision

handmaid *n* ***syn*** MAID 2, biddy, girl, hired girl, housemaid, maidservant

hand on *vb* ***syn*** HAND DOWN, bequeath, pass (on), transmit

hand out *vb* ***syn*** GIVE 1, bestow, devote, donate, give away, present

hand over *vb* **1** ***syn*** RELINQUISH, abandon, cede, give up, leave, resign, surrender, ‖turn up, waive, yield

2 ***syn*** GIVE 3, deliver, dispense, feed, find, hand, provide, supply, transfer, turn over

---

syn synonym(s) — *rel* related word(s)
idiom idiomatic equivalent(s) — *con* contrasted word(s)
ant antonym(s) — * vulgar
‖ use limited; if in doubt, see a dictionary

The first word in a synonym list when printed in SMALL CAPITALS shows where there is more information about the group. For a more efficient use of this book see Explanatory Notes.

3 ***syn*** COMMIT 1, commend, confide, consign, entrust, relegate, turn over

hand running *adv* ***syn*** TOGETHER 2, consecutively, continually, continuously, night and day, running, successively, unintermittedly, uninterruptedly

handsome *adj* **1** ***syn*** LIBERAL 1, bounteous, bountiful, free, freehanded, generous, munificent, openhanded, unsparing
con economical, frugal, sparing; scrimpy, skimpy
2 ***syn*** BEAUTIFUL, attractive, beauteous, ‖bonny, comely, fair, good-looking, lovely, pretty, pulchritudinous
rel august, majestic, noble, stately; chic, dashing, fashionable, modish, smart, stylish
con inelegant, unsightly
ant unhandsome

handwriting *n* writing in which the letters are formed by a hand-guided implement (as a pen) <legible *handwriting*>
syn calligraphy, chirography, ductus, fist, hand, penmanship, script
rel longhand

handy *adj* **1** ***syn*** CONVENIENT 2, adjacent, close-at-hand, close-by, near-at-hand, nearby
idiom at one's hand (*or* elbow), ready to hand
ant unhandy
2 ***syn*** PRACTICAL 2, functional, practicable, serviceable, useful, utile
rel adaptable, advantageous, beneficial, wieldy
con clumsy, cumbersome, cumbrous, unwieldy
ant unhandy
3 ***syn*** DEXTEROUS 1, adroit, clever, deft, neat-handed, nimble

hang *vb* **1** to place or be placed so as to be supported at one point or side usually at the top <*hang* the washing on the line>
syn dangle, depend, sling, suspend
rel attach, hook; fix, pin, tack (up); adhere, cling, stick
2 to put to death by suspending by the neck <was *hanged* for stealing a sheep>
syn gibbet, noose, scrag, string (up), turn off
rel execute, lynch
idiom bring to the gallows, hang by the neck, make dance on air (*or* nothing)
3 to remain poised or stationary as if suspended in midair <clouds *hanging* in the west>
syn float, hover, poise
4 to project outward or incline downward <children *hanging* out the windows to watch a parade>
syn beetle, bend (over), jut, lean (over), overhang
rel drape, droop, loll, lop, sag, trail

hang (on *or* upon) *vb* ***syn*** DEPEND (on *or* upon) 1, hinge (on *or* upon), ‖pend, stand (on *or* upon), turn (on *or* upon)

hang *n* the special method of doing, using, or dealing with something <can't get the *hang* of this gadget>
syn knack, swing, trick
rel art, craft, skill

hang around *vb* ***syn*** FREQUENT, affect, hang out, haunt, resort

hanger–on *n* ***syn*** PARASITE, barnacle, bloodsucker, freeloader, leech, lounge lizard, ‖spiv, sponge, sponger, sucker
rel bystander, follower, spectator, sycophant

hanging *adj* ***syn*** SUSPENDED, pendent, pendulant, pendulous, pensile

hang on *vb* ***syn*** PERSEVERE, carry on, go on, persist

hang out *vb* **1** ***syn*** RESIDE 1, abide, bide, ‖dig, dwell, live
2 ***syn*** FREQUENT, affect, hang around, haunt, resort

hangout *n* **1** ***syn*** RESORT 2, haunt, purlieu, rendezvous, stamping ground, watering hole
2 ***syn*** DIVE, barrelhouse, honky-tonk, joint

hang up *vb* ***syn*** DELAY 1, bog (down), decelerate, detain, embog, mire, retard, set back, slacken, slow (up *or* down)

hanker *vb* ***syn*** LONG, ache, crave, hunger, lust, pine, sigh, thirst, yearn, yen
rel covet, desire, wish

hankie *n* ***syn*** HANDKERCHIEF, kerchief, *snot-rag, ‖wipe, ‖wiper

hanky–panky *n* ***syn*** DECEPTION 1, chicane, chicanery, ‖dipsy-doodle, double-dealing, fourberie, fraud, highbinding, sharp practice, trickery

hap *n* ***syn*** ACCIDENT 1, chance, fortuity, luck
rel destiny, fate, lot, portion

hap *vb* ***syn*** HAPPEN 1, befall, betide, break, chance, come off, develop, go, occur, transpire

‖**hap** *vb* ***syn*** BUNDLE UP, muffle, wrap (up)

haphazard *adj* ***syn*** RANDOM, aimless, designless, desultory, hit-or-miss, indiscriminate, irregular, unaimed, unconsidered, unplanned
rel accidental; careless, helter-skelter, slipshod; unorganized, unsystematic
con deliberate, designed, intentional, voluntary, willful
ant planned

haphazard *adv* ***syn*** ABOUT 4, anyhow, any which way, anywise, around, at random, haphazardly, helter-skelter, random, randomly
rel accidentally, aimlessly, carelessly, casually, promiscuously

haphazardly *adv* ***syn*** ABOUT 4, anyhow, any which way, anywise, around, at random, haphazard, helter-skelter, random, randomly
rel accidentally, aimlessly, carelessly, casually, promiscuously

hapless *adj* ***syn*** UNLUCKY, ill-fated, ill-starred, luckless, misfortunate, star-crossed, unfortunate, unhappy, untoward
rel infelicitous; miserable, woeful, wretched

happen *vb* **1** to take place or come about <the incident *happened* at midnight>
syn befall, betide, break, chance, come, come off, develop, do, fall out, give, go, hap, occur, pass, rise, transpire
rel go off, turn out
idiom come to pass

---

syn synonym(s) ***rel*** related word(s)
idiom idiomatic equivalent(s) ***con*** contrasted word(s)
ant antonym(s) * vulgar
‖ use limited; if in doubt, see a dictionary
The first word in a synonym list when printed in SMALL CAPITALS shows where there is more information about the group. For a more efficient use of this book see Explanatory Notes.

2 to come by chance <he unexpectedly *happened* on a new method>
syn bump, chance, hit, light, luck, meet, stumble, tumble
rel befall

happening *n* ***syn*** OCCURRENCE, circumstance, episode, event, go, incident, occasion, thing

happify *vb* ***syn*** PLEASE 2, arride, delectate, delight, gladden, gratify, pleasure

happily *adv* ***syn*** WELL 5, favorably, fortunately, prosperously, satisfyingly, successfully, swimmingly

happiness *n* a state of well-being or pleasurable satisfaction <felt *happiness* at her husband's success>
syn beatitude, blessedness, bliss, blissfulness
rel content, contentedness, satisfaction; cheer, cheerfulness, felicity, gladness; gaiety, jollity, joy; delectation, delight, enjoyment, pleasure
con discontent, dissatisfaction, vexation; cheerlessness, despair, desperation, despondency, hopelessness; distress, misery, wretchedness
ant unhappiness

happy *adj* **1** ***syn*** LUCKY, fortunate, providential, ‖sonsy, well
rel accidental, casual, fortuitous, incidental; opportune, seasonable, timely
ant unhappy
2 ***syn*** FIT 1, appropriate, apt, befitting, felicitous, fitting, just, meet, proper, suitable
rel effective, effectual, efficacious, efficient; cogent, convincing, telling; pat, seasonable, well-timed; correct, nice, right
ant unhappy
3 ***syn*** GLAD 1, joyful, joyous, lighthearted
rel content, contented, satisfied
ant unhappy; disconsolate

happy-go-lucky *adj* disposed to accept cheerfully whatever happens <enjoyed a *happy-go-lucky* existence without needlessly worrying>
syn carefree, free-minded, insouciant, lighthearted, lightsome; *compare* COOL 2
rel casual, easy, easygoing; blithe, careless, cheerful, feckless, heedless, lackadaisical; debonair, nonchalant, unconcerned; devil-may-care, reckless
con careful, cautious, circumspect, discreet, guarded, prudent

happy hunting ground *n* ***syn*** HEAVEN 2, bliss, Canaan, Civitas Dei, elysium, empyrean, New Jerusalem, nirvana, paradise, Zion

hara–kiri *n* ***syn*** SUICIDE, felo-de-se, self-destruction, self-murder, self-slaughter, self-violence

harangue *n* ***syn*** TIRADE, diatribe, jeremiad, philippic

harangue *vb* ***syn*** ORATE, bloviate, declaim, mouth, perorate, rant, rave, soapbox

harass *vb* **1** ***syn*** RAID 1, foray, harry, maraud
2 ***syn*** WORRY 1, annoy, bedevil, beleaguer, gnaw, hagride, harry, pester, plague, tease
rel badger, bait, bullyrag, chivy, devil, heckle, hector, hound, ride
idiom give a bad (*or* hard) time
3 ***syn*** TRY 2, distress, irk, pain, strain, stress, trouble

harassed *adj* ***syn*** DISTRAUGHT, distracted, distrait, distressed, tormented, troubled, worried

harasser *n* ***syn*** BULLY 1, browbeater, bulldozer, harrier, hector, intimidator

harassment *n* ***syn*** ANNOYANCE 1, bothering, irking, provocation, provoking, vexation, vexing
rel aggravation, disturbance, exasperation, irritation, perturbation

harbinger *n* ***syn*** FORERUNNER 1, herald, outrider, precursor

harbinger *vb* ***syn*** ANNOUNCE 2, forerun, foreshow, herald, preindicate, presage

harbor *n* **1** ***syn*** SHELTER 1, asylum, cover, covert, harborage, haven, port, refuge, retreat, sanctuary
2 ***syn*** INLET, arm, bay, bight, cove, ‖creek, firth, gulf, ‖loch, ‖lough
3 a place where seacraft may ride secure <a yacht *harbor*>
syn anchorage, ‖chuck, harborage, haven, port, riding, road(s), roadstead

harbor *vb* **1** to provide with shelter or a refuge <*harbored* the refugees in our homes>
syn chamber, haven, house, roof, shelter, shield
rel cherish, foster, nurse, nurture; conceal, hide, secrete; guard, protect, safeguard, screen
idiom give shelter (*or* asylum) to
con eject, evict, expel, oust; banish, deport, exile; eliminate, exclude, shut out
2 to provide with a usually temporary place to live <the miners were *harbored* in camps>
syn accommodate, bestow, billet, board, bunk, domicile, domiciliate, entertain, house, hut, lodge, put up, quarter, room, roost
rel cabin, camp, encamp

harborage *n* ***syn*** SHELTER 1, asylum, cover, covert, harbor, haven, port, refuge, retreat, sanctuary
2 ***syn*** REFUGE 1, asylum, sanctuary, shelter
3 ***syn*** HARBOR 3, anchorage, ‖chuck, haven, port, riding, road(s), roadstead

hard *adj* **1** ***syn*** FIRM 2, solid
rel compacted, compressed, concentrated, consolidated, packed; callous, hardened, indurate, indurated, set; adamantine, flinty, granitic, iron, ironhard
con fluid, liquid; flabby, limp; ductile, malleable, pliable, pliant, plastic; elastic, flexible, limber, resilient, supple
ant soft
2 ***syn*** SPIRITUOUS, alcoholic, ardent, strong
ant soft
3 ***syn*** REALISTIC, down-to-earth, hard-boiled, hardheaded, matter-of-fact, practical, pragmatic, sober, unfantastic, unidealistic
4 ***syn*** INSENSIBLE 5, anesthetic, bloodless, dull, impassible, insensate, insensitive, rocky
5 ***syn*** INTENSIVE, blood-and-guts, deep, intense, profound
6 demanding great toil and effort <a *hard* but rewarding task>

---

syn synonym(s) ***rel*** related word(s)
idiom idiomatic equivalent(s) ***con*** contrasted word(s)
ant antonym(s) * vulgar
‖ use limited; if in doubt, see a dictionary
The first word in a synonym list when printed in SMALL CAPITALS shows where there is more information about the group. For a more efficient use of this book see Explanatory Notes.

syn arduous, difficile, difficult, effortful, formidable, heavy, knotty, labored, laborious, operose, rough, rugged, serious, severe, slavish, sticky, strenuous, terrible, toilful, toilsome, tough, uphill
rel burdensome, exacting, onerous; complex, complicated, intricate, involved, scabrous; backbreaking, distressing, exhausting, fatiguing, grinding, tiring, wearing, wearisome, wearying; bothersome, demanding, irksome, rocky, straining, troublesome, trying; merciless, unsparing
con effortless, facile, light, simple, smooth
ant easy
7 ***syn*** ACTUAL 2, absolute, factual, genuine, positive, sure-enough
8 ***syn*** GRIM 2, austere, bleak, dour, harsh, severe, stringent
9 ***syn*** SEVERE 3, bitter, brutal, harsh, inclement, intemperate, rigorous, rugged

hard *adv* **1** with great or utmost force <hit the nail *hard*>
syn energetically, forcefully, forcibly, hardly, might and main, mightily, powerfully, strongly, vigorously
rel actively, animatedly, briskly, snappily, spiritedly, sprightly, vivaciously; earnestly, intensely, keenly, seriously, urgently, wholeheartedly
idiom with all one's might
con faintly, feebly, nervelessly, softly, strengthlessly, unenergetically, weakly
ant easily, easy
2 in a violent manner <the wind blew *hard* all the next day>
syn fiercely, frantically, frenziedly, furiously, hardly, madly, stormily, tumultuously, turbulently, violently, wildly
rel boisterously, exuberantly, rowdily, uproariously: angrily, brutally, ferociously, savagely, viciously
idiom like a house afire, like fury, like mad
con gently, mildly, softly
3 with intentness and determination <made up his mind to study *hard*>
syn assiduously, dingdong, earnestly, exhaustively, intensely, intensively, painstakingly, thoroughly, unremittingly
rel conscientiously, meticulously, punctiliously
con carelessly, casually, desultorily, fitfully, haphazardly
4 in a fixed and intensive manner <stared *hard* at the offender>
syn closely, intently, searchingly, sharply
con casually, cursorily, idly, offhand
5 in such manner as to cause hardship, difficulty, or defeat <things will go *hard* with him if he doesn't reform>
syn badly, hardly, harshly, painfully, rigorously, roughly, severely; *compare* AMISS 2
rel cruelly; relentlessly; meanly, shabbily, unfairly
con comfortably, pleasantly, smoothly; acceptably, satisfactorily, satisfyingly
ant easily, easy
6 with great or excessive resentment or grief <don't take your setback so *hard*>
syn bitterly, hardly, keenly, rancorously, resentfully, sorely
con casually, lightly, nonchalantly, offhandedly
7 in a firm manner <hold on *hard*>
syn fast, firm, firmly, fixedly, solidly, steadfastly, tight, tightly
con easily, easy, loose, loosely, slackly
8 with difficulty <breathing *hard* after the climb>
syn arduously, burdensomely, difficultly, hardly, laboriously, onerously, toilsomely
rel exhaustingly, gruelingly, painfully, tiredly; awkwardly, cumbersomely, cumbrously, inconveniently, ponderously, unhandily, unwieldily
con effortlessly, evenly, handily, readily, smoothly
ant easily, easy
9 to the point of hardness <the pond is frozen *hard*>
syn firmly, hardly, solid, solidly
10 ***syn*** CLOSE, at close hand, near, nearby, nigh

hard–boiled *adj* **1** ***syn*** UNFEELING 2, callous, coldhearted, hardhearted, heartless, obdurate, stonyhearted, uncompassionate, unemotional, unsympathetic
rel coarse, crude, rough; seasoned, sophisticated, worldly-wise
idiom not born yesterday
con artless, guileless, naive, simple-hearted, unsophisticated; kindly, mild, soft
2 ***syn*** REALISTIC, down-to-earth, hard, hardheaded, matter-of-fact, practical, pragmatic, sober, unfantastic, unidealistic

harden *vb* **1** to make or become physically hard or solid <this substance *hardens* immediately on exposure to air>
syn cake, concrete, congeal, dry, indurate, set, solidify
rel compact, consolidate, densify, firm, stiffen; anneal, caseharden, temper; calcify, fossilize, lithify, ossify, petrify
con deliquesce, dissolve, fuse, liquefy, melt
ant soften
2 to make proof against hardship, strain, or exposure <frontier life *hardened* most men quickly to rough conditions>
syn acclimate, acclimatize, climatize, season, toughen
rel accustom, habituate, indurate, inure; accommodate, adapt, adjust, conform
con emasculate, enervate; debilitate, devitalize, enfeeble, sap, undermine, weaken
ant soften

hardened *adj* ***syn*** UNFEELING 2, callous, coldhearted, hard-boiled, hardhearted, heartless, obdurate, stonyhearted, uncompassionate, unemotional

hardfisted *adj* ***syn*** STINGY, close, closefisted, hardhanded, narrow-fisted, narrowhearted, niggardly, penny-pinching, tight, tightfisted
ant openhanded

---

hardhanded *adj* ***syn*** STINGY, closefisted, hardfisted, narrow-fisted, niggardly, penny-pinching, save-all, scrimy, tight, tightfisted
ant openhanded

hardheaded *adj* **1** ***syn*** OBSTINATE, bullheaded, headstrong, intractable, mulish, pertinacious, perverse, pigheaded, self-willed, stubborn
2 ***syn*** REALISTIC, down-to-earth, hard, hard-boiled, matter-of-fact, practical, pragmatic, sober, unfantastic, unidealistic

hardhearted *adj* ***syn*** UNFEELING 2, callous, coldhearted, hard-boiled, heartless, obdurate, stonyhearted, uncompassionate, unemotional, unsympathetic

hardihood *n* **1** ***syn*** TEMERITY, assurance, audacity, brashness, hardiness, nerve
rel boldness, intrepidity; brazenness, cockiness; fortitude, grit, guts, pluck, sand
ant cowardice; timidity
2 ***syn*** INSOLENCE, boldness, disrespect, impertinence, impudence, insolency, insolentness
3 ***syn*** ENERGY 2, birr, go, ||moxie, pep, potency, tuck, vigor

hardiness *n* ***syn*** TEMERITY, assurance, audacity, brashness, hardihood, nerve
ant cowardice; timidity

hard–line *adj* ***syn*** TOUGH 3, inflexible, uncompromising, unyielding

hardly *adv* **1** ***syn*** HARD 1, energetically, forcefully, forcibly, might and main, mightily, powerfully, strongly, vigorously
2 ***syn*** HARD 2, fiercely, frenziedly, furiously, madly, stormily, tumultuously, turbulently, violently, wildly
3 ***syn*** HARD 5, badly, harshly, painfully, rigorously, roughly, severely
4 ***syn*** HARD 6, bitterly, keenly, rancorously, resentfully, sorely
5 ***syn*** HARD 8, arduously, burdensomely, difficultly, laboriously, onerously, toilsomely
6 ***syn*** JUST 2, barely, scarce, scarcely
7 ***syn*** HARD 9, firmly, solid, solidly

hardly ever *adv* ***syn*** SELDOM, infrequently, little, rarely, unfrequently, unoften

hardness *n* ***syn*** DIFFICULTY 1, asperity, hardship, rigor, vicissitude
ant easiness

hardpan *n* ***syn*** BASE 1, basis, bed, bedrock, bottom, foundation, groundwork, infrastructure, seat, understructure

hardscrabble *adj* ***syn*** BARREN 2, infertile, unbearing, unfertile, unproductive

hard–shell *adj* ***syn*** INVETERATE 1, bred-in-the-bone, confirmed, deep-dyed, deep-rooted, deep-seated, dyed-in-the-wool, entrenched, settled, sworn

hardship *n* ***syn*** DIFFICULTY 1, asperity, hardness, rigor, vicissitude
rel adversity, mischance, misfortune; danger, hazard, peril; affliction, trial, tribulation; drudgery, toil, travail; discomfort, distress
con comfort, ease

hardy *adj* ***syn*** TOUGH 4, rugged
ant tender

harebrain *n* **1** ***syn*** SCATTERBRAIN, birdbrain, featherbrain, featherhead, flibbertigibbet, rattlebrain, rattlehead, shatterbrain
2 ***syn*** CRACKPOT, crackbrain, crank, cuckoo, ding-a-ling, kook, lunatic, nut, screwball

harebrained *adj* **1** ***syn*** GIDDY 1, dizzy, empty-headed, featherbrained, flighty, frivolous, rattlebrained, scatterbrained, silly, skittish
2 ***syn*** FOOLISH 2, absurd, ||balmy, crazy, insane, loony, ||potty, preposterous, silly, wacky

harefooted *adj* ***syn*** FAST 3, breakneck, expeditious, expeditive, fleet, hasty, quick, rapid, speedy, swift

hark *vb* ***syn*** LISTEN, attend, hear, hearken, heed
rel mark, mind, note, notice, remark
idiom be all ears, not miss a trick

harlequin *n* ***syn*** CLOWN 3, buffoon, merry-andrew, zany

harlot *n* **1** a woman who engages in unlawful or socially unacceptable sexual intercourse often for material gain <ply the trade of a *harlot*>
syn blowen, courtesan, demimondaine, demimonde, demirep, fancy woman, hetaera, kept woman, paphian, whore; *compare* DOXY, MISTRESS, PROSTITUTE, WANTON
2 ***syn*** PROSTITUTE, bawd, call girl, drab, fille de joie, ||hooker, hustler, meretrix, streetwalker, whore

harlotry *n* ***syn*** PROSTITUTION, oldest profession, (the) social evil, streetwalking, whoredom

harm *n* ***syn*** INJURY 1, damage, hurt, mischief, outrage, ruin
rel deleteriousness; banefulness, noxiousness, perniciousness; mischance, misfortune, misuse; impairment, marring
con aid, help; accommodation, benefaction; charity, favor, service
ant benefit

harm *vb* ***syn*** INJURE 1, blemish, damage, hurt, impair, mar, prejudice, spoil, tarnish, vitiate
rel abuse, ill-use, maltreat, mistreat, misuse, molest; dilapidate, ruin; discommode, incommode, inconvenience; sabotage, sap, undermine
idiom do violence to
con ameliorate, better, improve; avail, profit
ant benefit

harmful *adj* inflicting or capable of inflicting injury <a *harmful* drug>
syn bad, damaging, deleterious, detrimental, evil, hurtful, ill, injurious, mischievous, nocent, nocuous, prejudicial, prejudicious
rel baleful, baneful, malefic, malign, malignant, noisome, noxious, pernicious, toxic; insalubrious, unhealthful, unhealthy, unwholesome; dangerous, hazardous, risky, unsafe
con innocuous, inoffensive, nontoxic; beneficent, beneficial, benign, benignant, favorable, helpful, salutary, useful; safe, unhazardous

---

syn synonym(s) ***rel*** related word(s)
idiom idiomatic equivalent(s) ***con*** contrasted word(s)
ant antonym(s) * vulgar
|| use limited; if in doubt, see a dictionary
The first word in a synonym list when printed in SMALL CAPITALS shows where there is more information about the group. For a more efficient use of this book see Explanatory Notes.

ant harmless

harmless *adj* not having hurtful or injurious qualities < *harmless* pastimes >
syn innocent, innocuous, innoxious, inobnoxious, inoffensive, unoffending, unoffensive; *compare* SAFE 3
rel guiltless; nontoxic, painless, safe
con baneful, dangerous, malignant, noxious, pernicious, toxic, virulent; damaging, detrimental, destructive, hurtful, injurious; deadly, fell, ruinous; improper, unsuitable, wrong
ant harmful

harmonic *adj* ***syn*** HARMONIOUS 1, blending, chiming, consonant, musical, symphonic, symphonious

harmonious *adj* **1** musically concordant <a *harmonious* morning chorus of birds>
syn blending, chiming, consonant, harmonic, musical, symphonic, symphonious
rel canorous, dulcet, euphonious, melodious, mellifluous, mellisonant, musical, silvery, sonorous, sweet, tuneful; chordal, contrapuntal, counterpointed, polyphonic
idiom in concert, in tune
con clashing, discordant, dissonant, grating, harsh, jangling, jarring, raucous, shrill, strident, tuneless, unmusical, untuneful; atonal
ant disharmonious, inharmonious, unharmonious
2 having the parts agreeably related <a building with *harmonious* proportions>
syn accordant, concordant, congruous; *compare* CONSONANT 1
rel agreeable, pleasing, satisfying; concinnate, symmetrical
con clashing, incongruous, unsymmetrical; askew, distorted, skewed
ant inharmonious, unharmonious
3 marked by accord in sentiment or action <a *harmonious* effort to reach a practicable agreement>
syn amicable, amical, congenial, friendly
rel coactive, collaborative, cooperative; empathetic, empathic, simpatico, sympathetic; calm, irenic, pacific, peaceful
idiom of one accord
con incompatible, uncongenial, uncooperative, unfriendly, unsympathetic; belligerent, contentious, pugnacious
ant inharmonious, unharmonious

harmonize *vb* **1** ***syn*** AGREE 3, coincide, concert, concord, concur
rel cooperate, match, unite
con differ, disagree
ant clash; conflict
2 ***syn*** AGREE 4, accord, conform, correspond, dovetail, fit (in), go, jibe, square, tally
ant differ (from)
3 to bring into consonance or accord < *harmonize* the factions of a political party>
syn accommodate, attune, conform, coordinate, integrate, proportion, reconcile, reconciliate, tune
rel adapt, adjust, correlate; coapt, relate
con alienate, disrupt, estrange
ant disharmonize
4 to combine or adapt so as to achieve a desired effect < *harmonize* the elements of a story>
syn arrange, blend, integrate, orchestrate, symphonize, synthesize, unify
rel coordinate, correlate

harmonizing *n* ***syn*** RECONCILIATION, rapprochement, reconcilement

harmony *n* **1** musical agreement of sounds <singing in *harmony*>
syn accord, chorus, concert, concord, consonance, tune
rel mellifluousness, melodiousness, melody, musicality, sonority, tunefulness; diapason, polyphony
con cacophony, discord, discordance, discordancy, dissonance, harshness, inharmoniousness, jangle, stridency, tunelessness, unharmoniousness, unmusicalness, untunefulness; atonality
ant disharmony, inharmony
2 the effect produced when different things come together without clashing or disagreement <goals that are in *harmony* with our capabilities>
syn accord, agreement, chime, concord, concordance, consonance, tune; *compare* CONSISTENCY
rel conformance, conformity, correspondence; articulation, coaptation, compatibility, congruity; concatenation, concurrence, integration, oneness, togetherness, unity
con disagreement, discord, disparity, dissidence, disunity, variance
ant conflict
3 the state of persons who are in full and perfect agreement <friends who live in *harmony*>
syn concord, rapport, unity
rel affinity, empathy, fellow-feeling, kinship; peace, tranquillity
idiom meeting of minds
con contention, dissension, strife
ant discord
4 ***syn*** SYMMETRY, balance, proportion
rel concinnity, consonance; dignity, elegance, grace; integrity, unity
con asymmetry, discordance, discordancy, imbalance
ant inharmony

harness *vb* ***syn*** HITCH 2, couple, yoke

‖**harness bull** (*or* **cop**) *n* ***syn*** POLICEMAN, ‖bobby, ‖bull, ‖copper, ‖flatfoot, ‖fuzz, gumshoe, ‖heat, John Law, ‖pig

harpy *n* ***syn*** VIRAGO, amazon, fishwife, ogress, scold, shrew, termagant, vixen, Xanthippe

harrier *n* ***syn*** BULLY 1, browbeater, bulldozer, harasser, hector, intimidator

harrow *vb* ***syn*** AFFLICT, agonize, crucify, excruciate, martyr, rack, torment, torture, try, wring
rel fret, irritate, pester; badger, bait, bedevil, devil, heckle, hector, needle, tantalize, tease

harrowing *adj* ***syn*** EXCRUCIATING, agonizing, racking, tearing, tormenting, torturing, torturous

---

syn synonym(s) | *rel* related word(s)
idiom idiomatic equivalent(s) | *con* contrasted word(s)
ant antonym(s) | * vulgar
‖ use limited; if in doubt, see a dictionary
The first word in a synonym list when printed in SMALL CAPITALS shows where there is more information about the group. For a more efficient use of this book see Explanatory Notes.

harry *vb* **1** ***syn*** RAVAGE, depredate, desecrate, desolate, despoil, devastate, havoc, pillage, sack, spoliate
2 ***syn*** RAID 1, foray, harass, maraud
3 ***syn*** WORRY 1, annoy, bedevil, beleaguer, gnaw, hagride, harass, pester, plague, tease
rel disturb, irk, perturb, upset; badger, irritate

harsh *adj* **1** ***syn*** ROUGH 1, asperous, craggy, jagged, rugged, scabrous, scraggy, uneven, unlevel, unsmooth
rel coarse, granular, loose; bristly, scraggly, scratchy, shaggy, stubbly
con glossy, satiny, silken, silky, sleek, slick, velvety
2 ***syn*** ACRID, amaroidal, astringent, austere, bitter, sharp
rel acerb, acerbic, biting, burning, mordant; pungent, tangy; dry, sour, tart
con mild, smooth, sweet, velvety
3 disagreeable to the ear <many birds have *harsh* cries>
syn dry, grating, hoarse, jarring, rasping, raucous, rough, rugged, rusty, squawky, strident, stridulent, stridulous
rel discordant, dissonant, immelodious, ineuphonious, inharmonious, unmelodious, unmusical; grinding, jangling, scraping; blaring, brassy; ear-piercing, piercing, shrill, squeaky
con euphonious, harmonious, mellow, melodic, melodious, musical, sonorous, sweet; low, soft; agreeable, pleasing
4 ***syn*** UNCOMFORTABLE, comfortless, discomforting, uncomforting, uncomfy
5 ***syn*** GRIM 2, austere, bleak, dour, hard, severe, stringent
6 ***syn*** SEVERE 3, bitter, brutal, hard, inclement, intemperate, rigorous, rugged
ant mild

harshly *adv* ***syn*** HARD 5, badly, hardly, painfully, rigorously, roughly, severely
con considerately; gently, lightly, well; famously
ant smoothly

haruspex *n* ***syn*** PROPHET, augur, auspex, forecaster, foreseer, foreteller, Nostradamus, predictor, prognosticator, prophesier

harvest *n* **1** the act, process, or occasion of gathering a crop <the time of *harvest*>
syn cropping, gathering, harvesting, ingathering, reaping
rel garnering, storing
con planting, seedtime, sowing
2 the gathered produce of land <a bountiful *harvest* saved the settlers>
syn crop, fruitage
rel yield; bearing, vintage

harvest *vb* ***syn*** REAP, garner, gather, ingather
rel assemble, collect; accumulate, amass, bin, store (up), stow (away); cache, hide, hoard, squirrel, stash

harvesting *n* ***syn*** HARVEST 1, cropping, gathering, ingathering, reaping

hash *vb* ***syn*** CHOP 2, mince

hash *n* **1** ***syn*** MISCELLANY 1, assortment, gallimaufry, hodgepodge, jumble, medley, mélange, mishmash, patchwork, stew
2 ***syn*** CLUTTER 2, hugger-mugger, jumble, jungle, litter, mishmash, muddle, rummage, scramble, tumble
3 ***syn*** MESS 3, botch, botchery, mess-up, mix-up, muddle, mull, muss, shambles

‖**hashery** *n* ***syn*** EATING HOUSE, beanery, café, coffee shop, diner, ‖greasy spoon, ‖hash house, luncheonette, lunchroom, sandwich shop

‖**hash house** *n* ***syn*** EATING HOUSE, beanery, café, coffee shop, diner, ‖greasy spoon, ‖hashery, luncheonette, lunchroom, sandwich shop

hassle *n* **1** ***syn*** QUARREL, altercation, beef, bickering, dispute, miff, rhubarb, row, run-in, squabble
2 ***syn*** COMMOTION 4, clamor, hubbub, hurly-burly, pother, to-do, tumult, turmoil, uproar, whirl
3 ***syn*** ATTEMPT, endeavor, essay, striving, struggle, trial, try, undertaking

hassle *vb* ***syn*** ARGUE 2, argufy, bicker, dispute, quibble, squabble, wrangle
rel cavil; brawl, fight, spar, struggle

haste *n* **1** rapidity of motion or action <we finished our job with great *haste*>
syn celerity, dispatch, expedition, expeditiousness, hurry, hustle, rustle, speed, speediness, swiftness
rel fastness, fleetness, quickness, rapidity; pace, velocity; dash, drive
con languidness, languor, leisureliness, reluctance, slowness; lethargy, sluggishness, torpor
ant deliberateness, deliberation
2 rash or headlong action <oversights due to *haste*>
syn hastiness, hurriedness, precipitance, precipitancy, precipitateness, precipitation, rush
rel impetuosity, impetuousness, impulsiveness
con care, carefulness, circumspection, hastelessness, unhurriedness
ant deliberateness, deliberation

haste *vb* ***syn*** HURRY 2, barrel, beeline, bucket, hasten, highball, hotfoot, hustle, rocket, run

hasten *vb* ***syn*** SPEED 3, accelerate, hurry, quicken, shake up, step up, swiften
2 ***syn*** HURRY 2, barrel, fleet, flit, fly, haste, hotfoot, hustle, run, rush

hastily *adv* ***syn*** FAST 2, apace, expeditiously, flat-out, lickety-split, posthaste, quickly, rapidly, speedily, swiftly
rel agilely, nimbly; impetuously, impulsively, unpremeditatedly; carelessly, recklessly, thoughtlessly; precipitately, prematurely, suddenly
con carefully, designedly, studiedly, thoughtfully; gradually, leisurely, slowly, sluggishly
ant deliberately

hastiness *n* ***syn*** WASTE 2, hurriedness, precipitance, precipitancy, precipitateness, precipitation, rush

hasty *adj* **1** ***syn*** FAST 3, breakneck, expeditious, expeditive, fleet, harefooted, quick, rapid, speedy, swift
rel agile, brisk, nimble; hurried, quickened

---

syn synonym(s) ***rel*** related word(s)
idiom idiomatic equivalent(s) ***con*** contrasted word(s)
ant antonym(s) * vulgar
‖ use limited; if in doubt, see a dictionary
The first word in a synonym list when printed in SMALL CAPITALS shows where there is more information about the group. For a more efficient use of this book see Explanatory Notes.

con dilatory, laggard, leisured, leisurely

2 *syn* PRECIPITATE 1, abrupt, headlong, hurried, impetuous, precipitant, precipitous, rushing, subitaneous, sudden

ant deliberate

3 *syn* RASH 1, brash, hotheaded, ill-advised, incautious, inconsiderate, mad-brained, madcap, reckless, thoughtless

rel devil-may-care, slambang, slapdash

hatch *vb* **1** *syn* GENERATE 3, breed, cause, engender, get up, induce, occasion, produce, provoke, work up

2 *syn* GENERATE 1, create, father, make, originate, parent, procreate, produce, sire, spawn

hatch (up) *vb syn* CONTRIVE 2, concoct, cook (up), devise, dream up, formulate, frame, invent, make up, vamp (up)

hatchet man *n syn* ASSASSIN, bravo, cutthroat, gun, gunman, ‖gunsel, gunslinger, hit man, torpedo, triggerman

hate *n* **1** *syn* ABOMINATION 2, abhorrence, aversion, detestation, hatred, horror, loathing, repugnance, repulsion, revulsion

rel animosity, animus, antipathy, hostility, ill will, rancor; disgust, scorn, spite

con affection; toleration; adoration, veneration

ant love

2 *syn* ABOMINATION 1, anathema, bête noire, black beast, bugbear, detestation

rel bother, grievance, gripe, irritant, nuisance, ‖pain, trouble

ant delight

hate *vb* to feel extreme enmity or dislike <Cain *hated* his brother> <*hate* to meet strangers>

syn abhor, abominate, detest, execrate, loathe

rel contemn, despise, disdain, dislike, scorn; deprecate, disapprove; resent

con cherish, enjoy, fancy, like, relish; favor, prefer, prize; esteem, respect, revere; dote; idolize, worship

ant love

hateable *adj syn* HATEFUL 2, abhorrent, abominable, detestable, horrid, odious

ant lovable

hateful *adj* **1** *syn* MALICIOUS, bitchy, catty, despiteful, evil, malevolent, malign, nasty, spiteful, vicious

rel acrimonious, ill-natured; bitter, resentful; mean

con benevolent, charitable, cordial, genial, good-humored, good-natured, kind, kindly, pleasant

2 deserving of or arousing hate <found himself in a *hateful* situation>

syn abhorrent, abominable, detestable, hateable, horrid, odious

rel distasteful, distressing, obnoxious, repellent, repulsive; contemptible, despicable, execrable, opprobrious, reprehensible, scurvy; foul, infamous, vile; accursed, blasphemous, damnable, unspeakable

con compatible, congenial, consonant; alluring, appealing, attractive, charming, enchanting; agreeable, delectable, delightful, likable, pleasant, pleasing

ant lovable; sympathetic

hatred *n syn* ABOMINATION 2, abhorrence, aversion, detestation, hate, horror, loathing, repugnance, repulsion, revulsion

rel antipathy, dislike; animosity, enmity, hostility, rancor

con affability, benevolence, benignity, charitableness, cordiality

ant love; admiration

haughtiness *n syn* PRIDE 3, arrogance, disdain, disdainfulness, hauteur, loftiness, morgue, superbity, superciliousness

ant lowliness

haughty *adj syn* PROUD 1, arrogant, cavalier, disdainful, high-and-mighty, insolent, lordly, overbearing, supercilious, superior

rel aloof, detached, distant, indifferent, reserved; egotistic; contemptuous, scornful

con humble; obsequious, servile, subservient

ant lowly

haul *vb syn* PULL 2, drag, draw, lug, tow, tug

rel move, remove, shift; boost, elevate, hoist, lift, raise

haul *n syn* LOAD 1, burden, cargo, freight, lading, payload

haul up *vb syn* STOP 4, bring up, draw up, fetch up, halt, pull up

haunches *n pl syn* BUTTOCKS, backside, beam, fundament, hind end, hunkers, posterior, rear end, rump, tail

haunt *vb syn* FREQUENT, affect, hang around, hang out, resort

haunt *n* **1** *syn* RESORT 2, hangout, purlieu, rendezvous, stamping ground, watering hole

2 *syn* HABITAT, home, locality, range, site, stamping ground

3 *syn* APPARITION, ghost, phantasm, phantom, shade, shadow, specter, spirit, ‖spook, wraith

haunter *n syn* HABITUÉ 1, denizen, frequenter

hauteur *n syn* PRIDE 3, arrogance, disdain, disdainfulness, haughtiness, loftiness, morgue, superbity, superciliousness

ant lowliness

haut monde *n syn* ARISTOCRACY, blue blood, carriage trade, elite, gentry, optimacy, patriciate, quality, society, who's who

have *vb* **1** to keep, control, or experience as one's own <can't *have* your cake and eat it too>

syn enjoy, hold, own, possess, retain

idiom to be possessed of, have in hand

con lack, need, want

2 *syn* INCLUDE, comprehend, contain, embody, embrace, encompass, involve, subsume, take in

rel admit, compose, comprise

3 *syn* BEAR 3, carry, possess

4 *syn* GET 1, acquire, annex, chalk up, compass, gain, land, obtain, pick up, procure

5 *syn* EXPERIENCE 1, know, see, suffer, sustain, undergo

6 *syn* LET 2, allow, leave, permit, suffer

7 *syn* KNOW 1, appreciate, apprehend, cognize, comprehend, fathom, grasp, understand

---

8 ***syn*** OUTWIT, outfox, outgeneral, outjockey, outmaneuver, outreach, outslick, outsmart, overreach, undo
9 ***syn*** BRIBE, buy, buy off, fix, ‖lubricate, sop, square, tamper (with)
10 ***syn*** MUST 2, ‖mun, need

haven *n* **1** ***syn*** HARBOR 3, anchorage, ‖chuck, harborage, port, riding, road(s), roadstead
2 ***syn*** SHELTER 1, asylum, cover, covert, harbor, harborage, port, refuge, retreat, sanctuary

haven *vb* ***syn*** HARBOR 1, chamber, house, roof, shelter, shield

haversack *n* ***syn*** BACKPACK, knapsack, pack, packsack, rucksack

havoc *n* ***syn*** RUIN 3, confusion, destruction, devastation, loss, ruination
rel calamity, cataclysm, catastrophe; despoiling, pillaging, ravaging; vandalism

havoc *vb* ***syn*** RAVAGE, depredate, desecrate, desolate, despoil, devastate, harry, pillage, sack, spoliate

hawk *vb* ***syn*** PEDDLE 2, huckster, monger, vend

hawker *n* ***syn*** PEDDLER, ‖arab, cheap-jack (*or* cheap-john), ‖duffer, higgler, huckster, monger, outcrier, packman, vendor

hawk–eyed *adj* ***syn*** SHARP-EYED, eagle-eyed, lyncean, lynx-eyed, sharp-sighted

hawkshaw *n* ***syn*** DETECTIVE, dick, ‖eye, gumshoe, investigator, plainclothesman, Sherlock, Sherlock Holmes, sleuth, ‖tec

haymaker *n* ***syn*** CUFF, box, buffet, chop, clout, ‖paste, poke, punch, smack, sock

hayseed *n* ***syn*** RUSTIC, bucolic, bumpkin, clodhopper, hick, hillbilly, jake, provincial, rube, yokel
ant city slicker, slicker

hazard *n* **1** ***syn*** CHANCE 2, fortune, luck
2 ***syn*** DANGER, jeopardy, peril, risk

hazard *vb* **1** ***syn*** VENTURE 1, adventure, chance, risk, wager
2 ***syn*** GAMBLE 2, chance, risk, venture
3 ***syn*** ENDANGER, compromise, imperil, jeopard, jeopardize, jeopardy, menace, peril, risk

hazardous *adj* ***syn*** DANGEROUS 1, chancy, hairy, jeopardous, parlous, perilous, risky, unhealthy, unsound, wicked
ant safe; unhazardous

haze *vb* ***syn*** OBSCURE, becloud, befog, cloud, dim, fog, mist, murk, overcast, overcloud

haze *n* **1** an atmospheric condition that is characterized by the presence of fine particulate material in the air and that deprives the air of its transparency <*haze* obscured the distant hills>
syn brume, film, mist, smaze
rel cloud, ‖drisk, fog, murk, ‖smeech, smog, smoke, vapor; cloudiness, mistiness, murkiness, smokiness
2 a state of mental vagueness or obtuseness <lived in a *haze* of pleasant memories>
syn befuddlement, daze, fog, ‖maze, muddledness, muddleheadedness, muddlement
rel dream, reverie, stupor, trance; absentmindedness, abstraction, bemusement, preoccupation, woolgathering
con alertness, attentiveness, awareness

hazy *adj* obscured or made dim by or as if by haze <had only a *hazy* idea of where they were>
syn cloudy, foggy, misty, mushy, vague, vaporous, vapory
rel blurred, clouded, dim, indefinite, indistinct, murky, nebulous, obscure; bemused, dreamy, tranced, stuporous; dazed, ‖mazed, muzzy

he *n* ***syn*** MAN 3, ‖bloke, boy, buck, chap, fellow, ‖gee, gent, gentleman, guy

head *n* **1** the upper division of the body that contains the brain, the chief sense organs, and the mouth <put your hat on your *head*>
syn ‖bean, ‖belfry, ‖chump, ‖coco, ‖coconut, ‖conk, ‖dome, headpiece, noddle, noggin, noodle, ‖nut, ‖pallet, pate, poll, sconce
rel brainpan, cranium, crown, scalp
2 ***syn*** MIND 1, brain, gray matter, ‖upper story, ‖upperworks, wit
3 ***syn*** GIFT 2, aptness, bent, bump, faculty, flair, genius, knack, talent, turn
4 ***syn*** LEADER 2, boss, chief, chieftain, cock, dominator, headman, hierarch, honcho, master
con subordinate; aide, assistant, helper
5 ***syn*** PROMONTORY, beak, bill, cape, foreland, headland, naze, point
6 ***syn*** TOILET, ‖can, convenience, john, johnny, latrine, lavatory, ‖loo, privy, water closet
7 ***syn*** HEADLINE, heading
8 ***syn*** SUBJECT 2, argument, matter, motif, motive, point, subject matter, text, theme, topic

head *adj* ***syn*** FIRST 3, arch, champion, chief, foremost, leading, premier, principal

head *vb* **1** ***syn*** BEHEAD, decapitate, decollate, guillotine, neck
2 ***syn*** DIRECT 2, address, aim, cast, incline, level, point, train, turn, zero (in)
3 to commence to go in an indicated direction <the cowboys *headed* for town>
syn bear, light out, make, set out, strike out, take off
rel go, proceed, start
idiom make a beeline for
4 ***syn*** SPRING 1, arise, derive (from), emanate, flow, issue, originate, proceed, rise, stem

heading *n* ***syn*** HEADLINE, head

headland *n* ***syn*** PROMONTORY, beak, bill, cape, foreland, head, naze, point

headline *n* a word or group of words usually in large type introducing and summarizing a newspaper story <*headlines* that screamed the news of the president's death>
syn head, heading
rel banner, banner head, bannerline, scarehead, screamer, spreadhead

headlong *adj* ***syn*** PRECIPITATE 1, abrupt, hasty, hurried, impetuous, precipitant, precipitous, rushing, subitaneous, sudden

---

syn synonym(s) | *rel* related word(s)
idiom idiomatic equivalent(s) | *con* contrasted word(s)
ant antonym(s) | * vulgar
‖ use limited; if in doubt, see a dictionary
The first word in a synonym list when printed in SMALL CAPITALS shows where there is more information about the group. For a more efficient use of this book see Explanatory Notes.

rel daredevil, daring, foolhardy, rash, reckless

headman *n* ***syn*** LEADER 2, boss, chief, chieftain, cock, dominator, head, hierarch, honcho, master

headmost *adj* ***syn*** FIRST 1, foremost, inaugural, initial, leading

headpiece *n* ***syn*** HEAD 1, ‖bean, ‖belfry, ‖coco, ‖conk, ‖dome, noddle, noggin, noodle, poll

headshaker *n* ***syn*** SKEPTIC, doubter, doubting Thomas, Pyrrhonian, Pyrrhonist, unbeliever, zetetic

head start *n* ***syn*** ADVANTAGE 3, allowance, bulge, ‖deadwood, draw, edge, handicap, odds, start, vantage

headstone *n* ***syn*** TOMBSTONE, footstone, grave marker, gravestone, ledger, monument

headstrong *adj* ***syn*** OBSTINATE, bullheaded, mulish, pigheaded, refractory, self-willed, stiff-necked, stubborn, willful, wrongheaded
con subdued, tame; amenable, biddable, docile, meek, obedient, tractable

headway *n* **1** ***syn*** ADVANCE 2, advancement, anabasis, march, ongoing, proficiency, progress

heady *adj* ***syn*** SHREWD, argute, astucious, astute, cagey, perspicacious, sagacious, ‖savvy

heal *vb* ***syn*** CURE, remedy

healing *adj* ***syn*** CURATIVE, curing, remedial, remedying, restorative, sanative, sanatory, vulnerary, wholesome

health *n* the state of being sound in body or mind <the patient was nursed back to *health*>
syn haleness, healthiness, soundness, wholeness
rel stamina, vitality, well-being; euphoria
con debility, decrepitude, feebleness; ill health, illness, sickliness
ant disease, infirmity

healthful *adj* conducive or beneficial to the health or soundness of body or mind <regular exercise is a *healthful* practice>
syn good, healthy, hygienic, salubrious, salutary, salutiferous, wholesome
rel advantageous, beneficial, profitable, useful; corrective, curative, remedial; aiding, alleviative, helpful, mitigative, restorative, sanative
con insalubrious, unhealthy, unhygienic, unwholesome; damaging, deleterious, detrimental, harmful, injurious, mischievous, pernicious
ant unhealthful

healthiness *n* ***syn*** HEALTH, haleness, soundness, wholeness
ant unhealthiness

healthy *adj* **1** enjoying or manifesting health <a *healthy* baby>
syn ‖bunkum, fit, hale, right, sane, sound, well, well-conditioned, well-liking, whole, wholesome
rel hearty, iron, lusty, robust, thriving, vigorous; rugged, stalwart, strong, sturdy, tough; agile, chipper, spry; blooming, rosy, thriving
idiom fit as a fiddle, in (top) condition, in fine fettle, in shape, in trim, sound as a dollar, up to snuff
con decrepit, delicate, feeble, fragile, frail, weak; infirm, ‖poorly, sickly
ant unhealthy
2 ***syn*** HEALTHFUL, good, hygienic, salubrious, salutary, salutiferous, wholesome
ant unhealthful
3 ***syn*** SAFE 3, uninjurious, wholesome

heap *n* **1** ***syn*** PILE 1, bank, cock, drift, hill, mass, mound, mountain, stack, stockpile
rel congeries, gathering
2 ***syn*** MUCH, barrel, great deal, lot, mass, mountain, peck, pile, ‖power, ‖sight
3 ***syn*** SCAD, gob(s), jillion, load(s), million, oodles, quantities, slather(s), thousand, trillion
4 ***syn*** JALOPY, clunker, crate, dog, junker, wreck

heap *vb* **1** to throw or collect in a pile < *heap* up leaves for a bonfire>
syn bank, cock, drift, hill, mound, pile, stack
rel cord, ‖dess, rick, shock; bunch, clump, lumber, lump, mass; deposit, dump; accumulate, amass, assemble, collect, gather, group
con broadcast, disperse, distribute, scatter, separate, spread, strew
2 ***syn*** LOAD 3, charge, choke, fill, pack, pile

hear *vb* **1** ***syn*** LISTEN, attend, hark, hearken, heed
idiom get wind of
2 ***syn*** DISCOVER 3, ascertain, catch on, determine, find out, learn, see, tumble, unearth

hearing *n* **1** ***syn*** EARSHOT, sound
2 an opportunity to be heard <they finally obtained a *hearing* on their complaints>
syn audience, audition
rel conference, interview, meeting, parley; test, tryout; discussion, negotiation

hearken *vb* ***syn*** LISTEN, attend, hark, hear, heed

hearsay *n* ***syn*** REPORT 1, buzz, cry, gossip, grapevine, on-dit, rumble, rumor, scuttlebutt, talk

heart *n* **1** the seat or center of secret thoughts and emotions <in his *heart* he knew he was seriously in the wrong>
syn bosom, breast, soul
idiom bottom of the heart, cockles of the heart
2 ***syn*** COURAGE, cojones, dauntlessness, guts, mettle, ‖moxie, pluck, resolution, spirit, spunk
3 ***syn*** TASTE 4, gusto, palate, relish, zest
4 ***syn*** CENTER 2, focal point, focus, hub, nerve center, polestar, seat
5 ***syn*** CENTER 3, core, pith, quick, root

heartache *n* ***syn*** SORROW, affliction, anguish, care, ‖dole, grief, heartbreak, regret, rue, woe
idiom aching heart, heavy heart

heartbreak *n* **1** ***syn*** SORROW, affliction, anguish, care, ‖dole, grief, heartache, regret, rue, woe
rel agony, bale, torment
idiom bleeding heart

heartbreaking *adj* ***syn*** DEPLORABLE, afflictive, calamitous, dire, distressing, grievous, heartrending, lamentable, regrettable, unfortunate

hearten *vb* ***syn*** ENCOURAGE 1, animate, cheer, chirk (up), embolden, enhearten, inspirit, nerve, steel, strengthen

---

syn synonym(s) ***rel*** related word(s)
idiom idiomatic equivalent(s) ***con*** contrasted word(s)
ant antonym(s) * vulgar
‖ use limited; if in doubt, see a dictionary
The first word in a synonym list when printed in SMALL CAPITALS shows where there is more information about the group. For a more efficient use of this book see Explanatory Notes.

rel energize, enliven; arouse, rally, rouse, stir
con damp, dampen; weigh
ant dishearten

heartfelt *adj* ***syn*** SINCERE 1, hearty, unfeigned, wholehearted, whole-souled
rel bona fide, genuine, honest, true, unfeigned; deep, profound
con hypocritical, insincere; false, pretended

heartless *adj* ***syn*** UNFEELING 2, callous, coldhearted, hard-boiled, hardhearted, obdurate, stonyhearted, uncompassionate, unemotional, unsympathetic

heartrending *adj* ***syn*** DEPLORABLE, afflictive, calamitous, dire, distressing, grievous, heartbreaking, lamentable, regrettable, unfortunate

heart–searching *n* ***syn*** INTROSPECTION, self-contemplation, self-examination, self-observation, self-questioning, self-reflection, self-scrutiny, self-searching, soul-searching

heartsick *adj* ***syn*** DOWNCAST, blue, cast down, dejected, depressed, disconsolate, dispirited, down, downhearted, heartsore

heartsore *adj* ***syn*** DOWNCAST, blue, cast down, dejected, depressed, disconsolate, dispirited, down, downhearted, heartsick

heartthrob *n* ***syn*** SWEETHEART 1, beloved, darling, flame, honey, honeybunch, love, sweet, sweetling, turtledove

heart–whole *adj* **1** ***syn*** FREE 6, fancy-free
2 ***syn*** GENUINE 3, honest, real, sincere, true, undesigning, undissembled, unfeigned

hearty *adj* ***syn*** SINCERE 1, heartfelt, unfeigned, wholehearted, whole-souled
rel responsive, warm, warmhearted; deep, profound; exuberant, profuse
con cold, dispassionate, emotionless
ant hollow

‖**heat** *n* ***syn*** POLICEMAN, cop, ‖copper, ‖flatfoot, ‖fuzz, John Law, man, ‖paddy, peace officer, police

heated *adj* **1** ***syn*** HOT 1, ardent, baking, boiling, broiling, burning, fiery, scalding, scorching, sizzling
ant chilled
2 ***syn*** FEVERISH 2, burning, fervid, fevered, hectic
3 ***syn*** ANGRY, acrimonious, indignant, irate, ireful, mad, waxy, wrathful, wrathy, wroth

heathen *adj* of or relating to people who do not acknowledge the God of the Bible <ancient *heathen* sacrificial rites>
syn ethnic, gentile, infidel, infidelic, pagan, profane
rel heathenish, paganish

heave *vb* **1** ***syn*** THROW 1, ‖bung, cast, fire, fling, hurl, launch, pitch, sling, toss
2 ***syn*** TOSS 2, pitch, rock, roll
3 ***syn*** PANT 1, blow, gasp, huff, ‖pank, ‖pegh, puff
4 ***syn*** RETCH, gag, keck
‖**5** ***syn*** VOMIT, barf, ‖cascade, ‖cast, disgorge, *puke, spew, spit up, throw up, upchuck

heaven *n* **1** *usu* **heavens** *pl* ***syn*** SKY, empyrean, firmament, welkin
2 an abode of blissful spiritual life after death <the religious conceptions of *heaven* and hell>
syn Abraham's bosom, bliss, Canaan, Civitas Dei, elysium, empyrean, happy hunting ground, kingdom come, New Jerusalem, nirvana, paradise, Zion
rel afterworld, eternity, glory, hereafter, promised land; everlastingness, immortality
idiom Beulah Land (*or* Land of Beulah), City of God, Kingdom of God, Kingdom of Heaven
con earth, world; Gehenna, hades, inferno, netherworld, perdition, pit, Sheol, Tartarus, Tophet, underworld
ant hell
3 ***syn*** UTOPIA, arcadia, Cockaigne, fairyland, lubberland, paradise, promised land, Shangri-la, wonderland, Zion
4 ***syn*** ECSTASY, rapture, rhapsody, seventh heaven, transport

heavenly *adj* **1** ***syn*** CELESTIAL, empyreal, empyrean
con hadean, Tartarean
ant hellish
2 ***syn*** DELIGHTFUL, adorable, ambrosial, darling, delectable, delicious, luscious, lush, scrumptious, yummy

heavy *adj* **1** having great or relatively great weight <a *heavy* load>
syn hefty, massive, ponderous, weighty; *compare* UNWIELDY
rel awkward, bulky, clumsy, lumbering, lumbersome; unhandy, unmanageable, unwieldy; cumbersome, cumbrous
con airy, buoyant, weightless; handy, manageable, wieldy
ant light
2 ***syn*** FAT 2, corpulent, fleshy, gross, obese, overweight, porcine, portly, stout, weighty
3 ***syn*** SERIOUS 2, grave, severe, weighty
4 ***syn*** RECONDITE, abstruse, acroamatic, deep, esoteric, hermetic, occult, orphic, profound, secret
5 ***syn*** PREGNANT 1, big, childing, enceinte, expectant, expecting, gone, gravid, parous, parturient
6 ***syn*** LETHARGIC, comatose, dopey, hebetudinous, sluggish, slumberous, stupid, torpid
7 ***syn*** OVERCAST, cloudy, ‖dowly, dull, lowering (*or* louring), nubilous, overclouded
8 ***syn*** HARD 6, arduous, difficult, effortful, formidable, labored, laborious, strenuous, toilsome, tough
9 ***syn*** RICH 3

heavy–footed *adj* ***syn*** PONDEROUS 2, elephantine, heavy-handed, uninspired

heavy–handed *adj* **1** ***syn*** AWKWARD 2, bumbling, gauche, halting, ham-handed, inept, maladroit, unhandy, unhappy, wooden
2 ***syn*** PONDEROUS 2, elephantine, heavy-footed, uninspired

heavyhearted *adj* ***syn*** SAD 1, melancholy, mournful, saddened, sorry, unhappy
ant lighthearted

heavyheartedness *n* ***syn*** SADNESS, blues, dejection, depression, (the) dismals, dumps, gloom, melancholy, mournfulness, unhappiness

---

syn synonym(s) | *rel* related word(s)
idiom idiomatic equivalent(s) | *con* contrasted word(s)
ant antonym(s) | * vulgar
‖ use limited; if in doubt, see a dictionary
The first word in a synonym list when printed in SMALL CAPITALS shows where there is more information about the group. For a more efficient use of this book see Explanatory Notes.

ant lightheartedness
heavyset *adj* ***syn*** STOCKY, ‖chumpy, chunky, dumpy, squdgy, stubby, stumpy, thick, thick-bodied, thickset
heavyweight *n* ***syn*** NOTABLE 1, big boy, ‖big cheese, ‖biggie, big-timer, chief, ‖fat cat, leader, lion, VIP
con lightweight
hebetate *vb* ***syn*** DULL 5, blunt, stupefy
hebetude *n* ***syn*** LETHARGY 1, coma, dullness, languor, lassitude, sleep, slumber, stupor, torpidity, torpor
hebetudinous *adj* ***syn*** LETHARGIC, comatose, dopey, heavy, sluggish, slumberous, stupid, torpid
heckle *vb* **1** ***syn*** BAIT 2, badger, bullyrag, chivy, hector, hound, ride
rel plague, worry; discomfit, disconcert, embarrass, faze, rattle; tease, torment
2 ***syn*** MOLEST, bait, persecute, torment
hectic *adj* ***syn*** FEVERISH 2, burning, fervid, fevered, heated
hector *n* ***syn*** BULLY 1, browbeater, bulldozer, harasser, harrier, intimidator
hector *vb* **1** ***syn*** INTIMIDATE, bludgeon, browbeat, bulldoze, bully, bullyrag, cow, dragoon, strong-arm, terrorize
2 ***syn*** BAIT 2, badger, bullyrag, chivy, heckle, hound, ride
hedge *vb* **1** ***syn*** EQUIVOCATE 2, dodge, evade, pussyfoot, shuffle, sidestep, tergiversate, tergiverse, weasel
2 ***syn*** ENCLOSE 1, cage, coop, corral, fence, hem, immure, mew, mure, pen
hedonist *n* one given to the zealous pursuit of pleasure <lead the life of a *hedonist*>
syn carpet knight, pleasuremonger, sybarite
rel bon vivant, man-about-town; epicure, epicurean, gourmand, gourmet; debauchee, libertine, rake; sensualist, voluptuary; pleasure-seeker
ant ascetic
hedonistic *adj* ***syn*** SYBARITIC, onanistic, self-indulgent, sybaritical, sybaritish
con austere, self-denying, self-disciplined, self-restricted
ant ascetic
heebie–jeebies *n pl* ***syn*** JITTERS, ‖all-overs, dither, ‖jimjams, ‖jimmies, jumps, shakes, shivers, whim-whams, willies
heed *vb* ***syn*** LISTEN, attend, hark, hear, hearken
rel mark, mind, note; observe, see, watch
idiom give (*or* pay) heed to
heed *n* **1** ***syn*** NOTICE 1, attention, cognizance, mark, ‖mind, note, observance, observation, regard, remark
rel awareness, interest, mindfulness; audience, hearing
2 ***syn*** ATTENTION 1, application, concentration, consideration, debate, deliberation, study
rel concern, interest
con inattention, unconcern
3 ***syn*** CARE 4, carefulness, concern, consciousness, heedfulness, regard
heedful *adj* **1** ***syn*** ATTENTIVE 1, advertent, arrect, intentive, observant, regardful
ant heedless, unheeding
2 ***syn*** MINDFUL 2, observant, observative, observing, regardful, thoughtful
ant heedless, unheeding
3 ***syn*** CAREFUL 2, conscientious, conscionable, exact, fussy, meticulous, painstaking, punctilious, punctual, scrupulous
heedfully *adv* ***syn*** WELL 2, considerately, generously, kindly, thoughtfully
ant heedlessly, unheeding
heedfulness *n* ***syn*** CARE 4, carefulness, concern, consciousness, heed, regard
ant heedlessness
heedless *adj* ***syn*** CARELESS 1, feckless, inadvertent, irreflective, thoughtless, uncaring, unheeding, unrecking, unreflective, unthinking
ant heedful, heeding
heedlessness *n* ***syn*** APATHY 2, disinterest, disregard, indifference, insouciance, lassitude, lethargy, listlessness, unconcern, unmindfulness
ant heedfulness
hee–haw *vb* ***syn*** LAUGH, chortle, chuckle, giggle, guffaw, snicker, ‖sniggle, tehee, titter
heel *n* **1** ***syn*** REMAINDER, balance, leavings, remains, remanet, remnant, residual, residue, residuum, rest
2 ***syn*** VILLAIN 1, *bastard, blackguard, knave, lowlife, miscreant, rascal, rogue, scoundrel, *son of a bitch
heel *vb* ***syn*** SLANT 1, cant, incline, lean, list, recline, slope, tilt, tip
hefty *adj* **1** ***syn*** HEAVY 1, massive, ponderous, weighty
2 ***syn*** HUSKY 1, beefy, burly
3 ***syn*** BIG 1, considerable, extensive, large, large-scale, major, sizable
height *n* the distance a thing rises above the level on which it stands <the *height* of a building>
syn altitude, elevation
rel highness, loftiness, rise, tallness, stature
con lowness, profundity
ant depth
heighten *vb* **1** ***syn*** INCREASE 1, aggrandize, augment, boost, compound, enlarge, expand, extend, magnify, multiply
2 ***syn*** INCREASE 2, augment, build, enlarge, expand, mount, multiply, rise, upsurge, wax
rel elevate, lift, raise; better, improve; enlarge, increase
con diminish, lessen, shrink
3 ***syn*** INTENSIFY, aggravate, deepen, enhance, intensate, magnify, mount, redouble, rise, rouse
heinie (*or* **hiney**) *n* ***syn*** BUTTOCKS, *ass, behind, bottom, ‖butt, fanny, hunkers, nates, posterior, rump
heinous *adj* ***syn*** OUTRAGEOUS 2, atrocious, crying, desperate, monstrous, scandalous, shocking
con paltry, petty, trifling, trivial
ant venial
heinousness *n* ***syn*** ENORMITY 1, atrociousness, atrocity, monstrousness
heir *n* one who inherits <died without *heirs*>
syn heritor, inheritor
‖**heist** *vb* ***syn*** STEAL 1, ‖clout, ‖cop, hook, lift, nab, ‖nail, ‖nick, snitch, swipe

---

hell *n* a place or state of the dead or of the damned <went to *hell* for his sins>
syn abyss, barathrum, blazes, Gehenna, hades, inferno, netherworld, Pandemonium, perdition, pit, Sheol, Tophet
rel limbo, Styx, Tartarus
idiom the hot place, infernal regions, place of torment
ant heaven

hell *vb* *syn* REVEL 1, carouse, frolic, riot, roister, spree, wassail

hell–fired *adj* *syn* UTTER, absolute, all-fired, blasted, blessed, confounded, consummate, damned, infernal, outright

hellish *adj* *syn* INFERNAL 2, avernal, cimmerian, pandemoniac, plutonian, plutonic, stygian

helotry *n* *syn* BONDAGE, enslavement, peonage, serfdom, servitude, slavery, thrall, thralldom, villenage, yoke

help *n* **1** an act or instance of giving what will benefit or assist <the stranded travelers received *help* from passersby>
syn aid, assist, assistance, comfort, hand, lift, relief, secours, succor, support
rel benefit, cooperation, service
ant hindrance
2 something that is beneficial <the rain was a real *help* to late crops>
syn aid, support
rel benefit, use
3 *syn* HELPER, aid, ancilla, assistant, attendant, striker

help *vb* **1** to give assistance or support <*help* the children with their lessons>
syn abet, aid, assist, benefact, do for, help out, stead
rel back, bolster, boost, champion, second, support, uphold; avail, benefit, profit; advance, facilitate, forward, further, promote, serve; befriend, succor
idiom give a lift, lend a hand (*or* a helping hand), stand back of (*or* behind)
con bar, block, impede, obstruct, oppose; baffle, balk, foil, frustrate, thwart; discomfit, embarrass; damage, harm, hurt, injure
ant hinder
2 *syn* IMPROVE 1, ameliorate, amend, better, meliorate
rel alleviate, mitigate, palliate, relieve
con harm, impair, worsen

helper *n* one that helps <was made boss and assigned a dozen *helpers*>
syn aid, ancilla, assistant, attendant, help, striker
rel helpmate, helpmeet; auxiliary, deputy, subordinate; associate, follower; employee, laborer, servant, worker
idiom helping hand, right-hand man

helpful *adj* **1** of service or assistance <*helpful* suggestions>
syn aidant, aiding, assistive, serviceable
rel beneficial, effective, profitable, salutary, usable; constructive, practical, useful
con timeserving, uncooperative, unreliable; impractical, ineffectual
ant unhelpful
2 *syn* GOOD 1, advantageous, benefic, beneficial, brave, favorable, favoring, propitious, toward, useful

helpless *adj* **1** lacking protection or support <*helpless* nestlings>
syn defenseless, unprotected
rel abandoned, desolate, forlorn, forsaken, friendless; feeble, weak
2 *syn* POWERLESS, impotent

helplessly *adv* *syn* WILLY-NILLY, inescapably, inevitably, perforce, unavoidably, whether or no

help out *vb* *syn* HELP 1, abet, aid, assist, benefact, do for, stead

helter–skelter *adv* **1** *syn* PELL-MELL, hotfoot, hurry-scurry, impetuously, incontinently
2 *syn* ABOUT 4, anyhow, any which way, anywise, around, at random, haphazard, haphazardly, random, randomly

hem *n* *syn* BORDER 1, brim, brink, define, edge, fringe, perimeter, periphery, selvage, skirt, verge

hem *vb* **1** *syn* BORDER, bound, define, edge, fringe, margin, rim, skirt, surround, verge
2 *syn* ENCLOSE 1, cage, close in, corral, envelop, fence, hedge, immure, pen, shut
3 *syn* SURROUND 1, begird, beset, circle, encircle, encompass, gird, girdle, ring, round

hence *adv* **1** *syn* AWAY 1, thence
2 *syn* THEREFORE, accordingly, consequently, ergo, so, then, thereupon, thus

henceforth *adv* from this time forward <made up his mind to keep out of trouble *henceforth*>
syn henceforward, hereafter; *compare* THENCEFORTH
idiom from now on

henceforward *adv* *syn* HENCEFORTH, hereafter

henchman *n* *syn* FOLLOWER, adherent, cohort, disciple, partisan, satellite, sectary, sectator, supporter
rel attendant; lackey, minion, stooge

henpeck *vb* *syn* NAG, carp (at), fuss, peck (at)

hep *adj* *syn* WISE 4, canny, knowing, nimble-witted, quick, quick-witted, sharp, sharp-witted, slick, smart

herald *n* *syn* FORERUNNER 1, harbinger, outrider, precursor
rel courier, crier, messenger

herald *vb* **1** *syn* ANNOUNCE 2, forerun, foreshow, harbinger, preindicate, presage
2 *syn* TOUT, ballyhoo, trumpet

Herculean *adj* *syn* HUGE, colossal, enormous, gargantuan, giant, gigantic, immense, mammoth, titanic, vast

herd *n* *syn* DROVE 2, ‖drift, flock

herd *vb* *syn* DRIVE 3, ‖drove, run

here *adv* *syn* HITHERTO 2

hereafter *adv* *syn* HENCEFORTH, henceforward

hereafter *n* **1** *syn* FUTURE, aftertime, afterward, by-and-by, offing, to-be
2 an existence or place of existence after this life <buried pots and tools with the dead for use in the *hereafter*>
syn afterlife, afterworld, beyond, otherworld
idiom great beyond (*or* hereafter), life after death, next world (*or* life), world beyond the grave, world to come

con here and now

here and there *adv* *syn* SOMETIMES, at times, ||betimes, ever and again, ever and anon, now and again, now and then, once and again, ||otherwhile

heresy *n* defection from a dominant belief or ideology <the *heresy* of the flat-earth theory>
syn dissent, dissidence, heterodoxy, misbelief, nonconformism, nonconformity, schism, unorthodoxy
rel impiety, infidelity; apostasy, defection, revisionism; error, fallacy

heretic *n* one who is not orthodox in his beliefs <a *heretic* in religion>
syn dissenter, dissident, misbeliever, nonconformist, schismatic, schismatist, sectary, separatist
rel apostate, defector, iconoclast, recreant, recusant, renegade; infidel, unbeliever; deviationist, revisionist
ant orthodox

heretical *adj* of, relating to, or characterized by heresy <*heretical* beliefs>
syn dissident, heterodox, nonconformist, schismatic, sectarian, unorthodox
rel apostate, infidel, miscreant, revisionist; differing, disagreeing, dissentient, dissenting, dissentive, misbelieving, unbelieving
con conventional, established; agreeing, conforming, conformist
ant orthodox

heretofore *adv* *syn* BEFORE 2, already, earlier, erstwhile, formerly, once, previously

heritage *n* **1** something that one receives or is entitled to receive by succession (as from a parent) <the *heritage* of freedom>
syn birthright, heritance, inheritance, legacy, patrimony
2 *syn* TRADITION 1

heritance *n* *syn* HERITAGE 1, birthright, inheritance, legacy, patrimony

heritor *n* *syn* HEIR, inheritor

hermaphrodite *adj* *syn* BISEXUAL, androgynous, hermaphroditic

hermaphroditic *adj* *syn* BISEXUAL, androgynous, hermaphrodite

hermetic *adj* **1** *syn* RECONDITE, abstruse, acroamatic, deep, esoteric, heavy, occult, orphic, profound, secret
2 *syn* SECLUDED, cloistered, recluse, secluse, seclusive, sequestered

hermit *n* *syn* RECLUSE, solitary

heroic *adj* **1** *syn* BRAVE 1, bold, courageous, dauntless, fearless, intrepid, unafraid, undaunted, valiant, valorous
ant pusillanimous
2 *syn* HUGE, colossal, cyclopean, enormous, gigantic, Herculean, mighty, monumental, prodigious, titanic

heroism *n* conspicuous courage or bravery <received an award for *heroism*>
syn gallantry, prowess, valiance, valiancy, valor, valorousness
rel boldness, bravery, courage, doughtiness, fearlessness, intrepidity, spirit; chivalry, nobility
con cowardice, spiritlessness, timidity, timorousness, weakness
ant pusillanimity

hesitancy *n* *syn* HESITATION, indecision, indecisiveness, irresolution, silly-shally, to-and-fro, vacillation, wavering

hesitant *adj* **1** *syn* DISINCLINED, afraid, averse, backward, indisposed, loath, reluctant, shy, uneager, unwilling
con resolute, staunch, steadfast
2 *syn* VACILLATING 2, faltering, halting, irresolute, shilly-shallying, tentative, uncertain, vacillatory, wiggle-waggle, wobbly

hesitate *vb* to show irresolution or uncertainty <*hesitate* to buy a new car just now>
syn dither, falter, halt, shilly-shally, stagger, vacillate, waver, whiffle, wiggle-waggle
rel balk, boggle, demur, scruple, stick, stickle; fluctuate, oscillate, swing; dawdle, delay, dillydally, hang back, procrastinate, stall, temporize; pause

hesitating *adj* *syn* VACILLATING 2, faltering, halting, hesitant, indecisive, shilly-shallying, undecisive, vacillant, wavering, whiffling

hesitation *n* the act or action of hesitating <several persons volunteered without *hesitation*>
syn hesitancy, indecision, indecisiveness, irresolution, shilly-shally, to-and-fro, vacillation, wavering
rel doubt, dubiety, dubiosity, mistrust, uncertainty; dawdling, delay, procrastination; averseness, indisposition, reluctance
con alacrity, eagerness; courage, mettle, resolution, spirit, tenacity; aplomb, assurance, confidence

hetaera *n* *syn* HARLOT 1, blowen, courtesan, demimondaine, demimonde, demirep, fancy woman, kept woman, paphian, whore

heteroclite *adj* *syn* ABNORMAL 1, aberrant, anomalous, atypical, deviant, deviative, preternatural, unrepresentative, untypical

heterodox *adj* *syn* HERETICAL, dissident, nonconformist, schismatic, sectarian, unorthodox
ant orthodox

heterodoxy *n* *syn* HERESY, dissent, dissidence, misbelief, nonconformism, nonconformity, schism, unorthodoxy
ant orthodoxy

heterogeneous *adj* *syn* MISCELLANEOUS, assorted, chowchow, conglomerate, indiscriminate, mixed, motley, multifarious, promiscuous, varied
ant homogeneous

hew *vb* *syn* FELL 2, chop, cut

hex *vb* *syn* BEWITCH 1, charm, enchant, ensorcell, spell, voodoo, witch

hex *n* **1** *syn* JINX, hoodoo, Indian sign, voodoo, whammy
2 *syn* WITCH 1, bruja, enchantress, hag, lamia, sorceress, witchwoman

hiatus *n* *syn* GAP 3, breach, break, interim, interruption, interval, lacuna

hic jacet *n* *syn* EPITAPH

---

hick *n* ***syn*** RUSTIC, bucolic, bumpkin, clodhopper, hayseed, hillbilly, jake, provincial, rube, yokel

hick town *n* ***syn*** BURG, jerkwater town, mudhole, one-horse town, Podunk, tank town, whistle-stop

hidden *adj* ***syn*** ULTERIOR, buried, concealed, covert, guarded, obscured, privy, shrouded
ant open

hide *vb* to withdraw or withhold from sight or observation <they *hid* their loot in a cave>
syn bury, ‖bush up, cache, conceal, cover, ‖ditch, ensconce, occult, plant, screen, secrete, stash
rel mantle, mask, obscure, shade, shield; entomb, inter; cloak, curtain, shroud, veil; harbor, lodge, seclude, shelter
con bare, disclose, discover, display, exhibit, expose, reveal, show; uncover, unmask, unveil, unwrap; flaunt, parade, show off

hide *n* an animal skin <tanned *hides* for shoe leather>
syn fell, fur, jacket, pelt, skin

hide *vb* ***syn*** WHIP 1, flagellate, flog, ‖larrup, lash, lather, scourge, stripe, thrash, ‖wear out

hideaway *n* ***syn*** HIDEOUT, den, lair

hidebound *adj* ***syn*** ILLIBERAL, bigoted, brassbound, intolerant, narrow, narrow-minded, small-minded, unenlarged

hideous *adj* **1** ***syn*** UGLY 2, ill-favored, ill-looking, unbeautiful, uncomely, unsightly
ant lovely
2 ***syn*** OFFENSIVE, disgusting, horrible, horrid, loathsome, nasty, repellent, repugnant, repulsive, revolting
3 ***syn*** GHASTLY 1, grisly, gruesome, horrible, horrid, horrifying, lurid, macabre, terrible, terrifying

hideout *n* a place of retreat or concealment <a gangsters' *hideout*>
syn den, hideaway, lair
rel covert, haven, hermitage, refuge, retreat, sanctuary, shelter; robbers' roost

hie *vb* ***syn*** GO 1, fare, journey, pass, proceed, ‖process, push on, repair, travel, wend

hierarch *n* ***syn*** LEADER 2, boss, chief, chieftain, cock, dominator, head, headman, honcho, master

hieratic *adj* ***syn*** SACERDOTAL, priestal, priestish, priestlike, priestly, sacerdotical

higgle *vb* ***syn*** HAGGLE 2, bargain, chaffer, dicker, huckster, palter

higgler *n* ***syn*** PEDDLER, ‖arab, cheap-jack (*or* cheap-john), ‖duffer, hawker, huckster, monger, outcrier, packman, vendor

high *adj* **1** having a relatively great upward extension <a *high* building>
syn altitudinous, tall; *compare* LOFTY 6
rel aerial, eminent, lofty, soaring, towering; big, gigantic, grand, large, prominent
idiom tall (*or* high) as a steeple
con little, short, squat
ant low
2 ***syn*** COSTLY 1, dear, expensive
ant low
3 ***syn*** MALODOROUS 1, fetid, nidorous, olid, putrid, rancid, rank, reeking, smelly, whiffy
4 ***syn*** ELEVATED 4, eloquent, lofty
5 ***syn*** ACUTE 4, argute, piercing, piping, sharp, shrill, thin, treble
6 ***syn*** DRUGGED, doped, hopped-up, spaced-out, stoned, tripped out, turned on, ‖wiped out, zonked

high and low *adv* ***syn*** EVERYWHERE 1, all over, all round (*or* all around), everyplace, far and near, far and wide, overall, throughout

high–and–mighty *adj* ***syn*** PROUD 1, arrogant, cavalier, disdainful, haughty, insolent, lordly, overbearing, supercilious, superior

highball *vb* ***syn*** HURRY 2, barrel, fly, hotfoot, hustle, ‖nip, run, rush, speed, whiz

highbinding *n* ***syn*** DECEPTION 1, chicane, chicanery, dishonesty, double-dealing, fourberie, fraud, hanky-panky, sharp practice, trickery

highbrow *n* ***syn*** INTELLECTUAL 2, Brahmin, double-dome, egghead

highbrow *adj* ***syn*** INTELLECTUAL 2, cerebral, highbrowed, intellectualistic

highbrowed *adj* ***syn*** INTELLECTUAL 2, cerebral, highbrow, intellectualistic
ant lowbrow, low-browed

higher *adj* ***syn*** SUPERIOR 1, greater, over, overlying, superincumbent, superjacent

higher–up *n* ***syn*** SUPERIOR, better, brass hat, elder, senior

highest *adj* **1** ***syn*** TOP 1, apical, loftiest, topmost, uppermost
ant lowest
2 ***syn*** EXALTED 1, astral, highest-ranking, top-drawer, top-ranking

highest–ranking *adj* ***syn*** EXALTED 1, astral, highest, top-drawer, top-ranking

highfalutin *adj* ***syn*** RHETORICAL, aureate, bombastic, declamatory, florid, flowery, high-flown, magniloquent, oratorical, pompous
con down-to-earth, matter-of-fact

highfalutin *n* ***syn*** BOMBAST, fustian, lexiphanicism, rant, rhapsody, rhetoric, rodomontade

high–flown *adj* ***syn*** RHETORICAL, aureate, bombastic, declamatory, euphuistic, flowery, grandiloquent, magniloquent, overblown, swollen

high–handed *adj* ***syn*** MASTERFUL 1, bossy, domineering, imperative, imperial, imperious, magisterial, overbearing, peremptory

high hat *n* ***syn*** SNOB, snoot, snot

high–hat *adj* ***syn*** SNOBBISH, ‖dicty, potty, snobby, snooty

high–hearted *adj* ***syn*** SPIRITED 2, beany, fiery, gingery, high-spirited, mettlesome, peppery, spunky

high jinks *n pl* **1** ***syn*** HORSEPLAY, fooling, roughhouse, roughhousing, rowdiness, skylarking
2 ***syn*** REVELRY 2, revel, revelment, skylarking, wassail, whoop-de-do, whoopee, whoopla, whoop-up

highly *adv* ***syn*** VERY 1, exceedingly, exceptionally, extremely, hugely, notably, parlous, remarkably, strikingly, surpassingly

high–minded *adj syn* ELEVATED 2, moral, noble
ant low-minded

high–muck–a–muck *n syn* NOTABLE 1, big boy, ‖big cheese, ‖big chief, big shot, ‖big wheel, bigwig, mugwump, nabob, VIP

high–principled *adj syn* HONORABLE 1, estimable, noble, sterling, worthy

high roller *n syn* SPENDTHRIFT, prodigal, profligate, scattergood, spender, squanderer, unthrift, waster, waste-thrift, wastrel

high sign *n* **1** *syn* SIGN 1, signal
2 a private usually covert signal, warning, or cue <I gave him the *high sign* when I saw the police approaching>
syn ‖office
rel tip, tip-off, wink; nod; alarm, SOS, warning

high–sounding *adj syn* PRETENTIOUS 3, arty, arty-crafty, big, imposing, overblown

high–spirited *adj* **1** *syn* SPIRITED 2, beany, fiery, gingery, high-hearted, mettlesome, peppery, spunky
rel jolly, lighthearted, merry, mirthful
ant low-spirited
2 *syn* EXUBERANT 1, brash, ebullient, effervescent, vivacious

high–strung *adj* **1** *syn* TENSE 3, overstrung, taut, tight, unrelaxed, uptight
2 *syn* NERVOUS, fidgety, goosey, jittery, jumpy, nervy, spooky, twittery, unrestful

hightail *vb syn* GET OUT 1, begone, clear out, decamp, kite, scram, skedaddle, skiddoo, take off, ‖vamoose

highway *n syn* WAY 1, artery, avenue, boulevard, ‖drag, path, road, street, thoroughfare, track

high yellow *n syn* MULATTO, *brass ankle

hike *vb* **1** *syn* RAISE 9, boost, increase, jack (up), jump, put up, up
2 to travel about or through on foot <*hiked* through the woods>
syn tramp, tromp
rel footslog; stroll, walk; ramble, rove, wander; explore

hike *n* **1** *syn* TRAMP 3, walkabout
2 *syn* RISE 3, boost, breakthrough, increase, upgrade, wax

hilarity *n syn* MIRTH, glee, jocularity, jocundity, jollity, joviality, merriment

hill *n syn* PILE 1, bank, cock, drift, heap, mound, mountain, rick, shock, stack

hill *vb syn* HEAP 1, bank, cock, drift, mound, pile, stack

hillbilly *n syn* RUSTIC, backwoodsman, bucolic, bumpkin, clodhopper, hayseed, hick, hillman, rube, yokel

hillman *n syn* RUSTIC, backwoodsman, bucolic, bumpkin, clodhopper, hayseed, hick, hillbilly, rube, yokel

hind *adj syn* POSTERIOR 2, after, back, hinder, hindmost, rear, retral

hind end *n syn* BUTTOCKS, backside, beam, fundament, haunches, hunkers, posterior, rear end, rump, tail

hinder *vb* to put obstacles in the way of <their cause was *hindered* by the excesses of overzealous supporters>
syn bar, block, brake, dam, impede, obstruct, overslaugh; *compare* HAMPER
rel arrest, check, interrupt, retard; clog, entrammel, fetter, hamper, hog-tie, manacle, shackle, trammel; curb, deter, hamstring, inhibit, restrain, tie (down); embog, mire; burden, handicap, lumber; baffle, balk, frustrate, thwart
idiom bog down
con abet, advance, aid, assist, ease, encourage, facilitate, forward, promote; accelerate, hasten, quicken, speed
ant further, help

hinder *adj syn* POSTERIOR 2, after, back, hind, hindmost, rear, retral
ant fore, front

‖**hinder** *n syn* BUTTOCKS, *arse, backside, behind, bottom, *bum, ‖butt, fanny, nates, posterior

hindmost *adj* **1** *syn* POSTERIOR 2, after, back, hind, hinder, rear, retral
con foremost, headmost
2 *syn* LAST, closing, concluding, eventual, final, lag, latest, latter, terminal, ultimate

hindrance *n syn* ENCUMBRANCE, clog, cumbrance, impedance, impediment
ant help

hinge (on *or* upon) *vb syn* DEPEND (on *or* upon) 1, hang (on *or* upon), ‖pend, stand (on *or* upon), turn (on *or* upon)

hint *n* **1** a slight or indirect pointing out of something and especially of the way to an end <give me a *hint* on how you would deal with the matter>
syn clue, cue, indication, inkling, intimation, notion, suggestion, telltale, wind
rel innuendo, insinuation; inspiration, prompting; aiming, direction, pointing; key, pointer, tip; advice, assistance
con command, directive, instruction, order
2 a very small amount or admixture <add a *hint* of garlic to the salad>
syn breath, cast, dash, intimation, lick, shade, shadow, smack, smatch, smell, soupçon, spice, sprinkling, strain, streak, suggestion, suspicion, taste, tincture, tinge, touch, trace, trifle, twang, vein, whiff, whisper, wink; *compare* HAIR
rel adumbration, taint, vestige; particle, scintilla
con abundance, heap, lot
ant oodles
3 *syn* ASSOCIATION 4, connotation, implication, overtone, suggestion, undertone

hint *vb* **1** *syn* SUGGEST 1, connote, imply, insinuate, intimate
2 *syn* POINT 2, imply, indicate, suggest
3 *syn* ADUMBRATE 1, foreshadow, prefigurate, prefigure, shadow (forth)
4 to seek to obtain by sly or indirect means <kept *hinting* for an invitation to the party>
syn angle, fish
rel beg, coax, plead; importune, press; seek, solicit
con ask (for), demand, insist (on *or* upon)

---

syn synonym(s) — *rel* related word(s)
idiom idiomatic equivalent(s) — *con* contrasted word(s)
ant antonym(s) — * vulgar
‖ use limited; if in doubt, see a dictionary
The first word in a synonym list when printed in SMALL CAPITALS shows where there is more information about the group. For a more efficient use of this book see Explanatory Notes.

hinterland *n* ***syn*** FRONTIER 2, backcountry, backland, backwash, backwater, backwoods, ‖boondocks, bush, sticks, up-country

hipped *adj* **1** ***syn*** DOWNCAST, bad, blue, cast down, dejected, depressed, dispirited, down, downhearted, low
2 ***syn*** OBSESSED, hagridden, queer

hire *n* ***syn*** WAGE, emolument, fee, pay, pay envelope, salary, stipend

hire *vb* **1** to take or engage something or grant the use of something for a stipulated price or rate <*hire* a conveyance>
syn charter, lease, let, rent
rel contract (for), engage; sublease, sublet, subrent
2 ***syn*** EMPLOY 2, engage, put on, take on
ant fire

hired girl *n* ***syn*** MAID 2, biddy, girl, handmaid, housemaid, maidservant

hireling *n* ***syn*** HACK 2, drudge, grub, grubber, mercenary, slavey

hiring *n* ***syn*** EMPLOYMENT 4, engagement, engaging

hirsute *adj* ***syn*** HAIRY 1, fleecy, pileous, pilose, whiskered, woolly
ant hairless

hiss *vb* to make a sibilant sound <he thought he heard a snake *hiss*>
syn buzz, fizz, fizzle, sibilate, sizz, sizzle, swish, wheeze, whish, whisper, whiz, whoosh

hiss *n* ***syn*** RASPBERRY, bazoo, bird, boo, ‖Bronx cheer, catcall, hoot, pooh, pooh-pooh, ‖razz

history *n* **1** ***syn*** ACCOUNT 7, chronicle, narrative, report, story, version
2 a chronological record of events <a *history* of the American Revolution>
syn annals, chronicle
rel account, recital, relation, report; diary, journal, memoir; epic, saga, tale

histrionic *adj* ***syn*** DRAMATIC 1, dramaturgic, theatral, theatric, theatrical, thespian

hit *vb* **1** ***syn*** STRIKE 2, clout, ‖devel, ding, ‖nail, slog, ‖slosh, smite, sock, whack
rel buffet, pound, stroke
idiom give one a clip
2 ***syn*** OCCUR 2, strike
3 ***syn*** HAPPEN 2, bump, chance, light, luck, meet, stumble, tumble

hit (on *or* upon) *vb* ***syn*** FIND 1, catch, descry, detect, encounter, espy, meet (with), spot, turn up

hit *n* **1** a stroke delivered with a part of the body or an instrument <gave the disobedient boy a *hit* on the head with her ruler>
syn ‖conk, knock, lick, rap, swat, swipe, wipe; *compare* BLOW 1, CUFF
2 ***syn*** SMASH 6, bang, bell ringer, succès fou, ten-strike, wow

hitch *vb* **1** ***syn*** LIMP 1, halt, hobble
2 to attach as a means of motive power <*hitched* the team to a wagon>
syn couple, harness, yoke
idiom make fast
con free, release, unfasten; uncouple, unharness, unyoke
ant unhitch
‖**3** ***syn*** MARRY 2, mate, splice, tie, wed
4 ***syn*** HITCHHIKE, thumb

hitchhike *vb* to travel by securing free rides <*hitchhiked* to California>
syn hitch, thumb
idiom bum (*or* hook) a ride

hitherto *adv* **1** up to this particular point or time <imposed order upon what was *hitherto* haphazard>
syn as yet, earlier, so far, thus far, yet
rel before, formerly, heretofore, once, previously
idiom up to now (*or* then)
2 to this place <the appointed delegate shall come *hitherto*>
syn here

hit man *n* ***syn*** ASSASSIN, bravo, cutthroat, gun, gunman, ‖gunsel, gunslinger, hatchet man, torpedo, triggerman

hit-or-miss *adj* ***syn*** RANDOM, aimless, designless, desultory, haphazard, indiscriminate, irregular, unaimed, unconsidered, unplanned

hive *vb* ***syn*** ACCUMULATE, amass, cumulate, garner, lay up, roll up, stockpile, store (up), uplay

hoard *n* **1** ***syn*** ACCUMULATION, agglomeration, aggregation, amassment, collection, colluvies, conglomeration, cumulation, trove
2 ***syn*** RESERVE, backlog, inventory, nest egg, reservoir, stock, stockpile, store

hoard *vb* to store up beyond one's present or reasonable need <*hoarding* sugar during war>
syn squirrel, stash; *compare* ACCUMULATE, SAVE 4
rel ‖sock away; garner, lay by, lay up
idiom take all one can lay one's hands on

hoarse *adj* **1** rough or dry in sound <developed a *hoarse* cough>
syn croaking, croaky, gruff, husky
rel coarse, dry, guttural, thick
2 ***syn*** HARSH 3, dry, grating, jarring, rasping, raucous, rough, strident, stridulent, stridulous
con honeyed, mellifluent, mellifluous, smooth

hoary *adj* ***syn*** ANCIENT 1, aged, age-old, antediluvian, antique, Noachian, old, timeworn, venerable

hoax *vb* ***syn*** DUPE, bamboozle, befool, chicane, flimflam, fool, gull, hoodwink, hornswoggle, trick

hoax *n* ***syn*** IMPOSTURE, fake, flimflam, fraud, gyp, humbug, phony, put-on, sell, spoof

hobble *vb* **1** ***syn*** LIMP 1, halt, hitch
2 ***syn*** HAMPER, clog, curb, entrammel, fetter, hog-tie, leash, shackle, tie, trammel

hobo *n* ***syn*** VAGABOND, ‖bindle stiff, bum, derelict, drifter, floater, street arab, tramp, vag, vagrant

hoboism *n* ***syn*** VAGRANCY, vagabondage, vagabondia, vagabondism

hock *vb* ***syn*** PAWN, ‖dip, impignorate, mortgage, pledge, ‖pop, ‖spout

hocus-pocus *n* ***syn*** GIBBERISH 3, abracadabra, mumbo jumbo, mummery

---

syn synonym(s) — *rel* related word(s)
idiom idiomatic equivalent(s) — *con* contrasted word(s)
ant antonym(s) — * vulgar
‖ use limited; if in doubt, see a dictionary
The first word in a synonym list when printed in SMALL CAPITALS shows where there is more information about the group. For a more efficient use of this book see Explanatory Notes.

‖**hodge** *n* ***syn*** RUSTIC, bucolic, bumpkin, clodhopper, hick, hillbilly, joskin, peasant, provincial, yokel

hodgepodge *n* ***syn*** MISCELLANY 1, gallimaufry, hash, hotchpotch, jumble, medley, mélange, mishmash, patchwork, potpourri

hogback *n* ***syn*** RIDGE 1, chine, crest

hogshead *n* ***syn*** CASK, barrel, butt, keg, pipe, tun

hog–tie *vb* ***syn*** HAMPER, clog, curb, entrammel, fetter, hobble, leash, shackle, tie, trammel

hogwash *n* ***syn*** NONSENSE 2, ‖baloney, bilge, bosh, ‖bull, eyewash, hokum, hooey, ‖horsefeathers, poppycock

hoi polloi *n* ***syn*** RABBLE 2, dreg(s), mass(es), mob, other half, proletariat, ragtag and bobtail, riffraff, scum, trash

hoist *vb* ***syn*** LIFT 1, elevate, pick up, raise, rear, take up, uphold, uplift, upraise, uprear

hoity–toity *adj* ***syn*** GIDDY 1, dizzy, featherbrained, flighty, frivolous, harebrained, rattlebrained, scatterbrained, silly, skittish

hokum *n* ***syn*** NONSENSE 2, ‖baloney, bosh, ‖bull, bunkum, flimflam, hooey, jazz, malarkey, poppycock

hold *vb* **1** ***syn*** KEEP 5, detain, hold back, keep back, keep out, reserve, retain, withhold
2 ***syn*** ENTHRALL 2, catch up, fascinate, grip, mesmerize, spellbind
3 ***syn*** HAVE 1, enjoy, own, possess, retain
4 ***syn*** CONTAIN 2, accommodate
5 ***syn*** FEEL 3, believe, consider, credit, deem, sense, think

hold (with) *vb* ***syn*** APPROVE 1, accept, approbate, countenance, favor, go (for)

hold *n* the act or manner of grasping or holding <lost his *hold* on the side of the boat>
syn clamp, clasp, clench, clinch, clutch, grapple, grasp, grip, gripe, tenure
rel handclasp, handhold; purchase

hold back *vb* **1** ***syn*** RESTRAIN 1, bit, bridle, check, constrain, curb, hold down, hold in, inhibit, withhold
2 ***syn*** KEEP 5, detain, hold, keep back, keep out, reserve, retain, withhold
3 ***syn*** DENY 3, abstain, constrain, curb, refrain

hold down *vb* ***syn*** RESTRAIN 1, bit, bridle, check, constrain, curb, hold back, hold in, inhibit, withhold

holder *n* ***syn*** OWNER, possessor, proprietor

hold in *vb* ***syn*** RESTRAIN 1, bit, bridle, check, constrain, curb, hold back, hold down, inhibit, withhold

hold off *vb* **1** ***syn*** FEND (off), keep off, rebuff, rebut, repel, repulse, stave off, ward (off)
2 ***syn*** DEFER, adjourn, delay, postpone, prorogue, put off, remit, shelve, stay, suspend

hold out *vb* ***syn*** OFFER 1, extend, give, pose, present, proffer, tender

hold over *vb* ***syn*** DEFER, adjourn, delay, hold up, postpone, prorogue, put off, shelve, stay, suspend

hold up *vb* ***syn*** DEFER, delay, hold off, postpone, prorogue, put off, remit, stay, suspend, waive

hole *n* **1** ***syn*** APERTURE, opening, orifice, outlet, vent
2 ***syn*** GAP 1, breach, break, discontinuity, opening
3 a space within the substance of a body or mass <buried their trash in a *hole* in the ground>
syn cavity, hollow, vacuity, void
rel gap, hiatus, lacuna; cranny, interstice, niche; fissure, rent, rift; vacancy, vacuum
4 ***syn*** HOVEL, burrow
5 ***syn*** PREDICAMENT, box, corner, dilemma, fix, jam, pickle, plight, scrape, spot

hole *vb* ***syn*** OPEN 3, breach, disrupt, rupture

hole–and–corner *adj* ***syn*** SECRET 1, clandestine, covert, furtive, hugger-mugger, stealthy, surreptitious, undercover, ‖underneath, under-the-table

holiday *n* ***syn*** VACATION, leave

holiness *n* a state of spiritual soundness and unimpaired virtue <the *holiness* of the saints>
syn saintliness, sanctity
rel blessedness, divineness, divinity, sacredness; consecration, devotion, devoutness, piety, piousness, spirituality

holler *vb* ***syn*** CALL 1, cry, hallo, hollo, shout, vociferate, yell

hollo *vb* ***syn*** CALL 1, cry, hallo, holler, shout, vociferate, yell

hollow *adj* **1** having a muffled or reverberating quality <had a deep *hollow* gloomy voice>
syn cavernous, reverberant, sepulchral
rel echoing, resonant, resounding, reverberating, sounding
con dead, dull, flat, toneless
2 ***syn*** VAIN 1, empty, idle, nugatory, otiose

hollow *n* **1** ***syn*** DEPRESSION 2, basin, concavity, dip, sag, sink, sinkage, sinkhole
2 ***syn*** HOLE 3, cavity, vacuity, void

holocaust *n* ***syn*** FIRE 1, conflagration, inferno

holy *adj* **1** dedicated to the service of or set apart by religion <pilgrimages to *holy* places>
syn blessed, consecrated, hallowed, sacred, sanctified, unprofane; *compare* SACRED 2
rel adored, glorified, revered, reverenced, venerated, worshiped; divine, religious, spiritual
2 ***syn*** SAINTLY, angelic, godly
ant unholy
3 ***syn*** DEVOUT, godly, pietistic, pious, prayerful, religious

‖**Holy Joe** *n* ***syn*** CLERGYMAN, churchman, cleric, clerical, clerk, divine, ecclesiastic, minister, parson, preacher

holy place *n* ***syn*** SHRINE, sanctorium, sanctuary, sanctum

Holy Writ *n* ***syn*** BIBLE, Book, Sacred Writ, Scripture

homage *n* ***syn*** HONOR 1, deference, obeisance, reverence

home *n* **1** ***syn*** HABITATION 2, commorancy, domicile, dwelling, house, residence, residency
2 ***syn*** HABITAT, haunt, locality, range, site, stamping ground
3 ***syn*** COUNTRY, fatherland, homeland, land, mother country, motherland, soil

home *adj* **1** ***syn*** DOMESTIC 1, family, household
2 ***syn*** DOMESTIC 2, ‖inland, internal, intestine, municipal, national, native

---

syn synonym(s) ***rel*** related word(s)
idiom idiomatic equivalent(s) ***con*** contrasted word(s)
ant antonym(s) * vulgar
‖ use limited; if in doubt, see a dictionary
The first word in a synonym list when printed in SMALL CAPITALS shows where there is more information about the group. For a more efficient use of this book see Explanatory Notes.

homeland *n* ***syn*** COUNTRY, fatherland, home, land, mother country, motherland, soil

homely *adj* **1** ***syn*** PLAIN 1, dry, inelaborate, modest, simple, unelaborate, ungarnished, unornamented, unostentatious, unpretentious
rel commonplace, familiar, intimate
2 ***syn*** PLAIN 5, unalluring, unattractive, unbeauteous, unbeautiful, uncomely, unhandsome, unpretty
idiom homely as a mud (*or* hedge) fence, homely enough to sour milk
ant comely

homicidal *adj* ***syn*** MURDEROUS, bloodthirsty, bloody, murdering, sanguinary, sanguine, sanguineous

homicide *n* **1** ***syn*** MURDERER, killer, manslayer, slayer
2 ***syn*** MURDER, blood, ‖bump-off, foul play, killing, manslaughter

homilize *vb* ***syn*** PREACH 1, evangelize, sermonize

hominine *adj* ***syn*** HUMAN, mortal

hominoid *n* ***syn*** ANTHROPOID, anthropomorphic, anthropomorphous, manlike

homo *n* ***syn*** HOMOSEXUAL, fag, faggot, ‖fruit, invert, queer, uranian, uranist

homoerotic *adj* ***syn*** HOMOSEXUAL, gay, homophile, inverted, queer, uranian

homophile *adj* ***syn*** HOMOSEXUAL, gay, homoerotic, inverted, queer, uranian

Homo sapiens *n* ***syn*** MANKIND, flesh, humanity, humankind, man, mortality

homosexual *adj* relating to or exhibiting sexual desire toward a member of one's own sex < *homosexual* acts between consenting adults >
syn gay, homoerotic, homophile, inverted, queer, uranian
rel androgynous, bisexual, epicene; transvestite; lesbian, sapphic; effeminate, swishy

homosexual *n* one who is inclined to or practices homosexuality < a bar frequented by *homosexuals* >
syn fag, faggot, ‖fruit, homo, invert, queer, uranian, uranist
rel transvestite; fairy, nance, nancy, pansy, queen, ‖swish; dike, lesbian, sapphist; pederast, sodomite

homunculus *n* ***syn*** DWARF, hop-o'-my-thumb, lilliputian, manikin, midge, midget, peewee, pygmy, runt, Tom Thumb

honcho *n* ***syn*** LEADER 2, boss, chief, chieftain, cock, dominator, head, headman, hierarch, master

hone *vb* ***syn*** SHARPEN, edge, ‖sharp, whet

honed *adj* ***syn*** SHARP 1, keen, razor-sharp, unblunted, whetted

honest *adj* **1** ***syn*** GENUINE 3, heart-whole, real, sincere, true, undesigning, undissembled, unfeigned
rel reliable, unaffected, unimpeachable
2 ***syn*** UPRIGHT 2, conscientious, honorable, just, right, scrupulous, true
rel candid, forthright, frank, open, plain; dispassionate, objective; truthful, veracious
ant dishonest

honestness *n* ***syn*** HONESTY, honor, honorableness, incorruption, integrity
ant dishonesty

honesty *n* uprightness as evidenced in character and actions < he was generally known as a person of scrupulous *honesty* >
syn honestness, honor, honorableness, incorruption, integrity
rel conscientiousness, justness, probity, scrupulousness, uprightness; dependability, reliability, trustworthiness; goodness, morality, rectitude, virtue
con deceitfulness, mendaciousness, mendacity, untruthfulness; deceit, duplicity, guile
ant dishonesty

honey *n* **1** ***syn*** SWEETHEART 1, beloved, darling, dear, heartthrob, honeybunch, love, loveling, sweet, sweetling
2 ***syn*** GIRL FRIEND 2, ‖baby, beloved, flame, inamorata, ladylove, steady, sweetheart, sweetie, truelove

honey *vb* ***syn*** SUGARCOAT 1, candy, sugar (over), sweeten

honey (up) *vb* ***syn*** FAWN, apple-polish, bootlick, ‖brownnose, cower, cringe, grovel, kowtow, toady, truckle

honeybunch *n* ***syn*** SWEETHEART 1, beloved, darling, dear, honey, love, loveling, sweet, sweetling, turtledove

honeyed *adj* ***syn*** MELLIFLUOUS, golden, Hyblaean, liquid, mellifluent, mellow

honky–tonk *n* ***syn*** DIVE, barrelhouse, hangout, joint

honor *n* **1** respect or esteem shown one as his due or claimed by one as a right < received the *honor* due his rank >
syn deference, homage, obeisance, reverence
rel admiration, esteem; adoration, adulation, devotion, veneration, worship; acknowledgment, compliment, recognition, regard, respect
con contempt, despite, disdain, scorn; disregard, neglect, slighting
ant dishonor
2 an evidence or symbol of distinction < received many *honors* for his devoted public service >
syn accolade, award, badge, bays, decoration, distinction, kudos, laurels
rel deference, esteem, respect; admiration, approval
3 ***syn*** HONESTY, honestness, honorableness, incorruption, integrity
con disgrace, ignominy, shame
ant dishonor, dishonorableness

honor *vb* ***syn*** EXALT 1, aggrandize, dignify, distinguish, ennoble, erect, glorify, magnify, sublime, uprear
ant dishonor

honorable *adj* **1** deserving of or entitled to honor (as because of rank, achievements, or service) < medicine is an *honorable* profession >
syn estimable, high-principled, noble, sterling, worthy; *compare* VENERABLE 1
rel august, illustrious, reverend, venerable, worshipful
ant dishonorable
2 ***syn*** UPRIGHT 2, conscientious, honest, just, right, scrupulous, true
ant dishonorable

---

syn synonym(s) ***rel*** related word(s)
idiom idiomatic equivalent(s) ***con*** contrasted word(s)
ant antonym(s) * vulgar
‖ use limited; if in doubt, see a dictionary
The first word in a synonym list when printed in SMALL CAPITALS shows where there is more information about the group. For a more efficient use of this book see Explanatory Notes.

honorableness *n* ***syn*** HONESTY, honestness, honor, incorruption, integrity
ant dishonor, dishonorableness

‖**hooch** *n* **1** ***syn*** LIQUOR 2, alcohol, aqua vitae, booze, drink, firewater, grog, ‖juice, spirit(s), tipple
2 ***syn*** MOONSHINE 2, bathtub gin, ‖blockade, bootleg, ‖busthead, mountain dew, white lightning

‖**hood** *n* ***syn*** THUG 1, ‖gorilla, hoodlum, hooligan, ruffian, strong arm

hoodlum *n* ***syn*** THUG 1, ‖gorilla, ‖hood, hooligan, ruffian, strong arm

hoodoo *n* ***syn*** JINX, hex, Indian sign, voodoo, whammy

hoodwink *vb* ***syn*** DUPE, bamboozle, befool, chicane, flimflam, fool, gull, hoax, hornswoggle, trick

hooey *n* ***syn*** NONSENSE 2, ‖baloney, bilge, bosh, ‖bull, bunkum, claptrap, hogwash, hokum, malarkey

hoof *vb* ***syn*** WALK 1, ambulate, foot (it), pace, step, traipse, tread, troop

hoof (it) *vb* ***syn*** DANCE 1, foot (it), prance, step, tread

hoofer *n* ***syn*** DANCER, ballerina, ballet girl, coryphée, dancing girl, danseur, danseuse, figurant, figurante

hook *vb* ***syn*** STEAL 1, cabbage, ‖cop, lift, nab, ‖nail, ‖nick, nim, nip, pinch

‖**hooker** *n* ***syn*** PROSTITUTE, bawd, call girl, drab, fille de joie, harlot, hustler, nightwalker, streetwalker, whore

‖**hookshop** *n* ***syn*** BROTHEL, bagnio, bawdy house, bordello, cathouse, ‖joyhouse, parlor house, sporting house, stew, whorehouse

hookup *n* ***syn*** ASSOCIATION 1, affiliation, alliance, cahoots, combination, conjunction, connection, partnership, tie-up, togetherness

hooligan *n* ***syn*** THUG 1, ‖gorilla, ‖hood, hoodlum, ruffian, strong arm

‖**hoosegow** *n* ***syn*** JAIL, ‖calaboose, ‖can, ‖clink, cooler, jug, lockup, ‖pokey, prison, ‖stir

hoosier *n* ***syn*** RUSTIC, backwoodsman, bucolic, bumpkin, chawbacon, clodhopper, hayseed, hick, hillbilly, jake

hoot *n* **1** ***syn*** RASPBERRY, bazoo, bird, boo, ‖Bronx cheer, catcall, hiss, pooh, pooh-pooh, ‖razz
2 ***syn*** PARTICLE, damn, ‖dite, iota, jot, modicum, ounce, scrap, whit, whoop

‖**hootenanny** *n* ***syn*** DOODAD, dingus, dofunny, doohickey, gadget, gizmo, jigger, thingumajig, thingumbob, thingummy

hop *vb* **1** ***syn*** SKIP 1, lope, skitter, spring, trip
2 ***syn*** JUMP 1, bounce, bound, hurdle, leap, lop, saltate, spring, vault

‖**hop** *n* ***syn*** DRUG 2, dope, narcotic, opiate

hope *vb* ***syn*** EXPECT 1, await, count (on *or* upon), look

hope *n* ***syn*** TRUST 1, confidence, dependence, faith, reliance, stock

hopeful *adj* **1** full of hope or inclined to hope <the candidate was *hopeful* of winning>
syn hoping; *compare* CONFIDENT 1, EXPECTANT 1, OPTIMISTIC
rel anticipative, assured, satisfied, secure; cheerful, content, easy, undisturbed; fond, optimistic, Pollyannaish, rose-colored, sanguine, upbeat
con doubtful, insecure, pessimistic, uncertain; discouraged, disheartened, gloomy, glum
ant hopeless
2 exhibiting qualities that inspire hope <a *hopeful* prospect for improvement>
syn couleur de rose, encouraging, likely, promiseful, promising, roseate, rose-colored, rosy
rel advantageous, auspicious, propitious; bright, cheering, cheery, golden, halcyon, happy, sunny; budding, up-and-coming
con discouraging, disheartening, dismal, dreary, gloomy, pessimistic
ant hopeless

hopeful *n* ***syn*** CANDIDATE, applicant, aspirant, seeker

hopeless *adj* **1** ***syn*** DESPONDENT, despairing, desperate, desponding, forlorn
rel gloomy, glum, morose
con cheerful; assured, confident, optimistic, sanguine, sure
ant hopeful
2 offering no prospect of change for the better <his case was *hopeless* and beyond all human aid>
syn cureless, immedicable, impossible, incurable, insanable, irremediable, irreparable, uncorrectable, uncurable, unrecoverable
rel insoluble; incorrigible, irredeemable
idiom beyond hope (*or* remedy *or* repair), beyond human aid
con correctable, curable, medicable, remediable, reparable
ant hopeful

hoper *n* ***syn*** OPTIMIST, Pollyanna

hoping *adj* ***syn*** HOPEFUL 1

hop–o'–my–thumb *n* ***syn*** DWARF, homunculus, lilliputian, manikin, midge, midget, peewee, pygmy, runt, Tom Thumb

hopped–up *adj* ***syn*** DRUGGED, doped, high, spaced-out, stoned, tripped out, turned on, ‖wiped out, zonked

hopping *adj* ***syn*** BUSTLING, busy, fussy, humming, hustling, lively, popping

horde *n* ***syn*** CROWD 1, crush, drove, multitude, press, push, squash, throng

horizon *n* ***syn*** KEN, purview, range, reach

horn in *vb* **1** ***syn*** MEDDLE, busybody, butt in, fool, interfere, interlope, intermeddle, ‖make, monkey (with), tamper (with)
2 ***syn*** INTRUDE 1, butt in, chisel (in), cut in, intertrude, obtrude

‖**horning** *n* ***syn*** SHIVAREE, ‖belling, ‖bull band, ‖callithump, charivari, ‖riding, ‖skimmelton

hornswoggle *vb* ***syn*** DUPE, bamboozle, befool, chicane, flimflam, fool, gull, hoax, hoodwink, pigeon

*__horny__ *adj* ***syn*** LUSTFUL 2, concupiscent, goatish, hot, lascivious, libidinous, lickerish, passionate, prurient, satyric

horrible *adj* **1** ***syn*** GHASTLY 1, grim, grisly, gruesome, hideous, horrid, horrifying, lurid, terrible, terrifying

---

syn synonym(s) ***rel*** related word(s)
idiom idiomatic equivalent(s) ***con*** contrasted word(s)
ant antonym(s) * vulgar
‖ use limited; if in doubt, see a dictionary
The first word in a synonym list when printed in SMALL CAPITALS shows where there is more information about the group. For a more efficient use of this book see Explanatory Notes.

rel abhorrent, abominable, detestable, hateful; loathsome, obnoxious, offensive, repulsive, revolting
con gratifying, pleasing, soothing
2 *syn* FEARFUL 3, appalling, awful, dreadful, formidable, frightful, horrific, shocking, terrible, terrific
3 *syn* OFFENSIVE, disgusting, hideous, horrid, loathsome, nasty, repellent, repugnant, repulsive, revolting

horrid *adj* 1 *syn* GHASTLY 1, grim, grisly, gruesome, hideous, horrible, horrifying, lurid, terrible, terrifying
2 *syn* HATEFUL 2, abhorrent, abominable, detestable, hateable, odious
3 *syn* OFFENSIVE, disgusting, horrible, loathsome, nasty, repellent, repugnant, repulsive, revolting

horrific *adj syn* FEARFUL 3, appalling, awful, dreadful, formidable, frightful, horrible, shocking, terrible, terrific

horrify *vb syn* DISMAY 1, appall, consternate, daunt, shake

horrifying *adj syn* GHASTLY 1, grim, grisly, gruesome, hideous, horrid, horrible, lurid, terrible, terrifying

horror *n* 1 *syn* FEAR 1, alarm, consternation, dismay, dread, fright, panic, terror, trepidation, trepidity
rel distress, pain, shock, throe, wrench
2 *syn* ABOMINATION 2, abhorrence, aversion, detestation, hate, hatred, loathing, repugnance, repulsion, revulsion

hors d'oeuvre *n syn* APPETIZER, antipasto, whet, zakuska

horse *n syn* SAWHORSE, buck, sawbuck, trestle, workhorse

horse *vb syn* CUT UP 2, act up, carry on, horseplay

‖**horsefeathers** *n pl syn* NONSENSE 2, ‖baloney, bosh, ‖bull, bunkum, ‖crap, fudge, hooey, *horseshit, poppycock

horse opera *n syn* WESTERN, oater

horseplay *n* rough or boisterous play <their friendly *horseplay* almost ended in tragedy>
syn fooling, high jinks, roughhouse, roughhousing, rowdiness, skylarking
rel buffoonery, clowning

horseplay *vb syn* CUT UP 2, act up, carry on, horse

horse sense *n syn* SENSE 6, common sense, good sense, gumption, judgment, wisdom

***horseshit** *n syn* NONSENSE, balderdash, ‖baloney, *bullshit, ‖crap, hogwash, hooey, ‖horsefeathers, poppycock, rot

hospice *n syn* HOTEL, auberge, caravansary, hostel, hostelry, inn, lodge, public house, roadhouse, tavern

hospitable *adj syn* SOCIAL, companionable, convivial, cooperative, gregarious, sociable
ant inhospitable

host *n syn* MULTITUDE 1, army, cloud, crowd, flock, legion, rout, scores

hostage *n syn* PLEDGE, earnest, pawn, token

---

syn synonym(s) *rel* related word(s)
idiom idiomatic equivalent(s) *con* contrasted word(s)
ant antonym(s) * vulgar
‖ use limited; if in doubt, see a dictionary
The first word in a synonym list when printed in SMALL CAPITALS shows where there is more information about the group. For a more efficient use of this book see Explanatory Notes.

rel guaranty, security, surety

hostel *n syn* HOTEL, auberge, caravansary, hospice, hostelry, inn, lodge, public house, roadhouse, tavern

hostelry *n syn* HOTEL, auberge, caravansary, hospice, hostel, inn, lodge, public house, roadhouse, tavern

hostile *adj* 1 marked by lack of friendliness or by opposition <takes a *hostile* view of a tax increase> <*hostile* tribes>
syn ill, inimicable, inimical, unfriendly
rel argumentative, competitive, contrary, dim, disaffected, disapproving, opposed, opposite, unfavorable; dour, sour; bellicose, belligerent, contentious, pugnacious; militant, warlike
con amicable, benign, friendly
ant unhostile
2 *syn* BITTER 3, antagonistic, rancorous, virulent, vitriolic

hostility *n syn* ENMITY, animosity, animus, antagonism, antipathy, rancor

hot *adj* 1 marked by a notable amount of heat <a *hot* day>
syn ardent, baking, blistering, boiling, broiling, burning, fiery, heated, red-hot, scalding, scorching, sizzling, sultry, sweltering, sweltry, torrid, white-hot
rel febrile, fevered, feverish, feverous, hectic; summery, tropic, tropical; mild, warm
idiom hot as a firecracker (*or* furnace), hot as an oven, hot as hell
con chilly, cool, frigid, icy
ant cold
2 *syn* LUSTFUL 2, concupiscent, goatish, *horny, lascivious, libidinous, lickerish, passionate, prurient, satyric
3 *syn* MARVELOUS 2, ‖cool, ‖dandy, glorious, groovy, ‖keen, ‖neat, nifty, peachy, super
4 *syn* CONTRABAND, banned

hot air *n syn* NONSENSE 2, blather, bosh, bunkum, double-talk, flimflam, ‖gas, malarkey, poppycock, twaddle

hotbed *n syn* BREEDING GROUND, forcing bed, forcing house, hothouse

hot–blooded *adj syn* IMPASSIONED, ardent, blazing, burning, fervent, fiery, flaming, passionate, red-hot, white-hot
con callous, hard, unfeeling
ant cold-blooded

hotchpotch *n syn* MISCELLANY 1, gallimaufry, hash, hodgepodge, jumble, medley, mélange, mishmash, patchwork, potpourri

hot dog *n syn* FRANKFURTER, dog, frank, wiener, wienerwurst, ‖wienie

hotel *n* an establishment for the lodging and entertainment especially of transients <spent their vacation at a resort *hotel*>
syn auberge, caravansary, hospice, hostel, hostelry, inn, lodge, public house, roadhouse, tavern
rel boardinghouse, lodging house, pension, rooming house, spa; boatel, motel, motor inn; ‖fleabag, ‖flophouse

hotfoot *adv syn* PELL-MELL, helter-skelter, hurry-scurry, impetuously, incontinently

hotfoot *vb syn* HURRY 2, barrel, beeline, hasten, highball, hustle, rocket, rush, smoke, speed

hotheaded *adj* ***syn*** RASH 1, brash, hasty, ill-advised, incautious, inconsiderate, mad-brained, madcap, reckless, thoughtless
ant cool

hothouse *n* ***syn*** BREEDING GROUND, forcing bed, forcing house, hotbed

hot spot *n* ***syn*** NIGHTCLUB, cabaret, café, discotheque, nightery, night spot, nitery, supper club, watering hole, watering place

hot–tempered *adj* **1** ***syn*** ILL-TEMPERED, bad-tempered, dyspeptic, ill-humored, ill-natured, ‖rusty, tempersome
2 ***syn*** IRASCIBLE, choleric, cranky, passionate, quick-tempered, ratty, temperish, testy, tetchy, touchy

hot water *n* **1** ***syn*** PREDICAMENT, box, corner, deep water, dilemma, fix, hole, jam, pickle, quagmire
2 ***syn*** TROUBLE 3, Dutch

hound *n* **1** ***syn*** DOG 1, bowwow, canine, ‖pooch, tyke
2 ***syn*** ADDICT, aficionado, buff, devotee, fan, habitué, lover, votary

hound *vb* ***syn*** BAIT 2, badger, bullyrag, chivy, heckle, hector, ride

house *n* **1** ***syn*** HABITATION 2, abode, commorancy, domicile, dwelling, home, residence, residency
2 ***syn*** FAMILY 2, folks, household, ménage
3 ***syn*** FAMILY 1, clan, folk, kindred, lineage, race, stock, tribe
4 ***syn*** ENTERPRISE 3, business, company, concern, establishment, firm, outfit

house *vb* **1** ***syn*** HARBOR 1, chamber, haven, roof, shelter, shield
2 ***syn*** HARBOR 2, bestow, billet, board, domicile, entertain, hut, lodge, put up, quarter

housebreak *vb* to commit an act of breaking open and entering with a felonious purpose the dwelling of another by day or night <was arrested again in September for *housebreaking*>
syn break in; *compare* BURGLARIZE, ROB 1
rel knock over, rob; ransack, rifle
idiom break and enter

household *n* ***syn*** FAMILY 2, folks, house, ménage

household *adj* ***syn*** DOMESTIC 1, family, home

housemaid *n* ***syn*** MAID 2, biddy, girl, handmaid, hired girl, maidservant

houseman *n* ***syn*** BOUNCER 2, chucker, ‖chucker-out

house of God ***syn*** HOUSE OF WORSHIP, church, house of prayer, tabernacle, temple

house of prayer ***syn*** HOUSE OF WORSHIP, church, house of God, tabernacle, temple

house of worship a building for religious exercises <there are many *houses of worship* in this city>
syn church, house of God, house of prayer, tabernacle, temple
rel abbey, basilica, bethel, cathedral, chantry, chapel, conventicle, ‖fane, ‖kirk, masjid, meetinghouse, minster, mosque, oratory, pagoda, sanctuary, shrine, stupa, synagogue
idiom the Lord's house

housing *n* ***syn*** SHELTER 2, quarterage

hovel *n* a small wretched dwelling place <migrants forced to live in *hovels*>
syn burrow, hole; *compare* HUT
rel hut, hutch, shack, shanty; pigpen, pigsty, sty

hover *vb* **1** ***syn*** FLIT 2, dance, flicker, flitter, flutter
2 ***syn*** HANG 3, float, poise

howbeit *adv* ***syn*** HOWEVER, after all, nevertheless, nonetheless, notwithstanding, still, still and all, though, withal, yet

howbeit *conj* ***syn*** THOUGH, albeit, although, much as, when, whereas, while

however *conj* ***syn*** ONLY, but, except, save, yet

however *adv* in spite of that <I accept your decision; I cannot, *however*, approve of it>
syn after all, howbeit, nevertheless, nonetheless, notwithstanding, per contra, still, still and all, though, withal, yet
idiom all the same, be that as it may, for all that, on the other hand

howl *vb* **1** to utter or emit a loud sustained doleful sound or outcry <the dogs *howled* through the night>
syn bay, quest, ululate, wail
rel bark, growl, yelp; blubber, cry, keen, weep, whimper; bawl, squall, yowl
2 ***syn*** YELL 2, scream, squeal, yip, yowl
3 ***syn*** BAWL 2, squawl, wail, yowl

howl *n* ***syn*** RIOT 2, ‖panic, scream, sidesplitter

hoyden *n* ***syn*** TOMBOY, gamine

hub *n* ***syn*** CENTER 2, focal point, focus, heart, nerve center, polestar, seat

hubbub *n* **1** ***syn*** DIN, babel, clamor, hullabaloo, jangle, pandemonium, racket, tintamarre, tumult, uproar
2 ***syn*** COMMOTION 4, clamor, hassle, hurly-burly, pother, to-do, tumult, turmoil, uproar, whirl

‖**hubby** *n* ***syn*** HUSBAND, lord, man, ‖master, mister, Mr., ‖old man

hubristic *adj* ***syn*** PROUD 1, arrogant, cavalier, disdainful, haughty, high-and-mighty, insolent, overbearing, supercilious, superior

huckster *n* ***syn*** PEDDLER, ‖arab, cheap-jack (*or* cheap-john), ‖duffer, hawker, higgler, monger, outcrier, packman, vendor

huckster *vb* **1** ***syn*** HAGGLE 2, bargain, chaffer, dicker, higgle, palter
2 ***syn*** PEDDLE 2, hawk, monger, vend

huddle *vb* **1** ***syn*** CROUCH, ‖crooch, hunch, scrooch (down)
2 ***syn*** CONFER 2, advise, collogue, confab, confabulate, consult, parley, powwow, treat

huddle (on) *vb* ***syn*** DON 1, assume, draw on, get on, put on, slip (on), throw

huddle *n* ***syn*** CONFUSION 3, ataxia, ‖ballup, chaos, clutter, disarray, disorder, muddle, snarl, topsy-turviness

hue *n* ***syn*** COLOR 1, cast, shade, tinge, tint, tone

huff *vb* **1** ***syn*** PANT 1, blow, gasp, heave, ‖pank, ‖pegh, puff
2 ***syn*** IRRITATE, grate, inflame, nettle, peeve, pique, provoke, put out, rile, roil

---

huff *n* ***syn*** OFFENSE 2, dudgeon, miff, pique, resentment, ‖snuff, umbrage

huffy *adj* **1** ***syn*** PROUD 1, arrogant, cavalier, disdainful, haughty, high-and-mighty, insolent, overbearing, supercilious, superior
2 ***syn*** IRRITABLE, fractious, fretful, peevish, pettish, petulant, querulous, snappish, waspish, waspy

hug *vb* ***syn*** EMBRACE 1, clasp, ‖clinch, ‖clip, ‖coll, enfold, press, squeeze

huge *adj* exceedingly or excessively large < *huge* corporations > <ate a *huge* dinner>
syn Antaean, behemothic, Brobdingnagian, Bunyanesque, colossal, cyclopean, dinosauric, elephantine, enormous, gargantuan, giant, gigantean, gigantesque, gigantic, Herculean, heroic, immense, jumbo, leviathan, lusty, mammoth, massive, massy, mastodonic, mighty, monster, monstrous, monumental, mountainous, planetary, prodigious, pythonic, ‖swapping, Titan, titanic, tremendous, unfathomed, untold, vast, walloping, whacking, whaling, whopping; *compare* GRAND 1
rel bulky, extensive, great, immeasurable, magnificent, towering; outsize, oversize
con diminutive, little, miniature, minute, petite, small, teeny, tiny, wee, weeny

hugely *adv* ***syn*** VERY 1, exceedingly, exceptionally, extremely, highly, notably, parlous, remarkably, strikingly, surpassingly

hugeness *n* ***syn*** ENORMITY 2, enormousness, immensity, magnitude, tremendousness, vastness

hugger–mugger *n* **1** ***syn*** SECRECY, hugger-muggery, hush, hush-hush, secretiveness, secretness, silence
2 ***syn*** CLUTTER 2, hash, jumble, jungle, litter, mash, muddle, rummage, scramble, tumble

hugger–mugger *adv* ***syn*** SECRETLY, by stealth, clandestinely, covertly, furtively, in camera, privately, stealthily, sub rosa, surreptitiously

hugger–mugger *adj* ***syn*** SECRET 1, clandestine, covert, furtive, hole-and-corner, hush-hush, sub-rosa, undercover, ‖underneath, under-the-table

hugger–muggery *n* ***syn*** SECRECY, hugger-mugger, hush, hush-hush, secretiveness, secretness, silence

hull *n* an outer covering of a fruit or seed <peanut *hulls*>
syn case, husk, pod, shell, shuck, skin, ‖slough
rel chaff; bark, peel, rind

hull *vb* ***syn*** SHUCK, husk, shell

hullabaloo *n* ***syn*** DIN, babel, clamor, hubbub, jangle, pandemonium, racket, tintamarre, tumult, uproar

hum *vb* to make a low prolonged sound <the wind *hummed* in the chimney>
syn bombinate, ‖bum, bumble, buzz, drone, ‖sowf, strum, thrum
rel moan, murmur, purr, vibrate, whisper
con howl, roar, shriek

syn synonym(s) ***rel*** related word(s)
idiom idiomatic equivalent(s) ***con*** contrasted word(s)
ant antonym(s) * vulgar
‖ use limited; if in doubt, see a dictionary
The first word in a synonym list when printed in SMALL CAPITALS shows where there is more information about the group. For a more efficient use of this book see Explanatory Notes.

human *adj* of, relating to, or characteristic of mankind <problems of *human* relationships>
syn hominine, mortal
rel anthropological, ethnologic, ethological; anthropoid, hominid, hominoid
con angelic, divine, superhuman; animal, brute, subhuman

human *n* a member of the human race <every *human* has a right to live>
syn being, body, ‖character, creature, individual, life, man, mortal, party, person, personage, soul, wight; *compare* MAN 3, MANKIND

humane *adj* ***syn*** CHARITABLE 1, altruistic, benevolent, eleemosynary, good, humanitarian, philanthropic
rel chickenhearted, compassionate, kindhearted, soft-hearted; benevolent, gentle, kind, kindly, mild
ant inhuman, inhumane

humanitarian *adj* ***syn*** CHARITABLE 1, altruistic, benevolent, eleemosynary, good, humane, philanthropic

humanity *n* ***syn*** MANKIND, flesh, Homo sapiens, humankind, man, mortality

humankind *n* ***syn*** MANKIND, flesh, Homo sapiens, humanity, man, mortality

humanoid *adj* ***syn*** ANTHROPOID, anthropomorphic, anthropomorphous, manlike

humble *adj* **1** lacking all signs of pride, aggressiveness, or self-assertiveness <accepted his success with *humble* appreciation>
syn lowly, meek, modest, unassuming
rel simple, unobtrusive, unostentatious, unpretentious; acquiescent, compliant, resigned; quiet, subdued, submissive
con ostentatious, pretentious, showy; vain, vainglorious; arrogant, disdainful, haughty, lordly, overbearing, proud, toplofty
ant conceited
2 ***syn*** IGNOBLE 1, base, baseborn, low, lowborn, lowly, mean, plebeian, unennobled, unwashed

humble *vb* to make lower in status, prestige, or esteem <his devotion to duty *humbled* his critics>
syn abase, bemean, cast down, debase, degrade, demean, humiliate, lower, sink
rel chagrin, mortify; abash, discomfit, embarrass
idiom bring low, take down a peg or two
con aggrandize, exalt, magnify

humbug *n* **1** ***syn*** IMPOSTURE, fake, flimflam, fraud, gyp, hoax, phony, sell, sham, spoof
2 ***syn*** IMPOSTOR, fake, faker, fraud, phony, pretender
3 ***syn*** NONSENSE 2, balderdash, blatherskite, bosh, bunkum, flapdoodle, hokum, malarkey, piffle, rot

humbug *vb* ***syn*** DECEIVE, beguile, betray, bluff, delude, double-cross, illude, juggle, mislead, take in

humdinger *n* ***syn*** ‖DILLY, ‖corker, crackerjack, ‖daisy, dandy, jim-dandy, ‖lulu, nifty, peach, ‖pip

humdrum *adj* ***syn*** DULL 9, banausic, blah, ‖dim, dreary, monotone, monotonous, pedestrian, plodding, stodgy

humdrum *n* ***syn*** MONOTONY, monotone, monotonousness

humid *adj* containing or characterized by an uncomfortable amount of atmospheric warmth and moisture <a *humid* climate>
syn mucky, muggy, soggy, sticky, sultry; *compare* STIFLING 1, STUFFY 1

rel clammy, dank, sodden; close, oppressive, stuffy; sweltering
con arid, dry; cool, crisp, fresh

humiliate *vb syn* HUMBLE, abase, bemean, cast down, debase, degrade, demean, lower, sink

humming *adj syn* BUSTLING, busy, fussy, hopping, hustling, lively, popping

humor *n* **1** *syn* DISPOSITION 3, character, complexion, individualism, individuality, makeup, nature, personality, temper, temperament
2 *syn* MOOD 1, mind, strain, temper, tone, vein
3 *syn* CAPRICE, bee, boutade, conceit, crotchet, fancy, freak, megrim, vagary, whim
4 that quality or element which appeals to a sense of the ludicrous or incongruous <see the *humor* in a situation>
syn comedy, comicality, comicalness, drollery, drollness, funniness, humorousness, wittiness
rel jocosity, jocularity, jocundity, jocundness; flippancy, levity, lightness; banter, chaffing, jesting, joking, kidding
con earnestness, seriousness, solemnity; depth, profundity
5 something that is or is designed to be humorous <his heavy *humor* fell flat>
syn wit
rel banter, chitchat, pleasantry, repartee
6 *syn* WIT 5, esprit
ant humorlessness

humor *vb* **1** *syn* INDULGE 1, cater (to), gratify
2 *syn* BABY, cater (to), cocker, coddle, cosset, cotton, indulge, mollycoddle, pamper, spoil

humorist *n* **1** *syn* WAG 1, card, comedian, joker, zany
2 a person noted for or specializing in humor <a writer best known as a *humorist*>
syn comedian, comic, droll, funnyman, jester, joker, jokester, quipster, wag, wit
rel buffoon, card, clown, cutup, gagman, gagster, jokesmith, merry-andrew, prankster, punster, zany; banterer, kidder

humorous *adj syn* WITTY, facetious, jocose, jocular

humorousness *n syn* HUMOR 4, comedy, comicality, comicalness, drollery, drollness, funniness, wittiness

humorsome *adj syn* MOODY, temperamental

‖**hump** *vb syn* CARRY 1, bear, buck, convey, ferry, ‖jag, lug, pack, tote, transport

hunch *vb syn* CROUCH, ‖crooch, huddle, scrooch (down)

hunch *n syn* LUMP 1, chunk, clod, clump, gob, hunk, nugget, wad

hunger *vb syn* LONG, ache, crave, hanker, lust, pine, sigh, thirst, yearn, yen

hungry *adj* feeling distressed from lack of food <a group of *hungry* children>
syn famished, ‖peckish, ravenous, starved, starving
rel rapacious, voracious
con full, glutted, gorged, sated, satiated
ant surfeited

hunk *n syn* LUMP 1, chunk, clod, clump, gob, hunch, nugget, wad

hunker (down) *vb syn* SQUAT, ‖quat, ‖swat

hunkers *n pl syn* BUTTOCKS, backside, behind, bottom, ‖butt, fanny, haunches, nates, posterior, rump

hunks *n pl but sing or pl in constr syn* MISER, chuff, moneygrubber, muckworm, nabal, niggard, ‖nipcheese, scrooge, skinflint, stiff

hunky–dory *adj syn* MARVELOUS 2, ‖cool, ‖dandy, divine, ‖galluptious, glorious, groovy, hot, ‖keen, ‖neat

Hunnic *adj syn* BARBARIAN 1, barbarous, Gothic, Hunnish, rude, savage, uncivil, uncivilized, uncultivated, wild

Hunnish *adj syn* BARBARIAN 1, barbarous, Gothic, Hunnic, rude, savage, uncivil, uncivilized, uncultivated, wild

hunt *vb* **1** to search for or pursue (game or prey) for the purpose of capturing or killing <*hunted* deer in bow-and-arrow season only>
syn chase, run
rel dog, ferret, hawk, hound; course, drive, stalk, start, still-hunt, track; capture, kill, snare; gun, shoot
idiom go hunting
2 *syn* SEEK 1, cast about, ferret out, quest, search (for *or* out)

hunt (down *or* out *or* up) *vb syn* RUMMAGE 3, dig out, rout

hunting *n* the act or practice of seeking and taking wild and especially game animals <lived by *hunting* and fishing>
syn chase, venery
rel angling, coursing, falconry, fishing, gunning, hawking, shooting

hurdle *n syn* OBSTACLE, bar, hamper, impediment, mountain, obstruction, rub, snag, stumbling block, traverse

hurdle *vb* **1** *syn* CLEAR 8, leap, negotiate, over, overleap, surmount, vault
2 *syn* JUMP 1, bounce, bound, hop, leap, lop, saltate, spring, vault
3 *syn* OVERCOME 1, conquer, down, lick, master, surmount, throw

hurl *vb syn* THROW 1, ‖bung, cast, fire, fling, heave, launch, pitch, sling, toss

hurly–burly *n syn* COMMOTION 4, clamor, hassle, hubbub, pother, to-do, tumult, turmoil, uproar, whirl

hurrah *n* **1** *syn* PASSION 6, ardor, calenture, enthusiasm, fervor, fire, zeal
2 *syn* COMMOTION 3, ‖catouse, coil, furore, fuss, ruckus, rumpus, shindy, to-do, uproar
3 *syn* ARGUMENT 2, contention, controversy, dispute, rumpus

hurricane *n* a violent rotating storm or system of winds originating in the tropics and often moving into temperate latitudes <the *hurricane* struck the coast early today>
syn tropical cyclone, tropical storm, typhoon, ‖willy-willy; *compare* TORNADO, WHIRLWIND 1
rel williwaw

---

hurried *adj* ***syn*** PRECIPITATE 1, abrupt, hasty, headlong, impetuous, precipitant, precipitous, rushing, subitaneous, sudden

ant unhurried

hurriedness *n* ***syn*** HASTE 2, hastiness, precipitance, precipitancy, precipitateness, precipitation, rush

hurry *vb* **1** ***syn*** SPEED 3, accelerate, hasten, quicken, shake up, step up, swiften

2 to proceed or move with dispatch < *hurry* home after school >

syn barrel, barrelhouse, beeline, bucket, bullet, bustle, ‖dust, fleet, flit, fly, haste, hasten, highball, hotfoot, hustle, ‖nip, pelt, rock, rocket, run, rush, scoot, scour, ‖skeet, skin, smoke, speed, stave, ‖tatter, whirl, whish, whisk, whiz, zip; *compare* RUSH 1

rel jog, peg, skelp, trot; bowl (along), breeze; dig in; post

idiom get a move on, go (*or* move) like lightning, make tracks, step on it, step on the gas

con creep, dally, dawdle, drag, lag, linger, loiter, poke, saunter, stroll

hurry *n* ***syn*** HASTE 1, celerity, dispatch, expedition, expeditiousness, hustle, rustle, speed, speediness, swiftness

hurry-scurry *adv* ***syn*** PELL-MELL, helter-skelter, hotfoot, impetuously, incontinently

hurt *vb* **1** ***syn*** INJURE 1, blemish, damage, harm, impair, mar, prejudice, spoil, tarnish, vitiate

rel abuse, afflict, mistreat, misuse

ant benefit

2 ***syn*** INJURE 3, wound

3 ***syn*** DISTRESS 2, aggrieve, constrain, grieve, injure, pain

4 to experience or be the seat of sharp physical distress < my arm still *hurts* >

syn ache, pain, ‖suffer; *compare* SMART

hurt *n* ***syn*** INJURY 1, damage, harm, mischief, outrage, ruin

hurtful *adj* **1** ***syn*** HARMFUL, damaging, deleterious, detrimental, evil, injurious, mischievous, nocuous, prejudicial, prejudicious

con harmless, innocuous

2 ***syn*** PAINFUL 1, aching, afflictive, algetic, hurting, sore

hurting *adj* ***syn*** PAINFUL 1, aching, afflictive, algetic, hurtful, sore

husband *n* the male partner in a marriage < neglected his responsibilities as a *husband* >

syn ‖hubby, lord, man, ‖master, mister, Mr., ‖old man

rel consort, helpmate, helpmeet, mate, other half, spouse; benedict, bridegroom

husbanding *n* ***syn*** CONSERVATION 1, conservancy, preserval, preservation, salvation, saving

ant squandering

---

syn synonym(s) ***rel*** related word(s)

idiom idiomatic equivalent(s) ***con*** contrasted word(s)

ant antonym(s) * vulgar

‖ use limited; if in doubt, see a dictionary

The first word in a synonym list when printed in SMALL CAPITALS shows where there is more information about the group. For a more efficient use of this book see Explanatory Notes.

husbandry *n* **1** ***syn*** ECONOMY, forehandedness, frugality, providence, prudence, thrift, thriftiness

2 ***syn*** AGRICULTURE, farming

hush *vb* ***syn*** SILENCE, choke (off), quiet, ‖quieten, shush, shut up, still

hush (up) *vb* ***syn*** SUPPRESS 3, burke, stifle

hush *adj* ***syn*** STILL 3, hushful, noiseless, quiet, silent, soundless, stilly, whist

hush *n* **1** ***syn*** QUIET 1, calm, lull

2 ***syn*** SECRECY, hugger-mugger, hugger-muggery, hush-hush, secretiveness, secretness, silence

hushed *adj* **1** ***syn*** CALM 1, halcyon, placid, quiet, still, stilly, untroubled

2 ***syn*** PRIVATE 2, closet, confidential, inside

hushful *adj* ***syn*** STILL 3, hush, noiseless, quiet, silent, soundless, stilly, whist

hush-hush *adj* ***syn*** SECRET 1, clandestine, covert, hole-and-corner, hugger-mugger, sub-rosa, surreptitious, undercover, ‖underneath, under-the-table

hush-hush *n* ***syn*** SECRECY, hugger-mugger, hugger-muggery, hush, secretiveness, secretness, silence

husk *n* ***syn*** HULL, case, pod, shell, shuck, skin, ‖slough

husk *vb* ***syn*** SHUCK, hull, shell

husky *adj* ***syn*** HOARSE 1, croaking, croaky, gruff

husky *adj* **1** big and muscular < a *husky* man carried in the trunks >

syn beefy, burly, hefty

rel brawny, muscular, well-built; stalwart, stout, strapping, strong, sturdy; Herculean, mighty, powerful; Bunyanesque, gigantic

con delicate, fragile, frail; puny, scrawny, slight; elfin; mousey

2 ***syn*** LARGE 1, big, bull, fat, great, oversize

hussy *n* **1** ***syn*** WANTON, baggage, ‖bimbo, jade, jezebel, slattern, slut, tramp, trull, wench

2 ***syn*** MINX, jade, malapert, saucebox, slut, snip

hustle *vb* **1** ***syn*** PUSH 2, bulldoze, elbow, jostle, press, ‖shog, shoulder, shove

2 ***syn*** HURRY 2, bustle, ‖dust, fly, hasten, hotfoot, ‖nip, run, rush, speed

hustle *n* ***syn*** HASTE 1, celerity, dispatch, expedition, expeditiousness, hurry, rustle, speed, speediness, swiftness

hustler *n* **1** an alert enterprising individual < he's a *hustler,* eager to get ahead in the world >

syn dynamo, go-getter, live wire, peeler, rustler, self-starter

rel humdinger, hummer; new broom; doer, powerhouse

idiom busy bee

con dawdler, idler; slow coach, slowpoke, stick-in-the-mud

2 ***syn*** PROSTITUTE, bawd, call girl, drab, harlot, ‖hooker, moll, streetwalker, ‖tomato, whore

hustling *adj* ***syn*** BUSTLING, busy, fussy, hopping, humming, lively, popping

hut *n* a small, simply constructed dwelling often for temporary or intermittent occupancy < the shepherds lived in *huts* in the summer >

syn ‖box, cabin ‖caboose, camp, cot, cottage, lodge, shack, shanty; *compare* BUILDING, EDIFICE, HOVEL

rel cabana, chalet, crib, dacha, hovel, hutch, lean-to, shed, summer house

hut *vb* ***syn*** HARBOR 2, bestow, billet, board, domicile, entertain, lodge, quarter, room, roost

Hyblaean *adj* ***syn*** MELLIFLUOUS, golden, honeyed, liquid, mellifluent, mellow

hybrid *n* an offspring produced by parents of different strains, breeds, varieties, species, or genera <the mule is a *hybrid* of the ass and the horse>
syn bastard, cross, crossbred, crossbreed, half blood, half-breed, mongrel, mule
rel incross, incrossbred, outcross; combination, composite, mixture
con pureblood, purebred, thoroughbred

hybridize *vb* ***syn*** CROSS 4, crossbreed, cross-mate, interbreed, intercross

hydrant *n* ***syn*** FAUCET, cock, gate, petcock, spigot, stopcock, tap, valve

‖**hydro** *n* ***syn*** SPA 1, baths, springs, watering place, wells

hydroponics *n* the growing of plants in nutrient solution and without soil <tomatoes grown by *hydroponics*>
syn aquiculture, nutriculture
idiom soilless agriculture

hygienic *adj* ***syn*** HEALTHFUL, good, healthy, salubrious, salutary, salutiferous, wholesome
ant unhygienic

hymeneal *adj* ***syn*** MATRIMONIAL, conjugal, connubial, marital, married, nuptial, spousal, wedded

hymn *n* ***syn*** SONG 2, aria, descant, ditty, lay, lied

hymn *vb* **1** ***syn*** PRAISE 2, bless, celebrate, cry up, eulogize, extol, glorify, laud, magnify, panegyrize
2 ***syn*** SING, carol, chant, descant, intone, trill, troll, warble

hypaethral *adj* ***syn*** OUTDOOR, alfresco, open-air, out-of-door, outside

hyperbole *n* ***syn*** EXAGGERATION, coloring, embellishment, embroidering, overstatement
con depreciation, minimization, understatement
ant litotes

hypercritical *adj* ***syn*** CRITICAL 1, captious, carping, caviling, cavillous, censorious, critic, faultfinding, overcritical

hypercriticize *vb* ***syn*** QUIBBLE 1, cavil, chicane

hypnotic *adj* ***syn*** SOPORIFIC 1, narcotic, opiate, sleepy, somnifacient, somniferous, somnific, somnolent, somnorific, soporiferous

hypocorism *n* ***syn*** NICKNAME, byname, byword, ‖handle, ‖moniker, sobriquet

hypocrisy *n* the pretense or affectation of having virtues, principles, or beliefs that one does not actually have <political *hypocrisy*>
syn cant, hypocriticalness, pecksniffery, pharisaicalness, pharisaism, sanctimoniousness, sanctimony, sham, Tartuffery, Tartuffism
rel pietism, religiosity; casuistry, glibness, insincerity, self-righteousness, unctiousness; charlatanry, humbug, quackery
con candidness, fairness, openness; honesty, probity, truthfulness
ant sincerity

hypocrite *n* one who affects virtues, qualities, or attitudes he does not have <don't be a *hypocrite*—if you don't approve, say so>
syn dissembler, dissimulator, lip server, pharisee, Tartuffe, whited sepulcher
rel pietist; actor, attitudinizer, bluffer, charlatan, faker, four-flusher, fraud, humbug, impostor, masquerader, phony, poser, poseur, pretender, quack, sham

hypocritical *adj* **1** characterized by hypocrisy <*hypocritical* compliments>
syn canting, pecksniffian, pharisaic, pharisaical, sanctimonious, self-righteous
rel goody-goody, holier-than-thou, moralistic, pietistic, religiose; casuistic; affected, insincere; bland, glib, mealymouthed, oily, smooth, smooth-spoken, smooth-tongued, unctuous
con honest, open, straightforward
ant sincere
2 ***syn*** INSINCERE, ambidextrous, double, double-dealing, double-faced, doublehearted, double-minded, double-tongued, left-handed, mala fide

hypocriticalness *n* ***syn*** HYPOCRISY, cant, pecksniffery, pharisaicalness, pharisaism, sanctimoniousness, sanctimony, Tartuffery, Tartuffism
ant sincerity

hypostatize *vb* ***syn*** MATERIALIZE 2, entify, reify

hypothesis *n* ***syn*** THEORY 1, supposal

hypothetical *adj* **1** ***syn*** SUPPOSED 1, conjectural, putative, reputed, suppositional, suppositious, supposititious, suppositive, suppository
rel doubtful, problematic
2 ***syn*** ABSTRACT 1, ideal, theoretical, transcendent, transcendental

I

icky *adj* ***syn*** OFFENSIVE, disgusting, horrible, loathsome, nasty, noisome, repellent, revolting, sickening, vile

iconographic *adj* ***syn*** PICTORIAL 1, graphic, illustrational, illustrative, illustratory, pictoric

icy *adj* **1** ***syn*** COLD 1, arctic, chill, chilly, freezing, frigid, frosty, gelid, glacial, shivery
ant fiery
2 ***syn*** COLD 2, chill, emotionless, frigid, glacial, indifferent, unemotional
ant fiery

idea *n* what exists in the mind as a representation (as of something comprehended) or as a formulation (as of a plan) <that's not my *idea* of a good time>
syn apprehension, conceit, concept, conception, image, impression, intellection, notion, perception, thought
rel assumption, belief, conclusion, conviction, estimation, feeling, inclination, judgment, opinion, persuasion, presumption, reaction, reflection, sentiment, view; conjecture, guess, hypothesis, speculation, supposition, surmise, suspicion, theory; caprice, fancy, fantasy, vagary, whim, whimsy; brainstorm, inspiration

ideal *adj* **1** ***syn*** ABSTRACT 1, hypothetical, theoretical, transcendent, transcendental
ant actual
2 ***syn*** CONCEPTUAL, ideational, notional
3 constituting a standard (as of perfection or excellence) <the *ideal* man of letters>
syn flawless, indefectible, model
rel archetypal, archetypical, prototypal, prototypical
con average, normal, representative, typical
4 ***syn*** PERFECT 3, model, very
5 ***syn*** TYPICAL 1, classic, classical, exemplary, model, paradigmatic, prototypal, prototypical, quintessential, representative

ideal *n* **1** ***syn*** MODEL 2, archetype, beau ideal, ensample, example, exemplar, mirror, paradigm, pattern, standard
2 ***syn*** PARAGON, jewel, nonesuch, nonpareil, phoenix

idealist *n* ***syn*** DREAMER, castle-builder, ideologue, utopian, visionary

idealist *adj* ***syn*** IDEALISTIC, utopian, visionary

idealistic *adj* characterized by idealism <made an *idealistic* speech on human rights>
syn idealist, utopian, visionary
rel impractical, poetical, quixotic, romantic, starry, starry-eyed, unrealistic
con empirical, matter-of-fact, practical, pragmatic, rational, realistic
ant unidealistic

---

syn synonym(s) *rel* related word(s)
idiom idiomatic equivalent(s) *con* contrasted word(s)
ant antonym(s) * vulgar
‖ use limited; if in doubt, see a dictionary
The first word in a synonym list when printed in SMALL CAPITALS shows where there is more information about the group. For a more efficient use of this book see Explanatory Notes.

ideational *adj* ***syn*** CONCEPTUAL, ideal, notional

identic *adj* ***syn*** SAME 2, duplicate, equal, equivalent, identical, indistinguishable, tantamount
ant nonidentical

identical *adj* **1** ***syn*** SAME 1, exact, selfsame, very
2 ***syn*** SAME 2, duplicate, equal, equivalent, identic, indistinguishable, tantamount
ant nonidentical

identicalness *n* ***syn*** IDENTITY 1, oneness, sameness, selfsameness

identification *n* ***syn*** RECOGNITION 1, apperception, assimilation

identify *vb* to establish the identity of <the culprit was *identified* by his fingerprints>
syn determinate, diagnose, diagnosticate, distinguish, finger, pinpoint, place, recognize, spot
rel find; determine, establish, make out, pick out, select, separate (out)

identity *n* **1** the quality of being the same in all that constitutes the objective reality of separate things <the *identity* of the two texts is exact>
syn identicalness, oneness, sameness, selfsameness
rel agreement, likeness, resemblance, semblance, similarity, similitude; correspondence, equality, equivalence; uniformity
con dissimilarity, dissimilitude, unlikeness, unsimilarity
ant nonidentity
2 ***syn*** INDIVIDUALITY 4, ipseity, personality, seity, selfdom, selfhood, selfness, singularity

ideologue *n* ***syn*** DREAMER, castle-builder, idealist, utopian, visionary

ideology *n* an overall view of or attitude toward life <an *ideology* based on tolerance>
syn credo, creed, weltanschauung
rel outlook, philosophy, view

idiom *n* ***syn*** LANGUAGE 1, dialect, speech, tongue, vernacular

idiosyncratic *adj* **1** ***syn*** CHARACTERISTIC, diacritic, diagnostic, distinctive, individual, peculiar, proper
2 ***syn*** STRANGE 4, curious, eccentric, erratic, odd, oddball, peculiar, queer, singular, weird

idiot *n* **1** ***syn*** FOOL 1, ass, *damfool, donkey, imbecile, jackass, jerk, nincompoop, ninny, tomfool
2 ***syn*** FOOL 2, jester, motley
3 ***syn*** FOOL 4, ament, cretin, ‖feeb, half-wit, imbecile, moron, natural, simpleton, zany
4 ***syn*** DUNCE, dullard, dullhead, dumbbell, ‖dummkopf, dummy, ignoramus, moron, simpleton, stupid

idle *adj* **1** ***syn*** VAIN 1, empty, hollow, nugatory, otiose
2 ***syn*** VACANT 4, unused
3 ***syn*** INACTIVE, asleep, inert, passive, quiet, sleepy
ant busy

idle *vb* to spend time in idleness <people *idling* in the park>
syn ‖brogue, bum, dawdle, diddle, diddle-daddle, drone, goldbrick, ‖goof (off), ‖lallygag, laze, lazy, loaf, loiter, loll, lounge
rel relax, repose, rest; amble, linger, mooch, mosey,

saunter, stroll, tarry; hang around, sit around, sit back, sit by
idiom dog it, kill time, lie around, mark time

idleheaded *adj* ***syn*** FOOLISH 2, absurd, ‖balmy, crazy, harebrained, insane, loony, ‖potty, silly, wacky

idleness *n* ***syn*** SLOTH 1, indolence, laze, laziness, slothfulness, slouch, sluggishness

idler *n* ***syn*** SLUGGARD, bum, dolittle, do-nothing, faineant, lazybones, loafer, slouch, slug, slugabed

idolatry *n* ***syn*** ADORATION, idolization, worship

idolization *n* ***syn*** ADORATION, idolatry, worship

idolize *vb* ***syn*** ADORE 3, dote (on *or* upon), worship
idiom worship the ground one walks on

iffy *adj* ***syn*** UNCERTAIN 1, capricious, chancy, erratic, fluctuant, incalculable, unpredictable, whimsical

ignis fatuus *n* ***syn*** DELUSION 1, hallucination, illusion, mirage, phantasm

ignitable *adj* ***syn*** COMBUSTIBLE 1, burnable, flammable, inflammable

ignite *vb* ***syn*** LIGHT 1, enkindle, fire, inflame, kindle

ignited *adj* ***syn*** BURNING 1, ablaze, afire, aflame, alight, blazing, fiery, flaming, flaring, lighted

ignoble *adj* **1** belonging to or characteristic of socially or economically inferior classes <a person of *ignoble* antecedents>
syn base, baseborn, humble, low, lowborn, lowly, mean, plebeian, unennobled, unwashed
rel coarse, common, homely, inferior, inglorious, modest, ordinary, peasant, plain, poor, popular, simple, vulgar
con highborn, highbred, wellborn, well-bred; eminent, high, lofty, proud, superior
ant noble
2 ***syn*** BASE 3, abject, despicable, low, mean, scurvy, servile, sordid, vile, wretched
ant noble

ignominious *adj* ***syn*** DISREPUTABLE 1, discreditable, disgraceful, dishonorable, inglorious, shabby, shady, shameful, shoddy, unrespectable

ignominy *n* ***syn*** DISGRACE, discredit, disesteem, dishonor, disrepute, infamy, obloquy, odium, opprobrium, shame
rel contempt, despite, disdain, scorn; chagrin, mortification
con glory, honor; esteem, respect

ignoramus *n* ***syn*** DUNCE, dullard, dullhead, dumbbell, ‖dummkopf, dummy, idiot, moron, simpleton, stupid

ignorance *n* **1** the state of being unlearned <the blight of *ignorance*>
syn benightedness, illiteracy
rel callowness, greenness, inexperience, naiveté, rawness, simpleness, simplicity, uncouthness, uncultivation, unsophistication; empty-headedness, unintelligence, witlessness; know-nothingism, philistinism
con education, enlightenment, erudition, learning, literacy
2 the state of being unaware or uninformed <*ignorance* of the law>
syn innocence, inscience, nescience, unacquaintance, unacquaintedness, unawareness, unfamiliarity, unknowingness
con acquaintance, acquaintanceship, experience; awareness, familiarity, knowledgeableness

ignorant *adj* **1** lacking knowledge or education <an *ignorant* boy with no taste for school>
syn benighted, empty-headed, illiterate, know-nothing, rude, uneducated, uninstructed, unlettered, unschooled, untaught, untutored
rel lowbrow, uncultured, unintellectual; callow, green, inexperienced; crude, gross, raw, uncouth; ingenuous, naive, simple, unsophisticated
con educated, erudite, learned, literate
2 lacking information on or awareness of something <was *ignorant* of the circumstances surrounding the affair>
syn incognizant, inconversant, oblivious, unacquainted, unaware, unfamiliar, uninformed, uninstructed, unknowing, unwitting
idiom in the dark
con aware, conscious, conversant, informed, knowing, knowledgeable
3 ***syn*** BACKWARD 5, benighted, unenlightened, unprogressive

ignore *vb* ***syn*** NEGLECT, blink (at *or* away), discount, disregard, fail, forget, omit, overlook, overpass, slight
rel avoid, evade

ilk *n* ***syn*** TYPE, breed, character, description, kidney, kind, nature, sort, stripe, variety

ill *adj* **1** ***syn*** EVIL 5, bad, unfavorable
ant good
2 ***syn*** HARMFUL, bad, damaging, deleterious, detrimental, evil, hurtful, injurious, nocent, nocuous
3 ***syn*** SICK 1, down
4 ***syn*** RUDE 6, discourteous, disgracious, disrespectful, ill-bred, ill-mannered, impertinent, impolite, uncivil, ungracious
5 ***syn*** HOSTILE 1, inimicable, inimical, unfriendly

ill *n* **1** ***syn*** EVIL 1
ant benefit
2 ***syn*** DISEASE 1, affection, ailment, complaint, condition, disorder, infirmity, malady, sickness, syndrome

ill–adapted *adj* ***syn*** UNFIT 1, ill-suited, inappropriate, inapt, unfitted, unmeet, unsuitable, unsuited

ill–advised *adj* **1** ***syn*** RASH 1, brash, hasty, hotheaded, incautious, inconsiderate, mad-brained, madcap, reckless, thoughtless
2 ***syn*** INADVISABLE, impolitic, imprudent, inexpedient, unadvisable, unexpedient
ant well-advised
3 ***syn*** UNWISE, ill-judged, impolitic, imprudent, indiscreet, injudicious
ant well-advised

illation *n* **1** ***syn*** INFERENCE 1, deduction, judgment, ratiocination
2 ***syn*** INFERENCE 2, conclusion, deduction, judgment, ratiocination, sequitur

---

syn synonym(s) | *rel* related word(s)
idiom idiomatic equivalent(s) | *con* contrasted word(s)
ant antonym(s) | * vulgar
‖ use limited; if in doubt, see a dictionary
The first word in a synonym list when printed in SMALL CAPITALS shows where there is more information about the group. For a more efficient use of this book see Explanatory Notes.

ill–behaved *adj* ***syn*** NAUGHTY 1, bad, misbehaving, mischievous, paw

ill–boding *adj* ***syn*** OMINOUS, apocalyptic, baleful, baneful, dire, fateful, ill-omened, inauspicious, unlucky, unpropitious

ill–bred *adj* **1** ***syn*** BOORISH, churlish, cloddish, loutish, lowbred, rugged, uncivilized, uncultured, unpolished, unrefined
ant well-bred
2 ***syn*** RUDE 6, discourteous, disgracious, disrespectful, ill-mannered, impertinent, impolite, incivil, uncivil, ungracious
ant well-bred, well-mannered

ill–chosen *adj* ***syn*** INFELICITOUS, awkward, graceless, inept, unfortunate, unhappy

ill–defined *adj* ***syn*** FAINT 2, blear, bleary, dim, fuzzy, indistinct, shadowy, unclear, undefined, vague
ant well-defined

illegal *adj* ***syn*** UNLAWFUL, criminal, illegitimate, illicit, lawless, wrongful
rel banned, forbidden, interdicted, prohibited, proscribed, outlawed, unauthorized, unlicensed, unwarranted; felonious; contraband, hot; actionable, irregular
con authorized, lawful, licensed, licit, permitted, regular, right
ant legal

illegality *n* the quality or state of being illegal <the *illegality* of an act>
syn illegitimacy, illicitness, unlawfulness
rel badness, impropriety, wrongness
con lawfulness, legitimacy, licitness; propriety
ant legality

illegible *adj* incapable of being read or deciphered <an *illegible* signature>
syn indecipherable, undecipherable, unreadable
rel faint, indistinct, obscure, unclear
ant legible, readable

illegitimacy *n* **1** the state or condition of being born out of wedlock <he accepted the fact of his *illegitimacy*>
syn bastardy, illegitimateness, supposititiousness
rel bar sinister
ant legitimacy, legitimateness
2 ***syn*** ILLEGALITY, illicitness, unlawfulness
ant legitimacy, legitimateness

illegitimate *adj* **1** not recognized by law as lawful offspring <an *illegitimate* child>
syn baseborn, bastard, fatherless, misbegotten, natural, spurious, supposititious, unfathered
rel birthless; adulterine
ant legitimate
2 ***syn*** UNLAWFUL, criminal, illegal, illicit, lawless, wrongful
ant legitimate

---

syn synonym(s) *rel* related word(s)
idiom idiomatic equivalent(s) *con* contrasted word(s)
ant antonym(s) * vulgar
‖ use limited; if in doubt, see a dictionary
The first word in a synonym list when printed in SMALL CAPITALS shows where there is more information about the group. For a more efficient use of this book see Explanatory Notes.

illegitimate *n* ***syn*** BASTARD 1, by-blow, catch colt, chance child, come-by-chance, filius nullius, filius populi, love child, natural child, woods colt
ant legitimate

illegitimateness *n* ***syn*** ILLEGITIMACY 1, bastardy, supposititiousness
ant legitimacy, legitimateness

ill–famed *adj* ***syn*** INFAMOUS 1, notorious, opprobrious

ill–fated *adj* ***syn*** UNLUCKY, hapless, ill-starred, luckless, misfortunate, star-crossed, unfortunate, unhappy, untoward

ill–favored *adj* **1** ***syn*** UGLY 2, hideous, ill-looking, unbeautiful, uncomely, unsightly
ant well-favored
2 ***syn*** OBJECTIONABLE, exceptionable, inadmissible, unacceptable, undesirable, unwanted, unwelcome

ill–flavored *adj* ***syn*** UNPALATABLE 1, distasteful, flat, flavorless, insipid, savorless, tasteless, unappetizing, unsavory

ill–humored *adj* ***syn*** ILL-TEMPERED, bad-tempered, dyspeptic, hot-tempered, ill-natured, ‖rusty, tempersome
ant good-humored, good-natured

illiberal *adj* unwilling or unable to grasp the point of view of others <had the *illiberal* outlook of an old-time schoolmaster>
syn bigoted, brassbound, hidebound, intolerant, narrow, narrow-minded, small-minded, unenlarged
rel biased, jaundiced, one-sided, opinionated, partial, partisan, prejudiced; grudging, little, mean, paltry, petty, small, uncharitable, ungenerous; insular, parochial, provincial; rigid, rigorous, stringent
con broad-minded, open-minded, tolerant, unbigoted; advanced, progressive, radical
ant liberal

illicit *adj* ***syn*** UNLAWFUL, criminal, illegal, illegitimate, lawless, wrongful
ant licit

illicitness *n* ***syn*** ILLEGALITY, illegitimacy, unlawfulness

illimitable *adj* ***syn*** INFINITE 1, eternal, perdurable, sempiternal, supertemporal
rel endless, interminable
ant limitable; limited

illiteracy *n* ***syn*** IGNORANCE 1, benightedness

illiterate *adj* ***syn*** IGNORANT 1, benighted, empty-headed, know-nothing, rude, uneducated, uninstructed, unlettered, untaught, untutored
ant literate; erudite

illiterate *n* one who cannot read or write <the training of adult *illiterates*>
syn analphabet
rel functional illiterate, semiliterate, subliterate
ant literate

ill–judged *adj* ***syn*** UNWISE, ill-advised, impolitic, imprudent, indiscreet, injudicious

ill–kempt *adj* ***syn*** SLOVENLY 1, careless, disheveled, messy, slipshod, sloppy, uncombed, unkempt, unneat, untidy

ill–looking *adj* ***syn*** UGLY 2, hideous, ill-favored, unbeautiful, uncomely, unsightly
ant good-looking, ‖well-looked

ill–mannered *adj* ***syn*** RUDE 6, discourteous, disgracious, disrespectful, ill-bred, impertinent, impolite, incivil, uncivil, ungracious *ant* well-bred, well-mannered

ill–natured *adj syn* ILL-TEMPERED, bad-tempered, dyspeptic, hot-tempered, ill-humored, ‖rusty, tempersome
ant good-humored, good-natured

illness *n syn* SICKNESS 1, affliction, diseasedness, disorder, indisposition, infirmity, unhealth
ant health

illogical *adj* contrary to or devoid of logic <came to an *illogical* conclusion from the facts presented>
syn fallacious, invalid, irrational, mad, nonrational, reasonless, sophistic, unreasonable, unreasoned; *compare* FALSE 1
rel inconsistent; plausible, specious; unscientific, unsound; absurd, meaningless, senseless
idiom without rhyme or reason
con rational, reasonable, sensible; sane, sound, valid
ant logical

ill–omened *adj syn* OMINOUS, apocalyptic, baleful, baneful, dire, fateful, ill-boding, inauspicious, unlucky, unpropitious
ant auspicious

ill–seasoned *adj syn* UNSEASONABLE 1, ill-timed, inopportune, malapropos, mistimed, untimely
ant seasonable

ill–starred *adj syn* UNLUCKY, hapless, ill-fated, luckless, misfortunate, star-crossed, unfortunate, unhappy, untoward
rel bodeful, fateful, foreboding, ominous, portentous; baleful, malefic, malign, sinister; unfavorable, unpromising, unpropitious

ill–suited *adj syn* UNFIT 1, ill-adapted, inappropriate, inapt, unfitted, unmeet, unsuitable, unsuited

ill–tempered *adj* having a bad temper <an *ill-tempered* old man>
syn bad-tempered, dyspeptic, hot-tempered, ill-humored, ill-natured, ‖rusty, tempersome
rel crabbed, surly; fractious, huffy, irritable, peevish, petulant, querulous, snappish, sour, waspish; shrewish, vixenish
con calm, easy, placid, serene, tranquil; amiable, complaisant, considerate, good-natured, kindly, obliging, tolerant
ant good-tempered, sweet-tempered, well-tempered

ill–timed *adj* **1** *syn* UNSEASONABLE 1, ill-seasoned, inopportune, malapropos, mistimed, untimely
ant seasonable
2 *syn* IMPROPER 1, inappropriate, inept, malapropos, unbecoming, unbefitting, unseasonable, unseemly, unsuitable, untimely

ill–treat *vb syn* ABUSE 4, ill-use, maltreat, mistreat, misuse, outrage
rel aggrieve, harass, harry, molest
con befriend, relieve, succor; countenance, encourage, favor, patronize

illude *vb syn* DECEIVE, beguile, betray, bluff, delude, double-cross, humbug, juggle, mislead, take in

illume *vb* **1** *syn* ILLUMINATE 1, illumine, light, lighten
2 *syn* ILLUMINATE 2, edify, enlighten, illumine, improve, irradiate, uplift

illuminant *adj syn* ENLIGHTENING, illuminating, illuminative, illumining

illuminate *vb* **1** to supply with physical light <a room dimly *illuminated* by firelight>
syn illume, illumine, light, lighten
rel brighten; irradiate; floodlight, highlight, spotlight; fire, ignite, kindle
con blur, cloud, darken, dim, dull, obscure, pale
2 to supply with spiritual or intellectual light <the worth of a truly *illuminating* book>
syn edify, enlighten, illume, illumine, improve, irradiate, uplift
rel better, improve; ennoble, exalt, refine; finish, mature, perfect, polish
con becloud, cloud, darken, obfuscate, obscure, overshadow, shadow
3 *syn* CLARIFY 2, clear, clear up, elucidate, explain, illustrate
rel construe, define, dramatize, expound, express, gloss, interpret
idiom shed light on (*or* upon)
con baffle, confound, confuse, mystify, pose, puzzle, stump

illuminati *n pl syn* INTELLIGENTSIA, clerisy, intellectuals, literati

illuminating *adj syn* ENLIGHTENING, illuminant, illuminative, illumining

illuminative *adj syn* ENLIGHTENING, illuminant, illuminating, illumining

illumine *vb* **1** *syn* ILLUMINATE 1, illume, light, lighten
2 *syn* ILLUMINATE 2, edify, enlighten, illume, improve, irradiate, uplift

illumining *adj syn* ENLIGHTENING, illuminant, illuminating, illuminative

ill–use *vb syn* ABUSE 4, ill-treat, maltreat, mistreat, misuse, outrage
con befriend, relieve, succor; countenance, encourage, favor, patronize

illusion *n* **1** *syn* DELUSION 1, hallucination, ignis fatuus, mirage, phantasm
rel invention; bubble, chimera, dream, will-o'-the-wisp; appearance, seeming, semblance
2 *syn* PIPE DREAM, bubble, chimera, dream, fantasy (*or* phantasy), ‖pipe, rainbow

illusionist *n syn* MAGICIAN 2, conjurer, trickster

illusive *adj syn* APPARENT 2, Barmecidal, illusory, ostensible, seeming, semblant

illusory *adj* **1** *syn* FICTITIOUS 1, chimerical, fanciful, fantastic, fictional, fictive, imaginary, suppositious, supposititious, unreal
ant factual
2 *syn* APPARENT 2, Barmecidal, illusive, ostensible, seeming, semblant
rel chimerical, fanciful, fantastic, imaginary, unreal, visionary; deceptive, delusive, delusory, misleading
con actual, real, veritable; authentic, true, valid
ant factual

---

syn synonym(s) *rel* related word(s)
idiom idiomatic equivalent(s) *con* contrasted word(s)
ant antonym(s) * vulgar
‖ use limited; if in doubt, see a dictionary
The first word in a synonym list when printed in SMALL CAPITALS shows where there is more information about the group. For a more efficient use of this book see Explanatory Notes.

illustrate *vb* **1** ***syn*** CLARIFY 2, clear, clear up, elucidate, explain, illuminate
rel display, exhibit, expose, show; disclose, discover, reveal
con cloak, conceal, enshroud, mask, screen, shroud, veil
2 ***syn*** EXEMPLIFY 1, instance
rel elucidate, explain, expound, interpret; demonstrate, manifest, show; enliven, vivify
3 ***syn*** REPRESENT 2, body (forth), emblematize, embody, epitomize, exemplify, mirror, personify, symbolize, typify
4 ***syn*** SHOW 2, demonstrate, evidence, evince, exhibit, manifest, mark, ostend, proclaim

illustration *n* **1** ***syn*** EXAMPLE 3, ensample, problem
2 ***syn*** INSTANCE, case, case history, example, representative, sample, sampling, specimen

illustrational *adj* ***syn*** PICTORIAL 1, graphic, iconographic, illustrative, illustratory, pictoric

illustrative *adj* ***syn*** PICTORIAL 1, graphic, iconographic, illustrational, illustratory, pictoric

illustratory *adj* ***syn*** PICTORIAL 1, graphic, iconographic, illustrational, illustrative, pictoric

illustrious *adj* ***syn*** FAMOUS 2, celebrated, celebrious, distinguished, eminent, famed, great, notable, prominent, renowned
rel glorious, resplendent, splendid, sublime; conspicuous, lofty, outstanding, signal, striking
con abject, inglorious, mean; disgraceful, dishonorable, ignoble, ignominious, shameful
ant infamous

illustriousness *n* ***syn*** EMINENCE 1, distinction, kudos, preeminence, prestige, prominence, prominency, renown
ant infamy

ill will *n* ***syn*** MALICE, despite, grudge, malevolence, maliciousness, malignancy, malignity, spite, spitefulness, spleen
rel hostility, rancor, venom
ant goodwill

image *n* **1** one strikingly like another especially in appearance or manner <she was the *image* of her mother>
syn double, picture, portrait, ringer, simulacrum, spit, spitting image
rel counterpart, equal, equivalent, match
idiom chip off the old block, dead ringer, speaking likeness, spit and image
2 ***syn*** IDEA, apprehension, conceit, concept, conception, impression, intellection, notion, perception, thought

image *vb* **1** ***syn*** REPRESENT 1, delineate, depict, describe, interpret, limn, picture, portray, render
2 ***syn*** THINK 1, conceive, envisage, envision, fancy, feature, imagine, realize, vision, visualize

---

syn synonym(s) ***rel*** related word(s)
idiom idiomatic equivalent(s) ***con*** contrasted word(s)
ant antonym(s) * vulgar
‖ use limited; if in doubt, see a dictionary
The first word in a synonym list when printed in SMALL CAPITALS shows where there is more information about the group. For a more efficient use of this book see Explanatory Notes.

3 ***syn*** REFLECT 1, glass, mirror

imaginable *adj* ***syn*** THINKABLE 2, conceivable, supposable
ant unimaginable

imaginary *adj* **1** having no real existence but existing in imagination <elves are *imaginary* beings>
syn fancied, fanciful, imagined, notional, shadowy
rel imaginative; abstract, hypothetical, ideal, visionary; apparitional, chimerical, fantastic, figmental, hallucinatory, illusory, phantasmal, phantasmic, quixotic, spectral; unreal, unsubstantial
con genuine, true, valid
ant actual, real
2 ***syn*** FICTITIOUS 1, chimerical, fanciful, fantastic, fictional, fictive, illusory, suppositious, supposititious, unreal
ant actual, real

imagination *n* the power or function of the mind by which mental images are formed or the exercise of that power <children have great *imagination*>
syn fancy, fantasy (*or* phantasy), imaginativeness
rel creativity, inspiration, invention, inventiveness, visualization
con literalness, matter-of-factness, prosaism, unimaginativeness

imaginativeness *n* ***syn*** IMAGINATION, fancy, fantasy (*or* phantasy)
ant unimaginativeness

imagine *vb* **1** ***syn*** THINK 1, conceive, envisage, envision, fancy, feature, image, realize, vision, visualize
2 ***syn*** UNDERSTAND 3, assume, believe, expect, gather, ‖reckon, suppose, suspect, take, think

imagined *adj* ***syn*** IMAGINARY 1, fancied, fanciful, notional, shadowy
con known, recognized, seen

imbecile *adj* ***syn*** RETARDED, backward, dim-witted, dull, feebleminded, half-witted, moronic, simpleminded, slow, slow-witted

imbecile *n* **1** ***syn*** FOOL 4, ament, cretin, ‖feeb, half-wit, idiot, moron, natural, simpleton, zany
2 ***syn*** FOOL 1, ass, *damfool, donkey, idiot, jackass, jerk, nincompoop, ninny, tomfool

imbibe *vb* **1** ***syn*** ABSORB 1, assimilate, incorporate, inhaust, insorb
2 ***syn*** DRINK 1, quaff, sip, sup (off *or* up), swallow, toss
3 ***syn*** DRINK 3, booze, guzzle, liquor (up), soak, swig, swill, swizzle, tank up, tipple

imbricate *vb* ***syn*** OVERLAP, lap, overlie, override, ride, shingle

imbroglio *n* ***syn*** QUARREL, altercation, bickering, dispute, embroilment, falling-out, miff, row, spat, squabble

imbrued *adj* ***syn*** BLOODY 1, bloodstained, ensanguined, gory, sanguinary, sanguine, sanguineous

imbue *vb* ***syn*** INFUSE 1, ingrain, inoculate, invest, leaven, steep, suffuse

imitate *vb* **1** ***syn*** COPY, duplicate, reduplicate, replicate, reproduce
2 ***syn*** MIMIC, ape, burlesque, mock, parody, take off, travesty

imitation *adj* ***syn*** ARTIFICIAL 2, dummy, ersatz, false, mock, sham, simulated, spurious, substitute

ant real

imitation *n* something made or produced as an often inferior likeness of something else <usually wore *imitations* of her costly jewels>
syn copy, ersatz, simulacrum
rel counterfeit, fake, forgery, phony, sham, simulation; counterpart, duplicate, replica, reproduction; likeness, semblance
ant original

imitative *adj* **1** ***syn*** ONOMATOPOEIC, echoic, onomatopoetic
2 ***syn*** SLAVISH 3, apish, emulative

immaculate *adj* **1** ***syn*** CHASTE, clean, decent, modest, pure, spotless, stainless, unblemished, undefiled, unsullied
ant maculate
2 ***syn*** IMPECCABLE 1, errorless, exquisite, faultless, flawless, irreproachable
3 ***syn*** CLEAN 1, cleanly, spotless, taintless, unsoiled, unsullied

immalleable *adj* ***syn*** STIFF 1, impliable, incompliant, inelastic, inflexible, rigid, unbending, unflexible, unyielding
ant malleable

immaterial *adj* **1** not composed of matter < *immaterial* forces>
syn asomatous, bodiless, disbodied, discarnate, disembodied, incorporeal, insubstantial, metaphysical, nonmaterial, nonphysical, spiritual, unbodied, ‖uncorporal, unembodied, unfleshly, unmaterial, unphysical, unsubstantial
rel impalpable, imponderable; psychic, subjective; aerial, airy, ethereal; insensible, unearthly, unworldly; supernatural; celestial, heavenly; apparitional, ghostly, shadowy
con bodily, corporeal, fleshly, incarnate; material, objective, palpable, physical, substantial; mundane, terrestrial, worldly
ant material
2 ***syn*** IRRELEVANT, extraneous, foreign, impertinent, inapplicable, inapposite, irrelative
ant material

immature *adj* **1** ***syn*** YOUNG 1, callow, green, infant, juvenile, unfledged, unripe, youthful
rel premature, precocious
ant mature
2 ***syn*** CHILDISH, babyish, infantile, infantine, prekindergarten, puerile
ant mature

immeasurable *adj* **1** ***syn*** INCALCULABLE 1, inestimable, measureless, uncountable, unmeasurable, unmeasured, unreckonable
2 ***syn*** LIMITLESS, boundless, endless, indefinite, infinite, measureless, unbounded, unlimited, unmeasured

immediacy *n* ***syn*** PROXIMITY, appropinquity, contiguity, contiguousness, propinquity

immediate *adj* **1** ***syn*** DIRECT 4, firsthand, primary
ant distant (*of relatives*)
2 ***syn*** INSTANTANEOUS, hair-trigger, instant
3 ***syn*** CLOSE 6, near, near-at-hand, nearby, nigh, proximate

immediately *adv* **1** in direct connection without intermediary < *immediately* in front of the viewers>
syn contiguously, directly
2 ***syn*** AWAY 3, at once, directly, forthwith, instanter, instantly, now, PDQ, right away, straightway
rel anon, shortly, soon
idiom right now

immedicable *adj* ***syn*** HOPELESS 2, cureless, impossible, incurable, insanable, irremediable, irreparable, uncorrectable, uncurable, unrecoverable
ant medicable

immense *adj* ***syn*** HUGE, colossal, enormous, gigantic, mighty, monstrous, prodigious. titanic, tremendous, vast

immensely *adv* ***syn*** EVER 6, excessively, extremely, inordinately, over, overfull, overly, overmuch, too, unduly

immensity *n* ***syn*** ENORMITY 2, enormousness, hugeness, magnitude, tremendousness, vastness

immerse *vb* **1** ***syn*** DIP 1, douse, duck, dunk, souse, submerge, submerse
rel saturate, soak
2 ***syn*** BAPTIZE, asperse, christen, sprinkle
3 ***syn*** ENGAGE 4, busy, engross, occupy, soak

immersed *adj* ***syn*** INTENT, absorbed, deep, engaged, engrossed, preoccupied, rapt, wrapped, wrapped up

immigrant *n* ***syn*** EMIGRANT, migrant

imminent *adj* **1** about to take place <their departure is *imminent*>
syn impending, proximate
rel approaching, coming, nearing, upcoming; brewing, gathering; pending; likely, possible, probable; ineluctable, inescapable, inevasible, inevitable, unavoidable, unescapable
idiom in prospect, in store, in the cards, in the offing, in the wind, in view
con distant, far-off, remote
2 menacingly near <a thunderstorm was *imminent*>
syn lowering (*or* louring), lowery (*or* loury), menacing, overhanging, threatening
rel alarming, ominous, sinister; brewing, gathering; minatory

immingle *vb* ***syn*** MIX 1, blend, comingle, commingle, commix, immix, interblend, intermingle, intermix, meld

immix *vb* ***syn*** MIX 1, admix, commingle, commix, compound, interblend, interfuse, intermingle, intermix, mingle

immixture *n* ***syn*** MIXTURE, admixture, commixture, composite, compost, compound, fusion, intermixture, mix, mix-up

immobile *adj* **1** ***syn*** IMMOVABLE 1, fixed, immotile, immotive, irremovable, ‖sitfast, steadfast, unmovable
ant mobile, movable
2 ***syn*** STATIC, stagnant, stationary, unmoving

immobilize *vb* ***syn*** PARALYZE 1, cripple, disable, disarm, incapacitate, prostrate

---

syn synonym(s)	***rel*** related word(s)
idiom idiomatic equivalent(s)	***con*** contrasted word(s)
ant antonym(s)	* vulgar

‖ use limited; if in doubt, see a dictionary
The first word in a synonym list when printed in SMALL CAPITALS shows where there is more information about the group. For a more efficient use of this book see Explanatory Notes.

immoderate *adj* **1** ***syn*** EXCESSIVE 1, dizzy, exorbitant, extravagant, extreme, inordinate, towering, unconscionable, undue, unmeasurable
ant moderate
2 ***syn*** EXCESSIVE 2, inordinate, intemperate, overindulgent, unrestrained, untempered
ant moderate

immoderation *n* ***syn*** EXCESS 3, inordinateness, intemperance, overindulgence
ant moderation

immolate *vb* ***syn*** SACRIFICE 1, victimize

immoral *adj* **1** ***syn*** IMPURE 1, dirty, unchaste, unclean, uncleanly
ant moral
2 ***syn*** WRONG 1, bad, evil, iniquitous, reprobate, sinful, vicious, wicked
ant moral

immorality *n* ***syn*** VICE 1, corruption, depravity, wickedness
ant morality

immortal *adj* **1** not subject to death <the *immortal* gods>
syn deathless, undying; *compare* EVERLASTING 1
rel endless, enduring, imperishable, indestructible, perpetual, sempiternal, timeless
con ephemeral, evanescent, fleeting, fugitive, passing, short-lived, transient, transitory
ant mortal
2 ***syn*** EVERLASTING 1, amaranthine, ceaseless, endless, eternal, never-ending, unending, world-without-end

immortality *n* ***syn*** ETERNITY 2, afterlife, everlastingness, eviternity, world-without-end
ant mortality

immortalize *vb* ***syn*** PERPETUATE, eternalize, eternize

immotile *adj* ***syn*** IMMOVABLE 1, fixed, immobile, immotive, irremovable, ||sitfast, steadfast, unmovable
ant motile

immotive *adj* ***syn*** IMMOVABLE 1, fixed, immobile, immotile, irremovable, ||sitfast, steadfast, unmovable

immovable *adj* **1** incapable of moving or being moved <an *immovable* rock>
syn fixed, immobile, immotile, immotive, irremovable, ||sitfast, steadfast, unmovable
rel adamant, fast, rooted, stable, stationary, stuck, unmoving, unyielding
con portable, removable, transferable, transportable
ant movable
2 ***syn*** INFLEXIBLE 3, constant, fixed, immutable, inalterable, invariable, unalterable, unchangeable, unmodifiable, unmovable

immunity *n* ***syn*** EXEMPTION, impunity
ant susceptibility

immure *vb* **1** ***syn*** ENCLOSE 1, cage, coop, corral, fence, hedge, hem, mure, pen, wall
2 ***syn*** IMPRISON, bastille, confine, constrain, incarcerate, intern, jail, jug, ||prison, ||quod

immusical *adj* ***syn*** DISSONANT 1, cacophonic, cacophonous, discordant, disharmonic, disharmonious, inharmonic, inharmonious, unharmonious, unmusical
ant musical

immutable *adj* ***syn*** INFLEXIBLE 3, constant, fixed, immovable, inalterable, invariable, unalterable, unchangeable, unmodifiable, unmovable
ant mutable

imp *n* **1** a small demon, devil, or wicked spirit <the *imps* of hell>
syn deviling, devilkin
rel elf, gnome, goblin, gremlin, ||hob, hobgoblin, kobold, ouph, pixie, puck, sprite, troll
2 ***syn*** URCHIN, gamin, monkey

impact *n* a forcible or enforced contact between two or more things <a crater formed by the *impact* of a meteorite>
syn appulse, blow, bump, clash, collision, concussion, crash, impingement, jar, jolt, jounce, percussion, shock, smash, wallop
rel brunt; buffet, hit, pound, punch, rap, slap, smiting, strike, stroke; bounce, quake, quiver, rock, shake, tremble, tremor; encounter, meeting

impair *vb* ***syn*** INJURE 1, blemish, damage, harm, hurt, mar, prejudice, spoil, tarnish, vitiate
rel sap, undermine, weaken
con ameliorate, better
ant improve; repair

impaired *adj* ***syn*** DAMAGED, flawed, marred, spoiled

impale *vb* to pierce or fix with or as if with something pointed <an insect *impaled* on a pin>
syn lance, skewer, skiver, spear, spike, spit, transfix, transpierce
rel perforate, pierce, prick, punch, puncture, stab

impalpable *adj* **1** ***syn*** IMPERCEPTIBLE, imponderable, inappreciable, indiscernible, insensible, intangible, unapparent, unappreciable, unobservable, unperceivable
ant palpable
2 ***syn*** FINE 2, powdery, pulverized

imparity *n* ***syn*** DISPARITY, disproportion, inequality, unevenness
ant parity

impart *vb* ***syn*** COMMUNICATE 1, break, convey, pass on, transmit

impartial *adj* ***syn*** FAIR 4, dispassionate, equal, equitable, just, nondiscriminatory, objective, unbiased, uncolored, unprejudiced
ant partial

impartially *adv* ***syn*** EVENLY 2, equally

impassable *adj* **1** not allowing passage <an *impassable* barrier>
syn impenetrable, impermeable, imperviable, impervious, unpierceable
con penetrable, permeable, pervious
ant passable
2 ***syn*** INSUPERABLE, inconquerable, indomitable, insurmountable, invincible, unconquerable, unsurmountable

impasse *n* **1** ***syn*** DEAD END, blind alley, cul-de-sac, pocket
2 ***syn*** PREDICAMENT, box, corner, dilemma, fix, hole, jam, pickle, plight, scrape

---

syn synonym(s) — *rel* related word(s)
idiom idiomatic equivalent(s) — *con* contrasted word(s)
ant antonym(s) — * vulgar
|| use limited; if in doubt, see a dictionary
The first word in a synonym list when printed in SMALL CAPITALS shows where there is more information about the group. For a more efficient use of this book see Explanatory Notes.

impassible *adj* ***syn*** INSENSIBLE 5, anesthetic, bloodless, dull, hard, insensate, insensitive, rocky
rel cold, emotionless, passionless, unemotional, unfeeling; inert, unresponsive
ant passible

impassioned *adj* actuated by or showing intense feeling < *impassioned* oratory >
syn ardent, blazing, burning, dithyrambic, fervent, fervid, fiery, flaming, glowing, hot-blooded, overheated, passionate, perfervid, red-hot, torrid, white-hot
rel feverish, fierce, furious, intense, vehement, violent; deep, profound, warm, zealous; gushing, gushy, maudlin, melodramatic, mushy, overemotional, romantic, sentimental
con cold, cool, dispassionate, frigid, icy, unemotional; objective
ant unimpassioned

impassive *adj* **1** unresponsive to what might normally excite interest or emotion < *impassive* endurance of pain >
syn apathetic, dry, matter-of-fact, phlegmatic, stoic, stolid
rel calm, cold, cool; collected, composed, dispassionate, emotionless, imperturbable, inexcitable, unexcitable, unflappable; inexpressive, reserved, reticent, taciturn, unemotional, unexpressive; bovine, placid, passionless, spiritless, unconcerned, wooden; callous, hardened, indurated, insensible; cold-blooded, coldhearted, heartless
con compassionate, sympathetic, tender, warm, warmhearted
ant responsive
2 ***syn*** INSUSCEPTIBLE, insensitive, insentient, unimpressible, unimpressionable, unresponsive, unsusceptible

impassivity *n* ***syn*** APATHY 1, insensibility, phlegm, stoicism, stolidity, unresponsiveness

impatient *adj* **1** lacking power to endure hardship, distress, or opposition <married to an *impatient* self-centered man>
syn chafing, fretful, unpatient
rel abrupt, hasty, headlong, impetuous; anxious, edgy, itchy, nervous; irascible, irritable
idiom all of a stew
con enduring, forbearing, tolerant; self-controlled, Spartan, stoic
ant patient
2 ***syn*** INTOLERANT 1, unforbearing, unindulgent
rel demanding, harsh
3 ***syn*** EAGER, agog, anxious, appetent, ardent, athirst, avid, breathless, keen, thirsty
ant patient

impeach *vb* ***syn*** ACCUSE, arraign, charge, criminate, incriminate, inculpate, indict, tax

impeccable *adj* **1** absolutely correct and beyond criticism < *impeccable* manners >
syn errorless, exquisite, faultless, flawless, immaculate, irreproachable
rel accurate, clean, correct, exact, nice, perfect, precise, right; infallible, unerring
con defective, deficient, faulty; blameworthy, censurable, criticizable, culpable; cursory, shallow, superficial, uncritical
ant peccant
2 ***syn*** PERFECT 2, absolute, flawless, fleckless, indefectible, note-perfect, unflawed

impecunious *adj* ***syn*** POOR 1, destitute, dirt poor, impoverished, indigent, necessitous, needy, penurious, poverty-stricken, unprosperous
ant affluent; flush

impecuniousness *n* ***syn*** POVERTY 1, destitution, impoverishment, indigence, need, neediness, penury, poorness, privation, want
ant affluence; flushness

impedance *n* ***syn*** ENCUMBRANCE, clog, cumbrance, hindrance, impediment

impede *vb* ***syn*** HINDER, bar, block, brake, dam, obstruct, overslaugh
rel discomfit, disconcert, embarrass, faze, rattle
ant aid, assist

impediment *n* **1** ***syn*** ENCUMBRANCE, clog, cumbrance, hindrance, impedance
ant aid, assistance
2 ***syn*** OBSTACLE, bar, Chinese wall, hamper, hurdle, mountain, obstruction, rub, snag, stumbling block

impel *vb* ***syn*** MOVE 5, actuate, drive, mobilize, propel
rel compel, constrain, force; foment, incite, instigate; goad, spur; inspire, motivate
con check, curb, inhibit
ant restrain

impend *vb* ***syn*** LOOM 2, brew, forthcome, gather

impending *adj* ***syn*** IMMINENT 1, proximate

impenetrable *adj* **1** ***syn*** IMPASSABLE 1, impermeable, imperviable, impervious, unpierceable
rel firm, solid, substantial
ant penetrable
2 ***syn*** INCOMPREHENSIBLE 1, incognizable, uncomprehensible, unfathomable, ungraspable, unintelligible, unknowable
ant penetrable
3 ***syn*** MYSTERIOUS, arcane, cabalistic, inscrutable, mysterial, mystic, numinous, unaccountable, unguessed, unknowable

impenetrate *vb* ***syn*** PERMEATE, charge, compenetrate, impregnate, interpenetrate, penetrate, percolate, pervade, saturate, transfuse

impenitent *adj* ***syn*** REMORSELESS, regretless, uncontrite, unregretful, unremorseful, unrepentant, unsorry
ant penitent

imperative *adj* **1** ***syn*** MASTERFUL 1, bossy, domineering, high-handed, imperial, imperious, magisterial, overbearing, peremptory
rel bidding, commanding, ordering; harsh, stern
con begging, entreating, imploring; lenient, mild, soft
2 ***syn*** PRESSING, burning, clamant, clamorous, crying, exigent, importunate, insistent, instant, urgent
rel acute, critical, crucial

---

3 ***syn*** ESSENTIAL 4, indispensable, necessary, necessitous, prerequisite

rel basic, fundamental; claimed, demanded, exacted

4 ***syn*** MANDATORY, compulsatory, compulsory, imperious, obligatory, required

imperceptible *adj* incapable of being apprehended by the senses or intellect < *imperceptible* changes in temperature >

syn impalpable, imponderable, inappreciable, indiscernible, insensible, intangible, invisible, unapparent, unappreciable, undiscernible, unobservable, unperceivable

rel faint, inconspicuous, indistinct, indistinguishable, insignificant, obscure, undistinguishable, unnoticeable, vague; ephemeral, evanescent, fugitive, momentary; slight, trivial

con apparent, appreciable, discernible, observable, palpable, ponderable, sensible, visible

ant perceptible, perceivable

imperceptive *adj* lacking perception or insight < *imperceptive* criticism >

syn impercipient, unperceiving, unperceptive

rel unappreciative, undiscerning, unobservant; cursory, shallow, slapdash, superficial

con astute, discerning, discriminating, judicious, perspicacious; delicate, nice, refined, sensitive, subtle

ant perceiving, perceptive, percipient

impercipient *adj* ***syn*** IMPERCEPTIVE, unperceiving, unperceptive

ant perceiving, perceptive, percipient

imperfect *adj* ***syn*** FAULTY, amiss, defective, flawed, sick

ant perfect

imperfection *n* an instance of failure to reach a standard of excellence or perfection < watch for *imperfections* in the cloth >

syn deficiency, demerit, fault, shortcoming, sin

rel blemish, defect, flaw; failing, foible, frailty

ant perfection

imperial *adj* ***syn*** MASTERFUL 1, bossy, domineering, high-handed, imperative, imperious, magisterial, overbearing, peremptory

imperil *vb* ***syn*** ENDANGER, compromise, hazard, jeopard, jeopardize, jeopardy, menace, peril, risk

imperious *adj* 1 ***syn*** MASTERFUL 1, bossy, domineering, high-handed, imperative, imperial, magisterial, overbearing, peremptory

rel heavy-handed, oppressive, strict, stringent; absolute, arbitrary

con considerate, easy, gentle, kindly

2 ***syn*** MANDATORY, compulsatory, compulsory, imperative, obligatory, required

imperishable *adj* ***syn*** INDESTRUCTIBLE, incorruptible, inexterminable, inextinguishable, inextirpable, irrefragable, irrefrangible, quenchless, undestroyable, unperishable

impermanent *adj* ***syn*** TRANSIENT, ephemeral, evanescent, fleeting, fugacious, fugitive, momentary, passing, short-lived, transitory

ant permanent

impermeable *adj* ***syn*** IMPASSABLE 1, impenetrable, imperviable, impervious, unpierceable

ant permeable

impersonal *adj* 1 ***syn*** NEUTRAL, abstract, colorless, detached, disinterested, dispassionate, poker-faced, unpassioned

2 ***syn*** FAIR 4, dispassionate, equal, equitable, impartial, nondiscriminatory, objective, unbiased, uncolored, unprejudiced

3 ***syn*** MATTER-OF-FACT 3, cold, cold-blooded, emotionless, unimpassioned

impersonate *vb* ***syn*** ACT 1, discourse, do, enact, perform, personate, play, playact

impersonator *n* ***syn*** ACTOR 1, mime, mimic, mummer, performer, playactor, player, thespian, trouper

impertinence *n* ***syn*** INSOLENCE, boldness, disrespect, hardihood, impudence, insolency, insolentness

impertinent *adj* 1 ***syn*** IRRELEVANT, extraneous, foreign, immaterial, inapplicable, inapposite, irrelative

ant pertinent

2 going beyond what is proper or acceptable in thrusting oneself into the affairs of others < *impertinent* interference with her sister's family >

syn busy, intrusive, meddlesome, ‖nebby, obtrusive, officious, polypragmatic

rel arrogant, bold, brash, brazen, fresh, impudent, pert, presumptuous, saucy; inquisitive, interfering, meddling, nosy, prying; offensive, rude

con decent, decorous, proper, seemly; reserved, reticent, silent; apposite, germane, pertinent, relevant

3 ***syn*** RUDE 6, discourteous, disgracious, disrespectful, ill-bred, ill-mannered, impolite, uncalled-for, uncivil, ungracious

4 ***syn*** INSOLENT 2, audacious, bold, ‖boldacious, brazen, contumelious, impudent, procacious, saucy

imperturbability *n* ***syn*** EQUANIMITY, ataraxy, calmness, composure, coolness, phlegm, sangfroid, self-possession

imperturbable *adj* ***syn*** COOL 2, collected, composed, disimpassioned, nonchalant, unflappable, unruffled

rel complacent, self-satisfied, smug; unaffected, unmoved, untouched

con discomfited, disconcerted, fazed, rattled; irascible, splenetic, testy

ant choleric; touchy

imperviable *adj* ***syn*** IMPASSABLE 1, impenetrable, impermeable, impervious, unpierceable

impervious *adj* ***syn*** IMPASSABLE 1, impenetrable, impermeable, imperviable, unpierceable

ant pervious

impetuous *adj* ***syn*** PRECIPITATE 1, abrupt, hasty, headlong, hurried, precipitant, precipitous, rushing, subitaneous, sudden

rel spontaneous; restive; ardent, fervid, impassioned, passionate

con equable, even, steady; advised, considered, deliberate, planned, premeditated

---

syn synonym(s) *rel* related word(s)
idiom idiomatic equivalent(s) *con* contrasted word(s)
ant antonym(s) * vulgar
‖ use limited; if in doubt, see a dictionary
The first word in a synonym list when printed in SMALL CAPITALS shows where there is more information about the group. For a more efficient use of this book see Explanatory Notes.

impetuously *adv* ***syn*** PELL-MELL, helter-skelter, hotfoot, hurry-scurry, incontinently

impetus *n* ***syn*** STIMULUS, catalyst, goad, impulse, incentive, incitation, incitement, motivation, spur, stimulant

impignorate *vb* ***syn*** PAWN, ‖dip, hock, mortgage, pledge, ‖pop, ‖spout

impingement *n* ***syn*** IMPACT, appulse, clash, collision, concussion, jar, jolt, percussion, shock, smash

impious *adj* **1** lacking reverence for holy or sacred matters <made *impious* remarks about the church>
syn irreverent, irreverential, profane, ungodly, unhallowed, unholy
rel godless, iconoclastic, irreligious, sacrilegious, scandalous, undevout
con devout, godly, religious, spiritual
ant pious
2 lacking due respect (as toward one's parents) <an *impious* son>
syn unduteous, undutiful
rel disobedient, froward, unfaithful, wayward; contrary, perverse, wrongheaded
con duteous, dutiful

impish *adj* ***syn*** PLAYFUL 1, coltish, elvish, frolicsome, mischievous, pixieish, puckish, roguish, sportive, waggish
rel arch, pert, saucy; flippant, fresh, giddy; casual, devil-may-care, free and easy, offhand

impishness *n* ***syn*** MISCHIEVOUSNESS, devilment, devilry, deviltry, mischief, roguery, roguishness, sportiveness, waggery, waggishness

implacable *adj* ***syn*** GRIM 3, ironfisted, merciless, mortal, relentless, ruthless, unappeasable, unflinching, unrelenting, unyielding
con peaceable, tractable; kindly, tolerant
ant placable

implant *vb* to introduce into the mind <*implanted* worthy ideals in their children>
syn inculcate, infix, inseminate, instill
rel imbue, infuse, ingrain, inoculate, leaven, root; impenetrate, impregnate, penetrate, permeate, pervade, saturate; inspire

implausible *adj* not plausible or readily believable <an *implausible* explanation>
syn flimsy, improbable, inconceivable, incredible, thick, thin, unbelievable, unconceivable, unconvincing, unsubstantial, weak; *compare* TENUOUS 3
rel doubtful, dubious, fishy; problematic, puzzling, suspect
idiom a bit thick
con meaty, pithy; solid, sound, substantial; believable, conceivable, credible; likely, probable
ant plausible

implement *n* a usually relatively simple device for performing a mechanical or manual operation <spades, hoes, and other gardener's *implements*>
syn instrument, tool, utensil
rel apparatus, appliance; contrivance, device; contraption, gadget

implement *vb* **1** ***syn*** FULFILL 1, complete, execute, perform
2 ***syn*** ENFORCE, effect, invoke
rel actualize, materialize, realize

implemental *adj* ***syn*** INSTRUMENTAL, ministerial

impliable *adj* ***syn*** STIFF 1, immalleable, incompliant, inelastic, inflexible, rigid, unbending, unflexible, unyielding
ant pliable

implicate *vb* ***syn*** INVOLVE 1, embroil, mire, tangle
rel affect, concern; incriminate
con absolve, acquit, exculpate, exonerate

implicated *adj* ***syn*** INTERESTED, affected, concerned, involved

implication *n* ***syn*** ASSOCIATION 4, connotation, hint, overtone, suggestion, undertone

implicit *adj* **1** ***syn*** TACIT 1, implied, inarticulate, inferred, undeclared, understood, unexpressed, unsaid, unspoken, unuttered
idiom taken for granted
ant explicit
2 being such in essential character <our *implicit* freedom is better than your nominal liberty>
syn constructive, practical, virtual
rel absolute, complete, unqualified, wholehearted; genuine, real
ant spelled out

implied *adj* ***syn*** TACIT 1, implicit, inferred, undeclared, understood, unexpressed, unsaid, unspoken, unuttered, wordless

imploration *n* ***syn*** PRAYER, appeal, application, entreaty, imprecation, orison, petition, plea, suit, supplication

implore *vb* ***syn*** BEG, appeal, beseech, conjure, crave, entreat, importune, plead, pray, supplicate

imply *vb* **1** ***syn*** POINT 2, hint, indicate, suggest
2 ***syn*** SUGGEST 1, connote, hint, insinuate, intimate
con state; express; affirm, assert, declare

impolite *adj* ***syn*** RUDE 6, discourteous, disgracious, disrespectful, ill-bred, ill-mannered, incivil, uncivil, uncourteous, ungracious
ant polite

impolitic *adj* **1** ***syn*** UNWISE, ill-advised, ill-judged, imprudent, indiscreet, injudicious
ant politic
2 ***syn*** INADVISABLE, ill-advised, imprudent, inexpedient, unadvisable, unexpedient
ant politic
3 ***syn*** TACTLESS, brash, maladroit, undiplomatic, unpolitic, untactful

imponderable *adj* ***syn*** IMPERCEPTIBLE, impalpable, inappreciable, indiscernible, insensible, intangible, unapparent, unappreciable, unobservable, unperceivable
ant appreciable, ponderable

imponderous *adj* ***syn*** LIGHT 1, featherlight, featherweight, lightweight, unheavy, weightless
ant ponderous

---

syn synonym(s) | ***rel*** related word(s)
idiom idiomatic equivalent(s) | ***con*** contrasted word(s)
ant antonym(s) | * vulgar
‖ use limited; if in doubt, see a dictionary
The first word in a synonym list when printed in SMALL CAPITALS shows where there is more information about the group. For a more efficient use of this book see Explanatory Notes.

import *vb* **1** ***syn*** MEAN 2, add up (to), connote, denote, express, intend, signify, spell
2 ***syn*** MATTER, count, mean, signify, weigh

import *n* **1** ***syn*** MEANING 1, acceptation, intendment, message, purport, sense, significance, significancy, signification, understanding
rel construction, interpretation
2 ***syn*** IMPORTANCE, consequence, magnitude, moment, momentousness, pith, significance, ‖signification, weight, weightiness
rel value, worth; design, intent, object, objective, purpose; emphasis, stress

importance *n* the quality or state of being of notable worth or influence <persons of national and worldwide *importance*>
syn consequence, import, magnitude, moment, momentousness, pith, significance, ‖signification, weight, weightiness
rel conspicuousness; distinction, eminence, mark, prominence, salience; notability, note, noteworthiness, reputation, standing; substance, value, worth, worthiness; gravity, seriousness
con inconsequence, insignificance, paltriness, pettiness, triviality
ant unimportance

important *adj* **1** marked by or indicative of notable worth or consequence <an *important* discovery> <his manner was grave and *important*>
syn big, consequential, considerable, material, meaningful, momentous, significant, substantial, weighty
rel conspicuous, distinctive, exceptional, impressive, marked, memorable, notable, noteworthy, noticeable, outstanding, prominent, remarkable, salient, unusual; essential; valuable, worthwhile; worthy; effective, potent, powerful, telling; big-time, first-class, first-rate, front-page, top-notch; distinguished, eminent, famous, noted
con inconsiderable, little, minor, paltry, petty, slight, trivial
ant unimportant
2 ***syn*** POMPOUS 1, arrogant, bloated, magisterial, pontifical, puffy, self-important, stuffy, wiggy

importunate *adj* ***syn*** PRESSING, burning, clamant, clamorous, crying, exigent, imperative, insistent, instant, urgent
rel persevering, persistent; dogged, pertinacious

importune *vb* ***syn*** BEG, appeal, beseech, crave, entreat, implore, invoke, plead, pray, supplicate

impose *vb* **1** ***syn*** DICTATE, decree, lay down, ordain, prescribe, set
rel charge, command, enjoin, order; demand, exact, require; compel, constrain, oblige
2 ***syn*** LEVY, assess, exact, put (on *or* upon)

---

syn synonym(s) *rel* related word(s)
idiom idiomatic equivalent(s) *con* contrasted word(s)
ant antonym(s) * vulgar
‖ use limited; if in doubt, see a dictionary
The first word in a synonym list when printed in SMALL CAPITALS shows where there is more information about the group. For a more efficient use of this book see Explanatory Notes.

3 ***syn*** INFLICT 2, force (on *or* upon), visit, wreak, wreck
4 to force another to accept <*imposed* all the dirty jobs on her sister>
syn foist, wish; *compare* FOIST 3, INFLICT 2
rel burden, lade, saddle; fob, fob off, palm off
idiom take advantage of
5 to take usually unwarranted advantage <did not wish to *impose* by turning up unannounced>
syn infringe, intrude, obtrude, presume
rel encroach, trespass
idiom make free, take liberties

impose (on *or* upon) *vb* ***syn*** EXPLOIT 2, abuse, use

imposing *adj* **1** ***syn*** GRAND 1, august, baronial, grandiose, magnificent, majestic, noble, princely, royal, stately
rel impressive, moving; imperial, regal
ant unimposing
2 ***syn*** PRETENTIOUS 3, arty, arty-crafty, big, high-sounding, overblown

impossible *adj* **1** not capable of being realized or attained <*impossible* goals>
syn impracticable, impractical, infeasible, irrealizable, unattainable, unfeasible, unrealizable, unworkable
rel absurd, inexecutable, unobtainable, unreasonable, unthinkable
idiom out of the question
con attainable, feasible, realizable; practicable, practical, rational, reasonable
ant possible
2 ***syn*** HOPELESS 2, cureless, immedicable, incurable, insanable, irremediable, irreparable, uncorrectable, uncurable, unrecoverable

impost *n* ***syn*** TAX 1, assessment, ‖cess, duty, levy, tariff

impostor *n* one who passes himself off as something or someone he is not <the presumed heir was discovered to be an *impostor*>
syn fake, faker, fraud, humbug, phony, pretender; *compare* CHARLATAN
rel imitator, mimic; beguiler, deceiver, misleader; cheat, pettifogger, shyster, trickster; hypocrite; charlatan, mountebank, quack; bluffer, dissembler, four-flusher, shammer
idiom wolf in sheep's clothing

imposture *n* the act, practice, or an instance of imposing on another by use of an assumed character or name <his claims were based on *imposture*>
syn cheat, counterfeit, deceit, deception, fake, flam, flimflam, fraud, gyp, hoax, humbug, mare's nest, phony, put-on, ‖rig, sell, sham, spoof, swindle
rel copy, imitation; fabrication, forgery; artifice, feint, gambit, maneuver, ploy, ruse, sleight, stratagem, trick, wile; make-believe, pretense, pretension

impotent *adj* **1** ***syn*** POWERLESS, helpless
rel crippled, disabled, enfeebled
con able, capable, competent
ant potent
2 ***syn*** WEAK 4, boneless, emasculate, forceless, inadequate, ineffective, ineffectual, invertebrate, slack-spined, spineless
con forceful, powerful, puissant, strenuous, vigorous
ant potent
3 ***syn*** STERILE 1, barren, effete, infecund, infertile, unfruitful

impoverish *vb* **1** ***syn*** DEPLETE, bankrupt, drain, draw, draw down, exhaust, use up
ant enrich
2 ***syn*** RUIN 3, bankrupt, break, bust, fold up, pauper, pauperize

impoverished *adj* ***syn*** POOR 1, beggared, destitute, impecunious, indigent, necessitous, needy, penurious, poverty-stricken, stone-broke

impoverishment *n* ***syn*** POVERTY 1, destitution, impecuniousness, indigence, need, neediness, penury, poorness, privation, want

impracticable *adj* **1** ***syn*** IMPOSSIBLE 1, impractical, infeasible, irrealizable, unattainable, unfeasible, unrealizable, unworkable
ant feasible, practicable
2 incapable of being successfully used or turned to account <a route through the mountains that is *impracticable* in winter>
syn impractical, nonfunctional, unfunctional, unserviceable, unusable, unworkable, useless
rel disadvantageous, unacceptable, undesirable, unsatisfactory; awkward, inconvenient, troublesome
con functional, practical, serviceable, usable, useful, workable
ant practicable

impractical *adj* **1** incapable of dealing prudently with practical matters <a very *impractical* person whose checkbook never balanced>
syn ivory-tower, ivory-towered, ivory-towerish, nonrealistic, unpractical, unrealistic, viewy
rel idealistic, otherworldly, quixotic, romantic, starry-eyed, visionary
con commonsensible, commonsensical, realistic, sensible, worldly-wise
ant practical
2 ***syn*** IMPRACTICABLE 2, nonfunctional, unfunctional, unserviceable, unusable, unworkable, useless
ant practical
3 ***syn*** IMPOSSIBLE 1, impracticable, infeasible, irrealizable, unattainable, unfeasible, unrealizable, unworkable

imprecate *vb* ***syn*** SWEAR 3, bedamn, curse, cuss, damn, execrate

imprecation *n* **1** ***syn*** BLASPHEMY 1, cursing, cussing, execration, profanity, swearing
2 ***syn*** PRAYER, appeal, application, entreaty, imploration, orison, petition, plea, suit, supplication
3 ***syn*** CURSE 1, anathema, commination, malediction, malison
con blessing

impregnable *adj* ***syn*** INVINCIBLE 1, inconquerable, indomitable, inexpugnable, invulnerable, unassailable, unbeatable, unconquerable, undefeatable
rel safe, secure; defended, guarded, protected, safeguarded, shielded
con exposed, open, susceptible

impregnate *vb* **1** ***syn*** PERMEATE, charge, compenetrate, impenetrate, interpenetrate, penetrate, percolate, pervade, saturate, transfuse
rel inoculate, leaven
2 ***syn*** SOAK 1, drench, saturate, seethe, sodden, ‖sog, sop, souse, steep, waterlog

impress *vb* **1** ***syn*** ENGRAVE 2, etch, imprint, inscribe
2 ***syn*** AFFECT, carry, get, influence, inspire, move, strike, sway, touch
rel enthuse, electrify, thrill; excite, galvanize, pique, provoke, stimulate
idiom make (*or* leave) one's mark
3 to fix in the mind or memory by emphasis or repetition <the speaker *impressed* his principal thesis upon his audience>
syn drive, grave, hammer, pound, stamp
rel establish, fix, set
idiom drive home to one, fix in one's mind, get into one's head

impress *n* ***syn*** IMPRESSION 1, imprint, indentation, print, stamp

impressible *adj* ***syn*** SENTIENT 3, impressionable, responsive, sensible, sensile, sensitive, susceptible, susceptive

impression *n* **1** the perceptible trace or traces left by pressure <the *impression* made by a die>
syn impress, imprint, indentation, print, stamp
rel dent, dint, hollow; trace, track, vestige; mark, sign
2 ***syn*** IDEA, apprehension, conceit, concept, conception, image, intellection, notion, perception, thought
3 ***syn*** EDITION, printing, reissue, reprinting

impressionable *adj* ***syn*** SENTIENT 3, impressible, responsive, sensible, sensile, sensitive, susceptible, susceptive
rel affectable, influenceable

impressive *adj* **1** ***syn*** MOVING 2, affecting, poignant, touching
rel august, grand, imposing, majestic, noble; splendid, superb; arresting, notable, striking
ant unimpressive
2 ***syn*** GRAND 2, gorgeous, lavish, luxurious, splendid, sumptuous

imprint *vb* ***syn*** ENGRAVE 2, etch, impress, inscribe

imprint *n* ***syn*** IMPRESSION 1, impress, indentation, print, stamp

imprison *vb* to shut up closely so that escape is impossible or unlikely <the offender was quickly sentenced and *imprisoned*>
syn bastille, confine, constrain, immure, incarcerate, intern, jail, jug, ‖prison, ‖quod
rel circumscribe, limit, restrict; check, curb, restrain
idiom put under lock and key
con free, liberate, release

improbable *adj* **1** not likely to be true or to occur <the immediate success of their plan is *improbable*>
syn doubtful, dubious, questionable, unlikely
ant probable
2 ***syn*** IMPLAUSIBLE, flimsy, inconceivable, incredible, thin, unbelievable, unconceivable, unconvincing, unsubstantial, weak

impromptu *n* ***syn*** IMPROVISATION, autoschediasm, extemporization

---

syn synonym(s) | *rel* related word(s)
idiom idiomatic equivalent(s) | *con* contrasted word(s)
ant antonym(s) | * vulgar
‖ use limited; if in doubt, see a dictionary
The first word in a synonym list when printed in SMALL CAPITALS shows where there is more information about the group. For a more efficient use of this book see Explanatory Notes.

impromptu *adj* ***syn*** EXTEMPORANEOUS, autoschediastic, extemporary, extempore, improvised, offhand, spur-of-the-moment, unrehearsed, unstudied
rel prompt, quick

improper *adj* **1** unsuited to the circumstances or the occasion <wore quite *improper* dress for such a formal reception>
syn ill-timed, inadmissible, inappropriate, inapt, inept, intempestive, malapropos, unapt, unbecoming, unbefitting, uncomely, undue, unfitting, unseasonable, unseemly, unsuitable, untimely
rel infelicitous, unhappy; inapplicable, inapposite; fresh, impertinent, sassy; crude, gauche, tactless
idiom out of place, out of season
con apposite, appropriate, apropos, apt, becoming, befitting, felicitous, fitting, germane, happy, opportune, pat, pertinent, seasonable, suitable, timely, well-timed
ant proper
2 ***syn*** INDECOROUS, indecent, indelicate, malodorous, rough, unbecoming, undecorous, ungodly, unseemly, untoward
rel informal, unceremonious, unconventional
con correct, right
ant proper

impropriety *n* **1** the quality or state of being improper (as in social behavior) <was shocked by the *impropriety* of their actions>
syn incorrectness, indecorousness, indecorum, inelegance, unbecomingness, unmeetness, unseemliness, untowardness
rel inadmissibility, objectionableness, unacceptableness
con becomingness, decency, decorousness, decorum, meetness
ant propriety, seemliness
2 ***syn*** FAUX PAS, blooper, boner, ‖boo-boo, break, gaffe, indecorum, solecism; *compare* ERROR 2
3 ***syn*** BARBARISM, corruption, slangism, solecism, vernacularism, vernacularity, vulgarism

improve *vb* **1** to make more acceptable or bring nearer to some standard <studied hard to *improve* his chances of success>
syn ameliorate, amend, better, help, meliorate
rel cultivate, develop, perfect; correct, emend, rectify, reform, remedy; edit, revise; enhance, enrich, refine, rub up, upgrade
con diminish, downgrade, lessen, lower
2 ***syn*** ILLUMINATE 2, edify, enlighten, illume, illumine, irradiate, uplift
3 to grow or become better (as in health or well-being) <the invalid is steadily *improving*>
syn ameliorate, convalesce, gain, look up, mend, perk (up), recuperate
rel advance, better, progress; recover; rally, revive, strengthen
idiom gain ground, make progress
con decline, deteriorate, fail, flag, languish, run down, sink, weaken

improvident *adj* not foreseeing or providing for the future <an *improvident* way of life>
syn thriftless, unthrift, unthrifty
rel careless, heedless, imprudent; extravagant, prodigal, profligate, spendthrift; lavish, profuse, reckless; uneconomical, wasteful
con careful, economical, frugal, parsimonious, prudent, saving, sparing
ant provident, thrifty

improvisate *vb* ***syn*** IMPROVISE, ad-lib, extemporize

improvisation *n* something that is improvised <the pianist played several clever *improvisations*>
syn autoschediasm, extemporization, impromptu

improvise *vb* to perform or provide on the spur of the moment <*improvise* an excuse for being late>
syn ad-lib, extemporize, improvisate
rel concoct, contrive, devise, invent

improvised *adj* ***syn*** EXTEMPORANEOUS, autoschediastic, extemporary, extempore, impromptu, offhand, spur-of-the-moment, unrehearsed, unstudied

imprudent *adj* **1** ***syn*** UNWISE, ill-advised, ill-judged, impolitic, indiscreet, injudicious
ant prudent
2 ***syn*** INADVISABLE, ill-advised, impolitic, inexpedient, unadvisable, unexpedient
ant prudent

impudence *n* ***syn*** INSOLENCE, boldness, disrespect, hardihood, impertinence, insolency, insolentness

impudent *adj* **1** ***syn*** WISE 5, bold, cheeky, forward, fresh, nervy, pert, sassy, smart, smart-alecky
2 ***syn*** INSOLENT 2, audacious, bold, ‖boldacious, brazen, contumelious, impertinent, procacious, saucy
3 ***syn*** SHAMELESS, arrant, barefaced, blatant, brassy, brazen, brazenfaced, overbold, unabashed, unblushing

impugn *vb* ***syn*** DENY 4, contradict, contravene, cross, disaffirm, gainsay, negate, negative, traverse
rel assail, attack
idiom call in (*or* into) question (*or* doubt), throw doubt on
con back, support, uphold
ant advocate; authenticate

impugnable *adj* ***syn*** DOUBTFUL 1, borderline, doubtable, equivocal, fishy, problematic, shady, suspect, suspicious, uncertain

impulse *n* ***syn*** STIMULUS, catalyst, goad, impetus, incentive, incitation, incitement, motivation, spur, stimulant
rel excitant; lust, passion, urge; actuation, drive, impulsion

impulsive *adj* ***syn*** SPONTANEOUS, automatic, instinctive, involuntary, unmeditated, unpremeditated, unprompted, will-less
rel abrupt, hasty, headlong, impetuous, precipitate, sudden
con considered, designed, premeditated; calculating, cautious, circumspect
ant deliberate

impulsiveness *n* ***syn*** ABANDON 2, uninhibitedness, unrestraint

impunity *n* ***syn*** EXEMPTION, immunity

---

syn synonym(s)	***rel*** related word(s)
idiom idiomatic equivalent(s)	***con*** contrasted word(s)
ant antonym(s)	* vulgar

‖ use limited; if in doubt, see a dictionary
The first word in a synonym list when printed in SMALL CAPITALS shows where there is more information about the group. For a more efficient use of this book see Explanatory Notes.

impure *adj* **1** morally or mentally unclean <*impure* thoughts>
syn dirty, immoral, unchaste, unclean, uncleanly
rel belowstairs, carnal, immodest, indecent, indecorous, lascivious, lewd, lustful, prurient, scarlet, sensual; filthy, vile
con chaste, clean, cleanly, decent, decorous, immaculate, modest, virtuous; moral
ant pure
2 *syn* DIRTY 1, black, filthy, foul, grubby, nasty, soily, squalid, unclean, uncleanly
3 made unfit for ceremonial purposes <altars overturned and sacred vessels made *impure* by the touch of profane hands>
syn common, defiled, desecrated, polluted, profaned, unclean
rel unhallowed, unholy
con clean, consecrated, undefiled
ant pure
4 *syn* UNREFINED 3, crude, native, raw, run-of-mine, ungraded, unsorted

impute *vb syn* ASCRIBE, accredit, assign, attribute, charge, credit, lay, refer
rel accuse, indict; adduce; hint, insinuate, intimate

in *adj syn* STYLISH, a la mode, chic, fashionable, modish, swank, swish, tonish, ‖trendy, with-it

in *n syn* PULL 2, clout, ‖drag, influence

inability *n* lack of sufficient power, resources, or capacity to perform <suffered from an *inability* to make quick decisions>
syn inadequacy, incapability, incapacity, incompetence, ineffectiveness, ineffectualness, inefficacy
rel inadeptness, inaptitude, inaptness, inefficiency, ineptitude, ineptness
con adequacy, capability, capacity; competence, efficiency
ant ability

inaccessible *adj* not capable of being achieved <an *inaccessible* goal>
syn inapproachable, unapproachable, unattainable, un-come-at-able, ungetatable, unobtainable, unreachable
rel distant, far, faraway, far-off, out-of-the-way, remote
ant accessible

inaccurate *adj syn* FALSE 1, counterfactual, erroneous, incorrect, specious, unsound, untrue, wrong
con right, true
ant accurate

inaction *n* lack of action or activity <the delay was due to the committee's *inaction*>
syn inactiveness, inactivity
rel drift, idleness, indolence, inertness, lethargy, quiescence, slackness, slothfulness, torpidity
con activeness, activity

inactive *adj* not characterized by or engaged in usual or normal activity <forced by illness to lead an *inactive* life>
syn asleep, idle, inert, passive, quiet, sleepy
rel abeyant, dormant, inoperative, latent, quiescent; do-nothing, indolent, lethargic, lymphatic, slack, slothful, sluggish, torpid; motionless, sedentary, static; disengaged, jobless, unemployed, unoccupied, unworking; ossified
con busy, employed, engaged, occupied; energetic, strenuous, vigorous; animated, brisk, lively
ant active

inactiveness *n syn* INACTION, inactivity

inactivity *n syn* INACTION, inactiveness
ant activity

in addition *adv syn* AGAIN 4, additionally, also, besides, further, then

inadept *adj syn* UNSKILLFUL 1, inapt, inept, inexpert, unapt, undexterous, unfacile, unhandy, unproficient
ant adept

inadequacy *n* **1** *syn* INABILITY, incapability, incapacity, incompetence, ineffectiveness, ineffectualness, inefficacy
2 *syn* FAILURE 3, defalcation, deficiency, deficit, insufficience, insufficiency, lack, scantiness, shortage, underage
ant adequacy

inadequate *adj* **1** *syn* DEFICIENT 1, defective, ‖half-assed, incomplete, insufficient, lacking, uncomplete, wanting
ant adequate
2 *syn* SHORT 3, failing, insufficient, scant, scanty, scarce, shy, skimpy, unsufficient, wanting
ant adequate
3 *syn* MEAGER, inappreciable, inconsiderable, insufficient, scanty, scrimpy, skimpy
ant adequate
4 *syn* WEAK 4, boneless, emasculate, forceless, impotent, ineffective, ineffectual, invertebrate, slack-spined, spineless
ant adequate

inadmissible *adj* **1** *syn* IMPROPER 1, ill-timed, inappropriate, inapt, inept, malapropos, unapt, unbecoming, unseasonable, unseemly
2 *syn* OBJECTIONABLE, exceptionable, ill-favored, unacceptable, undesirable, unwanted, unwelcome
ant admissible

in advance *adv syn* BEFORE 1, ahead, ante, antecedently, beforehand, fore, forward, precedently, previous

in advance of *prep* **1** *syn* BEFORE 1, ahead of, ante, ere, preceding, prior to, to
2 *syn* UNTIL, before, prior to, till, to, up till, up to

inadvertent *adj* **1** *syn* CARELESS 1, feckless, heedless, irreflective, thoughtless, uncaring, unheeding, unrecking, unreflective, unthinking
ant advertent
2 *syn* UNINTENTIONAL, undesigned, undevised, unintended, unplanned, unpremeditated, unpurposed, unthought

inadvisable *adj* not likely to have a satisfactory outcome <it seemed *inadvisable* to go any farther because of threatening weather>
syn ill-advised, impolitic, imprudent, inexpedient, unadvisable, unexpedient

rel careless, inappropriate, incautious, rash, undesirable, unsensible; foolish, indiscreet, pointless, unwise; foolhardy, harebrained
con expedient, judicious, politic, prudent, sensible, wise
ant advisable

in all *adv* ***syn*** ALTOGETHER 2, all told, quite

in all probability *adv* ***syn*** PRESUMABLY, assumably, doubtless, likely, presumptively, probably

inalterable *adj* ***syn*** INFLEXIBLE 3, constant, fixed, immovable, immutable, invariable, unalterable, unchangeable, unmodifiable, unmovable
ant alterable

inamorata *n* **1** ***syn*** GIRL FRIEND 2, ‖baby, beloved, flame, honey, ladylove, steady, sweetheart, sweetie, truelove
2 ***syn*** MISTRESS, ‖doxy, girl friend, lover, paramour, woman

inamorato *n* ***syn*** BOYFRIEND 2, beau, beloved, flame, lover, steady, sweetheart, truelove

in and out *adv* ***syn*** THOROUGHLY 2, completely, detailedly, exhaustively, inside out, up and down

inane *adj* ***syn*** INSIPID 3, driveling, flat, innocuous, jejune, milk-and-water, namby-pamby, sapless, vapid, wishy-washy
rel asinine, fatuous, foolish, silly; idle, vain; blank, empty, hollow
con expressive, meaningful, pregnant, significant, weighty
ant deep, profound

inanimate *adj* **1** ***syn*** INSENSATE 1, insensible, insentient, senseless, unfeeling
ant animate
2 ***syn*** DEAD 1, asleep, cold, deceased, defunct, departed, exanimate, extinct, late, lifeless
ant animate; living

inanity *n* ***syn*** FOOLISHNESS, absurdity, craziness, dottiness, folly, insanity, preposterousness, senselessness, silliness, witlessness

inapplicable *adj* ***syn*** IRRELEVANT, extraneous, foreign, immaterial, impertinent, inapposite, irrelative
ant applicable

inapposite *adj* ***syn*** IRRELEVANT, extraneous, foreign, immaterial, impertinent, inapplicable, irrelative
ant apposite

inappreciable *adj* **1** ***syn*** IMPERCEPTIBLE, impalpable, imponderable, indiscernible, insensible, intangible, unapparent, unappreciable, unobservable, unperceivable
ant appreciable
2 ***syn*** MEAGER, inadequate, inconsiderable, insufficient, scanty, scrimpy, skimpy

inapproachable *adj* ***syn*** INACCESSIBLE, unapproachable, unattainable, un-come-at-able, ungetatable, unobtainable, unreachable
ant approachable

inappropriate *adj* **1** ***syn*** UNFIT 1, ill-adapted, ill-suited, inapt, unfitted, unmeet, unsuitable, unsuited
rel indecorous, unseemly; inconsonant
con felicitous, fitting, happy, meet, proper; fit, suitable
ant appropriate
2 ***syn*** IMPROPER 1, ill-timed, inept, malapropos, unbecoming, unbefitting, undue, unseasonable, unsuitable, untimely

inapt *adj* **1** ***syn*** UNFIT 1, ill-adapted, ill-suited, inappropriate, unfitted, unmeet, unsuitable, unsuited
rel awkward, clumsy, gauche, maladroit; banal, flat, insipid, jejune
con apposite, germane, pertinent, relevant
ant apt
2 ***syn*** IMPROPER 1, ill-timed, inappropriate, malapropos, unapt, undue, unfitting, unseasonable, unsuitable, untimely
ant apt
3 ***syn*** UNSKILLFUL 1, inadept, inept, inexpert, unapt, undexterous, unfacile, unhandy, unproficient
ant adept

inarguable *adj* ***syn*** POSITIVE 3, certain, incontestable, indisputable, indubitable, sure, uncontestable, uncontrovertible, undeniable, unquestionable
ant arguable

inarticulate *adj* **1** ***syn*** DUMB 1, mute, silent, speechless, unarticulate, voiceless
ant articulate
2 ***syn*** TACIT 1, implicit, implied, inferred, undeclared, unexpressed, unsaid, unspoken, unuttered, wordless
3 failing to give or incapable of giving clear or effective verbal expression to one's ideas or feelings <made some *inarticulate* explanation for being late> <was completely *inarticulate* when it came to expressing affection>
syn incoherent, maundering, tongue-tied, unvocal
rel faltering, halting, hesitating, mumbling, stammered, stammering; blurred, indistinct
con facile, glib, smooth
ant articulate

inartificial *adj* ***syn*** NATURAL 5, artless, ingenuous, naive, simple, unaffected, unartificial, unschooled, unsophisticated, unstudied
ant artificial

inasmuch as *conj* ***syn*** BECAUSE, as, as long as, ‖being, 'cause, considering, for, now, since, whereas

inattentive *adj* not paying proper attention <an *inattentive* pupil dozing at his desk>
syn inobservant, unheeding, unnoticing, unobservant, unobserving, unperceiving, unwatchful
rel distracted, distrait, distraught; careless, heedless, thoughtless, undiscerning, unmindful, unthinking; bored, ennuyé
ant attentive; observant

inaugural *adj* ***syn*** FIRST 1, foremost, headmost, initial, leading

inaugural *n* ***syn*** INITIATION, inauguration, induction, installation, investiture

inaugurate *vb* **1** ***syn*** INITIATE 3, induct, install, instate, invest
2 ***syn*** BEGIN 1, commence, enter, get off, initiate, jump (off), kick off, launch, open, start

---

syn synonym(s) — *rel* related word(s)
idiom idiomatic equivalent(s) — *con* contrasted word(s)
ant antonym(s) — * vulgar
‖ use limited; if in doubt, see a dictionary
The first word in a synonym list when printed in SMALL CAPITALS shows where there is more information about the group. For a more efficient use of this book see Explanatory Notes.

3 ***syn*** INTRODUCE 3, initiate, institute, launch, originate, set up, usher in

inauguration *n* ***syn*** INITIATION, inaugural, induction, installation, investiture

inauspicious *adj* **1** ***syn*** OMINOUS, baleful, baneful, dire, fateful, ill-boding, ill-omened, threatening, unlucky, unpropitious
ant auspicious
2 ***syn*** EVIL 6, bad

in between *prep* ***syn*** BETWEEN 2, ‖atween, ‖atwixt, ‖betwixt, tween, twixt

inborn *adj* **1** ***syn*** INNATE 1, congenital, connate, connatural, indigenous, inherited, native, natural, unacquired
ant acquired
2 ***syn*** INHERENT, congenital, constitutional, deep-seated, essential, inbred, indwelling, ingrained, innate, intrinsic

inbred *adj* ***syn*** INHERENT, congenital, connate, constitutional, deep-seated, inborn, indwelling, ingrained, innate, intrinsic

in brief *adv* ***syn*** BRIEFLY, concisely, in short, laconically, shortly, succinctly, tersely

incalculable *adj* **1** being great beyond calculation <*incalculable* damage>
syn immeasurable, inestimable, measureless, uncountable, unmeasurable, unmeasured, unreckonable
rel countless, innumerable, unnumbered, untold; boundless, enormous, infinite, limitless, vast
con minimal, slight, trivial
ant infinitesimal
2 ***syn*** UNCERTAIN 1, capricious, chancy, erratic, fluctuant, iffy, unpredictable, whimsical
ant calculable

in camera *adv* ***syn*** SECRETLY, by stealth, clandestinely, covertly, furtively, hugger-mugger, privately, stealthily, sub rosa, surreptitiously

incandescent *adj* ***syn*** BRIGHT 1, beaming, brilliant, effulgent, fulgent, lambent, lucent, luminous, radiant, refulgent

incantation *n* **1** ***syn*** SPELL, charm, conjuration, ‖devil-devil, rune
2 ***syn*** MAGIC 1, bewitchment, conjuring, enchantment, magicking, necromancy, sorcery, witchcraft, witchery, wizardry

incapability *n* ***syn*** INABILITY, inadequacy, incapacity, incompetence, ineffectiveness, ineffectualness, inefficacy
ant capability

incapable *adj* **1** ***syn*** UNFIT 2, disqualified, incompetent, ineligible, unequipped, unfitted, unqualified
ant capable
2 ***syn*** INEFFICIENT 2, incompetent, inept, inexpert, unexpert, unskilled, unskillful, unworkmanlike
ant capable

incapacitate *vb* **1** ***syn*** PARALYZE 1, cripple, disable, disarm, immobilize, prostrate
2 ***syn*** DISQUALIFY, disable, disenable
ant capacitate

incapacity *n* ***syn*** INABILITY, inadequacy, incapability, incompetence, ineffectiveness, ineffectualness, inefficacy
ant capacity

incarcerate *vb* ***syn*** IMPRISON, bastille, confine, constrain, immure, intern, jail, jug, ‖prison, ‖quod

incarnadine *vb* ***syn*** REDDEN 1, rubify, rubric, ruby, rud, ruddle, ruddy

incarnate *vb* ***syn*** EMBODY 1, exteriorize, externalize, manifest, materialize, objectify, personalize, personify, personize, substantiate

incarnation *n* ***syn*** EMBODIMENT, personification

incautious *adj* **1** lacking in caution <made an *incautious* prediction>
syn unalert, unguarded, unvigilant, unwary, unwatchful; *compare* CARELESS 1
rel imprudent, indiscreet, injudicious; bold, brash, impetuous, rash, reckless; neglectful, negligent, regardless, thoughtless, unmindful; hasty
idiom caught napping, off one's guard
con careful, circumspect, judicious, wary, watchful; discreet, judicious, prudent; sensible, thoughtful, wise
ant cautious
2 ***syn*** RASH 1, brash, hasty, hotheaded, ill-advised, inconsiderate, mad-brained, madcap, reckless, thoughtless
ant cautious
3 ***syn*** IRRESPONSIBLE, carefree, careless, feckless, reckless, uncareful, wild

incendiary *n* a person who deliberately and unlawfully sets fire to a building or other property <a fire set by an *incendiary*>
syn arsonist, firebug, torch
rel pyromaniac

incendiary *adj* ***syn*** INFLAMMATORY

incense *n* **1** ***syn*** FRAGRANCE, aroma, balm, bouquet, perfume, redolence, scent, spice
2 ***syn*** FLATTERY, adulation, blandishment, blarney, oil, soft soap

incense *vb* ***syn*** ANGER 1, enrage, infuriate, ire, mad, madden, steam up, umbrage
ant placate

incentive *n* ***syn*** STIMULUS, catalyst, goad, impetus, impulse, incitation, incitement, motivation, spur, stimulant

inception *n* ***syn*** SOURCE, derivation, fountain, origin, provenance, provenience, root, well, wellspring, whence
con closing, completion, conclusion
ant termination

inceptive *adj* ***syn*** INITIAL 1, beginning, incipient, initiative, initiatory, introductory, nascent
ant terminal

incertitude *n* ***syn*** UNCERTAINTY, concern, doubt, dubiety, dubiosity, mistrust, skepticism, suspicion, uncertitude, wonder
ant certitude

incessant *adj* ***syn*** CONTINUAL, ceaseless, constant, continuous, endless, everlasting, interminable, perpetual, timeless, unceasing
ant intermittent

inchoate *adj* **1** ***syn*** FORMLESS, amorphous, shapeless, unformed, unshaped

---

syn synonym(s) ***rel*** related word(s)
idiom idiomatic equivalent(s) ***con*** contrasted word(s)
ant antonym(s) * vulgar
‖ use limited; if in doubt, see a dictionary
The first word in a synonym list when printed in SMALL CAPITALS shows where there is more information about the group. For a more efficient use of this book see Explanatory Notes.

2 *syn* INCOHERENT 2, disconnected, discontinuous, disjointed, disordered, incohesive, muddled, unconnected, uncontinuous, unorganized

incident *n* *syn* OCCURRENCE, circumstance, episode, event, go, happening, occasion, things

incident *adj* 1 *syn* CONCOMITANT, accompanying, ancillary, attendant, attending, coincident, collateral, satellite
ant essential, fundamental
2 *syn* RELATED, affiliated, agnate, akin, allied, cognate, connate, connatural, consanguine, kindred

incidental *adj* *syn* ACCIDENTAL, casual, chance, contingent, fluky, fortuitous, odd
ant essential

incidentally *adv* 1 by chance <in this discussion grave questions were brought up *incidentally*>
syn accidentally, casually, fortuitously
ant deliberately
2 by way of interjection or digression <another leading industry, *incidentally*, has quadrupled its business in four years>
syn by the bye, by the way, in passing, obiter, parenthetically
idiom in the bygoing

incipient *adj* *syn* INITIAL 1, beginning, inceptive, initiative, initiatory, introductory, nascent

incise *vb* 1 *syn* CUT 1, gash, pierce, slash, slice, slit
2 *syn* ENGRAVE 1, etch, grave

incisive *adj* having, manifesting, or suggesting a keen alertness of mind <a man well known for his *incisive* wit>
syn biting, clear-cut, crisp, cutting, ingoing, penetrating, trenchant
rel acute, drilling, keen, sharp; acerb, acerbic, caustic, mordant, scathing, slashing, tart; concise, laconic, succinct, terse
con diffuse, prolix, verbose, wordy; feeble, limp, pithless, sapless
ant unincisive

incisiveness *n* *syn* EDGE 2, keenness, sharpness

incitation *n* *syn* STIMULUS, catalyst, goad, impetus, impulse, incentive, incitement, motivation, spur, stimulant

incite *vb* to aid or promote the activity or development of < *incite* a riot>
syn abet, foment, instigate, provoke, raise, set, set on, stir (up), whip (up)
rel forward, further, promote, stimulate; set off, trigger; agitate, solicit; encourage, motivate, motive; excite, inflame, rouse
con check, curb, discourage, inhibit, restrain; calm, quiet, subdue

incitement *n* *syn* STIMULUS, catalyst, goad, impetus, impulse, incentive, incitation, motivation, spur, stimulant

ant restraint; inhibition

inciter *n* *syn* INSTIGATOR, agitator, fomenter, mover

incivil *adj* *syn* RUDE 6, discourteous, disgracious, disrespectful, ill-bred, ill-mannered, impertinent, impolite, uncivil, ungracious
ant civil

inclement *adj* *syn* SEVERE 3, bitter, brutal, hard, harsh, intemperate, rigorous, rugged
ant clement

inclination *n* 1 *syn* LEANING 2, bent, disposition, inclining, penchant, predilection, predisposition, proclivity, propensity, tendency
ant disinclination
2 *syn* WILL 1, fancy, liking, mind, pleasure, velleity
ant disinclination
3 *syn* APPETITE 3, fondness, liking, soft spot, taste, weakness
ant disinclination
4 *syn* SLOPE, grade, gradient, incline, lean, leaning, slant, tilt

incline *vb* 1 *syn* TEND 1, lean, look
2 *syn* SLANT 1, cant, heel, lean, list, recline, slope, tilt, tip
rel deflect, turn
3 to have an attitude toward or to influence one to take an attitude < *inclined* to believe the story> <his argument *inclined* me to share his view>
syn bend, bias, dispose, predispose; *compare* PREJUDICE 2, TEND 1
rel affect, influence, prompt, sway; drive, impel, induce, move, persuade
ant disincline, indispose
4 *syn* DIRECT 2, address, aim, cast, lay, level, point, train, turn, zero (in)

incline *n* *syn* SLOPE, grade, gradient, inclination, lean, leaning, slant, tilt

inclined *adj* 1 *syn* WILLING 1, disposed, fain, minded, predisposed, prone, ready
ant disinclined
2 *syn* APT 1, given, liable, likely, prone
ant disinclined
3 sloping from the horizontal or perpendicular <cars running on an *inclined* track>
syn declivate, declivitous, inclining, leaning, oblique, pitched, pitching, sloped, sloping, tilted, tilting, tipped; *compare* DIAGONAL
rel dipping, graded, raked

inclining *n* *syn* LEANING 2, bent, disposition, inclination, penchant, predilection, predisposition, proclivity, propensity, tendency

inclining *adj* *syn* INCLINED 3, leaning, oblique, pitched, pitching, sloped, sloping, tilted, tilting, tipped

include *vb* to possess as an integral part of a whole <the park *includes* a zoo and a botanical garden>
syn comprehend, contain, embody, embrace, encompass, have, involve, subsume, take in
rel comprise, cover, encircle, enclose, hold; number; admit, receive
con leave out, omit; preclude, reject; debar; eliminate, rule out
ant exclude

inclusive *adj* 1 *syn* ALL-AROUND 2, comprehensive, general, global, overall, sweeping

2 ***syn*** ENCYCLOPEDIC, comprehensive
incogitable *adj* ***syn*** INCREDIBLE 1, inconceivable, insupposable, unbelievable, unimaginable, unthinkable
ant cogitable
incogitant *adj* ***syn*** RASH 1, brash, hasty, hotheaded, ill-advised, inconsiderate, mad-brained, reckless, thoughtless, unadvised
incognizable *adj* ***syn*** INCOMPREHENSIBLE 1, impenetrable, uncomprehensible, unfathomable, ungraspable, unintelligible, unknowable
ant cognizable
incognizant *adj* ***syn*** IGNORANT 2, inconversant, oblivious, unacquainted, unaware, unfamiliar, uninformed, uninstructed, unknowing, unwitting
ant cognizant
incoherent *adj* **1** ***syn*** LOOSE 3, nonadhesive
2 lacking cohesion or continuity <an *incoherent* presentation>
syn disconnected, discontinuous, disjointed, disordered, inchoate, incohesive, muddled, unconnected, uncontinuous, unorganized
rel discordant, incompatible, incongruous, inconsistent, inconsonant, inharmonious
con ordered, orderly; connected; organized, planned, plotted
ant coherent
3 ***syn*** INARTICULATE 3, maundering, tongue-tied, unvocal
incohesive *adj* ***syn*** INCOHERENT 2, disconnected, discontinuous, disjointed, disordered, inchoate, muddled, unconnected, uncontinuous, unorganized
ant cohesive
incombustible *adj* ***syn*** NONCOMBUSTIBLE, apyrous, nonflammable, noninflammable, uninflammable
ant combustible
income *n* ***syn*** REVENUE, coming(s) in, receipts
incommode *vb* ***syn*** INCONVENIENCE, discommode, ‖disconvenience, disoblige, put about, put out, trouble
rel block, hinder, impede, obstruct; annoy, bother, irk, vex
con favor, oblige; humor, indulge; gratify, please
ant accommodate
incommodious *adj* **1** ***syn*** INCONVENIENT, awkward, discommoding, discommodious, embarrassing
ant commodious
2 ***syn*** CRAMPED, confined, cramp, squeezy, ‖tucked up
ant commodious
incommunicable *adj* **1** ***syn*** UNUTTERABLE, indefinable, indescribable, ineffable, inenarrable, inexpressible, undescribable, unexpressible, unspeakable, untellable
ant communicable
2 ***syn*** RESERVED 1, constrained, noncommittal, restrained
ant communicable, communicative
incomparable *adj* ***syn*** SUPREME, preeminent, surpassing, towering, transcendent, ultimate, unequalable, unmatchable, unsurpassable
rel matchless
con common, commonplace, ordinary; indifferent, mediocre, medium, middling
ant average
incompatible *adj* ***syn*** INCONSONANT 1, conflicting, disconsonant, discordant, discrepant, dissonant, incongruent, incongruous, inconsistent, unmixable
rel adverse, antagonistic, counter; antipathetic; antipodal, antipodean, antithetical, contradictory, contrary, opposite; irreconcilable, unadaptable, unconformable
ant compatible
2 ***syn*** IRRECONCILABLE, inconformable, inconsistent
ant compatible
incompetence *n* ***syn*** INABILITY, inadequacy, incapability, incapacity, ineffectiveness, ineffectualness, inefficacy
incompetent *adj* **1** ***syn*** UNFIT 2, disqualified, incapable, ineligible, unequipped, unfitted, unqualified
ant competent
2 ***syn*** INEFFICIENT 2, incapable, inept, inexpert, unexpert, unskilled, unskillful, unworkmanlike
ant competent
incomplete *adj* **1** lacking a part or parts <an *incomplete* text of a speech>
syn fractional, fragmentary, part, partial
rel broken, deficient, incoherent, lacking, short, wanting; bitty, composite, scrappy
con intact, undamaged, whole
ant complete
2 ***syn*** DEFICIENT 1, defective, ‖half-assed, inadequate, insufficient, lacking, uncomplete, wanting
ant complete
incompliant *adj* **1** ***syn*** OBSTINATE, bullheaded, headstrong, intractable, mulish, pertinacious, perverse, pigheaded, self-willed, stubborn
ant compliant
2 ***syn*** STIFF 1, immalleable, impliable, inelastic, inflexible, rigid, unbending, unflexible, unyielding
incomprehensible *adj* **1** lying above or beyond the reach of the human mind <the *incomprehensible* universe>
syn impenetrable, incognizable, uncomprehensible, unfathomable, ungraspable, unintelligible, unknowable
rel inscrutable, mysterious, mystifying, unsearchable; cryptic, enigmatic, obscure, unclear; imperceptible, indistinguishable
con cognizable, fathomable, graspable, intelligible, knowable; clear, lucid, plain, simple, straightforward; rational, reasonable
ant comprehensible, understandable
2 ***syn*** INCONCEIVABLE 1, unimaginable, unknowable, ununderstandable
ant comprehensible, graspable
inconceivable *adj* **1** impossible to comprehend in the absence of actual experience or knowledge <color is *inconceivable* to those born blind>
syn incomprehensible, unimaginable, unknowable, ununderstandable
idiom beyond one's grasp
con comprehensible, imaginable, knowable, understandable
ant conceivable

---

syn synonym(s) ***rel*** related word(s)
idiom idiomatic equivalent(s) ***con*** contrasted word(s)
ant antonym(s) * vulgar
‖ use limited; if in doubt, see a dictionary
The first word in a synonym list when printed in SMALL CAPITALS shows where there is more information about the group. For a more efficient use of this book see Explanatory Notes.

2 *syn* INCREDIBLE 1, incogitable, insupposable, unbelievable, unimaginable, unthinkable
ant conceivable
3 *syn* IMPLAUSIBLE, flimsy, improbable, incredible, thin, unbelievable, unconceivable, unconvincing, unsubstantial, weak
con believable, convincing, credible, plausible
ant conceivable

inconclusive *adj* leading to no conclusion or definite result <the report was *inconclusive*>
syn indecisive
rel open, uncertain, undecided, unsettled; incomplete, unfinished
con clarifying, illuminating; decisive
ant conclusive

incondite *adj syn* RUDE 6, discourteous, disgracious, disrespectful, ill-bred, ill-mannered, impertinent, impolite, uncivil, ungracious

inconformable *adj syn* IRRECONCILABLE, incompatible, inconsistent
ant conformable

incongruent *adj syn* INCONSONANT 1, conflicting, disconsonant, discordant, discrepant, dissonant, incompatible, incongruous, inconsistent, unmixable
ant congruent, congruous

incongruous *adj syn* INCONSONANT 1, conflicting, disconsonant, discordant, discrepant, dissonant, incompatible, incongruent, inconsistent, unmixable
rel alien, extraneous, foreign; bizarre, fantastic, grotesque
idiom out of place
con appropriate, fit, fitting, meet, seemly, suitable
ant congruent, congruous

inconnu *n syn* STRANGER, alien, auslander, foreigner, outcomer, outlander, outsider

inconquerable *adj* 1 *syn* INVINCIBLE 1, impregnable, indomitable, inexpugnable, invulnerable, unassailable, unbeatable, unconquerable, undefeatable
2 *syn* INSUPERABLE, impassable, indomitable, insurmountable, invincible, unconquerable, unsurmountable

inconscient *adj syn* ABSTRACTED, absent, absent-minded, bemused, distrait, faraway, lost, preoccupied
ant conscient, conscious

inconscious *adj syn* INSENSIBLE 2, cold, comatose, senseless, unconscious
ant conscious

inconsequent *adj syn* PETTY 2, inconsequential, inconsiderable, measly, niggling, paltry, peanut, pettifogging, picayune, picayunish

inconsequential *adj syn* PETTY 2, inconsequent, inconsiderable, measly, paltry, picayune, picayunish, small, trifling, trivial
ant consequential

---

syn synonym(s) *rel* related word(s)
idiom idiomatic equivalent(s) *con* contrasted word(s)
ant antonym(s) * vulgar
‖ use limited; if in doubt, see a dictionary
The first word in a synonym list when printed in SMALL CAPITALS shows where there is more information about the group. For a more efficient use of this book see Explanatory Notes.

inconsiderable *adj* 1 *syn* LITTLE 3, casual, insignificant, light, minor, petty, shoestring, small-beer, trivial, unimportant
ant considerable
2 *syn* MEAGER, inadequate, inappreciable, insufficient, scanty, scrimpy, skimpy
ant considerable
3 *syn* PETTY 2, inconsequent, inconsequential, paltry, peanut, picayune, puny, small, trifling, unconsidered
ant considerable

inconsiderate *adj* 1 *syn* RASH 1, brash, hasty, hotheaded, ill-advised, incautious, madcap, reckless, thoughtless, unconsidered
ant considerate
2 *syn* SHORT 5, sharp, thoughtless, unceremonious, ungracious
ant considerate

inconsistent *adj* 1 *syn* INCONSTANT 1, capricious, changeable, fickle, lubricious, mercurial, temperamental, ticklish, uncertain, unstable
ant consistent
2 *syn* INCONSONANT 1, conflicting, disconsonant, discordant, discrepant, dissonant, incompatible, incongruent, incongruous, unmixable
ant consistent
3 *syn* IRRECONCILABLE, incompatible, inconformable
ant consistent

inconsolable *adj* incapable of being consoled <she was *inconsolable* over the loss of her child>
syn desolate, disconsolate, unconsolable
rel comfortless, dejected, forlorn, heartsick
ant consolable

inconsonant *adj* 1 not in agreement with one another or not agreeable one to the other <his actions are *inconsonant* with his words>
syn conflicting, disconsonant, discordant, discrepant, dissonant, incompatible, incongruent, incongruous, inconsistent, unmixable
rel ill-matched, ill-suited, mismated, uncongenial; inappropriate, unsuitable
con accordant, compatible, congenial, congruous, consistent
ant consonant
2 *syn* INHARMONIOUS 2, discordant, uncongenial, unharmonious
ant consonant

inconspicuous *adj* not readily noticeable <occupied an *inconspicuous* position>
syn obscure, unconspicuous, unemphatic, unnoticeable
rel indistinct, insignificant, unnoticeable, unobtrusive, vague
con eye-catching, showy, striking; distinct, noticeable
ant conspicuous, prominent

inconstant *adj* 1 lacking firmness or steadiness (as in purpose or devotion) <depended too much on an *inconstant* friend>
syn capricious, changeable, fickle, inconsistent, lubricious, mercurial, temperamental, ticklish, uncertain, unstable, variable, volatile; *compare* CHANGEABLE 1, MUTABLE 2, UNCERTAIN 1
rel changeful, mutable, protean, unsettled, unsteady; elusive, erratic, vacillating, vagrant, wavering, wayward; irresolute, shifty, shilly-shally; undependable, un-

reliable; disloyal, faithless, false, perfidious, traitorous, treacherous, untrue; frivolous, light, light-minded
con dependable, reliable, trustworthy, trusty; faithful, loyal, resolute, staunch, steadfast, true
ant constant
2 *syn* MUTABLE 2, changeable, shifty, slippery, uncertain, unstable, unsteady, variable
ant constant

incontestable *adj syn* POSITIVE 3, certain, indisputable, indubitable, irrefutable, sure, uncontestable, uncontrovertible, undeniable, unquestionable
ant contestable

incontinent *adj syn* LICENTIOUS 2, fast, lascivious, lecherous, lewd, libertine, libidinous, lustful, salacious, satyric
ant continent

incontinently *adv syn* PELL-MELL, helter-skelter, hotfoot, hurry-scurry, impetuously

incontrovertible *adj syn* POSITIVE 3, certain, incontestable, indisputable, indubitable, uncontestable, undeniable, undisputable, unequivocal, unquestionable
ant controvertible

inconvenience *n* the quality or state of being inconvenient <he hated the *inconvenience* of not having a telephone>
syn bother, bothersomeness, ‖disconvenience, troublesomeness
rel annoyance, aggravation, exasperation, trial; fuss, pother, stew
ant convenience

inconvenience *vb* to subject to disturbance or discomfort <was not seriously *inconvenienced* by the bad weather>
syn discommode, ‖disconvenience, disoblige, incommode, put about, put out, trouble
rel discompose, disturb; interfere, intermeddle, meddle; aggravate, exasperate, try
idiom put to trouble
ant convenience

inconvenient *adj* not conducive to physical, mental, or social ease and comfort <he came at an *inconvenient* time>
syn awkward, discommoding, discommodious, embarrassing, incommodious
rel bothersome, pestiferous, troublesome; inexpedient; detrimental, disadvantageous, prejudicial
con appropriate, becoming, fitting, suitable; acceptable, bearable, tolerable; advantageous, desirable, helpful
ant convenient

inconversable *adj syn* SILENT 3, close-lipped, close-mouthed, close-tongued, reserved, reticent, shut-mouthed, taciturn, tight-lipped, uncommunicative
ant conversable

inconversant *adj syn* IGNORANT 2, incognizant, oblivious, unacquainted, unaware, unfamiliar, uninformed, uninstructed, unknowing, unwitting
ant conversant

incorporate *vb* **1** *syn* ABSORB 1, assimilate, imbibe, inhaust, insorb
2 *syn* EMBODY 2, combine, integrate

incorporeal *adj syn* IMMATERIAL 1, asomatous, bodiless, discarnate, disembodied, metaphysical, nonmaterial, nonphysical, unembodied, unphysical
ant corporeal

incorrect *adj syn* FALSE 1, counterfactual, erroneous, inaccurate, specious, unsound, untrue, wrong
ant correct

incorrectly *adv syn* AMISS 1, faultily, wrongly
ant correctly

incorrectness *n syn* IMPROPRIETY 1, indecorousness, indecorum, inelegance, unbecomingness, unmeetness, unseemliness, untowardness
ant correctitude, correctness

incorruptible *adj syn* INDESTRUCTIBLE, imperishable, inexterminable, inextinguishable, inextirpable, irrefragable, irrefrangible, quenchless, undestroyable, unperishable
ant corruptible

incorruption *n syn* HONESTY, honestness, honor, honorableness, integrity
ant corruption

increase *vb* **1** to make greater or more numerous <*increase* crops by good cultural practices>
syn aggrandize, augment, beef (up), boost, build, compound, enlarge, expand, extend, heighten, magnify, manifold, multiply, plus, push
rel aggravate, enhance, intensify; amplify, dilate, distend, inflate, swell; elongate, lengthen, prolong, protract; reinforce, strengthen
con abate, abbreviate, condense, contract; depreciate, diminish, lessen, lower, reduce; curtail, shorten, shrink; minimize
ant decrease
2 to become greater or more numerous <his wealth *increased* over the years>
syn augment, build, burgeon, enlarge, expand, heighten, mount, multiply, rise, run up, snowball, upsurge, wax
rel dilate, distend, inflate, intensify, lengthen, strengthen, swell; pullulate, swarm, teem
con abate, condense, contract, diminish, lessen, lower, reduce, shorten, shrink; die off, die (out), end, terminate
ant decrease
3 *syn* RAISE 9, boost, hike, jack (up), jump, put up, up

increase *n* **1** *syn* ADDITION, accession, accretion, augmentation, increment, raise, rise
ant decrease
2 *syn* RISE 3, boost, breakthrough, hike, upgrade, wax

increate *adj syn* SELF-EXISTENT, self-existing, unbegotten, uncaused, uncreated, unoriginated
ant created

incredible *adj* **1** too extraordinary or improbable to admit of belief <an *incredible* story of privations overcome>

---

syn synonym(s)	*rel* related word(s)
idiom idiomatic equivalent(s)	*con* contrasted word(s)
ant antonym(s)	* vulgar

‖ use limited; if in doubt, see a dictionary
The first word in a synonym list when printed in SMALL CAPITALS shows where there is more information about the group. For a more efficient use of this book see Explanatory Notes.

syn incogitable, inconceivable, insupposable, unbelievable, unimaginable, unthinkable
rel absurd, outlandish, preposterous, ridiculous; impossible, untenable
idiom beyond belief, out of the question
con acceptable, believable, conceivable, likely, plausible, reasonable
ant credible
2 *syn* IMPLAUSIBLE, flimsy, improbable, inconceivable, thick, thin, unbelievable, unconvincing, unsubstantial, weak
ant credible

incredulity *n syn* UNBELIEF, disbelief, unbelievingness, unfaith
con gullibility, naiveté
ant credulity, credulousness

incredulous *adj* unwilling to admit or accept what is offered as true <his explanation met an *incredulous* response from his listeners>
syn aporetic, disbelieving, questioning, quizzical, show-me, skeptical, unbelieving
rel hesitant, suspicious, uncertain, wary; distrustful, distrusting, mistrustful; doubting, dubious, unconvinced, unsatisfied
con trustful, trusting; unsuspecting, unsuspicious, unwary; gullible, naive
ant credulous

increment *n syn* ADDITION, accession, accretion, augmentation, increase, raise, rise

incriminate *vb syn* ACCUSE, arraign, charge, criminate, impeach, inculpate, indict, tax
rel implicate, involve
ant exonerate

incrustate *vb syn* CAKE 1, crust, encrust (*or* incrust), rime

inculcate *vb syn* IMPLANT, infix, inseminate, instill
rel educate, instruct, teach; communicate, impart

inculpable *adj* 1 *syn* GOOD, ‖blameless, exemplary, guiltless, innocent, irreprehensible, irreproachable, pure, righteous, virtuous
ant culpable
2 *syn* INNOCENT 2, blameless, clean, crimeless, faultless, guiltless, unguilty
ant culpable

inculpate *vb syn* ACCUSE, arraign, charge, criminate, impeach, incriminate, indict, tax
ant exculpate

incult *adj syn* COARSE 3, crass, crude, gross, inelegant, low, rough, rude, uncouth, unrefined

incur *vb* to bring (something usually unpleasant) upon oneself <he foolishly *incurred* debts beyond his ability to pay>
syn contract
rel acquire, get; bring on, induce
idiom bring down on (*or* upon)
con avoid, elude, escape, eschew, evade, shun; discharge, pay, settle

incurable *adj syn* HOPELESS 2, cureless, immedicable, impossible, insanable, irremediable, irreparable, uncorrectable, uncurable, unrecoverable
ant curable

incurious *adj syn* INDIFFERENT 2, aloof, casual, detached, disinterested, remote, unconcerned, uncurious, uninterested, withdrawn
rel absent, absentminded, abstracted, distraught, preoccupied
con nosy, prying, snoopy; impertinent, intrusive, meddlesome; observant, observing
ant curious, inquisitive

incursion *n syn* INVASION, foray, inroad, irruption, raid

indebted *adj* owing gratitude or recognition (as for a favor or service rendered) <was *indebted* to the book for most of his information>
syn beholden, obligated, obliged
rel duty-bound, honor-bound

indebtedness *n* 1 a state of owing something <unable to escape from *indebtedness*>
syn arrearage, debt, liability, obligation; *compare* DEBT 3
rel delinquency, nonpayment; bankruptcy, failure, insolvency
con discharge, liquidation, satisfaction; exoneration, freeing, release
2 *syn* DEBT 3, arrear(s), arrearage, due, liability

indecent *adj* 1 *syn* INDECOROUS, improper, indelicate, malodorous, ridiculous, unbecoming, undecorous, ungodly, unseemly, untoward
ant decent
2 *syn* OBSCENE 2, coarse, dirty, filthy, foul, nasty, raunchy, scatological, smutty, vulgar
ant decent

indecipherable *adj syn* ILLEGIBLE, undecipherable, unreadable
ant decipherable

indecision *n syn* HESITATION, hesitancy, indecisiveness, irresolution, shilly-shally, to-and-fro, vacillation, wavering
ant decision, decisiveness

indecisive *adj* 1 *syn* INCONCLUSIVE
ant decisive
2 *syn* DOUBTFUL 1, borderline, dubious, equivocal, open, problematic, shaky, uncertain, unclear, undecided
con certain, incontrovertible, undebatable, unequivocal
ant decisive
3 *syn* VACILLATING 2, faltering, halting, hesitant, hesitating, irresolute, shilly-shallying, tentative, uncertain, undecisive
rel undecided, unsettled
idiom of two minds
con decided, determined, firm, positive, resolved, settled, unfaltering, unhesitant, unhesitating, unwavering
ant decisive

indecisiveness *n syn* HESITATION, hesitancy, irresolution, shilly-shally, to-and-fro, vacillation, wavering
ant indecision, indecisiveness

indecorous *adj* not conforming with accepted standards of propriety or good taste <they regarded argument in public as *indecorous*>

---

syn synonym(s) — *rel* related word(s)
idiom idiomatic equivalent(s) — *con* contrasted word(s)
ant antonym(s) — * vulgar
‖ use limited; if in doubt, see a dictionary
The first word in a synonym list when printed in SMALL CAPITALS shows where there is more information about the group. For a more efficient use of this book see Explanatory Notes.

syn improper, indecent, indelicate, malodorous, ridiculous, rough, unbecoming, undecorous, ungodly, unseemly, untoward
rel inappropriate, incorrect, unbefitting, unfit, unfitting; immodest, inelegant, undignified; coarse, gross, loose, offensive, shameful, tasteless, vulgar; discourteous, ill-mannered, impolite, rude, uncivil; irregular, unlawful
idiom in bad form
con becoming, courteous, decent, nice, proper, seemly; conventional, formal
ant decorous

indecorousness *n syn* IMPROPRIETY 1, incorrectness, indecorum, inelegance, unbecomingness, unmeetness, unseemliness, untowardness
ant decorousness

indecorum *n* **1** *syn* FAUX PAS, blooper, boner, ‖boo-boo, break, gaffe, impropriety, solecism
2 *syn* IMPROPRIETY 1, incorrectness, indecorousness, inelegance, unbecomingness, unmeetness, unseemliness, untowardness
ant decorum

indeed *adv* **1** *syn* WELL 7, doubtlessly, easily, really, truly, undoubtedly
2 *syn* EVEN 3, nay, truly, verily, yea

indefatigable *adj* capable of prolonged and arduous effort <a teacher who has *indefatigable* patience with slow learners>
syn inexhaustible, tireless, unflagging, untiring, unweariable, unwearying, weariless
rel assiduous, diligent, painstaking, sedulous; determined, dogged, patient, persevering, persistent, pertinacious, relentless, steadfast, stubborn, tenacious, unfaltering, unflinching, unrelenting, unwavering; energetic, strenuous, vigorous
con dawdling, dilatory, laggard, lagging, procrastinating; faineant, indolent, lackadaisical, lazy, slothful, sluggish
ant fatigable

indefectible *adj* **1** *syn* PERFECT 2, absolute, flawless, fleckless, impeccable, note-perfect, unflawed
2 *syn* IDEAL 3, flawless, model

indefensible *adj syn* INEXCUSABLE, inexpiable, unforgivable, unjustifiable, unpardonable, untenable
ant defensible

indefinable *adj syn* UNUTTERABLE, incommunicable, indescribable, ineffable, inenarrable, inexpressible, undescribable, unexpressible, unspeakable, untellable
ant definable

indefinite *adj* **1** having no exact limits <a region with *indefinite* boundaries>
syn indeterminate, indistinct, inexact, undeterminable
rel unclear, undefined, unfixed, unspecific; broad, loose, wide; general, obscure, vague
con exact, measured; known
ant definite
2 *syn* LIMITLESS, boundless, endless, immeasurable, infinite, measureless, unbounded, unlimited, unmeasured
ant definite

indelible *adj* that cannot be removed or erased <made an *indelible* impression on his hearers>
syn ineffaceable, ineradicable, inerasable, inexpungible, inextirpable, uneradicable, unerasable
rel indestructible, undestroyable; enduring, permanent
con eradicable, effaceable, erasable, removable; ephemeral, evanescent, passing, temporary, transitory
ant delible

indelicate *adj syn* INDECOROUS, improper, indecent, malodorous, rough, unbecoming, undecorous, ungodly, unseemly, untoward
rel callow, crude, rude, uncouth; lewd, wanton
con chaste, modest, pure
ant delicate

indemnification *n syn* REPARATION, amends, compensation, indemnity, quittance, recompense, redress, reprisal, restitution

indemnify *vb syn* COMPENSATE 3, pay, recompense, reimburse, remunerate, repay, requite

indemnity *n syn* REPARATION, amends, compensation, indemnification, quittance, recompense, redress, reprisal, restitution

indentation *n* **1** *syn* NOTCH 1, indenture, nick
2 *syn* IMPRESSION 1, impress, imprint, print, stamp

indenture *n syn* NOTCH 1, indentation, nick

indentured *adj syn* BOUND 2, apprenticed, articled

independent *adj* **1** *syn* FREE 1, autarchic, autarkic, autonomous, separate, sovereign
2 *syn* SELF-SUFFICIENT, closed, self-centered, self-contained, self-sufficing, self-supported, self-supporting, self-sustained, self-sustaining
ant dependent

independently *adv syn* APART 1, individually, one by one, separately, severally, singly
idiom on one's own

indescribable *adj syn* UNUTTERABLE, incommunicable, indefinable, ineffable, inenarrable, inexpressible, undescribable, unexpressible, unspeakable, untellable
ant describable

indestructible *adj* incapable of being destroyed <*indestructible* idealism>
syn imperishable, incorruptible, inexterminable, inextinguishable, inextirpable, irrefragable, irrefrangible, quenchless, undestroyable, unperishable
rel changeless, immutable, unalterable, unchangeable; deathless, immortal, perpetual, undying; durable, enduring, lasting, permanent; indelible, ineradicable; unextinguishable, unquenchable
con alterable, changeable, corruptible, impermanent, temporary, transient, unlasting; mortal, temporal; evanescent
ant destroyable, destructible, perishable

indeterminate *adj syn* INDEFINITE 1, indistinct, inexact, undeterminable
ant determinate

index *n syn* INDICATION 3, evidence, indicia, mark, sign, significant, symptom, token

Indian sign *n syn* JINX, hex, hoodoo, voodoo, whammy

---

syn synonym(s) | *rel* related word(s)
idiom idiomatic equivalent(s) | *con* contrasted word(s)
ant antonym(s) | * vulgar
‖ use limited; if in doubt, see a dictionary
The first word in a synonym list when printed in SMALL CAPITALS shows where there is more information about the group. For a more efficient use of this book see Explanatory Notes.

indicate *vb* **1** ***syn*** POINT 2, hint, imply, suggest
2 to give evidence of or serve as ground for a valid or reasonable inference <several polls *indicate* a landslide for the incumbent>
syn announce, argue, attest, bespeak, betoken, testify, witness
rel denote, import, mean, signify; demonstrate, prove; evidence, evince, manifest, show; display, exhibit, express, illustrate; connote, hint, imply, suggest
3 ***syn*** SHOW 5, mark, read, record, register, say

indication *n* **1** ***syn*** HINT 1, clue, cue, inkling, intimation, notion, suggestion, telltale, wind
2 ***syn*** EXPRESSION 3, gesture, reminder, sign, token
3 something that is an outward manifestation of something else <such *indications* of prosperity as second cars and color TVs>
syn evidence, index, indicia, mark, sign, significant, symptom, token; *compare* SYMBOL 1, TESTIMONY
rel expression, manifestation; hint, suggestion; proof; prefiguration, type

indicative *adj* serving to indicate <the roar of the crowd was *indicative* of its approval>
syn denotative, denotive, designative, exhibitive, indicatory, indicial, significative
rel characteristic, demonstrative, evidential, evincive, expressive, suggestive, symbolic, symptomatic, testatory

indicatory *adj* ***syn*** INDICATIVE, denotative, denotive, designative, exhibitive, indicial, significative

indicia *n pl* ***syn*** INDICATION 3, evidence, index, mark, sign, significant, symptom, token

indicial *adj* ***syn*** INDICATIVE, denotative, denotive, designative, exhibitive, indicatory, significative

indict *vb* ***syn*** ACCUSE, arraign, charge, criminate, impeach, incriminate, inculpate, tax

indifference *n* ***syn*** APATHY 2, disinterest, disregard, heedlessness, insouciance, lassitude, lethargy, listlessness, unconcern, unmindfulness

indifferent *adj* **1** ***syn*** FAIR 4, dispassionate, equal, equitable, impartial, impersonal, nondiscriminatory, objective, unbiased, unprejudiced
2 marked by a lack of interest or concern <was *indifferent* to suffering and poverty>
syn aloof, by-the-way, casual, detached, disinterested, incurious, numb, pococurante, remote, unconcerned, uncurious, uninterested, withdrawn; *compare* UNSOCIABLE
rel apathetic, impassive, insensible; dispassionate; careless, heedless, negligent, regardless, uncaring, unmindful; inattentive, unobserving
con attentive, considerate, heedful, interested, mindful, regardful, sympathetic
ant concerned
3 ***syn*** COLD 2, chill, emotionless, frigid, glacial, icy, unemotional

---

syn synonym(s) ***rel*** related word(s)
idiom idiomatic equivalent(s) ***con*** contrasted word(s)
ant antonym(s) * vulgar
‖ use limited; if in doubt, see a dictionary
The first word in a synonym list when printed in SMALL CAPITALS shows where there is more information about the group. For a more efficient use of this book see Explanatory Notes.

4 ***syn*** MEDIUM, average, fair, fairish, intermediate, mean, mediocre, middling, moderate, so-so

indigence *n* ***syn*** POVERTY 1, destitution, impecuniousness, impoverishment, indigency, need, neediness, penury, privation, want
ant affluence, opulence

indigency *n* ***syn*** POVERTY 1, destitution, impecuniousness, impoverishment, indigence, need, neediness, penury, privation, want
ant affluence, opulence

indigenous *adj* **1** ***syn*** NATIVE 2, aboriginal, autochthonous, endemic
con alien, extraneous, foreign
ant exotic; naturalized
2 ***syn*** INNATE 1, congenital, connate, connatural, inborn, inherited, native, natural, unacquired

indigent *adj* ***syn*** POOR 1, destitute, dirt poor, impecunious, impoverished, necessitous, needy, penniless, penurious, poverty-stricken
ant affluent, opulent

indignant *adj* ***syn*** ANGRY, acrimonious, heated, irate, mad, wrathful, wrathy, wroth, wrothful, wrothy
ant gratified

indignation *n* ***syn*** ANGER, fury, ire, mad, rage, wrath
ant gratification

indignity *n* ***syn*** AFFRONT, contumely, despite, insult, slap
rel grievance, injury, injustice, wrong

indirect *adj* **1** deviating from a direct line or straightforward course <made *indirect* inquiries about the new neighbor>
syn circuitous, circular, collateral, oblique, roundabout
rel circumlocutory, crooked, devious; meandering, serpentine, sinuous, tortuous, twisting, winding; errant, vagrant, wandering
ant direct; forthright, straightforward
2 ***syn*** UNDERHAND, devious, duplicitous, guileful, shifty, sneaking, sneaky, underhanded
ant straight

indirection *n* ***syn*** DECEPTION 1, cheat, chicane, chicanery, dirt, dishonesty, double-dealing, dupery, fraud, hanky-panky

indiscernible *adj* ***syn*** IMPERCEPTIBLE, impalpable, imponderable, inappreciable, insensible, intangible, unapparent, unappreciable, unobservable, unperceivable
ant discernible, distinguishable

indiscreet *adj* ***syn*** UNWISE, ill-advised, ill-judged, impolitic, imprudent, injudicious
ant discreet

indiscriminate *adj* **1** including all or nearly all within the range of choice, operation, or effectiveness <her charity was *indiscriminate* but generous>
syn indiscriminating, indiscriminative, sweeping, undiscriminated, undiscriminating, undistinguishing, wholesale
rel assorted, heterogeneous, miscellaneous, promiscuous; shallow, superficial, uncritical; broad, extensive, wide
con discretionary, discriminative; choosy, picky; critical, perfectionist
ant selective; discriminate, discriminated
2 ***syn*** RANDOM, aimless, designless, desultory, haphazard, hit-or-miss, purposeless, spot, unconsidered, unplanned

3 ***syn*** MISCELLANEOUS, assorted, chowchow, conglomerate, heterogeneous, mixed, motley, multifarious, promiscuous, varied

indiscriminating *adj* ***syn*** INDISCRIMINATE 1, indiscriminative, sweeping, undiscriminated, undiscriminating, undistinguishing, wholesale
ant discriminating

indiscriminative *adj* ***syn*** INDISCRIMINATE 1, indiscriminating, sweeping, undiscriminated, undiscriminating, undistinguishing, wholesale
ant discriminative

indispensable *adj* ***syn*** ESSENTIAL 4, imperative, necessary, necessitous, prerequisite
rel cardinal, fundamental
ant dispensable

indisposed *adj* **1** ***syn*** UNWELL, ailing, ‖donsie, low, mean, off-color, offish, poorly, sickly, underly
2 ***syn*** DISINCLINED, afraid, averse, backward, hesitant, loath, reluctant, uneager, unwilling, unwishful
rel antagonistic, antipathetic, hostile, inimical
con amicable, neighborly; responsive, sympathetic
ant disposed

indisposition *n* **1** ***syn*** DISLIKE, aversion, bad books, disfavor, disinclination, disliking, displeasure, disrelish, dissatisfaction, distaste
2 ***syn*** SICKNESS 1, affliction, diseasedness, disorder, illness, infirmity, unhealth

indisputable *adj* **1** ***syn*** POSITIVE 3, certain, incontestable, indubitable, irrefutable, sure, uncontestable, uncontrovertible, undeniable, unquestionable
ant disputable
2 ***syn*** REAL 3, actual, true, undeniable, unfabled, veridical

indistinct *adj* **1** ***syn*** INDEFINITE 1, indeterminate, inexact, undeterminable
ant distinct
2 ***syn*** FAINT 2, bleary, dim, ill-defined, obscure, shadowy, unclear, undefined, undetermined, vague
ant distinct

indistinguishable *adj* ***syn*** SAME 2, duplicate, equal, equivalent, identic, identical, tantamount
ant distinguishable

indite *vb* ***syn*** WRITE, engross, inscribe, scribe

individual *adj* **1** ***syn*** PERSONAL 1
ant common, popular
2 ***syn*** SPECIAL 1, especial, particular, specific
rel separate, single, sole
con generic, universal
ant general
3 ***syn*** CHARACTERISTIC, diacritic, diagnostic, distinctive, idiosyncratic, peculiar, proper
ant common
4 ***syn*** SEVERAL 1, individual, particular, respective, singular

individual *n* **1** ***syn*** ENTITY 1, being, existence, existent, something, thing
2 ***syn*** THING 4, being, entity, material, matter, object, stuff, substance
3 ***syn*** HUMAN, being, body, creature, man, mortal, party, person, personage, soul

individualism *n* **1** ***syn*** DISPOSITION 3, character, complexion, humor, individuality, makeup, nature, personality, temper, temperament
2 ***syn*** INDIVIDUALITY 3, distinctiveness, particularity, singularity

individualist *adj* ***syn*** EGOCENTRIC 1, individualistic

individualistic *adj* ***syn*** EGOCENTRIC 1, individualist

individuality *n* **1** ***syn*** DISPOSITION 3, character, complexion, humor, individualism, makeup, nature, personality, temper, temperament
2 ***syn*** UNITY 1, oneness, singleness, singularity, singularness
3 distinctive character <a person of marked *individuality*>
syn distinctiveness, individualism, particularity, singularity
rel character, personality
4 individual identity <a teacher who respects children's *individualities*>
syn identity, ipseity, personality, seity, selfdom, selfhood, selfness, singularity
rel independence, separateness, uniqueness; difference, dissimilarity, unlikeness
con likeness, resemblance, similarity

individualize *vb* ***syn*** CHARACTERIZE 2, distinguish, individuate, mark, qualify, signalize, singularize

individually *adv* ***syn*** APART 1, independently, one by one, separately, severally, singly

individuate *vb* ***syn*** CHARACTERIZE 2, distinguish, individualize, mark, qualify, signalize, singularize

indocile *adj* ***syn*** UNRULY 1, fractious, indomitable, intractable, recalcitrant, uncontrollable, undisciplined, ungovernable, unmanageable, wild
ant docile

indolence *n* ***syn*** SLOTH 1, idleness, laze, laziness, slothfulness, slouch, sluggishness
ant industry

indolent *adj* ***syn*** LAZY, drony, easygoing, faineant, slothful, slowgoing, work-shy
con active, diligent, energetic, vigorous
ant industrious

indomitable *adj* **1** ***syn*** INVINCIBLE 1, impregnable, inconquerable, inexpugnable, invulnerable, unassailable, unbeatable, unconquerable, undefeatable
ant domitable
2 ***syn*** INSUPERABLE, impassable, inconquerable, insurmountable, invincible, unconquerable, unsurmountable
rel dogged, pertinacious, stubborn; resolute, staunch, steadfast
ant domitable
3 ***syn*** UNRULY 1, fractious, indocile, intractable, recalcitrant, undisciplinable, undisciplined, ungovernable, unmanageable, wild

indoors *adv* in or into a building <stayed *indoors* during the storm>
syn inside, within, withindoors, withinside
con outdoors, outside, without, withoutdoors

---

ant outdoors

indubitable *adj* **1** *syn* POSITIVE 3, certain, incontestable, indisputable, irrefutable, sure, uncontestable, uncontrovertible, undeniable, unquestionable
ant dubitable, questionable
2 *syn* AUTHENTIC 2, blown-in-the-bottle, bona fide, genuine, real, sure-enough, true, undoubted, unquestionable, veritable
ant doubtful, dubious
3 *syn* DOWNRIGHT 2, flat, unquestionable, up-and-down

induce *vb* **1** to move another to do or agree to something <*induced* him to give up smoking for the sake of his health>
syn argue (into), bring around, convince, draw, draw in, draw on, get, oversway, persuade, prevail (on *or* upon), procure, prompt, talk (into), win (over)
rel influence, sway; abet, incite, lead; actuate, impel, move; activate, motivate
con check, curb, hold back, restrain
2 *syn* GENERATE 3, breed, cause, engender, get up, hatch, muster (up), occasion, produce, work up

inducible *adj syn* INDUCTIVE, a posteriori

induct *vb syn* INITIATE 3, inaugurate, install, instate, invest

induction *n syn* INITIATION, inaugural, inauguration, installation, investiture

inductive *adj* **1** derived or derivable by reasoning from a part to a whole, from particulars to generals, or from the individual to the universal <used an *inductive* approach to the problem>
syn a posteriori, inducible
rel Baconian, epagogic
2 *syn* PRELIMINARY, introductory, prefatial, prefatorial, prefatory, ‖prelim, preludial, prelusive, preparative, preparatory

indulge *vb* **1** to give free rein to (as curiosity or a desire) <*indulged* their taste for gourmet foods>
syn cater (to), gratify, humor
rel favor, oblige, satisfy; delight, please, regale
idiom give rein to
con bridle, check, constrain, curb, restrain
2 *syn* BABY, cater (to), cocker, coddle, cosset, humor, mollycoddle, ‖much, pamper, spoil
3 *syn* WALLOW 3, bask, luxuriate, revel, roll, rollick, welter

indulgence *n* **1** *syn* FORBEARANCE 2, clemency, lenience, leniency, mercifulness, tolerance, toleration
rel benignancy, benignity, benignness, kindliness, kindness; gentleness, mildness
con rigor, severity, sternness; rigidity, rigorousness; harshness
ant strictness

---

syn synonym(s) *rel* related word(s)
idiom idiomatic equivalent(s) *con* contrasted word(s)
ant antonym(s) * vulgar
‖ use limited; if in doubt, see a dictionary
The first word in a synonym list when printed in SMALL CAPITALS shows where there is more information about the group. For a more efficient use of this book see Explanatory Notes.

2 *syn* FAVOR 4, courtesy, dispensation, kindness, service

indulgent *adj syn* FORBEARING, charitable, clement, easy, lenient, merciful, tolerant
rel cosseting, pampering, permissive; condoning, excusing, forgiving, pardoning; benign, benignant, kind, kindly
con severe, stern; harsh, rigorous, stringent
ant strict

indurate *vb syn* HARDEN 1, cake, concrete, congeal, dry, set, solidify

industrious *adj syn* ASSIDUOUS, diligent, operose, sedulous
rel active, busy, live, dynamic; persevering, persistent
con idle, inactive; lethargic, sluggish
ant indolent, slothful; unindustrious

industry *n syn* BUSINESS 4, commerce, trade, traffic

indwell *vb syn* BELONG 3, inhere

indweller *n syn* INHABITANT, denizen, dweller, habitant, liver, occupant, resident, ‖residenter, resider

indwelling *adj syn* INHERENT, congenital, constitutional, deep-seated, essential, inborn, inbred, ingrained, innate, intrinsic

inebriant *n syn* LIQUOR 2, alcohol, aqua vitae, booze, drink, intoxicant, ‖joy-juice, ‖juice, ‖sauce, spirits

inebriate *n syn* DRUNKARD, bibber, boozer, drunk, lush, soak, sot, tippler, toper, tosspot

inebriated *adj syn* INTOXICATED 1, ‖boozy, ‖canned, disguised, drunk, ‖lushed, muddled, pixilated, ‖plastered, tight

inebrious *adj syn* INTOXICATED 1, ‖boozy, ‖canned, disguised, drunk, inebriated, ‖lushed, muddled, pixilated, ‖plastered

inedible *adj* not fit for food <an *inedible* plant>
syn inesculent, uneatable
rel indigestible, unwholesome; insipid, unappetizing; baneful, noxious, poisonous
con eatable, esculent; digestible, wholesome; appetizing, savory, tasty; harmless, innocuous, innoxious, nonpoisonous
ant edible

ineffable *adj syn* UNUTTERABLE, incommunicable, indefinable, indescribable, inenarrable, inexpressible, undescribable, unexpressible, unspeakable, untellable
rel celestial, empyreal, empyrean, heavenly; ethereal; divine, holy, sacred, spiritual; abstract, ideal, transcendent, transcendental
con expressible; utterable

ineffaceable *adj syn* INDELIBLE, ineradicable, inerasable, inexpungible, inextirpable, uneradicable, unerasable

ineffective *adj* **1** *syn* FUTILE, abortive, bootless, fruitless, ineffectual, unavailable, unavailing, unproductive, useless, vain
ant effective
2 *syn* WEAK 4, boneless, emasculate, forceless, impotent, inadequate, ineffectual, invertebrate, slack-spined, spineless
3 not producing or not capable of producing a required result <*ineffective* remedies>
syn ineffectual, inefficacious, inefficient
rel inadequate, incompetent, inferior; useless, worthless
con active, effectual, efficacious; esteemed, valuable

ant effective

ineffectiveness *n* ***syn*** INABILITY, inadequacy, incapability, incapacity, incompetence, ineffectualness, inefficacy
ant effectiveness

ineffectual *adj* **1** ***syn*** FUTILE, abortive, bootless, fruitless, ineffective, unavailable, unavailing, unproductive, useless, vain
ant effectual
2 ***syn*** INEFFECTIVE 3, inefficacious, inefficient
ant effectual
3 ***syn*** WEAK 4, boneless, emasculate, forceless, impotent, inadequate, ineffective, invertebrate, slack-spined, spineless
4 ***syn*** LITTLE 2, borné, limited, mean, narrow, paltry, set, small

ineffectualness *n* ***syn*** INABILITY, inadequacy, incapability, incapacity, incompetence, ineffectiveness, inefficacy
ant effectualness

inefficacious *adj* ***syn*** INEFFECTIVE 3, ineffectual, inefficient
ant efficacious

inefficacy *n* ***syn*** INABILITY, inadequacy, incapability, incapacity, incompetence, ineffectiveness, ineffectualness
ant efficacy

inefficient *adj* **1** ***syn*** INEFFECTIVE 3, ineffectual, inefficacious
ant efficient
2 incapable of the proper performance of duties < *inefficient* workmen >
syn incapable, incompetent, inept, inexpert, unexpert, unskilled, unskillful, unworkmanlike
rel careless, slipshod, slovenly; unfitted, unprepared, unqualified, untrained; unskilled, unskillful
con able, adept, capable, competent, expert, proficient, qualified, skilled, skillful, workmanlike
ant efficient

inelaborate *adj* ***syn*** PLAIN 1, modest, simple, unbeautified, undecorated, unelaborate, unembellished, unembroidered, unostentatious, unpretentious
ant elaborate

inelastic *adj* ***syn*** STIFF 1, immalleable, impliable, incompliant, inflexible, rigid, unbending, unflexible, unyielding
ant elastic

inelegance *n* ***syn*** IMPROPRIETY 1, incorrectness, indecorousness, indecorum, unbecomingness, unmeetness, unseemliness, untowardness
ant elegance

inelegant *adj* ***syn*** COARSE 3, crass, crude, gross, raw, rough, rude, uncouth, unrefined, vulgar

ineligible *adj* ***syn*** UNFIT 2, disqualified, incapable, incompetent, unequipped, unfitted, unqualified
ant eligible

ineluctable *adj* ***syn*** INEVITABLE, certain, ineludible, inescapable, inevasible, necessary, returnless, unavoidable, unescapable, unevadable
con doubtful, dubious, questionable; likely, possible, probable

ineludible *adj* ***syn*** INEVITABLE, certain, ineluctable, inescapable, inevasible, necessary, returnless, unavoidable, unescapable, unevadable

inenarrable *adj* ***syn*** UNUTTERABLE, incommunicable, indefinable, indescribable, ineffable, inexpressible, undescribable, unexpressible, unspeakable, untellable

inept *adj* **1** ***syn*** IMPROPER 1, ill-timed, inappropriate, inapt, malapropos, unapt, undue, unseasonable, unseemly, unsuitable
ant apt
2 ***syn*** INFELICITOUS, awkward, graceless, ill-chosen, unfortunate, unhappy
ant apropos, apt
3 ***syn*** AWKWARD 2, bumbling, clumsy, gauche, halting, ham-handed, lumbering, maladroit, unhandy, wooden
ant apt; adept
4 ***syn*** UNSKILLFUL 1, inadept, inapt, inexpert, unapt, undexterous, unfacile, unhandy, unproficient
ant able
5 ***syn*** INEFFICIENT 2, incapable, incompetent, inexpert, unexpert, unskilled, unskillful, unworkmanlike
ant competent, efficient

inequable *adj* ***syn*** INEQUITABLE, unequitable, unfair, unjust, unrighteous
ant equable

inequality *n* **1** the quality of being uneven <hampered by the *inequality* of the ground>
syn asperity, irregularity, roughness, unevenness
rel cragginess, jaggedness, ruggedness, rugosity
con equality, evenness, levelness, smoothness
2 ***syn*** DISPARITY, disproportion, imparity, unevenness
ant equality

inequitable *adj* not fair or just <an *inequitable* tax burden>
syn inequable, unequitable, unfair, unjust, unrighteous
rel undeserved, undue, unmerited; bad, wrong, wrongful; arbitrary, high-handed, oppressive
con fair, just
ant equitable

inequitableness *n* ***syn*** INJUSTICE 1, inequity, unfairness, unjustness, wrong
ant equitableness

inequity *n* ***syn*** INJUSTICE 1, inequitableness, unfairness, unjustness, wrong
ant equity

ineradicable *adj* ***syn*** INDELIBLE, ineffaceable, inerasable, inexpungible, inextirpable, uneradicable, unerasable
ant eradicable

inerasable *adj* ***syn*** INDELIBLE, ineffaceable, ineradicable, inexpungible, inextirpable, uneradicable, unerasable
ant erasable

inerrable *adj* ***syn*** INFALLIBLE 1, inerrant, sure, unerring
ant errable

inerrant *adj* ***syn*** INFALLIBLE 1, inerrable, sure, unerring

---

syn synonym(s)	***rel*** related word(s)
idiom idiomatic equivalent(s)	***con*** contrasted word(s)
ant antonym(s)	* vulgar

‖ use limited; if in doubt, see a dictionary
The first word in a synonym list when printed in SMALL CAPITALS shows where there is more information about the group. For a more efficient use of this book see Explanatory Notes.

rel accurate, correct, exact, precise; dependable, reliable, trustworthy
ant errant

inert *adj* ***syn*** INACTIVE, asleep, idle, passive, quiet, sleepy
rel impotent, powerless; apathetic, impassive, phlegmatic, stolid; dead, inanimate, lifeless
con animated, awake; alert, vigilant, watchful; live, operative
ant animated; dynamic

inerudite *adj* ***syn*** UNSCHOLARLY, unbookish, unlearned, unstudious
ant erudite, learned

inescapable *adj* ***syn*** INEVITABLE, certain, ineluctable, ineludible, inevasible, necessary, returnless, unavoidable, unescapable, unevadable
ant escapable

inescapably *adv* ***syn*** WILLY-NILLY, helplessly, inevitably, perforce, unavoidably, whether or no

inesculent *adj* ***syn*** INEDIBLE, uneatable
ant esculent

in essence *adv* **1** ***syn*** ESSENTIALLY 1, au fond, basically, fundamentally
2 ***syn*** VIRTUALLY, morally, practically

inessential *adj* ***syn*** UNNECESSARY, needless, uncalled-for, unessential, unneeded, unneedful, unrequired
ant crucial, essential

inestimable *adj* **1** ***syn*** INCALCULABLE 1, immeasurable, measureless, uncountable, unmeasurable, unmeasured, unreckonable
2 ***syn*** PRECIOUS 1, costly, invaluable, priceless, valuable

inevasible *adj* ***syn*** INEVITABLE, certain, ineluctable, ineludible, inescapable, necessary, returnless, unavoidable, unescapable, unevadable

inevitable *adj* incapable of being avoided or escaped <the effect of the scandal on the election was *inevitable*>
syn certain, ineluctable, ineludible, inescapable, inevasible, necessary, returnless, unavoidable, unescapable, unevadable
rel ineliminable, sure, unpreventable; decided, settled; destined, foreordained; inexorable, inflexible
idiom as sure to follow as night follows day, in the cards
con eludible, escapable, evadable
ant avoidable, evitable

inevitably *adv* ***syn*** WILLY-NILLY, helplessly, inescapably, perforce, unavoidably, whether or no

inexact *adj* ***syn*** INDEFINITE 1, indeterminate, indistinct, undeterminable
ant exact

inexcusable *adj* being without excuse or justification <an *inexcusable* blunder>
syn indefensible, inexpiable, unforgivable, unjustifiable, unpardonable, untenable
rel blamable, blameworthy, censurable, criticizable; impermissible, unallowable, unpermissible; intolerable, reprehensible
con allowable, blameless, defensible, forgivable, justifiable, pardonable, venial
ant excusable

inexhaustible *adj* ***syn*** INDEFATIGABLE, tireless, unflagging, untiring, unweariable, unwearying, weariless

inexorable *adj* ***syn*** INFLEXIBLE 2, adamant, dogged, obdurate, relentless, rigid, single-minded, unbending, uncompromising, unyielding
rel resolute; immobile, immovable
con compassionate, responsive, sympathetic, tender; clement, forbearing, indulgent, lenient

inexpedient *adj* ***syn*** INADVISABLE, ill-advised, impolitic, imprudent, unadvisable, unexpedient
ant expedient

inexpensive *adj* ***syn*** CHEAP 1, low, low-cost, low-priced, popular, reasonable, uncostly, undear
ant expensive

inexperience *n* lack or serious deficiency of practical wisdom <his failure was due to his *inexperience*>
syn callowness, freshness, greenness, rawness
rel ignorance, naiveté; amateurishness; unfamiliarity; unsophistication, verdancy
con grasp, understanding; polish, sophistication; skill, training
ant experience

inexperienced *adj* lacking knowledge, skill, or practice based on direct observation and participation <hired *inexperienced* help>
syn callow, fresh, green, inexpert, raw, rude, unconversant, unexperienced, unfleshed, unpracticed, unseasoned, untried, unversed, young
rel ignorant, immature, inept, naive; prentice, unacquainted, unfamiliar, unskilled, untrained
con expert, old, practiced, seasoned, skilled, versed, veteran
ant experienced

inexpert *adj* **1** ***syn*** INEXPERIENCED, callow, fresh, green, raw, unpracticed, unseasoned, untried, unversed, young
ant expert
2 ***syn*** UNSKILLFUL 1, inadept, inapt, inept, unapt, undexterous, unfacile, unhandy, unproficient
ant expert
3 ***syn*** INEFFICIENT 2, incapable, incompetent, inept, unexpert, unskilled, unskillful, unworkmanlike
ant expert
4 ***syn*** CRUDE 5, coarse, prentice

inexpiable *adj* ***syn*** INEXCUSABLE, indefensible, unforgivable, unjustifiable, unpardonable, untenable
ant expiable

inexplainable *adj* ***syn*** INEXPLICABLE, unaccountable, unexplainable
ant explainable, explicable

inexplicable *adj* not capable of being explained or accounted for <an *inexplicable* discrepancy in the accounts>
syn inexplainable, unaccountable, unexplainable; *compare* MYSTERIOUS

---

syn synonym(s) ***rel*** related word(s)
idiom idiomatic equivalent(s) ***con*** contrasted word(s)
ant antonym(s) * vulgar
‖ use limited; if in doubt, see a dictionary
The first word in a synonym list when printed in SMALL CAPITALS shows where there is more information about the group. For a more efficient use of this book see Explanatory Notes.

rel indecipherable, indescribable, inscrutable, undefinable, unfathomable, unsolvable; mysterious, odd, peculiar, strange
con clear, obvious, plain; comprehensible, graspable, intelligible
ant explainable, explicable

inexpressible *adj syn* UNUTTERABLE, incommunicable, indefinable, indescribable, ineffable, inenarrable, undescribable, unexpressible, unspeakable, untellable
ant expressible

inexpressive *adj syn* EXPRESSIONLESS, blank, deadpan, empty, unexpressive, vacant
ant expressive

inexpugnable *adj syn* INVINCIBLE 1, impregnable, inconquerable, indomitable, invulnerable, unassailable, unbeatable, unconquerable, undefeatable
rel irresistible, unopposable
con assailable, attackable
ant expugnable

inexpungible *adj syn* INDELIBLE, ineffaceable, ineradicable, inerasable, inextirpable, uneradicable, unerasable

inexterminable *adj syn* INDESTRUCTIBLE, imperishable, incorruptible, inextinguishable, inextirpable, irrefragable, irrefrangible, quenchless, undestroyable, unperishable

inextinguishable *adj syn* INDESTRUCTIBLE, imperishable, incorruptible, inexterminable, inextirpable, irrefragable, irrefrangible, quenchless, undestroyable, unperishable
ant extinguishable

inextirpable *adj* 1 *syn* INDESTRUCTIBLE, imperishable, incorruptible, inexterminable, inextinguishable, irrefragable, irrefrangible, quenchless, undestroyable, unperishable
2 *syn* INDELIBLE, ineffaceable, ineradicable, inerasable, inexpungible, uneradicable, unerasable

inextricable *adj syn* INSOLUBLE, insolvable, irresoluble, irresolvable, unsoluble, unsolvable
ant extricable

infallible *adj* 1 incapable of being in error <an *infallible* ear for pitch in music>
syn inerrable, inerrant, sure, unerring
rel faultless, flawless, impeccable, undeceivable; correct, exact, perfect
con deceivable, faulty, unsure; doubtful, dubious, questionable
ant fallible
2 not liable to mislead, deceive, or disappoint <an *infallible* remedy>
syn certain, sure, surefire, unfailing
rel effective, efficacious, efficient; handy, helpful, useful; acceptable, agreeable, satisfying; satisfactory
con doubtful, questionable, uncertain, unsure; useless, worthless; unacceptable, unsatisfying; unsatisfactory
ant fallible

infamous *adj* 1 having an extremely and deservedly bad reputation <one of the most *infamous* of the dictator's henchmen>
syn ill-famed, notorious, opprobrious
rel abominable, atrocious, evil, hateful, heinous, iniquitous, odious, scandalous, vile, villainous; contemptible, despicable, scurvy, sorry
con distinguished, eminent, esteemed, honored, illustrious, notable, prestigious, reputable
2 *syn* VICIOUS 2, corrupt, degenerate, flagitious, miscreant, nefarious, perverse, rotten, unhealthy, villainous
rel disgraceful, disreputable, ignominious, shameful
con glorious, splendid, sublime
ant illustrious

infamy *n syn* DISGRACE, discredit, disesteem, dishonor, disrepute, ignominy, obloquy, odium, opprobrium, shame
rel notoriety, notoriousness

infancy *n* 1 early childhood <the helplessness of *infancy*>
syn babyhood, infanthood
rel childhood, immaturity, juvenility, nonage
con adulthood, maturity, old age, senescence
2 the state or period of being under the age established by law for the attainment of full civil rights <his heirs were still in *infancy*>
syn minority, nonage
rel immaturity, juniority, juvenility
con adulthood, adultness, maturity, seniority
ant majority

infant *n syn* BABY 1, babe, bantling, neonate, newborn

infant *adj syn* YOUNG 1, callow, green, immature, juvenile, unfledged, unripe, youthful

infanthood *n syn* INFANCY 1, babyhood

infantile *adj syn* CHILDISH, babyish, immature, infantine, prekindergarten, puerile
ant adult

infantine *adj syn* CHILDISH, babyish, immature, infantile, prekindergarten, puerile
ant adult

infatuate *adj syn* INFATUATED, besotted, dotty, enamored

infatuated *adj* possessed with or marked by a strong attachment or foolish or unreasoning love or desire <*infatuated* with a woman he can't have>
syn besotted, dotty, enamored, infatuate
rel bewitched, captivated, enraptured, obsessed; foolish, silly
con detached, dispassionate, objective, undazzled, unprepossessed

infatuation *n* a strong and unreasoning but transitory attachment <went through a series of *infatuations* before he settled down>
syn béguin, crush, ‖pash, passion
rel ardor, craze, devotion, fascination, obsession, rage

in favor of *prep syn* FOR 1, pro, with

infeasible *adj syn* IMPOSSIBLE 1, impracticable, impractical, irrealizable, unattainable, unfeasible, unrealizable, unworkable
ant feasible

infectious *adj* 1 capable of causing infection <viruses and other *infectious* agents>
syn infective

---

syn synonym(s) *rel* related word(s)
idiom idiomatic equivalent(s) *con* contrasted word(s)
ant antonym(s) * vulgar
‖ use limited; if in doubt, see a dictionary
The first word in a synonym list when printed in SMALL CAPITALS shows where there is more information about the group. For a more efficient use of this book see Explanatory Notes.

rel mephitic, miasmic, noxious, pestilent, pestilential, poisonous, toxic, virulent
con healthful, hygienic, salutary, wholesome
2 transmissible by infection < *infectious* diseases >
syn catching, communicable, contagious
3 easily communicated or diffused <her enthusiasm was *infectious* >
syn catching, contagious, taking
rel irresistible, sympathetic

infective *adj* ***syn*** INFECTIOUS 1

infecund *adj* ***syn*** STERILE 1, barren, effete, impotent, infertile, unfruitful
ant fecund

infelicitous *adj* marked by a lack of appropriateness and grace of expression <made a very *infelicitous* remark>
syn awkward, graceless, ill-chosen, inept, unfortunate, unhappy
rel inappropriate, inapropos, inapt, malapropos, unapt; deplorable, gauche, regrettable
con fortunate, graceful, happy
ant felicitous

infer *vb* to arrive at by reasoning from evidence or from premises <we *inferred* from his questions that he was a stranger in the vicinity>
syn collect, conclude, deduce, deduct, derive, ‖dope out, draw, gather, judge, make, make out; *compare* CONJECTURE
rel induce; conjecture, glean, guess, reckon, speculate, surmise, think; ascertain, construe, interpret, reason, understand
idiom come to (*or* draw *or* reach) a conclusion; read between the lines

inference *n* **1** the deriving of a conclusion by reasoning <the answer was obtainable by *inference* >
syn deduction, illation, judgment, ratiocination
rel conjecture, guessing, reckoning, supposition, surmise
2 a determination arrived at by reasoning <a wrong *inference* based on incomplete evidence>
syn conclusion, deduction, illation, judgment, ratiocination, sequitur
rel assumption, conjecture, guess, presumption, reckoning, supposition, surmise

inferior *adj* **1** being or regarded as being below the level of another thing <the *inferior* latitudes of the northern hemisphere>
syn lesser, low, lower, nether, subjacent, under
rel junior, minor, secondary, subaltern, subordinate
con greater, higher, over, overlying
ant superior
2 of little or less importance, value, or merit <sold *inferior* goods at high prices>
syn common, déclassé, hack, low-grade, mean, poor, second-class, second-drawer, second-rate; *compare* CHEAP 2
rel average, fair, indifferent, mediocre, middling, ordinary; bad, base, paltry, punk, shoddy, sleazy, sorry, tawdry, tin-pot, wretched; good-for-nothing, lousy, ‖no-account, no-good, unworthy, valueless, worthless
con choice, excellent, first-class, first-rate, high-grade, prime
ant superior

inferior *n* one lower than another (as in station or worth) <a man inclined to be disdainful of his social *inferiors* >
syn poor relation, scrub, secondary, subaltern, subordinate, underling, understrapper
rel attendant, auxiliary, deputy; retainer, satrap, subject, vassal; hanger-on, heeler, henchman, hireling, minion, satellite, sycophant; adherent, disciple, follower
con chief, head, leader, master, principal
ant superior

infernal *adj* **1** of or relating to a nether world of the dead <the *infernal* regions>
syn chthonian, chthonic, Hadean, plutonian, plutonic, sulphurous, Tartarean
con celestial, elysian, Hesperidean, paradisaic, paradisal, paradisiacal
ant supernal
2 resembling or appropriate to hell or its inhabitants <an *infernal* glow in the sky>
syn avernal, cimmerian, hellish, pandemoniac, plutonian, plutonic, stygian
rel demoniac, devilish, diabolic, fiendish; sulphurous
ant celestial, heavenly
3 ***syn*** DAMNED 2, blamed, blasted, confounded, cursed, cussed, dad-burned, damnable, dashed, execrable
4 ***syn*** UTTER, absolute, all-fired, blasted, blessed, downright, out-and-out, outright, straight-out, thoroughgoing

inferno *n* **1** ***syn*** HELL, abyss, blazes, Gehenna, hades, netherworld, perdition, pit, Sheol, Tophet
2 ***syn*** FIRE 1, conflagration, holocaust

inferred *adj* ***syn*** TACIT 1, implicit, implied, undeclared, understood, unexpressed, unsaid, unspoken, unuttered, wordless

infertile *adj* **1** ***syn*** STERILE 1, barren, effete, impotent, infecund, unfruitful
rel depleted, drained, exhausted, impoverished
con breeding, generating, propagating, reproducing
ant fertile
2 ***syn*** BARREN 2, hardscrabble, unbearing, unfertile, unproductive
ant fertile

infest *vb* **1** to spread or swarm over in a troublesome manner <lawns *infested* with weeds>
syn beset, overrun, overspread, overswarm
rel abound, crawl, swarm, teem; annoy, harass, harry, pester, plague, worry
2 to live in or on as a parasite <a dog *infested* by fleas>
syn parasite, parasitize

infidel *adj* ***syn*** HEATHEN, ethnic, gentile, infidelic, pagan, profane

---

infidelic *adj* ***syn*** HEATHEN, ethnic, gentile, infidel, pagan, profane

infidelity *n* betrayal of a moral obligation <a leader guilty of *infidelity* to the responsibilities he had accepted>
syn disloyalty, faithlessness, falseness, falsity, perfidiousness, perfidy, unfaithfulness; *compare* TREACHERY
rel fickleness, inconstancy; treacherousness, treachery, treason
idiom bad faith
con devotion, faithfulness, fealty; constancy, loyalty, steadfastness
ant fidelity

infiltrate *vb* ***syn*** INSINUATE 3, edge in, foist, work in, worm

infinite *adj* **1** being without known limits <the idea of an *infinite* universe>
syn eternal, illimitable, perdurable, sempiternal, supertemporal
rel everlasting, perpetual
con bounded, circumscribed, limited, restricted
ant finite
2 ***syn*** LIMITLESS, boundless, endless, immeasurable, indefinite, measureless, unbounded, unlimited, unmeasured
ant finite

infinity *n* ***syn*** ETERNITY 1, sempiternity

infirm *adj* ***syn*** WEAK 1, decrepit, feeble, flimsy, fragile, frail, unsound, unsubstantial, ‖wanky, weakly
ant hale

infirmity *n* **1** the quality or state of being enfeebled and weakened in health <suffering from old age and attendant physical *infirmity*>
syn debility, decrepitude, disease, feebleness, infirmness, malaise, sickliness, unhealthiness; *compare* DISEASE 1, SICKNESS 1
rel debilitation, decay, enfeeblement, failing, frailty, weakening, weakness; diseasedness, unwellness; illness, indisposition, sickness, unhealth
ant haleness
2 ***syn*** DISEASE 1, affection, ailment, complaint, condition, disorder, ill, malady, sickness, syndrome
3 ***syn*** SICKNESS 1, affliction, diseasedness, disorder, illness, indisposition, unhealth

infirmness *n* ***syn*** INFIRMITY 1, debility, decrepitude, disease, feebleness, malaise, sickliness, unhealthiness

infix *vb* **1** ***syn*** ENTRENCH 1, embed, fix, ingrain, lodge, root
2 ***syn*** IMPLANT, inculcate, inseminate, instill

inflame *vb* **1** ***syn*** LIGHT 1, enkindle, fire, ignite, kindle
ant extinguish
2 ***syn*** IRRITATE, aggravate, burn (up), gall, get, grate, provoke, put out, rile, roil

inflammable *adj* ***syn*** COMBUSTIBLE 1, burnable, flammable, ignitable
ant nonflammable, noninflammable

inflammatory *adj* exciting or tending to excite anger, animosity, or disorder <*inflammatory* speeches designed to spark rebellion>
syn incendiary
rel exciting, incitive, instigative, provocative; revolutionary, seditionary, seditious
con calming, moderating, soothing, temperate

inflate *vb* ***syn*** EXPAND 3, amplify, dilate, distend, swell
ant deflate

inflated *adj* swollen with or as if with something insubstantial <had an *inflated* idea of his own importance>
syn dropsical, dropsied, flatulent, overblown, tumescent, tumid, turgid, windy
rel aureate, bombastic, flowery, grandiloquent, magniloquent, rhetorical; ostentatious, pretentious, showy; fustian, ranting, rhapsodical; diffuse, prolix, verbose, wordy
con compendious, concise, laconic, pithy, succinct, summary, terse

inflatus *n* ***syn*** INSPIRATION, afflation, afflatus

inflection *n* a particular manner of employing the sounds of the voice in speech <questions end on a rising *inflection*>
syn accent, intonation, tone
rel articulation, enunciation, pronunciation; timbre, tonality
idiom tone of voice

inflexible *adj* **1** ***syn*** STIFF 1, immalleable, impliable, incompliant, inelastic, rigid, unbending, unflexible, unyielding
rel immobile, immovable
con elastic, resilient, springy, supple; ductile, malleable, plastic, pliable, pliant; fluid, liquid
ant flexible
2 rigidly firm in will or purpose <a person of *inflexible* resolution>
syn adamant, adamantine, brassbound, dogged, inexorable, iron, obdurate, relentless, rigid, rockbound, rock-ribbed, single-minded, steadfast, stubborn, unbendable, unbending, uncompliant, uncompromising, unswayable, unyielding; *compare* STIFF 1
rel intractable, obstinate; indomitable, invincible, unconquerable; grim, hard, implacable, unrelenting; dyed-in-the-wool, fixed, set, ‖sot
con agreeable, amenable, compliant, docile, pliant, responsive, swayable, yielding; mild, open
ant flexible
3 incapable of changing or being changed <*inflexible* rules>
syn constant, determinate, fixed, immovable, immutable, inalterable, invariable, ironclad, unalterable, unchangeable, unmodifiable, unmovable
rel strict; rigorous; established, set, settled; changeless, unchanging
con adaptable, adjustable, alterable, changeable, mutable, variable
ant flexible
4 ***syn*** TOUGH 3, hard-line, uncompromising, unyielding

inflict *vb* **1** ***syn*** GIVE 10, administer, deal, deliver, strike
2 to cause one to endure (something damaging or painful) <*inflict* retribution>

---

syn synonym(s)	***rel*** related word(s)
idiom idiomatic equivalent(s)	***con*** contrasted word(s)
ant antonym(s)	* vulgar

‖ use limited; if in doubt, see a dictionary
The first word in a synonym list when printed in SMALL CAPITALS shows where there is more information about the group. For a more efficient use of this book see Explanatory Notes.

syn force (on *or* upon), impose, visit, wreak, wreck; *compare* IMPOSE 4
rel expose, subject
idiom lay open to, put on the spot
con guard, protect, shelter, shield

inflow *n* ***syn*** INFLUX, influxion, inpour, inpouring, inrush
ant outflow, outflux

influence *n* **1** power exerted over the minds or behavior of others <a person of great *influence* in national politics>
syn authority, credit, prestige, weight; *compare* PULL 2
rel command, domination, dominion, mastery; ascendancy, dominance, eminence, predominance; consequence, importance, moment; ‖drag, in, pull
2 ***syn*** PULL 2, clout, ‖drag, in

influence *vb* **1** ***syn*** AFFECT, carry, get, impress, inspire, move, strike, sway, touch
2 ***syn*** PREJUDICE 2, bias, prepossess

influenceable *adj* ***syn*** RECEPTIVE 1, acceptant, acceptive, persuadable, persuasible, responsive, suasible, swayable

influx *n* a flowing in <anticipated an *influx* of immigrants>
syn inflow, influxion, inpour, inpouring, inrush
rel accession, augmentation, increase; illapse
con outpour, outpouring, outrush; efflux, effluxion, exodus
ant outflow, outflux

influxion *n* ***syn*** INFLUX, inflow, inpour, inpouring, inrush
ant effluxion

inform *vb* **1** ***syn*** FIRE 2, animate, exalt, inspire
rel imbue, infuse, leaven, permeate; enlighten, illuminate; endow, endue
2 to make aware or cognizant of something <was kept *informed* of developments>
syn acquaint, advise, apprise, clue (*or* clew), fill in, notify, post, tell, warn, wise (up)
rel educate, enlighten, instruct, teach; familiarize; caution, forewarn
idiom keep posted
3 to give information about someone especially as an informer <his suspicions aroused, he *informed* on his neighbor to the police>
syn ‖nark, peach, ‖pimp, rat, ‖sing, snitch, squeak, squeal, ‖stool; *compare* TALK 6
rel blab, tattle, tell; betray, give away, turn in

informal *adj* **1** conducted or carried out without rigidly prescribed procedure <carried on an *informal* investigation>
syn irregular, unceremonious, unofficial
rel casual, spontaneous; unauthorized; unconventional; private, special
con authorized, ceremonious, conventional, official, regular
ant formal
2 ***syn*** EASYGOING 3, breezy, casual, ‖common, dégagé, low-pressure, relaxed, ‖sonsy, unconstrained, unfussy
rel familiar, natural, simple
con affected, mannered, prim, rigid, stiff, stilted
ant formal

information *n* **1** ***syn*** KNOWLEDGE 2, lore, science, wisdom
2 ***syn*** NEWS, advice, intelligence, speerings, tidings, word

informational *adj* ***syn*** INFORMATIVE, educational, educative, informatory, instructional, instructive

informative *adj* imparting information <gave an *informative* talk>
syn educational, educative, informational, informatory, instructional, instructive
rel edifying, elucidative, enlightening, explanatory, illuminating
ant uninformative

informatory *adj* ***syn*** INFORMATIVE, educational, educative, informational, instructional, instructive

informed *adj* ***syn*** FAMILIAR 3, abreast, acquainted, au courant, au fait, conversant, up, versant, versed
ant uninformed

informer *n* one who informs against another <his arrest was brought about by an *informer*>
syn betrayer, ‖canary, ‖fink, ‖nark, ‖pimp, snitch, squawker, ‖squeaker, squealer, stool, stoolie, stool pigeon, talebearer, tattler, tattletale, tipster; *compare* BUSYBODY, DETECTIVE, GOSSIP 1, SPY

infra *adv* **1** ***syn*** BELOW 2
ant above, supra
2 ***syn*** AFTER, afterward, afterwhile, behind, by and by, later, latterly, next, subsequently

infract *vb* ***syn*** VIOLATE 1, breach, break, contravene, infringe, offend, transgress

infraction *n* ***syn*** BREACH 1, contravention, infringement, transgression, trespass, violation
rel crime, offense, sin; error, faux pas, lapse, slip

infrastructure *n* **1** ***syn*** BASE 1, basis, bedrock, bottom, footing, foundation, groundwork, substructure, underpinning, understructure
ant superstructure
2 ***syn*** BASIS 1, base, bedrock, footing, foundation, ground, groundwork, root, substratum, underpinning

infrequent *adj* appearing, happening, or met with so seldom as to attract attention <held only *infrequent* press conferences>
syn few, occasional, rare, scarce, seldom, semioccasional, sporadic, uncommon, unfrequent
rel isolated, scattered; meager, scant, scanty, sparse; exceptional, limited, unusual; odd, spasmodic, stray
idiom few and far between
con abundant, common, numerous, regular; ordinary, routine
ant frequent

infrequently *adv* **1** ***syn*** SELDOM, hardly ever, little, rarely, unfrequently, unoften
ant frequently
2 ***syn*** OCCASIONALLY, irregularly, on occasion, sporadically, uncommonly

---

syn synonym(s) ***rel*** related word(s)
idiom idiomatic equivalent(s) ***con*** contrasted word(s)
ant antonym(s) * vulgar
‖ use limited; if in doubt, see a dictionary
The first word in a synonym list when printed in SMALL CAPITALS shows where there is more information about the group. For a more efficient use of this book see Explanatory Notes.

ant frequently

infringe *vb* **1** *syn* TRESPASS 2, encroach, entrench, invade

2 *syn* VIOLATE 1, breach, break, contravene, infract, offend, transgress

3 *syn* IMPOSE 5, intrude, obtrude, presume

infringement *n* *syn* BREACH 1, contravention, infraction, transgression, trespass, violation

infuriate *vb* *syn* ANGER 1, enrage, incense, ire, mad, madden, steam up, umbrage

infuse *vb* **1** to introduce one thing into another so as to change or affect it <a teacher who *infused* her pupils with the desire to learn>

syn imbue, ingrain, inoculate, invest, leaven, steep, suffuse

rel animate, fire, inform, inspire; implant, inculcate, instill; impregnate, permeate, pervade, saturate; indoctrinate

2 *syn* INTERFUSE 2, diffuse, interlard, intersow, intersperse, intersprinkle

ingather *vb* *syn* REAP, garner, gather, harvest

ingathering *n* *syn* HARVEST 1, cropping, gathering, harvesting, reaping

ingeminate *vb* *syn* REPEAT, iterate, reiterate, renew, reprise, resay

ingenerate *adj* *syn* INHERENT, born, built-in, congenital, constitutional, deep-seated, essential, inborn, inbred, intrinsic

ingenious *adj* **1** *syn* INVENTIVE, creative, demiurgic, deviceful, innovational, innovative, innovatory, original, originative

2 *syn* CLEVER 4, adroit, canny, ‖coony, cunning, dexterous, ‖sleighty, slim, sly

ingenuous *adj* *syn* NATURAL 5, artless, naive, simple, unaffected, unartful, unartificial, unschooled, unsophisticated, unstudied

con covert, furtive, stealthy, surreptitious, underhand; artful, crafty, foxy, guileful, insidious, sly, tricky, wily

ant disingenuous

ingest *vb* *syn* EAT 1, consume, devour, feed (on), meal, partake (of), take

inglorious *adj* *syn* DISREPUTABLE 1, discreditable, disgraceful, dishonorable, ignominious, shabby, shady, shameful, shoddy, unrespectable

ant glorious

ingoing *adj* *syn* INCISIVE, biting, clear-cut, crisp, cutting, penetrating, trenchant

ingot *n* *syn* BAR 1, billet, rod, slab, stick, strip

ingrain *vb* **1** *syn* ENTRENCH 1, embed, fix, infix, lodge, root

rel engrave, etch, grave, incise

2 *syn* INFUSE 1, imbue, inoculate, invest, leaven, steep, suffuse

ingrained *adj* *syn* INHERENT, built-in, congenital, constitutional, deep-seated, inborn, inbred, indwelling, innate, intrinsic

rel chronic, confirmed, deep-rooted, inveterate

con exterior, external, outer, outside, outward

ingratiating *adj* intended or designed to gain favor <an *ingratiating* smile>

syn deferential, disarming, ingratiatory, insinuating, insinuative, saccharine, silken, silky

rel adulatory; fawning, sycophantic

ingratiatory *adj* *syn* INGRATIATING, deferential, disarming, insinuating, insinuative, saccharine, silken, silky

ingredient *n* *syn* ELEMENT 2, component, constituent, factor

ingress *n* **1** *syn* ENTRANCE 1, entry, ingression

ant egress

2 *syn* DOOR 2, access, adit, admission, admittance, entrance, entrée, entry, way

ant egress

ingress *vb* *syn* ENTER 1, come (in), go in, penetrate

ant egress

ingression *n* *syn* ENTRANCE 1, entry, ingress

ant egression

ingroup *n* *syn* CLIQUE, cabal, camarilla, camp, circle, clan, coterie, mob, ring

ant outgroup

ingurgitate *vb* *syn* GULP, bolt, cram, englut, gobble, guzzle, slop, slosh, wolf

inhabit *vb* to dwell in as a place of settled residence <islands *inhabited* by Polynesians>

syn occupy, people, populate, tenant

rel settle; abide, dwell, live

inhabitable *adj* *syn* LIVABLE 1, habitable, lodgeable, occupiable, tenantable

ant uninhabitable

inhabitancy *n* *syn* HABITATION 1, inhabitation, occupancy, occupation, residence, settlement

inhabitant *n* one that occupies a particular place regularly <*inhabitants* of large cities>

syn denizen, dweller, habitant, indweller, liver, occupant, resident, ‖residenter, resider

rel aborigine, autochthon, indigene, native

inhabitation *n* *syn* HABITATION 1, inhabitancy, occupancy, occupation, residence, settlement

inhale *vb* to draw (as air) into the lungs <*inhaling* smoke>

syn breathe (in), inspire

ant exhale, expire

inharmonic *adj* *syn* DISSONANT 1, cacophonic, cacophonous, discordant, disharmonic, disharmonious, immusical, inharmonious, unharmonious, unmusical

ant harmonic

inharmonious *adj* **1** *syn* DISSONANT 1, cacophonic, cacophonous, discordant, disharmonic, disharmonious, immusical, inharmonic, unharmonious, unmusical

ant harmonious

2 lacking harmony especially in sentiment <the committee meeting was singularly *inharmonious*>

syn discordant, inconsonant, uncongenial, unharmonious

rel antagonistic, cat-and-dog, conflicting, conflictive, differing, disagreeing, incompatible, incongruous, quarrelsome

---

syn synonym(s)	*rel* related word(s)
idiom idiomatic equivalent(s)	*con* contrasted word(s)
ant antonym(s)	* vulgar

‖ use limited; if in doubt, see a dictionary

The first word in a synonym list when printed in SMALL CAPITALS shows where there is more information about the group. For a more efficient use of this book see Explanatory Notes.

con concordant, congenial, consonant; amiable, compatible; collaborative
ant harmonious

inharmony *n* ***syn*** DISCORD, conflict, contention, difference, disharmony, dispeace, dissension, dissent, dissonance, disunion
ant harmony

inhaust *vb* ***syn*** ABSORB 1, assimilate, imbibe, incorporate, insorb

inhere *vb* **1** ***syn*** CONSIST 1, dwell, exist, lie, reside
2 ***syn*** BELONG 3, indwell

inherent *adj* being a part, element, or quality of a thing's inmost being < *inherent* rights of every citizen >
syn born, built-in, congenital, connate, constitutional, deep-seated, elemental, essential, inborn, inbred, indwelling, ingenerate, ingrained, innate, intimate, intrinsic
rel inner, internal, inward, resident; basic, elementary, fundamental, immanent, integral; characteristic, distinctive, individual, peculiar; natural, normal, regular, typical; bred-in-the-bone
con shallow, superficial; accidental, fortuitous, incidental; alien, extraneous, extrinsic, foreign
ant adventitious

inheritance *n* **1** ***syn*** HERITAGE 1, birthright, heritance, legacy, patrimony
2 ***syn*** LEGACY 1, bequest, devise

inherited *adj* ***syn*** INNATE 1, congenital, connate, connatural, inborn, indigenous, native, natural, unacquired

inheritor *n* ***syn*** HEIR, heritor

inhibit *vb* **1** ***syn*** FORBID, ban, enjoin, interdict, outlaw, prohibit, taboo
rel avert, ward
ant allow
2 ***syn*** RESTRAIN 1, bit, bridle, check, constrain, curb, hold back, hold down, hold in, withhold
ant activate; animate

inhibited *adj* ***syn*** FRIGID 3, cold, passionless, undersexed, unresponsive
ant uninhibited

inhuman *adj* ***syn*** FIERCE 1, barbarous, cannibalic, cruel, fell, ferocious, inhumane, savage, truculent, wolfish
rel malicious, malign, malignant; implacable, relentless, unrelenting; devilish, diabolical, fiendish
con altruistic, benevolent, charitable, eleemosynary, humanitarian, philanthropic; compassionate, tender
ant humane

inhumane *adj* ***syn*** FIERCE 1, barbarous, cruel, fell, ferocious, grim, inhuman, savage, truculent, wolfish
ant humane

inhumation *n* ***syn*** BURIAL 2, entombment, interment, sepulture
ant exhumation

inhume *vb* ***syn*** BURY 1, entomb, inter, lay away, plant, put away, sepulcher, sepulture, tomb
ant disinhume, exhume

inimicable *adj* ***syn*** HOSTILE 1, ill, inimical, unfriendly

inimical *adj* ***syn*** HOSTILE 1, ill, inimicable, unfriendly

iniquitous *adj* ***syn*** WRONG 1, bad, evil, immoral, reprobate, sinful, vicious, wicked

iniquity *n* ***syn*** EVIL 3, crime, diablerie, sin, tort, wrong, wrongdoing

initial *adj* **1** marking a commencement or constituting a start < *initial* symptoms of the disease >
syn beginning, inceptive, incipient, initiative, initiatory, introductory, nascent
rel basic, elementary, first, fundamental; embryonic, germinal; early, infant; antecedent; earliest, introductory, primary
con closing; concluding, conclusive; terminal, terminative; last, ultimate
ant final
2 ***syn*** FIRST 2, earliest, maiden, original, pioneer, primary, prime
3 ***syn*** FIRST 1, foremost, headmost, inaugural, leading
ant final

initially *adv* **1** in the beginning < *initially* we were confused but soon enough we fully understood >
syn originally, primarily, primitively
rel first, firstly, incipiently
idiom at first, at the first go-off, from the word go
con lastly, ultimately
ant finally
2 ***syn*** FIRSTLY, first

initiate *vb* **1** ***syn*** BEGIN 1, commence, enter, get off, inaugurate, kick off, launch, open, start, take up
ant terminate
2 ***syn*** INTRODUCE 3, inaugurate, institute, launch, originate, set up, usher in
3 to put through the formalities for becoming a member or official < the club *initiated* four new members >
syn inaugurate, induct, install, instate, invest
rel institute; admit, enter, introduce, take in

initiation *n* the process or an instance of being formally introduced into an office or made a member of an organization < a fraternity *initiation* >
syn inaugural, inauguration, induction, installation, investiture
rel baptism; institution, introduction

initiative *adj* ***syn*** INITIAL 1, beginning, inceptive, incipient, initiatory, introductory, nascent

initiative *n* ***syn*** ENTERPRISE 4, ambition, drive, get-up-and-go, push

initiatory *adj* ***syn*** INITIAL 1, beginning, inceptive, incipient, initiative, introductory, nascent

injudicious *adj* ***syn*** UNWISE, ill-advised, ill-judged, impolitic, imprudent, indiscreet
ant judicious

injunction *n* ***syn*** COMMAND 1, behest, bidding, charge, dictate, mandate, order, word

injure *vb* **1** to deplete the soundness, strength, effectiveness, or perfection of something < *injured* his prestige by making rash statements >
syn blemish, damage, harm, hurt, impair, mar, prejudice, spoil, tarnish, vitiate
rel disserve; disadvantage; endamage, weaken; blight, queer; foul up, louse up; contort, deface, deform, dis-

---

syn synonym(s) *rel* related word(s)
idiom idiomatic equivalent(s) *con* contrasted word(s)
ant antonym(s) * vulgar
‖ use limited; if in doubt, see a dictionary
The first word in a synonym list when printed in SMALL CAPITALS shows where there is more information about the group. For a more efficient use of this book see Explanatory Notes.

figure, distort; bespatter, foul, smirch; disable, incapacitate
con assist, help, succor; better, enhance, improve; benefit; strengthen
ant aid
2 *syn* DISTRESS 2, aggrieve, constrain, grieve, hurt, pain
idiom do dirt to
3 to inflict bodily hurt on <was *injured* in an auto accident>
syn hurt, wound
rel damage, harm; afflict, torment, torture; batter, cripple, maim, mangle, mutilate
idiom draw blood

injurious *adj syn* HARMFUL, bad, damaging, deleterious, detrimental, evil, hurtful, mischievous, nocent, nocuous

injury *n* 1 an act or the result of inflicting something that causes loss or pain <we cannot forgive his *injury* of the painting> <his falsehood caused grave *injury* to his brother's reputation>
syn damage, harm, hurt, mischief, outrage, ruin
rel agony, discomfiture, distress, misery, suffering; pain, pang; detriment, disservice, loss; bad, evil, ill
2 *syn* INJUSTICE 2, grievance, wrong

injustice *n* 1 absence of justice <preached against *injustice*>
syn inequitableness, inequity, unfairness, unjustness, wrong
rel crime, malfeasance, malpractice, villainy, wrongdoing; favoritism, inequality, partiality, partisanship
con equity, fairness, right
ant justice, justness
2 an act or instance of unjustness <pointed out various *injustices* in the law> <you do him an *injustice* when you call him lazy>
syn grievance, injury, wrong
rel damage, harm, hurt, mischief, outrage, ruin; breach, infraction, infringement, tort, transgression, trespass, violation

ink *vb syn* SIGN 1, autograph, signature, subscribe

inkling *n syn* HINT 1, clue, cue, indication, intimation, notion, suggestion, telltale, wind

inky *adj syn* BLACK 1, atramentous, ebon, ebony, jet, jetty, pitch-black, pitch-dark, raven, sable

||**inland** *adj syn* DOMESTIC 2, home, internal, intestine, municipal, national, native
ant foreign

inlet *n* a recess in the shores of a body of water <*inlets* of lakes and rivers>
syn arm, bay, bayou, bight, cove, ||creek, firth, gulf, harbor, ||loch, ||lough, slough

inn *n syn* HOTEL, auberge, caravansary, hospice, hostel, hostelry, lodge, public house, roadhouse, tavern

innards *n pl syn* ENTRAILS, gut(s), insides, internals, inwards, ||pudding(s), stuffing, tripes, viscera

innate *adj* 1 existing in or belonging to an individual inherently <*innate* vigor>
syn congenital, connate, connatural, inborn, indigenous, inherited, native, natural, unacquired
rel constitutional, deep-seated, essential, ingrained, inherent, intrinsic; hereditary; normal, regular, standard, typical
con accidental, adventitious, fortuitous, incidental; affected, assumed, feigned, simulated; cultivated, fostered, nurtured
ant acquired
2 *syn* INHERENT, congenital, connate, constitutional, deep-seated, elemental, essential, inborn, inbred, intrinsic

inner *adj* 1 situated further in <the *inner* layers were less worn>
syn ||innermore, inside, interior, internal, intestine, inward
rel central, focal, middle, nuclear; close, familiar, intimate; constitutional, essential, inherent, intrinsic
con exterior, external, outside, outward
ant outer
2 arising from one's inmost self <*inner* thoughts and feelings>
syn gut, interior, internal, intimate, visceral, viscerous
rel individual, personal, private; concealed, hidden, secret
con exterior, outer; open, public

||**innermore** *adj syn* INNER 1, inside, interior, internal, intestine, inward

innervate *vb syn* PROVOKE 4, excite, galvanize, innerve, motivate, move, pique, quicken, rouse, stimulate

innerve *vb syn* PROVOKE 4, excite, galvanize, innervate, motivate, move, pique, quicken, rouse, stimulate

innholder *n syn* SALOONKEEPER, barkeeper, boniface, innkeeper, ||publican, saloonist, taverner

innkeeper *n syn* SALOONKEEPER, barkeeper, boniface, innholder, ||publican, saloonist, taverner

innocence *n syn* IGNORANCE 2, inscience, nescience, unacquaintance, unacquaintedness, unawareness, unfamiliarity, unknowingness

innocent *adj* 1 *syn* GOOD 11, blameless, exemplary, guiltless, inculpable, irreproachable, pure, righteous, unblamable, virtuous
rel unstained, unsullied, white, white-handed
2 free from legal guilt or fault <the defendant was found *innocent*>
syn blameless, clean, crimeless, faultless, guiltless, inculpable, unguilty
idiom in the clear
ant guilty
3 *syn* LAWFUL, legal, legitimate, licit
4 *syn* DEVOID, destitute, empty, void
5 *syn* NATURAL 5, artless, guileless, ingenuous, naive, unaffected, unartificial, unschooled, unsophisticated, unstudied
6 *syn* HARMLESS, innocuous, innoxious, inobnoxious, inoffensive, unoffending, unoffensive
con harmful, injurious, mischievous

innocuous *adj* 1 *syn* HARMLESS, innocent, innoxious, inobnoxious, inoffensive, unoffending, unoffensive

---

syn synonym(s) *rel* related word(s)
idiom idiomatic equivalent(s) *con* contrasted word(s)
ant antonym(s) * vulgar
|| use limited; if in doubt, see a dictionary
The first word in a synonym list when printed in SMALL CAPITALS shows where there is more information about the group. For a more efficient use of this book see Explanatory Notes.

con harmful, injurious; evil; troublesome
ant pernicious
2 ***syn*** INSIPID 3, banal, bland, driveling, flat, inane, jejune, milk-and-water, namby-pamby, sapless

innominate *adj* ***syn*** ANONYMOUS, nameless, undesignated, unnamed

innovation *n* ***syn*** CHANGE 2, mutation, novelty, permutation, sport, vicissitude
rel deviation, introduction, wrinkle

innovational *adj* ***syn*** INVENTIVE, creative, demiurgic, deviceful, ingenious, innovative, innovatory, original, originative

innovative *adj* ***syn*** INVENTIVE, creative, demiurgic, deviceful, ingenious, innovational, innovatory, original, originative

innovator *n* one who introduces something new <an *innovator* of bold ideas in the field of computers>
syn introducer, inventor, original, originator
rel author, creator, maker, producer; architect, builder, developer

innovatory *adj* ***syn*** INVENTIVE, creative, demiurgic, deviceful, ingenious, innovational, innovative, original, originative

innoxious *adj* ***syn*** HARMLESS, innocent, innocuous, inobnoxious, inoffensive, unoffending, unoffensive
ant noxious

innuendo *n* ***syn*** INSINUATION, insinuendo

innumerable *adj* too many to be counted <received *innumerable* requests for help>
syn countless, innumerous, numberless, uncountable, uncounted, unnumberable, unnumbered, untold
ant numberable, numerable

innumerous *adj* ***syn*** INNUMERABLE, countless, numberless, uncountable, uncounted, unnumberable, unnumbered, untold

inobnoxious *adj* ***syn*** HARMLESS, innocent, innocuous, innoxious, inoffensive, unoffending, unoffensive
ant obnoxious

inobservant *adj* ***syn*** INATTENTIVE, unheeding, unnoticing, unobservant, unobserving, unperceiving, unwatchful
ant observant

inobtrusive *adj* ***syn*** QUIET 4, restrained, subdued, tasteful, tasty, unobtrusive
ant obtrusive

inoculate *vb* ***syn*** INFUSE 1, imbue, ingrain, invest, leaven, steep, suffuse
rel admit, enter, introduce

inodorous *adj* ***syn*** ODORLESS, scentless, smell-less
ant odorous; smelly

inoffensive *adj* ***syn*** HARMLESS, innocent, innocuous, innoxious, inobnoxious, unoffending, unoffensive
con loathsome, repulsive, revolting; distasteful, obnoxious, repellent, repugnant

ant offensive

inopportune *adj* ***syn*** UNSEASONABLE 1, ill-seasoned, ill-timed, malapropos, mistimed, untimely
ant opportune

inordinate *adj* **1** ***syn*** EXCESSIVE 1, dizzy, exorbitant, extravagant, extreme, immoderate, towering, unconscionable, undue, unmeasurable
rel irrational, unreasonable; gratuitous, supererogatory, uncalled-for, wanton; extra, superfluous, surplus
con moderate, temperate; checked, curbed, inhibited, restrained
2 ***syn*** EXCESSIVE 2, immoderate, intemperate, overindulgent, unrestrained, untempered

inordinately *adv* ***syn*** EVER 6, excessively, extremely, immensely, over, overfull, overly, overmuch, too, unduly

inordinateness *n* ***syn*** EXCESS 3, immoderation, intemperance, overindulgence

in passing *adv* ***syn*** INCIDENTALLY 2, by the bye, by the way, obiter, parenthetically

in perpetuum *adv* ***syn*** EVER 2, always, eternally, evermore, forever, forevermore

inpour *n* ***syn*** INFLUX, inflow, influxion, inpouring, inrush
ant outpour, outpouring

inpouring *n* ***syn*** INFLUX, inflow, influxion, inpour, inrush
ant outpour, outpouring

inquest *n* ***syn*** INQUIRY 1, delving, inquisition, investigation, probe, probing, quest, research

inquietude *n* ***syn*** UNREST, ailment, disquiet, disquietude, ferment, restiveness, restlessness, storm and stress, Sturm und Drang, turmoil
rel anxiety, uneasiness
ant quiet, quietness, quietude

inquire *vb* ***syn*** ASK 1, catechize, examine, interrogate, query, question, quiz
rel investigate, probe, search; scrutinize, study

inquire (into) *vb* ***syn*** EXPLORE, delve (into), dig (into), go (into), investigate, look (into), probe, prospect, sift

inquiring *adj* ***syn*** INQUISITIVE 1, curious, disquisitive, investigative, questioning

inquiry *n* **1** the act or an instance of seeking truth, information, or knowledge about something <an exhaustive *inquiry* revealed no evidence of a conspiracy>
syn delving, inquest, inquisition, investigation, probe, probing, quest, research
rel catechizing, interrogation, questioning; audit, check, examination, inspection, scrutiny; hearing; inquirendo
2 a request for information <addressed his *inquiry* to the personnel director>
syn interrogation, interrogatory, query, question, questioning

inquisition *n* ***syn*** INQUIRY 1, delving, inquest, investigation, probe, probing, quest, research

inquisitive *adj* **1** given to examination or investigation <an *inquisitive* child who was interested in everything around him>
syn curious, disquisitive, inquiring, investigative, questioning
rel nosy, prying, snoopy
con indifferent, unconcerned, uninquisitive, uninterested

ant incurious
2 ***syn*** CURIOUS 2, inquisitorial, inquisitory, ||nibby, nosy, peery, prying, snoopy
ant incurious, uninquiring

inquisitorial *adj* ***syn*** CURIOUS 2, inquisitive, inquisitory, ||nibby, nosy, peery, prying, snoopy

inquisitory *adj* ***syn*** CURIOUS 2, inquisitive, inquisitorial, ||nibby, nosy, peery, prying, snoopy

in re *prep* ***syn*** APROPOS, about, as for, as regards, as respects, as to, concerning, re, regarding, respecting

in respect to *prep* ***syn*** APROPOS, about, as for, as regards, as respects, as to, concerning, re, regarding, respecting

in reverse *adv* ***syn*** ABOUT 6, again, around, back, backward, round, round about

inroad *n* ***syn*** INVASION, foray, incursion, irruption, raid

inroad *vb* ***syn*** INVADE 1, foray, overrun, overswarm, raid

inrush *n* ***syn*** INFLUX, inflow, influxion, inpour, inpouring
ant outrush

insalubrious *adj* ***syn*** UNWHOLESOME 1, insalutary, noisome, noxious, sickly, unhealthful, unhealthy, unsalutary
ant salubrious, salutary

insalutary *adj* ***syn*** UNWHOLESOME 1, insalubrious, noisome, noxious, sickly, unhealthful, unhealthy, unsalutary
ant salubrious, salutary

insanable *adj* ***syn*** HOPELESS 2, cureless, immedicable, impossible, incurable, irremediable, irreparable, uncorrectable, uncurable, unrecoverable

ins and outs *n pl* characteristic peculiarities or technicalities <soon learned the *ins and outs* of his job>
syn minutiae, ropes
rel details, incidentals, particulars; ramifications; oddities, peculiarities, quirks

insane *adj* **1** being afflicted by or manifesting unsoundness of mind or an inability to control one's rational processes <adjudged *insane* after a period of observation>
syn ||batty, bedlamite, ||bonkers, brainsick, ||buggy, ||bughouse, ||bugs, crackbrained, cracked, ||crackers, ||cracky, ||cranky, crazed, crazy, cuckoo, daffy, daft, demented, deranged, disordered, distraught, ||fruity, ||loco, lunatic, mad, maniac, ||mental, mindless, non compos mentis, nuts, nutsy, nutty, reasonless, screwy, teched, unbalanced, unsane, unsound, wacky, witless, wrong
rel irrational, unreasonable; bewildered, distracted; dotty, eccentric, off, rocky, strange, touched; ||dippy
idiom around the bend, crazy as a coot, not all there, not right in one's head, ||off one's dot, off one's nut (*or* rocker), ||off one's onion, out of (*or* off) one's head, out of one's mind, touched in the head
con judicious, sapient, sensible, wise; rational, reasonable; balanced; logical, subtle; healthy, sound; clear, lucid
ant sane
2 ***syn*** FOOLISH 2, absurd, ||balmy, crazy, harebrained, loony, ||potty, preposterous, silly, wacky
rel fanciful, fantastic, imaginary, visionary; impractical, unrealistic
con feasible, possible, practicable, usable; rational, reasonable, sane, sensible; practical, realistic

insaneness *n* ***syn*** INSANITY 1, aberration, alienation, derangement, distraction, lunacy, madness, psychopathy, unbalance
ant saneness, sanity

insanity *n* **1** grave disorder of mind that impairs one's capacity to function safely or normally in society <his *insanity* required confinement in a mental institution>
syn aberration, alienation, derangement, distraction, insaneness, lunacy, madness, psychopathy, unbalance
rel acromania; delirium, frenzy, hysteria; delusion, hallucination, illusion; irrationality, unreasonableness; dotage
con judiciousness, sageness, sensibility, wiseness; rationality, reasonableness; healthiness, soundness, wholesomeness
ant saneness, sanity
2 ***syn*** FOOLISHNESS, absurdity, craziness, dottiness, folly, inanity, preposterousness, senselessness, silliness, witlessness
rel asininity, fatuousness, stupidity; impracticality

insatiable *adj* incapable of being satisfied or appeased <an *insatiable* lust for glory>
syn insatiate, quenchless, unappeasable, unquenchable, unsatiate, unsatisfiable
rel unsatiated, unsatisfied; demanding, exigent, importunate, insistent, urgent; clamorous, crying, pressing, yearning
con appeasable, quenchable, satisfiable; satiate, satiated, satisfied; controlled, curbed, restrained
ant satiable

insatiably *adv* ***syn*** VERY 1, awfully, dreadfully, exceedingly, extremely, highly, hugely, mightily, strikingly, surpassingly

insatiate *adj* ***syn*** INSATIABLE, quenchless, unappeasable, unquenchable, unsatiate, unsatisfiable
ant satiate, satiated

inscience *n* ***syn*** IGNORANCE 2, innocence, nescience, unacquaintance, unacquaintedness, unawareness, unfamiliarity, unknowingness

inscribe *vb* **1** ***syn*** WRITE, engross, indite, scribe
rel engrave, enscroll
2 ***syn*** LIST 3, book, catalog, enroll
3 ***syn*** ENGRAVE 2, etch, impress, imprint

inscrutable *adj* ***syn*** MYSTERIOUS, arcane, cabalistic, impenetrable, mysterial, mystic, numinous, unaccountable, unguessed, unknowable

insecure *adj* **1** not confident or sure <feels very *insecure* about his future>
syn unassured, unconfident, unsure
rel hesitant, questioning, uncertain
idiom in suspense, up in the air
con assured, confident, self-assured, self-confident, sure
ant secure

---

syn synonym(s) — *rel* related word(s)
idiom idiomatic equivalent(s) — *con* contrasted word(s)
ant antonym(s) — * vulgar
|| use limited; if in doubt, see a dictionary
The first word in a synonym list when printed in SMALL CAPITALS shows where there is more information about the group. For a more efficient use of this book see Explanatory Notes.

2 ***syn*** WEAK 2, dickey, fluctuant, rootless, shaky, unstable, unsure, vacillating, wavering, wobbly
ant secure

inseminate *vb* ***syn*** IMPLANT, inculcate, infix, instill

insensate *adj* **1** lacking animate awareness or sensation <would often talk to stones and other *insensate* objects>
syn inanimate, insensible, insentient, senseless, unfeeling
rel exanimate, unanimated; anesthetic, insensitive
con aware, cognizant, conscious; feeling, sensible, sensient
ant sensate
2 ***syn*** SIMPLE 3, brainless, fatuous, foolish, mindless, nitwitted, senseless, sheepheaded, silly, witless
3 ***syn*** INSENSIBLE 5, anesthetic, bloodless, dull, hard, impossible, insensitive, rocky

insensibility *n* ***syn*** APATHY 1, impassivity, phlegm, stoicism, stolidity, unresponsiveness
ant sensibility

insensible *adj* **1** ***syn*** INSENSATE 1, inanimate, insentient, senseless, unfeeling
ant sensible
2 deprived of consciousness <knocked *insensible* by a sudden punch>
syn cold, comatose, inconscious, senseless, unconscious
idiom out cold
3 ***syn*** NUMB 1, anesthetized, asleep, benumbed, dead, deadened, insensitive, numbed, senseless, unfeeling
4 ***syn*** IMPERCEPTIBLE, impalpable, imponderable, inappreciable, indiscernible, intangible, unapparent, unappreciable, unobservable, unperceivable
ant sensible
5 devoid or insusceptible of emotion or passion <*insensible* to love or compassion>
syn anesthetic, bloodless, dull, hard, impassible, insensate, insensitive, rocky
rel blunt, obtuse; apathetic, impassive, phlegmatic, stoic, stolid; callous, hardened, indurated, pachydermatous, thick-skinned; absorbed, engrossed, intent, rapt
con alert, alive, awake, aware, cognizant, conscious; affected, impressed, influenced, touched
ant sensible

insensitive *adj* **1** ***syn*** INSENSIBLE 5, anesthetic, bloodless, dull, hard, impassible, insensate, rocky
rel aloof, incurious, indifferent, unconcerned
con compassionate, responsive, tender
ant sensitive
2 ***syn*** NUMB 1, anesthetized, asleep, benumbed, dead, deadened, insensible, numbed, senseless, unfeeling
ant sensitive
3 ***syn*** INSUSCEPTIBLE, impassive, insentient, unimpressible, unimpressionable, unresponsive, unsusceptible
ant sensitive

---

syn synonym(s) | ***rel*** related word(s)
idiom idiomatic equivalent(s) | ***con*** contrasted word(s)
ant antonym(s) | * vulgar
‖ use limited; if in doubt, see a dictionary
The first word in a synonym list when printed in SMALL CAPITALS shows where there is more information about the group. For a more efficient use of this book see Explanatory Notes.

insentient *adj* **1** ***syn*** INSENSATE 1, inanimate, insensible, senseless, unfeeling
ant sentient
2 ***syn*** INSUSCEPTIBLE, impassive, insensitive, unimpressible, unimpressionable, unresponsive, unsusceptible

insert *vb* ***syn*** INTRODUCE 6, fill in, insinuate, intercalate, interject, interpolate, interpose, throw in
rel interlope, intrude, obtrude; implant, inculcate, instill; admit, enter
con detach, disengage
ant abstract, extract

in short *adv* ***syn*** BRIEFLY, concisely, in brief, laconically, shortly, succinctly, tersely

inside *n* **1** ***syn*** INTERIOR, inward(s), within
ant outside
2 insides *pl* ***syn*** ENTRAILS, gut(s), innards, internals, inwards, ‖pudding(s), stuffing, tripes, viscera

inside *adj* **1** ***syn*** INNER 1, ‖innermore, interior, internal, intestine, inward
ant outside
2 ***syn*** PRIVATE 2, closet, confidential, hushed

inside *adv* ***syn*** INDOORS, within, withindoors, withinside
ant outside

inside out *adv* ***syn*** THOROUGHLY 2, completely, detailedly, exhaustively, in and out, up and down

insidious *adj* ***syn*** SLY 2, artful, astute, crafty, cunning, deep, foxy, guileful, tricky, wily
rel perfidious, treacherous; dangerous, perilous; gradual, subtle

insight *n* **1** ***syn*** SAGACITY, sagaciousness, sageness, sapience, wisdom
2 ***syn*** INTUITION, anschauung, intuitiveness

insighted *adj* ***syn*** WISE 1, discerning, gnostic, insightful, knowing, knowledgeable, perceptive, sagacious, sage, sophic

insightful *adj* ***syn*** WISE 1, discerning, gnostic, insighted, knowing, knowledgeable, perceptive, sagacious, sage, sophic
rel discriminating, penetrating; inseeing

insignia *n* a distinguishing mark of authority, office, or honor <wore a coronet with the strawberry leaf *insignia* of his ducal rank>
syn badge, emblem
rel decoration; regalia

insignificancy *n* ***syn*** NONENTITY, cipher, nobody, nothing, nullity, whiffet, whippersnapper, whipster, zero, zilch

insignificant *adj* **1** ***syn*** SENSELESS 5, meaningless, pointless, purportless, unmeaning
ant significant
2 ***syn*** MINOR 2, dinky, lesser, minor-league, secondary, small, small-fry, small-time
3 ***syn*** LITTLE 3, casual, inconsiderable, light, minor, petty, shoestring, small-beer, trivial, unimportant
ant significant

insincere *adj* not being or expressing what one appears to be or express <an *insincere* person who could not be trusted>
syn ambidextrous, double, double-dealing, double-faced, doublehearted, double-minded, double-tongued, hypocritical, left-handed, mala fide
rel deceitful, dishonest, lying, mendacious, untruthful; shifty, slippery, tricky

con candid, frank, open, plain; direct, forthright, straight, straightforward
ant sincere

insinuate *vb* **1** *syn* INTRODUCE 6, fill in, insert, intercalate, interject, interpolate, interpose, throw in
2 *syn* SUGGEST 1, connote, hint, imply, intimate
rel ascribe, impute
con affirm, assert, aver, avouch, avow, declare, profess; air, broach, express, state, voice
3 to introduce (as oneself) by stealthy, smooth, or artful means < *insinuated* himself into the confidence of others >
syn edge in, foist, infiltrate, work in, worm
rel insert, intercalate, interject, interpolate, interpose, introduce

insinuating *adj syn* INGRATIATING, deferential, disarming, ingratiatory, insinuative, saccharine, silken, silky

insinuation *n* a stealthy or indirect hinting or suggestion < *insinuations* about his opponent's probity >
syn innuendo, insinuendo
rel hint, hinting, implication, implying, intimation, suggestion; animadversion, aspersion, reflection; ascription, imputation

insinuative *adj syn* INGRATIATING, deferential, disarming, ingratiatory, insinuating, saccharine, silken, silky

insinuendo *n syn* INSINUATION, innuendo

insipid *adj* **1** *syn* UNPALATABLE 1, distasteful, flat, flavorless, ill-flavored, savorless, tasteless, unappetizing, unsavory
rel bland, mild
con appetizing, flavorable, tasty
ant sapid, savory
2 *syn* ARID 2, bromidic, dry, dryasdust, dull, dusty, tedious, uninteresting, weariful, wearisome
rel commonplace, ordinary, plain; mundane, prosaic, unimaginative
3 devoid of qualities that make for spirit and character <an *insipid* little story of teenage puppy love>
syn banal, bland, driveling, flat, inane, innocuous, jejune, milk-and-water, namby-pamby, sapless, swashy, vapid, waterish, watery, wishy-washy
rel slight, tenuous, thin; feeble, weak; subdued, tame; mild, soft; pointless
con piquant, poignant, pungent, racy, spicy; fiery, gingery, high-spirited, mettlesome, peppery, spirited, spunky; exciting, piquing, provocative, provoking
ant sapid

insistent *adj* **1** *syn* PERSISTENT 1, dogged, perseverant, perseverative, persevering, persisting, persistive
2 *syn* EMPHATIC, assertive, forceful, resounding
rel persevering, persistent, pressing; obtrusive
3 *syn* PRESSING, burning, clamant, clamorous, crying, dire, exigent, imperative, importunate, urgent

insociable *adj syn* UNSOCIABLE, aloof, distant, reserved, solitary, standoff, standoffish, touch-me-not-ish, uncompanionable, withdrawn
ant sociable

insolate *vb syn* SUN, bask

insolence *n* the quality, state, or an instance of being insulting or grossly lacking in respect <court-martialed because of *insolence* to an officer>
syn boldness, disrespect, hardihood, impertinence, impudence, insolency, insolentness; *compare* EFFRONTERY
rel brazenness; presumption; arrogance; rudeness; contempt
con deference; correctness, decency, decorum, decorousness, properness, seemliness
ant respect, respectfulness

insolency *n syn* INSOLENCE, boldness, disrespect, hardihood, impertinence, impudence, insolentness
ant respect, respectfulness

insolent *adj* **1** *syn* PROUD 1, arrogant, cavalier, disdainful, haughty, high-and-mighty, lofty, overbearing, supercilious, superior
rel imperative, peremptory; dictatorial, magisterial
ant deferential
2 exhibiting boldness or effrontery <an *insolent* child with no respect or regard for anyone>
syn audacious, bold, ‖boldacious, brazen, contumelious, impertinent, impudent, procacious, saucy
rel arrogant, disdainful, overbearing; discourteous, impolite, rude, uncivil, ungracious
con humble, lowly, meek, modest, unassertive; civil, courteous, polite
ant deferential

insolentness *n syn* INSOLENCE, boldness, disrespect, hardihood, impertinence, impudence, insolency
ant respect, respectfulness

insoluble *adj* admitting of no solution <seemingly *insoluble* problems faced the city council>
syn inextricable, insolvable, irresoluble, irresolvable, unsoluble, unsolvable
rel inexplicable, unexplainable; inconceivable, unaccountable; mysterious
con answerable, explicable, understandable; resolvable; clear, plain, straightforward
ant soluble, solvable

insolvable *adj syn* INSOLUBLE, inextricable, irresoluble, irresolvable, unsoluble, unsolvable
ant soluble, solvable

insomnia *n* prolonged inability to obtain adequate sleep <sleeping pills failed to relieve his *insomnia* >
syn insomnolence, sleeplessness
rel restlessness, wakefulness; stress, tension

insomnolence *n syn* INSOMNIA, sleeplessness

insorb *vb syn* ABSORB 1, assimilate, imbibe, incorporate, inhaust

insouciance *n syn* APATHY 2, disinterest, disregard, heedlessness, indifference, lassitude, lethargy, listlessness, unconcern, unmindfulness

insouciant *adj syn* HAPPY-GO-LUCKY, carefree, free-minded, lighthearted, lightsome

inspect *vb syn* SCRUTINIZE 1, canvass, check over, check up, con, examine, study, survey, vet, view
rel notice, observe; catechize, inquire, interrogate, question; review

---

syn synonym(s) *rel* related word(s)
idiom idiomatic equivalent(s) *con* contrasted word(s)
ant antonym(s) * vulgar
‖ use limited; if in doubt, see a dictionary
The first word in a synonym list when printed in SMALL CAPITALS shows where there is more information about the group. For a more efficient use of this book see Explanatory Notes.

inspection *n* ***syn*** EXAMINATION, analysis, check-over, checkup, perlustration, review, scan, scrutiny, survey, view
rel inquest, inquiry, inquisition, investigation, probe, research; oversight, supervision, surveillance

inspiration *n* a divine or seemingly divine imparting of knowledge or power <*inspiration* is the only plausible explanation for his exquisite work>
syn afflation, afflatus, inflatus
rel animus, genius, muse, vision; enlightenment, illumination; brainstorm, brainwave

inspire *vb* **1** ***syn*** INHALE, breathe (in)
ant expire
2 ***syn*** FIRE 2, animate, exalt, inform
rel quicken, stimulate; infect, infuse; endow, endue
3 ***syn*** ELATE, commove, excite, exhilarate, set up, spirit (up), stimulate
4 ***syn*** AFFECT, carry, get, impress, influence, move, strike, sway, touch

inspiring *adj* ***syn*** EXCITING, exhilarant, exhilarating, exhilarative, eye-popping, intoxicating, rousing, stimulating, stirring
ant uninspiring

inspirit *vb* ***syn*** ENCOURAGE 1, animate, cheer, chirk (up), embolden, enhearten, hearten, nerve, steel, strengthen
rel exalt, fire, inform, inspire
ant dispirit

in spite of *prep* ***syn*** AGAINST 4, despite, notwithstanding, regardless of

instability *n* the state or quality of not being firm or fixed <the *instability* of the economy>
syn precariousness, shakiness, unfixedness, unsettledness, unstability, unstableness, unsteadfastness, unsteadiness
rel undependability, unreliability; inconstancy, insecurity
con firmness, soundness, stoutness, sturdiness; fixity, solidity
ant stability, stableness

install *vb* **1** ***syn*** INITIATE 3, inaugurate, induct, instate, invest
2 ***syn*** ENSCONCE 2, settle

installation *n* ***syn*** INITIATION, inaugural, inauguration, induction, investiture

instance *n* an individual that clearly belongs to an indicated class <their rescue was an *instance* of great courage>
syn case, case history, example, illustration, representative, sample, sampling, specimen
rel ground, proof, reason; detail, item, particular; exponent

instance *vb* **1** ***syn*** EXEMPLIFY 1, illustrate
2 ***syn*** MENTION, cite, name, specify
rel exemplify, illustrate

instant *n* **1** an infinitesimal space of time <came not an *instant* too soon>
syn breathing, crack, flash, ‖jiff, jiffy, minute, moment, second, shake, split second, ‖tick, trice, twinkle, twinkling, wink
2 ***syn*** POINT 7, juncture, moment
3 ***syn*** OCCASION 5, moment, time, while

instant *adj* **1** ***syn*** PRESSING, burning, clamant, crying, dire, exigent, imperative, importunate, insistent, urgent
2 ***syn*** PRESENT, contemporary, current, existent, extant, present-day, todayish
3 ***syn*** INSTANTANEOUS, hair-trigger, immediate

instantaneous *adj* done, occurring, or acting without any perceptible duration of time <*instantaneous* answers to tough questions>
syn hair-trigger, immediate, instant; *compare* QUICK 2
rel spontaneous; fast, quick, rapid; momentary, transitory
con late, tardy; slow, sluggish

instanter *adv* ***syn*** AWAY 3, at once, directly, first off, forthwith, immediately, instantly, now, right, right away

instantly *adv* ***syn*** AWAY 3, at once, directly, first off, forthwith, immediately, instanter, now, right, right away
idiom in a flash, on a dime, on the spot

instate *vb* ***syn*** INITIATE 3, inaugurate, induct, install, invest

instead *adv* as an alternative to something expressed or implied <longed *instead* for a quiet country life>
syn alternately, alternatively, in lieu, rather

insteep *vb* ***syn*** SOAK 1, drench, impregnate, saturate, seethe, sodden, sop, souse, steep, waterlog

instigate *vb* ***syn*** INCITE, abet, foment, provoke, raise, set, set on, stir (up), whip (up)
rel activate, actuate; hint, insinuate, suggest; plan, plot, scheme; goad, urge; fire, inflame

instigation *n* ***syn*** STIMULUS, catalyst, goad, impetus, impulse, incentive, incitation, incitement, spur, stimulation

instigator *n* one that goads or urges forward <the *instigator* of the riot>
syn agitator, fomenter, inciter, mover
rel firebrand, incendiary, inflamer, rabble-rouser

instill *vb* ***syn*** IMPLANT, inculcate, infix, inseminate

instinctive *adj* **1** prompted by natural instinct or propensity <was quite unable to control her *instinctive* fear of snakes>
syn instinctual, intuitive, visceral
rel congenital, inborn, innate; ingrained, inherent, intrinsic; natural
ant reasoned
2 ***syn*** SPONTANEOUS, automatic, impulsive, involuntary, unmeditated, unpremeditated, unprompted, will-less
rel natural, normal, regular, typical
ant intentional

instinctual *adj* ***syn*** INSTINCTIVE 1, intuitive, visceral

institute *vb* **1** ***syn*** FOUND 2, constitute, create, establish, organize, set up, start
ant abrogate
2 ***syn*** INTRODUCE 3, inaugurate, initiate, launch, originate, set up, usher in

---

syn synonym(s) | *rel* related word(s)
idiom idiomatic equivalent(s) | *con* contrasted word(s)
ant antonym(s) | * vulgar
‖ use limited; if in doubt, see a dictionary
The first word in a synonym list when printed in SMALL CAPITALS shows where there is more information about the group. For a more efficient use of this book see Explanatory Notes.

institute *n* ***syn*** LAW 1, decree, decretum, edict, ordinance, precept, prescript, regulation, rule, statute

institution *n* something or someone well established in a customary relationship <he's been in the office so long that he has become an *institution*>
syn fixture
rel custom, habit; establishment, rite

instruct *vb* **1** ***syn*** TEACH, discipline, educate, school, train
rel acquaint, apprise, inform; engineer, guide, lead, pilot, steer
2 ***syn*** COMMAND, bid, charge, direct, enjoin, order, tell, warn
rel assign, define, prescribe

instruction *n* ***syn*** EDUCATION 1, schooling, teaching, training, tuition, tutelage

instructional *adj* ***syn*** INFORMATIVE, educational, educative, informational, informatory, instructive

instructive *adj* ***syn*** INFORMATIVE, educational, educative, informational, informatory, instructional
rel didactic, moralistic, moralizing

instrument *n* **1** ***syn*** MEAN 2, agency, agent, channel, instrumentality, instrumentation, medium, ministry, organ, vehicle
2 ***syn*** IMPLEMENT, tool, utensil
rel equipment, gear, machinery, paraphernalia, tackle

instrumental *adj* serving as a means, agent, or tool <was *instrumental* in organizing the strike>
syn implemental, ministerial
rel conducive, helpful; serviceable, useful

instrumentality *n* ***syn*** MEAN 2, agency, agent, channel, instrument, instrumentation, medium, ministry, organ, vehicle
rel energy, force, might, power

instrumentation *n* ***syn*** MEAN 2, agency, agent, channel, instrument, instrumentality, medium, ministry, organ, vehicle

insubordinate *adj* unwilling to submit to authority <*insubordinate* soldiers are court-martialed>
syn contumacious, factious, insurgent, mutinous, rebellious, seditious
rel intractable, recalcitrant, refractory, ungovernable, unruly; indocile, uncompliant, uncomplying; disaffected, dissentious
con amenable, biddable, docile, obedient, tractable; subdued, submissive, tame
ant subordinate

insubstantial *adj* **1** ***syn*** IMMATERIAL 1, bodiless, disembodied, incorporeal, metaphysical, nonmaterial, nonphysical, unembodied, unfleshly, unsubstantial
ant substantial
2 ***syn*** WEAK 1, decrepit, feeble, flimsy, fragile, frail, infirm, puny, unsound, unsubstantial
ant substantial
3 ***syn*** TENUOUS 3, feeble, unsubstantial
ant substantial

insuccess *n* ***syn*** FAILURE 2, defeat, nonsuccess, unsuccess, unsuccessfulness
ant success, successfulness

insufferable *adj* incapable of being endured <that man is an *insufferable* bore>
syn insupportable, intolerable, unbearable, unbrookable, unendurable, unsufferable, unsupportable
rel distressing, painful; unacceptable
ant sufferable

insufficience *n* **1** ***syn*** FAILURE 3, defalcation, deficiency, deficit, inadequacy, insufficiency, lack, scantiness, shortage, underage
ant sufficiency
2 ***syn*** SCARCITY, insufficiency, paucity, poverty, ‖scant, scarceness
ant sufficiency

insufficiency *n* **1** ***syn*** FAILURE 3, defalcation, deficiency, deficit, inadequacy, insufficience, lack, scantiness, shortage, underage
ant sufficiency
2 ***syn*** SCARCITY, insufficience, paucity, poverty, ‖scant, scarceness
ant sufficiency

insufficient *adj* **1** ***syn*** DEFICIENT 1, defective, ‖half-assed, inadequate, incomplete, lacking, uncomplete, wanting
ant sufficient
2 ***syn*** SHORT 3, deficient, failing, inadequate, scant, scanty, scarce, shy, unsufficient, wanting
ant sufficient

insular *adj* having the narrow and limited outlook characteristic of geographic isolation <the *insular* thinking of peasant communities>
syn local, ‖parish-pump, parochial, provincial, sectarian, small-town
rel regional, sectional; insulated, isolated, secluded; circumscribed, confined, limited, restricted; illiberal, narrow, narrow-minded
con broad-minded, liberal; cosmopolitan, metropolitan, urban

insulate *vb* ***syn*** ISOLATE, close off, cut off, enisle, island, segregate, separate, sequester

insult *vb* ***syn*** OFFEND 3, affront, outrage
rel abase, debase, degrade, humble, humiliate; fleer, flout, gibe, gird, jeer, scoff, sneer; deride, mock, ridicule, taunt; rump
con admire, esteem, respect
ant honor

insult *n* ***syn*** AFFRONT, contumely, despite, indignity, slap
rel abuse, invective, obloquy, vituperation; disgrace, ignominy, opprobrium, shame; disdainfulness, insolence, superciliousness; contempt, disdain, scorn; unpleasantry
con deference, homage, honor, obeisance, reverence

insuperable *adj* incapable of being surmounted, overcome, or passed over <they met with *insuperable* difficulties>
syn impassable, inconquerable, indomitable, insurmountable, invincible, unconquerable, unsurmountable

---

syn synonym(s) ***rel*** related word(s)
idiom idiomatic equivalent(s) ***con*** contrasted word(s)
ant antonym(s) * vulgar
‖ use limited; if in doubt, see a dictionary
The first word in a synonym list when printed in SMALL CAPITALS shows where there is more information about the group. For a more efficient use of this book see Explanatory Notes.

rel unachievable, unattainable; unsurpassable; impregnable, impenetrable, invulnerable
con surmountable; achievable, negotiable
ant superable

insupportable *adj syn* INSUFFERABLE, intolerable, unbearable, unbrookable, unendurable, unsufferable, unsupportable
ant bearable, supportable

insupposable *adj syn* INCREDIBLE 1, incogitable, inconceivable, unbelievable, unimaginable, unthinkable
ant supposable

insuppressible *adj syn* IRREPRESSIBLE, insuppressive, irrestrainable, uncontainable, uncontrollable, unrestrainable
ant suppressible

insuppressive *adj syn* IRREPRESSIBLE, insuppressible, irrestrainable, uncontainable, uncontrollable, unrestrainable

insure *vb syn* ENSURE, assure, cinch, secure
rel guard, protect, safeguard, shield

insurgent *n syn* REBEL, anarch, anarchist, frondeur, insurrectionist, malcontent, mutineer, revolter

insurgent *adj syn* INSUBORDINATE, contumacious, factious, mutinous, rebellious, seditious

insurmountable *adj syn* INSUPERABLE, impassable, inconquerable, indomitable, invincible, unconquerable, unsurmountable
ant surmountable

insurrect *vb syn* REVOLT 1, mutiny, rebel, rise (against)

insurrectionist *n syn* REBEL, anarch, anarchist, frondeur, insurgent, malcontent, mutineer, revolter

insusceptible *adj* incapable of being moved, affected, or impressed < *insusceptible* to flattery >
syn impassive, insensitive, insentient, unimpressible, unimpressionable, unresponsive, unsusceptible
con impressible, impressionable, responsive, sensitive, sentient
ant susceptible

intact *adj* **1** *syn* WHOLE 1, entire, flawless, perfect, unblemished, undamaged, unhurt, unimpaired, uninjured, unmarred
ant defective
2 *syn* VIRGIN 1, maiden, undeflowered, virginal
ant deflowered

intangible *adj* **1** *syn* IMPERCEPTIBLE, impalpable, imponderable, inappreciable, indiscernible, insensible, invisible, unapparent, unappreciable, unobservable
rel rare, tenuous, thin; slender, slight; aerial, aeriform, airy, ethereal; eluding, elusive, evading, evasive; touchless
ant tangible
2 *syn* ELUSIVE, elusory, evasive

integer *n syn* NUMBER, chiffer, cipher, digit, figure, numeral, whole number

---

syn synonym(s) — *rel* related word(s)
idiom idiomatic equivalent(s) — *con* contrasted word(s)
ant antonym(s) — * vulgar
‖ use limited; if in doubt, see a dictionary
The first word in a synonym list when printed in SMALL CAPITALS shows where there is more information about the group. For a more efficient use of this book see Explanatory Notes.

integral *adj syn* WHOLE 3, choate, complete, entire, full, perfect

integral *n syn* WHOLE 2, entity, integrate, sum, system, totality

integrate *n syn* WHOLE 2, entity, integral, sum, system, totality

integrate *vb* **1** *syn* HARMONIZE 4, arrange, blend, orchestrate, symphonize, synthesize, unify
2 *syn* HARMONIZE 3, accommodate, attune, conform, coordinate, proportion, reconcile, reconciliate, tune
3 to join together systematically <an economic system that successfully *integrates* private gain with public responsibility>
syn articulate, concatenate
rel combine, conjoin, link, unite; compact, concentrate, consolidate, unify; blend, coalesce, fuse, merge; organize, systematize
con disperse, dissipate, scatter; analyze, break down, resolve
ant disintegrate
4 *syn* UNIFY 1, compact, concentrate, consolidate
5 *syn* EMBODY 2, combine, incorporate

integrative *adj* tending to integrate < *integrative* forces in a fragmented society>
syn centralizing, centripetal, compacting, concentrating, consolidating, unifying
ant disintegrative

integrity *n* **1** *syn* HONESTY, honestness, honor, honorableness, incorruption
rel forthrightness, straightforwardness
2 the quality or state of being complete or undivided <trying to maintain the *integrity* of the empire>
syn completeness, entireness, perfection, wholeness
rel soundness, stability; absoluteness, purity, simplicity

intellect *n* **1** *syn* REASON 5, understanding
rel comprehension; intuition
2 a person with great intellectual powers <one of the great *intellects* of his time>
syn brain, intellectual, intelligence
rel genius; egghead, pundit; thinker

intellection *n syn* IDEA, apprehension, conceit, concept, conception, image, impression, notion, perception, thought

intellective *adj syn* MENTAL 1, cerebral, intellectual, psychic, psychical, psychological

intellectual *adj* **1** *syn* MENTAL 1, cerebral, intellective, psychic, psychical, psychological
con animal, fleshly, sensual
ant carnal
2 devoted to or engaged in the creative use of the intellect <the play appealed to the *intellectual* members of the audience>
syn cerebral, highbrow, highbrowed, intellectualistic

intellectual *n* **1** *syn* INTELLECT 2, brain, intelligence
2 a person who possesses or has pretensions of strong intellectual interest or superiority <accused of being an *intellectual* and a snob>
syn Brahmin, double-dome, egghead, highbrow
3 intellectuals *pl syn* INTELLIGENTSIA, clerisy, illuminati, literati

intellectualistic *adj syn* INTELLECTUAL 2, cerebral, highbrow, highbrowed

intelligence *n* **1** the ability to learn and to cope <what he lacked in education, he made up in *intelligence*>

syn brain(s), brainpower, mentality, mother wit, sense, wit
rel acumen, discernment, insight, judgment; perspicacity, sagacity, wisdom
2 *syn* INTELLECT 2, brain, intellectual
3 *syn* NEWS, advice, information, speerings, tidings, word

intelligent *adj* 1 *syn* RATIONAL, consequent, logical, reasonable, sensible, sound
con irrational, unreasonable
ant unintelligent
2 mentally keen or quick <quite *intelligent* for his age>
syn alert, brainy, bright, brilliant, clever, knowing, knowledgeable, quick-witted, ready-witted, sharp, smart; *compare* WISE 4
rel astute, perspicacious, sagacious, shrewd; acute, keen; adroit, cunning, ingenious
con foolish, idiotic, imbecilic, moronic; crass, dense, dull, dumb, slow, stupid
ant unintelligent

intelligentsia *n* a class of articulate persons devoted to intellectual, cultural, and social matters <the *intelligentsia* posed a threat to the new regime>
syn clerisy, illuminati, intellectuals, literati
rel avant-garde, vanguard

intelligible *adj syn* UNDERSTANDABLE, apprehensible, comprehendible, comprehensible, fathomable, graspable, knowable, lucid, luminous
ant unintelligible

intemperance *n syn* EXCESS 3, immoderation, inordinateness, overindulgence
rel drunkenness, insobriety; debauchery
ant temperance

intemperate *adj* 1 *syn* EXCESSIVE 2, immoderate, inordinate, overindulgent, unrestrained, untempered
rel bibacious, bibulous, crapulous, drunken; gluttonous
ant temperate, tempered
2 *syn* SEVERE 3, bitter, brutal, hard, harsh, inclement, rigorous, rugged
ant temperate

intempestive *adj syn* IMPROPER 1, ill-timed, inappropriate, inapt, malapropos, unapt, undue, unseasonable, unsuitable, untimely

intemporal *adj syn* ETERNAL 4, ageless, dateless, timeless
ant temporal

intend *vb* 1 *syn* MEAN 2, add up (to), connote, denote, express, import, signify, spell
2 to have in mind as a purpose < *intended* to read the book>
syn aim, contemplate, design, mean, ‖mind, plan, propose, purpose
rel attempt, endeavor, essay, strive, try; plot, scheme; assign, designate, destine
idiom figure on, have in mind to, look forward to

intendance *n syn* OVERSIGHT 1, care, charge, conduct, handling, management, running, superintendence, superintendency, supervision

intended *adj syn* ENGAGED 2, affianced, betrothed, contracted, plighted, ‖promised

intended *n syn* BETROTHED, affianced

intendment *n* 1 *syn* INTENTION, animus, design, intent, meaning, plan, purpose
2 *syn* MEANING 1, acceptation, import, intent, purport, sense, significance, significancy, signification, understanding

intensate *vb syn* INTENSIFY, aggravate, deepen, enhance, heighten, magnify, mount, redouble, rise, rouse

intense *adj* 1 extreme in degree, power, or effect < *intense* hatred>
syn concentrated, desperate, exquisite, fierce, furious, terrible, vehement, vicious, violent
rel aggravated, enhanced, heightened, intensified; accentuated, emphasized, stressed
ant subdued
2 *syn* INTENSIVE, blood-and-guts, deep, hard, profound
3 *syn* ARDENT 2, extreme
ant slight

intensely *adv* 1 *syn* HARD 3, assiduously, dingdong, earnestly, exhaustively, intensively, painstakingly, thoroughly, unremittingly
rel fiercely, furiously, vehemently, viciously, violently
2 *syn* SERIOUSLY 2, gravely, severely

intensify *vb* to increase markedly in measure or degree <both companies *intensified* their efforts to win the contract> <the pain *intensified* sharply>
syn aggravate, deepen, enhance, heighten, intensate, magnify, mount, redouble, rise, rouse
rel accent, accentuate, emphasize, stress; aggrandize, exalt; sharpen
con moderate, qualify; alleviate, ease, lighten, relieve; decrease, diminish, lessen, reduce
ant abate; allay, mitigate; temper

intensive *adj* highly concentrated <an *intensive* study of the causes of the war>
syn blood-and-guts, deep, hard, intense, profound
con casual, shallow, superficial

intensively *adv syn* HARD 3, assiduously, dingdong, earnestly, exhaustively, intensely, painstakingly, thoroughly, unremittingly

intent *n* 1 *syn* INTENTION, animus, design, intendment, meaning, plan, purpose
rel conation, volition, will
con chance, fortune, hap, hazard, luck
ant accident
2 *syn* MEANING 1, acceptation, import, intendment, purport, sense, significance, significancy, signification, understanding

intent *adj* 1 having one's mind or attention deeply fixed <the student was too *intent* on his work to hear the phone>
syn absorbed, deep, engaged, engrossed, immersed, preoccupied, rapt, wrapped, wrapped up
rel attending, attentive, minding, watching; concentrated, riveted

---

syn synonym(s) *rel* related word(s)
idiom idiomatic equivalent(s) *con* contrasted word(s)
ant antonym(s) * vulgar
‖ use limited; if in doubt, see a dictionary
The first word in a synonym list when printed in SMALL CAPITALS shows where there is more information about the group. For a more efficient use of this book see Explanatory Notes.

con absent, absent-minded, abstracted, bemused, faraway, preoccupied; daydreaming, napping, oblivious
ant distracted
2 *syn* DECIDED 2, bent, decisive, determined, resolute, resolved, set, settled

intention *n* what one purposes to accomplish or do <his *intention* was to finish by noon>
syn animus, design, intendment, intent, meaning, plan, purpose; *compare* AMBITION 2
rel project, scheme; desire, hope, wish

intentional *adj* *syn* VOLUNTARY, deliberate, unforced, unprescribed, willful, willing, witting
rel intended, meant, proposed, purposed; advised, considered, designed, designful, premeditated, studied
con accidental, casual, fortuitous; careless, heedless, inadvertent, thoughtless
ant unintentional

intentionally *adv* with intention <hurt her *intentionally*>
syn ‖apurpose, deliberately, designedly, on purpose, prepensely, purposedly, purposely, purposively
ant unintentionally

intentive *adj* *syn* ATTENTIVE 1, advertent, arrect, heedful, observant, regardful

intently *adv* *syn* HARD 4, closely, searchingly, sharply

intentness *n* *syn* EARNESTNESS, earnest, serious-mindedness, seriousness

inter *vb* *syn* BURY 1, entomb, inhume, lay away, plant, put away, sepulcher, sepulture, tomb
ant disinter

interact *vb* to act upon one another <humor and pathos *interacted* to make a moving drama>
syn coact, interplay, interreact
rel collaborate, cooperate; combine, join, merge, unite

interagent *n* *syn* GO-BETWEEN 2, broker, entrepreneur, interceder, intercessor, intermediary, intermediate, intermediator, mediator, middleman

interblend *vb* *syn* MIX 1, blend, comingle, commingle, fuse, immingle, interfuse, intermingle, intermix, mingle

interbreed *vb* *syn* CROSS 4, crossbreed, cross-mate, hybridize, intercross

intercalate *vb* *syn* INTRODUCE 6, fill in, insert, insinuate, interject, interpolate, interpose, throw in

intercede *vb* *syn* INTERPOSE 2, interfere, intermediate, intervene, mediate, step in

interceder *n* *syn* GO-BETWEEN 2, broker, entrepreneur, interagent, intercessor, intermediary, intermediate, intermediator, mediator, middleman

intercept *vb* to stop, seize, or interrupt in progress or course <*intercept* a forward pass>
syn block, catch, cut off
rel grab, seize, take; check, curb
con fumble, miss; loose, release

intercessor *n* *syn* GO-BETWEEN 2, broker, entrepreneur, interagent, interceder, intermediary, intermediate, intermediator, mediator, middleman

interchange *vb* *syn* EXCHANGE 3, handy
rel reverse, transpose

interchangeable *adj* permitting mutual substitution <*interchangeable* parts>
syn commutable, exchangeable, fungible, interconvertible, substitutable
rel changeable, convertible; reciprocal, reciprocative

interchurch *adj* *syn* NONSECTARIAN, intercreedal, interdenominational, undenominational, unsectarian

intercommunication *n* 1 *syn* COMMUNICATION 3, communion, converse, intercourse
2 *syn* CONTACT 2, commerce, communication, communion, intercourse

intercomparable *adj* *syn* LIKE, akin, alike, analogous, comparable, consonant, corresponding, equivalent, parallel, similar

interconnect *vb* *syn* INTERJOIN, anastomose, interlink, intertie

interconvertible *adj* *syn* INTERCHANGEABLE, commutable, exchangeable, fungible, substitutable

intercourse *n* 1 *syn* COMMERCE 2, communion, dealings, traffic, truck
2 *syn* COMMUNICATION 3, communion, converse, intercommunication
3 *syn* CONTACT 2, commerce, communication, communion, intercommunication

intercreedal *adj* *syn* NONSECTARIAN, interchurch, interdenominational, undenominational, unsectarian

intercross *vb* 1 *syn* INTERSECT, crisscross, cross, crosscut, decussate
2 *syn* CROSS 4, crossbreed, cross-mate, hybridize, interbreed

interdenominational *adj* *syn* NONSECTARIAN, interchurch, intercreedal, undenominational, unsectarian

interdict *vb* *syn* FORBID, ban, enjoin, inhibit, outlaw, prohibit, taboo
ant sanction

interdiction *n* *syn* TABOO, ban, forbiddance, prohibition, proscription
ant sanction

interest *n* 1 participation in advantage, profit, and responsibility <he owned a half *interest* in a furniture store>
syn claim, share, stake
2 *syn* WELFARE, advantage, benefit, good, prosperity, well-being
3 readiness to be concerned with or moved by something <had an *interest* in art>
syn concern, curiosity, interestedness, regard
rel enthusiasm, excitement, passion; attention, care, concernment; absorption, engrossment
con apathy, indifference, unconcern
ant disinterest

interest *vb* to engage the attention and interest of <his appeal failed to *interest* his listeners>
syn appeal, attract, excite, fascinate, intrigue
rel arouse, tantalize, titillate; lure, pull, snare, tempt; pique
ant bore

interested *adj* having a share or concern in some affair <all *interested* parties met for the reading of the will>

---

syn synonym(s) | *rel* related word(s)
idiom idiomatic equivalent(s) | *con* contrasted word(s)
ant antonym(s) | * vulgar
‖ use limited; if in doubt, see a dictionary
The first word in a synonym list when printed in SMALL CAPITALS shows where there is more information about the group. For a more efficient use of this book see Explanatory Notes.

syn affected, concerned, implicated, involved
rel biased, partial, partisan, prejudiced
con aloof, incurious, indifferent, unconcerned; apathetic, bored, ennuyé
ant detached, disinterested

interestedness *n* *syn* INTEREST 3, concern, curiosity, regard

interfere *vb* **1** *syn* INTERPOSE 2, intercede, intermediate, intervene, mediate, step in
rel bar, block, hinder, impede, obstruct
2 *syn* MEDDLE, busybody, butt in, fool, horn in, interlope, intermeddle, ‖make, monkey (with), tamper (with)
rel discommode, incommode, inconvenience, trouble; baffle, balk, foil, frustrate, thwart

interflow *vb* *syn* MIX 1, blend, comingle, commingle, fuse, immingle, immix, interblend, intermingle, intermix

interfuse *vb* **1** *syn* MIX 1, blend, compound, fuse, immingle, interblend, intermingle, intermix, meld, mingle
2 to cause to pass into or through <*interfused* illuminating anecdotes with the informative text>
syn diffuse, infuse, interlard, intersow, intersperse, intersprinkle
rel impenetrate, impregnate, interpenetrate, penetrate, pervade, saturate
3 *syn* PERMEATE, compenetrate, impenetrate, impregnate, interpenetrate, penetrate, percolate, pervade, saturate, transfuse

interfusion *n* *syn* MIXTURE, admixture, alloy, amalgam, amalgamation, blend, commixture, fusion, immixture, intermixture

interim *n* *syn* GAP 3, breach, break, hiatus, interruption, interval, lacuna

interim *adj* *syn* TEMPORARY, acting, ad interim, pro tem, pro tempore, supply

interior *adj* **1** *syn* INNER 1, ‖innermore, inside, internal, intestine, inward
con extraneous, extrinsic, foreign
ant exterior
2 *syn* INNER 2, gut, internal, intimate, visceral, viscerous

interior *n* the internal or inner part <the *interior* of the house>
syn inside, inward(s), within
rel center, heart; belly, bosom; innards, internals
ant exterior, outside

interject *vb* *syn* INTRODUCE 6, fill in, insert, insinuate, intercalate, interpolate, interpose, throw in

interjoin *vb* to join mutually <*interjoined* several stations into a new system>
syn anastomose, interconnect, interlink, intertie
rel interdigitate, interlace, interlock, interrelate
con disunite, part, separate, sunder
ant disjoin

interknit *vb* *syn* INTERWEAVE, interlace, intertwine, intertwist, intervolve, interwind, interwork, interwreathe, inweave

interlace *vb* *syn* INTERWEAVE, interknit, intertwine, intertwist, intervolve, interwind, interwork, interwreathe, inweave

interlard *vb* *syn* INTERFUSE 2, diffuse, infuse, intersow, intersperse, intersprinkle

interlink *vb* *syn* INTERJOIN, anastomose, interconnect, intertie

interlope *vb* **1** *syn* INTRUDE
2 *syn* MEDDLE, busybody, butt in, fool, horn in, interfere, intermeddle, ‖make, monkey (with), tamper (with)

interlude *n* an intervening or interruptive period or space <an *interlude* of happiness in a tragic story> <woodland broken by *interludes* of meadow>
syn break, intermission, interregnum, interval, parenthesis
rel breather, lull, pause, respite, rest; episode, idyll; meantime, meanwhile, spell; entr'acte

intermeddle *vb* *syn* MEDDLE, busybody, butt in, fool, horn in, interfere, interlope, ‖make, monkey (with), tamper (with)
rel encroach, entrench, invade, trespass

intermeddler *n* *syn* BUSYBODY, butt-in, ‖buttinsky, kibitzer, meddler, pragmatist, prier (*or* pryer), quidnunc, rubberneck, snoop

intermediary *adj* *syn* MIDDLE 2, center, central, intermediate, mean, medial, median, mid

intermediary *n* **1** *syn* GO-BETWEEN 2, broker, entrepreneur, interagent, interceder, intercessor, intermediate, intermediator, mediator, middleman
2 *syn* MEAN 2, agency, agent, channel, instrument, instrumentality, medium, ministry, organ, vehicle

intermediate *vb* *syn* INTERPOSE 2, intercede, interfere, intervene, mediate, step in

intermediate *adj* **1** *syn* MIDDLE 2, center, central, intermediary, mean, medial, median, mid
2 *syn* MEDIUM, average, fair, fairish, indifferent, mean, mediocre, middling, moderate, so-so

intermediate *n* *syn* GO-BETWEEN 2, broker, entrepreneur, interagent, interceder, intercessor, intermediary, intermediator, mediator, middleman

intermediator *n* *syn* GO-BETWEEN 2, broker, entrepreneur, interagent, interceder, intercessor, intermediary, intermediate, mediator, middleman

interment *n* *syn* BURIAL 2, entombment, inhumation, sepulture
ant disinterment

intermesh *vb* *syn* ENGAGE 1, mesh

interminable *adj* *syn* CONTINUAL, ceaseless, constant, continuous, endless, everlasting, perpetual, unceasing, unending, uninterrupted
rel eternal, infinite; lasting, permanent
con intermittent, periodic; discontinued, stopped; closed, completed, ended, finished, terminated

intermingle *vb* *syn* MIX 1, comingle, commingle, commix, immingle, immix, interblend, interfuse, intermix, mingle

intermission *n* **1** *syn* ABEYANCE, abeyancy, cold storage, doldrums, dormancy, interruption, latency, quiescence, quiescency, suspension
2 *syn* INTERLUDE, break, interregnum, interval, parenthesis

---

intermit *vb* ***syn*** DEFER, delay, hold off, hold over, hold up, postpone, prorogue, put off, stay, suspend
rel arrest, check, interrupt
con continue, persist; iterate, reiterate, repeat

intermittent *adj* occurring or appearing in interrupted sequence <they predict *intermittent* rain throughout the day>
syn alternate, isochronal, isochronous, periodic, periodical, recurrent, recurring
rel cyclic, cyclical, iterant, iterative, metrical, rhythmic, rhythmical, seasonal, serial; arrested, checked, interrupted; fitful, spasmodic; infrequent, occasional, sporadic; discontinuing, discontinuous
con constant, perpetual; everlasting, interminable
ant continual, continuous; incessant, unceasing

intermix *vb* ***syn*** MIX 1, admix, comingle, commingle, commix, immingle, immix, interblend, interfuse, intermingle

intermixture *n* ***syn*** MIXTURE, admixture, amalgam, amalgamation, blend, commixture, immixture, interfusion, mix, mix-up

intermutual *adj* ***syn*** COMMON 1, communal, conjoint, conjunct, joint, mutual, public, shared

intern *vb* ***syn*** IMPRISON, bastille, confine, constrain, immure, incarcerate, jail, jug, ‖prison, ‖quod

internal *adj* **1** ***syn*** INNER 1, ‖innermore, inside, interior, intestine, inward
ant external
2 ***syn*** INNER 2, gut, interior, intimate, visceral, viscerous
3 ***syn*** DOMESTIC 2, home, ‖inland, intestine, municipal, national, native
ant external

internals *n pl* ***syn*** ENTRAILS, gut(s), innards, insides, inwards, ‖pudding(s), stuffing, tripes, viscera

internuncio *n* ***syn*** MESSENGER, bearer, carrier, courier, emissary, envoy

interpenetrate *vb* ***syn*** PERMEATE, compenetrate, impenetrate, impregnate, interfuse, penetrate, percolate, pervade, saturate, transfuse

interplay *vb* ***syn*** INTERACT, coact, interreact

interpolate *vb* ***syn*** INTRODUCE 6, fill in, insert, insinuate, intercalate, interject, interpose, throw in
rel admit, enter; interlope, intrude; add, annex, append, superadd
con cancel, delete, erase, expunge

interpose *vb* **1** ***syn*** INTRODUCE 6, fill in, insert, insinuate, intercalate, interject, interpolate, throw in
rel cast, throw, toss; push, shove, thrust
2 to come between disagreeing elements <forced to *interpose* when the argument grew heated>
syn intercede, interfere, intermediate, intervene, mediate, step in
rel butt in, interlope, intrude, obtrude; intermeddle, meddle; arbitrate, moderate, negotiate

interpret *vb* **1** ***syn*** EXPLAIN 1, construe, explicate, expound, spell out
rel exemplify, illustrate; annotate, gloss; comment, commentate
con contort, deform, distort; garble, misrepresent; misconstrue, misunderstand
2 ***syn*** REPRESENT 1, delineate, depict, describe, image, limn, picture, portray, render

interpretation *n* **1** ***syn*** EXPLANATION 1, construal, construction, exegesis, explication, exposé, exposition
2 manner of artistic presentation in performance or adaptation or an instance of this <*interpretation* involves a re-creative effort by the performer>
syn reading, rendering, rendition, version

interpretive *adj* ***syn*** EXPLANATORY, exegetic, explanative, explicative, explicatory, expositional, expositive, expository

interreact *vb* ***syn*** INTERACT, coact, interplay

interregnum *n* ***syn*** INTERLUDE, break, intermission, interval, parenthesis

interrogate *vb* ***syn*** ASK 1, catechize, examine, inquire, query, question, quiz

interrogation *n* **1** ***syn*** CROSS-EXAMINATION, grill, grilling, third degree
2 ***syn*** INQUIRY 2, interrogatory, query, question, questioning

interrogatory *n* ***syn*** INQUIRY 2, interrogation, query, question, questioning

interrupt *vb* **1** ***syn*** ARREST 1, check, halt, stall, stay
rel defer, intermit, postpone, suspend
2 to ask questions or make remarks while another is speaking <a chatterbox who habitually *interrupts* everyone>
syn break in, chime in, chip in
rel cut in, put in
idiom break in on (*or* upon)

interruption *n* **1** ***syn*** GAP 3, breach, break, hiatus, interim, interval, lacuna
rel rent, rift, rupture, split
2 ***syn*** ABEYANCE, abeyancy, cold storage, doldrums, dormancy, intermission, latency, quiescence, quiescency, suspension

intersect *vb* to divide by passing through or across <parallel lines can never *intersect*>
syn crisscross, cross, crosscut, decussate, intercross
rel traverse; bisect

intersow *vb* ***syn*** INTERFUSE 2, diffuse, infuse, interlard, intersperse, intersprinkle

intersperse *vb* ***syn*** INTERFUSE 2, diffuse, infuse, interlard, intersow, intersprinkle

intersprinkle *vb* ***syn*** INTERFUSE 2, diffuse, infuse, interlard, intersow, intersperse

intertangle *vb* ***syn*** ENTANGLE 1, ensnarl, perplex, snarl, tangle

intertie *vb* ***syn*** INTERJOIN, anastomose, interconnect, interlink

intertrude *vb* ***syn*** INTRUDE 1, butt in, chisel (in), cut in, horn in, obtrude

intertwine *vb* ***syn*** INTERWEAVE, interknit, interlace, intertwist, intervolve, interwind, interwork, interwreathe, inweave

---

syn synonym(s) | ***rel*** related word(s)
idiom idiomatic equivalent(s) | ***con*** contrasted word(s)
ant antonym(s) | * vulgar
‖ use limited; if in doubt, see a dictionary
The first word in a synonym list when printed in SMALL CAPITALS shows where there is more information about the group. For a more efficient use of this book see Explanatory Notes.

intertwist *vb* ***syn*** INTERWEAVE, interknit, interlace, intertwine, intervolve, interwind, interwork, interwreathe, inweave

interval *n* **1** ***syn*** PAUSE, comma, lull, pausation

2 ***syn*** INTERLUDE, break, intermission, interregnum, parenthesis

3 ***syn*** GAP 3, breach, break, hiatus, interim, interruption, lacuna

intervene *vb* ***syn*** INTERPOSE 2, intercede, interfere, intermediate, mediate, step in

rel divide, part, separate, sever

intervolve *vb* ***syn*** INTERWEAVE, interknit, interlace, intertwine, intertwist, interwind, interwork, interwreathe, inweave

interweave *vb* to blend or unite intimately <joy and melancholy are often closely *interwoven*>

syn interknit, interlace, intertwine, intertwist, intervolve, interwind, interwork, interwreathe, inweave

rel associate, join, link; blend, fuse, mix

interwind *vb* ***syn*** INTERWEAVE, interknit, interlace, intertwine, intertwist, intervolve, interwork, interwreathe, inweave

interwork *vb* ***syn*** INTERWEAVE, interknit, interlace, intertwine, intertwist, intervolve, interwind, interwreathe, inweave

interwreathe *vb* ***syn*** INTERWEAVE, interknit, interlace, intertwine, intertwist, intervolve, interwind, interwork, inweave

intestinal fortitude *n* ***syn*** FORTITUDE, backbone, grit, guts, ‖moxie, nerve, sand, spunk

intestine *adj* **1** ***syn*** DOMESTIC 2, home, ‖inland, internal, municipal, national, native

2 ***syn*** INNER 1, ‖innermore, inside, interior, internal, inward

intimacy *n* ***syn*** ACQUAINTANCE 1, experience, familiarity, inwardness

intimate *vb* ***syn*** SUGGEST 1, connote, hint, imply, insinuate

rel attest, bespeak, betoken, indicate

con air, express, utter, vent, voice; affirm, assert, aver, avouch, declare, profess

intimate *adj* **1** ***syn*** INHERENT, deep-seated, elemental, essential, inborn, inbred, indwelling, ingrained, innate, intrinsic

2 ***syn*** INNER 2, gut, interior, internal, visceral, viscerous

3 ***syn*** FAMILIAR 1, chummy, close, confidential, thick

rel nearest, next; affectionate, devoted, fond, loving; privy, secret

con distant, remote

4 having or marked by a warm personal relation <*intimate* friends for many years> <an *intimate* friendship>

syn ‖buddy-buddy, chummy, cozy, pally, ‖palsy-walsy

idiom thick as thieves

intimate *n* ***syn*** FRIEND, acquaintance, amigo, cater-cousin, confident, familiar, mate

rel associate, companion, comrade, crony

con outsider, stranger

intimation *n* **1** ***syn*** HINT 1, clue, cue, indication, inkling, notion, suggestion, telltale, wind

2 ***syn*** HINT 2, breath, shade, shadow, strain, streak, suggestion, suspicion, tinge, trace

intimidate *vb* to frighten or coerce into submission or obedience <refused to be *intimidated* by the manager>

syn bludgeon, bluster, ‖bounce, browbeat, bulldoze, bully, bullyrag, cow, dragoon, hector, ‖ruffle, strong-arm, terrorize

rel alarm, disquiet, frighten, scare, terrify; badger, bait, chivy, hound, ride; coerce, compel, constrain, force, oblige; ‖ruffianize

con blandish, cajole, coax, wheedle; induce, persuade, prevail

intimidator *n* ***syn*** BULLY 1, browbeater, bulldozer, harasser, harrier, hector

into *prep* ***syn*** TO 1

intolerable *adj* ***syn*** INSUFFERABLE, insupportable, unbearable, unbrookable, unendurable, unsufferable, unsupportable

ant tolerable

intolerant *adj* **1** unwilling or unable to endure with composure <he was inclined to be very *intolerant* of interruption>

syn impatient, unforbearing, unindulgent

rel contemptuous, disdainful; fractious, irritable, snappish, waspish; indignant, irate, outraged, stuffy, upset, worked up

con forbearing, indulgent, long-suffering, patient; resigned, uncomplaining

ant tolerant

2 ***syn*** ILLIBERAL, bigoted, brassbound, hidebound, narrow, narrow-minded, small-minded, unenlarged

rel inflexible, obdurate; antipathetic, averse, unsympathetic

con forbearing, indulgent, lenient

ant tolerant

intonation *n* ***syn*** INFLECTION, accent, tone

in toto *adv* ***syn*** ALL 1, all in all, altogether, exactly, just, quite, stick, totally, utterly, wholly

intoxicant *n* ***syn*** LIQUOR 2, alcohol, aqua vitae, booze, drink, inebriant, ‖joy-juice, ‖juice, ‖sauce, spirits

intoxicated *adj* **1** significantly under the influence of alcoholic liquor <some people become *intoxicated* more easily than others>

syn alcoholized, ‖bagged, blind, ‖blotto, ‖boiled, ‖bombed, ‖boozed, ‖boozy, ‖buffy, ‖buzzed, ‖canned, ‖capernoited, cockeyed, ‖crocked, cut, ‖deleerit, disguised, drunk, drunken, fried, ‖half-seas over, inebriated, inebrious, ‖jagged, ‖juiced, ‖lit, ‖lit up, ‖loaded, looped, ‖lushed, muddled, ‖oiled, ‖organized, ‖pickled, ‖pie-eyed, ‖pipped, ‖pissed, pixilated, ‖plastered, polluted, ‖potted, rum-dum, ‖screwy, ‖shick, ‖shicker, ‖shot, slewed, slopped, sloppy, ‖smashed, soshed, sozzled, ‖spiflicated, squiffed, ‖stewed, stiff, ‖stinking, ‖stinko, stoned, ‖swacked, tanked, ‖tiddly, tight, unsober, wet, zonked

---

syn synonym(s) ***rel*** related word(s)
idiom idiomatic equivalent(s) ***con*** contrasted word(s)
ant antonym(s) * vulgar
‖ use limited; if in doubt, see a dictionary
The first word in a synonym list when printed in SMALL CAPITALS shows where there is more information about the group. For a more efficient use of this book see Explanatory Notes.

rel befuddled, bemused, besotted, dazed, dopey, fuddled, loopy, maudlin, sodden, soppy, sotted, tipsy
idiom disguised with drink, full as a tick, in drink (*or* liquor), in one's cups, in the bag, stewed to the gills, the worse for drink, three sheets in (*or* to) the wind, under the table, under the weather, with drink taken
con abstemious, abstinent, moderate, temperate
ant sober
2 profoundly and usually pleasantly moved < *intoxicated* with the beauty of the scene >
syn elated, excited, exhilarated, turned-on
rel affected, concerned, interested, moved; galvanized, piqued, quickened, stimulated
con disinterested, unconcerned; depressed, disheartened, distressed, saddened

intoxicating *adj* *syn* EXCITING, exhilarant, exhilarating, exhilarative, eye-popping, inspiring, rousing, stimulating, stirring

intoxication *n* *syn* EUPHORIA 2, elation, exaltation

intractable *adj* **1** *syn* UNRULY 1, fractious, indocile, indomitable, recalcitrant, undisciplinable, undisciplined, ungovernable, unmanageable, wild
ant tractable
2 *syn* OBSTINATE, bullheaded, headstrong, mulish, pertinacious, perverse, refractory, self-willed, stubborn, unyielding
ant tractable

intransigent *adj* *syn* OBSTINATE, incompliant, intractable, pertinacious, self-willed, tough, stubborn, willful, unpliable, unyielding

intrepid *adj* *syn* BRAVE 1, audacious, bold, courageous, dauntless, fearless, unafraid, undaunted, valiant, valorous
ant craven

intricate *adj* **1** *syn* COMPLEX 2, Byzantine, complicated, daedal, elaborate, gordian, involved, knotty, labyrinthine, sophisticated
rel arduous, difficult, hard
2 *syn* ELABORATE 2, complicated, fancy

intrigue *vb* **1** *syn* INTEREST, appeal, attract, excite, fascinate
2 *syn* PLOT, cogitate, ‖collogue, collude, connive, conspire, contrive, devise, machinate, scheme (out)

intrigue *n* **1** *syn* PLOT 2, cabal, conspiracy, covin, machination, practice, scheme
2 *syn* AMOUR 2, affair, liaison

intrinsic *adj* *syn* INHERENT, built-in, congenital, connate, constitutional, deep-seated, elemental, essential, indwelling, innate
con added, annexed, appended, superadded
ant extrinsic

intrinsically *adv* *syn* PER SE, as such

introduce *vb* **1** *syn* ENTER 2, admit
rel inaugurate, induct, install; bring forward
2 *syn* BROACH, bring up, moot, ventilate
3 to bring into practice or use < *introduce* reforms in the welfare system >
syn inaugurate, initiate, institute, launch, originate, set up, usher in
rel establish, found, organize; innovate, invent; unveil; pioneer
4 to cause to know each other personally < planned to *introduce* her to his mother >
syn acquaint, present, ‖quaint
5 *syn* PRECEDE 3, lead, preface, usher
6 to put among or between others < *introduced* several new lines of dialogue >
syn fill in, insert, insinuate, intercalate, interject, interpolate, interpose, throw in
rel inlay, inlet, inset; inject, instill; work in
con eject, evict, oust; eliminate, exclude
ant abstract; withdraw

introducer *n* *syn* INNOVATOR, inventor, original, originator

introduction *n* something that serves as a preliminary or antecedent < the crisis could be the *introduction* to a general war >
syn exordium, foreword, overture, preamble, preface, prelude, prelusion, proem, prolegomenon, prologue

introductory *adj* **1** *syn* PRELIMINARY, inductive, prefatial, prefatorial, prefatory, preludial, prelusive, preparative, preparatory, proemial
ant closing, concluding
2 *syn* INITIAL 1, beginning, inceptive, incipient, initiative, initiatory, nascent

introspection *n* the examination of one's own thought and feeling < a man much given to *introspection* >
syn heart-searching, self-contemplation, self-examination, self-observation, self-questioning, self-reflection, self-scrutiny, self-searching, soul-searching
rel contemplation, meditation, reflection; self-analysis
ant extrospection

intrude *vb* **1** to thrust or force in without permission, welcome, or fitness < constantly *intruded* himself into his sister's affairs >
syn butt in, chisel (in), cut in, horn in, intertrude, obtrude
rel encroach, entrench, infringe, invade, muscle, trespass; insinuate, intercalate, interject, interpolate, interpose, introduce; interfere, intervene; intermeddle, meddle; bother, disturb, pester
con retire, stand off, withdraw
2 *syn* IMPOSE 5, infringe, obtrude, presume

intrusive *adj* *syn* IMPERTINENT 2, busy, meddlesome, ‖nebby, obtrusive, officious, polypragmatic
rel butting in, intruding, obtruding
con bashful, coy, diffident, modest, retiring, shy
ant unintrusive

intuition *n* immediate apprehension or cognition < skeptical of the traditional woman's *intuition* >
syn anschauung, insight, intuitiveness
rel second sight, sixth sense
ant ratiocination

intuitive *adj* *syn* INSTINCTIVE 1, instinctual, visceral
rel direct, immediate, presentative
ant ratiocinative

intuitiveness *n* *syn* INTUITION, anschauung, insight

inumbrate *vb* ***syn*** SHADE, screen, shadow, umbrage
inundate *vb* ***syn*** DELUGE 1, drown, engulf, flood, overflow, overwhelm, submerge, swamp, whelm
inundation *n* ***syn*** FLOOD 2, cataclysm, cataract, deluge, flooding, niagara, overflow, pour, spate, torrent
inurbane *adj* ***syn*** RUDE 6, discourteous, disgracious, disrespectful, ill-bred, ill-mannered, impolite, incivil, mannerless, ungracious
ant urbane
inure *vb* ***syn*** ACCUSTOM, familiarize, habituate, use, wont
rel discipline, train
inutile *adj* ***syn*** WORTHLESS 1, draffy, drossy, good-for-nothing, ||no-account, no-good, nothing, unworthy, valueless
ant utile
invade *vb* **1** to enter for conquest or plunder <the Danes *invaded* England>
syn foray, inroad, overrun, overswarm, raid
rel loot, pillage, plunder, ravage
2 ***syn*** TRESPASS 2, encroach, entrench, infringe
rel impenetrate, interpenetrate, permeate, pervade
invalid *adj* **1** ***syn*** ILLOGICAL, fallacious, irrational, mad, nonrational, reasonless, sophistic, unreasonable, unreasoned
ant valid
2 ***syn*** NULL, bad, null and void, void
invalidate *vb* ***syn*** ABOLISH 1, abate, abrogate, annihilate, annul, circumduct, negate, nullify, quash, undo
rel counteract, counterbalance, negative, neutralize, offset; discredit
ant validate
invaluable *adj* ***syn*** PRECIOUS 1, costly, inestimable, priceless, valuable
ant worthless
invariable *adj* **1** ***syn*** INFLEXIBLE 3, constant, fixed, immovable, immutable, inalterable, unalterable, unchangeable, unmodifiable, unmovable
ant variable
2 ***syn*** SAME 3, consistent, constant, unchanging, unfailing, unvarying
ant variable, varying
invariably *adv* **1** ***syn*** ALWAYS 1, constantly, continually, ever, perpetually
2 ***syn*** EVER 3
invasion *n* a hostile entrance into the territory of another <Hitler's *invasion* of Poland>
syn foray, incursion, inroad, irruption, raid
rel aggression, attack, offense, offensive; breach, infraction, infringement, transgression, trespass, violation; encroachment, entrenchment
invective *adj* ***syn*** ABUSIVE, contumelious, opprobrious, scurrile, scurrilous, truculent, vituperative, vituperatory, vituperous
rel censorious, condemnatory, damnatory, denunciatory, reproachful
invective *n* ***syn*** ABUSE, billingsgate, contumely, obloquy, scurrility, vituperation
rel diatribe, jeremiad, philippic, tirade
inveigh (against) *vb* ***syn*** OBJECT 1, except, expostulate, kick, protest, remonstrate
inveigle *vb* ***syn*** LURE, allure, bait, decoy, entice, entrap, lead on, seduce, tempt, toll
inveiglement *n* ***syn*** LURE 2, allurement, bait, come-on, decoy, enticement, seducement, snare, temptation, trap
invent *vb* ***syn*** CONTRIVE 2, concoct, cook (up), devise, dream up, formulate, frame, hatch (up), make up, vamp (up)
rel conceive, envision, imagine; create, mint, produce, turn out; inaugurate, initiate
invention *n* a product of creative imagination <his most famous *invention* is the electric light bulb>
syn brainchild, coinage, contrivance
rel concoction, contraption, innovation, novelty; creation, opus, original
inventive *adj* adept or prolific at producing new things and ideas <had a very *inventive* turn of mind> <he was an *inventive* genius>
syn creative, demiurgic, deviceful, ingenious, innovational, innovative, innovatory, original, originative
rel fertile, fruitful, productive, teeming; causative, constructive, formative
con sterile, uncreative, unproductive
ant uninventive
inventor *n* **1** ***syn*** INNOVATOR, introducer, original, originator
2 ***syn*** FATHER 2, architect, author, creator, founder, generator, maker, originator, patriarch, sire
inventory *n* **1** ***syn*** SUPPLY, armamentarium, fund, stock, store
2 ***syn*** RESERVE, backlog, hoard, nest egg, reservoir, stock, stockpile, store
inventory *vb* **1** to make an itemized report or record of <will *inventory* all office supplies>
syn catalog, itemize, tally
rel list, record, register; enumerate, tabulate
idiom take account (*or* stock) of
2 ***syn*** ITEMIZE 1, enumerate, list, particularize, specialize, specify
3 ***syn*** EPITOMIZE 1, condense, digest, nutshell, sum, summarize, summate, sum up, synopsize
inveracity *n* ***syn*** LIE, falsehood, falsity, misrepresentation, misstatement, prevarication, tale, taradiddle, untruism, untruth
ant veracity
inverse *vb* ***syn*** REVERSE 1, change, invert, revert, transplace, transpose, turn
inversion *n* ***syn*** REVERSAL 1, about-face, changeabout, reverse, reversement, reversion, turn, turnabout, turning, volte-face
invert *vb* ***syn*** REVERSE 1, change, inverse, revert, transplace, transpose, turn
rel flip, turn down, turn over
invert *n* ***syn*** HOMOSEXUAL, fag, faggot, ||fruit, homo, queer, uranian, uranist

---

syn synonym(s) ***rel*** related word(s)
idiom idiomatic equivalent(s) ***con*** contrasted word(s)
ant antonym(s) * vulgar
|| use limited; if in doubt, see a dictionary
The first word in a synonym list when printed in SMALL CAPITALS shows where there is more information about the group. For a more efficient use of this book see Explanatory Notes.

invertebrate *n* ***syn*** WEAKLING, baby, doormat, jellyfish, milksop, Milquetoast, mollycoddle, namby-pamby, pantywaist, sissy

invertebrate *adj* ***syn*** WEAK 4, boneless, emasculate, forceless, impotent, inadequate, ineffective, ineffectual, slack-spined, spineless
rel disorganized, structureless

inverted *adj* **1** ***syn*** UPSIDE-DOWN 1, topsy-turvy
2 ***syn*** HOMOSEXUAL, gay, homoerotic, homophile, queer, uranian

invest *vb* **1** ***syn*** INITIATE 3, inaugurate, induct, install, instate
rel endow, endue; consecrate, honor
ant divest, strip
2 to make a formal grant of power or authority <the Constitution *invests* the Congress with taxation powers>
syn authorize, empower, vest
rel bequeath, endow
con hold back, keep back, reserve, withhold
ant divest
3 ***syn*** ENFOLD 1, enclose, enshroud, envelop, enwrap, shroud, veil, wrap
4 ***syn*** BESIEGE, beleaguer, beset, blockade
5 ***syn*** INFUSE 1, imbue, ingrain, inoculate, leaven, steep, suffuse

investigate *vb* ***syn*** EXPLORE, delve (into), dig (into), go (into), inquire (into), look (into), probe, prospect, sift
rel muckrake, poke, pry

investigation *n* ***syn*** INQUIRY 1, delving, inquest, inquisition, probe, probing, quest, research
rel observation, observing; sounding, survey, surveying

investigative *adj* ***syn*** INQUISITIVE 1, curious, disquisitive, inquiring, questioning

investigator *n* ***syn*** DETECTIVE, dick, ‖eye, gumshoe, hawkshaw, plainclothesman, Sherlock, Sherlock Holmes, sleuth, ‖tec

investiture *n* ***syn*** INITIATION, inaugural, inauguration, induction, installation

inveterate *adj* **1** firmly established or having something firmly established <the *inveterate* tendency to overlook the obvious>
syn bred-in-the-bone, confirmed, deep-dyed, deep-rooted, deep-seated, dyed-in-the-wool, entrenched, hard-shell, irradicable, settled, sworn
rel accustomed, addicted, chronic, habituated; customary, habitual, usual; hardened, indurated; established, fixed, set; inbred, innate; abiding, enduring, persistent, persisting
2 ***syn*** OLD 2, continuing, enduring, lifelong, long-lasting, long-lived, perennial

invidious *adj* **1** ***syn*** LIBELOUS, calumnious, defamatory, detracting, detractive, detractory, maligning, scandalous, slanderous, vilifying
2 ***syn*** ENVIOUS, envying, green-eyed, jealous
rel bitter; hateful
3 ***syn*** REPUGNANT 1, abhorrent, obnoxious, repellent, revulsive
rel abominable, detestable, hateful, odious
con agreeable, grateful, gratifying, pleasant, pleasing

invidiousness *n* ***syn*** ENVY, enviousness, jealousy

invigorate *vb* ***syn*** STRENGTHEN 2, energize, fortify, reinforce
rel refresh, rejuvenate, renew, restore; rally, rouse, stir; activate, animate, stimulate, vitalize, vitaminize
ant debilitate

invigorating *adj* having an enlivening effect <an *invigorating* discussion>
syn animating, bracing, exhilarating, exhilarative, quickening, stimulating, stimulative, tonic, vitalizing
rel brisk, lively; fascinating, interesting
con anesthetic, numbing, somniferous
ant deadening

invincible *adj* **1** incapable of being conquered <the team proved to be *invincible*>
syn impregnable, inconquerable, indomitable, inexpugnable, invulnerable, unassailable, unbeatable, unconquerable, undefeatable
rel inviolable, untouchable; unattackable
con conquerable, subduable, surmountable, vanquishable
ant vincible
2 ***syn*** INSUPERABLE, impassable, inconquerable, indomitable, insurmountable, unconquerable, unsurmountable
ant vincible

inviolable *adj* ***syn*** SACRED 3, inviolate, sacrosanct
rel consecrated, hallowed; blessed, divine, holy; chaste, pure
ant violable

inviolate *adj* ***syn*** SACRED 3, inviolable, sacrosanct
rel intact, perfect; faultless, flawless
con desecrated, profaned; defiled, polluted

invisible *adj* ***syn*** IMPERCEPTIBLE, impalpable, imponderable, inappreciable, indiscernible, insensible, unapparent, unappreciable, unobservable, unperceivable
rel hidden, unseeable
ant visible

invitation *n* ***syn*** PROPOSAL, proffer, proposition, suggestion

invite *vb* to request the presence or participation of <*invited* guests to dinner> <*invited* the major nations to confer>
syn ask, bid
rel call, call in, summon; court, solicit, woo; entice, inveigle, lure, tempt

invoice *n* ***syn*** BILL 1, account, reckoning, score, statement, tab

invoke *vb* **1** ***syn*** BEG, appeal, beseech, crave, entreat, implore, importune, plead, pray, supplicate
2 ***syn*** ENFORCE, effect, implement

involuntary *adj* ***syn*** SPONTANEOUS, automatic, impulsive, instinctive, unmeditated, unpremeditated, unprompted, will-less
rel unintended, unintentional, unwitting
ant voluntary

involve *vb* **1** to bring a person or thing into circumstances or a situation from which extrication is difficult <nations *involved* in war>
syn embroil, implicate, mire, tangle; *compare* ENTANGLE 3
rel catch up; draw (into)
2 *syn* INCLUDE, comprehend, contain, embody, embrace, encompass, have, subsume, take in

involved *adj* **1** *syn* COMPLEX 2, Byzantine, complicated, daedal, elaborate, gordian, intricate, knotty, labyrinthine, sophisticated
rel confused, muddled
con easy, facile, simple
2 *syn* INTERESTED, affected, concerned, implicated
rel enmeshed, entangled
ant uninvolved

involvement *n syn* ENTANGLEMENT 1, embroilment, enmeshment

invulnerable *adj syn* INVINCIBLE 1, impregnable, inconquerable, indomitable, inexpugnable, unassailable, unbeatable, unconquerable, undefeatable
ant vulnerable

inward *adj syn* INNER 1, ‖innermore, inside, interior, internal, intestine
con alien, extraneous, extrinsic, foreign
ant outward

inward *n* **1** *often* **inwards** *pl syn* INTERIOR, inside, within
2 inwards *pl syn* ENTRAILS, gut(s), innards, insides, internals, ‖pudding(s), stuffing, tripes, viscera

inwardness *n syn* ACQUAINTANCE 1, experience, familiarity, intimacy

inweave *vb syn* INTERWEAVE, interknit, interlace, intertwine, intertwist, intervolve, interwind, interwork, interwreathe

iota *n syn* PARTICLE, atom, bit, crumb, grain, mite, molecule, ounce, ray, smidgen

ipseity *n syn* INDIVIDUALITY 4, identity, personality, seity, selfdom, selfhood, selfness, singularity

irascible *adj* easily aroused to anger <an *irascible* fellow and hard to get along with>
syn choleric, cranky, cross, hot-tempered, ireful, passionate, peppery, quick-tempered, ratty, ‖stomachy, temperish, testy, tetchy, touchy; *compare* CANTANKEROUS, IRRITABLE
rel fractious, huffy, irritable, peevish, petulant, querulous, snappish, waspish; impatient, jittery, jumpy, nervous, restive; bristly, crabbed, surly
con amiable, complaisant, good-natured, obliging; calm, quiet, relaxed; long-suffering, patient, tolerant

irate *adj syn* ANGRY, choleric, ireful, mad, waxy, wrathful, wrathy, wroth, wrothful, wrothy

ire *n syn* ANGER, fury, indignation, mad, rage, wrath

ire *vb syn* ANGER 1, enrage, incense, infuriate, mad, madden, steam up, umbrage

ireful *adj* **1** *syn* ANGRY, choleric, irate, mad, waxy, wrathful, wrathy, wroth, wrothful, wrothy
2 *syn* IRASCIBLE, choleric, cranky, hot-tempered, passionate, quick-tempered, ratty, testy, tetchy, touchy

irenic *adj syn* PACIFIC, nonviolent, pacificatory, pacifist, peaceable, peaceful
ant acrimonious

irk *vb* **1** *syn* ANNOY 1, abrade, bother, ‖bug, exercise, fret, gall, provoke, ruffle, vex
rel discommode, incommode, inconvenience, trouble
2 *syn* TRY 2, distress, harass, pain, strain, stress, trouble

irking *n syn* ANNOYANCE 1, bothering, harassment, provocation, provoking, vexation, vexing

irksome *adj* tending to cause boredom or tedium <an *irksome* task>
syn boresome, boring, drudging, tedious, tiresome, tiring
rel dull, stupid; exhausting, fagging, fatiguing, wearisome
con exciting, inspiring, provocative, stimulative, stirring
ant absorbing, engrossing

iron *n, usu* **irons** *pl syn* SHACKLE, bond(s), chains, fetter(s), gyve(s)

iron *adj syn* INFLEXIBLE 2, adamant, adamantine, brassbound, inexorable, obdurate, relentless, rigid, unbending, unyielding

ironbound *adj syn* ROUGH 1, asperous, craggy, harsh, jagged, rugged, scabrous, scraggy, uneven, unsmooth

ironclad *adj syn* INFLEXIBLE 3, constant, fixed, immovable, immutable, inalterable, invariable, unalterable, unchangeable, unmodifiable

ironfisted *adj* **1** *syn* STINGY, ‖chinchy, close, closefisted, hardfisted, hardhanded, miserly, narrow-fisted, narrowhearted, tightfisted
2 *syn* GRIM 3, implacable, merciless, mortal, relentless, ruthless, unappeasable, unflinching, unrelenting, unyielding

ironhanded *adj syn* RIGID 3, draconian, rigorist, rigorous, strict, stringent, unpermissive

ironhead *n syn* DUNCE, blockhead, bonehead, dope, dumbbell, fathead, ignoramus, knucklehead, nitwit, numskull

ironhearted *adj syn* UNFEELING 2, callous, cold-blooded, hard-boiled, hardened, heartless, obdurate, stony, uncompassionate, unsympathetic
ant softhearted

ironic *adj syn* SARDONIC, cynical, wry
rel biting, cutting, incisive, trenchant; caustic, mordant, scathing

‖**ironman** *n syn* DOLLAR, bill, ‖bone, ‖buck, ‖fish, ‖frogskin, oner, ‖skin, ‖smacker, ‖smackeroo

irradiate *vb syn* ILLUMINATE 2, edify, enlighten, illume, illumine, improve, uplift

irradicable *adj syn* INVETERATE 1, confirmed, deep-dyed, deep-rooted, deep-seated, dyed-in-the-wool, entrenched, hard-shell, settled, sworn

irrational *adj syn* ILLOGICAL, fallacious, invalid, mad, nonrational, reasonless, sophistic, unreasonable, unreasoned
rel crazy, demented, insane
con logical, reasonable, sensible

---

ant rational
irrealizable *adj syn* IMPOSSIBLE 1, impracticable, impractical, infeasible, unattainable, unfeasible, unrealizable, unworkable
ant realizable
irrebuttable *adj syn* POSITIVE 3, certain, inarguable, incontestable, incontrovertible, indisputable, indubitable, irrefutable, sure, uncontestable
ant rebuttable
irreclaimable *adj syn* IRRECOVERABLE, irredeemable, irremediable, irreparable, irretrievable
ant reclaimable
irreconcilable *adj* incapable of being made consistent <the two versions of the story are completely *irreconcilable*>
syn incompatible, inconformable, inconsistent
rel discordant, discrepant, dissonant, inaccordant, incongruent, incongruous, inharmonious
ant reconcilable
irrecoverable *adj* not capable of being recovered, regained, remedied, or rectified <suffered an *irrecoverable* loss in the fire>
syn irreclaimable, irredeemable, irremediable, irreparable, irretrievable
ant recoverable
irredeemable *adj syn* IRRECOVERABLE, irreclaimable, irremediable, irreparable, irretrievable
ant redeemable
irreflective *adj syn* CARELESS 1, feckless, heedless, inadvertent, thoughtless, uncaring, unheeding, unrecking, unreflective, unthinking
ant reflective
irrefragable *adj syn* INDESTRUCTIBLE, imperishable, incorruptible, inexterminable, inextinguishable, inextirpable, irrefrangible, quenchless, undestroyable, unperishable
irrefrangible *adj syn* INDESTRUCTIBLE, imperishable, incorruptible, inexterminable, inextinguishable, inextirpable, irrefragable, quenchless, undestroyable, unperishable
irrefutable *adj syn* POSITIVE 3, certain, inarguable, incontestable, incontrovertible, indisputable, indubitable, irrebuttable, sure, uncontestable
ant refutable
irregular *adj* **1** not according with or explainable by law, rule, or custom <unusual problems require *irregular* solutions>
syn abnormal, anomalous, deviant, divergent, off-key, unnatural, unregular
rel aberrant, atypical; exceptional, odd, peculiar, queer, singular, strange, unique
con natural, normal, typical; accustomed, customary, habitual, usual, wonted
ant regular

syn synonym(s) — *rel* related word(s)
idiom idiomatic equivalent(s) — *con* contrasted word(s)
ant antonym(s) — * vulgar
‖ use limited; if in doubt, see a dictionary
The first word in a synonym list when printed in SMALL CAPITALS shows where there is more information about the group. For a more efficient use of this book see Explanatory Notes.

2 *syn* INFORMAL 1, unceremonious, unofficial
3 *syn* LOPSIDED, asymmetric, disproportionate, nonsymmetrical, off-balance, overbalanced, unbalanced, unequal, uneven, unsymmetrical
ant regular
4 *syn* RANDOM, aimless, designless, desultory, haphazard, hit-or-miss, indiscriminate, purposeless, unaimed, unconsidered
rel occasional, sporadic; erratic, fitful, spasmodic; inconstant, uneven, unsteady
5 *syn* SPOTTY 1, patchy, uneven
irregular *n syn* PARTISAN 2, guerrilla, patriot
irregularity *n syn* INEQUALITY 1, asperity, roughness, unevenness
ant regularity
irregularly *adv syn* OCCASIONALLY, infrequently, on occasion, sporadically, uncommonly
ant regularly
irrelative *adj syn* IRRELEVANT, extraneous, foreign, immaterial, impertinent, inapplicable, inapposite
ant relative
irrelevant *adj* not applicable or pertinent <age should be *irrelevant* to employability>
syn extraneous, foreign, immaterial, impertinent, inapplicable, inapposite, irrelative
rel inconsequential, insignificant, unimportant
idiom beside the point, neither here nor there, out of the question
con applicable, appurtenant, germane, material, pertinent, significant
ant relevant
irreligious *adj* lacking religious emotions, doctrines, or practices <an *irreligious* person but not openly hostile to organized religion>
syn godless, nonreligious, unreligious
rel indevout, undevout; ungodly, unholy, unsanctimonious; blasphemous, impious, profane, sacrilegious; amoral, unmoral
con devout, pious
ant religious
irremediable *adj* **1** *syn* IRRECOVERABLE, irreclaimable, irredeemable, irreparable, irretrievable
ant remediable
2 *syn* HOPELESS 2, cureless, immedicable, impossible, incurable, insanable, irreparable, uncorrectable, uncurable, unrecoverable
irremovable *adj syn* IMMOVABLE 1, fixed, immobile, immotile, immotive, ‖sitfast, steadfast, unmovable
ant removable
irreparable *adj* **1** *syn* IRRECOVERABLE, irreclaimable, irredeemable, irremediable, irretrievable
ant reparable
2 *syn* HOPELESS 2, cureless, immedicable, impossible, incurable, insanable, irremediable, uncorrectable, uncurable, unrecoverable
irreprehensible *adj syn* GOOD 11, blameless, exemplary, guiltless, inculpable, innocent, irreproachable, lily-white, pure, righteous
ant reprehensible
irrepressible *adj* impossible to repress, restrain, or control <an *irrepressible* joy over his brother's good fortune>
syn insuppressible, insuppressive, irrestrainable, uncontainable, uncontrollable, unrestrainable

rel bubbling over, effervescent, enthusiastic, rhapsodical
ant repressible

irreproachable *adj* **1** *syn* GOOD 11, blameless, exemplary, guiltless, inculpable, innocent, pure, righteous, unblamable, virtuous
2 *syn* IMPECCABLE 1, errorless, exquisite, faultless, flawless, immaculate

irresoluble *adj syn* INSOLUBLE, inextricable, insolvable, irresolvable, unsoluble, unsolvable
ant resoluble

irresolute *adj syn* VACILLATING 2, faltering, halting, hesitant, shilly-shallying, tentative, uncertain, vacillatory, wiggle-waggle, wobbly
ant resolute

irresolution *n syn* HESITATION, hesitancy, indecision, indecisiveness, shilly-shally, to-and-fro, vacillation, wavering
ant resolution

irresolvable *adj syn* INSOLUBLE, inextricable, insolvable, irresoluble, unsoluble, unsolvable
ant resolvable

irresponsible *adj* lacking in responsibility < *irresponsible* behavior >
syn carefree, careless, feckless, incautious, reckless, uncareful, wild
rel undependable, unreliable, untrustworthy; unaccountable, unanswerable
con careful, cautious, discreet, heedful; dependable, reliable, trustworthy
ant responsible

irrestrainable *adj syn* IRREPRESSIBLE, insuppressible, insuppressive, uncontainable, uncontrollable, unrestrainable
ant restrainable

irretrievable *adj syn* IRRECOVERABLE, irreclaimable, irredeemable, irremediable, irreparable
ant retrievable

irreverent *adj syn* IMPIOUS 1, irreverential, profane, ungodly, unhallowed, unholy
ant reverent

irreverential *adj syn* IMPIOUS 1, irreverent, profane, ungodly, unhallowed, unholy
ant reverential

irreversible *adj syn* IRREVOCABLE, nonreversible, unrepealable
ant reversible

irrevocable *adj* incapable of being recalled or revoked < an *irrevocable* decision of the Supreme Court >
syn irreversible, nonreversible, unrepealable
rel constant, established, fixed; immutable, unchangeable, unmodifiable
con repealable, reversible; alterable, changeable, modifiable
ant revocable

irritable *adj* easily exasperated < the miserable weather made us all *irritable* >
syn disagreeable, fractious, fretful, huffy, peevish, pettish, petulant, ‖pindling, prickish, prickly, querulent, querulential, querulous, raspish, raspy, snappish, snappy, twitty, waspish, waspy, whiny; *compare* CANTANKEROUS, IRASCIBLE
rel cranky, cross, testy, touchy; choleric, irascible, splenetic
con amiable, complaisant, good-natured, obliging; affable, cordial, genial, gracious, sociable
ant easygoing

irritant *n syn* ANNOYANCE 3, besetment, bother, botheration, botherment, exasperation, nuisance, pest, pester, plague

irritate *vb* to excite to angry annoyance < his rude interruptions really *irritated* her >
syn aggravate, burn (up), exasperate, gall, get, grate, huff, inflame, nettle, peeve, pique, provoke, put out, rile, roil; *compare* ANNOY 1
rel abrade, bother, ‖bug, chafe, exercise, fret, irk, ruffle, try, vex; anger, enrage, incense, infuriate, madden; affront, offend
con appease, conciliate, mollify, pacify, placate, propitiate; delight, gladden, gratify, please

irrupt *vb syn* ERUPT 1, belch, disgorge, eject, eruct, expel, spew

irruption *n syn* INVASION, foray, incursion, inroad, raid

Ishmael *n syn* OUTCAST, castaway, derelict, Ishmaelite, leper, offscouring, pariah, untouchable

Ishmaelite *n syn* OUTCAST, castaway, derelict, Ishmael, leper, offscouring, pariah, untouchable

island *vb syn* ISOLATE, close off, cut off, enisle, insulate, segregate, separate, sequester

isochronal *adj syn* INTERMITTENT, alternate, isochronous, periodic, periodical, recurrent, recurring

isochronous *adj syn* INTERMITTENT, alternate, isochronal, periodic, periodical, recurrent, recurring

isolate *vb* to set apart from others < the jury was *isolated* for several days >
syn close off, cut off, enisle, insulate, island, segregate, separate, sequester
rel quarantine; block (off); abstract, detach, disengage, remove; divide, part, sever, sunder
con associate, connect, join, link, unite

isolate *adj syn* ALONE 1, apart, detached, isolated, removed, unaccompanied

isolated *adj syn* ALONE 1, apart, detached, isolate, removed, unaccompanied
rel retired, secluded, withdrawn; abandoned, deserted, forsaken, stranded

isolation *n syn* SOLITUDE, aloneness, loneness, solitariness

issue *n* **1** *syn* OFFSPRING, ‖begats, brood, children, descendants, posterity, progeniture, progeny, scions, seed
2 *syn* EFFECT 1, causatum, consequence, end product, eventuality, outcome, result, sequel, upshot
3 *syn* PROBLEM 2, nut, question
rel matter; subject, topic

issue *vb* **1** *syn* SPRING 1, arise, birth, derive (from), emanate, flow, originate, proceed, rise, stem
2 *syn* EMIT 2, give off, give out, release, throw off, vent

---

syn synonym(s) *rel* related word(s)
idiom idiomatic equivalent(s) *con* contrasted word(s)
ant antonym(s) * vulgar
‖ use limited; if in doubt, see a dictionary
The first word in a synonym list when printed in SMALL CAPITALS shows where there is more information about the group. For a more efficient use of this book see Explanatory Notes.

3 ***syn*** PUBLISH 2, get out, put out

italicize *vb* ***syn*** EMPHASIZE, feature, play (up), stress, underline, underscore

itch *n* **1** ***syn*** DESIRE 1, appetite, appetition, craving, lust, passion, urge
2 ***syn*** LUST 2, aphrodisia, concupiscence, desire, eroticism, lickerishness, lustfulness, passion, prurience, pruriency

itch *vb* ***syn*** LONG, ache, crave, hanker, hunger, lust, pine, sigh, thirst, yearn

itchy *adj* ***syn*** COVETOUS, acquisitive, desirous, grabby, grasping, greedy, prehensile

item *adv* ***syn*** ALSO 2, additionally, along, well, besides, furthermore, likewise, more, moreover, too

item *n* ***syn*** POINT 1, article, detail, element, particular, thing
rel component, piece; incidental, minutia

itemize *vb* **1** to set down in detail or by particulars < *itemize* deductions on a tax form >
syn enumerate, inventory, list, particularize, specialize, specify; *compare* SPECIFY 3
rel circumstantiate, document; count, number; cite, instance, mention; spell out
ant summarize
2 ***syn*** INVENTORY, catalog, tally

itemized *adj* ***syn*** CIRCUMSTANTIAL, blow-by-blow, clocklike, detailed, full, minute, particular, particularized, thorough
ant summarized

iterate *vb* ***syn*** REPEAT, ingeminate, reiterate, renew, reprise, resay

itinerant *adj* traveling from place to place < *itinerant* preachers >
syn ambulant, ambulatory, deambulatory, itinerate, nomadic, perambulant, perambulatory, peripatetic, roving, vagabond, vagrant, wandering, wayfaring
rel rambling, ranging, roaming; moving, shifting

itinerate *adj* ***syn*** ITINERANT, ambulant, ambulatory, deambulatory, nomadic, peripatetic, roving, vagabond, vagrant, wandering

itsy–bitsy *adj* ***syn*** TINY, ‖bitsy, diminutive, itty-bitty, lilliputian, minute, teensy, teenty, teeny, wee

itty–bitty *adj* ***syn*** TINY, ‖bitsy, diminutive, itsy-bitsy, lilliputian, minute, teensy, teensy-weensy, teenty, teeny

‖**ivory** *n often* **ivories** *pl* ***syn*** DICE, ‖African dominoes, bones, ‖cubes, ‖devil's-bones, ‖tats

ivory–tower *adj* ***syn*** IMPRACTICAL 1, ivory-towered, ivory-towerish, nonrealistic, unpractical, unrealistic, viewy
ant down-to-earth

ivory–towered *adj* ***syn*** IMPRACTICAL 1, ivory-tower, ivory-towerish, nonrealistic, unpractical, unrealistic, viewy

ivory–towerish *adj* ***syn*** IMPRACTICAL 1, ivory-tower, ivory-towered, nonrealistic, unpractical, unrealistic, viewy

---

syn synonym(s) ***rel*** related word(s)
idiom idiomatic equivalent(s) ***con*** contrasted word(s)
ant antonym(s) * vulgar
‖ use limited; if in doubt, see a dictionary
The first word in a synonym list when printed in SMALL CAPITALS shows where there is more information about the group. For a more efficient use of this book see Explanatory Notes.

J

jab *vb syn* POKE 1, dig, jog, nudge, prod, punch

jab *n* **1** *syn* POKE 1, dig, punch, stab
2 *syn* PRICK 1, ‖jag, puncture, stab

jabber *vb syn* GIBBER, babble, chatter, gabble

jabber *n* **1** *syn* GIBBERISH 1, babble, drivel, Greek, jabberwocky, nonsense, skimble-skamble
2 *syn* CHATTER, babble, blabber, chat, clack, gab, gabble, palaver, prattle, yak

jabberer *n syn* CHATTERBOX, bandar-log, blabber, blabbermouth, blabmouth, chatterer, gabber, magpie, prater, prattler

jabberwocky *n syn* GIBBERISH 1, babble, drivel, Greek, jabber, nonsense, skimble-skamble

jack *n* **1** *syn* MARINER, jack-tar, sailor, sailorman, salt, seaman, tar, tarpaulin
2 *syn* FLAG, banner, bannerol, color, ensign, pendant, pennant, pennon, standard, streamer
‖**3** *syn* MONEY, ‖bread, cash, ‖coin, dough, ‖greenbacks, ‖mazuma, ‖scratch, ‖shekels, ‖wampum

jack (up) *vb syn* RAISE 9, boost, hike, increase, jump, put up, up

jackass *n* **1** *syn* DONKEY 1, ass, burro, donk, ‖moke, ‖neddy, ‖Rocky Mountain canary
2 *syn* FOOL 1, ass, *damfool, donkey, idiot, imbecile, jerk, nincompoop, ‖schmo, ‖schmuck

jacket *n syn* HIDE, fell, fur, pelt, skin

jackleg *adj syn* AMATEURISH, dabbling, dilettante, dilettantish, dilettantist, unaccomplished, unfinished, ungifted, unskilled

jackleg lawyer *n syn* PETTIFOGGER, shyster

jackpot *n syn* POT 3, kitty, pool

jack-tar *n syn* MARINER, jack, sailor, sailorman, salt, seaman, tar, tarpaulin

jade *n* **1** *syn* WANTON, ‖bimbo, hussy, jezebel, slattern, slut, strumpet, tramp, trollop, wench
2 *syn* MINX, hussy, malapert, saucebox, slut, snip

jade *vb* **1** *syn* TIRE 1, drain, fatigue, wear, wear down, weary
rel cloy, pall, sate, satiate, surfeit; emasculate, enervate, unman, unnerve; depress, oppress, weigh
con rejuvenate, renew, restore
ant refresh
2 *syn* SATIATE, cloy, fill, glut, gorge, pall, sate, ‖stall, stodge, surfeit

jaded *adj* **1** *syn* TIRED 1, fatigued, wearied, weary, worn, worn down
ant refreshed
2 *syn* SATIATED, full, glutted, gorged, sated, satiate, surfeited

‖**jag** *n syn* PRICK 1, jab, puncture, stab

jag *n syn* BINGE 1, bender, booze, bum, bust, drunk, soak, souse, spree, tear

‖**jag** *vb syn* CARRY 1, bear, buck, convey, ferry, ‖hump, lug, pack, tote, transport

jagged *adj syn* ROUGH 1, asperous, craggy, harsh, rugged, scabrous, scraggy, uneven, unlevel, unsmooth

‖**jagged** *adj syn* INTOXICATED 1, ‖boozy, ‖canned, disguised, drunk, inebriated, ‖lushed, muddled, pixilated, ‖plastered

jail *n* a building or institution for the confinement of persons held in lawful custody <sent to *jail* for perjury>
syn bastille, ‖big house, bridewell, ‖brig, ‖bucket, ‖caboose, ‖calaboose, ‖can, ‖carcel, ‖chokey, ‖clink, ‖college, cooler, coop, freezer, guardroom, ‖hoosegow, jug, keep, lockup, pen, penitentiary, ‖pokey, prison, reformatory, rock pile, skookum-house, slammer, ‖stir, stockade
idiom house of correction

jail *vb syn* IMPRISON, bastille, confine, constrain, immure, incarcerate, intern, jug, ‖prison, ‖quod
ant release

jailbird *n syn* CONVICT, ‖con, ‖lag, loser, prison bird

jake *n syn* RUSTIC, backwoodsman, bucolic, bumpkin, clodhopper, hayseed, hick, hillbilly, redneck, yokel

jakes *n pl but sing or pl in constr syn* PRIVY 1, backhouse, ‖biffy, ‖closet, *crapper, ‖necessary, ‖office, outhouse

jalopy *n* a dilapidated old automobile <bought a *jalopy* for $50>
syn clunker, crate, dog, heap, junker, wreck

jam *vb* **1** *syn* PRESS 1, bear, crowd, crush, push, ‖squab, squash, squeeze, squish, squush
rel tamp, wad
2 *syn* CRAM 1, jam-pack, ‖pang, ram, stuff, tamp
3 *syn* PRESS 7, cram, crowd, crush, squash, squeeze

jam *n syn* PREDICAMENT, box, corner, dilemma, fix, hole, pickle, plight, scrape, spot

jam *n* a rich spread prepared by boiling fruit and sugar until the mixture thickens <enjoyed his mother's tasty berry *jams*>
syn confiture, conserve, preserve
rel jelly, marmalade

jam-full *adj syn* FULL 1, brimful, brimming, chock-full, crammed, crowded, jammed, jam-packed, packed, stuffed

jammed *adj syn* FULL 1, brimful, brimming, chock-full, crammed, crowded, jam-full, jam-packed, packed, stuffed

jam-pack *vb syn* CRAM 1, jam, ‖pang, ram, stuff, tamp

jam-packed *adj syn* FULL 1, brimful, brimming, chock-full, crammed, crowded, jam-full, jammed, packed, stuffed

jangle *vb syn* CLASH 2, conflict, disaccord, discord, disharmonize, jar, mismatch

---

syn synonym(s) *rel* related word(s)
idiom idiomatic equivalent(s) *con* contrasted word(s)
ant antonym(s) * vulgar
‖ use limited; if in doubt, see a dictionary
The first word in a synonym list when printed in SMALL CAPITALS shows where there is more information about the group. For a more efficient use of this book see Explanatory Notes.

jangle *n* ***syn*** DIN, babel, clamor, hubbub, hullabaloo, pandemonium, racket, tintamarre, tumult, uproar

jape *n* ***syn*** JOKE 1, crack, drollery, gag, jest, quip, waggery, wisecrack, witticism, ‖yak

jar *vb* **1** ***syn*** CLASH 2, conflict, disaccord, discord, disharmonize, jangle, mismatch
2 ***syn*** SHAKE 2, quake, tremble, tremor, vibrate

jar *n* ***syn*** IMPACT, bump, clash, collision, concussion, crash, jolt, jounce, shock, smash
rel fluctuation, sway, vibration; agitation, disturbance, upset

jargon *n* **1** ***syn*** TERMINOLOGY, cant, dictionary, language, lexicon, palaver, vocabulary
2 ***syn*** DIALECT 2, argot, cant, lingo, patois, patter, slang, vernacular
rel idiom, speech; abracadabra, gibberish

jarring *adj* ***syn*** HARSH 3, dry, grating, hoarse, rasping, raucous, rough, strident, stridulent, stridulous
ant soothing

jaundiced *adj* ***syn*** BIASED 2, colored, one-sided, partial, partisan, prejudiced, prepossessed, tendentious, unindifferent, warped

jaunt *n* ***syn*** EXCURSION 1, junket, outing, roundabout, sally

‖**jaw** *n* ***syn*** BACK TALK, guff, lip, mouth, sass, sauce

jaw *vb* **1** ***syn*** SCOLD 1, baste, berate, ‖cample, ‖carpet, rail, rate, tongue-lash, upbraid, wig
2 ***syn*** CHAT 1, babble, chatter, clack, gab, gabble, prate, prattle, yak, yakety-yak

jay *n* ***syn*** RUSTIC, backwoodsman, bumpkin, clodhopper, clown, country jake, hayseed, hick, hillbilly, jake

jazz *n* ***syn*** NONSENSE 2, ‖baloney, ‖bull, bushwa, ‖crap, flimflam, guff, malarkey, moonshine, poppycock

jealous *adj* **1** intolerant of rivalry or unfaithfulness <her husband was *jealous* of her flirting with other men>
syn possessive, possessory
rel covetous, demanding; grasping, grudging; envious, green-eyed, invidious; mistrustful, suspicious; doubting, questioning
con tolerant, trusting, understanding
2 ***syn*** ENVIOUS, envying, green-eyed, invidious
3 ***syn*** SUSPICIOUS 2, distrustful, mistrustful

jealousy *n* ***syn*** ENVY, enviousness, invidiousness

jeer *vb* ***syn*** SCOFF, fleer, flout, gibe, gird, jest, quip (at), scout (at), sneer
con fawn, toady, truckle; approve, endorse, OK, sanction

jejune *adj* ***syn*** INSIPID 3, banal, bland, flat, inane, innocuous, milk-and-water, namby-pamby, sapless, vapid
rel slight, slim, tenuous, thin; arid, dry

jell *vb* ***syn*** COAGULATE, clot, congeal, gel, gelate, gelatinize, jellify, jelly, set
rel stiffen, thicken; cohere, stick

---

syn synonym(s)	***rel*** related word(s)
idiom idiomatic equivalent(s)	***con*** contrasted word(s)
ant antonym(s)	* vulgar

‖ use limited; if in doubt, see a dictionary
The first word in a synonym list when printed in SMALL CAPITALS shows where there is more information about the group. For a more efficient use of this book see Explanatory Notes.

jellify *vb* ***syn*** COAGULATE, clot, congeal, gel, gelate, gelatinize, jell, jelly, set

jelly *vb* ***syn*** COAGULATE, clot, congeal, gel, gelate, gelatinize, jell, jellify, set

jellyfish *n* ***syn*** WEAKLING, baby, doormat, invertebrate, milksop, Milquetoast, mollycoddle, pantywaist, sissy, sop

jeopard *vb* ***syn*** ENDANGER, compromise, hazard, imperil, jeopardize, jeopardy, menace, peril, risk

jeopardize *vb* ***syn*** ENDANGER, compromise, hazard, imperil, jeopard, jeopardy, menace, peril, risk

jeopardous *adj* ***syn*** DANGEROUS 1, chancy, hairy, hazardous, perilous, risky, treacherous, unhealthy, unsound, wicked

jeopardy *n* ***syn*** DANGER, hazard, peril, risk
rel exposure; liability, openness, sensitiveness, susceptibility; accident, chance, hap
ant safety

jeopardy *vb* ***syn*** ENDANGER, compromise, hazard, imperil, jeopard, jeopardize, menace, peril, risk

jeremiad *n* ***syn*** TIRADE, diatribe, harangue, philippic

jerk *vb* to act on with or make a sudden sharp quick movement <*jerked* to one side> <*jerk* a root from the ground>
syn lug, lurch, snap, twitch, vellicate, yank
rel drag, pull; fling, sling, throw, toss; wrench, wrest, wring

jerk *n* ***syn*** FOOL 1, ass, *damfool, idiot, jackass, nincompoop, ninny, ‖schmo, ‖schmuck, tomfool

jerkwater town *n* ***syn*** BURG, hick town, mudhole, one-horse town, Podunk, tank-town, whistle-stop

jerry–build *vb* ***syn*** THROW UP 1, run up

jest *n* **1** ***syn*** JOKE 1, crack, drollery, gag, jape, quip, waggery, wisecrack, witticism, ‖yak
rel banter, chaff, jolly; derision, ridicule, twit
2 ***syn*** FUN 1, game, joke, play, sport
con gravity, seriousness, soberness
ant earnest
3 ***syn*** LAUGHINGSTOCK, butt, derision, jestee, joke, mock, mockery, pilgarlic, sport

jest *vb* **1** ***syn*** SCOFF, fleer, flout, gibe, gird, jeer, quip (at), scout (at), sneer
2 ***syn*** BANTER, chaff, fun, ‖jive, joke, josh, kid, rag, razz, rib

jestee *n* ***syn*** LAUGHINGSTOCK, butt, derision, jest, joke, mock, mockery, pilgarlic, sport

jester *n* **1** ***syn*** FOOL 2, idiot, motley
2 ***syn*** HUMORIST 2, comedian, comic, droll, funnyman, joker, jokester, quipster, wag, wit

jet *adj* ***syn*** BLACK 1, atramentous, ebon, ebony, inky, jetty, pitch-black, pitch-dark, raven, sable

jet *vb* ***syn*** SQUIRT, splurt, sprit, ‖spritz, spurt, ‖squitter

jetsam *n* ***syn*** DRIFTWOOD, flotsam, wreckage

jet set *n* ***syn*** SMART SET, beautiful people, ton

jettison *n* ***syn*** DISPOSAL 2, discarding, disposition, dumping, junking, relegation, riddance, scrapping, throwing away

jettison *vb* ***syn*** DISCARD, abdicate, cashier, cast, junk, reject, scrap, shed, slough, throw away
ant salvage

jetty *n* ***syn*** WHARF, berth, dock, levee, pier, quay, slip

jetty *adj* ***syn*** BLACK 1, atramentous, ebon, ebony, inky, jet, pitch-black, pitch-dark, raven, sable

jewel *n syn* PARAGON, ideal, nonesuch, nonpareil, phoenix

jewel *vb syn* BEJEWEL, begem, beset, enjewel, gem

jezebel *n syn* WANTON, hussy, jade, slattern, slut, strumpet, tramp, trollop, trull, wench

jib *vb syn* DEMUR, balk, boggle, gag, scruple, shy, stick, stickle, strain, stumble

jibe *vb syn* AGREE 4, accord, conform, correspond, dovetail, fit (in), go, harmonize, square, tally

‖**jiff** *n syn* INSTANT 1, breathing, crack, flash, jiffy, minute, moment, second, shake, split second

jiffy *n syn* INSTANT 1, breathing, crack, flash, ‖jiff, minute, moment, second, shake, split second

jig *n syn* TRICK 1, device, feint, gambit, gimmick, play, ploy, ruse, whizzer, wile

jigger *n* **1** *syn* DOODAD, dingus, dofunny, doohickey, gizmo, ‖hootenanny, thingum, thingumajig, thingumbob, thingummy
2 *syn* GADGET 1, concern, gimmick, gizmo, widget

‖**jiggery–pokery** *n syn* NONSENSE 2, ‖applesauce, balderdash, blatherskite, claptrap, flummadiddle, malarkey, piffle, poppycock, twaddle

jiggle *vb syn* SHAKE 3, joggle

jillion *n syn* SCAD, gob(s), heap, load(s), million, oodles, quantities, slew, thousand, trillion

jim–dandy *n syn* ‖DILLY, ‖corker, crackerjack, ‖daisy, dandy, humdinger, knockout, ‖lalapalooza, ‖lulu, nifty

‖**jimjams** *n syn* JITTERS, ‖all-overs, dither, heebie-jeebies, ‖jimmies, jumps, shakes, shivers, whim-whams, willies

‖**jimmies** *n syn* JITTERS, ‖all-overs, dither, heebie-jeebies, ‖jimjams, jumps, shakes, shivers, whim-whams, willies

jimmy *vb syn* PRY, lever, prize

jingle *vb* to make a repeated sharp light ringing sound <the coins *jingled* in his pocket>
syn chink, chinkle, clink, tingle, tinkle
rel clack, clatter, rattle

jinx *n* something that is felt or meant to bring bad luck <his continual bad luck seemed due to a *jinx*>
syn hex, hoodoo, Indian sign, voodoo, whammy
rel charm, enchantment, spell; curse, evil eye

jitters *n pl* a sense of panic or extreme nervousness <got the *jitters* whenever he thought of the money he had lost>
syn ‖all-overs, dither, heebie-jeebies, ‖jimjams, ‖jimmies, jumps, shakes, shivers, whim-whams, willies

jittery *adj syn* NERVOUS, fidgety, goosey, high-strung, jumpy, nervy, spooky, twittery, unrestful

‖**jive** *vb syn* BANTER, fun, jest, joke, jolly, josh, kid, rag, razz, rib

job *n* **1** *syn* TASK 1, assignment, chare, chore, devoir, duty, stint
rel affair, concern, matter, thing
2 a regular remunerative employment <held two *jobs* to make ends meet>
syn appointment, berth, billet, connection, office, place, position, post, situation, spot; *compare* WORK 1
rel assignment, engagement, posting; calling, employment, occupation, pursuit; profession, trade, vocation; niche, opening, slot
3 *syn* WORK 1, business, calling, employment, line, occupation, pursuit, ‖racket
4 *syn* TASK 2, chore, effort, taskwork

job *vb syn* DUPE, bamboozle, befool, chicane, flimflam, fool, gull, hoax, pigeon, victimize

jobless *adj syn* UNEMPLOYED, workless

jockey *vb syn* MANIPULATE 2, beguile, exploit, finesse, maneuver, play

jocose *adj syn* WITTY, facetious, humorous, jocular
rel playful, roguish, sportive, waggish, whimsical; comic, comical, droll, laughable, ludicrous; blithe, jocund, jolly, jovial
con demure, earnest, grave, sedate, serious, sober, solemn, staid
ant lugubrious

jocular *adj syn* WITTY, facetious, humorous, jocose
rel jolly, jovial, merry; playful, sportive; comic, comical, droll, laughable, ludicrous
con earnest, grave, serious, sober, solemn

jocularity *n syn* MIRTH, glee, hilarity, jocundity, jollity, joviality, merriment

jocund *adj syn* MERRY, blithe, blithesome, festive, gay, gleeful, jolly, jovial, lighthearted, mirthful
rel mischievous, playful, sportive
con dour, gloomy, glum, morose, saturnine, sullen; grave, sedate, serious, solemn, somber, staid

jocundity *n syn* MIRTH, glee, hilarity, jocularity, jollity, joviality, merriment

jog *vb syn* POKE 1, dig, jab, nudge, prod, punch
rel agitate, shake

joggle *vb syn* SHAKE 3, jiggle

john *n syn* TOILET, ‖can, convenience, ‖donicker, head, johnny, latrine, lavatory, ‖loo, privy

John Law *n syn* POLICEMAN, cop, ‖flatfoot, ‖fuzz, ‖heat, man, officer, patrolman, ‖peeler, ‖pig

johnny *n syn* TOILET, ‖can, ‖donicker, head, john, latrine, lavatory, ‖loo, privy, water closet

join *vb* **1** to bring or come together into some manner of union <the couple were *joined* in marriage soon thereafter>
syn associate, bracket, coadunate, coagment, coalesce, combine, compound, concrete, conjoin, conjugate, connect, couple, link, marry, one, relate, unite, wed, yoke
rel agree, concur, cooperate; articulate, concatenate, integrate; affix, attach, fasten; knit, weave; bind, tie, tie up
con separate, sever, sunder; detach, disengage; disembarrass, disentangle, untangle
ant disjoin, part
2 *syn* ADJOIN, abut, border, butt (on *or* against), communicate, line, march, neighbor, touch, verge

join (up) *vb syn* ENTER 3, enlist, enroll, muster, sign, sign up

joining *n syn* JOINT 1, connection, coupling, junction, juncture, seam, union

---

syn synonym(s)
rel related word(s)
idiom idiomatic equivalent(s)
con contrasted word(s)
ant antonym(s)
* vulgar
‖ use limited; if in doubt, see a dictionary
The first word in a synonym list when printed in SMALL CAPITALS shows where there is more information about the group. For a more efficient use of this book see Explanatory Notes.

joint *n* **1** a place where two or more things are united <the leak was found at a *joint* in the pipeline>
syn connection, coupling, joining, junction, juncture, seam, union
rel crux, link, tie; interconnection; abutment, articulation, suture; concourse, confluence, meeting
2 *syn* DIVE, barrelhouse, hangout, honky-tonk

joint *adj syn* COMMON 1, communal, conjoint, conjunct, intermutual, mutual, public, shared

jointly *adv syn* TOGETHER 3, conjointly, mutually

joke *n* **1** a remark, story, or action intended to evoke laughter <had a good memory for *jokes*>
syn crack, drôlerie, drollery, gag, jape, jest, quip, sally, waggery, wisecrack, witticism, ‖yak
rel antic, caper, dido, monkeyshine, prank; bijouterie, bon mot; burlesque, caricature, parody, quiz, rib; badinage, persiflage, raillery; facetiousness, humorousness, jocoseness, jocularity, wittiness; humor, repartee, sarcasm, wit
2 *syn* FUN 1, game, jest, play, sport
3 *syn* LAUGHINGSTOCK, butt, derision, jest, jestee, mock, mockery, pilgarlic, sport

joke *vb syn* BANTER, fun, jest, ‖jive, jolly, josh, kid, rag, razz, rib

joker *n* **1** *syn* WAG 1, card, comedian, humorist, zany
2 *syn* HUMORIST 2, comedian, comic, droll, funnyman, jester, jokester, quipster, wag, wit
3 *syn* ZANY 2, clown, cutup, farceur, jokester, wag

jokester *n* **1** *syn* HUMORIST 2, comedian, comic, droll, funnyman, jester, joker, quipster, wag, wit
2 *syn* ZANY 2, clown, cutup, farceur, joker, wag

jollity *n* **1** *syn* MIRTH, glee, hilarity, jocularity, jocundity, joviality, merriment
rel blitheness; disport, frolic, gambol, play, rollick, romp, sport
con earnestness, gravity, sedateness, seriousness, solemnity, staidness
ant somberness
2 *syn* MERRYMAKING, festivity, gaiety, merriment, revel, reveling, revelment, revelry, whoopee

jolly *adj syn* MERRY, blithe, blithesome, festive, gay, gleeful, jocund, jovial, lighthearted, mirthful
rel frolicsome, mischievous, playful, roguish, sportive, waggish
con earnest, grave, sedate, serious, solemn, staid; doleful, dolorous, lugubrious, rueful
ant somber

jolly *vb syn* BANTER, chaff, fun, jest, ‖jive, josh, kid, rag, razz, rib
rel blandish, cajole

jolt *vb syn* SHOCK 2, startle

jolt *n* **1** *syn* IMPACT, bump, clash, collision, concussion, crash, jar, jounce, percussion, shock
2 *syn* DRAM, ‖caulker, drop, nip, shot, slug, snifter, snort, toothful, tot

jongleur *n syn* BARD 1, minstrel, troubadour

josh *vb syn* BANTER, chaff, fun, jest, ‖jive, jolly, kid, rag, razz, rib

joskin *n syn* RUSTIC, backwoodsman, bucolic, bumpkin, clodhopper, hayseed, hick, hillbilly, hillman, yokel

jostle *vb syn* PUSH 2, bulldoze, elbow, hustle, press, ‖shog, shoulder, shove

jot *n syn* PARTICLE, atom, bit, grain, iota, minim, modicum, speck, tittle, whit

jounce *n syn* IMPACT, bump, collision, concussion, impingement, jar, jolt, percussion, shock, wallop

journal *n* a publication that appears at regular intervals <a monthly scientific *journal*>
syn magazine, newspaper, organ, periodical, review

journey *n* passing or a passage from one place to another <at that time it was a four day *journey* from Boston to New York> <she was tired though their *journey* was barely begun>
syn expedition, peregrination(s), travel(s), trek, trip; *compare* TRIP 1
rel excursion, jaunt, junket, sally, tour; cruise, voyage; pilgrimage, progress, safari

journey *vb syn* GO 1, fare, hie, pass, proceed, ‖process, push on, repair, travel, wend

jovial *adj syn* MERRY, blithe, blithesome, festive, gay, gleeful, jocund, jolly, lighthearted, mirthful
rel facetious, humorous, jocose, jocular; affable, genial, sociable; amiable, good-natured; bantering, chaffing, jollying, joshing
con dour, gloomy, glum, morose, saturnine, sullen; grave, sedate, serious, solemn, staid

joviality *n syn* MIRTH, glee, hilarity, jocularity, jocundity, jollity, merriment

joy *n syn* PLEASURE 2, delectation, delight, enjoyment, fruition, joyance
rel ecstasy, rapture, transport
ant sorrow; misery

joyance *n syn* PLEASURE 2, delectation, delight, enjoyment, fruition, joy

joyful *adj syn* GLAD 1, happy, joyous, lighthearted
rel buoyant, effervescent, expansive
con despairing, desperate, despondent, forlorn, hopeless; depressed, oppressed, weighed down
ant joyless

‖**joy girl** *n syn* PROSTITUTE, call girl, ‖cruiser, fille de joie, harlot, ‖hooker, hustler, streetwalker, ‖tomato, whore

‖**joyhouse** *n syn* BROTHEL, bagnio, bawdy house, bordello, cathouse, ‖hookshop, parlor house, sporting house, stew, whorehouse

‖**joy–juice** *n syn* LIQUOR 2, alcohol, aqua vitae, booze, drink, firewater, grog, ‖hooch, ‖juice, ‖sauce

joyless *adj* **1** *syn* SAD 2, depressing, melancholic, melancholy, mournful, saddening, triste
2 *syn* GLOOMY 3, black, bleak, cheerless, depressant, dismal, dispiriting, dreary, oppressive, somber

joyous *adj syn* GLAD 1, happy, joyful, lighthearted
rel ecstatic, rapturous, transported
con doleful, dolorous, melancholy; miserable, wretched
ant lugubrious

jubilance *n syn* EXULTATION, exultance, jubilation, triumph

jubilant *adj* ***syn*** EXULTANT, cock-a-hoop, cock-a-whoop, exulting, triumphal, triumphant

jubilate *vb* ***syn*** EXULT, delight, glory, triumph

jubilation *n* ***syn*** EXULTATION, exultance, jubilance, triumph

judge *n* **1** a person who impartially decides unsettled questions or controversial issues <the *judge* declared the ruling invalid>
syn arbiter, arbitrator, referee, umpire
rel intermediary, mediator, negotiator; conciliator, peacemaker, reconciler
2 an official entrusted with administration of laws <the *judge* gave the defendant a suspended sentence>
syn ‖beak, court, justice, magistrate

judge *vb* **1** to decide something in dispute or controversy upon its merits and upon evidence <the committee will *judge* the truth of the testimony>
syn adjudge, adjudicate, arbitrate, referee, umpire
rel decide, determine, rule, settle
2 ***syn*** INFER, collect, conclude, deduce, deduct, derive, draw, gather, make, make out
rel demonstrate, prove, show; check, test, try
3 ***syn*** ESTIMATE 3, approximate, call, place, put, reckon

judgmatic *adj* ***syn*** WISE 2, judicious, prudent, sage, sane, sapient, sensible

judgment *n* **1** ***syn*** INFERENCE 1, deduction, illation, ratiocination
rel decision, determination, ruling; belief, conviction, opinion, persuasion, view
2 ***syn*** INFERENCE 2, conclusion, deduction, illation, ratiocination, sequitur
3 ***syn*** ESTIMATION 1, appraisal, appraisement, assessment, estimate, evaluation, stock
4 ***syn*** SENSE 6, common sense, good sense, gumption, horse sense, wisdom
rel astuteness, perspicacity, sagacity, shrewdness; acumen, discernment, insight, penetration

judicious *adj* ***syn*** WISE 2, judgmatic, prudent, sage, sane, sapient, sensible
rel rational, reasonable; dispassionate, equitable, fair, objective
con irrational, thoughtless, unreasonable; ill-considered
ant injudicious; asinine

jug *n* ***syn*** JAIL, ‖calaboose, ‖can, ‖clink, cooler, coop, ‖hoosegow, lockup, pen, ‖pokey

jug *vb* ***syn*** IMPRISON, bastille, confine, constrain, immure, incarcerate, intern, jail, ‖prison, ‖quod

juggle *vb* ***syn*** DECEIVE, beguile, betray, bluff, delude, double-cross, humbug, illude, mislead, take in

‖**juice** *n* ***syn*** LIQUOR 2, alcohol, aqua vitae, booze, drink, firewater, grog, ‖hooch, spirit(s), tipple

‖**juiced** *adj* ***syn*** INTOXICATED 1, ‖boozy, ‖canned, disguised, drunk, inebriated, ‖lushed, muddled, pixilated, ‖plastered

juicy *adj* ***syn*** SUCCULENT, ‖sappy

juju *n* ***syn*** CHARM 2, amulet, fetish, luck, mascot, periapt, phylactery, talisman, zemi

jumble *vb* **1** ***syn*** CONFUSE 5, foul up, mix up, muddle, ‖snafu, snarl up, tumble
2 ***syn*** DISORDER 1, derange, disarrange, disorganize, disturb, mess (up), mix up, muddle, muss (up), rummage

jumble *n* **1** ***syn*** CLUTTER 2, hash, jungle, litter, mishmash, muddle, rummage, scramble, shuffle, tumble
2 ***syn*** MISCELLANY 1, assortment, gallimaufry, medley, olio, omnium-gatherum, pastiche, patchwork, potpourri, salmagundi

jumbo *adj* ***syn*** HUGE, colossal, cyclopean, elephantine, enormous, giant, gigantic, mammoth, mighty, prodigious

jump *vb* **1** to move suddenly through space by or as if by muscular action <*jumped* across the open trench>
syn bounce, bound, hop, hurdle, leap, lop, saltate, spring, vault
2 ***syn*** START 1, bolt, spring, startle
3 ***syn*** RAISE 9, boost, hike, increase, jack (up), put up, up

jump (in *or* into) *vb* ***syn*** PITCH IN 1, buckle (down), fall to, set to, wade (in *or* into)

jump (off) *vb* ***syn*** BEGIN 1, commence, embark (on *or* upon), get off, inaugurate, initiate, kick off, launch, open, start

jumps *n pl* ***syn*** JITTERS, ‖all-overs, dither, heebie-jeebies, ‖jimjams, ‖jimmies, shakes, shivers, whim-whams, willies

jumpy *adj* ***syn*** NERVOUS, fidgety, goosey, high-strung, jittery, nervy, spooky, twittery, unrestful
idiom on pins and needles

junction *n* **1** ***syn*** CONCOURSE, concursion, confluence, gathering, meeting
2 ***syn*** JOINT 1, connection, coupling, joining, juncture, seam, union

juncture *n* **1** ***syn*** JOINT 1, connection, coupling, joining, junction, seam, union
2 a critical or crucial time or state of affairs <was at a *juncture* where he had to make a decision>
syn contingency, crisis, crossroad(s), emergency, exigency, pass, pinch, strait, turning point, zero hour
rel condition, posture, situation, state, status; plight, predicament, quandary
3 ***syn*** POINT 7, instant, moment

jungle *n* **1** ***syn*** CLUTTER 2, hash, hugger-mugger, jumble, litter, mash, mishmash, muddle, rummage, scramble
2 ***syn*** MAZE 1, knot, labyrinth, mesh, mizmaze, morass, skein, snarl, tangle, web

junk *n* ***syn*** REFUSE, ‖collateral, debris, garbage, kelter, litter, offal, rubbish, trash, waste

junk *vb* ***syn*** DISCARD, cashier, cast, jettison, reject, scrap, slough, throw away, throw out, wash out

junker *n* ***syn*** JALOPY, clunker, crate, dog, heap, wreck

junket *n* ***syn*** EXCURSION 1, jaunt, outing, roundabout, sally

junking *n* ***syn*** DISPOSAL 2, discarding, disposition, dumping, jettison, relegation, riddance, scrapping, throwing away

---

syn synonym(s) — ***rel*** related word(s)
idiom idiomatic equivalent(s) — ***con*** contrasted word(s)
ant antonym(s) — * vulgar
‖ use limited; if in doubt, see a dictionary
The first word in a synonym list when printed in SMALL CAPITALS shows where there is more information about the group. For a more efficient use of this book see Explanatory Notes.

Junoesque *adj* ***syn*** CURVACEOUS, ‖built, curvesome, curvilinear, curvy, rounded, ‖stacked, well-developed

jurisdiction *n* ***syn*** POWER 1, authority, command, control, domination, mastery, might, strings, sway
rel bounds, confines, limits; compass, range, reach, scope; bailiwick, domain, field, province, sphere, territory

just *adj* **1** ***syn*** WELL-FOUNDED, cogent, good, justified, well-grounded
2 ***syn*** TRUE 3, faithful, right, strict, undistorted, veracious, veridical
3 being what is called for by circumstances or accepted standards <punishments once considered fair and *just* are now held to be cruel, excessive, and unreasonable>
syn appropriate, condign, deserved, due, merited, requisite, rhadamanthine, right, rightful, suitable; *compare* FIT 1
rel fit, fitting, meet, proper
con farfetched, irrelevant, remote, unconnected; improper, inapplicable, inapposite, inappropriate; abusive, cruel, harsh
ant unjust
4 ***syn*** UPRIGHT 2, conscientious, honest, honorable, right, scrupulous, true
rel rigid, strict; dependable, reliable, tried, trustworthy
5 ***syn*** FAIR 4, dispassionate, equal, equitable, impartial, nondiscriminatory, objective, unbiased, uncolored, unprejudiced
rel aloof; condign, due, rightful
ant unjust
6 ***syn*** FIT 1, appropriate, apt, befitting, felicitous, fitting, happy, meet, proper, suitable

just *adv* **1** as stated or indicated without deviation <*just* six inches long>
syn accurately, bang, exactly, precisely, right, sharp, ‖smack-dab, spang, square, squarely
rel definitely, directly, expressly, unmistakably
con almost, nearly; approximately, imprecisely, inaccurately, inexactly, loosely
2 by a very small margin <*just* enough food for one meal>
syn barely, hardly, scarce, scarcely
rel almost, approximately, nearly
con copiously, fully, generously, lavishly, unstintedly, unstintingly
3 no more than <*just* a note to remind you>
syn but, merely, only, simply
idiom nothing but
4 ***syn*** ALL 1, all in all, altogether, completely, exactly, in toto, quite, totally, utterly, wholly
5 ***syn*** EVEN 1, as well, exactly, expressly, precisely

just about *adv* ***syn*** NEARLY, about, all but, almost, approximately, as good as, ‖nearabout, nigh, practically, well-nigh

justice *n* **1** the action, practice, or obligation of awarding each his just due <his *justice* was stern but absolutely fair>
syn equity
rel evenness, fairness, impartiality
con foul play, inequity, unjustness; bias, leaning, one-sidedness, partiality
ant injustice
2 ***syn*** JUDGE 2, ‖beak, court, magistrate

justifiable *adj* capable of being justified <thought her absence was not *justifiable*>
syn condonable, defensible, excusable, tenable, vindicable, warrantable
rel admissible, allowable, legitimate, reasonable; forgivable, pardonable, remissible
ant unjustifiable

justification *n* **1** ***syn*** EXPLANATION 2, account, rationale, rationalization, reason
2 ***syn*** APOLOGY 1, apologetic, apologia, defense

justified *adj* ***syn*** WELL-FOUNDED, cogent, good, just, well-grounded
ant unjustified

justify *vb* **1** ***syn*** MAINTAIN 2, argue, assert, claim, contend, defend, vindicate, warrant
rel demonstrate, prove; back, support, uphold
con confute, disprove, refute
2 ***syn*** CONFIRM 2, authenticate, bear out, corroborate, substantiate, validate, verify
3 ***syn*** EXPLAIN 3, account, explain away, rationalize
rel extenuate, gloss, gloze, palliate, whitewash
con accuse, arraign, incriminate, indict; blame, condemn, denounce
4 to constitute sufficient grounds <thought the storm warning *justified* his leaving early>
syn warrant
rel allow, permit; approve, authorize, sanction

justly *adv* ***syn*** WELL 1, befittingly, correctly, decently, decorously, fitly, fittingly, nicely, properly, rightly

jut *vb* **1** ***syn*** BULGE, beetle, overhang, poke, pouch, pout, project, protrude, stand out, stick out
rel elongate, extend, lengthen
2 ***syn*** HANG 4, beetle, bend (over), lean (over), overhang

jut *n* ***syn*** PROJECTION 1, bulge, outthrust, protrusion, protuberance

juvenile *adj* ***syn*** YOUNG 1, callow, green, immature, infant, unfledged, unripe, youthful
ant adult

juvenile *n* ***syn*** CHILD 1, chickabiddy, kid, moppet, ‖nipper, puss, youngling, young one, youngster, youth

juvenility *n* ***syn*** YOUTH 1, adolescence, greenness, puberty, pubescence, spring, springtide, springtime, youthfulness, youthhood

juxtaposed *adj* ***syn*** ADJACENT 3, abutting, adjoining, approximal, bordering, conterminous, contiguous, touching

---

syn synonym(s) ***rel*** related word(s)
idiom idiomatic equivalent(s) ***con*** contrasted word(s)
ant antonym(s) * vulgar
‖ use limited; if in doubt, see a dictionary
The first word in a synonym list when printed in SMALL CAPITALS shows where there is more information about the group. For a more efficient use of this book see Explanatory Notes.

K

‖**kale** *n* ***syn*** MONEY, dough, filthy lucre, ‖gelt, ‖greenbacks, ‖jack, ‖lettuce, ‖long green, loot, lucre

keck *vb* ***syn*** RETCH, gag, heave

keel (over) *vb* ***syn*** FALL 2, drop, go down, pitch, plunge, slump, topple, tumble

keen *adj* **1** ***syn*** SHARP 1, honed, razor-sharp, unblunted, whetted
2 ***syn*** ENTHUSIASTIC, ‖buggy, ‖bugs, gung ho, nutty, warm, zealous
3 ***syn*** EAGER, agog, anxious, appetent, ardent, athirst, avid, breathless, impatient, thirsty
rel fervent, fervid, perfervid; fierce, intense, vehement; fired
con apathetic, impassive, phlegmatic, stolid; languid, listless
4 ***syn*** SHARP 4, acute, penetrating, penetrative, quick-sighted, quick-witted, sharp-sighted, sharp-witted
5 ***syn*** ACUTE 3, perceptive, sensitive, sharp
con dull, obtuse
6 ***syn*** LIVELY 1, alert, animate, animated, ‖cant, ‖canty, gay, spirited, sprightly, vivacious
‖**7** ***syn*** MARVELOUS 2, ‖cool, ‖dandy, divine, ‖galluptious, glorious, groovy, hot, hunky-dory, ‖neat

keenly *adv* ***syn*** HARD 6, bitterly, hardly, rancorously, resentfully, sorely

keenness *n* **1** ***syn*** EDGE 2, incisiveness, sharpness
2 ***syn*** WIT 3, acumen, astuteness, clear-sightedness, discernment, discrimination, penetration, percipience, perspicacity, shrewdness

keep *vb* **1** ***syn*** OBEY, comply, conform, follow, mind, observe
ant neglect
2 to notice or honor a day, occasion, or deed <remember the Sabbath and *keep* it rightly>
syn celebrate, commemorate, observe, solemnize
rel regard, respect; bless, consecrate, sanctify; honor, laud, praise
idiom keep the faith
con disregard, forget, ignore, neglect, omit, overlook, slight; contravene, infringe, transgress, violate
ant break
3 ***syn*** STOCK, carry
4 ***syn*** RESTRAIN 1, bit, bridle, check, constrain, curb, hold back, hold down, hold in, inhibit
ant release
5 to hold in one's possession or under one's control <*kept* all the money for himself>
syn detain, hold, hold back, keep back, keep out, reserve, retain, withhold
rel conserve, preserve, save; enjoy, have, own, possess; conduct, control, direct, manage
con cast, discard, junk; refuse, reject, repudiate, spurn; abandon, resign, surrender, yield
ant relinquish
6 ***syn*** REFRAIN 1, abstain, forbear, withhold
7 ***syn*** CONDUCT 3, carry on, direct, manage, operate, ordain, run

keep *n* **1** ***syn*** LIVING, alimentation, alimony, bread, bread and butter, livelihood, maintenance, subsistence, support, sustenance
2 ***syn*** JAIL, ‖can, ‖clink, cooler, jug, lockup, pen, ‖pokey, prison, stir

keep back *vb* **1** ***syn*** KEEP 5, detain, hold, hold back, keep out, reserve, retain, withhold
2 ***syn*** DENY 2, disallow, refuse, withhold

keeper *n* ***syn*** CUSTODIAN, cerberus, claviger, ‖custodier, custos, guardian, warden, watchdog

keeping *n* **1** ***syn*** CUSTODY, care, guardianship, safekeeping, trust, ward
2 ***syn*** PRESERVATION 1, conservation, safekeeping, salvation, saving, sustentation

keep off *vb* ***syn*** FEND (off), hold off, rebuff, rebut, repel, repulse, stave off, ward (off)

keep out *vb* ***syn*** KEEP 5, detain, hold, hold back, keep back, reserve, retain, withhold

keepsake *n* ***syn*** REMEMBRANCE 3, memento, memorial, relic, remembrancer, reminder, souvenir, token, trophy

keep up *vb* ***syn*** MAINTAIN 1, preserve, save, sustain

keg *n* ***syn*** CASK, barrel, butt, hogshead, pipe, tun

‖**keister** *n* ***syn*** BUTTOCKS, behind, bottom, ‖can, ‖duff, heinie (*or* hiney), posterior, *prat, rump, ‖tokus

kelter *n* ***syn*** REFUSE, ‖collateral, debris, garbage, junk, litter, offal, rubbish, trash, waste

ken *n* the extent of one's recognition, comprehension, perception, understanding, or knowledge <abstractions that are beyond the *ken* of small children>
syn horizon, purview, range, reach
rel comprehension, grasp, perception, understanding

kept woman *n* ***syn*** HARLOT 1, blowen, courtesan, demimondaine, demimonde, demirep, fancy woman, hetaera, paphian, whore

kerchief *n* **1** a square of cloth used as a head covering or scarf <wore a *kerchief* around his neck>
syn babushka, bandanna
2 ***syn*** HANDKERCHIEF, hankie, *snot-rag, ‖wipe, ‖wiper

kernel *n* ***syn*** SUBSTANCE 2, core, crux, gist, matter, meat, nub, nubbin, sum and substance, upshot

key *n* ***syn*** PASSPORT, open sesame, password, ticket

kibitzer *n* ***syn*** BUSYBODY, butt-in, ‖buttinsky, intermeddler, meddler, pragmatist, prier (*or* pryer), quidnunc, rubberneck, snoop

kick *vb* **1** ***syn*** OBJECT 1, except, expostulate, inveigh (against), protest, remonstrate
rel combat, fight, oppose, resist, withstand; anathematize, condemn, curse, damn, execrate

---

syn synonym(s) ***rel*** related word(s)
idiom idiomatic equivalent(s) ***con*** contrasted word(s)
ant antonym(s) * vulgar
‖ use limited; if in doubt, see a dictionary
The first word in a synonym list when printed in SMALL CAPITALS shows where there is more information about the group. For a more efficient use of this book see Explanatory Notes.

idiom put up a fight (against)
2 ***syn*** COMPLAIN, fuss, murmur, repine, wail, whine

kick *n* ***syn*** THRILL, bang, boot, wallop

‖**kick around** *vb* ***syn*** DISCUSS 1, agitate, argue, canvass, debate, discept, dispute, moot, thrash out, toss (around)

kick back *vb* ***syn*** BACKFIRE, backlash, boomerang, bounce (back)

kicker *n* ***syn*** GROUCH, ‖bellyacher, complainer, crab, crank, griper, growler, grumbler, sorehead, sourpuss

‖**kick in** *vb* **1** ***syn*** CONTRIBUTE 1, chip in, come through, pitch in, subscribe
2 ***syn*** DIE 1, cash in, ‖check out, ‖croak, go, ‖kick off, pass, pass away, perish, pop off

kick off *vb* **1** ***syn*** BEGIN 1, commence, embark (on *or* upon), get off, inaugurate, initiate, jump (off), launch, open, start
‖**2** ***syn*** DIE 1, cash in, ‖check out, ‖croak, go, ‖kick in, pass, pass away, perish, pop off

kick out *vb* **1** ***syn*** DISMISS 3, ax, boot (out), bounce, ‖can, cashier, discharge, drop, fire, sack
2 ***syn*** EJECT 1, boot (out), chase, chuck, dismiss, evict, extrude, out, throw out

kickshaw *n* ***syn*** DELICACY, bonne bouche, dainty, goody, morsel, tidbit (*or* titbit), treat

kid *n* ***syn*** CHILD 1, bud, chickabiddy, juvenile, moppet, ‖nipper, youngling, young one, youngster, youth

kid *vb* **1** ***syn*** DUPE, bamboozle, befool, flimflam, fool, gull, hoax, hoodwink, hornswoggle, trick
2 ***syn*** BANTER, fun, jest, ‖jive, joke, jolly, josh, rag, razz, rib

kidnap *vb* to carry off a person surreptitiously for an illegal purpose <an ex-convict *kidnapped* the child for ransom>
syn abduct, ‖snatch, spirit (away)
rel shanghai, waylay; coax, decoy, entice, inveigh, lure, seduce
idiom make off with
con deliver, ransom, redeem, rescue; bring (back), give back, restore, return

kidney *n* ***syn*** TYPE, breed, character, description, feather, ilk, kind, nature, sort, stripe

kid stuff *n* ***syn*** SNAP 1, breeze, child's play, duck soup, picnic, pie, pushover, setup, ‖snip, soft touch

kill *vb* **1** to deprive of life <found it hard to *kill* animals>
syn carry off, cut off, destroy, dispatch, down, finish, lay low, put away, scrag, slay, take off; *compare* MURDER 1
rel butcher, choke, drown, massacre, poison, shoot, slaughter, suffocate; knife, sacrifice, stifle; annihilate, exterminate, ruin
idiom do (*or* make) away with, do for, put out of the way, put (*or* do) to death, put to sleep, take one's life
2 ***syn*** VETO, negative, ‖nix, non-placet

killer *n* ***syn*** MURDERER, homicide, manslayer, slayer

killing *n* ***syn*** MURDER, blood, ‖bump-off, foul play, homicide, manslaughter

kiln *vb* ***syn*** FIRE 6, bake, burn

kilter *n* ***syn*** ORDER 10, condition, fettle, fitness, repair, shape, trim

kin *n* **1** ***syn*** FAMILY, clan, folk, kindred, lineage, race, stock, tribe
2 the members of one's immediate or extended family <all our *kin* gathered to celebrate great grandma's birthday>
syn cousinage, cousinhood, kinfolk, kinsmen
3 ***syn*** RELATIVE, kinsman, kinswoman, relation

kind *n* ***syn*** TYPE, character, description, feather, ilk, kidney, nature, sort, stripe, way

kind *adj* showing or having a gentle considerate nature <mother was a *kind* person, always willing to help others>
syn benign, benignant, good-hearted, kindly
rel altruistic, benevolent, charitable, eleemosynary, humane, humanitarian, openhearted, philanthropic, propitious; compassionate, kindhearted, responsive, sympathetic, tender, warm, warmhearted; clement, forbearing, indulgent, lenient, merciful, tolerant; affable, amiable, cordial, genial, good-humored, good-natured, good-tempered, sweet-tempered; complaisant, obliging; gentle, good
con cruel, fell, fierce, inhuman, savage; hard, harsh, rough; grim, implacable, merciless, unrelenting
ant unkind

kindhearted *adj* ***syn*** TENDER, compassionate, responsive, softhearted, sympathetic, warm, warmhearted

kindle *vb* **1** ***syn*** LIGHT 1, enkindle, fire, ignite, inflame
rel blaze, flame, flare, glow; excite, provoke, stimulate; arouse, foment, incite, instigate, rouse, stir
ant smother
2 ***syn*** STIR 1, arouse, awaken, bestir, challenge, rally, rouse, wake, waken, whet
ant stifle

kindless *adj* ***syn*** ANTIPATHETIC 2, aversive, repellent, repugnant, uncongenial, ungenial, unsympathetic

kindliness *n* ***syn*** GOODWILL 1, amity, benevolence, comity, friendliness, friendship
ant unkindliness

kindly *adj* ***syn*** KIND, benign, benignant, good-hearted
rel gracious, sociable; friendly, neighborly; attentive, considerate, thoughtful
con malevolent, malicious, malign, spiteful
ant unkindly; acrid (*of temper, attitudes, comments*)

kindly *adv* ***syn*** WELL 2, considerately, generously, heedfully, thoughtfully

kindness *n* ***syn*** FAVOR 4, courtesy, dispensation, indulgence, service

kind of *adv* ***syn*** SOMEWHAT 2, fairly, moderately, more or less, pretty, rather, ratherish, some, something, sort of

kindred *n* ***syn*** FAMILY 1, clan, folk, house, lineage, race, stock, tribe

kindred *adj* ***syn*** RELATED, affiliated, agnate, akin, allied, cognate, connate, connatural, consanguine, incident
ant alien

---

syn synonym(s) *rel* related word(s)
idiom idiomatic equivalent(s) *con* contrasted word(s)
ant antonym(s) * vulgar
‖ use limited; if in doubt, see a dictionary
The first word in a synonym list when printed in SMALL CAPITALS shows where there is more information about the group. For a more efficient use of this book see Explanatory Notes.

kinfolk *n pl* ***syn*** KIN 2, cousinage, counsinhood, kinsmen

king *n* ***syn*** MAGNATE, baron, czar, merchant prince, mogul, prince, tycoon

kingdom come *n* ***syn*** HEAVEN 2, bliss, Canaan, Civitas Dei, elysium, empyrean, happy hunting ground, New Jerusalem, paradise, Zion

kinglike *adj* ***syn*** KINGLY, majestic, monarchal, monarchial, monarchical, regal, royal, sovereign

kingly *adj* of, relating to, or befitting a king <a *kingly* entourage>
syn kinglike, majestic, monarchal, monarchial, monarchical, regal, royal, sovereign
rel imperious, lordly, masterful, powerful, puissant; imperial, princely, queenly

kinky *adj* ***syn*** OUTLANDISH 3, far-out, outré, ultra

kinsman *n* **1** ***syn*** RELATIVE, kin, kinswoman, relation
2 kinsmen *pl* ***syn*** KIN 2, cousinage, cousinhood, kinfolk

kinswoman *n* ***syn*** RELATIVE, kin, kinsman, relation

kismet *n* ***syn*** FATE, circumstance, destiny, doom, lot, moira, portion, weird

kiss *vb* **1** to touch with the lips especially as a sign of affection < *kissed* his mother good night>
syn buss, lip, osculate, peck, smack, smooch, ||smoodge, ||smouch
2 ***syn*** BRUSH, glance, graze, shave, skim

||**kisser** *n* ***syn*** FACE 1, countenance, ||dial, features, ||map, mug, ||pan, phiz, ||puss, visage

kiss off *vb* ***syn*** DISMISS 5, pooh-pooh

kite *vb* ***syn*** GET OUT 1, begone, clear out, decamp, hightail, scram, skedaddle, skiddoo, take off, ||vamoose

kittenish *adj* ***syn*** PLAYFUL 1, coltish, elvish, frisky, frolicsome, impish, larkish, mischievous, prankish, roguish

kitty *n* ***syn*** POT 3, jackpot, pool

klutz *n* ***syn*** OAF 2, gawk, lobster, looby, lout, lubber, ||lug, lummox, lump, palooka

knack *n* **1** ***syn*** GIFT 2, aptness, bent, genius, head, nose, set, talent, turn
rel quickness, readiness
ant ineptitude
2 ***syn*** ABILITY 2, command, expertise, expertism, expertness, know-how, mastership, mastery, skill
3 ***syn*** HANG, swing, trick

knapsack *n* ***syn*** BACKPACK, haversack, pack, packsack, rucksack

knave *n* ***syn*** VILLIAN 1, *bastard, blackguard, heel, lowlife, miscreant, rascal, rogue, scoundrel, *son of a bitch

knavish *adj* ***syn*** DISHONEST, deceitful, lying, mendacious, roguish, shifty, unhonest, untruthful

knell *vb* ***syn*** RING, bell, bong, chime, peal, toll

knickknack *n* a small or trivial ornamental article <a collection of pretty *knickknacks* was displayed on the mantel>
syn bauble, bibelot, curio, dido, gewgaw, gimcrack, novelty, objet d'art, pretty-pretty, rattletrap(s), toy, trifle, trinket, whatnot, whigmaleerie
rel souvenir; bric-a-brac, virtu; miniature; kickshaw, notion; trumpery

knifelike *adj* ***syn*** SHARP 8, acute, piercing, shooting, stabbing
ant dull

knobkerrie *n* ***syn*** CUDGEL, bat, billy, billy club, bludgeon, club, mace, ||shillelagh, truncheon, war club

knock *vb* **1** ***syn*** TAP 1, bob, rap, tunk
2 ***syn*** CRITICIZE, blame, censure, condemn, denounce, denunciate, rap, reprehend, reprobate, skin
ant boost

knock *n* ***syn*** HIT 1, ||conk, lick, rap, swat, swipe, wipe

knock about *vb* ***syn*** MANHANDLE, mishandle, rough (up), roughhouse, slap around

knock down *vb* **1** ***syn*** FELL 1, bowl (down *or* over), bring down, down, drop, flatten, floor, ground, lay low, level
2 ***syn*** EARN 1, acquire, bring in, ||drag down, draw down, gain, get, make, win

knock–down–and–drag–out *n* **1** ***syn*** BRAWL, affray, broil, donnybrook, fight, fracas, fray, free-for-all, melee, ruction
2 ***syn*** QUARREL, altercation, bickering, brawl, dispute, fight, hassle, rhubarb, run-in, set-to

knocker *n* ***syn*** CRITIC, aristarch, carper, caviler, criticizer, faultfinder, momus, smellfungus, Zoilus

knock off *vb* **1** ***syn*** STOP 3, cease, desist, ||deval, discontinue, give over, halt, leave off, quit, surcease
2 ***syn*** DEDUCT 1, discount, draw back, substract, subtract, take, take away, take off, take out
3 ***syn*** MURDER 1, assassinate, ||bump off, cool, do in, ||dust off, execute, finish, liquidate, put away
||**4** ***syn*** ROB 1, knock over, loot, plunder, ransack, relieve, rifle, stick up

knock out *vb* ***syn*** EXHAUST 4, ||bugger, fag, frazzle, outtire, outwear, ||poop, prostrate, tucker, wear out

knockout *n* **1** ***syn*** ||DILLY, ||corker, crackerjack, ||daisy, dandy, humdinger, jim-dandy ||lalapalooza, ||lulu, peach
2 ***syn*** BEAUTY, ||beaut, eyeful, looker, lovely, stunner

knock over *vb* **1** ***syn*** FELL 1, bowl (down *or* over), bring down, down, drop, flatten, floor, ground, knock down, lay low
2 ***syn*** OVERTURN 1, overset, overthrow, tip (over), topple, turn over, upset
3 ***syn*** OVERWHELM 4, drown, overcome, overpower, prostrate, whelm
4 ***syn*** ROB 1, ||knock off, loot, plunder, ransack, relieve, rifle, stick up

knot *n* **1** ***syn*** BOND 3, ligament, ligature, link, nexus, tie, vinculum, yoke
2 ***syn*** BUMP 2, bunch, lump, ||pumpknot
3 ***syn*** MAZE 1, jungle, labyrinth, mesh, mizmaze, morass, skein, snarl, tangle, web

knothead *n* ***syn*** DUNCE, blockhead, bonehead, chucklehead, dummy, fathead, knucklehead, lunkhead, numskull, pinhead

knotty *adj* **1** ***syn*** COMPLEX 2, Byzantine, complicated, daedal, elaborate, gordian, intricate, involved, labyrinthine, sophisticated
2 ***syn*** HARD 6, difficult, effortful, formidable, rough, rugged, sticky, terrible, tough, uphill

---

know *vb* **1** to possess an intellectual hold of < *knows* several languages >
syn appreciate, apprehend, cognize, comprehend, fathom, grasp, have, understand
rel apperceive; differentiate, discern, discriminate, distinguish, realize
idiom have at one's fingertips, see through
2 *syn* EXPERIENCE 1, have, see, suffer, sustain, undergo
3 *syn* FEEL 2, experience, savor, taste
4 to recognize the differences between < *know* right from wrong >
syn difference, differentiate, discern, discrepate, discriminate, distinguish, extricate, separate, sever, severalize
con confound, mingle, mix
ant confuse, mix up
5 *syn* RECOGNIZE 1

knowable *adj syn* UNDERSTANDABLE, apprehensible, comprehendible, comprehensible, fathomable, graspable, intelligible, lucid, luminous
ant unknowable

know-how *n* **1** *syn* ABILITY 2, command, expertise, expertism, expertness, knack, mastership, mastery, skill
2 *syn* ART 1, adroitness, craft, cunning, dexterity, expertise, skill

knowing *adj* **1** *syn* INTELLIGENT 2, brainy, bright, brilliant, clever, knowledgeable, quick-witted, ready-witted, sharp, smart
rel vigilant, watchful; discerning, observant, perceptive
con blunt, obtuse
2 *syn* WISE 1, discerning, gnostic, insighted, insightful, knowledgeable, perceptive, sagacious, sage, sophic
3 *syn* WISE 4, canny, hep, nimble-witted, quick, quick-witted, sharp, sharp-witted, slick, smart
4 *syn* AWARE, alive, apprehensive, awake, cognizant, conscious, conversant, sensible, sentient, witting
5 *syn* SOPHISTICATED 2, blasé, disenchanted, disentranced, disillusioned, mondaine, sophisticate, worldly, worldly-wise, world-wise

know-it-all *n syn* SMART ALECK, *smartass, smarty, smarty-pants, wiseacre, wisecracker, wise guy, wisehead, wisenheimer

knowledge *n* **1** *syn* EDUCATION 2, erudition, learning, scholarship, science
ant ignorance
2 the body of things known about or in science < made major contributions to scientific *knowledge* >
syn information, lore, science, wisdom
rel advice, intelligence, news; data, evidence, facts

knowledgeable *adj* **1** *syn* INTELLIGENT 2, brainy, bright, brilliant, clever, knowing, quick-witted, ready-witted, sharp, smart
2 *syn* WISE 1, discerning, gnostic, insighted, insightful, knowing, perceptive, sagacious, sage, sophic

know-nothing *adj syn* IGNORANT 1, benighted, empty-headed, illiterate, rude, uneducated, uninstructed, unlettered, untaught, untutored

know-nothing *n syn* DUNCE, dimwit, dolt, dope, dummy, idiot, ignoramus, lackwit, pinhead, wantwit

knuckle *vb syn* YIELD 2, bow, buckle (under), capitulate, cave, defer, knuckle under, submit, succumb

knucklehead *n syn* DUNCE, blockhead, bonehead, clodpate, hammerhead, muttonhead, numskull, thickhead, thickskull, woodenhead

knuckle under *vb syn* YIELD 2, bow, buckle (under), capitulate, cave, defer, knuckle, submit, succumb

kook *n syn* CRACKPOT, crackbrain, crank, cuckoo, ding-a-ling, harebrain, lunatic, nut, screwball

kowtow *vb syn* FAWN, apple-polish, bootlick, ‖brown-nose, cower, cringe, grovel, honey (up), toady, truckle

kowtowing *adj syn* FAWNING, bootlicking, cowering, cringing, groveling, parasitic, sycophantic, toadying, toadyish, truckling

kudize *vb syn* COMMEND 2, acclaim, applaud, compliment, hail, praise, recommend, ‖roose

kudo *n syn* COMPLIMENT 1, bouquet, orchid(s)

kudos *n* **1** *syn* EMINENCE 1, distinction, illustriousness, preeminence, prestige, prominence, prominency, renown
2 *syn* HONOR 2, accolade, award, badge, bays, decoration, distinction, laurels

---

syn synonym(s) *rel* related word(s)
idiom idiomatic equivalent(s) *con* contrasted word(s)
ant antonym(s) * vulgar
‖ use limited; if in doubt, see a dictionary
The first word in a synonym list when printed in SMALL CAPITALS shows where there is more information about the group. For a more efficient use of this book see Explanatory Notes.

L

laager *vb* ***syn*** CAMP, bivouac, ‖bivvy, encamp, ‖maroon, tent

label *n* ***syn*** TICKET 1, tag
rel mark, marker

labor *n* **1** ***syn*** WORK 2, bullwork, donkeywork, drudgery, grind, moil, slavery, slogging, toil, travail
rel endeavor, struggle
con ease, leisure, relaxation, repose, rest; amusement, diversion, entertainment, recreation; idleness, inactivity, inertia, inertness, passiveness
2 the physical activities involved in parturition <first *labors* are sometimes difficult>
syn birth pang(s), childbearing, childbirth, travail

labor *vb* **1** to exert one's powers of mind or body especially with painful or strenuous effort <*labored* all day to make a living>
syn drive, moil, strain, strive, toil, tug, work
idiom break one's neck
con idle, laze, loaf, lounge; goof (off), shirk; dawdle, poke, putter
‖**2** ***syn*** TILL, cultivate, dress, tend, work

labored *adj* **1** ***syn*** HARD 6, arduous, difficult, effortful, heavy, laborious, operose, strenuous, toilsome, uphill
2 ***syn*** FORCED, farfetched, strained
rel heavy, ponderous, weighty; awkward, clumsy, inept, maladroit

laborer *n* ***syn*** WORKER, hand, ‖mozo, operative, roustabout, workhand, workingman, workman

laborious *adj* ***syn*** HARD 6, arduous, difficult, effortful, heavy, labored, operose, strenuous, toilsome, uphill
ant easy, effortless

laboriously *adv* ***syn*** HARD 8, arduously, burdensomely, difficultly, hardly, onerously, toilsomely
ant easily, effortlessly

labyrinth *n* ***syn*** MAZE 1, jungle, knot, mesh, mizmaze, morass, skein, snarl, tangle, web

labyrinthine *adj* ***syn*** COMPLEX 2, Byzantine, complicated, daedal, elaborate, gordian, intricate, involved, knotty, sophisticated

lacerated *adj* having jagged cuts or breaks <the *lacerated* area was badly swollen>
syn mangled, rent, torn
rel gashed, mutilated, ripped, slashed; jagged, ragged, saw-toothed, scalloped, scored; serrated

lachrymose *adj* ***syn*** TEARFUL, teary, weeping, weepy

lack *vb* to be without something and especially something essential or greatly needed <the building *lacks* a fire escape>
syn need, require, want
con enjoy, have, hold, own, possess

lack *n* **1** ***syn*** ABSENCE, dearth, default, defect, ‖miss, privation, want
2 ***syn*** FAILURE 3, defalcation, deficiency, deficit, inadequacy, insufficience, insufficiency, scantiness, shortage, underage

lackadaisical *adj* ***syn*** LANGUID, die-away, enervated, languishing, languorous, limp, listless, spiritless
rel incurious, indifferent, unconcerned; faineant, indolent, lazy, slothful; idle, passive; emasculated; romantic, sentimental
con energetic, lusty, strenuous, vigorous; active, dynamic, live

lacking *adj* **1** ***syn*** ABSENT 1, away, gone, missing, omitted, wanting
2 ***syn*** DEFICIENT 1, defective, ‖half-assed, inadequate, incomplete, insufficient, uncomplete, wanting

lacking *prep* ***syn*** WITHOUT 2, awanting, minus, sans, wanting

lackluster *adj* **1** ***syn*** DULL 7, blind, dead, dim, flat, lusterless, mat, muted
2 ***syn*** COLORLESS 2, drab, dull, flat, lifeless, lusterless, prosaic, prosy
rel dead, leaden, rusty, tarnished
con lustrous

lackwit *n* ***syn*** DUNCE, ‖cluck, dimwit, ‖dumb bunny, ‖dumb cluck, featherweight, nitwit, pinhead, simp, wantwit

laconic *adj* ***syn*** CONCISE, breviloquent, brief, compendiary, compendious, curt, short, short and sweet, succinct, terse
rel brusque
con garrulous, glib, loquacious, talkative
ant verbose, wordy

laconically *adv* ***syn*** BRIEFLY, concisely, in brief, in short, shortly, succinctly, tersely

lacuna *n* ***syn*** GAP 3, breach, break, hiatus, interim, interruption, interval

lad *n* ***syn*** BOY 1, laddie, shaveling, son, stripling, tad

laddie *n* ***syn*** BOY 1, lad, shaveling, son, stripling, tad

lade *vb* **1** ***syn*** BURDEN, charge, clog, cumber, encumber, load, saddle, tax, weigh, weight
2 ***syn*** DIP 2, bail, ladle, scoop

la-di-da *adj* **1** ***syn*** PRECIOUS 4, affected, alembicated, chichi, overnice, overrefined, précieux
2 ***syn*** GENTEEL 3, affected, ‖lardy-dardy, mincing, pretentious, stilted, too-too

ladies' man *n* ***syn*** WOLF, Casanova, chaser, Don Juan, lady-killer, masher, philander, philanderer, womanizer

lading *n* ***syn*** LOAD 1, burden, cargo, freight, haul, payload

ladle *vb* ***syn*** DIP 2, bail, lade, scoop

lady *n* ***syn*** WIFE, ‖ball and chain, ‖little woman, ‖missus, Mrs., ‖old lady, ‖old woman, ‖rib, ‖squaw, woman

lady friend *n* ***syn*** GIRL FRIEND 1, best girl, ‖chick, ‖doney, gal, girl, lass, mouse, popsy

---

syn synonym(s) ***rel*** related word(s)
idiom idiomatic equivalent(s) ***con*** contrasted word(s)
ant antonym(s) * vulgar
‖ use limited; if in doubt, see a dictionary
The first word in a synonym list when printed in SMALL CAPITALS shows where there is more information about the group. For a more efficient use of this book see Explanatory Notes.

lady–killer *n* ***syn*** WOLF, Casanova, chaser, Don Juan, ladies' man, masher, philander, philanderer, womanizer

ladylove *n* ***syn*** GIRL FRIEND 2, ‖baby, beloved, flame, honey, inamorata, steady, sweetheart, sweetie, truelove

lag *vb* ***syn*** DELAY 2, dally, dawdle, drag, loiter, poke, procrastinate, put off, tarry, trail
rel retard, slacken, slow; stay

lag *adj* ***syn*** LAST, closing, concluding, eventual, final, hindmost, latest, latter, terminal, ultimate

‖**lag** *vb* ***syn*** BANISH, cast out, deport, displace, exile, expatriate, expel, expulse, relegate, transport

‖**lag** *n* ***syn*** CONVICT, ‖con, jailbird, loser, prison bird

laggard *adj* ***syn*** SLOW 2, deliberate, dilatory, leisurely, unhasty, unhurried
rel dawdling, delaying, loitering, procrastinating; comatose, lethargic, sluggish; apathetic, impassive, phlegmatic
con alert, vigilant, watchful, wide-awake; expeditious, fast, fleet, speedy
ant prompt, quick

laggard *n* one that delays unnecessarily or falls behind <no room for *laggards* on the expedition>
syn dawdler, lingerer, loiterer, slow coach, slowpoke, straggler
rel lazybones, loafer
con dynamo, go-ahead, go-getter, hustler, live wire, rustler; eager beaver

lagniappe *n* ***syn*** GRATUITY, cumshaw, largess, ‖palm grease, ‖palm oil, ‖perk(s), perquisite, pourboire, tip

lair *n* **1** a resting or living place of a wild animal <photographed the wolf at the entrance to his *lair*>
syn burrow, couch, den, lodge
2 ***syn*** HIDEOUT, den, hideaway

‖**lalapalooza** *n* ***syn*** ‖DILLY, ‖corker, crackerjack, ‖daisy, dandy, humdinger, jim-dandy, ‖lulu, peach, ‖pip

‖**lallygag** *vb* ***syn*** IDLE, bum, dawdle, diddle-daddle, goldbrick, laze, loaf, loiter, loll, lounge

lam *vb* ***syn*** BEAT 1, batter, drub, hammer, paste, pelt, pound, pummel, thrash, wallop

lam *n* ***syn*** ESCAPE 1, breakout, escapement, escaping, flight, getaway, ‖scape, slip

lambaste *vb* **1** ***syn*** BEAT 1, baste, drub, hammer, paste, pelt, pound, pummel, thrash, wallop
2 ***syn*** WHIP 2, beat, ‖clobber, drub, lick, shellac, smear, smother, thrash, trim
3 to assail with withering oral or written denunciation <the senator has been publicly *lambasted* for taking bribes>
syn blister, castigate, ‖crawl, drub, excoriate, flay, lash (into), roast, scarify, scathe, scorch, score, scourge, slam, slap, slash, ‖slate; *compare* CRITICIZE, REPROVE, SCOLD 1
rel censure, criticize, denounce, pan; berate, scold, tongue-lash; assail, attack, squabash
idiom burn one's ears, ‖crawl all over, give (one) a roasting, pin one's ears back, rake (one) over the coals, read the riot act, rip into
con applaud, extol, praise; approve, countenance, endorse

lambent *adj* ***syn*** BRIGHT 1, beaming, brilliant, effulgent, incandescent, lucent, luminous, lustrous, radiant, refulgent

lame–brain *n* ***syn*** DUNCE, chowderhead, chucklehead, dope, ‖dumbhead, dunderhead, noddy, noodle, ‖schnook, ‖stupe

lament *vb* ***syn*** DEPLORE 1, bemoan, bewail, grieve, moan, weep
ant exult; rejoice

lamentable *adj* **1** ***syn*** DEPLORABLE, afflictive, calamitous, dire, distressing, grievous, heartbreaking, regrettable, unfortunate, woeful
2 ***syn*** MELANCHOLY 2, doleful, dolesome, dolorous, lugubrious, mournful, plaintive, rueful, sorrowful, woeful

lamia *n* ***syn*** WITCH 1, bruja, enchantress, hag, hex, sorceress, witchwoman

lamp *n* ***syn*** EYE 1, ocular, oculus, ‖ogle, orb, peeper, winker

lampoonery *n* ***syn*** SATIRE, raillery, satiricalness

lampooning *adj* ***syn*** SATIRIC, satirizing

lance *vb* ***syn*** IMPALE, skewer, skiver, spear, spike, spit, transfix, transpierce

land *n* **1** ***syn*** EARTH 2, dirt, dry land, ground, soil, terra firma
2 ***syn*** COUNTRY, fatherland, home, homeland, mother country, motherland, soil
3 ***syn*** ESTATE 3, acres, manor, quinta

land *vb* **1** ***syn*** DISEMBARK, debark
2 ***syn*** ALIGHT, light, perch, roost, set down, settle, sit down, touch down
3 ***syn*** GET 1, acquire, annex, gain, have, obtain, pick up, procure, secure, win

‖**lang syne** *n* ***syn*** PAST, foretime, yesterday, yesteryear, yore

language *n* **1** a body or system of words and phrases used by a large community or by a people, a nation, or a group of nations <the English and French *languages*>
syn dialect, idiom, speech, tongue, vernacular
rel argot, cant, jargon, lingo, patois, slang
2 ***syn*** TERMINOLOGY, cant, dictionary, jargon, lexicon, palaver, vocabulary

languid *adj* lacking in vim or energy <doing the job in a slow and *languid* manner>
syn die-away, enervated, lackadaisical, languishing, languorous, limp, listless, spiritless
rel comatose, lethargic, sluggish, torpid; apathetic, impassive, phlegmatic; inactive, inert, supine
con alert, awake, ‖fly, keen, lively, wide-awake
ant vivacious; chipper

languish *vb* ***syn*** FAIL 1, decline, deteriorate, ‖dwine, fade, flag, weaken
ant flourish

languishing *adj* ***syn*** LANGUID, die-away, enervated, lackadaisical, languorous, limp, listless, spiritless
rel debilitated, enfeebled, weakened; faineant, indolent; longing, pining, yearning

---

syn synonym(s) *rel* related word(s)
idiom idiomatic equivalent(s) *con* contrasted word(s)
ant antonym(s) * vulgar
‖ use limited; if in doubt, see a dictionary
The first word in a synonym list when printed in SMALL CAPITALS shows where there is more information about the group. For a more efficient use of this book see Explanatory Notes.

con hale, healthy, robust, sound; energetic, lusty, vigorous
ant flourishing, thriving; unaffected

languor *n* ***syn*** LETHARGY 1, coma, dullness, hebetude, lassitude, sleep, slumber, stupor, torpidity, torpor
rel exhaustion, fatigue, weariness; blues, depression, dumps; doldrums, ennui, tedium
con celerity, legerity; gusto, zest
ant alacrity

languorous *adj* ***syn*** LANGUID, die-away, enervated, lackadaisical, languishing, limp, listless, spiritless
rel dilatory, laggard, leisurely, slow; faineant, indolent, slothful; passive; lax, loose, relaxed, slack; indulged, pampered
ant vigorous; strenuous (*of times, seasons*)

lank *adj* ***syn*** LEAN, angular, bony, gaunt, lanky, rawboned, scraggy, scrawny, skinny, spare
rel attenuated, extenuated
con chubby
ant burly

lanky *adj* **1** ***syn*** GANGLING, gangly, rangy, spindling, spindly
2 ***syn*** LEAN, angular, bony, gaunt, lank, rawboned, scraggy, scrawny, skinny, spare

lap *vb* ***syn*** OVERLAP, imbricate, overlie, override, ride, shingle

lap *vb* **1** ***syn*** SLOSH 1, bubble, burble, gurgle, swash, wash
2 ***syn*** BATHE 2, lave, lip, wash

lapse *n* **1** ***syn*** ERROR 2, blooper, blunder, boner, bull, bungle, fluff, mistake, slip, trip
rel crime, offense, sin, vice; failing, foible, frailty; breach, transgression, trespass, violation
2 a temporary deviation or fall especially from a higher to a lower state <a *lapse* into nonproductiveness> <ashamed of his *lapse* from grace>
syn backsliding, relapse
rel decadence, declension, decline, degeneration, deterioration, devolution; recession, retrogradation; regression, retrogression
con advance, progress; development, maturation; amendment; betterment, improvement

lapse *vb* to fall from a better or higher state into a lower or poorer one <*lapsed* into his old vulgar ways>
syn backslide, recidivate, relapse
rel return, revert; slide, slip; decline, degenerate, deteriorate; subside; descend; recede, retrograde; apostatize
con advance, progress; develop, mature; amend, mend; better, improve

larcener *n* ***syn*** THIEF, filcher, larcenist, nimmer, pilferer, prig, purloiner, stealer

larcenist *n* ***syn*** THIEF, filcher, larcener, nimmer, pilferer, prig, purloiner, stealer

larcenous *adj* prone to committing larceny <*larcenous* employees were robbing the company blind>
syn sticky-fingered, thieving, thievish
rel burglarious; light-fingered

larceny *n* ***syn*** THEFT, lift, pinch, purloining, steal, stealage, stealing, thievery, thieving, ‖touch

‖**lardy–dardy** *adj* ***syn*** GENTEEL 3, affected, la-di-da, mincing, pretentious, stilted, too-too

lares and penates *n pl* ***syn*** POSSESSION 2, belongings, chattels, effects, goods, movables, things

large *adj* **1** above the average of its kind in magnitude <a *large* increase in the tax rate>
syn big, bull, fat, great, husky, oversize
rel colossal, enormous, gigantic, huge, immense, mammoth, vast, voluminous; monstrous, monumental, prodigious, stupendous, tremendous; excessive, exorbitant, extravagant, extreme, immoderate, inordinate
con diminutive, little, minute, tiny, wee; slender, slight, slim, thin
ant small
2 ***syn*** BIG 1, considerable, extensive, hefty, large-scale, major, sizable

largely *adv* ***syn*** GENERALLY 1, chiefly, mainly, mostly, overall, predominantly, primarily, principally

largeness *n* ***syn*** SIZE 2, amplitude, bigness, greatness, magnitude, sizableness

large–scale *adj* ***syn*** BIG 1, considerable, extensive, hefty, large, major, sizable

largess *n* **1** ***syn*** GIFT 1, benevolence, boon, ‖compliment, favor, present
2 ***syn*** GRATUITY, cumshaw, lagniappe, ‖palm grease, ‖palm oil, ‖perk(s), perquisite, pourboire, tip

largest *adj* ***syn*** BEST, better, bettermost, greater, most

lark *n* **1** ***syn*** ESCAPADE, caper, rollick
2 ***syn*** PRANK, antic, caper, dido(es), frolic, monkeyshine, shenanigan, shine(s), tomfoolery, trick

larkish *adj* ***syn*** PLAYFUL 1, antic, frisky, frolicsome, gamesome, impish, ‖mischiefful, mischievous, prankful, prankish

‖**larrup** *vb* **1** ***syn*** WHIP 1, flagellate, flog, hide, lash, lather, scourge, stripe, thrash, whale
2 ***syn*** WHIP 2, beat, ‖clobber, drub, dust, lambaste, lick, mop (up), overwhelm, shellac

‖**larruping** *adv* ***syn*** VERY 1, ‖big, exceedingly, extremely, greatly, hugely, mightily, ‖monstrous, whacking, whopping

lascivious *adj* **1** ***syn*** LICENTIOUS 2, fast, incontinent, lecherous, lewd, libertine, libidinous, lustful, salacious, satyric
rel coarse, gross, obscene
2 ***syn*** LUSTFUL 2, concupiscent, goatish, *horny, hot, libidinous, lickerish, passionate, prurient, satyric

lash *vb* **1** ***syn*** RUSH 1, boil, bolt, charge, chase, dash, fling, race, shoot, tear
2 ***syn*** POUR 3, drench, teem
3 ***syn*** WHIP 1, flagellate, flog, hide, lather, scourge, stripe, thrash, ‖wear out, whale
4 ***syn*** WAG, beat, switch, waggle, wave, woggle
5 ***syn*** SCOLD 1, baste, bawl out, ‖bless out, ‖chew out, jaw, tell off, tongue-lash, upbraid, vituperate

lash (into) *vb* ***syn*** LAMBASTE 3, blister, castigate, excoriate, flay, scarify, scathe, scorch, scourge, slash

lashings *n pl* ***syn*** MUCH, barrel, lot, lump, mass, ‖mess, mountain, peck, ‖power, ‖sight

---

syn synonym(s) — *rel* related word(s)
idiom idiomatic equivalent(s) — *con* contrasted word(s)
ant antonym(s) — * vulgar
‖ use limited; if in doubt, see a dictionary
The first word in a synonym list when printed in SMALL CAPITALS shows where there is more information about the group. For a more efficient use of this book see Explanatory Notes.

lass *n* **1** ***syn*** GIRL 1, damsel, gal, lassie, maid, maiden, miss, missy, ||quail, wench
2 ***syn*** GIRL FRIEND 1, best girl, ||chick, ||doney, gal, girl, lady friend, mouse, popsy

lassie *n* ***syn*** GIRL 1, damsel, gal, lass, maid, maiden, miss, missy, ||quail, wench

lassitude *n* **1** ***syn*** FATIGUE, exhaustion, tiredness, weariness
2 ***syn*** APATHY 2, disinterest, disregard, heedlessness, indifference, insouciance, lethargy, listlessness, unconcern, unmindfulness
3 ***syn*** LETHARGY 1, dullness, hebetude, languor, sleep, slumber, stupor, torpidity, torpidness, torpor
rel doldrums, ennui, tedium; blues, depression, dumps; impotence, powerlessness
con energy, force, might, power, strength
ant vigor

last *vb* ***syn*** CONTINUE 1, abide, carry through, endure, perdure, persist

last *adj* following all relevant others (as in time, order, or importance) <he was the *last* one in line>
syn closing, concluding, eventual, final, hindmost, lag, latest, latter, rearmost, terminal, terminating, ultimate
rel bottommost, end, extreme, furthest, outermost, remotest, utmost, uttermost
con beginning, inaugural, initial, introductory, original, primary, prime
ant first

lasting *adj* existing or continuing for so long a time as to seem fixed or established <his reading made a *lasting* impression on him>
syn diuturnal, durable, enduring, perdurable, perduring, permanent, stable; *compare* OLD 2
rel abiding, continuing, persisting; endless, everlasting, unceasing; continual, continuous, incessant, perennial, unremitting; eternal, sempiternal; indelible, indissoluble, inexhaustible, inexpugnable, inexpungible
con ephemeral, evanescent, fugitive, momentary, passing, short-lived, transient, transitory
ant fleeting

last word *n* ***syn*** APOTHEOSIS 1, epitome, quintessence, ultimate

late *adj* **1** ***syn*** TARDY, behindhand, belated, lated, overdue, unpunctual
con opportune, seasonable, well-timed
ant early; prompt, punctual
2 ***syn*** DEAD 1, asleep, cold, deceased, defunct, departed, exanimate, extinct, inanimate, lifeless
3 ***syn*** FORMER 2, bygone, erstwhile, old, once, onetime, past, quondam, sometime, whilom
4 ***syn*** MODERN 1, recent

lated *adj* ***syn*** TARDY, behindhand, belated, late, overdue, unpunctual

lately *adv* ***syn*** NEW, afresh, anew, newly, of late, recently

latency *n* ***syn*** ABEYANCE, abeyancy, cold storage, doldrums, dormancy, intermission, interruption, quiescence, quiescency, suspension

latent *adj* not now manifest or showing signs of existence or activity <a *latent* infection>
syn abeyant, dormant, lurking, potential, prepatent, quiescent
rel concealed, hidden; idle, inactive, inert; immature, unmatured, unripe
con active, dynamic, live, operative; activated, energized, vitalized
ant patent

later *adj* ***syn*** SUBSEQUENT 1, after, ensuing, posterior, postliminary, subsequential

later *adv* ***syn*** AFTER, afterward, afterwhile, behind, by and by, infra, latterly, next, subsequently
ant earlier

laterally *adv* ***syn*** SIDEWAYS 1, crabwise, sideling, ||sidelings, sidelong, sideward, sidewise

latest *adj* ***syn*** LAST, closing, concluding, eventual, final, hindmost, lag, latter, rearmost, terminal
ant earliest

lather *n* **1** ***syn*** FOAM, froth, spume, suds, yeast
2 ***syn*** COMMOTION 4, bustle, clamor, hassle, hubbub, hurly-burly, moil, rowdydow, storm, whoopla
3 ***syn*** COMMOTION 2, agitation, confusion, dither, flap, pother, stew, tumult, turbulence, turmoil

lather *vb* ***syn*** WHIP 1, flagellate, flog, hide, lash, scourge, stripe, thrash, ||wear out, whale

latitude *n* ***syn*** ROOM 3, elbowroom, leeway, margin, play, scope

latrine *n* ***syn*** TOILET, ||can, convenience, head, john, johnny, lavatory, ||loo, privy, water closet

latter *adj* ***syn*** LAST, closing, concluding, eventual, final, hindmost, lag, latest, rearmost, terminal
ant former

latterly *adv* ***syn*** AFTER, afterward, afterwhile, behind, by and by, infra, later, next, subsequently

laud *vb* ***syn*** PRAISE 2, bless, celebrate, cry up, eulogize, extol, glorify, hymn, magnify, panegyrize
rel adore, revere, reverence, venerate, worship; admire; flatter
con blame, condemn; anathematize, curse, damn, execrate, objurgate
ant revile

laudable *adj* ***syn*** WORTHY 1, admirable, commendable, deserving, estimable, meritable, meritorious, praisable, praiseworthy, thankworthy
ant illaudable

laudative *adj* ***syn*** EULOGISTIC, encomiastic, laudatory, panegyrical, praiseful

laudatory *adj* ***syn*** EULOGISTIC, encomiastic, laudative, panegyrical, praiseful

laugh *vb* to show mirth, joy, or scorn with a smile and a usually explosive sound <*laughed* at all the funny things that happened>
syn chortle, chuckle, giggle, guffaw, hee-haw, snicker, ||sniggle, tehee, titter
rel cachinnate, cackle, crow, roar, whoop; beam, grin, simper, smile, smirk

laughable *adj* provoking laughter or mirth <the *laughable* antics of the clowns>

---

syn synonym(s)	*rel* related word(s)
idiom idiomatic equivalent(s)	*con* contrasted word(s)
ant antonym(s)	* vulgar

|| use limited; if in doubt, see a dictionary
The first word in a synonym list when printed in SMALL CAPITALS shows where there is more information about the group. For a more efficient use of this book see Explanatory Notes.

syn comic, comical, droll, farcical, funny, gelastic, ludicrous, ridiculous, risible
rel amusing, diverting, entertaining, rich; facetious, humorous, jocose, jocular, witty; derisive, derisory, mocking
con grave, serious, solemn; boring, irksome, tedious, tiresome, wearisome; affecting, impressive, moving, pathetic, poignant, touching

laughingstock *n* an object of ridicule <totally unaware that he was the *laughingstock* of the entire office>
syn butt, derision, jest, jestee, joke, mock, mockery, pilgarlic, sport
rel gazingstock; mark, target

launch *vb* **1** *syn* THROW 1, ‖bung, cast, fire, fling, heave, hurl, pitch, sling, toss
2 *syn* BEGIN 1, commence, embark (on *or* upon), get off, inaugurate, initiate, jump (off), kick off, open, start
3 *syn* INTRODUCE 3, inaugurate, initiate, institute, originate, set up, usher in

laurels *n pl syn* HONOR 2, accolade, award, badge, bays, decoration, distinction, kudos

lavatory *n syn* TOILET, convenience, ‖donicker, head, john, johnny, latrine, ‖loo, privy, water closet

lave *vb syn* BATHE 2, lap, lip, wash

lavish *adj* **1** *syn* PROFUSE, exuberant, lush, luxuriant, opulent, prodigal, profusive, riotous
con scant, scanty; economical, frugal, thrifty; discreet, provident, prudent; miserly, niggardly, parsimonious, penurious, stingy
ant sparing
2 *syn* GRAND 2, gorgeous, impressive, luxurious, splendid, sumptuous

lavishness *n syn* EXTRAVAGANCE 2, extravagancy, overdoing, prodigality, squander, unthrift, waste, wastefulness
ant sparingness

law *n* **1** a principle governing conduct, action, or procedure <found it hard to live by outdated *laws*>
syn assize, canon, decree, decretum, edict, institute, ordinance, precept, prescript, prescription, regulation, rule, statute
rel command, dictate, mandate
2 *syn* PRINCIPLE 1, axiom, fundamental, principium, theorem
rel exigency, necessity
ant chance

lawbreaker *n syn* CRIMINAL, felon, malefactor, offender

lawcourt *n syn* COURT 2, bar, tribunal

lawful *adj* being in accordance with law <obtained *lawful* custody of the child>
syn innocent, legal, legitimate, licit
rel condign, due, rightful; allowable, permissible; justifiable, warrantable; bona fide
idiom of right
con flagitious, iniquitous, nefarious; improper, unjustifiable, wrong; criminal, guilty, peccant; illegitimate, illicit
ant lawless, unlawful

lawless *adj syn* UNLAWFUL, criminal, illegal, illegitimate, illicit, wrongful
ant lawful

lawlessness *n syn* ANARCHY 1, chaos, mobocracy, ochlocracy
rel conflict, contention, difference, discord, dissension, strife, variance

lawsuit *n syn* SUIT 1, action, case, cause

lawyer *n* a person authorized to practice law in the courts or to serve clients in the capacity of legal agent or adviser <took the problem to his family *lawyer*>
syn attorney, attorney-at-law; *compare* PETTIFOGGER
rel advocate, ‖barrister, counsel, counselor, ‖mouthpiece, pleader, ‖solicitor; jurisconsult, jurisprudent, jurist; legist

lax *vb syn* LOOSE 5, ease, ease off, loosen, relax, slack, slacken, untighten

lax *adj* **1** *syn* LOOSE 1, relaxed, slack
con firm, hard, solid; elastic, resilient, springy
ant rigid
2 *syn* NEGLIGENT, behindhand, careless, delinquent, derelict, disregardful, neglectful, regardless, remiss, slack
rel forgetful, oblivious, unmindful
con austere, severe, stern; rigid, rigorous; conscientious, honest, upright, scrupulous
ant strict, stringent

lay *vb* **1** *syn* SET 1, establish, fix, place, put, settle, stick
2 *syn* GAMBLE 1, bet, game, play, put (on), set, stake, wager
3 *syn* EVEN 1, flatten, flush, level, plane, smooth, smoothen
4 *syn* ASCRIBE, accredit, assign, attribute, charge, credit, impute, refer
5 *syn* DIRECT 2, address, aim, cast, incline, level, point, train, turn, zero (in)
6 *syn* SET 5, spread
7 *syn* ADDUCE, advance, allege, cite, offer, present

lay (for) *vb syn* SURPRISE 1, ambush, waylay

lay (open) *vb syn* EXPOSE 1, subject, uncover

lay *n* **1** *syn* MELODY, air, descant, diapason, measure, melisma, melodia, strain, tune, warble
2 *syn* SONG 2, aria, descant, ditty, hymn, lied

lay *adj syn* PROFANE 1, secular, temporal, unsacred
con professional

lay aside *vb* **1** *syn* DISCARD, cast, chuck, ditch, jettison, reject, scrap, shed, slough, throw away
2 *syn* SAVE 4, lay away, lay by, lay in, lay up, put by, salt away, ‖spare

lay away *vb* **1** *syn* SAVE 4, lay aside, lay by, lay in, lay up, put by, salt away, ‖spare
2 *syn* BURY 1, entomb, inhume, inter, plant, put away, sepulcher, sepulture, tomb

lay by *vb syn* SAVE 4, lay aside, lay away, lay in, lay up, put by, salt away, ‖spare

lay down *vb* **1** *syn* RELINQUISH, abandon, cede, give up, hand over, leave, resign, surrender, waive, yield
2 *syn* PRESCRIBE 2, assign, define
3 *syn* DICTATE, decree, impose, ordain, prescribe, set

---

syn synonym(s) — *rel* related word(s)
idiom idiomatic equivalent(s) — *con* contrasted word(s)
ant antonym(s) — * vulgar
‖ use limited; if in doubt, see a dictionary
The first word in a synonym list when printed in SMALL CAPITALS shows where there is more information about the group. For a more efficient use of this book see Explanatory Notes.

layer *n* ***syn*** BOOKMAKER, bookie

lay in *vb* ***syn*** SAVE 4, lay aside, lay away, lay by, lay up, put by, salt away, ‖spare

lay low *vb* **1** ***syn*** FELL 1, bowl (down *or* over), flatten, floor, ground, knock down, knock over, level, mow (down), throw down

2 ***syn*** KILL 1, cut off, destroy, dispatch, down, finish, put away, scrag, slay, take off

lay off *vb* ***syn*** REST 3, breathe, lie by, spell

lay out *vb* **1** ***syn*** DESIGN 3, arrange, map (out), plan, set out

2 ***syn*** SPEND 1, disburse, expend, fork (out), give, outlay, pay, shell out

lay over *vb* ***syn*** DEFER, delay, hold off, hold over, hold up, postpone, put off, shelve, stay, suspend

lay up *vb* **1** ***syn*** ACCUMULATE, amass, cumulate, garner, hive, roll up, stockpile, store (up), uplay

2 ***syn*** SAVE 4, lay aside, lay away, lay by, lay in, put by, salt away, ‖spare

laze *vb* ***syn*** IDLE, bum, dawdle, goldbrick, ‖goof (off), lazy, loaf, loiter, loll, lounge

con drudge, grind, labor, toil, travail, work

laze *n* ***syn*** SLOTH 1, idleness, indolence, laziness, slothfulness, slouch, sluggishness

laziness *n* ***syn*** SLOTH 1, idleness, indolence, laze, slothfulness, slouch, sluggishness

ant industriousness

lazy *adj* not easily aroused to action or activity <the hot humid weather made them *lazy*>

syn drony, easygoing, faineant, indolent, slothful, slowgoing, work-shy

rel idle, inactive, inert, passive, supine, trifling; comatose, lethargic, sluggish, torpid; lackadaisical, languid, languorous, listless, unenergetic, unindustrious; lax, neglectful, negligent, remiss, shiftless, slack

con diligent, hardworking; brisk, chipper, energetic, vigorous; active, animated, lively, spry, vivacious; prompt, quick, ready

ant industrious

lazy *vb* ***syn*** IDLE, bum, dawdle, goldbrick, ‖goof (off), laze, loaf, loiter, loll, lounge

lazybones *n* ***syn*** SLUGGARD, bum, dolittle, do-nothing, faineant, idler, loafer, slouch, slug, slugabed

lead *vb* **1** ***syn*** GUIDE, conduct, direct, escort, pilot, route, see, shepherd, show, steer

rel get, induce, persuade, prevail

con drive, impel; coerce, compel, constrain, force, oblige

ant follow

2 ***syn*** PRECEDE 3, introduce, preface, usher

3 ***syn*** CONVERT 1, bring, move, persuade

lead *n* ***syn*** LEADER 1, ‖bell cow, bellwether, dean, doyen, guide, pilot

---

syn synonym(s)	***rel*** related word(s)
idiom idiomatic equivalent(s)	***con*** contrasted word(s)
ant antonym(s)	* vulgar

‖ use limited; if in doubt, see a dictionary

The first word in a synonym list when printed in SMALL CAPITALS shows where there is more information about the group. For a more efficient use of this book see Explanatory Notes.

leader *n* **1** one that takes the lead or initiative <each group selected its own *leader* for the tour>

syn ‖bell cow, bellwether, dean, doyen, guide, lead, pilot

rel pacemaker, pacesetter; forerunner, harbinger, herald, precursor; conductor, director, rector

con adherent, dependent, hanger-on, henchman, satellite

ant follower

2 a person in whom resides authority or ruling power <the company had only one *leader*>

syn boss, chief, chieftain, cock, dominator, head, headman, hierarch, honcho, master

rel captain, commander, general; director, principal, superintendent, superior; foreman, manager, straw boss

con inferior, subaltern, subordinate, underling, understrapper

3 ***syn*** NOTABLE 1, big-timer, ‖big wheel, bigwig, chief, dignitary, eminence, lion, luminary, notability

leading *adj* **1** ***syn*** FIRST 1, foremost, headmost, inaugural, initial

2 ***syn*** FIRST 3, arch, champion, chief, foremost, head, premier, principal

ant subordinate

3 ***syn*** WELL-KNOWN, famous, noted, notorious, popular, prominent

lead off *vb* ***syn*** BEGIN 1, commence, embark (on *or* upon), enter, inaugurate, initiate, launch, open, set to, start

lead on *vb* **1** ***syn*** LURE, allure, bait, decoy, entice, entrap, inveigle, seduce, tempt, toll

2 ***syn*** TRIFLE 1, coquet, dally, flirt, fool, string along, toy, wanton

leaf (through) *vb* ***syn*** BROWSE, dip (into), flip (through), glance (at *or* over), riff (through), riffle (through), run (through *or* over), scan, skim (through), thumb (through)

leafage *n* ***syn*** FOLIAGE, umbrage, verdure

league *n* **1** ***syn*** ALLIANCE 2, anschluss, coalition, confederacy, confederation, federation, union

2 ***syn*** ASSOCIATION 2, brotherhood, club, fellowship, fraternity, guild, order, society, sodality, union

3 ***syn*** CLASS 1, category, grade, group, grouping, pigeonhole, tier

4 a group of sports clubs or teams that play one another competitively <the new baseball *league*>

syn association, circuit, conference, loop, wheel

rel division

league *vb* ***syn*** UNITE 2, band, coadjute, combine, concur, conjoin, cooperate

leak *vb* ***syn*** GET OUT 2, break, come out, out, transpire

lean *vb* **1** ***syn*** SLANT 1, cant, heel, incline, list, recline, slope, tilt, tip

rel bend, curve; deflect, divert, sheer, turn

2 ***syn*** TEND 1, incline, look

lean (over) *vb* ***syn*** HANG 4, beetle, bend (over), jut, overhang

lean *n* ***syn*** SLOPE, grade, gradient, inclination, incline, leaning, slant, tilt

lean *adj* thin because of absence of superfluous flesh <a *lean* strong horse>

syn angular, bony, gaunt, lank, lanky, meager, rawboned, scraggy, scrawny, skinny, spare; *compare* THIN 1

rel slender, slight, slim, spare-set, stringy, thin; cadaverous, haggard, pinched, wasted, worn; wizened
con brawny, burly, husky, muscular, sinewy; stalwart, stout, strong, sturdy; corpulent, fat, fatty, flabby, obese, plump, portly, rotund
ant fleshy

leaning *n* **1** *syn* SLOPE, grade, gradient, inclination, incline, lean, slant, tilt
2 an attraction to a particular activity, thing, or end <a strong *leaning* toward liberal views>
syn bent, bias, disposition, drift, inclination, inclining, lurch, partiality, penchant, predilection, predisposition, proclivity, propensity, sentiment, tendency; *compare* GIFT 2, PREJUDICE
rel favor, favoritism, odds
con avoidance, evasion, shunning; disdaining, scorning, scouting, spurning; disinterest, dislike, distaste

leaning *adj syn* INCLINED 3, inclining, oblique, pitched, pitching, sloped, sloping, tilted, tilting, tipped

leap *vb* **1** *syn* JUMP 1, bounce, bound, hop, hurdle, lop, saltate, spring, vault
rel arise, ascend, mount, rise, soar
con drop, fall, sink, slump
2 *syn* CLEAR 8, hurdle, negotiate, over, overleap, surmount, vault

learn *vb* **1** to acquire knowledge of or skill in by study and experience <*learn* a trade>
syn get, master, pick up
rel con, peruse, study
idiom make oneself master of
2 *syn* MEMORIZE, con, get
3 *syn* DISCOVER 3, ascertain, catch on, determine, find out, hear, see, tumble, unearth

learned *adj* possessing or manifesting unusually wide and deep knowledge <a most *learned* scholar in his field>
syn erudite, scholarly, scholastic
rel cultivated, cultured; academic, bookish, pedantic, professorial; abstruse, esoteric, polymath, recondite
con ignorant, illiterate, uneducated, unlearned, unlettered, untutored

learnedness *n syn* ERUDITION 2, eruditeness, scholarliness, scholarship

learning *n syn* EDUCATION 2, erudition, knowledge, scholarship, science

lease *vb syn* HIRE 1, charter, let, rent

leash *vb syn* HAMPER, clog, curb, entrammel, fetter, hobble, hog-tie, shackle, tie, trammel

least *adj syn* FIRST 4, slightest, smallest

leave *vb* **1** *syn* WILL, bequeath, devise, legate
rel commit, confide, consign, entrust; allot, apportion, assign
2 *syn* LET 2, allow, have, permit, suffer
3 *syn* GO 2, ||blow, depart, exit, get away, get off, pull out, quit, retire, withdraw
4 *syn* QUIT 6, drop, resign, terminate
5 *syn* RELINQUISH, abandon, cede, give up, hand over, resign, surrender, ||turn up, waive, yield

leave *n* **1** *syn* PERMISSION, allowance, authorization, consent, permit, sanction, sufferance
rel assent
con refusal, rejection; forbiddance, interdiction, prohibition
2 *syn* VACATION, holiday

leaven *vb syn* INFUSE 1, imbue, ingrain, inoculate, invest, steep, suffuse
rel moderate, qualify, temper; enliven, quicken, vivify

leave off *vb syn* STOP 3, cease, desist, ||deval, discontinue, give over, halt, knock off, quit, surcease

leave–taking *n syn* PARTING, adieu, congé, farewell, good-bye

leaving *n, usu* **leavings** *pl syn* REMAINDER, balance, heel, remains, remanet, remnant, residual, residue, residuum, rest
rel fragments, pieces, portions; discards, junk, scrap

lecherous *adj syn* LICENTIOUS 2, fast, incontinent, lascivious, lewd, libertine, libidinous, lustful, salacious, satyric

lecture *n syn* SPEECH 2, address, allocution, talk

lecture *vb syn* TALK 7, address, prelect, speak

ledger *n syn* TOMBSTONE, footstone, grave marker, gravestone, headstone, monument

leech *n syn* PARASITE, barnacle, bloodsucker, freeloader, hanger-on, lounge lizard, ||spiv, sponge, sponger, sucker

leer *vb syn* SNEER 1, fleer, ||sleer

lees *n pl syn* SEDIMENT, deposit, dreg(s), grounds, precipitate, precipitation, settlings

leeway *n syn* ROOM 3, elbowroom, latitude, margin, play, scope

left–handed *adj syn* INSINCERE, ambidextrous, double, double-dealing, double-faced, doublehearted, double-minded, double-tongued, hypocritical, mala fide

legacy *n* **1** a gift by will especially of money or personal property <received a *legacy* of $5,000 from her late uncle>
syn bequest, devise, inheritance
2 *syn* HERITAGE 1, birthright, heritance, inheritance, patrimony

legal *adj syn* LAWFUL, innocent, legitimate, licit
ant illegal

legal tender *n syn* MONEY, ||bread, cash, ||coin, currency, dough, ||greenbacks, ||jack, lucre, ||scratch

legate *vb syn* WILL, bequeath, devise, leave

legend *n* **1** *syn* MYTH 1, mythos, mythus
2 *syn* CAPTION, underline
3 *syn* LORE 2, folklore, myth, mythology, mythos, tradition

legendary *adj syn* MYTHICAL, fabulous, mythological

legerdemain *n syn* MAGIC 2, conjuring

legion *n syn* MULTITUDE 1, army, cloud, crowd, flock, host, rout, scores

legion *adj syn* MANY, multifarious, multitudinal, multitudinous, numerous, populous, ||several, sundry, various, voluminous

legitimate *adj* **1** *syn* LAWFUL, innocent, legal, licit
rel cogent, sound, valid; acknowledged, recognized; customary, usual; natural, normal, regular, typical

---

syn synonym(s) *rel* related word(s)
idiom idiomatic equivalent(s) *con* contrasted word(s)
ant antonym(s) * vulgar
|| use limited; if in doubt, see a dictionary
The first word in a synonym list when printed in SMALL CAPITALS shows where there is more information about the group. For a more efficient use of this book see Explanatory Notes.

ant illegitimate
2 ***syn*** TRUE 8, rightful
ant arbitrary

leisure *n* ***syn*** REST 1, ease, relaxation, repose, requiescence
con drudgery, grind, labor
ant toil

leisurely *adj* ***syn*** SLOW 2, deliberate, dilatory, laggard, unhasty, unhurried
rel lax, relaxed, slack; delayed, retarded, slackened; comfortable, easy, restful
con fast, hasty, quick, rapid, speedy; headlong, impetuous, precipitate
ant hurried; abrupt

leitmotiv *n* a dominant recurring thematic element or feature (as in a work of art) <the *leitmotiv* of man against nature often appears in his paintings>
syn motif
rel motive, theme

lemon *n* ***syn*** FAILURE 5, bomb, bust, dud, flop, loser

lend *vb* to give into another's keeping for temporary use on condition that the borrower return the same or its equivalent <I do not have another copy of the book to give, but I can *lend* you mine>
syn advance, loan
rel lease-lend, lend-lease; allow, furnish, give; accommodate, oblige

length *n* **1** ***syn*** DISTANCE 1, stretch
2 ***syn*** RANGE 2, compass, orbit, panorama, purview, radius, reach, realm, scope, stretch

lengthen *vb* ***syn*** EXTEND 3, draw, draw out, elongate, prolong, prolongate, protract, spin (out), stretch
ant shorten; abbreviate

lengthening *n* ***syn*** EXTENSION 1, elongation, production, prolongation, prolongment, protraction
ant shortening

lengthways *adv* ***syn*** LENGTHWISE, endways, endwise, longitudinally, longways, longwise
ant widthways, widthwise

lengthwise *adv* in the direction of the length <the students folded their papers *lengthwise*>
syn endways, endwise, lengthways, longitudinally, longways, longwise
con latitudinally, widthways; broadside, broadway, broadwise
ant widthways, widthwise

lengthy *adj* **1** ***syn*** LONG 2, dragging, drawn-out, ‖dreich, long-drawn-out, longsome, overlong, prolonged, protracted
ant short
2 ***syn*** LONG 1, elongate, elongated, extended

lenience *n* ***syn*** FORBEARANCE 2, clemency, indulgence, leniency, mercifulness, tolerance, toleration

leniency *n* ***syn*** FORBEARANCE 2, clemency, indulgence, lenience, mercifulness, tolerance, toleration

lenient *adj* **1** ***syn*** GENTLE 1, balmy, bland, faint, mild, smooth, soft
ant caustic
2 ***syn*** FORBEARING, charitable, clement, easy, indulgent, merciful, tolerant
rel condoning, excusing, forgiving, pardoning; benign, benignant, kindly; compassionate, tender; humoring, indulging, pampering, mollycoddling, spoiling
con rigid, rigorous, stringent; austere, severe
ant stern; exacting
3 ***syn*** AMIABLE 1, complaisant, easy, good-humored, good-natured, good-tempered, mild, obliging

lenity *n* ***syn*** MERCY, caritas, charity, clemency, grace
rel tenderness; benevolence, charitableness, humaneness
con rigidity, rigorousness, strictness, stringency; austerity, sternness
ant severity

leper *n* ***syn*** OUTCAST, castaway, derelict, Ishmael, Ishmaelite, offscouring, pariah, untouchable

lessen *vb* **1** ***syn*** ABRIDGE 1, curtail, diminish, minify
rel amputate, clip, crop, truncate
2 ***syn*** DECREASE, abate, ‖bate, close, diminish, drain (away), dwindle, reduce, taper, taper off
rel attenuate, dilute, thin, weaken

lesser *adj* **1** ***syn*** INFERIOR 1, low, lower, nether, subjacent, under
2 ***syn*** MINOR 2, dinky, insignificant, minor-league, secondary, small, small-fry, small-time

lesson *n* ***syn*** EXERCISE 4, study

lesson *vb* ***syn*** REPROVE, admonish, call down, chide, monish, rebuke, reprimand, reproach, ‖sneap, tick off

let *vb* **1** ***syn*** HIRE 1, charter, lease, rent
2 to neither forbid nor prevent <*let* the boy go to the movies>
syn allow, have, leave, permit, suffer
rel accredit, approve, certify, endorse, sanction; authorize, commission, license; concede, grant
con ban, enjoin, forbid, inhibit, interdict, prohibit; bar, block, hinder, impede, obstruct; circumvent, foil, frustrate, thwart

let down *vb* ***syn*** LOWER 3, couch, demit, depress, droop, sink

lethal *adj* ***syn*** DEADLY 1, deathly, fatal, mortal, mortiferous, pestilent, pestilential
con renewing, restorative, restoring

lethality *n* ***syn*** FATALITY 1, deadliness, mortality

lethargic *adj* deficient in alertness or activity <became *lethargic* after taking the drug>
syn comatose, dopey, heavy, hebetudinous, sluggish, slumberous, stupid, torpid
rel dormant, idle, inactive, inert, passive, supine; apathetic, impassive, phlegmatic, spiritless, stolid; lackadaisical, languid, languorous, listless; dilatory, laggard, slow
con alert, aware, responsive; apt, prompt, quick, ready; brisk, gingery, peppery, spirited
ant energetic

lethargy *n* **1** physical and mental inertness <disgusted, he sank into a state of *lethargy*>
syn coma, dullness, hebetude, languor, lassitude, sleep, slumber, stupor, torpidity, torpidness, torpor

---

syn synonym(s) ***rel*** related word(s)
idiom idiomatic equivalent(s) ***con*** contrasted word(s)
ant antonym(s) * vulgar
‖ use limited; if in doubt, see a dictionary
The first word in a synonym list when printed in SMALL CAPITALS shows where there is more information about the group. For a more efficient use of this book see Explanatory Notes.

rel comatoseness, sluggishness; indolence, laziness, sloth, slothfulness; idleness, inactivity, inertia, inertness, passiveness, supineness; apathy, impassivity, inanition, phlegm
con aptness, promptness, quickness, readiness; alertness, quick-wittedness
ant vigor
2 *syn* APATHY 2, disinterest, disregard, heedlessness, indifference, insouciance, lassitude, listlessness, unconcern, unmindfulness

lethe *n syn* OBLIVION, forgetfulness, obliviousness

let off *vb syn* EXEMPT, absolve, discharge, dispense, excuse, privilege (from), relieve, spare

let on *vb* **1** *syn* ACKNOWLEDGE 1, admit, allow, avow, concede, confess, fess (up), grant, own, own up
2 *syn* REVEAL 1, betray, disclose, divulge, give away, ‖let out, spill, tell, uncover, unveil

let out *vb* ‖**1** *syn* REVEAL 1, betray, blab (out), disclose, discover, divulge, give away, mouth, spill, tell
2 *syn* DISMISS 3, ax, boot (out), bounce, ‖can, cashier, discharge, drop, fire, terminate

letter *n* **1 letters** *pl syn* ALPHABET 1, ABC(s), christcross-row
2 a direct or personal written or printed message addressed to a person or organization <wrote several *letters* to his friends>
syn epistle, missive, note
rel dispatch, memorandum, message, report

‖**lettuce** *n syn* MONEY, dough, filthy lucre, ‖gelt, ‖greenbacks, ‖jack, ‖kale, ‖long green, loot, lucre

let up *vb syn* ABATE 4, die (down *or* away), ease off, ebb, fall, moderate, relent, slacken, subside, wane

levee *n* **1** *syn* WHARF, berth, dock, jetty, pier, quay, slip
2 *syn* RED-LIGHT DISTRICT, stew(s), tenderloin

level *vb* **1** *syn* EVEN 1, flatten, flush, lay, plane, smooth, smoothen
2 *syn* DIRECT 2, address, aim, cast, incline, lay, point, train, turn, zero (in)
3 *syn* FELL 1, bring down, down, drop, flatten, floor, ground, knock down, knock over, mow (down)

level *adj* having a surface without bends, curves, or irregularities <looked for a *level* spot to land the plane>
syn even, flat, flush, planate, plane, smooth
rel akin, alike, identical, like, parallel, similar, uniform; aligned; regular; equal, equivalent, same
con bumpy, irregular, lumpy, uneven; unaligned, unparallel; changing, varying; fluctuating, rolling, swaying, undulating; coarse, rough

lever *vb syn* PRY, jimmy, prize

leviathan *n syn* GIANT, behemoth, mammoth, monster, whale

leviathan *adj syn* HUGE, cyclopean, elephantine, enormous, gargantuan, giant, gigantic, immense, mammoth, monster

levity *n syn* LIGHTNESS, flightiness, flippancy, frivolity, light-mindedness, volatility
rel absurdity, folly, foolishness, silliness
con collection, quietude, sobriety
ant gravity

levy *n syn* TAX 1, assessment, ‖cess, duty, impost, tariff

levy *vb* to determine and require satisfaction of (as a tax or obligation) <several broad-based taxes were *levied*>
syn assess, exact, impose, put (on *or* upon)
rel extort, wrest, wring; charge, lay (on *or* upon), place, set
con remit; abate, diminish, lessen

lewd *adj syn* LICENTIOUS 2, fast, incontinent, lascivious, lecherous, libertine, libidinous, lustful, salacious, satyric
rel coarse, gross, obscene; improper, indecent, indelicate
con modest, proper, self-restrained; temperate
ant chaste

lexicon *n* **1** *syn* VOCABULARY 1, word-hoard, word*stock
2 *syn* TERMINOLOGY, cant, dictionary, jargon, language, palaver, vocabulary

lexiphanicism *n syn* BOMBAST, fustian, highfalutin, rant, rhapsody, rhetoric, rodomontade

liability *n* **1** *syn* DEBT 3, arrear(s), arrearage, due, indebtedness
ant asset
2 *syn* INDEBTEDNESS 1, arrearage, debt, obligation
3 *syn* EXPOSURE, openness, vulnerability, vulnerableness

liable *adj* **1** *syn* RESPONSIBLE, accountable, amenable, answerable
rel bound, tied
con exempt, immune; free, independent
2 being likely to be affected by some usually adverse contingency or action <without the heat shield he was *liable* to be burned>
syn exposed, obnoxious, open, prone, sensitive, subject, susceptible
rel assailable, penetrable, vulnerable; attackable, beatable, conquerable, vincible
ant unliable
3 *syn* APT 1, given, inclined, likely, prone
ant unliable

liaison *n syn* AMOUR 2, affair, intrigue

liar *n* one that tells lies <he is a compulsive *liar*>
syn Ananias, falsifier, fibber, fibster, perjurer, prevaricator, storyteller

libel *vb syn* MALIGN, asperse, calumniate, defame, denigrate, scandalize, slander, tear down, traduce, vilify
rel burlesque, caricature, travesty

libelous *adj* injurious to reputation <the campaign degenerated into an exchange of *libelous* statements>
syn backbiting, calumnious, defamatory, detracting, detractive, detractory, invidious, maligning, scandalous, slanderous, traducing, vilifying
rel depreciative, depreciatory, derogative, disparaging, pejorative; contumelious, debasing, malevolent, vituperative
con adulating, adulatory, applauding, commendatory, eulogistic, eulogizing, laudatory, praising

---

syn synonym(s) *rel* related word(s)
idiom idiomatic equivalent(s) *con* contrasted word(s)
ant antonym(s) * vulgar
‖ use limited; if in doubt, see a dictionary
The first word in a synonym list when printed in SMALL CAPITALS shows where there is more information about the group. For a more efficient use of this book see Explanatory Notes.

liberal *adj* **1** marked by generosity and openhandedness <a *liberal* allowance for his son>
syn bounteous, bountiful, free, freehanded, generous, handsome, munificent, openhanded, unsparing
rel exuberant, lavish, prodigal, profuse; benevolent, charitable, eleemosynary, philanthropic
con closefisted, miserly, niggardly, parsimonious, penurious, stingy, tight, tightfisted; meager, scanty
ant close
2 ***syn*** PLENTIFUL, abundant, ample, bounteous, bountiful, copious, generous, plenteous, plenty
3 not bound by authoritarianism, orthodoxy, or traditional forms <modern young people usually have a *liberal* attitude toward sex>
syn advanced, broad, broad-minded, progressive, radical, tolerant, wide
rel forbearing, indulgent, lenient
con rigid, rigorous, strict, stringent; dictatorial, doctrinaire, dogmatic, oracular; conservative, reactionary
ant authoritarian

liberate *vb* ***syn*** FREE, discharge, emancipate, loose, loosen, manumit, release, unbind, unchain, unshackle
rel detach, unhook; untangle; disembarrass
con bind, tie; ensnare, entrap, snare, trap; constrain, restrain, restrict

libertine *adj* ***syn*** LICENTIOUS 2, fast, incontinent, lascivious, lecherous, lewd, libidinous, lustful, salacious, satyric
con ethical; continent, sober, temperate
ant straitlaced

liberty *n* ***syn*** FREEDOM, license
rel autonomy, independence; delivery, emancipation, enfranchisement, liberation
con circumscription, confinement, limitation, restriction
ant restraint

libidinous *adj* **1** ***syn*** LICENTIOUS 2, fast, incontinent, lascivious, lecherous, lewd, libertine, lustful, salacious, satyric
rel coarse, gross, obscene
2 ***syn*** LUSTFUL 2, concupiscent, goatish, *horny, hot, lascivious, lickerish, passionate, prurient, satyric

library *n* a place in which literary, musical, artistic, or reference materials (as books or films) are kept for use but not for sale <planned to study all evening in the *library*>
syn archive(s), athenaeum
rel reading room

license *n* ***syn*** FREEDOM, liberty
rel laxity, looseness, relaxation, slackness
con duty, obligation; decency, propriety; continence, sobriety, temperance
ant decorum

---

syn synonym(s) — ***rel*** related word(s)
idiom idiomatic equivalent(s) — ***con*** contrasted word(s)
ant antonym(s) — * vulgar
‖ use limited; if in doubt, see a dictionary
The first word in a synonym list when printed in SMALL CAPITALS shows where there is more information about the group. For a more efficient use of this book see Explanatory Notes.

license *vb* ***syn*** AUTHORIZE 1, accredit, commission, empower, enable
rel allow, let, permit, suffer; certify, sanction
con check, curb, restrain
ant ban

licentious *adj* **1** ***syn*** ABANDONED 2, dissolute, profligate, reprobate, self-abandoned, unprincipled
2 disregarding sexual restraints <a coarse *licentious* man>
syn fast, incontinent, lascivious, lecherous, lewd, libertine, libidinous, lustful, randy, salacious, satyric
rel animal, carnal, fleshly, oversexed, sensual; abandoned, dissolute, profligate, reprobate; corrupt, debauched, depraved, scabrous; amoral, immoral, unmoral; lax, loose, relaxed
con chaste, decent, pure; moral, virtuous; rigid, strict; ascetic, austere, severe
ant continent

licit *adj* ***syn*** LAWFUL, innocent, legal, legitimate
rel approved, sanctioned; authorized, licensed
con banned, forbidden, inhibited, interdicted, prohibited
ant illicit

lick *vb* **1** ***syn*** WHIP 2, beat, ‖clobber, drub, lambaste, overwhelm, shellac, smear, smother, thrash
2 ***syn*** OVERCOME 1, conquer, down, hurdle, master, surmount, throw

lick *n* **1** ***syn*** HINT 2, cast, dash, smack, suggestion, taste, tinge, touch, trace, whiff
2 ***syn*** HIT 1, ‖conk, knock, rap, swat, swipe, wipe

lickerish *adj* ***syn*** LUSTFUL 2, concupiscent, goatish, *horny, hot, lascivious, libidinous, passionate, prurient, satyric

lickerishness *n* ***syn*** LUST 2, aphrodisia, concupiscence, desire, eroticism, itch, lustfulness, passion, prurience, pruriency

lickety-split *adv* ***syn*** FAST 2, apace, expeditiously, flat-out, hastily, posthaste, quickly, rapidly, speedily, swiftly

licking *n* ***syn*** DEFEAT 1, beating, debacle, defeasance, drubbing, overthrow, rout, shellacking, thrashing, vanquishment

lickspit *n* ***syn*** SYCOPHANT, bootlick, bootlicker, ‖clawback, footlicker, lickspittle, spaniel, toad, toady, truckler

lickspittle *n* ***syn*** SYCOPHANT, bootlick, bootlicker, ‖clawback, footlicker, lickspit, toad, toadeater, toady, truckler

lie *vb* **1** ***syn*** REST 1, lie down, recline, repose, stretch (out)
2 ***syn*** CONSIST 1, dwell, exist, inhere, reside

lie *vb* to be untruthful directly or indirectly <*lying* under oath is a crime>
syn equivocate, falsify, fib, palter, prevaricate
rel beguile, deceive, delude, misguide, misinform, misinstruct, mislead; distort, exaggerate, misstate

lie *n* a statement or declaration that is not true <was sued for printing *lies* about the candidate>
syn ‖bouncer, canard, cock-and-bull story, falsehood, falsity, fib, inveracity, misrepresentation, misstatement, prevarication, ‖rapper, story, tale, taradiddle, untruism, untruth

rel deceitfulness, dishonesty, distortion, fraudulence, inaccuracy, mendacity; fable, flam, myth; falsification, forgery, libel, perjury; fish story, song and dance
idiom *crock of shit
con veracity, verisimilitude, verity
ant truth

lie by *vb syn* REST 3, breathe, lay off, spell

lied *n syn* SONG 2, aria, descant, ditty, hymn, lay

lie down *vb syn* REST 1, lie, recline, repose, stretch (out)

liege *adj syn* FAITHFUL 1, allegiant, ardent, constant, ‖dinky-di, loyal, resolute, staunch, steadfast, true

lieutenant *n syn* ASSISTANT 2, aid, aide, aide-de-camp, coadjutant, coadjutor

life *n* **1** *syn* BIOGRAPHY, autobiography, bio, confessions, memoir
2 *syn* HUMAN, being, body, creature, individual, man, mortal, person, personage, soul
3 *syn* SPIRIT 5, animation, brio, dash, élan, esprit, oomph, verve, vim, zing

lifeless *adj* **1** *syn* DEAD 1, asleep, cold, deceased, defunct, departed, exanimate, extinct, inanimate, late
ant living
2 *syn* COLORLESS 2, drab, dull, flat, lackluster, lusterless, prosaic, prosy
ant lifeful

lifelong *adj syn* OLD 2, continuing, enduring, inveterate, long-lasting, long-lived, perennial

lifework *n syn* MISSION, calling, vocation

lift *vb* **1** to remove from a lower to a higher place or position < *lifted* the sack to his shoulder >
syn elevate, hoist, pick up, raise, rear, take up, uphold, uplift, upraise, uprear
rel arise, ascend, levitate, mount, rise, rocket, soar, surge, tower; aggrandize, exalt, magnify
con decrease, diminish, lessen, reduce; abase, debase, degrade, demean, humble, humiliate; depress, oppress, weigh
ant lower
2 *syn* REVOKE 2, dismantle, recall, repeal, rescind, reverse
ant invoke
3 *syn* STEAL 1, ‖cop, filch, hook, nip, pilfer, pinch, purloin, snitch, swipe
4 *syn* RISE 4, arise, ascend, aspire, mount, soar, up, uprear

lift *n* **1** *syn* THEFT, larceny, pinch, purloining, steal, stealage, stealing, thievery, thieving, ‖touch
2 *syn* HELP 1, aid, assist, assistance, comfort, hand, relief, secours, succor, support

lifted *adj syn* ELEVATED 1, raised, upheaved, uplifted, upraised, uprisen

ligament *n syn* BOND 3, knot, ligature, link, nexus, tie, vinculum, yoke

ligature *n syn* BOND 3, knot, ligament, link, nexus, tie, vinculum, yoke

light *n syn* DAWN 1, aurora, cockcrow, cockcrowing, dawning, daybreak, daylight, morn, morning, sunrise

light *adj syn* FAIR 3, blond

light *vb* **1** to cause something to start burning < *lighted* the fuse on the dynamite >
syn enkindle, fire, ignite, inflame, kindle
con douse, ‖dout, put out, quench, snuff; damp (down), smother, stamp (out)
ant extinguish
2 *syn* ILLUMINATE 1, illume, illumine, lighten

light *adj* **1** having little weight <the package was *light* >
syn featherlight, featherweight, imponderous, lightweight, unheavy, weightless
rel inconsequential, trifling, trivial; little, petty, small; flimsy, meager, slender, slight
idiom light as a feather
con bulky, burdensome, cumbersome, huge, massive, overweight, ponderous, portly, unwieldy, weighty
ant heavy
2 *syn* EASY 1, effortless, facile, royal, simple, smooth, untroublesome
ant arduous
3 *syn* FAST 7, easy, loose, ‖riggish, unchaste, wanton, whorish
4 *syn* GIDDY 1, bird-witted, dizzy, empty-headed, featherbrained, flighty, frivolous, harebrained, rattlebrained, skittish
5 *syn* LITTLE 3, casual, inconsiderable, insignificant, minor, petty, shoestring, small-beer, trivial, unimportant
6 *syn* DIZZY 2, giddy, light-headed, swimming, swimmy, vertiginous

light *vb* **1** *syn* ALIGHT, land, perch, roost, set down, settle, sit down, touch down
2 *syn* HAPPEN 2, bump, chance, hit, luck, meet, stumble, tumble

lighted *adj syn* BURNING 1, ablaze, afire, aflame, alight, blazing, fiery, flaming, flaring, ignited
ant unlighted, unlit

lighten *vb syn* ILLUMINATE 1, illume, illumine, light
ant darken

lighten *vb syn* RELIEVE 1, allay, alleviate, assuage, ease, mitigate, mollify
rel attenuate, dilute, extenuate, thin
con depress, oppress, weigh

light–headed *adj* **1** *syn* GIDDY 1, bird-witted, dizzy, empty-headed, featherbrained, flighty, frivolous, harebrained, rattlebrained, scatterbrained
2 *syn* DIZZY 2, giddy, light, swimming, swimmy, vertiginous

lighthearted *adj* **1** *syn* HAPPY-GO-LUCKY, carefree, free-minded, insouciant, lightsome
ant heavyhearted
2 *syn* GLAD 1, happy, joyful, joyous
rel buoyant, effervescent, expansive, resilient, volatile; high-spirited, spirited; gay, lively, sprightly, vivacious
con gloomy, glum, morose, sullen
ant despondent
3 *syn* MERRY, blithe, blithesome, festive, gay, gleeful, jocund, jolly, jovial, mirthful
ant heavyhearted

---

syn synonym(s) *rel* related word(s)
idiom idiomatic equivalent(s) *con* contrasted word(s)
ant antonym(s) * vulgar
‖ use limited; if in doubt, see a dictionary
The first word in a synonym list when printed in SMALL CAPITALS shows where there is more information about the group. For a more efficient use of this book see Explanatory Notes.

lighthouse *n* a building equipped to guide sea navigators by means of a powerful light <rowed out to the *lighthouse*>
syn beacon, pharos
rel direction, guidance

lightless *adj* ***syn*** DARK 1, caliginous, dim, dusk, dusky, gloomy, murky, obscure, tenebrous, unillumined
ant bright, ‖lightful

lightly *adv* ***syn*** EASILY 1, effortlessly, facilely, freely, readily, smoothly, well

light–mindedness *n* ***syn*** LIGHTNESS, flightiness, flippancy, frivolity, levity, volatility

lightness *n* gaiety or indifference where seriousness and attention are called for <a crisis that allowed no room for *lightness*>
syn flightiness, flippancy, frivolity, levity, light-mindedness, volatility
rel buoyancy, effervescence, elasticity, expansiveness, resiliency; gaiety, liveliness, vivacity; cheerfulness, lightheartedness
con earnestness, gravity, sedateness, soberness, somberness, staidness
ant seriousness

light–o'–love *n* ***syn*** DOXY 1, ‖chippy, floozy, grisette, nymph, nymphet, party girl, roundheel, tart, ‖tootsie

light out *vb* ***syn*** HEAD 3, bear, make, set out, strike out, take off

lightsome *adj* **1** ***syn*** CHEERFUL 1, blithe, cheery, ‖chirk, chirpy, chirrupy, sunbeamy, sunny
2 ***syn*** HAPPY-GO-LUCKY, carefree, free-minded, insouciant, lighthearted

lightweight *adj* ***syn*** LIGHT 1, featherlight, featherweight, imponderous, unheavy, weightless

like *vb* **1** ***syn*** ENJOY 1, ‖dig, go, ‖mind, relish
rel choose, elect, prefer, select; admire, esteem, regard, respect; approve, endorse; appreciate, comprehend, understand
ant dislike
2 ***syn*** WILL, choose, elect, please, wish

like *adj* being so similar as to appear to be the same or nearly the same (as in appearance, character, or quantity) <shirts of *like* design>
syn agnate, akin, alike, analogous, comparable, consonant, corresponding, equivalent, intercomparable, parallel, similar, such, suchlike, undifferenced, undifferentiated, uniform; *compare* SAME 2
rel equal, equivalent, identical, same, selfsame; allied, cognate, close, related, resembling; coextensive, commensurate
idiom of that ilk, on the order of
con different, disparate, divergent, diverse, various; dissimilar, distinct; discordant, discrepant, inconsistent, inconsonant
ant unlike

syn synonym(s) ***rel*** related word(s)
idiom idiomatic equivalent(s) ***con*** contrasted word(s)
ant antonym(s) * vulgar
‖ use limited; if in doubt, see a dictionary
The first word in a synonym list when printed in SMALL CAPITALS shows where there is more information about the group. For a more efficient use of this book see Explanatory Notes.

like *n* ***syn*** EQUAL, counterpart, equivalent, match

likely *adj* **1** ***syn*** PROBABLE, conceivable, earthly, mortal, possible
con problematic; certain, inevitable, necessary
ant unlikely
2 ***syn*** APT 1, given, inclined, liable, prone
ant unlikely
3 ***syn*** HOPEFUL 2, couleur de rose, encouraging, promiseful, promising, roseate, rose-colored, rosy

likely *adv* ***syn*** PRESUMABLY, assumably, doubtless, presumptively, probably

liken *vb* ***syn*** EQUATE 2, assimilate, compare, match, paragon, parallel

likeness *n* agreement or correspondence in details (as of appearance, structure, or quality) <the remarkable *likeness* of the two cousins>
syn affinity, alikeness, analogy, comparison, resemblance, semblance, similarity, simile, similitude
rel equality, equivalence, identicalness, identity, sameness; agreement, conformity, correspondence; analogousness, comparableness, parallelism, uniformity
con difference, dissimilarity, distinction, divergence, divergency; disaffinity, opposition
ant unlikeness

likewise *adv* **1** ***syn*** ALSO 1, correspondingly, similarly, so
2 ***syn*** ALSO 2, additionally, along, as well, besides, furthermore, more, moreover, too, withal

liking *n* **1** ***syn*** APPETITE 3, fondness, inclination, soft spot, taste, weakness
ant disliking
2 ***syn*** WILL 1, fancy, inclination, mind, pleasure, velleity

lilliputian *adj* ***syn*** TINY, diminutive, minute, teensy, teensy-weensy, teenty, teeny, teeny-weeny, wee, weeny
ant Brobdingnagian

lilliputian *n* ***syn*** DWARF, homunculus, hop-o'-my-thumb, manikin, midge, midget, peewee, pygmy, runt, Tom Thumb

lily–livered *adj* ***syn*** COWARDLY, ‖chicken, coward, craven, gutless, poltroonish, poor-spirited, pusillanimous, spunkless, unmanly

lily–white *adj* ***syn*** GOOD 11, blameless, exemplary, guiltless, inculpable, innocent, irreproachable, pure, righteous, virtuous

limb *n* **1** a member of a woody plant that is an outgrowth from a main stem or from one of its divisions <hung the swing from a tree's *limb*>
syn bough, branch
rel shoot, spray, sprig, switch, twig; arm
2 ***syn*** SCAMP, devil, enfant terrible, mischief, rapscallion, rascal, rogue, scalawag, skeezicks, villain

limber *adj* ***syn*** SUPPLE 3, lissome, lithe, lithesome
rel plastic, pliable, pliant; elastic, flexible, resilient, springy
con inflexible, rigid, stark, stiff, tense, wooden

limit *n* **1** a material or immaterial point beyond which something does not or cannot extend <there seemed no *limit* to the problems they faced>
syn bound, confine(s), end, limitation, term; *compare* ENVIRONS 1
rel circumscription, confinement, restriction, termination; border, brim, brink, edge, margin, rim, verge

2 limits *pl* ***syn*** ENVIRONS 1, bound(s), boundary, compass, confine(s), precinct(s), purlieus
3 ***syn*** EXTREME 2, extremity

limit *vb* **1** ***syn*** DEMARCATE 1, bound, delimit, delimitate, determine, mark (out), measure
2 to prescribe or serve as a restricting boundary < *limited* the naughty child to the house for three days> <ignorance that *limits* spiritual growth>
syn bar, circumscribe, confine, delimit, delimitate, prelimit, restrict
rel constrict, contract, lessen, narrow, pinch; check, curb, hinder, inhibit, restrain; appoint, assign, define, prescribe, set
con enlarge, expand, extend, increase, widen; develop, grow
ant broaden

limitation *n* **1** ***syn*** LIMIT 1, bound, confine(s), end, term
2 ***syn*** RESTRICTION 1, ‖ball and chain, circumscription, cramp, stint, stricture

limited *adj* **1** ***syn*** DEFINITE 1, circumscribed, determinate, fixed, narrow, precise, restricted
rel inexhaustive, inextensive
con boundless, infinite
ant unlimited
2 ***syn*** FINITE, bound, bounded
3 ***syn*** QUALIFIED 2, modified, reserved
4 ***syn*** LITTLE 2, borné, ineffectual, mean, narrow, paltry, set, small

limitless *adj* having no limits <the *limitless* black of deep space>
syn boundless, endless, immeasurable, indefinite, infinite, measureless, unbounded, unlimited, unmeasured
rel bottomless, countless, incalculable, incomprehensible, inexhaustible, innumerable, undrainable, unfathomable, vast, wasteless
con bound, bounded, finite, fixed, limited, measurable; comprehensible, fathomable; confined, restricted
ant limited

limn *vb* ***syn*** REPRESENT 1, delineate, depict, describe, image, interpret, picture, portray, render

limp *vb* **1** to walk lamely < *limped* across the floor after his fall>
syn halt, hitch, hobble
rel toddle, totter, waddle; falter, stagger, stumble, wobble
2 ***syn*** STUMBLE 6, muddle, shuffle

limp *adj* **1** deficient in firmness of texture, substance, or structure <plants going *limp* from lack of water>
syn flabby, flaccid, flimsy, floppy, sleazy
rel lax, loose, relaxed, slack; limber, supple
con inflexible, rigid, stark, stiff, tense, wooden; firm, hard, solid; brittle, crisp
2 ***syn*** LANGUID, die-away, enervated, lackadaisical, languishing, languorous, listless, spiritless

limpid *adj* ***syn*** TRANSPARENT 1, clear, pellucid, see-through, translucent

limpidity *n* ***syn*** CLARITY, clearness, lucidity, perspicuity, plainness

line *n* **1** ***syn*** WAY 2, course, passage, path, road, route
2 ***syn*** COURSE 3, policy, polity, procedure, program
3 ***syn*** WORK 1, business, calling, employment, job, line, occupation, pursuit, ‖racket
‖**4** ***syn*** SPIEL, pitch, song and dance
5 a series of things arranged in continuous or uniform order <a *line* of cars waiting at the light>
syn echelon, file, queue, rank, row, string, tier
rel column, progression, succession, train; sequence, series
6 ***syn*** OUTLINE, contour, delineation, figuration, lineament, lineation, profile, silhouette
7 ***syn*** MERCHANDISE, commodities, goods, vendible(s), wares

line *vb* **1** to arrange in a line or lines < *lined* the bottles along the shelf>
syn align, allineate, line up, range
rel arrange, array, marshal, order, ordinate
con derange, disarrange, disorder, disturb; disperse, dissipate, scatter
2 ***syn*** ADJOIN, abut, border, butt (on *or* against), communicate, join, march, neighbor, touch, verge

lineage *n* **1** ***syn*** ANCESTRY, blood, descent, extraction, origin, pedigree
2 ***syn*** FAMILY 1, clan, folk, house, kindred, race, stock, tribe

lineal *adj* ***syn*** DIRECT 1

lineament *n* ***syn*** OUTLINE, contour, delineation, figuration, line, lineation, profile, silhouette

lineation *n* ***syn*** OUTLINE, contour, delineation, figuration, line, lineament, profile, silhouette

line up *vb* ***syn*** LINE 1, align, allineate, range

linger *vb* **1** ***syn*** STAY 2, abide, bide, remain, stick around, tarry, wait
2 ***syn*** DELAY 2, dally, dawdle, drag, lag, loiter, poke, procrastinate, put off, tarry
3 ***syn*** SAUNTER, amble, bummel, drift, mope, mosey, ‖muck, stroll

lingerer *n* ***syn*** LAGGARD, dawdler, loiterer, slow coach, slowpoke, straggler

lingo *n* ***syn*** DIALECT 2, argot, cant, jargon, patois, patter, slang, vernacular

link *n* ***syn*** BOND 3, knot, ligament, ligature, nexus, tie, vinculum, yoke

link *vb* ***syn*** JOIN 1, associate, combine, conjoin, conjugate, connect, couple, link, relate, unite

lint *n* ***syn*** DOWN, floss, flue, fluff, fur, fuzz, pile

lion *n* ***syn*** NOTABLE 1, big boy, ‖biggie, big-timer, chief, eminence, high-muck-a-muck, leader, luminary, VIP

lionhearted *adj* ***syn*** BRAVE 1, bold, courageous, dauntless, fearless, intrepid, unafraid, undaunted, valiant, valorous

‖**lip** *n* ***syn*** BACK TALK, guff, jaw, mouth, sass, sauce

lip *vb* **1** ***syn*** KISS 1, buss, osculate, peck, smack, smooch, ‖smoodge, ‖smouch
2 ***syn*** BATHE 2, lap, lave, wash

lip server *n* ***syn*** HYPOCRITE, dissembler, dissimulator, pharisee, Tartuffe, whited sepulcher

---

syn synonym(s)	***rel*** related word(s)
idiom idiomatic equivalent(s)	***con*** contrasted word(s)
ant antonym(s)	* vulgar

‖ use limited; if in doubt, see a dictionary

The first word in a synonym list when printed in SMALL CAPITALS shows where there is more information about the group. For a more efficient use of this book see Explanatory Notes.

liquefy *vb* to convert or to become converted to a liquid state < *liquefy* a block of ice by heating >
syn deliquesce, dissolve, flux, fuse, liquesce, melt, run, thaw
rel soften; thin
con clot, coagulate, congeal; harden, set; gel, jellify, jelly; condense, inspissate, thicken
ant solidify

liquesce *vb syn* LIQUEFY, deliquesce, dissolve, flux, fuse, melt, run, thaw

liquid *adj syn* MELLIFLUOUS, golden, honeyed, Hyblaean, mellifluent, mellow

liquidate *vb* **1** *syn* CLEAR 5, clear off, discharge, pay, pay up, quit, satisfy, settle, square
2 *syn* PURGE 3, eliminate, remove
3 *syn* MURDER 1, assassinate, ‖bump off, cool, do in, ‖dust off, execute, finish, knock off, put away

liquor *n* **1** *syn* DRINK 1, beverage, drinkable, potable
2 an intoxicating beverage usually distilled after being fermented <belted down a slug of *liquor*>
syn alcohol, aqua vitae, booze, ‖budge, drink, firewater, grog, ‖hooch, inebriant, intoxicant, ‖joy-juice, ‖juice, ‖lush, ‖sauce, spirit(s), ‖strunt, tipple
idiom Demon Rum, the bottle

liquor (up) *vb syn* DRINK 3, booze, guzzle, imbibe, soak, swig, swill, swizzle, tank up, tipple

lissome *adj syn* SUPPLE 3, limber, lithe, lithesome

list *n* a series of items (as names) written down or printed especially as a memorandum or record <all the people on the *list* were present>
syn catalog, register, roll, roll call, roster, schedule
rel checklist, handlist; index; inventory

list *vb* **1** *syn* ENUMERATE 2, numerate, tick off
2 *syn* ITEMIZE 1, enumerate, inventory, particularize, specialize, specify
3 to enter in a list <his name was not *listed* in the telephone book>
syn book, catalog, enroll, inscribe
rel file, index, note, post, schedule, tabulate; record, register, roster
4 *syn* ENROLL 1, register

list *vb syn* SLANT 1, cant, heel, incline, lean, recline, slope, tilt, tip

listen *vb* to perceive by ear usually with careful or responsive attention <now hear me; *listen* to my words>
syn attend, hark, hear, hearken, heed
idiom give a hearing to, give ear to, hang upon the lips (*or* words) of, keep one's ears open, lend one's (*or* an) ear, prick up one's ears, strain one's ears

listless *adj syn* LANGUID, die-away, enervated, lackadaisical, languishing, languorous, limp, spiritless
rel careless, heedless, thoughtless

---

syn synonym(s) *rel* related word(s)
idiom idiomatic equivalent(s) *con* contrasted word(s)
ant antonym(s) * vulgar
‖ use limited; if in doubt, see a dictionary
The first word in a synonym list when printed in SMALL CAPITALS shows where there is more information about the group. For a more efficient use of this book see Explanatory Notes.

con agog, anxious, avid, keen; alert, vigilant, watchful; energetic, lusty, vigorous; prompt, quick, ready
ant eager

listlessness *n syn* APATHY 2, disinterest, disregard, heedlessness, indifference, insouciance, lassitude, lethargy, unconcern, unmindfulness

‖**lit** *adj syn* INTOXICATED 1, ‖boozy, ‖canned, disguised, drunk, inebriated, ‖lushed, muddled, pixilated, ‖plastered

literal *adj syn* VERBATIM, verbal, word-for-word

literally *adv syn* VERBATIM, direct, directly, literatim, word for word

literati *n pl syn* INTELLIGENTSIA, clerisy, illuminati, intellectuals

literatim *adv syn* VERBATIM, direct, directly, literally, word for word

lithe *adj syn* SUPPLE 3, limber, lissome, lithesome
rel slender, slight, slim, thin; lean, spare
con awkward, clumsy, gauche, inept, maladroit; inflexible, stiff, tense, wooden

lithesome *adj syn* SUPPLE 3, limber, lissome, lithe

litigious *adj syn* CONTENTIOUS 2, argumentative, controversial, disputatious, polemical

litter *n* **1** *syn* REFUSE, ‖collateral, debris, garbage, junk, kelter, offal, rubbish, trash, waste
2 *syn* CLUTTER 2, hash, jumble, jungle, mishmash, muddle, rummage, scramble, shuffle, tumble

little *adj* **1** *syn* SMALL 1, bantam, monkey, petite, smallish
ant big
2 contemptibly limited <men with *little* minds picking at flaws in a great leader>
syn borné, ineffectual, limited, mean, narrow, paltry, set, small
rel bigoted, hidebound, illiberal, narrow-minded, provincial; contemptible; niggard, niggardly, self-centered, selfish
ant great
3 lacking importance <the nagging *little* details of a job>
syn casual, inconsiderable, insignificant, light, minor, minute, petty, ‖potty, shoestring, small, small-beer, trivial, unimportant; *compare* PETTY 2
rel fortuitous; incidental; collateral, secondary, subordinate, subsidiary
con consequential, meaningful, significant, substantial, weighty; basal, basic, essential, foundational, fundamental
ant important

little *adv syn* SELDOM, hardly ever, infrequently, rarely, unfrequently, unoften
ant much

little by little *adv syn* GRADUALLY, bit by bit, piecemeal

‖**little woman** *n syn* WIFE, ‖ball and chain, lady, ‖missus, Mrs., ‖old lady, ‖old woman, ‖rib, ‖squaw, woman

‖**lit up** *adj syn* INTOXICATED 1, ‖boozy, ‖canned, disguised, drunk, inebriated, ‖lushed, muddled, pixilated, ‖plastered

liturgy *n* **1** *syn* FORM 2, ceremonial, ceremony, formality, rite, ritual
2 *syn* RITE 2, ceremonial, ceremony, formality, observance, ritual, service

livable *adj* **1** suitable for living <a very *livable* apartment>
syn habitable, inhabitable, lodgeable, occupiable, tenantable
rel cozy, homelike, homey, snug; acceptable, bearable, tolerable
ant unlivable
2 *syn* BEARABLE, endurable, sufferable, supportable, sustainable, tolerable

live *vb* **1** *syn* BE, breathe, exist, move, subsist
2 *syn* RESIDE 1, abide, bide, ‖dig, dwell, hang out

live *adj* *syn* ACTIVE 1, alive, dynamic, functioning, operative, running, working
rel effective, effectual, efficacious, efficient
ant inactive, inert; dormant (*as a volcano*); defunct (*as an institution, journal*)

livelihood *n* *syn* LIVING, alimentation, alimony, bread, bread and butter, keep, maintenance, subsistence, support, sustenance
rel art, craft, handicraft, profession, trade; emolument, fee, pay, salary, stipend, wage

lively *adj* **1** keenly alive and brisk <always thought of as a *lively* teacher>
syn alert, animate, animated, bright, ‖cant, ‖canty, chipper, ‖chirk, dashing, gay, keen, ‖peart, peppy, pert, rousing, spirited, ‖spirity, sprightful, sprightly, unpedantic, vivacious; *compare* CHEERFUL 1
rel agile, brisk, nimble, spry; buoyant, effervescent, elastic, expansive, resilient, volatile; blithe, cock-a-hoop, jocund, jolly, merry; gleeful, hilarious, mirthful; chirping, chirpy, chirrupy
con lethargic, sluggish, torpid; lackadaisical, languid, languorous, listless; apathetic, impassive, phlegmatic, stolid; boring, irksome, tedious
ant dull, unlively
2 *syn* AGILE, active, brisk, brisky, catty, nimble, sprightly, spry, yare, zippy
idiom full of pep
3 *syn* ENERGETIC 2, active, driving, enterprising
4 *syn* BUSTLING, busy, fussy, hopping, humming, hustling, popping
ant unanimated

liven *vb* *syn* QUICKEN 1, animate, enliven, vivificate, vivify

liver *n* *syn* INHABITANT, denizen, dweller, habitant, indweller, occupant, resident, ‖residenter, resider

live wire *n* *syn* HUSTLER 1, dynamo, go-getter, peeler, rustler, self-starter

livid *adj* **1** *syn* PALE 1, ashen, ashy, blanched, colorless, doughy, lurid, pallid, wan, waxen
rel grisly; dusky, gloomy, murky
con bright, brilliant, effulgent, lucent, luminous, lustrous, radiant
2 *syn* SENSATIONAL 2, lurid, sensationalistic, sensationist, sultry, tabloid

living *adj* **1** having or showing life <the *living* things of a locality>
syn alive, animate, animated, vital, zoetic
rel being, existing, subsisting; active, dynamic, live, operative
con dead, deceased, defunct, demised, departed, gone, inanimate
ant lifeless
2 *syn* EXTANT 1, alive, around, existent, existing

living *n* supplies or resources needed to live <kept trying to earn a *living* the honest way>
syn alimenation, alimony, bread, bread and butter, keep, livelihood, maintenance, salt, subsistence, support, sustenance
rel sustainment, sustentation

load *n* **1** something which is carried, conveyed, or transported from one place to another <a *load* of grain just arrived>
syn burden, cargo, freight, haul, lading, payload
rel bale, pack, parcel, shipment
2 something heavy <could not lift the *load*>
syn weight
3 a burdensome or laborious responsibility <considered taking care of the children a heavy *load*>
syn burden, charge, deadweight, duty, millstone, onus, task, tax, weight
rel care, liability, obligation, responsibility; drag, drain, pressure
idiom millstone around one's neck
con breeze, child's play, cinch, duck soup, picnic, ‖pipe, pushover, snap
ant sinecure
4 *usu* **loads** *pl* *syn* SCAD, gob(s), heap, oodles, quantities, ream(s), ‖rimption(s), slather(s), slew, wad(s)

load *vb* **1** *syn* BURDEN, charge, cumber, encumber, lade, saddle, task, tax, weigh, weight
rel bear, carry, convey, transport
ant unload
2 *syn* ADULTERATE, debase, doctor, dope (up), sophisticate, weight
3 to make full or overfull <a basket *loaded* with fresh fruit>
syn charge, choke, fill, heap, pack, pile; *compare* CRAM 1
rel glut, gorge, surfeit; flood, oversupply, swamp

loaded *adj* **1** *syn* FULL 1, brimful, brimming, chock-full, crammed, crowded, jammed, jam-packed, packed, stuffed
‖**2** *syn* INTOXICATED 1, ‖boozy, ‖canned, disguised, drunk, inebriated, ‖lushed, muddled, pixilated, ‖plastered

loaf *vb* *syn* IDLE, bum, dawdle, goldbrick, ‖goof (off), laze, lazy, loiter, loll, lounge
con labor, toil, travail, work

loafer *n* *syn* SLUGGARD, bum, dolittle, do-nothing, fainéant, idler, lazybones, slouch, slug, slugabed

loan *vb* *syn* LEND, advance

loan shark *n* one who lends money to individuals at exorbitant rates of interest <got involved with *loan sharks*>
syn Shylock, usurer
rel lender, loaner, moneylender; shark

---

syn synonym(s) — *rel* related word(s)
idiom idiomatic equivalent(s) — *con* contrasted word(s)
ant antonym(s) — * vulgar
‖ use limited; if in doubt, see a dictionary
The first word in a synonym list when printed in SMALL CAPITALS shows where there is more information about the group. For a more efficient use of this book see Explanatory Notes.

loath *adj* ***syn*** DISINCLINED, afraid, averse, backward, hesitant, indisposed, reluctant, uneager, unwilling, unwishful
ant anxious

loathe *vb* ***syn*** HATE, abhor, abominate, detest, execrate
rel decline, refuse, reject, repudiate, spurn
con covet, crave, desire, want, wish
ant tolerate

loathing *n* ***syn*** ABOMINATION 2, abhorrence, aversion, detestation, hate, hatred, horror, repugnance, repulsion, revulsion
ant tolerance

loathsome *adj* ***syn*** OFFENSIVE, disgusting, hideous, horrible, nasty, repellent, repugnant, repulsive, revolting, vile
rel hateful, invidious, obnoxious
con bearable, endurable, sufferable, supportable; engaging, inviting; alluring, bewitching, charming, enchanting, fascinating
ant tolerable

lobby *n* ***syn*** VESTIBULE, foyer

lobster *n* ***syn*** OAF 2, gawk, klutz, looby, lout, lubber, ‖lug, lummox, lump, palooka

local *adj* ***syn*** INSULAR, ‖parish-pump, parochial, provincial, sectarian, small-town
ant cosmopolitan

locale *n* ***syn*** SCENE 3, mise-en-scène, site
rel area, district, neighborhood, vicinage, vicinity

locality *n* **1** a more or less definitely circumscribed place or region <searched for the child in the *locality* of the waterfront>
syn area, district, neighborhood, vicinage, vicinity
rel belt, region, tract, zone; section, sector; bailiwick, domain, field, province, sphere, territory
idiom neck of the woods
2 ***syn*** HABITAT, haunt, home, range, site, stamping ground

located *adj* ***syn*** SITUATED, placed, positioned, set, sited, situate

location *n* ***syn*** PLACE 1, locus, point, position, site, situation, spot, station, where

‖**loch** *n* ***syn*** INLET, arm, bay, bight, cove, ‖creek, firth, gulf, harbor, ‖lough

lockup *n* ***syn*** JAIL, ‖calaboose, ‖can, ‖clink, cooler, coop, ‖hoosegow, jug, pen, ‖pokey

‖**loco** *adj* ***syn*** INSANE 1, ‖fruity, lunatic, mad, maniac, ‖mental, mindless, non compos mentis, nuts, nutsy

locum tenens *n* ***syn*** SUBSTITUTE, alternate, fill-in, pinch hitter, replacement, stand-in, sub, succedaneum, surrogate

locus *n* ***syn*** PLACE 1, location, point, position, site, situation, spot, station, where

locution *n* ***syn*** PHRASE 2, expression

---

syn synonym(s) ***rel*** related word(s)
idiom idiomatic equivalent(s) ***con*** contrasted word(s)
ant antonym(s) * vulgar
‖ use limited; if in doubt, see a dictionary
The first word in a synonym list when printed in SMALL CAPITALS shows where there is more information about the group. For a more efficient use of this book see Explanatory Notes.

lodge *vb* **1** ***syn*** HARBOR 2, bestow, billet, board, domicile, entertain, house, hut, put up, quarter
rel accept, admit, receive, take; accommodate, contain, hold
2 ***syn*** ENTRENCH 1, embed, fix, infix, ingrain, root

lodge *n* **1** ***syn*** HUT, ‖box, cabin, ‖caboose, camp, cot, cottage, shack, shanty
2 ***syn*** HOTEL, auberge, caravansary, hospice, hostel, hostelry, inn, public house, roadhouse, tavern
3 ***syn*** LAIR 1, burrow, couch, den

lodgeable *adj* ***syn*** LIVABLE 1, habitable, inhabitable, occupiable, tenantable

lodging *n* **1** ***syn*** ACCOMMODATIONS, lodgment, room and board
2 usu **lodgings** *pl* ***syn*** APARTMENT 1, ‖chambers, flat, rental, rooms, suite, tenement

lodgment *n* ***syn*** ACCOMMODATIONS, lodging, room and board

loftiest *adj* ***syn*** TOP 1, apical, highest, topmost, uppermost

loftiness *n* ***syn*** PRIDE 3, arrogance, disdain, disdainfulness, haughtiness, hauteur, morgue, superbity, superciliousness

lofty *adj* **1** ***syn*** PROUD 1, arrogant, cavalier, disdainful, haughty, high-and-mighty, insolent, overbearing, supercilious, superior
2 ***syn*** AMBITIOUS 2, grandiose, pretentious, utopian, visionary
3 ***syn*** GRAND 3, elevated, exalted, sublime, superb
4 ***syn*** GENEROUS 1, benevolent, big, chivalrous, considerate, greathearted, magnanimous
5 ***syn*** ELEVATED 4, eloquent, high
6 extending or rising high in the air so as to have great or imposing height <a *lofty* monument to human aspiration>
syn aerial, airy, skyscraping, soaring, spiring, topless, towering, towery; *compare* HIGH 1
rel elevated, lifted, raised; aggrandized, exalted, magnified; august, imposing, majestic, stately
con humble, low, modest

logical *adj* **1** ***syn*** RATIONAL, consequent, intelligent, reasonable, sensible, sound
ant illogical
2 having or showing skill in thinking or reasoning <a *logical* argument>
syn analytic, analytical, ratiocinative, subtle
rel cogent, compelling, convincing, sound, telling, valid; clear, lucid, perspicuous; rational, reasonable; discriminating
con instinctive, intuitive; irrational, unreasonable; casuistical, sophistical
ant illogical

logo *n* ***syn*** MARK 7, brand, logotype, trademark

logotype *n* ***syn*** MARK 7, brand, logo, trademark

loiter *vb* **1** ***syn*** DELAY 2, dally, dawdle, drag, lag, poke, procrastinate, put off, tarry, trail
2 ***syn*** IDLE, bum, dawdle, diddle, ‖goof (off), laze, lazy, loaf, loll, lounge

loiterer *n* ***syn*** LAGGARD, dawdler, lingerer, slow coach, slowpoke, straggler

loll *vb* **1** ***syn*** SLOUCH, droop, ‖lollop, lop, slump, trollop
2 ***syn*** IDLE, bum, dawdle, diddle, ‖goof (off), laze, lazy, loaf, loiter, lounge

‖**lollop** *vb* ***syn*** SLOUCH, droop, loll, lop, slump, trollop

lone *adj* **1** having no company <a *lone* figure walking through the snow>
syn alone, lonely, lonesome, solitary
rel single, sole, unique; abandoned, deserted, forsaken; isolated, secluded
con attended, chaperoned, companioned, convoyed, escorted
ant accompanied
2 ***syn*** ONLY 2, alone, singular, sole, solitary, solo, unexampled, unique, unrepeatable
3 ***syn*** SINGLE 2, one, only, particular, separate, sole, solitary, unique

lonely *adj* **1** ***syn*** LONE 1, alone, lonesome, solitary
2 ***syn*** FORLORN 1, lonesome, lorn

loneness *n* ***syn*** SOLITUDE, aloneness, isolation, solitariness

lonesome *adj* **1** ***syn*** LONE 1, alone, lonely, solitary
2 ***syn*** FORLORN 1, lonely, lorn
3 ***syn*** OBSCURE 2, devious, out-of-the-way, remote, removed, retired, secret

long *adj* **1** having considerable extension in space or time <a *long* road> <it has been a *long* time since we have seen you>
syn elongate, elongated, extended, lengthy
rel extensive, longish, outstretched
con brief, curtailed
ant short
2 unduly extended <went through many *long* days of misery>
syn dragging, drawn-out, ‖dreich, lengthy, long-drawn-out, longsome, overlong, prolonged, protracted
rel diffuse, diffusive, long-winded, prolix; flatulent, verbose, wordy
con ephemeral, evanescent, fleeting, fugacious, fugitive, impermanent, passing, short-lived, transient, transitory; abbreviated, abridged, curtailed, shortened
ant brief

long *n* ***syn*** AGE 2, aeon, blue moon, coon's age, dog's age, donkey's years, eternity

long *vb* to desire urgently <*long* for peace>
syn ache, crave, dream, hanker, hunger, itch, lust, pine, sigh, suspire, thirst, yearn, yen
rel aim, aspire, want; miss
idiom have an appetite (*or* a longing) for
con abhor, detest, dread, fear, loathe

longanimity *n* ***syn*** PATIENCE, forbearance, long-suffering, patientness, resignation, uncomplainingness

long-drawn-out *adj* ***syn*** LONG 2, dragging, drawn-out, ‖dreich, lengthy, longsome, overlong, prolonged, protracted
ant short; curtailed

‖**long green** *n* ***syn*** MONEY, dough, ‖greenbacks, ‖jack, ‖kale, ‖lettuce, loot, ‖mazuma, ‖moolah, needful

longitudinally *adv* ***syn*** LENGTHWISE, endways, endwise, lengthways, longways, longwise
ant horizontally

long-lasting *adj* ***syn*** OLD 2, continuing, enduring, inveterate, lifelong, long-lived, perennial
ant ephemeral

long-lived *adj* ***syn*** OLD 2, continuing, enduring, inveterate, lifelong, long-lasting, perennial
ant short-lived

longsome *adj* ***syn*** LONG 2, dragging, drawn-out, ‖dreich, lengthy, long-drawn-out, overlong, prolonged, protracted

long-suffering *n* ***syn*** PATIENCE, forbearance, longanimity, patientness, resignation, uncomplainingness
rel subduedness; humility, lowliness, meekness
con impatience, uneasiness; irksomeness, tediousness, wearisomeness; boredom, ennui, tedium

long suit *n* ***syn*** FORTE, eminency, medium, métier, oyster, strong suit
rel specialism, specialization, specialty

longtimer *n* ***syn*** VETERAN, old hand, old-timer, vet
con apprentice, neophyte, novice; newcomer, rookie, tenderfoot

‖**long tongue** *n* ***syn*** GOSSIP 1, carrytale, gossipmonger, newsmonger, quidnunc, rumormonger, scandalmonger, tabby, talebearer, telltale

longways *adv* ***syn*** LENGTHWISE, endways, endwise, lengthways, longitudinally, longwise

long-winded *adj* ***syn*** WORDY, diffuse, palaverous, prolix, redundant, verbose, windy
rel extended, lasting, lengthy, long, long-drawn-out, prolonged, protracted
con brief, close, compact

longwise *adv* ***syn*** LENGTHWISE, endways, endwise, lengthways, longitudinally, longways

‖**loo** *n* ***syn*** TOILET, convenience, ‖donicker, john, johnny, ‖pot, ‖potty, privy, ‖throne, water closet

looby *n* ***syn*** OAF 2, gawk, klutz, lobster, lout, lubber, ‖lug, lummox, lump, palooka

look *vb* **1** to make sure or take care (that something is or is not done) <*look* that you accuse no one unjustly>
syn mind, see, watch
rel attend, heed, tend; note, notice, observe; beware
2 ***syn*** SEE 2, ‖dekko, watch
rel note, notice, observe, spot
idiom get a load of, take a gander at
3 ***syn*** EXPECT 1, await, count (on *or* upon), hope
rel divine, forecast, foretell
ant despair (of)
4 to make apparent by the expression of the eyes or countenance <*looked* her annoyance at this interruption>
syn exhibit, show; *compare* SHOW 2
rel display, express, indicate, manifest
5 ***syn*** SEEM, appear, sound
idiom strike one as
6 ***syn*** FACE 1, front
7 to gaze in wonder or surprise <you should have seen them *look*>
syn eye, gape, ‖gaup (*or* gawp), gaze, goggle, ogle, rubberneck, stare; *compare* GAZE 1
rel gawk; glare, gloat, glower; peer

---

syn synonym(s) ***rel*** related word(s)
idiom idiomatic equivalent(s) ***con*** contrasted word(s)
ant antonym(s) * vulgar
‖ use limited; if in doubt, see a dictionary
The first word in a synonym list when printed in SMALL CAPITALS shows where there is more information about the group. For a more efficient use of this book see Explanatory Notes.

8 ***syn*** TEND 1, incline, lean

look (at *or* upon) *vb* ***syn*** EYE 1, consider, contemplate, gaze (upon), view

look (into) *vb* ***syn*** EXPLORE, delve (into), dig (into), go (into), inquire (into), investigate, probe, prospect, sift

look *n* **1** the directing of one's eyes in order to see <he wanted one last *look* before departing>
syn sight, view
rel glance, glimpse, peek, peep, squint; cast, slant; eye, ‖gander, ‖look-see, regard; eyeful, gaze, stare, survey
2 facial aspect especially as indicative of mood or feeling <you should have seen the *look* on her face>
syn cast, countenance, expression, face, visage
rel mug, physiognomy, ‖puss
3 ***syn*** APPEARANCE 1, aspect, mien, seeming

look down *vb* **1** ***syn*** OVERLOOK 2, dominate, overtop, tower (above *or* over)
2 ***syn*** DESPISE, abhor, contemn, disdain, scorn, scout
3 ***syn*** STARE DOWN, outstare

looker *n* ***syn*** BEAUTY, ‖beaut, eyeful, knockout, lovely, stunner

looker–on *n* ***syn*** SPECTATOR, beholder, by-sitter, bystander, eyewitness, observer, onlooker, viewer, watcher, witness

look in *vb* ***syn*** VISIT 2, call, come by, come over, drop (in *or* by), look up, pop (in), see, step in, stop (in *or* by)

look–in *n* ***syn*** OPPORTUNITY, break, chance, occasion, opening, shot, show, squeak, time

looking glass *n* ***syn*** MIRROR 1, glass, ‖seeing glass

look out *vb* ***syn*** BEWARE, mind, watch out

lookout *n* **1** ***syn*** GUARD 2, picket, sentinel, sentry, ward, watch, watchman
2 an elevated place affording a wide view for observation <guards posted at a *lookout* to watch for enemy troops entering the valley>
syn observatory, outlook, overlook
rel watchtower; crow's nest; cupola, widow's walk; firetower
3 a careful looking or watching <kept a constant *lookout* for new developments>
syn surveillance, tout, vigil, vigilance, watch, watch and ward
rel observance, observation
4 ***syn*** VISTA, outlook, perspective, prospect, scape
5 ***syn*** BUSINESS 8, affair, concern, occasions, palaver

look up *vb* **1** ***syn*** IMPROVE 3, ameliorate, convalesce, gain, mend, perk(up), recuperate
2 ***syn*** VISIT 2, call, come by, come over, drop (in *or* by), look in, pop (in), run in, see, step in

loom *vb* **1** ***syn*** APPEAR 1, emerge, show
2 to take shape as an impending occurrence <an international economic crisis *looms* ahead>
syn brew, forthcome, gather, impend
rel approach, come on, make up, near
con disappear, fade, pass, vanish; die (down *or* away), diminish, dwindle, wane; recede, retreat, withdraw
3 to appear in an impressively great or exaggerated form <the power of the enemy *loomed* in the soldiers' imagination>
syn bulk, stand out
rel lower, rear, threaten, tower
con die (down *or* away), diminish, dwindle, wane

loon *n* ***syn*** LUNATIC 1, bedlamite, dement, loony, madling, madman, maniac, non compos, nut, Tom o' Bedlam

loony *adj* ***syn*** FOOLISH 2, absurd, ‖balmy, crazy, harebrained, insane, ‖potty, preposterous, silly, wacky

loony *n* ***syn*** LUNATIC 1, bedlamite, dement, loon, madling, madman, maniac, non compos, nut, Tom o' Bedlam

loony bin *n* ***syn*** ASYLUM 3, booby hatch, ‖bughouse, crazy house, madhouse, ‖nuthouse

loop *n* **1** a curving or doubling of a line so as to form a closed or partly open curve <the transit makes a *loop* around town>
syn eye, ring
rel circlet, circuit, circumference, hoop, wreath; curve
2 a circular or curved piece used often to form a fastening or a handle <one of his belt *loops* is broken>
syn eye, ring, staple
rel hook
3 ***syn*** LEAGUE 4, association, circuit, conference, wheel

loop *vb* ***syn*** SURROUND 1, begird, beset, circle, compass, encircle, encompass, gird, girdle, ring
rel arc, arch, bend, coil, curve

looped *adj* ***syn*** INTOXICATED 1, ‖boozy, ‖canned, disguised, drunk, inebriated, ‖lushed, muddled, pixilated, ‖plastered

loopy *adj* ***syn*** FOOLISH 2, absurd, ‖balmy, crazy, fantastic, harebrained, insane, loony, ‖potty, wacky

loose *adj* **1** not tightly bound, held, restrained, or stretched <*loose* rope>
syn lax, relaxed, slack
rel detached, free; flabby, flaccid, limp; desultory, negligent, remiss
con rigid, rigorous, stringent, taut, tense; exact, precise; bound, checked, curbed, inhibited, restrained, tied
ant strict; tight
2 ***syn*** FREE 2, unconfined, unrestrained
rel clear; disconnected, unattached, unconnected, undone, unfastened
con fast
3 not dense, close, or compact in structure <*loose* soil>
syn incoherent, nonadhesive
rel disconnected, disjointed, separate, unconnected
con compressed, condensed, contracted; concentrated, crammed, crowded, localized; close, compact, dense, thick
4 ***syn*** FAST 7, easy, light, ‖riggish, unchaste, wanton, whorish
rel capricious, extravagant, free, inconstant, reckless, unrestrained

loose *vb* **1** ***syn*** FREE, discharge, disenthrall, emancipate, liberate, loosen, manumit, release, unbind, unchain
2 ***syn*** TAKE OUT (on), release, unleash, vent

---

syn synonym(s) ***rel*** related word(s)
idiom idiomatic equivalent(s) ***con*** contrasted word(s)
ant antonym(s) * vulgar
‖ use limited; if in doubt, see a dictionary
The first word in a synonym list when printed in SMALL CAPITALS shows where there is more information about the group. For a more efficient use of this book see Explanatory Notes.

3 to set free from a fastened or fixed condition < *loose* a knot >

syn disengage, unbind, undo, unfasten, unfix, unloose, unloosen

rel unbandage, unbar, unbolt, unbuckle, unbutton, unchain, unclasp, unglue, unhitch, unhook, unlace, unlash, unlatch, unlock, unpin, unscrew, unsnap, unstick, unstrap, untie

con bind, engage, fasten, fix, secure

4 ***syn*** SHOOT 1, discharge, fire

5 to make less rigid or tight < exercise *loosed* his muscles >

syn ease, ease off, lax, loosen, relax, slack, slacken, untighten

rel abate, alleviate, bate, lessen, let up, mitigate

con anchor, cement, clamp, clinch, fasten, knit, secure, set, tauten

ant tighten

loose–lipped *adj* ***syn*** TALKATIVE, babblative, chatty, gabby, garrulous, loose-tongued, loquacious, multiloquent, multiloquious, talky

ant closemouthed

loosen *vb* **1** ***syn*** LOOSE 5, ease, ease off, lax, relax, slack, slacken, untighten

ant tighten

2 ***syn*** FREE, discharge, disenthrall, emancipate, liberate, loose, manumit, release, unbind, unchain

loosen up *vb* ***syn*** RELAX 2, ease off, unbend, unlax, unwind

ant tighten (up)

loose–tongued *adj* ***syn*** TALKATIVE, babblative, chatty, gabby, garrulous, loose-lipped, loquacious, multiloquent, multiloquious, talky

ant closemouthed

loot *n* **1** ***syn*** SPOIL, boodle, booty, plunder, plunderage, prize, ||spreaghery, ||spulzie, swag

rel lift, pillage, seizure

2 ***syn*** MONEY, dough, filthy lucre, ||gelt, ||greenbacks, ||jack, ||lettuce, ||long green, lucre, ||moolah

loot *vb* ***syn*** ROB 1, ||knock off, knock over, plunder, ransack, relieve, rifle, stick up

looter *n* ***syn*** MARAUDER, forager, freebooter, pillager, plunderer, raider, ravager, ravisher, sacker, spoiler

lop *vb* **1** ***syn*** SLOUCH, droop, loll, ||lollop, slump, trollop

2 ***syn*** JUMP 1, bounce, bound, hop, hurdle, leap, saltate, spring, vault

lope *vb* ***syn*** SKIP 1, hop, skitter, spring, trip

rel run, sprint; romp, trip

||**lopper** *vb* ***syn*** CURDLE, ||clabber, ||cruddle, curd, turn

lopsided *adj* lacking in balance, symmetry, or proportion < the arrangement of the furniture was *lopsided* >

syn asymmetric, difform, disproportional, disproportionate, irregular, nonsymmetrical, off-balance, overbalanced, proportionless, unbalanced, unequal, uneven, unproportionate, unsymmetrical

rel cockeyed, crooked, top-heavy, unsteady

con balanced, even, regular, symmetrical

loquacious *adj* ***syn*** TALKATIVE, babblative, chatty, gabby, garrulous, loose-lipped, loose-tongued, multiloquent, multiloquious, talky

rel jabbering, overtalkative; prolix, verbose, wordy

con breviloquent, concise, succinct, taciturn, terse; abrupt, brusque, curt

lord *n* ***syn*** HUSBAND, ||hubby, man, ||master, mister, Mr., ||old man

lord *vb* to affect an air of superiority and authority < nouveau riche love to *lord* it >

syn cock, peacock, pontificate, swagger, swank, swell

rel affect, pretend, put on; boss, order (about *or* around), overawe, overbear; tyrannize

idiom put on airs

lordly *adj* **1** ***syn*** GRAND 1, august, grandiose, imposing, magnific, magnificent, majestic, noble, princely, stately

2 ***syn*** PROUD 1, arrogant, cavalier, disdainful, haughty, high-and-mighty, insolent, overbearing, supercilious, superior

rel egotistic, puffed; affected, snobbish, swollen; authoritarian, dictatorial, magisterial

con humble; abject, mean; subdued, submissive

lore *n* **1** ***syn*** KNOWLEDGE 2, information, science, wisdom

2 a body of traditions relating to a person, institution, or place < the Scottish highlands are rich in local *lore* >

syn folklore, legend, myth, mythology, mythos, tradition

rel custom, folkway, traditionalism; fable, old wives' tale, saga, superstition, tale

Lorelei *n* ***syn*** SIREN, femme fatale, seductress, temptress

lorn *adj* **1** ***syn*** DERELICT 1, abandoned, deserted, desolate, forsaken, solitary, uncouth

2 ***syn*** FORLORN 1, lonely, lonesome

lose *vb* **1** to suffer deprivation of < *lost* all his savings in a poor investment >

syn drop, forfeit, sacrifice

rel mislay, misplace, miss; give up, relinquish, surrender, yield

con cash in, profit; clear, make, realize, take in; obtain, win

ant gain

2 to fail to win, gain, or obtain < *lost* every contest she entered >

syn drop, lose out

rel decline, fall, succumb, yield

ant win

3 ***syn*** DEPRIVE 2, bereave, disinherit, dispossess, divest, oust, rob

4 ***syn*** SHAKE 5, slip, throw off

5 ***syn*** RID, clear, shake (off), throw off, unburden

lose out *vb* ***syn*** LOSE 2, drop

loser *n* **1** ***syn*** FAILURE 5, bomb, bust, dud, flop, lemon

rel also-ran, underdog

ant winner

2 ***syn*** CONVICT, ||con, jailbird, ||lag, prison bird

losing *n* ***syn*** LOSS 1, mislaying, misplacement, misplacing

---

syn synonym(s) ***rel*** related word(s)
idiom idiomatic equivalent(s) ***con*** contrasted word(s)
ant antonym(s) * vulgar
|| use limited; if in doubt, see a dictionary
The first word in a synonym list when printed in SMALL CAPITALS shows where there is more information about the group. For a more efficient use of this book see Explanatory Notes.

loss *n* **1** the action of having something go out of one's control or possession <took precautions against *loss* or theft of his property>
syn losing, mislaying, misplacement, misplacing; *compare* PRIVATION 2
rel forfeit, forfeiture, sacrifice; bereavement, deprivation, deprivement, dispossession, divestiture, divestment, privation
2 *syn* PRIVATION 2, deprivation, deprivement, dispossession, divestiture
3 *syn* RUIN 3, confusion, destruction, devastation, havoc, ruination

lost *adj* **1** *syn* DAMNED 1, condemned, doomed
rel incorrigible, irreclaimable, irredeemable, irreformable, unconverted, unregenerate; graceless
2 no longer possessed <earned his *lost* reputation by his outrageous behavior>
syn gone, missing
rel absent, lacking; passed; irrecoverable, irretrievable, irrevocable
con cherished, protected, treasured
3 *syn* EXTINCT 2, bygone, dead, defunct, departed, gone, vanished
4 *syn* ABSTRACTED, absent, absentminded, bemused, distrait, faraway, inconscient, preoccupied
rel absorbed; daydreamy, musing, unconscious

lot *n* **1** *syn* SHARE 1, allotment, allowance, bite, cut, part, partage, portion, quota, slice
2 *syn* FATE, circumstance, destiny, doom, kismet, moira, portion, weird
rel decree, fortune; foreordination, predestination, predetermination
3 a measured portion of land having fixed boundaries <building *lots*>
syn parcel, plat, plot, tract
rel clearing, field, patch; part, plottage; block, frontage, real estate
4 *syn* GROUP 3, array, batch, body, bunch, bundle, clump, cluster, clutch, set
rel aggregate, aggregation, conglomerate, conglomeration
5 *syn* SET 5, bunch, circle, crowd, group, push
6 *syn* TYPE, breed, character, feather, ilk, kidney, kind, sort, species, stripe
7 *syn* MUCH, barrel, great deal, heap, lump, mass, ‖mess, multiplicity, peck, ‖power

lot *vb* *syn* ALLOT, admeasure, allocate, allow, apportion, assign, give, mete (out)

‖**lot** (on *or* upon) *vb* *syn* RELY (on *or* upon), bank (on *or* upon), build (on), calculate (on *or* upon), count (on), depend (on *or* upon), reckon (on), trust (in *or* to)

lot (out) *vb* *syn* DISTRIBUTE 1, deal, disburse, dispense, disperse, divide, ‖divvy, dole (out), measure (out), partition

---

syn synonym(s) *rel* related word(s)
idiom idiomatic equivalent(s) *con* contrasted word(s)
ant antonym(s) * vulgar
‖ use limited; if in doubt, see a dictionary
The first word in a synonym list when printed in SMALL CAPITALS shows where there is more information about the group. For a more efficient use of this book see Explanatory Notes.

lothario *n* *syn* GALLANT 2, amorist, Casanova, Don Juan, paramour, Romeo

loud *adj* **1** marked by intensity or volume of sound <a *loud* blast on a trumpet>
syn blaring, earsplitting, full-mouthed, piercing, roaring, stentorian, stentorious, stentorophonic
rel booming, deafening, ear-piercing, fulminating, pealing, ringing, thunderous; resonant, resounding, sonorous; harsh, hoarse, raucous, stertorous, strident
con dulcet, gentle, mellifluous, mellow, quiet, smooth
ant low, soft
2 *syn* GAUDY, blatant, brazen, chintzy, flashy, garish, glaring, meretricious, tawdry, tinsel
rel brassy, vulgar; obnoxious, offensive; obtrusive

loudmouthed *adj* *syn* VOCIFEROUS, blatant, boisterous, clamorous, ‖dinsome, multivocal, obstreperous, openmouthed, strident, vociferant

‖**lough** *n* *syn* INLET, arm, bay, bight, cove, ‖creek, firth, gulf, harbor, ‖loch

lounge *vb* *syn* IDLE, bum, dawdle, goldbrick, ‖goof (off), laze, lazy, loaf, loiter, loll
rel drift, vegetate; dally, slack; lie, lie down, recline

lounge *n* *syn* BAR 5, barroom, buvette, cocktail lounge, drinkery, pothouse, pub, saloon, tap, taproom

lounge car *n* *syn* PARLOR CAR, chair car, club car, palace car, tavern car

lounge lizard *n* **1** *syn* FOP, Beau Brummel, blood, buck, coxcomb, dandy, dude, exquisite, macaroni, petit-maître
2 *syn* PARASITE, barnacle, bloodsucker, freeloader, hanger-on, leech, ‖spiv, sponge, sponger, sucker

louse *n* *syn* SNOT 1, cur, dog, rat, skunk, snake, stinker, toad, *turd, wretch

louse up *vb* *syn* BOTCH, bitch (up), bobble, bollix, bungle, goof (up), gum (up), mess, mucker, ‖screw (up)

lout *n* *syn* OAF 2, gawk, klutz, lobster, looby, lubber, ‖lug, lummox, lump, palooka
rel boor, bumpkin, churl, clodhopper, hayseed, hick, peasant, rube, rustic, yokel; dolt

lout *vb* *syn* RIDICULE, deride, mock, quiz, rally, razz, scout, taunt, twit

loutish *adj* *syn* BOORISH, churlish, cloddish, clodhopping, clownish, ill-bred, lowbred, uncivilized, uncultured, unrefined
rel awkward, bungling, clumsy, inept, maladroit, rusty; callow, crude, gauche, raw, rough, uncouth

lovable *adj* gifted with traits and qualities that attract affection <a *lovable* child>
syn adorable, lovesome
rel admirable, agreeable, attractive, desirable, genial, likable, pleasing, winning, winsome; alluring, appealing, bewitching, captivating, charming, enchanting, engaging, enthralling, entrancing, fetching, ravishing, seductive
con dislikable, displeasing, distasteful, unattractive, unlikable, unpleasing; odious, offensive; abhorrent, abominable, obnoxious, repellent; contemptible, despicable, detestable
ant hateful; unlovable

love *n* **1** the feeling which animates a person who is genuinely fond of someone or something <a mother's *love* for her child>
syn affection, attachment, devotion, fondness

rel like(s), liking, regard; adoration, idolatry, piety, worship; allegiance, fealty, fidelity, loyalty; emotion, sentiment; crush, infatuation, passion, yearning; ardency, ardor, enthusiasm, fervor, zeal
con antipathy, aversion; animosity, animus, enmity, hostility, rancor; abhorrence, detestation, hatred
ant hate
2 the affection and tenderness felt by lovers <the ability to distinguish between *love* and lust was the mark of her maturity>
syn amorousness, amour, passion
rel crush, infatuation; desire, lust, yearning; ardency, ardor, fervor
idiom (the) tender passion
3 ***syn*** LOVE AFFAIR, affair, amour, romance
4 ***syn*** SWEETHEART 1, beloved, darling, dear, honey, honeybunch, loveling, sweet, sweetling, turtledove

love *vb* **1** to like or desire actively <she *loves* her material possessions all too dearly>
syn adore, delight (in), ‖eat up
rel appreciate, cherish, prize, treasure, value; dote (on *or* upon), fancy
idiom hold dear
con abjure, give up, reject, relinquish
2 to feel a lover's passion, devotion, or tenderness for <in spite of all their misfortunes, they continued to *love* each other devotedly>
syn adore, affection, worship
rel deify, exalt, idolize, revere, venerate; cherish, dote (on *or* upon); admire, fancy, like
con avoid, disregard, ignore, neglect, overlook, shun, slight
3 ***syn*** CARESS, cosset, cuddle, dandle, fondle, pet

love affair *n* a romantic attachment or episode between lovers <saddened by the end of a summer *love affair*>
syn affair, amour, love, romance
rel flirtation, intrigue; triangle, ménage à trois

love child *n* ***syn*** BASTARD 1, by-blow, catch colt, chance child, come-by-chance, filius nullius, illegitimate, natural child, whoreson, woods colt

loved *adj* ***syn*** FAVORITE 1, beloved, blue-eyed, darling, dear, fair-haired, pet, precious, white-haired, white-headed

love letter *n* a letter expressing a lover's affection <she had never received a *love letter*>
syn billet-doux, mash note
rel valentine

loveling *n* ***syn*** SWEETHEART 1, beloved, darling, dear, honey, honeybunch, love, sweet, sweetling, turtledove

lovely *adj* ***syn*** BEAUTIFUL, attractive, beauteous, ‖bonny, comely, fair, good-looking, handsome, pretty, pulchritudinous
rel alluring, bewitching, captivating, charming, enchanting, engaging, entrancing, lovesome; delectable, delightful; dainty, delicate, exquisite, rare; graceful
ant hideous; unlovely

lovely *n* ***syn*** BEAUTY, ‖beaut, eyeful, knockout, looker, stunner

lover *n* **1** a man who is a woman's regular partner in nonmarital sexual activity
syn boyfriend, fancy man, man, master, paramour
rel cavalier servente, sugar daddy
2 ***syn*** BOYFRIEND 2, beau, beloved, flame, inamorato, steady, sweetheart, truelove
3 ***syn*** ADDICT, aficionado, buff, devotee, fan, habitué, hound, votary
4 ***syn*** MISTRESS, ‖doxy, girl friend, inamorata, paramour, woman

lovesome *adj* **1** ***syn*** LOVABLE, adorable
2 ***syn*** LOVING, affectionate, dear, devoted, doting, fond

lovey–dovey *adj* ***syn*** SENTIMENTAL, bathetic, maudlin, mawkish, mushy, romantic, slushy, ‖soppy, sticky, tear-jerking

loving *adj* feeling or expressing love <his *loving* son unfailingly waited upon him during his last years>
syn affectionate, dear, devoted, doting, fond, lovesome
rel adoring, attached, benevolent, cordial, kind, tender, warmhearted; attentive, caring, considerate, solicitous; amatory, amorous, erotic; enamored, infatuated; ardent, fervent, impassioned, passionate; faithful; bound up
con aloof, detached, indifferent, unconcerned; chilly, cold, frigid
ant unloving

low *adj* ‖**1** ***syn*** SHORT 2, low-set, low-statured
rel squatty; unelevated
2 ***syn*** INFERIOR 1, lesser, lower, nether, subjacent, under
3 ***syn*** POOR 1, beggared, broke, destitute, dirt poor, flat, impoverished, indigent, needy, penurious
4 ***syn*** IGNOBLE 1, base, baseborn, humble, lowborn, lowly, mean, plebeian, unennobled, unwashed
rel lowbred, rude
5 ***syn*** BASE 3, abject, despicable, ignoble, mean, scurvy, servile, sordid, vile, wretched
rel scrubby, scruffy; miserable, woebegone, woeful
con decent, decorous, proper, seemly; ethical, moral, noble; high, lofty
6 ***syn*** COARSE 3, crass, crude, gross, inelegant, raw, rough, rude, uncouth, vulgar
7 ***syn*** UNWELL, ailing, ‖donsie, indisposed, mean, off-color, offish, poorly, sickly, underly
rel declining, weak; dizzy, faint, feverish
8 ***syn*** DOWNCAST, bad, blue, cast down, crestfallen, dejected, depressed, down, downhearted, spiritless
9 of lesser degree, size, or amount than average or ordinary <the energy crisis resulted in *lower* speed limits for all vehicles>
syn subaverage, subnormal
rel fallen, reduced; brief, short; mediocre, moderate; atypical
10 ***syn*** CHEAP 1, inexpensive, low-cost, low-priced, popular, reasonable, uncostly, undear
rel economical; moderate, nominal; cut, cut-rate, marked down, slashed
con elevated, enhanced, increased, raised

---

syn synonym(s)	***rel*** related word(s)
idiom idiomatic equivalent(s)	***con*** contrasted word(s)
ant antonym(s)	* vulgar

‖ use limited; if in doubt, see a dictionary
The first word in a synonym list when printed in SMALL CAPITALS shows where there is more information about the group. For a more efficient use of this book see Explanatory Notes.

lowborn *adj* ***syn*** IGNOBLE 1, base, baseborn, humble, low, lowly, mean, plebeian, unennobled, unwashed
ant highborn

lowbred *adj* ***syn*** BOORISH, churlish, cloddish, ill-bred, loutish, lubberly, uncivilized, uncultured, unpolished, unrefined
ant highbred

low-cost *adj* ***syn*** CHEAP 1, inexpensive, low, low-priced, popular, reasonable, uncostly, undear

low-down *adj* ***syn*** BASE 3, despicable, ignoble, low, mean, scurvy, servile, ugly, vile, wretched

lower *vb* ***syn*** FROWN 1, gloom, glower, scowl
rel peer, stare; intimidate, menace, threaten

lower *adj* ***syn*** INFERIOR 1, lesser, low, nether, subjacent, under
ant higher

lower *vb* **1** ***syn*** FALL 1, descend, drop
ant rise
2 ***syn*** DEPRECIATE 1, decry, devaluate, devalue, downgrade, mark down, underprize, undervalue, write down, write off
rel demote; de-escalate, deflate
con raise
3 to cause or allow to descend < *lowered* the landing gear of the aircraft >
syn couch, demit, depress, droop, let down, sink
rel detrude, submerge; debase, reduce
con elevate, hoist, lift, pull up, raise
4 ***syn*** REDUCE 2, clip, cut, cut back, cut down, mark down, pare, shave, slash
ant raise
5 ***syn*** HUMBLE, abase, bemean, cast down, debase, degrade, demean, humiliate, sink
ant elevate

lowering (*or* **louring**) *adj* **1** ***syn*** IMMINENT 2, lowery (*or* loury), menacing, overhanging, threatening
rel frowning, gloomy, sullen; black, dark; foreboding, impending, portentous
2 ***syn*** OVERCAST, cloudy, ||dowly, dull, heavy, nubilous, overclouded

lowermost *adj* ***syn*** BOTTOMMOST, bottom, lowest, nethermost, rock-bottom, undermost
ant uppermost

lowery (*or* loury) *adj* ***syn*** IMMINENT 2, lowering (*or* louring), menacing, overhanging, threatening

lowest *adj* ***syn*** BOTTOMMOST, bottom, lowermost, nethermost, rock-bottom, undermost
ant highest

low-grade *adj* ***syn*** INFERIOR 2, common, déclassé, hack, mean, poor, second-class, second-drawer, second-rate

low-key *adj* ***syn*** SUBDUED 2, low-keyed, sober, soft, softened, toned down

low-keyed *adj* ***syn*** SUBDUED 2, low-key, sober, soft, softened, toned down

---

syn synonym(s) ***rel*** related word(s)
idiom idiomatic equivalent(s) ***con*** contrasted word(s)
ant antonym(s) * vulgar
|| use limited; if in doubt, see a dictionary
The first word in a synonym list when printed in SMALL CAPITALS shows where there is more information about the group. For a more efficient use of this book see Explanatory Notes.

lowlife *n* **1** ***syn*** WRETCH 1, ||blighter, mucker, no-good, worm, wormling
2 ***syn*** VILLAIN 1, *bastard, blackguard, heel, knave, miscreant, rascal, rogue, scoundrel, *son of a bitch

lowly *adj* **1** ***syn*** HUMBLE 1, meek, modest, unassuming
rel retiring, withdrawing; deferential, obeisant, reverential; obsequious, servile
ant haughty
2 ***syn*** IGNOBLE 1, base, baseborn, humble, low, lowborn, mean, plebeian, unennobled, unwashed
3 ***syn*** PROSAIC 3, commonplace, everyday, mundane, workaday, workday

low-pressure *adj* ***syn*** EASYGOING 3, casual, ||common, dégagé, informal, relaxed, ||sonsy, unconstrained, unfussy, unreserved
ant high-pressure

low-priced *adj* ***syn*** CHEAP 1, inexpensive, low, low-cost, popular, reasonable, uncostly, undear

||low-rate *vb* ***syn*** DECRY 2, abuse, belittle, depreciate, derogate, detract (from), diminish, discount, disparage, dispraise

low-set *adj* ***syn*** SHORT 2, ||low, low-statured

low-spirited *adj* ***syn*** DOWNCAST, blue, dejected, depressed, dispirited, down, downhearted, down-in-the-mouth, heartsore, woebegone
ant high-spirited

low-statured *adj* ***syn*** SHORT 2, ||low, low-set

loyal *adj* ***syn*** FAITHFUL 1, allegiant, ardent, constant, ||dinky-di, liege, resolute, staunch, steadfast, true
con faithless; alienated, disaffected, estranged; contumacious, factious, insubordinate, mutinous, rebellious, seditious
ant disloyal

loyalist *n* ***syn*** PATRIOT 1

loyalty *n* **1** ***syn*** FIDELITY 1, allegiance, ardor, devotion, faithfulness, fealty, piety
rel trueness, truth
ant disloyalty
2 ***syn*** ATTACHMENT 1, adherence, adhesion, constancy, faithfulness, fidelity

lubber *n* ***syn*** OAF 2, gawk, klutz, lobster, looby, lout, ||lug, lummox, lump, palooka

lubberland *n* ***syn*** UTOPIA, arcadia, Cockaigne, fairyland, heaven, paradise, promised land, Shangri-la, wonderland, Zion

lubberly *adj* ***syn*** BOORISH, cloddish, clodhopping, clownish, loutish, lowbred, lumpish, rugged, unpolished, unrefined

||lubricate *vb* ***syn*** BRIBE, buy, buy off, fix, have, sop, square, tamper (with)

lubricious *adj* **1** ***syn*** INCONSTANT 1, capricious, changeable, fickle, temperamental, ticklish, uncertain, unstable, variable, volatile
2 ***syn*** SLICK 1, greasy, ||sliddery, ||slipper, slippery, slippy, slithery

lucent *adj* **1** ***syn*** BRIGHT 1, beaming, brilliant, effulgent, fulgent, incandescent, lambent, luminous, radiant, refulgent
2 ***syn*** CLEAR 4, clear-cut, crystal, luminous, pellucid, translucent, transparent, transpicuous, unambiguous, unblurred

lucid *adj* **1** ***syn*** BRIGHT 1, beaming, brilliant, effulgent, incandescent, lambent, luminous, lustrous, radiant, refulgent

2 *syn* SANE 2, all there, compos mentis, normal, right
3 *syn* UNDERSTANDABLE, apprehensible, comprehendible, comprehensible, fathomable, graspable, intelligible, knowable, luminous
4 *syn* CLEAR 4, clear-cut, crystal, luminous, pellucid, translucent, transparent, transpicuous, unambiguous, unblurred
con dusky, gloomy, murky; muddy, turbid

lucidity *n* 1 *syn* CLARITY, clearness, limpidity, perspicuity, plainness
rel comprehensibility, intelligibility, understandability; distinctness, explicitness
ant ambiguity
2 *syn* WIT 2, ||marbles, mind, reason, saneness, sanity, sense(s), soundness

Lucifer *n syn* DEVIL 1, Apollyon, Beelzebub, diablo, fiend, Old Gooseberry, Old Nick, Old Scratch, Satan, serpent

luck *n* 1 *syn* CHANCE 2, fortune, hazard
rel break, occasion, opportunity
2 *syn* ACCIDENT 1, chance, fortuity, hap
3 success dependent on chance <he had all the *luck* in the world and was greatly envied by every one of his associates>
syn fortunateness, fortune, luckiness
rel advantage, break, fluke, godsend, opportunity, windfall; weal; hap, kismet
ant ill-fortune
4 *syn* CHARM 2, amulet, fetish, juju, mascot, periapt, phylactery, talisman, zemi

luck *vb syn* HAPPEN 2, bump, chance, hit, light, meet, stumble, tumble

luckiness *n syn* LUCK 3, fortunateness, fortune

luckless *adj syn* UNLUCKY, hapless, ill-fated, ill-starred, misfortunate, star-crossed, unfortunate, unhappy, untoward
rel miserable, wretched
ant lucky

lucky *adj* having a favorable outcome or an unforeseen or unpredictable success <he can only be described as *lucky*, as his success and fame are unearned>
syn fortunate, happy, providential, ||sonsy, well
rel auspicious, benign, favorable, propitious; advantageous, beneficial, profitable; felicitous
idiom in luck
con baleful, malefic, maleficent, malign, sinister
ant luckless, unlucky

lucrative *adj syn* ADVANTAGEOUS 1, gainful, good, moneymaking, paying, profitable, remunerative, well-paying, worthwhile

lucre *n* 1 *syn* PROFIT, earnings, gain, proceeds, return
2 *syn* MONEY, dough, filthy lucre, ||greenbacks, ||jack, ||kale, ||lettuce, ||long green, loot, ||mazuma

luculent *adj syn* CLEAR 4, clear-cut, crystal, lucent, lucid, luminous, pellucid, translucent, unambiguous, unblurred

ludicrous *adj syn* LAUGHABLE, comic, comical, droll, farcical, funny, gelastic, ridiculous, risible
rel absurd, foolish, preposterous, silly; antic, bizarre, fantastic, grotesque
con doleful, dolorous, lugubrious, melancholy

lug *vb* 1 *syn* PULL 2, drag, draw, haul, tow, tug
2 *syn* CARRY 1, bear, buck, convey, ferry, ||hump, ||jag, pack, tote, transport
3 *syn* JERK, lurch, snap, twitch, vellicate, yank

||**lug** *n syn* OAF 2, gawk, klutz, lobster, looby, lout, lubber, lummox, lump, palooka

||**lugs** *n pl syn* POSE 2, affectation, air(s), mannerism, prettyism

lugubrious *adj* 1 *syn* MELANCHOLY 2, doleful, dolesome, dolorous, lamentable, mournful, plaintive, rueful, sorrowful, woeful
rel depressing, oppressing, oppressive; dour, glum, morose, saturnine, sullen
con blithe, jocund, jolly, jovial, merry; cheerful, glad, joyful
ant facetious
2 *syn* GLOOMY 3, black, bleak, cheerless, depressant, dismal, dispiriting, dreary, joyless, somber

lukewarm *adj* 1 *syn* TEPID 1, milk-warm, warmish
2 *syn* TEPID 2, halfhearted, unenthusiastic
rel irresolute, irresolved, uncommitted, unresolved; hesitant, indecisive, uncertain, undecided; cool; wishy-washy
ant icy; boiling

lull *vb* 1 *syn* CALM, allay, balm, becalm, compose, quiet, settle, soothe, still, tranquilize
rel moderate, qualify, temper
ant agitate
2 *syn* ABATE 4, die (down *or* away), ease off, ebb, fall, let up, moderate, slacken, subside, wane

lull *n* 1 *syn* QUIET 1, calm, hush
2 *syn* PAUSE, comma, interval, pausation
rel abeyance, quiescence

lullaby *n* a song to quiet children or lull them to sleep <sang a *lullaby* to the baby every night>
syn berceuse, cradlesong

||**lulu** *n syn* ||DILLY, ||corker, crackerjack, ||daisy, dandy, humdinger, jim-dandy, ||lalapalooza, peach, ||pip

lumber *vb* to tread heavily or clumsily <the tired old man slowly *lumbered* home>
syn barge, clump, galumph, stumble, stump
rel plod, trudge; shamble, slog

lumber *vb syn* BURDEN, charge, clog, cumber, encumber, lade, load, saddle, tax, weigh

lumbering *adj* 1 *syn* CLUMSY 1, awkward, gawky, lumpish, splathering, splay, ungainly
rel cumbersome, cumbrous, ponderous; hulking, hulky
2 *syn* AWKWARD 2, bumbling, clumsy, gauche, halting, ham-handed, inept, maladroit, unhandy, wooden

luminary *n* 1 *syn* CELEBRITY 2, big name, ||celeb, name, notability, notable, somebody
rel leading light
2 *syn* NOTABLE 1, big, ||biggie, big-timer, eminence, leader, lion, nabob, notability, VIP

luminous *adj* 1 *syn* BRIGHT 1, beaming, brilliant, effulgent, fulgent, incandescent, lambent, lucent, radiant, refulgent

---

syn synonym(s)	*rel* related word(s)
idiom idiomatic equivalent(s)	*con* contrasted word(s)
ant antonym(s)	* vulgar

|| use limited; if in doubt, see a dictionary
The first word in a synonym list when printed in SMALL CAPITALS shows where there is more information about the group. For a more efficient use of this book see Explanatory Notes.

2 ***syn*** CLEAR 4, clear-cut, crystal, lucid, pellucid, translucent, transparent, transpicuous, unambiguous, unblurred

3 ***syn*** UNDERSTANDABLE, apprehensible, comprehendible, comprehensible, fathomable, graspable, intelligible, knowable, lucid

lummox *n* ***syn*** OAF 2, gawk, klutz, lobster, looby, lout, lubber, ‖lug, lump, palooka

lump *n* **1** a compact mass of indefinite size and shape <dropped a large *lump* of butter into the steaming chowder>
syn chunk, clod, clump, gob, hunch, hunk, nugget, wad
rel particle, piece, portion; batch, bunch, ‖swad; bit, chip, crumb, morsel, scrap; wedge; block, bulk
2 ***syn*** MUCH, barrel, heap, lot, mass, mountain, peck, pile, ‖power, ‖sight
3 ***syn*** BUMP 2, bunch, knot, ‖pumpknot
rel bulge, protuberance, swelling
4 ***syn*** OAF 2, gawk, klutz, lobster, looby, lout, lubber, ‖lug, lummox, palooka
5 lumps *pl* ***syn*** DUE 1, comeuppance, desert(s), deserving, merit, right(s)

lump *vb* ***syn*** BEAR 10, abide, brook, digest, endure, stand, stomach, swallow, take, tolerate

lumpish *adj* **1** ***syn*** BOORISH, cloddish, clodhopping, clownish, loutish, lowbred, lubberly, uncultured, unpolished, unrefined
2 ***syn*** CLUMSY 1, awkward, gawky, lumbering, splathering, splay, ungainly

lumpkin *n* ***syn*** OAF 2, ‖gaum, gawk, klutz, looby, lout, lubber, ‖lug, lummox, palooka

lumpy *adj* ***syn*** RUDE 1, crude, raw, rough, roughhewn, undressed, unfashioned, unfinished, unformed, unpolished

lunacy *n* **1** ***syn*** INSANITY 1, aberration, alienation, derangement, distraction, insaneness, madness, psychopathy, unbalance
rel absurdity, folly, foolery, foolishness; asininity, fatuity, inanity, ineptitude, stupidity
2 ***syn*** FOOLISHNESS, absurdity, craziness, folly, inanity, insanity, preposterousness, senselessness, silliness, witlessness

lunatic *adj* **1** ***syn*** INSANE 1, ‖batty, cracked, crazed, crazy, demented, deranged, mad, maniac, unsound
2 ***syn*** FOOLISH 2, absurd, ‖balmy, crazy, fantastic, insane, loony, ‖potty, preposterous, wacky

lunatic *n* **1** a person who is insane or of unsound mind <Bedlam was a famous old English asylum for *lunatics*>
syn bedlamite, dement, loon, loony, madling, madman, maniac, non compos, nut, Tom o' Bedlam
rel demoniac, energumen; raver; neuropath, neurotic, paranoid, psycho, psychoneurotic
2 ***syn*** CRACKPOT, crackbrain, crank, cuckoo, ding-a-ling, harebrain, kook, nut, screwball

lunch counter (*or* **bar**) *n* ***syn*** EATING HOUSE, beanery, café, coffee shop, diner, luncheonette, lunchroom, quick-lunch, sandwich shop, snack bar (*or* counter)

luncheonette *n* ***syn*** EATING HOUSE, beanery, café, coffee shop, ‖hash house, lunch counter (*or* bar), lunchroom, quick-lunch, sandwich shop, snack bar (*or* counter)

lunchroom *n* ***syn*** EATING HOUSE, beanery, café, coffee shop, ‖hash house, lunch counter (*or* bar), luncheonette, quick-lunch, sandwich shop, snack bar (*or* counter)

lunch wagon (*or* **cart**) *n* ***syn*** EATING HOUSE, beanery, café, coffee shop, lunch counter (*or* bar), luncheonette, lunchroom, quick-lunch, sandwich shop, snack bar (*or* counter)

lunge *vb* ***syn*** PLUNGE 2, burst, dive, drive, pitch, ‖splunge

lunk *n* ***syn*** DUNCE, blockhead, boob, chump, clod, dummy, ‖goon, moron, numskull, simpleton

lunkhead *n* ***syn*** DUNCE, boob, booby, chump, dolt, dolthead, fathead, goof, ‖goon, oaf

lupanar *n* ***syn*** BROTHEL, bagnio, bawdy house, bordello, cathouse, disorderly house, parlor house, sporting house, stew, whorehouse

lurch *n* ***syn*** LEANING 2, bent, disposition, inclination, penchant, predilection, predisposition, proclivity, propensity, tendency

lurch *vb* **1** ***syn*** SEESAW, pitch, swag, tilt, tilter, yaw
2 to move forward unsteadily while swaying from side to side <the sodden drunk *lurched* uncertainly toward the door>
syn careen, stagger, ‖stoit, ‖stoiter, ‖stot, sway, swing, weave, wobble; *compare* TEETER
rel reel, rock, roll, swag, toss, totter, whirl; bob; wave, waver
con march, stride
3 ***syn*** TEETER, falter, stagger, ‖stammer, stumble, topple, totter, wobble
rel pitch, plunge
4 ***syn*** JERK, lug, snap, twitch, vellicate, yank
5 ***syn*** WALLOW 2, blunder, flounder, stumble
6 ***syn*** STUMBLE 3, blunder, bumble, ‖snapper

lure *n* **1** ***syn*** ATTRACTION 1, allurement, appeal, attractiveness, call, draw, drawing power, pull, seduction
2 something that leads an individual into a place or situation from which escape is difficult <used her charm as a *lure* to trap the unsuspecting youth>
syn allurement, bait, come-on, decoy, enticement, inveiglement, seducement, siren song, snare, ‖stale, temptation, trap
rel appeal, attraction, incentive, inducement; con game, gimmick, suck-in, trick; ambush, blind, camouflage, delusion, fake, illusion
con caution, caveat, warning

lure *vb* to draw from a usual, desirable, or proper course or situation into one felt as unusual, undesirable, or wrong <the promise of money *lured* him away from his steady job>
syn allure, bait, decoy, entice, entrap, inveigle, lead on, seduce, tempt, toll, train
rel bag, capture, catch, draw in, ensnare, rope, snare, suck in; attract, beguile, bewitch, captivate, charm, en-

chant, fascinate, invite; draw, draw on; blandish, cajole, wheedle
idiom bait the hook, give the come-on
con drive (away *or* off), rebuff, repulse
ant repel

lurid *adj* **1** *syn* PALE 1, ashen, ashy, blanched, colorless, doughy, livid, pallid, wan, waxen
2 *syn* GHASTLY 1, grim, gruesome, hideous, horrible, horrid, horrifying, macabre, terrible, terrifying
rel ashen, ashy, livid, pale, pallid, wan; baleful, malefic, maleficent, malign, sinister
3 *syn* SENSATIONAL 2, livid, sensationalistic, sensationist, sultry, tabloid

luring *adj syn* ENTICING, Circean, fetching, tempting
ant repellent, repelling

lurk *vb syn* SNEAK, creep, gumshoe, pussyfoot, skulk, slide, slink, slip, ||snake, steal

lurking *adj syn* LATENT, abeyant, dormant, potential, prepatent, quiescent

luscious *adj* **1** *syn* DELIGHTFUL, adorable, ambrosial, darling, delectable, delicious, heavenly, lush, scrumptious, yummy
rel appetizing, flavorsome, nectarious, palatable, piquant; choice, distinctive, exquisite, rare, rich
ant austere
2 *syn* LUXURIOUS 3, Capuan, deluxe, lush, luxuriant, opulent, palatial, plush, sumptuous, upholstered
3 *syn* SENSUOUS, epicurean, lush, luxurious, sensual, sensualistic, voluptuous
4 *syn* ORNATE, baroque, flamboyant, florid, rich, rococo

lush *adj* **1** *syn* PROFUSE, exuberant, lavish, luxuriant, opulent, prodigal, profusive, riotous
rel luxurious, sumptuous
2 *syn* DELIGHTFUL, adorable, ambrosial, delectable, delicious, delightful, heavenly, luscious, scrumptious, yummy
3 *syn* SENSUOUS, epicurean, luscious, luxurious, sensual, sensualistic, voluptuous
4 *syn* LUXURIOUS 3, Capuan, deluxe, luscious, luxuriant, opulent, palatial, plush, sumptuous, upholstered

lush *n* ||**1** *syn* LIQUOR 2, alcohol, booze, ||budge, drink, firewater, grog, ||hooch, ||joy-juice, tipple
2 *syn* DRUNKARD, bibber, boozehound, boozer, drunk, inebriate, ||lusher, soak, sot, tippler

lush (up) *vb syn* DRINK 3, booze, guzzle, imbibe, liquor (up), soak, swig, swill, swizzle, tank up

||**lushed** *adj syn* INTOXICATED 1, ||boozed, ||boozy, drunken, inebriated, ||oiled, ||pie-eyed, ||spiflicated, ||stewed, tight

||**lusher** *n syn* DRUNKARD, ||bloat, ||blotter, boozehound, boozer, drunk, inebriate, lush, soak, sot

lust *n* **1** *syn* DESIRE 1, appetite, appetition, craving, itch, passion, urge
rel coveting, yearning, yen
2 sexual appetency <they mistakenly thought that *lust* was lasting love>
syn aphrodisia, concupiscence, desire, eroticism, itch, lickerishness, lustfulness, passion, prurience, pruriency
rel nymphomania, priapism, satyriasis, satyrism; excitement, heat, hunger, libido, rut; fervor; carnality, lasciviousness, lecherousness, lechery, lubricity, salacity

lust *vb syn* LONG, ache, crave, hanker, hunger, itch, pine, thirst, yearn, yen
rel desire, wish

luster *n* the quality or condition of shining by reflected light <the satiny *luster* of fine pearls>
syn glaze, glint, gloss, polish, sheen, shine
rel iridescence, opalescence; brilliance, brilliancy, effulgence, luminosity, radiance, refulgence; afterglow, gleam, glow; candescence, incandescence

lusterless *adj* **1** *syn* DULL 7, blind, dead, dim, flat, lackluster, mat, muted
ant lustrous
2 *syn* COLORLESS 2, drab, dull, flat, lackluster, lifeless, prosaic, prosy

lustful *adj* **1** *syn* LICENTIOUS 2, fast, incontinent, lascivious, lecherous, lewd, libertine, libidinous, salacious, satyric
2 sexually excited < *lustful* old man>
syn concupiscent, goatish, *horny, hot, lascivious, libidinous, lickerish, passionate, prurient, ruttish, rutty, satyric
rel burning, hot-blooded, itching; lecherous, salacious

lustfulness *n syn* LUST 2, aphrodisia, concupiscence, desire, eroticism, itch, lickerishness, passion, prurience, pruriency

lustral *adj syn* PURGATIVE, expiative, expiatory, expurgatorial, expurgatory, lustratory, propitiatory, purgatorial

lustrate *vb syn* PURIFY 2, cleanse, expurgate, purge

lustration *n syn* PURIFICATION, catharsis, cleansing, expurgation, purgation

lustratory *adj syn* PURGATIVE, expiative, expiatory, expurgatorial, expurgatory, lustral, propitiatory, purgatorial

lustrous *adj* **1** having a high gloss or shine <a *lustrous* star sapphire>
syn burnished, gleaming, glistening, glossy, polished, sheeny, shining, shiny
rel gleamy, glimmering, glinting, sparkling; radiant
con dull, flat, lackluster, mat
ant lusterless
2 *syn* BRIGHT 1, brilliant, effulgent, fulgent, incandescent, lambent, lucent, luminous, radiant, refulgent
rel glorious, resplendent, splendid

lusty *adj* **1** *syn* VIGOROUS, dynamic, energetic, red-blooded, strenuous, ||survigrous, vital
rel hale, healthy
ant effete
2 *syn* STRONG 3, concentrated, full-bodied, potent, robust
3 *syn* HUGE, enormous, immense, massive, mighty, prodigious, tremendous, vast, whacking, whopping

lusus *n syn* FREAK 2, abortion, miscreation, monster, monstrosity

luxuriant *adj* **1** *syn* PROFUSE, exuberant, lavish, lush, opulent, prodigal, profusive, riotous

---

syn synonym(s) *rel* related word(s)
idiom idiomatic equivalent(s) *con* contrasted word(s)
ant antonym(s) * vulgar
|| use limited; if in doubt, see a dictionary
The first word in a synonym list when printed in SMALL CAPITALS shows where there is more information about the group. For a more efficient use of this book see Explanatory Notes.

rel fecund, fertile, fruitful, prolific; rampant, rank
con barren, infertile, sterile, unfruitful
2 *syn* LUXURIOUS 3, Capuan, deluxe, luscious, lush, opulent, palatial, plush, sumptuous, upholstered

luxuriate *vb syn* WALLOW 3, bask, indulge, revel, roll, rollick, welter
rel overindulge, overdo; eat up, enjoy, feast, love, riot

luxurious *adj* **1** *syn* SENSUOUS, epicurean, luscious, lush, sensual, sensualistic, voluptuous
rel self-indulging, self-pampering; languishing, languorous
con self-abnegating, self-denying; austere, severe, stern
ant ascetic
2 *syn* GRAND 2, gorgeous, impressive, lavish, splendid, sumptuous
rel imposing, majestic, stately
3 ostentatiously rich or magnificent <the robber barons built *luxurious* homes which rivaled the palaces of Europe>
syn Capuan, deluxe, luscious, lush, luxuriant, opulent, palace, palatial, plush, plushy, sumptuous, upholstered
rel extravagant, grandiose, ostentatious, posh, pretentious, showy; awful, grand, imposing, magnificent, majestic, stately; Lucullan; elaborate, fancy; costly, expensive, precious
con economical, frugal, sparing, thrifty; exiguous, meager, scant, scanty, scrimpy, skimpy, spare

luxury *n* something adding to pleasure but not absolutely necessary <the poor cannot even afford the essentials, let alone occasional *luxuries*>
syn amenity, extravagance, frill, luxus, superfluity
rel comfort; embellishment, redundancy, self-indulgence; dainty, delicacy
con basics, essential(s), fundamental(s)

luxus *n syn* LUXURY, amenity, extravagance, frill, superfluity

lying *adj syn* DISHONEST, deceitful, knavish, mendacious, roguish, shifty, unhonest, untruthful
rel false, wrong; deceptive, delusive, delusory, misleading

lying-in *n syn* CONFINEMENT 2, accouchement, childbed

lyncean *adj syn* SHARP-EYED, eagle-eyed, hawk-eyed, lynx-eyed, sharp-sighted

lynx-eyed *adj syn* SHARP-EYED, eagle-eyed, hawk-eyed, lyncean, sharp-sighted

---

syn synonym(s) *rel* related word(s)
idiom idiomatic equivalent(s) *con* contrasted word(s)
ant antonym(s) * vulgar
|| use limited; if in doubt, see a dictionary
The first word in a synonym list when printed in SMALL CAPITALS shows where there is more information about the group. For a more efficient use of this book see Explanatory Notes.

M

ma *n* ***syn*** MOTHER 1, ‖mam, mama (*or* mamma), mammy, ‖mater, mom, mommy, mummy, ‖old lady, ‖old woman

macabre *adj* ***syn*** GHASTLY 1, grim, grisly, gruesome, hideous, horrible, horrid, horrifying, lurid, terrible
rel deadly, deathlike, deathly; ghostlike, ghostly

macaroni *n* ***syn*** FOP, Beau Brummel, blood, buck, coxcomb, dandy, dude, exquisite, lounge lizard, petit-maître

mace *n* ***syn*** CUDGEL, bat, baton, billy, billy club, bludgeon, club, knobkerrie, nightstick, ‖shillelagh

‖**mace** *n* ***syn*** SWINDLER, cheat, chiaus, con man, diddler, flimflammer, ‖grifter, gyp, mountebank, sharpie

‖**mace** *vb* ***syn*** CHEAT, beat, bilk, chisel, cozen, diddle, do, ‖duff, gyp, overreach

machinate *vb* **1** ***syn*** ENGINEER, finagle, maneuver, wangle
2 ***syn*** PLOT, cogitate, ‖collogue, collude, connive, conspire, contrive, devise, intrigue, scheme (out)

machination *n* ***syn*** PLOT 2, cabal, conspiracy, covin, intrigue, practice, scheme

machine *n* **1** ***syn*** CAR, auto, autocar, automobile, buggy, ‖bus, motor, motorcar
2 ***syn*** ROBOT 2, automaton, golem

machinery *n* ***syn*** EQUIPMENT, accouterment(s), apparatus, gear, habiliments, matériel, outfit, paraphernalia, tackle, tackling
rel agency, agent, channel, instrument, instrumentality, means, medium, organ, vehicle; contraption, contrivance, device, gadget; appliance, implement, instrument, tool, utensil

‖**mack** *n* ***syn*** PIMP 1, bully, cadet, ‖easy rider, fancy man, macquereau, pander

macquereau *n* ***syn*** PIMP 1, bully, cadet, ‖easy rider, fancy man, ‖mack, pander

macrocosm *n* ***syn*** UNIVERSE, cosmos (*or* kosmos), creation, macrocosmos, megacosm, nature, world
ant microcosm

macrocosmos *n* ***syn*** UNIVERSE, cosmos (*or* kosmos), creation, macrocosm, megacosm, nature, world
ant microcosm

mad *adj* **1** ***syn*** INSANE 1, ‖batty, cracked, crazy, daft, demented, deranged, lunatic, non compos mentis, unbalanced
rel delirious, frantic, frenetic, furious, rabid, wild
2 ***syn*** FOOLISH 2, absurd, ‖balmy, crazy, fantastic, insane, loony, ‖potty, preposterous, wacky
3 ***syn*** ILLOGICAL, fallacious, invalid, irrational, nonrational, reasonless, sophistic, unreasonable, unreasoned
4 ***syn*** ANGRY, acrimonious, choleric, heated, indignant, irate, ireful, waxy, wrathful, wroth
rel sore, worked up; affronted, offended, outraged
5 ***syn*** FURIOUS 2, corybantic, delirious, frantic, frenetic, frenzied, rabid, wild

mad *vb* ***syn*** ANGER 1, enrage, incense, infuriate, ire, madden, steam up, umbrage

mad *n* ***syn*** ANGER, fury, indignation, ire, rage, wrath

mad–brained *adj* ***syn*** RASH 1, brash, hasty, hotheaded, ill-advised, incautious, inconsiderate, madcap, reckless, thoughtless

madcap *adj* ***syn*** RASH 1, brash, hasty, hotheaded, ill-advised, incautious, inconsiderate, mad-brained, reckless, thoughtless

madden *vb* **1** to make insane <prolonged solitary confinement had *maddened* the prisoners>
syn craze, derange, distract, frenzy, unbalance, unhinge
rel shatter; possess
idiom drive insane (*or* mad *or* crazy)
2 ***syn*** ANGER 1, enrage, incense, infuriate, ire, mad, steam up, umbrage
con allay, assuage, mitigate, relieve

made–to–order *adj* ***syn*** CUSTOM-MADE, custom, custom-built, customized, custom-tailored, tailor-made

madhouse *n* ***syn*** ASYLUM 3, booby hatch, ‖bughouse, crazy house, loony bin, ‖nuthouse

madid *adj* ***syn*** WET 1, drenched, dripping, saturate, saturated, soaking, sodden, sopping, soppy, soused

madling *n* ***syn*** LUNATIC 1, bedlamite, dement, loon, loony, madman, maniac, non compos, nut, Tom o' Bedlam

madly *adv* ***syn*** HARD 2, fiercely, frantically, frenziedly, furiously, stormily, tumultuously, turbulently, violently, wildly
rel foolishly, insanely, irrationally; hastily, rashly

madman *n* **1** ***syn*** LUNATIC 1, bedlamite, dement, loon, loony, madling, maniac, non compos, nut, Tom o' Bedlam
2 ***syn*** FOOL 1, ass, *damfool, donkey, idiot, imbecile, jackass, jerk, nincompoop, ninny

madness *n* ***syn*** INSANITY 1, aberration, alienation, derangement, distraction, insaneness, lunacy, psychopathy, unbalance

maelstrom *n* ***syn*** EDDY, vortex, whirl, whirlpool
rel commotion, confusion, fury, storm, turmoil

magazine *n* **1** ***syn*** DEPOT 2, arsenal, depository, repository, store, storehouse
rel cache, lumber room
2 ***syn*** ARMORY, arsenal, depot, dump
3 ***syn*** JOURNAL, newspaper, organ, periodical, review
rel publication; digest, gazette; annual, bimonthly, biweekly, daily, monthy, quarterly, semiweekly, weekly

mage *n* ***syn*** MAGICIAN 1, charmer, conjurer, enchanter, magian, magus, necromancer, sorcerer, warlock, wizard

maggot *n* ***syn*** CAPRICE, bee, boutade, conceit, crotchet, fancy, freak, humor, notion, vagary

---

magian *n* ***syn*** MAGICIAN 1, charmer, conjurer, enchanter, mage, magus, necromancer, sorcerer, warlock, wizard

magian *adj* ***syn*** MAGIC, magical, mystic, necromantic, sorcerous, thaumaturgic, witchy, wizardly

magic *n* **1** the use of means (as charms or spells) believed to have supernatural power over natural forces <the practice of *magic*>
syn bewitchment, conjuring, conjury, enchantment, ensorcellment, incantation, magicking, necromancy, sorcery, thaumaturgy, witchcraft, witchery, witching, wizardry
rel abracadabra, alchemy, augury, charm, divining, exorcism, fortune-telling, mumbo jumbo, occultism, soothsaying, sortilege, voodooism; devilry, deviltry, diablerie, diabolism, satanism; wicca
2 the art of producing mysterious effects by illusion and sleight of hand <the club presented a program of clever *magic* to raise funds>
syn conjuring, legerdemain
idiom sleight of hand

magic *adj* having seemingly supernatural qualities or powers <modern medicine has developed a host of *magic* drugs>
syn magian, magical, mystic, necromantic, sorcerous, thaumaturgic, witchy, wizardly
rel extraordinary, marvelous, prodigious, remarkable, stupendous, unbelievable, unprecedented

magical *adj* ***syn*** MAGIC, magian, mystic, necromantic, sorcerous, thaumaturgic, witchy, wizardly

magician *n* **1** one who practices magical arts <a *magician* cast a spell over the child>
syn archimage, charmer, conjurer, enchanter, mage, magian, magus, necromancer, sorcerer, voodoo, voodooist, warlock, wizard; *compare* WITCH 1
rel augurer, brujo, diviner, exorciser, exorcist, invocator, thaumaturge, thaumaturgist; medicine man, shaman; prophet, seer, soothsayer; fortune-teller, medium; diabolist, satanist
2 one who practices tricks of illusion and sleight of hand <a *magician* performed tricks for the children at the party>
syn conjurer, illusionist, trickster

magicking *n* ***syn*** MAGIC 1, bewitchment, conjuring, enchantment, necromancy, sorcery, thaumaturgy, witchcraft, witchery, wizardry

magisterial *adj* **1** ***syn*** DICTATORIAL, authoritarian, authoritative, dictative, doctrinaire, dogmatic
rel disdainful, insolent, lordly, supercilious
2 ***syn*** MASTERFUL 1, bossy, domineering, high-handed, imperative, imperial, imperious, overbearing, peremptory
3 ***syn*** POMPOUS 1, arrogant, bloated, important, pontifical, puffy, self-important, stuffy, wiggy

magistrate *n* ***syn*** JUDGE 2, ‖beak, court, justice

magnanimous *adj* ***syn*** GENEROUS 1, benevolent, big, chivalrous, considerate, greathearted, lofty
rel altruistic, liberal, unselfish; great, highminded, knightly, noble, nobleminded, princely
con measly, paltry, petty, picayunish, picayune

magnate *n* a businessman of exceptional wealth, influence, or power <the oil and steel *magnates* who controlled whole nations>
syn baron, czar, king, merchant prince, mogul, prince, tycoon
rel figure, name, personage; ‖biggie, big gun, big-timer, ‖big wheel, fat cat, lion, nabob; plutocrat
idiom captain of industry

magnetic *adj* ***syn*** ATTRACTIVE 1, alluring, appealing, attracting, bewitching, captivating, drawing, enchanting, fascinating, seductive
rel arresting, irresistible; charismatic
con repellent, repugnant, repulsive

magnetism *n* ***syn*** CHARM 3, allure, appeal, charisma, fascination, glamour, witchcraft, witchery

magnetize *vb* ***syn*** ATTRACT 1, allure, bewitch, captivate, charm, draw, enchant, fascinate, take, wile

magnific *adj* ***syn*** GRAND 1, august, grandiose, imposing, lordly, magnificent, majestic, noble, princely, stately

magnificent *adj* **1** ***syn*** GRAND 1, august, grandiose, imposing, lordly, magnific, majestic, noble, princely, stately
rel glorious, resplendent, splendid, sublime, superb; luxurious, opulent, sumptuous
con abject, ignoble, mean, sordid; humble, lowly, meek; paltry
ant modest
2 ***syn*** SPLENDID 2, glorious, gorgeous, proud, resplendent, splendiferous, splendorous, sublime, superb
3 ***syn*** SUPERB 3, outstanding, standout, superexcellent, superlative

magnify *vb* **1** ***syn*** PRAISE 2, bless, celebrate, cry up, eulogize, extol, glorify, hymn, laud, panegyrize
2 ***syn*** EXALT 1, aggrandize, dignify, distinguish, ennoble, erect, glorify, honor, sublime, uprear
rel augment, enlarge, increase; amplify, dilate, distend, expand, inflate, swell
ant belittle, minimize
3 ***syn*** INCREASE 1, aggrandize, augment, beef (up), boost, enlarge, expand, extend, heighten, multiply
ant minify
4 ***syn*** INTENSIFY, aggravate, deepen, enhance, heighten, intensate, mount, redouble, rise, rouse
5 ***syn*** OVERPLAY 2, maximize, overemphasize, overstress
6 ***syn*** EMBROIDER, color, embellish, exaggerate, fudge, overcharge, overdraw, overpaint, overstate, pad

magniloquent *adj* ***syn*** RHETORICAL, aureate, bombastic, declamatory, euphuistic, flowery, grandiloquent, overblown, sonorous, swollen

magnitude *n* **1** ***syn*** ENORMITY 2, enormousness, hugeness, immensity, tremendousness, vastness
2 ***syn*** SIZE 1, admeasurement, dimension(s), dimensionality, extent, measure, proportion
3 ***syn*** SIZE 2, amplitude, bigness, greatness, largeness, sizableness

---

syn synonym(s) ***rel*** related word(s)
idiom idiomatic equivalent(s) ***con*** contrasted word(s)
ant antonym(s) * vulgar
‖ use limited; if in doubt, see a dictionary
The first word in a synonym list when printed in SMALL CAPITALS shows where there is more information about the group. For a more efficient use of this book see Explanatory Notes.

4 ***syn*** ORDER 4, extent, matter, neighborhood, range, tune, vicinity
5 ***syn*** IMPORTANCE, consequence, import, moment, momentousness, pith, significance, ‖signification, weight, weightiness

magnum opus *n* ***syn*** MASTERPIECE 1, chef d'oeuvre, classic, masterwork, tour de force

magpie *n* ***syn*** CHATTERBOX, bandar-log, blabber, blabbermouth, blabmouth, chatterer, gabber, jabberer, prater, prattler

magus *n* ***syn*** MAGICIAN 1, charmer, conjurer, enchanter, mage, magian, necromancer, sorcerer, warlock, wizard

mahogany *n* ***syn*** TABLE 1, board, dining table, dinner table, ‖table-board

maid *n* **1** ***syn*** GIRL 1, damsel, gal, lass, lassie, maiden, miss, missy, ‖quail, wench
2 a woman hired to do housework <in addition to her other duties the *maid* was expected to care for the baby>
syn biddy, girl, handmaid, hired girl, housemaid, maidservant
rel au pair girl; chambermaid, nursemaid, parlormaid; handmaiden; domestic, factotum, ‖muchacha, servant
idiom maid of all work

maiden *n* ***syn*** GIRL 1, damsel, gal, lass, lassie, maid, miss, missy, ‖quail, wench

maiden *adj* **1** ***syn*** VIRGIN 1, intact, undeflowered, virginal
rel husbandless; old-maidish, spinsterish, spinsterly
2 ***syn*** FIRST 2, earliest, initial, original, pioneer, primary, prime

maidenhead *n* ***syn*** VIRGINITY, ‖cherry, maidenhood

maidenhood *n* ***syn*** VIRGINITY, ‖cherry, maidenhead

maiden lady *n* ***syn*** SPINSTER, old maid, spinstress, ‖tabby

maidservant *n* ***syn*** MAID 2, biddy, girl, handmaid, hired girl, housemaid

maim *vb* to wound so severely as to deprive of the use of or to cause loss of a limb or member <an arm hanging useless, *maimed* in an auto accident>
syn cripple, dislimb, dismember, mayhem, mutilate; *compare* PARALYZE 1
rel disable, disfigure, hamstring; batter, break, ‖bung up, mangle, massacre, maul
con rehabilitate, restore, salvage; cure, fix, heal, mend, remedy, repair

main *n* ***syn*** OCEAN, blue, brine, ‖briny, deep, drink, sea

main *adj* ***syn*** CHIEF 2, capital, ‖cock, major, outstanding, predominant, preeminent, principal, star, stellar
rel foremost, head, leading, paramount; cardinal, controlling, essential, fundamental, vital; prevailing

‖**main** *adv* ***syn*** VERY 1, ‖awful, ‖big, ‖crazy, damned, ‖dreadful, exceedingly, extremely, ‖larruping, ‖monstrous

‖**mainline** *vb* ***syn*** SHOOT UP 2, shoot

mainly *adv* ***syn*** GENERALLY 1, chiefly, largely, mostly, overall, predominantly, primarily, principally

mainstay *n* a chief reliance <the *mainstay* of the organization held things together>
syn backbone, pillar, sinew(s)
rel brace, buttress, crutch, maintainer, prop, staff, standby, stay, support, supporter, sustainer, upholder

maintain *vb* **1** to keep in a state of repair, efficiency, or validity <he followed a careful regimen to *maintain* his good health>
syn keep up, preserve, save, sustain; *compare* SAVE 3
rel husband, manage; care (for), cultivate; guard, protect
con disregard, ignore, neglect, omit, overlook, slight
2 to uphold as true, right, proper, or acceptable often in the face of challenge or indifference <I *maintain* that his actions were justified by the circumstances>
syn argue, assert, claim, contend, defend, justify, vindicate, warrant
rel affirm, aver, avouch, avow, declare, profess, protest; emphasize, insist, persist, stress; correct, rectify, right
con contradict, deny, gainsay, traverse; challenge, query, question
3 ***syn*** SUPPORT 3, provide (for)

maintenance *n* ***syn*** LIVING, alimentation, alimony, bread, keep, livelihood, salt, subsistence, support, sustenance

majestic *adj* **1** ***syn*** GRAND 1, august, grandiose, imposing, lordly, magnific, magnificent, noble, princely, stately
rel courtly, dignified; ceremonious; imperial
2 ***syn*** KINGLY, kinglike, monarchal, monarchial, monarchical, regal, royal, sovereign

major *adj* **1** ***syn*** CHIEF 2, capital, ‖cock, main, outstanding, predominant, preeminent, principal, star, stellar
rel better, greater, higher, superior
2 ***syn*** BIG 1, considerable, extensive, hefty, large, large-scale, sizable
3 ***syn*** GRAVE 3, dangerous, fell, grievous, serious, ugly

make *vb* **1** ***syn*** EFFECT 1, bring about, cause, draw on, produce, secure
rel initiate, originate, start
2 ***syn*** GENERATE 1, create, father, hatch, originate, parent, procreate, produce, sire, spawn
rel brew
3 to bring something into being by forming, shaping, combining, or altering materials <*made* a dress from odd bits of material>
syn assemble, build, construct, erect, fabricate, fashion, forge, form, frame, manufacture, mold, produce, put together, shape; *compare* BUILD 1
4 ***syn*** DRAFT 3, draw up, formulate, frame, prepare
5 ***syn*** CONSTITUTE 1, compose, comprise, form, make up
6 ***syn*** PREPARE 1, fit, fix, get, make up, ready
7 ***syn*** DESIGNATE 2, appoint, finger, name, nominate, tap
8 ***syn*** ENACT 1, constitute, establish
9 ***syn*** INFER, collect, conclude, deduce, deduct, derive, ‖dope out, draw, gather, judge

---

syn synonym(s) *rel* related word(s)
idiom idiomatic equivalent(s) *con* contrasted word(s)
ant antonym(s) * vulgar
‖ use limited; if in doubt, see a dictionary
The first word in a synonym list when printed in SMALL CAPITALS shows where there is more information about the group. For a more efficient use of this book see Explanatory Notes.

10 ***syn*** EARN 1, acquire, bring in, ‖drag down, draw down, gain, get, knock down, win
rel harvest, reap
11 ***syn*** CLEAR 6, clean up, gain, net
12 ***syn*** FORCE 2, coerce, compel, concuss, constrain, oblige, shotgun
13 ***syn*** HEAD 3, bear, light out, set out, strike out, take off
rel break (for)
‖14 ***syn*** MEDDLE, busybody, butt in, fool, horn in, interfere, interlope, intermeddle, monkey (with), tamper (with)
15 ***syn*** RUN 8, extend, go, reach, stretch

make–believe *n* ***syn*** PRETENSE 2, charade, disguise, pageant, pretension, pretentiousness

make off *vb* ***syn*** RUN 2, bolt, flee, fly, scamper, scoot, ‖screw, skedaddle, skip, skirr
rel depart, go, leave, quit, retire, withdraw; abscond, decamp, escape

make out *vb* **1** ***syn*** APPREHEND 1, accept, catch, compass, comprehend, ‖dig, follow, grasp, see, take in
2 ***syn*** ESTABLISH 6, demonstrate, determine, prove, show
3 ***syn*** INFER, collect, conclude, deduce, deduct, derive, ‖dope out, draw, gather, judge
‖**4** ***syn*** SHIFT 5, do, do with, fare, get along, get by, get on, manage, muddle through, stagger (on *or* along)
5 ***syn*** SUCCEED 3, arrive, flourish, go, prosper, score, thrive

make over *vb* ***syn*** TRANSFER 4, abalienate, alien, alienate, assign, cede, convey, deed, remise, sign (over)

make–peace *n* ***syn*** PEACEMAKER, pacificator

maker *n* ***syn*** FATHER 2, architect, author, creator, founder, generator, inventor, originator, patriarch, sire
rel executor, operator; manufacturer

makeshift *n* ***syn*** RESOURCE 3, dernier ressort, expediency, expedient, recourse, refuge, resort, shift, stopgap, substitute

makeshift *adj* serving as a temporary expedient <forced to make *makeshift* plans>
syn provisional, rough-and-ready, rough-and-tumble, stopgap

make up *vb* **1** ***syn*** CONTRIVE 2, concoct, cook (up), devise, dream up, formulate, frame, hatch (up), invent, vamp (up)
2 ***syn*** MIX 1, blend, compound, fuse, interblend, interfuse, intermix, meld, merge, mingle
3 ***syn*** PREPARE 1, fit, fix, get, make, ready
4 ***syn*** CONSTITUTE 1, compose, comprise, form, make
5 ***syn*** COMPENSATE 1, atone (for), balance, counterbalance, counterpoise, countervail, offset, outweigh, redeem, set off

make up (to) *vb* ***syn*** ADDRESS 8, court, pursue, spark, sue, sweetheart, woo

syn synonym(s) ***rel*** related word(s)
idiom idiomatic equivalent(s) ***con*** contrasted word(s)
ant antonym(s) * vulgar
‖ use limited; if in doubt, see a dictionary
The first word in a synonym list when printed in SMALL CAPITALS shows where there is more information about the group. For a more efficient use of this book see Explanatory Notes.

makeup *n* **1** the way in which parts or constituents are related in an organized whole <the complex *makeup* of the eye>
syn architecture, composition, constitution, construction, design, formation
rel arrangement, ordering, organization, plan, setup; form, shape, style
2 ***syn*** DISPOSITION 3, character, complexion, humor, individualism, individuality, nature, personality, temper, temperament
rel cast, fiber, grain, mold, stamp, stripe, vein; constitution, frame
3 cosmetics used to color and beautify the face or body <with *makeup* on, she didn't look bad>
syn face, maquillage, paint, war paint
rel powder; blackface, grease paint

maladroit *adj* **1** ***syn*** AWKWARD 2, bumbling, clumsy, gauche, halting, ham-handed, heavy-handed, inept, lumbering, unhandy
rel blundering, floundering, stumbling, ungraceful; left-handed, unskilled
con deft, dexterous, handy; clever, cunning, ingenious
ant adroit
2 ***syn*** TACTLESS, brash, impolitic, undiplomatic, unpolitic, untactful

malady *n* ***syn*** DISEASE 1, affection, ailment, complaint, condition, disorder, ill, infirmity, sickness, syndrome

mala fide *adj* ***syn*** INSINCERE, ambidextrous, double, double-dealing, double-faced, doublehearted, double-minded, double-tongued, hypocritical, left-handed
ant bona fide

malaise *n* ***syn*** INFIRMITY 1, debility, decrepitude, disease, feebleness, infirmness, sickliness, unhealthiness

malapert *adj* ***syn*** SAUCY 1, arch, bantam, ‖cocket, pert

malapert *n* ***syn*** MINX, hussy, jade, saucebox, slut, snip

malapropos *adj* **1** ***syn*** IMPROPER 1, ill-timed, inappropriate, inapt, unbefitting, undue, unseasonable, unseemly, unsuitable, untimely
ant apropos
2 ***syn*** UNSEASONABLE 1, ill-seasoned, ill-timed, inopportune, mistimed, untimely

malarkey *n* ***syn*** NONSENSE 2, balderdash, blatherskite, bunkum, bushwa, guff, hogwash, hooey, poppycock, twaddle

malconformation *n* ***syn*** DEFORMITY, distortion, malformation, misshape

malcontent *n* **1** ***syn*** GROUCH, ‖bellyacher, complainer, crank, faultfinder, griper, growler, grumbler, kicker, sorehead
2 ***syn*** REBEL, anarch, anarchist, frondeur, insurgent, insurrectionist, mutineer, revolter

malcontent *adj* ***syn*** DISCONTENTED, discontent, disgruntled, dissatisfied, malcontented, uncontent, uncontented, ungratified
rel alienated, disaffected, estranged; disobedient, ungovernable, unruly; restless; contumacious, factious, insubordinate, mutinous, rebellious, seditious

malcontented *adj* ***syn*** DISCONTENTED, discontent, disgruntled, dissatisfied, malcontent, uncontent, uncontented, ungratified

male *adj* ***syn*** VIRILE 2, manlike, manly, masculine

malediction *n* ***syn*** CURSE 1, anathema, commination, imprecation, malison

ant benediction
malefactor *n* ***syn*** CRIMINAL, felon, lawbreaker, offender
rel blackguard, knave, miscreant, rascal, rogue, scoundrel; evildoer, sinner, wrongdoer
malefic *adj* ***syn*** SINISTER, baleful, maleficent, malign
ant benefic
maleficent *adj* ***syn*** SINISTER, baleful, malefic, malign
ant beneficent
malevolence *n* ***syn*** MALICE, despite, despitefulness, grudge, ill will, maliciousness, malignity, spite, spitefulness, spleen
rel antagonism, hostility; abhorrence, abomination, detestation
ant benevolence
malevolent *adj* ***syn*** MALICIOUS, bitchy, despiteful, evil, hateful, malign, malignant, spiteful, vicious, wicked
rel baleful, malefic, maleficent, sinister
con benign, benignant, kind, kindly
ant benevolent
malformation *n* ***syn*** DEFORMITY, distortion, malconformation, misshape
malice *n* a desiring or wishing pain, injury, or distress to another <they sought to ruin his reputation out of pure *malice*>
syn despite, despitefulness, grudge, ill will, malevolence, maliciousness, malignancy, malignity, spite, spitefulness, spleen
rel bane, poison, venom; bile; animosity, animus, antipathy, down, enmity; hate, hatefulness, hatred, invidiousness, meanness; bitterness, resentment, unbrage
con benevolence, benignancy, benignity, charity, kindliness, kindness
malicious *adj* having, showing, or indicative of intense often vicious ill will <the helpless victim of *malicious* rumors>
syn bitchy, catty, despiteful, evil, hateful, malevolent, malign, malignant, nasty, rancorous, spiteful, spitish, vicious, wicked
rel poisonous, poison-pen, venomous, virulent; baneful, deleterious, detrimental, noxious, pernicious; envious, green, green-eyed, jealous; mean, petty
con benevolent, charitable, friendly, kind, kindly; considerate, thoughtful
maliciousness *n* ***syn*** MALICE, despite, grudge, ill will, malevolence, malignancy, malignity, spite, spitefulness, spleen
malign *adj* **1** ***syn*** SINISTER, baleful, malefic, maleficent
rel baneful, deleterious, detrimental, injurious, noxious, pernicious
con auspicious, favorable, propitious; fortunate, happy, lucky, providential
ant benign
2 ***syn*** MALICIOUS, despiteful, evil, hateful, malevolent, malignant, rancorous, spiteful, vicious, wicked
rel antagonistic, antipathetic, hostile, inimical
con benignant, kind, kindly
ant benign
malign *vb* to speak evil of for the purpose of injuring and without regard for the truth <the candidates increasingly *maligned* each other as the campaign degenerated>
syn asperse, befoul, bespatter, blacken, calumniate, defame, denigrate, libel, ||scandal, scandalize, slander, slur, smear, spatter, tear down, traduce, vilify, villainize
rel decry, depreciate, derogate, detract, disparage; opprobriate, revile, vituperate; backbite, besmirch, defile, pollute, smirch, soil, stain, sully, taint, tarnish
idiom blow upon, cast aspersion(s) on (*or* upon)
con acclaim, applaud, eulogize, extol, laud, praise; defend, justify, maintain, vindicate
malignancy *n* ***syn*** MALICE, despite, grudge, ill will, malevolence, maliciousness, malignity, spite, spitefulness, spleen
malignant *adj* ***syn*** MALICIOUS, despiteful, evil, hateful, malevolent, malign, rancorous, spiteful, vicious, wicked
rel devilish, diabolical, fiendish
con altruistic, benevolent, charitable, humane
ant benignant
maligning *adj* ***syn*** LIBELOUS, backbiting, calumnious, defamatory, detracting, detractive, scandalous, slanderous, traducing, vilifying
malignity *n* ***syn*** MALICE, despite, grudge, ill will, malevolence, maliciousness, malignancy, spite, spitefulness, spleen
rel revengefulness, vengefulness, vindictiveness
ant benignity
malison *n* ***syn*** CURSE 1, anathema, commination, imprecation, malediction
ant benison
||**malkin** *n* ***syn*** SLATTERN 1, dowd, dowdy, drab, draggle-tail, slut, ||streel, traipse
malleable *adj* ***syn*** PLASTIC, adaptable, ductile, moldable, pliable, pliant, supple
rel governable, manageable; transformable
con intractable, recalcitrant, ungovernable, unmanageable, unruly
ant refractory
malleate *vb* ***syn*** HAMMER 1, beat, pound
malodorous *adj* **1** having an unpleasant smell <*malodorous* cheeses>
syn fetid, frowsy, funky, fusty, gamy, high, mephitic, musty, nidorous, noisome, olid, putrid, rancid, rank, reeking, reeky, ||smellful, smelly, stale, stenchful, stenchy, stinking, stinky, strong, whiffy; *compare* ODOROUS
rel bad, foul, offensive, nauseating, vile; decayed, decomposed, fuggy, off, rotten, spoiled, tainted; nasty, noxious, pestilential, poisonous, polluted
con clean, deodorized, fresh
ant fragrant, sweet
2 ***syn*** INDECOROUS, improper, indecent, indelicate, rough, unbecoming, undecorous, ungodly, unseemly, untoward
maltreat *vb* ***syn*** ABUSE 4, ill-treat, ill-use, mistreat, misuse, outrage
||**mam** *n* ***syn*** MOTHER 1, ma, mama (*or* mamma), mammy, ||mater, mom, mommy, mummy, ||old lady, ||old woman

---

syn synonym(s) ***rel*** related word(s)
idiom idiomatic equivalent(s) ***con*** contrasted word(s)
ant antonym(s) * vulgar
|| use limited; if in doubt, see a dictionary
The first word in a synonym list when printed in SMALL CAPITALS shows where there is more information about the group. For a more efficient use of this book see Explanatory Notes.

mama (*or* **mamma**) *n* ***syn*** MOTHER 1, ma, ‖mam, mammy, ‖mater, mom, mommy, mummy, ‖old lady, ‖old woman

‖**mammock** *vb* ***syn*** DISORDER 1, disarrange, disarray, dislocate, disorganize, disrupt, disturb, jumble, mess (up), mix up

mammoth *n* ***syn*** GIANT, behemoth, leviathan, monster, whale

mammoth *adj* ***syn*** HUGE, behemothic, colossal, elephantine, enormous, gargantuan, gigantic, leviathan, mastodonic, monstrous

mammy *n* ***syn*** MOTHER 1, ma, ‖mam, mama (*or* mamma), ‖mater, mom, mommy, mummy, ‖old lady, ‖old woman

man *n* **1** ***syn*** HUMAN, being, body, ‖character, creature, individual, mortal, person, personage, soul
2 ***syn*** MANKIND, flesh, Homo sapiens, humanity, humankind, mortality
3 a male human being <just an average *man* trying to get by>
syn ‖bloke, boy, buck, ‖cat, chap, cuss, fellow, galoot, ‖gee, gent, gentleman, guy, he, ‖mun, skate, snap, ‖stirra; *compare* HUMAN
4 ***syn*** HUSBAND, ‖hubby, lord, ‖master, mister, Mr., ‖old man
5 ***syn*** LOVER 1, boyfriend, fancy man, master, paramour
6 ***syn*** POLICEMAN, bluecoat, ‖bull, cop, ‖flatfoot, ‖fuzz, ‖heat, John Law, officer, ‖pig

manage *vb* **1** ***syn*** CONDUCT 3, carry on, direct, keep, operate, ordain, run
rel superintend; guide
2 ***syn*** GOVERN 3, control, direct, dominate, handle
3 ***syn*** SHIFT 5, do, fare, get along, get by, get on, ‖make out, muddle through, stagger (on *or* along)
rel bring about, carry out, contrive, effect, execute; accomplish, achieve, succeed
idiom sink or swim on one's own
con collapse, fail, fall down; give up, poop (out)

management *n* ***syn*** OVERSIGHT 1, care, charge, conduct, handling, intendance, running, superintendence, superintendency, supervision

manager *n* ***syn*** EXECUTIVE, administrator, exec, officer, official
rel handler, impresario, producer

man-at-arms *n* ***syn*** SOLDIER, fighter, fighting man, GI, serviceman, swad, ‖swaddy, ‖sweat, warrior

mancipium *n* ***syn*** SLAVE 1, bondman, bondslave, bondsman, chattel

mandarin *n* ***syn*** BUREAUCRAT

mandate *n* ***syn*** COMMAND 1, behest, bidding, charge, dictate, injunction, order, word
rel decree, fiat, imperative; authority, authorization

---

syn synonym(s) ***rel*** related word(s)
idiom idiomatic equivalent(s) ***con*** contrasted word(s)
ant antonym(s) * vulgar
‖ use limited; if in doubt, see a dictionary
The first word in a synonym list when printed in SMALL CAPITALS shows where there is more information about the group. For a more efficient use of this book see Explanatory Notes.

mandatory *adj* containing or constituting a command <*mandatory* entrance examinations>
syn compulsatory, compulsory, imperative, imperious, obligatory, required
rel essential, indispensable, irremissible, necessary, needful, requisite; binding, commanding, compelling, de rigueur; forced, involuntary
con discretionary, elective, voluntary
ant optional

maneuver *n* **1** ***syn*** MEASURE 7, move, procedure, proceeding, step
2 ***syn*** TRICK 1, artifice, device, feint, gambit, gimmick, jig, play, ploy, stratagem
rel contrivance, device; intrigue, machination, manipulation, plot; demarche, movement, plan; finesse, subterfuge

maneuver *vb* **1** ***syn*** ENGINEER, finagle, machinate, wangle
rel navigate; finesse; design
2 ***syn*** HANDLE 2, dispense, manipulate, ply, swing, wield
rel navigate
3 ***syn*** MANIPULATE 2, beguile, exploit, finesse, jockey, play

man Friday *n* ***syn*** RIGHT-HAND MAN, girl Friday, right hand

manful *adj* ***syn*** BRAVE 1, bold, courageous, dauntless, fearless, intrepid, unafraid, undaunted, valiant, valorous

mangle *vb* ***syn*** BATTER 1, ‖bung up, maul
rel damage, impair, injure, mar; deface, disfigure; contort, deform, distort; butcher, hack

mangled *adj* ***syn*** LACERATED, rent, torn

mangy *adj* ***syn*** SHABBY 1, decrepit, down-at-heel, moth-eaten, scruffy, seedy, sleazy, squalid, tagrag, tattered

manhandle *vb* to treat roughly <riot police *manhandled* innocent bystanders>
syn knock about, mishandle, rough (up), roughhouse, slap around
rel abuse, maltreat, mistreat; batter, ‖bung up, mangle, maul

mania *n* ***syn*** FETISH 2, fixation, obsession, thing
rel craze, enthusiasm, fancy, fascination, infatuation, passion; compulsion, fixed idea, hangup, idée fixe

maniac *adj* ***syn*** INSANE 1, ‖batty, cracked, crazed, crazy, demented, deranged, lunatic, mad, unsound
rel berserk, delirious, frantic, frenetic, frenzied, furious, rabid, raging, ranting, violent, wild

maniac *n* **1** ***syn*** LUNATIC 1, bedlamite, dement, loon, loony, madling, madman, non compos, nut, Tom o' Bedlam
2 ***syn*** ENTHUSIAST, bigot, bug, fanatic, fiend, freak, nut, zealot

manifest *adj* ***syn*** CLEAR 5, apparent, distinct, evident, obvious, palpable, patent, plain, straightforward, unambiguous
rel disclosed, divulged, revealed, told; evidenced, evinced, shown; noticeable, prominent
con implicit; obscure

manifest *vb* **1** ***syn*** EMBODY 1, exteriorize, externalize, incarnate, materialize, objectify, personalize, personify, personize, substantiate
2 ***syn*** SHOW 2, demonstrate, evidence, evince, exhibit, illustrate, mark, ostend, proclaim

rel display, expose; express, utter, vent, voice
con adumbrate, shadow
ant suggest

manifold *adj* comprehending or uniting various features <a *manifold* operation>
syn diverse, diversiform, multifarious, multifold, multiform, multiplex, multivarious
rel multiphase, polymorphic, polymorphous
con homogeneous, pure, uniform; plain, simple, straightforward, uncomplex, uncomplicated

manifold *vb syn* INCREASE 1, aggrandize, augment, beef (up), boost, compound, enlarge, expand, magnify, multiply

manikin *n syn* DWARF, homunculus, hop-o'-my-thumb, lilliputian, midge, midget, peewee, pygmy, runt, Tom Thumb

manipulate *vb* **1** *syn* HANDLE 2, dispense, maneuver, ply, swing, wield
2 to control or play upon by artful, unfair, or insidious means <the sycophant cleverly *manipulated* his master>
syn beguile, exploit, finesse, jockey, maneuver, play; *compare* ENGINEER
rel machinate, use; conduct, control, direct, engineer, manage

mankind *n* the human race <all *mankind* will benefit from this new discovery>
syn flesh, Homo sapiens, humanity, humankind, man, mortality; *compare* HUMAN

manlike *adj* **1** *syn* ANTHROPOID, anthropomorphic, anthropomorphous, humanoid
2 *syn* VIRILE 2, male, manly, masculine

manly *adj* **1** *syn* VIRILE 2, male, manlike, masculine
2 *syn* BRAVE 1, bold, courageous, dauntless, fearless, intrepid, unafraid, undaunted, valiant, valorous

man–made *adj syn* SYNTHETIC, artificial, factitious

manner *n* **1** *syn* HABIT 1, consuetude, custom, habitude, practice, trick, usage, use, way, wont
2 *syn* METHOD 1, fashion, mode, modus, system, technique, way, wise
rel custom, habit, habitude, practice, usage, use, wont; form, style
3 *syn* STYLE 4, way
4 *syn* VEIN 1, fashion, mode, style, tone
rel form, turn; affectation, affectedness, mannerism; idiosyncrasy, peculiarity
5 manners *pl* habitual conduct or deportment in social intercourse evaluated according to some conventional standard of politeness or civility <a person with impeccable *manners*>
syn amenities, civilities, decorum(s), etiquette, mores, proprieties
rel formalities, protocol; elegancies; bearing, behavior, demeanor, deportment, mien, p's and q's; mannerliness
idiom conduct becoming a gentleman
con mannerlessness, unmannerliness

mannered *adj syn* SELF-CONSCIOUS, affected, conscious

mannerism *n syn* POSE 2, affectation, air(s), lugs, prettyism
rel eccentricity, idiosyncrasy; oddness, peculiarity, queerness, singularity

mannerless *adj syn* RUDE 6, discourteous, disgracious, disrespectful, ill-bred, ill-mannered, impolite, uncivil, unmannered, unmannerly
ant mannerly

mannerly *adj syn* CIVIL 2, courteous, genteel, polite, well-mannered
ant mannerless, unmannerly

manor *n* **1** *syn* MANSION, castle, chateau, villa
2 *syn* ESTATE 3, acres, land, quinta

mansion *n* a large imposing residence <the governor's *mansion*>
syn castle, chateau, manor, villa
rel estate, hall, house

manslaughter *n syn* MURDER, blood, ‖bump-off, foul play, homicide, killing

manslayer *n syn* MURDERER, homicide, killer, slayer

mantic *adj syn* PROPHETIC, apocalyptic, Delphian, fatidic, oracular, prophetical, sibylline, vatic, vaticinal

mantle *vb syn* BLUSH, color, crimson, flush, glow, pink, pinken, redden, rose, rouge

man–to–man *adj syn* FRANK, candid, open, openhearted, straightforward, unconcealed, undisguised, undissembled, unreserved, unvarnished

manual *n syn* HANDBOOK, Baedeker, compendium, enchiridion, guide, guidebook, vade mecum
rel abecedarium, hornbook, primer; text, textbook

manufactory *n syn* FACTORY, mill, plant, works

manufacture *vb syn* MAKE 3, fabricate, fashion, forge, form, frame, mold, produce, put together, shape

manumit *vb syn* FREE, discharge, emancipate, liberate, loose, loosen, release, unbind, unchain, unshackle
ant enslave

many *adj* consisting of a goodly but indefinite number <*many* lives were lost in the flood>
syn legion, multifarious, multitudinal, multitudinous, numerous, populous, ‖several, sundry, various, voluminous
rel divers, manifold, multiple, multiplicate, multiplied, myriad; abounding, abundant, bounteous, bountiful, copious, plentiful
con meager, scant, scanty, sparse; only, sole
ant few

many *pron syn* SUNDRY, divers, ‖several, various

many–sided *adj* **1** *syn* MULTILATERAL
2 *syn* VERSATILE, adaptable, all-around, ambidextrous, mobile, myriad-minded

map *n* **1** *syn* CHART 1, graph
rel picture, portrayal; delineation, design, diagram, draft, outline, sketch, tracing
‖**2** *syn* FACE 1, countenance, ‖dial, features, ‖kisser, mug, ‖pan, phiz, ‖puss, visage

map (out) *vb syn* DESIGN 3, arrange, lay out, plan, set out

maquillage *n syn* MAKEUP 3, face, paint, war paint

mar *vb syn* INJURE 1, blemish, damage, harm, hurt, impair, prejudice, spoil, tarnish, vitiate
rel bruise, scar, scratch, warp; ruin, wreck

---

syn synonym(s) — *rel* related word(s)
idiom idiomatic equivalent(s) — *con* contrasted word(s)
ant antonym(s) — * vulgar
‖ use limited; if in doubt, see a dictionary
The first word in a synonym list when printed in SMALL CAPITALS shows where there is more information about the group. For a more efficient use of this book see Explanatory Notes.

con adorn, beautify, decorate, embellish; mend, patch, repair; amend, correct, emend, rectify, reform, revise

maraud *vb* ***syn*** RAID 1, foray, harass, harry

marauder *n* one who raids in search of plunder < *marauders* sacked village after village >
syn bandit, brigand, bummer, cateran, depredator, despoiler, forager, freebooter, looter, pillager, plunderer, raider, ravager, ravisher, sacker, spoiler, spoliator
rel buccaneer, desperado, pirate; wrecker

marblehearted *adj* ***syn*** UNFEELING 2, callous, cold-blooded, hard-boiled, hardened, heartless, obdurate, stony, uncompassionate, unsympathetic
ant softhearted

marbles *n pl* ***syn*** WIT 2, lucidity, mind, reason, saneness, sanity, sense(s), soundness

march *n* ***syn*** FRONTIER 1, border, borderland, marchland
rel boundary, periphery; territory; outlands, provinces

march *vb* ***syn*** ADJOIN, abut, border, butt (on *or* against), communicate, join, line, neighbor, touch, verge
rel fringe, hem, rim, skirt; extend; parallel

march *vb* **1** ***syn*** AGREE 4, accord, check, correspond, dovetail, fit (in), ||gee, go, square, tally
2 ***syn*** STRIDE 1, sling, stalk, ||striddle
3 ***syn*** ADVANCE 5, get along, get on, move, proceed, progress

march *n* ***syn*** ADVANCE 2, advancement, anabasis, headway, ongoing, proficiency, progress

marchland *n* ***syn*** FRONTIER 1, border, borderland, march

mare's nest *n* ***syn*** IMPOSTURE, cheat, flimflam, fraud, hoax, humbug, put-on, sell, spoof, swindle
rel babel, clamor, din, hubbub, hullabaloo, racket, uproar

margin *n* **1** ***syn*** BORDER 1, brim, brink, edge, hem, perimeter, periphery, selvage, skirt, verge
rel frame, trimming; shore; side
2 ***syn*** ROOM 3, elbowroom, latitude, leeway, play, scope
3 ***syn*** MINIMUM

margin *vb* ***syn*** BORDER 1, bound, edge, fringe, hem, outline, rim, skirt, surround, verge
rel abut, connect, join, line, neighbor, touch

marijuana *n* the dried leaves and flowering tops of the pistillate hemp plant sometimes smoked for their intoxicating effect < *marijuana* was smoked by several students at the party >
syn boo, cannabis, grass, ||Mary Jane, moocah, pot, ||tea, weed
rel joint, reefer; hash, hashish

marine *adj* **1** of or relating to the sea < *marine* biology >
syn maritime, oceanic, thalassic
rel hydrographic oceanographic; abyssal, bathyal, bathybic, bathysmal, benthic, dipsey, neritic, pelagic; aquatic, fluvial, fluviatile, lacustrine
2 of or relating to the navigation of the sea < *marine* charts and maps >
syn maritime, nautical, navigational
rel naval; seamanlike, seamanly; deep-sea, ocean-going, seafaring, seagoing

mariner *n* one engaged in sailing or handling a ship <the tanker crew was made up mostly of experienced *mariners*>
syn jack, jack-tar, sailor, sailorman, salt, seaman, tar, tarpaulin
rel bluejacket, gob, rating, ||swab, ||swabbie; ||lascar, ||limey; old salt, sea dog, shellback

marital *adj* ***syn*** MATRIMONIAL, conjugal, connubial, hymeneal, married, nuptial, spousal, wedded

maritime *adj* **1** ***syn*** MARINE 2, nautical, navigational
2 ***syn*** MARINE 1, oceanic, thalassic

mark *n* **1** ***syn*** AMBITION 2, aim, goal, objective, quaesitum, target
2 ***syn*** TARGET 1, butt, sitting duck
3 ***syn*** USE 4, duty, function, goal, object, objective, purpose, target
4 ***syn*** FOOL 3, chump, fall guy, fish, gudgeon, gull, pigeon, sap, sucker, victim
5 ***syn*** INDICATION 3, evidence, index, indicia, sign, significant, symptom, token
rel attribute, emblem, symbol, type; character, property, quality
6 ***syn*** QUALITY 1, affection, attribute, character, characteristic, feature, peculiarity, property, trait, virtue
7 a device (as a word) pointing distinctly to the origin or ownership of merchandise to which it is applied and legally reserved to the exclusive use of the owner <the company was brought to court for illegally using the *mark* of its rival>
syn brand, logo, logotype, trademark
rel label, stamp
idiom brand name
8 ***syn*** CHARACTER 1, sign, symbol
9 ***syn*** NOTICE 1, attention, cognizance, heed, ||mind, note, observance, observation, regard, remark

mark *vb* **1** ***syn*** CHOOSE 1, cull, elect, opt (for), optate, pick, pick out, prefer, select, single (out)
2 ***syn*** SHOW 5, indicate, read, record, register, say
3 ***syn*** SHOW 2, demonstrate, evidence, evince, exhibit, illustrate, manifest, ostend, proclaim
4 ***syn*** CHARACTERIZE 2, distinguish, individualize, individuate, qualify, signalize, singularize
rel bespeak, betoken, denote, signify
idiom set apart
5 ***syn*** SEE 1, behold, discern, distinguish, note, notice, observe, perceive, remark, view
rel record, register; attend, heed, regard

mark (out) *vb* ***syn*** DEMARCATE 1, bound, delimit, delimitate, determine, limit, measure
rel lay off, mark off; chart, lay out, map

mark down *vb* **1** ***syn*** REDUCE 2, clip, cut, cut back, cut down, lower, pare, shave, slash
ant mark up
2 ***syn*** DEPRECIATE 1, decry, devaluate, devalue, downgrade, lower, underprize, undervalue, write down, write off

---

syn synonym(s) *rel* related word(s)
idiom idiomatic equivalent(s) *con* contrasted word(s)
ant antonym(s) * vulgar
|| use limited; if in doubt, see a dictionary
The first word in a synonym list when printed in SMALL CAPITALS shows where there is more information about the group. For a more efficient use of this book see Explanatory Notes.

marked *adj* ***syn*** NOTICEABLE, arresting, conspicuous, outstanding, pointed, prominent, remarkable, salient, signal, striking
rel distinguished, noted; considerable

market *n* ***syn*** STORE 4, outlet, shop, showroom

market *vb* **1** ***syn*** SELL 3, merchandise, retail
rel wholesale
2 ***syn*** SELL 2, give, vend

marketable *adj* capable of being sold < *marketable* commodities >
syn merchandisable, merchantable, salable, sellable, trafficable, vendible
rel commercial; profitable, selling; fit, good, sound, wholesome
con unmerchantable, unsalable
ant unmarketable

‖**maroon** *vb* ***syn*** CAMP, bivouac, ‖bivvy, encamp, ‖laager, tent

marred *adj* ***syn*** DAMAGED, flawed, impaired, spoiled
rel banged-up, battered, bruised, mutilated; ruined, wrecked
ant unmarred

marriage *n* **1** the state of being united to a person of the opposite sex as husband or wife < *marriage* was not in the plans of this couple >
syn conjugality, connubiality, matrimony, wedlock
rel match, union
2 ***syn*** WEDDING, bridal, espousal(s), nuptial(s), spousal

marriage broker *n* one who arranges marriages <the old widow served as the town's *marriage broker* >
syn go-between, matchmaker
rel shadchan

marriage portion *n* ***syn*** DOWRY, dot, dower

married *adj* ***syn*** MATRIMONIAL, conjugal, connubial, hymeneal, marital, nuptial, spousal, wedded

marrow *n* ***syn*** ESSENCE 2, bottom, essentiality, pith, quintessence, quintessential, soul, stuff, substance, virtuality
rel core, heart, kernel, meat

marrowy *adj* ***syn*** PITTY, compact, epigrammatic, meaty

marry *vb* **1** to take as spouse <he *married* her for her money >
syn catch, espouse, wed
rel wive
idiom get hitched, get married, tie the knot
con annul, divorce, separate
2 to join in wedlock <the minister *married* all three daughters in one ceremony >
syn ‖hitch, mate, splice, tie, wed
idiom tie the knot, unite in marriage
3 ***syn*** JOIN 1, associate, combine, conjoin, conjugate, couple, link, one, relate, yoke

marsh *n* ***syn*** SWAMP, baygall, bog, fen, marshland, mire, morass, quag, quagmire, swampland

marshal *vb* **1** ***syn*** ORDER 1, arrange, array, dispose, methodize, organize, systematize
rel distribute, space; escort, guide, shepherd, usher
2 ***syn*** MOBILIZE 3, muster, organize, rally

marshland *n* ***syn*** SWAMP, bog, fen, marsh, mire, morass, ‖moss, quagmire, slough, swampland

martial *adj* belonging to, engaged in, or appropriate to the affairs of war <the reviewing officer saw the company standing in *martial* array >
syn military, warlike
rel bellicose, belligerent, combative, pugnacious; aggressive, militant; high-spirited, mettlesome, spirited
con civil, civilian; irenic, pacific, peaceable, peaceful
ant unmartial

martyr *vb* ***syn*** AFFLICT, agonize, crucify, excruciate, harrow, rack, torment, torture, try, wring

martyrize *vb* ***syn*** AFFLICT, agonize, crucify, excruciate, harrow, rack, torment, torture, try, wring

marvel *n* ***syn*** WONDER 1, miracle, phenomenon, portent, prodigy, sensation, stunner

marveling *n* ***syn*** WONDER 2, admiration, amaze, amazement, wonderment
rel surprise

marvelous *adj* **1** causing or exciting wonder <the way in which he could bring together opposing forces was truly *marvelous* >
syn amazing, astonishing, astounding, miraculous, prodigious, spectacular, staggering, strange, stupendous, surprising, wonderful, wondrous
rel awe-inspiring, awesome, awful, awing; incomprehensible, inconceivable, incredible, unimaginable; fabulous, phenomenal, supernatural; exceptional, extraordinary; bewildering, confounding, striking, stunning
con commonplace, ordinary, routine; blah, unexciting, uninteresting
2 superior or outstanding of its kind <had a *marvelous* weekend >
syn ‖cool, ‖dandy, divine, dreamy, ‖galluptious, glorious, groovy, hot, hunky-dory, ‖keen, ‖neat, nifty, peachy, ripping, sensational, super, swell, terrific, wonderful; *compare* EXCELLENT, SUPERIOR 4, SUPREME
rel agreeable, enjoyable, pleasant, pleasurable; rewarding, satisfying
con dreary, dull, humdrum, monotonous, tedious; inferior, low-grade, mean, poor, punk

‖**Mary Jane** *n* ***syn*** MARIJUANA, boo, cannabis, grass, moocah, pot, ‖tea, weed

mascot *n* ***syn*** CHARM 2, amulet, fetish, juju, luck, periapt, phylactery, talisman, zemi

masculine *adj* ***syn*** VIRILE 2, male, manlike, manly
ant effeminate, unmasculine

mash *n* ***syn*** CLUTTER 2, hash, hugger-mugger, jumble, jungle, litter, muddle, rummage, scramble, tumble

mash *vb* **1** ***syn*** CRUSH 2, becrush, bruise, ‖mush (up), pulp, squash
‖**2** ***syn*** PRESS 1, bear, crowd, crush, jam, push, ‖squab, squash, squeeze, squish

mashed *adj* ***syn*** ENAMORED 1, smitten, soft (on), spoony (over *or* on)

masher *n* ***syn*** WOLF, Casanova, chaser, Don Juan, ladies' man, lady-killer, philander, philanderer, womanizer

mash note *n* ***syn*** LOVE LETTER, billet-doux

---

syn synonym(s) | *rel* related word(s)
idiom idiomatic equivalent(s) | *con* contrasted word(s)
ant antonym(s) | * vulgar
‖ use limited; if in doubt, see a dictionary
The first word in a synonym list when printed in SMALL CAPITALS shows where there is more information about the group. For a more efficient use of this book see Explanatory Notes.

mask *n* **1** a cover or partial cover for the face that has openings for the eyes and is used especially for disguise <on Halloween he wore a pirate's *mask*>
syn domino, doughface, false face, visor, vizard
rel disguise, masquerade; veil
2 an outward appearance that seeks to obscure an underlying true character <he was able to maintain a *mask* of dignity and tranquillity in his time of anxiety>
syn cloak, color, coloring, cover, disguise, disguisement, facade, face, false front, front, guise, masquerade, muffler, pretense, pretext, put-on, semblance, show, veil, veneer, window dressing; *compare* APPEARANCE 2
rel affectation, air, pose, posture; fakery, sham; dissembling, dissimulation, seeming, simulation; appearance, aspect

mask *vb syn* DISGUISE, camouflage, cloak, dissemble, dissimulate, dress up
rel screen, secrete, veil; blur; defend, guard, protect, safeguard, shield

masquerade *n syn* MASK 2, cloak, color, cover, disguise, facade, face, front, show, veil

masquerade *vb syn* POSE 4, attitudinize, pass (as *or* for), pass off, posture

mass *n* **1** *syn* BODY 4, bulk, object, volume
2 *syn* PILE 1, bank, heap, hill, mound, mountain, pyramid, shock, stack, stockpile
3 *syn* BULK 1, volume
rel aggregate, aggregation, conglomerate, conglomeration; sum, whole
4 *syn* BODY 3, bulk, core, corpus, staple, substance
5 *syn* MUCH, great deal, heap, lot, lump, ‖mess, mountain, pack, peck, pile
6 *usu* **masses** *pl syn* RABBLE 2, canaille, dreg(s), mob, proletariat, ragtag and bobtail, riffraff, scum, trash, unwashed

massacre *vb syn* SLAUGHTER 3, annihilate, decimate, exterminate, wipe (out)

massacre *n* the act or an instance of killing a considerable number of human beings under circumstances of atrocity or cruelty <the *massacre* of the Indians by the soldiers and settlers>
syn bloodbath, bloodshed, butchery, carnage, slaughter
rel blood purge, decimation, genocide, pogrom; internecion; assassination, killing, murder, slaying

massive *adj* **1** *syn* HEAVY 1, cumbersome, cumbrous, hefty, ponderous, weighty
rel hulking, hulky, massy
2 *syn* HUGE, elephantine, gigantic, grand, immense, mighty, monumental, mountainous, tremendous, vast
3 *syn* MONSTROUS 1, cracking, fantastic, monumental, mortal, prodigious, stupendous, towering, tremendous

syn synonym(s) — *rel* related word(s)
idiom idiomatic equivalent(s) — *con* contrasted word(s)
ant antonym(s) — * vulgar
‖ use limited; if in doubt, see a dictionary
The first word in a synonym list when printed in SMALL CAPITALS shows where there is more information about the group. For a more efficient use of this book see Explanatory Notes.

massy *adj syn* HUGE, colossal, enormous, giant, gigantic, heroic, immense, jumbo, mammoth, massive

master *n* **1** *syn* EXPERT, artist, artiste, authority, past master, professional, proficient, virtuoso, whiz, wizard
rel maestro, savant; genius, mastermind; guru, swami
2 *syn* LEADER 2, boss, chief, chieftain, cock, dominator, head, headman, hierarch, honcho
rel overlord, overman, overseer
3 *syn* VICTOR 1, conqueror, defeater, subduer, subjugator, vanquisher
‖**4** *syn* HUSBAND, ‖hubby, lord, man, mister, Mr., ‖old man
5 *syn* LOVER 1, boyfriend, fancy man, man, paramour

master *vb* **1** *syn* OVERCOME 1, conquer, down, hurdle, lick, surmount, throw
2 *syn* DOMESTICATE, domesticize, domiciliate, tame
rel dominate, govern, predominate, rule
3 *syn* CONQUER 2, best, overcome, prevail, triumph
4 *syn* LEARN 1, get, pick up

master *adj* **1** *syn* DOMINANT 1, ascendant, overbearing, paramount, predominant, predominate, preponderant, prevalent, regnant, sovereign
2 *syn* PROFICIENT, adept, crack, crackerjack, expert, masterful, masterly, skilled, skillful

masterdom *n syn* SUPREMACY, ascendancy, ascendant, dominance, domination, dominion, preeminence, prepotence, prepotency, sovereignty

masterful *adj* **1** disposed to exercise or flaunt dictatorial authority in a way to override any protestation <the royal favorite was pompous and *masterful* when dealing with subordinates>
syn bossy, domineering, high-handed, imperative, imperial, imperious, magisterial, overbearing, peremptory
rel absolute, arbitrary, authoritarian, authoritative, dictative, dictatorial, doctrinaire, dogmatic; autocratic, despotic, tyrannical; high-and-mighty, self-willed
con humble, modest, unpretentious; indecisive, irresolute; submissive, yielding; feeble, weak
2 *syn* PROFICIENT, adept, crack, crackerjack, expert, master, masterly, skilled, skillful
rel adroit, deft, dexterous; preeminent, superlative, supreme, transcendent

master–hand *n syn* EXPERT, artiste, authority, ‖dabster, master, maven, past master, professional, virtuoso, whiz

masterly *adj syn* PROFICIENT, adept, crack, crackerjack, expert, master, masterful, skilled, skillful
rel preeminent, superlative, supreme, transcendent

masterpiece *n* **1** something done or made with extraordinary skill or brilliance <his latest work is unquestionably a *masterpiece*>
syn chef d'oeuvre, classic, magnum opus, masterwork, tour de force
rel objet d'art, masterstroke
con botch, disaster, fiasco
2 *syn* SHOWPIECE, chef d'oeuvre, pièce de résistance

mastership *n syn* ABILITY 2, command, expertise, expertism, expertness, knack, know-how, mastery, skill

masterwork *n syn* MASTERPIECE 1, chef d'oeuvre, classic, magnum opus, tour de force

mastery *n* **1** *syn* POWER 1, authority, command, control, domination, jurisdiction, might, strings, swag
2 *syn* ABILITY 2, command, expertise, expertism, expertness, knack, know-how, mastership, skill

masticate *vb* ***syn*** CHEW 1, champ, ‖chaw, chomp, chumble, chump, crunch, munch, ruminate, scrunch
rel bruise, crush, macerate, mash, pulp, pulpify, smash, squash

mastodonic *adj* ***syn*** HUGE, behemothic, elphantine, enormous, giant, gigantic, leviathan, mammoth, monster, monstrous

mat *adj* ***syn*** DULL 7, blind, dead, dim, flat, luckluster, lusterless, muted

matador *n* ***syn*** BULLFIGHTER, toreador, torero

match *n* **1** ***syn*** OPPONENT, adversary, antagonist, anti, con, opposer, oppugnant
2 ***syn*** EQUAL, counterpart, equivalent, like
rel analogue, parallel
3 ***syn*** MATE 5, companion, coordinate, double, duplicate, fellow, reciprocal, twin
4 ***syn*** PARALLEL, analogue, correlate, correspondent, counterpart, countertype
5 ***syn*** EVENT 5, meet
rel bout, engagement, game

match *vb* **1** ***syn*** OPPOSE 1, counter, pit, play (off), vie
2 ***syn*** EQUATE 2, assimilate, compare, liken, paragon, parallel
3 ***syn*** AMOUNT 2, approach, correspond (to), equal, partake (of), rival, touch
rel complement, supplement
4 ***syn*** EQUAL 3, measure up, meet, rival, tie, touch
rel compare, stack up
idiom hold a candle to

matched *adj* ***syn*** ASSORTED 2, adapted, conformable, fitted, suited
rel balanced, equated, evened, similar; coordinated, harmonized; coupled, joined, mated, paired, yoked
ant unmatched

matchless *adj* ***syn*** ALONE 3, only, peerless, unequaled, unique, unmatched, unparagoned, unparalleled, unrivaled
ant matchable

matchmaker *n* ***syn*** MARRIAGE BROKER, go-between

mate *n* **1** ***syn*** PARTNER, associate, cohort, confrere, consociate, copartner, fellow, ‖pard
2 ***syn*** ACCOMPANIMENT 2, associate, companion, concomitant, consort, fellow
3 ***syn*** FRIEND, acquaintance, amigo, cater-cousin, confidant, familiar, intimate
rel bedmate, classmate, co-mate, helpmate, playmate, roommate, schoolmate, teammate
4 ***syn*** SPOUSE, consort
rel match, parti
5 one of a pair matched in one or more qualities <the *mate* of a shoe>
syn companion, coordinate, double, duplicate, fellow, match, riciprocal, twin
rel alter ego, complement, sosie; compeer, equal, equivalent, peer

mate *vb* ***syn*** MARRY 2, ‖hitch, splice, tie, wed
rel breed, crossbreed, pair; generate, procreate

‖**mater** *n* ***syn*** MOTHER 1, ma, ‖mam, mama (*or* mamma), 'mammy, mom, mommy, mummy, ‖old lady, ‖old woman

material *adj* **1** of or belonging to actuality <for him the *material* world is the only world>
syn corporeal, gross, objective, phenomenal, physical, sensible, substantial, tangible
rel actual, real, true; appreciable, palpable, perceptible; earthly, worldly; animal, carnal, fleshly, sensual
con impalpable, imperceptible, intangible, unsubstantial; spiritual
ant immaterial, nonmaterial
2 ***syn*** IMPORTANT 1, big, consequential, considerable, meaningful, momentous, significant, substantial, weighty
ant immaterial
3 ***syn*** RELEVANT, ad rem, applicable, applicative, applicatory, apposite, apropos, germane, pertinent, pointful
rel consequential, important, momentous, significant; cardinal, essential, fundamental, vital
ant immaterial

material *n* **1** ***syn*** THING 4, being, entity, individual, matter, object, stuff, substance
rel component, constituent, element, ingredient; apparatus, equipment, machinery
2 *usu* **materials** *pl* ***syn*** EQUIPMENT, apparatus, gear, habiliments, machinery, matériel, outfit, paraphernalia, tackle, tackling

materialistic *adj* of or relating to a preoccupation with or stress upon material rather than intellectual or spiritual things <*materialistic* values characterize the modern age>
syn banausic, earthy, mundane, sensual, temporal, worldly
rel carnal, profane; earthly, terrestrial; secular, unspiritual
con intellectual, mental; spiritual, unfleshly, unworldly; heavenly

materiality *n* ***syn*** ACTUALITY 2, reality

materialize *vb* **1** ***syn*** EMBODY 1, exteriorize, externalize, incarnate, manifest, objectify, personalize, personify, personize, substantiate
rel appear, emerge, loom, show; issue, rise, spring
2 to convert mentally into something concrete <with the help of graphs and figures abstract ideas can be *materialized*>
syn entify, hypostatize, reify
rel actualize, pragmatize, realize; corporealize; symbolize, typify

matériel *n* ***syn*** EQUIPMENT, accouterment(s), apparatus, gear, habiliments, machinery, outfit, paraphernalia, tackle, tackling

matriarch *n* a dignified, usually elderly woman of some rank or authority <the local *matriarchs* controlled the town's social functions>
syn dame, dowager, grande dame, matron
rel materfamilias, mother

matrimonial *adj* of, relating to, or characteristic of marriage <the *matrimonial* bond between husband and wife>

---

syn synonym(s) | *rel* related word(s)
idiom idiomatic equivalent(s) | *con* contrasted word(s)
ant antonym(s) | * vulgar
‖ use limited; if in doubt, see a dictionary
The first word in a synonym list when printed in SMALL CAPITALS shows where there is more information about the group. For a more efficient use of this book see Explanatory Notes.

syn conjugal, connubial, hymeneal, marital, married, nuptial, spousal, wedded
rel bridal, epithalamic

matrimony *n* ***syn*** MARRIAGE 1, conjugality, connubiality, wedlock

matron *n* ***syn*** MATRIARCH, dame, dowager, grande dame

matter *n* **1** ***syn*** SUBJECT 2, argument, head, motif, motive, point, subject matter, text, theme, topic
2 ***syn*** AFFAIR 1, business, concern, shooting match, thing
rel complication, grievance, to-do, worry; circumstance, predicament
3 ***syn*** SUBSTANCE 2, amount, body, burden, core, gist, meat, pith, sense, upshot
4 ***syn*** THING 4, being, entity, individual, material, object, stuff, substance
5 ***syn*** ORDER 4, extent, magnitude, neighborhood, range, tune, vicinity

matter *vb* to be of importance <being your own self is what really *matters*>
syn count, import, mean, signify, weigh
idiom carry weight

matter-of-course *adj* ***syn*** GENERAL 1, common, commonplace, natural, normal, prevalent, regular, run-of-the-mill, typical, usual

matter-of-fact *adj* **1** ***syn*** REALISTIC, down-to-earth, earthy, hard-boiled, hardheaded, practical, pragmatic, sober, unidealistic, unsentimental
rel objective, sound
2 ***syn*** PROSAIC 1, prose, prosing, prosy
3 involving no display of emotion <the *matter-of-fact* reading of the judge masked his inner anguish>
syn cold, cold-blooded, emotionless, impersonal, unimpassioned
rel unaffected, unsentimental; prosaic
con emotional, impassioned, personal
4 ***syn*** IMPASSIVE 1, apathetic, dry, phlegmatic, stoic, stolid

maturate *vb* ***syn*** MATURE, age, develop, grow, grow up, mellow, ‖ripe, ripen

mature *adj* **1** having attained the normal peak of natural growth and development <*mature* plants ready to bear fruit>
syn adult, full-blown, full-fledged, full-grown, grown, grown-up, matured, ripe, ripened
rel developed, ready
idiom of age
con childish, childlike; boyish, green, juvenile, maiden, puerile, youthful
ant immature
2 ***syn*** DUE 2, payable
3 ***syn*** UNPAID 2, due, outstanding, overdue, owing, payable, unsettled

---

syn synonym(s) *rel* related word(s)
idiom idiomatic equivalent(s) *con* contrasted word(s)
ant antonym(s) * vulgar
‖ use limited; if in doubt, see a dictionary
The first word in a synonym list when printed in SMALL CAPITALS shows where there is more information about the group. For a more efficient use of this book see Explanatory Notes.

---

mature *vb* to become fully developed or ripe <she *matured* as an actress after several years of summer stock>
syn age, develop, grow, grow up, maturate, mellow, ‖ripe, ripen
rel blossom, flower; advance, progress, round; season; decline, deteriorate, olden, wane
idiom come of age

matured *adj* **1** ***syn*** MATURE 1, adult, full-blown, full-fledged, full-grown, grown, grown-up, ripe, ripened
rel completed, finished; advised, considered, deliberate, designed, premeditated, studied
con callow, crude, green, raw, rough, rude, uncouth
ant premature, unmatured
2 ***syn*** RIPE 3, aged, mellow, ripened

maudlin *adj* ***syn*** SENTIMENTAL, bathetic, lovey-dovey, mawkish, mushy, romantic, slushy, ‖soppy, sticky, tear-jerking
rel addled, befuddled, confused, fuddled, muddled; silly

maul *n* ***syn*** BRAWL 2, broil, dogfight, donnybrook, fracas, fray, melee, row, ruction, set-to

maul *vb* ***syn*** BATTER 1, ‖bung up, mangle
rel flagellate, flail, lash, whip; bang, bash, buffet, pound; abuse, maltreat, manhandle, molest, rough (up)

maunder *vb* ***syn*** WANDER 1, bat, circumambulate, drift, gad, gallivant, meander, mooch, ramble, range

maundering *adj* ***syn*** INARTICULATE 3, incoherent, tongue-tied, unvocal

maven *n* ***syn*** EXPERT, adept, authority, ‖dab, ‖dabster, master, past master, professional, proficient, virtuoso

maverick *n* ***syn*** BOHEMIAN, nonconformist

mawkish *adj* ***syn*** SENTIMENTAL, bathetic, lovey-dovey, maudlin, mushy, romantic, slushy, ‖soppy, sticky, tear-jerking
rel banal, flat; cloying, nauseating, sickening

maxim *n* a general truth or fundamental principle usually expressed sententiously <Francis Bacon is noted for his fondness for *maxims*>
syn aphorism, apothegm, axiom, brocard, dictum, gnome, moral, rule, truism
rel commonplace, motto, platitude; law, precept, prescript; theorem; proverb
idiom rule of thumb

maximal *adj* ***syn*** MAXIMUM, outside, top, topmost, utmost
ant minimal

maximize *vb* ***syn*** OVERPLAY 2, magnify, overemphasize, overstress
ant minimize

maximum *adj* greatest in quantity or highest in degree attainable or attained <apply *maximum* pressure above the point of injury>
syn maximal, outside, top, topmost, utmost; *compare* SUPREME
rel greatest, highest, largest
con least, lowest, slightest, smallest
ant minimum

maybe *adv* ***syn*** PERHAPS, perchance, possibly

mayhem *vb* ***syn*** MAIM, cripple, dislimb, dismember, mutilate

maze *n* **1** something intricately or confusingly elaborate or complicated <the landscape soon became a *maze* of superhighways>

syn jungle, knot, labyrinth, mesh, mizmaze, morass, skein, snarl, tangle, web
rel fog, haze; gordian knot; conglomeration, hodgepodge, miscellany, mishmash
‖**2** ***syn*** HAZE 2, befuddlement, daze, fog, muddledness, muddleheadedness, muddlement

‖**mazuma** *n* ***syn*** MONEY, ‖bread, cash, ‖chips, currency, dough, ‖greenbacks, ‖scratch, ‖shekels, ‖wampum

MD *n* ***syn*** PHYSICIAN, ‖croaker, doc, doctor, medical, mediciner, medico, ‖sawbones

meager *adj* **1** ***syn*** LEAN, angular, bony, gaunt, lank, lanky, rawboned, scraggy, scrawny, skinny
2 being smaller than what is normal, necessary, or desirable <the remains of dinner provided only a *meager* meal that evening>
syn exiguous, poor, scant, scanty, scrimp, scrimpy, skimp, skimpy, spare, sparse; *compare* SHORT 3
rel deficient, inadequate, insufficient; inappreciable, inconsiderable, slight; bare, mere, minimum; miserable, shabby
con adequate, enough, sufficient; appreciable, considerable; copious, plentiful
ant ample

meal *n* the portion of food taken at one time to satisfy appetite <the noonday dinner was the big *meal* of the day in those times>
syn ‖chow, feed, refection, repast
rel feast, spread; refreshment, regalement; collation, snack; fare, grub, meat, mess, victuals; board, table

meal *vb* ***syn*** EAT 1, consume, devour, feed (on), ingest, partake (of), take

mean *adj* **1** ***syn*** IGNOBLE 1, base, baseborn, humble, low, lowborn, lowly, plebeian, unennobled, unwashed
ant wellborn
2 ***syn*** INFERIOR 2, common, déclassé, hack, low-grade, poor, second-class, second-drawer, second-rate
3 ***syn*** LITTLE 2, borné, ineffectual, limited, narrow, paltry, set, small
4 ***syn*** CONTEMPTIBLE, beggarly, cheap, despicable, despisable, pitiable, pitiful, scummy, scurvy, shabby
5 ***syn*** CHEAP 2, base, common, paltry, poor, rubbishy, shoddy, sleazy, tatty, trashy
6 ***syn*** STINGY, miserly, narrow-fisted, niggard, niggardly, penurious, scrimpy, scrimy, tight, tightfisted
7 ***syn*** TROUBLESOME, pesky, troublous, ugly, vexatious, wicked
rel difficult, formidable, rough, rugged, tough
8 ***syn*** UNWELL, ailing, ‖donsie, indisposed, low, off-color, offish, poorly, sickly, underly

mean *vb* **1** ***syn*** INTEND 2, aim, contemplate, design, ‖mind, plan, propose, purpose
rel desire, want, wish
2 to convey (as an idea) to the mind <your answer *means* nothing to me>
syn add up (to), connote, denote, express, import, intend, signify, spell
rel designate, name; attest, betoken, indicate; hint, imply, intimate, suggest
3 ***syn*** MATTER, count, import, signify, weigh

mean *n* **1** ***syn*** AVERAGE, median, norm, par
2 *usu* **means** *sing or pl in constr* one by which work is accomplished or an end effected <careful planning is a major *means* of improving output> <use any *means* to secure peace>
syn agency, agent, channel, instrument, instrumentality, instrumentation, intermediary, medium, ministry, organ, vehicle
rel fashion, manner, method, mode, system, way; apparatus, equipment, machinery, paraphernalia
3 means *pl* one's total property including real property and intangibles <people of moderate *means* are feeling the effects of inflation worse>
syn assets, capital, resources, wealth
rel finances, fortune, funds, moneybags, pocket, purse; ‖bundle, nest egg, pile, reserves, savings; estate, holdings, possessions; intangibles

mean *adj* **1** ***syn*** MIDDLE 2, center, central, intermediary, intermediate, medial, median, mid
2 ***syn*** MEDIUM, average, fair, fairish, indifferent, intermediate, mediocre, middling, moderate, so-so

meander *vb* ***syn*** WANDER 1, drift, gallivant, ramble, range, roam, rove, stray, traipse, vagabond
rel snake, turn, twist, wind

meanderer *n* ***syn*** ROVER, drifter, rambler, roamer, rolling stone, wanderer

meandering *adj* ***syn*** WINDING, anfractuous, convoluted, flexuous, meandrous, serpentine, sinuous, snaky, tortuous

meandrous *adj* ***syn*** WINDING, anfractuous, convoluted, flexuous, meandering, serpentine, sinuous, snaky, tortuous

meaning *n* **1** the idea that something conveys to the mind <critics have endlessly debated the *meaning* of the poem>
syn acceptation, import, intendment, intent, message, purport, sense, significance, significancy, signification, sum and substance, understanding; *compare* SUBSTANCE 2, TENOR 1
rel drift, effect, essence, tenor; force, point, value; hint, implication, intimation, suggestion; connotation, denotation, definition
2 ***syn*** INTENTION, animus, design, intendment, intent, plan, purpose

meaningful *adj* **1** ***syn*** EXPRESSIVE, eloquent, facund, pregnant, rich, sententious, significant
ant meaningless
2 ***syn*** IMPORTANT 1, big, consequential, considerable, material, momentous, significant, substantial, weighty

meaningless *adj* **1** ***syn*** SENSELESS 5, insignificant, pointless, purportless, unmeaning
rel blank, empty, vacant
ant meaningful
2 ***syn*** FECKLESS 1, fustian, good-for-nothing, purposeless, unpurposed, useless, worthless

measly *adj* ***syn*** PETTY 2, niggling, paltry, pettifogging, picayune, picayunish, piddling, puny, trifling, trivial

measure *n* **1** ***syn*** RATION, allotment, allowance, apportionment, meed, part, portion, quantum, quota, share

---

syn synonym(s)	***rel*** related word(s)
idiom idiomatic equivalent(s)	***con*** contrasted word(s)
ant antonym(s)	* vulgar

‖ use limited; if in doubt, see a dictionary
The first word in a synonym list when printed in SMALL CAPITALS shows where there is more information about the group. For a more efficient use of this book see Explanatory Notes.

2 ***syn*** TEMPERANCE 1, moderateness, moderation
3 ***syn*** SIZE 1, admeasurement, dimension(s), dimensionality, extent, magnitude, proportion
4 ***syn*** MELODY, air, descant, diapason, lay, melisma, melodia, strain, tune, warble
5 ***syn*** RHYTHM, beat, cadence, cadency, meter, rhyme, rhythmus, swing
6 ***syn*** STANDARD 3, benchmark, criterion, gauge, touchstone, yardstick
7 an action planned or taken toward the accomplishment of a purpose <developed a new set of safety *measures*>
syn maneuver, move, procedure, proceeding, step
rel effort, project, proposal, proposition; expedient, makeshift, resort, resource, shift, stopgap

measure *vb* 1 ***syn*** DEMARCATE 1, bound, delimit, delimitate, determine, limit, mark (out)
2 to ascertain the quantity, mass, extent, or degree of in terms of a standard unit or fixed amount <*measure* the depth of the water>
syn gauge, scale
rel size, size up; calculate, compute, estimate, figure, reckon

measure (out) *vb* ***syn*** DISTRIBUTE 1, deal, disburse, dispense, disperse, divide, ‖divvy, dole (out), lot (out), partition

measureless *adj* 1 ***syn*** INCALCULABLE 1, immeasurable, inestimable, uncountable, unmeasurable, unmeasured, unreckonable
ant measurable
2 ***syn*** LIMITLESS, boundless, endless, immeasurable, indefinite, infinite, unbounded, unlimited, unmeasured
ant measurable

measure up *vb* ***syn*** EQUAL 3, match, meet, rival, tie, touch

meat *n* 1 ***syn*** FOOD 1, ‖chow, comestibles, ‖eats, edibles, foodstuff, nurture, provender, provisions, victuals
2 ***syn*** SUBSTANCE 2, burden, core, gist, matter, pith, sense, short, thrust, upshot

meathead *n* ***syn*** OAF 2, ‖gaum, gawk, klutz, lobster, looby, lout, lubber, lump, palooka

meaty *adj* ***syn*** PITHY, compact, epigrammatic, marrowy

mechanical *adj* ***syn*** PERFUNCTORY, automatic

meddle *vb* to concern oneself with officiously, impertinently, or indiscreetly <continually *meddling* in other people's affairs>
syn busybody, butt in, fool, horn in, interfere, interlope, intermeddle, ‖make, mess around, monkey (with), tamper (with)
rel intervene, intrude, invade, obtrude; pry, snoop, trespass
idiom put (*or* shove *or* stick) one's oar in, stick one's nose into

con disregard, ignore, neglect, omit, overlook, slight; avoid, eschew, shun

meddler *n* ***syn*** BUSYBODY, butt-in, ‖buttinsky, intermeddler, kibitzer, pragmatist, prier (*or* pryer), quidnunc, rubberneck, snoop

meddlesome *adj* ***syn*** IMPERTINENT 2, busy, intrusive, ‖nebby, obtrusive, officious, polypragmatic

Meddlesome Mattie *n* ***syn*** BUSYBODY, butt-in, intermeddler, kibitzer, nose, nosey Parker, Paul Pry, prier (*or* pryer), quidnunc, snoop

medial *adj* 1 ***syn*** MIDDLE 1, center, centermost, equidistant, halfway, median, mid, middlemost, midmost
2 ***syn*** MIDDLE 2, center, central, intermediary, intermediate, mean, median, mid
3 ***syn*** MEDIUM, average, fair, fairish, indifferent, intermediate, mean, mediocre, middling, moderate

median *n* ***syn*** AVERAGE, mean, norm, par
rel center, middle

median *adj* 1 ***syn*** MIDDLE 1, center, centermost, equidistant, halfway, medial, mid, middlemost, midmost
2 ***syn*** MIDDLE 2, center, central, intermediary, intermediate, mean, medial, mid

mediate *vb* ***syn*** INTERPOSE 2, intercede, interfere, intermediate, intervene, step in

mediator *n* 1 ***syn*** GO-BETWEEN 2, broker, entrepreneur, interagent, interceder, intercessor, intermediary, intermediate, intermediator, middleman
rel arbitrator, judge; conciliator, peacemaker; negotiator, troubleshooter
2 ***syn*** MODERATOR, arbitrator

medical *n* ***syn*** PHYSICIAN, ‖croaker, doc, doctor, mediciner, medico, ‖sawbones

medicament *n* ***syn*** REMEDY 1, cure, medicant, medication, medicine, pharmacon, physic

medicant *n* ***syn*** REMEDY 1, cure, medicament, medication, medicine, pharmacon, physic

medication *n* ***syn*** REMEDY 1, cure, medicament, medicant, medicine, pharmacon, physic

medicinal *n* ***syn*** DRUG 1, biologic, pharmaceutic, pharmaceutical

medicine *n* ***syn*** REMEDY 1, cure, medicament, medicant, medication, pharmacon, physic

mediciner *n* ***syn*** PHYSICIAN, ‖croaker, doc, doctor, MD, medical, medico, ‖sawbones

medico *n* ***syn*** PHYSICIAN, ‖croaker, doc, doctor, MD, medical, mediciner, ‖sawbones

mediocre *adj* ***syn*** MEDIUM, average, fair, fairish, indifferent, intermediate, mean, middling, moderate, so-so
rel bad, inferior, poor; common, commonplace, ordinary, unexceptional
idiom no great shakes, nothing to write home about

meditate *vb* ***syn*** PONDER 2, ‖chaw, deliberate, mull (over), muse, revolve, roll, ruminate, turn over

meditative *adj* 1 ***syn*** THOUGHTFUL 1, cogitative, contemplative, pensive, pondering, reflecting, reflective, ruminative, speculative, thinking
rel musing, ruminant; wistful
2 ***syn*** PENSIVE 2, ‖pensy, wistful

medium *adj* midway between the extremes of a scale, measurement, or evaluation <bought a suit of *medium* quality>
syn average, fair, fairish, indifferent, intermediate, mean, medial, mediocre, middle-rate, middling, moderate, run-of-mine, run-of-the-mill, so-so

rel median, par; passable, tolerable; neutral; popular, vulgar; normal, standard
idiom fair to middling
con inferior, low-grade, poor; excellent, first-class, high-grade, prime, superior

medium *n* **1** *syn* MEAN 2, agency, agent, channel, instrument, instrumentality, instrumentation, ministry, organ, vehicle
rel intermediate, intermedium
2 *syn* ENVIRONMENT, ambience, ambient, atmosphere, climate, milieu, mise-en-scène, surroundings
3 *syn* FORTE, eminency, long suit, métier, oyster, strong suit

medley *n syn* MISCELLANY 1, assortment, brew, gallimaufry, jumble, mélange, pasticcio, pastiche, patchwork, potpourri

‖**meech** *vb syn* SNEAK, creep, glide, gumshoe, lurk, pussyfoot, skulk, slink, slip, steal

meed *n* **1** *syn* REWARD, carrot, dividend, guerdon, plum, premium, prize
rel recompensing, satisfaction
2 *syn* RATION, allotment, allowance, apportionment, measure, part, portion, quantum, quota, share
rel desert, due, merit

meek *adj syn* HUMBLE 1, lowly, modest, unassuming
rel gentle, mild; tame; forbearing, lenient, tolerant; long-suffering, patient
con high-spirited, mettlesome, spirited, spunky; contumacious, insubordinate, rebellious
ant arrogant

meet *vb* **1** *syn* HAPPEN 2, bump, chance, hit, light, luck, stumble, tumble
2 *syn* CONFRONT 1, affront, encounter, face
3 *syn* ENGAGE 5, encounter, face, take on
rel brave, oppose
4 *syn* EQUAL 3, match, measure up, rival, tie, touch
5 *syn* SATISFY 5, answer, fill, fulfill
rel approach, equal, match, rival, tie, touch
6 to come together face-to-face or as if face-to-face <the two leaders agreed to *meet* in a series of summit talks>
syn close, encounter, face, front; *compare* CONFRONT 1
rel accost, greet, salute; bump, clash, collide, cross; grapple, tussle, wrestle; experience, suffer, sustain, undergo
con elude, escape, evade, shun
ant avoid
7 *syn* CONVERGE, concenter, concentrate, focus
8 *syn* CONVENE 1, open, sit

meet (with) *vb syn* FIND 1, catch, descry, detect, encounter, espy, hit (on *or* upon), spot, turn up

meet *n* **1** *syn* EVENT 5, match
2 *syn* CONTEST 2, competition, concours, conflict, meeting, rencontre

meet *adj* **1** *syn* FIT 1, applicable, appropriate, apt, felicitous, fitting, happy, just, proper, suitable
rel accommodated, conformed, reconciled; good, right; equitable, fair, just
ant unmeet
2 *syn* GOOD 2, appropriate, convenient, fit, proper, suitable, useful
ant unmeet

meeting *n* **1** *syn* CONTEST 2, competition, concours, conflict, meet, rencontre
2 *syn* CONCOURSE, concursion, confluence, gathering, junction
3 *syn* TALK 4, conference, parley, powwow
rel congress, moot

meetness *n syn* ORDER 11, appositeness, appropriateness, aptness, expediency, fitness, propriety, rightness, suitability, suitableness
ant unmeetness

megacosm *n syn* UNIVERSE, cosmos (*or* kosmos), creation, macrocosm, macrocosmos, nature, world
ant microcosm

megrim *n syn* CAPRICE, bee, boutade, conceit, crotchet, fancy, freak, humor, whim, whimsy
rel impulse, urge

melancholic *adj syn* SAD 2, depressing, joyless, melancholy, mournful, saddening, triste

melancholy *n syn* SADNESS, blues, dejection, depression, (the) dismals, dumps, gloom, heavyheartedness, mournfulness, unhappiness
rel miserableness, misery, wretchedness; despair, desperation; boredom, ennui, tedium
con hopefulness, optimism
ant exhilaration

melancholy *adj* **1** *syn* SAD 1, heavyhearted, mournful, saddened, sorry, unhappy
2 expressing or suggesting sorrow or mourning <the gloomy day led him to a *melancholy* train of thought>
syn doleful, dolesome, dolorous, lamentable, lugubrious, moanful, mournful, plaintive, rueful, sighful, sorrowful, wailful, woeful; *compare* SAD 1, SAD 2
rel pensive, reflective, thoughtful; discomposing, disquieting, disturbing, perturbing; dismal, dreary, funereal, gloomy, lachrymose, somber, sombrous
con cheerful, glad, happy, joyful, joyous, lighthearted; gay, lively, vivacious
3 *syn* SAD 2, depressing, joyless, melancholic, mournful, saddening, triste

mélange *n syn* MISCELLANY 1, assortment, gallimaufry, hodgepodge, jumble, medley, pasticcio, pastiche, patchwork, potpourri

meld *vb syn* MIX 1, amalgamate, blend, compound, fuse, interblend, interfuse, intermingle, merge, mingle

melding *n syn* UNIFICATION, coadunation, coalition, combination, consolidation, mergence, merger, merging, union

melee *n* **1** *syn* CLASH 2, affray, brush, fray, mellay, scrimmage, skirmish
rel dogfight, scuffle
2 *syn* BRAWL 2, affray, broil, donnybrook, fight, fracas, fray, free-for-all, knock-down-and-drag-out, ruction
3 *syn* MISCELLANY 1, hash, hodgepodge, jumble, medley, mélange, mishmash, pastiche, potpourri, stew

meliorate *vb syn* IMPROVE 1, ameliorate, amend, better, help

---

melisma *n* ***syn*** MELODY, air, descant, diapason, lay, measure, melodia, strain, tune, warble

mellay *n* **1** ***syn*** BRAWL 2, bobbery, broil, donnybrook, fracas, fray, free-for-all, row, ruction, set-to
2 ***syn*** CLASH 2, affray, brush, fray, melee, scrimmage, skirmish

mellifluent *adj* ***syn*** MELLIFLUOUS, golden, honeyed, Hyblaean, liquid, mellow

mellifluous *adj* having a smooth rich flow <his *mellifluous* voice held his audience in a trance>
syn golden, honeyed, Hyblaean, liquid, mellifluent, mellow; *compare* MELODIOUS 1
rel accordant, canorous, euphonic, euphonious, harmonious, mellisonant, silvery; golden-tongued, silver-tongued; dulcet, sweet; resonant, sonorous
con blatant, boisterous, clamorous, obstreperous, strident, vociferous; discordant, grating, harsh

mellisonant *adj* ***syn*** MELODIOUS 1, dulcet, euphonic, euphonious, melodic, sweet, tuneful

mellow *adj* **1** ***syn*** RIPE 3, aged, matured, ripened
2 ***syn*** MELLIFLUOUS, golden, honeyed, Hyblaean, liquid, mellifluent

mellow *vb* ***syn*** MATURE, age, develop, grow, grow up, maturate, ‖ripe, ripen

melodia *n* ***syn*** MELODY, air, descant, diapason, lay, measure, melisma, strain, tune, warble

melodic *adj* **1** ***syn*** MELODIOUS 2, musical, songful, tuned, tuneful
2 ***syn*** MELODIOUS 1, dulcet, euphonic, euphonious, mellisonant, sweet, tuneful

melodious *adj* **1** pleasing to the ear <*melodious* sounds of the forest>
syn dulcet, euphonic, euphonious, mellisonant, melodic, sweet, tuneful; *compare* MELLIFLUOUS
rel canorous, harmonious
con discordant, grating, harsh
ant unmelodious
2 containing, constituting, or characterized by melody <his voice shows marked improvement and a new richly *melodious* quality>
syn melodic, musical, songful, tuned, tuneful
rel cantabile, lyric, melic

melody *n* a rhythmic succession of single tones organized as an aesthetic whole <took out his flute and played a simple *melody*>
syn air, descant, diapason, lay, measure, melisma, melodia, strain, tune, warble; *compare* SONG 2
rel song; bel canto, canto, vocalise; lyrics

melt *vb* **1** ***syn*** LIQUEFY, deliquesce, dissolve, flux, fuse, liquesce, run, thaw
rel heat, warm
con coagulate, harden, set
ant freeze; solidify
2 ***syn*** BURN 3, bake, broil, cook, roast, scorch, swelter
rel perspire, sweat

member *n* ***syn*** PART 1, cut, division, moiety, parcel, piece, portion, section, segment

memento *n* **1** ***syn*** REMEMBRANCE 3, keepsake, memorial, relic, remembrancer, reminder, souvenir, token, trophy
2 ***syn*** VESTIGE 1, relic, shadow, trace

memo *n* **1** ***syn*** NOTE 2, chit, memorandum, notandum, notation
2 ***syn*** MEMORANDUM 2, directive, notice

memoir *n* **1** ***syn*** BIOGRAPHY, autobiography, bio, confessions, life
rel anecdote; memory, recollection, remembrance, reminiscence
2 ***syn*** DISCOURSE 2, disquisition, dissertation, monograph, monography, thesis, tractate, treatise

memoirist *n* ***syn*** BIOGRAPHER, autobiographer, autobiographist, Boswell

memorable *adj* ***syn*** NOTEWORTHY, ‖bodacious, nameable, notable, observable, red-letter, rubric
rel momentous, rememberable; deathless, unfadable, unforgettable
ant unmemorable

memorandum *n* **1** ***syn*** NOTE 2, chit, memo, notandum, notation
2 a communication that contains directive, advisory, or informative matter <the *memorandum* announced the holiday schedule>
syn directive, memo, notice
rel announcement, dispatch, minute; epistle, letter, missive, note; reminder, tickler; message; diary

memorial *adj* serving to preserve remembrance <a *memorial* plaque>
syn commemorative, commemoratory
rel celebrative, consecrative, dedicatory, enshrining

memorial *n* **1** ***syn*** REMEMBRANCE 3, keepsake, memento, relic, remembrancer, reminder, souvenir, token, trophy
2 ***syn*** MONUMENT 2, testimonial

memorialize *vb* **1** ***syn*** ADDRESS 4, accost, apply (to), approach, bespeak
2 to record or honor the memory of by or as if by a monument <the new library *memorializes* the late President>
syn commemorate, monument, monumentalize
rel etch, grave, impress, imprint; jog, nudge, remind
idiom bring to mind, fix in the (*or* one's) mind (*or* memory), impress on one's mind, treasure in one's heart
con forget, neglect, overlook

memorial park *n* ***syn*** CEMETERY, ‖boneyard, ‖boot hill, burial ground, burying ground, God's acre, graveyard, necropolis, polyandrium, potter's field

memorize *vb* to commit to memory <the actors hadn't even *memorized* their lines>
syn con, get, learn
rel study
idiom get (*or* learn) by heart, get (*or* learn) word for word
con forget

memory *n* **1** the power or process of reproducing or recalling what has been learned <blessed with a good *memory*>

---

syn synonym(s) — *rel* related word(s)
idiom idiomatic equivalent(s) — *con* contrasted word(s)
ant antonym(s) — * vulgar
‖ use limited; if in doubt, see a dictionary
The first word in a synonym list when printed in SMALL CAPITALS shows where there is more information about the group. For a more efficient use of this book see Explanatory Notes.

syn recollection, remembrance, reminiscence
rel reflection, retrospection; retention, retentiveness; mind, recall; mind's eye; awareness, cognizance, consciousness
con forgetfulness, obliviousness, unmindfulness; lethe, oblivion
2 a particular act of recalling <her *memory* of her wedding day remains vivid>
syn anamnesis, recall, recollection, remembrance, reminiscence
rel memento, souvenir

menace *vb* **1** ***syn*** THREATEN
rel alarm, frighten, scare; endanger, torment; loom, lower
2 ***syn*** ENDANGER, compromise, hazard, imperil, jeopard, jeopardize, jeopardy, peril, risk

menacing *adj* ***syn*** IMMINENT 2, lowering (*or* louring), lowery (*or* loury), overhanging, threatening

ménage *n* ***syn*** FAMILY 2, folks, house, household
rel ménage à trois

mend *vb* **1** ***syn*** CORRECT 1, amend, emend, rectify, right
2 to put into good shape or working order again <*mends* garments in her spare time>
syn doctor, do up, fix, overhaul, patch, rebuild, recondition, reconstruct, repair, revamp, ‖right, ‖rightle, vamp
rel condition, ready, service; refurbish, rejuvenate, renew, renovate, restore; correct, emend, rectify, redress, reform; heal
3 ***syn*** IMPROVE 3, ameliorate, convalesce, gain, look up, perk (up), recuperate

mendacious *adj* ***syn*** DISHONEST, deceitful, knavish, lying, roguish, shifty, unhonest, untruthful
rel false, wrong; erroneous, fallacious, spurious; equivocating, fibbing, paltering, prevaricating
ant veracious

mendaciousness *n* ***syn*** MENDACITY, falsehood, fibbery, truthlessness, untruthfulness, unveracity
ant veraciousness, veracity

mendacity *n* the practice or an instance of lying <he was ultimately caught by his own outrageous *mendacity*>
syn falsehood, fibbery, mendaciousness, truthlessness, untruthfulness, unveracity
rel boggling, caviling, dodging, equivocation, hedging, quibbling, shifting, sidestepping
ant veraciousness, veracity

mendicancy *n* the practice or act of begging <the city passed an ordinance against *mendicancy*>
syn beggary, bumming, cadging, mendicity, mooching, panhandling
rel sponging

mendicity *n* ***syn*** MENDICANCY, beggary, bumming, cadging, mooching, panhandling

menial *adj* ***syn*** SUBSERVIENT 2, obeisant, obsequious, servile, slavish

mental *adj* **1** of or relating to the mind <the *mental* aspects of the problem>
syn cerebral, intellective, intellectual, psychic, psychical, psychological
rel immaterial, inner, spiritual; telepathic; intelligent, rational, reasoning, thinking; ideological
con bodily, corporal, corporeal, physical, somatic; perceptive; sensual, sensuous
‖**2** ***syn*** INSANE 1, ‖fruity, ‖loco, lunatic, mad, maniac, mindless, non compos mentis, nuts, nutsy

mentality *n* ***syn*** INTELLIGENCE 1, brain(s), brainpower, mother wit, sense, wit

mention *vb* to refer to someone or something in a clear unmistakable manner <several donors were *mentioned* in the article>
syn cite, instance, name, specify
rel denominate, designate; detail; advert, allude, refer; quote
idiom make mention of
con disregard, ignore, neglect, overlook, pass by, pass over, slight

menu *n* a list of the dishes that may be ordered (as at a restaurant) or that are to be served (as at a banquet) <hoped to find something tasty on the *menu*> <he saved the elaborate *menu* as a souvenir of the awards banquet>
syn card, carte du jour
idiom bill of fare

Mephistophelian *adj* ***syn*** SATANIC 1, devilish, diabolic

mephitic *adj* **1** ***syn*** MALODOROUS 1, fetid, funky, musty, noisome, olid, reeking, smelly, stenchy, stinking
2 ***syn*** POISONOUS, poison, toxic, toxicant, venomous, virulent

mercenary *n* ***syn*** HACK 2, drudge, grub, grubber, hireling, slavey

mercenary *adj* ***syn*** CORRUPT 2, praetorian, unethical, unprincipled, unscrupulous, venal
ant unmercenary

merchandisable *adj* ***syn*** MARKETABLE, merchantable, salable, sellable, trafficable, vendible
ant unmerchantable, unsalable

merchandise *n* the products that are bought and sold in business <*merchandise* of inferior quality>
syn commodities, goods, line, vendible(s), wares
rel effects; job lot, stock; staples

merchandise *vb* ***syn*** SELL 3, market, retail
rel advertise, publicize

merchandiser *n* ***syn*** MERCHANT, businessman, dealer, trader, tradesman, trafficker

merchant *n* a buyer and seller of commodities for profit <a *merchant* of dry goods>
syn businessman, dealer, merchandiser, trader, tradesman, trafficker
rel jobber, retailer, wholesaler

merchantable *adj* ***syn*** MARKETABLE, merchandisable, salable, sellable, trafficable, vendible
ant unmerchantable, unsalable

merchant prince *n* ***syn*** MAGNATE, baron, czar, king, mogul, prince, tycoon

merciful *adj* ***syn*** FORBEARING, charitable, clement, easy, indulgent, lenient, tolerant

---

rel compassionate, pitiful, softhearted; benign, kind, kindly; condoning, forgiving, pardoning
ant merciless, unmerciful

mercifulness *n syn* FORBEARANCE 2, clemency, indulgence, lenience, leniency, tolerance, toleration
rel commiseration, pity, ruth
con severeness, severity, sternness
ant mercilessness, unmercifulness

merciless *adj* **1** *syn* PITILESS, unmerciful, unpitying
ant merciful
2 *syn* GRIM 3, implacable, ironfisted, mortal, relentless, ruthless, unappeasable, unflinching, unrelenting, unyielding
rel compassionless, cutthroat, pitiless; gratuitous, uncalled-for, wanton
con charitable, lenient, tolerant; easy, easygoing
ant merciful

mercurial *adj syn* INCONSTANT 1, capricious, changeable, fickle, lubricious, temperamental, ticklish, unstable, variable, volatile
rel buoyant, effervescent, elastic, expansive, resilient; mobile, movable; adroit, clever, cunning, ingenious
ant saturnine

mercy *n* a show of or a disposition to show kindness or compassion <the *mercy* of the Lord knows all seasons>
syn caritas, charity, clemency, grace, lenity; *compare* FORBEARANCE 2
rel commiseration, compassion, pity, ruth; benevolence, benignancy, benignity, kindliness, kindness; generosity, goodwill
con reprisal, retaliation, retribution, revenge, vengeance; castigation, chastening, chastisement, punishment

mere *adj syn* VERY 4, bare

merely *adv syn* JUST 3, but, only, simply

meretricious *adj syn* GAUDY, blatant, brazen, chintzy, flashy, garish, glaring, loud, tawdry, tinsel
rel deceptive, delusive, delusory, misleading, spurious; insincere

meretrix *n syn* PROSTITUTE, bawd, call girl, drab, harlot, ‖hooker, hustler, quean, streetwalker, whore

merge *vb syn* MIX 1, amalgamate, blend, compound, fuse, interblend, interfuse, intermingle, meld, mingle

mergence *n syn* UNIFICATION, coadunation, coalition, combination, consolidation, melding, merger, merging, union

merger *n* **1** *syn* CONSOLIDATION 2, amalgamation
2 *syn* UNIFICATION, coadunation, coalition, combination, consolidation, melding, mergence, merging, union

merging *n syn* UNIFICATION, coadunation, coalition, combination, consolidation, melding, mergence, merger, union

---

syn synonym(s) | *rel* related word(s)
idiom idiomatic equivalent(s) | *con* contrasted word(s)
ant antonym(s) | * vulgar
‖ use limited; if in doubt, see a dictionary
The first word in a synonym list when printed in SMALL CAPITALS shows where there is more information about the group. For a more efficient use of this book see Explanatory Notes.

meridian *n syn* APEX 2, acme, apogee, climax, comble, culmination, peak, pinnacle, summit, zenith

merit *n* **1** *syn* EXCELLENCE, arete, excellency, perfection, quality, virtue
ant fault
2 *syn* QUALITY 2, caliber, stature, value, virtue, worth
3 *syn* DUE 1, comeuppance, desert(s), deserving, lumps, right(s)
rel gaining(s), winning(s)

merit *vb syn* EARN 2, deserve, rate
rel award, reward; recompense, repay, requite; entitle, justify, warrant

meritable *adj syn* WORTHY 1, admirable, commendable, deserving, estimable, laudable, meritorious, praisable, praiseworthy, thankworthy
ant meritless

merited *adj syn* JUST 3, appropriate, condign, deserved, due, requisite, rhadamanthine, right, rightful, suitable
rel entitled, justified, warranted
ant unmerited

meritorious *adj syn* WORTHY 1, admirable, commendable, deserving, estimable, laudable, meritable, praisable, praiseworthy, thankworthy

merriment *n* **1** *syn* MIRTH, glee, hilarity, jocularity, jocundity, jollity, joviality
2 *syn* MERRYMAKING, festivity, gaiety, jollity, revel, reveling, revelment, revelry, whoopee

merry *adj* indicative of or marked by high spirits or lightheartedness <the *merry* life of the town folk was a joy to see>
syn blithe, blithesome, boon, festive, gay, gleeful, jocund, jolly, jovial, lighthearted, mirthful, riant
rel animated, lively, sprightly, vivacious; cheerful, glad, happy, joyful, joyous; hilarious, mad, unconstrained, wild
con gloomy, glum, melancholy; grave, sober, somber; earnest, sedate, serious, staid

merry–andrew *n syn* CLOWN 3, buffoon, harlequin, zany

merrymaking *n* gay or festive activity <a night of *merrymaking*>
syn festivity, gaiety, jollity, merriment, revel, reveling, revelment, revelry, whoopee
rel enjoyment, indulgence, pleasure, self-indulgence

mesh *n* **1** *usu* **meshes** *pl syn* WEB 2, cobweb, entanglement, toil(s)
2 *syn* MAZE 1, jungle, knot, labyrinth, mizmaze, morass, skein, snarl, tangle, web
rel net, network

mesh *vb syn* ENGAGE 1, intermesh

meshuggaas *n syn* NONSENSE 2, balderdash, ‖baloney, ‖bunk, claptrap, drivel, flummadiddle, guff, poppycock, twaddle

mesmeric *adj syn* ATTRACTIVE 1, alluring, bewitching, captivating, charming, drawing, enchanting, glamorous, magnetic, siren

mesmerize *vb syn* ENTHRALL 2, catch up, fascinate, grip, hold, spellbind
rel entrance, hypnotize

mess *n* ‖**1** *syn* MUCH, great deal, heap, lot, lump, mass, peck, pile, ‖power, ‖sight
2 *syn* EYESORE, desight, fright, monstrosity, sight

3 a confused or disordered state, condition, or situation <upon becoming president, he proceeded to make a *mess* of the government>
syn botch, botchery, hash, mess-up, mix-up, muddle, mull, muss, shambles; *compare* MISCELLANY 1
rel confusion, disorder; wreck, wreckage
idiom kettle of fish

mess *vb* **1** ***syn*** BOTCH, bitch (up), ‖blow, bobble, bollix, bungle, goof (up), gum (up), louse up, ‖screw (up)
rel confuse, disorder, jumble
idiom make a mess of
2 ***syn*** FIDDLE 2, doodle, mess around, potter, puddle, putter, tinker

mess (up) *vb* ***syn*** DISORDER 1, derange, disarrange, discompose, disorganize, disturb, jumble, rummage, unsettle, upset
rel damage, mar, ruin, spoil; ‖muck, mucker, muff

message *n* **1** something (as information) conveyed by writing, speech, or signals <left a *message* before he went out>
syn communication, directive, word
rel communiqué, dispatch, report; memo, memorandum; epistle, letter, missive, note
2 ***syn*** MEANING 1, acceptation, import, intendment, purport, sense, significance, significancy, signification, understanding

mess around *vb* **1** ***syn*** FIDDLE 2, doodle, mess, potter, puddle, putter, tinker
2 ***syn*** MEDDLE, busybody, butt in, fool, horn in, interfere, interlope, intermeddle, monkey (with), tamper (with)
3 ***syn*** PHILANDER, fool (around), play (around), wolf, womanize

messenger *n* one who bears a message or does an errand <blamed the *messenger* for the bad news he brought>
syn bearer, carrier, courier, emissary, envoy, internuncio
rel herald; go-between, intermediary, mediator; dispatcher, post

mess–up *n* ***syn*** MESS 3, botch, botchery, hash, mix-up, muddle, mull, muss, shambles

messy *adj* **1** ***syn*** SLOVENLY 1, disheveled, ill-kempt, raunchy, slipshod, sloppy, unfastidious, unkempt, unneat, untidy
rel dirty, grimy, grubby
con clean
ant neat
2 ***syn*** SLIPSHOD 3, botchy, careless, slapdash, sloppy, slovenly, unthorough, untidy

metagrobolize *vb* ***syn*** PUZZLE, befog, bewilder, ‖cap, confound, confuse, perplex, pose, stumble

metamorphize *vb* ***syn*** TRANSFORM, change, commute, convert, metamorphose, transfigure, transmogrify, transmute, transpose, transubstantiate

metamorphose *vb* ***syn*** TRANSFORM, change, commute, convert, transfigure, translate, transmogrify, transmute, transpose, transubstantiate
rel age, develop, mature, ripen

metanoia *n* ***syn*** CONVERSION 1, rebirth

metaphor *n* ***syn*** ANALOGY 2, simile, similitude
rel comparison, trope; allegory, personification
idiom figure of speech

metaphysical *adj* **1** ***syn*** IMMATERIAL 1, bodiless, discarnate, incorporeal, insubstantial, nonmaterial, nonphysical, spiritual, unfleshly, unphysical
rel supernatural, transcendent, transcendental
2 ***syn*** SUPERNATURAL 1, numinous, preternatural, superhuman, superior, supermundane, suprahuman, supramundane, supranatural, unearthly

mete (out) *vb* **1** ***syn*** ADMINISTER 2, apportion, deal (out), dispense, dole (out), portion (out), share out
rel measure
2 ***syn*** ALLOT, admeasure, allocate, allow, apportion, assign, give, lot

meter *n* ***syn*** RHYTHM, beat, cadence, cadency, measure, rhyme, rhythmus, swing

method *n* **1** the means or procedures used in attaining an end <he claimed that his ends justified his *methods*>
syn fashion, manner, mode, modus, system, technique, way, wise
rel design, plan, schema, scheme; form, style; course, line; modus operandi, practice, procedure, process, routine; wrinkle
2 ***syn*** ORDER 8, orderliness, pattern, plan, system

methodic *adj* ***syn*** ORDERLY 1, methodical, regular, systematic
ant desultory, unmethodical

methodical *adj* ***syn*** ORDERLY 1, methodic, regular, systematic
rel methodized, organized, systematized; analytical, logical; careful, meticulous, scrupulous
con casual, hit-or-miss, random; confused, jumbled
ant desultory, unmethodical

methodize *vb* ***syn*** ORDER 1, arrange, array, dispose, marshal, organize, systematize
rel establish, fix, set, settle

meticulous *adj* ***syn*** CAREFUL 2, conscientious, conscionable, exact, fussy, heedful, painstaking, punctilious, punctual, scrupulous
rel fastidious, pernickety, picky; cautious, strict, thorough; microscopic

métier *n* **1** ***syn*** TRADE 1, art, calling, craft, handicraft, profession, vocation
2 ***syn*** FORTE, eminency, long suit, medium, oyster, strong suit

metropolitan *adj* ***syn*** COSMOPOLITAN 1, urbane

mettle *n* ***syn*** COURAGE, cojones, dauntlessness, guts, heart, ‖moxie, pluck, resolution, spirit, spunk

mettlesome *adj* ***syn*** SPIRITED 2, beany, fiery, gingery, high-hearted, high-spirited, peppery, spunky
rel edgy, excitable, high-strung, skittish, startlish

mew *vb* ***syn*** ENCLOSE 1, cage, coop, corral, fence, hem, immure, mure, pen, shut in

---

syn synonym(s) · *rel* related word(s)
idiom idiomatic equivalent(s) · *con* contrasted word(s)
ant antonym(s) · * vulgar
‖ use limited; if in doubt, see a dictionary
The first word in a synonym list when printed in SMALL CAPITALS shows where there is more information about the group. For a more efficient use of this book see Explanatory Notes.

Mickey Mouse *adj* ***syn*** PETTY 2, measly, niggling, paltry, peanut, pettifogging, picayune, picayunish, piddling, puny

mid *adj* **1** ***syn*** MIDDLE 2, center, central, intermediary, intermediate, mean, medial, median
2 ***syn*** MIDDLE 1, center, centermost, equidistant, halfway, medial, median, middlemost, midmost

mid *prep* **1** ***syn*** AMID 1, among, midst
2 ***syn*** AMONG 1, amid, midst
3 ***syn*** DURING, amid, midst, over, throughout

middle *adj* **1** equally distant from the extremes <the *middle* finger>
syn center, centermost, equidistant, halfway, medial, median, mid, middlemost, midmost
2 being at neither extreme <paid a *middle* price for it>
syn center, central, intermediary, intermediate, mean, medial, median, mid

middle *n* ***syn*** CENTER 1, core, midpoint, midst

middlebrow *n* ***syn*** PHILISTINE, Babbitt, boeotian, boob

middleman *n* ***syn*** GO-BETWEEN 2, broker, entrepreneur, interagent, interceder, intercessor, intermediary, intermediate, intermediator, mediator

middlemost *adj* ***syn*** MIDDLE 1, center, centermost, equidistant, halfway, medial, median, mid, midmost

middle–of–the–road *adj* ***syn*** MODERATE 4, middle-road, soft-shell

middle–rate *adj* ***syn*** MEDIUM, average, fair, intermediate, mean, mediocre, middling, moderate, run-of-the-mill, so-so

middle–road *adj* ***syn*** MODERATE 4, middle-of-the-road, soft-shell

middling *adj* ***syn*** MEDIUM, average, fair, fairish, indifferent, intermediate, mean, mediocre, moderate, so-so
rel inferior, poor, second-rate

midge *n* ***syn*** DWARF, homunculus, hop-o'-my-thumb, lilliputian, manikin, midget, peewee, pygmy, runt, Tom Thumb

midget *n* ***syn*** DWARF, homunculus, hop-o'-my-thumb, lilliputian, manikin, midge, peewee, pygmy, runt, Tom Thumb

midget *adj* ***syn*** TINY, diminutive, dwarf, dwarfish, lilliputian, miniature, minikin, teensy, teeny, wee

midmost *adj* ***syn*** MIDDLE 1, center, centermost, equidistant, halfway, medial, median, mid, middlemost

midpoint *n* ***syn*** CENTER 1, core, middle, midst

midst *n* ***syn*** CENTER 1, core, middle, midpoint

midst *prep* **1** ***syn*** AMID 1, among, mid
2 ***syn*** AMONG 1, amid, mid
3 ***syn*** DURING, amid, mid, over, throughout

mid–Victorian *n* ***syn*** FOGY, antediluvian, fogram, fossil, fuddy-duddy, mossback, square, stick-in-the-mud
rel bluenose, goody-goody, Mrs. Grundy, prig, prude, puritan; Victorian

---

syn synonym(s) ***rel*** related word(s)
idiom idiomatic equivalent(s) ***con*** contrasted word(s)
ant antonym(s) * vulgar
|| use limited; if in doubt, see a dictionary
The first word in a synonym list when printed in SMALL CAPITALS shows where there is more information about the group. For a more efficient use of this book see Explanatory Notes.

---

mien *n* **1** ***syn*** BEARING 1, address, air, comportment, demeanor, deportment, port, presence, set
rel expression, manner, mannerism
2 ***syn*** APPEARANCE 1, aspect, look, seeming

miff *n* **1** ***syn*** OFFENSE 2, dudgeon, huff, pique, resentment, ||snuff, umbrage
rel conniption, fit
2 ***syn*** QUARREL, altercation, beef, dispute, falling-out, rhubarb, run-in, spat, squabble, tiff

might *n* **1** ***syn*** POWER 1, authority, command, control, domination, jurisdiction, mastery, strings, sway
2 ***syn*** POWER 4, arm, beef, energy, force, muscle, potency, sinew, strength, strong arm
rel energeticness, lustiness, strenuousness, vigor, vigorousness; forcefulness, forcibleness, powerfulness
3 ***syn*** ABILITY 1, adequacy, capability, capacity, competence, qualification, qualifiedness
4 ***syn*** MUSCLE 1, beef, brawn, thew

might and main *adv* ***syn*** HARD 1, energetically, forcefully, forcibly, hardly, mightily, powerfully, strongly, vigorously

mightily *adv* **1** ***syn*** HARD 1, energetically, forcefully, forcibly, hardly, might and main, powerfully, strongly, vigorously
rel arduously, laboriously, strenuously, toilsomely
2 ***syn*** VERY 1, ||big, exceedingly, extremely, greatly, highly, hugely, mighty, notably, surpassingly

mighty *adj* **1** ***syn*** POWERFUL 2, forceful, forcible, potent, puissant
2 ***syn*** STRONG 1, powerful, ||strengthy, wieldy
3 ***syn*** HUGE, enormous, gigantic, grand, heroic, immense, massive, monumental, prodigious, tremendous
rel eminent, illustrious, renowned; august, grand, imposing, impressive, moving

mighty *adv* ***syn*** VERY 1, ||big, exceedingly, extremely, hugely, mightily, rattling, surpassingly, whacking, whopping

migrant *adj* ***syn*** MIGRATORY, migrative, migratorial, mobile, transmigratory

migrant *n* ***syn*** EMIGRANT, immigrant
rel in-migrant, out-migrant; drifter, mover, nomad, traveler, wanderer

migrate *vb* to move from one country, place, or locality to another <his father had *migrated* to the Far West years before>
syn emigrate, transmigrate
rel immigrate, in-migrate, out-migrate, remigrate; drift, trek; nomadize, range, roam, rove, wander

migrative *adj* ***syn*** MIGRATORY, migrant, migratorial, mobile, transmigratory
ant nonmigratory

migratorial *adj* ***syn*** MIGRATORY, migrant, migrative, mobile, transmigratory
ant nonmigratory

migratory *adj* moving habitually or occasionally from one region or climate to another <the study of *migratory* birds>
syn migrant, migrative, migratorial, mobile, transmigratory
rel errant, nomad, nomadic, ranging, roving, wandering
ant nonmigratory

mild *adj* **1** ***syn*** GENTLE 1, balmy, bland, faint, lenient, smooth, soft

rel choice, dainty, delicate, exquisite; moderate, temperate; benign, benignant
con intense, severe, sharp, vehement
ant fierce, harsh
2 *syn* AMIABLE 1, complaisant, easy, good-humored, good-natured, good-tempered, lenient, obliging
rel docile, meek; subdued, submissive; deferential, obeisant, subservient

milepost *n syn* EVENT 2, milestone, occasion

milestone *n syn* EVENT 2, milepost, occasion

milieu *n syn* ENVIRONMENT, ambience, ambient, atmosphere, climate, medium, mise-en-scène, surroundings

militant *adj* 1 *syn* BELLIGERENT, bellicose, combative, contentious, gladiatorial, pugnacious, quarrelsome, scrappy, truculent, warlike
rel martial, military
2 *syn* AGGRESSIVE, assertive, assertory, pushful, pushing, pushy, self-assertive

military *adj syn* MARTIAL, warlike
rel chauvinistic, jingoistic, militaristic, warmongering; soldierlike, soldierly
ant unmilitary

military *n syn* TROOP 2, armed forces, forces, servicemen

militate *vb syn* WEIGH 3, count, tell

milk *vb* 1 *syn* FLEECE 1, bleed, mulct, rook, stick, sweat
rel exact, exploit, extort; drain, empty, exhaust, pump, suck, wring
2 *syn* EDUCE 1, elicit, evince, evoke, extort, extract

milk-and-water *adj syn* INSIPID 3, inane, innocuous, jejune, namby-pamby, sapless, vapid, waterish, watery, wishy-washy

milk-livered *adj syn* COWARDLY, ||chicken, coward, craven, gutless, lily-livered, poltroonish, pusillanimous, spunkless, unmanly

milksop *n syn* WEAKLING, baby, doormat, invertebrate, jellyfish, Milquetoast, mollycoddle, namby-pamby, pantywaist, sissy
rel effeminate; coward

milk-warm *adj syn* TEPID 1, lukewarm, warmish

mill *n syn* FACTORY, manufactory, plant, works

million *n syn* SCAD, gob(s), heap, jillion, load(s), ream(s), ||rimption(s), slather(s), slew, wad(s)

millstone *n syn* LOAD 3, burden, charge, deadweight, duty, onus, task, tax, weight

Milquetoast *n syn* WEAKLING, baby, doormat, invertebrate, jellyfish, milksop, mollycoddle, pantywaist, sissy, sop

mime *n syn* ACTOR 1, impersonator, mimic, mummer, performer, playactor, player, thespian, trouper

mimic *n syn* ACTOR 1, impersonator, mime, mummer, performer, playactor, player, thespian, trouper

mimic *vb* to copy or exaggerate (as manner or gestures) often by way of mockery <*mimicked* her halting speech>
syn ape, burlesque, imitate, mock, parody, take off, travesty
rel hit off, mime, mum; act, do, enact, impersonate, perform, personate, play; copycat; pantomime

mimicry *n* the art or practice of closely imitating another in speech, gestures, or manners <engaged in *mimicry* of café society>
syn apery
rel imitation, mimesis, mimetism; mock, mockery; caricature, parody

miminy-piminy *adj syn* NICE 1, dainty, delicate, fastidious, finical, finicking, finicky, fussy, ||mincy, old-maidish

mince *vb* 1 *syn* CHOP 2, hash
2 *syn* SASHAY, flounce, prance, ||prink, strut

mincing *adj syn* GENTEEL 3, affected, la-di-da, ||lardy-dardy pretentious, stilted, too-too
rel dainty, delicate, fastidious, finical, finicking, finicky, fussy, nice, particular, pernickety, persnickety, squeamish

||**mincy** *adj syn* NICE 1, dainty, delicate, fastidious, finical, finicky, fussy, miminy-piminy, old-maidish, squeamish

mind *n* 1 the element or complex of elements in an individual that feels, perceives, thinks, wills, and especially reasons <sad to see such a *mind* dulled by drink and drugs>
syn brain, gray matter, head, ||upper story, ||upperworks, wit
rel brainpower, intellect, intelligence; consciousness, mentality; faculty, function, power
2 *syn* WILL 1, fancy, inclination, liking, pleasure, velleity
rel disposition, temper, temperament
con aversion, disinclination, indisposition
3 *syn* WIT 2, lucidity, ||marbles, reason, saneness, sanity, sense(s), soundness
4 *syn* OPINION, belief, conviction, eye, feeling, persuasion, sentiment, view
5 *syn* MOOD 1, humor, strain, temper, tone, vein
||6 *syn* NOTICE 1, attention, cognizance, head, mark, note, observance, observation, regard, remark

mind *vb* ||1 *syn* REMEMBER, bethink, cite, recall, recollect, remind, reminisce, retain, retrospect, revive
||2 *syn* ENJOY 1, ||dig, go, like, relish
3 *syn* SEE 1, behold, descry, discern, espy, mark, note, notice, observe, perceive
||4 *syn* INTEND 2, aim, contemplate, design, mean, plan, propose, purpose
5 *syn* OBEY, comply, conform, follow, keep, observe
6 *syn* LOOK 1, see, watch
7 *syn* BEWARE, look out, watch out
8 *syn* TEND 2, attend, care (for), watch
rel oversee, superintend, supervise; discipline, govern
con forget, slight
9 *syn* CONSIDER 1, contemplate, excogitate, perpend, ponder, study, think (out *or* over), weigh

minded *adj syn* WILLING 1, disposed, fain, inclined, predisposed, prone, ready
rel contemplating, intending, planning, purposing

---

mindful *adj* **1** ***syn*** AWARE, alive, apprehensive, au courant, awake, cognizant, conscious, conversant, knowing, sensible
ant unmindful
2 inclined to be aware < *mindful* of the ever-changing social scene >
syn heedful, observant, observative, observing, regardful, thoughtful
rel attentive, conscientious; aware, cognizant, conscious, conversant, sensible; alert, vigilant, watchful
con heedless, inattentive
ant mindless, unmindful

mindless *adj* **1** ***syn*** SIMPLE 3, asinine, brainless, ‖buffle-headed, foolish, nitwitted, senseless, sheepheaded, silly, witless
2 ***syn*** INSANE 1, ‖fruity, ‖loco, lunatic, mad, maniac, ‖mental, non compos mentis, nuts, nutsy

mine *n* ***syn*** BONANZA, eldorado, Golconda, gold mine, treasure-house, treasure trove, treasury
rel lode, quarry, vein; spring, well, wellspring

mine *vb* to dig into for the purpose of obtaining items of use or value < *mined* manuscripts looking for undiscovered masterpieces >
syn delve, quarry
rel burrow, drill, excavate, sap, scoop; work

mingle *vb* **1** ***syn*** MIX 1, comingle, commingle, commix, immingle, intermingle, intermix, make up, meld, merge
2 ***syn*** SOCIALIZE

mingle–mangle *n* ***syn*** MISCELLANY 1, assortment, gallimaufry, hodgepodge, jumble, medley, olio, omnium-gatherum, pastiche, salad

mingy *adj* ***syn*** STINGY, ‖chinchy, closefisted, mean, miserly, niggardly, penurious, scrimpy, tight, ungiving

miniature *n* ***syn*** MODEL 1, pocket edition

miniature *adj* ***syn*** TINY, diminutive, itty-bitty, lilliputian, minute, teensy, teeny, teeny-weeny, wee, weeny
rel small-scale, subminiature
con large-scale

minify *vb* ***syn*** ABRIDGE 1, curtail, diminish, lessen
rel dwarf, miniaturize, shrink

minikin *adj* ***syn*** TINY, ‖bitsy, itsy-bitsy, itty-bitty, midget, minute, teensy, teenty, teeny, wee

minim *n* ***syn*** PARTICLE, atom, grain, iota, jot, mite, modicum, smidgen, smitch, speck

minimal *adj* constituting the least possible < *minimal* differences of opinion >
syn minimum
rel littlest, lowest, slightest, smallest; basal, basic, essential, fundamental
con maximum, topmost, utmost; greatest, highest, largest, most
ant maximal

syn synonym(s) — *rel* related word(s)
idiom idiomatic equivalent(s) — *con* contrasted word(s)
ant antonym(s) — * vulgar
‖ use limited; if in doubt, see a dictionary
The first word in a synonym list when printed in SMALL CAPITALS shows where there is more information about the group. For a more efficient use of this book see Explanatory Notes.

minimize *vb* ***syn*** DECRY 2, belittle, depreciate, derogate, detract (from), diminish, discount, disparage, dispraise, run down
rel dwarf, reduce
ant magnify, maximize

minimum *n* the least quantity assignable, admissible, or possible < testing the use of a *minimum* of security at the prison >
syn margin
rel dab, hair, iota, jot, modicum, particle, pittance, smidgen, speck, whit
con abundance, bushel(s), gob(s), ‖lashings, load(s), lot(s), mass(es), much, oodles, profusion, scads, slather(s), ton(s), world(s)
ant maximum

minimum *adj* ***syn*** MINIMAL
ant maximum

minion *n* ***syn*** SYCOPHANT, apple-polisher, bootlicker, ‖brownnoser, lickspittle, spaniel, toad, toadeater, truckler, yes-man

minister *n* ***syn*** CLERGYMAN, churchman, cleric, clerical, clerk, divine, ecclesiastic, parson, preacher, reverend

minister (to) *vb* to attend to the wants and comforts of someone < *minister* to the sick and dying >
syn care (for), mother, nurse, serve, wait (on)
rel cure, heal, remedy; doctor, treat; pander

ministerial *adj* ***syn*** INSTRUMENTAL, implemental

minister plenipotentiary *n* ***syn*** ENVOY 1, envoy extraordinary

ministry *n* ***syn*** MEAN 2, agency, agent, channel, instrument, instrumentality, instrumentation, medium, organ, vehicle

minor *adj* **1** ***syn*** LITTLE 3, casual, inconsiderable, insignificant, light, petty, shoestring, small-beer, trivial, unimportant
rel dependent; inferior, piddling, trifling; junior, lower
con meaningful, significant
ant major
2 lower in standing or reputation than others of the same class < a *minor* poet of the late eighteenth century >
syn dinky, insignificant, lesser, minor-league, secondary, small, small-fry, small-time
rel average, fair, indifferent, mediocre, medium, middling, second-rate, undistinguished, unnoticeable; trivial, unimportant
con chief, foremost, leading, principal
ant major

minor *n* ***syn*** INFANT 2

minority *n* ***syn*** INFANCY 2, nonage
ant majority

minor–league *adj* ***syn*** MINOR 2, dinky, insignificant, lesser, secondary, small, small-fry, small-time

minstrel *n* ***syn*** BARD 1, jongleur, troubadour
rel balladist, singer, wait

mint *n* ***syn*** FORTUNE 4, ‖bomb, boodle, bundle, packet, pile, pot, ‖roll, wad

mint *adj* ***syn*** BRAND-NEW, fire-new, spang-new, spanking-new, span-new, spick-and-span
rel intact, original, perfect, unmarred

minus *prep* ***syn*** WITHOUT 2, awanting, lacking, sans, wanting
ant plus

minute *n* ***syn*** INSTANT 1, breathing, crack, flash, ‖jiff, jiffy, moment, second, shake, split second

minute *adj* **1** ***syn*** TINY, diminutive, itty-bitty, lilliputian, miniature, teensy, teeny, teeny-weeny, wee, weeny
2 ***syn*** LITTLE 3, inconsiderable, insignificant, light, minor, petty, small, small-beer, trivial, unimportant
3 ***syn*** CIRCUMSTANTIAL, blow-by-blow, clocklike, detailed, full, itemized, particular, particularized, thorough
rel careful, meticulous, punctilious, scrupulous
con abstract; general, universal; comprehending, comprehensive, embracing, embracive, including, inclusive

minutely *adj* ***syn*** CONTINUAL, around-the-clock, ceaseless, constant, continuous, incessant, interminable, unceasing, unintermitted, uninterrupted

minutia *n, usu* **minutiae** *pl* **1** ***syn*** INS AND OUTS, ropes
2 ***syn*** TRIVIA, small beer, small change, small potato(es), triviality

minx *n* a pert girl <her rivals called her a brazen *minx*>
syn hussy, jade, malapert, saucebox, slut, snip
rel broad, brat, upstart; baggage, chippy, drab, floozy, strumpet, tart, trollop, trull

miracle *n* ***syn*** WONDER 1, marvel, phenomenon, portent, prodigy, sensation, stunner

miraculous *adj* **1** ***syn*** SUPERNATURAL 1, numinous, preternatural, superhuman, superior, supermundane, suprahuman, supramundane, supranatural, unearthly
2 ***syn*** MARVELOUS 1, amazing, astonishing, astounding, prodigious, spectacular, staggering, strange, wonderful, wondrous
con natural, normal

mirage *n* ***syn*** DELUSION 1, hallucination, ignis fatuus, illusion, phantasm

mire *n* ***syn*** SWAMP, baygall, bog, fen, marsh, morass, ‖moss, quag, quagmire, ‖sump
rel muck

mire *vb* **1** ***syn*** DELAY 1, bog (down), decelerate, detain, embog, hang up, retard, set back, slacken, slow (up *or* down)
rel bemire, sink; adhere, cleave, cling, cohere, stick; enmesh, ensnare, entangle, entrap, involve, snare, trap
2 ***syn*** INVOLVE 1, embroil, implicate, tangle

mirror *n* **1** a polished or smooth surface (as of glass) that forms images by reflection <spent hours looking at herself in the *mirror*>
syn glass, looking glass, ‖seeing glass
rel cheval glass, pier glass, reflector, speculum
2 ***syn*** MODEL 2, archetype, beau ideal, ensample, example, exemplar, ideal, paradigm, pattern, standard

mirror *vb* **1** ***syn*** REFLECT 1, glass, image
2 ***syn*** REPRESENT 2, body (forth), emblematize, embody, epitomize, exemplify, illustrate, personify, symbolize, typify

mirth *n* a mood or temper characterized by joy and high spirits and usually manifested in laughter and merrymaking <a man of contentment, but seldom of *mirth*>
syn glee, hilarity, jocularity, jocundity, jollity, joviality, merriment
rel cheer, cheerfulness, joyfulness, lightheartedness; gladness, happiness; frivolity, levity
con blues, dejection, depression, dumps, gloom, sadness; boredom, ennui, tedium; anguish, misery, woe; infelicity, wretchedness
ant melancholy

mirthful *adj* ***syn*** MERRY, blithe, blithesome, festive, gay, gleeful, jocund, jolly, jovial, lighthearted
ant mirthless

miry *adj* ***syn*** MUDDY 1, bemired, ‖claggy, ‖clarty, oozy

misadventure *n* **1** ***syn*** DISASTER, calamity, cataclysm, catastrophe, tragedy, woe(s)
2 ***syn*** ACCIDENT 2, casualty, mischance, mishap
rel blunder, boner, bull, error, faux pas, howler, lapse, slip

misanthropic *adj* ***syn*** ANTISOCIAL, eremitic, reclusive, reserved, solitary, standoffish
rel misogynic
con altruistic, benevolent, charitable, humane, humanitarian
ant philanthropic

misapply *vb* ***syn*** ABUSE 2, misemploy, mishandle, misimprove, misuse, pervert, prostitute
rel misappropriate, misdirect, mismanage

misapprehend *vb* **1** ***syn*** MISUNDERSTAND 1, miscomprehend, misknow, miss
ant apprehend
2 ***syn*** MISUNDERSTAND 2, misconceive, misconstrue, misinterpret, misread, mistake
ant apprehend

misappropriate *vb* ***syn*** EMBEZZLE, peculate

misbegotten *adj* ***syn*** ILLEGITIMATE 1, baseborn, bastard, fatherless, natural, spurious, supposititious, unfathered

misbehaving *adj* ***syn*** NAUGHTY 1, bad, ill-behaved, mischievous, paw
ant well-behaved

misbehavior *n* ***syn*** MISCONDUCT, misdoing, wrongdoing

misbelief *n* ***syn*** HERESY, dissent, dissidence, heterodoxy, nonconformism, nonconformity, schism, unorthodoxy

misbeliever *n* ***syn*** HERETIC, dissenter, dissident, nonconformist, schismatic, schismatist, sectary, separatist

miscalculate *vb* to calculate wrongly <*miscalculate* the distance> <he seriously *miscalculated* the effect of his remark>
syn misestimate, misjudge, misreckon
rel discount, disregard, overlook; misconstrue, misinterpret, misunderstand; overestimate, overprize, overrate, overvalue; understimate, underprize, underrate, undervalue

miscarry *vb* to go wrong or amiss <his plans *miscarried* almost from the start>
syn misfire, miss
rel abort; fail, flop

idiom fall through, miss fire, miss the mark
con come off, prevail, succeed

miscellaneous *adj* consisting of diverse things or members <gathered together a *miscellaneous* lot of books for sale>
syn assorted, chowchow, conglomerate, heterogeneous, indiscriminate, mixed, motley, multifarious, promiscuous, unassorted, unsorted, varied
rel different, disparate, divergent, diverse, various; divers, many, sundry; odd; commingled, jumbled, mingled, scrambled
con akin, alike, identical, like, parallel, similar, uniform

miscellany *n* **1** an unorganized mixture of various dissimilar items or elements <sold a *miscellany* of old household effects>
syn assortment, brew, chowchow, colluvies, gallimaufry, hash, hodgepodge, hotchpotch, jumble, medley, mélange, melee, mingle-mangle, mishmash, mixed bag, motley, odds and ends, olio, olla podrida, omnium-gatherum, pasticcio, pastiche, patchwork, porridge, potpourri, rumble-bumble, salad, salmagundi, smorgasbord, stew
rel mess, muddle; accumulation, aggregation, congeries, conglomeration, cumulation; combination, mix, mixture
2 *syn* ANTHOLOGY, album, ana, analects, florilegium, garland, omnibus, posy

mischance *n* **1** *syn* MISFORTUNE, adversity, contretemps, ‖dole, mishap, tragedy, ‖unluck
2 *syn* ACCIDENT 2, casualty, misadventure, mishap

mischief *n* **1** *syn* INJURY 1, damage, harm, hurt, outrage, ruin
rel difficulty, hardship, trouble
2 *syn* SCAMP, devil, enfant terrible, limb, rapscallion, rascal, rogue, scalawag, skeezicks, villain
3 *syn* MISCHIEVOUSNESS, devilment, devilry, deviltry, diablerie, roguery, roguishness, sportiveness, waggery, waggishness
4 *syn* DISCORD, conflict, contention, difference, disaccord, dissension, dissent, division, strife, variance

‖**mischieful** *adj* *syn* PLAYFUL 1, antic, impish, larkish, mischievous, prankful, prankish, pranky, roguish, wicked

mischief-maker *n* *syn* TROUBLEMAKER, bad actor

mischievous *adj* **1** *syn* HARMFUL, bad, damaging, deleterious, detrimental, evil, hurtful, ill, injurious, nocuous
rel dangerous, hazardous, perilous, precarious, risky
2 *syn* NAUGHTY 1, bad, ill-behaved, misbehaving, paw
rel annoying, bothering, bothersome, irking, irksome, vexatious, vexing
3 *syn* PLAYFUL 1, antic, frolicsome, impish, larkish, ‖mischieful, roguish, sportive, waggish, wicked
rel artful, foxy, insidious, sly, tricky

mischievousness *n* action or conduct that annoys or irritates without causing or meaning serious harm <a wag who was forever engaging in *mischievousness*>
syn devilment, devilry, deviltry, diablerie, impishness, mischief, roguery, roguishness, sportiveness, waggery, waggishness
rel doggery, odiousness, offensiveness; evil, harm, hurt, injury; annoying, pestering, teasing

miscolor *vb* *syn* MISREPRESENT, belie, color, distort, falsify, garble, misstate, pervert, twist, warp

miscomprehend *vb* *syn* MISUNDERSTAND 1, misapprehend, misknow, miss

misconceive *vb* *syn* MISUNDERSTAND 2, misapprehend, misconstrue, misinterpret, misread, mistake

misconduct *n* improper behavior <was charged with *misconduct*>
syn misbehavior, misdoing, wrongdoing
rel impropriety; malfeasance, malversation, misfeasance

misconstrue *vb* *syn* MISUNDERSTAND 2, misapprehend, misconceive, misinterpret, misread, mistake

miscreant *adj* *syn* VICIOUS 2, corrupt, degenerate, depraved, flagitious, infamous, nefarious, perverse, unhealthy, villainous

miscreant *n* *syn* VILLAIN 1, *bastard, blackguard, heel, knave, lowlife, rascal, rogue, scoundrel, *son of a bitch

miscreation *n* *syn* FREAK 2, abortion, lusus, monster, monstrosity
rel deformation, deformity

miscue *n* *syn* ERROR 2, blooper, blunder, fluff, lapse, misstep, mistake, slip, slipup, trip

misdate *n* *syn* ANACHRONISM 1, misdating, mistiming, parachronism

misdating *n* *syn* ANACHRONISM 1, misdate, mistiming, parachronism

misdeed *n* *syn* CRIME 1, offense

misdeem *vb* **1** *syn* MISJUDGE 2, misesteem, mistake
2 *syn* MISTAKE 1, confound, confuse, misidentify, mix, mix up

misdoing *n* *syn* MISCONDUCT, misbehavior, wrongdoing

misdoubt *vb* *syn* DISTRUST, doubt, mistrust, suspect, ‖suspicion
rel apprehend, dread, fear

mise-en-scène *n* **1** *syn* SCENE 1, scenery, set, setting, stage set, stage setting
2 *syn* SCENE 3, locale, site
3 *syn* ENVIRONMENT, ambience, ambient, atmosphere, climate, medium, milieu, surroundings

misemploy *vb* *syn* ABUSE 2, misapply, mishandle, misimprove, misuse, pervert, prostitute

miser *n* a mean grasping person <an old *miser* who loved only his bank account>
syn cheapskate, cheeseparer, chuff, hunks, moneygrubber, muckworm, nabal, niggard, ‖nipcheese, penny pincher, piker, scrooge, skin, skinflint, stiff, tightwad
rel glutton, hog, pig

miserable *adj* *syn* WOEFUL 1, afflicted, doleful, dolent, dolorous, rueful, ruthful, sorrowful, wretched
rel despairing, despondent, forlorn, hopeless; piteous, pitiable, pitiful; melancholy
con cheerful, glad, happy, joyful, joyous, lighthearted

miserly *adj* *syn* STINGY, cheeseparing, close, closefisted, niggardly, parsimonious, penny-pinching, penurious, tight, tightfisted

rel avaricious, covetous, grasping, greedy; abject, ignoble, sordid
con bountious, generous; altruistic, benevolent, charitable

misery *n* **1** a state of suffering and want that is the result of poverty or conditions beyond one's control <the poor learn to live with *misery*> <the utter *misery* in which the flood victims survived>
syn unhappiness, woe, wretchedness
rel agony, anguish; despondency, grief, sorrow; desolation, squalor
con beatitude, blessedness, bliss, felicity, happiness; content, ease, satisfaction
2 *syn* DISTRESS, agony, dolor, passion, suffering
rel adversity, misfortune; dejection, depression, melancholy, sadness
ant blessedness
‖**3** *syn* PAIN 1, ache, pang, stitch, throe, twinge

misesteem *vb syn* MISJUDGE 2, misdeem, mistake

misestimate *vb syn* MISCALCULATE, misjudge, misreckon

misfire *vb syn* MISCARRY, miss

misfortunate *adj syn* UNLUCKY, hapless, ill-fated, ill-starred, luckless, star-crossed, unfortunate, unhappy, untoward
ant fortunate

misfortune *n* adverse fortune or an instance of this <his hopes and dreams soon ended in *misfortune*> <unable to grasp why he had been struck by such a *misfortune*>
syn adversity, contretemps, ‖dole, mischance, mishap, tragedy, ‖unluck
rel calamity, cataclysm, catastrophe, disaster; accident, casualty; affliction, cross, trial, tribulation, visitation
con break, chance, luck, opportunity
ant fortune

misgiving *n syn* APPREHENSION 3, apprehensiveness, foreboding, premonition, prenotion, presage, presentiment
rel doubt, fear, qualm, suspicion; distrust, mistrust

misguided *adj syn* MISTAKEN, erroneous, wrong

mishandle *vb* **1** *syn* MANHANDLE, knock about, rough (up), roughhouse, slap around
2 *syn* ABUSE 2, misapply, misemploy, misimprove, misuse, pervert, prostitute

mishap *n* **1** *syn* MISFORTUNE, adversity, contretemps, ‖dole, mischance, tragedy, ‖unluck
2 *syn* ACCIDENT 2, casualty, misadventure, mischance

mishmash *n* **1** *syn* MISCELLANY 1, hodgepodge, hotchpotch, medley, mélange, omnium-gatherum, pasticcio, pastiche, patchwork, potpourri
2 *syn* CLUTTER 2, hash, jumble, jungle, litter, mash, muddle, rummage, scramble, tumble

misidentify *vb syn* MISTAKE 1, confound, confuse, misdeem, mix, mix up

misimprove *vb syn* ABUSE 2, misapply, misemploy, mishandle, misuse, pervert, prostitute

misinterpret *vb syn* MISUNDERSTAND 2, misapprehend, misconceive, misconstrue, misread, mistake

misjudge *vb* **1** *syn* MISCALCULATE, misestimate, misreckon
2 to have a mistaken opinion of <her first impression led her to *misjudge* the girl>
syn misdeem, misesteem, mistake
rel misapprehend, miscomprehend, misconceive, misconstrue, misinterpret, misunderstand
con catch on (to), penetrate, tumble (to), wise (up)

misknow *vb syn* MISUNDERSTAND 1, misapprehend, miscomprehend, miss

mislaying *n syn* LOSS 1, losing, misplacement, misplacing

mislead *vb syn* DECEIVE, beguile, betray, bluff, ‖bunk, delude, double-cross, illude, juggle, take in
rel lie, misguide, misinform; entice, inveigle, lure, seduce, tempt

misleading *adj* having an appearance or character that leads one astray or into error <the president made several *misleading* statements to the people>
syn beguiling, deceiving, deceptive, deluding, delusive, delusory, fallacious, false
rel casuistical, sophistical, specious; wrong; bewildering, confounding, distracting, perplexing, puzzling; deceitful, inaccurate
con clarifying, elucidative, explanatory, illuminating

‖**mismannered** *adj syn* RUDE 6, discourteous, disrespectful, ill-bred, ill-mannered, impolite, mannerless, uncourteous, uncouth, unmannered

mismatch *vb syn* CLASH 2, conflict, disaccord, discord, disharmonize, jangle, jar

misorder *n syn* CONFUSION 3, ataxia, ‖ballup, clutter, disarray, disorder, huddle, muddle, ‖mullock, snarl

misplacement *n syn* LOSS 1, losing, mislaying, misplacing

misplacing *n syn* LOSS 1, losing, mislaying, misplacement

misread *vb syn* MISUNDERSTAND 2, misapprehend, misconceive, misconstrue, misinterpret, mistake

misreckon *vb syn* MISCALCULATE, misestimate, misjudge

‖**misremember** *vb syn* FORGET 1, disremember, unknow

misrepresent *vb* to give a false, imperfect, or misleading representation of <the summary totally *misrepresents* the facts of the case>
syn belie, color, confuse, distort, falsify, garble, miscolor, misstate, pervert, twist, warp, wrench, wrest
rel dress, embellish, embroider, gild, gloss, varnish; camouflage, cloak, disguise, dissemble, mask; counterfeit, feign, simulate; equivocate, lie, palter, prevaricate, weasel
idiom give a false coloring, put a false construction (*or* appearance) on

misrepresentation *n syn* LIE, canard, falsehood, falsity, fib, prevarication, story, tale, untruism, untruth

misrule *n syn* DISORDER 2, anarchism, anarchy, distemper, riot

miss *vb* **1** *syn* NEGLECT, discount, disregard, fail, forget, ignore, omit, overlook, pass, slight

2 ***syn*** MISUNDERSTAND 1, misapprehend, miscomprehend, misknow
3 ***syn*** MISCARRY, misfire

‖**miss** *n* ***syn*** ABSENCE, dearth, default, defect, lack, privation, want

miss *n* ***syn*** GIRL 1, damsel, gal, lass, lassie, maid, maiden, missy, ‖quail, wench

misshape *vb* ***syn*** DEFORM, contort, distort, torture, warp, wind

misshape *n* ***syn*** DEFORMITY, distortion, malconformation, malformation

missing *adj* 1 ***syn*** ABSENT 1, away, gone, lacking, omitted, wanting
2 ***syn*** LOST 2, gone

mission *n* a continuing task or responsibility that one is destined or fitted to do or specially called upon to undertake <his *mission* in life was to serve humanity>
syn calling, lifework, vocation
rel goal, purpose; business, profession, trade

missionary *n* one who attempts to convert others to a specific way of life, set of ideas, or course of action <served as a *missionary* for the feminist cause>
syn apostle, colporteur, evangelist, missioner, propagandist
rel revivalist; promoter

missioner *n* ***syn*** MISSIONARY, apostle, colporteur, evangelist, propagandist

missish *adj* ***syn*** PRIM 1, prig, priggish, prissy, prudish, puritanical, straitlaced, stuffy, tight-laced, Victorian

missive *n* ***syn*** LETTER 2, epistle, note

Miss–Nancyish *adj* ***syn*** EFFEMINATE, epicene, pansified, prissy, sissified, sissy, unmanly

misstate *vb* ***syn*** MISREPRESENT, belie, color, distort, falsify, garble, miscolor, pervert, twist, warp

misstatement *n* ***syn*** LIE, falsehood, falsity, fib, misrepresentation, prevarication, tale, taradiddle, untruism, untruth

misstep *n* ***syn*** ERROR 2, blooper, boner, bull, fluff, lapse, miscue, mistake, slip, slipup

‖**missus** *n* ***syn*** WIFE, ‖ball and chain, lady, ‖little woman, Mrs., ‖old lady, ‖old woman, ‖rib, ‖squaw, woman

missy *n* ***syn*** GIRL 1, damsel, gal, lass, lassie, maid, maiden, miss, ‖quail, wench

mist *n* ***syn*** HAZE 1, brume, film, smaze

mist *vb* ***syn*** OBSCURE, becloud, befog, cloud, dim, fog, haze, murk, overcast, overcloud

mistake *vb* 1 to take one thing to be another <he *mistakes* sarcasm for wit>
syn confound, confuse, misdeem, misidentify, mix, mix up
rel misconceive, misknow; addle, jumble, muddle, tumble
con discern, distinguish, grasp, perceive; differentiate, separate
ant recognize
2 ***syn*** MISUNDERSTAND 2, misapprehend, misconceive, misconstrue, misinterpret, misread
3 ***syn*** MISJUDGE 2, misdeem, misesteem

mistake *n* 1 ***syn*** ERROR 2, blooper, blunder, boner, bull, bungle, fluff, lapse, slip, trip
rel confounding, confusion, mistaking; inadvertence; disregarding, neglect, neglecting, omission, omitting, slight, slighting
2 ***syn*** ERROR 1, x

mistaken *adj* acting, thinking, or judging in a manner at variance with truth or the facts <he is *mistaken* in his evaluation of the crisis>
syn erroneous, misguided, wrong
rel confounded, confused; deceived, deluded, misinformed
idiom all wet, off base, off the track
con accurate, correct, right, unerring; exact, precise

mister *n* ***syn*** HUSBAND, ‖hubby, lord, man, ‖master, Mr., ‖old man

mistimed *adj* ***syn*** UNSEASONABLE 1, ill-seasoned, ill-timed, inopportune, malapropos, untimely
ant well-timed

mistiming *n* ***syn*** ANACHRONISM 1, misdate, misdating, parachronism

mistreat *vb* ***syn*** ABUSE 4, ill-treat, ill-use, maltreat, misuse, outrage

mistress *n* a woman who is a man's regular partner in nonmarital sexual activity <gave up his *mistress* when he married>
syn ‖doxy, girl friend, inamorata, lover, paramour, woman; *compare* HARLOT 1
rel bedmate; concubine; kept woman; dulcinea

mistrust *n* ***syn*** UNCERTAINTY, concern, doubt, dubiety, dubiosity, incertitude, skepticism, suspicion, uncertitude, wonder
rel apprehension, foreboding, misgiving, presentiment
con dependence, faith, reliance
ant assurance, trust

mistrust *vb* 1 ***syn*** DISTRUST, doubt, misdoubt, suspect, ‖suspicion
rel anticipate, apprehend, foresee; alarm, frighten, scare; appall, dismay
ant trust
2 ***syn*** QUESTION 2, challenge, dispute, doubt

mistrustful *adj* ***syn*** SUSPICIOUS 2, distrustful, jealous
ant trustful, trusting

mistrustfully *adv* ***syn*** ASKANCE 2, distrustfully, doubtfully, skeptically, suspiciously
ant trustfully, trustingly

misty *adj* ***syn*** HAZY, cloudy, foggy, mushy, vague, vaporous, vapory

misunderstand *vb* 1 to fail to understand <he *misunderstood* the full meaning of the novel>
syn misapprehend, miscomprehend, misknow, miss
rel misconceive, misconstrue, misinterpret, misread, mistake
con apprehend, conceive, know, realize; fathom, follow, grasp, seize, take in
ant comprehend, understand
2 to interpret incorrectly < *misunderstood* the instructions>

---

syn synonym(s) — ***rel*** related word(s)
idiom idiomatic equivalent(s) — ***con*** contrasted word(s)
ant antonym(s) — * vulgar
‖ use limited; if in doubt, see a dictionary
The first word in a synonym list when printed in SMALL CAPITALS shows where there is more information about the group. For a more efficient use of this book see Explanatory Notes.

syn misapprehend, misconceive, misconstrue, misinterpret, misread, mistake
rel misexplain, mistranslate; miscomprehend, misknow
con fathom, follow, take in
ant understand

misuse *vb* **1** *syn* ABUSE 2, misapply, misemploy, mishandle, misimprove, pervert, prostitute
2 *syn* ABUSE 4, ill-treat, ill-use, maltreat, mistreat, outrage

mite *n syn* PARTICLE, atom, grain, iota, jot, minim, modicum, molecule, ounce, tittle

mitigate *vb syn* RELIEVE 1, allay, alleviate, assuage, ease, lighten, mollify
rel extenuate, palliate
con aggravate, enhance, heighten; augment, increase
ant intensify

mitigation *n syn* EASE 3, alleviation, easement, relief

mix *vb* **1** to combine or be combined into a more or less uniform whole <*mixed* the ingredients to make a thick sauce>
syn admix, amalgamate, blend, comingle, commingle, commix, compound, fuse, immingle, immix, interblend, interflow, interfuse, intermingle, intermix, make up, meld, merge, mingle
rel associate, combine, conjoin, inosculate, join, link, unite; braid, lump, work in; coalesce; blunge
con divide, part, separate, sever, sunder
2 *syn* MISTAKE 1, confound, confuse, misdeem, misidentify, mix up

mix *n syn* MIXTURE, admixture, amalgam, amalgamation, blend, commixture, fusion, immixture, interfusion, intermixture

mixed *adj syn* MISCELLANEOUS, assorted, chowchow, conglomerate, heterogeneous, indiscriminate, motley, multifarious, promiscuous, varied
rel amalgamated, blended, fused, merged, mingled

mixed bag *n syn* MISCELLANY 1, assortment, gallimaufry, hodgepodge, jumble, medley, olio, omnium-gatherum, pastiche, salad

mixologist *n syn* BARTENDER, barkeeper, ‖barmaid, barman, tapster

mixture *n* a product formed by the combination of two or more things <the tea is actually a *mixture* of several varieties>
syn admixture, alloy, amalgam, amalgamation, blend, commixture, composite, compost, compound, fusion, immixture, interfusion, intermixture, mix, mix-up
rel brew, concoction, confection, mélange

mix up *vb* **1** *syn* CONFUSE 2, addle, ball up, befuddle, bewilder, ‖bumfuzzle, distract, dizzy, fluster, fuddle
ant straighten (out)
2 *syn* CONFUSE 5, foul up, jumble, muddle, ‖snafu, snarl up, tumble
3 *syn* MISTAKE 1, confound, confuse, misdeem, misidentify, mix
4 *syn* DISORDER 1, derange, disarrange, dissarray, discompose, disjoint, disorganize, disrupt, distemper, mess (up)
ant straighten (out *or* up)

mix–up *n* **1** *syn* MESS 3, botch, botchery, hash, mess-up, muddle, mull, muss, shambles
2 *syn* MIXTURE, blend, commixture, composite, compound, fusion, immixture, interfusion, intermixture, mix

mizmaze *n syn* MAZE 1, jungle, knot, labyrinth, mesh, morass, skein, snarl, tangle, web

‖**mizzle** *vb syn* SPRINKLE 5, drizzle

‖**mizzle** *vb syn* CONFUSE 2, addle, ball up, befuddle, bewilder, distract, fluster, fuddle, mix up, throw off

moan *vb syn* DEPLORE 1, bemoan, bewail, grieve, lament, weep

moanful *adj syn* MELANCHOLY 2, doleful, lamentable, lugubrious, mournful, plaintive, rueful, sighful, sorrowful, wailful

mob *n* **1** *syn* RABBLE, canaille, dreg(s), mass(es), proletariat, ragtag and bobtail, riffraff, scum, trash, unwashed
2 a large disorderly crowd of people usually bent on riotous or destructive action <the *mob* screamed for a lynching>
syn rabble, rout
rel posse; crowd, crush, horde, press, push, throng; herd, swarm
3 *syn* CLIQUE, cabal, camarilla, camp, circle, clan, coterie, ingroup, ring

‖**mob** *vb syn* SCOLD 1, ‖bless out, ‖cample, ‖carpet, ‖chew out, lash, rail, rate, ‖row, ‖tongue-walk

mobile *adj* **1** *syn* MOVABLE, moving, unstable, unsteadfast, unsteady
rel fluid, liquid; protean; capricious, fickle, inconstant, mercurial
con immutable, invariable, unchangeable
ant immobile
2 *syn* CHANGEABLE 1, changeful, fluid, mutable, protean, unsettled, unstable, unsteady, variable, weathery
ant immobile, stable
3 *syn* VERSATILE, adaptable, all-around, ambidextrous, many-sided, myriad-minded
4 *syn* MIGRATORY, migrant, migrative, migratorial, transmigratory

mobilize *vb* **1** to put into movement or circulation <an increase in prices *mobilizes* the whole cycle of inflation>
syn actuate, circulate, set off
rel activate; impel, propel
idiom set in motion
con inactivate, slow (down *or* up)
ant immobilize
2 *syn* MOVE 5, actuate, drive, impel, propel
3 to assemble (as resources) and make ready for use or action <the president tried to *mobilize* support for the new proposal>
syn marshal, muster, organize, rally

mobocracy *n syn* ANARCHY 1, chaos, lawlessness, ochlocracy

mock *vb* **1** *syn* RIDICULE, deride, lout, quiz, rally, razz, scout, taunt, twit
rel buffoon, burlesque, caricature, parody, travesty

---

2 ***syn*** DECEIVE, beguile, betray, delude, double-cross, humbug, illude, juggle, mislead, sell out
3 ***syn*** MIMIC, ape, burlesque, imitate, parody, take off, travesty
rel affect, assume, counterfeit, feign, simulate

mock *n* **1** ***syn*** LAUGHINGSTOCK, butt, derision, jest, jester, joke, mockery, pilgarlic, sport
2 ***syn*** MOCKERY 2, burlesque, caricature, farce, sham, travesty

mock *adj* **1** ***syn*** ARTIFICIAL 2, dummy, ersatz, false, imitation, sham, simulated, spurious, substitute
rel pseudo, quasi, so-called
2 ***syn*** FICTITIOUS 2, fake, sham, simulated
rel bogus, phony

mockery *n* **1** ***syn*** LAUGHINGSTOCK, butt, derision, jest, jester, joke, mock, pilgarlic, sport
2 an insincere, contemptible, or impertinent imitation of something worthwhile <arbitrary methods that make a *mockery* of justice>
syn burlesque, caricature, farce, mock, sham, travesty
rel derision, ridicule, sport; parody, satire, take-off; joke, laughingstock

mode *n* **1** ***syn*** VEIN 1, fashion, manner, style, tone
2 ***syn*** METHOD 1, fashion, manner, modus, system, technique, way, wise
3 ***syn*** STATE 1, condition, posture, situation, status

mode *n* ***syn*** FASHION 3, chic, craze, cry, dernier cri, fad, furore, rage, style, vogue

model *n* **1** a miniature representation of something <a *model* of the dam that was accurate down to the last detail>
syn miniature, pocket edition
rel copy, mock-up, replica, reproduction; dummy, effigy
2 something set or held before one for guidance or imitation <Samuel Johnson's literary style is often used as a *model* for writers seeking precision and clarity>
syn archetype, beau ideal, ensample, example, exemplar, ideal, mirror, paradigm, pattern, standard; *compare* PARAGON
rel apotheosis, nonesuch, nonpareil, paragon; emblem, symbol, type; embodiment, epitome, quintessence; criterion, gauge, touchstone

model *adj* **1** ***syn*** IDEAL 3, flawless, indefectible
rel commendable, exemplary
2 ***syn*** PERFECT 3, ideal, very
3 ***syn*** TYPICAL 1, classic, classical, exemplary, ideal, paradigmatic, prototypal, prototypical, quintessential, representative

moderate *adj* **1** ***syn*** SOBER 3, temperate, unimpassioned
2 not excessive in degree, amount, or intensity <the new proposals were met with only *moderate* enthusiasm> <the snowfall is expected to be no more than *moderate*>
syn modest, reasonable, temperate
rel bland, gentle, mild, soft; inconsequential, inconsiderable, slight, small; paltry, piddling, trifling, trivial
con excessive, extreme, inordinate, intemperate, radical, unreasonable
ant immoderate
3 ***syn*** MEDIUM, average, fair, fairish, indifferent, intermediate, mean, mediocre, middling, so-so
rel constant, equable, even, steady
4 avoiding extreme political or social measures <party policy became increasingly *moderate*>
syn middle-of-the-road, middle-road, soft-shell
con conservative, right, tory; left, radical, red; extremist, fanatical, ultra
5 ***syn*** CONSERVATIVE 2, controlled, discreet, reasonable, restrained, temperate, unexcessive, unextreme

moderate *vb* **1** to modify as to avoid an extreme or keep within bounds <actors *moderate* their voices and gestures to fit the size of the theatre>
syn modulate, restrain, temper
rel abate, decrease, diminish, lessen, reduce; alleviate, cushion, lighten, mitigate, mollify, relieve, slacken, slow; constrain, control, qualify; chasten, cool, subdue, tone (down)
con aggravate, enhance, heighten, intensify; augment, increase
2 ***syn*** ABATE 4, die (down *or* away), ease off, ebb, fall, let up, relent, slacken, subside, wane

moderately *adv* **1** ***syn*** ENOUGH 2, averagely, fairly, passably, rather, so-so, tolerably
2 ***syn*** SOMEWHAT 2, fairly, kind of, more or less, pretty, rather, ratherish, some, something, sort of
ant extremely, immoderately

moderateness *n* ***syn*** TEMPERANCE 1, measure, moderation
ant immoderateness, immoderation

moderation *n* ***syn*** TEMPERANCE 1, measure, moderateness
ant immoderateness, immoderation

moderator *n* one who arbitrates <the labor dispute was finally referred to a *moderator*>
syn arbitrator, mediator
rel arbiter, judge; conciliator, negotiator, peacemaker

modern *adj* **1** having taken place, existed, or developed in times close to the present <*modern* concepts of engineering made the bridge possible>
syn late, recent
rel contemporary, present-day; latter
con antiquated, old-fashioned, old hat, outdated, outmoded, outworn
ant old-time
2 ***syn*** NEW 1, fresh, modernistic, neoteric, newfangled, new-fashioned, new-sprung, novel, recent
rel coincident, concomitant, concurrent, contemporaneous, contemporary; current, prevailing, prevalent
ant ancient, antique

modernistic *adj* ***syn*** NEW 1, fresh, modern, neoteric, newfangled, new-fashioned, new-sprung, novel, recent
rel futuristic
ant antiquated

modernize *vb* ***syn*** RENEW 1, refresh, refurbish, rejuvenate, renovate, restore, update

modest *adj* **1** ***syn*** HUMBLE 1, lowly, meek, unassuming

---

syn synonym(s) ***rel*** related word(s)
idiom idiomatic equivalent(s) ***con*** contrasted word(s)
ant antonym(s) * vulgar
|| use limited; if in doubt, see a dictionary
The first word in a synonym list when printed in SMALL CAPITALS shows where there is more information about the group. For a more efficient use of this book see Explanatory Notes.

rel moderate, temperate; retiring, withdrawing; unboastful; unpresuming, unpresumptuous, unpretending
con barefaced, brazen, impudent, shameless
ant ambitious
2 ***syn*** SHY 1, bashful, coy, demure, diffident, retiring, self-effacing, timid, unassertive, unassured
rel reticent, silent; nice, proper, seemly
3 ***syn*** CHASTE, clean, decent, immaculate, pure, spotless, stainless, unblemished, undefiled, unsullied
rel priggish, prim, prissy, prudish, puritanical, straitlaced, stuffy
con improper, indecent, indecorous, indelicate, unseemly
ant immodest
4 ***syn*** MODERATE 2, reasonable, temperate
5 ***syn*** PLAIN 1, discreet, dry, inelaborate, simple, unelaborate, unembellished, unembroidered, unornamented, unpretentious

modicum *n* ***syn*** PARTICLE, atom, grain, iota, jot, minim, molecule, ounce, scrap, whit

modification *n* ***syn*** CHANGE 1, alteration, mutation, turn, variation
rel conversion, metamorphosis, transformation, transmogrification; qualification, tempering

modified *adj* ***syn*** QUALIFIED 2, limited, reserved

modify *vb* ***syn*** CHANGE 1, alter, mutate, refashion, turn, vary
rel modulate, restrain, temper; qualify

modish *adj* ***syn*** STYLISH, chic, dashing, exclusive, fashionable, smart, swank, swish, ‖trendy, with-it
rel voguish

modulate *vb* ***syn*** MODERATE 1, restrain, temper

modus *n* ***syn*** METHOD 1, fashion, manner, mode, system, technique, way, wise

‖**mog** *vb* ***syn*** GO 2, ‖blow, depart, exit, get away, get off, leave, pull out, take off, withdraw

mogul *n* ***syn*** MAGNATE, baron, czar, king, merchant prince, prince, tycoon

moiety *n* ***syn*** PART 1, cut, division, member, parcel, piece, portion, section, segment

moil *vb* **1** ***syn*** LABOR 1, drive, strain, strive, toil, tug, work
‖**2** ***syn*** SEETHE 4, boil, bubble, churn, ferment, simmer, smolder, stir

moil *n* **1** ***syn*** WORK 2, drudge, drudgery, grind, labor, plugging, slavery, slogging, toil, travail
2 ***syn*** COMMOTION 4, bustle, clamor, hubbub, hurly-burly, lather, rowdydow, ruction, to-do, uproar

moira *n* ***syn*** FATE, circumstance, destiny, doom, kismet, lot, portion, weird

moist *adj* **1** ***syn*** DAMP, dampish, dank, moisty, wettish
2 ***syn*** SENTIMENTAL, drippy, gooey, maudlin, mushy, sappy, slushy, ‖soppy, soupy, sticky

moistureless *adj* ***syn*** DRY 1, arid, bone-dry, droughty, sere, thirsty, unwatered, waterless
ant moist

moisty *adj* ***syn*** DAMP, dampish, dank, moist, wettish

‖**moke** *n* ***syn*** DONKEY 1, ass, burro, donk, jackass, ‖neddy, ‖Rocky Mountain canary

mold *n* ***syn*** TYPE, cast, character, class, description, kind, lot, nature, sort, stamp

mold *vb* ***syn*** MAKE 3, build, construct, erect, fashion, forge, form, frame, put together, shape

moldable *adj* ***syn*** PLASTIC, adaptable, ductile, malleable, pliable, pliant, supple

molder *vb* ***syn*** DECAY, break down, crumble, decompose, disintegrate, putrefy, rot, spoil, taint, turn

moldy *adj* ***syn*** OLD-FASHIONED, antiquated, archaic, bygone, dated, moth-eaten, old hat, outdated, passé, rococo

mole *n* ***syn*** BIRTHMARK 1, nevus

molecule *n* ***syn*** PARTICLE, atom, bit, iota, jot, minim, modicum, ounce, ray, speck

molest *vb* to annoy or disturb with hostile intent or injurious effect <he was specifically warned by the court not to *molest* his former wife>
syn bait, heckle, persecute, torment
rel annoy, badger, bother, irk, pester; pother, tease; bedevil, beset, devil, trouble; harass, harry, vex

moll *n* ***syn*** PROSTITUTE, bawd, drab, fille de joie, harlot, hustler, meretrix, quean, streetwalker, whore

mollify *vb* **1** ***syn*** PACIFY, appease, assuage, conciliate, placate, propitiate, sweeten
rel lighten; temper; abate, decrease, lessen, reduce
ant exasperate
2 ***syn*** RELIEVE 1, allay, alleviate, assuage, ease, lighten, mitigate

‖**molly** *n* ***syn*** WEAKLING, doormat, invertebrate, jellyfish, milksop, Milquetoast, mollycoddle, namby-pamby, pantywaist, sop

mollycoddle *n* ***syn*** WEAKLING, baby, doormat, invertebrate, jellyfish, milksop, Milquetoast, ‖molly, pantywaist, sissy
rel ‖mollycot

mollycoddle *vb* ***syn*** BABY, cater (to), cocker, coddle, cosset, humor, indulge, ‖much, pamper, spoil
ant neglect; abuse

molt *vb* ***syn*** SHED 2, exuviate, slip, slough

mom *n* ***syn*** MOTHER 1, ma, ‖mam, mama (*or* mamma), mammy, ‖mater, mommy, mummy, ‖old lady, ‖old woman

‖**momble** *vb* ***syn*** CONFUSE 2, addle, ball up, befuddle, bewilder, distract, fluster, fuddle, mix up, throw off

moment *n* **1** ***syn*** INSTANT 1, breathing, crack, flash, ‖jiff, jiffy, minute, second, shake, split second
ant eternity
2 ***syn*** POINT 7, instant, juncture
3 ***syn*** OCCASION 5, instant, time, while
4 ***syn*** IMPORTANCE, consequence, import, magnitude, momentousness, pith, significance, ‖signification, weight, weightiness
rel advantage, avail, profit, use

momentaneous *adj* ***syn*** TRANSIENT, evanescent, fleeting, fugacious, fugitive, impermanent, momentary, passing, short-lived, transitory

---

syn synonym(s) *rel* related word(s)
idiom idiomatic equivalent(s) *con* contrasted word(s)
ant antonym(s) * vulgar
‖ use limited; if in doubt, see a dictionary
The first word in a synonym list when printed in SMALL CAPITALS shows where there is more information about the group. For a more efficient use of this book see Explanatory Notes.

momentary *adj* ***syn*** TRANSIENT, ephemeral, evanescent, fleeting, fugacious, fugitive, impermanent, short-lived, transitory, volatile
rel brief, quick, short; impulsive
ant agelong

momentous *adj* **1** ***syn*** IMPORTANT 1, big, consequential, considerable, material, meaningful, significant, substantial, weighty
ant trivial
2 ***syn*** EPOCHAL

momentousness *n* ***syn*** IMPORTANCE, consequence, import, magnitude, moment, pith, significance, ‖signification, weight, weightiness
ant triviality

mommy *n* ***syn*** MOTHER 1, ma, ‖mam, mama (*or* mamma), mammy, ‖mater, mom, mummy, ‖old lady, ‖old woman

momus *n* ***syn*** CRITIC, aristarch, carper, caviler, criticizer, faultfinder, knocker, smellfungus, Zoilus

monarchal *adj* ***syn*** KINGLY, kinglike, majestic, monarchial, monarchical, regal, royal, sovereign

monarchial *adj* ***syn*** KINGLY, kinglike, majestic, monarchal, monarchical, regal, royal, sovereign

monarchical *adj* ***syn*** KINGLY, kinglike, majestic, monarchal, monarchial, regal, royal, sovereign

mondaine *adj* ***syn*** SOPHISTICATED 2, blasé, disenchanted, disentranced, disillusioned, knowing, sophisticate, worldly, worldly-wise, world-wise

monetary *adj* ***syn*** FINANCIAL, fiscal, pecuniary, pocket
rel numismatic

money *n* something (as pieces of stamped metal or paper certificates) customarily and legally used as a medium of exchange <the only thing that he liked about his job was the *money*>
syn ‖blunt, ‖brass, ‖bread, ‖cabbage, cash, ‖chink, ‖chips, ‖coin, currency, ‖dibs, ‖dinero, ‖do-re-mi, dough, filthy lucre, ‖gelt, ‖greenbacks, ‖jack, ‖kale, legal tender, ‖lettuce, ‖long green, loot, lucre, ‖mazuma, ‖moolah, ‖mopus, needful, ‖ooftish, pelf, rhino, rocks, ‖scratch, ‖shekels, ‖smash, stuff, ‖stumpy, ‖sugar, swag, ‖wampum
rel bankroll, capital, coinage, finances, funds, mammon, resources, riches, treasure, wealth, wherewithal; boodle, hay; ‖stiff

moneyed *adj* ***syn*** RICH 1, affluent, ‖oofy, opulent, wealthy
ant penniless, unmoneyed

moneygrubber *n* ***syn*** MISER, cheapskate, chuff, muckworm, nabal, niggard, scrooge, skin, skinflint, stiff

moneymaking *adj* ***syn*** ADVANTAGEOUS 1, gainful, good, lucrative, paying, profitable, remunerative, well-paying, worthwhile

monger *n* ***syn*** PEDDLER, ‖arab, ‖duffer, hawker, higgler, huckster, mongerer, outcrier, packman, vendor

monger *vb* ***syn*** PEDDLE 2, hawk, huckster, vend

mongerer *n* ***syn*** PEDDLER, ‖arab, ‖duffer, hawker, higgler, huckster, monger, outcrier, packman, vendor

mongrel *n* ***syn*** HYBRID, bastard, cross, crossbred, crossbreed, half blood, half-breed, mule

‖**moniker** *n* **1** ***syn*** NAME 1, appellation, cognomen, compellation, denomination, designation, ‖handle, nomen, style, title
2 ***syn*** NICKNAME, byname, byword, ‖handle, hypocorism, sobriquet

monish *vb* ***syn*** REPROVE, admonish, call down, chide, lesson, ‖rack back, rebuke, reprimand, reproach, tick off

monition *n* ***syn*** WARNING, admonition, caution, caveat, commonition, forewarning

monitorial *adj* ***syn*** MONITORY, admonishing, admonitory, cautionary, cautioning, warning

monitory *adj* giving a warning <the parents wrote their son a *monitory* letter>
syn admonishing, admonitory, cautionary, cautioning, monitorial, warning
rel advisory, counseling; critical, expostulatory, remonstratory; exhortatory, hortatory; moralistic, moralizing, preachy

monkey *n* **1** ***syn*** FOOL 3, dupe, easy mark, fall guy, gull, mark, pigeon, sap, sucker, victim
2 ***syn*** URCHIN, gamin, imp

monkey *adj* ***syn*** SMALL 1, bantam, little, petite, smallish

monkey (with) *vb* ***syn*** MEDDLE, busybody, butt in, fool, horn in, interfere, interlope, intermeddle, ‖make, tamper (with)

monkeyshine *n* ***syn*** PRANK, antic, caper, dido(es), frolic, lark, shenanigan, shine(s), tomfoolery, trick

monocratic *adj* ***syn*** ABSOLUTE 4, arbitrary, autarchic, autocratic, despotic, tyrannical, tyrannous
con democratic

monogram *n* a sign of identity usually formed of the combined initials of a name <everything he owned had his *monogram* on it>
syn cipher
rel device, initials; John Hancock, signature

monograph *n* ***syn*** DISCOURSE 2, disquisition, dissertation, memoir, monography, thesis, tractate, treatise

monography *n* ***syn*** DISCOURSE 2, disquisition, dissertation, memoir, monograph, thesis, tractate, treatise

monopolize *vb* to take up completely <he would attempt to *monopolize* every conversation>
syn absorb, consume, engross, sew up
rel corner, hog; devour; have, hold, own, possess; employ, use, utilize; control, manage
con contribute, participate, share

monopolizing *adj* ***syn*** ENGROSSING, absorbing, consuming

monopoly *n* exclusive possession <neither party has a *monopoly* on morality>
syn corner
rel cartel, consortium, pool, syndicate, trust; copyright; ownership, possessorship, proprietorship

monotone *n* ***syn*** MONOTONY, humdrum, monotonousness

monotone *adj* ***syn*** DULL 9, banausic, blah, ‖dim, dreary, humdrum, monotonous, pedestrian, poky, stodgy

monotonous *adj* ***syn*** DULL 9, banausic, blah, ‖dim, dreary, humdrum, monotone, pedestrian, poky, stodgy

---

syn synonym(s) — *rel* related word(s)
idiom idiomatic equivalent(s) — *con* contrasted word(s)
ant antonym(s) — * vulgar
‖ use limited; if in doubt, see a dictionary
The first word in a synonym list when printed in SMALL CAPITALS shows where there is more information about the group. For a more efficient use of this book see Explanatory Notes.

rel samely, uniform, unvaried; repetitious; jogtrot, singsong
con changing, varying; fresh, new, novel; absorbing, engrossing, interesting

monotonousness *n syn* MONOTONY, humdrum, monotone

monotony *n* a tedious sameness or reiteration <the *monotony* of his job finally got to him>
syn humdrum, monotone, monotonousness
rel ennui, boredom, tedium; dryness, flatness, uniformity
con variability, variation; diversification, diversity, multifariousness, variety

monster *n* **1** *syn* FREAK 2, abortion, lusus, miscreation, monstrosity
rel demon, devil, fiend, hellhound; bandersnatch
2 *syn* GIANT, behemoth, leviathan, mammoth, whale

monster *adj syn* HUGE, behemothic, colossal, elephantine, enormous, gargantuan, gigantic, mammoth, monstrous, titanic

monstrosity *n* **1** *syn* FREAK 2, abortion, lusus, miscreation, monster
2 *syn* EYESORE, desight, fright, mess, sight

monstrous *adj* **1** extremely impressive <the traditional burial ceremonies turned into a *monstrous* spectacle>
syn cracking, fantastic, massive, monumental, mortal, prodigious, stupendous, towering, tremendous
rel grandiose, impressive, magnificent, showy, splendid, superb; colossal, enormous, huge, immense, mammoth, vast
con mean, petty, picayune, poky, small-time
2 *syn* HUGE, Brobdingnagian, colossal, elephantine, enormous, gargantuan, gigantic, mammoth, prodigious, titanic
3 *syn* OUTRAGEOUS 2, atrocious, crying, desperate, heinous, scandalous, shocking
rel glaring, rank; fateful, ominous, portentous; flagitious, infamous

‖**monstrous** *adv syn* VERY 1, ‖awful, awfully, ‖big, ‖dreadful, extremely, mightily, mighty, rattling, snapping

monstrousness *n syn* ENORMITY 1, atrociousness, atrocity, heinousness

monument *n* **1** *syn* DOCUMENT 2, archive(s), record
2 a lasting evidence or reminder of someone or something notable <the whole body of students who learned from him form his *monument*>
syn memorial, testimonial
rel memento, tribute
3 *syn* TOMBSTONE, footstone, grave marker, gravestone, headstone, ledger

monument *vb syn* MEMORIALIZE 2, commemorate, monumentalize

monumental *adj* **1** *syn* HUGE, enormous, gigantic, immense, mammoth, massive, mighty, mountainous, prodigious, vast
2 *syn* MONSTROUS 1, cracking, fantastic, massive, mortal, prodigious, stupendous, towering, tremendous
3 *syn* TOWERING 4, overwhelming

monumentalize *vb syn* MEMORIALIZE 2, commemorate, monument

moocah *n syn* MARIJUANA, boo, cannabis, grass, ‖Mary Jane, pot, ‖tea, weed

mooch *vb syn* WANDER 1, bat, drift, meander, ramble, range, roam, rove, straggle, stray

moocher *n syn* BEGGAR 1, bummer, cadger, panhandler, ‖schnorrer

mooching *n syn* MENDICANCY, beggary, bumming, cadging, mendicity, panhandling

mood *n* **1** a state of mind in which an emotion or set of emotions gains ascendancy <a melancholy *mood* induced by the sight of ancient ruins>
syn humor, mind, strain, temper, tone, vein
rel character, disposition, individuality, personality, temperament; soul, spirit; affection, emotion, feeling, response
2 *syn* TEMPER 1, spirit, timbre, tone
3 *syn* AIR 3, atmosphere, aura, feel, feeling, semblance

moody *adj* subject to moods <a *moody* person whose behavior was erratic and whose actions were unpredictable>
syn humorsome, temperamental
rel capricious, fickle, inconstant, mercurial, unstable, whimsical; broody
con calm, dispassionate, stable, steady, unexcitable; bovine, impassive, stolid

‖**moolah** *n syn* MONEY, ‖mazuma, needful, ‖ooftish, pelf, rhino, rocks, ‖scratch, ‖smash, stuff

mooncalf *n syn* FOOL 1, doodle, idiot, imbecile, jackass, jerk, madman, nincompoop, ninny, tomfool

‖**moonraker** *n syn* DUNCE, blockhead, boob, dimwit, dolt, dope, dumbbell, idiot, ignoramus, numskull

moonshine *n* **1** *syn* NONSENSE 2, balderdash, blatherskite, bosh, bunkum, eyewash, flapdoodle, hokum, humbug, malarkey
2 illegally distilled liquor <his death was caused by bad *moonshine*>
syn bathtub gin, ‖blockade, bootleg, ‖busthead, ‖hooch, mountain dew, white lightning
rel homebrew; ‖bug juice, grappa, ‖jake, smoke, squareface

moor *vb syn* FASTEN 2, anchor, catch, fix, secure

moot *vb* **1** *syn* BROACH, bring up, introduce, ventilate
2 *syn* DISCUSS 1, agitate, argue, canvass, debate, dispute, ‖kick around, thrash out, toss (around)

moot *adj* open to question <it is a *moot* point whether he would have been tried and convicted>
syn arguable, debatable, disputable, doubtful, dubious, mootable, problematic, questionable, uncertain; *compare* DOUBTFUL 1
rel controversial, suspect; unsettled
con confirmed, established, settled; inarguable, indisputable, undebatable, unproblematic, unquestionable; certain, sure

mootable *adj syn* MOOT, arguable, debatable, disputable, doubtful, dubious, problematic, questionable, uncertain

---

syn synonym(s) *rel* related word(s)
idiom idiomatic equivalent(s) *con* contrasted word(s)
ant antonym(s) * vulgar
‖ use limited; if in doubt, see a dictionary
The first word in a synonym list when printed in SMALL CAPITALS shows where there is more information about the group. For a more efficient use of this book see Explanatory Notes.

mooting *n* ***syn*** ARGUMENTATION, debate, dialectic, disputation, forensic

mop *vb* ***syn*** GRIMACE, mouth, mow, mug, ||mump

mop (up) *vb* ***syn*** WHIP 2, beat, ||clobber, drub, dust, lambaste, ||larrup, lick, overwhelm, shellac

mope *vb* **1** to become listless or dejected < *moped* for several days after the divorce >
syn brood, despond
rel ache, grieve, grump, pout, sulk
2 ***syn*** SAUNTER, amble, bummel, drift, linger, mosey, ||muck, stroll

mopes *n pl* ***syn*** SADNESS, blues, depression, (the) dismals, (the) dolefuls, dumps, heavyheartedness, melancholy, mournfulness, unhappiness

mopey *adj* ***syn*** DOWNCAST, bad, blue, cast down, dejected, depressed, dispirited, down, low, spiritless

moppet *n* ***syn*** CHILD 1, bud, chick, chit, juvenile, kid, youngling, young one, youngster, youth

||**mopus** *n* ***syn*** MONEY, ||lettuce, ||long green, loot, lucre, ||mazuma, ||moolah, needful, ||ooftish, pelf

moral *adj* **1** conforming to a standard of what is right and good < *moral* goodness may be distinguished from intellectual goodness >
syn ethical, moralistic, noble, principled, righteous, right-minded, virtuous
rel good, right; conscientious, honest, honorable, just, scrupulous, upright; chaste, decent, modest, pure
con amoral, nonmoral, unmoral
ant immoral
2 ***syn*** DIDACTIC, moralizing, preachy, schoolmasterish, sermonic, sermonizing, teachy
3 ***syn*** ELEVATED 2, high-minded, noble

moral *n* ***syn*** MAXIM, aphorism, apothegm, axiom, brocard, dictum, gnome, rule, truism

morale *n* a sense of common purpose or a degree of dedication to a common task regarded as characteristic of or dominant in a group < *morale* was high among the troops >
syn esprit, esprit de corps
rel drive, spirit, vigor; assurance, confidence, self-confidence, self-possession
con enervation; aimlessness, purposelessness; egoism, egotism, self-centeredness

moralistic *adj* ***syn*** MORAL 1, ethical, noble, principled, righteous, right-minded, virtuous
rel didactic

morality *n* **1** ***syn*** GOODNESS, probity, rectitude, righteousness, rightness, uprightness, virtue
rel godliness, saintliness
2 ***syn*** ETHIC 2, morals, mores

moralize *vb* to make moral reflections usually in an officious or tiresome manner <people avoided him as he was always *moralizing* >
syn preach, preachify, sermonize
rel lecture, pontificate

moralizing *adj* ***syn*** DIDACTIC, moral, preachy, schoolmasterish, sermonic, sermonizing, teachy

morally *adv* ***syn*** VIRTUALLY, in essence, practically

morals *n pl* **1** ***syn*** ETHIC 1
2 ***syn*** ETHIC 2, morality, mores
rel conduct, habits, standards

morass *n* **1** ***syn*** SWAMP, bog, fen, marsh, mire, ||moss, quag, quagmire, ||sump, ||vlei
2 ***syn*** MAZE 1, jungle, knot, labyrinth, mesh, mizmaze, skein, snarl, tangle, web
rel dunghill

moratorium *n* ***syn*** SUSPENSION 2, suspense

morbid *adj* abnormally susceptible to or characterized by gloomy or unwholesome feelings <his *morbid* poetry is the product of his lifelong frustrations>
syn morose, sick, sickly
rel gloomy, melancholic; psychotic; dark, moody, saturnine, sullen
con healthy, sound, well, wholesome; solid, stable, stolid, sturdy

mordacious *adj* ***syn*** CAUSTIC 1, mordant, salty, scathing, trenchant

mordancy *n* ***syn*** ACRIMONY, acerbity, asperity
rel incisiveness, pungency, trenchancy; acidity, acridity, causticity, mordacity

mordant *adj* ***syn*** CAUSTIC 1, mordacious, salty, scathing, trenchant

more *adj* ***syn*** ADDITIONAL, added, another, else, farther, fresh, further, new, other

more *adv* ***syn*** ALSO 2, additionally, along, as well, besides, furthermore, likewise, moreover, too, withal
2 to a greater or higher degree <were *more* evenly matched>
syn better

more or less *adv* **1** ***syn*** SOMEWHAT 2, fairly, kind of, moderately, pretty, rather, ratherish, some, something, sort of
2 ***syn*** NEARLY, about, all but, almost, approximately, as good as, just about, most, practically, well-nigh

moreover *adv* ***syn*** ALSO 2, additionally, as well, besides, furthermore, likewise, more, too, withal, yet

mores *n pl* **1** ***syn*** ETHIC 2, morality, morals
2 ***syn*** MANNER 5, amenities, civilities, decorum(s), etiquette, proprieties

morgue *n* ***syn*** PRIDE 3, arrogance, disdain, disdainfulness, haughtiness, hauteur, loftiness, superbity, superciliousness

moribund *adj* approaching death or a final end <found lying *moribund* in her bed> <fox hunting is a *moribund* sport>
syn dying
rel expiring, fading, going; decadent, deteriorating, regressing
idiom at death's door, on one's last legs, with one foot in the grave
con booming, flourishing, prospering, thriving; lively, viable

morn *n* **1** ***syn*** DAWN 1, aurora, cockcrow, dawning, daybreak, daylight, light, morning, sunrise, sunup
2 ***syn*** MORNING 2, forenoon

morne *adj* ***syn*** GLOOMY 3, black, bleak, cheerless, cold, depressant, depressing, depressive, desolate, dismal

morning *n* **1** ***syn*** DAWN 1, aurora, cockcrow, dawning, daybreak, daylight, light, morn, sunrise, sunup
con sundown, sunset
2 the time before noon <it rained most of the *morning*>
syn forenoon, morn
con afternoon, evening; day, night

moron *n* **1** ***syn*** FOOL 4, ament, cretin, ‖feeb, half-wit, idiot, imbecile, natural, simpleton, zany
2 ***syn*** DUNCE, dullard, dullhead, dumbbell, ‖dummkopf, dummy, idiot, ignoramus, simpleton, stupid

moronic *adj* ***syn*** RETARDED, backward, dim-witted, dull, feebleminded, half-witted, imbecile, simple, simpleminded, slow-witted

morose *adj* **1** ***syn*** SULLEN, crabbed, ‖dorty, dour, gloomy, glum, saturnine, sulky, surly, ugly
rel choleric, cranky, irascible, splenetic, testy; irritable, waspish; brusque, gruff
con jocund, jolly, jovial, merry
ant blithe
2 ***syn*** MORBID, sick, sickly

morsel *n* **1** a small piece or quantity of food <tossed a *morsel* of meat to the dog>
syn bit, bite, mouthful
rel taste; tidbit; crumb, ort, scrap
2 ***syn*** SNACK, ‖bait, ‖bever, bite, ‖chack, mug-up, ‖piece, tapa
3 ***syn*** DELICACY, bonne bouche, dainty, goody, kickshaw, tidbit (*or* titbit), treat

mort *n* ***syn*** CORPSE, body, cadaver, carcass, ‖cold meat, ‖deader, remains, stiff

‖**mortacious** *adv* ***syn*** VERY 1, ‖awful, ‖big, ‖crazy, damned, ‖dreadful, extremely, ‖monstrous, mortally, terribly

mortal *adj* **1** ***syn*** DEADLY 1, deathly, fatal, lethal, mortiferous, pestilent, pestilential
rel implacable, relentless, unrelenting
2 ***syn*** GRIM 3, implacable, ironfisted, merciless, relentless, ruthless, unappeasable, unflinching, unrelenting, unyielding
3 ***syn*** MONSTROUS 1, cracking, fantastic, massive, monumental, prodigious, stupendous, towering, tremendous
4 ***syn*** HUMAN, hominine
rel finite, temporal; frail, weak
5 ***syn*** PROBABLE, conceivable, earthly, likely, possible

mortal *n* ***syn*** HUMAN, being, body, ‖character, creature, individual, man, party, person, personage

mortality *n* **1** ***syn*** FATALITY 1, deadliness, lethality
2 ***syn*** MANKIND, flesh, Homo sapiens, humanity, humankind, man

mortally *adv* ***syn*** VERY 1, awfully, dreadfully, exceedingly, extremely, highly, ‖mortacious, pesky, terribly, vitally

mortgage *vb* ***syn*** PAWN, ‖dip, hock, impignorate, pledge, ‖pop, ‖spout

mortician *n* one whose business is to prepare the dead for burial and to arrange and manage funerals < *morticians* must be certified>
syn funeral director, undertaker
rel embalmer

mortiferous *adj* ***syn*** DEADLY 1, deathly, fatal, lethal, mortal, pestilent, pestilential

mortified *adj* **1** ***syn*** SEVERE 1, ascetic, astringent, austere, stern
2 ***syn*** ASHAMED, chagrined, shamed
rel annoyed, harassed, harried, worried

mortuary *adj* ***syn*** SEPULCHRAL 1, tumulary

mosey *vb* ***syn*** SAUNTER, amble, bummel, drift, linger, mope, ‖muck, stroll

‖**moss** *n* ***syn*** SWAMP, baygall, bog, fen, marsh, mire, morass, quag, ‖sump, ‖vlei

mossback *n* **1** ***syn*** RUSTIC, ‖backwoodser, backwoodsman, bumpkin, clodhopper, hayseed, hick, hillbilly, provincial, yokel
2 ***syn*** FOGY, antediluvian, fogram, fossil, fuddy-duddy, mid-Victorian, square, stick-in-the-mud

most *adj* ***syn*** BEST, better, ‖bettermost, greater, largest
rel greatest, highest, maximum, utmost, uttermost

most *adv* ***syn*** VERY 1, eminently, exceedingly, extremely, mightily, mortally, remarkably, super, surpassingly, too

most *adv* ***syn*** NEARLY, about, all but, almost, approximately, much, ‖nearabout, nigh, practically, well-nigh

mostly *adv* ***syn*** GENERALLY 1, chiefly, largely, mainly, overall, predominantly, primarily, principally
idiom for the most part

mote *n* ***syn*** POINT 11, dot, flyspeck, speck

moth-eaten *adj* **1** ***syn*** SHABBY 1, dilapidated, dingy, down-at-heel, faded, run-down, seedy, tagrag, tattered, threadbare
2 ***syn*** OLD-FASHIONED, antiquated, archaic, bygone, dated, moldy, old hat, outdated, passé, rococo

mother *n* **1** a female human parent <the *mother* of seven children>
syn ma, ‖mam, mama (*or* mamma), mammy, ‖mater, mom, mommy, ‖mum, mummy, ‖old lady, ‖old woman; *compare* FATHER 1
2 ***syn*** SOURCE, fount, fountainhead, origin, provenance, provenience, root, rootage, rootstock, wellspring

mother *vb* ***syn*** MINISTER (to), care (for), nurse, serve, wait (on)

mother country *n* ***syn*** COUNTRY, fatherland, home, homeland, land, motherland, soil

motherland *n* ***syn*** COUNTRY, fatherland, home, homeland, land, mother country, soil

mother-naked *adj* ***syn*** NUDE 2, au naturel, *bare-assed, buff-bare, naked, raw, stark-naked, stripped, unclothed, undressed

mother wit *n* ***syn*** INTELLIGENCE 1, brain(s), brainpower, mentality, sense, wit

motif *n* **1** ***syn*** LEITMOTIV
2 ***syn*** SUBJECT 2, argument, head, matter, motive, point, subject matter, text, theme, topic
3 ***syn*** FIGURE 3, design, device, motive, pattern

motion *n* **1** the act or an instance of moving <the *motion* of the planets>
syn move, movement, stir, stirring

---

syn synonym(s) ***rel*** related word(s)
idiom idiomatic equivalent(s) ***con*** contrasted word(s)
ant antonym(s) * vulgar
‖ use limited; if in doubt, see a dictionary
The first word in a synonym list when printed in SMALL CAPITALS shows where there is more information about the group. For a more efficient use of this book see Explanatory Notes.

rel agitation, fluctuation, oscillation, sway, swing, wavering; locomotion

con inertia, inertness, passivity

2 an impulse or inclination of the mind or will <a *motion* of the will toward what appears good>

syn movement

rel goad, impulse, incentive, inducement, motive, spring, spur

con inertia, stagnation, vegetation

motion *vb* ***syn*** SIGNAL, flag, gesture, sign, signalize

motionless *adj* being without motion <stood *motionless* so that he would remain undiscovered>

syn still, stock-still, stone-still

rel stagnant, static, stationary, unmoving; fixed, immobile, immotile, immotive, immovable, irremovable, ‖sitfast, steadfast, unmovable

con active, changing, mobile, moving

motion picture *n* ***syn*** MOVIE, cine, ‖cinema, film, flick, moving picture, photoplay, picture, picture show, show

motivate *vb* ***syn*** PROVOKE 4, excite, galvanize, innervate, innerve, move, pique, quicken, rouse, stimulate

motivation *n* ***syn*** STIMULUS, catalyst, impetus, impulse, incentive, incitation, incitement, instigation, spur, stimulant

motive *n* **1** the object influencing a choice or prompting an action <trying to discover what was his *motive* in killing the girl>

syn cause, consideration, reason, spring; *compare* STIMULUS

rel antecedent, determinant; emotion, feeling, passion; aim, end, intent, intention, purpose

2 ***syn*** FIGURE 3, design, device, motif, pattern

3 ***syn*** SUBJECT 2, argument, head, matter, motif, point, subject matter, text, theme, topic

motley *adj* **1** ***syn*** VARIEGATED, dappled, discolor, multicolor, multicolored, multihued, parti-colored, varicolored, versicolor, versicolored

2 ***syn*** MISCELLANEOUS, assorted, chowchow, conglomerate, heterogeneous, indiscriminate, mixed, multifarious, promiscuous, varied

rel discrepant, incompatible, incongruous, uncongenial

motley *n* **1** ***syn*** FOOL 2, idiot, jester

2 ***syn*** MISCELLANY 1, assortment, colluvies, gallimaufry, hodgepodge, jumble, medley, omnium-gatherum, pastiche, salad

motor *n* ***syn*** CAR, auto, autocar, automobile, buggy, ‖bus, machine, motorcar

motor *vb* **1** ***syn*** RIDE 1, auto

2 ***syn*** DRIVE 5, auto, charioteer, pilot, tool, wheel

motorcar *n* ***syn*** CAR, auto, autocar, automobile, buggy, ‖bus, machine, motor

motorist *n* a person who travels by automobile <the roads were crowded with *motorists* going to work>

syn autoist, automobilist, driver, operator

mottle *vb* ***syn*** SPLOTCH, blotch, ‖splodge

motto *n* ***syn*** BATTLE CRY, cry, rallying cry, war cry

rel byword, catchphrase, catchword, shibboleth, slogan, watchword, word

moue *n* ***syn*** FACE 6, grimace, mouth, mouthing, mow, mug

mound *vb* ***syn*** HEAP 1, bank, cock, drift, hill, pile, stack

mound *n* ***syn*** PILE 1, bank, cock, drift, heap, hill, mass, mountain, shock, stack

mount *n* ***syn*** MOUNTAIN 1, alp, peak

mount *vb* **1** ***syn*** INCREASE 2, augment, build, enlarge, expand, heighten, multiply, rise, upsurge, wax

2 ***syn*** ASCEND 1, climb, escalade, escalate, scale, upclimb, upgo

con descend, fall, lower

ant drop

3 ***syn*** RISE 4, arise, ascend, aspire, lift, soar, up, uprear

ant drop

4 ***syn*** INTENSIFY, aggravate, deepen, enhance, heighten, intensate, magnify, redouble, rise, rouse

5 to get on (something) as a means of conveyance <*mount* a horse>

syn back, bestride

rel seat, settle

ant dismount

‖**6** ***syn*** TESTIFY 2, depone, depose, swear

7 ***syn*** STAGE, produce, put on, show

mountain *n* **1** a relatively steep and high elevation of land <why are *mountains* in New England considered no more than hills in Colorado>

syn alp, mount, peak

rel butte, mesa; bald, dome; hill; bluff; volcano; sierra

con bottom, bottomland, dale, dell, vale, valley

2 ***syn*** PILE 1, bank, drift, heap, hill, mass, mound, pyramid, shock, stack

3 ***syn*** MUCH, barrel, great deal, heap, lot, lump, mass, peck, pile, ‖sight

4 ***syn*** OBSTACLE, bar, Chinese wall, hamper, hurdle, impediment, obstruction, rub, snag, stumbling block

mountain dew *n* ***syn*** MOONSHINE 2, bathtub gin, ‖blockade, bootleg, ‖busthead, ‖hooch, white lightning

mountaineer *n* ***syn*** RUSTIC, ‖backwoodser, backwoodsman, bumpkin, clodhopper, hayseed, hick, hillbilly, provincial, yokel

mountainous *adj* ***syn*** HUGE, enormous, gigantic, immense, mammoth, massive, mighty, monumental, prodigious, vast

mountebank *n* **1** ***syn*** CHARLATAN, quack, quacksalver, quackster, saltimbanque

2 ***syn*** SWINDLER, cheat, confidence man, con man, defrauder, diddler, double-dealer, flimflammer, gyp, sharper

mourn *vb* ***syn*** GRIEVE 2, sorrow

con delight, gladden, please, rejoice

mournful *adj* **1** ***syn*** SAD 1, heavyhearted, melancholy, saddened, sorry, unhappy

2 ***syn*** SAD 2, depressing, joyless, melancholic, melancholy, saddening, triste

3 ***syn*** MELANCHOLY 2, doleful, dolesome, dolorous, lamentable, lugubrious, plaintive, rueful, sorrowful, woeful

4 ***syn*** DEPLORABLE, afflictive, calamitous, dire, distressing, grievous, lamentable, regrettable, unfortunate, woeful

---

syn synonym(s) ***rel*** related word(s)
idiom idiomatic equivalent(s) ***con*** contrasted word(s)
ant antonym(s) * vulgar
‖ use limited; if in doubt, see a dictionary
The first word in a synonym list when printed in SMALL CAPITALS shows where there is more information about the group. For a more efficient use of this book see Explanatory Notes.

mournfulness *n syn* SADNESS, blues, dejection, depression, (the) dismals, dumps, gloom, heavyheartedness, melancholy, unhappiness

mouse *n* **1** *syn* GIRL FRIEND 1, best girl, ‖chick, ‖doney, gal, girl, lady friend, lass, popsy
2 *syn* BLACK EYE 1, shiner

mouse *vb* **1** *syn* SNOOP, busybody, nose, ‖piroot, poke, pry, ‖snook
2 *syn* STEAL 3, creep, glide, slide, slip

mousehole *n syn* CUBBYHOLE, cubby, pigeonhole

mousetrap *n syn* PITFALL, booby trap, deadfall, springe, trapfall

mouth *n* **1** the opening through which food passes into the body of an animal <the *mouth* in vertebrates is one of the features of the face>
syn ‖bazoo, gob, ‖mush, ‖row, ‖trap, ‖yap
rel mug, muzzle
2 *syn* FACE 6, grimace, moue, mouthing, mow, mug
3 *syn* SPOKESMAN, mouthpiece, speaker, spokesperson, spokeswoman
4 *syn* BACK TALK, guff, ‖jaw, ‖lip, sass, sauce
5 the place where a tributary enters a larger stream or body of water <the *mouth* of the Mississippi river is in the Gulf of Mexico>
syn embouchement, embouchure
rel estuary; delta

mouth *vb* **1** *syn* ORATE, bloviate, declaim, harangue, perorate, rant, rave, soapbox
2 *syn* BOAST, blow, brag, cock-a-doodle-doo, crow, gasconade, prate, puff, rodomontade, vaunt
3 *syn* REVEAL 1, betray, blab (out), disclose, discover, divulge, give away, spill, tell, unclose
4 *syn* GRIMACE, mop, mow, mug, ‖mump

mouthful *n syn* MORSEL 1, bit, bite

mouthing *n syn* FACE 6, grimace, moue, mouth, mow, mug

mouthpiece *n syn* SPOKESMAN, mouth, speaker, spokesperson, spokeswoman

mouth-watering *adj syn* PALATABLE, aperitive, appetizing, good-tasting, ‖gusty, relishing, savory, tasteful, tasty, toothy

‖**mouthy** *adj* **1** *syn* TALKATIVE, babblative, gabby, garrulous, loose-lipped, loose-tongued, loquacious, multiloquent, talky, tonguey
2 *syn* RHETORICAL, bombastic, declamatory, euphuistic, florid, flowery, high-flown, oratorical, overblown, pompous

movable *adj* capable of moving or of being moved <a device with a *movable* attachment>
syn mobile, moving, unstable, unsteadfast, unsteady
rel remotive, removable; motile; changeable, changeful, mutable, variable; roving
con immobile, immotile, immotive, irremovable, steadfast; established, fixed, set, settled; stagnant, static, unmoving

movables *n pl syn* POSSESSION 2, belongings, chattels, effects, goods, lares and penates, things

move *vb* **1** *syn* GO 2, ‖blow, depart, exit, get away, get off, leave, pull out, take off, withdraw
2 *syn* ADVANCE 5, get along, get on, march, proceed, progress
3 *syn* BE, breathe, exist, live, subsist
4 to change or cause to change from one place to another <he *moved* quickly down the staircase> <*move* the chair across the room>
syn dislocate, disturb, remove, shift, ship, transfer
rel displace, replace, supersede, supplant; bear, carry, convey, transmit, transport
5 to set or keep in motion or action <the mechanism that *moves* the locomotive>
syn actuate, drive, impel, mobilize, propel
rel activate, motivate
con bring up, draw up, fetch up, halt, haul up, pull up, stop
6 *syn* PROVOKE 4, excite, galvanize, innervate, innerve, motivate, pique, quicken, rouse, stimulate
7 *syn* AFFECT, carry, get, impress, influence, inspire, strike, sway, touch
rel induce, persuade, prevail
8 *syn* CONVERT 1, bring, lead, persuade
9 *syn* BEHAVE 1, acquit, act, bear, carry, comport, conduct, demean, deport, go on

move *n* **1** *syn* MEASURE 7, maneuver, procedure, proceeding, step
2 *syn* MOTION 1, movement, stir, stirring
rel alteration, change, modification, variation

movement *n* **1** *syn* MOTION 1, move, stir, stirring
rel action, act, deed; activity, dynamism, liveness, operation, operativeness
2 *syn* MOTION 2

mover *n syn* INSTIGATOR, agitator, fomenter, inciter

movie *n* a representation (as of a story) by means of motion pictures <tired old *movies* that appear on TV>
syn cine, ‖cinema, film, flick, motion picture, moving picture, photoplay, picture, picture show, show
rel cinematics, cinematography

moving *adj* **1** *syn* MOVABLE, mobile, unstable, unsteadfast, unsteady
2 having the power to excite deep and usually somber emotion <made a *moving* appeal for help for the orphaned children>
syn affecting, impressive, poignant, touching; *compare* EMOTIONAL 2
rel eloquent, expressive, facund, meaningful, pregnant, sententious, significant; arousing, awakening, rallying, rousing, stirring; exciting, provoking, quickening, stimulating; breathless, gripping
con unaffecting, unimpressive, untouching; casual, cold, formal
ant unmoving
3 *syn* EMOTIONAL 2, affective, emotive

moving picture *n syn* MOVIE, cine, ‖cinema, film, flick, motion picture, photoplay, picture, picture show, show

mow *n syn* PILE 1, bank, cock, drift, heap, hill, rick, ‖ruck, shock, stack

---

mow *vb* to cut down standing grass or grain with a tool or a machine < *mowed* the lawn every week >
syn clip, crop, cut
rel reap; pare, trim

mow (down) *vb syn* FELL 1, bowl (down *or* over), bring down, down, drop, floor, ground, knock down, level, throw down

mow *n syn* FACE 6, grimace, moue, mouth, mouthing, mug

mow *vb syn* GRIMACE, mop, mouth, mug, ‖mump

moxie *n* **1** *syn* ENERGY 2, birr, go, hardihood, pep, potency, tuck, vigor
2 *syn* COURAGE, cojones, dauntlessness, guts, heart, mettle, pluck, resolution, spirit, spunk
3 *syn* FORTITUDE, backbone, grit, guts, intestinal fortitude, nerve, sand, spunk

‖**mozo** *n syn* WORKER, hand, laborer, operative, roustabout, workhand, workingman, workman

Mr. *n syn* HUSBAND, ‖hubby, lord, man, ‖master, mister, ‖old man

Mrs. *n syn* WIFE, ‖ball and chain, lady, ‖little woman, ‖missus, ‖old lady, ‖old woman, ‖rib, ‖squaw, woman

Mrs. Grundy *n syn* PRUDE, bluenose, comstock, goody-goody, Grundy, nice Nelly, prig, puritan, ‖wowser

much *adv* **1** *syn* VERY 1, eminently, exceedingly, exceptionally, extremely, greatly, highly, hugely, notably, surpassingly
2 *syn* OFTEN, again and again, frequently, oft, oftentimes, ofttimes, over and over, repeatedly, time and again
3 *syn* NEARLY, about, all but, almost, approximately, most, ‖nearabout, nigh, practically, well-nigh

much *n* a great quantity, amount, extent, or degree <learned *much* worth remembering from his experiences in the army>
syn barrel, great deal, heap, lashings, lot, lump, mass, ‖mess, mountain, multiplicity, pack, peck, pile, plenty, ‖power, ‖sight; *compare* MULTITUDE 1, SCAD
rel excess, overage, oversupply, plethora, superfluity
idiom all kinds of
con bit, crumb, modicum, trifle; deficiency, inadequacy, insufficiency, undersupply
ant little

‖**much** *vb syn* BABY, cater (to), cocker, coddle, cosset, humor, indulge, mollycoddle, pamper, spoil

much as *conj syn* THOUGH, albeit, although, howbeit, when, whereas, while

muck *n* **1** *syn* SLIME, ‖slab, slum
2 *syn* REFUSE, debris, garbage, junk, litter, offal, rubbish, swill, trash, waste
3 *syn* GOO 1, gook, goop, gumbo, gunk

muck *vb* **1** *syn* SOIL 2, dirty, grime, ‖mucky, muddy, murk, smirch, smooch, smudge, smutch
‖**2** *syn* BOTCH, bitch (up), ‖blow, blunder, bobble, bollix, bungle, gum (up), louse up, mucker
‖**3** *syn* COMPLICATE, entangle, muddle, perplex, ravel, snarl, tangle
4 *syn* DRUDGE, grind, grub, plod, slave, slog, toil
‖**5** *syn* SAUNTER, amble, bummel, drift, linger, mope, mosey, stroll

‖**muckamuck** *n syn* FOOD 1, bread, ‖chow, ‖eats, edibles, foodstuff, grub, provisions, tack, victuals

muckamuck *n syn* NOTABLE 1, big shot, ‖big wheel, bigwig, dignitary, ‖fat cat, nabob, notability, somebody, VIP

mucker *vb syn* BOTCH, bitch (up), ‖blow, blunder, bobble, bollix, bungle, gum (up), louse up, ‖muck

mucker *n* **1** *syn* BOOR, ‖bosthoon, chuff, churl, clodhopper, clown, grobian
2 *syn* WRETCH 1, ‖blighter, lowlife, no-good, worm, wormling
3 *syn* TOUGH, ‖b'hoy, bullyboy, punk, rough, roughneck, rowdy, ruffian, toughie, yahoo

mucking *adj syn* DAMNED 2, blamed, blasted, bleeding, ‖blinking, *‖bloody, damnable, dang, *goddamn, infernal

muckworm *n syn* MISER, chuff, hunks, moneygrubber, nabal, niggard, scrooge, skinflint, stiff, tightwad

mucky *adj* **1** *syn* DIRTY 1, black, dungy, filthy, foul, grubby, nasty, sordid, squalid, unclean
2 *syn* MURKY 3, cloudy
3 *syn* HUMID, muggy, soggy, sticky, sultry

‖**mucky** *vb syn* SOIL 2, begrime, besoil, dirty, foul, grime, muck, muddy, murk, smutch

mucronate *adj syn* POINTED 1, acicular, aciculate, acuminate, acuminous, acute, cuspidate, peaked, piked, sharp

mud *vb syn* ROIL 1, muddle, muddy, rile

muddle *vb* **1** *syn* ROIL 1, mud, muddy, rile
2 *syn* MUMBLE, ‖chunter, fumble, ‖mump, murmur, mutter, swallow
3 *syn* CONFUSE 2, addle, ball up, befuddle, bewilder, distract, fluster, fuddle, mix up, throw off
4 *syn* DISORDER 1, disarrange, disarray, discompose, disorganize, jumble, mess (up), mix up, muss (up), unsettle
5 *syn* CONFUSE 5, foul up, jumble, mix up, ‖snafu, snarl up, tumble
6 *syn* COMPLICATE, entangle, ‖muck, perplex, ravel, snarl, tangle
7 *syn* STUMBLE 6, limp, shuffle

muddle (away) *vb syn* WASTE 2, blow, blunder (away), cast away, drivel, fritter, frivol away, squander, throw away, trifle (away)

muddle *n* **1** *syn* CONFUSION 3, ataxia, ‖ballup, clutter, disarray, disorder, huddle, ‖mullock, snarl, topsy-turviness
2 *syn* MESS 3, botch, botchery, hash, mess-up, mix-up, mull, muss, shambles
3 *syn* CLUTTER 2, hash, jumble, jungle, litter, mishmash, rummage, scramble, shuffle, tumble

muddled *adj* **1** *syn* INCOHERENT 2, disconnected, discontinuous, disjointed, disordered, inchoate, incohesive, unconnected, uncontinuous, unorganized
2 *syn* INTOXICATED 1, ‖boozy, ‖canned, disguised, drunk, inebriated, ‖lushed, pixilated, ‖plastered, tight

---

syn synonym(s) *rel* related word(s)
idiom idiomatic equivalent(s) *con* contrasted word(s)
ant antonym(s) * vulgar
‖ use limited; if in doubt, see a dictionary
The first word in a synonym list when printed in SMALL CAPITALS shows where there is more information about the group. For a more efficient use of this book see Explanatory Notes.

muddledness *n* ***syn*** HAZE 2, befuddlement, daze, fog, ‖maze, muddleheadedness, muddlement

muddlehead *n* ***syn*** DUNCE, blockhead, chowderhead, dimwit, dolt, dumbbell, fathead, idiot, moron, simpleton

muddleheadedness *n* ***syn*** HAZE 2, befuddlement, daze, fog, ‖maze, muddledness, muddlement

muddlement *n* ***syn*** HAZE 2, befuddlement, daze, fog, ‖maze, muddledness, muddleheadedness

muddle through *vb* ***syn*** SHIFT 5, do, fare, get along, get by, get on, ‖make out, manage, stagger (on *or* along)

muddy *adj* **1** having a great deal of mud <playing in the wet field, he got his shoes all *muddy*>
syn bemired, ‖claggy, ‖clarty, miry, oozy
rel black, dirty, dungy, filthy, foul, grubby, impure, nasty, soily, sordid, squalid, unclean, uncleanly; bedraggled, draggled
con clean, cleanly, immaculate, spotless, taintless, unsoiled, unsullied
ant mudless
2 ***syn*** TURBID, riley, roily
rel gloomy, murky; addled, confused, muddled
3 ***syn*** DULL 8, drab, murky, subfusc

muddy *vb* **1** ***syn*** SOIL 2, begrime, besoil, dirty, grime, smirch, smooch, smudge, smutch, tarnish
2 ***syn*** ROIL 1, mud, muddle, rile
3 ***syn*** DULL 1, dim, fade, pale, tarnish
4 ***syn*** CONFUSE 4, becloud, befog, blur, cloud, fog
rel conceal, hide, screen
con illuminate, illumine, light, lighten

mudhole *n* **1** ***syn*** POTHOLE, chuckhole
2 ***syn*** BURG, hick town, jerkwater town, one-horse town, Podunk, tank town, whistle-stop

muff *vb* ***syn*** BOTCH, ‖blow, bobble, bollix, bungle, flub, fluff, goof (up), louse up, ‖screw (up)

muffle *vb* **1** ***syn*** BUNDLE UP, ‖hap, wrap (up)
rel cover, envelop, overspread, shroud, veil
2 to dull the sound of <closed the door to *muffle* the outside noises>
syn dampen, deaden, mute, stifle
rel mellow, soften, soft-pedal, subdue, tone (down); smother
con amplify, enhance, heighten, magnify, reinforce, strengthen
3 ***syn*** SUPPRESS 2, ‖quelch, repress, shush, squelch, strangle

muffler *n* ***syn*** MASK 2, cloak, cover, disguise, disguisement, facade, guise, masquerade, veil, veneer

mug *n* **1** ***syn*** FACE 1, countenance, ‖dial, features, ‖kisser, ‖map, ‖pan, phiz, ‖puss, visage
2 ***syn*** FACE 6, grimace, moue, mouth, mouthing, mow
3 ***syn*** DUNCE, blockhead, boob, dimwit, dolt, dope, dumbbell, idiot, ignoramus, numskull
‖**4** ***syn*** FOOL 3, dupe, easy mark, fall guy, gull, mark, pigeon, sap, sucker, victim
5 ***syn*** TOUGH, bullyboy, mucker, plug-ugly, punk, rough, roughneck, rowdy, ruffian, thug

mug *vb* ***syn*** GRIMACE, mop, mouth, mow, ‖mump

‖**mug** (up) *vb* ***syn*** CRAM 4, bone (up)

muggins *n* ***syn*** DUNCE, blockhead, boob, dimwit, dolt, dope, dumbbell, idiot, ignoramus, numskull

muggy *adj* ***syn*** HUMID, mucky, soggy, sticky, sultry
rel damp, dampish, moist, moisty, wettish
con dry

mughouse *n* ***syn*** ALEHOUSE, beer garden, beer hall, ‖beerhouse, bierstube, stube

mug–up *n* ***syn*** SNACK, ‖bait, ‖bever, bite, ‖chack, morsel, ‖piece, tapa

mugwump *n* ***syn*** NOTABLE 1, big boy, ‖big chief, big shot, bigwig, heavyweight, high-muck-a-muck, leader, lion, nabob

mulatto *n* a person of mixed Caucasian and Negro ancestry <the special conflicts faced by *mulattoes* with both whites and blacks>
syn *brass ankle, high yellow
rel mulatta, mulattress; octoroon, quadroon; sambo, zambo; mustee; half-breed

mulct *n* ***syn*** FINE, amercement, forfeit, penalty

mulct *vb* **1** ***syn*** PENALIZE, amerce, fine
rel claim, demand, exact, require
2 ***syn*** FLEECE 1, bleed, milk, rook, stick, sweat

mule *n* ***syn*** HYBRID, bastard, cross, crossbred, crossbreed, half blood, half-breed, mongrel

muleheaded *adj* ***syn*** OBSTINATE, bullheaded, closed-minded, deaf, hardheaded, headstrong, intractable, muley, mulish, ‖sot

muley *adj* ***syn*** OBSTINATE, bullheaded, closed-minded, deaf, hardheaded, headstrong, intractable, muleheaded, mulish, ‖sot

mulish *adj* ***syn*** OBSTINATE, bullheaded, headstrong, perverse, pigheaded, refractory, self-willed, stiff-necked, stubborn, wrongheaded
rel ungovernable, unruly; fixed, set

mull *n* ***syn*** MESS 3, botch, botchery, hash, mess-up, mix-up, muddle, muss, shambles

mull *vb* **1** ***syn*** DEADEN 1, benumb, blunt, desensitize, dull, numb
2 ***syn*** CONFUSE 2, addle, ball up, befuddle, bewilder, discombobulate, distract, fuddle, muddle, throw off
3 ***syn*** DELAY 2, dally, dawdle, dillydally, linger, loiter, poke, procrastinate, put off, tarry

mull (over) *vb* ***syn*** PONDER 2, ‖chaw, deliberate, meditate, muse, revolve, roll, ruminate, turn over

mulligrubs *n pl* ***syn*** SULK, ‖dods, ‖dorts, grumps, mumps, pouts, sullens
rel blues, dejection, depression, (the) dismals, dumps, gloom, heavyheartedness, melancholy, mournfulness, sadness, unhappiness

‖**mullock** *n* **1** ***syn*** REFUSE, debris, garbage, junk, litter, offal, rubbish, swill, trash, waste
2 ***syn*** CONFUSION 3, ataxia, ‖ballup, clutter, disarray, disorder, huddle, misorder, muddle, snarl

multeity *n* ***syn*** VARIETY 1, diverseness, diversity, multifariousness, multiformity, multiplicity, variousness

multicolor *adj* ***syn*** VARIEGATED, dappled, discolor, motley, multicolored, multihued, parti-colored, varicolored, versicolor, versicolored

---

syn synonym(s) ***rel*** related word(s)
idiom idiomatic equivalent(s) ***con*** contrasted word(s)
ant antonym(s) * vulgar
‖ use limited; if in doubt, see a dictionary
The first word in a synonym list when printed in SMALL CAPITALS shows where there is more information about the group. For a more efficient use of this book see Explanatory Notes.

ant monotone

multicolored *adj* ***syn*** VARIEGATED, dappled, discolor, motley, multicolor, multihued, parti-colored, varicolored, versicolor, versicolored
ant monotone

multifarious *adj* **1** ***syn*** MANY, legion, multitudinal, multitudinous, numerous, populous, ‖several, sundry, various, voluminous
2 ***syn*** MANIFOLD, diverse, diversiform, multifold, multiform, multiplex, multivarious
3 ***syn*** MISCELLANEOUS, assorted, chowchow, conglomerate, heterogeneous, indiscriminate, mixed, motley, promiscuous, varied

multifariousness *n* ***syn*** VARIETY 1, diverseness, diversity, multeity, multiformity, multiplicity, variousness

multifold *adj* ***syn*** MANIFOLD, diverse, diversiform, multifarious, multiform, multiplex, multivarious

multiform *adj* ***syn*** MANIFOLD, diverse, diversiform, multifarious, multifold, multiplex, multivarious
ant uniform

multiformity *n* ***syn*** VARIETY 1, diverseness, diversity, multeity, multifariousness, multiplicity, variousness
ant uniformity

multihued *adj* ***syn*** VARIEGATED, dappled, discolor, motley, multicolor, multicolored, parti-colored, varicolored, versicolor, versicolored
ant monotone

multilateral *adj* having many sides <*multilateral* figures>
syn many-sided
ant one-sided, unilateral

multiloquent *adj* ***syn*** TALKATIVE, babblative, chatty, gabby, garrulous, loose-lipped, loose-tongued, loquacious, multiloquious, talky

multiloquious *adj* ***syn*** TALKATIVE, babblative, chatty, gabby, garrulous, loose-lipped, loose-tongued, loquacious, multiloquent, talky

multiplex *adj* ***syn*** MANIFOLD, diverse, diversiform, multifarious, multifold, multiform, multivarious

multiplicity *n* **1** ***syn*** VARIETY 1, diverseness, diversity, multeity, multifariousness, multiformity, variousness
ant unity
2 ***syn*** MUCH, barrel, great deal, lashings, lot, mass, ‖mess, peck, ‖power, ‖sight

multiply *vb* **1** ***syn*** INCREASE 1, aggrandize, augment, beef (up), boost, enlarge, expand, extend, heighten, magnify
2 ***syn*** INCREASE 2, augment, build, enlarge, expand, heighten, mount, rise, upsurge, wax
3 ***syn*** PROCREATE 1, bear, beget, breed, generate, produce, propagate, reproduce

multitude *n* **1** a very large number of individuals or things <that child always asks a *multitude* of questions>
syn army, cloud, crowd, flock, host, legion, rout, scores; *compare* CROWD 1, MUCH, SCAD
rel numbers, oodles, quantities
con few, handful, scattering, smatter, smattering, sprinkling
ant none
2 ***syn*** CROWD 1, crush, drove, horde, press, push, squash, throng

multitudinal *adj* ***syn*** MANY, legion, multifarious, multitudinous, numerous, populous, ‖several, sundry, various, voluminous
rel countless, innumerable, innumerous, numberless, uncountable, uncounted, unnumberable, unnumbered, untold

multitudinous *adj* ***syn*** MANY, legion, multifarious, multitudinal, numerous, populous, ‖several, sundry, various, voluminous
rel countless, innumerable, innumerous, numberless, uncountable, uncounted, unnumberable, unnumbered, untold

multivarious *adj* ***syn*** MANIFOLD, diverse, diversiform, multifarious, multifold, multiform, multiplex

multivocal *adj* ***syn*** VOCIFEROUS, blatant, boisterous, clamorous, ‖dinsome, loudmouthed, obstreperous, openmouthed, strident, vociferant

mum *adj* ***syn*** SILENT 2, dumb, ‖mumchance, mute, speechless, wordless

‖**mum** *n* ***syn*** MOTHER 1, ma, ‖mam, mama (*or* mamma), mammy, ‖mater, mom, mommy, mummy, ‖old woman

mumble *vb* to utter with a low inarticulate voice <embarrassed, he *mumbled* an apology>
syn ‖chunter, fumble, muddle, ‖mump, murmur, mutter, swallow
rel maunder; limp, shuffle, stumble; ‖hammer, stammer, ‖stut, stutter; speak, talk, utter, verbalize, vocalize, voice
idiom speak with mush in one's mouth
con speak out, speak up; clamor, cry out, shout, vociferate

mumble *n* ***syn*** MURMUR 1, mutter, rumor, susurration, undertone, whisper

mumblenews *n pl but sing or pl in constr* ***syn*** GOSSIP 1, carrytale, circulator, clack, gossipmonger, ‖long tongue, newsmonger, quidnunc, sieve, tabby

mumbo jumbo *n* ***syn*** GIBBERISH 3, abracadabra, hocus-pocus, mummery

‖**mumchance** *adj* ***syn*** SILENT 2, dumb, mum, mute, speechless, wordless

mummer *n* ***syn*** ACTOR 1, impersonator, mime, mimic, performer, playactor, player, thespian, trouper

mummery *n* ***syn*** GIBBERISH 3, abracadabra, hocus-pocus, mumbo jumbo

mummify *vb* ***syn*** WITHER, dry up, mummy, shrivel, welter, wilt, wizen

mummy *n* ***syn*** MOTHER 1, ma, ‖mam, mama (*or* mamma), mammy, ‖mater, mom, mommy, ‖old lady, ‖old woman

mummy *vb* ***syn*** WITHER, dry up, mummify, shrivel, welter, wilt, wizen

‖**mump** *vb* **1** ***syn*** MUMBLE, ‖chunter, fumble, muddle, murmur, mutter, swallow
2 ***syn*** GRIMACE, mop, mouth, mow, mug
3 ***syn*** SULK, ‖dort, grump, pet, pout, ‖sull

---

syn synonym(s) ***rel*** related word(s)
idiom idiomatic equivalent(s) ***con*** contrasted word(s)
ant antonym(s) * vulgar
‖ use limited; if in doubt, see a dictionary
The first word in a synonym list when printed in SMALL CAPITALS shows where there is more information about the group. For a more efficient use of this book see Explanatory Notes.

‖**mump** *vb* ***syn*** CHEAT, beat, bilk, chisel, chouse, cozen, defraud, diddle, do, ‖screw

mumpish *adj* ***syn*** SULLEN, ‖chuff, ‖chuffy, ‖dorty, dour, morose, saturnine, sulky, surly, ugly

mumps *n pl* ***syn*** SULK, ‖dods, ‖dorts, grumps, mulligrubs, pouts, sullens

‖**mun** *vb* ***syn*** MUST 2, have, need

‖**mun** *n* ***syn*** MAN 3, ‖bloke, boy, buck, chap, fellow, ‖gee, gent, gentleman, guy

munch *vb* ***syn*** CHEW 1, champ, ‖chaw, chomp, chumble, chump, crunch, masticate, ruminate, scrunch

mundane *adj* **1** ***syn*** EARTHLY 1, earthy, sublunary, tellurian, telluric, terrene, terrestrial, uncelestial, worldly
rel profane, secular, temporal
ant eternal
2 ***syn*** MATERIALISTIC, banausic, earthy, sensual, temporal, worldly
rel animal, carnal, fleshly
3 ***syn*** PROSAIC 3, commonplace, everyday, lowly, workaday, workday

municipal *adj* **1** ***syn*** DOMESTIC 2, home, ‖inland, internal, intestine, national, native
2 ***syn*** URBAN, burghal, city

munificent *adj* ***syn*** LIBERAL 1, bounteous, bountiful, free, freehanded, generous, handsome, openhanded, unsparing
con close, mean, niggard, ungiving

murder *n* the crime of killing a person <a *murder* occurred during a gang shoot-out>
syn blood, ‖bump-off, foul play, homicide, killing, manslaughter

murder *vb* **1** to kill (a human being) unlawfully and with premeditated malice <planned a safe way to *murder* his rival>
syn assassinate, ‖bump off, cool, do in, ‖dust off, execute, finish, knock off, liquidate, put away, rub out, scrag, slay; *compare* KILL 1
rel asphyxiate, behead, decapitate, electrocute, garrote, guillotine, hang, lynch, smother, strangle
idiom take for a ride
2 ***syn*** ANNIHILATE 2, abate, abolish, blot out, eradicate, exterminate, extinguish, root out, uncreate, uproot

murderer *n* one who kills a human being <a *murderer* who wouldn't hesitate to kill in cold blood>
syn homicide, killer, manslayer, slayer; *compare* ASSASSIN
rel butcher, slaughterer

murdering *adj* ***syn*** MURDEROUS, bloodthirsty, bloody, homicidal, sanguinary, sanguine, sanguineous

murderous *adj* characterized by or of a kind to cause murder or bloodshed <made a *murderous* assault on his former friend>
syn bloodthirsty, bloody, homicidal, murdering, sanguinary, sanguine, sanguineous
rel deadly; destructive, devastating, ruinous
con harmless, innocuous, trivial

mure *vb* ***syn*** ENCLOSE 1, cage, close in, envelop, fence, hedge, immure, pen, shut in, wall

murk *vb* **1** ***syn*** OBSCURE, becloud, bedim, cloud, darken, dim, gloom, haze, mist, obfuscate
2 ***syn*** SOIL 2, begrime, besoil, dirty, foul, grime, muddy, smirch, smudge, tarnish

murky *adj* **1** ***syn*** DARK 1, caliginous, dim, dun, dusk, dusky, gloomy, obscure, somber, tenebrous
rel glooming, glowering, lowering
con bright, brilliant, effulgent, radiant
2 ***syn*** OBSCURE 3, ambiguous, amphibological, double-edged, double-faced, dusky, equivocal, nubilous, opaque, sibylline
3 having visible material in suspension <a *murky* liquid>
syn cloudy, mucky
rel muddy, roily, turbid
con clear, limpid, lucent, translucent, transparent; clean, fresh, pure, unpolluted
4 ***syn*** DULL 8, drab, muddy, subfusc
5 ***syn*** DIRTY 1, black, filthy, foul, grubby, mucky, nasty, sordid, squalid, unclean

murmur *n* **1** a low indistinct but often continuous sound (as of voices) <could hear the *murmur* of the audience throughout the entire performance>
syn mumble, mutter, rumor, susurration, undertone, whisper
rel murmuration; buzz, drone, hum, purr; brool
2 ***syn*** REPORT 1, buzz, cry, gossip, grapevine, hearsay, rumble, rumor, scuttlebutt, talk

murmur *vb* **1** ***syn*** GRUMBLE 1, croak, grouch, grouse, ‖grunt, mutter, scold
2 ***syn*** COMPLAIN, fuss, kick, repine, wail, whine
3 ***syn*** MUMBLE, ‖chunter, fumble, muddle, ‖mump, mutter, swallow

muscle *n* **1** muscular strength <loading cargo calls for real *muscle*>
syn beef, brawn, might, sinew, thew
rel power, strength
con impotence
2 ***syn*** POWER 4, arm, beef, energy, force, might, potency, sinew, strength, strong arm

muscle–bound *adj* ***syn*** STIFF 4, buckram, cardboard, stilted, wooden

muscular *adj* **1** marked by good well-developed musculature <his arms were lean but *muscular*>
syn fibrous, ropy, sinewy, stringy, wiry
rel flexible, elastic, resilient, springy, supple
con flabby, flaccid, flimsy, floppy, limp, sleazy; feeble, weak
2 strong and powerful in build or action <a *muscular* lad who could wield an ax like a man>
syn athletic, brawny, sinewy; *compare* STRONG 1
rel stalwart, stout, strong, sturdy; well-built, well-knit, well-set; beefy, burly, husky; Herculean, mighty, powerful
con faint, fragile, frail; delicate, feeble, weak; ‖pindling, puny, slight

muse *vb* ***syn*** PONDER 2, ‖chaw, deliberate, meditate, mull (over), revolve, roll, ruminate, turn over
rel excogitate, study

muse *n* ***syn*** REVERIE, brown study, study, trance

---

muse *n* ***syn*** POET, bard, Parnassian

museum *n* a room, building, or locale where a collection of objects is put on exhibition <an art *museum* with a famous collection of jade>
syn gallery
rel salon; picture gallery, pinacotheka

‖**mush** *n* **1** ***syn*** MOUTH 1, ‖bazoo, gob, ‖row, ‖trap, ‖yap
2 ***syn*** FACE 1, countenance, ‖dial, features, ‖kisser, ‖map, mug, muzzle, ‖pan, ‖puss

‖**mush** (up) *vb* ***syn*** CRUSH 2, becrush, bruise, mash, pulp, squash

mushroom *vb* ***syn*** EXPLODE 1, blow up, burst, detonate, go off

mushy *adj* **1** ***syn*** SOFT 6, pappy, pulpous, pulpy, quaggy, spongy, squashy, squelchy, squishy, squushy
2 ***syn*** HAZY, cloudy, foggy, misty, vague, vaporous, vapory
3 ***syn*** SENTIMENTAL, bathetic, lovey-dovey, maudlin, mawkish, romantic, slushy, ‖soppy, sticky, tear-jerking

music *n* ***syn*** DIN, babel, clamor, hubbub, hullabaloo, jangle, pandemonium, racket, tumult, uproar

musical *adj* **1** ***syn*** HARMONIOUS 1, blending, chiming, consonant, harmonic, symphonic, symphonious
ant unmusical; musicless
2 ***syn*** MELODIOUS 2, melodic, songful, tuned, tuneful
ant unmusical; musicless

musician *n* one skilled in music <the one playing the sax is a real *musician*>
syn musicianer, ‖musicker, musico, virtuoso
rel performer, player

musicianer *n* ***syn*** MUSICIAN, ‖musicker, musico, virtuoso

‖**musicker** *n* ***syn*** MUSICIAN, musicianer, musico, virtuoso

musico *n* ***syn*** MUSICIAN, musicianer, ‖musicker, virtuoso

muskeg *n* ***syn*** SWAMP, baygall, bog, fen, marsh, mire, ‖moss, quag, slough, ‖swang

muss *n* ‖**1** ***syn*** BRAWL 2, broil, donnybrook, fracas, fray, free-for-all, knock-down-and-drag-out, melee, ruction, set-to
2 ***syn*** MESS 3, botch, botchery, hash, mess-up, mix-up, muddle, mull, shambles

muss (up) *vb* ***syn*** DISORDER 1, disarray, disorganize, disrupt, jumble, mess (up), mix up, muddle, rummage, upset
rel dishevel, rumple, wrinkle

mussy *adj* ***syn*** SLOVENLY 1, disheveled, ill-kempt, messy, slobbery, sloppy, sloven, unkempt, unneat, untidy

must *verbal auxiliary* **1** ***syn*** WANT 3, ought, should
2 — used to indicate requirement by immediate or future need or purpose <we *must* hurry if we want to catch the bus>
syn have, ‖mun, need
rel ought, should want
idiom have got to, must needs

must *n* **1** ***syn*** OBLIGATION 2, charge, commitment, committal, devoir, duty, need, ought, ‖right
2 ***syn*** ESSENTIAL 2, condition, necessity, precondition, prerequisite, requirement, requisite, sine qua non

muster *vb* **1** ***syn*** ENTER 3, enlist, enroll, join (up), sign on, sign up
2 ***syn*** MOBILIZE 3, marshal, organize, rally
3 ***syn*** GATHER 6, assemble, collect, congregate, congress, forgather, raise, rendezvous

muster (up) *vb* ***syn*** GENERATE 3, breed, cause, engender, get up, hatch, induce, occasion, produce, work up

muster *n* **1** ***syn*** GATHERING 2, aggregation, assemblage, assembly, collection, company, congeries, congregation, crowd, group
2 ***syn*** ROSTER 1, muster roll, roll

muster out *vb* ***syn*** DISCHARGE 7, ‖demob, demobilize, separate
ant call up, draft

muster roll *n* ***syn*** ROSTER 1, muster, roll

musty *adj* **1** ***syn*** MALODOROUS 1, fetid, frowsy, funky, fusty, noisome, rank, smelly, stale, whiffy
rel dirty, filthy, squalid
2 ***syn*** TRITE, old hat, shopworn, stale, stereotyped, stereotypical, threadbare, timeworn, tired, warmed-over

mutable *adj* **1** ***syn*** CHANGEABLE 1, changeful, fluid, mobile, protean, unsettled, unstable, unsteady, variable, weathery
rel fluctuating, swaying, swinging, wavering; fickle, inconstant, unstable
con equable, even, steady, uniform; durable, lasting, permanent, stable
ant immutable
2 liable to change or to be changed <a flexible and perhaps too *mutable* policy>
syn changeable, inconstant, shifty, slippery, uncertain, unstable, unsteady, variable; *compare* CHANGEABLE 1, INCONSTANT 1
rel changeful, protean, unsettled; capricious, fickle, inconsistent, lubricious, mercurial, temperamental, ticklish, volatile; fluctuating, shilly-shally, vacillating, wavering
con constant, established, fixed, immovable, inalterable, invariable, set, unalterable, unchangeable, unmodifiable, unmovable
ant immutable

mutate *vb* **1** ***syn*** TRANSFORM, change, commute, metamorphize, metamorphose, transfigure, transmogrify, transmute, transpose, transubstantiate
2 ***syn*** CHANGE 1, alter, modify, refashion, turn, vary

mutation *n* **1** ***syn*** CHANGE 1, alteration, modification, turn, variation
2 ***syn*** CHANGE 2, innovation, novelty, permutation, sport, vicissitude

mute *adj* **1** ***syn*** DUMB 1, inarticulate, silent, speechless, unarticulate, voiceless
2 ***syn*** SILENT 2, dumb, mum, ‖mumchance, speechless, wordless
con articulate, eloquent, fluent, glib, vocal, voluble

mute *vb* ***syn*** MUFFLE 2, dampen, deaden, stifle

muted *adj* ***syn*** DULL 7, blind, dead, dim, flat, lackluster, lusterless, mat

---

syn synonym(s) *rel* related word(s)
idiom idiomatic equivalent(s) *con* contrasted word(s)
ant antonym(s) * vulgar
‖ use limited; if in doubt, see a dictionary
The first word in a synonym list when printed in SMALL CAPITALS shows where there is more information about the group. For a more efficient use of this book see Explanatory Notes.

mutedly *adv* ***syn*** SOTTO VOCE, faintly, weakly

mutilate *vb* **1** ***syn*** MAIM, cripple, dislimb, dismember, mayhem
rel damage, hurt, injure, mar, spoil; deface
2 ***syn*** STERILIZE, alter, castrate, change, desexualize, fix, geld, neuter, unsex

mutineer *n* ***syn*** REBEL, anarch, anarchist, frondeur, insurgent, insurrectionist, malcontent, revolter

mutinous *adj* ***syn*** INSUBORDINATE, contumacious, factious, insurgent, rebellious, seditious
rel alienated, disaffected

mutiny *vb* ***syn*** REVOLT 1, insurrect, rebel, rise (against)

mutt *n* ***syn*** DUNCE, blockhead, boob, dimwit, dolt, dope, dumbbell, idiot, ignoramus, numskull

mutter *vb* **1** ***syn*** MUMBLE, ||chunter, fumble, muddle, ||mump, murmur, swallow
2 ***syn*** GRUMBLE 1, croak, grouch, grouse, ||grunt, murmur, scold
rel repine, wail

mutter *n* ***syn*** MURMUR 1, mumble, rumor, susurration, undertone, whisper

muttonchops *n pl* ***syn*** SIDE-WHISKERS, burnsides, dundrearies, sideboards, sideburns

muttonhead *n* ***syn*** DUNCE, blockhead, bonehead, clodpate, hammerhead, knucklehead, numskull, thickhead, thickskull, woodenhead

mutual *adj* ***syn*** COMMON 1, communal, conjoint, conjunct, intermutual, joint, public, shared
rel partaken, participated; associated, connected, related, united

mutually *adv* ***syn*** TOGETHER 3, conjointly, jointly

||**mux** *vb* ***syn*** DISORDER 1, disarrange, disarray, disorganize, disrupt, disturb, mess (up), mix up, muddle, muss (up)

muzzle *n* ***syn*** FACE 1, countenance, ||dial, features, ||kisser, ||map, mug, phiz, ||puss, visage

myopic *adj* affected by a condition in which the visual images come to a focus in front of the retina of the eye resulting especially in defective vision of distant objects <so *myopic* that he used glasses even to read>
syn nearsighted, shortsighted
rel presbyopic; astigmatic
ant farsighted, hyperopic, longsighted

myriad-minded *adj* ***syn*** VERSATILE, adaptable, all-around, ambidextrous, many-sided, mobile

mysterial *adj* ***syn*** MYSTERIOUS, arcane, cabalistic, impenetrable, inscrutable, mystic, numinous, unaccountable, unguessed, unknowable

mysterious *adj* being beyond one's powers to discover, understand, or explain <he had a *mysterious* sense of humor, laughing when other people did not>
syn arcane, cabalistic, impenetrable, inscrutable, mysterial, mystic, numinous, unaccountable, unexaminable, unguessed, unknowable; *compare* INEXPLICABLE, STRANGE 4
rel impenetrable, incognizable, incomprehensible, uncomprehensible, ungraspable, unintelligible, unknowable; abstruse, esoteric, occult, recondite; ambiguous, cryptic, enigmatic, equivocal, obscure
con explainable, explicable; apprehensible, comprehendible, comprehensible, fathomable, graspable, intelligible, knowable, lucid, scrutable; candid, frank, honest, straightforward
ant unmysterious

mystery *n* something which baffles or perplexes <the *mystery* of his disappearance has never been solved>
syn Chinese puzzle, closed book, conundrum, enigma, mystification, puzzle, puzzlement, riddle, why
rel poser, problem, stumper; perplexity; brainteaser, brain twister
con open book

mystic *adj* **1** ***syn*** MYSTICAL 1, anagogic, telestic
rel imaginary, visionary; quixotic
2 ***syn*** MYSTERIOUS, arcane, cabalistic, impenetrable, inscrutable, mysterial, numinous, unaccountable, unguessed, unknowable
3 ***syn*** MAGIC, magian, magical, necromantic, sorcerous, thaumaturgic, witchy, wizardly

mystical *adj* **1** having a spiritual meaning or reality that is neither apparent to the senses nor obvious to the intelligence <the *mystical* food of the sacrament>
syn anagogic, mystic, telestic
rel abysmal, deep, profound; absolute, categorical, ultimate; divine, holy, sacred, spiritual; miraculous, supernatural, supranatural
2 ***syn*** SECRET 1, clandestine, covert, furtive, hole-and-corner, hugger-mugger, hush-hush, sneak, stealthy, sub-rosa

mystification *n* ***syn*** MYSTERY, Chinese puzzle, closed book, conundrum, enigma, puzzle, puzzlement, riddle, why

mystifying *adj* ***syn*** CRYPTIC, dark, Delphian, enigmatic

myth *n* **1** a traditional story of ostensibly historical content whose origin has been lost <the various Greek *myths* that have come down to us>
syn legend, mythos, mythus; *compare* ALLEGORY 2
rel saga; fable, fabrication, fiction, figment; creation, invention
2 ***syn*** ALLEGORY 2, apologue, fable, parable
3 ***syn*** LORE 2, folklore, legend, mythology, mythos, tradition

mythical *adj* lacking factual basis or historical validity <a *mythical* account attributes the founding of the city to Noah>
syn fabulous, legendary, mythological
rel fictional, fictitious, fictive, imaginary, suppositious, unreal; fanciful, fantastic, visionary; created, invented
con actual, real, true; authentic, genuine, veritable; truthful, veracious, verisimilar
ant historical

mythological *adj* ***syn*** MYTHICAL, fabulous, legendary

mythology *n* ***syn*** LORE 2, folklore, legend, myth, mythos, tradition

mythos *n* **1** ***syn*** MYTH 1, legend, mythus
2 ***syn*** LORE 2, folklore, legend, myth, mythology, tradition

mythus *n* ***syn*** MYTH 1, legend, mythos

---

syn synonym(s)	***rel*** related word(s)
idiom idiomatic equivalent(s)	***con*** contrasted word(s)
ant antonym(s)	* vulgar

|| use limited; if in doubt, see a dictionary
The first word in a synonym list when printed in SMALL CAPITALS shows where there is more information about the group. For a more efficient use of this book see Explanatory Notes.

N

nab *vb* **1** ***syn*** ARREST 2, apprehend, ‖bust, detain, pick up, pinch, pull in, run in
2 ***syn*** SEIZE 2, catch, clutch, ‖cotch, grab, grapple, ‖nail, snatch, take
3 ***syn*** STEAL 1, cabbage, ‖clout, ‖cly, collar, ‖cop, hook, ‖nail, ‖nick, nip

‖**nab** *n* **1** ***syn*** POLICEMAN, ‖bobby, ‖bull, ‖constable, cop, ‖flatfoot, ‖fuzz, ‖heat, ‖paddy, ‖peeler
2 ***syn*** ARREST, apprehension, arrestation, arrestment, detention, pickup, pinch

nabal *n* ***syn*** MISER, chuff, hunks, moneygrubber, muckworm, niggard, scrooge, skinflint, stiff, tightwad

nabob *n* ***syn*** NOTABLE 1, ‖big chief, ‖biggie, bigwig, dignitary, eminence, ‖fat cat, high-muck-a-muck, nawob, notability

nada *n* ***syn*** NOTHINGNESS, nihility, nonexistence, nullity, vacuity

nadir *n* ***syn*** BOTTOM 3, base, foot
con acme, climax, culmination; peak, summit
ant apex, zenith

nag *vb* to find fault incessantly <stop *nagging* her over nothing>
syn carp (at), fuss, henpeck, peck (at)
rel annoy, harass, harry, pester, plague, tease, worry; bother, irk, vex; badger, bait, chivy, heckle, hector, hound, ride; egg, goad, needle, prod, urge
idiom give a bad (*or* hard) time, pick at (*or* on), take it out on
con commend, compliment, praise; acclaim, applaud, hail

nail *vb* **1** ***syn*** CATCH 1, bag, capture, collar, ‖cotch, get, prehend, secure, take
‖**2** ***syn*** SEIZE 2, catch, clutch, ‖cotch, grab, grapple, nab, snatch, take
‖**3** ***syn*** STEAL 1, cabbage, ‖clout, ‖cly, collar, hook, nab, ‖nick, nip, pinch
‖**4** ***syn*** STRIKE 2, ‖biff, clout, ‖devel, ding, hit, slog, ‖slosh, sock, whack

naive *adj* **1** ***syn*** NATURAL 5, artless, ingenuous, simple, unaffected, unartful, unartificial, unschooled, unsophisticated, unstudied
rel fresh, original
ant sophisticated
2 ***syn*** EASY 3, fleeceable, gullible, susceptible

naked *adj* **1** ***syn*** BARE 1, bald, nude
2 ***syn*** NUDE 2, au naturel, *bare-assed, buff-bare, raw, stark-naked, stripped, unclad, unclothed, undressed
3 ***syn*** OPEN 2, bare, denuded, exposed, peeled, stripped, uncovered

---

syn synonym(s) *rel* related word(s)
idiom idiomatic equivalent(s) *con* contrasted word(s)
ant antonym(s) * vulgar
‖ use limited; if in doubt, see a dictionary
The first word in a synonym list when printed in SMALL CAPITALS shows where there is more information about the group. For a more efficient use of this book see Explanatory Notes.

rel disclosed, discovered, revealed; evident, manifest, obvious, palpable; colorless, uncolored; pure, sheer, simple

namby–pamby *adj* **1** ***syn*** INSIPID 3, banal, bland, driveling, flat, inane, innocuous, jejune, milk-and-water, sapless
2 ***syn*** CHARACTERLESS, pantywaist, wishy-washy

namby–pamby *n* ***syn*** WEAKLING, baby, doormat, jellyfish, milksop, Milquetoast, mollycoddle, pantywaist, sissy, sop

name *n* **1** the word or combination of words by which something is called and by means of which it can be distinguished or identified <the *name* always given to the eldest son> <what is the *name* of that bird?>
syn appellation, appellative, cognomen, compellation, denomination, designation, ‖handle, ‖moniker, nomen, rubric, style, title
rel baptismal name, Christian name, font name, forename, personal name, prename; byname, byword, hypocorism, nickname, pet name, sobriquet; epithet, label, tag; alias, incognito, nom de guerre, nom de plume, pen name, pseudonym
2 ***syn*** REPUTATION 2, character, fame, ‖rep, report, repute
3 ***syn*** CELEBRITY 2, big name, ‖celeb, luminary, notability, notable, somebody

name *vb* **1** to give a name to <*named* the child for his grandfather>
syn baptize, call, christen, denominate, designate, dub, entitle, style, term, title
rel label, tag, ticket; nickname
idiom give a handle, pin a moniker on
2 ***syn*** DESIGNATE 2, appoint, finger, make, nominate, tap
rel advertise, announce, declare, publish
3 ***syn*** MENTION, cite, instance, specify
rel identify, recognize

nameable *adj* ***syn*** NOTEWORTHY, ‖bodacious, memorable, notable, observable, red-letter, rubric

nameless *adj* **1** ***syn*** OBSCURE 5, uncelebrated, unfamed, unheard-of, unknown, unnoted, unrenowned
2 ***syn*** ANONYMOUS, innominate, undesignated, unnamed
ant named

namely *adv* that is to say <understandably his wife disapproves of his bad habits, *namely* gambling and fornication>
syn scilicet, to wit, videlicet
rel especially, expressly, particularly, specially, specifically

nana *n* ***syn*** NURSEMAID, ‖amah, ‖ayah, ‖nanny, nurse, nurserymaid

‖**nanny** *n* ***syn*** NURSEMAID, ‖amah, ‖ayah, nana, nurse, nurserymaid

nap *n* a short sleep <generally took an hour's *nap* after lunch>
syn catnap, dog nap, ‖dover, forty winks, siesta, snooze; *compare* DOZE, SLEEP 1

rel dogsleep; break, interlude, intermission, let up, pause, respite, rest

nap *vb* to sleep briefly <*napped* for an hour after lunch>
syn catnap, ||caulk (off), siesta, snooze; *compare* DOZE, SLEEP
rel drowse; relax, rest, unlax
idiom catch a wink of sleep, catch forty winks, take a nap (*or* siesta *or* snooze)

narcissism *n syn* CONCEIT 2, amour propre, conceitedness, self-admiration, self-conceit, self-esteem, self-love, vainglory, vainness, vanity

narcissistic *adj syn* VAIN 3, conceited, ||conceity, self-conceited, stuck-up, vainglorious

narcotic *n* **1** *syn* DRUG 2, dope, ||hop, opiate
2 *syn* ANODYNE 2, nepenthe, opiate

narcotic *adj syn* SOPORIFIC 1, hypnotic, opiate, somnifacient, somniferous, somnific, somnolent, somnorific, soporiferous, soporifical

||**nark** *n syn* INFORMER, betrayer, ||canary, ||fink, snitch, ||squeaker, squealer, stool pigeon, talebearer, tipster

||**nark** *vb syn* INFORM 3, peach, ||pimp, rat, ||sing, snitch, squeak, squeal, ||stool

narrate *vb syn* RELATE 1, describe, recite, recount, rehearse, report, state
rel descant, dilate, discourse, expatiate

narration *n* **1** *syn* DESCRIPTION 2, recital, recountal, recounting
2 *syn* STORY 2, anecdote, narrative, tale, yarn

narrative *n* **1** *syn* STORY 2, anecdote, narration, tale, yarn
2 *syn* ACCOUNT 7, chronicle, history, report, story, version

narrow *adj* **1** *syn* DEFINITE 1, circumscribed, determinate, fixed, limited, precise, restricted
2 *syn* LITTLE 2, borné, ineffectual, limited, mean, paltry, set, small
3 *syn* ILLIBERAL, bigoted, brassbound, hidebound, intolerant, narrow-minded, small-minded, unenlarged
rel inexorable, inflexible, obdurate
con forbearing, indulgent, lenient, tolerant
ant broad
||**4** *syn* STINGY, ||chinchy, close, narrow-fisted, narrowhearted, niggard, niggardly, ||scant, scrimpy, tight

narrow *vb syn* CONSTRICT 2, constringe

narrow–fisted *adj syn* STINGY, closefisted, hardfisted, hardhanded, mean, miserly, ||narrow, narrowhearted, penny-pinching, tightfisted
ant openhanded

narrowhearted *adj syn* STINGY, closefisted, hardfisted, hardhanded, mean, miserly, ||narrow, narrow-fisted, niggardly, penurious
ant openhearted

narrow–minded *adj syn* ILLIBERAL, bigoted, brassbound, hidebound, intolerant, narrow, small-minded, unenlarged
ant broad-minded

nascent *adj syn* INITIAL 1, beginning, inceptive, incipient, initiative, initiatory, introductory

nasty *adj* **1** *syn* DIRTY 1, black, filthy, foul, grubby, impure, soily, squalid, unclean, uncleanly
rel coarse, gross, obscene, ribald, vulgar; improper, indecent, indecorous, indelicate, unseemly
2 *syn* OFFENSIVE, disgusting, foul, horrid, icky, loathsome, obscene, repugnant, repulsive, vile
3 *syn* OBSCENE 2, coarse, dirty, filthy, foul, indecent, raunchy, scatological, smutty, vulgar
4 *syn* MALICIOUS, evil, hateful, malevolent, malign, malignant, spiteful, spitish, vicious, wicked

nates *n pl syn* BUTTOCKS, backside, beam, behind, bottom, ||butt, derriere, fanny, rear end, rump

national *adj* **1** *syn* PUBLIC 1, civic, civil
2 *syn* DOMESTIC 2, home, ||inland, internal, intestine, municipal, native

national *n syn* CITIZEN 2, subject

native *adj* **1** *syn* INNATE 1, congenital, connate, connatural, inborn, indigenous, inherited, natural, unacquired
2 belonging to a locality by birth or origin <a *native* tradition> <delighted with the tasty *native* fruits>
syn aboriginal, autochthonous, endemic, indigenous
rel domestic, local
con adopted, introduced, naturalized
ant alien, foreign, nonnative
3 *syn* DOMESTIC 2, home, ||inland, internal, intestine, municipal, national
4 *syn* WILD 1, agrarian, agrestal, natural, uncultivated, undomesticated
5 *syn* UNREFINED 3, crude, impure, raw, run-of-mine, ungraded, unsorted

Nativity *n syn* CHRISTMAS, noel, Xmas, yule, yuletide

||**natter** *vb syn* CHAT 1, babble, chatter, clack, gab, jaw, prate, prattle, run on, yak

natty *adj syn* DAPPER, bandbox, doggish, doggy, sassy, sparkish, spiffy, spruce, sprucy, well-groomed

natural *adj* **1** *syn* ILLEGITIMATE 1, baseborn, bastard, fatherless, misbegotten, spurious, supposititious, unfathered
2 *syn* INNATE 1, congenital, connate, connatural, inborn, indigenous, inherited, native, unacquired
ant abnormal, unnatural
3 *syn* GENERAL 1, common, commonplace, matter-of-course, normal, prevalent, regular, typic, typical, usual
4 *syn* WILD 1, agrarian, agrestal, native, uncultivated, undomesticated
5 free from pretension or calculation <he spoke in a perfectly *natural* manner>
syn artless, guileless, inartificial, ingenuous, innocent, naive, simple, simplehearted, unaffected, unartful, unartificial, unschooled, unsophisticated, unstudied, untutored, unworldly; *compare* GENUINE 3
rel impulsive, instinctive, spontaneous; easy, unlabored; constitutional, ingrained, inherent; folksy, homespun, unpretentious; ignorant, primitive, undesigning; unconstrained, unembarrassed; candid, frank, open, plain; sincere, unfeigned; provincial, rustic
con ceremonial, ceremonious, conventional, formal; ostentatious, pretentious, showy; assumed, contrived,

---

counterfeited, feigned, pretended; artful, sophisticated, studied
ant affected; artificial, unnatural

natural *n* *syn* FOOL 4, ament, cretin, ‖feeb, half-wit, idiot, imbecile, moron, simpleton, zany

natural child *n* *syn* BASTARD 1, by-blow, catch colt, chance child, come-by-chance, filius nullius, illegitimate, love child, whoreson, woods colt

naturalness *n* *syn* UNCONSTRAINT, abandon, ease, spontaneity, unrestraint
ant unnaturalness

nature *n* **1** *syn* TYPE, character, description, ilk, kidney, kind, sort, stripe, variety, way
rel anatomy, framework, structure; conformation, figure, shape
2 *syn* ESSENCE 1, being, essentia, essentiality, texture
3 *syn* DISPOSITION 3, character, complexion, humor, individualism, individuality, makeup, personality, temper, temperament
4 *syn* UNIVERSE, cosmos (*or* kosmos), creation, macrocosm, macrocosmos, megacosm, world

naught (*or* **nought**) *n* **1** *syn* NOTHING 1, nil, ‖nix, wind
2 *syn* ZERO, aught (*or* ought), cipher, goose egg, nothing, zilch

naughty *adj* **1** guilty of misbehavior <a *naughty* boy who teased the cat and upset the milk>
syn bad, ill-behaved, misbehaving, mischievous, paw; *compare* DISOBEDIENT
rel contrary, froward, perverse, wayward; headstrong, intractable, recalcitrant, refractory, ungovernable, unruly, willful; disorderly, rowdy, ruffianly; evil, indecorous, wicked
con decorous, good, well-behaved; amenable, docile, obedient, tractable; amiable, complaisant, good-natured, obliging; polite, proper; considerate, kindly, thoughtful
2 *syn* DISOBEDIENT, obstreperous, unruly

nausea *n* a stomach distress with an urge to vomit <overcome with *nausea* as the boat continued to pitch and wallow>
syn qualmishness, queasiness, squeamishness

nauseate *vb* *syn* DISGUST, reluct, repel, repulse, revolt, sicken

nauseated *adj* affected with nausea <was *nauseated* after taking the drug>
syn nauseous, squeamish; *compare* SQUEAMISH 1
rel choking, gagging; heaving; barfing, upchucking, vomiting
idiom ready (*or* about) to lose one's cookies

nauseating *adj* *syn* OFFENSIVE, disgusting, foul, icky, loathsome, nasty, noisome, repugnant, repulsive, sickening
ant appetizing

nauseous *adj* *syn* NAUSEATED, squeamish

nautical *adj* *syn* MARINE 2, maritime, navigational

navigable *adj* *syn* PASSABLE, negotiable, travelable
ant unnavigable

navigational *adj* *syn* MARINE 2, maritime, nautical

nawob *n* *syn* NOTABLE 1, ‖big chief, ‖biggie, bigwig, dignitary, eminence, ‖fat cat, high-muck-a-muck, nabob, notability

nay *adv* **1** *syn* NO, ‖nit, ‖nix, ‖nope
2 *syn* EVEN 3, indeed, truly, verily, yea

naze *n* *syn* PROMONTORY, beak, bill, cape, foreland, head, headland, point

neanderthal *adj* *syn* OLD-FASHIONED, antiquated, antique, archaic, bygone, oldfangled, old-time, outdated, unmodern, vintage

near *adv* **1** *syn* CLOSE, at close hand, hard, nearby, nigh
ant far
2 *syn* ABOUT 5, near-at-hand, nearby

near *prep* **1** *syn* ABOUT 1, around, circa, close on, nearby, nigh
2 not far distant from <kept the boy *near* him>
syn ‖aside, beside, by, nearby, nigh, round
idiom close to, hard by, within earshot, within reach, within sight

near *adj* **1** *syn* CLOSE 6, immediate, near-at-hand, nearby, nigh, proximate
ant far
2 *syn* COMPARATIVE, approximate, relative

near *vb* *syn* APPROACH 1, approximate, nigh
rel equal, match, rival, touch
con alter, change, modify, vary; differ

‖**nearabout** *adv* *syn* NEARLY, about, all but, almost, approximately, most, much, nigh, practically, well-nigh

near–at–hand *adj* **1** *syn* NEIGHBORING, adjacent, close-at-hand, close-by, contiguous, nearby
2 *syn* CLOSE 6, immediate, near, nearby, nigh, proximate
3 *syn* CONVENIENT 2, adjacent, close-at-hand, close-by, handy, nearby

near–at–hand *adv* *syn* ABOUT 5, near, nearby

nearby *adv* **1** *syn* CLOSE, at close hand, hard, near, nigh
2 *syn* ABOUT 5, near, near-at-hand

nearby *prep* **1** *syn* NEAR 2, ‖aside, beside, by, nigh, round
2 *syn* ABOUT 1, around, circa, close on, near, nigh

nearby *adj* **1** *syn* CLOSE 6, immediate, near, near-at-hand, nigh, proximate
2 *syn* NEIGHBORING, adjacent, close-at-hand, close-by, contiguous, near-at-hand
3 *syn* CONVENIENT 2, adjacent, close-at-hand, close-by, handy, near-at-hand

nearing *adj* *syn* FORTHCOMING, approaching, coming, oncoming, upcoming

nearly *adv* very close to <our work is *nearly* done for today>
syn about, all but, almost, approximately, as good as, just about, more or less, most, much, ‖nearabout, nigh, practically, roughly, round, roundly, rudely, say, some, somewhere, well-nigh
rel virtually
idiom as near as never mind(s), in effect, in essence, in substance, in the main, nigh on (*or* onto *or* upon), to all (practical) intents and purposes

nearsighted *adj* *syn* MYOPIC, shortsighted

---

syn synonym(s) *rel* related word(s)
idiom idiomatic equivalent(s) *con* contrasted word(s)
ant antonym(s) * vulgar
‖ use limited; if in doubt, see a dictionary
The first word in a synonym list when printed in SMALL CAPITALS shows where there is more information about the group. For a more efficient use of this book see Explanatory Notes.

neat *adj* 1 ***syn*** STRAIGHT 3, plain, pure, unadulterated, undiluted, unmixed
2 manifesting care and orderliness <always kept a *neat* house>
syn chipper, orderly, prim, shipshape, snug, spick-and-span, tidy, trig, trim, uncluttered, well-groomed; *compare* DAPPER
rel clean, immaculate, spotless; dainty, fastidious, finicky, nice; methodical, regular, systematic; accurate, correct, exact, precise
idiom in good order, neat as a pin (*or* bandbox), neat as can be, neat as wax
con disheveled, disordered, slipshod, sloppy, slovenly, unkempt, untidy; dirty, filthy, foul, nasty; lax, negligent, remiss, slack
ant disorderly, messy
‖3 ***syn*** MARVELOUS 2, ‖cool, ‖dandy, glorious, groovy, hunky-dory, ‖keen, nifty, peachy, super

neat–handed *adj* ***syn*** DEXTEROUS 1, adroit, clever, deft, handy, nimble

neb *n* ***syn*** BILL 1, beak, nib, pecker

‖**nebby** *adj* ***syn*** IMPERTINENT 2, busy, intrusive, meddlesome, obtrusive, officious, polypragmatic

‖**necessary** *n* ***syn*** PRIVY 1, backhouse, ‖biffy, ‖closet, *crapper, jakes, ‖office, outhouse

necessary *adj* 1 ***syn*** ESSENTIAL 4, imperative, indispensable, necessitous, prerequisite
rel compelling, compulsory, constraining, mandatory, obligatory; important, momentous, significant; cardinal, fundamental
con insignificant, unessential, unimportant
ant unnecessary
2 ***syn*** INEVITABLE, certain, ineluctable, ineludible, inescapable, inevasible, returnless, unavoidable, unescapable, unevadable
rel inerrable, inerrant, infallible, unerring

necessitate *vb* ***syn*** DEMAND 2, ask, call (for), crave, require, take

necessitous *adj* 1 ***syn*** POOR 1, destitute, dirt poor, impecunious, impoverished, indigent, needy, penurious, poverty-stricken, strapped
rel depleted, drained, exhausted
2 ***syn*** ESSENTIAL 4, imperative, indispensable, necessary, prerequisite

necessity *n* 1 ***syn*** NEED 4, exigency
rel coercion, compulsion, constraint, duress, obligation; indispensableness, needfulness, requisiteness
2 ***syn*** OCCASION 3, call, cause, obligation
3 ***syn*** ESSENTIAL 2, condition, must, precondition, prerequisite, requirement, requisite, sine qua non

neck *vb* ***syn*** BEHEAD, decapitate, decollate, guillotine, head

necrology *n* ***syn*** OBITUARY, obit

necromancer *n* ***syn*** MAGICIAN 1, charmer, conjurer, enchanter, mage, magus, sorcerer, voodooist, warlock, wizard

necromancy *n* ***syn*** MAGIC 1, bewitchment, conjuring, enchantment, magicking, sorcery, thaumaturgy, witchcraft, witchery, wizardry

necromantic *adj* ***syn*** MAGIC, magian, magical, mystic, sorcerous, thaumaturgic, witchy, wizardly

necropolis *n* ***syn*** CEMETERY, ‖boneyard, ‖boot hill, burial ground, burying ground, God's acre, graveyard, memorial park, polyandrium, potter's field

necropsy *n* ***syn*** AUTOPSY, ‖post, postmortem, postmortem examination

‖**neddy** *n* ***syn*** DONKEY 1, ass, burro, donk, jackass, ‖moke, ‖Rocky Mountain canary

need *n* 1 ***syn*** OBLIGATION 2, charge, commitment, committal, devoir, duty, must, ought, ‖right
2 ***syn*** REQUIREMENT 1, demand, want
3 opportunity or requirement to employ <found little *need* for his rifle>
syn demand, occasion, use
rel call, claim, exaction
4 a pressing lack of something essential <he is in *need* of food>
syn exigency, necessity
rel deficiency, deficit, lack, shortage, want
con adequacy, enough, sufficiency
5 ***syn*** POVERTY 1, destitution, impecuniousness, impoverishment, indigence, neediness, penury, poorness, privation, want

need *vb* 1 ***syn*** LACK, require, want
rel claim, demand, exact; hanker, hunger, long, pine, thirst, yearn; covet, crave, desire, wish
2 ***syn*** MUST 2, have, ‖mun

needed *adj* ***syn*** NEEDFUL, required, requisite
ant unneeded

needful *adj* necessary for supply or relief <provided them with everything *needful*>
syn needed, required, requisite
rel essential, imperative, indispensable, necessary; lacked, wanted; cardinal, fundamental, vital
con excess, redundant, superfluous; nonessential, unessential; uncalled-for, unnecessary, unneeded
ant needless

needful *n* ***syn*** MONEY, ‖mazuma, ‖moolah, ‖ooftish, pelf, rhino, rocks, ‖scratch, ‖shekels, ‖smash

neediness *n* ***syn*** POVERTY 1, destitution, impecuniousness, impoverishment, indigence, need, penury, poorness, privation, want

needle *vb* ***syn*** WORRY 1, annoy, bedevil, dun, gnaw, hagride, harass, pester, plague, tease

needless *adj* ***syn*** UNNECESSARY, inessential, uncalled-for, unessential, unneeded, unneedful, unrequired
ant needful

needy *adj* ***syn*** POOR 1, destitute, dirt poor, impecunious, impoverished, indigent, necessitous, penurious, poverty-stricken, unprosperous

ne'er *adv* ***syn*** NEVER

ne'er–do–well *n* ***syn*** WASTREL 1, ‖bad lot, good-for-nothing, no-good, profligate, rounder, scapegrace, waster

nefarious *adj* ***syn*** VICIOUS 2, corrupt, degenerate, flagitious, infamous, miscreant, perverse, putrid, rotten, villainous

---

syn synonym(s) ***rel*** related word(s)
idiom idiomatic equivalent(s) ***con*** contrasted word(s)
ant antonym(s) * vulgar
‖ use limited; if in doubt, see a dictionary
The first word in a synonym list when printed in SMALL CAPITALS shows where there is more information about the group. For a more efficient use of this book see Explanatory Notes.

rel atrocious, heinous, monstrous, outrageous; flagrant, glaring, gross, rank
ant exemplary

negate *vb* **1** ***syn*** DENY 4, contradict, contravene, cross, disaffirm, gainsay, impugn, negative, traverse
ant affirm
2 ***syn*** ABOLISH 1, abate, abrogate, annihilate, annul, invalidate, nullify, quash, undo, vitiate
3 ***syn*** NEUTRALIZE, annul, cancel (out), counteract, countercheck, frustrate, negative, redress

negation *n* ***syn*** DENIAL 2, contradiction, gainsaying
ant affirmation

negative *adj* ***syn*** ADVERSE 2, detrimental, unfavorable

negative *vb* **1** ***syn*** VETO, kill, ‖nix, non-placet
2 ***syn*** DENY 4, contradict, contravene, cross, disaffirm, gainsay, impugn, negate, traverse
ant affirm
3 ***syn*** NEUTRALIZE, annul, cancel (out), counteract, countercheck, frustrate, negate, redress
rel abrogate, invalidate, nullify

neglect *vb* to pass over without giving due attention < *neglected* his family for the sake of his mistress >
syn blink (at *or* away), discount, disregard, elide, fail, forget, ignore, miss, omit, overleap, overlook, overpass, pass, pass by, pass over, pretermit, slight, slough over, slur (over)
rel brush (off *or* aside), disdain, dismiss, reject, scant, scorn, shrug away, shrug off
idiom pay no attention to, pay no heed (*or* mind), think little of
con appreciate, prize, treasure, value; cultivate, foster, nurse, nurture
ant cherish

neglect *n* ***syn*** FAILURE 1, default, delinquency, dereliction, oversight

neglected *adj* not properly or sufficiently attended to or cared for <the whole property had a *neglected* appearance>
syn run-down, uncared-for, untended
rel disregarded, ignored, overlooked, slighted, unheeded
con prized, treasured; fostered, tended; guarded, supervised, watched
ant cherished

neglectful *adj* ***syn*** NEGLIGENT, behindhand, careless, delinquent, derelict, disregardful, lax, regardless, remiss, slack
ant attentive

negligent *adj* failing to give proper attention or care < *negligent* in taking care of the children> <a *negligent* man, prone to forgetfulness>
syn behindhand, careless, delinquent, derelict, discinct, disregardful, lax, neglectful, regardless, remiss, slack

syn synonym(s) ***rel*** related word(s)
idiom idiomatic equivalent(s) ***con*** contrasted word(s)
ant antonym(s) * vulgar
‖ use limited; if in doubt, see a dictionary
The first word in a synonym list when printed in SMALL CAPITALS shows where there is more information about the group. For a more efficient use of this book see Explanatory Notes.

rel heedless, inadvertent, inattentive, inconsiderate, thoughtless, unheedful, unthinking; incurious, indifferent, unconcerned; slipshod, slovenly
con rigid, rigorous, strict; attentive, considerate, heedful, thoughtful; careful, exact, fussy, meticulous, punctilious, punctual, scrupulous
ant attentive

negligible *adj* ***syn*** REMOTE 4, ‖fat, off, outside, slender, slight, slim, small
ant significant

negotiable *adj* ***syn*** PASSABLE, navigable, travelable
ant nonnegotiable

negotiate *vb* **1** to bring about by mutual agreement < *negotiate* a treaty>
syn arrange, concert, settle
rel adjust, compose, transact; agree, bargain, contract, covenant
con break off, intermit, interrupt, suspend; differ, disagree, dissent
2 ***syn*** CLEAR 8, hurdle, leap, over, overleap, surmount, vault

neigh *vb* to make the cry typical of a horse <the frightened horse *neighed* and stamped>
syn nicker, whicker, ‖whinner, whinny

neighbor *vb* ***syn*** ADJOIN, abut, border, butt (on *or* against), communicate, join, line, march, touch, verge

neighborhood *n* **1** ***syn*** LOCALITY 1, area, district, vicinage, vicinity
2 ***syn*** ORDER 4, extent, magnitude, matter, range, tune, vicinity

neighboring *adj* not distant <the need for understanding between *neighboring* countries>
syn adjacent, close-at-hand, close-by, contiguous, near-at-hand, nearby; *compare* CLOSE 6
rel abutting, adjoining, bordering, conterminous, touching; close, near
con distant, far, faraway, far-off, remote, removed; parted, separated

neighborly *adj* ***syn*** AMICABLE, friendly
rel cooperative, gregarious, hospitable, social; cordial, gracious, sociable
ant unneighborly; ill-disposed

neonate *n* ***syn*** BABY 1, babe, bantling, infant, newborn

neophyte *n* ***syn*** NOVICE, apprentice, beginner, colt, freshman, newcomer, novitiate, rookie, tenderfoot, tyro

neoteric *adj* ***syn*** NEW 1, fresh, modern, modernistic, newfangled, new-fashioned, new-sprung, novel, recent

nepenthe *n* ***syn*** ANODYNE 2, narcotic, opiate

ne plus ultra *n* ***syn*** APEX 2, acme, apogee, capstone, climax, culmination, peak, pinnacle, summit, zenith

nerve *n* **1** ***syn*** FORTITUDE, backbone, grit, guts, intestinal fortitude, ‖moxie, sand, spunk
2 ***syn*** TEMERITY, assurance, audacity, brashness, hardihood, hardiness
3 ***syn*** EFFRONTERY, brashness, brass, cheek, confidence, ‖crust, face, gall, presumption

nerve *vb* ***syn*** ENCOURAGE 1, animate, cheer, chirk (up), embolden, enhearten, hearten, inspirit, steel, strengthen

nerve center *n* ***syn*** CENTER 2, focal point, focus, heart, hub, polestar, seat

nervous *adj* easily upset or irritated <a *nervous* fretful woman>
syn fidgety, goosey, high-strung, jittery, jumpy, nervy, spooky, twittery, unrestful

rel agitated, edgy, excitable, skittish, volatile; fretful, irritable, querulous, snappish, waspish
con calm, placid, serene, steady, tranquil; collected, composed, cool, imperturbable, inexcitable, poised, unflappable, unruffled
ant nerveless

nervous breakdown *n* an emotional disorder often characterized by depression, tenseness, irritability, headache, and susceptibility to fatigue <worked and worried himself into a *nervous breakdown*>
syn breakdown, collapse, crack-up, nervous prostration
rel neurasthenia; prostration

nervous prostration *n* ***syn*** NERVOUS BREAKDOWN, breakdown, collapse, crack-up

nervy *adj* **1** ***syn*** WISE 5, bold, cheeky, forward, fresh, impudent, pert, sassy, smart, smart-alecky
2 ***syn*** NERVOUS, fidgety, goosey, high-strung, jittery, jumpy, spooky, twittery, unrestful
rel excitable, fidgety, jerky, tense, twitchy
idiom tied up in knots
con composed, easy, relaxed
ant phlegmatic
3 ***syn*** TENSE 2, edgy, restive, uneasy, uptight

nescience *n* ***syn*** IGNORANCE 2, innocence, inscience, unacquaintance, unacquaintedness, unawareness, unfamiliarity, unknowingness

nest egg *n* ***syn*** RESERVE, backlog, hoard, inventory, reservoir, stock, stockpile, store

nestle *vb* ***syn*** SNUGGLE, burrow, ||croodle, cuddle, nuzzle, ||snudge, snug, ||snuzzle

net *vb* ***syn*** CLEAR 6, clean up, gain, make

nether *adj* ***syn*** INFERIOR 1, lesser, low, lower, subjacent, under

nethermost *adj* ***syn*** BOTTOMMOST, bottom, lowermost, lowest, rock-bottom, undermost
ant uppermost

netherwards *adv* ***syn*** DOWN 1, downward, downwardly, downwards
ant upwards

netherworld *n* ***syn*** HELL, abyss, blazes, hades, inferno, Pandemonium, perdition, pit, Sheol, underworld

nettle *vb* ***syn*** IRRITATE, exasperate, get, huff, peeve, pique, provoke, put out, rile, roil
rel agitate, discompose, disturb, perturb, upset

nettlesome *adj* ***syn*** THORNY, prickly, spiny

neuter *vb* ***syn*** STERILIZE, alter, castrate, change, desexualize, fix, geld, mutilate, unsex

neutral *adj* not experiencing or generating a strong emotional commitment or response <made a *neutral* response to his challenge>
syn abstract, colorless, detached, disinterested, dispassionate, impersonal, poker-faced, unpassioned
rel clinical, collected, composed, cool, nonchalant; calm, easy, relaxed; aloof, indifferent
con intemperate, loaded; fervent, impassioned, passionate, vehement

neutralize *vb* to make inoperative or ineffective usually by means of an opposite force, influence, or effect <attacked by the kind of propaganda that is difficult to *neutralize*>
syn annul, cancel (out), counteract, countercheck, frustrate, negate, negative, redress
rel balance, compensate, counterbalance, counterpoise, countervail, offset; abrogate, invalidate, nullify; conquer, defeat, overcome, subdue; override, overrule
con activate, animate, dynamize, vitalize

never *adv* not at any time <they had *never* seen him before>
syn ne'er
idiom never in all one's born days, never in one's life, never in the world, never on earth
con constantly, continuously, ever, invariably, perpetually
ant always

never–ending *adj* ***syn*** EVERLASTING 1, amaranthine, ceaseless, endless, eternal, immortal, unending, world-without-end
ant ended; transitory

never–failing *adj* ***syn*** SURE 2, abiding, enduring, firm, steadfast, steady, unfaltering, unqualified, unquestioning, wholehearted

nevertheless *adv* ***syn*** HOWEVER, after all, howbeit, nonetheless, notwithstanding, still, still and all, though, withal, yet

nevus *n* ***syn*** BIRTHMARK 1, mole

new *adj* **1** recently come into existence or use or a particular state or relation <*new* styles that flatter stout figures>
syn fresh, modern, modernistic, neoteric, newfangled, new-fashioned, new-sprung, novel, recent
rel first-hand, independent, primary
con dated, outdated, outmoded, out-of-date; shabby, worn; hackneyed, old hat, trite
ant old
2 ***syn*** UNFAMILIAR 1, strange, unaccustomed
3 ***syn*** ADDITIONAL, added, another, else, farther, fresh, further, more, other
4 ***syn*** REFRESHED, regenerated, reinvigorated, renewed, revived

new *adv* within recent time <the scent of *new*-mown grass>
syn afresh, anew, lately, newly, of late, recently
con aforetime, before, earlier, formerly; heretofore, hitherto
ant once

newborn *n* ***syn*** BABY 1, babe, bantling, infant, neonate

newcomer *n* ***syn*** NOVICE, apprentice, beginner, colt, freshman, neophyte, novitiate, rookie, tenderfoot, tyro

newfangled *adj* ***syn*** NEW 1, fresh, modern, modernistic, neoteric, new-fashioned, new-sprung, novel, recent
ant oldfangled

new–fashioned *adj* ***syn*** NEW 1, fresh, modern, modernistic, neoteric, newfangled, new-sprung, novel, recent
ant old-fashioned

---

syn synonym(s) — ***rel*** related word(s)
idiom idiomatic equivalent(s) — ***con*** contrasted word(s)
ant antonym(s) — * vulgar
|| use limited; if in doubt, see a dictionary
The first word in a synonym list when printed in SMALL CAPITALS shows where there is more information about the group. For a more efficient use of this book see Explanatory Notes.

New Jerusalem *n syn* HEAVEN 2, Abraham's bosom, bliss, Canaan, Civitas Dei, elysium, empyrean, nirvana, paradise, Zion

newly *adv syn* NEW, afresh, anew, lately, of late, recently

news *n pl but sing in constr* a report of events or conditions not previously known <her friend gave her the bad *news*>
syn advice, information, intelligence, speerings, tidings, word
rel announcement, report; dope, lowdown, ||poop; gossip, rumor, tattle

newsmonger *n syn* GOSSIP 1, carrytale, gossiper, gossipmonger, quidnunc, rumormonger, scandalmonger, tabby, talebearer, telltale

newspaper *n syn* JOURNAL, magazine, organ, periodical, review

new–sprung *adj syn* NEW 1, fresh, modern, modernistic, neoteric, newfangled, new-fashioned, novel, recent

next *adj* being the one that comes immediately after another <the *next* day>
syn coming, ensuing, following; *compare* CONSECUTIVE
rel proximate

next *adv syn* AFTER, afterward, afterwhile, behind, by and by, infra, later, latterly, subsequently

next *prep syn* AFTER 2, behind, below, following, since, subsequent to

next to *prep syn* BESIDE 1, alongside, by, ||fornent

nexus *n syn* BOND 3, knot, ligament, ligature, link, tie, vinculum, yoke

niagara *n syn* FLOOD 2, cataclysm, cataract, deluge, flooding, inundation, overflow, pour, spate, torrent

nib *n syn* BILL 1, beak, neb, pecker

||**nibby** *adj syn* CURIOUS 2, inquisitive, inquisitorial, inquisitory, nosy, peery, prying, snoopy

nice *adj* **1** having or displaying exacting standards <too *nice* about his food to like camp cooking>
syn ||choicy, choosy, clerkish, dainty, delicate, fastidious, finical, finicking, finicky, fussy, miminy-piminy, ||mincy, niminy-piminy, old-maidish, old-womanish, particular, pernickety, persnickety, picksome, picky, precious, squeamish, squeamy
rel discerning, discriminating, penetrating; overparticular; queasy; careful, meticulous, punctilious, scrupulous; judicious, sage, sapient, wise
con coarse, gross, vulgar; callow, crude, green, raw, uncouth; lax, neglectful, negligent, remiss, slack; careless, sloppy, slovenly
2 *syn* FINE 1, delicate, finespun, hairline, hairsplitting, refined, subtle
3 *syn* PLEASANT 1, agreeable, congenial, favorable, good, gratifying, pleasing, pleasurable, pleasureful, welcome
4 *syn* CORRECT 2, accurate, exact, precise, proper, right, rigorous
rel rigid, strict, stringent; exquisite, rare
con haphazard, happy-go-lucky, hit-or-miss, random; careless, heedless, inadvertent
5 *syn* DECOROUS 1, becoming, befitting, comme il faut, conforming, correct, decent, proper, right, seemly

nicely *adv syn* WELL 1, befittingly, correctly, decently, decorously, fitly, fittingly, justly, properly, rightly

nice Nelly *n* **1** *syn* PRUDE, bluenose, comstock, goody-goody, Grundy, Mrs. Grundy, prig, puritan, ||wowser
2 *syn* EUPHEMISM, nice-nellyism

nice–nellyism *n syn* EUPHEMISM, nice Nelly

niche *n syn* NOOK, byplace, cranny

nick *n syn* NOTCH 1, indentation, indenture

||**nick** *vb syn* STEAL 1, cabbage, ||clout, ||cly, hook, nab, ||nail, nim, nip, pinch

nicker *vb syn* NEIGH, whicker, ||whinner, whinny

nickname *n* a descriptive or familiar name that is used instead of or in addition to one's proper name <because he was a redhead his friends gave him the *nickname* "Red">
syn byname, byword, ||handle, hypocorism, ||moniker, sobriquet
rel first name, middle name; appellation, appellative, compellation, denomination, style; epithet, label, tag

nictate *vb syn* WINK, bat, blink, nictitate, twinkle

nictitate *vb syn* WINK, bat, blink, nictate, twinkle

nidorous *adj syn* MALODOROUS 1, fetid, high, noisome, olid, putrid, rancid, reeking, smelly, whiffy

nifty *adj syn* MARVELOUS 2, ||cool, ||dandy, groovy, ||keen, ||neat, peachy, super, swell, terrific

nifty *n syn* ||DILLY, ||corker, crackerjack, ||daisy, dandy, humdinger, jim-dandy, knockout, ||lalapalooza, peach

niggard *n syn* MISER, cheapskate, chuff, hunks, moneygrubber, muckworm, nabal, scrooge, skinflint, stiff

niggard *adj syn* STINGY, cheeseparing, close, mean, miserly, niggardly, penny-pinching, penurious, save-all, tight

niggardly *adj syn* STINGY, cheeseparing, close, closefisted, miserly, parsimonious, penny-pinching, penurious, tight, tightfisted
ant bounteous, bountiful

niggling *adj syn* PETTY 2, measly, Mickey Mouse, paltry, peanut, pettifogging, picayune, picayunish, piddling, trifling

nigh *adv* **1** *syn* CLOSE, at close hand, hard, near, nearby
2 *syn* NEARLY, about, all but, almost, approximately, most, much, ||nearabout, practically, well-nigh

nigh *adj syn* CLOSE 6, immediate, near, near-at-hand, nearby, proximate

nigh *prep* **1** *syn* NEAR 2, ||aside, beside, by, nearby, round
2 *syn* ABOUT 1, around, circa, close on, near, nearby

nigh *vb syn* APPROACH 1, near, approximate

night *n* the time from dusk to dawn <stayed up all *night*>
syn nighttide, nighttime
con day, daytime

night *adj syn* NIGHTLY, nocturnal

night and day *adv syn* TOGETHER 2, consecutively, continually, continuously, hand running, running, successively, unintermittedly, uninterruptedly

---

syn synonym(s) — *rel* related word(s)
idiom idiomatic equivalent(s) — *con* contrasted word(s)
ant antonym(s) — * vulgar
|| use limited; if in doubt, see a dictionary
The first word in a synonym list when printed in SMALL CAPITALS shows where there is more information about the group. For a more efficient use of this book see Explanatory Notes.

nightclub *n* a restaurant serving liquor and providing entertainment <Las Vegas *nightclubs*>
syn bistro, cabaret, café, discotheque, hot spot, nightery, night spot, nitery, supper club, watering hole, watering place

nightery *n syn* NIGHTCLUB, cabaret, café, discotheque, hot spot, night spot, nitery, supper club, watering hole, watering place

nightfall *n syn* EVENING 1, ||dimmet, ||dimps, ||dimpsy, dusk, ||dusk dark, eventide, gloaming, owl-light, twilight

nightly *adj* of, relating to, or associated with the night <*nightly* noises>
syn night, nocturnal
con daily, diurnal; matutinal, morning; evening, twilight, vespertine

nightmare *n syn* FANCY 4, daydream, dream, fantasy (*or* phantasy), phantasm, vision

night spot *n syn* NIGHTCLUB, cabaret, café, discotheque, hot spot, nightery, nitery, supper club, watering hole, watering place

nightstick *n syn* CUDGEL, bat, baton, billy, billy club, bludgeon, club, mace, ||shillelagh, truncheon

nighttide *n syn* NIGHT, nighttime

nighttime *n syn* NIGHT, nighttide

nightwalker *n syn* PROSTITUTE, fille de joie, harlot, ||hooker, hustler, moll, poule, streetwalker, ||tomato, whore

nihility *n syn* NOTHINGNESS, nada, nonexistence, nullity, vacuity

nil *n syn* NOTHING 1, naught (*or* nought), ||nix, wind

nim *vb syn* STEAL 1, hook, lift, nab, ||nail, ||nick, nip, pinch, snitch, swipe

nimble *adj* **1** *syn* AGILE, active, brisk, brisky, catty, lively, sprightly, spry, yare, zippy
rel light, lightsome; alert, vigilant, watchful, wide-awake
2 *syn* DEXTEROUS 1, adroit, clever, deft, handy, neat-handed

nimble-witted *adj syn* WISE 4, canny, hep, knowing, quick, quick-witted, sharp, sharp-witted, slick, smart
ant slow-witted

niminy–piminy *adj syn* NICE 1, ||choicy, choosy, dainty, fastidious, finicky, fussy, particular, pernickety, precious

nimmer *n syn* THIEF, filcher, larcener, larcenist, pilferer, prig, purloiner, stealer

nincom *n syn* FOOL 1, ass, *damfool, idiot, imbecile, jerk, nincompoop, ninny, ninnyhammer, tomfool

nincompoop *n syn* FOOL 1, ass, *damfool, donkey, idiot, imbecile, jackass, jerk, ninny, tomfool

ninny *n syn* FOOL 1, ass, *damfool, donkey, idiot, imbecile, jackass, jerk, nincompoop, tomfool

ninnyhammer *n syn* FOOL 1, ass, *damfool, idiot, imbecile, jerk, nincom, nincompoop, ninny, tomfool

nip *vb* **1** *syn* BLAST 1, blight, dash
rel arrest, check; press, squeeze; balk, frustrate, thwart
2 *syn* STEAL 1, cabbage, ||clout, hook, lift, nab, ||nail, ||nick, nim, pinch
||**3** *syn* HURRY 2, fleet, flit, fly, hasten, hotfoot, hustle, run, rush, zip

nip *n syn* DRAM, ||caulker, drop, jolt, shot, slug, snifter, snort, toothful, tot

nip *vb syn* DRINK 3, booze, guzzle, imbibe, liquor (up), soak, swig, swill, swizzle, tank up

||**nipcheese** *n syn* MISER, cheapskate, cheeseparer, nabal, niggard, scrooge, skin, skinflint, stiff, tightwad

||**nipper** *n syn* CHILD 1, bud, chick, chickabiddy, juvenile, kid, moppet, youngling, young one, youngster

nipping *adj syn* COLD 1, arctic, chill, chilly, cool, freezing, frosty, glacial, icy, shivery

nippy *adj syn* COLD 1, arctic, chill, chilly, cool, freezing, frosty, glacial, icy, shivery

nirvana *n syn* HEAVEN 2, bliss, Canaan, Civitas Dei, elysium, empyrean, happy hunting ground, New Jerusalem, paradise, Zion

nisse *n syn* FAIRY, brownie, elf, fay, pixie, sprite

||**nit** *adv syn* NO, nay, ||nix, ||nope

nitery *n syn* NIGHTCLUB, cabaret, café, discotheque, hot spot, nightery, night spot, supper club, watering hole, watering place

nitwit *n syn* DUNCE, ||cluck, dimwit, ||dumb bunny, ||dumb cluck, featherweight, lackwit, pinhead, simp, wantwit

nitwitted *adj syn* SIMPLE 3, brainless, foolish, mindless, senseless, sheepheaded, silly, unwitty, weak-minded, witless

||**nix** *n syn* NOTHING 1, naught (*or* nought), nil, wind

||**nix** *adv syn* NO, nay, ||nit, ||nope

||**nix** *vb syn* VETO, kill, negative, non-placet

no *adv* — used as a function word to express negation, dissent, denial, or refusal <*no*, you can't come with me>
syn nay, ||nit, ||nix, ||nope
idiom by no manner of means, by no means, in no case, no dice, not at any price, not for love or money, not for the life of me, not for the world, nothing doing, not on your life, on no account, on no condition, under no circumstances
ant yes

||**no-account** *adj syn* WORTHLESS 1, draffy, drossy, good-for-nothing, inutile, no-good, nothing, unworthy, valueless

Noachian *adj syn* ANCIENT 1, aged, age-old, antediluvian, antique, hoary, old, timeworn, venerable

noble *adj* **1** *syn* GRAND 1, august, baronial, grandiose, imposing, magnific, magnificent, majestic, princely, stately
rel eminent, illustrious
con beggarly, contemptible, despicable, scurvy, sorry
ant cheap, ignoble, unnoble
2 *syn* ELEVATED 2, high-minded, moral
ant base
3 *syn* HONORABLE 1, estimable, high-principled, sterling, worthy
ant ignoble

---

syn synonym(s) *rel* related word(s)
idiom idiomatic equivalent(s) *con* contrasted word(s)
ant antonym(s) * vulgar
|| use limited; if in doubt, see a dictionary
The first word in a synonym list when printed in SMALL CAPITALS shows where there is more information about the group. For a more efficient use of this book see Explanatory Notes.

4 ***syn*** MORAL 1, ethical, moralistic, principled, righteous, right-minded, virtuous

nobody *pron* ***syn*** NO ONE, no man, none
ant everybody; somebody

nobody *n* ***syn*** NONENTITY, cipher, insignificancy, nothing, nullity, whiffet, whippersnapper, whipster, zero, zilch
ant somebody

nocent *adj* ***syn*** HARMFUL, bad, damaging, deleterious, detrimental, hurtful, ill, injurious, mischievous, nocuous
ant innocent

nocturnal *adj* ***syn*** NIGHTLY, night
con daily, diurnal

nocuous *adj* ***syn*** HARMFUL, bad, damaging, deleterious, detrimental, hurtful, ill, injurious, mischievous, nocent
ant innocuous

nodding *adj* ***syn*** SLEEPY 1, dozy, drowsy, ||peepy, ||sloomy, slumberous, slumbery, snoozy, somnolent, soporific

noddle *n* ***syn*** HEAD 1, ||bean, ||belfry, ||coco, ||conk, ||dome, headpiece, noggin, noodle, poll

noddy *n* ***syn*** DUNCE, chowderhead, chucklehead, dope, ||dumbhead, dunderhead, lame-brain, noodle, ||schnook, ||stupe

noel *n* ***syn*** CHRISTMAS, Nativity, Xmas, yule, yuletide

noggin *n* ***syn*** HEAD 1, ||bean, ||belfry, ||chump, ||coco, ||conk, ||dome, noddle, noodle, poll

no-good *adj* ***syn*** WORTHLESS 1, draffy, drossy, good-for-nothing, inutile, ||no-account, nothing, unworthy, valueless

no-good *n* **1** ***syn*** WASTREL 1, ||bad lot, good-for-nothing, ne'er-do-well, profligate, rounder, scapegrace, waster
2 ***syn*** WRETCH 1, ||blighter, lowlife, mucker, worm, wormling

noise *n* ***syn*** SOUND 1, sonance
rel babel, clamor, din, hubbub, pandemonium, racket, uproar
con quiet, silence, stillness

noise (about *or* abroad) *vb* ***syn*** GOSSIP, blab, rumor, talk, tattle,

noiseful *adj* ***syn*** NOISY, clangorous, clattery, rackety, sonorous, uproarious
ant noiseless, silent

noiseless *adj* ***syn*** STILL 3, hush, hushful, quiet, silent, soundless, stilly, whist
con boisterous, clamorous, strident, vociferous
ant noiseful, noisy

noiselessness *n* ***syn*** SILENCE 1, quiet, quietness, quietude, soundlessness, still, stillness
ant noisiness

noisome *adj* **1** ***syn*** UNWHOLESOME 1, insalubrious, insalutary, noxious, sickly, unhealthful, unhealthy, unsalutary
ant wholesome
2 ***syn*** MALODOROUS 1, fetid, funky, fusty, musty, nidorous, putrid, rancid, rank, stinking
rel dirty, filthy, squalid; loathsome, revolting
ant balmy
3 ***syn*** OFFENSIVE, disgusting, foul, horrid, loathsome, nasty, nauseating, repulsive, sickening, vile

noisy *adj* making noise <the *noisiest* car you ever heard>
syn clangorous, clattery, noiseful, rackety, sonorous, uproarious
rel blatant, boisterous, clamorous, obstreperous, strepitous, strident, vociferous; tumultuous, turbulent
con quiet, silent, still, stilly
ant noiseless

nomadic *adj* ***syn*** ITINERANT, itinerate, perambulant, perambulatory, peripatetic, roving, vagabond, vagrant, wandering, wayfaring

no man *pron* ***syn*** NO ONE, nobody, none
ant everybody, everyman

nom de guerre *n* ***syn*** PSEUDONYM, alias, anonym

nomen *n* ***syn*** NAME 1, appellation, appellative, cognomen, compellation, denomination, designation, ||moniker, style, title

nominal *adj* being something in name or form only <the *nominal* head of his party>
syn formal, so-called, titular
rel apparent, ostensible, seeming; alleged, pretended, professed
idiom in name only
con genuine, real, true
ant actual

nominate *vb* ***syn*** DESIGNATE 2, appoint, finger, make, name, tap
rel intend, mean, propose, purpose; offer, present, proffer, tender

nonadhesive *adj* ***syn*** LOOSE 3, incoherent

nonage *n* ***syn*** INFANCY 2, minority
ant age

nonchalant *adj* ***syn*** COOL 2, collected, composed, disimpassioned, imperturbable, unflappable, unruffled
rel cheerful, glad, lighthearted; easy, effortless, light, smooth
con anxious, careful, concerned, solicitous, worried

noncombustible *adj* incapable of being burned <*noncombustible* material was used whenever possible>
syn apyrous, incombustible, nonflammable, noninflammable, uninflammable
rel fireproof, fire-resistant, fire-resistive, fire-retardant, flameproof
con flammable, inflammable
ant combustible

noncommittal *adj* ***syn*** RESERVED 1, constrained, incommunicable, restrained

noncompos *n* ***syn*** LUNATIC 1, bedlamite, dement, loon, loony, madling, madman, maniac, nut, Tom o' Bedlam

non compos mentis *adj* ***syn*** INSANE 1, ||batty, cracked, crazy, daft, demented, deranged, mad, unbalanced, unsound

---

syn synonym(s) ***rel*** related word(s)
idiom idiomatic equivalent(s) ***con*** contrasted word(s)
ant antonym(s) * vulgar
|| use limited; if in doubt, see a dictionary
The first word in a synonym list when printed in SMALL CAPITALS shows where there is more information about the group. For a more efficient use of this book see Explanatory Notes.

nonconformism *n syn* HERESY, dissent, dissidence, heterodoxy, misbelief, nonconformity, schism, unorthodoxy
ant conformism

nonconformist *n* **1** *syn* HERETIC, dissenter, dissident, misbeliever, schismatic, schismatist, sectary, separatist
ant conformist
2 *syn* BOHEMIAN, maverick
ant conformist

nonconformist *adj syn* HERETICAL, dissident, heterodox, schismatic, sectarian, unorthodox

nonconformity *n syn* HERESY, dissent, dissidence, heterodoxy, misbelief, nonconformism, schism, unorthodoxy
ant conformity

noncreative *adj syn* UNORIGINAL, sterile, uncreative, uninspired, uninventive, unoriginative
ant creative

nondiscriminatory *adj syn* FAIR 4, dispassionate, equal, equitable, impartial, just, objective, unbiased, uncolored, unprejudiced
ant discriminatory

none *pron syn* NO ONE, nobody, no man

nonentity *n* an utterly insignificant person <tired of dealing with subordinates and *nonentities*>
syn cipher, insignificancy, nobody, nothing, nullity, rushlight, whiffet, whippersnapper, whipster, zero, zilch
rel lightweight, obscurity, sad sack, small beer, small fry
idiom blank space in the rear rank, man in the street, no great shakes

nonesuch *n syn* PARAGON, ideal, jewel, nonpareil, phoenix
idiom one in a million

nonessential *adj syn* DISPENSABLE, unessential, unrequired
ant essential

nonetheless *adv syn* HOWEVER, after all, howbeit, nevertheless, notwithstanding, still, still and all, though, withal, yet

nonexistence *n syn* NOTHINGNESS, nada, nihility, nullity, vacuity
ant existence; reality

nonflammable *adj syn* NONCOMBUSTIBLE, apyrous, incombustible, noninflammable, uninflammable
ant flammable, inflammable

nonfunctional *adj syn* IMPRACTICABLE 2, impractical, unfunctional, unserviceable, unusable, unworkable, useless
ant functional

noninflammable *adj syn* NONCOMBUSTIBLE, apyrous, incombustible, nonflammable, uninflammable
ant flammable, inflammable

nonliterate *adj syn* PRIMITIVE 6, preliterate

nonmaterial *adj syn* IMMATERIAL 1, asomatous, discarnate, disembodied, incorporeal, insubstantial, metaphysical, nonphysical, unembodied, unphysical
ant material

nonobligatory *adj syn* OPTIONAL, discretionary, elective, facultative
ant obligatory

no-nonsense *adj syn* SERIOUS 1, earnest, grave, sedate, sober, sobersided, solemn, somber, staid, weighty

nonpareil *n syn* PARAGON, ideal, jewel, nonesuch, phoenix

nonpartisan *adj syn* FAIR 4, equitable, impartial, indifferent, just, nondiscriminatory, objective, uncolored, undistinctive, unprejudiced
ant partisan

nonphysical *adj syn* IMMATERIAL 1, asomatous, discarnate, disembodied, incorporeal, metaphysical, nonmaterial, spiritual, unfleshly, unphysical
ant physical

non-placet *vb syn* VETO, kill, negative, ‖nix

nonplus *vb* **1** to cause to be at a total loss as to how to act or decide <was totally *nonplussed* by the economic problems>
syn beat, buffalo, get, stick, stump; *compare* PUZZLE
rel baffle, frustrate, stymie, thwart; confound, perplex; mystify; dumbfound; overcome, throw; paralyze; confuse, flurry, fluster, muddle, rattle
idiom put (*or* drive) to one's wit's end, put up a tree (*or* stump), throw on one's beam end
2 *syn* STAGGER 5, boggle, dumbfound
rel faze, rattle; baffle, balk, frustrate

nonprofessional *n syn* AMATEUR 2, abecedarian, dabbler, dilettante, smatterer, tyro, uninitiate
ant professional

nonrational *adj syn* ILLOGICAL, fallacious, invalid, irrational, mad, reasonless, sophistic, unreasonable, unreasoned
ant rational

nonrealistic *adj syn* IMPRACTICAL 1, ivory-tower, ivory-towered, ivory-towerish, unpractical, unrealistic, viewy
ant realistic

nonreligious *adj syn* IRRELIGIOUS, godless, unreligious
rel lay, profane, secular, temporal
ant religious

nonresistant *adj syn* PASSIVE 2, acquiescent, nonresisting, resigned, submissive, unresistant, unresisting, yielding
ant resistant, resisting

nonresisting *adj syn* PASSIVE 2, acquiescent, nonresistant, resigned, submissive, unresistant, unresisting, yielding
ant resistant, resisting

nonreversible *adj syn* IRREVOCABLE, irreversible, unrepealable
ant reversible

nonsectarian *adj* not affiliated with or restricted to a particular religious group <the problems facing *nonsectarian* colleges>
syn interchurch, intercreedal, interdenominational, undenominational, unsectarian
con denominational
ant sectarian

---

syn synonym(s) *rel* related word(s)
idiom idiomatic equivalent(s) *con* contrasted word(s)
ant antonym(s) * vulgar
‖ use limited; if in doubt, see a dictionary
The first word in a synonym list when printed in SMALL CAPITALS shows where there is more information about the group. For a more efficient use of this book see Explanatory Notes.

nonsense *n* **1** ***syn*** GIBBERISH 1, babble, drivel, Greek, jabber, jabberwocky, skimble-skamble
2 something uttered or proposed that seems senseless or absurd <his theories are mere *nonsense*>
syn ‖applesauce, balderdash, ‖baloney, bilge, blague, blah, blather, blatherskite, bosh, ‖bull, *bullshit, ‖bunk, bunkum, bushwa, claptrap, ‖cock, ‖crap, double-talk, ‖drip, drivel, drool, eyewash, fiddle-faddle, fiddlesticks, flapdoodle, flimflam, flummadiddle, fudge, ‖gas, gook, guff, hogwash, hokum, hooey, ‖horsefeathers, *horseshit, hot air, humbug, jazz, ‖jiggery-pokery, malarkey, meshuggaas, moonshine, piffle, pishposh, poppycock, punk, rot, rubbish, *shit, slipslop, tomfoolery, tommyrot, tosh, trash, trumpery, twaddle, whangdoodle, windbaggery
idiom stuff and nonsense

nonsuccess *n* ***syn*** FAILURE 2, defeat, insuccess, unsuccess, unsuccessfulness
ant success, successfulness

nonsymmetrical *adj* ***syn*** LOPSIDED, asymmetric, disproportionate, irregular, off-balance, overbalanced, unbalanced, unequal, uneven, unsymmetrical
ant symmetrical

nonviolent *adj* ***syn*** PACIFIC, irenic, pacificatory, pacifist, peaceable, peaceful
ant violent

noodle *n* **1** ***syn*** DUNCE, chowderhead, chucklehead, dope, ‖dumbhead, dunderhead, lame-brain, noddy, ‖schnook, ‖stupe
2 ***syn*** HEAD 1, ‖bean, ‖belfry, ‖chump, ‖coco, ‖conk, ‖dome, noddle, noggin, poll

nook *n* a secluded or sheltered place <resting in a shady *nook*>
syn byplace, cranny, niche
rel alcove, recess; cubbyhole, hole

noon *n* ***syn*** APEX 2, acme, apogee, capstone, climax, culmination, meridian, peak, pinnacle, summit

no one *pron* no person <*no one* will be allowed to leave early>
syn nobody, no man, none
idiom never a one, nobody on earth, nobody under the sun, not a blessed soul, not a soul
con all, everyman; many, some
ant everybody, everyone

noontide *n* ***syn*** APEX 2, acme, apogee, capstone, climax, culmination, meridian, peak, pinnacle, summit

noose *vb* ***syn*** HANG 2, gibbet, scrag, string (up), turn off

‖**nope** *adv* ***syn*** NO, nay, ‖nit, ‖nix
ant ‖yep, ‖yup

norm *n* ***syn*** AVERAGE, mean, median, par

normal *adj* **1** ***syn*** SANE 2, all there, compos mentis, lucid, right
2 ***syn*** GENERAL 1, common, commonplace, customary, natural, prevalent, regular, typic, typical, usual

---

syn synonym(s) ***rel*** related word(s)
idiom idiomatic equivalent(s) ***con*** contrasted word(s)
ant antonym(s) * vulgar
‖ use limited; if in doubt, see a dictionary
The first word in a synonym list when printed in SMALL CAPITALS shows where there is more information about the group. For a more efficient use of this book see Explanatory Notes.

nose *n* **1** the prominent part of the human face that bears the nostrils and covers the nasal passage <had a large *nose*>
syn beak, ‖beezer, ‖boko, ‖conk, pecker, proboscis, ‖schnozzle, smeller, ‖sneezer, ‖snitch, snoot, snout
2 ***syn*** BUSYBODY, butt-in, kibitzer, meddler, Paul Pry, pragmatist, prier (*or* pryer), quidnunc, rubberneck, snoop
3 ***syn*** GIFT 2, aptness, bent, bump, faculty, flair, genius, head, knack, talent

nose *vb* **1** ***syn*** SMELL 1, scent, sniff, ‖snift, snuff
2 ***syn*** SNOOP, busybody, mouse, poke, pry, ‖piroot, ‖snook

nose-dive *vb* ***syn*** PLUMMET, dip, drop, fall, plunge, skid, tumble

nosegay *n* ***syn*** BOUQUET 1, posy

nosey Parker *n* ***syn*** BUSYBODY, butt-in, ‖buttinsky, intermeddler, kibitzer, nose, prier (*or* pryer), quidnunc, rubberneck, snoop

Nostradamus *n* ***syn*** PROPHET, augur, auspex, forecaster, foreseer, foreteller, haruspex, predictor, prognosticator, prophesier

nostrum *n* ***syn*** PANACEA, catholicon, cure-all, elixir

nosy *adj* ***syn*** CURIOUS 2, inquisitive, inquisitorial, inquisitory, ‖nibby, peery, prying, snoopy

notability *n* **1** ***syn*** NOTABLE 1, big shot, big-timer, chief, dignitary, eminence, leader, lion, luminary, VIP
2 ***syn*** CELEBRITY 2, big name, ‖celeb, luminary, name, notable, somebody

notable *adj* **1** ***syn*** NOTEWORTHY, ‖bodacious, memorable, nameable, observable, red-letter, rubric
2 ***syn*** FAMOUS 2, celebrated, celebrious, distinguished, eminent, famed, great, illustrious, prominent, renowned

notable *n* **1** a person of consequence or prominence <*notables* of Congress and the diplomatic corps>
syn big, big boy, ‖big bug, ‖big cheese, ‖big chief, ‖biggie, big gun, ‖big noise, big shot, big-timer, ‖big wheel, bigwig, character, chief, dignitary, eminence, ‖fat cat, great gun, heavyweight, high-muck-a-muck, leader, lion, luminary, muckamuck, mugwump, nabob, nawob, notability, personage, personality, pooh-bah, pot, somebody, VIP
rel figure; baron, czar, king, magnate, mogul, prince; light, star; power
idiom big-time operator, his nibs, Mr. Big
con cipher, nobody, nonentity; functionary, underling
2 ***syn*** CELEBRITY 2, big name, ‖celeb, luminary, name, notability, somebody,

notably *adv* ***syn*** VERY 1, eminently, exceedingly, exceptionally, extremely, greatly, highly, hugely, remarkably, strikingly

notandum *n* ***syn*** NOTE 2, chit, memo, memorandum, notation

notation *n* ***syn*** NOTE 2, chit, memo, memorandum, notandum

notch *n* **1** a usually V-shaped depression in an edge or surface <a *notch* in the table>
syn indentation, indenture, nick; *compare* DEPRESSION 2
rel cut, gash, incision, score, scratch; cleft, gap, nock
2 ***syn*** DEGREE 1, grade, rung, stage, step

note *vb* ***syn*** SEE 1, descry, discern, distinguish, mark, notice, observe, perceive, remark, view

note *n* **1** ***syn*** CALL 1, cry, song
2 a written reminder <made a *note* to return the call>
syn chit, memo, memorandum, notandum, notation
3 ***syn*** REMARK 2, comment, commentary, obiter dictum, observation
rel reminder
4 ***syn*** LETTER 2, epistle, missive
5 ***syn*** NOTICE 1, attention, cognizance, heed, mark, ‖mind, observance, observation, regard, remark

noted *adj* ***syn*** WELL-KNOWN, famous, leading, notorious, popular, prominent
ant unnoted

note-perfect *adj* ***syn*** PERFECT 2, absolute, flawless, fleckless, impeccable, indefectible, unflawed

noteworthy *adj* having a quality that attracts one's attention <a *noteworthy* event>
syn ‖bodacious, memorable, nameable, notable, observable, red-letter, rubric
rel conspicuous, noticeable, outstanding, prominent, remarkable; evident, manifest, patent; exceptional, extraordinary
con blah, common, commonplace, inconsequential, insignificant, ordinary, quotidian, unimportant, unremarkable
ant unnoteworthy

nothing *n* **1** something that does not exist <his hopes were based on *nothing*>
syn naught (*or* nought), nil, ‖nix, wind
idiom nothing at all, nothing whatever
con something
2 ***syn*** ZERO 1, aught(*or* ought), cipher, goose egg, naught (*or* nought), zilch
3 ***syn*** NONENTITY, cipher, insignificancy, nobody, nullity, whiffet, whippersnapper, whipster, zero, zilch
idiom (the) little end of nothing whittled down to a point

nothing *adj* ***syn*** WORTHLESS 1, draffy, drossy, good-for-nothing, inutile, ‖no-account, no-good, unworthy, valueless

nothingness *n* the quality or state of being nothing <the house was blown into *nothingness* by the force of the explosion>
syn nada, nihility, nonexistence, nullity, vacuity
rel emptiness; vacuum, void
con concreteness, solidity, substantiality; materiality, reality
ant somethingness

notice *n* **1** a noting of or concerning oneself with something <take *notice* of the gathering clouds>
syn attention, cognizance, ear, heed, mark, ‖mind, note, observance, observation, regard, remark
rel care, concern, consideration, thought; apprehension, grasp, understanding
con disinterest, disregard, indifference, unconcern; carelessness, heedlessness, unmindfulness; insouciance, negligence, recklessness
2 ***syn*** MEMORANDUM 2, directive, memo
3 ***syn*** CRITICISM, comment, critique, review, reviewal

notice *vb* ***syn*** SEE 1, descry, discern, distinguish, espy, mark, note, observe, perceive, remark
rel acknowledge, recognize; advert, allude, refer
con disregard, ignore, neglect, overlook, slight

noticeable *adj* attracting or compelling notice or attention <they both showed a *noticeable* aversion to his company>
syn arresting, arrestive, conspicuous, eye-catching, marked, outstanding, pointed, prominent, remarkable, salient, sensational, signal, striking
rel notable, noteworthy; evident, manifest, obvious, palpable, patent; spectacular
con obscure, vague; concealed, hidden, shrouded; insignificant, undistinguished
ant unnoticeable

notify *vb* ***syn*** INFORM 2, acquaint, advise, apprise, clue (*or* clew), fill in, post, tell, warn, wise (up)
rel announce, broadcast, declare, proclaim, promulgate, publish; disclose, discover, divulge, reveal

notion *n* **1** ***syn*** IDEA, apprehension, conceit, concept, conception, image, impression, intellection, perception, thought
2 ***syn*** CAPRICE, bee, boutade, conceit, crotchet, fancy, freak, humor, maggot, whim
3 ***syn*** HINT 1, clue, cue, indication, inkling, intimation, suggestion, telltale, wind

notional *adj* **1** ***syn*** CONCEPTUAL, ideal, ideational
2 ***syn*** IMAGINARY 1, fancied, fanciful, imagined, shadowy
ant real

notoriety *n* ***syn*** FAME 2, celebrity, éclat, renown, ‖rep, reputation, repute
rel ballyhoo, promotion, propaganda, publicity

notorious *adj* **1** ***syn*** WELL-KNOWN, famous, leading, noted, popular, prominent
2 ***syn*** INFAMOUS 1, ill-famed, opprobrious

notwithstanding *prep* ***syn*** AGAINST 4, despite, in spite of, regardless of

notwithstanding *adv* ***syn*** HOWEVER, after all, howbeit, nevertheless, nonetheless, still, still and all, though, withal, yet

nourish *vb* **1** ***syn*** NURSE 1, breast-feed, suckle
2 ***syn*** NURSE 2, cherish, cultivate, foster, nursle, nurture

nourishing *adj* ***syn*** NUTRITIOUS, nutrient, nutrimental, nutritive
ant unnourishing

nourishment *n* ***syn*** FOOD 2, aliment, nutriment, pabulum, pap, sustenance
rel keep, living, maintenance, support

nouveau riche *n* ***syn*** UPSTART, arriviste, parvenu, roturier

novel *adj* ***syn*** NEW 1, fresh, modern, modernistic, neoteric, newfangled, new-fashioned, new-sprung, recent
rel different, odd, peculiar, singular, special, strange, uncommon, unfamiliar, unique, unusual
con customary, habitual, usual; common, familiar, ordinary

---

syn synonym(s) ***rel*** related word(s)
idiom idiomatic equivalent(s) ***con*** contrasted word(s)
ant antonym(s) * vulgar
‖ use limited; if in doubt, see a dictionary
The first word in a synonym list when printed in SMALL CAPITALS shows where there is more information about the group. For a more efficient use of this book see Explanatory Notes.

novelty *n* **1** ***syn*** CHANGE 2, innovation, mutation, permutation, sport, vicissitude
con old story
2 ***syn*** KNICKKNACK, bauble, bibelot, curio, gewgaw, gimcrack, objet d'art, trifle, trinket, whatnot

novice *n* one who is just entering a field in which he has no previous experience <a *novice* in the theater —had never even had a walk-on role>
syn apprentice, beginner, boot, colt, fledgling, freshman, neophyte, newcomer, novitiate, prentice, punk, recruit, rookie, tenderfoot, tyro
rel amateur; cub; postulant, probationer; greenhorn, greeny; learner, student, trainee, undergraduate
con expert, pro, professional
ant doyen, old hand, old-timer, veteran

novitiate *n* ***syn*** NOVICE, apprentice, beginner, colt, freshman, neophyte, newcomer, rookie, tenderfoot, tyro

now *adv* **1** ***syn*** TODAY, nowadays, presently
ant then
2 ***syn*** AWAY 3, at once, directly, first off, forthwith, immediately, instanter, instantly, right away, straightway

now *conj* ***syn*** BECAUSE, as, as long as, 'cause, considering, for, inasmuch as, seeing, since, whereas

now *n* ***syn*** PRESENT, today

nowadays *adv* ***syn*** TODAY, now, presently

now and again *adv* ***syn*** SOMETIMES, at times, ‖betimes, ever and again, ever and anon, here and there, now and then, once and again, ‖otherwhile

now and then *adv* ***syn*** SOMETIMES, at times, ‖betimes, ever and again, ever and anon, here and there, now and again, once and again, ‖otherwhile

noxious *adj* **1** ***syn*** UNWHOLESOME 1, insalubrious, insalutary, noisome, sickly, unhealthful, unhealthy, unsalutary
ant wholesome; sanitary
2 ***syn*** PERNICIOUS, baneful, deadly, pestiferous, pestilent, pestilential
rel fetid, putrid, noisome, stinking
ant innocuous, innoxious

nuance *n* ***syn*** GRADATION, shade
rel dash, soupçon, suggestion, suspicion, tinge, touch; nicety, refinement, subtlety

nub *n* ***syn*** SUBSTANCE 2, core, crux, gist, kernel, meat, nubbin, pith, short, upshot

nubbin *n* ***syn*** SUBSTANCE 2, burden, core, crux, gist, kernel, matter, meat, nub, upshot

nubilous *adj* **1** ***syn*** OVERCAST, cloudy, ‖dowly, dull, heavy, lowering (*or* louring), overclouded
2 ***syn*** OBSCURE 3, ambiguous, double-edged, double-faced, equivocal, tenebrous, uncertain, unclear, unintelligible, vague

nucleus *n* ***syn*** SEED 2, bud, embryo, germ, spark

nude *adj* **1** ***syn*** BARE 1, bald, naked
con covered
2 not wearing any clothes <all the boys liked to swim *nude*>
syn au naturel, *bare-assed, buff-bare, mother-naked, naked, raw, stark, stark-naked, stripped, unclad, unclothed, undressed
rel peeled, uncovered; dishabille, garmentless, unattired, unrobed
idiom ‖buck naked, in a state of nature, in one's birthday suit, in one's skin, in the altogether, in the buff, in the raw, stripped to the buff, without a stitch on, without a stitch to one's name
con attired, robed; decent; covered
ant clad, clothed, dressed

nudge *vb* ***syn*** POKE 1, dig, jab, jog, prod, punch

nudnick *n* ***syn*** PEST 2, nuisance, pesterer

nugatory *adj* ***syn*** VAIN 1, empty, hollow, idle, otiose

nugget *n* ***syn*** LUMP 1, chunk, clod, clump, gob, hunch, hunk, wad

nuisance *n* **1** ***syn*** PEST 2, nudnick, pesterer
2 ***syn*** ANNOYANCE 3, besetment, bother, botheration, botherment, exasperation, irritant, pest, pester, plague

null *adj* having no legal or binding force or validity <a *null* ballot>
syn bad, invalid, null and void, void
rel ineffective, ineffectual, inefficacious, useless, worthless
con acceptable, good, valid

null and void *adj* ***syn*** NULL, bad, invalid, void

nullify *vb* ***syn*** ABOLISH 1, abate, abrogate, annihilate, annul, invalidate, negate, quash, undo, vitiate
rel counteract, neutralize; compensate, counterbalance, countervail, offset; confine, limit, restrict

nullity *n* **1** ***syn*** NOTHINGNESS, nada, nihility, nonexistence, vacuity
2 ***syn*** NONENTITY, cipher, insignificancy, nobody, nothing, whiffet, whippersnapper, whipster, zero, zilch

numb *adj* **1** devoid of sensation or feeling <my arm is *numb*>
syn anesthetized, asleep, benumbed, dead, deadened, insensible, insensitive, numbed, senseless, unfeeling
rel insensate, insentient, stupefied; comatose, unconscious
con alert; aware, conscious; sensitive
2 ***syn*** INDIFFERENT 2, aloof, casual, detached, disinterested, incurious, remote, unconcerned, uncurious, uninterested

numb *vb* ***syn*** DEADEN 1, benumb, blunt, desensitize, dull, mull
rel chill, freeze, frost

numbed *adj* ***syn*** NUMB 1, anesthetized, asleep, benumbed, dead, deadened, insensible, insensitive, senseless, unfeeling

number *n* a character by which an arithmetical value is designated <you must add the *numbers* of the first column>
syn chiffer, cipher, digit, figure, integer, numeral, whole number

number *vb* **1** ***syn*** COUNT 1, enumerate, numerate, tale, tally, tell

---

syn synonym(s) *rel* related word(s)
idiom idiomatic equivalent(s) *con* contrasted word(s)
ant antonym(s) * vulgar
‖ use limited; if in doubt, see a dictionary
The first word in a synonym list when printed in SMALL CAPITALS shows where there is more information about the group. For a more efficient use of this book see Explanatory Notes.

2 *syn* AMOUNT 1, add up, aggregate, come, run (to *or* into), sum (to *or* into), total

numberless *adj* *syn* INNUMERABLE, countless, innumerous, uncountable, uncounted, unnumberable, unnumbered, untold
ant numberable

number one *adj* 1 *syn* CHIEF 2, capital, ‖cock, dominant, main, major, outstanding, predominant, preeminent, stellar
2 *syn* EXCELLENT, A1, blue-ribbon, first-class, first-rate, first-string, five-star, front-rank, Grade A, superior

numeral *n* *syn* NUMBER, chiffer, cipher, digit, figure, integer, whole number

numerate *vb* 1 *syn* ENUMERATE 2, list, tick off
2 *syn* COUNT 1, enumerate, number, tale, tally, tell

numerous *adj* *syn* MANY, legion, multifarious, multitudinal, multitudinous, populous, ‖several, sundry, various, voluminous
rel big, great, large

numinous *adj* 1 *syn* SUPERNATURAL 1, miraculous, preternatural, superhuman, superior, supermundane, suprahuman, supramundane, supranatural, unearthly
2 *syn* SACRED 2, spiritual
3 *syn* SPIRITUAL 4
4 *syn* MYSTERIOUS, arcane, cabalistic, impenetrable, inscrutable, mysterial, mystic, unaccountable, unguessed, unknowable

numskull *n* *syn* DUNCE, blockhead, bonehead, clodpate, hammerhead, knucklehead, muttonhead, thickhead, thickskull, woodenhead

numskulled *adj* *syn* STUPID 1, beefheaded, beetleheaded, blockheaded, dense, fatheaded, hammerheaded, thick, thickheaded, thick-witted

nuptial *adj* *syn* MATRIMONIAL, conjugal, connubial, hymeneal, marital, married, spousal, wedded

nuptial *n, usu* **nuptials** *pl* *syn* WEDDING, bridal, espousal(s), marriage, spousal

nurse *n* *syn* NURSEMAID, ‖amah, ‖ayah, nana, ‖nanny, nurserymaid

nurse *vb* 1 to feed from the breast <decided to *nurse* her baby>
syn breast-feed, nourish, suckle
rel bottle-feed
2 to promote the growth, development, or progress of <*nursed* the flame into a blaze>
syn cherish, cultivate, foster, nourish, nursle, nurture
rel feed; advance, forward, further, promote; humor, indulge, pamper
con check, hold back, retard, slow
3 *syn* MINISTER (to), care (for), mother, serve, wait (on)

nursemaid *n* one who is regularly employed to look after children <the *nursemaid* had three children in her charge>
syn ‖amah, ‖ayah, nana, ‖nanny, nurse, nurserymaid
rel babysitter, ‖minder, sitter; chaperon; governess

nurserymaid *n* *syn* NURSEMAID, ‖amah, ‖ayah, nana, ‖nanny, nurse

nursle *vb* *syn* NURSE 2, cherish, cultivate, foster, nourish, nurture

nurture *n* *syn* FOOD 1, comestibles, ‖eats, edibles, feed, grub, provender, provisions, viands, victuals

nurture *vb* *syn* NURSE 2, cherish, cultivate, foster, nourish, nursle
rel bring up, raise, rear; discipline, educate, school, train; back, bolster, support, sustain, uphold
con disregard, ignore, neglect, overlook, pass over, slight

nut *n* 1 *syn* PROBLEM 2, issue, question
‖2 *syn* HEAD 1, ‖bean, ‖belfry, ‖coconut, ‖conk, ‖dome, noddle, noggin, noodle, poll
3 *syn* CRACKPOT, crackbrain, crank, cuckoo, ding-a-ling, harebrain, kook, lunatic, screwball
4 *syn* LUNATIC 1, bedlamite, dement, loon, loony, madling, madman, maniac, non compos, Tom o' Bedlam
5 *syn* ENTHUSIAST, bigot, bug, fanatic, fiend, freak, maniac, zealot

‖**nuthouse** *n* *syn* ASYLUM 3, booby hatch, ‖bughouse, crazy house, loony bin, madhouse

nutriculture *n* *syn* HYDROPONICS, aquiculture

nutrient *adj* *syn* NUTRITIOUS, nourishing, nutrimental, nutritive

nutriment *n* *syn* FOOD 2, aliment, nourishment, pabulum, pap, sustenance
rel bread, bread and butter, keep, livelihood, living, maintenance, subsistence, support

nutrimental *adj* *syn* NUTRITIOUS, nourishing, nutrient, nutritive

nutritional *adj* *syn* NUTRITIVE 1, alimentary, alimentative

nutritious *adj* promoting growth and repairing natural waste <*nutritious* food>
syn nourishing, nutrient, nutrimental, nutritive
rel good, healthful, salubrious, salutary, wholesome; balanced
con indigestible; bad, insalubrious, unhealthful, unwholesome
ant innutritious

nutritive *adj* 1 relating to or concerned with nutrition <*nutritive* organs of the body>
syn alimentary, alimentative, nutritional
rel digestive, metabolic; constructive, creative, formative, productive
2 *syn* NUTRITIOUS, nourishing, nutrient, nutrimental

nuts *adj* *syn* INSANE 1, ‖batty, cracked, crazy, daft, demented, mad, screwy, unbalanced, wacky

nutshell *vb* *syn* EPITOMIZE 1, condense, digest, inventory, sum, summarize, summate, sum up, synopsize

nutsy *adj* *syn* INSANE 1, ‖batty, bedlamite, cracked, crazed, crazy, daft, demented, lunatic, nuts

nutty *adj* 1 *syn* ENTHUSIASTIC, ‖buggy, ‖bugs, gung ho, keen, warm, zealous

---

syn synonym(s)	*rel* related word(s)
idiom idiomatic equivalent(s)	*con* contrasted word(s)
ant antonym(s)	* vulgar

‖ use limited; if in doubt, see a dictionary
The first word in a synonym list when printed in SMALL CAPITALS shows where there is more information about the group. For a more efficient use of this book see Explanatory Notes.

2 ***syn*** INSANE 1, ‖batty, bedlamite, cracked, crazed, crazy, daft, demented, lunatic, nuts

nuzzle *vb* ***syn*** SNUGGLE, burrow, ‖croodle, cuddle, nestle, ‖snudge, snug, ‖snuzzle

nymph *n* ***syn*** DOXY 1, ‖chippy, floozy, grisette, light-o'-love, nymphet, party girl, roundheel, tart, ‖tootsie

nymphet *n* ***syn*** DOXY 1, ‖chippy, floozy, grisette, light-o'-love, nymph, party girl, roundheel, tart, ‖tootsie

---

syn synonym(s) ***rel*** related word(s)
idiom idiomatic equivalent(s) ***con*** contrasted word(s)
ant antonym(s) * vulgar
‖ use limited; if in doubt, see a dictionary
The first word in a synonym list when printed in SMALL CAPITALS shows where there is more information about the group. For a more efficient use of this book see Explanatory Notes.

O

oaf *n* **1** ***syn*** DUNCE, boob, booby, chump, dolt, dolthead, fathead, goof, ||goon, lunkhead
2 a big clumsy, usually slow-witted person <an *oaf* who bumped into everything he passed>
syn bohunk, ||gaum, gawk, klutz, lobster, looby, lout, lubber, ||lug, lummox, lump, lumpkin, meathead, palooka, slouch
rel ||baboon, beast, bruiser, brute, bull, gorilla, hulk, missing link, ox; clod, clown, dub, galoot, slob; blunderbuss, blunderer, blunderhead

oar *vb* ***syn*** ROW, paddle, pull

oater *n* ***syn*** WESTERN, horse opera

oath *n* ***syn*** SWEARWORD, curse, cuss, cussword, expletive, swear

obdurate *adj* **1** ***syn*** UNFEELING 2, callous, coldhearted, hard-boiled, hardhearted, heartless, stonyhearted, uncompassionate, unemotional, unsympathetic
con tender
2 ***syn*** INFLEXIBLE 2, adamant, brassbound, dogged, inexorable, relentless, rigid, unbending, uncompromising, unyielding
rel mulish, stiff-necked; immovable
con relenting, submitting

obedient *adj* submissive to the will, guidance, or control of another <children should always be *obedient* to their parents>
syn amenable, biddable, docile, ||docious, tractable
rel acquiescent, compliant, sheeplike, submissive, yielding; duteous, dutiful, loyal; law-abiding; obeisant, subservient
con insubordinate, rebellious; contrary, froward, perverse, wayward, willful; headstrong, intractable, recalcitrant, refractory, uncontrollable, ungovernable, unruly
ant contumacious, disobedient

obeisance *n* ***syn*** HONOR 1, deference, homage, reverence
rel allegiance, fealty, loyalty

obeisant *adj* ***syn*** SUBSERVIENT 2, menial, obsequious, servile, slavish

obese *adj* ***syn*** FAT 2, corpulent, fleshy, gross, heavy, overweight, porcine, portly, stout, upholstered
ant skinny

obesity *n* a condition characterized by excessive bodily fat <could barely walk because of his *obesity*>
syn adiposity, corpulence, fatness, fleshiness
rel chubbiness, chunkiness, embonpoint, grossness, plumpness, portliness, pudginess, rotundity, stockiness, stoutness, tubbiness
con lankiness, leanness, scrawniness, slenderness, slimness
ant skinniness

obey *vb* to act or behave in conformity with (as an order) or in duty to (as a parent) <*obey* a superior's order>
syn comply, conform, follow, keep, mind, observe
rel bow, defer, submit, yield; accede, acquiesce, agree, assent; fulfill, satisfy; carry out; heed, regard
idiom abide by
con break, disregard, transgress, violate; command, order
ant disobey

obfuscate *vb* ***syn*** OBSCURE, adumbrate, becloud, befog, darken, dim, gloom, murk, overcast, shadow
ant clarify

obit *n* ***syn*** OBITUARY, necrology

obiter *adv* ***syn*** INCIDENTALLY 2, by the bye, by the way, in passing, parenthetically

obiter dictum *n* ***syn*** REMARK 2, comment, commentary, note, observation

obituary *n* a notice of a person's death usually with a short biographical account <always read the *obituaries* in the paper>
syn necrology, obit

object *n* **1** ***syn*** THING 3, article
rel doodad; gadget
2 ***syn*** THING 4, being, entity, individual, material, matter, stuff, substance
3 ***syn*** BODY 4, bulk, mass, volume
4 ***syn*** VIEW 6
5 ***syn*** USE 4, duty, function, goal, mark, objective, purpose, target

object *vb* **1** to oppose by arguing against <*objecting* because the evidence was unclear>
syn except, expostulate, inveigh (against), kick, protest, remonstrate
rel balk, boggle, demur, dissent, jib, stickle; complain; criticize; challenge; spurn; rail, rant, rave, storm
con accede, agree, assent, consent; accredit, approve, sanction
ant acquiesce
2 ***syn*** DISAPPROVE 1, deprecate, discommend, discountenance, disesteem, disfavor, frown

objectify *vb* ***syn*** EMBODY 1, exteriorize, externalize, incarnate, manifest, materialize, personalize, personify, personize, substantiate

objection *n* ***syn*** DEMUR 2, challenge, demurral, demurrer, difficulty, protest, question, remonstrance, remonstration

objectionable *adj* arousing or likely to arouse objection <the language in that movie is *objectionable*>
syn exceptionable, ill-favored, inadmissible, unacceptable, undesirable, unwanted, unwelcome
rel abhorrent, loathsome, offensive, repellent, repugnant, repulsive, revolting; disagreeable, distasteful, invidious, obnoxious, unpleasant; unfit, unsuitable; censurable, reprehensible

---

syn synonym(s) ***rel*** related word(s)
idiom idiomatic equivalent(s) ***con*** contrasted word(s)
ant antonym(s) * vulgar
|| use limited; if in doubt, see a dictionary
The first word in a synonym list when printed in SMALL CAPITALS shows where there is more information about the group. For a more efficient use of this book see Explanatory Notes.

con acceptable, agreeable, gratifying, pleasant, pleasing, welcome
ant unobjectionable

objective *adj* **1** ***syn*** MATERIAL 1, corporeal, gross, phenomenal, physical, sensible, substantial, tangible
rel external, outer, outside, outward
ant subjective
2 ***syn*** FAIR 4, dispassionate, equitable, impartial, impersonal, nondiscriminatory, unbiased, uncolored, unprejudiced, unprepossessed
ant subjective

objective *n* **1** ***syn*** AMBITION 2, aim, goal, mark, quaesitum, target
2 ***syn*** USE 4, duty, function, goal, mark, object, purpose, target

objectless *adj* ***syn*** RANDOM, aimless, designless, haphazard, hit-or-miss, indiscriminate, irregular, purposeless, unconsidered, unplanned

objet d'art *n* ***syn*** KNICKKNACK, bauble, bibelot, curio, gewgaw, gimcrack, novelty, trifle, trinket, whatnot

objurgate *vb* ***syn*** EXECRATE 1, anathematize, curse, damn
rel castigate, censure

obligated *adj* ***syn*** INDEBTED, beholden, obliged

obligation *n* **1** ***syn*** OCCASION 3, call, cause, necessity
2 something one is bound to do or forbear <it is our *obligation* to obey the law>
syn charge, commitment, committal, devoir, duty, must, need, ought, ‖right
rel compulsion, constraint, restraint; burden, requirement, responsibility; business, part, place
con choice, discretion, free will, option; decision, determination, pleasure, will
3 ***syn*** INDEBTEDNESS 1, arrearage, debt, liability

obligatory *adj* ***syn*** MANDATORY, compulsatory, compulsory, imperative, imperious, required
ant nonobligatory

oblige *vb* **1** ***syn*** FORCE 2, coerce, compel, concuss, constrain, make, shotgun
2 to do a service or courtesy <you will *oblige* me greatly if you will get there on time>
syn accommodate, convenience, favor
rel gratify, please; avail, benefit, profit; aid, assist, contribute, help
con bother, discommode, incommode, inconvenience, trouble
ant disoblige

obliged *adj* **1** ***syn*** GRATEFUL 1, thankful
2 ***syn*** INDEBTED, beholden, obligated

obliging *adj* ***syn*** AMIABLE 1, complaisant, easy, good-humored, good-natured, good-tempered, lenient, mild
ant disobliging

oblique *adj* **1** ***syn*** INCLINED 3, inclining, leaning, pitched, pitching, sloped, sloping, tilted, tilting, tipped
2 ***syn*** INDIRECT 1, circuitous, circular, collateral, roundabout
ant straight

obliquely *adv* ***syn*** ASIDE 1, aslant, aslope, sideways, sidewise, slantingly, slantly, slantways, slantwise, ‖slaunchways
ant straight

obliterate *vb* ***syn*** ERASE, black (out), blot out, cancel, delete, efface, expunge, wipe (out), x (out)

oblivion *n* a state of forgetting or the fact of having forgotten <the *oblivion* of sleep>
syn forgetfulness, lethe, obliviousness
rel nirvana; insensibleness
con alertness, awareness, consciousness; memory, recall, recalling, recollection, remembrance

oblivious *adj* **1** ***syn*** FORGETFUL, unmindful, unwitting
rel absorbed, unaware, unconscious
idiom turned off
2 ***syn*** IGNORANT 2, incognizant, inconversant, unacquainted, unaware, unfamiliar, uninformed, uninstructed, unknowing, unwitting

obliviousness *n* ***syn*** OBLIVION, forgetfulness, lethe

obloquy *n* **1** ***syn*** ABUSE, billingsgate, contumely, invective, scurrility, vituperation
2 ***syn*** ANIMADVERSION, aspersion, reflection, slam, slur, stricture
3 ***syn*** DISGRACE, discredit, disesteem, dishonor, disrepute, ignominy, infamy, odium, opprobrium, shame

obnoxious *adj* **1** ***syn*** LIABLE 2, exposed, open, prone, sensitive, subject, susceptible
ant unobnoxious
2 ***syn*** REPUGNANT 1, abhorrent, invidious, repellent, revulsive
con congenial, likable, simpatico
ant grateful; unobnoxious

obscene *adj* **1** ***syn*** OFFENSIVE, disgusting, hideous, horrible, nauseating, noisome, repellent, repugnant, sickening, vile
2 marked by the use of words regarded as taboo in polite usage <knew all the *obscene* expressions for the genitalia>
syn barnyard, coarse, crude, crusty, dirty, fescennine, filthy, foul, gross, indecent, nasty, paw, profane, rank, raunchy, ‖raw, rocky, scatological, scurrilous, smutty, vulgar; *compare* RISQUÉ
rel bawdy, ribald, smoking-room; impure, lascivious, lewd, warm; lurid, pornographic, salacious, scabrous, sultry; earthy, rich; unprintable; foulmouthed
con acceptable, proper, tolerable; appropriate, fit, suitable; clean, decent, decorous, seemly

obscure *adj* **1** ***syn*** DARK 1, caliginous, dim, dusk, dusky, gloomy, lightless, murky, tenebrous, unilluminated
rel clouded, cloudy, fuliginous; shadowy, shady, umbrageous
con clear, lucid; bright, brilliant, luminous
2 withdrawn from the main centers of human activity <was exiled to an *obscure* Siberian village>
syn devious, lonesome, out-of-the-way, remote, removed, retired, secret
rel distant, far, far-off; close, hidden, odd, secluded, sequestered, solitary; blind; inaccessible
idiom back of beyond, off the beaten track (*or* path), in the boondocks (*or* sticks)

---

syn synonym(s) — *rel* related word(s)
idiom idiomatic equivalent(s) — *con* contrasted word(s)
ant antonym(s) — * vulgar
‖ use limited; if in doubt, see a dictionary
The first word in a synonym list when printed in SMALL CAPITALS shows where there is more information about the group. For a more efficient use of this book see Explanatory Notes.

con central; urban; populous

3 not readily understood or grasped <an *obscure* textual reference>

syn ambiguous, amphibological, double-edged, double-faced, dusky, equivocal, murky, nubilous, opaque, sibylline, tenebrous, uncertain, unclear, unexplicit, unintelligible, vague; *compare* CRYPTIC, FAINT 2

rel difficult, incomprehensible, inexplicable, puzzling, unfathomable; illegible; abstruse, Delphian, enigmatic, esoteric, inscrutable, mysterious, mystic, mystical; inconclusive, indecisive, indefinite

con definite, explicit, obvious; clear, express, unambiguous, unequivocal

ant lucid

4 *syn* INCONSPICUOUS, unconspicuous, unemphatic, unnoticeable

rel humble, lowly, minor, unimportant

5 lacking the prominence, showiness, or worth by which attention might be attracted <an *obscure* Roman poet>

syn nameless, uncelebrated, unfamed, unheard-of, unknown, unnoted, unrenowned

rel inconspicuous; minor, undistinguished, unimportant

con celebrated, distinguished, named, notable, noted, noteworthy, renowned, well-known

ant famed, famous

6 *syn* FAINT 2, blear, bleary, dim, ill-defined, indistinct, shadowy, unclear, undefined, vague

ant clear

obscure *vb* to make dark, dim, or indistinct <fog *obscured* our view>

syn adumbrate, becloud, bedim, befog, cloud, darken, dim, dislimn, eclipse, fog, gloom, haze, mist, murk, obfuscate, overcast, overcloud, overshadow, shadow

rel blear, blur, fuzz; blind, conceal, dim out, hide, screen, shade, shroud; bemask, camouflage, cloak, cover, disguise, mask, veil; belie, falsify, misrepresent

con brighten, light (up), lighten; clarify, enlighten; elucidate, exemplify, explain

ant illuminate, illumine

obscured *adj syn* ULTERIOR, buried, concealed, covert, guarded, hidden, privy, shrouded

obsequious *adj syn* SUBSERVIENT 2, menial, obeisant, servile, slavish

rel deferential; parasitic, sycophantic, toadying

con self-assertive

observable *adj* **1** *syn* PERCEPTIBLE, appreciable, detectable, discernible, palpable, sensible, tangible

ant unobservable

2 *syn* NOTEWORTHY, ‖bodacious, memorable, nameable, notable, red-letter, rubric

observance *n* **1** *syn* RITE 2, ceremonial, ceremony, formality, liturgy, ritual, service

2 *syn* NOTICE 1, attention, cognizance, heed, mark, ‖mind, note, observation, regard, remark

ant nonobservance, unobservance

observant *adj* **1** *syn* ATTENTIVE 1, advertent, arrect, heedful, intentive, regardful

rel awake

ant unobservant

2 *syn* MINDFUL 2, heedful, observative, observing, regardful, thoughtful

observation *n* **1** *syn* NOTICE 1, attention, cognizance, heed, mark, ‖mind, note, observance, regard, remark

2 *syn* REMARK 2, comment, commentary, note, obiter dictum

observative *adj syn* MINDFUL 2, heedful, observant, observing, regardful, thoughtful

observatory *n syn* LOOKOUT 2, outlook, overlook

observe *vb* **1** *syn* OBEY, comply, conform, follow, keep, mind

2 *syn* KEEP 2, celebrate, commemorate, solemnize

rel revere, reverence, venerate

ant break, violate

3 *syn* SEE 1, behold, discern, distinguish, mark, mind, note, notice, perceive, view

4 *syn* REMARK 2, animadvert, comment, commentate

observer *n syn* SPECTATOR, beholder, by-sitter, bystander, eyewitness, looker-on, onlooker, viewer, watcher, witness

observing *adj syn* MINDFUL 2, heedful, observant, observative, regardful, thoughtful

ant unobserving

obsessed *adj* preoccupied intensely or abnormally <*obsessed* with cleanliness>

syn hagridden, hipped, queer

rel bewitched, dominated, gripped, held, possessed, prepossessed; bedeviled, beset, dogged, harassed, haunted, plagued, troubled; overcome

idiom have on the brain

con detached, unconcerned, uninterested; indifferent, neutral; cool, easy-going

obsession *n syn* FETISH 2, fixation, mania, thing

obsolesce *vb syn* OUTDATE, antiquate, obsolete, outmode, superannuate

obsolete *adj* no longer active or in use <*obsolete* social customs>

syn dead, disused, extinct, outmoded, outworn, passé, superseded; *compare* ANCIENT 1

rel old-fashioned, old hat, old-time, old-timey, out-of-date, unfashionable; dusty, fusty, moldy, moth-eaten, musty, stale, timeworn

idiom behind the times

con contemporary, modern, new-fashioned, up-to-date, up-to-the-minute; novel, original, unique

ant current

obsolete *vb syn* OUTDATE, antiquate, obsolesce, outmode, superannuate

obstacle *n* something that seriously hampers action or progress <lack of education is an *obstacle* to advancement>

syn bar, Chinese wall, crimp, hamper, hurdle, impediment, mountain, obstruction, rub, snag, stumbling block, traverse

---

rel clog, encumbrance, handicap, hindrance; bump, difficulty, hardship, vicissitude; catch, hitch; disincentive
con aid, assist, assistance, help
ant advantage

obstinate *adj* unwilling to submit (as to reason or control) <he had an *obstinate* determination to live as he pleased>
syn bullheaded, closed-minded, deaf, hardheaded, headstrong, incompliant, intractable, intransigent, muleheaded, muley, mulish, pertinacious, perverse, pervicacious, pigheaded, refractory, self-willed, ‖sot, stiff, stiff-necked, stubborn, tough, unpliable, unpliant, unyielding, willful, wrongheaded; *compare* UNRULY 1
rel resistant, unsubmissive, withstanding; contrary, crabbed, recalcitrant, renitent; inexorable, inflexible, obdurate; opinionated; resolute, staunch, steadfast, unbudging
con acquiescent, complaisant, compliant; submissive, yielding; agreeable, cooperative, willing
ant pliable, pliant

obstipated *adj syn* CONSTIPATED, astricted, bound, costive

obstreperous *adj* **1** *syn* VOCIFEROUS, blatant, boisterous, clamorous, ‖dinsome, loudmouthed, multivocal, openmouthed, strident, vociferant
2 *syn* DISOBEDIENT, naughty, unruly

obstruct *vb* **1** *syn* FILL 1, block, choke, clog, close, congest, occlude, plug, stop, stopper
2 *syn* HINDER, bar, block, brake, dam, impede, overslaugh
3 *syn* SCREEN 3, block out, close, shroud, shut off, shut out

obstruction *n syn* OBSTACLE, bar, Chinese wall, hamper, hurdle, impediment, mountain, rub, snag, stumbling block

obtain *vb syn* GET 1, acquire, annex, chalk up, gain, have, pick up, procure, secure, win

obtainable *adj* **1** *syn* AVAILABLE 1, attainable, disponible, gettable, procurable, securable
rel derivable
2 *syn* PURCHASABLE 1, available, on offer

obtrude *vb* **1** *syn* IMPOSE 5, infringe, intrude, presume
2 *syn* INTRUDE 1, butt in, chisel (in), cut in, horn in, intertrude

obtrusive *adj syn* IMPERTINENT 2, busy, intrusive, meddlesome, ‖nebby, officious, polypragmatic
ant unobtrusive

obtund *vb syn* DULL 3, blunt, disedge, turn

obtuse *adj syn* DULL 6, blunt

obviate *vb syn* PREVENT 2, avert, deter, forestall, forfend, preclude, rule out, stave off, ward
rel anticipate; interfere, interpose, intervene

---

syn synonym(s) *rel* related word(s)
idiom idiomatic equivalent(s) *con* contrasted word(s)
ant antonym(s) * vulgar
‖ use limited; if in doubt, see a dictionary
The first word in a synonym list when printed in SMALL CAPITALS shows where there is more information about the group. For a more efficient use of this book see Explanatory Notes.

obvious *adj syn* CLEAR 5, apparent, distinct, evident, manifest, palpable, patent, plain, unambiguous, unequivocal
ant abstruse, obscure; unobvious

occasion *n* **1** *syn* OPPORTUNITY, break, chance, look-in, opening, shot, show, squeak, time
2 *syn* CAUSE 1, antecedent, determinant, reason
3 something that provides a reason for something else <there is no *occasion* for alarm>
syn call, cause, necessity, obligation
rel basis, foundation, ground, warrant; justification, right; excuse
4 *syn* OCCURRENCE, circumstance, episode, event, go, happening, incident, thing
5 a particular point of time at which something takes place <we always spoke, but on that *occasion* we didn't>
syn instant, moment, time, while
idiom point in time
6 *syn* NEED 3, demand, use
7 occasions *pl syn* BUSINESS 8, affair, concern, lookout, palaver
8 *syn* EVENT 2, milepost, milestone

occasion *vb syn* GENERATE 3, breed, cause, engender, hatch, induce, muster (up), produce, provoke, work up

occasional *adj syn* INFREQUENT, few, rare, scarce, seldom, semioccasional, sporadic, uncommon, unfrequent
rel incidental; casual, random
con accustomed, habitual, usual; constant, continual, continuous
ant customary

occasionally *adv* on a few occasions <*occasionally* she'll walk instead of drive>
syn infrequently, irregularly, on occasion, sporadically, uncommonly; *compare* SOMETIMES
rel off and on, once or twice
idiom every now and then, from time to time, ‖once in a way, once in a while
con continually, continuously, frequently; commonly, customarily, habitually, often; hardly ever, rarely, scarcely, seldom; never
ant constantly

occlude *vb syn* FILL 1, block, choke, clog, close, congest, obstruct, plug, stop, stopper

occult *vb syn* HIDE, bury, ‖bush up, cache, conceal, ‖ditch, ensconce, screen, secrete, stash

occult *adj syn* RECONDITE, abstruse, acroamatic, deep, esoteric, heavy, hermetic, orphic, profound, secret
rel arcane, mysterious; cabalistic, mystical, supernatural; eerie, unearthly, weird

occupancy *n syn* HABITATION 1, inhabitancy, inhabitation, occupation, residence, settlement

occupant *n syn* INHABITANT, denizen, dweller, habitant, indweller, liver, resident, ‖residenter, resider

occupation *n* **1** *syn* WORK 1, business, calling, employment, job, line, pursuit, ‖racket
2 *syn* HABITATION 1, inhabitancy, inhabitation, occupancy, residence, settlement

occupiable *adj syn* LIVABLE 1, habitable, inhabitable, lodgeable, tenantable

occupied *adj syn* BUSY 1, employed, engaged, working
ant unoccupied

occupy *vb* **1** *syn* ENGAGE 4, busy, engross, immerse, soak

2 ***syn*** INHABIT, people, populate, tenant

occur *vb* **1** ***syn*** HAPPEN 1, befall, betide, chance, come off, develop, fall out, go, hap, transpire
2 to enter one's mind <it just *occurred* to me: she can't drive>
syn hit, strike
idiom come into one's head, come to mind, cross one's mind, flash across one's mind, go through one's head

occurrence *n* something that happens or takes place <the chance encounter turned out to be a fortunate *occurrence*>
syn circumstance, episode, event, go, happening, incident, occasion, thing
rel contingency, emergency, exigency, juncture, pass; condition, situation, state; adventure, experience

ocean *n* the body of water that covers nearly three-fourths of the earth <pulled the downed pilot from the *ocean*>
syn blue, brine, ||briny, deep, drink, main, sea

oceanic *adj* ***syn*** MARINE 1, maritime, thalassic

ochlocracy *n* ***syn*** ANARCHY 1, chaos, lawlessness, mobocracy

ocular *adj* **1** ***syn*** VISUAL 2, seeable, viewable, visible
2 ***syn*** VISUAL 1, optic, optical, visional

ocular *n* ***syn*** EYE 1, lamp, oculus, ||ogle, orb, peeper, winker

oculus *n* ***syn*** EYE 1, lamp, ocular, ||ogle, orb, peeper, winker

odd *adj* **1** being without a corresponding mate <had only an *odd* glove; the other was lost>
syn unmatched, unpaired
rel lone, only, single
con matched, paired
2 ***syn*** ACCIDENTAL, casual, chance, contingent, fluky, fortuitous, incidental
3 ***syn*** STRANGE 4, curious, eccentric, erratic, idiosyncratic, oddball, peculiar, queer, singular, unusual

oddball *n* ***syn*** ECCENTRIC, case, character, ||duck, oddity, original, quiz, ||spook, ||wack, zombie

oddball *adj* ***syn*** STRANGE 4, bizarre, curious, eccentric, idiosyncratic, odd, outlandish, peculiar, queer, weird

oddity *n* **1** ***syn*** ECCENTRIC, case, character, ||duck, oddball, original, quiz, ||spook, ||wack, zombie
2 ***syn*** CURIOSITY 2, conversation piece

oddments *n pl* ***syn*** SUNDRIES, etceteras, odds and ends, this and that(s)

odds *n pl* ***syn*** ADVANTAGE 3, allowance, bulge, ||deadwood, draw, edge, handicap, head start, start, vantage

odds and ends *n pl* **1** ***syn*** SUNDRIES, etceteras, oddments, this and that(s)
2 ***syn*** MISCELLANY 1, assortment, hodgepodge, jumble, medley, mélange, melee, motley, olio, potpourri

odiferous *adj* ***syn*** ODOROUS, odoriferous, scented

odious *adj* ***syn*** HATEFUL 2, abhorrent, abominable, detestable, hateable, horrid

odium *n* **1** ***syn*** DISGRACE, discredit, disesteem, dishonor, disrepute, ignominy, infamy, obloquy, opprobrium, shame
rel hate, hatred
ant honor
2 ***syn*** STIGMA, bar sinister, black eye, blot, blur, brand, onus, slur, spot, stain

odor *n* ***syn*** SMELL 1, aroma, scent

odoriferous *adj* ***syn*** ODOROUS, odiferous, scented

odorize *vb* ***syn*** SCENT 2, aromatize, perfume

odorless *adj* having no odor <*odorless* castor oil>
syn inodorous, scentless, smell-less
rel deodorant, deodorizing; unscented
con scented, smelly
ant odorous

odorous *adj* having or emitting an odor <*odorous* chemicals are often malodorous>
syn odiferous, odoriferous, scented; *compare* MALODOROUS 1, SWEET 2
rel redolent, reeking, smelling, smelly; heady, pungent, strong; olfactive, olfactory
ant inodorous, odorless, scentless

o'er *prep* ***syn*** OVER 1, above

oeuvre *n* a substantial body of work constituting the lifework of a writer, composer, or artist <one of the more popular operas in the Mozart *oeuvre*>
syn corpus, opera omnia
rel output

off *adv* ***syn*** AWAY 2, over

off *adj* **1** ***syn*** REMOTE 4, ||fat, negligible, outside, slender, slight, slim, small
2 ***syn*** SLOW 3, down, slack, sluggish

offal *n* ***syn*** REFUSE, debris, garbage, junk, litter, rubbish, spilth, sweepings, trash, waste

off–balance *adj* ***syn*** LOPSIDED, asymmetric, disproportionate, irregular, nonsymmetrical, unbalanced, unequal, uneven, unproportionate, unsymmetrical

off–center *adj* ***syn*** ECCENTRIC 1

off–color *adj* **1** ***syn*** UNWELL, ailing, ||donsie, indisposed, low, mean, offish, poorly, sickly, underly
2 ***syn*** RISQUÉ, blue, broad, purple, racy, salty, shady, spicy, suggestive, wicked

offend *vb* **1** ***syn*** TRESPASS 1, sin, transgress
2 ***syn*** VIOLATE 1, breach, break, contravene, infract, infringe, transgress
3 to cause hurt feelings or deep resentment <*offended* her by his cruel remark>
syn affront, insult, outrage
rel aggrieve, hurt, sting, wound; exasperate, gall, irritate, nettle; excite, provoke; appall, horrify, scandalize, shock; disoblige, displease, distress, disturb, miff, pique, upset
idiom hurt one's feelings, ruffle one's feathers, step (*or* tread) on one's toes
con delight, gratify, please, tickle; captivate, charm, enchant; flatter

offender *n* ***syn*** CRIMINAL, felon, lawbreaker, malefactor

offense *n* **1** ***syn*** ATTACK 1, aggression, assailment, assault, offensive, onfall, onset, onslaught
2 an emotional response to a slight or indignity <he is so sensitive that he takes *offense* at the slightest criticism>

---

syn synonym(s) ***rel*** related word(s)
idiom idiomatic equivalent(s) ***con*** contrasted word(s)
ant antonym(s) * vulgar
|| use limited; if in doubt, see a dictionary
The first word in a synonym list when printed in SMALL CAPITALS shows where there is more information about the group. For a more efficient use of this book see Explanatory Notes.

syn dudgeon, huff, miff, pique, resentment, ‖snuff, umbrage
rel affront, indignity, insult; anger, indignation; displeasure; catfit, conniption, fit, tantrum; pet, tizzy; explosion, flare-up, outburst, scene
con delight, pleasure
3 ***syn*** CRIME 1, misdeed

offensive *adj* utterly unpleasant or distasteful to the senses or sensibilities <the *offensive* odor of stale garbage> <her arrogant assurance was more than a little *offensive*>
syn atrocious, disgusting, evil, foul, hideous, horrible, horrid, icky, loathsome, nasty, nauseating, noisome, obscene, repellent, repugnant, repulsive, revolting, sickening, ungrateful, unwholesome, vile
rel abhorrent, bad, disagreeable, objectionable, uncongenial, unpleasant; abominable, detestable, fulsome, odious; rank; appalling, awful, beastly, dreadful, frightful, ghastly, grim, grisly, gruesome, lurid, shocking, terrible; unappetizing, unpalatable, unsavory
con agreeable, appealing, attractive, pleasant, pleasing; favorable, unobjectionable, welcome; appetizing, palatable, savory; divine
ant inoffensive, unoffensive

offensive *n* ***syn*** ATTACK 1, aggression, assailment, assault, offense, onfall, onset, onslaught

offer *vb* **1** to put something before another for acceptance or consideration <he was soon *offered* another job>
syn extend, give, hold out, pose, present, proffer, tender
rel display, exhibit, show
con accept, receive, take; decline, refuse, reject
2 ***syn*** ADDUCE, advance, allege, cite, lay, present
3 ***syn*** TRY 5, assay, attempt, endeavor, essay, seek, strive, struggle, undertake
4 ***syn*** SHOW 1, display

offering *n* **1** ***syn*** VICTIM 1, sacrifice
2 ***syn*** DONATION, alms, benefaction, beneficence, charity, contribution

offgoing *n* ***syn*** DEPARTURE 1, egress, egression, exit, exiting, exodus, setting-out, withdrawal

offhand *adj* ***syn*** EXTEMPORANEOUS, autoschediastic, extemporary, extempore, impromptu, improvised, spur-of-the-moment, unrehearsed, unstudied

office *n* **1** ***syn*** JOB 2, appointment, berth, billet, connection, place, position, post, situation, spot
2 ***syn*** FUNCTION 1, business, duty, province, role
‖**3** ***syn*** PRIVY 1, backhouse, ‖biffy, ‖closet, *crapper, jakes, ‖necessary, outhouse
‖**4** ***syn*** HIGH SIGN 2

officer *n* **1** ***syn*** POLICEMAN, ‖constable, cop, ‖gendarme, John Law, patrolman, peace officer, police, ‖police constable, police officer
2 ***syn*** EXECUTIVE, administrator, exec, manager, official

official *n* ***syn*** EXECUTIVE, administrator, exec, manager, officer

official *adj* derived from the proper office, officer, or authority <the mayor's office issued an *official* statement>
syn authoritative, ex cathedra, ex officio
rel approved, authorized, certified, cleared, endorsed, OK'd, sanctioned; canonical, cathedral
ant officious (*in diplomatic use*), unofficial

officially *adv* ***syn*** OSTENSIBLY, apparently, evidently, outwardly, professedly, seemingly

officiate *vb* ***syn*** ACT 4, function, serve

officious *adj* ***syn*** IMPERTINENT 2, busy, intrusive, meddlesome, ‖nebby, obtrusive, polypragmatic

offing *n* ***syn*** FUTURE, aftertime, afterward, by-and-by, hereafter, to-be

offish *adj* **1** ***syn*** UNSOCIABLE, aloof, distant, insociable, reserved, solitary, standoffish, unapproachable, unbending, withdrawn
2 ***syn*** UNWELL, ailing, ‖donsie, indisposed, low, mean, off-color, poorly, sickly, underly

off–key *adj* ***syn*** IRREGULAR 1, abnormal, anomalous, deviant, divergent, unnatural, unregular

off–load *vb* ***syn*** UNLOAD, disburden, discharge, unlade, unship, unstow

off–lying *adj* ***syn*** DISTANT 1, far, faraway, far-flung, far-off, outlying, remote, removed

offscouring *n* ***syn*** OUTCAST, castaway, derelict, Ishmael, Ishmaelite, leper, pariah, untouchable

offset *vb* ***syn*** COMPENSATE 1, atone (for), balance, counterbalance, counterpoise, countervail, make up, outweigh, redeem, set off
rel check, stop

offshoot *n* ***syn*** OUTGROWTH 2, by-product, derivative, descendant, spin-off

offspring *n pl* those who follow in direct parental line <a mother of numerous *offspring*>
syn ‖begats, brood, children, descendants, issue, posterity, progeniture, progeny, scions, seed
rel hatch, swarm; produce, spawn, young
con antecedents, ascendants, forebears, forefathers, progenitors
ant ancestors

offstage *adj or adv* ***syn*** BACKSTAGE
ant onstage

of late *adv* ***syn*** NEW, afresh, anew, lately, newly, recently

oft *adv* ***syn*** OFTEN, again and again, frequently, much, oftentimes, ofttimes, over and over, repeatedly, time and again

often *adv* many times <we called *often* but still could not reach you>
syn again and again, frequently, much, oft, oftentimes, ofttimes, over and over, repeatedly, time and again
idiom a number of times, many a time, many times over, time and time again
con infrequently, rarely; now and then, occasionally
ant seldom

oftentimes *adv* ***syn*** OFTEN, again and again, frequently, much, oft, ofttimes, over and over, repeatedly, time and again

---

syn synonym(s) *rel* related word(s)
idiom idiomatic equivalent(s) *con* contrasted word(s)
ant antonym(s) * vulgar
‖ use limited; if in doubt, see a dictionary
The first word in a synonym list when printed in SMALL CAPITALS shows where there is more information about the group. For a more efficient use of this book see Explanatory Notes.

ofttimes *adv* ***syn*** OFTEN, again and again, frequently, much, oft, oftentimes, over and over, repeatedly, time and again

ogle *vb* ***syn*** LOOK 7, eye, gape, ‖gaup (*or* gawp), gaze, goggle, rubberneck, stare

‖**ogle** *n* ***syn*** EYE 1, lamp, ocular, oculus, orb, peeper, winker

ogress *n* ***syn*** VIRAGO, amazon, fishwife, harpy, scold, shrew, termagant, vixen, Xanthippe

oil *n* ***syn*** FLATTERY, adulation, blandishment, blarney, incense, soft soap

‖**oiled** *adj* ***syn*** INTOXICATED 1, ‖boozy, ‖canned, disguised, drunk, inebriated, ‖lushed, muddled, pixilated, ‖plastered

oily *adj* **1** ***syn*** FATTY 2, greasy, oleaginous, unctuous
2 ***syn*** FULSOME, oleaginous, slick, smarmy, soapy, unctious, unctuous

ointment *n* a semisolid medicinal or cosmetic preparation for application to the skin <put *ointment* on the burned skin>
syn balm, cerate, chrism, cream, salve, unction, unguent
rel embrocation, liniment; demulcent, emollient; lotion; dressing

OK (*or* **okay**) *adv* ***syn*** YES 1, agreed, all right, aye, ‖okeydoke, yea, ‖yep

OK (*or* **okay**) *vb* ***syn*** APPROVE 2, accredit, certify, endorse, sanction

OK (*or* **okay**) *n* ***syn*** APPROBATION, approval, benediction, blessing, favor

‖**okeydoke** *adv* ***syn*** YES 1, agreed, all right, aye, OK (*or* okay), yea, ‖yep

old *adj* **1** ***syn*** ANCIENT 1, aged, age-old, antediluvian, antique, hoary, Noachian, timeworn, venerable
con contemporary, current, recent; advanced
ant new
2 of long standing <the ending of such an *old* friendship was tragic>
syn continuing, enduring, inveterate, lifelong, long-lasting, long-lived, perennial; *compare* LASTING
rel constant, perpetual, staying; established, firm, solid, steady
con newfound, recent; brief, short-lived; casual, temporary, transitory, weak
ant new
3 ***syn*** OLD-FASHIONED, antiquated, antique, archaic, dated, démodé, oldfangled, old-timey, outmoded, passé
rel primitive; traditional
con newish
ant modern, new
4 ***syn*** AGED 1, ancient, elderly, olden, oldish, overage
idiom along in years, getting on
con juvenile, young
ant youthful
5 ***syn*** EXPERIENCED, old-time, practical, practiced, seasoned, skilled, versed, vet, veteran
con young
ant new
6 ***syn*** FORMER 2, bygone, erstwhile, late, once, one-time, past, quondam, sometime, whilom

old age *n* the final stage of the normal life span <spent his *old age* in a nursing home>
syn age, caducity, elderliness, senectitude, senescence, years; *compare* DOTAGE
rel decrepitude, feebleness; infirmity
idiom advanced years, declining years, winter of life
ant youth

olden *adj* **1** ***syn*** ANCIENT 1, aged, age-old, antediluvian, antique, hoary, Noachian, old, timeworn, venerable
2 ***syn*** AGED 1, ancient, elderly, old

oldest profession *n* ***syn*** PROSTITUTION, harlotry, (the) social evil, streetwalking, whoredom

oldfangled *adj* ***syn*** OLD-FASHIONED, antiquated, antique, archaic, old, old hat, old-time, old-timey, out-of-date, vintage
ant newfangled

old–fashioned *adj* typical of an earlier time and often replaced by something more modern or fashionable <*old-fashioned* high-buttoned shoes>
syn antiquated, antique, archaic, belated, bygone, dated, démodé, demoded, dowdy, fusty, moldy, moth-eaten, neanderthal, old, oldfangled, old hat, old-time, old-timey, outdated, outmoded, out-of-date, passé, rococo, unmodern, vintage
rel aged, ancient; discarded, disused, obsolete; outworn, unfashionable; crusty, fogyish, fuddy-duddy, fusty, moss-backed, moss-grown, mossy, stodgy; Victorian; old-line
con modernistic, modish, newfangled, stylish, ‖trendy; current, recent, timely; new-fashioned, up-to-date, up-to-the-minute
ant contemporary; modern

Old Gooseberry *n* ***syn*** DEVIL 1, Apollyon, Beelzebub, diablo, fiend, Lucifer, Old Nick, Old Scratch, Satan, serpent

Old Guard *n* ***syn*** ESTABLISHMENT 2

old hand *n* ***syn*** VETERAN, longtimer, old-timer, vet

old hat *adj* **1** ***syn*** OLD-FASHIONED, antiquated, antique, archaic, dated, démodé, oldfangled, old-time, out-of-date, vintage
2 ***syn*** TRITE, cliché, clichéd, hackneyed, shopworn, stale, threadbare, timeworn, tired, well-worn

old lady *n* ‖**1** ***syn*** WIFE, ‖ball and chain, lady, ‖little woman, ‖missus, Mrs., ‖old woman, ‖rib, ‖squaw, woman
‖**2** ***syn*** MOTHER 1, ma, ‖mam, mama (*or* mamma), mammy, ‖mater, mom, mommy, mummy, ‖old woman
3 ***syn*** FUSSBUDGET, fuddy-duddy, fusser, fusspot, granny, old maid

old–line *adj* ***syn*** CONSERVATIVE 1, die-hard, fogyish, orthodox, reactionary, right, tory, traditionalistic

old liner *n* ***syn*** DIEHARD 1, bitter-ender, conservative, fundamentalist, right, rightist, right-winger, standpat, standpatter, tory

old maid *n* **1** ***syn*** SPINSTER, maiden lady, spinstress, ‖tabby
2 ***syn*** FUSSBUDGET, fuddy-duddy, fusser, fusspot, granny, old lady

---

syn synonym(s)	***rel*** related word(s)
idiom idiomatic equivalent(s)	***con*** contrasted word(s)
ant antonym(s)	* vulgar

‖ use limited; if in doubt, see a dictionary
The first word in a synonym list when printed in SMALL CAPITALS shows where there is more information about the group. For a more efficient use of this book see Explanatory Notes.

old–maidish *adj* ***syn*** NICE 1, choosy, fastidious, finicky, fussy, old-womanish, particular, persnickety, picky, squeamish

‖**old man** *n* **1** ***syn*** HUSBAND, ‖hubby, lord, man, ‖master, mister, Mr.
2 ***syn*** FATHER 1, dad, daddy, ‖governor, pa, papa, ‖pappy, ‖pater, pop, poppa

Old Nick *n* ***syn*** DEVIL 1, Apollyon, Beelzebub, diablo, fiend, Lucifer, Old Gooseberry, Old Scratch, Satan, serpent

Old Scratch *n* ***syn*** DEVIL 1, Apollyon, Beelzebub, diablo, fiend, Lucifer, Old Gooseberry, Old Nick, Satan, serpent

oldster *n* a person of advanced years <an *oldster* long retired from the business world>
syn ancient, elder, golden-ager, old-timer, senior, senior citizen; *compare* BELDAM 1, GAFFER
ant youngster, youth

old–time *adj* **1** ***syn*** OLD-FASHIONED, antiquated, antique, archaic, bygone, dated, oldfangled, old hat, old-timey, vintage
2 ***syn*** EXPERIENCED, old, practical, practiced, seasoned, skilled, versed, vet, veteran

old–timer *n* **1** ***syn*** VETERAN, longtimer, old hand, vet
2 ***syn*** OLDSTER, ancient, elder, golden-ager, senior, senior citizen

old–timey *adj* ***syn*** OLD-FASHIONED, antiquated, antique, archaic, bygone, dated, oldfangled, old hat, old-time, vintage

‖**old woman** *n* **1** ***syn*** WIFE, ‖ball and chain, lady, ‖little woman, ‖missus, Mrs., ‖old lady, ‖rib, ‖squaw, woman
2 ***syn*** MOTHER 1, ma, ‖mam, mama (*or* mamma), mammy, ‖mater, mom, mommy, mummy, ‖old lady

old–womanish *adj* ***syn*** NICE 1, choosy, fastidious, finicky, fussy, old-maidish, particular, persnickety, picky, squeamish

oleaginous *adj* **1** ***syn*** FATTY 2, greasy, oily, unctuous
2 ***syn*** FULSOME, oily, slick, smarmy, soapy, unctious, unctuous

olid *adj* ***syn*** MALODOROUS 1, fetid, funky, mephitic, putrid, rancid, rank, smelly, stenchy, stinking

olio *n* ***syn*** MISCELLANY 1, brew, hash, hodgepodge, medley, mishmash, olla podrida, omnium-gatherum, potpourri, stew

olla podrida *n* ***syn*** MISCELLANY 1, brew, hash, hodgepodge, medley, mishmash, olio, omnium-gatherum, potpourri, stew

omen *n* ***syn*** FORETOKEN, augury, bodement, boding, portent, presage, prognostic

omen *vb* ***syn*** AUGUR 2, betoken, bode, forebode, foreshadow, foreshow, foretoken, portend, presage, promise

ominous *adj* indicative of future misfortune or calamity <dark *ominous* clouds preceded the storm>
syn apocalyptic, baleful, baneful, dire, direful, doomful, fateful, ill-boding, ill-omened, inauspicious, threatening, unlucky, unpropitious; *compare* EVIL 5, SINISTER
rel portentous; malefic, maleficent, malign, sinister; comminatory, forbidding, grim, lowering, menacing; hostile, inhospitable, unfriendly
con auspicious, benign, favorable, promising, propitious; beneficial

omission *n* something omitted or missing <several *omissions* in the list>
syn blank, chasm, overlook, oversight, preterition, pretermission, skip
rel inadvertence, inadvertency, lapse, slip; break, gap, hiatus, lacuna
con inclusion; accession, addition, augmentation, increase, reinforcement; superaddition

omit *vb* ***syn*** NEGLECT, blink (at *or* away), discount, disregard, fail, forget, ignore, overlook, overpass, slight

omitted *adj* ***syn*** ABSENT 1, away, gone, lacking, missing, wanting
ant included

omnibus *n* ***syn*** ANTHOLOGY, album, ana, analects, florilegium, garland, miscellany, posy

omnipotent *adj* having virtually unlimited authority or influence <an *omnipotent* leader>
syn all-powerful, almighty
rel divine, godlike; unlimited, unrestricted
con impotent, powerless; limited, restricted

omnipresent *adj* present at all places at all times <*omnipresent* God>
syn allover, ubiquitous, universal
rel boundless, endless, immeasurable, infinite, limitless, unending
con bounded, finite, limited, restricted; cramped, straitened; narrow, strait

omnium–gatherum *n* ***syn*** MISCELLANY 1, assortment, gallimaufry, hodgepodge, mélange, mishmash, olio, pastiche, patchwork, stew

on *prep* **1** ***syn*** OVER 4, upon
2 ***syn*** OVER 3, about, upon, with

on *adv* ***syn*** ALONG 1, forth, forward, onward

on–again–off–again *adj* ***syn*** FITFUL, catchy, desultory, spasmodic, sporadic, spotty

onanism *n* ***syn*** SELF-GRATIFICATION, self-indulgence

onanistic *adj* ***syn*** SYBARITIC, hedonistic, self-indulgent, sybaritical, sybaritish

once *adv* **1** ***syn*** EVER 5, anyway, anywise, at all
2 ***syn*** BEFORE 2, already, earlier, erstwhile, formerly, heretofore, previously

once *adj* ***syn*** FORMER 2, bygone, erstwhile, late, old, onetime, past, quondam, sometime, whilom

once and again *adv* ***syn*** SOMETIMES, at times, ‖betimes, ever and again, ever and anon, here and there, now and again, now and then, ‖otherwhile

once more *adv* ***syn*** OVER 7, afresh, again, anew, de novo

oncoming *adj* ***syn*** FORTHCOMING, approaching, coming, nearing, upcoming

on–dit *n* ***syn*** REPORT 1, buzz, cry, gossip, grapevine, hearsay, rumble, rumor, scuttlebutt, talk

one *adj* ***syn*** SINGLE 2, lone, only, particular, separate, sole, solitary, unique

one *vb* ***syn*** JOIN 1, associate, coadunate, coagment, coalesce, connect, link, relate, unite, wed

---

syn synonym(s) | ***rel*** related word(s)
idiom idiomatic equivalent(s) | ***con*** contrasted word(s)
ant antonym(s) | * vulgar
‖ use limited; if in doubt, see a dictionary
The first word in a synonym list when printed in SMALL CAPITALS shows where there is more information about the group. For a more efficient use of this book see Explanatory Notes.

one by one *adv* ***syn*** APART 1, independently, individually, separately, severally, singly

one–horse town *n* ***syn*** BURG, hick town, jerkwater town, mudhole, Podunk, tank town, whistle-stop

oneness *n* **1** ***syn*** UNITY 1, individuality, singleness, singularity, singularness
ant multiplicity
2 ***syn*** UNIQUENESS, singleness, unicity, uniquity
3 ***syn*** ENTIRETY 1, allness, completeness, entireness, totality, wholeness
4 ***syn*** IDENTITY 1, identicalness, sameness, selfsameness

oner *n* ***syn*** DOLLAR, bill, ‖bone, ‖buck, ‖fish, ‖frogskin, ‖ironman, ‖skin, ‖smacker, ‖smackeroo

onerous *adj* imposing great hardship or strain <found the care of his old mother an *onerous* burden>
syn burdensome, demanding, exacting, exigent, grievous, oppressive, superincumbent, taxing, tough, trying, weighty
rel arduous, difficult, hard, laborious; heavy, hefty, ponderous; cumbersome, unruly, unwieldy; driving, heavy-handed
con easy, effortless; facile, light, simple, smooth, unexacting, untaxing

onerously *adv* ***syn*** HARD 8, arduously, burdensomely, difficultly, hardly, laboriously, toilsomely

one–sided *adj* ***syn*** BIASED 2, colored, jaundiced, partial, partisan, prejudiced, prepossessed, tendentious, unindifferent, warped
rel lopsided, weighted
con many-sided

one–sidedness *n* ***syn*** PREJUDICE, bias, partiality
con manysidedness

onetime *adj* ***syn*** FORMER 2, bygone, erstwhile, late, old, once, past, quondam, sometime, whilom

onfall *n* ***syn*** ATTACK 1, aggression, assailment, assault, offense, offensive, onset, onslaught

ongoing *n* ***syn*** ADVANCE 2, advancement, anabasis, headway, march, proficiency, progress
rel development, growth

onlooker *n* ***syn*** SPECTATOR, beholder, by-sitter, bystander, eyewitness, looker-on, observer, viewer, watcher, witness

only *adj* **1** ***syn*** ALONE 3, matchless, peerless, unequaled, unique, unmatched, unparagoned, unparalleled, unrivaled
2 being one or more of which there exist no others <the *only* survivors of the wreck>
syn alone, lone, singular, sole, solitary, solo, unexampled, unique, unrepeatable
rel incomparable, inimitable, matchless, peerless, transcendent, unequaled, unparalleled, unrivaled; companionless, separate, unaccompanied, unattended, uncompanied, uncompanioned
con divers, many, multifarious, numerous, sundry, various
3 ***syn*** SINGLE 2, lone, one, particular, separate, sole, solitary, unique

only *adv* **1** to the exclusion of any alternative or competitor <he will confess *only* to you>
syn alone, but, entirely, exclusively, solely
2 ***syn*** JUST 3, but, merely, simply

only *conj* in spite of which <it looks delicious, *only* I'm not hungry>
syn but, except, however, save, yet

on occasion *adv* ***syn*** OCCASIONALLY, infrequently, irregularly, sporadically, uncommonly

on offer *adj* ***syn*** PURCHASABLE 1, available, obtainable

onomatopoeic *adj* formed in imitation of a natural sound < *buzz* is an *onomatopoeic* word to describe the sound of bees>
syn echoic, imitative, onomatopoetic
rel emulative, simulative; mimetic, mimic, mimical

onomatopoetic *adj* ***syn*** ONOMATOPOEIC, echoic, imitative

on purpose *adv* ***syn*** INTENTIONALLY, ‖apurpose, deliberately, designedly, prepensely, purposedly, purposely, purposively

onset *n* **1** ***syn*** ATTACK 1, aggression, assailment, assault, offense, offensive, onfall, onslaught
2 ***syn*** BEGINNING, birth, commencement, dawn, dawning, opening, outset, outstart, setout, start

onslaught *n* ***syn*** ATTACK 1, aggression, assailment, assault, offense, offensive, onfall, onset

on the whole *adv* ***syn*** ALTOGETHER 3, all in all, by and large, en masse, generally

onus *n* **1** ***syn*** LOAD 3, burden, charge, deadweight, duty, millstone, task, tax, weight
2 ***syn*** BLAME, culpability, fault, guilt
3 ***syn*** STIGMA, bar sinister, black eye, blot, blur, brand, odium, slur, spot, stain

onward *adv* **1** ***syn*** AHEAD 2, alee, forth, forward
2 ***syn*** ALONG 1, forth, forward, on

onyx *adj* ***syn*** BLACK 1, atramentous, ebony, inky, jet, jetty, pitch-black, pitch-dark, raven, sable

oodles *n pl but sometimes sing in constr* ***syn*** SCAD, gob(s), heap, jillion, load(s), million, quantities, slew, thousand, trillion

‖**ooftish** *n* ***syn*** MONEY, ‖gelt, ‖mazuma, ‖moolah, needful, pelf, rhino, ‖scratch, ‖shekels, ‖smash

‖**oofy** *adj* ***syn*** RICH 1, affluent, moneyed, opulent, wealthy

ooid *adj* ***syn*** OVAL, ovate, oviform, ovoid

oomph *n* ***syn*** SPIRIT 5, animation, brio, dash, élan, esprit, gimp, life, verve, vim

ooze *vb* ***syn*** EXUDE, bleed, ‖screeve, seep, ‖sew, ‖sicker, strain, sweat, transude, weep

oozy *adj* ***syn*** MUDDY 1, bemired, ‖claggy, ‖clarty, miry

opaque *adj* ***syn*** OBSCURE 3, ambiguous, amphibological, equivocal, nubilous, tenebrous, uncertain, unclear, unintelligible, vague
ant transparent, transpicuous

ope *vb* ***syn*** OPEN 1, unblock, unclose, undo, unshut, unstop

open *adj* **1** not closed or obstructed <escaped through the *open* gate>
syn patent, unclosed, unobstructed

---

syn synonym(s)	*rel* related word(s)
idiom idiomatic equivalent(s)	*con* contrasted word(s)
ant antonym(s)	* vulgar

‖ use limited; if in doubt, see a dictionary
The first word in a synonym list when printed in SMALL CAPITALS shows where there is more information about the group. For a more efficient use of this book see Explanatory Notes.

rel agape, dehiscent, gaping, patulous, ringent, wide, yawning; ajar; unbarred, unbolted, unfastened, unlocked, unsealed; clear, unimpeded
con blocked, obstructed; constricted, cramped, narrow, strait
ant closed, shut
2 lacking a cover or covering <an *open* wound that continued to ooze blood> <his chest *open* to the sun>
syn bare, denuded, exposed, naked, peeled, stripped, uncovered
3 *syn* LIABLE 2, exposed, obnoxious, prone, sensitive, subject, susceptible
ant closed
4 not restricted to a particular group or situation <favored *open* enrollment in the schools>
syn accessible, open-door, public, unrestricted
rel attainable, available, obtainable, reachable, securable
idiom to be had, within reach
con limited, restricted; inaccessible, private
ant closed
5 available for use or consideration or decision <there are only two courses *open* to us>
syn accessible, employable, operative, practicable, usable
rel appropriate, fit, proper, suitable; acceptable, agreeable, pleasing
idiom within reach
con inaccessible, inoperative, unusable
ant closed
6 *syn* DOUBTFUL 1, ambiguous, dubious, dubitable, equivocal, indecisive, problematic, uncertain, undecided, unsettled
7 *syn* FRANK, candid, openhearted, plain, straightforward, unconcealed, undisguised, undissembled, undissembling, unvarnished
ant close; clandestine

open *vb* **1** to change from a closed to an open condition <*open* the window>
syn ope, unblock, unclose, undo, unshut, unstop
rel clear, free, release; bare, disclose, expose, reveal
idiom lay open, swing open, throw open
con block, occlude, stop
ant close, shut
2 to make physically or mentally visible <dawn *opened* a surprising scene to his startled eyes>
syn disclose, display, expose, reveal, unclothe, uncover, unveil
rel adumbrate, hint, shadow, suggest
idiom bring to light, bring to (*or* into) view, lay bare, make plain, show forth
con cloak, conceal, hide, screen, secrete, shroud
3 to make an opening in <decided to *open* a can of beans>
syn breach, disrupt, hole, rupture
rel break, broach, tap, undo; cut, gash, slash; perforate, pierce
idiom lay open
con occlude, shut; fasten, secure
ant close
4 to spread out <the falcon slowly *opened* her mighty wings>
syn expand, extend, fan (out), outspread, outstretch, spread, unfold
rel billow, dilate, distend, swell; cover, mantle, overspread
con collect, concentrate, contract, gather (in)
ant close
5 *syn* BEGIN 1, commence, embark (on *or* upon), get off, inaugurate, initiate, jump (off), kick off, launch, start
ant close
6 *syn* CONVENE 1, meet, sit

open *n syn* OUTDOORS, open air, out-of-doors, outside, without

open air *n syn* OUTDOORS, open, out-of-doors, outside, without

open–air *adj syn* OUTDOOR, alfresco, hypaethral, out-of-door, outside
con indoor, inside; enclosed

open–and–shut *adj syn* CLEAR 5, apparent, distinct, evident, manifest, obvious, palpable, patent, plain, straightforward

open–door *adj syn* OPEN 4, accessible, public, unrestricted

open–eyed *adj syn* WATCHFUL, alert, unsleeping, vigilant, wakeful, wide-awake

openhanded *adj* **1** *syn* LIBERAL 1, bounteous, bountiful, free, freehanded, generous, handsome, munificent, unsparing
ant closefisted, tightfisted
2 *syn* CLEAR 5, apparent, distinct, evident, manifest, obvious, palpable, patent, plain, straightforward

openhearted *adj syn* FRANK, candid, open, plain, straightforward, unconcealed, undisguised, undissembled, undissembling, unvarnished

opening *n* **1** *syn* BEGINNING, birth, commencement, dawn, dawning, onset, outset, outstart, setout, start
ant closing
2 *syn* APERTURE, hole, orifice, outlet, vent
3 *syn* GAP 1, breach, break, discontinuity, hole
4 *syn* OPPORTUNITY, break, chance, look-in, occasion, shot, show, squeak, time

opening gun *n syn* BEGINNING, alpha, commencement, dawn, onset, opening, outset, outstart, setout, start

openmouthed *adj syn* VOCIFEROUS, blatant, boisterous, clamorous, ||dinsome, loudmouthed, multivocal, obstreperous, strident, vociferant

openness *n syn* EXPOSURE, liability, vulnerability, vulnerableness

open sesame *n syn* PASSPORT, key, password, ticket

open up *vb syn* OPERATE 2, cut

opera omnia *n syn* OEUVRE, corpus

operate *vb* **1** *syn* ACT 5, behave, function, perform, react, take, work
2 to perform surgery <*operated* on him to remove a brain tumor>

---

syn synonym(s) *rel* related word(s)
idiom idiomatic equivalent(s) *con* contrasted word(s)
ant antonym(s) * vulgar
|| use limited; if in doubt, see a dictionary
The first word in a synonym list when printed in SMALL CAPITALS shows where there is more information about the group. For a more efficient use of this book see Explanatory Notes.

syn cut, open up
3 to cause to function <knew how to *operate* earth-moving equipment>
syn handle, run, use, work
rel play; manage, maneuver; drive, pilot, steer; ply, wield
idiom make go
4 ***syn*** CONDUCT 3, carry on, direct, keep, manage, ordain, run

operation *n* **1** ***syn*** EXERCISE 1, application, employment, exercising, exertion, use
2 ***syn*** USE 1, appliance, application, employment, play, usance

operative *adj* **1** ***syn*** ACTIVE 1, alive, dynamic, functioning, live, running, working
ant inoperative
2 ***syn*** OPEN 5, accessible, employable, practicable, usable

operative *n* **1** ***syn*** WORKER, hand, laborer, ‖mozo, roustabout, workhand, workingman, workman
2 ***syn*** PRIVATE DETECTIVE, Pinkerton, ‖private eye, ‖shamus

operator *n* ***syn*** MOTORIST, autoist, automobilist, driver

operose *adj* **1** ***syn*** HARD 6, arduous, difficult, effortful, formidable, laborious, severe, strenuous, toilsome, tough
2 ***syn*** ASSIDUOUS, diligent, industrious, sedulous

opiate *adj* ***syn*** SOPORIFIC 1, hypnotic, narcotic, sleepy, somnifacient, somniferous, somnific, somnorific, soporiferous, soporifical

opiate *n* **1** ***syn*** DRUG 2, dope, ‖hop, narcotic
2 ***syn*** ANODYNE 2, narcotic, nepenthe

opine *vb* to form or express an opinion <he *opined* that the story was true>
syn ‖opinion, opinionate
rel accept, believe, consider, hold, judge, regard, think, view; speculate
con deny, disclaim, disown, reject, repudiate; disbelieve, discredit, doubt

opinion *n* an idea or judgment held as true or valid <seek an expert *opinion* on the authenticity of the painting>
syn belief, conviction, eye, feeling, mind, persuasion, sentiment, view
rel attitude, impression, notion, think, thought; conclusion, estimate, estimation, judgment, reaction; assumption, conjecture, speculation, supposition, theory
idiom point of view
con disbelief, discredit, doubt, unbelief; distrust, mistrust, questioning, skepticism

‖**opinion** *vb* ***syn*** OPINE, opinionate

opinionate *vb* ***syn*** OPINE, ‖opinion

opponent *n* one who expresses or manifests opposition <his *opponent* in the debate>
syn adversary, antagonist, anti, con, match, opposer, oppugnant
rel enemy, foe; competitor, rival; assailant, combatant; counteragent
con ally, colleague, comrade, confederate, partner; advocate, champion
ant exponent, pro, proponent

opportune *adj* ***syn*** TIMELY 1, auspicious, favorable, propitious, prosperous, seasonable, timeous, well-timed
rel appropriate, felicitous, happy
ant inopportune

opportunity *n* a state of affairs or combination of circumstances favorable to some end <all he asked was an *opportunity* to show what he could do>
syn break, chance, look-in, occasion, opening, shot, show, squeak, time
rel room, space; leisure, liberty; relief, spell, turn; juncture, pass; dog's chance, hope, prayer

oppose *vb* **1** to place over against something to provide resistance or counterbalance <*oppose* one military force to another>
syn counter, match, pit, play (off), vie
rel array, confront, face
idiom set over against
2 ***syn*** RESIST, buck, combat, contest, dispute, duel, fight, repel, traverse, withstand

opposed *adj* ***syn*** ADVERSE 1, antagonistic, anti, antipathetic, opposing, oppugnant

opposer *n* ***syn*** OPPONENT, adversary, antagonist, anti, con, match, oppugnant

opposing *adj* ***syn*** ADVERSE 1, antagonistic, anti, antipathetic, opposed, oppugnant

opposite *n* something that is exactly opposed or contrary <virtue and vice are *opposites*>
syn antipode, antipole, antithesis, contra, contradictory, contrary, converse, counter, counterpole, reverse
rel contrast, counterpoint, foil; contrapositive, inverse, obverse; antonym
idiom the other extreme, the other side of the coin
con analogon, analogue, counterpart, like, parallel, similar; equal, equivalent; correlate, correlative; carbon copy, duplicate, replica
ant same

opposite *adj* being so far apart as to be or to seem irreconcilable <held *opposite* views on the solution of the problem>
syn antipodal, antipodean, antithetical, contradictory, contrary, converse, counter, diametric, polar, reverse
rel contrasting; contrapositive, inverse, obverse; antonymous; different, dissimilar, divergent, opposed, unalike, unlike, unsimilar; independent, separate, unconnected, unrelated
con alike, analogous, equivalent, like, parallel, similar; equal; correlative
ant same

opposite *prep* ***syn*** TO 6

oppositely *adv* ***syn*** AGAIN 5, contra, contrariwise, contrary, contrawise, conversely, vice versa

opposite number *n* one holding an equivalent or parallel position <the Secretary of State and his *opposite number,* the Foreign Minister>
syn coordinate, counterpart, vis-à-vis; *compare* EQUAL

---

syn synonym(s) ***rel*** related word(s)
idiom idiomatic equivalent(s) ***con*** contrasted word(s)
ant antonym(s) * vulgar
‖ use limited; if in doubt, see a dictionary
The first word in a synonym list when printed in SMALL CAPITALS shows where there is more information about the group. For a more efficient use of this book see Explanatory Notes.

rel complement, cousin, equal, equivalent, like, match, tally

opposition *n* ***syn*** ANTAGONISM 2, antithesis, con, contradistinction, contraposition, contrariety, opposure

opposure *n* ***syn*** ANTAGONISM 2, antithesis, con, contradistinction, contraposition, contrariety, opposure

oppress *vb* **1** ***syn*** WRONG, aggrieve, outrage, persecute

rel harass, harry; afflict, torment, torture; conquer, overcome, overthrow, subjugate

2 ***syn*** DEPRESS 2, press, sadden, weigh down

rel burden, distress, trouble

oppressive *adj* **1** ***syn*** ONEROUS, burdensome, demanding, exacting, exigent, grievous, superincumbent, taxing, tough, weighty

ant unoppressive

2 ***syn*** GLOOMY 3, black, bleak, depressing, depressive, discouraging, disheartening, dismal, dispiriting, somber

oppressor *n* ***syn*** TYRANT, despot, dictator, duce, strong man

opprobriate *vb* ***syn*** DECRY 2, abuse, belittle, depreciate, derogate, detract (from), diminish, discount, disparage, dispraise

opprobrious *adj* **1** ***syn*** ABUSIVE, contumelious, invective, scurrile, scurrilous, truculent, vituperative, vituperatory, vituperous

2 ***syn*** INFAMOUS 1, ill-famed, notorious

opprobrium *n* ***syn*** DISGRACE, discredit, disesteem, dishonor, disrepute, ignominy, infamy, obloquy, odium, shame

rel abuse, scurrility, vituperation

con credit, prestige

oppugn *vb* ***syn*** CONTEND 1, battle, fight, tug, war

oppugnant *adj* ***syn*** ADVERSE 1, antagonistic, anti, antipathetic, opposed, opposing

oppugnant *n* ***syn*** OPPONENT, adversary, antagonist, anti, con, match, opposer

opt (for) *vb* ***syn*** CHOOSE 1, cull, elect, mark, optate, pick, prefer, select, single (out), take

optate *vb* ***syn*** CHOOSE 1, cull, elect, mark, opt (for), pick, pick out, prefer, select, single (out)

optic *adj* ***syn*** VISUAL 1, ocular, optical, visional

optical *adj* ***syn*** VISUAL 1, ocular, optic, visional

optimacy *n* ***syn*** ARISTOCRACY, blue blood, carriage trade, elite, patriciate, quality, society, upper class, upper crust, who's who

optimism *n* an inclination to put the most favorable construction on actions and events or to anticipate the best possible outcome <was a practitioner of *optimism* in his everyday life>

syn Pollyannaism, rose-colored spectacles, sanguineness, sanguinity

rel brightness, buoyancy, happiness; idealism, positivism

con hopelessness; despair, gloom, melancholy; malism; defeatism, fatalism; cynicism

ant pessimism

optimist *n* one given to optimism <was a jaunty *optimist*>

syn hoper, Pollyanna

rel dreamer, idealist, positivist

con defeatist, fatalist; cynic, doubter, skeptic

ant pessimist

optimistic *adj* anticipating only the best to happen and minimizing all other possibilities <was *optimistic* about book sales that year>

syn fond, Pollyannaish, sanguine, upbeat; *compare* HOPEFUL 1

rel bright, cheerful, merry, sunny; hopeful, hoping; assured, confident

idiom feeling on top of the world, looking on the bright side, riding (*or* sitting) on cloud nine

con cynical; doubtful, uncertain

ant pessimistic

option *n* ***syn*** CHOICE 1, alternative, ||druthers, election, preference, selection

rel prerogative, privilege, right

optional *adj* not compulsory <attendance at the meeting is *optional*>

syn discretionary, elective, facultative, nonobligatory

rel free, voluntary; alternative

con demanded, imperative; enforced, involuntary; essential, necessary

ant compulsory, mandatory, obligatory, required

opulent *adj* **1** ***syn*** RICH 1, affluent, moneyed, ||oofy, wealthy

rel lavish, prodigal, profuse; extravagant, ostentatious, pretentious, showy; plush, swank

con modest, simple, unpretentious

2 ***syn*** LUXURIOUS 3, Capuan, deluxe, luscious, lush, luxuriant, palatial, plush, sumptuous, upholstered

3 ***syn*** PROFUSE, exuberant, lavish, lush, luxuriant, prodigal, profusive, riotous

oracle *n* ***syn*** REVELATION, apocalypse, prophecy, vision

oracular *adj* ***syn*** PROPHETIC, apocalyptic, Delphian, fatidic, mantic, prophetical, sibylline, vatic, vaticinal

oral *adj* **1** ***syn*** VOCAL 1, articulate, sonant, spoken, viva voce, voiced

2 expressed or transmitted vocally <stories of folk heroes kept alive in *oral* tradition>

syn spoken, traditional, unwritten, verbal, word-of-mouth

rel narrated, recounted, related, told

con chronicled, recorded, written, written down

orate *vb* to talk in a declamatory, grandiloquent, or impassioned manner <*orated* to the crowd about the flag and patriotism>

syn bloviate, declaim, harangue, mouth, perorate, rant, rave, soapbox

rel elocute; bombast, rodomontade, sermonize, speechify; blah-blah

oratorical *adj* ***syn*** RHETORICAL, aureate, bombastic, declamatory, euphuistic, flowery, grandiloquent, magniloquent, overblown, sonorous

oratory *n* the art of speaking in public eloquently and effectively <a politician who was a master at *oratory*>

---

syn synonym(s) — *rel* related word(s)
idiom idiomatic equivalent(s) — *con* contrasted word(s)
ant antonym(s) — * vulgar
|| use limited; if in doubt, see a dictionary
The first word in a synonym list when printed in SMALL CAPITALS shows where there is more information about the group. For a more efficient use of this book see Explanatory Notes.

syn elocution, rhetoric, speechcraft

orb *n* **1** *syn* BALL 1, globe, rondure, round, sphere
2 *syn* EYE 1, lamp, ocular, oculus, ‖ogle, peeper, winker

orbit *n syn* RANGE 2, ambit, compass, extension, extent, purview, radius, reach, scope, sweep

orchestra *n* a usually large group of musicians who perform together <a string *orchestra* played at the reception>
syn band, philharmonic, symphony
rel combo, ensemble

orchestrate *vb syn* HARMONIZE 4, arrange, blend, integrate, symphonize, synthesize, unify

orchidaceous *adj syn* SHOWY, chichi, flamboyant, ostentatious, peacockish, peacocky, pretentious, splashy, swank

orchids *n pl syn* COMPLIMENT 1, bouquet, kudo

ordain *vb* **1** *syn* CONDUCT 3, carry on, direct, keep, manage, operate, run
2 *syn* DICTATE, decree, impose, lay down, prescribe, set

ordeal *n syn* TRIAL 1, affliction, calvary, cross, crucible, tribulation, visitation

order *n* **1** *syn* ASSOCIATION 2, brotherhood, club, fellowship, fraternity, guild, league, society, sodality, union
2 *syn* TYPE, breed, description, feather, ilk, kidney, kind, nature, sort, stripe
rel bracket, branch, pigeonhole, set; estate, grade, rank, status
3 sequential occurrence in space or time <changed the *order* of the books on the shelf>
syn arrangement, disposal, disposition, distribution, ordering, sequence
rel array, arrayal, collocation; allocation, allotment, apportionment, arrayment, proration
con disarrangement, disordering; chaos, confusion, disorder, mix-up, muddle
4 general or approximate size or amount <a loss on the *order* of seven million dollars>
syn extent, magnitude, matter, neighborhood, range, tune, vicinity
rel approach, approximation, closeness, nearness, proximity
5 manner of being arranged in space or of occurring in time <tell everything in the *order* in which it happened>
syn consecution, procession, sequence, succession
rel consecutiveness, following, successiveness; chain, progression, series, train
6 *syn* SUCCESSION 2, alternation, chain, consecution, progression, row, sequel, sequence, series, train
7 orderly conduct <about to call the meeting to *order* when the interruption occurred>
syn correctitude, correctness, decorousness, decorum, orderliness, properness, propriety, seemliness
rel goodness, niceness, rightness; fitness, suitability; integrity, probity, rectitude, uprightness
con impropriety, indecorousness, indecorum, unseemliness
ant disorder
8 orderly arrangement or disposition <troubled by the lack of *order* in their daily lives>
syn method, orderliness, pattern, plan, system
con anarchy, chaos, confusion, muddle, ‖snafu
ant disorder
9 state with respect to quality, functioning, or status <the equipment was in very poor *order*>
syn case, condition, estate, repair, shape
rel fettle, fitness, kilter, trim
10 a state of soundness <had his car put in *order* for spring>
syn condition, fettle, fitness, kilter, repair, shape, trim
rel adjustment, amendment, correction, gear, rectification
idiom working order
con disrepair
11 the state of being appropriate to or required by the circumstances <that remark is definitely out of *order*>
syn appositeness, appropriateness, aptness, expediency, fitness, meetness, propriety, rightness, suitability, suitableness
rel opportuneness, seasonableness, timeliness; auspiciousness, favorableness; felicity, grace
con inappropriateness, unfitness, unsuitability, unsuitableness
12 *syn* COMMAND 1, behest, bidding, charge, dictate, injunction, mandate, word
rel authorization, permission

order *vb* **1** to bring about an orderly disposition of individuals, units, or elements <*ordered* his affairs in preparation for marriage>
syn arrange, array, dispose, marshal, methodize, organize, systematize
rel adjust, fix, regulate, right; align, line, line up, range; classify, codify, hierarchize; regiment, routine, routinize; streamline
idiom put (*or* set) in order, put in shape, put (*or* set) to rights, reduce to order, whip into shape (*or* order)
ant disorder
2 *syn* COMMAND, bid, charge, direct, enjoin, instruct, tell, warn

ordering *n syn* ORDER 3, arrangement, disposal, disposition, distribution, sequence

orderliness *n* **1** *syn* ORDER 7, correctitude, correctness, decorousness, decorum, properness, propriety, seemliness
ant disorderliness
2 *syn* ORDER 8, method, pattern, plan, system
ant disorderliness

orderly *adj* **1** following a set arrangement, design, or pattern <work out an *orderly* procedure and stick to it> <an *orderly* row of houses surrounded the village green>
syn methodic, methodical, regular, systematic

---

rel accurate, correct, exact, precise; alike, uniform; businesslike; conventional, formal
idiom in apple-pie order
con haphazard, irregular, unmethodical, unsystematic; careless, casual, free and easy
ant chaotic, disorderly
2 *syn* NEAT 2, chipper, shipshape, snug, spick-and-span, tidy, trig, trim, uncluttered, well-groomed
rel picked up
ant disordered; disorderly

order up *vb syn* CALL UP

ordinance *n syn* LAW 1, canon, decree, decretum, edict, precept, prescript, regulation, rule, statute

ordinarily *adv syn* USUALLY 2, as a rule, by ordinary, commonly, frequently, generally

ordinary *adj* 1 of the customary or common type encountered in the normal course of events <*ordinary* traffic had been stopped to let the marchers pass>
syn everyday, plain, plain Jane, quotidian, routine, unremarkable, usual, workaday
rel commonplace, natural, normal, regular; customary, familiar, frequent
con infrequent, rare, uncommon; accidental, casual, chance, fortuitous
ant extraordinary
2 *syn* COMMON 6, commonplace, prosaic, uneventful, unexceptional, unnoteworthy

organ *n* 1 *syn* MEAN 2, agency, agent, channel, instrument, instrumentality, instrumentation, medium, ministry, vehicle
2 *syn* JOURNAL, magazine, newspaper, periodical, review

organize *vb* 1 *syn* FOUND 2, constitute, create, establish, institute, set up, start
rel construct, put together
2 *syn* ORDER 1, arrange, array, dispose, marshal, methodize, systemize
rel coordinate, integrate
3 *syn* MOBILIZE 3, marshal, muster, rally

‖**organized** *adj syn* INTOXICATED 1, ‖boozy, ‖canned, disguised, drunk, inebriated, ‖lushed, muddled, pixilated, ‖plastered

orgulous *adj syn* PROUD 1, arrogant, cavalier, disdainful, haughty, high-and-mighty, insolent, overbearing, supercilious, superior

orgy *n* 1 *syn* BINGE 1, bat, blowoff, carousal, carouse, ran-tan, soak, spree, tear, wassail
2 an act or occasion of excessive indulgence in sex <the house detective investigated an *orgy* in the penthouse suite>
syn bacchanal, bacchanalia, debauch, party, saturnalia
3 *syn* SPREE 1, binge, fling, rampage, splurge

orifice *n syn* APERTURE, hole, opening, outlet, vent

oriflamme *n syn* FLAG, banner, bannerol, color, gonfalon, pendant, pennant, pennon, standard, streamer

origin *n* 1 *syn* ANCESTRY, blood, descent, extraction, lineage, pedigree
rel maternity, parentage, paternity
2 *syn* SOURCE, derivation, fountain, inception, provenance, provenience, root, well, wellspring, whence

original *n* 1 a first form from which copies or reproductions can be produced <students copying the da Vinci *original*>
syn archetype, protoplast, prototype
rel forerunner, mother, precursor; model, pattern; precedent
con dummy, imitation, simulacrum; counterfeit, fake, forgery
ant copy, reproduction
2 *syn* INNOVATOR, introducer, inventor, originator
3 *syn* ECCENTRIC, case, character, ‖duck, oddball, oddity, quiz, ‖spook, ‖wack, zombie

original *adj* 1 *syn* FIRST 2, earliest, initial, maiden, pioneer, primary, prime
rel archetypal, prototypal
2 *syn* PRIMARY 5, prime, primitive, underivative, underived
3 *syn* INVENTIVE, creative, demiurgic, deviceful, ingenious, innovational, innovative, innovatory, originative
con banal, trite; derivative, initative
ant unoriginal

originally *adv syn* INITIALLY 1, primarily, primitively

originate *vb* 1 *syn* GENERATE 1, create, father, hatch, make, parent, procreate, produce, sire, spawn
2 *syn* INTRODUCE 3, inaugurate, initiate, institute, launch, set up, usher in
3 *syn* SPRING 1, arise, birth, derive (from), emanate, flow, issue, proceed, rise, stem
4 *syn* BEGIN 2, arise, commence, start
5 to have one's origin or home base in <he *originates* from Ohio>
syn come (from), hail (from)
rel derive (from), spring (from), stem (from)

originative *adj syn* INVENTIVE, creative, demiurgic, deviceful, ingenious, innovational, innovative, innovatory, original
ant unoriginative

originator *n* 1 *syn* FATHER 2, architect, author, creator, founder, generator, inventor, maker, patriarch, sire
2 *syn* INNOVATOR, introducer, inventor, original

orison *n syn* PRAYER, appeal, application, entreaty, imploration, imprecation, petition, plea, suit, supplication

ornament *vb syn* ADORN, beautify, bedeck, deck, decorate, dress (up), embellish, garnish, prank, trim
rel enrich; embroider

ornate *adj* elaborately and often pretentiously decorated or designed <a very *ornate* room—all marble, gilt, and brocade>
syn baroque, flamboyant, florid, luscious, rich, rococo
rel elaborate, high-wrought, resplendent; labored, overdone, overelaborated, overembellished, overworked, overwrought; luxuriant, luxurious, opulent, sumptuous; aureate, gilded
con natural, plain, quiet, simple; severe, unembellished, unornamented, unostentatious, unpretentious; restrained, subdued

---

syn synonym(s) *rel* related word(s)
idiom idiomatic equivalent(s) *con* contrasted word(s)
ant antonym(s) * vulgar
‖ use limited; if in doubt, see a dictionary
The first word in a synonym list when printed in SMALL CAPITALS shows where there is more information about the group. For a more efficient use of this book see Explanatory Notes.

ant austere; chaste

ornery *adj* ||1 *syn* CHEAP 2, base, common, mean, paltry, poor, rubbishy, shoddy, sleazy, tatty

2 *syn* CANTANKEROUS, bearish, cankered, cranky, cross-grained, crotchety, vinegarish, vinegary, waspish, waspy

3 *syn* CONTRARY 3, balky, cross-grained, froward, perverse, restive, wayward, wrongheaded

orotund *adj* 1 *syn* RESONANT, consonant, plangent, resounding, ringing, rotund, round, sonorant, sonorous, vibrant

rel loud, stentorian

2 *syn* RHETORICAL, aureate, bombastic, declamatory, euphuistic, flowery, grandiloquent, magniloquent, oratorical, sonorous

orphan *adj* deprived by death of one and usually both parents <seeking homes for the countless *orphan* children from the disaster area>

syn orphaned, parentless, unparented

rel alone, solitary; abandoned, cast-off, forsaken, lost; disregarded, ignored, neglected, slighted

orphaned *adj syn* ORPHAN, parentless, unparented

orphic *adj syn* RECONDITE, abstruse, acroamatic, deep, esoteric, heavy, hermetic, occult, profound, secret

orthodox *adj* 1 conforming to doctrines or practices that are held to be right or true by an authority, standard, or tradition <those who still hold an *orthodox* view about evolution>

syn accepted, authoritative, canonical, received, sanctioned, sound

rel acknowledged, admitted, approved; customary, official, recognized, standard, traditional; correct, proper, right

con heretical, heterodox, unauthoritative, uncanonical

ant unorthodox

2 *syn* CONVENTIONAL 1, button-down, square, straight

3 *syn* CONSERVATIVE 1, die-hard, fogyish, old-line, reactionary, right, tory, traditionalistic

ant unorthodox

oscillate *vb syn* SWING 2, pendulate, sway

osculate *vb syn* KISS 1, bus, lip, peck, smack, smooch, ||smoodge, ||smouch

ostend *vb syn* SHOW 2, demonstrate, evidence, evince, exhibit, illustrate, manifest, mark, proclaim

ostensible *adj* 1 *syn* APPARENT 2, Barmecidal, illusive, illusory, seeming, semblant

2 *syn* ALLEGED, pretended, professed, purported, so-called, supposed

ostensibly *adv* to all outward appearances <*ostensibly* it was a business trip but actually it was all pleasure>

syn apparently, evidently, officially, outwardly, professedly, seemingly

rel externally, superficially; sensibly

idiom on the face of it, on the surface, to the eye

con genuinely, really, truly; au fond, basically

ostentatious *adj syn* SHOWY, chichi, flamboyant, orchidaceous, peacockish, peacocky, pretentious, splashy, swank

ant unostentatious

ostracism *n syn* EXILE 1, banishment, deportation, displacement, expulsion, relegation

ostracize *vb* 1 *syn* BANISH, cast out, deport, displace, exile, expatriate, expel, expulse, oust, throw out

con accept, entertain, receive, welcome; harbor, haven, refuge, shelter

2 *syn* CUT 7, cold-shoulder, snob, snub

other *adj* 1 *syn* DIFFERENT 1, disparate, dissimilar, distant, divergent, diverse, otherwise, unalike, unequal, unlike

2 *syn* ADDITIONAL, added, another, else, farther, fresh, further, more, new

||**othergates** *adv syn* OTHERWISE 1, differently, diversely, variously

other half *n syn* RABBLE 2, dreg(s), hoi polloi, mass(es), mob, proletariat, ragtag and bobtail, riffraff, scum, trash

otherness *n syn* DISSIMILARITY, alterity, difference, discrepancy, dissemblance, dissimilitude, distinction, divergence, divergency, unlikeness

||**otherways** *adv syn* OTHERWISE 2, else, ||elseways, elsewise

||**otherwhile** *adv syn* SOMETIMES, at times, ||betimes, ever and again, ever and anon, here and there, now and again, now and then, once and again

otherwise *adv* 1 in a different way or manner <he could not act *otherwise*>

syn differently, diversely, ||othergates, variously

ant likewise

2 under different conditions <might *otherwise* have left>

syn else, ||elseways, elsewise, ||otherways

otherwise *adj syn* DIFFERENT 1, disparate, dissimilar, distant, divergent, diverse, other, unalike, unequal, unlike

otherworld *n syn* HEREAFTER 2, afterlife, afterworld, beyond

otherworldly *adj* 1 of or relating to a world other than the actual world <believed in the existence of *otherworldly* phenomena>

syn transcendental, transmundane

rel exterrestrial, extramundane, extraterrestrial; unearthly, unworldly

2 *syn* DREAMY 1, astral, daydreaming, daydreamy, unworldly, visionary

otiose *adj syn* VAIN 1, empty, hollow, idle, nugatory

rel purposeless, useless; inexcusable; superfluous, supernumerary, surplus

oubliette *n syn* DUNGEON

ought *vb syn* WANT 3, must, should

ought *n syn* OBLIGATION 2, charge, commitment, committal, devoir, duty, must, need, ||right

ounce *n syn* PARTICLE, atom, crumb, doit, dram, drop, grain, minim, shred, smidgen

oust *vb* 1 *syn* DEPRIVE 2, bereave, disinherit, dispossess, divest, lose, rob

2 *syn* BANISH, cast out, deport, displace, expel, expulse, ||lag, ostracize, relegate, transport

---

syn synonym(s) *rel* related word(s)
idiom idiomatic equivalent(s) *con* contrasted word(s)
ant antonym(s) * vulgar
|| use limited; if in doubt, see a dictionary
The first word in a synonym list when printed in SMALL CAPITALS shows where there is more information about the group. For a more efficient use of this book see Explanatory Notes.

out *adv* ***syn*** OUTDOORS, out of doors, outside, without, withoutdoors

out *vb* **1** ***syn*** EJECT 1, boot (out), chase, chuck, dismiss, evict, extrude, kick out, throw out

2 ***syn*** EXTINGUISH 1, douse, ‖dout, put out, quench, ‖squench

3 ***syn*** GET OUT 2, break, come out, leak, transpire

out *n* ***syn*** SHOWING 1, show

out and away *adv* ***syn*** FAR AND AWAY, by all odds, by a long shot, by far, by long odds, by odds

out–and–out *adj* ***syn*** UTTER, absolute, complete, consummate, gross, outright, perfect, positive, straight-out, thoroughgoing

‖**outback** *n* ***syn*** FRONTIER 2, backcountry, backland, ‖backveld, backwash, backwater, backwoods, bush, hinterland, up-country

outbalance *vb* ***syn*** OUTWEIGH 1, overbalance, overweigh, overweight

outbloom *vb* ***syn*** BLOSSOM, bloom, blow, burgeon, effloresce, flower

outbreak *n* **1** a sudden or violent beginning of activity <an *outbreak* of new housing starts>

syn burst, eruption, flare, outburst; *compare* EPIDEMIC

rel beginning, commencement, dawn, onset, outset

2 ***syn*** EPIDEMIC, plague, rash

outbreathe *vb* ***syn*** EXHALE, breathe (out), expire

outburst *n* **1** a violent expression of emotion <an *outburst* of anger>

syn access, burst, eruption, explosion, flare-up, gust, sally

rel scene, storm, tantrum; frenzy, rapture, transport(s)

2 ***syn*** OUTBREAK 1, burst, eruption, flare

outcast *n* one who is cast out by society <a political *outcast*>

syn castaway, derelict, Ishmael, Ishmaelite, leper, offscouring, pariah, untouchable

rel hobo, tramp, vagabond, vagrant; displaced person; exile, expatriate; reprobate

con big name, bigwig, celebrity, lion, luminary, name, notable, personage, somebody

outcome *n* ***syn*** EFFECT 1, aftereffect, aftermath, causatum, consequence, event, issue, result, sequel, upshot

outcomer *n* ***syn*** STRANGER, alien, auslander, foreigner, inconnu, outlander, outsider

out–country *adj* ***syn*** RURAL, agrestic, bucolic, campestral, countrified, country, outland, pastoral, provincial, rustic

outcrier *n* ***syn*** PEDDLER, ‖arab, cheap-jack (*or* cheap-john), ‖duffer, hawker, higgler, huckster, monger, packman, vendor

outcry *n* ***syn*** COMMOTION 1, clamor, convulsion, ferment, tumult, upheaval, upturn

outdare *vb* ***syn*** FACE 3, ‖banter, beard, brave, challenge, dare, defy, front, outface, venture

---

syn synonym(s) ***rel*** related word(s)
idiom idiomatic equivalent(s) ***con*** contrasted word(s)
ant antonym(s) * vulgar
‖ use limited; if in doubt, see a dictionary
The first word in a synonym list when printed in SMALL CAPITALS shows where there is more information about the group. For a more efficient use of this book see Explanatory Notes.

outdate *vb* to make obsolete or out-of-date <the automobile *outdated* the horse and buggy>

syn antiquate, obsolesce, obsolete, outmode, superannuate

rel age, date, fossilize; replace, supersede

outdated *adj* ***syn*** OLD-FASHIONED, antiquated, antique, archaic, dated, démodé, old, outmoded, passé, vintage

ant up-to-the-minute

outdistance *vb* ***syn*** OUTSTRIP 1, distance, outpace, outrun, outspeed

outdo *vb* **1** ***syn*** SURPASS 1, beat, best, better, exceed, excel, outshine, outstrip, top, transcend

idiom out-Herod Herod, steal (*or* get) a march on

2 ***syn*** DEFEAT 2, best, down, ‖pip, worst

outdoor *adj* taking place, done, or existing in the open air <an *outdoor* restaurant>

syn alfresco, hypaethral, open-air, out-of-door, outside

ant indoor, inside

outdoors *adv* in or into the open air <went *outdoors* for some fresh air>

syn out, out of doors, outside, without, withoutdoors

ant indoors, inside, withindoors

outdoors *n pl but sing in constr* the space where air is unconfined <every night he let the dog run in the *outdoors*>

syn open, open air, out-of-doors, outside, without

idiom God's good (*or* green) earth

outer *adj* being or located outside something <the sheep's thick *outer* coat of wool>

syn exterior, external, outside, outward, over

rel extraneous, extrinsic, superficial, surface; outlying, remote

con inside, interior, internal, inward

ant inner

outermost *adj* ***syn*** EXTREME 5, farthest, furthermost, furthest, outmost, remotest, utmost, uttermost

ant inmost, innermost

outface *vb* ***syn*** FACE 3, ‖banter, beard, brave, challenge, dare, defy, front, outdare, venture

outfit *n* **1** ***syn*** EQUIPMENT, accouterment(s), apparatus, gear, habiliments, machinery, matériel, paraphernalia, tackle, tackling

2 ***syn*** COSTUME, dress, getup, guise, rig, setout, turnout

3 ***syn*** COMPANY 4, band, corps, party, troop, troupe

4 ***syn*** ENTERPRISE 3, business, company, concern, establishment, firm, house

outfit *vb* ***syn*** FURNISH 1, accouter, appoint, arm, equip, fit out, gear, rig, turn out

outfox *vb* ***syn*** OUTWIT, outgeneral, outjockey, outmaneuver, outreach, outslick, outsmart, outthink, overreach, undo

outgeneral *vb* ***syn*** OUTWIT, outfox, outjockey, outmaneuver, outreach, outslick, outsmart, outthink, overreach, undo

rel outfight, outflank, outgame

idiom steal a march

outgo *vb* ***syn*** SURPASS 1, best, better, exceed, outdo, outmatch, outshine, outstrip, pass, top

outgoing *adj* ***syn*** DEMONSTRATIVE, expansive, unconstrained, unreserved, unrestrained

ant aloof

outgrowth *n* **1** a projecting part of an organism <a warty *outgrowth* on the skin>

syn excrescence, excrescency, process, processus
rel enlargement, prolongation, swelling; offshoot, shoot
2 something that develops or grows directly out of something else <the new TV series was an *outgrowth* of a popular play>
syn by-product, derivative, descendant, offshoot, spin-off
rel branch, member; child, offspring, product; aftereffect, consequence, effect, issue, outcome, result
con origin, root, source; antecedent, cause, determinant

outhouse *n syn* PRIVY 1, backhouse, ||biffy, ||closet, *crapper, jakes, ||necessary, ||office

outing *n syn* EXCURSION 1, jaunt, junket, roundabout, sally

outjockey *vb syn* OUTWIT, outfox, outgeneral, outmaneuver, outreach, outslick, outsmart, outthink, overreach, undo

outland *adj syn* RURAL, agrestic, bucolic, campestral, countrified, country, out-country, pastoral, provincial, rustic

outlander *n syn* STRANGER, alien, auslander, foreigner, inconnu, outcomer, outsider

outlandish *adj* 1 *syn* BARBARIC 1, barbarian, barbarous, graceless, tasteless, vulgar, wild
rel foreign, strange
2 *syn* STRANGE 4, bizarre, curious, odd, peculiar, queer, singular, uncouth, unusual, weird
rel monstrous; outré
con commonplace, everyday
3 marked by sharp departure from the traditional or usual <men who wear beads, feathers, and other *outlandish* gear>
syn far-out, kinky, outré, ultra; *compare* EXTREME 3
rel bizarre, extravagant, outrageous, wild; unconventional, unorthodox
con conservative, conventional; compliant, conformable; moderate
4 *syn* BACK 1, frontier, remote, unsettled

outlast *vb syn* OUTLIVE, outwear, survive

outlaw *n* a criminal of the American western frontier <*outlaws* held up stagecoaches>
syn badman, ||bandido, bandit, desperado
rel gunman, gunslinger
idiom bad guy

outlaw *vb syn* FORBID, ban, enjoin, inhibit, interdict, prohibit, taboo

outlay *vb syn* SPEND 1, disburse, expend, fork (out), give, lay out, pay, shell out

outlay *n syn* EXPENSE 1, cost, disbursement, expenditure

outlet *n* 1 *syn* APERTURE, hole, opening, orifice, vent
2 *syn* EGRESS 2, exit
rel escape; release
3 *syn* STORE 4, market, shop, showroom

outline *n* the line that gives form or shape to a body or a figure <saw only a dark *outline* of the house through the gloom>
syn contour, delineation, figuration, line, lineament, lineation, profile, silhouette
rel configuration, conformation, figure, form, shape; skyline
con bulk, hulk, mass

outline *vb* 1 *syn* BORDER 1, bound, define, edge, fringe, hem, margin, rim, skirt, surround
2 *syn* SKETCH, adumbrate, block (out), chalk (out), characterize, draft, rough (out), skeleton, skeletonize

outlive *vb* to remain in existence longer than <the committee has *outlived* its usefulness>
syn outlast, outwear, survive
rel outstand, outstay

outlook *n* 1 *syn* LOOKOUT 2, observatory, overlook
2 *syn* VISTA, lookout, perspective, prospect, scape
3 *syn* VIEW 4, scene, sight
4 *syn* VIEWPOINT 2, angle, direction, side, slant, standpoint

outlying *adj syn* DISTANT 1, far, faraway, far-flung, far-off, off-lying, remote, removed

outmaneuver *vb syn* OUTWIT, outfox, outgeneral, outjockey, outreach, outslick, outsmart, outthink, overreach, undo
idiom steal a march (on)

outmatch *vb syn* SURPASS 1, beat, best, better, outdo, outgo, outshine, outstrip, pass, top

outmode *vb syn* OUTDATE, antiquate, obsolesce, obsolete, superannuate

outmoded *adj* 1 *syn* OLD-FASHIONED, antiquated, antique, archaic, démodé, demoded, old-timey, outdated, out-of-date, vintage
2 *syn* OBSOLETE, dead, disused, extinct, outworn, passé, superseded
3 *syn* TACKY 2, dowdy frumpish, frumpy, out-of-date, stodgy, unstylish

outmost *adj syn* EXTREME 5, farthest, furthermost, furthest, outermost, remotest, utmost, uttermost
ant inmost, innermost

out-of-date *adj* 1 *syn* OLD-FASHIONED, antiquated, antique, archaic, dated, démodé, old-time, outdated, passé, vintage
ant up-to-date
2 *syn* TACKY 2, dowdy, frumpish, frumpy, outmoded, stodgy, unstylish

out-of-door *adj syn* OUTDOOR, alfresco, hypaethral, open-air, outside

out-of-doors *n pl but sing in constr syn* OUTDOORS, open, open air, outside, without

out of doors *adv syn* OUTDOORS, out, outside, without, withoutdoors

out-of-the-way *adj syn* OBSCURE 2, devious, lonesome, remote, removed, retired, secret

outpace *vb syn* OUTSTRIP 1, distance, outdistance, outrun, outspeed

outplace *vb syn* REPLACE 3, supersede, supplant

output *n* the amount of something produced <an annual *output* of 3,000,000 units>
syn outturn, product, production, turnout, yield

---

syn synonym(s)	*rel* related word(s)
idiom idiomatic equivalent(s)	*con* contrasted word(s)
ant antonym(s)	* vulgar

|| use limited; if in doubt, see a dictionary
The first word in a synonym list when printed in SMALL CAPITALS shows where there is more information about the group. For a more efficient use of this book see Explanatory Notes.

rel gain, get, profit, take; crop, harvest
con input; raw material

outrage *n syn* INJURY 1, damage, harm, hurt, mischief, ruin

outrage *vb* **1** *syn* RAPE, defile, deflorate, deflower, force, ravish, spoil, violate
2 *syn* ABUSE 4, ill-treat, ill-use, maltreat, mistreat, misuse
3 *syn* WRONG, aggrieve, oppress, persecute
4 *syn* OFFEND 3, affront, insult

outrageous *adj* **1** exceeding the limits of what is normal or tolerable < *outrageous* prices that threaten our way of life >
syn barbarous, unchristian, uncivilized, unconscionable, ungodly, unholy, wicked
rel abominable, awful, beastly, dreadful, ghastly, horrible, horrid, impossible, intolerable, terrible, unreasonable; scandalous, shocking
con normal, reasonable, tolerable; acceptable, bearable, endurable, supportable
2 enormously or flagrantly bad or horrible < *outrageous* treatment of prisoners >
syn atrocious, crying, desperate, heinous, monstrous, scandalous, shocking
rel enormous, flagrant, gross; egregious, nefarious, notorious, villainous
con condonable, excusable, forgivable, pardonable; defensible, justifiable; legitimate, reasonable; comprehensible, plausible, understandable

outrank *vb syn* PRECEDE 1, rank

outré *adj syn* OUTLANDISH 3, far-out, kinky, ultra

outreach *vb syn* OUTWIT, outfox, outgeneral, outjockey, outmaneuver, outslick, outsmart, outthink, overreach, undo

outrecuidance *n syn* CONCEIT 2, amour propre, complacence, conceitedness, consequence, egoism, egotism, narcissism, self-esteem, vainglory

outrider *n syn* FORERUNNER 1, harbinger, herald, precursor

outright *adj* **1** *syn* UTTER, absolute, complete, consummate, downright, out-and-out, perfect, positive, thoroughgoing, unmitigated
2 *syn* WHOLE 4, all, complete, entire, gross, total

outrun *vb syn* OUTSTRIP 1, distance, outdistance, outpace, outspeed

outset *n syn* BEGINNING, birth, commencement, dawn, dawning, onset, opening, outstart, setout, start

outshine *vb syn* SURPASS 1, beat, best, better, exceed, excel, outdo, outstrip, top, transcend

outside *n syn* OUTDOORS, open, open air, out-of-doors, without

outside *adj* **1** *syn* OUTER, exterior, external, outward, over
rel alien, foreign
ant inside
2 *syn* OUTDOOR, alfresco, hypaethral, open-air, out-of-door
3 *syn* MAXIMUM, maximal, top, topmost, utmost
4 *syn* REMOTE 4, ‖fat, negligible, off, slender, slight, slim, small

outside *adv syn* OUTDOORS, out, out of doors, without, withoutdoors

outside *prep* **1** *syn* BEYOND 1, after, past, without
2 *syn* EXCEPT, apart from, aside from, bar, beside, but, excluding, exclusive of, save, saving

outside of *prep syn* EXCEPT, aside from, bar, barring, besides, but, excluding, exclusive of, save, saving

outsider *n syn* STRANGER, alien, auslander, foreigner, inconnu, outcomer, outlander
con insider

outskirt *n usu* **outskirts** *pl syn* ENVIRONS 2, purlieus, suburbs

outslick *vb syn* OUTWIT, outfox, outgeneral, outjockey, outmaneuver, outreach, outsmart, outthink, overreach, undo

outsmart *vb syn* OUTWIT, outfox, outgeneral, outjockey, outmaneuver, outreach, outslick, outthink, overreach, undo

outspeed *vb syn* OUTSTRIP 1, distance, outdistance, outpace, outrun

outspoken *adj* speaking without fear or reserve <quite *outspoken* in her views on child rearing>
syn free, free-spoken, round, vocal
rel candid, direct, forthright, frank, open, plain, plainspoken, straightforward, unreticent; bluff, blunt; explicit, point-blank, unequivocal; strident
con reserved, restrained, reticent; private, retiring, shrinking; unassertive

outspread *vb syn* OPEN 4, expand, extend, fan (out), outstretch, spread, unfold
ant folded (*of wings or a fan*)

outstanding *adj* **1** *syn* UNPAID 2, due, mature, overdue, owing, payable, unsettled
2 *syn* NOTICEABLE, arresting, arrestive, conspicuous, marked, prominent, remarkable, salient, signal, striking
3 *syn* CHIEF 2, capital, dominant, main, major, predominant, preeminent, principal, star, stellar
4 *syn* SUPERB 3, magnificent, standout, superexcellent, superlative

outstare *vb syn* STARE DOWN, look down

outstart *n syn* BEGINNING, birth, commencement, dawn, dawning, onset, opening, outset, setout, start

outstep *vb syn* EXCEED 1, overrun, overstep, surpass

outstretch *vb syn* OPEN 4, expand, extend, fan (out), outspread, spread, unfold

outstrip *vb* **1** to go faster than <could *outstrip* even the fastest horse>
syn distance, outdistance, outpace, outrun, outspeed
rel outfly, outsoar, outwing; outfoot, outrace, outride; outsail; outtravel; lose, shake off
con follow, trail; drag, hang back, lag
2 *syn* SURPASS 1, beat, best, better, exceed, excel, outdo, outshine, top, transcend

outsweepings *n pl syn* REFUSE, debris, ‖dust, garbage, junk, litter, rubbish, sweepings, trash, waste

outthink *vb syn* OUTWIT, outfox, outgeneral, outjockey, outmaneuver, outreach, outslick, outsmart, overreach, undo

---

outthrust *n* ***syn*** PROJECTION 1, bulge, jut, protrusion, protuberance

outtire *vb* ***syn*** EXHAUST 4, ‖bugger, fag, frazzle, knock out, outwear, ‖poop, prostrate, tucker, wear out

outturn *n* ***syn*** OUTPUT, product, production, turnout, yield

outward *adj* ***syn*** OUTER, exterior, external, outside, over
ant inward

outwardly *adv* ***syn*** OSTENSIBLY, apparently, evidently, officially, professedly, seemingly
ant inwardly

outwear *vb* **1** ***syn*** EXHAUST 4, ‖bugger, fag, frazzle, knock out, outtire, ‖poop, prostrate, tucker, wear out
2 ***syn*** OUTLIVE, outlast, survive
rel endure, hold up

outweigh *vb* **1** to exceed in weight, value, or importance <her brother *outweighed* her by nearly fifty pounds> <the facts *outweigh* his argument>
syn outbalance, overbalance, overweigh, overweight
rel overbear
2 ***syn*** COMPENSATE 1, atone (for), balance, counterbalance, counterpoise, countervail, make up, offset, redeem, set off

outweighing *adj* ***syn*** DOMINANT 1, ascendant, master, overbearing, paramount, predominant, preponderant, prevalent, regnant, sovereign

outwit *vb* to defeat or get the better of by superior cleverness or ingenuity <*outwitted* the enemy by taking a different route>
syn have, outfox, outgeneral, outjockey, outmaneuver, outreach, outslick, outsmart, outthink, overreach, undo; *compare* FRUSTRATE 1
rel bamboozle, befool, dupe, gull, hoax, hoodwink, outtrick, outtrump, trick; outdo; outguess

outworn *adj* ***syn*** OBSOLETE, dead, disused, extinct, outmoded, passé, superseded

oval *adj* having the shape of a longitudinal section of an egg <an *oval* pond>
syn ooid, ovate, oviform, ovoid
rel ovaloid; ellipsoidal, elliptic

ovate *adj* ***syn*** OVAL, ooid, oviform, ovoid

over *adv* **1** from one point to another across intervening space <sailed *over* to the island>
syn across, athwart, beyond, transversely
2 ***syn*** AWAY 2, off
3 ***syn*** EVER 6, excessively, extremely, immensely, inordinately, overfull, overly, overmuch, too, unduly
4 at a higher point <the plane was directly *over*>
syn above, aloft, overhead
idiom on high
ant under
5 at or to an end <it's all *over* between them>
syn by, through
6 ***syn*** THROUGH 1, around, round, throughout
7 yet another time <do the work *over*>
syn afresh, again, anew, de novo, once more
idiom over again

over *prep* **1** at a higher level <clouds hung *over* the town>
syn above, o'er
ant under
2 ***syn*** ACROSS, athwart, cross
3 with respect to <children squabbling *over* toys>
syn about, on, upon, with
4 so as to make contact with <hit him *over* the head>
syn on, upon
5 ***syn*** DURING, amid, mid, midst, throughout
6 as the result of <quarreled *over* money matters>
syn because of, due to, owing to, through

over *adj* **1** ***syn*** SUPERIOR 1, greater, higher, overlying, superincumbent, superjacent
ant under
2 ***syn*** OUTER, exterior, external, outside, outward

over *vb* ***syn*** CLEAR 8, hurdle, leap, negotiate, overleap, surmount, vault

overabounding *adj* ***syn*** SUPERABUNDANT, overabundant, overflowing

overabundance *n* ***syn*** EXCESS 1, overflow, overkill, overmuch, overplus, plethora, superfluity, surfeit, surplus, surplusage

overabundant *adj* ***syn*** SUPERABUNDANT, overabounding, overflowing

overact *vb* to exaggerate in acting especially on the stage or screen <was criticized for *overacting* the part>
syn overplay
rel ham, mug; declaim, rant, spout
idiom chew the scenery
ant underact, underplay

over against *prep* **1** ***syn*** AGAINST 1, contra, facing, fronting, toward, vis-à-vis
2 ***syn*** VERSUS 2, vis-à-vis

overage *n* ***syn*** EXCESS 2, overstock, oversupply, plus, surplus, surplusage
ant shortage, underage

overall *adv* **1** ***syn*** EVERYWHERE 1, all over, all round (*or* all around), everyplace, far and near, far and wide, high and low, throughout
2 ***syn*** GENERALLY 1, chiefly, largely, mainly, mostly, predominantly, primarily, principally

overall *adj* ***syn*** ALL-AROUND 2, comprehensive, general, global, inclusive, sweeping

over and above *prep* ***syn*** BESIDES 1, as well as, beside, beyond

over and over *adv* ***syn*** OFTEN, again and again, frequently, much, oft, oftentimes, ofttimes, repeatedly, time and again

overbalance *vb* ***syn*** OUTWEIGH 1, outbalance, overweigh, overweight

overbalanced *adj* ***syn*** LOPSIDED, asymmetric, disproportionate, irregular, nonsymmetrical, off-balance, unbalanced, unequal, uneven, unsymmetrical

overbalancing *adj* ***syn*** DOMINANT 1, ascendant, master, outweighing, overbearing, paramount, predominant, preponderant, regnant, sovereign

---

syn synonym(s)	***rel*** related word(s)
idiom idiomatic equivalent(s)	***con*** contrasted word(s)
ant antonym(s)	* vulgar

‖ use limited; if in doubt, see a dictionary
The first word in a synonym list when printed in SMALL CAPITALS shows where there is more information about the group. For a more efficient use of this book see Explanatory Notes.

overbearing *adj* **1** ***syn*** MASTERFUL 1, bossy, domineering, high-handed, imperative, imperial, imperious, magisterial, peremptory
2 ***syn*** DOMINANT 1, ascendant, master, paramount, predominant, predominate, preponderant, prevalent, regnant, sovereign
3 ***syn*** PROUD 1, arrogant, cavalier, disdainful, haughty, high-and-mighty, insolent, lordly, supercilious, superior
rel absolute, autocratic, despotic, tyrannical
con passive, unassertive; acquiescent, compliant, unresisting
ant subservient

overblown *adj* **1** ***syn*** FAT 2, corpulent, fleshy, gross, heavy, obese, overweight, porcine, portly, stout
2 ***syn*** INFLATED, dropsical, dropsied, flatulent, tumescent, tumid, turgid, windy
3 ***syn*** RHETORICAL, aureate, bombastic, declamatory, euphuistic, flowery, grandiloquent, magniloquent, oratorical, sonorous
4 ***syn*** PRETENTIOUS 3, arty, arty-crafty, big, high-sounding, imposing

overbold *adj* ***syn*** SHAMELESS, arrant, barefaced, blatant, brassy, brazen, brazenfaced, impudent, unabashed, unblushing

overbrim *vb* ***syn*** OVERFLOW 2, overfill, overrun, run over, spill, well over

overburden *vb* ***syn*** OVERLOAD, overcharge, overlade, overtax, overweigh, overweight

overcast *vb* **1** ***syn*** OBSCURE, adumbrate, becloud, cloud, darken, dim, haze, overcloud, overshadow, shadow
2 ***syn*** COVER 3, blanket, cap, crown, overlay, overspread

overcast *adj* clouded over <a gray *overcast* March day>
syn cloudy, ‖dowly, dull, heavy, lowering (*or* louring), nubilous, overclouded
rel brooding, dirty, oppressive, sullen
ant clear, cloudless

overcharge *vb* **1** to charge excessively for service or goods <a clip joint well known for *overcharging* customers>
syn clip, fleece, skin, soak, stick
ant undercharge
2 ***syn*** OVERLOAD, overburden, overlade, overtax, overweigh, overweight
3 ***syn*** EMBROIDER, color, embellish, exaggerate, fudge, magnify, overdraw, overpaint, overstate, pad

overcloud *vb* ***syn*** OBSCURE, adumbrate, becloud, cloud, darken, dim, haze, overcast, overshadow, shadow

overclouded *adj* ***syn*** OVERCAST, cloudy, ‖dowly, dull, heavy, lowering (*or* louring), nubilous

overcome *vb* **1** to get the better of <*overcome* a bad habit>
syn conquer, down, hurdle, lick, master, surmount, throw; *compare* CONQUER 2
rel beat, defeat; outlive, prevail
con adopt, embrace, take up; indulge
2 ***syn*** CONQUER 2, best, master, prevail, triumph
3 ***syn*** OVERWHELM 4, drown, knock over, overpower, prostrate, whelm
4 ***syn*** WIN 1, beat, prevail, triumph

overconfident *adj* ***syn*** PRESUMPTUOUS, brash, brassbound, confident, overweening, presuming, pushful, ‖pushy, self-assertive, uppity

overcritical *adj* ***syn*** CRITICAL 1, captious, carping, caviling, cavillous, censorious, critic, faultfinding, hypercritical

overdo *vb* to make excessive use or application of <he has *overdone* that joke to the point that it is no longer funny>
syn overplay, overuse, overwork
idiom go overboard, go to extremes, run into the ground

overdoing *n* ***syn*** EXTRAVAGANCE 2, extravagancy, lavishness, prodigality, squander, unthrift, waste, wastefulness

overdraw *vb* ***syn*** EMBROIDER, color, embellish, exaggerate, fudge, magnify, overcharge, overpaint, overstate, pad

overdue *adj* **1** ***syn*** UNPAID 2, due, mature, outstanding, owing, payable, unsettled
2 ***syn*** TARDY, behindhand, belated, late, lated, unpunctual
ant early

overearly *adj* ***syn*** EARLY 2, oversoon, premature, previous, ‖soon, untimely

overemphasize *vb* ***syn*** OVERPLAY 2, magnify, maximize, overstress
ant underemphasize

overesteem *vb* ***syn*** OVERVALUE, overestimate, overprize, overrate, overreckon

overestimate *vb* ***syn*** OVERVALUE, overesteem, overprize, overrate, overreckon
ant underestimate

overfill *vb* ***syn*** OVERFLOW 2, overbrim, overrun, run over, spill, well over

overflow *vb* **1** ***syn*** DELUGE 1, drown, engulf, flood, inundate, overwhelm, submerge, swamp, whelm
2 to flow over the brim <the river *overflowed* its banks>
syn overbrim, overfill, overrun, run over, spill, well over
rel brim, cascade, slop, slosh
con drop, recede, withdraw

overflow *n* **1** ***syn*** FLOOD 2, cataclysm, cataract, deluge, flooding, inundation, niagara, pour, spate, torrent
2 ***syn*** EXCESS 1, overabundance, overkill, overmuch, overplus, plethora, superfluity, surfeit, surplus, surplusage

overflowing *adj* **1** ***syn*** ALIVE 5, abounding, replete, rife, swarming, teeming, thronged
2 ***syn*** SUPERABUNDANT, overabounding, overabundant

overfull *adv* ***syn*** EVER 6, excessively, extremely, immensely, inordinately, over, overly, overmuch, too, unduly

overgrown *adj* covered with growth or herbage <a vacant lot *overgrown* with weeds>

---

syn synonym(s) — *rel* related word(s)
idiom idiomatic equivalent(s) — *con* contrasted word(s)
ant antonym(s) — * vulgar
‖ use limited; if in doubt, see a dictionary
The first word in a synonym list when printed in SMALL CAPITALS shows where there is more information about the group. For a more efficient use of this book see Explanatory Notes.

syn grown, rank
rel braky, brambly, brushy, copsy, jungly, thicketed, thickety; dense, overrun, thick; lush

‖**overhand** *n* ***syn*** ADVANTAGE 3, allowance, bulge, ‖deadwood, draw, edge, handicap, head start, odds, vantage

overhang *vb* **1** ***syn*** BULGE, beetle, jut, poke, pouch, pout, project, protrude, stand out, stick out
2 ***syn*** HANG 4, beetle, bend (over), jut, lean (over)

overhanging *adj* ***syn*** IMMINENT 2, lowering, (*or* louring), lowery (*or* loury), menacing, threatening

overhaul *vb* **1** ***syn*** MEND 2, doctor, do up, fix, patch, rebuild, recondition, reconstruct, repair, revamp
2 ***syn*** CATCH 7, ‖cotch, overtake, take

overhead *adv* ***syn*** OVER 4, above, aloft
ant underfoot

overheated *adj* ***syn*** IMPASSIONED, ardent, burning, fervent, fervid, fiery, flaming, hot-blooded, passionate, torrid

overindulgence *n* ***syn*** EXCESS 3, immoderation, inordinateness, intemperance

overindulgent *adj* ***syn*** EXCESSIVE 2, immoderate, inordinate, intemperate, unrestrained, untempered

overkill *n* ***syn*** EXCESS 1, overabundance, overflow, overmuch, overplus, plethora, superfluity, surfeit, surplus, surplusage

overlade *vb* ***syn*** OVERLOAD, overburden, overcharge, overtax, overweigh, overweight

overlap *vb* to extend over and cover a part of <each course of shingles should *overlap* the preceding course by several inches>
syn imbricate, lap, overlie, override, ride, shingle

overlay *vb* ***syn*** COVER 3, blanket, cap, crown, overcast, overspread

overleap *vb* **1** ***syn*** CLEAR 8, hurdle, leap, negotiate, over, surmount, vault
2 ***syn*** NEGLECT, blink (at *or* away), discount, disregard, fail, forget, ignore, omit, overlook, overpass

overlie *vb* ***syn*** OVERLAP, imbricate, lap, override, ride, shingle

overload *vb* to load to excess <*overload* a ship>
syn overburden, overcharge, overlade, overtax, overweigh, overweight
con lighten

overlong *adj* ***syn*** LONG 2, dragging, drawn-out, ‖dreich, lengthy, long-drawn-out, longsome, prolonged,. protracted

overlook *vb* **1** ***syn*** SURVEY 3, oversee
2 to rise above and afford a view of <the tower *overlooks* the city>
syn dominate, look down, overtop, tower (above *or* over)
rel oversee
3 ***syn*** NEGLECT, blink (at *or* away), discount, disregard, fail, forget, ignore, omit, overpass, slight
4 ***syn*** SUPERVISE, boss, chaperon, oversee, quarterback, superintend, survey

overlook *n* **1** ***syn*** OMISSION, blank, chasm, oversight, preterition, pretermission, skip
2 ***syn*** LOOKOUT 2, observatory, outlook

overly *adv* ***syn*** EVER 6, excessively, extremely, immensely, inordinately, over, overfull, overmuch, too, unduly

overlying *adj* ***syn*** SUPERIOR 1, greater, higher, over, superincumbent, superjacent
ant underlying

overmuch *n* ***syn*** EXCESS 1, overabundance, overflow, overkill, overplus, plethora, superfluity, surfeit, surplus, surplusage

overmuch *adv* ***syn*** EVER 6, excessively, extremely, immensely, inordinately, over, overfull, overly, too, unduly

overnice *adj* ***syn*** PRECIOUS 4, affected, alembicated, chichi, la-di-da, overrefined, précieux

overpaint *vb* ***syn*** EMBROIDER, color, embellish, exaggerate, fudge, magnify, overcharge, overdraw, overstate, pad

overpass *vb* ***syn*** NEGLECT, blink (at *or* away), discount, disregard, fail, forget, ignore, omit, overleap, overlook

overpeopled *adj* ***syn*** OVERPOPULATED
ant underpeopled

overplay *vb* **1** ***syn*** OVERACT
ant underact, underplay
2 to give undue attention or emphasis to <*overplaying* the ephemeral at the expense of the significant>
syn magnify, maximize, overemphasize, overstress
rel accent, accentuate, point up; dramatize, exaggerate, hyperbolize, overdraw, overstate, stretch; overvalue
idiom lay it on thick
con downgrade, downplay; minimize
3 ***syn*** OVERDO, overuse, overwork

overplus *n* ***syn*** EXCESS 1, overabundance, overflow, overkill, overmuch, plethora, superfluity, surfeit, surplus, surplusage

overpopulated *adj* populated too densely <*overpopulated* cities>
syn overpeopled
rel congested, dense, overcrowded
con empty, vacant, void; unpopulated
ant underpopulated

overpower *vb* **1** ***syn*** CONQUER 1, bear down, beat down, crush, defeat, reduce, subdue, subjugate, vanquish
2 ***syn*** OVERWHELM 4, drown, knock over, overcome, prostrate, whelm

overpress *vb* ***syn*** PRESSURE, press, push

overprize *vb* ***syn*** OVERVALUE, overesteem, overestimate, overrate, overreckon
ant underprize, undervalue

overrate *vb* ***syn*** OVERVALUE, overesteem, overestimate, overprize, overreckon
ant underrate

overreach *vb* **1** ***syn*** CHEAT, beat, bilk, chouse, cozen, defraud, diddle, do, flimflam, gyp
2 ***syn*** OUTWIT, have, outfox, outgeneral, outjockey, outmaneuver, outreach, outslick, outsmart, undo

---

syn synonym(s) ***rel*** related word(s)
idiom idiomatic equivalent(s) ***con*** contrasted word(s)
ant antonym(s) * vulgar
‖ use limited; if in doubt, see a dictionary
The first word in a synonym list when printed in SMALL CAPITALS shows where there is more information about the group. For a more efficient use of this book see Explanatory Notes.

overreckon *vb* ***syn*** OVERVALUE, overesteem, overestimate, overprize, overrate

overrefined *adj* ***syn*** PRECIOUS 4, affected, alembicated, chichi, la-di-da, overnice, précieux

override *vb* ***syn*** OVERLAP, imbricate, lap, overlie, ride, shingle

overriding *adj* ***syn*** CENTRAL 1, cardinal, overruling, pivotal, ruling
rel primary, principal

overripe *adj* ***syn*** EFFETE 3, decadent, decayed, degenerate

overrule *vb* ***syn*** GOVERN 1, reign, rule, sway

overruling *adj* ***syn*** CENTRAL 1, cardinal, overriding, pivotal, ruling

overrun *vb* **1** ***syn*** WHIP 2, beat, ‖clobber, drub, lambaste, lick, overwhelm, smear, thrash, trim
2 ***syn*** INVADE 1, foray, inroad, overswarm, raid
3 ***syn*** INFEST 1, beset, overspread, overswarm
4 ***syn*** EXCEED 1, outstep, overstep, surpass
5 ***syn*** OVERFLOW 2, overbrim, overfill, run over, spill, well over

oversea *adj* ***syn*** OVERSEAS, transmarine, ultramarine

overseas *adv* beyond or across the sea <served *overseas* for two years>
syn abroad
con stateside

overseas *adj* situated, originating in, or relating to lands overseas <attempting to tap the potential of *overseas* markets>
syn oversea, transmarine, ultramarine
rel alien, exotic, foreign, strange
con domestic, home; stateside

oversee *vb* **1** ***syn*** SURVEY 3, overlook
2 ***syn*** SUPERVISE, boss, chaperon, overlook, quarterback, superintend, survey

overset *vb* **1** ***syn*** OVERTURN 1, knock over, overthrow, tip (over), topple, turn over, upset
2 ***syn*** OVERTHROW 2, overturn, topple, tumble, unhorse

overshadow *vb* ***syn*** OBSCURE, adumbrate, becloud, cloud, darken, dim, haze, overcast, overcloud, shadow

oversight *n* **1** the function or duty of watching or guarding for the sake of proper direction or control <had *oversight* of the children as they played>
syn care, charge, conduct, handling, intendance, management, running, superintendence, superintendency, supervision
rel custody, guard, guardianship; keeping, maintenance; surveillance; aegis, tutelage; ciceronage; chaperonage; check, control
2 ***syn*** FAILURE 1, default, delinquency, dereliction, neglect
3 ***syn*** OMISSION, blank, chasm, overlook, preterition, pretermission, skip

---

syn synonym(s)
idiom idiomatic equivalent(s)
ant antonym(s)
rel related word(s)
con contrasted word(s)
* vulgar
‖ use limited; if in doubt, see a dictionary
The first word in a synonym list when printed in SMALL CAPITALS shows where there is more information about the group. For a more efficient use of this book see Explanatory Notes.

oversize *adj* ***syn*** LARGE 1, big, bull, fat, great, husky
ant undersized

overslaugh *vb* ***syn*** HINDER, bar, block, brake, dam, impede, obstruct

oversoon *adj* ***syn*** EARLY 2, overearly, premature, previous, ‖soon, untimely

oversoon *adv* ***syn*** EARLY 2, betimes, prematurely

overspread *vb* **1** ***syn*** COVER 3, blanket, cap, crown, overcast, overlay
2 ***syn*** INFEST 1, beset, overrun, overswarm

overstate *vb* ***syn*** EMBROIDER, color, embellish, exaggerate, fudge, magnify, overcharge, overdraw, overpaint, pad
ant understate

overstatement *n* ***syn*** EXAGGERATION, coloring, embellishment, embroidering, hyperbole
ant understatement

overstep *vb* ***syn*** EXCEED 1, outstep, overrun, surpass
rel infringe, transgress, trespass

overstock *n* ***syn*** EXCESS 2, overage, oversupply, plus, surplus, surplusage
ant understock

overstress *vb* ***syn*** OVERPLAY 2, magnify, maximize, overemphasize

oversupply *n* ***syn*** EXCESS 2, overage, overstock, plus, surplus, surplusage
ant undersupply

overswarm *vb* **1** ***syn*** INFEST 1, beset, overrun, overspread
2 ***syn*** INVADE 1, foray, inroad, overrun, raid

oversway *vb* ***syn*** INDUCE 1, argue (into), bring around, convince, draw, draw in, draw on, persuade, prevail (on *or* upon), prompt

overtake *vb* ***syn*** CATCH 7, ‖cotch, overhaul, take

overtax *vb* ***syn*** OVERLOAD, overburden, overcharge, overlade, overweigh, overweight

overthrow *vb* **1** ***syn*** OVERTURN 1, knock over, overset, tip (over), topple, turn over, upset
2 to cause the downfall of <*overthrow* the government>
syn overset, overturn, topple, tumble, unhorse; *compare* CONQUER 1
rel depose, dethrone, oust, remove, unseat; liquidate, purge; conquer, defeat, destroy, ruin
con create, establish, found, set up

overthrow *n* ***syn*** DEFEAT 1, beating, debacle, defeasance, drubbing, licking, rout, shellacking, trouncing, vanquishment

overtone *n* ***syn*** ASSOCIATION 4, connotation, hint, implication, suggestion, undertone

overtop *vb* ***syn*** OVERLOOK 2, dominate, look down, tower (above *or* over)

overture *n* **1** action intended to attract favorable attention <made friendly *overtures* to the new member of the class>
syn advance, approach
rel bid, proposal, proposition, tender
2 ***syn*** INTRODUCTION, exordium, foreword, preamble, preface, prelude, prelusion, proem, prolegomenon, prologue

overturn *vb* **1** to turn from an upright or level position <the embarrassed boy backed into the table and *overturned* a lamp>

syn knock over, overset, overthrow, tip (over), topple, turn over, upset
rel capsize, keel (over *or* up), upend, upturn; prostrate; down; roll (over)
con erect, right, set up, straighten (up)
2 *syn* OVERTHROW 2, overset, topple, tumble, unhorse

overturn *n syn* SHAKE-UP, reorganization, revolution, turnover

overuse *vb syn* OVERDO, overplay, overwork
ant underuse

overvalue *vb* to set too high a value on <inclined to *overvalue* his own charm>
syn overesteem, overestimate, overprize, overrate, overreckon
rel cherish, prize, treasure; adore, idolize, worship
con belittle, depreciate
ant underprize, undervalue

overweening *adj syn* PRESUMPTUOUS, brash, forward, presuming, pushful, ‖pushy, self-asserting, self-assertive, uppish, uppity

overweigh *vb* **1** *syn* OUTWEIGH 1, outbalance, overbalance, overweight
2 *syn* OVERLOAD, overburden, overcharge, overlade, overtax, overweight

overweighing *adj syn* DOMINANT 1, ascendant, master, outweighing, overbearing, paramount, predominant, preponderant, regnant, sovereign

overweight *vb* **1** *syn* OUTWEIGH 1, outbalance, overbalance, overweigh
2 *syn* OVERLOAD, overburden, overcharge, overlade, overtax, overweigh

overweight *adj syn* FAT 2, corpulent, fleshy, gross, heavy, obese, portly, stout, upholstered, weighty
ant underweight

overwhelm *vb* **1** *syn* DELUGE 1, drown, engulf, flood, inundate, overflow, submerge, swamp, whelm
2 *syn* DELUGE 3, flood, swamp, whelm
3 *syn* WHIP 2, beat, ‖clobber, drub, lick, shellac, smear, smother, thrash, trim
4 to subject to the grip of something overpowering and usually distressing or damaging <*overwhelmed* by the death of his only child> <human wants that tend to *overwhelm* environmental realities>
syn drown, knock over, overcome, overpower, prostrate, whelm
rel demoralize, devastate, dumbfound, shatter; floor, sink; disturb, upset; destroy, ruin, wreck; downgrade, lower, subordinate

overwhelmed *adj syn* AGHAST 2, agape, confounded, dismayed, dumbfounded, shocked, thunderstruck

overwhelming *adj syn* TOWERING 4, monumental

overwork *vb syn* OVERDO, overplay, overuse

oviform *adj syn* OVAL, ooid, ovate, ovoid

ovoid *adj syn* OVAL, ooid, ovate, oviform

owing *adj syn* UNPAID 2, due, mature, outstanding, overdue, payable, unsettled

owing to *prep syn* OVER 6, because of, due to, through

owl–light *n syn* EVENING 1, ‖dimmet, ‖dimps, ‖dimpsy, dusk, ‖dusk dark, eventide, gloaming, nightfall, twilight

own *vb* **1** *syn* HAVE 1, enjoy, hold, possess, retain
2 *syn* ACKNOWLEDGE 1, admit, allow, avow, concede, confess, fess (up), grant, let on, own up
con deny, disclaim
ant disown, repudiate

owner *n* one that has the legal or rightful title <*owner* of the shop>
syn holder, possessor, proprietor
rel lord, master
con lessee, renter, tenant; squatter; interloper, intruder, trespasser

ownership *n* lawful claim or title <would soon have *ownership* of the house>
syn dominion, possession, possessorship, property, proprietary, proprietorship
rel hand

own up *vb syn* ACKNOWLEDGE 1, admit, allow, avow, concede, confess, fess (up), grant, let on, own

oyster *n syn* FORTE, eminency, long suit, medium, métier, strong suit

---

syn synonym(s) | *rel* related word(s)
idiom idiomatic equivalent(s) | *con* contrasted word(s)
ant antonym(s) | * vulgar
‖ use limited; if in doubt, see a dictionary
The first word in a synonym list when printed in SMALL CAPITALS shows where there is more information about the group. For a more efficient use of this book see Explanatory Notes.

P

pa *n* ***syn*** FATHER 1, dad, daddy, ‖old man, ‖pap, papa, ‖pappy, ‖pater, pop, poppa

pablum *n* ***syn*** PAP 2, rubbish, slop

pabulum *n* ***syn*** FOOD 2, aliment, nourishment, nutriment, pap, sustenance

pace *n* **1** ***syn*** TEMPO, time
2 ***syn*** SPEED 2, ‖bat, celerity, gait, quickness, rapidity, rapidness, swiftness, velocity
3 ***syn*** ROUTINE, grind, groove, rote, rut, treadmill

pace *vb* **1** ***syn*** WALK 1, ambulate, foot (it), hoof, step, traipse, tread, troop
2 ***syn*** PRECEDE 2, antecede, antedate, forerun, predate

pacific *adj* affording or promoting peace <a *pacific* policy>
syn irenic, nonviolent, pacificatory, pacifist, peaceable, peaceful
rel appeasing, conciliating, conciliatory, pacifying, propitiating, propitiatory; dovelike, gentle, inoffensive
con belligerent, combative, contentious, pugnacious, quarrelsome; unpeaceable, unpeaceful; hawkish, violent, warlike
ant bellicose, unpacific

pacificator *n* ***syn*** PEACEMAKER, make-peace

pacificatory *adj* ***syn*** PACIFIC, irenic, nonviolent, pacifist, peaceable, peaceful

pacificist *n* ***syn*** PACIFIST, dove
idiom man of peace

pacifist *n* one who opposes war or violence as a means of settling disputes <*pacifists* who fight war with argument and propaganda>
syn dove, pacificist
rel satyagrahi; ‖conchie, conscientious objector; peacemonger
con belligerent, combatant; chauvinist, hawk, jingo, jingoist, warmonger
ant bellicist

pacifist *adj* ***syn*** PACIFIC, irenic, nonviolent, pacificatory, peaceable, peaceful
ant combative

pacify *vb* to allay anger or agitation <saw his mounting rage and tried to *pacify* him>
syn appease, assuage, conciliate, mollify, placate, propitiate, sweeten
rel dulcify, soften; allay, alleviate, mitigate, relieve; moderate, qualify, smooth (over), temper
idiom pour balm into, pour oil on (the) troubled waters
con arouse, stir (up)
ant anger

pack *n* **1** ***syn*** BACKPACK, haversack, knapsack, packsack, rucksack
2 ***syn*** MUCH, barrel, great deal, heap, lot, lump, ‖mess, multiplicity, peck, pile

pack *vb* **1** ***syn*** STOW, bestow, store, warehouse
2 ***syn*** LOAD 3, charge, choke, fill, heap, pile
3 ***syn*** CARRY 1, bear, buck, convey, ferry, ‖hump, ‖jag, lug, tote, transport

packed *adj* ***syn*** FULL 1, awash, brimful, brimming, chock-full, crammed, crowded, jammed, jam-packed, stuffed
idiom packed like sardines (*or* herrings)

‖**packed out** *adj* ***syn*** FULL 1, brimful, brimming, bung-full, chockablock, chock-full, crammed, crowded, jam-packed, packed

packet *n* ***syn*** FORTUNE 4, ‖bomb, boodle, bundle, mint, pile, pot, ‖roll, wad

packman *n* ***syn*** PEDDLER, ‖arab, cheap-jack (*or* cheap-john), hawker, higgler, huckster, outcrier, piepoudre, roadman, vendor

packsack *n* ***syn*** BACKPACK, haversack, knapsack, pack, rucksack

pact *n* **1** ***syn*** CONTRACT, agreement, bargain, bond, compact, convention, covenant, transaction
rel settlement
2 ***syn*** TREATY, agreement, concord, convention

‖**pad** *n* ***syn*** PROTECTION 2

pad *vb* ***syn*** EMBROIDER, embellish, exaggerate, fudge, magnify, overcharge, overdraw, overpaint, overstate, stretch

paddle *vb* ***syn*** ROW, oar, pull

‖**paddy** *n* ***syn*** POLICEMAN, ‖bluebottle, ‖bobby, ‖bull, ‖constable, ‖copper, ‖flatfoot, ‖gendarme, officer, ‖peeler

pagan *adj* ***syn*** HEATHEN, ethnic, gentile, infidel, infidelic, profane

pageant *n* ***syn*** PRETENSE 2, charade, disguise, make-believe, pretension, pretentiousness

pagoda *n* ***syn*** SUMMERHOUSE, alcove, belvedere, garden house, gazebo

pain *n* **1** a bodily sensation that causes acute discomfort or suffering <suffering from chest *pains*>
syn ache, ‖misery, pang, stitch, throe, twinge
rel discomfort, distress, hurt, suffering; agony, torment, torture
2 pains *pl* ***syn*** EFFORT 1, elbow grease, exertion, trouble, while
rel assiduousness, diligence, industry, sedulousness

pain *vb* **1** ***syn*** HURT 4, ache, ‖suffer
rel agonize, convulse, crucify, excruciate, harrow, lacerate
2 ***syn*** DISTRESS 2, aggrieve, constrain, grieve, hurt, injure
rel afflict; distress, upset; wound; anguish
idiom ‖hit one where one lives
3 ***syn*** TRY 2, distress, harass, irk, strain, stress, trouble

---

syn synonym(s) — *rel* related word(s)
idiom idiomatic equivalent(s) — *con* contrasted word(s)
ant antonym(s) — * vulgar
‖ use limited; if in doubt, see a dictionary
The first word in a synonym list when printed in SMALL CAPITALS shows where there is more information about the group. For a more efficient use of this book see Explanatory Notes.

painful *adj* **1** causing, marked by, or affected with pain <a *painful* wound>
syn aching, afflictive, algetic, hurtful, hurting, sore
rel raw; acute, piercing, sharp, shooting, stabbing, stinging; agonizing, excruciating, harrowing, racking, tormenting, torturous
ant painless, unpainful
2 *syn* BITTER 2, afflictive, distasteful, galling, grievous, unpalatable
rel unappetizing, unsavory
ant painless

painfully *adv syn* HARD 5, badly, hardly, harshly, rigorously, roughly, severely
ant painlessly

pain–killer *n syn* ANODYNE 1, analgesic, anesthetic

painstaking *adj syn* CAREFUL 2, conscientious, conscionable, exact, fussy, heedful, meticulous, punctilious, punctual, scrupulous

painstakingly *adv syn* HARD 3, assiduously, dingdong, earnestly, exhaustively, intensely, intensively, thoroughly, unremittingly
rel carefully, meticulously; lovingly

paint *n syn* MAKEUP 3, face, maquillage, war paint

pair *n syn* COUPLE, brace, doublet, duo, dyad, twosome

paired *adj syn* TWIN, double, dual

pal *n syn* ASSOCIATE 3, buddy, chum, comate, companion, comrade, crony, ‖cully, running mate

palace *adj syn* LUXURIOUS 3, Capuan, deluxe, luxuriant, opulent, palatial, plush, plushy, sumptuous, upholstered

palace car *n syn* PARLOR CAR, chair car, club car, lounge car, tavern car

palatable *adj* agreeable or pleasant especially to the sense of taste <a *palatable* meal>
syn aperitive, appetizing, flavorsome, good-tasting, ‖gusty, mouth-watering, relishing, sapid, saporous, savorous, savorsome, savory, tasteful, tasty, toothsome, toothy
rel delectable, delicious, delightful, luscious, scrumptious, yummy; tempting; saporific
con bad-tasting, disagreeable, distasteful, ill-flavored, unappetizing
ant unpalatable

palate *n syn* TASTE 4, gusto, heart, relish, zest

palatial *adj syn* LUXURIOUS 3, Capuan, deluxe, luscious, lush, luxuriant, opulent, plush, sumptuous, upholstered
rel noble, regal; monumental; impressive; rich, splendid

palaver *n* **1** *syn* CONFERENCE 2, colloquium, colloquy, rap session, seminar
rel dialogue, discussion; parley
2 *syn* CHATTER, babble, blab, blabber, chat, clack, gabble, jabber, prattle, yak
rel gas, guff, hot air
3 *syn* TERMINOLOGY, cant, dictionary, jargon, language, lexicon, vocabulary
4 *syn* BUSINESS 8, affair, concern, lookout, occasions

palaverous *adj syn* WORDY, diffuse, long-winded, prolix, redundant, verbose, windy

pale *adj* **1** deficient in color or in intensity of color <a *pale* face>
syn ashen, ashy, blanched, colorless, complexionless, doughy, livid, lurid, pallid, paly, wan, waxen
rel sallow, sick, sickly; gray, pasty, pasty-faced, waxlike; white, whitened; deathlike, ghastly
con flushed, ruddy; bright, colorful, florid
2 being weak and thin in substance or in vital qualities <a *pale,* inadequate foreign policy>
syn anemic, bloodless, pallid, waterish, watery
rel inane, insipid, jejune, wishy-washy; insubstantial, unsubstantial; ineffective, ineffectual; faint, feeble, weak
con strong, substantial; effective, effectual; bright, colorful
ant brilliant

pale *vb syn* DULL 1, dim, fade, muddy, tarnish

Pale Horse *n, used with the syn* DEATH 1, curtains, decease, defunction, demise, dissolution, passing, quietus, silence, sleep

palinode *vb syn* ABJURE, forswear, recall, recant, retract, take back, unsay, withdraw

pall *vb* **1** *syn* BORE, ennui, tire, weary
2 *syn* SATIATE, cloy, fill, glut, gorge, jade, sate, ‖stall, stodge, surfeit
rel disgust, weary

‖**pallet** *n syn* HEAD 1, ‖bean, ‖belfry, ‖chump, ‖coco, headpiece, noddle, noggin, noodle, sconce

palliate *vb* to give a speciously fine appearance to what is erroneous, base, or evil <did not try to conceal or *palliate* his errors>
syn blanch (over), extenuate, gloss (over), gloze (over), prettify, sugarcoat, varnish, veneer, white, whiten, whitewash
rel alleviate, lighten, mitigate; condone, excuse; moderate, qualify, soften, temper; camouflage, cloak, conceal, cover up, disguise, dissemble, mask; hush (up)
idiom paper over the cracks, put a good face on (*or* upon)

pallid *adj* **1** *syn* PALE 1, ashen, ashy, blanched, colorless, complexionless, doughy, lurid, wan, waxen
2 *syn* PALE 2, anemic, bloodless, waterish, watery

pally *adj syn* INTIMATE 4, ‖buddy-buddy, chummy, cozy, ‖palsy-walsy

palm (on *or* upon) *vb syn* FOIST 3, fob off, palm off, pass off, work off

‖**palm grease** *n syn* GRATUITY, cumshaw, lagniappe, largess, ‖palm oil, ‖perk(s), perquisite, pourboire, tip

palm off *vb syn* FOIST 3, fob off, palm (on *or* upon), pass off, work off

‖**palm oil** *n syn* GRATUITY, cumshaw, lagniappe, largess, ‖palm grease, ‖perk(s), perquisite, pourboire, tip

palooka *n syn* OAF 2, gawk, klutz, lobster, looby, lout, lubber, ‖lug, lummox, lump

palpable *adj* **1** *syn* TANGIBLE 1, tactile, touchable
2 *syn* PERCEPTIBLE, appreciable, detectable, discernible, observable, sensible, tangible
rel apparent, ostensible, seeming; believable, colorable, credible, plausible

---

syn synonym(s) *rel* related word(s)
idiom idiomatic equivalent(s) *con* contrasted word(s)
ant antonym(s) * vulgar
‖ use limited; if in doubt, see a dictionary
The first word in a synonym list when printed in SMALL CAPITALS shows where there is more information about the group. For a more efficient use of this book see Explanatory Notes.

3 ***syn*** CLEAR 5, apparent, distinct, evident, manifest, obvious, patent, plain, straightforward, unequivocal
rel certain, positive, sure; arresting, noticeable, remarkable, striking
con doubtful, dubious, problematic, questionable
ant impalpable

palpate *vb* ***syn*** TOUCH 1, feel, finger, handle, paw

palpation *n* ***syn*** TOUCH 2, taction

palpitate *vb* ***syn*** PULSATE, beat, pulse, throb
rel pitter-patter

‖**palsy–walsy** *adj* ***syn*** INTIMATE 4, ‖buddy-buddy, chummy, cozy, pally

palter *vb* **1** ***syn*** LIE, equivocate, falsify, fib, prevaricate
rel evade, fence
idiom play false, play fast and loose
2 ***syn*** HAGGLE 2, bargain, chaffer, dicker, higgle, huckster

paltry *adj* **1** ***syn*** CHEAP 2, base, common, mean, poor, rubbishy, shoddy, sleazy, tatty, trashy
rel beggarly, shabby; pitiful
2 ***syn*** LITTLE 2, borné, ineffectual, limited, mean, narrow, set, small
rel base, low, low-down, vile
3 ***syn*** PETTY 2, measly, Mickey Mouse, picayune, picayunish, piddling, puny, trifling, trivial, unconsequential
rel insignificant, unimportant

paly *adj* ***syn*** PALE 1, ashy, colorless, complexionless, doughy, livid, lurid, pallid, wan, waxen

pamper *vb* ***syn*** BABY, cater (to), cocker, coddle, cosset, humor, indulge, mollycoddle, ‖much, spoil
rel regale, tickle; caress, dandle, fondle, pet; overindulge

‖**pan** *n* ***syn*** FACE 1, countenance, ‖dial, features, ‖kisser, ‖map, mug, ‖phiz, ‖puss, visage

pan *vb* ***syn*** CRITICIZE, blame, censure, condemn, cut up, denounce, denunciate, knock, rap, reprehend

panacea *n* a remedy for all ills or difficulties <bicycles are not a *panacea* for the traffic problem>
syn catholicon, cure-all, elixir, nostrum
rel relief; remedy
idiom universal (*or* sovereign) remedy

pandect *n* ***syn*** COMPENDIUM 1, aperçu, digest, précis, sketch, survey, syllabus, sylloge

pandemoniac *adj* ***syn*** INFERNAL 2, avernal, cimmerian, hellish, plutonian, plutonic, stygian

pandemonium *n* **1** *cap* **Pandemonium** ***syn*** HELL, abyss, Gehenna, hades, inferno, netherworld, perdition, Sheol, Tophet, underworld
2 ***syn*** SINK 1, Augean stable, cesspit, cesspool, den, Sodom, sty
3 ***syn*** DIN, babel, clamor, hubbub, hullabaloo, jangle, racket, tintamarre, tumult, uproar

pander *n* ***syn*** PIMP 1, bully, cadet, ‖easy rider, fancy man, ‖mack, macquereau

syn synonym(s) ***rel*** related word(s)
idiom idiomatic equivalent(s) ***con*** contrasted word(s)
ant antonym(s) * vulgar
‖ use limited; if in doubt, see a dictionary
The first word in a synonym list when printed in SMALL CAPITALS shows where there is more information about the group. For a more efficient use of this book see Explanatory Notes.

idiom *ass peddler

panegyric *n* ***syn*** ENCOMIUM, citation, eulogy, salutation, tribute

panegyrical *adj* ***syn*** EULOGISTIC, encomiastic, laudative, laudatory, praiseful

panegyrize *vb* ***syn*** PRAISE 2, bless, celebrate, cry up, eulogize, extol, glorify, hymn, laud, magnify

pang *n* ***syn*** PAIN 1, ache, ‖misery, stitch, throe, twinge
rel prick, stab, ‖stang

‖**pang** *vb* ***syn*** CRAM 1, jam, jam-pack, ram, stuff, tamp

panhandler *n* ***syn*** BEGGAR 1, bummer, cadger, moocher, ‖schnorrer

panhandling *n* ***syn*** MENDICANCY, beggary, bumming, cadging, mendicity, mooching

panic *n* **1** ***syn*** FEAR 1, alarm, cold feet, consternation, dismay, dread, fright, horror, terror, trepidation
rel frenzy, hysteria; stampede
con composure, equanimity, sangfroid, self-possession
‖**2** ***syn*** RIOT 2, howl, scream, sidesplitter

‖**pank** *vb* ***syn*** PANT 1, blow, gasp, heave, huff, ‖pegh, puff

panoply *n* ***syn*** DISPLAY 2, array, fanfare, parade, pomp, shine, show

panorama *n* ***syn*** RANGE 2, compass, dimension(s), extent, orbit, purview, radius, reach, scope, sweep

pan out *vb* ***syn*** SUCCEED 2, click, come off, go, go over, prove out

pansified *adj* ***syn*** EFFEMINATE, epicene, Miss-Nancyish, prissy, sissified, sissy, unmanly

pant *vb* **1** to breathe quickly, spasmodically, or in a labored manner <was *panting* after running up the stairs>
syn blow, gasp, heave, huff, ‖pank, ‖pegh, puff
rel gulp; wheeze; wind; chuff
idiom be out of breath
2 ***syn*** AIM 2, aspire
rel hunger, long, pine, thirst; desire, want, wish
idiom be consumed with desire (for)

pantywaist *n* ***syn*** WEAKLING, baby, doormat, invertebrate, jellyfish, milksop, Milquetoast, mollycoddle, sissy, sissy-pants (*or* sissy-britches)

pantywaist *adj* ***syn*** CHARACTERLESS, namby-pamby, wishy-washy

pap *n* **1** ***syn*** FOOD 2, aliment, nourishment, nutriment, pabulum, sustenance
2 something (as reading matter) lacking in solid value or substance <the sentimental *pap* that he offered his readers>
syn pablum, rubbish, slop
rel garbage, trash

‖**pap** *n* ***syn*** FATHER 1, dad, daddy, ‖old man, pa, papa, ‖pappy, ‖pater, pop, poppa

papa *n* ***syn*** FATHER 1, dad, daddy, ‖old man, pa, ‖pap, ‖pappy, ‖pater, pop, poppa

paper *n* ***syn*** ESSAY 2, article, composition, theme

paphian *n* ***syn*** HARLOT 1, blowen, courtesan, demimondaine, demimonde, demirep, fancy woman, hetaera, kept woman, whore

pappy *adj* ***syn*** SOFT 6, mushy, pulpous, pulpy, spongy, squashy, squelchy, squishy, squushy, yielding

‖**pappy** *n* ***syn*** FATHER 1, dad, daddy, ‖old man, pa, ‖pap, papa, ‖pater, pop, poppa

par *n* **1** ***syn*** EQUIVALENCE, adequation, equality, equatability, equivalency, parity, sameness

2 *syn* AVERAGE, mean, median, norm
rel standard

parable *n syn* ALLEGORY 2, apologue, fable, myth
rel comparison, similitude

parachronism *n syn* ANACHRONISM 1, misdate, misdating, mistiming

parade *n syn* DISPLAY 2, array, fanfare, panoply, pomp, shine, show
rel exhibition

parade *vb syn* SHOW 4, brandish, display, disport, exhibit, expose, flash, flaunt, show off, trot out
rel disclose, divulge, reveal; advertise, declare, proclaim, publish; boast, brag, gasconade
idiom parade one's wares
con camouflage, cloak, disguise, dissemble, mask

paradigm *n syn* MODEL 2, archetype, beau ideal, ensample, example, exemplar, ideal, mirror, pattern, standard

paradigmatic *adj syn* TYPICAL 1, classic, classical, exemplary, ideal, model, prototypal, prototypical, quintessential, representative

paradise *n* 1 *syn* HEAVEN 2, bliss, Canaan, Civitas Dei, elysium, empyrean, happy hunting ground, New Jerusalem, nirvana, Zion
idiom the next world (*or* life)
2 *syn* UTOPIA, arcadia, Cockaigne, fairyland, heaven, lubberland, promised land, Shangri-la, wonderland, Zion

paragon *n* an individual of unequaled excellence often serving as a model <she is a *paragon* of a housewife>
syn ideal, jewel, nonesuch, nonpareil, phoenix; *compare* MODEL 2
rel apotheosis, epitome, last word, quintessence, ultimate; archetype, beau ideal, exemplar, pattern; ‖beaut, beauty, crackerjack, gem, love, lovely, peach, trump; champ, champion; cream, pick, tops

paragon *vb syn* EQUATE 2, assimilate, compare, liken, match, parallel

parallel *adj syn* LIKE, agnate, akin, alike, analogous, comparable, consonant, corresponding, similar, uniform
ant nonparallel, unparallel

parallel *n* one that corresponds to or closely resembles another <we seek in vain a *parallel* for this situation>
syn analogue, correlate, correspondent, counterpart, countertype, match; *compare* COUNTERPART 1, EQUAL
rel equivalent; double, duplicate, duplication

parallel *vb* 1 *syn* EQUATE 2, assimilate, compare, liken, match, paragon
2 to place (something) so as to be parallel with another <machines that combed and *paralleled* the fibers>
syn collimate, collocate, parallelize
rel align, line up

parallelize *vb syn* PARALLEL 2, collimate, collocate

paralyze *vb* 1 to render completely powerless, ineffective, or inert <a general strike that *paralyzed* the nation>
syn cripple, disable, disarm, immobilize, incapacitate, prostrate; *compare* MAIM, WEAKEN 1
rel deaden, enfeeble, weaken; close, shut (down); freeze; demolish, destroy, knock out
idiom bring to a grinding halt, tie hand and foot
2 *syn* DAZE 2, bedaze, bemuse, benumb, petrify, stun, stupefy
rel appall, daunt, dismay, horrify; cripple, disable, enfeeble, weaken; astound, flabbergast, nonplus
con animate, enliven, pep (up), stimulate
ant galvanize

paramount *adj syn* DOMINANT 1, ascendant, master, overbearing, predominant, predominate, preponderant, prevalent, regnant, sovereign
rel capital, headmost; commanding, controlling; cardinal, crowning

paramour *n* 1 *syn* GALLANT 2, amorist, Casanova, Don Juan, lothario, Romeo
2 *syn* LOVER 1, boyfriend, fancy man, man, master
3 *syn* MISTRESS, ‖doxy, girl friend, inamorata, lover, woman

parapet *n syn* BULWARK, bastion, breastwork, rampart

paraphernalia *n pl but sometimes sing in constr syn* EQUIPMENT 1, accouterment(s), gear, habiliments, machinery, material(s), matériel, outfit, tackle, tackling

paraphrase *n syn* VERSION 1, rendering, restatement, translation

paraphrase *vb* to express or interpret something (as a text or passage) in other words <*paraphrased* the complicated document>
syn rephrase, restate, reword, translate (into)
rel summarize; transcribe
con quote, reproduce

parasite *n* a person who is supported or seeks support from another without making an adequate return <lived as a *parasite* in his father's house>
syn barnacle, bloodsucker, freeloader, hanger-on, leech, lounge lizard, ‖spiv, sponge, sponger, sucker; *compare* SYCOPHANT
rel dependent; smell-feast; deadbeat, idler, laze

parasite *vb syn* INFEST 2, parasitize

parasitic *adj syn* FAWNING, bootlicking, cowering, cringing, groveling, kowtowing, sycophantic, toadying, toadyish, truckling
rel freeloading, leechlike, sponging

parasitize *vb syn* INFEST 2, parasite

parboil *vb syn* BOIL 2, seethe, simmer, stew

parcel *n* 1 *syn* PART 1, cut, division, member, moiety, piece, portion, section, segment
2 *syn* LOT 3, plat, plot, tract
3 *syn* GROUP 3, array, batch, body, bunch, clot, clump, cluster, clutch, lot

parcel *vb syn* APPORTION 2, divide, ‖divvy, portion, prorate, quota, ration, share, ‖shift
rel allocate, allot, assign; deal, disburse, disperse; dole (out), lot (out)

parch *vb syn* DRY 1, dehydrate, desiccate, exsiccate, sear

‖**pard** *n syn* PARTNER, associate, cohort, confrere, consociate, copartner, fellow, mate

pardon *n* a remission of penalty or punishment <the governor granted the prisoner a *pardon*>
syn absolution, amnesty

---

syn synonym(s) *rel* related word(s)
idiom idiomatic equivalent(s) *con* contrasted word(s)
ant antonym(s) * vulgar
‖ use limited; if in doubt, see a dictionary
The first word in a synonym list when printed in SMALL CAPITALS shows where there is more information about the group. For a more efficient use of this book see Explanatory Notes.

rel acquittal, exculpation, exoneration, indemnification, indemnity; forgiveness, remission; justification, vindication
con conviction; condemnation
ant punishment

pardon *vb syn* EXCUSE 1, condone, forgive, remit
rel justify; accept, tolerate; free, liberate, release
idiom let bygones be bygones, wipe the slate clean
con amerce, fine, mulct, penalize
ant punish

pardonable *adj syn* VENIAL, excusable, forgivable, remittable
ant unpardonable

pare *vb* **1** *syn* CUT 6, clip, crop, prune, shave, shear, skive, trim
rel flay, scalp, skin, strip
2 *syn* REDUCE 2, clip, cut, cut back, cut down, lower, mark down, shave, slash

parent *vb syn* GENERATE 1, create, father, hatch, make, originate, procreate, produce, sire, spawn

parenthesis *n* **1** *syn* DIGRESSION, aside, discursion, divagation, excursion, excursus
2 *syn* INTERLUDE, break, intermission, interregnum, interval

parenthetically *adv syn* INCIDENTALLY 2, by the bye, by the way, in passing, obiter

parentless *adj syn* ORPHAN, orphaned, unparented
ant parented

par excellence *adj syn* EXCELLENT, champion, classic, classical, famous, fine, first-class, number one, prime, superior

pariah *n syn* OUTCAST, castaway, derelict, Ishmael, Ishmaelite, leper, offscouring, untouchable
rel déclassé

‖**parish–pump** *adj syn* INSULAR, local, parochial, provincial, sectarian, small-town

parity *n syn* EQUIVALENCE, adequation, equality, equatability, equivalency, par, sameness
rel analogy, parallelism, similitude; approximation, closeness, nearness
ant disparity, imparity

parlance *n syn* WORDING, diction, phrase, phraseology, phrasing, verbalism, verbiage, wordage

parley *vb* **1** *syn* SPEAK 3, converse (in), talk, use
2 *syn* CONFER 2, advise, collogue, confab, confabulate, consult, huddle, powwow, treat

parley *n* **1** *syn* TALK 4, conference, meeting, powwow
rel rap session
2 *syn* CONVERSATION 1, chat, colloquy, confabulation, converse, dialogue

parlor car *n* a railroad passenger car equipped with individual revolving and reclining chairs and providing the services of an attendant
syn chair car, club car, lounge car, palace car, tavern car

parlor house *n syn* BROTHEL, bagnio, bawdy house, bordello, call house, cathouse, disorderly house, ‖joyhouse, sporting house, whorehouse
idiom flesh factory

parlous *adj syn* DANGEROUS 1, chancy, ‖dangersome, hairy, hazardous, jeopardous, perilous, risky, treacherous, wicked

parlous *adv syn* VERY 1, ‖awful, ‖big, damned, ‖dreadful, exceedingly, exceptionally, extremely, greatly, mighty

Parnassian *n syn* POET, bard, muse

parochial *adj syn* INSULAR, local, ‖parish-pump, provincial, sectarian, small-town
rel prejudiced; bigoted
con unprejudiced; uncircumscribed, unlimited; cosmic, universal
ant catholic

parody *n syn* CARICATURE 2, burlesque, takeoff, travesty
rel spoof, spoofery, rib, ridicule

parody *vb syn* MIMIC, ape, burlesque, imitate, mock, take off, travesty

paronomasia *n syn* PUN, calembour

parous *adj syn* PREGNANT 1, big, childing, enceinte, expectant, expecting, gone, gravid, heavy, parturient

parry *vb* **1** *syn* DODGE 1, duck, fence, shirk, sidestep
rel preclude, prevent; anticipate, forestall
2 *syn* WARD 1, deflect, fend

parsimonious *adj syn* STINGY, cheeseparing, close, closefisted, miserly, niggardly, penny-pinching, penurious, tight, tightfisted
idiom penny-wise and pound-foolish
ant prodigal

parson *n syn* CLERGYMAN, churchman, cleric, clerical, clerk, divine, ecclesiastic, minister, preacher, reverend

part *n* **1** something less than the whole to which it belongs <a *part* of the road was paved>
syn cut, division, member, moiety, parcel, piece, portion, section, segment
rel component, constituent, element, ingredient; detail, fraction, fragment; bit, chip, scrap
con aggregate, total; combination, complex; entirety, entity, totality, unity
ant whole
2 parts *pl syn* GENITALIA, genitals, private parts, privates, privities, privy parts, pudendum (*usu* pudenda *pl*), secrets
3 *syn* RATION, allotment, allowance, apportionment, measure, meed, portion, quantum, quota, share
4 *syn* SHARE 1, allotment, allowance, bite, cut, lot, partage, portion, quota, slice
rel chunk
5 *syn* SIDE 4

part *vb syn* SEPARATE 1, break up, dichotomize, disjoin, dissect, dissever, disunite, divide, sever, sunder
ant unite

part *adj syn* INCOMPLETE 1, fractional, fragmentary, partial

partage *n syn* SHARE 1, allotment, allowance, bite, cut, lot, part, portion, quota, slice

partake *vb syn* SHARE 2, participate

---

syn synonym(s) *rel* related word(s)
idiom idiomatic equivalent(s) *con* contrasted word(s)
ant antonym(s) * vulgar
‖ use limited; if in doubt, see a dictionary
The first word in a synonym list when printed in SMALL CAPITALS shows where there is more information about the group. For a more efficient use of this book see Explanatory Notes.

rel accept, receive, take
idiom take part in
partake (of) *vb* **1** *syn* EAT 1, consume, devour, feed (on), ingest, meal, take
2 *syn* AMOUNT 2, approach, correspond (to), equal, match, rival, touch
idiom bear resemblance (to)
partaker *n syn* PARTICIPANT, actor, participator, party, sharer
part and parcel *n syn* ESSENTIAL 1, basic, element, fundamental, rudiment
partial *adj* **1** *syn* BIASED 2, colored, jaundiced, one-sided, partisan, prejudiced, prepossessed, tendentious, unindifferent, warped
ant impartial
2 *syn* INCOMPLETE 1, fractional, fragmentary, part
rel halfway
ant whole
partiality *n* **1** *syn* PREJUDICE, bias, one-sidedness
2 *syn* LEANING 2, bent, inclination, inclining, penchant, predilection, predisposition, proclivity, propensity, tendency
participant *n* one that takes part in something <were *participants* in the uprising>
syn actor, partaker, participator, party, sharer
rel aide, assistant, helper; colleague, confrere, fellow, partner
con bystander, looker-on, nonparticipant, observer, onlooker, spectator, watcher
participate *vb syn* SHARE 2, partake
rel enter (into), join (in)
idiom be a party to, be in on, be (*or* get) in the act, have to do with
con observe, watch; retire, withdraw
participator *n syn* PARTICIPANT, actor, partaker, party, sharer
particle *n* a tiny or insignificant amount, part, or piece <not a *particle* of sense>
syn ace, atom, bit, crumb, damn, ‖dite, doit, dram, drop, fragment, grain, hoot, iota, jot, minim, mite, modicum, molecule, ounce, ray, ‖rissom, scrap, scruple, shred, smidgen, smitch, snap, speck, spot, syllable, tittle, whit, whoop
rel morsel; snip; dribbet, dribble; dot
parti-color *adj syn* VARIEGATED, discolor, motley, multicolor, multicolored, multihued, parti-colored, varicolored, versicolor, versicolored
parti-colored *adj syn* VARIEGATED, dappled, discolor, motley, multicolor, multicolored, multihued, varicolored, versicolor, versicolored
ant unicolor, unicolorous
particular *adj* **1** *syn* SINGLE 2, lone, one, only, separate, sole, solitary, unique
ant general
2 *syn* CIRCUMSTANTIAL, blow-by-blow, clocklike, detailed, full, itemized, minute, particularized, thorough
rel careful, meticulous, punctilious, scrupulous
3 *syn* SPECIAL 1, especial, individual, specific
rel appropriate; distinct; singular
ant universal
4 *syn* SEVERAL 1, individual, respective, singular
5 *syn* NICE 1, dainty, fastidious, finical, finicking, finicky, fussy, pernickety, persnickety, picky
particular *n syn* POINT 1, article, detail, element, item, thing
rel speciality, specific
con entirety
ant universal
particularity *n syn* INDIVIDUALITY 3, distinctiveness, individualism, singularity
particularize *vb* **1** *syn* SPECIFY 3, detail, specificate, specificize, stipulate
idiom draw it fine
2 *syn* ITEMIZE 1, enumerate, inventory, list, specialize, specify
particularized *adj syn* CIRCUMSTANTIAL, blow-by-blow, clocklike, detailed, full, itemized, minute, particular, thorough
ant generalized
particularly *adv syn* ESPECIALLY 1, distinctively, special, specially, specifically
parting *n* a mutual separation of two or more persons <saddened by their approaching *parting*>
syn adieu, congé, farewell, good-bye, leave-taking
rel separation; departure
con joining, meeting; return
ant reunion
parting *adj* given, taken, or performed during leave-taking <remembered his father's *parting* advice>
syn departing, farewell, good-bye, valedictory
rel final, last
partisan *n* **1** *syn* FOLLOWER, adherent, cohort, disciple, henchman, satellite, sectary, sectator, supporter
rel backer, champion, upholder; die-hard, stalwart
con adversary, antagonist, opponent
2 an irregular soldier who operates behind enemy lines <a train blown up by *partisans*>
syn guerrilla, irregular, patriot
partisan *adj syn* BIASED 2, colored, jaundiced, one-sided, partial, prejudiced, prepossessed, tendentious, unindifferent, warped
rel denominational, factional, sectarian; blind, devoted, die-hard, fanatic, unreasoning
con impartial, indifferent, unbiased, unprejudiced
ant nonpartisan
partition *n syn* SEPARATION 1, detachment, dissolution, disunion, division, divorce, divorcement, rupture, split-up
partition *vb syn* DISTRIBUTE 1, deal, disburse, dispense, disperse, divide, ‖divvy, dole (out), lot (out), measure (out)
partner *n* one that is associated in any action with another <*partners* in crime>
syn associate, cohort, confrere, consociate, copartner, fellow, mate, ‖pard
rel assistant, helper, sidekick; bedfellow, buddy, chum, companion, comrade, crony, pal

---

syn synonym(s) *rel* related word(s)
idiom idiomatic equivalent(s) *con* contrasted word(s)
ant antonym(s) * vulgar
‖ use limited; if in doubt, see a dictionary
The first word in a synonym list when printed in SMALL CAPITALS shows where there is more information about the group. For a more efficient use of this book see Explanatory Notes.

partnership *n syn* ASSOCIATION 1, affiliation, alliance, cahoots, combination, conjunction, connection, hookup, tie-up, togetherness
rel consociation, fellowship

parturient *adj syn* PREGNANT 1, big, childing, enceinte, expectant, expecting, gone, gravid, heavy, parous

parturition *n syn* BIRTH 1, bearing, ‖birthing, childbearing, childbirth, delivery

party *n* **1** *syn* COMBINATION 2, bloc, coalition, combine, faction, ring
rel alliance, union; side
2 *syn* PARTICIPANT, actor, partaker, participator, sharer
3 *syn* HUMAN, being, body, ‖character, creature, individual, man, mortal, person, personage
4 *syn* GROUP 1, assembly, band, bevy, bunch, cluster, covey, crew
5 *syn* COMPANY 4, band, corps, outfit, troop, troupe
6 *syn* ORGY 2, bacchanal, bacchanalia, debauch, saturnalia

party girl *n* **1** *syn* DOXY 1, ‖chippy, floozy, grisette, light-o'-love, nymph, nymphet, roundheel, tart, ‖tootsie
2 *syn* PROSTITUTE, call girl, ‖cruiser, harlot, ‖hooker, hustler, ‖joy girl, nightwalker, streetwalker, whore

parvenu *n syn* UPSTART, arriviste, nouveau riche, roturier
idiom codfish aristocrat, pig in clover

‖**pash** *vb syn* SHATTER 1, burst, fragment, rive, shiver, smash, ‖smatter, splinter, splinterize, splitter

‖**pash** *n syn* INFATUATION, béguin, crush, passion

pass *vb* **1** *syn* GO 1, ‖cruise, fare, hie, journey, proceed, push on, repair, travel, wend
rel jog, ‖mog
2 *syn* DIE 1, cash in, decease, demise, depart, drop, expire, pass away, perish, succumb
idiom pass on to the Great Beyond
con linger
3 to move or come to a termination or end <as time *passes,* the pain too will *pass*>
syn ELAPSE, expire, go, pass away
rel slip (by); roll (on); fade (away), peter (out); cease, close, discontinue, end, stop, terminate
con continue; linger
4 *syn* HAPPEN 1, come off, develop, fall out, give, go, hap, occur, rise, transpire
idiom come to pass
5 *syn* SURPASS 1, beat, exceed, outdo, outgo, outmatch, outshine, outstrip, top, transcend
idiom leave way behind, shoot ahead of
6 *syn* SPEND 3, while (away)
7 *syn* NEGLECT, blink (at *or* away), discount, disregard, fail, forget, ignore, omit, overlook, slight
8 *syn* PROMISE 1, engage, pledge, undertake
9 to transfer by hand from one person to another <*pass* the salt>
syn buck, hand, reach, ‖shoot
rel give; fork (over)

pass (as *or* for) *vb syn* POSE 4, attitudinize, masquerade, pass off, posture

pass (on) *vb syn* HAND DOWN, bequeath, hand on, transmit

pass (over) *vb syn* TRAVEL 2, cover, do, track, traverse

pass *n syn* JUNCTURE 2, contingency, crisis, crossroad(s), emergency, exigency, pinch, strait, turning point, zero hour

passable *adj* capable of being passed, crossed, or traveled <*passable* roads>
syn navigable, negotiable, travelable
rel open, unblocked; ‖motorable; accessible, attainable, reachable
con blocked, closed; unnavigable; inaccessible, unattainable, unreachable
ant impassable

passably *adv syn* ENOUGH 2, averagely, fairly, moderately, rather, so-so, tolerably

passage *n* **1** movement or transference from one place or point to another <air *passage* from New York to London> <the *passage* of current through a wire>
syn transit, travel
rel traject, trajet, traverse, traversing; transfer, transference, transmission, transmittal, transmittance
2 *syn* TRANSITION, alteration, shift, transit
3 *syn* WAY 2, course, line, path, road, route
4 a typically long narrow way connecting parts of a building <the office building contained endless *passages*>
syn corridor, couloir, hall, hallway, passageway
rel areaway

passageway *n syn* PASSAGE 3, corridor, couloir, hall, hallway

pass away *vb* **1** *syn* DIE 1, cash in, decease, demise, depart, drop, expire, pass, perish, succumb
2 *syn* PASS 3, elapse, expire, go

pass by *vb syn* NEGLECT, disregard, fail, forget, ignore, omit, overlook, overpass, pass, pass over

passé *adj* **1** *syn* OBSOLETE, dead, disused, extinct, outmoded, outworn, superseded
2 *syn* OLD-FASHIONED, antiquated, belated, dated, démodé, demoded, old hat, outdated, outmoded, out-of-date
ant a la mode

passed master *n syn* EXPERT, artist, artiste, authority, master, master-hand, maven, past master, virtuoso, wizard

passel *n syn* GROUP 3, array, batch, battery, body, bunch, bundle, clot, clump, cluster

passing *n syn* DEATH 1, curtains, decease, defunction, demise, dissolution, (the) Pale Horse, quietus, silence, sleep

passing *adj syn* TRANSIENT, ephemeral, evanescent, fleeting, fugacious, fugitive, impermanent, momentary, short-lived, transitory
con lingering

passion *n* **1** *syn* DISTRESS, agony, dolor, misery, suffering
2 *syn* DESIRE 1, appetite, appetition, craving, itch, lust, urge

---

syn synonym(s) *rel* related word(s)
idiom idiomatic equivalent(s) *con* contrasted word(s)
ant antonym(s) * vulgar
‖ use limited; if in doubt, see a dictionary
The first word in a synonym list when printed in SMALL CAPITALS shows where there is more information about the group. For a more efficient use of this book see Explanatory Notes.

rel coveting; aiming, aspiring, panting
3 ***syn*** FEELING 3, affection, affectivity, emotion, sentiment
ant dispassion
4 ***syn*** TEMPER 4
rel outbreak, outburst
5 ***syn*** LOVE 2, amorousness, amour
rel heartthrob
6 intense, high-wrought emotion that compels to action <the *passion* of an evangelist>
syn ardor, calenture, enthusiasm, fervor, fire, hurrah, zeal
rel dedication, devotion; eagerness, lust; lyricism; ecstasy, rapture, transport; fury, rage
7 ***syn*** LUST 2, aphrodisia, concupiscence, desire, eroticism, itch, lickerishness, lustfulness, prurience, pruriency
rel amorousness; sensuality, sensuousness
8 ***syn*** INFATUATION, béguin, crush, ||pash

passionate *adj* **1** ***syn*** IRASCIBLE, choleric, hot-tempered, peppery, quick-tempered, ratty, temperish, testy, tetchy, touchy
2 ***syn*** IMPASSIONED, ardent, blazing, burning, fervent, fervid, fiery, flaming, glowing, hot-blooded
rel excited, quickened, stimulated; high-powered, high-pressure, steamed up; headlong, impetuous, precipitate
ant dispassionate
3 ***syn*** LUSTFUL 2, concupiscent, goatish, *horny, hot, lascivious, libidinous, lickerish, prurient, satyric
rel steamy, sultry
ant passionless

passionless *adj* ***syn*** FRIGID 3, cold, inhibited, undersexed, unresponsive
rel detached, impassive, unsusceptible; unaffected, unmoved; apathetic, indifferent, uncaring, unconcerned, unfeeling; cold-blooded, coldhearted, frozen, heartless
ant passionate, passionful

passive *adj* **1** ***syn*** INACTIVE, asleep, idle, inert, quiet, sleepy
rel apathetic, impassive, phlegmatic, stolid
ant active
2 receiving or enduring without resistance <a *passive* acceptance of her fate>
syn acquiescent, nonresistant, nonresisting, resigned, submissive, unresistant, unresisting, yielding
rel bearing, enduring, patient; compliant, docile, tractable; nonviolent
con resistant, resisting, unresigned, unsubmissive, unyielding

pass off *vb* **1** ***syn*** FOIST 3, fob off, palm (on *or* upon), palm off, work off
2 ***syn*** POSE 4, attitudinize, masquerade, pass (as *or* for), posture

pass on *vb* ***syn*** COMMUNICATE 1, break, convey, impart, transmit

pass out *vb* **1** ***syn*** FAINT, black out, ||crap out, ||swarf, ||swelt, swoon
2 ***syn*** DIE 1, cash in, ||croak, decease, demise, depart, expire, ||kick off, pass away, succumb

pass over *vb* ***syn*** NEGLECT, disregard, fail, forget, ignore, omit, overlook, overpass, pass, pass by

passport *n* a means of entry into a desirable group, society, or condition of life <his skill at sports was a *passport* to fame and fortune>
syn key, open sesame, password, ticket

password *n* **1** a word or phrase that must be spoken by a person before he may pass a guard <give the *password* before entering the fort>
syn countersign, watchword, word
rel tessera
2 ***syn*** PASSPORT, key, open sesame, ticket
3 something (as a short phrase) used as a sign of recognition among members of the same society, class, or group <a fraternity that has secret handshakes and *passwords*>
syn watchword, word

past *adj* **1** ***syn*** PRECEDING, antecedent, anterior, foregoing, former, precedent, previous, prior
2 ***syn*** FORMER 2, bygone, erstwhile, late, old, once, onetime, quondam, sometime, whilom
rel bypast, gone-by; late, previous
ant present

past *prep* **1** ***syn*** BEYOND 1, after, outside, without
rel by
ant before
2 ***syn*** BEYOND 2, above

past *n* former time <reminisced about the *past*>
syn foretime, ||lang syne, yesterday, yesteryear, yore; *compare* PRESENT
rel antiquity
idiom bygone days (*or* times), days gone by, the good old days
con here and now; tomorrow
ant present; future

paste *vb* ***syn*** BEAT 1, baste, batter, belabor, drub, lambaste, pound, pummel, thrash, wallop
idiom give one a pasting

||paste *n* ***syn*** CUFF, box, buffet, ||bust, clout, haymaker, punch, smack, sock, ||swack

pasticcio *n* ***syn*** MISCELLANY 1, brew, gallimaufry, hash, medley, mélange, mishmash, omnium-gatherum, pastiche, salmagundi

pastiche *n* ***syn*** MISCELLANY 1, assortment, gallimaufry, hodgepodge, hotchpotch, medley, mélange, mishmash, omnium-gatherum, pasticcio

past master *n* ***syn*** EXPERT, artist, artiste, authority, master, professional, proficient, virtuoso, whiz, wizard

pastoral *adj* ***syn*** RURAL, agrestic, bucolic, campestral, countrified, country, out-country, outland, provincial, rustic
rel agrarian

patch *vb* ***syn*** MEND 2, doctor, do up, fix, overhaul, rebuild, recondition, reconstruct, repair, revamp

patchwork *n* ***syn*** MISCELLANY 1, hash, hodgepodge, hotchpotch, jumble, mishmash, olio, salad, salmagundi, stew

patchy *adj* ***syn*** SPOTTY 1, irregular, uneven

---

syn synonym(s) ***rel*** related word(s)
idiom idiomatic equivalent(s) ***con*** contrasted word(s)
ant antonym(s) * vulgar
|| use limited; if in doubt, see a dictionary
The first word in a synonym list when printed in SMALL CAPITALS shows where there is more information about the group. For a more efficient use of this book see Explanatory Notes.

pate *n* ***syn*** HEAD 1, ‖bean, ‖belfry, ‖chump, ‖coco, headpiece, noddle, noggin, noodle, sconce

patent *adj* **1** ***syn*** OPEN 1, unclosed, unobstructed
2 ***syn*** CLEAR 5, apparent, distinct, evident, manifest, obvious, palpable, plain, straightforward, unequivocal
rel prominent; flagrant, glaring, gross, rank
idiom patently obvious
con impalpable, imperceptible, insensible; concealed, hidden, secreted
ant latent

‖**pater** *n* ***syn*** FATHER 1, dad, daddy, ‖governor, ‖old man, pa, papa, ‖pappy, pop, poppa

path *n* **1** ***syn*** TRAIL, pathway, track, ‖trod
2 ***syn*** WAY 1, artery, avenue, boulevard, ‖drag, highway, road, street, thoroughfare, track
3 ***syn*** WAY 2, course, line, passage, road, route

pathetic *adj* ***syn*** PITIFUL 1, commiserable, piteous, pitiable, poor, rueful

pathos *n* a quality that moves one to pity and sorrow <the *pathos* of the play was rarely offset by moments of comedy>
syn poignance, poignancy
rel bathos

pathway *n* ***syn*** TRAIL, path, track, ‖trod

patience *n* the power or capacity to endure without complaint something difficult or disagreeable <it took a lot of *patience* to put up with him>
syn forbearance, longanimity, long-suffering, patientness, resignation, uncomplainingness
rel composure, cool, equanimity, impeturbability, self-control; endurance, sufferance, suffering, tolerance, toleration; nonresistance, passiveness, passivity, submission, submissiveness
con fretfulness; restiveness, restlessness; hastiness; rebellion, resistance
ant impatience

patientness *n* ***syn*** PATIENCE, forbearance, longanimity, long-suffering, resignation, uncomplainingness

patois *n* **1** ***syn*** VERNACULAR 3, colloquial, vulgate
2 ***syn*** DIALECT 2, argot, cant, jargon, lingo, patter, slang, vernacular

patriarch *n* **1** ***syn*** FATHER 2, architect, author, creator, founder, generator, inventor, maker, originator, sire
2 ***syn*** GAFFER, graybeard

patriarchal *adj* ***syn*** VENERABLE 1, revered, reverend, reverential

patrician *n* ***syn*** GENTLEMAN, aristo, aristocrat, blue blood
ant plebeian

patriciate *n* ***syn*** ARISTOCRACY, aristoi, blue blood, elite, flower, gentility, gentry, optimacy, quality, upper crust
ant plebs

---

syn synonym(s) ***rel*** related word(s)
idiom idiomatic equivalent(s) ***con*** contrasted word(s)
ant antonym(s) * vulgar
‖ use limited; if in doubt, see a dictionary
The first word in a synonym list when printed in SMALL CAPITALS shows where there is more information about the group. For a more efficient use of this book see Explanatory Notes.

patrimony *n* ***syn*** HERITAGE 1, birthright, heritance, inheritance, legacy

patriot *n* **1** a person who loves his country and supports its interests <*patriots* who asked what they could do for their country>
syn loyalist
rel nationalist
ant traitor
2 ***syn*** PATRIOTEER, flag-waver, superpatriot
3 ***syn*** PARTISAN 2, guerrilla, irregular

patrioteer *n* one who is ostentatiously and chauvinistically patriotic <bloodthirsty *patrioteers* immersed in political witch-hunts>
syn flag-waver, patriot, superpatriot
rel jingo, jingoist

patrolman *n* ***syn*** POLICEMAN, ‖constable, cop, ‖gendarme, John Law, officer, peace officer, police, ‖police constable, police officer

patron *n* **1** ***syn*** PATRON SAINT, avowry
2 ***syn*** SPONSOR, angel, backer, backer-up, guarantor, surety
ant client; protégé
3 ***syn*** CUSTOMER, client

patronage *n* **1** ***syn*** BACKING, aegis, auspices, sponsorship
rel benefaction, guardianship, protection; subsidy
2 commercial transactions of customers and patrons <developed a large *patronage* by offering fair prices and courteous service>
syn business, custom, trade, traffic
rel clientage, clientele
3 the power to make appointments to government jobs on a basis other than merit alone <ousted his enemies from office and used *patronage* to support his policies>
syn pork-barreling
rel cronyism

patron saint *n* a saint to whose protection and intercession a person, society, church, or place is dedicated <Saint Christopher is the *patron saint* of travelers>
syn avowry, patron
rel titular; guardian angel

patsy *n* **1** ***syn*** SCAPEGOAT, fall guy, goat, whipping boy
2 ***syn*** FOOL 3, chump, dupe, fall guy, gull, mark, pigeon, sap, sucker, victim

patter *vb* ***syn*** CHAT 1, babble, chatter, clack, gabble, jaw, prate, prattle, yak, yakety-yak

patter *n* ***syn*** DIALECT 2, argot, cant, jargon, lingo, patois, slang, vernacular

pattern *n* **1** ***syn*** MODEL 2, archetype, beau ideal, ensample, example, exemplar, ideal, mirror, paradigm, standard
rel original
2 ***syn*** FIGURE 3, design, device, motif, motive
rel patterning
3 ***syn*** ORDER 8, method, orderliness, plan, system
rel arrangement, constellation

paucity *n* ***syn*** SCARCITY, insufficience, insufficiency, poverty, ‖scant, scarceness
rel fewness

Paul Pry *n* ***syn*** BUSYBODY, butt-in, ‖buttinsky, intermeddler, meddler, pragmatist, prier (*or* pryer), quidnunc, rubberneck, snoop

paunch *n* **1** ***syn*** ABDOMEN, belly, ‖gut, stomach, tummy, venter
2 ***syn*** POTBELLY, bay window, corporation, pod, ‖pot

paunch *vb* ***syn*** EVISCERATE, bowel, disembowel, draw, embowel, exenterate, gut

pauper *n* a person having no financial resources except those derived from charity
syn beggar, down-and-out
rel have-not, indigent; ‖casual; almsman, lazarus
con millionaire, plutocrat

pauper *vb* ***syn*** RUIN 3, bankrupt, break, bust, fold up, impoverish, pauperize

pauperism *n* ***syn*** POVERTY 1, beggary, destitution, impecuniousness, impoverishment, indigence, need, neediness, penury, want

pauperize *vb* ***syn*** RUIN 3, bankrupt, break, bust, fold up, impoverish, pauper

pausation *n* ***syn*** PAUSE, comma, interval, lull

pause *n* a temporary cessation of activity or of an activity <a *pause* in the conversation>
syn comma, interval, lull, pausation; *compare* BREAK 4, GAP 3
rel caesura, hush, lapse, letup, suspension; interlude, intermission; recess, respite; wait; break, gap, interruption; cessation, ‖deval
con continuation, progression

paw *vb* ***syn*** TOUCH 1, feel, finger, handle, palpate

paw *adj* **1** ***syn*** NAUGHTY 1, bad, ill-behaved, misbehaving, mischievous
2 ***syn*** OBSCENE 2, coarse, dirty, filthy, foul, indecent, nasty, raunchy, smutty, vulgar

pawn *n* ***syn*** PLEDGE 1, earnest, security, token, warrant

pawn *vb* to give or deposit as security for the payment of a loan or debt or for the fulfillment of an obligation <had to *pawn* all her jewels>
syn ‖dip, hock, impignorate, mortgage, pledge, ‖pop, ‖spout
ant redeem

pawn *n* ***syn*** TOOL 2, cat's-paw, puppet, stooge

pay *vb* **1** to discharge an obligation to usually with money <*paid* the doctor for his services>
syn compensate, guerdon, remunerate
rel indemnify, recompense, satisfy; cough (up), plunk down, pony (up), pungle (up), remit, render, tender; pay off
2 ***syn*** CLEAR 5, clear off, discharge, liquidate, pay up, quit, satisfy, settle, square
3 ***syn*** SPEND 1, disburse, expend, fork (out), give, lay out, outlay, shell out
4 ***syn*** COMPENSATE 3, indemnify, recompense, reimburse, remunerate, repay, requite
idiom make up for
5 ***syn*** YIELD 5, bring in, return

pay *n* ***syn*** WAGE, emolument, fee, hire, pay envelope, salary, stipend

payable *adj* **1** ***syn*** DUE 2, mature
ant unpayable
2 ***syn*** UNPAID 2, due, mature, outstanding, overdue, owing, unsettled

pay envelope *n* ***syn*** WAGE, emolument, fee, hire, pay, salary, stipend

paying *adj* ***syn*** ADVANTAGEOUS 1, gainful, good, lucrative, moneymaking, profitable, remunerative, well-paying, worthwhile
rel productive; sound; solvent

payload *n* ***syn*** LOAD 1, burden, cargo, freight, haul, lading

pay up *vb* ***syn*** CLEAR 5, clear off, discharge, liquidate, pay, quit, satisfy, settle, square

PDQ *adv* ***syn*** AWAY 3, at once, directly, forthwith, immediately, instanter, instantly, right away, right off, straightway

peaceable *adj* ***syn*** PACIFIC, irenic, nonviolent, pacificatory, pacifist, peaceful
rel amicable, friendly, neighborly; amiable, complaisant
ant acrimonious; contentious; warlike

peaceful *adj* ***syn*** PACIFIC, irenic, nonviolent, pacificatory, pacifist, peaceable
rel collected, composed, cool, unruffled; constant, equable, steady
con agitated, discomposed, disquieted, disturbed, perturbed, upset

peacemaker *n* one that makes or seeks to make peace <a president who was remembered as a great *peacemaker*>
syn make-peace, pacificator
rel arbitrator, mediator, negotiator; placater; appeaser, peacemonger; peacekeeper
con chauvinist, jingo, jingoist, militarist, war dog, warmonger; peacebreaker

peace officer *n* ***syn*** POLICEMAN, ‖constable, cop, ‖gendarme, John Law, officer, patrolman, police, ‖police constable, police officer

peach *n* ***syn*** ‖DILLY, crackerjack, ‖daisy, dandy, humdinger, jim-dandy, ‖lalapalooza, ‖lulu, nifty, ‖pip
rel pearl

peach *vb* ***syn*** INFORM 3, ‖nark, ‖pimp, rat, ‖sing, snitch, squeak, squeal, ‖stool

peachy *adj* ***syn*** MARVELOUS 2, ‖cool, ‖dandy, divine, ‖galluptious, glorious, groovy, hot, hunky-dory, ‖neat

peacock *vb* ***syn*** LORD, cock, pontificate, swagger, swank, swell

peacockish *adj* ***syn*** SHOWY, chichi, flamboyant, orchidaceous, ostentatious, peacocky, pretentious, splashy, swank

peacocky *adj* ***syn*** SHOWY, chichi, flamboyant, orchidaceous, ostentatious, peacockish, pretentious, splashy, swank

peak *n* **1** ***syn*** VISOR 1, bill
2 ***syn*** TOP 1, apex, crest, crown, fastigium, roof, summit, vertex
3 ***syn*** MOUNTAIN 1, alp, mount
4 ***syn*** APEX 2, acme, apogee, capsheaf, capstone, meridian, ne plus ultra, pinnacle, summit, zenith

peak (out) *vb* ***syn*** DECREASE, abate, ‖bate, diminish, drain (away), dwindle, lessen, rebate, recede, taper off

---

syn synonym(s) *rel* related word(s)
idiom idiomatic equivalent(s) *con* contrasted word(s)
ant antonym(s) * vulgar
‖ use limited; if in doubt, see a dictionary
The first word in a synonym list when printed in SMALL CAPITALS shows where there is more information about the group. For a more efficient use of this book see Explanatory Notes.

peaked *adj* ***syn*** POINTED 1, acicular, aciculate, acuminate, acuminous, acute, cuspidate, peaky, piked, sharp

peaked *adj* ***syn*** SICKLY 2, ‖peaking, peaky, sick

‖**peaking** *adj* ***syn*** SICKLY 2, peaked, peaky, sick

peaky *adj* ***syn*** POINTED 1, acicular, aciculate, acuminate, acuminous, acute, cuspidate, peaked, piked, sharp

peaky *adj* ***syn*** SICKLY 2, peaked, ‖peaking, sick

peal *vb* ***syn*** RING, bell, bong, chime, knell, toll

peanut *adj* ***syn*** PETTY 2, inconsequential, measly, Mickey Mouse, paltry, picayune, piddling, puny, small, trifling

‖**peart** *adj* ***syn*** LIVELY 1, alert, animate, animated, bright, gay, keen, spirited, sprightly, vivacious

‖**pearten** (up) *vb* ***syn*** ENCOURAGE 1, cheer, chirk (up), embolden, enhearten, hearten, inspirit, nerve, steel, strengthen

peasant *n* ***syn*** RUSTIC, bumpkin, clodhopper, country jake, hayseed, hick, hillbilly, provincial, redneck, yokel

peck *n* ***syn*** MUCH, barrel, great deal, lashings, lot, lump, mass, ‖mess, pack, ‖power

peck *vb* **1** to strike at or pick up with the beak <a hen *pecking* the scattered grain from the ground>
syn beak, pick
2 ***syn*** KISS 1, buss, lip, osculate, smack, smooch, ‖smoodge, ‖smouch

peck (at) *vb* ***syn*** NAG, carp (at), fuss, henpeck

pecker *n* **1** ***syn*** BILL 1, beak, neb, nib
2 ***syn*** NOSE 1, beak, ‖beezer, ‖boko, ‖conk, proboscis, ‖schnozzle, ‖snitch, snoot, snout

‖**peckish** *adj* ***syn*** HUNGRY, famished, ravenous, starved, starving

pecksniffery *n* ***syn*** HYPOCRISY, cant, hypocriticalness, pharisaicalness, pharisaism, sanctimoniousness, sanctimony, Tartuffery, Tartuffism

pecksniffian *adj* ***syn*** HYPOCRITICAL, canting, pharisaic, pharisaical, sanctimonious, self-righteous

peculate *vb* ***syn*** EMBEZZLE, misappropriate

peculiar *adj* **1** ***syn*** CHARACTERISTIC, diacritic, diagnostic, distinctive, idiosyncratic, individual, proper
rel unique
2 ***syn*** STRANGE 4, bizarre, curious, eccentric, idiosyncratic, odd, oddball, queer, singular, weird
rel uncustomary
con normal

peculiarity *n* ***syn*** QUALITY 1, affection, attribute, character, characteristic, feature, mark, property, savor, trait

pecuniary *adj* ***syn*** FINANCIAL, fiscal, monetary, pocket

pedantic *adj* too narrowly concerned with scholarly matters <intellectual life that was *pedantic* rather than broad and humane>
syn academic, bookish, book-learned, booky, quodlibetic, scholastic
rel erudite, learned; didactic, donnish, inkhorn, schoolish, schoolteacherish; arid, dry, dryasdust, dull
ant unpedantic

peddle *vb* **1** ***syn*** PUSH 6, shove
2 to sell or offer for sale from place to place <*peddled* fish from a pushcart>
syn hawk, huckster, monger, vend
rel sell; push

peddler *n* one who travels about with merchandise to sell <*peddlers* were once common in rural areas>
syn ‖arab, cheap-jack (*or* cheap-john), ‖duffer, hawker, higgler, huckster, monger, mongerer, outcrier, packman, piepoudre, roadman, vendor
rel colporteur, costermonger; pusher

peddling *adj* ***syn*** PETTY 2, measly, Mickey Mouse, niggling, peanut, piddling, puny, trifling, trivial, inconsequential

pedestal *vb* ***syn*** EXALT 1, aggrandize, dignify, ennoble, glorify, honor, magnify, stellify, sublime, uproar

pedestrian *adj* ***syn*** DULL 9, banausic, blah, ‖dim, dreary, humdrum, monotone, monotonous, plodding, stodgy
rel commonplace, platitudinous, truistic; banal, inane, jejune, wishy-washy; heavy

pedigree *n* **1** ***syn*** GENEALOGY, ‖begats, family tree, stemma
2 ***syn*** ANCESTRY, blood, descent, extraction, lineage, origin

pedigree *adj* ***syn*** PUREBRED, full-blooded, pedigreed, pureblood, thoroughbred

pedigreed *adj* ***syn*** PUREBRED, full-blooded, pedigree, pureblood, thoroughbred

peek (in *or* out) *vb* ***syn*** PEEP

peek *n* ***syn*** PEEP, ‖gander, glance, glimpse

peel *vb* **1** ***syn*** SKIN 2, decorticate, excorticate, scale, strip
2 ***syn*** SCALE 2, desquamate, exfoliate, flake (off)

peeled *adj* ***syn*** OPEN 2, bare, denuded, exposed, naked, stripped, uncovered

peeler *n* **1** ***syn*** STRIPTEASER, ecdysiast, stripper, striptease, teaser
2 ***syn*** HUSTLER, dynamo, go-getter, live wire, rustler, self-starter

‖**peeler** *n* ***syn*** POLICEMAN, ‖bluebottle, ‖bobby, ‖bull, ‖constable, ‖copper, ‖flatfoot, ‖gendarme, officer, ‖paddy

peep *vb* ***syn*** CHIRP, cheep, chip, chipper, ‖chirm, chirrup, chitter, tweedle, tweet, twitter
rel pip

peep *vb* to peer through or as if through a hole or crevice <*peeped* cautiously under the bed>
syn peek (in *or* out)
rel glance; look; peer, stare
idiom take a peep (*or* peek)

peep *n* a brief and sometimes furtive look <take a *peep* at the new neighbors>
syn ‖gander, glance, glimpse, peek
rel look-over, look-see; oeillade, ogle; stare

peeper *n* **1** ***syn*** PEEPING TOM, voyeur
2 ***syn*** EYE 1, lamp, ocular, oculus, ‖ogle, orb, winker

peeping tom *n* a pruriently prying person <a *peeping tom* spying on the couple>
syn peeper, voyeur
rel prowler, snoop, snooper

---

syn synonym(s) ***rel*** related word(s)
idiom idiomatic equivalent(s) ***con*** contrasted word(s)
ant antonym(s) * vulgar
‖ use limited; if in doubt, see a dictionary
The first word in a synonym list when printed in SMALL CAPITALS shows where there is more information about the group. For a more efficient use of this book see Explanatory Notes.

idiom porch climber, window (*or* transom) peeper

‖**peepy** *adj* ***syn*** SLEEPY 1, dozy, drowsy, nodding, ‖sloomy, slumberous, slumbery, snoozy, somnolent, soporific

peer *vb* ***syn*** GAZE 1, bore, gape, ‖gaup (*or* gawp), gawk, glare, gloat, goggle, stare
rel eye, rubberneck; pry, snoop

peerless *adj* ***syn*** ALONE 3, matchless, only, unequaled, unique, unmatched, unparagoned, unparalleled, unrivaled
rel dominant, paramount, predominant, sovereign

peery *adj* ***syn*** CURIOUS 2, inquisitive, inquisitorial, inquisitory, ‖nibby, nosy, prying, snoopy

peeve *vb* ***syn*** IRRITATE, aggravate, exasperate, get, nettle, pique, provoke, put out, rile, roil
rel disturb; miff
idiom make one hot under the collar

peevish *adj* ***syn*** IRRITABLE, fractious, fretful, huffy, pettish, petulant, querulous, snappish, waspish, waspy
rel captious, carping, caviling, critical, faultfinding
idiom being in a peeve

peewee *n* ***syn*** DWARF, homunculus, hop-o'-my-thumb, lilliputian, manikin, midge, midget, pygmy, runt, Tom Thumb

peewee *adj* ***syn*** TINY, ‖bitsy, diminutive, dwarf, dwarfish, lilliputian, midget, miniature, minikin, pygmy

‖**peg** *n* ***syn*** DRINK 3, draft, drag, drain, drench, swig, swill

‖**pegh** *vb* ***syn*** PANT 1, blow, gasp, heave, huff, ‖pank, puff

peg out *vb* **1** ***syn*** COLLAPSE 2, break down, cave (in), drop, ‖flake out, give out, succumb, wilt
2 ***syn*** DIE 1, cash in, ‖check out, conk, ‖croak, depart, expire, go, ‖kick off, pass away

pejorative *adj* ***syn*** DEROGATORY, depreciative, depreciatory, detracting, disadvantageous, disparaging, dyslogistic, slighting, uncomplimentary
con acclaiming, extolling, lauding, praising; aggrandizing, exalting, magnifying

pelf *n* **1** ***syn*** MONEY, ‖mazuma, ‖moolah, needful, ‖ooftish, rhino, ‖scratch, ‖smash, stuff, ‖stumpy
‖**2** ***syn*** REFUSE, debris, garbage, junk, kelter, litter, offal, rubbish, trash, waste

pell–mell *adv* in or as if in confused haste <barged in *pell-mell* without thinking>
syn helter-skelter, hotfoot, hurry-scurry, impetuously, incontinently
rel hurriedly; indiscreetly; carelessly, heedlessly, rashly, thoughtlessly
idiom on the spur of the moment

pell–mell *n* ***syn*** CONFUSION 3, ataxia, ‖ballup, chaos, clutter, disarray, disorder, huddle, muddle, snarl

pell–mell *vb* ***syn*** STAMPEDE 2

pellucid *adj* **1** ***syn*** TRANSPARENT 1, clear, limpid, see-through, translucent
rel sheer
con muddy, roily, turbid
2 ***syn*** CLEAR 4, clear-cut, crystal, lucent, lucid, luminous, translucent, transparent, transpicuous, unblurred

pelt *n* ***syn*** HIDE, fell, fur, jacket, skin

pelt *vb* **1** ***syn*** BEAT 1, batter, belabor, drub, hammer, pound, pummel, thrash, wallop, whop
2 ***syn*** HURRY 2, barrel, beeline, fleet, fly, haste, highball, hotfoot, rush, scoot

pen *vb* ***syn*** ENCLOSE 1, cage, close in, coop, corral, fence, hedge, hem, mew, shut in
ant unpen

pen *n* ***syn*** JAIL, ‖calaboose, ‖can, ‖clink, cooler, coop, ‖hoosegow, penitentiary, ‖pokey, prison

penalize *vb* to inflict a penalty on <*penalize* a delinquent taxpayer with a stiff fine>
syn amerce, fine, mulct
rel castigate, chasten, chastise, correct, discipline, punish; condemn; judge

penalty *n* ***syn*** FINE, amercement, forfeit, mulct

penance *n* ***syn*** PENITENCE, attrition, compunction, contrition, penitency, remorse, remorsefulness, repentance, rue, ruth

penchant *n* ***syn*** LEANING 2, bent, disposition, inclination, inclining, predilection, predisposition, proclivity, propensity, tendency

‖**pend** *vb* ***syn*** DEPEND (on *or* upon) 1, hang (on *or* upon), hinge (on *or* upon), stand (on *or* upon), turn (on *or* upon)

pendant *n* **1** ***syn*** FLAG, banner, bannerol, color, ensign, jack, pennant, pennon, standard, streamer
2 ***syn*** COUNTERPART 1, complement, correlate

pendent *adj* **1** ***syn*** SUSPENDED, hanging, pendulant, pendulous, pensile
2 ***syn*** PENDING, undecided, undetermined, unsettled

pending *adj* not yet settled or decided <a claim still *pending*>
syn pendent, undecided, undetermined, unsettled
idiom hanging in the balance, in suspense, up in the air
con decided, determined, settled
ant closed

pendulant *adj* ***syn*** SUSPENDED, hanging, pendent, pendulous, pensile

pendulate *vb* ***syn*** SWING 2, oscillate, sway

pendulous *adj* **1** ***syn*** SUSPENDED, hanging, pendent, pendulant, pensile
2 ***syn*** VACILLATING 2, faltering, hesitating, shilly-shally, shilly-shallying, tentative, vacillatory, wavering, wiggle-waggle, wobbly

penetrable *adj* ***syn*** PERMEABLE, pervious, porose, porous
ant impenetrable

penetrate *vb* **1** ***syn*** ENTER 1, come (in), go in, ingress
rel encroach, invade, trespass
2 to enter or go through by or as if by overcoming resistance <the icy wind *penetrated* the heavy parka>
syn pierce
rel bore, perforate, prick, puncture; jab, knife, stab; drill, drive
3 ***syn*** PERMEATE, charge, compenetrate, impenetrate, impregnate, interpenetrate, percolate, pervade, saturate, transfuse

---

syn synonym(s) — ***rel*** related word(s)
idiom idiomatic equivalent(s) — ***con*** contrasted word(s)
ant antonym(s) — * vulgar
‖ use limited; if in doubt, see a dictionary
The first word in a synonym list when printed in SMALL CAPITALS shows where there is more information about the group. For a more efficient use of this book see Explanatory Notes.

rel insert, insinuate, interpolate, introduce

penetrating *adj* **1** *syn* INCISIVE, biting, clear-cut, crisp, cutting, ingoing, trenchant
rel penetrant, penetrative
2 *syn* SHARP 4, acute, keen, penetrative, quick-sighted, quick-witted, sharp-sighted, sharp-witted

penetration *n syn* WIT 3, acumen, astucity, astuteness, discernment, discrimination, keenness, percipience, perspicacity, shrewdness
rel penetrativeness

penetrative *adj syn* SHARP 4, acute, keen, penetrating, quick-sighted, quick-witted, sharp-sighted, sharp-witted

penitence *n* regret for sin or wrongdoing <forgiveness following true *penitence*>
syn attrition, compunction, contriteness, contrition, penance, penitency, remorse, remorsefulness, repentance, rue, ruth
rel qualm, scruple; self-accusation, self-castigation, self-punishment, self-reproach, self-reproof; anguish, distress, grief, regret, sadness, sorrow; debasement, degradation, humbling, humiliation
con adamancy, inexorableness, obduracy, obdurateness, stubbornness

penitency *n syn* PENITENCE, attrition, compunction, contriteness, contrition, penance, remorse, repentance, rue, ruth

penitent *adj syn* REMORSEFUL, apologetic, attritional, compunctious, contrite, penitential, regretful, repentant, sorry

penitential *adj syn* REMORSEFUL, apologetic, attritional, compunctious, contrite, penitent, regretful, repentant, sorry

penitentiary *n syn* JAIL, ||can, cooler, coop, ||hoosegow, keep, lockup, pen, reformatory, stockade
idiom correctional institution

penmanship *n syn* HANDWRITING, calligraphy, chirography, ductus, fist, hand, script

pennant *n syn* FLAG, banderole, banner, color, ensign, jack, pendant, pennon, standard, streamer

pennilessness *n syn* POVERTY 1, beggary, destitution, impecuniousness, impoverishment, indigence, neediness, pauperism, penury, poorness

pennon *n syn* FLAG, banderole, banner, bannerol, color, ensign, gonfalon, gonfanon, jack, oriflamme

penny dreadful *n syn* DIME NOVEL, dreadful, shilling shocker, yellowback

penny pincher *n syn* MISER, cheapskate, cheeseparer, moneygrubber, niggard, ||nipcheese, piker, skinflint, stiff, tightwad

penny–pinching *adj syn* STINGY, cheeseparing, close, closefisted, miserly, niggardly, parsimonious, penurious, tight, tightfisted

penny–wise *adj syn* STINGY, cheeseparing, close, closefisted, hardfisted, hardhanded, narrow-fisted, narrow-hearted, penny-pinching, save-all

pennyworth *n syn* BARGAIN, buy, closeout, steal

pensile *adj syn* SUSPENDED, hanging, pendent, pendulant, pendulous

pension (off) *vb syn* RETIRE 2, superannuate

pensive *adj* **1** *syn* THOUGHTFUL 1, cogitative, contemplative, meditative, pondering, reflecting, reflective, ruminative, speculative, thinking
rel musing, ruminating
2 being musingly sad and thoughtful <gazed out the window with a *pensive* expression on her face>
syn meditative, ||pensy, wistful
rel absorbed, abstracted, contemplative, musing, preoccupied, thoughtful, withdrawn; blue, melancholy, sad, saddened
con alert, aware, interested, outgoing

||**pensy** *adj* **1** *syn* PENSIVE 2, meditative, wistful
2 *syn* THOUGHTFUL 1, cogitative, contemplative, meditative, pensive, pondering, reflecting, ruminative, speculative, thinking
3 *syn* SQUEAMISH 1, qualmish, qualmy, queasy, queer, ||wambly

penumbra *n syn* SHADE 1, adumbration, shadow, umbra, umbrage

penurious *adj* **1** *syn* POOR 1, beggared, destitute, dirt poor, impecunious, impoverished, indigent, necessitous, needy, poverty-stricken
2 *syn* STINGY, cheeseparing, close, closefisted, miserly, niggardly, parsimonious, penny-pinching, tight, tightfisted

penury *n syn* POVERTY 1, destitution, impecuniousness, impoverishment, indigence, need, neediness, poorness, privation, want
ant luxury

peon *n syn* SLAVE 2, dray horse, drudge, galley slave, slavey, toiler, workhorse

peonage *n syn* BONDAGE, enslavement, helotry, serfdom, servitude, slavery, thrall, thralldom, villenage, yoke

people *n* **1** *syn* SOCIETY 3, community, public
2 *syn* COMMONALTY, commonage, commoners, common men, plebeians, plebes, plebs, populace, rank and file, third estate

people *vb syn* INHABIT, occupy, populate, tenant

pep *n* **1** *syn* ENERGY 2, birr, go, hardihood, ||moxie, potency, tuck, vigor
2 *syn* VIGOR 2, bang, getup, get-up-and-go, go, punch, push, snap, starch, vitality

pepper *vb syn* SPECKLE 1, bespeckle, dot, freckle, speck, sprinkle, stipple

peppery *adj* **1** *syn* PUNGENT, piquant, poignant, racy, snappy, spicy, zesty
2 *syn* IRASCIBLE, choleric, cranky, cross, hot-tempered, passionate, quick-tempered, ratty, ||stomachy, temperish
3 *syn* SPIRITED 2, beany, fiery, gingery, high-hearted, high-spirited, mettlesome, spunky
rel pepperish; alert, keen, lively, peppy

peppy *adj syn* LIVELY 1, alert, animate, animated, bright, gay, keen, spirited, sprightly, vivacious

per *prep syn* VIA 2, by, by dint of, by means of, by virtue of, by way of, through, with

---

syn synonym(s) *rel* related word(s)
idiom idiomatic equivalent(s) *con* contrasted word(s)
ant antonym(s) * vulgar
|| use limited; if in doubt, see a dictionary
The first word in a synonym list when printed in SMALL CAPITALS shows where there is more information about the group. For a more efficient use of this book see Explanatory Notes.

‖**per** *adv* ***syn*** APIECE, all, aside, each, per capita, per caput

perambulant *adj* ***syn*** ITINERANT, ambulant, ambulatory, deambulatory, itinerate, nomadic, perambulatory, peripatetic, roving, vagabond

perambulate *vb* ***syn*** TRAVERSE 5, walk

‖**perambulator** *n* ***syn*** BABY CARRIAGE, baby buggy, bassinet, ‖pram

perambulatory *adj* ***syn*** ITINERANT, ambulant, ambulatory, deambulatory, itinerate, nomadic, perambulant, vagabond, vagrant, wandering

per capita *adv* ***syn*** APIECE, all, aside, each, ‖per, per caput

per caput *adv* ***syn*** APIECE, all, aside, each, ‖per, per capita

perceive *vb* ***syn*** SEE 1, behold, descry, discern, distinguish, espy, mark, mind, note, observe
rel divine, identify, realize, recognize; grasp, seize, take; apprehend

perceptible *adj* apprehensible as real or existent <a *perceptible* change in attitude>
syn appreciable, detectable, discernible, observable, palpable, sensible, tangible; *compare* TANGIBLE 1
rel distinguishable, recognizable; cognizable, understandable; clear, lucid, perspicuous; conspicuous, noticeable, signal
con impalpable, indiscernible, intangible, invisible, unappreciable, undetectable, undiscernible, unnoticeable, unobservable
ant imperceptible

perception *n* ***syn*** IDEA, apprehension, conceit, concept, conception, image, impression, intellection, notion, thought

perceptive *adj* **1** ***syn*** ACUTE 3, keen, sensitive, sharp
rel responsive
ant imperceptive, unperceptive
2 ***syn*** WISE 1, discerning, gnostic, insighted, insightful, knowing, knowledgeable, sagacious, sage, sophic
rel prehensile, prehensive, prehensorial
ant imperceptive, unperceptive

perch *vb* ***syn*** ALIGHT, land, light, roost, set down, settle, sit down, touch down

perchance *adv* ***syn*** PERHAPS, maybe, possibly

percipience *n* ***syn*** WIT 3, acumen, astuteness, clear-sightedness, discernment, discrimination, keenness, penetration, perspicacity, shrewdness

percolate *vb* **1** ***syn*** PERMEATE, charge, compenetrate, impenetrate, impregnate, interpenetrate, penetrate, pervade, saturate, transfuse
2 ***syn*** EXUDE, bleed, ooze, ‖screeve, seep, ‖sicker, strain, sweat, transude, weep

per contra *adv* ***syn*** HOWEVER, after all, howbeit, nevertheless, nonetheless, notwithstanding, still, still and all, though, withal

percussion *n* ***syn*** IMPACT, bump, clash, collision, concussion, crash, impingement, jar, jolt, shock
rel percussiveness

perdition *n* ***syn*** HELL, abyss, barathrum, Gehenna, hades, inferno, netherworld, Pandemonium, pit, underworld

perdurable *adj* **1** ***syn*** LASTING, diuturnal, durable, enduring, perduring, permanent, stable
ant fleeting
2 ***syn*** INFINITE 1, eternal, illimitable, sempiternal, supertemporal

perdure *vb* ***syn*** CONTINUE 1, abide, carry through, endure, last, persist

perduring *adj* ***syn*** LASTING, diuturnal, durable, enduring, perdurable, permanent, stable
ant fleeting

peregrination *n, usu* **peregrinations** *pl* ***syn*** JOURNEY, expedition, travel(s), trek, trip

peremptory *adj* ***syn*** MASTERFUL 1, bossy, domineering, high-handed, imperative, imperial, imperious, magisterial, overbearing
rel certain, positive; decided, decisive; absolute, fixed, uncompromising; obstinate

perennial *adj* ***syn*** OLD 2, continuing, enduring, inveterate, lifelong, long-lasting, long-lived
rel durable, perdurable

perfect *adj* **1** ***syn*** WHOLE 1, entire, flawless, intact, sound, unblemished, unbroken, undamaged, unimpaired, uninjured
ant imperfect
2 being entirely without flaw and meeting supreme standards of excellence <a ballerina whose technique was *perfect*>
syn absolute, flawless, fleckless, impeccable, indefectible, note-perfect, unflawed; *compare* CONSUMMATE 1
rel excellent; consummate; expert, finished, masterful, masterly
con defective, faulty, flawed; deficient, inadequate, wanting; unfinished, unpolished; unsound
ant imperfect
3 precisely appropriate or right <found the *perfect* gift for him>
syn ideal, model, very
rel needed, required, requisite; appropriate, fit, proper, right, suitable; exact, express, precise
idiom being just the thing
con foolish, inappropriate, undesirable, unsuitable
4 ***syn*** PURE 2, absolute, sheer, simple, unadulterated, unalloyed, undiluted, unmitigated, unmixed, unqualified
5 ***syn*** WHOLE 3, choate, complete, entire, full, integral
rel consummate
6 ***syn*** UTTER, absolute, complete, consummate, downright, gross, outright, positive, rank, unmitigated

perfect *vb* ***syn*** POLISH 2, refine, round, sleek, slick, smooth

perfected *adj* ***syn*** CONSUMMATE 1, accomplished, finished, ripe, virtuosic
ant unperfected

perfectibilian *n* ***syn*** PERFECTIONIST, perfectibilist, perfectist

perfectibilist *n* ***syn*** PERFECTIONIST, perfectibilian, perfectist

---

syn synonym(s) ***rel*** related word(s)
idiom idiomatic equivalent(s) ***con*** contrasted word(s)
ant antonym(s) * vulgar
‖ use limited; if in doubt, see a dictionary
The first word in a synonym list when printed in SMALL CAPITALS shows where there is more information about the group. For a more efficient use of this book see Explanatory Notes.

perfection *n* **1** ***syn*** INTEGRITY 2, completeness, entireness, wholeness
2 ***syn*** EXCELLENCE, arete, excellency, merit, quality, virtue
ant imperfection

perfectionist *n* one that demands or works to achieve perfection <a *perfectionist* who rehearsed one scene fifty times>
syn perfectibilian, perfectibilist, perfectist
rel precisian, precisionist, stickler

perfectist *n* ***syn*** PERFECTIONIST, perfectibilian, perfectibilist

perfectly *adv* ***syn*** WELL 3, à fond, altogether, completely, entirely, fully, quite, thoroughly, utterly, wholly

perfervid *adj* ***syn*** IMPASSIONED, ardent, blazing, burning, fervent, fiery, flaming, glowing, hot-blooded, passionate
rel enhanced, heightened, intensified

perfidious *adj* ***syn*** FAITHLESS, disloyal, false, recreant, traitorous, treacherous, unfaithful, unloyal, untrue
rel mercenary, venal; alienated, estranged, disaffected; deceitful, dishonest

perfidiousness *n* **1** ***syn*** INFIDELITY, disloyalty, faithlessness, falseness, falsity, perfidy, unfaithfulness
2 ***syn*** TREACHERY, disloyalty, faithlessness, perfidy, treacherousness, treason

perfidy *n* **1** ***syn*** TREACHERY, disloyalty, faithlessness, perfidiousness, treacherousness, treason
rel foul play
idiom Judas' kiss
ant fealty
2 ***syn*** INFIDELITY, disloyalty, faithlessness, falseness, falsity, perfidiousness, unfaithfulness
rel betrayal, sellout

perforate *vb* to pierce through so as to leave a hole <*perforate* a sheet of postage stamps>
syn bore, drill, prick, ||pritch, punch, puncture
rel pit; probe; drive, penetrate, pierce

perforce *adv* ***syn*** WILLY-NILLY, helplessly, inescapably, inevitably, unavoidably, whether or no

perform *vb* **1** ***syn*** FULFILL 1, complete, execute, implement
2 to carry something (as a process) to a successful conclusion <*perform* a surgical procedure>
syn achieve, do, execute; *compare* EFFECT 2
rel accomplish, bring off; complete, end, finish, wind up
idiom carry to completion (*or* a successful conclusion), do to a turn, do up brown
3 ***syn*** ACT 1, discourse, do, enact, impersonate, personate, play, playact
4 ***syn*** ACT 5, behave, function, operate, react, take, work

---

syn synonym(s) ***rel*** related word(s)
idiom idiomatic equivalent(s) ***con*** contrasted word(s)
ant antonym(s) * vulgar
|| use limited; if in doubt, see a dictionary
The first word in a synonym list when printed in SMALL CAPITALS shows where there is more information about the group. For a more efficient use of this book see Explanatory Notes.

performance *n* ***syn*** EFFICIENCY 1, effectiveness, efficacy

performer *n* ***syn*** ACTOR 1, impersonator, mime, mimic, mummer, playactor, player, thespian, trouper

perfume *n* ***syn*** FRAGRANCE, aroma, balm, bouquet, incense, redolence, scent, spice

perfume *vb* ***syn*** SCENT 2, aromatize, odorize

perfumed *adj* ***syn*** SWEET 2, ambrosial, aromal, aromatic, balmy, fragrant, perfumy, redolent, savory, scented

perfumy *adj* ***syn*** SWEET 2, ambrosial, aromal, aromatic, balmy, fragrant, perfumed, redolent, savory, scented

perfunctory *adj* characterized by routine and often done merely as a duty <gave her his usual *perfunctory* nod>
syn automatic, mechanical
rel cursory, superficial; involuntary, unaware; routine, usual; standard, stock; cool, impersonal, indifferent; wooden; unconcerned, uninterested
con cordial, friendly, genial, hearty, warm

pergola *n* ***syn*** ARBOR, bower

perhaps *adv* conceivably but not certainly so <*perhaps* this is true, but I think it's debatable>
syn maybe, perchance, possibly
rel conceivably, feasibly, imaginably
idiom as it may be, as the case may be, for all one knows
con certainly, definitely, doubtlessly, surely, undoubtedly, unquestionably

perhaps *n* ***syn*** THEORY 2, conjecture, speculation, suppose, supposition

periapt *n* ***syn*** CHARM 2, amulet, fetish, juju, luck, mascot, phylactery, talisman, zemi

peril *n* ***syn*** DANGER, hazard, jeopardy, risk
rel exposure, liability, openness, subjection; endangerment
idiom cause for alarm, rocks (*or* breakers) ahead

peril *vb* ***syn*** ENDANGER, compromise, hazard, imperil, jeopard, jeopardize, jeopardy, menace, risk

perilous *adj* ***syn*** DANGEROUS 1, chancy, hairy, hazardous, jeopardous, risky, treacherous, unhealthy, unsound, wicked
rel shaky, tottery, unstable, unsteady; delicate, ticklish, touchy

perimeter *n* **1** ***syn*** CIRCUMFERENCE, ambit, circuit, compass, periphery
2 ***syn*** BORDER 1, brim, brink, edge, fringe, hem, margin, periphery, skirt, verge

period *n* **1** ***syn*** END 2, cessation, close, closing, closure, conclusion, discontinuance, ending, stop, termination
2 an extent of time set off or typified by someone or something <the Victorian *period*> <a *period* of expansion>
syn age, day(s), epoch, era, time

periodic *adj* ***syn*** INTERMITTENT, alternate, isochronal, isochronous, periodical, recurrent, recurring
rel on-again-off-again

periodical *adj* ***syn*** INTERMITTENT, alternate, isochronal, isochronous, periodic, recurrent, recurring

periodical *n* ***syn*** JOURNAL, magazine, newspaper, organ, review

peripatetic *adj* ***syn*** ITINERANT, ambulant, itinerate, nomadic, perambulant, roving, vagabond, vagrant, wandering, wayfaring

periphery *n* **1** ***syn*** CIRCUMFERENCE, ambit, circuit, compass, perimeter
2 ***syn*** BORDER 1, brim, brink, edge, fringe, hem, margin, perimeter, skirt, verge

periphrase *n* ***syn*** VERBIAGE 1, circumambages, circumbendibus, circumlocution, periphrasis, pleonasm, redundancy, roundabout, tautology, verbality

periphrasis *n* ***syn*** VERBIAGE 1, circumambages, circumbendibus, circumlocution, periphrase, pleonasm, redundancy, roundabout, tautology, verbality

perish *vb* **1** ***syn*** DIE 1, ||croak, decease, demise, depart, expire, go, pass, pass away, succumb
ant survive
2 to suffer spiritual or moral death <nations *perishing* for lack of true leaders>
syn die
rel decline; collapse, go under; expire, succumb; disappear, vanish; cease, end
con flourish, prosper, thrive
ant endure
||**3** ***syn*** DECAY, break down, corrupt, crumble, decompose, disintegrate, putrefy, rot, spoil, turn

perishing *adj* ***syn*** DAMNED 2, blamed, blankety-blank, blasted, blessed, confounded, cursed, dad-blamed, dang, dashed

perjure *vb* to make a false swearer of oneself by violating one's oath to tell the truth <a *perjured* witness>
syn forswear
rel equivocate; deceive, delude, mislead, trick; lie, prevaricate
idiom commit perjury, lie under oath, swear falsely

perjurer *n* ***syn*** LIAR, Ananias, falsifier, fibber, fibster, prevaricator, storyteller

perk (up) *vb* ***syn*** IMPROVE 3, ameliorate, convalesce, gain, look up, mend, recuperate

||**perk** *n, usu* **perks** *pl* ***syn*** GRATUITY, cumshaw, lagniappe, largess, ||palm grease, ||palm oil, perquisite, pourboire, tip

perlustrate *vb* ***syn*** SCRUTINIZE 1, ||case, check over, check up, con, examine, inspect, study, survey, vet

perlustration *n* ***syn*** EXAMINATION, analysis, audit, check-over, checkup, inspection, review, scrutiny, survey, view

permanent *adj* ***syn*** LASTING, diuturnal, durable, enduring, perdurable, perduring, stable
rel imperishable, invariable
ant temporary

permeable *adj* capable of being permeated especially by fluids <a *permeable* membrane>
syn penetrable, pervious, porose, porous
rel passable
con impassable, impenetrable, impervious
ant impermeable

permeate *vb* to pass or cause to pass through every part of a thing <air *permeated* with cigar smoke>
syn charge, compenetrate, impenetrate, impregnate, interfuse, interpenetrate, penetrate, percolate, pervade, saturate, transfuse
rel invade; imbrue, imbue, infiltrate, infuse, ingrain; diffuse, suffuse; drench, soak, steep; fill

permissible *adj* that may be permitted <a *permissible* error>
syn admissible, allowable
rel unforbidden, unprohibited; allowed, permitted, tolerated; approved, authorized, endorsed, sanctioned; acceptable, bearable, tolerable
con banned, forbidden, disallowed, prohibited, unpermitted, verboten; unacceptable, unbearable
ant impermissible

permission *n* a sanctioning to act or do something that is granted by one in authority <received *permission* to leave work early>
syn allowance, authorization, consent, leave, permit, sanction, sufferance
rel acceptance, acquiescence; approbation, approval; endorsement
ant prohibition

permit *vb* ***syn*** LET 2, allow, have, leave, suffer
rel tolerate
idiom give one his head
ant forbid, prohibit

permit *n* ***syn*** PERMISSION, allowance, authorization, consent, leave, sanction, sufferance

permutation *n* ***syn*** CHANGE 2, innovation, mutation, novelty, sport, vicissitude
rel alteration, modification

pernicious *adj* exceedingly harmful or destructive <*pernicious* gossip>
syn baneful, deadly, noxious, pestiferous, pestilent, pestilential; *compare* DEADLY 1
rel damaging, deleterious, detrimental, harmful, hurtful; baleful, malefic, maleficent, malign, sinister; miasmatic, miasmic, poisonous, toxic, venomous; malignant, swart, virulent; destructive, devastating, ruinous; fatal, killing, lethal, mortal
con harmless, uninjurious; nonmalignant, nonpoisonous, nontoxic
ant innocuous

pernickety *adj* ***syn*** NICE 1, choosy, clerkish, fastidious, finicky, fussy, miminy-piminy, ||mincy, persnickety, picky

perorate *vb* ***syn*** ORATE, bloviate, declaim, harangue, mouth, rant, rave, soapbox

perpend *vb* ***syn*** CONSIDER 1, contemplate, excogitate, mind, ponder, study, think (out *or* over), weigh

perpendicular *adj* ***syn*** VERTICAL, plumb, straight-up
rel stand-up, straight
ant horizontal

perpendicularity *n* ***syn*** VERTICALITY, plumbness, verticalism, verticalness
rel erectness, uprightness
ant horizontality

perpetrate *vb* ***syn*** COMMIT 2, pull
rel effect; inflict, wreak
idiom ||up and do

---

syn synonym(s) — *rel* related word(s)
idiom idiomatic equivalent(s) — *con* contrasted word(s)
ant antonym(s) — * vulgar
|| use limited; if in doubt, see a dictionary
The first word in a synonym list when printed in SMALL CAPITALS shows where there is more information about the group. For a more efficient use of this book see Explanatory Notes.

perpetual *adj* ***syn*** CONTINUAL, ceaseless, constant, continuous, endless, everlasting, interminable, unceasing, unending, unremitting
ant ephemeral, transient

perpetually *adv* ***syn*** ALWAYS 1, constantly, continuously, ever, invariably

perpetuate *vb* to make perpetual or cause to last indefinitely <*perpetuate* his memory for future generations>
syn eternalize, eternize, immortalize
rel bolster, conserve, keep, maintain, preserve, secure, support, sustain
con annihilate, blot out, erase, expunge
ant obliterate

perplex *vb* **1** ***syn*** PUZZLE, befog, bewilder, ||cap, confound, confuse, metagrobolize, pose, stumble
rel discompose, perturb; balk, thwart; astonish, astound, surprise
idiom put (*or* drive) to one's wit's end
2 ***syn*** COMPLICATE, entangle, ||muck, muddle, ravel, snarl, tangle
3 ***syn*** ENTANGLE 1, ensnarl, intertangle, snarl, tangle

perquisite *n* **1** ***syn*** GRATUITY, cumshaw, lagniappe, largess, ||palm grease, ||palm oil, ||perk(s), pourboire, tip
2 ***syn*** RIGHT 2, appanage, birthright, prerogative, privilege

per se *adv* by, of, or in itself or oneself or themselves <a lover of language *per se*>
syn as such, intrinsically
rel alone, independently, solely

persecute *vb* **1** ***syn*** WRONG, aggrieve, oppress, outrage
rel dragoon, rack, torment, torture
con back, champion, support, uphold
2 ***syn*** MOLEST, bait, heckle, torment
rel worry; hound, ride
con humor, indulge, pamper; accommodate, favor, oblige

perseverant *adj* ***syn*** PERSISTENT 1, dogged, insistent, perseverative, persevering, persisting, persistive

perseverative *adj* ***syn*** PERSISTENT 1, dogged, insistent, perseverant, persevering, persisting, persistive

persevere *vb* to continue in a state, enterprise, or undertaking in spite of counter influences, opposition, or discouragement <*persevered* in his unpopular economic policy>
syn carry on, go on, hang on, persist
rel continue, get on, press (on), proceed
idiom ||hang in there keep at it, keep driving, never say die, stick (*or* tough) it out
con falter, hesitate, vacillate, waver; renounce, surrender, yield
ant give up

persevering *adj* ***syn*** PERSISTENT 1, dogged, insistent, perseverant, perseverative, persisting, persistive

---

syn synonym(s) — *rel* related word(s)
idiom idiomatic equivalent(s) — *con* contrasted word(s)
ant antonym(s) — * vulgar
|| use limited; if in doubt, see a dictionary
The first word in a synonym list when printed in SMALL CAPITALS shows where there is more information about the group. For a more efficient use of this book see Explanatory Notes.

persiflage *n* ***syn*** BANTER, backchat, badinage, ||cross talk, repartee, snip-snap

persist *vb* **1** ***syn*** PERSEVERE, carry on, go on, hang on
con cease, discontinue, quit, stop
ant desist
2 ***syn*** CONTINUE 1, abide, carry through, endure, last, perdure
rel go on; linger; obtain, prevail
ant desist

persistence *n* **1** ***syn*** CONTINUATION 1, continuity, duration, endurance
2 ***syn*** RUN 2, continuance, continuation, duration
rel course

persistent *adj* **1** continuing in a course of action without regard to discouragement, opposition, or previous failure <a *persistent* suitor>
syn dogged, insistent, perseverant, perseverative, persevering, persisting, persistive
rel determined, steadfast, tenacious, unshakable; relentless, unremitting
con malleable, pliant, tractable, yielding; infirm, invertebrate, spineless; vacillating, wavery, wobbling
2 ***syn*** PRIMITIVE 3, archaic, undeveloped, unevolved

persisting *adj* ***syn*** PERSISTENT 1, dogged, insistent, perseverant, perseverative, persevering, persistive

persistive *adj* ***syn*** PERSISTENT 1, dogged, insistent, perseverant, perseverative, persevering, persisting

persnickety *adj* ***syn*** NICE 1, choosy, clerkish, fastidious, finicky, fussy, miminy-piminy, ||mincy, pernickety, picky

person *n* ***syn*** HUMAN, being, body, creature, life, individual, man, mortal, personage, soul
rel chap, ||cookie, coot, fellow, galoot, guy, specimen, stick

personage *n* **1** ***syn*** NOTABLE 1, big shot, chief, dignitary, eminence, nabob, notability, personality, somebody, VIP
2 ***syn*** HUMAN, being, body, creature, life, individual, man, mortal, person, soul

personal *adj* **1** of, relating to, or affecting a particular person <owed his *personal* allegiance to his wife>
syn individual
rel particular, peculiar, special
con general, universal; common, joint, mutual, shared; commonplace, everyday, ordinary
2 ***syn*** PRIVATE 1, privy

personal effects *n pl* privately owned items (as clothing and toilet articles) normally worn or carried on the person <packed his *personal effects* in a small bag>
syn ||plunder, stuff, things, traps, tricks
rel belongings, goods, possessions
idiom personal belongings

personality *n* **1** ***syn*** INDIVIDUALITY 4, identity, ipseity, seity, selfdom, selfhood, selfness, singularity
2 ***syn*** DISPOSITION 3, character, complexion, humor, individualism, individuality, makeup, nature, temper, temperament
3 ***syn*** NOTABLE 1, big shot, chief, dignitary, eminence, nabob, notability, personage, somebody, VIP

personalize *vb* **1** ***syn*** EMBODY 1, exteriorize, externalize, incarnate, manifest, materialize, objectify, personify, personize, substantiate
rel anthropomorphize

2 *syn* REPRESENT 2, emblematize, embody, epitomize, exemplify, illustrate, mirror, personate, personify, typify

personal name *n syn* GIVEN NAME, baptismal name, Christian name, font name, forename, prename

personate *vb* **1** *syn* ACT 1, discourse, do, enact, impersonate, perform, play, playact
2 *syn* REPRESENT 2, emblematize, embody, epitomize, exemplify, illustrate, mirror, personalize, personify, typify

personification *n syn* EMBODIMENT, incarnation

personify *vb* **1** *syn* EMBODY 1, exteriorize, externalize, incarnate, manifest, materialize, objectify, personalize, personize, substantiate
rel reincarnate
2 *syn* REPRESENT 2, body (forth), emblematize, embody, epitomize, exemplify, illustrate, mirror, symbolize, typify

personize *vb syn* EMBODY 1, exteriorize, externalize, incarnate, manifest, materialize, objectify, personalize, personify, substantiate

perspective *n syn* VISTA, lookout, outlook, prospect, scape

perspicacious *adj syn* SHREWD, argute, astucious, astute, cagey, heady, sagacious, ||savvy
rel quick-sighted, sharp-sighted, sharp-witted

perspicacity *n syn* WIT 3, acumen, astucity, astuteness, discernment, discrimination, keenness, penetration, percipience, shrewdness

perspicuity *n syn* CLARITY, clearness, limpidity, lucidity, plainness
rel intelligibility; explicitness

perspicuous *adj syn* CLEAR 4, clear-cut, crystal, lucent, lucid, luculent, luminous, pellucid, unambiguous, unblurred

perspiring *adj syn* SWEATY, asweat, perspiry, ||puggy, sweatful, sweating

perspiry *adj syn* SWEATY, asweat, perspiring, ||puggy, sweatful, sweating

persuadable *adj syn* RECEPTIVE 1, acceptant, acceptive, influenceable, persuasible, responsive, suasible, swayable
ant unpersuadable

persuade *vb* **1** *syn* INDUCE 1, argue (into), bring around, convince, draw, get, prevail (on *or* upon), prompt, talk (into), win (over)
rel affect, impress, touch; reason; convert
con discourage, hinder, prevent
ant dissuade
2 *syn* CONVERT 1, bring, lead, move
3 *syn* ASSURE 2, convince, satisfy
ant dissuade

persuasible *adj syn* RECEPTIVE 1, acceptant, acceptive, influenceable, persuadable, responsive, suasible, swayable
ant unpersuasible

persuasion *n* **1** *syn* OPINION, belief, conviction, eye, feeling, mind, sentiment, view
rel bias, partiality, predilection, prejudice, prepossession
2 *syn* RELIGION 1, creed, cult, faith
3 *syn* RELIGION 2, church, communion, connection, creed, cult, denomination, faith, sect
rel affiliation; order
4 *syn* TYPE, cast, character, class, description, ilk, lot, mold, nature, sort

pert *adj* **1** *syn* SAUCY 1, arch, bantam, ||cocket, malapert
rel bold, daring; audacious, brazen
con shy
ant coy
2 *syn* WISE 5, bold, cheeky, forward, fresh, impudent, nervy, sassy, smart, smart-alecky
rel disrespectful, rude
3 *syn* LIVELY 1, alert, animate, animated, bright, gay, keen, spirited, sprightly, vivacious

pertain *vb* **1** *syn* BELONG 2, appertain, vest
2 *syn* BEAR (on *or* upon), appertain, apply, relate
rel associate, combine, connect, join
idiom be pertinent (*or* relevant) to

pertinacious *adj syn* OBSTINATE, bullheaded, headstrong, mulish, perverse, refractory, self-willed, stubborn, willful, unyielding
rel fixed, unshakable; dogged, tenacious

pertinent *adj syn* RELEVANT, ad rem, applicable, applicative, applicatory, apposite, apropos, germane, material, pointful
rel pertaining
ant impertinent

perturb *vb syn* DISCOMPOSE 1, agitate, bother, discombobulate, dismay, disquiet, disturb, flurry, fluster, upset
rel trouble; unsettle
ant compose

pervade *vb syn* PERMEATE, charge, compenetrate, impenetrate, impregnate, interpenetrate, penetrate, percolate, saturate, transfuse
idiom spread through and through

perverse *adj* **1** *syn* VICIOUS 2, corrupt, degenerate, depraved, miscreant, nefarious, putrid, rotten, unhealthy, villainous
2 *syn* OBSTINATE, headstrong, mulish, pertinacious, refractory, self-willed, stiff-necked, stubborn, wrongheaded, unyielding
rel cranky, irritable, unreasonable
3 *syn* CONTRARY 3, balky, cross-grained, froward, ornery, restive, wayward, wrongheaded

pervert *vb* **1** *syn* DEBASE 1, animalize, bastardize, bestialize, brutalize, corrupt, debauch, demoralize, deprave, warp
rel abuse, maltreat, mistreat, misuse, outrage; ruin
2 *syn* ABUSE 2, misapply, misemploy, mishandle, misimprove, misuse, prostitute
rel ill-treat
3 *syn* MISREPRESENT, belie, color, distort, falsify, garble, miscolor, misstate, twist, warp

perverted *adj syn* DEBASED, corrupted, debauched, depraved, vitiate, vitiated
rel defiled, polluted, tainted; contorted, distorted, warped; abused, misused, outraged

---

syn synonym(s) *rel* related word(s)
idiom idiomatic equivalent(s) *con* contrasted word(s)
ant antonym(s) * vulgar
|| use limited; if in doubt, see a dictionary
The first word in a synonym list when printed in SMALL CAPITALS shows where there is more information about the group. For a more efficient use of this book see Explanatory Notes.

pervicacious *adj* ***syn*** OBSTINATE, bullheaded, closed-minded, deaf, headstrong, incompliant, mulish, pertinacious, self-willed, ‖sot

pervious *adj* ***syn*** PERMEABLE, penetrable, porose, porous
ant impervious

pesky *adj* ***syn*** TROUBLESOME, mean, troublous, ugly, vexatious, wicked

pesky *adv* ***syn*** VERY 1, ‖awful, awfully, damned, ‖dreadful, dreadfully, extremely, ‖monstrous, ‖mortacious, terribly

pessimist *n* one who emphasizes adverse aspects or conditions and expects the worst <*pessimists* predicting another depression>
syn calamity howler, Cassandra, crepehanger, worrywart
rel fussbudget; Job's comforter; defeatist; killjoy; cynic, misanthrope
con positivist; idealist; Pollyanna
ant optimist

pest *n* **1** ***syn*** ANNOYANCE 3, besetment, bother, botheration, botherment, exasperation, irritant, nuisance, pester, plague
rel bane, trouble, vexation, worry
idiom *pain in the ass, pain in the neck, pea in the shoe, thorn in the flesh
2 one who pesters or annoys <a little *pest* who constantly asked questions>
syn nudnick, nuisance, pesterer
rel badgerer, heckler, tormentor
idiom *pain in the ass, pain in the neck

pester *vb* ***syn*** WORRY 1, annoy, bedevil, beleaguer, hagride, harass, harry, plague, tantalize, tease
rel ride
idiom drive (one) crazy, drive (one) up the wall, pester to death

pester *n* ***syn*** ANNOYANCE 3, besetment, bother, botheration, botherment, exasperation, irritant, nuisance, pest, plague

pesterer *n* ***syn*** PEST 2, nudnick, nuisance

‖**pesterment** *n* ***syn*** ANNOYANCE 3, besetment, bother, botheration, botherment, exasperation, nuisance, pest, pester, plague

pesticide *n* a chemical agent used to destroy pests <the need to control indiscriminate use of *pesticides*>
syn biocide, economic poison
rel bactericide, fungicide, germicide, insecticide, microbicide, rodenticide, vermicide

pestiferous *adj* ***syn*** PERNICIOUS, baneful, deadly, noxious, pestilent, pestilential

pestilence *n* ***syn*** PLAGUE 1, curse, scourge

pestilent *adj* **1** ***syn*** DEADLY 1, deathly, fatal, lethal, mortal, mortiferous, pestilential
2 ***syn*** PERNICIOUS, baneful, deadly, noxious, pestiferous, pestilential

pestilential *adj* **1** ***syn*** DEADLY 1, deathly, fatal, lethal, mortal, mortiferous, pestilent
2 ***syn*** PERNICIOUS, baneful, deadly, noxious, pestiferous, pestilent

pet *adj* ***syn*** FAVORITE 1, beloved, blue-eyed, darling, dear, fair-haired, loved, precious, white-haired, white-headed

pet *vb* ***syn*** CARESS, cosset, cuddle, dandle, fondle, love
rel embrace, hug

pet *vb* ***syn*** SULK, ‖dort, grump, ‖mump, pout, ‖sull

petcock *n* ***syn*** FAUCET, cock, gate, hydrant, spigot, stopcock, tap, valve

peter (out) *vb* ***syn*** DECREASE, abate, ‖bate, diminish, drain (away), dwindle, lessen, rebate, recede, taper off

Peter Funk *n* ***syn*** SWINDLER, cheat, cheater, chiaus, confidence man, con man, defrauder, double-dealer, flimflammer, mountebank

petite *adj* ***syn*** SMALL 1, bantam, little, monkey, smallish
rel diminutive, dwarf, lilliputian, miniature, wee

petition *n* ***syn*** PRAYER, appeal, application, entreaty, imploration, imprecation, orison, plea, suit, supplication
rel request

petition *vb* to make an earnest, formal, and often written request <*petitioned* for a hearing before the labor board>
syn appeal, sue (for *or* to)
rel ask, request; beg, beseech, entreat, implore, plead, pray, supplicate
con claim, demand, exact, press (for)

petitioner *n* ***syn*** SUPPLIANT, asker, beggar, prayer, suitor, supplicant, supplicator

petit–maître *n* ***syn*** FOP, Beau Brummel, blood, buck, coxcomb, dandy, dude, exquisite, lounge lizard, macaroni

petrify *vb* ***syn*** DAZE 2, bedaze, bemuse, benumb, paralyze, stun, stupefy
rel alarm, frighten, startle, terrify; appall, dismay, horrify; numb
idiom turn to stone

pettifogger *n* an unscrupulous lawyer <done out of his rights by a slick *pettifogger*>
syn jackleg lawyer, shyster; *compare* LAWYER
rel ambulance chaser, Philadelphia lawyer; ‖bush lawyer

pettifogging *adj* ***syn*** PETTY 2, measly, Mickey Mouse, niggling, peanut, peddling, picayunish, piddling, trifling, unconsequential

pettish *adj* ***syn*** IRRITABLE, fractious, fretful, huffy, peevish, petulant, querulous, snappish, waspish, waspy

petty *adj* **1** ***syn*** LITTLE 3, casual, inconsiderable, insignificant, light, minor, shoestring, small-beer, trivial, unimportant
2 being often contemptibly insignificant or unimportant <*petty* quarrels and intrigues>
syn inconsequent, inconsequential, inconsiderable, measly, Mickey Mouse, niggling, paltry, peanut, peddling, pettifogging, picayune, picayunish, piddling, piffling, pimping, puny, small, trifling, trivial, unconsequential, unconsidered, ungenerous, unvital; *compare* LITTLE 3

---

syn synonym(s) — *rel* related word(s)
idiom idiomatic equivalent(s) — *con* contrasted word(s)
ant antonym(s) — * vulgar
‖ use limited; if in doubt, see a dictionary
The first word in a synonym list when printed in SMALL CAPITALS shows where there is more information about the group. For a more efficient use of this book see Explanatory Notes.

rel negligible, unimportant; hair-drawn, hairsplitting; impertinent, irrelevant
con consequential, considerable; big, gross; significant, vital
ant important, momentous

petulant *adj* ***syn*** IRRITABLE, fractious, fretful, huffy, peevish, pettish, querulous, snappish, waspish, waspy
rel grouchy, sulky

phantasm *n* **1** ***syn*** DELUSION 1, hallucination, ignis fatuus, illusion, mirage
rel fabrication, fiction, invention
2 ***syn*** APPARITION, eidolon, ghost, phantom, revenant, shade, shadow, specter, spectrum, spirit
3 ***syn*** FANCY 4, daydream, dream, fantasy (*or* phantasy), nightmare, vision

phantom *n* ***syn*** APPARITION, eidolon, ghost, phantasm, revenant, shade, shadow, specter, spectrum, spirit

pharisaic *adj* ***syn*** HYPOCRITICAL, canting, pecksniffian, pharisaical, sanctimonious, self-righteous

pharisaical *adj* ***syn*** HYPOCRITICAL, canting, pecksniffian, pharisaic, sanctimonious, self-righteous

pharisaicalness *n* ***syn*** HYPOCRISY, cant, hypocriticalness, pecksniffery, pharisaism, sanctimoniousness, sanctimony, Tartuffery, Tartuffism

pharisaism *n* ***syn*** HYPOCRISY, cant, hypocriticalness, pecksniffery, pharisaicalness, sanctimoniousness, sanctimony, Tartuffery, Tartuffism

pharisee *n* ***syn*** HYPOCRITE, dissembler, dissimulator, lip server, Tartuffe, whited sepulcher

pharmaceutic *n* ***syn*** DRUG 1, biologic, medicinal, pharmaceutical

pharmaceutical *n* ***syn*** DRUG 1, biologic, medicinal, pharmaceutic

pharmacist *n* ***syn*** DRUGGIST, apothecary, ‖chemist

pharmacon *n* ***syn*** REMEDY 1, cure, medicament, medicant, medication, medicine, physic

pharos *n* ***syn*** LIGHTHOUSE, beacon

phase *n* one of the possible ways of viewing or being presented to view <the moral *phase* of the problem>
syn angle, aspect, facet, hand, side
rel condition, situation, state; position, posture, view, viewpoint; appearance, look, semblance; color, complexion

phenomenal *adj* **1** ***syn*** MATERIAL 1, corporeal, gross, objective, physical, sensible, substantial, tangible
con ontic
ant noumenal
2 ***syn*** EXCEPTIONAL 1, extraordinary, rare, remarkable, singular, unimaginable, unique, unthinkable, unusual, unwonted

phenomenon *n* **1** ***syn*** FACT 2, event
rel experience; actuality, reality
2 ***syn*** WONDER 1, marvel, miracle, portent, prodigy, sensation, stunner
rel abnormality; anomaly, paradox; peculiarity, singularity, uniqueness, unusualness

philander *n* ***syn*** WOLF, Casanova, chaser, Don Juan, ladies' man, lady-killer, masher, philanderer, womanizer
idiom ‖skirt chaser

philander *vb* to have many love affairs <his reputation for *philandering* with married women>
syn fool (around), mess around, play (around), wolf, womanize
rel dally, flirt, trifle; chase, pursue; *cat (around), ‖tomcat (around)
idiom ‖chase skirts, play Don Juan, play the femmes

philanderer *n* ***syn*** WOLF, Casanova, chaser, Don Juan, ladies' man, lady-killer, masher, philander, womanizer

philanthropic *adj* ***syn*** CHARITABLE 1, altruistic, benevolent, eleemosynary, good, humane, humanitarian
rel bighearted, freehearted, greathearted, kindhearted, largehearted, openhearted; contributing, donating, freehanded, giving, magnanimous; civic-minded, public-spirited
ant misanthropic

philharmonic *n* ***syn*** ORCHESTRA, band, symphony

philippic *n* ***syn*** TIRADE, diatribe, harangue, jeremiad

philistine *n* a crass, prosaic, often priggish individual guided by material rather than artistic or intellectual values <*philistines* who opposed everything new and creative in art>
syn Babbitt, boeotian, boob, middlebrow
rel bourgeois; capitalist; materialist; boor, clown, lout, vulgarian
ant aesthete

phiz *n* ***syn*** FACE 1, countenance, ‖dial, features, ‖kisser, ‖map, mug, muzzle, ‖pan, ‖puss

phlegm *n* **1** ***syn*** APATHY 1, impassivity, insensibility, stoicism, stolidity, unresponsiveness
2 ***syn*** EQUANIMITY, ataraxy, calmness, composure, coolness, imperturbability, sangfroid, self-possession
rel nonchalance, unconcern

phlegmatic *adj* ***syn*** IMPASSIVE 1, apathetic, dry, matter-of-fact, stoic, stolid
rel calm, undemonstrative; aloof, incurious, indifferent, unconcerned; lethargic, sluggish

phoebus *n* ***syn*** SUN 1, daystar, Sol

phoenix *n* ***syn*** PARAGON, ideal, jewel, nonesuch, nonpareil

phonate *vb* ***syn*** ARTICULATE 2, enunciate, pronounce, say

phone *vb* ***syn*** TELEPHONE, ‖buzz, call, ‖ring (up)

phony *adj* ***syn*** COUNTERFEIT, bogus, brummagen, fake, false, pinchbeck, pseudo, sham, snide, spurious

phony *n* **1** ***syn*** IMPOSTURE, cheat, counterfeit, fake, fraud, hoax, humbug, put-on, spoof, swindle
2 ***syn*** IMPOSTOR, fake, faker, fraud, humbug, pretender

photo *vb* ***syn*** PHOTOGRAPH, shoot
idiom take a photo (of)

photog *n* ***syn*** PHOTOGRAPHER, cameraman, camerist, photographist, photoist

photograph *vb* to use a camera to make a picture, image, or likeness of <*photographed* the whole family>
syn photo, shoot
rel cinematize, ‖cinematograph, cinemize, film, filmize, picture; kodak, snap, snapshoot, snapshot; mug

---

syn synonym(s) ***rel*** related word(s)
idiom idiomatic equivalent(s) ***con*** contrasted word(s)
ant antonym(s) * vulgar
‖ use limited; if in doubt, see a dictionary
The first word in a synonym list when printed in SMALL CAPITALS shows where there is more information about the group. For a more efficient use of this book see Explanatory Notes.

idiom capture on film, take a picture (*or* photograph)
photographer *n* one who takes photographs <a newspaper *photographer*>
syn cameraman, camerist, photog, photographist, photoist
rel snapshooter, ‖snapshotter; shutterbug
photographic *adj syn* GRAPHIC 1, pictorial, picturesque, vivid
rel accurate, detailed, exact
photographist *n syn* PHOTOGRAPHER, cameraman, camerist, photog, photoist
photoist *n syn* PHOTOGRAPHER, cameraman, camerist, photog, photographist
photoplay *n syn* MOVIE, cine, ‖cinema, film, flick, motion picture, moving picture, picture, picture show, show
phrase *n* **1** *syn* WORDING, diction, parlance, phraseology, phrasing, verbalism, verbiage, wordage
rel styling
2 a group of words which, taken together, express a notion and may constitute part of a sentence <an adverbial *phrase*> <a trite *phrase*>
syn expression, locution
rel phrasing; idiom; catchword, slogan
3 *syn* CATCHWORD, byword, catchphrase, shibboleth, slogan, watchword
phrase *vb syn* WORD, couch, express, formulate, put
phraseology *n syn* WORDING, diction, parlance, phrase, phrasing, verbalism, verbiage, wordage
idiom choice of words
phrasing *n syn* WORDING, diction, parlance, phrase, phraseology, verbalism, verbiage, wordage
phthisis *n syn* TUBERCULOSIS, consumption, TB, white plague
phylactery *n syn* CHARM 2, amulet, fetish, juju, luck, mascot, periapt, talisman, zemi
physic *n syn* REMEDY 1, cure, medicament, medicant, medication, medicine, pharmacon
physical *adj* **1** *syn* MATERIAL 1, corporeal, gross, objective, phenomenal, sensible, substantial, tangible
rel natural; elemental, elementary
ant spiritual
2 *syn* BODILY, carnal, corporal, corporeal, fleshly, somatic
rel visceral; lusty; brute
ant mental
physician *n* a doctor of medicine <the shortage of *physicians* in rural areas>
syn ‖croaker, doc, doctor, MD, medical, mediciner, medico, ‖sawbones
rel medic; general practitioner, practitioner; surgeon; specialist
idiom medical doctor, medical man

---

syn synonym(s) — *rel* related word(s)
idiom idiomatic equivalent(s) — *con* contrasted word(s)
ant antonym(s) — * vulgar
‖ use limited; if in doubt, see a dictionary
The first word in a synonym list when printed in SMALL CAPITALS shows where there is more information about the group. For a more efficient use of this book see Explanatory Notes.

physique *n* bodily makeup or type <a muscular *physique*>
syn build, constitution, habit, habitus
rel anatomy, structure; configuration, shape; body, figure, form, frame
picaroon *n syn* PIRATE, buccaneer, corsair, freebooter, rover, sea dog, sea robber, sea rover, sea wolf
picayune *adj syn* PETTY 2, inconsequent, inconsequential, measly, niggling, paltry, picayunish, puny, trifling, trivial
picayunish *adj syn* PETTY 2, inconsequential, measly, niggling, paltry, picayune, piddling, puny, trifling, trivial
pick *vb* **1** *syn* CHOOSE 1, cull, elect, mark, opt (for), optate, prefer, select, single (out), take
idiom pick and choose
ant reject
2 *syn* PECK 1, beak
pick *n syn* BEST, choice, cream, elite, fat, flower, pride, prime, prize, top
pick *adj syn* SELECT 1, chosen, elect, exclusive, picked, selected
picked *adj syn* SELECT 1, chosen, elect, exclusive, pick, selected
picket *n syn* GUARD 2, lookout, sentinel, sentry, ward, watch, watchman
pickle *n syn* PREDICAMENT, box, corner, dilemma, fix, hole, jam, plight, scrape, spot
idiom pretty pickle, ‖sticky wicket, tight spot
‖**pickled** *adj syn* INTOXICATED 1, ‖boozy, ‖canned, disguised, drunk, inebriated, ‖lushed, muddled, pixilated, ‖plastered
pick out *vb syn* CHOOSE 1, cull, elect, mark, opt (for), optate, pick, prefer, select, single (out)
pickpocket *n* one who steals from pockets <his wallet was lifted by a *pickpocket*>
syn ‖cannon, cutpurse, ‖dip, ‖diver, purse cutter, ‖wire
rel ‖ganef, thief; ‖mobsman, ‖swell-mobsman
idiom ‖pocket prowler
picksome *adj syn* NICE 1, choosy, delicate, fastidious, finicky, fussy, particular, persnickety, picky, squeamish
pick up *vb* **1** *syn* LIFT 1, elevate, hoist, raise, rear, take up, uphold, uplift, upraise, uprear
2 *syn* GLEAN, cull, extract, garner, gather
3 *syn* GET 1, acquire, annex, chalk up, compass, gain, have, land, obtain, procure
4 *syn* LEARN 1, get, master
5 *syn* ARREST 2, apprehend, ‖bust, detain, nab, pinch, pull in, run in
rel book
idiom ‖take (someone) downtown
6 *syn* RESUME 2, continue, recommence, renew, reopen, restart, take up
idiom pick up the thread again
pickup *n syn* ARREST, apprehension, arrestation, arrestment, detention, ‖nab, pinch
rel booking
picky *adj syn* NICE 1, choosy, dainty, fastidious, finical, finicking, finicky, fussy, particular, persnickety
picnic *n syn* SNAP 1, breeze, child's play, cinch, duck soup, kid stuff, pie, ‖pipe, pushover, setup
pictorial *adj* **1** consisting of or relating to pictures <a collection of *pictorial* materials>

syn graphic, iconographic, illustrational, illustrative, illustratory, pictoric
rel photographic, pictographic
2 *syn* GRAPHIC 1, photographic, picturesque, vivid

pictoric *adj* *syn* PICTORIAL 1, graphic, iconographic, illustrational, illustrative, illustratory

picture *n* 1 *syn* REPRESENTATION, delineation, depiction, description, portraiture, portrayal, presentment
2 *syn* IMAGE 1, double, portrait, ringer, simulacrum, spit, spitting image
3 *syn* MOVIE, cine, ‖cinema, film, flick, motion picture, moving picture, photoplay, picture show, show

picture *vb* *syn* REPRESENT 1, delineate, depict, describe, image, interpret, limn, portray, render
rel draw

picture show *n* *syn* MOVIE, cine, ‖cinema, film, flick, motion picture, moving picture, photoplay, picture, show

picturesque *adj* *syn* GRAPHIC 1, photographic, pictorial, vivid

piddling *adj* *syn* PETTY 2, measly, Mickey Mouse, niggling, paltry, peanut, peddling, pettifogging, puny, trifling

pie *n* *syn* SNAP 1, breeze, child's play, cinch, duck soup, kid stuff, picnic, ‖pipe, pushover, setup

piece *n* 1 *syn* PART 1, cut, division, member, moiety, parcel, portion, section, segment
‖2 *syn* SNACK, ‖bait, ‖bever, bite, ‖chack, morsel, mug-up, tapa

pièce de résistance *n* *syn* SHOWPIECE, chef d'oeuvre, masterpiece

piecemeal *adv* *syn* GRADUALLY, bit by bit, little by little

piecemeal *adj* *syn* GRADUAL, step-by-step

‖**pie–eyed** *adj* *syn* INTOXICATED 1, ‖boozed, ‖boozy, drunk, inebriated, ‖lushed, ‖oiled, pixilated, ‖stewed, zonked

piepoudre *n* *syn* PEDDLER, ‖arab, ‖duffer, hawker, higgler, huckster, outcrier, packman, roadman, vendor

pier *n* 1 *syn* WHARF, berth, dock, jetty, levee, quay, slip
rel pierage, wharfage
2 *syn* PILLAR 1, column, pilaster

pierce *vb* 1 *syn* CUT 1, gash, incise, slash, slice, slit
rel penetrate, perforate
2 *syn* PENETRATE 2
rel run through

piercing *adj* 1 *syn* SHARP 8, acute, knifelike, shooting, stabbing
2 *syn* LOUD 1, blaring, earsplitting, full-mouthed, roaring, stentorian, stentorious, stentorophonic
3 *syn* ACUTE 4, argute, high, piping, sharp, shrill, thin, treble

pietistic *adj* *syn* DEVOUT, godly, holy, pious, prayerful, religious
rel reverencing, reverential

piety *n* *syn* FIDELITY 1, allegiance, ardor, devotion, faithfulness, fealty, loyalty
rel docility, obedience; enthusiasm, fervor, passion, zeal; holiness, sanctity

piffle *n* *syn* NONSENSE 2, balderdash, blatherskite, bosh, bunkum, flapdoodle, hooey, malarkey, pishposh, twaddle

piffling *adj* *syn* PETTY 2, measly, Mickey Mouse, niggling, peddling, pettifogging, piddling, pimping, trifling, trivial

‖**pig** *n* 1 *syn* WANTON, cyprian, hussy, jade, jezebel, slattern, slut, strumpet, tramp, trull
2 *syn* POLICEMAN, ‖bull, cop, ‖copper, ‖flatfoot, ‖fuzz, ‖heat, man, ‖nab, ‖paddy

pigeon *n* *syn* FOOL 3, chump, dupe, fall guy, fish, gudgeon, gull, mark, sap, sucker

pigeon *vb* *syn* DUPE, bamboozle, flimflam, fool, gull, hoax, hoodwink, hornswoggle, job, victimize

pigeonhole *n* 1 *syn* CUBBYHOLE, cubby, mousehole
2 *syn* CLASS 1, category, grade, group, grouping, league, tier
rel niche, slot

pigeonhole *vb* *syn* ASSORT, categorize, class, classify, group, sort
rel identify, label, name; place, rank, rate; catalog; break down, subdivide

pigeon house *n* *syn* DOVECOTE, columbary, culverhouse, dovehouse, pigeonry

pigeonry *n* *syn* DOVECOTE, columbary, culverhouse, dovehouse, pigeon house

pigheaded *adj* *syn* OBSTINATE, bullheaded, headstrong, intractable, mulish, perverse, self-willed, stiff-necked, stubborn, unyielding
idiom not to be moved (*or* budged)

pigment *n* *syn* COLOR 6, colorant, dye, dyestuff, stain, tincture

pigpen *n* *syn* STY 1, dump, pigsty

pigsty *n* *syn* STY 1, dump, pigpen

piked *adj* *syn* POINTED 1, acicular, aciculate, acuminate, acuminous, acute, cuspidate, peaked, peaky, sharp

piker *n* *syn* VAGABOND, bum, drifter, floater, roadster, street arab, ‖traveler, vag, vagrant, Weary Willie

piker *n* *syn* MISER, cheapskate, cheeseparer, moneygrubber, niggard, ‖nipcheese, penny pincher, skinflint, stiff, tightwad

pilaster *n* *syn* PILLAR 1, column, pier

pile *n* 1 a quantity of things heaped or stacked together <a *pile* of dirty clothes>
syn bank, ‖bing, cock, drift, heap, hill, mass, mound, mountain, mow, pyramid, rick, ‖rickle, ‖ruck, shock, stack, stockpile, windrow
rel barrow, pyre, tumulus; ‖dess, haycock, hayrick, haystack; accumulation, aggregate, aggregation, amassment, assemblage, collection, conglomeration, glomeration, hoard, jumble
2 *syn* MUCH, barrel, great deal, heap, lot, lump, mass, mountain, pack, peck
3 *syn* EDIFICE, erection, structure
4 *syn* FORTUNE 4, ‖bomb, boodle, bundle, mint, packet, pot, ‖roll, wad
idiom a pile of money

---

syn synonym(s)	*rel* related word(s)
idiom idiomatic equivalent(s)	*con* contrasted word(s)
ant antonym(s)	* vulgar

‖ use limited; if in doubt, see a dictionary
The first word in a synonym list when printed in SMALL CAPITALS shows where there is more information about the group. For a more efficient use of this book see Explanatory Notes.

pile *vb* **1** ***syn*** HEAP 1, bank, cock, drift, hill, mound, stack
2 ***syn*** LOAD 3, charge, choke, fill, heap, pack

pile (in) *vb* ***syn*** RETIRE 4, bed, ||flop, roll in, turn in

pile (out) *vb* ***syn*** ROLL OUT, arise, get up, rise, rise and shine, turn out, uprise
idiom ||get the lead out, ||shake it out

pile *n* ***syn*** DOWN, floss, flue, fluff, fur, fuzz, lint

pileous *adj* ***syn*** HAIRY 1, fleecy, hirsute, pilose, whiskered, woolly
con bare; pileless

pile up *vb* ***syn*** SHIPWRECK 1, beach, cast away, strand, wreck

pileup *n* ***syn*** CRASH 3, crack-up, ||prang, smash, smash-up, ||stramash, wreck

pilfer *vb* ***syn*** STEAL 1, appropriate, ||cop, filch, lift, pinch, purloin, snitch, swipe, thieve

pilferer *n* ***syn*** THIEF, filcher, larcener, larcenist, nimmer, prig, purloiner, stealer

pilgarlic *n* ***syn*** LAUGHINGSTOCK, butt, derision, jest, jestee, joke, mock, mockery, sport

||**pill** *n* ***syn*** CIGARETTE, ||butt, ||cig, ||coffin nail, fag, ||gasper, ||skag, smoke

pillage *vb* **1** ***syn*** RAVAGE, depredate, desecrate, desolate, despoil, devastate, devour, sack, spoliate, waste
rel encroach, invade, trespass; appropriate, arrogate, confiscate, usurp
idiom lay waste
2 ***syn*** STEAL 1, appropriate, filch, lift, nab, pilfer, pinch, purloin, swipe, thieve

pillager *n* ***syn*** MARAUDER, forager, freebooter, looter, plunderer, raider, ravager, ravisher, sacker, spoiler

pillar *n* **1** a firm upright support for a superstructure <stone *pillars* supported the ceiling>
syn column, pier, pilaster
rel prop; pedestal; post
2 ***syn*** MAINSTAY, backbone, sinew(s)

pilose *adj* ***syn*** HAIRY 1, fleecy, hirsute, pileous, whiskered, woolly

pilot *n* **1** ***syn*** LEADER 1, ||bell cow, bellwether, dean, doyen, guide, lead
2 one who flies or is qualified to fly an airplane <jet *pilots*>
syn airman, aviator, birdman, flier, fly-boy
rel aerialist

pilot *vb* **1** ***syn*** GUIDE, conduct, direct, escort, lead, route, see, shepherd, show, steer
2 ***syn*** DRIVE 5, auto, charioteer, motor, tool, wheel

pimp *n* **1** a man who solicits for a prostitute, lives off her earnings, and often lives with her <after dark, the *pimp* appeared on the street seeking clients for his girls>
syn bully, cadet, ||easy rider, fancy man, ||mack, macquereau, pander
rel procurer; white slaver
||**2** ***syn*** INFORMER, betrayer, ||canary, ||fink, ||nark, snitch, squawker, ||squeaker, stool, stoolie

||**pimp** *vb* ***syn*** INFORM 3, ||nark, peach, rat, ||sing, snitch, squeak, squeal, ||stool

pimping *adj* ***syn*** PETTY 2, measly, Mickey Mouse, niggling, paltry, peddling, piddling, piffling, trifling, trivial

pimple *n* ***syn*** ABSCESS, boil, carbuncle, furuncle, pustule
rel ||plouk

pimple *vb* ***syn*** SPOT 2, dot, speckle, sprinkle, stud

pin *n* ***syn*** BROOCH, broach, clip

pinch *vb* **1** ***syn*** EXTORT 1, exact, gouge, screw, shake down, squeeze, wrench, wrest, wring
2 ***syn*** STEAL 1, ||cop, filch, lift, nab, ||nick, nip, snitch, swipe, thieve
3 ***syn*** ARREST 2, apprehend, ||bust, detain, nab, pick up, pull in, run in
4 ***syn*** SCRIMP, scrape, screw, skimp, ||skinch, spare, stint

pinch *n* **1** ***syn*** JUNCTURE 2, contingency, crisis, crossroad(s), emergency, exigency, pass, strait, turning point, zero hour
2 ***syn*** THEFT, larceny, lift, purloining, steal, stealage, stealing, thievery, thieving, ||touch
3 ***syn*** ARREST, apprehension, arrestation, arrestment, detention, ||nab, pickup

pinchbeck *adj* ***syn*** COUNTERFEIT, bogus, brummagem, fake, false, phony, pseudo, sham, snide, spurious

pinched *adj* ***syn*** HAGGARD, careworn, drawn, worn
con stalwart, stout, strong, sturdy; healthy, robust

pinching *adj* ***syn*** STINGY, cheeseparing, hardfisted, ironfisted, mingy, ||narrow, niggardly, penny-pinching, pinchpenny, tight

pinch hitter *n* ***syn*** SUBSTITUTE, alternate, fill-in, locum tenens, replacement, stand-in, sub, succedaneum, surrogate

pinchpenny *adj* ***syn*** STINGY, close, costive, ironfisted, mingy, ||narrow, niggard, pinching, save-all, tight

||**pindling** *adj* ***syn*** IRRITABLE, fretful, huffy, peevish, pettish, petulant, prickish, prickly, querulous, raspish

pine *vb* ***syn*** LONG, ache, crave, dream, hanker, hunger, sigh, suspire, thirst, yearn
rel brood, fret, mope; grieve, mourn; agonize

pinhead *n* ***syn*** DUNCE, ||cluck, dimwit, ||dumb bunny, ||dumb cluck, featherweight, lackwit, nitwit, simp, wantwit

pinhead *adj* ***syn*** STUPID 1, beefheaded, beetleheaded, blockheaded, chuckleheaded, dense, doltish, fatheaded, hammerheaded, pinheaded

pinheaded *adj* ***syn*** STUPID 1, beefheaded, beef-witted, beetleheaded, blear-eyed, blear-witted, blockish, dull, dumb, duncical

pink *vb* ***syn*** BLUSH, color, crimson, flush, glow, mantle, pinken, redden, rose, rouge

pinken *vb* ***syn*** BLUSH, color, crimson, flush, glow, mantle, pink, redden, rose, rouge

Pinkerton *n* ***syn*** PRIVATE DETECTIVE, operative, ||private eye, ||shamus

pin money *n* ***syn*** POCKET MONEY, spending money

pinnacle *n* ***syn*** APEX 2, acme, apogee, capsheaf, climax, culmination, meridian, peak, summit, zenith

pinpoint *vb* ***syn*** IDENTIFY, determinate, diagnose, diagnosticate, distinguish, finger, place, recognize, spot

---

syn synonym(s) ***rel*** related word(s)
idiom idiomatic equivalent(s) ***con*** contrasted word(s)
ant antonym(s) * vulgar
|| use limited; if in doubt, see a dictionary
The first word in a synonym list when printed in SMALL CAPITALS shows where there is more information about the group. For a more efficient use of this book see Explanatory Notes.

pint–size *adj syn* TINY, diminutive, midget, miniature, pocket, pocket-size, teensy, teeny, wee, weeny

pioneer *adj syn* FIRST 2, earliest, initial, maiden, original, primary, prime
rel pilot

pious *adj syn* DEVOUT, godly, holy, pietistic, prayerful, religious
rel priestlike, priestly
ant impious

pip *vb* ‖**1** *syn* DEFEAT 2, best, down, outdo, worst
2 *syn* DIE 1, cash in, ‖check out, conk, ‖croak, depart, drop, ‖kick in, ‖kick off, pass away

‖**pip** *n syn* ‖DILLY, ‖corker, crackerjack, ‖daisy, dandy, humdinger, jim-dandy, ‖lalapalooza, ‖lulu, nifty

pipe *n* **1** *syn* CASK, barrel, butt, hogshead, keg, tun
‖**2** *syn* PIPE DREAM, bubble, chimera, dream, fantasy (*or* phantasy), illusion, rainbow
‖**3** *syn* SNAP 1, breeze, child's play, cinch, duck soup, kid stuff, picnic, pie, pushover, setup

pipe *vb* ‖**1** *syn* CRY 2, blub, blubber, boohoo, sob, wail, weep
2 *syn* CONDUCT 4, carry, channel, convey, funnel, siphon, traject, transmit

pipe down *vb syn* SHUT UP 2, dry up, dumb (up), ‖dummy (up), ‖ring off

pipe dream *n* an illusory or fantastic plan or hope <*pipe dreams* of universal peace>
syn bubble, chimera, dream, fantasy (*or* phantasy), illusion, ‖pipe, rainbow
rel expectation, hope, prospect

pipeline *n* a person through whom information is transmitted <she was his news *pipeline* from the mayor's office>
syn channel, conduit
rel grapevine; origin, source, wellspring; supplier; connection, contact

piping *adj syn* ACUTE 4, argute, high, piercing, sharp, shrill, thin, treble

‖**pipped** *adj syn* INTOXICATED 1, ‖boozy, ‖canned, disguised, drunk, inebriated, ‖lushed, muddled, pixilated, ‖plastered

pippin *n syn* ‖DILLY, ‖corker, crackerjack, dandy, ‖dinger, ‖doozer, humdinger, jim-dandy, ‖lalapalooza, ‖pip

piquant *adj syn* PUNGENT, peppery, poignant, racy, snappy, spicy, zesty
rel high-flavored, well-flavored; appetizing, sparkling
con inane, jejune
ant banal

pique *n syn* OFFENSE 2, dudgeon, huff, miff, resentment, ‖snuff, umbrage
rel annoyance, irk, irking, vexation; exasperation, irritation, provocation

pique *vb* **1** *syn* IRRITATE, aggravate, exasperate, get, nettle, peeve, provoke, put out, rile, roil
2 *syn* PROVOKE 4, excite, galvanize, innervate, innerve, motivate, move, quicken, rouse, stimulate
rel prick, punch; ignite
3 *syn* PRIDE, plume, preen

pirate *n* a robber on the high seas <little boys dreaming of sailing as *pirates*>
syn buccaneer, corsair, freebooter, picaroon, rover, sea dog, sea robber, sea rover, sea wolf
rel viking; privateer; looter, marauder, pillager, plunderer, raider

‖**pirl** *vb syn* SPIN 1, gyrate, gyre, pirouette, ‖purl, twirl, whirl, whirligig

‖**piroot** *vb syn* SNOOP, busybody, mouse, nose, poke, pry, ‖snook

pirouette *vb syn* SPIN 1, gyrate, gyre, ‖pirl, ‖purl, twirl, whirl, whirligig

pishposh *n syn* NONSENSE 2, balderdash, blatherskite, bosh, bunkum, flapdoodle, hooey, malarkey, piffle, twaddle

‖**piss away** *vb syn* WASTE 2, blow, blunder (away), dissipate, fritter, frivol (away), prodigalize, squander, throw away, trifle (away)

‖**pissed** *adj* **1** *syn* ANGRY, choleric, heated, irate, ireful, mad, shirty, waxy, wrathful, wroth
2 *syn* INTOXICATED 1, ‖boozy, ‖canned, disguised, drunk, inebriated, ‖lushed, muddled, pixilated, ‖plastered

‖**pissed off** *adj syn* ANGRY, choleric, heated, irate, ireful, mad, shirty, waxy, wrathful, wroth

pit *n* ‖**1** *syn* GRAVE, burial, sepulcher, sepulture, tomb
2 *syn* HELL, abyss, barathrum, Gehenna, hades, inferno, netherworld, Pandemonium, perdition, underworld

pit *vb syn* OPPOSE 1, counter, match, play (off), vie

pitch *vb* **1** *syn* THROW 1, ‖bung, cast, fire, fling, heave, hurl, launch, sling, toss
rel hoist, raise; move
2 *syn* THROW 2, buck (off), unhorse, unseat
‖**3** *syn* PLANT 1, put in, seed, sow
4 *syn* FALL 2, drop, go down, keel (over), plunge, slump, topple, tumble
idiom take a pitch
5 *syn* PLUNGE 2, burst, dive, drive, lunge, ‖splunge
rel drop, fall, sink
6 *syn* TOSS 2, heave, rock, roll
7 *syn* SEESAW, lurch, swag, tilt, tilter, yaw

pitch *n syn* SPIEL, ‖line, song and dance
rel persuasion

pitch–black *adj syn* BLACK 1, atramentous, ebon, ebony, inky, jet, jetty, pitch-dark, raven, sable

pitch–dark *adj syn* BLACK 1, atramentous, ebon, ebony, inky, jet, jetty, pitch-dark, raven, sable

pitched *adj syn* INCLINED 3, inclining, leaning, oblique, pitching, sloped, sloping, tilted, tilting, tipped

pitch in *vb* **1** to set about doing something energetically <had a lot to do and decided to *pitch in*>
syn buckle (down), fall to, jump (in *or* into), set to, wade (in *or* into)
rel attack, tackle; launch, tee off; begin, commence, start (off *or* out *or* up)

---

syn synonym(s) *rel* related word(s)
idiom idiomatic equivalent(s) *con* contrasted word(s)
ant antonym(s) * vulgar
‖ use limited; if in doubt, see a dictionary
The first word in a synonym list when printed in SMALL CAPITALS shows where there is more information about the group. For a more efficient use of this book see Explanatory Notes.

idiom fall to it, fall to work, get busy (*or* cracking), get down to it, get going, get (*or* have) with it, go to it, hop (*or* jump) to it
con dally, dawdle, procrastinate, stall; vacillate
2 ***syn*** CONTRIBUTE 1, chip in, come through, kick in, subscribe

pitching *adj* ***syn*** INCLINED 3, inclining, leaning, oblique, pitched, sloped, sloping, tilted, tilting, tipped

pitchy *adj* ***syn*** BLACK 1, atramentous, ebon, ebony, inky, jet, onyx, pitch-black, raven, sable

piteous *adj* ***syn*** PITIFUL 1, commiserable, pathetic, pitiable, poor, rueful
rel beseeching, entreating, imploring, supplicating; doleful, dolorous, melancholy, plaintive; ruined

pitfall *n* a hidden or obscure source of danger, error, or harm <*pitfalls* that trap the unwary investigator>
syn booby trap, deadfall, mousetrap, springe, trapfall
rel danger, hazard, peril, risk; cobweb, entanglement, mesh(es), toil(s), web; bait, lure, snare, trap

pith *n* **1** ***syn*** ESSENCE 2, bottom, essentiality, marrow, quintessence, quintessential, rock bottom, root, soul, virtuality
rel center, focus, nucleus; meaning, meaningfulness
2 ***syn*** SUBSTANCE 2, burden, core, gist, matter, meat, sense, short, thrust, upshot
idiom the long and (the) short
3 ***syn*** CENTER 3, core, heart, quick, root
rel fulcrum; hub
4 ***syn*** IMPORTANCE, consequence, import, magnitude, moment, momentousness, significance, ‖signification, weight, weightiness

pithy *adj* being rich in meaning and tersely cogent in expression <a *pithy* summary>
syn compact, epigrammatic, marrowy, meaty; *compare* CONCISE
rel brief, concise, lean, short, short and sweet, succinct; crisp, curt, terse; effective, forceful; meaningful, significant, substantial
idiom brief and to the point, down to brass tacks, right to the point
con flatulent, inflated, tumid, turgid; prolix, verbose, wordy
ant diffuse

pitiable *adj* **1** ***syn*** PITIFUL 1, commiserable, pathetic, piteous, poor, rueful
2 ***syn*** CONTEMPTIBLE, beggarly, cheap, despicable, despisable, pitiful, scummy, scurvy, shabby, sorry
rel miserable, wretched; deplorable, lamentable

pitiful *adj* **1** arousing or deserving pity <*pitiful* refugees driven from their homes>
syn commiserable, pathetic, piteous, pitiable, poor, rueful
rel affecting, moving, touching; miserable, woeful, wretched; heartrending

---

syn synonym(s) ***rel*** related word(s)
idiom idiomatic equivalent(s) ***con*** contrasted word(s)
ant antonym(s) * vulgar
‖ use limited; if in doubt, see a dictionary
The first word in a synonym list when printed in SMALL CAPITALS shows where there is more information about the group. For a more efficient use of this book see Explanatory Notes.

2 ***syn*** CONTEMPTIBLE, beggarly, cheap, despicable, despisable, pitiable, scummy, scurvy, shabby, sorry

pitiless *adj* devoid of or unmoved by pity <a *pitiless* concentration camp guard>
syn merciless, unmerciful, unpitying; *compare* UNFEELING 2
rel coldhearted, hardhearted, heartless, ironhearted, marblehearted, stony, stonyhearted, uncompassionate, unfeeling; barbarous, brutal, cruel, cutthroat, inhumane, savage
idiom lacking bowels of compassion, without an ounce of pity
con compassionate, humane, sympathetic; clement, merciful; tender, warmhearted
ant pitying

pittance *n* a small, often barely sufficient amount or allowance <a *pittance* of an education> <worked for a mere *pittance*>
syn dribble, driblet, ‖scrimption
rel bit, mite, scrap, smidgen, trace; inadequacy, insufficiency
idiom a drop in the bucket, cheeseparings and candle ends, ‖pinchgut money
con abundance, opulence, plenty, wealth

pity *n* sympathetic feeling for one suffering, distressed, or unhappy <felt the deepest *pity* for the prisoners>
syn commiseration, compassion, rue, ruth, sympathy
rel dejection, distress, melancholy, sadness, sorrow; charity, clemency, lenity, mercy
con contempt, disdain, disgust, scorn

pity *vb* ***syn*** COMPASSIONATE, ache, commiserate, feel (for), sympathize (with)

pivot *vb* ***syn*** TURN 6, avert, deflect, divert, sheer, veer, volte-face, wheel, whip, whirl

pivotal *adj* ***syn*** CENTRAL 1, cardinal, overriding, overruling, ruling
rel essential, vital; momentous; capital, principal

pixie *n* **1** ***syn*** FAIRY, brownie, elf, fay, nisse, sprite
2 ***syn*** SCAMP, devil, enfant terrible, mischief, rapscallion, rascal, rogue, scalawag, skeezicks, slyboots

pixie *adj* ***syn*** PLAYFUL 1, antic, coltish, elvish, gamesome, impish, pixieish, pixilated, prankish, puckish

pixieish *adj* ***syn*** PLAYFUL 1, antic, elvish, frisky, impish, kittenish, mischievous, pixie, pixilated, puckish

pixilated *adj* **1** ***syn*** PLAYFUL 1, elvish, frolicsome, larkish, pixie, pixieish, pranky, puckish, roguish, waggish
2 ***syn*** INTOXICATED 1, ‖boozy, ‖canned, disguised, drunk, inebriated, ‖lushed, muddled, ‖plastered, stoned

placard *n* ***syn*** POSTER, affiche, bill, handbill

placard *vb* ***syn*** POST, poster

placate *vb* ***syn*** PACIFY, appease, assuage, conciliate, mollify, propitiate, sweeten
rel comfort; tranquilize
idiom lay the dust
con anger, incense, infuriate, madden; excite, pique, provoke, stimulate
ant enrage

place *n* **1** the portion of space occupied by or chosen for something <the *place* where we'll meet>
syn location, locus, point, position, site, situation, spot, station, where
rel district, locality, vicinity; area, region, tract, zone; field, province, territory

2 *syn* STATUS 1, capacity, character, footing, position, rank, situation, standing, state, station
3 *syn* JOB 2, appointment, berth, billet, connection, office, position, post, situation, spot

place *vb* **1** *syn* SET 1, establish, fix, lay, put, settle, stick
2 *syn* ESTIMATE 3, approximate, call, judge, put, reckon
3 *syn* IDENTIFY, determinate, diagnose, diagnosticate, distinguish, finger, pinpoint, recognize, spot
rel know, tell; nail, peg
idiom put one's finger on

placed *adj* *syn* SITUATED, located, positioned, set, sited, situate
ant displaced

placid *adj* **1** *syn* CALM 1, halcyon, hushed, quiet, still, stilly, untroubled
rel irenic, peaceful, serene, unagitated, unstirring
ant roiled
2 *syn* CALM 2, collected, composed, easy, easygoing, poised, self-composed, self-possessed, serene, tranquil
rel detached, inexcitable, unmoved
con fidgety, jittery, jumpy, skittery; agitated
ant choleric

plague *n* **1** an epidemic disease causing a high mortality rate <smallpox finally ceased to be a *plague* in those nations>
syn curse, pestilence, scourge
rel infestation, invasion; affliction, disease; epidemic; ravage
2 *syn* ANNOYANCE 3, besetment, bother, botheration, botherment, exasperation, irritant, nuisance, pest, pester
rel bane, curse
3 *syn* EPIDEMIC, outbreak, rash

plague *vb* *syn* WORRY 1, annoy, bedevil, beleaguer, gnaw, hagride, harass, harry, tease, ||wherret
rel chafe, gall; badger, bait, hassle, hector, hound, ride; afflict, torment

plain *adj* **1** free from all ostentation or superficial embellishment <just give the *plain* facts>
syn discreet, dry, homely, inelaborate, modest, simple, unadorned, unbeautified, undecorated, unelaborate, unembellished, unembroidered, ungarnished, unornamented, unostentatious, unpretentious
rel muted, restrained; austere, bald, bare, severe, spartan, stark, unluxurious; homespun
con adorned, beautified, elaborate, embellished, embroidered, exaggerated; high-flown, ostentatious, pretentious; flamboyant, rococo
ant rich
2 *syn* STRAIGHT 3, neat, pure, unadulterated, undiluted, unmixed
3 *syn* CLEAR 5, apparent, distinct, evident, manifest, obvious, palpable, patent, unambiguous, unequivocal
rel broad, unmistakable; legible
ant abstruse
4 *syn* FRANK, candid, open, openhearted, straightforward, unconcealed, undisguised, undissembled, undissembling, unvarnished
rel unfeigned; abrupt
idiom plain and open
5 lacking allure without being positively ugly <a *plain* woman, drably dressed>
syn homely, unalluring, unattractive, unbeauteous, unbeautiful, uncomely, unhandsome, unpretty
rel plain-featured; inelegant; ordinary, plain Jane, unremarkable; ill-favored
idiom not much for looks, not much to look at, short on looks
con alluring, attractive, beautiful, comely, handsome; elegant; striking; knockout, sensational
6 *syn* ORDINARY 1, everyday, plain Jane, quotidian, routine, unremarkable, usual, workaday

plainclothesman *n* *syn* DETECTIVE, dick, ||eye, gumshoe, hawkshaw, investigator, Sherlock, Sherlock Holmes, sleuth, ||tec

plain dealing *adj* *syn* STRAIGHTFORWARD 2, aboveboard, forthright, straight

plain Jane *adj* *syn* ORDINARY 1, everyday, plain, quotidian, routine, unremarkable, usual, workaday

plainness *n* *syn* CLARITY, clearness, limpidity, lucidity, perspicuity
ant abstruseness

plainspoken *adj* *syn* FRANK, candid, direct, forthright, open, plain, straightforward, undisguised, undissembled, unvarnished

plaintive *adj* *syn* MELANCHOLY 2, doleful, dolesome, dolorous, lamentable, lugubrious, mournful, rueful, sorrowful, woeful
rel deploring, lamenting, wailing; piteous, pitiful; sad, saddening

plan *n* **1** a method devised for making or doing something or attaining an end <each company had a *plan* for increasing profits>
syn blueprint, design, game plan, project, scheme, strategy
rel conception, idea, notion; ground plan, projection, projet; intent, intention, platform, purpose; means, method, way
idiom course (*or* plan) of action
2 *syn* INTENTION, animus, design, intendment, intent, meaning, purpose
rel policy
3 *syn* ORDER 8, method, orderliness, pattern, system

plan *vb* **1** *syn* DESIGN 3, arrange, lay out, map (out), set out
2 to formulate a plan for arranging, realizing, or achieving something <*planned* next year's program>
syn arrange, blueprint, cast, chart, design, devise, ||dope out, project; *compare* DESIGN 3
rel contemplate, meditate; cut out, draft, outline, sketch; figure (out), think (out); formulate, work out; organize
3 *syn* INTEND 2, aim, contemplate, design, mean, ||mind, propose, purpose
idiom be planning (*or* counting) on, have all intentions of, have every intention of

---

syn synonym(s) *rel* related word(s)
idiom idiomatic equivalent(s) *con* contrasted word(s)
ant antonym(s) * vulgar
|| use limited; if in doubt, see a dictionary
The first word in a synonym list when printed in SMALL CAPITALS shows where there is more information about the group. For a more efficient use of this book see Explanatory Notes.

planate *n syn* LEVEL, even, flat, flush, plane, smooth

plane *vb syn* EVEN 1, flatten, flush, lay, level, smooth, smoothen

plane *adj syn* LEVEL, even, flat, flush, planate, smooth

planet *n, used with* the *syn* EARTH 1, globe, world

planetary *adj* **1** *syn* HUGE, Antaean, colossal, cyclopean, elephantine, enormous, gigantic, immense, jumbo, monumental
2 *syn* UNIVERSAL 2, catholic, cosmic, cosmopolitan, ecumenical, global, worldwide

plangent *adj syn* RESONANT, consonant, orotund, resounding, ringing, rotund, round, sonorant, sonorous, vibrant

plant *vb* **1** to put or set into the ground for growth < *plant* corn >
syn ||pitch, put in, seed, sow
rel drill; broadcast, dust, scatter; seed down
con crop, gather, harvest, reap
2 *syn* HIDE, bury, ||bush up, cache, conceal, cover, occult, screen, secrete, stash
3 *syn* BURY 1, entomb, inhume, inter, lay away, put away, sepulcher, sepulture, tomb

plant *n syn* FACTORY, manufactory, mill, works

plash *vb syn* SPLASH, douse, slop, slosh, spatter, splatter, splosh, splurge, spurtle, swash

plaster *vb syn* SMEAR 1, bedaub, besmear, dab, daub, ||smarm, smudge

||**plastered** *adj syn* INTOXICATED 1, ||boozy, ||canned, disguised, drunk, inebriated, ||lushed, muddled, pixilated, stoned

plastic *adj* susceptible of being modified in form or nature <the *plastic* quality of modeling clay> <the *plastic* affections of children>
syn adaptable, ductile, malleable, moldable, pliable, pliant, supple
rel elastic, flexible, resilient, supple, workable; impressionable, influenceable, suggestible, susceptible; amenable, bending, giving, tractable, yielding
con inflexible, rigid, stiff; accepted, customary, prevailing, set, standard, wonted

plat *n syn* LOT 3, parcel, plot, tract

plateau *n* a usually extensive level land area raised sharply above adjacent land on at least one side <the *plateaus* of central Bolivia>
syn table, tableland, upland
rel mesa
con dale, glen, vale, valley; bottom, bottomland, lowland

platitude *n syn* COMMONPLACE, banality, bromide, cliché, prosaicism, prosaism, rubber stamp, shibboleth, tag, truism
rel inanity, insipidity, vapidity; mawkishness, sentimentality

---

syn synonym(s) *rel* related word(s)
idiom idiomatic equivalent(s) *con* contrasted word(s)
ant antonym(s) * vulgar
|| use limited; if in doubt, see a dictionary
The first word in a synonym list when printed in SMALL CAPITALS shows where there is more information about the group. For a more efficient use of this book see Explanatory Notes.

---

platoon *n syn* GROUP 3, array, batch, battery, bunch, clump, cluster, lot, parcel, set

plaudit *n, usu* **plaudits** *pl syn* APPLAUSE, acclaim, acclamation
rel kudos

plausibility *n syn* VERISIMILITUDE, color, verisimility

plausible *adj syn* BELIEVABLE, colorable, credible, creditable
rel likely, possible, probable; presumable
con impossible, improbable, unlikely
ant implausible

play *n* **1** activity engaged in for amusement <children need periods of work and *play*>
syn disport, diversion, fun, recreation, sport
rel amusement, entertainment; frolic, gambol, romp; delectation, delight, enjoyment, pleasure
con business, duty, obligation; labor; drudgery
ant work
2 *syn* FUN 1, game, jest, joke, sport
rel sportiveness
ant earnest
3 *syn* TRICK 1, artifice, device, feint, gambit, gimmick, maneuver, ploy, stratagem, wile
4 *syn* USE 1, appliance, application, employment, operation, usance
5 *syn* ROOM 3, elbowroom, latitude, leeway, margin, scope

play *vb* **1** to engage in an activity for amusement or recreation <*played* outside for hours>
syn disport, recreate, sport
rel amuse, divert, engage, entertain; frolic, gambol, rollick, romp
con labor, toil, travail; drudge, fag, slave
ant work
2 *syn* FIDDLE 1, fidget, trifle, twiddle
3 *syn* TREAT 2, deal (with), handle, serve, take, use
4 *syn* MANIPULATE 2, beguile, exploit, finesse, jockey, maneuver
5 *syn* ACT 1, discourse, do, enact, impersonate, perform, personate, playact
6 *syn* GAMBLE 1, bet, game, lay, put (on), set, stake, wager

play (around) *vb syn* PHILANDER, fool (around), mess around, wolf, womanize

play (down) *vb syn* SOFT-PEDAL, de-emphasize
rel restrain; mute, soften
ant play (up)

play (off) *vb syn* OPPOSE 1, counter, match, pit, vie

play (up) *vb syn* EMPHASIZE, feature, italicize, stress, underline, underscore
idiom make a (big) production of
ant play (down)

playact *vb syn* ACT 1, discourse, do, enact, impersonate, perform, personate, play

playactor *n syn* ACTOR 1, impersonator, mime, mimic, mummer, performer, player, thespian, trouper

player *n syn* ACTOR 1, impersonator, mime, mimic, mummer, performer, playactor, thespian, trouper

playful *adj* **1** given to or characterized by play, jests, or tricks <in a *playful* mood>
syn antic, coltish, elvish, frisky, frolicsome, gamesome, impish, kittenish, larkish, ||mischiefful, mischievous, pixie, pixieish, pixilated, prankful, prankish, pranky, puckish, roguish, sportive, waggish, wicked

rel gay, lighthearted, whimsical; dashing, larking, lively, sprightly; blithe, jocund, jolly, jovial, merry; gleeful, hilarious, mirthful
idiom as playful as a kitten (*or* colt), feeling one's oats
con grim, stern, stolid; grave, serious
2 *syn* ANTIC 2, frolicsome, rollicking, sprightly

‖play–pretty *n syn* TOY 2, ‖die, plaything, ‖pretty

plaything *n syn* TOY 2, ‖die, ‖play-pretty, ‖pretty

playwright *n* one who writes plays <a famous Broadway *playwright*>
syn dramatist, dramatizer, dramaturge
rel librettist; scenarist

plaza *n syn* COMMON 2, green, square

plea *n* 1 *syn* EXCUSE 1, alibi, pretext, ‖right
rel extenuation, mitigation, palliation; apology; out; vindication
2 *syn* PRAYER, appeal, application, entreaty, imploration, imprecation, orison, petition, suit, supplication
rel overture; call, cry
idiom solemn entreaty (*or* plea)

plead *vb syn* BEG, appeal, beseech, brace, crave, entreat, implore, importune, pray, supplicate

pleasance *n syn* AMENITY 1, agreeability, agreeableness, amiability, cordiality, enjoyableness, geniality, gratefulness, pleasantness, sweetness and light

pleasant *adj* 1 highly acceptable to the mind or senses <a *pleasant* personality> <a *pleasant* respite>
syn agreeable, congenial, favorable, good, grateful, gratifying, nice, pleasing, pleasurable, pleasureful, welcome
rel cheerful, cheering, cheery, glad, joyful, joyous; alluring, attractive, charming, pretty; convivial, engaging
con displeasing, distasteful; harsh; obnoxious, repellent, repelling, repugnant, repulsive
ant unpleasant
2 *syn* FAIR 2, clarion, clear, cloudless, fine, sunny, sunshine, sunshiny, unclouded, undarkened

pleasantness *n syn* AMENITY 1, agreeability, agreeableness, amiability, cordiality, enjoyableness, geniality, gratefulness, pleasance, sweetness and light
rel goodness, niceness
ant unpleasantness

please *vb* 1 *syn* WILL, choose, elect, like, wish
2 to give or be a source of pleasure to <her work *pleased* him>
syn arride, delectate, delight, gladden, gratify, happify, pleasure
rel content, satisfy, suit; amuse, tickle, titillate; regale, rejoice; overjoy
con vex; annoy; anger
ant displease
3 *syn* SUIT 6, satisfy

pleasing *adj syn* PLEASANT 1, agreeable, congenial, favorable, good, grateful, gratifying, nice, pleasurable, welcome
rel satisfactory, suitable; enchanting, winning; adorable, darling, delightful
ant displeasing, repellent

pleasurable *adj syn* PLEASANT 1, agreeable, congenial, favorable, good, grateful, gratifying, nice, pleasing, welcome
ant unpleasurable

pleasure *n* 1 *syn* WILL 1, fancy, inclination, liking, mind, velleity
2 the agreeable emotion accompanying the expectation, acquisition, or possession of something good or desirable <the *pleasures* and pains of growing up>
syn delectation, delight, enjoyment, fruition, joy, joyance; *compare* ENJOYMENT 1
rel bliss, felicity, happiness; kick, thrill
con vexation; annoyance; anger; affliction, distress, sorrow, trouble
ant displeasure
3 *syn* ENJOYMENT 1, delectation, diversion, relish
ant displeasure

pleasure *vb syn* PLEASE 2, arride, delectate, delight, gladden, gratify, happify

pleasure dome *n syn* RESORT 3, spa, watering place

pleasureful *adj syn* PLEASANT 1, agreeable, congenial, favorable, good, gratifying, nice, pleasing, pleasurable, welcome

pleasuremonger *n syn* HEDONIST, carpet knight, sybarite

pleb *n* **plebs** *pl syn* COMMONALTY, commonage, commoners, common men, people, plebes, plebeians, populace, rank and file, third estate

plebeian *adj syn* IGNOBLE 1, base, baseborn, humble, low, lowborn, lowly, mean, unennobled, unwashed
ant patrician

plebeians *n pl syn* COMMONALTY, commonage, commoners, common men, people, plebes, plebs, populace, rank and file, third estate
ant patricians

plebs *n* **plebes** *pl syn* COMMONALTY, commonage, commoners, common men, people, plebeians, plebs, populace, rank and file, third estate
rel peasantry, peasants
ant patricians, patriciate

pledge *n* 1 something given or held as a sign of another's good faith or intentions <the new school is the *pledge* given by the community to its children>
syn earnest, pawn, security, token, warrant; *compare* GUARANTEE 1, PROMISE
rel bail, bond, guarantee, guaranty, surety, warranty; promise, word; oath, vow
2 *syn* WORD 8, assurance, guarantee, warrant

pledge *vb* 1 *syn* PAWN, ‖dip, hock, impignorate, mortgage, ‖pop, ‖spout
2 *syn* DRINK 2, toast
3 *syn* PROMISE 1, engage, pass, undertake
rel bind, tie; commit, confide, consign, entrust
idiom give (*or* make) a solemn pledge, pledge one's honor
4 *syn* VOW, covenant, plight, swear

plenteous *adj syn* PLENTIFUL, abundant, ample, bounteous, bountiful, copious, generous, liberal, plenty

---

syn synonym(s) — *rel* related word(s)
idiom idiomatic equivalent(s) — *con* contrasted word(s)
ant antonym(s) — * vulgar
‖ use limited; if in doubt, see a dictionary
The first word in a synonym list when printed in SMALL CAPITALS shows where there is more information about the group. For a more efficient use of this book see Explanatory Notes.

rel full, hearty; fruitful, galore, prolific; luxurious, opulent, sumptuous; lavish, prodigal, profuse, profusive, rampant, rife

plentiful *adj* being more than sufficient without being excessive <a *plentiful* harvest>
syn abundant, ample, bounteous, bountiful, copious, generous, liberal, plenteous, plenty
rel enough, sufficient; fulsome, rich, unstinted; excessive, extravagant, overabundant, overflowing, superabundant; abounding, bumper, bursting, swarming, swimming, teeming
con deficient, exiguous, meager, skimpy; inadequate, insufficient
ant scant, scanty

plenty *n* ***syn*** MUCH, great deal, heap, lot, ||mess, mountain, pack, peck, pile, ||sight
rel abundance, cornucopia

plenty *adj* ***syn*** PLENTIFUL, abundant, ample, bounteous, bountiful, copious, generous, liberal, plenteous

pleonasm *n* ***syn*** VERBIAGE 1, circumambages, circumbendibus, circumlocution, periphrase, periphrasis, redundancy, roundabout, tautology, verbality

plethora *n* ***syn*** EXCESS 1, overabundance, overflow, overkill, overmuch, overplus, superfluity, surfeit, surplus, surplusage
rel much, plenty; many; deluge, flood

pliable *adj* ***syn*** PLASTIC, adaptable, ductile, malleable, moldable, pliant, supple
rel manipulable, manipulatable
con unadaptable, unflexible, unmalleable, unpliant
ant unpliable

pliant *adj* ***syn*** PLASTIC, adaptable, ductile, malleable, moldable, pliable, supple
rel spongy
ant unpliant

plica *n* ***syn*** WRINKLE, corrugation, crease, crinkle, fold, furrow, ridge, rimple, rivel, ruck

plight *vb* ***syn*** VOW, covenant, pledge, swear
idiom plight one's honor

plight *n* ***syn*** PROMISE, engagement, word

plight *n* ***syn*** PREDICAMENT, box, corner, dilemma, fix, hole, jam, pickle, scrape, spot
rel quandary

plighted *adj* ***syn*** ENGAGED 2, affianced, betrothed, contracted, intended, ||promised

plink *vb* ***syn*** TINKLE 1, ting, tingle

plod *vb* **1** to walk laboriously and heavily <slowly *plodded* across the sodden field>
syn footslog, ||plodge, plunther, slog, slop, stodge, toil, ||trash, trudge; *compare* TRAMP 1
rel tramp, trample, tromp; stamp, stomp, stump; flounder, wallow
2 ***syn*** DRUDGE, grind, grub, ||muck, slave, slog, toil
idiom plug away at it

---

syn synonym(s) *rel* related word(s)
idiom idiomatic equivalent(s) *con* contrasted word(s)
ant antonym(s) * vulgar
|| use limited; if in doubt, see a dictionary
The first word in a synonym list when printed in SMALL CAPITALS shows where there is more information about the group. For a more efficient use of this book see Explanatory Notes.

plodding *adj* ***syn*** DULL 9, banausic, blah, ||dim, dreary, humdrum, monotone, monotonous, pedestrian, stodgy

||plodge *vb* ***syn*** PLOD 1, footslog, plunther, slog, slop, stodge, toil, ||trash, trudge

plot *n* **1** ***syn*** LOT 3, parcel, plat, tract
2 a secret plan for accomplishing a usually evil or unlawful end <an assassination *plot*>
syn cabal, conspiracy, covin, intrigue, machination, practice, scheme
rel design, plan; connivance, conniving; collusion, complicity; contraption, contrivance, device; artifice, maneuver, ruse, stratagem, trick

plot *vb* to work out a plan especially for something unlawful or wrong <*plotted* the overthrow of the government>
syn cogitate, ||collogue, collude, connive, conspire, contrive, devise, intrigue, machinate, scheme (out)
rel lay; brew, concoct, cook (up), hatch, set up; finagle, maneuver

plow *vb* to cut into and work the surface of (soil) <*plow* a field>
syn break, plow up, turn, turn over
rel cultivate, till; fallow; ||backset; furrow, list, ridge, trench; harrow, rake

plow up *vb* ***syn*** PLOW, break, turn, turn over
rel plow out

ploy *n* ***syn*** TRICK 1, artifice, device, feint, gambit, maneuver, play, ruse, stratagem, wile

pluck *n* ***syn*** COURAGE, cojones, dauntlessness, guts, heart, mettle, ||moxie, resolution, spirit, spunk

||plucked *adj* ***syn*** BRAVE 1, bold, chin-up, dauntless, doughty, fearless, game, ||gutsy, intrepid, spunky

plucky *adj* ***syn*** BRAVE 1, bold, courageous, dauntless, doughty, fearless, ||gutsy, spunky, undauntable, unfearing
idiom full of pluck (*or* spunk)
con feeble, weak
ant pluckless

plug *n* ***syn*** PUFF 3, blurb, puffing, write-up

plug *vb* **1** ***syn*** FILL 1, block, choke, clog, close, congest, obstruct, occlude, stop, stopper
rel pack; cork
2 ***syn*** PROMOTE 3, advertise, boost, push

plugging *n* ***syn*** WORK 2, bullwork, donkeywork, drudge, drudgery, grind, labor, moil, slavery, toil

plug–ugly *n* ***syn*** TOUGH, ||b'hoy, bullyboy, mucker, mug, roughneck, rowdy, ruffian, thug, yahoo

plum *n* ***syn*** REWARD, carrot, dividend, guerdon, meed, premium, prize
rel catch, find

||plumb *adv* ***syn*** WELL 3, completely, entirely, fully, perfectly, quite, ||slap, thoroughly, utterly, wholly

plumb *vb* ***syn*** SOUND, fathom, plumb-line

plumb *adj* ***syn*** VERTICAL, perpendicular, straight-up

plumbless *adj* ***syn*** BOTTOMLESS 2, abysmal, fathomless, plummetless, soundless, unfathomable
con plumbable

plumb–line *vb* ***syn*** SOUND, fathom, plumb

plumbness *n* ***syn*** VERTICALITY, perpendicularity, verticalism, verticalness

plume *vb* ***syn*** PRIDE, pique, preen

plummet *vb* to decrease suddenly and sharply in financial value or price <the stock *plummeted* 60 points when the story broke>

syn dip, drop, fall, nose-dive, plunge, skid, tumble
rel decline, decrease, descend, sink; dump; precipitate; collapse, crash
idiom take a sudden downturn (*or* downtrend)
con increase; rise; shoot up
ant skyrocket, soar

plummetless *adj syn* BOTTOMLESS 2, abysmal, fathomless, plumbless, soundless, unfathomable

plump *adj syn* ROTUND 2, chubby, plumpish, plumpy, podgy, pudgy, roly-poly, round, roundabout, tubby
rel fleshy, portly
idiom plump as a partridge
ant skinny

plumpish *adj syn* ROTUND 2, chubby, plump, plumpy, podgy, pudgy, roly-poly, round, roundabout, tubby
idiom like a butterball

plumpy *adj syn* ROTUND 2, chubby, plump, plumpish, podgy, pudgy, roly-poly, round, roundabout, tubby

plunder *vb syn* ROB 1, ||knock off, knock over, loot, ransack, relieve, rifle, stick up

plunder *n* **1** *syn* SPOIL, boodle, booty, loot, plunderage, prize, ||spreaghery, ||spulzie, swag
||**2** *syn* PERSONAL EFFECTS, stuff, things, traps, tricks

plunderage *n syn* SPOIL, boodle, booty, loot, plunder, prize, ||spreaghery, ||spulzie, swag

plunderer *n syn* MARAUDER, despoiler, forager, freebooter, looter, pillager, raider, ravager, ravisher, sacker

plunge *vb* **1** *syn* THRUST 2, dig, drive, ram, run, sink, stab, stick
2 to thrust or cast oneself or something into or as if into deep water <*plunged* into the crowd>
syn burst, dive, drive, lunge, pitch, ||splunge; *compare* RUSH 1
rel dip, immerse, submerge; plump, plunk; propel, push, shove, thrust; boil, charge, fling, rush, tear
idiom plunge headlong
con ease, glide, slide, slip
3 *syn* FALL 2, drop, go down, keel (over), pitch, slump, topple, tumble
idiom take a plunge
4 *syn* PLUMMET, dip, drop, fall, nose-dive, skid, tumble
idiom drop like a rock, take a downward plunge

plunther *vb syn* PLOD 1, footslog, ||plodge, slog, slop, stodge, toil, ||trash, trudge

plus *n syn* EXCESS 2, overage, overstock, oversupply, surplus, surplusage

plus *vb syn* INCREASE 1, aggrandize, augment, beef (up), boost, build, compound, enlarge, expand, magnify

plush *adj syn* LUXURIOUS 3, Capuan, deluxe, luscious, lush, luxuriant, opulent, palatial, sumptuous, upholstered
idiom fit for the gods

plushy *adj syn* LUXURIOUS 3, Capuan, deluxe, luxuriant, opulent, palace, palatial, plush, sumptuous, upholstered

plutonian *adj* **1** *syn* INFERNAL 1, chthonian, chthonic, Hadean, plutonic, sulphurous, Tartarean
2 *syn* INFERNAL 2, avernal, cimmerian, hellish, pandemoniac, plutonic, stygian

plutonic *adj* **1** *syn* INFERNAL 1, chthonian, chthonic, Hadean, plutonian, sulphurous, Tartarean
2 *syn* INFERNAL 2, avernal, cimmerian, hellish, pandemoniac, plutonian, stygian

ply *vb* **1** *syn* HANDLE 2, dispense, maneuver, manipulate, swing, wield
rel exercise; function
2 *syn* EXERT, exercise, put out, throw, wield

pneuma *n syn* SOUL 1, anima, animus, élan vital, psyche, spirit, vital force

pneumatic *adj syn* AIRY 1, aerial, atmospheric

pocket *n syn* DEAD END, blind alley, cul-de-sac, impasse

pocket *vb* **1** *syn* STEAL 1, abstract, appropriate, collar, filch, hook, lift, nab, pinch, swipe
2 *syn* ACCEPT 2, bear (with), endure, swallow, tolerate, tough (out)

pocket *adj* **1** *syn* TINY, diminutive, dwarfish, itsy-bitsy, miniature, minute, pint-size, pocket-size, wee, weeny
2 *syn* CONDENSED, canned, capsule, epitomized, potted
3 *syn* FINANCIAL, fiscal, monetary, pecuniary

pocket edition *n syn* MODEL 1, miniature

pocket money *n* money for small personal expenses or incidentals <he had spent all his *pocket money* on candy and snacks>
syn pin money, spending money
rel petty cash; change, small change
con fortune, resources; income

pocket-size *adj syn* TINY, diminutive, dwarfish, itsy-bitsy, midget, miniature, minute, peewee, pint-size, pocket

pococurante *adj syn* INDIFFERENT 2, aloof, by-the-way, detached, disinterested, incurious, numb, remote, unconcerned, withdrawn

pod *n* **1** *syn* HULL, case, husk, shell, shuck, skin, ||slough
2 *syn* POTBELLY, bay window, corporation, paunch, ||pot

podex *n syn* BUTTOCKS, backside, beam, behind, derriere, fanny, hunkers, nates, posterior, rear end

podgy *adj syn* ROTUND 2, chubby, plump, plumpish, plumpy, pudgy, roly-poly, round, roundabout, tubby

Podunk *n syn* BURG, hick town, jerkwater town, mudhole, one-horse town, tank town, whistle-stop

poem *n* a particular example of metrical writing <recited a *poem* by Robert Frost>
syn poesy, poetry, rhyme, rune, verse

poesy *n* **1** *syn* POEM, poetry, rhyme, rune, verse
2 *syn* POETRY 1, rhyme, song, verse

poet *n* a writer of verse <a *poet* to stir men's souls>
syn bard, muse, Parnassian
rel jongleur, rhapsodist, trouvère, trouveur; balladist, elegist, idyllist, lyricist, lyrist, odist, satirist, sonneteer, sonnetist

poetaster *n* a writer of mediocre or inferior verse <*poetasters* who churn out tasteless verse>

---

syn synonym(s) — *rel* related word(s)
idiom idiomatic equivalent(s) — *con* contrasted word(s)
ant antonym(s) — * vulgar
|| use limited; if in doubt, see a dictionary
The first word in a synonym list when printed in SMALL CAPITALS shows where there is more information about the group. For a more efficient use of this book see Explanatory Notes.

syn balladmonger, bardlet, bardling, poeticule, poetling, rhymer, rhymester, verseman, versemonger, verser, versesmith, versificator, versifier

poeticule *n* ***syn*** POETASTER, bardlet, bardling, rhymer, rhymester, verseman, versemonger, versesmith, versificator, versifier

poetling *n* ***syn*** POETASTER, bardlet, bardling, rhymer, rhymester, verseman, versemonger, versesmith, versificator, versifier

poetry *n* **1** metrical language or writing <studied the *poetry* of Milton>
syn poesy, rhyme, song, verse
2 ***syn*** POEM, poesy, rhyme, rune, verse

poignance *n* ***syn*** PATHOS, poignancy

poignancy *n* ***syn*** PATHOS, poignance

poignant *adj* **1** ***syn*** PUNGENT, peppery, piquant, racy, snappy, spicy, zesty
ant dull
2 ***syn*** MOVING 2, affecting, impressive, touching
rel agitating, disturbing, perturbing

point *n* **1** one unitary part of a whole made up of two or more parts <listened to each *point* of his opponent's argument>
syn article, detail, element, item, particular, thing; *compare* ELEMENT 2
rel characteristic, feature, trait; constituent, material, part; circumstantial, circumstantiality
con aggregate, sum, total, whole
2 ***syn*** CHARACTERISTIC 1, birthmark, character, feature, trait
3 the quality of an utterance that arouses interest and produces an effect <a book that lacks *point*>
syn cogency, effectiveness, force, punch, validity, validness
rel appositeness, convincement, significance, suggestiveness; appeal, attraction, charm, fascination, interest
4 ***syn*** SUBJECT 2, argument, head, matter, motif, motive, subject matter, text, theme, topic
5 ***syn*** TIP, pointer, steer, tip-off
6 ***syn*** PLACE 1, location, locus, position, site, situation, spot, station, where
7 a particular limited and often critical interval of time <at that *point* he was interrupted>
syn instant, juncture, moment
rel brink, threshold, verge
8 ***syn*** VERGE 2, brink, edge, threshold
9 a sharp or slender and tapering terminal part <the *point* of a sword>
syn apex, cusp, tip
rel awn, barb, jag, nib, prong, snag, spike, tag, tine
10 ***syn*** PROMONTORY, beak, bill, cape, foreland, head, headland, naze
11 a tiny mark or spot <saw a distant *point* of light>
syn dot, flyspeck, mote, speck
rel bit, fleck, iota, minim, mite, particle, scrap, tittle, trace

point *vb* **1** ***syn*** PUNCTUATE
2 to tend to show something as probable <all signs *point* to an economic recovery>
syn hint, imply, indicate, suggest; *compare* SUGGEST 1
idiom make (*or* give) promise of, lead one to expect, offer a good prospect of
3 ***syn*** DIRECT 2, address, aim, cast, head, lay, level, train, turn, zero (in)

point (out) *vb* ***syn*** REFER 3, advert, allude, bring up

point (to) *vb* ***syn*** TESTIFY 1, attest

pointed *adj* **1** tapering to a thin tip <a *pointed* rock>
syn acicular, aciculate, acuminate, acuminous, acute, cuspidate, mucronate, peaked, peaky, piked, pointy, sharp
con dull, rounded
ant blunt
2 ***syn*** NOTICEABLE, arresting, conspicuous, marked, outstanding, prominent, remarkable, salient, signal, striking

pointer *n* ***syn*** TIP, point, steer, tip-off

pointful *adj* ***syn*** RELEVANT, ad rem, applicable, applicative, applicatory, apposite, apropos, germane, material, pertinent

pointless *adj* ***syn*** SENSELESS 5, insignificant, meaningless, purportless, unmeaning

‖**pointsman** *n* ***syn*** POLICEMAN, ‖bobby, ‖bull, cop, ‖copper, ‖flatfoot, ‖fuzz, ‖gendarme, ‖paddy, ‖peeler

pointy *adj* ***syn*** POINTED 1, acicular, acuminate, acuminous, acute, cuspidate, peaked, peaky, piked, sharp

poise *vb* **1** ***syn*** STABILIZE, ballast, stabilify, stabilitate, steady
rel back, support, uphold
con agitate, disturb, upset; overthrow, overturn, subvert
2 ***syn*** HANG 3, float, hover

poise *n* **1** ***syn*** BALANCE 1, equilibrium, equipoise, equiponderation, stasis
2 ***syn*** TACT, address, delicatesse, diplomacy, savoir faire, tactfulness
rel aplomb, assurance, confidence, self-possession; calmness, serenity, tranquillity; dignity, elegance, grace

poised *adj* ***syn*** CALM 2, collected, composed, easy, easygoing, placid, possessed, self-possessed, serene, tranquil

poison *n* something that harms, interferes with, or destroys the activity, progress, or welfare of something else <the publicity was *poison* to them>
syn bane, contagion, venom, virus
rel adulteration, contamination, corruption, sophistication
con catholicon, elixir, panacea
ant antidote

poison *vb* ***syn*** DEBASE 1, animalize, bestialize, corrupt, debauch, demoralize, deprave, pervert, stain, warp

poison *adj* ***syn*** POISONOUS, mephitic, toxic, toxicant, venomous, virulent

poisonous *adj* having the properties or effect of poison <*poisonous* propaganda>
syn mephitic, poison, toxic, toxicant, venomous, virulent
rel miasmal, miasmatic, miasmic, pestilent, pestilential; deadly, fatal, lethal, mortal; baneful, deleterious, detrimental, nocuous, noxious, pernicious

---

syn synonym(s) ***rel*** related word(s)
idiom idiomatic equivalent(s) ***con*** contrasted word(s)
ant antonym(s) * vulgar
‖ use limited; if in doubt, see a dictionary
The first word in a synonym list when printed in SMALL CAPITALS shows where there is more information about the group. For a more efficient use of this book see Explanatory Notes.

con corrective, countervailing, emendatory, healing, remedial
ant antidotal

‖**poke** *n syn* BAG 1, pouch, sack

poke *vb* **1** to thrust something into so as to stir up, urge on, or attract attention <he *poked* the man in front of him to get his attention>
syn dig, jab, jog, nudge, prod, punch
rel push, shove, thrust; arouse, awaken, rouse, stir; excite, galvanize, provoke, quicken, stimulate
2 *syn* SNOOP, busybody, mouse, nose, ‖piroot, pry, ‖snook
3 *syn* DELAY 2, dally, dawdle, drag, lag, loiter, procrastinate, put off, tarry, trail
4 *syn* BULGE, beetle, jut, overhang, pouch, pout, project, protrude, stand out, stick out

poke *n* **1** a quick thrust with or as if with the hand <gave him a *poke* in the ribs with my finger>
syn dig, jab, punch, stab
rel bunt, butt; boost, push, shove
2 *syn* CUFF, box, buffet, chop, clout, ‖paste, punch, smack, sock, spank
3 *syn* DUNCE, blockhead, chump, dimwit, dolt, dope, dumbbell, idiot, ignoramus, moron

poker–faced *adj* **1** *syn* SERIOUS 1, earnest, grave, sedate, sober, sobersided, solemn, somber, staid, weighty
2 *syn* NEUTRAL, abstract, colorless, detached, disinterested, dispassionate, impersonal, unpassioned

‖**pokey** *n syn* JAIL, ‖calaboose, ‖can, ‖clink, cooler, ‖hoosegow, jug, lockup, prison, ‖stir

poky *adj syn* DULL 9, banausic, blah, ‖dim, dreary, humdrum, monotone, monotonous, pedestrian, stodgy

polar *adj syn* OPPOSITE, antipodal, antipodean, antithetical, contradictory, contrary, converse, counter, diametric, reverse

polemical *adj syn* CONTENTIOUS 2, argumentative, controversial, disputatious, litigious

polestar *n syn* CENTER 2, focal point, focus, heart, hub, nerve center, seat

police *n syn* POLICEMAN, ‖bull, cop, ‖copper, ‖fuzz, ‖heat, man, officer, peace officer, police officer

‖**police constable** *n syn* POLICEMAN, ‖bobby, ‖bull, ‖constable, ‖copper, ‖gendarme, John Law, officer, ‖paddy, ‖peeler

policeman *n* a member of a police force <ask the *policeman* for directions>
syn ‖bluebottle, bluecoat, ‖bobby, ‖bull, ‖constable, cop, ‖copper, Dogberry, ‖flatfoot, ‖fuzz, ‖gendarme, gumshoe, ‖harness bull (*or* cop), ‖heat, John Law, man, ‖nab, officer, ‖paddy, patrolman, peace officer, ‖peeler, ‖pig, ‖pointsman, police, ‖police constable, police officer, ‖rozzer, ‖trap

police officer *n syn* POLICEMAN, ‖bull, cop, ‖copper, ‖fuzz, ‖heat, man, officer, peace officer, police

policy *n syn* COURSE 3, line, polity, procedure, program

polish *vb* **1** to make smooth or glossy usually by friction <*polished* the silver>
syn buff, burnish, furbish, glance, glaze, gloss, rub, shine
rel brighten, scour, scrub
con roughen
2 to give an elegant finish to <attended classes to *polish* his manners>
syn perfect, refine, round, sleek, slick, smooth
rel better, improve, mend; brush up, furbish, touch up; mature, perfect

polish *n* **1** *syn* LUSTER, glaze, glint, gloss, sheen, shine
2 *syn* CULTURE, breeding, cultivation, refinement

polished *adj* **1** *syn* LUSTROUS 1, burnished, gleaming, glistening, glossy, sheeny, shining, shiny
2 *syn* SLEEK, glassy, glossy, ‖sleekit, sleeky, smarmy
3 *syn* GENTEEL 1, cultivated, cultured, distingué, refined, urbane, well-bred

polish off *vb* **1** *syn* CONSUME 5, punish, put away, put down, shift, swill
2 *syn* EAT UP 1, devour, dispatch

polite *adj syn* CIVIL 2, courteous, genteel, mannerly, well-mannered
rel attentive, considerate, thoughtful
ant impolite

politic *adj* **1** *syn* EXPEDIENT, advisable, prudent, tactical, wise
rel astute, perspicacious, sagacious, shrewd
2 *syn* TACTFUL, delicate, diplomatic, tactical
rel judicious, wise

polity *n syn* COURSE 3, line, policy, procedure, program

poll *n syn* HEAD 1, ‖bean, ‖belfry, ‖coco, ‖chump, ‖conk, ‖dome, noddle, noggin, noodle

pollard *vb syn* TOP 1, crop, detruncate, truncate

polloi *n syn* RABBLE 2, dreg(s), hoi polloi, mass(es), mob, other half, proletariat, riffraff, scum, trash

pollute *vb* **1** *syn* CONTAMINATE 1, defile, soil, taint
2 *syn* CONTAMINATE 2, befoul, foul

polluted *adj* **1** *syn* IMPURE 3, common, defiled, desecrated, profaned, unclean
2 *syn* INTOXICATED 1, ‖boozy, ‖canned, disguised, drunk, inebriated, ‖lushed, muddled, pixilated, ‖plastered

Pollyanna *n syn* OPTIMIST, hoper
rel daydreamer, wishful thinker

Pollyannaish *adj syn* OPTIMISTIC, fond, sanguine, upbeat

Pollyannaism *n syn* OPTIMISM, rose-colored spectacles, sanguineness, sanguinity

‖**polly–fox** *vb syn* SKIRT 3, burke, bypass, circumvent, sidestep

poltroon *n syn* COWARD, chicken, craven, dastard, funk, funker, quitter, yellowbelly

poltroon *adj syn* COWARDLY, ‖chicken, coward, craven, gutless, lily-livered, poltroonish, pusillanimous, spunkless, unmanly

poltroonish *adj syn* COWARDLY, ‖chicken, coward, craven, gutless, lily-livered, poltroon, pusillanimous, spunkless, unmanly

polyandrium *n syn* CEMETERY, ‖boneyard, ‖boot hill, burial ground, burying ground, God's acre, graveyard, memorial park, necropolis, potter's field

---

syn synonym(s) *rel* related word(s)
idiom idiomatic equivalent(s) *con* contrasted word(s)
ant antonym(s) * vulgar
‖ use limited; if in doubt, see a dictionary
The first word in a synonym list when printed in SMALL CAPITALS shows where there is more information about the group. For a more efficient use of this book see Explanatory Notes.

polychromatic *adj* ***syn*** VARIEGATED, discolor, motley, multicolor, multicolored, multihued, parti-color, parti-colored, varicolored, versicolor

polychrome *adj* ***syn*** VARIEGATED, discolor, multicolor, multicolored, multihued, parti-color, parti-colored, polychromatic, varicolored, versicolor

polypragmatic *adj* ***syn*** IMPERTINENT 2, busy, intrusive, meddlesome, ‖nebby, obtrusive, officious

polypragmatist *n* ***syn*** BUSYBODY, ‖buttinsky, intermeddler, Meddlesome Mattie, nose, nosey Parker, Paul Pry, prier (*or* pryer), quidnunc, snoop

pomp *n* ***syn*** DISPLAY 2, array, fanfare, panoply, parade, shine, show
rel ceremonial, ceremony, form, formality, liturgy, ritual

pom–pom girl *n* ***syn*** PROSTITUTE, call girl, ‖cruiser, harlot, ‖hooker, hustler, ‖joy girl, nightwalker, party girl, streetwalker

pompous *adj* **1** characterized by or exhibiting self-importance <a *pompous* old fool>
syn arrogant, bloated, important, magisterial, pontifical, puffy, self-important, stuffy, wiggy; *compare* EGOCENTRIC 2, PROUD 1
rel conceited, narcissistic, self-conceited, stuck-up, vain, vainglorious; affected, highfalutin, hoity-toity, pretentious; presumptuous, self-centered, selfish; flaunting, flossy, ostentatious
con natural, unaffected, unpretentious; humble, meek, plain, simple; modest, unassuming
2 ***syn*** RHETORICAL, aureate, bombastic, declamatory, euphuistic, flowery, grandiloquent, magniloquent, overblown, sonorous

ponder *vb* **1** ***syn*** CONSIDER 1, contemplate, excogitate, mind, perpend, study, think (out *or* over), weigh
rel appraise, evaluate
2 to consider or examine attentively or deliberately <*ponder* the best way to do it>
syn ‖chaw, deliberate, meditate, mull (over), muse, revolve, roll, ruminate, turn over
rel cogitate, reason, reflect, speculate, think; brood, debate, dwell

pondering *adj* ***syn*** THOUGHTFUL 1, cogitative, contemplative, meditative, pensive, ‖pensy, reflecting, reflective, ruminative, speculative

ponderous *adj* **1** ***syn*** HEAVY 1, cumbersome, cumbrous, hefty, massive, weighty
rel substantial; burdensome, onerous, oppressive
2 lacking all lightness and grace <a *ponderous* prose style>
syn elephantine, heavy-footed, heavy-handed, uninspired
rel dreary, dry, dull, humdrum, lifeless, monotonous, pedestrian, plodding, stodgy, stuffy; arid, barren; flat, insipid, savorless, vapid; buckram, cardboard, muscle-bound, stiff, stilted, wooden
con sparkling, vivid; easy, natural, relaxed, supple, unlabored
3 ***syn*** UNWIELDY, cumbersome, cumbrous, unhandy

pontifical *adj* ***syn*** POMPOUS 1, arrogant, bloated, important, magisterial, puffy, self-important, stuffy, wiggy

pontificate *vb* ***syn*** LORD, cock, peacock, swagger, swank, swell

pony *n* a literal translation of a foreign language text used especially surreptitiously by students in rendering a lesson <had his *pony* hidden in his lap>
syn crib, trot

‖**pooch** *n* ***syn*** DOG 1, bowwow, canine, hound, tyke

pooh *n* ***syn*** RASPBERRY, bazoo, bird, boo, ‖Bronx cheer, catcall, hiss, hoot, pooh-pooh, ‖razz

pooh–bah *n* ***syn*** NOTABLE 1, big boy, ‖big cheese, big gun, big shot, bigwig, chief, dignitary, eminence, notability

pooh–pooh *n* ***syn*** RASPBERRY, bazoo, bird, boo, ‖Bronx cheer, catcall, hiss, hoot, pooh, ‖razz

pooh–pooh *vb* ***syn*** DISMISS 5, kiss off

pool *n* a small body of standing liquid <saw the *pool* of blood on the floor>
syn puddle

pool *n* **1** ***syn*** POT 3, jackpot, kitty
2 ***syn*** SYNDICATE, cartel, chain, combine, conglomerate, group, trust

poop *n* ***syn*** FOOL 1, ass, *damfool, idiot, imbecile, jackass, jerk, nincompoop, ninny, tomfool

‖**poop** *vb* ***syn*** EXHAUST, ‖bugger, fag, frazzle, knock out, outtire, outwear, prostrate, tucker, wear out

poor *adj* **1** lacking money or material possessions <they were so *poor* that the children had no winter coats>
syn beggared, broke, destitute, dirt poor, flat, fortuneless, impecunious, impoverished, indigent, low, necessitous, needy, penurious, poverty-stricken, stone-broke, stony, strapped, unprosperous
rel distressed, embarrassed, pinched, reduced, straitened; bankrupt, bankrupted, insolvent; hardscrabble; moneyless, penceless, penniless, unmoneyed; beggarly, down-and-out, pauperized; underprivileged
idiom down to one's bottom dollar, flat broke, hard up, in need, in penury, in rags, in want, on one's beam-ends, on one's uppers, out at elbows, out of pocket, poor as a church mouse, unable to keep the wolf from the door, unable to make ends meet
con affluent, comfortable, moneyed, ‖oofy, opulent, pecunious, prosperous, wealthy, well-fixed, well-heeled, well-off, well-to-do
ant rich
2 ***syn*** MEAGER 2, exiguous, scant, scanty, scrimp, scrimpy, skimp, skimpy, spare, sparse
3 ***syn*** PITIFUL 1, commiserable, pathetic, piteous, pitiable, rueful
4 ***syn*** CHEAP 2, base, common, mean, paltry, rubbishy, shoddy, sleazy, tatty, trashy
5 ***syn*** INFERIOR 2, common, déclassé, hack, low-grade, mean, second-class, second-drawer, second-rate
6 ***syn*** BAD 1, amiss, ‖bum, ‖crappy, dissatisfactory, ‖punk, rotten, unsatisfactory, up, wrong

poorly *adj* ***syn*** UNWELL, ailing, ‖donsie, indisposed, low, mean, off-color, offish, sickly, underly

---

syn synonym(s)	***rel*** related word(s)
idiom idiomatic equivalent(s)	***con*** contrasted word(s)
ant antonym(s)	* vulgar

‖ use limited; if in doubt, see a dictionary
The first word in a synonym list when printed in SMALL CAPITALS shows where there is more information about the group. For a more efficient use of this book see Explanatory Notes.

poorness *n* ***syn*** POVERTY 1, destitution, impecuniousness, impoverishment, indigence, neediness, pauperism, penury, privation, want

poor relation *n* ***syn*** INFERIOR, scrub, secondary, subaltern, subordinate, underling, understrapper

poor–spirited *adj* ***syn*** COWARDLY, ‖chicken, coward, craven, gutless, lily-livered, poltroon, pusillanimous, spunkless, unmanly

pop *vb* **1** ***syn*** STRIKE 2, catch, ding, hit, ‖nail, slog, smite, sock, swat, whack
‖**2** ***syn*** PAWN, ‖dip, hock, impignorate, mortgage, pledge, ‖spout

pop *n* ***syn*** FLING 1, crack, go, shot, slap, stab, ‖stagger, try, whack, whirl

pop *n* ***syn*** FATHER 1, dad, dada, daddy, ‖governor, ‖old man, pa, ‖pap, papa, poppa

pop (in) *vb* ***syn*** VISIT 2, call, come by, come over, drop (in *or* by), look in, look up, run in, see, stop (in *or* by)

popinjay *n* ***syn*** FOP, Beau Brummel, blood, buck, coxcomb, dandy, dude, exquisite, lounge lizard, macaroni

pop off *vb* **1** ***syn*** GO 2, ‖blow, exit, get away, get off, leave, pull out, retire, run along, take off
2 ***syn*** DIE 1, cash in, ‖check out, ‖croak, ‖kick in, ‖kick off, pass, pass away, perish, succumb

poppa *n* ***syn*** FATHER 1, dad, dada, daddy, ‖governor, ‖old man, pa, ‖pap, papa, pop

popping *adj* ***syn*** BUSTLING, busy, fussy, hopping, humming, hustling, lively

poppycock *n* ***syn*** NONSENSE 2, balderdash, bilge, blatherskite, bunkum, fiddle-faddle, guff, hokum, malarkey, rot

popsy *n* ***syn*** GIRL FRIEND 1, best girl, ‖chick, ‖doney, gal, girl, lady friend, lass, mouse

populace *n* ***syn*** COMMONALTY, commonage, commoners, common men, people, plebeians, plebes, plebs, rank and file, third estate

popular *adj* **1** ***syn*** PUBLIC 4, general, vulgar
2 ***syn*** DEMOCRATIC, self-governing, self-ruling
3 ***syn*** CHEAP 1, inexpensive, low, low-cost, low-priced, reasonable, uncostly, undear
4 ***syn*** PREVAILING, current, prevalent, rampant, regnant, rife, ruling, widespread
5 ***syn*** FAVORITE 2, favored, preferred, well-liked
ant unpopular
6 ***syn*** WELL-KNOWN, famous, leading, noted, notorious, prominent
ant unpopular

populate *vb* ***syn*** INHABIT, occupy, people, tenant

populous *adj* ***syn*** MANY, legion, multifarious, multitudinal, multitudinous, numerous, ‖several, sundry, various, voluminous

porcine *adj* ***syn*** FAT 2, corpulent, fleshy, gross, heavy, obese, overblown, overweight, portly, stout

pork–barreling *n* ***syn*** PATRONAGE 3

porky *adj* ***syn*** FATTY 2, greasy, oily, oleaginous, unctuous

porose *adj* ***syn*** PERMEABLE, penetrable, pervious, porous

porous *adj* ***syn*** PERMEABLE, penetrable, pervious, porose

porridge *n* ***syn*** MISCELLANY 1, pasticcio, pastiche, patchwork, potpourri, rumble-bumble, salad, salmagundi, smorgasbord, stew

port *n* **1** ***syn*** HARBOR 3, anchorage, ‖chuck, harborage, haven, riding, road(s), roadstead
2 ***syn*** SHELTER 1, asylum, cover, covert, harbor, harborage, haven, refuge, retreat, sanctuary

port *n* ***syn*** BEARING 1, address, air, comportment, demeanor, deportment, mien, presence, set

portable *adj* capable of being carried or moved about <a *portable* TV>
syn carriageable, portative, transportable
rel convenient, handy, manageable, wieldy
con fixed, stationary

portal *n* ***syn*** DOOR 1, doorway, entrance, entranceway, entry, entryway

portative *adj* ***syn*** PORTABLE, carriageable, transportable

portend *vb* **1** ***syn*** AUGUR 2, betoken, bode, forebode, foreshadow, foreshow, foretoken, omen, presage, promise
2 ***syn*** FORETELL, adumbrate, augur, call, forecast, predict, presage, prognosticate, prophesy, vaticinate

portent *n* **1** ***syn*** FORETOKEN, augury, bodement, boding, omen, presage, prognostic
2 ***syn*** WONDER 1, marvel, miracle, phenomenon, prodigy, sensation, stunner

porter *n* ***syn*** BEARER 2, carrier, drogher

portion *n* **1** ***syn*** SHARE 1, allotment, allowance, bite, cut, lot, part, partage, quota, slice
2 ***syn*** FATE, circumstance, destiny, doom, kismet, lot, moira, weird
3 ***syn*** PART 1, cut, division, member, moiety, parcel, piece, section, segment
4 ***syn*** RATION, allotment, allowance, apportionment, measure, meed, part, quantum, quota, share

portion *vb* ***syn*** APPORTION 2, divide, ‖divvy, parcel, prorate, quota, ration, share, ‖shift

portion (out) *vb* ***syn*** ADMINISTER 2, apportion, deal (out), dispense, dole (out), mete (out), share out

portly *adj* ***syn*** FAT 2, corpulent, fleshy, heavy, obese, overblown, overweight, stout, upholstered, weighty

portrait *n* ***syn*** IMAGE 1, double, picture, ringer, simulacrum, spit, spitting image

portraiture *n* ***syn*** REPRESENTATION, delineation, depiction, description, picture, portrayal, presentment

portray *vb* ***syn*** REPRESENT 1, delineate, depict, describe, image, interpret, limn, picture, render
rel photograph; copy, duplicate, reproduce

portrayal *n* ***syn*** REPRESENTATION, delineation, depiction, description, picture, portraiture, presentment

pose *vb* **1** ***syn*** OFFER 1, extend, give, hold out, present, proffer, tender
2 ***syn*** PROPOSE 1, prefer, ‖propone, proposition, propound, put, suggest
rel ask, query, question; confound, puzzle; baffle
3 to assume a particular physical posture <they *posed* for a family portrait>

---

syn synonym(s) *rel* related word(s)
idiom idiomatic equivalent(s) *con* contrasted word(s)
ant antonym(s) * vulgar
‖ use limited; if in doubt, see a dictionary
The first word in a synonym list when printed in SMALL CAPITALS shows where there is more information about the group. For a more efficient use of this book see Explanatory Notes.

syn posture, sit
rel peacock, strut
4 to assume an artificial or pretended attitude or character usually to deceive or impress <*posed* as a salesman>
syn attitudinize, masquerade, pass (as *or* for), pass off, posture
rel fake, feign, pretend, sham; profess, purport; grandstand, show off

pose *n* **1** *syn* POSTURE 1, attitude, carriage, positure, stance
2 an adopted way of speaking or acting <his reticence is just a *pose*>
syn affectation, air(s), lugs, mannerism, prettyism
rel dog, prettiness; fake, pretense, pretension

pose *vb* *syn* OFFER 1, extend, give, hold out, present, proffer, tender

pose *vb* *syn* PUZZLE, befog, bewilder, ‖cap, confound, confuse, metagrobolize, perplex, stumble

posh *adj* *syn* STYLISH, a la mode, chic, exclusive, fashionable, modish, smart, swank, tony, ‖trendy

posit *vb* *syn* PRESUPPOSE, assume, postulate, premise, presume

posit *n* *syn* ASSUMPTION 2, apriorism, postulate, postulation, premise, presumption, presupposition, supposition, thesis

position *n* **1** a firmly held point of view or way of regarding something <took a conservative *position* on educational issues>
syn attitude, color, stance, stand; *compare* SIDE 4
rel belief, judgment, opinion, view; angle, slant, standpoint, viewpoint
2 *syn* PLACE 1, location, locus, point, site, situation, spot, station, where
3 *syn* STATUS 1, capacity, character, footing, place, rank, situation, standing, state, station
4 *syn* STATUS 2, cachet, consequence, dignity, prestige, rank, standing, state, stature
5 *syn* JOB 2, appointment, berth, billet, connection, office, place, post, situation, spot

positioned *adj* *syn* SITUATED, located, placed, set, sited, situate

positive *adj* **1** expressed clearly and usually peremptorily <her answer was a *positive* no>
syn categorical, decided, definite, unequivocal
rel clear, unmistakable; decisive, emphatic, energetic, firm, forceful, forcible; explicit, express, specific, unambiguous
con irresolute, uncertain, undecided, unsure
2 *syn* SURE 5, certain, cocksure, confident
ant doubtful
3 not subject to being disputed or called in question <gave *positive* proof that he had been there>
syn certain, inarguable, incontestable, incontrovertible, indisputable, indubitable, irrebuttable, irrefutable, sure, uncontestable, uncontrovertible, undeniable, undisputable, undoubtable, unequivocal, unquestionable; *compare* DOWNRIGHT 2
rel assured, clear, decisive
con contestable, controvertible, debatable, disputable, doubtful, dubious, inconclusive, questionable, unconvincing
4 *syn* UTTER, absolute, complete, consummate, downright, gross, outright, perfect, rank, unmitigated
5 *syn* ACTUAL 2, absolute, factual, genuine, hard, sure-enough
6 capable of being constructively applied <*positive* proposals for improving the city>
syn affirmative
rel practical, reasonable, sound
con impractical, unsound, unusable
ant negative
7 *syn* RIGHT-HANDED, clockwise, dextrorotatory

positively *adv* *syn* EASILY 2, absolutely, definitely, doubtless, doubtlessly, unequivocally, unquestionably

positure *n* *syn* POSTURE 1, attitude, carriage, pose, stance

possess *vb* **1** *syn* HAVE 1, enjoy, hold, own, retain
2 *syn* BEAR 3, carry, have

possessed *adj* *syn* CALM 2, collected, composed, easy, placid, poised, self-composed, self-possessed, serene, tranquil

possession *n* **1** *syn* OWNERSHIP, dominion, possessorship, property, proprietary, proprietorship
2 possessions *pl* things one owns usually excluding real property and intangibles <lost all their *possessions* in the fire>
syn belongings, chattels, effects, goods, lares and penates, movables, things,
rel appointments, fixtures, furnishings, furniture; accessories, appurtenances, baggage, ‖duds, duffle, equipment, impedimenta, paraphernalia, trappings, tricks; havings; tangibles

possessive *adj* *syn* JEALOUS 1, possessory

possessor *n* *syn* OWNER, holder, proprietor

possessorship *n* *syn* OWNERSHIP, dominion, possession, property, proprietary, proprietorship

possessory *adj* *syn* JEALOUS 1, possessive

possibilities *n pl* *syn* POTENTIAL, potentiality

possible *adj* **1** capable of being realized <a cure is still *possible*>
syn doable, feasible, practicable, viable, workable
rel advisable, expedient; achievable, attainable, available
con futile, hopeless, impracticable
ant impossible
2 *syn* PROBABLE, conceivable, earthly, likely, mortal
rel dormant, latent, potential
3 *syn* POTENTIAL 1

possibly *adv* *syn* PERHAPS, maybe, perchance

post *vb* to affix to a usual place (as a wall) for public notices <*posted* the notice on the bulletin board>
syn placard, poster

post *vb* *syn* INFORM 2, acquaint, advise, apprise, clue (*or* clew), fill in, notify, tell, warn, wise (up)

post *n* *syn* JOB 2, appointment, berth, billet, connection, office, place, position, situation, spot

post *vb* ***syn*** STATION, set

‖**post** *n* ***syn*** AUTOPSY, necropsy, postmortem, postmortem examination

poster *n* a notice or announcement for posting in a public place <nailed the *poster* to the side of the building>
syn affiche, bill, handbill, placard
rel advertisement, announcement, banner, broadside, notice, sign; billboard, signboard

poster *vb* ***syn*** POST, placard

posterior *adj* **1** ***syn*** SUBSEQUENT 1, after, ensuing, later, postliminary, subsequential
2 situated at or toward the back <the *posterior* part of the animal>
syn after, back, hind, hinder, hindmost, rear, retral
con fore, front
ant anterior

posterior *n* **1** ***syn*** BACK 1, rear, rearward
2 ***syn*** BUTTOCKS, backside, behind, rear, rear end, rump, seat, ‖stern, tail, tail end

posterity *n* ***syn*** OFFSPRING, ‖begats, brood, children, descendants, issue, progeniture, progeny, scions, seed
ant ancestry

posthaste *adv* ***syn*** FAST 2, flat-out, fleetly, full tilt, hastily, lickety-split, quickly, rapidly, speedily, swiftly

posthaste *adj* ***syn*** FAST 3, breakneck, expeditious, fleet, harefooted, hasty, quick, rapid, speedy, swift

posthumous *adj* occurring after one's death <*posthumous* fame>
syn postmortal, postmortem, post-obit, post-obituary
rel delayed, late, retarded
con opportune, seasonable, timely
ant antemortem

postliminary *adj* ***syn*** SUBSEQUENT 1, after, ensuing, later, posterior, subsequential

postmortal *adj* ***syn*** POSTHUMOUS, postmortem, post-obit, post-obituary

postmortem *adj* ***syn*** POSTHUMOUS, postmortal, post-obit, post-obituary
ant antemortem

postmortem *n* ***syn*** AUTOPSY, necropsy, ‖post, postmortem examination

postmortem examination *n* ***syn*** AUTOPSY, necropsy, ‖post, postmortem

post–obit *adj* ***syn*** POSTHUMOUS, postmortal, postmortem, post-obituary

post–obituary *adj* ***syn*** POSTHUMOUS, postmortal, postmortem, post-obit

postpone *vb* ***syn*** DEFER, delay, hold off, hold over, hold up, lay over, prorogue, put off, shelve, suspend

postulate *vb* **1** ***syn*** DEMAND 1, call, challenge, claim, exact, require, requisition, solicit
2 ***syn*** PRESUPPOSE, assume, posit, premise, presume
rel affirm, assert, aver, predicate

postulate *n* ***syn*** ASSUMPTION 2, apriorism, posit, postulation, premise, presumption, presupposition, supposition, thesis

postulation *n* ***syn*** ASSUMPTION 2, apriorism, posit, postulate, premise, presumption, presupposition, supposition, thesis

posture *n* **1** the position or bearing of the body <erect *posture*>
syn attitude, carriage, pose, positure, stance
rel bearing, deportment, mien
2 ***syn*** STATE 1, condition, mode, situation, status
rel promptness, quickness, readiness

posture *vb* **1** ***syn*** POSE 3, sit
2 ***syn*** POSE 4, attitudinize, masquerade, pass (as *or* for), pass off

posy *n* **1** ***syn*** FLOWER 1, bloom, blossom
2 ***syn*** BOUQUET 1, nosegay
3 ***syn*** ANTHOLOGY, album, ana, analects, florilegium, garland, miscellany, omnibus

pot *n* **1** ***syn*** FORTUNE 4, ‖bomb, boodle, bundle, mint, packet, pile, ‖roll, wad
2 ***syn*** BET, ante, stake, wager
3 the total of the bets at stake at one time <lost track of how much was in the *pot*>
syn jackpot, kitty, pool
4 ***syn*** POTSHOT, shy, sideswipe
‖**5** ***syn*** POTBELLY, bay window, corporation, paunch, pod
6 ***syn*** NOTABLE 1, ‖big cheese, ‖biggie, big shot, ‖big wheel, bigwig, high-muck-a-muck, leader, lion, notability
7 ***syn*** MARIJUANA, boo, cannabis, grass, ‖Mary Jane, moocah, ‖tea, weed
‖**8** ***syn*** TOILET, ‖can, *crapper, ‖donicker, john, johnny, ‖loo, ‖potty, ‖throne, water closet

potable *adj* suitable for drinking <*potable* water>
syn drinkable
rel clean, fresh, pure, uncontaminated, unpolluted
con dirty, foul, impure, polluted, unclean
ant impotable

potable *n* ***syn*** DRINK 1, beverage, drinkable, liquor

potbelly *n* an enlarged, swollen, or protruding abdomen <he had the biggest *potbelly* we had ever seen>
syn bay window, corporation, paunch, pod, ‖pot

potency *n* **1** ***syn*** POWER 4, energy, force, might, muscle, puissance, sinew, strength, vigor, virtue
ant impotence
2 ***syn*** EFFICACY 1, capability, effectiveness, efficiency
3 ***syn*** ENERGY 2, birr, go, hardihood, ‖moxie, pep, tuck, vigor
ant impotence

potent *adj* **1** ***syn*** POWERFUL 2, forceful, forcible, mighty, puissant
ant impotent
2 ***syn*** STRONG 3, concentrated, full-bodied, lusty, robust
3 able to copulate <a *potent* male>
syn virile
ant impotent

potential *adj* **1** existing in possibility <a *potential* site for the new factory>
syn possible

---

syn synonym(s) ***rel*** related word(s)
idiom idiomatic equivalent(s) ***con*** contrasted word(s)
ant antonym(s) * vulgar
‖ use limited; if in doubt, see a dictionary
The first word in a synonym list when printed in SMALL CAPITALS shows where there is more information about the group. For a more efficient use of this book see Explanatory Notes.

rel conceivable, imaginable, likely, plausible, probable, thinkable
idiom within the realm (*or* range) of possibility
con existent, extant; doubtful, impossible, questionable; impracticable, unsuitable
ant actual
2 *syn* LATENT, abeyant, dormant, lurking, prepatent, quiescent

potential *n* something that can develop or become actual <industrial *potential*>
syn possibilities, potentiality
ant actuality, reality

potentiality *n syn* POTENTIAL, possibilities
ant actuality

pother *n* **1** *syn* COMMOTION 4, clamor, hassle, hubbub, hurly-burly, to-do, tumult, turmoil, uproar, whirl
2 *syn* STIR 1, ado, bustle, flurry, furore, fuss, whirl, whirlpool, whirlwind
3 *syn* ANNOYANCE 2, aggravation, bother, botheration, exasperation
4 *syn* COMMOTION 2, agitation, confusion, dither, flap, lather, stew, tumult, turbulence, turmoil

pother *vb syn* WORRY 3, cark, fret, fuss, stew, ||tew

pothole *n* a hole, depression, or rut in a road surface <*potholes* all over that stretch of highway>
syn chuckhole, mudhole

pothouse *n syn* BAR 5, barroom, ||bucket shop, ||gin mill, ||grogshop, pub, ||public house, ||rum-hole, ||rum-mill, saloon

potpourri *n syn* MISCELLANY 1, assortment, hash, hodgepodge, medley, mélange, mishmash, pastiche, patchwork, salmagundi

potshot *n* a critical remark made in a random or sporadic manner <took a few *potshots* at his neighbor's argument>
syn pot, shy, sideswipe
rel cut, crack, dig; gibe, jeer; aspersion, criticism, insult

potted *adj* **1** *syn* CONDENSED, canned, capsule, epitomized, pocket
||**2** *syn* INTOXICATED 1, ||pickled, ||pie-eyed, ||pipped, ||pissed, pixilated, ||plastered, polluted, rum-dum, ||screwy

potter *vb syn* FIDDLE 2, doodle, mess, mess around, puddle, putter, tinker

potter (away) *vb syn* WASTE 2, blow, blunder (away), dissipate, fool (away), fritter, frivol away, muddle away, prodigalize, squander

potter's field *n syn* CEMETERY, ||boneyard, ||boot hill, burial ground, burying ground, God's acre, graveyard, memorial park, necropolis, polyandrium

potty *adj* ||**1** *syn* LITTLE 3, inconsiderable, insignificant, minor, petty, shoestring, small, small-beer, trivial, unimportant
||**2** *syn* FOOLISH 2, absurd, ||balmy, crazy, harebrained, insane, loony, preposterous, silly, wacky
3 *syn* SNOBBISH, ||dicty, high-hat, snobby, snooty

||**potty** *n syn* TOILET, ||can, *crapper, ||donicker, john, johnny, ||loo, ||pot, privy, ||throne

pouch *n syn* BAG 1, ||poke, sack

pouch *vb syn* BULGE, beetle, jut, overhang, poke, pout, project, protrude, stand out, stick out

pouf *n syn* QUILT, ||comfortable, comforter, puff

poule *n syn* PROSTITUTE, call girl, ||cruiser, fille de joie, harlot, ||hooker, hustler, nightwalker, streetwalker, whore

poultice *n* a soft, usually heated, and sometimes medicated mass spread on cloth and applied to sores or other lesions <slapped a bread *poultice* over the boil>
syn cataplasm
rel plaster; compress; dressing

pound *vb* **1** *syn* HAMMER 1, beat, malleate
2 *syn* BEAT 1, batter, belabor, buffet, drub, hammer, pelt, pummel, thrash, wallop
3 *syn* IMPRESS 3, drive, grave, hammer, stamp

pound *n syn* BLOW 1, bang, bash, bat, belt, biff, crack, slam, smack, sock

pour *vb* **1** *syn* DISCHARGE 5, disembogue, emit, flow, give off, void
2 to send forth or come forth abundantly <medical supplies *poured* into the stricken area>
syn flow, gush, roll, sluice, stream, surge
rel issue, proceed, spring; course, rill, run, rush, swarm; cascade, cataract; deluge, flood, inundate
3 to rain heavily <it *poured* for two solid days>
syn drench, lash, teem
rel beat; deluge, flood, stream
idiom come down in buckets (*or* torrents), rain cats and dogs

pour *n syn* FLOOD 2, cataclysm, cataract, deluge, flooding, inundation, niagara, overflow, spate, torrent

pourboire *n syn* GRATUITY, cumshaw, lagniappe, largess, ||palm grease, ||palm oil, ||perk(s), perquisite, tip

pout *vb* **1** *syn* SULK, ||dort, grump, ||mump, pet, ||sull
2 *syn* BULGE, beetle, jut, overhang, poke, pouch, project, protrude, stand out, stick out

pouts *n pl syn* SULK, ||dods, ||dorts, grumps, mulligrubs, mumps, sullens

poverty *n* **1** the state of one with insufficient resources <repeated crop failures had reduced the farmers to *poverty*>
syn beggary, borasca, destituteness, destitution, impecuniousness, impoverishment, indigence, indigency, need, neediness, pauperism, pennilessness, penury, poorness, privation, unprosperousness, want
rel exigency, necessity; juncture, pass, pinch, strait; difficulty, distress, embarrassment; hardship, suffering; mendicancy
idiom hand-to-mouth existence, straitened circumstances
con affluence, comfort, luxury, opulence, prosperity, richness, wealth
ant riches
2 *syn* SCARCITY, insufficience, insufficiency, paucity, ||scant, scarceness

poverty–stricken *adj syn* POOR 1, beggared, destitute, dirt poor, impecunious, impoverished, indigent, necessitous, needy, penurious

---

syn synonym(s) — *rel* related word(s)
idiom idiomatic equivalent(s) — *con* contrasted word(s)
ant antonym(s) — * vulgar
|| use limited; if in doubt, see a dictionary
The first word in a synonym list when printed in SMALL CAPITALS shows where there is more information about the group. For a more efficient use of this book see Explanatory Notes.

idiom *piss poor, *without a pot to piss in

powder *vb* **1** ***syn*** SPRINKLE 1, besprinkle, dust, ‖strinkle
2 ***syn*** PULVERIZE 1, bray, buck, comminute, contriturate, crush, triturate

powdering *n* ***syn*** DUSTING, dust, sprinkling

powdery *adj* ***syn*** FINE 2, impalpable, pulverized

power *n* **1** the right or prerogative of determining, ruling, or governing or the exercise of that right or prerogative <party in *power*>
syn authority, command, control, domination, jurisdiction, mastery, might, strings, sway
rel birthright, prerogative, privilege, right; direction, management; ascendancy, dominance, dominion, masterdom, sovereignty, supremacy; superiority; influence, prestige, weight; force, strength
con forcelessness, impotence, weakness
ant impuissance, powerlessness
‖**2** ***syn*** MUCH, barrel, lashings, lot, lump, mass, ‖mess, mountain, peck, ‖sight
3 the ability of a living being to perform in a given way or a capacity for a particular kind of performance <the *power* to think clearly>
syn faculty, function
rel ability, capability, capacity; aptitude, bent, turn; endowment, gift, talent
con inability, incapability, incapacity; inaptness, ineptitude
4 the ability to exert effort for a purpose <raised the productive *power* of the nation>
syn arm, beef, dint, energy, force, might, muscle, potency, puissance, sinew, steam, strength, strong arm, vigor, virtue
rel ability, capability, capacity; effectiveness; dynamism, powder, voltage; dynamis, potentiality; competence, qualification
con inability, incapability, incapacity; ineffectiveness; incompetence

powerful *adj* **1** ***syn*** STRONG 1, mighty, ‖strengthy, wieldy
2 having or manifesting power to effect great or striking results <a *powerful* leader>
syn forceful, forcible, mighty, potent, puissant
rel able, capable, competent; effective, effectual, efficacious, efficient; dynamic, energetic, strenuous, vigorous; convincing, great, invincible; authoritative, dominant, influential, weighty
con faulty, feeble, flawed; impotent, inadequate, incompetent, weak
ant powerless

powerfully *adv* ***syn*** HARD 1, energetically, forcefully, forcibly, hardly, might and main, mightily, strongly, vigorously

powerless *adj* unable to effect one's purpose, intention, or end <*powerless* to leave>
syn helpless, impotent
rel inactive, inert, passive, supine; decrepit, feeble, infirm, weak; incapable, incompetent, ineffective, unfit
con effective, effectual, efficient; able, capable, competent; potent, puissant
ant powerful

powwow ***syn*** TALK 4, conference, meeting, parley

powwow *vb* ***syn*** CONFER 2, advise, collogue, confab, confabulate, consult, huddle, parley, treat

‖**prabble** *n* ***syn*** QUARREL, altercation, beef, bickering, brabble, brannigan, dispute, falling-out, fracas, fuss

practic *adj* ***syn*** REALISTIC, down-to-earth, hard, matter-of-fact, practical, pragmatic, pragmatical, unidealistic, unromantic, utilitarian

practicable *adj* **1** ***syn*** POSSIBLE 1, doable, feasible, viable, workable
ant impracticable
2 ***syn*** PRACTICAL 2, functional, handy, serviceable, useful, utile
3 ***syn*** OPEN 5, accessible, employable, operative, usable
ant impracticable

practical *adj* **1** ***syn*** IMPLICIT 2, constructive, virtual
2 capable of being turned to use or account <had a *practical* rather than a theoretical acquaintance with mechanics>
syn functional, handy, practicable, serviceable, useful, utile
con abstract, academic, theoretical
ant impractical, unpractical
3 ***syn*** REALISTIC, down-to-earth, hard, hard-boiled, hardheaded, matter-of-fact, pragmatic, sober, unfantastic, unidealistic
ant impractical, unpractical
4 ***syn*** EXPERIENCED, old, old-time, practiced, seasoned, skilled, versed, vet, veteran

practically *adv* **1** ***syn*** VIRTUALLY, in essence, morally
2 ***syn*** ALMOST 2, all but, as good as, as much as, essentially, well-nigh
3 ***syn*** NEARLY, about, all but, almost, approximately, most, much, ‖nearabout, nigh, well-nigh

practice *vb* ***syn*** EXERCISE 3, drill, rehearse
rel execute, fulfill, perform; follow, pursue; iterate, repeat

practice *n* **1** ***syn*** HABIT 1, custom, habitude, manner, praxis, trick, usage, use, way, wont
rel procedure, proceeding, process; method, mode, system
2 ***syn*** PLOT 2, cabal, conspiracy, covin, intrigue, machination, scheme
3 ***syn*** EXERCISE 3, drill, drilling
rel use, usefulness, utility; convenance, convention, form, usage
ant theory; precept

practiced *adj* ***syn*** EXPERIENCED, old, old-time, practical, seasoned, skilled, versed, vet, veteran
ant unpracticed

praetorian *adj* ***syn*** CORRUPT 2, mercenary, unethical, unprincipled, unscrupulous, venal

praetorian *n* ***syn*** DIEHARD 1, bitter-ender, conservative, fundamentalist, old liner, rightist, right-winger, standpat, standpatter, tory

---

pragmatic *n* ***syn*** BUSYBODY, butt-in, ‖buttinsky, intermeddler, meddler, nose, prier (*or* pryer), quidnunc, rubberneck, snoop

pragmatic *adj* ***syn*** REALISTIC, down-to-earth, hard, hard-boiled, hardheaded, matter-of-fact, practical, sober, unfantastic, unidealistic

pragmatical *adj* ***syn*** REALISTIC, down-to-earth, hard, matter-of-fact, practic, practical, pragmatic, unidealistic, unromantic, utilitarian

pragmatist *n* ***syn*** BUSYBODY, butt-in, ‖buttinsky, intermeddler, kibitzer, meddler, prier (*or* pryer), quidnunc, rubberneck, snoop

praisable *adj* ***syn*** WORTHY 1, admirable, commendable, deserving, estimable, laudable, meritable, meritorious, praiseworthy, thankworthy

praise *vb* **1** ***syn*** COMMEND 2, acclaim, applaud, compliment, hail, kudize, recommend, ‖roose

ant censure, criticize

2 to glorify and exalt expecially in song or writing <*praised* God for all his blessings>

syn bless, celebrate, cry up, eulogize, extol, glorify, hymn, laud, magnify, panegyrize, psalm, psalmody, resound

rel aggrandize, dignify, distinguish, ennoble, erect, exalt, honor, sublime, uprear; enhance, heighten, intensify; apotheosize; proclaim

idiom sing the praises of

con asperse, calumniate, defame, libel, malign, traduce, vilify; belittle, decry, depreciate, derogate, detract (from), discount, disparage, minimize, opprobriate; censure, criticize, denounce, reprehend, reprobate; abuse, reproach, revile

ant dispraise; blame

praiseful *adj* ***syn*** EULOGISTIC, encomiastic, laudative, laudatory, panegyrical

praiseworthy *adj* ***syn*** WORTHY 1, admirable, commendable, deserving, estimable, laudable, meritable, meritorious, praisable, thankworthy

ant despicable

‖**pram** *n* ***syn*** BABY CARRIAGE, baby buggy, bassinet, ‖perambulator

prance *vb* **1** ***syn*** SASHAY, flounce, mince, ‖prink, strut

2 ***syn*** DANCE 1, foot (it), hoof (it), step, tread

‖**prang** *vb* ***syn*** BUMP 1, clash, collide

‖**prang** *n* ***syn*** CRASH 3, crack-up, pileup, smash, smashup, ‖stramash, wreck

prank *n* a mischievous or roguish act <he was always playing *pranks* on his sister>

syn antic, caper, dido(es), frolic, lark, monkeyshine, ‖rig, shenanigan, shine(s), ‖skite, tomfoolery, trick, wheeze; *compare* ESCAPADE, TRICK 1

rel fooling, high jinks, horseplay, roughhouse, roughhousing, rowdiness, skylarking; gambol, play, rollick, sport; frivolity, levity, lightness; caprice, conceit, fancy, freak, vagary, whim, whimsy

prank *vb* **1** ***syn*** ADORN, beautify, bedeck, deck, decorate, dress (up), embellish, garnish, ornament, trim

2 ***syn*** DRESS UP 1, deck (out), doll out, doll up, fix up, gussy up, primp, smarten (up), spiff, spruce (up)

prankful *adj* ***syn*** PLAYFUL 1, antic, impish, larkish, ‖mischiefful, mischievous, prankish, pranky, puckish, roguish

prankish *adj* ***syn*** PLAYFUL 1, antic, impish, larkish, ‖mischiefful, mischievous, prankful, pranky, roguish, wicked

pranky *adj* ***syn*** PLAYFUL 1, antic, impish, larkish, ‖mischiefful, mischievous, prankful, prankish, roguish, wicked

‖**prat** *n* ***syn*** TRICK 1, artifice, gimmick, maneuver, play, ploy, ruse, shenanigan, stratagem, wile

prat** *n* ***syn BUTTOCKS, *arse, *ass, backside, behind, bottom, *bum, ‖can, rear, tail

prate *vb* **1** ***syn*** CHAT 1, babble, chatter, clack, gab, gabble, jaw, prattle, yak, yakety-yak

2 ***syn*** BOAST, blow, brag, cock-a-doodle-doo, crow, gasconade, mouth, puff, redomontade, vaunt

3 ***syn*** BABBLE 2, blabber, blather, drivel, drool, gabble, prattle, twaddle, ‖waffle

prate *n* ***syn*** CHATTER, babble, blab, blabber, chat, gab, gabble, jabber, palaver, prattle

prater *n* ***syn*** CHATTERBOX, bandar-log, blabber, blabbermouth, blabmouth, chatterer, gabber, jabberer, magpie, prattler

prattle *vb* **1** ***syn*** CHAT 1, babble, chatter, clack, gab, gabber, jaw, prate, yak, yakety-yak

2 ***syn*** BABBLE 2, blabber, blather, drivel, drool, gabble, prate, twaddle, ‖waffle

prattle *n* ***syn*** CHATTER, babble, blab, blabber, chat, gab, gabble, jabber, palaver, yak

prattler *n* ***syn*** CHATTERBOX, bandar-log, blabber, blabbermouth, blabmouth, chatterer, gabber, jabberer, magpie, prater

praxis *n* ***syn*** HABIT 1, consuetude, custom, habitude, manner, practice, trick, usage, use, wont

pray *vb* ***syn*** BEG, appeal, beseech, brace, crave, entreat, implore, importune, plead, supplicate

prayer *n* an earnest and usually a formal request for something <the *prayer* in a bill in equity is the part that specifies the kind of relief sought>

syn appeal, application, entreaty, imploration, imprecation, orison, petition, plea, suit, supplication

rel begging, beseeching, imploring, pleading; adoration, worship

con claim, demand, exaction

prayer *n* ***syn*** SUPPLIANT, asker, beggar, petitioner, suitor, supplicant, supplicator

prayerful *adj* ***syn*** DEVOUT, godly, holy, pietistic, pious, religious

preach *vb* **1** to discourse publicly on a religious subject <*preached* at Sunday services>

syn evangelize, homilize, sermonize

rel minister, mission, missionary; prophesy; address, lecture, speak, talk

2 ***syn*** MORALIZE, preachify, sermonize

preach *n* ***syn*** SERMON, preaching, preachment, sermonizing

---

syn synonym(s) — *rel* related word(s)
idiom idiomatic equivalent(s) — *con* contrasted word(s)
ant antonym(s) — * vulgar
‖ use limited; if in doubt, see a dictionary
The first word in a synonym list when printed in SMALL CAPITALS shows where there is more information about the group. For a more efficient use of this book see Explanatory Notes.

preacher *n* ***syn*** CLERGYMAN, churchman, cleric, clerical, clerk, divine, ecclesiastic, minister, parson, reverend

preachify *vb* ***syn*** MORALIZE, preach, sermonize

preaching *n* ***syn*** SERMON, preach, preachment, sermonizing

preachment *n* ***syn*** SERMON, preach, preaching, sermonizing

preachy *adj* ***syn*** DIDACTIC, moral, moralizing, schoolmasterish, sermonic, sermonizing, teachy

preamble *n* ***syn*** INTRODUCTION, exordium, foreword, overture, preface, prelude, prelusion, proem, prolegomenon, prologue

precarious *adj* **1** ***syn*** DOUBTFUL 1, ambiguous, borderline, dubious, equivocal, impugnable, indecisive, open, problematic, uncertain
2 ***syn*** DELICATE 7, sensitive, ticklish, touchy, tricky

precariousness *n* ***syn*** INSTABILITY, shakiness, unfixedness, unsettledness, unstability, unstableness, unsteadfastness, unsteadiness

precaution *n* ***syn*** PRUDENCE 1, canniness, caution, discreetness, discretion, foresight, forethought, providence

precede *vb* **1** to go before in rank, dignity, or importance <the small countries at the conference were *preceded* by the large wealthy ones> <those who still feel that age should *precede* beauty>
syn outrank, rank
2 to go before in time <all-out war was *preceded* by many small raids>
syn antecede, antedate, forerun, pace, predate
rel announce, herald, foreshadow, harbinger, presage
con ensue, supervene
ant follow, succeed
3 to cause to be preceded <*preceded* his address with a welcome to the visitors>
syn introduce, lead, preface, usher
ant follow

precedence *n* ***syn*** PRIORITY, antecedence, precedency, previousness

precedency *n* ***syn*** PRIORITY, antecedence, precedence, previousness

precedent *adj* ***syn*** PRECEDING, antecedent, anterior, foregoing, former, past, previous, prior

precedently *adv* ***syn*** BEFORE 1, ahead, ante, antecedently, beforehand, fore, forward, in advance, previous

preceding *adj* being before especially in time or in arrangement <the *preceding* day>
syn antecedent, anterior, foregoing, former, past, precedent, previous, prior
rel other; preexistent; precursive, precursory; erstwhile, heretofore, hitherto
con coming, ensuing, next, sequent, sequential, subsequent, successive
ant following, succeeding

preceding *prep* ***syn*** BEFORE 1, ahead of, ante, ere, in advance of, prior to, to

precept *n* ***syn*** LAW 1, canon, decree, decretum, edict, ordinance, prescript, regulation, rule, statute
rel axiom, fundamental, principle; doctrine, dogma, tenet; behest, bidding, injunction
ant practice; counsel

précieux *adj* ***syn*** PRECIOUS 4, affected, alembicated, chichi, la-di-da, overnice, overrefined

precinct *n* **1** ***syn*** QUARTER 2, district, section, sector
2 ***syn*** FIELD, bailiwick, champaign, domain, dominion, province, region, sphere, territory, walk
3 precincts *pl* ***syn*** ENVIRONS 1, bound(s), boundary, compass, confine(s), limits, purlieus

precious *adj* **1** of such great value that a suitable price is hard to estimate <a *precious* twelfth century painting>
syn costly, inestimable, invaluable, priceless, valuable; *compare* COSTLY 1
rel choice, exquisite, rare, recherché; treasurable; rich; prizable
idiom of price
con base, common, mean, paltry, poor, rubbishy, shabby, trashy; contemptible, despicable, miserable; claptrap, gimcrack, trumpery
ant cheap; worthless
2 ***syn*** FAVORITE 1, beloved, blue-eyed, darling, dear, fair-haired, loved, pet, white-haired, white-headed
3 ***syn*** NICE 1, choosy, fastidious, finicky, fussy, miminy-piminy, particular, persnickety, picky, squeamish
4 excessively refined <too *precious* to mingle with the common people>
syn affected, alembicated, chichi, la-di-da, overnice, overrefined, précieux; *compare* GENTEEL 3
rel ostentatious, pretentious, showy; artful, sophisticated, studied
con artless, ingenuous, naive, natural, simple, unaffected, unartful, unschooled, unsophisticated, unstudied, untutored; down-to-earth, matter-of-fact, practical, pragmatic, rational

precipitance *n* ***syn*** HASTE 2, hastiness, hurriedness, precipitancy, precipitateness, precipitation, rush

precipitancy *n* ***syn*** HASTE 2, hastiness, hurriedness, precipitance, precipitateness, precipitation, rush

precipitant *adj* ***syn*** PRECIPITATE 1, abrupt, hasty, headlong, hurried, impetuous, precipitous, rushing, subitaneous, sudden

precipitate *n* **1** ***syn*** SEDIMENT, deposit, dreg(s), grounds, lees, precipitation, settlings
2 ***syn*** EFFECT 1, aftereffect, aftermath, causatum, consequence, event, issue, result, sequel, upshot

precipitate *adj* **1** characterized by impetuous or unexpected haste <beat a *precipitate* retreat>
syn abrupt, hasty, headlong, hurried, impetuous, precipitant, precipitous, rushing, subitaneous, sudden
rel breakneck, headstrong, hotheaded, impatient, impulsive, madcap, refractory, uncontrolled, willful; unanticipated, unexpected, unforeseen, unlooked-for; overhasty
con leisurely, slow, unhurried
ant deliberate
2 ***syn*** STEEP 1, abrupt, arduous, precipitous, sheer, sideling, steepdown, steep-to, steep-up, ‖stickle

---

precipitateness *n* ***syn*** HASTE 2, hastiness, hurriedness, precipitance, precipitancy, precipitation, rush

precipitation *n* **1** ***syn*** HASTE 2, hastiness, hurriedness, precipitance, precipitancy, precipitateness, rush
2 ***syn*** SEDIMENT, deposit, dreg(s), grounds, lees, precipitate, settlings

precipitous *adj* **1** ***syn*** PRECIPITATE 1, abrupt, hasty, headlong, hurried, impetuous, precipitant, rushing, subitaneous, sudden
2 ***syn*** STEEP 1, abrupt, arduous, precipitate, sheer, sideling, steepdown, steep-to, steep-up, ‖stickle

précis *n* ***syn*** COMPENDIUM 1, aperçu, digest, pandect, sketch, survey, syllabus, sylloge

precise *adj* **1** ***syn*** DEFINITE 1, circumscribed, determinate, fixed, limited, narrow, restricted
2 ***syn*** CORRECT 2, accurate, exact, nice, proper, right, rigorous
rel rigid, stringent
con careless, heedless; lax, slack
ant imprecise; loose
3 ***syn*** PRIM 1, genteel, missish, prig, priggish, prissy, prudish, puritanical, straitlaced, stuffy
4 distinguished from every other <arrived just at the *precise* moment when he was needed>
syn exact, very
rel specific; individual; particular
con general, inexact, nonspecific
ant imprecise

precisely *adv* **1** ***syn*** JUST 1, accurately, bang, exactly, right, sharp, ‖smack-dab, spang, square, squarely
idiom on the button
ant imprecisely; approximately
2 ***syn*** EVEN 1, as well, exactly, expressly, just
3 ***syn*** EXACTLY 3, yes

preciseness *n* ***syn*** PRECISION, accuracy, correctness, definiteness, definitiveness, definitude, exactitude, exactness
ant impreciseness

precisian *n* ***syn*** PURIST, precisionist, traditionalist

precision *n* the quality or character of what is precise <the *precision* involved in close-tolerance machining>
syn accuracy, correctness, definiteness, definitiveness, definitude, exactitude, exactness, preciseness
rel care, carefulness; attention, heed
con inaccuracy, incorrectness, indefiniteness, inexactness; obscurity, unclearness, vagueness; unreliability, untrustworthiness
ant imprecision

precisionist *n* ***syn*** PURIST, precisian, traditionalist

preclude *vb* ***syn*** PREVENT 2, avert, deter, forestall, forfend, obviate, rule out, stave off, ward
rel cease, discontinue, quit, stop

precocious *adj* exceptionally early in development <a *precocious* child, smart beyond his years>
syn advanced, forward; *compare* EARLY 2
rel ahead, early, overearly, oversoon, premature, previous, ‖soon; developed, mature
con backward, undeveloped; dull, slow, slow-witted, sluggish
ant retarded

precogitate *vb* ***syn*** PREMEDITATE, forethink, predetermine

preconception *n* an attitude, belief, or impression formed beforehand <had a lot of *preconceptions* about a man she'd never met>
syn prejudgment, prepossession; *compare* PREJUDICE
rel illusion; delusion
idiom preconceived notion (*or* idea *or* opinion)

precondition *n* ***syn*** ESSENTIAL 2, condition, must, necessity, prerequisite, requirement, requisite, sine qua non

precursor *n* **1** ***syn*** FORERUNNER 1, harbinger, herald, outrider
2 ***syn*** FORERUNNER 2, ancestor, antecedent, antecessor, foregoer, predecessor, prototype

predacious *adj* ***syn*** RAPACIOUS 1, predative, predatorial, predatory, raptorial, vulturine, vulturish, vulturous

predate *vb* ***syn*** PRECEDE 2, antecede, antedate, forerun, pace

predative *adj* ***syn*** RAPACIOUS 1, predacious, predatorial, predatory, raptorial, vulturine, vulturish, vulturous

predatorial *adj* ***syn*** RAPACIOUS 1, predacious, predative, predatory, raptorial, vulturine, vulturish, vulturous

predatory *adj* ***syn*** RAPACIOUS 1, predacious, predative, predatorial, raptorial, vulturine, vulturish, vulturous

predecessor *n* ***syn*** FORERUNNER 2, ancestor, antecedent, antecessor, foregoer, precursor, prototype

predestinate *vb* ***syn*** PREDESTINE 2, foredestine, foreordain, predetermine, preordain

predestine *vb* **1** to fix the future of in advance <his treasured scribblings were *predestined* to light a kitchen fire>
syn destine, determine, doom (to), fate, foreordain, predetermine, preform, preordain
rel predecide; prejudge; preestablish
2 to determine by or as if by divine decree or eternal purpose <some believe that God *predestines* individuals to eternal life or to eternal death>
syn foredestine, foreordain, predestinate, predetermine, preordain

predetermine *vb* **1** ***syn*** PREDESTINE 2, foredestine, foreordain, predestinate, preordain
2 ***syn*** PREMEDITATE, forethink, precogitate
3 ***syn*** PREDESTINE 1, destine, determine, doom (to), fate, foreordain, preform, preordain

predicament *n* a difficult, perplexing, or trying situation <was in a *predicament,* trying to decide whether or not to take the job>
syn box, corner, deep water, dilemma, fix, hole, hot water, impasse, jam, pickle, plight, quagmire, scrape, soup, spot
rel emergency, exigency, juncture, pass, pinch, strait; asperity, difficulty, hardness, hardship, rigor, vicissitude; Dutch, trouble; condition, posture, situation, state
idiom ‖in a bind

predicate *vb* **1** ***syn*** ASSERT 1, affirm, aver, avouch, avow, constate, declare, depose, profess, protest

---

syn synonym(s) *rel* related word(s)
idiom idiomatic equivalent(s) *con* contrasted word(s)
ant antonym(s) * vulgar
‖ use limited; if in doubt, see a dictionary
The first word in a synonym list when printed in SMALL CAPITALS shows where there is more information about the group. For a more efficient use of this book see Explanatory Notes.

2 *syn* BASE, bottom, establish, found, ground, rest, stay

predict *vb* **1** *syn* FORETELL, adumbrate, augur, forecast, portend, presage, prognosticate, prophesy, soothsay, vaticinate
2 to conjecture correctly <*predicted* the turn of the market months in advance>
syn call, guess
rel conjecture, presume, suppose, surmise, think; conclude, gather, infer, judge
idiom hazard a conjecture (*or* guess)

prediction *n* something that is predicted <the *prediction* was for a good outcome>
syn cast, forecast, foretelling, prevision, prognosis, prognostication, prophecy, weird
rel conjecture, guess, surmising

predictor *n* *syn* PROPHET, augur, auspex, forecaster, foreseer, foreteller, haruspex, Nostradamus, prognosticator, prophesier

predilection *n* *syn* LEANING 2, bent, disposition, inclination, inclining, penchant, predisposition, proclivity, propensity, tendency

predispose *vb* *syn* INCLINE 3, bend, bias, dispose
rel impress, strike, sway
con disaffect, disincline, disinterest, indispose

predisposed *adj* *syn* WILLING 1, disposed, fain, inclined, minded, prone, ready
ant indisposed

predisposition *n* *syn* LEANING 2, bent, disposition, inclination, inclining, penchant, predilection, proclivity, propensity, tendency
ant indisposition

predominant *adj* **1** *syn* DOMINANT 1, ascendant, master, overbearing, paramount, predominate, preponderant, prevalent, regnant, sovereign
ant subordinate
2 *syn* CHIEF 2, capital, dominant, main, major, number one, outstanding, preeminent, principal, star

predominantly *adv* *syn* GENERALLY 1, chiefly, largely, mainly, mostly, overall, primarily, principally

predominate *adj* *syn* DOMINANT 1, ascendant, master, overbearing, paramount, predominant, preponderant, prevalent, regnant, sovereign

predominate *vb* *syn* RULE 2, dominate, domineer, preponderate, prevail, reign

preeminence *n* **1** *syn* SUPREMACY, ascendancy, domination, dominion, masterdom, preponderance, preponderancy, prepotence, prepotency, sovereignty
2 *syn* EMINENCE 1, distinction, illustriousness, kudos, prestige, prominence, prominency, renown

preeminent *adj* **1** *syn* SUPREME, incomparable, surpassing, towering, transcendent, ultimate, unequalable, unmatchable, unsurpassable
2 *syn* CHIEF 2, capital, dominant, main, major, number one, outstanding, predominant, principal, stellar

preempt *vb* **1** *syn* APPROPRIATE 1, accroach, annex, arrogate, commandeer, confiscate, expropriate, seize, sequester, take
2 *syn* ARROGATE 1, accroach, appropriate, assume, commandeer, usurp

preen *vb* *syn* PRIDE, pique, plume

preengage *vb* **1** *syn* RESERVE 2, bespeak, book
2 *syn* PREPOSSESS 1, preoccupy

preface *n* *syn* INTRODUCTION, exordium, foreword, overture, preamble, prelude, prelusion, proem, prolegomenon, prologue

preface *vb* *syn* PRECEDE 3, introduce, lead, usher

prefatial *adj* *syn* PRELIMINARY, inductive, introductory, prefatorial, prefatory, ‖prelim, preludial, prelusive, preparatory, proemial

prefatorial *adj* *syn* PRELIMINARY, inductive, introductory, prefatial, prefatory, ‖prelim, preludial, prelusive, preparatory, proemial

prefatory *adj* *syn* PRELIMINARY, inductive, introductory, prefatial, prefatorial, ‖prelim, preludial, prelusive, preparatory, proemial

prefer *vb* **1** *syn* ADVANCE 2, elevate, promote, upgrade
2 *syn* CHOOSE 1, cull, elect, mark, opt (for), optate, pick, select, single (out), take
3 *syn* PROPOSE 1, pose, ‖propone, proposition, propound, put, suggest

preferable *adj* *syn* BETTER 2, ‖bettermost, superior

preference *n* **1** *syn* CHOICE 1, alternative, ‖druthers, election, option, selection
rel partiality, predilection, prepossession
2 *syn* ADVANCEMENT 1, elevation, preferment, prelation, promotion, upgrading

preferment *n* *syn* ADVANCEMENT 1, elevation, preference, prelation, promotion, upgrading

preferred *adj* *syn* FAVORITE 2, favored, popular, well-liked

prefigurate *vb* *syn* ADUMBRATE 1, foreshadow, hint, prefigure, shadow (forth)

prefigure *vb* *syn* ADUMBRATE 1, foreshadow, hint, prefigurate, shadow (forth)

preform *vb* *syn* PREDESTINE 1, destine, determine, doom (to), fate, foreordain, predetermine, preordain

pregnance *n* *syn* PREGNANCY, gestation, gravidity, situation

pregnancy *n* the condition of containing unborn young within the body <she was in the last trimester of her *pregnancy*>
syn gestation, gravidity, pregnance, situation

pregnant *adj* **1** containing unborn young within the body <she was *pregnant* with her second child>
syn big, childing, enceinte, expectant, expecting, gone, gravid, heavy, parous, parturient
idiom in an interesting condition, in the family way, with child (*or* young)
con barren, infertile; delivered; postpartum
2 *syn* EXPRESSIVE, eloquent, facund, meaningful, rich, sententious, significant
rel consequential, important, momentous, significant, weighty

prehend *vb* *syn* CATCH 1, bag, capture, collar, ‖cotch, get, nail, secure, take

---

syn synonym(s) | *rel* related word(s)
idiom idiomatic equivalent(s) | *con* contrasted word(s)
ant antonym(s) | * vulgar
‖ use limited; if in doubt, see a dictionary
The first word in a synonym list when printed in SMALL CAPITALS shows where there is more information about the group. For a more efficient use of this book see Explanatory Notes.

prehensile *adj* ***syn*** COVETOUS, acquisitive, desirous, grabby, grasping, greedy, itchy
preindicate *vb* ***syn*** ANNOUNCE 2, forerun, foreshow, harbinger, herald, presage
prejudgment *n* ***syn*** PRECONCEPTION, prepossession
prejudice *n* the inclination to take a stand (as in a conflict) usually without just grounds or sufficient information <could not review his competitor's work without *prejudice*>
syn bias, one-sidedness, partiality; *compare* LEANING 2, PRECONCEPTION
rel partisanship
idiom jaundiced eye
con detachment, dispassion, impartiality, indifference, neutrality
ant objectivity
prejudice *vb* **1** ***syn*** INJURE 1, blemish, damage, harm, hurt, impair, mar, spoil, tarnish, vitiate
2 to cause to have opinions formed without due knowledge or examination <*prejudice* a man against his neighbor by innuendo>
syn bias, influence, prepossess; *compare* INCLINE 3, SLANT 3
rel bend, dispose, incline, predispose; angle, skew, slant; prejudge
prejudiced *adj* ***syn*** BIASED 2, colored, jaundiced, one-sided, partial, partisan, prepossessed, tendentious, unindifferent, warped
ant unprejudiced; disinterested
prejudicial *adj* **1** ***syn*** HARMFUL, bad, damaging, deleterious, detrimental, evil, injurious, mischievous, nocuous, prejudicious
2 ***syn*** DISCRIMINATORY, differential, discriminative
prejudicious *adj* ***syn*** HARMFUL, bad, damaging, deleterious, detrimental, evil, injurious, mischievous, nocuous, prejudicial
prekindergarten *adj* ***syn*** CHILDISH, babyish, immature, infantile, infantive, puerile
preknow *vb* ***syn*** FORESEE, anticipate, apprehend, divine, forefeel, foreknow, previse, prevision, see, visualize
prelation *n* ***syn*** ADVANCEMENT 1, elevation, preference, preferment, promotion, upgrading
prelect *vb* ***syn*** TALK 7, address, lecture, speak
||**prelim** *adj* ***syn*** PRELIMINARY, inductive, introductory, prefatial, prefatorial, prefatory, preludial, prelusive, preparative, preparatory
preliminary *adj* serving to make ready the way for something that follows <held a *preliminary* discussion to set up the agenda of the conference>
syn inductive, introductory, prefatial, prefatorial, prefatory, ||prelim, preludial, prelusive, preparative, preparatory, proemial
rel primal, primary; elemental, elementary; basic, fundamental; fitting, preparing, readying
ant postliminary
prelimit *vb* ***syn*** LIMIT 2, bar, circumscribe, confine, delimit, delimitate, restrict
preliterate *adj* ***syn*** PRIMITIVE 6, nonliterate
prelude *n* ***syn*** INTRODUCTION, exordium, foreword, overture, preamble, preface, prelusion, proem, prolegomenon, prologue
preludial *adj* ***syn*** PRELIMINARY, inductive, introductory, prefatial, prefatorial, prefatory, ||prelim, prelusive, preparative, preparatory
prelusion *n* ***syn*** INTRODUCTION, exordium, foreword, overture, preamble, preface, prelude, proem, prolegomenon, prologue
prelusive *adj* ***syn*** PRELIMINARY, inductive, introductory, prefatial, prefatorial, prefatory, ||prelim, preludial, preparative, preparatory
premature *adj* ***syn*** EARLY 2, overearly, oversoon, previous, ||soon, untimely
prematurely *adv* ***syn*** EARLY 2, betimes, oversoon
premeditate *vb* to think on and revolve in the mind beforehand <carefully *premeditating* each step of his plan of campaign>
syn forethink, precogitate, predetermine
rel prearrange, preplan, set up; predecide; prepare
premeditated *adj* ***syn*** DELIBERATE 1, advised, aforethought, considered, designed, prepense, studied, studious, thought-out
ant unpremeditated; spontaneous
premier *adj* ***syn*** FIRST 3, arch, champion, chief, foremost, head, leading, principal
premise *n* ***syn*** ASSUMPTION 2, apriorism, posit, postulate, postulation, presumption, presupposition, supposition, thesis
premise *vb* ***syn*** PRESUPPOSE, assume, posit, postulate, presume
premium *n* ***syn*** REWARD, carrot, dividend, guerdon, meed, plum, prize
premium *adj* ***syn*** SUPERIOR 4, exceptional
premonition *n* ***syn*** APPREHENSION 3, apprehensiveness, foreboding, misgiving, prenotion, presage, presentiment
prename *n* ***syn*** GIVEN NAME, baptismal name, Christian name, font name, forename, personal name
prenotion *n* ***syn*** APPREHENSION 3, apprehensiveness, foreboding, misgiving, premonition, presage, presentiment
prentice *n* ***syn*** NOVICE, apprentice, beginner, boot, freshman, neophyte, newcomer, novitiate, recruit, rookie
prentice *adj* ***syn*** CRUDE 5, coarse, inexpert
preoccupied *adj* **1** ***syn*** INTENT, absorbed, deep, engaged, engrossed, immersed, rapt, wrapped, wrapped up
2 ***syn*** ABSTRACTED, absent, absentminded, bemused, distrait, faraway, inconscient, lost
rel absorbed; forgetful
ant unpreoccupied
preoccupy *vb* ***syn*** PREPOSSESS 1, preengage
preordain *vb* **1** ***syn*** PREDESTINE 1, destine, determine, doom (to), fate, foreordain, predetermine, preform
2 ***syn*** PREDESTINE 2, foredestine, foreordain, predestinate, predetermine
preparative *adj* ***syn*** PRELIMINARY, inductive, introductory, prefatial, prefatorial, prefatory, ||prelim, preludial, prelusive, preparatory

---

syn synonym(s) — *rel* related word(s)
idiom idiomatic equivalent(s) — *con* contrasted word(s)
ant antonym(s) — * vulgar
|| use limited; if in doubt, see a dictionary
The first word in a synonym list when printed in SMALL CAPITALS shows where there is more information about the group. For a more efficient use of this book see Explanatory Notes.

preparatory *adj* ***syn*** PRELIMINARY, inductive, introductory, prefatial, prefatorial, prefatory, ‖prelim, preludial, prelusive, preparative

prepare *vb* **1** to make ready in advance usually for a particular use or disposition <*prepared* rooms for the expected guests>
syn fit, fix, get, make, make up, ready
rel furnish, provide, supply; dower, endow, endue; equip, outfit; dispose, incline, predispose; prime
idiom set the stage (for)
ant unprepare
2 ***syn*** DRAFT 3, draw up, formulate, frame, make
3 ***syn*** GIRD 3, brace, fortify, ready, steel, strengthen

prepared *adj* ***syn*** READY 1, set
ant unprepared

prepatent *adj* ***syn*** LATENT, abeyant, dormant, lurking, potential, quiescent

prepense *adj* ***syn*** DELIBERATE 1, advised, aforethought, considered, designed, premeditated, studied, studious, thought-out

prepensely *adv* ***syn*** INTENTIONALLY, ‖apurpose, deliberately, designedly, on purpose, purposedly, purposely, purposively

preponderance *n* ***syn*** SUPREMACY, ascendancy, ascendant, dominance, domination, dominion, masterdom, preponderancy, preponderation, prepotence

preponderancy *n* ***syn*** SUPREMACY, ascendancy, dominance, domination, dominion, preponderance, preponderation, prepotence, prepotency, sovereignty

preponderant *adj* ***syn*** DOMINANT 1, ascendant, master, overbearing, paramount, predominant, predominate, prevalent, regnant, sovereign

preponderate *vb* ***syn*** RULE 2, dominate, domineer, predominate, prevail, reign

preponderation *n* ***syn*** SUPREMACY, dominance, domination, dominion, masterdom, preeminence, preponderance, preponderancy, prepotence, prepotency

prepossess *vb* **1** to influence or affect strongly beforehand <was *prepossessed* with the notion of his own superiority>
syn preengage, preoccupy
rel busy, engage, engross, immerse, occupy, soak; absorb, imbue, involve
2 ***syn*** PREJUDICE 2, bias, influence

prepossessed *adj* ***syn*** BIASED 2, colored, jaundiced, one-sided, partial, partisan, prejudiced, tendentious, unindifferent, warped
ant unprepossessed

prepossessing *adj* ***syn*** ATTRACTIVE 1, alluring, appealing, attracting, captivating, charming, drawing, enchanting, engaging, mesmeric

prepossession *n* ***syn*** PRECONCEPTION, prejudgment

preposterous *adj* **1** ***syn*** FOOLISH 2, absurd, ‖balmy, crazy, harebrained, insane, loony, ‖potty, silly, wacky
rel irrational, unreasonable
2 ***syn*** EXTRAVAGANT 1, fantastic, wild

preposterousness *n* ***syn*** FOOLISHNESS, absurdity, craziness, dottiness, folly, inanity, insanity, senselessness, silliness, witlessness

prepotence *n* ***syn*** SUPREMACY, ascendancy, dominance, domination, dominion, masterdom, preeminence, preponderance, prepotency, sovereignty

prepotency *n* ***syn*** SUPREMACY, ascendancy, dominance, domination, dominion, masterdom, preeminence, preponderance, preponderancy, prepotence

prerequisite *n* ***syn*** ESSENTIAL 2, condition, must, necessity, precondition, requirement, requisite, sine qua non

prerequisite *adj* ***syn*** ESSENTIAL 4, imperative, indispensable, necessary, necessitous

prerogative *n* ***syn*** RIGHT 2, appanage, birthright, perquisite, privilege
rel exemption, immunity

presage *n* **1** ***syn*** FORETOKEN, augury, bodement, boding, omen, portent, prognostic
2 ***syn*** APPREHENSION 3, apprehensiveness, foreboding, misgiving, premonition, prenotion, presentiment

presage *vb* **1** ***syn*** AUGUR 2, betoken, bode, forebode, foreshadow, foreshow, foretoken, omen, portend, promise
rel bespeak, indicate
2 ***syn*** ANNOUNCE 2, forerun, foreshow, harbinger, herald, preindicate
3 ***syn*** FORETELL, adumbrate, augur, forecast, portend, predict, prognosticate, prophesy, soothsay, vaticinate

prescribe *vb* **1** ***syn*** DICTATE, decree, impose, lay down, ordain, set
2 to fix arbitrarily or authoritatively for the sake of order or of a clear understanding <the Constitution *prescribes* the conditions under which it may be amended>
syn assign, define, lay down
rel establish, fix, set, settle; decide, determine; choose, pick out, select

prescript *n* ***syn*** LAW 1, decree, decretum, edict, institute, ordinance, precept, prescription, regulation, rule

prescription *n* ***syn*** LAW 1, decree, decretum, edict, institute, ordinance, precept, prescript, regulation, rule

presence *n* ***syn*** BEARING 1, address, air, comportment, demeanor, deportment, mien, port, set
rel appearance, aspect, look, seeming

present *n* ***syn*** GIFT 1, benevolence, boon, ‖compliment, favor, largess

present *vb* **1** ***syn*** INTRODUCE 4, acquaint, ‖quaint
2 ***syn*** GIVE 1, bestow, devote, donate, give away, hand out
3 ***syn*** OFFER 1, extend, give, hold out, pose, proffer, tender
4 ***syn*** ADDUCE, advance, allege, cite, lay, offer
5 ***syn*** DIRECT 2, address, aim, cast, head, incline, lay, level, point, train

present *adj* now existing or in progress <the *present* state of the economy seems to be shaky from all reports>
syn contemporary, current, existent, extant, instant, present-day, todayish

---

syn synonym(s)	***rel*** related word(s)
idiom idiomatic equivalent(s)	***con*** contrasted word(s)
ant antonym(s)	* vulgar

‖ use limited; if in doubt, see a dictionary
The first word in a synonym list when printed in SMALL CAPITALS shows where there is more information about the group. For a more efficient use of this book see Explanatory Notes.

rel contemporaneous, modern; newfashioned, up-to-date, up-to-the-minute
con bygone, erstwhile, late, old, once, onetime, quondam, sometime, whilom
ant past

present *n* the present time <the course covers U.S. history from 1900 to the *present*>
syn now, today; *compare* FUTURE, PAST
idiom here and now, this day and age
ant past; future

presentable *adj* *syn* RESPECTABLE 5, decent, tolerable

present–day *adj* *syn* PRESENT, contemporary, current, existent, extant, instant, todayish

presenter *n* *syn* DONOR, bestower, conferrer, donator, giver

presentiment *n* *syn* APPREHENSION 3, apprehensiveness, foreboding, misgiving, premonition, prenotion, presage
rel discomposing, discomposure, disquietude, disturbance, perturbation

presently *adv* **1** without undue time lapse <the results will be evident *presently*>
syn anon, by and by, directly, shortly, soon
2 *syn* TODAY, now, nowadays

presentment *n* *syn* REPRESENTATION, delineation, depiction, description, picture, portraiture, portrayal

preserval *n* *syn* CONSERVATION 1, conservancy, husbanding, preservation, salvation, saving

preservation *n* **1** the act of preserving or the state of being preserved <the *preservation* of peace in the world>
syn conservation, keeping, safekeeping, salvation, saving, sustentation
rel defense, guard, protection, safeguard, shield; care, guardianship, ward
2 *syn* CONSERVATION 1, conservancy, husbanding, preserval, salvation, saving

preserve *vb* **1** *syn* SAVE 3, conserve
2 *syn* MAINTAIN 1, keep up, save, sustain

preserve *n* *syn* JAM, confiture, conserve

preside *vb* to occupy the place of authority (as in an assembly) <the chief justice *presides* over the supreme court> <the *presiding* elders of the church>
syn chair
rel carry on, conduct, control, direct, keep, manage, operate, ordain, run; administer, handle, head, oversee, supervise

press *n* *syn* CROWD 1, crush, drove, horde, multitude, push, squash, throng

press *vb* **1** to act upon through steady pushing or thrusting force exerted in contact <*pressed* his nose against the window>
syn bear, compress, constrain, crowd, crush, jam, ‖mash, push, ‖squab, squash, squeeze, squish, squush
rel propel, shove, thrust; drive, impel, move
2 *syn* DEPRESS 2, oppress, sadden, weigh down
3 to squeeze out the juice or contents of <*press* grapes>
syn crush, express
rel compress, squeeze
4 *syn* PUSH 2, bulldoze, elbow, hustle, jostle, ‖shog, shoulder, shove
5 *syn* PRESSURE, overpress, push
6 *syn* EMBRACE 1, clasp, ‖clinch, ‖clip, ‖coll, enfold, hug, squeeze
7 to crowd closely against or around someone or something <hundreds *pressed* around the performer after the show>
syn cram, crowd, crush, jam, squash, squeeze; *compare* CRAM 1
rel pack, ram, stuff, tamp; mass, pile; assemble, collect, congregate, gather
8 to force or push one's way (as through a crowd or against obstruction) <had to *press* through the traffic to get to the other side of town>
syn bear, squeeze
rel force, push, shove

press–agent *vb* *syn* PUBLICIZE, advertise, build up, cry, puff

press–agentry *n* *syn* PUBLICITY, advertising, buildup, promotion, puffery

pressing *adj* demanding or claiming especially immediate attention <he was barely able to pay his most *pressing* debts>
syn burning, clamant, clamorous, crying, dire, exigent, imperative, importunate, insistent, instant, urgent
rel direct, immediate; claiming, demanding, exacting, requiring; compelling, constraining, forcing, obliging; acute, critical, crucial

pressure *n* *syn* STRESS 1, strain, tension

pressure *vb* to insist upon unduly <*pressured* him into making the wrong move>
syn overpress, press, push
rel drive, impel; rush

prestige *n* **1** *syn* STATUS 2, cachet, consequence, dignity, position, rank, standing, state, stature
2 *syn* INFLUENCE 1, authority, credit, weight
rel power, sway
3 *syn* EMINENCE 1, distinction, illustriousness, kudos, preeminence, prominence, prominency, renown

prestigious *adj* *syn* FAMOUS 2, celebrated, distinguished, eminent, famed, great, illustrious, notable, prominent, renowned

presto *adv* *syn* FAST 2, chop-chop, expeditiously, flat-out, full tilt, hastily, lickety-split, posthaste, quickly, rapidly

presumably *adv* by reasonable assumption <*presumably* the best qualified for the job should get it>
syn assumably, doubtless, likely, presumptively, probably
con indubitably, surely, undoubtedly, unquestionably

presume *vb* **1** *syn* CONJECTURE, guess, pretend, suppose, surmise, think
2 *syn* PRESUPPOSE, assume, posit, postulate, premise
3 *syn* IMPOSE 5, infringe, intrude, obtrude

presuming *adj* *syn* PRESUMPTUOUS, brash, forward, overweening, pushful, pushing, self-asserting, self-assertive, uppish, uppity *ant* unassuming, unpresuming

presumption *n* **1** *syn* EFFRONTERY, brashness, brass, cheek, confidence, ‖crust, face, gall, nerve

2 *syn* PRESUPPOSITION 1, assumption

3 *syn* ASSUMPTION 2, apriorism, posit, postulate, postulation, premise, presupposition, supposition, thesis

presumptively *adv* *syn* PRESUMABLY, assumably, doubtless, likely, probably

presumptuous *adj* marked by or based on bold and excessive self-confidence <in such company his demand for attention was utterly *presumptuous*>

syn brash, brassbound, confident, forward, gay, overconfident, overweening, presuming, pushful, pushing, ‖pushy, self-asserting, self-assertive, uppish, uppity

rel pretentious, self-assured, self-conceited; lofty, pompous, supercilious; complacent, self-satisfied, smug; inexcusable, outrageous

idiom above one's britches

con deferential, dutiful, respectful, submissive; appropriate, proper

presuppose *vb* to take something for granted or as true or existent especially as a basis for action or reasoning <a lecturer who talks above the heads of his listeners *presupposes* too extensive a knowledge on their part>

syn assume, posit, postulate, premise, presume

rel conjecture, guess, surmise; deduce, infer, judge; believe, expect, gather, imagine, reckon, suppose, suspect, take, think, understand; preconceive

presupposition *n* **1** an act of presupposing <going on his *presupposition* that they would succeed>

syn assumption, presumption

rel conjecture, guess, surmise; deduction, inference, judgment; belief, conviction, opinion, view

2 *syn* ASSUMPTION 2, apriorism, posit, postulate, postulation, premise, presumption, supposition, thesis

pretend *vb* **1** *syn* ASSUME 4, act, affect, bluff, counterfeit, fake, feign, put on, sham, simulate

rel beguile, deceive, delude, mislead; profess, purport

idiom make believe

2 *syn* CONJECTURE, guess, presume, suppose, surmise, think

pretended *adj* *syn* ALLEGED, ostensible, professed, purported, so-called, supposed

pretender *n* *syn* IMPOSTOR, fake, faker, fraud, humbug, phony

pretense *n* **1** *syn* CLAIM 1, ‖dibs, pretension, title

2 the offering of something false as real or true <there is too much *pretense* in his piety>

syn charade, disguise, make-believe, pageant, pretension, pretentiousness

rel deceit, deception, fake, fraud, humbug, imposture, sham; affectation, air, mannerism, pose

con sincereness; reality, soundness, substantiality, validity; fairness, honesty

ant sincerity

3 *syn* MASK 2, cloak, color, coloring, cover, facade, face, false front, guise, masquerade

pretension *n* **1** *syn* CLAIM 1, ‖dibs, pretense, title

2 *syn* AMBITION 1, ambitiousness, aspiration

3 *syn* PRETENSE 2, charade, disguise, make-believe, pageant, pretentiousness

pretentious *adj* **1** *syn* SHOWY, chichi, flamboyant, orchidaceous, ostentatious, peacockish, peacocky, splashy, swank

ant unpretentious

2 *syn* GENTEEL 3, affected, la-di-da, ‖lardy-dardy, mincing, stilted, too-too

ant unpretentious

3 flamboyant, turgid, or bombastic in manner or content <a *pretentious* literary style>

syn arty, arty-crafty, big, high-sounding, imposing, overblown

rel affected, feigned, put-on; pompier; aureate, bombastic, euphuistic, flowery, grandiloquent, magniloquent, rhetorical; inflated, tumid, turgid

con heartfelt, hearty, sincere, unfeigned, wholehearted, whole-souled; artless, genuine, natural, simple, unaffected

ant unpretentious

4 *syn* AMBITIOUS 2, grandiose, lofty, utopian, visionary

pretentiousness *n* *syn* PRETENSE 2, charade, disguise, make-believe, pageant, pretension

ant unpretentiousness

preterition *n* *syn* OMISSION, blank, chasm, overlook, oversight, pretermission, skip

pretermission *n* *syn* OMISSION, blank, chasm, overlook, oversight, preterition, skip

pretermit *vb* *syn* NEGLECT, disregard, fail, forget, ignore, miss, omit, overlook, pass over, slight

preternatural *adj* **1** *syn* SUPERNATURAL 1, miraculous, numinous, superhuman, superior, supermundane, suprahuman, supramundane, supranatural, unearthly

rel anomalous, unnatural; nonnatural

2 *syn* ABNORMAL 1, aberrant, anomalous, atypical, deviant, deviative, heteroclite, unrepresentative, untypical

ant natural

pretext *n* **1** *syn* EXCUSE 1, alibi, plea, ‖right

2 *syn* MASK 2, cloak, color, coloring, cover, face, front, guise, masquerade, pretense

prettify *vb* *syn* PALLIATE, blanch (over), extenuate, gloss (over), gloze (over), sugarcoat, varnish, veneer, whiten, whitewash

pretty *adj* **1** *syn* SKILLFUL 2, adroit, clever, good, ‖skilly, wicked, workmanlike, workmanly

2 *syn* BEAUTIFUL, attractive, beauteous, ‖bonny, comely, fair, good-looking, handsome, lovely, pulchritudinous

rel darling, ducky; cunning, cute

ant unpretty

pretty *adv* *syn* SOMEWHAT 2, fairly, kind of, moderately, more or less, rather, ratherish, some, something, sort of

idiom pretty much

‖**pretty** *n* *syn* TOY 2, ‖die, ‖play-pretty, plaything

prettyism *n* *syn* POSE 2, affectation, air(s), lugs, mannerism

---

syn synonym(s) *rel* related word(s)
idiom idiomatic equivalent(s) *con* contrasted word(s)
ant antonym(s) * vulgar
‖ use limited; if in doubt, see a dictionary
The first word in a synonym list when printed in SMALL CAPITALS shows where there is more information about the group. For a more efficient use of this book see Explanatory Notes.

pretty–pretty *n* ***syn*** KNICKKNACK, bauble, bibelot, curio, dido, gewgaw, objet d'art, toy, trifle, trinket

preux *adj* ***syn*** COURTLY, gallant, gracious, stately

prevail *vb* **1** ***syn*** CONQUER 2, best, master, overcome, triumph
2 ***syn*** WIN 1, beat, overcome, triumph
3 ***syn*** RULE 2, dominate, domineer, predominate, preponderate, reign

prevail (on *or* upon) *vb* ***syn*** INDUCE 1, argue (into), bring around, convince, draw, get, persuade, prompt, talk (into), win (over)
rel affect, impress

prevailing *adj* general (as in circulation, acceptance, or use) in a given place or at a given time <the *prevailing* point of view among farmers>
syn current, popular, prevalent, rampant, regnant, rife, ruling, widespread
rel dominant, predominant, preponderant; common, familiar, ordinary; general, universal
con exceptional, uncommon, unusual

prevalent *adj* **1** ***syn*** DOMINANT 1, ascendant, master, overbearing, paramount, predominant, predominate, preponderant, regnant, sovereign
2 ***syn*** PREVAILING, current, popular, rampant, regnant, rife, ruling, widespread
3 ***syn*** GENERAL 1, common, commonplace, natural, normal, regular, run-of-the-mill, typic, typical, usual
rel accustomed, customary, wonted

prevaricate *vb* ***syn*** LIE, equivocate, falsify, fib, palter
rel belie, garble, misrepresent

prevarication *n* ***syn*** LIE, ‖bouncer, canard, falsehood, falsity, fib, misrepresentation, ‖rapper, story, tale

prevaricative *adj* ***syn*** EVASIVE 1, equivocating, prevaricatory, shifty, shuffling

prevaricator *n* ***syn*** LIAR, Ananias, falsifier, fibber, fibster, perjurer, storyteller

prevaricatory *adj* ***syn*** EVASIVE 1, equivocating, prevaricative, shifty, shuffling

prevent *vb* **1** to be or get ahead of or to deal with beforehand <many problems are *prevented* easily if one plans wisely>
syn anticipate, forestall
rel baffle, balk, foil, frustrate, thwart; arrest, check, interrupt
2 to stop from advancing or occurring <take steps to *prevent* war> <measures designed to *prevent* the spread of disease>
syn avert, deter, forestall, forfend, obviate, preclude, rule out, stave off, ward
rel bar, block, dam, hinder, impede, obstruct; debar, shut out; forbid, inhibit, interdict, prohibit
con allow, leave, let, suffer
ant permit

---

syn synonym(s) ***rel*** related word(s)
idiom idiomatic equivalent(s) ***con*** contrasted word(s)
ant antonym(s) * vulgar
‖ use limited; if in doubt, see a dictionary
The first word in a synonym list when printed in SMALL CAPITALS shows where there is more information about the group. For a more efficient use of this book see Explanatory Notes.

previous *adj* **1** ***syn*** PRECEDING, antecedent, anterior, foregoing, former, past, precedent, prior
ant subsequent; consequent
2 ***syn*** EARLY 2, overearly, oversoon, premature, ‖soon, untimely

previous *adv* ***syn*** BEFORE 1, ahead, ante, antecedently, beforehand, fore, forward, in advance, precedently

previously *adv* ***syn*** BEFORE 2, already, earlier, erstwhile, formerly, heretofore, once
ant subsequently; consequently

previousness *n* ***syn*** PRIORITY, antecedence, precedence, precedency

previse *vb* ***syn*** FORESEE, anticipate, apprehend, divine, forefeel, foreknow, preknow, prevision, see, visualize

prevision *n* ***syn*** PREDICTION, cast, forecast, foretelling, prognosis, prognostication, prophecy, weird

prevision *vb* ***syn*** FORESEE, anticipate, apprehend, divine, forefeel, foreknow, preknow, previse, see, visualize

prey *n* **1** ***syn*** GAME 3, chase, quarry
2 ***syn*** VICTIM 2, bottom dog, casualty, underdog

‖**pribble** *n* ***syn*** QUARREL, altercation, ‖barney, beef, bickering, controversy, dispute, falling-out, fracas, fuss

price *n* **1** the quantity of one thing that is exchanged or demanded in barter or sale for another <what is the *price* of this book>
syn charge, cost, price tag, rate, tab, tariff
2 ***syn*** EXPENSE 2, cost, toll

priceless *adj* ***syn*** PRECIOUS 1, costly, inestimable, invaluable, valuable
rel cherished, prized, treasured, valued
idiom without price

price tag *n* ***syn*** PRICE 1, charge, cost, rate, tab, tariff

prick *n* **1** a mark or shallow hole made by or as if by a pointed tool <a needle *prick* in his arm>
syn jab, ‖jag, puncture, stab
rel prickle; hole
‖**2** ***syn*** SNOT 1, ‖bugger, scum, *shit, *shithead, skunk, snake, stinker, toad, *turd

prick *vb* **1** ***syn*** PERFORATE, bore, drill, ‖pritch, punch, puncture
rel enter; cut, slash, slit
2 ***syn*** URGE, egg (on), exhort, goad, prod, prompt, propel, sic, spur
rel excite, pique, stimulate

‖**prick** (up) *vb* ***syn*** DRESS UP 1, deck (out), doll out, doll up, fix up, gussy up, primp, slick, smarten (up), spruce (up)

prickish *adj* ***syn*** IRRITABLE, fractious, fretful, peevish, pettish, petulant, prickly, snappish, snappy, waspish

prickly *adj* **1** ***syn*** THORNY, nettlesome, spiny
rel annoying, bothersome
2 ***syn*** IRRITABLE, fractious, fretful, peevish, pettish, petulant, prickish, snappish, twitty, waspish

pride *n* **1** ***syn*** CONCEIT 2, egoism, egotism, self-consequence, self-glory, self-importance, self-opinion, self-pride, swellheadedness, vainglory
rel bighead, cockiness, overconfidence, self-assurance
idiom overweening pride
ant humility
2 a reasonable or justifiable sense of one's worth or position <inhumane treatment in prison caused him to lose his *pride*>
syn amour propre, self-esteem, self-regard, self-respect

rel dignity, face, pridefulness, self-confidence, self-trust
con humiliation, mortification; shamefacedness
ant shame
3 proud or disdainful behavior or actions <her snobbishness and overbearing *pride* were offensive>
syn arrogance, disdain, disdainfulness, haughtiness, hauteur, loftiness, morgue, superbity, superciliousness
rel condescension, snobbishness; contempt, scorn; insolence; smugness; pretentiousness
idiom haughty airs
con humbleness, modesty, unpretentiousness
ant humility
4 ***syn*** BEST, choice, cream, elite, fat, flower, pick, prime, prize, top
idiom pride of the herd

pride *vb* to congratulate (oneself) for something one is, has, or has done or achieved <he *prides* himself on his ancestry>
syn pique, plume, preen
rel boast, brag, crow, gasconade, vaunt; congratulate, felicitate
ant efface

‖**pridy** *adj* ***syn*** PROUD 1, arrogant, cavalier, disdainful, haughty, high-and-mighty, insolent, overbearing, supercilious, superior

prier (*or* **pryer**) *n* ***syn*** BUSYBODY, butt-in, ‖buttinsky, intermeddler, meddler, Paul Pry, pragmatist, quidnunc, rubberneck, snoop

priestal *adj* ***syn*** SACERDOTAL, hieratic, priestish, priestlike, priestly, sacerdotical

priestish *adj* ***syn*** SACERDOTAL, hieratic, priestal, priestlike, priestly, sacerdotical

priestlike *adj* ***syn*** SACERDOTAL, hieratic, priestal, priestish, priestly, sacerdotical

priestly *adj* ***syn*** SACERDOTAL, hieratic, priestal, priestish, priestlike, sacerdotical

‖**prig** *vb* ***syn*** STEAL 1, ‖clout, ‖cly, ‖cop, filch, ‖heist, ‖nab, ‖nick, pilfer, thieve

prig *n* ***syn*** THIEF, filcher, larcener, larcenist, nimmer, pilferer, purloiner, stealer

prig *n* ***syn*** PRUDE, bluenose, comstock, goody-goody, Grundy, Mrs. Grundy, nice Nelly, puritan, ‖wowser

prig *adj* ***syn*** PRIM 1, genteel, priggish, prissy, prudish, puritanical, straitlaced, stuffy, tight-laced, Victorian

priggish *adj* **1** ***syn*** COMPLACENT, self-complacent, self-contented, self-pleased, self-satisfied, smug
rel self-righteous; self-esteeming, self-loving
2 ***syn*** PRIM 1, genteel, prig, prissy, prudish, puritanical, straitlaced, stuffy, tight-laced, Victorian

prim *adj* **1** excessively concerned with what one regards as proper or right <a *prim* woman, easily shocked by vulgar language>
syn bluenosed, genteel, missish, precise, prig, priggish, prissy, proper, prudish, puritanical, straitlaced, stuffy, tight-laced, Victorian; *compare* GENTEEL 3
rel correct, nice, precise; decorous; rigid, stiff, wooden; ceremonial, ceremonious, conventional, formal, straight
idiom prim and proper
con lax, loose, slack; easy, easygoing, free
2 ***syn*** NEAT 2, chipper, orderly, shipshape, snug, spick-and-span, tidy, trim, uncluttered, well-groomed

prima facie *adj* ***syn*** SELF-EVIDENT, self-evidencing

primarily *adv* **1** ***syn*** GENERALLY 1, chiefly, largely, mainly, mostly, overall, predominantly, principally
2 ***syn*** INITIALLY 1, originally, primitively

primary *adj* **1** ***syn*** FIRST 2, earliest, initial, maiden, original, pioneer, prime
2 ***syn*** PRIMITIVE 4, primeval, primevous, primitial
3 ***syn*** FUNDAMENTAL 1, basal, basic, bottom, foundational, radical, underlying
4 ***syn*** DIRECT 4, firsthand, immediate
5 not based on or derived from something else <the *primary* studies in nuclear physics>
syn original, prime, primitive, underivative, underived
rel first, firsthand; basic, foundational, fundamental, principal, underlying
con derivate, derivational, derivative, derived; borrowed, secondhand
ant secondary

prime *n* **1** ***syn*** MORNING 1, aurora, cockcrow, dawn, daybreak, dayspring, morn, sunrise, sunup
2 ***syn*** YOUTH 1, adolescence, greenness, juvenility, puberty, pubescence, spring, springtide, springtime, youthfulness
3 ***syn*** BEST, choice, cream, elite, fat, flower, pick, pride, prize, top

prime *adj* **1** ***syn*** FIRST 2, earliest, initial, maiden, original, pioneer, primary
2 ***syn*** EXCELLENT, capital, ‖dandy, famous, fine, first-class, first-rate, first-string, superior, top
3 ***syn*** PRIMARY 5, original, primitive, underivative, underived

prime *vb* ***syn*** PROVOKE 4, excite, galvanize, innervate, innerve, motivate, move, pique, quicken, stimulate

primeval *adj* ***syn*** PRIMITIVE 4, primary, primevous, primitial

primevous *adj* ***syn*** PRIMITIVE 4, primary, primeval, primitial

primitial *adj* ***syn*** PRIMITIVE 4, primary, primeval, primevous

primitive *adj* **1** ***syn*** PRIMARY 5, original, prime, underivative, underived
2 ***syn*** EARLY 1, primordial
3 closely approximating an early ancestral type <the opossums are *primitive* mammals>
syn archaic, persistent, undeveloped, unevolved
ant advanced
4 of or relating to earlier ages of the world or of human history <archaeology is concerned especially with the study of *primitive* man>
syn primary, primeval, primevous, primitial
ant unprimitive
5 ***syn*** ELEMENTAL 1, basic, elementary, essential, fundamental, substratal, underlying
6 characterized by a lack of written language, simple technology, and a relatively simple social organization
syn nonliterate, preliterate
rel barbarian, uncivilized, uncultivated

---

syn synonym(s) *rel* related word(s)
idiom idiomatic equivalent(s) *con* contrasted word(s)
ant antonym(s) * vulgar
‖ use limited; if in doubt, see a dictionary
The first word in a synonym list when printed in SMALL CAPITALS shows where there is more information about the group. For a more efficient use of this book see Explanatory Notes.

con advanced, civilized, cultivated

primitively *adv syn* INITIALLY 1, originally, primarily

primogenitor *n syn* ANCESTOR 1, antecedent (used in pl.), ascendant, forebear, forefather, progenitor

primordial *adj* **1** *syn* EARLY 1, primitive
2 *syn* FIRST, primary, prime

primp *vb syn* DRESS UP 1, deck (out), doll out, doll up, fix up, gussy up, slick, smarten (up), spiff, spruce (up)

primrose *n syn* BEST, choice, cream, elite, fat, flower, pick, prime, prize, top

prince *n syn* MAGNATE, baron, czar, king, merchant prince, mogul, tycoon

princely *adj syn* GRAND 1, august, baronial, grandiose, imposing, lordly, magnificent, noble, royal, stately

principal *adj* **1** *syn* CHIEF 2, capital, dominant, main, major, outstanding, predominant, preeminent, star, stellar
2 *syn* FIRST 3, arch, champion, chief, foremost, head, leading, premier

principally *adv syn* GENERALLY 1, chiefly, largely, mainly, mostly, overall, predominantly, primarily

principium *n syn* PRINCIPLE 1, axiom, fundamental, law, theorem

principle *n* **1** a comprehensive and fundamental rule, doctrine, or assumption <the *principle* of free speech>
syn axiom, fundamental, law, principium, theorem
rel basis, foundation, ground; canon, precept, rule; convention, form, usage
2 principles *pl syn* ETHIC 3
3 principles *pl syn* ALPHABET 2, ABC's, elements, fundamentals, grammar, rudiments

principled *adj syn* MORAL 1, ethical, moralistic, noble, righteous, right-minded, virtuous
ant unprincipled

‖**prink** *vb syn* SASHAY, flounce, mince, prance, strut

prink (up) *vb syn* DRESS UP 1, deck (out), doll out, doll up, fix up, gussy up, primp, smarten (up), spiff, spruce (up)

print *n* **1** *syn* IMPRESSION 1, impress, imprint, indentation, stamp
2 printed state or form <to see his name in *print*>
syn black and white, writing

printing *n syn* EDITION, impression, reissue, reprinting

prior *adj syn* PRECEDING, antecedent, anterior, foregoing, former, past, precedent, previous
rel ahead, before, forward
con after, behind

priority *n* the act, the fact, or the right of preceding another <the right to inherit a title is dependent mainly on *priority* of birth>
syn antecedence, precedence, precedency, previousness
rel arrangement, order, ordering; ascendancy, supremacy; preeminence, transcendence

---

syn synonym(s)	*rel* related word(s)
idiom idiomatic equivalent(s)	*con* contrasted word(s)
ant antonym(s)	* vulgar

‖ use limited; if in doubt, see a dictionary
The first word in a synonym list when printed in SMALL CAPITALS shows where there is more information about the group. For a more efficient use of this book see Explanatory Notes.

prior to *prep* **1** *syn* BEFORE 1, ahead of, ante, ere, in advance of, preceding, to
2 *syn* UNTIL, before, in advance of, till, to, up till, up to

prison *n syn* JAIL, ‖can, cooler, ‖hoosegow, keep, lockup, pen, penitentiary, reformatory, stockade

‖**prison** *vb syn* IMPRISON, bastille, confine, constrain, immure, incarcerate, intern, jail, jug, ‖quod

prison bird *n syn* CONVICT, ‖con, jailbird, ‖lag, loser

prissy *adj* **1** *syn* PRIM 1, genteel, missish, priggish, prudish, puritanical, straitlaced, stuffy, tight-laced, Victorian
rel fastidious, finicky, squeamish
2 *syn* EFFEMINATE, epicene, Miss-Nancyish, pansified, sissified, sissy, unmanly

‖**pritch** *vb syn* PERFORATE, bore, drill, prick, punch, puncture

private *adj* **1** belonging to or concerning an individual person, company, or interest <*private* property>
syn personal, privy
rel intimate
con common, general, shared
ant public
2 known only to a select few <the group had *private* information about the strike>
syn closet, confidential, hushed, inside
rel secret; discreet; concealed, hidden
con common, general, open
ant public

private detective *n* a person concerned with the maintenance of lawful conduct or the investigation of crime either as a regular employee of a private interest (as a hotel) or as a contractor for fees <obtained a *private detective* to report on his wife's associates>
syn operative, Pinkerton, ‖private eye, ‖shamus; *compare* DETECTIVE

‖**private eye** *n syn* PRIVATE DETECTIVE, operative, Pinkerton, ‖shamus

privately *adv syn* SECRETLY, by stealth, clandestinely, covertly, furtively, hugger-mugger, in camera, stealthily, sub rosa, surreptitiously

private parts *n pl syn* GENITALIA, genitals, parts, privates, privities, privy parts, pudendum (*usu* pudenda *pl*), secrets

privates *n pl syn* GENITALIA, genitals, parts, private parts, privities, privy parts, pudendum (*usu* pudenda *pl*), secrets

privation *n* **1** *syn* ABSENCE, dearth, default, defect, lack, ‖miss, want
2 the state of one deprived of something previously or normally possessed <suffered great *privation* during the famine>
syn deprivation, deprivement, dispossession, divestiture, loss; *compare* LOSS 1
rel distress, misery, suffering; losing, mislaying, misplacement, misplacing
3 *syn* POVERTY 1, destitution, impecuniousness, impoverishment, indigence, need, neediness, penury, poorness, want

privilege *n syn* RIGHT 2, appanage, birthright, perquisite, prerogative
rel allowance, concession; boon, favor

privilege (from) *vb syn* EXEMPT, absolve, discharge, dispense, excuse, let off, relieve, spare

privities *n pl syn* GENITALIA, genitals, parts, private parts, privates, privy parts, pudendum (*usu* pudenda *pl*), secrets

privy *adj* **1** *syn* PRIVATE 1, personal
2 *syn* ULTERIOR, buried, concealed, covert, hidden, obscured, shrouded

privy *n* **1** an outdoor toilet <in less settled areas, *privies* often take the place of indoor plumbing>
syn backhouse, ||biffy, ||closet, *crapper, jakes, ||necessary, ||office, outhouse
2 *syn* TOILET, ||can, convenience, ||donicker, head, john, johnny, latrine, lavatory, water closet

privy parts *n pl syn* GENITALIA, genitals, parts, private parts, privates, privities, pudendum (*usu* pudenda *pl*), secrets

prize *n* **1** *syn* REWARD, carrot, dividend, guerdon, meed, plum, premium
2 *syn* BEST, choice, cream, elite, fat, flower, pick, pride, prime, top

prize *vb syn* APPRECIATE 1, apprize, cherish, esteem, treasure, value

prize *n syn* SPOIL, boodle, booty, loot, plunder, plunderage, ||spreaghery, ||spulzie, swag

prize *vb syn* PRY, jimmy, lever

prizefighting *n syn* BOXING, fisticuffs, pugilism, ring

pro *prep syn* FOR 2, in favor of, with
ant anti, con

pro *n syn* EXPERT, adept, authority, doyen, master, master-hand, professional, proficient, whiz, wiz

pro and con *vb syn* DISCUSS 1, agitate, argue, canvass, debate, discept, dispute, ||kick around, thrash out, toss (around)

probable *adj* being such as may become true or actual <seems to be a *probable* candidate>
syn conceivable, earthly, likely, mortal, possible
rel believable, colorable, credible, plausible; rational, reasonable; apparent, illusory, ostensible, seeming
con doubtful, dubious, questionable, unlikely
ant improbable, unprobable

probably *adv syn* PRESUMABLY, assumably, doubtless, likely, presumptively
ant improbably

probe *n syn* INQUIRY 1, delving, inquest, inquisition, investigation, probing, quest, research

probe *vb* **1** *syn* EXPLORE, delve (into), dig (into), go (into), inquire (into), investigate, look (into), prospect, sift
2 to try to find out (as by discreet questioning) the views or intentions of <*probed* the neighbors on the subject of political reform>
syn feel out, sound (out)
rel ask, catechize, examine, inquire, interrogate, query, quiz
idiom feel the pulse, put out a feeler, see how the land lies, see which way the wind blows
3 *syn* SCOUT, reconnoiter

probing *n syn* INQUIRY 1, delving, inquest, inquisition, investigation, probe, quest, research

probity *n syn* GOODNESS, morality, rectitude, righteousness, rightness, uprightness, virtue

problem *n* **1** *syn* EXAMPLE 3, ensample, illustration
2 something requiring thought and skill to arrive at a proper conclusion or decision <what to do now is a *problem*>
syn issue, nut, question
rel enigma, mystery, puzzle; bugaboo, bugbear; count, point
idiom a hard nut to crack

problematic *adj* **1** *syn* DOUBTFUL 1, ambiguous, dubious, dubitable, indecisive, open, precarious, suspect, uncertain, unsettled
ant unproblematic
2 *syn* MOOT, arguable, debatable, disputable, doubtful, dubious, mootable, questionable, uncertain
ant unproblematic

proboscis *n syn* NOSE 1, beak, ||beezer, ||boko, ||conk, ||schnozzle, smeller, ||sneezer, snoot, snout

procacious *adj* **1** *syn* INSOLENT 2, audacious, bold, ||boldacious, brazen, contumelious, impertinent, impudent, saucy
2 *syn* WISE 5, ||biggety, bold, cheeky, forward, fresh, impudent, nervy, pert, smart

procedure *n* **1** *syn* COURSE 3, line, policy, polity, program
2 *syn* MEASURE 7, maneuver, move, proceeding, step
3 *syn* PROCESS 1, proceeding

proceed *vb* **1** *syn* SPRING 1, arise, derive (from), emanate, flow, head, issue, originate, rise, stem
2 *syn* GO 1, fare, hie, journey, pass, ||process, push on, repair, travel, wend
3 *syn* ADVANCE 5, get along, get on, march, move, progress
ant recede

proceeding *n* **1** *syn* MEASURE 7, maneuver, move, procedure, step
2 *syn* PROCESS 1, procedure

proceeds *n pl syn* PROFIT, earnings, gain, lucre, return

process *n* **1** the series of actions, operations, or motions involved in the accomplishment of an end <the *process* of making sugar from sugarcane>
syn procedure, proceeding
rel fashion, manner, method, mode, modus, system, technique, way, wise; routine; operation
2 *syn* OUTGROWTH 1, excrescence, excrescency, processus

||**process** *vb syn* GO 1, ||cruise, fare, hie, journey, pass, proceed, push on, repair, travel

procession *n syn* ORDER 5, consecution, sequence, succession

processus *n syn* OUTGROWTH 1, excrescence, excrescency, process

proclaim *vb* **1** *syn* DECLARE 1, advertise, announce, annunciate, blaze (abroad), broadcast, bruit (about), disseminate, promulgate, publish
rel utter, vent, ventilate, voice
2 *syn* SHOW 2, demonstrate, evidence, evince, exhibit, illustrate, manifest, mark, ostend

---

syn synonym(s) — *rel* related word(s)
idiom idiomatic equivalent(s) — *con* contrasted word(s)
ant antonym(s) — * vulgar
|| use limited; if in doubt, see a dictionary
The first word in a synonym list when printed in SMALL CAPITALS shows where there is more information about the group. For a more efficient use of this book see Explanatory Notes.

proclamation *n* ***syn*** DECLARATION, advertisement, announcement, broadcast, promulgation, pronouncement, pronunciamento, publication

proclivity *n* ***syn*** LEANING 2, bent, disposition, inclination, inclining, penchant, predilection, predisposition, propensity, tendency

procrastinate *vb* ***syn*** DELAY 2, dally, dawdle, drag, lag, linger, loiter, poke, put off, tarry
rel defer, postpone, stay, suspend; prolong, protract

procreate *vb* **1** to produce offspring <*procreate* children>
syn bear, beget, breed, generate, multiply, produce, propagate, reproduce
rel mother; engender; hatch, spawn; proliferate
idiom give birth to, multiply the earth
2 ***syn*** GENERATE 1, create, father, hatch, make, originate, parent, produce, sire, spawn
3 ***syn*** FATHER 1, beget, breed, get, progenerate, sire

procumbent *adj* ***syn*** PRONE 4, decumbent, flat, prostrate, reclining, recumbent

procurable *adj* ***syn*** AVAILABLE 1, attainable, disponible, gettable, obtainable, securable

procure *vb* **1** ***syn*** GET 1, acquire, annex, compass, gain, have, land, obtain, pick up, secure
2 ***syn*** INDUCE 1, argue (into), bring around, convince, draw, draw in, draw on, persuade, prevail (on *or* upon), win (over)

prod *vb* **1** ***syn*** POKE 1, dig, jab, jog, nudge, punch
2 ***syn*** URGE, egg (on), exhort, goad, prick, prompt, propel, sic, spur
rel instigate; excite, pique, provoke, stimulate

prodigal *adj* ***syn*** PROFUSE, exuberant, lavish, lush, luxuriant, opulent, profusive, riotous
ant parsimonious

prodigal *n* ***syn*** SPENDTHRIFT, high roller, profligate, scattergood, spender, squanderer, unthrift, waster, wastethrift, wastrel

prodigality *n* ***syn*** EXTRAVAGANCE 2, extravagancy, lavishness, overdoing, squander, unthrift, waste, wastefulness
ant parsimoniousness

prodigalize *vb* ***syn*** WASTE 2, blow, blunder (away), dissipate, drivel, fool (away), fritter, frivol away, muddle away, squander

prodigious *adj* **1** ***syn*** MARVELOUS 1, amazing, astonishing, astounding, miraculous, spectacular, staggering, stupendous, surprising, wonderful
2 ***syn*** MONSTROUS 1, cracking, fantastic, massive, monumental, mortal, stupendous, towering, tremendous
3 ***syn*** HUGE, colossal, enormous, gigantic, immense, mammoth, massive, mighty, tremendous, vast

prodigy *n* ***syn*** WONDER 1, marvel, miracle, phenomenon, portent, sensation, stunner

syn synonym(s) ***rel*** related word(s)
idiom idiomatic equivalent(s) ***con*** contrasted word(s)
ant antonym(s) * vulgar
‖ use limited; if in doubt, see a dictionary
The first word in a synonym list when printed in SMALL CAPITALS shows where there is more information about the group. For a more efficient use of this book see Explanatory Notes.

produce *vb* **1** ***syn*** PROCREATE 1, bear, beget, breed, generate, multiply, propagate, reproduce
2 ***syn*** STAGE, mount, put on, show
3 ***syn*** EFFECT 1, bring about, cause, draw on, make, secure
4 ***syn*** GENERATE 1, create, father, hatch, make, originate, parent, procreate, sire, spawn
5 ***syn*** GENERATE 3, breed, cause, engender, get up, hatch, induce, muster (up), occasion, work up
6 ***syn*** MAKE 3, build, construct, erect, fabricate, fashion, form, frame, manufacture, put together
7 ***syn*** BEAR 9, turn out, yield
8 ***syn*** GIVE 7, yield
9 ***syn*** GROW 1, breed, cultivate, propagate, raise

produce *n* ***syn*** PRODUCT 1, production

product *n* **1** something produced by physical labor or intellectual effort <the literary *products* of the Age of Reason>
syn produce, production
rel handiwork; consequence, effect, offshoot, outcome, outgrowth, result; fruit, harvest
2 ***syn*** OUTPUT, outturn, production, turnout, yield

production *n* **1** ***syn*** PRODUCT 1, produce
2 ***syn*** EXTENSION 1, elongation, lengthening, prolongation, prolongment, protraction
3 ***syn*** OUTPUT, outturn, product, turnout, yield

productive *adj* ***syn*** FERTILE, childing, fecund, fruitful, proliferant, prolific, rich, spawning
ant unproductive

proem *n* ***syn*** INTRODUCTION, exordium, foreword, overture, preamble, preface, prelude, prelusion, prolegomenon, prologue

proemial *adj* ***syn*** PRELIMINARY, inductive, introductory, prefatial, prefatorial, prefatory, ‖prelim, preludial, prelusive, preparatory

profanation *n* a violation or misuse of something normally held sacred <the *profanation* of a religious ritual>
syn blasphemy, desecration, sacrilege, violation
rel contamination, defilement, pollution; corruption, debasement, perversion, vitiation; transgression, trespass
con glorification, hallowing, sanctification
ant purification; consecration

profane *adj* **1** not concerned with religion or religious purposes <he was speaking of *profane* history, not the history found in the Bible>
syn lay, secular, temporal, unsacred
rel earthly, mundane, terrestrial, worldly
con consecrated, hallowed, holy, sanctified; divine, religious, spiritual
ant sacred
2 ***syn*** HEATHEN, ethnic, gentile, infidel, infidelic, pagan
3 ***syn*** IMPIOUS 1, irreverent, irreverential, ungodly, unhallowed, unholy
4 ***syn*** SACRILEGIOUS, blasphemous
5 ***syn*** OBSCENE 2, coarse, dirty, filthy, foul, indecent, nasty, raunchy, smutty, vulgar

profaned *adj* ***syn*** IMPURE 3, common, defiled, desecrated, polluted, unclean
ant unprofaned

profanity *n* ***syn*** BLASPHEMY 1, cursing, cussing, execration, imprecation, swearing

profess *vb* ***syn*** ASSERT 1, affirm, aver, avouch, avow, constate, declare, depose, predicate, protest

professed *adj* ***syn*** ALLEGED, ostensible, pretended, purported, so-called, supposed

professedly *adv* ***syn*** OSTENSIBLY, apparently, evidently, officially, outwardly, seemingly

profession *n* ***syn*** TRADE 1, art, calling, craft, handicraft, métier, vocation

professional *n* ***syn*** EXPERT, adept, artist, artiste, authority, master, past master, proficient, virtuoso, whiz
ant amateur

proffer *vb* ***syn*** OFFER 1, extend, give, hold out, pose, present, tender

proffer *n* ***syn*** PROPOSAL, invitation, proposition, suggestion

proficiency *n* ***syn*** ADVANCE 2, advancement, anabasis, headway, march, ongoing, progress

proficient *adj* having or manifesting the knowledge, skill, and experience needed for sucess in a particular field or endeavor <a *proficient* glider pilot>
syn adept, crack, crackerjack, expert, master, masterful, masterly, skilled, skillful; *compare* EXPERIENCED, SKILLFUL 2
rel checked-out, drilled, exercised, practiced; effective, effectual, efficient; able, capable, competent, qualified; accomplished, consummate, finished
con ignorant, untaught, untrained; inexperienced; unskilled
ant incompetent

proficient *n* ***syn*** EXPERT, adept, artist, artiste, authority, master, past master, professional, virtuoso, whiz

profile *n* ***syn*** OUTLINE, contour, delineation, figuration, line, lineament, lineation, silhouette

profit *n* the excess of returns over expenditure in a transaction or a series of transactions <his *profits* from the business venture were rewarding>
syn earnings, gain, lucre, proceeds, return
rel cleaning, cleanup, killing; receipt(s); output, outturn, product, production, turnout, yield
con cost, expenditure, expense, outgo
ant loss

profit *vb* ***syn*** BENEFIT, advantage, avail, serve, work (for)
ant lose

profitable *adj* ***syn*** ADVANTAGEOUS 1, gainful, good, lucrative, moneymaking, paying, remunerative, well-paying, worthwhile
ant profitless, unprofitable

profligate *adj* ***syn*** ABANDONED 2, dissolute, licentious, reprobate, self-abandoned, unprincipled

profligate *n* **1** ***syn*** WASTREL 1, ‖bad lot, good-for-nothing, ne'er-do-well, no-good, rounder, scapegrace, waster
2 ***syn*** SPENDTHRIFT, high roller, prodigal, scattergood, spender, squanderer, unthrift, waster, wastethrift, wastrel

profound *adj* **1** ***syn*** RECONDITE, abstruse, acroamatic, deep, esoteric, heavy, hermetic, occult, orphic, secret
2 ***syn*** DEEP 1, abysmal
3 ***syn*** INTENSIVE, blood-and-guts, deep, hard, intense

profoundness *n* ***syn*** DEPTH 2, abyss, deepness, profundity

profundity *n* ***syn*** DEPTH 2, abyss, deepness, profoundness

profuse *adj* proffered in or characterized by great abundance <*profuse* apologies> <a *profuse* flow of blood>
syn exuberant, lavish, lush, luxuriant, opulent, prodigal, profusive, riotous
rel abundant, copious; abounding, swarming, teeming; excessive, extravagant, immoderate; bounteous, bountiful, generous, liberal, munificent, openhanded
con exiguous, meager, scrimpy, skimpy, slight, small, sparse
ant scant, scanty

profusive *adj* ***syn*** PROFUSE, exuberant, lavish, lush, luxuriant, opulent, prodigal, riotous

progenerate *vb* ***syn*** FATHER 1, beget, breed, get, procreate, sire

progenitor *n* ***syn*** ANCESTOR 1, antecedent (used in pl.), ascendant, forebear, forefather, primogenitor

progeniture *n* ***syn*** OFFSPRING, ‖begats, brood, children, descendants, issue, posterity, progeny, scions, seed

progeny *n* ***syn*** OFFSPRING, ‖begats, brood, children, descendants, issue, posterity, progeniture, scions, seed

prognosis *n* ***syn*** PREDICTION, cast, forecast, foretelling, prevision, prognostication, prophecy, weird

prognostic *n* ***syn*** FORETOKEN, augury, bodement, boding, omen, portent, presage

prognosticate *vb* ***syn*** FORETELL, adumbrate, augur, forecast, portend, predict, presage, prophesy, soothsay, vaticinate

prognostication *n* ***syn*** PREDICTION, cast, forecast, foretelling, prevision, prognosis, prophecy, weird

prognosticator *n* ***syn*** PROPHET, augur, auspex, forecaster, foreseer, foreteller, haruspex, Nostradamus, predictor, prophesier

program *n* **1** a formulated plan listing things to be done or to take place especially in their time order <the *program* of a concert>
syn agenda, calendar, card, docket, programma, schedule, sked, timetable
rel bill; slate; plan
idiom order of the day
2 ***syn*** COURSE 3, line, policy, polity, procedure

programma *n* ***syn*** PROGRAM 1, agenda, calendar, card, docket, schedule, sked, timetable

progress *n* **1** ***syn*** ADVANCE 2, advancement, anabasis, headway, march, ongoing, proficiency
ant regression, retrogression
2 a movement onward (as in time or space) <the *progress* of a disease> <they made slow *progress* toward their destination>
syn advance, course, progression
rel passage
3 ***syn*** DEVELOPMENT, evolution, evolvement, flowering, growth, progression, unfolding, upgrowth

progress *vb* ***syn*** ADVANCE 5, get along, get on, march, move, proceed

---

syn synonym(s) | ***rel*** related word(s)
idiom idiomatic equivalent(s) | ***con*** contrasted word(s)
ant antonym(s) | * vulgar
‖ use limited; if in doubt, see a dictionary
The first word in a synonym list when printed in SMALL CAPITALS shows where there is more information about the group. For a more efficient use of this book see Explanatory Notes.

ant retrogress

progression *n* **1** ***syn*** PROGRESS 2, advance, course
2 ***syn*** SUCCESSION 2, alternation, chain, consecution, order, row, sequel, sequence, series, train
3 ***syn*** DEVELOPMENT, evolution, evolvement, flowering, growth, progress, unfolding, upgrowth
ant regression, retrogression

progressive *adj* ***syn*** LIBERAL 3, advanced, broad, broad-minded, radical, tolerant, wide
ant reactionary

prohibit *vb* ***syn*** FORBID, ban, enjoin, inhibit, interdict, outlaw, taboo
ant permit

prohibited *adj* ***syn*** FORBIDDEN, banned, verboten

prohibition *n* ***syn*** TABOO, ban, forbiddance, interdiction, proscription
ant permission

project *n* **1** ***syn*** PLAN 1, blueprint, design, game plan, scheme, strategy
2 something (as a business operation) that one engages in or attempts <large-scale *projects* involving large sums of money>
syn enterprise, undertaking
rel affair, business, concern, matter, proposition, thing; adventure, emprise, exploit, feat, gest, venture

project *vb* **1** ***syn*** PLAN 2, arrange, blueprint, cast, chart, design, devise, ‖dope out
rel intend, propose, purpose; delineate, diagram
2 ***syn*** THINK 1, conceive, envisage, envision, feature, image, imagine, see, vision, visualize
‖**3** ***syn*** WANDER 1, circumambulate, drift, meander, mooch, ramble, range, rove, straggle, stray
4 ***syn*** BULGE, beetle, jut, overhang, poke, pouch, pout, protrude, stand out, stick out
rel extend, lengthen, prolong

projection *n* **1** something which extends beyond a level or a normal outer surface <buttresses are *projections* which serve to support a wall>
syn bulge, jut, outthrust, protrusion, protuberance
rel bump, bunch, swelling; extension, prolongation; hook, knob, point, spine, spur
ant depression
2 ***syn*** EMINENCE 3, prominence

prolegomenon *n* ***syn*** INTRODUCTION, exordium, foreword, overture, preamble, preface, prelude, prelusion, proem, prologue

proletariat *n* ***syn*** RABBLE 2, canaille, dreg(s), mass(es), mob, ragtag and bobtail, riffraff, scum, trash, unwashed

proliferant *adj* ***syn*** FERTILE, childing, fecund, fruitful, productive, prolific, rich, spawning

prolific *adj* ***syn*** FERTILE, childing, fecund, fruitful, productive, proliferant, rich, spawning
rel abounding, swarming; breeding, generating, propagating, reproducing, reproductive
ant barren, unfruitful

prolificacy *n* ***syn*** FERTILITY, fecundity, fruitfulness
ant barrenness, unfruitfulness

prolix *adj* ***syn*** WORDY, diffuse, long-winded, palaverous, redundant, verbose, windy
rel irksome, tedious, tiresome, wearisome; prolonged, protracted

prolixity *n* ***syn*** VERBOSITY, prolixness, verbalism, verboseness, windiness, wordiness

prolixness *n* ***syn*** VERBOSITY, prolixity, verbalism, verboseness, windiness, wordiness

prologue *n* ***syn*** INTRODUCTION, exordium, foreword, overture, preamble, preface, prelude, prelusion, proem, prolegomenon
ant epilogue

prolong *vb* ***syn*** EXTEND 3, draw, draw out, elongate, lengthen, prolongate, protract, spin (out), stretch
rel continue, endure, last, persist
con abbreviate, retrench, shorten
ant curtail

prolongate *vb* ***syn*** EXTEND 3, draw, draw out, elongate, lengthen, prolong, protract, spin (out), stretch

prolongation *n* ***syn*** EXTENSION 1, elongation, lengthening, production, prolongment, protraction

prolonged *adj* ***syn*** LONG 2, dragging, drawn-out, ‖dreich, lengthy, long-drawn-out, longsome, overlong, protracted
ant curtailed

prolongment *n* ***syn*** EXTENSION 1, elongation, lengthening, production, prolongation, protraction

prominence *n* **1** ***syn*** EMINENCE 1, distinction, illustriousness, kudos, preeminence, prestige, prominency, renown
2 ***syn*** EMINENCE 3, projection

prominency *n* ***syn*** EMINENCE 1, distinction, illustriousness, kudos, preeminence, prestige, prominence, renown

prominent *adj* **1** ***syn*** NOTICEABLE, arresting, arrestive, conspicuous, marked, outstanding, remarkable, salient, signal, striking
ant inconspicuous
2 ***syn*** FAMOUS 2, celebrated, celebrious, distinguished, eminent, famed, great, illustrious, notable, renowned
3 ***syn*** WELL-KNOWN, famous, leading, noted, notorious, popular

promiscuous *adj* **1** ***syn*** MISCELLANEOUS, assorted, chowchow, conglomerate, heterogeneous, indiscriminate, mixed, motley, multifarious, varied
2 ***syn*** RANDOM, aimless, designless, desultory, haphazard, hit-or-miss, indiscriminate, irregular, purposeless, unplanned

promise *vb* **1** to give one's word to do, bring about, or provide <*promised* to render all possible assistance to the flood victims>
syn engage, pass, pledge, undertake; *compare* VOW
rel accede, agree, assent, consent; bargain, compact, contract; covenant, plight, swear, vow; assure, ensure, insure; guarantee
idiom give (*or* make) a promise, pass one's word
2 ***syn*** AUGUR 2, betoken, bode, forebode, foreshadow, foreshow, foretoken, omen, portend, presage

---

syn synonym(s) — *rel* related word(s)
idiom idiomatic equivalent(s) — *con* contrasted word(s)
ant antonym(s) — * vulgar
‖ use limited; if in doubt, see a dictionary
The first word in a synonym list when printed in SMALL CAPITALS shows where there is more information about the group. For a more efficient use of this book see Explanatory Notes.

promise *n* a declaration that one will do or refrain from doing something specified <never gave a *promise* that he did not intend to keep>
syn engagement, plight, word; *compare* PLEDGE 1, WORD 8
rel earnest, guarantee, pawn, pledge, security, token; covenant, swear, vow; assurance, warrant
idiom word of honor

‖**promised** *adj* ***syn*** ENGAGED 2, affianced, betrothed, contracted, intended, plighted

promised land *n* ***syn*** UTOPIA, arcadia, Cockaigne, fairyland, heaven, lubberland, paradise, Shangri-la, wonderland, Zion

promiseful *adj* ***syn*** HOPEFUL 2, couleur de rose, encouraging, likely, promising, roseate, rose-colored, rosy

promising *adj* ***syn*** HOPEFUL 2, couleur de rose, encouraging, likely, promiseful, roseate, rose-colored, rosy
ant unpromising

promontory *n* a high point of land or rock projecting into a body of water beyond the line of coast <stood on the *promontory* watching boats come in with the tide>
syn beak, bill, cape, foreland, head, headland, naze, point

promote *vb* **1** ***syn*** ADVANCE 2, elevate, prefer, upgrade
con break, bust, declass, degrade, demerit, disgrade, disrate, downgrade, reduce
ant bump, demote
2 ***syn*** ADVANCE 1, encourage, forward, foster, further, serve
3 to encourage public acceptance of (as a policy or merchandise) through publicity <official attempts to *promote* energy conservation> <television helped *promote* the new smaller cars>
syn advertise, boost, plug, push; *compare* PUBLICIZE
rel ballyhoo, propagandize; build up, cry, press-agent, publicize, puff; communicate, impart
idiom make much of
con belittle, decry, depreciate, discredit, knock, run down
ant disparage

promotion *n* **1** ***syn*** ADVANCEMENT 1, elevation, preference, preferment, prelation, upgrading
ant demotion
2 ***syn*** PUBLICITY, advertising, buildup, press-agentry, puffery
rel advertisement

prompt *vb* **1** ***syn*** INDUCE 1, argue (into), bring around, convince, draw, get, persuade, prevail (on *or* upon), talk (into), win (over)
2 ***syn*** URGE, egg (on), exhort, goad, prick, prod, propel, sic, spur

prompt *adj* **1** ***syn*** QUICK 2, apt, ready
rel alert, vigilant, watchful, wide-awake; expeditious, speedy, swift
con lax, remiss, slack; dilatory
2 ***syn*** PUNCTUAL 2, timely

promptitude *n* ***syn*** ALACRITY, dispatch, expedition, goodwill, readiness

promptly *adv* ***syn*** FAST 2, expeditiously, flat-out, fleetly, hastily, lickety-split, posthaste, quickly, rapidly, swiftly

promulgate *vb* ***syn*** DECLARE 1, advertise, announce, annunciate, broadcast, disseminate, proclaim, publish, sound, toot

promulgation *n* ***syn*** DECLARATION, advertisement, announcement, broadcast, proclamation, pronouncement, pronunciamento, publication

prone *adj* **1** ***syn*** WILLING 1, disposed, fain, inclined, minded, predisposed, ready
2 ***syn*** LIABLE 2, exposed, obnoxious, open, sensitive, subject, susceptible
3 ***syn*** APT 1, given, inclined, liable, likely
4 lying down <lying *prone* on the floor>
syn decumbent, flat, procumbent, prostrate, reclining, recumbent
rel resupine, supine; level
con arrect, raised, stand-up, straight-up, upright, upstanding
ant erect

pronounce *vb* ***syn*** ARTICULATE 2, enunciate, phonate, say

pronounced *adj* ***syn*** DECIDED 1, assured, clear-cut, definite

pronouncement *n* ***syn*** DECLARATION, advertisement, announcement, broadcast, proclamation, promulgation, pronunciamento, publication

‖**pronto** *adv* ***syn*** FAST 2, flat-out, full tilt, hastily, lickety-split, posthaste, promptly, quickly, rapidly, speedily

pronunciamento *n* ***syn*** DECLARATION, advertisement, announcement, broadcast, proclamation, promulgation, pronouncement, publication

proof *n* **1** ***syn*** REASON 3, argument, ground, wherefore, why, whyfor
2 ***syn*** TESTIMONY, attestation, confirmation, evidence, testament, testimonial, witness

prop *n* ***syn*** SUPPORT 3, brace, buttress, column, shore, stay, underpinner, underpinning, underpropping

prop *vb* **1** ***syn*** SUPPORT 4, bear up, bolster, brace, buttress, carry, shore (up), sustain, upbear, uphold
2 ***syn*** SUPPORT 5, bolster, buoy (up), sustain, underprop, uphold

propagandist *n* ***syn*** MISSIONARY, apostle, colporteur, evangelist, missioner

propagate *vb* **1** ***syn*** PROCREATE 1, bear, beget, breed, generate, multiply, produce, reproduce
2 ***syn*** GROW 1, breed, cultivate, produce, raise
3 ***syn*** SPREAD 1, circulate, diffuse, disperse, disseminate, distribute, radiate, strew

propel *vb* **1** ***syn*** PUSH 1, drive, shove, thrust
2 ***syn*** MOVE 5, actuate, drive, impel, mobilize
3 ***syn*** URGE, egg (on), exhort, goad, prick, prod, prompt, sic, spur

propellant *n* ***syn*** STIMULUS, catalyst, impetus, impulse, incentive, incitation, motivation, provocative, spur, stimulant

propensity *n* ***syn*** LEANING 2, bent, disposition, inclination, inclining, penchant, predilection, predisposition, proclivity, tendency

---

ant antipathy

proper *adj* **1** *syn* FIT 1, applicable, appropriate, apt, felicitous, fitting, happy, just, meet, suitable
ant improper
2 *syn* TRUE 7, appropriate, desired, fitting
ant improper
3 *syn* DECOROUS 1, becoming, befitting, comely, comme il faut, conforming, correct, decent, nice, right
ant improper
4 *syn* ABLE, au fait, capable, competent, good, qualified, wicked
5 *syn* GOOD 2, appropriate, convenient, fit, meet, suitable, useful
ant improper
6 *syn* CHARACTERISTIC, diacritic, diagnostic, distinctive, idiosyncratic, individual, peculiar
‖**7** *syn* UTTER, absolute, arrant, blamed, complete, confounded, consummate, crashing, infernal, out-and-out
8 *syn* CORRECT 2, accurate, exact, nice, precise, right, rigorous
9 *syn* PRIM 1, genteel, missish, prig, priggish, prissy, prudish, puritanical, straitlaced, stuffy

properly *adv* **1** *syn* WELL 4, acceptably, adequately, amply, appropriately, becomingly, fittingly, right, satisfactorily, suitably
ant improperly
2 *syn* WELL 1, befittingly, correctly, decently, decorously, fitly, fittingly, justly, nicely, rightly
idiom by rights
ant improperly

properness *n* *syn* ORDER 7, correctitude, correctness, decorousness, decorum, orderliness, propriety, seemliness
ant improperness

property *n* **1** *syn* QUALITY 1, affection, attribute, character, characteristic, feature, mark, peculiarity, trait, virtue
2 *syn* WEALTH 2, fortune, resources, riches, substance, worth
3 *syn* OWNERSHIP, dominion, possession, possessorship, proprietary, proprietorship

prophecy *n* **1** *syn* REVELATION, apocalypse, oracle, vision
2 *syn* PREDICTION, cast, forecast, foretelling, prevision, prognosis, prognostication, weird

prophesier *n* *syn* PROPHET, augur, auspex, forecaster, foreseer, foreteller, haruspex, Nostradamus, predictor, prognosticator

prophesy *vb* *syn* FORETELL, adumbrate, augur, forecast, portend, predict, presage, prognosticate, soothsay, vaticinate

prophet *n* one who predicts events or developments <there have been many *prophets* foretelling the end of the world>
syn augur, auspex, forecaster, foreseer, foreteller, haruspex, Nostradamus, predictor, prognosticator, prophesier, seer, soothsayer

prophetic *adj* of, relating to, or characteristic of a prophet or prophecy <the old woman seemed to have *prophetic* powers>
syn apocalyptic, Delphian, fatidic, mantic, oracular, prophetical, sibylline, vatic, vaticinal
rel revelatory; interpretive; mysterious, mystic, strange, unexplainable
ant unprophetic

prophetical *adj* *syn* PROPHETIC, apocalyptic, Delphian, fatidic, mantic, oracular, sibylline, vatic, vaticinal

propinquity *n* *syn* PROXIMITY, appropinquity, contiguity, contiguousness, immediacy

propitiate *vb* *syn* PACIFY, appease, assuage, conciliate, mollify, placate, sweeten
rel adapt, adjust, conform, reconcile; content, satisfy; intercede, mediate

propitiatory *adj* *syn* PURGATIVE, expiative, expiatory, expurgatorial, expurgatory, lustral, lustratory, purgatorial

propitious *adj* **1** *syn* FAVORABLE 5, auspicious, benign, bright, dexter, fortunate, white
ant unpropitious; adverse
2 *syn* TIMELY 1, auspicious, favorable, opportune, prosperous, seasonable, timeous, well-timed
ant unpropitious
3 *syn* GOOD 1, advantageous, benefic, beneficial, brave, favorable, favoring, helpful, toward, useful
ant unpropitious; adverse

‖**propone** *vb* *syn* PROPOSE 1, pose, prefer, proposition, propound, put, suggest

proponent *n* *syn* EXPONENT, advocate, champion, expounder, supporter
ant opponent

proportion *n* **1** *syn* DEGREE 2, rate, ratio, scale
2 *syn* SYMMETRY, balance, harmony
ant disproportion
3 *syn* SIZE 1, admeasurement, dimension(s), dimensionality, extent, magnitude, measure

proportion *vb* *syn* HARMONIZE 3, accommodate, attune, conform, coordinate, integrate, reconcile, reconciliate, tune

proportional *adj* being in proportion <his weight is *proportional* to his size>
syn commensurable, commensurate, equal, symmetrical
rel correlative, corresponding, reciprocal; contingent, dependent, relative
con asymmetrical, disproportionate, irregular, lopsided, nonsymmetrical, off-balance, overbalanced, unbalanced, unequal, uneven, unsymmetrical
ant disproportional

proportionless *adj* *syn* LOPSIDED, asymmetric, difform, disproportional, disproportionate, nonsymmetrical, unequal, uneven, unproportionate, unsymmetrical

proposal *n* something which is proposed to another for consideration <his *proposal* for a new bussing plan>
syn invitation, proffer, proposition, suggestion
rel motion; recommendation; idea, plan, project; outline, scheme

propose *vb* **1** to set before the mind for consideration <he *proposed* Mr. Smith for secretary of the club>

---

syn synonym(s) — *rel* related word(s)
idiom idiomatic equivalent(s) — *con* contrasted word(s)
ant antonym(s) — * vulgar
‖ use limited; if in doubt, see a dictionary
The first word in a synonym list when printed in SMALL CAPITALS shows where there is more information about the group. For a more efficient use of this book see Explanatory Notes.

syn pose, prefer, ‖propone, proposition, propound, put, suggest
rel move (for); offer, present, submit, tender; ask, request, solicit
idiom put forth (*or* forward)
ant withdraw
2 ***syn*** INTEND 2, aim, contemplate, design, mean, ‖mind, plan, purpose

proposition *n* ***syn*** PROPOSAL, invitation, proffer, suggestion

proposition *vb* ***syn*** PROPOSE 1, pose, prefer, ‖propone, propound, put, suggest

propound *vb* ***syn*** PROPOSE 1, pose, prefer, ‖propone, proposition, put, suggest

proprietary *n* ***syn*** OWNERSHIP, dominion, possession, possessorship, property, proprietorship

proprietor *n* ***syn*** OWNER, holder, possessor

proprietorship *n* ***syn*** OWNERSHIP, dominion, possession, possessorship, property, proprietary

propriety *n* **1** ***syn*** ORDER 11, appositeness, appropriateness, aptness, expediency, fitness, meetness, rightness, suitability, suitableness
2 ***syn*** DECORUM 1, decency, dignity, etiquette, seemliness
ant impropriety
3 ***syn*** ORDER 7, correctitude, correctness, decorousness, decorum, orderliness, properness, seemliness
ant impropriety
4 proprieties *pl* ***syn*** MANNER 5, amenities, civilities, decorum(s), etiquette, mores

prorate *vb* ***syn*** APPORTION 2, divide, ‖divvy, parcel, portion, quota, ration, share, ‖shift

prorogate *vb* ***syn*** ADJOURN 2, dissolve, prorogue, recess, rise, terminate

prorogue *vb* **1** ***syn*** DEFER, delay, hold off, hold over, hold up, postpone, put off, remit, shelve, stay
2 ***syn*** ADJOURN 2, dissolve, prorogate, recess, rise, terminate

prosaic *adj* **1** belonging to or characteristic of prose as distinguished from poetry <his poetry is far more fanciful than his *prosaic* writings>
syn matter-of-fact, prose, prosing, prosy
rel actual, factual; literal
con figurative, metaphorical, symbolic; fanciful, florid, flowery, ornate
ant poetic
2 ***syn*** COLORLESS 2, drab, dull, flat, lackluster, lifeless, lusterless, prosy
3 belonging to or suitable to the everyday world <the *prosaic* business of day-to-day housekeeping>
syn commonplace, everyday, lowly, mundane, workaday, workday
rel practicable, practical; boring, irksome, tedious
4 ***syn*** COMMON 6, commonplace, ordinary, uneventful, unexceptional, unnoteworthy

prosaicism *n* ***syn*** COMMONPLACE, banality, bromide, cliché, platitude, prosaism, rubber stamp, shibboleth, tag, truism

prosaism *n* ***syn*** COMMONPLACE, banality, bromide, cliché, platitude, prosaicism, rubber stamp, shibboleth, tag, truism

proscribe *vb* ***syn*** SENTENCE, condemn, damn, doom

proscription *n* ***syn*** TABOO, ban, forbiddance, interdiction, prohibition

prose *n* ***syn*** CHAT 2, causerie, chin, rap, talk, yarn

prose *adj* ***syn*** PROSAIC 1, matter-of-fact, prosing, prosy

prosing *adj* ***syn*** PROSAIC 1, matter-of-fact, prose, prosy

prospect *n* ***syn*** VISTA, lookout, outlook, perspective, scape

prospect *vb* ***syn*** EXPLORE, delve (into), dig (into), go (into), inquire (into), investigate, look (into), probe, sift

prosper *vb* ***syn*** SUCCEED 3, arrive, flourish, go, make out, score, thrive
rel augment, increase, multiply; bear, produce, turn out, yield

prospering *adj* ***syn*** FLOURISHING, booming, prosperous, roaring, robust, thrifty, thriving

prosperity *n* **1** ***syn*** SUCCESS, arrival, ‖do, flying colors, go, successfulness
2 a state of good fortune and especially of financial success <his wise investments finally brought him a life of *prosperity*>
syn abundance, ease, easy street, prosperousness, thriving, well-being
rel affluence, riches, wealth
idiom bed of roses, comfortable (*or* easy) circumstances, life of ease, the good life
con misery, suffering; distress, embarrassment, indigence, poverty, straits
ant adversity
3 ***syn*** WELFARE, advantage, benefit, good, interest, well-being
4 a state of high general economic activity marked by relatively full employment <a war economy often generates *prosperity*>
syn boom, prosperousness
rel expansion; growth; inflation
con recession, slump, stagnation; bust
ant depression

prosperous *adj* **1** ***syn*** TIMELY 1, auspicious, favorable, opportune, propitious, seasonable, timeous, well-timed
rel appropriate, convenient, desirable; felicitous, fortunate, happy, lucky
con ill-seasoned, ill-timed, inauspicious, inopportune, unpropitious, unseasonable, untimely
ant unprosperous
2 ***syn*** SUCCESSFUL, thriving
3 enjoying or marked by economic well-being <in *prosperous* circumstances>
syn comfortable, easy, ‖snug, substantial, well, well-fixed, well-heeled, well-off, well-to-do
rel affluent, opulent, rich, wealthy; halcyon
idiom comfortably off, comfortably situated, in (the) clover, in good case
con impecunious, necessitous, needy, poor; failing, unfortunate, unsuccessful
ant unprosperous

---

syn synonym(s) *rel* related word(s)
idiom idiomatic equivalent(s) *con* contrasted word(s)
ant antonym(s) * vulgar
‖ use limited; if in doubt, see a dictionary
The first word in a synonym list when printed in SMALL CAPITALS shows where there is more information about the group. For a more efficient use of this book see Explanatory Notes.

4 *syn* FLOURISHING, booming, prospering, roaring, robust, thrifty, thriving
rel lusty, strong
con decrepit, feeble, spindling, weak

prosperously *adv* *syn* WELL 5, favorably, fortunately, happily, satisfyingly, successfully, swimmingly
ant unprosperously

prosperousness *n* 1 *syn* PROSPERITY 2, abundance, ease, easy street, thriving, well-being
ant unprosperousness
2 *syn* PROSPERITY 4, boom

prostitute *vb* *syn* ABUSE 2, misapply, misemploy, mishandle, misimprove, misuse, pervert
rel corrupt, debase, debauch, deprave, vitiate

prostitute *n* a woman who engages in promiscuous sexual intercourse especially for money <streets haunted by *prostitutes*>
syn bawd, ‖callet, call girl, camp follower, cocotte, ‖cruiser, drab, fille de joie, harlot, ‖hooker, hustler, ‖joy girl, meretrix, moll, nightwalker, party girl, pom-pom girl, poule, quean, sporting girl, street girl, streetwalker, ‖tomato, whore; *compare* DOXY, HARLOT 1, WANTON
rel bar girl, B-girl, pickup; V-girl, victory girl; cocodette
idiom lady of pleasure, lady of the evening, woman of the street (*or* streets), woman of the town

prostitution *n* the act or practice of engaging in promiscuous sexual intercourse especially for money <the problem of *prostitution* around military installations>
syn harlotry, oldest profession, (the) social evil, streetwalking, whoredom

prostrate *adj* *syn* PRONE 4, decumbent, flat, procumbent, reclining, recumbent

prostrate *vb* 1 *syn* FELL 1, bowl (down *or* over), down, drop, floor, ground, lay low, level, mow (down), throw down
2 *syn* PARALYZE 1, cripple, disable, disarm, immobilize, incapacitate
3 *syn* OVERWHELM 4, drown, knock over, overcome, overpower, whelm
4 *syn* EXHAUST 4, ‖bugger, fag, frazzle, knock out, outtire, outwear, ‖poop, tucker, wear out

prosy *adj* 1 *syn* PROSAIC 1, matter-of-fact, prose, prosing
2 *syn* COLORLESS 2, drab, dull, flat, lackluster, lifeless, lusterless, prosaic

protean *adj* *syn* CHANGEABLE 1, changeful, fluid, mobile, mutable, unsettled, unstable, unsteady, variable, weathery

protect *vb* *syn* DEFEND 1, bulwark, cover, fend, guard, safeguard, screen, secure, shield
rel conserve, preserve, save; harbor, shelter

protection *n* 1 *syn* DEFENSE 1, aegis, armament, armor, guard, safeguard, security, shield, ward
2 money paid under threat of depredation <offered *protection* to keep his store from being vandalized>
syn ‖pad
rel extortion, shakedown, squeeze; graft; bribe

pro tem *adj* *syn* TEMPORARY, acting, ad interim, interim, pro tempore, supply

pro tempore *adj* *syn* TEMPORARY, acting, ad interim, interim, pro tem, supply

protest *n* *syn* DEMUR 2, challenge, demurral, demurrer, difficulty, objection, question, remonstrance, remonstration

protest *vb* 1 *syn* ASSERT 1, affirm, aver, avouch, avow, constate, declare, depose, predicate, profess
2 *syn* OBJECT 1, except, expostulate, inveigh (against), kick, remonstrate
rel demonstrate; combat, fight, oppose, resist
ant agree

protoplast *n* *syn* ORIGINAL 1, archetype, prototype

prototypal *adj* *syn* TYPICAL 1, classic, classical, exemplary, ideal, model, paradigmatic, prototypical, quintessential, representative

prototype *n* 1 *syn* ORIGINAL 1, archetype, protoplast
2 *syn* FORERUNNER 2, ancestor, antecedent, antecessor, foregoer, precursor, predecessor

prototypical *adj* *syn* TYPICAL 1, archetypal, classic, classical, exemplary, ideal, model, prototypal, quintessential, representative

protract *vb* *syn* EXTEND 3, draw, draw out, elongate, lengthen, prolong, prolongate, spin (out), stretch
ant curtail

protracted *adj* *syn* LONG 2, dragging, drawn-out, ‖dreich, lengthy, long-drawn-out, longsome, overlong, prolonged
ant curtailed

protraction *n* *syn* EXTENSION 1, elongation, lengthening, production, prolongation, prolongment
rel dallying, dawdling, delay, lag; stay, suspension
ant curtailment

protrude *vb* *syn* BULGE, beetle, jut, overhang, poke, pouch, pout, project, stand out, stick out

protrusion *n* *syn* PROJECTION 1, bulge, jut, outthrust, protuberance

protuberance *n* *syn* PROJECTION 1, bulge, jut, outthrust, protrusion

protuberate *vb* *syn* BULGE, beetle, jut, poke, pouch, pout, project, protrude, stand out, stick out

proud *adj* 1 showing or feeling superiority toward others <a woman who was too *proud* to do her share of menial tasks>
syn arrogant, cavalier, disdainful, dismissive, haughty, high-and-mighty, hubristic, huffy, insolent, lofty, lordly, orgulous, overbearing, ‖pridy, proudhearted, supercilious, superior, toploftical, toplofty; *compare* POMPOUS 1, VAIN 3
rel contemptuous, scornful; misproud; ostentatious, pretentious; bloated, important, pompous, self-important, stuffy, wiggy; conceited, narcissistic, self-conceited, stuck-up, vain, vainglorious; domineering, high-handed, imperious, masterful
con lowly, meek, modest, unassuming; chagrined, mortified

---

syn synonym(s) *rel* related word(s)
idiom idiomatic equivalent(s) *con* contrasted word(s)
ant antonym(s) * vulgar
‖ use limited; if in doubt, see a dictionary
The first word in a synonym list when printed in SMALL CAPITALS shows where there is more information about the group. For a more efficient use of this book see Explanatory Notes.

ant humble
2 *syn* SPLENDID 2, glorious, gorgeous, magnificent, resplendent, splendiferous, splendorous, sublime, superb

proudhearted *adj syn* PROUD 1, arrogant, cavalier, disdainful, haughty, high-and-mighty, insolent, overbearing, supercilious, superior

prove *vb* **1** to establish a point by appropriate objective means <gathered evidence that *proved* the need for better controls>
syn demonstrate, test, try
rel confirm, corroborate, substantiate, verify; argue, attest, bespeak, betoken, indicate
ant disprove; refute
2 *syn* TRY 1, check, examine, test
3 *syn* ESTABLISH 6, demonstrate, determine, make out, show

provenance *n syn* SOURCE, derivation, fountain, inception, origin, provenience, root, well, wellspring, whence

provender *n syn* FOOD 1, ‖chow, comestibles, edibles, feed, grub, nurture, provisions, viands, victuals

provenience *n syn* SOURCE, derivation, fountain, inception, origin, provenance, root, well, wellspring, whence

prove out *vb syn* SUCCEED 2, click, come off, go, go over, pan out

proverb *n syn* SAYING, adage, byword, saw, word

provide *vb syn* GIVE 3, deliver, dispense, feed, furnish, hand, hand over, supply, transfer, turn over

provide (for) *vb syn* SUPPORT 3, maintain

providence *n* **1** *syn* ECONOMY, forehandedness, frugality, husbandry, prudence, thrift, thriftiness
ant improvidence
2 *syn* PRUDENCE 1, canniness, caution, discreetness, discretion, foresight, forethought, precaution
ant improvidence

provident *adj syn* SPARING, canny, chary, economical, frugal, saving, Scotch, stewardly, thrifty, unwasteful
ant improvident

providential *adj syn* LUCKY, fortunate, happy, ‖sonsy, well
rel benignant, kind, kindly

province *n* **1** *syn* FUNCTION 1, business, duty, office, role
rel calling, pursuit, work
2 *syn* FIELD, bailiwick, champaign, demesne, domain, dominion, sphere, terrain, territory, walk

provincial *n syn* RUSTIC, ‖backwoodser, backwoodsman, bucolic, bumpkin, clown, hayseed, hick, jake, peasant

provincial *adj* **1** *syn* RURAL, agrestic, bucolic, campestral, countrified, country, out-country, outland, pastoral, rustic
2 *syn* INSULAR, local, ‖parish-pump, parochial, sectarian, small-town
rel bigoted, hidebound
con cosmic, universal; progressive
ant catholic

provision *n syn* CONDITION 1, proviso, reservation, stipulation, strings, terms

provisional *adj* **1** *syn* CONDITIONAL 1, provisionary, provisory, tentative
rel temporary; contingent, dependent
ant definitive
2 *syn* MAKESHIFT, rough-and-ready, rough-and-tumble, stopgap

provisionary *adj syn* CONDITIONAL 1, provisional, provisory, tentative

provisions *n pl syn* FOOD 1, comestibles, ‖eats, edibles, feed, grub, nurture, provender, viands, victuals

proviso *n syn* CONDITION 1, provision, reservation, stipulation, strings, terms

provisory *adj syn* CONDITIONAL 1, provisional, provisionary, tentative

provocation *n syn* ANNOYANCE 1, bothering, harassment, irking, provoking, vexation, vexing

provocative *n syn* STIMULUS, goad, impetus, impulse, incentive, incitation, incitement, motivation, push, spur

provoke *vb* **1** *syn* IRRITATE, aggravate, gall, get, grate, inflame, pique, put out, rile, roil
rel insult, outrage
ant gratify
2 *syn* ANNOY 1, abrade, bother, ‖bug, chafe, exercise, fret, gall, irk, ruffle
rel anger, incense, madden
3 *syn* INCITE, abet, foment, instigate, raise, set, set on, stir (up), whip (up)
rel perturb, upset
4 to lead one into doing or feeling or to produce by so leading a person <was *provoked* into finding a solution to the problem> <this foolish answer *provoked* an outburst of rage>
syn excite, galvanize, innervate, innerve, motivate, move, pique, prime, quicken, rouse, ‖roust, stimulate, suscitate; *compare* FIRE 2, STIR 1
rel arouse, awaken, bestir, build up, challenge, kindle, rally, stir, wake, waken, whet; animate, exalt, fire, inform, inspire; electrify, enthuse, thrill; titillate, titivate
idiom bring (one) to one's feet
con calm, relax, soothe
5 *syn* GENERATE 3, breed, cause, engender, get up, hatch, induce, muster (up), occasion, produce

provoking *n syn* ANNOYANCE 1, bothering, harassment, irking, provocation, vexation, vexing

prowess *n* **1** *syn* HEROISM, gallantry, valiance, valiancy, valor, valorousness
2 *syn* ADDRESS 1, adroitness, deftness, dexterity, dexterousness, readiness, skill, sleight

proximate *adj* **1** *syn* CLOSE 6, immediate, near, near-at-hand, nearby, nigh
2 *syn* IMMINENT 1, impending
3 *syn* RUDE 3, approximate, rough
ant exact

proximity *n* the quality or state of being near <the two houses are in close *proximity*>
syn appropinquity, contiguity, contiguousness, immediacy, propinquity

---

syn synonym(s)	*rel* related word(s)
idiom idiomatic equivalent(s)	*con* contrasted word(s)
ant antonym(s)	* vulgar

‖ use limited; if in doubt, see a dictionary
The first word in a synonym list when printed in SMALL CAPITALS shows where there is more information about the group. For a more efficient use of this book see Explanatory Notes.

rel togetherness; closeness, nearness; adjacency, juxtaposition
con farness, remoteness
ant distance

proxy *n syn* AGENT 2, assignee, attorney, deputy, factor

prude *n* a person who is excessively or priggishly attentive to propriety or decorum <in that narrow atmosphere she hardened into a rigid, inhibited, censorious person—a thorough *prude*>
syn bluenose, comstock, goody-goody, Grundy, Mrs. Grundy, nice Nelly, prig, puritan, ‖wowser
rel spoilsport, stick-in-the-mud, wet blanket; fuddy-duddy, old fogy, stuffed shirt; fussbudget, old maid
con freethinker, latitudinarian, libertarian

prudence *n* **1** a quality in a person that allows him to choose the sensible course <displayed *prudence* in setting up his business>
syn canniness, caution, discreetness, discretion, foresight, forethought, precaution, providence; *compare* WIT 3
rel acumen, astucity, astuteness, clear-sightedness, discrimination, keenness, penetration, percipience, perspicacity, shrewdness, wit; insight, sagaciousness, sagacity, sageness, sapience, wisdom; advisableness, expediency; calculation, circumspection
con indiscretion, unreasonableness, unwiseness
ant imprudence
2 *syn* ECONOMY, forehandedness, frugality, husbandry, providence, thrift, thriftiness

prudent *adj* **1** *syn* WISE 2, judgmatic, judicious, sage, sane, sapient, sensible
ant imprudent
2 *syn* EXPEDIENT, advisable, politic, tactical, wise

prudish *adj syn* PRIM 1, genteel, priggish, prissy, proper, puritanical, straitlaced, stuffy, tight-laced, Victorian
rel strict; austere, severe, stern

prune *n syn* DUNCE, blockhead, chump, dimwit, dolt, dope, dumbbell, idiot, ignoramus, moron

prune *vb syn* CUT 6, clip, crop, pare, shave, shear, skive, trim
rel brash, lop; thin; eliminate, exclude

prurience *n syn* LUST 2, aphrodisia, concupiscence, desire, eroticism, itch, lickerishness, lustfulness, passion, pruriency

pruriency *n syn* LUST 2, aphrodisia, concupiscence, desire, eroticism, itch, lickerishness, lustfulness, passion, prurience

prurient *adj syn* LUSTFUL 2, concupiscent, goatish, *horny, hot, lascivious, libidinous, lickerish, passionate, satyric
rel bawdy, erotic, lewd; sensual

pry *vb syn* SNOOP, busybody, mouse, nose, ‖piroot, poke, ‖snook
idiom nose into

pry *vb* to raise, move, or pull apart with or as if with a pry <*pry* up a floorboard>
syn jimmy, lever, prize
rel elevate, hoist, lift, pick up, raise, rear, take up, uphold, uplift, upraise, uprear; turn, twist; disengage, disjoin, divide, separate

prying *adj syn* CURIOUS 2, inquisitive, inquisitorial, inquisitory, ‖nibby, nosy, peery, snoopy
rel obtrusive, officious

psalm *vb syn* PRAISE 2, celebrate, cry up, eulogize, extol, glorify, hymn, laud, magnify, psalmody

psalmody *vb syn* PRAISE 2, celebrate, cry up, eulogize, extol, glorify, hymn, laud, magnify, psalm

pseudo *adj syn* COUNTERFEIT, bogus, brummagem, fake, false, phony, pinchbeck, sham, snide, spurious
rel wrong

pseudonym *n* a fictitious or assumed name <used a *pseudonym* in many of his adventures>
syn alias, anonym, nom de guerre
rel ananym; nom de plume, pen name; stage name; incognito

psychal *adj syn* PSYCHIC 1, psychical, supersensible, supersensory

psyche *n syn* SOUL 1, anima, animus, élan vital, pneuma, spirit, vital force

psychic *adj* **1** sensitive to nonphysical forces and influences <because he foretold many things correctly, people regarded him as *psychic*>
syn psychal, psychical, supersensible, supersensory
rel telepathic; spiritual; impressible, impressionable, responsive, sensible, sensile, sensitive, sentient, susceptible, susceptive
2 *syn* MENTAL 1, cerebral, intellective, intellectual, psychical, psychological

psychical *adj* **1** *syn* PSYCHIC 1, psychal, supersensible, supersensory
2 *syn* MENTAL 1, cerebral, intellective, intellectual, psychic, psychological

psychological *adj syn* MENTAL 1, cerebral, intellective, intellectual, psychic, psychical

psychopathy *n syn* INSANITY 1, aberration, alienation, derangement, distraction, insaneness, lunacy, madness, unbalance

pub *n syn* BAR 5, barroom, drinkery, ‖groggery, ‖grogshop, pothouse, ‖public house, rummery, taproom, tavern

puberty *n syn* YOUTH 1, adolescence, greenness, juvenility, pubescence, spring, springtide, springtime, youthfulness, youthhood

pubescence *n syn* YOUTH 1, adolescence, greenness, juvenility, puberty, spring, springtide, springtime, youthfulness, youthhood

public *adj* **1** of, relating to, or affecting the people as an organized community <*public* affairs>
syn civic, civil, national
rel government, governmental; community; state; municipal, urban
2 *syn* OPEN 4, accessible, open-door, unrestricted
rel common, general, universal
con private
3 *syn* COMMON 1, communal, conjoint, conjunct, intermutual, joint, mutual, shared

con private
4 held by or applicable to the majority of the people <*public* opinion>
syn general, popular, vulgar
rel prevalent, usual, widespread
ant private

public *n* **1** *syn* SOCIETY 3, community, people
2 *syn* FOLLOWING 2, audience, clientage, clientele
rel hangers-on, suite

‖**publican** *n syn* SALOONKEEPER, barkeeper, boniface, innholder, innkeeper, saloonist, taverner

publication *n syn* DECLARATION, advertisement, announcement, broadcast, proclamation, promulgation, pronouncement, pronunciamento
rel dissemination

public house *n* **1** *syn* HOTEL, auberge, caravansary, hospice, hostel, hostelry, inn, lodge, roadhouse, tavern
‖**2** *syn* BAR 5, barroom, drinkery, ‖groggery, ‖grogshop, pothouse, pub, rummery, taproom, tavern

publicity *n* information with news value issued to gain public attention or support <$100,000 was allocated for new-product *publicity*>
syn advertising, buildup, press-agentry, promotion, puffery
rel broadcasting, promulgation, skywriting; réclame; announcement, write-up; blurb, commercial, plug, puff; ballyhoo, hoopla; propaganda; hard sell

publicize *vb* to give publicity to <*publicize* a new book>
syn advertise, build up, cry, press-agent, puff; *compare* PROMOTE 3
rel announce, broadcast, headline, promulgate, skywrite; advance, boost, plug, push; extol; bruit, tout, trumpet; propagandize
idiom bring into the limelight, throw the spotlight on

publish *vb* **1** *syn* DECLARE 1, advertise, announce, annunciate, blaze (abroad), broadcast, disseminate, proclaim, promulgate, toot
rel broach, express, utter, vent, ventilate
idiom bring to public notice, lay before the public, publish (*or* noise *or* spread) abroad, put forth
2 to produce for publication and allow to be distributed and sold <*published* a newspaper>
syn get out, issue, put out
rel produce; bring out; market; distribute

puckfist *n syn* BRAGGART, blower, blowhard, boaster, braggadocio, bragger, ‖gasbag, rodomont, rodomontade, vaunter

puckish *adj syn* PLAYFUL 1, antic, impish, larkish, mischievous, prankish, roguish, sportive, waggish, wicked

‖**pudding** *n, usu* **puddings** *pl syn* ENTRAILS, gut(s), innards, insides, internals, inwards, stuffing, tripes, viscera

puddle *n syn* POOL

puddle *vb syn* FIDDLE 2, doodle, mess, mess around, potter, putter, tinker

puddy *adj syn* ROTUND 2, chubby, plump, plumpish, plumpy, podgy, pudgy, roly-poly, spuddy, tubby

pudendum *n, usu* **pudenda** *pl syn* GENITALIA, genitals, parts, private parts, privates, privities, privy parts, secrets

pudgy *adj syn* ROTUND 2, chubby, plump, plumpish, plumpy, podgy, roly-poly, round, roundabout, tubby
rel ‖chuffy, ‖chumpy, squab, squdgy, ‖stuggy, stumpy, thick-bodied

puerile *adj syn* CHILDISH, babyish, immature, infantile, infantine, prekindergarten

puff *vb* **1** *syn* PANT 1, blow, gasp, heave, huff, ‖pank, ‖pegh
idiom huff and puff, pant and blow
2 *syn* BOAST, blow, brag, cock-a-doodle-doo, crow, gasconade, mouth, prate, rodomontade, vaunt
3 *syn* PUBLICIZE, advertise, build up, cry, press-agent

puff *n* **1** *syn* DRAW 1, drag, pull
rel inhalation, inhaling
2 *syn* QUILT, ‖comfortable, comforter, pouf
3 a commendatory and often extravagant publicity notice or review <this book fails to deliver what the *puff* promises>
syn blurb, plug, puffing, write-up
rel boost, buildup, push; laudation, praise

puffery *n syn* PUBLICITY, advertising, buildup, press-agentry, promotion

puffing *n syn* PUFF 3, blurb, plug, write-up

puffy *adj syn* POMPOUS 1, arrogant, bloated, important, magisterial, pontifical, self-important, stuffy, wiggy

‖**puggy** *adj syn* SWEATY, asweat, perspiring, perspiry, sweatful, sweating

pugilism *n syn* BOXING, fisticuffs, prizefighting, ring

pugnacious *adj syn* BELLIGERENT, bellicose, combative, contentious, gladiatorial, militant, quarrelsome, scrappy, truculent, warlike
rel pushing, pushy, self-assertive; defiant, rebellious; brawling
idiom itching for a fight, itching (*or* ready) to fight, ready to fight at the drop of a hat
con bland, easygoing, mild; calm, peaceful; quiet
ant pacific

pugnacity *n syn* ATTACK 2, aggression, aggressiveness, belligerence, combativeness, fight

puissance *n syn* POWER 4, energy, force, might, muscle, potency, sinew, strength, vigor, virtue
rel clout, influence, sway
con powerlessness, weakness
ant impuissance

puissant *adj syn* POWERFUL 2, forceful, forcible, mighty, potent
rel influential; commanding, ruling
con ineffectual, inefficacious, powerless
ant impuissant

***puke** *vb syn* VOMIT, barf, ‖cack, ‖cascade, ‖cast, ‖cat, ‖heave, shoot, spit up, upchuck

puke *n syn* SNOT 1, louse, ‖prick, scum, *shit, *shithead, stinkard, stinkaroo, *turd, wretch

pukka *adj syn* AUTHENTIC 2, bona fide, genuine, indubitable, questionless, real, right, simon-pure, sure-enough, true

---

syn synonym(s) *rel* related word(s)
idiom idiomatic equivalent(s) *con* contrasted word(s)
ant antonym(s) * vulgar
‖ use limited; if in doubt, see a dictionary
The first word in a synonym list when printed in SMALL CAPITALS shows where there is more information about the group. For a more efficient use of this book see Explanatory Notes.

pulchritudinous *adj* ***syn*** BEAUTIFUL, attractive, beauteous, ||bonny, comely, fair, good-looking, handsome, lovely, pretty

pule *vb* ***syn*** WHIMPER, whine

pull *vb* **1** ***syn*** EXTRACT 1, evulse, tear, yank
2 to cause to move toward or after an applied force <*pull* a trunk across the floor>
syn drag, draw, haul, lug, tow, tug
rel strain; heave; jerk, wrench, yank; drive, impel, push, shove
3 ***syn*** STRAIN 2
4 ***syn*** ROW, oar, paddle
idiom pull on the oar (*or* oars)
5 ***syn*** COMMIT 2, perpetrate
idiom ||go and do
6 ***syn*** DON 2, assume, put on, strike, take on
7 ***syn*** GET 1, chalk up, gain, have, land, obtain, pick up, procure, secure, win

pull *n* **1** ***syn*** DRAW 1, drag, puff
2 the power or ability to secure special favor or partiality <had lots of *pull* with the government>
syn clout, ||drag, in, influence; *compare* INFLUENCE 1
rel persuasion; wire-pulling
idiom backstairs influence
3 ***syn*** ATTRACTION 1, allurement, appeal, attractiveness, call, draw, drawing power, lure, seduction

pullback *n* ***syn*** DIEHARD 1, bitter-ender, conservative, fundamentalist, old liner, rightist, right-winger, standpat, standpatter, tory

pull down *vb* ***syn*** DESTROY 1, annihilate, decimate, demolish, destruct, dismantle, raze, ruin, tear down, wreck

pull in *vb* **1** ***syn*** RESTRAIN 1, bit, bridle, check, constrain, curb, hold back, hold down, hold in, inhibit
2 ***syn*** ARREST 2, apprehend, ||bust, detain, nab, pick up, pinch, run in

pull out *vb* ***syn*** GO 2, depart, exit, get off, leave, quit, retire, shove (off), take off, withdraw
ant pull in

pull through *vb* ***syn*** SURVIVE 2, come through, ride (out)

pullulate *vb* ***syn*** TEEM, abound, crawl, flow, ||sny, swarm

pull up *vb* ***syn*** STOP 4, bring up, draw up, fetch up, halt, haul up

pulp *vb* ***syn*** CRUSH 2, becrush, bruise, mash, ||mush (up), squash

pulpitarian *n* ***syn*** CLERGYMAN, ||blackcoat, cassock, churchman, cleric, clerk, divine, ||dominie, ecclesiastic, preacher

pulpiteer *n* ***syn*** CLERGYMAN, churchman, cleric, clerk, divine, ||dominie, ecclesiastic, minister, parson, preacher

pulpiter *n* ***syn*** CLERGYMAN, churchman, cleric, clerk, divine, ||dominie, ecclesiastic, minister, parson, preacher

pulpous *adj* ***syn*** SOFT 6, mushy, pappy, pulpy, spongy, squashy, squelchy, squishy, squushy, yielding

pulpy *adj* ***syn*** SOFT 6, mushy, pappy, quaggy, spongy, squashy, squelchy, squishy, squushy, yielding

pulsate *vb* to course or move with or as if with rhythmic strokes <blood *pulsating* through his veins>
syn beat, palpitate, pulse, throb
rel fluctuate, oscillate, vibrate; pump; drum, pound, roar, thrum

pulse *vb* ***syn*** PULSATE, beat, palpitate, throb

pulverize *vb* **1** to reduce (as by crushing, beating, or grinding) to minute particles <*pulverized* the ore in a stamp mill>
syn bray, buck, comminute, contriturate, crush, powder, triturate; *compare* SHATTER 1
rel break up; abrade, grate, grind; crumble, crunch, mull; levigate; atomize, fragment, fragmentalize, fragmentize, micronize; beat, shatter, smash, smatter, splinter; flour, mill
2 ***syn*** DESTROY 1, decimate, demolish, destruct, dynamite, rub out, ruin, shatter, tear down, wreck

pulverized *adj* ***syn*** FINE 2, impalpable, powdery
rel pulverous, pulverulent; dusty, granular, splintery
ant unpulverized

pummel *vb* ***syn*** BEAT 1, batter, belabor, buffet, drub, hammer, pelt, pound, thrash, wallop

pump *vb* ***syn*** DRAIN 1, draft, draw, draw off, siphon, tap

pumpkin head *n* ***syn*** DUNCE, cabbagehead, chowderhead, ||doughhead, dumbbell, dummy, goof, idiot, moron, muttonhead

||**pumpknot** *n* ***syn*** BUMP 2, bunch, knot, lump

pun *n* the humorous use of a word so as to suggest different meanings, or of words having the same or similar sound but different meanings <"mourning shall come with approaching day" is a *pun*>
syn calembour, paronomasia
rel double entendre
idiom play on words

punch *vb* **1** ***syn*** POKE 1, dig, jab, jog, nudge, prod
rel hit, slap, strike
2 ***syn*** PERFORATE, bore, drill, prick, ||pritch, puncture

punch *n* **1** ***syn*** CUFF, box, buffet, clout, ||paste, poke, smack, sock, ||spat, ||swack
2 ***syn*** POKE 1, dig, jab, stab
3 ***syn*** POINT 3, cogency, effectiveness, force, validity, validness
4 ***syn*** VIGOR 2, bang, drive, getup, go, pep, push, snap, starch, vitality

punctilious *adj* ***syn*** CAREFUL 2, conscientious, conscionable, exact, fussy, heedful, meticulous, painstaking, punctual, scrupulous
rel conventional, formal, observant; overconscientious, overscrupulous

punctual *adj* **1** ***syn*** CAREFUL 2, conscientious, conscionable, exact, fussy, heedful, meticulous, painstaking, punctilious, scrupulous
ant unpunctual
2 marked by exact adherence to an appointed time <a *punctual* arrival>
syn prompt, timely
rel quick, ready
idiom on the dot, on time

---

syn synonym(s) ***rel*** related word(s)
idiom idiomatic equivalent(s) ***con*** contrasted word(s)
ant antonym(s) * vulgar
|| use limited; if in doubt, see a dictionary
The first word in a synonym list when printed in SMALL CAPITALS shows where there is more information about the group. For a more efficient use of this book see Explanatory Notes.

con late, tardy
ant unpunctual

punctuate *vb* to mark or divide (written matter) with punctuation marks <*punctuated* the sentence>
syn point
rel divide, separate

puncture *n* ***syn*** PRICK 1, jab, ‖jag, stab
rel perforation

puncture *vb* **1** ***syn*** PERFORATE, bore, drill, prick, ‖pritch, punch
rel riddle
2 ***syn*** DISCREDIT 2, blow up, disprove, explode, shoot
idiom shoot full of holes

pungent *adj* sharp and stimulating to the mind or senses <his *pungent* wit>
syn peppery, piquant, poignant, racy, snappy, spicy, zesty
rel acute, keen, salt, salty, sharp; biting, bitter, cutting, hot, incisive, trenchant; exciting, provocative, stimulating; rich
con banal, corny, dull, flat, hackneyed, insipid, old hat, platitudinous, prosaic, prosy, stale, stodgy, tasteless, unimaginative, uninteresting
ant bland

punish *vb* **1** to inflict a penalty on in requital for a wrongdoing <*punished* the child for misbehaving>
syn castigate, chasten, chastise, correct, discipline
rel criticize, reprove; amerce, fine, mulct, penalize; avenge, fix, revenge; lambaste, scourge
con overlook; absolve, acquit, exculpate, exonerate, vindicate; let off, release
ant excuse, pardon
2 ***syn*** CONSUME 5, polish off, put away, put down, shift, swill

punishing *adj* ***syn*** PUNITIVE, castigatory, disciplinary, punitory

punishment *n* the act or an instance of punishing <a spanking was his *punishment*>
syn castigation, chastisement, correction, discipline, punition, rod
rel criticism, reproof; amercement, fine, mulct, penalty; avengement, revenge
idiom carrot-and-stick treatment, disciplinary action, dose of strap oil, what for
con overlooking; acquittal, exculpation, exoneration, vindication
ant excuse, pardon

punition *n* ***syn*** PUNISHMENT, castigation, chastisement, correction, discipline, rod
idiom punitive measures

punitive *adj* inflicting, involving, or constituting punishment <took *punitive* action against him>
syn castigating, disciplinary, punishing, punitory
rel correctional, penal

punitory *adj* ***syn*** PUNITIVE, castigatory, disciplinary, punishing

punk *n* **1** ***syn*** NONSENSE 2, balderdash, ‖baloney, bosh, ‖bunk, bunkum, claptrap, flummadiddle, hogwash, hot air
2 ***syn*** NOVICE, apprentice, beginner, colt, fledgling, neophyte, newcomer, novitiate, rookie, tenderfoot
3 ***syn*** TOUGH, ‖b'hoy, bullyboy, mucker, rough, roughneck, rowdy, ruffian, toughie, yahoo

‖**punk** *adj* ***syn*** BAD 1, amiss, ‖bum, ‖crappy, dissatisfactory, poor, rotten, unsatisfactory, up, wrong

puny *adj* **1** ***syn*** PETTY 2, measly, niggling, paltry, picayune, picayunish, piddling, trifling, trivial, unconsequential
rel feeble, weak
2 ***syn*** WEAK 1, decrepit, feeble, fragile, frail, infirm, unsound, unsubstantial, ‖wanky, weakly

pup *n* ***syn*** TWERP, puppy, sprat, squirt, ‖squit

puppet *n* ***syn*** TOOL 2, cat's-paw, pawn, stooge
rel dupe; slave

puppy *n* ***syn*** TWERP, pup, sprat, squirt, ‖squit

purblind *adj* partly blind <*purblind* with cataracts>
syn dim-sighted, half-blind
rel myopic, nearsighted, shortsighted; dim; blind, dark, sightless

purchasable *adj* **1** capable of being bought <*purchasable* goods>
syn available, obtainable, on offer
rel marketable, salable
idiom on (*or* for) sale, on the market, to be had
con rare; unavailable, unobtainable
ant unpurchasable
2 ***syn*** VENAL 1, bribable, buyable, corruptible
rel undependable, unreliable; slippery, tricky; treacherous

purchase *vb* ***syn*** BUY 1, take
idiom make a purchase
ant sell

purchaser *n* one to whom something is sold <instruction booklets for new-car *purchasers*>
syn buyer, emptor, vendee
rel marketer, shopper; client, customer, patron; consumer, user
con seller, vendor

pure *adj* **1** ***syn*** STRAIGHT 3, neat, plain, unadulterated, undiluted, unmixed
ant impure
2 being such and no other <his solution of the problem was *pure* genius>
syn absolute, perfect, pure and simple, sheer, simple, unadulterated, unalloyed, undiluted, unmitigated, unmixed, unqualified; *compare* UTTER
rel complete, plenary, total; authentic, genuine; classic; out-and-out, plain, utter
con mixed, qualified; doubtful, dubious, questionable, uncertain
3 ***syn*** UTTER, absolute, blasted, blessed, complete, confounded, gross, infernal, out-and-out, sheer
4 ***syn*** GOOD 11, blameless, exemplary, guiltless, inculpable, innocent, irreproachable, righteous, unblamable, virtuous
ant impure

---

syn synonym(s) ***rel*** related word(s)
idiom idiomatic equivalent(s) ***con*** contrasted word(s)
ant antonym(s) * vulgar
‖ use limited; if in doubt, see a dictionary
The first word in a synonym list when printed in SMALL CAPITALS shows where there is more information about the group. For a more efficient use of this book see Explanatory Notes.

5 ***syn*** CHASTE, clean, decent, immaculate, modest, spotless, stainless, unblemished, undefiled, unsullied

rel fresh, inviolate, unblighted, unprofaned

idiom as pure as the driven snow

con contaminated, dirty, sullied

ant immoral, impure

‖**pure** *adv* ***syn*** VERY 1, ‖awful, awfully, dreadfully, exceedingly, exceptionally, extremely, hugely, ‖larruping, thoroughly

pure and simple *adj* ***syn*** PURE 2, absolute, perfect, sheer, simple, unadulterated, unalloyed, unmitigated, unmixed, unqualified

pureblood *adj* ***syn*** PUREBRED, full-blooded, pedigree, pedigreed, thoroughbred

purebred *adj* being of unmixed ancestry <a *purebred* collie>

syn full-blooded, pedigree, pedigreed, pureblood, thoroughbred

rel registered

con bastard, hybrid, lowbred, mixed

ant mongrel

‖**puredee** (*or* **pure–D**) *adj* ***syn*** UTTER, absolute, arrant, blasted, complete, confounded, damned, dang, out-and-out, unmitigated

purely *adv* ***syn*** ALL 1, all in all, altogether, exactly, in toto, just, quite, totally, utterly, wholly

purgation *n* ***syn*** PURIFICATION, catharsis, cleansing, expurgation, lustration

purgative *adj* cleansing or purifying especially from sin <confession as a *purgative* ritual>

syn expiative, expiatory, expurgatorial, expurgatory, lustral, lustratory, propitiatory, purgatorial

purgatorial *adj* ***syn*** PURGATIVE, expiative, expiatory, expurgatorial, expurgatory, lustral, lustratory, propitiatory

‖**purgatory** *n* ***syn*** SWAMP, bog, fen, marsh, mire, morass, quag, quagmire, slough, ‖sump

purge *vb* **1** ***syn*** DISABUSE, undeceive, undelude

rel absolve, cleanse; clear, rid

2 ***syn*** PURIFY 2, cleanse, expurgate, lustrate

3 to get rid of often by exile, imprisonment, or murder <Stalin *purged* all the Party dissidents>

syn eliminate, liquidate, remove

rel debar, exclude, shut out; dismiss, eject, expel, oust; erase, expunge, wipe (out); exterminate

con rehabilitate; reinstate; repatriate; accept, bear (with), tolerate

ant depurge

purification *n* a freeing from something morally harmful, offensive, or sinful <sought *purification* through repentance>

syn catharsis, cleansing, expurgation, lustration, purgation

rel atonement, expiation; absolution, forgiveness; grace, redemption, salvation; rebirth, regeneration; sanctification

con contamination, defilement

purify *vb* **1** to free from material impurities or noxious matter <*purify* the water for drinking>

syn clarify, clean, cleanse, depurate

rel elutriate; filter; refine

con dirty, foul, soil

ant contaminate, pollute

2 to free from guilt or moral blemish (often ceremonially) <*purify* one's heart through confession>

syn cleanse, expurgate, lustrate, purge

rel atone, expiate; absolve, remit

con defile, sully, tarnish

purist *n* one who adheres strictly and often excessively to a tradition <*purists* who believe in prescriptive grammar>

syn precisian, precisionist, traditionalist

rel Atticist, classicist; bitter-ender, conservative, diehard, Puritan

con liberal, radical, young Turk

ant revisionist

puritan *n* ***syn*** PRUDE, bluenose, comstock, goody-goody, Grundy, Mrs. Grundy, nice Nelly, prig, ‖wowser

puritanical *adj* ***syn*** PRIM 1, blue-nosed, genteel, priggish, prissy, prudish, straitlaced, stuffy, tight-laced, Victorian

rel rigorous, strict; bigoted, hidebound, illiberal, intolerant, narrow, narrow-minded

con liberal, tolerant; modern

purl *vb* ***syn*** SWIRL, eddy, gurge, swoosh, whirl, whirlpool, whorl

‖**purl** *vb* ***syn*** SPIN 1, gyrate, gyre, ‖pirl, pirouette, twirl, whirl, whirligig

purlieu *n* **1** ***syn*** RESORT 2, hangout, haunt, rendezvous, stamping ground, watering hole

2 purlieus *pl* ***syn*** ENVIRONS 1, bound(s), boundary, compass, confine(s), limits, precinct(s)

3 purlieus *pl* ***syn*** ENVIRONS 2, outskirt(s), suburbs

purloin *vb* ***syn*** STEAL 1, appropriate, cabbage, ‖cop, filch, pilfer, pinch, snitch, swipe, thieve

purloiner *n* ***syn*** THIEF, filcher, larcener, larcenist, nimmer, pilferer, prig, stealer

purloining *n* ***syn*** THEFT, larceny, lift, pinch, steal, stealage, stealing, thievery, thieving, ‖touch

purple *adj* **1** ***syn*** RISQUÉ, blue, broad, off-color, racy, salty, shady, spicy, suggestive, wicked

2 ***syn*** RHETORICAL, bombastic, florid, flowery, high-flown, oratorical, overblown, pompous, stilted, turgid

purport *n* **1** ***syn*** MEANING 1, acceptation, import, intendment, message, sense, significance, significancy, signification, understanding

2 ***syn*** TENOR 1, drift, substance

rel connotation; implication

3 ***syn*** SUBSTANCE 2, burden, core, gist, matter, meat, pith, sense, thrust, upshot

purported *adj* ***syn*** ALLEGED, ostensible, pretended, professed, so-called, supposed

rel postulated, presupposed; suppositional, suppositive; academic, speculative, theoretical; reputed, rumored; suspected

---

syn synonym(s) — ***rel*** related word(s)
idiom idiomatic equivalent(s) — ***con*** contrasted word(s)
ant antonym(s) — * vulgar
‖ use limited; if in doubt, see a dictionary
The first word in a synonym list when printed in SMALL CAPITALS shows where there is more information about the group. For a more efficient use of this book see Explanatory Notes.

purportless *adj* ***syn*** SENSELESS 5, insignificant, meaningless, pointless, unmeaning

purpose *n* **1** ***syn*** INTENTION, animus, design, intendment, intent, meaning, plan
rel destination, direction; aim, goal, mission, objective, point; ambition, aspiration; proposal, proposition
2 ***syn*** USE 4, duty, function, goal, mark, object, objective, target
rel mission

purpose *vb* ***syn*** INTEND 2, aim, contemplate, design, mean, ‖mind, plan, propose
rel meditate, ponder; consider; conclude, decide, determine, resolve

purposedly *adv* ***syn*** INTENTIONALLY, ‖apurpose, deliberately, designedly, on purpose, prepensely, purposely, purposively

purposefulness *n* ***syn*** DECISION 2, decidedness, determination, firmness, purposiveness, resoluteness, resolution, resolve
rel certainty, confidence, sureness
con indecision, irresoluteness, irresolution, vacillation, waffling, wavering, weakness; aimlessness, indirection
ant purposelessness

purposeless *adj* **1** ***syn*** FECKLESS 1, fustian, good-for-nothing, meaningless, unpurposed, useless, worthless
rel unhelpful, unprofitable; purportless, senseless; nonsensical
con helpful, profitable
ant purposeful
2 ***syn*** RANDOM, aimless, designless, desultory, haphazard, hit-or-miss, indiscriminate, irregular, unaimed, unplanned
ant purposeful

purposely *adv* ***syn*** INTENTIONALLY, ‖apurpose, deliberately, designedly, on purpose, prepensely, purposedly, purposively
rel expressly; explicitly
con unintentionally
ant accidentally

purposively *adv* ***syn*** INTENTIONALLY, ‖apurpose, deliberately, designedly, on purpose, prepensely, purposedly, purposely

purposiveness *n* ***syn*** DECISION 2, decidedness, determination, firmness, purposefulness, resoluteness, resolution, resolve

purse cutter *n* ***syn*** PICKPOCKET, ‖cannon, cutpurse, ‖dip, ‖diver, ‖wire

pursual *n* ***syn*** PURSUIT 2, pursuance, pursuing, quest, search, seeking

pursuance *n* ***syn*** PURSUIT 2, pursual, pursuing, quest, search, seeking

pursue *vb* **1** ***syn*** FOLLOW 2, chase, chivy, trail
rel persevere, persist; oppress, persecute; badger, bait, hound, ride
idiom go in pursuit (of)
2 ***syn*** ADDRESS 8, court, make up (to), spark, sue, sweetheart, woo

pursuing *n* ***syn*** PURSUIT 2, pursual, pursuance, quest, search, seeking

pursuit *n* **1** ***syn*** WORK 1, business, calling, employment, job, line, occupation, ‖racket
2 a following with a view to reach, accomplish, or obtain <the *pursuit* of happiness>
syn pursual, pursuance, pursuing, quest, search, seeking
rel following; reaching; obtaining; accomplishing, accomplishment
idiom a going all out (after)

pursy *adj* ***syn*** FAT 2, corpulent, fleshy, gross, obese, overblown, overweight, porcine, stout, weighty

purview *n* **1** ***syn*** RANGE 2, ambit, compass, extension, extent, orbit, radius, reach, scope, sweep
2 ***syn*** KEN, horizon, range, reach

push *vb* **1** to use force so as to cause to move ahead or aside <*push* a wheelbarrow across the yard>
syn drive, propel, shove, thrust
rel launch; impel, move; force, ram
con brake, check, stay
ant pull
2 to do, effect, or accomplish by forcing aside obstacles or opposition <*pushed* his way through the crowd> <*pushed* the measure through congress>
syn bulldoze, elbow, hustle, jostle, press, ‖shog, shoulder, shove
rel dig, nudge; hunch; drive, force, thrust; bump, butt, ram
con ease, facilitate, slide (by), slip (through); expedite, help (along)
3 ***syn*** INCREASE 1, aggrandize, augment, beef (up), boost, build, compound, enlarge, expand, magnify
4 ***syn*** PRESSURE, overpress, press
5 ***syn*** PROMOTE 3, advertise, boost, plug
rel oversell
6 to engage in the illicit sale of (narcotics) <*pushing* drugs to teenagers>
syn peddle, shove
7 ***syn*** PRESS 1, bear, crowd, crush, jam, ‖squab, squash, squeeze, squish, squush

push *n* **1** ***syn*** ENTERPRISE 4, ambition, drive, get-up-and-go, initiative
2 ***syn*** VIGOR 2, bang, drive, getup, get-up-and-go, pep, punch, snap, starch, vitality
3 ***syn*** STIMULUS, goad, impetus, impulse, incentive, incitation, incitement, instigation, propellant, spur
4 ***syn*** CROWD 1, crush, drove, horde, multitude, press, squash, throng
5 ***syn*** SET 5, bunch, circle, crowd, group, lot

push around *vb* ***syn*** BAIT 2, badger, bullyrag, chivy, heckle, hector, hound, ride

pushful *adj* **1** ***syn*** AGGRESSIVE, assertive, assertory, militant, pushing, pushy, self-assertive
2 ***syn*** PRESUMPTUOUS, brash, forward, overweening, presuming, pushing, self-asserting, self-assertive, uppish, uppity
rel imposing, intrusive, obtruding, obtrusive, officious; assured, confident, self-confident

---

pushing *adj* **1** ***syn*** AGGRESSIVE, assertive, assertory, militant, pushful, pushy, self-assertive
idiom ‖not backward in going forward
2 ***syn*** PRESUMPTUOUS, brash, forward, overweening, presuming, pushful, self-asserting, self-assertive, uppish, uppity

push off *vb* ***syn*** GO 2, ‖blow, depart, exit, get away, get off, leave, pull out, quit, withdraw

push on *vb* ***syn*** GO 1, fare, hie, journey, pass, proceed, ‖process, repair, travel, wend

pushover *n* ***syn*** SNAP 1, breeze, child's play, cinch, duck soup, kid stuff, picnic, pie, ‖pipe, setup

pushy *adj* **1** ***syn*** AGGRESSIVE, assertive, assertory, militant, pushful, pushing, self-assertive
‖**2** ***syn*** PRESUMPTUOUS, brash, forward, overweening, presuming, pushful, self-asserting, self-assertive, uppish, uppity

pusillanimous *adj* ***syn*** COWARDLY, ‖chicken, coward, craven, gutless, lily-livered, poltroon, poltroonish, spunkless, unmanly

puss *n* ***syn*** CHILD 1, bud, chick, chickabiddy, juvenile, kid, moppet, ‖nipper, young one, youngster

‖**puss** *n* ***syn*** FACE 1, countenance, ‖dial, ‖kisser, ‖map, mug, muzzle, ‖pan, ‖phiz, visage

pussyfoot *vb* **1** ***syn*** SNEAK, creep, glide, gumshoe, lurk, skulk, slide, slink, slip, steal
2 ***syn*** EQUIVOCATE 2, dodge, evade, hedge, shuffle, sidestep, tergiversate, tergiverse, weasel

pustule *n* ***syn*** ABSCESS, boil, carbuncle, furuncle, pimple

put *vb* **1** ***syn*** SET 1, establish, fix, lay, place, settle, stick
2 ***syn*** FASTEN 3, concenter, concentrate, fix, fixate, focus, rivet
3 ***syn*** PROPOSE 1, pose, prefer, ‖propone, proposition, propound, suggest
4 ***syn*** WORD, couch, express, formulate, phrase
5 ***syn*** TRANSLATE 1, render, transpose, turn
6 ***syn*** EXPRESS 2, air, give, state, vent, ventilate
7 ***syn*** ESTIMATE 3, approximate, call, judge, place, reckon

put (back) *vb* ***syn*** RESTORE 5, give back, reinstate, replace, return

put (on) *vb* ***syn*** GAMBLE 1, bet, game, lay, play, set, stake, wager

put (on *or* upon) *vb* ***syn*** LEVY, assess, exact, impose

put *n* ***syn*** DUNCE, blockhead, boob, dimwit, dolt, dope, idiot, moron, nitwit, simpleton

put about *vb* ***syn*** INCONVENIENCE, discommode, ‖disconvenience, disoblige, incommode, put out, trouble

putative *adj* ***syn*** SUPPOSED 1, conjectural, hypothetical, reputed, suppositional, suppositious, supposititious, suppositive, suppository

put away *vb* **1** ***syn*** DIVORCE 2, dismiss, unmarry
2 ***syn*** CONSUME 5, polish off, punish, put down, shift, swill
3 ***syn*** MURDER 1, assassinate, ‖bump off, cool, do in, ‖dust off, execute, finish, knock off, liquidate
4 ***syn*** BURY 1, entomb, inhume, inter, lay away, plant, sepulcher, sepulture, tomb
5 ***syn*** KILL 1, carry off, cut off, destroy, dispatch, finish, lay low, scrag, slay, take off

put by *vb* ***syn*** SAVE 4, lay aside, lay away, lay by, lay in, lay up, salt away, ‖spare

put down *vb* **1** ***syn*** CRUSH 5, annihilate, extinguish, quash, quell, quench, squash, suppress
2 ***syn*** DEGRADE 1, break, bump, bust, declass, demerit, demote, disgrade, disrate, downgrade
3 ***syn*** CONSUME 5, polish off, punish, put away, shift, swill

put in *vb* ***syn*** PLANT 1, ‖pitch, seed, sow

put off *vb* **1** ***syn*** DELAY 2, dally, dawdle, dillydally, lag, linger, loiter, poke, tarry, trail
idiom drag one's feet
2 ***syn*** DEFER, adjourn, hold off, hold over, lay over, postpone, prorogue, shelve, stay, suspend
idiom lay on the table, let the matter stand
3 ***syn*** REMOVE 3, doff, douse, take off
ant put on

put on *vb* **1** ***syn*** DON 1, assume, draw on, get on, huddle (on), slip (on), throw (on)
ant put off
2 ***syn*** DON 2, assume, pull, strike, take on
rel affect, feign, sham, simulate; masquerade, pose
idiom make as if (*or* as though)
3 ***syn*** ASSUME 4, act, affect, bluff, counterfeit, fake, feign, pretend, sham, simulate
idiom put on a (false) front, put on an act
4 ***syn*** EMPLOY 2, engage, hire, take on
5 ***syn*** STAGE, mount, produce, show

put–on *adj* ***syn*** ARTIFICIAL 3, affected, assumed, feigned, spurious
rel mannered, posed; faked, sham

put–on *n* **1** ***syn*** IMPOSTURE, cheat, deceit, deception, fake, humbug, phony, sell, sham, spoof
2 ***syn*** MASK 2, cloak, cover, disguise, facade, face, false front, guise, masquerade, show

put out *vb* **1** ***syn*** EXERT, exercise, ply, throw, wield
2 ***syn*** EXTINGUISH 1, douse, ‖dout, out, quench, ‖squench
3 ***syn*** PUBLISH 2, get out, issue
4 ***syn*** IRRITATE, aggravate, burn (up), exasperate, gall, get, grate, inflame, rile, roil
5 ***syn*** INCONVENIENCE, discommode, ‖disconvenience, disoblige, incommode, put about, trouble
rel displease, dissatisfy; annoy, irritate
idiom put out of the way, put to it

put over *vb* ***syn*** DEFER, delay, hold off, hold over, hold up, lay over, postpone, put off, shelve, stand over

putrefy *vb* ***syn*** DECAY, break down, crumble, decompose, disintegrate, molder, rot, spoil, taint, turn

putresce *vb* ***syn*** DECAY, break down, corrupt, crumble, decompose, disintegrate, putrefy, rot, spoil, turn

putrid *adj* **1** ***syn*** BAD 5, decayed, rotten, spoiled
2 ***syn*** MALODOROUS 1, fetid, high, nidorous, noisome, olid, rancid, reeking, smelly, whiffy
3 ***syn*** VICIOUS 2, corrupt, degenerate, depraved, flagitious, nefarious, perverse, rotten, unhealthy, villainous

putter *vb* ***syn*** FIDDLE 2, doodle, mess, mess around, potter, puddle, tinker

---

syn synonym(s)	***rel*** related word(s)
idiom idiomatic equivalent(s)	***con*** contrasted word(s)
ant antonym(s)	* vulgar

‖ use limited; if in doubt, see a dictionary
The first word in a synonym list when printed in SMALL CAPITALS shows where there is more information about the group. For a more efficient use of this book see Explanatory Notes.

rel boondoggle; dawdle

‖**put to** *vb syn* CLOSE 1, shut

put together *vb syn* MAKE 3, build, construct, erect, fabricate, fashion, form, frame, produce, shape

put up *vb* **1** *syn* HARBOR 2, bestow, billet, board, bunk, domicile, house, hut, lodge, quarter
2 *syn* BUILD 1, construct, erect, raise, rear, uprear
rel forge, make, put together, shape
3 *syn* ERECT 3, raise, rear, set up
4 *syn* RAISE 9, boost, hike, increase, jack (up), jump, up
rel elevate, escalate

‖**puxy** *n syn* SWAMP, baygall, bog, fen, marsh, mire, ‖moss, slough, ‖sump, swampland

puzzle *vb* to baffle and disturb mentally <a persistent fever that *puzzled* her doctor>
syn befog, bewilder, ‖cap, confound, confuse, metagrobolize, perplex, pose, stumble; *compare* NONPLUS 1
rel baffle, foil, frustrate; befuddle, ‖bumfuzzle, fuddle; disconcert, distract, disturb, upset; addle, muddle; mystify; amaze, dumbfound, flabbergast
con enlighten, inform

puzzle *n syn* MYSTERY, Chinese puzzle, closed book, conundrum, enigma, mystification, puzzlement, riddle, why

puzzlement *n syn* MYSTERY, Chinese puzzle, closed book, conundrum, enigma, mystification, puzzle, riddle, why

puzzle out *vb syn* SOLVE 2, break, ‖cipher, clear up, decipher, ‖dope out, figure out, unfold, unravel, unriddle
idiom find the key to, pick the lock

pygmy *n syn* DWARF, homunculus, hop-o'-my-thumb, lilliputian, manikin, midge, midget, peewee, runt, Tom Thumb
ant giant

pygmy *adj syn* TINY, ‖bitsy, diminutive, dwarf, dwarfish, lilliputian, midget, minikin, peewee, pocket-size

pyramid *n syn* PILE 1, bank, drift, heap, hill, mass, mound, mountain, stack, windrow

Pyrrhonian *n syn* SKEPTIC, doubter, doubting Thomas, headshaker, Pyrrhonist, unbeliever, zetetic

Pyrrhonist *n syn* SKEPTIC, doubter, doubting Thomas, headshaker, Pyrrhonian, unbeliever, zetetic

pythonic *adj syn* HUGE, Antaean, colossal, cyclopean, elephantine, enormous, gigantic, immense, jumbo, monumental

---

syn synonym(s) — *rel* related word(s)
idiom idiomatic equivalent(s) — *con* contrasted word(s)
ant antonym(s) — * vulgar
‖ use limited; if in doubt, see a dictionary
The first word in a synonym list when printed in SMALL CAPITALS shows where there is more information about the group. For a more efficient use of this book see Explanatory Notes.

Q

quack *n* ***syn*** CHARLATAN, mountebank, quacksalver, quackster, saltimbanque
rel counterfeiter, pretender, shammer, simulator

||**quackle** *vb* ***syn*** SUFFOCATE, asphyxiate, choke, smother, stifle

quacksalver *n* ***syn*** CHARLATAN, mountebank, quack, quackster, saltimbanque

quackster *n* ***syn*** CHARLATAN, mountebank, quack, quacksalver, saltimbanque

quad *n* ***syn*** COURT 1, ||close, courtyard, curtilage, enclosure, quadrangle, yard

quadrangle *n* ***syn*** COURT 1, ||close, courtyard, curtilage, enclosure, quad, yard

quadrate *adj* ***syn*** SQUARE 1, foursquare, quadratic, quadratical

quadrate *vb* **1** ***syn*** AGREE 4, accord, check, comport, conform, correspond, dovetail, fit (in), go, harmonize
2 ***syn*** ADAPT, accommodate, adjust, conform, fit, reconcile, square, suit, tailor, tailor-make

quadratic *adj* ***syn*** SQUARE 1, foursquare, quadrate, quadratical

quadratical *adj* ***syn*** SQUARE 1, foursquare, quadrate, quadratic

quaesitum *n* ***syn*** AMBITION 2, aim, goal, mark, objective, target

quaff *vb* ***syn*** DRINK 1, imbibe, sip, sup (off *or* up), swallow, toss

quag *n* ***syn*** SWAMP, bog, fen, marsh, mire, morass, ||moss, quagmire, ||sump, ||vlei

quaggy *adj* ***syn*** SOFT 6, mushy, pappy, pulpy, spongy, squashy, squelchy, squishy, squushy, yielding

quagmire *n* **1** ***syn*** SWAMP, bog, fen, marsh, marshland, mire, morass, ||moss, quag, slough
2 ***syn*** PREDICAMENT, box, corner, dilemma, fix, hole, jam, pickle, plight, scrape

quail *n* ***syn*** GIRL 1, damsel, gal, lass, lassie, maid, maiden, miss, missy, ||quiff

quail *vb* ***syn*** RECOIL, blanch, blench, flinch, shrink, squinch, start, wince
rel cower, cringe

quaint *adj* ***syn*** STRANGE 4, curious, eccentric, idiosyncratic, odd, oddball, peculiar, queer, singular, unusual
rel droll, funny, laughable; antiquated, antique, archaic

||**quaint** *vb* ***syn*** INTRODUCE 4, acquaint, present

quake *vb* **1** ***syn*** SHAKE 2, jar, tremble, tremor, vibrate
rel fluctuate, waver
2 ***syn*** SHAKE 1, ||didder, dither, quaver, quiver, shiver, shudder, tremble, tremor, twitter

---

syn synonym(s) ***rel*** related word(s)
idiom idiomatic equivalent(s) ***con*** contrasted word(s)
ant antonym(s) * vulgar
|| use limited; if in doubt, see a dictionary
The first word in a synonym list when printed in SMALL CAPITALS shows where there is more information about the group. For a more efficient use of this book see Explanatory Notes.

quake *n* ***syn*** EARTHQUAKE, ||quaker, shake, shock, temblor (*or* tremblor), tremor

||**quaker** *n* ***syn*** EARTHQUAKE, quake, shake, shock, temblor (*or* tremblor), tremor

quaking *adj* ***syn*** TREMULOUS, aquake, aquiver, quaky, quivering, shaking, shaky, trembling, tremorous, tremulant

quaky *adj* ***syn*** TREMULOUS, aquake, quaking, quivering, quivery, shaking, shaky, shivering, shivery, trembling

qualification *n* ***syn*** ABILITY 1, adequacy, capability, capacity, competence, might, qualifiedness

qualified *adj* **1** ***syn*** ABLE, au fait, capable, competent, good, proper, wicked
rel disciplined, instructed, trained; catechized, examined, quizzed; proved, tested, tried
con incapable, incompetent, unequipped, unfit
ant disqualified, unqualified
2 not unlimited and complete <gave only a *qualified* endorsement to the project>
syn limited, modified, reserved
rel circumscribed, definite, determined, fixed, restricted; partial
con complete, entire, full, total, utter, whole; unlimited, unrestricted
ant absolute, unqualified

qualifiedness *n* ***syn*** ABILITY 1, adequacy, capability, capacity, competence, might, qualification

qualify *vb* **1** ***syn*** CHARACTERIZE 2, distinguish, individualize, individuate, mark, signalize, singularize
rel ascribe, assign, attribute, impute; predicate
2 ***syn*** ENTITLE 2, authorize

quality *n* **1** something inherent and distinctive <learned the special *qualities* of the native herbs>
syn affection, attribute, character, characteristic, feature, mark, peculiarity, property, savor, trait, virtue; *compare* CHARACTERISTIC 1
rel individuality; affirmation, predication; element, factor, parameter
2 a usually high level of merit or superiority <merchandise of *quality*>
syn caliber, merit, stature, value, virtue, worth
rel arete, excellence, excellency, perfection, superbness, superiority
con inferiority, meanness, mediocrity, poorness; inadequacy; deficiency
3 degree of excellence <upgrading the *quality* of incoming students>
syn caliber, class, grade
rel capacity, character, footing, place, position, rank, situation, standing, state, station, status
4 ***syn*** STATUS 1, capacity, character, footing, place, position, rank, standing, state, station
5 ***syn*** ARISTOCRACY, aristoi, blue blood, elite, flower, gentility, gentry, patriciate, society, upper class
6 ***syn*** EXCELLENCE, arete, excellency, merit, perfection, virtue

quality *adj* ***syn*** EXCELLENT, A1, blue-ribbon, fine, first-class, first-rate, five-star, Grade A, prime, superior

qualm *n* a misgiving about what one is going to do <had *qualms* about the secret meeting>
syn compunction, conscience, demur, scruple, squeam
rel apprehension, foreboding, misgiving, presentiment; doubt, mistrust, suspicion, uncertainty; agitation, insecurity, perturbation; objection, remonstrance; reluctance, unwillingness; impatience, nervousness, unease, uneasiness
con aplomb, assurance, confidence, self-assurance, self-confidence, self-possession; certainty, certitude, conviction

qualmish *adj* ***syn*** SQUEAMISH 1, ‖pensy, qualmy, queasy, queer, ‖wambly

qualmishness *n* ***syn*** NAUSEA, queasiness, squeamishness

qualmy *adj* ***syn*** SQUEAMISH 1, ‖pensy, qualmish, queasy, queer, ‖wambly

quantity *n* **1** ***syn*** BODY 5, aggregate, amount, budget, bulk, quantum, total
2 quantities *pl* ***syn*** SCAD, gob(s), heap, jillion, load(s), million, oodles, ream(s), thousand, trillion

quantum *n* **1** ***syn*** BODY 5, aggregate, amount, budget, bulk, quantity, total
2 ***syn*** RATION, allotment, allowance, apportionment, measure, meed, part, portion, quota, share

quarrel *n* a usually verbal dispute marked by anger or discord <a *quarrel* over who would drive the car>
syn altercation, ‖barney, beef, bickering, brabble, brannigan, brawl, controversy, difficulty, dispute, dust, dustup, embroilment, falling-out, feud, fight, fracas, fuss, hassle, imbroglio, knock-down-and-drag-out, miff, ‖prabble, ‖pribble, rhubarb, row, ruckus, run-in, set-to, spat, squabble, squall, tiff, to-and-fro, word(s), wrangle; *compare* BRAWL 2
rel battle royal, catfight; affray, bobbery, broil, donnybrook, fray, free-for-all, melee, ruction, rumpus, scrap, scrimmage, scuffle; conflict, contention, difference, discord, dissension, strife, variance; disagreement, misunderstanding
idiom ‖pribbles and prabbles
con accord, concord, harmony; agreement, likemindedness, understanding, unity

quarrel *vb* to contend noisily or captiously <with his belligerent personality he was always *quarreling* with someone>
syn altercate, bicker, brabble, brawl, ‖cast out, caterwaul, fall out, row, scrap, spat, squabble, tiff, wrangle; *compare* ARGUE 2
rel differ, disaccord, dissent, divide, vary; bump, clash, collide, conflict, thwart; battle, contend, fight, war
idiom have words with, pull caps
con agree, coincide, concur

quarrelsome *adj* **1** ***syn*** BELLIGERENT, bellicose, combative, contentious, gladiatorial, militant, pugnacious, ‖ructious, truculent, warlike
rel adverse, antagonistic, counter; antipathetic, hostile, inimical, rancorous
idiom having a chip on one's shoulder
2 apt or disposed to quarrel <when he's in a bad mood he becomes so *quarrelsome*>
syn battlesome, brawling, brawlsome, brawly, scrappy; *compare* BELLIGERENT
rel argumentative; disputatious; cankered, crabbed, irascible, irritable
con conciliatory, propitiatory

quarry *n* ***syn*** GAME 3, chase, prey

quarry *vb* ***syn*** MINE, delve

quarter *n* **1** one of four equal parts <ate one *quarter* of the pie>
syn fourth, quartern
rel quadrant
2 a division or part of a town or city <the market *quarter* in Paris>
syn district, precinct, section, sector
rel division, part; area; locality; barrio

quarter *vb* **1** ***syn*** HARBOR 2, board, bunk, domicile, domiciliate, entertain, house, hut, lodge, put up
2 ***syn*** BILLET 1, canton

quarterage *n* ***syn*** SHELTER 2, housing

quarterback *vb* ***syn*** SUPERVISE, boss, chaperon, overlook, oversee, superintend, survey

quartern *n* ***syn*** QUARTER 1, fourth

quarter–witted *adj* ***syn*** RETARDED, backward, dim-witted, dull, feebleminded, half-witted, imbecile, moronic, simpleminded, slow-witted

quartet *n* a group consisting of four individuals <a singing *quartet*>
syn four, foursome, quartetto, quaternion, quatuor, tetrad
rel quadruplet

quartetto *n* ***syn*** QUARTET, four, foursome, quaternion, quatuor, tetrad

quash *vb* **1** ***syn*** ANNUL 4, abrogate, discharge, dissolve, vacate, void
2 ***syn*** ABOLISH 1, abate, abrogate, annihilate, annul, invalidate, negate, nullify, undo, vitiate
3 ***syn*** CRUSH 5, annihilate, extinguish, put down, quell, quench, squash, suppress

quashing *n* ***syn*** REPRESSION 1, choking, extinguishment, quenching, smothering, squashing, squelching, stifling, strangling, suppression

‖**quat** *vb* ***syn*** SQUAT, hunker (down), ‖swat

quaternion *n* ***syn*** QUARTET, four, foursome, quartetto, quatuor, tetrad

quatuor *n* ***syn*** QUARTET, four, foursome, quartetto, quaternion, tetrad

quaver *vb* ***syn*** SHAKE 1, ‖didder, dither, quake, quiver, shiver, shudder, tremble, tremor, twitter
rel falter, hesitate, vacillate, waver

‖**quawk** *vb* ***syn*** SQUALL 1, caw, squark, squawk, yawp (*or* yaup)

quay *n* ***syn*** WHARF, berth, dock, jetty, levee, pier, slip

‖**queak** *vb* ***syn*** SQUEAK 1

quean *n* ***syn*** PROSTITUTE, bawd, drab, fille de joie, harlot, ‖hooker, hustler, meretrix, streetwalker, whore

queasiness *n* ***syn*** NAUSEA, qualmishness, squeamishness

---

queasy *adj* **1** *syn* DOUBTFUL 1, ambiguous, doubtable, dubious, fishy, indecisive, open, precarious, shady, unsettled
2 *syn* SQUEAMISH 1, ||pensy, qualmish, qualmy, queer, ||wambly

queer *adj* **1** *syn* STRANGE 4, bizarre, curious, eccentric, oddball, outlandish, peculiar, singular, unusual, weird
rel doubtful, dubious, questionable; droll, funny, laughable
2 *syn* OBSESSED, hagridden, hipped
3 *syn* HOMOSEXUAL, gay, homoerotic, homophile, inverted, uranian
4 *syn* SQUEAMISH 1, ||pensy, qualmish, qualmy, queasy, ||wambly

queer *n syn* HOMOSEXUAL, fag, faggot, ||fruit, homo, invert, uranian, uranist

||**quelch** *vb syn* SUPPRESS 2, muffle, repress, shush, squelch, strangle

quell *vb syn* CRUSH 5, annihilate, extinguish, put down, quash, quench, squash, suppress
rel conquer, overcome, subjugate, vanquish
con abet, incite, instigate
ant foment

quench *vb* **1** *syn* EXTINGUISH 1, douse, ||dout, out, put out, ||squench
2 *syn* CRUSH 5, annihilate, extinguish, put down, quash, quell, squash, suppress
rel end, terminate
3 *syn* DESTROY 1, annihilate, decimate, demolish, destruct, dismantle, raze, ruin, shatter, wreck
4 to bring (as thirst) to an end with or as if with a refreshing drink <after being in the hot sun, he found it difficult to *quench* his thirst>
syn slake, ||squench
rel appease, content, gratify, satisfy; sate, satiate; allay, alleviate, assuage, lighten, mitigate, relieve; decrease, diminish, lessen, reduce

quenching *n syn* REPRESSION 1, choking, extinguishment, quashing, smothering, squashing, squelching, stifling, strangling, suppression

quenchless *adj* **1** *syn* INSATIABLE, insatiate, unappeasable, unquenchable, unsatiate, unsatisfiable
2 *syn* INDESTRUCTIBLE, imperishable, incorruptible, inexterminable, inextinguishable, inextirpable, irrefragable, irrefrangible, undestroyable, unperishable

querulent *adj syn* IRRITABLE, disagreeable, fractious, fretful, querulential, querulous, raspish, snappish, twitty, waspish

querulential *adj syn* IRRITABLE, disagreeable, fractious, fretful, querulent, querulous, raspish, snappish, twitty, waspish

querulous *adj syn* IRRITABLE, fractious, fretful, huffy, peevish, pettish, petulant, snappish, waspish, waspy
rel blubbering, crying, wailing, weeping, whimpering; bemoaning, deploring, lamenting

query *n* **1** *syn* INQUIRY 2, interrogation, interrogatory, question, questioning
2 *syn* UNCERTAINTY, concern, doubt, dubiety, dubiosity, dubitancy, mistrust, skepticism, suspicion, uncertitude

query *vb syn* ASK 1, catechize, examine, inquire, interrogate, question, quiz

quest *n* **1** *syn* INQUIRY 1, delving, inquest, inquisition, investigation, probe, probing, research
2 *syn* PURSUIT 2, pursual, pursuance, pursuing, search, seeking

quest *vb* **1** *syn* HOWL 1, bay, ululate, wail
2 *syn* SEEK 1, cast about, ferret out, hunt, search (for *or* out)

question *n* **1** *syn* INQUIRY 2, interrogation, interrogatory, query, questioning
2 *syn* PROBLEM 2, issue, nut
3 *syn* DEMUR 2, challenge, demurral, demurrer, difficulty, objection, protest, remonstrance, remonstration

question *vb* **1** *syn* ASK 1, catechize, examine, inquire, interrogate, query, quiz
2 to express doubt about <*questioned* his decision to take a new job>
syn challenge, dispute, doubt, mistrust
rel suspect, ||suspicion; hesitate (over), puzzle (over), wonder (about)

questionable *adj* **1** *syn* IMPROBABLE 1, doubtful, dubious, unlikely
ant unquestionable
2 *syn* MOOT, arguable, debatable, disputable, doubtful, dubious, mootable, problematic, uncertain
rel refutable; equivocal, obscure, vague
con dependable, true, trustworthy, trusty; genuine, indubitable, real, undoubted, undubitable, veritable, very
ant authoritative; unquestionable, unquestioned
3 *syn* UNRELIABLE 1, dubious, fly-by-night, trustless, undependable, unsure, untrustworthy, untrusty

questioning *n syn* INQUIRY 2, interrogation, interrogatory, query, question

questioning *adj* **1** *syn* INCREDULOUS, aporetic, disbelieving, quizzical, show-me, skeptical, unbelieving
ant questionless, unquestioning
2 *syn* INQUISITIVE 1, curious, disquisitive, inquiring, investigative

questionless *adj syn* AUTHENTIC 2, bona fide, genuine, indubitable, pukka, real, right, simon-pure, sure-enough, true

queue *n syn* LINE 5, echelon, file, rank, row, string, tier

quibble *vb* **1** to find fault with something usually on minor grounds <was a peevish critic, always ready to *quibble*>
syn cavil, chicane, hypercriticize
rel carp, criticize
idiom split hairs
con applaud, commend, compliment, recommend; approve, endorse, sanction
2 *syn* ARGUE 2, argufy, bicker, dispute, hassle, squabble, wrangle

quick *adj* **1** *syn* FAST 3, breakneck, expeditious, expeditive, fleet, harefooted, hasty, rapid, speedy, swift
rel agile, brisk, nimble; abrupt, impetuous

---

syn synonym(s) *rel* related word(s)
idiom idiomatic equivalent(s) *con* contrasted word(s)
ant antonym(s) * vulgar
|| use limited; if in doubt, see a dictionary
The first word in a synonym list when printed in SMALL CAPITALS shows where there is more information about the group. For a more efficient use of this book see Explanatory Notes.

idiom quick on the trigger
con dilatory, laggard, leisurely, slow, unhasty, unhurried; comatose
ant sluggish
2 able to respond without delay or hesitation or indicative of such ability <very *quick* in perception> <his *quick* eye spotted the trouble>
syn apt, prompt, ready; *compare* INSTANTANEOUS
rel clever, intelligent, quick-witted, smart; adroit, deft, dexterous; acute, keen, sharp; able, capable, competent, effective, effectual
con comatose, lethargic, logy, poky, torpid; crass, dense, dull, dumb, stupid
ant slow; sluggish
3 ***syn*** WISE 4, canny, hep, knowing, nimble-witted, quick-witted, sharp, sharp-witted, slick, smart

quick *adv* ***syn*** FAST 2, apace, expeditiously, flat-out, hastily, lickety-split, posthaste, rapidly, speedily, swiftly

quick *n* ***syn*** CENTER 3, core, heart, pith, root

quicken *vb* **1** to make alive or lively <warm spring days that *quicken* the earth>
syn animate, enliven, liven, vivificate, vivify
rel activate, energize, vitalize; arouse, awaken, rouse, stir, wake
con blunt, dull; slow (down)
ant deaden
2 ***syn*** PROVOKE 4, excite, galvanize, innervate, innerve, motivate, move, pique, rouse, stimulate
rel activate, actuate, motivate; goad, induce, spur
con check, halt, interrupt, stall, stay; curb, inhibit, restrain
ant arrest
3 ***syn*** SPEED 3, accelerate, hasten, hurry, shake up, step up, swiften
con bog (down), detain, embog, hang up, mire
ant slacken

quickening *adj* ***syn*** INVIGORATING, animating, bracing, exhilarating, exhilarative, stimulating, stimulative, tonic, vitalizing

quick–lunch *n* ***syn*** EATING HOUSE, beanery, café, coffee shop, diner, ‖hash house, lunch counter (*or* bar), luncheonette, sandwich shop, snack bar (*or* counter)

quickly *adv* ***syn*** FAST 2, apace, expeditiously, flat-out, hastily, lickety-split, posthaste, rapidly, speedily, swiftly

quickness *n* ***syn*** SPEED 2, ‖bat, celerity, gait, pace, rapidity, rapidness, swiftness, velocity
ant slowness

quick–sighted *adj* ***syn*** SHARP 4, acute, keen, penetrating, penetrative, quick-witted, sharp-sighted, sharp-witted

quick–tempered *adj* ***syn*** IRASCIBLE, choleric, cranky, cross, hot-tempered, passionate, peppery, ratty, ‖stomachy, temperish

quick–witted *adj* **1** ***syn*** SHARP 4, acute, keen, penetrating, penetrative, quick-sighted, sharp-sighted, sharp-witted
2 ***syn*** INTELLIGENT 2, alert, brainy, bright, brilliant, clever, knowing, ready-witted, sharp, smart
rel apt, prompt, quick, ready
3 ***syn*** WISE 4, canny, hep, knowing, nimble-witted, quick, sharp, sharp-witted, slick, smart
rel acute, keen; facetious, humorous, witty
ant slow-witted

quidnunc *n* **1** ***syn*** BUSYBODY, butt-in, ‖buttinsky, intermeddler, kibitzer, meddler, pragmatist, prier (*or* pryer), rubberneck, snoop
2 ***syn*** GOSSIP 1, carrytale, gossiper, gossipmonger, newsmonger, rumormonger, scandalmonger, tabby, talebearer, telltale

quiescence *n* ***syn*** ABEYANCE, abeyancy, cold storage, doldrums, dormancy, intermission, interruption, latency, quiescency, suspension

quiescency *n* ***syn*** ABEYANCE, abeyancy, cold storage, doldrums, dormancy, intermission, interruption, latency, quiescence, suspension

quiescent *adj* ***syn*** LATENT, abeyant, dormant, lurking, potential, prepatent
rel calm, halcyon, hushed, placid, quiet, still, stilly, untroubled

quiet *n* **1** a period of intensified silence <the *quiet* before the storm>
syn calm, hush, lull
rel cessation, stop, termination
con din, hubbub, racket, uproar
2 ***syn*** SILENCE 1, noiselessness, quietness, quietude, soundlessness, still, stillness

quiet *adj* **1** ***syn*** CALM 1, halcyon, hushed, placid, still, stilly, untroubled
con harsh, rough; disquieted, disturbed, perturbed, upset
ant unquiet
2 ***syn*** INACTIVE, asleep, idle, inert, passive, sleepy
3 ***syn*** STILL 3, hush, hushful, noiseless, silent, soundless, stilly, whist
con blatant, boisterous, clamorous, strident, vociferous
4 not showy or obtrusive <always dressed in *quiet* good taste>
syn inobtrusive, restrained, subdued, tasteful, tasty, unobtrusive
rel homely, plain, simple, unpretentious
con blatant, brazen, flashy, garish, glaring, meretricious, tawdry, tinsel; elaborate
ant gaudy, loud

quiet *vb* **1** ***syn*** SILENCE, choke (off), hush, ‖quieten, shush, shut up, still
rel abate, decrease, lessen
con excite, provoke, quicken, stimulate; awaken, rally, stir
2 ***syn*** CALM, allay, becalm, compose, lull, ‖quieten, settle, soothe, still, tranquilize
con agitate; unhinge, untune
ant disquiet; excite

‖**quieten** *vb* **1** ***syn*** SILENCE, choke (off), hush, quiet, shush, shut up, still
2 ***syn*** CALM, allay, becalm, compose, lull, quiet, settle, soothe, still, tranquilize
ant arouse; excite

---

syn synonym(s) *rel* related word(s)
idiom idiomatic equivalent(s) *con* contrasted word(s)
ant antonym(s) * vulgar
‖ use limited; if in doubt, see a dictionary
The first word in a synonym list when printed in SMALL CAPITALS shows where there is more information about the group. For a more efficient use of this book see Explanatory Notes.

quietive *adj syn* SEDATIVE, calmant, calmative

quietness *n syn* SILENCE 1, noiselessness, quiet, quietude, soundlessness, still, stillness

quietude *n syn* SILENCE 1, noiselessness, quiet, quietness, soundlessness, still, stillness

quietus *n syn* DEATH 1, curtains, decease, defunction, demise, dissolution, (the) Pale Horse, passing, silence, sleep

‖**quiff** *n syn* GIRL 1, damsel, gal, lass, lassie, maid, maiden, miss, missy, ‖quail

quilt *n* a bed coverlet made of two layers of cloth with a stuffing (as of cotton, wool, or feathers) between <a warm *quilt* is nice on a winter night>
syn ‖comfortable, comforter, pouf, puff
rel bedcover, bedspread, counterpane; eiderdown

quinary *adj syn* QUINTUPLE, fivefold

quinta *n syn* ESTATE 3, acres, land, manor

quintessence *n* **1** *syn* ESSENCE 2, bottom, essentiality, marrow, pith, quintessential, soul, stuff, substance, virtuality
2 *syn* APOTHEOSIS 1, epitome, last word, ultimate

quintessential *adj syn* TYPICAL 1, archetypal, classic, classical, exemplary, ideal, model, prototypal, prototypical, representative

quintessential *n syn* ESSENCE 2, bottom, essentiality, marrow, pith, quintessence, soul, stuff, substance, virtuality

quintuple *adj* consisting of five <the problem is viewed as having *quintuple* aspects>
syn fivefold, quinary
rel quintuplicate

quip *n syn* JOKE 1, crack, drollery, gag, jape, jest, sally, wisecrack, witticism, ‖yak

quip (at) *vb syn* SCOFF, fleer, flout, gibe, gird, jeer, jest, scout (at), sneer

quipster *n syn* HUMORIST 2, comedian, comic, droll, funnyman, jester, joker, jokester, wag, wit

quit *vb* **1** *syn* CLEAR 5, clear off, discharge, liquidate, pay, pay up, satisfy, settle, square
2 *syn* BEHAVE 1, acquit, act, bear, carry, comport, conduct, demean, deport, go on
3 *syn* GO 2, ‖blow, depart, exit, get away, get off, leave, retire, take off, withdraw
4 *syn* ABANDON 1, chuck, desert, forsake, renounce, throw over
rel relinquish, resign, surrender
5 *syn* STOP 3, cease, desist, ‖deval, discontinue, give over, halt, knock off, leave off, surcease
6 to give up (as a habit, activity, or employment) especially with finality <*quit* a job> <determined to *quit* smoking>
syn drop, leave, resign, terminate
rel retire, secede, withdraw
idiom draw one's time, give notice
con hire on, hire out

quite *adv* **1** *syn* WELL 3, altogether, ‖cleverly, completely, entirely, fully, perfectly, thoroughly, utterly, wholly
2 *syn* ALTOGETHER 2, all told, in all
3 *syn* ALL 1, all in all, altogether, exactly, in toto, just, purely, totally, utterly, wholly
4 *syn* WELL 8, considerably, far, rather, significantly, somewhat

quittance *n syn* REPARATION, amends, compensation, indemnification, indemnity, recompense, redress, reprisal, restitution

quitter *n syn* COWARD, chicken, craven, dastard, funk, funker, poltroon, yellowbelly

quiver *n syn* FLASH 1, glance, gleam, glimmer, glint, glisten, glitter, shimmer, sparkle, twinkle

quiver *vb syn* SHAKE 1, ‖didder, dither, quake, quaver, shiver, shudder, tremble, tremor, twitter
rel beat, palpatate, pulsate, pulse, throb

quivering *adj syn* TREMULOUS, aquake, aquiver, quaking, shaking, shaky, shivering, trembling, tremorous, tremulant

quivery *adj syn* TREMULOUS, aquiver, ashake, quaking, quivering, shaking, shaky, trembling, tremorous, tremulant

quiz *n syn* ECCENTRIC, case, character, ‖duck, oddball, oddity, original, ‖spook, ‖wack, zombie

quiz *vb* **1** *syn* RIDICULE, deride, lout, mock, rally, razz, scout, taunt, twit
2 *syn* ASK 1, catechize, examine, inquire, interrogate, query, question

quizzical *adj syn* INCREDULOUS, aporetic, disbelieving, questioning, show-me, skeptical, unbelieving
rel curious, inquisitive; probing, searching

‖**quod** *vb syn* IMPRISON, bastille, confine, constrain, immure, incarcerate, intern, jail, jug, ‖prison

quodlibetic *adj syn* PEDANTIC, academic, bookish, book-learned, booky, scholastic

quondam *adj syn* FORMER 2, bygone, erstwhile, late, old, once, onetime, past, sometime, whilom

quota *n* **1** *syn* SHARE 1, allotment, allowance, bite, cut, lot, part, partage, portion, slice
2 *syn* RATION, allotment, allowance, apportionment, measure, meed, part, portion, quantum, share

quota *vb syn* APPORTION 2, divide, ‖divvy, parcel, portion, prorate, ration, share, ‖shift

quotidian *adj* **1** *syn* DAILY, diurnal
2 *syn* ORDINARY 1, everyday, plain, plain Jane, routine, unremarkable, usual, workaday

---

syn synonym(s) *rel* related word(s)
idiom idiomatic equivalent(s) *con* contrasted word(s)
ant antonym(s) * vulgar
‖ use limited; if in doubt, see a dictionary
The first word in a synonym list when printed in SMALL CAPITALS shows where there is more information about the group. For a more efficient use of this book see Explanatory Notes.

R

rabbity *adj* ***syn*** SHY 1, bashful, coy, demure, diffident, retiring, self-effacing, timid, unassertive, unassured

rabble *n* **1** ***syn*** MOB 2, rout

2 the lowest class of people <the *rabble* of the city>

syn canaille, doggery, dreg(s), hoi polloi, mass(es), mob, other half, polloi, proletariat, raff, ‖ragabash, ragtag, ragtag and bobtail, riffraff, roughscuff, rout, scum, scurf, tag and rag, tagrag and bobtail, trash, unwashed

rel bourgeoisie, commonalty, many, people, populace, public, rank and file

idiom the great unwashed, the scum of the earth, the submerged tenth

con aristocracy, aristoi, elite, Four Hundred, gentility, nobility, upper class, upper crust, upper ten, upper ten thousand

rabble–rouser *n* ***syn*** DEMAGOGUE

rabid *adj* **1** ***syn*** FURIOUS 2, corybantic, delirious, frantic, frenetic, frenzied, mad, wild

rel crazed, crazy, demented, deranged, insane

2 ***syn*** EXTREME 3, extremist, fanatic, radical, revolutional, revolutionary, revolutionist, ultra, ultraist

rel enthusiastic, keen, obsessed, zealous

race *n* ***syn*** CREEK 2, ‖branch, brook, ‖burn, gill, ‖rindle, rivulet, ‖run, runnel, stream

race *vb* **1** ***syn*** RUSH 1, boil, bolt, charge, chase, dash, fling, lash, shoot, tear

2 ***syn*** COURSE, career, chase, rush, speed, tear

race *n* ***syn*** FAMILY 1, clan, folk, house, kindred, lineage, stock, tribe

rel culture, nation, nationality, people; breed, type, variety

rachis *n* ***syn*** SPINE, back, backbone, spinal column, vertebrae, vertebral column

rachitic *adj* ***syn*** RICKETY, rackety, rattletrap, shaky, wobbly

racial *adj* ***syn*** ETHNIC 2

racialism *n* ***syn*** RACISM

racism *n* racial prejudice or discrimination <an act of overt *racism*>

syn racialism

rel discrimination, prejudice; illiberality, unfairness; bias, one-sidedness, partiality

con broad-mindedness, liberalness, open-mindedness, tolerance; indifference, neutrality

rack *vb* ***syn*** AFFLICT, agonize, crucify, excruciate, harrow, martyr, torment, torture, try, wring

rel distress, pain; oppress, persecute

‖**rack back** *vb* ***syn*** REPROVE, admonish, call down, chide, lesson, monish, rebuke, reprimand, reproach, tick off

racket *n* **1** ***syn*** DIN, babel, brouhaha, clamor, hubbub, hullabaloo, jangle, pandemonium, tumult, uproar

‖**2** ***syn*** WORK 1, business, calling, employment, job, line, occupation, pursuit

racketry *n* ***syn*** DIN, babel, clamor, hubbub, hullabaloo, jangle, pandemonium, racket, tumult, uproar

rackety *adj* **1** ***syn*** NOISY, clangorous, clattery, noiseful, sonorous, uproarious

2 ***syn*** RICKETY, rachitic, rattletrap, shaky, wobbly

racking *adj* ***syn*** EXCRUCIATING, agonizing, harrowing, tearing, tormenting, torturing, torturous

rel barbarous, cruel, ferocious, fierce, inhuman, savage

rack up *vb* ***syn*** GAIN 1, accomplish, achieve, attain, reach, realize, score, win

racy *adj* **1** ***syn*** PUNGENT, peppery, piquant, poignant, snappy, spicy, zesty

rel fiery, gingery, mettlesome, spirited

con banal, inane, jejune

2 ***syn*** RISQUÉ, blue, broad, off-color, purple, salty, shady, spicy, suggestive, wicked

radiant *adj* **1** ***syn*** BRIGHT 1, beaming, brilliant, effulgent, fulgent, incandescent, lambent, lucent, luminous, refulgent

2 ***syn*** GLAD 2, bright, cheerful, cheery

radiate *vb* **1** ***syn*** SHINE 1, beam, burn, gleam

2 ***syn*** SPREAD 1, circulate, diffuse, disperse, disseminate, distribute, propagate, strew

rel diverge

radical *adj* **1** ***syn*** FUNDAMENTAL 1, basal, basic, bottom, foundational, primary, underlying

rel cardinal, essential, vital; constitutional, inherent, intrinsic

ant superficial

2 ***syn*** EXTREME 3, extremist, fanatic, rabid, revolutional, revolutionary, revolutionist, ultra, ultraist

3 ***syn*** LIBERAL 3, advanced, broad, broad-minded, progressive, tolerant, wide

radical *n* one who favors rapid and sweeping changes <the *radicals* advocated overthrow of the government>

syn extremist, revolutionary, revolutionist, ultraist; *compare* REACTIONARY

rel liberal, progressive, reformer; agitator, insurgent, insurrectionist, rebel; anarchist, nihilist, red, subversive; out-and-outer; secessionist, separatist

con bitter-ender, diehard, fogy, intransigent, mossback, reactionary, rightist, standpatter

ant conservative

radius *n* ***syn*** RANGE 2, ambit, compass, extension, extent, orbit, purview, reach, scope, sweep

raff *n* ***syn*** RABBLE 2, dreg(s), mass(es), mob, other half, proletariat, ragtag and bobtail, riffraff, roughscuff, scum

raffish *adj* ***syn*** WILD 7, devil-may-care, fast, gay, rakehell, rakish, sporty

rag *vb* **1** ***syn*** SCOLD 1, baste, bawl out, ‖bless out, ‖carpet, ‖chew, ‖chew out, jaw, rail, rant

---

syn synonym(s) ***rel*** related word(s)
idiom idiomatic equivalent(s) ***con*** contrasted word(s)
ant antonym(s) * vulgar
‖ use limited; if in doubt, see a dictionary
The first word in a synonym list when printed in SMALL CAPITALS shows where there is more information about the group. For a more efficient use of this book see Explanatory Notes.

2 *syn* BANTER, fool, fun, ‖jive, joke, jolly, josh, kid, razz, rib

‖**ragabash** *n syn* RABBLE 2, canaille, dreg(s), mass(es), mob, proletariat, ragtag and bobtail, riffraff, roughscuff, scum

ragamuffin *n* a person dressed in ragged clothing <a poor *ragamuffin* found begging>
syn ragshag, scarecrow, tatterdemalion
rel hobo, tramp, vagabond, vagrant; bum, loafer, wastrel; orphan, waif
con buck, coxcomb, dandy, dude, fop

rage *n* **1** *syn* ANGER, fury, indignation, ire, mad, wrath
rel acerbity, acrimony, asperity; frenzy, hysteria, mania; agitation, perturbation, upset
2 *syn* FASHION 3, chic, craze, cry, dernier cri, fad, furore, mode, style, vogue
rel caprice, conceit, crotchet, fancy, freak, vagary, whim

rage *vb syn* ANGER 2, blow up, boil, boil over, bristle, burn, flare (up), fume, seethe

ragged *adj* torn or worn to tatters <never saw such *ragged* clothes>
syn frayed, frazzled, shreddy, tattered
rel rent, torn; battered, patched; dilapidated, dingy, faded, seedy, shabby, threadbare, worn-out

raging *adj syn* WILD 6, blustering, blustery, ‖coarse, dirty, furious, rough, stormy, tempestuous, turbulent

rags *n pl* **1** poor or ragged clothing <a beggar in *rags*>
syn ‖duds, tatters
rel odds and ends, ribbons, shreds
2 *syn* CLOTHES, apparel, attire, attirement, clothing, dress, duds, habiliment(s), raiment, things

ragshag *n syn* RAGAMUFFIN, scarecrow, tatterdemalion

ragtag *n syn* RABBLE 2, dreg(s), hoi polloi, mass(es), mob, proletariat, ragtag and bobtail, riffraff, tag and rag, unwashed

ragtag and bobtail *n syn* RABBLE 2, dreg(s), hoi polloi, mass(es), mob, proletariat, ragtag, riffraff, tagrag and bobtail, unwashed

raid *n* **1** *syn* INVASION, foray, incursion, inroad, irruption
rel assault, onset, onslaught
2 a sudden attack by officers of the law <a *raid* on a gambling joint>
syn ‖bust

raid *vb* **1** to make a raid on <Indians *raided* the settlers frequently>
syn foray, harass, harry, maraud
rel despoil, devastate, ravage, sack, spoliate, waste; loot, plunder, rifle, rob
2 *syn* INVADE 1, foray, inroad, overrun, overswarm

raider *n syn* MARAUDER, forager, freebooter, looter, pillager, plunderer, ravager, ravisher, sacker, spoiler

rail *n syn* RAILING, balustrade, banister

syn synonym(s) *rel* related word(s)
idiom idiomatic equivalent(s) *con* contrasted word(s)
ant antonym(s) * vulgar
‖ use limited; if in doubt, see a dictionary
The first word in a synonym list when printed in SMALL CAPITALS shows where there is more information about the group. For a more efficient use of this book see Explanatory Notes.

rail *vb syn* SCOLD 1, bawl out, berate, ‖chew out, jaw, rate, revile, tongue-lash, upbraid, vituperate

railing *n* a usually protective barrier consisting essentially of an elongated raised member <a staircase without a *railing*>
syn balustrade, banister, rail

raillery *n syn* SATIRE, lampoonery, satiricalness

railroad station *n* a building containing accommodations for railroad passengers or freight <an old *railroad station* fallen into disrepair>
syn depot, station, station house

raiment *n syn* CLOTHES, apparel, attire, attirement, clothing, dress, duds, habiliment(s), things, togs

raiment *vb syn* CLOTHE, apparel, array, attire, clad, dress, enclothe, garb, garment

rainbow *n syn* PIPE DREAM, bubble, chimera, dream, fantasy (*or* phantasy), illusion, ‖pipe

rainless *adj syn* FAIR 2, clarion, clear, cloudless, fine, pleasant, sunny, sunshiny, unclouded, undarkened
ant rainy

raise *vb* **1** *syn* LIFT 1, elevate, hoist, pick up, rear, take up, uphold, uplift, upraise, uprear
ant lower
2 *syn* INCITE, abet, foment, instigate, provoke, set, set on, stir (up), whip (up)
3 *syn* RESURRECT 1
4 *syn* ERECT 3, put up, rear, set up
5 *syn* BUILD 1, construct, erect, put up, rear, uprear
6 *syn* BRING UP 1, ‖fetch up, rear
7 *syn* GROW 1, breed, cultivate, produce, propagate
8 *syn* GATHER 6, assemble, collect, congregate, congress, forgather, muster, rendezvous
9 to make larger in amount <*raised* the rent>
syn boost, hike, increase, jack (up), jump, put up, up
rel inflate
idiom send through the roof
con cut back, decrease, drop, lessen, reduce, roll back; minimize
ant lower

raise *n syn* ADDITION, accession, accretion, augmentation, increase, increment, rise

raised *adj* **1** *syn* ELEVATED 1, lifted, upheaved, uplifted, upraised, uprisen
2 *syn* ERECT, arrect, stand-up, straight-up, upright, upstanding

rake *vb syn* SCOUR 2, beat, comb, finecomb, fine-tooth-comb, forage, grub, ransack, rummage, search

rakehell *adj syn* WILD 7, devil-may-care, fast, gay, raffish, rakish, sporty

raking *adj syn* FAST 3, breakneck, expeditious, fleet, harefooted, hasty, quick, rapid, speedy, swift

rakish *adj syn* WILD 7, devil-may-care, fast, gay, raffish, rakehell, sporty

rally *vb* **1** *syn* MOBILIZE 3, marshal, muster, organize
2 *syn* STIR 1, arouse, awaken, bestir, challenge, kindle, rouse, wake, waken, whet
rel fire; refresh, renew, restore
3 *syn* RECOVER 2, come round
rel brace (up), enliven, invigorate, perk (up), pick up

rally *vb syn* RIDICULE, deride, lout, mock, quiz, razz, scout, taunt, twit
rel harass, harry, tantalize, tease, worry

rallying cry *n syn* BATTLE CRY, cry, motto, war cry

ram *vb* **1** ***syn*** THRUST 2, dig, drive, plunge, run, sink, stab, stick
2 ***syn*** CRAM 1, jam, jam-pack, ||pang, stuff, tamp

ramble *vb* **1** ***syn*** WANDER 1, gad, gallivant, meander, range, roam, rove, straggle, stray, traipse
2 ***syn*** DIGRESS 2, depart, divagate, diverge, excurse, stray, wander
3 ***syn*** SPRAWL 2, scramble, sprangle, spread-eagle, straddle, straggle

ramble *n* ***syn*** WALK 1, constitutional, saunter, stroll, turn

rambler *n* ***syn*** ROVER, drifter, meanderer, roamer, rolling stone, wanderer

rambunctious *adj* ***syn*** TURBULENT 1, boisterous, raucous, rowdy, rowdydowdy, rowdyish, rumbustious, termagant, tumultuous, unruly

rampage *n* ***syn*** SPREE 1, binge, fling, orgy, splurge
rel turmoil, uproar

rampant *adj* **1** ***syn*** RANK 1
rel excessive, immoderate, inordinate
con moderate, temperate; checked, curbed, restrained
2 ***syn*** PREVAILING, current, popular, prevalent, regnant, rife, ruling, widespread

rampart *n* ***syn*** BULWARK, bastion, breastwork, parapet

rancid *adj* ***syn*** MALODOROUS 1, fetid, high, nidorous, noisome, olid, putrid, reeking, smelly, whiffy
rel ||reasty; loathsome, repulsive
ant sweet

rancor *n* ***syn*** ENMITY, animosity, animus, antagonism, antipathy, hostility
rel bitterness, vindictiveness, virulence

rancorous *adj* **1** ***syn*** MALICIOUS, despiteful, evil, hateful, malevolent, malign, malignant, spiteful, vicious, wicked
2 ***syn*** BITTER 3, antagonistic, hostile, virulent, vitriolic

rancorously *adv* ***syn*** HARD 6, bitterly, hardly, keenly, resentfully, sorely

random *adj* lacking a definite plan, purpose, or pattern <a *random* choice>
syn aimless, designless, desultory, haphazard, hit-or-miss, indiscriminate, irregular, objectless, promiscuous, purposeless, slapdash, spot, unaimed, unconsidered, unplanned; *compare* ACCIDENTAL
rel contingent, fluky, fortuitous, incidental, odd
con arranged, organized, planned; methodical, systematic; deliberate, purposeful
ant purposive

random *adv* ***syn*** ABOUT 4, anyhow, any which way, anywise, around, at random, haphazard, haphazardly, helter-skelter, randomly
ant orderly

randomly *adv* ***syn*** ABOUT 4, anyhow, any which way, anywise, around, at random, haphazard, haphazardly, helter-skelter, random
ant orderly

randy *adj* ***syn*** LICENTIOUS 2, fast, incontinent, lascivious, lecherous, lewd, libertine, libidinous, lustful, satyric

range *vb* **1** ***syn*** LINE 1, align, allineate, line up
rel assort, classify, sort; bias, dispose, incline, predispose
2 ***syn*** WANDER 1, circumambulate, drift, gallivant, meander, ramble, roam, rove, straggle, stray
3 to change or differ within limits <discounts *range* from 10% to 40%>
syn extend, go, run, vary
rel differ, fluctuate

range *n* **1** ***syn*** HABITAT, haunt, home, locality, site, stamping ground
2 sphere of action, expression, or influence <a political movement worldwide in its *range* and power>
syn ambit, circle, compass, confine(s), dimension(s), extension, extensity, extent, length, orbit, panorama, purview, radius, reach, realm, scope, stretch, sweep, width
rel area, space, span; domain, field, province, sphere, territory; amplitude, expanse, gamut, spread
3 ***syn*** KEN, horizon, purview, reach
rel compass
idiom range of comprehension
4 ***syn*** ORDER 4, extent, magnitude, matter, neighborhood, tune, vicinity

rangy *adj* ***syn*** GANGLING, gangly, lanky, spindling, spindly
ant compact

rank *adj* **1** growing or increasing at an immoderate rate <*rank* weeds>
syn rampant
rel exuberant, lavish, lush, luxuriant, profuse
con scanty, sparse, thin
2 ***syn*** OVERGROWN, grown
3 ***syn*** OBSCENE 2, coarse, dirty, filthy, foul, gross, indecent, raunchy, smutty, vulgar
4 ***syn*** EGREGIOUS, capital, flagrant, glaring, gross
rel conspicuous, noticeable, outstanding
5 ***syn*** UTTER, absolute, complete, consummate, downright, gross, outright, perfect, positive, unmitigated
6 ***syn*** MALODOROUS 1, fetid, funky, noisome, olid, putrid, rancid, reeking, smelly, stinking
rel dank, humid; loathsome, repulsive

rank *n* **1** ***syn*** LINE 5, echelon, file, queue, row, string, tier
2 ***syn*** ESTATE 2, grade
3 ***syn*** STATUS 1, capacity, character, footing, place, position, situation, standing, state, station
4 ***syn*** STATUS 2, cachet, consequence, dignity, position, prestige, standing, state, stature

rank *vb* **1** ***syn*** CLASS 2, classify, evaluate, grade, rate
rel arrange, order; assort, sort
2 ***syn*** PRECEDE 1, outrank

rank and file *n* ***syn*** COMMONALTY, commonage, commoners, common men, people, plebeians, plebes, plebs, populace, third estate

rankle *vb* to produce continual or progressive anger, irritation, or bitterness <this decision has long *rankled* as an act of injustice>
syn fester

---

syn synonym(s)	***rel*** related word(s)
idiom idiomatic equivalent(s)	***con*** contrasted word(s)
ant antonym(s)	* vulgar

|| use limited; if in doubt, see a dictionary
The first word in a synonym list when printed in SMALL CAPITALS shows where there is more information about the group. For a more efficient use of this book see Explanatory Notes.

rel annoy, bother, irk, vex; aggravate, exasperate, irritate; harass, obsess, plague, torment

ransack *vb* **1** ***syn*** SCOUR 2, beat, comb, finecomb, fine-tooth-comb, forage, grub, rake, rummage, search
2 ***syn*** ROB 1, ‖knock off, knock over, loot, plunder, relieve, rifle, stick up

ransom *vb* to liberate by paying a price <*ransomed* the king>
syn buy, redeem
rel recover, regain, retrieve; emancipate, free, liberate; extricate, release

rant *vb* **1** ***syn*** ORATE, bloviate, declaim, harangue, mouth, perorate, rave, soapbox
rel bluster, huff; rage, storm
2 ***syn*** SCOLD 1, bawl out, berate, jaw, lash, rag, rail, rate, ‖ream out, vituperate

rant *n* ***syn*** BOMBAST, fustian, highfalutin, lexiphanicism, rhapsody, rhetoric, rodomontade

ran–tan *n* ***syn*** BINGE 1, bat, brannigan, bust, carousal, carouse, jag, spree, tear, wassail

rantankerous *adj* ***syn*** CANTANKEROUS, bearish, cankered, cranky, cross-grained, crotchety, ornery, vinegarish, vinegary, waspish

rap *n* **1** ***syn*** HIT 1, ‖conk, knock, lick, swat, swipe, wipe
2 ***syn*** REBUKE, admonishment, admonition, chiding, reprimand, reproach, reproof, wig

rap *vb* **1** ***syn*** TAP 1, bob, knock, tunk
2 ***syn*** CRITICIZE, blame, censure, condemn, denounce, denunciate, knock, reprehend, reprobate, skin

rap *n* **1** ***syn*** CHAT 2, causerie, chin, prose, talk, yarn
2 ***syn*** CONFERENCE 1, confabulation, deliberation, discussion, ventilation

rapacious *adj* **1** subsisting on prey <the *rapacious* wolf seized the lamb>
syn predacious, predative, predatorial, predatory, raptorial, vulturine, vulturish, vulturous
2 ***syn*** VORACIOUS, edacious, gluttonous, ravening, ravenous
rel ferocious, fierce

rapacity *n* ***syn*** CUPIDITY, avarice, avariciousness, avidity, greed
rel claim, demand, exaction

rape *vb* to have sexual intercourse with a woman without her consent and chiefly by force or deception <*rape* a young girl>
syn defile, deflorate, deflower, force, outrage, ravish, spoil, violate
rel debauch, devirginate, dishonor, ruin; betray, deceive, mislead; entice, lure, seduce, tempt; compromise, shame, wrong

rapid *adj* ***syn*** FAST 3, breakneck, expeditious, expeditive, fleet, hasty, quick, rapid, speedy, swift
rel agile, brisk, nimble; hurried, quickened
ant deliberate; leisurely

rapidity *n* ***syn*** SPEED 2, ‖bat, celerity, gait, pace, quickness, rapidness, swiftness, velocity

rapidly *adv* ***syn*** FAST 2, expeditiously, flat-out, full tilt, hastily, lickety-split, posthaste, quickly, speedily, swiftly

rapidness *n* ***syn*** SPEED 2, ‖bat, celerity, gait, pace, quickness, rapidity, swiftness, velocity

‖**rapper** *n* ***syn*** LIE, ‖bouncer, canard, cock-and-bull story, falsehood, falsity, fib, misrepresentation, story, tale

rapport *n* ***syn*** HARMONY 3, concord, unity

rapprochement *n* ***syn*** RECONCILIATION, harmonizing, reconcilement

rapscallion *n* ***syn*** SCAMP, devil, enfant terrible, limb, mischief, rascal, rogue, scalawag, skeezicks, villain

rap session *n* ***syn*** CONFERENCE 2, colloquium, colloquy, palaver, seminar

rapt *adj* ***syn*** INTENT, absorbed, deep, engaged, engrossed, immersed, preoccupied, wrapped, wrapped up

raptorial *adj* ***syn*** RAPACIOUS 1, predacious, predative, predatorial, predatory, vulturine, vulturish, vulturous

rapture *n* ***syn*** ECSTASY, heaven, rhapsody, seventh heaven, transport

rare *adj* **1** ***syn*** THIN 2, attenuate, attenuated, rarefied, subtile, subtle, tenuous
2 ***syn*** CHOICE, dainty, delicate, elegant, exquisite, recherché, select, superior
rel excellent, fine, unique
3 ***syn*** INFREQUENT, few, occasional, scarce, seldom, semioccasional, sporadic, uncommon, unfrequent
con accustomed, customary, habitual, usual, wonted; abounding, profuse
4 ***syn*** EXCEPTIONAL 1, extraordinary, singular, uncommon, unimaginable, unique, unordinary, unthinkable, unusual, unwonted

rarefied *adj* ***syn*** THIN 2, attenuate, attenuated, rare, subtile, subtle, tenuous

rarefy *vb* ***syn*** THIN 2, attenuate

rarely *adv* **1** ***syn*** SELDOM, hardly ever, infrequently, little, unfrequently, unoften
2 ***syn*** EXTRA, extremely, ‖uncommon, uncommonly, unusually

raring *adj* ***syn*** EAGER, agog, anxious, ardent, athirst, avid, breathless, impatient, keen, thirsty

rascal *n* **1** ***syn*** VILLAIN 1, *bastard, blackguard, heel, knave, lowlife, miscreant, rogue, scoundrel, *son of a bitch
2 ***syn*** SCAMP, devil, enfant terrible, limb, mischief, rapscallion, rogue, scalawag, skeezicks, villain

rash *adj* **1** acting, done, or expressed with undue haste or disregard for consequences <don't do anything *rash*> <that was a very *rash* statement>
syn brash, hasty, hotheaded, ill-advised, incautious, incogitant, inconsiderate, mad-brained, madcap, reckless, thoughtless, unadvised, unconsidered, unwary; *compare* CARELESS 1
rel abrupt, headlong, impetuous, precipitate, precipitous, sudden; foolhardy, foolish, impulsive, silly; careless, heedless, imprudent, indiscreet, injudicious, unthinking, unwise
con careful, cautious, chary, circumspect, wary; advised, considered, deliberate, designed, premeditated, studied; calm, cool, level-headed

---

syn synonym(s) ***rel*** related word(s)
idiom idiomatic equivalent(s) ***con*** contrasted word(s)
ant antonym(s) * vulgar
‖ use limited; if in doubt, see a dictionary
The first word in a synonym list when printed in SMALL CAPITALS shows where there is more information about the group. For a more efficient use of this book see Explanatory Notes.

ant calculating
2 *syn* ADVENTUROUS, adventuresome, audacious, daredevil, daring, foolhardy, reckless, temerarious, venturesome, venturous

rash *n syn* EPIDEMIC, outbreak, plague

rasp *vb syn* SCRAPE 1, grate, scratch

raspberry *n* a sound of disapproval, contempt, or derision <the crowd gave the umpire a *raspberry*>
syn bazoo, bird, boo, ‖Bronx cheer, catcall, hiss, hoot, pooh, pooh-pooh, ‖razz

rasping *adj syn* HARSH 3, dry, grating, hoarse, jarring, raucous, rough, rugged, stridulent, stridulous

raspish *adj syn* IRRITABLE, peevish, pettish, petulant, prickish, prickly, raspy, snappish, snappy, waspish

raspy *adj syn* IRRITABLE, peevish, pettish, petulant, prickish, prickly, raspish, snappish, snappy, waspish

rat *n* **1** *syn* RENEGADE, apostate, defector, recreant, runagate, tergiversator, turnabout, turncoat
2 *syn* SNOT 1, cur, dog, louse, ‖prick, scum, *shithead, skunk, snake, toad

rat *vb* **1** *syn* DEFECT, apostatize, desert, renounce, repudiate, tergiversate, tergiverse, turn
2 *syn* INFORM 3, ‖nark, peach, ‖pimp, ‖sing, snitch, squeak, squeal, ‖stool

rate *vb syn* SCOLD 1, bawl out, berate, ‖chew out, jaw, rail, revile, tongue-lash, upbraid, vituperate

rate *n* **1** *syn* PRICE 1, charge, cost, price tag, tab, tariff
2 *syn* DEGREE 2, proportion, ratio, scale

rate *vb* **1** *syn* ESTIMATE 1, appraise, assay, assess, evaluate, set (at), survey, valuate, value
2 *syn* CLASS 2, classify, evaluate, grade, rank
3 *syn* EARN 2, deserve, merit

rather *adv* **1** *syn* ENOUGH 2, averagely, fairly, moderately, passably, so-so, tolerably
2 *syn* INSTEAD, alternately, alternatively, in lieu
3 *syn* SOMEWHAT 2, fairly, kind of, moderately, more or less, pretty, ratherish, some, something, sort of
4 *syn* WELL 8, considerably, far, quite, significantly, somewhat

ratherish *adv syn* SOMEWHAT 2, fairly, kind of, moderately, more or less, pretty, rather, some, something, sort of

ratify *vb* to make something legally valid or operative usually by formal approval or sanctioning <agreed to *ratify* the treaty>
syn confirm
rel accredit, authorize, commission, license; approve, endorse, sanction; authenticate, validate
con disown, reject, repudiate

ratio *n syn* DEGREE 2, proportion, rate, scale

ratiocination *n* **1** *syn* INFERENCE 1, deduction, illation, judgment
ant intuition
2 *syn* INFERENCE 2, conclusion, deduction, illation, judgment, sequitur

ratiocinative *adj syn* LOGICAL 2, analytic, analytical, subtle

ration *n* an amount allotted or made available especially from a limited supply <saved up their gasoline *ration* for a vacation trip>
syn allotment, allowance, apportionment, measure, meed, part, portion, quantum, quota, share; *compare* SHARE 1
rel assignment, consignment, distribution, division

ration *vb syn* APPORTION 2, divide, ‖divvy, parcel, portion, prorate, quota, share, ‖shift
rel allocate, allot, assign, mete (out)

rational *adj* agreeable to reason <offered a *rational* explanation>
syn consequent, intelligent, logical, reasonable, sensible, sound
rel calm, cool, level-headed, sober, stable; circumspect, judicious, prudent; lucid, normal, sane
con rash, reckless, wild; groundless, illogical, unreasonable, unreasoning, unsound; crazy, demented, deranged
ant animal, irrational; absurd

rationale *n syn* EXPLANATION 2, account, justification, rationalization, reason

rationalization *n syn* EXPLANATION 2, account, justification, rationale, reason

rationalize *vb syn* EXPLAIN 3, account, explain away, justify

rattle *vb* **1** to make a rapid succession of short sharp noises <the window *rattled* in the wind>
syn bicker, clack, clatter, clitter, ‖ruttle, shatter
2 *syn* CHAT 1, babble, chatter, clack, gab, gabble, jaw, prattle, run on, yak
3 *syn* EMBARRASS, abash, confound, confuse, discomfit, disconcert, discountenance, faze
rel addle, muddle; disturb, upset; bewilder, distract, perplex

rattlebrain *n syn* SCATTERBRAIN, birdbrain, featherbrain, featherhead, flibbertigibbet, harebrain, rattlehead, shatterbrain

rattlebrained *adj syn* GIDDY 1, dizzy, empty-headed, featherbrained, flighty, frivolous, harebrained, scatterbrained, silly, skittish

rattlehead *n syn* SCATTERBRAIN, birdbrain, featherbrain, featherhead, flibbertigibbet, harebrain, rattlebrain, shatterbrain

rattletrap *n, usu* **rattletraps** *pl syn* KNICKKNACK, bauble, dido, gewgaw, gimcrack, toy, trifle, trinket, whatnot, whigmaleerie

rattletrap *adj syn* RICKETY, rachitic, rackety, shaky, wobbly

rattling *adv syn* VERY 1, damned, exceedingly, extremely, mighty, parlous, snapping, spanking, whacking, whopping

ratty *adj syn* IRASCIBLE, choleric, cranky, cross, peppery, ‖stomachy, temperish, testy, tetchy, touchy

raucous *adj* **1** *syn* HARSH 3, dry, grating, hoarse, jarring, rough, squawky, strident, stridulent, stridulous
rel brusque, gruff
2 *syn* TURBULENT 1, boisterous, disorderly, rowdy, rowdydowdy, rowdyish, rumbustious, termagant, tumultuous, unruly

---

syn synonym(s) *rel* related word(s)
idiom idiomatic equivalent(s) *con* contrasted word(s)
ant antonym(s) * vulgar
‖ use limited; if in doubt, see a dictionary
The first word in a synonym list when printed in SMALL CAPITALS shows where there is more information about the group. For a more efficient use of this book see Explanatory Notes.

raunchy *adj* **1** ***syn*** SLOVENLY 1, disheveled, ill-kempt, messy, slipshod, ||slommacky, sloppy, unkempt, unneat, untidy
2 ***syn*** OBSCENE 2, coarse, dirty, filthy, foul, indecent, nasty, ||raw, smutty, vulgar

ravage *vb* to lay waste (as by plundering or destroying) <the countryside was *ravaged* by the invading soldiers>
syn deflower, depredate, desecrate, desolate, despoil, devast, devastate, devour, harry, havoc, pillage, sack, scourge, spoil, spoliate, strip, waste
rel demolish, destroy, raze; loot, plunder, ransack, rob; ruin, wreck; encroach, invade, trespass; crush, overpower, overrun, overthrow, overwhelm
idiom lay in ruins, lay waste
con build, improve, rehabilitate

ravager *n* ***syn*** MARAUDER, forager, freebooter, looter, pillager, plunderer, raider, ravisher, sacker, spoiler

rave *vb* **1** ***syn*** ORATE, bloviate, declaim, harangue, mouth, perorate, rant, soapbox
2 ***syn*** ENTHUSE 2, drool, rhapsodize, rhapsody

ravel *vb* ***syn*** COMPLICATE, entangle, ||muck, muddle, perplex, snarl, tangle

raven *adj* ***syn*** BLACK 1, atramentous, ebon, ebony, inky, jet, jetty, pitch-black, pitch-dark, sable

ravening *adj* ***syn*** VORACIOUS, edacious, gluttonous, rapacious, ravenous

ravenous *adj* **1** ***syn*** VORACIOUS, edacious, gluttonous, rapacious, ravening
2 ***syn*** HUNGRY, famished, ||peckish, starved, starving

ravine *n* a small narrow steep-sided valley <followed the *ravine* high up into the hills>
syn arroyo, chasm, cleft, clough, clove, gap, gorge, gulch
rel cut, notch; defile, pass; abyss, gulf; crevasse, crevice, fissure; ||dry wash, gully, gutter, ||wash; canyon

raving *adj* ***syn*** DELIRIOUS 1, wandering

ravish *vb* **1** ***syn*** TRANSPORT 2, enrapture, enravish, entrance, trance
2 ***syn*** RAPE, defile, deflorate, deflower, force, outrage, spoil, violate

ravisher *n* ***syn*** MARAUDER, despoiler, looter, pillager, plunderer, raider, ravager, sacker, spoiler, spoliator

raw *adj* **1** not cooked <a *raw* egg>
syn uncooked
2 ***syn*** UNREFINED 3, crude, impure, native, run-of-mine, ungraded, unsorted
3 ***syn*** RUDE 1, crude, rough, roughhewn, undressed, unfashioned, unfinished, unformed, unhewn, unpolished
4 ***syn*** NUDE 2, au naturel, *bare-assed, buff-bare, naked, stark-naked, stripped, unclad, unclothed, undressed
5 ***syn*** INEXPERIENCED, callow, fresh, green, unconversant, unpracticed, unseasoned, untried, unversed, young
rel untaught, untutored; unmatured, unripe
con drilled, exercised; hardened; adult, grown-up, mature, matured, ripe
6 ***syn*** COARSE 3, crass, crude, gross, inelegant, rough, rude, uncouth, unrefined, vulgar
||**7** ***syn*** OBSCENE 2, coarse, dirty, filthy, foul, indecent, nasty, rank, smutty, vulgar

rawboned *adj* ***syn*** LEAN, angular, bony, gaunt, lank, lanky, scraggy, scrawny, skinny, spare

rawhider *n* ***syn*** SLAVE DRIVER, Simon Legree, taskmaster

rawness *n* ***syn*** INEXPERIENCE, callowness, freshness, greenness

ray *n* **1** one of the lines of light that appear to radiate from a bright or luminous object <the *rays* of the sun>
syn beam, shaft, shoot
rel raylet; pencil, streak, stream; moonbeam, sunbeam
con gleam, glow, incandescence, shine
2 ***syn*** PARTICLE, atom, drop, iota, jot, minim, molecule, scrap, shred, smidgen

raze *vb* ***syn*** DESTROY 1, decimate, demolish, ruin, unbuild, undo, unframe, unmake, wrack, wreck

razor–sharp *adj* ***syn*** SHARP 1, honed, keen, unblunted, whetted

||**razz** *n* ***syn*** RASPBERRY, bazoo, bird, boo, ||Bronx cheer, catcall, hiss, hoot, pooh, pooh-pooh

razz *vb* **1** ***syn*** BANTER, fool, jest, ||jive, joke, jolly, josh, kid, rag, rib
2 ***syn*** RIDICULE, deride, lout, mock, quiz, rally, scout, taunt, twit

re *prep* ***syn*** APROPOS, as for, as regards, as respects, as to, concerning, in re, regarding, respecting, with respect to

reach *vb* **1** ***syn*** COME 1, arrive, ||blow in, get, get in, show, show up, turn up
2 ***syn*** GAIN 1, accomplish, achieve, attain, rack up, realize, score, win
3 to get into contact with especially intellectually or emotionally <there was no common ground on which she could *reach* him>
syn approach
rel affect, influence, sway; get, move, touch
idiom establish contact with, find a common denominator, get through to, get to, have a meeting of minds, make advances to, make overtures to, make up to, reach (*or* share) common ground
4 to communicate with <you can *reach* me at this number>
syn contact, get
idiom get in touch (*or* contact) with, get through to, get to, keep in touch (*or* contact) with, maintain connections with
5 ***syn*** PASS 9, buck, hand, ||shoot
6 ***syn*** RUN 8, extend, go, make, stretch

reach *n* **1** ***syn*** RANGE 2, ambit, compass, extension, extent, orbit, purview, radius, scope, sweep
2 ***syn*** KEN, horizon, purview, range

react *vb* **1** ***syn*** ACT 5, behave, function, operate, perform, take, work
2 ***syn*** RETURN 1, recrudesce, recur, revert, turn back

reactionarist *n* ***syn*** REACTIONARY, blimp, Bourbon, diehard, reactionist, royalist, ultraconservative, white

syn synonym(s) — *rel* related word(s)
idiom idiomatic equivalent(s) — *con* contrasted word(s)
ant antonym(s) — * vulgar
|| use limited; if in doubt, see a dictionary
The first word in a synonym list when printed in SMALL CAPITALS shows where there is more information about the group. For a more efficient use of this book see Explanatory Notes.

reactionary *adj* ***syn*** CONSERVATIVE 1, die-hard, fogyish, old-line, orthodox, right, tory, traditionalistic

reactionary *n* one who strongly resists change and often favors a prior condition <he is a staunch political *reactionary*>
syn blimp, Bourbon, diehard, reactionarist, reactionist, royalist, ultraconservative, white; *compare* DIEHARD 1, RADICAL
rel bitter-ender, conservative, intransigent, rightist, right-winger, standpatter; fogy, mossback
con extremist, radical, revolutionary, revolutionist, ultraist; liberal, progressive, reformer

reactionist *n* ***syn*** REACTIONARY, blimp, Bourbon, diehard, reactionarist, royalist, ultraconservative, white

reactivate *vb* ***syn*** REVIVE 3, rekindle, renew, renovate, resurrect, resuscitate, retrieve, revitalize, revivify

read *vb* ***syn*** SHOW 5, indicate, mark, record, register, say

readily *adv* ***syn*** EASILY 1, effortlessly, facilely, freely, lightly, smoothly, well

readiness *n* **1** ***syn*** ALACRITY, dispatch, expedition, goodwill, promptitude
2 ***syn*** ADDRESS 1, adroitness, deftness, dexterity, dexterousness, prowess, skill, sleight
3 the power of doing something without evidence of effort <his *readiness* in repartee>
syn ease, facility
rel eloquence, fluency, volubility
con effort, exertions, pains, trouble

reading *n* ***syn*** INTERPRETATION 2, rendering, rendition, version

readjust *vb* ***syn*** REORGANIZE, rearrange, reconstitute, reconstruct, reorder, reorient, reorientate, reshuffle, retool

ready *adj* **1** in a state of mental or physical fitness for some experience or action <*ready* to leave at a moment's notice>
syn prepared, set
rel adjusted, fit, qualified; primed
idiom all ready, all set, champing at the bit
con unprepared, unqualified
ant unready
2 ***syn*** WILLING 1, disposed, fain, inclined, minded, predisposed, prone
3 ***syn*** QUICK 2, apt, prompt
rel adept, expert, masterly, proficient, skilled, skillful; active, dynamic, live

ready *vb* **1** ***syn*** PREPARE 1, fit, fix, get, make, make up
2 ***syn*** GIRD 3, brace, fortify, prepare, steel, strengthen

ready-made *adj* made for general sale or use rather than prepared according to individual specifications <*ready-made* clothing>
syn bought, ‖boughten, ready-to-wear, store, store-bought, ‖store-boughten
idiom off the rack
con custom-built, made-to-order, tailor-made; handmade
ant custom-made

ready-to-wear *adj* ***syn*** READY-MADE, bought, ‖boughten, store, store-bought, ‖store-boughten

ready-witted *adj* ***syn*** INTELLIGENT 2, alert, brainy, bright, brilliant, clever, knowing, quick-witted, sharp, smart

real *adj* **1** ***syn*** AUTHENTIC 2, blown-in-the-bottle, bona fide, genuine, indubitable, sure-enough, true, undoubted, undubitable, unquestionable
ant bogus
2 ***syn*** GENUINE 3, heart-whole, honest, sincere, true, undesigning, undissembled, unfeigned
3 corresponding to known facts <discovered the *real* reason for his hasty departure>
syn actual, indisputable, true, undeniable, unfabled, veridical
rel being, existing, subsisting; certain, inevitable, necessary; sound, valid, well-grounded
idiom deniable, disputable, doubtful, questionable; improbable, uncertain, unlikely
ant unreal; apparent; imaginary

realistic *adj* having no illusions and facing reality squarely <he made a *realistic* appraisal of his chances for advancement>
syn down-to-earth, earthy, hard, hard-boiled, hardheaded, matter-of-fact, practic, practical, pragmatic, pragmatical, sober, unfantastic, unidealistic, unromantic, unsentimental, utilitarian
rel rational, reasonable, sane, sensible, sound; astute, prudent, shrewd; nonacademic
con dreamy, fantastic, imaginative; idealistic, impractical, irrational, romantic, visionary; theoretical
ant unrealistic; fanciful

reality *n* **1** ***syn*** FACT 1, actuality
2 ***syn*** ACTUALITY 2, materiality

realize *vb* **1** ***syn*** GAIN 1, accomplish, achieve, attain, rack up, reach, score, win
2 ***syn*** THINK 1, conceive, envisage, envision, fancy, feature, image, imagine, vision, visualize

really *adv* **1** ***syn*** VERY 2, actually, de facto, genuinely, truly, veritably
2 ***syn*** WELL 7, doubtlessly, easily, indeed, truly, undoubtedly

realm *n* ***syn*** RANGE 2, compass, dimension(s), extent, orbit, purview, radius, reach, scope, sweep

ream *n, usu* **reams** *pl* ***syn*** SCAD, gob(s), heap, load(s), oodles, quantities, ‖rimption(s), slather(s), slew, wad(s)

ream *vb* ***syn*** CHEAT, beat, bilk, chisel, cozen, diddle, do, gyp, ‖mace, ‖screw

‖**ream out** *vb* ***syn*** SCOLD 1, bawl out, ‖bless out, ‖cample, ‖chew out, jaw, lash, tell off, tongue-lash, ‖tongue-walk

reanimation *n* ***syn*** REVIVAL, rebirth, renaissance, renascence, resurgence, resurrection, resuscitation, revivification, reviviscence, risorgimento

reap *vb* to do the work of collecting ripened crops <storms hampered his *reaping*>
syn garner, gather, harvest, ingather
rel glean

---

syn synonym(s) ***rel*** related word(s)
idiom idiomatic equivalent(s) ***con*** contrasted word(s)
ant antonym(s) * vulgar
‖ use limited; if in doubt, see a dictionary
The first word in a synonym list when printed in SMALL CAPITALS shows where there is more information about the group. For a more efficient use of this book see Explanatory Notes.

reaping *n* ***syn*** HARVEST 1, cropping, gathering, harvesting, ingathering

reappearance *n* ***syn*** RECURRENCE, reoccurrence, return

rear *vb* **1** ***syn*** BUILD 1, construct, erect, put up, raise, uprear
2 ***syn*** ERECT 3, put up, raise, set up
3 ***syn*** LIFT 1, elevate, hoist, pick up, raise, take up, uphold, uplift, upraise, uprear
4 ***syn*** BRING UP 1, ‖fetch up, raise
rel foster, nurse, nurture; breed, propagate

rear *n* **1** ***syn*** BACK 1, posterior, rearward
ant front
2 ***syn*** BUTTOCKS, backside, behind, bottom, fanny, hind end, rear end, rump, seat, tail

rear *adj* ***syn*** POSTERIOR 2, after, back, hind, hinder, hindmost, retral
ant front

rear end *n* ***syn*** BUTTOCKS, backside, behind, bottom, fanny, hind end, rear, rump, seat, tail

rearmost *adj* ***syn*** LAST, closing, concluding, eventual, final, hindmost, latest, latter, terminal, ultimate

rearrange *vb* ***syn*** REORGANIZE, readjust, reconstitute, reconstruct, reorder, reorient, reorientate, reshuffle, retool

rearward *n* ***syn*** BACK 1, posterior, rear

reason *n* **1** ***syn*** EXPLANATION 2, account, justification, rationale, rationalization
2 ***syn*** MOTIVE 1, cause, consideration, spring
3 a point or points that support something open to question <he soon gave sensible *reasons* for the proposed change>
syn argument, ground, proof, wherefore, why, whyfor
rel explanation, justification, rationalization
4 ***syn*** CAUSE 1, antecedent, determinant, occasion
5 the power of the mind by which man attains truth or knowledge <we all must use *reason* to solve this problem>
syn intellect, understanding
rel inference, ratiocination
6 ***syn*** WIT 2, lucidity, ‖marbles, mind, saneness, sanity, sense(s), soundness

reason *vb* ***syn*** THINK 5, cerebrate, cogitate, deliberate, reflect, speculate

reasonable *adj* **1** ***syn*** CONSERVATIVE 2, controlled, discreet, moderate, restrained, temperate, unexcessive, unextreme
2 ***syn*** MODERATE 2, modest, temperate
3 ***syn*** CHEAP 1, inexpensive, low, low-cost, low-priced, popular, uncostly, undear
ant extravagant
4 ***syn*** RATIONAL, consequent, intelligent, logical, sensible, sound
ant unreasonable

reasoned *adj* ***syn*** DEDUCTIVE, a priori, deducible, derivable, dogmatic

reasonless *adj* **1** ***syn*** INSANE 1, ‖batty, bedlamite, cracked, crazed, crazy, daft, demented, deranged, lunatic
2 ***syn*** ILLOGICAL, fallacious, invalid, irrational, mad, nonrational, sophistic, unreasonable, unreasoned

reassume *vb* ***syn*** RESUME 1, reoccupy, repossess, retake

rebate *vb* ***syn*** DECREASE, abate, ‖bate, diminish, drain (away), dwindle, lessen, reduce, taper, taper off

rebate *n* ***syn*** DEDUCTION 1, abatement, discount, reduction, subtraction

rebel *n* one who breaks with or opposes constituted authority or the established order <he is a *rebel* among educators>
syn anarch, anarchist, frondeur, insurgent, insurrectionist, malcontent, mutineer, revolter
rel adversary, antagonist, opponent; assailant, attacker; extremist, radical, revolutionary, revolutionist, ultraist; debunker, iconoclast
con authoritarian, intransigent, traditionalist; conservative, reactionary, white

rebel *vb* ***syn*** REVOLT 1, insurrect, mutiny, rise (against)

rebellious *adj* ***syn*** INSUBORDINATE, contumacious, factious, insurgent, mutinous, seditious
rel alienated, disaffected, estranged
con acquiescent, resigned; submissive

rebirth *n* **1** ***syn*** CONVERSION 1, metanoia
2 ***syn*** REVIVAL, reanimation, renaissance, renascence, resurgence, resurrection, resuscitation, revivification, reviviscence, risorgimento

rebound *vb* ***syn*** RECOVER 3, bounce (back), snap back

rebuff *vb* ***syn*** FEND (off), hold off, keep off, rebut, repel, repulse, stave off, ward (off)
idiom give the cold shoulder

rebuild *vb* ***syn*** MEND 2, doctor, do up, fix, overhaul, patch, recondition, reconstruct, repair, revamp

rebuke *vb* ***syn*** REPROVE, admonish, call down, chide, lesson, monish, ‖rack back, reprimand, reproach, tick off

rebuke *n* an expression of strong disapproval <his bad behavior earned him a sharp *rebuke*>
syn admonishment, admonition, chiding, rap, reprimand, reproach, reproof, wig
rel dressing down, earful, lecture, lesson, scolding, talking-to, tongue-lashing
idiom a flea in one's ear, slap on the wrist
con applause, compliment, praise

rebut *vb* **1** ***syn*** FEND (off), hold off, keep off, rebuff, repel, repulse, stave off, ward (off)
2 ***syn*** DISPROVE 1, break, confound, confute, controvert, disconfirm, evert, refute

recalcitrance *n* ***syn*** DEFIANCE 2, contempt, contumacy, despite, stubbornness

recalcitrant *adj* ***syn*** UNRULY 1, fractious, indomitable, intractable, undisciplinable, undisciplined, ungovernable, unmanageable, untoward, wild
rel obstinate, stubborn; opposing, resisting, withstanding
ant amenable

recall *vb* **1** ***syn*** REMEMBER, bethink, cite, ‖mind, recollect, remind, reminisce, retain, retrospect, revive
rel educe, elicit, evoke, extract; arouse, awaken, rouse, stir, waken

---

syn synonym(s) ***rel*** related word(s)
idiom idiomatic equivalent(s) ***con*** contrasted word(s)
ant antonym(s) * vulgar
‖ use limited; if in doubt, see a dictionary
The first word in a synonym list when printed in SMALL CAPITALS shows where there is more information about the group. For a more efficient use of this book see Explanatory Notes.

2 *syn* ABJURE, forswear, palinode, recant, retract, take back, unsay, withdraw
3 *syn* REVOKE 2, dismantle, lift, repeal, rescind, reverse
4 *syn* RESTORE 1, reestablish, reinstate, reintroduce, renew, revive

recall *n syn* MEMORY 2, anamnesis, recollection, remembrance, reminiscence

recant *vb syn* ABJURE, forswear, palinode, recall, retract, take back, unsay, withdraw

recapitulation *n syn* SUMMARY, epitome, résumé, sum, summation, summing-up, sum-up

recede *vb* **1** to move backward <they will return after the floodwaters *recede*>
syn back, fall back, retract, retreat, retrocede, retrograde
rel regress, retrogress; depart, retire, withdraw
ant proceed; advance
2 *syn* DECREASE, abate, ‖bate, close, diminish, drain (away), dwindle, lessen, reduce, taper

receipts *n pl syn* REVENUE, coming(s) in, income

receive *vb syn* TAKE 10, admit, take in

received *adj syn* ORTHODOX 1, accepted, authoritative, canonical, sanctioned, sound

recension *n syn* REVISION 1, redraft, rescript, review, revisal, revise

recent *adj* **1** *syn* NEW 1, fresh, modern, modernistic, neoteric, newfangled, new-fashioned, new-sprung, novel
2 *syn* MODERN 1, late

recently *adv syn* NEW, afresh, anew, lately, newly, of late

receptive *adj* **1** open to ideas, impressions, or suggestions <he has a most *receptive* mind>
syn acceptant, acceptive, influenceable, persuadable, persuasible, responsive, suasible, swayable
rel open, open-minded; accessible, amenable, suggestible
con closed, closed-minded, inhospitable
ant unreceptive
2 *syn* SYMPATHETIC 2, friendly, ‖sib, well-disposed

recess *vb syn* ADJOURN 2, dissolve, prorogate, prorogue, rise, terminate

recession *n syn* DEPRESSION 3, slump, stagnation

recherché *adj syn* CHOICE, dainty, delicate, elegant, exquisite, rare, select, superior
rel fresh, new, novel, original; exotic, uncommon, unusual
ant commonplace

recidivate *vb syn* LAPSE, backslide, relapse

reciprocal *n syn* MATE 5, companion, coordinate, double, duplicate, fellow, match, twin

reciprocate *vb* to give back, usually in kind or quantity <they were glad of the chance to *reciprocate* her kindness>
syn recompense, requite, retaliate, return
rel exchange, interchange; compensate, repay; retort, serve out
con accept, acquire, pocket, take

recital *n syn* DESCRIPTION 2, narration, recountal, recounting
rel discourse, story; enumeration

recite *vb syn* RELATE 1, describe, narrate, recount, rehearse, report, state
rel count, enumerate, number, tell

reckless *adj* **1** *syn* ADVENTUROUS, adventuresome, audacious, daredevil, daring, foolhardy, rash, temerarious, venturesome, venturous
rel desperate, hopeless
2 *syn* RASH 1, brash, hasty, hotheaded, ill-advised, incautious, inconsiderate, mad-brained, madcap, thoughtless
ant calculating
3 *syn* IRRESPONSIBLE, carefree, careless, feckless, incautious, uncareful, wild

reckon *vb* **1** *syn* CALCULATE, cipher, compute, estimate, figure
rel count, enumerate, number; add, cast, foot, sum, total
2 *syn* CONSIDER 3, account, deem, regard, view
rel conjecture, guess, surmise
3 *syn* ESTIMATE 3, approximate, call, judge, place, put
‖4 *syn* UNDERSTAND 3, assume, believe, expect, gather, imagine, suppose, suspect, take, think

reckon (on) *vb syn* RELY (on *or* upon), bank (on *or* upon), build (on), calculate (on *or* upon), count (on), depend (on *or* upon), ‖lot (on *or* upon), trust (in *or* to)

reckoning *n* **1** *syn* BILL 1, account, invoice, score, statement, tab
2 *syn* COMPUTATION, arithmetic, calculation, ciphering, estimation, figuring

reclaim *vb syn* RESTORE 3, recondition, reconstruct, recover, rehabilitate, rejuvenate, restitute

recline *vb* **1** *syn* SLANT 1, cant, heel, incline, lean, list, slope, tilt, tip
2 *syn* REST 1, lie, lie down, repose, stretch (out)

reclining *adj syn* PRONE 4, decumbent, flat, procumbent, prostrate, recumbent

recluse *adj syn* SECLUDED, cloistered, hermetic, secluse, seclusive, sequestered

recluse *n* a person who leads a secluded or solitary life <a man who led the life of a *recluse* although living in a busy city>
syn hermit, solitary
rel anchorite, cenobite, eremite

reclusion *n syn* SECLUSION, retirement, sequestration

reclusive *adj syn* ANTISOCIAL, eremitic, misanthropic, reserved, solitary, standoffish

recognition *n* **1** a learning process that relates a perception of something new to knowledge already possessed <*recognition* of a genuine diamond>
syn apperception, assimilation, identification
rel cognizance, realization; awareness, consciousness, sensibility
ant irrecognition
2 *syn* CREDIT 4, acknowledgment
ant unrecognition

---

syn synonym(s) *rel* related word(s)
idiom idiomatic equivalent(s) *con* contrasted word(s)
ant antonym(s) * vulgar
‖ use limited; if in doubt, see a dictionary
The first word in a synonym list when printed in SMALL CAPITALS shows where there is more information about the group. For a more efficient use of this book see Explanatory Notes.

recognize *vb* **1** to make out as or perceive to be something previously known <said they would *recognize* that face anywhere>
syn know
rel recall, recollect, remember
2 ***syn*** IDENTIFY, determinate, diagnose, diagnosticate, distinguish, finger, pinpoint, place, spot
3 ***syn*** ACKNOWLEDGE 2, admit, agree
rel note, notice, observe, remark

recoil *vb* to draw back usually through fear or disgust <*recoiled* from the snake>
syn blanch, blench, flinch, quail, shrink, squinch, start, wince
rel falter, hesitate, waver; balk, shy, stick, stickle; dodge, duck, swerve; quake, shake, shudder, tremble; reel (back)
con advance, approach, near
ant confront; defy

re–collect *vb* ***syn*** COMPOSE 4, collect, control, cool, rein, repress, restrain, simmer down, smother, suppress

recollect *vb* ***syn*** REMEMBER, bethink, cite, ||mind, recall, remind, reminisce, retain, retrospect, revive
rel arouse, awaken, rally, rouse, stir, waken

recollection *n* **1** ***syn*** MEMORY 2, anamnesis, recall, remembrance, reminiscence
2 ***syn*** MEMORY 1, remembrance, reminiscence

recommence *vb* ***syn*** RESUME 2, continue, pick up, renew, reopen, restart, take up

recommend *vb* **1** ***syn*** COMMEND 2, acclaim, applaud, compliment, hail, kudize, praise, ||roose
ant discommend
2 ***syn*** COUNSEL, advise

recommendation *n* ***syn*** CREDENTIALS, character, reference, testimonial
rel approval, endorsement; commendation

recompense *vb* **1** ***syn*** COMPENSATE 3, indemnify, pay, reimburse, remunerate, repay, requite
rel accord, award, grant, vouchsafe; balance, offset
2 ***syn*** RECIPROCATE, requite, retaliate, return

recompense *n* ***syn*** REPARATION, amends, compensation, indemnification, indemnity, quittance, redress, reprisal, restitution

reconcile *vb* **1** ***syn*** HARMONIZE 3, accommodate, attune, conform, coordinate, integrate, proportion, reconciliate, tune
idiom bury the hatchet, make peace
ant estrange
2 ***syn*** ADAPT, accommodate, adjust, conform, fit, quadrate, square, suit, tailor, tailor-make

reconcilement *n* ***syn*** RECONCILIATION, harmonizing, rapprochement

reconciliate *vb* ***syn*** HARMONIZE 3, accommodate, attune, conform, coordinate, integrate, proportion, reconcile, tune

reconciliation *n* establishment of harmony <a *reconciliation* between the two countries was effected after ten years>
syn harmonizing, rapprochement, reconcilement
rel appeasement, conciliation, mollification, propitiation, satisfying
ant disagreement

recondite *adj* beyond the reach of the average intelligence <a *recondite* subject>
syn abstruse, acroamatic, deep, esoteric, heavy, hermetic, occult, orphic, profound, secret
rel erudite, learned, scholarly; academic, pedantic; difficult, hard; dark, enigmatic, obscure; anagogic, cabalistic, mystic, mystical; cryptic, runic, sibylline
con easy, facile, simple, straightforward

recondition *vb* **1** ***syn*** RESTORE 3, reclaim, reconstruct, recover, rehabilitate, rejuvenate, restitute
2 ***syn*** MEND 2, doctor, do up, fix, overhaul, patch, rebuild, reconstruct, repair, revamp

reconnoiter *vb* ***syn*** SCOUT, probe

reconsider *vb* to consider again with a view to changing or reversing <was asked to *reconsider* his decision>
syn reevaluate, reexamine, rethink, re-treat, review, reweigh, think (over)
rel draw off; sleep (on); amend, correct, revise
idiom revise one's thoughts, think better of, view in a new light

reconsideration *n* ***syn*** REVIEW 5, afterlight, reexamination, retrospect, retrospection, revision

reconstitute *vb* ***syn*** REORGANIZE, readjust, rearrange, reconstruct, reorder, reorient, reorientate, reshuffle, retool

reconstruct *vb* **1** ***syn*** MEND 2, doctor, do up, fix, overhaul, patch, rebuild, recondition, repair, revamp
2 ***syn*** REORGANIZE, readjust, rearrange, reconstitute, reorder, reorient, reorientate, reshuffle, retool
3 ***syn*** RESTORE 3, reclaim, recondition, recover, rehabilitate, rejuvenate, restitute

record *vb* ***syn*** SHOW 5, indicate, mark, read, register, say

record *n* ***syn*** DOCUMENT 2, archive(s), monument

recount *vb* ***syn*** RELATE 1, describe, narrate, recite, rehearse, report, state

recountal *n* ***syn*** DESCRIPTION 2, narration, recital, recounting

recounting *n* ***syn*** DESCRIPTION 2, narration, recital, recountal

recoup *vb* ***syn*** RECOVER 1, get back, recruit, regain, repossess, retrieve

recourse *n* ***syn*** RESOURCE 3, dernier ressort, expediency, expedient, makeshift, refuge, resort, shift, stopgap, substitute

recover *vb* **1** to obtain again <*recover* a lost watch>
syn get back, recoup, recruit, regain, repossess, retrieve
rel reclaim, redeem; reacquire, recapture, retake, rewin; reoccupy, resume; rediscover; balance, compensate, offset
con lose, mislay, misplace; forfeit, sacrifice
2 to regain health <*recovering* from a bout of pneumonia>
syn come round, rally
rel convalesce, improve, mend, recuperate; perk (up), revive; heal; refresh, rejuvenate, renew, restore

---

syn synonym(s) ***rel*** related word(s)
idiom idiomatic equivalent(s) ***con*** contrasted word(s)
ant antonym(s) * vulgar
|| use limited; if in doubt, see a dictionary
The first word in a synonym list when printed in SMALL CAPITALS shows where there is more information about the group. For a more efficient use of this book see Explanatory Notes.

idiom get back in shape, get better, sit up and take nourishment, take a turn for the better
con decline, fail, weaken, worsen; die, expire, perish
3 to regain a former or normal state <the textile industry was *recovering* quickly from the depression>
syn bounce (back), rebound, snap back
rel rally, revive
con decline, fail
ant worsen
4 ***syn*** RESTORE 3, reclaim, recondition, reconstruct, rehabilitate, rejuvenate, restitute
recreancy *n* ***syn*** DEFECTION, apostasy, desertion, falseness, tergiversation
recreant *adj* ***syn*** FAITHLESS, disloyal, false, perfidious, traitorous, treacherous, unfaithful, unloyal, untrue
recreant *n* ***syn*** RENEGADE, apostate, defector, rat, runagate, tergiversator, turnabout, turncoat
recreate *vb* **1** ***syn*** AMUSE, divert, entertain
rel refresh, rejuvenate, renew, restore
2 ***syn*** PLAY 1, disport, sport
recreation *n* **1** ***syn*** ENTERTAINMENT, amusement, dissipation, distraction, diversion, divertissement
rel ease, relaxation, repose; frolic, rollick; hilarity, jollity, mirth
2 ***syn*** PLAY 1, disport, diversion, fun, sport
recrementitious *adj* ***syn*** SUPERFLUOUS, de trop, excess, extra, spare, superfluent, supernumerary, surplus
recrudesce *vb* ***syn*** RETURN 1, react, recur, revert, turn back
rel refurbish, renew, renovate
con repress, suppress; cease, discontinue, stop
recruit *n* ***syn*** NOVICE, apprentice, beginner, fledgling, freshman, neophyte, newcomer, novitiate, rookie, tenderfoot
recruit *vb* ***syn*** RECOVER 1, get back, recoup, regain, repossess, retrieve
rel refresh, renew, renovate, restore; mend, rebuild, repair
rectify *vb* ***syn*** CORRECT 1, amend, emend, mend, right
rel rebuild, repair
rectitude *n* ***syn*** GOODNESS, morality, probity, righteousness, rightness, uprightness, virtue
rel conscientiousness, justness, scrupulousness
recumbent *adj* ***syn*** PRONE 4, decumbent, flat, procumbent, prostrate, reclining
ant erect, upright
recuperate *vb* ***syn*** IMPROVE 3, ameliorate, convalesce, gain, look up, mend, perk (up)
recur *vb* **1** ***syn*** RETURN 1, react, recrudesce, revert, turn back
rel iterate, reiterate, repeat
2 ***syn*** RESORT 2, apply, go, refer, repair, run, turn
recurrence *n* a periodic or frequent returning <the *recurrence* of the nightmare upset him>
syn reappearance, reoccurrence, return
rel repetition, reproduction; crebrity, frequency
recurrent *adj* ***syn*** INTERMITTENT, alternate, isochronal, isochronous, periodic, periodical, recurring
recurring *adj* ***syn*** INTERMITTENT, alternate, isochronal, isochronous, periodic, periodical, recurrent
Red *n* ***syn*** COMMUNIST, Bolshevik, ‖Bolshie, commie, comrade
red–blooded *adj* ***syn*** VIGOROUS, dynamic, energetic, lusty, strenuous, ‖survigrous, vital
redden *vb* **1** to make red <blood soon *reddened* the bandage>
syn incarnadine, rubify, rubric, ruby, rud, ruddle, ruddy
2 ***syn*** BLUSH, color, crimson, flush, glow, mantle, pink, pinken, rose, rouge
redeem *vb* **1** ***syn*** RANSOM, buy
2 ***syn*** FREE, disenthrall, disimprison, emancipate, liberate, loose, manumit, release, unbind, unchain
3 ***syn*** COMPENSATE 1, atone (for), balance, counterbalance, counterpoise, countervail, make up, offset, outweigh, set off
red–handed *adv* in the act of committing a misdeed <caught *red-handed*>
syn dead to rights, flagrante delicto
rel blatantly, openly
red–hot *adj* **1** ***syn*** HOT 1, blistering, boiling, burning, fiery, scalding, scorching, sizzling, sweltering, white-hot
2 ***syn*** IMPASSIONED, ardent, blazing, burning, fervid, fiery, flaming, glowing, passionate, white-hot
3 ***syn*** UP-TO-DATE, abreast, au courant, contemporary, down-to-date, up, up-to-the-minute
red–letter *adj* ***syn*** NOTEWORTHY, ‖bodacious, memorable, nameable, notable, observable, rubric
red–light district *n* a district characterized by brothels <sailors frequented the *red-light district*>
syn levee, stew(s), tenderloin
idiom street of fallen women
red–neck *n* ***syn*** RUSTIC, backwoodsman, bumpkin, hayseed, hick, hillbilly, peasant, provincial, rube, yokel
redolence *n* ***syn*** FRAGRANCE, aroma, balm, bouquet, incense, perfume, scent, spice
redolent *adj* **1** ***syn*** SWEET 2, ambrosial, aromal, aromatic, balmy, fragrant, perfumed, perfumy, savory, spicy
2 ***syn*** REMINISCENT, remindful
redouble *vb* ***syn*** INTENSIFY, aggravate, deepen, enhance, heighten, intensate, magnify, mount, rise, rouse
redoubt *n* ***syn*** FORT, citadel, fastness, fortress, stronghold
redoubtable *adj* **1** ***syn*** FEARFUL 3, appalling, awful, dreadful, formidable, frightful, horrible, horrific, shocking, terrible
2 ***syn*** FAMOUS 2, celebrated, distinguished, eminent, famed, great, illustrious, notable, prominent, renowned
redound *vb* ***syn*** CONTRIBUTE 2, conduce, tend
redraft *n* ***syn*** REVISION 1, recension, rescript, review, revisal, revise
redraft *vb* ***syn*** REVISE, redraw, restyle, revamp, rework, rewrite, work over
redraw *vb* ***syn*** REVISE, redraft, restyle, revamp, rework, rewrite, work over
redress *vb* **1** ***syn*** AVENGE, revenge, venge, vindicate

---

2 ***syn*** NEUTRALIZE, annul, cancel (out), counteract, countercheck, frustrate, negate, negative

redress *n* ***syn*** REPARATION, amends, compensation, indemnification, indemnity, quittance, recompense, reprisal, restitution

rel balancing, offsetting; retaliation, vengeance

reduce *vb* **1** ***syn*** DECREASE, abate, diminish, drain (away), dwindle, lessen, rebate, recede, taper, taper off

2 to decrease in amount <they decided to *reduce* prices to stimulate sales>

syn clip, cut, cut back, cut down, lower, mark down, pare, shave, slash

rel curtail, decrease, diminish, lessen; deflate, depreciate; scale (down), step down; roll back

con boost, hike, jack (up), jump, put up, raise, up

ant increase

3 ***syn*** CONQUER 1, bear down, beat down, crush, defeat, overpower, subdue, subjugate, vanquish

rel cripple, disable, enfeeble, undermine, weaken; debase, degrade, humble, humiliate

4 ***syn*** DEGRADE 1, break, bump, bust, declass, demerit, demote, disgrade, disrate, downgrade

ant advance

5 to lose body weight especially by dieting <ate no cake while *reducing*>

syn slenderize, slim (down)

rel bant, diet

idiom lose flesh, take off weight

ant fatten

reduction *n* **1** ***syn*** DEDUCTION 1, abatement, discount, rebate, subtraction

2 ***syn*** DEMOTION, degradation, downgrading

redundancy *n* ***syn*** VERBIAGE 1, circumambages, circumbendibus, circumlocution, periphrase, periphrasis, pleonasm, roundabout, tautology, verbality

rel flatulence, inflatedness, inflation, tumidity, turgidity

redundant *adj* ***syn*** WORDY, diffuse, long-winded, palaverous, prolix, verbose, windy

rel extra, spare, superfluous, supernumerary, surplus; iterating, reiterating, repetitious

ant concise

reduplicate *vb* ***syn*** COPY, duplicate, imitate, replicate, reproduce

reduplication *n* ***syn*** REPRODUCTION, carbon, carbon copy, copy, ditto, duplicate, facsimile, replica, replication

reedy *adj* ***syn*** THIN 1, attenuate, slender, slight, slim, squinny, stalky, tenuous, twiggy

reek *vb* ***syn*** SMELL 3, funk, stench, stink

reeking *adj* ***syn*** MALODOROUS 1, fetid, funky, fusty, noisome, putrid, rancid, rank, smelly, stinking

reeky *adj* ***syn*** MALODOROUS 1, putrid, rancid, rank, reeking, ||smellful, smelly, stale, stenchy, stinking

---

syn synonym(s) ***rel*** related word(s)
idiom idiomatic equivalent(s) ***con*** contrasted word(s)
ant antonym(s) * vulgar
|| use limited; if in doubt, see a dictionary
The first word in a synonym list when printed in SMALL CAPITALS shows where there is more information about the group. For a more efficient use of this book see Explanatory Notes.

reel *vb* **1** ***syn*** SPIN 2, swim, turn, whirl

2 to move uncertainly or uncontrollably (as in intoxication) <*reeled* down the street>

syn stagger, titubate, totter, wheel

rel careen, lurch, ||swaver, sway, swing, weave, wobble; falter, ||stammer, stumble, teeter, topple; bob, waver

reestablish *vb* ***syn*** RESTORE 1, recall, reinstate, reintroduce, renew, revive

reevaluate *vb* ***syn*** RECONSIDER, reexamine, rethink, re-treat, review, reweigh, think (over)

reexamination *n* ***syn*** REVIEW 5, afterlight, reconsideration, retrospect, retrospection, revision

reexamine *vb* ***syn*** RECONSIDER, reevaluate, rethink, re-treat, review, reweigh, think (over)

refashion *vb* ***syn*** CHANGE 1, alter, modify, mutate, turn, vary

refection *n* ***syn*** MEAL, ||chow, feed, repast

refer *vb* **1** ***syn*** ASCRIBE, accredit, assign, attribute, charge, credit, impute, lay

2 ***syn*** SUBMIT 2, hand in

3 to call or direct attention to something <no one *referred* to his recent divorce>

syn advert, allude, bring up, point (out)

rel insert, interpolate, introduce; cite, quote; instance, mention, name, specify; glance, touch

idiom make an allusion to

4 ***syn*** RESORT 2, apply, go, recur, repair, run, turn

rel advise, commune, confer, consult

referee *n* ***syn*** JUDGE 1, arbiter, arbitrator, umpire

referee *vb* ***syn*** JUDGE 1, adjudge, adjudicate, arbitrate, umpire

reference *n* ***syn*** CREDENTIALS, character, recommendation, testimonial

refine *vb* ***syn*** POLISH 2, perfect, round, sleek, slick, smooth

refined *adj* **1** ***syn*** GENTEEL 1, cultivated, cultured, distingué, polished, urbane, well-bred

ant earthy

2 ***syn*** FINE 1, delicate, finespun, hairline, hairsplitting, nice, subtle

refinement *n* ***syn*** CULTURE, breeding, cultivation, polish

rel finish, suavity, urbanity; civility, courtesy, politeness; dignity, elegance, grace

ant vulgarity

reflect *vb* **1** to reproduce or show as a mirror does <the trees on the shore were *reflected* in the water>

syn glass, image, mirror

rel repeat, reproduce

2 ***syn*** THINK 5, cerebrate, cogitate, deliberate, reason, speculate

rel study, weigh

reflecting *adj* ***syn*** THOUGHTFUL 1, cogitative, contemplative, meditative, pensive, pondering, reflective, ruminative, speculative, thinking

reflection *n* **1** ***syn*** ANIMADVERSION, aspersion, obloquy, slam, slur, stricture

rel assault, attack, onset, onslaught; depreciation, derogation, disparagement

2 ***syn*** THOUGHT 1, brainwork, cerebration, cogitation, deliberation, speculation

reflective *adj* ***syn*** THOUGHTFUL 1, cogitative, contemplative, meditative, pensive, pondering, reflecting, ruminative, speculative, thinking

reformatory *n* ***syn*** JAIL, ‖can, cooler, lockup, pen, penitentiary, ‖pokey, prison, ‖stir, stockade

refractory *adj* ***syn*** OBSTINATE, bullheaded, headstrong, intractable, mulish, perverse, self-willed, stiff-necked, stubborn, unyielding
ant malleable

refrain *vb* **1** to hold oneself back from doing or indulging in something < *refrained* from speaking out of turn >
syn abstain, forbear, keep, withhold
rel arrest, check, halt, interrupt, stop; curb, inhibit, restrain
2 ***syn*** DENY 3, abstain, constrain, curb, hold back

refresh *vb* ***syn*** RENEW 1, modernize, refurbish, rejuvenate, renovate, restore, update
rel animate, enliven, quicken, vivify; recover, recruit, regain; amuse, divert, recreate
con exhaust, tire
ant addle; jade

refreshed *adj* made or become fresh <awoke a *refreshed* man>
syn new, regenerated, reinvigorated, renewed, revived
rel recreated, renovated; animated, exhilarated, invigorated, stimulated
con exhausted, fagged, fatigued, jaded, tired, tuckered, wearied, worn-down, worn-out

refuge *n* **1** the state of being covered or protected <exiles seeking *refuge* in neutral countries>
syn asylum, harborage, sanctuary, shelter; *compare* SHELTER 1
rel protection, shield; immunity
con exposure, liability, openness; vulnerability
2 ***syn*** SHELTER 1, asylum, cover, covert, harbor, harborage, haven, port, retreat, sanctuary
3 ***syn*** RESOURCE 3, dernier ressort, expediency, expedient, makeshift, recourse, resort, shift, stopgap, substitute

refugee *n* one who flees for safety <the villagers fed and housed the *refugees* from the bombed city>
syn displaced person, DP, émigré, evacuee, fugitive
rel exile; emigrant, expatriate
idiom stateless person

refulgent *adj* ***syn*** BRIGHT 1, beaming, brilliant, effulgent, fulgent, incandescent, lambent, lucent, luminous, radiant

refurbish *vb* ***syn*** RENEW 1, modernize, refresh, rejuvenate, renovate, restore, update

refusal *n* ***syn*** DENIAL 1, disallowance, rejection

refuse *vb* **1** ***syn*** DECLINE 4, disapprove, dismiss, reject, reprobate, repudiate, spurn, turn down
2 ***syn*** DENY 2, disallow, keep back, withhold

refuse *n* matter that is regarded as worthless and fit only for throwing away <heaps of *refuse* left by the former tenant>
syn ‖collateral, debris, dreck, ‖dust, garbage, junk, kelter, litter, ‖muck, ‖mullock, offal, outsweepings, ‖pelf, riffraff, rubbish, ‖sculch, spilth, sweepings, swill, trash, waste
rel dump, dustheap; rejectamenta, scraps; lumber; offscouring(s)

refute *vb* ***syn*** DISPROVE 1, break, confound, confute, controvert, disconfirm, evert, rebut

regain *vb* ***syn*** RECOVER 1, get back, recoup, recruit, repossess, retrieve
rel achieve, attain, compass, gain, reach; reclaim, redeem, save; renew, restore

regal *adj* ***syn*** KINGLY, kinglike, majestic, monarchal, monarchial, monarchical, royal, sovereign
rel august, imposing, magnificent, stately; glorious, resplendent, splendid, sublime

regale *n* ***syn*** DINNER, banquet, feast, spread

regalia *n pl* ***syn*** FINERY, ‖best bib and tucker, bravery, frippery, full dress, ‖glad rags, Sunday best, war paint

regard *n* **1** ***syn*** NOTICE 1, attention, cognizance, heed, mark, ‖mind, note, observance, observation, remark
2 ***syn*** CONSIDERATION 3, concern, considerateness, solicitude
ant disregard
3 ***syn*** INTEREST 3, concern, curiosity, interestedness
4 a feeling of deferential approval and liking <held in high *regard* by his neighbors>
syn account, admiration, consideration, esteem, estimation, favor, respect
rel deference, homage, honor, reverence; appreciation, cherishing, prizing, valuing; approbation, approval, satisfaction
con deprecation, disapproval; disfavor, disgust, dislike, distaste; contempt, disdain, scorn; detestation, hate, hatred
ant despite
5 ***syn*** CARE 4, carefulness, concern, consciousness, heed, heedfulness

regard *vb* **1** ***syn*** ADMIRE 2, consider, esteem, respect
con reject, repudiate, scorn
ant despise
2 ***syn*** CONSIDER 3, account, deem, reckon, view
rel assay, assess, estimate, rate, value

regardful *adj* **1** ***syn*** ATTENTIVE 1, advertent, arrect, heedful, intentive, observant
2 ***syn*** MINDFUL 2, heedful, observant, observative, observing, thoughtful
3 ***syn*** RESPECTFUL, deferential, duteous, dutiful

regarding *prep* ***syn*** APROPOS, about, as regards, as respects, as to, concerning, in re, re, respecting, with respect to

regardless *adj* ***syn*** NEGLIGENT, behindhand, careless, delinquent, derelict, disregardful, lax, neglectful, remiss, slack

regardless of *prep* ***syn*** AGAINST 4, despite, in spite of, notwithstanding

regenerated *adj* ***syn*** REFRESHED, new, reinvigorated, renewed, revived

region *n* **1** ***syn*** AREA 1, belt, territory, tract, zone
rel neighborhood, vicinity; division, part, section, sector
2 ***syn*** FIELD, bailiwick, demesne, domain, dominion, province, sphere, terrain, territory, walk

---

register *n* ***syn*** LIST, catalog, roll, roll call, roster, schedule

register *vb* **1** ***syn*** ENROLL 1, list
2 ***syn*** SHOW 5, indicate, mark, read, record, say

regnant *adj* **1** ***syn*** DOMINANT 1, ascendant, master, outweighing, overbearing, paramount, predominant, predominate, preponderant, sovereign
2 ***syn*** PREVAILING, current, popular, prevalent, rampant, rife, ruling, widespread

regress *vb* ***syn*** REVERT 2, retrogress, throw back

regret *vb* to be very sorry for <*regrets* his mistakes> <*regret* the problems facing minorities>
syn deplore, repent, rue
rel bemoan, bewail, lament; grieve, mourn, sorrow; deprecate, disapprove

regret *n* **1** ***syn*** SORROW, affliction, anguish, care, ‖dole, grief, heartache, heartbreak, rue, woe
rel compunction, contrition, penitence, remorse, repentance; demur, qualm, scruple
2 regrets *pl* ***syn*** APOLOGY 2, excuse

regretful *adj* ***syn*** REMORSEFUL, apologetic, attritional, compunctious, contrite, penitent, penitential, repentant, sorry

regretless *adj* ***syn*** REMORSELESS, impenitent, uncontrite, unregretful, unremorseful, unrepentant, unsorry

regrettable *adj* ***syn*** DEPLORABLE, afflictive, calamitous, dire, distressing, grievous, heartbreaking, lamentable, unfortunate, woeful

regular *adj* **1** ***syn*** GENERAL 1, common, commonplace, natural, normal, prevalent, run-of-the-mill, typic, typical, usual
rel customary, ordinary
ant irregular
2 ***syn*** ORDERLY 1, methodic, methodical, systematic
rel fixed, set, settled; constant, equable, even, steady, uniform
ant irregular; sporadic
3 ***syn*** UTTER, absolute, complete, consummate, downright, gross, outright, perfect, positive, unmitigated

regulate *vb* ***syn*** ADJUST 2, fix, tune (up)
rel arrange, methodize, order, organize, systematize; moderate, temper

regulation *n* ***syn*** LAW 1, canon, decree, decretum, edict, ordinance, precept, prescript, rule, statute

rehabilitate *vb* ***syn*** RESTORE 3, reclaim, recondition, reconstruct, recover, rejuvenate, restitute

rehearse *vb* **1** ***syn*** RELATE 1, describe, narrate, recite, recount, report, state
rel iterate, reiterate, repeat
2 ***syn*** EXERCISE 3, drill, practice
rel run through

reify *vb* ***syn*** MATERIALIZE 2, entify, hypostatize

reign *vb* **1** ***syn*** GOVERN 1, overrule, rule, sway
idiom sit on the throne
2 ***syn*** RULE 2, dominate, domineer, predominate, preponderate, prevail

reimburse *vb* ***syn*** COMPENSATE 3, indemnify, pay, recompense, remunerate, repay, requite
rel recover; balance, compensate, offset
con default, dishonor, repudiate, welsh

rein *vb* ***syn*** COMPOSE 4, collect, control, cool, re-collect, repress, restrain, simmer down, smother, suppress

reinforce *vb* ***syn*** STRENGTHEN 2, energize, fortify, invigorate
rel augment, enlarge, increase, multiply; bolster, buttress, pillar, prop, sustain
ant undermine

reinstate *vb* **1** ***syn*** RESTORE 5, give back, put (back), replace, return
2 ***syn*** RESTORE 1, recall, reestablish, reintroduce, renew, revive

reintroduce *vb* ***syn*** RESTORE 1, recall, reestablish, reinstate, renew, revive

reinvigorated *adj* ***syn*** REFRESHED, new, regenerated, renewed, revived

reissue *n* ***syn*** EDITION, impression, printing, reprinting

reiterate *vb* ***syn*** REPEAT, ingeminate, iterate, renew, reprise, resay

reject *vb* **1** ***syn*** DECLINE 4, disapprove, dismiss, refuse, reprobate, repudiate, spurn, turn down
rel debar, eliminate, exclude, shut out
ant accept; choose, select
2 ***syn*** DISCARD, cashier, cast, jettison, junk, scrap, shed, slough, throw away, throw out

rejection *n* ***syn*** DENIAL 1, disallowance, refusal

rejoin *vb* ***syn*** ANSWER 1, come in, reply, respond, retort, return

rejoinder *n* ***syn*** ANSWER 1, antiphon, reply, respond, response, retort, return

rejuvenate *vb* **1** ***syn*** RENEW 1, modernize, refresh, refurbish, renovate, restore, update
2 ***syn*** RESTORE 3, reclaim, recondition, reconstruct, recover, rehabilitate, restitute

rekindle *vb* ***syn*** REVIVE 3, reactivate, renew, renovate, resurrect, resuscitate, retrieve, revitalize, revivify

relapse *n* ***syn*** LAPSE 2, backsliding

relapse *vb* ***syn*** LAPSE, backslide, recidivate

relate *vb* **1** to tell orally or in writing the details or circumstances of a situation <*related* the story of his life>
syn describe, narrate, recite, recount, rehearse, report, state
rel disclose, divulge, reveal, tell; detail, itemize, particularize; depict, express, render; pronounce
idiom make public
2 ***syn*** JOIN 1, associate, bracket, combine, conjoin, connect; couple, link, unite, yoke
rel ascribe, assign, credit, impute, refer
3 ***syn*** BEAR (on *or* upon), appertain, apply, pertain

related *adj* connected by or as if by family ties <persons *related* in the first degree> <physics and mathematics are closely *related*>
syn affiliated, agnate, akin, allied, cognate, connate, connatural, consanguine, incident, kindred
rel associated, connected; complementary, convertible, correlative, corresponding, reciprocal; alike, analogous, identical; germane, pertinent, relevant

---

syn synonym(s) — *rel* related word(s)
idiom idiomatic equivalent(s) — *con* contrasted word(s)
ant antonym(s) — * vulgar
‖ use limited; if in doubt, see a dictionary
The first word in a synonym list when printed in SMALL CAPITALS shows where there is more information about the group. For a more efficient use of this book see Explanatory Notes.

con different, dissimilar, divergent, unconnected, unlike
ant unrelated

relation *n* *syn* RELATIVE, kin, kinsman, kinswoman

relative *n* a person connected with another by blood <all of his *relatives* live out of state>
syn kin, kinsman, kinswoman, relation
rel brother, half brother, half sister, sib, sibling, sister; father, mother, parent; child, daughter, son; grandfather, grandmother, grandparent; grandchild, granddaughter, grandson; aunt, half aunt, half uncle, uncle; half nephew, half niece, nephew, niece; cousin, cross-cousin, half cousin, ortho-cousin; agnate, cognate

relative *adj* **1** *syn* DEPENDENT 1, conditional, contingent, reliant
2 *syn* COMPARATIVE, approximate, near

relax *vb* **1** *syn* LOOSE 5, ease, ease off, lax, loosen, slack, slacken, untighten
2 to become less tense or reserved <couldn't *relax* in crowds>
syn ease off, loosen up, unbend, unlax, unwind
rel calm (down), collect (oneself), compose (oneself), cool (off), simmer down
idiom be at ease, breathe easily, feel at home, make oneself at home
con rack (oneself), tense (up)
3 *syn* REST 2, rest up, unbend, unlax

relaxation *n* *syn* REST 1, ease, leisure, repose, requiescence
rel amusement, diversion, recreation; alleviation, assuagement, mitigation, relief
ant tension

relaxed *adj* **1** *syn* LOOSE 1, lax, slack
rel flexuous, sinuous; gentle, lenient, mild, soft
ant stiff
2 *syn* EASYGOING 3, breezy, casual, ‖common, informal, low-pressure, ‖sonsy, unconstrained, unfussy, unreserved
con ascetic, austere, severe, stern
ant tense

release *vb* **1** *syn* FREE, discharge, emancipate, liberate, loose, loosen, manumit, unbind, unchain, unshackle
rel acquit, exculpate, exonerate; relinquish, resign, surrender, yield
idiom cast loose, set at large
ant detain
2 *syn* EMIT 2, give off, give out, issue, throw off, vent
3 *syn* TAKE OUT (on), loose, unleash, vent
ant check

relegate *vb* **1** *syn* BANISH, deport, displace, exile, expatriate, expel, expulse, ‖lag, ostracize, transport
2 *syn* COMMIT 1, commend, confide, consign, entrust, hand over, turn over
rel accredit, charge, credit, refer

relegation *n* **1** *syn* EXILE 1, banishment, deportation, displacement, expulsion, ostracism
2 *syn* DISPOSAL 2, discarding, disposition, dumping, jettison, junking, riddance, scrapping, throwing away

relent *vb* *syn* ABATE 4, die (down *or* away), ease off, ebb, fall, let up, moderate, slacken, subside, wane

relentless *adj* **1** *syn* GRIM 3, implacable, ironfisted, merciless, mortal, ruthless, unappeasable, unflinching, unrelenting, unyielding
rel rigorous, strict, stringent; cruel, ferocious, fierce, inhuman
con submissive, yielding
2 *syn* INFLEXIBLE 2, adamant, dogged, inexorable, obdurate, rigid, single-minded, unbending, uncompromising, unyielding

relevance *n* *syn* USE 3, account, advantage, applicability, appropriateness, fitness, service, serviceability, usefulness, utility

relevant *adj* relating to or bearing upon the matter in hand < *relevant* testimony>
syn ad rem, applicable, applicative, applicatory, apposite, apropos, germane, material, pertinent, pointful
rel allied, cognate, related; appropriate, apt, fit, fitting, proper, suitable; important, significant, weighty; admissible, allowable
idiom in point, in question, to the point
con impertinent, inadmissible, inapplicable, inapposite, inappropriate; unallied, unassociated, unconnected, unrelated; alien, extrinsic, foreign
ant irrelevant; extraneous

reliable *adj* **1** having qualities that merit confidence or trust <a *reliable* friend>
syn dependable, secure, tried, tried and true, trustworthy, trusty
rel safe; inerrable, inerrant, infallible, unerring; apposite, cogent, compelling, convincing, meaningful, significant, sound, telling, valid; attested, authenticated, circumstantiated, confirmed, proven, validated, verified; unimpeachable, unquestionable
con doubtful, dubious, problematic, questionable, suspect; independable, undependable, untried, untrustworthy; unattested, unauthenticated, unconfirmed, unvalidated
ant unreliable
2 *syn* CERTAIN 3, accurate, authentic, dependable

reliance *n* *syn* TRUST 1, confidence, dependence, faith, hope, stock

reliant *adj* *syn* DEPENDENT 1, conditional, contingent, relative

relic *n* **1** *syn* REMEMBRANCE 3, keepsake, memento, memorial, remembrancer, reminder, souvenir, token, trophy
2 *syn* VESTIGE 1, memento, shadow, trace

relief *n* **1** *syn* EASE 3, alleviation, easement, mitigation
rel lightening, softening; allayment, appeasement, assuagement, mollification
ant anguish
2 *syn* HELP 1, aid, assist, assistance, comfort, hand, lift, secours, succor, support

relieve *vb* **1** to make less grievous or more tolerable <drugs that *relieve* pain>
syn allay, alleviate, assuage, ease, lighten, mitigate, mollify
rel comfort, console, solace; appease, palliate, relieve, soften; quiet, soothe, subdue; moderate, qualify, tem-

per; decrease, diminish, lessen, reduce; aid, benefit, help
con aggravate, enhance, heighten, sharpen; reinforce
ant intensify
2 *syn* ROB 1, ‖knock off, knock over, loot, plunder, ransack, rifle, stick up
3 to take the place of for a time <sent to *relieve* the sentry>
syn spell, take over
rel fill in, sub, substitute; replace, supply
4 *syn* EXEMPT, absolve, discharge, dispense, excuse, let off, privilege (from), spare

religion *n* **1** a system of religious belief <tolerant of all *religions*>
syn creed, cult, faith, persuasion
rel belief, doctrine
2 the body of persons who accept a system of religious belief <all the members of my *religion* strive for tolerance>
syn church, communion, connection, creed, cult, denomination, faith, persuasion, sect

religious *adj syn* DEVOUT, godly, holy, pietistic, pious, prayerful
rel faithful, staunch, steadfast, true; ethical, moral, noble, righteous, virtuous; honest, honorable, just, upright
con godless, ungodly
ant irreligious

relinquish *vb* to let out of one's possession or control completely <few leaders willingly *relinquish* power>
syn abandon, cede, give up, hand over, lay down, leave, resign, surrender, ‖turn up, waive, yield; *compare* ABDICATE 1
rel lay aside; quit, throw up; abdicate, renounce; desert, forsake; abnegate, forbear, forgo, sacrifice; cast, discard, shed
ant keep

relish *n* **1** *syn* TASTE 3, flavor, sapidity, sapor, savor, smack, tang
2 *syn* TASTE 4, gusto, heart, palate, zest
rel enjoying, liking, loving; bias, prejudice; flair, leaning, penchant, propensity
3 *syn* ENJOYMENT 1, delectation, diversion, pleasure

relish *vb* **1** *syn* ENJOY 1, ‖dig, go, like, ‖mind
2 to eat or drink with pleasure <so hungry that he will *relish* plain food>
syn savor
3 *syn* ADMIRE 1, appreciate, cherish, delight (in)

relishing *adj syn* PALATABLE, aperitive, appetizing, flavorsome, good-tasting, mouth-watering, sapid, savory, tasty, toothsome
rel delighting, gratifying, pleasing, regaling, rejoicing, tickling
con banal, flat, inane, insipid, jejune

---

syn synonym(s) *rel* related word(s)
idiom idiomatic equivalent(s) *con* contrasted word(s)
ant antonym(s) * vulgar
‖ use limited; if in doubt, see a dictionary
The first word in a synonym list when printed in SMALL CAPITALS shows where there is more information about the group. For a more efficient use of this book see Explanatory Notes.

reluct *vb syn* DISGUST, nauseate, repel, repulse, revolt, sicken

reluctant *adj syn* DISINCLINED, afraid, averse, backward, hesitant, indisposed, loath, shy, uneager, unwilling
rel calculating, cautious, chary, circumspect, wary

rely (on *or* upon) *vb* to place full confidence <*relied* on the doctor for an accurate diagnosis>
syn bank (on *or* upon), build (on), calculate (on *or* upon), count (on), depend (on *or* upon), ‖lot (on *or* upon), reckon (on), trust (in *or* to)
rel commit, confide, entrust; await, expect, hope, look
idiom put faith in, swear by
con distrust, mistrust

remain *vb syn* STAY 2, abide, bide, linger, stick around, tarry, wait
ant depart

remainder *n* a remaining group, part, or trace <he spent the *remainder* of his life in prison>
syn balance, heel, leavings, remains, remanet, remnant, residual, residue, residuum, rest
rel excess, surplus; hangover, leftover

remains *n pl* **1** *syn* REMAINDER, balance, heel, leavings, remanet, remnant, residual, residue, residuum, rest
2 *syn* CORPSE, body, cadaver, carcass, ‖cold meat, ‖deader, mort, stiff

remanet *n syn* REMAINDER, balance, heel, leavings, remains, remnant, residual, residue, residuum, rest

remark *vb* **1** *syn* SEE 1, behold, descry, discern, espy, mark, note, notice, observe, perceive
2 to make observations and pass on one's judgment <he *remarked* on the lack of modern paintings at the gallery>
syn animadvert, comment, commentate, observe
rel mention, note

remark *n* **1** *syn* NOTICE 1, attention, cognizance, heed, mark, ‖mind, note, observance, observation, regard
2 an expression of opinion or judgment <a *remark* that led to a vehement argument>
syn comment, commentary, note, obiter dictum, observation
rel assertion, reflection, saying, statement, utterance; clarification, elucidation, explanation, explication, exposition, interpretation; annotation, exegesis, gloss, postil, scholium

remarkable *adj* **1** *syn* NOTICEABLE, arresting, arrestive, conspicuous, marked, outstanding, prominent, salient, signal, striking
rel exceptional; important, momentous, significant, weighty; peculiar, singular, strange, unique
2 *syn* EXCEPTIONAL 1, extraordinary, rare, singular, uncommon, uncustomary, unique, unordinary, unusual, unwonted

remarkably *adv syn* VERY 1, awfully, eminently, exceedingly, exceptionally, extremely, greatly, highly, notably, strikingly

remedial *adj syn* CURATIVE, curing, healing, remedying, restorative, sanative, sanatory, vulnerary, wholesome

remedy *n* **1** something used for the treatment of disease <a cold *remedy*>
syn cure, medicament, medicant, medication, medicine, pharmacon, physic
rel biologic, drug, medicinal, pharmaceutical

2 something that corrects or counteracts <no easy *remedy* for discontent>
syn antidote, corrective, counteractant, counteractive, counteragent, countermeasure, counterstep, cure
rel cure-all, elixir, panacea; nostrum

remedy *vb* ***syn*** CURE, heal

remedying *adj* ***syn*** CURATIVE, curing, healing, remedial, restorative, sanative, sanatory, vulnerary, wholesome

remember *vb* to bring an image or idea from the past into the mind < *remembers* the old days>
syn bethink, cite, ||mind, recall, recollect, remind, reminisce, retain, retrospect, revive, revoke
rel look back (on *or* upon), think (of), treasure; relive; educe, elicit, evoke, extract
con disregard, ignore, neglect, overlook; disremember, lose
ant forget

remembrance *n* **1** ***syn*** MEMORY 1, recollection, reminiscence
2 ***syn*** MEMORY 2, anamnesis, recall, recollection, reminiscence
3 something that serves to keep a person or thing in mind <wanted to give her a small *remembrance*>
syn keepsake, memento, memorial, relic, remembrancer, reminder, souvenir, token, trophy
rel favor, gift, present

remembrancer *n* ***syn*** REMEMBRANCE 3, keepsake, memento, memorial, relic, reminder, souvenir, token, trophy

remind *vb* ***syn*** REMEMBER, bethink, cite, ||mind, recall, recollect, reminisce, retain, retrospect, revive
rel hint, imply, intimate, suggest; admonish, advise, warn; jog, prompt
idiom put in mind

reminder *n* **1** ***syn*** EXPRESSION 3, gesture, indication, sign, token
2 ***syn*** REMEMBRANCE 3, keepsake, memento, memorial, relic, remembrancer, souvenir, token, trophy
rel memo, memorandum, note, notice; hint, intimation, suggestion; admonition, warning

remindful *adj* ***syn*** REMINISCENT, redolent

reminisce *vb* ***syn*** REMEMBER, bethink, cite, ||mind, recall, recollect, remind, retain, retrospect, revive

reminiscence *n* **1** ***syn*** MEMORY 1, recollection, remembrance
2 ***syn*** MEMORY 2, anamnesis, recall, recollection, remembrance

reminiscent *adj* tending to remind <shoes *reminiscent* of those worn fifty years ago>
syn redolent, remindful
rel evocative, suggestive
idiom bringing to mind

remise *vb* ***syn*** TRANSFER 4, abalienate, alien, alienate, assign, cede, convey, deed, make over, sign (over)

remiss *adj* ***syn*** NEGLIGENT, behindhand, careless, delinquent, derelict, disregardful, lax, neglectful, regardless, slack
rel faineant, indolent, lazy, slothful
ant scrupulous

remit *vb* **1** ***syn*** EXCUSE 1, condone, forgive, pardon
2 ***syn*** DEFER, delay, hold off, hold up, intermit, postpone, prorogue, put off, shelve, stay
3 ***syn*** SEND 1, address, consign, dispatch, forward, route, ship, transmit

remittable *adj* ***syn*** VENIAL, excusable, forgivable, pardonable

remnant *n* ***syn*** REMAINDER, balance, heel, leavings, remains, remanet, residual, residue, residuum, rest

remonstrance *n* ***syn*** DEMUR 2, challenge, demurral, demurrer, difficulty, objection, protest, question, remonstration

remonstrate *vb* ***syn*** OBJECT 1, except, expostulate, inveigh (against), kick, protest
rel combat, fight, oppose, resist, withstand

remonstration *n* ***syn*** DEMUR 2, challenge, demurral, demurrer, difficulty, objection, protest, question, remonstrance

remorse *n* ***syn*** PENITENCE, attrition, compunction, contriteness, contrition, penance, penitency, remorsefulness, repentance, rue

remorseful *adj* motivated or marked by remorse <a *remorseful* confession>
syn apologetic, attritional, compunctious, contrite, penitent, penitential, regretful, repentant, sorry
rel mournful, rueful, sorrowful
con impenitent, regretless, unregretful; hard, obdurate
ant remorseless

remorsefulness *n* ***syn*** PENITENCE, compunction, contriteness, contrition, penance, penitency, remorse, repentance, rue, ruth

remorseless *adj* having no remorse <a *remorseless* villain>
syn impenitent, regretless, uncontrite, unregretful, unremorseful, unrepentant, unsorry
rel compassionless, merciless, pitiless, ruthless, uncompassionate, unmerciful
con penitent, regretful, sorry
ant remorseful

remote *adj* **1** ***syn*** DISTANT 1, far, faraway, far-flung, far-off, off-lying, outlying, removed
ant close; adjacent
2 ***syn*** BACK 1, frontier, outlandish, unsettled
3 ***syn*** OBSCURE 2, devious, lonesome, out-of-the-way, removed, retired, secret
4 small in degree <a *remote* possibility>
syn ||fat, negligible, off, outside, slender, slight, slim, small
con great, large; important, significant, weighty
5 ***syn*** INDIFFERENT 2, aloof, casual, detached, disinterested, incurious, unconcerned, uncurious, uninterested, withdrawn

remotest *adj* ***syn*** EXTREME 5, farthest, furthermost, furthest, outermost, outmost, utmost, uttermost

remove *vb* **1** ***syn*** MOVE 4, dislocate, disturb, shift, ship, transfer
2 to take something from a place or position <*removed* the book from the shelf>
syn take away, take off, take out, withdraw

---

syn synonym(s) ***rel*** related word(s)
idiom idiomatic equivalent(s) ***con*** contrasted word(s)
ant antonym(s) * vulgar
|| use limited; if in doubt, see a dictionary
The first word in a synonym list when printed in SMALL CAPITALS shows where there is more information about the group. For a more efficient use of this book see Explanatory Notes.

rel move, shift, transfer; extract
3 to take (as a hat) from one's person < *removed* her coat when she entered the house >
syn doff, douse, put off, take off
rel cast off, throw off
idiom off with
con don, put on, replace
4 to get rid of < *remove* the causes of poverty >
syn clear away, eliminate, take out
rel dispose (of), eradicate, exterminate, extirpate; blot out, efface, erase, expunge, obliterate
idiom do away with
5 *syn* PURGE 3, eliminate, liquidate

removed *adj* **1** *syn* DISTANT 1, far, faraway, far-flung, far-off, off-lying, outlying, remote
ant adjoining
2 *syn* OBSCURE 2, devious, lonesome, out-of-the-way, remote, retired, secret
3 *syn* ALONE 1, apart, detached, isolate, isolated, unaccompanied

remunerate *vb* **1** *syn* PAY 1, compensate, guerdon
rel accord, award, grant, vouchsafe
2 *syn* COMPENSATE 3, indemnify, pay, recompense, reimburse, repay, requite

remunerative *adj* *syn* ADVANTAGEOUS 1, gainful, good, lucrative, money-making, paying, profitable, well-paying, worthwhile

renaissance *n* *syn* REVIVAL, reanimation, rebirth, renascence, resurgence, resurrection, resuscitation, revivification, reviviscence, risorgimento

renascence *n* *syn* REVIVAL, reanimation, rebirth, renaissance, resurgence, resurrection, resuscitation, revivification, reviviscence, risorgimento

rencontre *n* *syn* CONTEST 2, competition, concours, conflict, meet, meeting

rend *vb* *syn* TEAR 1, cleave, rip, rive, split
rel divide, separate

render *vb* **1** *syn* RETURN 3
2 *syn* REPRESENT 1, delineate, depict, describe, image, interpret, limn, picture, portray
3 *syn* TRANSLATE 1, put, transpose, turn
4 *syn* ADMINISTER 1, administrate, carry out, execute, govern

rendering *n* **1** *syn* INTERPRETATION 2, reading, rendition, version
2 *syn* VERSION 1, paraphrase, restatement, translation

rendezvous *n* **1** *syn* ENGAGEMENT 3, appointment, assignation, date, tryst
2 *syn* RESORT 2, hangout, haunt, purlieu, stamping ground, watering hole

rendezvous *vb* *syn* GATHER 6, assemble, collect, congregate, congress, forgather, muster, raise

rendition *n* *syn* INTERPRETATION 2, reading, rendering, version

---

syn synonym(s) *rel* related word(s)
idiom idiomatic equivalent(s) *con* contrasted word(s)
ant antonym(s) * vulgar
‖ use limited; if in doubt, see a dictionary
The first word in a synonym list when printed in SMALL CAPITALS shows where there is more information about the group. For a more efficient use of this book see Explanatory Notes.

renegade *n* a person who forsakes his faith, party, cause, or allegiance and aligns himself with another < the *renegade* derided his former beliefs >
syn apostate, defector, rat, recreant, runagate, tergiversator, turnabout, turncoat
rel iconoclast, insurgent, rebel; abandoner, deserter, forsaker; heretic, schismatic
con liege man; disciple, follower
ant adherent

renege *vb* *syn* BACK DOWN, back off, back out, backpedal, backwater, crawfish (out), cry off, declare off, resile, welsh

renew *vb* **1** to make like new < rested to *renew* their strength >
syn modernize, refresh, refurbish, rejuvenate, renovate, restore, update
rel make over, remodel; mend, rebuild, repair; correct, rectify, reform, revise
con bankrupt, deplete, drain, exhaust, impoverish; consume
ant wear out
2 *syn* RESTORE 1, recall, reestablish, reinstate, reintroduce, revive
3 *syn* REVIVE 3, reactivate, rekindle, renovate, resurrect, resuscitate, retrieve, revitalize, revivify
4 *syn* REPEAT, ingeminate, iterate, reiterate, reprise, resay
5 *syn* RESUME 2, continue, pick up, recommence, reopen, restart, take up

renewed *adj* *syn* REFRESHED, new, regenerated, reinvigorated, revived

renounce *vb* **1** *syn* ABDICATE 1, demit, resign
ant arrogate
2 *syn* ABANDON 1, chuck, desert, forsake, quit, throw over
idiom wash one's hands of
3 *syn* DEFECT, apostatize, desert, rat, repudiate, tergiversate, tergiverse, turn

renouncement *n* *syn* RENUNCIATION, abnegation, denial, self-abnegation, self-denial, self-renunciation

renovate *vb* **1** *syn* REVIVE 3, reactivate, rekindle, renew, resurrect, resuscitate, retrieve, revitalize, revivify
2 *syn* RENEW 1, modernize, refresh, refurbish, rejuvenate, restore, update
rel clean, cleanse

renown *n* **1** *syn* FAME 2, celebrity, éclat, notoriety, ‖rep, reputation, repute
2 *syn* EMINENCE 1, distinction, illustriousness, kudos, preeminence, prestige, prominence, prominency

renowned *adj* *syn* FAMOUS 2, celebrated, celebrious, distinguished, eminent, famed, great, illustrious, notable, prominent
rel acclaimed, extolled, lauded, praised; outstanding, signal

rent *vb* *syn* HIRE 1, charter, lease, let

rent *adj* *syn* LACERATED, mangled, torn

rent *n* *syn* BREACH 3, break, fissure, fracture, rift, rupture, schism, split

rental *n* *syn* APARTMENT 1, ‖chambers, flat, lodging(s), rooms, suite, tenement

renunciation *n* voluntary surrender or putting aside of something desired or desirable < led a life of total *renunciation* as a monk >

syn abnegation, denial, renouncement, self-abnegation, self-denial, self-renunciation
rel abjurement, eschewing, forbearing, forgoing, forswearing, sacrifice, self-sacrifice; rejection, repudiation, surrender, yielding
con gripping, holding, keeping
ant retention

reoccupy *vb* ***syn*** RESUME 1, reassume, repossess, retake

reoccurrence *n* ***syn*** RECURRENCE, reappearance, return

reopen *vb* ***syn*** RESUME 2, continue, pick up, recommence, renew, restart, take up

reorder *vb* ***syn*** REORGANIZE, readjust, rearrange, reconstitute, reconstruct, reorient, reorientate, reshuffle, retool

reorganization *n* ***syn*** SHAKE-UP, overturn, revolution, turnover

reorganize *vb* to arrange in a different way < *reorganize* a bankrupt company >
syn readjust, rearrange, reconstitute, reconstruct, reorder, reorient, reorientate, reshuffle, retool
rel reestablish, refound, resettle; rebuild, regenerate, renovate
con disarrange, disorder, disorganize

reorient *vb* ***syn*** REORGANIZE, readjust, rearrange, reconstitute, reconstruct, reorder, reorientate, reshuffle, retool

reorientate *vb* ***syn*** REORGANIZE, readjust, rearrange, reconstitute, reconstruct, reorder, reorient, reshuffle, retool

‖**rep** *n* **1** ***syn*** FAME 2, celebrity, éclat, notoriety, renown, reputation, repute
2 ***syn*** REPUTATION 2, character, fame, name, report, repute

repair *vb* **1** ***syn*** GO 1, fare, hie, journey, pass, proceed, ‖process, push on, travel, wend
2 ***syn*** RESORT 2, apply, go, recur, refer, run, turn

repair *vb* ***syn*** MEND 2, doctor, do up, fix, overhaul, patch, rebuild, recondition, reconstruct, revamp

repair *n* **1** ***syn*** ORDER 9, case, condition, estate, shape
2 ***syn*** ORDER 10, condition, fettle, fitness, kilter, shape, trim

reparation *n* a return for something lost or suffered, usually through the fault of another < war *reparations* >
syn amends, compensation, indemnification, indemnity, quittance, recompense, redress, reprisal, restitution
rel atonement, expiation; remuneration, requital, retribution, reward; adjustment, settlement

repartee *n* **1** ***syn*** RETORT 2, back answer, comeback, riposte
2 ***syn*** BANTER, backchat, badinage, ‖cross talk, persiflage, snip-snap
rel humor, irony, sarcasm, satire, wit; rejoinder, response, retort

repast *n* ***syn*** MEAL, ‖chow, feed, refection

repay *vb* ***syn*** COMPENSATE 3, indemnify, pay, recompense, reimburse, remunerate, requite
rel balance, offset; accord, award

repeal *vb* ***syn*** REVOKE 2, dismantle, lift, recall, rescind, reverse
ant establish; enact

repeat *vb* to say or do again < *repeat* a command >
syn ingeminate, iterate, reiterate, renew, reprise, resay
rel recite, recount, rehearse, relate; hash over, recapitulate, rehash, restate, retell; chime, din, echo, harp, ring; duplicate, reproduce; copy, ditto, imitate; recrudesce, recur, return, revert

repeatedly *adv* ***syn*** OFTEN, again and again, frequently, much, oft, oftentimes, ofttimes, over and over, time and again
idiom day after day, day by day, day in and day out*

repel *vb* **1** ***syn*** FEND (off), hold off, keep off, rebuff, rebut, repulse, stave off, ward (off)
2 ***syn*** RESIST, buck, combat, contest, dispute, duel, fight, oppose, traverse, withstand
3 ***syn*** DISGUST, nauseate, reluct, repulse, revolt, sicken
ant allure; attract

repellent *adj* **1** ***syn*** REPUGNANT 1, abhorrent, invidious, obnoxious, revulsive
con alluring, bewitching, captivating, charming; enticing, luring, seductive, tempting
ant attractive; pleasing
2 ***syn*** OFFENSIVE, disgusting, foul, loathsome, nasty, noisome, repugnant, repulsive, revolting, vile
3 ***syn*** ANTIPATHETIC 2, aversive, kindless, repugnant, uncongenial, ungenial, unsympathetic

repent *vb* ***syn*** REGRET, deplore, rue

repentance *n* ***syn*** PENITENCE, attrition, compunction, contriteness, contrition, penance, penitency, remorse, rue, ruth
con complacency, self-complacency, self-satisfaction

repentant *adj* ***syn*** REMORSEFUL, apologetic, attritional, compunctious, contrite, penitent, penitential, regretful, sorry

rephrase *vb* ***syn*** PARAPHRASE, restate, reword, translate (into)

repine *vb* ***syn*** COMPLAIN, fuss, kick, murmur, wail, whine

replace *vb* **1** ***syn*** RETURN 4, restitute, restore, take back
2 ***syn*** RESTORE 5, give back, put (back), reinstate, return
3 to put out of a usual or proper place or into the place of another < the old bridge was *replaced* by a new one last year >
syn outplace, supersede, supplant
rel renew, restore; alter, change; recoup, recover, regain, retrieve
4 ***syn*** CHANGE 5, shift

replacement *n* ***syn*** SUBSTITUTE, alternate, fill-in, locum tenens, pinch hitter, stand-in, sub, succedaneum, surrogate

replete *adj* **1** ***syn*** ALIVE 5, abounding, overflowing, rife, swarming, teeming, thronged
2 ***syn*** FULL 1, awash, brimful, brimming, chock-full, crammed, crowded, jammed, loaded, stuffed

---

syn synonym(s)	***rel*** related word(s)
idiom idiomatic equivalent(s)	***con*** contrasted word(s)
ant antonym(s)	* vulgar

‖ use limited; if in doubt, see a dictionary
The first word in a synonym list when printed in SMALL CAPITALS shows where there is more information about the group. For a more efficient use of this book see Explanatory Notes.

replica *n* ***syn*** REPRODUCTION, carbon, carbon copy, copy, ditto, duplicate, facsimile, reduplication, replication

replicate *vb* ***syn*** COPY, duplicate, imitate, reduplicate, reproduce

replication *n* ***syn*** REPRODUCTION, carbon, carbon copy, copy, ditto, duplicate, facsimile, reduplication, replica

reply *vb* ***syn*** ANSWER 1, come in, rejoin, respond, retort, return

con accuse, charge, impeach, indict; address, greet, salute

reply *n* ***syn*** ANSWER 1, antiphon, rejoinder, respond, response, retort, return

con argument, dispute; greeting, salute

report *n* **1** common talk or an instance of it that spreads rapidly <spread a false *report*>

syn buzz, cry, gossip, grapevine, hearsay, murmur, on-dit, rumble, rumor, scuttlebutt, talk, tattle, tittle-tattle, whispering, word

rel conversation, speech; chat, chatter, chitchat, prating, small talk; canard, dirt, scandal; advice, intelligence, news, tidings

2 ***syn*** REPUTATION 2, character, fame, name, ‖rep, repute

3 ***syn*** ACCOUNT 7, chronicle, history, narrative, story, version

rel declaration, statement; comment, notice, review; brief, bulletin

report *vb* ***syn*** RELATE 1, describe, narrate, recite, recount, rehearse, state

rel communicate, impart

repose *vb* ***syn*** REST 1, lie, lie down, recline, stretch (out)

repose *n* ***syn*** REST 1, ease, leisure, relaxation, requiescence

rel refreshment, renewal, restoration

con strain, stress; agitation, discomposure, perturbation

repository *n* ***syn*** DEPOT 2, arsenal, depository, magazine, store, storehouse

repossess *vb* **1** ***syn*** RECOVER 1, get back, recoup, recruit, regain, retrieve

2 ***syn*** RESUME 1, reassume, reoccupy, retake

3 to resume possession of (an item purchased on installment) in default of payments due <*repossessed* the car>

syn take back

rel get back, reclaim, recover, retrieve

reprehend *vb* ***syn*** CRITICIZE, blame, censure, condemn, denounce, denunciate, knock, rap, reprobate, skin

rel admonish, chide, rebuke, reprimand, reproach, reprove; berate, rate, scold, upbraid

---

syn synonym(s) ***rel*** related word(s)
idiom idiomatic equivalent(s) ***con*** contrasted word(s)
ant antonym(s) * vulgar
‖ use limited; if in doubt, see a dictionary
The first word in a synonym list when printed in SMALL CAPITALS shows where there is more information about the group. For a more efficient use of this book see Explanatory Notes.

reprehensible *adj* ***syn*** BLAMEWORTHY, amiss, blamable, blameful, censurable, culpable, demeritorious, guilty, sinful, unholy

represent *vb* **1** to present an image or lifelike imitation of (as in art) <the painting *represents* a spring scene>

syn delineate, depict, describe, image, interpret, limn, picture, portray, render

rel express, realize, show; display, exhibit; hint, suggest; draft, outline, sketch; narrate, relate

con color, distort, falsify, garble, misinterpret, pervert, twist, warp

2 to serve as the counterpart or image of <a movie hero who *represents* the ideals of the culture>

syn body (forth), emblematize, embody, epitomize, exemplify, illustrate, mirror, personalize, personate, personify, symbolize, typify; *compare* EMBODY 1

rel denote, mean, signify; impersonate, substitute; copy, imitate, reproduce

con belie, distort, garble, twist, warp

ant misrepresent

representant *n* ***syn*** DELEGATE, catchpole, deputy, representative

representation *n* the act of delineating <an exponent of *representation* in art>

syn delineation, depiction, description, picture, portraiture, portrayal, presentment

rel demonstration, exemplification, illustration

representative *adj* ***syn*** TYPICAL 1, archetypal, classic, classical, exemplary, ideal, model, prototypal, prototypical, quintessential

ant atypical

representative *n* **1** ***syn*** INSTANCE, case, case history, example, illustration, sample, sampling, specimen

2 ***syn*** DELEGATE, catchpole, deputy, representant

repress *vb* **1** ***syn*** SUPPRESS 2, muffle, ‖quelch, shush, squelch, strangle

2 ***syn*** COMPOSE 4, collect, control, cool, re-collect, rein, restrain, simmer down, smother, suppress

repression *n* **1** the action or process of putting down by authority or force <*repression* of unpopular opinions>

syn choking, extinguishment, quashing, quenching, smothering, squashing, squelching, stifling, strangling, suppression, throttling

rel check, control, curb, restraint; crushing, quelling, subdual

con emboldening, encouragement, support

2 an instance of putting down by authority or force <racial *repressions*>

syn clampdown, crackdown, suppression

rel crushing, extinction, smothering; limitation, repression, restriction

reprieve *n* ***syn*** RESPITE 1

reprimand *n* ***syn*** REBUKE, admonishment, admonition, chiding, rap, reproach, reproof, wig

reprimand *vb* ***syn*** REPROVE, admonish, call down, chide, lesson, monish, ‖rack back, rebuke, reproach, tick off

reprinting *n* ***syn*** EDITION, impression, printing, reissue

reprisal *n* **1** ***syn*** REPARATION, amends, compensation, indemnification, indemnity, quittance, recompense, redress, restitution

2 ***syn*** RETALIATION, avengement, avenging, counterblow, requital, retribution, revanche, revenge, vengeance

reprise *vb* ***syn*** REPEAT, ingeminate, iterate, reiterate, renew, resay

reproach *n* ***syn*** REBUKE, admonishment, admonition, chiding, rap, reprimand, reproof, wig
rel blame, censure, discredit

reproach *vb* ***syn*** REPROVE, admonish, call down, chide, lesson, monish, ||rack back, rebuke, reprimand, tick off

reprobate *vb* **1** ***syn*** CRITICIZE, blame, censure, condemn, denounce, denunciate, knock, rap, reprehend, skin
2 ***syn*** DECLINE 4, disapprove, dismiss, refuse, reject, repudiate, spurn, turn down

reprobate *adj* **1** ***syn*** ABANDONED 2, dissolute, licentious, profligate, self-abandoned, unprincipled
2 ***syn*** WRONG 1, bad, evil, immoral, iniquitous, sinful, vicious, wicked

reprobate *n* ***syn*** VILLAIN 1, *bastard, blackguard, heel, lowlife, miscreant, roperipe, scoundrel, ||slubberdegullion, *son of a bitch

reproduce *vb* **1** ***syn*** PROCREATE 1, bear, beget, breed, generate, multiply, produce, propagate
2 ***syn*** COPY, duplicate, imitate, reduplicate, replicate

reproduction *n* one thing which closely or essentially resembles another that has already been made, produced, or written <printed *reproductions* of the great masters>
syn carbon, carbon copy, copy, ditto, duplicate, facsimile, reduplication, replica, replication
ant original

reproof *n* ***syn*** REBUKE, admonishment, admonition, chiding, rap, reprimand, reproach, wig

reprove *vb* to criticize adversely, especially in order to warn of or to correct a fault <*reproved* him for talking in class>
syn admonish, call down, chide, lesson, monish, ||rack back, rebuke, reprimand, reproach, ||sneap, tick off; *compare* CRITICIZE, LAMBASTE 3, SCOLD 1
rel counsel, warn; blame, censure, criticize, reprehend, reprobate; chasten, correct, discipline, punish
idiom haul over the coals, slap one's wrist, take to task

reptile *n* ***syn*** SYCOPHANT, ||clawback, creature, groveler, lickspittle, minion, toad, toadeater, toadier, toady

repudiate *vb* **1** ***syn*** DECLINE 4, disapprove, dismiss, refuse, reject, reprobate, spurn, turn down
con acknowledge, admit, avow, confess, own
ant adopt
2 ***syn*** DEFECT, apostatize, desert, rat, renounce, tergiversate, tergiverse, turn
3 ***syn*** DISCLAIM, deny, disacknowledge, disallow, disavow, disown
rel abandon, desert, forsake; cast, discard
con allow, concede, grant
ant own

repugnance *n* ***syn*** ABOMINATION 2, abhorrence, aversion, detestation, hate, hatred, horror, loathing, repugnancy, repulsion

repugnancy *n* ***syn*** ABOMINATION 2, abhorrence, aversion, detestation, hate, hatred, horror, loathing, repugnance, repulsion

repugnant *adj* **1** so alien or unlikable as to arouse antagonism and aversion <the idea of moving again became *repugnant* to her>
syn abhorrent, invidious, obnoxious, repellent, revulsive
rel alien, extraneous, extrinsic, foreign; incompatible, incongruous, inconsonant, uncongenial
con acceptable, bearable, tolerable; agreeable, gratifying, pleasant, pleasing, pleasurable
ant congenial
2 ***syn*** OFFENSIVE, disgusting, foul, loathsome, nasty, noisome, repellent, repulsive, revolting, vile
3 ***syn*** ANTIPATHETIC 2, aversive, kindless, repellent, uncongenial, ungenial, unsympathetic

repulse *vb* **1** ***syn*** FEND (off), hold off, keep off, rebuff, rebut, repel, stave off, ward (off)
2 ***syn*** DISGUST, nauseate, reluct, repel, revolt, sicken
ant captivate

repulsion *n* ***syn*** ABOMINATION 2, abhorrence, aversion, detestation, hate, hatred, horror, loathing, repugnance, repugnancy

repulsive *adj* ***syn*** OFFENSIVE, disgusting, foul, loathsome, nasty, noisome, repellent, repugnant, revolting, vile
ant alluring

reputable *adj* ***syn*** RESPECTABLE 1, creditable, estimable, reputed, well-thought-of

reputation *n* **1** ***syn*** FAME 2, celebrity, éclat, notoriety, renown, ||rep, repute
rel authority, credit, influence, prestige, weight
2 the estimation in which one is generally held <a good *reputation*>
syn character, fame, name, ||rep, report, repute

repute *n* **1** ***syn*** FAME 2, celebrity, éclat, notoriety, renown, ||rep, reputation
ant disrepute
2 ***syn*** REPUTATION 2, character, fame, name, ||rep, report

reputed *adj* **1** ***syn*** RESPECTABLE 1, creditable, estimable, reputable, well-thought-of
2 ***syn*** SUPPOSED 1, conjectural, hypothetical, putative, suppositional, suppositious, supposititious, suppositive, suppository

request *vb* ***syn*** ASK 2, bespeak, desire, solicit
rel appeal, petition, pray, sue

requiescence *n* ***syn*** REST 1, ease, leisure, relaxation, repose

require *vb* **1** ***syn*** DEMAND 1, call, challenge, claim, exact, postulate, requisition, solicit
2 ***syn*** DEMAND 2, ask, call (for), crave, necessitate, take
3 ***syn*** LACK, need, want

required *adj* **1** ***syn*** NEEDFUL, needed, requisite
2 ***syn*** MANDATORY, compulsatory, compulsory, imperative, imperious, obligatory
ant optional

---

syn synonym(s) ***rel*** related word(s)
idiom idiomatic equivalent(s) ***con*** contrasted word(s)
ant antonym(s) * vulgar
|| use limited; if in doubt, see a dictionary
The first word in a synonym list when printed in SMALL CAPITALS shows where there is more information about the group. For a more efficient use of this book see Explanatory Notes.

requirement *n* **1** something wanted or needed <production was not sufficient to satisfy *requirements* for cars>
syn demand, need, want
2 ***syn*** ESSENTIAL 2, condition, must, necessity, precondition, prerequisite, requisite, sine qua non

requisite *adj* **1** ***syn*** NEEDFUL, needed, required
2 ***syn*** JUST 3, appropriate, condign, deserved, due, merited, rhadamanthine, right, rightful, suitable

requisite *n* ***syn*** ESSENTIAL 2, condition, must, necessity, precondition, prerequisite, requirement, sine qua non

requisition *vb* ***syn*** DEMAND 1, call, challenge, claim, exact, postulate, require, solicit

requital *n* ***syn*** RETALIATION, avengement, avenging, counterblow, reprisal, retribution, revanche, revenge, vengeance

requite *vb* **1** ***syn*** RECIPROCATE, recompense, retaliate, return
rel content, satisfy; revenge
2 ***syn*** COMPENSATE 3, indemnify, pay, recompense, reimburse, remunerate, repay

resay *vb* ***syn*** REPEAT, ingeminate, iterate, reiterate, renew, reprise

rescind *vb* ***syn*** REVOKE 2, dismantle, lift, recall, repeal, reverse

rescript *n* ***syn*** REVISION 1, recension, redraft, review, revisal, revise

rescue *vb* to set free (as from confinement or risk) <*rescue* a drowning child>
syn deliver, save
rel emancipate, free, liberate, manumit, release; conserve, preserve; disembarrass, disentangle, extricate; recover, regain, retrieve; buy, ransom, redeem

research *n* ***syn*** INQUIRY 1, delving, inquest, inquisition, investigation, probe, probing, quest

resect *vb* ***syn*** EXCISE, cut out, exsect, extirpate

resemblance *n* ***syn*** LIKENESS, affinity, alikeness, analogy, comparison, semblance, similarity, simile, similitude
rel parallel
ant dissemblance

resemble *vb* to be like or similar to <he *resembles* his father>
syn favor, ‖feature, simulate
idiom be a dead ringer for, bear a resemblance to, be the spit and image of, be the very image of, bring to mind, have all the earmarks of, look like, put one in mind of, remind one of, take after
con differ, vary

resentfully *adv* ***syn*** HARD 6, bitterly, hardly, keenly, rancorously, sorely

resentment *n* ***syn*** OFFENSE 2, dudgeon, huff, miff, pique, ‖snuff, umbrage
rel animosity, animus, antagonism, antipathy, rancor; ill will, malice, malignancy, malignity, spite

reservation *n* ***syn*** CONDITION 1, provision, proviso, stipulation, strings, terms
rel circumscription

reserve *vb* **1** ***syn*** KEEP 5, detain, hold, hold back, keep back, keep out, retain, withhold
2 to set or have set aside or apart <*reserve* a hotel room>
syn bespeak, book, preengage
rel contract, engage, retain

reserve *n* something stored or kept available for future use or need <keep a *reserve* of canned foods on hand>
syn backlog, hoard, inventory, nest egg, reservoir, stock, stockpile, store
rel fund, supply
idiom something for a rainy day, something in the sock

reserved *adj* **1** inclined to cautious restraint in the expression of knowledge or opinions <too *reserved* to offer a spontaneous criticism>
syn constrained, incommunicable, noncommittal, restrained
rel bashful, diffident, modest, shy; ceremonious, conventional, formal
con demonstrative, expansive, unconstrained, unrestrained; boisterous, loud, ostentatious; extroverted, open, outgoing
ant unreserved
2 ***syn*** SILENT 3, close, close-lipped, closemouthed, close-tongued, reticent, taciturn, tight-lipped, tight-mouthed, uncommunicative
ant effusive
3 ***syn*** UNSOCIABLE, aloof, distant, insociable, offish, solitary, standoffish, unapproachable, uncompanionable, withdrawn
ant affable
4 ***syn*** ANTISOCIAL, eremitic, misanthropic, reclusive, solitary, standoffish
5 ***syn*** QUALIFIED 2, limited, modified

reservoir *n* ***syn*** RESERVE, backlog, hoard, inventory, nest egg, stock, stockpile, store

reshuffle *vb* ***syn*** REORGANIZE, readjust, rearrange, reconstitute, reconstruct, reorder, reorient, reorientate, retool

reside *vb* **1** to have as one's habitation or domicile <he *resides* in Boston>
syn abide, bide, ‖dig, dwell, hang out, live
rel inhabit, occupy, people, tenant; continue, endure
2 ***syn*** CONSIST 1, dwell, exist, inhere, lie

residence *n* **1** ***syn*** HABITATION 1, inhabitancy, inhabitation, occupancy, occupation, settlement
2 ***syn*** HABITATION 2, abode, commorancy, domicile, dwelling, home, house, residency

residency *n* ***syn*** HABITATION 2, abode, commorancy, domicile, dwelling, home, house, residence

resident *n* ***syn*** INHABITANT, denizen, dweller, habitant, indweller, liver, occupant, ‖residenter, resider

‖**residenter** *n* ***syn*** INHABITANT, denizen, dweller, habitant, indweller, liver, occupant, resident, resider

resider *n* ***syn*** INHABITANT, denizen, dweller, habitant, indweller, liver, occupant, resident, ‖residenter

---

syn synonym(s) — *rel* related word(s)
idiom idiomatic equivalent(s) — *con* contrasted word(s)
ant antonym(s) — * vulgar
‖ use limited; if in doubt, see a dictionary
The first word in a synonym list when printed in SMALL CAPITALS shows where there is more information about the group. For a more efficient use of this book see Explanatory Notes.

residual *n* ***syn*** REMAINDER, balance, heel, leavings, remains, remanet, remnant, residue, residuum, rest

residue *n* ***syn*** REMAINDER, balance, heel, leavings, remains, remanet, remnant, residual, residuum, rest

residuum *n* ***syn*** REMAINDER, balance, heel, leavings, remains, remanet, remnant, residual, residue, rest

resign *vb* **1** ***syn*** RELINQUISH, abandon, cede, give up, hand over, leave, surrender, ‖turn up, waive, yield
2 ***syn*** ABDICATE 1, demit, renounce
3 ***syn*** QUIT 6, drop, leave, terminate

resignation *n* **1** ***syn*** ACQUIESCENCE, compliance, conformity
rel humbleness, lowliness, meekness, modesty
2 ***syn*** PATIENCE, forbearance, longanimity, long-suffering, patientness, uncomplainingness

resigned *adj* ***syn*** PASSIVE 2, acquiescent, nonresistant, nonresisting, submissive, unresistant, unresisting, yielding
ant rebellious

resile *vb* ***syn*** BACK DOWN, back off, back out, backpedal, backwater, crawfish (out), cry off, declare off, renege, welsh

resilient *adj* **1** ***syn*** ELASTIC 1, flexible, springy, stretch, stretchy, supple, whippy
2 ***syn*** ELASTIC 2, airy, bouncy, buoyant, effervescent, expansive, volatile
ant flaccid

resist *vb* to stand firm against a person or influence <the criminal *resisted* the police> <we must learn to *resist* temptation>
syn buck, combat, contest, dispute, duel, fight, oppose, repel, traverse, withstand
rel assail, assault, attack; contradict, contravene, gainsay, impugn; baffle, balk, foil, frustrate, thwart; check, counter, hinder, obstruct, stem
con bow, capitulate, surrender
ant submit, yield

resolute *adj* **1** ***syn*** DECIDED 2, bent, decisive, determined, intent, resolved, set, settled
rel obstinate, pertinacious, stubborn
2 ***syn*** FAITHFUL 1, allegiant, ardent, constant, fast, loyal, staunch, steadfast, steady, true

resoluteness *n* ***syn*** DECISION 2, decidedness, determination, firmness, purposefulness, purposiveness, resolution, resolve

resolution *n* **1** ***syn*** ANALYSIS 1, breakdown, breakup, dissection
2 ***syn*** DECISION 1, conclusion, determination, settlement
3 ***syn*** DECISION 2, decidedness, determination, firmness, purposefulness, purposiveness, resoluteness, resolve
4 ***syn*** COURAGE, cojones, dauntlessness, guts, heart, mettle, ‖moxie, pluck, spirit, spunk

resolve *vb* **1** ***syn*** ANALYZE, anatomize, breakdown, decompose, decompound, dissect
ant blend
2 ***syn*** SOLVE 1, fix, work, work out
3 ***syn*** SOLVE 2, break, clear up, decipher, dissolve, ‖dope out, puzzle out, unfold, unravel, unriddle
rel dispel, disperse, dissipate; clear, disabuse, purge, rid
4 ***syn*** DECIDE, conclude, determine, figure, rule, settle

resolve *n* ***syn*** DECISION 2, decidedness, determination, firmness, purposefulness, purposiveness, resoluteness, resolution

resolved *adj* ***syn*** DECIDED 2, bent, decisive, determined, intent, resolute, set, settled

resonant *adj* marked by conspicuously full and rich sounds or tones (as of speech or music) <a deep *resonant* voice rang out>
syn consonant, fat, orotund, plangent, resounding, ringing, rotund, round, sonorant, sonorous, vibrant
rel full, mellow, rich; deep, profound; enhanced, heightened, intensified; earsplitting, loud, powerful, stentorian, strident; beating, pulsating, pulsing, throbbing; booming, clangorous, noisy, reverberant, reverberating, sounding, thundering, thunderous; electrifying, thrilling
con faint, low, murmurous, muted, smothered, soft, weak; flat, toneless, unmusical; cacophonous, discordant, inharmonious, off-key

resort *n* **1** ***syn*** RESOURCE 3, dernier ressort, expediency, expedient, makeshift, recourse, refuge, shift, stopgap, substitute
2 a place that is habitually frequented <a favorite *resort* of teenagers>
syn hangout, haunt, purlieu, rendezvous, stamping ground, watering hole
rel harbor, haven, refuge, retreat; den, nest
3 a place providing recreation and entertainment especially to vacationers <returned to the same *resort* every year>
syn pleasure dome, spa, watering place
rel hotel, inn, lodge; bath(s), hot spring(s), mineral spring(s), spring(s), thermal spring(s)

resort *vb* **1** ***syn*** FREQUENT, affect, hang around, hang out, haunt
ant avoid
2 to betake oneself or to have recourse when in need of help or relief <they were unwilling to *resort* to her parents for aid>
syn apply, go, recur, refer, repair run, turn
rel address, devote, direct, employ, use, utilize
idiom avail oneself of, fall back on (*or* upon)

resound *vb* ***syn*** PRAISE 2, bless, celebrate, cry up, eulogize, extol, glorify, hymn, laud, magnify

resounding *adj* **1** ***syn*** RESONANT, consonant, orotund, plangent, ringing, rotund, round, sonorant, sonorous, vibrant
2 ***syn*** EMPHATIC, assertive, forceful, insistent

resource *n* **1** **resources** *pl* ***syn*** MEAN 3, assets, capital, wealth
2 **resources** *pl* ***syn*** WEALTH 2, fortune, property, riches, substance, worth
3 something to which one turns for assistance in difficulty or need in the absence of a usual means or

---

source of supply <has exhausted every *resource* he can think of>
syn dernier ressort, expediency, expedient, makeshift, recourse, refuge, resort, shift, stopgap, string, substitute, surrogate
rel contraption, contrivance, device, lash-up; creation, invention; fashion, manner, method, mode, system, way; means, measure, step; artifice, dodge, stratagem, subterfuge; hope, opportunity, possibility, relief

respect *n* ***syn*** REGARD 4, account, admiration, consideration, esteem, estimation, favor
rel awe, fear, reverence; adoration, veneration, worship
ant scorn

respect *vb* ***syn*** ADMIRE 2, consider, esteem, regard
rel revere, reverence, venerate
ant abuse; misuse; scorn

respectable *adj* **1** worthy of esteem or deference <a *respectable* scientist>
syn creditable, estimable, reputable, reputed, well-thought-of
rel honorable, worthy
ant disreputable, unrespectable
2 ***syn*** DECOROUS 1, becoming, befitting, comely, conforming, correct, decent, done, nice, proper
3 ***syn*** DECENT 4, acceptable, adequate, all right, good, right, satisfactory, sufficient, tolerable, unexceptionable
4 ***syn*** CONSIDERABLE 2, good, ‖right smart, sensible, sizable, ‖smart
5 acceptable in appearance or standing <wore old but *respectable* clothes>
syn decent, presentable, tolerable; *compare* DECENT 4
rel adequate, satisfactory; acceptable, appropriate, proper, suitable
ant disreputable

respectful *adj* marked by or showing respect or deference <a *respectful* glance>
syn deferential, duteous, dutiful, regardful
rel reverent, reverential, venerating; attentive, civil, courteous, gracious, polite
con abusive, insolent, insulting, offensive; contemptuous, impudent, irreverent, rude
ant disrespectful

respecting *prep* ***syn*** APROPOS, about, as regards, as respects, as to, concerning, in re, regarding, touching, with respect to

respective *adj* ***syn*** SEVERAL 1, individual, particular, singular

respire *vb* ***syn*** BREATHE 3

respite *n* **1** a temporary suspension of the execution of a capital offender <the murderer won a *respite*>
syn reprieve
2 ***syn*** BREAK 4, blow, breath, breather, breathing space (*or* spell), ten
rel intermission, lull, pause, recess; ease, leisure, rest

---

syn synonym(s) ***rel*** related word(s)
idiom idiomatic equivalent(s) ***con*** contrasted word(s)
ant antonym(s) * vulgar
‖ use limited; if in doubt, see a dictionary
The first word in a synonym list when printed in SMALL CAPITALS shows where there is more information about the group. For a more efficient use of this book see Explanatory Notes.

resplendent *adj* ***syn*** SPLENDID 2, glorious, gorgeous, magnificent, proud, splendiferous, splendorous, sublime, superb
rel blazing, flaming, glowing

respond *n* ***syn*** ANSWER 1, antiphon, rejoinder, reply, response, retort, return

respond *vb* ***syn*** ANSWER 1, come in, rejoin, reply, retort, return
rel act, behave, react

response *n* ***syn*** ANSWER 1, antiphon, rejoinder, reply, respond, retort, return

responsible *adj* subject to an authority which may exact redress in case of default <he is *responsible* for the safe delivery of the goods>
syn accountable, amenable, answerable, liable
rel exposed, open, subject
con clear, exempt, immune; irresponsible, unaccountable, unanswerable, unliable
ant irresponsible

responsive *adj* **1** ***syn*** RECEPTIVE 1, acceptant, acceptive, influenceable, persuadable, persuasible, suasible, swayable
ant unresponsive
2 ***syn*** SENTIENT 3, impressible, impressionable, sensible, sensile, sensitive, susceptible, susceptive
rel answering, replying, responding
3 ***syn*** TENDER, compassionate, kindhearted, softhearted, sympathetic, warm, warmhearted
con cold, cool, indifferent

rest *n* **1** freedom from toil or strain <enjoyed his well-deserved *rest*>
syn ease, leisure, relaxation, repose, requiescence
rel deferring, intermission, suspension; quiet, silence, stillness; calm, peace, peacefulness, placidity, restfulness, serenity, tranquillity
con action, work; restlessness, strain
2 ***syn*** BASE 1, basis, bed, bottom, footing, foundation, ground, groundwork, seat, seating

rest *vb* **1** to dispose oneself at ease in order to relieve or avoid fatigue <she is *resting* in the bedroom after a hard day's work>
syn lie, lie down, recline, repose, stretch (out)
rel doze, nap, nod, sleep, slumber, snooze
2 to refrain from labor or exertion <planned to do nothing but *rest* during his vacation>
syn relax, rest up, unbend, unlax
rel loaf, loll, lounge; ease off, ease up, let down, let up, slacken, slack off
idiom take it easy, take life easy
con labor, toil, work; drudge, grind, slave
3 to allow an interval of rest from exertion <they *rested* for ten minutes before going back to work>
syn breathe, lay off, lie by, spell
idiom lie (*or* rest) on one's oars, stop for breath, take a break (*or* rest), take five (*or* ten), take time out
4 ***syn*** BASE, bottom, establish, found, ground, predicate, stay
rel depend, hang, hinge; count, rely

rest *n* ***syn*** REMAINDER, balance, heel, leavings, remains, remanet, remnant, residual, residue, residuum
rel excess, overplus, superfluity, surplus, surplusage

restart *vb* ***syn*** RESUME 2, continue, pick up, recommence, renew, reopen, take up

restate *vb* ***syn*** PARAPHRASE, rephrase, reword, translate (into)

restatement *n* ***syn*** VERSION 1, paraphrase, rendering, translation

restitute *vb* **1** ***syn*** RESTORE 3, reclaim, recondition, reconstruct, recover, rehabilitate, rejuvenate

2 ***syn*** RETURN 4, replace, restore, take back

restitution *n* ***syn*** REPARATION, amends, compensation, indemnification, indemnity, quittance, recompense, redress, reprisal

restive *adj* **1** ***syn*** CONTRARY 3, balky, cross-grained, froward, ornery, perverse, wayward, wrongheaded

2 ***syn*** TENSE 2, edgy, nervy, uneasy, uptight

restiveness *n* ***syn*** UNREST, ailment, disquiet, disquietude, ferment, inquietude, restlessness, storm and stress, Sturm und Drang, turmoil

restless *adj* lacking rest or giving no rest < the patient was *restless* from pain > < *restless* sleep >

syn uneasy, unpeaceful, unquiet, unrestful, unsettled, untranquil

rel agitated, disturbed, perturbed, troubled; fidgety, jittery, jumpy, nervous, restive; fitful, intermittent, spasmodic

con easy, peaceful, quiet, tranquil

ant restful

restlessness *n* ***syn*** UNREST, ailment, disquiet, disquietude, ferment, inquietude, restiveness, storm and stress, Sturm und Drang, turmoil

restorative *adj* **1** ***syn*** CURATIVE, curing, healing, remedial, remedying, sanative, sanatory, vulnerary, wholesome

2 ***syn*** TONIC 1, astringent, roborant

restore *vb* **1** to put or bring back (as into existence or use) < *restore* peace in the world >

syn recall, reestablish, reinstate, reintroduce, renew, revive

rel get back, recover, regain, retrieve, win (back)

2 ***syn*** RENEW 1, modernize, refresh, refurbish, rejuvenate, renovate, update

3 to put into a previous good state < made plans to *restore* slum areas >

syn reclaim, recondition, reconstruct, recover, rehabilitate, rejuvenate, restitute

rel redeem, rescue, save; amend, reform, revise; recoup, recruit, regain, retrieve; better, improve; correct, rectify, remedy, right; return

ant deteriorate

4 to help or cause to regain signs of life and vigor < *restore* him to health >

syn resuscitate, revive, revivify

rel cure, heal, remedy; arouse, rally, rouse, stir

5 to put again in possession of something < *restore* the king to his throne >

syn give back, put (back), reinstate, replace, return

6 ***syn*** RETURN 4, replace, restitute, take back

restrain *vb* **1** to prevent from or control in doing something < *restrained* the child from picking all the flowers >

syn bit, bridle, check, coarct, constrain, crimp, curb, hold back, hold down, hold in, inhibit, keep, pull in, withhold; *compare* HAMPER

rel arrest, interrupt, stop; prevent; forbear, refrain; block, hinder, impede, obstruct; gag, muzzle

idiom keep in line, put (*or* lay) under restraint

con countenance, encourage; incline, induce, move, prompt; persuade; allow, permit

ant impel; incite

2 ***syn*** COMPOSE 4, collect, control, cool, re-collect, rein, repress, simmer down, smother, suppress

ant abandon

3 ***syn*** MODERATE 1, modulate, temper

restrained *adj* **1** ***syn*** QUIET 4, inobtrusive, subdued, tasteful, tasty, unobtrusive

ant unrestrained

2 ***syn*** UNDEMONSTRATIVE, aseptic, retiring, shrinking, unaffable, unexpansive, withdrawn

3 ***syn*** RESERVED 1, constrained, incommunicable, noncommittal

4 ***syn*** CONSERVATIVE 2, controlled, discreet, moderate, reasonable, temperate, unexcessive, unextreme

ant extravagant

restraint *n* ***syn*** RESTRICTION 2, circumscription, confinement, constrainment, constraint, cramp

restrict *vb* ***syn*** LIMIT 2, bar, circumscribe, confine, delimit, delimitate, prelimit

rel bind, tie; shrink

restricted *adj* ***syn*** DEFINITE 1, circumscribed, determinate, fixed, limited, narrow, precise

restriction *n* **1** something that restricts or restrains < they both wanted to be free of the *restriction* of the school >

syn ‖ball and chain, circumscription, cramp, limitation, stint, stricture

rel brake, check, control, curb

2 an act of restricting or the condition of being restricted < undue *restriction* of children >

syn circumscription, confinement, constrainment, constraint, cramp, restraint

rest up *vb* ***syn*** REST 2, relax, unbend, unlax

restyle *vb* ***syn*** REVISE, redraft, redraw, revamp, rework, rewrite, work over

result *n* **1** ***syn*** EFFECT 1, aftereffect, aftermath, consequence, eventuality, issue, outcome, sequel, sequence, upshot

rel close, conclusion, end, finish, termination; product, production

con origin, root, source

2 ***syn*** ANSWER 2, solution

resume *vb* **1** to assume or take again < *resumed* her place in society >

syn reassume, reoccupy, repossess, retake

rel reclaim, recoup, recover, regain, retrieve

2 to return to or begin again after interruption < *resumed* her work >

syn continue, pick up, recommence, renew, reopen, restart, take up

rel carry on, go on, keep up

---

syn synonym(s)	***rel*** related word(s)
idiom idiomatic equivalent(s)	***con*** contrasted word(s)
ant antonym(s)	* vulgar

‖ use limited; if in doubt, see a dictionary

The first word in a synonym list when printed in SMALL CAPITALS shows where there is more information about the group. For a more efficient use of this book see Explanatory Notes.

con cease, discontinue, end, halt, postpone, quit, stop; check, intermit, interrupt

résumé *n* ***syn*** SUMMARY, epitome, recapitulation, sum, summation, summing-up, sum-up

resurgence *n* ***syn*** REVIVAL, reanimation, rebirth, renaissance, renascence, resurrection, resuscitation, revivification, reviviscence, risorgimento

resurrect *vb* **1** to restore to life <believed that his body would be literally *resurrected*>
syn raise
idiom raise from the dead
2 ***syn*** REVIVE 3, reactivate, rekindle, renew, renovate, resuscitate, retrieve, revitalize, revivify

resurrection *n* ***syn*** REVIVAL, reanimation, rebirth, renaissance, renascence, resurgence, resuscitation, revivification, reviviscence, risorgimento

resuscitate *vb* **1** ***syn*** RESTORE 4, revive, revivify
2 ***syn*** REVIVE 3, reactivate, rekindle, renew, renovate, resurrect, retrieve, revitalize, revivify

resuscitation *n* ***syn*** REVIVAL, reanimation, rebirth, renaissance, renascence, resurgence, resurrection, revivification, reviviscence, risorgimento

retail *vb* ***syn*** SELL 3, market, merchandise

retain *vb* **1** ***syn*** HAVE 1, enjoy, hold, own, possess
2 ***syn*** KEEP 5, detain, hold, hold back, keep back, keep out, reserve, withhold
con abdicate, resign; abjure, forswear, recant, renounce, retract
3 ***syn*** REMEMBER, bethink, cite, ‖mind, recall, recollect, remind, reminisce, retrospect, revive

retake *vb* ***syn*** RESUME 1, reassume, reoccupy, repossess

retaliate *vb* ***syn*** RECIPROCATE, recompense, requite, return
rel avenge, revenge
idiom even the score, get back at, get even with, give in kind, give one a dose of his own medicine, give one tit for tat, pay one in his own coin, settle (*or* square) accounts, turn the tables on

retaliation *n* the act of inflicting or the intent to inflict injury in return for injury <they had no opportunity for *retaliation*>
syn avengement, avenging, counterblow, reprisal, requital, retribution, revanche, revenge, vengeance
rel correction, discipline, punishment; indemnification, recompense, repayment; amends, indemnity, redress, reparation, restitution
idiom an eye for an eye, blow for blow, measure for measure, tit for tat
con clemency, grace, lenity, mercy; forgiveness, pardon, remission

retard *vb* ***syn*** DELAY 1, bog (down), decelerate, detain, embog, hang up, mire, set back, slacken, slow (up *or* down)
rel decrease, lessen, reduce; clog, fetter, hamper; baffle, balk
ant accelerate; advance

retarded *adj* limited in intellectual or emotional development <a *retarded* child>
syn backward, dim-witted, dull, feebleminded, half-witted, imbecile, moronic, quarter-witted, simple, simpleminded, slow, slow-witted; *compare* SIMPLE 3, STUPID 1
rel dim, ‖dough-baked, ‖dunny, opaque; exceptional, underachieving; touched
idiom not all there, soft in the head
con bright, capable, intelligent

retch *vb* to make an effort to vomit <started to *retch* after drinking it>
syn gag, heave, keck

rethink *vb* ***syn*** RECONSIDER, reevaluate, reexamine, retreat, review, reweigh, think (over)

reticent *adj* ***syn*** SILENT 3, close, close-lipped, closemouthed, close-tongued, reserved, taciturn, tight-lipped, tight-mouthed, uncommunicative
con candid, open, plain
ant frank, unreticent

retinue *n* ***syn*** ENTOURAGE, following, suite, train

retire *vb* **1** ***syn*** RETREAT 2, fall back, give back, withdraw
2 ***syn*** GO 2, depart, exit, get away, get off, leave, quit, run along, take off, withdraw
rel recede, retreat; abandon, relinquish, surrender, yield
ant advance
3 to cause to withdraw from one's position or occupation <all employees are automatically *retired* at age sixty-five>
syn pension (off), superannuate
rel discharge, dismiss; drop, leave, quit, resign, terminate, vacate
4 to go to bed <youngsters should always *retire* before midnight>
syn bed, ‖flop, pile (in), roll in, turn in
idiom go beddie-bye, go night-night, hit the hay (*or* sack)
con arise, get out, get up, pile (out), roll out, turn out, uprise
ant rise

retired *adj* ***syn*** OBSCURE 2, devious, lonesome, out-of-the-way, remote, removed, secret

retirement *n* ***syn*** SECLUSION, reclusion, sequestration

retiring *adj* **1** ***syn*** SHY 1, backward, bashful, demure, diffident, rabbity, self-effacing, timid, unassertive, unassured
ant assertive
2 ***syn*** UNDEMONSTRATIVE, aseptic, restrained, shrinking, unaffable, unexpansive, withdrawn
ant forward

retool *vb* ***syn*** REORGANIZE, readjust, rearrange, reconstitute, reconstruct, reorder, reorient, reorientate, reshuffle

retort *vb* ***syn*** ANSWER 1, come in, rejoin, reply, respond, return

retort *n* **1** ***syn*** ANSWER 1, antiphon, rejoinder, reply, respond, response, return
2 a quick, witty, or cutting reply <he made a very clever *retort*>

syn back answer, comeback, repartee, riposte
rel reprisal, retaliation, revenge; crack, gag, jape, jest, joke, quip, sally, wisecrack, witticism

retouch *vb* *syn* TOUCH UP, brush up, tease up

retract *vb* **1** *syn* RECEDE 1, back, fall back, retreat, retrocede, retrograde
ant protract
2 *syn* ABJURE, forswear, palinode, recall, recant, take back, unsay, withdraw
rel eliminate, exclude, rule out, suspend

retral *adj* **1** *syn* POSTERIOR 2, after, back, hind, hinder, hindmost, rear
2 *syn* BACKWARD 1, retrograde

retreat *n* *syn* SHELTER 1, asylum, cover, covert, harbor, harborage, haven, port, refuge, sanctuary

retreat *vb* **1** *syn* RECEDE 1, back, fall back, retract, retrocede, retrograde
rel quail, recoil, shrink
ant advance
2 to draw back from action or danger <the army *retreated* in disarray>
syn fall back, give back, retire, withdraw
rel abandon, depart, evacuate, go, leave, pull out, quit, vacate; decamp, escape, flee, fly; back down, back out, bow out, climb down
idiom beat a retreat, drop back, give ground, give way, sound a retreat
con advance, move, proceed, progress
ant attack

re–treat *vb* *syn* RECONSIDER, reevaluate, reexamine, rethink, review, reweigh, think (over)

retrench *vb* *syn* SHORTEN, abbreviate, abridge, curtail, cut, cut back, slash

retribution *n* *syn* RETALIATION, avengement, avenging, counterblow, reprisal, requital, revanche, revenge, vengeance
rel affliction, trial, tribulation, visitation

retrieve *vb* **1** *syn* RECOVER 1, get back, recoup, recruit, regain, repossess
2 *syn* REVIVE 3, reactivate, rekindle, renew, renovate, resurrect, resuscitate, revitalize, revivify

retrocede *vb* *syn* RECEDE 1, back, fall back, retract, retreat, retrograde

retrograde *adj* *syn* BACKWARD 1, retral

retrograde *vb* **1** *syn* RECEDE 1, back, fall back, retract, retreat, retrocede
rel return, revert; invert, reverse; backslide, lapse, relapse
2 *syn* DETERIORATE 1, decline, degenerate, descend, disimprove, disintegrate, rot, sink, worsen

retrogress *vb* *syn* REVERT 2, regress, throw back

retrospect *n* *syn* REVIEW 5, afterlight, reconsideration, reexamination, retrospection, revision

retrospect *vb* *syn* REMEMBER, bethink, cite, ‖mind, recall, recollect, remind, reminisce, retain, revive

retrospection *n* *syn* REVIEW 5, afterlight, reconsideration, reexamination, retrospect, revision

return *vb* **1** to go or come back (as to a person, place, or condition) <the converted sinner soon *returned* to his old ways>
syn react, recrudesce, recur, revert, turn back
rel advert; revolve, rotate, turn; renew, restore; recover, regain; rebound, reflect, repercuss, reverberate
con abandon, depart, leave, quit
ant forsake
2 *syn* ANSWER 1, come in, rejoin, reply, respond, retort
3 to bring back (as a writ or verdict) to an office or tribunal <*return* a verdict of not guilty>
syn render
4 to bring, send, or put back to a former or proper place <*return* the gun to its holster>
syn replace, restitute, restore, take back
ant remove
5 *syn* RESTORE 5, give back, put (back), reinstate, replace
6 *syn* YIELD 5, bring in, pay
7 *syn* RECIPROCATE, recompense, requite, retaliate
rel bestow, give

return *n* **1** *syn* RECURRENCE, reappearance, reoccurrence
2 *syn* ANSWER 1, antiphon, rejoinder, reply, respond, response, retort
3 *syn* PROFIT, earnings, gain, lucre, proceeds
ant outlay

returnless *adj* *syn* INEVITABLE, certain, ineluctable, ineludible, inescapable, inevasible, necessary, unavoidable, unescapable, unevadable

revamp *vb* **1** *syn* MEND 2, do up, fix, overhaul, patch, rebuild, recondition, reconstruct, repair, vamp
2 *syn* REVISE, redraft, redraw, restyle, rework, rewrite, work over

revanche *n* *syn* RETALIATION, avengement, avenging, counterblow, reprisal, requital, retribution, revenge, vengeance

reveal *vb* **1** to make known what has been or should be concealed <he solemnly promised he would not *reveal* the truth>
syn betray, blab (out), disclose, discover, divulge, give away, let on, ‖let out, mouth, spill, tell, unbosom, unclose, uncover, uncurtain, unveil
rel break, communicate, impart; announce, blow (about *or* abroad), broadcast, declare, give out, publish, vent; breathe, whisper; leak; acknowledge, admit, avow, confess, let on; peach, rat, ‖split, squeak, squeal (on), ‖stool, talk
idiom let slip, let the cat out of the bag, spill the beans
con cover (up), hide, obscure, veil
ant conceal
2 *syn* OPEN 2, disclose, display, expose, unclothe, uncover, unveil

revel *vb* **1** to be festive in a noisy or riotous manner <they *reveled* all night long>
syn carouse, frolic, hell, riot, roister, spree, wassail
idiom blow off steam, cut loose, kick up one's heels, let go, let loose, paint the town red, whoop it up

---

syn synonym(s) *rel* related word(s)
idiom idiomatic equivalent(s) *con* contrasted word(s)
ant antonym(s) * vulgar
‖ use limited; if in doubt, see a dictionary
The first word in a synonym list when printed in SMALL CAPITALS shows where there is more information about the group. For a more efficient use of this book see Explanatory Notes.

2 *syn* WALLOW 3, bask, indulge, luxuriate, roll, rollick, welter

revel *n* **1** *syn* MERRYMAKING, festivity, gaiety, jollity, merriment, reveling, revelment, revelry, whoopee
2 *syn* REVELRY 2, high jinks, revelment, skylarking, wassail, whoop-de-do, whoopee, whoopla, whoop-up

revelation *n* disclosure or something disclosed by or as if by divine or preternatural means <a *revelation* closely guarded by members of the sect>
syn apocalypse, oracle, prophecy, vision
ant adumbration

reveling *n* *syn* MERRYMAKING, festivity, gaiety, jollity, merriment, revel, revelment, revelry, whoopee

revelment *n* **1** *syn* MERRYMAKING, festivity, gaiety, jollity, merriment, revel, reveling, revelry, whoopee
2 *syn* REVELRY 2, high jinks, revel, skylarking, wassail, whoop-de-do, whoopee, whoopla, whoop-up

revelry *n* **1** *syn* MERRYMAKING, festivity, gaiety, jollity, merriment, revel, reveling, revelment, whoopee
2 boisterous partying <they were exhausted after the night of *revelry*>
syn high jinks, revel, revelment, skylarking, wassail, whoop-de-do, whoopee, whoopla, whoop-up

revenant *n* *syn* APPARITION, ghost, ‖haunt, phantasm, phantom, shade, shadow, specter, spirit, wraith

revenge *vb* *syn* AVENGE, redress, venge, vindicate
rel defend, justify
idiom get one's own back, have one's revenge, take an eye for an eye

revenge *n* *syn* RETALIATION, avengement, avenging, counterblow, reprisal, requital, retribution, revanche, vengeance

revengeful *adj* *syn* VINDICTIVE, vengeful, wreakful
rel adamant, inexorable, inflexible, obdurate

revenue *n* amount received or gained usually measured in money <still holds property that yields a good *revenue*>
syn coming(s) in, income, receipts
rel earnings, gains, salary, wages; proceeds, profit, returns, yield
con expenditure, expense(s), outgoings, outlay

reverberant *adj* *syn* HOLLOW 1, cavernous, sepulchral

revere *vb* to honor and admire profoundly and respectfully <he is *revered* for his wisdom>
syn adore, reverence, venerate, worship
rel admire, esteem, regard, respect; appreciate, cherish, prize, treasure, value; exalt, magnify; enjoy, love
con contemn, despise, disdain, scorn, scout; insult, mock, scoff
ant flout

revered *adj* *syn* VENERABLE 1, patriarchal, reverend, reverential

reverence *n* **1** *syn* HONOR 1, deference, homage, obeisance
rel devotion, fealty, loyalty, piety
2 the emotion inspired by what arouses one's deep respect or veneration <a deep *reverence* for honesty>
syn awe, fear
con contempt, despite, disdain, hatred, scorn; insult, mockery

reverence *vb* *syn* REVERE, adore, venerate, worship
idiom hold in reverence

reverend *adj* *syn* VENERABLE 1, patriarchal, revered, reverential

reverend *n* *syn* CLERGYMAN, churchman, cleric, clerical, clerk, divine, ecclesiastic, minister, parson, preacher

reverential *adj* *syn* VENERABLE 1, patriarchal, revered, reverend

reverie *n* the condition of being lost in thought <spent the day in *reverie* before the fire>
syn brown study, muse, study, trance
rel absorption, abstraction, preoccupation; contemplation, meditation, thought; castle-building, daydreaming, dreaming

reversal *n* **1** a causing to move or face in an opposite direction or to appear in an inverted position <a *reversal* in policy> <the *reversal* of objects seen through a simple lens>
syn about-face, changeabout, inversion, reverse, reversement, reversion, right-about, right-about-face, turn, turnabout, turning, volte-face
rel bouleversement, overturning
2 *syn* SETBACK, backset, check, reverse

reverse *adj* *syn* OPPOSITE, antipodal, antipodean, antithetical, contradictory, contrary, converse, counter, diametric, polar

reverse *vb* **1** to change to the contrary or opposite side or position <the chairman *reversed* the order in which they would speak>
syn change, inverse, invert, revert, transplace, transpose, turn
rel capsize, overturn, upset; exchange, interchange; shift, transfer
2 *syn* REVOKE 2, dismantle, lift, recall, repeal, rescind

reverse *n* **1** *syn* OPPOSITE, antipode, antipole, antithesis, contra, contradictory, contrary, converse, counter, counterpole
2 *syn* REVERSAL 1, about-face, changeabout, reversement, reversion, right-about, right-about-face, turn, turnabout, volte-face
3 *syn* SETBACK, backset, check, reversal

reversement *n* *syn* REVERSAL 1, about-face, changeabout, reverse, reversion, right-about, right-about-face, turn, turnabout, volte-face

reversion *n* **1** a return to an ancestral type or condition or an instance of such a return <the law was a shocking *reversion* to earlier times>
syn atavism, throwback
rel backsliding, lapse, relapse
con advance, amendment, bettering, betterment, improvement; reform
2 *syn* REVERSAL 1, about-face, changeabout, reverse, reversement, right-about, right-about-face, turn, turnabout, volte-face

revert *vb* **1** *syn* RETURN 1, react, recrudesce, recur, turn back
2 to come or go back to a lower or worse condition <*reverted* to savagery>

---

syn synonym(s) *rel* related word(s)
idiom idiomatic equivalent(s) *con* contrasted word(s)
ant antonym(s) * vulgar
‖ use limited; if in doubt, see a dictionary
The first word in a synonym list when printed in SMALL CAPITALS shows where there is more information about the group. For a more efficient use of this book see Explanatory Notes.

syn regress, retrogress, throw back
rel backslide, lapse, relapse; decline, degenerate, deteriorate, retrograde
con advance, progress
3 *syn* REVERSE 1, change, inverse, invert, transplace, transpose, turn

review *n* **1** *syn* REVISION 1, recension, redraft, rescript, revisal, revise
2 *syn* EXAMINATION, analysis, audit, check-over, checkup, inspection, scan, scrutiny, survey, view
3 *syn* CRITICISM, comment, critique, notice, reviewal
4 *syn* JOURNAL, magazine, newspaper, organ, periodical
5 a retrospective view of or meditation on past events <an occurrence that in *review* did not surprise him>
syn afterlight, reconsideration, reexamination, retrospect, retrospection, revision
rel reflection, study; second thought
con anticipation, contemplation, foreseeing

review *vb* *syn* RECONSIDER, reevaluate, reexamine, rethink, re-treat, reweigh, think (over)

reviewal *n* *syn* CRITICISM, comment, critique, notice, review

revile *vb* *syn* SCOLD 1, bawl out, berate, ‖chew out, jaw, rail, rate, tongue-lash, upbraid, vituperate
rel asperse, calumniate, defame, libel, malign, slander, traduce, vilify
con acclaim, eulogize, extol, praise
ant laud

revisal *n* *syn* REVISION 1, recension, redraft, rescript, review, revise

revise *vb* to make a new, amended, improved, or up-to-date version of <the many problems involved in *revising* a dictionary>
syn redraft, redraw, restyle, revamp, rework, rewrite, work over
rel overhaul, reorganize; perfect, polish, upgrade
con discard, disregard

revise *n* *syn* REVISION 1, recension, redraft, rescript, review, revisal

revision *n* **1** an act of revising <the *revision* of a manuscript>
syn recension, redraft, rescript, review, revisal, revise
rel amendment, correction, emendation, rectification
2 *syn* REVIEW 5, afterlight, reconsideration, reexamination, retrospect, retrospection

revitalize *vb* *syn* REVIVE 3, reactivate, rekindle, renew, renovate, resurrect, resuscitate, retrieve, revivify

revival *n* a renewal of life, activity, or prominence <a *revival* of weaving>
syn reanimation, rebirth, renaissance, renascence, resurgence, resurrection, resuscitation, revivification, reviviscence, risorgimento
rel regeneration, rejuvenation, renewal, restoration

revive *vb* **1** *syn* RESTORE 4, resuscitate, revivify
rel gain, improve, recuperate
2 *syn* RESTORE 1, recall, reestablish, reinstate, reintroduce, renew
3 to restore from a depressed, inactive, or unused state <*revived* his hope of escape>
syn reactivate, rekindle, renew, renovate, resurrect, resuscitate, retrieve, revitalize, revivify
rel reanimate, regenerate, reinvigorate, rejuvenate; arouse, galvanize, quicken, stimulate; activate, energize, vitalize
con extinguish, put down, put out, quell, quench, suppress; inhibit
4 *syn* REMEMBER, bethink, cite, ‖mind, recall, recollect, remind, reminisce, retain, retrospect

revived *adj* *syn* REFRESHED, new, regenerated, reinvigorated, renewed

revivification *n* *syn* REVIVAL, reanimation, rebirth, renaissance, renascence, resurgence, resurrection, resuscitation, reviviscence, risorgimento

revivify *vb* **1** *syn* REVIVE 3, reactivate, rekindle, renew, renovate, resurrect, resuscitate, retrieve, revitalize
2 *syn* RESTORE 4, resuscitate, revive

reviviscence *n* *syn* REVIVAL, reanimation, rebirth, renaissance, renascence, resurgence, resurrection, resuscitation, revivification, risorgimento

revoke *vb* **1** *syn* REMEMBER, bethink, cite, recall, recollect, remind, reminisce, retain, retrospect, revive
2 to annul by recalling or taking back <*revoke* a privilege>
syn dismantle, lift, recall, repeal, rescind, reverse
rel abrogate, annul, void; cancel, erase, expunge; invalidate, nullify; countermand, counterorder; abjure, forswear, recant, retract
ant confirm

revolt *vb* **1** to renounce allegiance or subjection <*revolted* against the king>
syn insurrect, mutiny, rebel, rise (against)
rel defy, oppose, resist; break, renounce, turn (against); boycott, strike; overthrow, overturn, riot
idiom kick over the traces, take up arms against
con obey, submit; aid, assist, help, succor, support; bolster, prop (up), sustain, uphold
2 *syn* DISGUST, nauseate, reluct, repel, repulse, sicken

revolter *n* *syn* REBEL, anarch, anarchist, frondeur, insurgent, insurrectionist, malcontent, mutineer

revolting *adj* *syn* OFFENSIVE, disgusting, foul, loathsome, nasty, noisome, repellent, repugnant, repulsive, vile

revolute *vb* *syn* REVOLUTIONIZE, revolution

revolution *n* **1** the action or an act of moving around an orbit or circular course <the *revolution* of the earth around the sun>
syn circuit, circulation, circumvolution, gyration, gyre, revolve, rotation, round, turn, wheel, whirl
rel cycle, pirouette, reel, roll, spin, twirl
2 *syn* SHAKE-UP, overturn, reorganization, turnover

revolution *vb* *syn* REVOLUTIONIZE, revolute

revolutional *adj* *syn* EXTREME 3, extremist, fanatic, rabid, radical, revolutionary, revolutionist, ultra, ultraist

---

syn synonym(s) | *rel* related word(s)
idiom idiomatic equivalent(s) | *con* contrasted word(s)
ant antonym(s) | * vulgar
‖ use limited; if in doubt, see a dictionary
The first word in a synonym list when printed in SMALL CAPITALS shows where there is more information about the group. For a more efficient use of this book see Explanatory Notes.

revolutionary *adj* ***syn*** EXTREME 3, extremist, fanatic, rabid, radical, revolutional, revolutionist, ultra, ultraist

revolutionary *n* ***syn*** RADICAL, extremist, revolutionist, ultraist

revolutionist *n* ***syn*** RADICAL, extremist, revolutionary, ultraist

revolutionist *adj* ***syn*** EXTREME 3, extremist, fanatic, rabid, radical, revolutional, revolutionary, ultra, ultraist

revolutionize *vb* to change fundamentally or completely <he *revolutionized* manufacturing processes>
syn revolute, revolution
rel alter, change, modify; recast, refashion, reform, remodel; redraw, restyle, revamp, revise; metamorphose, transfigure, transform, transmogrify; overthrow, overturn
idiom break with the past, make a clean sweep, make a radical change

revolve *vb* **1** ***syn*** PONDER 2, ‖chaw, deliberate, meditate, mull (over), muse, roll, ruminate, turn over
2 ***syn*** TURN 1, circle, circumduct, gyrate, gyre, roll, rotate

revolve *n* ***syn*** REVOLUTION 1, circuit, circulation, circumvolution, gyration, gyre, rotation, round, turn, wheel

revulsion *n* ***syn*** ABOMINATION 2, abhorrence, aversion, detestation, hate, hatred, horror, loathing, repugnance, repulsion

revulsive *adj* ***syn*** REPUGNANT 1, abhorrent, invidious, obnoxious, repellent

reward *n* something that is offered or given for some service or attainment <the miner received a *reward* for his hard work>
syn carrot, dividend, guerdon, meed, plum, premium, prize
rel compensation, recompense, remuneration, requital

reweigh *vb* ***syn*** RECONSIDER, reevaluate, reexamine, rethink, re-treat, review, think (over)

reword *vb* ***syn*** PARAPHRASE, rephrase, restate, translate (into)

rework *vb* ***syn*** REVISE, redraft, redraw, restyle, revamp, rewrite, work over

rewrite *vb* ***syn*** REVISE, redraft, redraw, restyle, revamp, rework, work over

rhadamanthine *adj* ***syn*** JUST 3, appropriate, condign, deserved, due, merited, requisite, right, rightful, suitable

rhapsodize *vb* ***syn*** ENTHUSE 2, drool, rave, rhapsody
rel acclaim, extol, praise
con blame, condemn, denounce; decry, derogate, detract, minimize

rhapsody *n* **1** ***syn*** BOMBAST, fustian, highfalutin, lexiphanicism, rant, rhetoric, rodomontade
2 ***syn*** ECSTASY, heaven, rapture, seventh heaven, transport

rhapsody *vb* ***syn*** ENTHUSE 2, drool, rave, rhapsodize

rhetoric *n* **1** ***syn*** ORATORY, elocution, speechcraft
2 ***syn*** BOMBAST, fustian, highfalutin, lexiphanicism, rant, rhapsody, rodomontade

rhetorical *adj* emphasizing style often at the expense of thought <the candidate was given to windy *rhetorical* speeches>
syn aureate, bombastic, declamatory, euphuistic, florid, flowery, grandiloquent, highfalutin, high-flown, magniloquent, ‖mouthy, oratorical, orotund, overblown, pompous, purple, sonorous, stilted, swelling, swollen, tumescent, tumid, turgid
rel chichi, orchidaceous, ostentatious, pretentious, showy; gassy, inflated, windy; exaggerated, overdone, overwrought; grand, grandiose, high-sounding, imposing; flamboyant, ornate; embellished; articulate, eloquent, fluent, glib, vocal, voluble
con homely, literal, plain, simple, unpretentious; unadorned, undecorated, unembellished, ungarnished, unornamented
ant unrhetorical

rhino *n* ***syn*** MONEY, ‖mazuma, ‖moolah, needful, ‖ooftish, pelf, ‖scratch, ‖smash, stuff, ‖stumpy

rhubarb *n* ***syn*** QUARREL, altercation, beef, bickering, controversy, dispute, falling-out, row, run-in, set-to

rhyme *n* **1** ***syn*** POETRY 1, poesy, song, verse
2 ***syn*** POEM, poesy, poetry, rune, verse
3 ***syn*** RHYTHM, beat, cadence, cadency, measure, meter, rhythmus, swing

rhyme *vb* ***syn*** AGREE 4, accord, check, cohere, comport, conform, consist, consort, correspond, dovetail

rhymer *n* ***syn*** POETASTER, balladmonger, bardlet, bardling, poeticule, poetling, rhymester, verseman, versemonger, versifier

rhymester *n* ***syn*** POETASTER, balladmonger, bardlet, bardling, poeticule, poetling, rhymer, verseman, versemonger, versifier

rhythm *n* the regular rise and fall in intensity of sounds that is associated chiefly with poetry and music <the *rhythm* of the music made it easy to dance to>
syn beat, cadence, cadency, measure, meter, rhyme, rhythmus, swing
rel lilt; accent

rhythmus *n* ***syn*** RHYTHM, beat, cadence, cadency, measure, meter, rhyme, swing

riant *adj* ***syn*** MERRY, blithe, boon, festive, gay, gleeful, jocund, jolly, jovial, mirthful

‖**rib** *n* ***syn*** WIFE, ‖ball and chain, lady, ‖little woman, ‖missus, Mrs., ‖old lady, ‖old woman, ‖squaw, woman

rib *vb* ***syn*** BANTER 1, chaff, fool, fun, jest, joke, josh, kid, rag, razz

ribald *n* ***syn*** SCAMP, devil, enfant terrible, mischief, rapscallion, rascal, rogue, scalawag, skeezicks, slyboots

ribbon *n* ***syn*** STRIP 1, band, bandeau, banding, fillet, stripe

rich *adj* **1** having goods, property, and money in abundance <he was a *rich* man, having accumulated his wealth in business>
syn affluent, moneyed, ‖oofy, opulent, wealthy
rel comfortable, easy, independent, prosperous, well-fixed, well-heeled, well-off, well-to-do; fat, flush
idiom flush with money, having money to burn, in the money, rich as Croesus, rolling in money

---

con destitute, indigent, penurious, poverty-stricken
ant poor
2 *syn* ORNATE, baroque, flamboyant, florid, luscious, rococo
3 highly seasoned and fatty, oily, or sweet <ate *rich* desserts every day>
syn heavy
rel cloying, oversweet; filling, satiating, sating; fat
con natural, simple, unseasoned
ant plain
4 *syn* FERTILE, childing, fecund, fruitful, productive, proliferant, prolific, spawning
5 *syn* EXPRESSIVE, eloquent, facund, meaningful, pregnant, sententious, significant

richen *vb syn* ENRICH

riches *n pl syn* WEALTH 2, fortune, property, resources, substance, worth

rick *n syn* PILE 1, bank, cock, drift, heap, hill, mow, ‖ruck, shock, stack

‖**rick** *vb syn* SPRAIN; turn, twist, wrench

rickety *adj* likely to give way or break down <a *rickety* old chair>
syn rachitic, rackety, rattletrap, shaky, wobbly; *compare* WEAK 2
rel unsound, unsteady
con firm, rugged, solid, sturdy, substantial, well-made
ant stable

‖**rickle** *n syn* PILE 1, bank, cock, drift, heap, hill, mass, mound, rick, ‖ruck

ricochet *vb syn* GLANCE 1, carom, dap, graze, skim, skip
rel bound, rebound, recoil

rid *vb* to set a person or thing free of something that encumbers <*rid* himself of his troubles>
syn clear, lose, shake (off), throw off, unburden
rel free, liberate, release; disembosom, unbosom; eradicate, exterminate, extirpate, remove, uproot; abolish, extinguish
con burden, charge, clog, cumber, encumber, lade, load, lumber, saddle, task, tax, weigh, weight
ant weigh down

riddance *n syn* DISPOSAL 2, discarding, disposition, dumping, jettison, junking, relegation, scrapping, throwing away

riddle *n syn* MYSTERY, Chinese puzzle, closed book, conundrum, enigma, mystification, puzzle, puzzlement, why

ride *vb* **1** to travel by automobile <often *rode* out to the countryside>
syn auto, motor
idiom go for a spin
2 *syn* DRIFT 1, float, wash
3 *syn* BAIT 2, badger, bullyrag, chivy, heckle, hector, hound
rel oppress, persecute; torment, torture
4 *syn* OVERLAP, imbricate, lap, overlie, override, shingle

ride (out) *vb syn* SURVIVE 2, come through, pull through

ride *n syn* DRIVE 1, spin, turn
rel excursion, expedition, journey, tour, trip

rider *n syn* APPENDIX 1, addendum, codicil, supplement

ridge *n* **1** a top or upper part especially when long and narrow <topped the mountain *ridge*>
syn chine, crest, hogback
2 *syn* WRINKLE, corrugation, crease, crinkle, fold, furrow, plica, rimple, rivel, ruck

‖**ridge runner** *n syn* RUSTIC, ‖backwoodser, backwoodsman, bumpkin, clodhopper, hayseed, hick, hillbilly, hillman, rube

ridicule *vb* to make an object of laughter <*ridiculed* him for his inability to perform the feat>
syn deride, lout, mock, quiz, rally, razz, scout, taunt, twit
rel ‖barrack, flout, gibe, jape, jeer, scoff, sneer; burlesque, caricature, mimic, travesty; haze, ride, roast
idiom laugh out of court, make fun (*or* game *or* sport) of, poke fun at

ridiculous *adj* **1** *syn* LAUGHABLE, comic, comical, droll, farcical, funny, gelastic, ludicrous, risible
rel absurd, foolish, preposterous, silly; antic, bizarre, fantastic, grotesque
2 *syn* INDECOROUS, improper, indecent, indelicate, malodorous, rough, unbecoming, undecorous, ungodly, unseemly

riding *n* **1** *syn* SHIVAREE, ‖belling, ‖bull band, ‖callithump, charivari, ‖horning, ‖skimmelton
2 *syn* HARBOR 3, anchorage, ‖chuck, harborage, haven, port, road(s), roadstead

rife *adj* **1** *syn* PREVAILING, current, popular, prevalent, rampant, regnant, ruling, widespread
2 *syn* ALIVE 5, abounding, overflowing, replete, swarming, teeming, thronged

riff (through) *vb syn* BROWSE, dip (into), flip (through), glance (at *or* over), leaf (through), riffle (through), run (through *or* over), scan, skim (through), thumb (through)

riffle *vb syn* RIPPLE, cockle, dimple, fret

riffle (through) *vb syn* BROWSE, dip (into), flip (through), glance (at *or* over), leaf (through), riff (through), run (through *or* over), scan, skim (through), thumb (through)

riffraff *n* **1** *syn* RABBLE 2, canaille, dreg(s), mass(es), mob, proletariat, ragtag and bobtail, scum, trash, unwashed
2 *syn* REFUSE, debris, garbage, junk, kelter, litter, offal, rubbish, trash, waste

rifle *vb syn* ROB 1, ‖knock off, knock over, loot, plunder, ransack, relieve, stick up

rift *n* **1** *syn* CRACK 3, chink, cleft, fissure, rima, rimation, rime, split
2 *syn* BREACH 3, break, fissure, fracture, rent, rupture, schism, split
rel gap, hiatus, interruption, interval

rig *vb syn* FURNISH 1, accouter, appoint, arm, equip, fit out, gear, outfit, turn out

rig *n syn* COSTUME, dress, getup, guise, outfit, setout, turnout

---

syn synonym(s) *rel* related word(s)
idiom idiomatic equivalent(s) *con* contrasted word(s)
ant antonym(s) * vulgar
‖ use limited; if in doubt, see a dictionary
The first word in a synonym list when printed in SMALL CAPITALS shows where there is more information about the group. For a more efficient use of this book see Explanatory Notes.

||**rig** *n* **1** ***syn*** IMPOSTURE, cheat, counterfeit, deception, flam, flimflam, fraud, gyp, hoax, humbug
2 ***syn*** PRANK, antic, caper, dido(es), frolic, lark, monkeyshine, shenanigan, shine(s), trick

||**rig** *vb* ***syn*** DUPE, bamboozle, chicane, con, flimflam, fool, gull, hoax, hoodwink, trick

rigamajig *n* ***syn*** DOODAD, business, dingus, dofunny, doohickey, gadget, gizmo, thingum, thingumajig, thingumbob

rigging *n* ***syn*** CLOTHES, apparel, attire, attirement, clothing, dress, duds, raiment, things, togs

||**riggish** *adj* ***syn*** FAST 7, easy, light, loose, unchaste, wanton, whorish

right *adj* **1** ***syn*** UPRIGHT 2, conscientious, honest, honorable, just, scrupulous, true
2 ***syn*** DECOROUS 1, becoming, befitting, comely, comme il faut, correct, decent, done, nice, proper
3 ***syn*** JUST 3, appropriate, condign, deserved, due, merited, requisite, rhadamanthine, rightful, suitable
4 ***syn*** TRUE 3, faithful, just, strict, undistorted, veracious, veridical
con specious, unsound; misguided, mistaken
ant unright, wrong
5 ***syn*** CORRECT 2, accurate, exact, nice, precise, proper, rigorous
6 ***syn*** FIT 1, applicable, appropriate, apt, befitting, felicitous, fitting, happy, proper, suitable
7 ***syn*** AUTHENTIC 2, bona fide, genuine, indubitable, real, simon-pure, sure-enough, true, undoubted, veritable
8 ***syn*** SANE 2, all there, compos mentis, lucid, normal
9 ***syn*** HEALTHY 1, ||bunkum, fit, hale, sane, well, well-conditioned, well-liking, whole, wholesome
10 ***syn*** CONSERVATIVE 1, die-hard, fogyish, old-line, orthodox, reactionary, tory, traditionalistic
11 ***syn*** DECENT 4, acceptable, adequate, all right, common, good, satisfactory, sufficient, tolerable, unexceptional

right *n* **1** qualities (as adherence to duty or obedience to lawful authority) that together constitute the ideal of moral propriety or merit moral approval <the *right* is not all on one side>
syn good, straight
rel correctitude, correctness, properness, propriety, rightness
con debt, sin, wickedness; improperness, impropriety, incorrectness, unrightness
ant unright, wrong
2 something to which one has a just claim <the *right* to life, liberty, and the pursuit of happiness>
syn appanage, birthright, perquisite, prerogative, privilege
rel claim, interest, title; freedom, liberty, license
3 *usu* **rights** *pl* ***syn*** DUE 1, comeuppance, desert(s), deserving, lumps, merit
4 ***syn*** DIEHARD 1, bitter-ender, conservative, fundamentalist, old liner, rightist, right-winger, standpat, standpatter, tory
||**5** ***syn*** OBLIGATION 2, charge, commitment, committal, devoir, duty, must, need, ought
||**6** ***syn*** EXCUSE 1, alibi, plea, pretext

right *adv* **1** ***syn*** JUST 1, accurately, bang, exactly, precisely, sharp, ||smack-dab, spang, square, squarely
2 ***syn*** WELL 4, acceptably, adequately, amply, appropriately, becomingly, fittingly, properly, satisfactorily, suitably
ant wrong, wrongly
3 ***syn*** DIRECTLY 1, dead, direct, due, straight, straightly, undeviatingly
4 ***syn*** WELL 3, altogether, clear, completely, entirely, fully, perfectly, quite, ||slap, utterly
5 ***syn*** AWAY 3, at once, directly, first off, forthwith, immediately, instanter, now, right away, straightaway
6 ***syn*** VERY 1, ||awful, ||big, exceedingly, extremely, highly, notably, parlous, remarkably, ||right smart

right *vb* **1** ***syn*** CORRECT 1, amend, emend, mend, rectify
||**2** ***syn*** MEND 2, fix, overhaul, patch, recondition, reconstruct, repair, revamp, ||rightle, vamp

right–about *n* ***syn*** REVERSAL 1, about-face, changeabout, reverse, reversement, reversion, right-about-face, turn, turnabout, volte-face

right–about–face *n* ***syn*** REVERSAL 1, about-face, changeabout, reverse, reversement, reversion, right-about, turn, turnabout, volte-face

right away *adv* ***syn*** AWAY 3, at once, directly, first off, forthwith, immediately, instanter, instantly, now, straightway

righteous *adj* **1** ***syn*** MORAL 1, ethical, moralistic, noble, principled, right-minded, virtuous
con corrupt, flagitious, nefarious; bad, evil, immoral, reprobate, sinful, vicious, wicked, wrong
ant iniquitous, unrighteous
2 ***syn*** GOOD 11, blameless, exemplary, guiltless, inculpable, innocent, irreproachable, pure, virtuous, unblamable
ant unrighteous

righteousness *n* ***syn*** GOODNESS, morality, probity, rectitude, rightness, uprightness, virtue
ant unrighteousness

rightful *adj* **1** ***syn*** JUST 3, appropriate, condign, deserved, due, merited, requisite, rhadamanthine, right, suitable
rel equitable, fair, impartial
ant unrightful
2 ***syn*** TRUE 8, legitimate
ant unrightful
3 ***syn*** FIT 1, applicable, appropriate, apt, befitting, fitting, just, proper, right, suitable

right hand *n* ***syn*** RIGHT-HAND MAN, girl Friday, man Friday

right–handed *adj* having the same direction or course as the movement of the hands of a watch viewed from in front <a *right-handed* propeller>
syn clockwise, dextrorotatory, positive

right–hand man *n* a reliable or indispensable person <the boss viewed his efficient assistant as his *right-hand man*>

---

syn synonym(s) — *rel* related word(s)
idiom idiomatic equivalent(s) — *con* contrasted word(s)
ant antonym(s) — * vulgar
|| use limited; if in doubt, see a dictionary
The first word in a synonym list when printed in SMALL CAPITALS shows where there is more information about the group. For a more efficient use of this book see Explanatory Notes.

syn girl Friday, man Friday, right hand

rightist *n* *syn* DIEHARD 1, bitter-ender, conservative, fundamentalist, old liner, right, right-winger, standpat, standpatter, tory
ant leftist

‖**rightle** *vb* *syn* MEND 2, fix, overhaul, patch, recondition, reconstruct, repair, revamp, ‖right, vamp

rightly *adv* *syn* WELL 1, befittingly, correctly, decently, decorously, fitly, fittingly, justly, nicely, properly

right-minded *adj* *syn* MORAL 1, ethical, moralistic, noble, principled, righteous, virtuous

rightness *n* **1** *syn* GOODNESS, morality, probity, rectitude, righteousness, uprightness, virtue
2 *syn* ORDER 11, appositeness, appropriateness, aptness, expediency, fitness, meetness, propriety, suitability, suitableness

right off *adv* *syn* AWAY 3, at once, directly, forthwith, immediately, instanter, now, right away, straight, straightway

‖**right smart** *adj* *syn* CONSIDERABLE 2, good, respectable, sensible, sizable, ‖smart

‖**right smart** *adv* *syn* VERY 1, ‖awful, ‖big, ‖dreadful, extremely, mighty, notably, parlous, remarkably, right

right wing *n* *syn* DIEHARD 1, bitter-ender, conservative, fundamentalist, old liner, right, rightist, right-winger, standpat, standpatter

right-winger *n* *syn* DIEHARD 1, bitter-ender, conservative, fundamentalist, old liner, right, rightist, standpat, standpatter, tory
ant left-winger

rigid *adj* **1** *syn* STIFF 1, immalleable, impliable, incompliant, inelastic, inflexible, unbending, unflexible, unyielding
rel firm, hard, solid
ant elastic
2 *syn* INFLEXIBLE 2, adamant, inexorable, obdurate, relentless, single-minded, unbending, uncompliant, uncompromising, unyielding
3 extremely severe or stern <was regarded as a *rigid* disciplinarian>
syn draconian, ironhanded, rigorist, rigorous, strict, stringent, unpermissive
rel austere, severe, stern; hard-line, inflexible, tough, uncompromising, unyielding; adamant, adamantine, inexorable, obdurate
con humoring, indulgent, pampering; loose, relaxed; easy, gentle, mild
ant lax

rigor *n* *syn* DIFFICULTY 1, asperity, hardness, hardship, vicissitude
rel austerity, severity, sternness; harshness, roughness; affliction, trial, tribulation, visitation
ant amenity

rigorist *adj* *syn* RIGID 3, draconian, ironhanded, rigorous, strict, stringent, unpermissive

rigorous *adj* **1** *syn* RIGID 3, draconian, ironhanded, rigorist, strict, stringent, unpermissive
rel inflexible, stiff; ascetic; burdensome, exacting, onerous, oppressive
con easy, effortless, facile, light, smooth
ant mild
2 *syn* SEVERE 3, bitter, brutal, hard, harsh, inclement, intemperate, rugged
rel drastic
con bland, faint, lenient, smooth
3 *syn* CORRECT 2, accurate, exact, nice, precise, proper, right

rigorously *adv* *syn* HARD 5, badly, hardly, harshly, painfully, roughly, severely

rile *vb* **1** *syn* ROIL 1, mud, muddle, muddy
2 *syn* IRRITATE, aggravate, grate, inflame, nettle, peeve, pique, provoke, put out, roil

riley *adj* *syn* TURBID, muddy, roily

rim *n* *syn* BORDER 1, brim, brink, edge, fringe, hem, margin, perimeter, periphery, verge

rim *vb* *syn* BORDER 1, bound, edge, fringe, hem, margin, outline, skirt, surround verge

rima *n* *syn* CRACK 3, chink, cleft, fissure, rift, rimation, rime, split

rimation *n* *syn* CRACK 3, chink, cleft, fissure, rift, rima, rime, split

rime *n* *syn* CRACK 3, chink, cleft, fissure, rift, rima, rimation, split

rime *vb* *syn* CAKE 1, crust, encrust (*or* incrust), incrustate

rimple *n* *syn* WRINKLE, corrugation, crease, crinkle, fold, furrow, plica, ridge, rivel, ruck

rimple *vb* *syn* CRUMPLE 1, crimp, crimple, crinkle, ruck (up), ‖ruckle, rumple, screw, scrunch, wrinkle

‖**rimption** *n*, *usu* **rimptions** *pl* *syn* SCAD, heap, load(s), oodles, quantities, ream(s), slather(s), slew, thousand, wad(s)

‖**rindle** *n* *syn* CREEK 2, ‖branch, brook, ‖burn, gill, race, rivulet, ‖run, runnel, stream

ring *n* **1** *syn* LOOP 2, eye, staple
2 *syn* LOOP 1, eye
3 *syn* BOXING, fisticuffs, prizefighting, pugilism
4 *syn* CLIQUE, cabal, camarilla, camp, circle, clan, coterie, ingroup, mob
5 *syn* COMBINATION 2, bloc, coalition, combine, faction, party

ring *vb* *syn* SURROUND 1, begird, circle, compass, encircle, encompass, gird, girdle, hem, round

ring *vb* to sound clearly and resonantly <the church bells were *ringing*>
syn bell, bong, chime, knell, peal, toll
rel resound, reverberate, sound

‖**ring** (up) *vb* *syn* TELEPHONE, ‖buzz, call, phone

ringer *n* *syn* IMAGE 1, double, picture, portrait, simulacrum, spit, spitting image

ringing *adj* *syn* RESONANT, consonant, orotund, plangent, resounding, rotund, round, sonorant, sonorous, vibrant

‖**ring off** *vb* *syn* SHUT UP 2, dry up, dumb (up), ‖dummy (up), pipe down

riot *n* **1** *syn* DISORDER 2, anarchism, anarchy, distemper, misrule

---

syn synonym(s) *rel* related word(s)
idiom idiomatic equivalent(s) *con* contrasted word(s)
ant antonym(s) * vulgar
‖ use limited; if in doubt, see a dictionary
The first word in a synonym list when printed in SMALL CAPITALS shows where there is more information about the group. For a more efficient use of this book see Explanatory Notes.

2 something or someone wildly amusing <the new comedy is a *riot*>
syn howl, ||panic, scream, sidesplitter
rel sensation, smash, wow

riot *vb* ***syn*** REVEL 1, carouse, frolic, hell, roister, spree, wassail

riot (away) *vb* ***syn*** WASTE 2, blow, blunder (away), dissipate, fool (away), fritter, frivol away, muddle away, prodigalize, squander

riotous *adj* ***syn*** PROFUSE, exuberant, lavish, lush, luxuriant, opulent, prodigal, profusive

rip *vb* ***syn*** TEAR 1, cleave, rend, rive, split

rip (out) *vb* ***syn*** SPUTTER 1, spit, splutter

ripe *adj* **1** ***syn*** MATURE 1, adult, full-blown, full-fledged, full-grown, grown, grown-up, matured, ripened
rel seasonable, timely, well-timed; overdue
con callow, crude, raw, rude; immature, unmatured, unmellow
ant unripe; green
2 ***syn*** CONSUMMATE 1, accomplished, finished, perfected, virtuosic
3 brought by aging to full flavor or the best state <*ripe* cheese>
syn aged, matured, mellow, ripened
rel ready
ant unripe

||**ripe** *vb* ***syn*** MATURE, age, develop, grow, grow up, maturate, mellow, ripen

ripen *vb* ***syn*** MATURE, age, develop, grow, grow up, maturate, mellow, ||ripe
rel better, improve; enhance, heighten, intensify, season

ripened *adj* **1** ***syn*** MATURE 1, adult, full-blown, full-fledged, full-grown, grown, grown-up, matured, ripe
ant unripened
2 ***syn*** RIPE 3, aged, matured, mellow

riposte *n* ***syn*** RETORT 2, back answer, comeback, repartee

ripper *n* ***syn*** ||DILLY, ||corker, crackerjack, dandy, ||dinger, humdinger, jim-dandy, ||lulu, nifty, peach

ripping *adj* ***syn*** MARVELOUS 2, divine, glorious, nifty, peachy, sensational, super, swell, terrific, wonderful

ripple *vb* to become fretted or lightly ruffled on the surface (as water) <the pond was *rippled* by rain>
syn cockle, dimple, fret, riffle

ripsnorter *n* ***syn*** ||DILLY, ||corker, crackerjack, ||daisy, dandy, ||dinger, ||doozer, humdinger, jim-dandy, ||lulu

rise *vb* **1** to assume an upright or standing position <he *rose* from his chair>
syn get up, stand up, uprise, upspring
rel sit up; straighten up
idiom come to one's feet
con lie, lounge, recline, sit; loll, sprawl
2 ***syn*** ROLL OUT, arise, get up, pile (out), rise and shine, turn out, uprise
ant retire
3 ***syn*** ADJOURN 2, dissolve, prorogate, prorogue, recess, terminate
ant sit
4 to move or come up from a lower to a higher level <smoke *rose* from the chimneys>
syn arise, ascend, aspire, lift, mount, soar, up, uprear
rel surge, tower; climb, scale; elevate, raise, rear
con descend, drop, lower; dip, plummet, sink
ant fall; decline
5 ***syn*** INTENSIFY, aggravate, deepen, enhance, heighten, intensate, magnify, mount, redouble, rouse
6 ***syn*** SURFACE
7 ***syn*** INCREASE 2, augment, build, enlarge, expand, heighten, mount, multiply, upsurge, wax
ant abate; fall
8 ***syn*** HAPPEN 1, befall, betide, chance, come, develop, fall out, go, occur, transpire
9 ***syn*** SPRING 1, arise, derive (from), emanate, flow, head, issue, originate, proceed, stem

rise (against) *vb* ***syn*** REVOLT 1, insurrect, mutiny, rebel

rise (to) *vb* ***syn*** APPLAUD 2, cheer, root

rise *n* **1** ***syn*** ASCENT, ascension, rising
ant fall
2 ***syn*** ADDITION, accession, accretion, augmentation, increase, increment, raise
3 an increment in amount, number, or volume <crime is on the *rise*>
syn boost, breakthrough, hike, increase, upgrade, wax
con declension, decline, lessening, letup, reduction, slump; decrement, loss
ant drop

rise and shine *vb* ***syn*** ROLL OUT, arise, get up, pile (out), rise, turn out, uprise

risible *adj* ***syn*** LAUGHABLE, comic, comical, droll, farcical, funny, gelastic, ludicrous, ridiculous
ant lachrymose, larmoyant

rising *n* ***syn*** ASCENT, ascension, rise
ant falling

risk *n* ***syn*** DANGER, hazard, jeopardy, peril
rel accident, chance, fortune, luck; exposedness, exposure, liability, liableness, openness

risk *vb* **1** ***syn*** ENDANGER, compromise, hazard, imperil, jeopard, jeopardize, jeopardy, menace, peril
rel beard, brave, dare, defy, face; confront, encounter, meet
idiom go out of one's depth
2 ***syn*** VENTURE 1, adventure, chance, hazard, wager
3 ***syn*** GAMBLE 2, chance, hazard, venture

riskless *adj* ***syn*** SAFE 2, secure

risky *adj* **1** ***syn*** DANGEROUS 1, chancy, hairy, hazardous, jeopardous, perilous, treacherous, unhealthy, unsound, wicked
rel delicate, precarious, sensitive, ticklish, touchy; speculative
idiom on thin ice
2 ***syn*** RISQUÉ, blue, broad, off-color, racy, salty, shady, spicy, suggestive, wicked

risorgimento *n* ***syn*** REVIVAL, reanimation, rebirth, renaissance, renascence, resurgence, resurrection, resuscitation, revivification, reviviscence

---

syn synonym(s) ***rel*** related word(s)
idiom idiomatic equivalent(s) ***con*** contrasted word(s)
ant antonym(s) * vulgar
|| use limited; if in doubt, see a dictionary
The first word in a synonym list when printed in SMALL CAPITALS shows where there is more information about the group. For a more efficient use of this book see Explanatory Notes.

risqué *adj* verging on impropriety or indecency <blushed at his *risqué* stories>
syn blue, broad, off-color, purple, racy, risky, salty, sexy, shady, spicy, suggestive, wicked; *compare* OBSCENE 2
rel naughty, warm; coarse, crude, earthy, gross, lewd, obscene, raunchy, raw, ribald, vulgar; dirty, foul; indecent, indecorous, indelicate, inelegant, unrefined
con clean, decent, proper; restrained; euphemistic

‖**rissom** *n syn* PARTICLE, bit, crumb, minim, mite, scrap, shred, smitch, speck, tittle

rite *n* **1** *syn* FORM 2, ceremonial, ceremony, formality, liturgy, ritual
2 forms (as religious rites) appropriate to a particular event <the marriage *rites*>
syn ceremonial, ceremony, formality, liturgy, observance, ritual, service
rel celebration, occasion, solemnity; sacrament, sacramental; form

‖**rithe** *n syn* CREEK 2, ‖branch, brook, ‖burn, gill, race, ‖rindle, rivulet, ‖run, stream

ritual *n* **1** *syn* RITE 2, ceremonial, ceremony, formality, liturgy, observance, service
2 *syn* FORM 2, ceremonial, ceremony, formality, liturgy, rite

rival *n* one of two or more striving for what only one can possess <political *rivals* for the nomination>
syn competition, competitor, corrival
rel contender, contestant, entrant; adversary, antagonist, opponent

rival *vb* **1** *syn* COMPETE 1, contend, contest, vie
2 to strive to equal or surpass <*rivaling* each other for the most work done>
syn compete, emulate, rivalize
rel attempt, strive, struggle, try; contend, fight
3 *syn* EQUAL 3, match, measure up, meet, tie, touch
4 *syn* AMOUNT 2, approach, correspond (to), equal, match, partake (of), touch

rivalize *vb syn* RIVAL 2, compete, emulate

rivalry *n syn* CONTEST 1, competition, conflict, emulation, strife, striving, tug-of-war, warfare

rive *vb* **1** *syn* TEAR 1, cleave, rend, rip, split
rel divide, separate; chop, hew
2 *syn* SHATTER 1, burst, fragment, ‖pash, shiver, smash, ‖smatter, splinter, splinterize, splitter

rivel *n syn* WRINKLE, corrugation, crease, crinkle, fold, furrow, plica, ridge, rimple, ruck

rivet *vb* **1** *syn* FASTEN 1, affix, attach, fix
2 *syn* FASTEN 3, concenter, concentrate, fix, fixate, focus, put

rivulet *n syn* CREEK 2, ‖branch, brook, ‖burn, gill, race, ‖rindle, ‖run, runnel, stream

road *n* **1** *often* **roads** *pl syn* HARBOR 3, anchorage, ‖chuck, harborage, haven, port, riding, roadstead
2 *syn* WAY 1, artery, avenue, boulevard, ‖drag, highway, path, street, thoroughfare, track
3 *syn* WAY 2, course, line, passage, path, route

roadblock *n syn* BAR 2, barricade, barrier, blank wall, block, blockade, fence, stop

roadhouse *n syn* HOTEL, auberge, caravansary, hospice, hostel, hostelry, inn, lodge, public house, tavern

roadman *n syn* PEDDLER, ‖arab, ‖duffer, hawker, higgler, huckster, monger, mongerer, packman, vendor

roadstead *n syn* HARBOR 3, anchorage, ‖chuck, harborage, haven, port, riding, road(s)

roadster *n syn* VAGABOND, bum, derelict, drifter, floater, hobo, runagate, street arab, tramp, ‖traveler

roam *vb syn* WANDER 1, bat, drift, gad, gallivant, meander, ramble, range, rove, vagabond

roamer *n syn* ROVER, drifter, meanderer, rambler, rolling stone, wanderer

roar *vb* to make a very loud and often a continuous or protracted noise <the crowd *roared* their disapproval of the speech>
syn bawl, bellow, bluster, clamor, rout; *compare* BAWL 2
rel rebound, repercuss, reverberate; shout, vociferate, yell; din
con breathe, murmur, mutter, whisper

roaring *adj* **1** *syn* LOUD 1, blaring, earsplitting, full-mouthed, piercing, stentorian, stentorious, stentorophonic
2 *syn* FLOURISHING, booming, prospering, prosperous, robust, thrifty, thriving

roast *vb* **1** *syn* BURN 3, bake, broil, cook, melt, scorch, swelter
2 *syn* LAMBASTE 3, blister, castigate, excoriate, flay, lash (into), scathe, scorch, score, slash

rob *vb* **1** to take possessions unlawfully <*rob* a bank> <he was mugged and *robbed*>
syn ‖knock off, knock over, loot, plunder, ransack, relieve, rifle, stick up; *compare* BURGLARIZE, HOUSEBREAK
rel ‖heist, hold up; jackroll, roll; strong-arm; filch, hijack, lift, pilfer, purloin, steal, thieve; cheat, defraud, hustle, swindle; despoil, pillage, ravage, sack
2 *syn* DEPRIVE 2, bereave, disinherit, dispossess, divest, lose, oust

robber *n* one who commits the crime of robbery <only one *robber* was involved in the holdup>
syn yegg; *compare* THIEF
rel hijacker; sandbagger; crook, swindler; cat burglar, cat man, housebreaker, raffles, second-story man; rifler; holdup man, stickup man; ‖bushranger, highwayman, ‖sticker-up

roborant *adj syn* TONIC 1, astringent, restorative

robot *n* **1** a machine that looks like a human being and performs various complex acts (as walking or talking) of a human being <a *robot* that performed household chores>
syn android, automaton
rel golem
2 an efficient, insensitive, often brutalized person <working on an assembly line can often turn a man into a *robot*>
syn automaton, golem, machine

---

syn synonym(s) *rel* related word(s)
idiom idiomatic equivalent(s) *con* contrasted word(s)
ant antonym(s) * vulgar
‖ use limited; if in doubt, see a dictionary
The first word in a synonym list when printed in SMALL CAPITALS shows where there is more information about the group. For a more efficient use of this book see Explanatory Notes.

robust *adj* **1** *syn* FLOURISHING, booming, prospering, prosperous, roaring, thrifty, thriving
2 *syn* STRONG 3, concentrated, full-bodied, lusty, potent

robustious *adj syn* BOORISH, churlish, clownish, ill-bred, loutish, lubberly, lumpish, rugged, unpolished, unrefined

rock *vb* **1** *syn* SHAKE 4, agitate, concuss, convulse
rel oscillate, sway, swing, undulate; quake, totter, tremble
2 *syn* TOSS 2, heave, pitch, roll
3 *syn* HURRY 2, barrel, bullet, fly, hotfoot, hustle, rocket, rush, speed, zip

rock *n* **1** *syn* ERROR 2, blooper, blunder, boner, bungle, fluff, miscue, misstep, slip, slipup
2 *syn* DOLLAR, bill, ‖bone, ‖buck, ‖fish, ‖frogskin, ‖ironman, oner, ‖skin, ‖smacker
3 rocks *pl syn* MONEY, ‖mazuma, ‖moolah, needful, ‖ooftish, pelf, rhino, ‖scratch, ‖shekels, ‖smash

rock bottom *n syn* ESSENCE 2, bottom, marrow, pith, quintessence, root, soul, stuff, substance, virtuality

rock–bottom *adj syn* BOTTOMMOST, bottom, lowermost, lowest, nethermost, undermost

rockbound *adj* **1** *syn* ROCKY 1, rock-ribbed
2 *syn* INFLEXIBLE 2, adamant, brassbound, inexorable, obdurate, rigid, single-minded, unbending, uncompromising, unyielding

rocket *vb* **1** *syn* SKYROCKET, shoot up, soar
rel arise, ascend, levitate, mount, surge, tower
2 *syn* HURRY 2, bullet, fly, haste, highball, ‖nip, smoke, whish, whiz, zip

rock pile *n syn* JAIL, ‖calaboose, ‖can, ‖carcel, ‖clink, cooler, coop, ‖hoosegow, lockup, prison

rock–ribbed *adj* **1** *syn* ROCKY 1, rockbound
2 *syn* INFLEXIBLE 2, adamant, brassbound, inexorable, obdurate, rigid, single-minded, unbending, uncompromising, unyielding

rocky *adj* **1** abounding in or consisting of rocks <a *rocky* shore>
syn rockbound, rock-ribbed
rel bebouldered, bouldery; stony
2 *syn* INSENSIBLE 5, anesthetic, bloodless, dull, hard, impassible, insensate, insensitive

rocky *adj* **1** *syn* UNSTABLE 2, ticklish, tricky
2 *syn* OBSCENE 2, barnyard, coarse, crude, crusty, gross, indecent, rank, scurrilous, smutty

‖**Rocky Mountain canary** *n syn* DONKEY 1, ass, burro, donk, jackass, ‖moke, ‖neddy

rococo *adj* **1** *syn* OLD-FASHIONED, antiquated, archaic, bygone, dated, moldy, moth-eaten, old hat, outdated, passé
2 *syn* ORNATE, baroque, flamboyant, florid, luscious, rich

rod *n* **1** *syn* BAR 1, billet, ingot, slab, stick, strip
2 *syn* PUNISHMENT, castigation, chastisement, correction, discipline, punition
idiom rod in pickle

rodomont *n syn* BRAGGART, blower, blowhard, boaster, braggadocio, bragger, ‖gasbag, puckfist, rodomontade, vaunter

rodomontade *n* **1** *syn* BOMBAST, fustian, highfalutin, lexiphanicism, rant, rhapsody, rhetoric
rel boasting, bragging, vaunting; pride, vainglory, vanity
2 *syn* BRAGGART, blower, blowhard, boaster, braggadocio, bragger, ‖gasbag, puckfist, rodomont, vaunter

rodomontade *vb syn* BOAST, blow, brag, cock-a-doodle-doo, crow, gasconade, mouth, prate, puff, vaunt

rodomontade *adj syn* BOASTFUL, braggadocian, braggart, braggy, self-glorifying, vaunting

rogue *n* **1** *syn* VILLAIN 1, *bastard, blackguard, heel, knave, lowlife, miscreant, rascal, scoundrel, *son of a bitch
rel culprit, delinquent
2 *syn* SWINDLER, cheat, cheater, chiaus, defrauder, gyp, mountebank, sharper, skin, trickster
3 *syn* SCAMP, devil, enfant terrible, limb, mischief, rapscallion, rascal, scalawag, skeezicks, villain

roguery *n syn* MISCHIEVOUSNESS, devilment, devilry, deviltry, diablerie, mischief, roguishness, sportiveness, waggery, waggishness

roguish *adj* **1** *syn* DISHONEST, deceitful, knavish, lying, mendacious, shifty, unhonest, untruthful
2 *syn* PLAYFUL 1, antic, impish, larkish, ‖mischiefful, mischievous, prankful, prankish, pranky, wicked
3 *syn* COY 2, arch, coquettish

roguishness *n syn* MISCHIEVOUSNESS, devilment, devilry, deviltry, diablerie, mischief, roguery, sportiveness, waggery, waggishness

roil *vb* **1** to make turbid <*roiled* the brook with his splashings>
syn mud, muddle, muddy, rile
rel befoul, contaminate, dirty, pollute
con clear, purify, settle
2 *syn* IRRITATE, aggravate, burn (up), exasperate, grate, inflame, nettle, peeve, provoke, rile

roily *adj syn* TURBID, muddy, riley

roister *vb syn* REVEL 1, carouse, frolic, hell, riot, spree, wassail

role *n* **1** characteristic exterior properties and aspects, style, and atmosphere in which something intangible is discerned <the moral *role* of the legislature>
syn character, clothing
rel appearance, face, guise, seeming, semblance, show; aspect, look
2 *syn* FUNCTION 1, business, duty, office, province

roll *n* **1** *syn* LIST, catalog, register, roll call, roster, schedule
2 *syn* ROSTER 1, muster, muster roll
‖**3** *syn* FORTUNE 4, ‖bomb, boodle, bundle, mint, packet, pile, pot, wad

roll *vb* **1** *syn* PONDER 2, ‖chaw, deliberate, meditate, mull (over), muse, revolve, ruminate, turn over
2 *syn* SWATHE, drape, enswathe, envelop, enwrap, swaddle, wrap (up)
3 to wrap around on itself or something else <this cloth *rolls* unevenly>

---

syn synonym(s) | *rel* related word(s)
idiom idiomatic equivalent(s) | *con* contrasted word(s)
ant antonym(s) | * vulgar
‖ use limited; if in doubt, see a dictionary
The first word in a synonym list when printed in SMALL CAPITALS shows where there is more information about the group. For a more efficient use of this book see Explanatory Notes.

syn furl
4 *syn* WALLOW 3, bask, indulge, luxuriate, revel, rollick, welter
5 *syn* TURN 1, circle, circumduct, gyrate, gyre, revolve, rotate
6 *syn* WANDER 1, drift, gad, gallivant, mooch, ramble, range, roam, rove, stray
7 *syn* POUR 2, flow, gush, sluice, stream, surge
8 *syn* RUMBLE, growl, grumble
9 *syn* TOSS 2, heave, pitch, rock

roll call *n syn* LIST, catalog, register, roll, roster, schedule

rollick *vb* 1 *syn* GAMBOL, caper, cavort, frisk, frolic, romp
2 *syn* WALLOW 3, bask, indulge, luxuriate, revel, roll, welter

rollick *n syn* ESCAPADE, caper, lark

rollicking *adj syn* ANTIC 2, frolicsome, playful, sprightly
rel cheerful, glad, happy, joyful, joyous, lighthearted

roll in *vb syn* RETIRE 4, bed, ||flop, pile (in), turn in
ant roll out

rolling stone *n syn* ROVER, drifter, meanderer, rambler, roamer, wanderer

roll out *vb* to leave one's bed < *rolled out* at dawn >
syn arise, get up, pile (out), rise, rise and shine, turn out, uprise
ant roll in

roll up *vb syn* ACCUMULATE, amass, cumulate, garner, hive, lay up, stockpile, store (up), uplay

roly-poly *adj syn* ROTUND 2, chubby, plump, plumpish, plumpy, podgy, pudgy, round, roundabout, tubby

romance *n syn* LOVE AFFAIR, affair, amour, love

romanesque *adj syn* EXOTIC 2, romantic, strange

romantic *adj syn* EXOTIC 2, romanesque, strange
2 *syn* SENTIMENTAL, bathetic, lovey-dovey, maudlin, mawkish, mushy, slushy, ||soppy, sticky, tear-jerking
rel fanciful, fantastic, imaginary, quixotic, visionary; created, invented
ant unromantic; matter-of-fact

Romeo *n syn* GALLANT 2, amorist, Casanova, Don Juan, lothario, paramour

romp *n syn* RUNAWAY, cakewalk, rout, walkaway, walkover

romp *vb syn* GAMBOL, caper, cavort, frisk, frolic, rollick
idiom cut capers, horse around

rondure *n syn* BALL 1, globe, orb, round, sphere

roof *n syn* TOP 1, apex, crest, crown, fastigium, peak, summit, vertex

roof *vb syn* HARBOR 1, chamber, haven, house, shelter, shield

rook *vb syn* FLEECE 1, bleed, milk, mulct, stick, sweat

rookie *n syn* NOVICE, apprentice, beginner, colt, freshman, neophyte, newcomer, novitiate, tenderfoot, tyro

room *n* 1 space in a building enclosed or set apart by a partition < the house had seven *rooms* >
syn apartment, chamber
2 **rooms** *pl syn* APARTMENT 1, ||chambers, flat, lodging(s), rental, suite, tenement
3 enough space or range for free movement < no *room* for hope >
syn elbowroom, latitude, leeway, margin, play, scope
rel clearance; license, range, rein, sway; rope

room *vb syn* HARBOR 2, billet, board, domicile, house, hut, lodge, put up, quarter, roost

room and board *n syn* ACCOMMODATIONS, lodging, lodgment

roomy *adj syn* SPACIOUS, ample, capacious, commodious, wide
ant cramped

||**roose** *vb syn* COMMEND 2, acclaim, applaud, complement, hail, kudize, praise, recommend

roost *vb* 1 *syn* ALIGHT, land, light, perch, set down, settle, sit down, touch down
2 *syn* HARBOR 2, billet, board, domicile, house, hut, lodge, put up, quarter, room

root *n* 1 *syn* SOURCE, derivation, fountain, fountainhead, inception, origin, provenance, provenience, well, wellhead
rel basis, foundation, ground
2 *syn* BASIS 1, base, bedrock, footing, foundation, ground, groundwork, infrastructure, substratum, underpinning
3 *syn* CENTER 3, core, heart, pith, quick
4 *syn* ESSENCE 2, bottom, essentiality, marrow, pith, quintessence, rock bottom, soul, stuff, substance

root *vb syn* ENTRENCH 1, embed, fix, infix, ingrain, lodge
ant uproot

root *vb syn* APPLAUD 2, cheer, rise (to)

rootage *n syn* SOURCE, derivation, fount, inception, origin, root, rootstock, spring, well, wellhead

rootless *adj syn* WEAK 2, dickey, fluctuant, insecure, shaky, unstable, unsure, vacillating, wavering, wobbly

root out *vb syn* ANNIHILATE 2, abate, abolish, blot out, eradicate, exterminate, extinguish, extirpate, uproot, wipe (out)
rel demolish, destroy, raze
ant enroot

rootstock *n syn* SOURCE, derivation, fount, inception, origin, provenance, provenience, root, rootage, whence

roperipe *n syn* VILLAIN 1, *bastard, blackguard, knave, lowlife, miscreant, reprobate, rogue, scoundrel, *son of a bitch

ropes *n pl syn* INS AND OUTS, minutiae

ropy *adj syn* MUSCULAR 1, fibrous, sinewy, stringy, wiry

rose *vb syn* BLUSH, color, crimson, flush, glow, mantle, pink, pinken, redden, rouge

roseate *adj syn* HOPEFUL 2, couleur de rose, encouraging, likely, promiseful, promising, rose-colored, rosy

rose-colored *adj syn* HOPEFUL 2, couleur de rose, encouraging, likely, promiseful, promising, roseate, rosy

rose-colored spectacles *n pl syn* OPTIMISM, Pollyannaism, sanguineness, sanguinity

roster *n* 1 a list of officers or enlisted men < an army *roster* >

---

syn synonym(s) *rel* related word(s)
idiom idiomatic equivalent(s) *con* contrasted word(s)
ant antonym(s) * vulgar
|| use limited; if in doubt, see a dictionary
The first word in a synonym list when printed in SMALL CAPITALS shows where there is more information about the group. For a more efficient use of this book see Explanatory Notes.

syn muster, muster roll, roll
2 *syn* LIST, catalog, register, roll, roll call, schedule

rosy *adj* *syn* HOPEFUL 2, couleur de rose, encouraging, likely, promiseful, promising, roseate, rose-colored

rot *vb* **1** *syn* DECAY, break down, crumble, decompose, disintegrate, molder, putrefy, spoil, taint, turn
rel corrupt, debase, vitiate
2 *syn* DETERIORATE 1, decline, degenerate, descend, disimprove, disintegrate, retrograde, sink, worsen
3 *syn* DEBASE 1, animalize, bestialize, corrupt, debauch, demoralize, deprave, pervert, stain, warp

rot *n* *syn* NONSENSE 2, bilge, bosh, ‖bull, ‖crap, hogwash, hooey, rubbish, tommyrot, trash

rotate *vb* **1** *syn* TURN 1, circle, circumduct, gyrate, gyre, revolve, roll
2 to succeed or cause to succeed each other in turn <the drivers in the car pool *rotated* each week>
syn alternate
rel bandy, exchange, interchange; ensue, follow, succeed; relieve, spell

rotation *n* *syn* REVOLUTION 1, circuit, circulation, circumvolution, gyration, gyre, round, turn, wheel, whirl

rote *n* *syn* ROUTINE, grind, groove, pace, rut, treadmill

rotten *adj* **1** *syn* BAD 5, decayed, putrid, spoiled
rel foul; tainted, touched; sour
2 *syn* VICIOUS 2, corrupt, degenerate, depraved, flagitious, nefarious, perverse, putrid, unhealthy, villainous
3 *syn* BAD 8, ‖chiselly, disagreeable, displeasing, sour, unhappy, unpleasant
4 *syn* BAD 1, amiss, ‖bum, ‖crappy, dissatisfactory, poor, ‖punk, unsatisfactory, up, wrong

rotter *n* *syn* CAD, bounder, cur, yellow dog

rotund *adj* **1** *syn* RESONANT, consonant, orotund, plangent, resounding, ringing, round, sonorant, sonorous, vibrant
2 rounded or swollen with fat <a wheezing *rotund* man lumbered by>
syn chubby, plump, plumpish, plumpy, podgy, puddy, pudgy, roly-poly, round, roundabout, spuddy, tubby; *compare* FAT 2
rel beefy, chunky, dumpy, heavyset, squat, stocky, stubby, thick, thickset; paunchy, potbellied; buxom, ‖crummy
idiom on the plump side
con angular, gaunt, lank, lanky, lean, rawboned, scrawny, skinny, spare; slender, slight, slim, thin

roturier *n* *syn* UPSTART, arriviste, nouveau riche, parvenu

rouge *vb* *syn* BLUSH, color, crimson, flush, glow, mantle, pink, pinken, redden, rose

rough *adj* **1** not smooth or even <a *rough* undressed block of stone>
syn asperous, cragged, craggy, hairy, harsh, ironbound, jagged, rugged, scabrous, scraggy, uneven, unlevel, unsmooth
rel bumpy, choppy; burred; firm, hard, solid; coarse, gross
con flat, flush, level, plain, plane
ant smooth
2 *syn* WILD 6, blustering, blustery, ‖coarse, furious, raging, stormful, stormy, tempestuous, turbulent
con calm, halcyon, peaceful, placid, serene, tranquil
3 *syn* TOUGH 8, bad
4 *syn* TIGHT 4, arduous, tricksy, trying
5 *syn* INDECOROUS, improper, indecent, indelicate, malodorous, ridiculous, unbecoming, undecorous, ungodly, unseemly
6 *syn* RUDE 1, crude, raw, roughhewn, undressed, unfashioned, unfinished, unformed, unhewn, unpolished
idiom in the rough
7 *syn* RUDE 3, approximate, proximate
8 *syn* HARSH 3, dry, grating, hoarse, jarring, rasping, raucous, rugged, stridulent, stridulous
9 *syn* COARSE 3, crass, crude, gross, inelegant, raw, rude, uncouth, unrefined, vulgar
rel discourteous, impolite, uncivil, ungracious
10 *syn* BLUFF, abrupt, blunt, brief, brusque, crusty, curt, gruff, short, short-spoken
11 *syn* HARD 6, difficult, formidable, heavy, knotty, laborious, operose, rugged, strenuous, tough

rough *n* *syn* TOUGH, ‖b'hoy, bullyboy, mucker, punk, roughneck, rowdy, ruffian, toughie, yahoo

rough (out) *vb* *syn* SKETCH, adumbrate, block (out), chalk (out), characterize, draft, outline, skeleton, skeletonize

rough (up) *vb* *syn* MANHANDLE, knock about, mishandle, roughhouse, slap around

rough–and–ready *adj* *syn* MAKESHIFT, provisional, rough-and-tumble, stopgap

rough–and–tumble *n* *syn* BRAWL 2, bobbery, broil, donnybrook, fracas, fray, melee, row, ruction, set-to

rough–and–tumble *adj* *syn* MAKESHIFT, provisional, rough-and-ready, stopgap

roughhewn *adj* *syn* RUDE 1, crude, rough, undressed, unfashioned, unfinished, unformed, unhewn, unpolished, unworked

roughhouse *n* *syn* HORSEPLAY, fooling, high jinks, roughhousing, rowdiness, skylarking

roughhouse *vb* *syn* MANHANDLE, knock about, mishandle, rough (up), slap around

roughhousing *n* *syn* HORSEPLAY, fooling, high jinks, roughhouse, rowdiness, skylarking

roughly *adv* **1** *syn* HARD 5, badly, hardly, harshly, painfully, rigorously, severely
ant smoothly
2 *syn* NEARLY, about, all but, almost, approximately, as good as, just about, most, practically, well-nigh

roughneck *n* *syn* TOUGH, ‖b'hoy, bullyboy, mucker, punk, rough, rowdy, ruffian, toughie, yahoo

roughness *n* *syn* INEQUALITY 1, asperity, irregularity, unevenness
ant smoothness

roughscuff *n* *syn* RABBLE 2, dreg(s), hoi polloi, mass(es), mob, other half, proletariat, ragtag and bobtail, riffraff, trash

---

syn synonym(s) — *rel* related word(s)
idiom idiomatic equivalent(s) — *con* contrasted word(s)
ant antonym(s) — * vulgar
‖ use limited; if in doubt, see a dictionary
The first word in a synonym list when printed in SMALL CAPITALS shows where there is more information about the group. For a more efficient use of this book see Explanatory Notes.

round *adj* **1** having every part of the circumference equally distant from a center within <flowers crowded in stiff *round* beds>
syn circular
rel annular, globular, orbed, orbicular, rounded, spherical, spiral
2 *syn* CURVED, arced, arched, arciform, arrondi, bent, bowed, curvilinear, rounded
3 *syn* ROTUND 2, chubby, plump, plumpish, plumpy, podgy, pudgy, roly-poly, roundabout, tubby
4 *syn* OUTSPOKEN, free, free-spoken, vocal
5 *syn* RESONANT, consonant, orotund, plangent, resounding, ringing, rotund, sonorant, sonorous, vibrant

round *adv* **1** *syn* ABOUT 1, around, round about
2 *syn* NEARLY, about, all but, almost, approximately, as good as, just about, most, practically, well-nigh
3 *syn* THROUGH 1, around, over, throughout
4 *syn* ABOUT 6, again, around, back, backward, in reverse, round about

round *prep* **1** *syn* NEAR 2, ‖aside, beside, by, nearby, nigh
2 *syn* ABOUT 4, through, throughout

round *n* **1** *syn* BALL 1, globe, orb, rondure, sphere
2 *syn* REVOLUTION 1, circuit, circulation, circumvolution, gyration, gyre, rotation, turn, wheel, whirl
3 *syn* TOUR 2, circuit, roundabout, round trip
4 *syn* CYCLE 1, circle, wheel
5 *syn* CURVE, arc, arch, bend, bow, curvation, curvature

round *vb* **1** *syn* BALL, conglobate, conglobe, ensphere, sphere
2 *syn* SURROUND 1, begird, circle, compass, encircle, encompass, gird, girdle, hem, ring
3 *syn* POLISH 2, perfect, refine, sleek, slick, smooth
4 *syn* CURVE, bend, bow, crook

round about *adv* **1** *syn* ABOUT 1, around, round
2 *syn* ABOUT 6, again, around, back, backward, in reverse, round
3 *syn* ABOUT 2, circuitously

roundabout *n* **1** *syn* DETOUR, runaround
2 *syn* VERBIAGE 1, circumambages, circumbendibus, circumlocution, periphrase, periphrasis, pleonasm, redundancy, tautology, verbality
3 *syn* TOUR 2, circuit, round, round trip
4 *syn* EXCURSION 1, jaunt, junket, outing, sally

roundabout *adj* **1** *syn* INDIRECT 1, circuitous, circular, collateral, oblique
2 *syn* ROTUND 2, chubby, plump, plumpish, plumpy, podgy, pudgy, roly-poly, round, tubby

rounded *adj* **1** *syn* CURVED, arced, arched, arciform, arrondi, bent, bowed, curvilinear, round
2 *syn* CURVACEOUS, ‖built, curvesome, curvilinear, curvy, Junoesque, ‖stacked, well-developed

rounder *n* *syn* WASTREL 1, ‖bad lot, good-for-nothing, ne'er-do-well, no-good, profligate, scapegrace, waster

roundheel *n* *syn* DOXY 1, ‖chippy, floozy, grisette, light-o'-love, nymph, nymphet, party girl, tart, ‖tootsie

roundly *adv* **1** *syn* WELL 3, à fond, altogether, completely, entirely, fully, perfectly, quite, utterly, wholly
2 *syn* NEARLY, about, all but, almost, approximately, as good as, just about, most, practically, well-nigh

round off *vb* *syn* CLIMAX, cap, crown, culminate, finish off, top off

round trip *n* *syn* TOUR 2, circuit, round, roundabout

round up *vb* *syn* GROUP 1, assemble, cluster, collect, gather

rouse *vb* **1** *syn* WAKE 1, awake, awaken, stir, waken
rel animate, enliven, quicken, vivify; excite, provoke, stimulate; foment, incite, instigate
con calm, compose, lull, quiet, quieten, settle, soothe, still, tranquilize
2 *syn* INTENSIFY, aggravate, deepen, enhance, heighten, intensate, magnify, mount, redouble, rise
3 *syn* PROVOKE 4, excite, galvanize, innervate, innerve, motivate, move, pique, quicken, stimulate
4 *syn* STIR 1, arouse, awaken, bestir, challenge, kindle, rally, wake, waken, whet

rouser *n* *syn* ‖DILLY, ‖corker, crackerjack, ‖daisy, dandy, ‖dinger, humdinger, jim-dandy, ‖lulu, ripper

rousing *adj* **1** *syn* EXCITING, exhilarant, exhilarating, exhilarative, eye-popping, inspiring, intoxicating, stimulating, stirring
2 *syn* LIVELY 1, alert, animate, animated, bright, dashing, gay, keen, spirited, sprightly

‖**roust** *vb* *syn* PROVOKE 4, excite, galvanize, innerve, motivate, move, pique, quicken, rouse, stimulate

roustabout *n* *syn* WORKER, hand, laborer, ‖mozo, operative, workhand, workingman, workman

rout *n* **1** *syn* MOB 2, rabble
2 *syn* RABBLE 2, dreg(s), hoi polloi, mass(es), mob, other half, proletariat, ragtag and bobtail, riffraff, trash
3 *syn* MULTITUDE 1, army, cloud, crowd, flock, host, legion, scores

rout *vb* *syn* ROAR, bawl, bellow, bluster, clamor

rout *vb* *syn* RUMMAGE 3, dig out, hunt (down *or* out *or* up)

rout *n* **1** *syn* DEFEAT 1, beating, debacle, defeasance, drubbing, licking, overthrow, shellacking, vanquishment, warming
2 *syn* RUNAWAY, cakewalk, romp, walkaway, walkover

rout *vb* **1** to put to precipitate flight <the army regrouped and *routed* the enemy>
syn derout, stampede
rel chase, dispel, drive, expel
idiom put to flight
2 *syn* WHIP 2, beat, ‖clobber, drub, ‖clean up (on), dust, lambaste, lick, shellac, wallop

route *n* *syn* WAY 2, course, line, passage, path, road

route *vb* **1** *syn* SEND 1, address, consign, dispatch, forward, remit, ship, transmit
2 *syn* GUIDE, conduct, direct, escort, lead, pilot, see, shepherd, show, steer

routine *n* habitual or mechanical and sometimes monotonous performance of an established procedure <settled into the *routine* of factory work>
syn grind, groove, pace, rote, rut, treadmill

---

syn synonym(s) *rel* related word(s)
idiom idiomatic equivalent(s) *con* contrasted word(s)
ant antonym(s) * vulgar
‖ use limited; if in doubt, see a dictionary
The first word in a synonym list when printed in SMALL CAPITALS shows where there is more information about the group. For a more efficient use of this book see Explanatory Notes.

rel squirrel cage; ||drill
idiom the beaten path, the drab monotony of habit

routine *adj* **1** *syn* ORDINARY 1, everyday, plain, plain Jane, quotidian, unremarkable, usual, workaday
2 *syn* USUAL 1, accepted, accustomed, chronic, customary, habitual, wonted

rove *vb syn* WANDER 1, drift, gallivant, meander, ramble, range, roam, stray, traipse, vagabond

rover *n syn* PIRATE, buccaneer, corsair, freebooter, picaroon, sea dog, sea robber, sea rover, sea wolf

rover *n* one who roams habitually <he spent most of his life as a *rover* always on the move>
syn drifter, meanderer, rambler, roamer, rolling stone, wanderer
rel gad, gadabout, gadder, runabout; itinerant, peripatetic; floater
idiom bird of passage
con homebody
ant stay-at-home

roving *adj syn* ITINERANT, itinerate, nomadic, perambulant, perambulatory, peripatetic, vagabond, vagrant, wandering, wayfaring

row *vb* to propel a boat by means of oars <*rowed* across the lake>
syn oar, paddle, pull
rel scull; punt; sail, scud

row *n* **1** *syn* LINE 5, echelon, file, queue, rank, string, tier
2 *syn* SUCCESSION 2, chain, consecution, order, progression, sequel, sequence, series, string, train

row *n* **1** *syn* BRAWL 2, affray, broil, fight, fracas, fray, knock-down-and-drag-out, melee, scrap, set-to
2 *syn* QUARREL, altercation, beef, bickering, dispute, falling-out, rhubarb, run-in, set-to, wrangle
3 *syn* MOUTH 1, ||bazoo, gob, ||mush, ||trap, ||yap

row *vb* ||**1** *syn* SCOLD 1, bawl out, berate, ||bless out, ||carpet, ||chew out, jaw, ||ream out, tongue-lash, ||tongue-walk
2 *syn* QUARREL, bicker, brabble, caterwaul, fall out, scrap, spat, squabble, tiff, wrangle

rowdiness *n syn* HORSEPLAY, fooling, high jinks, roughhouse, roughhousing, skylarking

rowdy *adj syn* TURBULENT 1, boisterous, disorderly, raucous, rowdydowdy, rowdyish, rumbustious, termagant, tumultuous, unruly

rowdy *n syn* TOUGH, ||b'hoy, bullyboy, mucker, punk, rough, roughneck, ruffian, toughie, yahoo

rowdydow *n* **1** *syn* COMMOTION 4, bustle, clamor, hubbub, hurly-burly, lather, moil, ruction, to-do, uproar
2 *syn* BRAWL 2, bobbery, broil, donnybrook, fracas, fray, free-for-all, melee, rough-and-tumble, set-to
3 *syn* BINGE 1, bat, bender, brannigan, bust, carousal, drunk, spree, tear, toot

rowdydowdy *adj syn* TURBULENT 1, boisterous, disorderly, rambunctious, raucous, rowdy, rowdyish, termagant, tumultuous, unruly

rowdyish *adj syn* TURBULENT 1, boisterous, disorderly, rambunctious, raucous, rowdy, rowdydowdy, termagant, tumultuous, unruly

royal *adj* **1** *syn* KINGLY, kinglike, majestic, monarchal, monarchial, monarchical, regal, sovereign
rel glorious, resplendent, splendid, superb; august, imposing, stately
2 *syn* EASY 1, effortless, facile, light, simple, smooth, untroublesome
3 *syn* GRAND 1, august, baronial, grandiose, imposing, lordly, magnificent, majestic, noble, stately
4 *syn* EXCELLENT, champion, classical, five-star, front-rank, number one, prime, sovereign, superior, top

royalist *n syn* REACTIONARY, blimp, Bourbon, diehard, reactionarist, reactionist, ultraconservative, white

||**rozzer** *n syn* POLICEMAN, ||bobby, ||bull, ||constable, ||copper, ||gendarme, John Law, ||paddy, ||peeler, police

rub *vb* **1** *syn* ABRADE 1, chafe, corrade, erode, gall, graze, ruffle, wear
2 *syn* CHAFE 3, abrade, excoriate, fret, gall
rel aggravate, exasperate, nettle, peeve, provoke, rile; annoy, bother, irk, vex
3 *syn* POLISH 1, buff, burnish, furbish, glance, glaze, gloss, shine

rub *n syn* OBSTACLE, bar, crimp, hamper, hurdle, impediment, obstruction, snag, stumbling block, traverse

rubber *n syn* BUSYBODY, butt-in, intermeddler, nose, nosey Parker, Paul Pry, quidnunc, rubberneck, snoop, ||stickybeak

rubberneck *n* **1** *syn* BUSYBODY, butt-in, ||buttinsky, intermeddler, kibitzer, meddler, pragmatist, prier (*or* pryer), quidnunc, snoop
2 *syn* TOURIST, sightseer, ||tripper

rubberneck *vb syn* LOOK 7, eye, gape, ||gaup (*or* gawp), gaze, goggle, ogle, stare

rubber stamp *n syn* COMMONPLACE, banality, bromide, cliché, platitude, prosaicism, prosaism, shibboleth, tag, truism

rubbish *n* **1** *syn* REFUSE, debris, garbage, junk, kelter, litter, offal, sweepings, trash, waste
2 *syn* NONSENSE 2, bilge, bosh, ||crap, hogwash, hooey, poppycock, rot, tommyrot, trash
3 *syn* PAP 2, pablum, slop

rubbishing *adj syn* CHEAP 2, base, cheesy, common, mean, ||ornery, paltry, poor, shoddy, sleazy

rubbishly *adj syn* CHEAP 2, base, cheesy, common, mean, ||ornery, paltry, poor, shoddy, sleazy

rubbishy *adj syn* CHEAP 2, base, common, mean, paltry, poor, shoddy, sleazy, tatty, trashy

rube *n syn* RUSTIC, backwoodsman, bucolic, bumpkin, clodhopper, hayseed, hick, hillbilly, provincial, redneck

rubicund *adj syn* RUDDY 1, florid, flush, flushed, full-blooded, glowing, sanguine

rubify *vb syn* REDDEN 1, incarnadine, rubric, ruby, rud, ruddle, ruddy

rub out *vb* **1** *syn* DESTROY 1, annihilate, decimate, demolish, destruct, raze, ruin, shatter, smash, wreck
2 *syn* MURDER 1, assassinate, ||bump off, cool, do in, ||dust off, finish, knock off, liquidate, put away

rubric *n* ***syn*** NAME 1, appellation, appellative, cognomen, compellation, denomination, designation, nomen, style, title

rubric *adj* ***syn*** NOTEWORTHY, ‖bodacious, memorable, nameable, notable, observable, red-letter

rubric *vb* ***syn*** REDDEN 1, incarnadine, rubify, ruby, rud, ruddle, ruddy

ruby *vb* ***syn*** REDDEN 1, incarnadine, rubify, rubric, rud, ruddle, ruddy

ruck *n* ‖**1** ***syn*** PILE 1, bank, ‖bing, cock, drift, heap, mass, mound, rick, stack
2 ***syn*** GATHERING 2, aggregation, assemblage, collection, company, congeries, congregation, crowd, group, muster

ruck *n* ***syn*** WRINKLE, corrugation, crease, crinkle, fold, furrow, plica, ridge, rimple, rivel

ruck (up) *vb* ***syn*** CRUMPLE 1, crimp, crimple, crinkle, rimple, ‖ruckle, rumple. screw, scrunch, wrinkle

‖**ruckle** *vb* ***syn*** CRUMPLE 1, crimp, crimple, crinkle, rimple, ruck (up), rumple, screw, scrunch, wrinkle

rucksack *n* ***syn*** BACKPACK, haversack, knapsack, pack, packsack

ruckus *n* **1** ***syn*** COMMOTION 3, ‖catouse, coil, furore, fuss, rumpus, shindig, shindy, to-do, uproar
rel brawl, broil, melee, scrap
2 ***syn*** QUARREL, altercation, bickering, controversy, dispute, falling-out, hassle, row, squabble, wrangle

ruction *n* **1** ***syn*** BRAWL 2, affray, broil, donnybrook, fight, fracas, fray, free-for-all, knock-down-and-drag-out, melee
2 ***syn*** COMMOTION 4, bustle, clamor, clatter, hassle, hubbub, hurly-burly, pother, storm, to-do

‖**ructious** *adj* ***syn*** BELLIGERENT, bellicose, combative, contentious, gladiatorial, militant, pugnacious, quarrelsome, truculent, warlike

rud *vb* ***syn*** REDDEN 1, incarnadine, rubify, rubric, ruby, ruddle, ruddy

ruddle *vb* ***syn*** REDDEN 1, incarnadine, rubify, rubric, ruby, rud, ruddy

ruddy *adj* **1** having a healthy reddish color <has a *ruddy* complexion after being out in the cold>
syn florid, flush, flushed, full-blooded, glowing, rubicund, sanguine
rel bronzed; blooming; blowsy
con ashen, ashy, livid, pale, pallid, wan, waxy; anemic, bloodless
*‖**2** ***syn*** DAMNED 2, blankety-blank, bleeding, ‖blinking, *‖bloody, ‖blooming, damnable, dashed, execrable, infernal
*‖**3** ***syn*** UTTER, absolute, *‖bloody, complete, gross, out-and-out, perfect, rank, thoroughgoing, unmitigated

ruddy *vb* ***syn*** REDDEN 1, incarnadine, rubify, rubric, ruby, rud, ruddle

rude *adj* **1** lacking in craftsmanship or artistic finish <a *rude* sketch>
syn angular, crude, lumpy, raw, rough, roughhewn, undressed, unfashioned, unfinished, unformed, unhewn, unpolished, unworked, unwrought
rel unlicked; unprocessed; primitive, rudimental, rudimentary
con dressed, fashioned, finished, formed, hewn, polished, worked, wrought
2 ***syn*** DISSONANT 1, cacophonic, cacophonous, discordant, disharmonic, disharmonious, immusical, inharmonic, inharmonious, unharmonious
3 hastily executed and admittedly imperfect or imprecise <*rude* estimates for the cost of building the house>
syn approximate, proximate, rough
rel crude, imperfect, imprecise, inexact
idiom ‖in the ball park
con accurate, correct; faultless, perfect; exact, precise; meticulous, scrupulous
4 ***syn*** COARSE 3, crass, crude, gross, inelegant, raw, rough, uncouth, unrefined, vulgar
5 ***syn*** IGNORANT 1, benighted, empty-headed, illiterate, know-nothing, uneducated, uninstructed, unlettered, unschooled, untaught
6 lacking in social refinement <gave a *rude* reply to a polite question>
syn discourteous, disgracious, disrespectful, ill, ill-bred, ill-mannered, impertinent, impolite, incivil, incondite, inurbane, mannerless, ‖mismannered, uncalled-for, uncivil, uncourteous, uncouth, ungracious, unhandsome, unmannered, unmannerly, unpolished
rel brusque, crusty, curt, gruff; harsh; intrusive, meddlesome; crabbed, surly; boorish, churlish, clownish, loutish
con courteous, genteel, mannerly, polite, well-mannered; bland, diplomatic, politic, smooth, suave; affable, considerate, gracious
ant civil; urbane
7 ***syn*** BARBARIAN 1, barbaric, barbarous, Gothic, Hunnish, savage, uncivil, uncivilized, uncultivated, wild
8 ***syn*** INEXPERIENCED, callow, fresh, green, inexpert, raw, unconversant, unfleshed, unpracticed, unversed

rudely *adv* ***syn*** NEARLY, about, all but, almost, approximately, as good as, just about, most, practically, well-nigh

rudiment *n* **1** ***syn*** ESSENTIAL 1, basic, element, fundamental, part and parcel
2 rudiments *pl* ***syn*** ALPHABET 2, ABC's, elements, fundamentals, grammar, principles

rudimental *adj* ***syn*** ELEMENTARY 1, basal, beginning, elemental, rudimentary, simplest

rudimentary *adj* ***syn*** ELEMENTARY 1, basal, beginning, elemental, rudimental, simplest

rue *vb* ***syn*** REGRET, deplore, repent

rue *n* **1** ***syn*** SORROW, affliction, anguish, care, ‖dole, grief, heartache, heartbreak, regret, woe
2 ***syn*** PENITENCE, compunction, contriteness, contrition, penance, penitency, remorse, remorsefulness, repentance, ruth
3 ***syn*** PITY, commiseration, compassion, ruth, sympathy

---

rueful *adj* **1** ***syn*** PITIFUL 1, commiserable, pathetic, piteous, pitiable, poor
2 ***syn*** WOEFUL 1, afflicted, doleful, dolent, dolorous, miserable, ruthful, sorrowful, wretched
3 ***syn*** MELANCHOLY 2, doleful, dolesome, dolorous, lamentable, lugubrious, mournful, plaintive, sorrowful, woeful
rel depressed, oppressed, weighed down; piteous, pitiful; despairing, despondent, hopeless

ruffian *n* **1** ***syn*** TOUGH, ‖b'hoy, bullyboy, mucker, punk, rough, roughneck, rowdy, toughie, yahoo
2 ***syn*** THUG 1, ‖gorilla, ‖hood, hoodlum, hooligan, strong arm

ruffle *vb* **1** ***syn*** BLOW 1, fan, wind, winnow
2 ***syn*** ABRADE 1, chafe, corrade, erode, gall, graze, rub, wear
3 ***syn*** ANNOY 1, abrade, bother, ‖bug, chafe, exercise, fret, gall, irk, provoke
‖**4** ***syn*** INTIMIDATE, bludgeon, bluster, browbeat, bulldoze, bully, bullyrag, cow, dragoon, strong-arm

rugged *adj* **1** ***syn*** ROUGH 1, asperous, craggy, harsh, jagged, scabrous, scraggy, uneven, unlevel, unsmooth
2 ***syn*** SEVERE 3, bitter, brutal, hard, harsh, inclement, intemperate, rigorous
rel arduous, difficult
3 ***syn*** HARSH 3, dry, grating, hoarse, jarring, rasping, raucous, rough, stridulent, stridulous
4 ***syn*** BOORISH, churlish, clownish, ill-bred, loutish, lubberly, lumpish, robustious, unpolished, unrefined
5 ***syn*** TOUGH 4, hardy
rel brawny, burly, husky, muscular
ant fragile
6 ***syn*** HARD 6, difficult, formidable, heavy, knotty, laborious, operose, rough, strenuous, tough

ruin *n* **1** ***syn*** DETERIORATION 1, atrophy, decadence, declension, decline, degeneracy, degeneration, devolution, downfall, downgrade
2 ***syn*** DOWNFALL 2, bane, destroyer, destruction, ruination, undoing
3 the bringing about of or the results of disaster <met *ruin* at the hands of the enemy>
syn confusion, destruction, devastation, havoc, loss, ruination
rel crumbling, disintegration; break up, dissolution; disrepair; wreck
con rebuilding, reconstruction, re-creation
4 ***syn*** INJURY 1, damage, harm, hurt, mischief, outrage

ruin *vb* **1** ***syn*** DESTROY 1, decimate, demolish, raze, unbuild, undo, unframe, unmake, wrack, wreck
rel deface, disfigure; maim, mangle, mutilate; depredate, desecrate, desolate, despoil, devastate, devour, pillage, sack, spoliate, waste
ant restore
2 to subject to forces that are destructive of soundness, worth, or usefulness <in danger of being *ruined* by prosperity>
syn bankrupt, dilapidate, do in, shipwreck, wreck
rel corrupt, debase, degenerate, vitiate
idiom play hob (*or* the devil) with
con rebuild, renew, restore; reclaim, redeem, retrieve, salvage
3 to overthrow the fortunes of <was *ruined* during the great crash>
syn bankrupt, break, bust, fold up, impoverish, pauper, pauperize
rel beggar, clean out, deplete, drain, draw, draw down, exhaust, use up; wipe (out); reduce
idiom go under, lose one's shirt (*or* pants), take to the cleaners
4 ***syn*** FRUSTRATE 1, baffle, balk, beat, bilk, circumvent, dash, disappoint, foil, thwart

‖**ruinate** *vb* ***syn*** DESTROY 1, annihilate, demolish, destruct, raze, ruin, smash, tear down, wrack, wreck

ruination *n* **1** ***syn*** RUIN 3, confusion, destruction, devastation, havoc, loss
2 ***syn*** DOWNFALL 2, bane, destroyer, destruction, ruin, undoing

ruinator *n* ***syn*** VANDAL, defacer, despoiler, destroyer, ruiner, wrecker

ruiner *n* ***syn*** VANDAL, defacer, despoiler, destroyer, ruinator, wrecker

ruinous *adj* **1** ***syn*** DESTRUCTIVE, annihilative, shattering, wrackful, wreckful
2 ***syn*** FATAL 2, calamitous, cataclysmic, catastrophic, disastrous, fateful

rule *n* **1** ***syn*** LAW 1, assize, canon, decree, decretum, edict, ordinance, precept, regulation, statute
rel order; axiom, fundamental, principle; decorum, etiquette, propriety
2 ***syn*** MAXIM, aphorism, apothegm, axiom, brocard, dictum, gnome, moral, truism
rel fundamental, principle

rule *vb* **1** ***syn*** GOVERN 1, overrule, reign, sway
rel guide, lead
2 to hold preeminence in (as by ability, strength, or position) <an actor who rightfully *rules* the Shakespearian stage>
syn dominate, domineer, predominate, preponderate, prevail, reign
rel guide, lead; preside
idiom be number one, take first place (in *or* on)
3 ***syn*** DECIDE, conclude, determine, figure, resolve, settle
rel deduce, gather, infer, judge

rule out *vb* **1** ***syn*** EXCLUDE, bar, bate, count out, debar, eliminate, except, suspend
2 ***syn*** PREVENT 2, avert, deter, forestall, forfend, obviate, preclude, stave off, ward

ruling *n* ***syn*** EDICT 1, decree, directive, ukase

ruling *adj* **1** ***syn*** CENTRAL 1, cardinal, overriding, overruling, pivotal
con peripheral
2 ***syn*** PREVAILING, current, popular, prevalent, rampant, regnant, rife, widespread

‖**rum** *adj* ***syn*** STRANGE 4, bizarre, curious, eccentric, idiosyncratic, odd, oddball, peculiar, queer, singular

---

syn synonym(s) ***rel*** related word(s)
idiom idiomatic equivalent(s) ***con*** contrasted word(s)
ant antonym(s) * vulgar
‖ use limited; if in doubt, see a dictionary
The first word in a synonym list when printed in SMALL CAPITALS shows where there is more information about the group. For a more efficient use of this book see Explanatory Notes.

rumble *vb* to make a low heavy rolling sound <thunder *rumbling* in the distance>
syn growl, grumble, roll
rel boom, roar, thunder; peal, resound; blast, burst, clap, crack, crash

rumble *n syn* REPORT 1, buzz, cry, gossip, grapevine, hearsay, on-dit, rumor, scuttlebutt, talk

rumble–bumble *n syn* MISCELLANY 1, assortment, colluvies, gallimaufry, hodgepodge, jumble, medley, omnium-gatherum, pastiche, salad

rumbustious *adj syn* TURBULENT 1, boisterous, disorderly, rambunctious, raucous, rowdy, rowdydowdy, rowdyish, termagant, unruly

rum–dum *adj syn* INTOXICATED 1, ‖boozy, ‖canned, disguised, drunk, inebriated, ‖lushed, muddled, pixilated, ‖plastered

rumdum *n syn* DRUNKARD, boozehound, boozer, drunk, guzzler, inebriate, lush, ‖lusher, swiller, tippler

‖**rum–hole** *n syn* BAR 5, barroom, cocktail lounge, drinkery, ‖gin mill, ‖groggery, ‖grogshop, ‖rum-mill, saloon, taproom

ruminate *vb* **1** *syn* PONDER 2, ‖chaw, deliberate, meditate, mull (over), muse, revolve, roll, turn over
rel consider, excogitate, weigh
2 *syn* CHEW 1, champ, ‖chaw, chomp, chumble, chump, crunch, masticate, munch, scrunch

ruminative *adj syn* THOUGHTFUL 1, cogitative, contemplative, meditative, pensive, pondering, reflecting, reflective, speculative, thinking

rummage *n syn* CLUTTER 2, hash, jumble, jungle, litter, mash, mishmash, muddle, scramble, tumble
rel conglomeration, hash, hotchpotch, miscellany, patchwork, potpourri

rummage *vb* **1** *syn* DISORDER 1, disarrange, disarray, discompose, disorganize, disrupt, disturb, jumble, mess (up), mix up
2 *syn* SCOUR 2, beat, comb, finecomb, fine-tooth-comb, forage, grub, rake, ransack, search
3 to produce by searching <*rummaged* an old dress out of the attic>
syn dig out, hunt (down *or* out *or* up), rout
rel ferret (out), find; fish, search (out), spy (out); poke

rummery *n syn* BAR 5, barroom, ‖boozer, drinkery, ‖gin mill, ‖groggery, rumshop, saloon, taproom, tavern

‖**rum–mill** *n syn* BAR 5, barroom, cocktail lounge, drinkery, ‖gin mill, ‖groggery, ‖grogshop, ‖rum-hole, saloon, taproom

rummy *adj syn* STRANGE 4, bizarre, curious, eccentric, odd, oddball, peculiar, queer, ‖rum, singular

rummy *n syn* DRUNKARD, boozehound, boozer, drunk, guzzler, inebriate, lush, ‖lusher, swiller, tippler

rumor *n* **1** *syn* REPORT 1, buzz, cry, gossip, grapevine, hearsay, on-dit, rumble, scuttlebutt, talk
2 *syn* MURMUR 1, mumble, mutter, susurration, undertone, whisper

rumor *vb syn* GOSSIP, blab, noise (about *or* abroad), talk, tattle

rumorer *n syn* GOSSIP 1, carrytale, clack, gossipmonger, ‖long tongue, mumblenews, newsmonger, quidnunc, sieve, tabby

rumormonger *n syn* GOSSIP 1, carrytale, gossiper, gossipmonger, newsmonger, quidnunc, scandalmonger, tabby, talebearer, telltale

rump *n syn* BUTTOCKS, backside, beam, bottom, derriere, fanny, haunches, posterior, rear, rear end

rumple *vb syn* CRUMPLE 1, crimp, crimple, crinkle, rimple, ruck (up), ‖ruckle, screw, scrunch, wrinkle

‖**rumpot** *n syn* DRUNKARD, boozehound, boozer, drunk, guzzler, inebriate, lush, ‖lusher, swiller, tippler

rumpus *n* **1** *syn* COMMOTION 3, ‖catouse, coil, foofaraw, furore, ruckus, shindig, shindy, to-do, uproar
2 *syn* ARGUMENT 2, contention, controversy, dispute, hurrah

rumshop *n syn* BAR 5, barroom, ‖boozer, drinkery, ‖gin mill, ‖groggery, rummery, saloon, taproom, tavern

run *vb* **1** to move at a fast springing gait in which both feet are momentarily off the ground in the course of each pace <the boy *ran* down the walk>
syn dash, scamper, scoot, scurry, shin, sprint; *compare* SCUTTLE
rel career, course, race; bustle, hurry, hustle, rush, speed; scorch
con crawl, creep, drag, inch, mosey, poke, saunter, stroll, toddle
2 to hasten away from something that frightens or perturbs <afraid to fight but ashamed to *run*>
syn bolt, flee, fly, make off, scamper, scoot, ‖screw, skedaddle, skip, skirr
idiom ‖dog it, make a break, run for it, show a clean pair of heels, take flight, take French leave, take to one's heels
3 *syn* HURRY 2, fleet, flit, fly, haste, highball, hotfoot, hustle, rush, speed
idiom go all out, go like (greased) lightning
4 *syn* RESORT 2, apply, go, recur, refer, repair, turn
5 *syn* FUNCTION 3, act, go, work
6 *syn* BECOME 1, come, ‖come over, get, go, grow, turn, wax
7 *syn* LIQUEFY, deliquesce, dissolve, flux, fuse, liquesce, melt, thaw
8 to lie in or take a certain course <the path *runs* along the crest of the hill>
syn extend, go, make, reach, stretch
9 *syn* RANGE 3, extend, go, vary
10 *syn* HUNT 1, chase
11 *syn* DRIVE 3, ‖drove, herd
12 *syn* THRUST 2, dig, drive, plunge, ram, sink, stab, stick
13 *syn* SMUGGLE, bootleg, contraband
14 *syn* OPERATE 3, handle, use, work
15 *syn* CONDUCT 3, carry on, direct, keep, manage, operate, ordain

run (through *or* over) *vb syn* BROWSE, dip (into), flip (through), glance (at *or* over), leaf (through), riff (through), riffle (through), scan, skim (through), thumb (through)

---

syn synonym(s) *rel* related word(s)
idiom idiomatic equivalent(s) *con* contrasted word(s)
ant antonym(s) * vulgar
‖ use limited; if in doubt, see a dictionary
The first word in a synonym list when printed in SMALL CAPITALS shows where there is more information about the group. For a more efficient use of this book see Explanatory Notes.

run (to *or* into) *vb* ***syn*** AMOUNT 1, add up, aggregate, come, number, sum (to *or* into), total

run *n* **1** ‖***syn*** CREEK 2, ‖branch, brook, ‖burn, gill, race, ‖rindle, rivulet, runnel, stream

2 an uninterrupted course of occurrence or repetition especially of like things or events <the play had a long *run*>

syn continuance, continuation, duration, persistence

rel continuity, endurance, prolongation

3 ***syn*** TENDENCY 1, current, drift, tenor, trend

rel course, set; bearing, direction, line, swing

4 ***syn*** TRIP 1

‖**5 runs** *pl but sing or pl in constr* ***syn*** DIARRHEA, ‖backdoor trots, dysentery, flux, scour(s), *shits, ‖squirts, *trots

runagate *n* **1** ***syn*** RENEGADE, apostate, defector, rat, recreant, tergiversator, turnabout, turncoat

2 ***syn*** VAGABOND, drifter, floater, hobo, roadster, street arab, tramp, ‖traveler, vag, vagrant

run along *vb* ***syn*** GO 2, ‖blow, depart, exit, get off, leave, pull out, quit, shove (off), take off

runaround *n* **1** ***syn*** DETOUR, roundabout

2 ***syn*** ESCAPE 2, avoidance, come-off, elusion, escaping, eschewal, evasion, shunning

run away *vb* ***syn*** ELOPE

runaway *n* a one-sided or overwhelming victory <the game was a *runaway,* the home team winning by 30 points>

syn cakewalk, romp, rout, walkaway, walkover

rel breather, cinch, duck soup, pushover; setup; shutout; conquest, triumph, victory, win

con photo finish, tossup

run down *vb* ***syn*** DECRY 2, belittle, depreciate, derogate, detract (from), diminish, disparage, dispraise, downcry, opprobriate

run–down *adj* **1** ***syn*** SHABBY 1, broken-down, dilapidated, dingy, down-at-heel, seedy, tacky, tagrag, tattered, tired

2 ***syn*** NEGLECTED, uncared-for, untended

rel abandoned, derelict, deserted, desolate, forsaken, lorn

rune *n* **1** ***syn*** SPELL, charm, conjuration, ‖devil-devil, incantation

2 ***syn*** POEM, poesy, poetry, rhyme, verse

rung *n* ***syn*** DEGREE 1, grade, notch, stage, step

run in *vb* **1** ***syn*** ARREST 2, apprehend, ‖bust, detain, nab, pick up, pinch, pull in

2 ***syn*** VISIT 2, come by, come over, drop (in *or* by), look in, look up, pop (in), see, step in, stop (in *or* by)

run–in *n* **1** ***syn*** ENCOUNTER, brush, set-to, skirmish, velitation

2 ***syn*** QUARREL, altercation, bickering, dispute, falling-out, fight, hassle, rhubarb, row, set-to

runnel *n* ***syn*** CREEK 2, ‖branch, brook, ‖burn, gill, race, ‖rindle, rivulet, ‖run, stream

running *n* ***syn*** OVERSIGHT 1, care, charge, conduct, handling, intendance, management, superintendence, superintendency, supervision

running *adj* **1** ***syn*** ACTIVE 1, alive, dynamic, functioning, live, operative, working

2 ***syn*** EASY 9, cursive, effortless, flowing, fluent, smooth

running *adv* ***syn*** TOGETHER 2, consecutively, continually, continuously, hand running, night and day, successively, unintermittedly, uninterruptedly

running mate *n* ***syn*** ASSOCIATE 3, buddy, chum, comate, companion, comrade, crony, ‖cully, pal

run–of–mine *adj* **1** ***syn*** UNREFINED 3, crude, impure, native, raw, ungraded, unsorted

2 ***syn*** MEDIUM, average, fair, indifferent, intermediate, mean, mediocre, middling, moderate, run-of-the-mill

run–of–the–mill *adj* **1** ***syn*** MEDIUM, average, fair, indifferent, intermediate, mean, mediocre, middling, moderate, run-of-mine

rel uncommon, unexceptional

2 ***syn*** GENERAL 1, common, commonplace, natural, normal, prevalent, regular, typic, typical, usual

run on *vb* ***syn*** CHAT 1, babble, chatter, clack, gab, gabble, jaw, prattle, rattle, yak

run out *vb* **1** ***syn*** FAIL 2, give out

2 ***syn*** BANISH, cast out, deport, displace, exile, expatriate, expel, ostracize, oust, transport

run over *vb* ***syn*** OVERFLOW 2, overbrim, overfill, overrun, spill, well over

runt *n* ***syn*** DWARF, homunculus, hop-o'-my-thumb, lilliputian, manikin, midge, midget, peewee, pygmy, Tom Thumb

runted *adj* ***syn*** STUNTED, runtish, runty, ‖scrunty, ‖stunt

run through *vb* ***syn*** GO 4, consume, exhaust, expend, finish, spend, use up, wash up

runtish *adj* ***syn*** STUNTED, runted, runty, ‖scrunty, ‖stunt

runty *adj* ***syn*** STUNTED, runted, runtish, ‖scrunty, ‖stunt

run up *vb* **1** ***syn*** INCREASE 2, augment, build, enlarge, expand, mount, multiply, rise, snowball, wax

2 ***syn*** THROW UP 1, jerry-build

rupture *n* **1** ***syn*** BREACH 3, break, fissure, fracture, rent, rift, schism, split

rel division, divorce, parting

2 ***syn*** SEPARATION 1, detachment, dissolution, disunion, division, divorce, divorcement, partition, split-up

rupture *vb* **1** ***syn*** OPEN 3, breach, disrupt, hole

rel divide, divorce, part, separate, sunder; cleave, rend, rive, split

2 ***syn*** SEPARATE 1, break up, disjoin, dissect, disunite, divide, divorce, sever, split (up), sunder

rural *adj* relating to or characteristic of the country <a peaceful *rural* scene>

syn agrestic, bucolic, campestral, countrified, country, out-country, outland, pastoral, provincial, rustic

rel arcadian, idyllic; natural, simple, unsophisticated

con metropolitan, municipal, oppidan; crammed, crowded, packed, populous; bustling, busy, hustling; artificial, mundane, sophisticated, worldly

ant urban; citified

ruse *n syn* TRICK 1, artifice, feint, gambit, gimmick, jig, maneuver, ploy, stratagem, wile

rush *vb* **1** to move or cause to move quickly, impetuously, and often heedlessly < *rushed* around madly trying to get things done>
syn boil, bolt, charge, chase, dash, fling, lash, race, shoot, ‖swither, tear; *compare* COURSE, HURRY 2, PLUNGE 2, STAMPEDE 2
rel hasten, hurry, speed; dart, fly, scud; break
idiom go off half-cocked, not look before one leaps
2 ***syn*** HURRY 2, bustle, fleet, flit, fly, haste, hasten, run, speed, whiz
3 ***syn*** COURSE, career, chase, race, speed, tear

rush *n* **1** ***syn*** HASTE 2, hastiness, hurriedness, precipitance, precipitancy, precipitateness, precipitation
2 ***syn*** FLOW, current, drift, flood, flux, spate, stream, tide

rushing *adj* ***syn*** PRECIPITATE 1, abrupt, hasty, headlong, hurried, impetuous, precipitant, precipitous, subitaneous, sudden

rushlight *n* ***syn*** NONENTITY, cipher, insignificancy, nobody, nothing, nullity, whiffet, whippersnapper, zero, zilch

rustic *adj* ***syn*** RURAL, agrestic, bucolic, campestral, countrified, country, out-country, outland, pastoral, provincial

rustic *n* an inhabitant of a rural or remote area who is usually characterized by an utter lack of sophistication and cultivation <an unbelieving *rustic* gawking at the skyscrapers>
syn ‖apple knocker, ‖backwoodser, backwoodsman, bucolic, bumpkin, chawbacon, clodhopper, clown, country jake, countryman, greenhorn, hayseed, hick, hillbilly, hillman, ‖hodge, hoosier, jake, jay, joskin, mossback, mountaineer, peasant, provincial, redneck, ‖ridge runner, rube, ‖wayback, woodsy, yap, ‖yob, yokel
rel rural; exurbanite, suburbanite; agriculturalist, farmer, granger, husbandman
con burgher, oppidan, townsman; cityite, urbanite; cosmopolitan, cosmopolite
ant city slicker

rustle *n* ***syn*** HASTE 1, celerity, dispatch, expedition, expeditiousness, hurry, hustle, speed, speediness, swiftness

rustler *n* ***syn*** HUSTLER 1, dynamo, go-getter, live wire, peeler, self-starter

rusty *adj* ***syn*** HARSH 3, dry, grating, hoarse, jarring, rasping, raucous, rough, rugged, strident

‖**rusty** *adj* ***syn*** ILL-TEMPERED, bad-tempered, dyspeptic, hot-tempered, ill-humored, ill-natured, tempersome

rut *n* ***syn*** ROUTINE, grind, groove, pace, rote, treadmill

ruth *n* **1** ***syn*** PITY, commiseration, compassion, rue, sympathy
2 ***syn*** PENITENCE, attrition, compunction, contrition, penance, penitency, remorse, remorsefulness, repentance, rue

ruthful *adj* ***syn*** WOEFUL 1, afflicted, doleful, dolent, dolorous, miserable, rueful, sorrowful, wretched

ruthless *adj* ***syn*** GRIM 3, implacable, ironfisted, merciless, mortal, relentless, unappeasable, unflinching, unrelenting, unyielding

ruttish *adj* ***syn*** LUSTFUL 2, concupiscent, goatish, *horny, hot, lascivious, libidinous, lickerish, rutty, satyric

‖**ruttle** *vb* ***syn*** RATTLE 1, bicker, clack, clatter, clitter, shatter

rutty *adj* ***syn*** LUSTFUL 2, concupiscent, goatish, *horny, hot, lascivious, libidinous, lickerish, ruttish, satyric

---

S

sable *adj* ***syn*** BLACK 1, atramentous, ebon, ebony, inky, jet, jetty, pitch-black, pitch-dark, raven
rel dark, dusky, murky; gloomy, somber

sabotage *n* willful effort by indirect means to hinder, prevent, undo, or discredit (as a plan or activity) < *sabotage* of the project by disgruntled officials >
syn subversion, undermining, wreckage, wrecking
rel subversiveness, subversivism; damage, impairment, injury

sabotage *vb* to practice sabotage on < *sabotaged* his opponent's campaign with rumors and smears >
syn subvert, undermine, wreck
rel frustrate, hamper, hinder; block, obstruct; damage; break up, destroy
idiom throw a monkey wrench into
con assist, back, support

saccharine *adj* ***syn*** INGRATIATING, deferential, disarming, ingratiatory, insinuating, insinuative, silken, silky
rel candied, cloying, honeyed, oversweet, sugar-candy, sugar-coated, sugared, sugary, sweet, syrupy

sacerdotal *adj* of, relating to, or belonging to priests or priesthood < *sacerdotal* vestments >
syn hieratic, priestal, priestish, priestlike, priestly, sacerdotical
rel churchly, ecclesiastical, religious; clerical, ministerial; apostolic, papal

sacerdotical *adj* ***syn*** SACERDOTAL, hieratic, priestal, priestish, priestlike, priestly

sack *n* ***syn*** BAG 1, ‖poke, pouch
rel container; pocket

sack *vb* ***syn*** DISMISS 3, ax, boot (out), bounce, ‖can, cashier, drop, fire, kick out, terminate
rel expel, ship; ‖bump, ‖chuck
idiom give one the sack, send packing

sack *vb* ***syn*** RAVAGE, depredate, desecrate, desolate, despoil, devastate, devour, pillage, spoliate, waste
rel forage, raid; strip

sacker *n* ***syn*** MARAUDER, despoiler, forager, freebooter, looter, pillager, plunderer, raider, ravager, ravisher

sacred *adj* **1** ***syn*** HOLY 1, blessed, consecrated, hallowed, sanctified, unprofane
rel sacramental; angelic, godly, saintly; cherished
con lay, secular, temporal; earthly; unhallowed
ant profane
2 dedicated to or hallowed by association with a deity < *sacred* songs >
syn numinous, spiritual; *compare* HOLY 1
rel hallowed, sanctified
3 protected (as by law, custom, or human respect) against abuse < a fund *sacred* to charity >
syn inviolable, inviolate, sacrosanct
rel defended, guarded, protected, shielded; immune, untouchable

Sacred Writ *n* ***syn*** BIBLE, Book, Holy Writ, Scripture
idiom Good Book

sacrifice *n* ***syn*** VICTIM 1, offering
rel burnt offering, oblation; sacrification; hecatomb; sin offering

sacrifice *vb* **1** to offer as a victim in sacrifice < Abraham about to *sacrifice* Isaac >
syn immolate, victimize
rel offer (up); consecrate, dedicate, devote; donate, give, yield
2 ***syn*** LOSE 1, drop, forfeit
idiom kiss good-bye
3 ***syn*** FORGO, eschew, forbear
rel cede, yield
idiom part with

sacrilege *n* ***syn*** PROFANATION, blasphemy, desecration, violation
rel irreverence; heresy; crime, impiety, offense, sin

sacrilegious *adj* involving or marked by debasement or defilement of what is sacred < *sacrilegious* despoilers of ancient churches >
syn blasphemous, profane
rel impious, irreverent, ungodly; evil, sinful, wicked; irreligious
con godly, pious, reverent; religious

sacrosanct *adj* ***syn*** SACRED 3, inviolable, inviolate
rel esteemed, regarded, respected

sad *adj* **1** affected with or expressing sadness < was *sad* to see him go >
syn heavyhearted, melancholy, mournful, saddened, sorry, unhappy; *compare* DOWNCAST, MELANCHOLY 2
rel blue, dejected, dispirited, down, downbeat, downcast, drear, dumpish, dumpy; grieving, unenjoying; depressed, morose; depressing, dismal, joyless, mirthless, saddening, triste; desolate
con happy, joyful, joyous; blithe, gay, lighthearted; exalted, fired, inspired, uplifted
ant glad
2 causing sadness < felt miserable after listening to that *sad* song >
syn depressing, joyless, melancholic, melancholy, mournful, saddening, triste; *compare* MELANCHOLY 2
rel dismal, gloomy; afflicting, doleful, dreary, lamentable, sorrowful; pathetic, tear-jerking
con bright, gay, lively; exhilarating, heartwarming, stimulating, stirring
ant happy

sadden *vb* ***syn*** DEPRESS 2, oppress, press, weigh down
idiom make blue, ‖put into a funk
ant gladden

saddened *adj* ***syn*** SAD 1, heavyhearted, melancholy, mournful, sorry, unhappy

---

syn synonym(s) ***rel*** related word(s)
idiom idiomatic equivalent(s) ***con*** contrasted word(s)
ant antonym(s) * vulgar
‖ use limited; if in doubt, see a dictionary
The first word in a synonym list when printed in SMALL CAPITALS shows where there is more information about the group. For a more efficient use of this book see Explanatory Notes.

saddening *adj* ***syn*** SAD 2, depressing, joyless, melancholic, melancholy, mournful, triste

saddle *vb* ***syn*** BURDEN, charge, cumber, encumber, lade, load, task, tax, weigh, weight
rel hamper, impede, restrict; impose, inflict
idiom hang like a millstone around one's neck

sadness *n* the quality, state, or an instance of being sad <her feelings of *sadness* and longing persisted long after he left>
syn blues, dejection, depression, dinge, (the) dismals, (the) dolefuls, dumps, dysphoria, gloom, heavyheartedness, melancholy, mopes, mournfulness, suds, unhappiness
rel dispiritedness, doldrums, downcastness, downheartedness, downs, ||funk, listlessness, moodiness; anguish, grief, sorrow, sorrowfulness, woe; desolation, disconsolateness, disconsolation, forlornness, misery, mourning; blue devils, despondency, hopelessness, megrims, melancholia
idiom slough of despond
con happiness, joy, joyfulness, joyousness; cheerfulness, cheeriness, gayness, lightheartedness, liveliness; exhilaration, ups
ant gladness

safe *adj* **1** having been freed from risk, danger, harm, or injury <refugees who found themselves *safe* at last in a neutral country>
syn scatheless, unharmed, unscathed
rel unhurt, uninjured; intact
idiom in (*or* with) a whole skin, out of harm's way, safe and sound
con damaged, harmed, hurt, injured
ant unsafe
2 affording security from threat of harm, injury, risk, or loss <found a *safe* place to hide>
syn riskless, secure
rel guarding, protecting, safeguarding, sheltering, shielding; defended, guarded, protected, sheltered, shielded; unthreatened; impregnable, inviolable, invulnerable, unassailable
idiom safe as a bank vault
con insecure, undefended, unguarded, unprotected, vulnerable; threatened; hazardous, risky
ant dangerous, unsafe
3 not threatening danger <it's *safe* to go there only in the daytime>
syn healthy, uninjurious, wholesome; *compare* HARMLESS
rel innocent, innocuous, inoffensive
con hazardous, perilous, precarious, risky; harmful, injurious, unhealthy
ant dangerous, unsafe
4 ***syn*** CAUTIOUS, calculating, careful, chary, circumspect, considerate, discreet, gingerly, guarded, wary

safeguard *n* ***syn*** DEFENSE 1, aegis, armament, armor, guard, protection, security, shield, ward
rel palladium; buffer, screen

safeguard *vb* ***syn*** DEFEND 1, bulwark, cover, fend, guard, protect, screen, secure, shield
rel conserve, preserve, save; assure, ensure, insure

safekeeping *n* **1** ***syn*** CUSTODY, care, guardianship, keeping, trust, ward
2 ***syn*** PRESERVATION 1, conservation, keeping, salvation, saving, sustentation

safeness *n* ***syn*** SAFETY, assurance, security

safety *n* the quality, state, or condition of being safe <there's *safety* in numbers>
syn assurance, safeness, security
rel cover, protection, shelter; defense; impregnability, inviolability, invulnerability
con hazard, jeopardy, peril, risk, threat; instability, vulnerability
ant danger

sag *vb* **1** ***syn*** SLIP 6, drop (off), fall (off *or* away), slide, slump
2 ***syn*** DROOP 3, flag, swag, wilt
rel bend, decline; dangle, flap, flop
idiom ||have a case of the sags
ant tauten

sag *n* **1** ***syn*** DEPRESSION 2, basin, concavity, dip, hollow, sink, sinkage, sinkhole
rel settling, sinking
2 ***syn*** DECLINE 3, dip, downslide, downswing, downtrend, downturn, drop, falloff, slip, slump

sagacious *adj* **1** ***syn*** WISE 1, discerning, gnostic, insighted, insightful, knowing, knowledgeable, perceptive, sage, sophic
rel clever, intelligent, smart; far-seeing; judicious, prudent, sapient
idiom wise as an owl
con dumb, stupid, unintelligent; ignorant, unlearned, untaught; unperceptive; unwise
2 ***syn*** SHREWD, argute, astucious, astute, cagey, heady, perspicacious, ||savvy
rel critical, discerning, discriminating
idiom wise in the ways of the world

sagaciousness *n* ***syn*** SAGACITY, insight, sageness, sapience, wisdom
rel judgment, wiseness

sagacity *n* intelligent application of knowledge <*sagacity* acquired from years of learning and experience>
syn insight, sagaciousness, sageness, sapience, wisdom
rel discernment, penetration, perception, perceptiveness, sensitivity; understanding; judiciousness, prudence; comprehension, grasp

sage *adj* **1** ***syn*** WISE 1, discerning, gnostic, insighted, insightful, knowing, knowledgeable, perceptive, sagacious, sophic
rel philosophic; learned; profound
2 ***syn*** WISE 2, judgmatic, judicious, prudent, sane, sapient, sensible
rel acute, penetrating, probing

sage *n* one distinguished for his breadth of knowledge, experience, wisdom, and sound judgment <was one of the renowned *sages* of constitutional law>
syn savant, scholar, wise man
rel expert, master

---

syn synonym(s) ***rel*** related word(s)
idiom idiomatic equivalent(s) ***con*** contrasted word(s)
ant antonym(s) * vulgar
|| use limited; if in doubt, see a dictionary
The first word in a synonym list when printed in SMALL CAPITALS shows where there is more information about the group. For a more efficient use of this book see Explanatory Notes.

sageness *n* ***syn*** SAGACITY, insight, sagaciousness, sapience, wisdom

said *adj* ***syn*** SUCH 1, aforementioned, aforesaid

sail *vb* **1** ***syn*** FLY 1, dart, float, scud, shoot, skim, skirr
2 ***syn*** FLY 4, fleet, flit, sweep, wing

sailor *n* ***syn*** MARINER, jack, jack-tar, sailorman, salt, seaman, tar, tarpaulin

sailorman *n* ***syn*** MARINER, jack, jack-tar, sailor, salt, seaman, tar, tarpaulin

saintliness *n* ***syn*** HOLINESS, sanctity
rel righteousness, worthiness

saintly *adj* being of deeply religious and wholly upright character <a *saintly* old couple>
syn angelic, godly, holy
rel righteous, upright, upstanding, virtuous, worthy; devout, God-fearing, pious; sainted; seraph, seraphic, seraphlike
idiom pure in mind and heart

salable *adj* ***syn*** MARKETABLE, merchandisable, merchantable, sellable, trafficable, vendible
ant unsalable

salacious *adj* ***syn*** LICENTIOUS 2, fast, incontinent, lascivious, lecherous, lewd, libertine, libidinous, lustful, satyric

salad *n* ***syn*** MISCELLANY 1, brew, hash, mélange, mishmash, pasticcio, pastiche, potpourri, salmagundi, stew

salary *n* ***syn*** WAGE, emolument, fee, hire, pay, pay envelope, stipend

salient *adj* ***syn*** NOTICEABLE, arresting, arrestive, conspicuous, marked, outstanding, prominent, remarkable, signal, striking
rel important, pertinent, significant, weighty; impressive, moving; obvious, pronounced; intrusive, obtrusive

saliferous *adj* ***syn*** SALTY 1, saline, salt

saline *adj* ***syn*** SALTY 1, saliferous, salt

saliva *n* a liquid secreted into the mouth and helpful to digestion <*saliva* drooled down the baby's chin>
syn slaver, spit, spittle, water
rel sputum

salivate *vb* ***syn*** DROOL 2, dribble, drivel, slabber, slaver, slobber

sally *n* **1** ***syn*** OUTBURST 1, access, burst, eruption, explosion, flare-up, gust
2 ***syn*** JOKE 1, crack, drollery, gag, jape, jest, quip, waggery, wisecrack, witticism
3 ***syn*** EXCURSION 1, jaunt, junket, outing, roundabout

salmagundi *n* ***syn*** MISCELLANY 1, gallimaufry, hodgepodge, jumble, medley, mélange, mishmash, pasticcio, pastiche, potpourri

salon *n* **1** a spacious elegant apartment or living room (as in a fashionable house) <her *salon* was decorated à la Louis XV>
syn drawing room, saloon
rel parlor; suite
2 a fashionable assemblage of notables held by custom at the home of a prominent person <was famous for her literary *salons*>
syn saloon
rel at home; reception; levee; evening, soiree

saloon *n* **1** ***syn*** SALON 1, drawing room
rel gallery; hall
2 ***syn*** SALON 2
rel gathering, party
3 ***syn*** BAR 5, barroom, ‖bucket shop, drinkery, ‖groggery, ‖rum-hole, ‖rum-mill, taproom, tavern, watering hole

saloonist *n* ***syn*** SALOONKEEPER, barkeeper, boniface, innholder, innkeeper, ‖publican, taverner

saloonkeeper *n* one who owns or manages a bar <the traditional image of the fat cigar-smoking *saloonkeeper*>
syn barkeeper, boniface, innholder, innkeeper, ‖publican, saloonist, taverner; *compare* BARTENDER
rel victualler

salt *n* **1** ***syn*** LIVING, alimentation, alimony, bread, keep, livelihood, maintenance, subsistence, support, sustenance
2 ***syn*** MARINER, jack, jack-tar, sailor, sailorman, seaman, tar, tarpaulin

salt *adj* ***syn*** SALTY 1, saliferous, saline

saltate *vb* ***syn*** JUMP 1, bounce, bound, hop, hurdle, leap, lop, spring, vault

salt away *vb* ***syn*** SAVE 4, lay aside, lay away, lay by, lay in, lay up, put by, ‖spare

saltimbanque *n* ***syn*** CHARLATAN, mountebank, quack, quacksalver, quackster
rel impostor, pretender; cheat, fraud

salty *adj* **1** of, relating to, or containing salt <*salty* deposits>
syn saliferous, saline, salt
rel brackish, briny, saltish; salted
ant saltless
2 ***syn*** RISQUÉ, blue, broad, off-color, purple, racy, shady, spicy, suggestive, wicked
3 ***syn*** CAUSTIC 1, mordacious, mordant, scathing, trenchant

salubrious *adj* ***syn*** HEALTHFUL, good, healthy, hygienic, salutary, salutiferous, wholesome
rel bracing, invigorating, stimulating
ant insalubrious

salutary *adj* ***syn*** HEALTHFUL, good, healthy, hygienic, salubrious, salutiferous, wholesome
rel restorative, sanative, sanatory, tonic
con debilitating, enfeebling, weakening; bad, evil
ant deleterious; unsalutary

salutation *n* **1** ***syn*** GREETING, salute
2 ***syn*** ENCOMIUM, citation, eulogy, panegyric, tribute

salute *vb* ***syn*** ADDRESS 7, accost, call (to), greet, hail

salute *n* ***syn*** GREETING, salutation

salutiferous *adj* ***syn*** HEALTHFUL, good, healthy, hygienic, salubrious, salutary, wholesome

salvage *vb* to rescue and save from wreckage, destruction, or loss <*salvaged* the torpedoed vessel>
syn salve
rel deliver, redeem, rescue, save; reclaim, recover, regain, retrieve; ransom
con dump, jettison

---

syn synonym(s) — *rel* related word(s)
idiom idiomatic equivalent(s) — *con* contrasted word(s)
ant antonym(s) — * vulgar
‖ use limited; if in doubt, see a dictionary
The first word in a synonym list when printed in SMALL CAPITALS shows where there is more information about the group. For a more efficient use of this book see Explanatory Notes.

salvation *n* **1** *syn* PRESERVATION 1, conservation, keeping, safekeeping, saving, sustentation
2 *syn* CONSERVATION 1, conservancy, husbanding, preserval, preservation, saving

salve *n* *syn* OINTMENT, balm, cerate, chrism, cream, unction, unguent
rel emollient, lubricant; counterirritant; aid, remedy

salve *vb* *syn* SALVAGE

salvo *n* **1** *syn* BARRAGE, bombardment, broadside, burst, cannonade, fusillade, hail, shower, storm, volley
rel discharge; spray
2 *syn* TESTIMONIAL 3, appreciation, tribute

same *adj* **1** being one rather than another or more <went to the *same* hotel each summer>
syn exact, identical, selfsame, very
rel comparable, like, similar
ant different
2 agreeing fundamentally or absolutely <all the family have the *same* dark eyes>
syn duplicate, equal, equivalent, identic, identical, indistinguishable, tantamount; *compare* LIKE
rel comparable, like, similar; coequal
ant different
3 not changing or fluctuating <treated everyone with the *same* courtesy>
syn consistent, constant, invariable, unchanging, unfailing, unvarying
con changeable, fluctuant, inconsistent, inconstant, irregular, variable, varying

sameness *n* **1** *syn* IDENTITY 1, identicalness, oneness, selfsameness
rel alikeness; uniformity, uniformness, unity
2 *syn* EQUIVALENCE, adequation, equality, equatability, equivalency, par, parity
rel analogy; resemblance, similarity

sample *n* *syn* INSTANCE, case, case history, example, illustration, representative, sampling, specimen
rel indication, sign; fragment, part, piece, portion, segment; constituent, element; individual, unit

sampling *n* *syn* INSTANCE, case, case history, example, illustration, representative, sample, specimen

sanative *adj* *syn* CURATIVE, curing, healing, remedial, remedying, restorative, sanatory, vulnerary, wholesome
rel healthful, hygienic, salutary, sanitary

sanatory *adj* *syn* CURATIVE, curing, healing, remedial, remedying, restorative, sanative, vulnerary, wholesome

sanctified *adj* *syn* HOLY 1, blessed, consecrated, hallowed, sacred, unprofane
rel canonized, deified, sainted
ant unsanctified

sanctify *vb* *syn* BLESS 1, consecrate, hallow

sanctimonious *adj* *syn* HYPOCRITICAL, canting, pecksniffian, pharisaic, pharisaical, self-righteous
rel deceiving, false; snuffling
ant unsanctimonious

sanctimoniousness *n* *syn* HYPOCRISY, cant, hypocriticalness, pecksniffery, pharisaicalness, pharisaism, sanctimony, Tartuffery, Tartuffism
idiom odor of sanctity
ant unsanctimoniousness

sanctimony *n* *syn* HYPOCRISY, cant, hypocriticalness, pecksniffery, pharisaicalness, pharisaism, sanctimoniousness, Tartuffery, Tartuffism

sanction *n* **1** explicit authoritative permission or recognition that gives validity to acts of a subordinate <a colonial governor acting under the *sanction* of the king>
syn endorsement, fiat
rel approval, authorization, consent, permission; approbation, confirmation, encouragement, ratification, recommendation, support
con restraint; debarment; interdict, prohibition; disapprobation, disapproval, objection
ant interdiction
2 *syn* PERMISSION, allowance, authorization, consent, leave, permit, sufferance

sanction *vb* *syn* APPROVE 2, accredit, certify, endorse, OK (*or* okay)
rel authorize, commission, license
con ban, disallow, forbid, prohibit
ant interdict

sanctioned *adj* *syn* ORTHODOX 1, accepted, authoritative, canonical, received, sound
ant unsanctioned

sanctity *n* *syn* HOLINESS, saintliness
rel godliness; righteousness, uprightness

sanctorium *n* *syn* SHRINE, holy place, sanctuary, sanctum

sanctuary *n* **1** *syn* SHRINE, holy place, sanctorium, sanctum
2 *syn* SHELTER 1, asylum, cover, covert, harbor, harborage, haven, port, refuge, retreat
rel bamah; oasis
3 *syn* REFUGE 1, asylum, harborage, shelter

sanctum *n* *syn* SHRINE, holy place, sanctorium, sanctuary

sand *n* *syn* FORTITUDE, backbone, grit, guts, intestinal fortitude, ‖moxie, nerve, spunk
rel *balls; chutzpah, gall
idiom true (*or* clear) grit

sandwich shop *n* *syn* EATING HOUSE, café, coffee shop, cookshop, diner, ‖greasy spoon, ‖hashery, ‖hash house, luncheonette, lunchroom

sane *adj* **1** *syn* HEALTHY 1, ‖bunkum, fit, hale, right, sound, well, well-conditioned, well-liking, wholesome
2 free from mental disorder <a thoroughly *sane* and well-balanced man>
syn all there, compos mentis, lucid, normal, right
rel balanced, oriented; levelheaded, rational, sensible, sober, sound
idiom of sound mind
con abnormal, unbalanced; neurotic, paranoid, psychopathic, psychotic, schizophrenic; balmy, crazy, ‖cuckoo, non compos, non compos mentis, nuts, screwy; deranged, lunatic, mad, wild
ant insane
3 *syn* WISE 2, judgmatic, judicious, prudent, sage, sapient, sensible

---

syn synonym(s) *rel* related word(s)
idiom idiomatic equivalent(s) *con* contrasted word(s)
ant antonym(s) * vulgar
‖ use limited; if in doubt, see a dictionary
The first word in a synonym list when printed in SMALL CAPITALS shows where there is more information about the group. For a more efficient use of this book see Explanatory Notes.

rel logical, rational, reasonable; good, right; cogent, compelling, convincing, sound
con imprudent, injudicious, unwise

saneness *n syn* WIT 2, lucidity, ‖marbles, mind, reason, sanity, sense(s), soundness
rel clear-mindedness, perception; comprehension, ‖smarts, understanding

sangfroid *n syn* EQUANIMITY, ataraxy, calmness, composure, coolness, imperturbability, phlegm, self-possession
rel self-containment, self-control; aloofness, coolheadedness, indifference, unconcern

sanguinary *adj* **1** *syn* MURDEROUS, bloodthirsty, bloody, homicidal, murdering, sanguine, sanguineous
2 *syn* BLOODY 1, bloodstained, ensanguined, gory, imbrued, sanguine, sanguineous
ant unsanguinary

sanguine *adj* **1** *syn* BLOODY 1, bloodstained, ensanguined, gory, imbrued, sanguinary, sanguineous
2 *syn* MURDEROUS, bloodthirsty, bloody, homicidal, murdering, sanguinary, sanguineous
3 *syn* RUDDY 1, florid, flush, flushed, full-blooded, glowing, rubicund
4 *syn* CONFIDENT 1, assured, secure, self-assured, self-confident, undoubtful
rel expectant; hopeful, undespairing
idiom full of hope
ant hopeless
5 *syn* OPTIMISTIC, fond, Pollyannaish, upbeat
ant unsanguine

sanguineness *n syn* OPTIMISM, Pollyannaism, rose-colored spectacles, sanguinity

sanguineous *adj* **1** *syn* BLOODY 1, bloodstained, ensanguined, gory, imbrued, sanguinary, sanguine
2 *syn* MURDEROUS, bloodthirsty, bloody, homicidal, murdering, sanguinary, sanguine

sanguinity *n syn* OPTIMISM, Pollyannaism, rose-colored spectacles, sanguineness

sanity *n syn* WIT 2, lucidity, ‖marbles, mind, reason, saneness, sense(s), soundness
rel intelligence; comprehension
idiom sound mind
ant insanity

sans *prep syn* WITHOUT 2, awanting, lacking, minus, wanting

sap *n syn* FOOL 3, chump, dupe, fall guy, gull, mark, pigeon, saphead, ‖schlemiel, sucker

sap *vb syn* WEAKEN 1, attenuate, blunt, cripple, debilitate, disable, enfeeble, unbrace, undermine, unstrengthen
rel deplete, drain, exhaust, knock out; ruin, wreck; destroy

saphead *n syn* FOOL 3, chump, dupe, fall guy, gull, mark, pigeon, sap, ‖schlemiel, sucker

rel ‖boob, jerk

sapid *adj syn* PALATABLE, aperitive, appetizing, flavorsome, mouth-watering, relishing, saporous, savory, tasty, toothsome
idiom fit for a king
con bland, tasteless; repulsive, unpalatable
ant insipid

sapidity *n syn* TASTE 3, flavor, relish, sapor, savor, smack, tang
ant insipidity

sapience *n syn* SAGACITY, insight, sagaciousness, sageness, wisdom

sapient *adj syn* WISE 2, judgmatic, judicious, prudent, sage, sane, sensible
rel erudite, learned, scholarly; thinking; discriminating, sapiential

sapless *adj syn* INSIPID 3, bland, driveling, flat, inane, innocuous, jejune, milk-and-water, namby-pamby, vapid

sapor *n syn* TASTE 3, flavor, relish, sapidity, savor, smack, tang

saporous *adj syn* PALATABLE, aperitive, appetizing, flavorsome, mouth-watering, relishing, sapid, savory, tasty, toothsome

sappy *adj* ‖**1** *syn* SUCCULENT, juicy
2 *syn* SENTIMENTAL, bathetic, drippy, maudlin, mawkish, mushy, slushy, ‖soppy, soupy, sticky
3 *syn* FOOLISH 2, absurd, ‖balmy, crazy, fantastic, harebrained, insane, loony, preposterous, silly

sarcasm *n* a savage bitter form of humor usually intended to hurt or wound <a speech full of personal jabs and *sarcasm*>
syn acerbity, causticity, corrosiveness, sarcasticness
rel humor, irony, raillery, satire, wit; jest, repartee; gibe, lampooning; mockery, ridicule, scorn, sneering; acrimony, invective; rancor, sharpness
con playfulness, waggishness, whimsicality

sarcastic *adj* marked by, expressive of, or given to sarcasm <a critic noted for his *sarcastic* comments on actors' performances>
syn acerb, acerbic, archilochian, caustic, corrosive, ‖sarky; *compare* CAUSTIC 1
rel dry; cynical, ironic, sardonic, satiric; jeering, mocking, scornful; biting, cutting, incisive; mordant, scathing, sharp, stinging; pungent, tart, trenchant
con droll, playful, sportive, waggish, whimsical

sarcasticness *n syn* SARCASM, acerbity, causticity, corrosiveness
rel bitingness, cuttingness, incisiveness, trenchancy; derision, mocking, taunting

sardonic *adj* characterized by or expressing disdainful, skeptical humor <had a *sardonic* smile that mirrored his fixed expectation of the worst from everyone>
syn cynical, ironic, wry
rel contemptuous, disdainful, scornful; derisive, jeering, mocking, saturnine, sneering; caustic, corrosive, sarcastic, satiric

‖**sarky** *adj syn* SARCASTIC, acerb, acerbic, archilochian, caustic, corrosive

sash *n syn* BELT 1, ceinture, cincture, girdle, waistband

sashay *vb* to move about often self-consciously and usually in a conspicuous manner <*sashaying* around, trying to walk like a model>

---

syn synonym(s) · *rel* related word(s)
idiom idiomatic equivalent(s) · *con* contrasted word(s)
ant antonym(s) · * vulgar
‖ use limited; if in doubt, see a dictionary
The first word in a synonym list when printed in SMALL CAPITALS shows where there is more information about the group. For a more efficient use of this book see Explanatory Notes.

syn flounce, mince, prance, ‖prink, strut
rel swagger

sass *n* *syn* BACK TALK, guff, ‖jaw, ‖lip, mouth, sauce
rel impertinence, insolence, sassiness

sassy *adj* **1** *syn* WISE 5, bold, cheeky, forward, fresh, impudent, nervy, pert, smart, smart-alecky
rel brazen, unabashed; audacious
2 *syn* DAPPER, bandbox, doggish, doggy, natty, sparkish, spiffy, spruce, sprucy, well-groomed

Satan *n* **1** *syn* DEVIL 1, Apollyon, Beelzebub, diablo, fiend, Lucifer, Old Gooseberry, Old Nick, Old Scratch, serpent
rel deuce; Mephistopheles; devil-god
idiom fallen angel, lord of the underworld, prince of darkness
2 *syn* DEVIL 2, archfiend, demon, fiend, succubus
rel renegade, villain; beast, viper

satanic *adj* **1** of, relating to, or characteristic of Satan <*Satanic* rites>
syn devilish, diabolic, Mephistophelian
rel saturnine
2 *syn* FIENDISH, demoniac, demonian, demonic, devilish, diabolic, diabolonian, serpentine, unhallowed
rel evil, wicked

satanism *n* the worship of Satan usually marked by the travesty of Christian rites <interpreted *satanism* as an offshoot of the belief in two coequal and coeternal principles of good and evil>
syn diabolism
rel Black Mass

sate *vb* *syn* SATIATE, cloy, fill, glut, gorge, jade, pall, ‖stall, stodge, surfeit
rel overfill, overstuff, stuff
idiom have (*or* give) a bellyful of, have (*or* give) an overdose of

sated *adj* *syn* SATIATED, full, glutted, gorged, jaded, satiate, surfeited
ant unsated

satellite *n* *syn* FOLLOWER, adherent, cohort, disciple, henchman, partisan, sectary, sectator, supporter
rel favorite, minion

satellite *adj* *syn* CONCOMITANT, accompanying, ancillary, attendant, attending, coincident, collateral, incident

satiate *adj* *syn* SATIATED, full, glutted, gorged, jaded, sated, surfeited
idiom stuffed to the gills
con insatiable, unsatiable
ant insatiate, unsatiate

satiate *vb* to satisfy fully or to repletion <tried to titillate rather than *satiate* his readers' interest>
syn cloy, fill, glut, gorge, jade, pall, sate, ‖stall, stodge, surfeit; *compare* SATISFY 3
rel content, fulfill, gratify, indulge, satisfy; overdose, stuff
con coax, court, invite, pique, tantalize, tempt, titillate

satiated *adj* filled to repletion <the mob, *satiated* with violence, finally dispersed>
syn full, glutted, gorged, jaded, sated, satiate, surfeited
rel fulfilled, gratified, indulged, satisfied
con avid, greedy, ravening; craving, hungering, hungry, lusting, thirsting, thirsty
ant unsatiated

satiny *adj* *syn* SOFT 3, cottony, silken, silky, velvety

satire *n* humorous ridicule often used to convey rebuke or criticism or to expose folly or vice <a brilliant writer noted for his *satire*>
syn lampoonery, raillery, satiricalness
rel banter, chaffing; causticity, irony; mockery, ridicule; pasquinade, persiflage, squib; parody, spoof, spoofery, takeoff

satiric *adj* of, relating to, characterized by, or based on satire <witty, eloquent, and *satiric* sermons>
syn lampooning, satirizing
rel bantering, chaffing; caustic, ironic; mocking, ridiculing; parodying, spoofing; farcical; Rabelaisian

satiricalness *n* *syn* SATIRE, lampoonery, raillery

satirizing *adj* *syn* SATIRIC, lampooning

satisfactorily *adv* *syn* WELL 4, acceptably, adequately, amply, appropriately, becomingly, fittingly, properly, right, suitably
rel competently, sufficiently
ant unsatisfactorily

satisfactory *adj* **1** *syn* SUFFICIENT 1, adequate, comfortable, competent, decent, enough, sufficing
ant unsatisfactory
2 *syn* VALID, cogent, convincing, satisfying, solid, sound, telling
ant unsatisfactory
3 *syn* DECENT 4, acceptable, adequate, all right, good, sufficient, tolerable, unexceptionable, unexceptional, unimpeachable
rel fair, goodish, passable
ant unsatisfactory

satisfy *vb* **1** *syn* CLEAR 5, clear off, discharge, liquidate, pay, pay up, quit, settle, square
2 *syn* SUIT 6, please
3 to satiate desires or longings <strove to *satisfy* his lust for money and power>
syn appease, content, gratify; *compare* SATIATE
rel gladden, humor, indulge, please; sate, satiate; pacify, placate
con tantalize, tease; excite, pique, provoke, stimulate; arouse
4 *syn* ASSURE 2, convince, persuade
rel induce, inveigle, win (over)
5 measure up to a set of criteria or requirements <courses taken to *satisfy* requirements for graduation>
syn answer, fill, fulfill, meet
rel comply (with), conform (to), serve; do, suffice
idiom fill the bill, make good

satisfying *adj* *syn* VALID, cogent, convincing, satisfactory, solid, sound, telling
ant unsatisfying

satisfyingly *adv* *syn* WELL 5, favorably, fortunately, happily, prosperously, successfully, swimmingly

---

syn synonym(s) — *rel* related word(s)
idiom idiomatic equivalent(s) — *con* contrasted word(s)
ant antonym(s) — * vulgar
‖ use limited; if in doubt, see a dictionary
The first word in a synonym list when printed in SMALL CAPITALS shows where there is more information about the group. For a more efficient use of this book see Explanatory Notes.

rel gratifyingly, pleasingly
ant unsatisfyingly

saturate *vb* **1** *syn* SOAK 1, drench, ‖drouk, impregnate, sodden, ‖sog, sop, souse, steep, waterlog
rel bathe, douche, wash; imbue, infuse, suffuse
2 *syn* PERMEATE, charge, compenetrate, impenetrate, impregnate, interpenetrate, penetrate, percolate, pervade, transfuse
rel pierce, probe; inoculate, instill

saturate *adj syn* WET 1, drenched, dripping, madid, saturated, soaked, soaking, sodden, sopping, soused

saturated *adj syn* WET 1, drenched, dripping, soaked, soaking, sodden, sopping, soppy, soused, wringing-wet

saturnalia *n syn* ORGY 2, bacchanal, bacchanalia, debauch, party

saturnine *adj syn* SULLEN, crabbed, ‖dorty, dour, gloomy, glum, morose, sulky, surly, ugly
rel grave, serious, solemn, somber, staid; moping; dark, funereal; reserved, silent, taciturn, uncommunicative
con cheerful, cheery, happy; cordial, polite
ant genial

satyric *adj* **1** *syn* LICENTIOUS 2, fast, incontinent, lascivious, lecherous, lewd, libertine, libidinous, lustful, salacious
2 *syn* LUSTFUL 2, concupiscent, goatish, *horny, hot, lascivious, libidinous, lickerish, passionate, prurient

sauce *n* **1** *syn* BACK TALK, guff, ‖jaw, ‖lip, mouth, sass
rel pertness, sauciness
‖**2** *syn* LIQUOR 2, alcohol, aqua vitae, booze, ‖budge, drink, firewater, grog, ‖hooch, ‖juice

saucebox *n syn* MINX, hussy, jade, malapert, slut, snip

saucy *adj* **1** flippant and bold in manner or attitude <a *saucy* little flirt>
syn arch, bantam, ‖cocket, malapert, pert
rel flippant, frivolous, light-minded, volatile; bold, brash, combative; impertinent, impudent, insolent; intrusive, meddlesome, obtrusive; smart, smart-alecky, wise
con gentle, meek, mild, quiet, subdued
ant deferential
2 *syn* INSOLENT 2, audacious, bold, ‖boldacious, brazen, contumelious, impertinent, impudent, procacious

sault *n syn* WATERFALL, cascade, cataract, chute, fall(s), ‖force, spout

saunter *vb* to walk slowly in an idle or leisurely manner <*sauntered* about the streets, stopping in at various shops>
syn amble, bummel, drift, linger, mope, mosey, ‖muck, stroll; *compare* WANDER 1
rel meander, ramble, roam, rove, spatiate, ‖stravage, wander; loiter, tarry
con bustle, chase, hustle, scurry, tear

saunter *n syn* WALK 1, constitutional, ramble, stroll, turn

savage *adj* **1** being undomesticated and often destructive or ferocious through lack of restraints or human control <*savage* dogs>
syn feral, vicious, wild; *compare* WILD 1
rel uncivilized, undomesticated, unsocialized; unbroken, unsubdued, untamed; bestial, brutal, brute; ferocious, fierce
con civilized, domesticated, socialized; broken, subdued, tamed; domestic, tame
2 *syn* FIERCE 1, barbarous, cruel, fell, ferocious, grim, inhuman, inhumane, truculent, wolfish
rel coldhearted, heartless, implacable, relentless, unrelenting; rapacious, ravenous, voracious; bloodthirsty, bloody, butcherly, murderous, rabid
3 *syn* BARBARIAN 1, barbaric, barbarous, Gothic, Hunnic, Hunnish, rude, uncivilized, uncultivated, wild
rel primeval, primitive; uncontrolled, unharnessed; harsh, rough, rugged

savant *n syn* SAGE, scholar, wise man

save *vb* **1** *syn* RESCUE, deliver
rel unchain, unshackle
idiom snatch from the jaws of death
con desert, leave; condemn, damn
2 *syn* MAINTAIN 1, keep up, preserve, sustain
3 to keep secure or maintain intact from injury, decay, or loss <regular painting helps *save* the wood>
syn conserve, preserve; *compare* MAINTAIN 1
rel defend, guard, protect, safeguard, shield
con draw (out), withdraw; consume, spend, use up
4 to accumulate and store up (a supply) for future use <*saved* his money for college>
syn lay aside, lay away, lay by, lay in, lay up, put by, salt away, ‖spare; *compare* HOARD
rel accumulate, cache, collect, stockpile, store (up); hoard, squirrel, stash (away); conserve, husband, manage; keep, reserve, set by; deposit, stow
idiom feather one's nest, keep as a nest egg, save for a rainy day, save to fall back on
con lose, squander, use up, waste
ant consume, spend
5 *syn* ECONOMIZE

save *prep syn* EXCEPT, aside from, bar, barring, bating, besides, but, excluding, exclusive of, saving

save *conj* **1** *syn* ONLY, but, except, however, yet
2 *syn* EXCEPT 1, but, saving, unless, ‖without

save–all *adj syn* STINGY, ‖chinchy, close, mean, miserly, ‖narrow, niggardly, parsimonious, penurious, tight

saving *n* **1** *syn* PRESERVATION 1, conservation, keeping, safekeeping, salvation, sustentation
2 *syn* CONSERVATION 1, conservancy, husbanding, preserval, preservation, salvation

saving *prep syn* EXCEPT, aside from, barring, bating, beside, besides, ‖cep, except for, excluding, save

saving *conj syn* EXCEPT 1, but, save, unless, ‖without

saving *adj syn* SPARING, canny, chary, economical, provident, Scotch, stewardly, thrifty, unwasteful, wary

savoir faire *n syn* TACT, address, delicatesse, diplomacy, poise, tactfulness
rel manners; dignity, elegance, grace; refinement, savoir vivre, taste; aplomb, confidence, self-assurance, self-possession; experience, blaséness, sophistication

---

con awkwardness, clumsiness, gaucherie, ineptness, maladroitness

savor *n* **1** ***syn*** TASTE 3, flavor, relish, sapidity, sapor, smack, tang
rel scent, tinge
2 ***syn*** QUALITY 1, affection, attribute, character, characteristic, feature, mark, property, trait, virtue

savor *vb* **1** ***syn*** SMACK, smell
2 ***syn*** FEEL 2, experience, know, taste
3 ***syn*** RELISH 2

savorless *adj* ***syn*** UNPALATABLE 1, distasteful, flat, flavorless, ill-flavored, insipid, tasteless, unappetizing, unsavory
rel bland; thin, watery, weak; unpleasing
con appetizing, pleasing, tempting; piquant, spicy
ant savory

savorous *adj* ***syn*** PALATABLE, flavorsome, good-tasting, sapid, saporous, savorsome, savory, tasteful, tasty, toothsome

savorsome *adj* ***syn*** PALATABLE, flavorsome, good-tasting, sapid, saporous, savorous, savory, tasteful, tasty, toothsome

savory *adj* **1** ***syn*** PALATABLE, aperitive, appetizing, flavorsome, relishing, sapid, savorous, savorsome, tasty, toothsome
rel pleasing, tempting; gustful
con acrid, sharp, strong
ant unsavory
2 ***syn*** SWEET 2, ambrosial, aromal, aromatic, balmy, fragrant, perfumed, perfumy, redolent, spicy

||**savvy** *adj* ***syn*** SHREWD, argute, astucious, astute, cagey, heady, perspicacious, sagacious

saw *n* ***syn*** SAYING, adage, byword, proverb, word

||**sawbones** *n* ***syn*** PHYSICIAN, ||croaker, doc, doctor, MD, medical, mediciner, medico

sawbuck *n* ***syn*** SAWHORSE, buck, horse, trestle, workhorse

saw–edged *adj* ***syn*** SERRATE, denticulate, sawtooth, saw-toothed, serrated, serried

sawhorse *n* a rack on which something (as a board) is laid for sawing <*sawhorses* in the carpentry shop>
syn buck, horse, sawbuck, trestle, workhorse

sawtooth *adj* ***syn*** SERRATE, denticulate, saw-edged, saw-toothed, serrated, serried

saw–toothed *adj* ***syn*** SERRATE, denticulate, saw-edged, sawtooth, serrated, serried

say *vb* **1** to express in words <learn to *say* what you mean>
syn bring out, chime in, come out (with), declare, deliver, state, tell, throw out, utter; *compare* EXPRESS 2
rel breathe; articulate, enunciate, pronounce; announce, proclaim; animadvert, comment, give, remark; cite, quote, recite, repeat; affirm, assert, aver, avow, protest
idiom out with, put in (*or* into) words, put it
2 ***syn*** ARTICULATE 2, enunciate, phonate, pronounce
rel speak, talk
3 ***syn*** SHOW 5, indicate, mark, read, record, register

say *n* ***syn*** VOICE 2, say-so
rel authority; decision

say *adv* ***syn*** NEARLY, about, almost, approximately, just about, most, much, ||nearabout, nigh, practically

saying *n* an oft-repeated statement usually involving common experience or observation <the old *saying* that ignorance is bliss>
syn adage, byword, proverb, saw, word
rel dictum, maxim; truism

say–so *n* ***syn*** VOICE 2, say

scabrous *adj* ***syn*** ROUGH 1, asperous, craggy, harsh, jagged, rugged, scraggy, uneven, unlevel, unsmooth
rel scabby, scaly, scurfy; downy; knobby, knotty; bristly, prickly, thorny
con bald, glabrescent
ant glabrous, smooth

scad *n, usu* **scads** *pl* a great number or abundance <*scads* of opportunities>
syn gob(s), heap, jillion, load(s), million, oodles, quantities, ream(s), ||rimption(s), slather(s), slew, thousand, trillion, wad(s); *compare* MUCH, MULTITUDE 1
rel great deal, lot
con few, handful, scattering, sprinkle, sprinkling

scalawag *n* ***syn*** SCAMP, devil, enfant terrible, limb, mischief, rapscallion, rascal, rogue, skeezicks, villain

scalding *adj* ***syn*** HOT 1, baking, broiling, burning, fiery, heated, red-hot, scorching, sizzling, white-hot
ant freezing

scale *vb* **1** ***syn*** SKIN 2, decorticate, excorticate, peel, strip
2 to shed scales or fragmentary surface matter <*scaling* skin>
syn desquamate, exfoliate, flake (off), peel
rel chip (off), spall (off)

scale *n* ***syn*** DEGREE 2, proportion, rate, ratio

scale *vb* **1** ***syn*** ASCEND 1, climb, escalade, escalate, mount, upclimb, upgo
2 ***syn*** MEASURE 2, gauge

||**scamble** *vb* ***syn*** SPRAWL 1, drape, ||spelder, spraddle, spread-eagle

scamp *n* a pleasantly mischievous person <what have those little *scamps* done now>
syn devil, enfant terrible, limb, mischief, pixie, rapscallion, rascal, ribald, rogue, scalawag, skeezicks, slyboots, villain
rel bird, chap, dog, ||duck; ||bleeder; joker, prankster
con sobersides

scamper *vb* **1** ***syn*** RUN 2, bolt, flee, fly, make off, scoot, ||screw, skedaddle, skip, skirr
rel hasten (off), hurry (away *or* off), light out, speed (away); dash (off), rush (off), shoot, tear (off), whip (off), whiz (off)
2 ***syn*** RUN 1, dash, scoot, scurry, shin, sprint
rel scud, scuddle, scuttle

scan *vb* ***syn*** BROWSE, dip (into), flip (through), glance (at *or* over), leaf (through), riff (through), riffle (through), run (through *or* over), skim (through), thumb (through)

---

syn synonym(s) ***rel*** related word(s)
idiom idiomatic equivalent(s) ***con*** contrasted word(s)
ant antonym(s) * vulgar
|| use limited; if in doubt, see a dictionary
The first word in a synonym list when printed in SMALL CAPITALS shows where there is more information about the group. For a more efficient use of this book see Explanatory Notes.

idiom pass one's eye over

scan *n syn* EXAMINATION, analysis, audit, check-over, inspection, perlustration, review, scrutiny, survey, view
rel perusal; observation, reconnaissance

scandal *n syn* DETRACTION, backbiting, backstabbing, belittlement, calumny, defamation, depreciation, disparagement, slander, tale
rel aspersion; reproach; discredit, disrepute

‖**scandal** *vb syn* MALIGN, asperse, calumniate, defame, denigrate, libel, scandalize, slander, slur, smear

scandalize *vb* **1** *syn* MALIGN, asperse, calumniate, defame, denigrate, libel, ‖scandal, slander, slur, smear
2 *syn* SHOCK 1

scandalizer *n syn* GOSSIP 1, carrytale, gossiper, gossipmonger, newsmonger, quidnunc, scandalmonger, tabby, talebearer, telltale
rel blabber, blabbermouth, talker

scandalmonger *n syn* GOSSIP 1, carrytale, gossiper, gossipmonger, newsmonger, quidnunc, scandalizer, tabby, talebearer, telltale
rel meddler, snoop; backbiter; muckraker

scandalous *adj* **1** *syn* LIBELOUS, backbiting, calumnious, defamatory, detracting, detractive, maligning, slanderous, traducing, vilifying
2 *syn* OUTRAGEOUS 2, atrocious, crying, desperate, heinous, monstrous, shocking

‖**scant** *n syn* SCARCITY, insufficience, insufficiency, paucity, poverty, scarceness

scant *adj* ‖**1** *syn* STINGY, ‖chinchy, close, ‖narrow, niggard, save-all, scrimpy, scrimy, tight, tightfisted
2 *syn* SHORT 3, deficient, failing, inadequate, insufficient, scanty, scarce, shy, unsufficient, wanting
3 *syn* MEAGER 2, exiguous, poor, scanty, scrimp, scrimpy, skimp, skimpy, spare, sparse
ant ample

scant *vb syn* SPARE 3, short, skimp, ‖skinch, stint

scantiness *n syn* FAILURE 3, defalcation, deficiency, deficit, inadequacy, insufficience, insufficiency, lack, shortage, underage
rel scarceness, scarcity; sparseness, sparsity
con excess, overage, surplus

scanty *adj* **1** *syn* MEAGER 2, exiguous, poor, scant, scrimp, scrimpy, skimp, skimpy, spare, sparse
rel scarce, wanting
con ample, enough; profuse
ant plentiful
2 *syn* SHORT 3, deficient, failing, inadequate, insufficient, scant, scarce, shy, unsufficient, wanting

scape *vb syn* ESCAPE 1, abscond, break, ‖bunk, decamp, flee, fly

‖**scape** *n syn* ESCAPE 1, breakout, escapement, escaping, flight, getaway, lam, slip

scape *n syn* VISTA, lookout, outlook, perspective, prospect

---

syn synonym(s) *rel* related word(s)
idiom idiomatic equivalent(s) *con* contrasted word(s)
ant antonym(s) * vulgar
‖ use limited; if in doubt, see a dictionary
The first word in a synonym list when printed in SMALL CAPITALS shows where there is more information about the group. For a more efficient use of this book see Explanatory Notes.

scapegoat *n* one that bears the blame for another or others <was made the *scapegoat* for his boss's errors>
syn fall guy, goat, patsy, whipping boy
rel mark, target; victim

scapegrace *n syn* WASTREL 1, ‖bad lot, good-for-nothing, ne'er-do-well, no-good, profligate, rounder, waster

scar *n* a mark left by the healing of injured tissue <still had *scars* from the operation>
syn cicatrix, scarification
rel blemish, defect, flaw; blister, pockmark, scab; disfigurement

scar *vb* to mark with a scar <burns that had *scarred* his face>
syn cicatrize, scarify
rel cut, score, scratch; blemish, disfigure, flaw, mar; damage, deface

scarce *adj* **1** *syn* SHORT 3, deficient, failing, inadequate, insufficient, scant, scanty, shy, unsufficient, wanting
rel curtailed, shortened, truncated
con adequate, sufficient, unwanting
ant abundant
2 *syn* INFREQUENT, few, occasional, rare, seldom, semioccasional, sporadic, uncommon, unfrequent
idiom scarce as ice water in hell, scarcer than hen's teeth, seldom met with

scarce *adv syn* JUST 2, barely, hardly, scarcely

scarcely *adv syn* JUST 2, barely, hardly, scarce
idiom just barely, only just

scarceness *n syn* SCARCITY, insufficience, insufficiency, paucity, poverty, ‖scant

scarcity *n* smallness of supply, quantity, or number in proportion to demand <a serious *scarcity* of grain>
syn insufficience, insufficiency, paucity, poverty, ‖scant, scarceness; *compare* FAILURE 3
rel deficiency, shortage, underage; meagerness; rareness, uncommonness; absence, dearth, lack
con sufficiency; great deal, much; overabundance, overage, oversupply, surplus
ant abundance

scare *vb syn* FRIGHTEN, affright, alarm, awe, fright, ‖spook, startle, terrify, terrorize
rel panic, shake up; freeze, paralyze, petrify
idiom give a scare to, *scare shitless, strike terror into the heart of, throw a scare into

scarecrow *n syn* RAGAMUFFIN, ragshag, tatterdemalion

scared *adj syn* AFRAID 1, aghast, anxious, ‖ascared, fearful, frightened, scary, terrified
rel startled; panicked, panicky, terror-stricken
con emboldened, heartened, reassured; aggressive, bold
ant unafraid, unscared

scarification *n syn* SCAR, cicatrix

scarify *vb* **1** *syn* SCAR, cicatrize
rel deform, disfigure, maim, mar
2 *syn* LAMBASTE 3, blister, castigate, excoriate, flay, lash (into), scathe, scorch, scourge, slash

scary *adj syn* AFRAID 1, aghast, anxious, ‖ascared, fearful, frightened, scared, terrified

scathe *vb syn* LAMBASTE 3, blister, castigate, excoriate, flay, lash (into), scarify, scorch, scourge, slash
idiom ‖give holy hell, give the business, rip (someone) up one side and down the other

scatheless *n syn* SAFE 1, unharmed, unscathed

scathing *adj syn* CAUSTIC 1, mordacious, mordant, salty, trenchant *rel* brutal; burning, scorching, searing, sulphurous

scatological *adj* *syn* OBSCENE 2, coarse, dirty, filthy, foul, indecent, nasty, raunchy, smutty, vulgar

scatter *vb* **1** to cause to separate or break up <the rain *scattered* the crowd>
syn dispel, disperse, dissipate
rel break up, shatter; disband; diverge, divide, part, separate, sever
con assemble, congregate, convene; accumulate, amass, collect, concentrate, crowd
ant gather
2 *syn* STREW 1, bestrew, broadcast, disject, disseminate, sow, straw
rel dispense, distribute; cast, discard, shed; besprinkle, sprinkle
con accumulate, amass, concentrate
ant collect

scatterbrain *n* a flighty thoughtless person <his wife is a *scatterbrain*>
syn birdbrain, featherbrain, featherhead, flibbertigibbet, harebrain, rattlebrain, rattlehead, shatterbrain
rel fool, goose, silly, simpleton

scatterbrained *adj* *syn* GIDDY 1, bird-witted, dizzy, empty-headed, featherbrained, flighty, frivolous, harebrained, rattlebrained, silly

scattergood *n* *syn* SPENDTHRIFT, high roller, prodigal, profligate, spender, squanderer, unthrift, waster, wastethrift, wastrel

scattering *n* *syn* FEW, handful, smatch, smatter, smattering, spatter, spattering, sprinkling

scene *n* **1** the total arrangement of the objects that form the scenic environment in which a drama is enacted <spectacle plays that attempt a realistic, three-dimensional *scene*>
syn mise-en-scène, scenery, set, setting, stage set, stage setting
rel hangings, scene cloth; ‖back cloth, backdrop, background; tableau
2 *syn* VIEW 4, outlook, sight
3 the place of an occurrence or action <the *scene* of the crime>
syn locale, mise-en-scène, site
rel locality, location, place, spot
4 a sphere of activity, interest, or controversy <the drug *scene*>
syn arena
rel compass, field, setting, sphere; culture, environment, milieu

scenery *n* *syn* SCENE 1, mise-en-scène, set, setting, stage set, stage setting
rel decor; furnishings, furniture; properties, props

scent *vb* **1** *syn* SMELL 1, nose, sniff, ‖snift, snuff
2 to imbue or fill with an odor <air *scented* with herbs>
syn aromatize, odorize, perfume

scent *n* **1** *syn* SMELL 1, aroma, odor
rel essence, whiff
2 *syn* FRAGRANCE, aroma, balm, bouquet, incense, perfume, redolence, spice

scented *adj* **1** *syn* SWEET 2, ambrosial, aromal, aromatic, fragrant, perfumed, perfumy, redolent, savory, spicy
2 *syn* ODOROUS, odiferous, odoriferous
ant scentless, unscented

scentless *adj* *syn* ODORLESS, inodorous, smell-less

schedule *n* **1** *syn* LIST, catalog, register, roll, roll call, roster
rel chart, table
2 *syn* PROGRAM 1, agenda, calendar, card, docket, programma, sked, timetable

schedule *vb* **1** to place in a schedule <*schedule* a new train>
syn card, sked
rel list, record, slate
2 *syn* TIME 1, book

scheme *n* **1** *syn* PLAN 1, blueprint, design, game plan, project, strategy
rel presentation, proposal, proposition, suggestion; arrangement, order, ordering; contrivance, device, expedient
2 *syn* PLOT 2, cabal, conspiracy, covin, intrigue, machination, practice

scheme (out) *vb* *syn* PLOT, cogitate, ‖collogue, collude, connive, conspire, contrive, devise, intrigue, machinate

schism *n* **1** *syn* BREACH 3, break, fissure, fracture, rent, rift, rupture, split
2 *syn* HERESY, dissent, dissidence, heterodoxy, misbelief, nonconformism, nonconformity, unorthodoxy
3 a division of a group into two discordant groups <a *schism* within a political party>
syn chasm, cleavage, cleft, split; *compare* BREACH 3
rel divergence, division, separation; breach, break, rupture; estrangement
con unification, unity; reconciliation

schismatic *n* *syn* HERETIC, dissenter, dissident, misbeliever, nonconformist, schismatist, sectary, separatist
rel protester; skeptic; radical, Young Turk

schismatic *adj* *syn* HERETICAL, dissident, heterodox, nonconformist, sectarian, unorthodox
rel rebellious; unconventional

schismatist *n* *syn* HERETIC, dissenter, dissident, misbeliever, nonconformist, schismatic, sectary, separatist

‖**schlemiel** *n* *syn* FOOL 3, chump, dupe, fall guy, gull, mark, pigeon, sap, saphead, sucker

‖**schmo** *n* *syn* FOOL 1, ass, *damfool, idiot, jackass, jerk, nincompoop, ninny, ‖schmuck, tomfool

‖**schmuck** *n* *syn* FOOL 1, ass, *damfool, idiot, jackass, jerk, nincompoop, ninny, ‖schmo, tomfool

‖**schnook** *n* *syn* DUNCE, chowderhead, chucklehead, dope, ‖dumbhead, dunderhead, lame-brain, noddy, noodle, ‖stupe

‖**schnorrer** *n* *syn* BEGGAR 1, bummer, cadger, moocher, panhandler

‖**schnozzle** *n* *syn* NOSE 1, beak, ‖beezer, pecker, proboscis, smeller, ‖sneezer, ‖snitch, snoot, snout

scholar *n* *syn* SAGE, savant, wise man
rel pupil, student; bookman; polymath

---

syn synonym(s) — *rel* related word(s)
idiom idiomatic equivalent(s) — *con* contrasted word(s)
ant antonym(s) — * vulgar
‖ use limited; if in doubt, see a dictionary
The first word in a synonym list when printed in SMALL CAPITALS shows where there is more information about the group. For a more efficient use of this book see Explanatory Notes.

scholarliness *n* ***syn*** ERUDITION 2, eruditeness, learnedness, scholarship
ant unscholarliness

scholarly *adj* ***syn*** LEARNED, erudite, scholastic
rel studious; intellectual, long-hair; educated, taught, trained
con untaught, untrained
ant unscholarly

scholarship *n* **1** ***syn*** EDUCATION 2, erudition, knowledge, learning, science
2 ***syn*** ERUDITION 2, eruditeness, learnedness, scholarliness

scholastic *adj* **1** ***syn*** PEDANTIC, academic, bookish, book-learned, booky, quodlibetic
rel lettered, literary; scholarly; formal
2 ***syn*** LEARNED, erudite, scholarly
rel conversant, versed
con unconversant, unscholarly

school *vb* ***syn*** TEACH, discipline, educate, instruct, train
rel inform; guide, lead, show; advance, cultivate; control, direct, manage

schooling *n* ***syn*** EDUCATION 1, instruction, teaching, training, tuition, tutelage
rel knowledge; book learning, booklore

schoolmasterish *adj* ***syn*** DIDACTIC, moral, moralizing, preachy, sermonic, sermonizing, teachy

science *n* **1** ***syn*** KNOWLEDGE 2, information, lore, wisdom
2 ***syn*** EDUCATION 2, erudition, knowledge, learning, scholarship

scilicet *adv* ***syn*** NAMELY, to wit, videlicet

scintillate *vb* ***syn*** FLASH 1, glance, gleam, glimmer, glint, glisten, glitter, shimmer, sparkle, twinkle

scintillating *adj* ***syn*** CLEVER 5, good, smart, sprightly

scintillation *n* ***syn*** FLASH 1, coruscation, glance, glimmer, glint, glisten, glitter, shimmer, sparkle, twinkle

scions *n pl* ***syn*** OFFSPRING, ‖begats, brood, children, descendants, issue, posterity, progeniture, progeny, seed

scoff *vb* to show contempt by derision or mockery <heard his tale and *scoffed* at it>
syn fleer, flout, gibe, gird, jeer, jest, quip (at), scout (at), sneer
rel pooh-pooh; deride, mock, rally, ridicule, taunt, twit; contemn, despise, disdain, scorn; boo
con accept, approve, commend; compliment; acclaim, laud, praise

scoff *n* ***syn*** FOOD 1, ‖chow, comestibles, ‖eats, edibles, feed, foodstuff, grub, provisions, victuals

scold *n* ***syn*** VIRAGO, amazon, fishwife, harpy, ogress, shrew, termagant, vixen, Xanthippe

scold *vb* **1** to reproach angrily and abusively <loudly *scolded* him for staying out late>
syn baste, bawl out, berate, ‖bless out, ‖cample, ‖carpet, ‖chew, ‖chew out, dress down, jaw, lash, ‖mob, rag, rail, rant, rate, ‖ream out, revile, ‖row, tell off, tongue, tongue-lash, ‖tongue-walk, upbraid, vituperate, wig; *compare* CRITICIZE, LAMBASTE 3, REPROVE
rel blame, censure, criticize, denounce, reprehend, reprobate; admonish, chide, rebuke, reprimand, reproach, reprove; execrate, objurate; brace, grill, harass, hound; blister, excoriate
idiom jump down one's throat, rake over the coals, read one the riot act, walk into
2 ***syn*** GRUMBLE 1, croak, grouch, grouse, ‖grunt, murmur, mutter

sconce *n* ***syn*** HEAD 1, ‖bean, ‖belfry, ‖chump, ‖coco, ‖conk, ‖dome, noggin, noodle, poll

scoop *n* a news story first obtained and reported by only one source (as a newspaper) <the story was a *scoop* by just a few hours>
syn beat, exclusive

scoop *vb* **1** ***syn*** DIP 2, bail, lade, ladle
rel gather; lift, pick up
2 ***syn*** DIG 2, dig out, excavate, shovel, spade
rel gouge, grub
3 to report a news item in advance of competitors <CBS *scooped* NBC on that story>
syn beat

scoot *vb* **1** ***syn*** HURRY 2, barrel, beeline, bustle, fleet, hasten, highball, hustle, rush, zip
2 ***syn*** RUN 1, dash, scamper, scurry, shin, sprint
3 ***syn*** RUN 2, bolt, flee, fly, make off, scamper, ‖screw, skedaddle, skip, skirr

scope *n* **1** ***syn*** ROOM 3, elbowroom, latitude, leeway, margin, play
2 ***syn*** RANGE 2, ambit, compass, extension, extent, orbit, purview, radius, reach, sweep
3 ***syn*** BREADTH 2, amplitude, comprehensiveness, fullness, wideness

scopic *adj* ***syn*** EXTENSIVE 1, broad, expansive, extended, scopious, wide

scopious *adj* ***syn*** EXTENSIVE 1, broad, expansive, extended, scopic, wide

scorch *vb* **1** ***syn*** LAMBASTE 3, blister, castigate, excoriate, flay, lash (into), scarify, scathe, scourge, slash
2 ***syn*** BURN 3, bake, broil, cook, melt, roast, swelter
rel seethe, simmer, stew; ‖plot

scorching *adj* ***syn*** HOT 1, baking, broiling, burning, fiery, red-hot, scalding, sizzling, torrid, white-hot
idiom scorching hot, sizzling hot

score *n* **1 scores** *pl* ***syn*** MULTITUDE 1, army, cloud, crowd, flock, host, legion, rout
2 a slight cut or line made with or as if with a sharp instrument <cut *scores* on the ham before baking it>
syn scotch, scratch
rel line, mark; nick, notch, serration; cut, slit; cleft, furrow, groove, indentation; gash
3 ***syn*** BILL 1, account, invoice, reckoning, statement, tab
4 an obligation or injury kept in mind for future reckoning <had a *score* to settle with him>
syn account
rel grudge
5 the number of points gained by contestants in a game or contest <a record *score* of 263 for 72 holes>
syn tally
rel account, record; summary, total

---

syn synonym(s) ***rel*** related word(s)
idiom idiomatic equivalent(s) ***con*** contrasted word(s)
ant antonym(s) * vulgar
‖ use limited; if in doubt, see a dictionary
The first word in a synonym list when printed in SMALL CAPITALS shows where there is more information about the group. For a more efficient use of this book see Explanatory Notes.

idiom the final count
score *vb* **1** *syn* LAMBASTE 3, castigate, excoriate, flay, lash (into), scarify, scathe, scorch, scourge, slash
rel ream out
idiom tear to pieces
2 *syn* GAIN 1, accomplish, achieve, attain, rack up, reach, realize, win
3 *syn* SUCCEED 3, arrive, flourish, go, make out, prosper, thrive
scorn *n syn* DESPITE 1, contempt, despisal, despisement, disdain, disparagement
rel flouting, gibing, jeering, scoffing; derision, mockery, ridicule, taunt, taunting
con consideration, respectfulness
ant respect
scorn *vb syn* DESPISE, abhor, contemn, disdain, look down, scout
rel flout, gibe, jeer, scoff; mock, ridicule, taunt
idiom hold in utter contempt
con accept, acknowledge, welcome
ant respect
scotch *n syn* SCORE 2, scratch
Scotch *adj syn* SPARING, canny, chary, economical, frugal, saving, stewardly, thrifty, unwasteful, wary
scoundrel *n syn* VILLAIN 1, *bastard, blackguard, heel, knave, lowlife, miscreant, rascal, rogue, *son of a bitch
scour *vb* **1** *syn* HURRY 2, beeline, bullet, fleet, flit, fly, highball, rocket, smoke, speed
2 to make a thorough search or examination of <*scoured* the neighborhood for the lost child>
syn beat, comb, finecomb, fine-tooth-comb, forage, grub, rake, ransack, rummage, search
rel rout; look (for), seek; fan, range; rifle; ferret (out), find
idiom beat the bushes, leave no stone unturned, look high and low, look up and down, turn inside out, turn upside down
scour *vb* **1** *syn* SCRUB 1
2 *syn* EAT 3, bite, corrode, eat away, erode, gnaw, wear away
scour *n, usu* **scours** *pl syn* DIARRHEA, ‖backdoor trots, dysentery, flux, ‖runs, *shits, ‖squirts, *trots
scourge *n syn* PLAGUE 1, curse, pestilence
scourge *vb* **1** *syn* WHIP 1, flagellate, flog, hide, lash, lather, stripe, thrash, ‖wear out, whale
rel hit; knout; frail, whop
idiom whip to ribbons
2 *syn* RAVAGE, depredate, desecrate, desolate, despoil, devastate, pillage, sack, spoliate, waste
3 *syn* LAMBASTE 3, blister, castigate, excoriate, flay, lash (into), scarify, scathe, scorch, slash
scout *vb* to explore in order to obtain information <forward observers *scouted* the terrain before the attack>
syn probe, reconnoiter
rel look (over), survey; observe; check out, examine; ‖case, inspect
idiom run reconnaissance
scout *vb* **1** *syn* RIDICULE, deride, lout, mock, quiz, rally, razz, taunt, twit
2 *syn* DESPISE, abhor, contemn, disdain, look down, scorn
rel mock, ridicule
scout (at) *vb syn* SCOFF, fleer, flout, gibe, gird, jeer, jest, quip (at), sneer
scowl *vb syn* FROWN 1, gloom, glower, lower
idiom look black as thunder, pull a face (*or* scowl)
scrabble *vb* **1** *syn* SCRIBBLE, scratch, scrawl, squiggle
2 *syn* SCRAMBLE 1, clamber, ‖spartle, ‖sprauchle
scrag *vb* **1** *syn* HANG 2, gibbet, noose, string (up), turn off
2 *syn* KILL 1, carry off, cut off, destroy, dispatch, finish, lay low, put away, slay, take off
3 *syn* MURDER 1, assassinate, ‖bump off, cool, do in, ‖dust off, execute, finish, knock off, liquidate
scraggy *adj* **1** *syn* ROUGH 1, asperous, craggy, harsh, jagged, rugged, scabrous, uneven, unlevel, unsmooth
2 *syn* LEAN, angular, bony, gaunt, lank, lanky, rawboned, scrawny, skinny, spare
rel gangling, spindling, spindly; skeletal; dwarfed, scrubby, stunted, undersize
scram *vb syn* GET OUT 1, begone, clear out, decamp, hightail, kite, skedaddle, skiddoo, take off, ‖vamoose
idiom ‖beat it, ‖cheese it, ‖get the hell out
scramble *vb* **1** to move or climb hastily on all fours <*scrambled* across the rocks>
syn clamber, scrabble, ‖spartle, ‖sprauchle
rel scurry, scuttle
2 *syn* SPRAWL 2, ramble, sprangle, spread-eagle, straddle, straggle
scramble *n syn* CLUTTER 2, hash, jumble, jungle, litter, mishmash, muddle, rummage, shuffle, tumble
rel conglomeration
scrap *n* **1** *syn* END 4, bit, fragment
rel chip, cutting; scrappage, waste
2 *syn* PARTICLE, bit, crumb, jot, shred, smitch, speck, tittle, whit, whoop
scrap *vb syn* DISCARD, cashier, cast, jettison, junk, reject, shed, slough, throw away, throw out
idiom consign to the scrap heap
scrap *n syn* BRAWL 2, affray, bobbery, broil, fight, fracas, fray, row, scuffle, set-to
scrap *vb syn* QUARREL, bicker, brabble, caterwaul, fall out, row, spat, squabble, tiff, wrangle
scrape *vb* **1** to rub or slide against something that is often harsh, rough, or sharp <chalk *scraping* on the blackboard>
syn grate, rasp, scratch
rel graze, rub, scuff; abrade, chafe, grind
2 *syn* SCRIMP, pinch, screw, skimp, ‖skinch, spare, stint
3 to make one's way with great difficulty or succeed by a narrow margin <the student barely *scraped* through the exam>
syn shave
rel struggle; get along, get by
idiom cut it (*or* the corner) pretty close, have a close shave

---

syn synonym(s) | *rel* related word(s)
idiom idiomatic equivalent(s) | *con* contrasted word(s)
ant antonym(s) | * vulgar
‖ use limited; if in doubt, see a dictionary
The first word in a synonym list when printed in SMALL CAPITALS shows where there is more information about the group. For a more efficient use of this book see Explanatory Notes.

scrape *n* ***syn*** PREDICAMENT, box, corner, dilemma, fix, hole, jam, pickle, plight, spot
rel trouble; discomfiture, embarrassment

scrapping *n* ***syn*** DISPOSAL 2, discarding, disposition, dumping, jettison, junking, relegation, riddance, throwing away

scrappy *adj* **1** ***syn*** QUARRELSOME 2, battlesome, brawling, brawlsome, brawly
2 ***syn*** BELLIGERENT, bellicose, combative, contentious, militant, pugnacious, quarrelsome, ‖ructious, truculent, warlike

scratch *vb* **1** ***syn*** SCRAPE 1, grate, rasp
rel squeak, squeal
2 ***syn*** SCRIBBLE, scrabble, scrawl, squiggle

scratch *n* **1** ***syn*** SCORE 2, scotch
‖**2** ***syn*** MONEY, ‖bread, cash, ‖chips, ‖coin, dough, ‖greenbacks, ‖jack, ‖mazuma, ‖wampum

scrawl *vb* ***syn*** SCRIBBLE, scrabble, scratch, squiggle
rel inscribe; doodle

scrawny *adj* ***syn*** LEAN, angular, bony, gaunt, lank, lanky, rawboned, scraggy, skinny, spare
idiom just (*or* nothing but) skin and bones
ant brawny

screak *vb* ***syn*** SQUEAL 2, scream, screech, shriek

scream *vb* **1** to voice a sudden piercing loud cry often in shock, terror, or pain <*screamed* at the sight of the accident and then fainted>
syn screech, shriek, shrill, squeal; *compare* SHOUT 1
rel screak, squeak; cry, yell; bellow, roar; caterwaul, howl, wail, ‖yawl
idiom let out a scream (*or* shriek *or* screech)
2 ***syn*** SQUEAL 2, screak, screech, shriek
3 ***syn*** YELL 2, howl, squeal, yip, yowl
rel complain, grumble, protest; blare
idiom raise a howl
4 to produce a vivid, blatant, or startling effect <clothes and furnishings that *screamed* nouveau riche>
syn blare, shout, shriek

scream *n* ***syn*** RIOT 2, howl, ‖panic, sidesplitter

screech *vb* **1** ***syn*** SCREAM 1, shriek, shrill, squeal
rel penetrate, pierce; vent, voice
2 ***syn*** SQUEAL 2, screak, scream, shriek

screen *vb* **1** ***syn*** DEFEND 1, bulwark, cover, fend, guard, protect, safeguard, secure, shield
2 ***syn*** SHADE, inumbrate, shadow, umbrage
3 to cut off from view by interposing something resembling a screen <*screen* a view with a tall hedge>
syn block out, close, obstruct, shroud, shut off, shut out
rel conceal, hide; separate, wall off; protect, seclude; embosk
idiom throw up a screen
con bare, disclose, expose, open, reveal

syn synonym(s)	***rel*** related word(s)
idiom idiomatic equivalent(s)	***con*** contrasted word(s)
ant antonym(s)	* vulgar

‖ use limited; if in doubt, see a dictionary
The first word in a synonym list when printed in SMALL CAPITALS shows where there is more information about the group. For a more efficient use of this book see Explanatory Notes.

4 ***syn*** HIDE, bury, ‖bush up, cache, conceal, cover, ‖ditch, ensconce, secrete, stash
rel defend, guard, protect, safeguard, shield; camouflage, cloak, cover up, disguise
5 to examine carefully and methodically in order to separate, select, or eliminate <the personnel department *screened* seventy candidates for ten jobs>
syn sieve, sift; *compare* SORT 2
rel choose, pick out, select; extract, filter (out), riddle, sort (out), winnow (out)
6 ***syn*** CENSOR, blip, bowdlerize, expurgate

‖**screeve** *vb* ***syn*** EXUDE, bleed, ooze, seep, ‖sew, ‖sicker, strain, sweat, transude, weep

‖**screw** *n* ***syn*** SHAFT 3, ‖screwing

screw *vb* **1** ***syn*** CRUMPLE 1, crimp, crimple, crinkle, rimple, ruck (up), ‖ruckle, rumple, scrunch, wrinkle
2 ***syn*** EXTORT 1, exact, gouge, pinch, shake down, squeeze, wrench, wrest, wring
‖**3** ***syn*** CHEAT, beat, bilk, chisel, cozen, defraud, diddle, do, gyp, ream
4 ***syn*** SCRIMP, pinch, scrape, skimp, ‖skinch, spare, stint
‖**5** ***syn*** RUN 2, bolt, flee, fly, make off, scamper, scoot, skedaddle, skip, skirr

‖**screw** (up) *vb* ***syn*** BOTCH, bitch (up), ‖blow, bobble, bungle, flub, goof (up), louse up, mess, muff
rel confuse, muddle, snafu; spoil

screwball *n* ***syn*** CRACKPOT, crackbrain, crank, cuckoo, ding-a-ling, harebrain, kook, lunatic, nut

‖**screwing** *n* ***syn*** SHAFT 3, ‖screw

screwy *adj* ‖**1** ***syn*** INTOXICATED 1, ‖boozy, ‖canned, disguised, drunk, inebriated, ‖lushed, muddled, pixilated, ‖plastered
2 ***syn*** INSANE 1, ‖batty, cracked, daft, lunatic, mad, nuts, unbalanced, unsound, wacky
idiom having a screw loose

scribble *vb* to write or draw hastily or roughly <*scribbled* a quick note to her on his way out>
syn scrabble, scratch, scrawl, squiggle
rel jot (down); scribe, write

scribe *vb* ***syn*** WRITE, engross, indite, inscribe

scrimmage *n* **1** ***syn*** CLASH 2, affray, brush, fray, melee, mellay, skirmish
rel scuffle; fight; free-for-all
2 ***syn*** BRAWL 2, affray, broil, donnybrook, fight, fracas, fray, free-for-all, scuffle, set-to

scrimp *adj* ***syn*** MEAGER 2, exiguous, poor, scant, scanty, scrimpy, skimp, skimpy, spare, sparse

scrimp *vb* to be extremely frugal and parsimonious in an effort to economize <*scrimped* all year to buy that fur coat>
syn pinch, scrape, screw, skimp, ‖skinch, spare, stint; *compare* SPARE 3
rel scamp; scratch; save (up)
idiom pinch pennies

‖**scrimption** *n* ***syn*** PITTANCE, dribble, driblet

scrimpy *adj* **1** ***syn*** MEAGER 2, exiguous, poor, scant, scanty, scrimp, skimp, skimpy, spare, sparse
2 ***syn*** SHORT 3, deficient, failing, inadequate, insufficient, scant, scanty, scarce, shy, wanting
3 ***syn*** STINGY, cheeseparing, ‖chinchy, close, mean, ‖narrow, niggardly, penny-pinching, save-all, scrimy

scrimy *adj* ***syn*** STINGY, cheeseparing, ||chinchy, mean, miserly, narrow-fisted, niggardly, penny-pinching, ||scant, scrimpy

script *n* ***syn*** HANDWRITING, calligraphy, chirography, ductus, fist, hand, penmanship

Scripture *n* ***syn*** BIBLE, Book, Holy Writ, Sacred Writ

scrooch (down) *vb* ***syn*** CROUCH, ||crooch, huddle, hunch

scrooge *n* ***syn*** MISER, cheapskate, chuff, hunks, money-grubber, muckworm, nabal, niggard, skinflint, tightwad

scrub *n* ***syn*** INFERIOR, poor relation, secondary, subaltern, subordinate, underling, understrapper

scrub *vb* **1** to clean by abrasive action <*scrubbed* the pots and pans>
syn scour
rel brush; rub; cleanse, wash; buff, polish
2 ***syn*** CANCEL 2, call off, drop

scrubby *adj* ***syn*** SHABBY 1, bedraggled, broken-down, dingy, down-at-heel, faded, run-down, scruffy, seedy, tacky

scruffy *adj* ***syn*** SHABBY 1, down-at-heel, moth-eaten, run-down, scrubby, seedy, tacky, tagrag, tattered, threadbare

scrumptious *adj* ***syn*** DELIGHTFUL, adorable, ambrosial, darling, delectable, delicious, heavenly, luscious, lush, yummy

scrunch *vb* **1** ***syn*** CHEW 1, champ, ||chaw, chomp, ||chonk, chump, crunch, masticate, munch, ruminate
2 ***syn*** CRUMPLE 1, crimp, crimple, crinkle, rimple, ruck (up), ||ruckle, rumple, screw, wrinkle

||**scrunty** *adj* ***syn*** STUNTED, runted, runtish, runty, ||stunt

scruple *n* ***syn*** PARTICLE, atom, bit, fragment, grain, iota, jot, modicum, scrap, shred

scruple *n* ***syn*** QUALM, compunction, conscience, demur, squeam
rel faltering, hesitancy, hesitation, pause; reconsideration, second thought

scruple *vb* ***syn*** DEMUR, balk, boggle, gag, jib, shy, stick, stickle, strain, stumble
rel question; fret, worry

scrupulous *adj* **1** ***syn*** UPRIGHT 2, conscientious, honest, honorable, just, right, true
rel fair-minded; strict; upstanding
con questionable; shifty, slippery; dishonorable, unprincipled; dishonest
ant unscrupulous
2 ***syn*** CAREFUL 2, conscientious, conscionable, exact, fussy, heedful, meticulous, painstaking, punctilious, punctual
rel critical, fastidious
con careless; undiscriminating, unparticular
ant remiss

scrutinize *vb* **1** to look at or over critically and searchingly <the jeweler *scrutinized* the diamonds to see if they were fakes>
syn canvass, ||case, check over, check up, con, examine, inspect, perlustrate, study, survey, vet, view
rel look over, overlook, peruse, pore (over), scan; consider, contemplate, weigh; penetrate, pierce, probe; analyze, dig (into), dissect; comb
idiom turn a careful (*or* heedful) eye to (*or* on)
2 ***syn*** EYE 2, eyeball, watch

scrutiny *n* **1** ***syn*** EXAMINATION, analysis, audit, check-over, inspection, perlustration, review, scan, survey, view
rel look-in, lookover, look-see
2 ***syn*** EYE 3, eagle eye, surveillance, tab, watch

scud *vb* ***syn*** FLY 1, dart, float, sail, shoot, skim, skirr

scuddle *vb* ***syn*** SCUTTLE, scurry, scutter

scuff *vb* ***syn*** SHUFFLE 3, scuffle, shamble, ||shool, shovel

scuffle *vb* **1** ***syn*** WRESTLE, grapple, tussle, ||wraxle
rel cuff, scuff
2 ***syn*** SHUFFLE 3, scuff, shamble, ||shool, shovel

scuffle *n* ***syn*** BRAWL 2, affray, bobbery, broil, fight, fracas, fray, row, scrap, set-to

||**sculch** *n* ***syn*** REFUSE, debris, ||dust, garbage, junk, litter, spilth, sweepings, trash, waste

sculp *vb* ***syn*** SCULPTURE, carve, chisel, sculpt

sculpt *vb* ***syn*** SCULPTURE, carve, chisel, sculp

sculpture *vb* to form an image or representation from solid material (as wood or stone) <*sculptured* a colossal statue of a horse>
syn carve, chisel, sculp, sculpt
rel cast, form; model, mold, shape

scum *n* **1** ***syn*** RABBLE 2, canaille, dreg(s), mass(es), mob, proletariat, ragtag and bobtail, riffraff, trash, unwashed
idiom scum of the earth
2 ***syn*** SNOT 1, cur, ||prick, *shit, *shithead, skunk, snake, stinker, toad, *turd

scummy *adj* ***syn*** CONTEMPTIBLE, beggarly, cheap, despicable, despisable, mean, pitiable, scurvy, shabby, sorry

scurf *n* ***syn*** RABBLE 2, canaille, hoi polloi, mass(es), mob, other half, proletariat, riffraff, scum, trash

scurrile *adj* ***syn*** ABUSIVE, contumelious, invective, opprobrious, scurrilous, truculent, vituperative, vituperatory, vituperous

scurrility *n* ***syn*** ABUSE, billingsgate, contumely, invective, obloquy, vituperation
rel scurrilousness; maligning, traducing, vilification

scurrilous *adj* **1** ***syn*** ABUSIVE, contumelious, invective, opprobrious, scurrile, truculent, vituperative, vituperatory, vituperous
rel coarse, gross; filthy, foul; insulting, offending, offensive, outrageous, outraging
2 ***syn*** OBSCENE 2, coarse, dirty, filthy, foul, indecent, nasty, raunchy, smutty, vulgar

scurry *vb* **1** ***syn*** SCUTTLE, scuddle, scutter
2 ***syn*** RUN 1, dash, scamper, scoot, shin, sprint
rel shoot, tear; dart, fly; scuffle, skelter

scurvy *adj* ***syn*** CONTEMPTIBLE, beggarly, cheap, despicable, despisable, mean, pitiable, scummy, shabby, sorry
rel base, low, vile

scutter *vb* ***syn*** SCUTTLE, scuddle, scurry

---

rel hasten, hurry, run, speed

scuttle *vb* to move with or as if with short rapidly alternating steps <armies of fiddler crabs *scuttled* across the road>
syn scuddle, scurry, scutter; *compare* RUN 1
rel scoot; scramble; scud

scuttlebutt *n* *syn* REPORT 1, buzz, cry, gossip, grapevine, hearsay, on-dit, rumble, rumor, talk

sea *n* *syn* OCEAN, blue, brine, ‖briny, deep, drink, main

sea dog *n* *syn* PIRATE, buccaneer, corsair, freebooter, picaroon, rover, sea robber, sea rover, sea wolf

seal *n* an adhesive-backed device bearing a symbolic, pictorial, or official design <the *seal* on a diploma>
syn stamp, sticker

seam *n* *syn* JOINT 1, connection, coupling, joining, junction, juncture, union
rel bond

seaman *n* *syn* MARINER, jack, jack-tar, sailor, sailorman, salt, tar, tarpaulin

sear *vb* **1** *syn* DRY 1, dehydrate, desiccate, exsiccate, parch
2 to burn or scorch with a sudden application of intense heat <*seared* the steaks in the broiler>
syn sizzle
rel scorch, shrivel, parch; burn (up)

search *vb* **1** *syn* SCOUR 2, beat, comb, finecomb, fine-tooth-comb, forage, grub, rake, ransack, rummage
rel run down, scout (around), scrimmage, skirmish
idiom search high and low
2 to subject (a person) to a thorough check for concealed or contraband articles <police *searching* the suspects for weapons>
syn ‖fan, frisk, shake down
rel check, examine; inspect, look over, scan, scrutinize, study

search (for *or* out) *vb* *syn* SEEK 1, cast about, ferret out, hunt, quest
rel pry (out), scout (out)

search *n* *syn* PURSUIT 2, pursual, pursuance, pursuing, quest, seeking

searchingly *adv* *syn* HARD 4, closely, intently, sharply

sea robber *n* *syn* PIRATE, buccaneer, corsair, freebooter, picaroon, rover, sea dog, sea rover, sea wolf

sea rover *n* *syn* PIRATE, buccaneer, corsair, freebooter, picaroon, rover, sea dog, sea robber, sea wolf

season *n* a particular period of the year <the Christmas *season*>
syn time
rel period, term

season *vb* *syn* HARDEN 2, acclimate, acclimatize, climatize, toughen
rel discipline, school, train; fit, prepare; case harden, steel

syn synonym(s) *rel* related word(s)
idiom idiomatic equivalent(s) *con* contrasted word(s)
ant antonym(s) * vulgar
‖ use limited; if in doubt, see a dictionary
The first word in a synonym list when printed in SMALL CAPITALS shows where there is more information about the group. For a more efficient use of this book see Explanatory Notes.

seasonable *adj* *syn* TIMELY 1, auspicious, favorable, opportune, propitious, prosperous, timeous, well-timed
rel apropos, pertinent, relevant; appropriate, apt; convenient
con irrelevant; inappropriate, inapt; ill-timed, inconvenient, inopportune
ant unseasonable

seasonably *adv* *syn* EARLY 1, betimes, soon, timely
ant unseasonably

seasoned *adj* *syn* EXPERIENCED, old, old-time, practical, practiced, skilled, versed, vet, veteran
rel acclimated, acclimatized, hardened, toughened; case-hardened, steeled
con inexperienced, unpracticed, unskilled, unversed; unacclimated, unacclimatized, unsteeled, untempered, untried
ant unseasoned

seat *n* **1** *syn* BUTTOCKS, backside, beam, behind, bottom, ‖can, derriere, ‖duff, fundament, posterior
2 *syn* CENTER 2, focal point, focus, heart, hub, nerve center, polestar
rel fulcrum
3 *syn* BASE 1, basement, basis, bed, bottom, footing, foundation, groundwork, rest, seating

seat *vb* to cause to be seated <an usher *seated* her in the third row>
syn sit
rel establish, place, put

seating *n* *syn* BASE 1, bedrock, ground, infrastructure, seat, substratum, substruction, substructure, underpinning, understructure

sea wolf *n* *syn* PIRATE, buccaneer, corsair, freebooter, picaroon, rover, sea dog, sea robber, sea rover

seclude *vb* to remove or separate (oneself or another) from external influences <in the convent she was *secluded* from secular life>
syn cloister, sequester
rel retire, separate, withdraw; closet, confine, enclose, immure, isolate; screen, shut off

secluded *adj* disposed to, living in, or characterized by seclusion <*secluded* monks> <they enjoyed *secluded* country living>
syn cloistered, hermetic, recluse, secluse, seclusive, sequestered
rel retired, withdrawn; close, hidden, private, screened, shy; alone, isolated, solitary
con communal, public

secluse *adj* *syn* SECLUDED, cloistered, hermetic, recluse, seclusive, sequestered

seclusion *n* the act or condition of secluding or of being secluded <the queen went into *seclusion* when her husband died>
syn reclusion, retirement, sequestration; *compare* SOLITUDE
rel detachment, separation, withdrawal; reclusiveness, seclusiveness; privacy, privateness; aloneness, isolation, separateness, solitude

seclusive *adj* *syn* SECLUDED, cloistered, hermetic, recluse, secluse, sequestered

second *n* *syn* INSTANT 1, flash, jiffy, minute, moment, split second, ‖tick, trice, twinkling, wink
idiom the flash of an eyelid

secondary *adj* **1** *syn* SUBORDINATE, collateral, dependent, sub, subject, tributary, under

rel accessory, subservient
con major, prime; first, first-ranking, first-string
ant primary
2 formed from something original, primary, or basic <a *secondary* historical analysis based on original archives>
syn derivate, derivational, derivative, derived
rel borrowed, secondhand; consequent, resultant, subsequent
con basic, principle; first, firsthand, original, uncopied, underived
ant primary
3 ***syn*** MINOR 2, dinky, insignificant, lesser, minor-league, small, small-fry, small-time

secondary *n* ***syn*** INFERIOR, poor relation, scrub, subaltern, subordinate, underling, understrapper
rel second fiddle, second-in-command

second childhood *n* ***syn*** DOTAGE, senility

second–class *adj* ***syn*** INFERIOR 2, common, déclassé, hack, low-grade, mean, poor, second-drawer, second-rate

second–drawer *adj* ***syn*** INFERIOR 2, common, déclassé, hack, low-grade, mean, poor, second-class, second-rate

second–rate *adj* ***syn*** INFERIOR 2, common, déclassé, hack, low-grade, mean, poor, second-class, second-drawer
ant first-rate

secours *n* ***syn*** HELP 1, aid, assist, assistance, comfort, hand, lift, relief, succor, support

secrecy *n* the practice or policy of keeping secrets or maintaining concealment <*secrecy* is an inherent feature of intelligence operations>
syn hugger-mugger, hugger-muggery, hush, hush-hush, secretiveness, secretness, silence
rel clandestineness, covertness, furtiveness; concealment, stealth, subterfuge; censorship, suppression
ant openness

secret *adj* **1** existing or done in such a way as to maintain concealment <was involved in *secret* negotiations with the enemy>
syn clandestine, covert, furtive, hole-and-corner, hugger-mugger, hush-hush, mystical, sneak, stealthy, sub-rosa, surreptitious, undercover, ||underneath, under-the-table; *compare* STEALTHY 2, UNDERHAND
rel underhand, underhanded; unacknowledged, unavowed, undeclared; concealed, hidden, screened; classified, confidential, ||eyes-only, restricted, top-secret
con acknowledged, avowed, declared, revealed; aboveboard, straightforward, unconcealed; declassified, unclassified, unrestricted; clear, evident, manifest, obvious, patent, plain
ant open, public
2 ***syn*** OBSCURE 2, devious, lonesome, out-of-the-way, remote, removed, retired
3 ***syn*** RECONDITE, abstruse, acroamatic, deep, esoteric, heavy, hermetic, occult, orphic, profound

secret *n* **secrets** *pl* ***syn*** GENITALIA, genitals, parts, private parts, privates, privities, privy parts, pudendum (*usu* pudenda *pl*)

secretaire *n* ***syn*** DESK, escritoire, secretary, writing desk

secretary *n* ***syn*** DESK, escritoire, secretaire, writing desk

secrete *vb* ***syn*** HIDE, bury, ||bush up, cache, conceal, cover, ensconce, plant, screen, stash
rel deposit; withhold

secretiveness *n* ***syn*** SECRECY, hugger-mugger, hugger-muggery, hush, hush-hush, secretness, silence

secretly *adv* in a secret manner <negotiated *secretly* with both sides>
syn by stealth, clandestinely, covertly, furtively, hugger-mugger, in camera, privately, stealthily, sub rosa, surreptitiously
rel confidentially; privatim, privily
idiom behind closed doors, on the qt, on the quiet, under the rose, under the table
con forthrightly, plainly, publicly; manifestly, overtly
ant openly

secretness *n* ***syn*** SECRECY, hugger-mugger, hugger-muggery, hush, hush-hush, secretiveness, silence

sect *n* ***syn*** RELIGION 2, church, communion, connection, creed, cult, denomination, faith, persuasion

sectarian *adj* **1** ***syn*** HERETICAL, dissident, heterodox, nonconformist, schismatic, unorthodox
rel splinter
con unified, united
ant nonsectarian
2 ***syn*** INSULAR, local, ||parish-pump, parochial, provincial, small-town

sectary *n* **1** ***syn*** HERETIC, dissenter, dissident, misbeliever, nonconformist, schismatic, schismatist, separatist
rel beatnik, Bohemian, hippie; maverick; liberal, radical, Young Turk; rebel, revolutionary
con advocate, conformist, follower
2 ***syn*** FOLLOWER, adherent, cohort, disciple, henchman, partisan, satellite, sectator, supporter
rel bigot

sectator *n* ***syn*** FOLLOWER, adherent, cohort, disciple, henchman, partisan, satellite, sectary, supporter

section *n* **1** ***syn*** PART 1, cut, division, member, moiety, parcel, piece, portion, segment
rel district, locality, subdivision, vicinity; area, belt, zone; region, tract; field, sphere, territory
2 ***syn*** QUARTER 2, district, precinct, sector

section *vb* to divide into sections <*sectioned* the class on the basis of ability>
syn sectionalize, sectionize; *compare* SEGMENT
rel break up, divide, separate, slice, split; sector, segment

sectionalize *vb* ***syn*** SECTION, sectionize

sectionize *vb* ***syn*** SECTION, sectionalize

sector *n* ***syn*** QUARTER 2, district, precinct, section

secular *adj* ***syn*** PROFANE 1, lay, temporal, unsacred
rel nonclerical, nonreligious
con clerical, ecclesiastical, ministerial, priestly, regular; eternal
ant religious

securable *adj* ***syn*** AVAILABLE 1, attainable, disponible, gettable, obtainable, procurable

---

syn synonym(s) — ***rel*** related word(s)
idiom idiomatic equivalent(s) — ***con*** contrasted word(s)
ant antonym(s) — * vulgar
|| use limited; if in doubt, see a dictionary
The first word in a synonym list when printed in SMALL CAPITALS shows where there is more information about the group. For a more efficient use of this book see Explanatory Notes.

rel convenient, handy, reachable, ready
idiom at one's disposal
con unavailable, unreachable

secure *adj* **1** ***syn*** CONFIDENT 1, assured, sanguine, self-assured, self-confident, undoubtful
2 ***syn*** SAFE 2, riskless
rel firm, stable, strong
con open, wide-open; assailable, weak; dangerous, precarious
ant insecure
3 ***syn*** RELIABLE 1, dependable, tried, tried and true, trustworthy, trusty
4 ***syn*** FAST 4, firm, fixed, set, tenacious, tight
rel strong; iron
5 ***syn*** STABLE 4, firm, solid, sound
6 ***syn*** SURE 1, fast, firm, stable, staunch, strong
rel established, settled; balanced
con precarious; unbalanced; unstable, wobbly
ant insecure

secure *vb* **1** ***syn*** DEFEND 1, bulwark, cover, fend, guard, protect, safeguard, screen, shield
2 ***syn*** ENSURE, assure, cinch, insure
rel underwrite
3 ***syn*** CATCH 1, bag, capture, collar, ||cotch, get, nail, prehend, take
4 ***syn*** FASTEN 2, anchor, catch, fix, moor
rel batten (down), clamp, clinch, pinion, rivet, tie down; cement
con unfasten, untie
5 ***syn*** GET 1, acquire, annex, chalk up, gain, have, land, obtain, pick up, procure
6 ***syn*** EFFECT 1, bring about, cause, draw on, make, produce

security *n* **1** ***syn*** SAFETY, assurance, safeness
ant insecurity
2 ***syn*** STABILITY, firmness, soundness, stableness, steadiness, strength
3 ***syn*** PLEDGE 1, earnest, pawn, token, warrant
4 ***syn*** GUARANTEE 1, bail, bond, guaranty, surety, warranty
rel assurance; certification; pledge
5 ***syn*** DEFENSE 1, aegis, armament, armor, guard, protection, safeguard, shield, ward

sedate *adj* ***syn*** SERIOUS 1, earnest, grave, no-nonsense, sober, sobersided, solemn, somber, staid, weighty
rel calm, placid, serene, tranquil; collected, composed, dispassionate, imperturbable, unruffled; decorous, dignified, proper, seemly
con indecorous, undignified, unseemly; airy, flippant, light
ant flighty

sedative *n* an agent or drug that relieves irritability, nervousness, or excitement <took a *sedative* to help her sleep>
syn calmant, calmative, quietive
rel balm; pacifier, tranquilizer; sleeping pill, sleeping tablet; depressant, ||downer
con energizer; stimulant; ||upper

sediment *n* matter which settles to the bottom of a liquid <rocks hidden by *sediment* spoiled the cove for diving>
syn deposit, dreg(s), grounds, lees, precipitate, precipitation, settlings
rel bottoms, dross, recrement, scoria, slag; draff, heeltap

sedition *n* an offense against official ruling authority (as a government or sovereign) to which one owes allegiance <considered the defense industry strike to be overt *sedition*>
syn seditiousness, treason
rel alienation, disaffection, estrangement; action, protest, strike; coup, coup d'etat, putsch; insurrection, mutiny, rebellion, revolt, revolution, uprising; quislingism
con allegiance, fealty, fidelity, loyalty; duty, respect, responsibility

seditious *adj* ***syn*** INSUBORDINATE, contumacious, factious, insurgent, mutinous, rebellious
rel alienated, disaffected, dissident; faithless, disloyal, perfidious, traitorous, treacherous; lawless, violent
con faithful, loyal, patriotic

seditiousness *n* ***syn*** SEDITION, treason

seduce *vb* **1** ***syn*** LURE, allure, bait, decoy, entice, entrap, inveigle, lead on, tempt, train
rel coax, tease; betray, deceive, delude, mislead; enslave, entrance; overpower, overwhelm
2 to persuade or entice into sexual partnership <lechers who *seduce* silly young girls>
syn debauch, undo
rel deflower; rape, ravish, violate; corrupt, degrade, pervert, ruin

seducement *n* **1** ***syn*** SEDUCTION 1
rel undoing
2 ***syn*** LURE 2, allurement, bait, come-on, decoy, enticement, inveiglement, snare, temptation, trap

seduction *n* **1** the act or an instance of seducing or being seduced into a sexual relationship <women who lay themselves open to *seduction*>
syn seducement
rel deflowering; rape, ravishment, violation; corruption, degradation, perversion, ruin
2 ***syn*** ATTRACTION 1, allurement, appeal, attractiveness, call, draw, drawing power, lure, pull
rel lorelei, siren song, temptation

seductive *adj* ***syn*** ATTRACTIVE 1, alluring, attracting, bewitching, captivating, drawing, enchanting, fascinating, magnetic, siren
rel desirable, mouth-watering, provocative

seductress *n* ***syn*** SIREN, femme fatale, Lorelei, temptress

sedulous *adj* ***syn*** ASSIDUOUS, diligent, industrious, operose
rel active; busy; hustling, persevering, persistent, unremitting

see *vb* **1** to take cognizance of by physical or mental vision <*saw* that the boat was being driven ashore> <the only one who *saw* the truth>

---

syn synonym(s) | *rel* related word(s)
idiom idiomatic equivalent(s) | *con* contrasted word(s)
ant antonym(s) | * vulgar
|| use limited; if in doubt, see a dictionary
The first word in a synonym list when printed in SMALL CAPITALS shows where there is more information about the group. For a more efficient use of this book see Explanatory Notes.

syn behold, descry, discern, distinguish, espy, mark, mind, note, notice, observe, perceive, remark, twig, view
rel sight; make out; examine, inspect, scan, scrutinize; penetrate, pierce, probe; consider, study; appraise, ponder, weigh
idiom fix one's eyes (*or* mind *or* thoughts) on, occupy oneself with, pay heed (*or* attention) to, take notice of
2 to perceive something by means of the eyes <she *sees* clearly with her new glasses>
syn ‖dekko, look, watch
rel gape, gaze, glare, peek, peep, peer, stare
idiom give the eye, hold in view, keep one's eye on, lay eyes on, turn one's eyes to
3 ***syn*** EXPERIENCE 1, have, know, suffer, sustain, undergo
4 ***syn*** DISCOVER 3, ascertain, catch on, determine, find out, hear, learn, tumble, unearth
5 ***syn*** THINK 1, conceive, envisage, envision, fancy, feature, imagine, realize, vision, visualize
6 ***syn*** APPREHEND 1, accept, catch, comprehend, ‖dig, follow, grasp, take, take in, understand
rel discern, discriminate, recognize
7 ***syn*** FORESEE, anticipate, apprehend, divine, forefeel, foreknow, preknow, previse, prevision, visualize
idiom see the day when
8 ***syn*** LOOK 1, mind, watch
rel look out, watch out
idiom see to it that
9 ***syn*** VISIT 2, call, come by, come over, drop (in *or* by), look in, look up, pop (in), step in, stop (in *or* by)
10 ***syn*** DATE, take out
11 ***syn*** GUIDE, conduct, direct, escort, lead, pilot, route, shepherd, show, steer
rel accompany, go (with); attend

seeable *adj* ***syn*** VISUAL 2, ocular, viewable, visible
ant unseeable

seed *n* **1** ***syn*** OFFSPRING, ‖begats, brood, children, descendants, issue, posterity, progeniture, progeny, scions
2 a beginning or source from which something (as a conception) may later develop <the growing *seeds* of suspicion in her mind>
syn bud, embryo, germ, nucleus, spark
rel rudiment; core, kernel; conceit, concept, conception, image, impression, notion

seed *vb* ***syn*** PLANT 1, ‖pitch, put in, sow

seedy *adj* ***syn*** SHABBY 1, bedraggled, decrepit, dingy, down-at-heel, faded, run-down, tattered, threadbare, tired
rel drooping, droopy, flagging, sagging, wilted, wilting; messy, slovenly, unkempt, untidy; neglected, overgrown
idiom gone to seed
con manicured, polished, shined

seeing *n* ***syn*** EYE 2, eyesight, sight, vision

seeing *conj* ***syn*** BECAUSE, as, as long as, ‖being, 'cause, considering, for, inasmuch as, since, whereas
idiom ‖being as how, in that

‖**seeing glass** *n* ***syn*** MIRROR 1, glass, looking glass

seek *vb* **1** to look for <has gone to *seek* a doctor>
syn cast about, ferret out, hunt, quest, search (for *or* out)
rel bird-dog, delve, dig, fish, mouse, nose, root, smell out, sniff
idiom go in quest (*or* search) of
2 ***syn*** TRY 5, assay, attempt, endeavor, essay, offer, strive, struggle, undertake

seeker *n* ***syn*** CANDIDATE, applicant, aspirant, hopeful
rel bidder; petitioner; solicitant; claimant

seeking *n* ***syn*** PURSUIT 2, pursual, pursuance, pursuing, quest, search

seem *vb* to give the impression of being without necessarily being so in fact <things are not always the way they *seem*>
syn appear, look, sound
rel resemble, suggest; hint, imply, insinuate, intimate
idiom have (*or* show) every sign of, have the earmarks of

seeming *n* **1** ***syn*** APPEARANCE 2, face, guise, semblance, show, showing, simulacrum
rel feigning, pretense, sham; facade; illusion
idiom false face (*or* front), outward show
2 ***syn*** APPEARANCE 1, aspect, look, mien
rel bearing, demeanor, posture; image, style; effect, impression

seeming *adj* ***syn*** APPARENT 2, Barmecidal, illusive, illusory, ostensible, semblant

seemingly *adv* ***syn*** OSTENSIBLY, apparently, evidently, officially, outwardly, professedly

seemliness *n* **1** ***syn*** ORDER 7, correctitude, correctness, decorousness, decorum, orderliness, properness, propriety
2 ***syn*** DECORUM 1, decency, dignity, etiquette, propriety
ant unseemliness

seemly *adj* ***syn*** DECOROUS 1, becoming, befitting, comme il faut, conforming, correct, decent, nice, proper, right
rel compatible, congenial, congruous, consistent, consonant; pleasing
con inappropriate, unfit, unseasonable, unsuitable, untimely; incompatible, uncongenial; displeasing, unpleasing
ant unseemly

seep *vb* ***syn*** EXUDE, bleed, ooze, ‖screeve, ‖sew, ‖sicker, strain, sweat, transude, weep
rel drip; leak; flow

seer *n* ***syn*** PROPHET, augur, auspex, forecaster, foreseer, foreteller, haruspex, Nostradamus, predictor, prognosticator

seesaw *vb* to move backward and forward or up and down from a central axis usually in a swaying often unsteady way <planes landing on the *seesawing* flight deck>
syn lurch, pitch, swag, tilt, tilter, yaw; *compare* TEETER, TOSS 2
rel cant, incline, lean, list; rock, roll, sway

seethe *vb* **1** ***syn*** BOIL 2, parboil, simmer, stew

---

syn synonym(s) | *rel* related word(s)
idiom idiomatic equivalent(s) | *con* contrasted word(s)
ant antonym(s) | * vulgar
‖ use limited; if in doubt, see a dictionary
The first word in a synonym list when printed in SMALL CAPITALS shows where there is more information about the group. For a more efficient use of this book see Explanatory Notes.

2 ***syn*** SOAK 1, drench, impregnate, saturate, sodden, ‖sog, sop, souse, steep, waterlog
3 ***syn*** ANGER 2, blow up, boil, boil over, bristle, burn, flare (up), fume, rage
idiom ‖do a slow burn
con calm (down), simmer (down)
ant cool (down)
4 to be in a state of internal and especially mental agitation, excitement, or turmoil <his brain *seethed* with unanswered questions>
syn boil, bubble, churn, ferment, ‖moil, simmer, smolder, stir
rel abound, swarm, teem; fret, fume, sizzle, steam; bubble over, erupt, overflow

see–through *adj* ***syn*** TRANSPARENT 1, clear, limpid, pellucid, translucent

segment *n* ***syn*** PART 1, cut, division, member, moiety, parcel, piece, portion, section

segment *vb* to separate into segments <tried to *segment* the poem into understandable units>
syn segmentalize, segmentize; *compare* SECTION
rel categorize, compartmentalize; divide, separate; isolate, seclude, set off

segmentalize *vb* ***syn*** SEGMENT, segmentize

segmentize *vb* ***syn*** SEGMENT, segmentalize

segregate *vb* ***syn*** ISOLATE, close off, cut off, enisle, insulate, island, separate, sequester
rel disconnect; choose, select, single
con mix
ant desegregate

segregation *n* the quality, state, or condition of being socially or racially excluded or separated <fought against racial *segregation* in the schools>
syn apartheid, separateness, separation, separatism
rel discrimination, jim crowism; ghettoization; isolation, seclusion
ant desegregation

seity *n* ***syn*** INDIVIDUALITY 4, identity, ipseity, personality, selfdom, selfhood, selfness, singularity

seize *vb* **1** ***syn*** APPROPRIATE 1, accroach, annex, arrogate, commandeer, confiscate, expropriate, preempt, sequester, take
rel occupy; usurp
2 to take possession or control of usually suddenly and forcibly <the cat *seized* the fish and made off> <*seized* the rope and dragged the boat ashore>
syn catch, clutch, ‖cotch, grab, grapple, nab, ‖nail, snatch, take; *compare* CATCH 1
rel fasten (onto), grasp, latch (onto), snap (at); apprehend, arrest; capture, secure, take over; abduct, carry off, kidnap, spirit (away *or* off)
idiom get into one's clutches, get one's hands (*or* paws) on, lay hold (on *or* of)
con free, loose, release
3 to affect especially as if by laying hold of <was *seized* with a coughing fit>
syn catch, strike, take
rel overtake; afflict

seizure *n* ***syn*** ATTACK 3, access, fit, spell, throe, turn
rel convulsion; breakdown

seldom *adv* in few instances <she *seldom* writes home anymore>
syn hardly ever, infrequently, little, rarely, unfrequently, unoften
rel occasionally; semioccasionally; irregularly, sporadically; hardly, scarcely
idiom once in a blue moon
con regularly; frequently; usually
ant often

seldom *adj* ***syn*** INFREQUENT, few, occasional, rare, scarce, semioccasional, sporadic, uncommon, unfrequent

select *adj* **1** singled out from a number or group by fitness or preference <this hotel caters to a *select* clientele>
syn chosen, elect, exclusive, pick, picked, selected
rel culled, screened, weeded (out), winnowed (out); favored, preferred; best, elite
con random; indiscriminate; average, commonplace, mediocre, run-of-the-mill
2 ***syn*** CHOICE, dainty, delicate, elegant, exquisite, rare, recherché, superior
rel blue-chip, fine; best; top
3 ***syn*** ECLECTIC 1, discriminating, selective

select *vb* ***syn*** CHOOSE 1, cull, elect, mark, opt (for), optate, pick, prefer, single (out), take
idiom make a choice (*or* selection)
con ignore, pass (over); drop
ant reject

selected *adj* ***syn*** SELECT 1, chosen, elect, exclusive, pick, picked
rel singled (out); appointed, tagged, tapped

selection *n* ***syn*** CHOICE 1, alternative, ‖druthers, election, option, preference
rel choosing, culling, draft, drafting, picking; acumen, discernment, discrimination, insight
ant rejection

selective *adj* ***syn*** ECLECTIC 1, discriminating, select
rel particular, scrupulous

self–abandoned *adj* ***syn*** ABANDONED 2, dissolute, licentious, profligate, reprobate, unprincipled

self–abnegating *adj* ***syn*** SELF-SACRIFICING, self-denying, self-giving, self-renouncing

self–abnegation *n* ***syn*** RENUNCIATION, abnegation, denial, renouncement, self-denial, self-renunciation
rel abandonment, relinquishment, resignation

self–absorbed *adj* ***syn*** EGOCENTRIC 2, egoistic, egomaniacal, egotistic, self-centered, self-concerned, self-interested, self-involved, selfish, self-serving
rel arrogant, cocky, self-important

self–abuse *n* ***syn*** SELF-REPROACH, self-accusation, self-criticism, self-recrimination, self-reproof

self–accusation *n* ***syn*** SELF-REPROACH, self-abuse, self-criticism, self-recrimination, self-reproof

self–admiration *n* ***syn*** CONCEIT 2, amour propre, conceitedness, narcissism, self-conceit, self-esteem, self-glory, self-love, vainglory, vainness

---

syn synonym(s) ***rel*** related word(s)
idiom idiomatic equivalent(s) ***con*** contrasted word(s)
ant antonym(s) * vulgar
‖ use limited; if in doubt, see a dictionary
The first word in a synonym list when printed in SMALL CAPITALS shows where there is more information about the group. For a more efficient use of this book see Explanatory Notes.

self–asserting *adj* ***syn*** PRESUMPTUOUS, forward, overweening, presuming, pushful, pushing, ||pushy, self-assertive, uppish, uppity
rel aggressive, militant
con meek, modest, unassuming; docile, passive
ant self-effacing

self–assertive *adj* **1** ***syn*** AGGRESSIVE, assertive, assertory, militant, pushful, pushing, pushy
rel impertinent, intrusive, meddlesome, obtrusive, officious; audacious, bold; cocksure, sure
2 ***syn*** PRESUMPTUOUS, forward, overweening, presuming, pushful, pushing, ||pushy, self-asserting, uppish, uppity

self–assurance *n* ***syn*** CONFIDENCE 2, aplomb, assurance, self-assuredness, self-confidence, self-trust
rel collectedness, coolness, imperturbability; composure, equanimity, sangfroid
con insecurity, uncertainness

self–assured *adj* ***syn*** CONFIDENT 1, assured, sanguine, secure, self-confident, undoubtful
rel self-satisfied, smug

self–assuredness *n* ***syn*** CONFIDENCE 2, aplomb, assurance, self-assurance, self-confidence, self-trust

self–centered *adj* **1** ***syn*** SELF-SUFFICIENT, closed, independent, self-contained, self-sufficing, self-supported, self-supporting, self-sustained, self-sustaining
2 ***syn*** EGOCENTRIC 2, egoistic, egomaniacal, egotistic, self-absorbed, self-concerned, self-interested, self-involved, selfish, self-serving
idiom wrapped up in oneself

self–centeredness *n* ***syn*** SELFISHNESS, self-concern, selfhood, self-interest, self-regard, self-seeking

self–command *n* ***syn*** WILL 3, discipline, self-control, self-discipline, self-government, self-mastery, self-restraint, willpower
rel self-containment, uncommunicativeness

self–complacency *n* ***syn*** CONCEIT 2, amour propre, complacency, conceitedness, consequence, egoism, egotism, narcissism, pride, vainglory

self–complacent *adj* ***syn*** COMPLACENT, priggish, self-contented, self-pleased, self-satisfied, smug

self–composed *adj* ***syn*** CALM 2, collected, composed, easy, placid, poised, possessed, self-possessed, serene, tranquil

self–conceit *n* ***syn*** CONCEIT 2, amour propre, conceitedness, egoism, egotism, narcissism, self-admiration, self-esteem, self-love, self-opinion

self–conceited *adj* ***syn*** VAIN 3, conceited, ||conceity, narcissistic, stuck-up, vainglorious

self–concern *n* ***syn*** SELFISHNESS, self-centeredness, selfhood, self-interest, self-regard, self-seeking

self–concerned *adj* ***syn*** EGOCENTRIC 2, egoistic, egomaniacal, egotistic, self-absorbed, self-centered, self-interested, self-involved, selfish, self-serving

self–confidence *n* ***syn*** CONFIDENCE 2, aplomb, assurance, self-assurance, self-assuredness, self-trust
rel sanguineness, sureness; cockiness, overconfidence
con diffidence, shyness; self-distrust; doubt, uneasiness
ant self-doubt

self–confident *adj* ***syn*** CONFIDENT 1, assured, sanguine, secure, self-assured, undoubtful

self–conscious *adj* aware of the scrutiny of others to the point of not appearing natural or spontaneous <felt *self-conscious* about wearing platform shoes>
syn affected, conscious, mannered
rel self-aware; anxious, ill at ease, uncomfortable, uneasy; formal, stiff, stilted; artificial; ||mim, prim; exhibitionist, flaunty, ostentatious
con unaware, unconcerned; blithe, easy; natural, spontaneous, unaffected

self–consequence *n* ***syn*** CONCEIT 2, egoism, egotism, pride, self-conceit, self-glory, self-importance, self-opinion, self-pride, swellheadedness

self–contained *adj* ***syn*** SELF-SUFFICIENT, closed, independent, self-centered, self-sufficing, self-supported, self-supporting, self-sustained, self-sustaining

self–contemplation *n* ***syn*** INTROSPECTION, heart-searching, self-examination, self-observation, self-questioning, self-reflection, self-scrutiny, self-searching, soul-searching

self–contented *adj* ***syn*** COMPLACENT, priggish, self-complacent, self-pleased, self-satisfied, smug

self–control *n* ***syn*** WILL 3, discipline, self-command, self-discipline, self-government, self-mastery, self-restraint, willpower
rel constraint, reserve, self-containedness; balance, stability; dignity
idiom presence of mind
ant self-abandonment

self–criticism *n* ***syn*** SELF-REPROACH, self-abuse, self-accusation, self-recrimination, self-reproof

self–deceit *n* ***syn*** SELF-DECEPTION, self-delusion

self–deception *n* the act or an instance of deceiving oneself or of being so deceived <to presume agreement where none exists is a dangerous form of *self-deception*>
syn self-deceit, self-delusion
rel misconception, misinterpretation, misunderstanding; deception, delusion, illusion
idiom kidding oneself

self–defense *n* an act, instance, or means of defending oneself, one's property, or a close relative <sought some measure of *self-defense* against society's lawless elements>
syn self-protection
rel self-preservation

self–delusion *n* ***syn*** SELF-DECEPTION, self-deceit

self–denial *n* ***syn*** RENUNCIATION, abnegation, denial, renouncement, self-abnegation, self-renunciation
rel abstaining, abstemiousness, abstinence; asceticism, selflessness, self-sacrifice, self-sacrificing; self-forgetful, self-forgetting
ant self-indulgence

self–denying *adj* ***syn*** SELF-SACRIFICING, self-abnegating, self-giving, self-renouncing

self–dependence *n* ***syn*** SELF-RELIANCE

self–destruction *n* ***syn*** SUICIDE, felo-de-se, hara-kiri, self-murder, self-slaughter, self-violence

---

syn synonym(s) ***rel*** related word(s)
idiom idiomatic equivalent(s) ***con*** contrasted word(s)
ant antonym(s) * vulgar
|| use limited; if in doubt, see a dictionary
The first word in a synonym list when printed in SMALL CAPITALS shows where there is more information about the group. For a more efficient use of this book see Explanatory Notes.

self–discipline *n* ***syn*** WILL 3, discipline, self-command, self-control, self-government, self-mastery, self-restraint, willpower

selfdom *n* ***syn*** INDIVIDUALITY 4, identity, ipseity, personality, seity, selfhood, selfness, singularity

self–educated *adj* ***syn*** SELF-TAUGHT, autodidactic, self-instructed

self–effacing *adj* ***syn*** SHY 1, backward, bashful, diffident, modest, rabbity, retiring, timid, unassertive, unassured

self–esteem *n* **1** ***syn*** PRIDE 2, amour propre, self-regard, self-respect
rel self-content, self-contentment; self-satisfaction
con self-distrust, self-doubt; self-contempt
ant self-hate
2 ***syn*** CONCEIT 2, amour propre, narcissism, self-admiration, self-consequence, self-glory, self-love, self-opinion, self-pride, vanity
rel self-flattery, self-glorification
con self-distrust, self-doubt; self-hate
ant self-contempt

self–evidencing *adj* ***syn*** SELF-EVIDENT, prima facie

self–evident *adj* evident in itself without need of argument or proof <*self-evident* truths>
syn prima facie, self-evidencing
rel clear, manifest, obvious, plain; unmistakable, unquestionable
con enigmatic, hidden, mysterious, obscure; doubtable, doubtful, questionable, uncertain

self–exaltation *n* ***syn*** CONCEIT 2, amour propre, complacency, conceitedness, consequence, egoism, egotism, narcissism, pride, vainglory

self–examination *n* ***syn*** INTROSPECTION, heart-searching, self-contemplation, self-observation, self-questioning, self-reflection, self-scrutiny, self-searching, soul-searching

self–existent *adj* existing of or by itself and having no antecedent cause <argues backward to a first great cause, which is itself *self-existent*>
syn increate, self-existing, unbegotten, uncaused, uncreated, unoriginated
rel self-generated, self-originated, self-produced
con consequent, resultant, sequential
ant derivative

self–existing *adj* ***syn*** SELF-EXISTENT, increate, unbegotten, uncaused, uncreated, unoriginated

self–explaining *adj* ***syn*** SELF-EXPLANATORY

self–explanatory *adj* capable of being understood without explanation <his actions are *self-explanatory:* he wants to resign>
syn self-explaining; *compare* CLEAR 5
rel clear, evident, obvious, manifest, plain, self-evident; comprehensible, understandable

---

syn synonym(s) ***rel*** related word(s)
idiom idiomatic equivalent(s) ***con*** contrasted word(s)
ant antonym(s) * vulgar
‖ use limited; if in doubt, see a dictionary
The first word in a synonym list when printed in SMALL CAPITALS shows where there is more information about the group. For a more efficient use of this book see Explanatory Notes.

con equivocal, obscure, uncertain, unclear, vague; complex; incomprehensible, mysterious; inexplicable, unexplainable

self–forgetful *adj* ***syn*** SELFLESS, self-forgetting, unselfish

self–forgetting *adj* ***syn*** SELFLESS, self-forgetful, unselfish

self–giving *adj* ***syn*** SELF-SACRIFICING, self-abnegating, self-denying, self-renouncing

self–glorifying *adj* ***syn*** BOASTFUL, braggadocian, braggart, braggy, rodomontade, vaunting

self–glory *n* ***syn*** CONCEIT 2, egoism, egotism, pride, self-consequence, self-importance, self-opinion, self-pride, swellheadedness, vainglory
rel self-aggrandizement, self-glorification

self–governing *adj* ***syn*** DEMOCRATIC, popular, self-ruling

self–government *n* ***syn*** WILL 3, discipline, self-command, self-control, self-discipline, self-mastery, self-restraint, willpower

self–gratification *n* the act of pleasing oneself or of satisfying one's desires <human beings driven by unconscious forces toward *self-gratification*>
syn onanism, self-indulgence
rel self-abandonment; self-pleasing, self-satisfaction; autotheism, narcissism, self-worship

selfhood *n* **1** ***syn*** INDIVIDUALITY 4, identity, ipseity, personality, seity, selfdom, selfness, singularity
2 ***syn*** SELFISHNESS, self-centeredness, self-concern, self-interest, self-regard, self-seeking

self–importance *n* **1** ***syn*** CONCEIT 2, egoism, egotism, pride, self-consequence, self-glory, self-opinion, self-pride, swellheadedness, vainglory
2 ***syn*** EGOTISM 1, egoism
rel arrogance, pomposity

self–important *adj* ***syn*** POMPOUS 1, arrogant, bloated, important, magisterial, pontifical, puffy, stuffy, wiggy

self–imposed *adj* imposed by oneself or itself <insists on working under *self-imposed* handicaps>
syn self-inflicted
rel self-generated, self-produced

self-indulgence *n* ***syn*** SELF-GRATIFICATION, onanism
rel indulgence; excess, intemperance, overindulgence
ant abstinence

self–indulgent *adj* ***syn*** SYBARITIC, hedonistic, onanistic, sybaritical, sybaritish

self–inflicted *adj* ***syn*** SELF-IMPOSED
rel self-determined; accepted; voluntary

self–instructed *adj* ***syn*** SELF-TAUGHT, autodidactic, self-educated

self–interest *n* ***syn*** SELFISHNESS, self-centeredness, self-concern, selfhood, self-regard, self-seeking

self–interested *adj* ***syn*** EGOCENTRIC 2, egoistic, egomaniacal, egotistic, self-absorbed, self-centered, self-concerned, selfish, self-seeking, self-serving

self–involved *adj* ***syn*** EGOCENTRIC 2, egoistic, egomaniacal, egotistic, self-absorbed, self-centered, self-concerned, self-interested, self-seeking, self-serving

selfish *adj* ***syn*** EGOCENTRIC 2, egoistic, egomaniacal, egotistic, self-absorbed, self-centered, self-concerned, self-interested, self-seeking, self-serving
idiom ‖looking out for number one
con self-denying, selfless, self-sacrificing; altruistic, benevolent, charitable, generous, magnanimous

ant unselfish

selfishness *n* a concern for one's own welfare at the expense of or in disregard of others <his *selfishness* was consummate: he cared for no one but himself>
syn self-centeredness, self-concern, selfhood, self-interest, self-regard, self-seeking
rel egoism, egotism, self-absorption; self, selfism, selfness; autotheism, self-worship
con self-denial, selflessness, self-sacrificing; benevolence, charity, generosity
ant unselfishness

self-knowledge *n* knowledge or understanding of one's own character, motivations, and capabilities <a poet whose verse reflected deep *self-knowledge* and honesty>
syn autognosis, self-understanding
rel self-awareness; introspection, self-examination, self-observation

selfless *adj* having no concern for oneself <*selfless* service to community, state, and nation>
syn self-forgetful, self-forgetting, unselfish
rel self-giving, self-sacrificing; self-renouncing; elevated, generous, high-minded, magnanimous
con self-devoted, self-loving, self-serving
ant self-centered, selfish

self–love *n* ***syn*** CONCEIT 2, amour propre, conceitedness, narcissism, self-admiration, self-conceit, self-esteem, vainglory, vainness, vanity
idiom the sixth insatiable sense
con self-abuse, self-accusation, self-reproach; self-forgetfulness, selflessness
ant self-hate

self–mastery *n* ***syn*** WILL 3, discipline, self-command, self-control, self-discipline, self-government, self-restraint, willpower

self–murder *n* ***syn*** SUICIDE, felo-de-se, hara-kiri, self-destruction, self-slaughter, self-violence

selfness *n* ***syn*** INDIVIDUALITY 4, identity, ipseity, personality, seity, selfdom, selfhood, singularity

self–observation *n* ***syn*** INTROSPECTION, heart-searching, self-contemplation, self-examination, self-questioning, self-reflection, self-scrutiny, self-searching, soul-searching

self–opinion *n* ***syn*** CONCEIT 2, conceitedness, egoism, egotism, pride, self-consequence, self-glory, self-importance, self-pride, swellheadedness

self–pleased *adj* ***syn*** COMPLACENT, priggish, self-complacent, self-contented, self-satisfied, smug

self–possessed *adj* ***syn*** CALM 2, collected, composed, easy, easygoing, placid, poised, self-composed, serene, tranquil
rel aloof, reserved; self-contained, self-controlled; self-assured

self–possession *n* ***syn*** EQUANIMITY, ataraxy, calmness, composure, coolness, imperturbability, phlegm, sangfroid

self–pride *n* ***syn*** CONCEIT 2, egoism, egotism, pride, self-consequence, self-esteem, self-glory, self-importance, self-opinion, vanity

self–proclaimed *adj* ***syn*** SELF-STYLED, soi-disant

self–protection *n* ***syn*** SELF-DEFENSE

self–questioning *n* ***syn*** INTROSPECTION, heart-searching, self-contemplation, self-examination, self-observation, self-reflection, self-scrutiny, self-searching, soul-searching

self–recrimination *n* ***syn*** SELF-REPROACH, self-abuse, self-accusation, self-criticism, self-reproof

self–reflection *n* ***syn*** INTROSPECTION, heart-searching, self-contemplation, self-examination, self-observation, self-questioning, self-scrutiny, self-searching, soul-searching

self–regard *n* **1** ***syn*** SELFISHNESS, self-centeredness, self-concern, selfhood, self-interest, self-seeking
2 ***syn*** PRIDE 2, amour propre, self-esteem, self-respect

self–reliance *n* reliance on one's own resources, efforts, and ability <a strong people characterized by bravery and *self-reliance*>
syn self-dependence
rel confidence, self-assurance, self-confidence; self-sufficiency, self-support

self–renouncing *adj* ***syn*** SELF-SACRIFICING, self-abnegating, self-denying, self-giving

self–renunciation *n* ***syn*** RENUNCIATION, abnegation, denial, renouncement, self-abnegation, self-denial

self–reproach *n* an act or instance of reproaching oneself <experienced both guilt and *self-reproach* after the quarrel>
syn self-abuse, self-accusation, self-criticism, self-recrimination, self-reproof
rel contrition, regret, remorse; self-castigation, self-condemnation, self-flagellation, self-punishment; self-contempt
con self-contentment, self-satisfaction; self-applause
ant self-approbation

self–reproof *n* ***syn*** SELF-REPROACH, self-abuse, self-accusation, self-criticism, self-recrimination

self–respect *n* ***syn*** PRIDE 2, amour propre, self-esteem, self-regard

self–restraining *adj* ***syn*** ABSTEMIOUS, abstentious, abstinent, continent, sober, temperate

self–restraint *n* ***syn*** WILL 3, discipline, self-command, self-control, self-discipline, self-government, self-mastery, willpower
ant abandon

self–righteous *adj* ***syn*** HYPOCRITICAL, canting, pecksniffian, pharisaic, pharisaical, sanctimonious

self–ruling *adj* ***syn*** DEMOCRATIC, popular, self-governing

self–sacrificing *adj* sacrificing or denying oneself for others <a *self-sacrificing* love>
syn self-abnegating, self-denying, self-giving, self-renouncing
rel selfless, unselfish; charitable, generous, kindly, philanthropic
con self-centered, selfish, self-seeking

selfsame *adj* ***syn*** SAME 1, exact, identical, very
rel alike, like

---

syn synonym(s) — *rel* related word(s)
idiom idiomatic equivalent(s) — *con* contrasted word(s)
ant antonym(s) — * vulgar
|| use limited; if in doubt, see a dictionary
The first word in a synonym list when printed in SMALL CAPITALS shows where there is more information about the group. For a more efficient use of this book see Explanatory Notes.

idiom (the) very same
con different, unalike
ant diverse

selfsameness *n* ***syn*** IDENTITY, identicalness, oneness, sameness
ant diverseness

self–satisfied *adj* ***syn*** COMPLACENT, priggish, self-complacent, self-contented, self-pleased, smug

self–scrutiny *n* ***syn*** INTROSPECTION, heart-searching, self-contemplation, self-examination, self-observation, self-questioning, self-reflection, self-searching, soul-searching

self–searching *n* ***syn*** INTROSPECTION, heart-searching, self-contemplation, self-examination, self-observation, self-questioning, self-reflection, self-scrutiny, soul-searching

self–seeking *n* ***syn*** SELFISHNESS, self-centeredness, self-concern, selfhood, self-interest, self-regard

self–seeking *adj* ***syn*** EGOCENTRIC 2, egoistic, egomaniacal, egotistic, self-absorbed, self-centered, self-concerned, self-interested, self-involved, self-serving

self–serving *adj* ***syn*** EGOCENTRIC 2, egoistic, egomaniacal, egotistic, self-absorbed, self-centered, self-concerned, self-interested, self-involved, self-seeking

self–slaughter *n* ***syn*** SUICIDE, felo-de-se, hara-kiri, self-destruction, self-murder, self-violence

self–starter *n* ***syn*** HUSTLER 1, dynamo, go-getter, live wire, peeler, rustler

self–styled *adj* given a specified designation or title by oneself often without justification <a department cluttered with *self-styled* experts>
syn self-proclaimed, soi-disant
rel self-appointed, self-created, self-given; so-called; quasi; would-be

self–sufficient *adj* maintaining or able to maintain oneself without outside aid <organisms are not *self-sufficient*, closed systems>
syn closed, independent, self-centered, self-contained, self-sufficing, self-supported, self-supporting, self-sustained, self-sustaining
rel self-dependent, self-reliant; self-subsistent, self-subsisting; individual, one-man, unit
idiom one's own man, sufficient unto oneself (*or* itself)
con dependent

self–sufficing *adj* ***syn*** SELF-SUFFICIENT, closed, independent, self-centered, self-contained, self-supported, self-supporting, self-sustained, self-sustaining

self–supported *adj* ***syn*** SELF-SUFFICIENT, closed, independent, self-centered, self-contained, self-sufficing, self-supporting, self-sustained, self-sustaining

self–supporting *adj* ***syn*** SELF-SUFFICIENT, closed, independent, self-centered, self-contained, self-sufficing, self-supported, self-sustained, self-sustaining

syn synonym(s) ***rel*** related word(s)
idiom idiomatic equivalent(s) ***con*** contrasted word(s)
ant antonym(s) * vulgar
‖ use limited; if in doubt, see a dictionary
The first word in a synonym list when printed in SMALL CAPITALS shows where there is more information about the group. For a more efficient use of this book see Explanatory Notes.

self–sustained *adj* ***syn*** SELF-SUFFICIENT, closed, independent, self-centered, self-contained, self-sufficing, self-supported, self-supporting, self-sustaining

self–sustaining *adj* ***syn*** SELF-SUFFICIENT, closed, independent, self-centered, self-contained, self-sufficing, self-supported, self-supporting, self-sustained

self–taught *adj* having knowledge or skills acquired by one's own efforts without formal instruction <a *self-taught* painter>
syn autodidactic, self-educated, self-instructed

self–trust *n* ***syn*** CONFIDENCE 2, aplomb, assurance, self-assurance, self-assuredness, self-confidence

self–understanding *n* ***syn*** SELF-KNOWLEDGE, autognosis

self–violence *n* ***syn*** SUICIDE, felo-de-se, hara-kiri, self-destruction, self-murder, self-slaughter

self–willed *adj* ***syn*** OBSTINATE, bullheaded, headstrong, intractable, mulish, pertinacious, pigheaded, refractory, stiff-necked, stubborn
con weak, weak-willed, wishy-washy; spineless

sell *vb* **1** ***syn*** BETRAY 2, cross, double-cross, sell out, ‖split
2 to give up (property) to another for money or other valuable consideration <can *sell* you the house now>
syn give, market, vend
ant buy, purchase
3 to deal in or offer (articles) for sale on a regular basis <he *sells* small appliances>
syn market, merchandise, retail
rel barter, deal (in), exchange, trade, traffic; hawk, peddle; vend
ant buy
4 to command a specified price <that coat *sells* for $300>
syn bring, bring in, fetch
rel command, draw; realize, return, yield; gross, net

sell *n* ***syn*** IMPOSTURE, cheat, deceit, deception, fake, flimflam, hoax, put-on, sham, spoof

sellable *adj* ***syn*** MARKETABLE, merchandisable, merchantable, salable, trafficable, vendible

sell off *vb* ***syn*** SELL OUT 1, close out, ‖sell up

sell out *vb* **1** to dispose of entirely by selling <*sold out* his share of the business>
syn close out, sell off, ‖sell up
rel dump, move, unload; sacrifice
2 ***syn*** DECEIVE, beguile, betray, ‖bunk, delude, double-cross, four-flush, humbug, mislead, take in
3 ***syn*** BETRAY 2, cross, double-cross, sell, ‖split

‖**sell up** *vb* ***syn*** SELL OUT 1, close out, sell off

selvage *n* ***syn*** BORDER 1, brim, brink, edge, fringe, hem, perimeter, periphery, skirt, verge

semblance *n* **1** ***syn*** AIR 3, atmosphere, aura, feel, feeling, mood
rel aspect, look
2 ***syn*** LIKENESS, affinity, alikeness, analogy, comparison, resemblance, similarity, simile, similitude
3 ***syn*** APPEARANCE 2, face, guise, seeming, show, showing, simulacrum
rel air, pose
4 ***syn*** MASK 2, disguise, facade, face, false front, front, guise, masquerade, veil, veneer

semblant *adj* ***syn*** APPARENT 2, Barmecidal, illusive, illusory, ostensible, seeming

seminar *n* ***syn*** CONFERENCE 2, colloquium, colloquy, palaver, rap session

semioccasional *adj* ***syn*** INFREQUENT, few, occasional, rare, scarce, seldom, sporadic, uncommon, unfrequent

sempiternal *adj* ***syn*** INFINITE 1, eternal, illimitable, perdurable, supertemporal

sempiternity *n* ***syn*** ETERNITY 1, infinity

send *vb* **1** to cause to go or be taken from one place, person, or condition to another < *send* a messenger to the bank > <his cold *sent* him to bed>
syn address, consign, dispatch, forward, remit, route, ship, transmit
rel allocate, assign, commit, delegate; advance, launch; expedite, rush
ant receive
2 ***syn*** THRILL, electrify, enthuse

senectitude *n* ***syn*** OLD AGE, age, caducity, elderliness, senescence, years

senescence *n* ***syn*** OLD AGE, age, caducity, elderliness, senectitude, years

senile *adj* exhibiting the weakness and loss of mental faculties often associated with old age <a *senile* professor now unable to lecture coherently>
syn doddering, doddery, ||doted, doting
rel aging, senescent; aged, ancient, old; enfeebled, feeble, weak; decrepit, doddered, shattered
idiom in one's second childhood

senility *n* ***syn*** DOTAGE, second childhood
rel decline; senescence

senior *n* **1** ***syn*** OLDSTER, ancient, elder, golden-ager, old-timer, senior citizen
2 one older than another <he was her *senior* by eight years>
syn elder
ant junior
3 ***syn*** SUPERIOR, better, brass hat, elder, higher-up
con inferior, subordinate, underling

senior citizen *n* ***syn*** OLDSTER, ancient, elder, golden-ager, old-timer, senior

sensation *n* **1** the power to respond or an act of responding to stimuli <the stage of *sensation* precedes that of rational comprehension>
syn feeling, sense, sensibility, sensitivity
rel susceptibility; consciousness; sensitiveness, sensitivity; impression, perception, response
2 ***syn*** WONDER 1, marvel, miracle, phenomenon, portent, prodigy, stunner
rel bomb, bombshell

sensational *adj* **1** ***syn*** SENSORY, sensatory, sensitive, sensorial, sensual
2 arousing or designed to arouse a quick, intense, and usually superficial emotional response < *sensational* crime reporting>
syn livid, lurid, sensationalistic, sensationist, sultry, tabloid
rel juicy, piquant, pungent; colored, extravagant; coarse, vulgar
con exact, factual; dignified, formal, proper, restrained
3 ***syn*** NOTICEABLE, arresting, conspicuous, marked, outstanding, pointed, prominent, remarkable, salient, signal
rel impressive, stunning
4 ***syn*** MARVELOUS 2, ||cool, ||dandy, divine, ||galluptious, glorious, groovy, hot, hunky-dory, ||keen
rel boffo, crashing, rousing, slambang, smash, smashing, superfine

sensationalistic *adj* ***syn*** SENSATIONAL 2, livid, lurid, sensationist, sultry, tabloid

sensationist *adj* ***syn*** SENSATIONAL 2, livid, lurid, sensationalistic, sultry, tabloid

sensatory *adj* ***syn*** SENSORY, sensational, sensitive, sensorial, sensual

sense *n* **1** ***syn*** MEANING 1, acceptation, import, intendment, message, purport, significance, significancy, signification, understanding
rel gist, pith, substance; center, core, focus, nucleus
2 ***syn*** SUBSTANCE 2, burden, core, gist, matter, meat, purport, short, thrust, upshot
3 ***syn*** SENSATION 1, feeling, sensibility, sensitivity
rel awareness, cognizance; discernment, discrimination, penetration; appreciation; recognition
4 *usu* **senses** *pl* ***syn*** WIT 2, lucidity, ||marbles, mind, reason, saneness, sanity, soundness
rel consciousness
5 ***syn*** INTELLIGENCE 1, brain(s), brainpower, mentality, mother wit, wit
6 ability to make intelligent choices and to reach intelligent conclusions or decisions <had enough *sense* to study something practical>
syn common sense, good sense, gumption, horse sense, judgment, wisdom
rel discretion, foresight, prudence; appreciation, comprehension, understanding; brains, intelligence, ||smarts, wit
ant folly

sense *vb* ***syn*** FEEL 3, believe, consider, credit, deem, hold, think
rel anticipate; know, realize

senseless *adj* **1** ***syn*** NUMB 1, anesthetized, asleep, benumbed, dead, deadened, insensible, insensitive, numbed, unfeeling
rel oblivious, unaware; inanimate, wooden
2 ***syn*** INSENSATE 1, inanimate, insensible, insentient, unfeeling
3 ***syn*** INSENSIBLE 2, cold, comatose, inconscious, unconscious
4 ***syn*** SIMPLE 3, brainless, foolish, mindless, nitwitted, silly, unwitty, weak-headed, weak-minded, witless
rel irrational, surd
5 having no meaning <an ancient custom, now outdated and *senseless*>
syn insignificant, meaningless, pointless, purportless, unmeaning
rel purposeless; trivial, unimportant
idiom without rhyme or reason
con purposeful; important, meaning, meaningful, significant

---

syn synonym(s) ***rel*** related word(s)
idiom idiomatic equivalent(s) ***con*** contrasted word(s)
ant antonym(s) * vulgar
|| use limited; if in doubt, see a dictionary
The first word in a synonym list when printed in SMALL CAPITALS shows where there is more information about the group. For a more efficient use of this book see Explanatory Notes.

senselessness *n* ***syn*** FOOLISHNESS, absurdity, craziness, dottiness, folly, inanity, insanity, preposterousness, silliness, witlessness
rel illogicality, stupidity

sensibility *n* ***syn*** SENSATION 1, feeling, sense, sensitivity
rel discernment, discrimination, insight, keenness, penetration, responsiveness; affection, emotion, heart
con apathy, indifference, insensibleness, insentience, unfeelingness, unresponsiveness
ant insensibility

sensibilize *vb* ***syn*** SENSITIZE

sensible *adj* **1** ***syn*** MATERIAL 1, corporeal, gross, objective, phenomenal, physical, substantial, tangible
rel concrete, solid
con immaterial, insubstantial; unreal
2 ***syn*** PERCEPTIBLE, appreciable, detectable, discernible, observable, palpable, tangible
rel imaginal, perceptual, sensational; weighable; evident, manifest, obvious, patent
con imperceptible; cloudy, unclear
ant insensible
3 ***syn*** CONSIDERABLE 2, good, respectable, ‖right smart, sizable, smart
4 ***syn*** SENTIENT 3, impressible, impressionable, responsive, sensile, sensitive, susceptible, susceptive
5 ***syn*** AWARE, alive, au courant, awake, cognizant, conscious, conversant, knowing, sentient, witting
rel sensitive, susceptible; noting, observing, perceiving, remarking, seeing; appreciating, comprehending, understanding; intelligent, knowing
con anesthetic, insensate, insensitive
ant insensible
6 ***syn*** RATIONAL, consequent, intelligent, logical, reasonable, sound
rel sensemaking
7 ***syn*** WISE 2, judgmatic, judicious, prudent, sage, sane, sapient
rel rational, reasonable; down-to-earth, matter-of-fact
con unreasonable, unsound, unwise; asinine, fatuous
ant absurd, foolish

sensile *adj* ***syn*** SENTIENT 3, impressible, impressionable, responsive, sensible, sensitive, susceptible, susceptive

sensitive *adj* **1** ***syn*** SENTIENT 3, impressible, impressionable, responsive, sensible, sensile, susceptible, susceptive
rel hypersensitive, supersensitive
con impervious, insensible, unfeeling, unimpressionable, unresponsive; wooden
ant insensitive, unsensitive
2 ***syn*** EMOTIONAL 1, emotionable, feeling, sentient
rel high-strung, irritable, nervous, tense; insultable, oversensitive, umbrageous; unstable
con impervious, insensate, insensible, unaffected, unemotional
ant insensitive, unsensitive
3 ***syn*** ACUTE 3, keen, perceptive, sharp
rel perceiving, seeing; aware, cognizant, conscious; knowing, understanding
4 ***syn*** LIABLE 2, exposed, obnoxious, open, prone, subject, susceptible
rel affected, impressed, influenced; disposed, inclined, predisposed
ant insensitive
5 ***syn*** DELICATE 7, precarious, ticklish, touchy, tricky
6 ***syn*** SENSORY, sensational, sensatory, sensorial, sensual

sensitivity *n* ***syn*** SENSATION 1, feeling, sense, sensibility

sensitize *vb* to cause to become sensitive or more sensitive < *sensitizing* corporate officers to social and environmental problems >
syn sensibilize
rel animate, excite, quicken, sharpen, stimulate, whet
ant desensitize

sensorial *adj* ***syn*** SENSORY, sensational, sensatory, sensitive, sensual

sensory *adj* of or relating to sensation or the senses < *sensory* perception >
syn sensational, sensatory, sensitive, sensorial, sensual
rel sensate; receptive

sensual *adj* **1** ***syn*** SENSORY, sensational, sensatory, sensitive, sensorial
2 ***syn*** CARNAL 2, animal, fleshly
rel irreligious, unspiritual
3 ***syn*** SENSUOUS, epicurean, luscious, lush, luxurious, sensualistic, voluptuous
4 ***syn*** MATERIALISTIC, banausic, earthy, mundane, temporal, worldly

sensualistic *adj* ***syn*** SENSUOUS, epicurean, luscious, lush, luxurious, sensual, voluptuous

sensuous *adj* producing or characterized by gratification of the senses < *sensuous* pleasures >
syn epicurean, luscious, lush, luxurious, sensual, sensualistic, voluptuous; *compare* CARNAL 2, SYBARITIC
rel bacchic, dionysiac, Dionysian, hedonistic, pleasure-loving, pleasure-seeking; self-indulgent, sybaritic; carnal, fleshly, fleshy
con ascetic, disciplined, restrained

sentence *vb* to decree the fate or punishment of one adjudged guilty, unworthy, or unfit < was *sentenced* to exile >
syn condemn, damn, doom, proscribe
rel adjudge, adjudicate, judge; ordain, rule; blame, denounce; penalize, punish; devote
idiom pass sentence on
con absolve, acquit, exculpate, exonerate, vindicate; discharge, free, liberate, release

sententious *adj* ***syn*** EXPRESSIVE, eloquent, facund, meaningful, pregnant, rich, significant
rel aphoristic, concise, crisp, epigrammatic, piquant, pithy, terse

sentient *adj* **1** ***syn*** AWARE, alive, au courant, awake, cognizant, conscious, conversant, knowing, sensible, witting
2 ***syn*** EMOTIONAL 1, emotionable, feeling, sensitive
3 capable of receiving and of being readily affected by external stimuli < deeply disturbed in the most *sentient* reaches of his mind >
syn impressible, impressionable, responsive, sensible, sensile, sensitive, susceptible, susceptive

rel sensate; open, receptive, susceptive; reactive
con insensate; closed, unreceptive; unreactive

sentiment *n* **1** *syn* LEANING 2, bias, disposition, inclination, inclining, partiality, penchant, predilection, predisposition, tendency
2 *syn* OPINION, belief, conviction, eye, feeling, mind, persuasion, view
rel leaning, predilection, propensity; position, posture
idiom way of thinking
3 *syn* FEELING 3, affection, affectivity, emotion, passion
rel conception; sensation; emotionalism, sentimentality

sentimental *adj* unduly or affectedly emotional <*sentimental* love stories>
syn bathetic, drippy, gooey, lovey-dovey, maudlin, mawkish, moist, mushy, romantic, sappy, slushy, sobby, sobful, soft-boiled, ‖soppy, soupy, sticky, syrupy, tear-jerking
rel dreamy, misty-eyed, moonstruck, nostalgic, oversentimental; inane, insipid, jejune, namby-pamby, schoolgirlish, vapid; rosewater, saccharine, soft, sugar-candy, sugary, sweet; loving, tender; affectionate, demonstrative, effusive; gushing, gushy; passionate
con unaffectionate, undemonstrative; dispassionate, emotionless, unemotional, unresponsive; unfeeling, unloving; dry
ant unsentimental

sentinel *n* *syn* GUARD 2, lookout, picket, sentry, ward, watch, watchman

sentry *n* *syn* GUARD 2, lookout, picket, sentinel, ward, watch, watchman

separate *vb* **1** to become or cause to become disunited or disjoined <forces that *separate* families>
syn break up, dichotomize, disjoin, disjoint, dissect, dissever, disunite, divide, divorce, part, rupture, sever, split (up), sunder, uncombine
rel alienate, discontinue, disunify, estrange; dislink, uncouple, unjoin, unlink; disaggregate, disassemble, disgregate, dispel, disperse, dissolve, scatter; detach, disengage, disrelate, dissociate; halve, quarter
con assemble, associate, blend, mingle, mix; connect, couple, join, link; unify, unite; agglutinate, bind, cement, fuse, weld
ant combine
2 *syn* KNOW 4, difference, differentiate, discern, discrepate, discriminate, distinguish, extricate, sever, severalize
3 *syn* SORT 2, comb, sift, winnow
rel compartment, compartmentalize
4 *syn* DISCHARGE 7, ‖demob, demobilize, muster out
5 *syn* ISOLATE, close off, cut off, enisle, insulate, island, segregate, sequester

separate *adj* **1** *syn* SINGLE 2, lone, one, only, particular, sole, solitary, unique
rel distinctive, peculiar; detached, disconnected, disengaged
2 *syn* FREE 1, autarchic, autarkic, autonomous, independent, sovereign
3 *syn* DISTINCT 1, different, discrete, diverse, several, various
rel free, independent

separately *adv* *syn* APART 1, independently, individually, one by one, severally, singly
rel distinctly; solely
con conjointly, jointly
ant together

separateness *n* *syn* SEGREGATION, apartheid, separation, separatism
ant togetherness

separation *n* **1** the act, process, or an instance of separating or of being separated <*separation* of church and state> <their *separation* was a sad occasion>
syn detachment, dissolution, disunion, division, divorce, divorcement, partition, rupture, split-up
rel disrelation, dissociation, disunity, parting, shedding; disconnection, disjointedness, disjointure; breakup, disjunction, dissection, sequestration; diffluence, dispersal; dichotomy, diremption, trichotomy
con combination; unification
ant union
2 *syn* SEGREGATION, apartheid, separateness, separatism

separatism *n* *syn* SEGREGATION, apartheid, separateness, separation

separatist *n* *syn* HERETIC, dissenter, dissident, misbeliever, nonconformist, schismatic, schismatist, sectary

sepulcher *n* *syn* GRAVE, burial, ‖pit, sepulture, tomb

sepulcher *vb* **1** *syn* ENTOMB 1, ensepulcher, sepulture, tomb
2 *syn* BURY 1, entomb, inhume, inter, lay away, plant, put away, sepulture, tomb

sepulchral *adj* **1** of, relating to, or serving as a sepulcher or a memorial to the dead <*sepulchral* inscriptions>
syn mortuary, tumulary
rel exequial, funebrial, funeral, funerary, funereal
2 *syn* HOLLOW 1, cavernous, reverberant

sepulture *n* **1** *syn* BURIAL 2, entombment, inhumation, interment
2 *syn* GRAVE, burial, ‖pit, sepulcher, tomb

sepulture *vb* **1** *syn* ENTOMB 1, ensepulcher, sepulcher, tomb
2 *syn* BURY 1, entomb, inhume, inter, lay away, plant, put away, sepulcher, tomb

sequel *n* **1** *syn* SUCCESSION 2, alternation, chain, consecution, order, progression, row, sequence, series, train
2 *syn* EFFECT 1, aftereffect, aftermath, causatum, consequence, eventuality, issue, outcome, result, upshot
rel end, ending, termination; close, closing, finish, finishing
3 *syn* EPILOGUE 2
rel continuation, development; aftermath, outcome, result

sequence *n* **1** *syn* SUCCESSION 2, alternation, chain, consecution, order, progression, row, sequel, series, train
rel arrangement, disposition, ordering; procession
2 *syn* ORDER 3, arrangement, disposal, disposition, distribution, ordering

---

rel classification, grouping; placement

3 ***syn*** EFFECT 1, aftereffect, aftermath, consequence, eventuality, issue, outcome, result, sequel, upshot

4 ***syn*** ORDER 5, consecution, procession, succession

sequent *adj* ***syn*** CONSECUTIVE, sequential, serial, subsequent, subsequential, succedent, succeeding, successional, successive

sequential *adj* ***syn*** CONSECUTIVE, sequent, serial, subsequent, subsequential, succedent, succeeding, successional, successive

sequester *vb* **1** ***syn*** ISOLATE, close off, cut off, enisle, insulate, island, segregate, separate

2 ***syn*** SECLUDE, cloister

rel hide, secrete

3 ***syn*** APPROPRIATE 1, accroach, annex, arrogate, commandeer, confiscate, expropriate, preempt, seize, take

rel attach; impound; dispossess

sequestered *adj* ***syn*** SECLUDED, cloistered, hermetic, recluse, secluse, seclusive

rel sheltered; closeted

sequestration *n* ***syn*** SECLUSION, reclusion, retirement

rel retreat

sequitur *n* ***syn*** INFERENCE 2, conclusion, deduction, illation, judgment, ratiocination

seraglio *n* ***syn*** BROTHEL, bagnio, bordello, cathouse, ‖joyhouse, lupanar, parlor house, sporting house, stew, whorehouse

sere *adj* ***syn*** DRY 1, arid, bone-dry, droughty, moistureless, thirsty, unwatered, waterless

serene *adj* ***syn*** CALM 2, collected, composed, easy, easygoing, placid, poised, self-composed, self-possessed, tranquil

rel noiseless, quiet, still; quiescent, resting; undisturbed

con agitated, disquieted, upset

serfage *n* ***syn*** BONDAGE, enslavement, helotry, peonage, serfdom, servility, servitude, slavery, thralldom, yoke

serfdom *n* ***syn*** BONDAGE, enslavement, helotry, peonage, serfage, servility, servitude, slavery, thralldom, yoke

serial *adj* ***syn*** CONSECUTIVE, sequent, sequential, subsequent, subsequential, succedent, succeeding, successional, successive

series *n* ***syn*** SUCCESSION 2, alternation, chain, consecution, progression, row, sequel, sequence, string, train

rel continuance, continuation, run; category, group, set; column, tier; gradation, scale

serious *adj* **1** not light or frivolous (as in disposition, appearance, or manner) <he was disturbed by her stern, *serious* look>

syn earnest, grave, no-nonsense, poker-faced, sedate, sober, sobersided, solemn, somber, staid, weighty

rel businesslike, ‖dern, determined, steady, steady-going; intent, serious-minded; contemplative, meditative, pensive, reflective, thoughtful; austere, severe, stern; humorless, unhumorous; grim

idiom serious as a judge

con flighty, ‖flip, flippant, frivolous, volatile; casual, easy, relaxed

ant light, unserious

2 expressing, involving, or characterized by seriousness or gravity (as of consequence) <a *serious* economic situation>

syn grave, heavy, severe, weighty

rel important, significant; sobering; unamusing, unfunny, unhumorous; grim

idiom no joke, no laughing matter

con inconsequential, insignificant, unimportant, unserious

ant trifling, trivial

3 ***syn*** HARD 6, arduous, difficult, formidable, heavy, laborious, operose, severe, strenuous, tough

4 ***syn*** GRAVE 3, dangerous, fell, grievous, major, ugly

rel menacing, threatening

seriously *adv* **1** in a serious manner <at last settled *seriously* to work>

syn actively, down, earnestly, for real

rel gravely, soberly, solemnly; intently; vigorously, zealously; determinedly, purposefully, resolutely; fervently, passionately

idiom all joking aside, in all seriousness, in earnest

con airily, casually, flippantly, lightly, unconcernedly; carelessly, haphazardly

2 to a serious extent <the cities are *seriously* overcrowded>

syn gravely, intensely, severely

rel decidedly, quite, very; dangerously; critically, deplorably, regrettably

serious–mindedness *n* ***syn*** EARNESTNESS, earnest, intentness, seriousness

rel thoughtfulness; sober-mindedness

seriousness *n* ***syn*** EARNESTNESS, earnest, intentness, serious-mindedness

rel sedateness, sobriety, solemnity, staidness

con gaiety, jollity; lightness

ant flippancy, frivolity

sermon *n* a religious discourse delivered in public by a clergyman as part of a worship service <preached his first *sermon* on Sunday>

syn preach, preaching, preachment, sermonizing

rel preachification; sermonary, sermonology; sermonette; exhortation, harangue, lecture, tirade

sermonic *adj* ***syn*** DIDACTIC, moral, moralizing, preachy, schoolmasterish, sermonizing, teachy

sermonize *vb* **1** ***syn*** PREACH 1, evangelize, homilize

2 ***syn*** DISCOURSE 1, descant, dilate (on *or* upon), discuss, dissert, dissertate, expatiate

3 ***syn*** MORALIZE, preach, preachify

sermonizer *n* ***syn*** CLERGYMAN, churchman, cleric, clerk, ‖devil-dodger, divine, ecclesiastic, minister, parson, preacher

sermonizing *n* ***syn*** SERMON, preach, preaching, preachment

sermonizing *adj* ***syn*** DIDACTIC, moral, moralizing, preachy, schoolmasterish, sermonic, teachy

serpent *n* ***syn*** DEVIL 1, Apollyon, Beelzebub, diablo, fiend, Lucifer, Old Gooseberry, Old Nick, Old Scratch, Satan

---

syn synonym(s) — *rel* related word(s)
idiom idiomatic equivalent(s) — *con* contrasted word(s)
ant antonym(s) — * vulgar
‖ use limited; if in doubt, see a dictionary
The first word in a synonym list when printed in SMALL CAPITALS shows where there is more information about the group. For a more efficient use of this book see Explanatory Notes.

serpentine *adj* 1 ***syn*** FIENDISH, demoniac, demonian, demonic, devilish, diabolic, diabolonian, satanic, unhallowed
2 ***syn*** WINDING, anfractuous, convoluted, flexuous, meandering, meandrous, sinuous, snaky, tortuous
rel serpentiform, serpentile, serpentlike, snakelike; crooked, devious

serrate *adj* notched or toothed on the edge <jagged peaks and *serrate* ridges>
syn denticulate, saw-edged, sawtooth, saw-toothed, serrated, serried
rel indented, notched, scored, toothed; serrulate

serrated *adj* ***syn*** SERRATE, denticulate, saw-edged, sawtooth, saw-toothed, serried

serried *adj* ***syn*** SERRATE, denticulate, saw-edged, sawtooth, saw-toothed, serrated

serve *vb* 1 ***syn*** BENEFIT, advantage, avail, profit, work (for)
2 ***syn*** ACT 4, function, officiate
3 to prove adequate or sufficient <will not *serve* as a true translation>
syn do, suffice, suit
rel service; function, work; fit; satisfy; make
idiom fill the bill
4 ***syn*** MINISTER (to), care (for), mother, nurse, wait (on)
5 to put in (a term of imprisonment) <*served* ten years for armed robbery>
syn do
rel put in, spend; undergo
idiom do a hitch (*or* stretch), serve (out) a sentence, serve time, ‖take a vacation
6 ***syn*** ADVANCE 1, encourage, forward, foster, further, promote
7 ***syn*** TREAT 2, deal (with), handle, play, take, use

service *n* 1 the performance of military duty in wartime and especially in a combat zone <saw a year's *service* in Vietnam>
syn action, combat
rel active duty, duty; fighting
2 ***syn*** FAVOR 4, courtesy, dispensation, indulgence, kindness
3 ***syn*** RITE 2, ceremonial, ceremony, formality, liturgy, observance, ritual
4 ***syn*** USE 3, account, advantage, applicability, appropriateness, avail, fitness, relevance, serviceability, usefulness

serviceability *n* ***syn*** USE 3, account, advantage, applicability, appropriateness, avail, fitness, relevance, service, usefulness
rel serviceableness; durability

serviceable *adj* 1 ***syn*** HELPFUL 1, aidant, aiding, assistive
ant unserviceable
2 ***syn*** PRACTICAL 2, functional, handy, practicable, useful, utile
ant unserviceable

serviceman *n* 1 ***syn*** SOLDIER, fighter, fighting man, GI, man-at-arms, swad, ‖swaddy, ‖sweat, warrior
2 **servicemen** *pl* ***syn*** TROOP 2, armed forces, forces, military

servile *adj* 1 ***syn*** SUBSERVIENT 2, menial, obeisant, obsequious, slavish
rel obedient, submissive; passive, unresisting; bootlicking, groveling, toadish
con aggressive
ant authoritative
2 ***syn*** BASE 3, abject, despicable, ignoble, low, mean, scurvy, sordid, ugly, vile

servility *n* ***syn*** BONDAGE, enslavement, helotry, peonage, serfage, serfdom, servitude, slavery, thralldom, yoke

servitude *n* ***syn*** BONDAGE, enslavement, helotry, peonage, serfdom, serfhood, servility, slavery, thralldom, yoke
con freedom, independence

set *vb* 1 to position (something) in a specified place <*set* the lamp on the table>
syn establish, fix, lay, place, put, settle, stick
rel bestow, deposit, park; emplace, ensconce, install; affix, anchor, wedge
con displace, replace, supplant; remove, take (away); uproot
2 ***syn*** DIRECT 2, aim, cast, head, lay, level, point, train, turn, zero (in)
idiom set one's sights on
3 ***syn*** STATION, post
4 ***syn*** DICTATE, decree, impose, lay down, ordain, prescribe
rel designate, direct, instruct, specify, stipulate; establish; make, name
5 to put in order for a meal <she quickly *set* the table for dinner>
syn lay, spread
rel fix, prepare, ready; arrange
ant clear
6 ***syn*** GAMBLE 1, bet, game, lay, play, put (on), stake, wager
7 ***syn*** INCITE, abet, foment, instigate, provoke, raise, set on, stir (up), whip (up)
‖8 ***syn*** SIT 1
9 ***syn*** BELONG 1, fit, go
10 ***syn*** COAGULATE, clot, congeal, gel, gelate, gelatinize, jell, jellify, jelly
11 *of a fowl* to incubate eggs by crouching upon them <a chicken house filled with hens *setting* on eggs>
syn brood, ‖clock, cover, sit
rel hatch, incubate; hover
12 *of a celestial body* to pass below the horizon <the sun *set* at seven o'clock>
syn decline, dip, go down, sink
rel descend, drop
con ascend, climb, come up
ant rise
13 ***syn*** HARDEN 1, cake, concrete, congeal, dry, indurate, solidify
rel crystallize, granulate; fix

---

syn synonym(s) | *rel* related word(s)
idiom idiomatic equivalent(s) | *con* contrasted word(s)
ant antonym(s) | * vulgar
‖ use limited; if in doubt, see a dictionary
The first word in a synonym list when printed in SMALL CAPITALS shows where there is more information about the group. For a more efficient use of this book see Explanatory Notes.

set (at) *vb* ***syn*** ESTIMATE 1, appraise, assay, assess, evaluate, rate, survey, valuate, value

set *adj* **1** ***syn*** SITUATED, located, placed, positioned, sited, situate
2 ***syn*** DECIDED 2, bent, decisive, determined, intent, resolute, resolved, settled
3 ***syn*** FIRM 4, certain, fixed, settled, stated, stipulated
rel confirmed, entrenched, established, inveterate, rooted, well-set, well-settled; prescribed, specified
4 ***syn*** LITTLE 2, borné, ineffectual, limited, mean, narrow, paltry, small
rel diehard, inflexible, obstinate, pigheaded, rigid, unbending, unyielding
5 ***syn*** FAST 4, firm, fixed, secure, tenacious, tight
rel fastened; close; sound
6 ***syn*** EXPRESS 2, especial, special, specific
7 ***syn*** READY 1, prepared

set *n* **1** ***syn*** GIFT 2, aptness, bent, bump, genius, head, knack, nose, talent, turn
2 ***syn*** BEARING 1, address, air, comportment, demeanor, deportment, mien, port, presence
3 ***syn*** SCENE 1, mise-en-scène, scenery, setting, stage set, stage setting
4 ***syn*** GROUP 3, array, batch, body, bunch, bundle, clump, cluster, clutch, lot
rel assortment, gaggle; kit, pack
5 a number of people having something (as habit, interest, occupation, or age) in common <the horsey *set* was gathered at the bar>
syn bunch, circle, crowd, group, lot, push; *compare* CLIQUE
rel clan, clique, crew, gang, mob; cénacle; camp, faction; company

set back *vb* ***syn*** DELAY 1, bog (down), decelerate, detain, embog, hang up, mire, retard, slacken, slow (up *or* down)

setback *n* a checking of progress <loss of his fellowship was a serious *setback* to his education>
syn backset, check, reversal, reverse; *compare* COMEDOWN
rel delay, retardation, slowdown; hindrance, impediment, obstacle, stumbling block; disappointment; rebuff; defeat; regress, regression
idiom reverse of fortune
con advancement, forwarding, progressing

set down *vb* ***syn*** ALIGHT, land, light, perch, roost, settle, sit down, touch down

set off *vb* **1** ***syn*** COMPENSATE 1, atone (for), balance, counterbalance, counterpoise, countervail, make up, offset, outweigh, redeem
2 ***syn*** MOBILIZE 1, actuate, circulate

set on *vb* ***syn*** INCITE, abet, foment, instigate, provoke, raise, set, stir (up), whip (up)

syn synonym(s) ***rel*** related word(s)
idiom idiomatic equivalent(s) ***con*** contrasted word(s)
ant antonym(s) * vulgar
‖ use limited; if in doubt, see a dictionary
The first word in a synonym list when printed in SMALL CAPITALS shows where there is more information about the group. For a more efficient use of this book see Explanatory Notes.

set out *vb* **1** ***syn*** DESIGN 3, arrange, lay out, map (out), plan
2 ***syn*** HEAD 3, bear, light out, make, strike out, take off
idiom set one's course for

setout *n* **1** ***syn*** COSTUME, dress, getup, guise, outfit, rig, turnout
2 ***syn*** BEGINNING, birth, commencement, dawn, dawning, onset, opening, outset, outstart, start

setting *n* ***syn*** SCENE 1, mise-en-scène, scenery, set, stage set, stage setting

setting–out *n* ***syn*** DEPARTURE 1, egress, egression, exit, exiting, exodus, offgoing, withdrawal

settle *vb* **1** ***syn*** ENSCONCE 2, install
2 ***syn*** CALM, allay, becalm, compose, lull, quiet, ‖quieten, soothe, still, tranquilize
rel assure, reassure
ant unsettle
3 ***syn*** SET 1, establish, fix, lay, place, put, stick
rel found, ground, lodge, seat
con dislodge, uproot, unseat
ant unsettle
4 ***syn*** DECIDE, conclude, determine, figure, resolve, rule
rel fix, seal
idiom come to a decision (*or* conclusion), form a judgment, make a decision
5 ***syn*** NEGOTIATE 1, arrange, concert
rel mediate, reconcile, straighten (out)
idiom bring to terms (*or* agreement)
6 ***syn*** CLEAR 5, clear off, discharge, liquidate, pay, pay up, quit, satisfy, square
idiom settle the score, settle up (*or* square) accounts
7 to put in order for final disposal <waiting to *settle* an estate>
syn clean up, wind up
8 ***syn*** ALIGHT, land, light, perch, roost, set down, sit down, touch down
rel flop (down), plop (down)

settled *adj* **1** ***syn*** FIRM 4, certain, fixed, set, stated, stipulated
rel decided, determined
con uncertain, undecided
ant unsettled
2 ***syn*** INVETERATE 1, bred-in-the-bone, confirmed, deep-dyed, deep-rooted, deep-seated, dyed-in-the-wool, entrenched, hard-shell, sworn
3 ***syn*** DECIDED 2, bent, decisive, determined, intent, resolute, resolved, set
rel certain, fixed
con irresolute, undecided, undetermined, unresolved, vacillating, wavering
ant unsettled

settlement *n* **1** ***syn*** HABITATION 1, inhabitancy, inhabitation, occupancy, occupation, residence
2 ***syn*** DECISION 1, conclusion, determination, resolution
rel showdown; quietus

settlings *n pl* ***syn*** SEDIMENT, deposit, dreg(s), grounds, lees, precipitate, precipitation

set to *vb* **1** ***syn*** BEGIN 1, commence, embark (on *or* upon), enter, get off, launch, open, start, take up, tee off

2 *syn* PITCH IN 1, buckle (down), fall to, jump (in *or* into), wade (in *or* into)

set–to *n* **1** *syn* BRAWL 2, affray, bobbery, broil, fight, fracas, fray, row, scrap, scuffle
2 *syn* QUARREL, altercation, bickering, dispute, falling-out, fight, hassle, rhubarb, row, run-in
3 *syn* ENCOUNTER, brush, run-in, skirmish, velitation

set up *vb* **1** *syn* ERECT 5, build up, construct, establish, hammer (out)
ant tear down
2 *syn* ELATE, commove, excite, exhilarate, inspire, spirit (up), stimulate
3 *syn* ERECT 3, put up, raise, rear
con disassemble, take down
4 *syn* FOUND 2, constitute, create, establish, institute, organize, start
rel generate, originate; start up; open
5 *syn* INTRODUCE 3, inaugurate, initiate, institute, launch, originate, usher in
6 *syn* TREAT 3, blow, ‖shout, stand

setup *n syn* SNAP 1, breeze, child's play, cinch, duck soup, kid stuff, picnic, pie, ‖pipe, pushover

seventh heaven *n syn* ECSTASY, heaven, rapture, rhapsody, transport
rel exhilaration; bliss, paradise
con sadness, unhappiness; blues, doldrums, dumps

sever *vb* **1** *syn* SEPARATE 1, break up, dichotomize, disjoint, dissect, dissever, divide, divorce, part, sunder
2 *syn* KNOW 4, difference, differentiate, discern, discrepate, discriminate, distinguish, extricate, separate, severalize
3 *syn* CUT 5, carve, cleave, dissect, dissever, slice, split, sunder

several *adj* **1** possessed by or attributed to a specific individual <the debaters expressed their *several* opinions>
syn individual, particular, respective, singular
rel independent; personal, special, specific
2 *syn* DISTINCT 1, different, discrete, diverse, separate, various
3 consisting of an indefinite number more than two and less than many <*several* days passed>
syn divers, some, sundry, various
rel particular, separate, single; few; considerable; many, numerous
idiom not a few
‖**4** *syn* MANY, legion, multifarious, multitudinal, multitudinous, numerous, populous, sundry, various, voluminous

‖**several** *pron syn* SUNDRY, divers, many, various

severalize *vb syn* KNOW 4, difference, differentiate, discern, discrepate, discriminate, distinguish, extricate, separate, sever

severally *adv syn* APART 1, independently, individually, one by one, separately, singly
rel discretely; exclusively
idiom one at a time

severe *adj* **1** given to or characterized by strict discipline and firm restraint <treated all the students with *severe* impartiality>
syn ascetic, astringent, austere, mortified, stern
rel exacting, heavy-handed, onerous, oppressive; disciplined, iron-willed, self-disciplined; inflexible, restrictive, rigid, rigorous, strict, stringent, uncompromising, unyielding
con easy, easygoing, gentle, mild, soft; clement, forbearing, indulgent, lax, lenient, merciful
ant tender, tolerant
2 *syn* GRIM 2, austere, bleak, dour, hard, harsh, stringent
rel serious, sober, stern
3 of a kind to cause discomfort or hardship <a *severe* winter storm>
syn bitter, brutal, hard, harsh, inclement, intemperate, rigorous, rugged
rel crimpy, unpleasant; forbidding, hostile, inhospitable; bleak, disagreeable, grim; painful, raw, sharp, smart; blistering, extreme, intense, savage; blustering, blustery, stormy, wintry
con balmy, calm, equable, gentle, moderate, soft, temperate
ant mild
4 *syn* HARD 6, arduous, difficult, effortful, heavy, laborious, serious, strenuous, toilsome, tough
5 *syn* SERIOUS 2, grave, heavy, weighty
rel consequential; dear, sore

severely *adv* **1** *syn* HARD 5, badly, hardly, harshly, painfully, rigorously, roughly
2 *syn* SERIOUSLY 2, gravely, intensely
rel markedly

‖**sew** *vb syn* EXUDE, bleed, ooze, ‖screeve, seep, ‖sicker, strain, sweat, transude, weep

sew up *vb* ‖**1** *syn* EXHAUST 4, ‖bugger, fag, frazzle, knock out, outtire, ‖poop, prostrate, tucker, wear out
2 *syn* MONOPOLIZE, absorb, consume, engross

sexy *adj syn* RISQUÉ, blue, broad, off-color, purple, racy, salty, shady, spicy, suggestive

shabby *adj* **1** being ill-kept and showing signs of wear and tear <a *shabby* neighborhood full of depressing tenements>
syn bedraggled, broken-down, decrepit, dilapidated, dingy, disreputable, down-at-heel, faded, mangy, moth-eaten, run-down, scrubby, scruffy, seedy, shoddy, sleazy, slipshod, squalid, tacky, tagrag, tattered, threadbare, tired
rel disfigured, dog-eared; decaying, deteriorated, deteriorating; ramshackle, ratty, rickety; bare, miserable, neglected, poor, poverty-stricken; sordid; worm-eaten; outworn, worn-out; abandoned, desolate, ruined, ruinous, wrecked
idiom gone to seed
con neat, spick-and-span, tidy, trig, trim, well-kept; brand-new, fresh, new; unused
ant spruce
2 *syn* CONTEMPTIBLE, beggarly, cheap, despicable, despisable, mean, pitiable, scummy, scurvy, sorry

---

syn synonym(s) *rel* related word(s)
idiom idiomatic equivalent(s) *con* contrasted word(s)
ant antonym(s) * vulgar
‖ use limited; if in doubt, see a dictionary
The first word in a synonym list when printed in SMALL CAPITALS shows where there is more information about the group. For a more efficient use of this book see Explanatory Notes.

3 ***syn*** DISREPUTABLE 1, discreditable, disgraceful, dishonorable, ignominious, inglorious, shady, shameful, shoddy, unrespectable

‖**shack** *n* ***syn*** VAGABOND, ‖bindle stiff, bum, derelict, drifter, floater, hobo, street arab, tramp, ‖traveler

shack *n* ***syn*** HUT, ‖box, cabin, ‖caboose, camp, cot, cottage, lodge, shanty

shackle *n, usu* **shackles** *pl* something that confines the legs or arms so as to prevent free movement <slaves in *shackles*>
syn bond(s), chains, fetter(s), gyve(s), iron(s)
rel anklet, bilbo, leg-iron, trammel; bracelet, handcuff, manacle; straitjacket; collar, garrote

shackle *vb* ***syn*** HAMPER, clog, curb, entrammel, fetter, hobble, hog-tie, leash, tie, trammel
rel lash, rope, strap; chain, enchain, manacle; handcuff; pinion, secure
con unchain, unfetter, untie
ant unshackle

shade *n* **1** comparative darkness or obscurity due to interception of light rays <trees providing *shade* from the sunlight>
syn adumbration, penumbra, shadow, umbra, umbrage
rel blackness, darkness, dimness, obscuration, obscurity; cover, shelter
con brightness, brilliancy, effulgence, radiance; blaze, glare, glow
2 ***syn*** APPARITION, bogey, ghost, ‖haunt, phantasm, phantom, shadow, specter, spirit, umbra
3 ***syn*** COLOR 1, cast, hue, tinge, tint, tone
rel intensity, saturation
4 ***syn*** GRADATION, nuance
rel difference, distinction, variation
5 ***syn*** HINT 2, cast, soupçon, spice, streak, suggestion, suspicion, tincture, tinge, trace

shade *vb* to cast into shadow by intercepting light rays <avenues *shaded* by large trees>
syn inumbrate, screen, shadow, umbrage
rel shelter; cover
con roast, scorch, swelter; expose

shaded *adj* ***syn*** SHADY 1, shadow, shadowed, shadowy, umbrageous, umbrous
ant unshaded

shadow *n* **1** ***syn*** SHADE 1, adumbration, penumbra, umbra, umbrage
2 ***syn*** APPARITION, eidolon, phantasm, phantom, revenant, shade, specter, spirit, umbra, wraith
3 ***syn*** VESTIGE 1, memento, relic, trace
4 ***syn*** HINT 2, breath, intimation, smack, suggestion, suspicion, tincture, tinge, touch, trace

shadow *vb* **1** ***syn*** SHADE, inumbrate, screen, umbrage
2 ***syn*** OBSCURE, adumbrate, becloud, bedim, cloud, dim, haze, overcast, overcloud, overshadow
3 ***syn*** TAIL, bedog, dog, tag, trail

shadow (forth) *vb* **1** ***syn*** SUGGEST 5, adumbrate
2 ***syn*** ADUMBRATE 1, foreshadow, hint, prefigurate, prefigure
rel forecast, foretell, predict

shadow *adj* ***syn*** SHADY 1, shaded, shadowed, shadowy, umbrageous, umbrous

shadowed *adj* ***syn*** SHADY 1, shaded, shadow, shadowy, umbrageous, umbrous
ant unshadowed

shadowy *adj* **1** ***syn*** IMAGINARY 1, fancied, fanciful, imagined, notional
2 ***syn*** GHASTLY 2, cadaverous, corpselike, deathlike, ghostlike, ghostly, spectral
3 ***syn*** FAINT 2, blear, bleary, dim, fuzzy, indistinct, obscure, unclear, undefined, undistinct
rel amorphous; foggy
4 ***syn*** SHADY 1, shaded, shadow, shadowed, umbrageous, umbrous
ant bright

shady *adj* **1** producing, affording, or abounding in shade <a *shady* day> <cool, *shady* streets>
syn shaded, shadow, shadowed, shadowy, umbrageous, umbrous
rel bosky, screened, sheltered; dusky; dark
con exposed, unshaded, unshadowed; unsheltered; bright, light
ant sunny
2 ***syn*** DOUBTFUL 1, clouded, equivocal, fishy, impugnable, indecisive, suspect, suspicious, uncertain, undecided
3 ***syn*** DISREPUTABLE 1, discreditable, disgraceful, dishonorable, ignominious, inglorious, shabby, shameful, shoddy, unrespectable
rel subreputable
4 ***syn*** RISQUÉ, blue, broad, off-color, purple, racy, salty, spicy, suggestive, wicked
rel disreputable, shameful

shaft *n* **1** ***syn*** RAY 1, beam, shoot
2 a scornful, cutting, or pithily critical remark <the target of his latest *shaft* is the president himself>
syn barb, dart
rel cut, jab, thrust; potshot
3 harsh or unfair treatment <he really got the *shaft:* he was fired without notice>
syn ‖screw, ‖screwing
rel short end
idiom ‖a royal screwing, the dirty end of the stick, ‖the royal shaft

shake *vb* **1** to move irregularly to and fro or up and down often in a wavering or oscillating manner <was so frightened that her hands *shook*>
syn ‖didder, dither, quake, quaver, quiver, shiver, shudder, tremble, tremor, twitter
rel palpitate, quail, waver; flicker, flit, flitter, flutter; fluctuate, oscillate; chatter, shimmy, vibrate
idiom shake like an aspen leaf
2 to undergo strong vibration especially as the result of a physical blow or shock <the platform *shook* as the train passed>
syn jar, quake, tremble, tremor, vibrate
rel bounce, jounce; chatter, quiver, shimmy; rock, stagger
3 to cause to move in a quick, jerky manner <rattling and *shaking* the latch>

---

syn synonym(s) ***rel*** related word(s)
idiom idiomatic equivalent(s) ***con*** contrasted word(s)
ant antonym(s) * vulgar
‖ use limited; if in doubt, see a dictionary
The first word in a synonym list when printed in SMALL CAPITALS shows where there is more information about the group. For a more efficient use of this book see Explanatory Notes.

syn jiggle, joggle
rel bounce, ||chounse, jounce; jostle; rattle; jerk
4 to cause to move to and fro or up and down violently <an earthquake that *shook* the whole coast>
syn agitate, concuss, convulse, rock
rel jog, jostle, rattle, ||shog; commove, discompose, disorder, jar, jolt, unsettle; disquiet, disturb, perturb, upset; churn, roil, ruffle, stir up, whip
5 to get or keep away from (a pursuer) <tried unsuccessfully to *shake* the man tailing him>
syn lose, slip, throw off; *compare* ESCAPE 2
rel avoid, elude; outwit
idiom get rid of, give (someone) the shake (*or* slip), slip from under the eye of
6 *syn* DISMAY 1, appall, consternate, daunt, horrify
rel disturb, jar, rattle, unsettle, upset; bother, worry; unnerve, unstring

shake (off) *vb syn* RID, clear, lose, throw off, unburden

shake *n* **1** *syn* EARTHQUAKE, quake, ||quaker, shock, temblor (*or* tremblor), tremor
2 shakes *pl syn* JITTERS, ||all-overs, dither, heebie-jeebies, ||jimjams, ||jimmies, jumps, shivers, whim-whams, willies
3 *syn* INSTANT 1, breathing, crack, flash, ||jiff, jiffy, minute, moment, second, split second
4 *syn* DEAL 2

shake down *vb* **1** *syn* EXTORT 1, exact, gouge, pinch, screw, squeeze, wrench, wrest, wring
2 *syn* SEARCH 2, ||fan, frisk

shake up *vb syn* SPEED 3, accelerate, hasten, hurry, quicken, step up, swiften

shake–up *n* an extensive and often drastic rearrangement <a personnel *shake-up* effected by new management>
syn overturn, reorganization, revolution, turnover
rel liquidation, purge; cleanout, cleanup, clearing out, clear-up; removal, riddance
idiom break with the past, clean sweep

shakiness *n syn* INSTABILITY, precariousness, unfixedness, unsettledness, unstability, unstableness, unsteadfastness, unsteadiness

shaking *adj syn* TREMULOUS, aquake, aquiver, ashake, quaking, quivering, shaky, trembling, tremorous, tremulant
rel unsettled, unstable, unsteady; tottering
con unshakable, unshaken

shaky *adj* **1** *syn* WEAK 2, dickey, fluctuant, insecure, rootless, unstable, unsure, vacillating, wavering, wobbly
rel unsettled; infirm, unsound, unsteady; precarious, tottering, tottery
2 *syn* DOUBTFUL 1, dubious, indecisive, precarious, problematic, suspect, uncertain, unclear, unsettled, unsure
3 *syn* TREMULOUS, aquake, aquiver, ashake, quaking, quivering, quivery, shaking, trembling, tremorous
4 *syn* RICKETY, rachitic, rackety, rattletrap, wobbly

shallow *adj* **1** lacking physical depth <buried in a *shallow* grave>
syn shoal, superficial
rel shallowish; surface
idiom as deep as a mud puddle, no deeper than a heavy dew, not deep enough to float a match
con bottomless, unfathomable
ant deep
2 *syn* SUPERFICIAL 2, cursory, depthless, sketchy, uncritical
rel paltry, petty, trifling, trivial; empty, hollow, idle, vain; bird-witted, featherbrained, flighty
con heavy, profound; discerning, penetrating
ant deep

shallow *n syn* SHOAL
ant deep

sham *n* **1** *syn* IMPOSTURE, cheat, deceit, deception, fake, flimflam, hoax, put-on, sell, spoof
rel facade, fakery, false front, Potemkin village
2 *syn* HYPOCRISY, cant, hypocriticalness, pecksniffery, pharisaicalness, pharisaism, sanctimoniousness, sanctimony, Tartuffery, Tartuffism
3 *syn* MOCKERY 2, burlesque, caricature, farce, mock, travesty

sham *vb syn* ASSUME 4, act, affect, bluff, counterfeit, fake, feign, pretend, put on, simulate
rel ape, copy, imitate, mock; create, invent; lie, mislead

sham *adj* **1** *syn* FICTITIOUS 2, fake, mock, simulated
rel affected, assumed, feigned; pseudo, so-called; make-believe, pretend
2 *syn* COUNTERFEIT, bogus, brummagem, fake, false, phony, pinchbeck, pseudo, snide, spurious
3 *syn* ARTIFICIAL 2, dummy, ersatz, false, imitation, mock, simulated, spurious, substitute
rel plaster, synthetic; adulterated; bogus

shamble *vb syn* SHUFFLE 3, scuff, scuffle, ||shool, shovel

shambles *n pl but usu sing in constr syn* MESS 3, botch, botchery, hash, mess-up, mix-up, muddle, mull, muss

shame *n syn* DISGRACE, discredit, disesteem, dishonor, disrepute, ignominy, infamy, obloquy, odium, opprobrium
rel chagrin, embarrassment; guilt, mortification, self-reproach, self-reproof
con pride, self-admiration, self-love, self-respect
ant glory

shamed *adj syn* ASHAMED, chagrined, mortified
rel crestfallen; shamefaced, shamefast; crushed, disgraced
idiom loaded (*or* bowed down) with shame
ant proud

shameful *adj syn* DISREPUTABLE 1, discreditable, disgraceful, dishonorable, ignominious, inglorious, shabby, shady, shoddy, unrespectable

shameless *adj* characterized by or exhibiting boldness and a lack of shame <a *shameless* hussy>
syn arrant, barefaced, blatant, brassy, brazen, brazenfaced, impudent, overbold, unabashed, unblushing
rel audacious, bold, cheeky, presumptuous; baldfaced, high-handed; abandoned, dissolute, profligate; immodest, lewd; disgraceful, outrageous
idiom bold as brass, dead (*or* lost) to shame

con bashful, diffident, mousy, shy; chaste, decent, modest, pure

‖**shamus** *n* ***syn*** PRIVATE DETECTIVE, operative, Pinkerton, ‖private eye

Shangri-la *n* ***syn*** UTOPIA, arcadia, Cockaigne, fairyland, heaven, lubberland, paradise, promised land, wonderland, Zion

shanty *n* ***syn*** HUT, ‖box, cabin, ‖caboose, camp, cot, cottage, lodge, shack

shape *vb* ***syn*** MAKE 3, assemble, build, construct, fabricate, fashion, forge, form, frame, mold
rel devise, plan, work up; tailor

shape *n* **1** ***syn*** FORM 1, cast, configuration, conformation, figure
rel appearance, aspect, look, semblance
2 ***syn*** ORDER 9, case, condition, estate, repair
3 ***syn*** ORDER 10, condition, fettle, fitness, kilter, repair, trim
rel state, whack

shapeful *adj* ***syn*** SHAPELY, clean-limbed, statuesque, trim, well-proportioned, well-turned
ant shapeless

shapeless *adj* ***syn*** FORMLESS, amorphous, inchoate, unformed, unshaped
rel unshapely; deformed, misshapen
con proportional, proportionate, proportioned, shapeful, symmetrical
ant shapeful, shapely

shapely *adj* having a regular or pleasing shape <a *shapely* girl>
syn clean-limbed, shapeful, statuesque, trim, well-proportioned, well-turned; *compare* CURVACEOUS
rel balanced, clean-cut, proportioned, regular, symmetrical; comely, pleasing; ‖built, full-figured, rounded, ‖stacked; buxom
con dumpy, squat, stumpy; angular, lank, lean; ill-favored, ill-looking
ant shapeless, unshapely

share *n* **1** something belonging to, assumed by, or falling to one (as in division or apportionment) <wanted his *share* of the prize money>
syn allotment, allowance, bite, cut, lot, part, partage, portion, quota, slice; *compare* RATION
rel proportion, quotient, quotum; commission, percentage; divide, ‖divvy; rake-off
idiom piece of the action, slice of the melon
2 ***syn*** RATION, allotment, allowance, apportionment, measure, meed, part, portion, quantum, quota
3 ***syn*** INTEREST 1, claim, stake

share *vb* **1** ***syn*** APPORTION 2, divide, ‖divvy, parcel, portion, prorate, quota, ration, ‖shift
rel assign, deal (out), dispense, dole (out), give out, mete (out)
idiom ‖go snucks, share and share alike
con retain, withhold; combine, unite
2 to have, get, or use in common with another or others <she *shared* her husband's fate>
syn partake, participate
rel experience
idiom have a share (*or* part) in, have (*or* take) a hand in

shared *adj* ***syn*** COMMON 1, communal, conjoint, conjunct, intermutual, joint, mutual, public
ant unshared

share out *vb* ***syn*** ADMINISTER 2, apportion, deal (out), dispense, dole (out), mete (out), portion (out)

sharer *n* ***syn*** PARTICIPANT, actor, partaker, participator, party

sharp *adj* **1** having a fine edge <a *sharp* knife makes a clean cut>
syn honed, keen, razor-sharp, unblunted, whetted
rel acute
idiom sharp as a razor blade
con blunted, dulled; unsharpened
ant blunt, dull
2 ***syn*** POINTED 1, acicular, aciculate, acuminate, acuminous, acute, cuspidate, peaked, peaky, piked
3 ***syn*** INTELLIGENT 2, alert, brainy, bright, brilliant, clever, knowing, quick-witted, ready-witted, smart
4 possessing or indicative of alert competence and clear understanding <people of *sharp* judgment and refined sensibilities>
syn acute, keen, penetrating, penetrative, quick-sighted, quick-witted, sharp-sighted, sharp-witted; *compare* SHREWD
rel alert, bright; clever, cute, ingenious, original, resourceful; fast, quick
idiom sharp as a knife (*or* tack)
con dull-witted; unintelligent; foolish, simple, slow, stupid
ant dull
5 ***syn*** ACUTE 3, keen, perceptive, sensitive
6 ***syn*** WISE 4, canny, hep, knowing, nimble-witted, quick, quick-witted, sharp-witted, slick, smart
rel adroit, nimble; clever, cute; sly, unethical
idiom nobody's fool
7 ***syn*** SHORT 5, inconsiderate, thoughtless, unceremonious, ungracious
rel acrimonious, biting, double-edged, incisive, penetrating, piercing, stabbing, stinging; caustic, virulent, vitriolic
8 causing intense mental or physical distress <a *sharp* pain>
syn acute, knifelike, piercing, shooting, stabbing
rel intense, severe, smart; biting, drilling, stinging; penetrating; agonizing, excruciating; paralyzing
9 ***syn*** ACRID, amaroidal, astringent, austere, bitter, harsh
rel odorous; strong-scented, strong-smelling; suffocating
10 ***syn*** ACUTE 4, argute, high, piercing, piping, shrill, thin, treble
11 ***syn*** STYLISH, ‖classy, dashing, snappy, swank, swish, tonish, tony, ‖trendy, trig

‖**sharp** *vb* ***syn*** SHARPEN, edge, hone, whet

sharp *adv* ***syn*** JUST 1, accurately, bang, exactly, precisely, right, ‖smack-dab, spang, square, squarely

sharpen *vb* to give a keen edge to < *sharpen* an ax >
syn edge, hone, ‖sharp, whet
rel dress, file, grind, stroke
idiom hone to a razor edge, hone to razor sharpness
ant blunt, dull

sharper *n syn* SWINDLER, cheat, con man, defrauder, diddler, double-dealer, ‖grifter, gyp, mountebank, trickster

sharp–eyed *adj* having keen vision < the *sharp-eyed* child found all the Easter eggs >
syn eagle-eyed, hawk-eyed, lyncean, lynx-eyed, sharp-sighted
rel alert, attentive, aware, keen, lynxlike, observant, sharp, vigilant, watchful
con myopic, nearsighted, shortsighted; dim-sighted, purblind; blind

sharpie *n syn* SWINDLER, cheat, con man, defrauder, diddler, double-dealer, ‖grifter, gyp, mountebank, trickster

sharply *adv syn* HARD 4, closely, intently, searchingly
rel intensely, penetratingly, piercingly

sharpness *n syn* EDGE 2, incisiveness, keenness
ant bluntness, dullness

sharp practice *n syn* DECEPTION 1, cheat, chicane, chicanery, double-dealing, fourberie, fraud, hanky-panky, highbinding, trickery

sharp–sighted *adj* **1** *syn* SHARP-EYED, eagle-eyed, hawk-eyed, lyncean, lynx-eyed
2 *syn* SHARP 4, acute, keen, penetrating, penetrative, quick-sighted, quick-witted, sharp-witted

sharp–witted *adj* **1** *syn* SHARP 4, acute, keen, penetrating, penetrative, quick-sighted, quick-witted, sharp-sighted
2 *syn* WISE 4, canny, hep, knowing, nimble-witted, quick, quick-witted, sharp, slick, smart

shatter *vb* **1** to break into small pieces by or as if by a blow < *shatter* a windowpane with a rock >
syn burst, fragment, ‖pash, rive, shiver, smash, ‖smatter, splinter, splinterize, splitter; *compare* PULVERIZE 1
rel break, crack, rend, snap, ‖spalt, split; crunch, crush; crash, dash; fragmentalize, fragmentize, pulverize; demolish, destroy, disintegrate, ruin, ‖total, wreck
idiom smash to smithereens (*or* bits)
2 *syn* DESTROY 1, annihilate, decimate, demolish, destruct, raze, ruin, shoot, wrack, wreck
3 *syn* RATTLE 1, bicker, clack, clatter, clitter, ‖ruttle

shatterable *adj syn* FRAGILE 1, breakable, delicate, fracturable, frail, frangible, shattery
ant shatterproof

shatterbrain *n syn* SCATTERBRAIN, birdbrain, featherbrain, featherhead, flibbertigibbet, harebrain, rattlebrain, rattlehead

shattering *adj syn* DESTRUCTIVE, annihilative, ruinous, wrackful, wreckful

shattery *adj syn* FRAGILE 1, breakable, delicate, fracturable, frail, frangible, shatterable
idiom as delicate as an eggshell

shave *vb* **1** *syn* SLIVER, shred
2 *syn* CUT 6, clip, crop, pare, prune, shear, skive, trim
rel shingle
3 *syn* REDUCE 2, clip, cut, cut back, cut down, lower, mark down, pare, slash
4 *syn* BRUSH, glance, graze, kiss, skim
idiom cut (*or* shave) it close
5 *syn* SCRAPE 3

shaveling *n syn* BOY 1, lad, laddie, son, stripling, tad

shear *vb syn* CUT 6, clip, crop, pare, prune, shave, skive, trim
rel mow; barb, barber; manicure, snip

sheath *n syn* SKIN 3, sheathing

sheathe *vb* to cover (a surface) with something that protects < a house *sheathed* with aluminum siding >
syn clad, face, side, skin
rel envelop, surround, wrap; case, cover, encase, jacket; panel
con bare, expose, strip

sheathing *n syn* SKIN 3, sheath

shed *vb* **1** *syn* DISCARD, cashier, cast, jettison, junk, reject, scrap, slough, throw away, throw out
rel drop; divest
2 to cast off (a body covering) in a periodic process of growth or renewal < a snake *shedding* its skin >
syn exuviate, molt, slip, slough
rel cast off, discard; doff, take off

sheen *n syn* LUSTER, glaze, glint, gloss, polish, shine
rel finish; shininess

sheeny *adj syn* LUSTROUS 1, burnished, gleaming, glistening, glossy, polished, shining, shiny

sheepheaded *adj syn* SIMPLE 3, brainless, ‖buffle-headed, fatuous, mindless, nitwitted, senseless, silly, unwitty, witless

sheer *adj* **1** *syn* FILMY, diaphanous, flimsy, gauzy, gossamer, tiffany, transparent
rel airy, chiffon, thin; see-through
2 *syn* UTTER, absolute, blasted, blessed, complete, confounded, gross, infernal, out-and-out, rank
3 *syn* PURE 2, absolute, perfect, simple, unadulterated, unalloyed, undiluted, unmitigated, unmixed, unqualified
rel arrant, bald-faced, complete, outright
4 *syn* STEEP 1, abrupt, arduous, precipitate, precipitous, sideling, steepdown, steep-to, steep-up, ‖stickle

sheer *vb* **1** *syn* TURN 6, avert, deflect, divert, pivot, veer, volte-face, wheel, whip, whirl
2 *syn* SWERVE 1, dip, skew, slue, train off, veer

‖shekels *n pl syn* MONEY, ‖bread, ‖chips, ‖coin, dough, ‖greenbacks, ‖jack, ‖mazuma, ‖scratch, ‖wampum

shell *n syn* HULL, case, husk, pod, shuck, skin, ‖slough

shell *vb* **1** *syn* SHUCK, hull, husk
2 *syn* BOMBARD, blitz, bomb, cannonade
rel pepper; rake
idiom open fire on

shellac *vb syn* WHIP 2, beat, ‖clobber, drub, lambaste, lick, smear, smother, thrash, trim

shellacking *n syn* DEFEAT 1, beating, debacle, defeasance, drubbing, licking, overthrow, rout, trouncing, vanquishment

---

syn synonym(s) *rel* related word(s)
idiom idiomatic equivalent(s) *con* contrasted word(s)
ant antonym(s) * vulgar
‖ use limited; if in doubt, see a dictionary
The first word in a synonym list when printed in SMALL CAPITALS shows where there is more information about the group. For a more efficient use of this book see Explanatory Notes.

rel ‖clobbering, whipping

shell out *vb* ***syn*** SPEND 1, disburse, expend, fork (out), give, lay out, outlay, pay

shelter *n* **1** something (as a structure or place) that covers or affords protection <a bomb *shelter*>
syn asylum, cover, covert, harbor, harborage, haven, port, refuge, retreat, sanctuary; *compare* REFUGE 1
rel buen retiro, den, hermitage, hide, hideaway, hideout, hidey-hole, retirement, tower
2 dwellings provided for numbers of people or for a community <*shelter* for the aged>
syn housing, quarterage
rel dwellings, lodging; roof
3 ***syn*** REFUGE 1, asylum, harborage, sanctuary

shelter *vb* ***syn*** HARBOR 1, chamber, haven, house, roof, shield

shelve *vb* ***syn*** DEFER, delay, hold off, hold over, hold up, postpone, prorogue, put off, stay, waive
rel dish, drop, give up
idiom put on the shelf

shenanigan *n* **1** ***syn*** TRICK 1, device, gimmick, maneuver, play, ploy, ruse, stratagem, whizzer, wile
rel fast one, game, legerdemain
2 ***syn*** PRANK, antic, caper, dido(es), frolic, lark, monkeyshine, shine(s), tomfoolery, trick
rel frolic; goings-on, mischievousness; stunt

Sheol *n* ***syn*** HELL, barathrum, Gehenna, hades, inferno, netherworld, Pandemonium, perdition, Tophet, underworld

shepherd *vb* ***syn*** GUIDE, conduct, direct, escort, lead, pilot, route, see, show, steer

Sherlock *n* ***syn*** DETECTIVE, dick, ‖eye, gumshoe, hawkshaw, investigator, plainclothesman, Sherlock Holmes, sleuth, ‖tec

Sherlock Holmes *n* ***syn*** DETECTIVE, dick, ‖eye, gumshoe, hawkshaw, investigator, plainclothesman, Sherlock, sleuth, ‖tec

shibboleth *n* **1** ***syn*** CATCHWORD, byword, catchphrase, phrase, slogan, watchword
rel platitude, truism
2 ***syn*** COMMONPLACE, banality, bromide, cliché, platitude, prosaicism, prosaism, rubber stamp, tag, truism

‖**shick** *adj* ***syn*** INTOXICATED 1, ‖boozy, ‖canned, disguised, drunk, inebriated, ‖lushed, muddled, pixilated, ‖plastered

‖**shicker** *adj* ***syn*** INTOXICATED 1, ‖boozy, ‖canned, disguised, drunk, inebriated, ‖lushed, muddled, pixilated, ‖plastered

‖**shicker** *n* ***syn*** DRUNKARD, ‖bloat, ‖blotter, boozehound, boozer, drunk, inebriate, soak, sot, tippler

shield *n* ***syn*** DEFENSE 1, aegis, armament, armor, guard, protection, safeguard, security, ward
rel buffer, bumper, screen

shield *vb* **1** ***syn*** HARBOR 1, chamber, haven, house, roof, shelter
idiom give cover (*or* shelter) to; take (*or* shield) under one's wing
ant expose
2 ***syn*** DEFEND 1, bulwark, cover, fend, guard, protect, safeguard, screen, secure

shift *vb* ‖**1** ***syn*** APPORTION 2, divide, ‖divvy, parcel, portion, prorate, quota, ration, share
2 ***syn*** CHANGE 5, replace
3 ***syn*** MOVE 4, dislocate, disturb, remove, ship, transfer
rel alter, change, vary; budge, stir; shuffle; relocate
idiom shift place
4 ***syn*** CONSUME 5, polish off, punish, put away, put down, swill
5 to carry on one's affairs independently and self-sufficiently often under difficult circumstances <had to *shift* for his own maintenance on very meager pay>
syn do, fare, get along, get by, get on, ‖make out, manage, muddle through, stagger (on *or* along)
rel contrive, survive; freelance; progress, succeed
idiom fend for oneself, make do, make it alone, make shift, paddle one's own canoe, stand on one's own two feet

shift *n* **1** ***syn*** CONVERSION 2, alteration, changeover, transformation
2 ***syn*** RESOURCE 3, dernier ressort, expediency, expedient, makeshift, recourse, refuge, resort, stopgap, substitute
rel gambit, maneuver, ploy, strategy
3 ***syn*** SPELL 1, bout, go, stint, time, tour, trick, turn
4 ***syn*** TRANSITION, alteration, passage, transit
5 ***syn*** TURN 2, bend, deflection, deviation, double, tack, yaw

shifty *adj* **1** ***syn*** EVASIVE 1, equivocating, prevaricative, prevaricatory, shuffling
rel dodging, elusive; cagey, collusive, conniving, crafty, cunning; furtive, shifty-eyed, sneaky, tricky; insidious, shady; deceitful, dishonest, fraudulent; treacherous
idiom shifty as the sand
2 ***syn*** DISHONEST, deceitful, knavish, lying, mendacious, roguish, unhonest, untruthful
3 ***syn*** UNDERHAND, devious, duplicitous, guileful, indirect, sneaking, sneaky, underhanded
4 ***syn*** MUTABLE 2, changeable, inconstant, slippery, uncertain, unstable, unsteady, variable

shill *n* ***syn*** DECOY 2, blind, ‖bonnet, ‖booster, capper, shillaber, stick

shillaber *n* ***syn*** DECOY 2, blind, ‖bonnet, ‖booster, capper, shill, stick

‖**shillelagh** *n* ***syn*** CUDGEL, bat, baton, billy, billy club, bludgeon, club, knobkerrie, mace, truncheon

shilling shocker *n* ***syn*** DIME NOVEL, dreadful, penny dreadful, shocker, yellowback

shilly–shally *adj* ***syn*** VACILLATING 2, faltering, halting, hesitating, shilly-shallying, vacillatory, wavering, whiffling, wiggle-waggle, wobbly

shilly–shally *n* ***syn*** HESITATION, hesitancy, indecision, indecisiveness, irresolution, to-and-fro, vacillation, wavering

shilly–shally *vb* ***syn*** HESITATE, dither, falter, halt, stagger, vacillate, waver, whiffle, wiggle-waggle

---

syn synonym(s) ***rel*** related word(s)
idiom idiomatic equivalent(s) ***con*** contrasted word(s)
ant antonym(s) * vulgar
‖ use limited; if in doubt, see a dictionary
The first word in a synonym list when printed in SMALL CAPITALS shows where there is more information about the group. For a more efficient use of this book see Explanatory Notes.

shilly–shallying *adj* ***syn*** VACILLATING 2, faltering, halting, indecisive, vacillant, vacillatory, wavering, whiffling, wiggle-waggle, wobbly
rel halfhearted, lukewarm

shimmer *vb* ***syn*** FLASH 1, coruscate, gleam, glimmer, glint, glisten, glitter, scintillate, sparkle, twinkle

shimmer *n* ***syn*** FLASH 1, coruscation, gleam, glimmer, glint, glisten, glitter, scintillation, sparkle, twinkle
rel blinking; spangle; spark, sparking

shin *vb* ***syn*** RUN 1, dash, scamper, scoot, scurry, sprint

shindig *n* **1** a large, festive, and often overly lavish party <threw the *shindig* of the year for the debs>
syn bash, ||blowout, shindy
rel fête, gala; ball, dance; party; affair, shebang; ||shivoo
2 ***syn*** COMMOTION 3, ||catouse, coil, foofaraw, furore, ruckus, rumpus, shindy, to-do, uproar

shindy *n* **1** ***syn*** SHINDIG 1, bash, ||blowout
2 ***syn*** COMMOTION 3, brouhaha, ||catouse, coil, foofaraw, furore, ruckus, rumpus, shindig, uproar

shine *vb* **1** to emit rays of light <the storm is over and the sun is *shining*>
syn beam, burn, gleam, radiate
rel glimmer, glow; incandesce, luminesce; flash, sparkle, twinkle; flare; glare
2 ***syn*** POLISH 1, buff, burnish, furbish, glance, glaze, gloss, rub

shine *n* **1** ***syn*** DISPLAY 2, array, fanfare, panoply, parade, pomp, show
2 ***syn*** LUSTER, glaze, glint, gloss, polish, sheen
rel finish
3 *usu* **shines** *pl* ***syn*** PRANK, antic, caper, dido(es), frolic, lark, monkeyshine, shenanigan, tomfoolery, trick

shiner *n* ***syn*** BLACK EYE 1, mouse

shingle *vb* ***syn*** OVERLAP, imbricate, lap, overlie, override, ride

shining *adj* ***syn*** LUSTROUS 1, burnished, gleaming, glistening, glossy, polished, sheeny, shiny

shiny *adj* ***syn*** LUSTROUS 1, burnished, gleaming, glistening, glossy, polished, sheeny, shining

ship *vb* **1** ***syn*** SEND 1, address, consign, dispatch, forward, remit, route, transmit
rel direct; freight; export
ant receive
2 ***syn*** MOVE 4, dislocate, disturb, remove, shift, transfer

shipshape *adj* ***syn*** NEAT 2, chipper, orderly, snug, spick-and-span, tidy, trig, trim, uncluttered, well-groomed

shipwreck *vb* **1** to destroy, disable, or seriously damage a ship (as by running aground or causing to founder) <the typhoon *shipwrecked* the entire fishing fleet>
syn beach, cast away, pile up, strand, wreck
rel break up; scuttle; founder; capsize; go down, sink
idiom go aground, go to the bottom (*or* Davy Jones's locker), run on the rocks
2 ***syn*** RUIN 2, bankrupt, dilapidate, do in, wreck

shirk *vb* **1** ***syn*** SNEAK, creep, gumshoe, lurk, pussyfoot, skulk, slink, slip, ||snake, steal
2 ***syn*** DODGE 1, duck, fence, parry, sidestep
rel bilk, burke; bypass, double, eschew, get around; shuffle off, shun

shirker *n* ***syn*** SLACKER, goldbrick, slinker, ||spiv

shirty *adj* ***syn*** ANGRY, choleric, heated, irate, ireful, mad, waxy, wrathful, wrathy, wroth

shit** *n* **1** ***syn NONSENSE 2, ||bull, *bullshit, ||crap, hogwash, hooey, *horseshit, poppycock, rot, rubbish
2 ***syn*** SNOT 1, cur, dog, ||prick, scum, *shithead, skunk, snake, toad, *turd
rel *asshole, bastard, son of a bitch
3 **shits** *pl* ***syn*** DIARRHEA, ||backdoor trots, dysentery, flux, ||runs, scour(s), ||squirts, *trots

shithead** *n* ***syn SNOT 1, cur, dog, ||prick, scum, *shit, skunk, snake, toad, *turd

shivaree *n* a noisy mock serenade to a newly married couple <*shivarees* and other such disappearing rural customs>
syn ||belling, ||bull band, ||callithump, charivari, ||horning, ||riding, ||skimmelton
rel entertainment, reception, welcome

shiver *vb* ***syn*** SHATTER 1, burst, fragment, ||pash, rive, smash, ||smatter, splinter, splinterize, splitter

shiver *vb* ***syn*** SHAKE 1, ||didder, dither, quake, quaver, quiver, shudder, tremble, tremor, twitter

||shivereens *n pl* ***syn*** SMITHEREENS, smithers

shivering *adj* ***syn*** TREMULOUS, ashake, ashiver, quaking, quivering, shaking, shaky, shivery, trembling, tremulant

shivers *n pl* ***syn*** JITTERS, ||all-overs, dither, heebie-jeebies, ||jimjams, ||jimmies, jumps, shakes, whim-whams, willies

shivery *adj* **1** ***syn*** TREMULOUS, aquake, aquiver, quaking, quivering, shaking, shaky, trembling, tremorous, tremulant
2 ***syn*** COLD 1, arctic, chill, chillsome, chilly, cool, freezing, frigid, frosty, nippy

shoal *adj* ***syn*** SHALLOW 1, superficial

shoal *n* a place where a body of water (as a sea or river) is not deep <dangerous *shoals* in uncharted waters>
syn shallow
rel barrier, barrier reef, coral reef, fringing reef, reef, sand reef; bank, bar, sandbank, sandbar, tombolo; hook, spit; seamount
con abyss, deep, depth

shock *n* ***syn*** PILE 1, bank, cock, hill, mound, pyramid, rick, ||ruck, stack, stockpile

shock *n* **1** ***syn*** IMPACT, bump, clash, collision, concussion, crash, jar, jolt, percussion, smash
2 ***syn*** EARTHQUAKE, quake, ||quaker, shake, temblor (*or* tremblor), tremor
3 ***syn*** TRAUMA, traumatism
rel prostration, stupefaction

shock *vb* **1** to offend the moral sense of <were *shocked* by pornography>
syn scandalize

---

syn synonym(s) *rel* related word(s)
idiom idiomatic equivalent(s) *con* contrasted word(s)
ant antonym(s) * vulgar
|| use limited; if in doubt, see a dictionary
The first word in a synonym list when printed in SMALL CAPITALS shows where there is more information about the group. For a more efficient use of this book see Explanatory Notes.

rel astonish, astound, startle, surprise; jar, jolt, shake up; insult, offend, outrage; appall, horrify; floor, knock out; disgust, nauseate, sicken
idiom stink in one's nostrils, turn one's stomach
2 to cause to undergo a physical or psychological shock <his slap *shocked* her out of hysterics>
syn jolt, startle
rel shake; jar; electrify

shocked *adj* ***syn*** AGHAST 2, agape, confounded, dismayed, dumbfounded, overwhelmed, thunderstruck
rel jarred, jolted, shaken up, ||shook up; offended, outraged; appalled, horrified

shocker *n* **1** ***syn*** THRILLER, chiller, thriller-diller
2 ***syn*** DIME NOVEL, dreadful, penny dreadful, shilling shocker, yellowback

shocking *adj* **1** ***syn*** FEARFUL 3, appalling, awful, direful, dreadful, formidable, frightful, horrible, horrific, terrible
rel heinous, monstrous
2 ***syn*** OUTRAGEOUS 2, atrocious, crying, desperate, heinous, monstrous, scandalous
rel burning, glaring; disgraceful, shameful; unspeakable

shoddy *adj* **1** ***syn*** CHEAP 2, base, common, mean, paltry, poor, rubbishy, sleazy, tatty, trashy
rel makeshift, scambling
2 ***syn*** SHABBY 1, broken-down, dilapidated, dingy, disreputable, down-at-heel, run-down, scruffy, seedy, tacky
3 ***syn*** DISREPUTABLE 1, discreditable, disgraceful, dishonorable, ignominious, inglorious, shabby, shady, shameful, unrespectable

shoeless *adj* ***syn*** BAREFOOT 1, unsandaled, unshod
ant shod

shoestring *adj* ***syn*** LITTLE 3, casual, inconsiderable, insignificant, light, minor, petty, small-beer, trivial, unimportant

||**shog** *vb* ***syn*** PUSH 2, bulldoze, elbow, hustle, jostle, press, shoulder, shove

shoo–in *n* ***syn*** SURE THING

||**shool** *vb* ***syn*** SHUFFLE, scuff, scuffle, shamble, shovel

shoot *vb* **1** to cause (a weapon) to drive a projectile forward <*shoot* an arrow at a target>
syn discharge, fire, loose
rel trigger; launch, project; expel; blast; poop
idiom let fly
2 ***syn*** DESTROY 1, annihilate, decimate, demolish, destruct, raze, ruin, shatter, wrack, wreck
3 ***syn*** DISCREDIT 2, blow up, disprove, explode, puncture
||**4** ***syn*** DISCARD, cashier, chuck, ditch, jettison, junk, reject, scrap, throw away, throw out
5 ***syn*** VOMIT, barf, ||cack, ||cascade, ||cast, disgorge, ||heave, spew, throw up, upchuck
||**6** ***syn*** PASS 9, buck, hand, reach
7 ***syn*** SHOOT UP 2, ||mainline
8 ***syn*** FLY 1, dart, float, sail, scud, skim, skirr
9 ***syn*** RUSH 1, boil, bolt, charge, chase, dash, fling, lash, race, tear
rel gallop, highball, hotfoot; spurt
10 ***syn*** PHOTOGRAPH, photo

shoot *n* ***syn*** RAY 1, beam, shaft

shooting *adj* ***syn*** SHARP 8, acute, knifelike, piercing, stabbing
ant stationary

shooting match *n* ***syn*** AFFAIR 1, business, concern, matter, thing

shoot up *vb* **1** ***syn*** SKYROCKET, rocket, soar
2 to take (a drug) by hypodermic needle <had been *shooting up* heroin for weeks>
syn ||mainline, shoot

shop *n* ***syn*** STORE 4, market, outlet, showroom
rel boutique

shoplift *vb* to steal displayed goods from a store <the manager caught them *shoplifting* records>
syn ||boost
rel bag, cop, ||nick, palm, pilfer, pinch, rip off, snitch, swipe

shopworn *adj* ***syn*** TRITE, cliché, clichéd, hackneyed, stale, sterotypical, timeworn, tired, well-worn, worn-out
rel overused, overworked, overworn

shore *n* the land bordering a usually large body of water <watched the ships while walking along the *shore*>
syn bank, beach, coast, strand
rel coastline, shoreline, waterfront, waterside; coastland, seacoast, seashore; foreshore, littoral, shoreface, shoreside; brink, embankment, riverbank, riverside

shore (up) *vb* ***syn*** SUPPORT 4, bear up, bolster, brace, buttress, carry, prop, sustain, upbear, uphold

shore *n* ***syn*** SUPPORT 3, brace, buttress, column, prop, stay, underpinner, underpinning, underpropping

short *adj* **1** having little length in space or time <a *short* visit>
syn brief
rel abbreviate, abbreviated, abridged, curtailed, decreased, diminished, lessened, shortened; curtate, decurtate
con extensive, lengthy; drawn-out, overlong; extended, prolonged, protracted
ant long
2 having small physical stature <he was the *shortest* boy present>
syn ||low, low-set, low-statured
rel chunky, dumpy, squat, squatty, stubby, thick, thickset
con gangling, gangly, lanky, rangy; elevated, high, lofty, spiring, towering
ant tall
3 not coming up to a measure or need <fuel was very *short* that year>
syn deficient, failing, inadequate, insufficient, scant, scanty, scarce, scrimpy, shy, skimpy, slender, unsufficient, wanting; *compare* MEAGER 2
rel lacking, needing; exiguous, meager, sparse
con abounding, overflowing, teeming; abundant, ample, copious, plenteous, plentiful
ant long
4 ***syn*** BLUFF, abrupt, blunt, breviloquent, brief, brusque, crusty, curt, snippety, snippy

---

ant expansive
5 lacking in graciousness or consideration <his manner was *short* and abrupt>
syn inconsiderate, sharp, thoughtless, unceremonious, ungracious
rel bluff, blunt, brusque, crusty, curt; short-spoken; gruff, irascible
con considerate, gracious, kindly; bland, smooth; ceremonious
6 readily breaking or crumbling <a rich *short* pastry>
syn brittle, crisp, crumbly, ‖crump, crunchy, friable
rel delicate, fragile
con soggy, tough
7 *syn* CONCISE, breviloquent, brief, compendiary, compendious, curt, laconic, succinct, summary, terse
rel compact; pointed
idiom to the point
con extended, protracted, spun-out
ant lengthy, long-drawn-out

short *adv* 1 without hesitation or delay <stopped *short*>
syn abruptly, asudden, forthwith, sudden, suddenly
con hesitantly; gradually, slowly
2 *syn* UNAWARES, aback, sudden, suddenly, unanticipatedly, unaware, unawaredly, unexpectedly

short *n syn* SUBSTANCE 2, amount, burden, core, gist, meat, pith, purport, thrust, upshot

short *vb syn* SPARE 3, scant, skimp, ‖skinch, stint

shortage *n syn* FAILURE 3, defalcation, deficiency, deficit, inadequacy, insufficience, insufficiency, lack, scantiness, underage
rel curtailment, pinch, tightness; shortfall
ant overage

short and sweet *adj syn* CONCISE, breviloquent, brief, compendiary, curt, laconic, short, succinct, summary, terse

shortcoming *n syn* IMPERFECTION, deficiency, demerit, fault, sin
idiom weak point
con forte, long suit

shortcut *n* a route shorter or more direct than the one ordinarily taken <they took a *shortcut* down the back roads>
syn cutoff
rel bypass
ant detour

shorten *vb* to reduce in extent (as of length or duration) <decided to *shorten* their visit> <*shorten* a skirt for summer wear>
syn abbreviate, abridge, curtail, cut, cut back, retrench, slash
rel decrease, diminish, elide, excerpt, lessen, reduce; compress, condense, contract, shrink; bobtail, clip, dock; minimize
idiom cut short
con draw out, protract
ant elongate; lengthen; extend, prolong

shorthanded *adj* short of the necessary number of people <the office was critically *shorthanded*>
syn underhanded, undermanned, understaffed
rel short, wanting
con overmanned, overstaffed

short–lived *adj syn* TRANSIENT, ephemeral, evanescent, fleeting, fugacious, fugitive, impermanent, momentary, passing, transitory
rel short-haul, short-run, short-term
con long-run, long-term
ant agelong; long-lived

shortly *adv* 1 *syn* BRIEFLY, concisely, in brief, in short, laconically, succinctly, tersely
2 *syn* PRESENTLY 1, anon, by and by, directly, soon
rel pronto, quickly

short–range *adj syn* TACTICAL 1
ant long-range

shortsighted *adj syn* MYOPIC, nearsighted
ant farsighted, longsighted

short–spoken *adj syn* BLUFF, abrupt, blunt, brief, brusque, crusty, curt, gruff, snippety, snippy
ant windy

shot *n* 1 *syn* FLING 1, crack, go, pop, slap, stab, ‖stagger, try, whack, whirl
2 *syn* OPPORTUNITY, break, chance, look-in, occasion, opening, show, squeak, time
3 *syn* DRAM, ‖caulker, drop, jolt, nip, slug, snifter, snort, toothful, tot

‖**shot** *adj syn* INTOXICATED 1, ‖boozy, ‖canned, disguised, drunk, inebriated, ‖lushed, muddled, pixilated, ‖plastered

shotgun *vb syn* FORCE 2, coerce, compel, concuss, constrain, make, oblige

should *vb syn* WANT 3, must, ought

shoulder *vb syn* PUSH 2, bulldoze, elbow, hustle, jostle, press, ‖shog, shove

shout *vb* 1 to utter a sudden loud cry (as to express joy or triumph or to attract attention) <the mob *shouted* for a speech>
syn cry, whoop, yell; *compare* CALL 1, SCREAM 1
rel exclaim; howl, scream, shriek; bawl, bellow, clamor, roar, vociferate
con murmur, whisper
2 *syn* SCREAM 4, blare, shriek
3 *syn* CALL 1, cry, hallo, holler, hollo, vociferate, yell
rel bark; bray
4 *syn* TREAT 3, blow, set up, stand

shove *vb* 1 *syn* PUSH 1, drive, propel, thrust
rel cram, jam; dig, jab, poke, prod
idiom push and shove
2 *syn* PUSH 2, bulldoze, elbow, hustle, jostle, press, ‖shog, shoulder
3 *syn* PUSH 6, peddle

shove (off) *vb syn* GO 2, ‖blow, depart, exit, get off, leave, pull out, quit, run along, take off
ant pull in

shovel *vb* 1 *syn* DIG 1, ‖delve, excavate, grub, spade
2 *syn* DIG 2, dig out, excavate, scoop, spade

shovel *vb syn* SHUFFLE, scuff, scuffle, shamble, ‖shool

---

syn synonym(s) *rel* related word(s)
idiom idiomatic equivalent(s) *con* contrasted word(s)
ant antonym(s) * vulgar
‖ use limited; if in doubt, see a dictionary
The first word in a synonym list when printed in SMALL CAPITALS shows where there is more information about the group. For a more efficient use of this book see Explanatory Notes.

show *vb* **1** to set out or place on view for customers <we're *showing* lots of long dresses this fall>
syn display, offer
rel afford, supply; exhibit; present, proffer, submit; deal (in), sell
2 to reveal outwardly or make apparent <asked a question or two to *show* his intelligence>
syn demonstrate, evidence, evince, exhibit, illustrate, manifest, mark, ostend, proclaim; *compare* LOOK 4
rel disclose, discover, divulge, lay out, reveal, unveil; present, project
con camouflage, conceal, dissemble, hide, obscure
ant disguise
3 ***syn*** STAGE, mount, produce, put on
4 to present in such a way as to invite notice, attention, and admiration <she loved to *show* her jewels to everyone>
syn brandish, display, disport, exhibit, expose, flash, flaunt, parade, show off, trot out
rel air, lay out, set out, spread; blazon, flourish, sport, vaunt
con belittle, deprecate, depreciate, minimize
5 to give an exact and usually automatic reading or indication of <the speedometer *shows* 70 MPH>
syn indicate, mark, read, record, register, say
rel point (to); ring up
6 ***syn*** LOOK 4, exhibit
rel lay out, reveal, unveil
7 ***syn*** GUIDE, conduct, direct, escort, lead, pilot, route, see, shepherd, steer
8 ***syn*** ESTABLISH 6, demonstrate, determine, make out, prove
rel present; plead; allege
9 ***syn*** APPEAR 1, emerge, loom
rel come, show up; materialize
10 ***syn*** COME 1, arrive, ||blow in, get, get in, reach, show up, turn up
idiom ||make the scene, put in an appearance, show one's face
11 ***syn*** TURN UP 3, show up

show *n* ***syn*** APPEARANCE 2, face, guise, seeming, semblance, showing, simulacrum
rel likeness; effect, impression
idiom outward show
2 ***syn*** MASK 2, color, coloring, disguise, facade, face, front, put-on, veneer, window dressing
3 ***syn*** DISPLAY 2, array, fanfare, panoply, parade, pomp, shine
4 ***syn*** OPPORTUNITY, break, chance, look-in, occasion, opening, shot, squeak, time
5 ***syn*** EXHIBITION 1, demonstration, display, spectacle
6 ***syn*** EXHIBITION 2, exhibit, exposition, fair
7 ***syn*** MOVIE, cine, ||cinema, film, flick, motion picture, moving picture, photoplay, picture, picture show
8 ***syn*** SHOWING 1, out

shower *n* ***syn*** BARRAGE, bombardment, broadside, burst, cannonade, drumfire, fusillade, hail, salvo, storm
rel shatter, spatter, spray

shower *vb* ***syn*** BATHE 1, ||bath, tub, wash

showing *n* **1** performance in a test of skill, power, or effectiveness <he made a good *showing* in the race>
syn out, show
rel record
2 ***syn*** APPEARANCE 2, face, guise, seeming, semblance, show, simulacrum

show–me *adj* ***syn*** INCREDULOUS, aporetic, disbelieving, questioning, quizzical, skeptical, unbelieving

show off *vb* ***syn*** SHOW 4, brandish, display, disport, exhibit, expose, flash, flaunt, parade, trot out
rel boast, brag, swagger

showpiece *n* a prime or outstanding example used or suitable for exhibition <a Fabergé Easter egg was the *showpiece* of the collection>
syn chef d'oeuvre, masterpiece, pièce de résistance
rel gem, jewel; prize
con claptrap, rubbish, trash, trivia, truck

showroom *n* ***syn*** STORE 4, market, outlet, shop

show up *vb* ***syn*** EXPOSE 4, debunk, discover, uncloak, undress, unmask, unshroud
rel discredit; invalidate
2 ***syn*** TURN UP 3, show
3 ***syn*** COME 1, arrive, ||blow in, get, get in, reach, show, turn up

showy *adj* given to or marked by excessive outward display <*showy* decorations>
syn chichi, flamboyant, orchidaceous, ostentatious, peacockish, peacocky, pretentious, splashy, swank
rel sporty; flashy, garish, gaudy, jazzy, meretricious, tawdry; gorgeous, resplendent; luxurious, opulent, ornate, sumptuous; overdone, overwrought; sensational
con muted, quiet, restrained, subdued; elegant, graceful, restrained; appropriate, seemly
ant unshowy

shred *n* ***syn*** PARTICLE, bit, crumb, iota, modicum, ounce, ray, scrap, smidgen, speck

shred *vb* ***syn*** SLIVER, shave

shreddy *adj* ***syn*** RAGGED, frayed, frazzled, tattered

shrew *n* ***syn*** VIRAGO, amazon, fishwife, harpy, ogress, scold, termagant, vixen, Xanthippe
rel she-devil, spitfire

shrewd *adj* marked by clever discerning awareness and hardheaded acumen <the captain was a *shrewd* judge of character>
syn argute, astucious, astute, cagey, heady, perspicacious, sagacious, ||savvy; *compare* SHARP 4, WISE 2, 4
rel canny, crafty, foxy, ingenious, ||pawky, slick, ||sly, tidy; clever, intelligent, knowing, quick-witted, smart; polite, smooth; judicious, prudent, sensible, wise; penetrating, piercing, probing; acute, keen, sharp; far-sighted, foresighted
con green, naive, simple, soft; foolable, gullible, slow

shrewdness *n* ***syn*** WIT 3, acumen, astuteness, astucity, discernment, discrimination, keenness, penetration, percipience, perspicacity
rel canniness, foxiness

shriek *vb* **1** ***syn*** SCREAM 1, screech, shrill, squeal
rel squawk, ||yarm

2 ***syn*** SQUEAL 2, screak, scream, screech
3 ***syn*** SCREAM 4, blare, shout

shrill *vb* ***syn*** SCREAM 1, screech, shriek, squeal

shrill *adj* ***syn*** ACUTE 4, argute, high, piercing, piping, sharp, thin, treble

shrine *n* a structure or place considered sacred by a religious group <pilgrims going to the *shrine* at Lourdes hoping to be healed>
syn holy place, sanctorium, sanctuary, sanctum
rel reliquary; enshrinement

shrink *vb* **1** ***syn*** CONTRACT 3, compress, concentrate, condense, constrict
rel shrivel (up), wither
con amplify, expand
ant swell
2 ***syn*** FAIL 3, dwindle, fall short, wane, waste (away), weaken
idiom shrink (*or* dwindle) down to nothing
3 ***syn*** RECOIL, blanch, blench, flinch, quail, squinch, start, wince
rel cower, cringe, crouch, huddle, slink; draw (back), recede, retire, retreat, withdraw; boggle, demur, scruple

shrinking *adj* ***syn*** UNDEMONSTRATIVE, aseptic, restrained, retiring, unaffable, unexpansive, withdrawn

shrivel *vb* ***syn*** WITHER, dry up, mummify, mummy, welter, wilt, wizen
rel parch; fossilize

shroud *vb* **1** ***syn*** ENFOLD 1, enclose, enshroud, envelop, enwrap, invest, veil, wrap
2 ***syn*** SCREEN 3, block out, close, obstruct, shut off, shut out

shrouded *adj* ***syn*** ULTERIOR, buried, concealed, covert, guarded, hidden, obscured, privy

shuck *n* ***syn*** HULL, case, husk, pod, shell, skin, ‖slough

shuck *vb* to strip, break off, or remove the enclosing case or cover of <*shuck* corn>
syn hull, husk, shell; *compare* SKIN 2
rel decorticate, peel, skin, strip

shuck (off) *vb* ***syn*** DISCARD, cast, chuck, ditch, jettison, junk, reject, scrap, shed, slough

shudder *vb* ***syn*** SHAKE 1, ‖didder, dither, quake, quaver, quiver, shiver, tremble, tremor, twitter
rel gyrate, shimmy

shuffle *vb* **1** ***syn*** DISORDER 1, disarrange, disarray, discompose, dislocate, disorganize, disrupt, disturb, jumble, mess (up)
2 ***syn*** EQUIVOCATE 2, dodge, evade, hedge, pussyfoot, sidestep, tergiversate, tergiverse, weasel
3 to walk awkwardly in a sliding, dragging way without lifting the feet <an old drunk *shuffling* along in filthy bedroom slippers>
syn scuff, scuffle, shamble, ‖shool, shovel
rel drag, pad, scrape, slipper, slip-slop, slur; draggle, straggle, trail (along)
4 ***syn*** STUMBLE 6, limp, muddle

shuffle *n* ***syn*** CLUTTER 2, hash, jumble, jungle, litter, mash, mishmash, muddle, rummage, tumble

shuffling *adj* ***syn*** EVASIVE 1, equivocating, prevaricative, prevaricatory, shifty

shun *vb* ***syn*** ESCAPE 2, avoid, bilk, double, duck, elude, eschew, evade, shy
rel decline, refuse, reject; snub; despise, disdain, scorn
idiom have nothing to do with, keep away from, stand aloof from, steer clear of, turn away from, turn one's back upon
con accept, adopt, welcome

shunning *n* ***syn*** ESCAPE 2, avoidance, come-off, elusion, escaping, eschewal, evasion, runaround

shunt *vb* **1** to push or turn off to one side <*shunt* a railroad car onto a siding>
syn sidetrack, switch; *compare* TURN 6
rel change, move, shift, transfer; avert, deflect, divert, head off
idiom push aside (*or* to the side)
2 ***syn*** SHUTTLE

shush *vb* **1** ***syn*** SILENCE, choke (off), hush, quiet, ‖quieten, shut up, still
2 ***syn*** SUPPRESS 2, muffle, ‖quelch, repress, squelch, strangle

shut *vb* ***syn*** CLOSE 1, ‖put to
rel lock, seal; batten (down)
ant open

‖shut–eye *n* ***syn*** SLEEP 1, ‖doss, slumber

shut in *vb* ***syn*** ENCLOSE 1, cage, close in, coop, envelop, hem, immure, mure, pen, wall
ant shut out

shut–in *adj* ***syn*** UNSOCIABLE, aloof, cool, distant, offish, reserved, standoffish, touch-me-not-ish, uncompanionable, withdrawn

shut–mouthed *adj* ***syn*** SILENT 3, close-lipped, closemouthed, close-tongued, reserved, reticent, taciturn, tight-lipped, tight-mouthed, uncommunicative
ant openmouthed

shut off *vb* ***syn*** SCREEN 3, block out, close, obstruct, shroud, shut out

shut out *vb* ***syn*** SCREEN 3, block out, close, obstruct, shroud, shut off

shuttle *vb* to travel back and forth frequently <*shuttled* between New York and Washington every week>
syn shunt
rel shuttlecock; alternate

shut up *vb* **1** ***syn*** SILENCE, choke (off), hush, quiet, ‖quieten, shush, still
2 to cease speaking <told the boy to sit down and *shut up*>
syn dry up, dumb (up), ‖dummy (up), pipe down, ‖ring off
rel hush, quiet (down), shush, soft-pedal
idiom button (*or* seal) one's lips, keep quiet

shy *adj* **1** disinclined to obtrude oneself <*shy* in the presence of strangers>
syn backward, bashful, coy, demure, diffident, modest, rabbity, retiring, self-effacing, timid, unassertive, unassured
rel backhanded, hesitant, reluctant; conscious, self-conscious, self-distrustful, shamefaced, sheepish; intro-

---

syn synonym(s) — *rel* related word(s)
idiom idiomatic equivalent(s) — *con* contrasted word(s)
ant antonym(s) — * vulgar
‖ use limited; if in doubt, see a dictionary
The first word in a synonym list when printed in SMALL CAPITALS shows where there is more information about the group. For a more efficient use of this book see Explanatory Notes.

versive, introvert, introverted, inturned; circumspect, reserved; cautious, chary, suspicious, wary; apprehensive, fearful, nervous, skittish, timorous
con brash, forward; aggressive, audacious, intrusive, obtruding, pushing, pushy; blunt, crass
ant bold, obtrusive
2 ***syn*** DISINCLINED, afraid, averse, backward, hesitant, indisposed, loath, reluctant, uneager, unwilling
3 ***syn*** SHORT 3, deficient, failing, inadequate, insufficient, scant, scanty, scarce, unsufficient, wanting
con excess, over, surplus

shy *vb* **1** ***syn*** DEMUR, balk, boggle, gag, jib, scruple, stick, stickle, strain, stumble
rel blench, quail, recoil, shrink
2 ***syn*** ESCAPE 2, avoid, bilk, double, duck, elude, eschew, evade, shun

shy *n* ***syn*** POTSHOT, pot, sideswipe

Shylock *n* ***syn*** LOAN SHARK, usurer

shyster *n* ***syn*** PETTIFOGGER, jackleg lawyer

‖**sib** *adj* ***syn*** SYMPATHETIC 2, friendly, receptive, well-disposed

sibilate *vb* ***syn*** HISS, buzz, fizz, fizzle, sizzle, swish, wheeze, whisk, whisper, whiz

sibylline *adj* **1** ***syn*** PROPHETIC, apocalyptic, Delphian, fatidic, mantic, oracular, prophetical, vatic, vaticinal
2 ***syn*** OBSCURE 3, ambiguous, amphibological, double-edged, double-faced, dusky, equivocal, murky, nubilous, opaque

sic *vb* ***syn*** URGE, egg (on), exhort, goad, prick, prod, prompt, propel, spur
rel agitate, catalyze, inspirit, instigate; abet, aid, countenance, favor

sick *adj* **1** affected with illness or disease <was *sick* with pneumonia>
syn down, ill; *compare* UNWELL
rel diseased, disordered, fevered; ailing, ‖cronk, ‖crook, funny, indisposed, unwell; debilitated, sickly, unhealthy; rocky, tottering, wobbly; confined, laid up; lousy, mean, rotten
idiom ‖on the sick list, sick as a dog
con healthy, strong
ant well
2 ***syn*** MORBID, morose, sickly
3 ***syn*** FED UP, disgusted, tired, weary
idiom ‖up to here with
4 ***syn*** FAULTY, amiss, defective, flawed, imperfect
5 ***syn*** SICKLY 2, peaked, ‖peaking, peaky

sick (up) *vb* ***syn*** VOMIT, barf, bring up, disgorge, ‖heave, shoot, spew, spit up, throw up, upchuck

sicken *vb* **1** ***syn*** UPSET 5, derange, disorder, turn, unhinge, unsettle
2 ***syn*** DISGUST, nauseate, reluct, repel, repulse, revolt

sicken (with *or* **of)** *vb* ***syn*** CONTRACT 1, catch, come down (with), get, take

---

syn synonym(s) ***rel*** related word(s)
idiom idiomatic equivalent(s) ***con*** contrasted word(s)
ant antonym(s) * vulgar
‖ use limited; if in doubt, see a dictionary
The first word in a synonym list when printed in SMALL CAPITALS shows where there is more information about the group. For a more efficient use of this book see Explanatory Notes.

sickening *adj* ***syn*** OFFENSIVE, disgusting, foul, icky, loathsome, nasty, nauseating, repugnant, repulsive, revolting

‖**sicker** *vb* ***syn*** EXUDE, bleed, ooze, ‖screeve, seep, ‖sew, strain, sweat, transude, weep

sickliness *n* ***syn*** INFIRMITY 1, debility, decrepitude, disease, feebleness, infirmness, malaise, unhealthiness

sickly *adj* **1** ***syn*** UNWELL, ailing, ‖donsie, indisposed, low, mean, off-color, offish, poorly, underly
rel ‖cranky, down
con hale, hearty; healthy, well
ant robust
2 accompanying, indicating, or suggesting sickness <a *sickly* complexion>
syn peaked, ‖peaking, peaky, sick
rel ‖pimping, puny, sickish, weak; diseased; unhealthy
con healthy, hearty
3 ***syn*** UNWHOLESOME 1, insalubrious, insalutary, noisome, noxious, unhealthful, unhealthy, unsalutary
4 ***syn*** MORBID, morose, sick

sickness *n* **1** the condition of being ill <finally recovered from her *sickness*>
syn affliction, diseasedness, disorder, illness, indisposition, infirmity, unhealth; *compare* DISEASE 1, INFIRMITY 1
rel indisposedness, unhealthfulness, unhealthiness, unwellness; affection, ailment, ill
idiom ill health
con haleness, healthiness, heartiness
ant health
2 ***syn*** DISEASE 1, affection, ailment, complaint, condition, disorder, ill, infirmity, malady, syndrome

side *n* **1** a place, space, or direction with respect to a center or a line of division <lived on the north *side* of the street> <the morning *side* of the hill> <turned to one *side*>
syn hand
rel direction, flank, sector
2 ***syn*** PHASE, angle, aspect, facet, hand
3 ***syn*** VIEWPOINT 2, angle, direction, outlook, slant, standpoint
4 the attitude, position, or action of one person or group as opposed to another <could understand her *side* as well as his in the quarrel>
syn part; *compare* POSITION 1
rel attitude, disposition; posture, stance, stand; position, standpoint, viewpoint

side *vb* ***syn*** SHEATHE, clad, face, skin

side (with) *vb* ***syn*** SUPPORT 2, advocate, back, backstop, champion, uphold

side action *n* ***syn*** SIDE EFFECT, side reaction

sideboards *n pl* ***syn*** SIDE-WHISKERS, burnsides, dundrearies, muttonchops, sideburns

sideburns *n pl* ***syn*** SIDE-WHISKERS, burnsides, dundrearies, muttonchops, sideboards

side effect *n* a secondary and usually adverse effect (as of a drug) <drowsiness is a common *side effect* of antihistimines>
syn side action, side reaction
rel effect; reaction, response

side–glance *n* a look or glance directed to one side <she shot an impatient *side-glance* at him>
syn side-look

rel glance; stare

sideling *adv* ***syn*** SIDEWAYS 1, crabwise, laterally, ‖sidelings, sidelong, sideward, sidewise

sideling *adj* ***syn*** STEEP 1, abrupt, arduous, precipitate, precipitous, sheer, steepdown, steep-to, steep-up, ‖stickle

‖**sidelings** *adv* ***syn*** SIDEWAYS 1, crabwise, laterally, sideling, sidelong, sideward, sidewise

sidelong *adv* ***syn*** SIDEWAYS 1, crabwise, laterally, sideling, ‖sidelings, sideward, sidewise

side–look *n* ***syn*** SIDE-GLANCE

side reaction *n* ***syn*** SIDE EFFECT, side action

sidereal *adj* ***syn*** STELLAR 1, astral, ‖starny, starry, stellular

sidesplitter *n* ***syn*** RIOT 2, howl, ‖panic, scream

sidestep *vb* **1** ***syn*** EQUIVOCATE 2, dodge, evade, hedge, pussyfoot, shuffle, tergiversate, tergiverse, weasel
2 ***syn*** SKIRT 3, burke, bypass, circumvent, ‖polly-fox
3 ***syn*** DODGE 1, duck, fence, parry, shirk

sideswipe *n* ***syn*** POTSHOT, pot, shy

sidetrack *vb* ***syn*** SHUNT 1, switch

sideward *adv* ***syn*** SIDEWAYS 1, crabwise, laterally, sideling, ‖sidelings, sidelong, sidewise

sideways *adv* **1** to, toward, or at one side <slipped *sideways* on the ice>
syn crabwise, laterally, sideling, ‖sidelings, sidelong, sideward, sidewise; *compare* ASIDE 1
rel obliquely; indirectly
con straight; directly
2 ***syn*** ASIDE 1, aslant, aslope, obliquely, sidewise, slantingly, slantly, slantways, slantwise, ‖slaunchways

side–whiskers *n pl* the usually shaped growth of whiskers on both sides of a man's face <grew *side-whiskers* and a moustache in order to look older>
syn burnsides, dundrearies, muttonchops, sideboards, sideburns

sidewise *adv* **1** ***syn*** SIDEWAYS 1, crabwise, laterally, sideling, ‖sidelings, sidelong, sideward
2 ***syn*** ASIDE 1, aslant, aslope, obliquely, sideways, slantingly, slantly, slantways, slantwise, ‖slaunchways

sidle *vb* to move sideways or obliquely especially in an unobtrusive or furtive manner <a suspicious-looking man *sidled* up to her>
syn edge, ‖slive
rel ease, slip

siege *n* a sometimes prolonged period of disorder or stress (as of body or mind) <endured a three-week *siege* of flu>
syn bout, go; *compare* ATTACK 3
rel attack, onslaught, seizure, spell

siesta *n* ***syn*** NAP, catnap, dog nap, ‖dover, forty winks, snooze

siesta *vb* ***syn*** NAP, catnap, ‖caulk (off), snooze

sieve *n* ***syn*** GOSSIP 1, clack, gossiper, ‖long tongue, quidnunc, rumormonger, scandalizer, scandalmonger, tabby, talebearer

sieve *vb* ***syn*** SCREEN 5, sift

sift *vb* **1** ***syn*** SCREEN 5, sieve
2 ***syn*** SORT 2, comb, separate, winnow
3 ***syn*** EXPLORE, delve (into), dig (into), go (into), inquire (into), investigate, look (into), probe, prospect

sigh *vb* **1** to take in and let out a deep audible breath (as in weariness, grief, or relief) <flopped down in the chair and *sighed* deeply>
syn ‖sock, sough, suspire
rel breathe, respire; exhale; gasp, pant, wheeze; groan, moan; sob
idiom heave a sigh
2 to make a sound like sighing <the wind *sighed* in the branches>
syn sough
rel blow; murmur, whisper; moan; whine; whistle; howl, roar
3 ***syn*** LONG, ache, crave, dream, hanker, hunger, lust, pine, suspire, thirst

sighful *adj* ***syn*** MELANCHOLY 2, doleful, lamentable, moanful, mournful, plaintive, rueful, sorrowful, wailful, woeful

sight *n* **1** ***syn*** EYESORE, desight, fright, mess, monstrosity
‖**2** ***syn*** MUCH, barrel, great deal, lashings, lot, lump, mass, ‖mess, peck, ‖power
3 ***syn*** EYE 2, eyesight, seeing, vision
4 ***syn*** LOOK 1, view
5 ***syn*** VIEW 4, outlook, scene
6 ***syn*** VIEW 5

sightless *adj* ***syn*** BLIND 1, ‖dark, eyeless, stone-blind, visionless
ant sighted

sightseer *n* ***syn*** TOURIST, rubberneck, ‖tripper

sign *n* **1** a motion, action, gesture, or word by which a command, thought, or wish is expressed <put a finger to her lips as a *sign* to keep quiet>
syn high sign, signal
rel gesticulation, gesture, motion; hint, indication, suggestion, warning
2 ***syn*** CHARACTER 1, mark, symbol
3 ***syn*** EXPRESSION 3, gesture, indication, reminder, token
rel symbolization; attestation, evidence, proof
4 ***syn*** INDICATION 3, evidence, index, indicia, mark, significant, symptom, token
rel earmark, exponent, indicator; exhibit, show

sign *vb* **1** to affix a signature to <he refused to *sign* a confession>
syn autograph, ink, signature, subscribe
idiom put one's John Hancock on, put one's John Henry down (*or* on)
2 ***syn*** SIGNAL, flag, gesture, motion, signalize

sign (over) *vb* ***syn*** TRANSFER 4, abalienate, alien, alienate, assign, cede, convey, deed, make over, remise

signal *n* ***syn*** SIGN 1, high sign
rel alarm, alert, tocsin; movement

signal *vb* to notify by or as if by a signal <*signaled* his wife to keep quiet>
syn flag, gesture, motion, sign, signalize
idiom give the high sign (to)

---

syn synonym(s) ***rel*** related word(s)
idiom idiomatic equivalent(s) ***con*** contrasted word(s)
ant antonym(s) * vulgar
‖ use limited; if in doubt, see a dictionary
The first word in a synonym list when printed in SMALL CAPITALS shows where there is more information about the group. For a more efficient use of this book see Explanatory Notes.

signal *adj* ***syn*** NOTICEABLE, arresting, arrestive, conspicuous, marked, outstanding, prominent, remarkable, salient, striking
rel characteristic, distinctive, individual, peculiar, significative; eminent, famous, illustrious, renowned

signalize *vb* **1** ***syn*** CHARACTERIZE 2, distinguish, individualize, individuate, mark, qualify, singularize
2 ***syn*** SIGNAL, flag, gesture, motion, sign

signature *vb* ***syn*** SIGN 1, autograph, ink, subscribe

significance *n* **1** ***syn*** MEANING 1, acceptation, import, intendment, message, purport, sense, significancy, signification, understanding
2 ***syn*** IMPORTANCE, consequence, import, magnitude, moment, momentousness, pith, ‖signification, weight, weightiness
rel authority, credit, influence, merit, prestige; excellence, perfection, virtue
con indifference; triviality, unimportance, worthlessness; irrelevance
ant insignificance

significancy *n* ***syn*** MEANING 1, acceptation, import, intendment, message, purport, sense, significance, signification, understanding

significant *adj* **1** ***syn*** EXPRESSIVE, eloquent, facund, meaningful, pregnant, rich, sententious
rel cogent, compelling, convincing, sound, telling, valid; forceful, powerful; important, momentous, weighty
con meaningless, unexpressive; unimportant
ant insignificant
2 ***syn*** IMPORTANT 1, big, consequential, considerable, material, meaningful, momentous, substantial, weighty
con inconsequential, meaningless, unimportant
ant insignificant

significant *n* ***syn*** INDICATION 3, evidence, index, indicia, mark, sign, symptom, token

significantly *adv* ***syn*** WELL 8, considerably, far, quite, rather, somewhat
ant insignificantly

signification *n* **1** ***syn*** MEANING 1, acceptation, import, intendment, message, purport, sense, significance, significancy, understanding
rel implying, signifying; construction, implication; essence, gist, substance
‖**2** ***syn*** IMPORTANCE, consequence, import, magnitude, moment, momentousness, pith, significance, weight, weightiness

significative *adj* ***syn*** INDICATIVE, denotative, denotive, designative, exhibitive, indicatory, indicial

signify *vb* **1** ***syn*** MEAN 2, add up (to), connote, denote, express, import, intend, spell
rel bear, carry, convey; bespeak, purport
2 ***syn*** MATTER, count, import, mean, weigh

---

syn synonym(s) ***rel*** related word(s)
idiom idiomatic equivalent(s) ***con*** contrasted word(s)
ant antonym(s) * vulgar
‖ use limited; if in doubt, see a dictionary
The first word in a synonym list when printed in SMALL CAPITALS shows where there is more information about the group. For a more efficient use of this book see Explanatory Notes.

sign on *vb* ***syn*** ENTER 3, enlist, enroll, join (up), muster, sign up

sign up *vb* ***syn*** ENTER 3, enlist, enroll, join (up), muster, sign on

silence *n* **1** absence of sound or noise <the heavy *silence* of the night>
syn noiselessness, quiet, quietness, quietude, soundlessness, still, stillness
rel calm, hush, lull
con din, uproar
ant noise
2 ***syn*** SECRECY, hugger-mugger, hugger-muggery, hush, hush-hush, secretiveness, secretness
3 ***syn*** DEATH 1, curtains, decease, defunction, demise, dissolution, (the) Pale Horse, passing, quietus, sleep

silence *vb* to compel or reduce to silence <*silenced* the courtroom chatter by pounding his gavel>
syn choke (off), hush, quiet, ‖quieten, shush, shut up, still
rel dampen, deaden, dumb, lull, muffle, mute; quash, quell, squash, squelch, suppress; gag, muzzle

silent *adj* **1** ***syn*** DUMB 1, inarticulate, mute, speechless, unarticulate, voiceless
2 characterized by absence of speech <was *silent* as he faced the altar>
syn dumb, mum, ‖mumchance, mute, speechless, wordless; *compare* DUMB 1
rel inarticulate, muted, tongue-tied, voiceless
con speaking, talking
3 showing marked restraint in speaking <a stern, *silent* man>
syn close, close-lipped, closemouthed, close-tongued, dumb, inconversable, reserved, reticent, shut-mouthed, silentious, speechless, taciturn, tight-lipped, tight-mouthed, uncommunicative, wordless
rel checked, curbed, inhibited, restrained; unconversational, unsociable; inarticulate, incoherent; mute, voiceless; mum, secretive
con articulate, fluent, glib, vocal, voluble; babblative, garrulous, loquacious, windy; blabbering, blabbery, chattering
ant talkative
4 ***syn*** STILL 3, hush, hushful, noiseless, quiet, soundless, stilly, whist
idiom silent as a post (*or* stone), silent as the grave (*or* tomb)
ant noisy
5 ***syn*** UNSPOKEN 1, tacit, unexpressed, unuttered, unvoiced, wordless

silentious *adj* ***syn*** SILENT 3, close-lipped, closemouthed, close-tongued, reserved, reticent, taciturn, tight-lipped, tight-mouthed, uncommunicative

silhouette *n* ***syn*** OUTLINE, contour, delineation, figuration, line, lineament, lineation, profile
rel ‖shade, shadow

silken *adj* **1** ***syn*** SOFT 3, cottony, satiny, silky, velvety
2 ***syn*** INGRATIATING, deferential, disarming, ingratiatory, insinuating, insinuative, saccharine, silky

silky *adj* **1** ***syn*** SOFT 3, cottony, satiny, silken, velvety
2 ***syn*** INGRATIATING, deferential, disarming, ingratiatory, insinuating, insinuative, saccharine, silken

silliness *n* ***syn*** FOOLISHNESS, absurdity, craziness, dottiness, folly, inanity, insanity, preposterousness, senselessness, witlessness

rel illogicality
con logic, logicality, logicalness, sanity, sensibleness; wisdom

silly *adj* **1** *syn* SIMPLE 3, asinine, fatuous, foolish, nitwitted, sheepheaded, unwitty, weak-headed, weak-minded, witless
rel empty, empty-headed, vacuous; irrational, unreasonable; ignorant, unintelligent, unwise
ant sensible
2 *syn* GIDDY 1, bird-witted, dizzy, empty-headed, featherbrained, flighty, harebrained, light-headed, rattlebrained, scatterbrained
rel ‖balmy, crazy, ‖dippy, irrational, off, ‖wacked-out
idiom silly as a goose
con level-headed, practical, rational, serious
ant sensible
3 *syn* FOOLISH 2, absurd, crazy, fantastic, harebrained, insane, loony, preposterous, sappy, wacky
rel funny, senseless

silvern *adj syn* SILVERY, argent, argentate, argenteous, argentine

silver–tongued *adj syn* GLIB, vocative, voluble, well*-hung

silvery *adj* relating to, containing, or resembling silver <repeated polishings gave the wood a *silvery* sheen>
syn argent, argentate, argenteous, argentine, silvern
rel silver; brilliant, glittering, shimmering, shining

similar *adj syn* LIKE, agnate, akin, alike, analogous, comparable, consonant, corresponding, parallel, uniform
rel complementary, correlative; reciprocal
idiom much of a muchness, much the same
con antithetical, antonymous, contradictory, contrary, opposite
ant dissimilar

similarity *n syn* LIKENESS, affinity, alikeness, analogy, comparison, resemblance, semblance, simile, similitude
rel approximation; collation, correlation; association, interrelation; parallel; closeness; coincidence, synonymity
con unlikeness, variance
ant dissimilarity

similarly *adv syn* ALSO 1, correspondingly, likewise, so
idiom by the same token

simile *n* **1** *syn* ANALOGY 2, metaphor, similitude
2 *syn* LIKENESS, affinity, alikeness, analogy, comparison, resemblance, semblance, similarity, similitude

similitude *n* **1** *syn* LIKENESS, affinity, alikeness, analogy, comparison, resemblance, semblance, similarity, simile
rel copy, image, replica
ant dissimilitude
2 *syn* ANALOGY 2, metaphor, simile

simmer *vb* **1** *syn* BOIL 2, parboil, seethe, stew
2 *syn* SEETHE 4, boil, bubble, churn, ferment, ‖moil, smolder, stir

simmer down *vb syn* COMPOSE 4, collect, control, cool, re-collect, rein, repress, restrain, smother, suppress
rel quiet (down), subside
idiom ‖cool it, take it easy
con boil, seethe; explode, fulminate
ant boil over

Simon Legree *n syn* SLAVE DRIVER, rawhider, taskmaster

simon–pure *adj syn* AUTHENTIC 2, blown-in-the-bottle, bona fide, genuine, indubitable, real, sure-enough, true, undoubted, veritable

simp *n syn* DUNCE, ‖cluck, dimwit, ‖dumb bunny, ‖dumb cluck, featherweight, lackwit, nitwit, pinhead, wantwit

simper *vb syn* SMIRK, ‖smirkle

simple *adj* **1** *syn* NATURAL 5, artless, ingenuous, naive, unaffected, unartful, unartificial, unschooled, unsophisticated, unstudied
rel childish, childlike; amateur, green, unexperienced; trusting; ‖square
2 *syn* PLAIN 1, discreet, inelaborate, modest, unbeautified, undecorated, unelaborate, unornamented, unostentatious, unpretentious
ant elaborate
3 actually or apparently deficient in intelligence <a poor *simple* woman easily duped>
syn asinine, brainless, ‖buffle-headed, fatuous, foolish, insensate, mindless, nitwitted, senseless, sheepheaded, silly, soft, spoony, unintelligent, unwitty, weak-headed, weak-minded, witless; *compare* RETARDED, STUPID 1
rel amateur, green, inexperienced, inexpert; credulous, gullible; childish, childlike, naive; ignorant, illiterate, uneducated, unschooled, untaught; crass, dense, dopey, dull, dumb, slow, stupid; doting, feebleminded, idiotic, retarded, simpleminded
con able, competent; alert, clever, keen; bright, intelligent, understanding
ant wise
4 *syn* RETARDED, backward, dim-witted, dull, feebleminded, half-witted, imbecile, moronic, simpleminded, slow-witted
5 *syn* PURE 2, absolute, perfect, pure and simple, sheer, unadulterated, unalloyed, unmitigated, unmixed, unqualified
rel inelaborate, stark; bald, bare, mere; fundamental, uncompounded
6 *syn* EASY 1, effortless, facile, light, royal, smooth, untroublesome
rel incomplex, incomplicate
idiom simple as ABC
ant complex, complicated

simple *n syn* FOOL 3, butt, chump, dupe, fall guy, gull, mark, pigeon, sap, sucker

simplehearted *adj syn* NATURAL 5, artless, inartificial, ingenuous, naive, simple, unaffected, unschooled, unsophisticated, unstudied

simpleminded *adj syn* RETARDED, dim-witted, dull, feebleminded, half-witted, imbecile, moronic, simple, slow, slow-witted

simplest *adj syn* ELEMENTARY 1, basal, beginning, elemental, rudimental, rudimentary

---

syn synonym(s) — *rel* related word(s)
idiom idiomatic equivalent(s) — *con* contrasted word(s)
ant antonym(s) — * vulgar
‖ use limited; if in doubt, see a dictionary
The first word in a synonym list when printed in SMALL CAPITALS shows where there is more information about the group. For a more efficient use of this book see Explanatory Notes.

simpleton *n* **1** ***syn*** FOOL 4, ament, cretin, ‖feeb, half-wit, idiot, imbecile, moron, natural, zany
2 ***syn*** DUNCE, dullard, dullhead, dumbbell, ‖dummkopf, dummy, idiot, ignoramus, moron, stupid
rel bungler, ‖clot

simplify *vb* to make simple or simpler <*simplify* a manufacturing process>
syn boil down, streamline
rel clarify, clean up, disentangle, disinvolve, straighten (out), unscramble; abridge, cut down, reduce, shorten; oversimplify
ant complicate

simply *adv* ***syn*** JUST 3, but, merely, only

simulacrum *n* **1** ***syn*** IMAGE 1, double, picture, portrait, ringer, spit, spitting image
2 ***syn*** IMITATION, copy, ersatz
3 ***syn*** APPEARANCE 2, face, guise, seeming, semblance, show, showing

simulate *vb* **1** ***syn*** ASSUME 4, act, affect, bluff, counterfeit, fake, feign, pretend, put on, sham
rel ape, copy, imitate, mimic; play-act, pose
idiom ‖make out like (*or* as if)
2 ***syn*** RESEMBLE, favor, ‖feature

simulated *adj* **1** ***syn*** FICTITIOUS 2, fake, mock, sham
ant genuine
2 ***syn*** ARTIFICIAL 2, dummy, ersatz, false, imitation, mock, sham, spurious, substitute
ant genuine

simultaneous *adj* ***syn*** CONTEMPORARY 1, coetaneous, coeval, coexistent, coexisting, concurrent, contemporaneous, synchronal, synchronic, synchronous
rel agreeing, concurring, coinciding

simultaneously *adv* ***syn*** TOGETHER 1, at once, coincidentally, coincidently, coinstantaneously, concurrently
idiom in one breath

sin *n* **1** ***syn*** EVIL 3, crime, diablerie, iniquity, tort, wrong, wrongdoing
2 ***syn*** EVIL 2, debt, wickedness, wrong
3 ***syn*** IMPERFECTION, deficiency, demerit, fault, shortcoming

sin *vb* ***syn*** TRESPASS 1, offend, transgress

since *prep* ***syn*** AFTER 2, behind, below, following, next, subsequent to
ant before

since *conj* ***syn*** BECAUSE, as, as long as, ‖being, 'cause, considering, for, inasmuch as, seeing, whereas

sincere *adj* **1** genuine in feeling or expression <had a *sincere* dislike for politics>
syn heartfelt, hearty, unfeigned, wholehearted, whole-souled; *compare* GENUINE 3
rel candid, frank, frankhearted, open, plain; faithful, honest, truthful; aboveboard, forthright, pretensionless, straightforward, unpretentious; dear, devout, heartful; meant, unaffected
con affected, artificial, feigned, put-on, unmeant
ant insincere
2 ***syn*** GENUINE 3, heart-whole, honest, real, true, undesigning, undissembled, unfeigned
rel authentic, bona fide; serious; actual
idiom honest to God
ant insincere

sincereness *n* ***syn*** GOOD FAITH, bona fides, sincerity, uberrima fides

sincerity *n* ***syn*** GOOD FAITH, bona fides, sincereness, uberrima fides
rel heart; goodwill; singleness, straightforwardness
con cunning, deceit, guile; ill will
ant insincerity

sine qua non *n* ***syn*** ESSENTIAL 2, condition, must, necessity, precondition, prerequisite, requirement, requisite

sinew *n* **1** ***syn*** POWER 4, arm, beef, energy, force, might, muscle, potency, strength, strong arm
2 *usu* **sinews** *pl* ***syn*** MAINSTAY, backbone, pillar

sinewy *adj* ***syn*** MUSCULAR 1, fibrous, ropy, stringy, wiry
rel strong, sturdy, tenacious, tough
ant flabby
2 ***syn*** MUSCULAR 2, athletic, brawny

sinful *adj* **1** ***syn*** WRONG 1, bad, evil, immoral, iniquitous, reprobate, vicious, wicked
rel base, low, vile; disgraceful, shameful; culpable, damnable
2 ***syn*** BLAMEWORTHY, amiss, blamable, blameful, censurable, culpable, demeritorious, guilty, reprehensible, unholy
ant sinless

sing *vb* **1** to utter words in musical tones and with musical inflections and modulations <children often can *sing* before they converse>
syn chant, tune, vocalize
rel descant; carol, serenade, troll; croon, hum, lull, lullaby; cantillate, hymn, intone; singsong; roar
2 ***syn*** TALK 6, squeak, squeal
‖**3** ***syn*** INFORM 3, ‖nark, peach, ‖pimp, rat, snitch, squeak, squeal, ‖stool

single *adj* **1** being without a spouse <enjoying life as a *single* girl>
syn sole, spouseless, unmarried, unwed
rel free, unattached, unfettered; celibate; maiden, virgin
idiom footloose and fancy-free
con attached; united; wed
ant married
2 one as distinguished from two or more or all others <a *single* instance of dishonesty has been cited>
syn lone, one, only, particular, separate, sole, solitary, unique
rel individual, singular; especial, special, specific; distinguished, singled-out; distinct
con several; manifold, many, numerous
ant multiple
3 ***syn*** FRANK, candid, open, plain, single-eyed, single-hearted, single-minded, straightforward, undissembled, unvarnished
4 ***syn*** SOLE 4, exclusive, unshared

single (out) *vb* ***syn*** CHOOSE 1, cull, elect, mark, opt (for), optate, pick, prefer, select, take

---

syn synonym(s) ***rel*** related word(s)
idiom idiomatic equivalent(s) ***con*** contrasted word(s)
ant antonym(s) * vulgar
‖ use limited; if in doubt, see a dictionary
The first word in a synonym list when printed in SMALL CAPITALS shows where there is more information about the group. For a more efficient use of this book see Explanatory Notes.

rel screen, winnow (out); accept, admit, receive

single–eyed *adj* ***syn*** FRANK, candid, open, plain, single, single-hearted, single-minded, straightforward, undissembled, unvarnished

single–hearted *adj* ***syn*** FRANK, candid, open, plain, single, single-eyed, single-minded, straightforward, undissembled, unvarnished

single–minded *adj* **1** ***syn*** FRANK, candid, open, plain, single, single-eyed, single-hearted, straightforward, undissembled, unvarnished
2 ***syn*** INFLEXIBLE 2, adamant, brassbound, inexorable, obdurate, relentless, rigid, unbending, uncompromising, unyielding
rel diehard; bigoted

singleness *n* **1** ***syn*** UNIQUENESS, oneness, unicity, uniquity
2 ***syn*** UNITY 1, individuality, oneness, singularity, singularness
ant multifariousness

singly *adv* ***syn*** APART 1, independently, individually, one by one, separately, severally
ant together

singular *adj* **1** ***syn*** SEVERAL 1, individual, particular, respective
rel discrete; certain, definite; exclusive
2 ***syn*** EXCEPTIONAL 1, extraordinary, rare, uncommon, unimaginable, unique, unordinary, unthinkable, unusual, unwonted
ant usual
3 ***syn*** ONLY 2, alone, lone, sole, solitary, solo, unexampled, unique, unrepeatable
idiom first and last, one and only, one only
4 ***syn*** STRANGE 4, bizarre, curious, odd, oddball, outlandish, peculiar, queer, unusual, weird
idiom passing strange

singularity *n* **1** ***syn*** INDIVIDUALITY 4, identity, ipseity, personality, seity, selfdom, selfhood, selfness
2 ***syn*** INDIVIDUALITY 3, distinctiveness, individualism, particularity
3 ***syn*** UNITY 1, individuality, oneness, singleness, singularness
ant multiplicity

singularize *vb* ***syn*** CHARACTERIZE 2, distinguish, individualize, individuate, mark, qualify, signalize

singularness *n* ***syn*** UNITY 1, individuality, oneness, singleness, singularity
ant multifariousness

sinister *adj* seriously threatening disaster <a *sinister* plot>
syn baleful, malefic, maleficent, malign; *compare* OMINOUS
rel fateful, ill-omened, inauspicious, ominous, portentous, unpropitious; apocalyptic, dire, doomful, ill-boding, threatening; lowering, menacing; evil, malicious
con harmless, innocent, innocuous

sink *vb* **1** to become submerged <the overloaded raft *sank* below the surface>
syn founder, go down, go under, submerge, submerse
rel capsize, overturn, tip (over); dive, plunge; scuttle; shipwreck, wreck
idiom go to Davy Jones's locker, go to the bottom, sink like a rock
con come up, rise
ant float
2 ***syn*** SET 12, decline, dip, go down
3 ***syn*** DETERIORATE 1, decline, degenerate, descend, disimprove, disintegrate, retrograde, rot, worsen
ant rise
4 ***syn*** STOOP 2, descend
5 ***syn*** LOWER 3, couch, demit, depress, droop, let down
6 ***syn*** THRUST 2, dig, drive, plunge, ram, run, stab, stick
7 ***syn*** HUMBLE, abase, bemean, cast down, debase, degrade, demean, humiliate, lower
ant uplift

sink *n* **1** a place marked by a staggering amount of corruption and filth <that area of the city was a *sink* of vice and crime>
syn Augean stable, cesspit, cesspool, den, pandemonium, Sodom, sty
rel hellhole; fleshpot
idiom Alsatian den, den of iniquity, sink of corruption
2 ***syn*** DEPRESSION 2, basin, concavity, dip, hollow, sag, sinkage, sinkhole

sinkage *n* ***syn*** DEPRESSION 2, basin, concavity, dip, hollow, sag, sink, sinkhole

sinkhole *n* ***syn*** DEPRESSION 2, basin, concavity, dip, hollow, sag, sink, sinkage

sinuous *adj* ***syn*** WINDING, anfractuous, convoluted, flexuous, meandering, meandrous, serpentine, snaky, tortuous
rel twisted; snake-shaped
idiom twisting and turning

sip *vb* ***syn*** DRINK 1, imbibe, quaff, sup (off *or* up), swallow, toss

siphon *vb* **1** ***syn*** CONDUCT 4, carry, channel, convey, funnel, pipe, traject, transmit
2 ***syn*** DRAIN 1, draft, draw, draw off, pump, tap

sire *n* ***syn*** FATHER 2, architect, author, creator, founder, generator, inventor, maker, originator, patriarch

sire *vb* **1** ***syn*** FATHER 1, beget, breed, get, procreate, progenerate
2 ***syn*** GENERATE 1, create, father, hatch, make, originate, parent, procreate, produce, spawn

siren *n* an enticingly attractive woman who lures men into dangerous or compromising situations <a slinky *siren* of the silent screen era>
syn femme fatale, Lorelei, seductress, temptress
rel charmer, vamp

siren *adj* ***syn*** ATTRACTIVE 1, alluring, attracting, bewitching, captivating, drawing, enchanting, fascinating, magnetic, seductive
rel sirenic

siren song *n* ***syn*** LURE 2, allurement, bait, come-on, decoy, enticement, seducement, snare, temptation, trap

---

syn synonym(s) | ***rel*** related word(s)
idiom idiomatic equivalent(s) | ***con*** contrasted word(s)
ant antonym(s) | * vulgar
|| use limited; if in doubt, see a dictionary
The first word in a synonym list when printed in SMALL CAPITALS shows where there is more information about the group. For a more efficient use of this book see Explanatory Notes.

sissified *adj* ***syn*** EFFEMINATE, epicene, Miss-Nancyish, pansified, prissy, sissy, unmanly

sissy *n* ***syn*** WEAKLING, baby, doormat, invertebrate, jellyfish, milksop, Milquetoast, mollycoddle, panty-waist, sissy-pants (*or* sissy-britches)

sissy *adj* ***syn*** EFFEMINATE, epicene, Miss-Nancyish, pansified, prissy, sissified, unmanly

sissy–pants (*or* **sissy-britches**) *n pl but sing or pl in constr* ***syn*** WEAKLING, baby, doormat, invertebrate, jellyfish, milksop, Milquetoast, mollycoddle, panty-waist, sissy

sit *vb* **1** to rest on the buttocks or haunches <she was *sitting* in a chair>
syn ‖set
rel perch, rest; ‖plop (down), seat, sit down; squat
con arise, get up, rise, stand, stand up
2 ***syn*** CONVENE 1, meet, open
3 ***syn*** POSE 3, posture
4 ***syn*** SET 11, brood, ‖clock, cover
5 ***syn*** SEAT
rel ensconce, install, settle

sit down *vb* ***syn*** ALIGHT, land, light, perch, roost, set down, settle, touch down

site *n* **1** ***syn*** PLACE 1, location, locus, point, position, situation, spot, station, where
2 ***syn*** SCENE 3, locale, mise-en-scène
3 a place where an archaeological excavation is made <a burial *site*>
syn dig
4 ***syn*** HABITAT, haunt, home, locality, range, stamping ground

sited *adj* ***syn*** SITUATED, located, placed, positioned, set, situate

‖**sitfast** *adj* ***syn*** IMMOVABLE 1, fixed, immobile, immotile, immotive, irremovable, steadfast, unmovable

sitting duck *n* ***syn*** TARGET 1, butt, mark
rel sitter

situate *adj* ***syn*** SITUATED, located, placed, positioned, set, sited

situated *adj* having a site, situation, or location <a town *situated* on a hill>
syn located, placed, positioned, set, sited, situate

situation *n* **1** ***syn*** PLACE 1, location, locus, point, position, site, spot, station, where
2 ***syn*** PREGNANCY, gestation, gravidity, pregnance
3 ***syn*** JOB 2, appointment, berth, billet, connection, office, place, position, post, spot
4 ***syn*** STATUS 1, capacity, character, footing, place, position, rank, standing, state, station
5 ***syn*** STATE 1, condition, mode, posture, status
rel bargain

sizable *adj* **1** ***syn*** CONSIDERABLE 2, good, respectable, ‖right smart, sensible, ‖smart
2 ***syn*** BIG 1, considerable, extensive, hefty, large, large-scale, major
rel man-sized; giant-sized

sizableness *n* ***syn*** SIZE 2, amplitude, bigness, greatness, largeness, magnitude

size *n* **1** the amount of measurable space or area occupied by or comprising a thing <the *size* of the card is 3″x 5″>
syn admeasurement, dimension(s), dimensionality, extent, magnitude, measure, proportion
rel area; body, bulk, mass, volume; height; extension, length; amplitude, breadth, expanse, spread, stretch, width; measurement
2 considerable amount, proportion, volume, character, or importance <left an estate of some *size*>
syn amplitude, bigness, greatness, largeness, magnitude, sizableness
rel dimension, extent
con littleness, smallness; minuteness, tininess

sizz *vb* ***syn*** HISS, buzz, fizz, fizzle, sibilate, sizzle, swish, whish, whisper, whiz

sizzle *vb* **1** ***syn*** SEAR 2
2 ***syn*** HISS, buzz, fizz, fizzle, sibilate, swish, wheeze, whish, whiz, whoosh

sizzling *adj* ***syn*** HOT 1, baking, broiling, burning, fiery, red-hot, scalding, scorching, torrid, white-hot

‖**skag** *n* ***syn*** CIGARETTE, ‖butt, ‖cig, ‖coffin nail, fag, ‖gasper, ‖pill, smoke

skate *n* ***syn*** MAN 3, ‖bloke, boy, buck, chap, fellow, gent, gentleman, guy, ‖mun

sked *n* ***syn*** PROGRAM 1, agenda, calendar, card, docket, programma, schedule, timetable

sked *vb* ***syn*** SCHEDULE 1, card

skedaddle *vb* **1** ***syn*** RUN 2, bolt, flee, fly, make off, scamper, scoot, ‖screw, skip, skirr
rel ‖split; cut out
2 ***syn*** GET OUT 1, begone, clear out, decamp, hightail, kite, scram, skiddoo, take off, ‖vamoose
idiom lift them up and set them down, *move one's ass, ‖take off like a bat out of hell

‖**skeet** *vb* ***syn*** HURRY 2, barrel, bucket, fleet, fly, hasten, highball, hustle, ‖nip, rush

skeezicks *n* ***syn*** SCAMP, devil, enfant terrible, limb, mischief, rapscallion, rascal, rogue, scalawag, villain

skein *n* ***syn*** MAZE 1, jungle, knot, labyrinth, mesh, mizmaze, morass, snarl, tangle, web

skeletal *adj* ***syn*** EMACIATED, cadaverous, gaunt, wasted

skeleton *vb* ***syn*** SKETCH, adumbrate, block (out), chalk (out), characterize, draft, outline, rough (out), skeletonize

skeletonize *vb* ***syn*** SKETCH, adumbrate, block (out), chalk (out), characterize, draft, outline, rough (out), skeleton

‖**sken** *vb* ***syn*** SQUINT, squinch, squinny

skeptic *n* a doubting or incredulous person <men of long experience are often *skeptics*>
syn doubter, doubting Thomas, headshaker, Pyrrhonian, Pyrrhonist, unbeliever, zetetic
rel questioner; agnostic; pessimist; scoffer; cynic, misanthrope; disbeliever
con accepter; apostle, disciple, follower; devotee, diehard
ant believer

---

syn synonym(s) ***rel*** related word(s)
idiom idiomatic equivalent(s) ***con*** contrasted word(s)
ant antonym(s) * vulgar
‖ use limited; if in doubt, see a dictionary
The first word in a synonym list when printed in SMALL CAPITALS shows where there is more information about the group. For a more efficient use of this book see Explanatory Notes.

skeptical *adj* ***syn*** INCREDULOUS, aporetic, disbelieving, questioning, quizzical, show-me, unbelieving
rel freethinking; dissenting; suspicious; cynical
idiom ‖from Missouri
ant believing

skeptically *adv* ***syn*** ASKANCE 2, distrustfully, doubtfully, mistrustfully, suspiciously
idiom with a grain of salt, with a note of skepticism, with a skeptical eye
con trustingly
ant gullibly

skepticism *n* ***syn*** UNCERTAINTY, concern, doubt, dubiety, dubiosity, incertitude, mistrust, suspicion, uncertitude, wonder
rel qualm, qualmishness
idiom question in one's mind, shadow of doubt
con belief, trust
ant gullibility

sketch *n* ***syn*** COMPENDIUM 1, aperçu, digest, pandect, précis, survey, syllabus, sylloge

sketch *vb* to present succinctly <let's *sketch* our plan of action>
syn adumbrate, block (out), chalk (out), characterize, draft, outline, rough (out), skeleton, skeletonize
rel depict; diagram, diagrammatize; blueprint, delineate, line; draw, plot, trace; design, develop; detail, lay out, map (out)

sketchy *adj* ***syn*** SUPERFICIAL 2, cursory, depthless, shallow, uncritical

skew *vb* **1** ***syn*** SLANT 3, angle, bias
2 ***syn*** SWERVE 1, dip, sheer, slue, train off, veer
rel skid, slide, slip

skewer *vb* ***syn*** IMPALE, lance, skiver, spear, spike, spit, transfix, transpierce

skid *vb* **1** ***syn*** SLIDE 3, ‖slidder, ‖slur
rel sheer, skew, slue, veer
idiom go into a skid
2 ***syn*** PLUMMET, dip, drop, fall, nose-dive, plunge, tumble

skiddoo *vb* ***syn*** GET OUT 1, begone, clear out, decamp, hightail, kite, scram, skedaddle, take off, ‖vamoose
idiom go (*or* take) off like a shot

skid road *n* ***syn*** SKID ROW, bowery

skid row *n* a city street or district notorious for cheap bars, flophouses, and homeless derelicts <boozy old men wandering the *skid row*>
syn bowery, skid road

skill *n* **1** ***syn*** ABILITY 2, command, expertise, expertism, expertness, knack, know-how, mastership, mastery
2 ***syn*** ART 1, adroitness, craft, cunning, dexterity, expertise, know-how
3 ***syn*** ADDRESS 1, adroitness, deftness, dexterity, dexterousness, prowess, readiness, sleight
rel ease, skillfulness

skilled *adj* **1** ***syn*** PROFICIENT, adept, crack, crackerjack, expert, master, masterful, masterly, skillful
con skill-less, unproficient
ant unskilled, unskillful
2 ***syn*** EXPERIENCED, old, old-time, practical, practiced, seasoned, versed, vet, veteran
rel prepared, primed, trained
con unfit, unqualified, untrained
ant unskilled

skillet *n* ***syn*** FRYING PAN, spider

skillful *adj* **1** ***syn*** PROFICIENT, adept, crack, crackerjack, expert, master, masterful, masterly, skilled
rel learned, versant, well-versed
ant unskillful
2 accomplished or done with proficiency or skill <his answer was a very *skillful* evasion>
syn adroit, clever, good, pretty, ‖skilly, wicked, workmanlike, workmanly; *compare* CLEVER 4, PROFICIENT
rel expert, masterful
con clumsy; unskilled
ant inept, unskillful

‖**skilly** *adj* ***syn*** SKILLFUL 2, adroit, clever, good, pretty, wicked, workmanlike, workmanly

skim *vb* **1** ***syn*** BRUSH, glance, graze, kiss, shave
2 ***syn*** GLANCE 1, carom, dap, graze, ricochet, skip
3 ***syn*** FLY 1, dart, float, sail, scud, shoot, skirr

skim (through) *vb* ***syn*** BROWSE, dip (into), flip (through), glance (at *or* over), leaf (through), riff (through), riffle (through), run (through *or* over), scan, thumb (through)
con examine, inspect, scrutinize

skimble–skamble *n* ***syn*** GIBBERISH 1, babble, drivel, Greek, jabber, jabberwocky, nonsense

‖**skimmelton** *n* ***syn*** SHIVAREE, ‖belling, ‖bull band, ‖callithump, charivari, ‖horning, ‖riding

skimp *adj* ***syn*** MEAGER 2, exiguous, poor, scant, scanty, scrimp, scrimpy, skimpy, spare, sparse

skimp *vb* **1** ***syn*** SCRIMP, pinch, scrape, screw, ‖skinch, spare, stint
2 ***syn*** SPARE 3, scant, short, ‖skinch, stint

skimpy *adj* **1** ***syn*** MEAGER 2, exiguous, poor, scant, scanty, scrimp, scrimpy, skimp, spare, sparse
2 ***syn*** SHORT 3, deficient, failing, inadequate, insufficient, scant, scarce, shy, unsufficient, wanting

skin *n* **1** ***syn*** HIDE, fell, fur, jacket, pelt
2 ***syn*** HULL, case, husk, pod, shell, shuck, ‖slough
3 a usually thin casing forming the outside surface of a structure or thing <aircraft *skins* made of aluminum alloys>
syn sheath, sheathing
rel facing, siding; case, casing, cover, jacket; shell
4 ***syn*** MISER, cheapskate, cheeseparer, nabal, niggard, ‖nipcheese, scrooge, skinflint, stiff, tightwad
5 ***syn*** SWINDLER, cheat, con man, defrauder, diddler, double-dealer, flimflammer, ‖grifter, gyp, sharper
‖**6** ***syn*** DOLLAR, bill, ‖bone, ‖buck, ‖fish, ‖frogskin, ‖ironman, oner, ‖smacker, ‖smackeroo

skin *vb* **1** ***syn*** SHEATHE, clad, face, side
2 to remove the surface, skin, or thin outer covering of <*skin* a Bermuda onion>
syn decorticate, excorticate, peel, scale, strip; *compare* SHUCK

---

syn synonym(s) ***rel*** related word(s)
idiom idiomatic equivalent(s) ***con*** contrasted word(s)
ant antonym(s) * vulgar
‖ use limited; if in doubt, see a dictionary
The first word in a synonym list when printed in SMALL CAPITALS shows where there is more information about the group. For a more efficient use of this book see Explanatory Notes.

rel cut off, pull off; pare, shave (off), trim; hull, husk, shuck; bark, rind; excoriate, flay, gall
3 *syn* OVERCHARGE 1, clip, fleece, soak, stick
4 *syn* CRITICIZE, blame, censure, condemn, denounce, denunciate, knock, rap, reprehend, reprobate
5 *syn* HURRY 2, barrel, beeline, bucket, bullet, fleet, haste, hasten, highball, hustle

‖**skinch** *vb* **1** *syn* SCRIMP, pinch, scrape, screw, skimp, spare, stint
2 *syn* SPARE 3, scant, short, skimp, stint

skinflint *n syn* MISER, cheapskate, cheeseparer, chuff, muckworm, nabal, niggard, ‖nipcheese, skin, tightwad

‖**skinhead** *n syn* BALDHEAD, baldpate, ‖baldy

skinny *adj syn* LEAN, angular, bony, gaunt, lank, lanky, rawboned, scraggy, scrawny, spare
rel twiggy, weedy; emaciated; skeletal
idiom mere skin and bones, skinny as a rail
ant fleshy

skip *vb* **1** to move or proceed with a light bounding step <children *skipping* home from school>
syn hop, lope, skitter, spring, trip
rel caper, cavort, curvet, frisk, gambol; bounce, hippety-hop; jump; leap; bound
con hobble, shamble, shuffle; hitch, limp, stagger, totter
2 *syn* GLANCE 1, carom, dap, graze, ricochet, skim
3 *syn* RUN 2, bolt, flee, fly, make off, scamper, scoot, ‖screw, skedaddle, skirr
idiom ‖split the scene

skip *n syn* OMISSION, blank, chasm, overlook, oversight, preterition, pretermission

skirmish *n* **1** *syn* CLASH 2, affray, brush, fray, melee, mellay, scrimmage
rel assault, attack; ambush
con pitched battle
2 *syn* ENCOUNTER, brush, run-in, set-to, velitation

skirr *vb* **1** *syn* RUN 2, bolt, flee, fly, make off, scamper, scoot, ‖screw, skedaddle, skip
2 *syn* FLY 1, dart, float, sail, scud, shoot, skim

skirt *n syn* BORDER 1, brim, brink, edge, fringe, hem, margin, perimeter, periphery, verge
rel skirting

skirt *vb* **1** *syn* BORDER 1, bound, define, edge, fringe, hem, margin, rim, surround, verge
2 to make a detour or circuit (as around a congested area) <*skirted* the city to avoid traffic>
syn bypass, circumnavigate, circumvent, detour
idiom go around
3 to avoid (as a topic or question) because of difficulty, complexity, controversy, or danger <*skirted* all touchy issues>
syn burke, bypass, circumvent, ‖polly-fox, sidestep; *compare* EQUIVOCATE 2, ESCAPE 2
rel avoid, dodge, duck, evade, hedge; elude, escape; ignore, skip
idiom get around
con confront, face, meet, take on

‖**skite** *n syn* PRANK, antic, caper, dido(es), frolic, lark, monkeyshine, shenanigan, shine(s), tomfoolery

skitter *vb syn* SKIP 1, hop, lope, spring, trip

skittery *adj syn* EXCITABLE, agitable, alarmable, combustible, edgy, skittish, startlish, volatile

skittish *adj* **1** *syn* GIDDY 1, bird-witted, dizzy, empty-headed, flighty, frivolous, harebrained, light-headed, rattlebrained, scatterbrained
rel irresponsible, undependable, unreliable
2 *syn* EXCITABLE, agitable, alarmable, combustible, edgy, skittery, startlish, volatile
rel restive; nervous

skive *vb syn* CUT 6, clip, crop, pare, prune, shave, shear, trim

skiver *vb syn* IMPALE, lance, skewer, spear, spike, spit, transfix, transpierce

skookum *adj syn* EXCELLENT, bang-up, ‖bunkum, capital, champion, ‖dandy, first-class, first-rate, first-string, front-rank

skookum–house *n syn* JAIL, ‖big house, bridewell, ‖brig, ‖calaboose, ‖can, ‖clink, cooler, coop, ‖hoosegow

skulk *vb syn* SNEAK, creep, gumshoe, lurk, pussyfoot, shirk, slink, slip, ‖snake, steal

skunk *n syn* SNOT 1, cur, dog, ‖prick, scum, *shit, *shithead, snake, toad, *turd

skunk *vb syn* WHIP 2, beat, ‖clobber, drub, lambaste, ‖larrup, lick, overwhelm, shellac, thrash

sky *n* the expanse of space surrounding the earth <blue *sky* crisscrossed with jet trails>
syn empyrean, firmament, heaven(s), welkin
rel azure; celestial sphere
idiom the wild blue yonder

sky–high *adv syn* APART 3, asunder

sky–high *adj syn* EXCESSIVE 1, dizzy, exorbitant, extravagant, extreme, inordinate, towering, unconscionable, undue, unmeasurable

skylarking *n* **1** *syn* HORSEPLAY, fooling, high jinks, roughhouse, roughhousing, rowdiness
idiom ‖making whoopee
2 *syn* REVELRY 2, high jinks, revel, revelment, wassail, whoop-de-do, whoopee, whoopla, whoop-up

sky pilot *n syn* CLERGYMAN, churchman, cleric, clerical, clerk, divine, ecclesiastic, minister, parson, preacher
rel chaplain; padre

skyrocket *vb* to rise abruptly and rapidly (as to an unprecedented level or amount) <when the election was over taxes and prices *skyrocketed*>
syn rocket, shoot up, soar
rel climb, rise; upsoar, upspring
con slide; fall; drop
ant crash, plummet

skyscraping *adj syn* LOFTY 6, aerial, airy, soaring, spiring, topless, towering, towery

slab *n syn* BAR 1, billet, ingot, rod, stick, strip
rel chunk, lump

‖**slab** *n syn* SLIME, muck, slum

slabber *vb syn* DROOL 2, dribble, drivel, salivate, slaver, slobber

---

syn synonym(s) — *rel* related word(s)
idiom idiomatic equivalent(s) — *con* contrasted word(s)
ant antonym(s) — * vulgar
‖ use limited; if in doubt, see a dictionary
The first word in a synonym list when printed in SMALL CAPITALS shows where there is more information about the group. For a more efficient use of this book see Explanatory Notes.

slack *adj* **1** ***syn*** NEGLIGENT, behindhand, careless, delinquent, derelict, disregardful, lax, neglectful, regardless, remiss
rel dilatory, lackadaisical, lethargic, sluggish; faineant, indolent, lazy, slothful; inert, stagnant
con assiduous, busy, diligent, industrious, sedulous
2 ***syn*** LOOSE 1, lax, relaxed
rel feeble, infirm, soft, unsteady, weak; inactive, inert, passive, supine; laggard, leisurely, slow
con tensed, tightened; constant, equable, even, steady, uniform; firm, hard
ant taut, tight
3 ***syn*** SLOW 3, down, off, sluggish

slack *vb* ***syn*** LOOSE 5, ease, ease off, lax, loosen, relax, slacken, untighten
idiom ‖cut some slack, make slack
ant tighten

slack *n* ***syn*** SLOWDOWN 1, slackening, slow-up

slacken *vb* **1** ***syn*** DELAY 1, bog (down), decelerate, detain, embog, hang up, mire, retard, set back, slow (up *or* down)
idiom keep back
ant quicken
2 ***syn*** ABATE 4, die (down *or* away), ease off, ebb, fall, let up, moderate, relent, subside, wane
3 ***syn*** LOOSE 5, ease, ease off, lax, loosen, relax, slack, untighten
ant tighten

slackening *n* ***syn*** SLOWDOWN 1, slack, slow-up

slacker *n* one who shirks work, responsibility, or an obligation <didn't want any *slackers* in his office>
syn goldbrick, shirker, slinker, ‖spiv
rel idler, loafer; slugabed, sluggard

slack–spined *adj* ***syn*** WEAK 4, boneless, emasculate, forceless, impotent, ineffective, ineffectual, invertebrate, spineless, wan

slake *vb* ***syn*** QUENCH 4, ‖squench

slam *n* **1** ***syn*** BLOW 1, bang, bash, bastinado, crack, ‖ding, pound, smack, smash, whack
2 ***syn*** BANG 2, blast, boom, burst, clap, crack, crash, smash, wham
3 ***syn*** ANIMADVERSION, aspersion, obloquy, reflection, slur, stricture
rel fling, swipe; crack, potshot; rap, slap; dig, jab

slam *vb* **1** to strike with extreme force or violence <*slammed* the ball out of the park> <the car *slammed* into the fence>
syn belt, blast, clobber, slug, smash, wallop; *compare* STRIKE 2
rel bang, bat, hit, knock, slap, swat, thwack; cudgel, hammer, mace; batter, beat, pound
2 ***syn*** LAMBASTE 3, castigate, drub, flay, lash (into), scathe, scourge, slap, slash, ‖slate

‖**slam** *adv* ***syn*** WELL 3, à fond, altogether, clear, completely, entirely, fully, quite, right, ‖slap

slammer *n* ***syn*** JAIL, ‖brig, ‖bucket, ‖calaboose, ‖can, ‖clink, cooler, jug, pen, prison

slander *n* ***syn*** DETRACTION, backbiting, backstabbing, belittlement, calumny, defamation, depreciation, disparagement, scandal, tale
rel black wash, muckraking, mud-slinging, roorback, scandal-mongering

slander *vb* ***syn*** MALIGN, asperse, calumniate, defame, denigrate, libel, slur, smear, tear down, traduce
rel assail, attack; damage, hurt, injure; blackwash, muckrake; belie, strumpet
idiom dish the dirt, run a smear campaign, sling the mud
ant panegyrize

slanderous *adj* ***syn*** LIBELOUS, backbiting, calumnious, defamatory, detracting, detractive, maligning, scandalous, traducing, vilifying
rel blackwashing, muckraking, scandal-mongering
ant panegyrical

slang *n* ***syn*** DIALECT 2, argot, cant, jargon, lingo, patois, patter, vernacular
rel slanginess, slanguage

slangism *n* ***syn*** BARBARISM, corruption, impropriety, solecism, vernacularism, vernacularity, vulgarism

slant *adv* ***syn*** ASIDE 1, aslant, aslope, obliquely, sideways, sidewise, slantingly, slantways, slantwise, ‖slaunchways

slant *vb* **1** to set or be set at an angle <*slanted* the ladder against the wall>
syn cant, heel, incline, lean, list, recline, slope, tilt, tip
rel bank, decline, descend; bend, deviate, diverge, splay, swerve, veer
2 to direct (written or spoken material) to the interests of a particular audience or group <a magazine *slanted* to farm families>
syn aim, angle
rel direct, orient, point, train; concentrate, focus; spoon-feed; bias, skew, warp
3 to orient (material) from objective presentation so as to favor a particular bias <accused the media of *slanting* the news against the president>
syn angle, bias, skew; *compare* PREJUDICE 2
rel influence, prejudice; color, distort, twist, warp
ant objectify, objectivize

slant *n* **1** ***syn*** SLOPE, grade, gradient, inclination, incline, lean, leaning, tilt
2 ***syn*** VIEWPOINT 2, angle, direction, outlook, side, standpoint
rel predilection, predisposition, prejudice

slanted *adj* ***syn*** DIAGONAL, bevel, beveled, bias, biased, slanting

slanting *adj* ***syn*** DIAGONAL, bevel, beveled, bias, biased, slanted

slantingly *adv* ***syn*** ASIDE 1, aslant, aslope, obliquely, sideways, sidewise, slantly, slantways, slantwise, ‖slaunchways

slantingways *adv* **1** ***syn*** ASIDE 1, aslant, aslope, obliquely, sideways, sidewise, slantingly, slantly, slantways, slantwise
2 ***syn*** DIAGONALLY, catercorner (*or* catty-corner *or* kitty-corner), cornerwise, slantways, slantwise, ‖slaunchways

---

syn synonym(s)	***rel*** related word(s)
idiom idiomatic equivalent(s)	***con*** contrasted word(s)
ant antonym(s)	* vulgar

‖ use limited; if in doubt, see a dictionary
The first word in a synonym list when printed in SMALL CAPITALS shows where there is more information about the group. For a more efficient use of this book see Explanatory Notes.

slantly *adv* ***syn*** ASIDE 1, aslant, aslope, obliquely, sideways, sidewise, slantingly, slantways, slantwise, ‖slaunchways

slantways *adv* **1** ***syn*** ASIDE 1, aslant, aslope, obliquely, sideways, sidewise, slantingly, slantly, slantwise, ‖slaunchways
2 ***syn*** DIAGONALLY, catercorner (*or* catty-corner *or* kitty-corner), cornerwise, slantingways, slantwise, ‖slaunchways

slantwise *adv* **1** ***syn*** ASIDE 1, aslant, aslope, obliquely, sideways, sidewise, slantingly, slantly, slantways, ‖slaunchways
2 ***syn*** DIAGONALLY, catercorner (*or* catty-corner *or* kitty-corner), cornerwise, slantingways, slantways, ‖slaunchways

slap *n* **1** ***syn*** CUFF, box, ‖bust, chop, clout, haymaker, poke, punch, smack, sock
2 ***syn*** AFFRONT, contumely, despite, indignity, insult
3 ***syn*** FLING 1, crack, go, pop, shot, stab, ‖stagger, try, whack, whirl

slap *vb* **1** to strike quickly and sharply with the hand < *slapped* the hysterical girl >
syn blip, box, buffet, cuff, smack, spank, ‖wherret; *compare* STRIKE 2
rel ‖biff, ding, hit, sock, swat, whack; ‖wap, wham; bash
2 ***syn*** LAMBASTE 3, castigate, drub, flay, lash (into), scathe, score, scourge, slam, slash

‖**slap** *adv* ***syn*** WELL 3, à fond, altogether, clear, completely, entirely, fully, perfectly, quite, utterly

slap around *vb* ***syn*** MANHANDLE, knock about, mishandle, rough (up), roughhouse

slapdash *adj* **1** ***syn*** RANDOM, aimless, designless, desultory, haphazard, hit-or-miss, indiscriminate, irregular, promiscuous, spot
2 ***syn*** SLIPSHOD 3, botchy, careless, messy, sloppy, slovenly, unthorough, untidy

‖**slap–up** *adj* ***syn*** EXCELLENT, bang-up, ‖boss, bully, capital, champion, famous, first-class, first-rate, five-star

slash *vb* **1** ***syn*** CUT 1, gash, incise, pierce, slice, slit
2 ***syn*** HACK, hackle, haggle
3 ***syn*** LAMBASTE 3, blister, castigate, excoriate, flay, lash (into), scarify, scathe, scorch, scourge
idiom ‖light into
4 ***syn*** REDUCE 2, clip, cut, cut back, cut down, lower, mark down, pare, shave
5 ***syn*** SHORTEN, abbreviate, abridge, curtail, cut, cut back, retrench

slate *n* ***syn*** TICKET 3

‖**slate** *vb* ***syn*** LAMBASTE 3, blister, castigate, ‖crawl, excoriate, lash (into), scarify, scathe, score, scourge

slather *n, often* **slathers** *pl* ***syn*** SCAD, gob(s), heap, load(s), million, oodles, quantities, ream(s), ‖rimption(s), wad(s)

slattern *n* **1** an untidy slovenly woman < two blowsy *slatterns* gossiping at the bar >
syn dowd, dowdy, drab, draggle-tail, ‖malkin, slut, ‖streel, traipse
rel frump; slob, ‖slommack, sloven; crone, gammer, hag, witch
2 ***syn*** WANTON, baggage, hussy, jade, slut, strumpet, tramp, trollop, trull, wench
rel prostitute, whore

slattern *adj* ***syn*** SLATTERNLY, blowsy, dowdy, draggletailed, frowsy, sordid

slatternly *adj* being habitually untidy and very dirty especially in dress or appearance < a filthy, *slatternly* old woman >
syn blowsy, dowdy, draggletailed, frowsy, slattern, sordid; *compare* SLOVENLY 1
rel careless, disordered, neglected, poky; bedraggled, disheveled, draggled, draggly, messy, mussy, slipshod, sloppy, slovenly, unkempt, untidy; dirty, filthy, foul, grimy, squalid
con clean, fresh, neat, tidy, trim; smart; immaculate, spotless
ant bandbox

slaughter *n* ***syn*** MASSACRE, bloodbath, bloodshed, butchery, carnage
rel slaughtery; annihilation, destruction

slaughter *vb* **1** to kill (animals) for food < *slaughtered* a beef for the winter >
syn butcher, slay
rel stick
2 to kill (a person) in an especially bloody or barbarous manner < Jack the Ripper *slaughtered* his victims with a knife >
syn butcher, slay
rel kill, murder, ‖total, ‖waste; maim, mangle, mutilate, torture
3 to kill (people) in large numbers < millions *slaughtered* in death camps >
syn annihilate, decimate, exterminate, massacre, wipe (out)

‖**slaunchways** *adv* **1** ***syn*** DIAGONALLY, catercorner (*or* catty-corner *or* kitty-corner), cornerwise, slantingways, slantways, slantwise
2 ***syn*** ASIDE 1, aslant, aslope, obliquely, sideways, sidewise, slantingly, slantly, slantways, slantwise

slave *n* **1** a person held in servitude or bondage < plantations worked by *slaves* >
syn bondman, bondslave, bondsman, chattel, mancipium
rel help, menial, retainer, servant; helot, serf, thrall, vassal
con freedman, freedwoman; ‖deditician
ant freeman
2 one who works at a hard, monotonous, usually menial task < *slaves* working all night on a senator's speech >
syn dray horse, drudge, galley slave, peon, slavey, toiler, workhorse
rel ‖coolie

slave *vb* ***syn*** DRUDGE, grind, grub, ‖muck, plod, slog, toil

---

syn synonym(s) *rel* related word(s)
idiom idiomatic equivalent(s) *con* contrasted word(s)
ant antonym(s) * vulgar
‖ use limited; if in doubt, see a dictionary
The first word in a synonym list when printed in SMALL CAPITALS shows where there is more information about the group. For a more efficient use of this book see Explanatory Notes.

idiom work like a slave

slave driver *n* a person in authority who exacts extreme effort from his subordinates <the chief proofreader was a real *slave driver*>
syn rawhider, Simon Legree, taskmaster
rel martinet
idiom a hard taskmaster

slaver *vb* **1** *syn* DROOL 2, dribble, drivel, salivate, slabber, slobber
2 *syn* FAWN, apple-polish, bootlick, cower, cringe, grovel, honey (up), kowtow, toady, truckle

slaver *n syn* SALIVA, spit, spittle, water

slavery *n* **1** *syn* WORK 2, bullwork, donkeywork, drudge, drudgery, grind, labor, moil, plugging, toil
2 *syn* BONDAGE, enslavement, helotry, peonage, serfdom, servitude, thrall, thralldom, villenage, yoke
idiom involuntary servitude, the yoke (*or* chains) of slavery

slavey *n* **1** *syn* SLAVE 2, dray horse, drudge, galley slave, peon, toiler, workhorse
2 *syn* HACK 2, drudge, grub, grubber, hireling, mercenary

slavish *adj* **1** *syn* HARD 6, difficult, formidable, heavy, knotty, laborious, operose, rough, rugged, strenuous
2 *syn* SUBSERVIENT 2, menial, obeisant, obsequious, servile
rel spineless, subdued, tame; miserable, wretched
ant independent
3 copying obsequiously something superior <the painting was a *slavish* copy of an old master>
syn apish, emulative, imitative
rel uninspired; unoriginal
con fresh, new, novel, original; fanciful, imaginative, ingenious, inspired; extravagant, high-flown

slay *vb* **1** *syn* KILL 1, carry off, cut off, destroy, dispatch, down, finish, lay low, put away, take off
2 *syn* MURDER 1, assassinate, ‖bump off, cool, do in, ‖dust off, execute, finish, knock off, liquidate
3 *syn* SLAUGHTER 2, butcher
4 *syn* SLAUGHTER 1, butcher

slayer *n syn* MURDERER, homicide, killer, manslayer

sleazy *adj* **1** *syn* LIMP 1, flabby, flaccid, flimsy, floppy
rel slight, tenuous, thin; gossamery
2 *syn* CHEAP 2, base, cheesy, common, mean, paltry, poor, shoddy, tatty, trashy
3 *syn* SHABBY 1, broken-down, dilapidated, dingy, disreputable, down-at-heel, run-down, seedy, shoddy, tacky

sleek *vb syn* POLISH 2, perfect, refine, round, slick, smooth

sleek *adj* having a very smooth or lustrous surface or texture <the car's *sleek* new paint job>
syn glassy, glossy, polished, ‖sleekit, sleeky, smarmy
rel smooth; glistening, lustrous

‖sleekit *adj syn* SLEEK, glassy, glossy, polished, sleeky, smarmy

sleeky *adj syn* SLEEK, glassy, glossy, polished, ‖sleekit, smarmy

sleep *n* **1** the natural periodic suspension of consciousness during which the powers of the body are restored <needed eight hours of *sleep* to function efficiently>
syn ‖doss, ‖shut-eye, slumber; *compare* DOZE, NAP
rel repose, rest; slumberland
idiom land of Nod, the arms of Morpheus
con wakefulness
2 *syn* LETHARGY 1, coma, dullness, hebetude, languor, lassitude, slumber, torpidity, torpidness, torpor
3 *syn* DEATH 1, curtains, decease, defunction, demise, dissolution, (the) Pale Horse, passing, quietus, silence

sleep *vb* to rest in a state of sleep <*slept* for over eight hours>
syn ‖doss, slumber; *compare* DOZE, NAP
rel relax, repose, rest; oversleep, sleep in
idiom be in the land of Nod, be sunk in sleep, pound one's ear, rest in the arms of Morpheus, sleep like a top (*or* log)
con arouse, awaken, wake (up)

sleeplessness *n syn* INSOMNIA, insomnolence

sleepy *adj* **1** having an inclination for or affected by sleep <was *sleepy* after the long day>
syn dozy, drowsy, nodding, ‖peepy, ‖sloomy, slumberous, slumbery, snoozy, somnolent, soporific
rel heavy, heavy-eyed, lethargic, sluggish, torpid; dazed, dopey, listless, oscitant, yawning; asleep, sleeping, slumbering; nepenthean, poppied; comatose, ‖out
con awake, conscious; restless, sleepless, unsleeping; alert, wide-awake
ant wakeful
2 *syn* INACTIVE, asleep, idle, inert, passive, quiet
3 *syn* SOPORIFIC 1, hypnotic, narcotic, opiate, slumberous, somnifacient, somniferous, somnific, somnolent, somnorific

‖sleer *vb syn* SNEER 1, fleer, leer

sleight *n* **1** *syn* ADDRESS 1, adroitness, deftness, dexterity, dexterousness, prowess, readiness, skill
2 *syn* TRICK 1, artifice, device, gimmick, maneuver, play, ploy, ruse, stratagem, wile

‖sleighty *adj syn* CLEVER 4, adroit, canny, ‖coony, cunning, dexterous, ingenious, slim, sly

slender *adj* **1** *syn* THIN 1, attenuate, reedy, slight, slim, squinny, stalky, tenuous, twiggy
rel slenderish, slimmish; lithe, svelte, trim
idiom slender as a reed
2 *syn* SHORT 3, deficient, inadequate, insufficient, scant, scanty, scarce, shy, unsufficient, wanting
3 *syn* REMOTE 4, ‖fat, negligible, off, outside, slight, slim, small

slenderize *vb syn* REDUCE 5, slim (down)

sleuth *n syn* DETECTIVE, dick, ‖eye, gumshoe, hawkshaw, investigator, plainclothesman, Sherlock, Sherlock Holmes, ‖tec

slew *n syn* SCAD, jillion, load(s), million, oodles, quantities, ‖rimption(s), slather(s), thousand, trillion

slewed *adj syn* INTOXICATED 1, ‖boozy, ‖canned, disguised, drunk, inebriated, ‖lushed, muddled, pixilated, ‖plastered

---

syn synonym(s) *rel* related word(s)
idiom idiomatic equivalent(s) *con* contrasted word(s)
ant antonym(s) * vulgar
‖ use limited; if in doubt, see a dictionary
The first word in a synonym list when printed in SMALL CAPITALS shows where there is more information about the group. For a more efficient use of this book see Explanatory Notes.

slice *n* ***syn*** SHARE 1, allotment, allowance, bite, cut, lot, part, partage, portion, quota
rel segment
idiom a slice of the pie (*or* melon)

slice *vb* **1** ***syn*** CUT 1, gash, incise, pierce, slash, slit
2 ***syn*** CUT 5, carve, cleave, dissect, dissever, sever, split, sunder

slick *vb* **1** ***syn*** POLISH 2, perfect, refine, round, sleek, smooth
2 ***syn*** DRESS UP 1, deck (out), doll out, doll up, ‖dude up, fix up, gussy up, smarten (up), spiff, spruce (up)
3 ***syn*** SLIDE 1, glide, glissade, slip, slither

slick *adj* **1** having a glassy surface that often offers insecure footing <a floor *slick* with wax>
syn greasy, lubricious, ‖sliddery, ‖slipper, slippery, slippy, slithery
rel oily; ‖slape, smooth; soapy
idiom slick as a greased pig
con coarse, gritty, rough, uneven
2 ***syn*** FULSOME, oily, oleaginous, smarmy, soapy, unctious, unctuous
rel glossy; slippery
3 ***syn*** WISE 4, canny, hep, knowing, nimble-witted, quick, quick-witted, sharp, sharp-witted, smart

slicker *n* ***syn*** SWINDLER, cheater, defrauder, diddler, double-dealer, flimflammer, ‖grifter, gypper, sharper, trickster

‖**slidder** *vb* **1** ***syn*** SLIDE 3, skid, slip, ‖slur
2 ***syn*** SLITHER 2, snake, undulate

‖**sliddery** *adj* ***syn*** SLICK 1, greasy, lubricious, ‖slipper, slippery, slippy, slithery

slide *vb* **1** to go or progress with a smooth continuous motion <goldfish *slid* across the pool>
syn glide, glissade, slick, slip, slither
rel flow, stream
2 ***syn*** SLIP 6, drop (off), fall (off *or* away), sag, slump
3 to fall or nearly fall because of loss of balance or footing <stumbled and *slid* on the ice>
syn skid, ‖slidder, slip, ‖slur
idiom take a slide (*or* a skid)
4 to shift or be shifted out of place or away from one's grasp <the packages *slid* from her arms>
syn slip
rel shift; move; fall, spill, tumble
5 ***syn*** CREEP 1, crawl, snake
6 to take a natural course <preferred to let the matter *slide* for a while>
syn coast, drift
rel glide
idiom run its course
7 ***syn*** STEAL 3, creep, glide, mouse, slip
8 ***syn*** SNEAK, creep, glide, lurk, shirk, skulk, slink, slip, ‖snake, steal

slide *n* ***syn*** DECLINE 3, dip, downslide, downswing, downtrend, downturn, drop, falloff, sag, slip

slight *adj* **1** ***syn*** THIN 1, attenuate, reedy, slender, slim, squinny, stalky, tenuous, twiggy
rel slightish, ‖slighty; smallish; pint-sized
2 ***syn*** DELICATE 5, flimsy
rel gossamery, sleazy
3 ***syn*** REMOTE 4, ‖fat, negligible, off, outside, slender, slim, small

slight *vb* ***syn*** NEGLECT, blink (at *or* away), discount, disregard, fail, forget, ignore, omit, overlook, overpass
rel skip; contemn, despise; flout, scoff

slightest *adj* ***syn*** FIRST 4, least, smallest
rel ‖fat, negligible

slighting *adj* ***syn*** DEROGATORY, depreciative, depreciatory, detracting, disadvantageous, disparaging, dyslogistic, pejorative, uncomplimentary

slim *adj* **1** ***syn*** THIN 1, attenuate, reedy, slender, slight, squinny, stalky, tenuous, twiggy
rel lissome, lithe, lithesome, svelte
ant chubby
2 ***syn*** CLEVER 4, adroit, canny, ‖coony, cunning, dexterous, ingenious, ‖sleighty, sly
3 ***syn*** REMOTE 4, ‖fat, negligible, off, outside, slender, slight, small

slim (down) *vb* ***syn*** REDUCE 5, slenderize

slime *n* a viscous and usually dirty or offensive substance <a layer of *slime* formed in the bottom of the pool>
syn muck, ‖slab, slum
rel ooze, ‖sleech, sludge; scum

sling *vb* **1** ***syn*** THROW 1, ‖bung, cast, fire, fling, heave, hurl, launch, pitch, toss
rel catapult; sock
2 ***syn*** STRIDE 1, march, stalk, ‖striddle

sling *vb* ***syn*** HANG 1, dangle, depend, suspend

slink *vb* ***syn*** SNEAK, creep, gumshoe, lurk, pussyfoot, shirk, skulk, slide, ‖snake, steal

slink *n* ***syn*** SNEAK, sneaker, sneaksby, weasel

slinker *n* ***syn*** SLACKER, goldbrick, shirker, ‖spiv

slip *vb* **1** ***syn*** SLIDE 1, glide, glissade, slick, slither
2 ***syn*** SNEAK, creep, gumshoe, lurk, pussyfoot, shirk, skulk, slide, slink, ‖snake
3 ***syn*** STEAL 3, creep, glide, mouse, slide
4 ***syn*** SLIDE 4
5 ***syn*** SLIDE 3, skid, ‖skidder, ‖slur
6 to decline gradually from a standard or accustomed level <sales in some lines *slipped*>
syn drop (off), fall (off *or* away), sag, slide, slump
rel erode, soften; decline, go down, sink; dip, drop; nose-dive, plummet, topple; crash
con better, gain, improve, rally, rebound; ascend, climb, rise; skyrocket, soar
7 ***syn*** SHAKE 5, lose, throw off
8 ***syn*** SHED 2, exuviate, molt, slough

slip (on) *vb* ***syn*** DON 1, assume, draw on, get on, huddle (on), put on, throw
ant slip (off)

slip *n* **1** ***syn*** WHARF, berth, dock, jetty, levee, pier, quay
2 ***syn*** ESCAPE 1, breakout, escapement, escaping, flight, getaway, lam, ‖scape
3 ***syn*** ERROR 2, blooper, blunder, boner, bull, bungle, fluff, lapse, mistake, trip

---

syn synonym(s) — *rel* related word(s)
idiom idiomatic equivalent(s) — *con* contrasted word(s)
ant antonym(s) — * vulgar
‖ use limited; if in doubt, see a dictionary
The first word in a synonym list when printed in SMALL CAPITALS shows where there is more information about the group. For a more efficient use of this book see Explanatory Notes.

4 ***syn*** DECLINE 3, dip, downslide, downswing, downtrend, downturn, drop, falloff, sag, slump

‖**slipper** *adj* ***syn*** SLICK 1, greasy, lubricious, ‖sliddery, slippery, slippy, slithery

slippery *adj* **1** ***syn*** SLICK 1, greasy, lubricious, ‖sliddery, ‖slipper, slippy, slithery

2 ***syn*** MUTABLE 2, changeable, inconstant, shifty, uncertain, unstable, unsteady, variable

slippy *adj* ***syn*** SLICK 1, greasy, lubricious, ‖sliddery, ‖slipper, slippery, slithery

slipshod *adj* **1** ***syn*** SHABBY 1, bedraggled, down-at-heel, scrubby, scruffy, shoddy, tacky, tagrag, tattered, threadbare

2 ***syn*** SLOVENLY 1, careless, disheveled, ill-kempt, messy, raunchy, sloppy, unkempt, unneat, untidy

3 marked by indifference to exactness, precision, and accuracy <a *slipshod* piece of research>

syn botchy, careless, messy, slapdash, sloppy, slovenly, unthorough, untidy

rel neglected, negligent; haphazard, slaphappy, unmeticulous; botched-up, fouled-up, messed-up, ‖screwed-up; faulty, imperfect, inaccurate, inexact

con fastidious, meticulous, neat; accurate, exact, precise; methodical, orderly, systematic; thorough

slipslop *n* ***syn*** NONSENSE 2, balderdash, ‖baloney, ‖bunk, claptrap, drivel, guff, hogwash, poppycock, twaddle

slipup *n* ***syn*** ERROR 2, blooper, blunder, boner, bungle, fluff, lapse, mistake, slip, trip

slit *vb* ***syn*** CUT 1, gash, incise, pierce, slash, slice

slither *vb* **1** ***syn*** SLIDE 1, glide, glissade, slick, slip

rel ‖sluther

2 to walk or move in a sinuous way <a slinky blonde *slithered* over from the bar>

syn ‖slidder, snake, undulate

rel creep, glide, sidle, steal; lurk, prowl, slink, sneak

slithery *adj* ***syn*** SLICK 1, greasy, lubricious, ‖sliddery, ‖slipper, slippery, slippy

‖**slive** *vb* ***syn*** SIDLE, edge

sliver *vb* to cut into very thin slices <*slivered* cheese>

syn shave, shred

rel carve, haggle, slice

con chop, dice, mince; comminute, powder, pulverize; crush, mash

slobber *vb* ***syn*** DROOL 2, dribble, drivel, salivate, slabber, slaver

slobbering *adj* ***syn*** EFFUSIVE, gushing, gushy, slobbery, sloppy

slobbery *adj* **1** ***syn*** EFFUSIVE, gushing, gushy, slobbering, sloppy

2 ***syn*** SLOVENLY 1, ill-kempt, messy, raunchy, ‖slommacky, sloppy, uncombed, unkempt, unneat, untidy

slog *vb* **1** ***syn*** STRIKE 2, catch, clout, ding, hit, ‖nail, ‖slosh, smite, sock, whack

2 ***syn*** PLOD 1, footslog, ‖plodge, plunther, slop, stodge, toil, ‖trash, trudge

3 ***syn*** DRUDGE, grind, grub, ‖muck, plod, slave, toil

slogan *n* ***syn*** CATCHWORD, byword, catchphrase, phrase, shibboleth, watchword

rel expression, idiom, locution

slogging *n* ***syn*** WORK 2, bullwork, donkeywork, drudgery, grind, labor, moil, slavery, sweat, toil

‖**slommacky** *adj* ***syn*** SLOVENLY 1, disheveled, ill-kempt, messy, raunchy, slobbery, sloppy, unkempt, unneat, untidy

‖**sloom** *n* ***syn*** DOZE, drowse, slumber

‖**sloom** *vb* ***syn*** DOZE, ‖dorm, drowse, slumber, ‖snoozle, ‖sog

‖**sloomy** *adj* ***syn*** SLEEPY 1, dozy, drowsy, nodding, ‖peepy, slumberous, slumbery, snoozy, somnolent, soporific

slop *n* ***syn*** PAP 2, pablum, rubbish

slop *vb* **1** ***syn*** SPILL 1, squab

2 ***syn*** SPLASH, douse, plash, slosh, spatter, splatter, splosh, splurge, spurtle, swash

3 ***syn*** GULP, bolt, cram, englut, gobble, guzzle, ingurgitate, slosh, wolf

4 ***syn*** PLOD 1, footslog, ‖plodge, plunther, slog, stodge, toil, ‖trash, trudge

slope *vb* ***syn*** SLANT 1, cant, heel, incline, lean, list, recline, tilt, tip

slope *n* a natural or artificial inclined surface <the steep *slope* of the hill>

syn grade, gradient, inclination, incline, lean, leaning, slant, tilt

rel acclivity, ascent, rise; declivity, descent; deflection, deviation, obliqueness, obliquity; pitch, swag, sway, tip; bend, skew

con champaign, flat, flatland, mesa, plain(s), plateau, tableland

ant level

sloped *adj* ***syn*** INCLINED 3, inclining, leaning, oblique, pitched, pitching, sloping, tilted, tilting, tipped

slopeways *adv* ***syn*** ASIDE 1, aslant, aslope, obliquely, sideways, sidewise, slantingways, slantways, slantwise, ‖slaunchways

sloping *adj* ***syn*** INCLINED 3, inclining, leaning, oblique, pitched, pitching, sloped, tilted, tilting, tipped

slopped *adj* ***syn*** INTOXICATED 1, ‖boozy, ‖canned, disguised, drunk, inebriated, ‖lushed, muddled, pixilated, ‖plastered

sloppy *adj* **1** ***syn*** SLIPSHOD 3, botchy, careless, messy, slapdash, slovenly, unthorough, untidy

rel amateurish; mediocre; awkward, clumsy; poor

ant exact, precise

2 ***syn*** SLOVENLY 1, careless, disheveled, ill-kempt, messy, slipshod, unfastidious, unkempt, unneat, untidy

3 ***syn*** EFFUSIVE, gushing, gushy, slobbering, slobbery

rel soft; oversentimental

4 ***syn*** INTOXICATED 1, ‖boozy, ‖canned, disguised, drunk, inebriated, ‖lushed, muddled, pixilated, ‖plastered

slosh *n* ***syn*** BLOW 1, bang, bash, bat, belt, crack, pound, slam, smack, wallop

---

syn synonym(s) ***rel*** related word(s)
idiom idiomatic equivalent(s) ***con*** contrasted word(s)
ant antonym(s) * vulgar
‖ use limited; if in doubt, see a dictionary
The first word in a synonym list when printed in SMALL CAPITALS shows where there is more information about the group. For a more efficient use of this book see Explanatory Notes.

slosh *vb* **1** *of a liquid* to move with a gentle lapping motion or sound <heard water *sloshing* in the bottom of the boat>
syn bubble, burble, gurgle, lap, swash, wash
rel babble; ripple; dash, plash, splash, tumble; bespatter, spatter; churn, whirl; gush, rush; roar
2 ***syn*** SPLASH, douse, plash, slop, spatter, splatter, splosh, splurge, spurtle, swash
3 ***syn*** GULP, bolt, cram, englut, gobble, guzzle, ingurgitate, slop, wolf
||**4** ***syn*** STRIKE 2, ||biff, catch, clout, ||devel, ||nail, slog, smite, sock, whack

sloth *n* **1** disinclination to action or labor <a bland *sloth*-provoking summer day>
syn idleness, indolence, laze, laziness, slothfulness, slouch, sluggishness
rel ergophobia, faineancy, idling, lazing, loafing; apathy, heaviness, languidness, languor, lassitude, lethargy, listlessness, torpidity; shiftlessness
con assiduity, assiduousness, busyness, diligence, sedulity, sedulousness
ant industriousness, industry
2 sluggishness and apathy in the practice of virtue <the deadly sin of *sloth*>
syn acedia
rel heedlessness, inattention, inattentiveness
con assiduity

slothful *adj* ***syn*** LAZY, drony, easygoing, faineant, indolent, slowgoing, work-shy
con assiduous, busy, diligent, sedulous
ant industrious

slothfulness *n* ***syn*** SLOTH 1, idleness, indolence, laze, laziness, slouch, sluggishness

slouch *n* **1** ***syn*** OAF 2, ||gaum, gawk, klutz, lobster, looby, lout, lubber, lump, meathead
2 ***syn*** SLUGGARD, bum, dolittle, do-nothing, faineant, idler, lazybones, loafer, slug, slugabed
3 ***syn*** SLOTH 1, idleness, indolence, laze, laziness, slothfulness, sluggishness

slouch *vb* to assume, have, or move with an awkwardly drooping posture, carriage, or gait <three drunks *slouched* across the room>
syn droop, loll, ||lollop, lop, slump, trollop
rel loaf, lounge, saunter, shamble, shuffle; bend, lean, stoop; sag, wilt
con erect, straighten (up); sit up, stand up

slough *n* **1** ***syn*** SWAMP, bog, fen, marsh, marshland, mire, morass, quagmire, ||sump, swampland
2 ***syn*** INLET, arm, bay, bayou, cove, ||creek, firth, gulf, harbor, ||lough

||**slough** *n* ***syn*** HULL, case, husk, pod, shell, shuck, skin

slough *vb* **1** ***syn*** SHED 2, exuviate, molt, slip
2 ***syn*** DISCARD, cashier, cast, jettison, junk, reject, scrap, shed, throw away, throw out
idiom ||get shut (*or* shed) of

slough over *vb* ***syn*** NEGLECT, blink (at *or* away), discount, disregard, fail, forget, ignore, omit, overlook, slight

sloven *adj* ***syn*** SLOVENLY 1, careless, disheveled, ill-kempt, messy, slipshod, sloppy, uncombed, unkempt, untidy

slovenly *adj* **1** negligent of or marked by lack of neatness and order especially in appearance or dress <*slovenly* attire>
syn careless, disheveled, ill-kempt, messy, mussy, raunchy, slipshod, slobbery, ||slommacky, sloppy, sloven, uncombed, unfastidious, unkempt, unneat, untidy; *compare* SLATTERNLY
rel down-at-heel, shabby, sleazy, sluttish, slutty; blowsy, dowdy, frowsy, frumpish
con fastidious, neat, tidy, trim; combed, groomed, well-groomed; immaculate
ant neat
2 ***syn*** SLIPSHOD 3, botchy, careless, messy, slapdash, sloppy, unthorough, untidy

slow *adj* **1** ***syn*** RETARDED, backward, dim-witted, dull, feebleminded, half-witted, imbecile, moronic, simple, slow-witted
rel limited; ||dunch
2 moving, flowing, or proceeding at less than the usual, desirable, or required speed <a *slow* advance toward mutual understanding>
syn deliberate, dilatory, laggard, leisurely, unhasty, unhurried
rel measured, slowish, steady; unhasting, unhurrying; slow-footed, slow-going, slow-paced; plodding, poky, rusty; dragging, flagging, halting, lagging, straggling; dawdling, delaying, postponing, procrastinating; leaden, sluggish; crawling, snaillike, snail-paced, ultra-slow
idiom as slow as a swamp turtle, as slow as molasses in January
con blitz, lightning, quick, rapid, swift; fast-going, fast-moving, fast-paced, rapid-paced
ant fast
3 marked by reduced economic activity (as in sales or patronage) <trading was *slow* on the commodity exchange today>
syn down, off, slack, sluggish
rel moderate; reduced; low; inactive, stagnant
con active; up; heavy

slow (up *or* down) *vb* ***syn*** DELAY 1, bog (down), decelerate, detain, embog, hang up, mire, retard, set back, slacken
rel moderate, qualify, temper; abate, decrease, lessen, reduce
ant speed

slow coach *n* ***syn*** LAGGARD, dawdler, lingerer, loiterer, slowpoke, straggler

slowdown *n* **1** a slowing or gradual decrease in activity <a *slowdown* in car sales this quarter>
syn slack, slackening, slow-up
rel decline, downtrend, downturn; drop, drop-off, fall-off; inactivity, stagnation; freeze
con increase, rise, upswing, upturn; acceleration, quickening
ant speedup

---

2 a deliberate slowing down by workers in the rate and quantity of production <air traffic snarled by a controllers' *slowdown*>
syn ||ca' canny
rel action; protest; slow-up; sit-down; strike, walkout; stoppage
ant speedup

slowgoing *adj* ***syn*** LAZY, drony, easygoing, faineant, indolent, slothful, work-shy

slowpoke *n* ***syn*** LAGGARD, dawdler, lingerer, loiterer, slow coach, straggler

slow–up *n* ***syn*** SLOWDOWN 1, slack, slackening

slow–witted *adj* ***syn*** RETARDED, backward, dim-witted, dull, feebleminded, half-witted, imbecile, moronic, simple, slow
ant quick-witted

||slubberdegullion *n* ***syn*** VILLAIN 1, *bastard, blackguard, heel, knave, lowlife, miscreant, rascal, rogue, scoundrel

slue *vb* ***syn*** SWERVE 1, dip, sheer, skew, train off, veer

slug *n* ***syn*** SLUGGARD, bum, dolittle, do-nothing, faineant, idler, lazybones, loafer, slouch, slugabed
rel slacker, sloven

slug *n* ***syn*** DRAM, ||caulker, drop, jolt, nip, shot, snifter, snort, toothful, tot

slug *vb* ***syn*** SLAM 1, belt, blast, clobber, smash, wallop

slugabed *n* ***syn*** SLUGGARD, bum, dolittle, do-nothing, faineant, idler, lazybones, loafer, slouch, slug

sluggard *n* an habitually lazy, shiftless, and inactive person <a *sluggard* who wanted to sleep all day>
syn bum, dolittle, do-nothing, faineant, idler, lazybones, loafer, slouch, slug, slugabed
rel lie-abed, sleepyhead; dawdler, laggard, slow coach, slowpoke; goldbrick, shirker
idiom ||his idleship, ||Weary Willie
con go-getter, hustler, live wire
ant dynamo

sluggish *adj* **1** ***syn*** LETHARGIC, comatose, dopey, heavy, hebetudinous, slumberous, stupid, torpid
rel dragging, draggy, leaden, lumpish; costive, stiff; apathetic, stupefied
con go-getting, hustling, vigorous; expeditious
ant brisk
2 ***syn*** SLOW 3, down, off, slack

sluggishness *n* ***syn*** SLOTH 1, idleness, indolence, laze, laziness, slothfulness, slouch

sluice *vb* ***syn*** POUR 2, flow, gush, roll, stream, surge
rel flush, wash; douse, drench, soak

slum *n* a densely populated usually urban area marked by run-down housing, poverty, and social disorganization <a *slum* full of vagrants, junkies, pimps, and pushers>
syn stew
rel slumdom, slumland; tobacco road; tenderloin; skid row; ghetto; hive, kennel, rookery, warren
idiom desolation row, the wrong side of the tracks

slum *n* ***syn*** SLIME, muck, ||slab

slumber *vb* **1** ***syn*** DOZE, ||dorm, drowse, ||sloom, ||snoozle, ||sog
2 ***syn*** SLEEP, ||doss

slumber *n* **1** ***syn*** SLEEP 1, ||doss, ||shut-eye
2 ***syn*** DOZE, drowse, ||sloom
3 ***syn*** LETHARGY 1, coma, dullness, hebetude, languor, lassitude, sleep, stupor, torpidity, torpor

slumberous *adj* **1** ***syn*** SLEEPY 1, dozy, drowsy, nodding, ||peepy, ||sloomy, slumbery, snoozy, somnolent, soporific
2 ***syn*** SOPORIFIC 1, hypnotic, narcotic, opiate, somnifacient, somniferous, somnific, somnolent, somnorific, soporiferous
3 ***syn*** LETHARGIC, comatose, dopey, heavy, hebetudinous, sluggish, stupid, torpid

slumbery *adj* ***syn*** SLEEPY 1, dozy, drowsy, nodding, ||peepy, ||sloomy, slumberous, snoozy, somnolent, soporific

slump *vb* **1** ***syn*** FALL 2, drop, go down, keel (over), pitch, plunge, topple, tumble
rel droop, flag, sag
idiom come down like a rock (*or* a ton of bricks)
2 ***syn*** SLOUCH, droop, loll, ||lollop, lop, trollop
rel cave in, collapse
3 ***syn*** SLIP 6, drop (off), fall (off *or* away), sag, slide

slump *n* **1** ***syn*** DECLINE 3, dip, downslide, downswing, downtrend, downturn, drop, falloff, sag, slip
2 ***syn*** DEPRESSION 3, recession, stagnation

slup *vb* ***syn*** SLURP

||slur *vb* ***syn*** SLIDE 3, skid, ||slidder, slip

slur *vb* ***syn*** MALIGN, befoul, bespatter, blacken, calumniate, defame, denigrate, smear, tear down, traduce

slur (over) *vb* ***syn*** NEGLECT, blink (at *or* away), discount, disregard, fail, forget, ignore, omit, overlook, slight

slur *n* **1** ***syn*** ANIMADVERSION, aspersion, obloquy, reflection, slam, stricture
2 ***syn*** STIGMA, bar sinister, black eye, blot, blur, brand, odium, onus, spot, stain

slurp *vb* to eat or drink noisily <*slurping* soup with a large spoon>
syn slup
rel guzzle, lap (up), slosh, swill; suck; wolf (down); smack
con nibble, pick (at); sip

slushy *adj* ***syn*** SENTIMENTAL, bathetic, lovey-dovey, maudlin, mawkish, mushy, romantic, ||soppy, sticky, tear-jerking

slut *n* **1** ***syn*** SLATTERN 1, dowd, dowdy, drab, draggletail, ||malkin, ||streel, traipse
2 ***syn*** WANTON, baggage, ||bimbo, hussy, jade, jezebel, strumpet, tramp, trollop, wench
idiom *easy piece (*or* lay)
3 ***syn*** MINX, hussy, jade, malapert, saucebox, snip

sly *adj* **1** ***syn*** CLEVER 4, adroit, canny, ||coony, cunning, dexterous, ingenious, ||sleighty, slim
rel smart; cagey; masterful
2 attaining or seeking to attain one's ends by devious means <a *sly* way of upping sales>

---

syn synonym(s) ***rel*** related word(s)
idiom idiomatic equivalent(s) ***con*** contrasted word(s)
ant antonym(s) * vulgar
|| use limited; if in doubt, see a dictionary
The first word in a synonym list when printed in SMALL CAPITALS shows where there is more information about the group. For a more efficient use of this book see Explanatory Notes.

syn artful, astute, crafty, cunning, deep, ‖downy, foxy, guileful, insidious, subdolous, subtle, tricky, vulpine, wily; *compare* UNDERHAND
rel disingenuous, unfrank; calculating, designing, Machiavellian, scheming; cagey, devious, shady, shifty, ‖slanter, slick, slippery, smooth; clandestine, covert, furtive, stealthy; underhand, underhanded, unscrupulous; predatory; crooked, dishonest
idiom crazy like a fox, cunning as a fox (*or* serpent), sly as a fox
con candid, forthright, frank, honest, open, sincere, straightforward

sly *vb* ***syn*** SNEAK, creep, gumshoe, lurk, skulk, slide, slink, ‖snake, ‖snook, steal

slyboots *n pl but sing in constr* ***syn*** SCAMP, devil, enfant terrible, mischief, rapscallion, rascal, rogue, scalawag, skeezicks, villain

slyness *n* ***syn*** CUNNING 2, art, artfulness, artifice, cageyness, canniness, craft, craftiness, foxiness, wiliness

smack *n* **1** ***syn*** TASTE 3, flavor, relish, sapidity, sapor, savor, tang
2 ***syn*** HINT 2, dash, lick, soupçon, sprinkling, suspicion, taste, tincture, tinge, trace

smack *vb* to have a trace, vestige, or suggestion of something <that plan *smacks* of radicalism>
syn savor, smell
rel resemble, suggest; reek, stink

smack *vb* **1** ***syn*** KISS 1, buss, lip, osculate, peck, smooch, ‖smoodge, ‖smouch
idiom ‖plant a juicy kiss on
2 ***syn*** SLAP 1, blip, box, buffet, cuff, spank, ‖wherret

smack *n* **1** ***syn*** CUFF, box, buffet, ‖bust, chop, clout, ‖paste, punch, slap, sock
2 ***syn*** BLOW 1, bash, bat, belt, biff, bop, crack, smash, sock, ‖welt

‖**smack–dab** *adv* ***syn*** JUST 1, accurately, bang, exactly, precisely, right, sharp, spang, square, squarely

‖**smacker** *n* ***syn*** DOLLAR, bill, ‖bone, ‖buck ‖fish, ‖frogskin, ‖ironman, oner, ‖skin, ‖smackeroo

‖**smackeroo** *n* ***syn*** DOLLAR, bill, ‖bone, ‖buck, ‖fish, ‖frogskin, ‖ironman, oner, ‖skin, ‖smacker

small *adj* **1** being the opposite of large <a *small* white house>
syn bantam, little, monkey, petite, smallish; *compare* TINY
rel cramped, limited, narrow, two-by-four; puny, undersized; paltry, petty, piddling, trivial
con big, great; considerable, sizable; enormous, huge, immense, vast
ant large
2 ***syn*** MINOR 2, dinky, insignificant, lesser, minor-league, secondary, small-fry, small-time
3 ***syn*** LITTLE 2, borné, ineffectual, limited, mean, narrow, paltry, set
4 ***syn*** LITTLE 3, inconsiderable, insignificant, light, minor, minute, petty, small-beer, trivial, unimportant
5 ***syn*** PETTY 2, inconsequent, inconsequential, inconsiderable, paltry, picayune, picayunish, puny, trifling, trivial
6 ***syn*** REMOTE 4, ‖fat, negligible, off, outside, slender, slight, slim

small beer *n* ***syn*** TRIVIA, minutia(e), small change, small potato(es), triviality

small–beer *adj* ***syn*** LITTLE 3, casual, inconsiderable, insignificant, light, minor, petty, shoestring, trivial, unimportant

small change *n* ***syn*** TRIVIA, minutia(e), small beer, small potato(es), triviality

smallest *adj* ***syn*** FIRST 4, least, slightest

small–fry *adj* ***syn*** MINOR 2, dinky, insignificant, lesser, minor-league, secondary, small, small-time

smallish *adj* ***syn*** SMALL 1, bantam, little, monkey, petite
ant largish

small–minded *adj* ***syn*** ILLIBERAL, bigoted, brassbound, hidebound, intolerant, narrow, narrow-minded, unenlarged
ant large-minded

small potato *n, usu* **small potatoes** *pl but sing or pl in constr* ***syn*** TRIVIA, minutia(e), small beer, small change, triviality

small talk *n* light or casual conversation <had to make *small talk* at the cocktail party>
syn bavardage, by-talk, chitchat, chitter-chatter, trifling
rel badinage, banter, repartee; babble, babbling, bibble-babble, chatter, prattle, prattling, prittle-prattle

small–time *adj* ***syn*** MINOR 2, dinky, insignificant, lesser, minor-league, secondary, small, small-fry
ant big-time

small–town *adj* ***syn*** INSULAR, local, ‖parish-pump, parochial, provincial, sectarian

‖**smarm** *vb* ***syn*** SMEAR 1, bedaub, besmear, dab, daub, plaster, smudge

smarmy *adj* **1** ***syn*** SLEEK, glassy, glossy, polished, ‖sleekit, sleeky
2 ***syn*** FULSOME, oily, oleaginous, slick, soapy, unctious, unctuous

smart *vb* ***syn*** HURT 4, ache, pain, suffer

smart *vb* to cause or produce a sharp stinging and usually localized pain <gave him a slap that was hard enough to *smart*>
syn bite, burn, ‖stang, sting; *compare* HURT 4
rel prick; tingle; hurt

smart *adj* **1** ***syn*** INTELLIGENT 2, alert, brainy, bright, brilliant, clever, knowing, quick-witted, ready-witted, sharp
ant stupid
2 ***syn*** WISE 4, canny, hep, knowing, nimble-witted, quick, quick-witted, sharp, sharp-witted, slick
idiom knowing the score, on the ball
ant dull, dumb
3 ***syn*** CLEVER 5, good, scintillating, sprightly
rel pert, saucy
4 ***syn*** WISE 5, ‖biggety, bold, cheeky, fresh, impudent, nervy, pert, sassy, smart-alecky
5 ***syn*** STYLISH, chic, dashing, exclusive, fashionable, modish, swank, swish, ‖trendy, with-it

---

syn synonym(s) — *rel* related word(s)
idiom idiomatic equivalent(s) — *con* contrasted word(s)
ant antonym(s) — * vulgar
‖ use limited; if in doubt, see a dictionary
The first word in a synonym list when printed in SMALL CAPITALS shows where there is more information about the group. For a more efficient use of this book see Explanatory Notes.

rel dapper, ‖dinky, spruce
ant dowdy
‖6 *syn* CONSIDERABLE 2, good, respectable, ‖right smart, sensible, sizable

smart aleck *n* an obnoxiously conceited and self-assertive person with pretensions to smartness or cleverness <was heckled by a *smart aleck* in the back row>
syn know-it-all, *smartass, smarty, smarty-pants, wiseacre, wisecracker, wise guy, wisehead, wisenheimer
rel blowhard, boaster, braggadocio, braggart, gasbag, windbag; exhibitionist, grandstander, show-off
idiom hot-air artist

smart–alecky *adj syn* WISE 5, ‖biggety, bold-faced, cheeky, fresh, impudent, nervy, procacious, sassy, smart

***smartass** *n syn* SMART ALECK, know-it-all, smarty, smarty-pants, wiseacre, wisecracker, wise guy, wisehead, wisenheimer

smarten (up) *vb syn* DRESS UP 1, deck (out), doll out, doll up, fix up, gussy up, primp, slick, spiff, spruce (up)

smart set *n* ultrafashionable often international society <the *smart set* that suns in Cannes and skis in St. Moritz>
syn beautiful people, jet set, ton
rel aristocracy, aristoi, blue bloods, bon ton, elite, Four Hundred, society, upper crust, who's who

smarty *n syn* SMART ALECK, know-it-all, *smartass, smarty-pants, wiseacre, wisecracker, wise guy, wisehead, wisenheimer

smarty–pants *n pl but sing in constr syn* SMART ALECK, know-it-all, *smartass, smarty, wiseacre, wisecracker, wise guy, wisehead, wisenheimer

smash *vb* **1** *syn* SHATTER 1, burst, fragment, ‖pash, rive, shiver, ‖smatter, splinter, splinterize, splitter
2 *syn* SLAM 1, belt, blast, clobber, slug, wallop
3 *syn* DESTROY 1, annihilate, decimate, demolish, destruct, raze, ruin, shatter, tear down, wreck

smash *n* **1** *syn* BLOW 1, bang, bash, bastinado, slam, sock, wallop, ‖welt, whack, whop
2 *syn* BANG 2, blast, boom, burst, clap, crack, crash, slam, wham
3 *syn* IMPACT, bump, clash, collision, crash, jar, jolt, percussion, shock, wallop
4 *syn* CRASH 3, crack-up, pileup, ‖prang, smashup, ‖stramash, wreck
5 *syn* COLLAPSE 2, breakdown, crack-up, crash, debacle, smashup, wreck
6 a striking success <the new musical was a box-office *smash*>
syn bang, bell ringer, hit, succès fou, ten-strike, wow
rel sensation; knockout
idiom howling (*or* roaring) success, smash hit
con disaster, dud, failure
ant flop

‖**smash** *n syn* MONEY, pelf, rhino, rocks, ‖scratch, ‖shekels, stuff, ‖stumpy, ‖sugar, ‖wampum

‖**smashed** *adj syn* INTOXICATED 1, ‖boozy, ‖canned, disguised, drunk, inebriated, ‖lushed, muddled, pixilated, ‖plastered

smashup *n* **1** *syn* COLLAPSE 2, breakdown, crack-up, crash, debacle, smash, wreck
2 *syn* CRASH 3, crack-up, pileup, ‖prang, smash, ‖stramash, wreck

smatch *n* **1** *syn* HINT 2, dash, shade, smack, suggestion, suspicion, tinge, touch, trace, trifle
2 *syn* FEW, handful, scattering, smatter, smattering, spatter, spattering, sprinkling

smatter *vb* ‖**1** *syn* SHATTER 1, burst, fragment, ‖pash, rive, shiver, smash, splinter, splinterize, splitter
2 *syn* CHAT 1, babble, cackle, chatter, clack, gab, ‖gas, jaw, prate, prattle

smatter *n syn* FEW, handful, scattering, smatch, smattering, spatter, spattering, sprinkling

smatterer *n syn* AMATEUR 2, abecedarian, dabbler, dilettante, nonprofessional, tyro, uninitiate

smattering *n syn* FEW, handful, scattering, smatch, smatter, spatter, spattering, sprinkling

smaze *n syn* HAZE 1, brume, film, mist

smear *vb* **1** to overspread with something unctuous, viscous, or adhesive <*smeared* the crack with wet concrete>
syn bedaub, besmear, dab, daub, plaster, ‖smarm, smudge
rel rub; coat, cover, overlay, overspread, spread; smirch, soil
2 *syn* TAINT 1, besmear, besmirch, defile, discolor, soil, stain, sully, tar, tarnish
3 *syn* MALIGN, asperse, befoul, bespatter, blacken, calumniate, defame, denigrate, slander, slur
idiom use smear tactics (on *or* against)
4 *syn* WHIP 2, beat, ‖clobber, drub, lambaste, lick, shellac, smother, thrash, trim
rel foil, frustrate; repulse
idiom mop up the floor (*or* earth) with

smell *vb* **1** to perceive by means of the olfactory organs <*smelled* a dead skunk>
syn nose, scent, sniff, ‖snift, snuff
rel detect, perceive, sense; whiff; ‖snaffle, snuffle
idiom get a whiff of
2 *syn* SMACK, savor
3 to have or emit an offensive odor <the canal *smells* today>
syn funk, reek, stench, stink
idiom offend the nostrils, smell (*or* stink) to high heaven

smell *n* **1** a quality that makes a thing perceptible to the olfactory sense <the *smell* of a ham cooking>
syn aroma, odor, scent
rel bouquet, fragrance, incense, perfume, redolence, spice; flavor, savor, stench, stink
2 *syn* HINT 2, intimation, smack, soupçon, strain, suggestion, suspicion, tincture, trace, whiff

smeller *n syn* NOSE 1, ‖beezer, ‖boko, ‖conk, pecker, ‖schnozzle, ‖sneezer, ‖snitch, snoot, snout

‖**smellful** *adj syn* MALODOROUS 1, putrid, rancid, rank, reeking, smelly, stale, stenchy, stinking, stinky
ant odorless, smell-less

---

smellfungus *n* ***syn*** CRITIC, aristarch, carper, caviler, criticizer, faultfinder, knocker, momus, Zoilus

smell–less *adj* ***syn*** ODORLESS, inodorous, scentless
ant ‖smellful, smelly

smelly *adj* ***syn*** MALODOROUS 1, fetid, funky, noisome, olid, putrid, rancid, rank, reeking, stinking
con odorless, scentless, smell-less; fragrant, fresh, sweet

smidgen *n* ***syn*** PARTICLE, atom, bit, iota, jot, minim, mite, ray, smitch, speck

smile *vb* to express amusement, satisfaction, or pleasure by brightening one's eyes and curving the corners of one's mouth upward < *smiled* as she greeted him >
syn beam, grin
rel simper, smirk
idiom break into a smile, crack a smile
con grimace; glare, glower, lower, scowl
ant frown

smirch *vb* ***syn*** SOIL 2, begrime, besoil, dirty, foul, grime, smooch, smudge, smutch, tarnish
rel discolor; smear

smirk *vb* to smile in an affected manner < *smirking* children imitating their teacher >
syn simper, ‖smirkle; *compare* SNEER 1
rel grin, smile; fleer, leer, sneer
idiom *have a shit-eating grin

‖**smirkle** *vb* ***syn*** SMIRK, simper

smitch *n* ***syn*** PARTICLE, crumb, iota, jot, modicum, scrap, shred, smidgen, speck, tittle

smite *vb* **1** ***syn*** STRIKE 2, catch, clout, ‖devel, ding, hit, slog, ‖slosh, sock, whack
rel bat, belt, clobber; dash
idiom smite a blow
2 ***syn*** AFFLICT, agonize, crucify, excruciate, harrow, martyr, strike, torment, torture, try

smithereens *n pl* very small particles or fragments < a house blown to *smithereens* by a bomb >
syn ‖shivereens, smithers
rel fragments, particles, pieces

smithers *n pl* ***syn*** SMITHEREENS, ‖shivereens

smitten *adj* ***syn*** ENAMORED 1, mashed, soft (on), spoony (over *or* on)
idiom bitten by the love bug

smoke *n* ***syn*** CIGARETTE, ‖butt, ‖cig, ‖coffin nail, fag, ‖gasper, ‖pill, ‖skag

smoke *vb* ***syn*** HURRY 2, bucket, bullet, fly, hasten, run, rush, speed, whiz, zip

smolder *vb* ***syn*** SEETHE 4, boil, bubble, churn, ferment, ‖moil, simmer, stir
rel burst, erupt, explode; fulminate

smooch *vb* ***syn*** SOIL 2, begrime, besoil, dirty, foul, grime, smirch, smudge, smutch, tarnish

smooch *vb* ***syn*** KISS 1, buss, lip, osculate, peck, smack, ‖smoodge, ‖smouch
idiom ‖plant a smooch on

‖**smoodge** *vb* ***syn*** KISS 1, buss, lip, osculate, peck, smack, smooch, ‖smouch

smooth *adj* **1** ***syn*** LEVEL, even, flat, flush, planate, plane
rel glossy, sleek, slick; rippleless, unbroken, unwrinkled
con harsh, rugged, scabrous, uneven
ant rough
2 ***syn*** HAIRLESS, bald, glabrous
3 ***syn*** EASY 9, cursive, effortless, flowing, fluent, running
4 ***syn*** EASY 1, effortless, facile, light, royal, simple, untroublesome
rel smooth-running
idiom smooth and easy
ant labored
5 ***syn*** SUAVE, bland, civilized, urbane
rel courteous, courtly, polite; smooth-faced, smooth-tongued
con bluff, blunt, brusque, crusty, curt, gruff, harsh
6 ***syn*** GENTLE 1, balmy, bland, faint, lenient, mild, soft
rel agreeable, soothing

smooth *vb* **1** ***syn*** EVEN 1, flatten, flush, lay, level, plane, smoothen
con corrugate; roughen; wrinkle
ant unsmooth
2 ***syn*** POLISH 2, perfect, refine, round, sleek, slick

smooth *adv* ***syn*** EVENLY 3, flatly, smoothly, uniformly

smoothen *vb* ***syn*** EVEN 1, flatten, flush, lay, level, plane, smooth

smoothly *adv* **1** ***syn*** EVENLY 3, flatly, smooth, uniformly
con unevenly, ununiformly
ant roughly
2 ***syn*** EASILY 1, effortlessly, facilely, freely, lightly, readily, well
ant unsmoothly

smooth–spoken *adj* ***syn*** VOCAL 3, articulate, eloquent, fluent
ant rough-spoken

smorgasbord *n* ***syn*** MISCELLANY 1, gallimaufry, hash, hodgepodge, jumble, medley, mélange, mishmash, pastiche, potpourri

smother *vb* **1** ***syn*** SUFFOCATE, asphyxiate, choke, ‖quackle, stifle
2 ***syn*** COMPOSE 4, collect, control, cool, re-collect, rein, repress, restrain, simmer down, suppress
rel hush up, muffle; cork; quash, quell, squelch; quench
3 ***syn*** WHIP 2, beat, ‖clobber, drub, lambaste, lick, shellac, smear, thrash, trim

smothering *adj* ***syn*** STIFLING 1, smothery, ‖smudgy, suffocating, suffocative

smothering *n* ***syn*** REPRESSION 1, choking, extinguishment, quashing, quenching, squashing, squelching, stifling, strangling, suppression

smothery *adj* ***syn*** STIFLING 1, smothering, ‖smudgy, suffocating, suffocative

‖**smouch** *vb* ***syn*** KISS 1, buss, lip, osculate, peck, smack, smooch, ‖smoodge

smouch *vb* ***syn*** STEAL 1, cabbage, ‖cly, filch, hook, lift, nab, ‖nick, pilfer, ‖snaffle

---

syn synonym(s) ***rel*** related word(s)
idiom idiomatic equivalent(s) ***con*** contrasted word(s)
ant antonym(s) * vulgar
‖ use limited; if in doubt, see a dictionary
The first word in a synonym list when printed in SMALL CAPITALS shows where there is more information about the group. For a more efficient use of this book see Explanatory Notes.

smudge *vb* **1** ***syn*** SOIL 2, begrime, besoil, dirty, foul, grime, smirch, smooch, smutch, tarnish
rel smear; blotch, splotch
2 ***syn*** SMEAR 1, bedaub, besmear, dab, daub, plaster, ‖smarm
3 ***syn*** TAINT 1, besmirch, defile, dirty, smut, smutch, soil, stain, sully, tarnish

‖**smudgy** *adj* ***syn*** STIFLING 1, smothering, smothery, suffocating, suffocative

smug *adj* ***syn*** COMPLACENT, priggish, self-complacent, self-contented, self-pleased, self-satisfied
idiom pleased with oneself

smug *vb* ***syn*** DRESS UP 1, deck (out), doll out, doll up, ‖dude up, gussy up, primp, slick, smarten (up), spruce (up)

smuggle *vb* to import or export secretly and in violation of the law < *smuggling* weapons into the country >
syn bootleg, contraband, run
idiom run contraband

smut *vb* **1** ***syn*** STAIN 1, bestain, blot, discolor
2 ***syn*** TAINT 1, besmirch, defile, dirty, discolor, smear, smudge, smutch, soil, stain

smutch *vb* **1** ***syn*** SOIL 2, begrime, besoil, dirty, foul, grime, smirch, smooch, smudge, tarnish
2 ***syn*** TAINT 1, besmirch, defile, dirty, discolor, smudge, smut, soil, stain, sully

smutty *adj* ***syn*** OBSCENE 2, coarse, dirty, filthy, foul, indecent, nasty, raunchy, scatological, vulgar

snack *n* food served or taken informally and usually in small amounts and typically under other circumstances than a regular meal < a milk-and-cookie *snack* after school >
syn ‖bait, ‖bever, bite, ‖chack, morsel, mug-up, ‖piece, tapa
rel collation, refreshment, tea
idiom bite to eat

snack bar (*or* **counter**) *n* ***syn*** EATING HOUSE, beanery, coffee shop, diner, ‖greasy spoon, ‖hashery, ‖hash house, luncheonette, lunchroom, quick-lunch

‖**snaffle** *vb* ***syn*** STEAL 1, ‖clout, ‖cly, ‖cop, ‖heist, hook, lift, ‖nail, pinch, purloin

‖**snafu** *vb* ***syn*** CONFUSE 5, foul up, jumble, mix up, muddle, snarl up, tumble

snag *n* ***syn*** OBSTACLE, bar, crimp, hamper, hurdle, impediment, obstruction, rub, stumbling block, traverse
rel brake, clog, curb, drag; hold-up
idiom ‖snags and sawyers

snake *n* ***syn*** SNOT 1, cur, dog, ‖prick, scum, *shit, *shithead, skunk, toad, *turd

snake *vb* ‖**1** ***syn*** STEAL 1, hook, lift, nab, ‖nail, ‖nick, nip, pinch, snitch, swipe
2 ***syn*** CREEP 1, crawl, slide
3 ***syn*** SLITHER 2, ‖slidder, undulate
‖**4** ***syn*** SNEAK, glide, lurk, pussyfoot, shirk, skulk, slide, slink, slip, steal

snaky *adj* ***syn*** WINDING, anfractuous, convoluted, flexuous, meandering, meandrous, serpentine, sinuous, tortuous

snap *vb* **1** to speak in a curt, biting tone < *snapped* at his subordinates for inefficiency >
syn bark, snarl
rel growl, grumble, grunt, snort; roar, yell
idiom bite one's head off, snap off one's head (*or* nose)
2 ***syn*** JERK, lug, lurch, twitch, vellicate, yank
rel clutch, grab, grasp, seize, snaffle, snatch

snap *n* **1** something easily managed or accomplished < that exam was a *snap* >
syn breeze, child's play, cinch, duck soup, kid stuff, picnic, pie, ‖pipe, pushover, setup, ‖snip, soft touch
rel sinecure
idiom a simple twist of the wrist, simplicity itself, soft snap
con difficulty, headache, problem, trouble; bother, inconvenience, pain
ant chore
2 ***syn*** PARTICLE, bit, dram, drop, fragment, grain, hoot, iota, jot, modicum
3 ***syn*** MAN 3, ‖bloke, boy, buck, chap, fellow, ‖gee, ‖mun, skate, ‖stirra
4 ***syn*** VIGOR 2, bang, drive, getup, go, pep, punch, push, starch, vitality

snap back *vb* ***syn*** RECOVER 3, bounce (back), rebound

‖**snapper** *vb* ***syn*** STUMBLE 3, blunder, bumble, lurch

snapping *adv* ***syn*** VERY 1, awfully, damned, dreadfully, extremely, hugely, rattling, spanking, whacking, whopping

snappish *adj* ***syn*** IRRITABLE, fractious, fretful, huffy, peevish, pettish, petulant, querulous, waspish, waspy
rel curt, short, ungracious; crabbed, morose, surly

snappy *adj* **1** ***syn*** IRRITABLE, disagreeable, fractious, huffy, petulant, prickish, raspish, raspy, snappish, twitty
2 ***syn*** FAST 3, breakneck, expeditious, fleet, harefooted, hasty, quick, rapid, speedy, swift
3 ***syn*** PUNGENT, peppery, piquant, poignant, racy, spicy, zesty
rel animated, lively, vivacious; prompt, quick, ready
4 ***syn*** STYLISH, ‖classy, dashing, sharp, smart, swank, swish, tony, ‖trendy, trig

snare *n* ***syn*** LURE 2, allurement, bait, come-on, decoy, enticement, inveiglement, seducement, temptation, trap
rel chicane, chicanery, deception; ensnarement, entrapment

snare *vb* ***syn*** CATCH 3, benet, catch up, ensnare, entangle, entrap, tangle, trap
rel seduce, tempt; involve; embrangle, enmesh, ensnarl, trammel

‖**snark** *vb* ***syn*** SNORE

snarl *n* **1** ***syn*** CONFUSION 3, ataxia, ‖ballup, chaos, clutter, disarray, disorder, huddle, muddle, topsy-turviness
rel entanglement, tangle; complexity, complication, intricacy, intricateness; labyrinth, maze; mishmash, swarm; jam
idiom tangled skein, wheels within wheels
2 ***syn*** MAZE 1, jungle, knot, labyrinth, mesh, mizmaze, morass, skein, tangle, web

---

syn synonym(s) ***rel*** related word(s)
idiom idiomatic equivalent(s) ***con*** contrasted word(s)
ant antonym(s) * vulgar
‖ use limited; if in doubt, see a dictionary
The first word in a synonym list when printed in SMALL CAPITALS shows where there is more information about the group. For a more efficient use of this book see Explanatory Notes.

snarl *vb* **1** ***syn*** ENTANGLE 1, ensnarl, intertangle, perplex, tangle
2 ***syn*** COMPLICATE, entangle, ‖muck, muddle, perplex, ravel, tangle

snarl *vb* ***syn*** SNAP 1, bark

snarl up *vb* ***syn*** CONFUSE 5, foul up, jumble, mix up, muddle, ‖snafu, tumble

snatch *vb* **1** ***syn*** SEIZE 2, catch, clutch, ‖cotch, grab, grapple, nab, ‖nail, take
rel jerk, wrench, yank; nip (up), whip (up)
‖**2** ***syn*** KIDNAP, abduct, spirit (away)

sneak *vb* to move or go stealthily and furtively <*sneaked* into the garage and stole the car>
syn creep, glide, gumshoe, lurk, ‖meech, pussyfoot, shirk, skulk, slide, slink, slip, sly, ‖snake, ‖snook, steal; *compare* STEAL 3
rel crawl, slither, worm, prowl
idiom go on (little) cat's feet, move under cover
con barge, strut, swagger; clump, stamp, stump; stride; march, parade

sneak *n* a person who behaves in a stealthy, furtive, or shifty manner <found out that he was a liar, a cheat, and a *sneak*>
syn slink, sneaker, sneaksby, weasel
rel blackguard, knave, scoundrel; cur, heel, louse, reptile, skunk, snake; *shithead, toad
idiom Jerry Sneak, *sneaky bastard

sneak *adj* ***syn*** SECRET 1, clandestine, covert, furtive, hole-and-corner, hush-hush, stealthy, sub-rosa, surreptitious, undercover

sneaker *n* ***syn*** SNEAK, slink, sneaksby, weasel

sneaking *adj* ***syn*** UNDERHAND, devious, duplicitous, guileful, indirect, shifty, sneaky, underhanded
ant forthright

sneaksby *n* ***syn*** SNEAK, slink, sneaker, weasel

sneaky *adj* ***syn*** UNDERHAND, devious, duplicitous, guileful, indirect, shifty, sneaking, underhanded

‖**sneap** *vb* ***syn*** REPROVE, admonish, call down, chide, lesson, monish, ‖rack back, rebuke, reprimand, reproach

sneer *vb* **1** to smile with attendant facial contortions expressing scorn or contempt <*sneered* haughtily at the beggar>
syn fleer, leer, ‖sleer; *compare* SMIRK
rel grin, smile
idiom curl one's lip, make a scornful (*or* mocking) face
2 ***syn*** SCOFF, fleer, flout, gibe, gird, jeer, jest, quip (at), scout (at)
rel belittle, detract, disparage, underrate
idiom cock a snook at, give the Bronx cheer to, give the raspberry, sneeze at, thumb one's nose at

‖**sneezer** *n* ***syn*** NOSE 1, ‖beezer, ‖boko, ‖conk, pecker, ‖schnozzle, smeller, ‖snitch, snoot, snout

---

syn synonym(s)	***rel*** related word(s)
idiom idiomatic equivalent(s)	***con*** contrasted word(s)
ant antonym(s)	* vulgar

‖ use limited; if in doubt, see a dictionary
The first word in a synonym list when printed in SMALL CAPITALS shows where there is more information about the group. For a more efficient use of this book see Explanatory Notes.

snicker *vb* ***syn*** LAUGH, chortle, chuckle, giggle, guffaw, hee-haw, ‖sniggle, tehee, titter
idiom have a case of the snickers

snide *adj* **1** ***syn*** COUNTERFEIT, bogus, brummagem, fake, false, phony, pinchbeck, pseudo, sham, spurious
2 ***syn*** CROOKED 2, corrupt, dishonest

sniff *vb* ***syn*** SMELL 1, nose, scent, ‖snift, snuff

‖**snift** *vb* ***syn*** SMELL 1, nose, scent, sniff, snuff
rel ‖snifter

snifter *n* ***syn*** DRAM, ‖caulker, drop, jolt, nip, shot, slug, snort, toothful, tot

‖**sniggle** *vb* ***syn*** LAUGH, chortle, chuckle, giggle, guffaw, hee-haw, snicker, tehee, titter

snip *n* **1** ***syn*** MINX, hussy, jade, malapert, saucebox, slut
‖**2** ***syn*** SNAP 1, breeze, child's play, cinch, duck soup, kid stuff, picnic, pie, ‖pipe, pushover

snippety *adj* ***syn*** BLUFF, abrupt, blunt, brief, brusque, crusty, curt, gruff, short, snippy
rel impolite, insolent, rude

snippy *adj* ***syn*** BLUFF, abrupt, blunt, brief, brusque, crusty, curt, gruff, short, snippety

snip–snap *n* ***syn*** BANTER, backchat, badinage, ‖cross talk, persiflage, repartee

snit *n* a state of agitation or excited irritation especially over a trivial matter <was in a *snit* because his secretary was one minute late>
syn fume, stew, sweat, swivet, tizzy
rel huff, pique; conniption, fit, frenzy, seizure, taking; dither, flap, panic, ‖swither

snitch *vb* **1** ***syn*** INFORM 3, ‖nark, peach, ‖pimp, rat, ‖sing, squeak, squeal, ‖stool
2 ***syn*** STEAL 1, ‖cop, filch, hook, lift, ‖nick, nip, pinch, purloin, swipe

snitch *n* ‖**1** ***syn*** NOSE 1, beak, ‖beezer, ‖boko, ‖conk, pecker, ‖schnozzle, smeller, ‖sneezer, snout
2 ***syn*** INFORMER, betrayer, ‖canary, ‖fink, ‖nark, ‖squeaker, squealer, stool pigeon, tattler, tipster

snob *n* one inclined to rebuff or ignore people or things that he regards as inferior (as in culture or social status) <appeals to real lovers of music rather than musical *snobs*>
syn high-hat, snoot, snot
rel name-dropper, snobling; bootlicker, hanger-on, lickspittle, sycophant, toady

snob *vb* ***syn*** CUT 7, cold-shoulder, ostracize, snub

snobbish *adj* of, relating to, or characteristic of a snob <a *snobbish* group of jet-set sophisticates>
syn ‖dicty, high-hat, potty, snobby, snooty
rel aloof, remote; high-flown, pretentious, snotty, supercilious; haughty, hoity-toity, pompous, ritzy; condescending, patronizing; insecure, uncertain, unconfident, unselfconfident, unsure
con certain, confident, secure, self-confident

snobby *adj* ***syn*** SNOBBISH, ‖dicty, high-hat, potty, snooty
rel snubbing, snubby

‖**snook** *vb* **1** ***syn*** SNOOP, busybody, mouse, nose, ‖piroot, poke, pry
2 ***syn*** SNEAK, creep, glide, lurk, pussyfoot, skulk, slink, slip, ‖snake, steal

snoop *vb* to look, inquire, or search impertinently or intrusively <he knew he had no right to *snoop* into her private life>

syn busybody, mouse, nose, ‖piroot, poke, pry, ‖snook
rel peek, peep, peer, stare; interfere, intrude, meddle, mess
idiom stick (*or* poke) one's nose into

snoop *n syn* BUSYBODY, butt-in, ‖buttinsky, intermeddler, meddler, Paul Pry, pragmatist, prier (*or* pryer), quidnunc, rubberneck

snoopy *adj syn* CURIOUS 2, inquisitive, inquisitorial, inquisitory, ‖nibby, nosy, peery, prying

snoot *n* **1** *syn* NOSE 1, beak, ‖beezer, ‖boko, ‖conk, pecker, ‖schnozzle, smeller, ‖sneezer, ‖snitch
2 *syn* SNOB, high-hat, snot

snooty *adj syn* SNOBBISH, ‖dicty, high-hat, potty, snobby

snooze *vb syn* NAP, catnap, ‖caulk (off), siesta

snooze *n syn* NAP, catnap, dog nap, ‖dover, forty winks, siesta

‖**snoozle** *vb syn* DOZE, ‖dorm, drowse, ‖sloom, slumber, ‖sog

snoozy *adj syn* SLEEPY 1, dozy, drowsy, nodding, ‖peepy, ‖sloomy, slumberous, slumbery, somnolent, soporific

snore *vb* to breathe during sleep with a rough hoarse noise due to vibration of the soft palate <driven to distraction by her sister's *snoring*>
syn ‖snark
rel wheeze; snuffle; snort, ‖snotter
idiom ‖drive pigs to market, ‖saw logs (*or* wood)

snort *n syn* DRAM, ‖caulker, drop, jolt, nip, shot, slug, snifter, toothful, tot

snorter *n syn* DRAM, ‖caulker, drop, jolt, nip, shot, slug, snifter, toothful, tot

snot *n* **1** an utterly contemptible person <a despicable *snot* whom everyone shunned>
syn ‖bugger, cur, dog, louse, ‖prick, puke, rat, scum, *shit, *shithead, skunk, snake, sod, stinkard, stinkaroo, stinker, toad, *turd, wretch; *compare* VILLAIN 1
rel ‖creep, ‖crumb, lowlife; knave, rogue, scoundrel, ‖skite; pig, reptile
2 *syn* SNOB, high-hat, snoot

***snot–rag** *n syn* HANDKERCHIEF, hankie, kerchief, ‖wipe, ‖wiper

snout *n syn* NOSE 1, beak, ‖beezer, ‖boko, ‖conk, pecker, ‖schnozzle, smeller, ‖sneezer, ‖snitch

snowball *vb syn* INCREASE 2, augment, build, expand, mount, multiply, rise, run up, upsurge, wax

snub *vb syn* CUT 7, cold-shoulder, ostracize, snob
rel high-hat, ‖ritz, swank; put down
idiom look coldly upon, turn a cold shoulder (on *or* upon)

‖**snudge** *vb syn* SNUGGLE, burrow, ‖croodle, cuddle, nestle, nuzzle, snug, ‖snuzzle

‖**snuff** *n syn* OFFENSE 2, dudgeon, huff, miff, pique, resentment, umbrage

snuff *vb syn* SMELL 1, nose, scent, sniff, ‖snift

‖**snuff** (out) *vb syn* DIE 1, cash in, ‖check out, conk, ‖croak, drop, ‖kick in, ‖kick off, pass out, pop off

snug *adj* **1** *syn* NEAT 2, chipper, orderly, shipshape, spick-and-span, tidy, trig, trim, uncluttered, well-groomed
2 *syn* COMFORTABLE 2, comfy, cozy, cushy, easeful, easy, soft
idiom snug as a bug in a rug
‖**3** *syn* PROSPEROUS 3, comfortable, easy, substantial, well, well-fixed, well-heeled, well-off, well-to-do

snug *vb syn* SNUGGLE, burrow, ‖croodle, cuddle, nestle, nuzzle, ‖snudge, ‖snuzzle

snuggle *vb* to assume or be in a warm comfortable position usually near another person or thing <a baby *snuggling* close to his mother>
syn burrow, ‖croodle, cuddle, nestle, nuzzle, ‖snudge, snug, ‖snuzzle
rel curl up; huddle; spoon
idiom snuggle up like a bug in a rug
con flinch, recoil, shrink

‖**snuzzle** *vb syn* SNUGGLE, burrow, ‖croodle, cuddle, nestle, nuzzle, ‖snudge, snug

‖**sny** *vb syn* TEEM, abound, crawl, flow, pullulate, swarm

so *adv* **1** *syn* ALSO 1, correspondingly, likewise, similarly
2 *syn* THUS 1, thus and so, thus and thus, thusly
3 *syn* VERY 1, ‖awful, awfully, exceedingly, exceptionally, extremely, much, parlous, whacking, whopping
4 *syn* THEREFORE, accordingly, consequently, ergo, hence, then, thereupon, thus

so *conj* with the purpose that <repeated it aloud *so* there'd be no mistake>
syn so as, so that
idiom in order that, to the end that, with the intent that

soak *vb* **1** to permeate or be permeated with or as if with water <*soak* a sponge with water> <rain *soaked* her to the skin>
syn drench, ‖drouk, impregnate, insteep, saturate, seethe, sodden, ‖sog, sop, souse, steep, waterlog; *compare* WET
rel dip, immerse, submerge; draw, infuse; infiltrate, penetrate, permeate, pervade; water-soak; drown
2 *syn* WET, deluge, douse, drench, drown, sop, souse
3 *syn* ENGAGE 4, busy, engross, immerse, occupy
4 *syn* OVERCHARGE 1, clip, fleece, skin, stick
5 *syn* DRINK 3, booze, guzzle, imbibe, liquor (up), swig, swill, swizzle, tank up, tipple
idiom ‖soak it up like a sponge

soak *n* **1** *syn* DRUNKARD, bibber, boozehound, boozer, drunk, guzzler, inebriate, lush, soaker, sot
2 *syn* BINGE 1, bender, booze, brannigan, bum, bust, drunk, jag, souse, tear

soaked *adj syn* WET 1, drenched, dripping, saturated, soaking, sodden, sopping, soppy, soused, wringing-wet

soaker *n syn* DRUNKARD, bibber, boozehound, boozer, drunk, guzzler, inebriate, lush, soak, sot

soaking *adj syn* WET 1, drenched, dripping, saturated, soaked, sodden, sopping, soppy, soused, wringing-wet
idiom soaking wet

---

syn synonym(s)	*rel* related word(s)
idiom idiomatic equivalent(s)	*con* contrasted word(s)
ant antonym(s)	* vulgar

‖ use limited; if in doubt, see a dictionary
The first word in a synonym list when printed in SMALL CAPITALS shows where there is more information about the group. For a more efficient use of this book see Explanatory Notes.

so–and–so *adj syn* DAMNED 2, blamed, blankety-blank, blasted, bleeding, cursed, dad-blamed, dad-blasted, dad-burned, dang

soapbox *vb syn* ORATE, bloviate, declaim, harangue, mouth, perorate, rant, rave

soapy *adj syn* FULSOME, oily, oleaginous, slick, smarmy, unctious, unctuous

soar *vb* **1** *syn* RISE 4, arise, ascend, aspire, lift, mount, up, uprear
rel climb; shoot
2 *syn* SKYROCKET, rocket, shoot up
ant plummet

soaring *adj syn* LOFTY 6, aerial, airy, skyscraping, spiring, topless, towering, towery
idiom high as the sky

so as *conj syn* SO, so that

sob *vb syn* CRY 2, blub, blubber, boohoo, ‖pipe, wail, weep

sobby *adj syn* SENTIMENTAL, drippy, mawkish, mushy, sappy, slushy, sobful, ‖soppy, soupy, tear-jerking

sober *adj* **1** *syn* ABSTEMIOUS, abstentious, abstinent, continent, self-restraining, temperate
rel controlled, restrained; self-possessed
con indulgent, overindulgent; uncontrolled, unrestrained; immoderate, intemperate; excessive; profligate
2 *syn* SERIOUS 1, earnest, grave, no-nonsense, sedate, sobersided, solemn, somber, staid, weighty
rel decorous, proper; calm, placid, serene, tranquil
con flippant, light, light-minded; unstable, volatile
ant gay
3 having or exhibiting self-control and avoiding extremes of behavior <his bearing was *sober,* his comments judicious>
syn moderate, temperate, unimpassioned; *compare* ABSTEMIOUS
rel rational, reasonable; calm, collected, composed, cool, imperturbable; constrained, disciplined, inhibited, reserved, restrained, self-controlled, self-disciplined; abstaining, forbearing, refraining; abnegating, eschewing, forgoing
con irrational, unreasonable; emotional, hotheaded, impassioned, overemotional, passionate; intemperate, uncontained, uncontrolled; excited; drunk, intoxicated; abandoned
ant unsober
4 *syn* SUBDUED 2, low-key, low-keyed, soft, softened, toned down
5 *syn* REALISTIC, down-to-earth, hard, hard-boiled, hardheaded, matter-of-fact, practical, pragmatic, unfantastic, unidealistic
rel sober-eyed, sober-minded

sobersided *adj syn* SERIOUS 1, earnest, grave, no-nonsense, sedate, sober, solemn, somber, staid, weighty

sobful *adj syn* SENTIMENTAL, drippy, mawkish, mushy, slushy, sobby, ‖soppy, soupy, sticky, tear-jerking

sobriety *n syn* TEMPERANCE 2, abstinence, continence
rel gravity, sedateness, seriousness, soberness
con excitement; drunkenness, intoxication; abandonment
ant insobriety

sobriquet *n syn* NICKNAME, byname, byword, ‖handle, hypocorism, ‖moniker

so–called *adj* **1** *syn* NOMINAL, formal, titular
2 *syn* ALLEGED, ostensible, pretended, professed, purported, supposed

sociable *adj* **1** *syn* SOCIAL 2, gregarious
ant nonsocial
2 *syn* GRACIOUS 1, affable, congenial, cordial, genial, ‖sonsy
rel companionable, convivial; gregarious; close, familiar, intimate; good-natured
ant unsociable
3 *syn* SOCIAL 1, companionable, convivial
ant unsociable, unsocial

social *adj* **1** conducive to, marked by, or passed in pleasant companionship with one's friends or associates <a relaxed, *social* evening>
syn companionable, convivial, sociable
rel amusing, entertaining, pleasant, pleasurable; cordial, friendly, genial, gracious, hospitable
con inimicable, inimical, unfriendly, unhospitable; eremitic, solitary
ant unsociable, unsocial
2 inclined by nature to association or community life with others of the same species <man is a *social* animal>
syn gregarious, sociable
rel social-minded; intersocial
con eremitic, solitary, unsociable; antisocial, asocial, unsocial; remote, withdrawn
ant nonsocial

social evil *n, used with the syn* PROSTITUTION, harlotry, oldest profession, streetwalking, whoredom

socialize *vb* to participate actively in a social group <*socializes* with his colleagues>
syn mingle
rel associate, mix

society *n* **1** *syn* COMPANY 1, companionship, fellowship
2 *syn* ASSOCIATION 2, brotherhood, club, fellowship, fraternity, guild, league, order, sodality, union
3 an organized aggregate of persons who are responsible for a prevailing social order <rules made in the interests of *society* rather than for the chosen few>
syn community, people, public
rel masses, populace
idiom people in general, society at large, the general public
4 *syn* ARISTOCRACY, aristoi, elite, flower, gentry, patriciate, quality, upper class, upper crust, who's who
idiom high society (*or* life)

sock *vb syn* STRIKE 2, ‖biff, clout, ‖devel, ding, hit, ‖nail, slog, ‖slosh, whack

sock *n* **1** *syn* BLOW 1, bash, belt, biff, bop, smack, smash, thwack, ‖welt, whack
2 *syn* CUFF, box, buffet, ‖bust, chop, clout, ‖paste, punch, slap, smack

---

‖**sock** *vb* ***syn*** SIGH 1, sough, suspire

sod *n* ***syn*** SNOT 1, ‖bugger, cur, dog, louse, puke, scum, skunk, snake, wretch

sodality *n* ***syn*** ASSOCIATION 2, brotherhood, club, fellowship, fraternity, guild, league, order, society, union

sodden *adj* ***syn*** WET 1, drenched, dripping, saturated, soaked, soaking, sopping, soppy, soused, wringing-wet

sodden *vb* ***syn*** SOAK 1, drench, impregnate, saturate, seethe, ‖sog, sop, souse, steep, waterlog

Sodom *n* ***syn*** SINK 1, Augean stable, cesspit, cesspool, den, pandemonium, sty
rel Babylon

so far *adv* ***syn*** HITHERTO 1, as yet, earlier, thus far, yet
idiom up till now

soft *adj* **1** ***syn*** GENTLE 1, balmy, bland, faint, lenient, mild, smooth
rel moderate, temperate
2 ***syn*** SUBDUED 2, low-key, low-keyed, sober, softened, toned down
ant loud
3 smooth or delicate in texture, grain, or fiber <the dog's fur was *soft*>
syn cottony, satiny, silken, silky, velvety
rel smooth; sleek
con coarse, rough
ant harsh
4 ***syn*** COMFORTABLE 2, comfy, cozy, cushy, easeful, easy, snug
ant rough
5 ***syn*** SIMPLE 3, ‖buffle-headed, fatuous, foolish, sheepheaded, silly, spoony, weak-headed, weak-minded, witless
idiom ‖soft in the head
6 giving way easily to physical touch or pressure <a *soft* cheese>
syn mushy, pappy, pulpous, pulpy, quaggy, spongy, squashy, squelchy, squishy, squushy, yielding
rel softish; compressible, malleable, pliable, pliant, workable; doughy, formless; flabby, fleshy
idiom soft as butter
con firm, solid; resistant, rigid, tough, unyielding; nail-hard, rock-hard
ant hard

soft (on) *adj* ***syn*** ENAMORED 1, mashed, smitten, spoony (over *or* on)

soft–boiled *adj* ***syn*** SENTIMENTAL, bathetic, maudlin, mushy, romantic, sappy, slushy, ‖soppy, soupy, sticky
ant hard-boiled

soften *vb* ***syn*** DEPRECIATE 1, decry, devaluate, devalue, lower, mark down, underrate, undervalue, write down, write off

softened *adj* ***syn*** SUBDUED 2, low-key, low-keyed, sober, soft, toned down

softhead *n* ***syn*** FOOL 4, cretin, ‖feeb, half-wit, idiot, imbecile, moron, natural, simpleton, zany

softhearted *adj* ***syn*** TENDER, compassionate, kindhearted, responsive, sympathetic, warm, warmhearted
ant hardhearted

soft–pedal *vb* to reduce the emphasis, importance, or effect of something (as an issue) <tried to *soft-pedal* military spending>
syn de-emphasize, play (down)
rel tone (down), tune (down); cushion, dampen, muffle, subdue; hush (up), silence, suppress; conceal, disguise
con emphasize, play (up); focus (on), spotlight

soft–shell *adj* ***syn*** MODERATE 4, middle-of-the-road, middle-road

soft soap *n* ***syn*** FLATTERY, adulation, blandishment, blarney, incense, oil
rel ‖snow job

soft–soap *vb* ***syn*** COAX, ‖banter, blandish, blarney, cajole, con, sweet-talk, wheedle

soft spot *n* **1** ***syn*** APPETITE 3, fondness, inclination, liking, taste, weakness
2 a vulnerable point <the major *soft spot* in the West's armor>
syn Achilles' heel
rel vulnerability, vulnerableness, weakness; chink, loophole
idiom heel of Achilles, weak link (*or* point), weak link in the chain
con impregnability, invulnerability; invincibility

soft touch *n* **1** someone who can be easily talked into giving help (as a loan) <recognized him as a *soft touch* when she was broke>
syn easy mark
rel softy; dupe, fool, pushover; sucker; mark, sitting duck, target
con cynic, doubting Thomas, hard case, skeptic
2 ***syn*** SNAP 1, breeze, child's play, cinch, picnic, pie, ‖pipe, pushover, setup, ‖snip

‖**sog** *vb* ***syn*** SOAK 1, drench, ‖drouk, impregnate, saturate, sodden, sop, souse, steep, waterlog

‖**sog** *vb* ***syn*** DOZE, ‖dorm, drowse, ‖sloom, slumber, ‖snoozle

soggy *adj* ***syn*** HUMID, mucky, muggy, sticky, sultry

soi–disant *adj* ***syn*** SELF-STYLED, self-proclaimed

soil *vb* **1** ***syn*** CONTAMINATE 1, defile, pollute, taint
ant purify
2 to make or become unclean <a shirt *soiled* with grease and grime>
syn begrime, besoil, dirty, foul, grime, muck, ‖mucky, muddy, murk, smirch, smooch, smudge, smutch, tarnish; *compare* STAIN 1
rel ‖becoom, ‖benasty, ‖nasty; bedaub, daub, smear; drabble, draggle; mess, spoil
con brighten, cleanse, freshen, renew; purify
ant clean
3 ***syn*** TAINT 1, besmear, besmirch, defile, discolor, smear, stain, sully, tar, tarnish

soil *n* **1** ***syn*** EARTH 2, dirt, dry land, ground, land, terra firma
2 ***syn*** COUNTRY, fatherland, home, homeland, land, mother country, motherland

---

syn synonym(s) *rel* related word(s)
idiom idiomatic equivalent(s) *con* contrasted word(s)
ant antonym(s) * vulgar
‖ use limited; if in doubt, see a dictionary
The first word in a synonym list when printed in SMALL CAPITALS shows where there is more information about the group. For a more efficient use of this book see Explanatory Notes.

soily *adj* ***syn*** DIRTY 1, black, filthy, foul, grubby, impure, nasty, squalid, unclean, uncleanly

soiree *n* ***syn*** EVENING 3

sojourn *n* a temporary but sometimes extended stay <a summer *sojourn* in Nice>
syn stopover, tarriance, visit
rel stay, stop; layover

sojourn *vb* ***syn*** VISIT 3, stay, stop (over), tarry
rel linger; abide

Sol *n* ***syn*** SUN 1, daystar, phoebus

solace *vb* ***syn*** COMFORT, buck up, cheer, console, upraise
idiom offer (*or* give) solace to, wipe one's tears away

soldier *n* a person engaged in military service <*soldiers* fighting and dying in futile wars>
syn fighter, fighting man, GI, man-at-arms, serviceman, swad, ‖swaddy, ‖sweat, warrior
rel dogface, doughboy, ‖doughfoot, infantryman; trooper; guerrilla, partisan; condottiere, free companion, free lance, mercenary, soldier of fortune

soldierly *adj* ***syn*** BRAVE 1, bold, boldhearted, courageous, dauntless, fearless, intrepid, unafraid, valiant, valorous
rel martial; aggressive, combative, militant, pugnacious, warlike
con unsoldierly

sole *n* ***syn*** BOTTOM 1, underneath, underside, undersurface

sole *adj* **1** ***syn*** SINGLE 1, spouseless, unmarried, unwed
2 ***syn*** SINGLE 2, lone, one, only, particular, separate, solitary, unique
3 ***syn*** ONLY 2, alone, lone, singular, solitary, solo, unexampled, unique, unrepeatable
idiom one and only
4 belonging, granted, or attributed to the one person or group <*sole* rights of publication>
syn exclusive, single, unshared
con multiple; shared

solecism *n* **1** ***syn*** ANACHRONISM 2
2 ***syn*** BARBARISM, corruption, impropriety, slangism, vernacularism, vernacularity, vulgarism
3 ***syn*** FAUX PAS, blooper, boner, ‖boo-boo, break, gaffe, impropriety, indecorum

solely *adv* ***syn*** ONLY 1, alone, but, entirely, exclusively

solemn *adj* **1** ***syn*** CEREMONIAL, ceremonious, conventional, formal, stately
rel full, plenary; august, grand, impressive, magnificent, majestic, overwhelming; ostentatious
2 ***syn*** SERIOUS 1, earnest, grave, no-nonsense, sedate, sober, sobersided, somber, staid, weighty
idiom as solemn as an owl, grave as an undertaker

solemnize *vb* ***syn*** KEEP 2, celebrate, commemorate, observe
rel dignify, honor, solemnify, venerate

---

syn synonym(s) ***rel*** related word(s)
idiom idiomatic equivalent(s) ***con*** contrasted word(s)
ant antonym(s) * vulgar
‖ use limited; if in doubt, see a dictionary
The first word in a synonym list when printed in SMALL CAPITALS shows where there is more information about the group. For a more efficient use of this book see Explanatory Notes.

solicit *vb* **1** to seek (as advertising, orders, or votes) especially on a large scale <*solicited* contributions all over the district>
syn canvass, drum, drum up
rel ask, request; beg, beseech, implore; claim, demand, exact
2 ***syn*** ASK 2, bespeak, desire, request
rel apply, go, refer, resort, turn
3 ***syn*** DEMAND 1, call, challenge, claim, exact, postulate, require, requisition

solicitous *adj* ***syn*** EAGER, anxious, appetent, ardent, athirst, avid, impatient, keen, raring, thirsty

solicitude *n* **1** ***syn*** CARE 2, anxiety, concern, concernment, disquiet, disquietude, unease, uneasiness, worry
rel attention, heed, watchfulness; presentiment; compunction, qualm, scruple
con carelessness, heedlessness, indifference, neglect, negligence
ant unmindfulness
2 ***syn*** CONSIDERATION 3, concern, considerateness, regard

solid *adj* **1** ***syn*** FIRM 2, hard
rel compacted, concentrated, consolidated
con spongy; disintegrated; fluid, liquid
2 ***syn*** STABLE 4, firm, secure, sound
3 ***syn*** VALID, cogent, convincing, satisfactory, satisfying, sound, telling
rel firm, hard
ant insubstantial
4 ***syn*** UNANIMOUS, consentaneous, consentient

solid *adv* ***syn*** HARD 9, firmly, hardly, solidly

solidarism *n* ***syn*** SOLIDARITY, cohesion, togetherness

solidarity *n* a feeling of unity (as in interests, standards, and responsibilities) that binds members of a group together <*solidarity* among union members is essential in negotiations>
syn cohesion, solidarism, togetherness
rel cohesiveness; oneness, singleness, undividedness; integrity, solidity, union, unity; esprit, esprit de corps; firmness, fixity
con separation; discord, dissension, schism; confusion, disorder, disorganization
ant division

solidify *vb* ***syn*** HARDEN 1, cake, concrete, congeal, dry, indurate, set
rel compress, contract
idiom make (*or* become) hard as a rock
con soften; disintegrate, dissolve
ant liquefy

solidly *adv* **1** ***syn*** HARD 9, firmly, hardly, solid
2 ***syn*** HARD 7, fast, firm, firmly, fixedly, steadfastly, tight, tightly

solitariness *n* ***syn*** SOLITUDE, aloneness, isolation, loneness

solitary *adj* **1** ***syn*** ANTISOCIAL, eremitic, misanthropic, reclusive, reserved, standoffish
ant gregarious
2 ***syn*** UNSOCIABLE, aloof, distant, insociable, offish, reserved, standoffish, unapproachable, uncompanionable, withdrawn
3 ***syn*** DERELICT 1, abandoned, deserted, desolate, forsaken, lorn, uncouth
4 ***syn*** LONE 1, alone, lonely, lonesome

rel companionless, unaccompanied, unattended
ant accompanied
5 *syn* SINGLE 2, lone, one, only, particular, separate, sole, unique
6 *syn* ONLY 2, alone, lone, singular, sole, solo, unexampled, unique, unrepeatable

solitary *n syn* RECLUSE, hermit

solitude *n* the state of one who is alone <a very social person who could not bear *solitude*>
syn aloneness, isolation, loneness, solitariness; *compare* SECLUSION
rel detachment, separateness; retirement, withdrawal; confinement, quarantine; loneliness, lonesomeness
con companionship, company

solo *adj syn* ONLY 2, alone, lone, singular, sole, solitary, unexampled, unique, unrepeatable

so long *interj syn* GOOD-BYE, adieu, by, bye-bye, ||cheerio, farewell, ||toodle-oo

solution *n syn* ANSWER 2, result

solve *vb* **1** to find an answer or solution for (a problem or difficulty) <mass transit partially *solved* the traffic problem>
syn fix, resolve, work, work out
rel decide, determine, settle
idiom hit upon a solution
2 to find an explanation or solution for something obscure, mysterious, or incomprehensible <the mystery of the missing cookies has been *solved*>
syn break, ||cipher, clear up, decipher, dissolve, ||dope out, figure out, puzzle out, resolve, unfold, unravel, unriddle
rel enlighten, illuminate; construe, elucidate, explain, interpret
idiom get to the bottom of, have it, put two and two together

somatic *adj syn* BODILY, carnal, corporal, corporeal, fleshly, physical

somber *adj* **1** *syn* DARK 1, caliginous, dim, dusk, dusky, gloomy, lightless, murky, obscure, tenebrous
2 *syn* GLOOMY 3, black, bleak, depressing, depressive, dismal, dispiriting, dreary, funereal, tenebrific
3 *syn* SERIOUS 1, earnest, grave, no-nonsense, sedate, sober, sobersided, solemn, staid, weighty
idiom as somber as an undertaker

some *adj* **1** *syn* CERTAIN 2, various
2 *syn* SEVERAL 3, divers, sundry, various

some *adv* **1** *syn* NEARLY, about, all but, almost, approximately, as good as, just about, most, practically, well-nigh
2 *syn* SOMEWHAT 2, fairly, kind of, moderately, more or less, pretty, rather, ratherish, something, sort of

somebody *pron* one or some individual of no certain or known identity <*somebody* should be home>
syn someone
rel anybody, one
con none
ant nobody, no one

somebody *n* **1** *syn* NOTABLE 1, ||big cheese, ||biggie, big-timer, ||big wheel, heavyweight, high-muck-a-muck, leader, lion, VIP
ant nobody
2 *syn* CELEBRITY 2, big name, ||celeb, luminary, name, notability, notable
ant nobody

someday *adv syn* YET 2, eventually, finally, sometime, somewhen, sooner or later, ultimately

||somegate *adv syn* SOMEHOW, someway, somewise

somehow *adv* in some way not yet known or specified <this thing must be done *somehow*>
syn ||somegate, someway, somewise
rel anyhow, anyway, anywise
idiom by hook or by crook, in one way or another, in some such way, somehow or other (*or* another)
con nohow, noway, nowise

someone *pron syn* SOMEBODY

someplace *adv syn* SOMEWHERE 1, ||somewheres
ant no place

something *adv syn* SOMEWHAT 2, fairly, kind of, moderately, more or less, pretty, rather, ratherish, some, sort of

something *n syn* ENTITY 1, being, existence, existent, individual, thing

sometime *adv syn* YET 2, eventually, finally, someday, somewhen, sooner or later, ultimately
idiom one of these days

sometime *adj syn* FORMER 2, bygone, erstwhile, late, old, once, onetime, past, quondam, whilom

sometimes *adv* at intervals <illustrated by beautiful and *sometimes* outstanding photographs>
syn at times, ||betimes, ever and again, ever and anon, here and there, now and again, now and then, once and again, ||otherwhile; *compare* OCCASIONALLY
rel intermittently, periodically, recurrently; frequently; consistently, constantly
idiom every now and then (*or* again), every once in a while, every so often, from time to time
con continually, continuously, unceasingly, uninterruptedly; endlessly, ever, interminably

someway *adv syn* SOMEHOW, ||somegate, somewise

somewhat *adv* **1** *syn* WELL 8, considerably, far, quite, rather, significantly
2 to some extent or in some degree <felt *somewhat* better but not fine>
syn fairly, kind of, moderately, more or less, pretty, rather, ratherish, some, something, sort of
rel adequately, bearably, tolerably; insignificantly, slightly
idiom rather more than less

somewhen *adv syn* YET 2, eventually, finally, someday, sometime, sooner or later, ultimately

somewhere *adv* **1** to, at, or in some unknown or unspecified location <lived on a farm *somewhere* in the Midwest>
syn someplace, ||somewheres
rel somewhither; elsewhere, otherwhere
idiom someplace or other

---

syn synonym(s)
rel related word(s)
idiom idiomatic equivalent(s)
con contrasted word(s)
ant antonym(s)
* vulgar
|| use limited; if in doubt, see a dictionary
The first word in a synonym list when printed in SMALL CAPITALS shows where there is more information about the group. For a more efficient use of this book see Explanatory Notes.

con anyplace, anywhere, ||anywheres; no place, ||nowheres
ant nowhere
2 *syn* NEARLY, about, all but, almost, approximately, as good as, just about, most, practically, well-nigh
||**somewheres** *adv syn* SOMEWHERE 1, someplace
ant ||nowheres
somewise *adv syn* SOMEHOW, ||somegate, someway
somnifacient *adj syn* SOPORIFIC 1, hypnotic, narcotic, opiate, somniferous, somnific, somnolent, somnorific, soporiferous, soporifical
somniferous *adj syn* SOPORIFIC 1, narcotic, sleepy, slumberous, somnifacient, somnific, somnolent, somnorific, soporiferous, soporifical
somnific *adj syn* SOPORIFIC 1, narcotic, sleepy, slumberous, somnifacient, somniferous, somnolent, somnorific, soporiferous, soporifical
somnolent *adj* 1 *syn* SOPORIFIC 1, narcotic, opiate, slumberous, somnifacient, somniferous, somnific, somnorific, soporiferous, soporifical
2 *syn* SLEEPY 1, dozy, drowsy, nodding, ||peepy, ||sloomy, slumberous, slumbery, snoozy, soporific
rel inactive, passive, supine
somnorific *adj syn* SOPORIFIC 1, hypnotic, narcotic, opiate, slumberous, somnifacient, somniferous, somnific, somnolent, soporiferous
so much as *adv syn* EVEN 4
son *n syn* BOY 1, lad, laddie, shaveling, stripling, tad
rel sonny; junior
sonance *n syn* SOUND 1, noise
sonant *adj syn* VOCAL 1, articulate, oral, spoken, viva voce, voiced
song *n* 1 *syn* POETRY 1, poesy, rhyme, verse
2 music or a piece of music intended for vocal expression <played and sang a *song*>
syn aria, descant, ditty, hymn, lay, lied; *compare* MELODY
rel lyric; piece
3 *syn* CALL 1, cry, note
song and dance *n syn* SPIEL, ||line, pitch
songful *adj syn* MELODIOUS 2, melodic, musical, tuned, tuneful
***son of a bitch** *n syn* VILLAIN 1, *bastard, blackguard, heel, knave, lowlife, miscreant, rascal, rogue, scoundrel
sonorant *adj syn* RESONANT, consonant, orotund, plangent, resounding, ringing, rotund, round, sonorous, vibrant
sonorous *adj* 1 *syn* RESONANT, consonant, orotund, plangent, resounding, ringing, rotund, round, sonorant, vibrant
2 *syn* RHETORICAL, aureate, bombastic, declamatory, euphuistic, flowery, grandiloquent, magniloquent, oratorical, overblown

3 *syn* NOISY, clangorous, clattery, noiseful, rackety, uproarious
||**sonsy** *adj* 1 *syn* LUCKY, fortunate, happy, providential, well
2 *syn* GRACIOUS 1, affable, congenial, cordial, genial, sociable
3 *syn* EASYGOING 3, breezy, casual, ||common, informal, low-pressure, relaxed, unconstrained, unfussy, unreserved
soon *adv* 1 *syn* PRESENTLY 1, anon, by and by, directly, shortly
rel forthwith, instantly, pronto, quickly
idiom in the near future
2 *syn* FAST 2, expeditiously, fleetly, hastily, lickety-split, posthaste, quick, quickly, rapidly, speedily
3 *syn* EARLY 1, betimes, seasonably, timely
||**soon** *adj syn* EARLY 2, overearly, oversoon, premature, previous, untimely
sooner *adv syn* BEFORE 3, beforehand, earlier
sooner or later *adv syn* YET 2, eventually, finally, someday, sometime, somewhen, ultimately
soothe *vb syn* CALM, allay, balm, becalm, compose, lull, ||quieten, settle, still, tranquilize
rel comfort, console; hush, subdue
con annoy, irritate, vex
ant excite
||**soother** *n syn* CALM, allay, balm, becalm, compose, lull, quiet, settle, soothe, still
soothsay *vb syn* FORETELL, adumbrate, augur, call, forecast, portend, predict, presage, prognosticate, prophesy
soothsayer *n syn* PROPHET, augur, auspex, forecaster, foreseer, foreteller, haruspex, predictor, prognosticator, prophesier
sop *n* 1 *syn* WEAKLING, doormat, invertebrate, jellyfish, milksop, Milquetoast, mollycoddle, namby-pamby, pantywaist, sissy
2 a conciliatory or propitiatory gift or advance <provided the $400 raise as a *sop*> <the new office was a *sop* to his wounded feelings>
syn sugarplum
rel douceur, gratuity; ||baksheesh, ||boodle, bribe, ||palm oil
idiom sop in the pan, sop to Cerberus
sop *vb* 1 *syn* WET, deluge, douse, drench, drown, soak, souse
2 *syn* SOAK 1, drench, impregnate, saturate, seethe, sodden, ||sog, souse, steep, waterlog
3 *syn* BRIBE, buy, buy off, fix, have, ||lubricate, square, tamper (with)
sophic *adj syn* WISE 1, discerning, gnostic, insighted, insightful, knowing, knowledgeable, perceptive, sagacious, sage
sophism *n syn* FALLACY 2, casuistry, deception, deceptiveness, delusion, equivocation, sophistry, speciousness, spuriousness
rel illogicality, irrationality; invalidity, unsoundness; claptrap
sophistic *adj syn* ILLOGICAL, fallacious, invalid, irrational, mad, nonrational, reasonless, unreasonable, unreasoned
sophisticate *adj syn* SOPHISTICATED 2, blasé, disenchanted, disentranced, disillusioned, knowing, mondaine, worldly, worldly-wise, world-wise

---

syn synonym(s) *rel* related word(s)
idiom idiomatic equivalent(s) *con* contrasted word(s)
ant antonym(s) * vulgar
|| use limited; if in doubt, see a dictionary
The first word in a synonym list when printed in SMALL CAPITALS shows where there is more information about the group. For a more efficient use of this book see Explanatory Notes.

sophisticate *vb* ***syn*** ADULTERATE, debase, doctor, dope (up), load, weight

sophisticated *adj* **1** ***syn*** COMPLEX 2, Byzantine, complicated, daedal, elaborate, gordian, intricate, involved, knotty, labyrinthine
ant unsophisticated
2 being experienced in the ways of the world <a *sophisticated,* well-traveled man>
syn blasé, disenchanted, disentranced, disillusioned, knowing, mondaine, sophisticate, worldly, worldly-wise, world-wise; *compare* COSMOPOLITAN 1
rel adult, mature; experienced, practiced, schooled, seasoned; salty, uncelestial; couth, well-bred; smooth, suave, svelte, urbane; bored, jaded, world-weary; brittle; cynical, skeptical
con artless, gee-whiz, ingenuous, natural; green, inexperienced, unseasoned, virginal; unworldly
ant naive, unsophisticated

sophistry *n* ***syn*** FALLACY 2, casuistry, deception, deceptiveness, delusion, equivocation, sophism, speciousness, spuriousness
rel ambiguity, tergiversation

soporiferous *adj* ***syn*** SOPORIFIC 1, hypnotic, narcotic, opiate, somnifacient, somniferous, somnific, somnolent, somnorific, soporifical

soporific *adj* **1** tending to induce sleep <a *soporific* drug> <*soporific* prose>
syn hypnotic, narcotic, opiate, sleepy, slumberous, somnifacient, somniferous, somnific, somnolent, somnorific, soporiferous, soporifical
rel calming, quietening, sedative, tranquilizing; anesthetic, deadening, numbing
con arousing, waking; invigorating, stimulating
2 ***syn*** SLEEPY 1, dozy, drowsy, nodding, ||peepy, ||sloomy, slumberous, slumbery, snoozy, somnolent

soporifical *adj* ***syn*** SOPORIFIC 1, opiate, sleepy, slumberous, somnifacient, somniferous, somnific, somnolent, somnorific, soporiferous

sopping *adj* ***syn*** WET 1, drenched, dripping, saturated, soaked, soaking, sodden, soppy, soused, wringing-wet

soppy *adj* **1** ***syn*** WET 1, drenched, dripping, saturated, soaked, soaking, sodden, sopping, soused, wringing-wet
||**2** ***syn*** SENTIMENTAL, bathetic, lovey-dovey, maudlin, mawkish, mushy, romantic, slushy, sticky, tear-jerking

sorcerer *n* ***syn*** MAGICIAN 1, charmer, conjurer, enchanter, mage, magus, necromancer, voodooist, warlock, wizard

sorceress *n* ***syn*** WITCH 1, bruja, enchantress, hag, hex, lamia, witchwoman

sorcerous *adj* ***syn*** MAGIC, magian, magical, mystic, necromantic, thaumaturgic, witchy, wizardly

sorcery *n* ***syn*** MAGIC 1, bewitchment, conjuring, enchantment, incantation, necromancy, thaumaturgy, witchcraft, witching, wizardry

sordid *adj* **1** ***syn*** DIRTY 1, black, filthy, foul, grubby, impure, nasty, squalid, unclean, uncleanly
2 ***syn*** SLATTERNLY, blowsy, dowdy, draggletailed, frowsy, slattern
3 ***syn*** BASE 3, despicable, ignoble, low, low-down, mean, scurvy, servile, vile, wretched
rel foul, nasty, seamy, sodden

sore *adj* ***syn*** PAINFUL 1, aching, afflictive, algetic, hurtful, hurting

sorehead *n* ***syn*** GROUCH, ||bellyacher, complainer, crab, griper, grouser, growler, grumbler, malcontent, sourpuss

sorely *adv* ***syn*** HARD 6, bitterly, hardly, keenly, rancorously, resentfully

sorrow *n* distress of mind <felt great *sorrow* at the loss of her friend>
syn affliction, anguish, care, ||dole, grief, heartache, heartbreak, regret, rue, woe
rel mournfulness, sadness, sorrowfulness, unhappiness; grieving, lamentation, mourning, sorrowing; dejection, depression, melancholy; agony, distress, dolor, misery, suffering, wretchedness
con cheerfulness, gaiety, gladness, happiness, joyfulness; ecstasy
ant joy

sorrow *vb* ***syn*** GRIEVE 2, mourn
rel groan, moan, sob
idiom break one's heart over, eat one's heart out
ant rejoice

sorrowful *adj* **1** ***syn*** WOEFUL 1, afflicted, doleful, dolent, dolorous, miserable, rueful, ruthful, wretched
rel sorrow-laden, sorrow-stricken, sorrow-struck
idiom full of (*or* filled with) sorrow
con sorrowless
ant joyful
2 ***syn*** MELANCHOLY 2, doleful, dolesome, dolorous, lamentable, lugubrious, mournful, plaintive, rueful, woeful
ant gay

sorry *adj* **1** ***syn*** SAD 1, heavyhearted, melancholy, mournful, saddened, unhappy
rel bad, regretful, remorseful; miserable, wretched
ant glad
2 ***syn*** REMORSEFUL, apologetic, attritional, compunctious, contrite, penitent, penitential, regretful, repentant
3 ***syn*** CONTEMPTIBLE, beggarly, cheap, despicable, despisable, mean, pitiable, scummy, scurvy, shabby
rel inadequate, paltry, poor, trifling; cheesy, scruffy, shoddy; disgraceful

sort *n* **1** ***syn*** TYPE, character, class, description, ilk, kind, order, species, stripe, variety
2 ***syn*** GROUP 3, array, batch, battery, body, clutch, lot, parcel, set, suite

sort *vb* **1** ***syn*** ASSORT, categorize, class, classify, group, pigeonhole
2 to analyze and assort (as individuals or things) to obtain those desired or required <he knew he must *sort* out facts from fancy>
syn comb, separate, sift, winnow; *compare* SCREEN 5
rel riddle, screen; choose, cull, pick, select
con consolidate, join, lump, merge; aggregate, amalgamate, blend, fuse, mix; unify

---

syn synonym(s) ***rel*** related word(s)
idiom idiomatic equivalent(s) ***con*** contrasted word(s)
ant antonym(s) * vulgar
|| use limited; if in doubt, see a dictionary
The first word in a synonym list when printed in SMALL CAPITALS shows where there is more information about the group. For a more efficient use of this book see Explanatory Notes.

sort of *adv* ***syn*** SOMEWHAT 2, fairly, kind of, moderately, more or less, pretty, rather, ratherish, some, something

SOS *n* ***syn*** ALARM 1, alert, tocsin

soshed *adj* ***syn*** INTOXICATED 1, ||boozy, ||canned, disguised, drunk, inebriated, ||lushed, muddled, pixilated, ||plastered

so–so *adv* ***syn*** ENOUGH 2, averagely, fairly, moderately, passably, rather, tolerably

so–so *adj* ***syn*** MEDIUM, average, fair, fairish, indifferent, mediocre, middling, moderate, run-of-mine, run-of-the-mill

sot *n* ***syn*** DRUNKARD, bibber, boozehound, boozer, drunk, guzzler, inebriate, lush, soak, tippler

||**sot** *adj* ***syn*** OBSTINATE, bullheaded, closed-minded, deaf, hardheaded, headstrong, intractable, muleheaded, muley, mulish

so that *conj* ***syn*** SO, so as

sotto voce *adv* in an inaudible or barely audible voice <made a snide remark to her *sotto voce*>
syn faintly, mutedly, weakly
rel low, quietly, softly; muffledly; mutteringly; aside, privately
idiom below one's breath, between one's teeth, in an aside, in an undertone, in a whisper, out of earshot, under one's breath
con aloud, out, out loud

sough *vb* **1** ***syn*** SIGH 2
2 ***syn*** SIGH 1, ||sock, suspire

soul *n* **1** an animating essence or principle held to be inseparably associated with life or living beings <philosophers who teach that life is a manifestation of *soul*>
syn anima, animus, élan vital, pneuma, psyche, spirit, vital force
rel life, vitality
idiom breath of life
2 the immortal part of man believed to have permanent individual existence <into God's hands I commit my *soul*>
syn spirit
rel life; noumenon
idiom one's immortal soul
con flesh
ant body
3 ***syn*** HEART 1, bosom, breast
rel character, personality, psyche; conscience; spirit
idiom heart of hearts, heart's core, one's inmost soul (*or* mind), one's secret (*or* inner) self, (the) secret recesses of the heart
4 ***syn*** ESSENCE 2, bottom, essentiality, marrow, pith, quintessence, quintessential, stuff, substance, virtuality
5 ***syn*** HUMAN, being, ||character, creature, individual, man, mortal, person, personage, wight

---

syn synonym(s) ***rel*** related word(s)
idiom idiomatic equivalent(s) ***con*** contrasted word(s)
ant antonym(s) * vulgar
|| use limited; if in doubt, see a dictionary
The first word in a synonym list when printed in SMALL CAPITALS shows where there is more information about the group. For a more efficient use of this book see Explanatory Notes.

soul–searching *n* ***syn*** INTROSPECTION, heart-searching, self-contemplation, self-examination, self-observation, self-questioning, self-reflection, self-scrutiny, self-searching

soul–sick *adj* ***syn*** DOWNCAST, bad, blue, cast down, dejected, depressed, dispirited, heartsick, heartsore, low

sound *adj* **1** ***syn*** HEALTHY 1, ||bunkum, fit, hale, right, sane, well, well-conditioned, well-liking, wholesome
rel intact, unimpaired; perfect
idiom sound as a bell (*or* whistle), sound of mind and body
con impaired; unfit
ant unsound
2 ***syn*** WHOLE 1, flawless, intact, unblemished, unbroken, undamaged, unhurt, unimpaired, uninjured, unmarred
3 ***syn*** STABLE 4, firm, secure, solid
ant unsound
4 ***syn*** VALID, cogent, convincing, satisfactory, satisfying, solid, telling
rel errorless, faultless, flawless, impeccable; accurate, correct, exact, precise; rational, reasonable; well-founded, well-grounded
con questionable, shaky; invalid
ant unsound
5 ***syn*** ORTHODOX 1, accepted, authoritative, canonical, received, sanctioned
6 ***syn*** RATIONAL, consequent, intelligent, logical, reasonable, sensible
rel right-minded, sober, sober-minded, sound-minded
ant unsound

sound *n* **1** a sensation or effect resulting from stimulation of the auditory receptors <the *sound* of thunder>
syn noise, sonance
rel vibration; resonance; sonancy; reverberation
con quiet, soundlessness
ant silence
2 ***syn*** EARSHOT, hearing

sound *vb* **1** ***syn*** SEEM, appear, look
2 ***syn*** DECLARE 1, advertise, announce, annunciate, blaze (abroad), broadcast, disseminate, proclaim, promulgate, publish

sound *vb* to measure the depth of (as a body of water) typically with a weighted line <*sounding* the distance to the bottom>
syn fathom, plumb, plumb-line
idiom ||cast (*or* sling) the lead, make a sounding, take soundings

sound (out) *vb* ***syn*** PROBE 2, feel out

soundless *adj* ***syn*** BOTTOMLESS 2, abysmal, fathomless, plumbless, plummetless, unfathomable
ant soundable

soundless *adj* ***syn*** STILL 3, hush, hushful, noiseless, quiet, silent, stilly, whist

soundlessness *n* ***syn*** SILENCE 1, noiselessness, quiet, quietness, quietude, still, stillness

soundness *n* **1** ***syn*** HEALTH, haleness, healthiness, wholeness
ant unsoundness
2 ***syn*** STABILITY, firmness, security, stableness, steadiness, strength
3 ***syn*** WIT 2, lucidity, ||marbles, mind, reason, saneness, sanity, sense(s)

rel level-headedness, sensibleness
idiom sound mind, soundness of mind
ant unsoundness

sound off *vb* ***syn*** SPEAK UP, speak out

soup *n* ***syn*** PREDICAMENT, box, corner, dilemma, fix, hole, jam, pickle, plight, scrape

soupçon *n* ***syn*** HINT 2, dash, intimation, smack, sprinkling, streak, suggestion, taste, trace, whiff

soupy *adj* ***syn*** SENTIMENTAL, drippy, maudlin, mawkish, mushy, slushy, sobby, ‖soppy, sticky, tear-jerking

sour *adj* **1** causing or characterized by the one of the basic taste sensations produced chiefly by acids < *sour* pickles >
syn acerb, acerbic, acetose, acid, acidulous, dry, tart
rel keen, sharp, tangy; ‖blinky, sourish; fermented, soured, turned; acrid, bitter, vinegary
ant sweet
2 ***syn*** BAD 8, ‖chiselly, disagreeable, displeasing, rotten, unhappy, unpleasant

source *n* the point at which something begins its course or existence <the *source* of his wisdom was long practical experience>
syn derivation, fount, fountain, fountainhead, inception, mother, origin, provenance, provenience, root, rootage, rootstock, spring, well, wellhead, wellspring, whence
rel birthplace; beginning, commencement, dawn, dawning, onset, opening, start, starting; authorship, origination, rise, rising; antecedent, cause, determinant; parent, paternity
con end, ending, terminus
ant termination; outcome

sourpuss *n* ***syn*** GROUCH, ‖bellyacher, complainer, crab, crank, crosspatch, griper, grouser, kicker, sorehead
rel killjoy

souse *vb* **1** ***syn*** DIP 1, douse, duck, dunk, immerse, submerge, submerse
2 ***syn*** WET, deluge, douse, drench, drown, soak, sop
3 ***syn*** SOAK 1, drench, impregnate, saturate, seethe, sodden, ‖sog, sop, steep, waterlog

souse *n* ***syn*** BINGE 1, bender, booze, brannigan, bum, bust, drunk, jag, soak, tear

soused *adj* ***syn*** WET 1, drenched, dripping, saturated, soaked, soaking, sodden, sopping, soppy, wringing-wet

souvenir *n* ***syn*** REMEMBRANCE 3, keepsake, memento, memorial, relic, remembrancer, reminder, token, trophy
idiom token of remembrance

sovereign *adj* **1** ***syn*** FREE 1, autarchic, autarkic, autonomous, independent, separate
rel self-determined, self-governed
2 ***syn*** DOMINANT 1, ascendant, master, overbearing, paramount, predominant, predominate, preponderant, prevalent, regnant
rel commanding, directing, guiding; highest, loftiest
3 ***syn*** EXCELLENT, blue-ribbon, capital, champion, classical, fine, first-class, five-star, number one, royal
4 ***syn*** KINGLY, kinglike, majestic, monarchal, monarchial, monarchical, regal, royal

sovereignty *n* ***syn*** SUPREMACY, ascendancy, ascendant, dominance, domination, dominion, masterdom, preeminence, prepotence, prepotency

sow *vb* **1** ***syn*** PLANT 1, ‖pitch, put in, seed
2 ***syn*** STREW 1, bestrew, broadcast, disject, disseminate, scatter, straw
rel fling, toss; drill

‖sowf *vb* ***syn*** HUM, bombinate, ‖bum, bumble, buzz, drone, strum, thrum

sozzled *adj* ***syn*** INTOXICATED 1, ‖boozy, ‖canned, disguised, drunk, inebriated, ‖lushed, muddled, pixilated, ‖plastered

spa *n* **1** a locality featuring mineral springs or water cures <hoped a week at a *spa* would help his arthritis>
syn baths, ‖hydro, springs, watering place, wells
rel waters
idiom health spa
2 ***syn*** RESORT 3, pleasure dome, watering place

space *n* **1** ***syn*** WHILE 1, bit, spell, stretch, time, ‖whet
rel lapse; interval, term; duration
2 ***syn*** EXPANSE, amplitude, breadth, distance, expansion, spread, stretch
rel room, roomage; spaciousness

spaced–out *adj* ***syn*** DRUGGED, doped, high, hopped-up, stoned, tripped out, turned on, ‖wiped out, zonked

spacious *adj* larger in extent or capacity than the average <a mansion with *spacious* rooms and gardens>
syn ample, capacious, commodious, roomy, wide
rel big, generous, great, large, spacy; enormous, immense, vast; expansive, extended, extensive; boundless, spaceless
con circumscribed, confined, cramped, limited, narrow, restricted; small, tiny
ant strait

spade *vb* **1** ***syn*** DIG 2, dig out, excavate, scoop, shovel
2 ***syn*** DIG 1, ‖delve, excavate, grub, shovel

span *n* ***syn*** TERM 2, duration, time
rel interval; space

spang *adv* ***syn*** JUST 1, accurately, bang, exactly, precisely, right, sharp, ‖smack-dab, square, squarely

spangle *vb* **1** to adorn with small brilliant objects <a tutu *spangled* with sequins>
syn bespangle, glitter
rel adorn, decorate, ornament, trim
2 ***syn*** FLASH 1, coruscate, gleam, glimmer, glisten, glitter, scintillate, shimmer, sparkle, twinkle

spang–new *adj* ***syn*** BRAND-NEW, fire-new, mint, spanking-new, span-new, spick-and-span

spaniel *n* ***syn*** SYCOPHANT, bootlicker, ‖clawback, footlicker, lickspit, lickspittle, toad, toadeater, toady, truckler

spank *vb* ***syn*** SLAP 1, blip, box, buffet, cuff, smack, ‖wherret

spank *n* ***syn*** CUFF, box, buffet, ‖bust, clout, ‖paste, punch, slap, smack, sock
idiom a sound spank

spanking *adv* ***syn*** VERY 1, awfully, damned, dreadfully, extremely, mightily, rattling, snapping, whacking, whopping

---

syn synonym(s)
idiom idiomatic equivalent(s)
ant antonym(s)
rel related word(s)
con contrasted word(s)
* vulgar
‖ use limited; if in doubt, see a dictionary
The first word in a synonym list when printed in SMALL CAPITALS shows where there is more information about the group. For a more efficient use of this book see Explanatory Notes.

spanking–new *adj* ***syn*** BRAND-NEW, fire-new, mint, spang-new, span-new, spick-and-span

span–new *adj* ***syn*** BRAND-NEW, fire-new, mint, spang-new, spanking-new, spick-and-span

spare *vb* **1** ***syn*** EXEMPT, absolve, discharge, dispense, excuse, let off, privilege (from), relieve
2 ***syn*** SAVE 4, lay aside, lay away, lay by, lay in, lay up, put by, salt away
3 to refrain from the free use or consumption of <don't *spare* the syrup on my pancakes>
syn scant, short, skimp, ‖skinch, stint; *compare* SCRIMP
rel pinch
4 ***syn*** SCRIMP, pinch, scrape, screw, skimp, ‖skinch, stint

spare *adj* **1** ***syn*** SUPERFLUOUS, de trop, excess, extra, recrementitious, superfluent, supernumerary, surplus
idiom enough and to spare, more than enough
2 ***syn*** LEAN, angular, bony, gaunt, lank, lanky, rawboned, scraggy, scrawny, skinny
ant corpulent
3 ***syn*** MEAGER 2, exiguous, poor, scant, scanty, scrimp, scrimpy, skimp, skimpy, sparse
ant profuse

sparing *adj* careful in the use of money, goods, or resources <was *sparing* in his expenditures>
syn canny, chary, economical, frugal, provident, saving, Scotch, stewardly, thrifty, unwasteful, wary; *compare* STINGY
rel parsimonious, ‖scant, tight, tightfisted, ungiving
con exuberant, liberal, prodigal, profuse
ant lavish, unsparing

spark *n* ***syn*** SEED 2, bud, embryo, germ, nucleus

spark *n* ***syn*** SUITOR 2, sparker, swain, wooer

spark *vb* ***syn*** ADDRESS 8, court, make up (to), pursue, sue, sweetheart, woo

sparker *n* ***syn*** SUITOR 2, spark, swain, wooer

sparkish *adj* ***syn*** DAPPER, bandbox, doggish, doggy, natty, sassy, spiffy, spruce, sprucy, well-groomed

sparkle *vb* ***syn*** FLASH 1, coruscate, glance, gleam, glimmer, glint, glitter, scintillate, shimmer, twinkle

sparkle *n* ***syn*** FLASH 1, coruscation, gleam, glimmer, glint, glisten, glitter, scintillation, shimmer, twinkle

sparse *adj* ***syn*** MEAGER 2, exiguous, poor, scant, scanty, scrimp, scrimpy, skimp, skimpy, spare
rel dispersed, scattered; infrequent, occasional, sporadic; rare, scarce, uncommon
con close, compact, thick

‖spartle *vb* ***syn*** SCRAMBLE 1, clamber, scrabble, ‖sprauchle

spasmodic *adj* ***syn*** FITFUL, catchy, desultory, on-again-off-again, sporadic, spotty
rel spurtive
con continual, continuous, uninterrupted

spat *n* **1** ***syn*** QUARREL, altercation, beef, bickering, dispute, falling-out, fight, hassle, miff, tiff
‖**2** ***syn*** CUFF, box, buffet, ‖burst, chop, ‖paste, punch, slap, smack, ‖swack

spat *vb* ***syn*** QUARREL, bicker, brabble, caterwaul, fall out, row, scrap, squabble, tiff, wrangle

spate *n* **1** ***syn*** FLOOD 2, cataclysm, cataract, deluge, flooding, inundation, niagara, overflow, pour, torrent
rel progression, series, succession; rain, river, spurt
2 ***syn*** FLOW, current, drift, flood, flux, rush, stream, tide

spatter *vb* **1** ***syn*** SPLASH, douse, plash, slop, slosh, splatter, splosh, splurge, spurtle, swash
rel sparge
2 ***syn*** SPOT 1, bespatter, bespot
3 ***syn*** MALIGN, asperse, befoul, bespatter, blacken, defame, denigrate, slur, smear, traduce
4 ***syn*** SPUTTER 2, spit, splutter

spatter *n* ***syn*** FEW, handful, scattering, smatch, smatter, smattering, spattering, sprinkling

spattering *n* ***syn*** FEW, handful, scattering, smatch, smatter, smattering, spatter, sprinkling

spawn *vb* ***syn*** GENERATE 1, create, father, hatch, make, originate, parent, procreate, produce, sire

spawning *adj* ***syn*** FERTILE, childing, fecund, fruitful, productive, proliferant, prolific, rich

speak *vb* **1** to articulate words in order to express thoughts <always *speak* clearly>
syn talk, utter, verbalize, vocalize, voice
rel drawl, gasp, mouth, mumble, murmur, mutter, shout, splutter, spout, whisper; descant, dilate (on *or* upon), expatiate, perorate; converse, discourse; allege, assert, aver, convey, declare, tell
idiom break silence, give voice (*or* tongue *or* utterance) to, let fall, make public (*or* known), open one's mouth (*or* lips), put in (*or* into) words, say one's say, speak one's piece
con gabble, gibber, jabber; maunder, mumble, mutter; mispronounce, misspeak
2 ***syn*** TALK 7, address, lecture, prelect
3 to have oral command of (a language) <he *speaks* fluent German>
syn converse (in), parley, talk, use
idiom be at ease in
con falter, hesitate, stumble

speaker *n* ***syn*** SPOKESMAN, mouth, mouthpiece, spokesperson, spokeswoman

speaking *n* ***syn*** SPEECH 1, discourse, talk, utterance, verbalization

speak out *vb* ***syn*** SPEAK UP, sound off

speak up *vb* to speak strongly, boldly, or vigorously <we'll never know how you feel if you don't *speak up*>
syn sound off, speak out
idiom come out with it, have one's say, let one's voice be heard, make oneself heard, speak one's mind, stand up and be counted

spear *vb* ***syn*** IMPALE, lance, skewer, skiver, spike, spit, transfix, transpierce
rel stick; bore, drill, penetrate, pierce; gouge, ream

special *adj* **1** of or relating to one thing or class <*special* soap for infants>
syn especial, individual, particular, specific

---

syn synonym(s) ***rel*** related word(s)
idiom idiomatic equivalent(s) ***con*** contrasted word(s)
ant antonym(s) * vulgar
‖ use limited; if in doubt, see a dictionary
The first word in a synonym list when printed in SMALL CAPITALS shows where there is more information about the group. For a more efficient use of this book see Explanatory Notes.

rel characteristic, distinctive, peculiar; exceptional, occasional, rare, uncommon; unique
con common, familiar, ordinary; customary, habitual, usual
2 *syn* EXPRESS 2, especial, set, specific
rel defined, determinate; designated, earmarked

special *adv syn* ESPECIALLY 1, distinctively, particularly, specially, specifically

specialize *vb syn* ITEMIZE 1, enumerate, inventory, list, particularize, specify

specially *adv* **1** *syn* ESPECIALLY 1, distinctively, particularly, special, specifically
2 *syn* EXPRESSLY 2, especially, in specie, specifically

species *n syn* TYPE, breed, class, kidney, kind, nature, order, sort, stripe, variety

specific *adj* **1** *syn* SPECIAL 1, especial, individual, particular
rel limited, reserved, restricted, specialized
con general, generic
ant nonspecific, unspecific
2 *syn* EXPLICIT, categorical, clean-cut, clear-cut, definite, definitive, express, unambiguous
con ambiguous, cloudy, indefinite, uncertain, unexplicit, unspecified, vague
ant nonspecific, unspecific
3 *syn* EXPRESS 2, especial, set, special
ant nonspecific, unspecific

specifically *adv* **1** *syn* EXPRESSLY 2, especially, in specie, specially
2 *syn* ESPECIALLY 1, distinctively, particularly, special, specially
3 *syn* EXPRESSLY 1, categorically, definitely, explicitly

specificate *vb syn* SPECIFY 3, detail, particularize, specificize, stipulate

specificize *vb syn* SPECIFY 3, detail, particularize, specificate, stipulate

specify *vb* **1** *syn* MENTION, cite, instance, name
2 *syn* ITEMIZE 1, enumerate, inventory, list, particularize, specialize
3 to make something (as a condition or requirement) specific <his will *specified* how the money would be divided>
syn detail, particularize, specificate, specificize, stipulate; *compare* ITEMIZE 1
rel determine, establish, fix, settle; condition, limit, set; pin (down); enumerate, list; precise

specimen *n syn* INSTANCE, case, case history, example, illustration, representative, sample, sampling
rel sort, species, type, variety

specious *adj syn* FALSE 1, counterfactual, erroneous, inaccurate, incorrect, unsound, untrue, wrong
rel apparent, seeming; colorable, plausible; beguiling; illogical, spurious; empty, hollow, idle, nugatory, vain
ant valid

speciousness *n syn* FALLACY 2, casuistry, deception, deceptiveness, delusion, equivocation, sophism, sophistry, spuriousness
rel speciosity
ant validity

speck *n* **1** *syn* POINT 11, dot, flyspeck, mote
rel pinpoint; tick
2 *syn* PARTICLE, atom, bit, crumb, grain, iota, jot, mite, molecule, smitch

speck *vb syn* SPECKLE 1, bespeckle, dot, freckle, pepper, sprinkle, stipple

speckle *vb* **1** to produce on or mark with small spots, speckles, or blemishes <a *speckled* egg>
syn bespeckle, dot, freckle, pepper, speck, sprinkle, stipple; *compare* SPOT 1
rel dapple, flake, fleck
2 *syn* SPOT 2, dot, pimple, sprinkle, stud

spectacle *n syn* EXHIBITION 1, demonstration, display, show

spectacled *adj syn* BESPECTACLED

spectacular *adj syn* MARVELOUS 1, amazing, astonishing, astounding, miraculous, prodigious, staggering, stupendous, wonderful, wondrous
rel eye-popping, sensational, striking, thrilling; dramatic, histrionic, stagy, theatrical
ant unspectacular

spectator *n* one who sees or looks upon something <sports *spectators*>
syn beholder, by-sitter, bystander, eyewitness, looker-on, observer, onlooker, stander-by, viewer, watcher, witness
rel gazer; perceiver; seer

specter *n syn* APPARITION, eidolon, ghost, phantasm, phantom, revenant, shade, shadow, spirit, umbra

spectral *adj syn* GHASTLY 2, cadaverous, corpselike, deathlike, ghostlike, ghostly, shadowy
rel phantom, phantomlike, shadowlike; disembodied, unearthly; spooky

spectrum *n syn* APPARITION, bogey, eidolon, ghost, ‖haunt, phantasm, revenant, shade, spirit, ‖spook

speculate *vb syn* THINK 5, cerebrate, cogitate, deliberate, reason, reflect
rel excogitate, review, study, weigh
idiom ‖beat one's brains, turn over in one's mind, ‖use the gray matter

speculation *n* **1** *syn* THOUGHT 1, brainwork, cerebration, cogitation, deliberation, reflection
rel excogitation, review, studying, weighing
2 *syn* THEORY 2, conjecture, perhaps, suppose, supposition

speculative *adj* **1** *syn* THEORETICAL 1, academic, closet
2 *syn* THOUGHTFUL 1, cogitative, contemplative, meditative, pensive, ‖pensy, reflecting, reflective, ruminative, thinking
rel musing, ruminating; curious, inquiring, questioning
ant unspeculative

speech *n* **1** communication, expression, or interchange of thoughts in spoken words <considered *speech* as a means of reproducing for one's listeners the images in one's mind>
syn discourse, speaking, talk, utterance, verbalization; *compare* VOCALIZATION

---

rel articulation, uttering, vocalization, vocalizing, voice, voicing; expressing, expression; language
idiom oral communication, vocal expression
2 a usually formal discourse delivered to an audience <a televised *speech* to the nation>
syn address, allocution, lecture, talk
rel debate, parlance, parley; declamation, harangue, oration, speechification
3 ***syn*** LANGUAGE 1, dialect, idiom, tongue, vernacular

speechcraft *n* ***syn*** ORATORY, elocution, rhetoric

speechless *adj* **1** ***syn*** DUMB 1, inarticulate, mute, silent, unarticulate, voiceless
rel aphonic
2 ***syn*** SILENT 2, dumb, mum, ||mumchance, mute, wordless
3 ***syn*** SILENT 3, closemouthed, close-tongued, dumb, reserved, taciturn, tight-lipped, tight-mouthed, uncommunicative, wordless

speed *n* **1** ***syn*** HASTE 1, celerity, dispatch, expedition, expeditiousness, hurry, hustle, rustle, speediness, swiftness
rel alacrity, legerity; headway
con dilatoriness, tardiness
2 rate of movement, performance, or occurrence <ran through the exercise at a high *speed*>
syn ||bat, celerity, gait, pace, quickness, rapidity, rapidness, swiftness, velocity; *compare* TEMPO
rel fastness, fleetness; clip, hickory

speed *vb* **1** ***syn*** HURRY 2, barrel, bucket, fly, hasten, highball, hustle, run, rush, whiz
idiom make haste
ant slow (up *or* down)
2 ***syn*** COURSE, career, chase, race, rush, tear
3 to cause to move fast or faster <*sped* our craft forward>
syn accelerate, hasten, hurry, quicken, shake up, step up, swiften
rel advance, aid, ease, encourage, expedite, facilitate, forward, further, help (along), smooth; cheer (on), drive (on), goad (on), spur (on); burn (up)
idiom ||get the lead out
con hamper, restrain, retard; check, stay; delay, postpone, put off
ant slow (up *or* down)

speedily *adv* ***syn*** FAST 2, flat-out, fleetly, full tilt, hastily, lickety-split, posthaste, quickly, rapidly, swiftly
idiom against the clock, hell-bent for leather, like a bat out of hell, like all forty, ||like all get-out, on the double, to beat the band
con deliberately, languidly, leisurely; lazily, lethargically, sluggishly; crawlingly, creepingly
ant slow, slowly

speediness *n* ***syn*** HASTE 1, celerity, dispatch, expedition, expeditiousness, hurry, hustle, rustle, speed, swiftness

ant slowness

speedy *adj* ***syn*** FAST 3, breakneck, expeditious, fleet, harefooted, hasty, quick, raking, rapid, swift
rel agile, brisk, nimble; prompt, ready
idiom fast as greased lightning, speedy as an arrow
ant dilatory; slow

speerings *n pl* ***syn*** NEWS, advice, information, intelligence, tidings, word

||**spelder** *vb* ***syn*** SPRAWL 1, drape, ||scamble, spraddle, spread-eagle

spell *n* a spoken word or set of words believed to have magic power <cause death by muttering *spells* over her>
syn charm, conjuration, ||devil-devil, incantation, rune
rel bewitching, enchanting, hexing

spell *vb* ***syn*** BEWITCH 1, charm, enchant, ensorcell, hex, voodoo, witch

spell *vb* ***syn*** MEAN 2, add up (to), connote, denote, express, import, intend, signify

spell *vb* **1** ***syn*** RELIEVE 3, take over
2 ***syn*** REST 3, breathe, lay off, lie by

spell *n* **1** a limited period or amount of activity <each *spell* of work was followed by a brief rest>
syn bout, go, shift, stint, time, tour, trick, turn
rel streak; ||patch, period; stretch; relay
2 ***syn*** WHILE 1, bit, space, stretch, time, ||whet
3 ***syn*** ATTACK 3, access, fit, seizure, throe, turn

spellbind *vb* ***syn*** ENTHRALL 2, catch up, fascinate, grip, hold, mesmerize

spell out *vb* ***syn*** EXPLAIN 1, construe, explicate, expound, interpret

spend *vb* **1** to distribute or consume in payment or expenditure <*spent* fifty dollars for that dress>
syn disburse, expend, fork (out), give, lay out, outlay, pay, shell out
rel blow, drop, hand out; contribute; consume, dissipate, lavish, squander, throw away, waste
ant save
2 ***syn*** GO 4, consume, exhaust, expend, finish, run through, use up, wash up
3 to cause or permit to elapse <*spent* the summer at the beach>
syn pass, while (away)

spender *n* ***syn*** SPENDTHRIFT, high roller, prodigal, profligate, scattergood, squanderer, unthrift, waster, wastethrift, wastrel
ant saver

spending money *n* ***syn*** POCKET MONEY, pin money

spendthrift *n* one who dissipates his resources foolishly and wastefully <a *spendthrift* who lost his estate through gambling>
syn high roller, prodigal, profligate, scattergood, spender, squanderer, unthrift, waster, wastethrift, wastrel
con hoarder, miser, saver

spent *adj* ***syn*** EFFETE 2, all in, bleary, depleted, drained, exhausted, far-gone, used up, washed-out, worn-out

spew *vb* **1** ***syn*** VOMIT, bring up, ||cack, ||cascade, disgorge, ||heave, *puke, spit up, throw up, upchuck
2 ***syn*** ERUPT 1, belch, disgorge, eject, eruct, expel, irrupt
rel flood, gush

sphere *n* **1** ***syn*** BALL 1, globe, orb, rondure, round
2 ***syn*** FIELD, bailiwick, champaign, demesne, domain, dominion, province, terrain, territory, walk

---

syn synonym(s) ***rel*** related word(s)
idiom idiomatic equivalent(s) ***con*** contrasted word(s)
ant antonym(s) * vulgar
|| use limited; if in doubt, see a dictionary
The first word in a synonym list when printed in SMALL CAPITALS shows where there is more information about the group. For a more efficient use of this book see Explanatory Notes.

rel circle, jurisdiction, realm

sphere *vb* *syn* BALL, conglobate, conglobe, ensphere, round

spice *n* **1** *syn* HINT 2, cast, dash, lick, smack, smell, taste, tinge, touch, trace
2 *syn* FRAGRANCE, aroma, balm, bouquet, incense, perfume, redolence, scent

spick–and–span *adj* **1** *syn* BRAND-NEW, fire-new, mint, spang-new, spanking-new, span-new
2 *syn* NEAT 2, chipper, orderly, shipshape, snug, tidy, trig, trim, uncluttered, well-groomed

spicy *adj* **1** *syn* SWEET 2, ambrosial, aromal, aromatic, fragrant, perfumed, perfumy, redolent, savory, scented
2 *syn* PUNGENT, peppery, piquant, poignant, racy, snappy, zesty
rel fiery, gingery, high-spirited, spirited, zestful
3 *syn* RISQUÉ, blue, broad, off-color, purple, racy, salty, shady, suggestive, wicked
rel sophisticated; piquant

spider *n* *syn* FRYING PAN, skillet

spiel *n* voluble, glib, or extravagant talk often intended to impress, persuade, or deceive <gave her a long sales *spiel*>
syn ‖line, pitch, song and dance
rel demagoguery; dramatics, pyrotechnics, sensationalism

‖**spieler** *n* *syn* SWINDLER, cheater, defrauder, diddler, double-dealer, flimflammer, ‖grifter, gypper, sharper, slicker

spiff *vb* *syn* DRESS UP 1, deck (out), doll out, doll up, ‖dude up, fix up, gussy up, slick, smarten (up), spruce (up)

spiffy *adj* *syn* DAPPER, bandbox, doggish, doggy, natty, sassy, sparkish, spruce, sprucy, well-groomed

‖**spiflicated** *adj* *syn* INTOXICATED 1, ‖boozed, ‖boozy, drunk, ‖lushed, ‖oiled, ‖pie-eyed, ‖stewed, tight, zonked

spigot *n* *syn* FAUCET, cock, gate, hydrant, petcock, stopcock, tap, valve

spike *vb* *syn* IMPALE, lance, skewer, skiver, spear, spit, transfix, transpierce

spill *vb* **1** to cause or allow (something) to fall, flow, or run out and be lost or wasted <accidentally dropped the cup and *spilled* his tea>
syn slop, squab
rel dribble, drip, drop; spatter, splash, spray
2 *syn* OVERFLOW 2, overbrim, overfill, overrun, run over, well over
3 *syn* REVEAL 1, betray, blab (out), disclose, discover, divulge, give away, mouth, tell, unclose

spilth *n* *syn* REFUSE, debris, ‖dust, garbage, junk, litter, ‖sculch, sweepings, trash, waste

spin *vb* **1** to turn or cause to turn rapidly <pinwheels *spinning* in the wind>
syn gyrate, gyre, ‖pirl, pirouette, ‖purl, twirl, whirl, whirligig; *compare* TURN 1
rel revolve, rotate, wheel; swirl; oscillate, pendulate, vibrate
idiom spin like a top
2 to feel as if revolving <her head was *spinning* with figures>
syn reel, swim, turn, whirl
rel dizzy, giddy; fluster, mix up, muddle
idiom be in a whirl

spin (out) *vb* *syn* EXTEND 3, draw, draw out, elongate, lengthen, prolong, prolongate, protract, stretch

spin *n* *syn* DRIVE 1, ride, turn

spinal column *n* *syn* SPINE, back, backbone, rachis, vertebrae, vertebral column

spindling *adj* *syn* GANGLING, gangly, lanky, rangy, spindly

spindly *adj* *syn* GANGLING, gangly, lanky, rangy, spindling

spine *n* the articulated column of bones that is the central and axial feature of a vertebrate skeleton <fractured his *spine*>
syn back, backbone, rachis, spinal column, vertebrae, vertebral column
rel spinal cord

spineless *adj* *syn* WEAK 4, boneless, emasculate, forceless, impotent, inadequate, ineffective, ineffectual, invertebrate, slack-spined
rel weak-kneed, weak-willed
idiom as spineless as an amoeba
con self-willed, strong-willed

spin–off *n* *syn* OUTGROWTH 2, by-product, derivative, descendant, offshoot

spinster *n* a woman who is past the common age for marrying or who seems unlikely ever to marry <a gentle *spinster*, happy in her solitary life>
syn maiden lady, old maid, spinstress, ‖tabby

spinstress *n* *syn* SPINSTER, maiden lady, old maid, ‖tabby

spiny *adj* *syn* THORNY, nettlesome, prickly

spiral *vb* *syn* WIND 2, coil, corkscrew, curl, entwine, twine, twist, wreathe

spiring *adj* *syn* LOFTY 6, aerial, airy, skyscraping, soaring, topless, towering, towery

spirit *n* **1** *syn* SOUL 1, anima, animus, élan vital, pneuma, psyche, vital force
2 *syn* APPARITION, eidolon, phantasm, phantom, revenant, shade, shadow, specter, umbra, wraith
3 *syn* SOUL 2
4 *syn* TEMPER 1, mood, timbre, tone
5 a lively or brisk quality in a person or his actions <a man of great *spirit* and courage>
syn animation, brio, dash, élan, esprit, gimp, life, oomph, verve, vim, zing; *compare* VIGOR 2
rel ardor, briskness, enthusiasm, liveliness; drive, get-up-and-go, ginger, go, pep, snap, starch, vigor, vitality, zip; character, force, substance
6 *syn* COURAGE, cojones, dauntlessness, guts, heart, mettle, ‖moxie, pluck, resolution, spunk
rel ardor, fervor, passion, zeal; energy, force, might, power, strength
7 *often* **spirits** *pl* *syn* LIQUOR, aqua vitae, booze, drink, firewater, grog, ‖hooch, ‖juice, ‖sauce, tipple

spirit (away) *vb* *syn* KIDNAP, abduct, ‖snatch

---

syn synonym(s) *rel* related word(s)
idiom idiomatic equivalent(s) *con* contrasted word(s)
ant antonym(s) * vulgar
‖ use limited; if in doubt, see a dictionary
The first word in a synonym list when printed in SMALL CAPITALS shows where there is more information about the group. For a more efficient use of this book see Explanatory Notes.

spirit (up) *vb* ***syn*** ELATE, commove, excite, exhilarate, inspire, set up, stimulate

spirited *adj* **1** ***syn*** LIVELY 1, alert, animate, animated, bright, ‖cant, chipper, keen, sprightly, vivacious
rel sharp; fiery, gingery, peppery
idiom full of life (*or* go)
ant spiritless
2 having or manifesting a high degree of vitality, spirit, and daring <the lawyer gave a *spirited* defense of his client>
syn beany, fiery, gingery, high-hearted, high-spirited, mettlesome, peppery, spunky
rel game, gritty, resolute; audacious, bold, brave, courageous, dauntless, fearless, intrepid, nervy, plucky, valiant; avid, eager, hot, keen; ardent, enthusiastic, fervent, hot, passionate, peppy, zealous
con unenthusiastic; flabby, languid, limp; boneless, spineless
ant spiritless

spiritless *adj* **1** ***syn*** DEAD 1, asleep, cold, deceased, defunct, departed, exanimate, extinct, lifeless, unanimated
2 ***syn*** DOWNCAST, blue, cast down, dejected, depressed, disconsolate, dispirited, down, downhearted, low
idiom down in the dumps
3 ***syn*** LANGUID, die-away, enervated, lackadaisical, languishing, languorous, limp, listless
rel tame; broken, subdued, submissive
ant spirited

spiritual *adj* **1** ***syn*** IMMATERIAL 1, bodiless, discarnate, disembodied, incorporeal, metaphysical, nonmaterial, nonphysical, unfleshly, unphysical
rel supernatural, supramundane
ant physical
2 ***syn*** SACRED 2, numinous
3 ***syn*** ECCLESIASTICAL, church, churchly, churchmanly
4 appealing to, coming from, or related to the higher emotions or to the aesthetic senses <man's *spiritual* and intellectual life as opposed to his animal instincts>
syn numinous
rel cerebral, intellectual, mental; elevated, high, high-minded, lofty; saintly
con low, lower; base
ant animal

spirituous *adj* containing a considerable amount of alcohol <*spirituous* liquors>
syn alcoholic, ardent, hard, strong
rel spiked; inebriating, intoxicating, intoxicative; heady
con nonalcoholic, nonintoxicating, soft

‖**spirity** *adj* ***syn*** LIVELY 1, alert, animate, animated, dashing, rousing, spirited, sprightful, sprightly, vivacious

---

syn synonym(s) ***rel*** related word(s)
idiom idiomatic equivalent(s) ***con*** contrasted word(s)
ant antonym(s) * vulgar
‖ use limited; if in doubt, see a dictionary
The first word in a synonym list when printed in SMALL CAPITALS shows where there is more information about the group. For a more efficient use of this book see Explanatory Notes.

spit *vb* ***syn*** IMPALE, lance, skewer, skiver, spear, spike, transfix, transpierce

spit *n* **1** ***syn*** SALIVA, slaver, spittle, water
2 ***syn*** IMAGE 1, double, picture, portrait, ringer, simulacrum, spitting image
rel counterpart; look-alike; twin

spit *vb* **1** ***syn*** SPUTTER 1, rip (out), splutter
2 ***syn*** SPUTTER 2, spatter, splutter

spite *n* ***syn*** MALICE, despite, despitefulness, grudge, ill will, malevolence, maliciousness, malignancy, spitefulness, spleen
rel rancor; revenge, revengefulness, vengeance, vengefulness, vindictiveness
con sympathy; affection, love, tenderness

spiteful *adj* ***syn*** MALICIOUS, despiteful, evil, hateful, malevolent, malign, malignant, rancorous, vicious, wicked
rel antagonistic, hostile; revengeful, vengeful, vindictive
con charitable; sympathetic; affectionate, loving
ant spiteless

spitefulness *n* ***syn*** MALICE, despite, despitefulness, grudge, ill will, malevolence, maliciousness, malignancy, spite, spleen

spitish *adj* ***syn*** MALICIOUS, catty, despiteful, hateful, malevolent, malign, malignant, spiteful, vicious, wicked

spitting image *n* ***syn*** IMAGE 1, double, picture, portrait, ringer, simulacrum, spit
rel mirror image

spittle *n* ***syn*** SALIVA, slaver, spit, water

spit up *vb* ***syn*** VOMIT, barf, bring up, ‖cascade, ‖cast, disgorge, ‖heave, spew, throw up, upchuck

‖**spiv** *n* **1** ***syn*** PARASITE, barnacle, bloodsucker, freeloader, hanger-on, leech, lounge lizard, sponge, sponger, sucker
2 ***syn*** SLACKER, goldbrick, shirker, slinker

splash *vb* to dash a liquid or semiliquid substance upon or against <*splashed* water onto her face>
syn douse, plash, slop, slosh, spatter, splatter, splosh, splurge, spurtle, swash
rel dash, throw; spray; sprinkle; ‖sprent, squirt; drench, drown, soak, sop, wet

splashy *adj* ***syn*** SHOWY, chichi, flamboyant, orchidaceous, ostentatious, peacockish, peacocky, pretentious, swank

splathering *adj* ***syn*** CLUMSY 1, awkward, gawky, lumbering, lumpish, splay, ungainly

splatter *vb* ***syn*** SPLASH, douse, plash, slop, slosh, spatter, splosh, splurge, spurtle, swash

splay *adj* ***syn*** CLUMSY 1, awkward, gawky, lumbering, lumpish, splathering, ungainly

spleen *n* ***syn*** MALICE, despite, despitefulness, grudge, ill will, malevolence, maliciousness, malignancy, spite, spitefulness
rel revenge, revengefulness, vindictiveness; wrath

splendid *adj* **1** ***syn*** GRAND 2, gorgeous, impressive, lavish, luxurious, sumptuous
rel baroque, flamboyant
2 extraordinarily or transcendently impressive <a *splendid* new city>
syn glorious, gorgeous, magnificent, proud, resplendent, splendiferous, splendorous, sublime, superb
rel eminent, illustrious; grand, impressive, lavish, luxurious, royal, sumptuous; divine, exquisite, lovely; incomparable, matchless, peerless, superlative, supreme, unparalleled, unsurpassed; surpassing, transcendent

con common, ordinary, run-of-the-mill
ant unimpressive

splendiferous *adj syn* SPLENDID 2, glorious, gorgeous, magnificent, proud, resplendent, splendorous, sublime, superb
rel dazzling, marvelous; smashing, walloping; rattling, ripping, screaming, terrific

splendorous *adj syn* SPLENDID 2, glorious, gorgeous, magnificent, proud, resplendent, splendiferous, sublime, superb

splice *vb syn* MARRY 2, ‖hitch, mate, tie, wed

splinter *vb syn* SHATTER 1, burst, fragment, ‖pash, rive, shiver, smash, ‖smatter, splinterize, splitter

splinterize *vb syn* SHATTER 1, burst, fragment, ‖pash, rive, shiver, smash, ‖smatter, splinter, splitter

split *vb* **1** *syn* CUT 5, carve, cleave, dissect, dissever, sever, slice, sunder
rel crack, rive
2 *syn* TEAR 1, cleave, rend, rip, rive
‖**3** *syn* BETRAY 2, cross, double-cross, sell, sell out

split (up) *vb syn* SEPARATE 1, break (up), dichotomize, disjoin, dissever, divide, divorce, part, sever, sunder

split *n* **1** *syn* CRACK 3, chink, cleft, fissure, rift, rima, rimation, rime
2 *syn* SCHISM 3, chasm, cleavage, cleft
3 *syn* BREACH 3, break, fissure, fracture, rent, rift, rupture, schism
rel alienating, estranging

split second *n syn* INSTANT 1, breathing, flash, jiffy, minute, moment, second, shake, trice, twinkling

splitter *vb syn* SHATTER 1, burst, fragment, ‖pash, rive, shiver, smash, ‖smatter, splinter, splinterize

split–up *n syn* SEPARATION 1, detachment, dissolution, disunion, division, divorce, divorcement, partition, rupture

‖**splodge** *vb syn* SPLOTCH, blotch, mottle

splosh *vb syn* SPLASH, douse, plash, slop, slosh, spatter, splatter, splurge, spurtle, swash

splotch *vb* to mark or spot with irregular patches especially of contrasting color <a pallid face *splotched* with red>
syn blotch, mottle, ‖splodge
rel blot, stain; dapple, fleck, marble, motley, variegate; bespot, spot; harlequin

‖**splunge** *vb syn* PLUNGE 2, burst, dive, drive, lunge, pitch

splurge *n syn* SPREE 1, binge, fling, orgy, rampage
rel extravagance; splash

splurge *vb syn* SPLASH, douse, plash, slop, slosh, spatter, splatter, splosh, spurtle, swash

splurt *vb syn* SQUIRT, jet, sprit, ‖spritz, spurt, ‖squitter

splutter *vb* **1** *syn* SPUTTER 2, spatter, spit
2 *syn* SPUTTER 1, rip (out), spit

spoil *n* something taken from another by force or craft <gold, jewels, and paintings are often *spoils* of war>
syn boodle, booty, loot, plunder, plunderage, prize, ‖spreaghery, ‖spulzie, swag
rel acquisition, grab, haul, take; pickings, stealings; pillage, spoliation

spoil *vb* **1** *syn* RAVAGE, depredate, desecrate, desolate, despoil, devastate, pillage, sack, spoliate, waste
2 *syn* INJURE 1, blemish, damage, harm, hurt, impair, mar, prejudice, tarnish, vitiate
rel ‖snafu; ruin, wreck; demolish, destroy
3 *syn* RAPE, defile, deflorate, deflower, force, outrage, ravish, violate
4 *syn* BABY, cater (to), cocker, coddle, cosset, humor, indulge, mollycoddle, ‖much, pamper
rel accommodate, favor, oblige
idiom spoil (one) rotten, spoil to death
5 *syn* DECAY, break down, crumble, decompose, disintegrate, molder, putrefy, rot, taint, turn

spoiled *adj* **1** *syn* DAMAGED, flawed, impaired, marred
ant unspoiled
2 *syn* BAD 5, decayed, putrid, rotten
rel off, tainted; putrefying, rotting
ant unspoiled

spoiler *n syn* MARAUDER, depredator, despoiler, pillager, plunderer, raider, ravager, ravisher, sacker, spoliator

spoken *adj* **1** *syn* ORAL 2, traditional, unwritten, verbal, word-of-mouth
ant written
2 *syn* VOCAL 1, articulate, oral, sonant, viva voce, voiced
ant unspoken

spokesman *n* one who speaks as a representative of another <selected as *spokesman* for the party's views>
syn mouth, mouthpiece, speaker, spokesperson, spokeswoman
rel delegate, deputy, representative; champion, protagonist; prophet

spokesperson *n syn* SPOKESMAN, mouth, mouthpiece, speaker, spokeswoman

spokeswoman *n syn* SPOKESMAN, mouth, mouthpiece, speaker, spokesperson

spoliate *vb syn* RAVAGE, depredate, desecrate, desolate, despoil, devastate, devour, pillage, sack, waste
rel raid; maraud; gut, ravish, sweep

spoliator *n syn* MARAUDER, despoiler, looter, pillager, plunderer, raider, ravager, ravisher, sacker, spoiler

sponge *n* **1** *syn* DRUNKARD, bibber, ‖blotter, boozer, drunk, guzzler, inebriate, lush, sot, tippler
2 *syn* PARASITE, barnacle, bloodsucker, freeloader, hanger-on, leech, lounge lizard, ‖spiv, sponger, sucker

sponger *n syn* PARASITE, barnacle, bloodsucker, freeloader, hanger-on, leech, lounge lizard, ‖spiv, sponge, sucker

spongy *adj syn* SOFT 6, mushy, pappy, pulpous, pulpy, quaggy, squashy, squelchy, squishy, yielding
idiom as soft as a sponge

sponsor *n* one that accepts responsibility for another person or thing <the major *sponsor* of this project is the government>
syn angel, backer, backer-up, guarantor, patron, surety
rel advocate, champion, mainstay, supporter, upholder; preferrer, promoter; benefactor, Maecenas

---

syn synonym(s) *rel* related word(s)
idiom idiomatic equivalent(s) *con* contrasted word(s)
ant antonym(s) * vulgar
‖ use limited; if in doubt, see a dictionary
The first word in a synonym list when printed in SMALL CAPITALS shows where there is more information about the group. For a more efficient use of this book see Explanatory Notes.

sponsorship *n syn* BACKING, aegis, auspices, patronage

spontaneity *n syn* UNCONSTRAINT, abandon, ease, naturalness, unrestraint
rel extemporaneousness, offhandedness, unpremeditatedness

spontaneous *adj* acting or activated without apparent thought or deliberation <a *spontaneous* burst of applause>
syn automatic, impulsive, instinctive, involuntary, unmeditated, unpremeditated, unprompted, will-less
rel unconstrained, unforced; unreasoned, unstudied; extemporaneous, extempore, impromptu, improvised, offhand; natural, simple, unsophisticated
con deliberate, intended, intentional, planned, predetermined, preplanned, studied, thought-out, voluntary, willed, willful; forced, prompted; conventional, formal, stylized
ant premeditated

spontoon *n syn* CUDGEL, bat, baton, billy, billy club, bludgeon, club, mace, nightstick, truncheon

spoof *vb syn* DUPE, bamboozle, befool, chicane, flimflam, fool, hoax, hoodwink, hornswoggle, trick

spoof *n syn* IMPOSTURE, cheat, deceit, deception, fake, flimflam, phony, put-on, sell, sham

spook *n* ‖**1** *syn* APPARITION, bogey, eidolon, ghost, ‖haunt, phantom, shade, shadow, specter, spirit
‖**2** *syn* ECCENTRIC, case, character, ‖duck, oddball, oddity, original, quiz, ‖wack, zombie
3 *syn* SPY, agent, undercover man

‖**spook** *vb* **1** *syn* FRIGHTEN, affright, alarm, awe, fright, scare, startle, terrify, terrorize
2 *syn* GHOSTWRITE, ghost

spooky *adj* **1** *syn* WEIRD 1, eerie, uncanny, unearthly
rel spookish; ominous
2 *syn* NERVOUS, fidgety, goosey, high-strung, jittery, jumpy, nervy, twittery, unrestful

‖**spoon** *n syn* DUNCE, blockhead, ‖cluck, dimwit, dope, ‖goon, ignoramus, moron, numskull, simpleton

spoony *adj syn* SIMPLE 3, ‖buffle-headed, fatuous, foolish, sheepheaded, silly, unwitty, weak-headed, weak-minded, witless

spoony (over *or* on) *adj syn* ENAMORED 1, mashed, smitten, soft (on)

spoor *n syn* FOOTPRINT, footstep, step, track, tract, vestige

sporadic *adj* **1** *syn* FITFUL, catchy, desultory, on-again-off-again, spasmodic, spotty
ant regular
2 *syn* INFREQUENT, few, occasional, rare, scarce, seldom, semioccasional, uncommon, unfrequent
rel separate, single
ant frequent

sporadically *adv syn* OCCASIONALLY, infrequently, irregularly, on occasion, uncommonly
ant regularly

sport *vb syn* PLAY 1, disport, recreate

sport *n* **1** *syn* PLAY 1, disport, diversion, fun, recreation
2 sports *pl syn* ATHLETICS, games
3 *syn* FUN 1, game, jest, joke, play
rel jollification; antics, high jinks, horseplay
4 *syn* LAUGHINGSTOCK, butt, derision, jest, jestee, joke, mock, mockery, pilgarlic
5 *syn* CHANGE 2, innovation, mutation, novelty, permutation, vicissitude

sporting girl *n syn* PROSTITUTE, call girl, ‖cruiser, fille de joie, harlot, ‖hooker, hustler, nightwalker, party girl, pom-pom girl

sporting house *n syn* BROTHEL, bawdy house, bordello, call house, cathouse, disorderly house, ‖joyhouse, parlor house, seraglio, whorehouse

sportive *adj syn* PLAYFUL 1, antic, frisky, frolicsome, gamesome, impish, larkish, mischievous, roguish, waggish

sportiveness *n syn* MISCHIEVOUSNESS, devilment, devilry, deviltry, impishness, mischief, roguery, roguishness, waggery, waggishness

sportsmanlike *adj syn* FAIR 5, clean, sportsmanly
ant unsporting, unsportsmanlike

sportsmanly *adj syn* FAIR 5, clean, sportsmanlike
ant unsporting, unsportsmanlike

sporty *adj syn* WILD 7, devil-may-care, fast, gay, raffish, rakehell, rakish

spot *n* **1** *syn* STIGMA, bar sinister, black eye, blot, blur, brand, odium, onus, slur, stain
2 *syn* DRAM, dollop, drop, jolt, nip, shot, slug, snort, snorter, tot
3 *syn* PARTICLE, atom, doit, iota, jot, mite, molecule, smidgen, speck, whit
4 *syn* PLACE 1, location, locus, point, position, site, situation, station, where
rel scene; section, sector
5 *syn* JOB 2, appointment, berth, billet, connection, office, place, position, post, situation
idiom job slot
6 *syn* PREDICAMENT, box, corner, dilemma, fix, hole, jam, pickle, plight, scrape

spot *vb* **1** to mark or stain (something) with spots <a white dress *spotted* with red mud>
syn bespatter, bespot, spatter; *compare* SPECKLE 1
rel blot, blotch, mottle; fleck, marble, streak, stripe; dot, pepper, speck, speckle, sprinkle, stipple; splash; dirty, soil, stain
2 to form or appear as spots on <a bleak landscape *spotted* with cottages>
syn dot, pimple, speckle, sprinkle, stud
rel intersperse
3 *syn* IDENTIFY, determinate, diagnose, diagnosticate, distinguish, finger, pinpoint, place, recognize
rel ascertain; see
4 *syn* FIND 1, catch, descry, detect, encounter, espy, hit (on *or* upon), meet (with), turn up

spot *adj syn* RANDOM, aimless, designless, haphazard, hit-or-miss, irregular, slapdash, unaimed, unconsidered, unplanned

spotless *adj* **1** *syn* CLEAN 1, cleanly, immaculate, taintless, unsoiled, unsullied
rel hygienic, sanitary

---

syn synonym(s) — *rel* related word(s)
idiom idiomatic equivalent(s) — *con* contrasted word(s)
ant antonym(s) — * vulgar
‖ use limited; if in doubt, see a dictionary
The first word in a synonym list when printed in SMALL CAPITALS shows where there is more information about the group. For a more efficient use of this book see Explanatory Notes.

2 *syn* CHASTE, clean, decent, immaculate, modest, pure, stainless, unblemished, undefiled, unsullied
ant spotted

spotty *adj* **1** lacking uniformity <*spotty* illumination>
syn irregular, patchy, uneven
rel unequal; flickering, fluctuating
con equal, even, regular, uniform
2 *syn* FITFUL, catchy, desultory, on-again-off-again, spasmodic, sporadic

spousal *n syn* WEDDING, bridal, espousal(s), marriage, nuptial(s)

spousal *adj syn* MATRIMONIAL, conjugal, connubial, hymeneal, marital, married, nuptial, wedded

spouse *n* a marriage partner <consulted with her *spouse* before buying the dress>
syn consort, mate

spouseless *adj syn* SINGLE 1, sole, unmarried, unwed
con espoused

||**spout** *vb syn* PAWN, ||dip, hock, impignorate, mortgage, pledge, ||pop

spout *n syn* WATERFALL, cascade, cataract, chute, fall(s), ||force, sault

spraddle *vb syn* SPRAWL 1, drape, ||scamble, ||spelder, spread-eagle

sprain *vb* to injure (a joint) by a sudden twisting motion that stretches and lacerates the ligaments <*sprained* her ankle>
syn ||rick, turn, twist, wrench
rel pull, strain, stretch; tear; dislocate, throw; break, fracture

sprangle *vb syn* SPRAWL 2, ramble, scramble, spread-eagle, straddle, straggle

sprat *n syn* TWERP, pup, puppy, squirt, ||squit

||**sprauchle** *vb syn* SCRAMBLE 1, clamber, scrabble, ||spartle

sprawl *vb* **1** to lie or sit with arms and legs stretched out carelessly and awkwardly <the dog lay *sprawled* out on the sofa>
syn drape, ||scamble, ||spelder, spraddle, spread-eagle
rel loll, lounge; slouch, slump
2 to grow, develop, or spread irregularly and without apparent design or plan <the city *sprawls* down the whole coast>
syn ramble, scramble, sprangle, spread-eagle, straddle, straggle
rel extend, stretch; spread

spread *vb* **1** to extend or cause to extend over a considerable area or space <they *spread* the news far and wide> <clouds *spread* over the sky>
syn circulate, diffuse, disperse, disseminate, distribute, propagate, radiate, strew; *compare* STREW 1
rel deal, dispense; broadcast, communicate, pass (on), transmit; dissipate, scatter, sow; peddle, push, retail
idiom spread abroad (*or* far and wide)
con hold (in); contain; compress
2 *syn* OPEN 4, expand, extend, fan (out), outspread, outstretch, unfold
con fold; close
3 *syn* SET 5, lay

spread *n* **1** *syn* EXPANSION 2, enlargement, extension
rel diffusion; profusion; stretch, sweep
2 *syn* EXPANSE, amplitude, breadth, distance, expansion, space, stretch
3 *syn* DINNER, banquet, feast, regale
4 *syn* BEDSPREAD, bedcover, counterpane, coverlet, ||coverlid

spread–eagle *vb* **1** *syn* SPRAWL 1, drape, ||scamble, ||spelder, spraddle
2 *syn* SPRAWL 2, ramble, scramble, sprangle, straddle, straggle

||**spreaghery** *n syn* SPOIL, boodle, booty, loot, plunder, plunderage, prize, ||spulzie, swag

spree *n* **1** an unrestrained indulgence in or outburst of an activity <a shopping *spree*>
syn binge, fling, orgy, rampage, splurge
2 *syn* BINGE 1, bat, bender, bust, carousal, carouse, jag, ran-tan, tear, wassail

spree *vb syn* REVEL 1, carouse, frolic, hell, riot, roister, wassail

sprightful *adj syn* LIVELY 1, alert, animate, animated, dashing, rousing, spirited, ||spirity, sprightly, vivacious

sprightly *adj* **1** *syn* LIVELY 1, alert, animate, animated, ||canty, gay, keen, spirited, unpedantic, vivacious
rel perky; breezy
2 *syn* ANTIC 2, frolicsome, playful, rollicking
rel sportive; coltish, frisky
3 *syn* AGILE, active, brisk, brisky, lively, nimble, spry, volant, yare, zippy
4 *syn* CLEVER 5, good, scintillating, smart
rel pungent, sharp; keen-witted, quick-witted

spring *vb* **1** to have something as a source <the primitive cultures from which civilization *springs*>
syn arise, birth, come (from), derive (from), emanate, flow, head, issue, originate, proceed, rise, stem, upspring; *compare* BEGIN 2
rel appear, emerge, come out, loom; arrive, come; begin, commence, hatch, start
2 *syn* SKIP 1, hop, lope, skitter, trip
3 *syn* JUMP 1, bounce, bound, hop, hurdle, leap, lop, saltate, vault
4 *syn* START 1, bolt, jump, startle
||**5** *syn* FREE, discharge, emancipate, liberate, loose, manumit, release, unbind, unchain, unshackle

spring *n* **1** *usu* **springs** *pl syn* SPA 1, baths, ||hydro, watering place, wells
2 *syn* SOURCE, fount, fountain, fountainhead, origin, root, well, wellhead, wellspring, whence
3 *syn* YOUTH 1, adolescence, greenness, juvenility, puberty, pubescence, springtide, springtime, youthfulness, youthhood
ant autumn
4 *syn* MOTIVE 1, cause, consideration, reason
rel excitant, impetus, incitement, stimulant, stimulus
5 the season between winter and summer <planting flowers in the *spring*>
syn budtime, springtide, springtime
rel ||blackberry winter

---

idiom prime of the year
con autumn, fall

spring *adj* ***syn*** VERNAL, springlike

springe *n* ***syn*** PITFALL, booby trap, deadfall, mousetrap, trapfall

springlike *adj* ***syn*** VERNAL, spring

springtide *n* **1** ***syn*** SPRING 5, budtime, springtime
2 ***syn*** YOUTH 1, adolescence, greenness, juvenility, puberty, pubescence, spring, springtime, youthfulness, youthhood
ant autumn

springtime *n* **1** ***syn*** SPRING 5, budtime, springtide
2 ***syn*** YOUTH 1, adolescence, greenness, juvenility, puberty, pubescence, spring, springtide, youthfulness, youthhood
ant autumn

springy *adj* ***syn*** ELASTIC 1, flexible, resilient, stretch, stretchy, supple, whippy
rel rebounding, recoiling
ant rigid; springless

sprinkle *vb* **1** to scatter (something) in small drops or particles <*sprinkle* chocolate shot on whipped cream>
syn besprinkle, dust, powder, ||strinkle; *compare* STREW 1
rel shake; scatter; pepper; sparge
2 ***syn*** SPECKLE 1, bespeckle, dot, freckle, pepper, speck, stipple
3 ***syn*** SPOT 2, dot, pimple, speckle, stud
4 ***syn*** BAPTIZE, asperse, christen, immerse
5 to rain lightly <it's only *sprinkling*, so we can still take our walk>
syn drizzle, ||mizzle
rel mist; shower; spit
con pour, stream

sprinkling *n* **1** ***syn*** HINT 2, dash, lick, spice, strain, streak, taste, tinge, touch, trace
2 ***syn*** DUSTING, dust, powdering
3 ***syn*** FEW, handful, scattering, smatch, smatter, smattering, spatter, spattering

sprint *vb* ***syn*** RUN 1, dash, scamper, scoot, scurry, shin

sprit *vb* ***syn*** SQUIRT, jet, splurt, ||spritz, spurt, ||squitter

sprite *n* ***syn*** FAIRY, brownie, elf, fay, nisse, pixie

||**spritz** *vb* ***syn*** SQUIRT, jet, splurt, sprit, spurt, ||squitter

spruce *adj* ***syn*** DAPPER, bandbox, doggish, doggy, natty, sassy, sparkish, spiffy, sprucy, well-groomed
ant slouchy

spruce (up) *vb* ***syn*** DRESS UP 1, deck (out), doll out, doll up, ||dude up, fix up, gussy up, slick, smarten (up), spiff

sprucy *adj* ***syn*** DAPPER, bandbox, doggish, doggy, natty, sassy, sparkish, spiffy, spruce, well-groomed

spry *adj* ***syn*** AGILE, active, brisk, brisky, lively, nimble, sprightly, volant, yare, zippy

---

syn synonym(s) — ***rel*** related word(s)
idiom idiomatic equivalent(s) — ***con*** contrasted word(s)
ant antonym(s) — * vulgar
|| use limited; if in doubt, see a dictionary
The first word in a synonym list when printed in SMALL CAPITALS shows where there is more information about the group. For a more efficient use of this book see Explanatory Notes.

rel prompt, quick, ready; energetic, vigorous; healthy, robust, sound
ant doddering

spuddy *adj* ***syn*** ROTUND 2, chubby, plump, plumpish, plumpy, podgy, puddy, pudgy, roly-poly, tubby

||**spulzie** *n* ***syn*** SPOIL, boodle, booty, loot, plunder, plunderage, prize, ||spreaghery, swag

spume *n* ***syn*** FOAM, froth, lather, suds, yeast

spunk *n* **1** ***syn*** FORTITUDE, backbone, grit, guts, intestinal fortitude, ||moxie, nerve, sand
rel bulldoggedness, doggedness
idiom clear (*or* true) grit
ant funk
2 ***syn*** COURAGE, cojones, dauntlessness, guts, heart, mettle, ||moxie, pluck, resolution, spirit

spunkless *adj* ***syn*** COWARDLY, ||chicken, coward, craven, gutless, lily-livered, poltroon, poltroonish, pusillanimous, unmanly
ant spunky

spunky *adj* **1** ***syn*** BRAVE 1, bold, courageous, dauntless, doughty, fearless, ||gutsy, plucky, undauntable, unfearing
idiom full of spunk
ant spunkless; funky
2 ***syn*** SPIRITED 2, beany, fiery, gingery, high-hearted, high-spirited, mettlesome, peppery
ant funky

spur *n* ***syn*** STIMULUS, catalyst, goad, impetus, impulse, incentive, incitation, incitement, motivation, stimulant
rel excitant; activation, actuation
ant checkrein, curb

spur *vb* ***syn*** URGE, egg (on), exhort, goad, prick, prod, prompt, propel, sic
rel rowel; arouse, awaken, rally, rouse, stir; instigate; countenance, favor
ant curb

spurious *adj* **1** ***syn*** ILLEGITIMATE 1, baseborn, bastard, fatherless, misbegotten, natural, supposititious, unfathered
2 ***syn*** ARTIFICIAL 2, dummy, ersatz, false, imitation, mock, sham, simulated, substitute
3 of doubtful authenticity <claimed they had bought a *spurious* painting>
syn apocryphal, bastard, unauthentic, ungenuine; *compare* ARTIFICIAL 2, COUNTERFEIT
rel bogus, counterfeit, fake, phony, pseudo, sham; false, unreal
idiom not what (*or* all) it's cracked up to be
con actual, real, true; bona fide, genuine, veritable
ant authentic
4 ***syn*** ARTIFICIAL 3, affected, assumed, feigned, put-on
rel make-believe, pretend, pretended, pseudo
5 ***syn*** COUNTERFEIT, bogus, brummagem, fake, false, phony, pinchbeck, pseudo, sham, snide

spuriousness *n* ***syn*** FALLACY 2, casuistry, deception, deceptiveness, delusion, equivocation, sophism, sophistry, speciousness

spurn *vb* ***syn*** DECLINE 4, disapprove, dismiss, refuse, reject, reprobate, repudiate, turn down
rel conspue, contemn, despise, disdain, scorn, scout; flout, scoff, sneer
con crave, desire, want
ant embrace

spur–of–the–moment *adj* *syn* EXTEMPORANEOUS, autoschediastic, extemporary, extempore, impromptu, improvised, offhand, unrehearsed, unstudied

spurt *vb* *syn* SQUIRT, jet, splurt, sprit, ‖spritz, ‖squitter

spurtle *vb* *syn* SPLASH, douse, plash, slop, slosh, spatter, splatter, splosh, splurge, swash

sputter *vb* **1** to utter (words or ejaculations) hastily, explosively, and sometimes indistinctly <pompously *sputtering* his objections>
syn rip (out), spit, splutter
rel ejaculate, eject, throw (out); gibber, jabber; bluster, heckle, hector, rage, rant, rave, storm
2 to make a series of sudden short crackling or popping sounds <bacon *sputtering* in the pan>
syn spatter, spit, splutter
rel crackle, pop; hiss

spy (on *or* upon) *vb* to make furtive, stealthy, or secret observations of <had private detectives *spying* on his wife>
syn ‖stag
rel stake out; watch

spy *n* one who keeps secret watch to obtain information <was convicted on evidence produced by a *spy*>
syn agent, spook, undercover man; *compare* INFORMER
rel detective, investigator, sleuth; scout; beagle
idiom inside man, secret agent

spying *n* *syn* ESPIONAGE

squab *adj* *syn* STOCKY, ‖chuffy, ‖chumpy, dumpy, squdgy, stubby, ‖stuggy, stumpy, thick, thickset

‖**squab** *vb* *syn* PRESS 1, bear, crowd, crush, jam, push, squash, squeeze, squish, squush

squab *vb* *syn* SPILL 1, slop

squabble *n* *syn* QUARREL, altercation, beef, bickering, controversy, dispute, fight, hassle, row, tiff

squabble *vb* **1** *syn* QUARREL, bicker, brabble, caterwaul, fall out, row, scrap, spat, tiff, wrangle
rel clash, encounter
idiom have a squabble over
2 *syn* ARGUE 2, argufy, bicker, dispute, hassle, quibble, wrangle
idiom get into (*or* have) a hassle, have a verbal wrestling match

squalid *adj* **1** *syn* DIRTY 1, black, filthy, foul, grubby, impure, nasty, soily, unclean, uncleanly
rel disheveled, slipshod, sloppy, slovenly, unkempt; frowzy, slatternly; dingy, shoddy, sleazy
2 *syn* SHABBY 1, broken-down, dilapidated, dingy, disreputable, run-down, scrubby, seedy, shoddy, sleazy
3 *syn* BASE 3, despicable, ignoble, low, low-down, mean, scurvy, ugly, vile, wretched

squall *vb* **1** to make a raucous noise <angry street urchins fighting and *squalling* at each other>
syn caw, ‖quawk, squark, squawk, yawp (*or* yaup)
rel bellow, howl, roar, shout, yell; bark, yap, yip; croak
2 *syn* BAWL 2, howl, wail, yowl
rel squeal; screech, shriek; yelp

squall *n* *syn* QUARREL, altercation, beef, bickering, brawl, dispute, falling-out, feud, fight, hassle

squander *vb* *syn* WASTE 2, blow, consume, dissipate, fool (away), fritter, frivol away, prodigalize, throw away, trifle (away)
idiom make ducks and drakes of, play ducks and drakes with

squander *n* *syn* EXTRAVAGANCE 2, extravagancy, lavishness, overdoing, prodigality, unthrift, waste, wastefulness

squanderer *n* *syn* SPENDTHRIFT, high roller, prodigal, profligate, scattergood, spender, unthrift, waster, wastethrift, wastrel

square *n* **1** *syn* COMMON 2, green, plaza
2 *syn* FOGY, antediluvian, fogram, fossil, fuddy-duddy, mid-Victorian, mossback, stick-in-the-mud

square *adj* **1** having four equal sides and four right angles <a large *square* Georgian mansion>
syn foursquare, quadrate, quadratic, quadratical
rel boxlike, boxy, squarish
2 *syn* EVEN 5, exact
3 *syn* FAIR 4, equal, equitable, impartial, impersonal, just, nonpartisan, objective, unbiased, unprejudiced
4 *syn* CONVENTIONAL 1, button-down, orthodox, straight

square *vb* **1** *syn* ADAPT, accommodate, adjust, conform, fit, quadrate, reconcile, suit, tailor, tailor-make
2 *syn* CLEAR 5, clear off, discharge, liquidate, pay, pay up, quit, satisfy, settle
3 *syn* BRIBE, buy, buy off, fix, have, ‖lubricate, sop, tamper (with)
4 *syn* AGREE 4, accord, check out, conform, correspond, dovetail, fit (in), ‖gee, harmonize, jibe
rel balance; coincide

square *adv* *syn* JUST 1, accurately, bang, exactly, precisely, right, sharp, ‖smack-dab, spang, squarely

squarehead *n* *syn* DUNCE, blockhead, bonehead, chowderhead, chucklehead, dolt, dope, dumbbell, fathead, knucklehead

squarely *adv* **1** *syn* EVENLY 1, equally, fifty-fifty
2 *syn* JUST 1, accurately, bang, exactly, precisely, right, sharp, ‖smack-dab, spang, square

squark *vb* *syn* SQUALL 1, caw, ‖quawk, squawk, yawp (*or* yaup)

squash *vb* **1** *syn* PRESS 1, bear, crowd, crush, jam, push, ‖squab, squeeze, squish, squush
2 *syn* CRUSH 2, becrush, bruise, mash, ‖mush (up), pulp
3 *syn* CRUSH 5, annihilate, extinguish, put down, quash, quell, quench, suppress
4 *syn* PRESS 7, cram, crowd, crush, jam, squeeze

squash *n* **1** *syn* SQUELCH, squidge, squish
2 *syn* CROWD 1, crush, drove, horde, multitude, press, push, throng

squashing *n* *syn* REPRESSION 1, choking, extinguishment, quashing, quenching, smothering, squelching, stifling, strangling, suppression

squashy *adj* *syn* SOFT 6, mushy, pappy, pulpy, quaggy, spongy, squelchy, squishy, squushy, yielding

---

syn synonym(s) *rel* related word(s)
idiom idiomatic equivalent(s) *con* contrasted word(s)
ant antonym(s) * vulgar
‖ use limited; if in doubt, see a dictionary
The first word in a synonym list when printed in SMALL CAPITALS shows where there is more information about the group. For a more efficient use of this book see Explanatory Notes.

ant firm

squat *vb* to sit on one's haunches <they were *squatting* around the fire>
syn hunker (down), ‖quat, ‖swat; *compare* CROUCH
rel crouch; hunch; stoop

squat *adj* ***syn*** STOCKY, chunky, dumpy, heavyset, squdgy, stubby, ‖stuggy, thick, thick-bodied, thickset
rel squattish, squatty
con long, tall; twiggy
ant lanky

‖squaw *n* ***syn*** WIFE, ‖ball and chain, lady, ‖little woman, ‖missus, Mrs., ‖old lady, ‖old woman, ‖rib, woman

squawk *vb* **1** ***syn*** SQUALL 1, caw, ‖quawk, squark, yawp (*or* yaup)
2 ***syn*** GRIPE, ‖beef, ‖bellyache, ‖bitch, bleat, crab, ‖crib, fuss, yammer yawp (*or* yaup)
rel yap, yip

squawker *n* ***syn*** INFORMER, betrayer, ‖canary, ‖fink, ‖nark, snitch, squealer, stool, stool pigeon, tipster

squawky *adj* ***syn*** HARSH 3, dry, grating, hoarse, jarring, rasping, raucous, rough, rusty, strident
con liquid, mellow, smooth

squdgy *adj* ***syn*** STOCKY, ‖chumpy, chunky, dumpy, squat, stubby, ‖stuggy, stumpy, thick-bodied, thickset

squeak *vb* **1** to utter or make a short shrill cry or noise <mice *squeaking* in the barn>
syn ‖queak; *compare* SQUEAL 2
rel creak, grate, screak, screech, squeal; pipe; scream
2 ***syn*** TALK 6, sing, squeal
3 ***syn*** INFORM 3, ‖nark, peach, ‖pimp, rat, ‖sing, snitch, squeal, ‖stool

squeak *n* ***syn*** OPPORTUNITY, break, change, look-in, occasion, opening, shot, show, time

‖squeaker *n* ***syn*** INFORMER, betrayer, ‖canary, ‖fink, ‖nark, snitch, squealer, stoolie, stool pigeon, tipster

squeal *vb* **1** ***syn*** SCREAM 1, screech, shriek, shrill
idiom squeal like a stuck pig
2 to make a harsh piercing sometimes rasping noise <tires *squealing* on wet pavement>
syn screak, scream, screech, shriek; *compare* SQUEAK 1
rel creak, grate, rasp
3 ***syn*** INFORM 3, ‖nark, peach, ‖pimp, rat, ‖sing, snitch, squeak, ‖stool
4 ***syn*** TALK 6, sing, squeak
5 ***syn*** YELL 2, howl, scream, yip, yowl
rel bitch, bleat, complain, gripe, squawk
idiom raise a howl, scream bloody murder

squealer *n* ***syn*** INFORMER, betrayer, ‖canary, ‖fink, ‖nark, snitch, ‖squeaker, stool pigeon, talebearer, tipster

squeam *n* ***syn*** QUALM, compunction, conscience, demur, scruple

squeamish *adj* **1** inclined to become nauseated <felt *squeamish* after the heavy meal on the ship>
syn ‖pensy, qualmish, qualmy, queasy, queer, ‖wambly; *compare* NAUSEATED
rel unsettled, upset; dizzy, shaky, vertiginous
2 ***syn*** NAUSEATED, nauseous
idiom sick at (*or* to) one's stomach
3 ***syn*** NICE 1, dainty, fastidious, finical, finicking, finicky, fussy, particular, pernickety, persnickety

squeamishness *n* ***syn*** NAUSEA, qualmishness, queasiness

squeamy *adj* ***syn*** NICE 1, choosy, dainty, delicate, fastidious, particular, picksome, picky, precious, squeamish

squeeze *vb* **1** ***syn*** PRESS 1, bear, crowd, crush, jam, push, ‖squab, squash, squish, squush
rel contract, ‖scruze
2 ***syn*** EMBRACE 1, clasp, ‖clinch, ‖clip, ‖coll, enfold, hug, press
3 ***syn*** EXTORT 1, exact, gouge, pinch, screw, shake down, wrench, wrest, wring
4 ***syn*** EKE OUT 2, extract, scratch, wring
5 ***syn*** PRESS 8, bear
6 ***syn*** PRESS 7, cram, crowd, crush, jam, squash

squeezy *adj* ***syn*** CRAMPED, confined, cramp, incommodious, ‖tucked up

squelch *n* a sound of or as if of semiliquid matter under suction <the *squelch* of his feet in the mud>
syn squash, squidge, squish

squelch *vb* ***syn*** SUPPRESS 2, muffle, ‖quelch, repress, shush, strangle

squelching *n* ***syn*** REPRESSION 1, choking, extinguishment, quashing, quenching, smothering, squashing, stifling, strangling, suppression

squelchy *adj* ***syn*** SOFT 6, mushy, pappy, pulpy, quaggy, spongy, squashy, squishy, squushy, yielding

‖squench *vb* **1** ***syn*** EXTINGUISH 1, douse, ‖dout, out, put out, quench
2 ***syn*** QUENCH 4, slake

squidge *n* ***syn*** SQUELCH, squash, squish

squiffed *adj* ***syn*** INTOXICATED 1, ‖boozy, ‖canned, disguised, drunk, inebriated, ‖lushed, muddled, pixilated, ‖plastered

squiggle *vb* **1** ***syn*** WRIGGLE, squirm, wiggle, worm, writhe
2 ***syn*** SCRIBBLE, scrabble, scratch, scrawl

squinch *vb* **1** ***syn*** RECOIL, blanch, blench, flinch, quail, shrink, start, wince
2 ***syn*** SQUINT, ‖sken, squinny

squinny *vb* ***syn*** SQUINT, ‖sken, squinch

squinny *adj* ***syn*** THIN 1, attenuate, reedy, slender, slight, slim, stalky, tenuous, twiggy

squint *vb* to look or peer with the eyes partly closed <*squinted* in the bright sunlight>
syn ‖sken, squinch, squinny
idiom look asquint, screw up one's eyes
ant goggle

squirm *vb* **1** ***syn*** WRIGGLE, squiggle, wiggle, worm, writhe
2 ***syn*** WRITHE 1, agonize, toss

squirrel *vb* ***syn*** HOARD, stash

squirt *vb* to come forth in a sudden rapid usually narrow stream <water *squirting* from the hose>
syn jet, splurt, sprit, ‖spritz, spurt, ‖squitter
rel pour, stream, surge; spatter; spray

---

syn synonym(s) — ***rel*** related word(s)
idiom idiomatic equivalent(s) — ***con*** contrasted word(s)
ant antonym(s) — * vulgar
‖ use limited; if in doubt, see a dictionary
The first word in a synonym list when printed in SMALL CAPITALS shows where there is more information about the group. For a more efficient use of this book see Explanatory Notes.

con dribble, drip, trickle

squirt *n* ||**1 squirts** *pl* ***syn*** DIARRHEA, ||backdoor trots, dysentery, flux, ||runs, scour(s), *shits, *trots

2 ***syn*** TWERP, pup, puppy, sprat, ||squit

squish *n* **1** ***syn*** PRESS 1, bear, crowd, crush, jam, push, ||squab, squash, squeeze, squush

2 ***syn*** SQUELCH, squash, squidge

squishy *adj* ***syn*** SOFT 6, mushy, pulpous, pulpy, quaggy, spongy, squashy, squelchy, squushy, yielding

||**squit** *n* ***syn*** TWERP, pup, puppy, sprat, squirt

||**squitter** *vb* ***syn*** SQUIRT, jet, splurt, sprit, ||spritz, spurt

squush *vb* ***syn*** PRESS 1, bear, crowd, crush, jam, push, ||squab, squash, squeeze, squish

squushy *adj* ***syn*** SOFT 6, mushy, pappy, pulpy, quaggy, spongy, squashy, squelchy, squishy, yielding

stab *n* **1** ***syn*** PRICK 1, jab, ||jag, puncture

2 ***syn*** POKE 1, dig, jab, punch

3 ***syn*** FLING 1, crack, go, pop, shot, slap, ||stagger, try, whack, whirl

stab *vb* ***syn*** THRUST 2, dig, drive, plunge, ram, run, sink, stick

rel dagger, dirk, poniard, prong

stabbing *adj* ***syn*** SHARP 8, acute, knifelike, piercing, shooting

stabile *adj* ***syn*** STEADY 2, constant, equable, even, stable, unchanging, unfluctuating, uniform, unvarying

stabilify *vb* ***syn*** STABILIZE, ballast, poise, stabilitate, steady

stabilitate *vb* ***syn*** STABILIZE, ballast, poise, stabilify, steady

stability *n* the ability to withstand force or stress without alteration of position and without material change <the structural *stability* of the bridge>

syn firmness, security, soundness, stableness, steadiness, strength

rel dependability, durability, reliability; solidity, solidness, sturdiness; cohesion, toughness

con insecurity, undependability, unreliability, unsoundness, unsteadiness; weakness

ant instability, unstability

stabilize *vb* to make or keep stable, steadfast, or firm <a policy that *stabilized* the economy>

syn ballast, poise, stabilify, stabilitate, steady

rel balance, counterbalance, counterpoise, equalize, equipoise; prop, support, sustain; fix, secure, set, settle

ant unstabilize

stable *adj* **1** ***syn*** SURE 1, fast, firm, secure, staunch, strong

rel balanced, poised; fixed, set, solid, sound, steadfast

con wobbling, wobbly

ant instable, unstable

2 ***syn*** STEADY 2, constant, equable, even, stabile, unchanging, unfluctuating, uniform, unvarying

3 ***syn*** LASTING, diuturnal, durable, enduring, perdurable, perduring, permanent

rel constant, steady; safe, secure, sound; staunch, steadfast, resolute

4 marked by solidity, firmness, and stability especially in design or construction <a *stable* foundation for the building>

syn firm, secure, solid, sound; *compare* FAST 4, SURE 1

rel strong, sturdy; unassailable, unshakable

idiom as firm as (the rock of) Gibraltar, solid as a rock

con insecure, shaky, unsound, weak, wobbling, wobbly

ant instable, unstable

stableness *n* ***syn*** STABILITY, firmness, security, soundness, steadiness, strength

ant unstableness

stack *n* ***syn*** PILE 1, bank, ||bing, cock, drift, heap, hill, mass, mound, pyramid

stack *vb* ***syn*** HEAP 1, bank, cock, drift, hill, mound, pile

||**stacked** *adj* ***syn*** CURVACEOUS, ||built, curvesome, curvilinear, curvy, Junoesque, rounded, well-developed

stade *n* ***syn*** STADIUM, bowl, coliseum

stadium *n* a large usually unroofed structure with tiered seats enclosing a field used especially for sports <a football *stadium*>

syn bowl, coliseum, stade

rel arena, garden, gymnasium

||**stag** *vb* ***syn*** SPY (on *or* upon)

stage *n* **1** *used with* the ***syn*** DRAMA, boards, footlights, theater

2 ***syn*** DEGREE 1, grade, notch, rung, step

rel level; phase; period

stage *vb* to present on the stage <*staged* a play>

syn mount, produce, put on, show

rel bring out, open; give, present; do, execute, perform, play

stage set *n* ***syn*** SCENE 1, mise-en-scène, scenery, set, setting, stage setting

stage setting *n* ***syn*** SCENE 1, mise-en-scène, scenery, set, setting, stage set

stagger *vb* **1** ***syn*** REEL 2, titubate, totter, wheel

2 ***syn*** LURCH 2, careen, ||stoit, ||stoiter, ||stot, sway, swing, weave, wobble

idiom pitch and plunge

3 ***syn*** TEETER, falter, lurch, ||stammer, stumble, topple, totter, wobble

rel ||stiver, ||stoit, ||stoiter, ||stot

4 ***syn*** HESITATE, dither, falter, halt, shilly-shally, vacillate, waver, whiffle, wiggle-waggle

5 to affect with great wonder or bewilderment <a plot so bizarre as to *stagger* the imagination>

syn boggle, dumbfound, nonplus

rel perplex, puzzle, stump; amaze, astonish, astound, flabbergast; bowl (over), floor, knock over; devastate, overpower, overwhelm, shatter; paralyze

idiom take (one) aback

stagger (on *or* along) *vb* ***syn*** SHIFT 5, do, fare, get along, get by, get on, ||make out, manage, muddle through

||**stagger** *n* ***syn*** FLING 1, crack, go, pop, shot, slap, stab, try, whack, whirl

staggering *adj* ***syn*** MARVELOUS 1, amazing, astonishing, astounding, miraculous, spectacular, strange, surprising, wonderful, wondrous

---

stagnant *adj* ***syn*** STATIC, immobile, stationary, unmoving

stagnate *vb* **1** ***syn*** VEGETATE
2 ***syn*** STULTIFY, constipate, stifle, trammel

stagnation *n* ***syn*** DEPRESSION 3, recession, slump

staid *adj* ***syn*** SERIOUS 1, earnest, grave, no-nonsense, sedate, sober, sobersided, solemn, somber, weighty
rel decorous, formal; collected, composed, cool; priggish, smug; starchy, stuffy
con breezy, devil-may-care, easy, frivolous; debonair, jaunty; playful, sportive; hoydenish, rakish; fresh, irreverent; uncontrolled, unrestrained
ant unstaid

stain *vb* **1** to soil often permanently with foreign matter <a shirt *stained* with grease>
syn bestain, blot, discolor, smut; *compare* SOIL 2
rel tinge; bedaub, daub, smear; besmirch, smirch, smudge, smutch
2 ***syn*** TAINT 1, besmear, besmirch, defile, discolor, smear, soil, sully, tar, tarnish
3 ***syn*** DEBASE 1, animalize, bastardize, bestialize, brutalize, corrupt, debauch, demoralize, deprave, pervert

stain *n* **1** ***syn*** STIGMA, bar sinister, black eye, blot, blur, brand, odium, onus, slur, spot
rel blemish, defect, flaw
idiom blot on the escutcheon
2 ***syn*** COLOR 6, colorant, dye, dyestuff, pigment, tincture

stainless *adj* ***syn*** CHASTE, clean, decent, immaculate, modest, pure, spotless, unblemished, undefiled, unsullied
con tainted, tarnished
ant stained

stake *n* **1** ***syn*** BET, ante, pot, wager
2 ***syn*** INTEREST 1, claim, share

stake *vb* **1** ***syn*** GAMBLE 1, bet, game, lay, play, put (on), set, wager
rel stake down
2 ***syn*** CAPITALIZE, back, bankroll, finance, grubstake

stale *adj* **1** ***syn*** MALODOROUS 1, fetid, fusty, musty, noisome, rank, reeking, smelly, stenchy, stinking
2 ***syn*** TRITE, cliché, clichéd, commonplace, hackneyed, shopworn, stereotyped, threadbare, timeworn, tired
rel dusty, fusty; dead
ant fresh

‖**stale** *n* ***syn*** LURE 2, allurement, bait, come-on, decoy, enticement, seducement, snare, temptation, trap

stalemate *n* ***syn*** DRAW 4, deadlock, dogfall, standoff, tie

stalk *vb* **1** to pursue (game) stealthily or under cover <*stalk* deer>
syn still-hunt
rel follow, track; drive, chase, pursue; walk up; flush (out); ambush
2 ***syn*** STRIDE 1, march, sling, ‖striddle

stalky *adj* ***syn*** THIN 1, attenuate, reedy, slender, slight, slim, squinny, tenuous, twiggy

stall *vb* ‖**1** ***syn*** SATIATE, cloy, fill, glut, gorge, jade, pall, sate, stodge, surfeit
2 ***syn*** ARREST 1, check, halt, interrupt, stay
rel brake, slow (down); hold off, put off, stand off; suspend; shut down
idiom pull the checkstring
con spur

stalwart *adj* **1** ***syn*** STRONG 2, stout, sturdy, tenacious, tough
rel athletic, brawny, husky, muscular, sinewy
2 ***syn*** BRAVE 1, bold, courageous, dauntless, fearless, intrepid, unafraid, undaunted, valiant, valorous

stamina *n* ***syn*** TOLERANCE 1, endurance, toleration

stammer *vb* **1** to make involuntary stops and repetitions in uttering syllables and words <the frightened child *stammered* and fell silent>
syn ‖hammer, ‖stut, stutter
rel falter, hesitate; stumble; splutter, sputter; gibber, jabber
‖**2** ***syn*** TEETER, falter, lurch, stagger, stumble, topple, totter, wobble

stamp *vb* **1** ***syn*** TRAMPLE 2, stomp, tramp, tromp
rel clomp, clump, stump
2 ***syn*** IMPRESS 3, drive, grave, hammer, pound
rel etch, imprint, infix, inscribe, print
idiom impress on the mind

stamp *n* **1** ***syn*** IMPRESSION 1, impress, imprint, indentation, print
2 ***syn*** TYPE, cast, character, description, ilk, kind, lot, mold, sort, stripe
3 ***syn*** SEAL, sticker

stampede *vb* **1** ***syn*** ROUT 1, derout
2 to take to sudden headlong flight in panic <cattle *stampeding* across the plain>
syn pell-mell; *compare* RUSH 1
rel bolt, charge, chase, crash, dash, fling, hurry, rush, shoot, tear
idiom run like a pack of scalded dogs

stamping ground *n* **1** ***syn*** HABITAT, haunt, home, locality, range, site
2 ***syn*** RESORT 2, hangout, haunt, purlieu, rendezvous, watering hole

stance *n* **1** ***syn*** POSTURE 1, attitude, carriage, pose, posture
2 ***syn*** POSITION 1, attitude, color, stand

stanch *vb* ***syn*** STEM, stop

stand *vb* **1** ***syn*** BEAR 10, abide, brook, endure, lump, stomach, suffer, swallow, take, tolerate
idiom ‖hack it, take lying down
2 ***syn*** TREAT 3, blow, set up, ‖shout

stand (on *or* upon) *vb* ***syn*** DEPEND (on *or* upon) 1, hang (on *or* upon), hinge (on *or* upon), ‖pend, turn (on *or* upon)
idiom be contingent on

stand *n* ***syn*** POSITION 1, attitude, color, stance

standard *n* **1** ***syn*** FLAG, banderole, banner, bannerol, color, ensign, jack, pennant, pennon, streamer
2 ***syn*** MODEL 2, archetype, beau ideal, ensample, example, exemplar, ideal, mirror, paradigm, pattern
3 a means of determining what a thing should be <each generation has its own *standards* of morality>

---

syn synonym(s)	***rel*** related word(s)
idiom idiomatic equivalent(s)	***con*** contrasted word(s)
ant antonym(s)	* vulgar

‖ use limited; if in doubt, see a dictionary

The first word in a synonym list when printed in SMALL CAPITALS shows where there is more information about the group. For a more efficient use of this book see Explanatory Notes.

syn benchmark, criterion, gauge, measure, touchstone, yardstick
rel average, mean, median, norm, par; axiom, belief, fundamental, principle; law, rule; exemplar, model, pattern
idiom rule of thumb
4 a fixed, customary, or official measure (as of quantity, quality, or price) <governmental *standards* of weights and measures>
syn assize
rel ‖dick

stander–by *n syn* SPECTATOR, by-sitter, bystander, eyewitness, looker-on, observer, onlooker, viewer, watcher, witness

stand–in *n syn* SUBSTITUTE, alternate, fill-in, locum tenens, pinch hitter, replacement, sub, succedaneum, surrogate
rel second; assistant

standing *n* **1** *syn* TERM 5, footing
2 *syn* STATUS 1, capacity, character, footing, place, position, rank, situation, state, station
3 *syn* STATUS 2, cachet, consequence, dignity, position, prestige, rank, state, stature

standoff *adj syn* UNSOCIABLE, aloof, distant, insociable, reserved, solitary, standoffish, touch-me-not-ish, uncompanionable, withdrawn

standoff *n syn* DRAW 4, deadlock, dogfall, stalemate, tie

standoffish *adj* **1** *syn* UNSOCIABLE, aloof, distant, insociable, reserved, solitary, standoff, touch-me-not-ish, uncompanionable, withdrawn
2 *syn* ANTISOCIAL, eremitic, misanthropic, reclusive, reserved, solitary

stand out *vb* **1** *syn* BULGE, beetle, jut, overhang, poke, pouch, pout, project, protrude, stick out
2 *syn* LOOM 3, bulk

standout *adj syn* SUPERB 3, magnificent, outstanding, superexcellent, superlative

stand over *vb syn* DEFER, delay, hold off, hold over, hold up, lay over, postpone, put off, shelve, stay

standpat *n syn* DIEHARD 1, bitter-ender, conservative, fundamentalist, old liner, right, rightist, right-winger, standpatter, tory

standpatter *n syn* DIEHARD 1, bitter-ender, conservative, fundamentalist, old liner, right, rightist, right-winger, standpat, tory

standpoint *n syn* VIEWPOINT 2, angle, direction, outlook, side, slant

standstill *n* cessation of movement <the car came to a *standstill* in the mud>
syn stay, stillstand, stop
rel arrest, check; pause; cessation, halt
con start; movement
ant start-up

stand up *vb syn* RISE 1, get up, uprise, upspring

stand–up *adj syn* ERECT, arrect, raised, straight-up, upright, upstanding
con lowered; flat, horizontal

‖stang *vb syn* SMART, bite, burn, sting

staple *n syn* LOOP 2, eye, ring

staple *n syn* BODY 3, bulk, core, corpus, mass, substance

star *n syn* CHIEF 2, capital, ‖cock, dominant, main, major, outstanding, predominant, preeminent, principal

starch *n syn* VIGOR 2, bang, drive, getup, go, pep, punch, push, snap, vitality

star–crossed *adj syn* UNLUCKY, hapless, ill-fated, ill-starred, luckless, misfortunate, unfortunate, unhappy, untoward

stare *vb* **1** *syn* LOOK 7, eye, gape, ‖gaup (*or* gawp), gaze, goggle, ogle, rubberneck
idiom ‖take a gander at
2 *syn* GAZE 1, bore, gape, ‖gaup (*or* gawp), gawk, glare, gloat, goggle, peer
idiom fix (*or* rivet) one's eyes on

stare down *vb* to overcome (someone) by or as if by staring <the teacher could not *stare* the boy *down*>
syn look down, outstare
rel glare; master, quell, subdue, suppress; overcome, overwhelm

stark *adj* **1** *syn* UTTER, absolute, blasted, blessed, complete, confounded, gross, infernal, out-and-out, rank
2 *syn* NUDE 2, au naturel, *bare-assed, buff-bare, naked, raw, stark-naked, stripped, unclad, unclothed
3 *syn* EMPTY 1, bare, clear, vacant, vacuous, void

stark–naked *adj syn* NUDE 2, au naturel, *bare-assed, buff-bare, naked, raw, stripped, unclad, unclothed, undressed
idiom bare (*or* naked) as a newborn babe, ‖naked as a jaybird, naked as the day one was born

‖starny *adj syn* STELLAR 1, astral, sidereal, starry, stellular

starry *adj syn* STELLAR 1, astral, sidereal, ‖starny, stellular

start *vb* **1** to move suddenly and violently from a state of stillness or rest <*started* from his bed at the sound of shots>
syn bolt, jump, spring, startle
rel dart; bounce; bound, leap; draw (back), flinch, recoil
idiom jump out of one's skin, start aside
ant stay
2 *syn* RECOIL, blanch, blench, flinch, quail, shrink, squinch, wince
3 *syn* BEGIN 2, arise, commence, originate
rel proceed, spring
ant end
4 *syn* FOUND 2, constitute, create, establish, institute, organize, set up
5 *syn* BEGIN 1, commence, embark (on *or* upon), enter, get off, inaugurate, initiate, open, take up, tee off
ant stop

start *n* **1** *syn* BEGINNING, alpha, commencement, dawn, dawning, genesis, onset, opening, outset, setout
ant finish
2 *syn* ADVANTAGE 3, allowance, bulge, ‖deadwood, draw, edge, handicap, head start, odds, vantage

startle *vb* **1** *syn* START 1, bolt, jump, spring

---

syn synonym(s) *rel* related word(s)
idiom idiomatic equivalent(s) *con* contrasted word(s)
ant antonym(s) * vulgar
‖ use limited; if in doubt, see a dictionary
The first word in a synonym list when printed in SMALL CAPITALS shows where there is more information about the group. For a more efficient use of this book see Explanatory Notes.

2 *syn* SHOCK 2, jolt
3 *syn* FRIGHTEN, affright, alarm, awe, fright, scare, ‖spook, terrify, terrorize
rel astonish, surprise
idiom make one jump out of one's skin, ‖scare the pants off

startlish *adj syn* EXCITABLE, agitable, alarmable, combustible, edgy, skittery, skittish, volatile

starved *adj syn* HUNGRY, famished, ‖peckish, ravenous, starving
rel underfed, undernourished; weakened; half-famished, half-starved
con fed, nourished; overfed
ant well-fed

starving *adj syn* HUNGRY, famished, ‖peckish, ravenous, starved
rel craving, famishing, hungering; dying, perishing
idiom crazy for food

stash *vb* **1** *syn* HOARD, squirrel
2 *syn* HIDE, bury, ‖bush up, cache, conceal, ‖ditch, ensconce, plant, screen, secrete
rel hoard, squirrel

stasis *n syn* BALANCE 1, equilibrium, equipoise, equiponderation, poise

state *n* **1** the way in which one manifests existence or the circumstances under which one exists or by which one is given distinctive character <remained in a weakened *state* for weeks>
syn condition, mode, posture, situation, status
rel circumstances; attitude, position, stand
idiom state of being
2 *syn* STATUS 1, capacity, character, footing, place, position, rank, situation, standing, station
3 *syn* STATUS 2, cachet, consequence, dignity, position, prestige, rank, standing, stature

state *vb* **1** *syn* RELATE 1, describe, narrate, recite, recount, rehearse, report
rel elucidate, explain, expound, interpret; set forth
2 *syn* ENUNCIATE 1, enounce
3 *syn* SAY 1, bring out, chime in, come out (with), declare, deliver, tell, throw out, utter
4 *syn* EXPRESS 2, air, give, put, vent, ventilate
ant imply

stated *adj syn* FIRM 4, certain, fixed, set, settled, stipulated

stately *adj* **1** *syn* CEREMONIAL, ceremonious, conventional, formal, solemn
rel dignified, grand, noble; imperial, kingly, princely, regal, royal
2 *syn* COURTLY, gallant, gracious, preux
3 *syn* GRAND 1, august, grandiose, imposing, lordly, magnific, magnificent, majestic, noble, princely
con lowly, poor; shabby; cheap

statement *n* **1** *syn* EXPRESSION 1, utterance, vent, voice
rel outgiving; articulation, presentation, presentment, verbalization, vocalization
2 *syn* WORD 1, utterance
rel description, narrative, recital
3 *syn* BILL 1, account, invoice, reckoning, score, tab

static *adj* characterized by relatively little or no movement, progression, or change (as in conditions) <a *static* economy>
syn immobile, stagnant, stationary, unmoving; *compare* STEADY 2
rel constant, stabile, stable, unchanging, unfluctuating; fixed, immovable, rigid, sticky; inactive, inert; stalled, stopped, stuck
idiom at a standstill, standing still
con active, changing, mobile, moving, progressing; erratic, fluctuating, inconstant, unstable
ant dynamic

station *n* **1** *syn* PLACE 1, location, locus, point, position, site, situation, spot, where
2 *syn* RAILROAD STATION, depot, station house
3 *syn* STATUS 1, capacity, character, footing, place, position, rank, situation, standing, state

station *vb* to appoint or assign to an office or duty <*stationed* guards around the camp>
syn post, set
rel appoint, assign; place, position

stationary *adj syn* STATIC, immobile, stagnant, unmoving
rel motionless, stock-still
ant moving

station house *n syn* RAILROAD STATION, depot, station

statuesque *adj syn* SHAPELY, clean-limbed, shapeful, trim, well-proportioned, well-turned

stature *n* **1** *syn* QUALITY 2, caliber, merit, value, virtue, worth
rel prestige, standing, status; ability, capacity; competence, qualification
2 *syn* STATUS 2, cachet, consequence, dignity, position, prestige, rank, standing, state

status *n* **1** rating or positioning in relation to others (as in a social order, community, class, or profession) <his *status* as a slave>
syn capacity, character, footing, place, position, quality, rank, situation, standing, state, station
rel rating
2 social or professional importance or distinction <a lawyer of international *status*>
syn cachet, consequence, dignity, position, prestige, rank, standing, state, stature
rel caliber, merit, worth; distinction, renown; eminence, prominence
con inconsequence, insignificance, unimportance
3 *syn* STATE 1, condition, mode, posture, situation
rel status quo
idiom state of affairs

statute *n syn* LAW 1, assize, canon, decree, decretum, edict, ordinance, precept, regulation, rule
rel act, enactment

staunch *adj* **1** *syn* SURE 1, fast, firm, secure, stable, strong
2 *syn* FAITHFUL 1, allegiant, ardent, constant, fast, liege, loyal, resolute, steadfast, true
rel firm, strong

idiom as staunch as an oak, tried and true
con mercurial; shaky, unsteady

stave *vb* ***syn*** HURRY 2, barrel, barrelhouse, bucket, bullet, haste, hasten, highball, hotfoot, hustle

stave off *vb* **1** ***syn*** FEND (off), hold off, keep off, rebuff, rebut, repel, repulse, ward (off)
rel beat off, drive (off), fight (off); block, parry
2 ***syn*** PREVENT 2, avert, deter, forestall, forfend, obviate, preclude, rule out, ward

staving *adv* ***syn*** VERY 1, exceedingly, exceptionally, extremely, highly, rattling, snapping, spanking, whacking, whopping
ant barely

stay *vb* **1** ***syn*** ARREST 1, check, halt, interrupt, stall
rel postpone, prorogue, put off
2 to continue to be in one place for a noticeable time < *stayed* late at the office >
syn abide, bide, linger, remain, stick around, tarry, wait
rel dally, delay, dillydally, lag, procrastinate; hang around, loiter; outstay, stay out
ant go
3 ***syn*** VISIT 3, sojourn, stop (over), tarry
rel bide, dwell, live
4 ***syn*** DEFER, adjourn, hold over, intermit, postpone, prorogue, put off, remit, shelve, suspend

stay *n* ***syn*** STANDSTILL, stillstand, stop

stay *n* ***syn*** SUPPORT 3, brace, buttress, column, prop, shore, underpinner, underpinning, underpropping

stay *vb* ***syn*** BASE, bottom, establish, found, ground, predicate, rest

stead *vb* ***syn*** HELP 1, abet, aid, assist, benefact, do for, help out

steadfast *adj* **1** ***syn*** IMMOVABLE 1, fixed, immobile, immotile, immotive, irremovable, ||sitfast, unmovable
2 ***syn*** INFLEXIBLE 2, adamant, inexorable, obdurate, relentless, rigid, single-minded, stubborn, unbending, unyielding
ant unsteadfast, vacillating
3 ***syn*** SURE 2, abiding, enduring, firm, never-failing, steady, unfaltering, unqualified, unquestioning, wholehearted
ant capricious
4 ***syn*** FAITHFUL 1, allegiant, ardent, constant, fast, liege, loyal, resolute, staunch, true
rel unfaltering, unflinching, unquestioning, unwavering

steadfastly *adv* ***syn*** HARD 7, fast, firm, firmly, fixedly, solidly, tight, tightly
rel staunchly, strongly

steadiness *n* ***syn*** STABILITY, firmness, security, soundness, stableness, strength
ant unsteadiness

steady *adj* **1** ***syn*** SURE 2, abiding, enduring, never-failing, steadfast, unfaltering, unqualified, unquestioning, unshaken, wholehearted
rel unswerving; eternal, never-ending
2 being neither markedly varying nor variable in course or extent < a *steady* rain > < *steady* prices >
syn constant, equable, even, stabile, stable, unchanging, unfluctuating, uniform, unvarying; *compare* STATIC
rel steady-going; certain, changeless, fixed, set, sure, unchangeable; unflickering, unwavering; durable, reliable
con inconstant, uneven, unstable; changeable; changing, fluctuating, uncertain, undependable, undulating, unsure, varying, wavering
ant unsteady
3 ***syn*** FAITHFUL 1, allegiant, ardent, constant, fast, liege, loyal, resolute, staunch, steadfast

steady *vb* ***syn*** STABILIZE, ballast, poise, stabilify, stabilitate

steady *n* **1** ***syn*** BOYFRIEND 2, beau, beloved, flame, inamorato, lover, sweetheart, truelove
2 ***syn*** GIRL FRIEND 2, ||baby, beloved, flame, honey, inamorata, ladylove, sweetheart, sweetie, truelove

steal *vb* **1** to take another's possession illegally and without his knowledge < *stole* a car >
syn abstract, annex, appropriate, cabbage, ||clout, ||cly, collar, ||coon, ||cop, ||crook, filch, ||heist, hook, lift, nab, ||nail, ||nick, nim, nip, pilfer, pillage, pinch, pocket, ||prig, purloin, smouch, ||snaffle, ||snake, snitch, swipe, thieve, vulture
rel mooch; fleece, frisk; grab, grasp, seize, snatch, take; hijack, shanghai; poach, rustle; burglarize, rob; loot, plunder, rifle
idiom make off (*or* away) with, run away (*or* off) with
2 ***syn*** SNEAK, gumshoe, lurk, pussyfoot, shirk, skulk, slide, slink, slip, ||snake
3 to move or go quietly so as not to disturb < *stole* out of the sickroom on tiptoe >
syn creep, glide, mouse, slide, slip; *compare* SNEAK
rel tiptoe
con clump, stamp, stomp, stump

steal *n* **1** ***syn*** THEFT, larceny, lift, pinch, purloining, stealage, stealing, thievery, thieving, ||touch
2 ***syn*** BARGAIN 1, buy, closeout, pennyworth

stealage *n* ***syn*** THEFT, larceny, lift, pinch, purloining, steal, stealing, thievery, thieving, ||touch

stealer *n* ***syn*** THIEF, filcher, larcener, larcenist, nimmer, pilferer, prig, purloiner

stealing *n* ***syn*** THEFT, larceny, lift, pinch, purloining, steal, stealage, thievery, thieving, ||touch

stealthily *adv* ***syn*** SECRETLY, by stealth, clandestinely, covertly, furtively, hugger-mugger, in camera, privately, sub rosa, surreptitiously
ant openly

stealthy *adj* **1** ***syn*** SECRET 1, clandestine, covert, furtive, hole-and-corner, hugger-mugger, hush-hush, sub-rosa, surreptitious, undercover
rel crafty, cunning, sly, wily; skulking, slinking, sneaking; catlike
con direct, straight, straightforward
ant open
2 being so quiet, slow, and deliberate in movement as to escape observation < the *stealthy* movements of the cat burglar >
syn catlike, catty, feline, furtive; *compare* SECRET 1

---

rel noiseless, pantherine, pantherish, quiet, silent; shifty, skulking, sly, sneak, sneaking, sneaky

steam *n* ***syn*** POWER 4, beef, energy, force, might, muscle, potency, puissance, sinew, strength

steamroller *vb* ***syn*** WHIP 2, beat, blast, ‖clobber, ‖cream, drub, lambaste, lick, overwhelm, wallop

steam up *vb* ***syn*** ANGER 1, enrage, incense, infuriate, ire, mad, madden, umbrage

steel *vb* **1** ***syn*** GIRD 3, brace, fortify, prepare, ready, strengthen
rel rally; nerve; buck up; reinforce
idiom grit one's teeth, set one's jaw, take the bit in one's teeth
ant unsteel
2 ***syn*** ENCOURAGE 1, animate, cheer, chirk (up), embolden, enhearten, hearten, inspirit, nerve, strengthen

steep *adj* **1** having an incline approaching the perpendicular <a *steep* trail up the mountain>
syn abrupt, arduous, precipitate, precipitous, sheer, sideling, steepdown, steep-to, steep-up, ‖stickle
rel elevated, lifted, raised; steepish; high, lofty; prerupt; perpendicular, straight-up; breakneck
con easy, gentle, gradual, moderate; shelfy, shelving, shelvy
2 ***syn*** EXCESSIVE 1, dizzy, exorbitant, extreme, immoderate, inordinate, stiff, towering, undue, unmeasurable

steep *vb* **1** ***syn*** SOAK 1, drench, impregnate, insteep, saturate, sodden, ‖sog, sop, souse, waterlog
2 ***syn*** INFUSE 1, imbue, ingrain, inoculate, invest, leaven, suffuse

steepdown *adj* ***syn*** STEEP 1, abrupt, arduous, precipitate, precipitous, sheer, sideling, steep-to, steep-up, ‖stickle

steep–to *adj* ***syn*** STEEP 1, abrupt, arduous, precipitate, precipitous, sheer, sideling, steepdown, steep-up, ‖stickle

steep–up *adj* ***syn*** STEEP 1, abrupt, arduous, precipitate, precipitous, sheer, sideling, steepdown, steep-to, ‖stickle

steer *vb* ***syn*** GUIDE, conduct, direct, escort, lead, pilot, route, see, shepherd, show
idiom steer one's course

steer *n* ***syn*** TIP, point, pointer, tip-off

stellar *adj* **1** of, relating to, or suggestive of a star or group of stars <*stellar* light>
syn astral, sidereal, ‖starny, starry, stellular
rel gleaming, luminous, lustrous, shining, starlike, twinkling; star-spangled
con starless
2 ***syn*** CHIEF 2, capital, ‖cock, dominant, main, major, outstanding, predominant, preeminent, principal

stellify *vb* ***syn*** EXALT 1, aggrandize, dignify, distinguish, ennoble, glorify, honor, magnify, sublime, uprear

stellular *adj* ***syn*** STELLAR 1, astral, sidereal, ‖starny, starry

---

syn synonym(s)	***rel*** related word(s)
idiom idiomatic equivalent(s)	***con*** contrasted word(s)
ant antonym(s)	* vulgar

‖ use limited; if in doubt, see a dictionary
The first word in a synonym list when printed in SMALL CAPITALS shows where there is more information about the group. For a more efficient use of this book see Explanatory Notes.

stem *vb* ***syn*** SPRING 1, arise, derive (from), emanate, flow, head, issue, originate, proceed, rise

stem *vb* to hinder or prevent by or as if by damming <*stem* the flow of blood>
syn stanch, stop
rel arrest, check, control

stemma *n* ***syn*** GENEALOGY, ‖begats, family tree, pedigree

stench *vb* ***syn*** SMELL 3, funk, reek, stink

stenchful *adj* ***syn*** MALODOROUS 1, reeking, reeky, ‖smellful, smelly, stale, stenchy, stinking, stinky, strong

stenchy *adj* ***syn*** MALODOROUS 1, fetid, nidorous, noisome, olid, putrid, rancid, reeking, smelly, stinking

stentorian *adj* ***syn*** LOUD 1, blaring, earsplitting, full-mouthed, piercing, roaring, stentorious, stentorophonic
rel orotund; clamorous, vociferous; gravelly, rough; clarion-voiced, loudmouthed, loud-voiced, trumpet-tongued

stentorious *adj* ***syn*** LOUD 1, blaring, earsplitting, full-mouthed, piercing, roaring, stentorian, stentorophonic
rel orotund; clamorous, vociferous; gravelly, rough; clarion-voiced, loudmouthed, loud-voiced, trumpet-tongued

stentorophonic *adj* ***syn*** LOUD 1, blaring, earsplitting, full-mouthed, piercing, roaring, stentorian, stentorious

step *n* **1** ***syn*** FOOTPRINT, footstep, spoor, track, tract, vestige
2 ***syn*** DEGREE 1, grade, notch, rung, stage
3 ***syn*** MEASURE 7, maneuver, move, procedure, proceeding
rel act, action; motion

step *vb* **1** ***syn*** WALK 1, ambulate, foot (it), hoof, pace, traipse, tread, troop
2 ***syn*** DANCE 1, foot (it), hoof (it), prance, tread

step–by–step *adj* ***syn*** GRADUAL, piecemeal

step in *vb* **1** ***syn*** VISIT 2, call, come by, come over, drop (in *or* by), look in, look up, pop (in), run in, stop (in *or* by)
2 ***syn*** INTERPOSE 2, intercede, interfere, intermediate, intervene, mediate

step up *vb* ***syn*** SPEED 3, accelerate, hasten, hurry, quicken, shake up, swiften
ant step down

stereotyped *adj* ***syn*** TRITE, cliché, clichéd, commonplace, hackneyed, stale, threadbare, tired, well-worn, worn-out
idiom worn thin

stereotypical *adj* ***syn*** TRITE, bathetic, cliché, clichéd, commonplace, hack, hackneyed, shopworn, stale, time-worn
ant original

sterile *adj* **1** lacking the power to bear offspring or produce fruit <a hybrid that is completely *sterile*>
syn barren, effete, impotent, infecund, infertile, unfruitful
rel sterilized; fallow, fruitless, unproductive; unprolific; arid, bare, dry; dead, desolate
con potent, productive, rich; bearing, fruiting, fruitive, producing, turning out, yielding; fecund, fruitful, prolific, teeming
ant fertile
2 ***syn*** UNORIGINAL, noncreative, uncreative, uninspired, uninventive, unoriginative

rel flat, insipid, jejune, vapid; stale; effete, worn-out; impotent
con fertile, fruitful, potent, producing, productive, prolific
ant fecund

sterlize *vb* to make incapable of producing offspring < *sterilizing* animals in medical experiments >
syn alter, castrate, change, desexualize, fix, geld, mutilate, neuter, unsex
rel emasculate; caponize, poulardize; spay

sterling *adj* ***syn*** HONORABLE 1, estimable, high-principled, noble, worthy
rel pure, true

stern *adj* ***syn*** SEVERE 1, ascetic, astringent, austere, mortified
rel grim, implacable, unrelenting; inexorable, inflexible
ant lenient, soft

‖**stern** *n* ***syn*** BUTTOCKS, backside, beam, behind, bottom, ‖butt, ‖can, derriere, rump, tail

stew *n* **1** ***syn*** BROTHEL, bagnio, bawdy house, bordello, cathouse, ‖hookshop, ‖joyhouse, seraglio, sporting house, whorehouse
2 *usu* **stews** *pl* ***syn*** RED-LIGHT DISTRICT, levee, tenderloin
3 ***syn*** SLUM
4 ***syn*** MISCELLANY 1, brew, hash, jumble, medley, mélange, mishmash, olio, pasticcio, potpourri
5 ***syn*** SNIT, fume, sweat, swivet, tizzy
rel boil
6 ***syn*** COMMOTION 2, agitation, confusion, dither, flap, lather, pother, tumult, turbulence, turmoil

stew *vb* **1** ***syn*** BOIL 2, parboil, seethe, simmer
2 ***syn*** WORRY 3, cark, fret, fuss, pother, ‖tew
idiom be in a stew

stewardly *adj* ***syn*** SPARING, canny, chary, economical, frugal, provident, saving, Scotch, thrifty, unwasteful

‖**stewed** *adj* ***syn*** INTOXICATED 1, ‖boozed, ‖canned, drunken, inebriated, ‖lushed, ‖oiled, ‖pie-eyed, ‖plastered, ‖spiflicated

stick *n* **1** ***syn*** BAR 1, billet, ingot, rod, slab, strip
2 ***syn*** DECOY 2, blind, ‖bonnet, ‖booster, capper, shill, shillaber
3 **sticks** *pl, used with* the ***syn*** FRONTIER 2, backcountry, backland, backwash, backwater, backwoods, ‖boondocks, ‖boonies, bush, hinterland
idiom the middle of nowhere

stick *adv* ***syn*** ALL 1, altogether, exactly, in toto, just, purely, quite, totally, utterly, wholly

stick *vb* **1** ***syn*** THRUST 2, dig, drive, plunge, ram, run, sink, stab
2 to become or cause to become closely and firmly attached < papers all *stuck* together >
syn adhere, cleave, cling, cohere
rel affix, attach, fasten, fix; glue; cement; fuse, weld; braze, solder
idiom stick close, stick like a wet shirt, stick like the paper on the wall, stick like wax, stick to like a barnacle (*or* leech)
con loosen; detach, disengage
ant unstick
3 ***syn*** SET 1, establish, fix, lay, place, put, settle
4 ***syn*** NONPLUS 1, beat, buffalo, get, stump
5 ***syn*** FLEECE 1, bleed, milk, mulct, rook, sweat
6 ***syn*** OVERCHARGE 1, clip, fleece, skin, soak
‖**7** ***syn*** BEAR 10, abide, brook, endure, go, lump, stand, stomach, suffer, support
8 ***syn*** DEMUR, balk, boggle, gag, jib, scruple, shy, stickle, strain, stumble

stickage *n* ***syn*** ADHERENCE 1, adhesion, bond, cling, clinging, coherence, cohesion, sticking

stick around *vb* ***syn*** STAY 2, abide, bide, linger, remain, tarry, wait

stick–at–nothing *adj* ***syn*** UNSCRUPULOUS, conscienceless, unconscionable, unprincipled

sticker *n* ***syn*** SEAL, stamp

sticking *n* ***syn*** ADHERENCE 1, adhesion, bond, cling, clinging, coherence, cohesion, stickage

stick–in–the–mud *n* ***syn*** FOGY, antediluvian, fogram, fossil, fuddy-duddy, mid-Victorian, mossback, square

‖**stickle** *adj* ***syn*** STEEP 1, abrupt, arduous, precipitate, precipitous, sheer, sideling, steepdown, steep-to, steep-up

stickle *vb* ***syn*** DEMUR, balk, boggle, gag, jib, scruple, shy, stick, strain, stumble
rel hold out, stall; contend, kick, object, protest

stick out *vb* **1** ***syn*** BULGE, beetle, jut, overhang, poke, pouch, pout, project, protrude, stand out
rel outstretch, outthrust, protend, push
2 ***syn*** STRIKE 1, walk out
3 ***syn*** BEAR 10, abide, brook, endure, go, stand, stomach, support, take, tolerate

stick up *vb* ***syn*** ROB 1, ‖knock off, knock over, loot, plunder, ransack, relieve, rifle

sticky *adj* **1** having the quality of sticking by or as if by adhesion < *sticky* syrup >
syn adhesive, ‖claggy, ‖clarty, cloggy, gluey, gooey, gummy, stodgy
rel tacky; viscid, viscous
2 ***syn*** HUMID, mucky, muggy, soggy, sultry
3 ***syn*** HARD 6, difficult, formidable, heavy, knotty, laborious, operose, rough, rugged, strenuous
4 ***syn*** SENTIMENTAL, bathetic, lovey-dovey, maudlin, mawkish, mushy, romantic, slushy, ‖soppy, tear-jerking

‖**stickybeak** *n* ***syn*** BUSYBODY, butt-in, ‖buttinsky, intermeddler, meddler, Paul Pry, prier (*or* pryer), quidnunc, rubberneck, snoop

sticky–fingered *adj* ***syn*** LARCENOUS, thieving, thievish

stiff *adj* **1** incapable of or highly resistant to bending or flexing < a *stiff* cardboard packing box >
syn immalleable, impliable, incompliant, inelastic, inflexible, rigid, unbending, unflexible, unyielding; *compare* INFLEXIBLE 2
rel stiffish; hard, resistant; hardened, petrified; stark
idiom stiff as a board (*or* poker)
con soft, softened; yielding; bendable, pliable, pliant; limber, supple, willowy
ant flexible, flexile

---

syn synonym(s) — *rel* related word(s)
idiom idiomatic equivalent(s) — *con* contrasted word(s)
ant antonym(s) — * vulgar
‖ use limited; if in doubt, see a dictionary
The first word in a synonym list when printed in SMALL CAPITALS shows where there is more information about the group. For a more efficient use of this book see Explanatory Notes.

2 ***syn*** INTOXICATED 1, ‖boozy, ‖canned, disguised, drunk, inebriated, ‖lushed, muddled, pixilated, ‖plastered

3 ***syn*** OBSTINATE, bullheaded, closed-minded, hardheaded, headstrong, intractable, mulish, pertinacious, self-willed, ‖sot

4 characterized by a lack of ease, grace, or spontaneity especially in style <a play whose dialogue and characters were *stiff* and perfunctory>

syn buckram, cardboard, muscle-bound, stilted, wooden

rel rigid, set, studied; machine-made, mechanical, stereotyped, stock; arid, dry, dull

con expressive, graphic, vivid; easy, fluent, graceful, smooth

5 ***syn*** EXCESSIVE 1, exorbitant, extravagant, extreme, immoderate, inordinate, steep, towering, unconscionable, undue

stiff *n* **1** ***syn*** CORPSE, body, cadaver, carcass, ‖cold meat, ‖deader, mort, remains

2 ***syn*** DRUNKARD, boozehound, boozer, drunk, guzzler, inebriate, lush, ‖lusher, sponge, swiller

3 ***syn*** MISER, cheapskate, muckworm, nabal, niggard, ‖nipcheese, scrooge, skin, skinflint, tightwad

stiff-necked *adj* ***syn*** OBSTINATE, headstrong, intractable, mulish, pertinacious, pigheaded, refractory, self-willed, willful, unyielding

stifle *vb* **1** ***syn*** SUFFOCATE, asphyxiate, choke, ‖quackle, smother

2 ***syn*** MUFFLE 2, dampen, deaden, mute

3 ***syn*** SUPPRESS 3, burke, hush (up)

4 ***syn*** STULTIFY, constipate, stagnate, trammel

stifling *adj* **1** producing or seeming to produce suffocation <*stifling* heat>

syn smothering, smothery, ‖smudgy, suffocating, suffocative; *compare* HUMID, STUFFY 1

rel oppressive, overpowering; unbearable, unendurable

2 ***syn*** STUFFY 1, airless, breathless, close, stivy, suffocating, sultry

stifling *n* ***syn*** REPRESSION 1, choking, extinguishment, quashing, quenching, smothering, squashing, squelching, strangling, suppression

stigma *n* a mark of shame or discredit <the *stigma* of personal cowardice>

syn bar sinister, black eye, blot, blur, brand, odium, onus, slur, spot, stain

rel besmirchment, disfigurement, smudge, smutch, taint, tainting; disgrace, dishonor, shame

con credit, distinction, glory, honor; bay(s), crown, laurel(s)

still *adj* **1** ***syn*** MOTIONLESS, stock-still, stone-still

2 ***syn*** CALM 1, halcyon, hushed, placid, quiet, stilly, untroubled

rel peaceful, unperturbed

con roiled, roily, turbid

3 devoid of or making no stir, sound, or noise <the streets were *still* at 3:00 A.M.>

syn hush, hushful, noiseless, quiet, silent, soundless, stilly, whist

rel calm, hushed, peaceful, placid, serene, tranquil; deathlike, deathly

idiom deathly still, still as death

ant noisy

still *vb* **1** ***syn*** CALM, allay, balm, becalm, compose, lull, quiet, ‖quieten, settle, tranquilize

ant agitate

2 ***syn*** SILENCE, choke (off), hush, quiet, ‖quieten, shush, shut up

still *adv* **1** ***syn*** HOWEVER, after all, howbeit, nevertheless, nonetheless, notwithstanding, still and all, though, withal, yet

2 ***syn*** YET 1, even

idiom still (*or* even) more

3 ***syn*** ALSO 2, additionally, along, as well, besides, furthermore, likewise, more, moreover, too

still *n* ***syn*** SILENCE 1, noiselessness, quiet, quietness, quietude, soundlessness, stillness

still and all *adv* ***syn*** HOWEVER, after all, howbeit, nevertheless, nonetheless, notwithstanding, still, though, withal, yet

still-hunt *vb* ***syn*** STALK 1

stillness *n* ***syn*** SILENCE 1, noiselessness, quiet, quietness, quietude, soundlessness, still

stillstand *n* ***syn*** STANDSTILL, stay, stop

stilly *adj* **1** ***syn*** STILL 3, hush, hushful, noiseless, quiet, silent, soundless, whist

con agitated, disturbed, noisy

ant noiseful

2 ***syn*** CALM 1, halcyon, hushed, placid, quiet, still, untroubled

stilted *adj* **1** ***syn*** RHETORICAL, aureate, bombastic, declamatory, euphuistic, flowery, grandiloquent, magniloquent, overblown, sonorous

2 ***syn*** STIFF 4, buckram, cardboard, muscle-bound, wooden

3 ***syn*** GENTEEL 3, affected, la-di-da, ‖lardy-dardy, mincing, pretentious, too-too

rel conventional, formal; decorous; prim

stimulant *n* ***syn*** STIMULUS, catalyst, goad, impetus, impulse, incentive, incitation, incitement, motivation, spur

stimulate *vb* **1** ***syn*** PROVOKE 4, excite, galvanize, innervate, innerve, motivate, move, pique, quicken, rouse

rel enliven, vivify; activate, dynamize, energize, vitalize

idiom build a fire under, get one started (*or* moving)

con unnerve; deaden

2 ***syn*** ELATE, commove, excite, exhilarate, inspire, set up, spirit (up)

stimulating *adj* **1** ***syn*** EXCITING, exhilarant, exhilarating, exhilarative, eye-popping, inspiring, intoxicating, rousing, stirring

rel enlivening, lively; provocative, seminal, suggestive; incitory, stimulative, stimulatory

2 ***syn*** INVIGORATING, animating, bracing, exhilarating, exhilarative, quickening, stimulative, tonic, vitalizing

stimulative *adj* ***syn*** INVIGORATING, animating, bracing, exhilarating, exhilarative, quickening, stimulating, tonic, vitalizing

---

syn synonym(s) ***rel*** related word(s)
idiom idiomatic equivalent(s) ***con*** contrasted word(s)
ant antonym(s) * vulgar
‖ use limited; if in doubt, see a dictionary
The first word in a synonym list when printed in SMALL CAPITALS shows where there is more information about the group. For a more efficient use of this book see Explanatory Notes.

stimulus *n* something that rouses the mind or spirits or incites to activity <the war proved a *stimulus* to the economy> <sought a *stimulus* to take her mind off her own troubles>
syn catalyst, goad, impetus, impulse, incentive, incitation, incitement, instigation, motivation, propellant, provocative, push, spur, stimulant; *compare* MOTIVE 1
rel boost, encouragement, inducement, invitation, urging; cause, motive; excitement, piquing, provocation, stimulation

sting *vb* ***syn*** SMART, bite, burn, ||stang

stingy *adj* being unwilling or showing unwillingness to share with others <too *stingy* to tip the waiter>
syn cheeseparing, ||chinchy, close, closefisted, costive, hardfisted, hardhanded, ironfisted, mean, mingy, miserly, ||narrow, narrow-fisted, narrowhearted, niggard, niggardly, parsimonious, penny-pinching, penny-wise, penurious, pinching, pinchpenny, save-all, ||scant, scrimpy, scrimy, tight, tightfisted, ungenerous, ungiving; *compare* SPARING
rel economical, frugal, Scotch, sparing, thrifty; scaly, screwy
idiom as close as a vise, as close (*or* tight) as paper on a wall, as tightfisted as a kulak, near (*or* close *or* tight) as the bark on a tree
con bountiful, giving, liberal, munificent, open-handed, philanthropic, unsparing, unstinting; prodigal
ant generous

stink *vb* **1** ***syn*** SMELL 3, funk, reek, stench
2 to be extremely or disgustingly unpleasant or objectionable <that advertising just *stinks*>
syn *suck
rel smell
idiom be rotten (*or* lousy)

stinkard *n* ***syn*** SNOT 1, ||prick, scum, *shit, *shithead, skunk, snake, stinkaroo, stinker, toad

stinkaroo *n* ***syn*** SNOT 1, ||prick, scum, *shit, *shithead, skunk, snake, stinkard, stinker, *turd

stinker *n* ***syn*** SNOT 1, cur, dog, scum, *shit, skunk, snake, stinkard, stinkaroo, *turd

stinking *adj* **1** ***syn*** MALODOROUS 1, fetid, funky, noisome, olid, rank, reeking, smelly, stenchy, whiffy
idiom stinking to high heaven
||**2** ***syn*** INTOXICATED 1, ||boozy, ||canned, disguised, drunk, inebriated, ||lushed, muddled, pixilated, ||plastered

||**stinko** *adj* ***syn*** INTOXICATED 1, ||boozy, ||canned, disguised, drunk, inebriated, ||lushed, muddled, pixilated, ||plastered

stinky *adj* ***syn*** MALODOROUS 1, fetid, funky, noisome, olid, rank, reeking, smelly, stenchy, whiffy

stint *vb* **1** ***syn*** SCRIMP, pinch, scrape, screw, skimp, ||skinch, spare
2 ***syn*** SPARE 3, scant, short, skimp, ||skinch

stint *n* **1** ***syn*** RESTRICTION 1, ||ball and chain, circumscription, cramp, limitation, stricture
2 ***syn*** TASK 1, assignment, chare, chore, devoir, duty, job
rel amount, quantity; allotment, apportionment; participation, share
3 ***syn*** SPELL 1, bout, go, shift, time, tour, trick, turn

stipend *n* ***syn*** WAGE, emolument, fee, hire, pay, pay envelope, salary
rel award, consideration, payment

stipple *vb* ***syn*** SPECKLE 1, bespeckle, dot, freckle, pepper, speck, sprinkle

stipulate *vb* ***syn*** SPECIFY 3, detail, particularize, specificate, specificize
rel designate; state; provide

stipulated *adj* ***syn*** FIRM 3, certain, fixed, set, settled, stated
rel designated, pinned down
con implied, unstated, unwritten

stipulation *n* ***syn*** CONDITION 1, provision, proviso, reservation, strings, terms
rel specification; circumscription, limit

stir *vb* **1** to cause to shift from quiescence or torpor into activity <a teacher who *stirred* the minds of his most sluggish students>
syn arouse, awaken, bestir, challenge, kindle, rally, rouse, wake, waken, whet; *compare* PROVOKE 4
rel excite, galvanize, inspire, provoke, quicken, stimulate; agitate, foment, incite, instigate; activate, energize, vitalize; actuate, drive, move, impel; ||roust, rout
idiom make (*or* have) an impact on, set astir, set on fire
2 ***syn*** WAKE 1, awake, awaken, rouse, waken
3 ***syn*** SEETHE 4, boil, bubble, churn, ferment, ||moil, simmer, smolder

stir (up) *vb* ***syn*** INCITE, abet, foment, instigate, provoke, raise, set, set on, whip (up)
idiom add fuel to the flame, apply the torch, feed the fire, pour oil on the fire, stir the embers

stir *n* **1** signs of excited activity, hurry, or commotion <noticed a *stir* within the crowd>
syn ado, bustle, flurry, furore, fuss, pother, whirl, whirlpool, whirlwind; *compare* COMMOTION 4
rel agitation, disquiet, stir-up; commotion, disturbance; din, hubbub, pandemonium, stirabout, tumult
con calm, peace, placidity; inaction, inactivity
ant tranquillity
2 ***syn*** MOTION 1, move, movement, stirring

||**stir** *n* ***syn*** JAIL, ||calaboose, ||can, ||clink, cooler, ||hoosegow, jug, keep, pen, ||pokey

||**stirra** *n* ***syn*** MAN 3, ||bloke, boy, chap, fellow, gent, guy, ||mun, skate, snap

stirring *n* ***syn*** MOTION 1, move, movement, stir

stirring *adj* ***syn*** EXCITING, exhilarant, exhilarating, exhilarative, eye-popping, inspiring, intoxicating, rousing, stimulating
rel heart-stirring, soul-stirring

stitch *n* ***syn*** PAIN 1, ache, ||misery, pang, throe, twinge

stivy *adj* ***syn*** STUFFY 1, airless, breathless, close, stifling, suffocating, sultry

stock *n* **1** ***syn*** FAMILY 1, clan, folk, house, kindred, lineage, race, tribe

---

syn synonym(s) | *rel* related word(s)
idiom idiomatic equivalent(s) | *con* contrasted word(s)
ant antonym(s) | * vulgar
|| use limited; if in doubt, see a dictionary
The first word in a synonym list when printed in SMALL CAPITALS shows where there is more information about the group. For a more efficient use of this book see Explanatory Notes.

2 ***syn*** ESTIMATION 1, appraisal, appraisement, assessment, estimate, evaluation, judgment
3 ***syn*** TRUST 1, confidence, dependence, faith, hope, reliance
4 ***syn*** SUPPLY, armamentarium, fund, inventory, store
5 ***syn*** RESERVE, backlog, hoard, inventory, nest egg, reservoir, stockpile, store

stock *vb* to equip, furnish, supply, or have material requisites (as for sale) <a bar that *stocks* all the best brands of liquor>
syn carry, keep
rel have; furnish, supply
idiom have (*or* keep) in stock, keep on hand

stockade *n* ***syn*** JAIL, ‖calaboose, ‖can, cooler, coop, guardroom, ‖hoosegow, jug, lockup, prison

stockpile *n* **1** ***syn*** PILE 1, bank, drift, heap, hill, mass, mound, mountain, pyramid, stack
2 ***syn*** RESERVE, backlog, hoard, inventory, nest egg, reservoir, stock, store

stockpile *vb* ***syn*** ACCUMULATE, amass, cumulate, garner, hive, lay up, roll up, store (up), uplay

stock–still *adj* ***syn*** MOTIONLESS, still, stone-still

stocky *adj* being compact and broad in build and often short in stature <a *stocky* but quick and hard-hitting catcher>
syn ‖chuffy, ‖chumpy, chunky, dumpy, heavyset, squab, squat, squdgy, stubby, ‖stuggy, stumpy, thick, thick-bodied, thickset
rel plump, stout; bunty, low-set, short; lumpish, lumpy, pudgy; corpulent, fat
con lean, skinny, thin, wiry

stodge *vb* **1** ***syn*** SATIATE, cloy, fill, glut, gorge, jade, pall, sate, ‖stall, surfeit
2 ***syn*** PLOD 1, footslog, ‖plodge, plunther, slog, slop, toil, ‖trash, trudge

stodgy *adj* **1** ***syn*** STICKY 1, adhesive, ‖claggy, ‖clarty, cloggy, gluey, gooey, gummy
2 ***syn*** DULL 9, banausic, blah, ‖dim, dreary, humdrum, monotone, monotonous, pedestrian, plodding
rel unexciting; pedantic; heavy, ponderous, weighty
3 ***syn*** TACKY 2, dowdy, frumpish, frumpy, outmoded, out-of-date, unstylish

stoic *adj* ***syn*** IMPASSIVE 1, apathetic, dry, matter-of-fact, phlegmatic, stolid
rel aloof, detached, indifferent, unconcerned; self-controlled, Spartan; indomitable, unassailable; long-suffering, patient, resigned

stoicism *n* ***syn*** APATHY 1, impassivity, insensibility, phlegm, stolidity, unresponsiveness
rel backbone, fortitude, grit, guts, pluck, sand

‖**stoit** *vb* ***syn*** LURCH 2, careen, stagger, ‖stoiter, ‖stot, sway, swing, weave, wobble

‖**stoiter** *vb* ***syn*** LURCH 2, careen, stagger, ‖stoit, ‖stot, sway, swing, weave, wobble

---

syn synonym(s) ***rel*** related word(s)
idiom idiomatic equivalent(s) ***con*** contrasted word(s)
ant antonym(s) * vulgar
‖ use limited; if in doubt, see a dictionary
The first word in a synonym list when printed in SMALL CAPITALS shows where there is more information about the group. For a more efficient use of this book see Explanatory Notes.

stolid *adj* ***syn*** IMPASSIVE 1, apathetic, dry, matter-of-fact, phlegmatic, stoic
rel blunt, dull, obtuse; dense, dull, dumb, slow, stupid; inactive, inert, passive, supine
ant sensitive

stolidity *n* ***syn*** APATHY 1, impassivity, insensibility, phlegm, stoicism, unresponsiveness
rel dullness, dumbness, slowness, stupidity; inactiveness, inactivity, inertia, passivity
con aptness, quickness, readiness; animation, enlivening, quickening; ardor, enthusiasm, fervor, passion, zeal; fire
ant sensitivity

stomach *n* **1** ***syn*** ABDOMEN, belly, ‖gut, paunch, tummy, venter
2 ***syn*** APPETITE 1, appetence, taste

stomach *vb* ***syn*** BEAR 10, abide, brook, digest, endure, go, stand, swallow, take, tolerate

stomachache *n* abdominal pain <she has a terrible *stomachache*>
syn bellyache, colic, collywobbles, gripe(s)
rel distress, misery

‖**stomachy** *adj* ***syn*** IRASCIBLE, choleric, cranky, cross, peppery, ratty, temperish, testy, tetchy, touchy

stomp *vb* ***syn*** TRAMPLE 2, stamp, tramp, tromp

stone–blind *adj* ***syn*** BLIND 1, ‖dark, eyeless, sightless, visionless

stone–broke *adj* ***syn*** POOR 1, beggared, broke, destitute, dirt poor, flat, necessitous, penurious, stony, strapped

stoned *adj* **1** ***syn*** INTOXICATED 1, ‖boozy, ‖canned, disguised, drunk, inebriated, ‖lushed, muddled, pixilated, ‖plastered
2 ***syn*** DRUGGED, doped, high, hopped-up, spaced-out, tripped out, turned on, ‖wiped out, zonked

stone–still *adj* ***syn*** MOTIONLESS, still, stock-still

stony *adj* **1** ***syn*** UNFEELING 2, callous, cold-blooded, coldhearted, hard-boiled, hardened, heartless, obdurate, uncompassionate, unsympathetic
ant soft
2 ***syn*** POOR 1, beggared, broke, destitute, dirt poor, flat, fortuneless, needy, stone-broke, strapped

stonyhearted *adj* ***syn*** UNFEELING 2, callous, coldhearted, hardhearted, heartless, ironhearted, obdurate, stony, uncompassionate, unsympathetic
rel flinty, hard, stonelike
idiom as cold as marble
ant softhearted

stooge *n* **1** one who plays a subordinate or compliant role to a principal <an executive who was only a *stooge* with no real power>
syn Charlie McCarthy, dummy, yes-man
2 ***syn*** TOOL 2, cat's-paw, pawn, puppet

stool *n* ***syn*** INFORMER, betrayer, ‖canary, ‖fink, ‖nark, snitch, squawker, squealer, stool pigeon, tipster

‖**stool** *vb* ***syn*** INFORM 3, ‖nark, peach, ‖pimp, rat, ‖sing, snitch, squeak, squeal

stoolie *n* ***syn*** INFORMER, betrayer, ‖canary, ‖fink, ‖nark, snitch, squealer, stool pigeon, tattler, tipster

stool pigeon *n* ***syn*** INFORMER, betrayer, ‖canary, ‖fink, ‖nark, snitch, squealer, stoolie, tattler, tipster

stoop *vb* **1** to descend from one's level (as of rank or dignity) usually to do something <a king who would not *stoop* to consider the common people>

syn condescend, deign
rel relax, thaw, unbend; accord, concede; accommodate, favor, oblige
idiom be so good as to, come (*or* get) down from one's high horse, lower oneself
2 to drop in status or dignity by indulgence in pettiness or unworthy behavior <a man who would not *stoop* to tell a lie>
syn descend, sink
idiom act beneath oneself, debase (*or* demean) oneself, lower oneself
3 *syn* DUCK 2, dip

stop *vb* **1** *syn* STEM, stanch
2 *syn* FILL 1, block, choke, clog, close, congest, obstruct, occlude, plug, stopper
rel disrupt, hinder, interrupt; cut off, shut off, turn off
ant unstop
3 to suspend or cause to suspend activity <the conversation *stopped*>
syn cease, desist, ‖deval, discontinue, give over, halt, knock off, leave off, quit, surcease; *compare* ARREST 1
rel ‖can, refrain (from); arrest, check, cut off, interrupt; stay, suspend; ‖cheese, lay off; break off, break up, end, terminate
con continue, go on, keep (on), keep up, persist
ant start
4 to come to a standstill <the car *stopped* at the intersection>
syn bring up, draw up, fetch up, halt, haul up, pull up
con start; move; pull out
ant go

stop (in *or* by) *vb syn* VISIT 2, call, come by, come over, drop (in *or* by), look in, pop (in), run in, see, step in

stop (over) *vb syn* VISIT 3, sojourn, stay, tarry
idiom make a stopover

stop *n* **1** *syn* END 2, cease, cessation, close, closing, conclusion, desistance, discontinuance, ending, termination
ant start
2 *syn* BAR 2, barricade, barrier, blank wall, block, blockade, fence, roadblock, wall
3 *syn* STANDSTILL, stay, stillstand

stopcock *n syn* FAUCET, cock, gate, hydrant, petcock, spigot, tap, valve

stopgap *adj syn* MAKESHIFT, provisional, rough-and-ready, rough-and-tumble

stopgap *n syn* RESOURCE 3, dernier ressort, expediency, expedient, makeshift, recourse, refuge, resort, shift, substitute

stopover *n syn* SOJOURN, tarriance, visit

stopper *vb syn* FILL 1, block, choke, clog, close, congest, obstruct, occlude, plug, stop
ant unstopper

store *vb syn* STOW, bestow, pack, warehouse

store (up) *vb syn* ACCUMULATE, amass, cumulate, garner, hive, lay up, roll up, stockpile, uplay
rel deposit; cache

store *n* **1** *syn* RESERVE, backlog, hoard, inventory, nest egg, reservoir, stock, stockpile
2 *syn* SUPPLY, armamentarium, fund, inventory, stock
3 *syn* DEPOT 2, arsenal, depository, magazine, repository, storehouse
4 a business establishment where goods are shown for sale <a food *store*>
syn market, outlet, shop, showroom
rel discounter, discount house, discount store, emporium

store *adj syn* READY-MADE, bought, ‖boughten, ready-to-wear, store-bought, ‖store-boughten

store–bought *adj syn* READY-MADE, bought, ‖boughten, ready-to-wear, store, ‖store-boughten

‖**store–boughten** *adj syn* READY-MADE, bought, ‖boughten, ready-to-wear, store, store-bought

storehouse *n syn* DEPOT 2, arsenal, depository, magazine, repository, store

storm *n* **1** *syn* COMMOTION 4, bustle, clamor, clatter, hassle, hubbub, hurly-burly, pother, ruction, to-do
2 *syn* BARRAGE, bombardment, broadside, burst, cannonade, drumfire, fusillade, hail, salvo, volley

storm *vb syn* ATTACK 1, aggress, assail, assault, beset, fall (on *or* upon), strike

storm and stress *n syn* UNREST, ailment, disquiet, disquietude, ferment, inquietude, restiveness, restlessness, Sturm und Drang, turmoil

stormful *adj syn* WILD 6, blustering, blustery, dirty, furious, raging, rough, stormy, tempestuous, turbulent
rel threatening; dusty, murky; foul; howling, riproaring, roaring
ant calm

stormily *adv syn* HARD 2, fiercely, frantically, frenziedly, furiously, madly, tumultuously, turbulently, violently, wildly

stormy *adj syn* WILD 6, blustering, blustery, dirty, furious, raging, rough, stormful, tempestuous, turbulent
rel threatening; dusty, murky; foul; howling, riproaring, roaring
ant calm

story *n* **1** *syn* ACCOUNT 7, chronicle, history, narrative, report, version
2 a recital of real or imaginary happenings that is less elaborate than a novel <told the *story* of his escape> <a simple *story* of heartwarming devotion>
syn anecdote, narration, narrative, tale, yarn; *compare* ACCOUNT 7
rel conte; description; fable; folktale, legend, märchen; Canterbury tale, cock-and-bull story, fabrication, fairy tale, fiction
3 *syn* LIE, canard, falsehood, falsity, fib, misrepresentation, prevarication, tale, untruism, untruth

storyteller *n syn* LIAR, Ananias, falsifier, fibber, fibster, perjurer, prevaricator

‖**stot** *vb syn* LURCH 2, careen, stagger, ‖stoit, ‖stoiter, sway, swing, weave, wobble

stout *adj* **1** *syn* BRAVE 1, bold, bravehearted, courageous, fearless, heroic, intrepid, stalwart, valiant, valorous
idiom bold as a lion
con irresolute; fainthearted
2 *syn* STRONG 2, stalwart, sturdy, tenacious, tough

---

syn synonym(s) *rel* related word(s)
idiom idiomatic equivalent(s) *con* contrasted word(s)
ant antonym(s) * vulgar
‖ use limited; if in doubt, see a dictionary
The first word in a synonym list when printed in SMALL CAPITALS shows where there is more information about the group. For a more efficient use of this book see Explanatory Notes.

rel resolute, steadfast; hard; indomitable, invincible
idiom as strong (*or* stalwart) as an English oak
3 *syn* FAT 2, corpulent, fleshy, heavy, obese, overweight, porcine, portly, upholstered, weighty
rel thick-bodied; ‖plenitudinous
ant spare

stouthearted *adj* *syn* BRAVE 1, bold, courageous, dauntless, doughty, fearless, intrepid, unafraid, undaunted, valiant

stow *vb* to put (articles) into a storage space <*stowed* his gear belowdecks>
syn bestow, pack, store, warehouse
ant unstow

straddle *vb* 1 *syn* BESTRIDE 2, ‖striddle, stride
2 *syn* SPRAWL 2, ramble, scramble, sprangle, spread-eagle, straggle

straggle *vb* 1 *syn* WANDER 1, drift, maunder, meander, mooch, ramble, range, roam, rove, stray
2 *syn* SPRAWL 2, ramble, scramble, sprangle, spread-eagle, straddle

straggler *n* *syn* LAGGARD, dawdler, lingerer, loiterer, slow coach, slowpoke

straight *adv* 1 *syn* AWAY 3, at once, directly, first off, forthwith, immediately, instanter, now, right away, straightaway
2 *syn* DIRECTLY 1, dead, direct, due, right, straightly, undeviatingly

straight *adj* 1 *syn* DIRECT 2, straightforward, through, uninterrupted
idiom as straight as an arrow
ant circuitous
2 *syn* STRAIGHTFORWARD 2, aboveboard, forthright, plain dealing
3 free from admixture or extraneous matter <a shot of *straight* liquor>
syn neat, plain, pure, unadulterated, undiluted, unmixed
rel unmodified; concentrated; strong
con adulterated, blended, mixed; watered-down; weak
4 *syn* CONVENTIONAL 1, button-down, orthodox, square

straight *n* *syn* RIGHT 1, good

straightaway *adv* *syn* AWAY 3, at once, directly, first off, forthwith, immediately, instanter, now, right away, straight

straightforward *adj* 1 *syn* DIRECT 2, straight, through, uninterrupted
2 free from all that is dishonest or secretive <a *straightforward* answer>
syn aboveboard, forthright, plain dealing, straight; *compare* FRANK
rel pretenseless; honest, honorable, just, upright, upstanding; candid, frank, open, plain, unequivocal; direct, outspoken
con equivocal, evasive, shuffling; indirect; prevaricative; dishonest, untruthful
ant devious
3 *syn* FRANK, candid, open, openhearted, plain, unconcealed, undisguised, undissembled, undissembling, unvarnished
rel barefaced, straight-from-the-shoulder
4 *syn* CLEAR 5, apparent, distinct, evident, manifest, palpable, patent, plain, unambiguous, unequivocal

straightly *adv* *syn* DIRECTLY 1, dead, direct, due, right, straight, undeviatingly

straight off *adv* *syn* AWAY 3, at once, directly, first off, forthwith, immediately, instanter, now, right away, straight

straight–out *adj* *syn* UTTER, absolute, complete, downright, gross, out-and-out, outright, rank, thoroughgoing, unmitigated

straight–up *adj* 1 *syn* ERECT, arrect, raised, stand-up, upright, upstanding
2 *syn* VERTICAL, perpendicular, plumb

straightway *adv* *syn* AWAY 3, at once, directly, first off, forthwith, immediately, instanter, instantly, now, right away

strain *n* 1 *syn* HINT 2, shade, soupçon, streak, suggestion, suspicion, tinge, touch, trace, vein
2 *syn* MELODY, air, descant, diapason, lay, measure, melisma, melodia, tune, warble
3 *syn* MOOD 1, humor, mind, temper, tone, vein

strain *vb* 1 *syn* TRY 2, distress, harass, irk, pain, stress, trouble
rel stretch
idiom put a strain on
2 to injure (as a body part) by overuse or misuse <*strained* a muscle while lifting weights>
syn pull
3 *syn* LABOR 1, drive, moil, strive, toil, tug, work
4 *syn* EXUDE, bleed, ooze, ‖screeve, seep, ‖sew, ‖sicker, sweat, transude, weep
5 *syn* DEMUR, balk, boggle, gag, jib, scruple, shy, stick, stickle, stumble

strain *n* *syn* STRESS 1, pressure, tension

strained *adj* *syn* FORCED, farfetched, labored
rel taut, tense, tight
con unforced, unlabored; unconstrained
ant unstrained

strait *n* *syn* JUNCTURE 2, contingency, crisis, crossroad(s), emergency, exigency, pass, pinch, turning point, zero hour
rel bind, squeeze; difficulty, hardship, rigor, vicissitude; bewilderment, mystification, perplexity

straitlaced *adj* *syn* PRIM 1, genteel, prig, priggish, prissy, prudish, puritanical, stuffy, tight-laced, Victorian
rel hidebound, intolerant, narrow, narrow-minded; rigorous, strict
idiom prim and proper
con easygoing, relaxed; broadminded, liberal, liberal-minded; libertine

strake *vb* *syn* STREAK, striate, stripe

‖**stramash** *n* *syn* CRASH 3, crack-up, pileup, ‖prang, smash, smashup, wreck

strand *n* *syn* SHORE, bank, beach, coast

strand *vb* *syn* SHIPWRECK 1, beach, cast away, pile up, wreck

---

syn synonym(s) | *rel* related word(s)
idiom idiomatic equivalent(s) | *con* contrasted word(s)
ant antonym(s) | * vulgar
‖ use limited; if in doubt, see a dictionary
The first word in a synonym list when printed in SMALL CAPITALS shows where there is more information about the group. For a more efficient use of this book see Explanatory Notes.

stranded *adj* ***syn*** AGROUND, beached, grounded
idiom high and dry, run aground

strange *adj* **1** ***syn*** EXOTIC 2, romanesque, romantic
2 ***syn*** UNFAMILIAR 1, new, unaccustomed
rel unknown; alien
3 ***syn*** MARVELOUS 1, amazing, astonishing, astounding, miraculous, spectacular, stupendous, surprising, wonderful, wondrous
4 deviating from what is ordinary, usual, or to be expected <a *strange*, unpredictable man>
syn bizarre, curious, eccentric, erratic, idiosyncratic, odd, oddball, outlandish, peculiar, quaint, queer, ‖rum, rummy, singular, uncouth, unusual, weird; *compare* EXCEPTIONAL 1, MYSTERIOUS
rel aberrant, abnormal, atypical, off, off-the-wall; fishy, funny; far-out, freaky, ‖kinky, kooky, offbeat, outré, ‖scatty; crazy, nutty; fantastic, grotesque
idiom as strange as they come
con common, ordinary, unexceptional, usual; expected, predictable
ant familiar

stranger *n* a nonresident or an unknown person in a community <he felt he had become a *stranger* in a foreign land>
syn alien, auslander, foreigner, inconnu, outcomer, outlander, outsider
rel out-of-stater, outstater; transient; visitor; immigrant; wanderer
idiom stranger within the gates
con inhabitant, resident; aboriginal, aborigine, autochthon, indigene, native

strangle *vb* **1** ***syn*** CHOKE 1, throttle
2 ***syn*** SUPPRESS 2, muffle, ‖quelch, repress, shush, squelch

strangling *n* ***syn*** REPRESSION 1, choking, extinguishment, quashing, quenching, smothering, squashing, squelching, stifling, suppression

strapped *adj* ***syn*** POOR 1, beggared, broke, destitute, dirt poor, flat, fortuneless, penurious, stone-broke, stony

stratagem *n* ***syn*** TRICK 1, artifice, device, feint, gambit, maneuver, play, ploy, ruse, wile
rel conspiracy, intrigue, machination, plot

strategy *n* ***syn*** PLAN 1, blueprint, design, game plan, project, scheme

stratospheric *adj* ***syn*** EXCESSIVE 1, dizzy, exorbitant, extravagant, immoderate, sky-high, steep, stiff, unconscionable, unmeasurable

straw *adj* ***syn*** BLOND 1, flaxen, golden
rel strawish, strawy

straw *vb* ***syn*** STREW 1, bestrew, broadcast, disject, disseminate, scatter, sow

stray *vb* **1** ***syn*** WANDER 1, gad, gallivant, meander, ramble, range, roam, rove, straggle, traipse
2 ***syn*** ERR, deviate, wander
idiom stray from the straight and narrow
3 ***syn*** DIGRESS 2, depart, divagate, diverge, excurse, ramble, wander
idiom get off the track, get sidetracked

stray *adj* ***syn*** ERRATIC 1, devious, errant, wandering
rel random, sporadic

streak *n* ***syn*** HINT 2, intimation, shade, strain, suggestion, suspicion, tincture, tinge, touch, trace

streak *vb* to make irregular lines or stripes of contrasting colors on or in <hair *streaked* with gray>
syn strake, striate, stripe
rel dapple, fleck, spot; marble, variegate, vein

stream *n* **1** ***syn*** CREEK 2, ‖branch, brook, ‖burn, gill, race, ‖rindle, rivulet, ‖run, runnel
2 ***syn*** FLOW, current, drift, flood, flux, rush, spate, tide

stream *vb* ***syn*** POUR 2, flow, gush, roll, sluice, surge

streamer *n* ***syn*** FLAG, banner, bannerol, color, ensign, jack, pendant, pennant, pennon, standard

streamline *vb* ***syn*** SIMPLIFY, boil down

‖**streel** *n* ***syn*** SLATTERN 1, dowd, dowdy, drab, draggletail, ‖malkin, slut, traipse

street *n* ***syn*** WAY 1, artery, avenue, boulevard, ‖drag, highway, path, road, thoroughfare, track
rel ruelle, streetlet; drive

street arab *n* ***syn*** VAGABOND, bum, derelict, drifter, floater, hobo, tramp, tramper, vag, vagrant

street girl *n* ***syn*** PROSTITUTE, call girl, ‖cruiser, harlot, ‖hooker, hustler, ‖joy girl, nightwalker, sporting girl, streetwalker

streetwalker *n* ***syn*** PROSTITUTE, bawd, ‖cruiser, harlot, ‖hooker, hustler, moll, nightwalker, ‖tomato, whore

streetwalking *n* ***syn*** PROSTITUTION, harlotry, oldest profession, (the) social evil, whoredom

strength *n* **1** ***syn*** POWER 4, arm, beef, energy, force, might, muscle, potency, sinew, strong arm
rel brawn; sturdiness, toughness; healthiness, soundness
con feebleness
ant weakness
2 ***syn*** STABILITY, firmness, security, soundness, stableness, steadiness
3 ***syn*** SUBSTANCE 2, body, burden, core, gist, meat, pith, purport, sense, sum and substance

strengthen *vb* **1** ***syn*** ENCOURAGE 1, animate, cheer, chirk (up), embolden, enhearten, hearten, inspirit, nerve, steel
2 to make strong or stronger <exercise is needed to *strengthen* the body>
syn energize, fortify, invigorate, reinforce
rel brace, support, undergird; anneal, ruggedize, sinew, tone (up), toughen; cheer, embolden, encourage, enhearten, ensteel, hearten, inspirit, nerve, steel
con cripple, debilitate, disable, enfeeble, tear down, undermine; deject, discourage, dishearten, dispirit; emasculate, enervate, unman, unnerve
ant weaken
3 ***syn*** GIRD 3, brace, fortify, prepare, ready, steel
idiom gather one's resources, recruit one's strength

‖**strengthy** *adj* ***syn*** STRONG 1, mighty, powerful, wieldy

strenuous *adj* **1** ***syn*** VIGOROUS, dynamic, energetic, lusty, red-blooded, ‖survigrous, vital

---

syn synonym(s)	***rel*** related word(s)
idiom idiomatic equivalent(s)	***con*** contrasted word(s)
ant antonym(s)	* vulgar

‖ use limited; if in doubt, see a dictionary
The first word in a synonym list when printed in SMALL CAPITALS shows where there is more information about the group. For a more efficient use of this book see Explanatory Notes.

2 *syn* HARD 6, arduous, difficult, effortful, laborious, operose, toilful, toilsome, tough, uphill
rel breathless, energy-consuming; mean, wicked; Herculean
idiom a long hard pull, an uphill climb, tough going
con comfortable, cushy, light, unburdensome
ant effortless

stress *n* the action or effect of force exerted within or upon a thing <the bridge trusses slowly yielded to *stress* and buckled under the weight of the deck>
syn pressure, strain, tension
rel pinch; burden, weight
2 *syn* EMPHASIS, accent, accentuation
rel import, importance

stress *vb* 1 *syn* TRY 2, distress, harass, irk, pain, strain, trouble
2 *syn* EMPHASIZE, feature, italicize, play (up), underline, underscore

stretch *vb* 1 *syn* RUN 8, extend, go, make, reach
rel range, roll
2 *syn* EXTEND 3, draw, draw out, elongate, lengthen, prolong, prolongate, protract, spin (out)
con abbreviate, shorten; condense, curtail, cut, trim
3 *syn* EMBROIDER, embellish, exaggerate, fudge, magnify, overcharge, overdraw, overpaint, overstate, pad

stretch (out) *vb syn* REST 1, lie, lie down, recline, repose

stretch *n* 1 *syn* RANGE 2, compass, dimension(s), extent, orbit, purview, radius, reach, scope, sweep
2 *syn* DISTANCE 1, length
3 *syn* EXPANSE, amplitude, breadth, distance, expansion, space, spread
rel area, region, tract
4 *syn* WHILE 1, bit, space, spell, time, ‖whet

stretch *adj syn* ELASTIC 1, flexible, resilient, springy, stretchy, supple, whippy

stretchy *adj syn* ELASTIC 1, flexible, resilient, springy, stretch, supple, whippy

strew *vb* 1 to spread (something) loosely or at intervals usually over a substantial area <*strew* seed for birds>
syn bestrew, broadcast, disject, disseminate, scatter, sow, straw; *compare* SPREAD 1, SPRINKLE 1
rel dust, pepper; dissipate; cover
2 *syn* SPREAD 1, circulate, diffuse, disperse, disseminate, distribute, propagate, radiate

striate *vb syn* STREAK, strake, stripe

strict *adj* 1 *syn* RIGID 3, draconian, ironhanded, rigorist, rigorous, stringent, unpermissive
rel exacting, oppressive, unsparing; dour, forbidding, grim, hard-boiled, harsh, tough
idiom not to be trifled (*or* messed) with
con easy, easygoing; lax, loose; permissive
ant lenient
2 *syn* TRUE 3, faithful, just, right, undistorted, veracious, veridical

---

syn synonym(s) *rel* related word(s)
idiom idiomatic equivalent(s) *con* contrasted word(s)
ant antonym(s) * vulgar
‖ use limited; if in doubt, see a dictionary
The first word in a synonym list when printed in SMALL CAPITALS shows where there is more information about the group. For a more efficient use of this book see Explanatory Notes.

stricture *n* 1 *syn* RESTRICTION 1, ‖ball and chain, circumscription, cramp, limitation, stint
2 *syn* ANIMADVERSION, aspersion, obloquy, reflection, slam, slur

‖striddle *vb* 1 *syn* BESTRIDE 2, straddle, stride
2 *syn* STRIDE 1, march, sling, stalk

stride *vb* 1 to move or walk with long often purposeful steps <*strode* to the door and slammed it>
syn march, sling, stalk, ‖striddle
rel clump, stamp, stomp, tramp, tromp
2 *syn* BESTRIDE, straddle, ‖striddle

strident *adj* 1 *syn* HARSH 3, grating, hoarse, jarring, rasping, raucous, squawky, stridulent, stridulous
rel loud, stentorian, stertorous
2 *syn* VOCIFEROUS, blatant, boisterous, clamorous, ‖dinsome, loudmouthed, multivocal, obstreperous, openmouthed, vociferant

stridulent *adj syn* HARSH 3, dry, grating, hoarse, jarring, rasping, raucous, rough, strident, stridulous

stridulous *adj syn* HARSH 3, grating, hoarse, jarring, rasping, rough, rugged, squawky, strident, stridulent

strife *n* 1 *syn* DISCORD, conflict, contention, difference, disaccord, dissension, dissent, dissidence, disunity, variance
rel argument, controversy, dispute; altercation, quarrel, squabble, wrangle; brawl, broil, fracas; affray, combat, fight, fray
ant accord
2 *syn* CONTEST 1, competition, conflict, emulation, rivalry, striving, tug-of-war, warfare

strike *vb* 1 to engage in a temporary work stoppage to effect compliance with demands made on an employer <they *struck* for higher wages>
syn stick out, walk out
idiom go (*or* be) on strike
2 to deliver (a blow) in a strong, vigorous manner <angrily *struck* the boy>
syn ‖biff, catch, clout, ‖devel, ding, hit, ‖nail, pop, slog, ‖slosh, smite, sock, swat, whack; *compare* SLAM 1, SLAP 1
rel beat, pummel, ‖slat, ‖swap, ‖wap, whop; cudgel, hammer, mace; ‖plug, poke, ‖puck, punch; bang, bash, crash, ‖pandy, slam; ‖stoush, thrash
idiom hang one on, let one fly
3 *syn* GIVE 10, administer, deal, deliver, inflict
4 *syn* AFFLICT, excruciate, harrow, martyr, rack, smite, torment, torture, try, wring
5 *syn* SEIZE 3, catch, take
6 *syn* ATTACK 1, aggress, assail, assault, beset, fall (on *or* upon), storm
7 *syn* OCCUR 2, hit
8 *syn* AFFECT, carry, get, impress, influence, inspire, move, sway, touch
9 *syn* DON 2, assume, pull, put on, take on

strike *n syn* DISCOVERY, detection, espial, find, unearthing

strike out *vb syn* HEAD 3, bear, light out, make, set out, take off

striker *n syn* HELPER, aid, ancilla, assistant, attendant, help

striking *adj syn* NOTICEABLE, arresting, arrestive, conspicuous, marked, outstanding, prominent, remarkable, salient, signal *rel* showy; forceful, powerful; cogent, compelling, telling

strikingly *adv syn* VERY 1, eminently, exceedingly, exceptionally, extremely, highly, notably, remarkably, surpassingly, vitally

string *n* **1** *syn* LINE 5, echelon, file, queue, rank, row, tier

2 *syn* RESOURCE 3, dernier ressort, expedient, makeshift, recourse, refuge, resort, shift, stopgap, substitute

3 *syn* SUCCESSION 2, chain, consecution, order, progression, row, sequel, sequence, series, train

4 strings *pl syn* POWER 1, authority, command, control, domination, jurisdiction, mastery, might, sway

string (up) *vb syn* HANG 2, gibbet, noose, scrag, turn off

string along *vb syn* TRIFLE 1, coquet, dally, flirt, fool, lead on, toy, wanton

idiom keep (someone) dangling

stringent *adj* **1** *syn* RIGID 3, draconian, ironhanded, rigorist, rigorous, strict, unpermissive

rel binding, confining, drawing

2 *syn* GRIM 2, austere, bleak, dour, hard, harsh, severe

strings *n pl syn* CONDITION 1, provision, proviso, reservation, stipulation, terms

stringy *adj syn* MUSCULAR 1, fibrous, ropy, sinewy, wiry

‖**strinkle** *vb syn* SPRINKLE 1, besprinkle, dust, powder

strip *vb* **1** to remove the clothing of <guards *stripped* and searched the prisoners>

syn denude, disrobe, unclothe, undress

rel doff, peel, take off; bare, denudate, expose, uncover; disfrock, unfrock

idiom strip to the buff

con clothe, dress, robe; cover

2 to take something (as honors, privileges, functions, or trappings) away from <an exiled king now *stripped* of his power>

syn bankrupt, bare, denudate, denude, deprive, dismantle, disrobe, divest; *compare* DEPRIVE 2

rel bereave; deplenish, disfurnish, ‖displenish, dispossess; despoil, rob

con clothe, endow, furnish, grant, vest; install

ant invest

3 *syn* RAVAGE, depredate, desecrate, desolate, despoil, devastate, pillage, sack, spoliate, waste

4 *syn* SKIN 2, decorticate, excorticate, peel, scale

strip *n syn* STRIPTEASE, stripping

strip *n* **1** a relatively long and narrow piece or section <tear old linen into *strips* for bandages>

syn band, bandeau, banding, fillet, ribbon, stripe

rel piece; section; segment; shred

2 *syn* BAR 1, billet, ingot, rod, slab, stick

stripe *vb syn* WHIP 1, flagellate, flog, hide, lash, lather, scourge, thrash, whale, ‖yerk

stripe *n* **1** *syn* STRIP 1, band, bandeau, banding, fillet, ribbon

2 *syn* TYPE, breed, feather, ilk, kidney, kind, order, sort, species, variety

stripe *vb syn* STREAK, strake, striate

stripling *n syn* BOY 1, lad, laddie, shaveling, son, tad

stripped *adj* **1** *syn* NUDE 2, au naturel, *bare-assed, buff-bare, naked, raw, stark-naked, unclad, unclothed, undressed

con attired; covered

ant clothed, dressed

2 *syn* OPEN 2, bare, denuded, exposed, naked, peeled, uncovered

con covered, unexposed; protected

stripper *n syn* STRIPTEASER, ecdysiast, peeler, stripteuse, teaser

stripping *n syn* STRIPTEASE, strip

striptease *n* entertainment in which a female performer removes her clothing piece by piece in view of an audience <a nightclub featuring *striptease*>

syn strip, stripping

idiom exotic dancing

stripteaser *n* one who performs a striptease <worked part-time as a model and *stripteaser*>

syn ecdysiast, peeler, stripper, stripteuse, teaser

idiom exotic dancer, ‖pantie peeler, ‖strip-and-shake artist, strip artist

stripteuse *n syn* STRIPTEASER, ecdysiast, peeler, stripper, teaser

strive *vb* **1** *syn* LABOR 1, drive, moil, strain, toil, tug, work

2 *syn* TRY 5, assay, attempt, endeavor, essay, offer, seek, struggle, undertake

rel labor, toil, travail, work; drive, strain

striving *n* **1** *syn* CONTEST 1, competition, conflict, emulation, rivalry, strife, tug-of-war, warfare

rel contending; combat, fight

2 *syn* ATTEMPT, endeavor, essay, hassle, struggle, trial, try, undertaking

rel labor, toil, travail, work

stroll *vb syn* SAUNTER, amble, bummel, drift, linger, mope, mosey, ‖muck

stroll *n syn* WALK 1, constitutional, ramble, saunter, turn

strong *adj* **1** having great physical strength <had the *strong* hands and arms of a wrestler>

syn mighty, powerful, ‖strengthy, wieldy; *compare* MUSCULAR 2

rel firm, robust, stark, strapping, sturdy, two-handed; able-bodied, tough; brawny, muscular, sinewy; lusty, vigorous

idiom strong as a bull (*or* ox)

con feeble, frail; puny, weak-bodied; forceless, impotent, powerless, strengthless

ant weak

2 having or manifesting great force or power (as in acting or resisting) <a *strong* constitution>

syn stalwart, stout, sturdy, tenacious, tough

rel hardy, robust, rugged, strapping; firm, solid, staunch; durable, enduring; forceful, potent, powerful; lusty, vigorous

con frail; forceless, impotent, powerless, strengthless; depleted, failing

---

syn synonym(s) | *rel* related word(s)
idiom idiomatic equivalent(s) | *con* contrasted word(s)
ant antonym(s) | * vulgar
‖ use limited; if in doubt, see a dictionary

The first word in a synonym list when printed in SMALL CAPITALS shows where there is more information about the group. For a more efficient use of this book see Explanatory Notes.

ant weak

3 being rich in a characteristic ingredient < *strong* coffee >

syn concentrated, full-bodied, lusty, potent, robust

rel strong-flavored, strong-tasting; straight, undiluted, unmixed; rich; heroic, large, powerful

con diluted, mixed, watered-down

ant weak

4 ***syn*** SPIRITUOUS, alcoholic, ardent, hard

5 ***syn*** SURE 1, fast, firm, secure, stable, staunch

rel solid, substantial, unmoving, unyielding

6 ***syn*** MALODOROUS 1, fetid, high, nidorous, noisome, olid, rancid, rank, stenchy, stinking

strong arm *n* **1** ***syn*** POWER 4, arm, beef, energy, force, might, muscle, potency, sinew, strength

2 ***syn*** THUG 1, ‖gorilla, ‖hood, hoodlum, hooligan, ruffian

strong–arm *vb* ***syn*** INTIMIDATE, bludgeon, ‖bounce, browbeat, bulldoze, bully, bullyrag, dragoon, hector, terrorize

stronghold *n* ***syn*** FORT, citadel, fastness, fortress, redoubt

strongly *adv* ***syn*** HARD 1, energetically, forcefully, forcibly, hardly, might and main, mightily, powerfully, vigorously

ant weakly

strong man *n* ***syn*** TYRANT, despot, dictator, duce, oppressor

strong suit *n* ***syn*** FORTE, eminency, long suit, medium, métier, oyster

structure *n* **1** ***syn*** BUILDING, fabric

rel construction, erection, pile

2 ***syn*** EDIFICE, erection, pile

3 something made up of more or less interdependent elements and having a definite organizational pattern < the complex bureaucratic *structure* of modern government >

syn framework

rel anatomy, skeleton; build, construction, frame; arrangement, composition, form, format, makeup, morphology; complex, network, system

struggle *vb* ***syn*** TRY 5, assay, attempt, endeavor, essay, offer, seek, strive, undertake

rel compete, vie

idiom make a valiant attempt (*or* try)

ant give up

struggle *n* ***syn*** ATTEMPT, endeavor, essay, hassle, striving, trial, try, undertaking

strum *vb* ***syn*** HUM, bombinate, ‖bum, bumble, buzz, drone, ‖sowf, thrum

strumpet *n* ***syn*** WANTON, hussy, jade, jezebel, slattern, slut, tramp, trollop, trull, wench

‖**strunt** *vb* ***syn*** STRUT 2, swagger

syn synonym(s) ***rel*** related word(s)
idiom idiomatic equivalent(s) ***con*** contrasted word(s)
ant antonym(s) * vulgar
‖ use limited; if in doubt, see a dictionary
The first word in a synonym list when printed in SMALL CAPITALS shows where there is more information about the group. For a more efficient use of this book see Explanatory Notes.

‖**strunt** *n* ***syn*** LIQUOR 2, alcohol, aqua vitae, booze, firewater, grog, ‖lush, ‖sauce, spirit(s), tipple

strut *vb* **1** ***syn*** SASHAY, flounce, mince, prance, ‖prink

2 to walk with an air of pomposity or affected dignity < a pompous general *strutting* off the parade ground >

syn ‖strunt, swagger

rel flaunt, parade

con cower, cringe; slink

stubborn *adj* **1** ***syn*** OBSTINATE, bullheaded, headstrong, intractable, mulish, pigheaded, refractory, stiff-necked, willful, unyielding

rel contumacious, insubordinate, rebellious; cantankerous, ornery; ‖stunkard, ‖stunt

idiom set in one's ways, stubborn as a mule

con adaptable, pliable, pliant; amenable, tractable

ant docile

2 ***syn*** INFLEXIBLE 2, adamant, inexorable, obdurate, relentless, rigid, single-minded, steadfast, unbending, unyielding

stubbornness *n* ***syn*** DEFIANCE 2, contempt, contumacy, despite, recalcitrance

rel cantankerousness, orneriness

stubby *adj* ***syn*** STOCKY, ‖chumpy, chunky, dumpy, heavyset, squat, squdgy, ‖stuggy, ‖stumpy, thick-bodied

stube *n* ***syn*** ALEHOUSE, beer garden, beer hall, ‖beerhouse, bierstube, mughouse

stuck–up *adj* ***syn*** VAIN 3, conceited, conceity, narcissistic, self-conceited, vainglorious

idiom too big for one's breeches, wise in one's own conceit

stud *vb* ***syn*** SPOT 2, dot, pimple, speckle, sprinkle

studied *adj* ***syn*** DELIBERATE 1, advised, aforethought, considered, designed, premeditated, prepense, studious, thought-out

rel thoughtful; intentional, voluntary, willful, willing

con natural, offhand

ant unstudied

studio *n* the working place of an artist (as a painter) < moved to a larger *studio* >

syn atelier, bottega

rel shop, workroom, workshop

studious *adj* ***syn*** DELIBERATE 1, advised, aforethought, considered, designed, premeditated, prepense, studied, thought-out

ant impromptu

study *n* **1** ***syn*** REVERIE, brown study, muse, trance

2 ***syn*** ATTENTION 1, application, concentration, consideration, debate, deliberation, heed

rel contemplation, weighing; abstraction, meditation, musing, pondering, rumination

3 ***syn*** EXERCISE 4, lesson

study *vb* **1** ***syn*** CONSIDER 1, contemplate, excogitate, mind, perpend, ponder, think (out *or* over), weigh

idiom give careful study to

2 ***syn*** SCRUTINIZE 1, canvass, check over, check up, con, examine, inspect, survey, vet, view

stuff *n* **1** ***syn*** PERSONAL EFFECTS, ‖plunder, things, traps, tricks

2 ***syn*** MONEY, dough, pelf, rhino, rocks, ‖scratch, ‖shekels, ‖smash, ‖stumpy, ‖sugar

3 ***syn*** THING 4, being, entity, individual, material, matter, object, substance

4 ***syn*** ESSENCE 2, bottom, essentiality, marrow, quintessence, quintessential, soul, substance, pith, virtuality

stuff *vb* ***syn*** CRAM 1, jam, jam-pack, ‖pang, ram, tamp
rel overfill, overstuff
idiom fill to overflowing, fill to the brim

stuffed *adj* ***syn*** FULL 1, awash, brimful, brimming, chock-full, crammed, crowded, jammed, loaded, replete

stuffed shirt *n* a smug usually pompous person with an inflexibly conservative or reactionary outlook <a *stuffed shirt* with a starched mind>
syn Blimp, Colonel Blimp, fuddy-duddy
rel diehard; prig, prude, smug
con freethinker, latitudinarian, liberal, libertarian, libertine; avant garde

stuffing *n* ***syn*** ENTRAILS, gut(s), innards, insides, internals, inwards, ‖pudding(s), tripes, viscera
rel ‖tar

stuffy *adj* **1** marked by a heavy oppressive quality of air <a *stuffy* room that needed airing>
syn airless, breathless, close, stifling, stivy, suffocating, sultry; *compare* HUMID, STIFLING 1
rel heavy, oppressive, thick; stagnant; shut-up, unventilated
con airy, breezy; open, ventilated; bracing, invigorating, refreshing, stimulating
2 ***syn*** PRIM 1, genteel, priggish, prissy, proper, prudish, puritanical, straitlaced, tight-laced, Victorian
rel dull, humdrum, stodgy; hidebound, illiberal, narrow, narrow-minded
3 ***syn*** POMPOUS 1, arrogant, bloated, important, magisterial, pontifical, puffy, self-important, wiggy

‖**stuggy** *adj* ***syn*** STOCKY, ‖chumpy, chunky, dumpy, squat, squdgy, stubby, stumpy, thick, thick-bodied

stultify *vb* to deprive of vitality and render futile especially by enfeebling or repressive influences <artistic creativity *stultified* by the intrusion of propaganda>
syn constipate, stagnate, stifle, trammel
rel discourage, inhibit, restrain; check, stunt; enfeeble, impair, weaken; deaden, dull; repress, smother, suffocate, suppress; invalidate, nullify
con encourage, foster, nourish; pique, provoke, stimulate

stultiloquence *n* ***syn*** CHATTER, babble, blab, blabber, cackle, ‖chin music, clack, gab, gabble, jabber

stumble *vb* **1** ***syn*** WALLOW 2, blunder, flounder, lurch
rel falter, waver; trip; fall
2 ***syn*** DEMUR, balk, boggle, gag, jib, scruple, shy, stick, stickle, strain
3 to move so clumsily and awkwardly as to lose one's balance or trip and fall <*stumbled* across the darkened room and fell>
syn blunder, bumble, lurch, ‖snapper; *compare* WALLOW 2
rel reel, stagger, totter; trip; pitch, topple
4 ***syn*** LUMBER, barge, clump, galumph, stump
5 ***syn*** TEETER, falter, lurch, stagger, ‖stammer, topple, totter, wobble
rel careen, swing
6 to act, proceed, or execute in a hesitant and clumsily faltering manner <*stumbled* through his Latin translation>
syn limp, muddle, shuffle
rel falter, hesitate, wobble; blunder, bumble; botch, bungle, ‖muck
ant breeze
7 ***syn*** HAPPEN 2, bump, chance, hit, light, luck, meet, tumble
idiom come (*or* run) up against, fall upon, stub one's toe upon (*or* on)
8 ***syn*** PUZZLE, befog, bewilder, ‖cap, confound, confuse, metagrobolize, perplex, pose

stumblebum *n* a clumsy inept or blundering person <a staff consisting of third-raters and *stumblebums*>
syn blunderbuss, blunderer, bungler
rel incompetent
con crackerjack, ‖dab, ‖darb, expert, topnotcher, whiz; natural; professional

stumbling block *n* ***syn*** OBSTACLE, bar, Chinese wall, hamper, hurdle, impediment, mountain, obstuction, rub, snag

stump *vb* **1** ***syn*** NONPLUS 1, beat, buffalo, get, stick
2 ***syn*** LUMBER, barge, clump, galumph, stumble

stump *n* ***syn*** DEFIANCE 1, cartel, challenge, dare, defi, defy

stumpy *adj* ***syn*** STOCKY, ‖chumpy, chunky, dumpy, squat, squdgy, stubby, ‖stuggy, thick-bodied, thickset

‖**stumpy** *n* ***syn*** MONEY, cash, rhino, rocks, ‖scratch, ‖shekels, ‖smash, stuff, ‖sugar, ‖wampum

stun *vb* ***syn*** DAZE 2, bedaze, bemuse, benumb, paralyze, petrify, stupefy
rel nonplus; amaze, astound, flabbergast; knock out
idiom strike dumb (*or* dead)

stunner *n* **1** ***syn*** WONDER 1, marvel, miracle, phenomenon, portent, prodigy, sensation
2 ***syn*** BEAUTY, ‖beaut, eyeful, knockout, looker, lovely

stunning *adj* **1** ***syn*** EXCELLENT, famous, fine, first-class, first-rate, first-string, number one, royal, superior, top
2 ***syn*** BEAUTIFUL, attractive, beauteous, ‖bonny, comely, fair, handsome, lovely, pretty, pulchritudinous

‖**stunpoll** *n* ***syn*** DUNCE, blockhead, boob, dimwit, dolt, dope, dumbbell, idiot, ignoramus, numskull

‖**stunt** *adj* ***syn*** STUNTED, runted, runtish, runty, ‖scrunty

stunt *vb* to hinder the normal growth and development of <the inhospitable climate had *stunted* all vegetation>
syn dwarf, suppress
rel check, curb, hold back; impair

stunt *n* ***syn*** TRICK 3, feat

stunted *adj* having had one's growth and development hindered or arrested <the children were *stunted* from malnutrition>
syn runted, runtish, runty, ‖scrunty, ‖stunt
rel undersized; dwarf
con able-bodied, robust well-set, well-set-up; giant, oversize; healthy, strong, sturdy, vigorous

‖**stupe** *n* ***syn*** DUNCE, chowderhead, chucklehead, dope, ‖dumbhead, dunderhead, lame-brain, noddy, noodle, ‖schnook

stupefy *vb* **1** ***syn*** DULL 5, blunt, hebetate

---

syn synonym(s) ***rel*** related word(s)
idiom idiomatic equivalent(s) ***con*** contrasted word(s)
ant antonym(s) * vulgar
‖ use limited; if in doubt, see a dictionary
The first word in a synonym list when printed in SMALL CAPITALS shows where there is more information about the group. For a more efficient use of this book see Explanatory Notes.

2 ***syn*** DAZE 2, bedaze, bemuse, benumb, paralyze, petrify, stun
rel addle, faze, rattle; nonplus

stupendous *adj* **1** ***syn*** MARVELOUS 1, amazing, astonishing, astounding, miraculous, prodigious, spectacular, staggering, wonderful, wondrous
2 ***syn*** MONSTROUS 1, cracking, fantastic, massive, monumental, mortal, prodigious, towering, tremendous

stupid *adj* **1** lacking in or exhibiting a lack of power to absorb ideas or impressions <a willing boy but too *stupid* to succeed in school>
syn beefheaded, beef-witted, beetleheaded, blear-eyed, blear-witted, blockheaded, blockish, chuckleheaded, dense, doltish, dull, dumb, duncical, fatheaded, goosey, hammerheaded, numskulled, pinhead, pinheaded, thick, thickheaded, thick-witted; *compare* RETARDED, SIMPLE 3
rel asinine, fatuous, foolish, silly, simple; brute, brutish, dummel, lumbering, oafish, slow, slow-witted, sluggish; ||half-assed; crass; backward, half-witted, retarded; idiotic, imbecilic
idiom ||dead above (*or* between) the ears, ||dead from the neck up, having a block for a head, having cotton between the ears, ||muscle-bound between the ears
con acute, alert, bright, clever, keen, knowing, quick, quick-witted, sharp, smart; sage, wise; brilliant; able, competent
ant intelligent
2 ***syn*** LETHARGIC, comatose, dopey, heavy, hebetudinous, sluggish, slumberous, torpid

stupid *n* ***syn*** DUNCE, dullard, dullhead, dumbbell, ||dummkopf, dummy, idiot, ignoramus, moron, simpleton

stupor *n* ***syn*** LETHARGY 1, coma, dullness, hebetude, languor, lassitude, sleep, slumber, torpidity, torpor
rel sopor; anesthesia, insensibility

sturdy *adj* ***syn*** STRONG 2, stalwart, stout, tenacious, tough
rel sound, substantial
ant decrepit

Sturm und Drang *n* ***syn*** UNREST, ailment, disquiet, disquietude, ferment, inquietude, restiveness, restlessness, storm and stress, turmoil

||**stut** *vb* ***syn*** STAMMER 1, ||hammer, stutter

stutter *vb* ***syn*** STAMMER 1, ||hammer, ||stut

sty *n* **1** an extremely unkempt or filthy place <the basement was a rat-infested *sty*>
syn dump, pigpen, pigsty
2 ***syn*** SINK 1, Augean stable, cesspit, cesspool, den, pandemonium, Sodom

stygian *adj* ***syn*** INFERNAL 2, avernal, cimmerian, hellish, pandemoniac, plutonian, plutonic

style *n* **1** ***syn*** VEIN 1, fashion, manner, mode, tone
2 ***syn*** NAME 1, appellation, appellative, cognomen, compellation, denomination, designation, ||moniker, nomen, title
3 ***syn*** FASHION 3, chic, craze, dernier cri, fad, mode, rage, thing, ||twig, vogue
4 an individual's characteristic attitudes and taste as expressed or indicated in his way of life <she liked the man's sophisticated *style*>
syn manner, way
rel behavior; bearing, carriage; characteristic, trait; idiosyncrasy, peculiarity

style *vb* ***syn*** NAME 1, baptize, call, christen, denominate, designate, dub, entitle, term, title

stylish *adj* being in accordance with or conforming to current fashion <she was a *stylish* dresser>
syn a la mode, chic, ||classy, dashing, exclusive, fashionable, in, modish, posh, sharp, smart, snappy, swank, swish, tonish, tony, ||trendy, trig, ultrafashionable, with-it; *compare* DAPPER
rel new, new-day, newfangled, new-fashioned; modern, modernistic, up-to-date; chichi, doggish, doggy, natty, rakish, sassy, swagger; ostentatious, pretentious, ritzy, showy, swell; sleek, slick
idiom in fashion, in the mode
con styleless; old-fashioned, outmoded, out-of-date; drab, tasteless
ant dowdy, unstylish

suasible *adj* ***syn*** RECEPTIVE 1, acceptant, acceptive, influenceable, persuadable, persuasible, responsive, swayable

suave *adj* being conspicuously and ingratiatingly tactful and well-mannered <a man of *suave*, well-bred equanimity>
syn bland, civilized, smooth, urbane; *compare* TACTFUL
rel affable, cordial, genial, gracious, sociable; courteous, courtly, polite; diplomatic, politic; cultivated, cultured, distingué, polished, refined, well-bred; sophisticated, worldly; ingratiating, soft, soft-spoken; fulsome, slick, unctuous
con clumsy, unpolished, unskilled; tactless, undiplomatic, untactful
ant bluff

sub *adj* ***syn*** SUBORDINATE, collateral, dependent, secondary, subject, tributary, under

sub *n* ***syn*** SUBSTITUTE, alternate, fill-in, locum tenens, pinch hitter, replacement, stand-in, succedaneum, surrogate

subaltern *n* ***syn*** INFERIOR, poor relation, scrub, secondary, subordinate, underling, understrapper

subaquatic *adj* ***syn*** SUBMARINE, subaqueous, underwater

subaqueous *adj* ***syn*** SUBMARINE, subaquatic, underwater

subaverage *adj* ***syn*** LOW 9, subnormal

subconscious *n* mental activities that occur just below the threshold of consciousness <a motive probably rooted in his *subconscious*>
syn underconsciousness, undersense
rel subconsciousness; subliminal self
idiom subconscious (*or* submerged) mind
con consciousness; awareness

subdolous *adj* ***syn*** SLY 2, artful, crafty, cunning, deep, foxy, guileful, insidious, tricky, wily

---

syn synonym(s) · *rel* related word(s)
idiom idiomatic equivalent(s) · *con* contrasted word(s)
ant antonym(s) · * vulgar
|| use limited; if in doubt, see a dictionary
The first word in a synonym list when printed in SMALL CAPITALS shows where there is more information about the group. For a more efficient use of this book see Explanatory Notes.

subdue *vb* ***syn*** CONQUER 1, bear down, beat down, crush, defeat, overpower, reduce, subjugate, vanquish
rel extinguish, put down, quash, quell, quench, squelch, suppress

subdued *adj* **1** ***syn*** QUIET 4, inobtrusive, restrained, tasteful, tasty, unobtrusive
2 reduced or lacking in force, intensity, or vividness < *subdued* colors > < she answered his questions in a timid *subdued* voice >
syn low-key, low-keyed, sober, soft, softened, toned down
rel moderated, tempered; controlled, restrained; mellow; neutral; quiet
con enlivened, intensified; bright, intense, strong; brilliant, vivid; saturated; blaring, glaring, harsh, screaming
3 ***syn*** TAME, domestic, domesticated, domitae naturae, submissive
ant unsubdued

subduer *n* ***syn*** VICTOR 1, conqueror, defeater, master, subjugator, vanquisher

subfusc *adj* ***syn*** DULL 8, drab, muddy, murky

subitaneous *adj* ***syn*** PRECIPITATE 1, abrupt, hasty, headlong, hurried, impetuous, precipitant, precipitous, rushing, sudden

subjacent *adj* ***syn*** INFERIOR 1, lesser, low, lower, nether, under
ant superjacent

subject *n* **1** ***syn*** CITIZEN 2, national
2 the basic idea or the principal object of attention in a discourse or artistic composition < the Puritans as soldiers of Christ was the *subject* of her paper >
syn argument, head, matter, motif, motive, point, subject matter, text, theme, topic
rel material, substance; problem, question; leitmotiv; core, meat
con elaboration, enlargement, enlarging, expatiation; development, explication

subject *adj* **1** ***syn*** SUBORDINATE, collateral, dependent, secondary, sub, tributary, under
rel servile, slavish, subservient
ant dominant, sovereign
2 ***syn*** LIABLE 2, exposed, obnoxious, open, prone, sensitive, susceptible
rel apt, likely

subject *vb* ***syn*** EXPOSE 1, lay (open), uncover

subjective *adj* peculiar to a particular individual as modified by individual bias and limitations < *subjective* judgments >
syn unobjective
rel biased, prejudiced; abstract, nonobjective, nonrepresentational, nonrepresentative
ant objective

subject matter *n* ***syn*** SUBJECT 2, argument, head, matter, motif, motive, point, text, theme, topic

subjoin *vb* ***syn*** ADD 1, annex, append, superadd, take on
rel combine, conjoin, unite
con part, separate, sever

subjugate *vb* **1** ***syn*** CONQUER 1, bear down, beat down, crush, defeat, overpower, reduce, subdue, vanquish
rel compel, coerce, force
2 ***syn*** ENSLAVE, enthrall
ant liberate

subjugator *n* ***syn*** VICTOR 1, conqueror, defeater, master, subduer, vanquisher

sublease *vb* ***syn*** SUBLET, underlease, underlet

sublet *vb* to turn over to another one's right of occupancy of (rented or leased housing) < *sublet* her apartment to a friend >
syn sublease, underlease, underlet

sublime *vb* ***syn*** EXALT 1, aggrandize, dignify, distinguish, ennoble, erect, glorify, honor, magnify, uprear

sublime *adj* **1** ***syn*** GRAND 3, elevated, exalted, lofty, superb
2 ***syn*** SPLENDID 2, glorious, gorgeous, magnificent, proud, resplendent, splendiferous, spendorous, superb
rel abstract, ideal, transcendent, transcendental; divine, holy, sacred, spiritual; august, majestic, noble, stately

sublimity *n* ***syn*** APEX 2, acme, apogee, capstone, climax, culmination, meridian, peak, pinnacle, summit

sublunary *adj* ***syn*** EARTHLY 1, earthy, mundane, tellurian, telluric, terrene, terrestrial, uncelestial, worldly

submarine *adj* being, acting, growing, or used under water < a *submarine* camera >
syn subaquatic, subaqueous, underwater

submerge *vb* **1** ***syn*** DIP 1, douse, duck, dunk, immerse, souse, submerse
rel drench, impregnate, saturate, soak
2 ***syn*** DELUGE 1, drown, engulf, flood, inundate, overflow, overwhelm, swamp, whelm
3 ***syn*** SINK 1, founder, go down, go under, submerse

submerse *vb* **1** ***syn*** DIP 1, douse, duck, dunk, immerse, souse, submerge
2 ***syn*** SINK 1, founder, go down, go under, submerge

submission *n* ***syn*** SURRENDER, capitulation, dedition
rel bowing, submitting; acquiescence, compliance, resignation; cringing, servility; prostration
ant resistance

submissive *adj* **1** ***syn*** TAME, domestic, domesticated, domitae naturae, subdued
rel complying, conformable, obeying; bowing down, unerect; menial, servile, slavish, subservient
ant rebellious
2 ***syn*** PASSIVE 2, acquiescent, nonresistant, nonresisting, resigned, unresistant, unresisting, yielding

submit *vb* **1** ***syn*** YIELD 2, bow, buckle (under), capitulate, cave, defer, knuckle, knuckle under, succumb
ant resist, withstand
2 to offer or commit (something) for consideration, study, or decision < *submitted* his report directly to the general >
syn hand in, refer
rel bring, deliver, present; offer, proffer, tender; send in; provide
3 ***syn*** SUGGEST 4, theorize
4 ***syn*** FALL 3, go down, go under, succumb, surrender

---

syn synonym(s) — ***rel*** related word(s)
idiom idiomatic equivalent(s) — ***con*** contrasted word(s)
ant antonym(s) — * vulgar
‖ use limited; if in doubt, see a dictionary
The first word in a synonym list when printed in SMALL CAPITALS shows where there is more information about the group. For a more efficient use of this book see Explanatory Notes.

ant hold out, resist

subnormal *adj* ***syn*** LOW 9, subaverage
rel subpar

subordinate *adj* placed in or occupying a lower class, rank, or status <making the executive *subordinate* to the legislative branch>
syn collateral, dependent, secondary, sub, subject, tributary, under
rel adjuvant, auxiliary, contributory, subsidiary; satellite; inferior, subaltern, subalternate; accessory, parergal, supplementary
con chief, first, leading, main; dominant, master, superior

subordinate *n* ***syn*** INFERIOR, poor relation, scrub, secondary, subaltern, underling, understrapper

sub rosa *adv* ***syn*** SECRETLY, by stealth, clandestinely, covertly, furtively, hugger-mugger, in camera, privately, stealthily, surreptitiously
ant aboveboard

sub–rosa *adj* ***syn*** SECRET 1, clandestine, covert, hugger-mugger, hush-hush, stealthy, surreptitious, undercover, ||underneath, under-the-table
ant aboveboard

subscribe *vb* **1** ***syn*** SIGN 1, autograph, ink, signature
2 ***syn*** CONTRIBUTE 1, chip in, come through, kick in, pitch in
3 ***syn*** ASSENT, accede, acquiesce, agree, consent, yes
rel approve, endorse, favor, sanction

subsequent *adj* **1** being, occurring, or carried out at a time after something else <*subsequent* events disproved his predictions>
syn after, ensuing, later, posterior, postliminary, subsequential
rel following, next, succeeding; consequential, resultant, resulting
con exordial, introductory, prefatory, preliminary, preludial; anterior, precedent, preceding, prior
ant antecedent
2 ***syn*** CONSECUTIVE, sequent, sequential, serial, subsequential, succedent, succeeding, successional, successive
ant antecedent

subsequential *adj* **1** ***syn*** SUBSEQUENT 1, after, ensuing, later, posterior, postliminary
2 ***syn*** CONSECUTIVE, sequent, sequential, serial, subsequent, succedent, succeeding, successional, successive
ant antecedent

subsequently *adv* ***syn*** AFTER, afterward, afterwhile, behind, by and by, infra, later, latterly, next
ant antecedently, priorly

subsequent to *prep* ***syn*** AFTER 2, behind, below, following, next, since

subservient *adj* **1** ***syn*** AUXILIARY, accessory, adjuvant, ancillary, appurtenant, collateral, contributory, subsidiary
2 showing extreme compliance or abject obedience <a *subservient* minor bureaucrat>
syn menial, obeisant, obsequious, servile, slavish
rel acquiescent, compliant, resigned, submissive; cowering, cringing, fawning, truckling; abject, ignoble, mean
idiom as obedient as a dog
con aggressive; arrogant, haughty; rebellious; independent, irrepressible, uncontainable
ant domineering, overbearing

subside *vb* ***syn*** ABATE 4, die (down *or* away), ease off, ebb, fall, let up, lull, moderate, slacken, wane
idiom dwindle down

subsidiary *adj* ***syn*** AUXILIARY, accessory, adjuvant, ancillary, appurtenant, collateral, contributory, subservient
rel back-up; minor, tributary

subsidize *vb* ***syn*** ENDOW 2, finance, fund
rel back; promote; help

subsidy *n* ***syn*** APPROPRIATION, grant, subvention
rel subsidization; gift, reward

subsist *vb* ***syn*** BE, breathe, exist, live, move

subsistence *n* ***syn*** LIVING, alimentation, alimony, bread, bread and butter, keep, maintenance, salt, support, sustenance

substance *n* **1** ***syn*** TENOR 1, drift, purport
rel import, meaning
idiom the general drift
2 the inner significance or central meaning of something written or said <just give me the *substance* of his speech>
syn amount, body, burden, core, crux, gist, kernel, matter, meat, nub, nubbin, pith, purport, sense, short, strength, sum and substance, sum total, thrust, upshot; *compare* BODY 3, ESSENCE 2, MEANING 1, TENOR 1
rel center, focus, heart, nucleus; point; import, meaningfulness
3 ***syn*** BODY 3, bulk, core, corpus, mass, staple
rel drift, tenor
4 ***syn*** ESSENCE 2, bottom, essentiality, marrow, pith, quintessence, quintessential, soul, stuff, virtuality
5 ***syn*** THING 4, being, entity, individual, material, matter, object, stuff
6 ***syn*** WEALTH 2, fortune, property, resources, riches, worth

substantial *adj* **1** ***syn*** MATERIAL 1, corporeal, gross, objective, phenomenal, physical, sensible, tangible
con airy, ethereal
ant unsubstantial
2 ***syn*** IMPORTANT 1, big, consequential, considerable, material, meaningful, momentous, significant, weighty
rel key, principal; strong; serious
3 ***syn*** PROSPEROUS 3, comfortable, easy, ||snug, well, well-fixed, well-heeled, well-off, well-to-do
rel solid, solvent

substantiate *vb* **1** ***syn*** EMBODY 1, exteriorize, externalize, incarnate, manifest, materialize, objectify, personalize, personify, personize
rel substantialize, substantify
2 ***syn*** CONFIRM 2, authenticate, bear out, corroborate, justify, validate, verify
rel demonstrate, prove, test, try

substitutable *adj* ***syn*** INTERCHANGEABLE, commutable, exchangeable, fungible, interconvertible

---

substitute *n* **1** a person who takes the place of or acts instead of another <found a *substitute* for the sick teacher>
syn alternate, fill-in, locum tenens, pinch hitter, replacement, stand-in, sub, succedaneum, surrogate
rel relay, relief; deputy, procurator, proxy; supply; double, understudy
2 *syn* RESOURCE 3, dernier ressort, expediency, expedient, makeshift, recourse, refuge, resort, stopgap, surrogate

substitute *vb syn* EXCHANGE 2, change, swap, switch, trade

substitute *adj* **1** serving or fitted for use as a substitute <a *substitute* driver was needed for the long trip>
syn alternate, alternative, surrogate
rel additional, another; other, second; back-up, reserve; supplemental, supplementary, suppletory
2 *syn* ARTIFICIAL 2, dummy, ersatz, false, imitation, mock, sham, simulated, spurious

substract *vb syn* DEDUCT 1, discount, draw back, knock off, subtract, take, take away, take off, take out

substratal *adj syn* ELEMENTAL 1, basic, elementary, essential, fundamental, primitive, underlying

substratum *n* **1** *syn* BASIS 1, base, bedrock, footing, foundation, ground, groundwork, infrastructure, root, underpinning
rel core, meat, stuff, substance
2 *syn* BASE 1, basis, bottom, foundation, groundwork, infrastructure, seat, substruction, substructure, understructure

substruction *n syn* BASE 1, basis, bottom, foundation, groundwork, infrastructure, seat, substratum, substructure, understructure

substructure *n syn* BASE 1, basis, bottom, foundation, groundwork, infrastructure, seat, substratum, substruction, understructure
ant superstructure

subsume *vb syn* INCLUDE, comprehend, contain, embody, embrace, encompass, have, involve, take in

subterfuge *n syn* DECEPTION 1, cheat, chicane, chicanery, dishonesty, double-dealing, dupery, fraud, highbinding, trickery

subterrane *n syn* CAVE, cavern, grotto, subterranean

subterranean *adj* being, lying, functioning, or operating under the surface of the earth <*subterranean* hot springs that emerge as geysers>
syn subterrestrial, underearth, underfoot, underground
con aboveground, surface, surficial

subterranean *n syn* CAVE, cavern, grotto, subterrane

subterrestrial *adj syn* SUBTERRANEAN, underearth, underfoot, underground

subtile *adj syn* THIN 2, attenuate, attenuated, rare, rarefied, subtle, tenuous

subtle *adj* **1** *syn* THIN 2, attenuate, attenuated, rare, rarefied, subtile, tenuous
2 *syn* FINE 1, delicate, finespun, hairline, hairsplitting, nice, refined
ant unsubtle
3 *syn* LOGICAL 2, analytic, analytical, ratiocinative
rel dexterous, skillful
con blunt; dense
4 *syn* SLY 2, artful, astute, crafty, cunning, deep, foxy, guileful, insidious, wily
ant unsubtle

subtract *vb syn* DEDUCT 1, discount, draw back, knock off, substract, take, take away, take off, take out
ant add

subtraction *n syn* DEDUCTION 1, abatement, discount, rebate, reduction
ant addition

suburbs *n pl syn* ENVIRONS 2, outskirt(s), purlieus
rel fringes; suburbia

subvention *n syn* APPROPRIATION, grant, subsidy

subversion *n syn* SABOTAGE, undermining, wreckage, wrecking
rel demolishing, destroying, destruction

subvert *vb syn* SABOTAGE, undermine, wreck
rel overthrow, overturn, upset; demolish, destroy, ruin; corrupt, debase, deprave, pervert
con sustain, uphold

succedaneum *n syn* SUBSTITUTE, alternate, fill-in, locum tenens, pinch hitter, replacement, stand-in, sub, surrogate

succedent *adj syn* CONSECUTIVE, sequent, sequential, serial, subsequent, subsequential, succeeding, successional, successive

succeed *vb* **1** *syn* FOLLOW 1, ensue, supervene
ant precede
2 to result favorably according to plans and desires <that advertising campaign really *succeeded*>
syn click, come off, go, go over, pan out, prove out
rel catch on; prevail
idiom go over big, go over with a bang, hit the mark, make a hit, turn out well
ant fail, flop
3 to attain or be attaining a desired end <how to *succeed* in big business>
syn arrive, flourish, go, make out, prosper, score, thrive
rel ‖dow; get ahead; boom; achieve, attain, gain, reach; accomplish, effect, fulfill; conquer, prevail, triumph, win (out)
idiom do all right by oneself, do well, gain one's end, get places, get somewhere, get to the top of the ladder, make a success, make it (big), make one's mark, ‖make the big time, make the grade
con dwindle, languish; fall down, flounder, founder; lose (out); bust
ant fail

succeeding *adj syn* CONSECUTIVE, sequent, sequential, serial, subsequent, subsequential, succedent, successional, successive

succès fou *n syn* SMASH 6, bang, bell ringer, hit, ten*strike, wow

success *n* a succeeding fully or in accordance with one's desires <attributed his business *success* to hard work and attention to detail>

---

syn arrival, ||do, flying colors, go, prosperity, successfulness
rel accomplishment, achievement, attainment; triumph, victory
ant failure; nonsuccess, unsuccessfulness

successful *adj* resulting in or having gained success <a *successful* business venture>
syn prosperous, thriving; *compare* FLOURISHING
rel extraordinary, notable, noteworthy, outstanding, smash, smashing
idiom crowned (*or* blessed *or* flushed) with success, ||out front
con failing, thriveless, unprosperous; defeated, disappointed, failed, frustrated; bankrupt, broken, destroyed, ruined
ant successless, unsuccessful

successfully *adv* *syn* WELL 5, favorably, fortunately, happily, prosperously, satisfyingly, swimmingly
ant unsuccessfully

successfulness *n* *syn* SUCCESS, arrival, ||do, flying colors, go, prosperity
ant nonsuccess, unsuccessfulness

succession *n* **1** *syn* ORDER 5, consecution, procession, sequence
2 a number of things that follow each other in some order <another *succession* of price hikes>
syn alternation, chain, consecution, course, order, progression, row, sequel, sequence, series, string, suite, train; *compare* CYCLE 1
rel successiveness; round, round robin

successional *adj* *syn* CONSECUTIVE, sequent, sequential, serial, subsequent, subsequential, succedent, succeeding, successive

successive *adj* *syn* CONSECUTIVE, sequent, sequential, serial, subsequent, subsequential, succedent, succeeding, successional
rel alternating, rotating

successively *adv* *syn* TOGETHER 2, consecutively, continually, continuously, hand running, night and day, running, unintermittedly, uninterruptedly

succinct *adj* *syn* CONCISE, breviloquent, brief, compendiary, compendious, curt, laconic, short, summary, terse
rel blunt, brusque
idiom right to the point
ant discursive

succinctly *adv* *syn* BRIEFLY, concisely, in brief, in short, laconically, shortly, tersely
ant discursively

succor *n* *syn* HELP 1, aid, assist, assistance, comfort, hand, lift, relief, secours, support
rel ministration, ministry; maintenance, nourishment, sustenance

succubus *n* *syn* DEVIL 2, archfiend, demon, fiend, Satan

---

syn synonym(s) *rel* related word(s)
idiom idiomatic equivalent(s) *con* contrasted word(s)
ant antonym(s) * vulgar
|| use limited; if in doubt, see a dictionary
The first word in a synonym list when printed in SMALL CAPITALS shows where there is more information about the group. For a more efficient use of this book see Explanatory Notes.

succulent *adj* full of juice <a *succulent* roast>
syn juicy, ||sappy

succumb *vb* **1** *syn* YIELD 2, bow, buckle (under), capitulate, cave, defer, knuckle, knuckle under, submit
rel abandon, relinquish, resign
2 *syn* FALL 3, go down, go under, submit, surrender
idiom hand over one's sword, meet one's Waterloo, show (*or* wave) the white flag, strike (*or* haul down) one's colors
3 *syn* COLLAPSE 2, break down, cave (in), drop, ||flake out, give out, peg out, wilt
idiom bite the dust, ||take the count
4 *syn* DIE 1, cash in, decease, demise, depart, drop, expire, pass, pass away, perish
idiom yield one's breath

such *adj* **1** being previously characterized or specified <authorized to seize illegally parked cars and impound *such* vehicles>
syn aforementioned, aforesaid, said
2 being of so extreme a degree or quality <*such* nonsense as I had never heard before>
syn that
3 *syn* LIKE, akin, alike, analogous, comparable, corresponding, equivalent, parallel, similar, suchlike

such *pron* **1** *syn* SUCH A ONE
2 *syn* SUCHLIKE
idiom the like

such a one *pron* someone or something that has been, is being, or will be stated, implied, or exemplified <the area is full of caverns; *such a one* may be found here>
syn such

suchlike *adj* *syn* LIKE, akin, alike, analogous, comparable, corresponding, equivalent, parallel, similar, such

suchlike *pron* a person or thing of the same or similar kind <airplanes, missiles, rockets, and *suchlike*>
syn such

***suck** *vb* *syn* STINK 2

||**suck** *n* *syn* SYCOPHANT, bootlicker, footlicker, lickspit, lickspittle, reptile, toad, toadeater, truckler, yes-man

sucker *n* **1** *syn* PARASITE, barnacle, bloodsucker, freeloader, hanger-on, leech, lounge lizard, ||spiv, sponge, sponger
2 *syn* FOOL 3, chump, dupe, fall guy, gull, mark, pigeon, sap, saphead, ||schlemiel
idiom easy pickings

sucker *vb* *syn* CHEAT, beat, bilk, cozen, defraud, diddle, do, gyp, overreach, take

suck in *vb* *syn* DECEIVE, beguile, betray, ||bitch, ||bunk, delude, double-cross, four-flush, sell out, take in

||**suck–in** *n* *syn* DECEPTION 1, cheat, chicane, chicanery, dishonesty, double-dealing, dupery, fraud, sharp practice, trickery

suckle *vb* *syn* NURSE 1, breast-feed, nourish

sudden *adj* *syn* PRECIPITATE 1, abrupt, hasty, headlong, hurried, impetuous, precipitant, precipitous, rushing, subitaneous
rel accelerated, quickened, speeded; expeditious, fast, fleet, rapid, swift

sudden *adv* **1** *syn* UNAWARES, aback, short, suddenly, unanticipatedly, unaware, unawaredly, unexpectedly
2 *syn* SHORT 1, abruptly, asudden, forthwith, suddenly

suddenly *adv* **1** *syn* SHORT 1, abruptly, asudden, forthwith, sudden

2 ***syn*** UNAWARES, aback, short, sudden, unanticipatedly, unaware, unawaredly, unexpectedly
idiom of (*or* on) a sudden, on the sudden

suds *n pl but sing or pl in constr* **1** ***syn*** SADNESS, blues, dinge, (the) dismals, (the) dolefuls, dumps, gloom, heavy-heartedness, mopes, unhappiness
2 ***syn*** FOAM, froth, lather, spume, yeast

sue *vb* ***syn*** ADDRESS 8, court, make up (to), pursue, spark, sweetheart, woo
idiom make (*or* pay) suit to, press one's suit

sue (for *or* to) *vb* ***syn*** PETITION, appeal

suffer *vb* **1** ***syn*** BEAR 10, abide, brook, endure, lump, stand, stomach, swallow, take, tolerate
rel accept, admit, receive
idiom grin and abide
2 ***syn*** EXPERIENCE 1, have, know, see, sustain, undergo
3 ***syn*** LET 2, allow, have, leave, permit
rel countenance; accept, admit, receive; acquiesce, bow, submit, yield
‖**4** ***syn*** HURT 4, ache, pain

sufferable *adj* ***syn*** BEARABLE, endurable, livable, supportable, sustainable, tolerable
ant insufferable

sufferance *n* ***syn*** PERMISSION, allowance, authorization, consent, leave, permit, sanction

suffering *n* ***syn*** DISTRESS, agony, dolor, misery, passion
rel adversity, misfortune

suffice *vb* ***syn*** SERVE 3, do, suit

sufficiency *n* ***syn*** ENOUGH, adequacy, competence, sufficient
ant insufficiency

sufficient *adj* **1** being what is requisite or needed especially without superfluity <there is *sufficient* bread left for breakfast>
syn adequate, comfortable, competent, decent, enough, satisfactory, sufficing; *compare* DECENT 4
rel ample, plenteous, plentiful, plenty; commensurable, commensurate, due, proportionate; acceptable, agreeable, pleasing
con inadequate, unsufficing; deficient; failing, lacking, missing, wanting
ant insufficient
2 ***syn*** DECENT 4, acceptable, adequate, all right, common, satisfactory, tolerable, unexceptionable, unexceptional, unobjectionable
idiom fair to middling

sufficient *n* ***syn*** ENOUGH, adequacy, competence, sufficiency

sufficiently *adv* ***syn*** ENOUGH 1, adequately
ant insufficiently

sufficing *adj* ***syn*** SUFFICIENT 1, adequate, comfortable, competent, decent, enough, satisfactory

suffocate *vb* to stop the respiration of (as by asphyxiation) <the child was *suffocated* in an old refrigerator>
syn asphyxiate, choke, ‖quackle, smother, stifle; *compare* CHOKE 1
rel stive; strangle

suffocating *adj* **1** ***syn*** STIFLING 1, smothering, smothery, ‖smudgy, suffocative
2 ***syn*** STUFFY 1, airless, breathless, close, stifling, stivy, sultry

suffocative *adj* ***syn*** STIFLING 1, smothering, smothery, ‖smudgy, suffocating

suffrage *n* the right, privilege, or power of expressing one's choice or wish (as in an election or in the determination of policy) <universal *suffrage*>
syn ballot, franchise, vote
rel voice

suffuse *vb* ***syn*** INFUSE 1, imbue, ingrain, inoculate, invest, leaven, steep
rel interject, interpose, introduce

‖**sugar** *n* ***syn*** MONEY, ‖bread, rhino, rocks, ‖scratch, ‖shekels, ‖smash, stuff, ‖stumpy, ‖wampum

sugar (over) *vb* ***syn*** SUGARCOAT 1, candy, honey, sweeten

sugarcoat *vb* **1** to make (something difficult or unpleasant) superficially easy or attractive <*sugarcoated* the reproach with a smile>
syn candy, honey, sugar (over), sweeten
rel edulcorate
2 ***syn*** PALLIATE, blanch (over), extenuate, gloss (over), gloze (over), varnish, veneer, white, whiten, whitewash

sugarplum *n* ***syn*** SOP 2

suggest *vb* **1** to convey an idea indirectly <designing attractive books with jackets that truly *suggest* their contents>
syn connote, hint, imply, insinuate, intimate; *compare* POINT 2
rel advert, allude, refer; denote
idiom bring to mind
con demonstrate, display, exhibit, manifest, set out, show
ant express
2 ***syn*** POINT 2, hint, imply, indicate
rel promise
idiom be the sign of, point in the direction of
3 ***syn*** PROPOSE 1, pose, prefer, ‖propone, proposition, propound, put
4 to offer (as an idea or theory) for consideration <this, I *suggest,* is what really happened>
syn submit, theorize
rel conjecture; imagine
5 to represent another thing indirectly, figuratively, and sometimes obscurely by evoking a thought, image, or conception of it <the meaning of a poem is often *suggested* in its title>
syn adumbrate, shadow (forth); *compare* ADUMBRATE 1
rel outline, sketch; betoken, symbolize; typify
con display, flaunt, parade
ant manifest

suggestion *n* **1** ***syn*** PROPOSAL, invitation, proffer, proposition
2 ***syn*** HINT 1, clue, cue, indication, inkling, intimation, notion, telltale, wind
rel implication, innuendo

---

3 ***syn*** ASSOCIATION 4, connotation, hint, implication, overtone, undertone
rel allusion; reminder
con demonstration, display, exhibition, manifestation, show
ant expression
4 ***syn*** HINT 2, intimation, shade, smack, soupçon, strain, suspicion, tinge, trace, vein

suggestive *adj* **1** ***syn*** EVOCATIVE, evocatory
rel significative
2 ***syn*** RISQUÉ, blue, broad, off-color, purple, racy, salty, shady, spicy, wicked
rel erotic, sexy

suicide *n* the act or an instance of taking one's own life voluntarily and intentionally <committed *suicide* by shooting herself>
syn felo-de-se, hara-kiri, self-destruction, self-murder, self-slaughter, self-violence

suit *n* **1** a legal proceeding instituted for the sake of demanding justice or enforcing a right <filed a *suit* to recover her property>
syn action, case, cause, lawsuit
2 ***syn*** PRAYER, appeal, application, entreaty, imploration, imprecation, orison, petition, plea, supplication
rel asking, request, requesting, solicitation, soliciting

suit *vb* **1** ***syn*** AGREE 4, accord, check, check out, conform, ‖gee, go, jibe, square, tally
idiom be in accord with, check out to the letter
2 ***syn*** SERVE 3, do, suffice
3 ***syn*** ADAPT, accommodate, adjust, conform, fit, quadrate, reconcile, square, tailor, tailor-make
4 to be suitable for or to <the right word is the one that *suits* the occasion>
syn agree (with), become, befit, fit, go (together *or* with); *compare* SUIT 6
rel harmonize (with); benefit; please, satisfy
idiom answer a need (*or* the purpose), hit the spot
con clash, conflict, disaccord, disagree
5 ***syn*** FLATTER, become, enhance
6 to meet the needs or desires of <this arrangement *suits* me fine>
syn please, satisfy; *compare* SUIT 4
con discontent, displease, dissatisfy; disappoint, fail, let down

suitability *n* ***syn*** ORDER 11, appositeness, appropriateness, aptness, expediency, fitness, meetness, propriety, rightness, suitableness
ant unsuitability

suitable *adj* **1** ***syn*** GOOD 2, appropriate, convenient, fit, meet, proper, useful
ant unsuitable
2 ***syn*** JUST 3, appropriate, condign, deserved, due, merited, requisite, rhadamanthine, right, rightful
rel reasonable; advisable, expedient, politic

syn synonym(s) — ***rel*** related word(s)
idiom idiomatic equivalent(s) — ***con*** contrasted word(s)
ant antonym(s) — * vulgar
‖ use limited; if in doubt, see a dictionary
The first word in a synonym list when printed in SMALL CAPITALS shows where there is more information about the group. For a more efficient use of this book see Explanatory Notes.

ant unsuitable
3 ***syn*** FIT 1, applicable, appropriate, apt, felicitous, fitting, happy, just, meet, proper
rel nice, presentable, seemly
ant unbecoming, unsuitable
4 ***syn*** ELIGIBLE, fit
ant unsuitable

suitableness *n* ***syn*** ORDER 11, appositeness, appropriateness, aptness, expediency, fitness, meetness, propriety, rightness, suitability
ant unsuitableness

suitably *adv* ***syn*** WELL 4, acceptably, adequately, amply, appropriately, becomingly, fittingly, properly, right, satisfactorily
ant unsuitably

suite *n* **1** ***syn*** ENTOURAGE, following, retinue, train
2 ***syn*** GROUP 3, array, batch, battery, body, clutch, lot, parcel, set, sort
3 ***syn*** APARTMENT 1, ‖chambers, flat, lodging(s), rental, rooms, tenement
4 ***syn*** SUCCESSION 2, chain, consecution, progression, row, sequel, sequence, series, string, train

suited *adj* ***syn*** ASSORTED 2, adapted, conformable, fitted, matched
ant unsuited

suitor *n* **1** ***syn*** SUPPLIANT, asker, beggar, petitioner, prayer, supplicant, supplicator
2 one who courts a woman or seeks to marry her <a *suitor* for the king's daughter>
syn spark, sparker, swain, wooer
rel beau, boyfriend; cavalier, gallant; lover, man, paramour

sulk *vb* to be sullen or morose in mood usually because of a grievance <*sulked* all day when he didn't call>
syn ‖dort, grump, ‖mump, pet, pout, ‖sull
rel frown, glower, lower, scowl; brood, gloom, mope, take on
idiom be in a sulk, have the sulks, ‖take the dods

sulk *n, often* **sulks** *pl* the state, condition, or mood of one sulking <sat in a *sulk* all day after being reprimanded>
syn ‖dods, ‖dorts, grumps, mulligrubs, mumps, pouts, sullens
rel sourness, sulkiness, surliness; glumness, grouchiness
idiom a case of the sulks

sulky *adj* ***syn*** SULLEN, ‖chuffy, crabbed, ‖dorty, dour, gloomy, glum, morose, saturnine, surly
rel cranky, testy, touchy; cantankerous, irritable, querulous
idiom having the sulks

‖**sull** *vb* ***syn*** SULK, ‖dort, grump, ‖mump, pet, pout

sullen *adj* showing a forbidding or disagreeable mood <stalked out in *sullen* silence>
syn ‖chuff, ‖chuffy, crabbed, crabby, ‖dorty, dour, gloomy, glum, morose, mumpish, saturnine, sulky, surly, ugly
rel moody; tenebrific, tenebrose, tenebrous; frowning, glowering, lowering, scowling; cross, fretful, grumpy, ill-humored, peevish, petulant, pouting, pouty, sour, sourpussed; black, hostile, malevolent, malicious, malign, mean, ‖runty; cynical, pessimistic
con easy, gay, high-spirited, insouciant, lighthearted, smiling

sullens *n pl* ***syn*** SULK, ‖dods, ‖dorts, grumps, mulligrubs, mumps, pouts

sully *vb* ***syn*** TAINT 1, besmear, besmirch, defile, discolor, smear, soil, stain, tar, tarnish
rel disgrace, shame

sulphurous *adj* ***syn*** INFERNAL 1, chthonian, chthonic, Hadean, plutonian, plutonic, Tartarean

sultry *adj* **1** ***syn*** HUMID, mucky, muggy, soggy, sticky
rel smothering, smothery, ‖smudgy, stifling, suffocating
2 ***syn*** STUFFY 1, airless, breathless, close, stifling, stivy, suffocating
3 ***syn*** HOT 1, baking, broiling, burning, red-hot, scorching, sizzling, sweltering, sweltry, torrid
idiom hot as Hades, ‖hot as old Billy Hell
4 ***syn*** SENSATIONAL 2, livid, lurid, sensationalistic, sensationist, tabloid

sum *n* **1** ***syn*** WHOLE 1, aggregate, all, be-all and end-all, entirety, gross, sum total, tale, total, totality
2 ***syn*** WHOLE 2, entity, integral, integrate, system, totality
rel body, bulk, mass; structure
3 ***syn*** SUMMARY, epitome, recapitulation, résumé, summation, summing-up, sum-up

sum *vb* **1** ***syn*** ADD 2, cast, figure, foot, summate, tot, total, totalize, tote
2 ***syn*** EPITOMIZE 1, condense, digest, inventory, nutshell, summarize, summate, sum up, synopsize

sum (to *or* into) *vb* ***syn*** AMOUNT 1, add up, aggregate, come, number, run (to *or* into), total

sum and substance *n* **1** ***syn*** SUBSTANCE 2, amount, core, gist, meat, pith, purport, short, sum total, upshot
2 ***syn*** MEANING 1, acceptation, import, intendment, intent, message, purport, sense, significance, significancy

summarize *vb* ***syn*** EPITOMIZE 1, condense, digest, inventory, nutshell, sum, summate, sum up, synopsize
rel recapitulate, résumé, retrograde

summary *adj* **1** ***syn*** CONCISE, breviloquent, brief, compendiary, compendious, curt, laconic, short, succinct, terse
rel compact, compacted
ant circumstantial
2 done or executed on the spot and without formality <a *summary* trial and speedy execution>
syn drumhead

summary *n* a short restatement of the main points <a *summary* of the news>
syn epitome, recapitulation, résumé, sum, summation, summing-up, sum-up
rel outline; run-through; roundup; inventory
con amplification, elaboration, enlargement, expansion

summate *vb* **1** ***syn*** ADD 2, cast, figure, foot, sum, tot, total, totalize, tote
2 ***syn*** EPITOMIZE 1, condense, digest, inventory, nutshell, sum, summarize, sum up, synopsize

summation *n* ***syn*** SUMMARY, epitome, recapitulation, résumé, sum, summing-up, sum-up

summative *adj* ***syn*** CUMULATIVE, accumulative, additive, additory, chain

summer *n* the season between spring and autumn <liked to swim during the *summer*>
syn summertide, summertime
rel midsummer

summerhouse *n* a covered structure in a garden or park designed to provide a shady resting place <watched the sea from the *summerhouse*>
syn alcove, belvedere, garden house, gazebo, pagoda

summertide *n* ***syn*** SUMMER, summertime

summertime *n* ***syn*** SUMMER, summertide

summing–up *n* ***syn*** SUMMARY, epitome, recapitulation, résumé, sum, summation, sum-up

summit *n* **1** ***syn*** TOP 1, apex, crest, crown, fastigium, peak, roof, vertex
2 ***syn*** APEX 2, acme, apogee, capsheaf, capstone, climax, culmination, meridian, pinnacle, zenith

summon *vb* **1** ***syn*** CONVOKE, assemble, call, convene
2 to demand or request the presence or service of <were *summoned* to the principal's office>
syn call, call in, convene, summons; *compare* CONVOKE
rel bid, command, enjoin, order; cite, subpoena
idiom bid come

summons *vb* ***syn*** SUMMON 2, call, call in, convene

‖**sump** *n* ***syn*** SWAMP, bog, fen, marsh, mire, morass, quag, quagmire, slough, swampland

sumptuous *adj* **1** ***syn*** LUXURIOUS 3, Capuan, deluxe, luscious, lush, luxuriant, opulent, palatial, plush, upholstered
rel gorgeous, resplendent, splendid, superb; lavish, rich
2 ***syn*** GRAND 2, gorgeous, impressive, lavish, luxurious, splendid
rel awe-inspiring, grandiose, imposing

sum total *n* **1** ***syn*** WHOLE 1, aggregate, all, be-all and end-all, entirety, gross, sum, tale, total, totality
2 ***syn*** SUBSTANCE 2, amount, body, gist, meat, purport, sense, sum and substance, thrust, upshot

sum up *vb* ***syn*** EPITOMIZE 1, condense, digest, inventory, nutshell, sum, summarize, summate, synopsize

sum–up *n* ***syn*** SUMMARY, epitome, recapitulation, résumé, sum, summation, summing-up

sun *n* **1** the heavenly body about which the earth rotates <up in time to see the *sun* rise>
syn daystar, phoebus, Sol
rel celestial body, luminary, orb, star
idiom old Sol
2 the radiation of the sun <enjoying the warm spring *sun*>
syn sunlight, sunshine
rel daylight; radiance, radiation

sun *vb* to expose to sunshine <*sunned* himself too long and got badly burned>
syn bask, insolate
rel sunbathe; sunburn, sun-cure, sun-dry, tan

sunbeamy *adj* ***syn*** CHEERFUL 1, blithe, cheery, ‖chirk, chirpy, chirrupy, lightsome, sunny

---

syn synonym(s) — *rel* related word(s)
idiom idiomatic equivalent(s) — *con* contrasted word(s)
ant antonym(s) — * vulgar
‖ use limited; if in doubt, see a dictionary
The first word in a synonym list when printed in SMALL CAPITALS shows where there is more information about the group. For a more efficient use of this book see Explanatory Notes.

Sunday best *n* ***syn*** FINERY, ||best bib and tucker, bravery, frippery, full dress, ||glad rags, regalia, war paint
idiom Sunday-go-to-meeting clothes

sunder *vb* **1** ***syn*** SEPARATE 1, break up, dichotomize, disjoin, disjoint, dissever, disunite, divide, divorce, part
rel cleave, rend, rive
2 ***syn*** CUT 5, carve, cleave, dissect, dissever, sever, slice, split

||**sundowner** *n* ***syn*** VAGABOND, ||bindle stiff, drifter, floater, hobo, roadster, tramp, ||traveler, vag, Weary Willie

sundries *n pl* miscellaneous small articles, details, or items <supplied such *sundries* as needles, pins, and thread>
syn etceteras, oddments, odds and ends, this and that(s)
rel notions

sundry *adj* **1** ***syn*** MANY, legion, multifarious, multitudinal, multitudinous, numerous, populous, ||several, various, voluminous
idiom all and sundry
2 ***syn*** SEVERAL 3, divers, some, various
idiom all sorts of

sundry *pron, pl in constr* an indeterminate number of more than one or two <*sundry* were interviewed; a few were selected>
syn divers, many, ||several, various
idiom all and sundry, quite a few

sunk *adj* ***syn*** DOWNCAST, blue, cast down, crestfallen, dejected, depressed, downhearted, down-in-the-mouth, droopy, low

sunlight *n* ***syn*** SUN 2, sunshine

sunny *adj* **1** ***syn*** FAIR 2, clarion, clear, cloudless, fine, pleasant, rainless, sunshiny, unclouded, undarkened
rel bright, brilliant
idiom bright and sunny
2 ***syn*** CHEERFUL 1, blithe, cheery, ||chirk, chirpy, chirrupy, lightsome, sunbeamy

sunrise *n* ***syn*** DAWN 1, aurora, cockcrow, dawning, daybreak, daylight, light, morn, morning, sunup

sunset *n* ***syn*** EVENING 2, twilight

sunshine *n* ***syn*** SUN 2, sunlight

sunshine *adj* ***syn*** FAIR 2, clarion, clear, cloudless, fine, pleasant, rainless, sunny, sunshining, sunshiny

sunshining *adj* ***syn*** FAIR 2, clarion, clear, cloudless, fine, pleasant, rainless, sunny, sunshine, sunshiny

sunshiny *adj* ***syn*** FAIR 2, clarion, clear, cloudless, fine, pleasant, rainless, sunny, sunshine, sunshining

sunup *n* ***syn*** DAWN 1, aurora, cockcrow, dawning, daybreak, daylight, light, morn, morning, sunrise

sup (off *or* up) *vb* ***syn*** DRINK 1, imbibe, quaff, sip, swallow, toss

super *adj* ***syn*** MARVELOUS 2, ||cool, divine, groovy, hot, ||keen, ||neat, sensational, terrific, wonderful
idiom out of this world

super *adv* **1** ***syn*** VERY 1, damned, exceedingly, exceptionally, extremely, highly, hugely, rattling, strikingly, surpassingly
2 ***syn*** EVER 6, excessively, immensely, inordinately, over, overfull, overly, overmuch, too, unduly

superabundant *adj* abounding to a great, abnormal, or excessive degree <*superabundant* harvests had brought down prices>
syn overabounding, overabundant, overflowing
rel abounding, abundant, cornucopian, plenteous, plentiful; excess, excessive, overmuch, surplus; crawling, teeming; overspilling; epidemic, rampant

superadd *vb* ***syn*** ADD 1, annex, append, subjoin, take on

superannuate *vb* **1** ***syn*** OUTDATE, antiquate, obsolesce, obsolete, outmode
2 ***syn*** RETIRE 2, pension (off)

superb *adj* **1** ***syn*** GRAND 3, elevated, exalted, lofty, sublime
rel noble; majestic
2 ***syn*** SPLENDID 2, glorious, gorgeous, magnificent, proud, resplendent, splendiferous, splendorous, sublime
rel imposing, stately; opulent
3 consummately impressive and supremely excellent of its kind <the writer's style is brilliant and his command of words and imagery, *superb*>
syn magnificent, outstanding, standout, superexcellent, superlative; *compare* SUPREME
rel gorgeous, glorious, marvelous, resplendent; crashing, rousing, sensational, slambang, super, superfine, wonderful; best, optimal, optimum, prime; sublime
idiom very best
con inferior, mediocre, poor, substandard; atrocious, awful, dreadful, shocking; deplorable, dismal, lamentable, pitiful, woeful; abominable, execrable, outrageous, shameful
ant wretched

superbity *n* ***syn*** PRIDE 3, arrogance, disdain, disdainfulness, haughtiness, hauteur, loftiness, morgue, superciliousness

supercilious *adj* ***syn*** PROUD 1, arrogant, cavalier, disdainful, haughty, high-and-mighty, insolent, lordly, overbearing, superior
rel sniffish, sniffy, snifty, snippy, snuffy; sneering

superciliousness *n* ***syn*** PRIDE 3, arrogance, disdain, disdainfulness, haughtiness, hauteur, loftiness, morgue, superbity

supererogant *adj* ***syn*** SUPEREROGATORY, gratuitous, supererogative, unasked, uncalled-for, wanton

supererogative *adj* ***syn*** SUPEREROGATORY, gratuitous, supererogant, unasked, uncalled-for, wanton

supererogatory *adj* given or done without compulsion, need, or warrant <people who offer *supererogatory* advice>
syn gratuitous, supererogant, supererogative, unasked, uncalled-for, wanton
rel nonessential, superfluous, supernumerary, unnecessary, unneeded
con essential, indispensible, vital; compulsory, obligatory; called-for, needful, required, requisite, sought, wanted

superexcellent *adj* ***syn*** SUPERB 3, magnificent, outstanding, standout, superlative

---

syn synonym(s) ***rel*** related word(s)
idiom idiomatic equivalent(s) ***con*** contrasted word(s)
ant antonym(s) * vulgar
|| use limited; if in doubt, see a dictionary
The first word in a synonym list when printed in SMALL CAPITALS shows where there is more information about the group. For a more efficient use of this book see Explanatory Notes.

rel incomparable, matchless, unparalleled, unsurpassed

superficial *adj* **1** ***syn*** SHALLOW 1, shoal
2 lacking in depth, solidity, and comprehensiveness <wrote only a *superficial* report on the situation>
syn cursory, depthless, shallow, sketchy, uncritical
rel bird's-eye, general; one-dimensional, skin-deep; smattery
con comprehensive, full, inclusive; deep, detailed, in-depth, thorough; critical
ant exhaustive

superficies *n* ***syn*** TOP 2, face, surface

superfluent *adj* ***syn*** SUPERFLUOUS, de trop, excess, extra, recrementitious, spare, supernumerary, surplus

superfluity *n* **1** ***syn*** EXCESS 1, overabundance, overflow, overkill, overmuch, overplus, plethora, surfeit, surplus, surplusage
rel overflowing, swarming, teeming
2 ***syn*** LUXURY, amenity, extravagance, frill, luxus

superfluous *adj* exceeding what is needed or indispensable <omitted all *superfluous* information>
syn de trop, excess, extra, recrementitious, spare, superfluent, supernumerary, surplus
rel unnecessary, unneeded, unwanted; needless, useless; dispensable, nonessential; gratuitous, supererogatory, unasked, uncalled-for
con critical, crucial, imperative; essential, fundamental, vital; consequential, important, momentous, notable, noteworthy; defective, inadequate
ant deficient

superhuman *adj* **1** ***syn*** SUPERNATURAL 1, miraculous, numinous, preternatural, superior, supermundane, suprahuman, supramundane, supranatural, unearthly
2 ***syn*** SUPERNATURAL 2, supernormal, superordinary, supranormal, uncanny, unnatural

superhuman *n* ***syn*** SUPERMAN, demigod

superincumbent *adj* **1** ***syn*** SUPERIOR 1, greater, higher, over, overlying, superjacent
2 ***syn*** ONEROUS, burdensome, demanding, exacting, exigent, grievous, oppressive, taxing, tough, weighty

superintend *vb* ***syn*** SUPERVISE, boss, chaperon, overlook, oversee, quarterback, survey

superintendence *n* ***syn*** OVERSIGHT 1, care, charge, conduct, handling, intendance, management, running, superintendency, supervision
rel direction, presidence

superintendency *n* ***syn*** OVERSIGHT 1, care, charge, conduct, handling, intendance, management, running, superintendence, supervision
rel direction, presidence

superior *adj* **1** being or regarded as being above the level of another <the new assistant received a *superior* rating for his work>
syn greater, higher, over, overlying, superincumbent, superjacent
rel major, primary, senior
con lesser, lower, nether, under
ant inferior
2 ***syn*** SUPERNATURAL 1, miraculous, numinous, preternatural, superhuman, supermundane, suprahuman, supramundane, supranatural, unearthly
3 ***syn*** BETTER 2, ‖bettermost, preferable
ant inferior
4 being of higher quality, accomplishment, or merit <a class of *superior* students>
syn exceptional, premium; *compare* MARVELOUS 2
rel noteworthy, remarkable, unusual
con commonplace, ordinary, unexceptional, unremarkable
ant average
5 ***syn*** CHOICE, dainty, delicate, elegant, exquisite, rare, recherché, select
6 ***syn*** EXCELLENT, capital, ‖dandy, famous, fine, first-class, first-rate, first-string, five-star, prime
ant inferior
7 ***syn*** PROUD 1, arrogant, cavalier, disdainful, haughty, high-and-mighty, insolent, lofty, overbearing, supercilious

superior *n* one standing above another in a hierarchy of rank <was always respectful to his *superiors* in the department>
syn better, brass hat, elder, higher-up, senior
rel heavyweight
ant inferior

superiority *n* ***syn*** BETTER 2, advantage, upper hand, victory, whip hand
rel ascendancy, dominance, supremacy
ant inferiority

superjacent *adj* ***syn*** SUPERIOR 1, greater, higher, over, overlying, superincumbent
ant subjacent

superlative *adj* ***syn*** SUPERB 3, magnificent, outstanding, standout, superexcellent
rel accomplished, consummate, finished

superman *n* a person of extraordinary power or achievement <a space program run by scientific *supermen*>
syn demigod, superhuman
idiom Triton among the minnows
con also-ran, loser, underdog
ant subhuman

supermundane *adj* ***syn*** SUPERNATURAL 1, miraculous, numinous, preternatural, superhuman, superior, suprahuman, supramundane, supranatural, unearthly

supernatural *adj* **1** of, relating to, or proceeding from an order of existence beyond the visible observable universe <many then believed in a *supernatural* force that directs history>
syn metaphysical, miraculous, numinous, preternatural, superhuman, superior, supermundane, suprahuman, supramundane, supranatural, unearthly
rel paranormal, rare, unusual; spiritual; celestial, heavenly; divine
2 being much more than is natural or normal <had a *supernatural* ability to win money>
syn superhuman, supernormal, superordinary, supranormal, uncanny, unnatural
rel extraordinary, outstanding, phenomenal, remarkable; paranormal

---

syn synonym(s) ***rel*** related word(s)
idiom idiomatic equivalent(s) ***con*** contrasted word(s)
ant antonym(s) * vulgar
‖ use limited; if in doubt, see a dictionary
The first word in a synonym list when printed in SMALL CAPITALS shows where there is more information about the group. For a more efficient use of this book see Explanatory Notes.

3 ***syn*** EXCESSIVE 1, exorbitant, extravagant, extreme, immoderate, inordinate, stratospheric, towering, unconscionable, unmeasurable

supernormal *adj* ***syn*** SUPERNATURAL 2, superhuman, superordinary, supranormal, uncanny, unnatural
ant subnormal

supernumerary *adj* ***syn*** SUPERFLUOUS, de trop, excess, extra, recrementitious, spare, superfluent, surplus

superordinary *adj* ***syn*** SUPERNATURAL 2, superhuman, supernormal, supranormal, uncanny, unnatural
ant ordinary

superpatriot *n* ***syn*** PATRIOTEER, flag-waver, patriot

superscribe *vb* ***syn*** ADDRESS 6, direct

supersede *vb* ***syn*** REPLACE 3, outplace, supplant
rel reject, repudiate; abandon, desert, forsake; discard

superseded *adj* ***syn*** OBSOLETE, dead, disused, extinct, outmoded, outworn, passé

supersensible *adj* ***syn*** PSYCHIC 1, psychal, psychical, supersensory

supersensory *adj* ***syn*** PSYCHIC 1, psychal, psychical, supersensible

supertemporal *adj* ***syn*** INFINITE 1, eternal, illimitable, perdurable, sempiternal

supervene *vb* ***syn*** FOLLOW 1, ensue, succeed

supervenient *adj* ***syn*** ADVENTITIOUS, adscititious, advenient, advential

supervise *vb* to have or exercise the charge, direction, and oversight of < *supervised* the construction of the new stadium >
syn boss, chaperon, overlook, oversee, quarterback, superintend, survey
rel guide, steer; administer, conduct, direct; manage, run; control; monitor, proctor

supervision *n* ***syn*** OVERSIGHT 1, care, charge, conduct, handling, intendance, management, running, superintendence, superintendency

supper club *n* ***syn*** NIGHTCLUB, cabaret, café, discotheque, hot spot, nightery, night spot, nitery, watering hole, watering place

supplant *vb* **1** to supersede (another) by or as if by force, trickery, or treachery <a wife who found herself *supplanted* by another woman >
syn cut out, displace, usurp
rel crowd (out), force (out); bounce, cast (out), eject, expel, oust
idiom give the bum's rush, give the old heave-ho, step into the shoes of
2 ***syn*** REPLACE 3, outplace, supersede

supple *adj* **1** ***syn*** ELASTIC 1, flexible, resilient, springy, stretch, stretchy, whippy
ant stiff
2 ***syn*** PLASTIC, adaptable, ductile, malleable, moldable, pliable, pliant
3 showing freedom and ease of bodily movement (as in bending or twisting) <the light *supple* spring of a cat >
syn limber, lissome, lithe, lithesome
rel agile, graceful, willowy, wiry, withy
con awkward, clumsy, gawky, maladroit, unhandy; ungraceful; arthritic, creaky, decrepit
ant stiff

supplement *n* **1** ***syn*** COMPLEMENT 1
2 ***syn*** APPENDIX 1, addendum, codicil, rider

suppliant *n* one who asks (as for a favor or gift) humbly <a room full of *suppliants* waiting to see the king >
syn asker, beggar, petitioner, prayer, suitor, supplicant, supplicator
rel solicitant, solicitor

supplicant *n* ***syn*** SUPPLIANT, asker, beggar, petitioner, prayer, suitor, supplicator

supplicate *vb* ***syn*** BEG, appeal, beseech, crave, entreat, implore, importune, invoke, plead, pray
idiom ask on bended knee, ‖come down on one's marrowbones

supplication *n* ***syn*** PRAYER, appeal, application, entreaty, imploration, imprecation, orison, petition, plea, suit

supplicator *n* ***syn*** SUPPLIANT, asker, beggar, petitioner, prayer, suitor, supplicant

supply *vb* ***syn*** GIVE 3, deliver, dispense, feed, find, hand, hand over, provide, transfer, turn over
rel fulfill, outfit, provision

supply *n* an accumulation of something that is a source from which things may be drawn <an unending *supply* of new talent >
syn armamentarium, fund, inventory, stock, store
rel accumulation; reserve, reservoir, stockpile, surplus; hoard

supply *adj* ***syn*** TEMPORARY, acting, ad interim, interim, pro tem, pro tempore

support *vb* **1** ***syn*** BEAR 10, abide, brook, endure, go, stand, ‖stick, stomach, swallow, take
2 to favor actively in the face of opposition < *support* an unpopular economic policy >
syn advocate, back, backstop, champion, side (with), uphold
rel applaud, approve, endorse, favor, plunk (for), pull (for), root; adopt, embrace, espouse; defend, maintain, sustain
idiom align oneself with, be on (someone's) side, take (someone's) side
con battle, combat, counter, fight, oppose; withstand
ant buck
3 to supply what is needed for sustenance < *support* his family >
syn maintain, provide (for)
idiom boil the pot, bring home the bacon, make a living for, take care of
4 to hold up in position by serving as a foundation or base for <pillars *supporting* an arch >
syn bear up, bolster, brace, buttress, carry, prop, shore (up), sustain, upbear, uphold
rel stand
5 to keep from yielding, sinking, or losing courage or stability <her friends *supported* her during the crisis >
syn bolster, buoy (up), prop, sustain, underprop, uphold; *compare* ENCOURAGE 1

---

rel encourage; fortify, stiffen, strengthen

support *n* **1** *syn* HELP 1, aid, assist, assistance, comfort, hand, lift, relief, secours, succor
2 *syn* HELP 2, aid
3 a supporting means, agency, medium, or device <girders as structural *supports*> <strong economic *support* for the government>
syn brace, buttress, column, prop, shore, stay, underpinner, underpinning, underpropping
rel base, foundation; sustentation
4 *syn* LIVING, alimentation, alimony, bread, keep, livelihood, maintenance, salt, subsistence, sustenance

supportable *adj syn* BEARABLE, endurable, livable, sufferable, sustainable, tolerable
ant insupportable, unsupportable

supporter *n* **1** *syn* FOLLOWER, adherent, cohort, disciple, henchman, partisan, satellite, sectary, sectator
2 *syn* EXPONENT, advocate, champion, expounder, proponent
ant antagonist

supposable *adj syn* THINKABLE 2, conceivable, imaginable
ant insupposable

supposal *n syn* THEORY 1, hypothesis

suppose *vb* **1** *syn* UNDERSTAND 3, assume, believe, expect, gather, imagine, ||reckon, suspect, take, think
rel presuppose
2 *syn* CONJECTURE, guess, presume, pretend, surmise, think

suppose *n syn* THEORY 2, conjecture, perhaps, speculation, supposition

supposed *adj* **1** accepted or advanced as true or real on the basis of less than conclusive evidence <the *supposed* efficiency of the new machine>
syn conjectural, hypothetical, putative, reputed, suppositional, suppositious, supposititious, suppositive, suppository; *compare* ALLEGED
rel assumed, postulated, postulatory, presumed, presupposed; provisional, tentative; academic, speculative, theoretical; alleged
con sure; known, proved, proven; ascertained, demonstrated, observed, recognized
ant certain
2 *syn* ALLEGED, ostensible, pretended, professed, purported, so-called
ant proved, proven

supposition *n* **1** *syn* ASSUMPTION 2, apriorism, posit, postulate, postulation, premise, presumption, presupposition, thesis
2 *syn* THEORY 2, conjecture, perhaps, speculation, suppose

suppositional *adj syn* SUPPOSED 1, conjectural, hypothetical, putative, reputed, suppositious, supposititious, suppositive, suppository

suppositious *adj* **1** *syn* FICTITIOUS 1, chimerical, fanciful, fantastic, fictional, fictive, illusory, imaginary, supposititious, unreal
2 *syn* SUPPOSED 1, conjectural, hypothetical, putative, reputed, suppositional, supposititious, suppositive, suppository
rel doubtful, dubious, questionable; pretended, simulated

supposititious *adj* **1** *syn* ILLEGITIMATE 1, baseborn, bastard, fatherless, misbegotten, natural, spurious, unfathered
2 *syn* FICTITIOUS 1, chimerical, fanciful, fantastic, fictional, fictive, illusory, imaginary, suppositious, unreal
3 *syn* SUPPOSED 1, conjectural, hypothetical, putative, reputed, suppositional, suppositious, suppositive, suppository

supposititiousness *n syn* ILLEGITIMACY 1, bastardy, illegitimateness

suppositive *adj syn* SUPPOSED 1, conjectural, hypothetical, putative, reputed, suppositional, suppositious, supposititious, suppository

suppository *adj syn* SUPPOSED 1, conjectural, hypothetical, putative, reputed, suppositional, suppositious, supposititious, suppositive

suppress *vb* **1** *syn* CRUSH 5, annihilate, extinguish, put down, quash, quell, quench, squash
idiom ride roughshod over
2 to hold back more or less forcefully someone or something that seeks an outlet <management tried to *suppress* the workers' discontent> <there was no way to *suppress* her short of murder>
syn muffle, ||quelch, repress, shush, squelch, strangle; *compare* CRUSH 5
rel curb, restrain; arrest, check, interrupt; put down, slap down; quash, quell, squash; cut off, spike; abolish, annihilate, extinguish
idiom bring to naught, crack (*or* clamp) down on, put the kibosh on
3 to keep from public knowledge <*suppress* all news from the front>
syn burke, hush (up), stifle
rel repress; censor; silence
idiom put the lid on
con disclose, divulge, leak, ||let out, reveal; broadcast, circulate, diffuse, publish, spread
4 *syn* COMPOSE 4, collect, control, cool, re-collect, rein, repress, restrain, simmer down, smother
rel drown; swallow
5 *syn* STUNT, dwarf

suppression *n* **1** *syn* REPRESSION 1, choking, extinguishment, quashing, quenching, smothering, squashing, squelching, stifling, strangling
2 *syn* REPRESSION 2, clampdown, crackdown

supra *adv syn* ABOVE 2
ant infra

suprahuman *adj syn* SUPERNATURAL 1, miraculous, numinous, preternatural, superhuman, superior, supermundane, supramundane, supranatural, unearthly

supramundane *adj syn* SUPERNATURAL 1, miraculous, numinous, preternatural, superhuman, superior, supermundane, suprahuman, supranatural, unearthly

---

supranatural *adj* ***syn*** SUPERNATURAL 1, miraculous, numinous, preternatural, superhuman, superior, supermundane, suprahuman, supramundane, unearthly

supranormal *adj* ***syn*** SUPERNATURAL 2, superhuman, supernormal, superordinary, uncanny, unnatural

supremacy *n* the position of being first (as in rank, power, or influence) <Britain once enjoyed *supremacy* on the seas>
syn ascendancy, ascendant, dominance, domination, dominion, masterdom, preeminence, preponderance, preponderancy, preponderation, prepotence, prepotency, sovereignty
rel authority, control, driver's seat, power, sway; mastership, mastery, principality, superiority; transcendence

supreme *adj* developed to the utmost and not exceeded by any other in degree, quality, or intensity <dying for one's principles is an example of *supreme* sacrifice>
syn incomparable, preeminent, surpassing, towering, transcendent, ultimate, unequalable, unmatchable, unsurpassable; *compare* ALONE 3, EXCELLENT, MARVELOUS 2, MAXIMUM, SUPERB 3
rel crowning, master, sovereign; unequaled, unmatched, unparalleled, unrivaled, unsurpassed; final, last; absolute, perfect

surcease *vb* ***syn*** STOP 3, cease, desist, ‖deval, discontinue, give over, halt, knock off, leave off, quit

sure *adj* **1** firmly settled or established <trying to find a *sure* footing on the rugged slope>
syn fast, firm, secure, stable, staunch, strong; *compare* FAST 4, STABLE 4
2 free from doubt, hesitation, or fear <upheld a *sure* faith>
syn abiding, enduring, firm, fixed, never-failing, steadfast, steady, unfaltering, unqualified, unquestioning, unshakable, unshaken, unwavering, wholehearted
rel assured, changeless, constant, unchangeable, unchanging, uncompromising, unfailing, unvarying; certain, fixed, set
con insecure, uncertain, unreliable; feeble, infirm, shaky, unsound; doubtful, dubious, hesitant
ant unsure
3 ***syn*** INFALLIBLE 1, inerrable, inerrant, unerring
4 ***syn*** INFALLIBLE 2, certain, surefire, unfailing
5 marked by unwavering assurance especially as to the rightness of one's views or actions <was *sure* he knew the answer>
syn certain, cocksure, confident, positive
rel assured, self-assured, self-possessed, self-satisfied; arrogant, cocky, pert; decided, decisive
con doubtful, hesitant, uncertain
ant unsure
6 ***syn*** POSITIVE 3, certain, incontestable, incontrovertible, indisputable, indubitable, uncontestable, undeniable, unequivocal, unquestionable
rel convincing, telling; absolute, definite; genuine, real, valid

sure–enough *adj* **1** ***syn*** ACTUAL 2, absolute, factual, genuine, hard, positive
2 ***syn*** AUTHENTIC 2, blown-in-the-bottle, bona fide, indubitable, true, undoubted, undubitable, unquestionable, veritable, very

surefire *adj* ***syn*** INFALLIBLE 2, certain, sure, unfailing

sureness *n* ***syn*** CERTAINTY, assurance, assuredness, certitude, confidence, conviction, surety
ant unsureness

sure thing *n* one that is bound to be successful <was deemed a *sure thing* in the race>
syn shoo-in
rel certainty; winner

surety *n* **1** ***syn*** CERTAINTY, assurance, assuredness, certitude, confidence, conviction, sureness
2 ***syn*** GUARANTEE 1, bail, bond, guaranty, security, warranty
3 ***syn*** SPONSOR, angel, backer, backer-up, guarantor, patron

surface *n* ***syn*** TOP 2, face, superficies
rel exterior, outside; cover, covering
con body, mass; inside, interior; lining

surface *vb* to come to the surface (as of water) <a submarine *surfaced* outside the harbor>
syn rise
rel come up
con go down, go under; submerge; dive

surfeit *n* ***syn*** EXCESS 1, overabundance, overflow, overkill, overmuch, overplus, plethora, superfluity, surplus, surplusage

surfeit *vb* ***syn*** SATIATE, cloy, fill, glut, gorge, jade, pall, sate, ‖stall, stodge
rel overfill, overindulge
idiom have all one can take (*or* stand)
ant whet

surfeited *adj* ***syn*** SATIATED, full, glutted, gorged, jaded, sated, satiate
ant unsatisfied

surge *vb* ***syn*** POUR 2, flow, gush, roll, sluice, stream

surly *adj* ***syn*** SULLEN, ‖chuffy, crabbed, ‖dorty, dour, glum, morose, saturnine, sulky, ugly
rel discourteous, ill-mannered, rude, ungracious; bearish, boorish, churlish; fractious, irritable, snappish, waspish
idiom as surly as a bear
con affable, cordial, genial, gracious
ant amiable

surmise *vb* ***syn*** CONJECTURE, guess, presume, pretend, suppose, think
rel consider, regard; hypothesize, theorize
idiom risk assuming, venture a guess

surmount *vb* **1** ***syn*** OVERCOME 1, conquer, down, hurdle, lick, master, throw
rel best, better, outdo, outstrip, outtop, outtower, surpass
idiom rise superior to
2 ***syn*** CLEAR 8, hurdle, leap, negotiate, over, overleap, vault

3 to stand or lie at the top of <a cross *surmounts* the cupola>
syn cap, crest, crown, top
rel finish; terminate
4 *syn* TOP, clear

surpass *vb* **1** to be or become greater than or superior to <*surpassed* all his fellows in scholarship>
syn ‖bang, beat, best, better, cap, cob, ding, exceed, excel, outdo, outgo, outmatch, outshine, outstrip, pass, top, transcend, trump
rel distance, outdistance, outpace, outperform, outpoint, outrange, outrival, outrun, outvie; eclipse, outrank, outtop, outtower, outweigh, overshadow, overtop, rank
idiom have it all over, put to shame
2 *syn* EXCEED 1, outstep, overrun, overstep

surpassing *adj syn* SUPREME, incomparable, preeminent, towering, transcendent, ultimate, unequalable, unmatchable, unsurpassable

surpassingly *adv syn* VERY 1, exceedingly, exceptionally, extremely, greatly, hugely, mightily, remarkably, strikingly, vitally

surplus *n* **1** *syn* EXCESS 1, overabundance, overflow, overkill, overmuch, overplus, plethora, superfluity, surfeit, surplusage
ant deficiency
2 *syn* EXCESS 2, overage, overstock, oversupply, plus, surplusage
ant shortage

surplus *adj syn* SUPERFLUOUS, de trop, excess, extra, recrementitious, spare, superfluent, supernumerary

surplusage *n* **1** *syn* EXCESS 2, overage, overstock, oversupply, plus, surplus
ant shortage, underage
2 *syn* EXCESS 1, overabundance, overflow, overkill, overmuch, overplus, plethora, superfluity, surfeit, surplus
ant shortage

surprise *vb* **1** to attack unawares <hijackers *surprised* the truck driver and took his cargo>
syn ambush, lay (for), waylay
rel bushwhack, dry-gulch; capture, catch; grab, grasp, seize, take
2 to impress forcibly through unexpectedness, startlingness, or unusualness <was *surprised* by his violent jealousy>
syn amaze, astonish, astound, dumbfound, flabbergast
rel startle; bewilder, confound, discomfit, disconcert, dismay, nonplus, ‖swan; faze, rattle, rock; bowl (over), floor, stagger; stun, stupefy
idiom leave open-mouthed (*or* aghast), take aback (*or* by surprise)

surprising *adj syn* MARVELOUS 1, amazing, astonishing, astounding, miraculous, prodigious, spectacular, staggering, stupendous, wondrous
rel unexpected, unforeseen, unlooked-for; eye-opening, eye-popping

surrender *vb* **1** *syn* RELINQUISH, abandon, cede, give up, hand over, leave, resign, ‖turn up, waive, yield
rel commit, consign, entrust
2 *syn* FALL 3, go down, go under, submit, succumb
rel give in, give up
idiom haul down one's colors, strike the (*or* one's) flag

surrender *n* the yielding of one's person, forces, or possessions to another <the victors demanded unconditional *surrender*>
syn capitulation, dedition, submission
rel appeasement, Munich; relenting, succumbing, yielding; white flag

surreptitious *adj syn* SECRET 1, clandestine, covert, furtive, hole-and-corner, hush-hush, stealthy, sub-rosa, undercover, under-the-table
rel skulking, slinking, slinky, sneaking, sneaky
con obvious, open, overt
ant brazen

surreptitiously *adv syn* SECRETLY, by stealth, clandestinely, covertly, furtively, hugger-mugger, in camera, privately, stealthily, sub rosa
con openly, overtly, plainly
ant brazenly

surrogate *n* **1** *syn* SUBSTITUTE, alternate, fill-in, locum tenens, pinch hitter, replacement, stand-in, sub, succedaneum
2 *syn* RESOURCE 3, dernier ressort, expediency, expedient, makeshift, recourse, refuge, resort, stopgap, substitute

surrogate *adj syn* SUBSTITUTE 1, alternate, alternative

surround *vb* **1** to close in or as if in a ring about something <a crowd *surrounded* the accident victim>
syn begird, beset, circle, compass, encircle, encompass, environ, gird, girdle, hem, loop, ring, round
rel embosom, enclave, enclose, envelop; circumscribe, circumvent, confine, limit
2 *syn* BORDER 1, bound, edge, fringe, hem, margin, outline, rim, skirt, verge

surroundings *n pl syn* ENVIRONMENT, ambience, ambient, atmosphere, climate, medium, milieu, mise-en-scène

surveillance *n* **1** *syn* EYE 3, eagle eye, scrutiny, tab, watch
idiom peeled eye
2 *syn* LOOKOUT 3, tout, vigil, vigilance, watch, watch and ward
rel surveyance
idiom watchful (*or* weather) eye

survey *vb* **1** *syn* ESTIMATE 1, appraise, assay, assess, evaluate, rate, set (at), valuate, value
rel measure, size, size up
2 *syn* SUPERVISE, boss, chaperon, overlook, oversee, quarterback, superintend
3 to view from or as if from a high place or position <*surveyed* the view from his penthouse window>
syn overlook, oversee
4 *syn* SCRUTINIZE 1, canvass, check over, check up, con, examine, inspect, study, vet, view

---

syn synonym(s)　*rel* related word(s)
idiom idiomatic equivalent(s)　*con* contrasted word(s)
ant antonym(s)　* vulgar
‖ use limited; if in doubt, see a dictionary
The first word in a synonym list when printed in SMALL CAPITALS shows where there is more information about the group. For a more efficient use of this book see Explanatory Notes.

survey *n* **1** *syn* EXAMINATION, analysis, audit, check* over, inspection, perlustration, review, scan, scrutiny, view

2 *syn* COMPENDIUM 1, aperçu, digest, pandect, précis, sketch, syllabus, sylloge

‖**survigrous** *adj* *syn* VIGOROUS, dynamic, energetic, lusty, red-blooded, strenuous, vital

survive *vb* **1** *syn* OUTLIVE, outlast, outwear

2 to continue to exist or function in spite of a usually adverse condition or development <a company that managed to *survive* the recession>

syn come through, pull through, ride (out)

rel carry on, carry through, continue, endure, last, persist; live down, outlast, outlive; recover, revive

idiom come out of it, live to fight again, make it through, ride out (*or* weather) the storm

con collapse, crash, fold, fold up, go down, go under; founder, sink; close (down), close up; bankrupt, bust

ant perish

susceptible *adj* **1** *syn* LIABLE 2, exposed, obnoxious, open, prone, sensitive, subject

rel disposed, inclined, predisposed

ant immune, unsusceptible

2 *syn* EASY 3, fleeceable, gullible, naive

rel nonresistant, soft; movable, persuadable

ant unsusceptible

3 *syn* SENTIENT 3, impressible, impressionable, responsive, sensible, sensile, sensitive, susceptive

rel affected, impressed, influenced, swayed, touched; aroused, roused, stirred

ant unsusceptible

susceptive *adj* *syn* SENTIENT 3, impressible, impressionable, responsive, sensible, sensile, sensitive, susceptible

suscitate *vb* *syn* PROVOKE 4, excite, galvanize, innervate, innerve, motivate, move, pique, quicken, stimulate

suspect *adj* *syn* DOUBTFUL 1, doubtable, dubious, open, problematic, shaky, suspicious, uncertain, unclear, unsure

idiom ‖a bit thin (*or* thick), open to suspicion

suspect *vb* **1** *syn* DISTRUST, doubt, misdoubt, mistrust, ‖suspicion

idiom have doubts about

2 *syn* UNDERSTAND 3, assume, believe, conceive, expect, gather, imagine, ‖reckon, suppose, think

idiom be inclined to think

suspend *vb* **1** *syn* EXCLUDE, bar, bate, count out, debar, eliminate, except, rule out

2 *syn* DEFER, delay, hold off, hold up, intermit, postpone, prorogue, put off, shelve, stay

rel arrest, check, interrupt; cease, discontinue, stop

idiom lay on the table, put on the shelf

3 *syn* HANG 1, dangle, depend, sling

suspended *adj* hung or seeming as if hung from a support <bunches of grapes *suspended* from the vines>

syn hanging, pendent, pendulant, pendulous, pensile

rel dangling, swinging

suspenders *n pl* a pair of supporting bands worn across the shoulders to support trousers, skirt, or belt <*suspenders* are out of style>

syn braces, ‖gallows, ‖galluses

suspense *n* *syn* SUSPENSION 2, moratorium

suspension *n* **1** *syn* ABEYANCE, abeyancy, cold storage, doldrums, dormancy, intermission, interruption, latency, quiescence, quiescency

2 a temporary withholding of action or cessation of activity <asked for *suspension* of judgment until all the evidence was in>

syn moratorium, suspense

rel cessation, concluding, conclusion, end, ending, finish, period, termination

con resumption; continuance

suspicion *n* **1** *syn* UNCERTAINTY, concern, doubt, dubiety, dubiosity, incertitude, mistrust, skepticism, uncertitude, wonder

rel apprehension, foreboding, misgiving, presentiment; distrust

2 *syn* HINT 2, cast, intimation, shade, smell, suggestion, tinge, touch, trace, whiff

‖**suspicion** *vb* *syn* DISTRUST, doubt, misdoubt, mistrust, suspect

suspicious *adj* **1** *syn* DOUBTFUL 1, borderline, doubtable, dubious, open, problematic, shaky, suspect, uncertain, unsure

rel questionable; queer

2 given or prone to suspicion <was *suspicious* of everyone's motives>

syn distrustful, jealous, mistrustful

rel careful, cautious; leery, wary, watchful; skeptical, unbelieving

con trustful, trusting, unsuspecting; naive; dupable, easy, exploitable, gullible

ant unsuspicious

suspiciously *adv* *syn* ASKANCE 2, distrustfully, doubtfully, mistrustfully, skeptically

rel distrustingly, mistrustingly

ant unsuspiciously

suspire *vb* **1** *syn* SIGH 1, ‖sock, sough

idiom draw a long breath

2 *syn* LONG, ache, crave, dream, hanker, hunger, lust, pine, sigh, thirst

sustain *vb* **1** *syn* MAINTAIN 1, keep up, preserve, save

rel nourish, support; prolong

2 *syn* SUPPORT 4, bear up, bolster, brace, buttress, carry, prop, shore (up), upbear, uphold

rel lug, pack, tote

3 *syn* SUPPORT 5, bolster, buoy (up), prop, underprop, uphold

rel befriend, favor

idiom stand by

con abandon, forsake; ignore

4 *syn* BEAR 10, abide, brook, digest, endure, go, lump, stand, stomach, tolerate

5 *syn* EXPERIENCE 1, have, know, see, suffer, undergo

rel bear, endure

sustainable *adj* *syn* BEARABLE, endurable, livable, sufferable, supportable, tolerable

ant unsustainable

---

syn synonym(s)	*rel* related word(s)
idiom idiomatic equivalent(s)	*con* contrasted word(s)
ant antonym(s)	* vulgar

‖ use limited; if in doubt, see a dictionary

The first word in a synonym list when printed in SMALL CAPITALS shows where there is more information about the group. For a more efficient use of this book see Explanatory Notes.

sustenance *n* **1** ***syn*** FOOD 2, aliment, nourishment, nutriment, pabulum, pap
idiom bodily sustenance
2 ***syn*** LIVING, alimentation, alimony, bread, keep, livelihood, maintenance, salt, subsistence, support

sustentation *n* ***syn*** PRESERVATION 1, conservation, keeping, safekeeping, salvation, saving

susurration *n* ***syn*** MURMUR 1, mumble, mutter, rumor, undertone, whisper

‖**swack** *n* ***syn*** CUFF, box, buffet, chop, clout, ‖paste, punch, slap, smack, sock

‖**swacked** *adj* ***syn*** INTOXICATED 1, ‖boozy, ‖canned, disguised, drunk, inebriated, ‖lushed, muddled, pixilated, ‖plastered

swad *n* ***syn*** SOLDIER, fighter, fighting man, GI, man-at-arms, serviceman, ‖swaddy, ‖sweat, warrior

swaddle *vb* ***syn*** SWATHE, drape, enswathe, envelop, enwrap, roll, wrap (up)
rel ‖sweel
ant unswaddle

‖**swaddy** *n* ***syn*** SOLDIER, fighter, fighting man, GI, man-at-arms, serviceman, swad, ‖sweat, warrior

swag *vb* **1** ***syn*** SEESAW, lurch, pitch, tilt, tilter, yaw
2 ***syn*** DROOP 3, flag, sag, wilt

swag *n* **1** ***syn*** SPOIL, boodle, booty, loot, plunder, plunderage, prize, ‖spreaghery, ‖spulzie
2 ***syn*** MONEY, rhino, rocks, ‖scratch, ‖shekels, ‖smash, stuff, ‖stumpy, ‖sugar, ‖wampum

swagger *vb* **1** ***syn*** LORD, cock, peacock, pontificate, swank, swell
rel swash, swashbuckle
2 ***syn*** STRUT 2, ‖strunt
rel bluster, brandish, flourish
con blench, quail; shrink, wince; truckle

‖**swagger** *n* ***syn*** VAGABOND, ‖bindle stiff, drifter, ‖gangrel, hobo, roadster, ‖shack, ‖sundowner, ‖swagman, ‖traveler

‖**swagman** *n* ***syn*** VAGABOND, ‖bindle stiff, drifter, floater, hobo, roadster, ‖shack, tramp, ‖traveler, vag

swain *n* **1** ***syn*** BOYFRIEND 1, beau, gentleman friend, young man
2 ***syn*** SUITOR 2, spark, sparker, wooer

swainish *adj* ***syn*** BOORISH, churlish, cloddish, clodhopping, clownish, ill-bred, loutish, lowbred, lubberly, lumpish

swallow *vb* **1** to receive through the esophagus into the stomach < *swallowed* the pills easily with a sip of water >
syn down, take
rel drop, gulp, ‖quilt, toss; ingest, ingurgitate
2 ***syn*** DRINK 1, imbibe, quaff, sip, sup (off *or* up), toss
3 ***syn*** BELIEVE 1, accept, ‖buy
idiom swallow (something) hook, line, and sinker
4 ***syn*** BEAR 10, abide, brook, digest, endure, go, stand, stomach, take, tolerate
5 ***syn*** ACCEPT 2, bear (with), endure, pocket, tolerate, tough (out)
6 ***syn*** MUMBLE, ‖chunter, fumble, muddle, ‖mump, murmur, mutter

swamp *n* wet spongy land saturated and sometimes partially covered with water <hunted alligators in the Florida *swamps* >
syn baygall, bog, fen, marsh, marshland, mire, morass, ‖moss, muskeg, ‖purgatory, ‖puxy, quag, quagmire, slough, ‖sump, swampland, ‖swang, ‖vlei
rel bottoms, ‖holm; ‖glade; jheel; quake ooze; shaking prairie, trembling prairie

swamp *vb* **1** ***syn*** DELUGE 1, drown, engulf, flood, inundate, overflow, overwhelm, submerge, whelm
2 ***syn*** DELUGE 3, flood, overwhelm, whelm

swampland *n* ***syn*** SWAMP, bog, fen, marsh, marshland, morass, quag, quagmire, slough, ‖sump

‖**swang** *n* ***syn*** SWAMP, baygall, bog, fen, marsh, ‖moss, quag, slough, swampland, ‖vlei

swank *vb* ***syn*** LORD, cock, peacock, pontificate, swagger, swell

swank *adj* **1** ***syn*** SHOWY, chichi, flamboyant, orchidaceous, ostentatious, peacockish, peacocky, pretentious, splashy
2 ***syn*** STYLISH, ‖classy, sharp, snappy, swish, tonish, tony, ‖trendy, trig, with-it

swap *vb* **1** ***syn*** EXCHANGE 2, change, substitute, switch, trade
2 ***syn*** TRADE 1, bargain, barter, exchange, traffic, truck
idiom ‖swap horses, swap out of

‖**swap** *n* ***syn*** BLOW 1, bang, bash, belt, biff, crack, pound, slam, smack, sock

‖**swapping** *adj* ***syn*** HUGE, colossal, enormous, giant, gigantic, immense, jumbo, mammoth, tremendous, whopping

‖**swarf** *vb* ***syn*** FAINT, black out, ‖crap out, pass out, ‖swelt, swoon

swarm *vb* ***syn*** TEEM, abound, crawl, flow, pullulate, ‖sny
idiom gather (*or* swarm) like bees

swarming *adj* ***syn*** ALIVE 5, abounding, overflowing, replete, rife, teeming, thronged

swart *adj* ***syn*** DARK 3, bistered, black-a-vised, brunet, dark-skinned, dusky, swarth, swarthy

swarth *adj* ***syn*** DARK 3, bistered, black-a-vised, brunet, dark-skinned, dusky, swart, swarthy

swarthy *adj* ***syn*** DARK 3, bistered, black-a-vised, brunet, dark-skinned, dusky, swart, swarth

swash *vb* **1** ***syn*** SLOSH 1, bubble, burble, gurgle, lap, wash
2 ***syn*** SPLASH, douse, plash, slop, slosh, spatter, splatter, splosh, splurge, spurtle

swashy *adj* ***syn*** INSIPID 3, banal, bland, driveling, inane, milk-and-water, sapless, vapid, waterish, watery

swat *vb* ‖**1** ***syn*** SQUAT, hunker (down), ‖quat
2 ***syn*** STRIKE 2, ‖biff, clout, ‖devel, ding, hit, slog, smite, sock, whack
rel blip, box, buffet, cuff, smack; belt, clobber, slug, smash, wallop

swat *n* ***syn*** HIT 1, ‖conk, knock, lick, rap, swipe, wipe

---

syn synonym(s) | ***rel*** related word(s)
idiom idiomatic equivalent(s) | ***con*** contrasted word(s)
ant antonym(s) | * vulgar
‖ use limited; if in doubt, see a dictionary
The first word in a synonym list when printed in SMALL CAPITALS shows where there is more information about the group. For a more efficient use of this book see Explanatory Notes.

swathe *vb* to cover or bind completely with clothing or material <legs *swathed* in bandages> <the baby was *swathed* in a warm shawl>
syn drape, enswathe, envelop, enwrap, roll, swaddle, wrap (up); *compare* ENFOLD 1
rel enfold; encase; cover
con bare, denude, expose, strip, uncover, unswaddle, unwrap
ant unswathe

sway *vb* **1** *syn* SWING 2, oscillate, pendulate
2 *syn* LURCH 2, careen, stagger, ‖stoit, ‖stoiter, ‖stot, swing, weave, wobble
3 *syn* GOVERN 1, overrule, reign, rule
4 *syn* AFFECT, carry, get, impress, influence, inspire, move, strike, touch
rel bias, dispose, incline, predispose; conduct, control, direct, manage; govern, rule

sway *n* *syn* POWER 1, authority, command, control, domination, jurisdiction, mastery, might, strings
rel range, reach, scope, sweep; amplitude, expanse, spread, stretch

swayable *adj* *syn* RECEPTIVE 1, acceptant, acceptive, influenceable, persuadable, persuasible, responsive, suasible

swear *vb* **1** *syn* VOW, covenant, pledge, plight
idiom swear on a stack of Bibles, swear to God, swear up and down
2 *syn* TESTIFY 2, depone, depose, ‖mount
3 to use profane, blasphemous, or obscene language <*swore* when the horse threw him>
syn bedamn, curse, cuss, damn, execrate, imprecate
rel blaspheme; rail, rant; abuse, revile, vilify, vituperate
idiom ‖chew the dirty rag, curse and swear, fall a-cursing, ‖let out religion, make the air blue, rip (*or* rap) out an oath, swear like a sailor (*or* trooper), use language

swear *n* *syn* SWEARWORD, curse, cuss, cussword, expletive, oath

swearing *n* *syn* BLASPHEMY 1, cursing, cussing, execration, imprecation, profanity

swearword *n* a profane, blasphemous, or obscene word <let loose with a string of *swearwords*>
syn curse, cuss, cussword, expletive, oath, swear
rel four-letter word, obscenity, scurrility
idiom blue word, one-horse oath, raw one, ripe (*or* juicy) word, sailor's blessing, six-cornered oath, strong word

sweat *vb* **1** *syn* EXUDE, bleed, ooze, ‖screeve, seep, ‖sew, ‖sicker, strain, transude, weep
2 *syn* FLEECE 1, bleed, milk, mulct, rook, stick

sweat *n* **1** *syn* WORK 2, bullwork, donkeywork, drudgery, grind, labor, moil, slavery, toil, travail
2 *syn* SNIT, fume, stew, swivet, tizzy
‖**3** *syn* SOLDIER, fighter, fighting man, GI, man-at-arms, serviceman, swad, ‖swaddy, warrior

sweatful *adj* *syn* SWEATY, asweat, perspiring, perspiry, ‖puggy, sweating

sweating *adj* *syn* SWEATY, asweat, perspiring, perspiry, ‖puggy, sweatful

sweat out *vb* *syn* BEAR 10, abide, brook, endure, go, lump, stand, stomach, take, tolerate

sweaty *adj* producing, accompanied by, or characterized by sweat <he still held the racket tight in *sweaty* hands>
syn asweat, perspiring, perspiry, ‖puggy, sweatful, sweating
rel clammy; sticky; wet
idiom bathed in sweat, covered with sweat, drenched with (*or* in) sweat, in a muck of a sweat, wet with sweat (*or* perspiration)

sweep *vb* *syn* FLY 4, fleet, flit, sail, wing

sweep *n* *syn* RANGE 2, ambit, compass, extension, extent, orbit, purview, radius, reach, scope

sweeping *n* **sweepings** *pl* *syn* REFUSE, debris, ‖dust, garbage, junk, litter, outsweepings, rubbish, trash, waste

sweeping *adj* **1** *syn* ALL-AROUND 2, comprehensive, general, global, inclusive, overall
rel all-embracing, all-encompassing
2 *syn* INDISCRIMINATE 1, indiscriminating, indiscriminative, undiscriminated, undiscriminating, undistinguishing, wholesale
rel all-out, out-and-out, whole-hog; across-the-board, blanket

sweet *adj* **1** distinctly pleasing or charming <a *sweet* smile>
syn dulcet, engaging, winning, winsome
rel agreeable, pleasant, pleasing; beautiful, fair, lovely; delectable, delicious, delightful, luscious; angelic, heavenly
con disagreeable, unpleasant; displeasing, obnoxious, repulsive
ant bitter
2 having a pleasant smell <the *sweet* odor of flowers and incense>
syn ambrosial, aromal, aromatic, balmy, fragrant, perfumed, perfumy, redolent, savory, scented, spicy; *compare* ODOROUS
rel clean, fresh; sweetish
con funky, fusty, musty, noisome, putrid, rancid, rotten, stale, stinking, strong, whiffy; fetid, foul, olid, rank, smelly
ant malodorous
3 *syn* MELODIOUS 1, dulcet, euphonic, euphonious, mellisonant, melodic, tuneful

sweet *n* *syn* SWEETHEART 1, beloved, darling, dear, honey, honeybunch, love, loveling, sweetling, turtledove

sweeten *vb* **1** *syn* PACIFY, appease, assuage, conciliate, mollify, placate, propitiate
2 *syn* SUGARCOAT 1, candy, honey, sugar (over)

sweetheart *n* **1** one who is dearly beloved — often used as a term of endearment <was her childhood *sweetheart*> <*sweetheart*, you know I'll wait>
syn beloved, darling, dear, flame, heartthrob, honey, honeybunch, love, loveling, sweet, sweetling, turtledove
rel ‖cutie pie, deary, pigsney; pet, puggy
2 *syn* GIRL FRIEND 2, ‖baby, beloved, flame, honey, inamorata, ladylove, steady, sweetie, truelove

---

syn synonym(s) *rel* related word(s)
idiom idiomatic equivalent(s) *con* contrasted word(s)
ant antonym(s) * vulgar
‖ use limited; if in doubt, see a dictionary
The first word in a synonym list when printed in SMALL CAPITALS shows where there is more information about the group. For a more efficient use of this book see Explanatory Notes.

rel doll baby, lovey-dovey, ||tootsie
3 *syn* BOYFRIEND 2, beau, beloved, flame, inamorato, lover, steady, truelove
rel paramour; ||dreamboat

sweetheart *vb syn* ADDRESS 8, court, make up (to), pursue, spark, sue, woo

sweetie *n syn* GIRL FRIEND 2, ||baby, beloved, flame, honey, inamorata, ladylove, steady, sweetheart, truelove
rel sweetie pie

sweetling *n syn* SWEETHEART 1, beloved, darling, dear, honey, honeybunch, love, loveling, sweet, turtledove

sweetness and light *n syn* AMENITY 1, agreeability, agreeableness, amiability, cordiality, enjoyableness, geniality, gratefulness, pleasance, pleasantness

sweet–talk *vb syn* COAX, ||banter, blandish, blarney, cajole, con, soft-soap, wheedle

swell *vb* **1** *syn* EXPAND 3, amplify, dilate, distend, inflate
rel balloon, belly, bloat, blow up, bosom; pouch, pout; overblow
con compress, condense, constrict, contract
ant shrink
2 *syn* LORD, cock, peacock, pontificate, swagger, swank
rel puff
idiom act the grand seigneur, swell it

swell *n syn* EXPERT, ||dab, ||dabster, master, masterhand, passed master, past master, pro, whiz, wiz

swell *adj syn* MARVELOUS 2, ||cool, ||dandy, groovy, ||keen, ||neat, nifty, super, terrific, wonderful

swelled head *n syn* CONCEIT 2, amour propre, complacency, conceitedness, consequence, egoism, egotism, narcissism, pride, vainglory

swellheadedness *n syn* CONCEIT 2, egoism, egotism, pride, self-glory, self-importance, self-opinion, self-pride, vainglory, vanity

swelling *adj syn* RHETORICAL, aureate, bombastic, euphuistic, flowery, grandiloquent, magniloquent, swollen, tumescent, tumid

||swelt *vb* **1** *syn* DIE 1, ||check out, conk, ||croak, decease, depart, drop, expire, go, perish
2 *syn* FAINT, black out, ||crap out, pass out, ||swarf, swoon

swelter *vb syn* BURN 3, bake, broil, cook, melt, roast, scorch

sweltering *adj syn* HOT 1, baking, broiling, burning, fiery, scorching, sizzling, sultry, sweltry, torrid
idiom ||hot as the hinges of hell
ant frigid

sweltry *adj syn* HOT 1, baking, broiling, burning, fiery, scorching, sizzling, sultry, sweltering, torrid

swerve *vb* **1** to turn or be turned away abruptly from a straight line or course <*swerved* the car to avoid collision>
syn dip, sheer, skew, slue, train off, veer
2 to be deflected from a fixed or right course of action or conduct <never *swerved* from the concept of duty, honor, country>
syn depart, deviate, digress, diverge
rel shift; waver; err, stray, wander
idiom deviate from the straight and narrow, get off the proper course (*or* path)

swift *adj syn* FAST 3, breakneck, fleet, harefooted, hasty, quick, raking, rapid, snappy, speedy
rel headlong, precipitate, sudden; double-quick; supersonic
ant sluggish

swift *adv syn* FAST 2, flat-out, fleetly, full tilt, promptly, quick, quickly, rapidly, speedily, swiftly
ant sluggishly

swiften *vb syn* SPEED 3, accelerate, hasten, hurry, quicken, shake up, step up

swiftly *adv syn* FAST 2, expeditiously, flat-out, fleetly, full tilt, hastily, posthaste, quickly, rapidly, speedily
con slowly
ant sluggishly

swiftness *n* **1** *syn* SPEED 2, ||bat, celerity, gait, pace, quickness, rapidity, rapidness, velocity
ant sluggishness
2 *syn* HASTE 1, celerity, dispatch, expedition, expeditiousness, hurry, hustle, rustle, speed, speediness
ant slowness

swig *n syn* DRINK 3, draft, drag, drain, drench, ||peg, swill

swig *vb syn* DRINK 3, booze, guzzle, imbibe, liquor (up), soak, swill, swizzle, tank up, tipple

swill *vb* **1** *syn* DRINK 3, booze, guzzle, ||lush (up), soak, swig, swizzle, tank up, tipple, tope
2 *syn* CONSUME 5, polish off, punish, put away, put down, shift

swill *n* **1** *syn* REFUSE, debris, garbage, junk, litter, offal, rubbish, spilth, trash, waste
2 *syn* DRINK 3, draft, drag, drain, drench, ||peg, swig

swillbowl *n syn* DRUNKARD, bibber, boozer, drunk, guzzler, inebriate, lush, soak, sot, tippler

swiller *n syn* DRUNKARD, bibber, boozer, drunk, guzzler, inebriate, lush, soak, sot, tippler

swim *vb syn* SPIN 2, reel, turn, whirl
idiom have one's head swim

swimming *adj syn* DIZZY 2, giddy, light, light-headed, swimmy, vertiginous
rel fluctuating, swaying, wavering

swimmingly *adv syn* WELL 5, favorably, fortunately, happily, prosperously, satisfyingly, successfully

swimmy *adj syn* DIZZY 2, giddy, light, light-headed, swimming, vertiginous

swindle *vb syn* CHEAT, beat, bilk, chouse, cozen, defraud, diddle, do, flimflam, gyp
rel rogue; victimize
idiom sell one a bill of goods, take for a ride, take for a sucker

swindle *n syn* IMPOSTURE, cheat, fake, fraud, gyp, hoax, humbug, phony, sell, sham

swindler *n* one who defrauds usually of money and especially by imposture or by gaining the victim's confi-

---

syn synonym(s) *rel* related word(s)
idiom idiomatic equivalent(s) *con* contrasted word(s)
ant antonym(s) * vulgar
|| use limited; if in doubt, see a dictionary
The first word in a synonym list when printed in SMALL CAPITALS shows where there is more information about the group. For a more efficient use of this book see Explanatory Notes.

dence <lost their savings to *swindlers* in a get-rich-quick scheme>
syn bunco steerer, cheat, cheater, chiaus, come-on, confidence man, con man, defrauder, diddler, double-dealer, flimflammer, ‖grifter, gyp, gypper, ‖mace, mountebank, Peter Funk, rogue, sharper, sharpie, skin, slicker, ‖spieler, trickster
rel bilk, bilker, blackleg, charlatan, chiseler, crook, deceiver, dodger, fraud, gouger, harpy, highbinder, hoaxer, operator, rook, shark, sharp, sharpster, tricker; scoundrel

swing *vb* **1** ***syn*** HANDLE 2, dispense, maneuver, manipulate, ply, wield
2 to move rhythmically to and fro, up and down, or back and forth <the clock's pendulum *swung* slowly>
syn oscillate, pendulate, sway
rel undulate, wave; rock, roll; revolve, rotate, switch, wheel; jiggle, wag, waggle, wiggle, wigwag
3 ***syn*** TURN 6, avert, deflect, divert, pivot, sheer, veer, volte-face, wheel, whirl
4 ***syn*** LURCH 2, careen, stagger, ‖stoit, ‖stoiter, ‖stot, sway, weave, wobble

swing *n* **1** ***syn*** RHYTHM, beat, cadence, cadency, measure, meter, rhyme, rhythmus
2 ***syn*** HANG, knack, trick

‖**swingeing** *adj* ***syn*** EXCELLENT, bully, capital, champion, famous, prime, stunning, superior, top, whiz-bang

swinish *adj* ***syn*** BRUTISH, animal, beastly, bestial, brutal, brute, feral, ferine

swipe *n* ***syn*** HIT 1, ‖conk, knock, lick, rap, swat, wipe

swipe *vb* ***syn*** STEAL 1, ‖cop, ‖heist, hook, lift, nab, ‖nail, ‖nick, pinch, snitch

swirl *vb* to move swiftly in circles, eddies, or undulations <water *swirled* into the storm drains>
syn eddy, gurge, purl, swoosh, whirl, whirlpool, whorl
rel boil, roil; gush, surge

swish *vb* ***syn*** HISS, buzz, fizz, fizzle, sibilate, sizzle, wheeze, whish, whiz, whoosh

swish *adj* ***syn*** STYLISH, ‖classy, exclusive, in, smart, swank, tonish, tony, ‖trendy, with-it

switch *vb* **1** ***syn*** WAG, beat, lash, waggle, wave, woggle
2 ***syn*** EXCHANGE 2, change, substitute, swap, trade
3 ***syn*** SHUNT 1, sidetrack

‖**swither** *vb* ***syn*** RUSH 1, bolt, charge, chase, dash, fling, lash, race, shoot, tear

swivet *n* ***syn*** SNIT, fume, stew, sweat, tizzy

swizzle *vb* ***syn*** DRINK 3, booze, guzzle, imbibe, liquor (up), soak, swig, swill, tank up, tipple

swollen *adj* ***syn*** RHETORICAL, aureate, bombastic, euphuistic, flowery, grandiloquent, magniloquent, swelling, tumescent, tumid

swoon *vb* ***syn*** FAINT, black out, ‖crap out, pass out, ‖swarf, ‖swelt
rel die away, drown

swoon *n* ***syn*** FAINT, blackout, coma, syncope

swoosh *vb* ***syn*** SWIRL, eddy, gurge, purl, whirl, whirlpool, whorl

sworn *adj* ***syn*** INVETERATE 1, bred-in-the-bone, confirmed, deep-dyed, deep-rooted, deep-seated, dyed-in-the-wool, entrenched, hard-shell, settled

sybarite *n* ***syn*** HEDONIST, carpet knight, pleasure-monger

sybaritic *adj* marked by or given to luxury or voluptuous living <the *sybaritic* grandeur of a sultan's harem> <a man of *sybaritic* and self-indulgent habits>
syn hedonistic, onanistic, self-indulgent, sybaritical, sybaritish; *compare* SENSUOUS
rel apolaustic, pleasure-loving; epicurean, luxurious; carnal, sensual, voluptuous

sybaritical *adj* ***syn*** SYBARITIC, hedonistic, onanistic, self-indulgent, sybaritish

sybaritish *adj* ***syn*** SYBARITIC, hedonistic, onanistic, self-indulgent, sybaritical

sycophancy *n* ***syn*** DETRACTION, backbiting, backstabbing, belittlement, calumny, defamation, depreciation, disparagement, scandal, slander

sycophant *n* a base or servilely attentive flatterer and self-seeker <*sycophants* who slavishly curried favor with the king>
syn apple-polisher, bootlick, bootlicker, ‖brownnose, ‖brownnoser, ‖clawback, creature, ‖easy rider, footlicker, groveler, lickspit, lickspittle, minion, reptile, spaniel, ‖suck, toad, toadeater, toadier, toady, truckler, yes-man; *compare* PARASITE
rel flunky, gopher, lackey, slave, stooge; flatterer, self-seeker; snob, tuft-hunter

sycophant *adj* ***syn*** FAWNING, bootlicking, cowering, cringing, groveling, kowtowing, parasitic, toadying, toadyish, truckling

sycophantic *adj* ***syn*** FAWNING, bootlicking, cowering, cringing, groveling, kowtowing, parasitic, toadying, toadyish, truckling

sycophantical *adj* ***syn*** FAWNING, bootlicking, cowering, cringing, groveling, kowtowing, parasitic, toadying, toadyish, truckling

sycophantish *adj* ***syn*** FAWNING, bootlicking, cowering, cringing, groveling, kowtowing, parasitic, toadying, toadyish, truckling

syllable *n* ***syn*** PARTICLE, atom, bit, crumb, iota, jot, modicum, ounce, shred, whit

syllabus *n* ***syn*** COMPENDIUM 1, aperçu, digest, pandect, précis, sketch, survey, sylloge

sylloge *n* ***syn*** COMPENDIUM 1, aperçu, digest, pandect, précis, sketch, survey, syllabus

symbol *n* **1** something that stands for something else by reason of relationship, association, convention, or accidental resemblance <the lion is often used as a *symbol* of courage>
syn attribute, emblem; *compare* INDICATION 3
rel indication, token, type; badge, mark, note, sign, stamp; character, design, device, figure, motif, pattern; representation
2 ***syn*** CHARACTER 1, mark, sign

symbolism *n* ***syn*** ALLEGORY 1, figuration, symbolization, typification

symbolization *n* ***syn*** ALLEGORY 1, figuration, symbolism, typification

---

syn synonym(s) *rel* related word(s)
idiom idiomatic equivalent(s) *con* contrasted word(s)
ant antonym(s) * vulgar
‖ use limited; if in doubt, see a dictionary
The first word in a synonym list when printed in SMALL CAPITALS shows where there is more information about the group. For a more efficient use of this book see Explanatory Notes.

symbolize *vb syn* REPRESENT 2, body (forth), emblematize, embody, epitomize, exemplify, illustrate, mirror, personify, typify

symmetrical *adj syn* PROPORTIONAL, commensurable, commensurate, equal

symmetry *n* beauty of form or arrangement arising from balanced proportions <the superb *symmetry* of the design>
syn balance, harmony, proportion
rel arrangement, order; agreement, conformity; equality, evenness, regularity; rhythm; finish
con asymmetry, dissymmetry; disproportion, imbalance, irregularity, unbalance

sympathetic *adj* **1** *syn* CONSONANT 1, agreeable, compatible, congenial, congruous, consistent
ant unsympathetic
2 favorably inclined <found his hearers *sympathetic* to his proposal>
syn friendly, receptive, ‖sib, well-disposed
rel agreeable, congenial, favorable; amenable, open, open-minded, receptive, responsive
con ill-disposed, unfriendly, unreceptive; cool, indifferent, lukewarm; neutral
ant unsympathetic
3 *syn* TENDER, compassionate, kindhearted, responsive, softhearted, warm, warmhearted
rel benign, benignant, kind, kindly; appreciating, comprehending, understanding
ant unsympathetic

sympathize (with) *vb syn* COMPASSIONATE, ache, commiserate, feel (for), pity
rel appreciate, comprehend, understand

sympathy *n* **1** *syn* ATTRACTION 2, affinity
ant antipathy
2 a feeling for or a capacity for sharing in the interests of another <he was in *sympathy* with her desire to succeed>
syn compassion, empathy, fellow feeling
rel responsiveness, sensitivity; feelings, heart; tenderness, warmheartedness, warmth; benignancy, benignness, kindliness, kindness
con disinterest, unconcern
3 *syn* PITY, commiseration, compassion, rue, ruth

symphonic *adj syn* HARMONIOUS 1, blending, chiming, consonant, harmonic, musical, symphonious

symphonious *adj syn* HARMONIOUS 1, blending, chiming, consonant, harmonic, musical, symphonic

symphonize *vb syn* HARMONIZE 4, arrange, blend, integrate, orchestrate, synthesize, unify

symphony *n syn* ORCHESTRA, band, philharmonic
rel concert band, symphony band; symphony orchestra

symptom *n syn* INDICATION 3, evidence, index, indicia, mark, sign, significant, token

synchronal *adj syn* CONTEMPORARY 1, coetaneous, coeval, coexistent, coexisting, concurrent, contemporaneous, simultaneous, synchronic, synchronous

synchronic *adj syn* CONTEMPORARY 1, coetaneous, coeval, coexistent, coexisting, concurrent, contemporaneous, simultaneous, synchronal, synchronous

synchronous *adj syn* CONTEMPORARY 1, coetaneous, coeval, coexistent, coexisting, concurrent, contemporaneous, simultaneous, synchronal, synchronic

syncope *n syn* FAINT, blackout, coma, swoon

syndicate *n* a combination of interlocked companies or enterprises <a large newspaper *syndicate*>
syn cartel, chain, combine, conglomerate, group, pool, trust
rel association, organization; partnership, union

syndrome *n syn* DISEASE 1, affection, ailment, complaint, condition, disorder, ill, infirmity, malady, sickness

synergetic *adj syn* COOPERATIVE, coacting, coactive, coefficient, conjoint, synergic
ant counteractive

synergic *adj syn* COOPERATIVE, coacting, coactive, coefficient, conjoint, synergetic
ant counteractive

synopsis *n syn* ABRIDGMENT, abstract, boildown, breviary, breviate, brief, condensation, conspectus, epitome

synopsize *vb syn* EPITOMIZE 1, condense, digest, inventory, nutshell, sum, summarize, summate, sum up
idiom hit the high spots, put it in a nutshell

synthesize *vb syn* HARMONIZE 4, arrange, blend, integrate, orchestrate, symphonize, unify

synthetic *adj* formed or developed by human art, skill, or effort and not by natural processes <*synthetic* plastics>
syn artificial, factitious, man-made; *compare* ARTIFICIAL 2
rel manufactured; constructed, fabricated, made
con natural

syrupy *adj syn* SENTIMENTAL, drippy, gooey, maudlin, moist, mushy, sappy, slushy, sobby, sticky

system *n* **1** an organized integrated whole made up of diverse but interrelated and interdependent parts <the capitalist *system*>
syn complex; *compare* WHOLE 2
rel aggregation, array; mesh, network; arrangement, disposition, scheme, setup; order, pattern
con disorganization; chaos
2 *syn* WHOLE 2, entity, integral, integrate, sum, totality
3 *syn* ORDER 8, method, orderliness, pattern, plan
rel proceeding, procedure, process
4 *syn* METHOD 1, fashion, manner, mode, modus, technique, way, wise

systematic *adj syn* ORDERLY 1, methodic, methodical, regular
rel arranged, ordered, organized, systematized; analytical, logical
con disorganized; chaotic
ant unsystematic

systematize *vb syn* ORDER 1, arrange, array, dispose, marshal, methodize, organize
rel contrive, frame
con confuse, disorder, jumble

T

tab *n* **1** ***syn*** EYE 3, eagle eye, scrutiny, surveillance, watch
2 ***syn*** BILL 1, account, invoice, reckoning, score, statement
3 ***syn*** CHECK 2, bill
4 ***syn*** PRICE 1, charge, cost, price tag, rate, tariff

tabby *n* **1** ***syn*** GOSSIP 1, carrytale, gossiper, gossipmonger, newsmonger, quidnunc, rumorer, scandalmonger, talebearer, telltale
‖**2** ***syn*** SPINSTER, maiden lady, old maid, spinstress

tabernacle *n* ***syn*** HOUSE OF WORSHIP, church, house of God, house of prayer, temple

table *n* **1** a piece of furniture on which food is customarily served <a feast on the *table*>
syn board, dining table, dinner table, mahogany, ‖table-board
rel bar, buffet, counter, sideboard
2 a condensed ordered enumeration of items usually arranged in columns <a *table* of weights and measures>
syn chart, tabulation
rel list; diagram
3 ***syn*** PLATEAU, tableland, upland

‖**table–board** *n* ***syn*** TABLE 1, board, dining table, dinner table, mahogany

tableland *n* ***syn*** PLATEAU, table, upland

tabloid *adj* ***syn*** SENSATIONAL 2, livid, lurid, sensationalistic, sensationist, sultry

taboo *n* a restraint imposed by social usage or as a protective measure <a society rife with antiquated moral *taboos*>
syn ban, forbiddance, interdiction, prohibition, proscription
rel inhibition, limitation, reservation, restraint, restriction; regulation, sanction; don't
con acceptance, toleration; approval, authorization, permission, permit, permittance

taboo *vb* ***syn*** FORBID, ban, enjoin, inhibit, interdict, outlaw, prohibit

tabulation *n* ***syn*** TABLE 2, chart

tacit *adj* **1** expressed or conveyed without words, speech, or forthright reference <they made a *tacit* agreement to work together>
syn implicit, implied, inarticulate, inferred, undeclared, understood, unexpressed, unsaid, unspoken, unuttered, wordless
rel alluded (to), hinted (at), intimated, suggested; assumed
con expressed, spoken, verbal; categorical, explicit, express, unequivocal
2 ***syn*** UNSPOKEN 1, silent, unexpressed, unuttered, unvoiced, wordless

taciturn *adj* ***syn*** SILENT 3, close, close-lipped, close-mouthed, reserved, reticent, silentious, tight-lipped, uncommunicative, wordless
rel laconic, unexpressive; brooding, dour
con chatty, communicative, loquacious, talkative; convivial, uninhibited, unreserved, unrestrained
ant garrulous

tack *n* ***syn*** TURN 2, bend, deflection, deviation, double, shift, yaw
rel alteration; digression, tangent; swerve, zigzag

tackle *n* ***syn*** EQUIPMENT, accouterment(s), apparatus, gear, habiliments, machinery, matériel, outfit, paraphernalia, tackling

tackle *vb* ***syn*** ATTACK 2, bang away (at)
rel take on, undertake; plunge into, set about
idiom get on the job, put one's shoulder to the wheel, start the ball rolling
con avoid, delay, hesitate, put off

tackling *n* ***syn*** EQUIPMENT, accouterment(s), apparatus, gear, habiliments, machinery, matériel, outfit, paraphernalia, tackle

tacky *adj* **1** ***syn*** SHABBY 1, broken-down, dilapidated, dingy, down-at-heel, faded, run-down, seedy, tagrag, threadbare
rel dowdy, outmoded, unstylish; messy, sloppy, slovenly, unkempt, untidy; blowsy, frowzy, frumpish
idiom gone to seed
2 marked by a lack of style or good taste <an old *tacky* scarf spoiled her outfit>
syn dowdy, frumpish, frumpy, outmoded, out-of-date, stodgy, unstylish
rel unbecoming; crude, inelegant, tasteless; incorrect, unsuitable; cheap, gaudy
con ‖mod, modern, modish, smart, stylish, tasteful; elegant

tact *n* skill and grace in dealing with others <handled the embarrassing situation with great *tact*>
syn address, delicatesse, diplomacy, poise, savoir faire, tactfulness; *compare* ADDRESS 1
rel control, head, presence, repose; amenity, courtesy, gallantry; policy, politicness, smoothness, suavity, urbanity; adroitness, deftness, skill; acumen, finesse, perception, sensitivity
con abruptness, bluntness, coarseness, discourtesy, rudeness
ant tactlessness

tactful *adj* marked by or exhibiting tact <his *tactful* skill in handling negotiations>
syn delicate, diplomatic, politic, tactical; *compare* SUAVE
rel polished, suave, urbane; adroit, deft, skilled, skillful; perceptive, sensitive
con clumsy, unpolished, unskilled; discourteous, impolite, rude; undiplomatic

---

syn synonym(s) ***rel*** related word(s)
idiom idiomatic equivalent(s) ***con*** contrasted word(s)
ant antonym(s) * vulgar
‖ use limited; if in doubt, see a dictionary
The first word in a synonym list when printed in SMALL CAPITALS shows where there is more information about the group. For a more efficient use of this book see Explanatory Notes.

ant blunt, tactless, untactful

tactfulness *n* ***syn*** TACT, address, delicatesse, diplomacy, poise, savoir faire
rel civility, civilness, politeness; polish
ant tactlessness

tactic *adj* ***syn*** TACTILE 2, tactual

tactical *adj* **1** made or carried out with only a limited or immediate end in view <had time only for *tactical* decisions and not strategic planning>
syn short-range
con long-range
ant strategic
2 ***syn*** EXPEDIENT, advisable, politic, prudent, wise
3 ***syn*** TACTFUL, delicate, diplomatic, politic

tactile *adj* **1** ***syn*** TANGIBLE 1, palpable, touchable
2 of or relating to the sense of touch < *tactile* responses>
syn tactic, tactual

tactility *n* ***syn*** TOUCH 3, feel

taction *n* ***syn*** TOUCH 2, palpation

tactless *adj* marked by a lack of tact <his *tactless* remark hurt her>
syn brash, impolitic, maladroit, undiplomatic, unpolitic, untactful
rel impolite, inconsiderate, indelicate, rude; bungling, inept
con diplomatic, polite, tactical
ant tactful

tactual *adj* ***syn*** TACTILE 2, tactic

tad *n* ***syn*** BOY 1, lad, laddie, shaveling, son, stripling

tag *n* **1** ***syn*** COMMONPLACE, banality, bromide, cliché, platitude, prosaicism, prosaism, rubber stamp, shibboleth, truism
2 ***syn*** TICKET 1, label

tag *vb* ***syn*** TAIL, bedog, dog, shadow, trail

tag and rag *n* ***syn*** RABBLE 2, dreg(s), hoi polloi, mass(es), mob, proletariat, ragtag, riffraff, tagrag and bobtail, unwashed

tag end *n* ***syn*** TAIL END 2

tagrag *adj* ***syn*** SHABBY 1, bedraggled, dilapidated, dingy, down-at-heel, faded, run-down, seedy, tacky, threadbare

tagrag and bobtail *n* ***syn*** RABBLE 2, dreg(s), hoi polloi, mass(es), mob, proletariat, ragtag and bobtail, riffraff, tag and rag, unwashed

tail *n* ***syn*** BUTTOCKS, *arse, *ass, backside, ||butt, hind end, posterior, rear, rear end, tail end

tail *vb* to follow (someone) for purposes of surveillance <detectives *tailing* the suspects>
syn bedog, dog, shadow, tag, trail; *compare* EYE 2, FOLLOW 2
rel hound, pursue

tail end *n* **1** ***syn*** BUTTOCKS, *arse, *ass, backside, ||butt, hind end, posterior, rear, rear end, tail
2 the hindmost end of something <watched the *tail end* of the parade march off>
syn tag end

tailor *vb* ***syn*** ADAPT, accommodate, adjust, conform, fit, quadrate, reconcile, square, suit, tailor-make
rel style; dovetail; shape up

tailor-made *adj* ***syn*** CUSTOM-MADE, custom, custom-built, customized, custom-tailored, made-to-order

tailor-make *vb* ***syn*** ADAPT, accommodate, adjust, conform, fit, quadrate, reconcile, square, suit, tailor

taint *vb* **1** to touch or affect with something bad or undesirable <his good reputation was *tainted* by the scandal>
syn besmear, besmirch, blur, cloud, defile, dirty, discolor, smear, smudge, smut, smutch, soil, stain, sully, tar, tarnish; *compare* CONTAMINATE 1
rel discredit; brand, stigmatize; blacken; damage, harm, hurt
idiom cast a slur upon; give a bad name to, give a black mark to
con brighten, cleanse, clear
2 ***syn*** DECAY, break down, crumble, decompose, disintegrate, molder, putrefy, rot, spoil, turn
rel befoul, contaminate, foul
3 ***syn*** CONTAMINATE 1, defile, pollute, soil

taintless *adj* ***syn*** CLEAN 1, cleanly, immaculate, spotless, unsoiled, unsullied
ant tainted

take *vb* **1** ***syn*** CATCH 1, bag, capture, collar, ||cotch, get, nail, prehend, secure
2 ***syn*** SEIZE 2, catch, clutch, ||cotch, grab, grapple, nab, ||nail, snatch
idiom make off with
con drop, dump, give up, relinquish, surrender
3 ***syn*** APPROPRIATE 1, accroach, annex, arrogate, commandeer, confiscate, expropriate, preempt, seize, sequester
con relinquish, yield
4 to lay hold of (as with the hands or an instrument) < *took* the ax by the handle>
syn clasp, grasp, grip
rel hold; handle
idiom take hold of
con drop, release
5 ***syn*** SEIZE 3, catch, strike
rel contract, get; harrow, reach, torment
6 ***syn*** CATCH 7, ||cotch, overhaul, overtake
7 ***syn*** ATTRACT 1, allure, bewitch, captivate, charm, draw, enchant, fascinate, magnetize, wile
8 ***syn*** SWALLOW 1, down
9 ***syn*** EAT 1, consume, devour, feed (on), ingest, meal, partake (of)
10 to bring into and accept in a particular capacity or relationship < *took* his son as a member of the firm>
syn admit, receive, take in
rel bring; accept; have, include
11 ***syn*** BUY 1, purchase
12 ***syn*** CHOOSE 1, cull, elect, mark, opt (for), optate, pick, prefer, select, single (out)
13 ***syn*** DEMAND 2, ask, call (for), crave, necessitate, require
14 to obtain from another source by means of derivation < *takes* his name from his father's>
syn derive, draw

---

syn synonym(s) ***rel*** related word(s)
idiom idiomatic equivalent(s) ***con*** contrasted word(s)
ant antonym(s) * vulgar
|| use limited; if in doubt, see a dictionary
The first word in a synonym list when printed in SMALL CAPITALS shows where there is more information about the group. For a more efficient use of this book see Explanatory Notes.

rel get, obtain; borrow
15 *syn* BEAR 10, abide, brook, endure, go, stand, stomach, suffer, swallow, tolerate
rel withstand; undergo; ||hack
idiom take it lying down, take it on the chin
16 *syn* CONTRACT 1, catch, come down (with), get, sicken (with *or* of)
idiom take sick with
17 *syn* APPREHEND 1, accept, catch, compass, comprehend, follow, grasp, see, take in, understand
18 *syn* UNDERSTAND 3, assume, believe, expect, gather, imagine, ||reckon, suppose, suspect, think
19 *syn* DEDUCT 1, discount, draw back, knock off, substract, subtract, take away, take off, take out
20 *syn* TREAT 2, deal (with), handle, play, serve, use
21 *syn* CHEAT, beat, bilk, chouse, cozen, defraud, diddle, do, flimflam, gyp
rel bamboozle, hoodwink
idiom take for a ride
22 *syn* ACT 5, behave, function, operate, perform, react, work

take (from) *vb syn* DECRY 2, belittle, depreciate, derogate, detract (from), diminish, disparage, minimize, take away, write off

take (to) *vb syn* HABITUATE 2, addict, adjust, confirm (in), devote (to)
rel enjoy, fancy, favor, like
idiom get used to

take away *vb* **1** *syn* REMOVE 2, take off, take out, withdraw
rel separate
2 *syn* DEDUCT 1, discount, draw back, knock off, substract, subtract, take, take off, take out
3 *syn* DECRY 2, belittle, depreciate, derogate, detract (from), diminish, disparage, minimize, take (from), write off

take back *vb* **1** *syn* RETURN 4, replace, restitute, restore
2 *syn* REPOSSESS 3
3 *syn* ABJURE, forswear, palinode, recall, recant, retract, unsay, withdraw

take down *vb syn* DISMOUNT, disassemble, dismantle, dismember

take in *vb* **1** *syn* TAKE 10, admit, receive
2 *syn* INCLUDE, comprehend, contain, embody, embrace, encompass, have, involve, subsume
3 *syn* APPREHEND 1, accept, catch, compass, comprehend, follow, grasp, see, take, understand
rel perceive; ||savvy; absorb, assimilate, digest
4 *syn* DECEIVE, beguile, betray, bluff, delude, double-cross, four-flush, humbug, illude, juggle
rel flimflam, take; trick

take off *vb* **1** *syn* REMOVE 2, take away, take out, withdraw
2 *syn* REMOVE 3, doff, douse, put off
3 *syn* DEDUCT 1, discount, draw back, knock off, substract, subtract, take, take away, take out
4 *syn* KILL 1, cut off, destroy, dispatch, down, finish, lay low, put away, scrag, slay
5 *syn* MIMIC, ape, burlesque, imitate, mock, parody, travesty
idiom do a takeoff on
6 *syn* GET OUT 1, begone, clear out, decamp, hightail, kite, scram, skedaddle, skiddoo, ||vamoose
7 *syn* HEAD 3, bear, light out, make, set out, strike out
idiom hit the road (*or* trail)
8 *syn* GO 2, ||blow, depart, exit, get away, get off, leave, pull out, quit, withdraw

takeoff *n syn* CARICATURE 2, burlesque, parody, travesty

take on *vb* **1** *syn* DON 2, assume, pull, put on, strike
2 *syn* ADD 1, annex, append, subjoin, superadd
3 to proceed to deal with < *took on* a new job with more responsibilities >
syn take up, undertake
rel begin, commence, enter (upon); attempt, endeavor, try; launch, venture
idiom set about, take upon oneself
con abandon, drop, forsake
ant give up
4 *syn* ENGAGE 5, encounter, face, meet
5 *syn* EMPLOY 2, engage, hire, put on
6 *syn* ADOPT, embrace, espouse, take up
ant give up

take out *vb* **1** *syn* REMOVE 2, take away, take off, withdraw
2 *syn* REMOVE 4, clear away, eliminate
3 *syn* DEDUCT 1, discount, draw back, knock off, substract, subtract, take, take away, take off
4 *syn* DATE, see

take out (on) *vb* to find release for (as emotions) < *took out* his anger on the dog >
syn loose, release, unleash, vent
idiom give vent to, let loose (*or* fly)
con control, govern, restrain; bottle (up), check, keep down, quell, smother; repress, suppress

take over *vb syn* RELIEVE 3, spell

take up *vb* **1** *syn* LIFT 1, elevate, hoist, pick up, raise, rear, uphold, uplift, upraise, uprear
2 *syn* BEGIN 1, commence, enter, get off, initiate, kick off, open, set to, start, tee off
3 *syn* TAKE ON 3, undertake
rel assume; tackle
idiom address oneself to
4 *syn* ADOPT, embrace, espouse, take on
rel support; affiliate
5 *syn* RESUME 2, continue, pick up, recommence, renew, reopen, restart

taking *adj syn* INFECTIOUS 3, catching, contagious

tale *n* **1** *syn* STORY 2, anecdote, narration, narrative, yarn
rel myth, saga
2 *syn* DETRACTION, backbiting, backstabbing, belittlement, calumny, defamation, depreciation, disparagement, scandal, slander
3 *syn* LIE, canard, falsehood, falsity, fib, misrepresentation, prevarication, story, untruism, untruth

---

syn synonym(s) *rel* related word(s)
idiom idiomatic equivalent(s) *con* contrasted word(s)
ant antonym(s) * vulgar
|| use limited; if in doubt, see a dictionary
The first word in a synonym list when printed in SMALL CAPITALS shows where there is more information about the group. For a more efficient use of this book see Explanatory Notes.

rel fiction; yarn

4 ***syn*** WHOLE 1, aggregate, all, be-all and end-all, entirety, sum, sum total, total, totality, ‖tote

tale *vb* ***syn*** COUNT 1, enumerate, number, numerate, tally, tell

talebearer *n* **1** ***syn*** INFORMER, ‖canary, ‖fink, ‖nark, snitch, ‖squeaker, squealer, stool pigeon, tattler, tipster

2 ***syn*** GOSSIP 1, carrytale, gossiper, newsmonger, quidnunc, rumorer, rumormonger, scandalmonger, tabby, telltale

talent *n* ***syn*** GIFT 2, aptness, bent, bump, faculty, flair, genius, nose, set, turn

rel art, craft, skill; endowment; expertise, forte

talisman *n* ***syn*** CHARM 2, amulet, fetish, juju, luck, mascot, periapt, phylactery, zemi

idiom good-luck piece, lucky piece (*or* charm)

talk *vb* **1** ***syn*** SPEAK 3, converse (in), parley, use

2 ***syn*** SPEAK 1, utter, verbalize, vocalize, voice

3 ***syn*** CONVERSE, chat, chin, colloque, visit, yarn

4 ***syn*** CHAT 1, babble, chatter, gab, gabble, patter, prate, prattle, run on, yak

rel palaver, spout off

idiom talk one's arm (*or* ear *or* leg) off, flap (*or* wag) the (*or* one's) tongue

5 ***syn*** GOSSIP, blab, noise (about *or* abroad), rumor, tattle

6 to reveal secret or confidential information usually concerning illegal acts <at last the suspect *talked* to the police>

syn sing, squeak, squeal; *compare* INFORM 3

rel inform (on); divulge, reveal; confess

idiom spill one's guts, spill the beans, tell all

7 to give a talk <he *talks* to community groups on ecology>

syn address, lecture, prelect, speak

rel declaim, harangue, hold forth, perorate, speechify, spout

talk (into) *vb* ***syn*** INDUCE 1, argue (into), bring around, convince, draw, get, persuade, prevail (on *or* upon), prompt, win (over)

talk *n* **1** ***syn*** SPEECH 1, discourse, speaking, utterance, verbalization

2 ***syn*** CONVERSATION 2, colloquy, confabulation, dialogue

3 ***syn*** CHAT 2, causerie, chin, prose, rap, yarn

4 a formal or prearranged discussion, exchange, or negotiation usually of a political nature <summit *talks* on nuclear arms>

syn conference, meeting, parley, powwow

rel dialogue, discussion, exchange; negotiation; deliberation

5 ***syn*** REPORT 1, buzz, cry, gossip, grapevine, hearsay, on-dit, rumble, rumor, scuttlebutt

6 ***syn*** SPEECH 2, address, allocution, lecture

rel spiel; conference, discussion

talkative *adj* given to talk or talking <a *talkative,* sociable man>

syn babblative, chatty, gabby, garrulous, loose-lipped, loose-tongued, loquacious, mouthy, multiloquent, multiloquious, talky, tonguey; *compare* GLIB

rel articulate, eloquent, fluent; vocal, voluble; buzzy, gossipy

con closemouthed, laconic, reserved, reticent, uncommunicative; speechless

ant silent

talkee–talkee *n* ***syn*** CHATTER, babble, blab, blabber, chat, clack, gabble, jabber, palaver, yakety-yak

talky *adj* ***syn*** TALKATIVE, babblative, chatty, gabby, garrulous, loose-lipped, loose-tongued, loquacious, multiloquent, multiloquious

tall *adj* ***syn*** HIGH 1, altitudinous

rel high-reaching, sky-high, skyscraping

idiom higher than a cat's back

con abbreviated, truncated; low

ant short

tally *n* ***syn*** SCORE 5

tally *vb* **1** ***syn*** INVENTORY, catalog, itemize

2 ***syn*** COUNT 1, enumerate, number, numerate, tale, tell

3 ***syn*** AGREE 4, accord, conform, correspond, fit (in), ‖gee, go, harmonize, jibe, square

rel equal, match; balance, complement

con conflict (with), differ (from), disagree (with)

tame *adj* docilely tractable <a *tame* lion>

syn domestic, domesticated, domitae naturae, subdued, submissive

rel broken (in), ‖busted, housebroken, trained; amenable, biddable, docile, obedient, tractable; pliable, pliant; meek, mild

idiom gentle as a lamb

con fierce, savage, tameless; undomesticated, untrained; unbridled, unbroken

ant untamed, wild

tame *vb* ***syn*** DOMESTICATE, domesticize, domiciliate, master

tamp *vb* ***syn*** CRAM 1, jam, jam-pack, ‖pang, ram, stuff

rel fill up (*or* in), plug up; concentrate

tamper (with) *vb* **1** ***syn*** BRIBE, buy, buy off, fix, have, ‖lubricate, sop, square

2 ***syn*** MEDDLE, busybody, butt in, fool, horn in, interfere, interlope, intermeddle, ‖make, monkey (with)

rel interpose, intervene; doctor, manipulate

tang *n* ***syn*** TASTE 3, flavor, relish, sapidity, sapor, savor, smack

rel bite, nip, piquancy, twang; aroma, pungency; spiciness, tanginess

tangible *adj* **1** capable of being perceived especially by the sense of touch <primitives who find *tangible* expression of divinity in idols>

syn palpable, tactile, touchable; *compare* PERCEPTIBLE

rel corporeal, physical; embodied, material, real, substantial

con ethereal, spiritual, unreal

ant intangible

2 ***syn*** MATERIAL 1, corporeal, gross, objective, phenomenal, physical, sensible, substantial

3 ***syn*** PERCEPTIBLE, appreciable, detectable, discernible, observable, palpable, sensible

---

syn synonym(s) ***rel*** related word(s)
idiom idiomatic equivalent(s) ***con*** contrasted word(s)
ant antonym(s) * vulgar
‖ use limited; if in doubt, see a dictionary
The first word in a synonym list when printed in SMALL CAPITALS shows where there is more information about the group. For a more efficient use of this book see Explanatory Notes.

rel distinct, evident, manifest, obvious, patent, plain
con clouded, cloudy, imperceptible, indistinct, unclear
ant intangible

tangle *vb* **1** *syn* INVOLVE 1, embroil, implicate
idiom make a party to
ant untangle
2 *syn* CATCH 3, benet, catch up, ensnare, entangle, entrap, snare, trap
ant untangle
3 *syn* ENTANGLE 1, ensnarl, intertangle, perplex, snarl
rel foul up, mix up
4 *syn* COMPLICATE, entangle, ‖muck, muddle, perplex, ravel, snarl
ant untangle

tangle *n syn* MAZE 1, jungle, knot, labyrinth, mesh, mizmaze, morass, skein, snarl, web

tanked *adj syn* INTOXICATED 1, ‖boozy, ‖canned, disguised, drunk, inebriated, ‖lushed, muddled, pixilated, ‖plastered

tank town *n syn* BURG, hick town, jerkwater town, mudhole, one-horse town, Podunk, whistle-stop

tank up *vb syn* DRINK 3, booze, guzzle, imbibe, liquor (up), soak, swig, swill, swizzle, tipple

tantalize *vb syn* WORRY 1, annoy, bedevil, beleaguer, gnaw, hagride, harass, harry, pester, plague
rel badger, bait; frustrate

tantamount *adj syn* SAME 2, duplicate, equal, equivalent, identic, identical, indistinguishable
rel alike, like, uniform; selfsame, very
idiom as much as to say

tap *n* **1** *syn* FAUCET, cock, gate, hydrant, petcock, spigot, stopcock, valve
2 *syn* BAR 5, barroom, cocktail lounge, drinkery, ‖groggery, ‖grogshop, pothouse, pub, ‖public house, taproom

tap *vb syn* DRAIN 1, draft, draw, draw off, pump, siphon

tap *vb* **1** to strike or hit audibly and usually lightly < *tapped* her pencil on the desk >
syn bob, knock, rap, tunk
rel bang, beat, hammer, hit, pound, smite, strike, thud, thump
2 *syn* DESIGNATE 2, appoint, finger, make, name, nominate

tapa *n syn* SNACK, ‖bait, ‖bever, bite, ‖chack, morsel, mug-up, ‖piece

taper *vb syn* DECREASE, abate, ‖bate, close, diminish, drain (away), dwindle, lessen, reduce, taper off

taper off *vb syn* DECREASE, abate, ‖bate, close, diminish, drain (away), dwindle, lessen, reduce, taper

taproom *n syn* BAR 5, barroom, drinkery, ‖groggery, ‖grogshop, pothouse, pub, ‖public house, saloon, tap

tapster *n syn* BARTENDER, barkeeper, ‖barmaid, barman, mixologist

---

syn synonym(s) — *rel* related word(s)
idiom idiomatic equivalent(s) — *con* contrasted word(s)
ant antonym(s) — * vulgar
‖ use limited; if in doubt, see a dictionary
The first word in a synonym list when printed in SMALL CAPITALS shows where there is more information about the group. For a more efficient use of this book see Explanatory Notes.

tar *n syn* MARINER, jack, jack-tar, sailor, sailorman, salt, seaman, tarpaulin

tar *vb syn* TAINT 1, besmear, besmirch, defile, discolor, smear, soil, stain, sully, tarnish

taradiddle *n syn* LIE, ‖bouncer, canard, cock-and-bull story, falsehood, falsity, fib, misrepresentation, prevarication, story

tardy *adj* not arriving, occurring, or done at the set, due, or expected time < be *tardy* for school >
syn behindhand, belated, late, lated, overdue, unpunctual
rel delayed, detained; dilatory, laggard, slow; delinquent
con beforehand, early; convenient, opportune, seasonable, timely; precise, punctilious
ant prompt, punctual

target *n* **1** an object of ridicule, attack, or abuse < made him the chief *target* of political satire >
syn butt, mark, sitting duck
rel victim; fall guy, scapegoat, whipping boy
2 *syn* AMBITION 2, aim, goal, mark, objective, quaesitum
3 *syn* USE 4, duty, function, goal, mark, object, objective, purpose

tariff *n* **1** *syn* TAX 1, assessment, ‖cess, duty, impost, levy
2 *syn* PRICE 1, charge, cost, price tag, rate, tab

‖**tarnation** *adj syn* UTTER, blasted, blessed, confounded, dad-burned, downright, goldarn, infernal, outright, unmitigated

tarnish *vb syn* DULL 1, dim, fade, muddy, pale
2 *syn* SOIL 2, begrime, besoil, dirty, foul, grime, smirch, smooch, smudge, smutch
rel contaminate, defile, pollute, stain, taint
con clean, cleanse; shine (up)
ant polish
3 *syn* INJURE 1, blemish, damage, harm, hurt, impair, mar, prejudice, spoil, vitiate
4 *syn* TAINT 1, besmear, besmirch, defile, discolor, smear, soil, stain, sully, tar
rel defame, disgrace, embarrass; slander

tarpaulin *n syn* MARINER, jack, jack-tar, sailor, sailorman, salt, seaman, tar

tarriance *n syn* SOJOURN, stopover, visit

tarry *vb* **1** *syn* DELAY 2, dally, dawdle, drag, lag, loiter, poke, procrastinate, put off, trail
rel falter, flag
2 *syn* STAY 2, abide, bide, linger, remain, stick around, wait
rel dawdle; sojourn
3 *syn* VISIT 3, sojourn, stay, stop (over)

tart *adj syn* SOUR 1, acerb, acerbic, acetose, acid, acidulous, dry
rel piquant, pungent
ant flat

tart *n syn* DOXY 1, ‖chippy, floozy, grisette, light-o'-love, nymph, nymphet, party girl, roundheel, ‖tootsie

Tartarean *adj syn* INFERNAL 1, chthonian, chthonic, Hadean, plutonian, plutonic, sulphurous

Tartuffe *n syn* HYPOCRITE, dissembler, dissimulator, lip server, pharisee, whited sepulcher

Tartuffery *n syn* HYPOCRISY, cant, hypocriticalness, pecksniffery, pharisaicalness, pharisaism, sanctimoniousness, sanctimony, Tartuffism

Tartuffism *n* ***syn*** HYPOCRISY, cant, hypocriticalness, pecksniffery, pharisaicalness, pharisaism, sanctimoniousness, sanctimony, Tartuffery

task *n* **1** a piece of work assigned or to be done <laboratory *tasks* assigned to chemistry students>
syn assignment, chare, chore, devoir, duty, job, stint
rel enterprise, project, undertaking; errand, labor, toil, work; charge, function, mission, office, province; business, calling, employment, occupation, vocation
2 a necessary undertaking that is usually difficult, dull, disagreeable, or problematic <deciphering his handwriting is a real *task*>
syn chore, effort, job, taskwork
rel burden, onus, strain, tax; bother, headache, nuisance, pain, trouble
idiom a hard (*or* long) row to hoe
con child's play, cinch, duck soup, picnic, ‖pipe, sinecure, snap
3 ***syn*** LOAD 3, burden, charge, deadweight, duty, millstone, onus, tax, weight

task *vb* ***syn*** BURDEN, charge, encumber, lade, load, lumber, saddle, tax, weigh, weight

taskmaster *n* ***syn*** SLAVE DRIVER, rawhider, Simon Legree

taskwork *n* ***syn*** TASK 2, chore, effort, job

taste *vb* ***syn*** FEEL 2, experience, know, savor
idiom be exposed to, run up against

taste *n* **1** ***syn*** HINT 2, dash, smack, sprinkling, tincture, tinge, touch, trifle, whiff, wink
rel bit, sample, sampling
2 ***syn*** APPETITE 1, appetence, stomach
3 the property of a substance which makes it perceptible to the gustatory sense <children often dislike the *taste* of olives>
syn flavor, relish, sapidity, sapor, savor, smack, tang
4 a liking for or enjoyment of something because of the pleasure it gives <had a *taste* for fast cars>
syn gusto, heart, palate, relish, zest
rel appreciation, comprehension, understanding; partiality, predilection, prepossession; disposition, inclination, predisposition
con dislike, disrelish; allergy, aversion, repugnance, repulsion
ant antipathy; distaste
5 ***syn*** APPETITE 3, fondness, inclination, liking, soft spot, weakness
ant distaste
6 the power or practice of discerning and enjoying whatever constitutes excellence (as in the fine arts) <a room whose decoration reflected her exquisite *taste*>
syn tastefulness
rel correctness; finesse, polish, refinement; elegance, grace
con gracelessness, inelegance, unrefinement; incorrectness, vulgarity
ant tastelessness

tasteful *adj* **1** ***syn*** PALATABLE, appetizing, flavorsome, good-tasting, mouth-watering, relishing, sapid, savory, tasty, toothsome
rel rich
ant savorless, tasteless
2 ***syn*** QUIET 4, inobtrusive, restrained, subdued, tasty, unobtrusive
ant tasteless

tastefulness *n* ***syn*** TASTE 6
ant tastelessness

tasteless *adj* **1** ***syn*** UNPALATABLE 1, distasteful, flat, flavorless, ill-flavored, insipid, savorless, unappetizing, unsavory
rel bland, dull, stale, vapid; unflavored; uninteresting
con flavorful, pleasing
ant tasteful, tasty
2 ***syn*** BARBARIC 1, barbarian, barbarous, graceless, outlandish, vulgar, wild
rel inelegant, unpolished, unrefined
idiom in bad taste
ant tasteful, tasty

tasty *adj* **1** ***syn*** PALATABLE, appetizing, flavorsome, good-tasting, relishing, sapid, savory, tasteful, toothsome, toothy
idiom fit for a king
con unsavory; bland, flavorless, unpalatable
ant savorless, tasteless
2 ***syn*** QUIET 4, inobtrusive, restrained, subdued, tasteful, unobtrusive
ant tasteless

‖**tats** *n pl* ***syn*** DICE, ‖African dominoes, bones, ‖cubes, ‖devil's bones, ‖ivory

‖**tatter** *vb* ***syn*** HURRY 2, barrel, beeline, bullet, fly, haste, hasten, highball, ‖nip, rocket

tatterdemalion *n* ***syn*** RAGAMUFFIN, ragshag, scarecrow

tattered *adj* **1** ***syn*** RAGGED, frayed, frazzled, shreddy
2 ***syn*** SHABBY 1, bedraggled, broken-down, dilapidated, dingy, run-down, seedy, tacky, tagrag, threadbare

tatters *n pl* ***syn*** RAGS 1, ‖duds

tattle *vb* ***syn*** GOSSIP, blab, noise (about *or* abroad), rumor, talk
idiom tell tales out of school

tattle *n* ***syn*** REPORT 1, buzz, cry, gossip, grapevine, hearsay, rumble, rumor, scuttlebutt, talk

tattler *n* ***syn*** INFORMER, ‖canary, ‖fink, ‖nark, snitch, ‖squeaker, squealer, stool pigeon, talebearer, tipster

tattletale *n* ***syn*** INFORMER, betrayer, ‖fink, snitch, ‖squeaker, squealer, stool pigeon, talebearer, tattler, tipster

tatty *adj* ***syn*** CHEAP 2, base, common, mean, paltry, poor, rubbishy, shoddy, sleazy, trashy

taunt *vb* ***syn*** RIDICULE, deride, lout, mock, quiz, rally, razz, scout, twit
rel banter, chaff; provoke; upbraid; disdain, scorn; affront, insult, offend, outrage

taut *adj* ***syn*** TIGHT 3, close, tense
rel firm, trim; stretched
con flabby; relaxed
ant slack

---

tautology *adj syn* VERBIAGE 1, circumambages, circumbendibus, circumlocution, periphrase, periphrasis, pleonasm, redundancy, roundabout, verbality
rel reiteration, repetition, repetitiousness; padding

tavern *n* **1** *syn* BAR 5, barroom, drinkery, ||grog shop, pub, public house, saloon, taproom, watering hole
2 *syn* HOTEL, auberge, caravansary, hospice, hostel, hostelry, inn, lodge, public house, roadhouse

tavern car *n syn* PARLOR CAR, chair car, club car, lounge car, palace car

taverner *n syn* SALOONKEEPER, barkeeper, boniface, innholder, innkeeper, ||publican, saloonist

tawdry *adj syn* GAUDY, blatant, brazen, chintzy, flashy, garish, glaring, loud, meretricious, tinsel
rel common, sleazy; flaring, screaming

tax *vb* **1** *syn* BURDEN, charge, cumber, encumber, lade, load, saddle, task, weigh, weight
rel overtax
idiom press hard upon, tax the strength of, weigh heavy on (*or* upon)
2 *syn* ACCUSE, arraign, charge, criminate, impeach, incriminate, inculpate, indict

tax *n* **1** a charge usually of money imposed by authority upon persons or property for public purposes <federal, state, and local *taxes* bear heavily on the thrifty>
syn assessment, ||cess, duty, impost, levy, tariff
rel tithe, tribute; boodle, boondoggle, giveaway, pork barrel
2 *syn* LOAD 3, burden, charge, deadweight, duty, millstone, onus, task, weight
rel difficulty, strain; demand, imposition

taxi *n syn* TAXICAB, cab, hack

taxicab *n* an automobile that carries passengers for a fare <took a *taxicab* from the airport to his hotel>
syn cab, hack, taxi
rel ||crawler, nighthawk

taxing *adj syn* ONEROUS, burdensome, demanding, exacting, exigent, grievous, oppressive, tough, trying, weighty
rel wearing; tedious, troublesome

TB *n syn* TUBERCULOSIS, consumption, phthisis, white plague

||**tea** *n syn* MARIJUANA, boo, cannabis, grass, ||Mary Jane, moocah, pot, weed

teach *vb* to cause to acquire knowledge or skill <*teach* a child to read>
syn discipline, educate, instruct, school, train
rel communicate, impart; implant, inculcate, instill; edify, enlighten, indoctrinate; fit, ground, prepare, rear; drill, exercise, practice; coach, tutor; lesson
idiom give instruction

teaching *n syn* EDUCATION 1, instruction, schooling, training, tuition, tutelage

teachy *adj syn* DIDACTIC, moral, moralizing, preachy, schoolmasterish, sermonic, sermonizing

tear *vb* **1** to separate (one part of a substance or object from another) forcibly <*tore* a chunk from the loaf on the table>
syn cleave, rend, rip, rive, split
rel cut, gash, incise, slash, slit; devil, pull (apart), rift, sever, sunder; ribbon, shred; break, crack, rupture; damage, impair, injure
2 *syn* EXTRACT 1, evulse, pull, yank
3 *syn* RUSH 1, boil, bolt, charge, chase, dash, fling, lash, race, shoot
4 *syn* COURSE, career, chase, race, rush, speed

tear *n syn* BINGE 1, bat, bender, booze, bust, carousal, carouse, drunk, spree, wassail

tear down *vb* **1** *syn* DESTROY 1, annihilate, demolish, destruct, raze, ruin, shatter, unbuild, wrack, wreck
ant build up
2 *syn* MALIGN, asperse, calumniate, defame, denigrate, ||scandal, scandalize, slander, slur, smear
ant build up

teardrops *n pl syn* TEARS, water

tearful *adj* flowing with or accompanied by tears <*tearful* entreaties>
syn lachrymose, teary, weeping, weepy
rel lamenting, mournful; sniveling; bawling, blubbering, crying, sobbing
con dry-eyed
ant tearless

tearing *adj syn* EXCRUCIATING, agonizing, harrowing, racking, tormenting, torturing, torturous

tear–jerking *adj syn* SENTIMENTAL, bathetic, lovey-dovey, maudlin, mawkish, mushy, romantic, slushy, ||soppy, sticky

tears *n pl* a profuse secretion of saline fluid that overflows the eyelids and dampens the face <a blow that brought *tears* to his eyes>
syn teardrops, water

teary *adj syn* TEARFUL, lachrymose, weeping, weepy
ant tearless

tease *vb syn* WORRY 1, annoy, bedevil, beleaguer, gnaw, harass, harry, pester, plague, ||wherret
rel disturb, importune
idiom give a bad time

teaser *n syn* STRIPTEASER, ecdysiast, peeler, stripper, stripteuse

tease up *vb syn* TOUCH UP, brush up, retouch

||**tec** *n syn* DETECTIVE, dick, ||eye, gumshoe, hawkshaw, investigator, plainclothesman, Sherlock, Sherlock Holmes, sleuth

teched *adj syn* INSANE 1, ||batty, bedlamite, cracked, crazed, crazy, daft, demented, deranged, lunatic

technique *n syn* METHOD 1, fashion, manner, mode, modus, system, way, wise

tedious *adj* **1** *syn* IRKSOME, boresome, boring, drudging, tiresome, tiring
2 *syn* ARID 2, bromidic, dry, dryasdust, dull, dusty, insipid, uninteresting, weariful, wearisome
rel dragging, mortal, slow, tiresome

tedium *n* a state of dissatisfaction and weariness <incessant routine without variety breeds *tedium*>
syn boredom, doldrums, ennui, yawn
rel irksomeness, tediousness, tiresomeness, wearisomeness; dullness, monotony

---

syn synonym(s) *rel* related word(s)
idiom idiomatic equivalent(s) *con* contrasted word(s)
ant antonym(s) * vulgar
|| use limited; if in doubt, see a dictionary
The first word in a synonym list when printed in SMALL CAPITALS shows where there is more information about the group. For a more efficient use of this book see Explanatory Notes.

con enlivenment, interest, invigoration, refreshment

teem *vb* to be abundantly stocked or provided <rivers *teeming* with fish>
syn abound, crawl, flow, pullulate, ‖sny, swarm
rel bristle, bustle; cram, crowd, jam, pack; overbrim, overflow, overrun
con lack, want

teem *vb syn* POUR 3, drench, lash

teeming *adj syn* ALIVE 5, abounding, overflowing, replete, rife, swarming, thronged
rel multitudinous, populous, pregnant; bristling
con rare, sparse, uncommon; empty, lacking, void, wanting

teensy *adj syn* TINY, diminutive, lilliputian, miniature, minute, teensy-weensy, teenty, teeny, teeny-weeny, wee

teensy–weensy *adj syn* TINY, lilliputian, miniature, minute, teensy, teenty, teeny, teeny-weeny, wee, weeny

teenty *adj syn* TINY, diminutive, miniature, minute, teensy, teensy-weensy, teeny, teeny-weeny, wee, weeny

teeny *adj syn* TINY, diminutive, lilliputian, minute, teensy, teensy-weensy, teenty, teeny-weeny, wee, weeny

teeny–weeny *adj syn* TINY, lilliputian, miniature, minute, teensy, teensy-weensy, teenty, teeny, wee, weeny

tee off *vb syn* BEGIN 1, commence, enter, get off, initiate, kick off, lead off, open, start, take up

teeter *vb* to progress (as by walking) unsteadily <*teetered* along on 4-inch heels>
syn falter, lurch, stagger, ‖stammer, stumble, topple, totter, wobble; *compare* LURCH 2, SEESAW
rel sway, weave

teethy *adj syn* TOOTHY 1

teetotal *adj syn* DRY 3, bone-dry

tehee *vb syn* LAUGH, chortle, chuckle, giggle, guffaw, hee-haw, snicker, ‖sniggle, titter

telephone *vb* to communicate with (a person) by telephone <*telephoned* him yesterday>
syn ‖buzz, call, phone, ‖ring (up)
idiom ‖get (one) on the horn, give (one) a buzz (*or* ring)

telestic *adj syn* MYSTICAL 1, anagogic, mystic

tell *vb* **1** *syn* COUNT 1, enumerate, number, numerate, tale, tally
2 *syn* SAY 1, bring out, chime in, come out (with), declare, deliver, state, throw out, utter
rel communicate, convey, impart
3 *syn* REVEAL 1, betray, blab (out), disclose, discover, divulge, give away, mouth, spill, unclose
rel recite, recount, rehearse, relate; acquaint, apprise, inform
4 *syn* INFORM 2, acquaint, advise, apprise, clue (*or* clew), fill in, notify, post, warn, wise (up)
5 *syn* COMMAND, bid, charge, direct, enjoin, instruct, order, warn
6 *syn* WEIGH 3, count, militate

telling *adj syn* VALID, cogent, convincing, satisfactory, satisfying, solid, sound
rel power-packed; influential, weighty; significant, striking

tell off *vb syn* SCOLD 1, bawl out, berate, ‖chew out, jaw, rail, revile, tongue-lash, upbraid, vituperate
rel call down; denounce
idiom give (one) a piece of one's mind, tell (one) a thing or two, tell (one) where to get off

telltale *n* **1** *syn* GOSSIP 1, carrytale, clack, gossiper, gossipmonger, newsmonger, quidnunc, scandalmonger, tabby, talebearer
2 *syn* HINT 1, clue, cue, indication, inkling, intimation, notion, suggestion, wind

tellurian *adj syn* EARTHLY 1, earthy, mundane, sublunary, telluric, terrene, terrestrial, uncelestial, worldly

telluric *adj syn* EARTHLY 1, earthy, mundane, sublunary, tellurian, terrene, terrestrial, uncelestial, worldly

temblor (*or* **tremblor**) *n syn* EARTHQUAKE, quake, quaker, shake, shock, tremor

temerarious *adj syn* ADVENTUROUS, adventuresome, audacious, daredevil, daring, foolhardy, rash, reckless, venturesome, venturous
rel heedless, imprudent, incautious, injudicious

temerity *n* conspicuous or flagrant boldness (as in speech, behavior, or action) <had the *temerity* to order an attack when hopelessly outnumbered>
syn assurance, audacity, brashness, hardihood, hardiness, nerve
rel daring, foolhardiness, heedlessness, rashness, recklessness, venturesomeness; impetuosity, precipitateness; impertinence, intrusiveness
con deliberation, judgment, judiciousness, prudence; heed, heedfulness
ant caution

temper *vb syn* MODERATE 1, modulate, restrain
rel dilute, season; ease, pacify, soften; adjust, modify; curb, tune down
idiom take the edge off

temper *n* **1** a general or prevailing quality or characteristic (as of moral or social attitudes and behavior) <riots reflected the *temper* of the times>
syn mood, spirit, timbre, tone
rel atmosphere, aura, climate; orientation, outlook; disposition, drift, leaning, tendency, trend; character, nature, peculiarity
2 *syn* DISPOSITION 3, character, complexion, humor, individualism, individuality, makeup, nature, personality, temperament
rel condition, posture, state; attribute, property, quality; style, type, way
idiom turn of mind
3 *syn* MOOD 1, humor, mind, strain, tone, vein
idiom frame (*or* state) of mind
4 an outbreak or display of anger <a childish fit of *temper*>
syn passion
rel anger, fury, ire, rage; conniption, fit, outburst, tantrum

temperament *n syn* DISPOSITION 3, character, complexion, humor, individualism, individuality, makeup, nature, personality, temper
rel mentality, mind; kind, type, way

---

syn synonym(s) *rel* related word(s)
idiom idiomatic equivalent(s) *con* contrasted word(s)
ant antonym(s) * vulgar
‖ use limited; if in doubt, see a dictionary
The first word in a synonym list when printed in SMALL CAPITALS shows where there is more information about the group. For a more efficient use of this book see Explanatory Notes.

idiom inner nature

temperamental *adj* **1** *syn* MOODY, humorsome
2 *syn* INCONSTANT 1, capricious, changeable, fickle, mercurial, ticklish, uncertain, unstable, variable, volatile
ant steady

temperance *n* **1** an avoidance of extremes (as in action, thought, or feeling) <a man who knew no *temperance* in his opinions>
syn measure, moderateness, moderation
rel reasonableness; constraint, restraint
idiom happy medium
con extremeness, radicalness; excess, excessiveness; immoderateness, immoderation, unconstraint, unreasonableness, unrestraint
ant intemperance, intemperateness
2 strict habitual and usually complete self-denial in the gratification of appetites or passions <an ascetic who practiced complete *temperance*>
syn abstinence, continence, sobriety
rel abnegation, eschewal, forbearance, forgoing, refrainment, sacrifice, self-denial, self-deprivation; control, restraint, self-control, self-discipline; asceticism, austerity, mortification
con intemperance, intemperancy, intemperateness, prodigality
ant excess

temperate *adj* **1** *syn* MODERATE 2, modest, reasonable
rel constant, equable, even, steady; checked, curbed, regulated, restrained
ant intemperate
2 *syn* ABSTEMIOUS, abstentious, abstinent, continent, self-restraining, sober
rel indulgent; self-indulgent
con intemperate; dissipated, prodigal, profligate
ant excessive
3 *syn* CONSERVATIVE 2, controlled, discreet, moderate, reasonable, restrained, unexcessive, unextreme
4 *syn* SOBER 3, moderate, unimpassioned

temperish *adj syn* IRASCIBLE, choleric, cranky, cross, hot-tempered, peppery, quick-tempered, ||stomachy, testy, touchy

tempersome *adj syn* ILL-TEMPERED, bad-tempered, dyspeptic, hot-tempered, ill-humored, ill-natured, ||rusty

tempestuous *adj syn* WILD 6, blustering, blustery, ||coarse, dirty, furious, raging, rough, stormy, turbulent
rel tumultuous, unbridled, unrestrained, violent
ant calm, quiet

temple *n syn* HOUSE OF WORSHIP, church, house of God, house of prayer, tabernacle

tempo *n* rate of performance or delivery <increased sales and production *tempo*>
syn pace, time; *compare* SPEED 2
rel speed; momentum

temporal *adj* **1** *syn* MATERIALISTIC, banausic, earthy, mundane, sensual, worldly
ant nontemporal
2 *syn* PROFANE 1, lay, secular, unsacred
rel material, physical; nonsacred, nonspiritual, unhallowed, unsanctified, unspiritual
con celestial, heavenly
ant spiritual

temporary *adj* lasting, continuing, or serving for a limited time <was *temporary* president of the company for nine months>
syn acting, ad interim, interim, pro tem, pro tempore, supply; *compare* TRANSIENT
rel alternate, substitute; interimistic, provisional, provisory; jackleg, make-do, makeshift, stopgap
ant permanent

tempt *vb syn* LURE, allure, bait, decoy, entice, entrap, inveigle, lead on, seduce, train
rel provoke, rouse; court, invite, solicit, vamp, woo
idiom whet the appetite
con discourage; dissuade; repel, repulse, revolt

temptation *n syn* LURE 2, allurement, bait, come-on, decoy, enticement, inveiglement, seducement, snare, trap

tempting *adj syn* ENTICING, Circean, fetching, luring
rel appetizing, mouth-watering; provoking, rousing, tantalizing
con repellent, repulsive
ant untempting

temptress *n syn* SIREN, femme fatale, Lorelei, seductress

ten *n syn* BREAK 4, blow, breath, breather, breathing space (*or* spell), respite

tenable *adj* **1** capable of being defended against attack <the platoon's position was no longer *tenable*>
syn defendable, defensible
rel impregnable, secure
con insecure, vulnerable; defenseless, helpless, unprotected; dangerous, precarious, risky
ant untenable
2 *syn* JUSTIFIABLE, condonable, defensible, excusable, vindicable, warrantable
rel believable, credible, maintainable, plausible
con indefensible, inexcusable, unbelievable, unjustifiable
ant untenable

tenacious *adj* **1** *syn* STRONG 2, stalwart, stout, sturdy, tough
rel bulldogged, bulldoggish, bulldoggy, dogged, obstinate, pertinacious, stubborn; resolute, steadfast, true; persevering, persisting
2 *syn* VISCOUS, tough, viscid, viscose
rel cohesive; tacky; sticky
3 *syn* FAST 4, firm, fixed, secure, set, tight
con lax, slack

tenant *vb syn* INHABIT, occupy, people, populate

tenantable *adj syn* LIVABLE 1, habitable, inhabitable, lodgeable, occupiable
idiom fit to live in
con uninhabitable

tend *vb* **1** *syn* TILL, cultivate, dress, ||labor, work
2 to supervise or take charge of <employed a girl to *tend* the children each day>

---

syn synonym(s) — *rel* related word(s)
idiom idiomatic equivalent(s) — *con* contrasted word(s)
ant antonym(s) — * vulgar
|| use limited; if in doubt, see a dictionary
The first word in a synonym list when printed in SMALL CAPITALS shows where there is more information about the group. For a more efficient use of this book see Explanatory Notes.

syn attend, care (for), mind, watch
rel cherish, cultivate, foster, minister, nurse, nurture, serve; defend, guard, protect, safeguard, shield; supervise
idiom look after, see after, see to, take care of, take under one's wing
con disregard, ignore, neglect

tend *vb* **1** to have or exhibit an inclination or tendency <he *tends* to praise people too highly>
syn incline, lean, look; *compare* INCLINE 3
idiom be disposed
2 *syn* CONTRIBUTE 2, conduce, redound

tendency *n* **1** a movement or course having a particular direction and character <a growing *tendency* to underestimate the potential strength of that nation>
syn current, drift, run, tenor, trend
rel curve, inclination, leaning, propensity; turn; shift; custom, habit, usage, way
2 *syn* LEANING 2, bent, disposition, inclination, inclining, penchant, predilection, predisposition, proclivity, propensity

tendentious *adj* *syn* BIASED 2, colored, jaundiced, one-sided, partial, partisan, prejudiced, prepossessed, unindifferent, warped

tender *adj* showing or expressing affectionate interest in another <his mother was very *tender* with her wayward son>
syn compassionate, kindhearted, responsive, softhearted, sympathetic, warm, warmhearted
rel gentle, lenient, mild, soft, yielding; considerate, solicitous, thoughtful; affectionate, fond, loving; benevolent, charitable, humane, mild; commiserative; forgiving, merciful, tolerant
con callous, hard, harsh; inhumane, uncharitable, unfeeling
ant rough, severe

tender *vb* *syn* OFFER 1, extend, give, hold out, pose, present, proffer
rel propose, purpose, submit, suggest

tenderfoot *n* *syn* NOVICE, apprentice, beginner, colt, freshman, neophyte, newcomer, novitiate, rookie, tyro

tenderloin *n* *syn* RED-LIGHT DISTRICT, levee, stew(s)

tenebrific *adj* *syn* GLOOMY 3, black, bleak, disheartening, dismal, dispiriting, dreary, funereal, oppressive, somber

tenebrous *adj* **1** *syn* DARK 1, caliginous, dim, dusk, dusky, gloomy, lightless, murky, obscure, unilluminated
2 *syn* OBSCURE 3, ambiguous, amphibological, equivocal, sibylline, uncertain, unclear, unexplicit, unintelligible, vague

tenement *n* *syn* APARTMENT 1, ‖chambers, flat, lodging(s), rental, rooms, suite

tenet *n* *syn* DOCTRINE, canon, dogma
rel belief, conviction, persuasion, view

tenor *n* **1** the course of thought that is retained through something spoken or written <the *tenor* of the book is first expressed in the introduction>
syn drift, purport, substance; *compare* BODY 3, MEANING 1, SUBSTANCE 2
rel intent; inclination, trend; mood, tone; core, gist, meat, stuff
2 *syn* TENDENCY 1, current, drift, run, trend

tense *adj* **1** *syn* TIGHT 3, close, taut
rel strained, stretched
ant relaxed
2 feeling or showing nervous tension <the soldiers were *tense* as they waited for the order to advance>
syn edgy, nervy, restive, uneasy, uptight
rel queasy; jittery, rusty, unquiet; anxious, concerned, overanxious
con easy; calm, cool, ‖loose, placid, unconcerned; firm, nerveless, unshaken
ant relaxed

tension *n* **1** *syn* STRESS 1, pressure, strain
rel tautness, tenseness, tightness
idiom stress and strain
ant relaxation
2 emotional strain <was suffering from nervous *tension*>
syn unease, uptightness
rel strain, stress; anxiety, nerves, nervousness, uneasiness; agitation, discomfort, disquiet, misease

ten–strike *n* *syn* SMASH 6, bang, bell ringer, hit, succès fou, wow

tent *vb* *syn* CAMP, bivouac, ‖bivvy, encamp, ‖laager, ‖maroon

tentative *adj* **1** *syn* CONDITIONAL 1, provisional, provisionary, provisory
rel acting, ad interim, makeshift, temporary; probationary; experimental, test, trial
con conclusive, decisive, definitive
ant final
2 *syn* VACILLATING 2, faltering, halting, hesitant, irresolute, shilly-shallying, uncertain, vacillatory, wiggle-waggle, wobbly
rel disinclined, reluctant

tenue *n* *syn* BEHAVIOR, comportment, conduct, deportment

tenuous *adj* **1** *syn* THIN 2, attenuate, attenuated, rare, rarefied, subtile, subtle
2 *syn* THIN 1, attenuate, reedy, slender, slight, slim, squinny, stalky, twiggy
rel aerial, airy, ethereal, fine
con abundant
ant dense
3 having little substance or strength and usually not firmly based <only a *tenuous* link in the chain of evidence>
syn feeble, insubstantial, unsubstantial; *compare* IMPLAUSIBLE
rel flimsy, weak; insignificant
con significant, sound, strong
ant substantial

tenure *n* *syn* HOLD, clamp, clasp, clench, clinch, clutch, grapple, grasp, grip, gripe

tepid *adj* **1** moderately warm <a *tepid* bath>

---

syn synonym(s) *rel* related word(s)
idiom idiomatic equivalent(s) *con* contrasted word(s)
ant antonym(s) * vulgar
‖ use limited; if in doubt, see a dictionary
The first word in a synonym list when printed in SMALL CAPITALS shows where there is more information about the group. For a more efficient use of this book see Explanatory Notes.

syn lukewarm, milk-warm, warmish
rel mild, temperate, warm
con cold, cool, freezing, frozen; heated, hot, steaming
2 lacking in animation, force, passion, conviction, or commitment <gave only a *tepid* endorsement to the candidate>
syn halfhearted, lukewarm, unenthusiastic; *compare* ARID 2
rel indifferent; colorless, dull, lifeless, unlively; feeble, marrowless, pithless, sapless, spiritless; dim, faint, forceless, weak
con animated, forceful; fiery, impassioned, passionate, spirited

tergiversate *vb* **1** *syn* DEFECT, apostatize, desert, rat, renounce, repudiate, tergiverse, turn
idiom fall away from
2 *syn* EQUIVOCATE 2, dodge, evade, hedge, pussyfoot, shuffle, sidestep, tergiverse, weasel
idiom beg the question

tergiversation *n* **1** *syn* DEFECTION, apostasy, desertion, falseness, recreancy
rel about-face, reversal, reverse; denial, disavowal, forswearing, renunciation, repudiation
2 *syn* AMBIGUITY, amphibology, double entendre, double meaning, equivocality, equivocation, equivoque

tergiversator *n* *syn* RENEGADE, apostate, defector, rat, recreant, runagate, turnabout, turncoat

tergiverse *vb* **1** *syn* DEFECT, apostatize, desert, rat, renounce, repudiate, tergiversate, turn
2 *syn* EQUIVOCATE 2, dodge, evade, hedge, pussyfoot, shuffle, sidestep, tergiversate, weasel

term *n* **1** *syn* LIMIT 1, bound, confine(s), end, limitation
rel terminus
2 a limited, definite, or measurable extent of time during which something exists, lasts, or is in progress <the office has a *term* of four years>
syn duration, span, time
rel phase; go, period, spell, stretch; hitch, tour, turn; standing
3 *syn* WORD 2, vocable
4 terms *pl syn* CONDITION 1, provision, proviso, reservation, stipulation, strings
rel detail, item, particular, point; limit
5 terms *pl* mutual social relationship or relative position <fight on equal *terms*> <the two were on *terms* of great intimacy>
syn footing, standing
rel coequality, equipollence, status; equality, equivalence, par, parity; balance

term *vb* *syn* NAME 1, baptize, call, christen, denominate, designate, dub, entitle, style, title

termagant *n* *syn* VIRAGO, amazon, fishwife, harpy, ogress, scold, shrew, vixen, Xanthippe

termagant *adj* *syn* TURBULENT 1, boisterous, disorderly, raucous, rowdy, rowdydowdy, rowdyish, rumbustious, tumultuous, unruly

terminable *adj* liable to be terminated or subject to termination <marriage is a *terminable* institution>
syn determinable, endable
rel finite, limited; limitable

terminal *adj* *syn* LAST, closing, concluding, eventual, final, hindmost, lag, latest, latter, ultimate
con beginning, starting
ant initial

terminate *vb* **1** *syn* CLOSE 3, complete, conclude, determine, end, finish, halt, ultimate, wind up, wrap up
rel abolish, extinguish; discontinue, wind down
idiom put the lid on
ant initiate
2 *syn* ADJOURN 2, dissolve, prorogate, prorogue, recess, rise
3 *syn* DISMISS 3, ax, boot (out), bounce, cashier, discharge, drop, fire, kick out, sack
4 *syn* QUIT 6, drop, leave, resign

terminated *adj* *syn* COMPLETE 4, completed, concluded, done, down, ended, finished, through

terminating *adj* *syn* LAST, closing, concluding, eventual, final, lag, latest, latter, terminal, ultimate
ant initial

termination *n* *syn* END 2, cease, cessation, conclusion, desistance, ending, finish, period, stop, terminus
rel issue, outcome, ‖pay-off, result
con source; beginning, start
ant initiation

terminology *n* the specialized or technical terms and expressions peculiar to a field, subject, or trade <the *terminology* of the plastics industry>
syn cant, dictionary, jargon, language, lexicon, palaver, vocabulary; *compare* DIALECT 2
rel shoptalk; gibberish, gobbledygook

terminus *n* *syn* END 2, cease, cessation, conclusion, desistance, ending, finish, period, stop, termination

terra firma *n* *syn* EARTH 2, dirt, dry land, ground, land, soil

terrain *n* **1** the physical configuration and features of a tract of land <made an analysis of the *terrain* via aerial photos>
syn topography
rel contour, form, profile, shape
2 an area devoted to a specified activity <the whole county had become breeding and racing *terrain*>
syn territory, turf
3 *syn* FIELD, bailiwick, champaign, demesne, domain, dominion, province, sphere, territory, walk

terrene *adj* **1** *syn* EARTHLY 1, earthy, mundane, sublunary, tellurian, telluric, terrestrial, uncelestial, worldly
2 *syn* EARTHY 1, earthlike, terrestrial

terrestrial *adj* **1** *syn* EARTHLY 1, earthy, mundane, sublunary, tellurian, telluric, terrene, uncelestial, worldly
rel earthbound, prosaic; profane, secular, unspiritual
ant empyreal
2 *syn* EARTHY 1, earthlike, terrene

terrible *adj* **1** *syn* FEARFUL 3, appalling, awful, dreadful, formidable, frightful, horrible, horrific, shocking, terrific
2 *syn* HARD 6, arduous, difficult, formidable, heavy, laborious, severe, strenuous, toilsome, tough

---

syn synonym(s) *rel* related word(s)
idiom idiomatic equivalent(s) *con* contrasted word(s)
ant antonym(s) * vulgar
‖ use limited; if in doubt, see a dictionary
The first word in a synonym list when printed in SMALL CAPITALS shows where there is more information about the group. For a more efficient use of this book see Explanatory Notes.

3 ***syn*** INTENSE 1, concentrated, desperate, exquisite, fierce, furious, vehement, vicious, violent
4 ***syn*** GHASTLY 1, grim, grisly, gruesome, hideous, horrible, horrid, horrifying, macabre, terrifying

terribly *adv* ***syn*** VERY 1, awfully, dreadfully, exceedingly, extremely, greatly, highly, mightily, remarkably, strikingly

terrific *adj* **1** ***syn*** FEARFUL 3, appalling, awful, dreadful, formidable, frightful, horrible, horrific, shocking, terrible
rel terrorizing; agitating, disquieting, upsetting
2 ***syn*** MARVELOUS 2, divine, glorious, groovy, hot, ‖keen, sensational, super, swell, wonderful
rel magnificent, superb; rattling, screaming

terrified *adj* ***syn*** AFRAID 1, aghast, anxious, ‖ascared, fearful, frightened, scared, scary
rel horrified, shocked; terrorized; frozen, paralyzed
con unfearful, unfearing, unfrightened
ant unafraid

terrify *vb* ***syn*** FRIGHTEN, affright, alarm, awe, fright, scare, ‖spook, startle, terrorize
rel freeze, paralyze, petrify, stun, stupefy
idiom put the fear of God into, *scare shitless, strike fear into the heart of

terrifying *adj* ***syn*** GHASTLY 1, grim, grisly, gruesome, hideous, horrible, horrid, horrifying, macabre, terrible
ant unterrifying

territory *n* **1** ***syn*** AREA 1, belt, region, tract, zone
2 ***syn*** FIELD, bailiwick, champaign, demesne, domain, dominion, province, sphere, terrain, walk
3 ***syn*** TERRAIN 2, turf

terror *n* ***syn*** FEAR 1, alarm, consternation, dismay, dread, fright, horror, panic, trepidation, trepidity
rel awe, fearfulness

terroristic *adj* characterized by or practicing terror as a means of coercion <used torture and other *terroristic* tactics to extract confessions>
syn gestapo
rel coercive, strong-arm; brutal, cruel, merciless; immoral, improper, unsanctioned

terrorize *vb* **1** ***syn*** FRIGHTEN, affright, alarm, awe, fright, scare, ‖spook, startle, terrify
idiom scare to death
2 ***syn*** INTIMIDATE, bludgeon, browbeat, bulldoze, bully, bullyrag, cow, dragoon, hector, strong-arm
idiom use gestapo tactics on

terse *adj* ***syn*** CONCISE, breviloquent, brief, compendiary, compendious, curt, laconic, short, succinct, summary
rel close, compact; lean, precise; clear-cut, crisp, incisive; taut
con circuitous; pleonastic, redundant, repetitious

tersely *adv* ***syn*** BRIEFLY, concisely, in brief, in short, laconically, shortly, succinctly
rel closely, compactly; crisply, incisively, precisely; abruptly, curtly
idiom in as few words as possible
ant prolixly

test *n* ***syn*** EXPERIMENT, experimentation, trial, trial and error, trial run
rel inspection, scrutiny; confirmation, corroboration, substantiation, verification

test *vb* **1** ***syn*** TRY 1, check, examine, prove
rel assay, essay; confirm, substantiate, verify
idiom bring to test
2 ***syn*** PROVE 1, demonstrate, try

test (out) *vb* ***syn*** EXPERIMENT, experimentalize, experimentize, try (out), try on

test *adj* ***syn*** EXPERIMENTAL 2, experimentative, trial
rel proving, testing, trying; probationary, speculative

testament *n* ***syn*** TESTIMONY, attestation, confirmation, evidence, proof, testimonial, witness

testify *vb* **1** to serve as evidence of <present conditions *testify* to the accuracy of his predictions>
syn attest, point (to)
rel affirm; demonstrate, show; prove
con discredit, disprove, invalidate; confute, refute
2 to make a solemn declaration under oath for the purpose of establishing a fact (as in court) <*testified* against the defendant>
syn depone, depose, ‖mount, swear
idiom give testimony
3 ***syn*** INDICATE 2, announce, argue, attest, bespeak, betoken, witness

testimonial *n* **1** ***syn*** TESTIMONY, attestation, confirmation, evidence, proof, testament, witness
rel indication, manifestation, show, sign, symbol, token
2 ***syn*** CREDENTIALS, character, recommendation, reference
3 an expression of great approval and high esteem <a dinner was planned as a *testimonial* in his honor>
syn appreciation, salvo, tribute
rel salute; triumph; jubilee; commemoration, memorialization, remembrance
4 ***syn*** MONUMENT 2, memorial

testimony *n* something that serves as tangible verification <the results are remarkable *testimony* to the accuracy of his predictions>
syn attestation, confirmation, evidence, proof, testament, testimonial, witness; *compare* INDICATION 3
rel demonstration, illustration; affirmation, corroboration, documentation, substantiation, verification

testy *adj* ***syn*** IRASCIBLE, choleric, cranky, cross, quick-tempered, ratty, ‖stomachy, temperish, tetchy, touchy
rel annoyed, exasperated, grouchy, irritable, *pissed off

tetchy *adj* ***syn*** IRASCIBLE, choleric, cranky, cross, quick-tempered, ratty, ‖stomachy, temperish, testy, touchy
rel ill-humored; cantankerous

tête-à-tête *n* a private conversation between two people <had a *tête-à-tête* with her in a quiet corner>
syn vis-à-vis
rel causerie, chat, coze; conversation, talk; argument, discussion

tetrad *n* ***syn*** QUARTET, four, foursome, quartetto, quaternion, quatuor

---

syn synonym(s) ***rel*** related word(s)
idiom idiomatic equivalent(s) ***con*** contrasted word(s)
ant antonym(s) * vulgar
‖ use limited; if in doubt, see a dictionary
The first word in a synonym list when printed in SMALL CAPITALS shows where there is more information about the group. For a more efficient use of this book see Explanatory Notes.

‖**tew** *vb* ***syn*** WORRY 3, cark, fret, fuss, pother, stew
text *n* ***syn*** SUBJECT 2, argument, head, matter, motif, motive, point, subject matter, theme, topic
rel consideration, issue; fundamentals; idea
texture *n* **1** ***syn*** ESSENCE 1, being, essentia, essentiality, nature
2 a basic often highly complex underlying scheme, structure, or pattern <war destroys the very *texture* of a society>
syn fabric, fiber, web
rel framework, structure; composition, constitution, makeup; pattern, scheme
thalassic *adj* ***syn*** MARINE 1, maritime, oceanic
thankful *adj* ***syn*** GRATEFUL 1, obliged
con unappreciative, ungrateful
ant thankless, unthankful
thankless *adj* **1** not inclined to give thanks <a *thankless* guest>
syn unappreciative, ungrateful, unthankful
rel self-centered; careless, heedless, thoughtless; unappreciative, ungrateful, unmindful
con appreciative, grateful, mindful; careful, heedful, thoughtful
ant thankful
2 not likely to obtain thanks <a *thankless* job>
syn unappreciated, ungrateful, unthankful
rel disagreeable, distasteful, unpleasant; miserable, wretched
con thankworthy
thanks *n pl* ***syn*** GRACE 1, benediction, blessing, thanksgiving
thanksgiving *n* ***syn*** GRACE 1, benediction, blessing, thanks
thankworthy *adj* ***syn*** WORTHY 1, admirable, commendable, deserving, estimable, laudable, meritable, meritorious, praisable, praiseworthy
thank-you-ma'am *n* ***syn*** BUMP 3, ‖cahot
that *adj* **1** being the other <we argued it this way and we argued it *that* way>
syn another
ant this
2 ***syn*** SUCH 2
thaumaturgic *adj* ***syn*** MAGIC, magian, magical, mystic, necromantic, sorcerous, witchy, wizardly
thaumaturgy *n* ***syn*** MAGIC 1, bewitchment, conjuring, enchantment, incantation, necromancy, sorcery, witchcraft, witchery, wizardry
thaw *vb* ***syn*** LIQUEFY, deliquesce, dissolve, flux, fuse, liquesce, melt, run
theater *n* ***syn*** DRAMA, boards, footlights, (the) stage
theatral *adj* ***syn*** DRAMATIC 1, dramaturgic, histrionic, theatric, theatrical, thespian
theatric *adj* ***syn*** DRAMATIC 1, dramaturgic, histrionic, theatral, theatrical, thespian

syn synonym(s) ***rel*** related word(s)
idiom idiomatic equivalent(s) ***con*** contrasted word(s)
ant antonym(s) * vulgar
‖ use limited; if in doubt, see a dictionary
The first word in a synonym list when printed in SMALL CAPITALS shows where there is more information about the group. For a more efficient use of this book see Explanatory Notes.

theatrical *adj* **1** ***syn*** DRAMATIC 1, dramaturgic, histrionic, theatral, theatric, thespian
2 having qualities resembling a stage play or an actor's performance <he slowly made an exaggerated *theatrical* bow>
syn dramatic
rel histrionic, melodramatic, staged; affected, artificial, exaggerated, mannered, unnatural
theft *n* the unlawful taking and carrying away of property without the consent of its owner <was found guilty of auto *theft*>
syn larceny, lift, pinch, purloining, steal, stealage, stealing, thievery, thieving, ‖touch
rel filching, pilferage, pilfering, swiping; robbery, robbing, ‖stouth, ‖stouthrief; ‖score
theme *n* **1** ***syn*** SUBJECT 2, argument, head, matter, motif, motive, point, subject matter, text, topic
2 ***syn*** ESSAY 2, article, composition, paper
then *adv* **1** at another time <science as it was taught *then*>
syn again, anon, when; *compare* BEFORE 2
rel before, formerly
2 ***syn*** AGAIN 4, additionally, also, besides, further, in addition
3 ***syn*** THEREFORE, accordingly, consequently, ergo, hence, so, thereupon, thus
thence *adv* **1** ***syn*** AWAY 1, hence
2 ***syn*** THEREFROM, thereof
thenceforth *adv* from that time forward <the island which was *thenceforth* to be their home>
syn thenceforward, thereafter; *compare* HENCEFORTH
idiom from then on
thenceforward *adv* ***syn*** THENCEFORTH, thereafter
theorem *n* ***syn*** PRINCIPLE 1, axiom, fundamental, law, principium
theoretical *adj* **1** concerned principally with abstractions and theories <*theoretical* versus applied physics>
syn academic, closet, speculative
rel conjectural, hypothetical, notional, suppositional, unproved; analytical, problematical
con practical; factual; proved
ant applied
2 ***syn*** ABSTRACT 1, hypothetical, ideal, transcendent, transcendental
rel idealized, ivory-tower
ant concrete
theorize *vb* ***syn*** SUGGEST 4, submit
theory *n* **1** a belief, policy, or procedure proposed or followed as the basis of action <an educational system that was based on the *theory* that men learn best by experience>
syn hypothesis, supposal; *compare* ASSUMPTION 2
rel base, basis, grounds, position, premise, understanding
ant practice
2 something taken for granted especially on trivial or inadequate grounds <her *theory* that the house was haunted>
syn conjecture, perhaps, speculation, suppose, supposition
rel guess, guesswork, surmise; feeling, hunch, impression, presentiment, suspicion
con assurance, certainty, knowledge

there *adv* to or into that place <they seldom go *there* anymore>
syn thither, thitherward, yon
rel yonder
ant here

thereafter *adv* ***syn*** THENCEFORTH, thenceforward

thereby *adv* in consequence of that <lied to the jury, *thereby* negating his testimony>
syn therethrough; *compare* THEREFROM

therefore *adv* for this or that reason <I think, *therefore* I am>
syn accordingly, consequently, ergo, hence, so, then, thereupon, thus
rel thence, therefrom

therefrom *adv* from that thing, fact, or circumstance <public opinion and a policy deriving *therefrom*>
syn thence, thereof; *compare* THEREBY

thereof *adv* ***syn*** THEREFROM, thence

thereon *adv* on or upon that <knew both the text and commentary *thereon*>
syn thereupon
rel therein, thereof, thereto

therethrough *adv* ***syn*** THEREBY

theretofore *adv* up to that time <*theretofore* obscure communities>
syn thereuntil
rel ‖afore, before, previously
idiom before then

thereuntil *adv* ***syn*** THERETOFORE
idiom until then

thereupon *adv* **1** ***syn*** THEREON
2 ***syn*** THEREFORE, accordingly, consequently, ergo, hence, so, then, thus

thesis *n* **1** a position assumed or a point made especially in controversy <his *thesis* about the assassination was arguable>
syn contention, contestation
rel point, position; argument; belief, opinion, sentiment(s), view(s)
2 ***syn*** ASSUMPTION 2, apriorism, posit, postulate, postulation, premise, presumption, presupposition, supposition
3 ***syn*** DISCOURSE 2, disquisition, dissertation, memoir, monograph, monography, tractate, treatise
rel exposition; argument, argumentation

thespian *adj* ***syn*** DRAMATIC 1, dramaturgic, histrionic, theatral, theatric, theatrical

thespian *n* ***syn*** ACTOR 1, impersonator, mime, mimic, mummer, performer, playactor, player, trouper

thew *n* ***syn*** MUSCLE 1, beef, brawn, might

thick *adj* **1** ***syn*** STOCKY, ‖chumpy, chunky, dumpy, heavyset, squat, stubby, stumpy, thick-bodied, thickset
rel broad, wide; bulky, burly, husky; blubber, blubbery, massive, obese
con slender, slight, slim; lanky, spare; skeletal
2 ***syn*** CLOSE 4, compact, crowded, dense, tight
rel concentrated, crammed; localized
con dispersed, scattered
ant diffuse
3 ***syn*** STUPID 1, beef-witted, blockish, dense, doltish, dull, dumb, duncical, numskulled, thickheaded
4 ***syn*** FAMILIAR 1, chummy, close, confidential, intimate
idiom hand in glove, thick as thieves
5 ***syn*** IMPLAUSIBLE, flimsy, improbable, inconceivable, incredible, thin, unbelievable, unconceivable, unconvincing, unsubstantial
idiom a little too thick

thick–bodied *adj* ***syn*** STOCKY, ‖chumpy, chunky, dumpy, heavyset, squat, stubby, stumpy, thick, thickset

thickhead *n* ***syn*** DUNCE, blockhead, bonehead, clodpate, hammerhead, knucklehead, muttonhead, numskull, thickskull, woodenhead
rel ‖clot

thickheaded *adj* ***syn*** STUPID 1, beefheaded, beetleheaded, blockheaded, chuckleheaded, fatheaded, hammerheaded, numskulled, thick, thick-witted

thickset *adj* ***syn*** STOCKY, ‖chumpy, chunky, dumpy, heavyset, squat, stubby, stumpy, thick, thick-bodied
rel fleshy, portly

thickskull *n* ***syn*** DUNCE, blockhead, bonehead, clodpate, hammerhead, knucklehead, muttonhead, numskull, thickhead, woodenhead
rel lout

thick–witted *adj* ***syn*** STUPID 1, beef-witted, blear-witted, blockish, dense, doltish, dull, dumb, thick, thickheaded

thief *n* one who steals <a *thief* took her money>
syn filcher, larcener, larcenist, nimmer, pilferer, prig, purloiner, stealer; *compare* ROBBER
rel burglar, cat burglar, cat man, housebreaker; hijacker, robber; ‖booster, ‖dip, lifter, shoplifter; nip, pickpocket

thieve *vb* ***syn*** STEAL 1, filch, hook, lift, nip, pilfer, pinch, purloin, snitch, swipe

thievery *n* ***syn*** THEFT, larceny, lift, pinch, purloining, steal, stealage, stealing, thieving, ‖touch

thieving *adj* ***syn*** LARCENOUS, sticky-fingered, thievish

thieving *n* ***syn*** THEFT, larceny, lift, pinch, purloining, steal, stealage, stealing, thievery, ‖touch

thievish *adj* ***syn*** LARCENOUS, sticky-fingered, thieving

thin *adj* **1** not thick, heavy, or broad (as in configuration or physique) <a *thin* body>
syn attenuate, reedy, slender, slight, slim, squinny, stalky, tenuous, twiggy; *compare* LEAN
rel lank, lanky, lathy, lean, macilent, spare; cadaverous, gaunt, pinched, skeletal, wasted; meager, puny, small, twiglike
con broad, wide; compact, dense, solid; heavy, massive; corpulent, fat, obese
ant thick
2 characterized by wide separation of component particles <*thin* air at high altitudes>
syn attenuate, attenuated, rare, rarefied, subtile, subtle, tenuous
rel diffuse, diluted, dispersed; fine, refined
con heavy, thick

---

syn synonym(s) *rel* related word(s)
idiom idiomatic equivalent(s) *con* contrasted word(s)
ant antonym(s) * vulgar
‖ use limited; if in doubt, see a dictionary
The first word in a synonym list when printed in SMALL CAPITALS shows where there is more information about the group. For a more efficient use of this book see Explanatory Notes.

ant dense
3 ***syn*** DILUTE, diluted, washy, watered-down, waterish, watery, weak
4 ***syn*** ACUTE 4, argute, high, piercing, piping, sharp, shrill, treble
rel high-pitched
con low, low-pitched; guttural; deep
5 ***syn*** IMPLAUSIBLE, flimsy, improbable, inconceivable, incredible, thick, unbelievable, unconvincing, unsubstantial, weak
rel vapid; transparent; questionable; untenable
idiom a bit thin
con believable, convincing, sound, substantial

thin *vb* **1** to make thin or thinner <a once powerful frame *thinned* by privation>
syn attenuate, extenuate, wiredraw
rel diminish, reduce; weaken
con broaden, enlarge; strengthen
ant thicken
2 to make or become less dense <the air *thinned* at high altitudes>
syn attenuate, rarefy
ant densify
3 ***syn*** DILUTE, cut, weaken

thing *n* **1** ***syn*** AFFAIR 1, business, concern, matter, shooting match
2 ***syn*** OCCURRENCE, circumstance, episode, event, go, happening, incident, occasion
3 ***syn*** ACTION 1, accomplishment, act, deed, doing
rel exploit, feat, stunt
4 whatever is apprehended as having actual, distinct, and demonstrable existence <there is a place for each *thing* in the lab>
syn article, object
rel entity, item
5 that which can be known as having existence in space or time <virtue is not a *thing,* but an attribute of a *thing*>
syn being, entity, individual, material, matter, object, stuff, substance
rel item, particular
con attribute, characteristic, property, quality
6 ***syn*** ENTITY 1, being, existence, existent, individual, something
ant nonentity, nonexistence
7 things *pl* ***syn*** POSSESSION 2, belongings, chattels, effects, goods, lares and penates, movables
8 things *pl* ***syn*** PERSONAL EFFECTS, ‖plunder, stuff, traps, tricks
9 things *pl* ***syn*** CLOTHES, apparel, attire, attirement, clothing, dress, duds, habiliment(s), raiment, togs
10 ***syn*** POINT 1, article, detail, element, item, particular
11 ***syn*** FASHION 3, craze, cry, dernier cri, fad, furore, mode, rage, style, vogue
12 ***syn*** FETISH 2, fixation, mania, obsession

thingum *n* ***syn*** DOODAD, dingus, dofunny, doohickey, gadget, gizmo, ‖hootenanny, jigger, thingumajig, thingumbob

thingumajig *n* ***syn*** DOODAD, dingus, dofunny, doohickey, gadget, gizmo, ‖hootenanny, jigger, thingum, thingumbob

thingumbob *n* ***syn*** DOODAD, dingus, dofunny, gadget, gizmo, ‖hootenanny, jigger, thingum, thingumajig, thingummy

thingummy *n* ***syn*** DOODAD, dingus, doohickey, gadget, gizmo, ‖hootenanny, jigger, thingum, thingumajig, thingumbob

think *vb* **1** to form an idea of something in the mind <try to *think* exactly how the accident happened>
syn conceive, envisage, envision, fancy, feature, image, imagine, project, realize, see, vision, visualize
rel consider, contemplate, study, weigh; appreciate, comprehend, understand; cerebrate, ideate; conjecture, guess, surmise
2 ***syn*** UNDERSTAND 3, assume, believe, expect, gather, imagine, ‖reckon, suppose, suspect, take
3 ***syn*** CONJECTURE, guess, presume, pretend, suppose, surmise
4 ***syn*** FEEL 3, believe, consider, credit, deem, hold, sense
rel estimate; regard
5 to use one's powers of conception, judgment, or inference <the power to *think* sets humans apart from other animals>
syn cerebrate, cogitate, deliberate, reason, reflect, speculate
rel consider, contemplate; brood, meditate, mull, muse, ponder, ruminate; intellectualize, logicalize, logicize, rationalize; conclude, deduce, infer, judge
idiom put on one's thinking cap, set one's brain to work, use one's head, use the old bean

think (out *or* over) *vb* ***syn*** CONSIDER 1, contemplate, excogitate, mind, perpend, ponder, study, weigh

think (over) *vb* ***syn*** RECONSIDER, reevaluate, reexamine, rethink, re-treat, review, reweigh

thinkable *adj* **1** capable of being thought about <concepts that are easy enough to be *thinkable*>
syn cogitable
rel imaginable, presumable, supposable; comprehendible, comprehensible
con unimaginable; incomprehensible, uncomprehensible
ant unthinkable
2 capable of being made actual <nationalism at this time would be scarcely *thinkable*>
syn conceivable, imaginable, supposable
rel likely, possible; convincing, plausible; feasible, practicable, practical
con inconceivable, unimaginable; impossible, unlikely; implausible; impractical, unfeasible
ant unthinkable

thinking *adj* ***syn*** THOUGHTFUL 1, cogitative, contemplative, meditative, pensive, pondering, reflecting, reflective, ruminative, speculative
ant unthinking

third degree *n* ***syn*** CROSS-EXAMINATION, grill, grilling, interrogation

---

syn synonym(s) ***rel*** related word(s)
idiom idiomatic equivalent(s) ***con*** contrasted word(s)
ant antonym(s) * vulgar
‖ use limited; if in doubt, see a dictionary
The first word in a synonym list when printed in SMALL CAPITALS shows where there is more information about the group. For a more efficient use of this book see Explanatory Notes.

third estate *n* ***syn*** COMMONALTY, commonage, commoners, common men, people, plebeians, plebes, plebs, populace, rank and file

thirst *vb* ***syn*** LONG, ache, crave, hanker, hunger, itch, lust, pine, yearn, yen
rel covet; desire, wish

thirsting *adj* ***syn*** THIRSTY 1, athirst, dry

thirsty *adj* **1** experiencing a desire for drink <the long hot walk had made him *thirsty*>
syn athirst, dry, thirsting
rel juiceless, parched, sapless
2 ***syn*** DRY 1, arid, bone-dry, droughty, moistureless, sere, unwatered, waterless
3 ***syn*** EAGER, agog, anxious, appetent, ardent, athirst, avid, breathless, impatient, keen
idiom hungry for, itching for, wild for
ant sated, satiated

this and that *n, often* **this and thats** *pl* ***syn*** SUNDRIES, etceteras, oddments, odds and ends

thither *adv* ***syn*** THERE, thitherward, yon
ant hither

thitherward *adv* ***syn*** THERE, thither, yon
ant hitherward

thorny *adj* bristling with perplexities, points of controversy, or other conflicting elements <the *thorny* question of states' rights>
syn nettlesome, prickly, spiny
rel troublesome, vexatious; difficult; tricky

thorough *adj* **1** ***syn*** EXHAUSTIVE, complete, full-dress, thoroughgoing, whole-hog
rel absolute
2 ***syn*** CIRCUMSTANTIAL, blow-by-blow, clocklike, detailed, full, itemized, minute, particular, particularized

thoroughbred *adj* ***syn*** PUREBRED, full-blooded, pedigree, pedigreed, pureblood
con mixed, mongrel

thoroughfare *n* ***syn*** WAY 1, artery, avenue, boulevard, ‖drag, highway, path, road, street, track

thoroughgoing *adj* **1** ***syn*** EXHAUSTIVE, complete, full-dress, thorough, whole-hog
2 ***syn*** UTTER, absolute, complete, consummate, gross, out-and-out, outright, rank, straight-out, unmitigated

thoroughly *adv* **1** ***syn*** WELL 3, altogether, completely, entirely, fully, perfectly, ‖plumb, quite, utterly, wholly
2 in a detailed and complete manner <*thoroughly* investigated the accusations>
syn completely, detailedly, exhaustively, in and out, inside out, up and down
idiom item by item, to the last detail
con casually, offhandedly, sketchily, superficially
ant cursorily
3 ***syn*** VERY 1, exceedingly, exceptionally, extremely, highly, hugely, notably, rattling, remarkably, strikingly
4 ***syn*** HARD 3, assiduously, dingdong, earnestly, exhaustively, intensely, intensively, painstakingly, unremittingly

though *adv* ***syn*** HOWEVER, after all, howbeit, nevertheless, nonetheless, notwithstanding, still, still and all, withal, yet

though *conj* in spite of the fact that <*though* they know the war is lost, they continue to fight>
syn albeit, although, howbeit, much as, when, whereas, while

thought *n* **1** the act or process of thinking <sat immersed in deep *thought*>
syn brainwork, cerebration, cogitation, deliberation, reflection, speculation
rel contemplation; meditation, musing, pondering, rumination
2 ***syn*** IDEA, apprehension, conceit, concept, conception, image, impression, intellection, notion, perception

thoughtful *adj* **1** characterized by or exhibiting the power to think <the doctor had a shrewd rather than a *thoughtful* face>
syn cogitative, contemplative, meditative, pensive, ‖pensy, pondering, reflecting, reflective, ruminative, speculative, thinking
rel analytical, calculating, logical, rational; earnest, grave, melancholy, serious, sober, studious; brainy, intellectual; deep, inseeing, introspective
con irrational; dull, slow, stupid, unthinking; empty-headed, shallow, vacuous
ant thoughtless
2 ***syn*** MINDFUL 2, heedful, observant, observative, observing, regardful
3 mindful of others <the thank-you note was a *thoughtful* gesture>
syn attentive, considerate
rel anxious, careful, concerned, heedful, mindful, solicitous; chivalrous, civil, courteous, gallant, gracious, polite, well-bred
con careless, heedless, inattentive, negligent, remiss, unconcerned, unmindful, unthinking; inconsiderate; discourteous, impolite
ant thoughtless, unthoughtful

thoughtfully *adv* ***syn*** WELL 2, considerately, generously, heedfully, kindly
rel courteously, politely, solicitously
con discourteously, impolitely; inconsiderately, heedlessly, unkindly
ant thoughtlessly, unthoughtfully

thoughtless *adj* **1** ***syn*** RASH 1, brash, hasty, hotheaded, ill-advised, incautious, inconsiderate, mad-brained, madcap, reckless
2 ***syn*** CARELESS 1, feckless, heedless, inadvertent, irreflective, uncaring, unheeding, unrecking, unreflective, unthinking
con mindful
ant thoughtful
3 ***syn*** SHORT 5, inconsiderate, sharp, unceremonious, ungracious
rel discourteous, impolite, rude; selfish
ant thoughtful

thought-out *adj* ***syn*** DELIBERATE 1, advised, aforethought, considered, designed, premeditated, prepense, studied, studious
rel investigated; analyzed

---

syn synonym(s) ***rel*** related word(s)
idiom idiomatic equivalent(s) ***con*** contrasted word(s)
ant antonym(s) * vulgar
‖ use limited; if in doubt, see a dictionary
The first word in a synonym list when printed in SMALL CAPITALS shows where there is more information about the group. For a more efficient use of this book see Explanatory Notes.

idiom thought over (*or* through)

thousand *n* ***syn*** SCAD, gob(s), heap, jillion, load(s), million, oodles, quantities, ream(s), trillion

thrall *n* ***syn*** BONDAGE, enslavement, helotry, peonage, serfdom, servitude, slavery, thralldom, villenage, yoke

thralldom *n* ***syn*** BONDAGE, enslavement, helotry, peonage, serfdom, servitude, slavery, thrall, villenage, yoke

thrash *vb* **1** ***syn*** BEAT 1, batter, belabor, buffet, lambaste, paste, pelt, pound, pummel, wallop
2 ***syn*** WHIP 2, beat, ||clobber, drub, lambaste, lick, shellac, smear, smother, trim
3 ***syn*** WHIP 1, flagellate, flog, hide, lash, scourge, stripe, thrash, ||wear out, whale
rel strike; paddywhack, ||pail

thrashing *n* ***syn*** DEFEAT 1, beating, debacle, defeasance, drubbing, licking, overthrow, rout, shellacking, trouncing

thrash out *vb* ***syn*** DISCUSS 1, agitate, argue, canvass, debate, discept, dispute, ||kick around, moot, toss (around)

threadbare *adj* **1** ***syn*** SHABBY 1, dilapidated, dingy, down-at-heel, faded, run-down, seedy, tacky, tagrag, tattered
rel damaged, impaired, injured; frayed, ragged; shopworn, timeworn, worn
idiom the worse for wear, worn to rags (*or* threads)
2 ***syn*** TRITE, bathetic, cliché, clichéd, commonplace, hack, stale, tired, well-worn, worn-out
rel common, familiar; imitative, uncreative; set, stock; banal, corny
con fresh, new; different, novel, original, unconventional, unusual; memorable

threaten *vb* to announce or forecast impending danger or evil <bullies *threatening* the child with a beating>
syn menace
rel browbeat, bulldoze, cow, intimidate; augur, forebode, portend, presage; caution, forewarn, warn
idiom make (*or* utter) threats against

threatening *adj* **1** ***syn*** IMMINENT 2, lowering (*or* louring), lowery (*or* loury), menacing, overhanging
rel impending; forthcoming, upcoming; close, near
2 ***syn*** OMINOUS, apocalyptic, baleful, baneful, dire, fateful, ill-boding, inauspicious, unlucky, unpropitious

threesome *n* ***syn*** TRIAD, trine, trinity, trio, triple, triumvirate, triune, troika

threshold *n* ***syn*** VERGE 2, brink, edge, point

thrift *n* ***syn*** ECONOMY, forehandedness, frugality, husbandry, providence, prudence, thriftiness
rel austerity, economizing; saving; parsimony
ant waste

thriftiness *n* ***syn*** ECONOMY, forehandedness, frugality, husbandry, providence, prudence, thrift
ant thriftlessness

thriftless *adj* ***syn*** IMPROVIDENT, unthrift, unthrifty

---

syn synonym(s) — *rel* related word(s)
idiom idiomatic equivalent(s) — *con* contrasted word(s)
ant antonym(s) — * vulgar
|| use limited; if in doubt, see a dictionary
The first word in a synonym list when printed in SMALL CAPITALS shows where there is more information about the group. For a more efficient use of this book see Explanatory Notes.

---

ant thrifty

thrifty *adj* **1** ***syn*** FLOURISHING, booming, prospering, prosperous, roaring, robust, thriving
rel blooming, burgeoning; growing
2 ***syn*** SPARING, canny, chary, economical, frugal, provident, saving, Scotch, stewardly, unwasteful
rel foresighted, prudent; conserving, preserving
con extravagant, improvident
ant wasteful

thrill *vb* to fill with emotions that stir or excite or to be so excited <an audience *thrilled* by the brilliant spectacle>
syn electrify, enthuse, send
rel animate, excite, galvanize, move, quicken, stimulate; arouse, inspire, rally, rouse, stir
idiom thrill to pieces (*or* to bits)
con bore, ennui, weary

thrill *n* sudden emotional stimulation, excitement, or enjoyment <they both got a *thrill* out of small-boat racing>
syn bang, boot, kick, wallop
rel excitement, lift, stimulation, titillation

thriller *n* a work of fiction or drama designed to hold the interest by use of a high degree of intrigue, adventure, or suspense <wrote cheap detective *thrillers*>
syn chiller, shocker, thriller-diller
rel gothic, mystery; dime novel, penny dreadful, shilling shocker

thriller–diller *n* ***syn*** THRILLER, chiller, shocker

thrive *vb* **1** ***syn*** BOOM, flourish
rel come on, develop, grow; increase; prosper
con stagnate; fail; bust
2 ***syn*** SUCCEED 3, arrive, flourish, go, make out, prosper, score
rel advance, progress
idiom make a go, turn out well

thriving *adj* **1** ***syn*** FLOURISHING, booming, prospering, prosperous, roaring, robust, thrifty
rel blooming, growing; advancing, progressing
idiom going strong
con shriveling; dying
2 ***syn*** SUCCESSFUL, prosperous

thriving *n* ***syn*** PROSPERITY 2, abundance, ease, easy street, prosperousness, well-being

throb *vb* ***syn*** PULSATE, beat, palpitate, pulse
rel thump; resonate

throe *n* **1** ***syn*** ATTACK 3, access, fit, seizure, spell, turn
rel convulsion
2 ***syn*** PAIN 1, ache, ||misery, pang, stitch, twinge
rel stab

throne *n* ***syn*** TOILET, ||can, *crapper, ||donicker, head, john, johnny, ||loo, ||pot, ||potty

throng *n* ***syn*** CROWD 1, crush, drove, horde, multitude, press, push, squash
rel assemblage, assembly, collection, congregation, gathering; bunch, flock, group, pack

thronged *adj* ***syn*** ALIVE 5, abounding, overflowing, replete, rife, swarming, teeming
rel crawling

throttle *vb* ***syn*** CHOKE 1, strangle
rel garrote

throttling *n* ***syn*** REPRESSION 1, choking, extinguishment, quashing, smothering, squashing, squelching, stifling, strangling, suppression

through *prep* **1** ***syn*** VIA 1, by, by way of
2 ***syn*** VIA 2, by, by dint of, by means of, by virtue of, by way of, per, with
3 ***syn*** OVER 6, because of, due to, owing to
4 ***syn*** ABOUT 4, round, throughout
idiom clear through

through *adv* **1** from beginning to end <the region has a mild climate the whole year *through*>
syn around, over, round, throughout
2 ***syn*** OVER 5, by

through *adj* **1** ***syn*** DIRECT 2, straight, straightforward, uninterrupted
con obstructed; interrupted
2 ***syn*** COMPLETE 4, completed, concluded, done, down, ended, finished, terminated
3 having no further value, strength, or resources <when he lost his voice, his singing career was *through*>
syn done for, finished, washed-up
rel ended; over
4 being at the very end of a course, concern, or relationship <was *through* with his wife>
syn done, washed-up
rel finished

through–and–through *adv* ***syn*** DOWN 2, completely, fully

throughout *adv* **1** ***syn*** EVERYWHERE 1, all over, everyplace, far and near, far and wide, high and low, overall
2 ***syn*** THROUGH 1, around, over, round

throughout *prep* **1** ***syn*** ABOUT 4, round, through
2 ***syn*** DURING, amid, mid, midst, over

throw *vb* **1** to cause to move swiftly through space by a propulsive movement or a propelling force <*throw* a ball to first base>
syn ‖bung, cast, fire, fling, heave, hurl, launch, pitch, sling, toss
rel ding, drive, impel, precipitate, shoot; project, propel, push, shove, thrust; flick, flip; ‖chuck, shy, tumble; lift, lob
2 to dislodge from one's seat especially in horseback riding <was *thrown* while taking a hurdle>
syn buck (off), pitch, unhorse, unseat
rel ding (off), fling (off)
3 ***syn*** OVERCOME 1, conquer, down, hurdle, lick, master, surmount
4 ***syn*** DON 1, assume, draw on, get on, huddle (on), put on, slip (on)
5 ***syn*** EXERT, exercise, ply, put out, wield
6 ***syn*** ADDRESS 3, apply, bend, buckle (down), devote, direct, give, turn

throw away *vb* **1** ***syn*** DISCARD, cashier, cast, jettison, junk, reject, scrap, shed, slough, throw out
ant salvage
2 ***syn*** WASTE 2, blow, blunder (away), consume, dissipate, fool (away), fritter, frivol away, squander, trifle (away)
con lay away, lay by, lay up

throw back *vb* ***syn*** REVERT 2, regress, retrogress

throwback *n* ***syn*** REVERSION 1, atavism

throw down *vb* ***syn*** FELL 1, bowl (down *or* over), bring down, down, knock down, knock over, lay low, level, mow (down), prostrate
rel cast down

throw in *vb* ***syn*** INTRODUCE 6, fill in, insert, insinuate, intercalate, interject, interpolate, interpose
rel contribute

throwing away *n* ***syn*** DISPOSAL 2, discarding, disposition, dumping, jettison, junking, relegation, riddance, scrapping
ant salvaging

throw off *vb* **1** ***syn*** RID, clear, lose, shake (off), unburden
2 ***syn*** SHAKE 5, lose, slip
3 ***syn*** EMIT 2, give off, give out, issue, release, vent
rel disgorge, eject, exhaust, expel
4 ***syn*** CONFUSE 2, addle, ball up, befuddle, bewilder, distract, dizzy, fluster, mix up, throw out

throw out *vb* **1** ***syn*** EJECT 1, boot (out), chase, chuck, dismiss, evict, extrude, kick out, out
2 ***syn*** DISCARD, cashier, cast, jettison, junk, reject, scrap, shed, slough, throw away
3 ***syn*** SAY 1, bring out, chime in, come out (with), declare, deliver, state, tell, utter
4 ***syn*** CONFUSE 2, addle, ball up, befuddle, bewilder, ‖bumfuzzle, distract, fluster, mix up, throw off

throw over *vb* ***syn*** ABANDON 1, chuck, desert, forsake, quit, renounce

throw up *vb* **1** to construct or erect hastily and often carelessly <makeshift buildings *thrown up* almost overnight>
syn jerry-build, run up
rel roughcast, roughhew
idiom slap together, throw together
2 ***syn*** VOMIT, barf, bring up, ‖cast, disgorge, ‖heave, *puke, spew, spit up, upchuck

thrum *vb* ***syn*** HUM, bombinate, ‖bum, bumble, buzz, drone, ‖sowf, strum
rel birr, purr

thrust *vb* **1** ***syn*** PUSH 1, drive, propel, shove
rel crowd, jam; bump, elbow, jostle, nudge, prod, shoulder
2 to cause (as a pointed instrument) to penetrate forcibly <*thrust* the dagger through her heart>
syn dig, drive, plunge, ram, run, sink, stab, stick
rel jab, shove; impale; pierce; embed; put

thrust *n* ***syn*** SUBSTANCE 2, burden, core, gist, meat, pith, purport, sense, short, upshot

thud *vb* to make a dull sound by or as if by striking a surface with something thick and heavy <heard footsteps *thudding* down the hall>
syn clonk, clunk, thump
rel tunk; hit, smite, strike; beat, pound

thug *n* **1** a person inclined or hired to treat another roughly, brutally, or murderously <was beaten and robbed by *thugs*>
syn ‖gorilla, ‖hood, hoodlum, hooligan, ruffian, strong arm; *compare* TOUGH

---

syn synonym(s)	***rel*** related word(s)
idiom idiomatic equivalent(s)	***con*** contrasted word(s)
ant antonym(s)	* vulgar

‖ use limited; if in doubt, see a dictionary
The first word in a synonym list when printed in SMALL CAPITALS shows where there is more information about the group. For a more efficient use of this book see Explanatory Notes.

rel bully, ‖larrikan, plug-ugly, roughneck, rowdy, tough; punk; cutthroat, gangster, gunman, mobster; goon, hatchet man
2 *syn* TOUGH, mucker, mug, plug-ugly, punk, rough, roughneck, rowdy, ruffian, yahoo

thumb *vb syn* HITCHHIKE, hitch
idiom thumb a ride

thumb (through) *vb syn* BROWSE, dip (into), flip (through), glance (at *or* over), leaf (through), riff (through), riffle (through), run (through *or* over), scan, skim (through)

thump *vb syn* THUD, clonk, clunk
rel hammer, knock

thunder *n* the sound that follows a flash of lightning and is caused by sudden expansion of the air in the path of the electrical discharge <he was more afraid of *thunder* than of lightning>
syn thunderclap, thundercrack, thundering
rel fulmination

thunderbolt *n* a single discharge of lightning with the accompanying thunder <he was startled by the *thunderbolt*>
syn bolt, thunderstroke

thunderclap *n syn* THUNDER, thundercrack, thundering

thundercrack *n syn* THUNDER, thunderclap, thundering

thundering *n syn* THUNDER, thunderclap, thundercrack

thunderstroke *n syn* THUNDERBOLT, bolt

thunderstruck *adj syn* AGHAST 2, agape, confounded, dismayed, dumbfounded, overhwhelmed, shocked
rel bewildered, staggered; breathless, stunned
idiom struck dumb

thus *adv* **1** in this or that manner <summoned his counselors and spoke *thus* to them>
syn so, thus and so, thus and thus, thusly
2 *syn* THEREFORE, accordingly, consequently, ergo, hence, so, then, thereupon

thus and so *adv syn* THUS 1, so, thus and thus, thusly

thus and thus *adv syn* THUS 1, so, thus and so, thusly

thus far *adv syn* HITHERTO 1, as yet, earlier, so far, yet

thusly *adv syn* THUS 1, so, thus and so, thus and thus

thwack *n syn* BLOW 1, biff, bop, crack, pound, smack, sock, ‖welt, whack, whop

thwart *adj syn* TRANSVERSE, crossing, crosswise, transversal, traverse

thwart *vb syn* FRUSTRATE 1, baffle, balk, beat, bilk, circumvent, dash, disappoint, foil, ruin
rel curb, restrain, scotch; cross; foul up, gum up, queer; stymie
con aid, assist, help, support; abet, encourage

‖**tick** *n syn* INSTANT 1, minute, moment, second, shake, split second, trice, twinkle, twinkling, wink

ticket *n* **1** a slip giving information (as of ownership, identity, or price) <the price of the iron is on the *ticket*>
syn label, tag
rel card; slip; sticker
2 a card of admission <theater *tickets*>
syn carte d'entrée
rel pass
3 a list of candidates for appointment, nomination, or election <vote the party *ticket*>
syn slate
rel choice; lineup; list
4 *syn* BALLOT 1, vote
5 *syn* PASSPORT, key, open sesame, password

ticklish *adj* **1** *syn* UNSTABLE 2, rocky, tricky
2 *syn* DELICATE 7, precarious, sensitive, touchy, tricky
rel critical
3 *syn* INCONSTANT 1, capricious, changeable, fickle, mercurial, temperamental, uncertain, unstable, variable, volatile

tick off *vb* **1** *syn* ENUMERATE 2, list, numerate
2 *syn* REPROVE, admonish, call down, chide, lesson, monish, ‖rack back, rebuke, reprimand, reproach

tidbit (*or* **titbit**) *n syn* DELICACY, bonne bouche, dainty, goody, kickshaw, morsel, treat

‖**tiddly** *adj syn* INTOXICATED 1, ‖boozy, ‖canned, disguised, drunk, inebriated, ‖lushed, muddled, pixilated, ‖plastered

tide *n syn* FLOW, current, drift, flood, flux, rush, spate, stream

tidings *n pl syn* NEWS, advice, information, intelligence, speerings, word

tidy *adj syn* NEAT 2, chipper, orderly, shipshape, snug, spick-and-span, trig, trim, uncluttered, well-groomed
rel sleek, spruce
ant untidy

tie *n* **1** *syn* BOND 3, knot, ligament, ligature, link, nexus, vinculum, yoke
rel fastener, fastening; attachment
2 *syn* DRAW 4, deadlock, dogfall, stalemate, standoff

tie *vb* **1** to make fast and secure <*tie* a bundle with strong cord>
syn bind, tie up
rel attach, fasten; connect, join, link; anchor, moor, rivet, secure; lash, truss (up); band, cinch, gird, rope
con loose, loosen; disconnect
ant untie
2 *syn* MARRY 2, ‖hitch, mate, splice, wed
3 *syn* HAMPER, clog, curb, entrammel, fetter, hobble, hog-tie, leash, shackle, trammel
idiom tie hand and foot, tie one's hands
ant untie
4 *syn* EQUAL 3, match, measure up, meet, rival, touch

tier *n* **1** *syn* LINE 5, echelon, file, queue, rank, row, string
rel layer
2 *syn* CLASS 1, category, grade, group, grouping, league, pigeonhole

tie up *vb* **1** *syn* TIE 1, bind
2 *syn* HAMPER, clog, curb, entrammel, fetter, hobble, hog-tie, leash, shackle, tie

tie–up *n syn* ASSOCIATION 1, affiliation, alliance, cahoots, combination, conjunction, connection, hookup, partnership, togetherness
rel linkup

tiff *n syn* QUARREL, altercation, bickering, dispute, falling-out, miff, rhubarb, run-in, spat, squabble

---

syn synonym(s) | *rel* related word(s)
idiom idiomatic equivalent(s) | *con* contrasted word(s)
ant antonym(s) | * vulgar
‖ use limited; if in doubt, see a dictionary
The first word in a synonym list when printed in SMALL CAPITALS shows where there is more information about the group. For a more efficient use of this book see Explanatory Notes.

tiff *vb* ***syn*** QUARREL, bicker, brabble, caterwaul, fall out, row, scrap, spat, squabble, wrangle

tiffany *adj* ***syn*** FILMY, diaphanous, flimsy, gauzy, gossamer, sheer, transparent

tight *adj* **1** ***syn*** FAST 4, firm, fixed, secure, set, tenacious
rel clasped; solid, steadfast
con lax, limp; shaky
ant loose
2 ***syn*** CLOSE 4, compact, crowded, dense, thick
ant loose
3 fitting, drawn, or stretched so that there is no slackness or looseness <a *tight* drumhead>
syn close, taut, tense
rel skintight; constricted, contracted, drawn, tightened; inflexible, rigid, stiff
con loosened, slack, unconstricted
ant loose
4 difficult to cope with, get through, or circumvent <a very *tight* diplomatic situation>
syn arduous, rough, tricksy, trying
rel difficult; exacting; tense; critical; punishing; distressing, disturbing, upsetting
5 ***syn*** STINGY, cheeseparing, close, closefisted, miserly, niggardly, parsimonious, penny-pinching, penurious, tightfisted
6 ***syn*** INTOXICATED 1, ‖boozed, ‖boozy, drunk, drunken, inebriated, ‖loaded, ‖oiled, ‖plastered, ‖stewed
idiom tight as a tick

tight *adv* ***syn*** HARD 7, fast, firm, firmly, fixedly, solidly, steadfastly, tightly

tightfisted *adj* ***syn*** STINGY, cheeseparing, close, closefisted, miserly, niggardly, parsimonious, penny-pinching, penurious, tight
rel grudging, mean, shabby

tight-laced *adj* ***syn*** PRIM 1, genteel, prig, priggish, prissy, prudish, puritanical, straitlaced, stuffy, Victorian

tight-lipped *adj* ***syn*** SILENT 3, close, close-lipped, closemouthed, close-tongued, reserved, reticent, taciturn, tight-mouthed, uncommunicative
idiom with one's lips sealed

tightly *adv* ***syn*** HARD 7, fast, firm, firmly, fixedly, solidly, steadfastly, tight

tight-mouthed *adj* ***syn*** SILENT 3, close, close-lipped, closemouthed, close-tongued, reserved, reticent, taciturn, tight-lipped, uncommunicative

tightwad *n* ***syn*** MISER, cheapskate, cheeseparer, nabal, niggard, ‖nipcheese, scrooge, skin, skinflint, stiff

till *prep* ***syn*** UNTIL, before, in advance of, prior to, to, up till, up to

till *conj* up to the time when <be sure to wait *till* I come>
syn until

till *vb* to prepare (soil) for the raising of crops <*till* the soil>
syn cultivate, dress, ‖labor, tend, work
rel harrow, hoe, mulch, plow, turn; plant, sow

tillable *adj* ***syn*** ARABLE, cultivable, cultivatable
ant untillable

tilt *vb* **1** ***syn*** SLANT 1, cant, heel, incline, lean, list, recline, slope, tip
2 ***syn*** SEESAW, lurch, pitch, swag, tilter, yaw

tilt *n* ***syn*** SLOPE, grade, gradient, inclination, incline, lean, leaning, slant

tilted *adj* ***syn*** INCLINED 3, inclining, leaning, oblique, pitched, pitching, sloped, sloping, tilting, tipped

tilter *vb* ***syn*** SEESAW, lurch, pitch, swag, tilt, yaw

tilting *adj* ***syn*** INCLINED 3, inclining, leaning, oblique, pitched, pitching, sloped, sloping, tilted, tipped

timber *n* **1** ***syn*** FOREST, timberland, weald, wood(s), woodland
2 a large squared or dressed piece of wood <roof *timbers*>
syn balk, beam
rel girder, rafter

timberland *n* ***syn*** FOREST, timber, weald, wood(s), woodland

timbre *n* ***syn*** TEMPER 1, mood, spirit, tone

time *n* **1** ***syn*** WHILE 1, bit, space, spell, stretch, ‖whet
rel season
2 ***syn*** OCCASION 5, instant, moment, while
3 ***syn*** OPPORTUNITY, break, chance, look-in, occasion, opening, shot, show, squeak
idiom the proper moment
4 ***syn*** PERIOD 2, age, day(s), epoch, era
5 ***syn*** TERM 2, duration, span
6 ***syn*** SEASON
7 ***syn*** TEMPO, pace
8 ***syn*** SPELL 1, bout, go, shift, stint, tour, trick, turn
‖**9** ***syn*** BINGE 1, bender, brannigan, bust, carousal, carouse, compotation, jag, ran-tan, spree

time *vb* **1** to arrange or set the time of <*timed* his visits to coincide with her vacations>
syn book, schedule
rel plan, program, set up
2 to ascertain or record the time, duration, or rate of <*timed* the car at 100 mph>
syn clock
idiom hold the clock on

time and again *adv* ***syn*** OFTEN, again and again, frequently, much, oft, oftentimes, ofttimes, over and over, repeatedly

timeless *adj* **1** ***syn*** CONTINUAL, ceaseless, endless, everlasting, interminable, perpetual, unceasing, unending, uninterrupted, unremitting
2 ***syn*** ETERNAL 4, ageless, dateless, intemporal

timely *adv* ***syn*** EARLY 1, betimes, seasonably, soon

timely *adj* **1** done or occurring at a suitable time <await a more *timely* moment>
syn auspicious, favorable, opportune, propitious, prosperous, seasonable, timeous, well-timed
rel appropriate, fit, fitting, meet, proper, suitable; likely, promising
con improper, inappropriate, unfitting; inauspicious, inopportune, unfavorable, unpropitious, unsuitable; ill-timed
ant untimely
2 ***syn*** PUNCTUAL 2, prompt

---

syn synonym(s) ***rel*** related word(s)
idiom idiomatic equivalent(s) ***con*** contrasted word(s)
ant antonym(s) * vulgar
‖ use limited; if in doubt, see a dictionary
The first word in a synonym list when printed in SMALL CAPITALS shows where there is more information about the group. For a more efficient use of this book see Explanatory Notes.

timeous *adj* ***syn*** TIMELY 1, auspicious, favorable, opportune, propitious, prosperous, seasonable, well-timed

timetable *n* ***syn*** PROGRAM 1, agenda, calendar, card, docket, programma, schedule, sked

rel table; plan

timeworn *adj* **1** ***syn*** ANCIENT 1, aged, age-old, antediluvian, antique, hoary, Noachian, old, venerable

2 ***syn*** TRITE, clichéd, commonplace, hack, hackneyed, shopworn, stale, threadbare, well-worn, worn-out

timid *adj* **1** ***syn*** SHY 1, bashful, coy, demure, diffident, modest, rabbity, retiring, unassertive, unassured

rel humble; shrinking

ant bold

2 marked by or exhibiting a lack of boldness, courage, or determination <was too *timid* to ski>

syn timorous, ‖timorsome, undaring

rel gentle, mild, milk-toast, milky; cautious, chary, wary; jumpy, nervous, skittish; afraid, apprehensive, fainthearted, fearful; chicken, chickenhearted, henhearted, mouselike, mousy, pigeonhearted; cowardly, yellow; funky, panicky

con audacious, brave, courageous, daring, doughty, fearless, intrepid, lionhearted, unafraid, valiant, valorous

ant bold

3 ***syn*** VACILLATING 2, faltering, halting, hesitant, irresolute, shilly-shallying, tentative, uncertain, vacillatory, wiggle-waggle

timorous *adj* ***syn*** TIMID 2, ‖timorsome, undaring

rel quailing, recoiling, shrinking; quivering, shivering, shuddering, trembling

ant assured

‖**timorsome** *adj* ***syn*** TIMID 2, timorous, undaring

tincture *n* **1** ***syn*** COLOR 6, colorant, dye, dyestuff, pigment, stain

2 ***syn*** HINT 2, cast, intimation, shade, strain, streak, suggestion, tinge, touch, trace

rel smattering

tincture *vb* ***syn*** TINT, complexion, tinge

rel pigment; stain

ting *vb* ***syn*** TINKLE 1, plink, tingle

tinge *vb* ***syn*** TINT, complexion, tincture

rel streak

tinge *n* **1** ***syn*** COLOR 1, cast, hue, shade, tint, tone

rel coloration, coloring, tincture; stain

2 ***syn*** HINT 2, intimation, shade, sprinkling, strain, streak, suggestion, tincture, touch, trace

tingle *vb* **1** ***syn*** TINKLE 1, plink, ting

rel chime

2 ***syn*** JINGLE, chink, chinkle, clink, tinkle

tinker *vb* ***syn*** FIDDLE 2, doodle, mess, mess around, potter, puddle, putter

idiom play around

---

syn synonym(s) — *rel* related word(s)
idiom idiomatic equivalent(s) — *con* contrasted word(s)
ant antonym(s) — * vulgar
‖ use limited; if in doubt, see a dictionary
The first word in a synonym list when printed in SMALL CAPITALS shows where there is more information about the group. For a more efficient use of this book see Explanatory Notes.

tinkle *vb* **1** to make a repeated light high-pitched ringing sound <wind-bells *tinkling* in the breeze>

syn plink, ting, tingle

rel clink, jangle, jingle

2 ***syn*** JINGLE, chink, chinkle, clink, tingle

3 ***syn*** CHAT 1, babble, chatter, clack, gab, ‖gas, jaw, prattle, rattle, yak

tinsel *adj* ***syn*** GAUDY, blatant, brazen, chintzy, flashy, garish, glaring, loud, meretricious, tawdry

tint *n* ***syn*** COLOR 1, cast, hue, shade, tinge, tone

rel tincture, touch; coloration, pigmentation; dye, stain, wash

tint *vb* to color with a slight shade or stain <white blossoms *tinted* with pale pink>

syn complexion, tincture, tinge

rel color, dye; shade, touch (up); stain, wash

tintamarre *n* ***syn*** DIN, babel, clamor, hubbub, hullabaloo, jangle, pandemonium, racket, tumult, uproar

tiny *adj* exceptionally or remarkably small <the first *tiny* buds of spring flowers>

syn ‖bitsy, diminutive, dwarf, dwarfish, itsy-bitsy, itty-bitty, lilliputian, midget, miniature, minikin, minute, peewee, pint-size, pocket, pocket-size, pygmy, teensy, teensy-weensy, teenty, teeny, teeny-weeny, wee, weensy, weeny; *compare* SMALL 1

rel minuscular, minuscule; infinitesimal, microscopic, minim

con colossal, enormous, gigantic, immense, mammoth, vast

ant huge

tip *n* ***syn*** POINT 9, apex, cusp

tip *vb* ***syn*** SLANT 1, cant, heel, incline, lean, list, recline, slope, tilt

tip *vb* ***syn*** TIPTOE, toe

rel creep, mince, pussyfoot, steal

tip (over) *vb* ***syn*** OVERTURN 1, knock over, overset, overthrow, topple, turn over, upset

idiom turn upside down

tip *n* ***syn*** GRATUITY, cumshaw, lagniappe, largess, ‖palm grease, ‖palm oil, ‖perk(s), perquisite, pourboire

tip *n* a piece of advice or confidential information given by one thought to have access to special or inside sources <gave him a *tip* on which horse would win>

syn point, pointer, steer, tip-off

rel advice; information; clue, cue, hint; forecast, prediction

idiom a bit of inside advice, a bug in the ear, a word to the wise

tip-off *n* ***syn*** TIP, point, pointer, steer

tipped *adj* ***syn*** INCLINED 3, inclining, leaning, oblique, pitched, pitching, sloped, sloping, tilted, tilting

tipple *vb* ***syn*** DRINK 3, booze, guzzle, imbibe, liquor (up), soak, swig, swill, swizzle, tank up

idiom drown one's cares (*or* sorrows)

tipple *n* ***syn*** LIQUOR 2, aqua vitae, booze, ‖budge, drink, firewater, grog, ‖hooch, ‖juice, spirit(s)

tippler *n* ***syn*** DRUNKARD, bibber, boozer, drunk, inebriate, lush, soak, sot, toper, tosspot

tipster *n* ***syn*** INFORMER, betrayer, ‖canary, ‖fink, ‖nark, snitch, squealer, stool pigeon, talebearer, tattler

tipsy *adj* ***syn*** INTOXICATED 1, ‖boozed, ‖boozy, drunk, drunken, inebriated, ‖oiled, ‖stewed, ‖tiddly, tight

rel dazed, unsteady

tiptoe *vb* to walk or proceed quietly on or as if on the ends of the toes <*tiptoed* through the dark house>
syn tip, toe
rel creep, gumshoe, pussyfoot, steal
con clomp, clump, stamp, stomp, stump

tirade *n* a violent, often protracted, and usually denunciatory speech or writing <lashed out with a vicious *tirade* of angry protest>
syn diatribe, harangue, jeremiad, philippic
rel rant, rodomontade, screed; abuse, invective, revilement, vituperation; censure, condemnation, denunciation; berating, tongue-lashing; lecture, sermon

tire *vb* **1** to deplete the strength and energy of <the plane trip *tired* him>
syn drain, fatigue, jade, wear, wear down, weary; *compare* EXHAUST 4
rel debilitate, enervate, enfeeble, sap, weaken; exhaust, wear out
con brace (up), invigorate, strengthen; animate, energize, enliven, pep (up), quicken, stimulate, vitalize
2 *syn* BORE, ennui, pall, weary
rel jade, wear; irk; disgust, nauseate, sicken
idiom make one tired, put one to sleep

tired *adj* **1** being depleted of strength and energy <was too *tired* to go on>
syn fatigued, jaded, wearied, weary, worn, worn down
rel overtaxed, overworked; drained, run-down; ‖beat, ‖bushed, dog-tired, exhausted, fagged, frazzled, overworn, ‖pooped, ‖tucked up, tuckered, worn-out; collapsing, consumed, knocked out, prostrate, spent
idiom worn to a frazzle
con active, energetic, lively, strong, tireless
ant rested; fresh, untired
2 *syn* SHABBY 1, bedraggled, broken-down, decrepit, down-at-heel, faded, run-down, seedy, tattered, threadbare
3 *syn* FED UP, disgusted, sick, weary
rel annoyed, bothered, displeased, irked
idiom having a bellyful of, having about enough of
4 *syn* TRITE, clichéd, commonplace, hack, hackneyed, shopworn, stale, threadbare, well-worn, worn-out

tiredness *n* *syn* FATIGUE, exhaustion, lassitude, weariness
rel collapse, prostration

tireless *adj* *syn* INDEFATIGABLE, inexhaustible, unflagging, untiring, unwearіable, unwearying, weariless
rel active, enthusiastic
con inactive, listless, tired, unenergetic, unenthusiastic, weak

tiresome *adj* *syn* IRKSOME, boresome, boring, drudging, tedious, tiring
rel dull; jading; burdensome, onerous, oppressive; difficult, hard

tiring *adj* *syn* IRKSOME, boresome, boring, drudging, tedious, tiresome

Titan *adj* *syn* HUGE, Antaean, colossal, cyclopean, gargantuan, gigantic, Herculean, mighty, monstrous, titanic

titanic *adj* *syn* HUGE, colossal, cyclopean, enormous, gargantuan, gigantic, Herculean, mighty, monstrous, tremendous

title *n* **1** *syn* CLAIM 1, ‖dibs, pretense, pretension
rel argument, ground, justification, proof, reason; desert, due, merit
2 *syn* NAME 1, appellation, appellative, cognomen, compellation, denomination, designation, ‖moniker, nomen, style

title *vb* *syn* NAME 1, baptize, call, christen, denominate, designate, dub, entitle, style, term

titter *vb* *syn* LAUGH, chortle, chuckle, giggle, guffaw, hee-haw, snicker, ‖sniggle, tehee
rel twitter
idiom laugh behind (*or* in) one's hand, laugh in one's beard

tittle *n* *syn* PARTICLE, atom, bit, ‖dite, iota, jot, minim, mite, smidgen, smitch
rel fleck, flyspeck, speck; crumb, grain, scrap, snippet

tittle–tattle *n* **1** *syn* CHATTER, babble, bibble-babble, blabber, chat, chitter-chatter, gabble, gibble-gabble, jabber, palaver
2 *syn* REPORT 1, buzz, cry, gossip, grapevine, hearsay, rumble, rumor, scuttlebutt, talk

titubate *vb* *syn* REEL 2, stagger, totter, wheel

titular *adj* *syn* NOMINAL, formal, so-called

tizzy *n* *syn* SNIT, fume, stew, sweat, swivet

to *prep* **1** in the direction of and as far as <was driving *to* the city>
syn into
rel toward
ant from
2 *syn* AGAINST 2, touching
rel on, over, upon
3 *syn* BEFORE 1, ahead of, ante, ere, in advance of, preceding, prior to
4 *syn* UNTIL, before, in advance of, prior to, till, up till, up to
5 for the particular purpose of <a market study tailored *to* your needs>
syn for
idiom in contemplation (*or* consideration) of, with an eye to, with a view to
6 in complement to <played Romeo *to* her Juliet>
syn opposite

toad *n* *syn* SNOT 1, dog, ‖prick, scum, *shit, *shithead, skunk, snake, stinker, *turd

toad *n* *syn* SYCOPHANT, bootlicker, ‖clawback, footlicker, lickspit, lickspittle, spaniel, toadeater, toady, truckler

toadeater *n* *syn* SYCOPHANT, bootlick, bootlicker, ‖clawback, footlicker, lickspit, lickspittle, toad, toady, truckler

toadier *n* *syn* SYCOPHANT, apple-polisher, ‖brownnose, ‖brownnoser, footlicker, lickspittle, spaniel, toad, toadeater, toady

toady *n* *syn* SYCOPHANT, bootlick, bootlicker, ‖clawback, footlicker, lickspit, lickspittle, toad, toadeater, truckler

---

syn synonym(s) *rel* related word(s)
idiom idiomatic equivalent(s) *con* contrasted word(s)
ant antonym(s) * vulgar
‖ use limited; if in doubt, see a dictionary
The first word in a synonym list when printed in SMALL CAPITALS shows where there is more information about the group. For a more efficient use of this book see Explanatory Notes.

toady *vb* ***syn*** FAWN, apple-polish, bootlick, ‖brownnose, cower, cringe, grovel, honey (up), kowtow, truckle
rel follow, tag, tail, trail
idiom *kiss ass

toadying *adj* ***syn*** FAWNING, bootlicking, cowering, cringing, groveling, kowtowing, parasitic, sycophantic, toadyish, truckling

toadyish *adj* ***syn*** FAWNING, bootlicking, cowering, cringing, groveling, kowtowing, parasitic, sycophantic, toadying, truckling

to–and–fro *n* **1** ***syn*** HESITATION, hesitancy, indecision, indecisiveness, irresolution, shilly-shally, vacillation, wavering
2 ***syn*** QUARREL, altercation, beef, bickering, dispute, fight, hassle, row, run-in, set-to

toast *n* ***syn*** DRINK 2, pledge

to–be *n* ***syn*** FUTURE, aftertime, afterward, by-and-by, hereafter, offing

tocsin *n* ***syn*** ALARM 1, alert, SOS
rel sign, signal

today *adv* at the present time <youth *today* do not know what poverty is>
syn now, nowadays, presently
idiom in this day and age, these days
con then, yesteryear

today *n* ***syn*** PRESENT, now

todayish *adj* ***syn*** PRESENT, contemporary, current, existent, extant, instant, present-day

to–do *n* **1** ***syn*** COMMOTION 4, clamor, hassle, hubbub, hurly-burly, pother, tumult, turmoil, uproar, whirl
2 ***syn*** COMMOTION 3, ‖catouse, coil, furore, fuss, hurrah, ruckus, rumpus, shindy, uproar

toe *vb* ***syn*** TIPTOE, tip

tog (out *or* up) *vb* ***syn*** DRESS UP 1, deck (out), doll out, doll up, fix up, gussy up, slick, smarten (up), spiff, spruce (up)

together *adv* **1** at one and the same time <events that occurred *together*>
syn at once, coincidentally, coincidently, coinstantaneously, concurrently, simultaneously
idiom all at once, all together
ant separately
2 in succession usually without intermission <was moody for days *together*>
syn consecutively, continually, continuously, hand running, night and day, running, successively, unintermittedly, uninterruptedly
idiom on end
3 in or by combined action or effort <students and faculty protested *together*>
syn conjointly, jointly, mutually
rel collectively, concertedly, unanimously
idiom in one breath, in the same breath, with one accord, with one voice
ant separately

togetherness *n* **1** ***syn*** ASSOCIATION 1, affiliation, alliance, cahoots, combination, conjunction, connection, hookup, partnership, tie-up
2 ***syn*** SOLIDARITY, cohesion, solidarism

‖**toggle** *vb* ***syn*** DRESS UP 1, deck (out), doll out, doll up, fix up, gussy up, slick, smarten (up), spiff, spruce (up)

togs *n pl* ***syn*** CLOTHES, apparel, attire, attirement, clothing, dress, duds, habiliment(s), raiment, things

toil *n* ***syn*** WORK 2, bullwork, drudge, drudgery, grind, labor, moil, slogging, sweat, travail
idiom sweat of one's brow, toil and trouble

toil *vb* **1** ***syn*** LABOR 1, drive, moil, strain, strive, tug, work
2 ***syn*** DRUDGE, grind, grub, ‖muck, plod, slave, slog
3 ***syn*** PLOD 1, footslog, ‖plodge, plunther, slog, slop, stodge, ‖trash, trudge

toil *n, usu* **toils** *pl* ***syn*** WEB 2, cobweb, entanglement, mesh(es)

toiler *n* ***syn*** SLAVE 2, dray horse, drudge, galley slave, peon, slavey, workhorse

toilet *n* a fixture for defecation and urination
syn ‖can, convenience, *crapper, ‖donicker, head, john, johnny, latrine, lavatory, ‖loo, ‖pot, ‖potty, privy, ‖throne, water closet
rel hopper

toilful *adj* ***syn*** HARD 6, arduous, difficult, effortful, labored, laborious, operose, strenuous, toilsome, uphill

toilsome *adj* ***syn*** HARD 6, arduous, difficult, effortful, labored, laborious, operose, strenuous, toilful, uphill

toilsomely *adv* ***syn*** HARD 8, arduously, burdensomely, difficultly, hardly, laboriously, onerously

token *n* **1** ***syn*** INDICATION 3, evidence, index, indicia, mark, sign, significant, symptom
rel harbinger, omen, portent; characteristic, earmark; indicator, smack
2 ***syn*** REMEMBRANCE 3, keepsake, memento, memorial, relic, remembrancer, reminder, souvenir, trophy
3 ***syn*** EXPRESSION 3, gesture, indication, reminder, sign
4 ***syn*** PLEDGE 1, earnest, pawn, security, warrant

‖**tokus** *n* ***syn*** BUTTOCKS, bottom, breech, ‖butt, ‖can, ‖duff, ‖hinder, hunkers, ‖keister, ‖stern

tolerable *adj* **1** ***syn*** BEARABLE, endurable, livable, sufferable, supportable, sustainable
ant intolerable
2 ***syn*** RESPECTABLE 5, decent, presentable
3 ***syn*** DECENT 4, acceptable, adequate, all right, common, satisfactory, sufficient, unexceptionable, unexceptional, unimpeachable
rel fair, goodish, OK, tidy
idiom better than nothing, good enough
ant intolerable

tolerably *adv* ***syn*** ENOUGH 2, averagely, fairly, moderately, passably, rather, so-so

tolerance *n* **1** the capacity to bear something unpleasant, painful, or difficult <had always had a high *tolerance* to pain>
syn endurance, stamina, toleration
rel fortitude, grit, guts; strength, vigor; long-suffering, patience, sufferance; steadfastness, steadiness; opposition, resistance
ant intolerance

---

syn synonym(s) ***rel*** related word(s)
idiom idiomatic equivalent(s) ***con*** contrasted word(s)
ant antonym(s) * vulgar
‖ use limited; if in doubt, see a dictionary
The first word in a synonym list when printed in SMALL CAPITALS shows where there is more information about the group. For a more efficient use of this book see Explanatory Notes.

2 *syn* FORBEARANCE 2, clemency, indulgence, lenience, leniency, mercifulness, toleration
rel liberality, liberalness, open-mindedness, permissiveness
con narrow-mindedness; prejudice; dogmatism; bigotry
ant intolerance

tolerant *adj* 1 *syn* LIBERAL 3, advanced, broad, broad-minded, progressive, radical, wide
rel open-minded; permissive
con narrow, narrow-minded; prejudiced; dogmatic; bigoted
ant intolerant
2 *syn* FORBEARING, charitable, clement, easy, indulgent, lenient, merciful
rel benevolent, humane; condoning, excusing, forgiving, sympathetic, understanding
con severe, stern; uncompromising, unforgiving, unsympathetic
ant intolerant

tolerate *vb* 1 *syn* ACCEPT 2, bear (with), endure, pocket, swallow, tough (out)
rel condone, countenance; allow, consent (to), permit; have, hear (to)
2 *syn* BEAR 10, abide, brook, endure, go, stand, stomach, suffer, swallow, take
rel sustain

toleration *n* 1 *syn* FORBEARANCE 2, clemency, indulgence, lenience, leniency, mercifulness, tolerance
2 *syn* TOLERANCE 1, endurance, stamina

toll *n syn* EXPENSE 2, cost, price

toll *vb syn* LURE, allure, bait, decoy, entice, entrap, inveigle, lead on, seduce, tempt

toll *vb syn* RING, bell, bong, chime, knell, peal

‖**tomato** *n syn* PROSTITUTE, bawd, call girl, drab, fille de joie, harlot, ‖hooker, meretrix, moll, poule

tomb *n syn* GRAVE, burial, ‖pit, sepulcher, sepulture
rel box, coffin, ‖trough

tomb *vb* 1 *syn* BURY 1, entomb, inhume, inter, lay away, plant, put away, sepulcher, sepulture
ant untomb
2 *syn* ENTOMB 1, ensepulcher, sepulcher, sepulture
ant disentomb, untomb

tomboy *n* a girl exhibiting boyish behavior <a *tomboy* who still rode, fished, and fought with her brothers>
syn gamine, hoyden
rel romp

tombstone *n* an inscribed memorial stone set at a place of interment <read the epitaph on the *tombstone* of her ancestor>
syn footstone, grave marker, gravestone, headstone, ledger, monument
rel memorial; cenotaph

tome *n syn* BOOK 1, volume

tomfool *n syn* FOOL 1, ass, *damfool, donkey, idiot, imbecile, jackass, jerk, nincompoop, ninny

tomfool *adj syn* FOOLISH 2, absurd, ‖balmy, crazy, fantastic, harebrained, insane, loony, preposterous, silly

tomfoolery *n* 1 *syn* NONSENSE 2, balderdash, ‖baloney, blatherskite, claptrap, hogwash, malarkey, poppycock, rubbish, twaddle
2 *syn* PRANK, antic, caper, dido(es), frolic, lark, monkeyshine, shenanigan, shine(s), trick

tommyrot *n syn* NONSENSE 2, bilge, bosh, ‖bull, ‖crap, hogwash, hooey, rot, rubbish, trash

Tom o' Bedlam *n syn* LUNATIC 1, bedlamite, dement, loon, loony, madling, madman, maniac, non compos, nut

Tom Thumb *n syn* DWARF, homunculus, hop-o'-my-thumb, lilliputian, manikin, midge, midget, peewee, pygmy, runt

ton *n* 1 *syn* FASHION 3, chic, craze, cry, dernier cri, fad, furore, mode, rage, style
2 *syn* SMART SET, beautiful people, jet set

tone *n* 1 *syn* INFLECTION, accent, intonation
2 *syn* VEIN 1, fashion, manner, mode, style
3 *syn* COLOR 1, cast, hue, shade, tinge, tint
rel blend
4 the state of a living body or any of its organs or parts in which the functions are healthy and performed with due vigor <diet and exercise contributed to his good muscle *tone*>
syn tonicity, tonus
rel health, healthiness; elasticity, resiliency; strength, vigor
5 *syn* TEMPER 1, mood, spirit, timbre
rel current, movement
idiom (the) state of things
6 *syn* MOOD 1, humor, mind, strain, temper, vein

toned down *adj syn* SUBDUED 2, low-key, low-keyed, sober, soft, softened

tongue *n syn* LANGUAGE 1, dialect, idiom, speech, vernacular

tongue *vb syn* SCOLD 1, baste, berate, ‖bless out, ‖carpet, ‖chew out, jaw, rail, rate, upbraid

tongue–lash *vb syn* SCOLD 1, bawl out, berate, ‖bless out, ‖chew out, lash, rail, tell off, upbraid, wig
idiom give one the rough side of one's tongue

tongue–tied *adj syn* INARTICULATE 3, incoherent, maundering, unvocal
con loose-lipped, loose-tongued

‖**tongue–walk** *vb syn* SCOLD 1, bawl out, berate, ‖bless out, ‖chew out, lash, rail, tell off, tongue, tongue-lash
idiom give one the rough side of one's tongue

tonguey *adj syn* TALKATIVE, babblative, chatty, gabby, loose-lipped, loose-tongued, loquacious, multiloquent, multiloquious, talky

tonic *adj* 1 increasing or restoring physical or mental tone <the *tonic* effect of a vacation>
syn astringent, restorative, roborant
rel invigorating, refreshing, renewing, strengthening; bracing, sharp
con debilitating, enfeebling, weakening; enervating; exhausting, grueling, sapping
2 *syn* INVIGORATING, animating, bracing, exhilarating, exhilarative, quickening, stimulating, stimulative, vitalizing

tonicity *n syn* TONE 4, tonus

---

tonish *adj* ***syn*** STYLISH, chic, ||classy, exclusive, fashionable, in, modish, tony, ||trendy, with-it

tonus *n* ***syn*** TONE 4, tonicity

tony *adj* ***syn*** STYLISH, a la mode, chic, exclusive, fashionable, in, modish, swank, swish, tonish

too *adv* **1** ***syn*** ALSO 2, additionally, along, as well, besides, furthermore, likewise, more, moreover, withal
2 ***syn*** EVER 6, excessively, extremely, immensely, inordinately, over, overfull, overly, overmuch, unduly
rel exorbitantly, immoderately, unconscionably, unmeasurably
3 ***syn*** VERY 1, awfully, exceedingly, exceptionally, extremely, greatly, highly, notably, remarkably, strikingly

||**toodle–oo** *interj* ***syn*** GOOD-BYE, adieu, by, bye-bye, ||cheerio, farewell, so long

tool *n* **1** ***syn*** IMPLEMENT, instrument, utensil
rel machine, mechanism
2 one used or manipulated by another to accomplish his purposes <had no intention of being used as a *tool* by either faction>
syn cat's-paw, pawn, puppet, stooge
rel agent, hireling, vehicle; chump, sucker

tool *vb* ***syn*** DRIVE 5, auto, charioteer, motor, pilot, wheel

toot *vb* ***syn*** DECLARE 1, advertise, announce, annunciate, blaze (abroad), broadcast, disseminate, proclaim, publish, sound

toot *n* ***syn*** BINGE 1, bat, bender, blowoff, bust, carouse, drunk, jag, spree, tear

toothful *n* ***syn*** DRAM, ||caulker, drop, jolt, nip, shot, slug, snifter, snort, tot

toothsome *adj* ***syn*** PALATABLE, appetizing, flavorsome, good-tasting, relishing, sapid, savory, tasteful, tasty, toothy
rel agreeable, pleasant, pleasing

toothy *adj* **1** having or showing prominent teeth <a wide *toothy* grin>
syn teethy
2 ***syn*** PALATABLE, appetizing, flavorsome, good-tasting, relishing, sapid, savory, tasteful, tasty, toothsome

too–too *adj* ***syn*** GENTEEL 3, affected, la-di-da, ||lardy-dardy, mincing, pretentious, stilted
rel chichi

||**tootsie** *n* ***syn*** DOXY 1, ||chippy, floozy, grisette, light-o'-love, nymph, nymphet, party girl, roundheel, tart

top *n* **1** the highest point <hiked to the *top* of the mountain>
syn apex, crest, crown, fastigium, peak, roof, summit, vertex
rel acme, climax, culmination, height, pinnacle; cusp, head, point, tip
con base, foot, sole; nadir
ant bottom
2 the outer or upper part <the *top* of the table>
syn face, superficies, surface
3 ***syn*** BEST, choice, cream, elite, fat, flower, pick, pride, prime, prize
ant bottom

top *vb* **1** to remove or cut back the top of <*top* a tree>
syn crop, detruncate, pollard, truncate
rel clip, dock, prune, trim; curtail, shorten
2 ***syn*** SURPASS 1, beat, best, better, exceed, excel, outdo, outshine, outstrip, transcend
3 ***syn*** SURMOUNT 3, cap, crest, crown

top *adj* **1** of, relating to, or being at the top <the *top* floor of the house>
syn apical, highest, loftiest, topmost, uppermost
con bottommost, lowest
ant bottom
2 ***syn*** EXCELLENT, capital, fine, first-class, first-rate, first-string, five-star, prime, superior, top-notch
3 ***syn*** MAXIMUM, maximal, outside, topmost, utmost

top–drawer *adj* ***syn*** EXALTED 1, astral, highest, highest-ranking, top-ranking

tope *vb* ***syn*** DRINK 3, booze, guzzle, imbibe, liquor (up), nip, soak, swizzle, tank up, tipple

toper *n* ***syn*** DRUNKARD, bibber, boozer, drunk, inebriate, lush, soak, sot, tippler, tosspot

Tophet *n* ***syn*** HELL, barathrum, blazes, Gehenna, hades, inferno, Pandemonium, perdition, Sheol, underworld

topic *n* ***syn*** SUBJECT 2, argument, head, matter, motif, motive, point, subject matter, text, theme
rel proposition; issue

topless *adj* ***syn*** LOFTY 6, aerial, airy, skyscraping, soaring, spiring, towering, towery

toplofical *adj* ***syn*** PROUD 1, arrogant, cavalier, disdainful, haughty, high-and-mighty, insolent, overbearing, supercilious, superior

toplofty *adj* ***syn*** PROUD 1, arrogant, cavalier, disdainful, haughty, high-and-mighty, insolent, overbearing, supercilious, superior
rel inflated, puffed; egotistic
con crestfallen

topmost *adj* **1** ***syn*** TOP 1, apical, highest, loftiest, uppermost
ant bottommost
2 ***syn*** MAXIMUM, maximal, outside, top, utmost

top–notch *adj* ***syn*** EXCELLENT, capital, fine, first-class, first-rate, first-string, five-star, prime, superior, top

top off *vb* ***syn*** CLIMAX, cap, crown, culminate, finish off, round off

topography *n* ***syn*** TERRAIN 1

topple *vb* **1** ***syn*** FALL 2, drop, go down, keel (over), pitch, plunge, slump, tumble
2 ***syn*** TEETER, falter, lurch, stagger, ||stammer, stumble, totter, wobble
3 ***syn*** OVERTURN 1, knock over, overset, overthrow, tip (over), turn over, upset
4 ***syn*** OVERTHROW 2, overset, overturn, tumble, unhorse

top–ranking *adj* ***syn*** EXALTED 1, astral, highest, highest-ranking, top-drawer

topsy–turviness *n* ***syn*** CONFUSION 3, ataxia, ||ballup, chaos, clutter, disarray, disorder, huddle, muddle, snarl

topsy–turvy *adj* **1** ***syn*** UPSIDE-DOWN 1, inverted
2 ***syn*** UPSIDE-DOWN 2, arsy-varsy, downside-up
rel cockeyed, disarranged, disjointed, disordered, unhinged

---

syn synonym(s) ***rel*** related word(s)
idiom idiomatic equivalent(s) ***con*** contrasted word(s)
ant antonym(s) * vulgar
|| use limited; if in doubt, see a dictionary
The first word in a synonym list when printed in SMALL CAPITALS shows where there is more information about the group. For a more efficient use of this book see Explanatory Notes.

torch *n syn* INCENDIARY, arsonist, firebug

toreador *n syn* BULLFIGHTER, matador, torero

torero *n syn* BULLFIGHTER, matador, toreador

torment *vb* **1** *syn* AFFLICT, agonize, crucify, excruciate, harrow, rack, smite, torture, try, wring
rel distress, trouble; hurt, pain, punish
2 *syn* MOLEST, bait, heckle, persecute

tormented *adj syn* DISTRAUGHT, distracted, distrait, distressed, harassed, troubled, worried

tormenting *adj syn* EXCRUCIATING, agonizing, harrowing, racking, tearing, torturing, torturous

torn *adj syn* LACERATED, mangled, rent

tornado *n* a violent destructive whirling wind accompanied by a funnel-shaped cloud extending downward from a cumulonimbus cloud <the *tornado* caused extensive destruction>
syn cyclone, twister; *compare* HURRICANE, WHIRLWIND 1

torpedo *n syn* ASSASSIN, bravo, cutthroat, gun, gunman, ‖gunsel, gunslinger, hatchet man, hit man, triggerman

torpid *adj syn* LETHARGIC, comatose, dopey, heavy, hebetudinous, sluggish, slumberous, stupid
rel dull, leaden, sodden; motionless, static; numb
con lively; frisky, sprightly, vigorous; fast
ant active

torpidity *n syn* LETHARGY 1, coma, dullness, hebetude, languor, lassitude, sleep, stupor, torpidness, torpor
rel listlessness, passivity, stagnation

torpidness *n syn* LETHARGY 1, coma, dullness, hebetude, languor, lassitude, sleep, stupor, torpidity, torpor
ant activeness

torpor *n syn* LETHARGY 1, coma, dullness, hebetude, languor, lassitude, sleep, stupor, torpidity, torpidness
rel stolidity; passivity
ant activity; animation

torrent *n syn* FLOOD 2, cataclysm, cataract, deluge, flooding, inundation, niagara, overflow, pour, spate
rel flux, rush

torrid *adj* **1** *syn* HOT 1, broiling, burning, fiery, heated, red-hot, scalding, scorching, sizzling, sweltering
idiom burning hot, hot enough to roast an ox
ant arctic
2 *syn* IMPASSIONED, ardent, blazing, burning, fervid, flaming, hot-blooded, passionate, red-hot, white-hot
rel sultry
ant frigid

tort *n syn* EVIL 3, crime, diablerie, iniquity, sin, wrong, wrongdoing

tortuous *adj syn* WINDING, anfractuous, convoluted, flexuous, meandering, meandrous, serpentine, sinuous, snaky
rel involute, vermiculate; cranky; involved

torture *vb* **1** *syn* AFFLICT, agonize, crucify, excruciate, harrow, rack, smite, torment, try, wring
rel oppress, persecute, wrong; hurt, wound; maim, mangle, mutilate
idiom put on the rack, put to torture
2 *syn* DEFORM, contort, distort, misshape, warp, wind

torturing *adj syn* EXCRUCIATING, agonizing, harrowing, racking, tearing, tormenting, torturous

torturous *adj syn* EXCRUCIATING, agonizing, harrowing, racking, tearing, tormenting, torturing

tory *n syn* DIEHARD 1, bitter-ender, conservative, fundamentalist, old liner, right, rightist, right-winger, standpat, standpatter
rel loyalist, traditionalist

tory *adj syn* CONSERVATIVE 1, die-hard, fogyish, old-line, orthodox, reactionary, right, traditionalistic

tosh *n syn* NONSENSE 2, ‖applesauce, ‖baloney, bilge, bosh, bunkum, eyewash, hooey, malarkey, pishposh

toss *vb* **1** *syn* THROW 1, ‖bung, cast, fire, fling, heave, hurl, launch, pitch, sling
2 to rise and fall often rhythmically or with alternate motions <a small boat *tossing* in heavy seas>
syn heave, pitch, rock, roll; *compare* SEESAW
rel bob; sway
3 *syn* DRINK 1, imbibe, quaff, sip, sup (off *or* up), swallow
4 *syn* WRITHE 1, agonize, squirm
idiom toss and turn

toss (around) *vb syn* DISCUSS 1, agitate, argue, canvass, debate, discept, dispute, ‖kick around, moot, thrash out
rel bandy (about)

tosspot *n syn* DRUNKARD, bibber, boozer, drunk, inebriate, lush, soak, sot, tippler, toper

tot *n syn* DRAM, ‖caulker, drop, jolt, nip, shot, slug, snifter, snort, toothful

tot *vb syn* ADD 2, cast, figure, foot, sum, summate, total, totalize, tote

total *adj* **1** *syn* WHOLE 4, all, complete, entire, gross, outright
rel overall; comprehensive, full, inclusive, plenary; teetotal
ant partial
2 *syn* UTTER, absolute, complete, consummate, out-and-out, outright, perfect, positive, thoroughgoing, unmitigated
3 *syn* TOTALITARIAN 1, authoritarian, totalistic
rel authoritative; absolute, arbitrary, despotic; omnipotent
4 *syn* TOTALITARIAN 2
rel monopolistic
5 concentrating and employing all resources on a single objective <a *total* offensive>
syn all-out, full-blown, full-out, full-scale, totalitarian, unlimited
rel out-and-out, unreserved, unrestricted
con hampered, impeded, trammeled; restrained, restricted; stinted
ant limited

total *n* **1** *syn* WHOLE 1, aggregate, all, be-all and end-all, entirety, gross, sum, sum total, tale, totality
2 *syn* BODY 5, aggregate, amount, budget, bulk, quantity, quantum

---

syn synonym(s) *rel* related word(s)
idiom idiomatic equivalent(s) *con* contrasted word(s)
ant antonym(s) * vulgar
‖ use limited; if in doubt, see a dictionary
The first word in a synonym list when printed in SMALL CAPITALS shows where there is more information about the group. For a more efficient use of this book see Explanatory Notes.

total *vb* **1** ***syn*** ADD 2, cast, figure, foot, sum, summate, tot, totalize, tote
2 ***syn*** AMOUNT 1, add up, aggregate, come, number, run (to *or* into), sum (to *or* into)
rel comprise, consist (of); stack up; equal, result (in), yield
idiom mount up to, pile up to
3 to make a total wreck of < *totaled* his car when he hit the wall >
syn demolish, wreck; *compare* DESTROY 1
rel crack up, smash

totalistic *adj* ***syn*** TOTALITARIAN 1, authoritarian, total
con democratic; individualistic

totalitarian *adj* **1** of or relating to centralized control by one autocratic leader or party considered to be infallible < Nazi Germany was a *totalitarian* state >
syn authoritarian, total, totalistic; *compare* ABSOLUTE 4, DICTATORIAL
con democratic, popular; constitutional
2 having or exercising dictatorial powers often tending toward monopoly < antitrust legislation reversing the trend toward the *totalitarian* collectivism of big business >
syn total
3 ***syn*** TOTAL 5, all-out, full-blown, full-out, full-scale, unlimited

totalitarianism *n* ***syn*** TYRANNY, autocracy, despotism, dictatorship

totality *n* **1** ***syn*** WHOLE 1, aggregate, all, be-all and end-all, entirety, gross, sum, sum total, tale, total
2 ***syn*** ENTIRETY 1, allness, completeness, entireness, oneness, wholeness
3 ***syn*** WHOLE 2, entity, integral, integrate, sum, system
rel configuration, form

totalize *vb* ***syn*** ADD 2, cast, figure, foot, sum, summate, tot, total, tote

totally *adv* ***syn*** ALL 1, all in all, altogether, completely, exactly, in toto, just, quite, utterly, wholly

tote *vb* ***syn*** CARRY 1, bear, buck, convey, ferry, ‖hump, ‖jag, lug, pack, transport
rel cart, haul; shoulder

‖**tote** *n* ***syn*** WHOLE 1, aggregate, all, be-all and end-all, entirety, gross, sum, sum total, tale, total

tote *vb* ***syn*** ADD 2, cast, figure, foot, sum, summate, tot, total, totalize

totter *vb* **1** ***syn*** TEETER, falter, lurch, stagger, ‖stammer, stumble, topple, wobble
rel shimmy
2 ***syn*** REEL 2, stagger, titubate, wheel
rel blunder, stumble, trip; dodder, ‖dotter; flounder

touch *vb* **1** to probe with a sensitive part of the body (as a finger) so as to get or produce a sensation often in the course of examining or exploring < *touch* an iron to test its temperature >
syn feel, finger, handle, palpate, paw
rel brush, graze; caress, fondle, rub, stroke, toy (with); palm, thumb; examine, inspect, probe, scrutinize; investigate
2 ***syn*** ADJOIN, abut, border, butt (on *or* against), communicate, join, line, march, neighbor, verge
3 ***syn*** EQUAL 3, match, measure up, meet, rival, tie
4 ***syn*** AFFECT, carry, get, impress, influence, inspire, move, strike, sway
rel arouse, stir; excite, quicken, stimulate
idiom touch a chord
5 ***syn*** AMOUNT 2, approach, correspond (to), equal, match, partake (of), rival
rel come (to), verge (on)

touch *n* **1** ***syn*** CONTACT 1, contingence
rel junction; communication
2 an act of touching or feeling < woke her with a light *touch* on her hand >
syn palpation, taction
rel brush, pat, stroke; contact
3 tactile sensitivity < a blanket soft to the *touch* >
syn feel, tactility
rel feeling
4 a specified sensation conveyed through the tactile receptors < the velvety *touch* of a fabric >
syn feel, feeling
5 ***syn*** HINT 2, dash, shade, smack, soupçon, streak, suggestion, suspicion, tincture, tinge
6 distinctive manner or method < this house needs a woman's *touch* >
syn hand
rel manner, style, way
‖**7** ***syn*** THEFT, larceny, lift, pinch, purloining, steal, stealage, stealing, thievery, thieving

touchable *adj* ***syn*** TANGIBLE 1, palpable, tactile
ant untouchable

touch down *vb* ***syn*** ALIGHT, land, light, perch, roost, set down, settle, sit down

touching *prep* **1** ***syn*** AGAINST 2, to
idiom up against
2 ***syn*** APROPOS, about, against, anent, as for, as regards, as respects, as to, concerning, in re

touching *adj* **1** ***syn*** ADJACENT 3, abutting, adjoining, approximal, bordering, conterminous, contiguous, juxtaposed
rel meeting; impinging; overlapping
2 ***syn*** MOVING 2, affecting, impressive, poignant
rel compassionate, responsive, sympathetic, tender; piteous, pitiable, pitiful, tear-jerking

touch–me–not–ish *adj* ***syn*** UNSOCIABLE, aloof, distant, insociable, reserved, solitary, standoff, standoffish, uncompanionable, withdrawn

touchstone *n* ***syn*** STANDARD 3, benchmark, criterion, gauge, measure, yardstick
rel check, test, trial; barometer, scale; demonstration, proof

touch up *vb* to improve or perfect by small additional strokes or alterations < *touch up* a picture >
syn brush up, retouch, tease up
rel improve, perfect, polish; do (up), fix (up)
idiom put finishing touches on

touchy *adj* **1** ***syn*** IRASCIBLE, choleric, cranky, cross, quick-tempered, ratty, ‖stomachy, temperish, testy, tetchy

---

rel hypersensitive, oversensitive, sensitive, thin-skinned; temperamental, volatile; miffy
ant imperturbable
2 *syn* DELICATE 7, precarious, sensitive, ticklish, tricky
rel dicey, risky, unpredictable; harmful, hazardous, unsafe

tough *adj* **1** *syn* STRONG 2, stalwart, stout, sturdy, tenacious
rel flinty, hard, unyielding; resistant, unbreakable, withstanding
idiom tough as leather (*or* nails)
con breakable; brittle; yielding
ant fragile
2 *syn* VISCOUS, tenacious, viscid, viscose
3 advocating a persistently firm course of action <a *tough* foreign policy>
syn hard-line, inflexible, uncompromising, unyielding
rel stiff, taut; fixed, confirmed, hard-shell, narrow, rigid; arbitrary, immutable, unalterable; hard-boiled, hardened, obdurate; harsh, procrustean, rigorous, severe, strict; drastic
con liberal, relaxed; compromising, flexible, laissez-faire, yielding
ant soft
4 having or exhibiting great physical endurance (as to strain, hardship, or labor) <the rigorous climate created a *tough* people>
syn hardy, rugged
rel conditioned, hard-bitten, hardened, seasoned, steeled; fit, healthy, lusty, robust, vigorous; stalwart, strong, sturdy
con delicate, fragile, frail, tender; half-hardy, puny; weakened
ant weak
5 *syn* OBSTINATE, bullheaded, headstrong, intractable, mulish, pertinacious, pigheaded, refractory, self-willed, stubborn
rel hardfisted, hardhanded, hardheaded, tough-minded
6 *syn* HARD 6, arduous, difficult, effortful, labored, laborious, strenuous, toilful, toilsome, uphill
ant soft
7 *syn* ONEROUS, burdensome, demanding, exacting, exigent, grievous, oppressive, taxing, trying, weighty
ant soft
8 frequented by rowdy or criminal elements <lived in a *tough* neighborhood>
syn bad, rough
rel disorderly, rowdy; dangerous, unsafe; ghetto, inner-city, underprivileged
con orderly, quiet, safe

tough (out) *vb* *syn* ACCEPT 2, bear (with), endure, pocket, swallow, tolerate

tough *n* a rough or unruly person often taking part in bullying or violent behavior <attacked by a gang of *toughs*>
syn ‖b'hoy, bullyboy, mucker, mug, plug-ugly, punk, rough, roughneck, rowdy, ruffian, thug, toughie, yahoo; *compare* BULLY 1, THUG 1
rel goon, hood, hoodlum, hooligan

toughen *vb* *syn* HARDEN 2, acclimate, acclimatize, climatize, season
rel develop, strengthen
ant weaken

toughie *n* *syn* TOUGH, ‖b'hoy, bullyboy, mucker, punk, rough, roughneck, rowdy, ruffian, yahoo
rel ‖heavy

tour *n* **1** *syn* SPELL, bout, go, shift, stint, time, trick, turn
2 a journey in which one eventually returns to the starting point <made a quick *tour* of all the bars>
syn circuit, round, roundabout, round trip; *compare* TRIP 1
rel turn; circle tour

tour de force *n* **1** *syn* FEAT 2, achievement, deed, exploit
2 *syn* MASTERPIECE 1, chef d'oeuvre, classic, magnum opus, masterwork

tourist *n* one who makes a tour for pleasure or culture <*tourists* going through the castle>
syn rubberneck, sightseer, ‖tripper
rel day-tripper, excursionist; traveler; visitor

tout *n* *syn* LOOKOUT 3, surveillance, vigil, vigilance, watch, watch and ward

tout *vb* to overly publicize <was *touted* as the world's most modern shopping center>
syn ballyhoo, herald, trumpet
rel proclaim, publicize; plug, promote; acclaim, laud, praise
idiom praise to the skies

tow *vb* *syn* PULL 2, drag, draw, haul, lug, tug
rel propel; push
idiom take in tow

toward *adj* *syn* GOOD 1, advantageous, benefic, beneficial, brave, favorable, favoring, helpful, propitious, useful
ant untoward

toward *prep* **1** *syn* APROPOS, about, against, anent, as for, as to, concerning, in re, re, regarding
2 *syn* AGAINST 1, contra, facing, fronting, over against, vis-à-vis

tower (above *or* over) *vb* *syn* OVERLOOK 2, dominate, look down, overtop

towering *adj* **1** *syn* LOFTY 6, aerial, airy, skyscraping, soaring, spiring, topless, towery
rel altitudinous, high, tall; stratospheric
2 *syn* SUPREME, incomparable, preeminent, surpassing, transcendent, ultimate, unequalable, unmatchable, unsurpassable
3 *syn* MONSTROUS 1, cracking, fantastic, massive, monumental, mortal, prodigious, stupendous, tremendous
4 reaching a high point of greatness, intensity, or violence <a *towering* rage>
syn monumental, overwhelming
rel ‖crashing; overpowering; mind-blowing
con minor, petty, piddling, puny, trivial

---

syn synonym(s) — *rel* related word(s)
idiom idiomatic equivalent(s) — *con* contrasted word(s)
ant antonym(s) — * vulgar
‖ use limited; if in doubt, see a dictionary
The first word in a synonym list when printed in SMALL CAPITALS shows where there is more information about the group. For a more efficient use of this book see Explanatory Notes.

5 ***syn*** EXCESSIVE 1, dizzy, exorbitant, extravagant, extreme, immoderate, inordinate, unconscionable, undue, unmeasurable

towery *adj* ***syn*** LOFTY 6, aerial, airy, skyscraping, soaring, spiring, topless, towering

to wit *adv* ***syn*** NAMELY, scilicet, videlicet

towner *n* ***syn*** TOWNSMAN, burgher, cit, citizen, townman, towny

townish *adj* of, relating to, or characteristic of a town or of urban life <enjoyed a fast-paced, competitive, *townish* life-style>
syn towny
rel city, metropolitan, urban
con bucolic, rural; isolated, lonely, solitary

townman *n* ***syn*** TOWNSMAN, burgher, cit, citizen, towner, towny

townsman *n* a town dweller <population composed mostly of *townsmen* and a few countrymen>
syn burgher, cit, citizen, towner, townman, towny

towny *n* ***syn*** TOWNSMAN, burgher, cit, citizen, towner, townman

towny *adj* ***syn*** TOWNISH

tow–row *n* ***syn*** COMMOTION 4, bustle, clamor, hassle, hubbub, hurly-burly, pother, to-do, tumult, uproar

toxic *adj* ***syn*** POISONOUS, mephitic, poison, toxicant, venomous, virulent
ant nontoxic

toxicant *adj* ***syn*** POISONOUS, mephitic, poison, toxic, venomous, virulent

toy *n* **1** ***syn*** KNICKKNACK, bauble, bibelot, curio, gewgaw, gimcrack, novelty, trifle, trinket, whatnot
2 something for a child to play with <games, dolls, and other *toys*>
syn ‖die, ‖play-pretty, plaything, ‖pretty

toy *vb* ***syn*** TRIFLE 1, coquet, dally, flirt, fool, lead on, string along, wanton
rel disport, frolic, play, sport; fiddle (with), tease; caress, cosset, cuddle, dandle, pet
idiom fool (*or* mess) around with

trace *n* **1** ***syn*** TRACK 1, tread
rel evidence, proof
2 ***syn*** VESTIGE 1, memento, relic, shadow
rel mark, token
3 ***syn*** HINT 2, intimation, shade, smell, soupçon, strain, streak, suspicion, tinge, whiff

trace *vb* ***syn*** TRACK 1, trail

track *n* **1** detectable evidence that something has passed <the *track* of a sleigh in the snow>
syn trace, tread
rel impress, imprint, mark, print; sign, vestige
2 ***syn*** TRAIL, path, pathway, ‖trod
rel footpath, footway, walk
idiom beaten path
3 ***syn*** WAY 1, artery, avenue, boulevard, ‖drag, highway, path, road, street, thoroughfare
rel roadway, trackway
4 ***syn*** FOOTPRINT, footstep, spoor, step, tract, vestige
rel scent, slot

track *vb* **1** to follow the tracks or traces of <*track* a wounded deer>
syn trace, trail
rel follow; dog, shadow, tail; chase, pursue; find, hunt (down), smell (out)
idiom be hot on the trail of
2 ***syn*** TRAVEL 2, cover, do, pass (over), traverse

tract *n* **1** ***syn*** AREA 1, belt, region, territory, zone
rel amplitude, spread, stretch; part, portion, section, sector
2 ***syn*** LOT 3, parcel, plat, plot
3 ***syn*** FOOTPRINT, footstep, spoor, step, track, vestige

tractable *adj* ***syn*** OBEDIENT, amenable, biddable, docile, ‖docious
rel flexible, pliable, pliant; manageable; subdued
con headstrong, unmanageable, willful; obstinate, refractory, stubborn
ant intractable, unruly

tractate *n* ***syn*** DISCOURSE 2, disquisition, dissertation, memoir, monograph, monography, thesis, treatise

trade *n* **1** a pursuit followed as an occupation or means of livelihood and requiring technical knowledge and skill <the *trade* of a carpenter>
syn art, calling, craft, handicraft, métier, profession, vocation
rel employment, occupation, pursuit, work
con avocation, hobby
2 ***syn*** BUSINESS 4, commerce, industry, traffic
rel market
3 ***syn*** PATRONAGE 2, business, custom, traffic

trade *vb* **1** to give one thing in return for another with an expectation of gain <*traded* furs for tobacco and rum>
syn bargain, barter, exchange, swap, traffic, truck; *compare* EXCHANGE 2
rel market, merchandise, sell; deal; argue, chaffer, dicker, haggle, wrangle
idiom make (*or* strike) a bargain, make a deal
2 ***syn*** EXCHANGE 2, change, substitute, swap, switch

trademark *n* ***syn*** MARK 7, brand, logo, logotype

trader *n* ***syn*** MERCHANT, businessman, dealer, merchandiser, tradesman, trafficker

tradesman *n* ***syn*** MERCHANT, businessman, dealer, merchandiser, trader, trafficker

tradition *n* **1** an inherited or established way of thinking, feeling, or doing <America's Puritan *tradition* is still very much alive>
syn heritage
rel culture; convention, custom, ethic, form; birthright, inheritance, legacy
2 ***syn*** LORE 2, folklore, legend, myth, mythology, mythos

traditional *adj* **1** of or relating to tradition <a *traditional* interpretation of the Bible>
syn conventional, tralatitious; *compare* CONVENTIONAL 1
rel ancestral, immemorial, old; customary, habitual, usual; acknowledged, established, establishmentarian, fixed; common, popular

con new; unconventional, unusual; individualistic, original, personal
2 ***syn*** ORAL 2, spoken, unwritten, verbal, word-of-mouth
traditionalist *n* ***syn*** PURIST, precisian, precisionist
traditionalistic *adj* ***syn*** CONSERVATIVE 1, die-hard, fogyish, old-line, orthodox, reactionary, right, tory
traduce *vb* ***syn*** MALIGN, asperse, calumniate, defame, denigrate, libel, scandalize, slander, vilify, villainize
rel mock; disgrace; betray; violate
traducing *adj* ***syn*** LIBELOUS, backbiting, calumnious, defamatory, detracting, detractive, maligning, scandalous, slanderous, vilifying
traffic *n* **1** ***syn*** BUSINESS 4, commerce, industry, trade
2 ***syn*** COMMERCE 2, communion, dealings, intercourse, truck
rel relations, relationship; closeness, connection, familiarity, intimacy
3 ***syn*** PATRONAGE 2, business, custom, trade
4 the number or volume of vehicles or pedestrians moving along a route <freeway *traffic* is heavy during the rush hour>
syn travel
traffic *vb* **1** ***syn*** TRADE 1, bargain, barter, exchange, swap, truck
2 to engage in illegal or disreputable business or activity <*trafficked* in drugs>
syn truck
rel deal (in), push, shove; black-market; bootleg, moonshine; fence
idiom handle (*or* deal in) under the counter
trafficable *adj* ***syn*** MARKETABLE, merchandisable, merchantable, salable, sellable, vendible
trafficker *n* ***syn*** MERCHANT, businessman, dealer, merchandiser, trader, tradesman
tragedy *n* **1** ***syn*** DISASTER, calamity, cataclysm, catastrophe, misadventure, woe(s)
rel blow, shock
2 ***syn*** MISFORTUNE, adversity, contretemps, ‖dole, mischance, mishap, ‖unluck
rel unluckiness; curse, lot; woe(s)
con prosperity, success
ant triumph
trail *vb* **1** ***syn*** DRAG 3, draggle, traipse
2 ***syn*** DELAY 2, dally, dawdle, drag, lag, linger, loiter, poke, procrastinate, tarry
rel plod, trudge; falter, flag; halt
3 ***syn*** TRACK 1, trace
rel nose (out), sniff (out)
idiom follow a scent
4 ***syn*** TAIL, bedog, dog, shadow, tag
5 ***syn*** FOLLOW 2, chase, chivy, pursue
trail *n* a rough course or way formed by or as if by repeated chance footsteps <an old Indian *trail*>
syn path, pathway, track, ‖trod
rel footpath, footwalk, footway
train *vb* ***syn*** LURE, allure, bait, decoy, entice, inveigle, lead on, seduce, tempt, toll
train *n* **1** ***syn*** ENTOURAGE, following, retinue, suite
2 ***syn*** SUCCESSION 2, alternation, chain, consecution, order, progression, row, sequel, sequence, series
rel course, run; line, thread; gradation, scale, tier
train *vb* **1** ***syn*** TEACH, discipline, educate, instruct, school
rel cultivate, develop, shape; accustom, habituate; harden, season
2 ***syn*** DIRECT 2, aim, cast, head, incline, lay, level, point, turn, zero (in)
training *n* ***syn*** EDUCATION 1, instruction, schooling, teaching, tuition, tutelage
train off *vb* ***syn*** SWERVE 1, dip, sheer, skew, slue, veer
traipse *vb* **1** ***syn*** WANDER 1, drift, gad, gallivant, meander, mooch, ramble, range, roam, rove
2 ***syn*** WALK 1, ambulate, foot (it), hoof, pace, step, tread, troop
3 ***syn*** DRAG 3, draggle, trail
traipse *n* ***syn*** SLATTERN 1, dowd, dowdy, drab, draggle-tail, ‖malkin, slut, ‖streel
trait *n* **1** ***syn*** QUALITY 1, affection, attribute, character, characteristic, feature, mark, property, savor, virtue
2 ***syn*** CHARACTERISTIC 1, birthmark, character, feature, point
rel denominator; attribute, quality
traitorous *adj* ***syn*** FAITHLESS, disloyal, false, perfidious, recreant, treacherous, unfaithful, unloyal, untrue
rel apostate, renegade; mutinous, rebellious, seditious; alienated, disaffected, estranged; unpatriotic
con faithful; patriotic
traject *vb* ***syn*** CONDUCT 4, carry, channel, convey, funnel, pipe, siphon, transmit
tralatitious *adj* ***syn*** TRADITIONAL 1, conventional
idiom handed down from time immemorial
tralucent *adj* ***syn*** TRANSLUCENT 3, clear, translucid, transparent
trammel *vb* **1** ***syn*** ENTANGLE 3, embrangle, enmesh, ensnarl
2 ***syn*** HAMPER, clog, curb, entrammel, fetter, hobble, hog-tie, leash, shackle, tie
rel circumscribe, confine, limit; bind, enchain, handcuff, manacle
3 ***syn*** STULTIFY, constipate, stagnate, stifle
tramp *vb* **1** to walk, tread, or step especially heavily <heard hobnailed boots *tramping* across the square>
syn trample, tromp; *compare* PLOD 1
rel march; thud; footslog, stodge, trudge; stamp, stomp
2 ***syn*** HIKE 2, tromp
3 ***syn*** TRAMPLE 2, stamp, stomp, tromp
tramp *n* **1** ***syn*** VAGABOND, derelict, drifter, floater, hobo, street arab, tramper, vag, vagrant, Weary Willie
2 ***syn*** WANTON, baggage, ‖bim, ‖bimbo, hussy, jade, jezebel, slattern, slut, strumpet
3 a journey on foot or a walking trip <took a long *tramp* through the woods>
syn hike, walkabout
rel ramble, saunter, stroll, walk; traipse
tramper *n* ***syn*** VAGABOND, bum, derelict, drifter, floater, hobo, street arab, tramp, vag, vagabond

---

syn synonym(s) ***rel*** related word(s)
idiom idiomatic equivalent(s) ***con*** contrasted word(s)
ant antonym(s) * vulgar
‖ use limited; if in doubt, see a dictionary
The first word in a synonym list when printed in SMALL CAPITALS shows where there is more information about the group. For a more efficient use of this book see Explanatory Notes.

trample *vb* **1** *syn* TRAMP 1, tromp
2 to tread on forcibly and repeatedly so as to crush or injure <was *trampled* to death by his horse>
syn stamp, stomp, tramp, tromp
rel ‖stoach, ‖stramp, ‖stunt; pound; tread (on); override

trance *vb syn* TRANSPORT 2, enrapture, enravish, entrance, ravish

trance *n syn* REVERIE, brown study, muse, study

tranquil *adj syn* CALM 2, collected, composed, easy, easygoing, placid, poised, possessed, self-possessed, serene
rel irenic, pacific, peaceful; quiet, still; stable, steady
con stirred up, troubled
ant agitated

tranquilize *vb syn* CALM, balm, becalm, compose, lull, quiet, ‖quieten, settle, soothe, still
rel hush; sedate; subdue
idiom pour oil on troubled waters
ant agitate

transaction *n syn* CONTRACT, agreement, bargain, bond, compact, convention, covenant, pact

transcend *vb syn* SURPASS 1, beat, best, better, exceed, excel, outdo, outshine, outstrip, top
idiom go beyond, rise above

transcendent *adj* **1** *syn* SUPREME, incomparable, preeminent, surpassing, towering, ultimate, unequalable, unmatchable, unsurpassable
rel accomplished, consummate, finished; entire, intact, perfect, whole
2 *syn* ABSTRACT 1, hypothetical, ideal, theoretical, transcendental
rel absolute, ultimate; boundless, eternal, infinite

transcendental *adj* **1** *syn* OTHERWORLDLY 1, transmundane
2 *syn* ABSTRACT 1, hypothetical, ideal, theoretical, transcendent
rel supernatural, supranatural, ultimate

transfer *vb* **1** *syn* MOVE 4, dislocate, disturb, remove, shift, ship
rel carry, convey; relocate
2 *syn* GIVE 3, deliver, dispense, feed, find, hand, hand over, provide, supply, turn over
rel convey, transmit
3 *syn* TRANSFORM, change, convert, metamorphose, transfigure, translate, transmogrify, transmute, transpose, transubstantiate
4 to shift the title of (property) from one owner to another <to preserve the farm intact he *transfers* it to a single heir>
syn abalienate, alien, alienate, assign, cede, convey, deed, make over, remise, sign (over)

transfigure *vb syn* TRANSFORM, change, commute, convert, metamorphose, translate, transmogrify, transmute, transpose, transubstantiate

transfix *vb syn* IMPALE, lance, skewer, skiver, spear, spike, spit, transpierce

transform *vb* to make over to a radically different form, composition, state, or disposition <the interaction of social forces *transforms* custom and produces a new tradition>
syn change, commute, convert, metamorphize, metamorphose, mutate, transfer, transfigure, translate, transmogrify, transmute, transpose, transubstantiate; *compare* CHANGE 1
rel alter; denature

transformation *n syn* CONVERSION 2, alteration, changeover, shift

transfuse *vb syn* PERMEATE, charge, impenetrate, impregnate, interfuse, interpenetrate, penetrate, percolate, pervade, saturate

transgress *vb* **1** *syn* VIOLATE 1, breach, break, contravene, infract, infringe, offend
2 *syn* TRESPASS 1, offend, sin

transgression *n syn* BREACH 1, contravention, infraction, infringement, trespass, violation
rel erring, error, lapse, slip; overstepping; misbehavior, misstepping

transient *adj* lasting or staying only a short time <features of a *transient* culture now extinct>
syn ephemeral, evanescent, fleeting, fugacious, fugitive, impermanent, momentaneous, momentary, passing, short-lived, transitory, volatile; *compare* TEMPORARY
rel deciduous, flitting, unstable; temporal, temporary; insubstantial
idiom as transient as the clouds, here today and gone tomorrow
con lasting, perdurable, permanent, substantial; durable, stable
ant perpetual

transit *n* **1** *syn* PASSAGE 1, travel
2 *syn* TRANSITION, alteration, passage, shift
3 *syn* TRANSPORTATION 1, carriage, carrying, conveyance, transport, transporting
4 public conveyance of passengers or goods as a commercial enterprise <mass *transit*>
syn transport, transportation

transition *n* passage from one state or condition to another <the *transition* from boyhood to manhood>
syn alteration, passage, shift, transit
rel change, conversion, metamorphosis, transformation; development, evolution; growth, progress

transitional *adj* involving or characterized by passage from one stage, condition, or state to another <a *transitional* phase of social development>
syn transitive, transitory
rel developing, evolving; altering, changing, shifting
idiom being in a state of flux

transitive *adj syn* TRANSITIONAL, transitory

transitory *adj* **1** *syn* TRANSIENT, ephemeral, fleeting, fugacious, fugitive, impermanent, momentary, passing, short-lived, volatile
rel changeable; nonpermanent, unenduring; brief, short-term
2 *syn* TRANSITIONAL, transitive

---

syn synonym(s) — *rel* related word(s)
idiom idiomatic equivalent(s) — *con* contrasted word(s)
ant antonym(s) — * vulgar
‖ use limited; if in doubt, see a dictionary
The first word in a synonym list when printed in SMALL CAPITALS shows where there is more information about the group. For a more efficient use of this book see Explanatory Notes.

translate *vb* **1** to make a version of in another language < *translated* many secret documents from French to English >
syn put, render, transpose, turn
rel transliterate; transcribe; interpret; metaphrase, paraphrase
2 ***syn*** TRANSFORM, change, commute, convert, metamorphose, transfigure, transmogrify, transmute, transpose, transubstantiate

translate (into) *vb* ***syn*** PARAPHRASE, rephrase, restate, reword

translation *n* ***syn*** VERSION 1, paraphrase, rendering, restatement

translucent *adj* **1** ***syn*** TRANSPARENT 1, clear, limpid, pellucid, see-through
2 ***syn*** CLEAR 4, clear-cut, crystal, lucent, lucid, luminous, pellucid, transparent, transpicuous, unblurred
rel apparent, obvious, unmistakable
3 admitting and diffusing light so that objects beyond cannot be clearly distinguished < *translucent* amber >
syn clear, tralucent, translucid, transparent; *compare* TRANSPARENT 1
rel lucent, lucid

translucid *adj* ***syn*** TRANSLUCENT 3, clear, tralucent, transparent

transmarine *adj* ***syn*** OVERSEAS, oversea, ultramarine

transmigrate *vb* ***syn*** MIGRATE, emigrate

transmigratory *adj* ***syn*** MIGRATORY, migrant, migrative, migratorial, mobile

transmit *vb* **1** ***syn*** SEND 1, address, consign, dispatch, forward, remit, route, ship
rel convey, transport
2 ***syn*** COMMUNICATE 1, break, convey, impart, pass on
3 ***syn*** HAND DOWN, bequeath, hand on, pass (on)
rel instill; transfuse, translate
4 ***syn*** CONDUCT 4, carry, channel, convey, funnel, pipe, siphon, traject

transmogrify *vb* ***syn*** TRANSFORM, change, commute, convert, metamorphose, transfigure, translate, transmute, transpose, transubstantiate

transmundane *adj* ***syn*** OTHERWORLDLY 1, transcendental

transmute *vb* ***syn*** TRANSFORM, change, commute, convert, metamorphose, transfigure, translate, transmogrify, transpose, transubstantiate

transparent *adj* **1** admitting light without appreciable diffusion or distortion so that objects beyond are entirely visible <a sheet of *transparent* plastic>
syn clear, limpid, pellucid, see-through, translucent; *compare* TRANSLUCENT 3
rel crystal, crystalline, glassy; diaphanous
idiom clear as glass (*or* crystal)
con dark, smoky; cloudy, foggy hazy, misty, nubilous
ant opaque
2 ***syn*** FILMY, diaphanous, flimsy, gauzy, gossamer, sheer, tiffany
3 ***syn*** TRANSLUCENT 3, clear, tralucent, translucid
4 ***syn*** CLEAR 4, clear-cut, crystal, lucent, lucid, luminous, pellucid, translucent, transpicuous, unblurred
rel distinguishable, recognizable; articulate, distinct, plain; unambiguous, unequivocal
con muddy, turbid

transpicuous *adj* ***syn*** CLEAR 4, clear-cut, crystal, lucent, lucid, luminous, pellucid, translucent, transparent, unblurred

transpierce *vb* ***syn*** IMPALE, lance, skewer, skiver, spear, spike, spit, transfix

transpire *vb* **1** ***syn*** GET OUT 2, break, come out, leak, out
2 ***syn*** HAPPEN 1, befall, betide, chance, come off, develop, fall out, go, hap, occur
rel eventuate, result

transplace *vb* ***syn*** REVERSE 1, change, inverse, invert, revert, transpose, turn
rel remove; rearrange

transport *vb* **1** ***syn*** CARRY 1, bear, buck, convey, ferry, ‖hump, ‖jag, lug, pack, tote
2 to carry away by strong and usually pleasant emotion < *transported* with ecstasy >
syn enrapture, enravish, entrance, ravish, trance
rel excite, move, provoke, quicken, stimulate; agitate, inflame, stir (up); elevate, uplift; carry away, delight, imparadise, ‖send, slay, thrill, ‖wow
3 ***syn*** BANISH, cast out, deport, displace, exile, expel, expulse, ‖lag, oust, relegate

transport *n* **1** ***syn*** TRANSPORTATION 1, carriage, carrying, conveyance, transit, transporting
2 ***syn*** ECSTASY, heaven, rapture, rhapsody, seventh heaven
rel ardor, enthusiasm, fervor, passion; happiness
3 ***syn*** VEHICLE 3, conveyance, transportation
4 ***syn*** TRANSIT 4, transportation

transportable *adj* ***syn*** PORTABLE, carriageable, portative

transportation *n* **1** an act, process, or instance of transporting or being transported <arranged for the *transportation* of his luggage>
syn carriage, carrying, conveyance, transit, transport, transporting
rel hauling, moving
2 ***syn*** VEHICLE 3, conveyance, transport
3 ***syn*** TRANSIT 4, transport

transporting *n* ***syn*** TRANSPORTATION 1, carriage, carrying, conveyance, transit, transport

transpose *vb* **1** ***syn*** TRANSFORM, change, commute, convert, metamorphose, transfigure, translate, transmogrify, transmute, transubstantiate
2 ***syn*** TRANSLATE 1, put, render, turn
3 ***syn*** REVERSE 1, change, inverse, invert, revert, transplace, turn

transubstantiate *vb* ***syn*** TRANSFORM, change, commute, convert, metamorphose, transfigure, translate, transmogrify, transmute, transpose

transude *vb* ***syn*** EXUDE, bleed, ooze, ‖screeve, seep, ‖sew, ‖sicker, strain, sweat, weep

---

syn synonym(s) ***rel*** related word(s)
idiom idiomatic equivalent(s) ***con*** contrasted word(s)
ant antonym(s) * vulgar
‖ use limited; if in doubt, see a dictionary
The first word in a synonym list when printed in SMALL CAPITALS shows where there is more information about the group. For a more efficient use of this book see Explanatory Notes.

transversal *adj* ***syn*** TRANSVERSE, crossing, crosswise, thwart, traverse
rel bent; intersecting

transverse *vb* ***syn*** TRAVERSE 4, cross

transverse *adj* extended or lying in a direction across something else <the *transverse* arches of the cathedral ceiling>
syn crossing, crosswise, thwart, transversal, traverse
rel diagonal, oblique; across, crossed
con perpendicular
ant longitudinal

transversely *adv* ***syn*** OVER 1, across, athwart, beyond

transversely *adv* ***syn*** OVER 1, across, athwart, beyond

trap *n* **1** ***syn*** LURE 2, allurement, bait, come-on, decoy, enticement, inveiglement, seducement, snare, temptation
rel artifice, feint, gambit, maneuver, ploy, ruse, stratagem, wile; birdlime, net; ambuscade, ambush; conspiracy, intrigue, machination, plot
‖**2** ***syn*** POLICEMAN, ‖bobby, ‖bull, ‖constable, ‖copper, ‖gendarme, John Law, ‖paddy, ‖peeler, police
‖**3** ***syn*** MOUTH 1, ‖bazoo, gob, ‖mush, ‖row, ‖yap

trap *vb* ***syn*** CATCH 3, benet, catch up, ensnare, entangle, entrap, snare, tangle
rel mousetrap, snag

trapfall *n* ***syn*** PITFALL, booby trap, deadfall, mousetrap, springe

traps *n pl* ***syn*** PERSONAL EFFECTS, ‖plunder, stuff, things, tricks

trash *n* **1** ***syn*** REFUSE, debris, garbage, junk, kelter, litter, offal, rubbish, sweepings, waste
rel leavings
2 ***syn*** NONSENSE 2, bilge, bosh, bunkum, claptrap, ‖crap, hokum, malarkey, rot, rubbish
3 ***syn*** RABBLE 2, canaille, dreg(s), mass(es), mob, proletariat, ragtag and bobtail, riffraff, scum, unwashed

‖**trash** *vb* ***syn*** VANDALIZE, wreck

trash *vb* ***syn*** PLOD 1, footslog, ‖plodge, plunther, slog, slop, stodge, toil, trudge

trashy *adj* ***syn*** CHEAP 2, base, common, mean, paltry, poor, rubbishy, shoddy, sleazy, tatty
rel third-rate

trauma *n* intense mental, emotional, or physical disturbance resulting from stress <a broken home may produce persistent *trauma* in children>
syn shock, traumatism
rel blow, stress; traumatization; derangement, disturbance, upset; collapse

traumatism *n* ***syn*** TRAUMA, shock

travail *n* **1** ***syn*** WORK 2, bullwork, drudge, drudgery, grind, labor, moil, plugging, slavery, toil
rel task; struggle
idiom toil and trouble
con relaxation, rest
2 ***syn*** LABOR 2, birth pang(s), childbearing, childbirth
rel contractions, pains
idiom birth throe

travel *vb* **1** ***syn*** GO 1, fare, hie, journey, pass, proceed, ‖process, push on, repair, wend
rel move (on); voyage; roam, trek; explore
2 to journey over (as by conveyance) <certain roads can be *traveled* only on horseback>
syn cover, do, pass (over), track, traverse
rel cross

travel *n* **1** ***syn*** PASSAGE 1, transit
2 *often* **travels** *pl* ***syn*** JOURNEY, expedition, peregrination(s), trek, trip
3 ***syn*** TRAFFIC 4

travelable *adj* ***syn*** PASSABLE, navigable, negotiable

‖**traveler** *n* ***syn*** VAGABOND, ‖bindle stiff, bum, drifter, floater, roadster, ‖shack, street arab, tramp, vag

traverse *n* ***syn*** OBSTACLE, bar, Chinese wall, hamper, hurdle, impediment, obstruction, rub, snag, stumbling block

traverse *vb* **1** ***syn*** RESIST, buck, combat, contest, dispute, duel, fight, oppose, repel, withstand
2 ***syn*** DENY 4, contradict, contravene, cross, disaffirm, gainsay, impugn, negate, negative
rel oppose; dismiss; squash, squelch
3 ***syn*** TRAVEL 2, cover, do, pass (over), track
4 to extend or lie across (something) <a highway *traversing* the entire state>
syn cross, transverse
rel crisscross, intersect, quarter
idiom cut across
5 to pass over, along, or to and fro especially on foot <deep in thought he *traversed* the terrace again and again>
syn perambulate, walk
rel peregrinate; track, tread; pace

traverse *adj* ***syn*** TRANSVERSE, crossing, crosswise, thwart, transversal

travesty *n* **1** ***syn*** CARICATURE 2, burlesque, parody, take off
rel mimicry; distortion, exaggeration; ridicule
2 ***syn*** MOCKERY 2, burlesque, caricature, farce, mock, sham

travesty *vb* ***syn*** MIMIC, ape, burlesque, imitate, mock, parody, take off

treacherous *adj* **1** ***syn*** FAITHLESS, disloyal, false, perfidious, recreant, traitorous, unfaithful, unloyal, untrue
rel undependable, unreliable, untrustworthy; betraying, deceptive, double-crossing, falsehearted, misleading, Punic
ant dependable; trustworthy
2 ***syn*** DANGEROUS 1, chancy, hairy, hazardous, jeopardous, perilous, risky, unhealthy, unsound, wicked
rel deceptive, ticklish, tricky; precarious

treacherousness *n* ***syn*** TREACHERY, disloyalty, faithlessness, perfidiousness, perfidy, treason
ant dependability; trustworthiness

treachery *n* betrayal of a trust or confidence <corruption in public office is little short of *treachery*>
syn disloyalty, faithlessness, perfidiousness, perfidy, treacherousness, treason; *compare* INFIDELITY
rel falseheartedness, falseness; double cross, double-dealing; sellout

---

syn synonym(s) ***rel*** related word(s)
idiom idiomatic equivalent(s) ***con*** contrasted word(s)
ant antonym(s) * vulgar
‖ use limited; if in doubt, see a dictionary
The first word in a synonym list when printed in SMALL CAPITALS shows where there is more information about the group. For a more efficient use of this book see Explanatory Notes.

idiom dirty pool, dirty work at the crossroads
con incorruptibility, reliability; probity, rectitude, uprightness; constancy, fidelity, loyalty, staunchness
ant dependability; trustworthiness

tread *vb* **1** ***syn*** DANCE 1, foot (it), hoof (it), prance, step
2 ***syn*** WALK 1, ambulate, foot (it), hoof, pace, step, traipse, troop
rel march, stride; tromp

tread *n* ***syn*** TRACK 1, trace

treadmill *n* ***syn*** ROUTINE, grind, groove, pace, rote, rut

treason *n* **1** ***syn*** TREACHERY, disloyalty, faithlessness, perfidiousness, perfidy, treacherousness
rel deceit, deceitfulness; duplicity; Machiavellianism
idiom breach of trust (*or* faith)
con allegiance, loyalty
ant staunchness
2 ***syn*** SEDITION, seditiousness
rel disloyalty, treacherousness, treachery; high treason; misprision
ant allegiance

treasure *n* ***syn*** FIND 1, treasure trove
rel catch, plum, prize; pearl

treasure *vb* ***syn*** APPRECIATE 1, apprize, cherish, esteem, prize, value
rel conserve, guard, preserve, save; idolize, revere, reverence, venerate, worship
idiom hold dear

treasure–house *n* **1** ***syn*** TREASURY 1
2 ***syn*** BONANZA, eldorado, Golconda, gold mine, mine, treasure trove, treasury

treasure trove *n* **1** ***syn*** FIND 1, treasure
2 ***syn*** BONANZA, eldorado, Golconda, gold mine, mine, treasure-house, treasury

treasury *n* **1** a place (as a room or building) where valuables are kept <priceless gold candlesticks kept in the *treasury* of the cathedral>
syn treasure-house
rel archive(s), gallery, museum; depository, repository, storehouse
idiom treasure room
2 the place of deposit, retention, and disbursement of collected funds <the union *treasury* held emergency strike funds>
syn chest, coffer, exchequer, war chest
rel depositary, depository
3 ***syn*** BONANZA, eldorado, Golconda, gold mine, mine, treasure-house, treasure trove

treat *vb* **1** ***syn*** CONFER 2, advise, collogue, confab, confabulate, consult, huddle, parley, powwow
rel consider, study, weigh; deliberate, reason, think
2 to have to do with or behave toward (a person or thing) in a specified manner <*treat* all employees fairly and impartially>
syn deal (with), handle, play, serve, take, use
rel conduct, do with, manage, ‖wield; regard, respect; account, consider, hold; appraise, estimate, evaluate, rate, value
idiom act with regard to, conduct oneself toward, do by
3 to pay for another's entertainment <*treated* her to a few drinks>
syn blow, set up, ‖shout, stand
rel stake
idiom go treat, pick up the tab for, stand treat
4 to give medical treatment to <was *treated* by an eye specialist>
syn doctor
rel attend, care (for), minister (to), nurse

treat *n* ***syn*** DELICACY, bonne bouche, dainty, goody, kickshaw, morsel, tidbit (*or* titbit)

treatise *n* ***syn*** DISCOURSE 2, disquisition, dissertation, memoir, monograph, monography, thesis, tractate
rel writing; book; argument, discussion, exposition

treaty *n* a formal, usually written, arrangement made by negotiation between two or more political authorities <the two nations finally signed an arms-limitation *treaty*>
syn agreement, concord, convention, pact; *compare* CONTRACT
rel arrangement, entente, understanding; bargain, contract; charter, compact, concordat, covenant; alliance, cartel, league; accord, reconciliation, settlement

treble *adj* ***syn*** ACUTE 4, argute, high, piercing, piping, sharp, shrill, thin
ant bass

tree *vb* ***syn*** CORNER, bottle (up), collar

trek *n* ***syn*** JOURNEY, expedition, peregrination(s), travel(s), trip

tremble *vb* **1** ***syn*** SHAKE 1, ‖didder, dither, quake, quaver, quiver, shiver, shudder, tremor, twitter
rel shrink, wince
idiom tremble like a leaf
2 ***syn*** SHAKE 2, jar, quake, tremor, vibrate

trembling *adj* ***syn*** TREMULOUS, aquake, aquiver, quaking, quivering, shaking, shaky, shivering, tremorous, tremulant
ant steady

tremendous *adj* **1** ***syn*** FEARFUL 3, appalling, awful, dreadful, formidable, frightful, horrible, shocking, terrible, terrific
2 ***syn*** MONSTROUS 1, cracking, fantastic, massive, monumental, mortal, prodigious, stupendous, towering
3 ***syn*** HUGE, colossal, enormous, gigantic, immense, mighty, monstrous, prodigious, titanic, vast
rel amazing, astounding, flabbergasting; terrific
idiom great big
ant minute

tremendousness *n* ***syn*** ENORMITY 2, enormousness, hugeness, immensity, magnitude, vastness
rel bigness, largeness

tremor *n* ***syn*** EARTHQUAKE, quake, ‖quaker, shake, shock, temblor (*or* tremblor)

tremor *vb* **1** ***syn*** SHAKE 1, ‖didder, dither, quake, quaver, quiver, shiver, shudder, tremble, twitter
2 ***syn*** SHAKE 2, jar, quake, tremble, vibrate

---

syn synonym(s) ***rel*** related word(s)
idiom idiomatic equivalent(s) ***con*** contrasted word(s)
ant antonym(s) * vulgar
‖ use limited; if in doubt, see a dictionary
The first word in a synonym list when printed in SMALL CAPITALS shows where there is more information about the group. For a more efficient use of this book see Explanatory Notes.

tremorous *adj* ***syn*** TREMULOUS, aquake, aquiver, quaking, quivering, shaking, shaky, shivery, trembling, tremulant

tremulant *adj* ***syn*** TREMULOUS, aquake, aquiver, quaking, quivering, shaking, shaky, shivery, trembling, tremorous

tremulous *adj* characterized by or affected with trembling or tremors <her *tremulous* hands could scarcely hold the book>
syn aquake, aquiver, ashake, ashiver, quaking, quaky, quivering, quivery, shaking, shaky, shivering, shivery, trembling, tremorous, tremulant
rel aguish; aspen; palpitating; vibrating
idiom having the shakes
con firm, settled, stable, steady, unmoving

trench *n* a long narrow furrow in the ground <dig a *trench* for a sewer pipe>
syn cut, ditch
rel gully; drill, furrow; fosse; trough; drain, sink

trench *vb* ***syn*** BORDER 3, approach, verge

trenchant *adj* **1** ***syn*** INCISIVE, biting, clear-cut, crisp, cutting, ingoing, penetrating
rel piercing, probing, razor-sharp; sarcastic, sardonic, satiric; acrid; piquant, poignant, pungent
2 ***syn*** CAUSTIC 1, mordacious, mordant, salty, scathing
rel scalding, scorching

trend *n* **1** ***syn*** TENDENCY 1, current, drift, run, tenor
rel movement; flow; direction, orientation; swing, wind; progression
2 ***syn*** FASHION 3, craze, cry, dernier cri, fad, furore, mode, rage, style, vogue

||**trendy** *adj* ***syn*** STYLISH, a la mode, fashionable, in, modish, swank, swish, tonish, tony, with-it
rel ultramodern
con dated, outmoded

trepidation *n* ***syn*** FEAR 1, alarm, consternation, dismay, dread, fright, horror, panic, terror, trepidity
ant unapprehensiveness

trepidity *n* ***syn*** FEAR 1, alarm, consternation, dismay, dread, fright, horror, panic, terror, trepidation
ant intrepidity, intrepidness

trespass *n* ***syn*** BREACH 1, contravention, infraction, infringement, transgression, violation
rel encroachment, entrenchment, invasion; intrusion, obtrusion

trespass *vb* **1** to commit an offense <exhibited scrupulous fairness even to those who *trespassed* against him>
syn offend, sin, transgress
rel deviate, err, lapse
idiom do wrong by
2 to make inroads on the property, territory, or rights of another <warned the hunters not to *trespass* on his land>
syn encroach, entrench, infringe, invade
rel enter, penetrate, pierce, probe; interlope, intermeddle, intrude; transgress
idiom crash the gate

trestle *n* ***syn*** SAWHORSE, buck, horse, sawbuck, workhorse

triad *n* a union or group of three often closely related individuals or things <a *triad* of deities>
syn threesome, trine, trinity, trio, triple, triumvirate, triune, troika; *compare* TRIUMVIRATE 1

trial *n* **1** the state or fact of being tested (as by suffering) <the Vietnam war period was a time of great national *trial*>
syn affliction, calvary, cross, crucible, ordeal, tribulation, visitation
rel agony, distress, misery, suffering; anguish, grief, heartbreak, sorrow, woe; adversity, misfortune; difficulty, hardship, rigor, vicissitude
idiom crown of thorns, fiery ordeal, trial and tribulation
2 a source of vexation or annoyance <living in a crowded hotel is a real *trial*>
syn care, trouble, worry
rel complication, difficulty; annoyance, distress, misfortune; ordeal
3 ***syn*** EXPERIMENT, experimentation, test, trial and error, trial run
4 ***syn*** ATTEMPT, endeavor, essay, hassle, striving, struggle, try, undertaking

trial *adj* ***syn*** EXPERIMENTAL 2, experimentative, test

trial and error *n* ***syn*** EXPERIMENT, experimentation, test, trial, trial run

trial balloon *n* ***syn*** FEELER
rel trial

trial run *n* ***syn*** EXPERIMENT, experimentation, test, trial, trial and error

tribe *n* ***syn*** FAMILY 1, clan, folk, house, kindred, lineage, race, stock

tribulation *n* ***syn*** TRIAL 1, affliction, calvary, cross, crucible, ordeal, visitation
rel oppression, persecution, wronging

tribunal *n* ***syn*** COURT 2, bar, lawcourt

tributary *adj* ***syn*** SUBORDINATE, collateral, dependent, secondary, sub, subject, under
rel conquered, subdued, subjugated, vanquished; accessory, minor; satellite

tribute *n* **1** ***syn*** TESTIMONIAL 3, appreciation, salvo
rel recognition; monument
2 ***syn*** ENCOMIUM, citation, eulogy, panegyric, salutation

trice *n* ***syn*** INSTANT 1, minute, moment, second, shake, split second, ||tick, twinkle, twinkling, wink

trick *n* **1** an indirect, ingenious, and often cunning means to gain an end <used every *trick* in the bag to cover up the scandal>
syn artifice, chouse, device, feint, gambit, gimmick, jig, maneuver, play, ploy, ||prat, ruse, shenanigan, sleight, stratagem, whizzer, wile; *compare* PRANK
rel contrivance, craft, expediency; blind, bluff, diversion, dodge, dodgery, red herring; curve, deception, sham, stall; fraud, ||rort, scheme, shift, skin game
2 ***syn*** PRANK, antic, caper, dido(es), frolic, lark, monkeyshine, shenanigan, shine(s), tomfoolery

---

syn synonym(s) ***rel*** related word(s)
idiom idiomatic equivalent(s) ***con*** contrasted word(s)
ant antonym(s) * vulgar
|| use limited; if in doubt, see a dictionary
The first word in a synonym list when printed in SMALL CAPITALS shows where there is more information about the group. For a more efficient use of this book see Explanatory Notes.

rel boutade; escapade; practical joke
3 an ingenious or dexterous act or procedure designed to puzzle or amuse <a juggler's *trick*>
syn feat, stunt
rel accomplishment
4 **tricks** *pl* *syn* PERSONAL EFFECTS, ‖plunder, stuff, things, traps
5 *syn* HANG, knack, swing
6 *syn* HABIT 1, custom, habitude, manner, practice, praxis, usage, use, way, wont
7 *syn* SPELL, bout, go, shift, stint, time, tour, turn

trick *adj* somewhat defective and inclined to function abnormally on occasion <a *trick* lock that doesn't always catch>
syn tricky, undependable
rel catchy, touchy; unreliable, untrustworthy; insecure, shaky, unstable; defective, dysfunctioning, malfunctioning

trick *vb* *syn* DUPE, bamboozle, chicane, flimflam, fool, gull, hoax, hoodwink, hornswoggle, victimize
rel outtrick, outtrump, outwit; have
idiom take (someone) for a ride

trick (off, out, *or* up) *vb* *syn* DRESS UP 1, deck (out), doll out, doll up, ‖dude up, fix up, gussy up, slick, smarten (up), spruce (up)

trickery *n* *syn* DECEPTION 1, cheat, chicane, chicanery, double-dealing, fourberie, fraud, hanky-panky, highbinding, sharp practice
rel double-cross; underhandedness
idiom underhand dealing

trickle *vb* *syn* DRIP, distill, drib, dribble, drop, trill, weep
ant gush

trickster *n* 1 *syn* SWINDLER, cheat, cheater, con man, defrauder, diddler, double-dealer, flimflammer, grifter, sharper
idiom gyp artist
2 *syn* MAGICIAN 2, conjurer, illusionist

tricksy *adj* *syn* TIGHT 4, arduous, rough, trying

tricky *adj* 1 *syn* SLY 2, artful, astute, crafty, cunning, deep, foxy, guileful, insidious, wily
rel deceptive, delusive; delusory, misleading; deceitful, dishonest
2 *syn* UNSTABLE 2, rocky, ticklish
rel catchy, difficult, trappy; quirky
3 *syn* DELICATE 7, precarious, sensitive, ticklish, touchy
4 *syn* TRICK, undependable

tried *adj* *syn* RELIABLE 1, dependable, secure, tried and true, trustworthy, trusty
rel constant, faithful, staunch, steadfast; demonstrated, proved, tested; approved, certified
ant untried

tried and true *adj* *syn* RELIABLE 1, dependable, secure, tried, trustworthy, trusty

trifle *n* 1 *syn* KNICKKNACK, bauble, bibelot, curio, gewgaw, gimcrack, novelty, objet d'art, trinket, whatnot
rel rope yarn
2 *syn* HINT 2, dash, shade, smack, soupçon, spice, suggestion, suspicion, touch, trace

trifle *vb* 1 to behave amorously without serious intent <was interested only in *trifling* with her, not marrying her>
syn coquet, dally, flirt, fool, lead on, string along, toy, wanton
rel play (with); mess around, ‖muck, mucker; philander; mash
2 *syn* FIDDLE 1, fidget, play, twiddle

trifle (away) *vb* *syn* WASTE 2, consume, dissipate, fool (away), fritter, frivol away, potter (away), prodigalize, squander, throw away
rel misuse; burn (up), use up
con retain, save

trifling *n* *syn* SMALL TALK, bavardage, by-talk, chitchat, chitter-chatter

trifling *adj* *syn* PETTY 2, inconsequential, measly, Mickey Mouse, niggling, paltry, picayune, picayunish, puny, trivial
rel banal, inane, insipid, jejune, vapid; empty, frivolous, hollow, idle, nugatory, otiose, vain; insignificant, unimportant

trig *adj* 1 *syn* NEAT 2, chipper, orderly, shipshape, snug, spick-and-span, tidy, trim, uncluttered, well-groomed
2 *syn* STYLISH, chic, ‖classy, dashing, fashionable, modish, sharp, smart, snappy, swank
‖3 *syn* FULL 1, brimful, brimming, chockablock, crammed, crowded, jam-full, jammed, loaded, packed

triggerman *n* *syn* ASSASSIN, bravo, cutthroat, gun, gunman, ‖gunsel, gunslinger, hatchet man, hit man, torpedo

trill *vb* *syn* DRIP, distill, drib, dribble, drop, trickle, weep

trillion *n* *syn* SCAD, gob(s), heap, jillion, load(s), million, oodles, quantities, thousand, wad(s)

trim *vb* 1 *syn* ADORN, beautify, bedeck, deck, decorate, dress (up), embellish, garnish, ornament, prank
2 *syn* WHIP 2, beat, ‖clobber, drub, lambaste, lick, shellac, smear, smother, thrash
rel ‖skin
3 *syn* CUT 6, clip, crop, pare, prune, shave, shear, skive

trim *adj* 1 *syn* NEAT 2, chipper, orderly, shipshape, snug, spick-and-span, tidy, trig, uncluttered, well-groomed
rel clean, clean-cut, fit, spruce; shapely, streamlined, symmetrical
con disordered, shapeless, straggly
ant frowsy
2 *syn* SHAPELY, clean-limbed, shapeful, statuesque, well-proportioned, well-turned

trim *n* *syn* ORDER 10, condition, fettle, fitness, kilter, repair, shape
rel commission; whack

trine *n* *syn* TRIAD, threesome, trinity, trio, triple, triumvirate, triune, troika

trinity *n* *syn* TRIAD, threesome, trine, trio, triple, triumvirate, triune, troika

---

syn synonym(s) *rel* related word(s)
idiom idiomatic equivalent(s) *con* contrasted word(s)
ant antonym(s) * vulgar
‖ use limited; if in doubt, see a dictionary
The first word in a synonym list when printed in SMALL CAPITALS shows where there is more information about the group. For a more efficient use of this book see Explanatory Notes.

trinket *n* ***syn*** KNICKKNACK, bauble, bibelot, curio, gewgaw, gimcrack, novelty, objet d'art, trifle, whatnot
rel plaything; frippery, showpiece, tinsel; trinketry, trinkums

trio *n* ***syn*** TRIAD, threesome, trine, trinity, triple, triumvirate, triune, troika

trip *vb* ***syn*** SKIP 1, hop, lope, skitter, spring

trip *n* **1** a single passage of a vehicle between two points or to a point and return <a regular bus *trip* to and from the city>
syn run; *compare* DRIVE 1, JOURNEY, TOUR 2
rel drive; progress
2 ***syn*** JOURNEY, expedition, peregrination(s), travel(s), trek
rel run
3 ***syn*** ERROR 2, blooper, blunder, boner, bull, bungle, fluff, lapse, mistake, slip

tripes *n pl* ***syn*** ENTRAILS, gut(s), innards, insides, internals, inwards, ‖pudding(s), stuffing, viscera

triple *n* ***syn*** TRIAD, threesome, trine, trinity, trio, triumvirate, triune, troika

tripped out *adj* ***syn*** DRUGGED, doped, high, hopped-up, spaced-out, stoned, turned on, ‖wiped out, zonked

‖**tripper** *n* ***syn*** TOURIST, rubberneck, sightseer

triste *adj* ***syn*** SAD 2, depressing, joyless, melancholic, melancholy, mournful, saddening

trite *adj* used or occurring so often as to have lost interest, freshness, or force <unrequited love has become a *trite* theme>
syn bathetic, chain, cliché, clichéd, commonplace, corny, hack, hackneyed, musty, old hat, shopworn, stale, stereotyped, stereotypical, threadbare, timeworn, tired, twice-told, warmed-over, well-worn, worn-out
rel common, ordinary; banal, dull, flat, jejune, mildewed, vapid; bedridden, drained, exhausted, used-up; bromidic, platitudinous, prosaic, ready-made, set, stock
con first, new, seminal; novel, unique; creative, imaginative; uncopied; memorable; distinctive
ant fresh, original

triturate *vb* ***syn*** PULVERIZE 1, bray, buck, comminute, contriturate, crush, powder

triumph *n* **1** ***syn*** VICTORY 1, conquest, win
rel ascendancy, gain; surmounting, vanquishing, vanquishment
ant defeat
2 ***syn*** EXULTATION, exultance, jubilance, jubilation
rel joy; festivity, merriment, reveling

triumph *vb* **1** ***syn*** EXULT, delight, glory, jubilate
rel gloat
2 ***syn*** WIN 1, beat, overcome, prevail
rel prosper, succeed; conquer, surmount
idiom get the best (*or* better) of
con lose
ant fail
3 ***syn*** CONQUER 2, best, master, overcome, prevail

triumphal *adj* ***syn*** EXULTANT, cock-a-hoop, cock-a-whoop, exulting, jubilant, triumphant

triumphant *adj* ***syn*** EXULTANT, cock-a-hoop, cock-a-whoop, exulting, jubilant, triumphal
rel rejoicing, triumphing

triumvirate *n* **1** an administrative or ruling body of three <a monarchy replaced by a *triumvirate* of generals>
syn troika; *compare* TRIAD
rel junta
2 ***syn*** TRIAD, threesome, trine, trinity, trio, triple, triune, troika

triune *n* ***syn*** TRIAD, threesome, trine, trinity, trio, triple, triumvirate, troika

trivia *n pl but sometimes sing in constr* unimportant matters <they became bored with the *trivia* of everyday life>
syn minutia(e), small beer, small change, small potato(es), triviality

trivial *adj* **1** ***syn*** LITTLE 3, casual, inconsiderable, insignificant, light, minor, petty, shoestring, small-beer, unimportant
rel slight; negligible
idiom no great shakes
con considerable
ant momentous, weighty
2 ***syn*** PETTY 2, inconsequential, measly, Mickey Mouse, paltry, picayune, picayunish, puny, trifling, unconsequential
rel captious, fribbling, frivolous; shallow, superficial

triviality *n* ***syn*** TRIVIA, minutia(e), small beer, small change, small potato(es)
rel shallowness, superficiality, unimportance
con basic(s), essential(s), fundamental(s)

‖**trod** *n* ***syn*** TRAIL, path, pathway, track

troika *n* **1** ***syn*** TRIUMVIRATE 1
2 ***syn*** TRIAD, threesome, trine, trinity, trio, triple, triumvirate, triune

trollop *n* ***syn*** WANTON, baggage, hussy, jade, jezebel, slattern, slut, strumpet, tramp, wench
idiom (a) fast number

trollop *vb* ***syn*** SLOUCH, droop, loll, ‖lollop, lop, slump

tromp *vb* **1** ***syn*** TRAMP 1, trample
2 ***syn*** HIKE 2, tramp
rel slog, trudge
3 ***syn*** TRAMPLE 2, stamp, stomp, tramp
4 ***syn*** BEAT 1, batter, belabor, buffet, drub, lambaste, pelt, pound, pummel, thrash

troop *n* **1** ***syn*** COMPANY 4, band, corps, outfit, party, troupe
rel assemblage, assembly, collection, gathering; army, host, legion, multitude
2 troops *pl* members of a nation's military units <Marines, GI's, and Seabees were among the *troops* sent to war>
syn armed forces, forces, military, servicemen
rel combatants; soldiers, troopers
idiom fighting men

troop *vb* ***syn*** WALK 1, ambulate, foot (it), hoof, pace, step, traipse, tread

trophy *n* ***syn*** REMEMBRANCE 3, keepsake, memento, memorial, relic, remembrancer, reminder, souvenir, token

---

syn synonym(s) ***rel*** related word(s)
idiom idiomatic equivalent(s) ***con*** contrasted word(s)
ant antonym(s) * vulgar
‖ use limited; if in doubt, see a dictionary
The first word in a synonym list when printed in SMALL CAPITALS shows where there is more information about the group. For a more efficient use of this book see Explanatory Notes.

tropic *adj* ***syn*** TROPICAL
rel baking, broiling, scorching, sweltering
con arctic

tropical *adj* of, relating to, or occurring in the tropics < *tropical* fruits >
syn tropic
rel equatorial, semitropical, subtropical; warm; hot, sultry, torrid
con temperate

tropical cyclone *n* ***syn*** HURRICANE, tropical storm, typhoon, ‖willy-willy

tropical storm *n* ***syn*** HURRICANE, tropical cyclone, typhoon, ‖willy-willy

trot *n* **1** ***syn*** HAG 2, ‖bag, ‖bat, beldam, biddy, crone, drab, witch
2 ***syn*** PONY, crib
3 trots** *pl* ***syn DIARRHEA, ‖backdoor trots, dysentery, flux, ‖runs, scour(s), *shits, ‖squirts

troth *n* ***syn*** ENGAGEMENT 2, betrothal, betrothing, betrothment, espousal

trot out *vb* ***syn*** SHOW 4, brandish, display, disport, exhibit, expose, flash, flaunt, parade, show off

troubadour *n* ***syn*** BARD 1, jongleur, minstrel
rel balladist; rhymer, rhymester

trouble *vb* **1** to cause to be uneasy or upset < sorrows that *trouble* the strongest of men >
syn ail, cark, distress, upset, worry
rel agitate, concern, discompose, disquiet, disturb, perturb, rowel, ‖worrit; annoy, bother, fret, irk, vex; ‖destroy, haunt
2 ***syn*** TRY 2, distress, harass, irk, pain, strain, stress
rel upset, worry; discompose, disconcert, disturb; harry, irritate; afflict, torment
3 ***syn*** INCONVENIENCE, discommode, ‖disconvenience, disoblige, incommode, put about, put out
rel annoy, pester, plague, worry; impose (on *or* upon), intrude

trouble *n* **1** ***syn*** TRIAL 2, care, worry
2 ***syn*** EFFORT 1, elbow grease, exertion, pains, while
rel ado, bustle, flurry, fuss, pother; bother, inconvenience; difficulty, hardship, rigor; strain, stress
3 a condition of annoyance, disturbance, or distress < got him into *trouble* by repeating gossip >
syn Dutch, hot water
rel bind, difficulty, predicament

troubled *adj* ***syn*** DISTRAUGHT, distracted, distrait, distressed, harassed, tormented, worried

troublemaker *n* a person who consciously or unconsciously causes trouble < a *troublemaker* who set father against daughter >
syn bad actor, mischief-maker
rel agitator, inciter, inflamer, instigator

troublesome *adj* giving trouble or anxiety < a *troublesome* infection >
syn mean, pesky, troublous, ugly, vexatious, wicked
rel annoying, bothersome, vexing; alarming, disquieting, disturbing, upsetting; infestive; painful
con untroublesome
ant innocuous

troublesomeness *n* ***syn*** INCONVENIENCE, bother, bothersomeness, ‖disconvenience
rel difficulty; irritation, vexation

troublous *adj* ***syn*** TROUBLESOME, mean, pesky, ugly, vexatious, wicked
rel troubling

trounce *vb* ***syn*** WHIP 2, beat, ‖clobber, drub, overwhelm, shellac, thrash, trim, wallop, whomp
idiom walk all over

trouncing *n* ***syn*** DEFEAT 1, beating, debacle, defeasance, drubbing, licking, overthrow, rout, shellacking, thrashing

troupe *n* ***syn*** COMPANY 4, band, corps, outfit, party, troop

trouper *n* ***syn*** ACTOR 1, impersonator, mime, mimic, mummer, performer, playactor, player, thespian
rel entertainer; artiste

trove *n* ***syn*** ACCUMULATION, agglomeration, aggregation, amassment, collection, colluvies, conglomeration, cumulation, hoard

truce *n* a suspension of or an agreement for suspending hostilities < the high command ordered a *truce* for the holidays >
syn armistice, cease-fire
rel break, ‖breather, letup, lull, pause, respite; de-escalation, ‖wind-down; accord, reconciliation; peace

truck *vb* **1** ***syn*** TRADE 1, bargain, barter, exchange, swap, traffic
rel handle; peddle, retail
2 ***syn*** TRAFFIC 2
idiom have truck with

truck *n* ***syn*** COMMERCE 2, communion, dealings, intercourse, traffic

truckle *vb* ***syn*** FAWN, apple-polish, bootlick, ‖brownnose, cower, cringe, grovel, honey (up), kowtow, toady
rel knuckle down, knuckle under, succumb; follow, tag, tail, trail
idiom *kiss ass, kiss (*or* lick) one's boots, lick the feet of, make a doormat of oneself

truckler *n* ***syn*** SYCOPHANT, bootlicker, ‖clawback, footlicker, lickspit, lickspittle, spaniel, toad, toadeater, toady

truckling *adj* ***syn*** FAWNING, bootlicking, cowering, cringing, groveling, kowtowing, parasitic, sycophantic, toadying, toadyish

truculent *adj* **1** ***syn*** FIERCE 1, barbarous, cruel, fell, ferocious, grim, inhuman, inhumane, savage, wolfish
rel browbeating, bullying, cowing, intimidating; frightening, terrifying, terrorizing
2 ***syn*** ABUSIVE, contumelious, invective, opprobrious, scurrile, scurrilous, vituperative, vituperatory, vituperous
rel caustic, mordacious, mordant, scathing, sharp, trenchant; harsh, rough, severe; vitriolic
3 ***syn*** BELLIGERENT, bellicose, combative, contentious, gladiatorial, militant, pugnacious, quarrelsome, scrappy, warlike

trudge *vb* ***syn*** PLOD 1, footslog, ‖plodge, plunther, slog, slop, stodge, toil, ‖trash

---

true *adj* **1** *syn* FAITHFUL 1, allegiant, ardent, constant, ‖dinky-di, liege, loyal, resolute, staunch, steadfast
rel sincere, unfeigned, whole-hearted, whole-souled
ant false, fickle
2 *syn* UPRIGHT 2, conscientious, honest, honorable, just, right, scrupulous
rel creditable, estimable, worthy; high-principled, right-minded, truehearted
3 conformable to fact or to a standard, rule, or model <gave a *true* account of the accident>
syn faithful, just, right, strict, undistorted, veracious, veridical
rel careful, conscientious, meticulous, punctilious, scrupulous; finicky, fussy, overnice; accurate, precise; absolute, mathematical
idiom true to the letter
con imprecise, inaccurate, incorrect, inexact; erroneous, false
ant untrue
4 *syn* GENUINE 3, heart-whole, honest, real, sincere, undesigning, undissembled, unfeigned
con deceitful
5 *syn* AUTHENTIC 2, bona fide, genuine, indubitable, real, sure-enough, undoubted, unquestionable, veritable, very
rel genuine, kosher; sincere, unfaked, unfeigned
con artificial, fake, faked, feigned; insincere
ant false
6 *syn* REAL 3, actual, indisputable, undeniable, unfabled, veridical
rel natural, normal, regular, typical
ant false
7 being such as it should be <meanings presented in their *true* relationship>
syn appropriate, desired, fitting, proper
rel acceptable; applicable, befitting, likely, suitable
con inappropriate, unfitting
8 being such by right <the *true* heir>
syn legitimate, rightful
rel lawful, legal, proper
con illegitimate, spurious, supposititious
ant false
9 that can be relied on <polls can provide a *true* projection of public sentiment>
syn authoritative, dependable, trustable, trustworthy
rel meaningful, significant; expressive, indicative, suggestive
con independable, undependable, untrustworthy; doubtful, questionable

truelove *n* **1** *syn* GIRL FRIEND 2, ‖baby, beloved, flame, honey, inamorata, ladylove, steady, sweetheart, sweetie
2 *syn* BOYFRIEND 2, beau, beloved, flame, inamorata, lover, steady, sweetheart
idiom one and only

true–tongued *adj syn* TRUTHFUL, truth-speaking, truth-telling, veracious, veridical

truism *n* **1** *syn* VERACITY 2, gospel, truth, verity
2 *syn* MAXIM, aphorism, apothegm, axiom, brocard, dictum, gnome, moral, rule
3 *syn* COMMONPLACE, banality, bromide, cliché, platitude, prosaicism, prosaism, rubber stamp, shibboleth, tag

trull *n syn* WANTON, baggage, hussy, jade, slattern, slut, strumpet, tramp, trollop, wench

truly *adv* **1** *syn* VERY 2, actually, de facto, genuinely, really, veritably
rel absolutely, positively
2 *syn* EVEN 3, indeed, nay, verily, yea
rel confidently, really
3 *syn* WELL 7, doubtlessly, easily, indeed, really, undoubtedly
rel probably; surely

trump *n syn* TRUMP CARD, clincher

trump *vb syn* SURPASS 1, beat, best, better, cap, excel, outdo, outstrip, pass, top

trump card *n* something decisive or telling often held in reserve <kept a political *trump card* up his sleeve till election eve>
syn clincher, trump
rel ace; coup, coup de grace, coup de main
idiom ace in the hole

trumpery *n syn* NONSENSE 2, bilge, bunkum, bushwa, claptrap, double-talk, flimflam, hokum, malarkey, twaddle

trumpery *adj syn* CHEAP 2, base, cheesy, common, mean, paltry, poor, rubbishy, shoddy, trashy

trumpet *vb syn* TOUT, ballyhoo, herald

truncate *vb syn* TOP 1, crop, detruncate, pollard
rel abbreviate, abridge; cut off, lop; shear

truncheon *n syn* CUDGEL, bat, billy, billy club, bludgeon, club, knobkerrie, mace, nightstick, ‖shillelagh

trust *n* **1** complete assurance and certitude regarding the character, ability, strength, or truth of someone or something <they continue to have *trust* in his judgment>
syn confidence, dependence, faith, hope, reliance, stock
rel assurance, certainty, certitude, conviction; belief, credence, credit; positiveness, sureness; entrustment; overconfidence, oversureness
con doubt, dubiety, dubiosity, skepticism, suspicion, uncertainty
ant mistrust
2 *syn* SYNDICATE, cartel, chain, combine, conglomerate, group, pool
3 *syn* CUSTODY, care, guardianship, keeping, safekeeping, ward

trust *vb syn* ENTRUST 1, charge
rel commit, consign, hand over

trust (in *or* to) *vb syn* RELY (on *or* upon), bank (on *or* upon), build (on), calculate (on *or* upon), count (on), depend (on *or* upon), ‖lot (on *or* upon), reckon (on)
rel assume, imagine, presume
idiom have no reservations

trustable *adj syn* TRUE 9, authoritative, dependable, trustworthy
ant trustless

trustless *adj* ***syn*** UNRELIABLE 1, dubious, fly-by-night, questionable, undependable, unsure, untrustworthy, untrusty
rel unworthy; unfaithful; suspect, suspicious; dishonest; deceitful; treacherous
ant trustable, trustworthy

trustworthy *adj* **1** ***syn*** RELIABLE 1, dependable, secure, tried, tried and true, trusty
rel veracious, truthful; honest, scrupulous, upright
con deceitful; dishonest
ant untrustworthy
2 ***syn*** TRUE 9, authoritative, dependable, trustable
rel accurate, exact; valid; realistic
con inaccurate, inexact; invalid; unrealistic; suspect
ant untrustworthy
3 ***syn*** AUTHENTIC 1, convincing, credible, faithful, trusty

trusty *adj* **1** ***syn*** RELIABLE 1, dependable, secure, tried, tried and true, trustworthy
rel predictable, stable; firm, sound; responsible, ‖straight
con capricious
ant untrusty
2 ***syn*** AUTHENTIC 1, convincing, credible, faithful, trustworthy
ant untrusty

truth *n* **1** ***syn*** VERACITY 1, truthfulness, veraciousness, veridicality, verity
rel precision, rightness, trueness; authenticity, genuineness, veritableness; candor
idiom unvarnished truth (*or* truthfulness)
con equivocation, evasion, hedging; deception, deceptiveness, falseness
ant falsity, untruth
2 ***syn*** VERACITY 2, gospel, truism, verity
rel reality
idiom (the) gospel truth, (the) truth of the matter
ant lie, untruth

truthful *adj* observant of or telling the truth <a *truthful* witness>
syn true-tongued, truth-speaking, truth-telling, veracious, veridical
rel candid, frank, honest, sincere; accurate, factual; real, realistic
con false, insincere, truthless, uncandid; inaccurate; unrealistic
ant untruthful

truthfulness *n* ***syn*** VERACITY 1, truth, veraciousness, veridicality, verity
ant untruthfulness

truthlessness *n* ***syn*** MENDACITY, falsehood, fibbery, mendaciousness, untruthfulness, unveracity

truth–speaking *adj* ***syn*** TRUTHFUL, true-tongued, truth-telling, veracious, veridical

truth–telling *adj* ***syn*** TRUTHFUL, true-tongued, truth-speaking, veracious, veridical

try *vb* **1** to subject to testing <*try* the door to be sure it's locked>
syn check, examine, prove, test
rel inspect, scrutinize; appraise, judge, weigh
idiom make trial of, put to proof, put to the test
2 to subject to stress <the fine print *tried* her eyes>
syn distress, harass, irk, pain, strain, stress, trouble
rel annoy, bother, vex
3 ***syn*** AFFLICT, agonize, crucify, excruciate, harrow, martyr, rack, torment, torture, wring
4 ***syn*** PROVE 1, demonstrate, test
5 to make an effort to do or accomplish something <the baby is *trying* to walk>
syn assay, attempt, endeavor, essay, offer, seek, strive, struggle, undertake
rel aim, aspire, hope, strike
idiom do one's best (*or* utmost) to, have a go at

try (out) *vb* ***syn*** EXPERIMENT, experimentalize, experimentize, test (out), try on
rel examine, inspect, scrutinize; demonstrate, prove
idiom cut and try, put to trial, try for size

try *n* **1** ***syn*** ATTEMPT, endeavor, essay, hassle, striving, struggle, trial, undertaking
2 ***syn*** FLING 1, crack, go, pop, shot, slap, stab, ‖stagger, whack, whirl
rel dab, jab

trying *adj* **1** ***syn*** TIGHT 4, arduous, rough, tricksy
rel annoying, bothersome, irksome, irritating, troublesome, vexing; strenuous; sticky, tricky
2 ***syn*** ONEROUS, burdensome, demanding, exacting, exigent, oppressive, superincumbent, taxing, tough, weighty

try on *vb* ***syn*** EXPERIMENT, experimentalize, experimentize, test (out), try (out)

tryst *n* ***syn*** ENGAGEMENT 3, appointment, assignation, date, rendezvous

‖**tub** *n* ***syn*** FATTY, blimp, butterball, dumpling, ‖fatso

tub *vb* ***syn*** BATHE 1, ‖bath, shower, wash

tubby *adj* ***syn*** ROTUND 2, chubby, plump, plumpish, plumpy, podgy, pudgy, roly-poly, roundabout, tubby
idiom plump as a dumpling (*or* partridge)

tuberculosis *n* a communicable bacterial disease typically marked by wasting, fever, and formation of cheesy tubercles often in the lungs <Victorian heroines fading away with *tuberculosis*>
syn consumption, phthisis, TB, white plague

tuck (in) *vb* ***syn*** BED
rel snug (down *or* up), snuggle

‖**tuck** *n* ***syn*** FOOD 1, bread, chow, eats, feed, grub, meat, provender, scoff, viands

tuck *n* ***syn*** ENERGY 2, birr, go, hardihood, ‖moxie, pep, potency, vigor

‖**tucked up** *adj* ***syn*** CRAMPED, confined, cramp, incommodious, squeezy

tucker *vb* ***syn*** EXHAUST 3, ‖bugger, fag, frazzle, knock out, outtire, outwear, ‖poop, prostrate, wear out
rel gruel; wilt; drop
idiom take the tuck out of

tug *vb* **1** ***syn*** CONTEND 1, battle, fight, oppugn, war
2 ***syn*** LABOR 1, drive, moil, strain, strive, toil, work
3 ***syn*** PULL 2, drag, draw, haul, lug, tow

---

syn synonym(s) | ***rel*** related word(s)
idiom idiomatic equivalent(s) | ***con*** contrasted word(s)
ant antonym(s) | * vulgar
‖ use limited; if in doubt, see a dictionary
The first word in a synonym list when printed in SMALL CAPITALS shows where there is more information about the group. For a more efficient use of this book see Explanatory Notes.

tug–of–war *n syn* CONTEST 1, competition, conflict, emulation, rivalry, strife, striving, warfare

tuition *n syn* EDUCATION 1, instruction, schooling, teaching, training, tutelage

tumble *vb* **1** *syn* FALL 2, drop, go down, keel (over), pitch, plunge, slump, topple
rel trip; come (down), descend
2 *syn* PLUMMET, dip, drop, fall, nose-dive, plunge, skid
rel depreciate; sag, slump
idiom take a downward spiral, take a nosedive
3 *syn* HAPPEN 2, bump, chance, hit, light, luck, meet, stumble
4 *syn* DISCOVER 3, ascertain, catch on, determine, find out, hear, learn, see, unearth
5 *syn* OVERTHROW 2, overset, overturn, topple, unhorse
6 *syn* FELL 1, bowl (down *or* over), bring down, down, drop, flatten, floor, knock down, knock over, level
7 *syn* CONFUSE 5, foul up, jumble, mix up, muddle, ‖snafu, snarl up
8 *syn* DISORDER 1, disarrange, disarray, discompose, disturb, jumble, mess (up), muss (up), unsettle, upset

tumble (to) *vb syn* APPREHEND 1, accept, catch, compass, comprehend, ‖dig, follow, grasp, see, take in

tumble *n syn* CLUTTER 2, hash, jumble, litter, mash, mishmash, muddle, rummage, scramble, shuffle

tumescent *adj* **1** *syn* INFLATED, dropsical, dropsied, flatulent, overblown, tumid, turgid, windy
rel bloated; bulging
2 *syn* RHETORICAL, aureate, bombastic, euphuistic, flowery, grandiloquent, magniloquent, swelling, swollen, tumid

tumid *adj* **1** *syn* INFLATED, dropsical, dropsied, flatulent, overblown, tumescent, turgid, windy
rel dilated, distended, expanded, swollen
2 *syn* RHETORICAL, aureate, bombastic, euphuistic, flowery, grandiloquent, magniloquent, swelling, swollen, tumescent

tummy *n syn* ABDOMEN, belly, ‖gut, paunch, stomach, venter

tumulary *adj syn* SEPULCHRAL 1, mortuary

tumult *n* **1** *syn* COMMOTION 1, clamor, convulsion, ferment, outcry, upheaval, upturn
rel disturbance, turmoil, uproar
2 *syn* COMMOTION 4, clamor, hassle, hubbub, hurly-burly, pother, to-do, turmoil, uproar, whirl
rel babel, din, hullabaloo, pandemonium, racket
con calm, hush, lull, quietude
3 *syn* COMMOTION 2, agitation, confusion, dither, flap, lather, pother, stew, turbulence, turmoil
rel seething; disorder, unsettlement; ferment, maelstrom, paroxysm

syn synonym(s)
rel related word(s)
idiom idiomatic equivalent(s)
con contrasted word(s)
ant antonym(s)
* vulgar
‖ use limited; if in doubt, see a dictionary
The first word in a synonym list when printed in SMALL CAPITALS shows where there is more information about the group. For a more efficient use of this book see Explanatory Notes.

4 *syn* DIN, babel, clamor, hubbub, hullabaloo, jangle, pandemonium, racket, tintamarre, uproar
rel noise; ‖corroboree
idiom ‖all hell broken loose

tumultuous *adj syn* TURBULENT 1, boisterous, disorderly, raucous, rowdy, rowdydowdy, rowdyish, rumbustious, termagant, unruly

tumultuously *adv syn* HARD 2, fiercely, frantically, frenziedly, furiously, madly, stormily, turbulently, violently, wildly

tun *n syn* CASK, barrel, butt, hogshead, keg, pipe
rel vat

tune *n* **1** *syn* MELODY, air, descant, diapason, lay, measure, melisma, melodia, strain, warble
rel carol; composition, number, piece
2 *syn* HARMONY 1, accord, chorus, concert, concord, consonance
3 *syn* HARMONY 2, accord, agreement, chime, concord, concordance, consonance
4 *syn* ORDER 4, extent, magnitude, matter, neighborhood, range, vicinity

tune *vb* **1** *syn* SING 1, chant, vocalize
2 *syn* HARMONIZE 3, accommodate, attune, conform, coordinate, integrate, proportion, reconcile, reconciliate
rel fix, regulate
3 to adjust with respect to resonance < *tune* a TV set to a local station >
syn dial

tune (up) *vb syn* ADJUST 2, fix, regulate

tuned *adj syn* MELODIOUS 2, melodic, musical, songful, tuneful

tuneful *adj* **1** *syn* MELODIOUS 2, melodic, musical, songful, tuned
2 *syn* MELODIOUS 1, dulcet, euphonic, euphonious, mellisonant, melodic, sweet
ant tuneless

tunk *vb syn* TAP 1, bob, knock, rap

turbid *adj* clouded with or as if with roiled sediment <a *turbid* stream>
syn muddy, riley, roily
rel dark, dense, obscure; mucky, thick; clouded, cloudy, murky, opaque, smoky; dull
con translucent; lucid, pellucid, transparent; crystal, crystalline; clean, pure, undefiled
ant clear, limpid

turbulence *n syn* COMMOTION 2, agitation, confusion, dither, flap, lather, pother, stew, tumult, turmoil
rel babel, din, pandemonium, uproar; unruliness; fracas, fight
con calmness, composure, placidity, quiet

turbulent *adj* **1** given to insubordination and disorder <a *turbulent* and irresponsible group>
syn boisterous, disorderly, rambunctious, raucous, rowdy, rowdydowdy, rowdyish, rumbustious, termagant, tumultuous, unruly; *compare* UNRULY 1
rel mutinous; fast, roisterous, uncontrollable, uninhibited, wild; clamorous, loudmouthed; brawling, quarrelsome, rough, roughhouse; hell-for-leather, rip-roaring, tempestuous
con calm, placid, quiet, tranquil; controlled, orderly, peaceful, restrained
2 *syn* WILD 6, blustering, blustery, ‖coarse, furious, raging, rough, stormful, stormy, tempestuous

rel agitated, convulsed, moiling, stirred up; boiling, roily, ruffled, swirling; howling, riotous, roaring; tempest-tossed

turbulently *adv* *syn* HARD 2, fiercely, frantically, frenziedly, furiously, madly, stormily, tumultuously, violently, wildly
rel blusteringly

***turd** *n* *syn* SNOT, cur, dog, ‖prick, scum, *shit, *shithead, skunk, snake, toad

turf *n* *syn* TERRAIN 2, territory
rel area, region, sphere

turgid *adj* **1** *syn* INFLATED, dropsical, dropsied, flatulent, overblown, tumescent, tumid, windy
rel swelling, turgescent
2 *syn* RHETORICAL, aureate, bombastic, euphuistic, flowery, grandiloquent, magniloquent, swelling, swollen, tumid

turmoil *n* **1** *syn* COMMOTION 2, agitation, confusion, dither, flap, lather, pother, stew, tumult, turbulence
rel jitteriness, nervousness, restlessness, unease, uneasiness; disorder, disruption; moil; riot, strife, uproar
2 *syn* UNREST, ailment, disquiet, disquietude, ferment, inquietude, restiveness, restlessness, storm and stress, Sturm und Drang
rel distress; anxiety, anxiousness
ant tranquillity
3 *syn* COMMOTION 4, clamor, hassle, hubbub, hurly-burly, pother, to-do, tumult, uproar, whirl

turn *vb* **1** to move or cause to move in a curved or circular path on or as if on an axis <*turned* the wheel sharply to avoid a collision>
syn circle, circumduct, gyrate, gyre, revolve, roll, rotate; *compare* SPIN 1
rel orbit; pirouette, spin, twirl, whirl; twist, weave, wind; circulate, eddy, swirl; oscillate, sway, swing, vibrate
2 *syn* SPRAIN, ‖rick, twist, wrench
3 *syn* REVERSE 1, change, inverse, invert, revert, transplace, transpose
4 *syn* PLOW, break, plow up, turn over
5 *syn* UPSET 5, derange, disorder, sicken, unhinge, unsettle
rel discompose, undo; unbalance
6 to change or cause to change course or direction <*turned* his car down a side road>
syn avert, deflect, divert, pivot, sheer, swing, veer, volte-face, wheel, whip, whirl; *compare* SHUNT 1
rel depart, detract, deviate, digress, diverge; move, shift; switch, swivel, twist, zigzag; call off, double (back), reverse; shunt, sidetrack; bend, curve, sway; detour, rechannel, turn away
7 *syn* DIRECT 2, address, aim, cast, head, lay, level, point, train, zero (in)
con call off, detract (from), distract, divert (from), draw (away)
8 *syn* ADDRESS 3, apply, bend, buckle (down), devote, direct, give, throw
rel employ, use; plunge (into), undertake
idiom turn one's hand (*or* energies) to
con avoid, dodge, shy (away)
9 *syn* CURDLE, ‖clabber, ‖cruddle, curd, ‖lopper
10 *syn* DECAY, break down, crumble, decompose, disintegrate, molder, putrefy, rot, spoil, taint
11 *syn* CHANGE 1, alter, modify, mutate, refashion, vary
12 *syn* TRANSLATE 1, put, render, transpose
13 *syn* DULL 3, blunt, disedge, obtund
14 *syn* SPIN 2, reel, swim, whirl
15 *syn* DEFECT, apostatize, desert, rat, renounce, repudiate, tergiversate, tergiverse
16 *syn* RESORT 2, apply, go, recur, refer, repair, run
17 *syn* BECOME 1, come, ‖come over, get, go, grow, run, wax
rel change (into), pass (into)

turn (on *or* upon) *vb* *syn* DEPEND (on *or* upon) 1, hang (on *or* upon), hinge (on *or* upon), ‖pend, stand (on *or* upon)

turn *n* **1** *syn* REVOLUTION 1, circuit, circulation, circumvolution, gyration, gyre, rotation, round, wheel, whirl
2 an often sudden change in course or trend <his health took a *turn* for the better>
syn bend, deflection, deviation, double, shift, tack, yaw
rel course, drift, trend
3 *syn* REVERSAL 1, about-face, changeabout, reverse, reversement, reversion, right-about, turnabout, turning, volte-face
4 a point at which a change of course takes place <hidden by a *turn* in the road>
syn angle, bend, bow, flection, flexure, turning
rel curve, twist; corner
5 *syn* WALK 1, constitutional, ramble, saunter, stroll
6 *syn* DRIVE 1, ride, spin
7 *syn* SPELL 1, bout, go, shift, stint, time, tour, trick
8 *syn* CHANGE 1, alteration, modification, mutation, variation
9 *syn* GIFT 2, aptness, bent, bump, faculty, flair, genius, head, knack, talent
rel bias, disposition, predisposition
10 an unusual, unexpected, or special interpretation or construction <gave a new *turn* to the old joke>
syn twist
rel construction, interpretation; device, gimmick, trick
11 *syn* ATTACK 3, access, fit, seizure, spell, throe

turnabout *n* **1** *syn* REVERSAL 1, about-face, changeabout, reverse, reversement, reversion, right-about, turn, turning, volte-face
2 *syn* RENEGADE, apostate, defector, rat, recreant, runagate, tergiversator, turncoat
rel backslider, coward, quitter, turnback

turn back *vb* *syn* RETURN 1, react, recrudesce, recur, revert

turncoat *n* *syn* RENEGADE, apostate, defector, rat, recreant, runagate, tergiversator, turnabout
rel deserter, straggler; betrayer, quisler, quisling, traitor; spy

---

turn down *vb* ***syn*** DECLINE 4, disapprove, dismiss, refuse, reject, reprobate, repudiate, spurn

turned on *adj* ***syn*** DRUGGED, doped, high, hopped-up, spaced-out, stoned, tripped out, ‖wiped out, zonked

turn in *vb* ***syn*** RETIRE 4, bed, ‖flop, pile (in), roll in
ant turn out

turning *n* **1** ***syn*** TURN 4, angle, bend, bow, flection, flexure
2 ***syn*** DEVIATION 1, aberration, deflection, departure, divergence, diversion
rel detour
3 ***syn*** REVERSAL 1, about-face, changeabout, reverse, reversement, reversion, right-about, turn, turnabout, volte-face

turning point *n* ***syn*** JUNCTURE 2, contingency, crisis, crossroad(s), emergency, exigency, pass, pinch, strait, zero hour
rel climax, culmination, peak
idiom moment of truth

turnip *n* ***syn*** DUNCE, blockhead, boob, chump, dolt, dope, dumbbell, idiot, moron, nitwit

turn off *vb* **1** ***syn*** DISMISS 3, ax, boot (out), bounce, ‖can, cashier, discharge, drop, kick out, terminate
2 ***syn*** HANG 2, gibbet, noose, scrag, string (up)

turn out *vb* **1** ***syn*** FURNISH 1, accouter, appoint, arm, equip, fit out, gear, outfit, rig
rel deck, dress (out)
2 ***syn*** BEAR 9, produce, yield
3 ***syn*** ROLL OUT, arise, get up, pile (out), rise, rise and shine, uprise

turnout *n* **1** ***syn*** COSTUME, dress, getup, guise, outfit, rig, setout
2 ***syn*** OUTPUT, outturn, product, production, yield

turn over *vb* **1** ***syn*** OVERTURN 1, knock over, overset, overthrow, tip (over), topple, upset
2 ***syn*** PLOW, break, plow up, turn
3 ***syn*** PONDER 2, ‖chaw, deliberate, meditate, mull (over), muse, revolve, roll, ruminate
idiom turn over in one's mind
4 ***syn*** GIVE 3, deliver, feed, find, furnish, hand, hand over, provide, supply, transfer
rel assign, confer, consign, convey, delegate, relegate; give up, relinquish, ‖turn up
idiom come across with, put into the hands of
con get back, reclaim, recover, regain, retrieve, take back
5 ***syn*** COMMIT 1, commend, confide, consign, entrust, hand over, relegate

turnover *n* ***syn*** SHAKE-UP, overturn, reorganization, revolution

turn up *vb* **1** ***syn*** FIND 1, catch, descry, detect, encounter, espy, hit (on *or* upon), meet (with), spot
rel see; uncover, unearth; track (down)
idiom come across
‖**2** ***syn*** RELINQUISH, abandon, cede, give up, hand over, leave, resign, surrender, waive, yield
3 to arrive when or where expected <*turned up* for dinner promptly at seven o'clock>
syn show, show up
rel appear, arrive, come, materialize; blow in, pop (in), punch in, roll (in), weigh in
idiom make one's appearance, put in an appearance
4 ***syn*** COME 1, arrive, ‖blow in, get, get in, reach, show, show up

turtledove *n* ***syn*** SWEETHEART 1, beloved, darling, dear, flame, heartthrob, honey, honeybunch, sweet, sweetling

tussle *vb* ***syn*** WRESTLE, grapple, scuffle, ‖wraxle
rel scrap, skirmish, spar; hassle
idiom get into a tussle

tutelage *n* ***syn*** EDUCATION 1, instruction, schooling, teaching, training, tuition

twaddle *n* ***syn*** NONSENSE 2, balderdash, blather, bosh, claptrap, drivel, hot air, malarkey, poppycock, tommyrot
rel gabble; wish-wash

twaddle *vb* **1** ***syn*** BABBLE 2, blabber, blather, drivel, drool, gabble, prate, prattle, ‖waffle
2 ***syn*** CHAT 1, babble, chatter, clack, dither, gabble, jaw, prattle, run on, yak

twang *n* ***syn*** HINT 2, dash, intimation, shade, streak, suspicion, tinge, touch, trace, whiff

‖**twat** *n* ***syn*** BUTTOCKS, *ass, bottom, ‖butt, ‖can, fanny, heinie (*or* hiney), *prat, tail, ‖tokus

tweedle *vb* ***syn*** CHIRP, cheep, chip, chipper, ‖chirm, chirrup, chitter, peep, tweet, twitter

tween *prep* ***syn*** BETWEEN 2, ‖atween, ‖atwixt, ‖betwixt, in between, twixt

tweet *vb* ***syn*** CHIRP, cheep, chip, chipper, ‖chirm, chirrup, chitter, peep, tweedle, twitter

twerp *n* a usually young or insignificant upstart who meddles beyond his competence or concern <ignored the protests of that insolent *twerp*>
syn pup, puppy, sprat, squirt, ‖squit
rel upstart; ‖squib; fool, jerk, ‖twit; brat
idiom small-time big shot

twice–told *adj* ***syn*** TRITE, cliché, clichéd, hackneyed, old hat, stale, stereotyped, stereotypical, timeworn, worn-out

twiddle *vb* ***syn*** FIDDLE 1, fidget, play, trifle
rel finger, manipulate, palpate; monkey (with), toy (with)
idiom twiddle around with

twiddle *vb* ***syn*** CHAT 1, babble, cackle, chatter, gab, ‖gas, jaw, prattle, rattle, yak

twig *vb* **1** ***syn*** SEE 1, descry, discern, distinguish, espy, mark, note, notice, observe, perceive
2 ***syn*** APPREHEND 1, accept, catch, comprehend, ‖dig, grasp, see, take, take in, understand

‖**twig** *n* ***syn*** FASHION 3, craze, cry, dernier cri, fad, furore, mode, rage, style, vogue

twiggy *adj* ***syn*** THIN 1, attenuate, reedy, slender, slight, slim, squinny, stalky, tenuous

twilight *n* **1** ***syn*** EVENING 1, ‖dimmet, ‖dimps, ‖dimpsy, dusk, ‖dusk dark, eventide, gloaming, nightfall, owl-light
rel afterglow, afterlight

---

syn synonym(s) ***rel*** related word(s)
idiom idiomatic equivalent(s) ***con*** contrasted word(s)
ant antonym(s) * vulgar
‖ use limited; if in doubt, see a dictionary
The first word in a synonym list when printed in SMALL CAPITALS shows where there is more information about the group. For a more efficient use of this book see Explanatory Notes.

2 ***syn*** EVENING 2, sunset
rel decline; end

twin *adj* made up of two very closely matched or identical aspects, elements, individuals, or parts <the *twin* threats of inflation and recession>
syn double, dual, paired
rel bifold, binary, twofold; identical, matched, matching; like, similar
con independent, separate; dissimilar, unlike

twin *n* ***syn*** MATE 5, companion, coordinate, double, duplicate, fellow, match, reciprocal

twine *vb* ***syn*** WIND 2, coil, corkscrew, curl, entwine, spiral, twist, wreathe
rel interweave; undulate; enmesh, entangle, tangle

twinge *n* ***syn*** PAIN 1, ache, ‖misery, pang, stitch, throe

twinkle *vb* **1** ***syn*** BLINK 2, flash, flicker
rel illuminate, light, light up; shine
2 ***syn*** FLASH 1, coruscate, gleam, glimmer, glint, glisten, glitter, scintillate, shimmer, sparkle
3 ***syn*** WINK, bat, blink, nictate, nictitate

twinkle *n* **1** ***syn*** INSTANT 1, minute, moment, second, shake, split second, ‖tick, trice, twinkling, wink
2 ***syn*** FLASH 1, coruscation, gleam, glimmer, glint, glisten, glitter, scintillation, shimmer, sparkle

twinkling *n* ***syn*** INSTANT 1, minute, moment, second, shake, split second, ‖tick, trice, twinkle, wink
idiom the twinkling of an eye

twirl *vb* ***syn*** SPIN 1, gyrate, gyre, ‖pirl, pirouette, ‖purl, whirl, whirligig

twist *vb* **1** ***syn*** SPRAIN, ‖rick, turn, wrench
2 ***syn*** MISREPRESENT, belie, color, distort, falsify, garble, miscolor, misstate, pervert, warp
3 ***syn*** WIND 2, coil, corkscrew, curl, entwine, spiral, twine, wreathe
ant untwist

twist *n* ***syn*** TURN 10

twister *n* ***syn*** TORNADO, cyclone

twisting *adj* ***syn*** CROOKED 1, bending, curving, devious

twit *vb* ***syn*** RIDICULE, deride, lout, mock, quiz, rally, razz, scout, taunt
rel jive, josh, tease; chide, reproach, reprove; blame, censure, reprehend

twitch *vb* ***syn*** JERK, lug, lurch, snap, vellicate, yank
rel clutch, grasp, pluck, snatch; nip, pinch

twitter *vb* **1** ***syn*** CHIRP, cheep, chip, chipper, ‖chirm, chirrup, chitter, peep, tweedle, tweet
2 ***syn*** CHAT 1, babble, cackle, chatter, gab, ‖gas, jaw, prattle, rattle, run on
3 ***syn*** SHAKE 1, ‖didder, dither, quake, quaver, quiver, shiver, shudder, tremble, tremor

twittery *adj* ***syn*** NERVOUS, fidgety, goosey, high-strung, jittery, jumpy, nervy, spooky, unrestful
rel flustered; twittering
idiom all atwitter, all fluttery, all of a twitter

twitty *adj* ***syn*** IRRITABLE, peevish, pettish, petulant, raspish, raspy, snappish, snappy, waspish, waspy

twixt *prep* ***syn*** BETWEEN 2, ‖atween, ‖atwixt, ‖betwixt, in between, tween

twofold *adj* **1** having two parts, elements, or aspects <the problem is *twofold:* to find gasoline and to be able to pay for it>
syn bifold, binary, double, double-barreled, dual, dualistic, duple, duplex
rel dyadic; paired, twin
con distinct, separate
2 being twice as large, as great, or as many <a *twofold* increase in enrollment>
syn double, double-barreled
idiom twice over

two-handed *adj* **1** designed for or requiring the use of both hands <a *two-handed* sword>
syn bimanual
2 having or being efficient with two hands <*two-handed* tennis players are rare>
syn ambidextrous, bimanual

twosome *n* ***syn*** COUPLE, brace, doublet, duo, dyad, pair

two-time *vb* ***syn*** DECEIVE, beguile, bluff, delude, double-cross, humbug, illude, juggle, mislead, take in

two-wheeler *n* ***syn*** BICYCLE, bike, cycle, velocipede

tycoon *n* ***syn*** MAGNATE, baron, czar, king, merchant prince, mogul, prince

tyke *n* ***syn*** DOG 1, bowwow, canine, hound, ‖pooch

type *n* a number of individuals thought of as a group because of a common quality or qualities <political radicals of whatever *type*>
syn breed, cast, character, class, cut, description, feather, ilk, kidney, kind, lot, mold, nature, order, persuasion, sort, species, stamp, stripe, variety, way
rel blazon, brand, form; sample, specimen; category, group, rubric

typhoon *n* ***syn*** HURRICANE, tropical cyclone, tropical storm, ‖willy-willy

typic *adj* ***syn*** GENERAL 1, common, commonplace, natural, normal, prevalent, regular, run-of-the-mill, typical, usual
rel average, ordinary

typical *adj* **1** constituting or having the nature of a type <a *typical* instance of guilt by association>
syn archetypal, classic, classical, exemplary, ideal, model, paradigmatic, prototypal, prototypical, quintessential, representative
rel characteristic; emblematic, symbolic; absolute, consummate, perfect
con uncharacteristic; unusual
ant atypical, untypical
2 ***syn*** GENERAL 1, common, commonplace, matter-of-course, natural, normal, prevalent, regular, typic, usual
rel old hat, unexceptional; collective, quintessential, representative; characteristic, specific
idiom being the rule and not the exception
con distinctive; exceptional, extraordinary, unusual; abnormal
ant atypical, untypical

typification *n* ***syn*** ALLEGORY 1, figuration, symbolism, symbolization

---

syn synonym(s) — ***rel*** related word(s)
idiom idiomatic equivalent(s) — ***con*** contrasted word(s)
ant antonym(s) — * vulgar
‖ use limited; if in doubt, see a dictionary
The first word in a synonym list when printed in SMALL CAPITALS shows where there is more information about the group. For a more efficient use of this book see Explanatory Notes.

typify *vb* **1** ***syn*** REPRESENT 2, body (forth), emblematize, embody, epitomize, exemplify, illustrate, mirror, personify, symbolize
2 ***syn*** EPITOMIZE 2, exemplify
rel model

tyrannical *adj* ***syn*** ABSOLUTE 4, arbitrary, autarchic, autocratic, despotic, monocratic, tyrannous
rel brutal, harsh, oppressive; roughshod

tyrannize *vb* to exercise arbitrary power over often with unjust and oppressive severity <a country *tyrannized* by a dictator and his secret police>
syn despotize
rel dictate, dominate, domineer, overlord; crush, oppress, trample; shackle; terrorize

tyrannous *adj* ***syn*** ABSOLUTE 4, arbitrary, autarchic, autocratic, despotic, monocratic, tyrannical
rel lordly; fascistic, totalitarian

tyranny *n* absolute government in which unlimited power is vested in a single usually severe and oppressive ruler <the *tyranny* of Hitler>
syn autocracy, despotism, dictatorship, totalitarianism
rel monocracy; absolutism, authoritarianism, fascism; domination, oppression, totality; terrorism
idiom iron heel (*or* boot)
con democracy; freedom; anarchy

tyrant *n* a ruler who exercises absolute power oppressively and brutally <Hitler and Stalin as twentieth-century *tyrants*>
syn despot, dictator, duce, oppressor, strong man
rel autocrat, totalitarian
idiom man on horseback

tyro *n* **1** ***syn*** AMATEUR 2, abecedarian, dabbler, dilettante, nonprofessional, smatterer, uninitiate
2 ***syn*** NOVICE, apprentice, beginner, colt, freshman, neophyte, newcomer, novitiate, rookie, tenderfoot

---

syn synonym(s) — ***rel*** related word(s)
idiom idiomatic equivalent(s) — ***con*** contrasted word(s)
ant antonym(s) — * vulgar
‖ use limited; if in doubt, see a dictionary
The first word in a synonym list when printed in SMALL CAPITALS shows where there is more information about the group. For a more efficient use of this book see Explanatory Notes.

U

uberrima fides *n syn* GOOD FAITH, bona fides, sincereness, sincerity
ubiquitous *adj syn* OMNIPRESENT, allover, universal
ugly *adj* **1** *syn* GRAVE 3, dangerous, fell, grievous, major, serious
2 unpleasing to the sight <an *ugly* decaying neighborhood>
syn hideous, ill-favored, ill-looking, unbeautiful, uncomely, unsightly
rel homely, plain; bizarre, grotesque; repelling, repugnant, repulsive; unattractive, uninviting, unpleasing, unprepossessing
idiom homely as a mud (*or* hedge) fence, not much to look at, short on looks
con comely, fair, good-looking, handsome, lovely, pretty; attractive, prepossessing
ant beautiful
3 *syn* BASE 3, despicable, ignoble, low, low-down, servile, sordid, ugly, vile, wretched
4 *syn* TROUBLESOME, mean, pesky, troublous, vexatious, wicked
5 *syn* SULLEN, ‖chuffy, crabbed, dour, gloomy, glum, morose, saturnine, sulky, surly
ukase *n syn* EDICT 1, decree, directive, ruling
ulterior *adj* lying behind what is manifest or avowed <an *ulterior* motive>
syn buried, concealed, covert, guarded, hidden, obscured, privy, shrouded
rel ambiguous, cryptic, dark, enigmatic, equivocal, obscure
idiom hidden under the rug, kept behind a screen, under cover, under wraps
con clear, open, overt, plain, straightforward; explicit, expressed
ultimate *adj* **1** *syn* LAST, closing, concluding, eventual, final, hindmost, lag, latest, latter, terminal
2 *syn* SUPREME, incomparable, preeminent, surpassing, towering, transcendent, unequalable, unmatchable, unsurpassable
3 being so fundamental as to stand at the extreme limit of the actually or conceivably knowable <*ultimate* realities>
syn absolute, categorical
rel empyreal, empyrean, sublime, transcendental; exalted, grand, lofty
ultimate *n syn* APOTHEOSIS 1, epitome, last word, quintessence
ultimate *vb syn* CLOSE 3, complete, conclude, consummate, determine, end, finish, terminate, wind up, wrap up
ultimately *adv syn* YET 2, eventually, finally, someday, sometime, somewhere, sooner or later
ultra *adj* **1** *syn* EXTREME 3, extremist, fanatic, rabid, radical, revolutional, revolutionary, revolutionist, ultraist
2 *syn* OUTLANDISH 3, far-out, kinky, outré
ultraconservative *n syn* REACTIONARY, blimp, Bourbon, diehard, reactionarist, reactionist, royalist, white
ultrafashionable *adj syn* STYLISH, a la mode, chic, exclusive, in, modish, swank, tonish, tony, ‖trendy
ultraist *n syn* RADICAL, extremist, revolutionary, revolutionist
ultraist *adj syn* EXTREME 3, extremist, fanatic, rabid, radical, revolutional, revolutionary, revolutionist, ultra
ultramarine *adj syn* OVERSEAS, oversea, transmarine
ululate *vb syn* HOWL 1, bay, quest, wail
rel bewail, lament
umbra *n* **1** *syn* APPARITION, eidolon, ghost, ‖haunt, phantasm, phantom, revenant, shade, shadow, ‖spook
2 *syn* SHADE 1, adumbration, penumbra, shadow, umbrage
umbrage *n* **1** *syn* SHADE 1, adumbration, penumbra, shadow, umbra
2 *syn* FOLIAGE, leafage, verdure
3 *syn* OFFENSE 2, dudgeon, huff, miff, pique, resentment, ‖snuff
rel annoyance, irking, vexation; exasperation, irritation, nettling, provoking; fury, ire, rage, wrath
umbrage *vb* **1** *syn* SHADE, inumbrate, screen, shadow
2 *syn* ANGER 1, enrage, incense, infuriate, ire, mad, madden, steam up
umbrageous *adj syn* SHADY 1, shaded, shadow, shadowed, shadowy, umbrous
umbrous *adj syn* SHADY 1, shaded, shadow, shadowed, shadowy, umbrageous
umpire *n syn* JUDGE 1, arbiter, arbitrator, referee
umpire *vb syn* JUDGE 1, adjudge, adjudicate, arbitrate, referee
unabashed *adj syn* SHAMELESS, arrant, barefaced, blatant, brassy, brazen, brazenfaced, impudent, overbold, unblushing
ant abashed
unabbreviated *adj syn* UNABRIDGED, complete, uncondensed, uncut, undocked, whole-length
ant abbreviated
unabridged *adj* not shortened by omission of parts (as words) <published an *unabridged* edition of Shakespeare's plays>
syn complete, unabbreviated, uncondensed, uncut, undocked, whole-length
rel entire, intact, whole
con condensed, cropped, curtailed, cut, incompleted, shortened, trimmed
ant abridged
unacceptable *adj syn* OBJECTIONABLE, exceptionable, ill-favored, inadmissible, undesirable, unwanted, unwelcome

---

syn synonym(s) — *rel* related word(s)
idiom idiomatic equivalent(s) — *con* contrasted word(s)
ant antonym(s) — * vulgar
‖ use limited; if in doubt, see a dictionary
The first word in a synonym list when printed in SMALL CAPITALS shows where there is more information about the group. For a more efficient use of this book see Explanatory Notes.

ant acceptable

unaccompanied *adj syn* ALONE 1, apart, detached, isolate, isolated, removed
ant accompanied, companioned

unaccomplished *adj syn* AMATEURISH, dabbling, dilettante, dilettantish, dilettantist, jackleg, unfinished, ungifted, unskilled
ant accomplished, skilled

unaccountable *adj* 1 *syn* INEXPLICABLE, inexplainable, unexplainable
ant accountable
2 *syn* MYSTERIOUS, arcane, cabalistic, impenetrable, inscrutable, mysterial, mystic, numinous, unguessed, unknowable

unaccustomed *adj syn* UNFAMILIAR 1, new, strange
ant accustomed, familiar

unacquaintance *n syn* IGNORANCE 2, innocence, inscience, nescience, unacquaintedness, unawareness, unfamiliarity, unknowingness
ant acquaintance

unacquainted *adj syn* IGNORANT 2, incognizant, inconversant, oblivious, unaware, unfamiliar, uninformed, uninstructed, unknowing, unwitting
ant acquainted

unacquaintedness *n syn* IGNORANCE 2, innocence, inscience, nescience, unacquaintance, unawareness, unfamiliarity, unknowingness
ant acquaintance

unacquired *adj syn* INNATE 1, congenital, connate, connatural, inborn, indigenous, inherited, native, natural
ant acquired

unadorned *adj syn* PLAIN 1, unbeautified, undecorated, unelaborate, unembellished, unembroidered, ungarnished, unornamented, unostentatious, unpretentious
ant adorned

unadulterated *adj* 1 *syn* PURE 2, absolute, perfect, sheer, simple, unalloyed, undiluted, unmitigated, unmixed, unqualified
2 *syn* STRAIGHT 3, neat, plain, pure, undiluted, unmixed
ant adulterated

unadvisable *adj syn* INADVISABLE, ill-advised, impolitic, imprudent, inexpedient, unexpedient
ant advisable

unadvised *adj syn* RASH 1, brash, hasty, hotheaded, ill-advised, incautious, inconsiderate, reckless, thoughtless, unconsidered
ant advised, thought-out

unaffable *adj syn* UNDEMONSTRATIVE, aseptic, restrained, retiring, shrinking, unexpansive, withdrawn
ant affable

unaffected *adj syn* NATURAL 5, artless, ingenuous, naive, simple, unartificial, unschooled, unsophisticated, unstudied, untutored
ant affected, artificial

unafraid *adj syn* BRAVE 1, audacious, bold, courageous, dauntless, fearless, intrepid, undaunted, valiant, valorous
rel composed, cool, imperturbable; assured, confident, sure
con apprehensive, fearful
ant afraid

unaimed *adj syn* RANDOM, aimless, designless, desultory, haphazard, hit-or-miss, indiscriminate, purposeless, unconsidered, unplanned

unalert *adj syn* INCAUTIOUS 1, unguarded, unvigilant, unwary, unwatchful
ant alert

unalike *adj syn* DIFFERENT 1, disparate, dissimilar, distant, divergent, diverse, unequal, unlike, unsimilar, various
ant alike

unalloyed *adj syn* PURE 2, absolute, perfect, sheer, simple, unadulterated, undiluted, unmitigated, unmixed, unqualified

unalluring *adj syn* PLAIN 5, homely, unattractive, unbeauteous, unbeautiful, uncomely, unhandsome, unpretty
ant alluring, attractive

unalterable *adj syn* INFLEXIBLE 3, constant, fixed, immovable, immutable, inalterable, invariable, unchangeable, unmodifiable, unmovable
ant alterable

unambiguous *adj* 1 *syn* CLEAR 4, clear-cut, crystal, lucid, luminous, pellucid, translucent, transparent, transpicuous, unblurred
ant ambiguous, obscure
2 *syn* EXPLICIT, categorical, clean-cut, clear-cut, definite, definitive, express, specific
ant ambiguous
3 *syn* CLEAR 5, apparent, distinct, evident, manifest, obvious, palpable, patent, plain, straightforward

unanimated *adj syn* DEAD 1, asleep, cold, deceased, defunct, departed, exanimate, extinct, inanimate, late

unanimous *adj* being of one mind <they were *unanimous* in their determination to win>
syn consentaneous, consentient, solid
rel agreed, agreeing, concordant, concurrent, harmonious
idiom of one accord, of one (*or* the same) mind, with one voice
con differing, disagreed, disagreeing, discordant, inharmonious

unanticipatedly *adv syn* UNAWARES, aback, short, sudden, suddenly, unaware, unawaredly, unexpectedly

unapparent *adj syn* IMPERCEPTIBLE, impalpable, imponderable, inappreciable, indiscernible, insensible, intangible, unappreciable, unobservable, unperceivable
ant apparent, detectable

unappeasable *adj* 1 *syn* INSATIABLE, insatiate, quenchless, unquenchable, unsatiate, unsatisfiable
ant appeasable
2 *syn* GRIM 3, implacable, ironfisted, merciless, mortal, relentless, ruthless, unflinching, unrelenting, unyielding
ant appeasable, placable

---

syn synonym(s) — *rel* related word(s)
idiom idiomatic equivalent(s) — *con* contrasted word(s)
ant antonym(s) — * vulgar
|| use limited; if in doubt, see a dictionary
The first word in a synonym list when printed in SMALL CAPITALS shows where there is more information about the group. For a more efficient use of this book see Explanatory Notes.

unappetizing *adj* ***syn*** UNPALATABLE 1, distasteful, flat, flavorless, ill-flavored, insipid, savorless, tasteless, unsavory
ant appetizing

unappreciable *adj* ***syn*** IMPERCEPTIBLE, impalpable, imponderable, inappreciable, indiscernible, insensible, intangible, unapparent, unobservable, unperceivable
ant appreciable

unappreciated *adj* ***syn*** THANKLESS 2, ungrateful, unthankful
ant appreciated

unappreciative *adj* ***syn*** THANKLESS 1, ungrateful, unthankful
ant appreciative

unapproachable *adj* **1** ***syn*** INACCESSIBLE, inapproachable, unattainable, un-come-at-able, ungetatable, unobtainable, unreachable
ant approachable, attainable
2 ***syn*** UNSOCIABLE, aloof, distant, insociable, offish, reserved, standoffish, unbending, uncommunicative, withdrawn
ant accessible, approachable

unapt *adj* **1** ***syn*** IMPROPER 1, inappropriate, inapt, malapropos, unbefitting, undue, unseasonable, unseemly, unsuitable, untimely
2 ***syn*** UNSKILLFUL 1, inadept, inapt, inept, inexpert, undexterous, unfacile, unhandy, unproficient
ant apt

unarm *vb* ***syn*** DISARM 2, unsteel, win (over)

unartful *adj* ***syn*** NATURAL 5, artless, ingenuous, naive, simple, unaffected, unartificial, unschooled, unsophisticated, unstudied
ant artful

unarticulate *adj* ***syn*** DUMB 1, inarticulate, mute, silent, speechless, voiceless
ant articulate

unartificial *adj* ***syn*** NATURAL 5, artless, inartificial, ingenuous, naive, simple, unaffected, unschooled, unsophisticated, unstudied
ant affected, artificial

unasked *adj* **1** not asked or invited <annoyed by his *unasked* advice>
syn unbidden, uninvited, unrequested, unsought
rel arrogant, impudent, overbearing, presumptuous; spontaneous, voluntary; unacceptable, unwanted, unwelcome
con desired, invited, sought, wanted; acceptable, welcome
ant asked
2 ***syn*** SUPEREROGATORY, gratuitous, supererogant, supererogative, uncalled-for, wanton

unassailable *adj* ***syn*** INVINCIBLE 1, impregnable, inconquerable, indomitable, inexpugnable, invulnerable, unbeatable, unconquerable, undefeatable
rel stalwart, stout, strong, sturdy, tenacious, tough
ant assailable

unassertive *adj* ***syn*** SHY 1, backward, bashful, diffident, modest, rabbity, retiring, self-effacing, timid, unassured
ant aggressive, assertive

unassorted *adj* ***syn*** MISCELLANEOUS, assorted, heterogeneous, indiscriminate, mixed, motley, multifarious, promiscuous, unsorted, varied

unassuming *adj* ***syn*** HUMBLE 1, lowly, meek, modest
ant assuming, presumptuous

unassured *adj* **1** ***syn*** UNSAFE, undependable, unreliable, untrustworthy
2 ***syn*** SHY 1, backward, bashful, diffident, modest, rabbity, retiring, self-effacing, timid, unassertive
ant assured
3 ***syn*** INSECURE 1, unconfident, unsure

unattainable *adj* **1** ***syn*** INACCESSIBLE, inapproachable, unapproachable, un-come-at-able, ungetatable, unobtainable, unreachable
ant attainable
2 ***syn*** IMPOSSIBLE 1, impracticable, impractical, infeasible, irrealizable, unfeasible, unrealizable, unworkable

unattractive *adj* ***syn*** PLAIN 5, homely, unalluring, unbeauteous, unbeautiful, uncomely, unhandsome, unpretty
ant alluring, attractive

unauthentic *adj* ***syn*** SPURIOUS 3, apocryphal, bastard, ungenuine
ant authentic, genuine

unavailable *adj* ***syn*** FUTILE, abortive, bootless, fruitless, ineffective, ineffectual, unavailing, unproductive, useless, vain

unavailing *adj* ***syn*** FUTILE, abortive, bootless, fruitless, ineffective, ineffectual, unavailable, unproductive, useless, vain

unavoidable *adj* ***syn*** INEVITABLE, certain, ineluctable, ineludible, inescapable, inevasible, necessary, returnless, unescapable, unevadable
ant avoidable

unavoidably *adv* ***syn*** WILLY-NILLY, helplessly, inescapably, inevitably, perforce, whether or no

unaware *adv* ***syn*** UNAWARES, aback, short, sudden, suddenly, unanticipatedly, unawaredly, unexpectedly

unaware *adj* ***syn*** IGNORANT 2, incognizant, inconversant, oblivious, unacquainted, unfamiliar, uninformed, uninstructed, unknowing, unwitting
ant aware, conscious

unawaredly *adv* ***syn*** UNAWARES, aback, short, sudden, suddenly, unanticipatedly, unaware, unexpectedly

unawareness *n* ***syn*** IGNORANCE 2, innocence, inscience, nescience, unacquaintance, unacquaintedness, unfamiliarity, unknowingness
ant awareness, consciousness

unawares *adv* without warning <caught *unawares* by company>
syn aback, short, sudden, suddenly, unanticipatedly, unaware, unawaredly, unexpectedly
rel unprepared, unready
idiom like a bolt from the blue, off base, out of a clear sky, out of the blue

unbalance *vb* ***syn*** MADDEN 1, craze, derange, distract, frenzy, unhinge

---

syn synonym(s) ***rel*** related word(s)
idiom idiomatic equivalent(s) ***con*** contrasted word(s)
ant antonym(s) * vulgar
|| use limited; if in doubt, see a dictionary
The first word in a synonym list when printed in SMALL CAPITALS shows where there is more information about the group. For a more efficient use of this book see Explanatory Notes.

unbalance *n* ***syn*** INSANITY 1, aberration, alienation, derangement, distraction, insaneness, lunacy, madness, psychopathy
rel disorientation, instability

unbalanced *adj* **1** ***syn*** LOPSIDED, asymmetric, disproportionate, irregular, nonsymmetrical, off-balance, overbalanced, unequal, uneven, unsymmetrical
ant balanced
2 ***syn*** INSANE 1, ‖batty, crazed, daft, demented, deranged, mad, non compos mentis, unsound, wacky

unbearable *adj* ***syn*** INSUFFERABLE, insupportable, intolerable, unbrookable, unendurable, unsufferable, unsupportable
ant bearable, supportable

unbearing *adj* ***syn*** BARREN 2, hardscrabble, infertile, unfertile, unproductive

unbeatable *adj* ***syn*** INVINCIBLE 1, impregnable, inconquerable, indomitable, inexpugnable, invulnerable, unassailable, unconquerable, undefeatable
ant beatable, defeatable

unbeauteous *adj* ***syn*** PLAIN 5, homely, unalluring, unattractive, unbeautiful, uncomely, unhandsome, unpretty
ant beauteous

unbeautified *adj* ***syn*** PLAIN 1, homely, simple, unadorned, undecorated, unembellished, unembroidered, ungarnished, unornamented, unostentatious
ant beautified, embellished

unbeautiful *adj* **1** ***syn*** PLAIN 5, homely, unalluring, unattractive, unbeauteous, uncomely, unhandsome, unpretty
ant beautiful
2 ***syn*** UGLY 2, hideous, ill-favored, ill-looking, uncomely, unsightly
ant beautiful

unbecoming *adj* **1** ***syn*** INDECOROUS, improper, indecent, indelicate, malodorous, rough, undecorous, ungodly, unseemly, untoward
rel awkward, clumsy, gauche, inept, maladroit
ant becoming, seemly
2 ***syn*** IMPROPER 1, inappropriate, inapt, inept, malapropos, unbefitting, undue, unseasonable, unsuitable, untimely

unbecomingness *n* ***syn*** IMPROPRIETY 1, incorrectness, indecorousness, indecorum, inelegance, unmeetness, unseemliness, untowardness
ant becomingness, seemliness

unbefitting *adj* ***syn*** IMPROPER 1, inappropriate, inapt, inept, malapropos, unbecoming, uncomely, undue, unseasonable, unsuitable
ant apropos, befitting

unbegotten *adj* ***syn*** SELF-EXISTENT, increate, self-existing, uncaused, uncreated, unoriginated

---

syn synonym(s) ***rel*** related word(s)
idiom idiomatic equivalent(s) ***con*** contrasted word(s)
ant antonym(s) * vulgar
‖ use limited; if in doubt, see a dictionary
The first word in a synonym list when printed in SMALL CAPITALS shows where there is more information about the group. For a more efficient use of this book see Explanatory Notes.

unbelief *n* the attitude or state of mind of one who does not believe <after so much deception, so many lies, she could offer nothing but *unbelief* to his words>
syn disbelief, incredulity, unbelievingness, unfaith
rel doubt, dubiety, dubiosity, skepticism, uncertainty; distrust, mistrust, suspicion; apprehension, misgiving, qualm
con assurance, certitude, security, trust; dependence, reliance, stock, store
ant belief

unbelievable *adj* **1** ***syn*** INCREDIBLE 1, incogitable, inconceivable, insupposable, unimaginable, unthinkable
ant believable, credible
2 ***syn*** IMPLAUSIBLE, flimsy, improbable, inconceivable, incredible, thick, thin, unconvincing, unsubstantial, weak
ant believable, credible

unbelieve *vb* ***syn*** DISBELIEVE, discredit
ant believe, credit

unbeliever *n* ***syn*** SKEPTIC, doubter, doubting Thomas, headshaker, Pyrrhonian, Pyrrhonist, zetetic
ant believer

unbelieving *adj* ***syn*** INCREDULOUS, aporetic, disbelieving, questioning, quizzical, show-me, skeptical
ant believing

unbelievingness *n* ***syn*** UNBELIEF, disbelief, incredulity, unfaith

unbend *vb* **1** ***syn*** RELAX 2, ease off, loosen up, unlax, unwind
2 ***syn*** REST 2, relax, rest up, unlax

unbendable *adj* ***syn*** INFLEXIBLE 2, brassbound, inexorable, obdurate, relentless, rigid, single-minded, unbending, uncompromising, unyielding
ant bendable

unbending *adj* **1** ***syn*** STIFF 1, immalleable, impliable, incompliant, inelastic, inflexible, rigid, unflexible, unyielding
ant bendable
2 ***syn*** INFLEXIBLE 2, brassbound, inexorable, obdurate, relentless, rigid, single-minded, uncompromising, unswayable, unyielding
3 ***syn*** UNSOCIABLE, aloof, distant, insociable, offish, reserved, standoffish, unapproachable, uncommunicative, withdrawn

unbiased *adj* ***syn*** FAIR 4, dispassionate, equal, equitable, impartial, just, nondiscriminatory, objective, uncolored, unprejudiced
rel aloof, uninterested
ant biased

unbidden *adj* ***syn*** UNASKED, uninvited, unrequested, unsought

unbind *vb* **1** ***syn*** LOOSE 3, disengage, undo, unfasten, unfix, unloose, unloosen
ant bind
2 ***syn*** FREE, discharge, emancipate, liberate, loose, loosen, manumit, release, unchain, unshackle
ant bind

unblamable *adj* ***syn*** GOOD 11, blameless, exemplary, guiltless, inculpable, innocent, irreprehensible, pure, righteous, virtuous
ant blamable, blameworthy

unblemished *adj* **1** ***syn*** WHOLE 1, flawless, intact, perfect, sound, undamaged, unhurt, unimpaired, uninjured, unmarred

ant blemished, flawed
2 ***syn*** CHASTE, clean, decent, immaculate, modest, pure, spotless, stainless, undefiled, unsullied

unblenched *adj* ***syn*** BRAVE 1, audacious, bold, courageous, dauntless, fearless, intrepid, undaunted, valiant, valorous

unblenching *adj* ***syn*** BRAVE 1, audacious, bold, courageous, dauntless, fearless, intrepid, undaunted, valiant, valorous

unblock *vb* ***syn*** OPEN 1, ope, unclose, undo, unshut, unstop
ant block

unblunted *adj* ***syn*** SHARP 1, honed, keen, razor-sharp, whetted
ant blunt, blunted

unblurred *adj* ***syn*** CLEAR 4, clear-cut, crystal, lucid, luminous, pellucid, translucent, transparent, transpicuous, unambiguous
ant blurred

unblushing *adj* ***syn*** SHAMELESS, arrant, barefaced, blatant, brassy, brazen, brazenfaced, impudent, overbold, unabashed

unbodied *adj* ***syn*** IMMATERIAL 1, bodiless, discarnate, disembodied, incorporeal, insubstantial, metaphysical, nonmaterial, nonphysical, unembodied
ant bodied, incarnate

unbookish *adj* ***syn*** UNSCHOLARLY, inerudite, unlearned, unstudious
ant bookish

unbosom *vb* ***syn*** REVEAL 1, betray, disclose, discover, divulge, tell, unclose, uncover, uncurtain, unveil

unbounded *adj* ***syn*** LIMITLESS, boundless, endless, immeasurable, indefinite, infinite, measureless, unlimited, unmeasured
ant bounded, limited

unbrace *vb* ***syn*** WEAKEN 1, attenuate, blunt, cripple, debilitate, disable, enfeeble, sap, undermine, unstrengthen
ant brace, reinforce

unbroken *adj* ***syn*** WHOLE 1, entire, intact, perfect, sound, undamaged, unhurt, unimpaired, uninjured, unmarred
ant broken

unbrookable *adj* ***syn*** INSUFFERABLE, insupportable, intolerable, unbearable, unendurable, unsufferable, unsupportable

unbuild *vb* ***syn*** DESTROY 1, decimate, demolish, raze, ruin, undo, unframe, unmake, wrack, wreck
ant build

unburden *vb* ***syn*** RID, clear, lose, shake (off), throw off
rel discharge, disencumber, unload
con encumber, lade, load, saddle, tax, weight
ant burden

unbury *vb* ***syn*** EXHUME, disinhume, disinter, exhumate, uncharnel
ant bury

uncalled–for *adj* **1** ***syn*** UNNECESSARY, inessential, needless, unessential, unneeded, unneedful, unrequired
ant required
2 ***syn*** SUPEREROGATORY, gratuitous, supererogant, supererogative, unasked, wanton
3 ***syn*** BASELESS, bottomless, foundationless, gratuitous, groundless, unfounded, ungrounded, unwarranted
rel absurd, foolish, preposterous, silly; impertinent, intrusive, officious
ant well-founded
4 ***syn*** RUDE 6, discourteous, disgracious, disrespectful, ill-mannered, impertinent, impolite, incivil, uncivil, ungracious

uncandid *adj* ***syn*** DISINGENUOUS, unfrank
ant candid

uncanny *adj* **1** ***syn*** WEIRD 1, eerie, spooky, unearthly
2 ***syn*** SUPERNATURAL 2, superhuman, supernormal, superordinary, supranormal, unnatural

uncared–for *adj* ***syn*** NEGLECTED, run-down, untended
ant cared-for

uncareful *adj* ***syn*** IRRESPONSIBLE, carefree, careless, feckless, incautious, reckless, wild
ant careful

uncaring *adj* ***syn*** CARELESS 1, feckless, heedless, inadvertent, irreflective, thoughtless, unheeding, unrecking, unreflective, unthinking
ant careful

uncaused *adj* ***syn*** SELF-EXISTENT, increate, self-existing, unbegotten, uncreated, unoriginated

unceasing *adj* ***syn*** CONTINUAL, ceaseless, constant, continuous, endless, interminable, perpetual, unending, uninterrupted, unremitting

uncelebrated *adj* ***syn*** OBSCURE 5, nameless, unfamed, unheard-of, unknown, unnoted, unrenowned
ant celebrated, noted

uncelestial *adj* ***syn*** EARTHLY 1, earthy, mundane, sublunary, tellurian, telluric, terrene, terrestrial, worldly
ant celestial

unceremonious *adj* **1** ***syn*** INFORMAL 1, irregular, unofficial
ant ceremonious
2 ***syn*** SHORT 5, inconsiderate, sharp, thoughtless, ungracious

uncertain *adj* **1** not stable, consistent, or predictable <was in very *uncertain* health>
syn capricious, chancy, erratic, fluctuant, iffy, incalculable, unpredictable, whimsical; *compare* INCONSTANT 1
rel questionable, undependable, unsettled; fickle, inconstant, insecure, unstable, unsure; changeable, mutable, protean, variable; unexpectable, unforeseeable
idiom in a state of uncertainty, in suspense
2 ***syn*** INCONSTANT 1, capricious, changeable, fickle, lubricious, mercurial, temperamental, ticklish, unstable, volatile
3 ***syn*** MUTABLE 2, changeable, inconstant, shifty, slippery, unstable, unsteady, variable
4 ***syn*** DOUBTFUL 1, borderline, dubious, indecisive, open, precarious, suspect, undecided, unsettled, unsure
ant certain

---

syn synonym(s)	***rel*** related word(s)
idiom idiomatic equivalent(s)	***con*** contrasted word(s)
ant antonym(s)	* vulgar

‖ use limited; if in doubt, see a dictionary
The first word in a synonym list when printed in SMALL CAPITALS shows where there is more information about the group. For a more efficient use of this book see Explanatory Notes.

5 ***syn*** MOOT, arguable, debatable, disputable, doubtful, dubious, mootable, problematic, questionable
ant certain
6 ***syn*** OBSCURE 3, ambiguous, amphibological, equivocal, sibylline, tenebrous, unclear, unexplicit, unintelligible, vague
7 ***syn*** VACILLATING 2, faltering, halting, hesitant, irresolute, shilly-shallying, tentative, vacillatory, wiggle-waggle, wobbly
idiom at a loss
ant certain, set

uncertainty *n* a feeling of unsureness about someone or something <troubled by a growing *uncertainty* about the future>
syn concern, doubt, doubtfulness, dubiety, dubiosity, dubitancy, incertitude, mistrust, query, skepticism, suspicion, uncertitude, wonder
rel anxiety, bother, disquiet, trouble, worry; agitation, distress, perturbation, uneasiness; disfaith, distrust; hesitation, reserve, salt
con assurance, certitude, confidence, conviction; complacency, content, satisfaction
ant certainty

uncertitude *n* ***syn*** UNCERTAINTY, concern, doubt, dubiety, dubiosity, incertitude, mistrust, skepticism, suspicion, wonder
ant certitude

unchain *vb* ***syn*** FREE, discharge, emancipate, liberate, loose, loosen, manumit, release, unbind, unshackle
ant chain

unchangeable *adj* ***syn*** INFLEXIBLE 3, constant, fixed, immovable, immutable, inalterable, invariable, unalterable, unmodifiable, unmovable
ant changeable

unchanging *adj* 1 ***syn*** STEADY 2, constant, equable, even, stabile, stable, unfluctuating, uniform, unvarying
2 ***syn*** SAME 3, consistent, constant, invariable, unfailing, unvarying
ant changeable, changing

uncharnel *vb* ***syn*** EXHUME, disinhume, disinter, exhumate, unbury

unchaste *adj* 1 ***syn*** IMPURE 1, dirty, immoral, unclean, uncleanly
ant chaste
2 ***syn*** FAST 7, easy, light, loose, ||riggish, wanton, whorish
ant chaste

unchristian *adj* ***syn*** OUTRAGEOUS 1, barbarous, uncivilized, unconscionable, ungodly, unholy, wicked
ant ||Christian

uncivil *adj* 1 ***syn*** BARBARIAN 1, barbaric, barbarous, Gothic, Hunnish, rude, savage, uncivilized, uncultivated, wild
2 ***syn*** RUDE 6, discourteous, disgracious, disrespectful, ill-mannered, impertinent, impolite, incivil, uncourteous, ungracious
rel coarse, crass, crude
con polished, smooth, urbane
ant civil

uncivilized *adj* 1 ***syn*** BARBARIAN 1, barbaric, barbarous, Gothic, Hunnic, Hunnish, rude, savage, uncultivated, wild
ant civilized
2 ***syn*** BOORISH, churlish, cloddish, ill-bred, loutish, lowbred, rugged, uncultured, unpolished, unrefined
ant civilized
3 ***syn*** OUTRAGEOUS 1, barbarous, unchristian, unconscionable, ungodly, unholy, wicked

unclad *adj* ***syn*** NUDE 2, au naturel, *bare-assed, buff-bare, naked, raw, stark-naked, stripped, unclothed, undressed

unclean *adj* 1 ***syn*** IMPURE 1, dirty, immoral, unchaste, uncleanly
ant clean, pure
2 ***syn*** DIRTY 1, black, filthy, foul, grubby, impure, nasty, soily, squalid, uncleanly
ant clean, cleanly
3 ***syn*** IMPURE 3, common, defiled, desecrated, polluted, profaned
ant clean; purified

uncleanly *adj* 1 ***syn*** IMPURE 1, dirty, immoral, unchaste, unclean
ant cleanly
2 ***syn*** DIRTY 1, black, filthy, foul, grubby, impure, nasty, soily, squalid, unclean
ant clean, cleanly

unclear *adj* 1 ***syn*** OBSCURE 3, ambiguous, amphibological, equivocal, opaque, tenebrous, uncertain, unexplicit, unintelligible, vague
ant clear
2 ***syn*** FAINT 2, blear, bleary, dim, ill-defined, indistinct, obscure, shadowy, undefined, vague
ant clear, distinct
3 ***syn*** DOUBTFUL 1, ambiguous, dubious, equivocal, open, problematic, suspect, uncertain, unsettled, unsure
ant clear

uncloak *vb* ***syn*** EXPOSE 4, debunk, discover, show up, undress, unmask, unshroud
ant cloak

unclose *vb* 1 ***syn*** OPEN 1, ope, unblock, undo, unshut, unstop
ant close
2 ***syn*** REVEAL 1, betray, disclose, discover, divulge, tell, unbosom, uncover, uncurtain, unveil

unclosed *adj* ***syn*** OPEN 1, patent, unobstructed
ant closed

unclothe *vb* 1 ***syn*** STRIP 1, denude, disrobe, undress
ant clothe, dress
2 ***syn*** OPEN 2, disclose, display, expose, reveal, uncover, unveil

unclothed *adj* ***syn*** NUDE 2, au naturel, *bare-assed, buff-bare, naked, raw, stark-naked, stripped, unclad, undressed
ant clothed, dressed

unclouded *adj* ***syn*** FAIR 2, clarion, clear, cloudless, fine, pleasant, rainless, sunny, sunshiny, undarkened *ant* clouded, cloudy

uncluttered *adj* ***syn*** NEAT 2, chipper, orderly, shipshape, snug, spick-and-span, tidy, trig, trim, well-groomed
ant cluttered

uncolored *adj* ***syn*** FAIR 4, dispassionate, equal, equitable, impartial, just, nondiscriminatory, objective, unbiased, unprejudiced
ant colored, partial

uncombed *adj* ***syn*** SLOVENLY 1, disheveled, ill-kempt, messy, slipshod, sloppy, unfastidious, unkempt, unneat, untidy

uncombine *vb* ***syn*** SEPARATE 1, dichotomize, disjoin, disjoint, dissever, disunite, divide, part, sever, sunder
ant combine

un–come–at–able *adj* ***syn*** INACCESSIBLE, inapproachable, unapproachable, unattainable, ungetatable, unobtainable, unreachable
ant come-at-able

uncomely *adj* **1** ***syn*** IMPROPER 1, inappropriate, inapt, inept, malapropos, unbecoming, unbefitting, undue, unsuitable, untimely
2 ***syn*** PLAIN 5, homely, unalluring, unattractive, unbeauteous, unbeautiful, unhandsome, unpretty
ant comely
3 ***syn*** UGLY 2, hideous, ill-favored, ill-looking, unbeautiful, unsightly
ant comely

uncomfortable *adj* causing or likely to cause discomfort <kept an *uncomfortable* chair for uninvited callers>
syn comfortless, discomforting, harsh, uncomforting, uncomfy
rel distressing, easeless, uneasy
con comforting, easy, soothing
ant comfortable

uncomforting *adj* ***syn*** UNCOMFORTABLE, comfortless, discomforting, harsh, uncomfy
ant comforting

uncomfy *adj* ***syn*** UNCOMFORTABLE, comfortless, discomforting, harsh, uncomforting
ant comfy

uncommon *adj* **1** ***syn*** INFREQUENT, few, occasional, rare, scarce, seldom, semioccasional, sporadic, unfrequent
con commonplace, everyday, ordinary
ant common
2 ***syn*** EXCEPTIONAL 1, extraordinary, rare, singular, unimaginable, unique, unordinary, unthinkable, unusual, unwonted
ant common, commonplace

‖**uncommon** *adv* ***syn*** EXTRA, extremely, rarely, uncommonly, unusually

uncommonly *adv* **1** ***syn*** OCCASIONALLY, infrequently, irregularly, on occasion, sporadically
ant commonly
2 ***syn*** EXTRA, extremely, rarely, ‖uncommon, unusually

uncommunicative *adj* **1** ***syn*** SILENT 3, close, close-lipped, closemouthed, close-tongued, reserved, reticent, taciturn, tight-lipped, tight-mouthed
ant communicative
2 ***syn*** UNSOCIABLE, aloof, distant, insociable, offish, reserved, standoffish, unapproachable, unbending, withdrawn

uncompanionable *adj* ***syn*** UNSOCIABLE, aloof, distant, insociable, offish, reserved, solitary, standoffish, uncommunicative, withdrawn
ant companionable

uncompassionate *adj* ***syn*** UNFEELING 2, callous, coldhearted, hard-boiled, hardhearted, heartless, obdurate, stonyhearted, unemotional, unsympathetic
ant compassionate

uncompensated *adj* ***syn*** UNPAID 1, unrecompensed, unremunerated
ant compensated

uncomplainingness *n* ***syn*** PATIENCE, forbearance, longanimity, long-suffering, patientness, resignation
ant complainingness, discontent

uncomplete *adj* ***syn*** DEFICIENT 1, defective, ‖half-assed, inadequate, incomplete, insufficient, lacking, wanting
ant complete

uncompliant *adj* ***syn*** INFLEXIBLE 2, brassbound, inexorable, obdurate, rigid, single-minded, unbending, uncompromising, unswayable, unyielding
ant compliant

uncomplimentary *adj* ***syn*** DEROGATORY, depreciative, depreciatory, detracting, disadvantageous, disparaging, dyslogistic, pejorative, slighting
ant complimentary

uncomprehensible *adj* ***syn*** INCOMPREHENSIBLE 1, impenetrable, incognizable, unfathomable, ungraspable, unintelligible, unknowable
ant comprehensible, graspable

uncompromising *adj* **1** ***syn*** INFLEXIBLE 2, brassbound, inexorable, obdurate, relentless, rigid, single-minded, unbending, uncompliant, unyielding
2 ***syn*** TOUGH 3, hard-line, inflexible, unyielding

unconcealed *adj* ***syn*** FRANK, candid, open, openhearted, plain, straightforward, undisguised, undissembled, undissembling, unvarnished

unconceivable *adj* ***syn*** IMPLAUSIBLE, flimsy, improbable, inconceivable, incredible, thin, unbelievable, unconvincing, unsubstantial, weak
ant conceivable

unconcern *n* ***syn*** APATHY 2, disinterest, disregard, heedlessness, indifference, insouciance, lassitude, lethargy, listlessness, unmindfulness
ant concern

unconcerned *adj* ***syn*** INDIFFERENT 2, aloof, casual, detached, disinterested, incurious, remote, uncurious, uninterested, withdrawn
rel collected, composed, cool, nonchalant
con anxious, careful, solicitous, worried
ant concerned

uncondensed *adj* ***syn*** UNABRIDGED, complete, unabbreviated, uncut, undocked, whole-length
ant condensed

unconfident *adj* ***syn*** INSECURE 1, unassured, unsure

---

ant confident
unconfined *adj* ***syn*** FREE 2, loose, unrestrained
ant confined
uncongenial *adj* **1** ***syn*** ANTIPATHETIC 2, aversive, kindless, repellent, repugnant, ungenial, unsympathetic
rel displeasing, unattractive, unlikable, unpleasing
ant congenial
2 ***syn*** INHARMONIOUS 2, discordant, inconsonant, unharmonious
unconnected *adj* ***syn*** INCOHERENT 2, disconnected, discontinuous, disjointed, disordered, inchoate, incohesive, muddled, uncontinuous, unorganized
ant connected, ordered
unconquerable *adj* **1** ***syn*** INVINCIBLE 1, impregnable, inconquerable, indomitable, inexpugnable, invulnerable, unassailable, unbeatable, undefeatable
rel insuperable, unsurmountable; proof, resistant, secure, tight
idiom more than a match for
con beatable, vincible; expugnable, pregnable, vulnerable; insecure, open, unprotected
ant conquerable
2 ***syn*** INSUPERABLE, impassable, inconquerable, indomitable, insurmountable, invincible, unsurmountable
ant conquerable
unconscionable *adj* **1** ***syn*** UNSCRUPULOUS, conscienceless, stick-at-nothing, unprincipled
ant conscientious, conscionable
2 ***syn*** EXCESSIVE 1, dizzy, exorbitant, extravagant, extreme, immoderate, inordinate, towering, undue, unmeasurable
3 ***syn*** UNREASONABLE 2, undue, unjustifiable, unwarrantable, unwarranted
4 ***syn*** OUTRAGEOUS 1, barbarous, unchristian, uncivilized, ungodly, unholy, wicked
unconscious *adj* ***syn*** INSENSIBLE 2, cold, comatose, inconscious, senseless
ant conscious
unconsequential *adj* ***syn*** PETTY 2, inconsequent, inconsequential, inconsiderable, paltry, picayune, picayunish, small, trifling, trivial
ant consequential
unconsidered *adj* **1** ***syn*** PETTY 2, inconsequent, inconsequential, inconsiderable, paltry, picayune, puny, small, trifling, trivial
2 ***syn*** RANDOM, aimless, designless, desultory, haphazard, hit-or-miss, indiscriminate, objectless, promiscuous, unplanned
ant considered, planned
3 ***syn*** RASH 1, brash, hasty, hotheaded, ill-advised, incautious, inconsiderate, reckless, thoughtless, unadvised
ant considered
unconsolable *adj* ***syn*** INCONSOLABLE, desolate, disconsolate
ant consolable
unconspicuous *adj* ***syn*** INCONSPICUOUS, obscure, unemphatic, unnoticeable
ant conspicuous
unconstrained *adj* **1** ***syn*** EASYGOING 3, casual, ‖common, dégagé, informal, low-pressure, relaxed, ‖sonsy, unfussy, unreserved
2 ***syn*** DEMONSTRATIVE, expansive, outgoing, unreserved, unrestrained
ant constrained
unconstraint *n* freedom from constraint or pressure <had always been used to the *unconstraint* of a happy affectionate family>
syn abandon, ease, naturalness, spontaneity, unrestraint; *compare* ABANDON 2
rel impulsiveness, instinctiveness; ingenuousness, naiveté, simplicity, unsophistication
con pressure, strain, stress, tension; formality, rigidity; sophistication
ant constraint
uncontainable *adj* ***syn*** IRREPRESSIBLE, insuppressible, insuppressive, irrestrainable, uncontrollable, unrestrainable
uncontent *adj* ***syn*** DISCONTENTED, discontent, disgruntled, dissatisfied, malcontent, malcontented, uncontented, ungratified
ant content, contented
uncontented *adj* ***syn*** DISCONTENTED, discontent, disgruntled, dissatisfied, malcontent, malcontented, uncontent, ungratified
ant content, contented
uncontestable *adj* ***syn*** POSITIVE 3, certain, incontestable, incontrovertible, indisputable, indubitable, undeniable, undisputable, unequivocal, unquestionable
ant contestable
uncontinuous *adj* ***syn*** INCOHERENT 2, disconnected, discontinuous, disjointed, disordered, inchoate, incohesive, muddled, unconnected, unorganized
uncontrite *adj* ***syn*** REMORSELESS, impenitent, regretless, unregretful, unremorseful, unrepentant, unsorry
ant contrite
uncontrollable *adj* **1** ***syn*** UNRULY 1, fractious, indocile, indomitable, intractable, recalcitrant, undisciplinable, undisciplined, unmanageable, wild
ant controllable
2 ***syn*** IRREPRESSIBLE, insuppressible, insuppressive, irrestrainable, uncontainable, unrestrainable
ant controllable
uncontrovertible *adj* ***syn*** POSITIVE 3, certain, inarguable, incontestable, indisputable, indubitable, sure, undeniable, unequivocal, unquestionable
ant controvertible, disputable
unconversant *adj* ***syn*** INEXPERIENCED, callow, green, raw, unfleshed, unpracticed, unseasoned, untried, unversed, young
ant conversant, versed
unconvincing *adj* ***syn*** IMPLAUSIBLE, flimsy, improbable, inconceivable, incredible, thick, thin, unbelievable, unsubstantial, weak
ant convincing
uncooked *adj* ***syn*** RAW 1
ant cooked

||**uncorporal** *adj* ***syn*** IMMATERIAL 1, bodiless, discarnate, disembodied, incorporeal, insubstantial, metaphysical, nonmaterial, nonphysical, unembodied

uncorrectable *adj* ***syn*** HOPELESS 2, cureless, immedicable, impossible, incurable, insanable, irremediable, irreparable, uncurable, unrecoverable
ant correctable

uncostly *adj* ***syn*** CHEAP 1, inexpensive, low, low-cost, low-priced, popular, reasonable, undear
ant costly

uncountable *adj* **1** ***syn*** INNUMERABLE, countless, innumerous, numberless, uncounted, unnumberable, unnumbered, untold
ant countable
2 ***syn*** INCALCULABLE 1, immeasurable, inestimable, measureless, unmeasurable, unmeasured, unreckonable

uncounted *adj* ***syn*** INNUMERABLE, countless, innumerous, numberless, uncountable, unnumberable, unnumbered, untold

uncouple *vb* ***syn*** DETACH, abstract, disassociate, disconnect, disengage, dissociate, unfix
ant couple

uncourteous *adj* ***syn*** RUDE 6, discourteous, disgracious, disrespectful, ill-mannered, impertinent, impolite, uncalled-for, uncivil, ungracious
ant courteous

uncouth *adj* **1** ***syn*** STRANGE 4, bizarre, curious, eccentric, erratic, odd, oddball, quaint, queer, rummy
2 ***syn*** DERELICT 1, abandoned, deserted, desolate, forsaken, lorn, solitary
3 ***syn*** COARSE 3, crass, crude, gross, inelegant, raw, rough, rude, unrefined, vulgar
ant couth
4 ***syn*** RUDE 6, discourteous, disgracious, disrespectful, ill-bred, ill-mannered, impertinent, impolite, uncalled-for, uncivil

uncover *vb* **1** ***syn*** REVEAL 1, betray, disclose, discover, divulge, tell, unbosom, unclose, uncurtain, unveil
2 ***syn*** EXPOSE 1, lay (open), subject
3 ***syn*** OPEN 2, disclose, display, expose, reveal, unclothe, unveil
ant cover

uncovered *adj* ***syn*** OPEN 2, bare, denuded, exposed, naked, peeled, stripped

uncreate *vb* ***syn*** ANNIHILATE 2, abate, abolish, blot out, eradicate, exterminate, extinguish, extirpate, root out, wipe (out)

uncreated *adj* ***syn*** SELF-EXISTENT, increate, self-existing, unbegotten, uncaused, unoriginated
ant created

uncreative *adj* ***syn*** UNORIGINAL, noncreative, sterile, uninspired, uninventive, unoriginative
ant creative

uncritical *adj* ***syn*** SUPERFICIAL 2, cursory, depthless, shallow, sketchy
rel imprecise, inaccurate, inexact; careless, casual, offhand, perfunctory, slipshod
con accurate, exact, precise; careful; discerning, discriminating, penetrating
ant critical

uncrown *vb* ***syn*** DEPOSE 1, dethrone, discrown, disenthrone, displace, disthrone, unmake
ant coronate, crown

unction *n* ***syn*** OINTMENT, balm, cerate, chrism, cream, salve, unguent

unctious *adj* ***syn*** FULSOME, oily, oleaginous, slick, smarmy, soapy, unctuous

unctuous *adj* **1** ***syn*** FATTY 2, greasy, oily, oleaginous
2 ***syn*** FULSOME, oily, oleaginous, slick, smarmy, soapy, unctious

uncultivated *adj* **1** ***syn*** COARSE 3, crass, crude, gross, incult, inelegant, raw, rough, rude, uncultured
ant cultivated
2 ***syn*** BARBARIAN 1, barbaric, barbarous, Gothic, Hunnish, rude, savage, uncivil, uncivilized, wild
ant cultivated
3 ***syn*** WILD 1, agrarian, agrestal, native, natural, undomesticated
ant cultivated

uncultured *adj* **1** ***syn*** BOORISH, churlish, cloddish, clodhopping, ill-bred, loutish, lowbred, uncivilized, unpolished, unrefined
ant cultured
2 ***syn*** COARSE 3, crass, crude, gross, incult, raw, rough, uncouth, unrefined, vulgar

uncurable *adj* ***syn*** HOPELESS 2, cureless, immedicable, impossible, incurable, insanable, irremediable, irreparable, uncorrectable, unrecoverable
ant curable

uncurbed *adj* ***syn*** AUDACIOUS 4, ungoverned, unhampered, uninhibited, unrestrained, untrammeled
ant curbed

uncurious *adj* ***syn*** INDIFFERENT 2, aloof, casual, detached, disinterested, incurious, remote, unconcerned, uninterested, withdrawn
ant curious

uncurtain *vb* ***syn*** REVEAL 1, betray, disclose, discover, divulge, tell, unbosom, unclose, uncover, unveil

uncustomary *adj* ***syn*** EXCEPTIONAL 1, extraordinary, rare, singular, uncommon, unique, unordinary, unthinkable, unusual, unwonted
ant customary

uncut *adj* ***syn*** UNABRIDGED, complete, unabbreviated, uncondensed, undocked, whole-length
ant cut

undamaged *adj* ***syn*** WHOLE 1, flawless, intact, sound, unblemished, unbroken, unhurt, unimpaired, uninjured, unmarred
ant damaged

undaring *adj* ***syn*** TIMID 2, timorous, ||timorsome
ant daring

undarkened *adj* ***syn*** FAIR 2, clarion, clear, cloudless, fine, pleasant, rainless, sunny, sunshiny, unclouded

undauntable *adj* ***syn*** BRAVE 1, audacious, bold, courageous, dauntless, fearless, intrepid, undaunted, valiant, valorous

---

syn synonym(s) ***rel*** related word(s)
idiom idiomatic equivalent(s) ***con*** contrasted word(s)
ant antonym(s) * vulgar
|| use limited; if in doubt, see a dictionary
The first word in a synonym list when printed in SMALL CAPITALS shows where there is more information about the group. For a more efficient use of this book see Explanatory Notes.

undaunted *adj* ***syn*** BRAVE 1, audacious, bold, courageous, dauntless, fearless, intrepid, undauntable, valiant, valorous
ant daunted

undear *adj* ***syn*** CHEAP 1, inexpensive, low, low-cost, low-priced, popular, reasonable, uncostly
ant dear

undeceive *vb* ***syn*** DISABUSE, purge, undelude
ant deceive

undecided *adj* **1** ***syn*** PENDING, pendent, undetermined, unsettled
ant decided
2 ***syn*** DOUBTFUL 1, borderline, dubious, equivocal, indecisive, open, uncertain, unclear, unsettled, unsure

undecipherable *adj* ***syn*** ILLEGIBLE, indecipherable, unreadable
ant decipherable

undecisive *adj* ***syn*** VACILLATING 2, faltering, halting, hesitant, hesitating, indecisive, irresolute, tentative, vacillant, wavering
ant decisive

undeclared *adj* ***syn*** TACIT 1, implicit, implied, inferred, understood, unexpressed, unsaid, unspoken, unuttered, wordless

undecorated *adj* ***syn*** PLAIN 1, homely, inelaborate, simple, unadorned, unbeautified, unembellished, unembroidered, ungarnished, unornamented
ant decorated

undecorous *adj* ***syn*** INDECOROUS, improper, indecent, indelicate, malodorous, rough, unbecoming, ungodly, unseemly, untoward
ant decorous

undefeatable *adj* ***syn*** INVINCIBLE 1, impregnable, inconquerable, indomitable, inexpugnable, invulnerable, unassailable, unbeatable, unconquerable
ant defeatable

undefiled *adj* ***syn*** CHASTE, clean, decent, immaculate, modest, pure, spotless, stainless, unblemished, unsullied

undefined *adj* ***syn*** FAINT 2, bleary, dim, ill-defined, indistinct, obscure, shadowy, unclear, undetermined, vague
ant defined

undeflowered *adj* ***syn*** VIRGIN 1, intact, maiden, virginal
ant deflowered

undelude *vb* ***syn*** DISABUSE, purge, undeceive
ant delude

undemonstrated *adj* ***syn*** UNTRIED 1, unpracticed, unproved, untested
ant demonstrated

undemonstrative *adj* not socially outgoing <a shy *undemonstrative* person yet capable of deep feeling>
syn aseptic, restrained, retiring, shrinking, unaffable, unexpansive, withdrawn; *compare* UNSOCIABLE
rel chill, cold, frigid, glacial, icy; emotionless, indifferent, unemotional, uninterested; aloof, distant, reserved, standoffish
con free and easy, hail-fellow-well-met, outgiving, outgoing, palsy-walsy; sociable
ant demonstrative

undeniable *adj* **1** ***syn*** POSITIVE 3, inarguable, incontestable, incontrovertible, indisputable, indubitable, uncontestable, undisputable, unequivocal, unquestionable
ant deniable
2 ***syn*** REAL 3, actual, indisputable, true, unfabled, veridical

undenominational *adj* ***syn*** NONSECTARIAN, interchurch, intercreedal, interdenominational, unsectarian
ant denominational

undependable *adj* **1** ***syn*** UNRELIABLE 1, dubious, fly-by-night, questionable, trustless, unsure, untrustworthy, untrusty
ant dependable
2 ***syn*** UNSAFE, unassured, unreliable, untrustworthy
ant dependable
3 ***syn*** TRICK, tricky
ant dependable

under *adv* ***syn*** BELOW 1, beneath, underneath
ant above, over

under *prep* ***syn*** BELOW 1, beneath, underneath
ant over

under *adj* **1** ***syn*** INFERIOR 1, lesser, low, lower, nether, subjacent
2 ***syn*** SUBORDINATE, collateral, dependent, secondary, sub, subject, tributary

underage *n* ***syn*** FAILURE 3, defalcation, deficiency, deficit, inadequacy, insufficience, insufficiency, lack, scantiness, shortage
ant overage

underconsciousness *n* ***syn*** SUBCONSCIOUS, undersense

undercover *adj* ***syn*** SECRET 1, clandestine, covert, furtive, hole-and-corner, hugger-mugger, hush-hush, sub-rosa, ‖underneath, under-the-table

undercover man *n* ***syn*** SPY, agent, spook

undercroft *n* ***syn*** CRYPT, catacomb, vault

underdeveloped *adj* ***syn*** BACKWARD 6, behindhand, undeveloped, unprogressive

underdog *n* ***syn*** VICTIM 2, bottom dog, casualty, prey
ant overdog, top dog

underearth *adj* ***syn*** SUBTERRANEAN, subterrestrial, underfoot, underground

underfoot *adj* **1** ***syn*** SUBTERRANEAN, subterrestrial, underearth, underground
2 ***syn*** DOWNTRODDEN, abject

undergo *vb* ***syn*** EXPERIENCE 1, have, know, see, suffer, sustain
rel abide, bear, endure, tolerate; bow, defer, submit, yield

underground *adj* ***syn*** SUBTERRANEAN, subterrestrial, underearth, underfoot

underhand *adj* characterized by sly unobtrusive craft or deceit <ready to use the most *underhand* methods to gain his ends>
syn devious, duplicitous, guileful, indirect, shifty, sneaking, sneaky, underhanded; *compare* SECRET 1, SLY 2
rel deceitful, dishonest; crooked, oblique; crafty, cunning, insidious, sly, tricky, wily; furtive, hangdog

---

syn synonym(s)	*rel* related word(s)
idiom idiomatic equivalent(s)	*con* contrasted word(s)
ant antonym(s)	* vulgar

‖ use limited; if in doubt, see a dictionary
The first word in a synonym list when printed in SMALL CAPITALS shows where there is more information about the group. For a more efficient use of this book see Explanatory Notes.

con candid, frank, open, plain; forthright, straight-forward
ant aboveboard

underhanded *adj* **1** *syn* UNDERHAND, devious, duplicitous, guileful, indirect, shifty, sneaking, sneaky
ant aboveboard
2 *syn* SHORTHANDED, undermanned, understaffed

underivative *adj syn* PRIMARY 5, original, prime, primitive, underived
ant derivative

underived *adj syn* PRIMARY 5, original, prime, primitive, underivative
ant derived

underlease *vb syn* SUBLET, sublease, underlet

underlet *vb syn* SUBLET, sublease, underlease

underline *vb syn* EMPHASIZE, feature, italicize, play (up), stress, underscore

underline *n syn* CAPTION, legend

underling *n syn* INFERIOR, poor relation, scrub, secondary, subaltern, subordinate, understrapper

underly *adj syn* UNWELL, ailing, ‖donsie, indisposed, low, mean, off-color, offish, poorly, sickly

underlying *adj* **1** *syn* FUNDAMENTAL 1, basal, basic, bottom, foundational, primary, radical
rel cardinal, essential, vital; critical, crucial; indispensable, necessary, needful
2 *syn* ELEMENTAL 1, basic, elementary, essential, fundamental, primitive, substratal

undermanned *adj syn* SHORTHANDED, underhanded, understaffed
ant overmanned

undermine *vb* **1** *syn* WEAKEN 1, attenuate, blunt, cripple, debilitate, disable, enfeeble, sap, unbrace, unstrengthen
rel ruin, wreck; foil, frustrate, thwart
idiom bore from within
ant reinforce
2 *syn* SABOTAGE, subvert, wreck

undermining *n syn* SABOTAGE, subversion, wreckage, wrecking

undermost *adj syn* BOTTOMMOST, bottom, lowermost, lowest, nethermost, rock-bottom
ant uppermost

underneath *prep syn* BELOW 1, beneath, under

underneath *adv syn* BELOW 1, beneath, under

‖**underneath** *adj syn* SECRET 1, clandestine, covert, furtive, hole-and-corner, stealthy, sub-rosa, surreptitious, undercover, under-the-table

underneath *n syn* BOTTOM 1, sole, underside, undersurface

underpinner *n syn* SUPPORT 3, brace, buttress, column, prop, shore, stay, underpinning, underpropping

underpinning *n* **1** *syn* BASIS 1, base, bedrock, footing, foundation, ground, groundwork, infrastructure, root, substratum
2 *syn* BASE 1, footing, foundation, groundwork, infrastructure, seat, seating, substruction, substructure, understructure
3 *syn* SUPPORT 3, brace, buttress, column, prop, shore, stay, underpinner, underpropping

underprivileged *adj* deficient in basic economic and social resources <the role of the school in bettering the lot of *underprivileged* children>
syn depressed, deprived, disadvantaged
rel handicapped; hapless, ill-fated, ill-starred, unfortunate, unlucky; impoverished, needy, poor
idiom badly off, in adverse circumstances, out of luck
con advantaged, fortunate, privileged; coddled, indulged, spoiled

underprize *vb syn* DEPRECIATE 1, decry, devalorize, devaluate, devalue, lower, mark down, undervalue, write down, write off
ant overprize

underprop *vb syn* SUPPORT 5, bolster, buoy (up), prop, sustain, uphold

underpropping *n syn* SUPPORT 3, brace, buttress, column, prop, shore, stay, underpinner, underpinning

underrate *vb syn* DEPRECIATE 1, decry, devalorize, devaluate, devalue, lower, mark down, undervalue, write down, write off
ant overrate

underscore *vb syn* EMPHASIZE, feature, italicize, play (up), stress, underline

undersense *n syn* SUBCONSCIOUS, underconsciousness

undersexed *adj syn* FRIGID 3, cold, inhibited, passionless, unresponsive
ant oversexed

underside *n syn* BOTTOM 1, sole, underneath, undersurface

understaffed *adj syn* SHORTHANDED, underhanded, undermanned
ant overstaffed

understand *vb* **1** *syn* APPREHEND 1, accept, catch, comprehend, ‖dig, follow, grasp, see, take, take in
idiom get the drift
ant misunderstand
2 *syn* KNOW 1, appreciate, apprehend, cognize, comprehend, fathom, grasp, have
idiom get the hang of
3 to view as plausible or likely <I *understand* he is expected home soon>
syn assume, believe, ‖conceit, conceive, expect, gather, imagine, ‖reckon, suppose, suspect, take, think, ‖wit; *compare* CONJECTURE
rel conclude, deduce, infer; conjecture, guess, presume, surmise; fancy; consider
con know; challenge, doubt, question

understandable *adj* of a kind to be readily understood <her style was smooth and easy, her language *understandable*>
syn apprehensible, comprehendible, comprehensible, fathomable, graspable, intelligible, knowable, lucid, luminous; *compare* CLEAR 4, 5
rel clear-cut, unambiguous, unblurred; plain, simple, straightforward; exoteric, lay, popular
con mysterious, obscure, strange, vague; cryptic, esoteric, hidden

---

syn synonym(s) *rel* related word(s)
idiom idiomatic equivalent(s) *con* contrasted word(s)
ant antonym(s) * vulgar
‖ use limited; if in doubt, see a dictionary
The first word in a synonym list when printed in SMALL CAPITALS shows where there is more information about the group. For a more efficient use of this book see Explanatory Notes.

understanding *n* **1** ***syn*** REASON 5, intellect
rel discernment, discrimination, insight, penetration; awareness, intuition; apprehension, comprehension, grasp
2 ***syn*** AGREEMENT 2, accord, deal
3 ***syn*** MEANING 1, acceptation, import, intendment, message, purport, sense, significance, significancy, signification

understood *adj* ***syn*** TACIT 1, implicit, implied, inferred, undeclared, unexpressed, unsaid, unspoken, unuttered, wordless

understrapper *n* ***syn*** INFERIOR, poor relation, scrub, secondary, subaltern, subordinate, underling

understructure *n* ***syn*** BASE 1, basement, basis, bed, bottom, foundation, groundwork, infrastructure, substruction, substructure
ant superstructure

undersurface *n* ***syn*** BOTTOM 1, sole, underneath, underside

undertake *vb* **1** ***syn*** TRY 5, assay, attempt, endeavor, essay, offer, seek, strive, struggle
rel begin, commence, start
idiom put (*or* set) one's hand to
2 ***syn*** TAKE ON 3, take up
3 ***syn*** PROMISE 1, engage, pass, pledge
rel certify, warrant
idiom stand back of (*or* behind)

undertaker *n* **1** ***syn*** ENTREPRENEUR 1
2 ***syn*** MORTICIAN, funeral director

undertaking *n* **1** ***syn*** ATTEMPT, endeavor, essay, hassle, striving, struggle, trial, try
2 ***syn*** PROJECT 2, enterprise

under–the–table *adj* ***syn*** SECRET 1, clandestine, covert, furtive, hole-and-corner, stealthy, sub-rosa, surreptitious, undercover, ‖underneath
ant aboveboard

undertone *n* **1** ***syn*** MURMUR 1, mumble, mutter, rumor, susurration, whisper
2 ***syn*** ASSOCIATION 4, connotation, hint, implication, overtone, suggestion

undervalue *vb* ***syn*** DEPRECIATE 1, decry, devalorize, devaluate, devalue, lower, mark down, underprize, write down, write off
ant overvalue

underwater *adj* ***syn*** SUBMARINE, subaquatic, subaqueous

underwit *n* ***syn*** FOOL 4, cretin, ‖feeb, half-wit, idiot, imbecile, moron, natural, simpleton, zany

underworld *n* ***syn*** HELL, abyss, barathrum, Gehenna, hades, inferno, netherworld, Pandemonium, Sheol, Tophet

undescribable *adj* ***syn*** UNUTTERABLE, incommunicable, indefinable, indescribable, ineffable, inenarrable, inexpressible, unexpressible, unspeakable, untellable
ant describable

undesignated *adj* ***syn*** ANONYMOUS, innominate, nameless, unnamed

undesigned *adj* ***syn*** UNINTENTIONAL, inadvertent, undevised, unintended, unplanned, unpremeditated, unpurposed, unthought
ant designed

undesigning *adj* ***syn*** GENUINE 3, heart-whole, honest, real, sincere, true, undissembled, unfeigned
ant designing

undesirable *adj* ***syn*** OBJECTIONABLE, exceptionable, ill-favored, inadmissible, unacceptable, unwanted, unwelcome
ant desirable

undesired *adj* ***syn*** UNWELCOME 1, unsought, unwanted, unwished
ant desired

undestroyable *adj* ***syn*** INDESTRUCTIBLE, imperishable, incorruptible, inexterminable, inextinguishable, inextirpable, irrefragable, irrefrangible, quenchless, unperishable
ant destroyable, destructible

undeterminable *adj* ***syn*** INDEFINITE 1, indeterminate, indistinct, inexact
ant determinable

undetermined *adj* **1** ***syn*** PENDING, pendent, undecided, unsettled
ant determined
2 ***syn*** FAINT 2, bleary, dim, ill-defined, indistinct, obscure, shadowy, unclear, undefined, vague

undeveloped *adj* **1** ***syn*** BACKWARD 6, behindhand, underdeveloped, unprogressive
ant developed
2 ***syn*** PRIMITIVE 3, archaic, persistent, unevolved
ant advanced

undeviatingly *adv* ***syn*** DIRECTLY 1, dead, direct, due, right, straight, straightly

undevised *adj* ***syn*** UNINTENTIONAL, inadvertent, undesigned, unintended, unplanned, unpremeditated, unpurposed, unthought
ant devised

undexterous *adj* ***syn*** UNSKILLFUL 1, inadept, inapt, inept, inexpert, unapt, unfacile, unhandy, unproficient
ant dexterous

undifferenced *adj* ***syn*** LIKE, akin, alike, analogous, comparable, consonant, corresponding, parallel, similar, undifferentiated

undifferentiated *adj* ***syn*** LIKE, agnate, akin, alike, analogous, comparable, consonant, corresponding, parallel, similar
ant differentiated

undiluted *adj* **1** ***syn*** STRAIGHT 3, neat, plain, pure, unadulterated, unmixed
ant diluted
2 ***syn*** PURE 2, absolute, perfect, sheer, simple, unadulterated, unalloyed, unmitigated, unmixed, unqualified

undiplomatic *adj* ***syn*** TACTLESS, brash, impolitic, maladroit, unpolitic, untactful
ant diplomatic

undiscernible *adj* ***syn*** IMPERCEPTIBLE, inappreciable, indiscernible, insensible, intangible, invisible, unapparent, unappreciable, unobservable, unperceivable
ant discernible

undisciplinable *adj* ***syn*** UNRULY 1, fractious, intractable, recalcitrant, uncontrollable, undisciplined, ungovernable, unmanageable, untoward, wild

undisciplined *adj* ***syn*** UNRULY 1, fractious, intractable, recalcitrant, uncontrollable, undisciplinable, ungovernable, unmanageable, untoward, wild
ant disciplined

undiscriminated *adj* ***syn*** INDISCRIMINATE 1, indiscriminating, indiscriminative, sweeping, undiscriminating, undistinguishing, wholesale
ant discriminate, discriminated

undiscriminating *adj* ***syn*** INDISCRIMINATE 1, indiscriminating, indiscriminative, sweeping, undiscriminated, undistinguishing, wholesale

undisguised *adj* ***syn*** FRANK, candid, open, openhearted, plain, straightforward, unconcealed, undissembled, undissembling, unvarnished

undisputable *adj* ***syn*** POSITIVE 3, certain, incontestable, incontrovertible, indisputable, indubitable, uncontestable, undeniable, unequivocal, unquestionable
ant controvertible, disputable

undissembled *adj* **1** ***syn*** GENUINE 3, heart-whole, honest, real, sincere, true, undesigning, unfeigned
ant dissembled, feigned
2 ***syn*** FRANK, candid, open, openhearted, plain, straightforward, unconcealed, undisguised, undissembling, unvarnished

undissembling *adj* ***syn*** FRANK, candid, open, openhearted, plain, straightforward, unconcealed, undisguised, undissembled, unvarnished
ant dissembling

undistinct *adj* ***syn*** FAINT 2, dim, ill-defined, indistinct, obscure, shadowy, unclear, undefined, undetermined, vague
ant clear, distinct

undistinctive *adj* ***syn*** FAIR 4, dispassionate, equitable, impartial, just, nondiscriminatory, objective, unbiased, uncolored, unprejudiced

undistinguishing *adj* ***syn*** INDISCRIMINATE 1, indiscriminating, indiscriminative, sweeping, undiscriminated, undiscriminating, wholesale

undistorted *adj* ***syn*** TRUE 3, faithful, just, right, strict, veracious, veridical
ant distorted

undistracted *adj* ***syn*** WHOLE 5, concentrated, exclusive, fixed, undivided, unswerving

undivided *adj* ***syn*** WHOLE 5, concentrated, exclusive, fixed, undistracted, unswerving
ant divided

undo *vb* **1** ***syn*** LOOSE 3, disengage, unbind, unfasten, unfix, unloose, unloosen
2 ***syn*** OPEN 1, ope, unblock, unclose, unshut, unstop
rel loose, untie
3 ***syn*** ABOLISH 1, abate, abrogate, annihilate, annul, invalidate, negate, nullify, quash, vitiate
4 ***syn*** DESTROY 1, decimate, demolish, raze, ruin, unbuild, unframe, unmake, wrack, wreck
5 ***syn*** OUTWIT, have, outfox, outgeneral, outjockey, outmaneuver, outreach, outslick, outsmart, overreach
idiom bring down (*or* low), bring to naught
6 ***syn*** SEDUCE 2, debauch

undocked *adj* ***syn*** UNABRIDGED, complete, unabbreviated, uncondensed, uncut, whole-length
ant docked

undoing *n* ***syn*** DOWNFALL 2, bane, destroyer, destruction, ruin, ruination

undomesticated *adj* ***syn*** WILD 1, agrarian, agrestal, native, natural, uncultivated
ant domesticated

undoubtable *adj* ***syn*** POSITIVE 3, inarguable, incontestable, incontrovertible, indisputable, indubitable, sure, uncontestable, undeniable, unquestionable
ant doubtable, questionable

undoubted *adj* ***syn*** AUTHENTIC 2, bona fide, genuine, indubitable, real, sure-enough, true, unquestionable, veritable, very
ant doubtful, questionable

undoubtedly *adv* ***syn*** WELL 7, doubtlessly, easily, indeed, really, truly

undoubtful *adj* ***syn*** CONFIDENT 1, assured, sanguine, secure, self-assured, self-confident
ant doubtful

undress *vb* **1** ***syn*** STRIP 1, denude, disrobe, unclothe
ant dress
2 ***syn*** EXPOSE 4, debunk, discover, show up, uncloak, unmask, unshroud
ant dress up

undressed *adj* **1** ***syn*** NUDE 2, au naturel, *bare-assed, buff-bare, naked, raw, stark-naked, stripped, unclad, unclothed
ant dressed
2 ***syn*** RUDE 1, crude, rough, roughhewn, unfashioned, unfinished, unformed, unhewn, unpolished, unworked
ant dressed, finished

undubitable *adj* ***syn*** AUTHENTIC 2, bona fide, genuine, indubitable, real, sure-enough, true, undoubted, unquestionable, veritable
ant dubitable

undue *adj* **1** ***syn*** IMPROPER 1, ill-timed, inappropriate, inapt, inept, unapt, unfitting, unseasonable, unsuitable, untimely
2 ***syn*** EXCESSIVE 1, dizzy, exorbitant, extravagant, extreme, immoderate, inordinate, towering, unconscionable, unmeasurable
3 ***syn*** UNREASONABLE 2, unconscionable, unjustifiable, unwarrantable, unwarranted

undulate *vb* ***syn*** SLITHER 2, ‖slidder, snake

unduly *adv* ***syn*** EVER 6, excessively, extremely, immensely, inordinately, over, overfull, overly, overmuch, too
ant duly

unduteous *adj* ***syn*** IMPIOUS 2, undutiful
ant duteous

undutiful *adj* ***syn*** IMPIOUS 2, unduteous
ant dutiful

undying *adj* ***syn*** IMMORTAL 1, deathless

---

syn synonym(s) — *rel* related word(s)
idiom idiomatic equivalent(s) — *con* contrasted word(s)
ant antonym(s) — * vulgar
‖ use limited; if in doubt, see a dictionary
The first word in a synonym list when printed in SMALL CAPITALS shows where there is more information about the group. For a more efficient use of this book see Explanatory Notes.

rel continuing, persistent; interminable, unceasing; inextinguishable, unquenchable
ant mortal

uneager *adj* ***syn*** DISINCLINED, afraid, averse, backward, hesitant, indisposed, loath, reluctant, shy, unwilling
ant eager

unearth *vb* ***syn*** DISCOVER 3, ascertain, catch on, determine, find out, hear, learn, see, tumble
rel exhibit, expose, show; disclose, reveal; delve, dig

unearthing *n* ***syn*** DISCOVERY, detection, espial, find, strike

unearthly *adj* **1** ***syn*** SUPERNATURAL 1, miraculous, numinous, preternatural, superhuman, superior, supermundane, suprahuman, supramundane, supranatural
2 ***syn*** WEIRD 1, eerie, spooky, uncanny
3 ***syn*** FOOLISH 2, absurd, ||balmy, crazy, fantastic, insane, loony, preposterous, silly, wacky

unease *n* **1** ***syn*** CARE 2, anxiety, concern, concernment, disquiet, disquietude, solicitude, uneasiness, worry
2 ***syn*** TENSION 2, uptightness
3 ***syn*** EMBARRASSMENT, abashment, confusion, discomfiture, discomposure, disconcertion, disconcertment, uneasiness
ant ease, easiness

uneasiness *n* **1** ***syn*** CARE 2, anxiety, concern, concernment, disquiet, disquietude, solicitude, uneasiness, worry
2 ***syn*** EMBARRASSMENT, abashment, confusion, discomfiture, discomposure, disconcertion, disconcertment, unease
ant ease, easiness

uneasy *adj* **1** ***syn*** TENSE 2, edgy, nervy, restive, uptight
rel anxious, careful, concerned, solicitous, worried; agitated, disquieted, disturbed, perturbed
idiom on pins and needles
ant easy
2 ***syn*** RESTLESS, unpeaceful, unquiet, unrestful, unsettled, untranquil
3 ***syn*** DOUBTFUL 1, ambiguous, borderline, doubtable, precarious, shaky, suspect, uncertain, unsettled, unsure

uneatable *adj* ***syn*** INEDIBLE, inesculent
ant eatable

uneducated *adj* ***syn*** IGNORANT 1, benighted, empty-headed, illiterate, know-nothing, rude, uninstructed, unlettered, untaught, untutored
ant educated, lettered

unelaborate *adj* ***syn*** PLAIN 1, homely, inelaborate, modest, simple, unbeautified, unembellished, ungarnished, unostentatious, unpretentious
ant elaborate

unembellished *adj* ***syn*** PLAIN 1, unadorned, unbeautified, undecorated, unelaborate, unembroidered, ungarnished, unornamented, unostentatious, unpretentious
ant embellished

unembodied *adj* ***syn*** IMMATERIAL 1, asomatous, bodiless, discarnate, disembodied, incorporeal, nonmaterial, nonphysical, unfleshly, unphysical

unembroidered *adj* ***syn*** PLAIN 1, inelaborate, simple, unadorned, unelaborate, unembellished, ungarnished, unornamented, unostentatious, unpretentious

unemotional *adj* **1** ***syn*** COLD 2, chill, emotionless, frigid, glacial, icy, indifferent
rel dispassionate; unfeeling; impassive
con affective, feeling; affectionate, demonstrative
ant emotional
2 ***syn*** UNFEELING 2, callous, coldhearted, hard-boiled, hardhearted, heartless, obdurate, stonyhearted, uncompassionate, unsympathetic

unemphatic *adj* ***syn*** INCONSPICUOUS, obscure, unconspicuous, unnoticeable

unemployed *adj* lacking a gainful occupation <the problems of *unemployed* workers>
syn jobless, workless
rel free, unengaged, unoccupied; underemployed; fired, laid off
idiom at liberty, let go, on layoff, out of work
ant employed

unending *adj* **1** ***syn*** EVERLASTING 1, amaranthine, ceaseless, endless, eternal, immortal, never-ending, world-without-end
2 ***syn*** CONTINUAL, ceaseless, constant, continuous, endless, everlasting, interminable, perpetual, uninterrupted, unremitting

unendurable *adj* ***syn*** INSUFFERABLE, insupportable, intolerable, unbearable, unbrookable, unsufferable, unsupportable
ant endurable

unenlarged *adj* ***syn*** ILLIBERAL, bigoted, brassbound, hidebound, intolerant, narrow, narrow-minded, small-minded

unenlightened *adj* ***syn*** BACKWARD 5, benighted, ignorant, unprogressive
ant enlightened

unennobled *adj* ***syn*** IGNOBLE 1, base, baseborn, humble, low, lowborn, lowly, mean, plebeian, unwashed
ant ennobled, noble

unentangle *vb* ***syn*** EXTRICATE 2, disembarrass, disembroil, disencumber, disentangle, disentwine, unscramble, untangle, untie, untwine
ant entangle

unenthusiastic *adj* ***syn*** TEPID 2, halfhearted, lukewarm
ant enthusiastic

unequal *adj* **1** ***syn*** DIFFERENT 1, disparate, dissimilar, distant, divergent, diverse, unalike, unlike, unsimilar, various
2 ***syn*** LOPSIDED, asymmetric, disproportionate, irregular, nonsymmetrical, off-balance, overbalanced, uneven, unproportionate, unsymmetrical

unequalable *adj* ***syn*** SUPREME, incomparable, preeminent, surpassing, towering, transcendant, ultimate, unmatchable, unsurpassable

unequaled *adj* ***syn*** ALONE 3, matchless, only, peerless, unique, unmatched, unparagoned, unparalleled, unrivaled
ant equaled

unequipped *adj* ***syn*** UNFIT 2, disqualified, incapable, incompetent, ineligible, unfitted, unqualified

---

syn synonym(s) *rel* related word(s)
idiom idiomatic equivalent(s) *con* contrasted word(s)
ant antonym(s) * vulgar
|| use limited; if in doubt, see a dictionary
The first word in a synonym list when printed in SMALL CAPITALS shows where there is more information about the group. For a more efficient use of this book see Explanatory Notes.

unequitable *adj* ***syn*** INEQUITABLE, inequable, unfair, unjust, unrighteous
ant equitable

unequivocal *adj* **1** ***syn*** CLEAR 5, apparent, distinct, evident, manifest, obvious, palpable, patent, plain, univocal
ant equivocal
2 ***syn*** POSITIVE 1, categorical, decided, definite
ant equivocal
3 ***syn*** POSITIVE 3, certain, incontestable, incontrovertible, indisputable, indubitable, uncontestable, undeniable, undisputable, unquestionable

unequivocally *adv* ***syn*** EASILY 2, absolutely, definitely, doubtless, doubtlessly, positively, unquestionably

uneradicable *adj* ***syn*** INDELIBLE, ineffaceable, ineradicable, inerasable, inexpungible, inextirpable, unerasable
ant eradicable

unerasable *adj* ***syn*** INDELIBLE, ineffaceable, ineradicable, inerasable, inexpungible, inextirpable, uneradicable
ant erasable

unerring *adj* ***syn*** INFALLIBLE 1, inerrable, inerrant, sure

unescapable *adj* ***syn*** INEVITABLE, certain, ineluctable, ineludible, inescapable, inevasible, necessary, returnless, unavoidable, unevadable
ant escapable

unessential *adj* **1** ***syn*** UNNECESSARY, inessential, needless, uncalled-for, unneeded, unneedful, unrequired
ant essential
2 ***syn*** DISPENSABLE, nonessential, unrequired
ant essential

unethical *adj* ***syn*** CORRUPT 2, mercenary, praetorian, unprincipled, unscrupulous, venal
ant ethical

unevadable *adj* ***syn*** INEVITABLE, certain, ineluctable, ineludible, inescapable, inevasible, necessary, returnless, unavoidable, unescapable
ant evadable

uneven *adj* **1** ***syn*** ROUGH 1, asperous, craggy, harsh, jagged, rugged, scabrous, scraggy, unlevel, unsmooth
ant even
2 ***syn*** LOPSIDED, asymmetric, disproportionate, irregular, nonsymmetrical, off-balance, overbalanced, unbalanced, unequal, unsymmetrical
ant even
3 ***syn*** SPOTTY 1, irregular, patchy
rel differing, disparate, unequal; discrepant, inconsistent
con consistent, equal, regular

unevenness *n* **1** ***syn*** DISPARITY, disproportion, imparity, inequality
2 ***syn*** INEQUALITY 1, asperity, irregularity, roughness

uneventful *adj* ***syn*** COMMON 6, commonplace, ordinary, prosaic, unexceptional, unnoteworthy
ant eventful

unevolved *adj* ***syn*** PRIMITIVE 3, archaic, persistent, undeveloped
ant advanced, evolved

unexaminable *adj* ***syn*** MYSTERIOUS, arcane, cabalistic, impenetrable, inscrutable, mysterial, mystic, unaccountable, unguessed, unknowable

unexampled *adj* ***syn*** ONLY 2, alone, lone, singular, sole, solitary, solo, unique, unrepeatable

unexceptionable *adj* ***syn*** DECENT 4, acceptable, adequate, all right, common, satisfactory, sufficient, tolerable, unexceptional, unimpeachable
ant exceptionable

unexceptional *adj* **1** ***syn*** DECENT 4, acceptable, adequate, all right, common, satisfactory, sufficient, tolerable, unexceptionable, unimpeachable
2 ***syn*** COMMON 6, commonplace, ordinary, prosaic, uneventful, unnoteworthy
ant exceptional

unexcessive *adj* ***syn*** CONSERVATIVE 2, controlled, discreet, moderate, reasonable, restrained, temperate, unextreme
ant excessive

unexpansive *adj* ***syn*** UNDEMONSTRATIVE, aseptic, restrained, retiring, shrinking, unaffable, withdrawn
ant expansive

unexpectedly *adv* ***syn*** UNAWARES, aback, short, sudden, suddenly, unanticipatedly, unaware, unawaredly

unexpedient *adj* ***syn*** INADVISABLE, ill-advised, impolitic, imprudent, inexpedient, unadvisable
ant expedient

unexperienced *adj* ***syn*** INEXPERIENCED, callow, fresh, green, raw, unfleshed, unpracticed, unseasoned, untried, unversed
ant experienced

unexpert *adj* ***syn*** INEFFICIENT 2, incapable, incompetent, inept, inexpert, unskilled, unskillful, unworkmanlike
ant expert

unexplainable *adj* ***syn*** INEXPLICABLE, inexplainable, unaccountable
ant explainable, explicable

unexplicit *adj* ***syn*** OBSCURE 3, ambiguous, amphibological, equivocal, nubilous, tenebrous, uncertain, unclear, unintelligible, vague
ant explicit

unexpressed *adj* **1** ***syn*** UNSPOKEN 1, silent, tacit, unuttered, voiceless, wordless
ant expressed
2 ***syn*** TACIT 1, implicit, implied, inferred, undeclared, understood, unsaid, unspoken, unuttered, wordless
ant expressed

unexpressible *adj* ***syn*** UNUTTERABLE, incommunicable, indefinable, indescribable, ineffable, inenarrable, inexpressible, undescribable, unspeakable, untellable
ant expressible

unexpressive *adj* ***syn*** EXPRESSIONLESS, blank, deadpan, empty, inexpressive, vacant
ant expressive

unextreme *adj* ***syn*** CONSERVATIVE 2, controlled, discreet, moderate, reasonable, restrained, temperate, unexcessive

---

syn synonym(s)	***rel*** related word(s)
idiom idiomatic equivalent(s)	***con*** contrasted word(s)
ant antonym(s)	* vulgar

‖ use limited; if in doubt, see a dictionary
The first word in a synonym list when printed in SMALL CAPITALS shows where there is more information about the group. For a more efficient use of this book see Explanatory Notes.

unfabled *adj* ***syn*** REAL 3, actual, indisputable, true, undeniable, veridical
ant fabled

unfacile *adj* ***syn*** UNSKILLFUL 1, inadept, inapt, inept, inexpert, unapt, undexterous, unhandy, unproficient

unfailing *adj* **1** ***syn*** SAME 3, consistent, constant, invariable, unchanging, unvarying
2 ***syn*** INFALLIBLE 2, certain, sure, surefire
ant fallible

unfair *adj* ***syn*** INEQUITABLE, inequable, unequitable, unjust, unrighteous
ant fair

unfairness *n* ***syn*** INJUSTICE 1, inequitableness, inequity, unjustness, wrong
ant fairness

unfaith *n* ***syn*** UNBELIEF, disbelief, incredulity, unbelievingness
ant faith

unfaithful *adj* ***syn*** FAITHLESS, disloyal, false, perfidious, recreant, traitorous, treacherous, unloyal, untrue
ant faithful

unfaithfulness *n* ***syn*** INFIDELITY, disloyalty, faithlessness, falseness, falsity, perfidiousness, perfidy
ant faithfulness

unfaltering *adj* ***syn*** SURE 2, abiding, enduring, firm, never-failing, steadfast, steady, unqualified, unquestioning, wholehearted

unfamed *adj* ***syn*** OBSCURE 5, nameless, uncelebrated, unheard-of, unknown, unnoted, unrenowned
ant famed

unfamiliar *adj* **1** not well known <trying to find her way about the *unfamiliar* room in the dark>
syn new, strange, unaccustomed
rel exotic, foreign; curious, peculiar, remarkable; unknown
con accustomed, commonplace, customary, ordinary, usual, wonted
ant familiar
2 ***syn*** IGNORANT 2, incognizant, inconversant, oblivious, unacquainted, unaware, uninformed, uninstructed, unknowing, unwitting
ant familiar

unfamiliarity *n* ***syn*** IGNORANCE 2, innocence, inscience, nescience, unacquaintance, unacquaintedness, unawareness, unknowingness

unfantastic *adj* ***syn*** REALISTIC, down-to-earth, hard, hard-boiled, hardheaded, matter-of-fact, practical, pragmatic, sober, unidealistic
ant fantastic

unfashioned *adj* ***syn*** RUDE 1, crude, rough, roughhewn, undressed, unfinished, unformed, unhewn, unpolished, unworked

unfasten *vb* ***syn*** LOOSE 3, disengage, unbind, undo, unfix, unloose, unloosen
ant fasten

unfastidious *adj* ***syn*** SLOVENLY 1, careless, ill-kempt, messy, slipshod, sloppy, uncombed, unkempt, unneat, untidy
ant fastidious

unfathered *adj* ***syn*** ILLEGITIMATE 1, baseborn, bastard, fatherless, misbegotten, natural, spurious, supposititious

unfathomable *adj* **1** ***syn*** BOTTOMLESS 2, abysmal, fathomless, plumbless, plummetless, soundless
ant fathomable
2 ***syn*** INCOMPREHENSIBLE 1, impenetrable, incognizable, uncomprehensible, ungraspable, unintelligible, unknowable
ant fathomable

unfathomed *adj* ***syn*** HUGE, colossal, enormous, immense, massive, mighty, monstrous, prodigious, tremendous, vast

unfavorable *adj* **1** ***syn*** ADVERSE 2, detrimental, negative
ant favorable
2 ***syn*** EVIL 5, bad, ill

unfavorably *adv* ***syn*** AMISS 2, afield, astray, awry, badly, wrong

unfearful *adj* ***syn*** BRAVE 1, audacious, bold, courageous, dauntless, fearless, intrepid, undaunted, valiant, valorous
ant fearful

unfearing *adj* ***syn*** BRAVE 1, audacious, bold, courageous, dauntless, fearless, intrepid, undaunted, valiant, valorous
ant fearing

unfeasible *adj* ***syn*** IMPOSSIBLE 1, impracticable, impractical, infeasible, irrealizable, unattainable, unrealizable, unworkable
ant feasible, practicable

unfeeling *adj* **1** ***syn*** INSENSATE 1, inanimate, insensible, insentient, senseless
ant feeling
2 lacking in normal human sympathy <an *unfeeling* response to a plea for help>
syn callous, cold-blooded, coldhearted, compassionless, hard-boiled, hardened, hardhearted, heartless, ironhearted, marblehearted, obdurate, stony, stonyhearted, uncompassionate, unemotional, unsympathetic; *compare* PITILESS
rel brutal, cruel, indurated, merciless, roughhearted, ruthless, tough; exacting, severe; unamiable, uncordial, unkind; cantankerous, churlish, crotchety, curmudgeonly, surly
idiom hard of heart
con considerate, gentle, thoughtful; kind, merciful; compassionate, sympathetic, warmhearted
ant feeling
3 ***syn*** NUMB 1, anesthetized, asleep, benumbed, dead, deadened, insensible, insensitive, numbed, senseless

unfeigned *adj* **1** ***syn*** SINCERE 1, heartfelt, hearty, wholehearted, whole-souled
ant feigned
2 ***syn*** GENUINE 3, heart-whole, honest, real, sincere, true, undesigning, undissembled
ant dissembled, feigned

unfertile *adj* ***syn*** BARREN 2, hardscrabble, infertile, unbearing, unproductive
ant fertile

---

syn synonym(s)	*rel* related word(s)
idiom idiomatic equivalent(s)	*con* contrasted word(s)
ant antonym(s)	* vulgar

|| use limited; if in doubt, see a dictionary

The first word in a synonym list when printed in SMALL CAPITALS shows where there is more information about the group. For a more efficient use of this book see Explanatory Notes.

unfinished *adj* **1** ***syn*** RUDE 1, crude, rough, roughhewn, undressed, unfashioned, unformed, unhewn, unpolished, unworked
ant dressed, finished
2 ***syn*** AMATEURISH, dabbling, dilettante, dilettantish, dilettantist, jackleg, unaccomplished, ungifted, unskilled
ant finished

unfit *adj* **1** not adapted or appropriate to a particular end <land *unfit* for farming>
syn ill-adapted, ill-suited, inappropriate, inapt, unfitted, unmeet, unsuitable, unsuited
rel discordant, inharmonious; improper, infelicitous, unbecoming; incompatible, incongruous, uncongenial
idiom out of drawing, out of one's element, out of place
con adapted, appropriate, apt, suitable, suited; congruous, harmonious
ant fit
2 lacking essential qualifications <politicians *unfit* to govern>
syn disqualified, incapable, incompetent, ineligible, unequipped, unfitted, unqualified
rel awkward, blundering, bungling; butterfingered, heavyhanded, maladjusted, maladroit, unhandy; inefficient, inexpert, unproficient, unskillful
con capable, competent, qualified; adroit, dexterous, handy; expert, skilled

unfitted *adj* **1** ***syn*** UNFIT 1, ill-adapted, ill-suited, inappropriate, inapt, unmeet, unsuitable, unsuited
2 ***syn*** UNFIT 2, disqualified, incapable, incompetent, ineligible, unequipped, unqualified
ant fitted

unfitting *adj* ***syn*** IMPROPER 1, inappropriate, inapt, inept, malapropos, unapt, unbecoming, unbefitting, unseemly, unsuitable
ant fitting

unfix *vb* **1** ***syn*** LOOSE 3, disengage, unbind, undo, unfasten, unloose, unloosen
ant fix
2 ***syn*** DETACH, abstract, disassociate, disconnect, disengage, dissociate, uncouple

unfixedness *n* ***syn*** INSTABILITY, precariousness, shakiness, unsettledness, unstability, unstableness, unsteadfastness, unsteadiness

unflagging *adj* ***syn*** INDEFATIGABLE, inexhaustible, tireless, untiring, unweariable, unwearying, weariless
rel constant, steady
ant flagging

unflappable *adj* ***syn*** COOL 2, collected, composed, disimpassioned, imperturbable, nonchalant, unruffled
rel easy, relaxed

unflawed *adj* ***syn*** PERFECT 2, absolute, flawless, fleckless, impeccable, indefectible, note-perfect
ant flawed

unfledged *adj* ***syn*** YOUNG 1, callow, green, immature, infant, juvenile, unripe, youthful
ant fledged

unfleshed *adj* ***syn*** INEXPERIENCED, callow, fresh, green, raw, unpracticed, unseasoned, untried, unversed, young

unfleshly *adj* ***syn*** IMMATERIAL 1, asomatous, bodiless, discarnate, disembodied, incorporeal, nonmaterial, nonphysical, unembodied, unphysical
ant fleshly

unflexible *adj* ***syn*** STIFF 1, immalleable, impliable, incompliant, inelastic, inflexible, rigid, unbending, unyielding
ant flexible

unflinching *adj* ***syn*** GRIM 3, implacable, ironfisted, merciless, mortal, relentless, ruthless, unappeasable, unrelenting, unyielding

unfluctuating *adj* ***syn*** STEADY 2, constant, equable, even, stabile, stable, unchanging, uniform, unvarying
ant fluctuant, fluctuating

unfold *vb* **1** ***syn*** OPEN 4, expand, extend, fan (out), outspread, outstretch, spread
ant fold
2 ***syn*** SOLVE 2, clear up, decipher, dissolve, ‖dope out, figure out, puzzle out, resolve, unravel, unriddle
3 to disclose by degrees to the sight or understanding <shyly she *unfolded* her hopes for the future>
syn develop, elaborate, evolve
rel demonstrate, evidence, evince, manifest, show; disclose, display, exhibit, expose, reveal

unfolding *n* ***syn*** DEVELOPMENT, evolution, evolvement, flowering, growth, progress, progression, upgrowth

unforbearing *adj* ***syn*** INTOLERANT 1, impatient, unindulgent
ant forbearing

unforced *adj* ***syn*** VOLUNTARY, deliberate, intentional, unprescribed, willful, willing, witting
ant forced

unforgivable *adj* ***syn*** INEXCUSABLE, indefensible, inexpiable, unjustifiable, unpardonable, untenable
ant forgivable

unformed *adj* **1** ***syn*** FORMLESS, amorphous, inchoate, shapeless, unshaped
rel unfinished
ant formed
2 ***syn*** RUDE 1, crude, rough, roughhewn, undressed, unfashioned, unfinished, unhewn, unpolished, unworked

unfortunate *adj* **1** ***syn*** UNLUCKY, hapless, ill-fated, ill-starred, luckless, misfortunate, star-crossed, unhappy, untoward
rel infelicitous; deplorable, miserable, sad, wretched; malefic
con auspicious, favorable, propitious
ant fortunate
2 ***syn*** INFELICITOUS, awkward, graceless, ill-chosen, inept, unhappy
3 ***syn*** DEPLORABLE, afflictive, calamitous, dire, distressing, grievous, heartbreaking, lamentable, regrettable, woeful

unfounded *adj* ***syn*** BASELESS, bottomless, foundationless, gratuitous, groundless, uncalled-for, ungrounded, unwarranted

---

syn synonym(s) ***rel*** related word(s)
idiom idiomatic equivalent(s) ***con*** contrasted word(s)
ant antonym(s) * vulgar
‖ use limited; if in doubt, see a dictionary
The first word in a synonym list when printed in SMALL CAPITALS shows where there is more information about the group. For a more efficient use of this book see Explanatory Notes.

rel deceptive, misleading; dishonest, mendacious, untruthful
ant well-founded

unframe *vb* ***syn*** DESTROY 1, decimate, demolish, raze, ruin, unbuild, undo, unmake, wrack, wreck

unfrank *adj* ***syn*** DISINGENUOUS, uncandid
ant frank

unfrequent *adj* ***syn*** INFREQUENT, few, occasional, rare, scarce, seldom, semioccasional, sporadic, uncommon
ant frequent

unfrequently *adv* ***syn*** SELDOM, hardly ever, infrequently, little, rarely, unoften
ant frequently

unfriendly *adj* ***syn*** HOSTILE 1, ill, inimicable, inimical
ant friendly

unfruitful *adj* ***syn*** STERILE 1, barren, effete, impotent, infecund, infertile
con fecund, fertile
ant fruitful, prolific

unfunctional *adj* ***syn*** IMPRACTICABLE 2, impractical, nonfunctional, unserviceable, unusable, unworkable, useless
ant functional

unfussy *adj* ***syn*** EASYGOING 3, casual, ‖common, dégagé, informal, low-pressure, relaxed, ‖sonsy, unconstrained, unreserved
ant fussy

ungainly *adj* ***syn*** CLUMSY 1, awkward, gawky, lumbering, lumpish, splathering, splay
rel blundering, lubberly, maladroit
con graceful, supple, willowy; gainly

ungarnished *adj* ***syn*** PLAIN 1, dry, inelaborate, modest, simple, unadorned, unelaborate, unembellished, unembroidered, unornamented
ant garnished

ungenerous *adj* **1** ***syn*** PETTY 2, inconsequent, inconsequential, inconsiderable, paltry, peanut, picayune, puny, small, trifling
ant generous
2 ***syn*** STINGY, close, mean, miserly, niggardly, parsimonious, penny-pinching, penurious, tight, ungiving
ant generous

ungenial *adj* ***syn*** ANTIPATHETIC 2, aversive, kindless, repellent, repugnant, uncongenial, unsympathetic
ant genial

ungenuine *adj* ***syn*** SPURIOUS 3, apocryphal, bastard, unauthentic
ant genuine

ungetatable *adj* ***syn*** INACCESSIBLE, inapproachable, unapproachable, unattainable, un-come-at-able, unobtainable, unreachable
ant getatable

---

syn synonym(s) ***rel*** related word(s)
idiom idiomatic equivalent(s) ***con*** contrasted word(s)
ant antonym(s) * vulgar
‖ use limited; if in doubt, see a dictionary
The first word in a synonym list when printed in SMALL CAPITALS shows where there is more information about the group. For a more efficient use of this book see Explanatory Notes.

ungifted *adj* ***syn*** AMATEURISH, dabbling, dilettante, dilettantish, dilettantist, jackleg, unaccomplished, unfinished, unskilled
ant gifted

ungiving *adj* ***syn*** STINGY, close, mean, miserly, niggardly, parsimonious, penurious, save-all, tight, tightfisted

ungodly *adj* **1** ***syn*** IMPIOUS 1, irreverent, irreverential, profane, unhallowed, unholy
ant godly
2 ***syn*** INDECOROUS, improper, indecent, indelicate, malodorous, rough, unbecoming, undecorous, unseemly, untoward
3 ***syn*** OUTRAGEOUS 1, barbarous, unchristian, uncivilized, unconscionable, unholy, wicked

ungovernable *adj* ***syn*** UNRULY 1, fractious, intractable, recalcitrant, uncontrollable, undisciplinable, undisciplined, unmanageable, untoward, wild
ant governable

ungoverned *adj* ***syn*** AUDACIOUS 4, uncurbed, unhampered, uninhibited, unrestrained, untrammeled

ungracious *adj* **1** ***syn*** RUDE 6, discourteous, disgracious, disrespectful, ill-mannered, impertinent, impolite, uncalled-for, uncivil, uncourteous
ant gracious
2 ***syn*** SHORT 5, inconsiderate, sharp, thoughtless, unceremonious
ant gracious

ungraded *adj* ***syn*** UNREFINED 3, crude, impure, native, raw, run-of-mine, unsorted

ungraspable *adj* ***syn*** INCOMPREHENSIBLE 1, impenetrable, incognizable, uncomprehensible, unfathomable, unintelligible, unknowable
ant comprehensible, graspable

ungrateful *adj* **1** ***syn*** THANKLESS 1, unappreciative, unthankful
ant grateful
2 ***syn*** THANKLESS 2, unappreciated, unthankful
3 ***syn*** OFFENSIVE, disgusting, foul, hideous, horrible, loathsome, repellent, repugnant, repulsive, revolting

ungratified *adj* ***syn*** DISCONTENTED, discontent, disgruntled, dissatisfied, malcontent, malcontented, uncontent, uncontented
ant gratified

ungrounded *adj* ***syn*** BASELESS, bottomless, foundationless, gratuitous, groundless, uncalled-for, unfounded, unwarranted

unguarded *adj* ***syn*** INCAUTIOUS 1, unalert, unvigilant, unwary, unwatchful
ant guarded

unguent *n* ***syn*** OINTMENT, balm, cerate, chrism, cream, salve, unction

unguessed *adj* ***syn*** MYSTERIOUS, arcane, cabalistic, impenetrable, inscrutable, mysterial, mystic, numinous, unaccountable, unknowable

unguilty *adj* ***syn*** INNOCENT 2, blameless, clean, crimeless, faultless, guiltless, inculpable
ant guilty

unhallowed *adj* **1** ***syn*** IMPIOUS 1, irreverent, irreverential, profane, ungodly, unholy
2 ***syn*** FIENDISH, demoniac, demonian, demonic, devilish, diabolic, diabolonian, satanic, serpentine

unhampered *adj* ***syn*** AUDACIOUS 4, uncurbed, ungoverned, uninhibited, unrestrained, untrammeled

ant hampered

unhandsome *adj* **1** ***syn*** PLAIN 5, homely, unalluring, unattractive, unbeauteous, unbeautiful, uncomely, unpretty
ant handsome
2 ***syn*** RUDE 6, discourteous, disgracious, disrespectful, ill-bred, ill-mannered, impertinent, impolite, uncivil, ungracious

unhandy *adj* **1** ***syn*** UNWIELDY, cumbersome, cumbrous, ponderous
2 ***syn*** UNSKILLFUL 1, inadept, inapt, inept, inexpert, unapt, undexterous, unfacile, unproficient
ant handy
3 ***syn*** AWKWARD 2, bumbling, clumsy, gauche, halting, ham-handed, inept, maladroit, unhappy, wooden
ant handy

unhappiness *n* **1** ***syn*** MISERY 1, woe, wretchedness
ant happiness
2 ***syn*** SADNESS, blues, dejection, depression, (the) dismals, dumps, gloom, heavyheartedness, melancholy, mournfulness
ant happiness

unhappy *adj* **1** ***syn*** UNLUCKY, hapless, ill-fated, ill-starred, luckless, misfortunate, star-crossed, unfortunate, untoward
ant happy
2 ***syn*** INFELICITOUS, awkward, graceless, ill-chosen, inept, unfortunate
ant happy
3 ***syn*** AWKWARD 2, bumbling, clumsy, gauche, halting, heavy-handed, inept, maladroit, unhandy, wooden
4 ***syn*** SAD 1, heavyhearted, melancholy, mournful, saddened, sorry
ant happy
5 ***syn*** BAD 8, ||chiselly, disagreeable, displeasing, rotten, sour, unpleasant
6 ***syn*** GLOOMY 3, black, bleak, cheerless, depressant, dismal, dispiriting, dreary, joyless, oppressive

unharmed *adj* ***syn*** SAFE 1, scatheless, unscathed

unharmonious *adj* **1** ***syn*** DISSONANT 1, cacophonic, cacophonous, discordant, disharmonic, disharmonious, immusical, inharmonic, inharmonious, unmusical
ant harmonious
2 ***syn*** INHARMONIOUS 2, discordant, inconsonant, uncongenial
ant harmonious

unhasty *adj* ***syn*** SLOW 2, deliberate, dilatory, laggard, leisurely, unhurried
ant hasty

unhealth *n* ***syn*** SICKNESS 1, affliction, diseasedness, disorder, illness, indisposition, infirmity
ant health

unhealthful *adj* ***syn*** UNWHOLESOME 1, insalubrious, insalutary, noisome, noxious, sickly, unhealthy, unsalutary
ant healthful

unhealthiness *n* ***syn*** INFIRMITY 1, debility, decrepitude, disease, feebleness, infirmness, malaise, sickliness
ant healthiness

unhealthy *adj* **1** ***syn*** UNWHOLESOME 1, insalubrious, insalutary, noisome, noxious, sickly, unhealthful, unsalutary
ant healthy
2 ***syn*** DANGEROUS 1, chancy, hairy, hazardous, jeopardous, perilous, risky, treacherous, unsound, wicked
3 ***syn*** VICIOUS 2, corrupt, degenerate, depraved, flagitious, nefarious, perverse, putrid, rotten, villainous

unheard–of *adj* ***syn*** OBSCURE 5, nameless, uncelebrated, unfamed, unknown, unnoted, unrenowned

unheavy *adj* ***syn*** LIGHT 1, featherlight, featherweight, imponderous, lightweight, weightless
ant heavy

unheeding *adj* **1** ***syn*** INATTENTIVE, inobservant, unnoticing, unobservant, unobserving, unperceiving, unwatchful
ant heedful, heeding
2 ***syn*** CARELESS 1, feckless, heedless, inadvertent, irreflective, thoughtless, uncaring, unrecking, unreflective, unthinking
ant heedful, heeding

unhewn *adj* ***syn*** RUDE 1, crude, rough, roughhewn, undressed, unfashioned, unfinished, unformed, unpolished, unworked

unhinge *vb* **1** ***syn*** UPSET 5, derange, disorder, sicken, turn, unsettle
2 ***syn*** MADDEN 1, craze, derange, distract, frenzy, unbalance
3 ***syn*** DISCOMPOSE 1, agitate, bother, disquiet, disturb, flurry, fluster, perturb, untune, upset

unholy *adj* **1** ***syn*** IMPIOUS 1, irreverent, irreverential, profane, ungodly, unhallowed
ant holy
2 ***syn*** BLAMEWORTHY, amiss, blamable, blameful, censurable, culpable, demeritorious, guilty, reprehensible, sinful
3 ***syn*** OUTRAGEOUS 1, barbarous, unchristian, uncivilized, unconscionable, ungodly, wicked

unhonest *adj* ***syn*** DISHONEST, deceitful, knavish, lying, mendacious, roguish, shifty, untruthful
ant honest

unhorse *vb* **1** ***syn*** THROW 2, buck (off), pitch, unseat
2 ***syn*** OVERTHROW 2, overset, overturn, topple, tumble

unhurried *adj* ***syn*** SLOW 2, deliberate, dilatory, laggard, leisurely, unhasty
ant hurried

unhurt *adj* ***syn*** WHOLE 1, entire, intact, perfect, sound, unbroken, undamaged, unimpaired, uninjured, unmarred

unicity *n* ***syn*** UNIQUENESS, oneness, singleness, uniquity

unidealistic *adj* ***syn*** REALISTIC, down-to-earth, hard, hard-boiled, hardheaded, matter-of-fact, practical, pragmatic, sober, unfantastic
ant idealistic

unification *n* a bringing together or being brought together into an integrated whole < *unification* of mass transit facilities is increasingly needed >

---

syn synonym(s) ***rel*** related word(s)
idiom idiomatic equivalent(s) ***con*** contrasted word(s)
ant antonym(s) * vulgar
|| use limited; if in doubt, see a dictionary
The first word in a synonym list when printed in SMALL CAPITALS shows where there is more information about the group. For a more efficient use of this book see Explanatory Notes.

syn coadunation, coalition, combination consolidation, melding, mergence, merger, merging, union; *compare* ALLIANCE 2
rel affiliation, connection, interlocking, joining, linkage; coupling, hookup
con dissociation, disunion, division, parting, partition, separation
ant disunification

uniform *adj* **1** ***syn*** LIKE, agnate, akin, alike, analogous, comparable, consonant, corresponding, parallel, undifferentiated
ant various
2 ***syn*** STEADY 2, constant, equable, even, stabile, stable, unchanging, unfluctuating, unvarying
rel compatible, consistent, consonant; ordered, orderly, regular
ant multiform

uniformly *adv* ***syn*** EVENLY 3, flatly, smooth, smoothly
ant variably

unify *vb* **1** to gather or combine parts or elements into a close mass or a coherent whole <minorities that are *unified* by persecution>
syn compact, concentrate, consolidate, integrate; *compare* UNITE 2
rel articulate, concatenate; order, organize, systematize; bind, tie
idiom make one
con divide, part, scatter; disorder, disorganize; disunite, divide, separate
ant break up, disunify
2 ***syn*** HARMONIZE 4, arrange, blend, integrate, orchestrate, symphonize, synthesize
ant disunify

unifying *adj* ***syn*** INTEGRATIVE, centralizing, centripetal, compacting, concentrating, consolidating
ant disunifying

unilluminated *adj* ***syn*** DARK 1, caliginous, dim, dusk, dusky, gloomy, lightless, murky, obscure, tenebrous
ant illuminated

unimaginable *adj* **1** ***syn*** INCONCEIVABLE 1, incomprehensible, unknowable, ununderstandable
ant imaginable
2 ***syn*** EXCEPTIONAL 1, extraordinary, rare, singular, uncommon, unique, unordinary, unthinkable, unusual, unwonted
3 ***syn*** INCREDIBLE 1, incogitable, inconceivable, insupposable, unbelievable, unthinkable

unimpaired *adj* ***syn*** WHOLE 1, entire, intact, perfect, sound, unbroken, undamaged, unhurt, uninjured, unmarred
ant impaired

unimpassioned *adj* **1** ***syn*** MATTER-OF-FACT 3, cold, cold-blooded, emotionless, impersonal
ant impassioned
2 ***syn*** SOBER 3, moderate, temperate
rel impassive, phlegmatic, stoic, stolid; calm, placid, tranquil
con ardent, fervent, fervid, heated, keen
ant impassioned, passionate

unimpeachable *adj* ***syn*** DECENT 4, acceptable, adequate, all right, common, satisfactory, sufficient, tolerable, unexceptionable, unexceptional

unimportant *adj* ***syn*** LITTLE 3, casual, inconsiderable, insignificant, light, minor, petty, shoestring, small-beer, trivial
ant important

unimpressible *adj* ***syn*** INSUSCEPTIBLE, impassive, insensitive, insentient, unimpressionable, unresponsive, unsusceptible
ant impressible

unimpressionable *adj* ***syn*** INSUSCEPTIBLE, impassive, insensitive, insentient, unimpressible, unresponsive, unsusceptible
ant impressionable

unindifferent *adj* ***syn*** BIASED 2, colored, jaundiced, one-sided, partial, partisan, prejudiced, prepossessed, tendentious, unneutral
ant indifferent

unindulgent *adj* ***syn*** INTOLERANT 1, impatient, unforbearing
ant indulgent

uninflammable *adj* ***syn*** NONCOMBUSTIBLE, apyrous, incombustible, nonflammable, noninflammable
ant flammable, inflammable

uninformed *adj* ***syn*** IGNORANT 2, incognizant, inconversant, oblivious, unacquainted, unaware, unfamiliar, uninstructed, unknowing, unwitting
ant informed

uninhibited *adj* ***syn*** AUDACIOUS 4, uncurbed, ungoverned, unhampered, unrestrained, untrammeled
ant inhibited

uninhibitedness *n* ***syn*** ABANDON 2, impulsiveness, unrestraint

uninitiate *n* ***syn*** AMATEUR 2, abecedarian, dabbler, dilettante, nonprofessional, smatterer, tyro

uninjured *adj* ***syn*** WHOLE 1, entire, intact, perfect, sound, unbroken, undamaged, unhurt, unimpaired, unmarred
ant injured

uninjurious *adj* ***syn*** SAFE 3, healthy, wholesome

uninspired *adj* **1** ***syn*** UNORIGINAL, noncreative, sterile, uncreative, uninventive, unoriginative
ant inspired
2 ***syn*** PONDEROUS 2, elephantine, heavy-footed, heavy-handed
ant inspired

uninstructed *adj* **1** ***syn*** IGNORANT 2, incognizant, inconversant, oblivious, unacquainted, unaware, unfamiliar, uninformed, unknowing, unwitting
2 ***syn*** IGNORANT 1, benighted, empty-headed, illiterate, know-nothing, rude, uneducated, unlettered, untaught, untutored

unintelligent *adj* ***syn*** SIMPLE 3, brainless, fatuous, foolish, insensate, mindless, senseless, weak-headed, weak-minded, witless
ant intelligent

unintelligible *adj* 1 ***syn*** INCOMPREHENSIBLE 1, impenetrable, incognizable, uncomprehensible, unfathomable, ungraspable, unknowable
ant intelligible
2 ***syn*** OBSCURE 3, ambiguous, amphibological, equivocal, opaque, tenebrous, uncertain, unclear, unexplicit, vague
ant intelligible

unintended *adj* ***syn*** UNINTENTIONAL, inadvertent, undesigned, undevised, unplanned, unpremeditated, unpurposed, unthought
ant intended

unintentional *adj* not the result of intent or design <her slight of the newcomer was quite *unintentional*>
syn inadvertent, undesigned, undevised, unintended, unplanned, unpremeditated, unpurposed, unthought; *compare* ACCIDENTAL, EXTEMPORANEOUS
rel causeless, chance, haphazard, purposeless, random; unanticipated, unexpected, unforeseen, unlooked-for; unthinking, unwitting
con deliberate, designed, devised, intended, planned, premeditated, purposed
ant intentional

uninterested *adj* ***syn*** INDIFFERENT 2, aloof, casual, detached, disinterested, incurious, remote, unconcerned, uncurious, withdrawn
ant interested

uninteresting *adj* ***syn*** ARID 2, bromidic, dry, dryasdust, dull, dusty, insipid, tedious, weariful, wearisome
ant interesting

unintermitted *adj* ***syn*** CONTINUAL, around-the-clock, ceaseless, constant, continuous, incessant, unceasing, unintermittent, uninterrupted, unremitting
ant intermitted, intermittent

unintermittedly *adv* ***syn*** TOGETHER 2, consecutively, continually, continuously, hand running, night and day, running, successively, uninterruptedly

unintermittent *adj* ***syn*** CONTINUAL, around-the-clock, ceaseless, constant, continuous, incessant, unceasing, unending, unintermitted, uninterrupted
ant intermitted, intermittent

uninterrupted *adj* 1 ***syn*** CONTINUAL, ceaseless, constant, continuous, endless, interminable, perpetual, unceasing, unending, unremitting
ant interrupted
2 ***syn*** DIRECT 2, straight, straightforward, through

uninterruptedly *adv* ***syn*** TOGETHER 2, consecutively, continually, continuously, hand running, night and day, running, successively, unintermittedly
ant interruptedly

uninventive *adj* ***syn*** UNORIGINAL, noncreative, sterile, uncreative, uninspired, unoriginative
ant inventive

uninvited *adj* ***syn*** UNASKED, unbidden, unrequested, unsought
ant invited

union *n* 1 ***syn*** UNIFICATION, coadunation, coalition, combination, consolidation, melding, mergence, merger, merging
ant disunion
2 ***syn*** ASSOCIATION 2, brotherhood, club, congress, fellowship, guild, league, order, society, sodality
3 ***syn*** JOINT 1, connection, coupling, joining, junction, juncture, seam
4 ***syn*** ALLIANCE 2, anschluss, coalition, confederacy, confederation, federation, league

unique *adj* 1 ***syn*** ONLY 2, alone, lone, singular, sole, solitary, solo, unexampled, unrepeatable
2 ***syn*** SINGLE 2, lone, one, only, particular, separate, sole, solitary
3 ***syn*** ALONE 3, matchless, only, peerless, unequaled, unmatched, unparagoned, unparalleled, unrivaled
4 ***syn*** EXCEPTIONAL 1, extraordinary, rare, singular, uncommon, unimaginable, unordinary, unthinkable, unusual, unwonted

uniqueness *n* the quality or state of standing alone and without a peer <the time she rode in an old-time sleigh — never would she forget the *uniqueness* of that experience>
syn oneness, singleness, unicity, uniquity
rel curiousness, oddity, peculiarity, quaintness, singularity, strangeness; import, mark, moment, note, significance; memorability, notability, remarkableness, unusualness
con commonness, commonplaceness, ordinariness, routineness; monotony, sameness, tediousness

uniquity *n* ***syn*** UNIQUENESS, oneness, singleness, unicity

unite *vb* 1 ***syn*** JOIN 1, associate, combine, conjoin, connect, couple, link, marry, relate, wed
rel amalgamate, blend, merge, mix
ant alienate; disunite, divide
2 to join forces especially in order to act more effectively <citizen groups *uniting* to further the fight against crime>
syn band, coadjute, combine, concur, conjoin, cooperate, league; *compare* UNIFY 1
rel affiliate, ally, associate, confederate; coalesce, commingle, fuse, mingle, weld
idiom draw together, hook up with, join forces (with), make common cause (with), throw in with
con break up, disband, separate, split (up)
ant disunite, part

unity *n* 1 the condition of being or consisting of one <*unity* — the idea conveyed by whatever we visualize as one thing>
syn individuality, oneness, singleness, singularity, singularness
rel identity, selfsameness, soleness, uniqueness, uniquity
ant multiplicity
2 ***syn*** HARMONY 3, concord, rapport
rel agreement, identity, oneness, union; solidarity; conformance, congruity
ant disunity

universal *adj* 1 ***syn*** OMNIPRESENT, allover, ubiquitous
2 present or significant throughout the world <*universal* aspirations for a better world>

---

syn catholic, cosmic, cosmopolitan, ecumenical, global, planetary, worldwide
rel all-embracing, all-inclusive; broad, extensive, sweeping; all, entire, total, whole
con narrow, petty, provincial
ant parochial
3 ***syn*** GENERAL 2, common, generic
ant particular

universe *n* the totality of physical entities <theories of the expanding *universe*>
syn cosmos (*or* kosmos), creation, macrocosm, macrocosmos, megacosm, nature, world

univocal *adj* ***syn*** CLEAR 5, apparent, distinct, evident, manifest, obvious, palpable, patent, plain, unequivocal
ant ambiguous

unjust *adj* ***syn*** INEQUITABLE, inequable, unequitable, unfair, unrighteous
ant just

unjustifiable *adj* **1** ***syn*** UNREASONABLE 2, unconscionable, undue, unwarrantable, unwarranted
ant justifiable
2 ***syn*** INEXCUSABLE, indefensible, inexpiable, unforgivable, unpardonable, untenable
ant justifiable

unjustness *n* ***syn*** INJUSTICE 1, inequitableness, inequity, unfairness, wrong
ant justice, justness

unkempt *adj* ***syn*** SLOVENLY 1, disheveled, ill-kempt, messy, slipshod, sloppy, uncombed, unfastidious, unneat, untidy
ant kempt

unknow *vb* ***syn*** FORGET 1, disremember, ||misremember

unknowable *adj* **1** ***syn*** INCOMPREHENSIBLE 1, impenetrable, incognizable, uncomprehensible, unfathomable, ungraspable, unintelligible
ant knowable
2 ***syn*** INCONCEIVABLE 1, incomprehensible, unimaginable, ununderstandable
ant knowable
3 ***syn*** MYSTERIOUS, arcane, cabalistic, impenetrable, inscrutable, mysterial, mystic, numinous, unexaminable, unguessed

unknowing *adj* ***syn*** IGNORANT 2, incognizant, inconversant, oblivious, unacquainted, unaware, unfamiliar, uninformed, uninstructed, unwitting
ant knowing

unknowingness *n* ***syn*** IGNORANCE 2, innocence, inscience, nescience, unacquaintance, unacquaintedness, unawareness, unfamiliarity
ant knowingness

unknown *adj* ***syn*** OBSCURE 5, nameless, uncelebrated, unfamed, unheard-of, unnoted, unrenowned
ant well-known

unlade *vb* ***syn*** UNLOAD, disburden, discharge, off-load, unship, unstow
ant lade, load

unlawful *adj* contrary to or prohibited by law <the spread of *unlawful* wiretapping>
syn criminal, illegal, illegitimate, illicit, lawless, wrongful
rel flagitious, iniquitous, nefarious; black-market, bootleg, under-the-counter; exceptionable, improper, intolerable, objectionable
idiom against the law
con condign, due, rightful; allowable, justifiable, permissible
ant lawful

unlawfulness *n* ***syn*** ILLEGALITY, illegitimacy, illicitness
ant lawfulness

unlax *vb* **1** ***syn*** RELAX 2, ease off, loosen up, unbend, unwind
2 ***syn*** REST 2, relax, rest up, unbend

unlearned *adj* ***syn*** UNSCHOLARLY, inerudite, unbookish, unstudious
ant erudite, learned

unleash *vb* ***syn*** TAKE OUT (on), loose, release, vent

unless *conj* ***syn*** EXCEPT 1, but, save, saving, ||without

unlettered *adj* ***syn*** IGNORANT 1, benighted, empty-headed, illiterate, rude, uneducated, uninstructed, unschooled, untaught, untutored
ant educated, lettered

unlevel *adj* ***syn*** ROUGH 1, asperous, craggy, harsh, jagged, rugged, scabrous, scraggy, uneven, unsmooth
ant level

unlike *adj* ***syn*** DIFFERENT 1, disparate, dissimilar, distant, divergent, diverse, unalike, unequal, unsimilar, various
ant like

unlikely *adj* ***syn*** IMPROBABLE 1, doubtful, dubious, questionable
ant likely

unlikeness *n* ***syn*** DISSIMILARITY, alterity, difference, discrepancy, dissemblance, dissimilitude, distinction, divergence, divergency, otherness
rel incompatibility, incongruousness, inconsistence
ant likeness

unlimited *adj* **1** ***syn*** LIMITLESS, boundless, endless, immeasurable, indefinite, infinite, measureless, unbounded, unmeasured
ant limited, measured
2 ***syn*** TOTAL 5, all-out, full-blown, full-out, full-scale, totalitarian
ant limited

unload *vb* to remove cargo or the cargo of <*unload* cattle from a truck>
syn disburden, discharge, off-load, unlade, unship, unstow
rel disencumber, dump, jettison, lighten; stevedore; debark, disembark, land
idiom break bulk
ant lade, load

unloose *vb* ***syn*** LOOSE 3, disengage, unbind, undo, unfasten, unfix, unloosen

unloosen *vb* ***syn*** LOOSE 3, disengage, unbind, undo, unfasten, unfix, unloose

unloyal *adj* ***syn*** FAITHLESS, disloyal, false, perfidious, recreant, traitorous, treacherous, unfaithful, untrue

---

syn synonym(s) — ***rel*** related word(s)
idiom idiomatic equivalent(s) — ***con*** contrasted word(s)
ant antonym(s) — * vulgar
|| use limited; if in doubt, see a dictionary
The first word in a synonym list when printed in SMALL CAPITALS shows where there is more information about the group. For a more efficient use of this book see Explanatory Notes.

ant loyal

‖**unluck** *n* ***syn*** MISFORTUNE, adversity, contretemps, ‖dole, mischance, mishap, tragedy
ant luck

unlucky *adj* **1** ***syn*** OMINOUS, apocalyptic, baleful, baneful, dire, direful, doomful, fateful, ill-boding, ill-omened
2 involving or suffering misfortune that results from chance <in spite of careful planning the expedition was *unlucky* from the start>
syn hapless, ill-fated, ill-starred, luckless, misfortunate, star-crossed, unfortunate, unhappy, untoward
rel calamitous, cataclysmic, catastrophic, dire, disastrous, tragical
idiom down on one's luck, out of luck
con fortunate, happy, providential; prosperous, successful; coming, made
ant lucky

unmake *vb* **1** ***syn*** DESTROY 1, decimate, demolish, raze, ruin, unbuild, undo, unframe, wrack, wreck
2 ***syn*** DEPOSE 1, dethrone, discrown, disenthrone, displace, disthrone, uncrown
ant make

unman *vb* ***syn*** UNNERVE, castrate, emasculate, enervate, unstring
rel deplete, drain, exhaust, impoverish; abase, degrade; disqualify, paralyze, prostrate, unfit
idiom knock the bottom (*or* stuffing) out of
con brace, fortify
ant man

unmanageable *adj* ***syn*** UNRULY 1, fractious, indocile, indomitable, intractable, recalcitrant, undisciplinable, undisciplined, ungovernable, wild
ant manageable

unmanly *adj* **1** ***syn*** COWARDLY, ‖chicken, coward, craven, gutless, lily-livered, poltroon, poor-spirited, pusillanimous, spunkless
ant manly
2 ***syn*** EFFEMINATE, epicene, Miss-Nancyish, pansified, prissy, sissified, sissy
ant manly

unmannered *adj* **1** ***syn*** RUDE 6, discourteous, disgracious, disrespectful, ill-bred, ill-mannered, impolite, uncivil, ungracious, unmannerly
2 ***syn*** FRANK, candid, man-to-man, open, openhearted, plain, straightforward, undisguised, undissembled, unvarnished

unmannerly *adj* ***syn*** RUDE 6, discourteous, disgracious, disrespectful, ill-bred, ill-mannered, impolite, uncivil, ungracious, unmannered
ant mannerly

unmarred *adj* ***syn*** WHOLE 1, entire, intact, perfect, sound, unbroken, undamaged, unhurt, unimpaired, uninjured
ant marred

unmarried *adj* ***syn*** SINGLE 1, sole, spouseless, unwed
ant married, wed

unmarry *vb* ***syn*** DIVORCE 2, dismiss, put away

unmask *vb* ***syn*** EXPOSE 4, debunk, discover, show up, uncloak, undress, unshroud

unmatchable *adj* ***syn*** SUPREME, incomparable, preeminent, surpassing, towering, transcendent, ultimate, unequalable, unsurpassable

unmatched *adj* **1** ***syn*** ALONE 3, matchless, only, peerless, unequaled, unique, unparagoned, unparalleled, unrivaled
2 ***syn*** ODD 1, unpaired
ant matched

unmaterial *adj* ***syn*** IMMATERIAL 1, bodiless, discarnate, disembodied, incorporeal, insubstantial, metaphysical, nonmaterial, nonphysical, unembodied
ant material

unmeaning *adj* ***syn*** SENSELESS 5, insignificant, meaningless, pointless, purportless
ant meaningful

unmeasurable *adj* **1** ***syn*** INCALCULABLE 1, immeasurable, inestimable, measureless, uncountable, unmeasured, unreckonable
ant measurable
2 ***syn*** EXCESSIVE 1, dizzy, exorbitant, extravagant, extreme, immoderate, inordinate, towering, unconscionable, undue

unmeasured *adj* **1** ***syn*** INCALCULABLE 1, immeasurable, inestimable, measureless, uncountable, unmeasurable, unreckonable
ant measurable
2 ***syn*** LIMITLESS, boundless, endless, immeasurable, indefinite, infinite, measureless, unbounded, unlimited
ant limited, measured

unmeditated *adj* ***syn*** SPONTANEOUS, automatic, impulsive, instinctive, involuntary, unpremeditated, unprompted, will-less
ant meditated

unmeet *adj* ***syn*** UNFIT 1, ill-adapted, ill-suited, inappropriate, inapt, unfitted, unsuitable, unsuited
ant meet

unmeetness *n* ***syn*** IMPROPRIETY 1, incorrectness, indecorousness, indecorum, inelegance, unbecomingness, unseemliness, untowardness

unmellowed *adj* ***syn*** YOUNG 1, callow, green, immature, infant, juvenile, unfledged, unripe, youthful
con developed, matured, ripened
ant mellow, mellowed

unmerciful *adj* ***syn*** PITILESS, merciless, unpitying
ant merciful

unmindful *adj* ***syn*** FORGETFUL, oblivious, unwitting
con anxious, careful, concerned
ant mindful; solicitous

unmindfulness *n* ***syn*** APATHY 2, disinterest, disregard, heedlessness, indifference, insouciance, lassitude, lethargy, listlessness, unconcern
ant mindfulness

unmistakable *adj* ***syn*** CLEAR 5, apparent, distinct, evident, manifest, palpable, patent, plain, straightforward, univocal
ant mistakable

---

unmitigated *adj* **1** ***syn*** PURE 2, absolute, perfect, sheer, simple, unadulterated, unalloyed, undiluted, unmixed, unqualified
2 ***syn*** UTTER, absolute, complete, damned, gross, out-and-out, outright, rank, straight-out, thoroughgoing

unmixable *adj* ***syn*** INCONSONANT 1, conflicting, disconsonant, discordant, discrepant, dissonant, incompatible, incongruent, incongruous, inconsistent

unmixed *adj* **1** ***syn*** STRAIGHT 3, neat, plain, pure, unadulterated, undiluted
ant blended, mixed
2 ***syn*** PURE 2, absolute, perfect, sheer, simple, unadulterated, unalloyed, undiluted, unmitigated, unqualified

unmodern *adj* ***syn*** OLD-FASHIONED, antiquated, antique, archaic, dated, old, oldfangled, old-time, out-of-date, vintage
ant modern

unmodifiable *adj* ***syn*** INFLEXIBLE 3, constant, fixed, immovable, immutable, inalterable, invariable, unalterable, unchangeable, unmovable
ant modifiable

unmovable *adj* **1** ***syn*** IMMOVABLE 1, fixed, immobile, immotile, immotive, irremovable, ‖sitfast, steadfast
ant mobile, movable
2 ***syn*** INFLEXIBLE 3, constant, fixed, immovable, immutable, inalterable, invariable, unalterable, unchangeable, unmodifiable

unmoving *adj* ***syn*** STATIC, immobile, stagnant, stationary
ant mobile

unmusical *adj* ***syn*** DISSONANT 1, cacophonic, cacophonous, discordant, disharmonic, disharmonious, immusical, inharmonic, inharmonious, unharmonious
ant musical

unnamed *adj* ***syn*** ANONYMOUS, innominate, nameless, undesignated

unnatural *adj* **1** ***syn*** IRREGULAR 1, abnormal, anomalous, deviant, divergent, off-key, unregular
2 ***syn*** SUPERNATURAL 2, superhuman, supernormal, superordinary, supranormal, uncanny
ant natural

unneat *adj* ***syn*** SLOVENLY 1, careless, ill-kempt, messy, slipshod, sloppy, uncombed, unfastidious, unkempt, untidy
ant neat

unnecessary *adj* not needed or unavoidable < *unnecessary* loss of life >
syn inessential, needless, uncalled-for, unessential, unneeded, unneedful, unrequired
rel excess, redundant, superfluous, surplus; lavish, prodigal, profuse; gratuitous, supererogatory
con essential, needed, required, vital; inevitable, unescapable
ant necessary; unavoidable

---

syn synonym(s) ***rel*** related word(s)
idiom idiomatic equivalent(s) ***con*** contrasted word(s)
ant antonym(s) * vulgar
‖ use limited; if in doubt, see a dictionary
The first word in a synonym list when printed in SMALL CAPITALS shows where there is more information about the group. For a more efficient use of this book see Explanatory Notes.

unneeded *adj* ***syn*** UNNECESSARY, inessential, needless, uncalled-for, unessential, unneedful, unrequired
ant needed; unavoidable

unneedful *adj* ***syn*** UNNECESSARY, inessential, needless, uncalled-for, unessential, unneeded, unrequired
ant needful; unavoidable

unnerve *vb* to deprive of strength, spirit, and vigor <a man so *unnerved* as to be bereft of sense and judgment>
syn castrate, emasculate, enervate, unman, unstring
rel enfeeble, sap, undermine, weaken; bewilder, confound, distract; agitate, perturb, upset
con brace (up), inspirit, invigorate, reinforce, strengthen; encourage, hearten, steel
ant nerve

unneutral *adj* ***syn*** BIASED 2, colored, jaundiced, one-sided, partial, partisan, prejudiced, prepossessed, tendentious, warped
ant neutral

unnoted *adj* ***syn*** OBSCURE 5, nameless, uncelebrated, unfamed, unheard-of, unknown, unrenowned
rel unconsidered, unobserved, unremarked
ant noted

unnoteworthy *adj* ***syn*** COMMON 6, commonplace, ordinary, prosaic, uneventful, unexceptional
ant noteworthy

unnoticeable *adj* ***syn*** INCONSPICUOUS, obscure, unconspicuous, unemphatic
ant noticeable

unnoticing *adj* ***syn*** INATTENTIVE, inobservant, unheeding, unobservant, unobserving, unperceiving, unwatchful
ant noticing

unnumberable *adj* ***syn*** INNUMERABLE, countless, innumerous, numberless, uncountable, uncounted, unnumbered, untold

unnumbered *adj* ***syn*** INNUMERABLE, countless, innumerous, numberless, uncountable, uncounted, unnumberable, untold
ant numbered

unobjectionable *adj* ***syn*** DECENT 4, adequate, all right, common, good, satisfactory, sufficient, tolerable, unexceptionable, unexceptional
ant objectionable

unobjective *adj* ***syn*** SUBJECTIVE
ant objective

unobservable *adj* ***syn*** IMPERCEPTIBLE, impalpable, imponderable, inappreciable, indiscernible, insensible, intangible, unapparent, unappreciable, unperceivable

unobservant *adj* ***syn*** INATTENTIVE, inobservant, unheeding, unnoticing, unobserving, unperceiving, unwatchful
ant observant, observing

unobserving *adj* ***syn*** INATTENTIVE, inobservant, unheeding, unnoticing, unobservant, unperceiving, unwatchful
ant observant, observing

unobstructed *adj* ***syn*** OPEN 1, patent, unclosed
con clogged, plugged
ant obstructed

unobtainable *adj* ***syn*** INACCESSIBLE, inapproachable, unapproachable, unattainable, un-come-at-able, ungetatable, unreachable

unobtrusive *adj* ***syn*** QUIET 4, inobtrusive, restrained, subdued, tasteful, tasty
ant obtrusive

unoffending *adj* ***syn*** HARMLESS, innocent, innocuous, innoxious, inobnoxious, inoffensive, unoffensive
ant offending

unoffensive *adj* ***syn*** HARMLESS, innocent, innocuous, innoxious, inobnoxious, inoffensive, unoffending
ant offensive

unofficial *adj* ***syn*** INFORMAL 1, irregular, unceremonious

unoften *adv* ***syn*** SELDOM, hardly ever, infrequently, little, rarely, unfrequently
ant often

unordinary *adj* ***syn*** EXCEPTIONAL 1, extraordinary, rare, singular, uncommon, unimaginable, unique, unthinkable, unusual, unwonted
ant ordinary

unorganized *adj* ***syn*** INCOHERENT 2, disconnected, discontinuous, disjointed, disordered, inchoate, incohesive, muddled, unconnected, uncontinuous
ant organized

unoriginal *adj* lacking or manifesting a lack of capacity for originality <a good man but with a mind stolid and *unoriginal*>
syn noncreative, sterile, uncreative, uninspired, uninventive, unoriginative; *compare* ARID 2
rel arid, barren, dry; dull, prosaic, staid, stodgy, stuffy, unfired
con creative, inspired, inventive, originative; alert, aware, keen; constructive, productive
ant original

unoriginated *adj* ***syn*** SELF-EXISTENT, increate, self-existing, unbegotten, uncaused, uncreated

unoriginative *adj* ***syn*** UNORIGINAL, noncreative, sterile, uncreative, uninspired, uninventive
ant originative

unornamented *adj* ***syn*** PLAIN 1, dry, inelaborate, simple, unadorned, unbeautified, unelaborate, unembellished, unembroidered, ungarnished

unorthodox *adj* ***syn*** HERETICAL, dissident, heterodox, nonconformist, schismatic, sectarian
ant orthodox

unorthodoxy *n* ***syn*** HERESY, dissent, dissidence, heterodoxy, misbelief, nonconformism, nonconformity, schism
ant orthodoxy

unostentatious *adj* ***syn*** PLAIN 1, discreet, inelaborate, modest, simple, unbeautified, unelaborate, unembellished, unembroidered, unpretentious
ant ostentatious

unpaid *adj* **1** serving without pay <a charity manned by *unpaid* assistants>
syn uncompensated, unrecompensed, unremunerated
rel freewill, gratuitous, voluntary, volunteer
con compensated, recompensed, remunerated
ant paid
2 not cleared by payment <an *unpaid* bill>
syn due, mature, outstanding, overdue, owing, payable, unsettled
idiom in arrears
con cleared, discharged, liquidated, settled
ant paid

unpaired *adj* ***syn*** ODD 1, unmatched
ant paired

unpalatable *adj* **1** lacking appeal to the sense of taste <threw together a greasy *unpalatable* meal>
syn distasteful, flat, flavorless, ill-flavored, insipid, savorless, tasteless, unappetizing, unsavory
rel loathsome, nauseous, sickening; thin, washy, watery, weak
con appetizing, delectable, delicious, flavorsome, sapid, savory, tasty
ant palatable
2 ***syn*** BITTER 2, afflictive, distasteful, galling, grievous, painful

unparagoned *adj* ***syn*** ALONE 3, matchless, only, peerless, unequaled, unique, unmatched, unparalleled, unrivaled
ant paragoned

unparalleled *adj* ***syn*** ALONE 3, matchless, only, peerless, unequaled, unique, unmatched, unparagoned, unrivaled
ant paralleled

unpardonable *adj* ***syn*** INEXCUSABLE, indefensible, inexpiable, unforgivable, unjustifiable, untenable
ant pardonable

unparented *adj* ***syn*** ORPHAN, orphaned, parentless

unpassioned *adj* ***syn*** NEUTRAL, abstract, colorless, detached, disinterested, dispassionate, impersonal, poker-faced
ant impassioned, passionate

unpatient *adj* ***syn*** IMPATIENT 1, chafing, fretful
ant patient

unpeace *n* ***syn*** DISCORD, conflict, contention, difference, disaccord, dispeace, dissension, dissent, strife, variance
ant peace

unpeaceful *adj* ***syn*** RESTLESS, uneasy, unquiet, unrestful, unsettled, untranquil
ant peaceful

unpedantic *adj* ***syn*** LIVELY 1, alert, animate, animated, ‖cant, gay, keen, spirited, sprightly, vivacious
ant pedantic

unperceivable *adj* ***syn*** IMPERCEPTIBLE, impalpable, imponderable, inappreciable, indiscernible, insensible, intangible, unapparent, unappreciable, unobservable

unperceiving *adj* **1** ***syn*** IMPERCEPTIVE, impercipient, unperceptive
ant perceiving, perceptive, percipient
2 ***syn*** INATTENTIVE, inobservant, unheeding, unnoticing, unobservant, unobserving, unwatchful

unperceptive *adj* ***syn*** IMPERCEPTIVE, impercipient, unperceiving
ant perceiving, perceptive, percipient

unperishable *adj* ***syn*** INDESTRUCTIBLE, imperishable, incorruptible, inexterminable, inextinguishable, inextirpable, irrefragable, irrefrangible, quenchless, undestroyable

---

syn synonym(s) ***rel*** related word(s)
idiom idiomatic equivalent(s) ***con*** contrasted word(s)
ant antonym(s) * vulgar
‖ use limited; if in doubt, see a dictionary
The first word in a synonym list when printed in SMALL CAPITALS shows where there is more information about the group. For a more efficient use of this book see Explanatory Notes.

ant perishable

unpermissive *adj* ***syn*** RIGID 3, draconian, ironhanded, rigorist, rigorous, strict, stringent
ant permissive

unphysical *adj* ***syn*** IMMATERIAL 1, asomatous, bodiless, discarnate, disembodied, incorporeal, metaphysical, nonmaterial, nonphysical, unembodied
ant physical

unpierceable *adj* ***syn*** IMPASSABLE 1, impenetrable, impermeable, imperviable, impervious
ant pierceable

unpitying *adj* ***syn*** PITILESS, merciless, unmerciful
ant pitying

unplanned *adj* **1** ***syn*** RANDOM, aimless, designless, desultory, haphazard, hit-or-miss, indiscriminate, purposeless, unaimed, unconsidered
ant planned
2 ***syn*** UNINTENTIONAL, inadvertent, undesigned, undevised, unintended, unpremeditated, unpurposed, unthought
ant planned

unpleasant *adj* ***syn*** BAD 8, ||chiselly, disagreeable, displeasing, rotten, sour, unhappy

unpliable *adj* ***syn*** OBSTINATE, bullheaded, headstrong, intractable, mulish, pertinaceous, perverse, pigheaded, self-willed, stubborn
ant pliable, pliant

unpliant *adj* ***syn*** OBSTINATE, bullheaded, headstrong, intractable, mulish, pertinaceous, perverse, pigheaded, self-willed, stubborn
ant pliable, pliant

unpolished *adj* **1** ***syn*** RUDE 1, crude, rough, roughhewn, undressed, unfashioned, unfinished, unformed, unhewn, unworked
idiom in the rough
ant polished
2 ***syn*** RUDE 6, discourteous, disgracious, disrespectful, ill-bred, ill-mannered, impolite, incivil, uncivil, ungracious
3 ***syn*** BOORISH, churlish, cloddish, clodhopping, ill-bred, loutish, lowbred, uncivilized, uncultured, unrefined
ant polished

unpolitic *adj* ***syn*** TACTLESS, brash, impolitic, maladroit, undiplomatic, untactful
ant politic

unpractical *adj* ***syn*** IMPRACTICAL 1, ivory-tower, ivory-towered, ivory-towerish, nonrealistic, unrealistic, viewy
ant practical

unpracticed *adj* **1** ***syn*** UNTRIED 1, undemonstrated, unproved, untested
2 ***syn*** INEXPERIENCED, callow, fresh, green, raw, unconversant, unfleshed, unseasoned, untried, unversed
ant practiced

---

syn synonym(s) — *rel* related word(s)
idiom idiomatic equivalent(s) — *con* contrasted word(s)
ant antonym(s) — * vulgar
|| use limited; if in doubt, see a dictionary
The first word in a synonym list when printed in SMALL CAPITALS shows where there is more information about the group. For a more efficient use of this book see Explanatory Notes.

---

unpredictable *adj* ***syn*** UNCERTAIN 1, capricious, chancy, erratic, fluctuant, iffy, incalculable, whimsical
ant predictable

unprejudiced *adj* ***syn*** FAIR 4, dispassionate, equal, equitable, impartial, just, nondiscriminatory, objective, unbiased, uncolored
ant prejudiced

unpremeditated *adj* **1** ***syn*** SPONTANEOUS, automatic, impulsive, instinctive, involuntary, unmeditated, unprompted, will-less
2 ***syn*** UNINTENTIONAL, inadvertent, undesigned, undevised, unintended, unplanned, unpurposed, unthought
ant premeditated

unprepossessed *adj* ***syn*** FAIR 4, dispassionate, equitable, impartial, just, nondiscriminatory, objective, unbiased, uncolored, unprejudiced
ant prepossessed

unprescribed *adj* ***syn*** VOLUNTARY, deliberate, intentional, unforced, willful, willing, witting
ant prescribed

unpretentious *adj* ***syn*** PLAIN 1, discreet, inelaborate, modest, simple, unbeautified, unelaborate, unembellished, ungarnished, unostentatious
ant pretentious

unpretty *adj* ***syn*** PLAIN 5, homely, unalluring, unattractive, unbeauteous, unbeautiful, uncomely, unhandsome
ant pretty

unprevailing *adj* ***syn*** FUTILE, abortive, bootless, fruitless, ineffective, ineffectual, unavailable, unavailing, useless, vain

unprincipled *adj* **1** ***syn*** UNSCRUPULOUS, conscienceless, stick-at-nothing, unconscionable
ant principled
2 ***syn*** ABANDONED 2, dissolute, licentious, profligate, reprobate, self-abandoned
rel corrupt, crooked, unscrupulous; dishonest, unconscientious, unethical
3 ***syn*** CORRUPT 2, mercenary, praetorian, unethical, unscrupulous, venal
ant principled

unproductive *adj* **1** ***syn*** BARREN 2, hardscrabble, infertile, unbearing, unfertile
rel impotent, infecund, unprolific
ant productive
2 ***syn*** FUTILE, abortive, bootless, fruitless, ineffective, ineffectual, unavailable, unavailing, useless, vain
ant productive

unprofane *adj* ***syn*** HOLY 1, blessed, consecrated, hallowed, sacred, sanctified
ant profane

unproficient *adj* ***syn*** UNSKILLFUL 1, inadept, inapt, inept, inexpert, unapt, undexterous, unfacile, unhandy
ant proficient, skilled

unprogressive *adj* **1** ***syn*** BACKWARD 6, behindhand, underdeveloped, undeveloped
ant progressive
2 ***syn*** BACKWARD 5, benighted, ignorant, unenlightened
ant progressive

unprompted *adj* ***syn*** SPONTANEOUS, automatic, impulsive, instinctive, involuntary, unmeditated, unpremeditated, will-less

unpropitious *adj* ***syn*** OMINOUS, baleful, baneful, dire, fateful, ill-boding, ill-omened, inauspicious, threatening, unlucky
rel adverse, antagonistic, counter
con cheering, encouraging, reassuring
ant propitious

unproportionate *adj* ***syn*** LOPSIDED, asymmetric, difform, disproportional, disproportionate, nonsymmetrical, proportionless, unequal, uneven, unsymmetrical
ant proportionate

unprosperous *adj* ***syn*** POOR 1, broke, destitute, fortuneless, impecunious, impoverished, indigent, low, needy, penurious
ant prosperous

unprosperousness *n* ***syn*** POVERTY 1, destitution, impecuniousness, impoverishment, indigence, need, neediness, penury, poorness, privation
ant prosperousness

unprotected *adj* ***syn*** HELPLESS 1, defenseless
rel undefended, unguarded, unsheltered, unshielded; insecure, unsafe
ant protected

unproved *adj* ***syn*** UNTRIED 1, undemonstrated, unpracticed, untested
ant proved

unpunctual *adj* ***syn*** TARDY, behindhand, belated, late, lated, overdue
ant punctual

unpurposed *adj* **1** ***syn*** UNINTENTIONAL, inadvertent, undesigned, undevised, unintended, unplanned, unpremeditated, unthought
2 ***syn*** FECKLESS 1, fustian, good-for-nothing, meaningless, purposeless, useless, worthless

unqualified *adj* **1** ***syn*** UNFIT 2, disqualified, incapable, incompetent, ineligible, unequipped, unfitted
rel unskilled; unsuitable
ant qualified
2 ***syn*** SURE 2, abiding, enduring, firm, never-failing, steadfast, steady, unfaltering, unquestioning, wholehearted
rel unconditional, unlimited, unreserved; clear, explicit, express; entire, perfect, utter
ant qualified
3 ***syn*** UTTER, absolute, blasted, blessed, complete, confounded, gross, infernal, out-and-out, rank
4 ***syn*** PURE 2, absolute, perfect, sheer, simple, unadulterated, unalloyed, undiluted, unmitigated, unmixed

unquenchable *adj* ***syn*** INSATIABLE, insatiate, quenchless, unappeasable, unsatiate, unsatisfiable
ant quenchable

unquestionable *adj* **1** ***syn*** AUTHENTIC 2, bona fide, genuine, indubitable, real, sure-enough, true, undoubted, veritable, very
ant doubtable, questionable
2 ***syn*** POSITIVE 3, certain, incontestable, incontrovertible, indisputable, indubitable, uncontestable, undeniable, undisputable, unequivocal
rel dependable, reliable; established, well-founded, well-grounded
ant doubtable, questionable
3 ***syn*** DOWNRIGHT 2, flat, indubitable, up-and-down

unquestionably *adv* ***syn*** EASILY 2, absolutely, definitely, doubtless, doubtlessly, positively, unequivocally
ant questionably

unquestioning *adj* ***syn*** SURE 2, abiding, enduring, firm, fixed, never-failing, steadfast, steady, unshakable, unshaken
ant questioning

unquiet *adj* ***syn*** RESTLESS, uneasy, unpeaceful, unrestful, unsettled, untranquil
ant quiet

unravel *vb* ***syn*** SOLVE 2, break, decipher, dissolve, ||dope out, figure out, puzzle out, resolve, unfold, unriddle
rel disentangle, extricate, untangle

unreachable *adj* ***syn*** INACCESSIBLE, inapproachable, unapproachable, unattainable, un-come-at-able, ungetatable, unobtainable
ant reachable

unreadable *adj* ***syn*** ILLEGIBLE, indecipherable, undecipherable
ant legible, readable

unreal *adj* ***syn*** FICTITIOUS 1, chimerical, fanciful, fantastic, fictional, fictive, illusory, imaginary, suppositious, supposititious
ant real

unrealistic *adj* ***syn*** IMPRACTICAL 1, ivory-tower, ivory-towered, ivory-towerish, nonrealistic, unpractical, viewy
ant realistic

unrealizable *adj* ***syn*** IMPOSSIBLE 1, impracticable, impractical, infeasible, irrealizable, unattainable, unfeasible, unworkable
ant realizable

unreasonable *adj* **1** ***syn*** ILLOGICAL, fallacious, invalid, irrational, mad, nonrational, reasonless, sophistic, unreasoned
rel incongruous, loose, self-contradictory
ant reasonable
2 exceeding the bounds of reason or right <the constitutional guarantees against *unreasonable* searches and seizures>
syn unconscionable, undue, unjustifiable, unwarrantable, unwarranted
rel arbitrary, peremptory; excessive, immoderate, inordinate, overmuch; improper, unlawful, unrightful, wrongful
con lawful, licit; proper, right, tolerable
ant reasonable

unreasoned *adj* ***syn*** ILLOGICAL, fallacious, invalid, irrational, mad, nonrational, reasonless, sophistic, unreasonable
ant reasoned

unrecking *adj* ***syn*** CARELESS 1, feckless, heedless, inadvertent, irreflective, thoughtless, uncaring, unheeding, unreflective, unthinking

unreckonable *adj* ***syn*** INCALCULABLE 1, immeasurable, inestimable, measureless, uncountable, unmeasurable, unmeasured

---

syn synonym(s) ***rel*** related word(s)
idiom idiomatic equivalent(s) ***con*** contrasted wor
ant antonym(s) * vulgar
|| use limited; if in doubt, see a dictionary
The first word in a synonym list when printed i out
CAPITALS shows where there is more informat Ex-
the group. For a more efficient use of this bo
planatory Notes.

unrecompensed *adj* ***syn*** UNPAID 1, uncompensated, unremunerated
ant recompensed

unrecoverable *adj* ***syn*** HOPELESS 2, cureless, immedicable, impossible, incurable, insanable, irremediable, irreparable, uncorrectable, uncurable

unrefined *adj* **1** ***syn*** BOORISH, churlish, cloddish, clodhopping, ill-bred, loutish, lowbred, uncivilized, uncultured, unpolished
ant refined
2 ***syn*** COARSE 3, crass, crude, gross, inelegant, raw, rough, rude, uncouth, vulgar
ant refined
3 not freed from unwanted material <shipped the *unrefined* ore>
syn crude, impure, native, raw, run-of-mine, ungraded, unsorted
rel rough, roughcast, roughhewn; coarse, natural, undressed, unprocessed
idiom in the rough
con dressed, processed
ant refined

unreflective *adj* ***syn*** CARELESS 1, feckless, heedless, inadvertent, irreflective, thoughtless, uncaring, unheeding, unrecking, unthinking

unregretful *adj* ***syn*** REMORSELESS, impenitent, regretless, uncontrite, unremorseful, unrepentant, unsorry
ant regretful

unregular *adj* ***syn*** IRREGULAR 1, abnormal, anomalous, deviant, divergent, off-key, unnatural
ant regular

unrehearsed *adj* ***syn*** EXTEMPORANEOUS, autoschediastic, extemporary, extempore, impromptu, improvised, offhand, spur-of-the-moment, unstudied
ant rehearsed

unrelenting *adj* ***syn*** GRIM 3, implacable, ironfisted, merciless, mortal, relentless, ruthless, unappeasable, unflinching, unyielding
ant relenting

unreliable *adj* **1** not to be counted on <it is certain that much of the testimony was *unreliable*>
syn dubious, fly-by-night, questionable, trustless, undependable, unsure, untrustworthy, untrusty
rel fickle, inconstant, unstable, vacillating; faithless, false, untrue; falsehearted, perfidious; shifty, slick, slippery, tricky; inaccurate, inexact, unfaithful
idiom not to be depended (*or* relied) on
con dependable, trustworthy, trusty; constant; faithful, true
ant reliable
2 ***syn*** UNSAFE, unassured, undependable, untrustworthy
ant reliable

unreligious *adj* ***syn*** IRRELIGIOUS, godless, nonreligious
ant religious

unremarkable *adj* ***syn*** ORDINARY 1, everyday, plain, plain Jane, quotidian, routine, usual, workaday

unremitting *adj* ***syn*** CONTINUAL, ceaseless, constant, endless, everlasting, interminable, perpetual, unceasing, unending, uninterrupted

unremittingly *adv* ***syn*** HARD 3, assiduously, dingdong, earnestly, exhaustively, intensely, intensively, painstakingly, thoroughly

unremorseful *adj* ***syn*** REMORSELESS, impenitent, regretless, uncontrite, unregretful, unrepentant, unsorry
ant remorseful

unremunerated *adj* ***syn*** UNPAID 1, uncompensated, unrecompensed
ant remunerated

unrenowned *adj* ***syn*** OBSCURE 5, nameless, uncelebrated, unfamed, unheard-of, unknown, unnoted
ant renowned

unrepealable *adj* ***syn*** IRREVOCABLE, irreversible, nonreversible
ant repealable

unrepeatable *adj* ***syn*** ONLY 2, alone, lone, singular, sole, solitary, solo, unexampled, unique

unrepentant *adj* ***syn*** REMORSELESS, impenitent, regretless, uncontrite, unregretful, unremorseful, unsorry
ant repentant

unrepresentative *adj* ***syn*** ABNORMAL 1, aberrant, anomalous, atypical, deviant, deviative, heteroclite, preternatural, untypical

unrequested *adj* ***syn*** UNASKED, unbidden, uninvited, unsought

unrequired *adj* **1** ***syn*** UNNECESSARY, inessential, needless, uncalled-for, unessential, unneeded, unneedful
ant required
2 ***syn*** DISPENSABLE, nonessential, unessential
ant required

unreserved *adj* **1** ***syn*** FRANK 1, candid, open, openhearted, plain, straightforward, unconcealed, undisguised, undissembled, unvarnished
ant reserved
2 ***syn*** DEMONSTRATIVE, expansive, outgoing, unconstrained, unrestrained
ant reserved
3 ***syn*** EASYGOING 3, breezy, casual, dégagé, informal, low-pressure, relaxed, ‖sonsy, unconstrained, unfussy

unresistant *adj* ***syn*** PASSIVE 2, acquiescent, nonresistant, nonresisting, resigned, submissive, unresisting, yielding
ant resistant, resisting

unresisting *adj* ***syn*** PASSIVE 2, acquiescent, nonresistant, nonresisting, resigned, submissive, unresistant, yielding
ant resistant, resisting

unresolved *adj* ***syn*** VACILLATING 2, faltering, hesitant, hesitating, indecisive, irresolute, shilly-shally, uncertain, undecisive, wavering
ant resolved

unrespectable *adj* ***syn*** DISREPUTABLE 1, discreditable, disgraceful, dishonorable, ignominious, inglorious, shabby, shady, shameful, shoddy
ant respectable

unresponsive *adj* **1** ***syn*** INSUSCEPTIBLE, impassive, insensitive, insentient, unimpressible, unimpressionable, unsusceptible

---

syn synonym(s) ***rel*** related word(s)
idiom idiomatic equivalent(s) ***con*** contrasted word(s)
nt antonym(s) * vulgar
se limited; if in doubt, see a dictionary
first word in a synonym list when printed in SMALL
ALS shows where there is more information about
up. For a more efficient use of this book see Ex-
Notes.

ant responsive
2 ***syn*** FRIGID 3, cold, inhibited, passionless, undersexed

unresponsiveness *n* ***syn*** APATHY 1, impassivity, insensibility, phlegm, stoicism, stolidity
ant responsiveness

unrest *n* a disturbed uneasy state <that popular *unrest* that, unchecked, can lead to insurrection and anarchy>
syn ailment, disquiet, disquietude, ferment, inquietude, restiveness, restlessness, storm and stress, Sturm und Drang, turmoil
rel agitation, commotion, confusion, convulsion, tumult, turbulence, upheaval; anarchy, chaos, disorder
con calm, easiness, peace, quiet

unrestful *adj* **1** ***syn*** RESTLESS, uneasy, unpeaceful, unquiet, unsettled, untranquil
ant restful
2 ***syn*** NERVOUS, fidgety, goosey, high-strung, jittery, jumpy, nervy, spooky, twittery

unrestrainable *adj* ***syn*** IRREPRESSIBLE, insuppressible, insuppressive, irrestrainable, uncontainable, uncontrollable
ant restrainable

unrestrained *adj* **1** ***syn*** EXCESSIVE 2, immoderate, inordinate, intemperate, overindulgent, untempered
2 ***syn*** FREE 2, loose, unconfined
ant restrained
3 ***syn*** AUDACIOUS 4, uncurbed, ungoverned, unhampered, uninhibited, untrammeled
rel candid, frank, open; forthright, plainspoken, straightforward; bluff, blunt, brusque
ant restrained
4 ***syn*** DEMONSTRATIVE, expansive, outgoing, unconstrained, unreserved
ant restrained

unrestraint *n* **1** ***syn*** UNCONSTRAINT, abandon, ease, naturalness, spontaneity
ant restraint
2 ***syn*** ABANDON 2, impulsiveness, uninhibitedness

unrestricted *adj* ***syn*** OPEN 4, accessible, open-door, public

unriddle *vb* ***syn*** SOLVE 2, break, ‖cipher, decipher, ‖dope out, figure out, puzzle out, resolve, unfold, unravel

unrighteous *adj* ***syn*** INEQUITABLE, inequable, unequitable, unfair, unjust
ant righteous

unripe *adj* ***syn*** YOUNG 1, callow, green, immature, infant, juvenile, unfledged, youthful

unrivaled *adj* ***syn*** ALONE 3, matchless, only, peerless, unequaled, unique, unmatched, unparagoned, unparalleled

unromantic *adj* ***syn*** REALISTIC, down-to-earth, hard, hard-boiled, hardheaded, matter-of-fact, practical, pragmatic, sober, unsentimental
ant romantic

unruffled *adj* ***syn*** COOL 2, collected, composed, disimpassioned, imperturbable, nonchalant, unflappable
ant discomposed, ruffled

unruly *adj* **1** resistant to discipline or control <a stubborn *unruly* boy>
syn fractious, indocile, indomitable, intractable, recalcitrant, uncontrollable, undisciplinable, undisciplined, ungovernable, unmanageable, untoward, wild; *compare* OBSTINATE, TURBULENT 1
rel contumacious, incorrigible, insubordinate, rebellious; contrary, froward, perverse, wayward; boisterous, obstreperous, rampageous; disorderly, raffish, rambunctious, rowdy, turbulent
idiom out of hand
con controlled, easy, mild, restrained; disciplined, governable, manageable; amenable, biddable, obedient; correct, proper
ant docile, tractable
2 ***syn*** TURBULENT 1, boisterous, disorderly, raucous, rowdy, rowdydowdy, rowdyish, rumbustious, termagant, tumultuous
rel hard, ruffianly, tough
3 ***syn*** DISOBEDIENT, naughty, obstreperous

unsacred *adj* ***syn*** PROFANE 1, lay, secular, temporal
ant sacred

unsafe *adj* not to be depended on or trusted <an *unsafe* investment>
syn unassured, undependable, unreliable, untrustworthy
rel insecure, shaky, tottery, unsound, unstable; chancy, hazardous, risky; dangerous, jeopardous, perilous; erratic, uncertain
con dependable, trustworthy; secure, sound, stable, substantial
ant safe

unsaid *adj* ***syn*** TACIT 1, implicit, implied, inferred, undeclared, understood, unexpressed, unspoken, unuttered, wordless

unsalutary *adj* ***syn*** UNWHOLESOME 1, insalubrious, insalutary, noisome, noxious, sickly, unhealthful, unhealthy
ant salutary

unsandaled *adj* ***syn*** BAREFOOT 1, shoeless, unshod
ant sandaled

unsane *adj* ***syn*** INSANE 1, bedlamite, cracked, crazed, crazy, daft, demented, deranged, unbalanced, unsound
ant sane

unsatiate *adj* ***syn*** INSATIABLE, insatiate, quenchless, unappeasable, unquenchable, unsatisfiable
ant satiate, satiated

unsatisfactory *adj* ***syn*** BAD 1, amiss, ‖bum, ‖crappy, dissatisfactory, poor, ‖punk, rotten, up, wrong
ant satisfactory

unsatisfiable *adj* ***syn*** INSATIABLE, insatiate, quenchless, unappeasable, unquenchable, unsatiate
ant satisfiable

unsavory *adj* ***syn*** UNPALATABLE 1, distasteful, flat, flavorless, ill-flavored, insipid, savorless, tasteless, unappetizing
ant savory

---

unsay *vb* ***syn*** ABJURE, forswear, palinode, recall, recant, retract, take back, withdraw

unscathed *adj* ***syn*** SAFE 1, scatheless, unharmed

unscholarly *adj* not devoted to scholarly pursuits <*unscholarly* concerns>
syn inerudite, unbookish, unlearned, unstudious
rel unenlightened, uninformed, uninitiated; callow, green, unripe; inexperienced, naive
con bookish, erudite, learned; enlightened, informed; experienced
ant scholarly

unschooled *adj* **1** ***syn*** IGNORANT 1, benighted, empty-headed, illiterate, know-nothing, uneducated, uninstructed, unlettered, untaught, untutored
2 ***syn*** NATURAL 5, artless, ingenuous, naive, simple, unaffected, unartificial, unsophisticated, unstudied, untutored

unscramble *vb* ***syn*** EXTRICATE 2, disembarrass, disembroil, disencumber, disentangle, disentwine, unentangle, untangle, untie, untwine

unscrupulous *adj* **1** lacking in moral scruples <*unscrupulous* conduct of political leaders>
syn conscienceless, stick-at-nothing, unconscionable, unprincipled
rel crafty, deceitful, scheming; improper, unseemly, wrongful; corrupt, crooked, dishonest; questionable, shady, sinister, underhand
con conscientious, dutiful, proper, upright; dependable, reliable, responsible
ant scrupulous
2 ***syn*** CORRUPT 2, mercenary, praetorian, unethical, unprincipled, venal
con meticulous, particular, punctilious, strict
ant scrupulous

unseasonable *adj* **1** involving or occurring at an inappropriate or unexpected time <his wife's sudden return proved most *unseasonable*>
syn ill-seasoned, ill-timed, inopportune, malapropos, mistimed, untimely
rel deplorable, inappropriate, inconvenient, unsuitable; inauspicious, infelicitous, undesirable, unfavorable, unfortunate
con apropos, opportune, timely, well-timed
ant seasonable
2 ***syn*** IMPROPER 1, ill-timed, inappropriate, inapt, inept, malapropos, unapt, unbecoming, undue, untimely

unseasoned *adj* ***syn*** INEXPERIENCED, callow, fresh, green, raw, unfleshed, unpracticed, untried, unversed, young
ant seasoned

unseat *vb* ***syn*** THROW 2, buck (off), pitch, unhorse

unsectarian *adj* ***syn*** NONSECTARIAN, interchurch, intercreedal, interdenominational, undenominational
ant sectarian

---

syn synonym(s) ***rel*** related word(s)
idiom idiomatic equivalent(s) ***con*** contrasted word(s)
ant antonym(s) * vulgar
‖ use limited; if in doubt, see a dictionary
The first word in a synonym list when printed in SMALL CAPITALS shows where there is more information about the group. For a more efficient use of this book see Explanatory Notes.

unseemliness *n* ***syn*** IMPROPRIETY 1, incorrectness, indecorousness, indecorum, inelegance, unbecomingness, unmeetness, untowardness
ant propriety, seemliness

unseemly *adj* **1** ***syn*** INDECOROUS, improper, indecent, indelicate, malodorous, rough, unbecoming, undecorous, ungodly, untoward
rel coarse, crude, inelegant, unrefined; raffish, rowdy, ruffianly
con prim, restrained, starchy, stiff, stilted; elegant, gracious, polished, refined
ant seemly
2 ***syn*** IMPROPER 1, ill-timed, inappropriate, inapt, inept, malapropos, unapt, unbecoming, unbefitting, unsuitable
ant seemly

unselfish *adj* ***syn*** SELFLESS, self-forgetful, self-forgetting
ant selfish

unsentimental *adj* ***syn*** REALISTIC, down-to-earth, hard, hard-boiled, hardheaded, matter-of-fact, practical, pragmatic, sober, unromantic
ant sentimental

unserviceable *adj* ***syn*** IMPRACTICABLE 2, impractical, nonfunctional, unfunctional, unusable, unworkable, useless
ant serviceable

unsettle *vb* **1** ***syn*** DISORDER 1, derange, disarrange, disarray, discompose, disorganize, disturb, jumble, rummage, upset
rel agitate, disquiet, perturb; discommode, incommode, trouble
con calm, ease, quiet, stabilize, steady
ant settle
2 ***syn*** UPSET 5, derange, disorder, sicken, turn, unhinge
ant settle
3 ***syn*** DISCOMPOSE 1, agitate, bother, disquiet, disturb, flurry, fluster, perturb, unhinge, upset

unsettled *adj* **1** ***syn*** RESTLESS, uneasy, unpeaceful, unquiet, unrestful, untranquil
2 ***syn*** CHANGEABLE 1, changeful, fluid, mobile, mutable, protean, unstable, unsteady, variable, weathery
ant settled
3 ***syn*** DOUBTFUL 1, clouded, dubious, dubitable, indecisive, open, problematic, uncertain, unclear, undecided
4 ***syn*** PENDING, pendent, undecided, undetermined
ant settled
5 ***syn*** BACK 1, frontier, outlandish, remote
6 ***syn*** UNPAID 2, due, mature, outstanding, overdue, owing, payable
ant settled

unsettledness *n* ***syn*** INSTABILITY, precariousness, shakiness, unfixedness, unstability, unstableness, unsteadfastness, unsteadiness

unsex *vb* ***syn*** STERILIZE, alter, castrate, change, desexualize, fix, geld, mutilate, neuter

unshackle *vb* ***syn*** FREE, discharge, emancipate, liberate, loose, loosen, manumit, release, unbind, unchain
ant shackle

unshakable *adj* ***syn*** SURE 2, abiding, firm, fixed, never-failing, steadfast, steady, unfaltering, unquestioning, unwavering
ant shakable

unshaken *adj* ***syn*** SURE 2, abiding, firm, fixed, never-failing, steadfast, steady, unfaltering, unquestioning, unwavering
ant shaken

unshaped *adj* ***syn*** FORMLESS, amorphous, inchoate, shapeless, unformed
ant shaped

unshared *adj* ***syn*** SOLE 4, exclusive, single
ant shared

unship *vb* ***syn*** UNLOAD, disburden, discharge, off-load, unlade, unstow

unshod *adj* ***syn*** BAREFOOT 1, shoeless, unsandaled
ant shod

unshroud *vb* ***syn*** EXPOSE 4, debunk, discover, show up, uncloak, undress, unmask
ant shroud

unshut *vb* ***syn*** OPEN 1, ope, unblock, unclose, undo, unstop
ant shut

unsightly *adj* ***syn*** UGLY 2, hideous, ill-favored, ill-looking, unbeautiful, uncomely
rel ill-shaped, unshapely; unesthetic; drab, dull, lackluster
ant sightly

unsimilar *adj* ***syn*** DIFFERENT 1, disparate, dissimilar, distant, divergent, diverse, unalike, unequal, unlike, various
ant similar

unskilled *adj* **1** ***syn*** AMATEURISH, dabbling, dilettante, dilettantish, dilettantist, jackleg, unaccomplished, unfinished, ungifted
ant skilled
2 ***syn*** INEFFICIENT 2, incapable, incompetent, inept, inexpert, unexpert, unskillful, unworkmanlike
ant skilled

unskillful *adj* **1** lacking in skill or proficiency <an ardent but *unskillful* home mechanic>
syn inadept, inapt, inept, inexpert, unapt, undexterous, unfacile, unhandy, unproficient
rel incapable, incompetent; unfitted, unqualifed, unready
con adept, apt, dexterous, expert, handy, proficient
ant skillful
2 ***syn*** INEFFICIENT 2, incapable, incompetent, inept, inexpert, unexpert, unskilled, unworkmanlike

unsleeping *adj* ***syn*** WATCHFUL, alert, open-eyed, vigilant, wakeful, wide-awake
ant sleeping

unsmooth *adj* ***syn*** ROUGH 1, asperous, craggy, harsh, jagged, rugged, scabrous, scraggy, uneven, unlevel
ant smooth

unsober *adj* ***syn*** INTOXICATED 1, ‖boozy, ‖canned, disguised, drunk, inebriated, ‖lushed, muddled, pixilated, ‖plastered
ant sober

unsociable *adj* disinclined to active social intercourse <tried to hide his basically shy *unsociable* nature under a professional heartiness of manner>
syn aloof, cool, distant, insociable, offish, reserved, shut-in, solitary, standoff, standoffish, touch-me-not-ish, unapproachable, unbending, uncommunicative, uncompanionable, withdrawn; *compare* INDIFFERENT 2, UNDEMONSTRATIVE
rel self-contained, self-sufficient; exclusive, inaccessible, remote; prickly, sensitive; brooding, secretive; diffident, shy, timid
con cordial, genial, hearty, outgoing; companionable, friendly, gregarious
ant sociable, social

unsoiled *adj* ***syn*** CLEAN 1, cleanly, immaculate, spotless, taintless, unsullied
ant soiled, sullied

unsoluble *adj* ***syn*** INSOLUBLE, inextricable, insolvable, irresoluble, irresolvable, unsolvable
ant soluble, solvable

unsolvable *adj* ***syn*** INSOLUBLE, inextricable, insolvable, irresoluble, irresolvable, unsoluble
ant soluble, solvable

unsophisticated *adj* ***syn*** NATURAL 5, artless, naive, simple, unaffected, unartificial, unschooled, unstudied, untutored, unworldly
rel authentic, bona fide, genuine; callow, crude, green, uncouth
con finished, polished, smooth, suave
ant sophisticated

unsorry *adj* ***syn*** REMORSELESS, impenitent, regretless, uncontrite, unregretful, unremorseful, unrepentant
ant sorry

unsorted *adj* **1** ***syn*** MISCELLANEOUS, assorted, heterogeneous, indiscriminate, mixed, motley, multifarious, promiscuous, unassorted, varied
2 ***syn*** UNREFINED 3, crude, impure, native, raw, run-of-mine, ungraded
ant sorted

unsought *adj* **1** ***syn*** UNASKED, unbidden, uninvited, unrequested
2 ***syn*** UNWELCOME 1, undesired, unwanted, unwished

unsound *adj* **1** ***syn*** INSANE 1, ‖batty, cracked, crazed, daft, demented, deranged, lunatic, mad, unbalanced
ant sound
2 ***syn*** WEAK 1, decrepit, flimsy, fragile, frail, infirm, insubstantial, unsubstantial, ‖wanky, weakly
rel damaged, faulty, flawed, imperfect
con solid, strong, substantial
ant sound
3 ***syn*** FALSE 1, counterfactual, erroneous, inaccurate, incorrect, specious, untrue, wrong
ant sound
4 ***syn*** DANGEROUS 1, chancy, hairy, hazardous, jeopardous, perilous, risky, treacherous, unhealthy, wicked

unsparing *adj* ***syn*** LIBERAL 1, bounteous, bountiful, free, freehanded, generous, handsome, munificent, openhanded, unsparing
ant close, sparing

unspeakable *adj* ***syn*** UNUTTERABLE, incommunicable, indefinable, indescribable, ineffable, inenarrable, inexpressible, undescribable, unexpressible, untellable

---

syn synonym(s) *rel* related word(s)
idiom idiomatic equivalent(s) *con* contrasted word(s)
ant antonym(s) * vulgar
‖ use limited; if in doubt, see a dictionary
The first word in a synonym list when printed in SMALL CAPITALS shows where there is more information about the group. For a more efficient use of this book see Explanatory Notes.

rel loathsome, offensive, repulsive, revolting; abominable, detestable, hateful, odious; distasteful, obnoxious, repellent, repugnant; atrocious, disgusting, outrageous

unspoiled *adj* ***syn*** VIRGIN 2, untapped, untouched, virginal

unspoken *adj* **1** not put into words <met regularly by a sort of *unspoken* agreement>
syn silent, tacit, unexpressed, unuttered, unvoiced, wordless
rel implicit, implied, understood; hinted, intimated, suggested; mute, unsaid, unstated
con mentioned, said, stated, told, voiced
ant spoken
2 ***syn*** TACIT 1, implicit, implied, inferred, undeclared, understood, unexpressed, unsaid, unuttered, wordless
ant spoken

unstability *n* ***syn*** INSTABILITY, precariousness, shakiness, unfixedness, unsettledness, unstableness, unsteadfastness, unsteadiness
ant stability

unstable *adj* **1** ***syn*** MOVABLE, mobile, moving, unsteadfast, unsteady
ant stable
2 difficult to manage because of lack of physical steadiness <the canoe is an inherently *unstable* craft>
syn rocky, ticklish, tricky
rel insecure, uncertain, unsteady
con secure, steady
ant stable
3 ***syn*** WEAK 2, dickey, fluctuant, insecure, rootless, shaky, unsure, vacillating, wavering, wobbly
ant stable
4 ***syn*** INCONSTANT 1, capricious, changeable, fickle, lubricious, mercurial, temperamental, ticklish, variable, volatile
rel buoyant, effervescent, elastic, resilient; freakish
ant stable
5 ***syn*** CHANGEABLE 1, changeful, fluid, mobile, mutable, protean, unsettled, unsteady, variable, weathery
ant stable
6 ***syn*** MUTABLE 2, changeable, inconstant, shifty, slippery, uncertain, unsteady, variable
ant stable
7 ***syn*** DOUBTFUL 1, ambiguous, borderline, dubious, precarious, shaky, suspect, uncertain, unsettled, unsure

unstableness *n* ***syn*** INSTABILITY, precariousness, shakiness, unfixedness, unsettledness, unstability, unsteadfastness, unsteadiness
ant stability, stableness

unsteadfast *adj* ***syn*** MOVABLE, mobile, moving, unstable, unsteady
ant steadfast

syn synonym(s)
idiom idiomatic equivalent(s)
ant antonym(s)
rel related word(s)
con contrasted word(s)
* vulgar
‖ use limited; if in doubt, see a dictionary
The first word in a synonym list when printed in SMALL CAPITALS shows where there is more information about the group. For a more efficient use of this book see Explanatory Notes.

unsteadfastness *n* ***syn*** INSTABILITY, precariousness, shakiness, unfixedness, unsettledness, unstability, unstableness, unsteadiness
ant steadfastness

unsteadiness *n* ***syn*** INSTABILITY, precariousness, shakiness, unfixedness, unsettledness, unstability, unstableness, unsteadfastness
ant steadiness

unsteady *adj* **1** ***syn*** MOVABLE, mobile, moving, unstable, unsteadfast
2 ***syn*** CHANGEABLE 1, changeful, fluid, mobile, mutable, protean, unsettled, unstable, variable, weathery
ant steady
3 ***syn*** MUTABLE 2, changeable, inconstant, shifty, slippery, uncertain, unstable, variable
ant steady

unsteel *vb* ***syn*** DISARM 2, unarm, win (over)

unstop *vb* ***syn*** OPEN 1, ope, unblock, unclose, undo, unshut
ant stop

unstow *vb* ***syn*** UNLOAD , disburden, discharge, off-load, unlade, unship

unstrengthen *vb* ***syn*** WEAKEN 1, attenuate, blunt, cripple, debilitate, disable, enfeeble, sap, unbrace, undermine
ant strengthen

unstring *vb* ***syn*** UNNERVE, castrate, emasculate, enervate, unman

unstudied *adj* **1** ***syn*** NATURAL 5, artless, ingenuous, naive, simple, unaffected, unartificial, unschooled, unsophisticated, untutored
ant studied
2 ***syn*** EXTEMPORANEOUS, autoschediastic, extemporary, extempore, impromptu, improvised, offhand, spur-of-the-moment, unrehearsed

unstudious *adj* ***syn*** UNSCHOLARLY, inerudite, unbookish, unlearned
ant studious

unstylish *adj* ***syn*** TACKY 2, dowdy, frumpish, frumpy, outmoded, out-of-date, stodgy
ant stylish

unsubstantial *adj* **1** ***syn*** TENUOUS 3, feeble, insubstantial
ant substantial
2 ***syn*** IMPLAUSIBLE, flimsy, improbable, inconceivable, incredible, thick, thin, unbelievable, unconvincing, weak
3 ***syn*** IMMATERIAL 1, bodiless, incorporeal, insubstantial, metaphysical, nonmaterial, nonphysical, spiritual, unembodied, unphysical
ant substantial
4 ***syn*** WEAK 1, decrepit, feeble, flimsy, fragile, frail, infirm, unsound, ‖wanky, weakly
rel insecure, shaky, undependable
ant substantial

unsuccess *n* ***syn*** FAILURE 2, defeat, insuccess, nonsuccess, unsuccessfulness
ant success, successfulness

unsuccessfulness *n* ***syn*** FAILURE 2, defeat, insuccess, nonsuccess, unsuccess
ant success, successfulness

unsufferable *adj* ***syn*** INSUFFERABLE, insupportable, intolerable, unbearable, unbrookable, unendurable, unsupportable *ant* sufferable

unsufficient *adj* ***syn*** SHORT 3, deficient, inadequate, insufficient, scant, scanty, scarce, scrimpy, shy, wanting
ant sufficient

unsuitable *adj* **1** ***syn*** UNFIT 1, ill-adapted, ill-suited, inappropriate, inapt, unfitted, unmeet, unsuited
rel undesirable, unhappy
ant suitable
2 ***syn*** IMPROPER 1, ill-timed, inappropriate, inapt, inept, unbecoming, unbefitting, undue, unseasonable, untimely
ant suitable

unsuited *adj* ***syn*** UNFIT 1, ill-adapted, ill-suited, inappropriate, inapt, unfitted, unmeet, unsuitable
rel inadmissible, objectionable, unacceptable; disappointing, inadequate
ant suited

unsullied *adj* **1** ***syn*** CHASTE, clean, decent, immaculate, modest, pure, spotless, stainless, unblemished, undefiled
ant sullied
2 ***syn*** CLEAN 1, cleanly, immaculate, spotless, taintless, unsoiled
ant soiled, sullied

unsupportable *adj* ***syn*** INSUFFERABLE, insupportable, intolerable, unbearable, unbrookable, unendurable, unsufferable
ant bearable, supportable

unsure *adj* **1** ***syn*** INSECURE 1, unassured, unconfident
ant sure
2 ***syn*** WEAK 2, dickey, fluctuant, insecure, rootless, shaky, unstable, vacillating, wavering, wobbly
3 ***syn*** DOUBTFUL 1, borderline, dubious, indecisive, open, problematic, suspicious, uncertain, unclear, undecided
ant sure
4 ***syn*** UNRELIABLE 1, dubious, fly-by-night, questionable, trustless, undependable, untrustworthy, untrusty

unsurmountable *adj* ***syn*** INSUPERABLE, impassable, inconquerable, indomitable, insurmountable, invincible, unconquerable
ant surmountable

unsurpassable *adj* ***syn*** SUPREME, incomparable, preeminent, surpassing, towering, transcendent, ultimate, unequalable, unmatchable
ant surpassable

unsusceptible *adj* ***syn*** INSUSCEPTIBLE, impassive, insensitive, insentient, unimpressible, unimpressionable, unresponsive
ant susceptible

unsuspecting *adj* ***syn*** CREDULOUS, unsuspicious, unwary
ant suspecting, suspicious

unsuspicious *adj* ***syn*** CREDULOUS, unsuspecting, unwary
ant suspecting, suspicious

unswayable *adj* ***syn*** INFLEXIBLE 2, inexorable, obdurate, relentless, rigid, single-minded, unbendable, uncompliant, uncompromising, unyielding
ant suasible

unswerving *adj* ***syn*** WHOLE 5, concentrated, exclusive, fixed, undistracted, undivided
rel constant, steadfast, steady, unremitting; firm, unfaltering, unwavering

unsymmetrical *adj* ***syn*** LOPSIDED, asymmetric, disproportionate, irregular, nonsymmetrical, off-balance, overbalanced, unequal, uneven, unproportionate
ant symmetrical

unsympathetic *adj* **1** ***syn*** ANTIPATHETIC 2, aversive, kindless, repellent, repugnant, uncongenial, ungenial
rel dislikable, unlikable; displeasing, unpleasant, unpleasing
con appealing, congenial, likable; pleasant, pleasing
ant sympathetic
2 ***syn*** UNFEELING 2, callous, coldhearted, hard-boiled, hardhearted, heartless, obdurate, stonyhearted, uncompassionate, unemotional
rel cold, cool, frigid; disinterested, halfhearted, indifferent, lukewarm
ant sympathetic

untactful *adj* ***syn*** TACTLESS, brash, impolitic, maladroit, undiplomatic, unpolitic
ant tactful

untangle *vb* ***syn*** EXTRICATE 2, discumber, disembarrass, disembroil, disencumber, disentangle, disentwine, unentangle, unscramble, untwine
ant entangle, tangle

untapped *adj* ***syn*** VIRGIN 2, unspoiled, untouched, virginal

untaught *adj* ***syn*** IGNORANT 1, benighted, empty-headed, illiterate, know-nothing, uneducated, uninstructed, unlettered, unschooled, untutored

untellable *adj* ***syn*** UNUTTERABLE, incommunicable, indefinable, indescribable, ineffable, inenarrable, inexpressible, undescribable, unexpressible, unspeakable
ant expressible

untempered *adj* ***syn*** EXCESSIVE 2, immoderate, inordinate, intemperate, overindulgent, unrestrained
ant temperate, tempered

untenable *adj* ***syn*** INEXCUSABLE, indefensible, inexpiable, unforgivable, unjustifiable, unpardonable

untended *adj* ***syn*** NEGLECTED, run-down, uncared-for

untested *adj* ***syn*** UNTRIED 1, undemonstrated, unpracticed, unproved
ant tested, tried

unthankful *adj* **1** ***syn*** THANKLESS 2, unappreciated, ungrateful
2 ***syn*** THANKLESS 1, unappreciative, ungrateful
ant thankful

unthinkable *adj* **1** ***syn*** EXCEPTIONAL 1, extraordinary, rare, singular, uncommon, unimaginable, unique, unordinary, unusual, unwonted
2 ***syn*** INCREDIBLE 1, incogitable, inconceivable, insupposable, unbelievable, unimaginable
ant thinkable

unthinking *adj* ***syn*** CARELESS 1, feckless, heedless, inadvertent, irreflective, thoughtless, uncaring, unheeding, unrecking, unreflective

---

syn synonym(s) ***rel*** related word(s)
idiom idiomatic equivalent(s) ***con*** contrasted word(s)
ant antonym(s) * vulgar
‖ use limited; if in doubt, see a dictionary
The first word in a synonym list when printed in SMALL CAPITALS shows where there is more information about the group. For a more efficient use of this book see Explanatory Notes.

unthorough *adj* ***syn*** SLIPSHOD 3, botchy, careless, messy, slapdash, sloppy, slovenly, untidy
ant thorough

unthought *adj* ***syn*** UNINTENTIONAL, inadvertent, undesigned, undevised, unintended, unplanned, unpremeditated, unpurposed
ant aforethought

unthrift *n* **1** ***syn*** EXTRAVAGANCE 2, extravagancy, lavishness, overdoing, prodigality, squander, waste, wastefulness
ant thrift
2 ***syn*** SPENDTHRIFT, high roller, prodigal, profligate, scattergood, spender, squanderer, waster, wastethrift, wastrel

unthrift *adj* ***syn*** IMPROVIDENT, thriftless, unthrifty

unthrifty *adj* ***syn*** IMPROVIDENT, thriftless, unthrift
ant thrifty

untidy *adj* **1** ***syn*** SLOVENLY 1, disheveled, ill-kempt, messy, slipshod, sloppy, uncombed, unfastidious, unkempt, unneat
ant tidy
2 ***syn*** SLIPSHOD 3, botchy, careless, messy, slapdash, sloppy, slovenly, unthorough

untie *vb* ***syn*** EXTRICATE 2, disembarrass, disembroil, disencumber, disentangle, disentwine, unentangle, unscramble, untangle, untwine

untighten *vb* ***syn*** LOOSE 5, ease, ease off, lax, loosen, relax, slack, slacken
ant tighten

until *prep* up to a stipulated time <we never met him *until* last night>
syn before, in advance of, prior to, till, to, up till, up to; *compare* BEFORE 1

until *conj* ***syn*** TILL

untimely *adj* **1** ***syn*** EARLY 2, overearly, oversoon, premature, previous, ‖soon
ant timely
2 ***syn*** UNSEASONABLE 1, ill-seasoned, ill-timed, inopportune, malapropos, mistimed
con opportune, pat, seasonable, well-timed
ant timely
3 ***syn*** IMPROPER 1, ill-timed, inappropriate, inapt, intempestive, malapropos, unapt, undue, unseasonable, unsuitable
ant timely

untiring *adj* ***syn*** INDEFATIGABLE, inexhaustible, tireless, unflagging, unweariable, unwearying, weariless
con casual, disinterested, intermittent

untold *adj* **1** ***syn*** HUGE, enormous, gigantic, immense, mammoth, mighty, monstrous, prodigious, titanic, vast
2 ***syn*** INNUMERABLE, countless, innumerous, numberless, uncountable, uncounted, unnumberable, unnumbered

untouchable *n* ***syn*** OUTCAST, castaway, derelict, Ishmael, Ishmaelite, leper, offscouring, pariah
rel déclassé, outcaste, outsider

untouched *adj* **1** ***syn*** WHOLE 1, entire, flawless, good, intact, perfect, sound, unblemished, undamaged, unmarred
2 ***syn*** VIRGIN 2, unspoiled, untapped, virginal

untoward *adj* **1** ***syn*** UNRULY 1, fractious, indocile, intractable, recalcitrant, undisciplinable, undisciplined, ungovernable, unmanageable, wild
2 ***syn*** UNLUCKY, hapless, ill-fated, ill-starred, luckless, misfortunate, star-crossed, unfortunate, unhappy
3 ***syn*** INDECOROUS, improper, indecent, indelicate, malodorous, rough, unbecoming, undecorous, ungodly, unseemly

untowardness *n* ***syn*** IMPROPRIETY 1, incorrectness, indecorousness, indecorum, inelegance, unbecomingness, unmeetness, unseemliness

untrammeled *adj* ***syn*** AUDACIOUS 4, uncurbed, ungoverned, unhampered, uninhibited, unrestrained

untranquil *adj* ***syn*** RESTLESS, uneasy, unpeaceful, unquiet, unrestful, unsettled

untried *adj* **1** not subjected to test or proof (as by experience or use) <the fledgling's *untried* wings>
syn undemonstrated, unpracticed, unproved, untested
rel inexperienced, unseasoned; callow, green, immature; fresh, half-baked, unripe
con practiced, proven, tested; accomplished, finished, skilled; initiated
ant tested, tried
2 ***syn*** INEXPERIENCED, callow, fresh, green, raw, unconversant, unfleshed, unpracticed, unseasoned, unversed

untroubled *adj* ***syn*** CALM 1, halcyon, hushed, placid, quiet, still, stilly
ant troubled

untroublesome *adj* ***syn*** EASY 1, effortless, facile, light, royal, simple, smooth

untrue *adj* **1** ***syn*** FAITHLESS, disloyal, false, perfidious, recreant, traitorous, treacherous, unfaithful, unloyal
ant true
2 ***syn*** FALSE 1, counterfactual, erroneous, inaccurate, incorrect, specious, unsound, wrong
rel imprecise, inexact, unprecise; forsworn, perjured
con exact, precise
ant true

untruism *n* ***syn*** LIE, ‖bouncer, canard, falsehood, fib, misrepresentation, prevarication, story, tale, untruth
ant truism

untrustworthy *adj* **1** ***syn*** UNRELIABLE 1, dubious, fly-by-night, questionable, trustless, undependable, unsure, untrusty
ant trustworthy
2 ***syn*** UNSAFE, unassured, undependable, unreliable
ant trustworthy

untrusty *adj* ***syn*** UNRELIABLE 1, dubious, fly-by-night, questionable, trustless, undependable, unsure, untrustworthy
ant trusty

untruth *n* **1** ***syn*** FALLACY 1, erroneousness, error, fallaciousness, falsehood, falseness, falsity
ant truth
2 ***syn*** LIE, canard, falsehood, falsity, fib, misrepresentation, prevarication, story, tale, untruism

ant truth

untruthful *adj* *syn* DISHONEST, deceitful, knavish, lying, mendacious, roguish, shifty, unhonest
rel deceptive, delusive, delusory, misleading; false, wrong; inaccurate, incorrect
ant truthful

untruthfulness *n* *syn* MENDACITY, falsehood, fibbery, mendaciousness, truthlessness, unveracity
ant truthfulness

untune *vb* *syn* DISCOMPOSE 1, agitate, bother, disquiet, disturb, flurry, fluster, perturb, unhinge, upset

untutored *adj* **1** *syn* IGNORANT 1, benighted, empty-headed, illiterate, know-nothing, uneducated, uninstructed, unlettered, unschooled, untaught
2 *syn* NATURAL 5, artless, ingenuous, naive, simple, unaffected, unartificial, unschooled, unsophisticated, unstudied

untwine *vb* *syn* EXTRICATE 2, disembarrass, disembroil, disencumber, disentangle, disentwine, unentangle, unscramble, untangle, untie

untypical *adj* *syn* ABNORMAL 1, aberrant, anomalous, atypical, deviant, deviative, heteroclite, preternatural, unrepresentative
ant typical

ununderstandable *adj* *syn* INCONCEIVABLE 1, incomprehensible, unimaginable, unknowable
ant understandable

unusable *adj* *syn* IMPRACTICABLE 2, impractical, nonfunctional, unfunctional, unserviceable, unworkable, useless
ant usable

unused *adj* *syn* VACANT 4, idle

unusual *adj* **1** *syn* EXCEPTIONAL 1, extraordinary, rare, singular, uncommon, unimaginable, unique, unordinary, unthinkable, unwonted
idiom the exception rather than the rule
ant usual
2 *syn* STRANGE 4, bizarre, curious, eccentric, odd, oddball, outlandish, peculiar, quaint, singular
ant usual

unusually *adv* *syn* EXTRA, extremely, rarely, ||uncommon, uncommonly

unutterable *adj* being beyond human power to tell or describe < *unutterable* spiritual bliss >
syn incommunicable, indefinable, indescribable, ineffable, inenarrable, inexpressible, undescribable, unexpressible, unspeakable, untellable
rel inconceivable, incredible, unbelievable, unimaginable; awesome, awful, marvelous, prodigious, wonderful, wondrous
idiom beyond expression
con commonplace, humdrum, ordinary; monotonous, samely, unvarying

unuttered *adj* **1** *syn* UNSPOKEN 1, silent, tacit, unexpressed, unvoiced, wordless
ant uttered
2 *syn* TACIT 1, implicit, implied, inferred, undeclared, understood, unexpressed, unsaid, unspoken, wordless
ant uttered

unvarnished *adj* *syn* FRANK, candid, open, openhearted, plain, straightforward, unconcealed, undisguised, undissembled, undissembling

unvarying *adj* **1** *syn* STEADY 2, constant, equable, even, stabile, stable, unchanging, unfluctuating, uniform
ant varying
2 *syn* SAME 3, consistent, constant, invariable, unchanging, unfailing
ant variable, varying

unveil *vb* **1** *syn* OPEN 2, disclose, display, expose, reveal, unclothe, uncover
ant veil
2 *syn* REVEAL 1, betray, disclose, discover, divulge, tell, unbosom, unclose, uncover, uncurtain
ant veil

unveracity *n* *syn* MENDACITY, falsehood, fibbery, mendaciousness, truthlessness, untruthfulness
ant veracity

unversed *adj* *syn* INEXPERIENCED, callow, fresh, green, raw, unconversant, unfleshed, unpracticed, unseasoned, untried
ant versed

unvigilant *adj* *syn* INCAUTIOUS 1, unalert, unguarded, unwary, unwatchful
ant vigilant

unvital *adj* *syn* PETTY 2, inconsequent, inconsequential, paltry, peanut, pettifogging, piddling, trifling, trivial, unconsequential
ant vital

unvocal *adj* *syn* INARTICULATE 3, incoherent, maundering, tongue-tied
ant vocal

unvoiced *adj* *syn* UNSPOKEN 1, silent, tacit, unexpressed, unuttered, wordless
ant voiced

unwanted *adj* **1** *syn* UNWELCOME 1, undesired, unsought, unwished
ant wanted
2 *syn* OBJECTIONABLE, exceptionable, ill-favored, inadmissible, unacceptable, undesirable, unwelcome

unwarrantable *adj* *syn* UNREASONABLE 2, unconscionable, undue, unjustifiable, unwarranted
ant warrantable

unwarranted *adj* **1** *syn* BASELESS, bottomless, foundationless, gratuitous, groundless, uncalled-for, unfounded, ungrounded
2 *syn* UNREASONABLE 2, unconscionable, undue, unjustifiable, unwarrantable

unwary *adj* **1** *syn* INCAUTIOUS 1, unalert, unguarded, unvigilant, unwatchful
ant wary
2 *syn* CREDULOUS, unsuspecting, unsuspicious
3 *syn* RASH 1, brash, hasty, hotheaded, ill-advised, incautious, inconsiderate, reckless, thoughtless, unadvised
ant wary

unwashed *adj* *syn* IGNOBLE 1, base, baseborn, humble, low, lowborn, lowly, mean, plebeian, unennobled

---

syn synonym(s) *rel* related word(s)
idiom idiomatic equivalent(s) *con* contrasted word(s)
ant antonym(s) * vulgar
|| use limited; if in doubt, see a dictionary
The first word in a synonym list when printed in SMALL CAPITALS shows where there is more information about the group. For a more efficient use of this book see Explanatory Notes.

unwashed *n* ***syn*** RABBLE 2, canaille, dreg(s), mass(es), mob, proletariat, ragtag and bobtail, riffraff, scum, trash

unwasteful *adj* ***syn*** SPARING, canny, chary, economical, frugal, provident, saving, Scotch, stewardly, thrifty
ant wasteful

unwatchful *adj* **1** ***syn*** INATTENTIVE, inobservant, unheeding, unnoticing, unobservant, unobserving, unperceiving
ant watchful
2 ***syn*** INCAUTIOUS 1, unalert, unguarded, unvigilant, unwary
ant watchful

unwatered *adj* ***syn*** DRY 1, arid, bone-dry, droughty, moistureless, sere, thirsty, waterless
ant watered

unwavering *adj* ***syn*** SURE 2, abiding, enduring, firm, fixed, never-failing, steadfast, steady, unfaltering, unqualified
ant wavering

unweariable *adj* ***syn*** INDEFATIGABLE, inexhaustible, tireless, unflagging, untiring, unwearying, weariless
ant weariable

unwearying *adj* ***syn*** INDEFATIGABLE, inexhaustible, tireless, unflagging, untiring, unweariable, weariless
rel constant, steady; interminable, unceasing

unwed *adj* ***syn*** SINGLE 1, sole, spouseless, unmarried
ant married, wed

unwelcome *adj* **1** not of a kind to be welcome <an *unwelcome* interruption that scattered his train of thought>
syn undesired, unsought, unwanted, unwished
rel distasteful, obnoxious, repellent; unasked; undesirable, unpleasant, unpleasing
con desired, sought, wanted; agreeable, desirable, pleasant, pleasing
ant welcome
2 ***syn*** OBJECTIONABLE, exceptionable, ill-favored, inadmissible, unacceptable, undesirable, unwanted
ant welcome

unwell *adj* somewhat disordered in health <had felt *unwell* from the moment she got up>
syn ailing, ‖donsie, indisposed, low, mean, off-color, offish, poorly, sickly, underly; *compare* SICK 1
rel rocky, shaky, wobbly; feeble, frail, infirm, weakly; ill, sick; qualmish, queasy, squeamish
idiom out of sorts, under the weather
ant well

unwholesome *adj* **1** likely to be detrimental to physical, mental, or moral health <an *unwholesome* crime-ridden neighborhood>
syn insalubrious, insalutary, noisome, noxious, sickly, unhealthful, unhealthy, unsalutary
rel baneful, deleterious, detrimental, pernicious; harmful, hurtful, injurious, mischievous
con healthful, hygienic, salubrious, salutary
ant wholesome
2 ***syn*** OFFENSIVE, disgusting, foul, hideous, horrible, loathsome, noisome, obscene, repellent, repulsive
ant wholesome

unwieldy *adj* clumsy and difficult to handle usually because of excessive weight and awkward form <a massive *unwieldy* sledgehammer>
syn cumbersome, cumbrous, ponderous, unhandy; *compare* HEAVY 1
rel awkward, inconvenient; uncontrollable, unmanageable; bulky, clumsy, lumbering, massive; burdensome, encumbering, onerous
con compact, neat, trig, trim; adaptable, convenient, handy; easy, facile, light
ant wieldy

unwilling *adj* ***syn*** DISINCLINED, afraid, averse, backward, hesitant, indisposed, loath, reluctant, uneager, unwishful
ant willing

unwind *vb* ***syn*** RELAX 2, ease off, loosen up, unbend, unlax

unwise *adj* not marked by or according with good sense or sound judgment <his decision to quit school was most *unwise*>
syn ill-advised, ill-judged, impolitic, imprudent, indiscreet, injudicious
rel senseless, thoughtless, witless; impractical, unsound; fatuous, inane, inept; inappropriate, undesirable, unfortunate; foolish, misguided, unintelligent; childish, immature, naive
idiom penny-wise and pound-foolish
con discreet, judicious, prudent; sane, sensible, sound; appropriate, apt, desirable
ant wise

unwished *adj* ***syn*** UNWELCOME 1, undesired, unsought, unwanted

unwishful *adj* ***syn*** DISINCLINED, afraid, averse, backward, hesitant, indisposed, loath, reluctant, uneager, unwilling
ant wishful

unwitting *adj* **1** ***syn*** FORGETFUL, oblivious, unmindful
ant witting
2 ***syn*** IGNORANT 2, incognizant, inconversant, oblivious, unacquainted, unaware, unfamiliar, uninformed, uninstructed, unknowing
ant witting

unwitty *adj* ***syn*** SIMPLE 3, asinine, brainless, fatuous, foolish, mindless, silly, weak-headed, weak-minded, witless
ant ‖witty

unwonted *adj* ***syn*** EXCEPTIONAL 1, extraordinary, rare, singular, uncommon, unimaginable, unique, unordinary, unthinkable, unusual
ant wonted

unworkable *adj* **1** ***syn*** IMPOSSIBLE 1, impracticable, impractical, infeasible, irrealizable, unattainable, unfeasible, unrealizable
2 ***syn*** IMPRACTICABLE 2, impractical, nonfunctional, unfunctional, unserviceable, unusable, useless
ant workable

---

syn synonym(s) — *rel* related word(s)
idiom idiomatic equivalent(s) — *con* contrasted word(s)
ant antonym(s) — * vulgar
‖ use limited; if in doubt, see a dictionary
The first word in a synonym list when printed in SMALL CAPITALS shows where there is more information about the group. For a more efficient use of this book see Explanatory Notes.

unworked *adj* ***syn*** RUDE 1, crude, rough, roughhewn, undressed, unfashioned, unfinished, unformed, unhewn, unpolished
ant worked, wrought

unworkmanlike *adj* ***syn*** INEFFICIENT 2, incapable, incompetent, inept, inexpert, unexpert, unskilled, unskillful
ant workmanlike, workmanly

unworldly *adj* **1** ***syn*** DREAMY 1, astral, daydreaming, daydreamy, otherworldly, visionary
2 ***syn*** NATURAL 5, artless, ingenuous, naive, simple, unaffected, unartificial, unschooled, unstudied, untutored
ant worldly

unworthy *adj* ***syn*** WORTHLESS 1, draffy, drossy, good-for-nothing, inutile, ‖no-account, no-good, nothing, valueless
ant worthy

unwritten *adj* ***syn*** ORAL 2, spoken, traditional, verbal, word-of-mouth
ant written

unwrought *adj* ***syn*** RUDE 1, crude, rough, roughhewn, undressed, unfashioned, unfinished, unformed, unhewn, unworked
ant worked, wrought

unyielding *adj* **1** ***syn*** STIFF 1, immalleable, impliable, incompliant, inelastic, inflexible, rigid, unbending, unflexible
ant yielding
2 ***syn*** OBSTINATE, bullheaded, headstrong, intractable, mulish, pertinacious, pigheaded, refractory, self-willed, stubborn
rel firm, fixed, rigid
ant yielding
3 ***syn*** GRIM 3, implacable, ironfisted, merciless, mortal, relentless, ruthless, unappeasable, unflinching, unrelenting
4 ***syn*** TOUGH 3, hard-line, inflexible, uncompromising
ant yielding
5 ***syn*** INFLEXIBLE 2, inexorable, obdurate, relentless, rigid, single-minded, unbending, uncompliant, uncompromising, unswayable

up *adj* **1** ***syn*** BAD 1, amiss, ‖bum, ‖crappy, dissatisfactory, poor, ‖punk, rotten, unsatisfactory, wrong
2 ***syn*** FAMILIAR 3, abreast, acquainted, au courant, au fait, conversant, informed, versant, versed
3 ***syn*** UP-TO-DATE, abreast, au courant, contemporary, down-to-date, red-hot, up-to-the-minute

up *vb* **1** ***syn*** RISE 4, arise, ascend, aspire, lift, mount, soar, uprear
2 ***syn*** RAISE 9, boost, hike, increase, jack (up), jump, put up

up–and–coming *adj* ***syn*** ENTERPRISING 2, go-ahead, gumptious
rel alert, eager, keen, ready

up and down *adv* ***syn*** THOROUGHLY 2, completely, detailedly, exhaustively, in and out, inside out

up–and–down *adj* ***syn*** DOWNRIGHT 2, flat, indubitable, unquestionable

upbear *vb* ***syn*** SUPPORT 4, bear up, bolster, brace, buttress, carry, prop, shore (up), sustain, uphold

upbeat *adj* ***syn*** OPTIMISTIC, fond, Pollyannaish, sanguine

upbraid *vb* ***syn*** SCOLD 1, bawl out, berate, ‖bless out, ‖chew out, lash, rate, revile, tongue-lash, vituperate

upchuck *vb* ***syn*** VOMIT, barf, bring up, ‖cast, disgorge, ‖heave, *puke, spew, spit up, throw up

upclimb *vb* ***syn*** ASCEND 1, climb, escalade, escalate, mount, scale, upgo

upcoming *adj* ***syn*** FORTHCOMING, approaching, coming, nearing, oncoming
rel foreseen, prospective
idiom in prospect, on the horizon

up–country *n* ***syn*** FRONTIER 2, backcountry, backland, backwash, backwater, backwoods, ‖boondocks, bush, hinterland, sticks

update *vb* ***syn*** RENEW 1, modernize, refresh, refurbish, rejuvenate, renovate, restore

upend *vb* ***syn*** WHIP 2, beat, ‖clobber, drub, lick, overwhelm, shellac, trim, trounce, wallop

upgo *vb* ***syn*** ASCEND 1, climb, escalade, escalate, mount, scale, upclimb

upgrade *vb* ***syn*** ADVANCE 2, elevate, prefer, promote
ant downgrade

upgrade *n* ***syn*** RISE 3, boost, breakthrough, hike, increase, wax

upgrading *n* ***syn*** ADVANCEMENT 1, elevation, preference, preferment, prelation, promotion
ant downgrading

upgrowth *n* ***syn*** DEVELOPMENT, evolution, evolvement, flowering, growth, progress, progression, unfolding

upheaval *n* ***syn*** COMMOTION 1, clamor, convulsion, ferment, outcry, tumult, upturn
rel cataclysm, catastrophe, disaster; alteration, change; churning, heaving, stirring

upheaved *adj* ***syn*** ELEVATED 1, lifted, raised, uplifted, upraised, uprisen
ant downthrown

uphill *adj* ***syn*** HARD 6, arduous, difficult, effortful, labored, laborious, operose, rugged, strenuous, toilsome

uphold *vb* **1** ***syn*** SUPPORT 5, bolster, buoy (up), prop, sustain, underprop
rel defend, justify, maintain, vindicate; aid, assist, help
ant contravene; subvert
2 ***syn*** SUPPORT 2, advocate, back, backstop, champion, side (with)
3 ***syn*** SUPPORT 4, bear up, bolster, brace, buttress, carry, prop, shore (up), sustain, upbear
4 ***syn*** LIFT 1, elevate, hoist, pick up, raise, rear, take up, uplift, upraise, uprear

upholstered *adj* **1** ***syn*** LUXURIOUS 3, Capuan, deluxe, luscious, lush, luxuriant, opulent, palatial, plush, sumptuous
2 ***syn*** FAT 2, corpulent, fleshy, gross, obese, overweight, porcine, portly, stout, weighty

upland *n* ***syn*** PLATEAU, table, tableland

---

syn synonym(s) | *rel* related word(s)
idiom idiomatic equivalent(s) | *con* contrasted word(s)
ant antonym(s) | * vulgar
‖ use limited; if in doubt, see a dictionary
The first word in a synonym list when printed in SMALL CAPITALS shows where there is more information about the group. For a more efficient use of this book see Explanatory Notes.

uplay *vb* ***syn*** ACCUMULATE, amass, cumulate, garner, hive, lay up, roll up, stockpile, store (up)

uplift *vb* **1** ***syn*** LIFT 1, elevate, hoist, pick up, raise, rear, take up, uphold, upraise, uprear
2 ***syn*** ILLUMINATE 2, edify, enlighten, illume, illumine, improve, irradiate
ant degrade

uplifted *adj* ***syn*** ELEVATED 1, lifted, raised, upheaved, upraised, uprisen

upon *prep* **1** ***syn*** OVER 3, about, on, with
2 ***syn*** OVER 4, on

upper class *n* ***syn*** ARISTOCRACY, blue blood, elite, flower, gentility, gentry, quality, society, upper crust, who's who

upper crust *n* ***syn*** ARISTOCRACY, blue blood, elite, flower, gentility, gentry, quality, society, upper class, who's who
rel (the) Four Hundred

upper hand *n* ***syn*** BETTER 2, advantage, superiority, victory, whip hand

uppermost *adj* ***syn*** TOP 1, apical, highest, loftiest, topmost
ant lowermost

‖**upper story** *n* ***syn*** MIND 1, brain, gray matter, head, ‖upperworks, wit

‖**upperworks** *n pl* ***syn*** MIND 1, brain, gray matter, head, ‖upper story, wit

uppish *adj* ***syn*** PRESUMPTUOUS, brash, forward, overweening, presuming, pushful, pushing, self-asserting, self-assertive, uppity

uppity *adj* ***syn*** PRESUMPTUOUS, brash, forward, overweening, presuming, pushful, pushing, self-asserting, self-assertive, uppish

upraise *vb* **1** ***syn*** LIFT 1, elevate, hoist, pick up, raise, rear, take up, uphold, uplift, uprear
2 ***syn*** COMFORT, buck up, cheer, console, solace
ant depress

upraised *adj* ***syn*** ELEVATED 1, lifted, raised, upheaved, uplifted, uprisen

uprear *vb* **1** ***syn*** LIFT 1, elevate, hoist, pick up, raise, rear, take up, uphold, uplift, upraise
2 ***syn*** BUILD 1, construct, erect, put up, raise, rear
3 ***syn*** EXALT 1, aggrandize, dignify, distinguish, ennoble, erect, glorify, honor, magnify, sublime
con bust, demote, downgrade
ant degrade
4 ***syn*** RISE 4, arise, ascend, aspire, lift, mount, soar, up

upright *adj* **1** ***syn*** ERECT, arrect, raised, stand-up, straight-up, upstanding
2 having or manifesting a strict regard for what is morally right <an *upright* man ready to give even the devil his due>
syn conscientious, honest, honorable, just, right, scrupulous, true
rel ethical, moral, principled, righteous, virtuous; equitable, fair, impartial; elevated, high-minded, noble; blameless, exemplary, good, pure
con crooked, devious, oblique; depraved; base, low, vile; ignoble, mean
ant corrupt

uprightness *n* ***syn*** GOODNESS, morality, probity, rectitude, righteousness, rightness, virtue
rel nobility, reputability, worthiness; honesty, integrity
ant corruption

uprise *vb* **1** ***syn*** RISE 1, get up, stand up, upspring
2 ***syn*** ROLL OUT, arise, get up, pile (out), rise, rise and shine, turn out

uprisen *adj* ***syn*** ELEVATED 1, lifted, raised, upheaved, uplifted, upraised

uproar *n* **1** ***syn*** DIN, babel, clamor, hubbub, hullabaloo, jangle, pandemonium, racket, tintamarre, tumult
rel chaos, confusion, disorder; brawl, broil, fracas, melee; commotion, confusion, turbulence, turmoil
con calm, peace, quiet
2 ***syn*** COMMOTION 4, clamor, hassle, hubbub, hurly-burly, pother, to-do, tumult, turmoil, whirl
3 ***syn*** COMMOTION 3, ‖catouse, coil, foofaraw, furore, ruckus, rumpus, shindig, shindy, to-do

uproarious *adj* ***syn*** NOISY, clangorous, clattery, noiseful, rackety, sonorous

uproot *vb* ***syn*** ANNIHILATE 2, abate, abolish, blot out, eradicate, exterminate, extirpate, root out, uncreate, wipe (out)
rel demolish, destroy; overthrow, overturn, subvert; displace, replace, supersede, supplant; move, shift, transplant
ant establish; inseminate

upset *vb* **1** ***syn*** OVERTURN 1, knock over, overset, overthrow, tip (over), topple, turn over
rel invert, reverse; bend, curve, turn
2 ***syn*** DISCOMPOSE 1, agitate, bother, discombobulate, disquiet, disturb, flurry, fluster, perturb, unhinge
rel bewilder, confound, distract; unman, unnerve
idiom rock the boat
3 ***syn*** TROUBLE 1, ail, cark, distress, worry
4 ***syn*** DISORDER 1, derange, disarrange, disarray, jumble, mix up, muddle, rummage, tumble, unsettle
5 to disturb the normal functioning especially of body or mind <her stomach was badly *upset* by too many sweets>
syn derange, disorder, sicken, turn, unhinge, unsettle
rel afflict, indispose, lay up; ail, suffer; debilitate, incapacitate, invalid

upshot *n* **1** ***syn*** EFFECT 1, aftereffect, aftermath, consequence, event, eventuality, issue, outcome, result, sequel
rel ending, termination; climax, culmination; completion, conclusion, finish
2 ***syn*** SUBSTANCE 2, burden, core, gist, meat, pith, purport, sense, short, thrust

upside-down *adj* **1** having the upper and lower parts reversed in position <*upside-down* letters>
syn inverted, topsy-turvy
rel reversed
2 confused utterly even to the point of inversion of the normal or reasonable <*upside-down* logic that confused cause with effect>

---

syn arsy-varsy, downside-up, topsy-turvy
rel inverted, reversed; chaotic, confused, helter-skelter, jumbled, mixed-up; fouled-up, haywire, ||snafu
con orderly, well-ordered; logical, reasonable, sensible, sound; legitimate, plausible

upspring *vb* **1** *syn* SPRING 1, arise, derive (from), emanate, flow, head, issue, originate, proceed, rise
2 *syn* RISE 1, get up, stand up, uprise

upstanding *adj* *syn* ERECT, arrect, raised, stand-up, straight-up, upright

upstart *n* a usually crude and pushing person who has recently reached a position of prominence, power, or wealth <declared the new executive an *upstart* lacking all breeding and culture>
syn arriviste, nouveau riche, parvenu, roturier
rel bounder, cad, outsider; guttersnipe, mucker, slob, vulgarian; boor, lout, roughneck, rowdy; comer; social climber

upsurge *vb* *syn* INCREASE 2, augment, build, enlarge, expand, heighten, mount, multiply, rise, wax

uptight *adj* *syn* TENSE 2, edgy, nervy, restive, uneasy

uptightness *n* *syn* TENSION 2, unease

up till *prep* *syn* UNTIL, before, in advance of, prior to, till, to, up to

up to *prep* *syn* UNTIL, before, in advance of, prior to, till, to, up till

up-to-date *adj* completely modern (as in style or outlook) <using *up-to-date* methods of study>
syn abreast, au courant, contemporary, down-to-date, red-hot, up, up-to-the-minute
rel convenient, opportune, timely; expedient, fitting, suitable; advanced, modern, stylish; a la mode, dashing, modish
idiom abreast of the times
con dusty, rusty, stale, timeworn; antiquated, outmoded, superannuated
ant out-of-date; archaic

up-to-the-minute *adj* *syn* UP-TO-DATE, abreast, au courant, contemporary, down-to-date, red-hot, up

upturn *n* *syn* COMMOTION 1, clamor, convulsion, ferment, outcry, tumult, upheaval

uranian *adj* *syn* HOMOSEXUAL, gay, homoerotic, homophile, inverted, queer

uranian *n* *syn* HOMOSEXUAL, fag, faggot, ||fruit, homo, invert, queer, uranist

uranist *n* *syn* HOMOSEXUAL, fag, faggot, ||fruit, homo, invert, queer, uranian

urban *adj* of, relating to, or characteristic of a city <*urban* disorders>
syn burghal, city, municipal
rel inner city; metropolitan; civic, popular, public; oppidan, town, village
ant rural

urbane *adj* **1** *syn* COSMOPOLITAN 1, metropolitan
2 *syn* SUAVE, bland, civilized, smooth
rel balanced, poised
ant bucolic, clownish
3 *syn* GENTEEL 1, cultivated, cultured, distingué, polished, refined, well-bred
rel affable, civil, courteous, gracious, obliging
ant rude

urchin *n* a pert or roguish youngster <*urchins* pilfering apples on their way from school>
syn gamin, imp, monkey
rel brat, bratling, cub, dickens, pup, whelp, whippersnapper; guttersnipe, mudlark, ragamuffin, street arab; hobbledehoy

urge *vb* to press or impel to action, effort, or speed <his conscience *urged* him to tell the truth>
syn egg (on), exhort, goad, prick, prod, prompt, propel, sic, spur
rel hurry, hustle, push, rush, shove; blandish, cajole, coax, encourage, incite, needle, solicit, wheedle; constrain, drive, high-pressure, press, pressure; provoke, set (on), tar (on)
idiom bring pressure to bear on, twist one's arm
con brake, check, constrain, curb, hold back, inhibit, restrain

urge *n* *syn* DESIRE 1, appetite, appetition, craving, itch, lust, passion
rel goad, incentive, motive, spring, spur

urgent *adj* *syn* PRESSING, burning, clamant, clamorous, crying, exigent, imperative, importunate, insistent, instant
rel driving, impelling; demanding

usable *adj* *syn* OPEN 5, accessible, employable, operative, practicable
ant unusable

usage *n* **1** *syn* HABIT 1, custom, habitude, manner, practice, praxis, trick, use, way, wont
rel choice, preference; procedure, proceeding, process; guidance, guiding, lead
2 *syn* FORM 3, convenance, convention
rel ceremony, formality

usance *n* *syn* USE 1, appliance, application, employment, operation, play

use *n* **1** the act or practice of using something or the state of being used <all tools must be kept ready for instant *use*>
syn appliance, application, employment, operation, play, usance; *compare* EXERCISE 1
con desuetude, disuse
ant nonuse
2 *syn* EXERCISE 1, application, employment, exercising, exertion, operation
3 the quality of being appropriate or valuable to some end <even the scraps had some *use*>
syn account, advantage, applicability, appropriateness, avail, fitness, relevance, service, serviceability, usefulness, utility
rel adaptability, availability, benefit, efficacy; profit, value, worth
con inadequacy, inapplicability, inappropriateness, insufficiency, unfitness, unserviceability, uselessness, worthlessness
4 a particular service or end <industrial *uses* of atomic energy>

---

syn synonym(s) *rel* related word(s)
idiom idiomatic equivalent(s) *con* contrasted word(s)
ant antonym(s) * vulgar
|| use limited; if in doubt, see a dictionary
The first word in a synonym list when printed in SMALL CAPITALS shows where there is more information about the group. For a more efficient use of this book see Explanatory Notes.

syn duty, function, goal, mark, object, objective, purpose, target
5 *syn* HABIT 1, custom, habitude, manner, practice, praxis, trick, usage, way, wont
rel ceremony, formality
6 *syn* NEED 3, demand, occasion

use *vb* **1** *syn* ACCUSTOM, familiarize, habituate, inure, wont
2 to put into action or service <it is necessary to *use* resources wisely>
syn apply, bestow, employ, exercise, exploit, handle, utilize
rel manipulate, operate, ply, wield; control, govern, manage, regulate
idiom avail oneself of, bring into play, fall back (on *or* upon), make use of, press into service, put into action, put to use
con dissipate, exhaust, use up; waste
3 *syn* OPERATE 3, handle, run, work
4 *syn* SPEAK 3, converse (in), parley, talk
5 *syn* EXPLOIT 2, abuse, impose (on *or* upon)
idiom make the most of, make use of
6 *syn* TREAT 2, deal (with), handle, play, serve, take

used up *adj syn* EFFETE 2, all in, bleary, depleted, drained, exhausted, far-gone, spent, washed-out, worn-out

useful *adj* **1** *syn* PRACTICAL 2, functional, handy, practicable, serviceable, utile
2 *syn* GOOD 1, advantageous, benefic, beneficial, brave, favorable, favoring, helpful, propitious, toward
ant useless
3 *syn* GOOD 2, appropriate, convenient, fit, meet, proper, suitable
ant useless

usefulness *n syn* USE 3, account, advantage, applicability, appropriateness, fitness, relevance, service, serviceability, utility
ant uselessness

useless *adj* **1** *syn* FUTILE, abortive, bootless, fruitless, ineffective, ineffectual, unavailable, unavailing, unproductive, vain
ant useful
2 *syn* IMPRACTICABLE 2, impractical, nonfunctional, unfunctional, unserviceable, unusable, unworkable
ant useful
3 *syn* FECKLESS 1, fustian, good-for-nothing, meaningless, purposeless, unpurposed, worthless

use up *vb* **1** *syn* CONSUME 1, devour, eat, eat up, exhaust
2 *syn* GO 4, consume, exhaust, expend, finish, run through, spend, wash up
3 *syn* DEPLETE, bankrupt, drain, draw, draw down, exhaust, impoverish

usher *vb syn* PRECEDE 3, introduce, lead, preface

usher in *vb syn* INTRODUCE 3, inaugurate, initiate, institute, launch, originate, set up

usual *adj* **1** familiar through frequent or regular repetition <the sort that would perform her *usual* chores while waiting for the end of the world>
syn accepted, accustomed, chronic, customary, habitual, routine, wonted
rel natural, normal, regular, typical; common, familiar, ordinary; current, prevailing, prevalent, rife
idiom that make up one's daily round
con exceptional, rare, unaccustomed; remarkable, strange, unexpected
ant unusual
2 *syn* GENERAL 1, common, commonplace, matter-of-course, natural, normal, prevalent, regular, typic, typical
3 *syn* ORDINARY 1, everyday, plain, plain Jane, quotidian, routine, unremarkable, workaday

usually *adv* **1** by or in accord with habit or custom <establishments of a kind *usually* restricted to back streets>
syn as usual, consistently, customarily, habitually, wontedly
2 more often than not <he is *usually* late for work>
syn as a rule, by ordinary, commonly, frequently, generally, ordinarily
rel now and again (*or* now and then), occasionally, once and again, sometimes
idiom for the most part, in the main
con infrequently, seldom, uncommonly
ant rarely

usurer *n syn* LOAN SHARK, Shylock

usurp *vb* **1** *syn* ARROGATE 1, accroach, appropriate, assume, commandeer, preempt
ant abdicate
2 *syn* SUPPLANT 1, cut out, displace

utensil *n syn* IMPLEMENT, instrument, tool

utile *adj syn* PRACTICAL 2, functional, handy, practicable, serviceable, useful
ant inutile

utilitarian *adj syn* REALISTIC, down-to-earth, hard, matter-of-fact, practic, practical, pragmatic, pragmatical, unidealistic, unromantic

utility *n syn* USE 3, account, advantage, applicability, appropriateness, fitness, relevance, service, serviceability, usefulness
ant inutility

utilize *vb syn* USE 2, apply, bestow, employ, exercise, exploit, handle
rel advance, forward, further, promote

utmost *adj* **1** *syn* EXTREME 5, farthest, furthermost, furthest, outermost, outmost, remotest, uttermost
2 *syn* MAXIMUM, maximal, outside, top, topmost
3 *syn* EXTREME 1, uttermost

utopia *n* an often imaginary place or situation of perfection and delight <able to make an enduring *utopia* of the humblest house>
syn arcadia, Cockaigne, fairyland, heaven, lubberland, paradise, promised land, Shangri-la, wonderland, Zion
rel dreamland, dreamworld, never-never

utopian *adj* **1** *syn* IDEALISTIC, idealist, visionary
rel abstract, ideal, transcendental
2 *syn* AMBITIOUS 2, grandiose, lofty, pretentious, visionary

---

syn synonym(s) *rel* related word(s)
idiom idiomatic equivalent(s) *con* contrasted word(s)
ant antonym(s) * vulgar
‖ use limited; if in doubt, see a dictionary
The first word in a synonym list when printed in SMALL CAPITALS shows where there is more information about the group. For a more efficient use of this book see Explanatory Notes.

rel impossible, impracticable, unfeasible; arcadian, edenic, millennial, otherworldly

utopian *n* ***syn*** DREAMER, castle-builder, idealist, ideologue, visionary

utter *adj* being such without qualification — used especially to intensify the noun modified <acted like an *utter* idiot>

syn absolute, all-fired, arrant, black, blamed, blank, blankety-blank, blasted, bleeding, blessed, blighted, blinding, ‖blinking, blithering, *‖bloody, ‖blooming, blue, complete, confounded, ‖consarned, consummate, crashing, dad-blamed, dad-blasted, dad-burned, damned, dang, darn (*or* durn), dashed, deuced, doggone, double-distilled, double-dyed, downright, flat-out, *fucking, *goddamn, goldarn, gross, hell-fired, infernal, out-and-out, outright, perfect, positive, ‖proper, pure, ‖puredee (*or* pure-D), rank, regular, *‖ruddy, sheer, stark, straight-out, ‖tarnation, thoroughgoing, total, unmitigated, unqualified; *compare* PURE 2

utter *vb* **1** ***syn*** SPEAK 1, talk, verbalize, vocalize, voice

idiom give utterance to

2 ***syn*** SAY 1, bring out, chime in, come out (with), declare, deliver, state, tell, throw out

utterance *n* **1** ***syn*** WORD 1, statement

2 ***syn*** VOCALIZATION, articulation, uttering, vocalism

3 ***syn*** EXPRESSION 1, statement, vent, voice

4 ***syn*** SPEECH 1, discourse, speaking, talk, verbalization

uttering *n* ***syn*** VOCALIZATION, articulation, utterance, vocalism

utterly *adv* **1** ***syn*** WELL 3, à fond, completely, entirely, fully, perfectly, ‖plumb, quite, thoroughly, wholly

2 ***syn*** ALL 1, all in all, altogether, exactly, in toto, just, purely, quite, totally, wholly

uttermost *adj* **1** ***syn*** EXTREME 5, farthest, furthermost, furthest, outermost, outmost, remotest, utmost

2 ***syn*** EXTREME 1, utmost

---

syn synonym(s) ***rel*** related word(s)
idiom idiomatic equivalent(s) ***con*** contrasted word(s)
ant antonym(s) * vulgar
‖ use limited; if in doubt, see a dictionary
The first word in a synonym list when printed in SMALL CAPITALS shows where there is more information about the group. For a more efficient use of this book see Explanatory Notes.

V

vacancy *n* ***syn*** VACUITY 2, blankness, emptiness, vacuousness, voidness
rel desertedness
ant occupancy

vacant *adj* **1** ***syn*** EMPTY 1, bare, clear, stark, vacuous, void
rel tenantless, unfilled, unoccupied, untaken
con inhabited, tenanted
ant occupied
2 ***syn*** VACUOUS 2, empty-headed
3 ***syn*** EXPRESSIONLESS, blank, deadpan, empty, inexpressive, unexpressive
rel empty-headed, inane, thoughtless, witless
4 not being put to normal or appropriate use < *vacant* land >
syn idle, unused
rel bare, empty; unfilled, unoccupied
con filled; used
ant occupied

vacate *vb* **1** ***syn*** ANNUL 4, abrogate, discharge, dissolve, quash, void
rel repeal, rescind, retract, reverse, revoke
idiom declare null and void
2 to make something (as an office, post, or dwelling) vacant or empty < *vacate* a house >
syn clear, empty, void
rel abandon, give up, part (with *or* from), relinquish; leave, quit

vacation *n* a period spent away from one's usual activity or work often in travel or recreation <took a two-week *vacation* to Florida>
syn holiday, leave
rel break, breathing space (*or* breathing spell), intermission, recess; time off; respite, rest; furlough

vacillant *adj* ***syn*** VACILLATING 2, faltering, halting, hesitating, shilly-shallying, vacillatory, wavering, whiffling, wiggle-waggle, wobbly

vacillate *vb* ***syn*** HESITATE, dither, falter, halt, shilly-shally, stagger, waver, whiffle, wiggle-waggle
rel swag, sway, ‖swither; alternate, seesaw, teeter, teeter-totter, wag, waggle, wigwag, wobble; dally, dawdle, fiddle-faddle
idiom blow hot and cold, hem and haw, swing from one thing to another
con decide, resolve, settle

vacillating *adj* **1** ***syn*** WEAK 2, dickey, fluctuant, insecure, rootless, shaky, unstable, unsure, wavering, wobbly
rel unfixed; unsettled, unsteady; changeable, fickle, inconstant; eccentric, erratic, mercurial, volatile
con constant, steady, unchanging; strong
2 given to or manifesting hesitation or vacillation <a *vacillating* witness>
syn double-minded, faltering, halting, hesitant, hesitating, indecisive, irresolute, pendulous, shilly-shally, shilly-shallying, tentative, timid, uncertain, undecisive, unresolved, vacillant, vacillatory, wavering, weak-kneed, whiffling, wiggle-waggle, wobbly
rel doubtful, doubting, unsure; fluctuating, oscillating, shifting; dallying, dawdling, demurring, dillydallying, stalling
con certain, decisive, resolute, resolved, sure; definite, positive

vacillation *n* ***syn*** HESITATION, hesitancy, indecision, indecisiveness, irresolution, shilly-shally, to-and-fro, wavering
rel dallying, demurral, dillydallying, stalling

vacillatory *adj* ***syn*** VACILLATING 2, faltering, halting, hesitant, irresolute, shilly-shallying, tentative, uncertain, wiggle-waggle, wobbly
rel alternating, seesawing, varying; indecisive, irresolute, uncertain

vacuity *n* **1** ***syn*** HOLE 3, cavity, hollow, void
2 the condition, fact, or quality of being vacuous <the utter *vacuity* of his expression>
syn blankness, emptiness, vacancy, vacuousness, voidness
rel bareness, barrenness, bleakness, desolateness, hollowness; dullness, inaneness, inanity, stupidity
3 ***syn*** NOTHINGNESS, nada, nihility, nonexistence, nullity

vacuous *adj* **1** ***syn*** EMPTY 1, bare, clear, stark, vacant, void
2 characterized by a lack of substance, thought, or intellectual content <a *vacuous* mind>
syn empty-headed, vacant; *compare* STUPID 1
rel shallow, superficial; blank, empty; dull, foolish, inane, silly

vacuousness *n* ***syn*** VACUITY 2, blankness, emptiness, vacancy, voidness

vade mecum *n* ***syn*** HANDBOOK, Baedeker, compendium, enchiridion, guide, guidebook, manual

vag *n* ***syn*** VAGABOND, ‖bindle stiff, bum, derelict, drifter, floater, hobo, street arab, tramp, vagrant

vagabond *adj* ***syn*** ITINERANT, itinerate, nomadic, perambulant, perambulatory, peripatetic, roving, vagrant, wandering, wayfaring
rel vagabondish

vagabond *n* a person who wanders at will or as a habit <a park full of *vagabonds* sleeping on benches>
syn arab, ‖bindle stiff, bum, canter, clochard, derelict, drifter, floater, ‖gangrel, hobo, piker, roadster, runagate, ‖shack, street arab, ‖sundowner, ‖swagger, ‖swagman, tramp, tramper, ‖traveler, vag, vagrant, Weary Willie

---

syn synonym(s)	***rel*** related word(s)
idiom idiomatic equivalent(s)	***con*** contrasted word(s)
ant antonym(s)	* vulgar

‖ use limited; if in doubt, see a dictionary
The first word in a synonym list when printed in SMALL CAPITALS shows where there is more information about the group. For a more efficient use of this book see Explanatory Notes.

rel roamer, rover, wanderer; boomer, migrant, runabout, straggler, stray, transient; bohemian, gypsy, picaro, picaroon; ||casual; stiff; beggar, rogue
idiom knight of the road

vagabond *vb* ***syn*** WANDER 1, drift, meander, ramble, range, roam, rove, straggle, stray, traipse

vagabondage *n* ***syn*** VAGRANCY, hoboism, vagabondia, vagabondism

vagabondia *n* ***syn*** VAGRANCY, hoboism, vagabondage, vagabondism

vagabondism *n* ***syn*** VAGRANCY, hoboism, vagabondage, vagabondia

vagabondize *vb* ***syn*** WANDER 1, drift, meander, ramble, range, roam, rove, straggle, stray, traipse

vagarious *adj* ***syn*** ARBITRARY 1, capricious, erratic, freakish, whimsical, whimsied
rel unreasonable; kinky

vagary *n* ***syn*** CAPRICE, bee, boutade, conceit, crotchet, fancy, freak, humor, megrim, whim
rel daydream, dream, fantasy; kink, quirk
idiom passing fancy

vagrancy *n* the act or state of wandering from place to place usually with no means of support <dropped out of society and lived a life of *vagrancy*>
syn hoboism, vagabondage, vagabondia, vagabondism
rel itineracy, itinerancy, nomadism; rambling, roaming, roving, wandering

vagrant *n* ***syn*** VAGABOND, ||bindle stiff, bum, derelict, drifter, floater, hobo, street arab, tramp, vag

vagrant *adj* ***syn*** ITINERANT, itinerate, nomadic, perambulant, perambulatory, peripatetic, roving, vagabond, wandering, wayfaring
rel aimless, errant, erratic; straying; sauntering, strolling

vague *adj* **1** ***syn*** OBSCURE 3, ambiguous, amphibological, equivocal, opaque, tenebrous, uncertain, unclear, unexplicit, unintelligible
rel indeterminate, indistinct, unplain; cloudy, dim, hazy, nebulous; muddy
con clear, distinct
ant express
2 ***syn*** FAINT 2, blear, bleary, dim, ill-defined, indistinct, obscure, shadowy, unclear, undetermined
rel nebulous, unsubstantial; indefinite, unplain; uncertain, unrecognizable; dreamlike, dreamy
3 ***syn*** HAZY, cloudy, foggy, misty, mushy, vaporous, vapory
rel bleared, bleary, blurry

vain *adj* **1** devoid of worth or significance <the *vain* pursuits of a luxurious life>
syn empty, hollow, idle, nugatory, otiose
rel profitless, unprofitable, useless, valueless, void, worthless; ineffective, ineffectual, inefficacious; bootless, fruitless; abortive, futile
con useful, valuable, worthy; effective, effectual, efficacious
2 ***syn*** FUTILE, abortive, bootless, fruitless, ineffective, ineffectual, unavailable, unavailing, unproductive, useless
rel paltry, petty, puny, trifling, trivial; delusive, delusory, misleading
3 having or exhibiting undue or excessive pride especially in one's appearance or achievements <was *vain* about his clothes>
syn conceited, ||conceity, narcissistic, self-conceited, stuck-up, vainglorious; *compare* PROUD 1
rel arrogant, egocentric, egoistic, haughty, ||pensy, proud, self-important, swollen-headed; boastful, self-exalting; coxcombical, dandyish, foppish
idiom stuck on oneself
con humble, meek, modest; bashful, diffident, retiring, shy

vainglorious *adj* ***syn*** VAIN 3, conceited, ||conceity, narcissistic, self-conceited, stuck-up
rel boastful, bragging, vaunting; disdainful, insolent, supercilious

vainglory *n* ***syn*** CONCEIT 2, egoism, egotism, pride, self-consequence, self-glory, self-importance, self-opinion, self-pride, swellheadedness
rel arrogance, haughtiness; boastfulness, bombast; exhibition, flaunting, parading
con lowliness, meekness; bashfulness, diffidence, self-effacement, shyness; modesty
ant humility

vainness *n* ***syn*** CONCEIT 2, conceitedness, egoism, narcissism, self-admiration, self-conceit, self-esteem, self-love, vainglory, vanity

vale *n* ***syn*** VALLEY, ||combe, dale, glen

valedictory *adj* ***syn*** PARTING, departing, farewell, good-bye

valiance *n* ***syn*** HEROISM, gallantry, prowess, valiancy, valor, valorousness
con feebleness, ineffectiveness; fear

valiancy *n* ***syn*** HEROISM, gallantry, prowess, valiance, valor, valorousness
con feebleness, ineffectiveness; fear

valiant *adj* ***syn*** BRAVE 1, audacious, bold, courageous, dauntless, doughty, fearless, intrepid, undaunted, valorous
ant pusillanimous

valid *adj* having the power to impress others as right and well-founded <a *valid* conclusion>
syn cogent, convincing, satisfactory, satisfying, solid, sound, telling
rel persuasive, potent, strong; attested, confirmed, corroborated, demonstrated, determined, established, substantiated, validated, verified; lawful, legal, licit; effective, effectual; conclusive, decisive, definitive, determinative; acceptable
con groundless, shaky, unconvincing, unfounded, unsound; fallacious, false, misleading, sophistical; counterfeit, fictitious
ant invalid

validate *vb* ***syn*** CONFIRM 2, authenticate, bear out, corroborate, justify, substantiate, verify
rel approve, endorse, legalize, ratify, rubber-stamp, sanction
con abolish, abrogate, annul, cancel, repeal; void

---

ant invalidate

validity *n* ***syn*** POINT 3, cogency, effectiveness, force, punch, validness
rel efficacy, gravity, soundness; persuasiveness, potency
con inconsistency; unsoundness; fallacy, falsity
ant invalidity, invalidness

validness *n* ***syn*** POINT 3, cogency, effectiveness, force, punch, validity
ant invalidity, invalidness

valley *n* an elongate depression of the earth's surface commonly situated between ranges of hills or mountains <small farms dotted the floor of the *valley*>
syn ||combe, dale, glen, vale
rel dell, dingle, hollow; ||rincon; canyon

valor *n* ***syn*** HEROISM, gallantry, prowess, valiance, valiancy, valorousness
rel mettle, resolution, spirit, tenacity; indomitableness, invincibility, unconquerableness; backbone, fortitude, guts, sand
con cowardliness, fear
ant pusillanimity, pusillanimousness

valorous *adj* ***syn*** BRAVE 1, audacious, bold, courageous, dauntless, doughty, fearless, intrepid, undaunted, valiant
ant pusillanimous

valorousness *n* ***syn*** HEROISM, gallantry, prowess, valiance, valiancy, valor
rel chivalrousness, chivalry; manliness
con cowardliness
ant pusillanimity, pusillanimousness

valuable *adj* ***syn*** PRECIOUS 1, costly, inestimable, invaluable, priceless
rel dear, expensive; appreciated, prized, treasured, valued; admired, esteemed, respected
idiom of great value
con cheap, inexpensive, trashy; unmarketable, unsalable; unworthy
ant valueless, worthless

valuate *vb* ***syn*** ESTIMATE 1, appraise, assay, assess, evaluate, rate, set (at), survey, value

valuation *n* **1** ***syn*** ESTIMATE 1, appraisal, appraisement, assessment, estimation, evaluation
rel judgment, opinion, rating
2 ***syn*** WORTH 1, account, value
rel charge, cost, price

value *n* **1** ***syn*** WORTH 1, account, valuation
rel appraisal, assessment; charge, cost, expense, price
2 ***syn*** QUALITY 2, caliber, merit, stature, virtue, worth

value *vb* **1** ***syn*** ESTIMATE 1, appraise, assay, assess, evaluate, rate, set (at), survey, valuate
rel compute, figure, gauge, reckon
idiom place a value (*or* price) on
2 ***syn*** APPRECIATE 1, apprize, cherish, esteem, prize, treasure
rel care (for); revere, reverence, venerate
idiom set much by

valueless *adj* ***syn*** WORTHLESS 1, draffy, drossy, good-for-nothing, inutile, ||no-account, no-good, nothing, unworthy
ant valuable

valve *n* ***syn*** FAUCET, cock, gate, hydrant, petcock, spigot, stopcock, tap
rel shutoff

||vamoose *vb* ***syn*** GET OUT 1, begone, clear out, decamp, hightail, kite, scram, skedaddle, skiddoo, take off

vamp *vb* ***syn*** MEND 2, do up, fix, overhaul, patch, rebuild, recondition, reconstruct, repair, revamp
rel brush up, fix up, touch up; furbish, refurbish

vamp (up) *vb* ***syn*** CONTRIVE 2, concoct, cook (up), devise, dream up, formulate, frame, hatch (up), invent, make up

vamp *n* ***syn*** FLIRT, coquette
rel charmer, enchantress, enticer, femme fatale, gold digger, inveigler, seductress, siren, temptress

vandal *n* one who willfully destroys or mars something valuable <*vandals* had knocked off the head of the statue>
syn defacer, despoiler, destroyer, ruinator, ruiner, wrecker
rel hoodlum, hooligan, lout, ruffian; devastator, ravager, spoiler, spoliator; looter, pillager, plunderer; iconoclast

vandalize *vb* to destroy or deface (as public or private property) willfully or maliciously <youths *vandalized* the shop>
syn ||trash, wreck
rel ||rip off; destroy, tear up

vanish *vb* to pass from view or out of existence <the moon *vanished* behind a cloud>
syn clear, disappear, evanesce, evanish, evaporate, fade
rel dematerialize, dissolve, melt (away); die
idiom do the vanishing act, vanish from sight, vanish into thin air, vanish like a dream
con arise, break out (*or* through), come (forth *or* out), emerge, issue, loom (up), materialize, show (up)
ant appear

vanished *adj* ***syn*** EXTINCT 2, bygone, dead, defunct, departed, gone, lost
rel expired, passed away; annihilated, no more, perished

vanity *n* ***syn*** CONCEIT 2, amour propre, conceitedness, narcissism, self-admiration, self-conceit, self-esteem, self-love, vainglory, vainness
rel autotheism, self-worship

vanquish *vb* ***syn*** CONQUER 1, bear down, beat down, crush, defeat, overpower, reduce, subdue, subjugate
rel surmount; overturn, subvert; humble, trample

vanquisher *n* ***syn*** VICTOR 1, conqueror, defeater, master, subduer, subjugator
rel champ, champion
con loser

vanquishment *n* ***syn*** DEFEAT 1, beating, debacle, defeasance, drubbing, licking, overthrow, rout, shellacking, trouncing
rel mastery, subdual, subjugation

---

syn synonym(s) *rel* related word(s)
idiom idiomatic equivalent(s) *con* contrasted word(s)
ant antonym(s) * vulgar
|| use limited; if in doubt, see a dictionary
The first word in a synonym list when printed in SMALL CAPITALS shows where there is more information about the group. For a more efficient use of this book see Explanatory Notes.

vantage *n* ***syn*** ADVANTAGE 3, allowance, bulge, ‖deadwood, draw, edge, handicap, head start, odds, start
ant disadvantage

vapid *adj* ***syn*** INSIPID 3, driveling, flat, inane, innocuous, jejune, milk-and-water, namby-pamby, sapless, wishy-washy
rel flavorless, milk-toast, tasteless, weak; dull, unimaginative, uninteresting
idiom neither hot nor cold, neither one thing nor the other
con brisk, lively, tangy, zesty; crisp, forceful, incisive, trenchant; expressive, meaningful, pregnant, significant, telling

vaporous *adj* **1** ***syn*** HAZY, cloudy, foggy, misty, mushy, vague, vapory
2 ***syn*** AIRY 3, aerial, ethereal, vapory
rel unsubstantial, wispy; illusory, unreal

vapory *adj* **1** ***syn*** HAZY, cloudy, foggy, misty, mushy, vague, vaporous
2 ***syn*** AIRY 3, aerial, ethereal, vaporous
rel gaseous

variable *adj* **1** ***syn*** CHANGEABLE 1, changeful, fluid, mobile, mutable, protean, unsettled, unstable, unsteady, weathery
rel fitful, spasmodic; irregular, unequable, unequal, ununiform
con unchanging, unvarying; immobile, stable, unmoving; equable, equal, uniform
ant constant, invariable
2 ***syn*** MUTABLE 2, changeable, inconstant, shifty, slippery, uncertain, unstable, unsteady
3 ***syn*** INCONSTANT 1, capricious, changeable, fickle, mercurial, temperamental, ticklish, uncertain, unstable, volatile

variance *n* **1** the quality, state, or fact of being variable <a daily *variance* of 1°F.>
syn difference, variation
rel change, deviation, fluctuation
ant invariance
2 ***syn*** DISCORD, conflict, contention, difference, disaccord, dissension, dissent, dissidence, disunity, strife
rel division, separation, severing, sundering

variation *n* **1** ***syn*** CHANGE 1, alteration, modification, mutation, turn
rel difference, dissimilarity; deflection, discrepancy
con stability, unchangeableness
2 ***syn*** VARIANCE 1, difference
rel shift; divergence; discrepancy, disparity
con uniformity

varicolored *adj* ***syn*** VARIEGATED, dappled, discolor, motley, multicolor, multicolored, multihued, parti-colored, versicolor, versicolored
ant solid

varied *adj* ***syn*** MISCELLANEOUS, assorted, chowchow, conglomerate, heterogeneous, indiscriminate, mixed, motley, multifarious, promiscuous

variegated *adj* having a pattern involving different colors or shades of color < *variegated* leaves >
syn dappled, discolor, motley, multicolor, multicolored, multihued, parti-color, parti-colored, polychromatic, polychrome, varicolored, versicolor, versicolored
rel checked, checkered; piebald, pied, skewbald; freaked, streaked; flecked; stippled; marbled; mottle, mottled, spattered, speckled, spotted; calico; pinto
ant solid

variety *n* **1** the quality or state of being composed of different parts, elements, or individuals <the *variety* of the city's cultural life>
syn diverseness, diversity, multeity, multifariousness, multiformity, multiplicity, variousness
rel diversification, heterogeneity, variation
2 a collection of different things, forms, or qualities especially of a particular class <had a great *variety* of jobs in his lifetime>
syn assortment
rel conglomeration, medley, miscellany
3 ***syn*** TYPE, character, description, ilk, kidney, kind, nature, sort, species, stripe
rel classification; grade, rank

various *adj* **1** ***syn*** MANY, legion, multifarious, multitudinal, multitudinous, numerous, populous, ‖several, sundry, voluminous
rel assorted, heterogeneous, miscellaneous, omnifarious, omnigenous
2 ***syn*** DIFFERENT 1, disparate, dissimilar, distant, divergent, diverse, unalike, unequal, unlike, unsimilar
rel changing, variant, varied, varying; distinct, separate; distinctive, individual, peculiar
ant uniform
3 ***syn*** SEVERAL 3, divers, some, sundry
ant many, numerous
4 ***syn*** DISTINCT 1, different, discrete, diverse, separate, several
5 ***syn*** CERTAIN 2, some

various *pron, pl in constr* ***syn*** SUNDRY, divers, many, ‖several

variously *adv* ***syn*** OTHERWISE 1, differently, diversely, ‖othergates

variousness *n* ***syn*** VARIETY 1, diverseness, diversity, multeity, multifariousness, multiformity, multiplicity

varnish *vb* ***syn*** PALLIATE, blanch (over), extenuate, gloss (over), gloze (over), sugarcoat, veneer, white, whiten, whitewash

vary *vb* **1** ***syn*** CHANGE 1, alter, modify, mutate, refashion, turn
rel modulate, qualify
2 ***syn*** DIFFER 1, disagree
3 ***syn*** DIFFER 2, disaccord, disagree, discord, dissent, divide
rel depart, deviate, digress, diverge; divide, part, separate
ant agree
4 ***syn*** RANGE 3, extend, go, run

vast *adj* ***syn*** HUGE, colossal, enormous, giant, gigantic, immense, monumental, titanic, tremendous, whopping
rel big, large; ample, capacious, spacious; broad, expansive, far-flung, wide, widespread; astronomical, cosmic

---

syn synonym(s) ***rel*** related word(s)
idiom idiomatic equivalent(s) ***con*** contrasted word(s)
ant antonym(s) * vulgar
‖ use limited; if in doubt, see a dictionary
The first word in a synonym list when printed in SMALL CAPITALS shows where there is more information about the group. For a more efficient use of this book see Explanatory Notes.

con confined, limited, narrow, restricted

vastness *n* ***syn*** ENORMITY 2, enormousness, hugeness, immensity, magnitude, tremendousness

vatic *adj* ***syn*** PROPHETIC, apocalyptic, Delphian, fatidic, mantic, oracular, prophetical, sibylline, vaticinal

vaticinal *adj* ***syn*** PROPHETIC, apocalyptic, Delphian, fatidic, mantic, oracular, prophetical, sibylline, vatic

vaticinate *vb* ***syn*** FORETELL, adumbrate, augur, call, forecast, portend, predict, presage, prognosticate, prophesy

vault *n* ***syn*** CRYPT, catacomb, undercroft

vault *vb* **1** ***syn*** JUMP 1, bounce, bound, hop, hurdle, leap, lop, saltate, spring
rel upleap, upspring; overjump, overleap; clear; rise, soar; ascend, mount; surmount
2 ***syn*** CLEAR 8, hurdle, leap, negotiate, over, overleap, surmount

vaulting *adj* ***syn*** AMBITIOUS 1, aspiring, emulous
rel enthusiastic; opportunistic

vaunt *vb* ***syn*** BOAST, blow, brag, cock-a-doodle-doo, crow, gasconade, mouth, prate, puff, rodomontade
rel brandish, display, exhibit, expose, flaunt, parade, show off
idiom puff oneself

vaunter *n* ***syn*** BRAGGART, blower, blowhard, boaster, braggadocio, bragger, ‖gasbag, puckfist, rodomont, rodomontade

vaunting *adj* ***syn*** BOASTFUL, braggadocian, braggart, braggy, rodomontade, self-glorifying

vector *n* an agent capable of transmitting a pathogen from one organism to another <fleas are *vectors* of bubonic plague>
syn carrier, vehicle

veer *vb* **1** ***syn*** TURN 6, avert, deflect, divert, pivot, sheer, volte-face, wheel, whip, whirl
2 ***syn*** SWERVE 1, dip, sheer, skew, slue, train off
rel depart, deviate, digress, diverge; angle off, bear off; twist; pivot, turn, wheel

vegetate *vb* to lead a passive existence without exertion of body or mind <he never really lived his life—he merely *vegetated*>
syn stagnate
rel idle; languish; hibernate
idiom idle life away, live the life of a clam, pass the time

vehement *adj* ***syn*** INTENSE 1, concentrated, desperate, exquisite, fierce, furious, terrible, vicious, violent
rel emphatic, pronounced; energetic, hearty, lively, zealous; forceful, potent, powerful; ardent, fervent, fervid, heated, impassioned, passionate, perfervid; delirious, frantic, furious, rabid, wild

vehicle *n* **1** ***syn*** VECTOR, carrier
rel agent
2 ***syn*** MEAN 2, agency, agent, channel, instrument, instrumentality, intermediary, medium, ministry, organ
rel implement, tool
3 a means of transporting goods or passengers <his *vehicle* was an old battered coupe>
syn conveyance, transport, transportation

veil *n* ***syn*** MASK 2, cloak, color, coloring, cover, disguise, facade, false front, front, guise

veil *vb* ***syn*** ENFOLD 1, enclose, enshroud, envelop, enwrap, invest, shroud, wrap
rel mantle, overspread, spread (over); blanket, curtain; camouflage, cloak, cover (up), disguise, mask; conceal, hide, screen, secrete
con exhibit, lay (open), open up, reveal, uncover, unmask; bare, expose, show
ant unveil

vein *n* **1** a distinctive method of expression <wrote his speech in the proper *vein* for a very sophisticated audience>
syn fashion, manner, mode, style, tone
rel way; line; mood, tenor
2 ***syn*** HINT 2, shade, strain, streak, suggestion, suspicion, tincture, tinge, touch, trace
3 ***syn*** MOOD 1, humor, mind, strain, temper, tone
rel complexion, disposition, fettle, temperament; character, nature, spirit

velitation *n* ***syn*** ENCOUNTER, brush, run-in, set-to, skirmish

velleity *n* ***syn*** WILL 1, fancy, inclination, liking, mind, pleasure
rel volition; wish

vellicate *vb* ***syn*** JERK, lug, lurch, snap, twitch, yank
rel nip, pinch; fidget, jig, jiggle

velocipede *n* ***syn*** BICYCLE, bike, cycle, two-wheeler

velocity *n* ***syn*** SPEED 2, ‖bat, celerity, gait, pace, quickness, rapidity, rapidness, swiftness
rel headway, impetus, momentum; dispatch, expedition, haste, hurry

velutinous *adj* ***syn*** VELVETY, velvetlike

velvetlike *adj* ***syn*** VELVETY, velutinous
idiom soft as velvet

velvety *adj* **1** having the extreme softness associated with the surface or appearance of velvet <wore a *velvety* red flower in her hair>
syn velutinous, velvetlike
rel plush, plushy, smooth, soft; glossy, sleek, slick; satiny, silken, silky
2 ***syn*** SOFT 3, cottony, satiny, silken, silky

venal *adj* **1** open to corrupt influence and especially bribery <a *venal* legislator>
syn bribable, buyable, corruptible, purchasable; *compare* CORRUPT 2, CROOKED 2
rel corrupt, flagitious, infamous, iniquitous, nefarious, vicious; hack, hireling, mercenary, paid; ignoble, sordid; unethical, unprincipled, unscrupulous
2 ***syn*** CORRUPT 2, mercenary, praetorian, unethical, unprincipled, unscrupulous

vend *vb* **1** ***syn*** SELL 2, give, market
2 ***syn*** PEDDLE 2, hawk, huckster, monger
3 ***syn*** DECLARE 1, advertise, announce, blazon, broadcast, proclaim, promulgate, publish, sound, toot

vendee *n* ***syn*** PURCHASER, buyer, emptor

---

syn synonym(s) ***rel*** related word(s)
idiom idiomatic equivalent(s) ***con*** contrasted word(s)
ant antonym(s) * vulgar
‖ use limited; if in doubt, see a dictionary
The first word in a synonym list when printed in SMALL CAPITALS shows where there is more information about the group. For a more efficient use of this book see Explanatory Notes.

vendetta *n* a prolonged mutual enmity marked by bitter hostility and conflict <a long-standing *vendetta* between two rival gangs>
syn feud
rel dispute, quarrel; rhubarb, row, wrangle; conflict, fight, set-to; blood feud, blood vengeance

vendible *adj* ***syn*** MARKETABLE, merchandisable, merchantable, salable, sellable, trafficable
ant unvendible

vendible *n, usu* **vendibles** *pl* ***syn*** MERCHANDISE, commodities, goods, line, wares

vendor *n* ***syn*** PEDDLER, ‖arab, cheap-jack (*or* cheap-john), ‖duffer, hawker, higgler, huckster, outcrier, packman, roadman

veneer *n* ***syn*** MASK 2, cover, disguise, facade, face, false front, front, show, veil, window dressing

veneer *vb* ***syn*** PALLIATE, blanch (over), extenuate, gloss (over), gloze (over), sugarcoat, varnish, white, whiten, whitewash

venerable *adj* **1** deserving to be venerated usually by reason of prolonged testing (as of character) <a *venerable* judge with an impressive knowledge of the law>
syn patriarchal, revered, reverend, reverential; *compare* HONORABLE 1
rel dignified, imposing, stately; admirable, estimable; honored, reverenced; worshipful; sacred
ant unvenerable
2 ***syn*** ANCIENT 1, aged, age-old, antediluvian, antique, hoary, Noachian, old, timeworn
rel elderly; patriarchal, reverenced, reverend, venerated
con contemporary, current; fresh, inexperienced, new, untried, unused

venerate *vb* ***syn*** REVERE, adore, reverence, worship
rel honor; idolize
idiom put on a pedestal

venery *n* ***syn*** HUNTING, chase

venge *vb* ***syn*** AVENGE, redress, revenge, vindicate
idiom even (up) the score, repay in kind, settle accounts (*or* an account)

vengeance *n* ***syn*** RETALIATION, avengement, avenging, counterblow, reprisal, requital, retribution, revanche, revenge
rel return; repayment; revengefulness, vengefulness

vengeful *adj* ***syn*** VINDICTIVE, revengeful, wreakful
rel antagonistic, hostile, inimical, rancorous
con charitable, forgiving, kind; benevolent, benign, inoffensive

venial *adj* of a kind that can be remitted and that does not warrant punishment or penalty <the *venial* indiscretions of youth>
syn excusable, forgivable, pardonable, remittable
rel allowable, unobjectionable; insignificant, minor, trifling, trivial; harmless, tolerable
con criminal, damning, deadly, mortal; grievous, outrageous, serious; inexcusable, unforgivable, unpardonable, unremittable
ant heinous

venom *n* ***syn*** POISON, bane, contagion, virus
rel ill will, malignity, rancor, venomousness, virulence, vitriol
con antidote, remedy

venomous *adj* ***syn*** POISONOUS, mephitic, poison, toxic, toxicant, virulent
rel malevolent, malign, malignant; baleful, malefic, maleficent; viperish, viperlike, viperous

vent *vb* **1** ***syn*** EMIT 2, give off, give out, issue, release, throw off
rel cast out, discharge, exhaust
2 ***syn*** EXPRESS 2, air, give, put, state, ventilate
rel utter, voice; assert, declare
idiom come out with, give vent to
con check, curb, inhibit, restrain; repress, suppress
3 ***syn*** TAKE OUT (on), loose, release, unleash

vent *n* **1** ***syn*** APERTURE, hole, opening, orifice, outlet
2 ***syn*** EXPRESSION 1, statement, utterance, voice
rel articulation, verbalization, vocalization

venter *n* ***syn*** ABDOMEN, belly, ‖gut, paunch, stomach, tummy

ventilate *vb* **1** ***syn*** BROACH, bring up, introduce, moot
2 ***syn*** EXPRESS 2, air, give, put, state, vent
rel go into, take up; debate, deliberate, discourse (about), discuss, ‖rap (about), talk over (*or* of *or* about), thresh out; advertise, broadcast, publish
idiom chew the fat (*or* the rag)

ventilation *n* ***syn*** CONFERENCE 1, confabulation, deliberation, discussion, rap

venture *vb* **1** to expose to risk or loss <*ventured* their capital in foreign trade>
syn adventure, chance, hazard, risk, wager; *compare* GAMBLE 2
rel endanger, imperil, jeopard, jeopardize, jeopardy, peril; expose, lay (open)
idiom take chances (*or* risks) on (*or* with)
2 ***syn*** GAMBLE 2, chance, hazard, risk
rel bet, operate, play (for), speculate, stake; jeopard, jeopardize, jeopardy
idiom luck it
3 ***syn*** FACE 3, ‖banter, beard, brave, challenge, dare, defy, front, outdare, outface

venture *n* ***syn*** ADVENTURE, emprise, enterprise, exploit, feat, gest
rel attempt, undertaking; crack, fling; dare, gamble, risk, speculation
idiom leap in the dark

venturesome *adj* ***syn*** ADVENTUROUS, adventuresome, audacious, daredevil, daring, foolhardy, rash, reckless, temerarious, venturous
rel stalwart, stout, sturdy; brave; overbold
con timid, timorous; afraid, apprehensive, fearful

venturous *adj* ***syn*** ADVENTUROUS, adventuresome, audacious, daredevil, daring, foolhardy, rash, reckless, temerarious, venturesome
rel aggressive, enterprising, hustling

veracious *adj* **1** ***syn*** TRUTHFUL, true-tongued, truth-speaking, truth-telling, veridical
rel direct; undeceitful, undeceptive

---

syn synonym(s) ***rel*** related word(s)
idiom idiomatic equivalent(s) ***con*** contrasted word(s)
ant antonym(s) * vulgar
‖ use limited; if in doubt, see a dictionary
The first word in a synonym list when printed in SMALL CAPITALS shows where there is more information about the group. For a more efficient use of this book see Explanatory Notes.

con equivocal; deceitful, dishonest, insincere; false, untruthful
ant unveracious
2 *syn* TRUE 3, faithful, just, right, strict, undistorted, veridical
rel unquestionable, valid
con illusory, invalid, wrong
ant unveracious

veraciousness *n syn* VERACITY 1, truth, truthfulness, veridicality, verity
rel artlessness, openness; trustworthiness
con falseness, insincerity

veracity *n* **1** the quality or state of keeping close to fact and avoiding distortion or misrepresentation <questions the *veracity* of that witness>
syn truth, truthfulness, veraciousness, veridicality, verity
rel accuracy, correctness, exactness, factualness; frankness, honesty
con inaccuracy, incorrectness; deception, dishonesty, untruth, untruthfulness
ant unveracity
2 something that is true <can make lies sound like *veracities*>
syn gospel, truism, truth, verity
rel verisimilitude; actuality; fact
con lie, untruth
ant unveracity

verbal *adj* **1** *syn* ORAL 2, spoken, traditional, unwritten, word-of-mouth
2 *syn* VERBATIM, literal, word-for-word

verbalism *n* **1** *syn* WORDING, diction, parlance, phrase, phraseology, phrasing, verbiage, wordage
rel styling
2 *syn* VERBOSITY, prolixity, prolixness, verboseness, windiness, wordiness

verbality *n syn* VERBIAGE 1, circumambages, circumbendibus, circumlocution, periphrase, periphrasis, pleonasm, redundancy, roundabout, tautology
rel verbalism, verboseness, verbosity, wordiness

verbalization *n syn* SPEECH 1, discourse, speaking, talk, utterance

verbalize *vb syn* SPEAK 1, talk, utter, vocalize, voice
rel air, express, give, say, state, vent, ventilate, word
idiom couch in terms, find words to express

verbatim *adv* in the same words <repeated their earlier conversation *verbatim*>
syn direct, directly, literally, literatim, word for word
rel accurately, exactly, precisely
idiom to the letter
con basically, essentially, in essence; carelessly, imprecisely, inaccurately, inexactly

verbatim *adj* using the same words <court stenographers took down the *verbatim* testimony>
syn literal, verbal, word-for-word
rel close, faithful, strict; exact, precise
idiom following the letter, true to the letter
con careless, imprecise, inaccurate, inexact

verbiage *n* **1** a stylistic fault involving excessive wordiness that obscures or unduly complicates expression <the florid *verbiage* of the dissertation>
syn circumambages, circumbendibus, circumlocution, periphrase, periphrasis, pleonasm, redundancy, roundabout, tautology, verbality; *compare* VERBOSITY
rel nimiety; repetition; expansiveness, floridity, floridness; longiloquence, long-windedness
idiom purple prose
con breviloquence, brevity, briefness, terseness
ant concision
2 *syn* WORDING, diction, parlance, phrase, phraseology, phrasing, verbalism, wordage

verbose *adj syn* WORDY, diffuse, long-winded, palaverous, prolix, redundant, windy
rel flowery, grandiloquent, magniloquent; circumlocutory, periphrastic, pleonastic, tautologous
con precise; close, compact, lean, tight
ant concise; laconic

verboseness *n syn* VERBOSITY, prolixity, prolixness, verbalism, windiness, wordiness
ant conciseness

verbosity *n* the quality or state or an instance of being wordy <his two-hour lecture was the epitome of *verbosity*> <flowery *verbosities* weakened his speech>
syn prolixity, prolixness, verbalism, verboseness, windiness, wordiness; *compare* VERBIAGE 1
rel bombast, grandiloquence; long-windedness; redundancy
con conciseness, preciseness, succinctness, terseness; leanness, tightness

verboten *adj syn* FORBIDDEN, banned, prohibited
rel disallowed, disapproved; unauthorized, unlicensed, unsanctioned; outlawed, taboo
con allowed, permitted; authorized, licensed; approved, endorsed, sanctioned

verdure *n syn* FOLIAGE, leafage, umbrage

verge *n* **1** *syn* BORDER 1, brim, brink, edge, fringe, hem, margin, rim, selvage, skirt
2 a time interval or set of circumstances marking the imminent beginning of a new state, condition, or action <on the *verge* of war>
syn brink, edge, point, threshold
rel border line

verge *vb* **1** *syn* BORDER 1, bound, edge, fringe, hem, margin, outline, rim, skirt, surround
rel approach; incline, lean, tend (to *or* toward); touch (on *or* upon)
2 *syn* ADJOIN, abut, border, butt (on *or* against), communicate, join, line, march, neighbor, touch
3 *syn* BORDER 3, approach, trench

veridical *adj* **1** *syn* TRUTHFUL, true-tongued, truth-speaking, truth-telling, veracious
2 *syn* REAL 3, actual, indisputable, true, undeniable, unfabled
3 *syn* TRUE 3, faithful, just, right, strict, undistorted, veracious
rel uncolored, undistorted, unvarnished; actual, real
con invalid; illusory, unreal

---

syn synonym(s) *rel* related word(s)
idiom idiomatic equivalent(s) *con* contrasted word(s)
ant antonym(s) * vulgar
‖ use limited; if in doubt, see a dictionary
The first word in a synonym list when printed in SMALL CAPITALS shows where there is more information about the group. For a more efficient use of this book see Explanatory Notes.

veridicality *n* ***syn*** VERACITY 1, truth, truthfulness, veraciousness, verity
rel genuineness

verificatory *adj* ***syn*** CORROBORATIVE, adminicular, collateral, confirmative, confirmatory, corroboratory

verify *vb* ***syn*** CONFIRM 2, authenticate, bear out, corroborate, justify, substantiate, validate
rel demonstrate, prove, test, try; document, establish, settle

verily *adv* ***syn*** EVEN 3, indeed, nay, truly, yea

verisimilitude *n* the quality of a representation that causes it to appear true <his characters are too stilted for *verisimilitude*>
syn color, plausibility, verisimility
rel authenticity, genuineness, veritableness; likeness, resemblance, similarity

verisimility *n* ***syn*** VERISIMILITUDE, color, plausibility

veritable *adj* ***syn*** AUTHENTIC 2, bona fide, genuine, indubitable, real, sure-enough, true, undoubted, unquestionable, very
rel undenied, unrefuted; actual, factual
con doubtful, questionable; imaginary, unreal, untrue; artificial, factitious; counterfeit, false, spurious

veritably *adv* ***syn*** VERY 2, actually, de facto, genuinely, really, truly

verity *n* **1** ***syn*** VERACITY 2, gospel, truism, truth
ant falsity
2 ***syn*** VERACITY 1, truth, truthfulness, veraciousness, veridicality

vernacular *adj* of or relating to everyday speech <*vernacular* Welsh differs greatly from literary Welsh>
syn colloquial, vulgar, vulgate

vernacular *n* **1** ***syn*** LANGUAGE 1, dialect, idiom, speech, tongue
rel mother tongue
idiom native tongue
2 ***syn*** DIALECT 2, argot, cant, jargon, lingo, patois, patter, slang
3 a commonly spoken as opposed to a prestige variety of a language <literary Chinese and the various *vernaculars*>
syn colloquial, patois, vulgate; *compare* DIALECT 2
rel dialect, lingo, slang

vernacularism *n* ***syn*** BARBARISM, corruption, impropriety, slangism, solecism, vernacularity, vulgarism

vernacularity *n* ***syn*** BARBARISM, corruption, impropriety, slangism, solecism, vernacularism, vulgarism

vernal *adj* of, relating to, or resembling the spring of the year <*vernal* sunshine>
syn spring, springlike

versant *adj* ***syn*** FAMILIAR 3, abreast, acquainted, au courant, au fait, conversant, informed, up, versed
ant unversed

versatile *adj* having a wide range of skills, aptitudes, or interests <a *versatile* artist, who is at home in any medium>
syn adaptable, all-around, ambidextrous, many-sided, mobile, myriad-minded
rel elastic, flexible, plastic, pliable; adroit, dexterous, facile; able, skilled, skillful; accomplished, conversant; gifted, talented; well-rounded
con inadequate, limited

verse *n* **1** ***syn*** POETRY 1, poesy, rhyme, song
2 ***syn*** POEM, poesy, poetry, rhyme, rune
rel jingle; ballad, lay; sonnet; lyric; ode; epic

versed *adj* **1** ***syn*** EXPERIENCED, old, old-time, practical, practiced, seasoned, skilled, vet, veteran
rel competent
con incompetent
ant unversed
2 ***syn*** FAMILIAR 3, abreast, acquainted, au courant, au fait, conversant, informed, up, versant
ant unversed

verseman *n* ***syn*** POETASTER, bardlet, bardling, poeticule, rhymer, rhymester, verser, versesmith, versificator, versifier

versemonger *n* ***syn*** POETASTER, balladmonger, bardling, poetling, rhymester, verseman, verser, versesmith, versificator, versifier

verser *n* ***syn*** POETASTER, bardlet, bardling, poetling, rhymer, rhymester, verseman, versesmith, versificator, versifier

versesmith *n* ***syn*** POETASTER, bardling, poeticule, poetling, rhymer, rhymester, verseman, verser, versificator, versifier

versicolor *adj* ***syn*** VARIEGATED, dappled, discolor, motley, multicolor, multicolored, multihued, parti-colored, varicolored, versicolored

versicolored *adj* ***syn*** VARIEGATED, dappled, discolor, motley, multicolor, multicolored, multihued, parti-colored, varicolored, versicolor

versificator *n* ***syn*** POETASTER, bardlet, bardling, rhymer, rhymester, verseman, versemonger, verser, versesmith, versifier

versifier *n* ***syn*** POETASTER, balladmonger, poetling, rhymer, rhymester, verseman, versemonger, verser, versesmith, versificator

version *n* **1** a restating often in simpler language of something previously stated or written <a simple *version* of Beowulf for the use of children>
syn paraphrase, rendering, restatement, translation
rel rendition; clarification, interpretation; condensation, simplification; rewording; restipulation
2 ***syn*** ACCOUNT 7, chronicle, history, narrative, report, story
rel tale
3 ***syn*** INTERPRETATION 2, reading, rendering, rendition

versus *prep* **1** in conflict with <the case of John Doe *versus* Richard Roe>
syn against
rel con, contra
idiom at cross-purposes with (*or* to), at odds with, at outs with, at variance with, on the outs with
2 in contrast with <the age-old argument about free trade *versus* protection>
syn over against, vis-à-vis

---

syn synonym(s)
idiom idiomatic equivalent(s)
ant antonym(s)
rel related word(s)
con contrasted word(s)
* vulgar
‖ use limited; if in doubt, see a dictionary
The first word in a synonym list when printed in SMALL CAPITALS shows where there is more information about the group. For a more efficient use of this book see Explanatory Notes.

idiom as opposed to

vertebrae *n* ***syn*** SPINE, back, backbone, rachis, spinal column, vertebral column

vertebral column *n* ***syn*** SPINE, back, backbone, rachis, spinal column, vertebrae

vertex *n* ***syn*** TOP 1, apex, crest, crown, fastigium, peak, roof, summit
rel cap; tip-top; apogee, zenith
idiom upper extremity

vertical *adj* situated at right angles to the plane of the horizon or extending from that plane at such an angle < *vertical* walls >
syn perpendicular, plumb, straight-up
rel erect, upright; steep, up-and-down
con flat, plane
ant horizontal

verticalism *n* ***syn*** VERTICALITY, perpendicularity, plumbness, verticalness

verticality *n* the quality or state of being vertical < the soaring *verticality* of the spires >
syn perpendicularity, plumbness, verticalism, verticalness
rel erectness, uprightness
con flatness, lowness
ant horizontality

verticalness *n* ***syn*** VERTICALITY, perpendicularity, plumbness, verticalism

vertiginous *adj* ***syn*** DIZZY 2, giddy, light, light-headed, swimming, swimmy

verve *n* ***syn*** SPIRIT 5, animation, brio, dash, élan, esprit, life, oomph, vim, zing
rel liveliness, vivacity; bounce, buoyancy, elasticity, resiliency, spring; fire, gusto, zest

very *adj* **1** ***syn*** AUTHENTIC 2, bona fide, genuine, indubitable, real, sure-enough, true, undoubted, unquestionable, veritable
rel hundred-percent, perfect; correct, exact, right
con fake, fraudulent, mock, sham
2 ***syn*** PRECISE 4, exact
rel especial, express, special
3 ***syn*** PERFECT 3, ideal, model
4 being as stated without addition or superfluity < the *very* thought of it makes me ill >
syn bare, mere
5 ***syn*** SAME 1, exact, identical, selfsame
idiom (the) very same

very *adv* **1** to a high or exceptional degree < a *very* successful meeting >
syn ‖awful, awfully, ‖big, ‖crazy, damned, ‖dreadful, dreadfully, eminently, exceedingly, exceptionally, extremely, greatly, highly, hugely, insatiably, ‖larruping, ‖main, mightily, mighty, ‖monstrous, ‖mortacious, mortally, most, much, notably, parlous, pesky, ‖pure, rattling, remarkably, right, ‖right smart, snapping, so, spanking, staving, strikingly, super, surpassingly, terribly, thoroughly, too, vitally, whacking, whopping
rel passing, quite, somewhat; perfectly, seriously, significantly, tellingly
idiom nothing if not
con inconsiderably, little, scarcely, slightly
2 in actual fact < told the *very* same story >
syn actually, de facto, genuinely, really, truly, veritably
rel exactly, precisely; almost, nearly, practically, well-nigh
idiom in point of fact, in truth
con apparently, ostensibly, outwardly, seemingly

vest *vb* **1** ***syn*** INVEST 2, authorize, empower
2 ***syn*** BELONG 2, appertain, pertain

vestibule *n* an entrance chamber between the outer door and the interior of a building < the *vestibule* of a theater >
syn foyer, lobby
rel entrance hall, entry, entryway; portal, portico; antechamber, anteroom; narthex

vestige *n* **1** something (as a mark or visible sign) left by a material thing formerly present but now lost or unknown < digging for the *vestiges* of past civilizations >
syn memento, relic, shadow, trace
rel remainder, remains; rag, remnant, scrap, tag
2 ***syn*** FOOTPRINT, footstep, spoor, step, track, tract
rel path; trail

vet *vb* ***syn*** SCRUTINIZE 1, canvass, check over, check up, con, examine, inspect, study, survey, view
idiom go over with a fine-tooth comb

vet *adj* ***syn*** EXPERIENCED, old, old-time, practical, practiced, seasoned, skilled, versed, veteran

vet *n* ***syn*** VETERAN, longtimer, old hand, old-timer

veteran *n* one having knowledge or ability gained through long experience < was a political campaign *veteran* of long standing >
syn longtimer, old hand, old-timer, vet
rel expert, master, past master
con amateur, freshman, youngster
ant novice

veteran *adj* ***syn*** EXPERIENCED, old, old-time, practical, practiced, seasoned, skilled, versed, vet
rel wise; sophisticated, worldly
idiom dry behind the ears, not born yesterday, wise in the ways of the world
con inexperienced, unpracticed, unversed; unqualified, unskilled, untrained

veto *vb* to refuse to admit or approve < the President *vetoed* the bill >
syn kill, negative, ‖nix, non-placet
rel decline, deny, disallow, forbid, prohibit, refuse, reject; defeat
idiom put one's veto on
con admit, approve, assent (to); pass

vex *vb* ***syn*** ANNOY 1, abrade, bother, ‖bug, chafe, exercise, fret, gall, irk, provoke
rel ‖chaw, embarrass; plague; anger, infuriate
con appease, mollify, pacify, propitiate, smooth (over); please, regale
ant soothe

vexation *n* ***syn*** ANNOYANCE 1, bothering, harassment, irking, provocation, provoking, vexing

rel aggravation, irritation

vexatious *adj* ***syn*** TROUBLESOME, mean, pesky, troublous, ugly, wicked

vexing *n* ***syn*** ANNOYANCE 1, bothering, harassment, irking, provocation, provoking, vexation

via *prep* **1** over a route that passes through <shipped to New York *via* the Panama Canal>

syn by, by way of, through

rel along; over

2 using as a means of approach or action <reached the voters *via* mass-media advertising>

syn by, by dint of, by means of, by virtue of, by way of, per, through, with

idiom through the medium of

viable *adj* ***syn*** POSSIBLE 1, doable, feasible, practicable, workable

viands *n pl* ***syn*** FOOD 1, comestibles, ‖eats, edibles, feed, grub, nurture, provender, provisions, victuals

rel fare

vibrant *adj* ***syn*** RESONANT, consonant, orotund, plangent, resounding, ringing, rotund, round, sonorant, sonorous

vibrate *vb* ***syn*** SHAKE 2, jar, quake, tremble, tremor

vice *n* **1** degrading or immoral habits and practices <an exposé of *vice* and crime in the city>

syn corruption, depravity, immorality, wickedness

rel decay, rot, squalor; evil, ill, sin, wrong; indecency, unchastity; debasement, debauchery, licentiousness, perversion

con morality; respectability; uprightness

ant virtue

2 ***syn*** FAULT 2, failing, foible, frailty

rel shortcoming

idiom weak point

3 ***syn*** BLEMISH, defect, flaw

vice versa *adv* ***syn*** AGAIN 5, contra, contrariwise, contrary, contrawise, conversely, oppositely

vicinage *n* ***syn*** LOCALITY 1, area, district, neighborhood, vicinity

vicinity *n* **1** ***syn*** LOCALITY 1, area, district, neighborhood, vicinage

2 ***syn*** ORDER 4, extent, magnitude, matter, neighborhood, range, tune

vicious *adj* **1** ***syn*** WRONG 1, bad, evil, immoral, iniquitous, reprobate, sinful, wicked

2 highly offensive or reprehensible in character, nature, or conduct < *vicious* parents who were a bad influence on their children>

syn corrupt, degenerate, depraved, flagitious, infamous, miscreant, nefarious, perverse, putrid, rotten, unhealthy, villainous

rel bad, faulty, poor, unsound; opprobrious, reprehensible; contaminated, obnoxious, septic

con good, moral, righteous, right-minded

ant virtuous

3 ***syn*** SAVAGE 1, feral, wild

rel brutish; bloodthirsty

4 ***syn*** MALICIOUS, despiteful, evil, hateful, malevolent, malign, malignant, rancorous, spiteful, wicked

5 ***syn*** INTENSE 1, concentrated, desperate, exquisite, fierce, furious, terrible, vehement, violent

rel severe

vicissitude *n* **1** ***syn*** CHANGE 2, innovation, mutation, novelty, permutation, sport

rel alternation; reversal; transposition; progression; diversity, variety

2 ***syn*** DIFFICULTY 1, asperity, hardness, hardship, rigor

rel chop and change, ups and downs; adversity, mischance, misfortune; affliction, trial, tribulation

victim *n* **1** a living being sacrificed (as in a religious rite) <offered up human *victims* to appease their bloodthirsty gods>

syn offering, sacrifice

2 one subjected to oppression, loss, or suffering < *victims* of social injustice>

syn bottom dog, casualty, prey, underdog

rel quarry

3 ***syn*** FOOL 3, butt, chump, dupe, fall guy, gudgeon, gull, mark, pigeon, sucker

idiom easy mark, easy pickings

victimize *vb* **1** ***syn*** SACRIFICE 1, immolate

2 ***syn*** DUPE, bamboozle, flimflam, fool, gull, hoax, hoodwink, hornswoggle, pigeon, trick

victor *n* **1** one that defeats an enemy <the Allies were the *victors* of World War II>

syn conqueror, defeater, master, subduer, subjugator, vanquisher

rel winner

con conquered, defeated, subjugated; loser

ant vanquished

2 a successful contender <emerged as *victor* in the swimming meet>

syn winner

rel champ, champion; first, top

idiom conquering hero

ant loser

Victorian *adj* ***syn*** PRIM 1, genteel, prig, priggish, prissy, prudish, puritanical, straitlaced, stuffy, tight-laced

rel old-fashioned, old-maidish; hidebound; starchy

con easy going; trendy, with-it

victory *n* **1** the overcoming of an opponent <won a knockout *victory* in the first round>

syn conquest, triumph, win

rel command, control, dominion, mastery, subjugation; superiority, supremacy; walkaway, walkover

idiom a feather in one's cap

con loss; bust, failure, fizzle, flop, ‖floperoo, washout; comedown, cropper

ant defeat

2 ***syn*** BETTER 2, advantage, superiority, upper hand, whip hand

victuals *n pl* ***syn*** FOOD 1, ‖chow, comestibles, ‖eats, edibles, feed, grub, provender, provisions, viands

videlicet *adv* ***syn*** NAMELY, scilicet, to wit

vie *vb* **1** ***syn*** COMPETE 1, contend, contest, rival

rel challenge; match; outvie

2 ***syn*** OPPOSE 1, counter, match, pit, play (off)

---

syn synonym(s) ***rel*** related word(s)

idiom idiomatic equivalent(s) ***con*** contrasted word(s)

ant antonym(s) * vulgar

‖ use limited; if in doubt, see a dictionary

The first word in a synonym list when printed in SMALL CAPITALS shows where there is more information about the group. For a more efficient use of this book see Explanatory Notes.

view *n* **1** ***syn*** LOOK 1, sight
rel examination, inspection, scan, scrutiny
2 ***syn*** EXAMINATION, analysis, audit, check-over, inspection, perlustration, review, scan, scrutiny, survey
3 ***syn*** EYE 4, viewpoint
4 what is revealed to the vision or can be seen <the *view* from the window>
syn outlook, scene, sight
rel panorama, picture, prospect, vista
5 extent or range of vision <there were still no ships in *view*>
syn sight
rel look; apprehension, scan
6 something (as an aim, end, or motive) to or by which the mind is directed <kept this *view* in mind while negotiating>
syn object
rel intent, intention, purpose; aim, ambition, goal, objective; design, plan, project; consideration, notion; expectation
7 ***syn*** OPINION, belief, conviction, eye, feeling, mind, persuasion, sentiment
rel concept, conception; deduction, inference

view *vb* **1** ***syn*** SCRUTINIZE 1, canvass, check over, check up, con, examine, inspect, study, survey, vet
2 ***syn*** EYE 1, consider, contemplate, gaze (upon), look (at *or* upon)
rel observe
3 ***syn*** SEE 1, behold, descry, discern, distinguish, espy, mark, notice, observe, perceive
4 ***syn*** CONSIDER 3, account, deem, reckon, regard

viewable *adj* ***syn*** VISUAL 2, ocular, seeable, visible

viewer *n* ***syn*** SPECTATOR, beholder, by-sitter, bystander, eyewitness, looker-on, observer, onlooker, watcher, witness

viewpoint *n* **1** ***syn*** EYE 4, view
2 the position or attitude that determines how something is seen, presented, or evaluated <from this *viewpoint* the picture looks askew> <consider totalitarianism from the German *viewpoint*>
syn angle, direction, outlook, side, slant, standpoint; *compare* EYE 4
rel estimation; attitude, position, posture, stand; long view, perspective
idiom frame of reference, point of view, vantage point

viewy *adj* ***syn*** IMPRACTICAL 1, ivory-tower, ivory-towered, ivory-towerish, nonrealistic, unpractical, unrealistic

vigil *n* ***syn*** LOOKOUT 3, surveillance, tout, vigilance, watch, watch and ward

vigilance *n* ***syn*** LOOKOUT 3, surveillance, tout, vigil, watch, watch and ward

vigilant *adj* ***syn*** WATCHFUL, alert, open-eyed, unsleeping, wakeful, wide-awake
rel agog, anxious, avid, eager, keen; acute, sharp, sharp-eyed; attentive
idiom on one's guard, with a weather eye open
con lax, neglectful, negligent, remiss, slack; forgetful, oblivious, unmindful

vigor *n* **1** ***syn*** POWER 4, beef, energy, force, might, muscle, potency, puissance, steam, strength
2 a quality of physical or mental force or forcefulness <the *vigor* of youth>
syn bang, drive, getup, get-up-and-go, go, pep, punch, push, snap, starch, vitality; *compare* ENERGY 2, ENTERPRISE 4, SPIRIT 5
rel bounce, energy, force, might, muscularity, power, strength; healthiness, soundness; lustiness, manliness, virility
con slowness, sluggishness
ant weakness
3 ***syn*** ENERGY 2, birr, go, hardihood, ‖moxie, pep, potency, tuck
rel dash, drive, dynamism, fire, punch, starch, steam, vim, zing, zip; ability, capability, capacity
con ineffectiveness; impotence; incompetence, uselessness, worthlessness

vigorous *adj* having or manifesting great vitality and force <seemed as *vigorous* as a youth half his age>
syn dynamic, energetic, lusty, red-blooded, strenuous, ‖survigrous, vital
rel brisk, dashing, lively, slashing; exuberant, mettlesome, proud, spirited; driving, hard-driving, hard-hitting, robust, rough-and-ready, zealous; bouncing, hardy, healthy, hearty, masterful, potent, powerful, strong, tough; rude, stout, sturdy; athletic, husky, muscular, sinewy
con languorous, unenergetic; decrepit, feeble, infirm, weak; impotent
ant lethargic

vigorously *adv* ***syn*** HARD 1, energetically, forcefully, forcibly, hardly, might and main, mightily, powerfully, strongly
rel alertly, eagerly; boldly, firmly, purposefully, resolutely, unfalteringly, zealously; lustily, robustly
con aimlessly, languorously; falteringly, indecisively; impotently

vile *adj* **1** ***syn*** BASE 3, despicable, ignoble, low, low-down, servile, sordid, squalid, ugly, wretched
rel corrupted, debased, debauched, depraved, perverted; coarse, gross, obscene, vulgar; disgusting, foul, nasty; abhorrent, contemptible, loathsome, offensive, repulsive, revolting
2 ***syn*** OFFENSIVE, disgusting, evil, foul, horrid, loathsome, nasty, noisome, repugnant, repulsive

vilify *vb* ***syn*** MALIGN, asperse, calumniate, defame, denigrate, libel, slander, tear down, traduce, villainize
rel abuse, mistreat, misuse, outrage; assail, attack, berate; denounce
con commend, compliment; acclaim, exalt; celebrate, glorify, honor; adore, worship
ant eulogize

vilifying *adj* ***syn*** LIBELOUS, backbiting, calumnious, defamatory, detracting, detractive, maligning, scandalous, slanderous, traducing

villa *n* ***syn*** MANSION, castle, chateau, manor

---

syn synonym(s) — *rel* related word(s)
idiom idiomatic equivalent(s) — *con* contrasted word(s)
ant antonym(s) — * vulgar
‖ use limited; if in doubt, see a dictionary
The first word in a synonym list when printed in SMALL CAPITALS shows where there is more information about the group. For a more efficient use of this book see Explanatory Notes.

villain *n* **1** a low, mean, reprehensible person utterly lacking in principle <was an insufferable bully, a tyrant, and a *villain* in general>
syn *bastard, blackguard, heel, knave, lowlife, miscreant, rascal, reprobate, rogue, roperipe, scoundrel, ‖slubberdegullion, *son of a bitch; *compare* SNOT 1, DEVIL 2
rel meanie; evildoer, offender, sinner; criminal, malefactor
2 ***syn*** SCAMP, devil, enfant terrible, limb, mischief, rapscallion, rascal, rogue, scalawag, skeezicks

villainize *vb* ***syn*** MALIGN, asperse, calumniate, defame, denigrate, libel, slander, tear down, traduce, vilify
ant eulogize

villainous *adj* ***syn*** VICIOUS 2, corrupt, degenerate, flagitious, infamous, miscreant, nefarious, perverse, putrid, rotten
rel contrary, detestable, objectionable, offensive; debased, perverted; atrocious, heinous, outrageous; abandoned, dissolute, profligate

villenage *n* ***syn*** BONDAGE, enslavement, helotry, peonage, serfdom, servitude, slavery, thrall, thralldom, yoke

vim *n* ***syn*** SPIRIT 5, animation, brio, dash, élan, esprit, life, oomph, verve, zing
rel pepper; kick, push

vinculum *n* ***syn*** BOND 3, knot, ligament, ligature, link, nexus, tie, yoke

vindicable *adj* ***syn*** JUSTIFIABLE, condonable, defensible, excusable, tenable, warrantable
rel inoffensive, unobjectionable, venial
con indefensible, unjustifiable; inexcusable, unforgivable; heinous, mortal

vindicate *vb* **1** ***syn*** AVENGE, redress, revenge, venge
2 ***syn*** MAINTAIN 2, argue, assert, claim, contend, defend, justify, warrant
rel advocate, plead (for), second, support, uphold; rationalize; bear out, prove
3 ***syn*** EXCULPATE, absolve, acquit, clear, disculpate, exonerate
rel confute, disprove, refute; defend, guard, protect, shield
con accuse, attack, calumniate
ant convict

vindictive *adj* showing or motivated by a desire for vengeance < *vindictive* hatred for his brother>
syn revengeful, vengeful, wreakful
rel grim, implacable, merciless, relentless, unrelenting; malicious, malign, malignant, spiteful
con charitable, forgiving, merciful, relenting
ant unvindictive

vinegarish *adj* ***syn*** CANTANKEROUS, bearish, cankered, cranky, cross-grained, crotchety, ornery, vinegary, waspish, waspy

vinegary *adj* ***syn*** CANTANKEROUS, bearish, cankered, cranky, cross-grained, crotchety, ornery, vinegarish, waspish, waspy

vintage *adj* **1** being of old, recognized, and enduring interest, importance, or quality <a *vintage* comedy from the silent movie era>
syn classic, classical
2 ***syn*** OLD-FASHIONED, antiquated, antique, archaic, dated, démodé, old, outdated, outmoded, passé

violate *vb* **1** to fail to keep <people who thoughtlessly *violate* the law>
syn breach, break, contravene, infract, infringe, offend, transgress
rel disregard, trample (on *or* upon); err, sin; overpass, trespass
con abide by, carry out, fulfill, submit (to); heed, keep, mind
ant observe; obey
2 ***syn*** RAPE, defile, deflorate, deflower, force, outrage, ravish, spoil

violation *n* **1** ***syn*** BREACH 1, contravention, infraction, infringement, transgression, trespass
rel break; encroachment; illegality, misdemeanor, offense, wrong
ant observance
2 ***syn*** PROFANATION, blasphemy, desecration, sacrilege
rel defacement, defacing

violence *n* ***syn*** FORCE 4, coercion, compulsion, constraint, duress
rel frenzy, fury, savagery; assault, attack, clash, foul play, onslaught, rampage, struggle, tumult, uproar
con passiveness, passivity; peace, peacefulness
ant nonviolence

violent *adj* ***syn*** INTENSE 1, concentrated, desperate, exquisite, fierce, furious, terrible, vehement, vicious
rel forceful, forcible, mighty, potent, powerful, strong; extreme, immoderate, inordinate; acute, cutting, piercing, splitting
con calm, moderate, peaceful
ant nonviolent

violently *adv* ***syn*** HARD 2, fiercely, frantically, frenziedly, furiously, madly, stormily, tumultuously, turbulently, wildly
rel combatively; destructively, ruinously
idiom like fury, with a vengeance

VIP *n* ***syn*** NOTABLE 1, ‖big cheese, ‖biggie, big shot, ‖big wheel, bigwig, ‖fat cat, leader, lion, luminary

virago *n* a woman of extremely pugnacious temperament <an overbearing *virago* who screamed at her children and squabbled with her neighbors>
syn amazon, fishwife, harpy, ogress, scold, shrew, termagant, vixen, Xanthippe
rel cat; dragon; fury

virgin *adj* **1** never having had sexual relations < *virgin* girls were sacrificed>
syn intact, maiden, undeflowered, virginal
rel innocent, untouched; single, spouseless, unmarried, unwed; abstinent, celibate
2 not marred or altered from a natural or original state <a *virgin* forest>
syn unspoiled, untapped, untouched, virginal
rel primeval, pristine; fresh, new; unmarred, unsullied

virginal *adj* **1** ***syn*** VIRGIN 1, intact, maiden, undeflowered
2 ***syn*** VIRGIN 2, unspoiled, untapped, untouched

---

syn synonym(s) | *rel* related word(s)
idiom idiomatic equivalent(s) | *con* contrasted word(s)
ant antonym(s) | * vulgar
‖ use limited; if in doubt, see a dictionary
The first word in a synonym list when printed in SMALL CAPITALS shows where there is more information about the group. For a more efficient use of this book see Explanatory Notes.

virginity *n* the quality or state of being a virgin <lost her *virginity*>
syn ||cherry, maidenhead, maidenhood
rel chasteness, chastity, purity

virile *adj* **1** ***syn*** POTENT 3
2 characterized by the energy and drive considered typical of a man or of men <developed a strong *virile* prose style>
syn male, manlike, manly, masculine
rel manful, mannish; decisive, driving, forceful; energetic, potent, robust; ultramasculine
con effeminate, womanish; emasculated, weak, weakened; impotent

virtual *adj* ***syn*** IMPLICIT 2, constructive, practical
rel basic, essential, fundamental
ant actual

virtuality *n* ***syn*** ESSENCE 2, bottom, essentiality, marrow, pith, quintessence, quintessential, soul, stuff, substance

virtually *adv* not absolutely or actually, yet so nearly so that the difference is negligible <that request is *virtually* an order>
syn in essence, morally, practically; *compare* ALMOST 2
rel basically, essentially, fundamentally; absolutely, actually
idiom for all practical purposes, in effect, in substance, to all intents and purposes

virtue *n* **1** ***syn*** GOODNESS, morality, probity, rectitude, righteousness, rightness, uprightness
rel fealty, fidelity, loyalty, piety; virtuousness
con dishonesty; disloyalty, infidelity; evil; immorality; depravity
ant vice
2 ***syn*** EXCELLENCE, arete, excellency, merit, perfection, quality
rel attribute, characteristic, feature, property; effectiveness, effectualness, efficacy; force, might, power, strength
3 ***syn*** QUALITY 1, affection, attribute, character, characteristic, feature, mark, property, savor, trait
4 ***syn*** QUALITY 2, caliber, merit, stature, value, worth
5 ***syn*** POWER 4, dint, energy, force, might, potency, puissance, sinew, strength, vigor

virtuosic *adj* ***syn*** CONSUMMATE 1, accomplished, finished, perfected, ripe

virtuoso *n* **1** ***syn*** EXPERT, artist, artiste, authority, ||dabster, master, past master, professional, whiz, wizard
2 ***syn*** MUSICIAN, musicianer, ||musicker, musico

virtuous *adj* **1** ***syn*** EFFECTIVE, effectual, efficacious, efficient
ant virtueless
2 ***syn*** MORAL 1, ethical, moralistic, noble, principled, righteous, right-minded
rel spotless, unsullied, untainted, untarnished; worthy
con dishonest; unjust; unworthy; impure, tainted; immodest, immoral, indecent; vicious, wicked
ant unvirtuous, virtueless
3 ***syn*** GOOD 11, blameless, exemplary, guiltless, inculpable, innocent, irreprehensible, pure, righteous, unblamable
rel faultless, sinless
idiom innocent as a lamb, in the clear, without reproach
con bad, impure, unrighteous
ant unvirtuous, virtueless; vicious

virulent *adj* **1** ***syn*** POISONOUS, mephitic, poison, toxic, toxicant, venomous
rel malign, malignant
2 ***syn*** BITTER 3, antagonistic, hostile, rancorous, vitriolic
rel biting, cutting, scathing, sharp, stabbing; hateful, spiteful, unfriendly

virus *n* ***syn*** POISON, bane, contagion, venom
rel corruption, taint

visage *n* **1** ***syn*** FACE 1, countenance, ||dial, features, ||kisser, ||map, mug, ||pan, phiz, ||puss
2 ***syn*** LOOK 2, cast, countenance, expression, face

vis-à-vis *n* **1** ***syn*** OPPOSITE NUMBER, coordinate, counterpart
2 ***syn*** TÊTE-À-TÊTE

vis-à-vis *prep* **1** ***syn*** AGAINST 1, contra, facing, fronting, over against, toward
rel opposite
2 ***syn*** VERSUS 2, over against

viscera *n pl* ***syn*** ENTRAILS, guts, innards, insides, internals, inwards, ||puddings, stuffing

visceral *adj* **1** ***syn*** INNER 2, gut, interior, internal, intimate, viscerous
2 ***syn*** INSTINCTIVE 1, instinctual, intuitive

viscerous *adj* ***syn*** INNER 2, gut, interior, internal, intimate, visceral

viscid *adj* ***syn*** VISCOUS, tenacious, tough, viscose
rel jellylike, slabby

viscose *adj* ***syn*** VISCOUS, tenacious, tough, viscid
rel smeary

viscous *adj* having a glutinous adhesive consistency or quality <a *viscous* scum covered the surface of the platter>
syn tenacious, tough, viscid, viscose
rel ||slab, slimy, thick; glutinous, gummy, ropy, sticky; semifluid; stiff

visibility *n* the quality or state of being visible <very poor *visibility* due to fog>
syn visuality

visible *adj* ***syn*** VISUAL 2, ocular, seeable, viewable
rel seen

vision *n* **1** ***syn*** REVELATION, apocalypse, oracle, prophecy
rel apparition, phenomenon, presence
2 ***syn*** FANCY 4, daydream, dream, fantasy (*or* phantasy), nightmare, phantasm
rel muse
idiom phantom of the mind
3 ***syn*** EYE 2, eyesight, seeing, sight

vision *vb* ***syn*** THINK 1, conceive, envisage, envision, fancy, feature, image, imagine, realize, visualize

visional *adj* ***syn*** VISUAL 1, ocular, optic, optical

---

visionary *adj* **1** ***syn*** DREAMY 1, astral, daydreaming, daydreamy, otherworldly, unworldly
rel abstracted, introspective, musing; impractical
idiom out of this world, up in the clouds
2 ***syn*** IDEALISTIC, idealist, utopian
rel exalted, grandiose, lofty, noble, pretentious
ant pragmatic, pragmatical
3 ***syn*** AMBITIOUS 2, grandiose, lofty, pretentious, utopian
rel radical

visionary *n* ***syn*** DREAMER, castle-builder, idealist, ideologue, utopian
ant pragmatist

visionless *adj* ***syn*** BLIND 1, ‖dark, eyeless, sightless, stone-blind

visit *vb* **1** ***syn*** INFLICT 2, force (on *or* upon), impose, wreak, wreck
rel afflict, bother, pain, trouble; avenge, punish
idiom bring down upon
2 to make a social call upon < *visited* friends briefly in the evening >
syn call, come by, come over, drop (in *or* by), look in, look up, pop (in), run in, see, step in, stop (in *or* by)
3 to reside with temporarily as a guest < *visited* with friends in the country for a few weeks >
syn sojourn, stay, stop (over), tarry
rel frequent; reside
4 ***syn*** CONVERSE, chat, chin, colloque, talk, yarn

visit *n* **1** a coming to stay with another temporarily and usually briefly < pay a *visit* to friends >
syn call, visitation
2 ***syn*** SOJOURN, stopover, tarriance

visitant *n* ***syn*** VISITOR 1, caller, guest

visitation *n* **1** ***syn*** VISIT 1, call
2 ***syn*** TRIAL 1, affliction, calvary, cross, crucible, ordeal, tribulation
rel mischance; calamity, catastrophe, disaster

visitor *n* **1** one who visits another < there are *visitors* in the living room >
syn caller, guest, visitant; *compare* COMPANY 2
rel invitee
2 visitors *pl* ***syn*** COMPANY 2, guests

visor *n* **1** a projecting front brim on a cap or hat for shading the eyes < the *visor* kept out the sun >
syn bill, peak
rel eyeshade
2 ***syn*** MASK 1, domino, doughface, false face, vizard

vista *n* an extensive or distant view < a long flat tree-lined *vista* >
syn lookout, outlook, perspective, prospect, scape
rel panorama, scene, sight, view; range, scope, survey
idiom long view

visual *adj* **1** of or relating to or used in vision < the *visual* sense >
syn ocular, optic, optical, visional
2 capable of being seen < *visual* objects >
syn ocular, seeable, viewable, visible
rel discernible, perceivable, perceptible

visuality *n* ***syn*** VISIBILITY

visualize *vb* **1** ***syn*** THINK 1, conceive, envisage, envision, fancy, feature, image, imagine, realize, vision
rel picture, view; objectify; call up, conjure (up)
idiom bring (*or* call) to mind, conjure up a mental image (*or* picture) of, see in the mind's eye
2 ***syn*** FORESEE, anticipate, apprehend, divine, forefeel, foreknow, preknow, previse, prevision, see

vital *adj* **1** ***syn*** LIVING 1, alive, animate, animated, zoetic
rel breathing
2 ***syn*** VIGOROUS, dynamic, energetic, lusty, red-blooded, strenuous, ‖survigrous
3 ***syn*** ESSENTIAL 2, cardinal, constitutive, fundamental
rel indispensable, needed, needful, required, requisite; integral, prerequisite

vital force *n* ***syn*** SOUL 1, anima, animus, élan vital, pneuma, psyche, spirit

vitality *n* ***syn*** VIGOR 2, bang, drive, getup, get-up-and-go, go, pep, punch, snap, starch
rel animation, life, liveliness, pulse; endurance, energy, spirit, vim

vitalize *vb* to arouse to activity, animation, or life < atomic energy is a force that can *vitalize* or destroy human civilization >
syn actify, activate, activize, energize
rel animate, enliven, invigorate, quicken, vivify; dynamize, excite, galvanize, provoke, stimulate; pep up, strengthen
idiom put life into
con eviscerate, weaken
ant atrophy; devitalize

vitalizing *adj* ***syn*** INVIGORATING, animating, bracing, exhilarating, exhilarative, quickening, stimulating, stimulative, tonic
ant devitalizing

vitally *adv* ***syn*** VERY 1, exceedingly, exceptionally, extremely, hugely, notably, parlous, remarkably, strikingly, surpassingly

vitiate *adj* ***syn*** DEBASED, corrupted, debauched, depraved, perverted, vitiated
ant purified

vitiate *vb* **1** ***syn*** INJURE 1, blemish, damage, harm, hurt, impair, mar, prejudice, spoil, tarnish
rel twist, warp
2 ***syn*** DEBASE 1, bastardize, bestialize, brutalize, corrupt, debauch, demoralize, deprave, pervert, warp
rel defile, soil, sully, taint; prostitute; contaminate
idiom drive to the dogs
ant purify
3 ***syn*** ABOLISH 1, abate, abrogate, annihilate, annul, invalidate, negate, nullify, quash, undo

vitiated *adj* ***syn*** DEBASED, corrupted, debauched, depraved, perverted, vitiate
rel contaminated, defiled, polluted, tainted; impaired, injured, spoiled
ant purified

vitriolic *adj* ***syn*** BITTER 3, antagonistic, hostile, rancorous, virulent

---

syn synonym(s) ***rel*** related word(s)
idiom idiomatic equivalent(s) ***con*** contrasted word(s)
ant antonym(s) * vulgar
‖ use limited; if in doubt, see a dictionary
The first word in a synonym list when printed in SMALL CAPITALS shows where there is more information about the group. For a more efficient use of this book see Explanatory Notes.

vituperate *vb* ***syn*** SCOLD 1, bawl out, berate, ‖chew out, lash, rail, rate, revile, tongue-lash, upbraid
rel condemn, lambaste; asperse, calumniate, malign, traduce; bark (at), growl (at), yell (at); abuse, curse
idiom rip into
con applaud, commend, compliment; eulogize, extol, praise
ant acclaim

vituperation *n* ***syn*** ABUSE, billingsgate, contumely, invective, obloquy, scurrility
rel blame, censure, revilement, scolding, tongue-lashing
con eulogy, extolment
ant acclaim, praise

vituperative *adj* ***syn*** ABUSIVE, contumelious, invective, opprobrious, scurrile, scurrilous, truculent, vituperatory, vituperous
rel censorious, critical; severe; railing, scolding

vituperatory *adj* ***syn*** ABUSIVE, contumelious, invective, opprobrious, scurrile, scurrilous, truculent, vituperative, vituperous
rel censorious, critical; severe; railing, scolding

vituperous *adj* ***syn*** ABUSIVE, contumelious, invective, opprobrious, scurrile, scurrilous, truculent, vituperative, vituperatory
rel censorious, critical; severe; railing, scolding

vivacious *adj* **1** ***syn*** LIVELY 1, alert, animate, animated, ‖cant, ‖canty, gay, keen, spirited, sprightly
rel breezy, vibrant, zesty; frolicsome, playful, sportive
idiom gay as a lark
ant languid
2 ***syn*** EXUBERANT 1, brash, ebullient, effervescent, high-spirited

viva voce *adj* ***syn*** VOCAL 1, articulate, oral, sonant, spoken, voiced

vivid *adj* **1** ***syn*** COLORFUL, brave, bright, colory, gay
2 ***syn*** GRAPHIC 1, photographic, pictorial, picturesque
rel acute, intense, keen, sharp; dramatic, dramaturgic, theatrical; eloquent, expressive, meaningful, rich; animated, lively, spirited, vigorous

vivificate *vb* ***syn*** QUICKEN 1, animate, enliven, liven, vivify
rel revive

vivify *vb* ***syn*** QUICKEN 1, animate, enliven, liven, vivificate
rel refresh, renew, restore; excite, galvanize
idiom give life to, imbue with life, put new life into

vivres *n pl* ***syn*** FOOD 1, bread, ‖chow, comestibles, ‖eats, edibles, feed, grub, provisions, victuals

vixen *n* ***syn*** VIRAGO, amazon, fishwife, harpy, ogress, scold, shrew, termagant, Xanthippe

vizard *n* ***syn*** MASK 1, domino, doughface, false face, visor

‖**vlei** *n* ***syn*** SWAMP, baygall, bog, fen, marsh, mire, ‖moss, quag, slough, ‖sump

---

syn synonym(s) ***rel*** related word(s)
idiom idiomatic equivalent(s) ***con*** contrasted word(s)
ant antonym(s) * vulgar
‖ use limited; if in doubt, see a dictionary
The first word in a synonym list when printed in SMALL CAPITALS shows where there is more information about the group. For a more efficient use of this book see Explanatory Notes.

vocable *n* ***syn*** WORD 2, term
rel verbalism

vocabulary *n* **1** the sum or set of words employed by a language, group, individual, or work or in relation to a subject <Latin contributes heavily to the *vocabulary* of English>
syn lexicon, word-hoard, word-stock
idiom stock of words
2 ***syn*** TERMINOLOGY, cant, dictionary, jargon, language, lexicon, palaver
rel phraseology

vocal *adj* **1** uttered by the voice or having to do with such utterance <the infant's primitive *vocal* sounds from which language develops>
syn articulate, oral, sonant, spoken, viva voce, voiced
rel intonated; expressed, uttered
con unexpressed, unuttered, unvoiced
ant nonvocal
2 ***syn*** VOCALIC, vowel, vowely
ant consonantal
3 being able to express oneself clearly or easily <he was hardly *vocal:* he could scarcely express the simplest concepts>
syn articulate, eloquent, fluent, smooth-spoken
rel expressing, voicing; expressive; outspoken, stentorian, venting
con faltering, halting, hesitant, stumbling
4 ***syn*** OUTSPOKEN, free, free-spoken, round

vocalic *adj* marked by, consisting of, or functioning as a vowel or vowels < *vocalic* and consonantal sounds>
syn vocal, vowel, vowely
rel vowellike

vocalism *n* ***syn*** VOCALIZATION, articulation, utterance, uttering

vocalization *n* the exercise of the vocal organs in song or speech <his *vocalization* of a previously unstated thought>
syn articulation, utterance, uttering, vocalism; *compare* SPEECH 1
rel mouth, mouthing; sounding, voice, voicing; diction, enunciation, verbalization; speaking, speech

vocalize *vb* **1** ***syn*** SPEAK 1, talk, utter, verbalize, voice
rel emit, let out; express; enunciate, pronounce; communicate, convey, impart
idiom execute vocally
2 ***syn*** SING 1, chant, tune

vocation *n* **1** ***syn*** TRADE 1, art, calling, craft, handicraft, métier, profession
2 ***syn*** MISSION, calling, lifework

vocative *adj* ***syn*** GLIB, silver-tongued, voluble, well-hung
rel chatty, garrulous, loquacious, talkative, windy; slick, smooth

vociferant *adj* ***syn*** VOCIFEROUS, blatant, boisterous, clamorous, ‖dinsome, loudmouthed, multivocal, obstreperous, openmouthed, strident

vociferate *vb* ***syn*** CALL 1, cry, hallo, holler, hollo, shout, yell

vociferous *adj* so loud, noisy, and insistent as to compel attention <the crowd made *vociferous* protests against the speaker's statement>
syn blatant, boisterous, clamorous, ‖dinsome, loudmouthed, multivocal, obstreperous, openmouthed, strident, vociferant

rel distracting; loud, noisy, shrill
con close-lipped, reserved, silent, uncommunicative; noiseless, quiet, still

vogue *n syn* FASHION 2, chic, craze, cry, dernier cri, fad, furore, mode, rage, style, trend
rel bon ton, fashionableness, stylishness

voice *n* **1** *syn* EXPRESSION 1, statement, utterance, vent
rel speech
2 the right to express a wish, choice, or opinion or to influence a situation <even the youngest had a *voice* in planning the party>
syn say, say-so

voice *vb syn* SPEAK 1, talk, utter, verbalize, vocalize
rel sound; articulate, enunciate, pronounce; formulate, phrase, present, put; recount, tell

voiced *adj syn* VOCAL 1, articulate, oral, sonant, spoken, viva voce

voiceless *adj syn* DUMB 1, inarticulate, mute, silent, speechless, unarticulate

void *adj* **1** *syn* EMPTY 1, bare, clear, vacant, vacuous
ant full
2 *syn* DEVOID, destitute, empty, innocent
rel scant, short, shy; bare, bereft, denuded, deprived
3 *syn* NULL, bad, invalid, null and void
rel negated

void *n syn* HOLE 3, cavity, hollow, vacuity

void *vb* **1** *syn* VACATE 2, clear, empty
rel evacuate; deplete, drain, eliminate; eject, remove, throw out
2 *syn* DISCHARGE 5, disembogue, emit, flow, give off, pour

void *vb syn* ANNUL 4, abrogate, discharge, dissolve, quash, vacate
idiom declare (*or* make) null and void

voidness *n syn* VACUITY 2, blankness, emptiness, vacancy, vacuousness
ant fullness

volage *adj syn* GIDDY 1, bird-witted, dizzy, empty-headed, featherbrained, flighty, frivolous, harebrained, rattlebrained, scatterbrained

volant *adj syn* AGILE, active, brisk, catty, lively, nimble, sprightly, spry, yare, zippy

volatile *adj* **1** *syn* ELASTIC 2, airy, bouncy, buoyant, effervescent, expansive, resilient
rel capricious, fickle, inconstant, mercurial, unstable; flighty, flippant, frivolous, light-minded; changeable, protean, variable
2 *syn* EXCITABLE, agitable, alarmable, edgy, skittery, skittish, startlish
rel explosive
3 *syn* INCONSTANT 1, capricious, changeable, fickle, lubricious, mercurial, temperamental, ticklish, unstable, variable
4 *syn* TRANSIENT, ephemeral, evanescent, fleeting, fugacious, fugitive, impermanent, momentary, short-lived, transitory

volatility *n syn* LIGHTNESS, flightiness, flippancy, frivolity, levity, light-mindedness
rel animation, sprightliness; inconstancy, instability, mercurialness; changeability, variability

volition *n syn* WILL 2
rel choice, election, option, selection; desire, preference
con coercion, compulsion, duress, force

volley *n syn* BARRAGE, bombardment, broadside, burst, cannonade, drumfire, fusillade, hail, shower, storm

volte–face *n syn* REVERSAL 1, about-face, changeabout, reverse, reversement, reversion, right-about, right-about-face, turn, turnabout

volte–face *vb syn* TURN 6, avert, deflect, divert, pivot, sheer, veer, wheel, whip, whirl
rel about-face, face (about), right-about-face

voluble *adj syn* GLIB, silver-tongued, vocative, well-hung

volume *n* **1** *syn* BOOK 1, tome
2 *syn* BULK 1, mass
rel amount, content, quantity
3 *syn* BODY 4, bulk, mass, object

voluminous *adj syn* MANY, legion, multifarious, multitudinal, multitudinous, numerous, populous, ‖several, sundry, various

voluntary *adj* consisting of or proceeding from an exercise of free will <the law requires that a confession be *voluntary*>
syn deliberate, intentional, unforced, unprescribed, willful, willing, witting
rel chosen, elected, opted, volitional; autonomous, free, independent
con coerced, compelled, forced; unintentional, unplanned, unwilling, unwitting
ant involuntary

voluptuous *adj syn* SENSUOUS, epicurean, luscious, lush, luxurious, sensual, sensualistic
rel indulgent, self-gratifying; abandoned, dissipated, dissolute, excessive, wanton
con self-contained, self-denying
ant ascetic

vomit *vb* to discharge the contents of the stomach through the mouth <the churning seas made several passengers *vomit*>
syn barf, bring up, ‖cack, ‖cascade, ‖cast, ‖cat, disgorge, ‖heave, *puke, shoot, sick (up), spew, spit up, throw up, upchuck
rel gag, regurgitate, retch; keck; eject, expel
idiom ‖blow one's lunch, holler New York, lose one's cookies

voodoo *n* **1** *syn* MAGICIAN 1, conjurer, enchanter, mage, magus, necromancer, sorcerer, voodooist, warlock, wizard
2 *syn* JINX, hex, hoodoo, Indian sign, whammy

voodoo *vb syn* BEWITCH 1, charm, enchant, ensorcell, hex, spell, witch

voodooist *n syn* MAGICIAN 1, charmer, conjurer, enchanter, mage, magus, necromancer, sorcerer, warlock, wizard

voracious *adj* excessively greedy (as in appetite, reactions, or behavior) <the wolverine is an extremely *voracious* eater>

---

syn synonym(s) — *rel* related word(s)
idiom idiomatic equivalent(s) — *con* contrasted word(s)
ant antonym(s) — * vulgar
‖ use limited; if in doubt, see a dictionary
The first word in a synonym list when printed in SMALL CAPITALS shows where there is more information about the group. For a more efficient use of this book see Explanatory Notes.

syn edacious, gluttonous, rapacious, ravening, ravenous
rel acquisitive, covetous, grasping, greedy; devouring, gorging, satiating, sating, surfeiting; avid, insatiable

vortex *n* *syn* EDDY, maelstrom, whirl, whirlpool
rel spiral, spout

votary *n* **1** *syn* ADDICT, aficionado, buff, devotee, fan, habitué, hound, lover
rel disciple; freak
2 *syn* AMATEUR 1, admirer, devotee, fan, fancier
rel hound

vote *n* **1** *syn* BALLOT 1, ticket
2 *syn* SUFFRAGE, ballot, franchise

vote (in) *vb* *syn* ELECT 2, ballot
rel choose, decide
idiom cast one's vote for

vouch *vb* *syn* CERTIFY 1, attest, witness
rel support, uphold; confirm, corroborate, prove, substantiate, verify; assure, guarantee

vouchsafe *vb* *syn* GRANT 1, accord, award, concede
rel condescend, deign, stoop; accommodate, favor, oblige

vow *vb* to promise solemnly < *vowed* never to leave each other >
syn covenant, pledge, plight, swear; *compare* PROMISE 1
rel assert, declare, ‖swan; promise
idiom give (*or* make) a solemn promise, give one's word of honor

vowel *adj* *syn* VOCALIC, vocal, vowely

vowely *adj* *syn* VOCALIC, vocal, vowel

voyage *n* a journey by water <took the new ship on a long *voyage*>
syn cruise
rel journey, tour, trip

voyeur *n* *syn* PEEPING TOM, peeper

vulgar *adj* **1** *syn* VERNACULAR, colloquial, vulgate
rel conversational, spoken; idiomatic
2 *syn* PUBLIC 4, general, popular
3 *syn* COARSE 3, crass, crude, gross, inelegant, raw, rough, rude, uncouth, unrefined
4 *syn* OBSCENE 2, barnyard, dirty, gross, indecent, nasty, profane, ribald, scatological, smutty
rel base, low, vile; loathsome, offensive, repulsive, revolting; indecorous, indelicate, uncouth
con decent, delicate, refined; high-minded, lofty, noble
5 *syn* BARBARIC 1, barbarian, barbarous, graceless, outlandish, tasteless, wild
rel inelegant, ungraceful; improper, incorrect, unseemly; uncouth, unpolished, unrefined
idiom in very poor taste
con elegant, graceful; correct, proper, seemly

vulgarism *n* *syn* BARBARISM, corruption, impropriety, slangism, solecism, vernacularism, vernacularity

vulgate *adj* *syn* VERNACULAR, colloquial, vulgar

vulgate *n* *syn* VERNACULAR 3, colloquial, patois

vulnerability *n* *syn* EXPOSURE, liability, openness, vulnerableness
rel vincibility

vulnerableness *n* *syn* EXPOSURE, liability, openness, vulnerability
rel weakness

vulnerary *adj* *syn* CURATIVE, curing, healing, remedial, remedying, restorative, sanative, sanatory, wholesome

vulpine *adj* *syn* SLY 2, artful, astute, crafty, cunning, foxy, guileful, insidious, tricky, wily

vulture *vb* *syn* STEAL 1, ‖cly, ‖cop, filch, ‖heist, hook, lift, pinch, snitch, swipe

vulturine *adj* *syn* RAPACIOUS 1, predacious, predative, predatorial, predatory, raptorial, vulturish, vulturous

vulturish *adj* *syn* RAPACIOUS 1, predacious, predative, predatorial, predatory, raptorial, vulturine, vulturous

vulturous *adj* *syn* RAPACIOUS 1, predacious, predative, predatorial, predatory, raptorial, vulturine, vulturish

---

syn synonym(s) *rel* related word(s)
idiom idiomatic equivalent(s) *con* contrasted word(s)
ant antonym(s) * vulgar
‖ use limited; if in doubt, see a dictionary
The first word in a synonym list when printed in SMALL CAPITALS shows where there is more information about the group. For a more efficient use of this book see Explanatory Notes.

W

‖**wack** *n* ***syn*** ECCENTRIC, case, character, ‖duck, oddball, oddity, original, quiz, ‖spook, zombie

wacky *adj* **1** ***syn*** FOOLISH 2, absurd, ‖balmy, crazy, harebrained, insane, loony, ‖potty, preposterous, silly
2 ***syn*** INSANE 1, ‖batty, cracked, crazed, crazy, demented, deranged, lunatic, mad, nuts

wad *n* **1** ***syn*** LUMP 1, chunk, clod, clump, gob, hunch, hunk, nugget
2 *often* **wads** *pl* ***syn*** SCAD, gob(s), heap, jillion, load(s), oodles, ream(s), ‖rimption(s), slather(s), slew
3 ***syn*** FORTUNE 4, ‖bomb, boodle, bundle, mint, packet, pile, pot, ‖roll

wade (in *or* into) *vb* ***syn*** PITCH IN 1, buckle (down), fall to, jump (in *or* into), set to

‖**waffle** *vb* ***syn*** BABBLE 2, blabber, blather, drivel, drool, gabble, prate, prattle, twaddle

wag *vb* to move to and fro <the dog *wagged* his tail briskly>
syn beat, lash, switch, waggle, wave, woggle
rel shake, twitch, wiggle; oscillate; wigwag

wag *n* **1** a person full of sportive humor <a gay young *wag,* always full of fun>
syn card, comedian, humorist, joker, zany
rel clown, cutup, madcap, prankster, show-off; jester, kidder, quipster, wisecracker, wit
idiom life of the party
2 ***syn*** ZANY 2, clown, cutup, farceur, joker, jokester
3 ***syn*** HUMORIST 2, comedian, comic, droll, funnyman, jester, joker, jokester, quipster, wit

wage *n, often* **wages** *pl* the price paid a person for his labor or services <high *wages* are often seen as a factor in inflation>
syn emolument, fee, hire, pay, pay envelope, salary, stipend
rel compensation, recompense, remuneration, reward; earnings, income, receipts, return(s), take

wager *n* ***syn*** BET, ante, pot, stake

wager *vb* **1** ***syn*** VENTURE 1, adventure, chance, hazard, risk
2 ***syn*** GAMBLE 1, bet, game, lay, play, put (on), set, stake
idiom lay a wager

waggery *n* **1** ***syn*** MISCHIEVOUSNESS, devilment, devilry, deviltry, impishness, mischief, roguery, roguishness, sportiveness, waggishness
2 ***syn*** JOKE 1, crack, drollery, gag, jape, jest, quip, wisecrack, witticism, ‖yak

waggish *adj* ***syn*** PLAYFUL 1, antic, frolicsome, impish, ‖mischiefful, mischievous, prankish, puckish, roguish, sportive
rel facetious, humorous, jocose, jocular, witty; comic, comical, droll, funny, laughable, ludicrous; arch, pert, saucy
con earnest, grave, sedate, serious, sober, staid

waggishness *n* ***syn*** MISCHIEVOUSNESS, devilment, devilry, deviltry, impishness, mischief, roguery, roguishness, sportiveness, waggery

waggle *vb* ***syn*** WAG, beat, lash, switch, wave, woggle
rel sway, waddle, wobble

wail *vb* **1** ***syn*** CRY 2, blub, blubber, boohoo, ‖pipe, sob, weep
idiom make an outcry
2 ***syn*** HOWL 1, bay, quest, ululate
3 ***syn*** BAWL 2, howl, squall, yowl
4 ***syn*** COMPLAIN, fuss, kick, murmur, repine, whine

wailful *adj* ***syn*** MELANCHOLY 2, doleful, dolesome, lamentable, lugubrious, mournful, plaintive, rueful, sorrowful, woeful

waistband *n* ***syn*** BELT 1, ceinture, cincture, girdle, sash

wait *vb* ***syn*** STAY 2, abide, bide, linger, remain, stick around, tarry
rel anticipate, foresee; await, expect
idiom bide one's time, cool one's heels, look forward to, mark time
con depart, go, leave

wait (on) *vb* ***syn*** MINISTER (to), care (for), mother, nurse, serve

waive *vb* **1** ***syn*** RELINQUISH, abandon, cede, give up, hand over, leave, resign, surrender, ‖turn up, yield
rel allow, concede, grant
con claim, demand, exact, require; assert, defend, maintain
2 ***syn*** DEFER, delay, hold off, hold over, hold up, postpone, put off, shelve, stay, suspend

wake *vb* **1** to stop sleeping <she usually *woke* before dawn>
syn awake, awaken, rouse, stir, waken
rel arise, get up, roll out
con catnap, doze, drowse, nap, nod, snooze; sleep, slumber
2 ***syn*** STIR 1, arouse, awaken, bestir, challenge, kindle, rally, rouse, waken, whet
rel freshen, renew
con calm, ease, mollify, relax

waken *vb* **1** ***syn*** STIR 1, arouse, awaken, bestir, challenge, kindle, rally, rouse, wake, whet
rel freshen, renew
con calm, ease, mollify, relax
2 ***syn*** WAKE 1, awake, awaken, rouse, stir

wale *n* ***syn*** WHEAL, weal, welt, whelk, ‖whelp

walk *vb* **1** to advance on foot step by step <often *walked* to work on pleasant mornings>
syn ambulate, foot (it), hoof, pace, step, traipse, tread, troop
rel circumambulate, perambulate, promenade, ramble, stroll; hike, tramp; lumber, plod, slog, stride, stump, trudge; leg, race, run

---

syn synonym(s) ***rel*** related word(s)
idiom idiomatic equivalent(s) ***con*** contrasted word(s)
ant antonym(s) * vulgar
‖ use limited; if in doubt, see a dictionary
The first word in a synonym list when printed in SMALL CAPITALS shows where there is more information about the group. For a more efficient use of this book see Explanatory Notes.

idiom beat one's feet, heel and toe it, ride shanks' mare
con drive, ride
2 *syn* TRAVERSE 5, perambulate

walk *n* **1** a usually brief journey on foot for pleasure or exercise <always took a *walk* before breakfast>
syn constitutional, ramble, saunter, stroll, turn
rel hike, march, tramp; deambulation, parade, promenade; airing, stretch
2 *syn* FIELD, bailiwick, champaign, demesne, domain, dominion, province, sphere, terrain, territory

walkabout *n syn* TRAMP 3, hike

walkaway *n syn* RUNAWAY, cakewalk, romp, rout, walkover

walk out *vb syn* STRIKE 1, stick out

walkover *n syn* RUNAWAY, cakewalk, romp, rout, walkaway

wall *n syn* BAR 2, barricade, barrier, block, blockade, fence, roadblock, stop

wall *vb syn* ENCLOSE 1, cage, close in, coop, corral, envelop, fence, hedge, hem, immure

wallop *n* **1** *syn* BLOW 1, bash, bat, belt, bop, slam, smack, smash, thwack, whop
2 *syn* IMPACT, bump, clash, collision, crash, jar, jolt, percussion, shock, smash
3 *syn* THRILL, bang, boot, kick

wallop *vb* **1** *syn* BEAT 1, baste, belabor, buffet, drub, paste, pelt, pound, pummel, thrash
2 *syn* WHIP 2, beat, ‖clobber, drub, lambaste, lick, shellac, thrash, trim, trounce
3 *syn* SLAM 1, belt, blast, clobber, slug, smash

walloping *adj syn* HUGE, colossal, enormous, gargantuan, giant, gigantic, immense, mammoth, monster, prodigious

wallow *vb* **1** to roll or move in an indolent and ungainly yet comfortable fashion <hogs *wallowing* in a cool mudhole>
syn welter
rel flounder, roll, tumble; cuddle, nestle, snuggle
2 to move or progress unsteadily and clumsily as if beset by obstacles <*wallowed* through the mire for miles trying to get help>
syn blunder, flounder, lurch, stumble; *compare* STUMBLE 3
rel reel, stagger, sway, totter, wamble, welter
idiom make heavy weather (of)
3 to become deeply or excessively involved in or with something subjectively felt as pleasant <*wallowing* in luxury>
syn bask, indulge, luxuriate, revel, roll, rollick, welter
rel baby, humor, pamper, spoil; appreciate, delight (in), enjoy, relish
con abstain, refrain; avoid, eschew, shun

waltz *vb syn* BREEZE, zip

---

syn synonym(s) *rel* related word(s)
idiom idiomatic equivalent(s) *con* contrasted word(s)
ant antonym(s) * vulgar
‖ use limited; if in doubt, see a dictionary
The first word in a synonym list when printed in SMALL CAPITALS shows where there is more information about the group. For a more efficient use of this book see Explanatory Notes.

‖**wambly** *adj syn* SQUEAMISH 1, ‖pensy, qualmish, qualmy, queasy, queer

‖**wampum** *n syn* MONEY, cash, ‖coin, currency, dough, ‖greenbacks, ‖jack, legal tender, lucre, ‖mazuma

wan *adj* **1** *syn* PALE 1, ashen, ashy, blanched, colorless, complexionless, doughy, livid, pallid, waxen
rel cadaverous, haggard, worn; blanched, bleached, washed-out; anemic, bloodless
2 *syn* WEAK 4, boneless, emasculate, forceless, impotent, ineffective, ineffectual, invertebrate, slack-spined, spineless

wander *vb* **1** to move about from place to place more or less aimlessly and without obvious plan <*wandering* through the forest>
syn bat, circumambulate, drift, gad, gallivant, maunder, meander, mooch, ‖project, ramble, range, roam, roll, rove, straggle, stray, traipse, vagabond, vagabondize; *compare* SAUNTER
rel amble, saunter, stroll; divagate, diverge; trail; boom, bum, tramp
2 *syn* DIGRESS 2, depart, divagate, diverge, excurse, ramble, stray
3 *syn* ERR, deviate, stray

wanderer *n syn* ROVER, drifter, meanderer, rambler, roamer, rolling stone

wandering *adj* **1** *syn* ITINERANT, ambulant, itinerate, nomadic, perambulant, perambulatory, roving, vagabond, vagrant, wayfaring
2 *syn* ERRATIC 1, devious, errant, stray
3 *syn* DELIRIOUS 1, raving

wane *vb* **1** *syn* ABATE 4, die (down *or* away), ease off, ebb, fall, let up, moderate, relent, slacken, subside
ant wax
2 *syn* FAIL 3, dwindle, fall short, shrink, waste (away), weaken
ant wax

wangle *vb syn* ENGINEER, finagle, machinate, maneuver
rel outflank, outgeneral, outmaneuver, overreach

waning *n syn* FAILURE 4, declination, decline, deterioration, ebbing
ant waxing

‖**wanky** *adj syn* WEAK 1, decrepit, feeble, flimsy, fragile, frail, infirm, unsound, unsubstantial, weakly

want *vb* **1** *syn* LACK, need, require
idiom be found wanting, fall short, feel the want of
2 *syn* DESIRE 1, ‖choose, covet, crave, desiderate, wish
rel choose, prefer
idiom could do with, have a mind (*or* an eye) to
3 to have as a duty or responsibility <you *want* to behave yourself>
syn must, ought, should
rel become, befit, behoove; need (to)
idiom be wise to, had better (*or* best)

want *n* **1** *syn* ABSENCE, dearth, default, defect, lack, ‖miss, privation
rel exigency, necessity, need
con sufficiency
2 *syn* POVERTY 1, destitution, impecuniousness, impoverishment, indigence, need, neediness, penury, poorness, privation
rel exiguousness, meagerness, scantiness, skimpiness; inadequacy, insufficiency
con riches

3 ***syn*** REQUIREMENT 1, demand, need

wanting *adj* ***syn*** ABSENT 1, away, gone, lacking, missing, omitted
2 ***syn*** SHORT 3, deficient, failing, inadequate, insufficient, scant, scanty, scarce, shy, unsufficient
3 ***syn*** DEFICIENT 1, defective, ‖half-assed, inadequate, incomplete, insufficient, lacking, uncomplete

wanting *prep* ***syn*** WITHOUT 2, awanting, lacking, minus, sans

wanton *adj* **1** ***syn*** FAST 7, easy, light, loose, ‖riggish, unchaste, whorish
rel lax, slack, wayward
idiom of easy virtue, of loose morals
con austere, puritanical, restrained, self-restrained
ant chaste
2 ***syn*** SUPEREROGATORY, gratuitous, supererogant, supererogative, unasked, uncalled-for
rel malevolent, malicious, spiteful; contrary, perverse, wayward

wanton *n* a woman who engages in lewd unseemly conduct <giddy *wantons* flaunting themselves in bars>
syn baggage, ‖bim, ‖bimbo, cyprian, hussy, jade, jezebel, ‖pig, slattern, slut, strumpet, tramp, trollop, trull, wench; *compare* DOXY, HARLOT 1, PROSTITUTE
idiom loose woman

wanton *vb* ***syn*** TRIFLE 1, coquet, dally, flirt, fool, lead on, string along, toy

wantwit *n* ***syn*** DUNCE, ‖cluck, dimwit, ‖dumb bunny, ‖dumb cluck, featherweight, lackwit, nitwit, pinhead, simp

war *vb* ***syn*** CONTEND 1, battle, fight, oppugn, tug
rel attempt, endeavor, essay, strive, struggle; challenge, engage, take on
idiom draw the sword against, lift one's hand against, take up the cudgels

warble *n* ***syn*** MELODY, air, descant, diapason, lay, measure, melisma, melodia, strain, tune

war chest *n* ***syn*** TREASURY 2, chest, coffer, exchequer

war club *n* ***syn*** CUDGEL, bat, baton, billy club, bludgeon, club, knobkerrie, mace, ‖shillelagh, truncheon

war cry *n* ***syn*** BATTLE CRY, cry, motto, rallying cry

ward *n* **1** ***syn*** GUARD 2, lookout, picket, sentinel, sentry, watch, watchman
2 ***syn*** DEFENSE 1, aegis, armament, armor, guard, protection, safeguard, security, shield
3 ***syn*** CUSTODY, care, guardianship, keeping, safekeeping, trust

ward *vb* **1** to cause to miss an objective by or as if by turning aside <*warded* the stroke of his enemy's sword with his shield>
syn deflect, fend, parry
rel block, check, halt, stay, stymie; avert, divert, turn
idiom keep at arm's length, turn aside
2 ***syn*** PREVENT 2, avert, deter, forestall, forfend, obviate, preclude, rule out, stave off
rel balk, foil, frustrate, thwart; check, interrupt
ant conduce (to)

ward (off) *vb* ***syn*** FEND (off), hold off, keep off, rebuff, rebut, repel, repulse, stave off
ant bring on

warden *n* ***syn*** CUSTODIAN, cerberus, claviger, ‖custodier, custos, guardian, keeper, watchdog

ware *adj* ***syn*** AWARE, alive, apprehensive, au courant, awake, cognizant, conscious, conversant, knowing, sensible

warehouse *vb* ***syn*** STOW, bestow, pack, store
rel accommodate; guard, protect, shelter

wares *n pl* ***syn*** MERCHANDISE, commodities, goods, line, vendible(s)

warfare *n* ***syn*** CONTEST 1, competition, conflict, emulation, rivalry, strife, striving, tug-of-war

warhorse *n* ***syn*** COURSER, charger

warlike *adj* **1** ***syn*** BELLIGERENT, bellicose, combative, contentious, gladiatorial, militant, pugnacious, quarrelsome, ‖ructious, truculent
ant peaceable
2 ***syn*** MARTIAL, military
rel battling, contending, fighting, warring
ant unwarlike

warlock *n* ***syn*** MAGICIAN 1, charmer, conjurer, enchanter, mage, magus, necromancer, sorcerer, voodooist, wizard

warm *adj* **1** ***syn*** ENTHUSIASTIC, ‖buggy, ‖bugs, gung ho, keen, nutty, zealous
2 ***syn*** TENDER, compassionate, kindhearted, responsive, softhearted, sympathetic, warmhearted
rel ardent, fervent, passionate; affable, cordial, gracious; heartfelt, hearty, sincere, wholehearted
ant cool; austere

warmed-over *adj* ***syn*** TRITE, clichéd, hackneyed, old hat, shopworn, stale, timeworn, tired, twice-told, well-worn

warmhearted *adj* ***syn*** TENDER, compassionate, kindhearted, responsive, softhearted, sympathetic, warm
rel benign, benignant, kind, kindly, outgoing
con austere, cold, cool, frigid, frosty, severe, stern
ant coldhearted

warming *n* ***syn*** DEFEAT 1, beating, debacle, defeasance, drubbing, licking, overthrow, rout, shellacking, thrashing

warmish *adj* ***syn*** TEPID 1, lukewarm, milk-warm

warn *vb* **1** to let one know of approaching danger or risk <police and the weather service join to *warn* travelers of hazardous road conditions>
syn caution, forewarn
rel advise, alert, apprise, inform, notify, tip; counsel, direct, guide
idiom address a warning to, give warning, put a flea in one's ear, put one on guard
2 ***syn*** INFORM 2, acquaint, advise, apprise, clue (*or* clew), fill in, notify, post, tell, wise (up)
3 ***syn*** COMMAND, bid, charge, direct, enjoin, instruct, order, tell

warning *n* something and especially a statement that warns or is intended to warn <gave them *warning* that disobedience would lead to punishment>

---

syn synonym(s)	***rel*** related word(s)
idiom idiomatic equivalent(s)	***con*** contrasted word(s)
ant antonym(s)	* vulgar

‖ use limited; if in doubt, see a dictionary
The first word in a synonym list when printed in SMALL CAPITALS shows where there is more information about the group. For a more efficient use of this book see Explanatory Notes.

syn admonition, caution, caveat, commonition, forewarning, monition
rel advice, counsel, guidance, recommendation; hint, suggestion, tip
idiom flea (*or* word) in the ear, word to the wise

warning *adj syn* MONITORY, admonishing, admonitory, cautionary, cautioning, monitorial

warp *vb* **1** *syn* DEBASE 1, bastardize, bestialize, brutalize, corrupt, debauch, demoralize, deprave, pervert, vitiate
rel contort, crook, distort, twist
con disentangle, rectify, straighten, unkink
2 *syn* DEFORM, contort, distort, misshape, torture, wind
rel bend, crook, kink, twist
3 *syn* MISREPRESENT, color, confuse, distort, garble, miscolor, pervert, twist, wrench, wrest

war paint *n* **1** *syn* FINERY, ‖best bib and tucker, bravery, frippery, full dress, ‖glad rags, regalia, Sunday best
2 *syn* MAKEUP 3, face, maquillage, paint

warped *adj syn* BIASED 2, colored, jaundiced, one-sided, partial, partisan, prejudiced, prepossessed, tendentious, unindifferent
ant unwarped

warrant *n* **1** *syn* PLEDGE 1, earnest, pawn, security, token
2 *syn* BASIS 3, foundation
3 *syn* WORD 8, assurance, guarantee, pledge

warrant *vb* **1** *syn* MAINTAIN 2, argue, assert, claim, contend, defend, justify, vindicate
rel state; assure, ensure, insure
2 to give assurance of the worth of something especially in respect to quality, quantity, or condition < *warranted* the merchandise to be exactly as described in the catalog >
syn certify, guarantee, guaranty
rel assure, insure, secure; back, sponsor, stipulate; affirm, claim, state
idiom stand behind
3 *syn* JUSTIFY 4
rel endorse; call (for), need, require

warrantable *adj syn* JUSTIFIABLE, condonable, defensible, excusable, tenable, vindicable
ant unwarrantable

warranty *n syn* GUARANTEE 1, bail, bond, guaranty, security, surety

warrior *n syn* SOLDIER, fighter, fighting man, GI, man-at-arms, serviceman, swad, ‖swaddy, ‖sweat

wary *adj* **1** *syn* CAUTIOUS, calculating, careful, chary, circumspect, considerate, discreet, gingerly, guarded, safe
rel distrustful, doubting, leery, suspicious; vigilant, watchful
idiom on one's guard

con careless, heedless, thoughtless; devil-may-care, reckless, venturesome
ant foolhardy; unwary
2 *syn* SPARING, canny, chary, frugal, provident, saving, Scotch, stewardly, thrifty, unwasteful

wash *vb* **1** *syn* BATHE 1, ‖bath, shower, tub
2 *syn* BATHE 2, lap, lave, lip
3 *syn* DRIFT 1, float, ride
4 *syn* SLOSH 1, bubble, burble, gurgle, lap, swash

washed–out *adj syn* EFFETE 2, all in, bleary, depleted, drained, exhausted, far-gone, spent, used up, worn-out

washed–up *adj* **1** *syn* THROUGH 3, done for, finished
2 *syn* THROUGH 4, done

wash out *vb* **1** *syn* FAIL 4, ‖flop, flummox
2 *syn* DISCARD, cashier, cast, jettison, junk, reject, scrap, shed, slough, throw away

wash up *vb syn* GO 4, consume, exhaust, expend, finish, run through, spend, use up

washy *adj syn* DILUTE, diluted, thin, watered-down, waterish, watery, weak

waspish *adj* **1** *syn* IRRITABLE, fractious, fretful, huffy, peevish, pettish, petulant, querulous, snappish, waspy
rel contrary, impatient, perverse; malicious, sharp, spiteful; crabbed, cross-grained
2 *syn* CANTANKEROUS, bearish, cankered, cranky, cross-grained, crotchety, ornery, vinegarish, vinegary, waspy

waspy *adj* **1** *syn* IRRITABLE, fractious, fretful, huffy, peevish, pettish, petulant, querulous, snappish, waspish
rel contrary, impatient, perverse; malicious, sharp, spiteful; crabbed, cross-grained
2 *syn* CANTANKEROUS, bearish, cankered, cranky, cross-grained, crotchety, ornery, vinegarish, vinegary, waspish

wassail *n* **1** *syn* BINGE 1, bat, bender, bust, carousal, carouse, ran-tan, soak, spree, tear
2 *syn* REVELRY 2, high jinks, revel, revelment, skylarking, whoop-de-do, whoopee, whoopla, whoop-up

wassail *vb syn* REVEL 1, carouse, frolic, hell, riot, roister, spree

waste *n* **1** an area of the earth unsuitable for cultivation or general habitation <the scattered dwellers of southern Africa's dry *wastes* >
syn badland, barren, desert, wasteland, wild, wilderness, wild land, wildness
rel brush, brushland, bush; jungle
2 *syn* EXTRAVAGANCE 2, extravagancy, lavishness, overdoing, prodigality, squander, unthrift, wastefulness
3 *syn* REFUSE, debris, garbage, junk, kelter, litter, offal, rubbish, sweepings, trash
rel rubble, rummage

waste *vb* **1** *syn* RAVAGE, depredate, desecrate, desolate, despoil, devastate, devour, pillage, sack, spoliate
idiom reduce to a shambles
ant conserve
2 to spend or expend freely and usually foolishly or futilely < *wasted* his inheritance on women and gambling > < *waste* one's time on trifles >
syn blow, blunder (away), cast away, consume, dissipate, dribble (away), drivel, fool (away), fritter, frivol away, muddle (away), ‖piss away, potter (away), prodigalize, riot (away), squander, throw away, trifle (away)

---

syn synonym(s) *rel* related word(s)
idiom idiomatic equivalent(s) *con* contrasted word(s)
ant antonym(s) * vulgar
‖ use limited; if in doubt, see a dictionary
The first word in a synonym list when printed in SMALL CAPITALS shows where there is more information about the group. For a more efficient use of this book see Explanatory Notes.

rel disburse, expend, spend; dispense, distribute; deplete, drain, exhaust, impoverish; dispel, disperse, scatter; misspend
idiom let slip through one's fingers, pour down the drain, throw good money after bad
ant save; conserve

waste (away) *vb syn* FAIL 3, dwindle, fall short, shrink, wane, weaken

wasted *adj syn* EMACIATED, cadaverous, gaunt, skeletal, worn
rel meager; shriveled, withered, wizened
con healthy, robust; stalwart, stout, strong, sturdy

wastefulness *n syn* EXTRAVAGANCE 2, extravagancy, lavishness, overdoing, prodigality, squander, unthrift, waste
ant frugality

wasteland *n syn* WASTE 1, badland, barren, desert, wild, wilderness, wild land, wildness

waster *n* **1** *syn* SPENDTHRIFT, high roller, prodigal, profligate, scattergood, spender, squanderer, unthrift, wastethrift, wastrel
rel dissipater, fritterer; idler, loafer, lounger
2 *syn* WASTREL 1, ‖bad lot, good-for-nothing, ne'er-do-well, no-good, profligate, rounder, scapegrace

wastethrift *n syn* SPENDTHRIFT, high roller, prodigal, profligate, scattergood, spender, squanderer, unthrift, waster, wastrel

wastrel *n* **1** a worthless, self-indulgent, and reprehensible person <loafers and other *wastrels* lounging on the corner>
syn ‖bad lot, good-for-nothing, ne'er-do-well, no-good, profligate, rounder, scapegrace, waster
rel lecher, libertine, rake, rip, roué; blackguard, black sheep, knave, rascal, rogue, scoundrel; rapscallion, scalawag, scamp
idiom sad case
2 *syn* SPENDTHRIFT, high roller, prodigal, profligate, scattergood, spender, squanderer, unthrift, waster, wastethrift
rel dissipater, fritterer; idler, loafer, lounger

watch *vb* **1** *syn* SEE 2, ‖dekko, look
rel examine, follow, inspect, scan, scrutinize
idiom keep an eye on, keep tabs on
2 *syn* EYE 2, eyeball, scrutinize
3 *syn* TEND 2, attend, care (for), mind
idiom keep watch over
4 *syn* LOOK 1, mind, see

watch *n* **1** *syn* LOOKOUT 3, surveillance, tout, vigil, vigilance, watch and ward
2 *syn* GUARD 2, lookout, picket, sentinel, sentry, ward, watchman
3 *syn* EYE 3, eagle eye, scrutiny, surveillance, tab

watch and ward *n syn* LOOKOUT 3, surveillance, tout, vigil, vigilance, watch

watchdog *n syn* CUSTODIAN, cerberus, claviger, ‖custodier, custos, guardian, keeper, warden

watcher *n syn* SPECTATOR, beholder, by-sitter, bystander, eyewitness, looker-on, observer, onlooker, viewer, witness

watchfire *n syn* BEACON 1, balefire

watchful *adj* paying close attention usually with a view to anticipating approaching danger or opportunity <adopted a policy of *watchful* waiting>
syn alert, open-eyed, unsleeping, vigilant, wakeful, wide-awake
rel cautious, chary, circumspect, wary; prompt, quick, ready
idiom keeping one's eyes peeled (*or* open), on the watch (*or* lookout)
con careless, heedless, thoughtless; inadvertent; absent-minded, abstracted, faraway
ant unwatchful

watchman *n syn* GUARD 2, lookout, picket, sentinel, sentry, ward, watch

watch out *vb syn* BEWARE, look out, mind

watchword *n* **1** *syn* PASSWORD 1, countersign, word
2 *syn* PASSWORD 3, word
3 *syn* CATCHWORD, byword, catchphrase, phrase, shibboleth, slogan

water *n* **1** *syn* TEARS, teardrops
2 *syn* SALIVA, slaver, spit, spittle

water *vb syn* DROOL 1

water closet *n syn* TOILET, convenience, head, john, johnny, latrine, lavatory, ‖loo, privy, ‖throne

watercourse *n syn* CHANNEL 1, aqueduct, canal, conduit, course, duct

watered-down *adj syn* DILUTE, diluted, thin, washy, waterish, watery, weak

waterfall *n* a precipitous descent of water or the site of this <heard the roar of the *waterfall*>
syn cascade, cataract, chute, fall(s), ‖force, sault, spout
rel rapid(s), riffle, shoot; eddy, surge, vortex, whirlpool

watering hole *n* **1** *syn* RESORT 2, hangout, haunt, purlieu, rendezvous, stamping ground
2 *syn* BAR 5, barroom, ‖boozer, cocktail lounge, drinkery, ‖gin mill, lounge, pub, saloon, tavern
3 *syn* NIGHTCLUB, cabaret, café, discotheque, hot spot, nightery, nightspot, nitery, supper club, watering place

watering place *n* **1** *syn* SPA 1, baths, ‖hydro, springs, wells
2 *syn* RESORT 3, pleasure dome, spa
3 *syn* BAR 5, barroom, ‖boozer, cocktail lounge, drinkery, ‖gin mill, lounge, pub, saloon, tavern
4 *syn* NIGHTCLUB, cabaret, café, discotheque, hot spot, nightery, night spot, nitery, supper club, watering hole

waterish *adj* **1** *syn* DILUTE, diluted, thin, washy, watered-down, watery, weak
2 *syn* PALE 2, anemic, bloodless, pallid, watery
3 *syn* INSIPID 3, inane, innocuous, jejune, milk-and-water, namby-pamby, sapless, vapid, watery, wishy-washy

waterless *adj syn* DRY 1, arid, bone-dry, droughty, moistureless, sere, thirsty, unwatered
ant watered

---

syn synonym(s) *rel* related word(s)
idiom idiomatic equivalent(s) *con* contrasted word(s)
ant antonym(s) * vulgar
‖ use limited; if in doubt, see a dictionary
The first word in a synonym list when printed in SMALL CAPITALS shows where there is more information about the group. For a more efficient use of this book see Explanatory Notes.

waterlog *vb* ***syn*** SOAK 1, drench, impregnate, insteep, saturate, sodden, ‖sog, sop, souse, steep

watery *adj* **1** ***syn*** DILUTE, diluted, thin, washy, watered-down, waterish, weak
2 ***syn*** PALE 2, anemic, bloodless, pallid, waterish
3 ***syn*** INSIPID 3, banal, bland, jejune, milk-and-water, namby-pamby, sapless, vapid, waterish, wishy-washy

wave *vb* ***syn*** WAG, beat, lash, switch, waggle, woggle

waver *vb* ***syn*** HESITATE, dither, falter, halt, shilly-shally, stagger, vacillate, whiffle, wiggle-waggle
rel palter, shift, trim; seesaw, teeter
idiom back and fill, hem and haw

wavering *n* ***syn*** HESITATION, hesitancy, indecision, irresolution, shilly-shally, to-and-fro, vacillation

wavering *adj* **1** ***syn*** VACILLATING 2, faltering, halting, hesitating, shilly-shallying, vacillant, vacillatory, whiffling, wiggle-waggle, wobbly
ant unwavering
2 ***syn*** WEAK 2, dickey, fluctuant, insecure, rootless, shaky, unstable, unsure, vacillating, wobbly

wax *vb* **1** ***syn*** INCREASE 2, augment, build, enlarge, expand, heighten, mount, multiply, rise, upsurge
ant wane
2 ***syn*** BECOME 1, come, ‖come over, get, go, grow, run, turn

wax *n* ***syn*** RISE 3, boost, breakthrough, hike, increase, upgrade
ant wane

waxen *adj* ***syn*** PALE 1, ashen, ashy, blanched, colorless, complexionless, doughy, livid, pallid, wan

waxy *adj* ***syn*** ANGRY, heated, indignant, irate, ireful, mad, wrathful, wrathy, wroth, wrothful

way *n* **1** a public and unobstructed passage leading from one place to another <tracing the remains of an old lumberman's *way*>
syn artery, avenue, boulevard, ‖drag, highway, path, road, street, thoroughfare, track
rel course, line, passage, route; alley, byway, lane, ride, row
2 that along which one passes in going from one place to another <his *way* led through wooded hills>
syn course, line, passage, path, road, route
3 ***syn*** DOOR 2, access, adit, admission, admittance, entrance, entrée, entry, ingress
4 ***syn*** METHOD 1, fashion, manner, mode, modus, system, technique, wise
rel custom, habit, habitude, practice, usage, use, wont
5 ***syn*** STYLE 4, manner
6 ***syn*** HABIT 1, consuetude, habitude, manner, practice, praxis, trick, usage, use, wont
7 ***syn*** DISTANCE 2, ways
8 ***syn*** TYPE, breed, class, ilk, kidney, kind, order, sort, species, variety

---

syn synonym(s) — ***rel*** related word(s)
idiom idiomatic equivalent(s) — ***con*** contrasted word(s)
ant antonym(s) — * vulgar
‖ use limited; if in doubt, see a dictionary
The first word in a synonym list when printed in SMALL CAPITALS shows where there is more information about the group. For a more efficient use of this book see Explanatory Notes.

‖wayback *n* ***syn*** RUSTIC, ‖appleknocker, backwoodsman, bumpkin, clodhopper, hayseed, hick, redneck, rube, yokel

wayfaring *adj* ***syn*** ITINERANT, itinerate, nomadic, perambulant, perambulatory, peripatetic, roving, vagabond, vagrant, wandering

waylay *vb* ***syn*** SURPRISE 1, ambush, lay (for)
rel lurk, prowl, skulk, slink
idiom lay wait for, lie in wait for

ways *n pl but sing in constr* ***syn*** DISTANCE 2, way

wayward *adj* **1** ***syn*** CONTRARY 3, balky, cross-grained, froward, ornery, perverse, restive, wrongheaded
rel capricious, fickle, inconstant, unstable, variable
con complaisant, good-natured
2 ***syn*** ARBITRARY 1, capricious, erratic, freakish, vagarious, whimsical, whimsied

weak *adj* **1** lacking physical, mental, or moral strength <a *weak* spirit in a *weak* body>
syn decrepit, feeble, flimsy, fragile, frail, infirm, insubstantial, puny, unsound, unsubstantial, ‖wanky, weakly
rel debilitated, enfeebled, sickly, spindly, weakened; forceless, impotent, impuissant, powerless
con stalwart, stout, sturdy, tenacious, tough; dynamic, energetic, forceful, vigorous
ant strong
2 deficient in stability <a love too *weak* to bear the trials of daily life>
syn dickey, fluctuant, insecure, rootless, shaky, unstable, unsure, vacillating, wavering, wobbly; *compare* RICKETY
rel hesitant, irresolute, trimming, uncertain; insubstantial, undependable, unreliable
con certain, secure, solid, stable, sure; dependable, reliable, substantial
ant strong
3 ***syn*** IMPLAUSIBLE, flimsy, improbable, inconceivable, incredible, thick, thin, unbelievable, unconvincing, unsubstantial
4 not equal to the requirements and demands of a situation <a *weak* executive>
syn boneless, emasculate, forceless, impotent, inadequate, ineffective, ineffectual, invertebrate, slack-spined, spineless, wan
rel unfit, unqualified, unsuitable; bungling, incompetent, inept
con able, competent, effective, efficient; adequate, fit, qualified, satisfactory, sufficient, suitable; manly, masculine, virile
ant strong
5 ***syn*** DILUTE, diluted, thin, washy, watered-down, waterish, watery
ant strong

weaken *vb* **1** to lose or cause to lose strength, vigor, or energy <his hesitation *weakened* the force of his argument>
syn attenuate, blunt, cripple, debilitate, disable, enfeeble, sap, unbrace, undermine, unstrengthen; *compare* PARALYZE 1
rel emasculate, enervate, incapacitate, unman, unnerve; damage, impair, injure; lessen, minimize, reduce; dilute, thin
con better, improve; activate, energize, invigorate, vitalize

ant strengthen
2 *syn* FAIL 1, decline, deteriorate, ||dwine, fade, flag, languish
3 *syn* FAIL 3, dwindle, fall short, shrink, wane, waste (away)
4 *syn* DILUTE, cut, thin

weak–headed *adj syn* SIMPLE 3, ||buffle-headed, fatuous, mindless, nitwitted, senseless, sheepheaded, unwitty, weak-minded, witless

weak–kneed *adj syn* VACILLATING 2, double-minded, faltering, irresolute, timid, uncertain, wavering, whiffling, wiggle-waggle, wobbly

weakling *n* a person lacking in stamina and character <his speech deplored the characterless *weaklings* in critical positions>
syn baby, doormat, invertebrate, jellyfish, milksop, Milquetoast, ||molly, mollycoddle, namby-pamby, pantywaist, sissy, sissy-pants (*or* sissy-britches), sop
rel butt, mark, pushover, sucker; drip, mama's boy, misfit, mother's boy, sad sack, weak sister
idiom shrinking violet

weakly *adv syn* SOTTO VOCE, faintly, mutedly
ant strongly

weakly *adj syn* WEAK 1, decrepit, feeble, flimsy, fragile, frail, infirm, insubstantial, unsound, unsubstantial

weak–minded *adj syn* SIMPLE 3, brainless, ||buffle-headed, foolish, mindless, nitwitted, sheepheaded, silly, unwitty, weak-headed

weakness *n syn* APPETITE 3, fondness, inclination, liking, soft spot, taste

weal *n syn* WHEAL, wale, welt, whelk, ||whelp

weald *n syn* FOREST, timber, timberland, wood(s), woodland

wealth *n* **1** *syn* MEAN 3, assets, capital, resources
2 one's worldly possessions <at that point his *wealth* consisted of the clothes he stood in and a solitary quarter>
syn fortune, property, resources, riches, substance, worth
rel assets, estate, goods, holdings, possessions

wealthy *adj syn* RICH 1, affluent, moneyed, ||oofy, opulent
con impoverished, penniless, poor
ant indigent

wean *vb syn* ESTRANGE, alien, alienate, disaffect, disunify, disunite
ant addict

wear *vb* **1** *syn* ABRADE 1, chafe, corrade, erode, gall, graze, rub, ruffle
2 *syn* TIRE 1, drain, fatigue, jade, wear down, weary

wear (away) *vb syn* EAT 3, bite, corrode, eat away, erode, gnaw, scour

wear down *vb syn* TIRE 1, drain, fatigue, jade, wear, weary

wearied *adj syn* TIRED 1, fatigued, jaded, weary, worn, worn down
ant refreshed; unwearied, unweary

weariful *adj syn* ARID 2, bromidic, dry, dryasdust, dull, dusty, insipid, tedious, uninteresting, wearisome

weariless *adj syn* INDEFATIGABLE, inexhaustible, tireless, unflagging, untiring, unweariable, unwearying

weariness *n syn* FATIGUE, exhaustion, lassitude, tiredness

2 *syn* ARID 2, bromidic, dry, dryasdust, dull, dusty, insipid, tedious, uninteresting, weariful

wear out *vb* **1** *syn* EXHAUST 4, ||bugger, fag, frazzle, knock out, outtire, outwear, ||poop, prostrate, tucker
||2 *syn* WHIP 1, flagellate, flog, hide, ||larrup, lash, scourge, stripe, thrash, whale

weary *vb* **1** *syn* TIRE 1, drain, fatigue, jade, wear, wear down
rel debilitate, enfeeble, weaken; depress, oppress, weigh
con animate, energize, vitalize; enliven, quicken, vivify
ant refresh
2 *syn* BORE, ennui, pall, tire

weary *adj* **1** *syn* TIRED 1, fatigued, jaded, wearied, worn, worn down
ant refreshed, unwearied, unweary
2 *syn* FED UP, disgusted, sick, tired

Weary Willie *n syn* VAGABOND, bum, derelict, drifter, floater, hobo, street arab, tramper, vag, vagrant

weasel *n syn* SNEAK, slink, sneaker, sneaksby

weasel *vb syn* EQUIVOCATE 2, dodge, evade, hedge, pussyfoot, shuffle, sidestep, tergiversate, tergiverse

weathery *adj syn* CHANGEABLE 1, changeful, fluid, mobile, mutable, protean, unsettled, unstable, unsteady, variable

weave *vb syn* LURCH 2, careen, stagger, ||stoit, ||stoiter, ||stot, sway, swing, wobble

web *n* **1** *syn* TEXTURE 2, fabric, fiber
2 something by which one is ensnared, held fast, or inextricably involved <diplomacy caught in its own *web* of double-dealing>
syn cobweb, entanglement, mesh(es), toil(s); *compare* ENTANGLEMENT 1
rel complexity, complication; labyrinth, maze, morass, skein, snarl, tangle; embroilment, enmeshment, ensnarement, entrapment, involvement
idiom a tangled web
3 *syn* MAZE 1, jungle, knot, labyrinth, mesh, mizmaze, morass, skein, snarl, tangle

wed *vb* **1** *syn* MARRY 1, catch, espouse
2 *syn* MARRY 2, ||hitch, mate, splice, tie
3 *syn* JOIN 1, associate, combine, conjoin, connect, link, marry, relate, unite, yoke

wedded *adj syn* MATRIMONIAL, conjugal, connubial, hymeneal, marital, married, nuptial, spousal
con unwed, unwedded

wedding *n* the marriage ceremony usually with its accompanying festivities <one of the most elaborate *weddings* of the social season>
syn bridal, espousal(s), marriage, nuptial(s), spousal

wedlock *n syn* MARRIAGE 1, conjugality, connubiality, matrimony

---

syn synonym(s) — *rel* related word(s)
idiom idiomatic equivalent(s) — *con* contrasted word(s)
ant antonym(s) — * vulgar
|| use limited; if in doubt, see a dictionary
The first word in a synonym list when printed in SMALL CAPITALS shows where there is more information about the group. For a more efficient use of this book see Explanatory Notes.

wee *adj* ***syn*** TINY, diminutive, lilliputian, miniature, minute, teensy, teensy-weensy, teeny, teeny-weeny, weensy

weed *n* ***syn*** MARIJUANA, boo, cannabis, grass, ‖Mary Jane, moocah, pot, ‖tea

weensy *adj* ***syn*** TINY, diminutive, lilliputian, miniature, minute, teensy, teensy-weensy, teeny, teeny-weeny, wee

weeny *adj* ***syn*** TINY, diminutive, lilliputian, miniature, minute, teensy, teensy-weensy, teeny, teeny-weeny, wee

weep *vb* **1** ***syn*** DEPLORE 1, bemoan, bewail, grieve, lament, moan
2 ***syn*** EXUDE, bleed, ooze, ‖screeve, seep, ‖sew, ‖sicker, strain, sweat, transude
3 ***syn*** CRY 2, blub, blubber, boohoo, ‖pipe, sob, wail
4 ***syn*** DRIP, distill, drib, dribble, drop, trickle, trill

weeping *adj* ***syn*** TEARFUL, lachrymose, teary, weepy

weepy *adj* ***syn*** TEARFUL, lachrymose, teary, weeping

weigh *vb* **1** ***syn*** CONSIDER 1, contemplate, excogitate, mind, perpend, ponder, study, think (out *or* over)
rel appraise, evaluate, rate
2 ***syn*** BURDEN, charge, cumber, encumber, lade, load, lumber, saddle, tax, weight
3 to carry intellectual weight <this evidence *weighed* heavily against him>
syn count, militate, tell
rel import, matter, register, signify
idiom amount to some shucks, be something, carry weight, cut (some) ice
4 ***syn*** MATTER, count, import, mean, signify

weigh down *vb* ***syn*** DEPRESS 2, oppress, press, sadden
ant raise (*one's spirits*)

weight *n* **1** ***syn*** LOAD 2
2 ***syn*** IMPORTANCE, consequence, import, magnitude, moment, momentousness, pith, significance, ‖signification, weightiness
3 ***syn*** INFLUENCE 1, authority, credit, prestige
rel effectiveness, efficacy; forcefulness, forcibleness, potency, powerfulness
4 ***syn*** LOAD 3, burden, charge, deadweight, duty, millstone, onus, task, tax

weight *vb* **1** ***syn*** ADULTERATE, debase, doctor, dope (up), load, sophisticate
rel burden, cumber, encumber; contaminate, corrupt, foul up, spoil
2 ***syn*** BURDEN, charge, cumber, encumber, lade, load, lumber, saddle, tax, weigh

weightiness *n* ***syn*** IMPORTANCE, consequence, import, magnitude, moment, momentousness, pith, significance, ‖signification, weight

weightless *adj* ***syn*** LIGHT 1, featherlight, featherweight, imponderous, lightweight, unheavy
ant weighty

---

syn synonym(s) — ***rel*** related word(s)
idiom idiomatic equivalent(s) — ***con*** contrasted word(s)
ant antonym(s) — * vulgar
‖ use limited; if in doubt, see a dictionary
The first word in a synonym list when printed in SMALL CAPITALS shows where there is more information about the group. For a more efficient use of this book see Explanatory Notes.

weighty *adj* **1** ***syn*** IMPORTANT 1, big, consequential, considerable, material, meaningful, momentous, significant, substantial
2 ***syn*** SERIOUS 1, earnest, grave, no-nonsense, sedate, sober, sobersided, solemn, somber, staid
3 ***syn*** SERIOUS 2, grave, heavy, severe
4 ***syn*** HEAVY 1, cumbersome, cumbrous, hefty, massive, ponderous
ant weightless
5 ***syn*** FAT 2, corpulent, fleshy, gross, heavy, obese, overweight, porcine, portly, stout
6 ***syn*** ONEROUS, burdensome, demanding, exacting, exigent, grievous, oppressive, superincumbent, taxing, tough

weird *n* **1** ***syn*** FATE, circumstance, destiny, doom, kismet, lot, moira, portion
2 ***syn*** PREDICTION, cast, forecast, foretelling, prevision, prognosis, prognostication, prophecy

weird *adj* **1** fearfully and mysteriously strange or fantastic <shuddered at the *weird* unearthly glow that swept across the sky>
syn eerie, spooky, uncanny, unearthly
rel creepy, haunting, unnatural; preternatural, supernatural; supernal; curious, odd, peculiar, queer, strange; inscrutable, mysterious; awe-inspiring, awful, dreadful, fearful, horrific
con common, commonplace, everyday, quotidian; natural, normal, ordinary
2 ***syn*** STRANGE 4, bizarre, curious, eccentric, oddball, outlandish, peculiar, queer, singular, uncouth

welcome *adj* ***syn*** PLEASANT 1, agreeable, congenial, favorable, good, gratifying, nice, pleasing, pleasurable, pleasureful
rel congenial, cordial, genial, sympathetic; contenting, satisfying
ant unwelcome

welfare *n* a state of thriving and progress <parents who seek their children's *welfare*>
syn advantage, benefit, good, interest, prosperity, well-being
rel fortune, luck, success; contentment, felicity, happiness, satisfaction
ant illfare

welkin *n* ***syn*** SKY, empyrean, firmament, heaven(s)

well *n* **1 wells** *pl* ***syn*** SPA 1, baths, ‖hydro, springs, watering place
2 ***syn*** SOURCE, fountain, fountainhead, inception, origin, provenance, provenience, root, wellhead, wellspring

well *adv* **1** in a good, proper, or acceptable manner <the children behaved very *well* at the party>
syn aright, befittingly, correctly, decently, decorously, fitly, fittingly, justly, nicely, properly, rightly
rel bearably, passably, tolerably, unobjectionably; considerately, pleasantly, thoughtfully, white; appropriately
con badly, improperly, objectionably, obnoxiously, outrageously
ant ill
2 in a pleasant, cooperative, or thoughtful manner <he speaks *well* of your new proposal>
syn considerately, generously, heedfully, kindly, thoughtfully
rel concernedly, interestedly; approvingly

con contemptuously, disdainfully, scornfully
3 to a full extent or degree <you are *well* aware of the problems we face>
syn à fond, altogether, clear, ||cleverly, completely, entirely, fully, perfectly, ||plumb, quite, right, roundly, ||slam, ||slap, thoroughly, utterly, wholly
rel certainly, obviously, surely, undoubtedly, unquestionably; sublimely
idiom all the way
con barely, hardly, scarcely
4 in an adequate or appropriate manner <any large box will answer our need very *well*>
syn acceptably, adequately, amply, appropriately, becomingly, fittingly, properly, right, satisfactorily, suitably
5 in a desirable or pleasing manner <everything went *well* on the trip>
syn favorably, fortunately, happily, prosperously, satisfyingly, successfully, swimmingly
rel comfortably, easily, smoothly
con amiss, wrong
ant badly
6 ***syn*** EASILY 1, effortlessly, facilely, freely, lightly, readily, smoothly
7 in all likelihood <the fighting may *well* continue for years>
syn doubtlessly, easily, indeed, really, truly, undoubtedly
rel conceivably, perhaps, possibly; likely, probably
8 to a considerable extent or degree <they landed *well* beyond the wharf>
syn considerably, far, quite, rather, significantly, somewhat
idiom by a long way, by a wide margin

well *adj* **1** ***syn*** PROSPEROUS 3, comfortable, easy, ||snug, substantial, well-fixed, well-heeled, well-off, well-to-do
2 ***syn*** HEALTHY 1, ||bunkum, fit, hale, right, sane, sound, well-conditioned, well-liking, wholesome
ant ill, unwell
3 ***syn*** LUCKY, fortunate, happy, providential, ||sonsy

well–behaved *adj* ***syn*** GOOD 13, decorous

well–being *n* **1** ***syn*** PROSPERITY 2, abundance, ease, easy street, prosperousness, thriving
ant ill-being
2 ***syn*** WELFARE, advantage, benefit, good, interest, prosperity
ant ill-being

well–bred *adj* ***syn*** GENTEEL 1, cultivated, cultured, distingué, polished, refined, urbane
ant ill-bred

well–conditioned *adj* ***syn*** HEALTHY 1, ||bunkum, fit, hale, right, sane, sound, well, well-liking, wholesome

well–developed *adj* ***syn*** CURVACEOUS, ||built, curvesome, curvilinear, curvy, Junoesque, rounded, ||stacked

well–disposed *adj* ***syn*** SYMPATHETIC 2, friendly, receptive, ||sib
ant ill-disposed

well–favored *adj* ***syn*** BEAUTIFUL, attractive, beauteous, comely, fair, good-looking, handsome, lovely, pretty, pulchritudinous
ant ill-favored

well–fixed *adj* ***syn*** PROSPEROUS 3, comfortable, easy, ||snug, substantial, well, well-heeled, well-off, well-to-do
ant badly off

well–founded *adj* having a firm foundation in fact or logic <offered *well-founded* arguments to support his position>
syn cogent, good, just, justified, well-grounded
rel sound, substantial, telling, valid; rational, reasonable, reasoned; fundamental, meaty, pithy
con unjustified; insubstantial, invalid, unsound; irrational, unreasonable

well–groomed *adj* **1** ***syn*** NEAT 2, chipper, orderly, shipshape, snug, spick-and-span, tidy, trig, trim, uncluttered
2 ***syn*** DAPPER, bandbox, doggish, doggy, natty, sassy, sparkish, spiffy, spruce, sprucy

well–grounded *adj* ***syn*** WELL-FOUNDED, cogent, good, just, justified

wellhead *n* ***syn*** SOURCE, fountain, fountainhead, inception, origin, provenance, provenience, root, well, wellspring

well–heeled *adj* ***syn*** PROSPEROUS 3, comfortable, easy, ||snug, substantial, well, well-fixed, well-off, well-to-do
ant badly off

well–hung *adj* ***syn*** GLIB, silver-tongued, vocative, voluble

well–known *adj* much talked about <a *well-known* hospital>
syn famous, leading, noted, notorious, popular, prominent; *compare* FAMOUS 2
rel conspicuous, important, outstanding
idiom on everyone's tongue
con inconspicuous, obscure, unheard-of, unimportant, unnoted, unpopular
ant unknown

well–liked *adj* ***syn*** FAVORITE 2, favored, popular, preferred

well–liking *adj* ***syn*** HEALTHY 1, ||bunkum, fit, hale, right, sane, sound, well, well-conditioned, wholesome

well–mannered *adj* ***syn*** CIVIL 2, courteous, genteel, mannerly, polite
ant ill-mannered

well–nigh *adv* **1** ***syn*** NEARLY, about, all but, almost, approximately, most, much, ||nearabout, nigh, practically
2 ***syn*** ALMOST 2, all but, as good as, as much as, essentially, practically

well–off *adj* ***syn*** PROSPEROUS 3, comfortable, easy, ||snug, substantial, well, well-fixed, well-heeled, well-to-do
ant badly off

well over *vb* ***syn*** OVERFLOW 2, overbrim, overfill, overrun, run over, spill

well–paying *adj* ***syn*** ADVANTAGEOUS 1, gainful, good, lucrative, moneymaking, paying, profitable, remunerative, worthwhile

---

syn synonym(s) *rel* related word(s)
idiom idiomatic equivalent(s) *con* contrasted word(s)
ant antonym(s) * vulgar
|| use limited; if in doubt, see a dictionary
The first word in a synonym list when printed in SMALL CAPITALS shows where there is more information about the group. For a more efficient use of this book see Explanatory Notes.

well–proportioned *adj* ***syn*** SHAPELY, clean-limbed, shapeful, statuesque, trim, well-turned

wellspring *n* ***syn*** SOURCE, fountain, fountainhead, inception, origin, provenance, provenience, root, well, wellhead

well–thought–of *adj* ***syn*** RESPECTABLE 1, creditable, estimable, reputable, reputed

well–timed *adj* ***syn*** TIMELY 1, auspicious, favorable, opportune, propitious, prosperous, seasonable, timeous
con premature, untimely; behindhand, late, tardy
ant ill-timed

well–to–do *adj* ***syn*** PROSPEROUS 3, comfortable, easy, ||snug, substantial, well, well-fixed, well-heeled, well-off
ant badly off

well–turned *adj* ***syn*** SHAPELY, clean-limbed, shapeful, statuesque, trim, well-proportioned

well–worn *adj* ***syn*** TRITE, commonplace, hackneyed, shopworn, stale, stereotyped, threadbare, timeworn, tired, worn-out

welsh *vb* ***syn*** BACK DOWN, back off, back out, backpedal, backwater, crawfish (out), cry off, declare off, renege, resile

welt *n* **1** ***syn*** WHEAL, wale, weal, whelk, ||whelp
||**2** ***syn*** BLOW 1, bash, bat, belt, bop, pound, smack, smash, wallop, whack

weltanschauung *n* ***syn*** IDEOLOGY, credo, creed

welter *vb* **1** ***syn*** WALLOW 1
rel strive, struggle; toss, tumble, writhe; grovel
2 ***syn*** WALLOW 3, bask, indulge, luxuriate, revel, roll, rollick

welter *vb* ***syn*** WITHER, dry up, mummify, mummy, shrivel, wilt, wizen

wench *n* **1** ***syn*** GIRL 1, damsel, gal, lass, lassie, maid, maiden, miss, missy, ||quail
2 ***syn*** WANTON, hussy, jade, jezebel, slattern, slut, strumpet, tramp, trollop, trull

wend *vb* ***syn*** GO 1, fare, hie, journey, pass, proceed, ||process, push on, repair, travel

western *n* a motion picture or radio or television play with its scene laid in the western U.S. and having cowboys as its main characters <young boys delighting in Saturday morning *westerns*>
syn horse opera, oater
rel shoot-'em-up

wet *vb* to make wet by or as if by saturating with water <they were *wet* thoroughly by the pouring rain>
syn deluge, douse, drench, drown, soak, sop, souse; *compare* SOAK 1
rel damp, dampen, moisten; humidify, humify; fill, impregnate, saturate; irrigate; lave, rinse, wash
ant desiccate, dry

wet *adj* **1** containing or impregnated with liquid <change *wet* clothing for dry>
syn drenched, dripping, madid, saturate, saturated, soaked, soaking, sodden, sopping, soppy, soused, wringing-wet
rel soggy, water-logged; damp, dank, moist, wettish
idiom dripping (*or* soaking *or* sopping) wet
con bone-dry, dehydrated, desiccated, parched, sere, waterless
ant dry
2 ***syn*** INTOXICATED 1, ||boozy, ||canned, disguised, drunk, inebriated, ||lushed, pixilated, ||plastered, slopped

||**wet** *n* ***syn*** DRAM, drop, jolt, nip, shot, slug, snifter, snort, toothful, tot

wettish *adj* ***syn*** DAMP, dampish, dank, moist, moisty

whack *vb* ***syn*** STRIKE 2, ||biff, catch, ||devel, ding, hit, ||nail, slog, ||slosh, sock

whack *n* **1** ***syn*** BLOW 1, bash, bat, crack, smack, smash, sock, thwack, wallop, whop
2 ***syn*** FLING 1, crack, go, pop, shot, slap, stab, ||stagger, try, whirl

whacking *adj* ***syn*** HUGE, colossal, enormous, gargantuan, gigantic, immense, mighty, prodigious, whaling, whopping

whacking *adv* ***syn*** VERY 1, ||awful, awfully, ||big, damned, exceedingly, highly, hugely, much, whopping

whale *n* ***syn*** GIANT, behemoth, leviathan, mammoth, monster

whale *vb* ***syn*** WHIP 1, flagellate, flog, hide, ||larrup, lash, scourge, stripe, thrash, ||wear out

whaling *adj* ***syn*** HUGE, colossal, enormous, gargantuan, gigantic, immense, mighty, prodigious, whacking, whopping

wham *n* ***syn*** BANG 2, blast, boom, burst, clap, crack, crash, slam, smash

whammy *n* ***syn*** JINX, hex, hoodoo, Indian sign, voodoo

whangdoodle *n* ***syn*** NONSENSE 2, balderdash, ||baloney, blather, bosh, ||bunk, claptrap, drivel, guff, malarkey

wharf *n* a structure used by boats and ships for taking on or landing cargo and passengers <brought the boat alongside the *wharf* and moored her>
syn berth, dock, jetty, levee, pier, quay, slip

what–do–you–call–it *n* a thing or person that the speaker cannot (as from not knowing or from forgetting) name <hand me one of those little *what-do-you-call-its*> <went to *what-do-you-call-her's* house last week>
syn what-is-it, whatsis, what's its name, what-you-call-it, what-you-may-call-it, whatyoumayjigger; *compare* DOODAD, GADGET 1

what–is–it *n* ***syn*** WHAT-DO-YOU-CALL-IT, whatsis, what's its name, what-you-call-it, what-you-may-call-it, whatyoumayjigger

whatnot *n* ***syn*** KNICKKNACK, bauble, bibelot, curio, gewgaw, gimcrack, novelty, objet d'art, trifle, trinket

whatsis *n* ***syn*** WHAT-DO-YOU-CALL-IT, what-is-it, what's its name, what-you-call-it, what-you-may-call-it, whatyoumayjigger

what's its name *n* ***syn*** WHAT-DO-YOU-CALL-IT, what-is-it, whatsis, what-you-call-it, what-you-may-call-it, whatyoumayjigger

what–you–call–it *n* ***syn*** WHAT-DO-YOU-CALL-IT, what-is-it, whatsis, what's its name, what-you-may-call-it, whatyoumayjigger

---

syn synonym(s) ***rel*** related word(s)
idiom idiomatic equivalent(s) ***con*** contrasted word(s)
ant antonym(s) * vulgar
|| use limited; if in doubt, see a dictionary
The first word in a synonym list when printed in SMALL CAPITALS shows where there is more information about the group. For a more efficient use of this book see Explanatory Notes.

what–you–may–call–it *n* ***syn*** WHAT-DO-YOU-CALL-IT, what-is-it, whatsis, what's its name, what-you-call-it, whatyoumayjigger

whatyoumayjigger *n* ***syn*** WHAT-DO-YOU-CALL-IT, what-is-it, whatsis, what's its name, what-you-call-it, what-you-may-call-it

wheal *n* a ridge raised on the skin by or as if by a stroke of a lash <the convict's back was covered with *wheals* and old scars>
syn wale, weal, welt, whelk, ‖whelp
rel strake, streak, stripe

wheedle *vb* ***syn*** COAX, ‖banter, blandish, blarney, cajole, con, soft-soap, sweet-talk

wheel *n* **1** ***syn*** CYCLE 1, circle, round
2 ***syn*** REVOLUTION 1, circuit, circulation, circumvolution, gyration, gyre, rotation, round, turn, whirl
3 ***syn*** LEAGUE 4, association, circuit, conference, loop

wheel *vb* **1** ***syn*** REEL 2, stagger, titubate, totter
2 ***syn*** DRIVE 5, auto, charioteer, motor, pilot, tool
3 ***syn*** TURN 6, avert, deflect, divert, pivot, sheer, veer, volte-face, whip, whirl

wheeze *vb* ***syn*** HISS, buzz, fizz, fizzle, sibilate, sizzle, swish, whisper, whiz, whoosh

wheeze *n* ***syn*** PRANK, antic, caper, dido(es), frolic, lark, monkeyshine, shenanigan, shine(s), trick

whelk *n* ***syn*** WHEAL, wale, weal, welt, ‖whelp

whelm *vb* **1** ***syn*** DELUGE 1, drown, engulf, flood, inundate, overflow, overwhelm, submerge, swamp
2 ***syn*** DELUGE 3, flood, overwhelm, swamp
3 ***syn*** OVERWHELM 4, drown, knock over, overcome, overpower, prostrate

‖whelp *n* ***syn*** WHEAL, wale, weal, welt, whelk

when *adv* ***syn*** THEN 1, again, anon

when *conj* ***syn*** THOUGH, albeit, although, howbeit, much as, whereas, while

whence *n* ***syn*** SOURCE, derivation, fountain, inception, origin, provenance, provenience, root, well, wellspring

where *adv* **1** ***syn*** WHEREVER, everywhere
2 ***syn*** WHITHER 1, whereabouts, ‖whereaway

where *n* ***syn*** PLACE 1, location, locus, point, position, site, situation, spot, station

whereabouts *adv* ***syn*** WHITHER 1, where, ‖whereaway
con hereabouts, thereabouts

whereas *conj* **1** ***syn*** BECAUSE, as, as long as, 'cause, considering, for, inasmuch as, now, seeing, since
2 ***syn*** THOUGH, albeit, although, howbeit, much as, when, while

‖whereaway *adv* ***syn*** WHITHER 1, where, whereabouts

wherefore *n* ***syn*** REASON 3, argument, ground, proof, why, whyfor

whereto *adv* ***syn*** WHITHER 2, whereunto

whereunto *adv* ***syn*** WHITHER 2, whereto

wherever *adv* at, in, or to any or every place in or to which <he goes *wherever* he is needed>
syn everywhere, where
con here, there

‖wherret *vb* ***syn*** SLAP 1, blip, box, buffet, cuff, smack, spank

‖wherret *vb* ***syn*** WORRY 1, annoy, bedevil, beleaguer, hagride, harass, harry, pester, plague, tease

whet *vb* **1** ***syn*** SHARPEN, edge, hone, ‖sharp
2 ***syn*** STIR 1, arouse, awaken, bestir, challenge, kindle, rally, rouse, wake, waken

whet *n* ‖**1** ***syn*** WHILE 1, bit, space, spell, stretch, time
2 ***syn*** APPETIZER, antipasto, hors d'oeuvre, zakuska

whether or no *adv* ***syn*** WILLY-NILLY, helplessly, inescapably, inevitably, perforce, unavoidably

whetted *adj* ***syn*** SHARP 1, honed, keen, razor-sharp, unblunted

whicker *vb* ***syn*** NEIGH, nicker, ‖whinner, whinny

whiff *n* ***syn*** HINT 2, breath, dash, shade, smack, soupçon, tincture, tinge, trace, trifle

whiffet *n* ***syn*** NONENTITY, cipher, insignificancy, nobody, nothing, nullity, whippersnapper, whipster, zero, zilch

whiffle *vb* ***syn*** HESITATE, dither, falter, halt, shilly-shally, stagger, vacillate, waver, wiggle-waggle

whiffling *adj* ***syn*** VACILLATING 2, faltering, halting, hesitating, shilly-shallying, vacillant, vacillatory, wavering, wiggle-waggle, wobbly

whiffy *adj* ***syn*** MALODOROUS 1, fetid, funky, nidorous, noisome, olid, rank, reeking, smelly, stinking

whigmaleerie *n* **1** ***syn*** CAPRICE, boutade, conceit, crotchet, fancy, freak, humor, megrim, vagary, whim
2 ***syn*** KNICKKNACK, bauble, bibelot, curio, gewgaw, gimcrack, objet d'art, trifle, trinket, whatnot

while *n* **1** a somewhat indefinite period of time <sat down to rest for a *while*>
syn bit, space, spell, stretch, time, ‖whet
2 ***syn*** OCCASION 5, instant, moment, time
3 ***syn*** EFFORT 1, elbow grease, exertion, pains, trouble

while *conj* ***syn*** THOUGH, albeit, although, howbeit, much as, when, whereas

while *vb* to pass time and especially leisure time without boredom or in pleasant ways <*whiled* odd hours away in dreaming>
syn beguile, fleet, wile
rel amuse, divert, entertain; brighten, enliven, lighten

while (away) *vb* ***syn*** SPEND 3, pass

whilom *adj* ***syn*** FORMER 2, bygone, erstwhile, late, old, once, onetime, past, quondam, sometime

whim *n* ***syn*** CAPRICE, bee, boutade, conceit, crotchet, fancy, freak, humor, megrim, vagary
rel idea; disposition, inclination, thought; dream, fantasy, vision

whimper *vb* to cry feebly and often plaintively or peevishly <a baby *whimpering* in its sleep>
syn pule, whine; *compare* CRY 2

whimsical *adj* **1** ***syn*** ARBITRARY 1, capricious, erratic, freakish, vagarious, wayward, whimsied
2 ***syn*** UNCERTAIN 1, capricious, chancy, erratic, fluctuant, iffy, incalculable, unpredictable

whimsied *adj* ***syn*** ARBITRARY 1, capricious, erratic, freakish, vagarious, wayward, whimsical

whimsy *n* ***syn*** CAPRICE, boutade, conceit, crotchet, fancy, freak, humor, megrim, vagary, whim

---

rel idea; disposition, inclination, thought; dream, fantasy, vision

whim–whams *n pl* ***syn*** JITTERS, ‖all-overs, dither, heebie-jeebies, ‖jimjams, ‖jimmies, jumps, shakes, shivers, willies

whine *vb* **1** ***syn*** WHIMPER, pule
2 ***syn*** COMPLAIN, fuss, kick, murmur, repine, wail

‖**whinner** *vb* ***syn*** NEIGH, nicker, whicker, whinny

whinny *vb* ***syn*** NEIGH, nicker, whicker, ‖whinner

whiny *adj* ***syn*** IRRITABLE, peevish, querulous, raspish, raspy, snappish, snappy, twitty, waspish, waspy

whip *vb* **1** to strike repeatedly with or as if with a lash or rod < *whip* a dog for stealing from the table>
syn flagellate, flog, hide, ‖larrup, lash, lather, scourge, stripe, thrash, ‖wear out, whale, ‖yerk
rel beat, belabor, drub, wallop; bastinado, birch, bludgeon, cane, cudgel, quirt, switch
2 to defeat utterly < *whipped* their traditional rival by a score of 40 to 7>
syn beat, blast, ‖bowl (down *or* out), ‖clean up (on), ‖clobber, ‖cream, curry, drub, dust, lambaste, ‖larrup, lick, mop (up), overrun, overwhelm, rout, shellac, skunk, smear, smother, steamroller, thrash, trim, trounce, upend, wallop, whomp; *compare* CONQUER 1, DEFEAT 2
rel conquer, defeat, overcome, subdue, vanquish
idiom cook one's goose, deal a crushing defeat, settle one's hash, snow one under
3 to agitate with an instrument so as to stiffen and increase the bulk of by incorporation of air < *whip* cream for a shortcake>
syn beat, whisk
4 ***syn*** TURN 6, avert, deflect, divert, pivot, sheer, veer, volte-face, wheel, whirl

whip (up) *vb* ***syn*** INCITE, abet, foment, instigate, provoke, raise, set, set on, stir (up)
ant calm (down)

whip hand *n* ***syn*** BETTER 2, advantage, superiority, upper hand, victory

whippersnapper *n* ***syn*** NONENTITY, cipher, insignificancy, nobody, nothing, nullity, whiffet, whipster, zero, zilch

whipping boy *n* ***syn*** SCAPEGOAT, fall guy, goat, patsy

whippy *adj* ***syn*** ELASTIC 1, flexible, resilient, springy, stretch, stretchy, supple

whipster *n* ***syn*** NONENTITY, cipher, insignificancy, nobody, nothing, nullity, whiffet, whippersnapper, zero, zilch

whirl *vb* **1** ***syn*** SPIN 1, gyrate, gyre, ‖pirl, pirouette, ‖purl, twirl, whirligig
2 ***syn*** SWIRL, eddy, gurge, purl, swoosh, whirlpool, whorl
3 ***syn*** TURN 6, avert, deflect, divert, pivot, sheer, veer, volte-face, wheel, whip
4 ***syn*** HURRY 2, barrel, bullet, fleet, flit, speed, stave, whish, whisk, whiz
5 ***syn*** SPIN 2, reel, swim, turn

whirl *n* **1** ***syn*** REVOLUTION 1, circuit, cirulation, circumvolution, gyration, gyre, rotation, round, turn, wheel
2 ***syn*** EDDY, maelstrom, vortex, whirlpool
3 ***syn*** COMMOTION 4, clatter, hassle, hubbub, hurly-burly, moil, rowdydow, ruction, storm, whoopla
4 ***syn*** STIR 1, ado, bustle, flurry, furore, fuss, pother, whirlpool, whirlwind
5 ***syn*** FLING 1, crack, go, pop, shot, slap, stab, ‖stagger, try, whack

whirlblast *n* ***syn*** WHIRLWIND 1, ‖whirlpuff, whirly

whirligig *vb* ***syn*** SPIN 1, gyrate, gyre, ‖pirl, pirouette, ‖purl, twirl, whirl

whirlpool *n* **1** ***syn*** EDDY, maelstrom, vortex, whirl
2 ***syn*** STIR 1, ado, bustle, flurry, furore, fuss, pother, whirl, whirlwind

whirlpool *vb* ***syn*** SWIRL, eddy, gurge, purl, swoosh, whirl, whorl

‖**whirlpuff** *n* ***syn*** WHIRLWIND 1, whirlblast, whirly

whirlwind *n* **1** a rotating windstorm of limited extent that is often accompanied by a column of dust or vapor < *whirlwinds* moved across the plowed land>
syn whirlblast, ‖whirlpuff, whirly; *compare* HURRICANE, TORNADO
rel dust devil, rainspout, sand column, sand spout, waterspout
2 ***syn*** STIR 1, ado, bustle, flurry, furore, fuss, pother, whirl, whirlpool

whirly *n* ***syn*** WHIRLWIND 1, whirlblast, ‖whirlpuff

whish *vb* **1** ***syn*** HISS, buzz, fizz, fizzle, sibilate, sizzle, swish, wheeze, whisper, whiz
2 ***syn*** HURRY 2, bullet, fleet, flit, fly, speed, stave, whirl, whisk, whiz

whisk *vb* **1** ***syn*** HURRY 2, barrel, bullet, flit, fly, ‖nip, speed, whish, whiz, zip
2 ***syn*** WHIP 3, beat

whisker *n* ***syn*** HAIR, ace, hairbreadth

whiskered *adj* **1** ***syn*** BEARDED, barbate, bewhiskered
2 ***syn*** HAIRY 1, fleecy, hirsute, pileous, pilose, woolly

whiskers *n pl* ***syn*** BEARD, beaver

whisper *vb* **1** ***syn*** HISS, buzz, fizz, fizzle, sibilate, sizzle, swish, wheeze, whiz, whoosh
2 ***syn*** CONFIDE 1, breathe

whisper *n* **1** ***syn*** MURMUR 1, mumble, mutter, rumor, susurration, undertone
2 ***syn*** HINT 2, breath, dash, shade, soupçon, suspicion, tinge, touch, trace, whiff

whispering *n* ***syn*** REPORT 1, buzz, cry, gossip, grapevine, hearsay, rumble, rumor, scuttlebutt, talk

whist *adj* ***syn*** STILL 3, hush, hushful, noiseless, quiet, silent, soundless, stilly

whistle–stop *n* ***syn*** BURG, hick town, jerkwater town, mudhole, one-horse town, Podunk, tank town

whit *n* ***syn*** PARTICLE, atom, bit, damn, hoot, iota, jot, modicum, shred, whoop

white *adj* ***syn*** FAVORABLE 5, auspicious, benign, bright, dexter, fortunate, propitious
ant black

white *n* ***syn*** REACTIONARY, blimp, Bourbon, diehard, reactionarist, reactionist, royalist, ultraconservative
ant red

---

syn synonym(s) ***rel*** related word(s)
idiom idiomatic equivalent(s) ***con*** contrasted word(s)
ant antonym(s) * vulgar
‖ use limited; if in doubt, see a dictionary
The first word in a synonym list when printed in SMALL CAPITALS shows where there is more information about the group. For a more efficient use of this book see Explanatory Notes.

white *vb* **1** ***syn*** WHITEN 1, blanch, bleach, blench, decolor, decolorize
2 ***syn*** PALLIATE, blanch (over), extenuate, gloss (over), gloze (over), sugarcoat, varnish, veneer, whiten, whitewash

whited sepulcher *n* ***syn*** HYPOCRITE, dissembler, dissimulator, lip server, pharisee, Tartuffe

white–haired *adj* ***syn*** FAVORITE 1, beloved, blue-eyed, darling, dear, fair-haired, loved, pet, precious, white*headed

white–headed *adj* ***syn*** FAVORITE 1, beloved, blue-eyed, darling, dear, fair-haired, loved, pet, precious, white*haired

white–hot *adj* **1** ***syn*** HOT 1, baking, broiling, burning, fiery, heated, scalding, scorching, sizzling, torrid
2 ***syn*** IMPASSIONED, ardent, blazing, burning, fervid, fiery, flaming, glowing, passionate, red-hot

white lightning *n* ***syn*** MOONSHINE 2, bathtub gin, ‖blockade, bootleg, ‖busthead, ‖hooch, mountain dew

white–livered *adj* ***syn*** COWARDLY, ‖chicken, coward, craven, gutless, lily-livered, milk-livered, poltroon, spunkless, yellow

whiten *vb* **1** to free from color and make white or whiter < *whiten* linen in the sun >
syn blanch, bleach, blench, decolor, decolorize, white
rel dim, dull, fade, lighten, pale; etiolate; frost, grizzle, silver
con color, darken
ant blacken
2 ***syn*** PALLIATE, blanch (over), extenuate, gloss (over), gloze (over), sugarcoat, varnish, veneer, white, whitewash

white plague *n* ***syn*** TUBERCULOSIS, consumption, phthisis, TB

whitewash *vb* ***syn*** PALLIATE, blanch (over), extenuate, gloss (over), gloze (over), sugarcoat, varnish, veneer, white, whiten

whither *adv* **1** to what place < *whither* did they go? >
syn where, whereabouts, ‖whereaway
2 to what point, conclusion, or end < *whither* is our nation drifting? >
syn whereto, whereunto

whiz *vb* **1** ***syn*** HISS, buzz, fizz, fizzle, sibilate, sizzle, swish, wheeze, whisper, whoosh
2 ***syn*** HURRY 2, bullet, ‖dust, flit, fly, speed, whirl, whish, whisk, zip

whiz *n* ***syn*** EXPERT, adept, ‖dab, ‖dabster, master, past master, professional, virtuoso, wiz, wizard
ant dub, dud, duffer

whiz–bang *adj* ***syn*** EXCELLENT, bang-up, capital, ‖dandy, first-class, first-rate, first-string, five-star, top, top-notch

whizzer *n* ***syn*** TRICK 1, device, feint, gambit, gimmick, jig, play, ruse, stratagem, wile

whole *adj* **1** free from damage, defect, or flaw < feared the eggs were broken but found them *whole* >
syn entire, flawless, good, intact, perfect, sound, unblemished, unbroken, undamaged, unhurt, unimpaired, uninjured, unmarred, untouched
rel complete, plenary; healthy, well
con broken, damaged, defective, impaired, injured, marred
2 ***syn*** HEALTHY 1, ‖bunkum, fit, hale, right, sane, well, well-conditioned, well-liking, wholesome
3 lacking nothing that properly belongs to it < the effect of the *whole* mural >
syn choate, complete, entire, full, integral, perfect
rel orbicular, rounded, well-rounded
ant partial
4 including every constituent element or individual < the *whole* community rose to his defense >
syn all, complete, entire, gross, outright, total
ant partial
5 not scattered or dispersed < gave the matter his *whole* attention >
syn concentrated, exclusive, fixed, undistracted, undivided, unswerving

whole *n* **1** the total supply or amount < the *whole* of our creative literature >
syn aggregate, all, be-all and end-all, entirety, gross, sum, sum total, tale, total, totality, ‖tote
rel amount, supply; result, resultant, summation; bulk, mass, quantity, quantum
con detail, division, fraction, fragment, portion, section, segment, share
ant part
2 an organized array of parts or elements forming or functioning as a unit < stars, planets, galaxies — all but parts of one stupendous *whole*, the universe >
syn entity, integral, integrate, sum, system, totality; *compare* SYSTEM 1
rel being, organism, organization; coherence, cohesion, linkage; unity
con accumulation, aggregation, heap, pile, mass; section, segment; selection
ant part; agglomeration

wholehearted *adj* **1** ***syn*** SURE 2, abiding, enduring, never-failing, steadfast, steady, unfaltering, unqualified, unquestioning, unwavering
2 ***syn*** SINCERE 1, heartfelt, hearty, unfeigned, whole*souled
rel ardent, fervent, impassioned, passionate; earnest, serious; authentic, bona fide, genuine

whole–hog *adj* ***syn*** EXHAUSTIVE, complete, full-dress, thorough, thoroughgoing

whole–length *adj* ***syn*** UNABRIDGED, complete, unabbreviated, uncondensed, uncut, undocked

wholeness *n* **1** ***syn*** HEALTH, haleness, healthiness, soundness
rel integrity; heartiness, robustness, vigor
2 ***syn*** ENTIRETY 1, allness, completeness, entireness, oneness, totality
3 ***syn*** INTEGRITY 2, completeness, entireness, perfection

whole number *n* ***syn*** NUMBER, chiffer, cipher, digit, figure, integer, numeral

---

syn synonym(s) | ***rel*** related word(s)
idiom idiomatic equivalent(s) | ***con*** contrasted word(s)
ant antonym(s) | * vulgar
‖ use limited; if in doubt, see a dictionary
The first word in a synonym list when printed in SMALL CAPITALS shows where there is more information about the group. For a more efficient use of this book see Explanatory Notes.

wholesale *adj* ***syn*** INDISCRIMINATE 1, indiscriminating, indiscriminative, sweeping, undiscriminated, undiscriminating, undistinguishing

wholesome *adj* **1** ***syn*** HEALTHFUL, good, healthy, hygienic, salubrious, salutary, salutiferous
ant noxious; unwholesome
2 ***syn*** CURATIVE, curing, healing, remedial, remedying, restorative, sanative, sanatory, vulnerary
3 ***syn*** HEALTHY 1, ‖bunkum, fit, hale, right, sane, sound, well, well-conditioned, well-liking
4 ***syn*** SAFE 3, healthy, uninjurious
ant noxious

whole-souled *adj* ***syn*** SINCERE 1, heartfelt, hearty, unfeigned, wholehearted
rel ardent, fervent, impassioned; earnest, intense, serious

wholly *adv* **1** ***syn*** WELL 3, altogether, completely, entirely, fully, perfectly, quite, roundly, thoroughly, utterly
2 ***syn*** ALL 1, all in all, altogether, exactly, in toto, just, purely, quite, totally, utterly

whomp *vb* ***syn*** WHIP 2, beat, ‖clobber, drub, lambaste, shellac, smear, thrash, trounce, wallop

whoop *vb* ***syn*** SHOUT 1, cry, yell

whoop *n* ***syn*** PARTICLE, ace, damn, hoot, iota, jot, modicum, ray, shred, whit

whoop-de-do *n* ***syn*** REVELRY 2, high jinks, revel, revelment, skylarking, wassail, whoopee, whoopla, whoop-up

whoopee *n* **1** ***syn*** REVELRY 2, high jinks, revel, revelment, skylarking, wassail, whoop-de-do, whoopla, whoop-up
2 ***syn*** MERRYMAKING, festivity, gaiety, jollity, merriment, revel, reveling, revelment, revelry

whoopla *n* **1** ***syn*** COMMOTION 4, clamor, hassle, hurly-burly, pother, to-do, tumult, turmoil, uproar, whirl
2 ***syn*** REVELRY 2, high jinks, revel, revelment, skylarking, wassail, whoop-de-do, whoopee, whoop-up

whoop-up *n* ***syn*** REVELRY 2, high jinks, revel, revelment, skylarking, wassail, whoop-de-do, whoopee, whoopla

whoosh *vb* ***syn*** HISS, buzz, fizz, fizzle, sibilate, sizzle, swish, wheeze, whisper, whiz

whop *vb* ***syn*** BEAT 1, baste, batter, belabor, buffet, drub, hammer, lambaste, pound, pummel

whop *n* ***syn*** BLOW 1, bash, bat, biff, bop, smack, sock, thwack, wallop, whack

whopping *adj* ***syn*** HUGE, colossal, enormous, gargantuan, gigantic, immense, mighty, prodigious, whacking, whaling

whopping *adv* ***syn*** VERY 1, ‖awful, awfully, ‖big, damned, exceedingly, highly, hugely, much, whacking

syn synonym(s) ***rel*** related word(s)
idiom idiomatic equivalent(s) ***con*** contrasted word(s)
ant antonym(s) * vulgar
‖ use limited; if in doubt, see a dictionary
The first word in a synonym list when printed in SMALL CAPITALS shows where there is more information about the group. For a more efficient use of this book see Explanatory Notes.

whore *n* **1** ***syn*** HARLOT 1, blowen, courtesan, demimondaine, demimonde, demirep, fancy woman, hetaera, kept woman, paphian
2 ***syn*** PROSTITUTE, bawd, call girl, drab, harlot, ‖hooker, meretrix, moll, nightwalker, streetwalker

whoredom *n* ***syn*** PROSTITUTION, harlotry, oldest profession, (the) social evil, streetwalking

whorehouse *n* ***syn*** BROTHEL, bagnio, bawdy house, bordello, cathouse, ‖hookshop, ‖joyhouse, parlor house, sporting house, stew

whoreson *n* ***syn*** BASTARD 1, by-blow, catch colt, chance child, come-by-chance, filius nullius, illegitimate, love child, natural child, woods colt

whorish *adj* ***syn*** FAST 7, easy, light, loose, ‖riggish, unchaste, wanton

whorl *vb* ***syn*** SWIRL, eddy, gurge, purl, swoosh, whirl, whirlpool

who's who *n* ***syn*** ARISTOCRACY, elite, flower, gentility, gentry, optimacy, quality, society, upper class, upper crust

why *n* **1** ***syn*** REASON 3, argument, ground, proof, wherefore, whyfor
2 ***syn*** MYSTERY, Chinese puzzle, closed book, conundrum, enigma, mystification, puzzle, puzzlement, riddle

whyfor *n* ***syn*** REASON 3, argument, ground, proof, wherefore, why

wicked *adj* **1** ***syn*** WRONG 1, bad, evil, immoral, iniquitous, reprobate, sinful, vicious
ant upright
2 ***syn*** PLAYFUL 1, antic, impish, larkish, ‖mischiefful, mischievous, prankful, prankish, pranky, roguish
3 ***syn*** RISQUÉ, blue, broad, off-color, purple, racy, salty, shady, spicy, suggestive
4 ***syn*** MALICIOUS, despiteful, evil, hateful, malevolent, malign, malignant, rancorous, spiteful, vicious
5 ***syn*** DANGEROUS 1, chancy, hairy, hazardous, jeopardous, perilous, risky, treacherous, unhealthy, unsound
6 ***syn*** TROUBLESOME, mean, pesky, troublous, ugly, vexatious
7 ***syn*** OUTRAGEOUS 1, barbarous, unchristian, uncivilized, unconscionable, ungodly, unholy
8 ***syn*** SKILLFUL 2, adroit, clever, good, pretty, ‖skilly, workmanlike, workmanly
9 ***syn*** ABLE, au fait, capable, competent, good, proper, qualified

wickedness *n* **1** ***syn*** EVIL 2, debt, sin, wrong
2 ***syn*** VICE 1, corruption, depravity, immorality

wide *adj* **1** ***syn*** SPACIOUS, ample, capacious, commodious, roomy
2 ***syn*** EXTENSIVE 1, broad, expansive, extended, scopic, scopious
3 ***syn*** LIBERAL 3, advanced, broad, broad-minded, progressive, radical, tolerant

wide-awake *adj* ***syn*** WATCHFUL, alert, open-eyed, unsleeping, vigilant, wakeful
rel alive, awake, aware, conscious, sensible

widen *vb* ***syn*** BROADEN, breadthen

wideness *n* ***syn*** BREADTH 2, amplitude, comprehensiveness, fullness, scope

widespread *adj* ***syn*** PREVAILING, current, popular, prevalent, rampant, regnant, rife, ruling

widget *n* ***syn*** GADGET 1, concern, gimmick, gizmo, jigger

width *n* ***syn*** RANGE 2, ambit, circle, compass, extension, length, orbit, panorama, radius, scope

wield *vb* **1** ***syn*** HANDLE 2, dispense, maneuver, manipulate, ply, swing
rel conduct, control
2 ***syn*** EXERT, exercise, ply, put out, throw

wieldy *adj* ***syn*** STRONG 1, mighty, powerful, ‖strengthy

wiener *n* ***syn*** FRANKFURTER, dog, frank, hot dog, ‖wienie, wienerwurst

wienerwurst *n* ***syn*** FRANKFURTER, dog, frank, hot dog, wiener, ‖wienie

‖**wienie** *n* ***syn*** FRANKFURTER, dog, frank, hot dog, wiener, wienerwurst

wife *n* the female partner in a marriage < *wives* unwilling to share responsibility >
syn ‖ball and chain, lady, ‖little woman, ‖missus, Mrs., ‖old lady, ‖old woman, ‖rib, ‖squaw, woman
rel consort, helpmate, helpmeet, mate, other half, spouse; bride, dowager, matron; concubine
idiom better half
con maid, maiden; widow

wig *n* ***syn*** REBUKE, admonishment, admonition, chiding, rap, reprimand, reproach, reproof

wig *vb* ***syn*** SCOLD 1, bawl out, berate, ‖chew out, jaw, rail, rate, revile, tongue-lash, upbraid

wiggle *vb* ***syn*** WRIGGLE, squiggle, squirm, worm, writhe

wiggle–waggle *adj* ***syn*** VACILLATING 2, faltering, halting, hesitant, irresolute, shilly-shallying, tentative, uncertain, vacillatory, wobbly

wiggle–waggle *vb* ***syn*** HESITATE, dither, falter, halt, shilly-shally, stagger, vacillate, waver, whiffle

wiggy *adj* ***syn*** POMPOUS 1, arrogant, bloated, important, magisterial, pontifical, puffy, self-important, stuffy

wight *n* ***syn*** HUMAN, being, body, creature, individual, man, mortal, person, personage, soul

wild *adj* **1** living and growing in a state of nature and without human intervention <lived on *wild* plants and game animals>
syn agrarian, agrestal, native, natural, uncultivated, undomesticated; *compare* SAVAGE 1
rel escaped, feral; unsubdued, untamed
ant cultivated, domesticated
2 ***syn*** SAVAGE 1, feral, vicious
ant tame, tamed
3 ***syn*** IRRESPONSIBLE, carefree, careless, feckless, incautious, reckless, uncareful
rel adventurous, audacious, daring, dashing; brash, cocksure, rash
4 ***syn*** FURIOUS 2, corybantic, delirious, frantic, frenetic, frenzied, mad, rabid
rel bewildered, distracted, perplexed; agitated, perturbed, upset; addled, confused, muddled; crazy, demented, deranged, mad
con easy, relaxed
5 ***syn*** UNRULY 1, fractious, intractable, recalcitrant, uncontrollable, undisciplinable, undisciplined, ungovernable, unmanageable, untoward
6 marked by turmoil and fury especially of natural elements <a *wild* night of howling winds and driving snow>
syn blustering, blustery, ‖coarse, dirty, furious, raging, rough, stormful, stormy, tempestuous, turbulent
rel blatant, boisterous, clamorous, ungovernable, unruly; brutal, harsh, severe
con calm, peaceful, placid, quiet, stormless; halcyon, irenic, serene
7 given to unrestrained self-indulgence and pursuit of pleasure <her son got in with a *wild* bunch and took to drink>
syn devil-may-care, fast, gay, raffish, rakehell, rakish, sporty
rel boisterous, roisterous, rollicking, swaggering; careless, heedless, irresponsible, thoughtless; lewd, loose, unchaste, wanton
con moderate, restrained, sober, sparing, temperate; bridled, controlled, curbed; self-controlled
8 ***syn*** EXTRAVAGANT 1, fantastic, preposterous
9 ***syn*** BARBARIAN 1, barbaric, barbarous, Gothic, Hunnish, rude, savage, uncivil, uncivilized, uncultivated
ant cultivated, cultured
10 ***syn*** BARBARIC 1, barbarian, barbarous, graceless, outlandish, tasteless, vulgar

wild *n* ***syn*** WASTE 1, badland, barren, desert, wasteland, wilderness, wild land, wildness

wilderness *n* ***syn*** WASTE 1, badland, barren, desert, wasteland, wild, wild land, wildness
rel backcountry, backland(s), hinterland
idiom back of beyond

wild land *n* ***syn*** WASTE 1, badland, barren, desert, wasteland, wild, wilderness, wildness

wildly *adv* ***syn*** HARD 2, fiercely, frantically, frenziedly, furiously, madly, stormily, tumultuously, turbulently, violently

wildness *n* ***syn*** WASTE 1, badland, barren, desert, wasteland, wild, wilderness, wild land

wile *n* ***syn*** TRICK 1, artifice, device, feint, gambit, gimmick, maneuver, ploy, ruse, stratagem
rel chicane, chicanery, trickery; cunning, deceit, dissimulation, guile
con candor, frankness, openness, plain dealing, straightforwardness, unconstraint; artlessness, naturalness, sincerity

wile *vb* **1** ***syn*** ATTRACT 1, allure, bewitch, captivate, charm, draw, enchant, fascinate, magnetize, take
2 ***syn*** WHILE, beguile, fleet

wiliness *n* ***syn*** CUNNING 2, art, artfulness, artifice, cageyness, canniness, craft, craftiness, foxiness, slyness

will *vb* to be inclined <you may decide whichever way you *will*>
syn choose, elect, like, please, wish
rel crave, desire, want
idiom have a mind to, see (*or* think) fit

will *n* **1** a desire to act in a particular way or have a particular thing <I've no *will* to be sociable tonight>
syn fancy, inclination, liking, mind, pleasure, velleity
rel appetite, desire, passion, urge; hankering, longing, pining, yearning
idiom heart's desire

---

syn synonym(s) ***rel*** related word(s)
idiom idiomatic equivalent(s) ***con*** contrasted word(s)
ant antonym(s) * vulgar
‖ use limited; if in doubt, see a dictionary
The first word in a synonym list when printed in SMALL CAPITALS shows where there is more information about the group. For a more efficient use of this book see Explanatory Notes.

con aversion, dislike, distaste, repugnance, repulsion, revulsion
2 the aspect of mind involved in choosing or deciding <problems arise when one's *will* and judgment come in conflict>
syn volition
rel design, intent, purpose, wishes; character, disposition, temper
3 power of controlling one's actions, impulses, or emotions <a self-indulgent man of feeble character and little *will*>
syn discipline, self-command, self-control, self-discipline, self-government, self-mastery, self-restraint, willpower
rel aplomb, assurance, confidence, poise, self-possession; control, discretion, restraint
con gratification, indulgence, self-indulgence

will *vb* to give to another by will <*will* family treasures to a relative>
syn bequeath, devise, leave, legate

willful *adj* **1** ***syn*** OBSTINATE, headstrong, intractable, mulish, pertinacious, perverse, pigheaded, self-willed, stiff-necked, wrongheaded
rel contumacious, factious
idiom having the bit in one's teeth, not yielding an inch
con amenable, docile, obedient, tractable
ant biddable
2 ***syn*** VOLUNTARY, deliberate, intentional, unforced, unprescribed, willing, witting
rel intentional, purposive; decided, determined, resolved; dogged, obstinate, pertinacious, stubborn
con accidental, chance, involuntary, unintentional, unplanned

willies *n pl* ***syn*** JITTERS, ‖all-overs, dither, heebie-jeebies, ‖jimjams, ‖jimmies, jumps, shakes, shivers, whim-whams

willing *adj* **1** prepared in mind or by disposition <*willing* to help>
syn disposed, fair, inclined, minded, predisposed, prone, ready
rel agreeable, compliant, favorable; forward, game, prompt
idiom in the mood
con averse, disinclined, indisposed, loath, reluctant, unminded
ant unwilling
2 ***syn*** VOLUNTARY, deliberate, intentional, unforced, unprescribed, willful, witting
rel disposed, inclined, predisposed; open, prone

will–less *adj* ***syn*** SPONTANEOUS, automatic, impulsive, instinctive, involuntary, unmeditated, unpremeditated, unprompted

---

syn synonym(s) *rel* related word(s)
idiom idiomatic equivalent(s) *con* contrasted word(s)
ant antonym(s) * vulgar
‖ use limited; if in doubt, see a dictionary
The first word in a synonym list when printed in SMALL CAPITALS shows where there is more information about the group. For a more efficient use of this book see Explanatory Notes.

willpower *n* ***syn*** WILL 3, discipline, self-command, self-control, self-discipline, self-government, self-mastery, self-restraint

willy–nilly *adv* surely and without regard to plans or inclination <it seems that we must drift *willy-nilly* toward disaster>
syn helplessly, inescapably, inevitably, perforce, unavoidably, whether or no
idiom as a matter of course, come what may, of necessity, without let or choice

‖**willy–willy** *n* ***syn*** HURRICANE, tropical cyclone, tropical storm, typhoon

wilt *vb* **1** ***syn*** WITHER, dry up, mummify, mummy, shrivel, welter, wizen
2 ***syn*** COLLAPSE 2, break down, cave (in), drop, ‖flake out, give out, peg out, succumb
3 ***syn*** DROOP 3, flag, sag, swag

wily *adj* ***syn*** SLY 2, artful, astute, crafty, cunning, deep, foxy, guileful, insidious, tricky
rel sagacious, shrewd; clever, knowing
con aboveboard, forthright, straightforward; guileless, open, trusting

win *vb* **1** to gain the victory <the home team *won* by a wide margin>
syn beat, overcome, prevail, triumph; *compare* CONQUER 1
idiom bear off the palm (*or* prize), bring home the bacon, carry the day, come out first (*or* ahead), finish in front
ant lose
2 ***syn*** GAIN 1, accomplish, achieve, attain, rack up, reach, realize, score
3 ***syn*** EARN 1, acquire, bring in, ‖drag down, draw down, gain, get, knock down, make
rel produce, yield
4 ***syn*** GET 1, acquire, annex, chalk up, gain, have, obtain, pick up, procure, secure
ant lose

win (over) *vb* **1** ***syn*** DISARM 2, unarm, unsteel
2 ***syn*** INDUCE 1, argue (into), bring around, convince, draw, get, persuade, prevail (on *or* upon), prompt, talk (into)

win *n* ***syn*** VICTORY 1, conquest, triumph

wince *vb* ***syn*** RECOIL, blanch, blench, flinch, quail, shrink, squinch, start
rel dodge, duck, jib, sheer, swerve, turn; cower, cringe

wind *n* **1** ***syn*** NOTHING 1, naught (*or* nought), nil, ‖nix
2 ***syn*** HINT 1, clue, cue, indication, inkling, intimation, notion, suggestion, telltale

wind *vb* ***syn*** BLOW 1, fan, ruffle, winnow

wind *vb* **1** ***syn*** DEFORM, contort, distort, misshape, torture, warp
2 to follow a circular, spiral, or writhing course <the vine *wound* its way up the pillar>
syn coil, corkscrew, curl, entwine, spiral, twine, twist, wreathe; *compare* CURVE
rel bend, curve, meander, weave; circle, encircle, enlace, gird, girdle, surround; enclose, envelop

windbaggery *n* ***syn*** NONSENSE 2, balderdash, bash, blather, double-talk, ‖gas, hooey, hot air, malarkey, poppycock

windiness *n* ***syn*** VERBOSITY, prolixity, prolixness, verbalism, verboseness, wordiness

winding *adj* curving repeatedly first one way then another <a *winding* country road>
syn anfractuous, convoluted, flexuous, meandering, meandrous, serpentine, sinuous, snaky, tortuous; *compare* CROOKED 1
rel bending, curving, twisting; crooked, devious; circuitous, indirect, roundabout
con direct, straight

window dressing *n* ***syn*** MASK 2, color, coloring, disguise, facade, face, front, put-on, show, veneer

windrow *n* ***syn*** PILE 1, bank, drift, heap, hill, mass, mound, mountain, pyramid, stack

wind up *vb* **1** ***syn*** CLOSE 3, complete, conclude, determine, do, end, finish, halt, terminate, wrap up
2 ***syn*** SETTLE 7, clean up

windup *n* ***syn*** FINALE, close, conclusion, end, ending, finish

windy *adj* **1** marked by more wind than usual <a *windy* March day>
syn airy, blowy, breezy, gusty
rel brisk, fresh; drafty
con breathless, motionless, still
ant windless
2 ***syn*** INFLATED, dropsical, dropsied, flatulent, overblown, tumescent, tumid, turgid
3 ***syn*** WORDY, diffuse, long-winded, palaverous, prolix, redundant, verbose

wing *n* ***syn*** ANNEX, arm, block, ell, extension
rel expansion, prolongation; bulge, projection, protrusion, protuberance

wing *vb* ***syn*** FLY 4, fleet, flit, sail, sweep

wink *vb* to close and open the eyelids quickly <*winking* involuntarily as the light struck his eyes>
syn bat, blink, nictate, nictitate, twinkle
rel squinch, squinny, squint; flutter

wink (at) *vb* ***syn*** CONNIVE 1, blink (at)

wink *n* **1** ***syn*** INSTANT 1, minute, moment, second, shake, split second, ‖tick, trice, twinkle, twinkling
2 ***syn*** HINT 2, dash, intimation, shade, smack, soupçon, suggestion, suspicion, touch, trace

winker *n* ***syn*** EYE 1, lamp, ocular, oculus, ‖ogle, orb, peeper

winner *n* ***syn*** VICTOR 2
ant loser

winning *adj* ***syn*** SWEET 1, dulcet, engaging, winsome

winnow *vb* **1** ***syn*** BLOW 1, fan, ruffle, wind
2 ***syn*** SORT 2, comb, separate, sift

winsome *adj* ***syn*** SWEET 1, dulcet, engaging, winning
rel adorable, lovable, lovesome

wipe (out) *vb* **1** ***syn*** ERASE, annul, black (out), blot out, cancel, delete, efface, expunge, obliterate, x (out)
2 ***syn*** ANNIHILATE 2, abate, abolish, blot out, eradicate, exterminate, extinguish, extirpate, root out, uproot
3 ***syn*** SLAUGHTER 3, annihilate, decimate, exterminate, massacre

wipe *n* **1** ***syn*** HIT 1, ‖conk, knock, lick, rap, swat, swipe
‖**2** ***syn*** HANDKERCHIEF, hankie, kerchief, *snot-rag, ‖wiper

‖**wiped out** *adj* ***syn*** DRUGGED, doped, high, hopped-up, spaced-out, stoned, tripped out, turned on, zonked

‖**wiper** *n* ***syn*** HANDKERCHIEF, hankie, kerchief, *snot-rag, ‖wipe

‖**wire** *n* ***syn*** PICKPOCKET, ‖cannon, cutpurse, ‖dip, ‖diver, purse cutter

wiredraw *vb* ***syn*** THIN 1, attenuate, extenuate

wiry *adj* ***syn*** MUSCULAR 1, fibrous, ropy, sinewy, stringy

wisdom *n* **1** ***syn*** KNOWLEDGE 2, information, lore, science
2 ***syn*** SAGACITY, insight, sagaciousness, sageness, sapience
3 ***syn*** SENSE 6, common sense, good sense, gumption, horse sense, judgment
rel judiciousness, sageness, saneness, sapience; perspicacity, sagacity, shrewdness
ant folly

wise *n* ***syn*** METHOD 1, fashion, manner, mode, modus, system, technique, way

wise *adj* **1** having or exhibiting a capacity for discernment and the intelligent application of knowledge <to be *wise* is to use knowledge well>
syn discerning, gnostic, insighted, insightful, knowing, knowledgeable, perceptive, sagacious, sage, sophic, wisehearted
rel aware, grasping, intuitive, sensing; acute, keen, perspicacious; cogitative, contemplative, reflective, thoughtful; astute, sharp, shrewd
con dull, obtuse, slow, slow-witted; insensitive, unaware, unknowing
ant unwise
2 exercising or involving sound judgment <*wise* management of scarce resources>
syn judgmatic, judicious, prudent, sage, sane, sapient, sensible; *compare* SHREWD
rel canny, discreet, foresighted, provident; astute, perspicacious, sagacious, shrewd; alert, bright, intelligent, keen, smart
con careless, heedless, injudicious; improvident, imprudent, indiscreet, short-sighted
ant foolish, unwise
3 ***syn*** EXPEDIENT, advisable, politic, prudent, tactical
4 shrewdly aware and subtly resourceful <a *wise* operator with his eye always on the main chance>
syn canny, hep, knowing, nimble-witted, quick, quick-witted, sharp, sharp-witted, slick, smart; *compare* INTELLIGENT 2, SHREWD
rel cagey, foresighted, shrewd; artful, crafty, cunning, slippery, smooth, tricky, wily; steel-trap
idiom in the groove, not born yesterday, on the beam
con narrow, prim, puritanical, straitlaced; conservative, plodding, ‖square
5 presumptuously confident and self-assured <a bunch of *wise* kids tearing up the neighborhood>
syn ‖biggety, bold, bold-faced, cheeky, forward, fresh, impudent, nervy, pert, procacious, sassy, smart, smart-alecky

---

syn synonym(s) — ***rel*** related word(s)
idiom idiomatic equivalent(s) — ***con*** contrasted word(s)
ant antonym(s) — * vulgar
‖ use limited; if in doubt, see a dictionary
The first word in a synonym list when printed in SMALL CAPITALS shows where there is more information about the group. For a more efficient use of this book see Explanatory Notes.

rel arrogant, brash, cocky, insolent; flip, flippant, impertinent, lippy, saucy
con demure, mannerly, modest, proper; dull, priggish, stuffy

wise (up) *vb* ***syn*** INFORM 2, acquaint, advise, apprise, clue (*or* clew), fill in, notify, post, tell, warn

wiseacre *n* ***syn*** SMART ALECK, know-it-all, *smartass, smarty, smarty-pants, wisecracker, wise guy, wisehead, wisenheimer

wisecrack *n* ***syn*** JOKE 1, crack, gag, jape, jest, quip, sally, waggery, witticism, ‖yak

wisecracker *n* ***syn*** SMART ALECK, know-it-all, *smartass, smarty, smarty-pants, wiseacre, wise guy, wisehead, wisenheimer

wise guy *n* ***syn*** SMART ALECK, know-it-all, *smartass, smarty, smarty-pants, wiseacre, wisecracker, wisehead, wisenheimer

wisehead *n* ***syn*** SMART ALECK, know-it-all, *smartass, smarty, smarty-pants, wiseacre, wisecracker, wise guy, wisenheimer

wisehearted *adj* ***syn*** WISE 1, discerning, gnostic, insighted, insightful, knowing, knowledgeable, perceptive, sagacious, sage

wise man *n* ***syn*** SAGE, savant, scholar

wisenheimer *n* ***syn*** SMART ALECK, know-it-all, *smartass, smarty, smarty-pants, wiseacre, wisecracker, wise guy, wisehead

wish *vb* **1** ***syn*** DESIRE 1, ‖choose, covet, crave, desiderate, want
rel expect, hope; fancy
2 ***syn*** WILL, choose, elect, like, please
3 ***syn*** IMPOSE 4, foist

wishy–washy *adj* **1** ***syn*** INSIPID 3, banal, bland, jejune, milk-and-water, namby-pamby, sapless, vapid, waterish, watery
rel enervated, languid, listless, spiritless; flavorless, savorless
idiom neither flesh, fowl, nor good red herring, neither one thing nor the other
2 ***syn*** CHARACTERLESS, namby-pamby, pantywaist

wistful *adj* ***syn*** PENSIVE 2, meditative, ‖pensy

‖**wit** *vb* ***syn*** UNDERSTAND 3, assume, believe, ‖conceit, conceive, gather, imagine, ‖reckon, suppose, think

wit *n* **1** ***syn*** MIND 1, brain, gray matter, head, ‖upper story, ‖upperworks
rel perspicacity, sagacity; apprehension, awareness, comprehension
2 *often* **wits** *pl* mental soundness and health <frightened nearly out of her *wits*>
syn lucidity, ‖marbles, mind, reason, saneness, sanity, sense(s), soundnesss
rel balance, rationality
con aberration; craziness, derangement, insanity, lunacy, madness, mania
ant witlessness
3 acuteness of perception or judgment <had the *wit* to know that he was out of his depth in such a discussion>
syn acumen, astucity, astuteness, clear-sightedness, discernment, discrimination, keenness, penetration, percipience, perspicacity, shrewdness; *compare* PRUDENCE 1
rel awareness, comprehension, grasp, insight, perception, understanding; prudence, sagaciousness, sagacity, sageness, sapience, wisdom; clairvoyance, divination, ESP, sensing
con aridity, dullness, prosaicness, unimaginativeness; fatuity, foolishness, inanity, silliness, stupidity
4 ***syn*** INTELLIGENCE 1, brain(s), brainpower, mentality, mother wit, sense
5 a talent for banter or persiflage <a jolly man, noted for his kindly *wit*>
syn esprit, humor
rel alertness, keenness, quick-wittedness; brilliance, cleverness, intelligence, smartness
6 ***syn*** HUMOR 5
7 ***syn*** HUMORIST 2, comedian, comic, droll, funnyman, jester, joker, jokester, quipster, wag

witch *n* **1** a woman who practices the black arts <ancient laws against *witches*>
syn bruja, enchantress, hag, hex, lamia, sorceress, witchwoman; *compare* MAGICIAN 1
2 ***syn*** HAG 2, ‖bag, ‖bat, beldam, biddy, crone, drab, trot

witch *vb* ***syn*** BEWITCH 1, charm, enchant, ensorcell, hex, spell, voodoo

witchcraft *n* **1** ***syn*** MAGIC 1, bewitchment, conjuring, enchantment, incantation, necromancy, sorcery, thaumaturgy, witchery, wizardry
2 ***syn*** CHARM 3, allure, appeal, charisma, fascination, glamour, magnetism, witchery

witchery *n* **1** ***syn*** MAGIC 1, bewitchment, conjuring, enchantment, incantation, magicking, necromancy, sorcery, witchcraft, wizardry
2 ***syn*** CHARM 3, allure, appeal, charisma, fascination, glamour, magnetism, witchcraft

witching *n* ***syn*** MAGIC 1, bewitchment, conjuring, enchantment, ensorcellment, incantation, necromancy, sorcery, witchcraft, witchery

witchwoman *n* ***syn*** WITCH 1, bruja, enchantress, hag, hex, lamia, sorceress

witchy *adj* ***syn*** MAGIC, magian, magical, mystic, necromantic, sorcerous, thaumaturgic, wizardly

with *prep* **1** ***syn*** OVER 3, about, on, upon
2 ***syn*** FOR 2, in favor of, pro
3 ***syn*** VIA 2, by, by dint of, by means of, by virtue of, by way of, per, through

withal *adv* **1** ***syn*** ALSO 2, additionally, as well, besides, furthermore, more, moreover, too, yea, yet
2 ***syn*** HOWEVER, after all, howbeit, nevertheless, nonetheless, notwithstanding, per contra, still, though, yet

withdraw *vb* **1** ***syn*** REMOVE 2, take away, take off, take out
ant deposit
2 ***syn*** ABJURE, forswear, palinode, recall, recant, retract, take back, unsay
3 ***syn*** GO 2, ‖blow, depart, exit, get away, get off, leave, quit, retire, run along

rel quail, recoil, retreat, shrink; recede
idiom give ground, give way
con advance, progress; arrive, come
4 *syn* RETREAT 2, fall back, give back, retire
ant advance

withdrawal *n syn* DEPARTURE 1, egress, egression, exit, exiting, exodus, offgoing, setting-out
ant approach

withdrawn *adj* **1** *syn* UNDEMONSTRATIVE, aseptic, restrained, retiring, shrinking, unaffable, unexpansive
ant outgiving
2 *syn* INDIFFERENT 2, aloof, casual, detached, disinterested, incurious, remote, unconcerned, uncurious, uninterested
3 *syn* UNSOCIABLE, aloof, cool, distant, insociable, offish, reserved, solitary, standoffish, uncompanionable
ant outgoing

wither *vb* to lose substance and freshness by or as if by loss of natural moisture <projects that *wither* and die from lack of popular interest>
syn dry up, mummify, mummy, shrivel, welter, wilt, wizen
rel cave in, collapse, deflate, fold; constrict, contract, shrink; decline, wane
con freshen, revive, revivify; develop, grow, increase, wax
ant flourish

withhold *vb* **1** *syn* RESTRAIN 1, bit, bridle, check, constrain, curb, hold back, hold down, hold in, inhibit
2 *syn* KEEP 5, detain, hold, hold back, keep back, keep out, reserve, retain
con award, concede, grant, vouchsafe
ant accord
3 *syn* DENY 2, disallow, keep back, refuse
4 *syn* REFRAIN 1, abstain, forbear, keep

within *adv syn* INDOORS, inside, withindoors, withinside
ant without

within *n syn* INTERIOR, inside, inward(s)
ant without

withindoors *adv syn* INDOORS, inside, within, withinside
ant withoutdoors

withinside *adv syn* INDOORS, inside, within, withindoors
ant withoutside

with–it *adj syn* STYLISH, a la mode, fashionable, in, modish, swank, swish, tonish, tony, ‖trendy

without *prep* **1** *syn* BEYOND 1, after, outside, past
2 not having <living *without* decent housing or adequate food>
syn awanting, lacking, minus, sans, wanting

without *adv syn* OUTDOORS, out, out of doors, outside, withoutdoors
ant within

without *n syn* OUTDOORS, open, open air, out-of-doors, outside

‖**without** *conj syn* EXCEPT 1, but, save, saving, unless

withoutdoors *adv syn* OUTDOORS, out, out of doors, outside, without
ant indoors, withindoors

with respect to *prep syn* APROPOS, as for, as regards, as respects, as to, concerning, re, regarding, respecting, touching

withstand *vb syn* RESIST, buck, combat, contest, dispute, duel, fight, oppose, repel, traverse
rel bear, endure, stand, suffer, tolerate
con capitulate, submit, yield

witless *adj* **1** *syn* SIMPLE 3, asinine, brainless, mindless, nitwitted, senseless, silly, unwitty, weak-headed, weak-minded
2 *syn* INSANE 1, ‖batty, bedlamite, cracked, crazed, crazy, daft, demented, deranged, reasonless

witlessness *n syn* FOOLISHNESS, absurdity, craziness, dottiness, folly, inanity, insanity, preposterousness, senselessness, silliness

witness *n* **1** *syn* TESTIMONY, attestation, confirmation, evidence, proof, testament, testimonial
2 *syn* SPECTATOR, beholder, by-sitter, bystander, eyewitness, looker-on, observer, onlooker, viewer, watcher

witness *vb* **1** *syn* CERTIFY 1, attest, vouch
rel affirm; endorse, subscribe
2 *syn* INDICATE 2, announce, argue, attest, bespeak, betoken, testify

witticism *n syn* JOKE 1, crack, drollery, gag, jape, jest, quip, waggery, wisecrack, ‖yak

wittiness *n syn* HUMOR 4, comedy, comicality, comicalness, drollery, drollness, funniness, humorousness

witting *adj* **1** *syn* AWARE, alive, apprehensive, awake, cognizant, conscious, knowing, sensible, sentient, ware
ant unwitting
2 *syn* VOLUNTARY, deliberate, intentional, unforced, unprescribed, willful, willing
ant unwitting

witty *adj* provoking or intended to provoke mirth <a whimsical *witty* discussion on the foreignness of honesty to politics>
syn facetious, humorous, jocose, jocular
rel amusing, diverting, entertaining; scintillating, sparkling; penetrating, piercing, probing; funny, ridiculous, risible
con foolish, senseless, silly; brash, cheeky, fresh; earnest, serious, sober, solemn
ant unwitty

wiz *n syn* EXPERT, artist, authority, master, past master, professional, proficient, virtuoso, whiz, wizard
ant dub, dud, duffer

wizard *n* **1** *syn* MAGICIAN 1, archimage, conjurer, enchanter, mage, magician, magus, necromancer, sorcerer, warlock
2 *syn* EXPERT, artist, authority, master, past master, professional, proficient, virtuoso, whiz, wiz
ant dub, dud, duffer

wizardly *adj syn* MAGIC, magian, magical, mystic, necromantic, sorcerous, thaumaturgic, witchy

wizardry *n syn* MAGIC 1, bewitchment, conjuring, enchantment, incantation, magicking, necromancy, sorcery, witchcraft, witchery

---

syn synonym(s) — *rel* related word(s)
idiom idiomatic equivalent(s) — *con* contrasted word(s)
ant antonym(s) — * vulgar
‖ use limited; if in doubt, see a dictionary
The first word in a synonym list when printed in SMALL CAPITALS shows where there is more information about the group. For a more efficient use of this book see Explanatory Notes.

wizen *vb* ***syn*** WITHER, dry up, mummify, mummy, shrivel, welter, wilt

rel decrease, diminish, dwindle, reduce

wobble *vb* **1** ***syn*** LURCH 2, careen, stagger, ‖stoit, ‖stoiter, ‖stot, sway, swing, weave

2 ***syn*** TEETER, falter, lurch, stagger, ‖stammer, stumble, topple, totter

3 ***syn*** SHAKE, dither, quake, quaver, quiver, shimmy, shiver, shudder, teeter, totter

wobbly *adj* **1** ***syn*** RICKETY, rachitic, rackety, rattletrap, shaky

2 ***syn*** WEAK 2, dickey, fluctuant, insecure, rootless, shaky, unstable, unsure, vacillating, wavering

3 ***syn*** VACILLATING 2, faltering, halting, hesitant, irresolute, shilly-shallying, tentative, uncertain, vacillatory, wiggle-waggle

woe *n* **1** ***syn*** SORROW, affliction, anguish, care, ‖dole, grief, heartache, heartbreak, regret, rue

rel bemoaning, bewailing, deploring, lamentation

con bliss, felicity, happiness

2 ***syn*** MISERY 1, unhappiness, wretchedness

3 *usu* **woes** *pl* ***syn*** DISASTER, calamity, cataclysm, catastrophe, misadventure, tragedy

woebegone *adj* **1** ***syn*** DOWNCAST, blue, crestfallen, dejected, depressed, disconsolate, dispirited, down, downhearted, low

rel lugubrious, melancholy

con alert, concerned, interested, spirited; lively, vigorous; avid, eager, keen

2 ***syn*** GLOOMY 3, black, bleak, depressing, dismal, dispiriting, dreary, funereal, oppressive, tenebrific

rel dilapidated, outworn, shabby, worn

con bright, crisp, fresh, gay

woeful *adj* **1** full of or expressive of woe <a *woeful* countenance>

syn afflicted, doleful, dolent, dolorous, miserable, rueful, ruthful, sorrowful, wretched

rel harrowed, racked, tortured, wrung; crushed, overcome, stricken; disconsolate, heartsick, inconsolable; dejected, depressed, dispirited, downcast, downhearted, low-spirited

idiom cut to the heart, cut up, in the dumps (*or* depths *or* doldrums), on the rack

con content, satisfied; easy, peaceful, quiet; cheerful, gay, lighthearted

ant joyful

2 ***syn*** MELANCHOLY 2, doleful, dolesome, dolorous, lamentable, lugubrious, mournful, plaintive, rueful, sorrowful

3 ***syn*** DEPLORABLE, afflictive, calamitous, dire, distressing, grievous, heartbreaking, lamentable, regrettable, unfortunate

rel dismal, grave, sad; unprecedented

woggle *vb* ***syn*** WAG, beat, lash, switch, waggle, wave

---

syn synonym(s) *rel* related word(s)
idiom idiomatic equivalent(s) *con* contrasted word(s)
ant antonym(s) * vulgar
‖ use limited; if in doubt, see a dictionary
The first word in a synonym list when printed in SMALL CAPITALS shows where there is more information about the group. For a more efficient use of this book see Explanatory Notes.

---

wolf *n* a man forward, direct, and zealous in amorous pursuit of women <known far and wide as a lecherous old *wolf*>

syn Casanova, chaser, Don Juan, ladies' man, lady-killer, masher, philander, philanderer, womanizer

rel amorist; lecher, libertine, Lothario, profligate, rip, roué, rounder

idiom man on the make, skirt chaser

wolf *vb* **1** ***syn*** GULP, bolt, cram, englut, gobble, guzzle, ingurgitate, slop, slosh

2 ***syn*** PHILANDER, fool (around), mess around, play (around), womanize

wolfish *adj* ***syn*** FIERCE 1, barbarous, cruel, fell, ferocious, grim, inhuman, inhumane, savage, truculent

woman *n* **1** ***syn*** WIFE, ‖ball and chain, lady, ‖little woman, ‖missus, Mrs., ‖old lady, ‖old woman, ‖rib, ‖squaw

2 ***syn*** MISTRESS, ‖doxy, girl friend, inamorata, lover, paramour

womanize *vb* ***syn*** PHILANDER, fool (around), mess around, play (around), wolf

womanizer *n* ***syn*** WOLF, Casanova, chaser, Don Juan, ladies' man, lady-killer, masher, philander, philanderer

wonder *n* **1** something that causes fascinated astonishment or admiration <the seven *wonders* of the ancient world>

syn marvel, miracle, phenomenon, portent, prodigy, sensation, stunner

rel curiosity, cynosure, gazingstock, spectacle

idiom one for the book(s), something to shout (*or* write home) about

2 the complex emotion aroused by the strange and incomprehensible and especially the awe-inspiring <stood gazing in wide-eyed *wonder* at the scene unveiled before her>

syn admiration, amaze, amazement, marveling, wonderment

rel awe, fear, reverence; bewilderment, perplexity, puzzlement; astonishment, marvel, shock

con disinterest, incuriosity, indifference, unconcern; dispassion, impassivity; casualness, offhandedness; boredom, ennui

3 ***syn*** UNCERTAINTY, concern, doubt, dubiety, dubiosity, incertitude, mistrust, skepticism, suspicion, uncertitude

rel assailability, vulnerability

con unconcern

wonderful *adj* **1** ***syn*** MARVELOUS 1, amazing, astonishing, astounding, miraculous, staggering, strange, stupendous, surprising, wondrous

2 ***syn*** MARVELOUS 2, ‖cool, divine, glorious, groovy, peachy, sensational, super, swell, terrific

ant lousy

wonderland *n* ***syn*** UTOPIA, arcadia, Cockaigne, fairyland, heaven, lubberland, paradise, promised land, Shangri-la, Zion

wonderment *n* ***syn*** WONDER 2, admiration, amaze, amazement, marveling

wondrous *adj* ***syn*** MARVELOUS 1, amazing, astonishing, astounding, miraculous, spectacular, strange, stupendous, surprising, wonderful

wont *n* ***syn*** HABIT 1, consuetude, custom, habitude, manner, practice, trick, usage, use, way

wont *vb* ***syn*** ACCUSTOM, familiarize, habituate, inure, use

wonted *adj* ***syn*** USUAL 1, accepted, accustomed, chronic, customary, habitual, routine
ant unwonted

wontedly *adv* ***syn*** USUALLY 1, as usual, consistently, customarily, habitually
ant unwontedly

woo *vb* ***syn*** ADDRESS 8, court, make up (to), pursue, spark, sue, sweetheart
idiom bill and coo, pitch woo

wood *n, often* **woods** *pl but sing or pl in constr* ***syn*** FOREST, timber, timberland, weald, woodland

wooden *adj* **1** ***syn*** STIFF 4, buckram, cardboard, muscle-bound, stilted
rel awkward, clumsy; heavy, ponderous, weighty
con limber, supple; plastic, pliable, pliant
2 ***syn*** AWKWARD 2, bumbling, gauche, halting, ham-handed, heavy-handed, inept, maladroit, unhandy, unhappy

woodenhead *n* ***syn*** DUNCE, blockhead, bonehead, clodpate, hammerhead, knucklehead, muttonhead, numskull, thickhead, thickskull

woodland *n* ***syn*** FOREST, timber, timberland, weald, wood(s)

woods colt *n* ***syn*** BASTARD 1, by-blow, chance child, come-by-chance, filius nullius, filius populi, illegitimate, love child, natural child, whoreson

woodsy *n* ***syn*** RUSTIC, ||backwoodser, backwoodsman, bumpkin, clodhopper, hayseed, hick, hillbilly, jake, rube

wooer *n* ***syn*** SUITOR 2, spark, sparker, swain

woolly *adj* ***syn*** HAIRY 1, fleecy, hirsute, pileous, pilose, whiskered

word *vb* to convey (as an impression, a thought, or a need) in words <seemed scarcely to know how to *word* her appeal>
syn couch, express, formulate, phrase, put; *compare* EXPRESS 2
rel convey, offer, submit; say, state, tell

word *n* **1** something that is said <didn't tell a *word* about his plans>
syn statement, utterance
rel announcement, declaration, pronouncement
2 a pronounceable sound or combination of sounds that expresses and symbolizes an idea <be sure you learn the meaning of each *word*>
syn term, vocable
rel expression, idiom, locution, phrase
3 ***syn*** COMMAND 1, behest, bidding, charge, dictate, injunction, mandate, order
4 ***syn*** NEWS, advice, information, intelligence, speerings, tidings
5 ***syn*** REPORT 1, buzz, cry, gossip, hearsay, rumble, rumor, scuttlebutt, talk, tattle
6 ***syn*** MESSAGE 1, communication, directive
7 ***syn*** SAYING, adage, byword, proverb, saw
8 a statement whose weight or worth depends on the truthfulness or authority of its maker <had the doctor's *word* that no operation would be needed>
syn assurance, guarantee, pledge, warrant; *compare* PROMISE
rel commitment, engagement, undertaking; oath, vow; promise
9 ***syn*** PROMISE, engagement, plight
10 *usu* **words** *pl* ***syn*** QUARREL, altercation, beef, bickering, dispute, fight, hassle, row, run-in, set-to
11 ***syn*** PASSWORD 3, watchword
12 ***syn*** PASSWORD 1, countersign, watchword

wordage *n* ***syn*** WORDING, diction, parlance, phrase, phraseology, phrasing, verbalism, verbiage

word for word *adv* ***syn*** VERBATIM, direct, directly, literally, literatim

word–for–word *adj* ***syn*** VERBATIM, literal, verbal

word–hoard *n* ***syn*** VOCABULARY 1, lexicon, word-stock

wordiness *n* ***syn*** VERBOSITY, prolixity, prolixness, verbalism, verboseness, windiness
con crispness, pithiness, trenchancy
ant laconicism, laconism

wording *n* manner or style of verbal expression <take care with the *wording* of a formal invitation>
syn diction, parlance, phrase, phraseology, phrasing, verbalism, verbiage, wordage
rel language, mode, style

wordless *adj* **1** ***syn*** TACIT 1, implicit, implied, inferred, undeclared, understood, unexpressed, unsaid, unspoken, unuttered
2 ***syn*** SILENT 2, dumb, mum, ||mumchance, mute, speechless
3 ***syn*** SILENT 3, close, close-lipped, dumb, reserved, reticent, speechless, tight-lipped, tight-mouthed, uncommunicative
4 ***syn*** UNSPOKEN 1, silent, tacit, unexpressed, unuttered, unvoiced
ant wordy

word–of–mouth *adj* ***syn*** ORAL 2, spoken, traditional, unwritten, verbal

word–stock *n* ***syn*** VOCABULARY 1, lexicon, word-hoard

wordy *adj* using or marked by the use of more words than are needed to express an idea <tired of dull *wordy* editorials>
syn diffuse, long-winded, palaverous, prolix, redundant, verbose, windy
rel flatulent, inflated, tumid, turgid; garrulous, glib, loquacious, talkative, voluble; bombastic, highfalutin, rhetorical
con compendious, concise, pithy, succinct, summary, terse; lean, taut
ant laconic

work *n* **1** the activity that affords one his livelihood <laborers hurrying to *work* at dawn>
syn business, calling, employment, job, line, occupation, pursuit, ||racket; *compare* JOB 2
rel art, craft, handicraft, métier, profession, trade, vocation, walk
2 strenuous activity that involves difficulty and effort and usually affords no pleasure <had done much hard *work* during his life>

---

syn synonym(s) ***rel*** related word(s)
idiom idiomatic equivalent(s) ***con*** contrasted word(s)
ant antonym(s) * vulgar
|| use limited; if in doubt, see a dictionary
The first word in a synonym list when printed in SMALL CAPITALS shows where there is more information about the group. For a more efficient use of this book see Explanatory Notes.

syn bullwork, donkeywork, drudge, drudgery, grind, labor, moil, plugging, slavery, slogging, sweat, toil, travail
rel effort, exertion, pains, trouble; chore, duty, job; elucubration; striving; spadework
ant play
3 works *pl syn* FACTORY, manufactory, mill, plant
work *vb* **1** *syn* OPERATE 3, handle, run, use
2 *syn* TILL, cultivate, dress, ‖labor, tend
3 *syn* SOLVE 1, fix, resolve, work out
4 *syn* LABOR 1, drive, moil, strain, strive, toil, tug
5 *syn* FUNCTION 3, act, go, run
6 *syn* ACT 5, behave, function, operate, perform, react, take
work (for) *vb syn* BENEFIT, advantage, avail, profit, serve
workable *adj syn* POSSIBLE 1, doable, feasible, practicable, viable
rel applicable, exploitable, usable
ant unworkable
workaday *adj* **1** *syn* PROSAIC 3, commonplace, everyday, lowly, mundane, workday
2 *syn* ORDINARY 1, everyday, plain, plain Jane, quotidian, routine, unremarkable, usual
workday *adj syn* PROSAIC 3, commonplace, everyday, lowly, mundane, workaday
worker *n* one who earns a living by labor and especially by manual labor <weary *workers* straggling home each night>
syn hand, laborer, ‖mozo, operative, roustabout, workhand, workingman, workman
rel artisan, craftsman, handicraftsman, mechanic; employee
ant idler
workhand *n syn* WORKER, hand, laborer, ‖mozo, operative, roustabout, workingman, workman
workhorse *n* **1** *syn* SLAVE 2, dray horse, drudge, galley slave, peon, slavey, toiler
2 *syn* SAWHORSE, buck, horse, sawbuck, trestle
work in *vb syn* INSINUATE 3, edge in, foist, infiltrate, worm
working *adj* **1** *syn* ACTIVE 1, alive, dynamic, functioning, live, operative, running
2 *syn* BUSY 1, employed, engaged, occupied
workingman *n syn* WORKER, hand, laborer, ‖mozo, operative, roustabout, workhand, workman
workless *adj syn* UNEMPLOYED, jobless
workman *n syn* WORKER, hand, laborer, ‖mozo, operative, roustabout, workhand, workingman
workmanlike *adj syn* SKILLFUL 2, adroit, clever, good, pretty, ‖skilly, wicked, workmanly
ant unworkmanlike
workmanly *adj syn* SKILLFUL 2, adroit, clever, good, pretty, ‖skilly, wicked, workmanlike

---

syn synonym(s) *rel* related word(s)
idiom idiomatic equivalent(s) *con* contrasted word(s)
ant antonym(s) * vulgar
‖ use limited; if in doubt, see a dictionary
The first word in a synonym list when printed in SMALL CAPITALS shows where there is more information about the group. For a more efficient use of this book see Explanatory Notes.

work off *vb syn* FOIST 3, fob off, palm (on *or* upon), palm off, pass off
work out *vb syn* SOLVE 1, fix, resolve, work
work over *vb syn* REVISE, redraft, redraw, restyle, revamp, rework, rewrite
work-shy *adj syn* LAZY, drony, easygoing, faineant, indolent, slothful, slowgoing
work up *vb syn* GENERATE 3, breed, cause, engender, get up, hatch, induce, muster (up), occasion, produce
world *n* **1** *syn* EARTH 1, globe, (the) planet
2 *syn* UNIVERSE, cosmos (*or* kosmos), creation, macrocosm, macrocosmos, megacosm, nature
worldly *adj* **1** *syn* EARTHLY 1, earthy, mundane, sublunary, tellurian, telluric, terrene, terrestrial, uncelestial
ant otherworldly
2 *syn* MATERIALISTIC, banausic, earthy, mundane, sensual, temporal
ant otherworldly, unworldly
3 *syn* SOPHISTICATED 2, blasé, disenchanted, disentranced, disillusioned, knowing, mondaine, sophisticate, worldly-wise, world-wise
ant unworldly
worldly-wise *adj syn* SOPHISTICATED 2, blasé, disenchanted, disentranced, disillusioned, knowing, mondaine, sophisticate, worldly, world-wise
rel callous, hard-boiled, hardened
con naive, unsophisticated, unworldly
worldwide *adj syn* UNIVERSAL 2, catholic, cosmic, cosmopolitan, ecumenical, global, planetary
con parochial
world-wise *adj syn* SOPHISTICATED 2, blasé, disenchanted, disentranced, disillusioned, knowing, mondaine, sophisticate, worldly, worldly-wise
world-without-end *adj syn* EVERLASTING 1, amaranthine, ceaseless, endless, eternal, immortal, never-ending, unending
world-without-end *n syn* ETERNITY 2, afterlife, everlastingness, eviternity, immortality
worm *n syn* WRETCH 1, ‖blighter, lowlife, mucker, no-good, wormling
worm *vb* **1** *syn* INSINUATE 3, edge in, foist, infiltrate, work in
2 *syn* WRIGGLE, squiggle, squirm, wiggle, writhe
wormling *n syn* WRETCH 1, ‖blighter, lowlife, mucker, no-good, worm
worn *adj* **1** *syn* TIRED 1, fatigued, jaded, wearied, weary, worn down
2 *syn* HAGGARD, careworn, drawn, pinched
worn down *adj syn* TIRED 1, fatigued, jaded, wearied, weary, worn
worn-out *adj* **1** *syn* EFFETE 2, all in, bleary, depleted, drained, exhausted, far-gone, spent, used up, washed-out
2 *syn* TRITE, clichéd, hackneyed, shopworn, stale, stereotyped, threadbare, timeworn, tired, well-worn
worried *adj syn* DISTRAUGHT, distracted, distrait, distressed, harassed, tormented, troubled
ant unworried
worry *vb* **1** to disturb one or destroy one's peace of mind by repeated or persistent tormenting attacks <vain regrets that *worry* his spirit>
syn annoy, bedevil, beleaguer, dun, gnaw, hagride, harass, harry, needle, pester, plague, tantalize, tease, ‖wherret

rel beset, bother, fret, pelt, trouble, vex; goad, test, try; afflict, torment, torture; aggrieve, oppress, persecute, wrong
idiom give one gyp
con comfort, console, solace; alleviate, assuage, ease, relieve
2 *syn* TROUBLE 1, ail, cark, distress, upset
3 to experience concern, disquietude, or anxiety < *worrying* over her children's health >
syn cark, fret, fuss, pother, stew, ‖tew
rel carry on, take on; despair, give up; bother, concern (oneself); agitate, disquiet, disturb, trouble
idiom be upset, bite one's nails
con accept, submit; abide, bear, endure, stand, support; disregard, ignore, overlook, pass over

worry *n* **1** *syn* CARE 2, anxiety, concern, concernment, disquiet, disquietude, solicitude, unease, uneasiness
rel presentiment; doubt, mistrust, uncertainty; anguish, heartache, woe
con composure, equanimity, sangfroid; assurance, certainty, certitude, confidence, security
2 *syn* TRIAL 2, care, trouble

worrywart *n* *syn* PESSIMIST, calamity howler, Cassandra, crepehanger

worsen *vb* *syn* DETERIORATE 1, decline, degenerate, descend, disimprove, disintegrate, retrograde, rot, sink
rel blast, blight, debase, degrade, humble, lower; corrupt, foul, taint
idiom get worse, grow worse
ant better

worship *n* *syn* ADORATION, idolatry, idolization

worship *vb* **1** *syn* REVERE, adore, reverence, venerate
con contemn, despise, disdain, flout, scorn; curse, execrate, vilify
2 *syn* ADORE 3, dote (on *or* upon), idolize
ant abominate; scorn
3 *syn* LOVE 2, adore, affection

worst *vb* *syn* DEFEAT 2, best, down, outdo, ‖pip

worth *n* **1** equivalence in good qualities (as utility, importance, or desirability) express or implied <impossible to estimate the *worth* of such a man to the community>
syn account, valuation, value
rel class, excellence, merit, perfection, quality, virtue; rate; use, usefulness, utility; consequence, importance, mark, moment, note, significance, weight
con baseness, meanness, paltriness, poorness
ant worthlessness
2 *syn* QUALITY 2, caliber, merit, stature, value, virtue
3 *syn* WEALTH 2, fortune, property, resources, riches, substance

worthless *adj* **1** lacking all excellence or value <gave me a *worthless* check>
syn draffy, drossy, good-for-nothing, inutile, ‖no-account, no-good, nothing, unworthy, valueless
rel inferior, mediocre, poor, second-rate; defective, flawed, imperfect; bootless, ineffectual, unavailing, useless; contemptible, dusty, mean, sad, sorry
idiom dear at any price, of no earthly value (*or* worth)
con esteemed, precious; useful, valuable, worthwhile; invaluable, priceless
ant worthful
2 *syn* FECKLESS 1, fustian, good-for-nothing, meaningless, purposeless, unpurposed, useless
rel incapable, incompetent, unqualified

worthwhile *adj* *syn* ADVANTAGEOUS 1, gainful, good, lucrative, moneymaking, paying, profitable, remunerative, well-paying

worthy *adj* **1** having worth or merit <a *worthy* custom handed down from our ancestors>
syn admirable, commendable, deserving, estimable, laudable, meritable, meritorious, praisable, praiseworthy, thankworthy
rel invaluable, precious, priceless; desirable, pleasing, satisfying; divine
con good-for-nothing, ‖no-account, no-good, valueless; contemptible, sad, sorry
ant worthless
2 *syn* HONORABLE 1, estimable, high-principled, noble, sterling
ant unworthy

wound *vb* *syn* INJURE 3, hurt

wow *n* *syn* SMASH 6, bang, bell ringer, hit, succès fou, ten-strike

‖**wowser** *n* *syn* PRUDE, bluenose, comstock, goody-goody, Grundy, Mrs. Grundy, nice Nelly, prig, puritan

wrack *vb* *syn* DESTROY 1, decimate, demolish, raze, ruin, unbuild, undo, unframe, unmake, wreck

wrackful *adj* *syn* DESTRUCTIVE, annihilative, ruinous, shattering, wreckful

wraith *n* *syn* APPARITION, ghost, ‖haunt, phantasm, phantom, shade, shadow, specter, spirit, ‖spook

wrangle *vb* **1** *syn* QUARREL, bicker, brabble, caterwaul, fall out, row, scrap, spat, squabble, tiff
2 *syn* ARGUE 2, argufy, bicker, dispute, hassle, quibble, squabble

wrangle *n* *syn* QUARREL, altercation, bickering, dispute, fight, fracas, hassle, row, squabble, tiff

wrap *vb* *syn* ENFOLD 1, enclose, enshroud, envelop, enwrap, invest, shroud, veil
rel camouflage, cloak, mask
ant unwrap

wrap (up) *vb* **1** *syn* BUNDLE UP, ‖hap, muffle
2 *syn* SWATHE, drape, enswathe, envelop, enwrap, roll, swaddle

wrapped *adj* *syn* INTENT, absorbed, deep, engaged, engrossed, immersed, preoccupied, rapt, wrapped up

wrapped up *adj* *syn* INTENT, absorbed, deep, engaged, engrossed, immersed, preoccupied, rapt, wrapped

wrap up *vb* *syn* CLOSE 3, complete, conclude, determine, end, finish, halt, terminate, ultimate, wind up

wrath *n* *syn* ANGER, fury, indignation, ire, mad, rage
rel acerbity, acrimony, asperity; offense, resentment

wrathful *adj* *syn* ANGRY, heated, irate, ireful, mad, waxy, wrathy, wroth, wrothful, wrothy

wrathy *adj* *syn* ANGRY, heated, irate, ireful, mad, waxy, wrathful, wroth, wrothful, wrothy

‖**wraxle** *vb* *syn* WRESTLE, grapple, scuffle, tussle

---

wreak *vb* ***syn*** INFLICT 2, force (on *or* upon), impose, visit, wreck

wreakful *adj* ***syn*** VINDICTIVE, revengeful, vengeful

wreath *n* a circlet of intertwined leaves or flowers worn upon the head as an ornament or as a mark of honor or esteem <received the laurel *wreath* of victory from the emperor's own hand>
syn anadem, chaplet, coronal, coronet, crown, garland
rel bay(s), laurel

wreathe *vb* ***syn*** WIND 2, coil, corkscrew, curl, entwine, spiral, twine, twist

wreck *n* **1** ***syn*** CRASH 3, crack-up, pileup, ‖prang, smash, smashup, ‖stramash
2 ***syn*** COLLAPSE 2, breakdown, crack-up, crash, debacle, smash, smashup
3 ***syn*** JALOPY, clunker, crate, dog, heap, junker

wreck *vb* **1** ***syn*** VANDALIZE, ‖trash
2 ***syn*** DESTROY 1, decimate, demolish, raze, ruin, unbuild, undo, unframe, unmake, wrack
rel despoil, loot, plunder, ravage; cripple, disable
3 ***syn*** TOTAL 3, demolish
4 ***syn*** SABOTAGE, subvert, undermine
5 ***syn*** SHIPWRECK 1, beach, cast away, pile up, strand
6 ***syn*** RUIN 2, bankrupt, dilapidate, do in, shipwreck
7 ***syn*** INFLICT 2, force (on *or* upon), impose, visit, wreak

wreckage *n* **1** ***syn*** SABOTAGE, subversion, undermining, wrecking
2 ***syn*** DRIFTWOOD, flotsam, jetsam

wrecker *n* ***syn*** VANDAL, defacer, despoiler, destroyer, ruinator, ruiner

wreckful *adj* ***syn*** DESTRUCTIVE, annihilative, ruinous, shattering, wrackful

wrecking *n* ***syn*** SABOTAGE, subversion, undermining, wreckage

wrench *vb* **1** to shift the position of or move by or as if by vigorous twisting <suddenly *wrenched* her around to face him>
syn wrest, wring, wry
rel bend, twist; coerce, compel, constrain, force; drag, rend, tear; contort, distort
2 ***syn*** SPRAIN, ‖rick, turn, twist
3 ***syn*** MISREPRESENT, color, confuse, distort, garble, miscolor, pervert, twist, warp, wrest
4 ***syn*** EXTORT 1, exact, gouge, pinch, screw, shake down, squeeze, wrest, wring

wrest *vb* **1** ***syn*** WRENCH 1, wring, wry
rel arrogate, confiscate, usurp; elicit, extort, extract
2 ***syn*** EXTORT 1, exact, gouge, pinch, screw, shake down, squeeze, wrench, wring
3 ***syn*** MISREPRESENT, color, confuse, distort, garble, miscolor, pervert, twist, warp, wrench

wrestle *vb* to struggle with an opponent at close quarters <determined to solve the problem if he had to *wrestle* with it all night>
syn grapple, scuffle, tussle, ‖wraxle
rel contend, fight, struggle; endeavor, essay; labor, moil, toil, travail, work; exert, strain, stretch, strive

wretch *n* **1** a worthless and often vicious or contemptible person <a treacherous drink-sodden *wretch*>
syn ‖blighter, lowlife, mucker, no-good, worm, wormling
rel good-for-naught, good-for-nothing, ne'er-do-well; blackguard, caitiff, devil, knave, rapscallion, rascal, rogue, rotter, scalawag, scoundrel, villain
idiom sad case
2 ***syn*** SNOT 1, cur, dog, scum, skunk, snake, stinkard, stinkaroo, stinker, toad

wretched *adj* **1** ***syn*** WOEFUL 1, afflicted, doleful, dolent, dolorous, miserable, rueful, ruthful, sorrowful
rel melancholy; abject, mean, sordid; piteous, pitiable, pitiful; despairing, despondent, forlorn, hopeless
con animated, gay, lively; content, contented, satisfied; gratified, pleased
2 ***syn*** BASE, abject, despicable, ignoble, low, mean, scurvy, servile, sordid, vile

wretchedness *n* ***syn*** MISERY 1, unhappiness, woe

wriggle *vb* to move or advance with wormlike motions <the attackers *wriggled* stealthily through the underbrush>
syn squiggle, squirm, wiggle, worm, writhe
rel flow, glide, ooze, slide, slip

wring *vb* **1** ***syn*** EXTORT 1, exact, gouge, pinch, screw, shake down, squeeze, wrench, wrest
2 ***syn*** WRENCH 1, wrest, wry
rel press, squeeze
3 ***syn*** AFFLICT, agonize, crucify, excruciate, harrow, martyr, rack, torment, torture, try

wringing–wet *adj* ***syn*** WET 1, drenched, dripping, saturated, soaked, soaking, sodden, sopping, soppy, soused

wrinkle *n* a small linear prominence or depression on a surface <a benign old face netted with *wrinkles*>
syn corrugation, crease, crinkle, fold, furrow, plica, ridge, rimple, rivel, ruck
rel crow's foot; pleat, pucker

wrinkle *vb* ***syn*** CRUMPLE 1, crimp, crimple, crinkle, rimple, ruck (up), ‖ruckle, rumple, screw, scrunch

write *vb* to form characters or words on a surface (as of paper) usually with pen or pencil <learned to *write* at an early age>
syn engross, indite, inscribe, scribe
rel dot (down), jot, note; chalk, pen, pencil; scratch, scrawl, scribble; draft, draw, make out; write down, write up
idiom push one's pen, put in writing, take down

write down *vb* ***syn*** DEPRECIATE 1, decry, devaluate, devalue, downgrade, lower, mark down, underrate, undervalue, write off
ant write up

write off *vb* **1** ***syn*** DEPRECIATE 1, decry, devaluate, devalue, downgrade, lower, mark down, underrate, undervalue, write down
2 ***syn*** DECRY 2, belittle, depreciate, derogate, detract (from), discount, disparage, downcry, minimize, run down

---

syn synonym(s) — *rel* related word(s)
idiom idiomatic equivalent(s) — *con* contrasted word(s)
ant antonym(s) — * vulgar
‖ use limited; if in doubt, see a dictionary
The first word in a synonym list when printed in SMALL CAPITALS shows where there is more information about the group. For a more efficient use of this book see Explanatory Notes.

write–up *n syn* PUFF 3, blurb, plug, puffing

writhe *vb* **1** to twist and turn in physical or mental distress <*writhing* in anguish with a throbbing toothache>
syn agonize, squirm, toss
rel blench, flinch, recoil, shrink, wince; contort, distort; bend, twist; thrash, tumble
2 *syn* WRIGGLE, squiggle, squirm, wiggle, worm

writing *n syn* PRINT 2, black and white

writing desk *n syn* DESK, escritoire, secretaire, secretary

wrong *n* **1** *syn* INJUSTICE 2, grievance, injury
2 *syn* EVIL 2, debt, sin, wickedness
3 *syn* EVIL 3, crime, diablerie, iniquity, sin, tort, wrongdoing
4 *syn* INJUSTICE 1, inequitableness, inequity, unfairness, unjustness

wrong *adj* **1** rejecting or deviating from the dictates of moral or divine law <had a *wrong* outlook on life> <*wrong* principles of conduct>
syn bad, evil, immoral, iniquitous, reprobate, sinful, vicious, wicked
rel blamable, blameworthy, censurable, reprehensible; corrupt, debauched, depraved; abandoned, dissolute, infamous, villainous; blasphemous, unholy, unrighteous; accursed, unblessed
con ethical, high-principled, moral, righteous, upright; chaste, innocent, pure, virtuous
ant right
2 *syn* FALSE 1, counterfactual, erroneous, inaccurate, incorrect, specious, unsound, untrue
idiom at fault, barking up the wrong tree, in error, on the wrong track
con exact, precise
ant right
3 *syn* BAD 1, amiss, ‖bum, ‖crappy, dissatisfactory, poor, ‖punk, rotten, unsatisfactory, up
rel improper, inappropriate, inapt, infelicitous, unfit, unfitting, unhappy, unsuitable
con appropriate, fit, fitting, proper, suitable
4 *syn* MISTAKEN, erroneous, misguided
ant right
5 *syn* INSANE 1, ‖batty, cracked, crazed, crazy, daft, demented, deranged, lunatic, unsound

wrong *adv syn* AMISS 2, afield, astray, awry, badly, unfavorably
ant right

wrong *vb* to inflict injury on another without justification <these men who have *wronged* the public trust deserve no consideration>
syn aggrieve, oppress, outrage, persecute
rel abuse, ill-treat, maltreat, mistreat; harm, hurt, injure; offend
idiom do wrong to (*or* by)
con guard, protect, safeguard; care (for), cherish; honor, love, respect

wrongdoing *n* **1** *syn* EVIL 3, crime, diablerie, iniquity, sin, tort, wrong
2 *syn* MISCONDUCT, misbehavior, misdoing

wrongful *adj syn* UNLAWFUL, criminal, illegal, illegitimate, illicit, lawless
ant rightful

wrongheaded *adj* **1** *syn* OBSTINATE, bullheaded, headstrong, mulish, pertinacious, perverse, pigheaded, self-willed, stiff-necked, stubborn
2 *syn* CONTRARY 3, balky, cross-grained, froward, ornery, perverse, restive, wayward

wrongly *adv syn* AMISS 1, faultily, incorrectly
ant rightly

wroth *adj syn* ANGRY, heated, irate, ireful, mad, waxy, wrathful, wrathy, wrothful, wrothy

wrothful *adj syn* ANGRY, heated, irate, ireful, mad, waxy, wrathful, wrathy, wroth, wrothy

wrothy *adj syn* ANGRY, heated, irate, ireful, mad, waxy, wrathful, wrathy, wroth, wrothful

wry *vb syn* WRENCH 1, wrest, wring

wry *adj syn* SARDONIC, cynical, ironic

XYZ

x *n syn* ERROR 1, mistake

x (out) *vb syn* ERASE, annul, black (out), blot out, cancel, delete, efface, expunge, obliterate, wipe (out)

Xanthippe *n syn* VIRAGO, amazon, fishwife, harpy, ogress, scold, shrew, termagant, vixen

Xmas *n syn* CHRISTMAS, Nativity, noel, yule, yuletide

yahoo *n syn* TOUGH, ‖b'hoy, bullyboy, mucker, punk, rough, roughneck, rowdy, ruffian, toughie

yak *n syn* CHATTER, babble, blab, blabber, chat, clack, gabble, jabber, palaver, prattle

yak *vb syn* CHAT 1, babble, chatter, clack, gab, gabble, jaw, prate, prattle, yakety-yak

‖**yak** *n syn* JOKE 1, crack, gag, jape, jest, quip, waggery, wisecrack, witticism

yakety–yak *n syn* CHATTER, babble, blab, blabber, chat, clack, gabble, jabber, palaver, prattle

yakety–yak *vb syn* CHAT 1, babble, chatter, clack, gab, gabble, jaw, prate, prattle, yak

yak–yak *n syn* CHATTER, babble, blab, blabber, chat, clack, gabble, jabber, palaver, prattle

yak–yak *vb syn* CHAT, babble, chatter, clack, gab, gabble, jaw, prate, prattle, yakety-yak

---

syn synonym(s) *rel* related word(s)
idiom idiomatic equivalent(s) *con* contrasted word(s)
ant antonym(s) * vulgar
‖ use limited; if in doubt, see a dictionary
The first word in a synonym list when printed in SMALL CAPITALS shows where there is more information about the group. For a more efficient use of this book see Explanatory Notes.

yammer *vb* **1** ***syn*** GRIPE, ‖beef, ‖bellyache, ‖bitch, bleat, ‖blow off, crab, fuss, squawk, yawp (*or* yaup)
2 ***syn*** CHAT 1, babble, chatter, clack, gab, gabble, jaw, prattle, yak, yakety-yak

yank *vb* **1** ***syn*** JERK, lug, lurch, snap, twitch, vellicate
rel tug; clutch, grab, snatch
2 ***syn*** EXTRACT 1, evulse, pull, tear

yap *n* **1** ***syn*** RUSTIC, backwoodsman, bumpkin, clodhopper, clown, hayseed, hick, hillybilly, jake, provincial
‖**2** ***syn*** MOUTH 1, ‖bazoo, gob, ‖mush, ‖row, ‖trap

yard *n* ***syn*** COURT 1, ‖close, courtyard, curtilage, enclosure, quad, quadrangle

yardstick *n* ***syn*** STANDARD 3, benchmark, criterion, gauge, measure, touchstone

yare *adj* ***syn*** AGILE, active, brisk, brisky, catty, lively, nimble, sprightly, spry, volant

yarn *n* **1** ***syn*** STORY 2, anecdote, narration, narrative, tale
2 ***syn*** CHAT 2, causerie, chin, prose, rap, talk

yarn *vb* ***syn*** CONVERSE, chat, chin, colloque, talk, visit

yatter *n* ***syn*** CHATTER, babble, ‖chin music, chitchat, clack, gabble, jabber, palaver, stultiloquence, talkee-talkee

yatter *vb* ***syn*** CHAT 1, babble, burble, cackle, chatter, clack, gab, ‖gas, jaw, ‖natter

yaw *n* ***syn*** TURN 2, bend, deflection, deviation, double, shift, tack

yaw *vb* ***syn*** SEESAW, lurch, pitch, swag, tilt, tilter

yaw *vb* ***syn*** YAWN, gape

yawn *vb* to breathe deeply with jaws widespread usually in reaction to fatigue or boredom < *yawned* again and again in the stuffy room >
syn gape, yaw
rel doze, drowse, nap, snooze

yawn *n* ***syn*** TEDIUM, boredom, doldrums, ennui

yawning *adj* ***syn*** CAVERNOUS 1, chasmal, gaping

yawp (*or* **yaup**) *vb* **1** ***syn*** SQUALL 1, caw, ‖quawk, squark, squawk
2 ***syn*** GRIPE, ‖beef, ‖bellyache, ‖bitch, bleat, ‖blow off, crab, fuss, squawk, yammer

yea *adv* **1** ***syn*** ALSO 2, additionally, along, as well, besides, likewise, more, moreover, too, yet
2 ***syn*** YES 1, agreed, all right, aye, OK (*or* okay), ‖okeydoke, ‖yep
3 ***syn*** EVEN 3, indeed, nay, truly, verily

yearbook *n* a book issued yearly to chronicle a particular part of the preceding year's activities < sports editor of his school *yearbook* >
syn annual, annuary

yearn *vb* ***syn*** LONG, ache, crave, dream, hanker, hunger, lust, pine, thirst, yen
rel covet, desire, wish; pant
ant dread

years *n pl* ***syn*** OLD AGE, age, caducity, elderliness, senectitude, senescence

yeast *n* ***syn*** FOAM, froth, lather, spume, suds

yeasty *adj* ***syn*** GIDDY 1, dizzy, featherbrained, flighty, fribbling, frivolous, harebrained, light, light-headed, scatterbrained

yegg *n* ***syn*** ROBBER

yell *vb* **1** ***syn*** SHOUT 1, cry, whoop
2 to complain vigorously or vociferously < let the opposition *yell;* we got the vote >
syn howl, scream, squeal, yip, yowl
rel cry, lament, squall, wail, weep; bemoan, bewail, deplore
idiom beat one's breast, make an outcry, tear one's hair, yell to high heaven
con acclaim, applaud, cheer, hail
3 ***syn*** CALL 1, cry, hallo, holler, hollo, shout, vociferate

yellow *adj* ***syn*** COWARDLY, ‖chicken, coward, craven, gutless, lily-livered, pusillanimous, spunkless, unmanly, white-livered

yellowback *n* ***syn*** DIME NOVEL, dreadful, penny dreadful, shilling shocker, shocker

yellowbelly *n* ***syn*** COWARD, chicken, craven, dastard, funk, funker, poltroon, quitter
rel fink, rat, stinker

yellow dog *n* ***syn*** CAD, bounder, cur, rotter

yen *vb* ***syn*** LONG, ache, crave, hanker, hunger, lust, pine, sigh, thirst, yearn

‖**yep** *adv* ***syn*** YES 1, agreed, all right, aye, OK (*or* okay), ‖okeydoke, yea
ant ‖nope

‖**yerk** *vb* ***syn*** WHIP 1, flagellate, flog, hide, lash, lather, scourge, stripe, thrash, whale

yes *adv* **1** —used as a function word to express assent, agreement, understanding, or acceptance < *yes,* I can do that >
syn agreed, all right, aye, OK (*or* okay), ‖okeydoke, yea, ‖yep
rel assuredly, certainly, gladly, willingly; undoubtedly, unquestionably
idiom beyond a doubt, beyond any shade (*or* shadow) of doubt, with all my heart, without the least doubt
2 ***syn*** EXACTLY 3, precisely

yes *vb* ***syn*** ASSENT, accede, acquiesce, agree, consent, subscribe

yes–man *n* **1** ***syn*** STOOGE 1, Charlie McCarthy, dummy
2 ***syn*** SYCOPHANT, bootlick, bootlicker, ‖brownnose, ‖brownnoser, groveler, minion, spaniel, toady, truckler

yesterday *n* ***syn*** PAST, foretime, ‖lang syne, yesteryear, yore
ant tomorrow

yesteryear *n* ***syn*** PAST, foretime, ‖lang syne, yesterday, yore

yet *adv* **1** beyond this — used as an intensive to stress the comparative degree < in spite of her protest he went *yet* faster >
syn even, still
2 at some future time < just wait, we'll get there *yet* >
syn eventually, finally, someday, sometime, somewhen, sooner or later, ultimately
idiom after a while, in due course, in the course of time

---

syn synonym(s)	***rel*** related word(s)
idiom idiomatic equivalent(s)	***con*** contrasted word(s)
ant antonym(s)	* vulgar

‖ use limited; if in doubt, see a dictionary
The first word in a synonym list when printed in SMALL CAPITALS shows where there is more information about the group. For a more efficient use of this book see Explanatory Notes.

3 *syn* ALSO 2, additionally, along, as well, besides, furthermore, likewise, more, moreover, too
4 *syn* HITHERTO 1, as yet, earlier, so far, thus far
5 *syn* HOWEVER, after all, howbeit, nevertheless, nonetheless, notwithstanding, still, still and all, though, withal

yet *conj syn* ONLY, but, except, however, save

yield *vb* **1** *syn* RELINQUISH, abandon, cede, give up, hand over, leave, resign, surrender, ‖turn up, waive
con appropriate, arrogate, confiscate
2 to give way before a force that one cannot longer resist <*yielded* to temptation>
syn bow, buckle (under), capitulate, cave, defer, knuckle, knuckle under, submit, succumb
rel accord, award, concede, grant; cede, surrender, waive; break, fail
idiom give ground, give place, give way
con bear up, hold out, resist
ant withstand
3 *syn* BEAR 9, produce, turn out
4 *syn* GIVE 7, produce
rel discharge, eject, emit, vent
5 to produce as return or revenue <an investment that *yields* 10 percent>
syn bring in, pay, return
rel afford, furnish, provide, supply; hold out, offer, proffer, tender
idiom afford (*or* give *or* provide) a return of, put at one's disposal
6 *syn* GIVE 12, bend, break, cave, collapse, crumple, fold up, go

yield *n syn* OUTPUT, outturn, product, production, turnout

yielding *adj* **1** *syn* SOFT 6, mushy, pappy, pulpy, quaggy, spongy, squashy, squelchy, squishy, squushy
ant unyielding
2 *syn* PASSIVE 2, acquiescent, nonresistant, nonresisting, resigned, submissive, unresistant, unresisting

yip *vb syn* YELL 2, howl, scream, squeal, yowl

‖**yob** *n syn* RUSTIC, backwoodsman, bumpkin, clodhopper, clown, hayseed, hick, hillbilly, provincial, rube

yoke *n* **1** *syn* BONDAGE, enslavement, helotry, peonage, serfage, serfdom, servility, servitude, slavery, thralldom
2 *syn* BOND 3, knot, ligament, ligature, link, nexus, tie, vinculum

yoke *vb* **1** *syn* HITCH 2, couple, harness
2 *syn* JOIN 1, associate, combine, conjoin, conjugate, connect, couple, link, unite, wed

yokel *n syn* RUSTIC, backwoodsman, bucolic, bumpkin, chawbacon, clodhopper, hayseed, hick, hillbilly, jake

yon *adv* **1** *syn* BEYOND 1, farther, further, yonder
2 *syn* THERE, thither, thitherward

yonder *adv syn* BEYOND 1, farther, further, ‖yon

yore *n syn* PAST, foretime, ‖lang syne, yesterday, yesteryear

young *adj* **1** being in an early stage of life, growth, or development <*young* shoots of new grass>
syn callow, green, immature, infant, juvenile, unfledged, unripe, youthful
rel fresh, new; crude, raw, unfinished, unformed
con full-grown, grown-up, mature, ripe; aged, elderly, superannuated
ant old; adult
2 *syn* INEXPERIENCED, callow, fresh, green, raw, unfleshed, unpracticed, unseasoned, untried, unversed

youngling *n syn* CHILD 1, bud, chick, chit, juvenile, kid, moppet, young one, youngster, youth

young man *n syn* BOYFRIEND 1, beau, gentleman friend, swain

young one *n syn* CHILD 1, bud, chick, chit, juvenile, kid, moppet, youngling, youngster, youth

youngster *n syn* CHILD 1, bud, chick, chit, juvenile, kid, moppet, youngling, young one, youth

youth *n* **1** the period of life in which one passes from childhood to maturity <the thought of regaining one's *youth*>
syn adolescence, greenness, juvenility, prime, puberty, pubescence, spring, springtide, springtime, youthfulness, youthhood
rel callowness, immaturity, inexperience, unripeness; dewiness
idiom awkward age, flower (*or* springtime *or* May) of life, salad days
ant age
2 *syn* CHILD 1, bud, chick, chit, juvenile, kid, moppet, youngling, young one, youngster

youthful *adj syn* YOUNG 1, callow, green, immature, infant, juvenile, unfledged, unripe
rel beardless, boyish, puerile; maiden, virgin, virginal
con adult, matured
ant aged, elderly

youthfulness *n syn* YOUTH 1, adolescence, greenness, juvenility, puberty, pubescence, spring, springtide, springtime, youthhood

youthhood *n syn* YOUTH, adolescence, greenness, juvenility, puberty, pubescence, spring, springtide, springtime, youthfulness

yowl *vb* **1** *syn* YELL 2, howl, scream, squeal, yip
2 *syn* BAWL 2, howl, squall, wail

yule *n syn* CHRISTMAS, Nativity, noel, Xmas, yuletide

yuletide *n syn* CHRISTMAS, Nativity, noel, Xmas, yule

yummy *adj syn* DELIGHTFUL, adorable, ambrosial, darling, delectable, delicious, heavenly, luscious, lush, scrumptious

zakuska *n syn* APPETIZER, antipasto, hors d'oeuvre, whet

zany *n* **1** *syn* CLOWN 3, buffoon, harlequin, merry-andrew
rel comic, farceur, funnyman
2 one who makes an exhibition of himself for the amusement of others <tired of having her parties spoiled by drunken *zanies*>
syn clown, cutup, farceur, joker, jokester, wag
rel practical joker, pranker, prankster, trickster; exhibitionist, show-off
3 *syn* WAG 1, card, comedian, humorist, joker
4 *syn* FOOL 4, ament, cretin, ‖feeb, half-wit, idiot, imbecile, moron, natural, simpleton

---

syn synonym(s) *rel* related word(s)
idiom idiomatic equivalent(s) *con* contrasted word(s)
ant antonym(s) * vulgar
‖ use limited; if in doubt, see a dictionary
The first word in a synonym list when printed in SMALL CAPITALS shows where there is more information about the group. For a more efficient use of this book see Explanatory Notes.

zeal *n* ***syn*** PASSION 6, ardor, calenture, enthusiasm, fervor, fire, hurrah
rel energy, gusto, spirit, zest; fierceness, intensity, vehemence; avidity, keenness, readiness, urgency; earnestness, seriousness, sincerity
con coolness, halfheartedness, indifference, lukewarmness; carelessness, heedlessness, insouciance, negligence, unmindfulness; disinterest, lackadaisy, unconcern
ant apathy

zealot *n* ***syn*** ENTHUSIAST, bigot, bug, fanatic, fiend, freak, maniac, nut
rel adherent, disciple, follower, partisan, sectary

zealous *adj* ***syn*** ENTHUSIASTIC, ‖buggy, ‖bugs, gung ho, keen, nutty, warm
rel afire, ardent, fervent, fervid, fired; avid, eager; dedicated, fanatic, frenetic, rabid, wild-eyed; infatuated, obsessed, possessed
con cool, halfhearted, indifferent, lukewarm; careless, heedless, insouciant, negligent, unmindful; disinterested, lackadaisical, uninterested
ant apathetic

zemi *n* ***syn*** CHARM 2, amulet, fetish, juju, luck, mascot, periapt, phylactery, talisman

zenith *n* ***syn*** APEX 2, acme, apogee, capstone, climax, culmination, meridian, peak, pinnacle, summit
ant nadir

zero *n* **1** a numerical symbol 0 denoting the absence of all magnitude or quantity <wrote a row of *zeros* after the decimal point>
syn aught (*or* ought), cipher, goose egg, naught (*or* nought), nothing, zilch
rel blank, nil, void
2 ***syn*** NONENTITY, cipher, insignificancy, nobody, nothing, nullity, whiffet, whippersnapper, whipster, zilch

zero (in) *vb* ***syn*** DIRECT 2, address, aim, cast, head, lay, level, point, train, turn

zero hour *n* ***syn*** JUNCTURE 2, contingency, crisis, crossroad(s), emergency, exigency, pass, pinch, strait, turning point

zest *n* ***syn*** TASTE 4, gusto, heart, palate, relish
rel ardor, eagerness, enthusiasm, fervor, passion, zeal; delectation, delight, enjoyment, pleasure, satisfaction; bliss, ecstasy, elation

zesty *adj* ***syn*** PUNGENT, peppery, piquant, poignant, racy, snappy, spicy

zetetic *n* ***syn*** SKEPTIC, doubter, doubting Thomas, headshaker, Pyrrhonian, Pyrrhonist, unbeliever

zilch *n* **1** ***syn*** ZERO 1, aught (*or* ought), cipher, goose egg, naught (*or* nought), nothing
2 ***syn*** NONENTITY, cipher, insignificancy, nobody, nothing, nullity, whiffet, whippersnapper, whipster, zero

zing *n* **1** ***syn*** EAGERNESS, ardor, enthusiasm
2 ***syn*** SPIRIT 5, animation, brio, dash, élan, esprit, life, oomph, verve, vim

Zion *n* **1** ***syn*** HEAVEN 2, Abraham's bosom, bliss, Canaan, Civitas Dei, elysium, empyrean, New Jerusalem, nirvana, paradise
2 ***syn*** UTOPIA, arcadia, Cockaigne, fairyland, heaven, lubberland, paradise, promised land, Shangri-la, wonderland

zip *vb* **1** ***syn*** BREEZE, waltz
2 ***syn*** HURRY 2, bustle, fly, hasten, hustle, ‖nip, rush, speed, whisk, whiz

zippy *adj* ***syn*** AGILE, active, brisk, brisky, catty, lively, nimble, sprightly, spry, yare
rel alert, keen, ready; dynamic, forceful, intense

zoetic *adj* ***syn*** LIVING 1, alive, animate, animated, vital

Zoilus *n* ***syn*** CRITIC, aristarch, carper, caviler, criticizer, faultfinder, knocker, momus, smellfungus

zombie *n* **1** ***syn*** DUNCE, boob, chump, clod, dolt, dullard, ‖goon, moron, nitwit, oaf
2 ***syn*** ECCENTRIC, case, character, ‖duck, oddball, oddity, original, quiz, ‖spook, ‖wack

zone *n* ***syn*** AREA 1, belt, region, territory, tract
rel section, sector, segment

zonked *adj* **1** ***syn*** INTOXICATED 1, ‖boozy, ‖crocked, drunk, drunken, inebriated, ‖pie-eyed, ‖pissed, ‖stewed, tight
2 ***syn*** DRUGGED, doped, high, hopped-up, spaced-out, stoned, tripped out, turned on, ‖wiped out